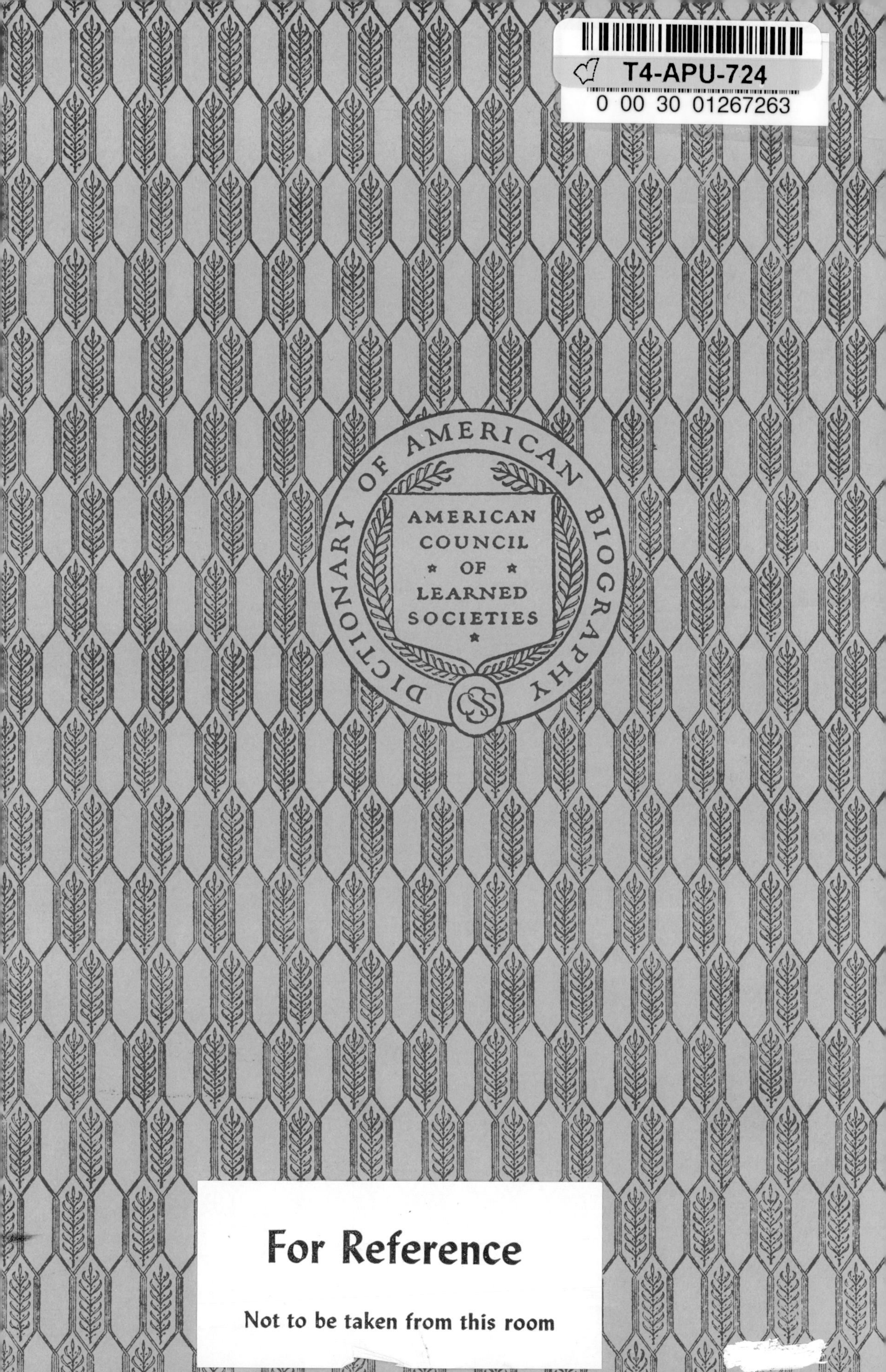
DICTIONARY OF AMERICAN BIOGRAPHY
AMERICAN COUNCIL OF LEARNED SOCIETIES
CSS

DICTIONARY
OF AMERICAN BIOGRAPHY

The *Dictionary of American Biography* was published originally in twenty volumes. Supplementary volumes were added in 1944 and 1958. This edition of the work combines all twenty-two volumes.

The present Volume I (Abbe–Brazer) contains Volumes I and II of the original edition, but these are now denominated "Part 1" and "Part 2" of the Volume. Volumes II through XI are arranged similarly, the Second Part in each instance representing a volume of the original series. For ease in reference, although the articles follow one another in strict alphabetical order, each Second Part is preceded by a half-title page which relates that Part to its place in the original numbering of the volumes.

The Errata list at the head of Volume I contains corrections of fact and additional data which have come to the attention of the Editors from the first publication of the work up to the present. Minor typographical corrections have been made in many instances directly on the plates.

PUBLISHED UNDER THE AUSPICES OF THE AMERICAN COUNCIL OF LEARNED SOCIETIES

The American Council of Learned Societies, organized in 1919 for the purpose of advancing the study of the humanities and of the humanistic aspects of the social sciences, is a nonprofit federation comprising forty-five national scholarly groups. The Council represents the humanities in the United States in the International Union of Academies, provides fellowships and grants-in-aid, supports research-and-planning conferences and symposia, and sponsors special projects and scholarly publications.

MEMBER ORGANIZATIONS

AMERICAN PHILOSOPHICAL SOCIETY, 1743
AMERICAN ACADEMY OF ARTS AND SCIENCES, 1780
AMERICAN ANTIQUARIAN SOCIETY, 1812
AMERICAN ORIENTAL SOCIETY, 1842
AMERICAN NUMISMATIC SOCIETY, 1858
AMERICAN PHILOLOGICAL ASSOCIATION, 1869
ARCHAEOLOGICAL INSTITUTE OF AMERICA, 1879
SOCIETY OF BIBLICAL LITERATURE, 1880
MODERN LANGUAGE ASSOCIATION OF AMERICA, 1883
AMERICAN HISTORICAL ASSOCIATION, 1884
AMERICAN ECONOMIC ASSOCIATION, 1885
AMERICAN FOLKLORE SOCIETY, 1888
AMERICAN DIALECT SOCIETY, 1889
AMERICAN PSYCHOLOGICAL ASSOCIATION, 1892
ASSOCIATION OF AMERICAN LAW SCHOOLS, 1900
AMERICAN PHILOSOPHICAL ASSOCIATION, 1901
AMERICAN ANTHROPOLOGICAL ASSOCIATION, 1902
AMERICAN POLITICAL SCIENCE ASSOCIATION, 1903
BIBLIOGRAPHICAL SOCIETY OF AMERICA, 1904
ASSOCIATION OF AMERICAN GEOGRAPHERS, 1904
HISPANIC SOCIETY OF AMERICA, 1904
AMERICAN SOCIOLOGICAL ASSOCIATION, 1905
AMERICAN SOCIETY OF INTERNATIONAL LAW, 1906
ORGANIZATION OF AMERICAN HISTORIANS, 1907
AMERICAN ACADEMY OF RELIGION, 1909
COLLEGE ART ASSOCIATION OF AMERICA, 1912
HISTORY OF SCIENCE SOCIETY, 1924
LINGUISTIC SOCIETY OF AMERICA, 1924
MEDIAEVAL ACADEMY OF AMERICA, 1925
AMERICAN MUSICOLOGICAL SOCIETY, 1934
SOCIETY OF ARCHITECTURAL HISTORIANS, 1940
ECONOMIC HISTORY ASSOCIATION, 1940
ASSOCIATION FOR ASIAN STUDIES, 1941
AMERICAN SOCIETY FOR AESTHETICS, 1942
AMERICAN ASSOCIATION FOR THE ADVANCEMENT OF SLAVIC STUDIES, 1948
METAPHYSICAL SOCIETY OF AMERICA, 1950
AMERICAN STUDIES ASSOCIATION, 1950
RENAISSANCE SOCIETY OF AMERICA, 1954
SOCIETY FOR ETHNOMUSICOLOGY, 1955
AMERICAN SOCIETY FOR LEGAL HISTORY, 1956
AMERICAN SOCIETY FOR THEATRE RESEARCH, 1956
SOCIETY FOR THE HISTORY OF TECHNOLOGY, 1958
AMERICAN COMPARATIVE LITERATURE ASSOCIATION, 1960
AMERICAN SOCIETY FOR EIGHTEENTH-CENTURY STUDIES, 1969
ASSOCIATION FOR JEWISH STUDIES, 1969

DICTIONARY
OF
American Biography

VOLUME VI
LARNED-MILLINGTON

Edited by

DUMAS MALONE

Charles Scribner's Sons *New York*

Prompted solely by a desire for public service the New York Times Company and its President, Mr. Adolph S. Ochs, have made possible the preparation of the manuscript of the Dictionary of American Biography through a subvention of more than $500,000 and with the understanding that the entire responsibility for the contents of the volumes rests with the American Council of Learned Societies.

ISBN 0-684-14143-4

Published simultaneously in Canada
by Collier Macmillan Canada, Inc.

13 15 17 19 B/C 20 18 16 14

Printed in the United States of America

The paper in this book meets the guidelines for
permanence and durability of the Committee on
Production Guidelines for Book Longevity of the
Council on Library Resources.

VOLUME VI, PART 1

LARNED - MacCRACKEN

(VOLUME XI OF THE ORIGINAL EDITION)

CROSS REFERENCES FROM THIS VOLUME ARE MADE TO THE VOLUME NUMBERS OF THE ORIGINAL EDITION.

CONTRIBUTORS
VOLUME VI, PART I

Kathryn T. Abbey . . . . . K. T. A.
Thomas P. Abernethy . . . . T. P. A.
Adeline Adams . . . . . . A. A.
James Truslow Adams . . . . J. T. A.
Randolph G. Adams . . . . . R. G. A—s.
Raymond Adams . . . . R. A.
Cyrus Adler . . . . C. A.
Robert Greenhalgh Albion . R. G. A—n.
Carroll S. Alden . . . . . . C. S. A.
Edmund Kimball Alden . . . E. K. A.
John Lincoln Alger . . . . . J. L. A.
Francis G. Allinson . . . . F. G. A.
William H. Allison . . . . . W. H. A.
Lewis Flint Anderson . . . . L. F. A.
John Clark Archer . . . . . J. C. Ar—r.
Percy M. Ashburn . . . . . P. M. A.
Frederick W. Ashley . . . . F. W. A.
Charles B. Atwell . . . . . C. B. A.
Joseph Cullen Ayer . . . . J. C. Ay—r.
John Bakeless . . . . J. B.
Hayes Baker-Crothers . . . H. B-C.
Thomas S. Barclay . . . . . T. S. B.
Gilbert H. Barnes . . . . . G. H. B.
Claribel R. Barnett . . . . C. R. B.
Anna Barrows . . . . A. B.
Harold K. Barrows . . . . . H. K. B.
Robert Duncan Bass . . . . R. D. B.
Ernest Sutherland Bates . . E. S. B.
William G. Bean . . . . . . W. G. B.
Percy W. Bidwell . . . . . P. W. B.
Bruce M. Bigelow . . . . . B. M. B.
Franklin C. Bing . . . . . F. C. B.
Edith R. Blanchard . . . . E. R. B.
Arthur R. Blessing . . . . . A. R. B.
Louise Pearson Blodget . . . L. P. B.
Lansing B. Bloom . . . . . . L. B. B.
Robert W. Bolwell . . . . . R. W. B.
Witt Bowden . . . . W. B—n.
Sarah G. Bowerman . . . . . S. G. B.
William K. Boyd . . . . . . W. K. B.
William Bridgwater . . . . W. B—r.
W. C. Bronson . . . . W. C. B.
Robert Preston Brooks . . . R. P. B.
Elmer Ellsworth Brown . . E. E. B.
Margaret Louise Brown . . M. L. B.
John S. Brubacher . . . . . J. S. B.
Paul H. Buck . . . . P. H. B.
Roberta B. Burnet . . . . . R. B. B.
Edmund C. Burnett . . . . . E. C. B.
Walter Lincoln Burrage . . W. L. B.
Huntington Cairns . . . . . H. Ca—s.
Isabel M. Calder . . . . . . I. M. C.
James M. Callahan . . . . J. M. C.
Killis Campbell . . . . . . K. C.
Charles F. Carey . . . . . . C. F. C.
Harry J. Carman . . . . . . H. J. C.
William S. Carpenter . . . . W. S. C.
Arthur E. Case . . . . A. E. C.
Zechariah Chafee, Jr. . . . . Z. C., Jr.
Will Grant Chambers . . . . W. G. C.
Francis A. Christie . . . . . F. A. C.
George H. Clark . . . . . . G. H. C.
R. C. Clark . . . . R. C. C.
Harry Clemons . . . . H. Cl—s.
Oral Sumner Coad . . . . . O. S. C.
Frederick W. Coburn . . . . F. W. C.
William E. Colby . . . . . . W. E. C.
Fannie L. Gwinner Cole . F. L. G. C.
Rossetter Gleason Cole . . R. G. C—e.
Christopher B. Coleman . . C. B. C.
R. V. Coleman . . . . R. V. C.
Theodore Collier . . . . . . T. C.
John R. Commons . . . . . . J. R. C.
Robert Spencer Cotterill . R. S. C.
Walter J. Couper . . . . . . W. J. C.
Jesse H. Coursault . . . . . J. H. C.
Theodore S. Cox . . . . . . T. S. C.
Katharine Elizabeth Crane . K. E. C.
Merle E. Curti . . . . M. E. C.
Edward E. Curtis . . . . . . E. E. C.
Robert E. Cushman . . . . . R. E. C.
Charles William Dabney . . C. W. D.
Frank Burnett Dains . . . . F. B. D.
Edward E. Dale . . . . E. E. D.
Harrison C. Dale . . . . . . H. C. D.
Ralph Davol . . . . R. D.
D. Bryson Delavan . . . . . D. B. D.
William H. S. Demarest . . . W. H. S. D.
Herman J. Deutsch . . . . . H. J. D.
Irving Dilliard . . . . I. D.
A. Imrie Dixon . . . . A. I. D.
Dorothy Anne Dondore . . . D. A. D.
Elizabeth Donnan . . . . . E. D.
William Howe Downes . . . W. H. D.
Stella M. Drumm . . . . . . S. M. D.
Edward A. Duddy . . . . . . E. A. D.
Raymond S. Dugan. . . . . . R. S. D.
Walter Prichard Eaton . . . W. P. E.

Contributors

H. J. Eckenrode . . . . . . H. J. E.
George H. Edgell . . . . . G. H. E—l.
Edwin Francis Edgett . . . E. F. E.
J. A. Estes . . . . J. A. E.
Paul D. Evans . . . . P. D. E.
George Henry Ewing . . . . G. H. E—g.
Charles Fairman . . . . . . C. F.
Paul Patton Faris. . . . . . P. P. F.
Hallie Farmer . . . . H. F.
Harold U. Faulkner. . . . . H. U. F.
Albert B. Faust . . . . . . A. B. F.
Mary Elizabeth Fittro . . . M. E. F.
Blanton Fortson . . . . . . B. F.
Louis H. Fox . . . . L. H. F.
L. Webster Fox . . . . L. W. F.
John H. Frederick. . . . . . J. H. F.
Douglas S. Freeman . . . . D. S. F.
John C. French . . . . J. C. F.
Robert D. French . . . . . R. D. F.
William L. Frierson . . . . W. L. F.
John F. Fulton . . . . J. F. F.
Elmer H. Funk . . . . E. H. F.
Ralph H. Gabriel . . . . . . R. H. G.
Samuel W. Geiser . . . . . . S. W. G.
George Harvey Genzmer . . G. H. G.
Margaret Wadsworth Genzmer . . . . M. W. G.
W. J. Ghent . . . . W. J. G.
Harley L. Gibb . . . . H. L. G.
Blake-More Godwin . . . . B–M. G.
Robert W. Goodloe . . . . . R. W. G.
Armistead Churchill Gordon, Jr. . . . . A. C. G., Jr.
Kenneth M. Gould . . . . . K. M. G.
Gladys Graham . . . . G. G.
Walter Granger . . . . . . W. G.
A. W. Greely . . . . A. W. G.
Ferris Greenslet . . . . . . F. G.
Anne King Gregorie. . . . . A. K. G.
Charles Burton Gulick . . . C. B. G.
Sidney Gunn . . . . S. G.
William James Hail . . . . . W. J. H.
Edward E. Hale . . . . . . E. E. H.
J. Evetts Haley . . . . . . J. E. H.
Edwin H. Hall . . . . E. H. H.
J. G. deR Hamilton . . . . . J. G. deR. H.
Talbot Faulkner Hamlin . . T. F. H.
Alvin F Harlow . . . . . . A. F. H.
Freeman H. Hart . . . . . . F. H. H.
Mary Bronson Hartt . . . . M. B. H.
Doremus A. Hayes . . . . . D. A. H.
Robert C. Hayes . . . . . . R. C. H.
Fred E. Haynes . . . . F. E. H.
Marshall DeLancey Haywood M. DeL. H.
John Grier Hibben . . . . . J. G. H.
Edward M. Hinton . . . . . E. M. H.
Arthur H. Hirsch . . . . . . A. H. H.
M. M. Hoffman . . . . M. M. H.
Arthur N. Holcombe . . . . A. N. H.
Raymond Holden . . . . R. H.
John Haynes Holmes . . . . J. H. H.
Oliver W. Holmes . . . . . . O. W. H.
Henry D. Hooker . . . . . . H. D. H.
Stephen Henry Horgan . . . S. H. H.
Leland Ossian Howard . . . L. O. H.
M. A. DeWolfe Howe . . . . M. A. DeW. H.
William T. Hutchinson . . . W. T. H.
Albert Hyma . . . . A. H.
Augustus E. Ingram . . . . . A. E. I.
Asher Isaacs . . . . A. I.
Theodore H. Jack . . . . . . T. H. J.
George Stuyvesant Jackson . G. S. J.
Joseph Jackson . . . . J. J.
Willis L. Jepson . . . . . . W. L. J.
Cecil Johnson . . . . C. J.
David Starr Jordan . . . . . D. S. J.
Louis C. Karpinski . . . . . L. C. K.
Paul Kaufman . . . . P. K.
Herbert Anthony Kellar . . H. A. K.
Louise Phelps Kellogg . . . L. P. K.
W. W. Kemp . . . . W. W. K.
Fiske Kimball . . . . F. K.
Gustav A. Kleene . . . . . . G. A. K.
Grant C. Knight . . . . . . G. C. K.
Edwin W. Kopf . . . . E. W. K.
John A. Krout . . . . J. A. K.
Wilmer Krusen . . . . W. K.
Leonard W. Labaree . . . . L. W. L.
William Palmer Ladd . . . . W. P. L.
Fred Landon . . . . F. L.
Barnes F. Lathrop . . . . . B. F. L.
Kenneth S. Latourette . . . K. S. L.
Algernon Lee . . . . A. L.
William Ellery Leonard . . W. E. L.
Anna Lane Lingelbach . . . A. L. L.
Ella Lonn . . . . E. L.
John Livingston Lowes . . . J. L. L.
Robert Luce . . . . R. L.
Harry Miller Lydenberg . . H. M. L.
Alexander McAdie . . . . . A. M.
N. E. McClure . . . . N. E. M.
Thomas McCrae . . . . . . T. M.
Arthur S. McDaniel . . . . A. S. M.
Reginald C. McGrane . . . . R. C. M.
Warren B. Mack . . . . . . W. B. M—k
Oliver McKee, Jr. . . . . . O. M., Jr.
Donald L. McMurry . . . . D. L. M.
William Francis Magie . . . W. F. M.
Bruce E. Mahan . . . . . . B. E. M.
James C. Malin . . . . J. C. M.
W. C. Mallalieu . . . . . . W. C. M.
Robert S. Mann . . . . . . R. S. M.
H. A. Marmer . . . . H. A. M—r.
William B. Marshall . . . . W. B. M—l
Lawrence S. Mayo . . . . . L. S. M.
Robert Douthat Meade . . . R. D. M.

Contributors

Donald H. Menzel	D. H. M.	Lowell Joseph Ragatz	L. J. R.
Robert L. Meriwether	R. L. M—r.	Charles W. Ramsdell	C. W. R.
George P. Merrill	G. P. M.	James G. Randall	J. G. R.
Frank J. Metcalf	F. J. M.	Belle Rankin	B. R.
Carl W. Mitman	C. W. M.	Albert G. Rau	A. G. R.
Conrad Henry Moehlman	C. H. M.	P. O. Ray	P. O. R.
E. V. Moffett	E. V. M.	John Henry Reynolds	J. H. R.
Frank Monaghan	F. M.	Charles Dudley Rhodes	C. D. R.
Robert E. Moody	R. E. M.	George L. Richardson	G. L. R.
Ross H. Moore	R. H. M.	Irving B. Richman	I. B. R.
Herbert M. Morais	H. M. M.	David A. Robertson	D. A. R.
Hugh A. Moran	H. A. M—n.	Doane Robinson	D. R.
Samuel Eliot Morison	S. E. M.	Edgar E. Robinson	E. E. R.
Richard B. Morris	R. B. M.	William A. Robinson	W. A. R.
Jarvis M. Morse	J. M. M.	Carl B. Roden	C. B. R.
Richard L. Morton	R. L. M—n.	J. Magnus Rohne	J. M. R.
Dana C. Munro	D. C. M.	Virginia Ronsaville	V. R.
William B. Munro	W. B. M—o.	Marvin B. Rosenberry	M. B. R.
H. Edward Nettles	H. E. N.	Frank Edward Ross	F. E. R.
Allan Nevins	A. N.	Herbert W. Schneider	H. W. S—r.
Lyman C. Newell	L. C. N.	Montgomery Schuyler	M. S.
A. R. Newsome	A. R. N.	Horace Wells Sellers	H. W. S—s.
Robert Hastings Nichols	R. H. N.	Thorsten Sellin	T. S.
Roy F. Nichols	R. F. N.	Edwin B. Shaw	E. B. S.
Walter B. Norris	W. B. N.	William Bristol Shaw	W. B. S.
William Notz	W. N.	Augustus H. Shearer	A. H. S.
Frank M. O'Brien	F. M. O.	Jay J. Sherman	J. J. S.
Robert B. Osgood	R. B. O.	Fred W. Shipman	F. W. S.
Winthrop J. V. Osterhout	W. J. V. O.	Lester B. Shippee	L. B. S.
Victor H. Paltsits	V. H. P.	George N. Shuster	G. N. S.
Henry K. Pancoast	H. K. P.	Wilbur H. Siebert	W. H. S.
John I. Parcel	J. I. P.	David Eugene Smith	D. E. S.
George W. Paré	G. W. P.	Edgar Fahs Smith	E. F. S.
J. Parmly Paret	J. P. P.	Fred M. Smith	F. M. S.
Stanley M. Pargellis	S. M. P.	Marion Parris Smith	M. P. S.
John C. Parish	J. C. P.	William Roy Smith	W. R. S.
Frances Fenton Park	F. F. P.	George Franklin Smythe	G. F. S.
Charles O. Paullin	C. O. P.	E. Wilder Spaulding	E. W. S.
Frederic Logan Paxson	F. L. P.	Oliver L. Spaulding, Jr.	O. L. S., Jr.
Charles E. Payne	C. E. P.	Thomas M. Spaulding	T. M. S.
Haywood J. Pearce, Jr.	H. J. P., Jr.	Charles Worthen Spencer	C. W. S.
C. C. Pearson	C. C. P.	Harris Elwood Starr	H. E. S.
Morton E. Peck	M. E. P.	George M. Stephenson	G. M. S.
James H. Peeling	J. H. P.	George Stewart	G. S.
Frederick T. Persons	F. T. P.	Witmer Stone	W. S.
A. Everett Peterson	A. E. P.	Tracy E. Strevey	T. E. S.
James M. Phalen	J. M. P—n.	James Sullivan	J. S.
Francis S. Philbrick	F. S. P.	William U. Swan	W. U. S.
David Philipson	D. P.	William W. Sweet	W. W. S.
David deSola Pool	D. deS. P.	Charles S. Sydnor	C. S. S.
John M. Poor	J. M. P—r.	Frank A. Taylor	F. A. T.
Charles Shirley Potts	C. S. P.	William A. Taylor	W. A. T.
Anne S. Pratt	A. S. P.	Marten ten Hoor	M. ten H.
Julius W. Pratt	J. W. P.	Edward Larocque Tinker	E. L. T.
Edward Preble	E. P.	Payson J. Treat	P. J. T.
Herbert I. Priestley	H. I. P.	Robert B. Tunstall	R. B. T.
Leon C. Prince	L. C. P.	William T. Utter	W. T. U.
Richard J. Purcell	R. J. P.	John G. Van Deusen	J. G. V-D.

Contributors

H. M. Varrell	H. M. V.
Henry R. Viets	H. R. V.
Oswald Garrison Villard	O. G. V.
John Martin Vincent	J. M. V.
Eugene M. Violette	E. M. V.
John D. Wade	J. D. W.
James Elliott Walmsley	J. E. W.
Louis B. Wehle	L. B. W.
Frank Weitenkampf	F. W.
Allan Westcott	A. W.
Edward M. Weyer	E. M. W.
George F. Whicher	G. F. W.
Thomas K. Whipple	T. K. W.
Melvin J. White	M. J. W.
Harry Emerson Wildes	H. E. W.
James F. Willard	J. F. W.
Clarence Russell Williams	C. R. W.
William F. Willoughby	W. F. W.
Helen Sumner Woodbury	H. S. W.
Maude H. Woodfin	M. H. W.
Mary E. Woolley	M. E. W.
Herbert F. Wright	H. F. W.
Lawrence C. Wroth	L. C. W.
John C. Wyllie	J. C. W.
Donovan Yeuell	D. Y.
Kimball Young	K. Y.

DICTIONARY OF

AMERICAN BIOGRAPHY

Larned — MacCracken

LARNED, JOSEPH GAY EATON (Apr. 29, 1819–June 3, 1870), lawyer, inventor, industrialist, was born at Thompson, Conn., the son of George and Anna Spalding (Gay) Larned, and a descendant of William and Goodith Learned who were in Charlestown, Mass., in 1632. His early education was received in the local public and preparatory schools, and he graduated from Yale College with the class of 1839, receiving the degree of B.A. He then taught the classics at Chatham Academy, Savannah, Ga., for a year, and in the fall of 1840 became a private teacher in Charleston, S. C. Early in 1841 he returned to his home and began studying law, but the following year he took charge of an academy at Waterloo, N. Y., and in November 1842 was called to a tutorship in Yale College. He continued in this capacity for some five years. In 1846 he initiated a project for raising money by subscription to purchase for the Yale law school the library of Judge Hitchcock of New Haven, then recently deceased; and during his vacations he devoted himself to this undertaking. Becoming interested in public affairs he assisted in the organization of the Free-Soil party of New Haven and published several articles in the *New Englander* (July, October 1845, April 1846) upon "Massachusetts and South Carolina." Late in 1847 he was admitted to the bar in New Haven and began the practice of law. His professional interest was gradually directed toward patent law, and thence to the financial support and development of certain inventions which came to his attention. In consequence, he withdrew from the practice of his profession about 1852, and in 1854 removed to New York City. There he soon became acquainted with Wellington Lee, who was engaged in the perfection of a steam fire engine, and in 1855 they formed a partnership to manufacture steam fire engines at the Novelty Iron Works, New York. Fire engines were then looked upon as novelties merely, and to introduce them into New York City for practical use was a difficult task. Beginning in April 1856, when one of their first engines was demonstrated in City Hall Park, Lee and Larned exhibited one after another of their successively improved engines and through their perseverance were at last rewarded by having their products put into service, not only in New York but also in several other cities in the United States and Europe. In November 1858 they first demonstrated their self-propelled steam fire engine, which weighed 5½ tons, raised steam to a working pressure of 150 pounds in from six to ten minutes, and was capable of discharging over 700 gallons of water per minute through a 1⅝-inch nozzle to a horizontal distance of 267 feet and a vertical height of nearly 200 feet. The machine incorporated the rotary pump invented by J. C. Cary, driven by a reciprocating steam engine, and Lee's and Larned's patented annular boiler. For an improvement in the boiler, Larned received patent No. 23,093, on Mar. 1, 1859. The boiler then consisted of rows of upright water tubes set side by side and connected to a steam dome above the fire and to a water bottom below in such a way as to form a water-jacketed fire-box. By 1860 Lee and Larned were manufacturing and selling steam fire engines of several different sizes, the smallest being designed for hand drawing and for use in small villages and towns. One of these, however, was on duty at the Valley Forge Hose Company stationed in Thirty-seventh Street, New York. It weighed about 3,700 pounds, and was a four-wheeled affair, about ten feet long, with the vertical boiler between the rear wheels. In 1863 Lee and Larned went out of business because their enterprise ceased to be profitable. Larned thereupon became assistant inspector of ironclads for the Navy Department and had charge of work in progress at Green Point, Brooklyn, N. Y. At the close of the Civil War he returned to the practice of law in New York City. During his leisure he began to collect and compile genealogical records of his ancestors, and in 1865 he published *A Quarter-Century Record of the Class of 1839, Yale College* (1865). He was married May 9, 1859, to Helen Lee, a sister of his business partner. She survived him at the time of his sudden death in New York City.

[*Obit. Record Grads. Yale Coll.*, 1870; W. L. Learned, *The Learned Family* (1882; 2nd ed., 1898); *Scientific American*, Apr. 5, 1856, Nov. 27, 1858, Apr. 7, 1860; *Sen. Ex. Doc. No. 12*, 36 Cong., 1 Sess.; Patent Office records; *New-Eng. Hist. and Geneal. Reg.*, Oct. 1874; *N. Y. Times*, June 4, 1870.] C. W. M.

LARNED, JOSEPHUS NELSON (May 11, 1836–Aug. 15, 1913), librarian, author, a descendant of William Learned who came to Massachusetts about 1632, was the son of Henry Sherwood and Mary Ann (Nelson) Larned. He was born in Chatham, Ont., while his parents, both citizens of the United States, were temporarily residents of Canada. During his boyhood they moved to Buffalo, where he attended public school until he was about seventeen. He was well schooled, but his further education was gained largely through his own efforts. He always regretted his lack of college training, but he appeared to his contemporaries as better informed than many college men. He became first a bookkeeper, then a clerk, and in the fall of 1857 was given a position on the Buffalo *Republic*. In 1859 he joined the editorial staff of the *Buffalo Express*, with which he remained until 1872, writing able editorials in behalf of the Union cause during the Civil War. In the office of the *Express* he was associated for about a year with Mark Twain. Larned had a financial interest in the paper from 1866 to 1877.

In the fall of 1871 Larned was elected superintendent of education, and for five years directed his efforts, unsuccessfully, toward removing the schools from politics. In 1877 he was appointed superintendent of the Buffalo Young Men's Association with the understanding that he would reorganize the library, thereafter known as the Buffalo Library. Finding the books not classified, he investigated different systems, and finally adopted Melvil Dewey's decimal classification. The Buffalo Library was the first to be completely classified under that system, since so widely adopted. Larned planned and established a children's room, one of the first in the country. He issued free tickets to children in the schools, started a school room in the library, and established an open-shelf room. In 1886 he moved the library into a new building which it occupied jointly with other cultural organizations. He was one of the early members of the American Library Association and its president in 1893–94. After he had directed the Buffalo Library for twenty years it was taken over by the city, in 1897, as a public circulating library. Although this step was directly in line with Larned's policy, he was not in sympathy with the new board and felt compelled to resign.

Thenceforth he devoted himself to literary and civic affairs. He will perhaps be longest remembered for his *History for Ready Reference* (5 vols., 1894–95; supplements in 1901 and 1910), an alphabetical arrangement, by historical subjects, of extracts from the writings of "the best historians, biographers, and specialists." His *Primer of Right and Wrong, for Young People* appeared in 1902; his *Seventy Centuries of the Life of Mankind* (1905), was later republished as *Larned's History of the World* (1915). His *History of England* (for schools) appeared in 1900, *A History of the United States for Secondary Schools*, in 1903, and *A History of Buffalo* (2 vols.), in 1911. He edited *The Literature of American History: A Bibliographical Guide*, in 1902, for the American Library Association, and published a number of other books and papers. Larned was active in the Civil Service Reform Association, the Municipal League, the School Association, and the Buffalo Peace and Arbitration Society. He was a member of the Liberal Club, an honorary member of the Saturn Club (1897), and a member of the Thursday Club (1899). On Apr. 29, 1861, he married Frances Anne Kemble McCrea, daughter of Walter McCrea, judge of the Algoma district in Ontario. He died in 1913, survived by his wife and their three children, and was buried in Forest Lawn, Buffalo.

[*Buffalo Express*, Aug. 16, 1913; sketch by J. B. Olmsted in *Buffalo Hist. Soc. Pubs.*, XIX (1915), 3–33; bibliography of Larned's publications, *Ibid.*, 133–36; W. L. Learned, *The Learned Family* (1898); book of clippings at the Buffalo Public Library, covering the period of his connection with the library and after; interviews with associates at Buffalo Public Library and in Young Men's Association, and with members of his family.] A. H. S.

LARNED, WILLIAM AUGUSTUS (Dec. 30, 1872–Dec. 16, 1926), lawn tennis player, seven times national champion, was born in Summit, N. J., and lived most of his life in that state and in New York. He was the son of William Zebedee and Katharine (Penniman) Larned, and a descendant of William Learned who emigrated to Massachusetts before 1632. He studied at Cornell University but did not graduate. During the Spanish-American War he was a private in Troop A of Roosevelt's "Rough Riders," and took part in the battle of San Juan Hill. For several years thereafter he suffered from the effects of West Indian fever. Soon after the United States entered the World War, having earlier learned to pilot an airplane, he was commissioned captain in the aviation section of the Signal Corps, and stationed in Washington as head of an examining board for officers in the air service. In October 1917 he sailed for France and later went to England where he was first assistant, and then aviation officer, Base Section, No. 3. He left the service in June 1919 with the rank of lieutenant-colonel.

Although he excelled at many sports, prominent among them being golf and ice-hockey, his greatest interest always centered in lawn tennis. His first big success was the winning of the intercollegiate championship in October 1892, when he represented Cornell; and during the next twenty years until his retirement in 1912 he won scores of championship titles in various sections of the country. He was officially ranked among the first ten players of the United States nineteen times within those twenty years, the only missing season being that of 1898 when he was in Cuba. During that period he was rated No. 1, eight years; No. 2 five years; No. 3 four years; No. 5 one year and No. 6 one year. In the international matches for the Davis Cup, he represented the United States on six different occasions, winning nine matches and losing five. For the famous Longwood Bowl at Boston he played seventeen years, winning twelve times. He perhaps surpassed all the other American lawn tennis players in mastery of ground-strokes, and it was his ability in this aspect of the game that gave him his fame. No player has excelled him in the ease and facility with which he executed them, particularly those on the backhand side, generally a weak point in other players; and none showed a wider range or more brilliant placing ability. In attack, he was supreme and at times invincible, but in defense his skill did not equal that of some others of his time, particularly R. D. Wrenn and the famous Doherty brothers of England. Allowed to play the game in his own way, he swept everything before him, but opposed by a perfect defense or the strategic tactics of the best court generals, he was beaten sometimes by men ranked officially below him. Furthermore, he never fully conquered an erratic tendency to be upset by small annoyances, which would throw him off his game at times.

Larned's health was poor during the last part of his life. He suffered a nervous breakdown two years before his death, and later an attack of spinal meningitis, which compelled him to depend upon a cane. He chafed under the consequent limitation to his activities, and in a period of despondency shot himself with an army revolver at the Knickerbocker Club, New York, some time between 11 P.M., Dec. 15, and 10 A.M., Dec. 16, 1926. He was the inventor of the steel-framed racket that came into wide use. A bronze tablet dedicated to his memory has been placed in the concrete wall of the stadium of the West Side Tennis Club at Forest Hills, N. Y., where many of the Davis Cup matches have been played. He never married.

[W. L. Learned, *The Learned Family* (1898); *War Records of the Knickerbocker Club 1914–1918* (1922); *Am. Lawn Tennis*, Jan. 15, 1927; S. W. Merrihew, *The Quest of the Davis Cup* (1928); *Spalding's Official Lawn Tennis Annual* and its predecessors, 1892–1912; *Literary Digest*, Jan. 15, 1927; *N. Y. Times*, Dec. 17, 20, 1926.]

J. P. P.

LAROCHE, RENÉ (Sept. 23, 1795–Dec. 9, 1872), physician, was born in Philadelphia, the only son of René and Marie Jeanne (de la Condemine) LaRoche. His father, a graduate of the ancient school of medicine at Montpellier in France, had practised his profession in Santo Domingo before coming to Philadelphia. During his teens young LaRoche served in the War of 1812 as a captain of volunteers in Colonel Biddle's regiment. At twenty-two he entered the University of Pennsylvania, from which he was graduated with the degree of M.D. in 1820. For a short period after graduation he was a teacher in the summer school of medicine. In 1824 he was married to Mary Jane Ellis, daughter of Col. John Ellis.

LaRoche's principal contribution to medicine was in the field of medical literature. It was stated in the *Transactions of the American Medical Association*, shortly after his death, that there was scarcely a medical journal in the land which had not, at some time or other, published contributions from his pen (*Transactions*, 1873, p. 380), and an eminent contemporary, Dr. Samuel D. Gross [*q.v.*], called him "one of the most erudite medical writers which our country has produced," adding: "Simplicity and directness were among his chief excellencies" (*Autobiography*, II, 376). His best-known work, *Yellow Fever, Considered in Its Historical, Pathological, Etiological, and Therapeutical Relations* (2 vols., 1855), is a medical classic. His library on yellow fever embraced the literature of many countries and constituted an invaluable collection. When it was sold at auction, after his death, a portion was secured by the College of Physicians of Philadelphia.

He was active in professional organizations, notably in the College of Physicians, the Pathological Society of Philadelphia (of which he was an original member and at one time president), and state and county medical societies. He was one of the editors of the *North American Medical and Surgical Journal* which flourished in Philadelphia from 1826 until 1831.

LaRoche was greatly interested in music and collected a large and valuable music library, much of which ultimately passed into the hands of J. W. Drexel [*q.v.*]. Haydn's Third Mass was sung with orchestral accompaniment for the first time in Philadelphia at St. Joseph's Church, under his direction as choir-master. Gross, who knew him intimately, said: "He never seemed so happy as when he was in his library up to his elbow in his manuscripts. . . . He was a charming conversationalist, always instructive and free from affectation and pedantry" (*Ibid.*, II, 375–76). He was of frail build, and yet could endure much physical exertion.

[*Trans. Am. Medic. Asso.*, 1873; S. D. Gross, *Hist. of Am. Medic. Lit. from 1776 to the Present Time* (1876); *Autobiog. of Samuel D. Gross with Sketches of his Contemporaries* (1887), II, 374–77; *Records Am. Cath. Hist. Soc. of Phila.*, vols. III (1891), XXIX (1918); *The Biog. Encyc. of Pa.* (1874); *Pub. Ledger* (Phila.), Dec. 11, 1872.] E. H. F.

LA RONDE, LOUIS DENIS, Sieur de (1675–March 1741), French naval officer and American prospector, was Canadian-born, son of Pierre Denis de la Ronde and Catherine Le Neuf of Quebec. At the early age of thirteen he entered the French navy and served therein for forty years as midshipman, lieutenant, and later as captain of a naval vessel. In 1689 he was a subordinate officer on the ship that carried James II to Ireland in his futile effort to regain his crown and took part in two naval contests off the Irish coast. In 1692 La Ronde cruised along the New England coast, and three years later he was captured in a sea fight and spent a year in an Irish prison. In 1697 he was with his fellow countryman Iberville [*q.v.*] on his desperate adventure in Hudson Bay and in 1700–01 accompanied his chief to Louisiana where he explored the Mississippi. In Queen Anne's War he took part in several naval battles, was wounded and shipwrecked. In 1711 he was sent on a secret mission to Boston. Twelve years later he again visited Boston as an envoy and spent the winter there. Parkman states that he spoke English and made himself agreeable to the British colonists. For this service he received the cross of the order of St. Louis.

In 1727 La Ronde, then captain in the Canadian army, was sent to command a post in Lake Superior on an island now called Madeline, in Chequamegon Bay. There he learned of the existence of copper mines in the vicinity and made proposals to the government to work them. It was 1733 before permission came from France and the next year La Ronde built at Sault Ste. Marie a sailing vessel of twenty-five tons, coasted along the lake shore, and sent samples of ore to Quebec. In 1736 he went thither in person to see his ore assayed and persuaded the government to send him from Europe two competent miners, who in 1739 made a favorable report of the prospects. Meanwhile at Fort La Pointe, Madeline Island, La Ronde and his sons had built a substantial log enclosure, had imported cattle and horses, and had made the beginning of a settlement. All their plans were brought to naught by an Indian war which broke out in 1740. La Ronde went to Quebec and there died. His widow, Marie Louise Chartier La Ronde, whom he had married on July 20, 1709, was granted the monopoly of Fort La Pointe and in 1744 leased it to a firm of fur-traders. La Ronde's life, full of adventure and incident, speaks of his energy and ability. At the time of his death he was senior captain in Canada and had been in the King's service over fifty years.

[See *Wis. Hist. Colls.*, XVII (1906), 299–306, 309–12; E. D. Neill, "Sieur de la Ronde, the First Navigator of Lake Superior in a Sailing Vessel, and the Pioneer in Copper Mining," *Macalester Coll. Contributions*, 1 ser. (1890), pp. 183–98; Cyprien Tanguay, *Dict. Généal. des Familles Canadiennes*, vol. I (1871). See also L. P. Kellogg, *French Régime in Wis. and the Northwest* (Madison, 1925), pp. 351–57, where it is erroneously stated that La Ronde was a native of France.]
L. P. K.

LARPENTEUR, CHARLES (May 8, 1807–Nov. 15, 1872), fur-trader, author, was born near Fontainebleau, France. The earlier birthdate assumed in the inscription on his tombstone is apparently incorrect as to the year but probably correct as to the month and day. The father was a Bonapartist who fled to America and in 1818 settled with his family on a farm near Baltimore. Young Larpenteur, who seems to have been reared as a farmer's boy, probably had little schooling. At the age of twenty-one he left for the West. After working for several years in St. Louis and making a journey up the Mississippi, he engaged as a clerk with Sublette and Campbell for the Rocky Mountain Fur Company's expedition of the spring of 1833. From the Green River rendezvous, which was reached in July, he accompanied Campbell to the vicinity of the

American Fur Company's post, Fort Union, at the mouth of the Yellowstone, where Sublette and Campbell for a year attempted to maintain an opposition. On the failure of the attempt Larpenteur engaged with the dominant company. As clerk, trader, fort-builder, chief factor, sutler, and for a brief time as farmer, he spent the remainder of his life, except for occasional journeys to the settlements, on the upper and middle Missouri, and no man of his time and place had a wider range of adventurous experiences. He married an Assiniboine woman, and after her death in 1837 he married another, by whom he had several children. In 1851 he bought a land claim on the Little Sioux, in the present Harrison County, Iowa, where he developed a farm which he named "Fontainebleau." For the following twenty years, however, he lived there only at intervals; his residence shifted from post to post in the Indian country. In the winter of 1853–54 his second wife was murdered by a roving band of Omahas. On Apr. 12, 1855, he married Rebecca (White) Bingham, a white woman, who survived him by more than twenty-five years. In May 1871, ousted from a good business as a sutler at Fort Buford by the Federal law prohibiting more than one sutler at a post, he gave up the Indian country and returned to his farm. At Fort Union, in 1834, he had started a journal, which except for occasional lapses he kept until the last year of his life. On his retirement he wrote an autobiography, sending it, five months before his death, to Washington Matthews. Twenty-five years later Matthews sent it to Elliott Coues, by whom it was edited and published.

Larpenteur died at a neighbor's house, several miles from his farm. He is described as a small, spare, wiry man of distinct Gallic type, intelligent, informed, and vivacious and witty in conversation. Though in the main kindly and amiable, he was not above harboring resentments, and he writes disparagingly of many of his associates. His life was crowded with disasters, and he believed himself born under a baleful star. His autobiography, with its many inaccuracies corrected by Coues from the entries in the journal, is probably the most valuable contemporary document extant upon the fur trade of the Missouri.

[*Forty Years a Fur Trader on the Upper Mo.: The Personal Narrative of Chas. Larpenteur, 1833–72* (2 vols., 1898), ed. by Elliott Coues; A. L. Larpenteur, "Recollections of the City and People of St. Paul, 1843–98," *Colls. Minn. Hist. Soc.*, vol. IX (1901); *Annals of Iowa*, July 1902, July 1908.] W. J. G.

LARRABEE, CHARLES HATHAWAY (Nov. 9, 1820–Jan. 20, 1883), lawyer, soldier, judge, son of Maj. Charles Larrabee of the regular army and Elizabeth (Hathaway) Larrabee, was born at Rome, Oneida County, N. Y. His father was probably of Huguenot stock; his mother was descended from John Haynes [*q.v.*], colonial governor of Massachusetts and later of Connecticut, while Judge Joshua Hathaway, her father, at sixteen, was one of six brothers, who, with their father, carried muskets at Bennington under Gen. John Stark. Charles attended Springfield Academy and Granville College, now Denison University, Ohio, then read law in the offices of Samson Mason and W. A. Rogers in Springfield, Ohio. In 1841 he went to Pontotoc, Miss., as a civil engineer. Here he made an unsuccessful attempt at farming but was admitted to the bar. Finding the climate of Mississippi harmful to him, he removed to Chicago in July 1844, entered upon the practice of his profession, and was elected city attorney. On May 13, 1846, he was married to Minerva Norton and in March 1847, they settled at Horicon, Wis. Here Larrabee erected mills and developed a fine water power.

He was chosen in October 1847, by an overwhelming majority, one of three members to represent Dodge County in the second constitutional convention of the territory of Wisconsin. He was a strong and ardent advocate of provisions against a state debt and for a homestead exemption, both of which were embodied in the constitution. In 1848 he was chosen circuit judge of the third circuit, made up of six large counties. As a circuit judge he became, upon the adoption of the constitution, *ex officio* a member of the supreme court and served in that capacity until the separate organization of the supreme court five years later. He was a strong supporter of Stephen A. Douglas and at the latter's solicitation resigned from the bench to become a successful candidate for Congress at the fall election in 1858, overcoming a strong Republican majority in his district. He went down with Douglas, however, when in 1860 he was a candidate for reëlection. He rendered creditable service in Congress and at the close of his term offered his services in April 1861 to Gov. A. W. Randall and Gen. Rufus King. He was commissioned a major of the 5th Wisconsin Infantry May 28, 1861, and with his regiment saw much hard service in the Army of the Potomac. He proved himself to be an excellent officer but his friends felt that his chances of promotion were diminished because of his former political affiliations. On July 25, 1862, by appointment of Governor Salomon, Larrabee became colonel of the 24th Wisconsin Infantry.

As a commanding officer he rendered distinguished service but he fell a victim to a disease contracted in the swamps of the Chickahominy and on Aug. 27, 1863, he retired from the service. After leaving the army, in the hope of regaining his health, he settled in California. He lived also for a short time at Seattle and here, almost exactly thirty years after he had served as a member of the Wisconsin Constitutional Convention, he became a member of a convention to frame a constitution for Washington Territory. This constitution was, however, rejected. Subsequently he settled at San Bernardino, in Southern California, where he resumed the practice of his profession. While on his way from San Francisco to Los Angeles on Jan. 20, 1883, he was killed in a railway accident. The distinguished services which he rendered in so many fields did not win adequate recognition because of his rather nomadic life. In a letter which he wrote two or three years before his death he said: "Being born in the army, I never had a particle of State pride. All States seem to me like so many Counties. Nor have I love of locality. Cities I hate. I am happiest in building up new homes, introducing new fruits, and other light productions of the soil" (Draper, *post,* p. 388).

[Lyman C. Draper's sketch of Larrabee in *Wis. Hist. Colls.*, vol. IX (1882), is the most complete and accurate history of his life. See also: H. A. Tenney and David Atwood, *Memorial Record of the Fathers of Wis.* (1880); P. M. Reed, *The Bench and Bar of Wis.* (1882); J. R. Berryman, *Hist. of the Bench and Bar of Wis.* (2 vols., 1898); *Biog. Dir. Am. Cong.* (1928); "Biographical Sketches of the Judges of the First Supreme Court of the State of Wisconsin," 3 *Pinney's Wis. Reports,* 617; G. T. Ridlon, *Saco Valley Settlements and Families* (1895); *Daily Examiner* (San Francisco), Jan. 21, 22, 1883.] M. B. R.

LARRABEE, WILLIAM (Jan. 20, 1832–Nov. 16, 1912), twelfth governor of Iowa, son of Capt. Adam and Hannah Gallup (Lester) Larrabee, was born at Ledyard, Conn. He was descended from Greenfield Larrabee who was in New London, Conn., in 1637. His father graduated from West Point in 1811 and served in the War of 1812. The family lived on a farm and William Larrabee received a common-school education. In 1853 he moved to Iowa, taught school for a time, and was foreman on a farm for a few years. In 1857 he bought a flour mill in the town of Clermont, in Fayette County, and remained in that business until 1874, when he sold out and went to Europe for three months. Afterward he engaged in banking and farming and became one of the largest landowners in the state. He married, on Sept. 12, 1861, Anna M. Appleton, whose family had emigrated from Connecticut to Iowa in 1854 and had settled on a farm near Clermont. During the Civil War Larrabee raised a company of soldiers, but he was not accepted for service because he had lost the sight of one eye in his youth. In 1868 he was elected to the state Senate and remained a member until he resigned to accept the nomination for governor in 1885. He was four times reëlected to the Senate without opposition in a district which sent Democrats after his retirement. During most of the time of his service in the Senate, he was chairman of the committee on ways and means.

He was elected governor by a vote of 175,504 against 168,525 for his Democratic and fusion opponent, and he was reëlected two years later by a vote of 169,595 to 153,706. These were the years when the third-party movements were reducing the Republican vote and increasing the Democratic support. The railroad question had been an active issue for a number of years. Larrabee's experience with the building of the Chicago, Milwaukee & St. Paul across the northern part of the state from 1857 to 1878 had called his attention to the need of railroad legislation. His election to the Senate was due to the long delay in railroad construction in his portion of the state. In his second inaugural address in 1888, he declared that he believ d transportation charges were far too high and that they bore little relation to the cost of the service. He recommended that the railroad commission "should be authorized and required to exercise full and complete supervision over the railroads, compelling them to comply with the laws and to furnish adequate facilities at reasonable compensation." Such a message and such recommendations were far in advance of the times and his position was all the more remarkable inasmuch as he was a successful business man and a banker. In his book, *The Railroad Question* (1893), he set forth many ideas which he lived to see incorporated in state and federal legislation. His administration is generally regarded as one of the strongest in the history of the state.

Larrabee was a man of great industry, honesty and generosity. As a miller he often worked twenty hours a day for months at a time. He was a great reader. He had collected a large library and his years of retirement were occupied with the care of his estate, "Montauk," and with wide reading. He contributed to the support of the local churches, and a school building costing $100,000, the gift of the Larrabees, was almost completed at the time of his death. He had a high sense of public duty and he did not hesitate to break close friendships if he deemed it necessary. In 1906 and 1908 he supported Albert B. Cummins in his gubernatorial and senatorial campaigns, when the controversies in Iowa between the conservative and progressive wings of his party were most bitter.

[The memorial address by Wm. S. Kenyon before the legislature of Iowa, Mar. 20, 1913, printed in the Senate *Journal*, 1913, pp. 1125–39, was privately printed in pamphlet form in 1913 (*Wm. Larrabee: Memorial Address by Senator Wm. S. Kenyon*) and partially reprinted in the *Register and Leader* (Des Moines), Mar. 21, 1913. See also B. F. Shambaugh, *The Messages and Proclamations of the Governors of Iowa*, vol. VI (1904); F. E. Haynes, *Third Party Movements Since the Civil War* (1916); Cyrenus Cole, *A Hist. of the People of Iowa* (1921); B. F. Gue, *Hist. of Iowa* (1903), vols. III and IV; E. R. Harlan, *A Narrative Hist. of the People of Iowa* (1931), vol. II; G. T. Ridlon, *Saco Valley Settlements and Families* (1895); and the *Register and Leader* (Des Moines), Jan. 23, 1906, Nov. 17, 18, 19, 1912.]

F. E. H.

LARRABEE, WILLIAM CLARK (Dec. 23, 1802–May 5, 1859), Methodist Episcopal clergyman, educator, was a descendant of Stephen Larrabee, one of the pioneers of North Yarmouth, Me. William's grandparents were Jonathan and Alice (Davis) Larrabee, and he was born at Cape Elizabeth, Me., his father, a sea captain, dying soon after the boy's birth. From his seventh year, he lived with his grandparents, and with his uncle Jonathan, at Durham, Me., working on the farm and attending school. Frequenting Methodist meetings, then just being introduced into that locality, he soon professed conversion, and in June 1821 was licensed to preach. In his youth he was associated with Eliphalet Clark, who became a lifelong friend, and from whom he adopted his middle name. After being licensed, he attended New Market Academy in New Hampshire, and later, Farmingham Academy, Maine, where he was prepared to enter the sophomore class at Bowdoin College, from which he graduated in 1828. From 1828 to 1830 he was principal of Alfred Academy, Maine, and in 1830 he was appointed tutor of a preparatory school at Middletown, Conn., which was the forerunner of Wesleyan University. The next year he was made the principal of Oneida Conference Seminary, Cazenovia, N. Y., and in 1832 was admitted to membership in the Oneida Conference of the Methodist Episcopal Church. After four successful years at Cazenovia, he became the principal of Maine Wesleyan Seminary, Kents Hill, where he enlarged his reputation as an educator. In 1837–38 he also assisted in the first geological survey of the state.

He was a delegate to the General Conference of the Methodist Episcopal Church at Baltimore in 1840, and there met Matthew Simpson [*q.v.*], the young president of a new Methodist institution, Indiana Asbury University (De Pauw University), just established at Greencastle. Simpson persuaded Larrabee to accept the professorship of mathematics and natural science, and from 1841 to 1852 he was not only a leading member of the faculty, but from 1848 to 1849, was the acting president, introducing numerous reforms in the course of study and doing much to raise educational standards. In 1848 he was one of the board of visitors at the United States Military Academy, West Point, and later was offered, but declined, several important educational positions, among them the presidency of Indiana and of Iowa universities. Elected in 1852 editor of the *Ladies' Repository*, a Methodist magazine published in Cincinnati, he soon resigned to accept nomination, on the Democratic ticket, for the superintendency of public instruction in the state of Indiana, to which he was elected. The new state constitution (1851) made provision for a uniform system of public schools, and Larrabee, the first state superintendent, was in a sense the founder of the Indiana public-school system. In 1854 he was defeated for reëlection, but in 1856 was again chosen to that office and devoted his second term to a reconstruction of the school system, the former school laws having been declared unconstitutional. He retired from office in January 1859 and died the following May.

He was married, Sept. 28, 1828, to Harriet, daughter of Col. William Dunn, and was the father of four children. He named his house at Greencastle "Rosabower" in memory of a daughter who died in infancy and was buried in the grounds, which are now a part of the campus of De Pauw University. His writings include: *Lectures on the Scientific Evidences of Natural and Revealed Religion* (1850); *Wesley and His Coadjutors* (2 vols., 1851); *Asbury and His Coadjutors* (2 vols., 1853); and a little volume of essays entitled *Rosabower* (1854), consisting of articles published in the *Ladies' Repository*. The first essay is a fanciful description of the grounds about his Indiana home and the death of his little daughter.

[*New-Eng. Hist. and Geneal. Reg.*, July 1859, reprints obituary from *Indianapolis Sentinel*, May 5, 1859; G. T. Ridlon, *Saco Valley Settlements and Families* (1895); F. C. Holliday, *Ind. Methodism* (1873); *Minutes of Conferences of the M. E. Ch.*, vols. II and III (1840); *First Fifty Years of Cazenovia Sem. 1825–1875* (n.d.); H. M. Skinner, *Biog. Sketches of the Supts. of Pub. Instruction of the State of Ind.* (1884); Logan Esarey, *A Hist. of Indiana*, vol. II (1918).]

W. W. S.

LARRAZOLO, OCTAVIANO AMBROSIO (Dec. 7, 1859–Apr. 7, 1930), jurist, governor of New Mexico, United States senator, was born at Allende in southern Chihuahua, Mexico, the son of Octaviano and Donaciana (Corral) Larrazolo. His boyhood memories were of the tragic years of the Reform and the French intervention in

Mexico. In 1870 he went to Tucson as the protégé of Bishop J. B. Salpointe, and when the latter became archbishop of Santa Fé (1875), young Larrazolo accompanied him to that city and studied at St. Michael's College. For a year he taught school in Tucson, and from 1879 to 1884 was a high-school principal in El Paso County, Tex. In the latter year he became clerk of the district at El Paso, serving until 1888, when he was admitted to the bar. He was elected district attorney for western Texas in 1890, and again in 1892. In January 1895 he moved to Las Vegas, N. Mex. During these early years he was a Democrat, and was the Democratic nominee for delegate to Congress from New Mexico in three different elections (1900, 1906, 1908). Each time he ran well but was defeated.

Throughout the Southwest, Larrazolo early came to be recognized as a brilliant orator in both English and Spanish, and also as a champion of the native people, who then constituted about half the voting population of the territory. When New Mexico was preparing for statehood (1910), he was instrumental in having written into the state constitution "strong provisions guaranteeing the rights of the Spanish-speaking voters against disfranchisement and protecting them against discrimination on account of language or racial descent. It assured the use of the Spanish language officially, together with English, for years to come" (Walter, *post*, p. 101). Hoping to better himself and his people politically, he became a Republican in 1911 and, in a dramatic speech at the party convention that fall, presented for governor a native New Mexican. His candidate was not nominated, but for the next twenty years Larrazolo was an important factor in New Mexican politics, and Spanish-Americans received greater recognition from both leading parties. Larrazolo himself was elected the first post-war governor (1918). When the coal miners' strike became general in the Rocky Mountain region in 1918, he invoked martial law and prevented the strike from spreading into New Mexico. He advocated federal aid to farmers and stockmen, and indorsed the idea of giving the public lands to the states in which they were situated, his proposal including the ownership of subsoil as well as surface. As Republican nominee for justice of the state supreme court, he was defeated in 1924; but in the fall of 1928 he was elected to the United States Senate.

Larrazolo will long be remembered as a fine example of the Spanish-American race; he was tall, of vigorous frame, and handsome, with the proud, courtly, and punctilious bearing of a Spanish gentleman. He was an ardent patriot of his adopted country and one of the most effective representatives of the native people of the Southwest. He was twice married: first in 1881 to Rosalia Cobos, who died ten years later, having borne him two children; and second, Aug. 4, 1892, to María García, by whom he had five children. His death occurred in Albuquerque.

[R. E. Twitchell, *Leading Facts of New Mexican Hist.* (1912), vol. II; *Albuquerque Morning Jour.*, Apr 8 and 10, 1930; *Santa Fé New Mexican*, Apr. 8, May 12, 1930; P. A. F. Walter, *New Mexico Hist. Rev.* Apr. 1932; personal acquaintance.] L. B. B.

LARRÍNAGA, TULIO (Jan. 15, 1847–Apr. 28, 1917), second resident commissioner for Puerto Rico in the United States, was born at Trujillo Alto, Puerto Rico, and died of heart trouble at Santurce, a suburb of San Juan. He studied at the Seminario Conciliar of San Ildefonso in San Juan before coming to the United States, where he studied civil engineering at the Rensselaer Polytechnic Institute, Troy, N. Y. (1865–68). He is said to have taken part in the preparation of the topographical map of Kings County (Brooklyn) and as a member of the technical department of Badger & Company to have worked on the construction of the Grand Central Station, New York.

Returning to Puerto Rico, he was later appointed architect for the city of San Juan, and is reputed to have designed the first building with steel framework erected in that city. On June 22, 1879, he married Bertha Goyro Saint Victor, whose father was a Spaniard but whose mother was French. They had five children. In 1880 he built the first railroad in Puerto Rico, introducing American rolling stock on the island. For almost a decade (1880–89) he was engineer for the Provincial Deputation, being prominent in the construction work in San Juan harbor, and in directing the extensive road construction of the island. Under the autonomous government, granted Puerto Rico by Spain in 1898, he was sub-secretary of public works. After the American occupation, he again assumed direction of construction work in San Juan harbor. While the Foraker Bill was being discussed, he came to Washington with a political delegation, asking for home rule. In 1902 he was elected a delegate to the insular legislature for the district of Arecibo. Here he advocated important measures favoring agriculture. He was elected resident commissioner for Puerto Rico in 1904 and twice reëlected, serving from Mar. 4, 1905, to Mar. 3, 1911. In 1905 he interceded for the continuance of the Puerto Rican regiment, which was to be suppressed, and in 1906 presented a law project for the amending of the Foraker Bill. He represented the United States at the Third Pan-

American Congress in Brazil (1906) and the United States Congress at conferences of the Interparliamentary Union at Berlin (1908) and Brussels (1910). In 1905 President Wilson appointed him a member of the Executive Council of Puerto Rico.

As one of the founders of the Ateneo, which played a considerable part in the intellectual leadership of the island, as one who gave free instruction in English to poor young men, as a member of the insular library commission, and in other ways, he influenced the educational life of Puerto Rico. He was also president of the agricultural commission.

[*El Libro de Puerto Rico: The Book of Porto Rico* (1923), ed. by E. Fernandez Garcia; *Biog. Dir. Am. Cong.* (1928); *La Correspondencia de Puerto-Rico* (San Juan), Apr. 30, 1917; *La Democracia*, Apr. 30, 1917; *El Tiempo*, Apr. 30, 1917; *N. Y. Times*, May 1, 1917; information from relatives and friends.] C. R. W.

LARSEN, PETER LAURENTIUS (Aug. 10, 1833–Mar. 1, 1915), pioneer Norwegian Lutheran clergyman and educator, was born at Christiansand, Norway, the son of Herman Larsen, an army officer, and Elen Else Marie (Oftedahl), daughter of a member of the Norwegian constitutional assembly held in 1814 at Eidsvold. When he was nine years old, the boy entered the Lancaster school at Christiansand, and in 1850, the university at Christiania (now Oslo), where he came under the influence of two of Norway's most celebrated theologians, Carl Paul Caspari and Gisle Johnson. After the completion of his studies there in 1855, when he graduated in theology, he remained in Christiania as teacher of German, French, and Hebrew.

Hearing the Macedonian call from his recently emigrated fellow countrymen in America, he went over to help them, and preached his first sermon in the United States near Rush River, Wis., on Nov. 2, 1857. Always a zealous missionary, he traveled far and wide, establishing congregations at such places as St. Paul and Red Wing, Minn. In 1859 the Norwegian Synod arranged for a theological professorship at Concordia Seminary, St. Louis, Mo., and Larsen was called to fill the position. When the Civil War broke out, he and the Norwegian students left St. Louis, whereupon the Synod established Luther College, presently located at Decorah, Iowa. Larsen was elected professor and president of the school, serving in the first capacity for fifty years and in the latter for forty-one. In 1913 he became professor emeritus. On Christmas Eve of that year he suffered a slight stroke, from which he rallied, but two years later one more severe brought on his death.

As president of a pioneer Norwegian Lutheran college, he faced many difficulties. His constituents had been in America in considerable numbers for less than twenty years when they were called upon to build a college in war times at a cost of $87,000. This expense fell upon a group which at the outset numbered seventeen pastors and sixty-nine congregations, and the successful completion of the project rested largely on the shoulders of Larsen. When fire gutted the "Old Main" on May 19, 1889, he again had to step into the breach, but by this time the idea of Christian education had been too firmly established in the people's minds for them to permit the building to lie in ruins. Other problems confronting the young American college with its somewhat European-minded constituency he met with tact and firmness. As a concession to American demands, he changed the curriculum from a six-year to an eight-year course, but the aim of the school to prepare men for the ministry always remained uppermost in his mind.

As a churchman he was a conspicuous figure. He became the center of two notable controversies, in which he himself contended that slavery is an evil rather than a sin (1861–68) and that there is powerful impartation of the forgiveness of sins in absolution (1861–1906). As editor of *Kirkelig Maanedstidende* ("Church Monthly") from 1868 to 1873, and of its successor, *Evangelisk Luthersk Kirketidende* ("Evangelical Lutheran Church Times"), from 1874 to 1889 and from 1902 to 1912, he was called upon to voice the official opinion of the Norwegian Synod on many difficult questions, chief of which were those connected with the predestination controversy. Throughout it all, Larsen succeeded in maintaining his reputation for mental and spiritual honesty, his thorough hatred of sham and subterfuge removing him from the temptations to resort to "church politics" trickery. Besides being editor and college president, he was vice-president of the Iowa district of the Norwegian Synod (1876–79), vice-president of the Norwegian Synod (1876–93), and chairman of the Lutheran Synodical Conference (1881–83). He served on many committees, being chairman of the Foreign Mission Committee for several years. From 1882 to 1884 he was also pastor of the Norwegian Lutheran congregation in Decorah.

At many Luther College banquets he was guest of honor, and tributes in verse and prose have been offered him by prominent alumni. On Oct. 22, 1884, and again in 1909, his students and fellow teachers celebrated his twenty-fifth and fiftieth anniversaries as teacher. The house which was his home for the last eighteen years of his life was a gift from former students. In 1908 he was made knight of the first class of the Order of St. Olav by King Haakon VII of Norway. He was twice married: first, July 23, 1855, to Karen Neuberg; second, Aug. 20, 1872, to Ingeborg Astrup; and he was the father of twelve children.

[O. M. Norlie, *Norsk Lutherske Prester i Amerika* (Minneapolis, 1914); L. S. Swenson, "Prof. Dr. Laur. Larsen, De Norsk-Amerikanske Skolemänds Nestor," in *Symra* (Decorah, Iowa), 5th *bind, 4 de hefte*, 1909; F. E. Peterson, "Presidents and Principals," in O. M. Norlie, O. A. Tingelstad, and K. T. Jacobsen, *Luther Coll. Through Sixty Years* (1922); J. M. Rohne, *Norwegian Am. Lutheranism Up To 1872* (1926); O. J. Kvale, *The Soul of Luther College* (1927); Gisle Bothne, *Det Norske Luther Coll.* (Decorah, Iowa, 1897); Karen Larsen, "A Contribution to the Study of the Adjustment of a Pioneer Pastor to American Conditions: Laur. Larsen, 1857–1880," in *Norwegian-American Hist. Asso. Studies and Records*, vol. IV (1929); Rasmus Malmin, O. M. Norlie, O. A. Tingelstad, *Who's Who Among Pastors in All the Norwegian Lutheran Synods in America 1843–1927* (1928); *Who's Who in America*, 1914–15.] J. M. R.

LA SALLE, ROBERT CAVELIER, Sieur de (November 1643–Mar. 19, 1687), explorer, was the second son of Jean Cavelier, a wealthy burgher of Rouen, where this child was baptized in the parish church of St. Herbland, Nov. 22, 1643. His mother was Catherine Geest, and one of her relatives was the boy's godfather. His title La Salle came from a family seigniory in the neighborhood of Rouen. He studied at the Jesuit college at Rouen, which was later the Lycée Corneille, and at the urgent desire of his father entered the Society of Jesus as a novice. The training he received was antagonistic to his independent, adventurous nature, and upon his father's death, when he was twenty-two years old, he left the Jesuits, apparently without ill will on either side. Through this or other experiences, however, he had acquired a dislike for the order and all its members which often broke out into open hostility. By the law of the time, when he took his first vows he lost his share of the paternal estate, and was dependent upon the allowance his relatives chose to make him.

His elder brother, Jean Cavelier, a member of the order of St. Sulpice, before the father's death had gone to New France, where the Sulpicians held the seigniory of Montreal. Possibly the connection of an uncle with the Hundred Associates for New France had interested the Caveliers in the colony of Canada, for in the summer of 1666 Robert followed his brother thither. From the Sulpicians he received a grant of land on the western end of the island of Montreal and there he erected several buildings, traded with the natives, and lived for two years the life of a pioneer farmer. His estate afterwards received the name of "La Chine" in derision of his fruitless efforts to range from there to China.

During the winter of 1668–69 La Salle entertained at his manor house two Iroquois Indians, who informed him of westward-flowing waters and awakened in him a desire for exploration. The next summer he sold his seigniory back to the convent of St. Sulpice at Montreal and entered upon the career which brought him fame. The Sulpicians were at this time sending two members of their order to begin missions in the West; on the advice of the Superior, La Salle attached himself to this expedition, which left Montreal July 6, 1669, with seven canoes, four of them conducted for La Salle. The expedition ascended the St. Lawrence River to Lake Ontario, coasted its southern shore to Irondequoit Bay, and there beached the canoes and went into the interior to obtain guides from the Iroquois. La Salle had boasted of his knowledge of the language, but once among the Indians he could not make himself understood. By means of a Dutch interpreter, however, who spoke a little French, the explorers obtained information concerning the geography of the country west of the Iroquois villages and again skirted the lake shore to the mouth of the Niagara River, where they could hear the noise of the great falls. They did not visit the falls, but went inland, where in a village at the western end of Lake Ontario they met Louis Jolliet [*q.v.*] returning from a visit to the Ottawa country.

Jolliet's report made the Sulpicians decide to visit the Northwest, but La Salle adhered to his purpose of seeking the Ohio, the headwaters of which the Iroquois had reported to be near at hand. He had been ill and made an excuse of his illness to leave the party. Whether he at that time finally reached the Ohio and sailed down it to the falls at Louisville, as he later claimed, is a moot question. That he did not discover the Ohio and saw it for the first time when he passed its mouth in 1682 seems by far the greater probability.

What occupied the young explorer from 1669 to 1673 is not known; one narrator speaks of meeting him in 1670 hunting on the Ottawa River. Meanwhile Jolliet had discovered the upper reaches of the Mississippi and had found that it descended to the Gulf of Mexico, and a furor for western exploration was in the air. About this time a new governor arrived at Quebec who pacified the Iroquois and built a fort on the north shore of Lake Ontario to which he gave his own name of Frontenac. In the Count de Frontenac La Salle found a kindred soul; their spirits leaped together to do some great thing for France. Frontenac sent La Salle to court to obtain permission for the monopoly of the fur trade on which they hoped to build their structure of expansion.

The young Norman, bronzed by years in the open, with his imaginative description of life in the wilderness, quickly gained favor and obtained a grant of Fort Frontenac as a seigniory with exclusive permission for trade. Coming back to Canada with his future companion, Friar Louis Hennepin [*q.v.*], as a fellow passenger, La Salle made plans with Frontenac to exploit the concession and to arrange for future discovery. After three years at Fort Frontenac, during which it is probable that La Salle first visited the upper Great Lakes, he went again to France to obtain fresh privileges. Again he was successful in winning favor at court. He was granted a title of nobility and a patent permitting him to explore and exploit the regions of the West and to deal in buffalo and lesser furs, but not in beaver: an exception which he constantly ignored.

Upon his arrival in the summer of 1678 in New France, accompanied by his faithful lieutenant, Tonty of the iron hand, he and Frontenac made plans for opening the West and beginning therein an empire for Louis XIV. These plans required the building of a sailing vessel above Niagara Falls: La Salle had already two barks on Lake Ontario. A shipyard was established near Buffalo on the Niagara River and there the *Griffon* (named for Frontenac's heraldic device) was launched in the early summer of 1679. La Salle had already sent traders into the West to gather peltry for the expenses of his expedition. He also sent Tonty [*q.v.*] in advance to gather furs in the Detroit region. Thence they went together to Michilimackinac, where they arrived at the end of August. Sailing on to Green Bay, the *Griffon* awakened fear and consternation among the savages, who saw in it an emblem of the overmastering power of the white men.

At Green Bay La Salle found that his traders had gathered a great store of furs, which he loaded onto his vessel to go back to Fort Frontenac. He and his men then took canoes to continue their journey. The *Griffon* was never seen or heard from after that time; its fate has remained a mystery to this day. Advancing up Lake Michigan, the adventurers entered St. Joseph River, portaged to the Kankakee, and sailed down the Illinois to Lake Peoria, where early in January was built Fort Crèvecœur. Thence La Salle sent three men, including Father Hennepin, to explore the upper Mississippi and gather furs. He himself, leaving Tonty in charge, started overland on foot for Fort Frontenac in pursuit of some deserters and in order to settle with his creditors, who were seizing the fort and stopping supplies. This terrible journey, during the melting weather of early spring, over an unknown route, he accomplished in sixty-five days. At the fort he was detained until late autumn, and on going back to the Illinois he found only the ruins of his enterprise; most of his men had deserted and Tonty and the missionaries had fled before an invasion of hostile Iroquois. At Mackinac in June 1681 the two explorers were reunited and returned again to the Illinois country, rebuilt their fort, this time on the upper Illinois River, on the summit of a rock near the present Ottawa. La Salle now sought to settle around his post a great confederation of western Indians, as a defense against the encroachments of the Iroquois. From this post he and Tonty set forth early in 1682 to explore the Mississippi. On their arrival at the Gulf, on Apr. 9, they took possession of all the river valley for the king of France and named it in his honor Louisiana. (*Collections of the State Historical Society of Wisconsin*, vol. XI, 1888, pp. 33–36.)

This was the climax of La Salle's career. Hitherto he had been supported by Governor Frontenac, but in 1682 Frontenac was replaced by a nominee of the Jesuit party, Antoine Lefebre, Sieur de la Barre. La Barre deprived La Salle of the command of his fort in the Illinois country and summoned him to Quebec to answer for misdemeanors. La Salle, who was on his way to Canada when he heard of this catastrophe, sent Tonty to deliver Fort St. Louis to La Barre's appointee while he continued his voyage to France, disdaining to reply to the governor's charge. In France he was at once the hero of the hour. He narrated his adventures, described the vast and wonderful country he had explored, and was restored by the King to all his commands and honors in New France.

He asked for an expedition to colonize the mouth of the Mississippi, and accordingly a fleet was prepared for this enterprise, with four ships, two hundred colonists, and many supplies. He was named viceroy of North America and given command from Illinois to the Spanish borders. The expedition sailed July 24, 1684, but by some inadvertence missed the mouth of the Mississippi and landed on the coast of Texas. The ships sailed home Mar. 12, 1685, and La Salle, now aware that he was not on the Mississippi, made heroic efforts to find it. He was on his final journey toward that river when on the Brazos River just above the mouth of the Navasota his men mutinied and shot him. His brother Jean, who had accompanied him, and his aide, Henri Joutel [*q.v.*], made their way to Tonty in the

Illinois country and thence to France without revealing the news of the death of La Salle.

La Salle's great projects and plans, his ambitious ideas and hopes, have blinded his biographers to the fact that most of his failures were due to his own defects. He was a dreamer without adequate executive power to carry out his schemes. He could not control the natives; he alienated his own men by his haughty bearing and lack of sympathy; he showed uncertainty and vacillation at critical moments. Yet his lack of success should not obscure his accomplishments both as an explorer and a publicity agent for the interior of North America. He was undoubtedly the first of the French explorers to trace the Mississippi to its mouth; he appreciated the possibilities of the Mississippi Valley, and anticipated its future greatness. In any judgment of him, his mistakes and failures must be subordinated to his vision, which encompassed an empire for France in the heart of America.

[La Salle was a voluminous writer. His many letters and journals were collected and published by Pierre Margry, in *Découvertes et Établissements des Français dans l'Ouest et dans le Sud de l'Amérique Septentrionale* (Paris, 1876–86). La Salle was Margry's hero, around the documents of whose career he built most of his six volumes. Other accounts are those of Tonty (see L. P. Kellogg, *Early Narratives of the Northwest*, 1917, pp. 283–322); Louis Hennepin, in *Description de la Louisiane* (1683), translated by J. G. Shea in 1880, and *Nouvelle Découverte* (1697), edited, in translation, by R. G. Thwaites as *A New Discovery of a Vast Country in America* (2 vols., 1903); Zénobe Membre in Chrétien Le Clercq, *Établissement de la Foy dans la Nouvelle France* (Paris, 2 vols., 1691), tr. by J. G. Shea, as *First Establishment of the Faith in New France* (2 vols., 1881). Translations of several of these accounts, including those by Jean Cavelier and Henri Joutel of the last expedition, are published in I. J. Cox, *The Journeys of René Robert Cavelier Sieur de La Salle* (2 vols., 1905). Francis Parkman, *La Salle and the Discovery of the Great West* (1879) is the best-known modern work. See also Marc de Villiers, *L'Expédition de Cavelier de La Salle dans le Golfe du Mexique, 1684–1687* (1931); Gabriel Gravier, *Découvertes et Établissements de Cavelier de La Salle de Rouen dans l'Amérique du Nord* (1870); Benjamin Sulte, "La Mort de Cavelier de La Salle," in *Proc. and Trans. Royal Soc. of Canada*, 2 ser. IV (1898). H. E. Bolton identifies the Texas sites of La Salle's colony and place of death in *Miss. Valley Hist. Rev.*, Sept. 1915.]

L. P. K.

LASATER, EDWARD CUNNINGHAM (Nov. 5, 1860–Mar. 20, 1930), cattleman, business man, and member of the United States Food Administration, was born in Goliad County, Tex. His parents, Albert H. and Sarah Jane (Cunningham) Lasater, moved to Texas from Arkansas in the late fifties. Edward's education was limited to the meager facilities of the Texas frontier, and an early ambition for law was forgotten in his love of the soil. He farmed and ranched until the drouths and depression of the early nineties left him without property and heavily involved. About this time, grasping the possibilities of the undeveloped land between the Nueces and the Rio Grande, he secured credit for the purchase of a ranch of 380,000 acres, and in time stocked it with 20,000 head of beef cattle. In anticipation of the advance of the farming settler into "the brush country," he encouraged the extension of the San Antonio & Aransas Pass Railway, founded the town of Falfurrias, and within twenty-five years sold land to more than six hundred farmers. His 2,500 Jersey cows, ranging a 40,000-acre dairy pasture, were reputed to be the largest herd of that breed in existence, and his registered stock were among the prize winners in the greatest cattle shows of the world.

Lasater was a slight, energetic, aggressive man, whose entire public enterprise was devoted to the problems of the men of the soil. He worked long and hard for clean politics on the Rio Grande, in the face of many threats against his life. In 1912 he was nominated for governor of Texas by the Progressive party. For two years, 1911–12, he served as president of the Texas and Southwestern Cattle Raisers Association. In the interests of the producers of agricultural products, he waged a long fight against various practices of the packers, the speculators, the bankers, and pernicious legislative trends.

On July 25, 1917, Herbert Hoover asked Lasater to serve with the Food Administration as chief of the department of live stock and animal food products. Lasater was soon at odds with Hoover's policies. He and Gifford Pinchot fought to remove speculation from the hog market by establishing the value of a hundred pounds of hog in its equivalent in bushels of corn. He attacked the campaign of "eat no lamb, eat no veal" as subversive of the Administration's attempt to stimulate production. Disagreeing with Hoover upon various other questions of fundamental importance to agriculture, he tendered his resignation from the Administration, Oct. 20, 1917. His published defense, including *Facts Affecting the United States Food Administration* (1917), *Reply to Mr. Hoover, U. S. Food Administrator* (1918), and a report to the Market Committee of the American National Live Stock Association, *As Showing that the Policies and Practices of Mr. Hoover, as Food Administrator are "Harmful to the Common Welfare"* (1918), alleges much floundering on the part of the Administration.

For twelve years more Lasater continued an active authority upon the problems of the range. In 1918 he published a paper on "Live Stock Marketing Conditions" in *Proceedings of the*

American National Live Stock Association, and in 1920 his testimony before the House Committee on Agriculture, under the title, *Meat Packer Legislation.* He died at Ardmore, Okla., but was buried in Texas. His first wife, Martha Noble Bennett, daughter of John M. Bennett, whom he married Dec. 28, 1892, died Aug. 19, 1900. On Oct. 29, 1902, he married Mary Gardner Miller, daughter of Garland Burleigh Miller, who survived him.

[*Who's Who in America,* 1930–31; Lasater's articles mentioned above; *N. Y. Times,* Nov. 13, 18, 1917, Jan. 27, Mar. 31, 1918, Mar. 22, 1930; *Tulsa Daily World,* Mar. 21, 1930; *Daily Oklahoman* (Oklahoma City), Mar. 21, 1930; *San Antonio Express,* Mar. 21, 1930; MSS., special articles, and memoranda in the hands of Mrs. Mary Lasater, Falfurrias, Tex.]

J. E. H.

LATHAM, MILTON SLOCUM (May 23, 1827–Mar. 4, 1882), United States senator from California, was born in Columbus, Ohio, the third son of Bela and Juliana (Sterritt) Latham. His father, a native of New Hampshire, was a practising lawyer in Ohio. The son attended schools in Ohio, and graduated in 1845 from Jefferson College, Canonsburg, Pa. He then spent some time in Russell County, Ala., where he taught school, studied law, was admitted to the bar, and served for a while as clerk of a circuit court. These experiences in the South seem to have influenced him in the friendships and opinions of later years. In 1850 he went to San Francisco, where, after holding briefly the office of district attorney for Sacramento County, he was elected to Congress, taking his seat in December 1853. He served only one term, declining renomination. By appointment of President Pierce, he became collector of the port at San Francisco (1855–57). His conduct of that office aroused considerable antagonism, partly because of the local conflicts made pointed by the activity of the Vigilance committee, partly because of the rivalry of the two factions of the Democratic party, one led by David C. Broderick and the other by William M. Gwin [*qq.v.*], both of them United States senators.

Latham was his own faction, and made a successful campaign for the governorship in 1859, winning by a large majority in spite of the savage opposition of Broderick. In his brief term as governor he transmitted to Buchanan the action of the preceding legislature agreeing to a division of the state of California, and presented at length the constitutional questions arising out of the proposal. Two days after his inauguration (Jan. 9, 1860), he was chosen by the legislature to fill the vacancy in the United States Senate created by the death of Broderick. He resigned the governorship Jan. 14, 1860, and accepted the new position gladly—in fact he had directed the legislative canvas through his secretary. In Washington he was made much of by the administration, although his relations with his colleague Gwin were strained. On Apr. 16, he made a powerful speech on "Labor and Capital," defending slavery, and attacking the capacities of the negro, the economic motives of the North, and the morals of the Republican party. In the course of this address he said that, in the event of the dissolution of the Union, "We in California would have reasons to induce us to become members neither of the southern confederacy nor of the northern confederacy, and would be able to sustain for ourselves the relations of a free and independent state" (*Congressional Globe,* 36 Cong., 1 Sess., p. 1728). He supported Breckinridge in the presidential contest of 1860, and when later taunted with the "independent California" prophecy, denied that he was ever other than a stanch Union man. For two more years he served as a member of the helpless minority in the Senate, usually supporting the war measures, but denouncing the conduct of the administration. He was not reëlected and retired from public life, Mar. 3, 1863, upon the expiration of his term. The next twenty years were spent in Europe, in California, and in New York. He became manager of the London and San Francisco Bank (1865–78). Going to New York in 1880, he became president of the New York Mining and Stock Exchange, which occupied his attention until shortly before his death.

Sanguine in temperament, ambitious for power, Latham possessed abilities which brought him success in politics and business—for a time. Skilful in manipulation of both men and principles, he made attempts at the formulation of policies which deserved a better fate. His choice language and a strain of mysticism in his nature gave distinction and beauty to some of his addresses. He was married at San Francisco in 1853 to Sophie Birdsall, daughter of Lewis A. Birdsall. She died in 1867, and in 1870 he married Mary W. McMullin, who survived him, as did one son.

[Journal of Milton S. Latham (Jan. 1–May 6, 1860), MS. in Stanford Univ. Lib.; W. J. Davis, *Hist. of Political Conventions in Cal.* (1893); *Biog. Dir. Am. Cong.* (1928); *Biog. and Hist. Cat. of Washington and Jefferson College* (1902); *Evening Bulletin* (San Francisco), May 11, 1861, Mar. 6, 1882; *Morning Call* (San Francisco), Mar. 5, 7, 1882; *N. Y. Times,* Mar. 5, 1882].

E. E. R.

LATHBURY, MARY ARTEMISIA (Aug. 10, 1841–Oct. 20, 1913), author, hymn-writer, daughter of the Rev. John Lathbury, a Methodist minister, and Betsy Shepherd (Jones) Lathbury, was born at Manchester, N. Y. The family was of English descent. Her childhood environment was one in which religious observances had an important place and her temperament fitted the environment. She was educated first in the school at Manchester and at eighteen went to an art school at Worcester, Mass. The following year she taught drawing, painting, and French at the Methodist Conference Seminary, Newbury, Vt. For the next five years she taught at the Fort Edward (New York) Institute and for six years she was at the Drew Ladies' Seminary at Carmel, N. Y. As a child she had written poems and illustrated them and during her teaching years she wrote occasionally for her own pleasure, but her real work as an author began in 1874, when Bishop John H. Vincent engaged her as assistant editor for some Sunday School publications in connection with the Chautauqua movement, among them the *Picture Lesson Paper.* Editorial work gave her an impetus toward creative writing and she was soon producing juvenile stories and poems, usually illustrated by herself, which were published in *St. Nicholas, Harper's Young People, Wide Awake,* and various church papers and magazines. Some of these were later published in small collections, including *Fleda and the Voice* (1876), fairy tales; *Out of Darkness into Light* (1878), poems; *Idyls of the Months* (1885), poems; *The Child's Life of Christ; Stories from the Bible* (1898); and *The Child's Story of the Bible* (1898). Her work in connection with Chautauqua included the founding of the Chautauqua Look Up Legion, suggested by Edward Everett Hale's motto "Look Up and not Down." She and Hale were close friends and she cooperated with him in founding the Ten Times One clubs. For several years she was superintendent of a Chinese Sunday School in New York City. Her hymns are her most valuable and enduring work. Edward Everett Hale said of her as a hymn-writer: "She has marvelous lyric force which not five people in a century show." Her best-known hymns are "Day Is Dying in the West," called Chautauqua's vesper hymn, "Break Thou the Bread of Life," and "Arise and Shine." If not notable as literature, they show a deep devotional spirit and lyric quality. For the last two years of her life she was an invalid and she died at her home in East Orange, N. J.

[*Who's Who in America,* 1912–13; Frances E. Willard, sketch in *Poems of Mary Artemisia Lathbury, Chautauqua Laureate* (1915); Kate F. Kimball, article in the *Chautauquan,* Nov. 8, 1913; obituaries in the *N. Y. Times,* Oct. 21, 1913, and the *N. Y. Tribune,* Oct. 22, 1913.] S. G. B.

LATHROP, FRANCIS AUGUSTUS (June 22, 1849–Oct. 18, 1909), mural painter, eldest son of Dr. George Alfred and Frances Maria (Smith) Lathrop, was born at sea during a voyage which his parents were making from the Atlantic coast to Honolulu by way of Cape Horn. His father, a descendant of John Lothropp and of Samuel Holden Parsons [*qq.v.*], was a young physician and had been appointed head of the then new naval hospital at Honolulu. The family remained there nine years, returning in 1858 to the mainland on the sloop-of-war *St. Mary's,* commanded by Captain Davis, afterward Admiral Davis. The voyage took three weeks owing to tempestuous weather. From San Francisco to New York the journey was continued by way of the Isthmus of Panama. In New York, Francis and his brother, George Parsons Lathrop [*q.v.*], attended a private school until 1861, when the family went to Europe and traveled for eight months. After the return the boys entered the Columbia Grammar school where Francis stood at the head of his class for three years. He entered Columbia College, but before the end of his freshman year he and his brother started for Germany with the intention of entering the University of Leipzig. They began preparatory study of the German language in Dresden. Francis then determined to begin work in the Royal Art Academy there, but James Whistler urged him to go to London and study with him; thus, after four months in Dresden, the young man went to London. He had no sooner reached that city than he was summoned to return to New York owing to his father's business reverses. For the time being study had to be abandoned and money earned, and during the ensuing year he gave lessons in drawing. When his father's circumstances had improved, he went again to London, took lodgings in Chelsea, and began work in Whistler's studio. He found, however, that his master could not give the requisite time and energy to teaching him, and it was arranged that the young man should work under Madox Brown. A little later he obtained admission to the studio of Edward Burne-Jones where he worked as assistant, making cartoons for stained-glass windows and executing other decorative work. He also worked for a time as assistant to William Morris and R. Spencer Stanhope.

After three years of this life in London he was once more recalled home in 1873 by his father whose affairs were in a critical condition. Francis found himself again obliged to be the bread-winner. He conducted a painting class at Cooper Institute; made illustrations for Clarence Cook's *House Beautiful* (1878); painted portraits; and before long obtained work as a mural painter, a specialty to which thenceforth he devoted most of his time and attention. He was one of the young men who assisted John La Farge in the interior decoration of Trinity Church, Boston, in 1878. He painted an important wall panel for the chapel of Bowdoin College, Brunswick, Me., "Moses Giving the Law to the Children of Israel," in which the figure of Aaron was a portrait of Professor Jonathan B. Sewall. This panel was given by the Bowdoin class of 1877. For the same chapel he painted copies of Raphael's "Transfiguration," "Paul at Mars Hill," "Peter and John at the Beautiful Gate," and Carlo Maratti's "Baptism of Jesus." Other decorative works are his "Light of the World" on the reredos of St. Bartholomew's Church, Madison Avenue, New York; "Apollo," over the proscenium of the Metropolitan Opera House, New York; the marble mosaic of "Widows and Orphans" in the building of the Equitable Life Assurance Company, New York; a stained-glass window representing the miracle at the pool of Bethesda, in the chancel of Bethesda Church, Saratoga, N. Y.; the Marquand memorial window in the chapel of Princeton University; the decorations in the music room of the Collis P. Huntington residence, Fifth Avenue, New York; and others. In all of his works Lathrop showed the influence of his Pre-Raphaelite masters, but aside from this there is in his decorative essays a personal stamp of imagination and an admirable instinct for design, qualities that are especially to be noticed in his Bowdoin College panel and his altarpiece in St. Bartholomew's.

Lathrop was never married. His New York studio was the tower room of the old University building in Washington Square, where S. F. B. Morse and Winslow Homer had been his illustrious predecessors. He was a charter member of the Society of American Artists, an associate of the National Academy of Design, a member of many other societies, and the recipient of a number of medals and honors. His death took place at his home at Woodcliffe Lake, N. J.

[Lathrop left an autobiographical fragment which is now in the possession of his cousin. Printed sources include: *Who's Who in America*, 1908–09; *Am. Art Annual*, 1910–11; J. D. Champlin and C. C. Perkins, *Cyc. of Painters and Paintings*, vol. III (1888); E. B. Huntington, *Geneal. Memoir of the Lo-Lathrop Family* (1884); *N. Y. Times*, Oct. 19, 1909.]

W. H. D.

LATHROP, GEORGE PARSONS (Aug. 25, 1851–Apr. 19, 1898), author and editor, was born near Honolulu, Oahu, Hawaiian Islands, the youngest son of Dr. George Alfred and Frances Maria (Smith) Lathrop, and a descendant of the Rev. John Lothropp [*q.v.*]. He was educated in private schools in New York and, from 1867 to 1870, in Dresden, Germany, where he met Rose Hawthorne, daughter of Nathaniel Hawthorne. Returning to America in 1870, he entered Columbia Law School in New York City for a term, but soon decided to leave the law for a literary career. On Sept. 11, 1871, he and Miss Hawthorne were married in St. Peter's Church, Chelsea, London. In 1875 Lathrop became associate editor of the *Atlantic Monthly* during the editorship of William Dean Howells. In 1877 he left the *Atlantic* to become editor for two years of the Boston Sunday *Courier*. In 1881, after the death of their only child, Francis Hawthorne Lathrop, he and his wife went to Europe, where he wrote "Spanish Vistas," travel essays later published in book form, for *Harper's Monthly*. Lathrop founded the American Copyright League in 1883 and acted as its secretary until the summer of 1885; later he organized as an auxiliary the Western Copyright League in Chicago. After a seven years' campaign, the international copyright law came into being, substantially as Lathrop had at first proposed it. During this time he had been literary editor of the New York *Star* and in 1887 had seen his dramatization of Tennyson's "Elaine," written in collaboration with Henry Edwards, presented in Madison Square Theatre, New York. Later in 1887 the play was presented in Boston and Chicago.

Converted to Roman Catholicism, Lathrop and his wife were received into the Church in March 1891 by the Paulist priest, Alfred Young. As a Catholic, Lathrop had an active part in two enterprises: the founding of the Catholic Summer School of America at New London, Conn., in 1892, an institution which was transferred in 1893 to its present location on Lake Champlain; and the Paulist inauguration of the Apostolate of the Press which he supported with his pen. He was the author of fifteen books of which *Rose and Roof-tree* (1875), poems; *A Study of Hawthorne* (1876); and *Spanish Vistas* (1883) are noteworthy. He edited in 1878 *A Masque of Poets* and in 1883 the Riverside edition of Hawthorne's works, with introductory notes and a biographical sketch of Hawthorne. He also adapted Hawthorne's *Scarlet Letter* for Walter Damrosch's opera of the same name, which was produced with great success in New York in 1896. With Mrs. Lathrop he wrote *A Story of Courage* (1894), a history of the Order of the Sisters of the Visitation. After his death in New York City, his widow became a nun, and as Mother Alphonsa [*q.v.*] organized a community of Dominican tertiaries, the Servants of Relief for Incurable Cancer Patients, with two hospitals in New York City.

[See "Death of George Parsons Lathrop, LL.D.," *Cath. Reading Circle Rev.*, Apr.–Sept. 1898; E. B. Huntington, *A Geneal. Memoir of the Lo-Lathrop Family* (1884); *Theatre*, Dec. 12, 1887; *N. Y. Tribune*, Apr. 29, May 1, 1887, Apr. 20, 1898.] R. A.

LATHROP, JOHN (Jan. 13, 1772–Jan. 30, 1820), lawyer and poet, was born at Boston, Mass., the son of the Rev. John and Mary (Wheatley) Lathrop. His father was for many years the minister of the Second Church in Boston and a direct descendant of the Rev. John Lothropp [*q.v.*] who was the first minister of Scituate and later of Barnstable, Mass. At Harvard Lathrop was distinguished for his scholarship. Upon graduating in 1789 he read law in the office of Christopher Gore with considerable assiduity, but the public came to know him more as a poet than as a lawyer. At Harvard Commencement in 1792 he delivered a poem and received the degree of A.M. He practised law at Boston and also at Dedham, Mass., where he enjoyed the society of Fisher Ames. In 1798 he was appointed clerk of the courts for Norfolk County, but the work was uncongenial and he soon returned to Boston. There he became identified with the wits and versifiers of the day, notably Robert Treat Paine and Charles Prentiss. This association did not help him in the legal profession and in 1799 he embarked for India where he hoped to make a fortune. Taking up his residence in Calcutta he opened a school and wrote frequently for the newspapers, the *Hircarrah* and the *Post*. To the Marquis Wellesley, governor-general of India, he submitted a plan of an institution of learning in which the youth of India might be educated without going to England to study. He urged his cause with fervency and eloquence, but his Lordship is said to have replied, "No, no, Sir, India is and ever ought to be a Colony of Great Britain; the seeds of Independence must not be sown here. Establishing a seminary in New England at so early a period of time hastened your revolution half a century" (Knapp, *post*, p. 180).

Returning to the United States in 1809 he entertained thoughts of founding a literary journal in his native country, but the times were not favorable. There was little left for him to do except to teach. For a number of years he superintended a school in Boston, edited almanacs, delivered a course of scientific lectures, and occasionally made speeches. Later he continued some of these pursuits at Washington and Georgetown, D. C., and finally obtained a position in the post-office. He died at Georgetown in 1820. His reputation rests chiefly upon *The Speech of Caunonicus*, a poem first printed in Calcutta in 1802 and reprinted in Boston in the following year. To the *Polyanthos*, a Boston magazine, he contributed (1812–14) a series of papers under the title "The Moral Censor," and also a course of lectures on natural philosophy which he had delivered in Calcutta in 1807–08 and in Boston in 1811. Modest and affectionate by nature, Lathrop made and retained many friends who easily forgave his lack of prudence and occasional negligence of duty. He was married thrice: in 1792 to Ann Pierce; about 1801 to Jane Thompson; and about 1808 to Grace Eleanor Harrison. John Lothrop Motley [*q.v.*], the historian, was his nephew.

[The best sketch of Lathrop's life is to be found in S. L. Knapp, *Biog. Sketches of Eminent Lawyers, Statesmen, and Men of Letters* (1821). See also Samuel Kettell, *Specimens of Am. Poetry, with Critical and Biog. Notices* (1829), II, 101–08; John Lathrop, "Biographical Memoir of the Rev. John Lothropp," *Mass. Hist. Soc. Colls.*, 2 ser. I (1814); E. B. Huntington, *Geneal. Memoir of the Lo-Lathrop Family* (1884); J. T. Buckingham, *Personal Memoirs* (1852), vol. I, and Thos. Bridgman, *The Pilgrims of Boston* (1856). A poem by Lathrop delivered at Harvard Commencement in 1792 is printed in the *Mass. Mag.*, July 1792. His fourth of July orations at Boston (1796) and at Dedham (1798) were printed separately in the years in which they were pronounced.] L. S. M.

LATHROP, JOHN HIRAM (Jan. 22, 1799–Aug. 2, 1866), pioneer in higher education in the Middle West, first and fifth president of the University of Missouri, and president of the universities of Wisconsin and Indiana, was born in Sherburne, Chenango County, N. Y. His parents, John and Prudence Elizabeth (Hatch) Lathrop were of Puritan ancestry; his father was a descendant of the Rev. John Lothropp [*q.v.*]. After preparatory study under a neighboring clergyman, he entered Hamilton College, Clinton, N. Y., in 1815, and two years later was admitted to the junior class at Yale, from which institution he was graduated in 1819. He then taught for three years, first in the grammar school at Farmington, Conn., and then in Monroe Academy at Weston. From 1822 until 1826 he was a tutor at Yale and at the same time studied law. Admitted to the bar in the latter year, he opened a law office at Middletown, Conn., but soon returned to educational work, in which he now was convinced he should make his career. He became an instructor in the Military Academy at Norwich, Vt., and later was principal of the Gardiner Lyceum at Gardiner, Me. In 1829 he became professor of mathematics and natural philosophy at Hamilton College and six years later was promoted to the Maynard professorship of law, civil polity, and political economy. He had married, in 1833, Frances E. Lothrop of Utica, N. Y.

Lathrop's career as a pioneer in higher education in the undeveloped Middle West began on Mar. 11, 1841, when, after a six weeks' journey by stage and boat to Columbia, Mo., he became the first president of the University of Missouri. His task as president was to lead in developing a university for the benefit of which Congress had appropriated land, and to which the citizens of Boone County had voluntarily given from their meager resources $117,900. The cornerstone of the first university building had been laid July 4, preceding his arrival, but the edifice was not completed until 1843. His work included overseeing the sale of lands, supervising the erection of buildings, maturing plans for curricula and teaching, and advising the legislature with regard to the nature and needs of a real university. In this work he necessarily faced difficulties arising from lack of funds, and from religious sectarianism and partisan politics. He was embarrassed, too, by the increasing controversy about slavery and could not escape the antagonism of many who knew his acceptance of the doctrine that "all men are born free."

Although the curators of the University of Missouri desired him to continue as president, he decided in 1849 to accept the chancellorship of the University of Wisconsin, where he again became a pioneer university builder for ten years. Then, after two invitations, he became president of Indiana University. When the University of Missouri was reorganized, he accepted, in 1860, a call to return to this institution as professor of English literature. His welcome was enthusiastic. During the years 1863–65, his title was chairman of the faculty and professor of moral, mental, and political philosophy. He helped to guide the university during the precarious conditions of civil war, and in 1865 he was for the second time officially made president. In the following year he died and was buried in a cemetery near the campus. He was a man of attractive personality, wide scholarship, and ability both in teaching and in educational administration. Well-grounded in the social philosophy of his time, he believed that education should be practical and that the university should provide training in agriculture and in the various professions and arts. He believed that the profession of education should be as clearly separated from that of theology as the profession of law is separated from that of medicine, and that the remuneration of the successful teacher should be equivalent to that of the successful man in other learned professions. Deeply religious, but without sectarian bias, he regularly attended and contributed to the support of church services. Late in life he became a member of the Episcopal Church. He said that the ideal professor should be "too intensely American to be partisan, too profoundly Christian to be sectarian." This ideal was largely realized in his own life.

[See W. B. Davis and D. S. Durrie, *Illustrated Hist. of Mo.* (1876); H. L. Conard, ed., *Encyc. of the Hist. of Mo.* (1901), vol. III; W. F. Switzler, "History of the University of Missouri," in the archives of the university; Lathrop's *Address Delivered in the Chapel of the Univ. . . . of Mo. on the Occasion of the Dedication of the Edifice* (1843); *Obit. Record of the Grads. of Yale Coll. Deceased During the Academic Year Ending July 1867*; E. B. Huntington, *A Geneal. Memoir of the Lo-Lathrop Family* (1884). There is an oil portrait of Lathrop in the library of the University of Missouri, and a bronze portrait on the gateway to Francis Quadrangle.]

J. H. C.

LATHROP, ROSE HAWTHORNE [See ALPHONSA, MOTHER, 1851–1926].

LATIL, ALEXANDRE (Oct. 6, 1816–March 1851), Louisiana poet, was born in New Orleans, La., of a family whose ancestors came from France and in early colonial days were sailors and *coureurs de bois.* Young Alexandre attended Les Écoles Centrale et Primaires, and later, the Collège d'Orléans. When he was only fifteen he fell in love with the pretty daughter of a Creole and they became engaged. Their families thought them too young to marry and insisted that they wait a few years. From then on Latil's life paralleled all the horrors of a Greek tragedy. He developed unmistakable signs of leprosy, which the neighbors attributed to the mating of one of his *coureur-de-bois* forebears with a *sauvagesse,* for it was then commonly believed that the mixture of French with Indian blood was responsible for this disease. In those days lepers were allowed to remain at home, so Latil continued to live with his parents. He released his fiancée from their engagement, but this did not change her devotion, for she visited him daily in an effort to bring some cheer into his hopeless situation. Finally when the ravages of his disease had become too terrible, Latil was sent to a small cabin out on Bayou St. John in the *"Terre aux Lepreux,"* where his fiancée followed him. No scandal ever attached to her name although she took entire charge of the sufferer and nursed him tenderly. So great was her love that she desired to be his wife in spite of his illness and finally succeeded in overcoming his scruples. After their marriage she continued her nursing, forced to watch the relentless progress of his disease, the repulsive scaly blanching of his face, and the torturing disintegration of his limbs.

During these years of suffering poetry had been Latil's great solace. He tried to forget his agony in reading Béranger, Barthélemy, and

Delavigne, and was finally inspired to write French verse himself. It was good and some of the verses were printed in the Creole newspapers and literary magazines. The beauty of their resigned despair impressed the local literati and they urged him to collect and publish them in book form. He did this at his own expense and in 1841 *Les Éphémères,* a small collection of twenty-four of his poems, appeared. In a pathetic foreword this boy of only twenty-five regretted that the state of his health and his failing eyesight kept him from finishing some other verses which he had wished to include. The remaining years of his life were an inferno of suffering. He became completely bedridden and blind and his fingers dropped off at the palms so he could not hold a pen. Finally, death came as a merciful release in March 1851. His wife remained with him until the end, and it seems unjust that the name of this self-sacrificing woman cannot be perpetuated; only her initials—E. T.—are known.

[E. L. Tinker, *Les Écrits de Langue Française en Louisiane au XIX*[e] *Siècle* (1932); death notice in *L'Orléanais* (New Orleans), Mar. 18, 1851; Charles Testut, "Ange et Poète," in *Veillées Louisianaises* (1849), vol. I, p. 409, and by the same author *Fleurs d'Été* (1851), containing on p. 121 a poem on Latil's death, and *Portraits Littéraires* (1850).] E. L. T.

LATIMER, MARY ELIZABETH WORMELEY (July 26, 1822–Jan. 4, 1904), author, daughter of Rear Admiral Ralph Randolph Wormeley of the British navy and Caroline (Preble) Wormeley, was born in London, England. Her father was sixth in descent from Ralphe Wormeley, who received a grant of land in Virginia in 1649, and fourth from Ralph Wormeley of "Rosegill," Middlesex County, Va., one of the first trustees of the College of William and Mary. He was taken to England in childhood and became a British citizen. His wife was the daughter of a Boston East-India merchant and a niece of Commodore Edward Preble [*q.v.*], who won distinction in the early American navy. The childhood of the four Wormeley children was not monotonous. The family vibrated from London to Paris, to Boston, to Newport, to Virginia. Mary Elizabeth's studies were conducted in a desultory way by tutors, and she was for a time a "parlor boarder" in the school of Mrs. Cockle of Ipswich, Mass. The education of travel compensated for defects in formal study, and was of the greatest advantage to her in her career as a writer. She attended the funeral of William IV and saw Victoria enter Westminster Abbey for her coronation. She witnessed the funeral of Napoleon when his remains were brought to Paris from St. Helena, and made her début at the balls of Louis Philippe. A young man named William Makepeace Thackeray was one of the friends whom the family knew in Paris. The winter of 1842 she spent in Boston. where the families of George Ticknor, William H. Prescott, and Julia (Ward) Howe were among her friends and encouraged her to begin writing. Her first printed work was the translation of a Mexican poem for the appendix of Prescott's *History of the Conquest of Mexico* (pt. 2, vol. III, 1844). Not long after its publication the family removed permanently to the United States and thenceforth resided in Boston and in Newport, R. I.

In 1852 her father died and in the same year her first novel, *Amabel,* was published in London and New York. In 1856 she published *Our Cousin Veronica* and was married to Randolph Brandt Latimer of Baltimore. For twenty years thereafter she devoted herself to the cares of a home and three children. During the Civil War she took part in the nursing of soldiers. In 1876 she resumed writing, with the determination to make it her chief work. Though her eyes were never strong, she read and wrote indefatigably, and between 1880 and 1903 produced a large number of volumes. Her stories are not noteworthy; her best work is to be found in her series of popular histories: *France in the Nineteenth Century* (1892), and similar volumes dealing with Russia and Turkey (1893), England (1894), Europe in Africa (1895), Spain (1897); *Italy in the Nineteenth Century and the Making of Austro-Hungary and Germany* (1896); *My Scrap Book of the French Revolution* (1898); *Judea from Cyrus to Titus; 537 B.C.–70 A.D.* (1899); and *The Last Years of the Nineteenth Century* (1900). These books reveal much study and considerable understanding of national and world development. They abound in anecdotes and are written in a vivacious style. She was engaged upon a history of Germany in the nineteenth century when her own failing health and her husband's death, Dec. 24, 1903, permanently ended her work. In addition to original writing, she published the following translations: *A History of the People of Israel* (1888–96), in collaboration with J. H. Allen from the French of Ernest Renan; *The Steel Hammer* (1888) and *For Fifteen Years* (1888), from Louis Ulbach; *Nanon* (1890), from George Sand; *The Italian Republics* (1901), by J. C. L. de Sismondi; *The Love Letters of Victor Hugo, 1820–22* (1901); *Talks of Napoleon at St. Helena with General Baron Gourgaud* (1903). She died at her home in Baltimore and was buried in Greenmount Cemetery.

[Sara Andrew Shafer, in *The Dial,* Feb. 1, 1904; *Who's Who in America,* 1903–05; F. E. Willard and M. A. Livermore, *Am. Women* (1897); H. E. Hayden, *Va. Geneals.* (1891); G. H. Preble, *Geneal. Sketch of the First Three Generations of Rebels in America* (1868); *New-Eng. Hist. and Geneal. Reg.,* Oct. 1868; *Baltimore American,* Jan. 3, 4, 7, 1904; the *Sun* (Baltimore), Jan. 4, 5, 1904.] S. G. B.

LA TOUR, LE BLOND de (d. Oct. 14, 1723), chief engineer of the French colony of Louisiana, was born in France in the latter part of the seventeenth century. During the War of the Spanish Succession, he was sent as a draftsman to Portugal in 1702, appointed engineer in 1703, and served with the army in Spain from 1704 to 1708. He was taken prisoner at Alcantara in 1705 and exchanged the next year. He participated in the siege of Marchienne and served as noncommissioned officer at the sieges of Douai, Quesnoy, and Bouchain in 1712, and of Freiburg in 1713. He was decorated with the Cross of the Royal and Military Order of St. Louis in 1715 and was named reserve captain of the Piedmont regiment and then corporal of his Majesty's Engineers. In 1720 he was appointed engineer-in-chief of the province of Louisiana which was at that time under the control of Law's Company of the West. He arrived at Old Biloxi, the capital of the province, in December of that year with a corps of assistants to superintend the construction of whatever public buildings and works might be needed. The most pressing question before the council of the province at that time was whether to rebuild Old Biloxi, which had been almost wiped out by fire the year before, or transfer the capital to some other place. Bienville [*q.v.*], the governor of the province, was very eager that the capital should be moved to New Orleans, which he had founded in 1718. But the council, acting under the advice of La Tour, decided to move the capital to a point a short distance to the west of Old Biloxi and to give it the name of New Biloxi. La Tour drew up an elaborate plan for the new capital, which included a fortress and a port on Ship Island which stood a few miles opposite in the Mississippi Sound. (The plan is reproduced in Villiers du Terrage, *Les Dernières Années de la Louisiane Française,* 1904, p. 9.) In September 1721 the transfer was made. New Biloxi developed into the Biloxi of today.

Meanwhile La Tour had been ordered to send his assistant, Adrien de Pauger [*q.v.*], to New Orleans to examine the site and transfer the settlement to a more suitable spot, if he should deem it necessary to avoid the inundations of the river. Pauger went to New Orleans in March 1721, and seeing no reason for changing the site, he surveyed the place and in a few weeks finished drawing up plans for a city of about a mile square. He sent the plans to La Tour, but instead of forwarding them to Paris, La Tour is said to have pigeonholed them for fear the capital would be moved from New Biloxi to New Orleans. Bienville had anticipated this action on the part of La Tour, and having procured a copy of Pauger's plans, he sent them on to Paris. Soon thereafter the board of liquidation, which had taken over the affairs of the company after it had collapsed in the latter part of 1720, ordered the capital of Louisiana transferred to New Orleans. Not until then did La Tour give his official approval of Pauger's plans of the city.

La Tour claimed in a letter written Dec. 9, 1721, that he had drawn up the plan of New Orleans, and most of the historians of that city, especially the earlier ones, have accepted his claim. But Villiers du Terrage (*Histoire, post,* p. 88) declares that La Tour did not see New Orleans until nearly six months after making this claim, and that probably the only part he had in the matter was to trace on paper in advance a number of little squares. He may have intended, however, that these little squares should be situated far away from the Mississippi River, probably on the Bayou St. John which flowed into Lake Ponchartrain north of New Orleans. La Tour favored establishing an inland settlement on Lake Ponchartrain rather than on the Mississippi River, on the ground that it would be easier of access from the towns along the Gulf Coast.

On June 10, 1722, La Tour and Pauger left New Biloxi for New Orleans, arriving at their destination on July 7. Other boats followed, and under La Tour's supervision the new city began to take form and shape. A church and several houses were built, a cemetery was laid out, levees were thrown up—the first on the Lower Mississippi—ditches were dug, and a canal was constructed in the rear of the city for drainage purposes. The city, as laid out by Pauger and developed by La Tour, constitutes the French Quarter or the Vieux Carré of the present city of New Orleans. (See the plan of the city in 1725, Villiers du Terrage, *Histoire, post,* facing p. 118.) Before leaving New Biloxi, La Tour was made lieutenant-general of the province, much to the disgust and chagrin of Bienville. But Bienville submitted to higher authority and formally presented La Tour in his new rôle to the troops. La Tour died in New Orleans about eighteen months after going there. As far as is known, he left no heirs or descendants.

[The best account of La Tour is contained in Baron Marc de Villiers du Terrage, *Histoire de la Fondation de la Nouvelle-Orléans (1717–22)* (Paris, 1917). A translation of this monograph appeared in the *La. Hist. Quart.*, Apr. 1920. Scattered references to him are to be found in the *Journal Historique de l'Établissement des Français à la Louisiane* (New Orleans and Paris, 1831); Pierre Heinrich, *La Louisiane sous la Compagnie des Indies, 1717–31* (n.d.), and Grace E. King, *Jean Baptiste Le Moyne, Sieur de Bienville* (1892). The brief sketches of Fort Maurepas, Fort Louis de la Mobile, and Biloxi in Alcée Fortier, *Louisiana*, vol. I (1914), are helpful in tracing the changes in the capitals of Louisiana in its earlier years.] E. M. V.

LATROBE, BENJAMIN HENRY (May 1, 1764–Sept. 3, 1820), architect, engineer, traced the French name which marked him professionally as a "foreigner" from Henri Boneval de la Trobe, a French Protestant who, according to tradition, emigrated to Holland after the revocation of the edict of Nantes, followed the Prince of Orange to England, was wounded in the Battle of the Boyne, and settled finally in Dublin (*Brief Notices of the Latrobe Family*, London, 1864). Henry Boneval's grandson, Benjamin, joined the Moravians and was their minister at the settlement of Fulneck near Leeds. Here he married Anna Margaret Antes, who had been sent to Fulneck School. The daughter of Henry Antes [*q.v.*], of Germantown, Pa., she was related to the Rittenhouses and brought to her descendants the mathematical talent of that family. Her third child and second son, Benjamin Henry, born at Fulneck, spent his boyhood in England and his youth in Germany, where he received an excellent education. Family tradition attributes to him a service in the Prussian hussars before his return to England about 1786. In the years immediately following he printed two translations of some pretensions, the admiring *Characteristic Anecdotes, and Miscellaneous Authentic Papers, Tending to Illustrate the Character of Frederick II, Late King of Prussia* (1788) and the *Authentic Elucidation of the History of Counts Struensee and Brandt, and of the Revolution in Denmark in the Year 1772* (1789). Meanwhile he studied architecture under Samuel Pepys Cockerell, a pioneer of the Greek revival, and engineering under Smeaton, builder of the Eddystone lighthouse, for whom he investigated the scouring-works of Lincolnshire and Cambridgeshire.

His first independent work, "Hammerwood Lodge," East Grinstead, Sussex, was followed by a house at Ashdown Park, buildings at Frimley, Surrey, and the superintendence of a canal in Surrey. His father's connections and his own varied talents were bringing him influential friends, such as Sir Charles Middleton, and he was offered an appointment as surveyor of the police office of London, with bright prospects of professional advancement. In 1790 he married Lydia Sellon, daughter of the rector of St. James, Clerkenwell, by whom he had two children, Henry and Lydia. The death of his wife in 1793, during her third confinement, was followed by a period of distress and confusion in his affairs which led him to emigrate, not without fortune, to America.

He landed in Norfolk, Va., in March 1796, with letters which assured him a friendly reception, and spent the next two and a half years in Virginia. At first, as he wrote soon after landing, he was "idly engaged . . . designing a staircase for Mr. A's new house, a house and offices for Captain P——, tuning a pianoforte for Mrs. W——, scribbling doggerel for Mrs. A——, tragedy for her mother, and Italian songs for Mrs. T——" (*Journal of Latrobe, post,* p. xv), but he was soon employed on important works. He was first consulted on improving the navigation of the Appomattox, then of the James around the falls at Richmond, then on the Dismal Swamp improvements. In 1797 his design for the penitentiary at Richmond, one of the earliest prisons on the principle of solitary confinement, was adopted, and he removed from Norfolk to Richmond to supervise its construction at a salary of £200 per annum. Here he also completed the exterior of Jefferson's Virginia state capitol, substituting for the Louis XVI ornaments of the model a more severe treatment *à l'antique* (Fiske Kimball, *Thomas Jefferson and the First Monument of the Classical Revival in America*, 1915, p. 41). Another architectural work, in 1797, was the long arcade and portico of "Greenspring," near Williamsburg (drawing at the Virginia Historical Society).

In March 1798 he went for the first time to Philadelphia, with introductions to Jefferson and others. A month before, the Bank of Pennsylvania had authorized the construction of a new banking house, which its president, Samuel M. Fox, was determined should be a handsome one. Latrobe left a sketch with Fox and went back to Richmond. It was not long before he learned that his design had been adopted, and he was pressed to return and supervise the execution. This was a principal inducement to him to wind up his Virginia affairs and remove to Philadelphia in December. A site was secured on Second Street, and the building, begun in April 1799, was occupied early in 1801. It stood until after the Civil War, when it was demolished to make room for the Appraisers' Stores. Study of the architect's drawings and of old photographs reveals what posterity has lost. The building, very simple and all of marble, was fronted with two porticoes of six Ionic columns, their details modeled on those of the Erechtheum. Although the general form was thus that of a temple, it was not a slavish imitation—less so perhaps than the classical enthusiasm of laymen on the bank board would have welcomed. The interior, vaulted throughout, had a circular banking room, crowned by a low dome and a lantern. The building was the first monument of the Greek revival in America. (Kimball, "The Bank of Pennsylvania, 1799," in *Architectural Record,* August 1918.)

Latrobe's abilities were also called into requisition in the project for a city water supply, the first in America, stimulated by the epidemic of yellow fever a few years before. His *View of the Practicability and Means of Supplying the City of Philadelphia with Wholesome Water* (published 1799) is dated Dec. 29, 1798, only a few days after his arrival in the city. It advocated the raising of water from the Schuylkill River, using pumps operated by steam-engines, to an elevated reservoir on Center Square. His plan was so practical that it led to the immediate abandonment of other schemes, and its official adoption by the City. Work was begun in March 1799, with Latrobe as engineer, under a contract which guaranteed successful operation. The engines, much the largest among the very few yet built in America, were built by Nicholas James Roosevelt [*q.v.*] at his works on the Passaic in New Jersey. Public ignorance and the delays and increased expense incident to such a pioneer undertaking had occasioned the greatest skepticism as to its success. Latrobe's son has recorded how on the night of Jan. 21, 1801, his father, "with three gentlemen, his friends, and one of his workmen, kindled a fire under the boiler, and set the ponderous machinery in motion while the city was buried in sleep," so that in the morning "the streets of Philadelphia were flowing with water from the gushing hydrants" (*Journal of Latrobe,* p. xxi). The works continued in operation until Sept. 7, 1815, when, no longer adequate, they were superseded by larger ones designed by one of Latrobe's pupils. The marble "Center House," on the general model of the *villa rotunda,* with Greek porticoes and a dome over the elevated tank, was a familiar landmark until its demolition in 1827. With William Rush's fountain, "The Nymph of the Schuylkill," it figures in John Lewis Krimmel's "Centre Square, Philadelphia, in 1812," one of the earliest American genre paintings. (Drawings by Latrobe of the house and its engines, reproduced in the *Architectural Record,* July 1927, pp. 18–22, are preserved by the Historical Society of Pennsylvania, which also has a very complete file of the early reports and pamphlets.)

In September 1801 the improvement of navigation of the Susquehanna was undertaken. The Pennsylvania portion of the survey was intrusted to Latrobe's American uncle, Col. Frederick Antes, who died at the beginning of the work. Latrobe carried it to completion, and by the end of the year had cleared the channel for downstream navigation from Columbia to tidewater. His report was published in *Report of the Governor and Directors to the Proprietors of the Susquehanna Canal* (1802). His very large and beautifully executed map is still preserved by the Maryland Historical Society, and has been authoritative in modern lawsuits. Perhaps to this period is to be referred also his undated pamphlet, *American Copper-Mines,* with its acute observations.

During these years he planned several houses in Philadelphia. "Sedgley," built for William Cramond on land acquired in March 1799 in what is now Fairmount Park, was the first design of the Gothic revival in America. Its little lodge still survives. In 1800 Latrobe designed for Robert Liston, the British minister, a house which was never built, intended for Fairmount itself. It was to be circular in plan, and represented an abstract ideal of form not realized in America until long afterwards. The Burd house at Chestnut and Ninth streets, with its broad wall surfaces and arched windows, was until its demolition a notable landmark of the city.

As early as 1800 Latrobe was at work on projects for the federal government. A design for a military academy, requested of him by the secretary of war, was furnished on Jan. 26 of that year. In November 1802, President Jefferson called him to Washington to make drawings, surveys, and estimates for a dry dock to preserve twelve frigates ready for sea. The design, dated Dec. 4, is in the possession of the Library of Congress. It shows a great vaulted hangar open at the sides and ends, and is so admirably worked out that we can well understand why the select committee of Congress was unanimous in its favor, and that this most derided of the Philosopher-President's ideas, defeated by a sectional vote, was by no means wholly impractical. (Kimball, "Benjamin Henry Latrobe and the Beginnings of Architectural and Engineering Practice in America," *Michigan Technic,* December 1917.)

When funds had been appropriated toward the completion of the federal buildings in Washington, Jefferson created for Latrobe, on Mar. 6, 1803, the post of surveyor of the public buildings. His salary was fixed at $1700 a year. The immediate task in hand was the erection of the south wing of the Capitol, to contain the Hall of Representatives. The north wing, containing the Senate Chamber, which was already complete, determined the exterior design of its fellow. Foundations had been laid, establishing an internal form for the structure in accordance with a design of William Thornton [*q.v.*], whose original plan had won the competition of 1792–93. Latrobe, like his predecessors in office, raised very sound objections to the design on both practical and artistic grounds. The old struggle between the tenacious amateur and his professional critics, in which Thornton had destroyed Hallet and George Hadfield [*qq.v.*], was renewed. It even rocked Congress, and threatened the loss of appropriations. But Jefferson, although counseling stability of plan and seeking to avoid a direct issue for political reasons, kept his architect in authority. Thornton had at last met his match. It was in the person of Jefferson himself, rather than Thornton, that the ideas of the amateur in architecture continued to embarrass Latrobe. The Roman tendencies of the pioneer of American classicism sometimes came in conflict with the Greek predilections of the younger man, and the President's orders were sometimes difficult to reconcile with structural considerations and elegancies of planning. With mutual concessions and mutual respect, however, the two men, by the close of Jefferson's administration, had brought the wings of the building to a worthy completion. (The controversial pamphlets of Thornton and Latrobe are listed by Glenn Brown, *post,* II, 225.)

In the south wing was the Hall of Representatives, with its circular ends and its twenty-four stone Corinthian columns, their capitals designed after the Greek example of the Monument of Lysicrates. For the carving two Italian sculptors, Giovanni Andrei and Giuseppi Franzoni, had been brought over in 1806. Franzoni's eagle above the speaker's desk was among the earliest American works of monumental sculpture. Many of the rooms in this wing were vaulted in masonry. In the north wing, much interior rebuilding had been undertaken, to raise the standard of construction. Here, for the east basement vestibule, Latrobe devised in 1809 his "American order" of maize, with what were promptly christened by admiring members of Congress the "corn-cob capitals."

Much other work for the federal government came meanwhile from Latrobe's hands. For the President's House he executed Jefferson's scheme of colonnaded terraces, and in 1807 made designs for the remodeling and development of the house itself (Kimball, *Thomas Jefferson, Architect,* pp. 66–67, 175–76). These showed the semicircular portico toward the river suggested by Jefferson, and proposed the north portico, both of which were executed in the rebuilding after Latrobe's final retirement from the government service in 1817. Construction of the Washington City Canal, on which he had first advised in 1802, was actively pursued in 1803 and 1810. In 1804 he was called "engineer of the Navy Department," and in the following years he designed much work at the yards in Washington, New York, and elsewhere. In 1810 he was building fireproofs for the State Department, and, by an irony of fate, remodeling the Patent Office, presided over by his old antagonist, Thornton. In 1812 he drew plans for the Marine Hospital in Washington.

His activity was not exhausted by the labors of his official post. In 1804, he was consulted by Bishop John Carroll [*q.v.*] about the building of a cathedral in Baltimore for his diocese, which then had a national scope. Invited to submit a plan, Latrobe gave his services without any remuneration. They were to extend from 1805 to 1818, and to involve the making of seven or eight successive and distinct designs. The first two plans offered the trustees, for the first time in America, a choice between the Gothic and classic styles. One was the earliest American church design of the Gothic revival; the other was of a Roman magnificence hitherto unknown in American ecclesiastical buildings. This classical plan, which was preferred, underwent gradual transformation to its final form—a Latin cross, with a great circular crossing embracing both nave and aisles, crowned by a low Roman dome. The exterior was of broad simplicity. The portico, six columns wide, of the Greek Ionic order, was first executed in 1860–63, when the choir was also extended eastward. Building committee and builders alike were little prepared to understand or sympathize with the monumental character of the design, and many difficulties arose in its execution; but, with the support of the Bishop, Latrobe persevered, and on his final departure from Baltimore received from the trustees such a letter of testimonial as few architects could show: "It is true that objections were sometimes made to parts of your plans, the propriety and connection of which their inexperience did not permit them at the time to discern clearly, but now that the various details of the building form one grand and beautiful whole, they are fully convinced of the propriety of having on such occasions given way to your greater experience and better judgment." (Kimball, "Latrobe's Designs for the Cathedral of Balti-

more," *Architectural Record,* December 1917, January 1918.)

During all these years there was an increasing flood of private commissions. In 1803 Latrobe was concerned with the reroofing of Nassau Hall at Princeton; in 1804, designing the first building, West College, for Dickinson College, Carlisle, Pa.; in 1805, the first Pennsylvania Academy of the Fine Arts, at Tenth and Chestnut streets, Philadelphia; in 1806, the additions which adapted the building once intended for the "President's House" in Philadelphia to the use of the University of Pennsylvania. Following his custom of giving gratuitous service to religious and educational institutions, he supplied the plans for these without charge. The wing of the Chestnut Street Theatre was from his design. The Bank of Philadelphia, a Gothic structure of brick and marble, was executed under the supervision of his pupil Robert Mills in 1807. That same year Latrobe built the Waln house, esteemed the finest in the city, and two years later the Markoe house—both with a rich variety of interior spatial effects. He added the portico to "Bellevue" (now Dumbarton House) in Georgetown, D. C.

His engineering work also continued. In February 1804 he was appointed engineer of the Chesapeake & Delaware Canal, for which he had made a first reconnaissance in 1799. His surveys were completed by the end of the year: a route from Welch Point on the Elk River (an arm of the Chesapeake) to Christiana Creek on the Delaware was adopted, providing for a canal twenty miles long, eighty feet wide and eight deep, fed by a branch six miles long, three and a half feet deep, and twenty-six feet wide, susceptible of extension by the valley of the Elk River and Octoraro Creek to the iron region of Pennsylvania. Work was first undertaken on the feeder, that it might be used in transportation of materials not found on the main line, and it was nearly finished in 1805, when failure of subscribers to pay caused the project to be suspended. (Documentary information regarding this project may be found in the published *Annual Reports,* and in Latrobe's letter of Jan. 4, 1808, in *Letters to the Honorable Albert Gallatin . . . and other Papers Relative to the Chesapeake and Delaware Canal,* 1808.)

Aaron Burr, in 1805, had invited Latrobe to go to Kentucky as engineer for a canal around the falls of the Ohio at Louisville, and to recruit five hundred men for the work. Latrobe's testimony to this effect was given weight by the government in Burr's trial. He was also consulted by the City of New York as to a system of drainage for the city; by the Philadelphia Chamber of Commerce in 1807 on the removal of the bar at the mouth of the Schuylkill; and by the House of Representatives as to the navigation of the Potomac. In general these projects were themselves beyond the resources of the time, and Latrobe's high standard of permanence in construction made him reluctant to employ the makeshifts by which the first of such works were later brought within the means of their proponents.

On the outbreak of the war of 1812 and the suspension of his government work, Latrobe entered partnership with Robert Fulton, Robert R. Livingston, and Nicholas J. Roosevelt, now his son-in-law, to build a steamboat adapted to navigation of the Ohio River above the falls. He removed with his family to Pittsburgh in the autumn of 1813. The war increased the costs, which the underwriters had difficulty in meeting, and the death of Fulton in 1815 brought the work to a standstill, to be finished later under other auspices. In this enterprise all Latrobe's private means were swept away. Even before going west, Latrobe had furnished designs for houses beyond the mountains, such as "Belvedere," the home of John Barker Church and his wife, Angelica Schuyler, in the upper Genesee Valley, and Henry Clay's house at Ashland, Ky. While in Pittsburgh, and later, he supplied plans for several others, the Robertson house in Pittsburgh, Governor Taylor's in Newport, Ky., the house of Governor Cass in Michigan.

On Aug. 24, 1814, following the capture of Washington by the British, the Capitol and the President's House were set on fire. The British officer charged with the task of destroying the Hall of Representatives said it was "a pity to burn anything so beautiful" (Brown, *post,* I, 39). The close of the war brought Latrobe an invitation (Mar. 14, 1815) to take charge of the rebuilding of the Capitol, and he returned to Washington in April. The external walls remained, but the interior, which had been destroyed, was now completely remodeled. The stately semicircular chambers of the House and Senate (now Statuary Hall and the Supreme Court room) were the fruit of Latrobe's activity at this time. For the vestibule of the Senate chamber he designed, as a pendant to the corn capitals, capitals composed from the flowers and leaves of the tobacco plant. Before the central Rotunda could be undertaken, difficulties had arisen with the commissioner, Samuel Lane, which made Latrobe's position insupportable, and he resigned, Nov. 20, 1817.

Among his private works in Washington during this period was St. John's Church, built orig-

inally in the form of a Greek cross. Latrobe, a member of the congregation, himself wrote the dedicatory hymn. Other works included the Van Ness house, long the finest in the city, the house of Commodore Decatur, the tower of Christ Church in Alexandria, Va., and the Court House in Hagerstown, Md. His advice had been sought by Jefferson in June 1817, in regard to the University of Virginia, and his sketches and drawings sent to Jefferson in July and October of that year were influential in the design of Pavilions V and III, and especially in the adoption, for the head of the plan, of a domed building of importance (Kimball, *Thomas Jefferson, Architect*, pp. 76–79, 187–92).

Harassed by the debts on the steamboat, he decided before leaving Washington to take advantage of the new insolvency act, the ceremony being performed, as he wrote, on Jan. 1, 1818. Penned in the margin of one of his printed notices of insolvency are the words: "Your claim on me is of a nature which no legal release can absolve . . . the field of productive activity before me is such, as to assure me,—if I live,—of the certainty of not disappointing your confidence in me" (Dreer Collection, Historical Society of Pennsylvania). With the friendly support of Gen. Robert Goodloe Harper [*q.v.*], he removed to Baltimore, where, besides the Cathedral, he had other important buildings under construction. He had undertaken, with Maximilian Godefroy [*q.v.*], designs for the Exchange in Baltimore which were adopted in February 1816, over those of Joseph Ramé. With the Exchange were incorporated the Bank of the United States and the Custom House, the whole making a large, simple, coherent building with a Roman dome some 115 feet in height. The building has been long since destroyed, but its aspect is preserved by a perspective drawing of Latrobe, belonging to the Maryland Historical Society. In the course of its execution difficulties arose between Latrobe and Godefroy which left the former arrayed against his friend, as well as his pupils, in competition for the next great prize.

The second Bank of the United States had been chartered Apr. 10, 1816, and, in anticipation of the erection of its main banking house in Philadelphia, Latrobe had made efforts, while still in the public service, to be entrusted outright with the commission. A competition was finally decided on, however, the advertisement, dated May 12, 1818, specifying that the building should be of rectangular form, with a portico on each front, "exhibiting a chaste imitation of Grecian architecture, in its simplest and least expensive form" (*United States Gazette,* July 9, 1818). Besides Latrobe, among the competitors were Mills, Strickland, Godefroy, and Hugh Bridport. Mills submitted a design fronted by six Greek Doric columns; Latrobe went further and proposed an imitation of the octastyle front of the Parthenon itself. His design, preserved in the office of the supervising architect of the Treasury, would seem to have carried the day, for there exists a later plan, reduced in size to meet the demands of the directors, who were alarmed by the threatening general financial conditions. By November a national panic had occurred, and hope for any early beginning of construction was abandoned. Thus it was only after Latrobe's final removal to New Orleans that the undertaking was resumed under the direction of Strickland. Latrobe was justified in saying that the design followed was his, but that the principal room was a departure from it. The cornerstone was laid Apr. 19, 1819; the building was occupied by the Bank from 1824 until the liquidation of 1841, and, since its purchase by the federal government in 1844, has been the Philadelphia Custom House. In it the enthusiasm of American classicism outran corresponding developments abroad. It antedated the European imitations of the Parthenon by a dozen years, and attracted an attention which was international (Kimball, "The Bank of the United States, 1818–24," *Architectural Record,* December 1925).

As early as 1809 Latrobe had been consulted in regard to a water supply for New Orleans, and the next year had sent his son Henry, who had graduated from St. Mary's College in Baltimore, to pursue the project. A year later the legislature of Louisiana granted the Latrobes exclusive privileges for twenty years from May 1813, the date at which it was thought the works could be completed. The war delayed the enterprise and Henry, who had taken part in the defense of the city and had begun the important lighthouse at Franks Island at the mouth of the Mississippi, died of yellow fever in 1817, leaving over $40,000 invested in the unfinished water works. His father determined to go himself to New Orleans. His contract successfully renewed, he brought his family overland early in 1820 and was actively pushing the work to completion when he too was attacked by yellow fever and died, on Sept. 3. As in Philadelphia, the main building of the water works was of excellent classical design, here with a pedimented portico (painting preserved in the Cabildo). Other work which he did in New Orleans included the tower of the Cathedral, erected in

1820. At the time of his death he was in negotiation with Rudolph Ackermann in London for the publication of his designs, but in the end only a single plate appeared, that of the Hall of Representatives in Washington.

Latrobe found architecture in America a polite accomplishment of the gentleman amateurs such as Jefferson, Thornton, and the young Charles Bulfinch, and a part of the business of superior builders and craftsmen such as McIntire, Hoban, and McComb. He left it a profession, with professional standards and practices, largely in the hands of his own pupils. The architect was no longer a dilettante, or a builder expected to contract for the execution of his design and tied to the building for his whole time. The foreign professionals who came before him, Hallet and Hadfield, had been borne under by existing conditions. Latrobe did not accomplish the change without bitter struggles against inertia and misunderstanding, which it took great stamina to overcome; nor without many mortifications to his proud and sensitive spirit. Few American architects before the great organizations of the past generation have had so wide and varied a practice. To compass it at that period meant constant days in the saddle, or coaching by miserable roads, and nights in more miserable ordinaries, where many of the vast mass of his drawings and letters were produced. Apprenticeship in his office constituted the first important professional training in engineering and architecture in America. Frederick Graff [*q.v.*], who was his pupil and assistant in the first Philadelphia water works, was in charge of their replacement by the remarkable works at Fairmount. Robert Mills and William Strickland, the principal later masters of the Greek revival, learned under him both architecture and engineering. It was his pupils who built the first American railroads. His style continued to dominate American building down to the Civil War.

He was personally accomplished and of most varied attainments. An excellent Latinist and Grecian, he knew also German, French, Spanish, and Italian, and his professional library contained works in all these languages. He drew with great facility and accuracy: many of his water colors of American scenes survive, and his rough pen sketches of important political figures, such as Washington, Edmund Randolph, and Patrick Henry, are of value as likenesses (*Magazine of American History,* August 1881). His reports on engineering and architectural projects are models of technical exposition. In design and construction he had the greatest facility and resource. During the wearisome hours of journeys or of illness—he had contracted malarial fever while on an Alpine expedition at the age of seventeen—he filled his notebooks with scientific observations, genre sketches, and fragments of romances. His scientific and artistic attainments brought him election to the American Philosophical Society (1799) and to the American Antiquarian Society (1815) as well as to the Society of Artists, before which he delivered the anniversary oration of 1811 (*Port Folio,* June 1811).

Portraits of Latrobe are reproduced in *The Journal of Latrobe* and Brown's *History of the United States Capitol* (*post*). His son described him as "6 feet 2 inches, of erect and military carriage" (Semmes, *post,* p. 6). By his devoted second wife, Mary Elizabeth Hazlehurst, whom he married in Philadelphia, May 2, 1800, he was the founder of a distinguished family. Of his two surviving sons, John Hazlehurst Boneval Latrobe [*q.v.*] became counsel of the Baltimore & Ohio Railroad, and Benjamin Henry Latrobe [*q.v.*] became its chief engineer.

[Latrobe's papers still remain chiefly in the hands of his descendants, the largest collection being in the possession of Ferdinand C. Latrobe. Transcripts of letters relating to the Capitol are in the MSS. Div. Lib. of Cong. Other Latrobe material is found in the Henley Smith Papers, Lib. of Cong.; the District of Columbia Papers, Dept. of State; and the papers of the Office of Public Buildings and Grounds, War Dept. (see list in Glenn Brown, *post,* II, 224). Much of this material is published in *Doc. Hist. of the Construction and Development of the U. S. Capitol* (1904). Many of Latrobe's drawings of the Capitol are preserved in the Lib. of Cong., and in the office of the superintendent of the Capitol. Extracts from his diaries and notebooks were published as *The Journal of Latrobe* (1905), with a biographical introduction by J. H. B. Latrobe, written in 1876. See also *Md. Hist. Mag.,* Sept. 1909; *Proc. Am. Inst. of Architects,* Nov. 16, 1881; *International Rev.,* Nov. 1874; *Repository of Arts,* etc. (London), Jan. 1, 1821; Wm. Dunlap, *Hist. of the Rise and Progress of the Arts of Design in the U. S.* (2 vols., 1834); *La. Courier* (New Orleans), Sept. 4, 1820; *Daily National Intelligencer* (Washington), Oct. 2, 1820; *American and Commercial Daily Advertiser* (Baltimore), Oct. 3, 1820; J. E. Semmes, *John H. B. Latrobe and His Times* (1917). Discussions of his relation to the Capitol include those of Peter B. Wight and Adolf Cluss in *Proc. Am. Inst. of Architects,* 1875 and 1876; G. A. Townsend, *Washington Outside and Inside* (1873); Glenn Brown, *Hist. of the U. S. Capitol* (2 vols., 1900–03); W. B. Bryan, *A Hist. of the National Capital* (2 vols., 1914–16); Fiske Kimball, *Thomas Jefferson, Architect* (1916).]

F. K.

LATROBE, BENJAMIN HENRY (Dec. 19, 1806–Oct. 19, 1878), civil engineer, was born at Philadelphia, Pa., the son of Benjamin Henry Latrobe [*q.v.*] and his second wife, Mary Elizabeth (Hazlehurst). His mother gave him his first schooling, and when he was eight he was placed with his elder brother, John H. B. Latrobe [*q.v.*], in Georgetown College. In 1817 the father took the family to Baltimore, and soon after that to New Orleans, where in 1820 he died. Returning with his mother to Baltimore, Latrobe attended St. Mary's College as a day student, 1821–23, taking high honors in mathematics. He then read law and practised a short time with his brother before going to Allowaystown, N. J., to act as agent for a parcel of land owned there by his mother and his uncle. Soon forced by ill health to leave Allowaystown, he returned to Baltimore, making his home with his brother and again associating with him in practice. The profession was not to his taste, however, and in 1831, through the influence of his brother, he obtained a position in the engineer corps of the Baltimore & Ohio Railroad.

Advancement was rapid on the new road for men with mathematical training and Benjamin Latrobe was soon principal assistant to Jonathan Knight [*q.v.*], the chief engineer. In 1832 he was in charge of the survey that located the line from Baltimore to Washington and he later designed and built the outstanding bit of construction of that branch, the Thomas Viaduct at Relay House, nine miles southwest of Baltimore. This stone-arch bridge, named for the first president of the road, was long known as "Latrobe's Folly." It has since been recognized as one of the finest pieces of railroad architecture in the country (Hungerford, *post,* I, 166), and, still in use, is now one of the oldest railroad viaducts in the world, successfully carrying modern equipment. In 1835 Latrobe left the Baltimore & Ohio to become chief engineer of the Baltimore & Port Deposit Railroad, for which he built the thirty-four difficult miles of road from Baltimore to Havre de Grace, Md. The ferries that he employed at Havre de Grace were probably the first of the present type of railroad ferries. Returning then to the Baltimore & Ohio, he directed the survey of the line from Point of Rocks to Harpers Ferry, and as engineer of location and construction (1836), built the road through the mountains from Harpers Ferry to Cumberland. Upon the completion of this part of the road, Knight resigned as chief engineer, Sept. 30, 1842, and Latrobe was appointed to his position.

In 1847 the extension to Wheeling, Va. (W. Va.), on the Ohio River was authorized, and Latrobe with three corps of engineers started in July of that year to lay out the line, completing the survey to the Ohio the next year. The construction of this road was probably his major work. With 5,000 men and 1,250 horses, drilling and loading by hand, blasting with black powder, and hauling with horses, he built 200 miles of road, including 113 bridges and eleven tunnels (one of the longest in the country at the time), in less than four years. The masonry wall construction which still carries the road along the slopes of the hills in the Cheat River Valley and the Kingswood Tunnel (4,100 feet) were the dramatic features of the task. To permit the opening of the line before the completion of the tunnel a temporary line two miles long with a grade of 10 per cent. (528 feet rise in a mile) was built and operated for passenger service for six months (T. C. Clarke, "The Building of a Railway," *Scribner's Magazine,* June 1888). Latrobe next built the Northwestern Virginia Railroad (1851–52) for the Baltimore & Ohio Railroad Company, and in 1871, as chief engineer of the Pittsburg & Connellsville Railroad, he drove the gold spike that completed this road and the Baltimore & Ohio to Pittsburgh. He originated the railroad unit of work, the "ton mile" (*Baltimore & Ohio Annual Report,* 1847), and was the authority for the maximum permissible grade of 116 feet to the mile, prescribed in the charters of the transcontinental railroads; he indorsed the proposal of the Magnetic Telegraph Company to lay the first line of the Morse telegraph along the Washington Branch of the Baltimore & Ohio; and he was a member of the committee to which Roebling submitted the plans of the Brooklyn Bridge. He retired from the railroad in 1875, and died at Baltimore three years later, after a short illness.

On Mar. 12, 1833, at Salem, N. J., he married a cousin, Maria Eleanor Hazlehurst. They were the parents of five children, one of whom, Charles Hazlehurst Latrobe [*q.v.*], attained distinction in his father's profession.

[J. E. Semmes, *John H. B. Latrobe and His Times* (1917); various reports by Latrobe, in Lib. of Cong.; Paul Winchester, *The Baltimore & Ohio Railroad,* vol. I (1927); Edward Hungerford, *The Story of the Baltimore & Ohio Railroad, 1827–1927* (1928), vol. I; C. B. Stuart, *Lives and Works of Civil and Military Engineers of America* (1871); *Railway Age,* Oct. 31, 1878; *Railroad Gazette,* Oct. 25, 1878; *Sun* (Baltimore), Oct. 21, 1878.] F. A. T.

LATROBE, CHARLES HAZLEHURST (Dec. 25, 1834–Sept. 19, 1902), civil engineer, was born in Baltimore, the eldest of the five children of Benjamin Henry Latrobe, the second [*q.v.*], and his wife, Maria Eleanor Hazlehurst. He attended St. Mary's College, in his native city, learned the rudiments of his profession in his father's office—which was probably the best school of its kind in the United States—and graduated thence into the service of the Baltimore & Ohio Railroad. A few years later he went to Florida as the youthful but very capable chief engineer in charge of construction on the Pensacola & Georgia Railroad. Stationed at Tallahassee when the state seceded from the Union, he promptly threw in his lot with the South and, as a lieutenant of engineers in the Confederate army, completed the grading, bridge-building, and rail-laying on the last twenty miles of the Pensacola & Georgia. The road proved of considerable military use. At the close of the war Latrobe returned to Baltimore, which was his home for the rest of his life. From 1866 to 1877 he was associated with his father and with Charles Shaler Smith in the Baltimore Bridge Company. This firm erected bridges in many parts of the eastern United States. Latrobe's own work, which was of a high order, was noted especially for its structural beauty. He was appointed engineer of the Jones Falls commission in Baltimore in 1875, when his cousin, Ferdinand Claiborne Latrobe, entered on his first term as mayor of the city; and he remained in the city employ until 1889. He designed and built the great retaining walls along the Falls and designed and constructed the iron bridges across the valley at St. Paul Street, Calvert Street, and Guilford Avenue. He built a number of other bridges in Baltimore, laid out the terraced gardens along Mount Royal Avenue, and was in charge of the improvements and extensions in Mount Royal, Druid Hill, and Patterson parks. He also executed several commissions for the Peruvian government. At Arequipa he constructed an aqueduct 1,300 feet long and sixty-five feet high; and at Verrugas, on the Callao-Oroya-Huancayo railway, he built the most famous of his bridges. Spanning one of the deepest gorges in the Andes, it was 575 feet in length and had a central wrought-iron pier 252 feet high. It was said to be the tallest bridge in the world. It was framed in the United States, then taken apart for shipment, and was reërected in ninety days. During his latter years Latrobe was consulting engineer for several railroads. He was married three times: in 1861 to a widow, Letitia Breckenridge (Gamble) Holliday, who bore him two daughters and a son and died in 1867; in 1869 to Rosa Wirt Robinson, who died the next year; and in 1881 to Louise, widow of Isaac McKim. Latrobe possessed the engaging social qualities as well as the engineering and artistic genius of his family. He died in Baltimore after an illness of a year and was buried in Greenmount Cemetery.

[*Baltimore American,* Sept. 20, 22, 1902; the *Sun* (Baltimore), Sept. 20, 21, 1902; *War of the Rebellion: Official Records (Army)*, 4 ser. I, 777–79; *Baltimore: Its Hist. and Its People* (1912), II, 400–02; J. E. Semmes, *John H. B. Latrobe and his Times 1803–91* (1917).]

G. H. G.

LATROBE, JOHN HAZLEHURST BONEVAL (May 4, 1803–Sept. 11, 1891), lawyer, inventor, public servant, was the elder son of Benjamin H. Latrobe [*q.v.*], and Mary Elizabeth (Hazlehurst) Latrobe. He was born in Philadelphia, but, with his brother Benjamin [*q.v.*], received his earlier educational training at Georgetown College in the District of Columbia and at St. Mary's College, Baltimore. Expecting to become an architect, he spent the years 1818–21 as a cadet at West Point, then the only school of engineering in the country, but resigned upon the death of his father shortly before the end of his fourth year. Returning to Baltimore, he entered the law office of Robert Goodloe Harper [*q.v.*], and was admitted to the bar in 1824. While waiting for his law practice, he pressed into service his talent as writer and artist to increase the meager income of the family. Under the pseudonym of Godfrey Wallace he made a yearly contribution to *The Atlantic Souvenir,* Mathew Carey's gift annual; in 1826 he published *The Justices' Practice under the Laws of Maryland,* begun at the suggestion of a Baltimore editor during his student days; to John Sanderson's *Biography of the Signers to the Declaration of Independence* (vol. VII, 1827) he contributed the sketch of Charles Carroll.

In 1827 he helped to draft the charter of the Baltimore & Ohio Railroad and the following year was retained by the road to secure its right of way from Point of Rocks to Williamsport, Md., services which marked his establishment in his profession. From that time until his death he was connected with the Baltimore & Ohio, and he attained wide recognition as a railroad lawyer. In 1857–58 while visiting Europe he was successful in securing from the Czar of Russia allowance for claims for a railroad from St. Petersburg to Moscow, for which he received the princely fee of $60,000. He argued many important cases in the state and federal supreme courts, and was in special demand as a patent lawyer, partly because of the engineering training he had received at West Point. His technical understanding enabled him to recognize at once the value of the Morse telegraph, and to recommend it to the president of the Baltimore & Ohio Railroad, who granted Morse the privilege of stringing the first line between Baltimore and Washington along the railroad's right of way. In response to his wife's complaint that the stoves in use claimed too much space he devised the popular Latrobe stove, to fit into the fireplace and heat not only the room in which it was installed but also the room above. It was characteristic of him that he shrank from taking credit for this useful invention, thinking it not in accord with the dignity of his profession, for although he continued to act in patent cases throughout his career, he desired to be known first as a master of legal principles. At the age of eighty-six he revised and published the eighth edition of his *Justices' Practices,* which he had begun before his admission to the bar.

Throughout his life Latrobe wielded pencil and brush with such enthusiasm that he filled his home with his works. From time to time he ventured into literature, noteworthy among his writings being *The Baltimore & Ohio Railroad: Personal Recollections* (1868); *Odds and Ends* (1876), a slight volume of poems printed for private circulation, which contained verses of grace and some merit; and *Reminiscences of West Point* (1887). In 1825 he produced the winning design for the Kościuszko monument at West Point. He also designed a number of other monuments, several structures for the Baltimore parks, and the "Baltimore Cottages" at White Sulphur Springs. It is perhaps as a patron, however, that he made a more permanent contribution to the arts. Inspired by the Franklin Institute at Philadelphia, he founded the Maryland Institute for the Promotion of the Mechanic Arts (chartered 1825), with which he kept his connection for years. He served the Academy of Art as its president before its absorption into the Peabody Institute. He was one of a committee which awarded a prize to Edgar Allan Poe for "A MS. Found in a Bottle," and a prize for a clay model to the sculptor Rinehart.

In the field of philanthropy his most conspicuous service was given to the cause of African colonization. While still in the office of General Harper he prepared the first map of Liberia for the American Colonization Society, of which his preceptor was an active leader. He was instrumental in getting a state appropriation for transportation of emigrants, helped to found the Maryland State Colonization Society, and drafted the constitution for the separate colony of Maryland in Liberia at Cape Palmas. In 1853 he was elected to succeed Henry Clay as president of the national society, in which post he continued thirty-seven years. He was one of two Americans invited by the King of the Belgians in 1876 to represent the United States at the first meeting of the International Association for the Exploration and Colonisation of Central Africa, and became the president of the American branch of that society. He rendered other public services as member of the Board of Visitors of the United States Military Academy, regent for the University of Maryland, founder and almost life president (1871–91) of the Maryland Historical Society, member of the Park Commission to which Baltimore owes Druid Hill Park; member of the Board of the Centennial Exposition at Philadelphia. He was repeatedly selected to deliver addresses on significant public occasions.

He was married twice: on Nov. 29, 1828, to Margaret Stuart of Baltimore, who died two years later, leaving one child; and on Dec. 6, 1832, to Charlotte Virginia Claiborne of Mississippi, by whom he had seven children. His son Ferdinand Claiborne Latrobe (1833–1911) was seven times mayor of Baltimore (*Who's Who in America,* 1910–11). Latrobe's friends knew him as a gentle, courteous, wonderfully vigorous man, whose clearness of perception, versatility, systematic precision, and prodigious industry enabled him to march through his manifold labors with military discipline. Active almost to the end, he died at his home in Baltimore in his eighty-ninth year.

[See J. E. Semmes, *John H. B. Latrobe and His Times* (1917); *Baltimore American* and Baltimore *Sun,* Sept. 12, 1891; M. P. Andrews, *Tercentenary Hist. of Md.* (1925); *Baltimore: Its Hist. and Its People* (1912), vol. II; G. W. Howard, *The Monumental City* (1873); C. W. Sams and E. S. Riley, *The Bench and Bar of Md.* (1901); H. E. Shepherd, *The Representative Authors of Md.* (1911); R. H. Spencer, *Geneal. and Memorial Encyc. of the State of Md.* (1919), vol. II; *Proc. Md. Hist. Soc. in Commemoration of the Late Hon. John H. B. Latrobe* (1891); Paul Winchester, *The Baltimore and Ohio Railroad,* vol. I (1927); Edward Hungerford, *The Story of the Baltimore and Ohio Railroad* (1928), vol. I. Some of Latrobe's papers are deposited with the Md. Hist. Soc. as the Latrobe and Semmes Papers, but others are still in the possession of the family.] E. L.

LATTA, ALEXANDER BONNER (June 11, 1821–Apr. 28, 1865), inventor, manufacturer, was born on a farm near Chillicothe, Ross County, Ohio, the youngest of the six children of John and Rebecca (Bonner) Latta. When he was five years old his father was killed in an accident, leaving his widow penniless. Consequently, after attending the country school for a few winters, the boy was obliged, at the age of ten, to go to work in a cotton factory; subsequently he became an apprentice in a machine shop. Becoming an expert machinist, he settled in Cincinnati, Ohio, in the early forties, where he was foreman in the Harkness machine shop. In 1845, under his directions, the first locomotive west of the Alleghany Mountains was built and had its trial trip from Cincinnati to Columbus and return, Latta acting as engineer. Subsequently, he designed and built a locomotive for the Boston & Maine Railroad. This machine had an extra pair of steam cylinders under the water tank, the steam being taken back and the exhaust being brought forward again through pipes fitted with ball joints. Between 1847 and the time of his death he secured a number of patents for improvements on steam engines, boilers, and locomotives, but by far his greatest inventive and manufacturing work was concerned with the development of the steam fire engine. He completed his first engine in 1852 and sold it to Cincinnati, the first city in the United States to adopt the steamer as a part of its fire-department apparatus. Latta's engines were designed to be drawn by men or horses, but he perfected, also, a self-propelled machine. One of his patents for the latter type was granted May 22, 1855, Patent No. 12,912 (*Senate Executive Document No. 20,* 34 Cong., 1 Sess.). It consisted of a three-wheeled chassis, the rear wheels being connected by rods to the same steam cylinders which furnished power to the water pumps. Upon arrival at the scene of a fire the engine was raised off the ground and supported by means of screws on the sides of the boiler, so that the rear wheels might be used as flywheels. The boiler in Latta's fire engines was constructed of two square chambers, one within the other, the space between being the steam and water space. The inner chamber, which was the firebox, was filled with a series of horizontal layers of tubes arranged diagonally over each other but forming one continuous coil. The water entered this coil at the lower end and passed upward into the annular area, where it was evaporated. As his business developed, he formed a partnership with his brother, and by 1858 six out of the seven horse-drawn fire engines in Cincinnati had been made by them. They built all told about thirty, the last, in 1860, were ordered for the cities of Nashville and Memphis, Tenn. These were not delivered until the Federal troops were in full control there. For his fire-engine improvements Latta was awarded a gold medal by the Ohio Mechanics Institute Fair in 1854. He retired from active business in 1862, but was engaged in inventive work at the time of his death. He was married to Elizabeth Ann Pawson of Cincinnati in 1847, and was survived by two children. His death occurred in Ludlow, Ky.

[Patent Office records; *Scientific Artisan* (Cincinnati), Oct. 21, 1858; E. W. Byrn, *The Progress of Invention in the Nineteenth Century* (1900); H. A. and K. B. Ford, *Hist. of Cincinnati, Ohio* (1881), pp. 328, 386; *The Great Industries of the U. S.* (1872); *Cincinnati Daily Commercial,* Apr. 29, 1865; family records.] C. W. M.

LATTIMORE, WILLIAM (Feb. 9, 1774–Apr. 3, 1843), physician, delegate to Congress from Mississippi, was born near Norfolk, Va., the son of Charles Lattimore. He and his brother, David, attended medical school and in 1801 settled at Natchez, Mississippi Territory. The brothers soon built up a thriving practice and Governor Claiborne put them in charge of the smallpox camp during the epidemic of 1801. They were able to persuade many of the people to submit to vaccination and thus soon had the malady under control. After a residence of less than a year in Natchez, William Lattimore moved to the eastern part of Wilkinson County, now known as Amite. He became interested in politics and was appointed to the territorial council by President Jefferson in 1802. The following year he was elected territorial delegate to Congress. Governor Claiborne describes him at this time as "a young man of promising Talents, & *a firm* & Genuine *republican.*" In 1805 he was reëlected, but George Poindexter defeated him in 1807, and Lattimore retired to his medical practice feeling that as delegate he had received "but little of the support which I expected from the territory." In 1813 he again represented the territory in Congress, was reëlected in 1815, and served until 1817, when Mississippi became a state. He then returned to his home and represented his county in the constitutional convention.

The most important problem with which he was concerned while in Congress was the controversy over the division of the Mississippi Territory in preparation for statehood. The inhabitants along the Mississippi River wished to have the entire territory admitted as a state, while those along the Tombigbee insisted that the territory be divided into a western and an eastern state. Lattimore was at first an anti-divisionist, but when he saw that there was little possibility that the Senate would permit the creation of so large a state, he pointed out the desirability of the formation of two states and proposed that the boundary line be drawn in such a way as to give Mobile and the mouth of the Tombigbee to the western state. The inhabitants of the eastern portion of the territory strenuously objected to this and demanded the Pascagoula River as a boundary. Lattimore proposed a compromise boundary which was accepted and is the present division between Mississippi and Alabama. In this matter Lattimore had fairly represented the whole of the territory, but the people in the western section denounced the compromise, as it involved the surrender of Mobile, their only port. As a result Lattimore was not reëlected and he was never able to regain his popularity. He entered the campaign for governor against Walter Leake, in 1823, but was defeated. His last service to his state was in 1821, when he was appointed one of three commissioners to choose a site for the seat of the state government. This commission selected a location on the Pearl River near the center of the state, to which the legislature gave the name Jackson, the present capital of the state. Lattimore died at his home in Amite County, Apr. 3, 1843. He was twice married. His first wife was Cecilia (Lea) Lattimore; his second wife was Sabrina Lattimore who survived him.

[J. F. H. Claiborne, *Miss. as a Province, Territory and State*, vol. I (1880); Dunbar Rowland, ed., *Official Letter Books of W. C. C. Claiborne* (1917), vol. I, and *Miss. Territorial Archives, 1798–1803*, vol. I (1905); F. L. Riley, "Location of the Boundaries of Mississippi," *Pubs. Miss. Hist. Soc.*, vol. III (1900); newspapers in the Dept. of Archives and History of the state government, Jackson, Miss.] R. H. M.

LAUDONNIÈRE, RENÉ GOULAINE de (fl. 1562–1582), a French Huguenot who was sent to establish a colony in Florida, is little known except for the narratives of his expedition. He was of a noble family of Poitou and had apparently seen service in the navy (Le Moyne, Perkins translation, *post,* p. 4). In 1562, Admiral Coligny, head of the French Huguenot party, determined to found a colony in the New World. Since he was then in favor at Court, he persuaded the King to allow him to send out several shiploads of colonists under the charge of Jean Ribaut [*q.v.*], whom Laudonnière accompanied as his lieutenant. Entering St. John's River, Florida, early in June, the expedition moved up the coast and settled at the present Port Royal, S. C., naming their colony Charlesfort. Then Ribaut and Laudonnière returned to France, where they entered the port of Dieppe July 20, 1562. The religious wars in France and perhaps other matters hindered Coligny from sending aid to his colony in 1563, but in April 1564 Laudonnière was sent out with three ships and three hundred colonists. Meanwhile, however, the settlers at Charlesfort, having become discouraged, had killed their commander, built a ship, and set sail for France. Learning that the settlement was abandoned, Laudonnière decided to found a colony on St. John's River, then called Rivière de May, where he built Fort Caroline, named for King Charles IX.

Although the French were kindly received by the Indians of the region, Laudonnière forfeited the friendship of their chief by establishing relations with an enemy chief who had access to a supply of gold. Dissensions within the colony arose when rations were reduced, and when the nobles in the group protested against the labor required of them. Some threescore mutineers, with two barques, sailed for the Spanish colonies. Most of them were captured by the Spaniards; a few returned to Fort Caroline, where Laudonnière promptly hanged the ringleaders. In spite of all these difficulties, however, the fort was maintained for over a year. On Aug. 3, 1565, the fleet of Sir John Hawkins entered the river. Laudonnière, his colony sadly reduced by famine, gave Hawkins four pieces of artillery and a supply of ammunition in exchange for a vessel in which to take his people home. They were ready to sail on Aug. 15, but were delayed by contrary winds. Meanwhile Ribaut had been sent to their aid with a large fleet and many supplies. His ships were sighted Aug. 28 and arrived Aug. 29, bearing orders for Laudonnière to return to France, to reply to criticisms of his care of his colony. Before he could sail, a Spanish fleet appeared off the coast and Ribaut with most of the able-bodied men sailed in pursuit, leaving Fort Caroline almost defenseless. On Sept. 20, a Spanish force under Menendez came overland from St. Augustine, fell upon the fort, and massacred most of the inhabitants. Laudonnière, although wounded, escaped, made his way to one of Ribaut's ships, and sailed for Europe. After being wrecked and cast ashore in Wales, he finally reached France in January 1566. Coldly received by the royal authorities, he retired to his estates, where he lived quietly, engaged in writing an account of the expeditions to Florida. It was published under the title *L'Histoire notable de la Floride* (Paris, 1586), after the author's death.

In Laudonnière's company was an artist, Jacques Le Moyne, whose drawings of natives and animals are among the best and earliest made of the New World. Le Moyne thus characterizes his chief: "of varied abilities, though experienced not so much in military as in naval affairs . . . a man too easily influenced by others" (Perkins translation, *post,* pp. 1, 4). His mistakes were due to his lack of judgment and the poor quality of the colonists whom he took with him; his misfortunes were the result of international jealousies, for which he was not responsible.

[Laudonnière's *Histoire notable de la Floride*, ed. in 1586 by Basanier, translated by Richard Hakluyt, and published as *A Notable Historie Containing Foure Voyages Made by Certayne French Captaynes into Florida* (1587) and reprinted in the second edition of Hakluyt's *Principal Navigations, Voyages*, etc. (vol. III, 1600). This translation appears in B. F. French, *Hist. Colls. of La. and Fla.*, n.s. I (1869), 165–362. Jacques Le Moyne's *Brevis Narratio*, etc. (1591), was published as pt. II of Theodore de Bry's series, *Collectio Peregrinationum* or Great Voyages, and has been translated into English by F. B. Perkins, under the title *Narrative of Le Moyne* (1875), and into French by C. G. M. B. de La Roncière, as *La Floride Française* (1928). Le Moyne's drawings and part of Laudonnière's text, modernized, appear in L. Ningler, *Voyages en Virginie et en Floride* (1927). The original of Le Moyne's engraving of the Indians worshiping Ribaut's column was found in 1901 in a château near Paris; the French officer is thought to be Laudonnière. See Jeannette T. Connor, in *Jean Ribaut, The Whole & True Discoverye of Terra Florida* (Fla. State Hist. Soc., 1927). A good modern account is that of Francis Parkman, in *Pioneers of France in the New World* (1865).] L. P. K.

LAUNITZ, ROBERT EBERHARD SCHMIDT VON DER (Nov. 4, 1806–Dec. 13, 1870), sculptor, was born in Riga, Russia, and came to the United States about 1828. One of his five brothers was a bishop, one a field-marshal, and three were generals. Robert received an excellent classical and military education and was intended for the army, but his native inclination was toward art. As a young man he went to Rome, where one of his uncles, a sculptor, was employed. He studied at first with his uncle, and later, for four years, under Thorvaldsen. On arriving in New York, he was seriously handicapped. Though talented and agreeable, he was friendless. He could speak Russian, German, French, Italian, and Spanish, but knew very little English. As a result of Roman fever, he was deaf. Thus circumstanced, he was glad to work as journeyman for John Frazee [*q.v.*], then in the marble business in New York City. With far more education in art than his employer, he soon became indispensable. In 1831 they formed a partnership, and Launitz's name appeared in the city directory as sculptor, 591 Broadway. His knowledge of European languages enabled him to employ and train the best of the foreign carvers arriving as immigrants, and he therefore played an important part in developing the carving industry in this country. He turned out excellent workmen. Under him, Thomas Crawford [*q.v.*] learned to handle the chisel. After Frazee received the commission for the New York Custom House (1839), Launitz took entire charge of the Broadway shop. All his life he was artist rather than business man and in his contracts often underestimated costs. His gains were at times so meager that to eke out a living, he turned small objects in alabaster.

His gifts and training won him a welcome among the artists. In 1833 he was made a member of the National Academy of Design on his bas-relief, "Venus and Cupid." For many years his output from the marble shop was confined to mantelpieces, gravestones, and the like. His first outstanding public work, the memorial portrait statue of Charlotte Canda, in Greenwood Cemetery (1845), together with his New York Firemen's monument, also in Greenwood, brought him wide recognition. Other large cemeteries ordered his designs; these his rivals often pirated in meaner material and workmanship. In 1848 the Kentucky legislature contracted with him for a fifteen-thousand-dollar monument "to those who had fallen in defense of their country." This tribute, placed in the center of the "Bivouac of the Dead," in the State Cemetery, Frankfort, Ky., was a female figure of War, sixty-two feet high, carved in Italian marble. It cost Launitz $17,500, but with characteristic probity, he chose to abide by his contract and declined the $2,500 proffered by the legislature to reimburse him. His last important monument was the statue of Pulaski, erected in Savannah, Ga. (1854). At the close of the Civil War, Launitz found it impossible to compete successfully with the mushroom monument firms scattering stone soldiers from coast to coast, and his influence declined.

[*Coll. of Monuments and Headstones, Designed by R. E. Launitz, N. Y.* (L. Prang and Company, 1866); Truman H. Bartlett, "Early Settler Memorials," *Am. Architect and Building News*, Aug. 6, Sept. 3, 1887; Clara Erskine Clement Waters and Laurence Hutton, *Artists of the Nineteenth Century* (1885); *N. Y. Daily Tribune*, Dec. 14, 1870.] A. A.

LAURANCE, JOHN (1750–Nov. 11, 1810), Revolutionary soldier, judge and United States senator, was born near Falmouth, England, and emigrated to New York in 1767. He studied law in the office of Lieutenant-Governor Colden and was admitted to the bar in 1772. In spite of this environment of his law-student days he married, probably in 1774 or early in 1775, Elizabeth, daughter of the flaming patriot, Alexander Macdougall [*q.v.*]. In 1775–76 he was second lieutenant in one of the regiments, raised by the Provincial Congress for Continental service, which participated in the Canada expedition. On the promotion of Macdougall to the rank of brigadier-general in August 1776, Laurance was appointed as his aide-de-camp and thus saw service in the actions in the vicinity of New York. On Apr. 11, 1777, he succeeded William Tudor as judge advocate-general on the staff of the Commander-in-Chief, and this position he held till June 1782. It was said that his record was one of "great uprightness, diligence and ability, by which he has acquired the esteem of the army and merited the consideration of his country" (*Journals of the Continental Congress*, Nov. 9, 1780). At the trial of André it was admitted by all that he combined competent performance of his duty in preparing and conducting the case against the prisoner with the dictates of "humanity and sensibility."

After the war his civil career in New York was active and varied. He made an excellent reputation for legal learning. He was associated with Robert R. Livingston in the movement to provide a water supply for the city, and in 1784 he was elected vestryman of Trinity Church and trustee of Columbia College. Political preferment also came to him. He was delegate to the Congress of the Confederation, 1785–87, and served in the state Senate, 1788–90. Owing to his handsome and dignified presence and enthusiastically Federalist sympathies, his selection, with John Cozine and Robert Troup, as bearer of the Constitution in the grand procession of July 23, 1788, preceding the ratification of that instrument, was altogether appropriate. He became New York City's "first Congressman," receiving an overwhelming vote from the city and Westchester County in the election to the House of Representatives. In the constructive activity of the First and Second congresses, 1789–93, he took a conspicuous part, to the effectiveness of which tribute was paid by the harsh comments in the diary of William Maclay. He is said to have been urged by Washington to accept the appointment, May 6, 1794, as judge of the United States district court because of his reputation in admiralty law. He held the position until Nov. 8, 1796. Upon this date he was elected to the United States Senate as successor to his friend and associate, Rufus King, retaining his seat in this body until his resignation in August 1800. The whole of his successful career in national politics is thus coincident with the period of Federalist dominance.

Laurance's first wife died on Aug. 16, 1790, and on June 30, 1791, he was married to Elizabeth Lawrence, widow of James Allen, of Philadelphia. To the children of these two marriages he left what was in those times a substantial fortune. His real estate included, besides extensive holdings in the interior of New York state, part of the D. M. Clarkson property in the city, purchased in 1784 in association with Rufus King, and a summer residence in Newark, N. J. He was reputed to be especially careful in all matters affecting title to real estate. He appears to have been a director of the Bank of the United States in 1794 (*The Life and Correspondence of Rufus King*, I, 540–41) and may also have been a director of the New York branch. After a stroke of paralysis in 1809, followed by partial recovery, he died in New York, Nov. 11, 1810.

[There is a sketch of Laurance by G. C. McWhorter in the library of the N. Y. Hist. Soc. For printed sources see: Richard Hildreth, *The Hist. of the U. S.*, 2 ser. II (1851); *Biog. Dir. Am. Cong.* (1928); E. A. Werner, *Civil List and Constitutional Hist. of the Colony and State of N. Y.* (1889); *N. Y. Geneal. and Biog. Record*, Jan. 1880; C. R. King, *The Life and Correspondence of Rufus King* (6 vols., 1894–1900), in which the subject's name is spelled *Lawrance*; J. C. Hamilton, *The Works of Alexander Hamilton*, vol. VI (1851); C. P. Keith, *The Provincial Councillors of Pa.* (1883), p. 451; *Calendar of N. Y. Colonial MSS. Endorsed Land Papers* (1864); E. S. Maclay, *Jour. of Wm. Maclay* (1890); *Commercial Advertiser* (N. Y.), Nov. 12, 1810. The spelling of Laurance's name follows manuscript signatures in the Library of the N. Y. Hist. Soc.] C. W. S.

LAURENS, HENRY (Mar. 6, 1724–Dec. 8, 1792), merchant, planter, Revolutionary statesman, came from pure Huguenot stock. His grandfather, André Laurens, fled from Rochelle in 1682 at the beginning of the persecutions, settled for a while in England and Ireland, then emigrated to New York City, and finally moved to Charleston, S. C., shortly before his death about 1715. His son, Jean Samuel, later called John, married in New York Hester or Esther Grasset, who also came from a Huguenot refugee family. Henry, the third of their six children and their eldest son, was born at Charleston. John Laurens became a saddler, building up the largest business of its kind in the colony, and bequeathing a considerable estate to Henry as his residuary legatee upon his death in 1747. Henry received the best education available in the colony, deficient in the classics, but well suited to the needs of a colonial gentleman-merchant. In 1744 he was sent to London by his father, in order to receive further commercial training and to make business contacts. Three years later, a letter offering him a partnership in a London commercial house missed him by five hours at Portsmouth, perhaps thus altering his whole career. When he returned to England after settling his father's estate, the vacant position had been filled and Laurens accepted instead a Charleston partnership with George Austin, later joined by George Appleby. This firm, conducting a general commission business, became one of the most active in the important South Carolina trade, and when it was dissolved in 1762, Laurens continued alone as probably the leading merchant of Charleston.

The business consisted mainly of exporting rice, deerskins, and indigo, and importing wine, slaves, and indentured servants. Probably the most common form of trade was the exchange of rice for slaves. The firm occasionally undertook ventures of its own, but in general it handled transactions for others, charging a commission of five per cent. on all but the "Guinea business" in slaves, which paid double that amount. Laurens finally withdrew from this last phase of the business, almost apologizing for his humanitarian motives. Most of the firm's trade was with London, Liverpool, and Bristol, but from time to time, Laurens also had correspondents in Glasgow, Rotterdam, Oporto, Lisbon, Madrid, and in the British, French, and Spanish West Indies. He owned a part interest in several vessels, but the southern colonies as a whole were far behind the northern in ship-building and ship-owning. After 1764 he gradually withdrew from the commission business, though still continuing some of his mercantile operations. His interest shifted to the acquiring and managing of plantations. He doubtless hoped to strengthen his already secure social position by becoming a landed proprietor. His principal holding was "Mepkin," a beautiful three-thousand-acre estate on the Cooper River some thirty miles above Charleston, where he raised rice and indigo. He raised indigo also on his "Mt. Tacitus" and "Wambaw" estates in the Santee region. He owned several rice plantations on the Georgia coast and a large unsettled tract around Ninety Six in the back country of Carolina. His entire holdings totaled some 20,000 acres and were becoming very profitable at the outbreak of the Revolution.

The year 1764 marks a turning point in Laurens' life. The previous twenty years had been spent almost entirely in overseas commerce, a field for which he was eminently adapted; during the next twenty years, he not only became a planter, but he also became increasingly involved in the preliminaries and events of the Revolution. At forty he was one of the wealthy men of the province. Short and rather swarthy in appearance, he looked "aggressive and just a bit cock-sure." His health was good, but later he was tortured with recurrent visitations of gout. His personal morality was unquestioned and he was a strong "family man." He enjoyed a high reputation for business sagacity and honesty. He had keen insight, great ingenuity, methodical habits, and unusual industry, frequently rising before dawn to handle his correspondence. He was a merciful creditor, never imprisoning and seldom suing for debt, though he was strict with the slack and the slippery. He was a humane and considerate slave-owner. On several occasions he showed great personal courage in taking an unpopular stand. He had, however, some less fortunate qualities. He lacked a genial and expansive nature, except possibly with social intimates. He was inclined to be self-satisfied, self-righteous, and sensitive about his dignity and honor. He could be brusque and insolent on occasion. Though he generally maintained strong self-control, he sometimes showed a merciless sarcasm with tongue or pen in debate or pamphlet dispute. More than once he became involved in duels, in which he refused to fire a shot. It was his misfortune that his public services in the Revolutionary period were more in the legislative and diplomatic field, where the less amiable qualities of his nature often handicapped him, than in executive, administrative positions for which he was so well adapted (Wallace, *post,* p. 432). His public career had started before 1764. He was elected to the provincial Commons House of Assembly in 1757 and was reëlected regularly, with one exception, from that time until the Revolution. In 1764 he declined a seat in the provincial Council on the ground that it was being degraded by the inclusion of royal placemen. He served as a lieutenant-colonel of militia against the Cherokees in 1761 and supported the colonel of British regulars in his subsequent quarrel with the militia colonel.

Laurens naturally became involved in the problems which strained Anglo-American relations in the decade before the Revolution. Then, as later, he took a middle ground between the radicals like Gadsden and the conservatives who favored little if any action. He believed in an attitude of "constitutional stubbornness" against the policy of the British ministry, but he feared the colonial mob element. This feeling was strengthened during the Stamp Act crisis when an armed mob searched his Charleston home, seeking the stamps, in spite of his contemptuous defiance. He declared that he never knowingly violated the Navigation Acts, but when the royal customs officials seized two of his vessels on frivolous technical charges, he tweaked the nose of the collector of customs and challenged Leigh, the apparently corrupt vice-admiralty judge, to a duel, justifying his conduct in a pamphlet full of incisive invective. (See *Extracts from the Proceedings of the High Court of Vice-Admiralty in Charleston, in 1767 and 1768,* 1769, and *An Appendix to the Extracts,* etc., 1769.) He approved of South Carolina's non-importation agreement of July 3, 1769, in opposition to the Townshend Acts, and supported the action of the provincial Assembly in sending money for the support of John Wilkes. He had married "the beautiful Eleanor Ball," daughter of Elias Ball, on July 6, 1750, and she had borne him at least a dozen children, only four of whom reached maturity, before her death in 1770. Their daughter Martha married David Ramsay [*q.v.*] and their daughter Eleanor married Gen. Charles Pinckney [*q.v.*]. In 1771 Laurens went to London for three years for the education of his sons John [*q.v.*] and Henry. Residing at Westminster, and associating chiefly with merchants, he used every opportunity for arguing in the interests of South Carolina and the other colonies. He became thoroughly disgusted with the corruption of the English ruling classes and removed his sons to schools in the stricter atmosphere of Geneva.

Late in 1774 he returned to America, arriving at Charleston in December. Four weeks later he was elected to the first Provincial Congress. His ability and standing gave him a commanding position in the province. He quickly became president of the executive General Committee, and in June 1775 he succeeded Charles Pinckney as president of the first Provincial Congress. In that position he boldly denounced the proposed persecution of those who would not sign the "Association." Later in June he became president of the powerful Council of Safety. In November 1775 he was in the second Provincial Congress. He was president of the second Council of Safety and a member of the so-called "dictatorship committee." In February 1776 he helped to draft South Carolina's temporary constitution and became vice-president when John Rutledge was elected president. He took a very active part in the successful defense of Charleston against the British attack in June 1776 and did what he could to avert the bitter civil war which threatened to break out in the Carolinas.

The following year, he moved from the provincial to the national sphere of politics. Elected to the Continental Congress on Jan. 10, 1777, he took his seat on July 22 and was soon actively engaged on several important committees. He was unanimously elected to succeed John Hancock as president of the Congress on Nov. 1, 1777, holding that office until Dec. 9, 1778. The Congress was at a low ebb during much of that time. The active membership at times was barely fifteen. Yet, small as it was, it was torn with factions. Laurens, racked with gout and sometimes working twenty hours a day, remained partly but not completely above these cliques, tending at times to side with the Adams-Lee group. He was active in securing the suspension of the Saratoga Convention on Jan. 8, 1778, angered at Burgoyne's charges of broken faith and hoping to force Parliament into recognizing Congress as a sovereign body. In the Conway Cabal, he exposed some of the plotting and strongly supported Washington, though he was accused, apparently falsely, of favoring Gates at the outset. He was skeptical of the motives of the French, calling them "artful specious half friends" (Wallace, *post,* p. 276), but he fully realized the value of the alliance. He did not favor, however, leaning too heavily on French loans. When the British sent the fruitless peace commission of 1778, Laurens was unsuccessfully approached with a letter from his British merchant friend, Richard Oswald. Laurens descended to partisan levels in the controversy between Silas Deane and Arthur Lee, arising from the mission to France. He sided with Lee, supporting the recall of Deane and treating him with suspicion upon his arrival. Angered at Deane's appeal to the public, which he considered an affront to the dignity of Congress and himself, he moved to suspend hearings with Deane pending a committee investigation. The motion failed and Laurens resigned his presidency on Dec. 9, 1778, declaring his disapproval of "the manner in which business is transacted here." His friends failed to reinstate him and the presidency fell to his opponent, John Jay.

Laurens continued in Congress for another eleven months. He rose above provincial lines in 1779 when he urged continuation of the war until fishing rights off Newfoundland should be granted; and he advocated a constitutional convention. At the same time, he descended to lower partisan levels. He suspiciously investigated the semi-official commercial dealings of Robert Morris; he also quarreled with his young colleague Drayton. He barely escaped a vote of censure when the British published his captured letter to the governor of Georgia, referring to the "venality, peculation and fraud" in the government. Finally, he was elected to negotiate a loan of $10,000,000 and a treaty of amity and commerce with the Dutch. He left Congress for Charleston on Nov. 9, 1779, after more than two years in that body. The impending British attack on Charleston prevented his sailing from there, and he finally set out from Philadelphia on Aug. 13, 1780, in the little brigantine *Mercury.* Three weeks later she was captured off Newfoundland by the British, who fished out of the sea a sack of papers which Laurens had thrown overboard too late. Among these was the Lee-Van Berkel draft of a projected treaty with Holland, which served as a pretext for the British declaration of war on the Dutch (Dec. 20, 1780).

Laurens was taken to England and, after a trying meeting with the ministers, was confined in the Tower of London on Oct. 6, 1780, remaining there until Dec. 31, 1781. His claims to diplomatic immunity were ignored, and his status as a state prisoner on suspicion of high treason prevented his exchange as a military prisoner of war. His treatment seems to have been unnecessarily harsh at times; his health was poor, and he was charged for rent, living, and even for the wages of his warders. He was able to smuggle out frequent communications to the "rebel press." He resisted the efforts of British friends to seduce him from his American allegiance, in spite of threats of hanging, but he felt completely neglected by Congress. The most discreditable incident in his career was the rather subservient petition which he addressed to the three secretaries of state on June 23, 1781, with merely the request for pen and paper to write a draft and for permission to see his son. In this so-called "submission," Laurens declared that he had "never lost his affection to Great Britain" and reviewed his career, giving to almost every incident a pro-British slant, stating that he had been called a "King's Man" and that he had done what he could to avert the struggle. On Dec. 1, 1781, he made a briefer petition, in the same vein, to the Commons. In these petitions he did nothing which technically compromised his position as a citizen of the United States, but it was naturally distasteful to the Americans to see an accredited envoy and former president of the Continental Congress using so submissive a tone. Madison felt that Laurens' diplomatic commission should be annulled, but Congress on Sept. 20, 1782, refused to recall him. By that time Laurens was free. The efforts of Franklin and Burke had finally secured his release on heavy bail on Dec. 31, 1781, and he was at last cleared in exchange for Cornwallis four months later. He went to Bath for his health and later held conferences with Shelburne.

He had been appointed a peace commissioner in May 1782 but was about to return home in November when he received definite instructions to join Franklin, Adams, and Jay at Paris. He reached there only two days before the signing of the preliminary articles, but during that brief time he used his influence to secure the fishing rights and the stipulation that the British should not carry away negroes and other American property. He seems to have been more worried than Jay about making peace independently of the French. For the next year and a half he acted as a sort of unofficial minister to England, frequently crossing the Channel to confer with the ministry on commercial and other matters. He happened to be absent on one of these missions when the final peace treaty was signed. He finally arrived in New York on Aug. 3, 1784, just four years after he had left America. He reported to Congress and was mentioned for another term as president. He reached Charleston early in 1785 and retired to "Mepkin" for the remaining seven years of his life. His health had been broken by his rigorous experiences; he was saddened by the death of his son John, one of the last casualties of the war; his property had suffered heavily, and he estimated his war losses at 40,000 guineas. He received several political honors from South Carolina, including election to the federal constitutional convention in 1787, but he remained at his estate, where he died after a prolonged period of feeble health. He was one of the first Americans to be cremated, having stipulated this disposal of his body in his will. In addition to the controversial pamphlets already mentioned, he wrote *Mr. Laurens's True State of the Case, by Which his Candor to Mr. Edmund Jennings is Manifested,* etc. (1783). Among his writings subsequently published are "A Narrative of the Capture of Henry Laurens, of his Confinement in the Tower of London" (*South Carolina Historical Society Collections,* I, 1857, pp. 18–68); *Correspondence of Henry Laurens, of South Carolina, 1776–82* (1861), and *A South Carolina Protest against Slavery* (1861).

[The best biography is D. D. Wallace, *Life of Henry Laurens* (1915), a very detailed, intimate account, thoroughly documented, and based on the several collections of Laurens papers, particularly the "Laurens Papers," in the S. C. Hist. Soc., and also those in the Library of Congress, N. Y. Public Library, Long Island Hist. Soc., and Hist. Soc. of Pa. It contains a detailed bibliography and the frontispiece is a Copley portrait of Laurens. See also: David Ramsay, *The Hist. of S. C.* (2 vols., 1809) and *Memoirs of the Life of Martha Laurens Ramsay* (1811); Freeman Hunt, *Lives of Am. Merchants* (1858), vol. I; Francis Wharton, *The Revolutionary Diplomatic Correspondence of the U. S.* (6 vols., 1889); E. C. Burnett, *Letters of Members of the Continental Cong.,* vol. I–V (1921–31); Elizabeth Donnan, "The Slave Trade into South Carolina before the Revolution," *Am. Hist. Rev.,* July 1928; *S. C. Hist. and Geneal. Mag.,* Apr. 1902–Oct. 1905, Jan. 1906–Oct. 1908, Jan. 1923–Apr. 1924, July 1927–July 1930.]

R. G. A—n.

LAURENS, JOHN (Oct. 28, 1754–Aug. 27, 1782), Revolutionary soldier, envoy to France, was born at Charleston, S. C., the son of Henry Laurens [*q.v.*] and Eleanor Ball. He studied under several tutors in Charleston and under the Rev. Richard Clarke, of Islington, London, then attended school at Geneva, Switzerland. On Sept. 16, 1772, he was admitted to the Middle Temple (London), where he began the study of law (E. A. Jones, *American Members of the Inns of Court,* 1924, pp. 117–20. In October 1776 he married Martha, daughter of William Manning of London, a friend of his father; she died at Lille, France, in 1781. Desiring to take part in the Revolution, Laurens returned to America in 1777 and joined Washington's staff as a volunteer aide. Congress later commissioned him lieutenant-colonel. He fought at Brandywine and Monmouth and was wounded at Germantown. In addition to active service

Washington frequently detached him for secret missions. At Valley Forge he kept his father, then president of Congress, informed of the movements of the conspirators involved in the Conway Cabal. He helped to soothe D'Estaing in 1778 when the latter was piqued by Maj.-Gen. John Sullivan [*q.v.*]. Angered by the "constant personal abuse" of Washington by Maj.-Gen. Charles Lee [*q.v.*], he challenged and wounded Lee in a duel fought Dec. 23, 1778 ("The Lee Papers," *Collections of the New-York Historical Society for the Year 1873*, 1874, pp. 283–85). He was elected to the South Carolina Assembly (1779) but withdrew to resume soldiering when Prevost invaded the state, first under Brig.-Gen. William Moultrie [*q.v.*], then under Maj.-Gen. Benjamin Lincoln [*q.v.*]. With the capitulation of Charleston (1780) he became a prisoner. Paroled and exchanged, he was commissioned by Congress envoy extraordinary to France (December 1780) at the age of twenty-six. He was not intended to supersede Benjamin Franklin [*q.v.*], minister to France, but it was thought that a soldier "could speak knowingly of the State of the Army" and obtain much-needed money and supplies from the French government (A. H. Smyth, *The Writings of Benjamin Franklin*, VIII, 1906, p. 251). Arriving in Paris in March 1781, he at once began negotiating with the Comte de Vergennes, minister of foreign affairs. Making no headway, he presented a memorial to Louis XVI at a reception and was soon able to forward to America four transports, three of which arrived safely, loaded with money and military supplies. He then left France, as Franklin wrote, "thoroughly possess'd of my Esteem," though the good doctor added, with justice, that Laurens "*brusqu'd* the Ministers too much" (Smyth, *supra*, VIII, 251, 295; Jared Sparks, *The Writings of George Washington*, VIII, 1835, pp. 526–27). In Philadelphia Laurens reported to Congress, then rejoined the army. He stormed a British redoubt at Yorktown, and with Viscount de Noailles, negotiated the terms of capitulation, a pleasant duty inasmuch as Cornwallis was constable of the Tower of London, where the elder Laurens lay confined. Turning homeward, he sat in the Jacksonborough legislature of January 1782, but his "intrepidity bordering upon rashness," which Washington noted (Sparks, *supra*, IX, 1836, p. 100), soon manifested itself, and he recklessly engaged in the irregular warfare that still persisted in South Carolina. There he fell, on a field so unimportant and nameless that Maj.-Gen. Nathanael Greene [*q.v.*] wrote mournfully: "The love of military glory made him seek it upon occasions unworthy of his rank" (William Johnson, *Sketches of the Life and Correspondence of Nathanael Greene*, 1822, II, 342).

[Sources include: Laurens MSS., L. I. Hist. Soc.; Wm. G. Simms, "The Army Correspondence of Col. John Laurens in the Year 1777–8 . . . with a Memoir," *Bradford Club Series No. 7* (1867); D. D. Wallace, *The Life of Henry Laurens, with a Sketch of the Life of Lieut-Col. John Laurens* (1915); Laurens' reports to Congress, printed in Jared Sparks, *The Diplomatic Correspondence of the Am. Revolution*, IX (1830), 193–249; *Secret Jours. of the Acts and Proc. of Cong.*, Dec. 11, 23, 26, 27, 1780, Sept. 5, 24, 1781; "The Mission of Col. John Laurens to Europe in 1781," *S. C. Hist. and Geneal. Mag.*, Jan. 1900–Apr. 1901; Laurens letters, father and son, *Ibid.*, Apr. 1902–Oct. 1904; *Jours. of Cong.*, Nov. 5, 6, 1778, Mar. 29, Sept. 29, Dec. 15, 1779; Philip Freneau, "On the Death of Col. Laurens," *Freeman's Jour.* (Phila.), Oct. 17, 1787, reprinted in *The Miscellaneous Works of Mr. Philip Freneau* (1788); obituary in the *Royal Gazette* (Charleston), Sept. 7, 1782. The many errors in the account by Wm. Jackson, Laurens' secretary, in Alex. Garden, *Anecdotes of the Am. Revolution* (2 ser., 1828), were perpetuated by Jas. Barnes in "The Man for the Hour," *McClure's Mag.*, Dec. 1899.]

F. E. R.

LAURIE, JAMES (May 9, 1811–Mar. 16, 1875), civil engineer, was born at Bells Quarry, near Edinburgh, Scotland. At an early age he was apprenticed to a maker of mathematical and engineering instruments in his native city, with whom he remained until about 1832. He then worked for a year in the office of a civil engineer, and while thus employed became acquainted with James P. Kirkwood, whom he accompanied to Massachusetts when Kirkwood was called to the position of chief engineer of construction of the Norwich & Worcester Railroad. Laurie obtained appointment as an associate engineer with the same company and in 1835 succeeded Kirkwood as chief engineer and superintendent of construction. Upon the completion of the road, he engaged in general practice, advising railroads and canal companies on locations and directing surveys for water power and harbor developments. In July 1848 he was one of the group of engineers that founded the Boston Society of Civil Engineers. He moved his office to New York City in 1852 and in October of that year sent out letters, signed by himself and two others, inviting all engineers in the neighborhood to attend a meeting to organize a society of civil engineers in the city of New York. At this gathering, Nov. 5, 1852, the American Society of Civil Engineers was formed, with Laurie as its first president. At the first regular meeting he presented a paper, "The Relief of Broadway," proposing the use of elevated railway tracks, the discussion of which was continued in the next meeting. Interest in the Society soon flagged, however, and it did not meet during the twelve years following 1855. Laurie retained his title of president during this time, and finally called a meeting, Oct. 12, 1867, at which the Society was revived, a new president was elected, and a resolution was adopted thanking Laurie for his efforts to reëstablish the organization.

In 1855 and 1856 he was employed by the State of New York to examine railroad bridges, and in 1858 he was engaged by the government of Nova Scotia to examine and report fully on the condition of the Nova Scotia Railroad, particularly in regard to the cost of construction and operation. He then served two years as chief engineer of that road. Subsequently, he reported on the condition of the Troy & Greenfield Railroad for the State of Massachusetts and was employed for several years by that state as its consultant on the Hoosac Tunnel. He was at the same time chief engineer of the New Haven, Hartford & Springfield Railroad, and designed and built its bridge across the Connecticut River at Warehouse Point. By this time he had accumulated considerable property and thenceforth, except for one or two examinations of engineering structures, he lived in retirement at Hartford until his death. He never married.

[C. W. Hunt, *Hist. Sketch of the Am. Soc. of Civil Engrs.* (1897); *Trans. Am. Soc. Civil Engrs.*, vol. XXXVII (1897); *Railway World*, Mar. 20, 1875; *Hartford Daily Courant*, Mar. 17, 1875.] F. A. T.

LA VERENDRYE, PIERRE GAULTIER DE VARENNES, Sieur de (Nov. 17, 1685–Dec. 6, 1749), explorer, was born at Three Rivers, Canada, where his father, René Gaultier, Sieur de Varennes, was governor. His mother, Marie, was a daughter of Pierre Boucher, first historian of New France. La Vérendrye was the fourth son, and his maternal grandfather was his godfather. His father died when the boy was but four years old, and at the age of twelve he entered the colonial army. He took part in several raids, notably that at Deerfield, Mass., in 1704. Three years later he was sent to France, where as lieutenant in the Régiment de Bretagne he saw hard service, was wounded nine times, and in 1709 was left for dead on the battlefield of Malplaquet. In 1711 he returned to Canada, and the next year was commissioned ensign in the local forces. On Oct. 29, 1712, he married Marie-Anne Dandonneau du Sablé, daughter of Louis Dandonneau du Sablé, Sieur de l'Ile du Pas. She bore him four sons: Jean Baptiste, Pierre, François, and Louis Joseph.

In 1726 La Vérendrye obtained the command of a post on Lake Nipigon, north of Lake Superior, and there heard from the Indians accounts of far western regions and the routes thither. One Ochagah drew for him a map of a westward-flowing river (see *Collections of the State Historical Society of Wisconsin*, vol. XVII, 1906, pp. 102–03 and *passim*), which so impressed La Vérendrye that in 1729 he went to Quebec to obtain permission from the governor to search overland for the Western Sea. Governor Beauharnois sent him to France, where he secured permission to explore at his own expense. The promise of a monopoly of the fur trade in the regions he might discover encouraged him to attempt the exploration. In 1731 he started west with his three eldest sons and his nephew, La Jemmeraye. Pushing west from Lake Superior by the Grand Portage route, they reached Rainy Lake, where Fort St. Pierre was built. The next year they erected Fort St. Charles on Lake of the Woods. During La Vérendrye's absence in Canada, his sons penetrated further into the wilderness, and in 1734 built Fort Maurepas on Lake Winnipeg.

The year 1736 was one of disaster: in May La Jemmeraye died; and in the summer Jean Baptiste La Vérendrye, Father Aulneau, and nineteen companions were murdered by the Sioux Indians on Massacre Island, Lake of the Woods. (The site was identified in 1909.) Nevertheless, La Vérendrye continued his advance, building in 1738 Fort La Reine on Assiniboin River and Fort Rouge on the site of Winnipeg, Manitoba. From Fort La Reine the explorers made their way overland to the Mandan villages on the upper Missouri. Thence four years later two of the sons with two voyageurs pushed west to mountains, variously identified as the Black Hills and as a portion of the Rocky Mountains. On their return they buried a leaden plate, which was found in 1913 at Fort Pierre, S. D., dated to correspond with the explorers' journal (*Proceedings of the State Historical Society of Wisconsin, 1913*, 1914, pp. 146–50). In 1744 La Vérendrye for the fourth time returned to Montreal to meet his creditors and to ask aid to continue his explorations. To his disappointment, however, he was kept on duty in Canada, while his posts were assigned to another officer. In 1746 he was promoted to a captaincy and in 1749 received the cross of St. Louis for his services. In that year a new governor granted him permission to return to the west, and he was making preparations for an expedition when he died. His sons were not allowed to continue his work.

Persistence in the face of great discouragements enabled La Vérendrye to enter the far West and to be the discoverer of Manitoba, the Dakotas, the western plains of Minnesota, the northwest territories of Canada, and probably part of Montana. He and his sons were the first white men to see the Red River of the North, the Assiniboin, probably the Saskatchewan, and great stretches of the upper Missouri. His discoveries opened a vast region for the French fur trade and pointed the way to the overland route to the Pacific.

[*Journals and Letters of Pierre Gaultier de Varennes de la Vérendrye and his Sons,* edited by L. J. Burpee, is published by the Champlain Society (Toronto, 1927); the introduction contains a good biographical sketch and there is an excellent bibliography. L. J. Burpee, *Pathfinders of the Great Plains* (Chronicles of Canada, vol. XIX, 1914), epitomizes these explorations. See also *Quart. of the Ore. Hist. Soc.,* June 1925; *S. Dak. Hist. Colls.,* vol. VII (1914); L. J. Burpee, "The Lake of the Woods Tragedy," *Proc. and Trans. Royal Soc. of Canada,* 2 ser., IX (1903); L. A. Prud'Homme, "Pierre Gaultier de Varennes, Sieur de la Vérendrye," *Ibid.,* XI (1906).] L. P. K.

LAW, ANDREW (March 1748/49–July 13, 1821), composer, compiler and pioneer teacher of sacred music, was born in Milford, Conn., the son of Jahleel and Ann (Baldwin) Hollingsworth Law. He was a grandson of Jonathan Law [*q.v.*], and Abigail Andrew, daughter of the Rev. Samuel Andrew. In 1753 the family removed to Cheshire, where the parents were admitted to the church in 1769. After graduating from Rhode Island College in 1775, Andrew studied theology with the Rev. Levi Hart of Preston, Conn., and was ordained in Hartford on Sept. 8, 1787. For a time he was connected with the presbyteries of Philadelphia and Baltimore, but preaching was not to be his life work. In 1767, when he was only nineteen years old, he had compiled *A Select Number of Plain Tunes Adapted to Congregational Worship.* By 1790 he had issued at least six books of hymns or tunes and was advertising in the *Maryland Journal* and *Baltimore Advertiser,* in November of that year, that these books could be obtained of the author who was then situated in the Maryland city. How long he remained in Baltimore is uncertain, but books of his music were printed there until 1795. In 1799 some of his books were printed in Philadelphia, and in 1814 his *Essays on Music* was printed there. In the meantime he had traveled into Vermont, where his *Christian Harmony* was printed in Windsor in 1805. From 1795 to 1797 he was in Salem and its neighborhood conducting classes in singing.

In 1781 Law petitioned the Assembly of Connecticut for the exclusive right to imprint and sell his collection of tunes. The petition was granted but the list of tunes which he proposed to publish was never used in its entirety in any one book. The patent, however, carried protection for the use of any or all of the tunes named. In 1802 he patented a new plan for printing music without the use of the staff, employing four different shapes of notes, which he afterward increased to seven different characters. In comparing his new plan with the old he pointed out that his system had only seven characters, while the old plan with its lines and spaces, and different keys, totaled 196 signs to learn. This new system, however, was not accepted by singers, and only a few of his books were published in it. His aim in teaching music was to have it very soft, slow, and solemn. For a time his music was quite popular, but most of the tunes dropped out as taste changed. "Archdale," which he believed to be his best composition, was the last to hold a place in hymn books.

Law published numerous hymnals, under varying titles. His first, the *Plain Tunes,* sixteen pages in length, contained fifty-four tunes, being those in common use at that period. In 1779 the *Select Harmony* made its appearance—one hundred pages of engraved music printed in New Haven, and containing some tunes of his own composition. *The Musical Primer* (1780) was advertised as "suitable for learners at their first setting out." *A Collection of the Best and Most Approved Tunes and Anthems* was printed in 1779. A number of his books were printed in Cheshire by his brother William. *The Art of Singing* (1792), in one volume, was made up of *The Musical Primer,* the *Christian Harmony,* and *The Musical Magazine.* Other works included *The Rudiments of Music* (1783 and later editions); *Harmonic Companion* (1807); *The Art of Playing the Organ* (1807), and *Essays on Music* (1814). According to his definition, in the first essay, the musician must be "a linguist, an orator, a poet, a painter, a mathematician, a philosopher, an architect, a christian, a friend to God and man." He died in Cheshire, Conn., at the home of his brother William. He had never married.

[N. H. Allen, "Old Time Music and Musicians," the *Conn. Quart.,* Jan.–Feb.–Mar. 1897; F. J. Metcalf, *Am. Writers and Compilers of Sacred Music* (1925); *The Diary of Wm. Bentley, D.D.,* vol. II (1907); *Musical Herald,* Aug. 1882; *Hist. Cat. of Brown Univ., 1764–1914* (1914); C. C. Baldwin, *The Baldwin Geneal. from 1500 to 1881* (1881); *Conn. Courant,* July 17, 1821; information as to certain facts from Joseph P. Beach, historian of Cheshire, Conn.] F. J. M.

LAW, EVANDER McIVOR (Aug. 7, 1836–Oct. 31, 1920), Confederate soldier, educator, was born in Darlington, S. C., the son of E. Augustus and Elizabeth (McIvor) Law. In 1856 he was graduated from the Citadel, in Charleston, where he had been assistant professor of belles-lettres during his senior year. The following five years he spent in teaching, first at the King's Mountain Military Academy at Yorkville, S. C., and later, at the Military High School, Tuskegee,

Ala., of which he was joint-founder with Robert Parks. In 1861 he recruited a company largely from his school and as captain took it into action at Pensacola. He served in all of the most important campaigns of the war in the East including Gettysburg, where he claimed that the result might have been otherwise had Lee followed the advice of himself and of two other colleagues regarding the seizure of Round Top. After having been wounded at Cold Harbor, he transferred from the Army of Virginia to a cavalry brigade in Johnston's command. Just prior to the surrender he became major-general.

Immediately after the war he administered the estate of William A. Latta, wealthy planter and railroad man, whose daughter, Jane Elizabeth, Law had married on Mar. 9, 1863. He then lived as a planter for a while in Tuskegee and Yorkville, resumed connections with the King's Mountain Military Academy until it closed in 1884, and dabbled in engineering and newspaper work. Finally he moved to Bartow, Fla., to fulfil a long-cherished plan of opening a school modeled after the Citadel and the Virginia Military Institute. After a year's existence as a private institution, this school was established as the South Florida Military and Educational Institute and received state aid through a system of county scholarships. It was a pioneer venture; the attendance was always small and the resources meager. The students aided in the upkeep and, during the first year, no fixed salaries were guaranteed to the teachers. Nevertheless, high standards were maintained and Law exercised a lasting influence on the students. In 1903 he resigned from the Institute to devote the rest of his life to newspaper work, as editor of the *Bartow Courier-Informant* (1905–15), and to his duties as trustee of Sumerlin Institute (1905–12) and as a member of the Polk County Board of Education (1912–20). He was especially interested in all state activities commemorating the Civil War. He served as commander of the Florida division of the Confederate Veterans (1899–1903) and aided in organizing the Bartow chapter of the Daughters of the Confederacy. Several articles on the campaigns in which he fought stand to his credit. When he died he was the last of the major-generals of the Confederacy. His reputation does not rest on his military record, however, for his most lasting achievement was his part in the establishment of the foundations of the educational system of his adopted state.

[See *Who's Who in America*, 1914–15; *Confed. Mil. Hist.* (1899), VII, 422–24; *Battles and Leaders of the Civil War* (4 vols., 1887–88); T. M. Owen, *Hist. of Ala. and Dict. of Ala. Biog.*, vol. IV (1921); *Makers of America: Fla. Edition*, vol. III (1909); *Bi-ennial Reports of the Supt. of Pub. Instruction of the State of Fla.*, 1895–1903; *Acts and Resolutions Adopted by the Legislature of Fla.*, 1895, 1897, 1901; files of the *Bartow Courier-Informant*; *Pensacola Jour.*, Nov. 1, 1920; and *Confed. Veteran*, Apr. 1914. Information as to certain facts was supplied by Law's daughter, Mrs. Francis Parker Winthrop, and by former associates.] K. T. A.

LAW, GEORGE (Oct. 25, 1806–Nov. 18, 1881), contractor, transportation promoter, was born in Jackson (now Shushan), N. Y., between Saratoga and the Vermont border, one of the five children of John Law, a native of the County Down in Ireland who had come to America in 1784 and become a dairyman-farmer. George learned the "three R's" at winter night school and became an omniverous reader. In 1824 the approaching completion of the Erie Canal tempted him away from the cows and churns. He trudged to Troy to seek his fortune. Starting as a hod-carrier, he soon learned stone-cutting and masonry. The mania for canal construction gave him a series of opportunities and he worked in turn on the Dismal Swamp, Morris, Harlem, and Delaware & Hudson canals. At the age of twenty-one he undertook his first work as a contractor, building a small lock and aqueduct. Then he constructed an inclined plane for the Lehigh Canal. By 1830 he had saved $2,800. This was increased tenfold in the next four years by successful contracting in canal and railroad construction in eastern Pennsylvania. In 1834 he married a Miss Anderson in Philadelphia. Three years later he moved to New York City, which became his home for the rest of his life. He secured two contracts for work near Tarrytown on the new Croton Water Works and in 1839 undertook his greatest piece of contracting, the High Bridge. His experience had revealed financial as well as engineering ability. Turning from contracting, he thenceforth applied his capital and skill to other fields. Elected president of the Dry Dock Bank in 1842, he rescued it from the brink of insolvency. Then, for a while, he devoted his attention to railroads. He helped to extend the Harlem Railroad twelve miles from Williamsbridge to White Plains, nearly doubling its earnings in two years and raising the value of its stock from five to seventy-five. He then took over the Mohawk & Hudson, doing away with its inclined planes, improving its roadbed and trebling the value of its stock. His next and most spectacular venture was in ocean steamships, which promised to become profitable with the federal policy of mail subsidies. In 1847, with Marshall O. Roberts and Bowes R. McIlvaine as junior partners, he formed the United States Mail Steamship Company and took over the federal contract awarded to A. G. Sloo for a biweekly mail service between New York, Havana, New Orleans, and Chagres. The company was to provide five ships and receive $290,000 annually. Their first ship reached Chagres in 1848, with passengers for California. The gold rush gave a tremendous impetus to the business; but the opposition developed when William H. Aspinwall's Pacific Mail Steamship Company started a rival line from New York to Chagres. Thereupon, Law secured four ships to compete with the Pacific Mail between Panama and San Francisco in 1850. A year later, the companies divided spheres of influence, Law keeping the Atlantic, and Aspinwall the Pacific. Law was also actively interested in the Panama Railroad. Several of his ships became involved in the Cuban troubles and in 1852 he sprang into fame. One Smith, purser of his *Crescent City*, had furnished the *New York Herald* with material which angered the captain-general of Cuba who forbade any ship bearing Smith aboard to enter Havana harbor. Though urged by President Fillmore to avoid trouble and penalized by the removal of the mails, Law sent the ship with Smith aboard into Havana time and again. This started a presidential "boom" for Law. Though only one generation removed from County Down, he was prominently associated with the Know-Nothing party and in 1855 received the support of the Pennsylvania legislature for that party's presidential nomination. When Fillmore received it instead in 1856, Law supported Frémont and attacked Fillmore in two widely circulated "North American" Letters. By that time he was a millionaire. He had sold his steamships just before the slump in the American merchant marine set in and had shifted from liners to prosaic but profitable horse cars. When the Eighth Avenue Railroad in New York City faced forfeiture of its contract in 1854 unless it completed its five miles of track within ten weeks, Law advanced some $800,000, completed the road within the given time, secured fifty cars, and then served as president of the road until his death. The road paid dividends averaging twelve per cent. during all that period. He was also promoter and president of the Ninth Avenue Railroad, started in 1859, but that line paid almost nothing. During his later years, his son took over the active management of the lines, and also of the Brooklyn and Staten Island ferries which he acquired. Law died at his home on Fifth Avenue after a period of failing health.

[The principal source is the eulogistic, anonymous campaign biography, *A Sketch of Events in the Life of Geo. Law, published in Advance of his Biog.* (1855). An uncomplimentary description of Law appeared in M. H. Smith, *Sunshine and Shadow in N. Y.* (1868). A pamphlet entitled *"North American" Docs.* (1856) contains two of his anti-Fillmore letters. The *N. Y. Herald*, Nov. 19, 1881, contained a long obituary. Details of his steamship activities are in the lengthy *House Executive Doc. 91*, 32 Cong., 1 Sess. Results of his railroad and traction activity are in H. V. Poor, *Hist. of the Railroads and Canals of the U. S.* (1860), pp. 267, 268, 288, 291, and in the successive editions of H. V. Poor, *Manual of the Railroads of the U. S.*, 1868 ff.]

R. G. A—n.

LAW, JOHN (Oct. 28, 1796–Oct. 7, 1873), judge, congressman, son of Lyman and Elizabeth (Learned) Law, was born in New London, Conn. His paternal grandfather was Richard Law [*q.v.*], and his great-grandfather, Jonathan Law [*q.v.*]. He graduated from Yale College in 1814, read law with his father, and was admitted to the bar in 1817. The same year he went west by way of Philadelphia and the Ohio River, taking up his residence as an attorney at Vincennes, Ind. This was his home until 1851, when he moved to a tract of land near Evansville, Ind., now in the city, which he and his associates laid out as the town of Lamasco, a venture which made him at least moderately wealthy. On Nov. 24, 1822, he married Sarah, daughter of Nathaniel and Anne Ewing, of Vincennes. Thirteen children were born to them. Law was prosecuting attorney in the first judicial circuit of Indiana in 1818 and again from 1825 to 1828. In 1823–24 he served one term in the state House of Representatives. The title of judge, by which he was universally known, came from his service as judge of the seventh circuit, 1830–31, and 1844–50. He was receiver of public money at Vincennes, 1838–42, and judge of the federal court of land claims there, 1855–57, by appointment of President Pierce. By his knowledge of the law, his patience and thoroughness in dealing with the complicated land titles of the region about Vincennes, and his fairness as a judge, he made a permanent reputation in the bar of the state. A Whig from the formation of that party until the late forties, he then became, and remained till his death, a Democrat. He represented his district in the national House of Representatives in the Thirty-seventh and in the Thirty-eighth congresses (1861–65), where he supported the administration in all war measures but opposed emancipation and all steps toward "radical" reconstruction of the seceding states. In 1865 he retired from public life and from the active practice of his profession.

Law devoted much time to historical matters, especially to the history of Vincennes and to the campaigns of George Rogers Clark culminating in the capture of Fort Sackville. For fourteen years, 1859–73, he was president of the Indiana Historical Society. His *Colonial History of Vincennes, under the French, British and Ameri-*

can Governments (1858), which was an enlarged edition of an address published in 1839, long ranked as the most authoritative account of the subject. A lecture, "Jesuit Missionaries in the North-West," was printed in the *Third Annual Report and Collections of the State Historical Society of Wisconsin* (1857). His historical and personal interests, as well as his innate sense of justice, led him to take up the prosecution of the claims for reimbursement of Francis Vigo, whose advances of money and supplies had made George Rogers Clark's success possible, and who was a resident of Vincennes from the close of the American Revolution till his death in 1836. It has been called "a centennial law suit," for it dragged on from one hearing to another till 1876, forty years after Vigo's death in relative poverty and three years after Law himself had died, when $49,898.50 was paid to Vigo's heirs. Law was a commanding, dignified figure. His genial disposition and the charm of his conversation made him popular in social circles both in his state and in Washington. He died at Evansville, Oct. 7, 1873, and was buried in Greenlawn Cemetery, Vincennes.

[Charles Denby, "Judge John Law," *Ind. Hist. Soc. Pubs.*, vol. I, no. 7 (1897); Wm. W. Woollen, *Biog. and Hist. Sketches of Early Ind.* (1883), pp. 332–34; F. A. Myers, "John Law of Indiana," *Mag. of Am. Hist.*, May 1891; *Early Ind. Trials and Sketches; Reminiscences by Hon. O. H. Smith* (1858); F. B. Dexter, *Biog. Sketches of the Grads. of Yale Coll.*, vol. VI (1912); the *Indianapolis Sentinel*, Oct. 8, 1873; manuscript letters of Law to Lyman C. Draper, Draper MSS., 2J51–69, Wis. State Hist. Lib.] C. B. C.

LAW, JONATHAN (Aug. 6, 1674–Nov. 6, 1750), colonial lawyer and governor, was born in Milford, Conn., the only son of Jonathan and Sarah (Clark) Law, and the grandson of Richard Law, an emigrant from England, who settled at Wethersfield in 1638 and in 1641 was one of the founders of Stamford, Conn. He was graduated from Harvard in 1695 and received the degree of A.M. from that institution in 1729. He applied himself to the practice of law, in which field he won a reputation for great skill and ability. He was one of the first men to be admitted to the Connecticut bar in 1708 after the passage of an act regulating attorneys. In the next year the Assembly appointed him justice of the peace and of the quorum for New Haven County. Except for one interval of two years he held judicial office continuously until he became governor in 1741, serving successively as judge of the county court, as assistant judge of the superior courts, and from 1725 to 1741, as chief judge of the superior courts, to which office Law like other deputy governors was annually appointed. The most important case with which he was connected, as judge, as deputy governor, and as governor, was that of *Clark* vs. *Tousey*. His judgment in the case, eventually sustained by the privy council of Great Britain (1745), went far to reëstablish the validity of the Connecticut procedure with regard to intestate estates, which had been declared contrary to English law in the earlier case of *Winthrop* vs. *Lechmere*. (See C. M. Andrews, "The Connecticut Intestacy Law," *Yale Review,* November 1894, 261–94.) Law's first elective office was that of deputy to the Assembly from Milford in 1706, an office which he filled intermittently until 1717, serving occasionally as clerk or as speaker of the lower house. His continuous nomination to the magistracy from 1710 on bore fruit in his election as assistant in 1717. Thereafter he advanced rapidly in seniority until, in 1724, his name stood sixth on the lists of assistants. On the death of Gov. Gurdon Saltonstall and the advancement of Deputy-Gov. Joseph Talcott to the vacancy in 1724, Law was elected deputy governor over the heads of the five senior assistants. The choice bore striking testimony to his popularity with the voters. He was annually reëlected until October 1741, when, following the death of Talcott, he was chosen governor. He continued to hold this office until his death in 1750. As Law's governorship covered the period of the War of the Austrian Succession, he was associated with the successful Louisbourg expedition of 1745 and the abortive Canadian expeditions of 1746 and 1747, although his rôle was that of organizer and director of Connecticut's military activities rather than that of direct participant. In religious matters he was thoroughly orthodox and showed little sympathy for the "New Lights" during the period of the Great Awakening. As a public official, he was typical of the conservative governing classes of his colony and age. Little is known of his private life and personality. He was married five times: in 1698 to Ann Eliot; in 1704/05 to Abigail Arnold; in 1706 to Abigail Andrew; in 1726 to Mrs. Sarah Burr; and in 1730 to Eunice (Hall) Andrew. He was survived by his fifth wife and by seven children, one of whom was Richard Law [*q.v.*].

[See *Pub. Records of the Colony of Conn.*, vols. IV–IX (1868–76); "The Talcott Papers," *Colls. of the Conn. Hist. Soc.*, vols. IV and V (1892–96); "The Law Papers," *Colls. of the Conn. Hist. Soc.*, vols. XI (1907), XIII (1911), and XV (1914). The best sketch of Law's life is that by Albert C. Bates in "The Law Papers." See also *New-Eng. Hist. and Geneal. Reg.*, Apr. 1847, pp. 188–90, and Ezra Stiles, *Oratio Funebris pro Exequiis Celebrandis Viri Perillustris Jonathan Law* (1751).] L. W. L.

LAW, RICHARD (Mar. 7, 1733–Jan. 26, 1806), Connecticut patriot and jurist, born in Milford,

Conn., was the son of Jonathan Law [*q.v.*] by his fifth and last wife, Eunice (Hall) Andrew Law. Richard graduated in 1751 from Yale, read law with Jared Ingersoll, was admitted to the bar in 1755, and moved two years later to New London. Here he attended the First Church (Congregational) and on Sept. 21, 1760, married Ann, the daughter of Capt. John Prentise. He seems to have been a thorough student of jurisprudence, a master of argument, if not of the art of persuasion, and a highly successful lawyer. His public career commenced in 1765 with his appointment as justice of the peace and with his election to the General Court. He was clerk of the latter during his last two years of membership and until his appointment as assistant, a position he held from 1776 to 1786. A faithful patriot, he joined in the protest against the Townshend duties and later against the Boston Port Bill, was a member of the Connecticut Council of Safety of 1776, and was one of the two delegates sent to New York to confer with Washington on the defense of the colony (1776). He was chosen a delegate to the Continental Congress in 1774, 1776, 1777, and from 1780 to 1783, but the state of his health seems to have prevented his attendance in 1774 and 1776, for he served only in the sessions of 1777, 1781, and 1782, and then without distinction.

More distinguished was his judicial career in Connecticut. In 1773 he became chief judge of the New London county court, a position that he held until 1784 when he was elevated to the bench of the superior court of which two years later he was made chief judge. In 1789 he was appointed by Washington United States district judge. Early in the Revolution the Council of Safety had requested him to compile a code of maritime law. In 1783–84 he, with the assistance of Roger Sherman, also a superior court judge, codified the statute law of the state, published as *Acts and Laws of the State of Connecticut, in America* (1784). The task brought them no little renown. In 1784 the freemen of New London unanimously elected Law the first mayor of the newly chartered city. This position, with his federal judgeship, he held until his death.

Law was generally Federalist in politics. At the Connecticut Convention of 1788 at Hartford, which so quickly ratified the federal Constitution, he spoke in favor of that document. A year later he was a member of the first electoral college from Connecticut. Yet in the spring elections of 1801 the Republicans named him their candidate for governor. Law declined the nomination, urging his age and disinclination for the office (*Connecticut Courant,* Apr. 6, 1801), but no other Republican nomination was made. Consequently he received only 1,056 votes to 11,156 for Governor Trumbull, and ran behind his own ticket. Five years later he died at his home in New London.

[F. B. Dexter, *Biog. Sketches of the Grads. of Yale Coll.,* vol. II (1896); *New-Eng. Hist. and Geneal. Reg.,* July 1847; F. M. Caulkins, *Hist. of New London, Conn.* (1852); *The Pub. Records of the Colony of Conn.,* vols. XII to XV (1881–90); *The Pub. Records of the State of Conn.,* vols. I and II (1894–95); Timothy Alden, *A Coll. of Am. Epitaphs and Inscriptions* (1814), IV, 130; the *Conn. Courant* (Hartford), Feb. 5, 1806.]

E. W. S.

LAW, SALLIE CHAPMAN GORDON (Aug. 27, 1805–June 28, 1894), "mother of the Confederacy," was born in Wilkes County, N. C., daughter of Chapman Gordon, of Virginian descent, and his wife Charity King of South Carolina. From both sides of her house she inherited martial blood, but especially from her father, who while in his teens had fought at King's Mountain and had served throughout the rest of the Revolutionary War under Generals Marion and Sumter. She married, June 28, 1825, near Eatonton, Ga., Dr. John S. Law, and settled with him in Forsythe, Ga., where they dwelt until 1834 when they removed to Columbia, Tenn. Ten years later, after her husband's death, Mrs. Law moved to Memphis in order to obtain better advantages for her seven children, and there passed the remainder of her long life.

She was self-reliant, charitable, unselfish, and devout, as her family and social relations had already proved her, and the outbreak of war offered a broader field for her executive ability and strength of will. Although she was thoroughly identified with the Confederacy by family ties, with more than two score near kinsmen—most distinguished of whom was her nephew, Gen. John B. Gordon—in the ranks and on the official list, she chafed at having only one son to lend to the Confederate armies and was quick to dedicate her own energies to the aid of her section. She was active in organizing in Memphis, in April 1861, the Southern Mothers' Hospital, which under her leadership expanded from its original twelve-bed capacity to an institution that, after the battle of Shiloh, cared for hundreds of wounded. Before this she had, at her own expense, twice journeyed to Columbus, Ky., conveying food and clothing from her hospital to the sick soldiers there. Upon the breaking up of the Memphis hospitals the money in the Southern Mothers' treasury was invested in quinine, morphine, and opium, which Mrs. Law carried into the Confederacy on her person, distributing it chiefly in the hospitals at LaGrange, Ga., where she had the compliment of having a hospital named for her. At Columbus, Ga., having learned of the destitution in Gen. Joseph E. Johnston's division at Dalton, she was instrumental in collecting hundreds of blankets, socks, and underclothing, which she went in person to see distributed to the soldiers. Officers and men idolized her for her intrepidity and cheerful confidence, and General Johnston ordered a review of thirty thousand troops in recognition of her services. After the war the hospital organization became the Southern Mothers' Association, one of the earliest memorial societies; and until shortly before her death Mrs. Law, as its only president, continued her labors in memory of the Confederacy and its sons, cooperating with other groups in erecting monuments, marking graves, and disseminating historical material about the Southern cause and its conduct. In her sixteen-page pamphlet, *Reminiscences of the War of the Sixties Between the North and South* (1892), she recounts a few of her many wartime experiences, revealing without ostentation how naturally, lovingly, and gratuitously she gave herself to the Confederacy during the war years and afterward.

[*Confed. Veteran*, Apr., July 1894; *Confederated Memorial Assos. of the South* (1904); *Memphis Commercial*, June 29, 1894; and obituary in the *Memphis Appeal-Avalanche*, June 30, 1894, reprinted in the *Southern Hist. Soc. Papers*, vol. XXII (1894).]

A. C. G., Jr.

LAWLEY, GEORGE FREDERICK (Dec. 8, 1848–Mar. 20, 1928), yacht-builder, was born in London. His father, George Lawley, had already acquired some knowledge of boat-building when he and his family emigrated to the United States in 1851, and he soon found employment in the yard of Donald McKay in East Boston. The son's earliest recollections were those of his wanderings among the chips and shavings of some of the mightiest ships of the clipper era. When he was less than twenty years old he helped his father establish a small boat yard at Scituate, where they began to build modest craft for Boston yachtsmen. Within a few years they gained a reputation for skilled and honest workmanship and established a larger yard at South Boston. World-wide fame came to them in 1885 when they built for a syndicate of Boston yachtsmen the wooden sloop *Puritan*, designed by Edward Burgess [*q.v.*], which defeated the English cutter *Genesta* in the fifth match for the *America's* Cup. The next year the firm built another cup defender, the *Mayflower*, designed by Burgess for Gen. Charles J. Paine, which defeated the British cutter *Galatea*. Although the builders had no facilities for constructing their own boats of iron, they rigged and outfitted the third Boston yacht to contend for the cup, the iron sloop *Volunteer*, which raced successfully against the Scotch cutter *Thistle*.

Orders came to the Lawley company from all parts of the world for pleasure craft, cruisers, and racers. Among the larger craft constructed during the period of the eighties and nineties were the schooners *Sachem, Idler, Savarona, Latona*, and *Margaret*. Owing to the demand for iron and steel construction, the plant was moved to Neponset, another suburb of Boston. With this move the elder Lawley retired from the business. In the yard at Neponset some of the largest yachts flying the American ensign were fashioned, including the steel schooners *Guinevere* and *Speejacks*, the composite yacht *Sea Call*, and large power boats such as the *Taormina* and the *Athero II*. Having brought the company to a high state of efficiency George F. Lawley retired from active work in 1925 but continued his energetic interest in the plant which his son, Frederick Damon Lawley, had established in Quincy. Lawley died in his eightieth year at his home in South Boston and was survived by his wife, Hannah (Damon) Lawley.

[W. M. Thompson and T. W. Lawson, *The Lawson Hist. of the America's Cup* (1902); H. L. Stone, *The "America's" Cup Races* (1914); *Yachting* (N. Y.), May 1928; *Power Boating* (Cleveland), May 1928; *Boston Globe, Boston Herald, Boston Transcript*, Mar. 21, 1928.]

W. U. S.

LAWRANCE, JOHN [See LAURANCE, JOHN, 1750–1810].

LAWRANCE, MARION [See LAWRANCE, URIAH MARION, 1850–1924].

LAWRANCE, URIAH MARION (Oct. 2, 1850–May 1, 1924), promoter of organized Sunday-school activity, was the son of Elonson Lawrance, a farmer and country school teacher of Winchester, Preble County, Ohio, and his wife, Amanda Melvina (Irwin). Named for the family hero, General Francis Marion, he chose to be known as Marion rather than as Uriah. In 1854 the Lawrances moved to Yellow Springs, and here the father kept the Antioch College bookstore. The enterprise proving a failure, Marion was thrown on his own resources at an early age. After experience as a farmer, storekeeper, and teacher, he entered Antioch College. At the end of a year, to his lifelong regret, ill health compelled him to give up his course. He then engaged in various business ventures till 1889, first in Syracuse, N. Y., and then in Toledo, Ohio.

At sixteen he had been an active Sunday-school worker in his family church, which was of the Christian denomination. In 1876 he became superintendent of the Sunday-school of the Washington Street Congregational Church, Toledo, which under his guidance developed into the model school of the country. Made secretary of the Ohio Sunday School Association in 1889, he brought it to a high degree of efficiency. In 1899 he became general secretary of the International Sunday School Association, which he shaped into a closely knit organization, with cooperating branches in every state. This body became affiliated with similar ones in other countries and there resulted the World's Sunday School Association, of which, also, he served as secretary from 1910 to 1914. After the latter date, he devoted his entire time to the International Association, which largely owed to him its compact organization, its use of uniform lessons, its teacher-training courses and summer conferences. In 1922 it was completely reorganized as the International Council of Religious Education, becoming broadly interdenominational. Of this new organization, for whose perfection Lawrance was largely responsible, he was made secretary emeritus. His death at Portland, Ore., resulted from over-exertion while on an extended speaking tour.

Lawrance was probably the best-known Sunday school man of his day. He was an able platform speaker and convention leader and had great skill in answering questions from the floor. He attended many world conventions and was especially prominent in those at Jerusalem, 1904, Rome, 1907, Washington, 1910, Zurich, 1913, and Tokyo, 1920. He made a speaking tour through the British Isles in 1911 as the guest of the British and World's Sunday School associations, at the close of which he was tendered a luncheon in the Parliament buildings at which many distinguished officials were present. His best-known work, *How to Conduct a Sunday-School* (1905, 1915), had a larger sale than any other work on the subject and has been translated into a dozen languages. Among his other publications are: *The Working Manual of a Successful Sunday-School* (1908); *Training the Teacher* (1908), with others; *Housing the Sunday-School* (1911); *The Sunday-School Organized for Service* (1914); *Special Days in the Sunday-School* (1916); *The Church-school Blue-Print* (1924); *My Message to Sunday-School Workers* (1924). He was also a voluminous contributor to periodicals. On Oct. 15, 1874, he was married to Flora Gaines. Their family consisted of one son and one daughter, who survived their parents.

[H. G. Lawrance, *Marion Lawrance; a Memorial Biog.* (1925); *Who's Who in America*, 1916–17; *Congregationalist*, May 15, 29, 1924; *Toledo News-Bee*, May 2, 1924; *Morning Oregonian* (Portland), May 3, 1924; information as to certain facts from son.]

F. T. P.

LAWRENCE, ABBOTT (Dec. 16, 1792–Aug. 18, 1855), merchant, manufacturer, diplomat, statesman, and philanthropist, was the seventh child and fifth son of Samuel and Susanna Parker Lawrence of Groton, Mass., where he was born and brought up on the paternal farm. Amos and William Lawrence [*qq.v.*] were his brothers. His father was of the sixth generation in descent from John Lawrence of Wisset, Suffolk County, England, who settled in Watertown, Mass., in 1635. In 1660, John Lawrence removed to Groton, then recently erected into a plantation or township by order of the General Court, and became one of its leading men. The Lawrence family continued to reside in Groton, where Samuel, the father of Abbott, was born on Apr. 24, 1754. Samuel Lawrence was one of the minute men who fought at Bunker Hill and lived to take part in the celebration there fifty years later at the laying of the corner-stone of the monument. He served through the Revolutionary War, rising to the rank of major, and, returning to Groton, settled down on his farm where he spent the rest of his life. He was a deacon of the First Congregational Church for forty years and was also one of the founders and for thirty-three years a trustee of Groton Academy. During Shays's Rebellion and all through the troubles of that period, he stood firm in support of the government, and in the advocacy of the supremacy of the laws. He is described as "a devout man, strict in all religious observances, firm, almost rigid, in the discipline of his family," and at the same time "cheerful, joyous, benignant, and given to hospitality." The mother of Abbott Lawrence was the daughter of William Parker, a Groton farmer who removed to Concord, where she witnessed the battle in 1775. She is described as having "strict notions of obedience, with deeply seated religious principles, which she succeeded in communicating to her children," and is said to have had "probably greater influence than her husband in forming their characters."

In 1808 Abbott was sent to Boston and apprenticed to his brother, Amos, who had recently established himself there as a merchant. In 1814, when he came of age, he was admitted to partnership, and the firm of A. & A. Lawrence was founded, which, as one biographer put it, "for the next half-century was to stand as a tower of strength among the business men of Boston." After the virtual retirement of the senior partner in 1831 on account of ill health

Abbott Lawrence became the principal member of the firm and so continued until his death nearly a quarter-century later. He was quick of decision and prompt in action. To these qualities were joined a sanguine and buoyant disposition and extraordinary physical energy. In short, he was the leading Boston merchant during the period when Massachusetts enterprise and capital were turning inland from the sea, and manufacturing was supplanting trade and navigation as the leading interest of New England.

The business of A. & A. Lawrence was at first the importation of English manufactures, especially drygoods. In 1815, as soon as peace was restored, Abbott Lawrence hastened to England and purchased a large stock of goods of which there had long been a dearth in America. Through superior enterprise, he was able to get them to Boston ahead of his competitors, where they were sold at a handsome profit. For the next ten years the firm continued to be importers of English manufactures. Gradually also the partners became interested in the sale of the products of the new cotton and woolen mills which had been established in New England since the war, and eventually they became agents exclusively for domestic manufactures. In 1830 they commenced also to be interested in manufacturing as well as selling domestic cottons and woolens. Associating themselves with the Lowells, Appletons, Jacksons, and other rising manufacturers, they presently became very active in the development of New England industry. In 1845 Abbott Lawrence took the lead in the foundation of the textile city, which bears the family name, and in the establishment of the great mills there, which soon made Lawrence the principal rival of Lowell, founded a quarter-century earlier, in the manufacture of cotton and woolen cloth.

Abbott Lawrence was also one of the first to appreciate the importance of steam railroads and to promote their construction. In 1835, in the face of widespread public indifference and scepticism, he took the lead in advocating the extension of the Boston & Worcester road over the Berkshire mountains to Albany, and the success of the Western Railroad, as it was called, presently attested the farsightedness and courage of its enterprising promoters. He took an equal interest in local improvements, where they seemed likely to be of public benefit, and gave his time and strength freely to foster promising public works in Boston. Thus in 1845 he was active in promoting the construction of municipal water works, despite the opposition of those interested in the private exploitation of the supply of water, and after a sharp contest the advocates of municipal ownership prevailed to the great gain of the city.

Abbott Lawrence's business efficiency, aptitude for affairs, and public spirit made him a favorite representative of the Boston merchants and manufacturers, whenever their special interests required the services of a business man in politics. The Lawrences, like most of the Boston merchants who turned to manufacturing in the period following the Napoleonic wars, were slow to abandon their early belief in the wisdom of a policy of freedom of trade, but after the adoption of the protective tariff act of 1824, convinced that it was useless to oppose longer what then appeared to be the favorite policy of the rest of the country, they decided to accept the system of protection and make the best of it. "The American system," Abbott Lawrence wrote long afterward, in a letter opposing the low tariff of 1846, "was forced upon us, and was adopted for the purpose of creating a home market for the products of the soil of the South and West; we resisted the adoption of a system which, we honestly believed, would greatly injure our navigation, and drive us from our accustomed employments into a business we did not understand. We came into it, however, reluctantly, and soon learned that with the transfer of our capital we acquired skill and knowledge in the use of it. . . . Those who . . . were the strongest opponents of the protective tariff among us have given up their theories. . . . We have gone forward steadily, till many descriptions of manufactures are as well settled in New England as the raising of potatoes" (Hill, *post,* p. 28).

In 1827 he was one of a delegation of seven Massachusetts business men sent to the famous Harrisburg Convention to discuss measures for promoting the interests of domestic manufactures, and in 1834 and again in 1838 he accepted election to Congress as the representative of Boston. In Congress he was an active and influential member of the committee on ways and means. He was an ardent Whig and, becoming more interested in politics, he attended the national convention of 1844 as a delegate and in 1848 was a leading candidate for the vice-presidential nomination. Taking an active part in the ensuing campaign, he was subsequently offered by President Taylor a place in his cabinet but declined both the secretaryship of the navy and that of the interior. Eventually he was prevailed upon to accept an appointment as minister to Great Britain, and for three years represented the United States at the Court of St. James's with efficiency and dignity. In 1852 he resigned in order to give more attention to his private business and did not again hold public office. He was dissatisfied with the failure of the Whig party to oppose the further extension of slavery, and, according to his biographer, would have been one of the original members of the Republican party, if death had not claimed him.

Like his brothers, Abbott Lawrence was a man of firm religious principles and became greatly interested in works of education and charity. On first going to Boston he joined one of the liberal Congregational churches and participated in the religious movement which produced New England Unitarianism. He remained to the end of his life an active member of that denomination. He was a generous benefactor of the academy at Groton, where he received his early education, and toward the close of his life he became deeply interested in the promotion of education in science, especially at Harvard College. He took a leading part in supporting the work of Louis Agassiz and in the founding of chairs at Harvard for the teaching of natural science. In 1847 he gave fifty thousand dollars to the establishment of a school of science and by his will he added another fifty thousand dollars to its endowment. This school was called in his honor the Lawrence Scientific School. Lawrence was also deeply interested in the improvement of the living conditions of the laboring population and bequeathed fifty thousand dollars for the construction of model lodging houses for wage-earners in Boston. His domestic life supported his public character as a popular and successful man of affairs. His wife, whom he married June 28, 1819, was Katherine Bigelow, the eldest daughter of Timothy Bigelow of Medford, Mass., a distinguished lawyer, who served for many years as speaker of the Massachusetts House of Representatives, and Lucy Prescott Bigelow. There were seven children, five sons and two daughters, of whom all but two sons survived their father.

[The principal life of Abbott Lawrence is Hamilton Andrews Hill, *Memoir of Abbott Lawrence* (1883). At a public memorial meeting in Boston, held immediately after his death, addresses were delivered by Edward Everett and Robert C. Winthrop, which have been preserved. Other sources include: W. H. Prescott, *Memoirs of the Hon. Abbott Lawrence* (1856); Nathan Appleton, memoir in the *Mass. Hist. Soc. Colls.*, 4 ser. IV (1858), 495–507; F. W. Ballard, *The Stewardship of Wealth, as Illustrated in the Lives of Amos and Abbott Lawrence* (1865); Freeman Hunt, *Lives of Am. Merchants*, vol. II (1858); John Lawrence, *The Geneal. of the Family of John Lawrence of Wisset, in Suffolk, England* (1869); R. M. Lawrence, *The Descendants of Maj. Samuel Lawrence* (1904); *Boston Daily Jour.*, Aug. 20, 1855. Selections from Abbott Lawrence's diplomatic correspondence were published at Boston as well as occasional pamphlets on the tariff, the currency, and other public questions. Many of these were reprinted in the Appendices of Hill's *Memoir* noted above.]

A. N. H.

LAWRENCE, AMOS (Apr. 22, 1786–Dec. 31, 1852), merchant and philanthropist, brother of Abbott and William Lawrence [*qq.v.*], was one of the leaders in the early development of the New England textile industry. He was distinguished not only for his business efficiency and success but even more for his philanthropic character and many public benefactions. He was the fourth child of Samuel and Susanna Parker Lawrence of Groton, Mass., the parents of a family of six sons and three daughters. Five of the sons grew to manhood, of whom four became successful merchants, one a successful lawyer. (See Abbott Lawrence, for account of ancestry.) Amos Lawrence was apprenticed at the age of thirteen to a merchant in Dunstable and at the age of twenty-one, having served his apprenticeship, went to Boston, where, after working a short period as a clerk, he set up in business for himself. In the following year (1808) he took in his younger brother, Abbott, as an apprentice and in 1814, when he became of age, made him a partner. The firm of A. & A. Lawrence, as it was called, soon became the most successful mercantile firm of its time.

Amos Lawrence was the head of the firm until the year 1831, when his health broke down and forced his retirement from active business. He was an invalid for the remaining twenty-one years of his life. From early youth he had been exceptionally industrious, thrifty, and temperate. Before leaving Groton for Boston, he had formed the habits of total abstinence from alcoholic liquor and tobacco, which he maintained throughout his life and, as soon as his means permitted, he showed a deep sense of the obligations of men of wealth toward the poor and needy. His invalidism in early middle life caused him to make a business of philanthropy at an age when most successful business men are still absorbed in the accumulation of wealth. It was his practice to give money, food, clothing, books, and other necessaries day by day, wherever it seemed to him that they were likely to do good. He kept a supply of such commodities always on hand in his house and devoted much time to personal supervision of their distribution. A memorandum, which he prepared in the last year of his life, shows that during the preceding ten years he had given away approximately five-sixths of his entire income during that period. The amount of these gifts, which was over half a million dollars, was exceeded by the benefactions of other rich men in his day, but in no case were more pains taken to make the gifts appropriate and helpful.

Much of Amos Lawrence's giving was in small amounts, and not a little of it anonymous. The principal recipients of the larger sums were educational institutions. He was always loyal to the academy at Groton, in which he secured his early education, and left a substantial endowment by his will in addition to many gifts during his lifetime. He was also a generous benefactor of Williams College, in which he became interested through his admiration for its president, Mark Hopkins. He took a deep interest also in the erection of Bunker Hill Monument and was the principal contributor to the building fund. Along with his benefactions went much good advice, often in the form of letters carefully written out by his own hand. After his death, those were collected by one of his sons and, at the request of members of the Boston Young Men's Christian Union and the Boston Young Men's Christian Association as well as of students at Williams College, many of them were published under the title, *Extracts from the Diary and Correspondence of the Late Amos Lawrence* (1855). This book gained wide popularity among the young men of the time.

Amos Lawrence was a man of strong religious feeling. Brought up in the old Puritan tradition, he joined the Brattle Street church on removing to Boston and always remained a member of that congregation. But he was not wholly satisfied with the rather cold and intellectual type of Unitarianism which flourished in Boston at that period, and in his benefactions he confined himself to no creed. He took much less interest in politics than in religion. He was originally a Federalist of the school of Hamilton and Jay, and in later life was a loyal Whig. Like so many Boston merchants, he was a strong admirer of Daniel Webster, whom he presented with a service of silver in evidence of his appreciation, not long after the great debate with Senator Hayne of South Carolina. But he had no desire to hold public office himself. He was a Whig presidential elector in 1852, but he refused to contribute to the campaign fund of his brother Abbott in 1848, when the latter was a candidate for the vice-presidential nomination on the ticket with General Taylor, saying that "if my vote would make my brother Vice-President, I would not give it, as I think it lowering his good name to accept office of any sort, by employing such means as are now needful to get votes." Later he rejoiced when his brother refused a place in General Taylor's cabinet, though he had supported "Old Zach" for president.

Amos Lawrence was twice married. His first wife, Sarah Richards, daughter of Giles Richards of Boston, whom he married June 6, 1811, died in 1819. Two years later he married Nancy (Means) Ellis, widow of Judge Ellis of Claremont, N. H., and daughter of Robert Means of Amherst, N. H. He had three sons and a daughter, one of whom, Amos Adams Lawrence [*q.v.*], also attained distinction as a merchant and philanthropist.

[The best source of information on Amos Lawrence's life and character is *Extracts from the Diary and Correspondence of the Late Amos Lawrence*, edited by his son, William R. Lawrence. See also: *Memorial Biogs. of the New-Eng. Hist. Geneal. Soc.*, vol. I (1880); Mark Hopkins, *A Discourse Commemorative of Amos Lawrence* (1853); F. W. Ballard, *The Stewardship of Wealth, as Illustrated in the Lives of Amos and Abbott Lawrence* (1865), a lecture delivered before the Y. M. C. A., New York; Chas. Adams, *Sketch of Amos Lawrence* (1883); Mary C. Crawford, *Famous Families of Mass.*, vol. II (1930); Freeman Hunt, *Lives of Am. Merchants*, vol. II (1858); John Lawrence, *The Geneal. of the Family of John Lawrence of Wisset, in Suffolk, England* (1869); *Boston Commonwealth*, Jan. 1, 3, 4, 5, 1853.] A. N. H.

LAWRENCE, AMOS ADAMS (July 31, 1814–Aug. 22, 1886), merchant and philanthropist, was the second son of Amos Lawrence [*q.v.*], a leading Boston merchant and philanthropist, and Sarah (Richards) Lawrence. He was educated at Franklin Academy, North Andover, and at Harvard College, where he graduated in 1835. Entering business for himself, after graduating from college, as a commission merchant, he formed a partnership in 1843 with Robert M. Mason, under the firm name of Mason & Lawrence. Mason ceased after a few years to be active in the firm and Lawrence continued to be the principal partner for forty years. The firm was very successful, holding the selling agency for several important textile mills and eventually acquiring the selling agency for the Pacific Mills at Lawrence, which for many years was the largest plant of its kind in the United States. Lawrence also engaged independently in manufacturing textiles, his principal venture being the Ipswich Mills, which he acquired in 1860 for the manufacture of cotton hosiery and other knit goods. This was then a new industry in the United States. Although for many years he operated the mill at a loss, he ultimately succeeded in making it profitable and established the industry on a sound basis, becoming the largest manufacturer of knit goods in the country. He took an active part in promoting the interests of the textile industry, being for many years an ardent advocate of a protective tariff and in later life serving as president of the American Association of Knit Goods Manufacturers and also of the National Association of Cotton Manufacturers and Planters.

His father's philanthropic activities naturally brought the son many opportunities for charitable work. While still a young man he became a trustee of the Massachusetts General Hospital and took a great interest in the hospital and in the McLean Asylum for the Insane. He became interested also in the colonization of free negroes in Africa. With increasing years he became more and more interested in education. He established Lawrence University, named after him, in Appleton, Wis., in connection with a large real-estate speculation, in which he became a reluctant partner, and another college at Lawrence, Kan., which afterward was taken over by the state and became the nucleus of the state university. He served for several years as treasurer of Harvard College, and for many years as treasurer of the Episcopal Theological School in Cambridge. He was a generous benefactor of both institutions.

His most distinguished public service was that which he rendered in connection with the New England Emigrant Aid Company, of which he was treasurer. This company was founded in 1854 by Eli Thayer of Worcester, Mass., an ardent but impecunious anti-slavery man, for the purpose of excluding slavery from the territory of Kansas by colonizing it with freemen. Thayer's scheme was to organize a company on a strictly business basis, which would finance settlers and by their success earn profits for the stockholders. A charter was secured and funds raised by the sale of stock. Lawrence had no faith in the Emigrant Aid Company as a business venture, never regarding it in any other light than as a patriotic and charitable enterprise, and seems to have sold the stock on that basis. (See Samuel A. Johnson, "The Genesis of the New England Emigrant Aid Society," in the *New England Quarterly*, January 1930.) To his zeal, aptitude, and business efficiency the success of the enterprise must be largely ascribed. After victory was in sight for the free-state forces, he withdrew from the management of the company, though retaining his interest in the university at Lawrence and in other public institutions in Kansas.

Despite Lawrence's hostility to slavery and his strenuous efforts to keep the "peculiar institution" from spreading onto free soil, he was a conservative in politics. Brought up as a Whig, he never joined the Free Soilers and was opposed to the radical Republican party in the campaigns of 1856 and 1860. In 1856 he was nominated for the governorship of Massachusetts on the Fillmore ticket, but declined. Two years later he accepted a similar nomination and was defeated. In 1860 he was the candidate of the Constitutional Union party and ran unsuccessfully on the ticket with Bell and Everett. After the secession of South Carolina he continued to work for the maintenance of the union by peaceful means and joined Everett and Robert C. Winthrop in a trip to Washington to support the Crittenden compromise. When war broke out, he gave the Lincoln administration unwavering support to the end. He took the lead in raising a regiment of mounted troops, the 2nd Massachusetts Cavalry, but the condition of his health prevented him from taking personal command.

Like his father, Lawrence was more interested in religion than in politics. The Unitarianism which his father and uncles adopted in place of their ancestral Puritanism on moving in to the city from the country failed to satisfy the religious needs of the next generation of Lawrences, and several of them became members of the Episcopal Church. Amos Adams Lawrence was one of these and in 1842 he was confirmed at St. Paul's, together with his wife and his brother. It was his strong religious feeling rather than his politics which made him an admirer of John Brown. Brown's forceful methods he never fully approved and the raid on Harpers Ferry he condemned as the act of a lawless fanatic. The rifles which had once belonged to the Emigrant Aid Company and which were used on Brown's raid were not so used with Lawrence's consent, but Lawrence did give money to Brown and he contributed toward the purchase of the farm at North Elba for Brown's family and toward the employment of counsel at his trial after the raid on Harpers Ferry. He foresaw that Brown would be lauded by the Abolitionists as a martyr and predicted that his death would hasten the end of slavery. Lawrence died suddenly, of heart disease, in August 1886. He had married, Mar. 31, 1842, Sarah Elizabeth Appleton, daughter of William Appleton, a leading Boston merchant. She, together with six of their seven children, survived him.

[There is an excellent biography, *Life of Amos A. Lawrence with Extracts from His Diary and Correspondence* (1888), by Lawrence's son, Wm. Lawrence. Additional material of much interest will be found in the same author's *Memories of a Happy Life* (1926). An obituary appeared in the *Boston Transcript*, Aug. 23, 1886.]

A. N. H.

LAWRENCE, GEORGE NEWBOLD (Oct. 20, 1806–Jan. 17, 1895), ornithologist and wholesale druggist, was born in New York City where his entire life was spent. His parents were John Burling Lawrence and Hannah Newbold. Through his father he traced his ancestry to William Lawrence, who emigrated from Hertfordshire, England, in 1635, and settled first at Plymouth. John Burling Lawrence was engaged in the wholesale drug and chemical business, having formed a partnership with Jacob Schieffelin in 1781. George entered this establishment at the age of sixteen, later becoming a partner and in 1835 head of the firm. He had married, in 1834, Mary Ann Newbold, the daughter of George Newbold of New York City. In later life he retired in order to devote all of his time to his ornithological studies which had hitherto been a hobby to be enjoyed only as business cares permitted. From early boyhood he seems to have been interested in birds. At the age of fourteen he was allowed to have a gun and soon began collecting specimens—the nucleus of the collection of some 8,000 skins which later became the property of the American Museum of Natural History. At this time the Lawrences lived at their country home, "Forest Hill," some eight miles north of the New York City Hall, from which an unbroken forest extended to Fort Washington Point. Not far from them was the home of John James Audubon and while, at the time of young Lawrence's boyhood, the famous painter-naturalist was nearing the close of his eventful life, Lawrence became well acquainted with his sons, Victor and John, and this association doubtless stimulated his interest in ornithology.

Lawrence's early studies dealt entirely with the birds of the United States but about 1858 he turned his attention to neotropical ornithology, especially to the study of the birds of the West Indies and Central America, upon which he soon became an authority. While his knowledge was broad and comprehensive, his publications were almost entirely limited to descriptions of new species or to lists of collections submitted to him for study. In 1841 he made the acquaintance of Spencer F. Baird, the future secretary of the Smithsonian Institution, whose magnetic enthusiasm doubtless did much to clinch Lawrence's determination to devote himself to the serious study of ornithology. A little later he met John Cassin, the noted ornithologist of Philadelphia. Together they assisted Baird in the preparation of the study on North American birds published by the War Department in the series of *Reports of Explorations and Surveys to Ascertain the . . . Route for a Railroad from the Mississippi River to the Pacific Ocean* (vol. IX, 1858). Lawrence contributed the accounts of many of the groups of water birds. In later life he became one of the founders of the American Ornithologists' Union and was soon after made an honorary member. He was similarly honored by the Zoological Society of London, the British Ornithologists' Union, and many of the scientific societies of America. He was also one of the founders of the College of Pharmacy of the City of New York. Those who knew him in the last years of his long life saw in him a typical gentleman of the old school in both manners and appearance.

[D. G. Elliot, "In Memoriam: Geo. Newbold Lawrence," *The Auk*, Jan. 1896; L. S. Foster, "The Published Writings of Geo. Newbold Lawrence," *Bull. U. S. Nat. Museum*, No. 40 (1892), with portrait and biographical sketch; Thomas Lawrence, *Hist. Geneal. of the Lawrence Family* (1858); *N. Y. Tribune*, Jan. 19, 1895; personal acquaintance.] W. S.

LAWRENCE, JAMES (Oct. 1, 1781–June 4, 1813), naval officer, great-grandson of Elisha Lawrence, who was established as a merchant in Monmouth County, N. J., at the end of the seventeenth century, was born in Burlington, N. J. He was the son of John (or John Brown) Lawrence, a lawyer of considerable ability, and his second wife, Martha (Tallman) Lawrence. After receiving an elementary education in the grammar school of his native town, James began the study of law, but, on evincing a distaste for his father's profession, he was permitted to choose his own calling, that of the sea, and was given instruction in navigation and naval tactics. On Sept. 4, 1798, he entered the navy as a midshipman on the *Ganges* and some two years later was made acting lieutenant on the *Adams*. Retained under Jefferson's peace establishment as a midshipman, he was on Sept. 1, 1801, promoted sailing master, and some months later, lieutenant, taking rank from Apr. 6, 1802. In the war with Tripoli, 1801–05, he was, successively, first lieutenant of the *Enterprise*, commander of the same, first lieutenant of the *John Adams*, and commander of *Gunboat No. 6*. He established a reputation for gallantry as second in command in the two most daring operations of the war, Porter's boat attack on Tripoli and the burning of the *Philadelphia*. His service in connection with the first of these exploits was highly commended by Porter. Notice of the second was taken by Congress in a resolution expressing its appreciation and granting to the participants two months' extra pay. So inadequate was the pecuniary reward that Lawrence declined to receive his share of it.

He next served as first lieutenant of the *Constitution* and then commanded, successively, the *Vixen, Wasp, Argus,* and *Hornet.* He was promoted to the rank of master commandant in December 1811. Twice he carried dispatches to Europe for the State Department—on the *Wasp* in 1809, and on the *Hornet* in 1811–12. The unsatisfactory character of the messages that he brought to America in May 1812 precipitated the war of that year.

The *Hornet* was one of the vessels of the squadron of Commodore John Rodgers [*q.v.*] that put to sea from New York on the declaration of war, and she captured three of the prizes taken during this initial venture, which was on the whole rather fruitless. Lawrence's second cruise was made in company with Commodore Bainbridge in the South Atlantic Ocean. At Bahia he blockaded the British sloop of war *Bonne Citoyenne* for several days and then challenged her to single combat. For various reasons the British commander, quite properly, declined to fight. Lawrence continued the blockade until driven into port by the *Montagu,* 74 guns. Escaping under cover of darkness, he cruised to the northward, and off Pernambuco captured the merchantman *Resolution,* 10 guns. On Feb. 24, 1813, at the mouth of the Demerara River, he encountered the British brig of war *Peacock,* about the same size as the *Hornet* but with an armament only two-thirds that of the American ship. A hot, close action ensued, ending in the surrender of the *Peacock,* some fifteen minutes after the first shot was fired. She was so badly injured that she sank before all her crew could be taken off. Her loss in the fight was thirty-four, including her commander, who was killed; that of the *Hornet,* three (Mahan, *post,* II, 8). This great difference is good evidence of the superior fighting and seamanship of the Americans. The *Hornet* arrived at New York Mar. 24, 1813.

Lawrence was promoted captain Mar. 3, 1813, before news of his victory had reached America. On Mar. 31, the Common Council of New York thanked him for his victory and voted to present him with the freedom of the city, together with a piece of plate, and a week later it gave him and his crew a public dinner. On May 1, 1813, he was placed in command of the navy yard at New York. He expected next to go to sea on the *Constitution,* but on May 6 he was ordered to relieve the commander of the *Chesapeake* at Boston. His instructions were to proceed to sea as soon as the weather and the force and position of the enemy would permit and to intercept the British storeships and transports bound to Canada. This was an objective of the highest importance, but Lawrence abandoned it to fight a ship duel that could not have greatly affected the course of the war had he been successful. His judgment has been severely censured by recent naval historians (Mahan, *post,* II, 131–33; Chadwick, *post,* pp. 206–07). He took command of the *Chesapeake* on May 20 and went to sea on June 1, with the intention of fighting the British frigate *Shannon,* 38 guns, then blockading Boston. In guns the ships were well matched. In number of crew the *Chesapeake* had the advantage, but in organization, seamanship, and gunnery practice, the *Shannon* was much the superior. Even so, Lawrence had a chance of success and must be acquitted of foolhardiness. The action lasted less than fifteen minutes. Lawrence and his first lieutenant, Augustus Ludlow [*q.v.*], fell mortally wounded. The flag of the *Chesapeake* was hauled down by the enemy. Her loss was 145; that of the *Shannon,* 82.

On June 8 Lawrence was buried at Halifax with military honors. In the following August Capt. George Crowninshield [*q.v.*], a shipowner of Salem, Mass., sailing under a flag of truce, brought the body to Salem, where it was given funeral honors with a eulogy pronounced by Justice Joseph Story [*q.v.*]. Thence it was conveyed to New York, where on Sept. 16, 1813 it was buried in Trinity Churchyard. The words, "Don't give up the ship," which the mortally wounded hero is said to have uttered when carried below, became a popular rallying cry of the navy.

In 1808 Lawrence was married to Julia Montaudevert, the daughter of a New York City merchant of French descent. There were two children, a daughter who later married a naval officer, and a posthumous son who died in infancy. All recognition of Lawrence's achievements by the federal government came after his death. On July 13, 1813, in accordance with a recommendation of the President, Congress voted $25,000 to the officers and crew of the *Hornet* as prize money. In January 1814, it adopted a resolution requesting the President to present to the nearest male relative of Lawrence a gold medal as a testimony of its appreciation of his victory and to communicate to his nearest relative its sense of the loss sustained by the navy in his death.

[Record of Officers, 1798–1817, Bureau of Navigation, Navy Dept.; Albert Gleaves, *James Lawrence* (1904); articles in *Port Folio* (Philadelphia), Sept. 1813, Jan., Feb. 1817; *Biography of James Lawrence, Esq.,* etc. (1813); Thomas Lawrence, *Hist. Geneal. of the Lawrence Family* (1858); J. F. Cooper, *The Hist. of the Navy of the U. S. A.* (2 vols., 1839); A. T.

Mahan, *Sea Power in Its Relations to the War of 1812* (1919), vol. II; F. E. Chadwick, "The American Navy, 1775–1815," *Proc. Mass. Hist. Soc.*, vol. XLVI (1913).]
C. O. P.

LAWRENCE, RICHARD SMITH (Nov. 22, 1817–Mar. 10, 1892), inventor, gunsmith, tool-manufacturer, was the son of Richard and Susan (Smith) Lawrence, both of English descent, and was born on his father's farm in Chester, Vt. When he was two years old the family moved to Jefferson County, N. Y., and for nineteen years Lawrence lived in the vicinity of Watertown, attending school for three years, doing farm work, laboring in a wood-working shop, and spending his spare time in a custom gun shop. After serving for three months in the army during the Canadian Rebellion he went in 1838 to live with relatives in Windsor, Vt. Here he found work with N. Kendall & Company, a firm that was making guns at the Windsor prison. In six months he had so mastered the manufacturing processes that he was put in charge of the work, continuing in this capacity until 1842, when gun-making was stopped. He then remained at the prison for a time in charge of the carriage shop. In 1843, in partnership with Kendall, he opened a gun shop in Windsor. The following year, with the help of S. E. Robbins, a business man, they obtained a contract for 10,000 rifles from the federal government, and a new company, Robbins, Kendall & Lawrence, was formed and a factory built at Windsor. After three prosperous years Robbins and Lawrence purchased Kendall's holdings and for the next four years the two partners continued successfully. Lawrence supervised the design and production of the guns and was constantly improving the methods of manufacture. He devised the barrel-drilling and rifling machines, built a plain milling machine—the forerunner of the Lincoln miller—and invented the split pulley. In 1850 he introduced the practice of lubricating bullets with tallow, which made possible the success of the repeating rifle. By 1851 the partners had built up a wide reputation and were engaged to furnish all of the machinery for the Enfield Armory in England and, in addition, were awarded a large contract for British Enfield rifles. In 1852 they contracted to manufacture Sharps carbines and rifles, the former at Windsor and the latter in a new plant at Hartford, Conn. Production had hardly got under way, however, when the partners experienced serious financial difficulties induced by their unsuccessful attempt in 1850 to undertake the manufacture of railroad cars, and they failed with a loss of nearly a quarter of a million dollars. The Sharps Rifle Company thereupon bought the Robbins and Lawrence enterprise in Hartford and employed Lawrence as superintendent. He continued with the company from 1856 to 1872 when he resigned to accept a position with the city of Hartford. Until his death he served on the water board, the board of aldermen, the council board, and on the fire board. He had married Mary Ann Finney in Philadelphia on May 22, 1842, and at the time of his death in Hartford was survived by a son.

[Jos. W. Roe, *English and Am. Tool Builders* (1916, 1926); Guy Hubbard, "Development of Machine Tools in New England," *Am. Machinist*, Oct. 15, 1923, Mar. 20, 1924; *Hartford Courant*, Mar. 11, 1892; family records.]
C. W. M.

LAWRENCE, WILLIAM (Sept. 7, 1783–Oct. 14, 1848), merchant and philanthropist, brother of Amos and Abbott Lawrence [*qq.v.*], was one of the leaders in the early development of the New England textile industry. He was born in Groton, Mass., the third son of Samuel and Susanna Parker Lawrence, and a descendant of John Lawrence who emigrated from Suffolk County, England, and settled in Watertown, Mass., in 1635. He originally intended to be a farmer, but poor health caused him to leave home in 1809 and spend the winter with his brother, Amos, in Boston, where the latter had recently established himself in business. Finding business to his liking, William set up for himself in the following year as a commission merchant and prospered. In 1822 he took into partnership his younger brother, Samuel, forming the firm of W. & S. Lawrence. In 1825, the brothers, who had previously been chiefly importers, became interested in domestic manufactures. It was through their agency that the first incorporated company for the manufacture of woolen goods was formed, the Middlesex Manufacturing Company, with a plant at Lowell, then recently formed. Lawrence continued in active business, principally in the woolen commission business, until 1842, when he retired with what is described as "an ample fortune." His wife, Susan Ruggles Bordman, born Apr. 29, 1787, whom he married May 20, 1813, was the daughter of one of Boston's leading citizens and contributed a substantial patrimony to the family fortune. Nine children were born, of whom four survived their father.

William Lawrence's most important public service was his part in the establishment of the so-called "Suffolk Bank System." This bank, designed to put the currency of New England on a sound basis, was chartered in 1818, and Lawrence served on the board of directors from its organization to his death, thirty years later. He was also active in the promotion of public improvements in Boston, and a generous contributor to local charities. His most significant benefaction was the endowment of Groton Academy, the name of which, in recognition of his benefactions and those of his brother Amos, was changed to Lawrence Academy in 1846. One of a remarkable group of brothers, distinguished alike for their business efficiency and for their practical philanthropy, he was a leader in the generation of Boston merchants which guided New England through its industrial revolution.

[S. K. Lothrop, *Memoir of Wm. Lawrence* (1856), reprinted from the *Am. Jour. of Educ.*, July 1856; Freeman Hunt, *Lives of Am. Merchants*, vol. II (1858); Mary C. Crawford, *Famous Families of Mass.*, vol. II (1930); John Lawrence, *The Geneal. of the Family of John Lawrence of Wisset, in Suffolk, England* (1869); *Boston Transcript*, Oct. 16, 1848.] A. N. H.

LAWRENCE, WILLIAM (June 26, 1819–May 8, 1899), jurist and Ohio congressman, the son of Joseph and Temperance (Gilchrist) Lawrence, was born in Mount Pleasant, Ohio. He received his early educational training in the village schools and in Tidball's Academy, near Steubenville. In 1838 he graduated with high honors from Franklin College at New Athens and, that autumn, entered the law office of James L. Gage of Morgan County. While pursuing his legal studies he taught school in Pennsville and at MacConnelsville, Ohio. In 1839 he entered the Cincinnati law school and the following March received his degree. In 1840 he began the practice of law, first in Zanesville, then in MacConnelsville and, the next year, settled at Bellefontaine. In 1842 he was appointed by the United States district court to be commissioner of bankruptcy for Logan County. On Dec. 20, 1843, he married Cornelia, the daughter of William Hawkins of MacConnelsville, who died three months after their marriage, and on Mar. 20, 1845, he married Caroline, the daughter of Henry Miller of Bellefontaine. In 1845 he became prosecuting attorney of Logan County and, from 1845 to 1847, was the editor of the *Logan Gazette*. He was a member of the Ohio House of Representatives in 1846 and 1847 and of the state Senate in 1849, 1850, and 1854. In the Ohio legislature he took an active part in obtaining the adoption of measures providing for reform schools for juvenile delinquents and for district school libraries. He also brought about the passage of a measure that gave greater security to real-estate interests in Ohio and was the author of the Ohio free banking law of 1851. In 1851 he was reporter for the Ohio supreme court, and he published the twentieth volume of *Reports of Cases Argued and Determined in the Supreme Court of Ohio*, which was favorably commented upon for its logical arrangement of decisions, interspersed with the author's comments on previous cases both in Ohio and elsewhere. In 1859 he became editor of the *Western Law Monthly* and served three years. From February 1857 to September 1864 he was judge of the common-pleas court and district court. During the Civil War he was colonel, for three months, of the 84th Ohio Volunteers, serving in Maryland, and, in 1863, Lincoln appointed him district judge of Florida, but he declined to accept.

From 1865 to 1877, excluding one term from 1871 to 1873, he was a member of Congress. During his ten years' service he was an earnest advocate of all measures designed to secure civil and political equality. In 1869 he made a report on the New York election frauds, which resulted in important state and federal legislation. He was the virtual author of the law that created the Department of Justice. He also drafted the measure that gave each soldier one hundred and sixty acres of the alternate reserved sections in the railroad land grants. In the interest of the settlers, he became one of the early advocates of prohibiting the sale of public lands by authority of an Indian treaty rather than by act of Congress, and his efforts led to the passage of the act of Mar. 3, 1871. In the face of strenuous opposition, he ably defended, against the railroad attorneys before the judiciary committee, a bill requiring the Pacific railroad companies to indemnify the government to the extent of one hundred and fifty million dollars and, on July 7, 1876, carried his measure through the House of Representatives. The next year the secretary of the interior, Carl Schurz, heartily indorsed the principles of the "Lawrence Bill" in his annual report. From 1880 to 1885 Lawrence held the office of first comptroller of the United States Treasury Department and was the first of the comptrollers to print his decisions. His legal acumen won for him universal recognition. He often appeared before the United States Supreme Court in important land cases such as *Morton* vs. *Nebraska* (21 *Wall*, 660–75), *Holden* vs. *Joy* (17 *Wall*, 211–53), and *Leavenworth, Lawrence and Galveston Railroad Company* vs. *United States* (92 *U. S.*, 733–60). His firm grasp of the fundamentals of the law, his keen analysis of the salient points at issue, his quick perception of the weakness in his opponents' arguments, and his frankness made him respected and feared. In the impeachment of Johnson he prepared a brief of authorities to support the legal argument of Benjamin F. Butler (appendix to *Proceedings in the Trial of Andrew Johnson,* 1868). He appeared before the Electoral Commission in 1877 to argue the case of Oregon and South Carolina (*Congressional Record,* 44 Cong., 2 Sess., pt. 4, pp. 4, 185). He was also a recognized authority on wool and became the president of the state association of wool growers in 1891 and of the national association in 1893. He died at Kenton, Ohio.

[Files of the Congressional Joint Committee on Printing; *A Biog. Cyc. and Portrait Gallery . . . of Ohio* (1879); Henry Howe, *Hist. Colls. of Ohio,* vol. II (1891); *The Biog. Annals of Ohio,* 1902–03; *Who's Who in America,* 1899; *Biog. Dir. of the Am. Cong.* (1928); *Ohio State Journal,* May 9, 1899.] R. C. M.

LAWRENCE, WILLIAM BEACH (Oct. 23, 1800–Mar. 26, 1881), public official, writer on international law, was born in New York City, the son of Isaac and Cornelia (Beach) Lawrence. His earliest American paternal ancestor, Thomas Lawrence, emigrated from England and had settled in Newtown, L. I., by 1656. His maternal grandfather was for many years assistant rector of Trinity Church, New York. From birth he had the advantages of opulence and social station. His father was a man of wealth and influence, a presidential elector in 1820 and one-time president of the New York branch of the Bank of the United States. The boy was by nature studious and precocious, and in 1818 he was graduated with high honors from Columbia College. After graduation he studied law in the famous law school in Litchfield, Conn. During a winter in the South he spent a few days at "Monticello," as the guest of Jefferson. In 1821 he married Esther, daughter of Archibald Gracie [*q.v.*]. The years 1821–23 he spent in Europe, where he enjoyed the entrée into the most exclusive circles, thanks to letters of introduction to Lord Holland, Lafayette, and others. Few young Americans have ever been accorded a more distinguished reception abroad. In Paris he pursued studies in law at the Sorbonne and the École de Droit and attended the lectures of Say on political economy. It was at this time that he conceived the interest in international law that was to be the absorbing concern of his life and the field of his greatest achievement. For three years after his return to America he practised law in New York. In 1826 he was appointed secretary of legation in London, and in 1827, as chargé d'affaires, he conducted the correspondence regarding the northeast boundary.

For the next twenty years Lawrence lived in New York, practising his profession, pursuing his investigations in jurisprudence and public law, writing, and lecturing. Among the products of this period may be noted the *Two Lectures on Political Economy* (1831); *The Bank of the United States* (1831), an argument for its constitutionality and utility, reprinted from the *North American Review,* April 1831; *The Origin and Nature of the Representative and Federative Institutions of the United States* (1832); "The Public Distress" (*American Quarterly Review,* June 1834); a *History of the Negotiations in Reference to the Eastern and Northeastern Boundaries of the United States* (1841); an address on the *Colonisation and Subsequent History of New Jersey* (1843); and an unpublished memoir of Albert Gallatin. His celebrated argument in the case of the German Reformed Church, by which he obtained a reversal of the Chancellor's decision, was published in 1845. In 1850 he took up his residence in Newport, R. I. In 1851 he was elected lieutenant-governor of Rhode Island, and in 1852, during the administration of Philip Allen, he served as acting governor. Among other measures, he urged the abolition of imprisonment for debt and opposed, on constitutional grounds, the enactment of a law prohibiting the sale of liquor. In 1855 appeared his annotated edition of the *Elements of International Law,* by Henry Wheaton, his long-time and intimate friend, a work of extraordinary erudition, which at once took rank as a standard textbook and an authoritative commentary. Three years later he published a treatise entitled *Visitation and Search.* The political issues of the fifties also enlisted his interest. While not defending slavery, he condoned it as an economic necessity and vehemently denounced abolitionists as dangerous fanatics. He stood for state's rights, but not for secession, yet he opposed coercion and after the Civil War protested against the attempt to "hold the South in vassalage." (See his *L'Industrie Française et L'Esclavage des Nègres aux États Unis,* 1860; and two addresses: *No North, No South!,* 1856, and *The Issues of the Hour,* 1868.)

In 1863 Lawrence brought out his second edition of Wheaton. Although his learning was universally recognized, his political views gave offense in certain quarters and an attempt was made to discredit his work as "disloyal." Richard Henry Dana, Jr., 1815–1882 [*q.v.*], was engaged to prepare a "loyal" edition. Lawrence charged Dana with piracy and was sustained in his contention by an opinion of the Court to the effect that many of the notes in the Dana edition infringed his rights. In 1866 he attended the Social Science Congress at Bristol and was named a member of a commission to compile a code of international law, a project which, together with an international court, he strongly advocated. Two years later appeared the first volume of the *Commentaire sur les Éléments du Droit International.* Later three other volumes followed. Lawrence published in 1866 a pamphlet on the *Disabilities of American Women Married Abroad*; in 1871, *The Treaty of Washington; Letters from Hon. William Beach Lawrence*; and in 1874, *Administration of Equity Jurisprudence.* Meanwhile he was contributing to the *Revue de Droit International,* the *London Law Magazine,* the *Transactions of the Social Science Association,* and other periodicals, and also lecturing on international law in Columbian University, Washington. In 1873 he defended the case of the steamship *Circassian* before the Joint High Commission, obtaining a reversal of the decision of the Supreme Court. His argument, published under the title *Belligerent and Sovereign Rights as Regards Neutrals During the War of Secession* (1873), was considered both in England and America as an authoritative exposition of certain important points of public law. In temperament and manner Lawrence combined the courtliness of the aristocrat with the candor and directness of the democrat. In literary style he was inclined to be diffuse. He was an omnivorous reader and an indefatigable student. Everything that came from his pen testifies to a prodigious memory, to a penetrating mind, and to analytical and reasoning powers of the first order.

[*Biog. Cyc. of Representative Men of R. I.* (1881), I, 287–89; Chas. H. Hart, *A Discourse Commemorative of the Life and Services of the Late Wm. Beach Lawrence* (1881); J. G. Wilson, *Gov. Wm. Beach Lawrence, an Address Delivered Before the N. Y. Hist. Soc.* (1882); J. S. Hart, *Manual of Am. Lit.* (1873); Thos. Lawrence, *Hist. Geneal. of the Lawrence Family* (1858); Isaac Lawrence, memoir in *N. Y. Geneal. and Biog. Record,* Apr. 1895; *N. Y. Times,* Mar. 26, 1881.]
T. C.

LAWRIE, ALEXANDER (Feb. 25, 1828–Feb. 15, 1917), painter and crayon portrait draftsman, was born in New York City, the son of Alexander Lawrie, merchant, and his wife, Sarah Coombe. According to one account, he was apprenticed to an engraver at fifteen. He studied in the life and antique classes of the National Academy of Design, and between the years 1850 and 1854 was living in Philadelphia and showing crayon portrait heads, among them one of Thomas Sully, at the Pennsylvania Academy of the Fine Arts. In 1854 he went abroad for three years' study under E. Leutze, at Düsseldorf, under Picot in Paris, and under Greek and Italian painters in Florence. Returning to America in 1858, he opened a studio in Philadelphia, where he regularly exhibited work in oils—portraits, landscapes, genre—until 1864. At the outbreak of the Civil War he enlisted (Apr. 18, 1861) in the 17th Regiment, Pennsylvania Volunteer Infantry. He was discharged in August and reënlisted Sept. 5, becoming captain of Company B, 121st Pennsylvania Volunteers. Early in 1863 he was disabled and was discharged the following June.

On his recovery he again went abroad to study, but before 1866 returned to New York, where he spent the best years of his professional life. For a decade his work was a regular feature of the annual exhibitions of the Academy, to which he contributed ideal figure pieces, portraits in oil and crayon, and landscapes painted in the Adirondacks or the highlands of the Hudson. In 1868 he was elected an associate of the National Academy of Design. To the Centennial Exhibition he sent two canvases, "A Monk Playing a Violoncello," and "Autumn in the Hudson Highlands." Among the best of his crayon portraits, of which he is said to have executed "upwards of a thousand," are those of Richard Henry Stoddard, Thomas Buchanan Read, and George Henry Boker. His portraits in oil include one of Judge Sutherland painted for the American Bar Association, and one of Gen. Zealous B. Tower, for the United States Military Academy at West Point. The erroneous statement, repeated in more than one biographical work, that Lawrie did engraving is probably due to his having been confused with one Robert Lawrie, an English engraver.

Lawrie, who was unmarried, disappeared from public life about 1876. Twenty years later he was living in Chalmers, Ind., and in 1902 he was admitted to the Indiana State Soldiers' Home at Lafayette, where he remained until his death. At the age of seventy-six, he undertook the painting of a series of portraits of the generals who served in the Civil War, many of them done partly from memory. The task occupied twelve years. He completed 158 portraits, which he bequeathed to the state of Indiana. The series, now hanging in the library of the Soldiers' Home where he died, will probably in time be placed in the State House at Indianapolis.

[C. E. Clement and Laurence Hutton, *Artists of the Nineteenth Century* (2 vols., 1907); Theodore Bolton, *Early Am. Portrait Draughtsmen in Crayon* (1923); S. P. Bates, *Hist. of Pa. Volunteers,* vols. I (1869), IV (1870); *Am. Art Annual,* 1917; *Am. Art News,* Mar. 3, 1917; *Indianapolis Star,* Feb. 16, 1917; information as to certain facts from a nephew, Robert Telfer, Brookston, Ind.]
M. B. H.

LAWS, SAMUEL SPAHR (Mar. 23, 1824–Jan. 9, 1921), educator, was born in Ohio County, Va., the son of James and Rachel (Spahr) Laws. His ancestors had come from England to Maryland in 1672. Having acquired the rudiments of his education in an old-field school in Virginia, he entered Miami University at Oxford, Ohio, where he was graduated in 1848 as the valedictorian of his class. He then was a student for three years in Princeton Theological Seminary, graduating in 1851 with highest honors. In the same year he was ordained and became pastor of West Church in St. Louis. His career as an educator began in 1854, when he became professor of physical science at Westminster College, Fulton, Mo. He was made president of this institution in the following year and served in this capacity until 1861, when, on account of difficulties resulting from his sympathy with the South in the Civil War, he resigned and began making a translation of Aristotle. As a Southern sympathizer he was arrested by Union authorities and confined in several prisons but eventually he was paroled. He then spent some time abroad, mostly in Paris. Before the close of the war he obtained a position as vice-president of the New York Gold Exchange, an office which he filled with recognized efficiency. After resigning this position, he invented and introduced the "ticker" by which market reports could be telegraphed simultaneously.

In New York he studied law at Columbia College and in 1870 he was granted the degree of LL.B. He had already been admitted, in 1869, to the New York bar. His interests then led him to become a student in the Bellevue Hospital Medical College, where in 1875 he received the degree of M.D. Called to the University of Missouri by unanimous action of the curators, he became on July 4, 1876, president of this institution and professor of mental and moral philosophy and of the evidences of Christianity. He served in this position until July 1, 1889. In his plans for the development of the university he displayed clear foresight. He believed that the university should be an integral part of the public-school system of the state, a fact which he forcefully brought before the legislature in 1887. After leaving the University, Laws engaged privately in scholarly work until 1893, when he accepted a position in the Presbyterian Theological Seminary, Columbia, S. C., as Perkins Professor of Natural Science in Connection with Revelation and Christian Apologetics. He retired from this position in 1898, at the age of seventy-four, moving to Richmond, Va., and later to Washington, D. C.

Laws was a solidly built man of medium height, revealing in his appearance a strong, vigorous character, tempered with geniality, but capable of brusqueness on occasion. In his inaugural address at the University of Missouri, he said: "*The authority of government in a school is not derived from the pupils nor is it dependent upon them in any sense whatever.* . . . It does not come up from them, but it comes down upon them. . . . The only alternative to a pupil in school is to obey or leave, willingly or by restraint. . . . Any other theory works its own inevitable destruction" (*Inauguration of S. S. Laws, post,* pp. 60–61). Although he was thoroughly honest in motive, his legalistic point of view, positive convictions, forceful will, and directness of word and act in discipline and in other administrative matters undoubtedly resulted in antagonisms which greater tact might have mitigated or even have avoided. His equally outstanding characteristics were his breadth of interests and his extensive and thorough scholarship. With an unusual memory, he had at command a definite, comprehensive, and well-organized stock of knowledge. A scholar in the classics and in Hebrew, he had an extensive knowledge of the sciences; an able student and writer in the field of theology, he was successful in business and made a notable mechanical invention; a teacher and investigator, he was also an educational administrator. His most profound interest appeared to be in theology, as evidenced by his teaching and writings. The latter, although brief, reveal a well-disciplined, logical mind and an extensive acquaintance with the literature in their respective fields. His published works include: *A Letter by the Rev. S. S. Laws, LL.D. to the Synod of Missouri* (*O. S.*) (1872); *Metaphysics: A Lecture* (1879); *Life and Labors of Louis Pasteur* (1886); *Christianity: Its Nature* (1903); *Polygamy and Citizenship in Church and State* (1906); and *The At-onement by the Christian Trinity* (1919). Laws was married, on Jan. 19, 1860, to Ann Maria (Broadwell) Doubleday, daughter of William Broadwell of Fulton, Mo. He died at Asheville, N. C., in his ninety-seventh year.

[*Hist. of Boone County, Mo.* (1882); *Inauguration of S. S. Laws, LL.D., as President of the Univ. of Mo.* (1876); brief obituary in *Mo. Hist. Rev.*, Jan. 1921; J. M. Greenwood, sketch in *Educ. Rev.*, Mar. 1903; *Mo. Alumni Tribute to Dr. Samuel Spahr Laws* (1901); Wm. F. Switzler, unpublished "History of the University of Missouri," in the archives of the University; *Princeton Theol. Sem. Necrological Report*, Aug. 1921; M. M. Fisher and J. J. Rice, *Hist. of Westminster Coll.* (1903); *Testimony Taken Before the Univ. Investigating Committee, Thirty-Fifth Gen. Assembly of the State of Mo.* (1889); records in the archives of the University.]

J. H. C.

LAWSON, ALEXANDER (Dec. 19, 1773–Aug. 22, 1846), line-engraver, was born on a farm at Ravenstruthers, Lanarkshire, Scotland. Leaving school at fifteen, he went to assist a brother who was in business in Liverpool, but after a year's experience, removed to Manchester. There he became interested in the prints hung in the windows of a bookseller's shop, and determined to became an engraver. He began with a penknife and a smooth halfpenny to cut designs, but the scratched result did not satisfy him, so he had a blacksmith fashion an engraver's tool for him, and with this continued his experiments. He was charmed by the French engravings of the period, and when he was twenty, determined to go to France to learn the art. Upon discovering that because of the French Revolution, then in progress, he could not go from England to France, he took passage for the United States in 1794. In Philadelphia he found employment with Thackara & Vallance, then at work upon plates for Thomas Dobson's *Encyclopaedia* (18 vols., 1790–98), which was the first American edition of the *Britannica.* While learning to engrave, he spent his free hours in the study of drawing, and after two years with his employers he set up in business for himself.

His first independent work was a series of four plates (1797) to illustrate Thomson's *Seasons.* When Joel Barlow saw Lawson's plates he expressed his regret at not having had *The Columbiad* illustrated in the United States (Ward, *post*). Lawson also engraved plates for the supplemental volumes (1803) of Dobson's *Encyclopaedia.* For a short time he was in partnership with J. J. Barralet, and engraved the plates for *The Powers of Genius* (2nd ed., 1802), by the Rev. John Blair Linn [*q.v.*], from designs by Barralet. Probably the most important incident in his career was his meeting with a fellow Scotsman, Alexander Wilson [*q.v.*], the naturalist. The friendship between the two men, begun in 1798, continued until Wilson's death. As it ripened Wilson confessed his ambition to issue a work on American birds, and Lawson finally agreed to engrave the plates for a little less than a dollar a day. He afterward explained his generosity by saying he did it "for the honor of the old country" (*Ibid.*). Wilson's *American Ornithology* was issued in nine volumes between 1808 and 1814. Lawson's plates, some of which he colored himself, attracted the attention of artists, engravers and naturalists in Europe, and the work established his reputation as an engraver. He was an industrious worker and applied himself closely, producing a great number of plates for maps, charts, and book illustrations. He engraved a portrait of Washington, after Stuart; one of Burns, after Nasmyth; and several designs after paintings by John Lewis Krimmel [*q.v.*], to whom he acted as guide and patron. His reputation was further enhanced by his plates for Charles Lucien Bonaparte's *American Ornithology; or, The Natural History of Birds Inhabiting the United States not Given by Wilson* (4 vols.. 1825–33). George Ord wrote from Paris in 1830, after seeing the third volume, that the naturalists in London "united in declaring such work could not be produced in England" (Ward, *post*). Lawson was married, June 6, 1805, to Elizabeth Scaife, a native of Cumberland, England. He had a son who became an artist and two daughters who also displayed artistic talents. He continued to work until ten days before his death, which occurred in Philadelphia. In 1928 he was represented in the exhibition of one hundred notable American engravers at the New York Public Library.

[Townsend Ward, "Alexander Lawson," in *Pa. Mag. of Hist. and Biog.*, Apr. 1904; D. M. Stauffer, *Am. Engravers upon Copper and Steel* (2 vols., 1907); W. S. Baker, *Am. Engravers* (1875); Wm. Dunlap, *Hist. of the Rise and Progress of the Arts of Design in the U. S.* (2 vols., 1834), quoting an autobiographical letter from Lawson, which gives 1773 as the year of his birth, instead of 1772, the year usually given; obituary in *Pub. Ledger* (Phila.), Aug. 24, 1846.]

J. J.

LAWSON, JAMES (Nov. 9, 1799–Mar. 24, 1880), author, editor, and insurance expert, was born in Glasgow, Scotland, the son of James Lawson, a merchant of that city. Matriculating in 1812, he studied at the University of Glasgow, but late in 1815, emigrated to New York, where he worked as an accountant in the office of his uncle, Alexander Thomson, and in 1822 became a partner in the firm of Alexander Thomson & Company. Having as a young man acquired an interest in literature, in 1821 he selected American writers for representation in John Mennons' *Literary Coronal* and, later, for similar miscellanies. Duyckinck credits him with the introduction of the best American authors to the British reading public. His first small book, *Ontwa, the Son of the Forest* (1822), a verse narrative of Indian warfare, was reprinted in *The Columbian Lyre, or Specimens of Transatlantic Poetry* (1828), published in Glasgow. In this early period he formed the lasting and wide-spread contacts with men of letters which give color to his life. He contributed to the *New York Literary Gazette and American Athenaeum,* and in this weekly reviewed the first appearance of Edwin Forrest in New York (November 1826). The two men became intimate and lasting friends, and Lawson was a helpful critic and adviser to Forrest in personal as well as professional matters. (See many references in W. R. Alger's *Life of Edwin Forrest,* 1877; also in Lawrence Barrett's *Edwin Forrest,* 1881.)

About 1826 the mercantile business in which Lawson was a partner failed, and he turned to journalism. With John B. Skilman and James G. Brooks of the *Literary Gazette,* he edited the *Morning Courier* (1827–29), leaving this newspaper when it was combined with Noah's *Enquirer.* He then joined with Amos Butler in editing the *Mercantile Advertiser* until 1833. His newspaper interests did not thwart his literary activity. He wrote a romantic tragedy, *Giordano,* which was played three times at the Park Theatre (November and December 1828), with no great success (G. C. D. Odell, *Annals of the New York Stage,* vol. III, 1928, p. 384); it was published in 1832. In 1830 his *Tales and Sketches, by a Cosmopolite,* a collection of sentimental stories of Scottish background, written in stilted, formal prose, appeared. He informed his reader that "there is not a passage in them, that contains a vicious or poisonous thought." Three later volumes came from his pen, all privately printed: *Poems: Gleanings from Spare Hours of a Business Life* (1857); *Liddesdale, or the Border Chief* (Library of Congress copy, privately printed, 1874), a tragedy in blank verse, faintly reminiscent of *Macbeth*; and *The Maiden's Oath* (1877), a domestic drama. That not one of Lawson's books bore his name in print is a token of both his modesty and his literary judgment. He was one of the committee with Bryant, Halleck, and others, which selected John Augustus Stone's *Metamora* as the prize play for Forrest in 1829, and helped in the same way to bring James K. Paulding's *The Lion of the West,* with its leading character, Nimrod Wildfire, to Hackett in 1831. One of his intimate friends was William Gilmore Simms whom he introduced to the Harpers and assisted in many literary and personal matters. Simms visited him many times in New York and later in Yonkers, and Lawson in 1859 journeyed to South Carolina to see his friend, whose daughter, Mary Lawson Simms, was named for him (W. P. Trent, *William Gilmore Simms,* 1892, pp. 70 ff., 99, 154). Poe also was a friend and frequent visitor in Lawson's home and included him with affectionate comment in the series of articles on "The Literati of New York City" (*Godey's Lady's Book,* August 1846; G. E. Woodberry, *Edgar Allan Poe,* 1885, p. 258).

In 1833 Lawson entered the marine insurance business, but kept literature and its pleasant personal associations to grace his leisure hours. He became important in New York's mercantile life as an adjuster and statistician. He continued to write occasional articles and verse, however, which appeared in the *American Monthly Magazine,* the *Knickerbocker,* the *Southern Literary Messenger,* and Sargent's *New Monthly* (Duyckinck, *post*). He married Mary Eliza Donaldson (died Jan. 28, 1886), and acquired a home in Yonkers, where he continued to live after he retired from business—an esteemed and public-spirited citizen. The closing years of his long life were marred by sickness.

[E. A. and G. L. Duyckinck, *Cyc. of Am. Lit.* (2nd ed., 1875), vol. II; J. G. Wilson, *The Poets and Poetry of Scotland* (1876), vol. II; W. M. MacBean, *Biog. Reg. of St. Andrew's Soc. of the State of N. Y.,* vol. II (1925); *Notes and Queries,* Jan. 31, Mar. 13, 1880; *N. Y. Times,* Mar. 25, 1880.] R. W. B.

LAWSON, JOHN (d. 1711), traveler, author, claims remembrance only on the authorship of one book, a so-called history of North Carolina. Nothing is known of his parentage or early life, though it has been conjectured that he was of Yorkshire descent. In 1700, being in a mood for travel, he "accidentally met with a gentleman . . . well acquainted with the ways of living in both Indies" who assured him "that Carolina was the best country to visit" (Introduction to Lawson's *History*). Immediately he took passage, and after stopping in New York, arrived in Charleston, S. C., in August. In December he started on an overland journey to the northern colony, his party consisting of six Englishmen and four Indians. The latter were soon dismissed and without guide Lawson and his comrades explored the Carolina wilderness, following Indian trails and finally taking the famous Trading Path which ran from Georgia to Bermuda Hundred, Virginia. Reaching the site of Hillsboro, N. C., the party left the Trading Path and made for the white settlements of Eastern Carolina. There Lawson remained for some years, being in 1705 one of the persons who secured the incorporation of the town of Bath. In the political dissensions of the time he took no part; apparently he was engaged in literary work, for in 1709 there appeared *A New Voyage to Carolina, Containing the Exact Description and Natural History of that Country; Together with the Present State thereof and A Journal of a Thousand Miles, traveled thro' several Nations of Indians, Giving a particular Account of their Customs, Manners; etc. By John Lawson, Gent'. Surveyor General of North Carolina, London: Printed in the Year 1709.* The book was the second volume of John

Stevens' *New Collection of Voyages and Travels.* In 1714 and again in 1718 it was republished with a new title, beginning *The History of Carolina.* In 1712 and 1722 German editions were published in Hamburg from the press of M. Vischer. Apparently the lords proprietors were interested in the publication, for they subscribed twenty pounds to Lawson "for maps of North and South Carolina." The work is a vivid and sprightly description of life on the frontier, especially valuable for its account of Indian life and customs. For this reason Lawson is more often cited by ethnologists than by formal historians.

It was probably while in England seeing his book through the press that the author was made surveyor-general of North Carolina (1708), for which office he was recommended in a petition of the North Carolina Assembly to the lords proprietors. In London, also, he met Christopher de Graffenried [*q.v.*], Swiss adventurer and colonizer, and joined him in the scheme to establish in North Carolina a colony of Swiss and German Palatines; in fact Lawson was one of three men who supervised the migration of some six hundred Palatines, of which the direct result was the foundation of New Bern, N. C. The new settlement soon aroused the enmity of the Indians and in September 1711 De Graffenried and Lawson, while on an exploring expedition, were seized by the Tuscaroras. De Graffenried through his power of persuasion was released, but Lawson was put to death. His will, which was made in 1708 and probated soon after his death, left a house, land, and one-third of his personal property to his "dearly beloved Hannah Smith," the remainder to be divided, share alike, between his daughter Isabella and "the brother and sister (which her mother is with child of at present)."

[The essential facts regarding John Lawson are summarized in S. B. Weeks, "Libraries and Literature in North Carolina in the Eighteenth Century," *Ann. Report of the Am. Hist. Asso.*, 1895, pp. 224–32. Contemporary references may be found in W. L. Saunders, *Colonial Records of N. C.*, vols. I and II (1886), and H. V. Todd, *Christoph von Graffenried's Account of the Founding of New Bern* (1920). The Sloan MSS., British Museum, contain three letters from Lawson to Sir Hans Sloan. J. C. Pilling, *Bibliog. of the Iroquoian Languages* (U. S. Bureau of American Ethnology, Bulletin No. 6, 1888), gives the best collation of the various editions of Lawson's *History.*] W. K. B.

LAWSON, LEONIDAS MERION (Sept. 10, 1812–Jan. 21, 1864), physician, was born in Nicholas Co., Ky., to the Rev. Jeremiah Lawson, a native of Virginia, and Hannah Chancellor. His early education was obtained from his father's instruction and from the primary school of what afterward became Augusta College. Beginning the study of medicine at the age of eighteen under a thoroughly incompetent preceptor, he so far overcame this handicap that two years later he passed the examination before the licensing board of the first medical district of Ohio at Cincinnati. He settled for practice in Mason County, Ky., and while there took a course at the Transylvania University and was given the degree of M.D. in 1838. He removed to Cincinnati in 1841 and the following year he founded the *Western Lancet* which he conducted until 1855. For one year (1844) he also edited the *Journal of Health.* Following a winter spent in study at Guy's Hospital in London and in Paris, he moved to Lexington in 1845 to fill a teaching appointment at Transylvania University. In 1847 he returned to Cincinnati to accept the chair of materia medica and pathology in the Medical College of Ohio. In 1853 he was transferred to the professorship of principles and practice of medicine. He went to Louisville in 1854 where he gave two courses of lectures in the Kentucky School of Medicine, returning to Cincinnati in 1856. Again in 1859 he left to fill the chair of clinical medicine at the University of Louisiana, but after one year he returned to the Cincinnati school as professor of the theory and practice of medicine, a position he occupied until his death at the early age of fifty-one. Although he was a subject of tuberculosis, he continued his duties up to within a month of the end. Many of the most profound students of tuberculosis have been victims of the disease and the later years of Lawson's life were occupied with the preparation of his treatise on *Phthisis Pulmonalis* which appeared in 1861. This work was as complete and accurate as anything on the subject up to that time, showing remarkable knowledge of the literature of the disease. It had a long and popular vogue as a college text. Other writings include monographs on cholera and pneumonia, and several addresses introductory to the college courses. Lawson was a forceful and pleasing lecturer, wholly devoted to his teaching and professional duties. His portrait taken in his later years shows a long thin serious face already marked by the inroads of disease. He was twice married. His first wife was Louise Cailey of Felicity, Ohio, who died in 1846 leaving three daughters. He later married Eliza Robinson of Wilmington, Del., who with two sons and five daughters survived him.

[*Trans. Ohio State Medic. Soc.*, 1865; *Cincinnati Lancet and Observer*, Feb. 1864; H. A. Kelly and W. L. Burrage, *Am. Medic. Biogs.* (1920); *Cincinnati Daily Commercial*, Jan. 22, 1864.] J. M. P—n.

LAWSON, THOMAS (*c.* 1781 or 1785–May 15, 1861), surgeon-general of the United States army, was born in Virginia. Definite information in regard to him begins with his appointment, from Virginia, as surgeon's mate in the navy on Mar. 11, 1809. Two years on shipboard satisfied his longings for sea life and in January 1811 he resigned. In February he was appointed garrison surgeon's mate in the army. In May 1813 he was promoted to the surgeoncy of the 6th Infantry, which position he retained throughout the War of 1812. Upon the reorganization and reduction of the army in 1815 he became surgeon of the 7th Infantry. When the medical department was reorganized in 1821 and regimental and post surgeons were placed on one list, instead of being carried separately as before, he became the senior surgeon and remained such until his appointment in 1836 as surgeon-general. Although reputed to be a "ladies' man," Lawson never married.

He was a positive character and did much for his corps. He was a good doctor, according to the standards of his day, the day of bleeding, blisters, salivation and tartar emetic. He was a good observer and wrote vigorously and forthrightly. His descriptions of "bilious intermittant" fever, which was apparently pernicious malaria, of cholera, yellow fever, and other diseases, were intelligent. He did not hesitate to point out military laxity as a cause of disease. Thus he wrote that moral as well as physical causes could be considered as having had an agency in producing the prostration of the 7th Infantry. His ability to see through theories to facts was sometimes marked, as when he wrote of cholera in New Orleans: "Whether the cause of this mysterious disease was wafted to us in a current of air down the river, or was brought among us pent up in a steamer, or whether the atmosphere of the city, which had been throughout the season very insalubrious, had reached its acme of pestilential explosion, we know not; but one thing is certain, that cholera, at least in that dreadful form which it afterwards assumed, was unknown among us until the steamer 'Constitution' arrived in port" (*Statistical Report on the Sickness and Mortality in the Army,* 1840, p. 263). Incidental to his description of this epidemic, he wrote: "The disease seized me on the third morning after its appearance among the troops. . . . On the following day the hospital steward was attacked; two acting stewards took the disease successively, and all the attendants were at one period or another affected with the disease. I am just now regaining my health; the hospital steward is not yet well, and the two acting stewards and four of the six attendants, died" (*Ibid.*, p. 265).

He was even more a soldier than a physician, and his administration was marked by concern for the military status of his department. He obtained for it military rank, two increases in numbers, proper uniform, stewards enlisted in the department, and increase of pay for other soldiers detailed to it for duty. He twice had line commands, once a regiment, and he served at other times as quartermaster and as adjutant. He was in the field in every war in which the army was engaged from 1811 to the Civil War, except the Black Hawk War. At that time he applied for field service and it was refused. In 1848 he was brevetted brigadier-general for meritorious conduct in the Mexican War. He died at Norfolk on May 15, 1861, as the result of a stroke of apoplexy. The general order announcing his death described him as "full of military fire, which not even the frosts of age could quench." He is an important figure in the history of the medical department of the army. His publication of the statistical reports on the sickness and mortality of the army (1840, 1856, 1860) and of the army meteorological registers (1840, 1851, 1855), was a service of great value.

[Jas. E. Pilcher, "Brevet Brig.-Gen. Thos. Lawson, Surgeon-Gen. of the U. S. Army, 1836–61," *Jour. Asso. Mil. Surgeons of the U. S.*, June 1904, reprinted in *The Surgeon-Generals of the U. S. Army* (1905); H. A. Kelly and W. L. Burrage, *Am. Medic. Biogs.* (1920); *Evening Star* (Wash., D. C.), May 20, 1861.]

P. M. A.

LAWSON, THOMAS WILLIAM (Feb. 26, 1857–Feb. 8, 1925), stockbroker and author, was born in Charlestown, Mass., the son of Thomas and Anna Maria (Loring) Lawson, who had emigrated from Nova Scotia a few years before. The father, a carpenter, died when young Thomas was only eight years old; and at twelve the boy, unwilling to be a burden on his mother any longer, slipped away from school one day and found work as an office boy with a brokerage firm in Boston, almost across the street from the location of his own sumptuous offices in later years. Early in his career he speculated in stocks. He made a considerable "killing" in railroad shares when he was only seventeen but lost his profits a few days later in another deal. At twenty-one he married Jeannie Augusta Goodwillie, his boyhood sweetheart, and shortly afterward became a broker on his own account. He is said to have accumulated a million dollars by the time he was thirty. He celebrated the occasion by writing a *History of the Republican Party,* which he published at his own expense, and of which he had four copies specially printed on satin. Despite his lack of formal education, he acquired by his own efforts an excellent command of English and a considerable degree of literary culture.

He spent his life in Boston, where he not only acted as agent and promoter for New York and other financiers and corporations but speculated for himself. He loved a fight when in his prime, and few men in the stock market have had so stormy a career. He assisted the Addicks interests to wrest the control of Bay State Gas from Standard Oil in 1894, though Addicks lost it again shortly afterward.

Lawson's ability was recognized by the Standard Oil magnates, and thereafter for several years he was their ally. For many years in the latter part of his life he was president of the Bay State Gas Company of Delaware. By 1900 he was worth at least fifty millions and had created a handsome estate, "Dreamwold," near Boston, which cost $6,000,000. He paid a florist $30,000 for a carnation bearing Mrs. Lawson's name. He was a lover of art, literature, and nature, and his large private office was crowded with bronzes, paintings, books, and masses of fresh flowers. These as adjuncts to the brilliant, dynamic, spectacular, faultlessly garbed but erratic personality behind the desk, rendered it unique among business offices. When Sir Thomas Lipton, the British yachtsman, challenged again for the *America's* Cup in 1901, Lawson, seeing here an opportunity for both sport and publicity, built a yacht of his own, *Independence,* to compete in the trial heats with the New York Yacht Club's two boats. But the Yacht Club practically barred his boat from competition, and he acquired a grudge against certain wealthy members of the club which long endured. He had in 1897 become connected with the promotion of Amalgamated Copper, the name under which Standard Oil capitalists reorganized the great Anaconda mine and allied properties. On this stock they now made a handsome profit, with Lawson acting as their chief broker. The stock thereafter rapidly declined in price and many holders of it suffered heavy losses.

In 1902, when Lawson, with Winfield M. Thompson, published *The Lawson History of the America's Cup,* the editor of *Everybody's Magazine,* learning of his grievance, induced him to write the allegedly true story of Amalgamated Copper, which he did under the title of "Frenzied Finance"—one of the most sensational successes in magazine history. The entire edition of the magazine containing the first instalment was exhausted in three days. To journalistic instinct, Lawson added an easy, slashing style and a knack for colorful phrasing which made his rough-and-tumble attack on the "money kings" vastly popular, even though readers regarded him as belonging in the same category. During the course of the articles (1904–05), the writer also assailed the large insurance companies and performed a public service by bringing about the insurance investigation of 1905; but his "remedies" for the correction of stock-market gambling were not adopted. *Frenzied Finance* was published in book form and was followed by a novel, *Friday, the Thirteenth* (1907), also attacking the stock market, but this was less popular. Later books were *The Remedy* (1912); *The High Cost of Living* (1913); and *The Leak* (1919). The enmity aroused by his *Frenzied Finance* was costly to him. He lost clients and good will thereby and many serious losses were wilfully inflicted upon him by antagonists. During the last fifteen years of his life he seemed to lose his old knack for success, and his fortunes declined steadily. He lost his magnificent estate, even his automobile, and died a comparatively poor man.

[*The Lawson History of the America's Cup* (1902) and *The High Cost of Living* (1913) contain important references to the writer's history, and "Frenzied Finance" as it ran in *Everybody's* with the supplementary department, "Lawson and his Critics," has some interesting personal material. See also *Who's Who in America,* 1924–25; *Nation,* Aug. 14, 1902, Dec. 21, 1905; *Independent,* May 18, 1905; *Arena,* Sept. 1905; the *Bookman,* Apr. 1907; *Current Lit.,* Mar. 1908; *Outlook,* Sept. 5, 1908; *New Eng. Mag.,* Mar. 1909; *Boston Herald, Boston Transcript,* Feb. 9, 1925.] A. F. H.

LAWSON, VICTOR FREEMONT (Sept. 9, 1850–Aug. 19, 1925), journalist, was born in Chicago, Ill., the son of Iver and Melinda (Nordvig) Lawson. Both parents were Norwegian, the father having been born in Norway, the mother in Illinois. Iver Lawson accumulated a considerable fortune in Chicago real estate, most of which was lost, however, in the Chicago fire of 1871. He died in 1873 leaving the residue of his estate to his son Victor. Young Lawson had been educated in the Chicago public schools and at Phillips Academy at Andover, Mass. Ill health put an end to further study. After a brief period of life in the open he returned to Chicago to take active charge of his father's estate. He inherited with other property an interest in the daily *Skandinaven* which his father and others had established. His interest in newspaper work had developed when he was employed as a boy in the circulation department of the *Chicago Evening Journal.* By a curious coincidence, the publication of a new newspaper, the *Chicago Daily News,* was begun in the same building with the *Skandinaven* in January 1876. This new publication, the first penny newspaper in the West, was sponsored by Melville E. Stone, William H. Dougherty, and Percy Meggy. Within six months the owners of the struggling paper had sold out to Lawson who retained Stone as editor and later took him into partnership. Under the efficient management of Lawson, the *Daily News* made rapid progress. In 1878 the *Evening Post* was taken over with its Associated Press franchise. In 1881 a morning edition was brought out which later became the *Chicago Record* and eventually the *Record-Herald,* when it was merged with the *Times-Herald.* The *Record-Herald* ceased publication in 1914 because of Lawson's reluctance to be connected with a paper publishing on Sunday. He had assumed editorial duties upon Stone's retirement in 1888.

At a critical moment Lawson took up the cause of the Associated Press which was rivaled by the United Press, a news service organized on a commercialized rather than a cooperative basis. As president of the organization from 1894 to 1900, he was supported by his former partner, Melville E. Stone, at this time manager of the Associated Press. He remained as director from 1893 until his death. In 1898 he turned his attention to the development of a foreign news service. The Spanish-American War had shown the need of an unbiased handling of foreign news affecting American interest. Up to this time cable news received by American newspapers was supplied by correspondents representing the British or other foreign papers. At the close of the war, Lawson placed his own correspondents in the leading European capitals and in the Orient. The example of the *Daily News* was widely followed by other papers and press associations. Another of Lawson's pioneering activities was his strong advocacy of postal savings-banks. Both by financial assistance and the use of his publishing organization, he consolidated support for the bill which was finally passed in 1910. To him, President Taft sent the pen with which the bill was signed.

The independent policy of the *Daily News* in politics and in civic reform made the paper a powerful influence in Chicago. At the same time the editor was exposed to furious attacks by corrupt agents of corporations seeking to exploit the city government. But nothing could swerve him from what he conceived to be his duty—the support of all civic reform movements. He gave generously to support a system of free lectures in public-school halls, to found a fresh air sanitarium, to maintain "better government associations," to support the Y.M.C.A., to endow the Chicago Theological Seminary, and to provide homes for the symphony orchestras, and for leading clubs of which he was a member. He was a life-time member of the New England Congregational Church of Chicago, and it was in connection with his work in the church that he met Jessie S. Bradley, daughter of W. H. Bradley of Chicago, whom he married in 1880. She it was who guided much of his humanitarian work for the relief of the poor, particularly members of the colored race. She died in 1914 leaving no children. Lawson combined the practical talents of business with ideals of good citizenship. He was religious in the strictest sense. Quiet determination, dislike of publicity, personal friendliness, and humanity marked his character and bearing. His genius as a newspaper editor consisted in making his paper a constructive force in the life of the community in which he lived and worked.

[*Who's Who in America,* 1924–25; A. N. Marquis, *The Book of Chicagoans* (1917); "Victor Freemont Lawson," *Am. Mag.*, Nov. 1909; Melville E. Stone, *Fifty Years a Journalist* (1921); *M. E. S.: His Book* (1918), a memorial to Melville E. Stone; *Chicago Daily News, Chicago Tribune*, Aug. 20, 1925.] E. A. D.

LAWTON, ALEXANDER ROBERT (Nov. 4, 1818–July 2, 1896), Confederate soldier, lawyer, was born in St. Peter's Parish, Beaufort District, S. C. His parents were Alexander James and Martha (Mosse) Lawton. At sixteen he was appointed to the United States Military Academy, where he graduated in 1839, and was assigned as second lieutenant to the 1st Artillery. He resigned in 1841, entered the Harvard Law School, graduated in 1842, and the following year settled permanently in Savannah, Ga., where he practised his profession, with certain interludes, until his death. In 1849–54 he was president of the Augusta & Savannah Railroad; in 1855–56, a member of the Georgia House of Representatives, and in 1860, state senator.

He was a leading advocate of secession, and as a member of the state Senate supported a resolution favoring immediate withdrawal from the Union. Before the ordinance had passed, as colonel of the 1st Volunteer Regiment, acting under the orders of Governor Brown, he seized Fort Pulaski, thus committing the first overt act of war in Georgia. Commissioned brigadier-general in 1861, he was placed in charge of the Georgia coast. He organized a brigade and in June 1862 was transferred with 5,000 men to Virginia, where, under Jackson, he took part in the Valley campaigns and distinguished himself in the Seven Days' fight around Richmond. In the second battle of Manassas, when Ewell fell wounded, Lawton took charge of his division and commanded it during the advance into Maryland. At the battle of Sharpsburg he was seriously wounded, and was disabled until May 1863. In August of that year, against his own strenuous objection, he was made quartermaster-general of the Confederacy. His management of this most difficult branch of the army was highly successful (Avery, *post,* pp. 295–97).

Returning to Savannah on the close of the war, Lawton resumed his practice of law and became an important factor in politics. He entered the lower house of the legislature and served from 1870 to 1875, was chairman of the state electoral college in 1876, member and president *pro tempore* of the state constitutional convention of 1877, and leader of the Georgia delegation to the National Democratic Convention in 1880 and 1884. In 1880 he was a candidate for the United States Senate, but was defeated in a spectacular campaign by former Governor Joseph E. Brown [*q.v.*], who had become a Republican and a supporter of the congressional reconstruction policies. Brown's election was a foregone conclusion; Lawton consented to be sacrificed in order that the conservative principles for which his element stood should not appear to be acquiescing, without a struggle, in the new régime. A contemporary writer regarded this contest as "the last close struggle for supremacy between the spirit that ruled the old South and the spirit of the new South" (see Avery, *post,* p. 603).

A mere chronicle of the various public services of General Lawton fails to provide an adequate picture of the man. His erect, well-set-up figure, his intellectual force, the culture and good breeding that were evident to all, his ability as a soldier, business man, and lawyer, marked him as an eminent member of the ruling aristocracy of his time. He stood in the front rank of Southern lawyers. His high professional standing in his own state was attested by impressive tributes at the time of his death. His election as president of the American Bar Association in 1882 indicates that the bar as a whole indorsed the judgment of his fellow Georgians. His last public service was performed in the capacity of minister to Austria (1887–89), a post to which he was appointed by President Cleveland.

On Nov. 5, 1845, Lawton married Sarah Hillhouse Alexander, sister of Gen. E. P. Alexander [*q.v.*]. They had four children, and celebrated their golden wedding in 1895. Lawton died at Clifton Springs, N. Y., less than eight months later, in the seventy-eighth year of his age.

[I. W. Avery, *The Hist. of the State of Ga. from 1850 to 1881* (1881); memorial of the Savannah Bar Asso., 99 *Ga. Reports,* 825; *Atlanta Constitution,* July 3, 1896; *Atlanta Journal,* July 2, 1896; L. L. Knight, *A Standard Hist. of Ga. and Georgians* (1917), vols. I, II; C. C. Jones, Jr., and others, *Hist. of Savannah, Ga.* (1890); *Report of the Fourteenth Annual Session of the Ga. Bar. Asso.* (1897); *Report of the Nineteenth Ann. Meeting of the Am. Bar Asso.* (1896); *Twenty-eighth Ann. Reunion Asso. Grads. U. S. Mil. Acad.* (1897); C. A. Evans, *Confed. Mil. Hist.* (1899), vols. I, VI; W. J. Northen, *Men of Mark in Ga.* (1911), III, 185–91.]

R. P. B.

LAWTON, HENRY WARE (Mar. 17, 1843–Dec. 19, 1899), soldier, was born at Manhattan, near Toledo, Ohio, a son of George and Catherine (Daley) Lawton. He received his education in the Fort Wayne Methodist Episcopal College at Fort Wayne, Ind., to which place his family had moved in his fifth year. His parents died when he was nine years old, and thereafter he lived with an uncle. At the opening of the Civil War he enlisted in the 9th Indiana Infantry, and on Aug. 20, 1861, was made first lieutenant in the newly raised 30th Indiana Infantry, with which regiment he served in the western armies throughout the war, rising to the rank of lieutenant-colonel. In the later campaigns of 1864, he commanded his regiment. On Nov. 25, 1865, he was mustered out with the brevet rank of colonel, and later was awarded the Medal of Honor for gallantry at Atlanta.

He entered upon the study of law at Harvard, but left there May 4, 1867, to accept a commission as second lieutenant in the 41st Infantry (colored), with rank from July 28, 1866. His promotion to first lieutenant came almost immediately, July 31, 1867. In 1869 his regiment was consolidated with another colored regiment and renumbered as the 24th. In 1871 he was transferred to the 4th Cavalry, and served under Gen. Ranald S. Mackenzie in the Indian wars, becoming captain Mar. 20, 1879. In 1886, under the orders of General Miles, he led the column that pursued Geronimo for thirteen hundred miles through the mountains of Arizona and Mexico, and received his surrender. On Sept. 17, 1888, he entered the Inspector-General's Department as major, was promoted lieutenant-colonel Feb. 18, 1889, and colonel July 7, 1898. During the Spanish-American War he served in Cuba as brigadier-general and major-general of volunteers, commanding the 2nd Division, V Army Corps, in the actions before Santiago. He was one of the commissioners to receive the surrender of that place, and became military governor of the city and province. Returning to the mainland, he accompanied the president in his tour of the states, and then took command of the IV Army Corps at Huntsville, Ala.

Ordered to the Philippines, he reached Manila Mar. 18, 1899, and was placed in command of the 1st Division, VIII Army Corps. On Apr. 9 he made an expedition up the Pasig River and across the Laguna de Bay to Santa Cruz. Immediately upon his return he moved upon San Isidro, on the Rio Grande de Pampanga, to break up insurgent forces which were threatening the communications of General MacArthur's division operating north of Malolos. Next, on June 1, he made a brief expedition into the district of Morong, north of the Laguna; then, on June 10, commenced his Cavite campaign, which opened with a spirited engagement at Zapote Bridge, and which pushed the "south line" far back from Manila.

In October began the decisive campaign against Aguinaldo's main force in the north. General MacArthur advanced west of Mount Arayat, to Tarlac; Lawton east of it, through San Isidro into the mountain country. Turning over his command to General Wheaton on Dec. 16, Lawton returned to Manila, and on the 18th started for the Mariquina Valley, east of the city, where the insurgents had a fortified line to keep open their communications between their northern and southern forces. On Dec. 19, while disposing his troops opposite San Mateo to force a crossing of the river, he was shot through the heart and died almost instantly.

Lawton was a striking and soldierly figure—six feet four inches tall, erect and well built. He was quick and energetic in manner and speech, a fine organizer, a thoroughly practical field soldier, and a highly competent commander, respected and loved by superiors and subordinates alike. He was married Dec. 12, 1881, to Mary Craig, daughter of Alexander and Annie (McCown) Craig of Louisville, Ky. He had seven children, three of whom died in infancy. His wife and the surviving children accompanied him to the Philippines and were in Manila at the time of his death.

[F. B. Heitman, *Hist. Reg. and Dict. U. S. Army* (1903), vol. I; O. O. Howard, "Gen. Henry W. Lawton," in *Rev. of Revs.* (N. Y.), Feb. 1900; D. C. Worcester, in *McClure's Mag.*, May 1900; R. G. Carter, *Pursuit of Kicking Bird* (1920); Otto Klemme, *General Lawton's Tod; eine Episode von den Philippinen, von Einem der dabei gewesen* (Leipzig, 1907), by a sergeant who was beside him when he fell; *Manila Times* and *N. Y. Tribune*, Dec. 20, 1899; personal and family information from Mrs. Lawton.] O. L. S., Jr.

LAY, BENJAMIN (1677–Feb. 3, 1759), Quaker reformer, was born in Colchester, Essex, England. He was deformed, and when full grown was hump-backed and only four feet seven inches in height, with a large head and slender legs that seemed almost unequal to bearing the weight of his body. Along with his physical deficiencies went mental peculiarities which had a determining influence upon the course of his later life. As a youth, after engaging in various occupations ashore, he went to sea, and on one voyage visited Syria, but about 1710 returned to Colchester, where he married and remained for several years. His assertiveness made him so troublesome in the affairs of the Quaker meeting that about 1717 he was removed from membership. He did not, however, either then or later, regard himself as cut off from the Society, and throughout his later life continued to be associated with the Friends. In 1718 he migrated to Barbados and engaged in business. The large black-slave population at once attracted his interest and stirred him to humanitarian efforts. He gathered the slaves about him on Sundays, feeding them and talking to them about religion. Suspicion and animosity aroused by his concern for the blacks and his constant readiness to argue on slavery caused him to leave the island in 1731 and go to Pennsylvania, where he settled near Philadelphia. In this colony he was able to bear his testimony against slavery without hindrance and it is from this period that most records of his eccentricities have come. He once attempted to imitate Christ by fasting for forty days. This act brought him near death, and only great care by friends restored his health. He feigned suicide in a Quaker meeting house, appearing to stab himself and causing a quantity of red fluid resembling blood to stream forth. Those present were greatly alarmed. He understood the value of a dramatic protest, and on one occasion stationed himself at the gateway to a meeting house with one leg bared and half buried in deep snow. To those who remonstrated he answered: "Ah, you pretend compassion for me, but you do not feel for the poor slaves in your fields, who go all winter half clad" (Vaux, *post*, p. 28). His eccentricities attracted much public attention and he was once visited by Governor Penn, Benjamin Franklin, and other gentlemen, before whom he set a plain meal of fruits and vegetables, since the use of animal products for either food or clothing was another matter upon which he bore testimony against prevailing practice. Franklin printed one of his numerous pamphlets against slavery, *All Slave-keepers that Keep the Innocent in Bondage, Apostates Pretending to Lay Claim to the Pure & Holy Christian Religion*, etc. (1737). From time to time Lay made public condemnation of the use of liquors, tobacco, and tea, and also advocated a more humane criminal code. After 1740 he lived with John Phipps near Abington Friends' meeting house, and there he died in February 1759, being buried in the Friends' burial ground. His wife, Sarah, who predeceased him, like himself was small of stature, and deformed. She is described as an intelligent and pious woman, an approved minister in the Society of Friends, who supported her husband at all times in his anti-slavery activities. Despite his eccentricities, Lay exercised considerable influence upon the Quaker attitude towards slavery and shortly before his death had the satisfaction of learning that the Society had resolved to disown slave-holding members.

[Roberts Vaux, *Memoirs of the Lives of Benjamin Lay and Ralph Sandiford* (1815); Lydia Maria (Francis) Child, *Memoir of Benjamin Lay* (1842); Benjamin Rush, "Biographical Anecdotes of Benjamin Lay," *The Annual Monitor*, vol. I (1813); Joseph Smith, *A Descriptive Cat. of Friends' Books* (1867), II, 92–93; *Biog. Cat. . . . London Friends' Institute* (1888); W. A. J. Archbold, in *Dict. Nat. Biog.*] F. L.

LAY, HENRY CHAMPLIN (Dec. 6, 1823–Sept. 17, 1885), Protestant Episcopal bishop, was born in Richmond, Va. His father, John Olmstead Lay, was a native of Connecticut, a descendant of John Lay who was living in Lyme, Conn., as early as 1648; his mother, Lucy Anne Fitzhugh (May), was of old Virginia stock. He received his education in his native state, graduating at the University of Virginia, Charlottesville, in 1842, and at the Theological Seminary in Virginia, Alexandria, in 1846. Following his graduation in theology he was at once ordained deacon by the Rt. Rev. William Meade, bishop of Virginia. On May 13, 1847, he was married to Elizabeth Withers Atkinson. After a short pastorate at Lynnhaven Parish, Va., he removed to Huntsville, Ala., where he became rector of the Church of the Nativity. In this parish he was made priest, July 12, 1848, by the Rt. Rev. Nicholas Hamner Cobbs, bishop of Alabama. Here Lay remained as rector until made bishop. He was elected missionary bishop of the Southwest at the General Convention of 1859, held in Richmond, and immediately after the close of the convention was consecrated (Oct. 23) in Richmond. The territory to which he was appointed included Arkansas, Indian Territory, and parts adjacent. Hardly had he removed to his jurisdiction when the Civil War broke out, and the state of Arkansas soon joined the Confederacy. The Protestant Episcopal Church in the Confederate States was regarded as having ceased to be a part of the Church in the United States, and the various dioceses were organized into an entirely independent church. This was a logical application of the principle underlying the establishment of the Protestant Episcopal Church in the United States as independent of the Church of England. Further, in the application of the Southern conception of local independence, Lay became bishop of Arkansas, not missionary bishop. It was "states rights" in matters ecclesiastical. At the close of the Civil War, Lay and Bishop Atkinson of North Carolina were the first Southern bishops to join with bishops of the Northern dioceses at the General Convention held in Philadelphia 1865 in reëstablishing the unity of the denomination which had been interrupted by the war. In the reunited church he became once more missionary bishop, but with his jurisdiction limited to Arkansas. In 1868 the Eastern Shore of Maryland was established as an independent diocese and to this charge Lay was elected as bishop of Easton, assuming office Apr. 1, 1869. Here he worked until his death. He published *Letters to a Man Bewildered among Many Counselors* (1853); *Tracts for Missionary Use* (1860); *Studies in the Church* (1872); *The Church in the Nation* (1885), being the Bishop Paddock Lectures; as well as many sermons and articles on sociological topics. He died at the Church Home, Baltimore, and was buried at Easton, Md.

[*Churchman*, Sept. 26, 1885; *Sun* (Baltimore), Sept. 18, 1885; E. E. and E. M. Salisbury, *Family-Histories and Genealogies* (1892); information gathered in part from Lay's family and from Convention Journals.] J. C. Ay—r.

LAY, JOHN LOUIS (Jan. 14, 1832–Apr. 17, 1899), inventor, son of John and Frances (Atkins) Lay, was born in Buffalo, N. Y. He was descended from Robert Lay who emigrated from England to America in 1635, settling first in Lynn, Mass., and then in Saybrook, Conn. Lay's father was long a prominent business man of Buffalo, N. Y., and the boy accordingly received a well-rounded education in the city schools. He developed an especial interest in mechanics as he grew to manhood, and was engaged in various engineering enterprises in Buffalo when the Civil War began. In July 1861 he enlisted in the United States Navy as a second assistant engineer, becoming first assistant in 1863. His mechanical aptitude quickly attracted attention and he was given every opportunity to develop his inventive talents. He perfected a torpedo for offensive warfare and communicated his plan for its use to Lieut. William Barker Cushing [*q.v.*]. Shortly afterward (Oct. 27, 1864), Cushing, with a Lay torpedo aboard, succeeded in blowing up the Confederate ram *Albemarle* by driving his boat against its bow. Lay conducted further work on torpedoes at the Philadelphia Navy Yard, and on Mar. 14, 1865, he and W. W. W. Wood secured a series of four patents, Nos. 46,850 to 46,853, describing not only apparatus for operating torpedoes but the design and equipment of a picket boat from which to discharge them. The patentees assigned these patents to Donald McKay [*q.v.*], the noted ship-builder of East Boston, Mass., but there is no record of the further development of the invention. Resigning from the navy in 1865, Lay was engaged by the Peruvian government to prepare fixed mines and place suspended torpedoes in the harbor of Callao, in order to forestall the threatened attack of a Spanish fleet. After returning to the United States in 1867, he devoted considerable time, at his home in Buffalo, to the perfection of what he called the "Lay Moveable Torpedo Submarine." He also secured a series of six patents for a steam-engine on July 23, 1867, and one for a locomotive on Oct. 29, 1867. The Lay movable torpedo was of two lengths, sixteen and twenty-three feet respectively, and consisted of a cylindrical body with conical ends, carrying in the forward end 100 to 200 pounds of explosives. It was electrically propelled and was controlled as to both direction and time of firing through a wire within a rope attached to the torpedo and paid out from its place of launching, either the shore or a vessel. The torpedo's cruising range was one and one-half miles and its speed ten to twelve miles an hour. The inventor set forth its merits in a pamphlet entitled *Submarine Warfare; Fixed Mines and Torpedos. The Lay Moveable Torpedo: Its Superiority over All other Implements of Submarine Warfare* (n.d.). Though the United States Navy purchased but two of his torpedoes, he received large sums of money from Russia and Turkey for the rights to his invention. He took up his residence in Europe about 1870, but subsequently lost his fortune, and after thirty years abroad returned to the United States in the hope of disposing of some later inventions. He died, however, homeless and penniless, in Bellevue Hospital, New York, survived by two children living in Europe.

[F. H. Severance, "The Journeys and Journals of an Early Buffalo Merchant," *Pubs. Buffalo Hist. Soc.*, vol. IV (1896); H. P. Smith, *Hist. of the City of Buffalo and Erie County* (1884), vol. II; E. A. Hill, "The Descendants of Robert Lay of Saybrook, Conn.," *New Eng. Hist. and Geneal. Reg.*, Apr., July 1908; *House Ex. Doc. No. 52*, 39 Cong., 1 Sess.; *House Ex. Doc. No. 96*, 40 Cong., 2 Sess.; *War of the Rebellion: Official Records (Navy)*, ser. 1 and 2; *N. Y. Times*, Apr. 21, 1899; *Army and Navy Jour.*, Apr. 22, 1899.]

C. W. M.

LAZARUS, EMMA (July 22, 1849–Nov. 19, 1887), poet, essayist, was born in New York City of pure Sephardic stock, the daughter of Moses and Esther (Nathan) Lazarus. A member of a large, wealthy, and devoted family, she passed a pleasant youth, with winters in New York City and summers by the sea. She was educated entirely by private tutors. Very precocious, in 1866 she had a volume entitled *Poems and Translations*, containing verses written between the ages of fourteen and sixteen, printed for private circulation. This collection, with additions, was published in 1867. The verses were preoccupied with the conventionally romantic and vaguely melancholy themes congenial to youth, but they breathed an unusually lofty spirit and showed a pleasing fancy and considerable command of rhythm. They attracted the attention of Ralph Waldo Emerson, who became interested in the young poet, invited her to spend a week in the Emerson home at Concord, and kept up a lifelong correspondence with her. She proudly dedicated her second volume, *Admetus and Other Poems* (1871), "To my friend, Ralph Waldo Emerson." In 1874 she published her first prose work, *Alide: an Episode of Goethe's Life*, dealing with the Fredericke Brion incident, and, in 1876, *The Spagnoletto*, a five-act poetic drama with its scene laid in seventeenth-century Italy. During this decade she also contributed numerous poems to *Scribner's Monthly* and to *Lippincott's Magazine*. Thus far, she had shown little interest in the life of her own people. Although she had made a thorough study of Jewish history and literature, she was internationally minded and trained too critically to regard with great reverence the dogmas of the orthodox church to which she outwardly belonged. In declining to contribute to a Jewish hymn book, she said, "I feel no religious fervour within me" (Rachel Cohen, *post*, p. 185). Even as late as 1881, when her *Poems and Ballads of Heinrich Heine* appeared, in the introduction to this excellent translation she considered Heine as a German almost more than as a Jew. But the persecution of Russian Jews during 1879–83 turned her from a pleasing litterateur into an ardent patriot. When the refugees began to crowd into Ward's Island in 1881, she became prominent in organizing efforts for their relief. Then, the next year, in the same number of the *Century Magazine* (April 1882) which carried her critical study, "Was the Earl of Beaconsfield a Representative Jew?" there appeared an opprobrious article by a Russian journalist, Mme. Z. Ragozin, "Russian Jews and Gentiles," in which the author attempted to defend the pogroms. Miss Lazarus replied in the next number with a crushing rejoinder, "Russian Christianity *versus* Modern Judaism." Henceforth she stood as the leading American champion of her race. In 1882 she published *Songs of a Semite*, containing "The Dance to Death"—written earlier, a powerful poetic drama of fourteenth-century Jewish life—and a number of other strong and impassioned poems. In February 1883 she contributed a noteworthy article on "The Jewish Problem" to the *Century Magazine*. Later followed a series of poems in prose called "By the Waters of Babylon" (*Cen-*

tury Magazine, March 1887), and another prose series entitled "An Epistle to the Hebrews," published in the *American Hebrew.* All this work was characterized by a prophetic quality of stern moral indignation and unbending courage. Racial enthusiasm was united in Emma Lazarus with a firm faith in America as the home of the oppressed. Her sonnet to the Statue of Liberty was fittingly chosen to be placed on the pedestal of the statue in 1886. On a trip to Europe three years earlier she had been received everywhere with tokens of an international reputation. Then, at the height of her powers, she was stricken with cancer. After a second trip to Europe in 1885–87, she returned home to die at the age of thirty-eight.

[Biographical sketch and appreciation in the *Century Mag.,* Oct. 1888, reprinted as introduction to *The Poems of Emma Lazarus* (2 vols., 1889); Philip Cowen, "Recollections of Emma Lazarus," *Am. Hebrew,* July 5, 1929; Rachel Cohen, "Emma Lazarus," in *Reform Advocate,* Sept. 24, 1927, repr. from *London Jewish Chronicle*; Mary M. Cohen, in *Poet-Lore,* June–July 1893; W. J. Price, in *Forum,* Mar. 1912; *Reflex,* Mar. 1930; *Am. Hebrew,* Nov. 25, Dec. 9, 1887; *Critic,* Dec. 10, 1887; *Evening Post* (N. Y.), Nov. 21, 1887; article in *Jewish Encyc.,* with additional references.] G. G.

LAZEAR, JESSE WILLIAM (May 2, 1866–Sept. 25, 1900), physician, who sacrificed his life in the work of the United States Army Yellow Fever Commission, was born in Baltimore County, Md. He was the son of William Lyons Lazear and Charlotte Pettigrew. After preliminary studies at Trinity Hall, a private school in Pennsylvania, he entered Johns Hopkins University, from which he was graduated with the degree of A.B. in 1889. Following three years at Columbia College, New York City, he received the degree of M.D. in 1892. After two years of interneship in Bellevue Hospital and a year of European study, he settled for practice in Baltimore in 1895. While in Europe he had spent some time in the Pasteur Institute in Paris and had become especially interested in bacteriology. He was appointed to the medical staff of Johns Hopkins Hospital, while he was also assistant in clinical microscopy at the university and in the laryngological department of the hospital clinic. He displayed brilliant promise in research work and is credited with being the first in the United States to isolate the diplococcus of Neisser from the circulating blood. He was also among the first to make a study of the structure of the malarial parasite.

In February 1900 he was appointed acting assistant surgeon in the army and was assigned to laboratory duty at Columbia Barracks at Quemados near Havana, Cuba. When, later in the year, the Yellow Fever Commission was organized, he was made a member together with Maj. Walter Reed and Doctors James Carroll and Aristides Agramonte. From the time of his arrival in Cuba, he had devoted much attention to the pathology and bacteriology of yellow fever. He was able to say with confidence to the commission that research along these lines offered little promise. With the decision to investigate the possible transmission of the disease by mosquitoes, Lazear was made responsible for the care and handling of the insects, including their application to fever patients and volunteers for experimentation. He and Carroll, together with some others, allowed supposedly infected mosquitoes to bite them, but without results. Carroll later succeeded in infecting himself and suffered a sharp attack of the disease. In September, while Lazear was engaged in placing mosquitoes upon patients in a fever ward, a free mosquito alighted upon his hand and, though seen, was allowed to take its feed of blood. Five days later he was taken ill and was removed to the yellow fever hospital at Quemados, where he died September 25, after seven days' illness. His body was returned to Baltimore and lies in Loudon Park Cemetery. A memorial tablet to his memory has been placed in Johns Hopkins Hospital.

Carroll's illness and Lazear's death went far to convince the commission that they were on the right path. Their subsequent work was convincing to the world. Though Lazear's name appears on but one of the published works of the commission, Major Reed insisted that Lazear should have equal honor for whatever credit was accorded the work of the Yellow Fever Commission. In the latter's untimely death, medical research lost a man of unusual promise. With an education and mental equipment far above the average, he well might have made a high place in American medicine. He was admired by his colleagues of Johns Hopkins Hospital for his keen perception and patient industry in research, and for his simple high-minded character and likable personality. He was, however, reticent in speech and somewhat diffident in his contact with new acquaintances. He was married, in 1896, to Mabel Houston of Baltimore, who survived him with two children, one of whom he never saw.

[Obituary notices with incomplete biography appeared in the *Jour. Am. Medic. Asso.,* Oct. 6, 1900, in the *Johns Hopkins Hospital Bull.,* Nov. 1900, and in *Science,* Dec. 14, 1900. See also H. A. Kelly, *Walter Reed and Yellow Fever* (1906). The most authoritative account of the Yellow Fever Commission is found in *Senate Document 822,* 61 Cong., 3 Sess., entitled "Yellow Fever," which contains portraits of all members of the commission.] J. M. P—n.

LEA, HENRY CHARLES (Sept. 19, 1825–Oct. 24, 1909), publisher, publicist, historian, was born and died in Philadelphia. His father was Isaac Lea [*q.v.*], a descendant of John Lea, an English Quaker who came to America in 1699. His mother, Frances Anne, daughter of Mathew Carey [*q.v.*], was bred a Catholic. Henry Charles Carey [*q.v.*] and Thomas Gibson Lea were his uncles. Students of heredity and environment might note from these relationships the most striking characteristics of Henry C. Lea: love of truth, interest in science, impatience of injustice or cruelty, intense patriotism, belief in the power of the pen to influence his countrymen. At the age of six he learned the letters of the Greek alphabet at his mother's bedside. When seven he spent a short time at a school in Paris, where he laid the foundation for his mastery of French. His formal education in the classics and mathematics was directed by a certain Eugenius Nulty, to whom he recited an hour a day. He had special masters in French, Italian, drawing, and writing. He and his elder brother, Mathew Carey Lea [*q.v.*], on Saturdays tramped fifteen or twenty miles, collecting flowers which they analyzed the following day. He was interested also in conchology, his father's specialty, and when he was just past his fifteenth birthday he contributed a paper on fossil shells to Silliman's *American Journal of Science and Arts* (January 1841). This was soon followed by an article on a chemical subject in the same journal (April 1842). He was also interested in literature and, after the panic of 1837, when he could not afford to buy a copy of Anacreon he copied it in full in order to possess it.

In his eighteenth year, early in 1843, he entered his father's publishing house. He worked hard mastering the business; evenings and early mornings he still studied and wrote. Among his publications of this period are articles on conchology, on Greek epitaphs, on Tennyson, and other poets; in four years he contributed at least sixteen long articles, besides reviews. In 1844, during the Anti-Catholic riot, Lea shouldered a gun and acted as defender of the nearest Catholic church. At twenty-two his health broke down and then ensued what he described as a period of "intellectual leisure," which was to turn his attention to his life work. For a time he had to give up business and traveled. On May 27, 1850, he married his first cousin, Anna Caroline Jaudon, from Cincinnati, who was of Huguenot ancestry. During this period, for recreation he had turned to French memoirs. While reading Froissart he wondered how accurate the account was in depicting the times and sent to Paris for books which might answer his query. This was in 1849 and for the ensuing sixty years history was his chief intellectual interest. To this avocation he brought his scientific training.

His interest turned early to legal institutions and his first historical article, published in January 1859 in the *North American Review,* was later reworked as part of his first volume, *Superstition and Force* (1866). "The history of jurisprudence," he believed, "is the history of civilization. The labors of the lawgiver embody not only the manners and customs of his time, but also its innermost thoughts and beliefs, laid bare for our examination with a frankness that admits of no concealment. These afford the surest outlines for a trustworthy picture of the past, of which the details are supplied by the records of the chronicler" (*Superstition and Force,* 1878, 1892, Preface). His studies led him to realize the importance of the church, the greatest medieval institution; in 1867 he published *An Historical Sketch of Sacerdotal Celibacy,* and in 1869, *Studies in Church History.*

This fecundity was amazing since in this decade from 1860 to 1870 he was also active in his publishing business, which after 1865 he conducted alone, and deeply interested in public affairs. When the Civil War began he became one of the early members of the Union League, for which he wrote many widely circulated pamphlets. He served on its military committee, on the finance and executive committee, on the committee on colored enlistments, which raised several regiments and helped to break down the prejudice against employing colored troops, and as bounty commissioner. This was the only public office which Lea ever held, but he was constantly engaged in public affairs. In the period immediately following the war he was still an ardent Republican but as he witnessed the orgy of corruption, culminating in Philadelphia in 1870 in the creation of the Public Buildings Commission, he discarded partisanship and organized the Municipal Reform Association, of which for several years he was president. He resigned from the Union League because it refused to throw its influence on the side of reform. He was an active member of the Committee of One Hundred, formed in 1880 for the purification of politics, and president of the Reform Club. He was one of the first to support civil service reform, aiding the cause by his contributions and writings. He was the author of the Chace copyright act. Throughout his life he was interested in good government in city, state, and nation and wrote editorials, articles, and pamphlets whenever he felt that he could contribute to the right decision of public matters.

With the formation of the firm of Henry C. Lea's Son & Company in 1880, Lea, though remaining a special partner until 1885, in effect retired from the publishing business. This action, which he had long contemplated, was precipitated by another breakdown due to overwork which led to four years of comparative leisure. In 1882 he printed privately *Translations and Other Rhymes.* A few years later his health was still so precarious that he consulted Dr. S. Weir Mitchell, who prescribed a "schedule of life" to which he conformed rigidly and thus was enabled to prolong his work for more than a score of years. Every day he took a constitutional, making this an opportunity to oversee his real-estate operations, which were very extensive. He did little traveling; during his life he made only three short trips to Europe. Summers he spent at Cape May, where he could, on his daily walks, enjoy the flowers characteristic of the seashore. The remainder of the day was spent in revising his notes, planning his work, or reading proof. In the late spring and early autumn he usually spent a few days at the Delaware Water Gap to enjoy the mountain flowers. Botany had been a favorite avocation from his youth and in his later years he always had flowers about him and frequently a rare or especially beautiful one on his desk. He was also interested in Japanese bronzes, of which he made a collection.

In the last twenty-five years of his life, his chief interest was in study and writing. The great work on which he had long been engaged, *A History of the Inquisition of the Middle Ages,* was published in three volumes in 1888. It is still the one indispensable work on the subject. This was followed in rapid succession by: *Chapters from the Religious History of Spain Connected with the Inquisition* (1890); *A Formulary of the Papal Penitentiary in the Thirteenth Century* (1892), edited by Lea; *A History of Auricular Confession and Indulgences* (3 vols., 1896); *The Moriscos of Spain, their Conversion and Expulsion* (1901); *A History of the Inquisition of Spain* (4 vols., 1906–07); *The Inquisition in the Spanish Dependencies* (1908). At the time of his death he was busy on a history of witchcraft. The mass of notes which he had copied for this work will eventually be published and even in its incomplete form illustrates his method of work. This method was first to collect the primary sources. In his rapidly growing library he gathered such as had been printed, although not always in the latest and best editions. He kept copyists busy in several of the great archives of Europe and South America, especially in Spain. He found it necessary to learn German at sixty, and Dutch at eighty. After collecting his material he studied it and whenever he found any passage which concerned his subject copied it. He never employed a secretary. He was careful to include not only the portion which he might wish to quote but all the context, however lengthy, necessary for its elucidation. When he had exhausted all the sources he made an analytical index of his notes. This dictated the scope and contents of his work, as it showed what material there was on each subject. Until this index was completed he refused to form any judgments. When he found a disproportionate amount of material on any subject he published it in a separate article in order not to cumber the prospective volume. Then began the task of writing and rewriting. When he had finished the first volume of his *History of Auricular Confession and Indulgences* and was ready to send it to the printer he found new material which necessitated rewriting the whole work. In 1904 when he had finished his *History of the Inquisition of Spain* he felt that it was too long and rewrote it, reducing it to four volumes. His purpose was to tell the truth exactly as he found it from the study of the contemporary documents. He felt that "no serious historical work is worth the writing or the reading unless it conveys a moral, but to be useful the moral must develop itself in the mind of the reader without being obtruded upon him. . . . I have not paused to moralize, but I have missed my aim if the events narrated are not so presented as to teach their appropriate lesson" (*A History of the Inquisition of the Middle Ages,* Preface, p. iv). Occasionally he did point a conclusion, as, for example, "that the attempt of man to control the conscience of his fellows reacts upon himself" (*A History of the Inquisition of Spain,* IV, 1907, p. 533), but in most of his later works there is less of this tendency.

In 1899, at the time of the Dreyfus trial, liberals in France were seeking material for propaganda. Salomon Reinach asked the privilege of translating the *History of the Inquisition of the Middle Ages.* This had been advised by August Molinier, the foremost French scholar on the subject. Lea consented and revised the work, so that the French translation (3 vols., 1900–02) is superior to the earlier English version. This was circulated in a cheap edition to influence public opinion in the struggle between the Church and State. Chapters were reprinted for ten centimes each and were used, not only in

France, but also by the Belgian and Spanish liberals. A similar use was made of the diverting article on Leo Taxil and Diana Vaughan, which first appeared in *Lippincott's Monthly Magazine* (December 1900), and of the pamphlet, *The Dead Hand: A Brief Sketch of the Relations between Church and State with Regard to Ecclesiastical Property* (1900), which Lea wrote when the question of the disposition of the ecclesiastical properties in the Philippines was confronting the American government. Much of the latter was quoted by Waldeck-Rousseau in a speech which was published in the *Journal Officiel* and thus obtained a wide circulation. In France, references became frequent to "M. Léa, the grand old man." Many honors came to him. He received degrees from Harvard, Pennsylvania, Princeton, and was elected president of the American Historical Association. His presidential address, "Ethical Values in History," appeared in the *American Historical Review,* January, 1904. He was better known, however, to the scholars of Europe than in his own country. He received the degree of Doctor of Theology from the University of Giessen, was made a fellow of the Imperial University of Moscow, and an honorary member of learned societies in Germany, Italy, and Great Britain. His friends and correspondents included leading historians, in many countries. Bryce sought his aid in writing *The American Commonwealth.* Acton asked him to write the chapter on "The Eve of the Reformation" for the *Cambridge Modern History* (vol. I, 1902, pp. 653–92). Döllinger and Giesebrecht in Germany, Frédéricq in Belgium, Balzani and Villari in Italy, Maitland in England joined in doing him honor. There was hostile criticism, especially from some Roman Catholics in the United States, but it is significant that the most scholarly estimate of his work by a Roman Catholic abroad speaks of him as *"ce bon ouvrier de vérité"* (Alphandéry, *post,* p. 131).

Throughout, Lea remained the modest, retiring scholar. Frail in health, small in stature, kindly in nature, with a keen sense of humor, he worked on steadily. When eighty-one he wrote: "As regards an autobiography, I am like Canning's knife-grinder—'Story, Lord bless you sir, I've none to tell.' I only followed my convictions and worked as they led me. Besides, I have no time to waste. Every day shortens the little term left to me, and I have two books under way, to be finished after the Spanish Inquisition is off of my hands, and I am revising my volume on 'Celibacy' for another edition. So you see my program is a pretty full one, especially as age is beginning to tell on me, and I find that my power of labor is not what it was a half-century ago" (letter to D. C. M.). He was generous, and wise in giving. Many of the benefactions will never be known but among those which necessarily became known were the Institute of Hygiene for the University of Pennsylvania, a new wing for the Library Company building in Philadelphia, an epileptic farm, contributions to Jefferson Medical School and for the increase of salaries at the University of Pennsylvania, and finally the gift of his library with an endowment to that institution. He was always the genial host and served as dean of the Wistar Association from 1886, when he succeeded his father, until his death.

[A preliminary memoir, *Henry Charles Lea, 1825–1909* (1910), was privately printed by the family. Edward S. Bradley, *Henry C. Lea* (1931), is an authorized biography. Information may be obtained from *Proc. Am. Philosophical Soc.,* Jan.–Apr. 1911, vol. L, no. 198, reprinted as *Addresses Delivered at a Meeting Held in Memory of H. C. Lea, by E. P. Cheyney and Others* (1911); and *Proc. Mass. Hist. Soc.,* Dec. 1909 (1910), pp. 183–88, an address by C. H. Haskins. Papers and letters are in the Henry Charles Lea Lib. of the Univ. of Pa. Part of the material in this article was derived from conversations with Lea. For criticisms of his work, see Acton, in *Eng. Hist. Rev.,* Oct. 1888, pp. 773–88; Maitland, *Ibid.,* Oct. 1893, pp. 755–56; P. M. Baumgarten, *Henry Charles Lea's Hist. Writings: An Inquiry into their Method and Merit* (1909); P. M. Alphandéry, in *Revue de l'Histoire des Religions,* Jan.–Feb. 1910; Felice Tocco, *Henry Charles Lea e la Storia dell' Inquisizione Spagnuola* (Florence, 1911).]

D. C. M.

LEA, HOMER (Nov. 17, 1876–Nov. 1, 1912), soldier and author, was born at Denver, Colo., the son of Alfred Erskine and Hersa (Coberly) Lea. He was educated in public schools, the University of the Pacific, Occidental College, and at The Leland Stanford Junior University, which he attended from 1897 to 1899. As a student he studied military tactics and the principal wars of history, particularly those of Napoleon. He was wont to declare to his friends that he was destined to become a great military commander, a boast which was received with scoffing incredulity since he was an undersized and frail hunchback. In college days, also, he became deeply interested in the disturbances in China, and, in 1899, he adventurously crossed the Pacific, arriving in time to join the relief of Peking during the Boxer uprising. He never married nor developed strong ties within his own country. Instead, the rest of his life is a part of the history of the country with which he had thrown in his fortunes. So deep an impression did he make upon the Chinese with his daring persistence and obvious grasp of military science that by 1909 he rose to a generalship and became the associate of the reformer K'ang

Yu-Wei. Later, in the revolution of 1911–12, he became the confidential adviser of Sun Yat Sen. During these years he experienced extraordinary adventures and a number of almost incredible escapes from death.

In the midst of these activities he found time to write several books which created a widespread sensation at the time. These include *The Vermilion Pencil,* a novel published in 1908, *The Valor of Ignorance* (1909), a startling description of the menace of a Japanese invasion of the United States, and *The Day of the Saxon* (1912), which similarly gave warning of attacks by Oriental peoples upon the British Empire. Stricken with paralysis, he struggled to finish this last book only a few days before his death at Ocean Park, near Los Angeles. He was also engaged upon a history of politics and of the development of Chinese civilization.

The materials for the proper appraisal of his character and ability are all too meager. He has been hailed as one of the greatest military geniuses of history, and he unquestionably impressed some observers with the right to this title. No one can doubt his uncanny skill in organizing and leading the forces of the Chinese people. Opinions differ concerning his motives, and it is not easy to determine whether he was an unselfish enthusiast fascinated by the cause of Chinese freedom, or whether he seized an opportunity to satisfy his passion for military experience. At all events he is one of the most picturesque personalities of his generation and, perhaps, the most gifted American who ever joined a foreign legion.

[See *Harper's Weekly*, Jan. 4, 1913; *Literary Digest*, Nov. 16, 1912; *Who's Who in America*, 1912–13. Robert Young, "The Impudence of Charlatanism," *World Peace Foundation Pamphlet Series*, vol. II (1912), reprinted from *Japan Chronicle* (Kobe), Feb. 11, 1912, with letter from David Starr Jordan, gives the more unfavorable view of Lea's character and motives. See also *New York Times* and *New York Tribune*, Nov. 2, 1912.] P. K.

LEA, ISAAC (Mar. 4, 1792–Dec. 8, 1886), malacologist, publisher, of Quaker stock, fifth son of James and Elizabeth (Gibson) Lea, was born at Wilmington, Del., to which place his great-great-grandfather, John Lea, had come from Gloucestershire, England, in 1699. When Isaac was fifteen the family moved to Philadelphia, and he entered the wholesale and importing establishment of his eldest brother. About this time he formed a friendship with Lardner Vanuxem [*q.v.*], with whom he made jaunts about Philadelphia, collecting minerals and rocks. Science at that day had not progressed very far, and it was difficult for the boys to obtain information about the specimens they gathered; although later they had access to a collection of minerals owned by Dr. Adam Seybert, then the only collection of its kind in the city. They were both early members (1815) of the Academy of Natural Sciences of Philadelphia. In 1814 they joined a volunteer rifle company and offered service against the British, then in possession of Washington. Although the company was not called into action, the enlistment cost Lea his birthright in the Society of Friends. In 1821 he married Frances Anne Carey, daughter of Mathew Carey [*q.v.*]. She died after a happy married life of fifty-two years, leaving two sons, Mathew Carey and Henry Charles Lea [*qq.v.*], and one daughter. Upon his marriage Lea became a member of the firm of M. Carey & Sons, the most extensive publishing house of its day in the United States. He remained with this firm and its successors until his retirement in 1851.

Lea's first scientific article (*Journal of the Academy of Natural Sciences of Philadelphia,* December 1818) was "An Account of the Minerals at Present Known to Exist in the Vicinity of Philadelphia"; his second article (*American Journal of Science and Arts,* vol. V, 1822, p. 155) was a "Notice of a Singular Impression in Sand-stone." He continued writing until 1876, his work covering a period of fifty-eight years. His style was plain but fluent; his bibliography includes 279 titles; and his papers deal with a wide range of subjects: mineralogy, hibernation, the Northwest Passage, halos with parhelia, geology, fossils, land, fresh-water, and marine *Mollusca.* After 1827 he gave most of his attention to studies of the fresh-water mollusks, becoming a recognized authority in his field. Most of his papers appeared in the *Proceedings* or *Transactions* of the American Philosophical Society, or in the *Proceedings* or *Journal* of the Academy of Natural Sciences of Philadelphia. From time to time they were republished in his *Observations on the Genus Unio,* issued between 1827 and 1874 in thirteen quarto volumes, with many lithographic plates illustrating all the species described. He described more than 1,800 species of mollusks, recent and fossil. Of pearly fresh-water mussels, the group for which he is most famous, he described 901 recent and ten fossil species. Of many he described not only the shell but also the soft parts and the glochidium (the minute embryonic shells in the gills of the mother). Among other mollusks his interest centered chiefly in fresh-water snails belonging to the genera *Melania, Goniobasis, Pleurocera, Anculosa,* and others of that group. He described a few miscellaneous fresh-water species, and about seventy-five terrestrial species.

As his studies of the *Mollusca* progressed he received specimens from correspondents in all parts of the world, who sought his aid in classifying them. Thus he acquired many species which he described as new, the types of which in most cases were retained for his collection. He received also many species already known which helped to build up his valuable series. His collections were bequeathed to the United States National Museum.

Self-confident, of strong will, successful in business, the leading authority on the fresh-water mussels, he did not take kindly to the work of Conrad and Rafinesque in this line, and his criticism of their work was sometimes very severe. In his eighty-fifth year he prepared and published *Catalogue of the Published Works of Isaac Lea, LL.D. from 1817 to 1876* (1876). Honors bestowed upon him included the presidency of the American Association for the Advancement of Science (1860); presidency of the Academy of Natural Sciences of Philadelphia (1858–63); vice-presidency of the American Philosophical Society; membership or honorary membership in numerous learned societies in America and abroad. In 1832 and again in 1853 he spent several months touring Europe and was an honored guest of many of the scientists of England, France, Germany, and other countries.

[Lea's *Catalogue of the Published Works of Isaac Lea, LL.D.* (1876); N. P. Scudder, *Published Writings of Isaac Lea, LL.D.* (Bull. 23, U. S. Nat. Museum, 1885), with a biographical sketch; *Proc. Am. Philosophical Soc.*, vol. XXIV (1887); W. H. Dall, in *Science*, Dec. 17, 1886; *Am. Jour. Sci.*, Jan. 1887; *Conchologists' Exchange*, Dec. 1886; W. J. Youmans, *Pioneers of Science in America* (1896); J. H. and G. H. Lea, *The Ancestry and Posterity of John Lea* (1906); the *Press* (Phila.), Dec. 9, 1886.]

W. B. M—l.

LEA, MATHEW CAREY (Aug. 18, 1823–Mar. 15, 1897), chemist, was born in Philadelphia, the son of Isaac Lea [*q.v.*] and Frances Anne (Carey) Lea, daughter of Mathew Carey [*q.v.*], political economist, publisher, and writer. Educated at home, he showed an especial taste for languages, literature, and mathematics. He traveled abroad with his parents during his boyhood, coming into personal contact with the European scientists of his father's acquaintance. With his younger brother, Henry Charles Lea [*q.v.*], he studied chemistry in the laboratory of James C. Booth [*q.v.*], in Philadelphia, and after devoting some time to the study of law, which he was forced to abandon on account of his health, he returned to the laboratory of Booth, Garrett and Blair to continue work in his chosen science. His later research was done almost entirely in his private laboratory at his home, Chestnut Hill, Philadelphia.

He had a decided preference for chemical theory and speculated considerably on the properties of the atoms. Their numerical relations led him to believe that "the number 44.45 plays an important part in the science of stoichiometry," since he found this relation to extend to forty-eight of the elements ("On Numerical Relations Existing between the Equivalent Numbers of Elementary Bodies," *American Journal of Science,* 2 ser. XXIX, 1860, pp. 98, 349, quoted by Barker, *post,* p. 159). He did much in synthetic organic chemistry, and through his study of the platinum metals greatly enriched analytical chemistry, but it was in photochemistry that he was a real pioneer. Foreign chemists were the first to recognize his efforts in this new field of physico-chemical research. His published contributions, dealing with "colloid silver" and "photohaloids" were translated into European languages and were heralded as epoch-making. The beautiful forms of amorphous silver, which he discovered, continued to enkindle enthusiasm wherever and whenever exhibited.

Possessed of ample means and handicapped throughout life by precarious health, he rarely mingled with men but in quiet worked unceasingly in his private laboratory until his contributions to photographic chemistry numbered three hundred and his communications on special chemical topics more than one hundred. His papers were published chiefly in photographic journals and in the *American Journal of Science.* The only book he ever wrote, *A Manual of Photography* (1868), dealt with photochemistry. He was also active as an investigator in the domain of pure physics. He was a member of the Franklin Institute and of the National Academy of Sciences. To the Chemical Section of the Franklin Institute he bequeathed his scientific books and apparatus, together with a fund to provide for the future purchase of books on physical and chemical subjects. He was married, July 14, 1852, to his cousin Elizabeth Lea Jaudon, sister of his brother Henry's wife and widow of William Woodhouse Bakewell. She died Mar. 19, 1881, leaving him one son, and he later married Eva Lovering, daughter of Prof. Joseph Lovering [*q.v.*]. He died at his home in Philadelphia.

[Edgar Fahs Smith, *M. Carey Lea—Chemist* (1923); G. F. Barker, in *Nat. Acad. Sci. Biog. Memoirs,* vol. V (1905), with bibliography of Lea's most important papers; *Jour. Franklin Inst.*, Feb. 1898; *Pub. Ledger* (Phila.), Mar. 16, 1897.] E. F. S.

LEACH, ABBY (May 28, 1855–Dec. 29, 1918), classicist, was born in Brockton, Mass., the daughter of Marcus and Eliza Paris (Bourne) Leach. She was a descendant of Lawrence Leach who emigrated from England to Salem, Mass., in 1629. At a time when opportunities for the higher education of women were limited, and when courses for advanced study were for them non-existent, she went to Cambridge and induced several professors at Harvard to give her private instruction. It is difficult to realize the courage and tact then required to overcome not only masculine and even feminine prejudices against such instruction, but also the many practical difficulties which impeded liberal-minded men like William W. Goodwin and James B. Greenough [*qq.v.*] in their desire to help her. Her own belief in the necessity of such work, inherited from her New England ancestors, joined to the ability and good sense that she displayed from the beginning, had its reward. Her example inspired other young women, and her residence in Cambridge (1879–82) became the direct cause of the founding of Radcliffe College, then known popularly and somewhat derisively as "The Harvard Annex."

She was teacher of Greek and Latin languages at Vassar College in 1883 and obtained the degrees of A.B. and A.M. there in 1885. She became associate professor in 1888 and in 1889 was elected professor and chief of the newly organized department of Greek, a post which she held until her death. A teacher of force and originality, with a personal bearing and address which won a large following, she made it an object of emulation among her students to be accepted as members of her beginners' course in Greek. This was one of the first of its kind to be introduced into an American college of high rank, since she was among the first to recognize the importance of maintaining the college study of Greek literature at a period when it was declining in the preparatory schools, and she carried her classes upward through the drama and into Plato and Aristotle. Her own experience as a pioneer, and the wide acquaintance which she had formed among scholars, made her invaluable in aiding young women to satisfy their ambition for advanced work in graduate schools. Her influence thus extended far beyond her own field of Greek. Her services outside the college were numerous and notable. She was president of the American Philological Association (1899–1900); member of the Managing Committee of the American School of Classical Studies at Athens; of the Council of the Archaeological Institute of America; of the Classical Association of England and Wales, and the Classical Association of the Middle States and Maryland; and president of the Association of Collegiate Alumnae (1899–1901). In 1908 the Emperor of Japan presented her with a gold cup in recognition of her services to education. She was an occasional contributor to the *American Journal of Philology* and to the *Classical Review*; and to Lane Cooper's work on *The Greek Genius and its Influence* (1917) she contributed a chapter on "Fate and Free Will in Greek Literature."

[Samuel Chessman, *Leach Family Record* (1898); Bradford Kingman, *Hist. of Brockton, Plymouth County, Mass., 1656–1894* (1895); *Cat. of the Officers and Students of Vassar Coll.*, 1882–90; *Who's Who in America*, 1918–19; *Vassarion*, 1910; *Vassar Quart.*, Feb. 1919; *N. Y. Times*, Dec. 30, 1918; personal acquaintance.]

C. B. G.

LEACH, DANIEL DYER (June 12, 1806–May 16, 1891), Episcopal clergyman, educator, author of textbooks, one of the six children of Apollos and Chloe (Dyer) Leach, was a descendant by several lines from many of the first settlers of his birthplace, Bridgewater, Plymouth County, Mass. His father, a carpenter and builder, owned a profitable farm. Daniel's early education in the school near his home, under the direction of George Chipman, was supplemented by the varied activities presented by the home life of the period. He was a studious, self-reliant, and original boy. When sixteen years of age he left the Bridgewater Academy and engaged for a time in business in Boston. He was graduated from Brown University in 1830, studied divinity at Andover Theological Seminary, was ordained an Episcopal clergyman in 1833, preached for five years in Quincy, Mass., and retired from this parish to take up what proved to be his life work in education. From 1838 to 1842 he was principal of the Classical High School in Roxbury, Mass., and from 1842 to 1848 he conducted a private school. His interest in popular education led to his employment as an agent of the Massachusetts State Board of Education from 1848 to 1855. While holding this position he inspected more than a thousand schools and schoolhouses, noting their defects, and advising with local committees regarding ways and means for betterment. In the *Seventeenth Annual Report of the* [*Massachusetts*] *Board of Education* (1854) Leach presented plans for an improved system of ventilation which was soon widely installed. This episode emphasized one of his characteristics. To him the recognition of an undesirable condition was a direct challenge to his resourcefulness in devising means for improvement.

In 1855 he was appointed superintendent of

schools for Providence, R. I. At this time the Providence school system consisted of a committee numbering at times sixty-three, a staff of two men and one hundred women teachers, a clerk, and about seven thousand children. With his horse and chaise the superintendent was able to keep in close touch with all of his classrooms. In this little laboratory of practical pedagogy Leach dealt at first hand with the perennial problems of school administration. With insight, resource, and a rare grasp of psychological principles, he initiated experiments, created methods, and set standards that had a constructive effect upon the schools of his own and later times. His textbooks on arithmetic, geography, and spelling were widely used as standard texts for elementary schools. His reports to the Providence school committee, extending through thirty years, reveal educational insight and vision that make them profitable reading to a later generation of educators. A series of pamphlets, *Directions to Teachers* (1873), "embracing the best methods of teaching reading, spelling, object lessons, etc., with judicious counsel on the administration of discipline" contributed to the advancement of teaching over a wide area. His methods for teaching spelling resounded even in the English Parliament in the reports of an inspector sent by the British government to observe the schools of the United States and Canada (James Fraser, *Report . . . on the Common School System of the United States and . . . Upper and Lower Canada,* 1866). From 1870 to 1889 he was a member of the Rhode Island State Board of Education, and in 1877 he was elected a trustee of Brown University for life. In methods of public-school administration he was a pioneer, making his way along untried paths in a profession lacking traditions and having few precedents. In 1834 Leach married Mary H. Lawton, daughter of Capt. Robert and Penelope (Brown) Lawton, of Newport, R. I. There were three children. A memorial tablet in honor of Daniel Leach and of his brother, Col. Franklin Leach, was placed in the memorial building of the Old Bridgewater Historical Society with appropriate historical addresses of dedication on Nov. 26, 1927.

[Leach's reports to the Providence School Committee, 1855–83; files of *Providence Jour.* for June 1891; Thos. Bicknell, *Hist. of the State of R. I. and Providence Plantations* (1920); Horace S. Tarbell, address at the centennial celebration of the establishment of the public schools of Providence, R. I., printed in the *Report of the School Committee, 1899–1900 Centennial, Providence, R. I.*; F. P. Leach, *Lawrence Leach of Salem, Mass., and Some of His Descendants,* vol. II (1925); *Providence Jour.*, May 18, 1891.]

J. L. A.

LEACH, SHEPHERD (Apr. 30, 1778–Sept. 19, 1832), iron founder, capitalist, was descended in the fifth generation from Lawrence Leach who settled at Salem, Mass., in 1629 and is said to have been connected with the establishment (at Lynn, Mass.) of the first iron works in the New England colonies. The son of Abisha Leach, an iron founder and Revolutionary soldier, by his wife, Patience Woods, Shepherd Leach was born in Easton, Mass. One of the oldest and most prosperous of Easton's industries was the smelting and casting of iron, for which the local supplies of bog ore furnished the raw material and local and neighboring manufacturers of nails and kitchen ware, the market. Young Leach early displayed business ability. At twenty-four he bought his father's iron works, to which he added within a few years the furnace of his chief competitor in Easton. In the sales contract the latter agreed not to operate any iron works within a distance of twenty miles. Leach, as the agreement indicates, was ambitious to become a captain of industry. He promptly undertook to enlarge the output of the combined businesses. To supply increased power he constructed a large reservoir, and by the purchase of several hundred acres of bog land and the lease of mining privileges on other lands, secured adequate supplies of raw material.

During the decade 1820–30, increased demand for heavy castings for engines and machinery for the new textile and other factories in southern New England generated a wave of prosperity for the iron works of southern Massachusetts. Believing that this prosperity would last, Leach expanded his business still further by buying out a number of competitors in Easton and nearby towns. Soon he was operating seven furnaces in Easton alone. His profits seem to have been greater than the iron industry could absorb, for he invested in other local enterprises: spinning-mills, a gristmill, and a sawmill. In 1832 his Easton iron works employed 100 workmen, producing 200 tons of pig iron and 600 tons of castings annually.

Leach became the wealthiest man in the community, which in 1830 numbered 1,756 persons, and took a leading part in a variety of local activities. His greatest distinction, outside of business, was attained in the Massachusetts militia, in which he held a major-general's commission. On muster days he cut a fine figure. He "was large, fleshy, of a commanding appearance, a fine officer on the field, and seemed to enjoy his position as general" (Chaffin, *post,* p. 516). He was a strong supporter of the local "evangelical society" and a bosom friend of its pastor. Avoiding as far as possible the strife between opposing factions which embittered religious life in Easton as well as in many other New England communities in his day, he gave his interest in church affairs a practical turn. "On stormy Sundays he would get out an immense covered wagon that he owned, and drive from house to house until it was filled with church-goers, and then . . . to meeting. . . . Though not much of a singer himself, General Leach was very fond of singing, and would lead the choir, standing with his back to the audience and beating time in the most approved style" (*Ibid.*, 517–18). He had the reputation of being open-handed in his charities and liberal in his business dealings. His capitalistic ambitions resulted disastrously. He acquired more property than he could profitably manage, and after his death, which was the result of a fall from his chaise, his affairs were found to be in bad condition. His wife, formerly Phoebe Torrey, whom he married in 1804, survived him.

[W. L. Chaffin, *Hist. of the Town of Easton, Mass.* (1886); "Documents Relative to the Manufactures in the U. S." (2 vols., 1833), *House Doc. No. 308, 22* Cong., 1 Sess.; F. P. Leach, *Lawrence Leach of Salem, Mass., and Some of His Descendants*, vol. I (1924).]

P. W. B.

LEAMING, JACOB SPICER (Apr. 2, 1815–May 12, 1885), Ohio farmer, producer of the famous Leaming corn, was the son of Christopher and Margaret Leaming, who, early in the nineteenth century, left Cape May, New Jersey, and moved to a farm on the Little Miami River near Madisonville, Ohio. There Leaming was born and reared. From his father he acquired an interest in corn culture, for Christopher Leaming was more than an average farmer. He raised twice as much corn per acre as his neighbors because he insisted on selection of his seed, deep planting, and careful cultivation. On Mar. 1, 1839, Leaming married Lydia Ann Van Middlesworth by whom he had nine children, seven of them boys. For sixteen years after his marriage he lived in the old homestead. A chance drive along the Bullskin Run in Hamilton County in the fall of 1855 gave him the idea which later made him famous. In need of feed for his horses, he stopped at a wayside corn field and bought some corn. Impressed by the beautiful yellow color of the corn and its early maturity, he purchased a bushel for seed. The next year he moved his family to a farm two miles from Wilmington, and here he raised corn until 1884. In the spring of 1856 he planted the corn he had bought the previous autumn and by careful attention was rewarded by a yield in excess of one hundred bushels per acre. Farmers regarded it as a phenomenal achievement and began to visit his farm to buy seed. This they planted next season and referred to it as "Leaming corn." In 1857 Leaming was advised by a country physician interested in scientific agriculture to devote his entire attention to corn cultivation. He did so, and by careful, intensive cultivation, with the aid of his sons, he began to produce superior corn. He selected his seed from the standing corn, choosing tapering ears because he believed they matured earliest. Stripped of part of the husks, these seed ears were hung in a crib to dry. The following spring a second selection was made, again from tapering ears. By this method he developed corn which matured early. Leaming was, perhaps, the first to plant corn in shallow drills, "one grain in a place, 12 to 14 inches apart in rows 4 feet apart." At the Paris Exposition in 1878, the popularity of Leaming corn was enhanced by the prizes it won. The demand for it became so pressing that Leaming advertised his seed and soon developed a flourishing seed business. The variety which he developed became well known and widely used in corn-producing sections.

[W. A. Lloyd, "J. S. Leaming and His Corn," *Ann. Report of the Ohio Corn Improvement Asso. . . . for the Year 1910* (1911), republished in *J. S. Leaming and His Corn* (n.d.); Ohio Agricultural Experiment Station, *Circular No. 117* (1911); H. A. Wallace and E. N. Bressman, *Corn and Corn-Growing* (1923).]

R. C. M.

LEAMING, JEREMIAH (1717–Sept. 15, 1804), clergyman, was the eldest son of Jeremiah and Abigail (Turner) Leaming, and the grandson of Christopher Leaming of Southampton, L. I., who settled in New Jersey. The record of his baptism on May 12, 1717, in Durham, Conn., indicates that he was born in or near that town, possibly in Middletown. Soon after his graduation from Yale College in 1745 he transferred from the Congregational to the Episcopal Church and under the direction of Dr. Samuel Johnson, minister of Stratford, Conn., he became a lay reader in Norwalk. In 1746 Trinity Church, Newport, R. I., having received a bequest from Nathaniel Kay to provide for a schoolmaster and catechist, episcopally ordained, was advised by the Society for the Propagation of the Gospel to apply to Dr. Johnson "for one of the young gentlemen educated at New Haven." As a consequence Leaming was sent to England at the expense of the Newport church, was ordained in 1748, and returned the same year to take up his work at Newport as head of the parochial school and assistant to the Rev. James Honyman. After the death of the latter in 1750 he had charge of the church until the appointment of another minister four years later. In 1758 he returned to Norwalk as minister of St. Paul's parish. At the outbreak of the Revolution he suffered severely for his Loyalist sympathies. All his considerable landed property in Connecticut was confiscated and he was for a time confined in the Fairfield county jail and so harshly treated that he contracted a rheumatic trouble which left him permanently lame. In July 1779 when British troops under General Tryon burned Norwalk, having lost all his books and household effects, Leaming decided to accompany the British to New York. He remained there until 1784, when he returned to Connecticut to become rector of the church at Stratford.

In March 1783 the clergy of Connecticut met in Woodbury to choose a presbyter who might seek Episcopal orders in England. Leaming had always been a strong advocate of a bishop for the colonies. By reason of his sufferings during the war which had gained him the reputation of a "confessor," no less than by his age and character, he was the leading presbyter among the Connecticut clergy. It was thus natural that he should be their first choice for bishop, but he declined to serve on the score of physical infirmity. In the following critical years Leaming worked effectively for the establishment of the Connecticut church and for its union with that of Pennsylvania and the other Southern dioceses. He objected (unsuccessfully) to the adoption of the word protestant by the Episcopal Church, and his Loyalist sympathies led him to protest (successfully) against the inclusion of a service for Independence Day in the new prayer-book. In 1765 he had received an honorary degree of M.A. from King's College and in 1789 the same institution conferred upon him the degree of S.T.D. In 1790 he retired from Stratford and from the active ministry and took up his residence in New York. The closing period of his life, however, was spent in New Haven at the home of the widow of James A. Hillhouse. Some years later a grand-niece, Mary Hillhouse, wrote: "He rises to my mind, the very ideal of age and decrepitude—a small, emaciated old man, very lame, his ashen and withered features surmounted sometimes by a cap, and sometimes by a small wig—always quiet and gentle in his manner, and uniformly kind and inoffensive. . . . He said little; spent most of his time in his own room, and never entertained his younger auditors with stirring tales of his earlier manhood" (Sprague, *post*, p. 130). He was twice married: but had no children. His first wife was Ann Leaming, his second, Elizabeth (Peck) Leaming. His published works consist of various sermons and controversial theological pamphlets which have little interest today.

[See E. E. Beardsley, *The Rev. Jeremiah Leaming, His Life and Services* (1885), reprinted from the *Churchman*, Feb. 21, 28, 1885; *The Hist. of the Episc. Ch. in Conn.* (2 vols., 1866–68), and *Life and Correspondence of the Right Rev. Samuel Seabury, D.D.* (1881); F. B. Dexter, *Biog. Sketches of the Grads. of Yale Coll.*, vol. II (1896); W. B. Sprague, *Annals. Am. Pulpit*, vol. V (1859); and the *Conn. Jour.* (New Haven), Sept. 20, 1804. Many of Leaming's letters have been printed; some unpublished ones are in the possession of Dr. H. C. Robbins of New York.]

W. P. L.

LEAMING, THOMAS (Sept. 1, 1748–Oct. 29, 1797), Revolutionary patriot, soldier, lawyer, merchant, was born in Cape May County, N. J., a descendant of Christopher Leaming, an Englishman, who moved from Southampton, L. I., to Cape May in 1692, and the son of Thomas and Elizabeth (Leaming) Leaming, who owned extensive property in South Jersey. He received his education and training in Philadelphia and was associated with that city during the greater part of his career. Soon after completing his scholastic education he was placed in the office of John Dickinson [*q.v.*] to study law and was admitted to the bar of Philadelphia. His association with Dickinson made him one of the most earnest of practical patriots. He gave his time and his money to the Revolutionary cause, and, by his ardent espousal of it, exposed his estate to confiscation by the British. Early in the year 1776 he had detected the danger in which South Jersey lay from attack by the British forces, and at the expense of himself and some wealthy neighbors, he organized a battalion of militia in Cape May County. On Apr. 15, 1776, he petitioned the Continental Congress to supply powder and lead to the battalion, a prayer that was granted with the addition of the clause, "he paying for the same."

Before the Cape May Battalion was actually called into action, the Provincial Assembly of the state of New Jersey opened its sessions, June 10, 1776, and Leaming was among the deputies sent to it from his county. A week later he resigned his office as adjutant of the battalion. He remained a member of the Assembly until its sessions for the year were ended, being present on July 2, 1776, when it voted for independence. He had joined the troop of Light Horse of the City of Philadelphia, now known as the First City Troop of Philadelphia City Cavalry, in 1775, and as soon as he was relieved of his legislative duties he returned to this little command which was composed entirely of well-to-do young men who furnished their own horses and equipment. They acted as Washington's escort, and as scouts, throughout the campaigns from 1776 to 1779. Leaming was with the troop at the battles of Princeton, Trenton, Germantown, and Brandywine, and was elected to its honorary roll in 1787.

In 1777 Leaming founded the firm of Bunner, Murray & Company, which in 1780 subscribed heavily to the Pennsylvania Bank (in 1781 the Bank of North America). The firm of Thomas Leaming & Company, which may have been a branch of the same house, began in 1777 to fit out privateers, and between May of that year and 1780, eleven vessels, varying in size from eighteen-gun ships to a four-gun schooner, were put on the seas, their masters bearing letters of marque. Fifty prizes and 1,000 prisoners were taken by these privateers. The schooner *Mars,* under Capt. Yelverton Taylor, took, in three vessels which it captured, 500 British and Hessian soldiers. At the close of the war, the firm was dissolved and Leaming returned to the practice of law in Philadelphia. He married Rebecca Fisher in Christ Church, in that city, Aug. 19, 1779, and his two sons, Thomas Fisher Leaming and Jeremiah Fisher Leaming, became well-known merchants in Philadelphia. Leaming was a victim of the yellow-fever epidemic which devastated the city in 1797, dying from that disease on Oct. 29. His remains were interred in the burial ground of Christ Church.

[P. S. Howe, *Mayflower Pilgrim Descendants in Cape May County, N. J.* (1921), p. 106; *Hist. of the First Troop, Phila. City Cavalry* (1874); S. N. Winslow, *Biogs. of Successful Phila. Merchants* (1864), pp. 69–72; Henry Simpson, *Lives of Eminent Philadelphians* (1859); Maurice Beasly, "Sketch of the Early History of the County of Cape May," *Geol. of the County of Cape May, State of N. J.* (1857); E. L. Clark, *A Record of the Inscriptions . . . in the Burial-Grounds of Christ Church, Phila.* (1864), p. 605; *Jours. of the Continental Cong.,* vol. IV (1906), vol. X (1908); *Pa. Archives,* 5 ser., I (1906); *Minutes of the Provincial Cong. and the Council of Safety of the State of N. J.* (1879).] J. J.

LEAR, TOBIAS (Sept. 19, 1762–Oct. 11, 1816), consular officer, was born at Portsmouth, N. H., the son of Col. Tobias Lear and Mary (Stilson) Lear. His father's prosperity as a shipmaster and later as a farmer enabled the son to graduate at Harvard, in 1783, and to travel and study in Europe. This preparation led to his engagement as private secretary to General Washington after his retirement to Mount Vernon in 1785. Lear held that enviable position for seven years, during which time there is every evidence that he greatly endeared himself to Washington and his family, becoming a life-long friend as well as a valued employee. While living at Mount Vernon he published *Observations on the River Potomack, the Country Adjacent, and the City of Washington* (1793), probably the earliest separate monograph on the District of Columbia. In 1790 he had married Mary Long of Portsmouth, N. H., and after her death in 1793 he went abroad, carrying letters of introduction from Washington and Jefferson. Returning in 1794, he settled in Alexandria, Va. He was elected president of the Potomac Canal Company in 1795 and on Aug. 22 of that year married Frances (Bassett) Washington, a niece of Martha Washington and the widow of Washington's nephew, George Augustine. On her death, he married Frances Dandridge Henley, another niece of Mrs. Washington. When war was imminent in 1798 Washington appointed him his military secretary, with rank of colonel, and from that time Lear remained with him until his death. Tradition says that he was the last person to whom Washington spoke; it is certain that he received a substantial legacy from his chief in appreciation of his services.

The fact that he was honored by Washington was largely responsible for his appointment by President Jefferson, in 1801, as consul at Santo Domingo. This post presented great difficulties at that time, for Toussaint L'Ouverture was rapidly becoming independent ruler there, while Jefferson still considered the island a French possession. Faced with these conditions, Lear conducted himself with great caution and tact, and upheld with energy the rights of American citizens during a period of bloodshed and horror. His task became hopeless after the arrival of General LeClerc, sent by Napoleon to take possession of the island, preparatory to extending the empire to Louisiana. In April 1802 LeClerc declined longer to allow Lear to remain, and he was forced to return to America. Upon his arrival in Washington his conduct was commended by the President, and he was shortly afterward named consul general at Algiers, with powers to negotiate a treaty with Tripoli in cooperation with the squadron commander, also to adjust affairs with any of the Barbary rulers.

It is evident that Lear possessed the qualities necessary to deal with the vacillating potentates, for between 1803 and 1805 he assisted in making a treaty with Morocco, in keeping a precarious peace with Algiers, and in adjusting affairs in Tunis. With Tripoli, matters were complicated in many ways: by the plight of three hundred Americans imprisoned since the loss of the *Philadelphia*; by the ill-health of Commodore Barron, with whom Lear was to cooperate; by a military expedition against the de facto authorities led by William Eaton [*q.v.*], "Navy Agent to the Barbary States"; and by Lear's own ardent desire for peace. Plans for a treaty had been discussed for two years, when suddenly, on June 4, 1805, Lear signed an agreement with the Pasha which, although otherwise desirable, acceded to ransom for the prisoners. Although this treaty was upheld by the government, it became a political issue. Opponents of the administration held that in view of the fleet in the Mediterranean and the land operations in progress under Eaton, no money should have been promised. Mystery surrounds Lear's motive for making this hasty treaty: explanations that have been suggested are the seemingly groundless fear of the naval officers for the safety of the prisoners, Lear's "passion for peace," and the fact that at that time he felt certain of securing liberal terms.

Beset by many difficulties, he remained as consul in Algiers until the beginning of the War of 1812, at which time the Dey, expecting the United States to be defeated by Great Britain, gave him summary orders to leave. Arriving in Washington under the cloud of the ill-timed treaty with Tripoli, Lear found his diplomatic career at an end. He was made an accountant in the War Department, and on Oct. 11, 1816, he committed suicide, leaving no explanation of his deed.

[C. W. Brewster, *Rambles about Portsmouth, First Series* (1859); H. H. Bennett, *Vignettes of Portsmouth* (1913); T. L. Tullock, "Col. Tobias Lear," *Granite Mo.*, Oct., Nov. 1882; *Letters from George Washington to Tobias Lear* (1905); *Letters and Recollections of George Washington, Being Letters to Tobias Lear and Others* (1906); Jared Sparks, *The Writings of George Washington* (12 vols., 1834–37); J. C. Fitzpatrick, *The Diaries of George Washington* (1925), vol. IV; *Am. State Papers, Foreign Relations*, vol. II (1832); C. O. Paullin, *Commodore John Rodgers* (1910); G. W. Allen, *Our Navy and the Barbary Corsairs* (1905); R. W. Irwin, *The Diplomatic Relations of the U. S. with the Barbary Powers, 1776–1816* (1931); F. J. R. Rodd, *Gen. Wm. Eaton* (1932); *Daily National Intelligencer*, Oct. 12, 1816; manuscript material in Lib. of Cong., Dept. of State, and Navy Dept.]
R. B. B.

LEARNED, EBENEZER (Apr. 18, 1728–Apr. 1, 1801), Revolutionary soldier, was born at Oxford, Mass., the son of Col. Ebenezer Learned and his wife, Deborah Haynes. He was descended from William Learned who was admitted to the First Church in Charlestown, in 1632, and in 1640 was one of the first settlers of Woburn. During part of the French and Indian War he served as captain of a company of Oxford men in Colonel Ruggles' regiment. He was one of the leading spirits in the Revolutionary movement in his native town. On Sept. 29, 1774, he was chosen delegate to the Provincial Congress at Concord, and on Jan. 12, 1775, to that at Cambridge. Shortly after the battle of Lexington he arrived in Cambridge at the head of a body of minute-men and was assigned, Apr. 21, 1775, to the right wing of the American army. While he was not present on the field of Bunker Hill, his men were under fire at Roxbury during the course of the action. On Jan. 1, 1776, he was commissioned colonel of the 3rd Continental Infantry. He helped to arrange the understanding between Washington and Howe respecting the evacuation of Boston, and on Mar. 17, 1776, he unbarred the gates with his own hands to admit the patriot forces. While the British fleet lingered in the harbor, his men were detailed to keep nightly watch upon it with the use of whale-boats. His regiment was presently ordered to New York, but on account of ill-health he resigned in May 1776.

Returning to Oxford, he continued to render various services to the Revolutionary cause. Not content to sniff the smoke of battle from afar, he accepted a commission, voted by Congress Apr. 2, 1777, as brigadier-general, and was ordered to join the northern army under Gates and Schuyler. After collecting the militia at Fort Edward and Fort Anne, he helped to remove valuable stores from Ticonderoga to prevent them from falling into enemy hands. He accompanied Arnold on his expedition to the relief of Fort Stanwix and took a noteworthy part in the battles of Sept. 19 and Oct. 7, 1777, his brigade being publicly thanked by Gates for its valiant behavior in the first-mentioned action. After Burgoyne's surrender he was ordered to the southward. On Mar. 24, 1778, he was again forced to resign his commission by reason of physical disability. Returning to Oxford, he served the town in civil capacity, representing it at the state constitutional convention in 1779 and as member of the legislature in 1783.

Learned was twice married: on Oct. 5, 1749, to Jerusha Baker, and on May 23, 1800, to Eliphal Putnam. For a time he kept a public house on his farm. He was at one time or another selectman, assessor, justice of the peace, and moderator of town-meeting, and was active in church affairs. His courage is attested not only by the incidents of his military career but by the fact that when most of his family and neighbors espoused the cause of Daniel Shays in 1786, he supported the constituted authorities even at the risk of his life. He died at Oxford.

[G. F. Daniels, *Hist. of the Town of Oxford, Mass.* (1892); J. Wilkinson, *Memoirs of My Own Times*, 3 vols. (1816); M. de W. Freeland, *The Records of Oxford, Mass.* (1894); F. B. Heitman, *Hist. Reg. of Officers of the Continental Army* (1893); Peter Nelson, "Learned's Expedition to the Relief of Fort Stanwix," *Quart. Jour. of the N. Y. State Hist. Asso.*, Oct. 1928; W. L. Learned, *The Learned Family* (2nd ed., 1898); *Columbian Centinel* (Boston, Mass.), Apr. 11, 1801.]

E. E. C.

LEARNED, MARION DEXTER (July 10, 1857–Aug. 1, 1917), German philologist, historian, editor, was born near Dover, Del., the son of Hervey Dexter and Mary Elizabeth (Griffith) Learned. He was descended from William Learned, who was admitted to the First Church in Charlestown, Mass., in 1632. The Griffiths settled on the Eastern Shore of Maryland about 1675. Marion Dexter Learned received his college education at Dickinson College (Carlisle, Pa.), was awarded the degree of A.B. in 1880, and then taught languages in the Williamsport Dickinson Seminary from 1880 to 1884. He visited Germany in 1885 for the study of Germanic philology and completed his graduate work at the Johns Hopkins University, where he received the degree of Ph.D. in 1887. He had been appointed instructor in German in 1886 and soon advanced to the associate professorship in the same department. On June 26, 1890, he married Annie Mosser of New Cumberland, Pa.

In 1895 Learned was called to the University of Pennsylvania as head of the German department, which, during more than twenty years of devoted service, he developed into one of the leading centers of Germanic studies. The call was a recognition of the scientific value of his philological work, *The Pennsylvania German Dialect* (1889), completed while at Johns Hopkins and originally published in the *American Journal of Philology* (vols. IX–X, 1888–89). Professor Oswald Seidensticker, Learned's predecessor in the chair of German at the University of Pennsylvania, had already revealed the fact that the Pennsylvania Germans had had a history, fascinating and important in the development of the American commonwealth. Learned became the continuator of this work of historical investigation and combined with it advanced philological and literary studies that attracted graduate students of ability. Their work, with the cooperation and under the guidance of their leader, resulted in a series of publications on German and American interrelations which were a contribution of lasting value. For the advancement of such studies he founded in 1897 a quarterly called the *Americana Germanica*, which after four years appeared monthly under the new name, *German American Annals*, "devoted to the comparative study of the historical, literary, linguistic, and educational relations of Germany and America." The journal was not confined to local investigations, but invited a wide range of contributors, and aimed to be national in its interests. His own contributions to the journal were numerous, and some of his studies were republished separately, including *Philip Waldeck's Diary of the American Revolution* (1907) and *The American Ethnographical Survey* (1911), in which he attempted to catch as it were in a drag-net, all the historical and literary materials still existing in the Pennsylvania-German counties of Pennsylvania. His most elaborate work, first published in the *Annals*, was his *Life of Francis Daniel Pastorius* (1908), which was a documentary history, furnishing as nearly as possible an exhaustive collection of all the documents available on the subject after a most painstaking search in Europe and America. These materials were published verbatim, in the original languages, ancient and modern, without translation and frequently without comment. He scorned the popular demand for readable books as something unworthy, tending to lower scientific standards. He preferred to "let truth unadorned radiate from the documents."

Another work of historical value was his *Guide to the Manuscript Materials Relating to American History in the German State Archives* (1912), undertaken under the direction of the department of historical research of the Carnegie Institution. Among other works should be mentioned: *The German-American Turner Lyric* (1896); *The Saga of Walther of Aquitaine* (1892); *A New German Grammar* (1903); and *Abraham Lincoln, An American Migration, Family English not German* (1909). He continued to edit the *German American Annals* until the year of his death. By that time nineteen volumes had been published and the monographs (most of them written by his students), published separately in the series called the *Americana Germanica*, numbered thirty-two. His graduate students felt an affectionate personal regard for him. He cared for them like a father when they needed aid in securing a position, and he was eminently successful in placing his men. He had the courage of his convictions, however, was quick to give them utterance, and would grow hotly indignant if the occasion provoked it. Then his high-pitched voice would ring out like a clarion. He was president of the Modern Language Association of America in 1909, member of the American Philosophical Society, and Knight of the Royal Prussian Order of the Red Eagle.

["In Memoriam: The Late Professor Learned," *German-Am. Annals,* Sept.–Dec. 1917; "The President's Address," *Modern Language Asso. of America Pubs.,* n.s. vol. XVIII (1910), pp. xlvi–lxv; W. L. Learned, *The Learned Family* (2nd ed., 1898); *Old Penn,* Oct. 5, 1917; *Philadelphia Inquirer,* Aug. 2, 1917.]
A. B. F.

LEARY, JOHN (Nov. 1, 1837–Feb. 8, 1905), capitalist, was born at St. John, New Brunswick, Canada. As a young man he engaged successfully in shipping, lumbering, and general merchandising at St. John and Woodstock, New Brunswick, and at Houlton, Me. Business reverses, however, induced him to migrate to the Far West, and he arrived at Seattle, Washington Territory, in 1869. A couple of years later he was admitted to the bar, and, after having been associated with two law firms, he withdrew from practice in 1882. Business enterprises of most varied character, but generally identified with Seattle and the Puget Sound country, absorbed his energies for the remainder of his life. Beginning as part owner in the Talbot coal mines, he extended these interests, opening the Leary mines, and establishing his own town of Leary. From mining he turned to real estate and became one of the largest holders of real property in Seattle. His financial interests in public utilities were large; in the city gas plant, in the company to furnish the city's water, in street railway and cable lines. He was also a promoter of elevator and warehouse companies. When it seemed as if the Northern Pacific would discriminate against Seattle, Leary organized, 1873, the Seattle & Walla Walla Railroad to connect his city with the transcontinental line. In 1891, he established the Columbia River & Puget Sound Navigation Company, which soon operated a fleet of coasters and ferry boats. James P. Ludlow was enabled through Leary's aid to secure the contract to carry mail from Puget Sound to Alaska and intermediate points, a privilege formerly enjoyed by a Portland concern. This versatile individual was also part owner of the *Seattle Post,* 1882, which was amalgamated with the *Seattle Post Intelligencer.* Later he held shares in the *Morning Journal,* which in 1891 was absorbed by the *Seattle Telegraph.* He was a founder of the Seattle Chamber of Commerce (April 1882) and for two terms its president. From 1884 to 1886 he was mayor of Seattle. He strongly advocated free public education, including provision for free textbooks for all children; and he was a regent of the University of Washington. His membership in the governing council of the Irish National League of America indicated a more cosmopolitan interest. He was twice married: first to Mary Blanchard; and second, Apr. 21, 1892, to Eliza P. Ferry, daughter of Elisha P. Ferry, first governor of the state of Washington. Leary died at Riverside, Cal.

[C. B. Bagley, *Hist. of King County, Wash.* (1929), vol. II; F. J. Grant, *Hist. of Seattle, Wash., with Illustrations and Biog. Sketches of Some of its Prominent Men and Pioneers* (1891); *Seattle and Environs* (1924), vol. II; *Seattle Daily Times,* Feb. 8, 10, 13, 14, 15, 25, 1905; *Seattle Post Intelligencer,* Feb. 9, 15, 16, 1905.]
H. J. D.

LEAVENWORTH, FRANCIS PRESERVED (Sept. 3, 1858–Nov. 12, 1928), astronomer and teacher, was born at Mount Vernon, Ind., the son of Seth Marshall and Sarah (Nettleton) Leavenworth. He was a descendant of Thomas Leavenworth who emigrated from England to America after 1664 and died at Woodbury, Conn., Aug. 3, 1683. Francis had a public-school education, and entered the University of Indiana in 1876, graduating in 1880 with the degree of B.A. At the university he came into contact with Prof. Daniel Kirkwood [*q.v.*], the astronomer, and after graduation he spent a year of study under Ormond Stone at the Cincinnati Observatory. In 1881, when Stone became director of the new Leander McCormick Observatory of the University of Virginia, he took Leavenworth with him as assistant. Leavenworth held this position from 1881 to 1887, doing also some graduate work in the university. On Oct. 11, 1883, he married Jennie Campbell of Louisville, Ky. They had three children.

In 1887 he was called to Haverford College as director of the observatory, for which a 10-inch telescope had been recently acquired. From Haverford, he was called in 1892 to the University of Minnesota as professor of astronomy and director of the new observatory, which was to have, as its chief instrument, a 10½-inch telescope. Here he remained until his retirement in 1927. During the second semester of 1918 he was in Duluth on leave of absence to teach navigation in the Shipping Board's nautical school. His main career was in teaching, for which profession he was well suited. Several of his many students went on to do graduate work in other institutions and became professional astronomers. He found time, however, for some valuable research. The observation of double stars was evidently his chief interest, and this he carried on at Cincinnati, McCormick, Haverford, and Minnesota observatories, as well as at Goodsell and Yerkes, where he spent several summers. His other observations include the discovery and measurement of 250 nebulae; the visual observation of four double stars for relative parallax; photographic observation of the asteroid Eros in the 1901 campaign to determine the parallax of the sun; the observation of brightness of Nova Aquilae No. 3, and of many variable stars. His observations are published in the *Haverford College Studies,* the *Astronomical Journal,* and the *Sidereal Messenger.* He was a fellow of the Royal Astronomical Society and a member of the American Astronomical Society.

[E. W. Leavenworth, *A Geneal. of the Leavenworth Family in the U. S.* (1873); W. O. Beal, in *Popular Astronomy,* Mar. 1929; *Monthly Notices of the Royal Astronomical Soc.,* Feb. 1929; *Pubs. of the Astronomical Observatory, Univ. of Minn.,* vol. I (1930); *Who's Who in America,* 1928–29; *Minneapolis Morning Tribune* and *Minneapolis Jour.,* Nov. 13, 1928.]

R. S. D.

LEAVENWORTH, HENRY (Dec. 10, 1783–July 21, 1834), soldier, was born in New Haven, Conn., the son of Jesse and Catharine (Conkling) Frisbie Leavenworth. His father was a graduate of Yale and a Revolutionary soldier who attained the rank of colonel. The parents moved to Danville, Vt., when he was a child, and later separated, the youth accompanying his father to Delhi, N. Y. Here he studied law and in 1804 was admitted to the bar. On Apr. 25, 1812, he was made a captain of the 25th Infantry and on Aug. 15, 1813, a major in the 9th Infantry. For distinguished services at Chippewa, July 5, and at Niagara, July 25, 1814, he was brevetted respectively a lieutenant-colonel and a colonel. He was transferred to the 2nd Infantry, May 17, 1815, and on a leave of absence granted at the end of the year served a term in the New York legislature. On Feb. 10, 1818, he was made lieutenant-colonel of the 5th Infantry. With a part of his regiment he arrived at the junction of the Minnesota and the Mississippi, Aug. 14, 1819, where he at once began the building of a cantonment, later named Fort Snelling, for many years the most northerly outpost of the frontier. On Oct. 1, 1821, he was transferred to the 6th Infantry and made commandant at Fort Atkinson (Calhoun), in the present Nebraska. In the summer of 1823, following the treacherous attack on Ashley's party, he led a punitive expedition against the Arikaras, though with results so dubious that they have been a matter of controversy ever since.

On July 25 of the following year he was brevetted a brigadier-general, and on Dec. 16, was made colonel of the 3rd Infantry, then stationed at Green Bay, Wis., but in the late summer of 1826 transferred to Jefferson Barracks, near St. Louis. In the summer of 1827 he built the post named, by the War Department, Cantonment (subsequently Fort) Leavenworth, near which the city of Leavenworth grew up. Two years later he became post commander at Jefferson Barracks. Early in 1834 he was put in command of the whole southwestern frontier, with instructions to negotiate peace among its warring tribes. With 500 troopers he set out from Fort Gibson, June 15. Illness decimated the ranks of his command, and in July he was himself stricken with a bilious fever. At Camp Smith, on the Washita near its junction with the Red, he died. The body was taken to Delhi for burial, and in 1902 was reburied at Fort Leavenworth. A monument to his memory was erected by the members of the 3rd Infantry.

Leavenworth was married three times—to Elizabeth Eunice Morrison, from whom he was divorced; at Delhi in 1810 to Electa Knapp, who died on June 12 of the following year, and in the winter of 1813–14 to Harriet Lovejoy, who accompanied him to the frontier and who survived him for twenty years. A son by his first wife, Jesse Henry Leavenworth (1807–1885), was a graduate of West Point, served for eighteen months in frontier service as a colonel in the Civil War, and for three years, 1864–67, was Indian agent for the Kiowas, Comanches, and Apaches. He was a severe critic of the military for what he termed their provocative conduct toward the Indians. Henry Leavenworth was a man of broad and varied culture. Major Davis credits him with the exercise of a profound influence upon the development of the standards of duty and discipline of the army during its formative period, and the *Military and Naval Magazine of the United States* for October 1834 pays tribute to his clearness of judgment and energy in action. In the military annals of the early frontier he holds a place second only to that of Henry Atkinson.

[F. B. Heitman, *Hist. Reg. and Dict. of the U. S. Army* (1903), vol. I; Geo. B. Davis, memoir of Leavenworth in *Jour. of the U. S. Cavalry Asso.,* Dec. 1895; V. M. Porter, "Journal of Stephen Watts Kearny," *Mo. Hist. Soc. Colls.,* vol. III, no. 2 (Apr. 1908); H. M. Chittenden, *The Am. Fur Trade of the Far West* (1902); E. W. Leavenworth, *A Geneal. of the Leavenworth Family* (1873); Thos. Forsyth, "Fort Snelling: Col. Leavenworth's Expedition to It in 1819," *Minn. Hist. Soc. Colls.,* vol. III, pt. 2 (1874); Grant Foreman, *Pioneer Days in the Early Southwest* (1926); Doane Robinson, "Official Correspondence of the Leavenworth Expedition into South Dakota in 1823," *S. D. Hist. Colls.,* I (1902), 181–256.]

W. J. G.

LEAVITT, DUDLEY (May 23, 1772–Sept. 15, 1851), almanac-maker, mathematician, author, and teacher, was born in Exeter, N. H., the eldest child of Joshua and Elizabeth (James)

Leavitt. On Apr. 7, 1795, he was married to Judith Glidden of Gilmanton, N. H., and to that place he moved in 1800. Soon afterward he began to publish a newspaper, the *Gilmanton Gazette.* He had issued his first almanac, printed by Elijah Russell at Concord, N. H., in 1797, and is said to have printed one number from his own press in Gilmanton. In 1806, having decided that he might devote summers to farming and winter evenings to teaching pupils and to making calculations for future almanacs, he bought a farm at Meredith, N. H., and thereafter made that his home. He also wrote school books and edited textbooks for publishers. From 1811 to 1817 he compiled the annual issues of the *New Hampshire Register* and for a time prepared calendars for the *Free-Will Baptist Register.*

The name of Leavitt's almanac was frequently changed. In 1815 it was called *Leavitt's Genuine, Improved New-England Farmer's Almanack, and Agricultural Register*; in 1830 it was *Leavitt's Farmer's and Scholar's Almanack*; in 1833 it was *Leavitt's the New England Farmer's and Scholar's Almanack*; and in 1850 he settled upon *Leavitt's Farmer's Almanack and Miscellaneous Year Book.* Usually he described himself as "Teacher of Mathematics and Astronomy," but sometimes as "Teacher of Mathematics and Natural Philosophy." His almanacs were usually well printed and always contained both original and reprinted articles of permanent interest, as well as mathematical problems, the solutions of which appeared the following year. In his almanac for 1847 he gave a short history of the almanac-makers of New England. Several numbers were calculated principally for amusement, and little effort was made to circulate them widely. The sale gradually increased, however, so that in 1846 60,000 copies were printed in two editions. The issue for 1853, published in Boston by Edward Livermore, was the first one printed after Leavitt's death. It carried an "Address to Patrons," in which it is stated that "at the time of his death, Mr. Leavitt had in his hands, perfectly prepared for the printer, the manuscripts of his almanac for every year up to 1857, inclusive. Besides the incalculable labor required to bring these manuscripts into their present perfect shape, Mr. Leavitt had prepared tables for his almanac from 1858 to 1899 inclusive. By so doing he has placed it in the power of those to whom he left his manuscripts to continue the publication of *Leavitt's Farmer's Almanack and Miscellaneous Year Book,* either by themselves or others to the close of this nineteenth century."

[Leavitt's *Almanacs,* of which he issued more than fifty, have been used for many of the facts, especially the issue for 1853 and the centennial number, that for 1896, which contained a sketch of Leavitt by Hon. Joseph A. Walker, and a portrait by Walter Ingalls, the original of which is in the library of the New Hampshire Historical Society. Other sources are: J. N. McClintock, *Colony: Province: State: 1623–1888. Hist. of N. H.* (1889); *New-Eng. Hist. and Geneal. Reg.,* Oct. 1851; Dean Dudley, *Hist. of the Dudley Family,* no. VII (1892), p. 802; G. W. Chamberlain and L. G. Strong, *The Descendants of Chas. Glidden of Portsmouth and Exeter, N. H.* (1925); *N. H. Statesman* (Concord), Sept. 20, 1851. Information as to certain facts was supplied by Clarence S. Brigham, librarian, American Antiquarian Society, Worcester, Mass.]

J. J.

LEAVITT, ERASMUS DARWIN (Oct. 27, 1836–Mar. 11, 1916), mechanical engineer, the son of Erasmus Darwin and Almira (Fay) Leavitt, was born in Lowell, Mass. After receiving a common-school education he entered the Lowell Machine Shop as an apprentice at the age of sixteen. Here he served three years and then was employed for one year in the firm of Corliss & Nightingale in Providence, R. I. He returned to Boston in 1856 and found employment at the City Point Works, becoming two years later an assistant foreman in charge of the construction of the engine of the United States flagship *Hartford.* In 1859 he returned to Providence as chief draftsman for Thurston, Gardner & Company, builders of high-class steam-engines, and served until the beginning of the Civil War when he entered the United States navy. Between 1861 and 1863 he was attached to the gunboat *Sagamore* in the Eastern Gulf Squadron. Later he was promoted to second assistant engineer and assigned to construction duty at Baltimore, Boston, and Brooklyn. In 1865 he was detailed to the Naval Academy at Annapolis as an instructor in steam-engineering, but he resigned in 1867 to take up the practice of mechanical engineering, specializing in pumping and mining machinery. He was recognized as an engineer of ability when, shortly thereafter, he installed the pumping engine at the waterworks of Lynn, Mass. This engine, which he designed, was of the beam compound type and its efficiency marked an advance in the economic operation of pumping engines. Following this work he designed and installed a pair of similar engines for the waterworks of Lawrence, Mass.

In 1874 Leavitt was appointed consulting and mechanical engineer for the Calumet & Hecla Mining Company, which position he held until 1904. During this connection he designed and superintended the building of the enormous equipment to be used at the company's mines in Michigan. This equipment included heavy machinery for pumping, air compression, hoisting, stamping, and general power purposes. While engaged in this work he was frequently called upon for assistance by other industrialists and municipalities as well. He advised Henry R. Worthington regarding the construction of high-duty, direct-acting pumping engines and the Bethlehem Steel Company in the introduction of the hydraulic forging process. He designed the first engines used for the cable railway of the Brooklyn Bridge, and the three great sewage pumping engines for the city of Boston. The waterworks pumping engines for Louisville, Ky., New Bedford, Boston, and Cambridge, Mass., also were designed by him. After 1888 he made frequent trips to Europe where his reputation as a consulting engineer had already spread. It is said that, as a machinery designer, he did more than any other engineer in the United States "to establish sound principles and propriety in design," and that he was "among the very first engineers . . . to appreciate the importance of weight in machinery." He was honored with the degree of Doctor of Engineering by Stevens Institute of Technology in 1884 and was the first recipient of this degree from the Institute. He was affiliated with the American Society of Mechanical Engineers (president, 1883), the American Institute of Mining and Metallurgical Engineers, the American Society of Naval Engineers, the Boston Society of Civil Engineers, and the Institution of Civil Engineers and Institution of Mechanical Engineers of Great Britain. Outside of his consulting work his chief interest lay in the Y. M. C. A. of Cambridge. He was married on June 5, 1867, to Annie Elizabeth Pettit of Philadelphia, Pa., and at the time of his death in Cambridge, Mass., was survived by three daughters.

[*Who's Who in America*, 1916–17; *Trans. Am. Soc. Mech. Engineers*, vol. XXXVIII (1917); *Boston Transcript*, Mar. 11, 1916.] C. W. M.

LEAVITT, FRANK McDOWELL (Mar. 3, 1856–Aug. 6, 1928), mechanical engineer, inventor, was born in Athens, Ohio, the son of the Rev. John McDowell and Bithia (Brooks) Leavitt. Shortly after his birth his parents moved to New York and later to Orange, N. J., where he attended the public schools and prepared for college. He entered Stevens Institute of Technology, Hoboken, N. J., at the age of fifteen years, studied engineering, and graduated four years later with the class of 1875. His first year out of college was spent with Frederick E. Sickels in New York, working on the design of steam steering apparatus for the United States navy. He then became chief draftsman for Bliss & Williams, Brooklyn, N. Y., manufacturers of sheet-metal-working machinery. After serving five years with this company he accepted the position of master mechanic of the Texas Division of the Mexican National Railway Company, but resigned after a year to become superintendent of the Graydon & Denton Manufacturing Company in Jersey City, N. J. Two years later, in 1884, he returned to E. W. Bliss & Company, successor to Bliss & Williams, in Brooklyn, as assistant superintendent, and remained with the company, with the exception of two years, 1900–02, for the rest of his life.

From the beginning of his career Leavitt showed a marked ingenuity in conceiving and designing mechanisms to accomplish a given purpose. He possessed, too, an unusual ability to visualize a problem, so that with his great knowledge of mechanical motions and forces he could design in detail the most difficult mechanism in the simplest forms. Over three hundred patents were granted to him between 1875 and 1921. The first six years of his service with E. W. Bliss & Company were taken up chiefly with the perfection of sheet-metal-working machinery. He was the first to build a successful automatic tin-can body-making machine. He invented, too, the toggle drawing press for making kitchen utensils and other articles. This type of press was the forerunner of the huge power presses used in making automobile bodies, frames, and similar pieces of equipment produced in quantity. After he had risen to the position of superintendent of the Bliss company he was called upon to install all of the machinery in the plant of the United States Projectile Company for the manufacture of shells and other "common" projectiles. Later, as chief engineer of his company, he made an extended tour abroad visiting the British, German, and Austrian torpedo and projectile plants. While abroad he purchased the American rights to the Whitehead submarine torpedo. He did not, however, purchase any torpedo manufacturing machinery and upon his return to the United States he undertook first to design machinery of this type. He continued, too, his work in sheet-metal machinery until about 1900. From that time until his death he was concerned primarily with the improvement of torpedoes. For two years he worked independently, then he returned to the Bliss company to continue the work, becoming also director of the organization. All of his patents acquired between 1900 and 1910 were purchased by the company. They included patents for the introduction of steel for the air flask; Curtis turbines for propulsion; the combustion of fuel in the air supply and the generation of steam in connection with that combustion; a new and dependable gyroscope steering apparatus, and a host of other innovations. His improved Whitehead torpedo became known as the Bliss-Leavitt and became standard equipment in the United States navy. Under Leavitt's leadership the torpedo was still further improved in succeeding years so that at the beginning of the World War it measured twenty-one inches in diameter and more than twenty-one feet in length; possessed a reliable range of 13,500 yards; was controlled by a superheated steam and combustion gas turbine, and carried over two hundred pounds of high explosive. During the war and for two years afterward Leavitt, as "a dollar-a-year man," was in charge of the Committee on Experimental Power of the Bureau of Steam Engineering of the Navy Department at Washington and worked continuously on the problem of developing a steam plant for the propulsion of aircraft. The result of this work was the design of an aircraft steam boiler which, with all appurtenances, control apparatus and necessary water, delivered about 1,000 horse-power and weighed but a little over 2,000 pounds. This was his last engineering work. He was married on Nov. 8, 1893, to Gertrude Goodsell of New York, who with a daughter survived him at the time of his death in Scarsdale, N. Y.

[*Trans. Soc. Naval Architects and Marine Engineers*, vol. XXXVI (1928); *Who's Who in America*, 1926–27; *N. Y. Times*, *N. Y. Herald Tribune*, *Brooklyn Daily Eagle*, Aug. 7, 1928; Patent Office records.]
C. W. M.

LEAVITT, HENRIETTA SWAN (July 4, 1868–Dec. 12, 1921), astronomer, was born in Lancaster, Mass. Her father was the Rev. George Roswell Leavitt, who was descended from early settlers in Hingham, Mass. Her mother was Henrietta Kendrick, who also came from colonial stock. After graduation from Radcliffe College (then the Society for the Collegiate Instruction of Women) in 1892 she spent several years in travel and teaching and as an advanced student and volunteer research assistant in the Harvard College Observatory, becoming a permanent member of the staff of the Observatory in 1902. At that time Edward Charles Pickering was directing the activities of the Observatory toward the determination of the photographic magnitudes of the stars. Assigned, as an assistant, to the study of the brightness of variable stars on the large number of photographic plates already accumulating, she soon became, by reason of her originality and intelligent industry, the head of the department of photographic stellar photometry. Her principal achievements in this field were her determination of the magnitudes of the stars in sequences near the North Pole and in other regions; her discoveries of variable stars; and her studies of variable stars in the Magellanic Clouds which led to her discovery of the "period-luminosity" law.

The photographic study of variable stars and any attempts at a systematic photometry of the stars with photographic plates called imperatively for standards of reference. Owing to the different colors of different stars, visual magnitudes, no matter how good, would not suffice. A sequence of stars, ranging from the second magnitude to the faintest star easily photographed, was charted near the North Pole. Methods had to be developed for the determination of the photographic magnitudes of these stars. Miss Leavitt was assigned to this work. The results were published in the *Harvard College Observatory Circular 170*, Feb. 21, 1912, and in the *Annals of the Astronomical Observatory of Harvard College*, vol. LXXI (1917). They have since been in constant use by many astronomers. She followed this work with similar measurements of sequences of stars in the forty-eight "Standard Regions" (*Annals*, Vol. LXXI, 1917) and of sequences (*Annals*, Vol. LXXXV, 1919) for use in connection with the international campaign of the Astrographic Catalogue. Much of her time in her last years was devoted to the determination of standards in the Kapteyn "Selected Areas."

Miss Leavitt's discoveries include four novae and twenty-four hundred variable stars—more than half as many as are listed in the catalogue of variable stars for 1930. Her study of the light-curves of ten variables of the Algol type appeared in the *Annals* (Vol. LX, 1908). The most powerful method of measuring distance developed from her discovery that the brightest of the "cluster" variables in the Magellanic Clouds had the longest periods of variation. With the calibration of this relation between period and luminosity it has become possible to estimate distance from period and apparent brightness wherever variables of this type are found.

[Solon I. Bailey, "Henrietta Swan Leavitt," *Popular Astronomy*, Apr. 1922; *Boston Transcript*, Dec. 13, 1921.]
R. S. D.

LEAVITT, HUMPHREY HOWE (June 18, 1796–Mar. 15, 1873), Ohio congressman and jurist, was born in Suffield, Conn., the son of

John Leavitt and his wife, née Fitch. He was a distant cousin of Joshua Leavitt [*q.v.*] and a descendant of John Leavitt, of Hingham, England, who emigrated to Boston in 1628 and, later, settled in Hingham, Mass. In 1800 the Leavitts removed to Ohio and located near Warren, Trumbull County, where he spent his boyhood and received a classical education in a grammar school. For some time he attended an academy in western Pennsylvania but, at sixteen, discontinued his studies. He taught school and worked as a clerk in a retail store. In the fall of 1814 he began to study law, first, with Benjamin Ruggles of St. Clairsville, Ohio, and, later, with John C. Wright of Steubenville. Two years later he was admitted to the bar and commenced to practise in Cadiz but, in 1819, moved to Steubenville, where for four years he was the partner of John M. Goodenow. In December 1821, he married Maria Antoinette, daughter of Dr. John McDowell of Steubenville. He was appointed, by the court of common pleas, prosecutor for Jefferson County and held this office from 1823 to 1829. In 1825 he was elected to the Ohio House of Representatives. Two years later he was elected to the state Senate. His election was contested on the ground that he was disqualified for membership because he was holding the office of prosecuting attorney. With but one dissenting vote, the Senate decided, however, to allow him to take his seat. At the conclusion of his term in the Senate he was appointed clerk of the common pleas and supreme courts of Jefferson County. In 1830 he was elected to Congress, as a Jacksonian Democrat, to fill the unexpired term of his former partner, John M. Goodenow. He was one of the three Ohio representatives who voted against rechartering the Bank of the United States, because he doubted the constitutionality of the bank and also the expediency of perpetuating the institution. In later life he questioned the correctness of these views. In 1832 he was reëlected to Congress.

On June 30, 1834, Jackson appointed him federal judge of the district court for Ohio, in which capacity he continued to serve for almost forty years. When, in 1855, the state of Ohio was divided into judicial districts he was assigned to the southern district and, in April of that year, moved to Cincinnati. Many of his opinions are printed in L. H. Bond, *Reports of Cases Decided in the Circuit and District Courts of the United States within the Southern District of Ohio* (2 vols., 1852), John McLean, *Reports of Cases Argued and Decided in the Circuit Court of the United States for the Seventh Circuit* (6 vols., 1840–56), and in S. S. Fisher, *Reports of Cases arising upon Letters Patent* (6 vols., 1867–74). Although he entertained anti-slavery views he rigorously maintained the constitutionality of the Fugitive-slave Law. For this he was severely criticized by the Anti-Slavery party. In 1858 in a charge to a jury in one of these cases he said: "Christian charity was not the meaning or intent of the fugitive slave law, and it would not therefore answer as a defence for violating the law" (Howe, *post*, p. 268). His most conspicuous case was the suit of Clement L. Vallandigham [*q.v.*] in 1863. Vallandigham, found guilty by a military commission, applied for a writ of *habeas corpus*. Contrary to the usual procedure of issuing the writ as "of right" and letting General Burnside reply thereto, Leavitt at once invited Burnside to present a statement and then refused the writ upon the grounds that the arrest was legal, and that, even though it had been illegal, the writ would not be obeyed. In 1871 he resigned and moved to Springfield, where he died.

[Files of the Congressional Joint Committee on Printing; *Cincinnati, Past and Present*, pub. by Maurice Joblin (1872); J. B. Doyle, *20th Century Hist. of Steubenville and Jefferson County* (1910), p. 139; *Hist. of Cincinnati and Hamilton County* (1894); Henry Howe, *Hist. Colls. of Ohio*, vol. II (1891); J. G. Randall, *Constitutional Problems under Lincoln* (1926); J. L. Vallandigham, *A Life of Clement L. Vallandigham* (1872); H. S. Sheldon, *Documentary Hist. of Suffield* (1879); *Cincinnati Enquirer*, Mar. 17, 18, 20, 1873.]

R. C. M.

LEAVITT, JOSHUA (Sept. 8, 1794–Jan. 16, 1873), clergyman, reformer, abolitionist, editor, was born at Heath, Mass., the son of Roger Smith Leavitt, a leading citizen, and Chloe Maxwell, daughter of Col. Hugh Maxwell, an Irish soldier in the American Revolution. His paternal grandfather was the Rev. Jonathan Leavitt, of Suffield, Conn. Early distinguished by good scholarship, young Leavitt entered Yale in 1810 and graduated in 1814. He then served as preceptor at Wethersfield Academy, whence he went to Northampton, Mass., to study law. He was admitted to the bar in 1819. The following year he was married to Sarah, daughter of the Rev. Solomon Williams of Northampton, Mass. He practised a short time at Heath and at Putney, Vt., but in 1823 returned to Yale and completed a two-year divinity course in a year. He was ordained and installed, February 1825, as Congregational minister at Stratford, Conn. Three years later he went to New York to be secretary of the Seamen's Friend Society and editor of the *Sailor's Magazine*. Known among New York friends as "the sturdy Puritan of New England," he entered upon strenuous literary and reformatory activities. He founded sailors' missions in several cities, and he was one of the first lecturers of the American Temperance Society. "Possessing," as he wrote, "no musical skill beyond that of ordinary plain singers," he compiled an evangelical hymnal, *The Christian Lyre,* which went into many editions. As early as 1825 he wrote for the *Christian Spectator* in opposition to slavery. His name appears also in the *Journal of Public Morals* as an editor and chairman of the executive committee of the American Seventh Commandment Society.

Having a vigorous physique and, according to his *Independent* associate, Henry E. Bowen, "rare confidence in his own judgment," Leavitt undertook publication, in 1831, of the *Evangelist,* an organ of religious revivals, temperance, anti-slavery, and other causes. He was a member for a time of the Colonization Society, but he differed with William Lloyd Garrison as to its policies. When the New York Anti-Slavery Society was founded in 1833 Leavitt was a member of its executive committee and was instrumental in merging it into the National Anti-Slavery Society. He was among those who fled from physical violence when Dr. Lewis Tappan's house, an abolitionist rendezvous, was mobbed. The financial depression of 1837 forced Leavitt to sell the *Evangelist,* but he reappeared as editor of the *Emancipator.* Before the election of 1840 he also edited the *Ballot Box,* which supported the party headed by J. G. Birney. Soon after this he moved the *Emancipator* to Boston where he opposed the Mexican War and espoused, besides anti-slavery, many causes, such as temperance, cheap postage, and free trade. He wrote vigorously and sometimes abusively. In 1848, when the pioneer work of the abolitionists was complete, and the *Emancipator* was visibly struggling for existence, Leavitt had an offer to return to New York as assistant editor of the *Independent,* then about to appear. He hesitated, but his friend, J. G. Whittier, advised: "Not all that thee might wish, Joshua, but a good harbor for thy old age." Such it proved to be. As office editor of the *Independent* for nearly twenty-five years Leavitt disappointed the expectations of those who predicted that he would be fiery and troublesome. He wrote millions of words of lucid editorial comment, handled correspondence, and won the affection and respect of his younger associates. He was in honor in Great Britain where, in 1869, the Cobden Club awarded him a gold medal for his work in behalf of free trade. His editorial labor continued until a few days before his death, which followed a stroke of paralysis.

[The journals edited by Leavitt contain much autobiographical material, not yet collated. See F. B. Dexter, *Biog. Sketches of the Grads. of Yale Coll.,* vol. VI (1912); obituary in *Independent,* Jan. 23, 1873; Elizur Wright, "The Father of the Liberty Party," *Ibid.,* Jan. 30, 1873; C. G. Finney, "Dr. Leavitt's Death," *Ibid.,* Feb. 6, 1873; Leonard Bacon, "Reminiscences of Joshua Leavitt," *Ibid.,* Feb. 13, 1873; J. P. Thompson, "Personal Recollections of Dr. Leavitt," *Ibid.,* Mar. 6, 1873; J. P. Bretz, "The Economic Background of the Liberty Party," *Am. Hist. Rev.,* Jan. 1929; L. H. Everts, *Hist. of the Conn. Valley in Mass.* (1879), vol. II; *N. Y. Geneal. and Biog. Record,* Apr. 1873; *N. Y. Times,* Jan. 17, 1873. In 1916 the Massachusetts Historical Society acquired a collection of free-soil papers assembled by Leavitt.]

F. W. C.

LEAVITT, MARY GREENLEAF CLEMENT (Sept. 22, 1830–Feb. 5, 1912), temperance advocate, was born in Hopkinton, N. H. She was the daughter of the Rev. Joshua and Eliza (Harvey) Clement. Her father was a Baptist clergyman who was generally called "Father" Clement because of his occupation, and also because of his marked resemblance to George Washington. Mary Greenleaf Clement attended the district schools of Hopkinton and Thetford (Vt.) Academy, after which she taught in country schools in Vermont and New Hampshire. She entered the Massachusetts State Normal School at Framingham and graduated from it in 1851, and then she taught in the Boylston Grammar School in Boston till 1857, when she married Thomas H. Leavitt of Greenfield, Mass., in Thetford, Vt. In 1867 she established a private school of her own in Boston which she conducted till 1881. She was interested in the meetings held by Moody and Sankey in Boston in 1876, and her interest in religious and temperance work made her active in the organization of the Massachusetts W.C.T.U. In 1883 she became a traveling representative of the national W.C.T.U. and undertook a campaign of education and organization under its auspices. She spent nine months in the United States and then sailed to the Sandwich Islands, after which she visited Australia, New Zealand, Japan, China, India, many parts of Africa (including the island of Madagascar, which she crossed escorted only by sixteen native bearers), the British Isles, and much of the continent of Europe. She did not return till 1891, and many times she spoke as often as three times a day, employing something like 229 interpreters in forty-seven different languages. The amount of money she expended was extremely small, and all but sixteen hundred dollars of it was "collected from those for whom she labored," that is, from offerings at the meetings she addressed. Soon after her return from her first trip, she started on another journey through South America, and it was attended with equal success. Her activities led to the organization of the World's W.C.T.U. and it, at a meeting in Boston in 1891, made her an honorary officer for life. She died in Boston and was survived by three daughters. Her publications include only a few tracts on the liquor question, so her distinction is due to her powers as a speaker and organizer. She is credited with forming eighty-six branches of the W.C.T.U., twenty-four temperance societies, and twenty-three branches of the White Cross in her travels; but what is perhaps more significant is the fact that the motto of the W.C.T.U. was changed from "For God and Home and Native Land" to "For God and Home and Every Land" largely because of her work, thus giving a wider outlook to a movement that was at most national, if not sectarian in its inception.

[Some of the details of this account have been secured from Mrs. Leavitt's family, but there are obituary notices of her in the reports of the Massachusetts and World's W.C.T.U. for 1912, and in the *Boston Transcript* for Feb. 5, 1912. Much that she wrote or supplied the information for about foreign temperance work appeared in the *Union Signal,* the publication of the World's W.C.T.U., during the period of her activity. See also: *Who's Who in America,* 1910–11; Clara C. Chapin, *Thumb Nail Sketches of White Ribbon Women* (1895); Elizabeth Putnam Gordon, *Women Torch Bearers* (1924); and *Our Message,* the organ of the Massachusetts W.C.T.U., Mar. 1912.] S. G.

LE BRUN, NAPOLÉON EUGÈNE HENRY CHARLES (Jan. 2, 1821–July 9, 1901), architect, was born in Philadelphia, Pa., of French ancestry, the son of Charles and Adelaide Le Brun. His father, who first came to the United States on a secret diplomatic mission while Jefferson was president, returned some years later to settle permanently. Napoléon early showed an aptitude for art and engineering and it was decided to educate him as an architect. Accordingly, he was sent in 1836 to study under Thomas U. Walter [*q.v.*], who in the fifties was architect of the Capitol extension. Walter had been the pupil of William Strickland [*q.v.*], in his day the leading architect of Philadelphia, who, in turn, had been the disciple of Benjamin H. Latrobe [*q.v.*], who came from England in 1796 and became the architect of the Capitol by appointment of Jefferson in 1803. In 1841 Le Brun began to practise for himself in Philadelphia, where he remained until he removed to New York City in 1864. On Dec. 20, 1845, he married Adèle Louise Lajus, youngest daughter of Paul Lajus, a merchant of Philadelphia. They had three sons and two daughters. The eldest and youngest sons followed their father's career and with him formed the firm of N. Le Brun & Sons in the early eighties. Le Brun was elected a fellow of the American Institute of Architects and president of the New York Chapter. He was also president of the Willard Architectural Commission.

Among his notable contributions to the architecture of Philadelphia were the Seventh or Tabernacle Presbyterian Church on Broad Street, the Academy of Music, the Girard Estate Building, several county structures, and the interior of the Roman Catholic Cathedral of Saints Peter and Paul. The latter is noteworthy as his only application of the Renaissance style to church work. In the Romanesque style he designed the Church of the Epiphany, Second Avenue near Twenty-first Street, New York City, modeled after the church of San Zeno in Verona. The Episcopal Church of St. Mary the Virgin, in West Forty-sixth Street, New York, is an example, not wholly successful, of his work in French Gothic. When it was built, in 1895, it was called the "Chicago Church" because it was an early specimen of steel construction. A much better example of Le Brun's Gothic work was the earlier Church of St. John Baptist (1872), in West Thirtieth Street. The firm of N. Le Brun & Sons designed for the fire department of New York City the headquarters in East Sixty-seventh Street, an example of Romanesque, and the engine house in Old Slip near the foot of Wall Street, an imitation of the old Dutch Renaissance, particularly appropriate to a building within the boundaries of the Dutch town of New Amsterdam. Other engine houses by this firm were those in Eighteenth Street near Broadway and at White and Lafayette Streets, the latter in the French château style. The Home Life Insurance Building on Broadway and the San Francisco office of the Metropolitan Life Insurance Company are examples of office buildings by the firm, but its most conspicuous success was the home office building and the tower of the Metropolitan Life at Madison Square, New York (1889–1909). The main edifice constituted one of the early experiments in tall buildings and one of the early uses of the "column" for skyscraper construction; the tower and addition, designed after the elder Le Brun's death, received the award of the New York Chapter of the American Institute of Architects "for the most meritorious work of 1909" in solving "one of the most difficult problems now presented to American architects."

[*N. Y. Times,* July 10, 1901; *Am. Architect and Building News,* July 20, 1901; *Proc. of the Thirty-fifth Ann. Conv. of the Am. Inst. of Architects, 1901* (1902); Montgomery Schuyler, "The Work of N. Le Brun and Sons," *Arch. Record,* May 1910; obituary of Pierre L. Le Brun, in *The Am. Architect and the Arch. Rev.*, Apr. 9, 1924.] M. S.

LECHFORD, THOMAS (fl. 1629–1642), was the first professional lawyer in the colony of Massachusetts Bay. The names of his parents and the details of his early life are unknown, but he was probably a member of the Lechford family of Surrey, England. At some time before 1629 he was living in London and was the auditor of Hugh Peter, lecturer at St. Sepulchre's. He was a member of Clement's Inn, and acquired some little skill in chirography. He was in Ireland with Lord Deputy Wentworth, but for how long and in what capacity are unknown. He opposed episcopacy and solicited the cause of William Prynne, for which he "suffered imprisonment, and a kind of banishment." He declined preferment at the court of George Rákóczy, prince of Transylvania and lord of lower Hungary, refused place and preferment from the Providence Company, and emigrated to New England, arriving at Boston June 27, 1638. He mentions his wife in an entry in his notebook (Trumbull, *post*) in 1639, but whether he married in England or in Massachusetts is uncertain. Her Christian name was Elizabeth, but her family name is unknown. Lechford soon found himself out of sympathy with the leaders of Massachusetts Bay. His manuscript writings, the title of only one of which, "Of Prophesie," has been preserved, were declared heretical by Deputy Governor Thomas Dudley (*Proceedings of the Massachusetts Historical Society,* III, 1859, 311–12; *Collections,* 4 ser. VII, 1865, 111–12); he was never received into church membership, and consequently could neither vote nor hold office in the colony. In the summer of 1639 he hoped to be employed as clerk and notary public by the Massachusetts General Court but, because of the distrust with which he was regarded, he was refused all preferment and forced to earn a meager living as a copyist and by drafting petty legal documents, a record of which is preserved in his notebook. For trying to influence the jury out of court in the case of William and Elizabeth Cole *vs.* Francis Doughty, Lechford in September 1639 was debarred from pleading in the courts of Massachusetts Bay. As early as July 28, 1640, he was thinking of returning to England or Ireland. In March 1640/41, he wrote to one "of no mean rank," complaining of his sufferings and asking to be sent for, and it was supposed that Prynne sent him money for his passage home. On Aug. 3, 1641, Lechford sailed from Boston, leaving his wife and household goods worth £6.13s.10d. in Massachusetts (*New-England Historical and Genealogical Register,* April 1876, pp. 201–02), and by Nov. 16, 1641, was once more at Clement's Inn, a much stronger supporter of monarchy and episcopacy than he had been before his sojourn in New England. In 1642 he published *Plain Dealing: or, Nevves from New-England,* which was reissued in 1644 under the title *New-Englands Advice of Old-England.* (It was republished under the original title in *Collections of the Massachusetts Historical Society,* 3 ser. III, 1833, and again, with an introduction and notes by J. H. Trumbull, in *Library of New England History,* No. IV, 1867). Lechford died soon after its first publication. His widow in New England married Samuel Wilbore some time before Nov. 29, 1645, and, after Wilbore's death in 1656, married Henry Bishop (*A Report of the Record Commissioners Containing Boston Births, Baptisms, Marriages and Deaths, 1630–1699,* 1883, pp. 56, 58).

["Note-Book Kept by Thomas Lechford . . . June 27, 1638, to July 29, 1641," with a sketch of his life by J. H. Trumbull, in *Trans. and Colls. Am. Antiq. Soc.*, vol. VII (1885); *Records of the Governor and Company of the Mass. Bay in New England,* vols. I and II (1853); John Cotton, *The Way of Congregational Churches Cleared* (1648).] I. M. C.

LE CLEAR, THOMAS (Mar. 11, 1818–Nov. 26, 1882), portrait and genre painter, was born at Owego, N. Y., the son of Louis Le Clear (or Le Clere). He was a veritable infant phenomenon, for without instruction, at the age of nine, he painted acceptable portraits of his schoolmates, and at twelve he produced a surprisingly good picture of St. Matthew, of which replicas were in brisk demand at $2.50 each. In 1832 the family moved to London, Ontario, where the youth of fourteen continued to paint portraits, his most influential patron being the Hon. John Wilson, a former member of the Canadian Parliament. Two years later he was at Goderich, Ontario, painting decorative panels for a Lake Huron steamboat. Thence he found his way to Norfolk, N. Y., and after two years there to Green Bay, Wis., "sketching Indians on the way." His subsequent wanderings in search of employment took him to Elmira and Rochester, N. Y., and finally in 1839 (*ætat* twenty-one), to New York City, where he was soon able to support himself "with comfort and respectability."

In 1844 he married a daughter of Russell R. Wells of Boston, Mass., and a year or more later, with his wife, he went to Buffalo, N. Y., where he worked busily on portraits and genre pieces. Returning to New York City in 1860, he passed the rest of his life there. In 1863 he was made a member of the National Academy of Design. He made two or three short trips abroad and exhibited several of his works in the Royal Academy, London, including his fine portrait of his colleague William Page (1876), now in the Corcoran Gallery, Washington, a canvas which was warmly praised by the English and American critics.

During his stay in Buffalo he had painted several successful genre pictures such as the "Marble-Players," which was bought by the Art Union, "Young America," and "The Itinerants," which was exhibited at the National Academy of 1862. These episodic canvases are well composed, agreeable in color, and manifest a distinct talent for the expression of juvenile character. But Le Clear's more significant achievements are his portraits of men, which are among the best made in America in the middle nineteenth century. Among his best-known sitters, besides Page, were Presidents Fillmore and Grant, George Bancroft, William Cullen Bryant, Bayard Taylor, Edwin Booth, Parke Godwin, Daniel S. Dickinson, and Joseph Henry, the last-named likeness belonging to the National Gallery of Art, Washington. Le Clear's first wife died in 1869 and he later married the daughter of James S. King of New York. He died at his home in Rutherford Park, N. J., in his sixty-fifth year.

[Henry T. Tuckerman's *Book of the Artists* (1867) contains the most complete account of Le Clear's life. Other sources include L. W. Kingman, *Early Owego* (1907); the *Art Jour.*, July 1878; the *Am. Art News*, Oct. 29, 1921; R. Rathbun, *The Nat. Gallery of Art* (1909); Algernon Graves, *The Royal Acad. of Arts*, vol. V (1906); *N. Y. Times*, *N. Y. Daily Tribune*, Nov. 28, 1882.]

W. H. D.

LECONTE, JOHN (Dec. 4, 1818–Apr. 29, 1891), scientist, teacher, brother of Joseph and first cousin of John Lawrence LeConte [*qq.v.*], was born in Liberty County, Ga. He was of French Huguenot descent, his earliest American ancestor being Guillaume LeConte, a native of Rouen. Louis LeConte, father of John, was a graduate of Columbia College in New York, and later a student of medicine, without, however, graduating in that profession. About 1810 he removed to Liberty County, Ga., to take possession of a plantation left him by his father. Here he married Ann Quarterman and of this marriage John was the fourth child and the second son. The father, in addition to the general management of the plantation, developed a "passionate pursuit of science," fitting up a chemical laboratory in the attic of the plantation house and setting aside a tract of land for a botanical garden. He also accumulated a large library of scientific books and periodicals. The boys of the family were trained to be naturalists and to put into organized form their knowledge of bird and animal life. John's early formal education was provided in a local private school supported by a small group of planters. One teacher only seems worthy of mention as a possible influence. This was Alexander H. Stephens [*q.v.*], who was to figure so prominently in the history of the South. In 1835 LeConte, then seventeen, was sent to Franklin College (later the University of Georgia), graduating with high honor in 1838. From Franklin he went to the College of Physicians and Surgeons in New York City. Attaining the degree of doctor of medicine in 1841, he made plans to continue his medical training at Paris; but the death of his eldest brother changed the current of events and he returned to Georgia. On July 20, 1841, he had married Eleanor Josephine Graham, whom he had met in New York. She is described as one possessed of rare intelligence, spirit, force of character, and beauty—qualities giving her assured social recognition. "No other influence," said his brother, Joseph LeConte, "so greatly affected the whole course of his life as that of his wife" ("Memoir," *post*, p. 375).

For a number of years he lived in Savannah, practising his profession but taking time to pursue scientific studies. In 1846 he became professor of physics and chemistry in Franklin College, resigning in 1855 to accept the chair of chemistry in the College of Physicians and Surgeons. His strong preferment for the subject of physics led him, within the year, to change to the professorship of physics in the South Carolina College (University of South Carolina), which he held until 1869. During the Civil War he served the Confederate government as superintendent of the niter works located in the vicinity of the college. At the time of Sherman's march through the South, LeConte witnessed not only the destruction of this plant, but the destruction of his own property. In spite of these experiences his zeal for scientific research continued and some of the more important of his studies are of this period. In 1868 he was elected to the chair of physics in the University of California, beginning work there in 1869. For the first year he acted as president of the institution in connection with his professorship. He again became president in 1875 and continued in the dual position until 1881. After that date he confined himself to the chair of physics. His contributions on scientific subjects over a period of fifty years amount to about one hundred papers. One of his earliest researches resulted in "Experiments Illustrating the Seat of Volition in the Alligator" (*New York Journal of*

Medicine and Collateral Sciences, November 1845). In 1850 he wrote a paper on the exudation of ice from the stems of certain plants and the protrusion of icy columns from certain soils (*Philosophical Magazine,* May 1850). In 1858 he developed an explanation of the phenomenon of sensitive flames, making clear the analogy of sound and light and introducing a new method of research made use of later by scientists in the study of acoustics ("On the Influence of Musical Sounds on the Flame of a Jet of Coal-gas," *American Journal of Science and Arts,* January 1858). In 1863 he wrote a paper on "The Adequacy of Laplace's Explanation to Account for the Discrepancy between the Computed and the Observed Velocity of Sound in Air and Gases" (*Philosophical Magazine,* January 1864). His paper, "On Sound Shadows in Water" (*American Journal of Science and Arts,* January 1882) contained the description and discussion of unique experiments on the propagation of vibrations through water. The results recorded attracted much attention in Europe. He wrote an exhaustive discussion of the whole subject of colored media of all kinds, under the title, "Physical Studies of Lake Tahoe" (*Overland Monthly,* November, December 1883 and January 1884). "This paper," said Joseph LeConte, "is in fact a perfect model of what a popular scientific article ought to be, for it is simple in style and yet thoroughly scientific in matter" ("Memoir," p. 383).

[Joseph LeConte, "Memoir of John LeConte 1818–1891," *Nat. Acad. Sci. Biog. Memoirs,* vol. III (1895), with list of LeConte's more important publications; Joseph LeConte, *The Autobiog. of Joseph LeConte* (1903); T. H. Hittell, "In Memory of Professor John LeConte," *Cal. Educ. Rev.,* May 1891; Frederick Slate, "In Memory of Professor John LeConte," *Ibid.*; *Popular Science Mo.,* Nov. 1889; *San Francisco Call,* Apr. 30, 1891.] W. W. K.

LECONTE, JOHN LAWRENCE (May 13, 1825–Nov. 15, 1883), entomologist, physician, was born in New York City, the son of John Eatton and Mary Anne H. (Lawrence) LeConte. John and Joseph LeConte [*qq.v.*] were his first cousins. They were of French Huguenot stock, being descended from Guillaume LeConte, who was born at Rouen in 1659 and migrated to Holland, and thence to America, after the peace of Ryswick in 1698. John Lawrence LeConte was educated at Mount Saint Mary's College, graduating in 1842, and at the College of Physicians and Surgeons in New York, graduating in 1846. He never practised medicine for a livelihood, since he possessed independent means. A taste for science seems to have been inherent in the family. His father, a major of engineers in the United States army, was both a zoölogist and a botanist. He seems to have been especially interested in the *Coleoptera* and published especially upon the family *Histeridae.* He was an excellent delineator of insects. It was natural, then, that John Lawrence, who was the constant companion of his father after the death of his mother in his infancy, should have shared his tastes. While at Saint Mary's College, he collected extensively, and while a medical student, at the age of nineteen, he published his first descriptive paper, on certain *Carabidae* (*Proceedings of the Academy of Natural Sciences of Philadelphia,* April 1844). He soon became interested in the subject of geographic distribution of species, and in one of his early papers wrote of the *Coleoptera* common to North America and Europe (*Annals of the Lyceum of Natural History of New York,* vol. IV, 1848, pp. 159–63). Later he studied the distribution of insects in the United States and made broad generalizations applying to other forms of life. He was the first biologist to map the faunal areas of the western part of the United States. It has been said, however, that his very important contributions to zoo-geography were "but accessories to his main work, the overflow of a mind charged with resources" (Scudder, *post*).

Although at first his taxonomic studies resulted in miscellaneous descriptions, he soon began to prepare synopses and monographs. Despite the wealth of material, he worked systematically and carefully. His patient and original investigation may be said to have culminated in his monographic revision of the *Rhynchophora* ("The *Rhynchophora* of America North of Mexico," *Proceedings of the American Philosophical Society,* vol. XV, 1876), and in his *Classification of the Coleoptera of North America* (Smithsonian Miscellaneous Collections, vol. XXVI, 1883). In both of these great undertakings he was associated with George H. Horn [*q.v.*]; but to the first Horn contributed only a single family, the *Otiorhynchidae.* In addition to studies in entomology, LeConte published essays dealing with mineralogy, geology, radiates, recent fossil mammals, and ethnology. He kept up with the advance of science, and his breadth of knowledge added authority to his special contributions to entomological science. He was recognized at home and abroad as the greatest entomologist America had produced. European entomologists visited him for consultation, and he was an honorary member of all the older and larger entomological societies in Europe. He was one of the incorporators of the National Academy of Sciences, and was president of the American Association for the Advancement of

Science in 1874. He visited Europe several times. His style was rather scholastic, and his philosophy was rather conservative, although he readily adopted evolutionary thought. During the Civil War he entered the army medical corps as surgeon of volunteers, and was promoted to the grade of lieutenant-colonel and medical inspector, in which capacity he served until the inspectors were mustered out in 1865. On Jan. 10, 1861, he married Helen S. Grier of Philadelphia. In 1878 he received strong indorsements for the post of United States commissioner of agriculture, but President Hayes chose William G. LeDuc [*q.v.*], giving LeConte the post of chief clerk of the United States Mint at Philadelphia, which position he held until his death.

[Memoir of LeConte by S. H. Scudder, in *Biog. Memoirs, Nat. Acad. Sci.*, vol. II (1886), repr. in *Trans. Am. Entomological Soc.*, vol. XI (1884), with a portrait and an appendix on his ancestry; *The Entomological Writings of John L. LeConte* (1878), listing his writings up to Nov. 18, 1878, published by the Cambridge Entomological Society as Dimmock's Special Bibliography, no. 1; G. H. Horn, in *Science*, Dec. 21, 1883, and in *Proc. Am. Philosophical Soc.*, vol. XXI (1884); C. V. Riley, in *Psyche*, Nov.–Dec. 1883; F. W. True, *A Hist. of the First Half Century of the Nat. Acad. of Sci.* (1913); David Sharp, in *Entomologist's Monthly Mag.* (London), Jan. 1884; the *Press* (Phila.), Nov. 16, 1883.]

L. O. H.

LECONTE, JOSEPH (Feb. 26, 1823–July 6, 1901), geologist, the fifth child and youngest son of Louis and Ann (Quarterman) LeConte, and brother of John [*q.v.*], was born on the Woodmanston plantation in Liberty County, Ga. His early schooling is said to have been scanty, but among his teachers was Alexander H. Stephens [*q.v.*], subsequently prominent in national affairs. The boy's vacations and holidays were spent in hunting, fishing, and other sports for which the country afforded abundant facilities. In 1838 his father died and shortly afterward he entered Franklin College (later the University of Georgia) at Athens, Ga., whence he was graduated in August 1841. Accompanied by a brother and sister, he toured the northern states, but returned to spend the winter on the Georgia plantation. In the fall of 1843 he entered upon the four months' winter course at the College of Physicians and Surgeons in New York. During the following season, in company with his cousin John Lawrence LeConte [*q.v.*], he made an excursion into what was then the Far West, visiting the region of the headwaters of the Mississippi River by way of Niagara, Buffalo, Detroit, and the Great Lakes. Returning to New York in the fall, he resumed his medical studies and graduated in April 1845, having meanwhile made the acquaintance of Audubon, Spencer F. Baird, and Jacob Post Girard. He spent the next two years in local travel and the carefree life of a country gentleman. In January 1847 he married Caroline Elizabeth Nisbet and settled down for a time to the practice of medicine in Macon. Concluding, after some years, that he had not yet "found himself," he went to Cambridge, Mass., in August 1850 and entered upon a course of study under Louis Agassiz which included six weeks' stay at Key West, Fla. In the following June at the suggestion of Agassiz, he presented a thesis and obtained the degree of S.B. from the newly established Lawrence Scientific School. Returning to Georgia in October 1851, he soon received a call to the professorship of all the sciences at Oglethorpe University, Midway, Ga. Here he remained but a year, resigning to accept a like position in the University of Georgia at Athens, where he remained until 1856. During this period he published a number of papers, the most important being "On the Agency of the Gulf Stream in the Formation of the Peninsula of Florida" (*Proceedings of the American Association for the Advancement of Science* for 1856, vol. X, 1857), based upon his Florida experiences with Agassiz. Administrative difficulties led him to resign his professorship at Athens, and he applied for and was elected in 1857 to the chair of geology in the College of South Carolina, Columbia, where his brother John was teaching.

LeConte remained in the South during the Civil War, although the College ceased to function in the summer of 1862. It does not appear that he took a particularly active part in the struggle, although he served for a time as chemist of the Niter and Mining Bureau, in which capacity he explored a number of "niter" caves in the Gulf States and iron deposits at Shelbyville, Ala. With the close of hostilities, he resumed his college duties and also his outside connections, in 1866–67 delivering a series of six lectures on coal and petroleum in the Peabody Institute of Baltimore. Conditions in the South were hard, at best, however, and accordingly, with the establishment of the University of California at Berkeley, he and his brother John both made successful application, in 1866, for positions on the teaching force there, and moved to California in 1869. Here, in an atmosphere that developed his full usefulness, he remained for the rest of his days, resigning from the teaching of undergraduates in 1896.

As a teacher and educator, LeConte was one of the most beloved and admired of men. Having a naturally joyous disposition, unusual talent, culture, and refinement, he possessed a rare faculty for friendship. His fecundity as a scientist is suggested by the following selection of titles (out of many) taken in the order of their appearance: "The Correlation of Physical, Chemical, and Vital Force, and the Conservation of Force in Vital Phenomena" (*Proceedings of the American Association for the Advancement of Science* for 1859, vol. XIII, 1860); "On the Law of Sexes, or the Production of the Sexes at Will" (*Nashville Journal of Medicine and Surgery,* October 1866); "On Some Phenomena of Binocular Vision" (*American Journal of Science and Arts,* 1869, 1871, 1875, 1877); "A Theory of the Formation of the Great Features of the Earth's Surface" (*Ibid.,* November, December 1872; see also June 1873); "On the Great Lava-Flood of the Northwest, and on the Structure and Age of the Cascade Mountains" (*Ibid.,* April 1874); "On the Evidences of Horizontal Crushing in the Formation of the Coast Range of California" (*Ibid.,* April 1876); "On Critical Periods in the History of the Earth and Their Relation to Evolution; and on the Quaternary as Such a Period" (*Ibid.,* August 1877), commonly considered as one of his best articles; "Some Thoughts on the Glycogenic Functions of the Liver" (*Ibid.,* February 1878); "The Genesis of Sex" (*Popular Science Monthly,* December 1879); "On the Genesis of Metalliferous Veins" (*American Journal of Science,* July 1883); *Evolution and its Relation to Religious Thought* (book, 1888); "Evolution and Human Progress" (*The Open Court,* Apr. 23, 1891); "Theories of the Origin of Mountain Ranges" (*Journal of Geology,* September-October 1893), which must be read in connection with the paper by James Dwight Dana [*q.v.*] on a similar subject for its value to be estimated; "The Ozarkian and its Significance in Theoretical Geology" (*Ibid.,* September-October 1899); "The Larynx as an Instrument of Music" (*Science,* May 17, 1901), and lastly, "What is Life?" (*Ibid.,* June 21, 1901).

From his youth LeConte was an ardent lover of camping and all sorts of outdoor sports. The experiences thus gained stood him in good stead when the pursuit of science rather than hunting or fishing brought him into similar conditions of life. He traveled widely over the Western states, often under most primitive conditions, and saw, and thought, and wrote of what he saw, with tireless energy. Passionately fond of outdoor life, he died, as he would doubtless have wished, while on a trip with the Sierra Club into the Yosemite.

[*The Autobiography of Joseph LeConte* (1903) ed. by W. D. Armes; E. W. Hilgard, memoir in *Biog. Memoirs Nat. Acad. Sci.,* vol. VI (1909); *San Francisco Call,* July 7, 1901; personal recollections.]

G. P. M.

LEDERER, JOHN (fl. 1669–1670), traveler and explorer, came to Virginia from Germany in 1668. Little is known about his antecedents but he must have had educational advantages, for he was familiar with several languages. From Governor Berkeley of Virginia who desired to find a passage through the mountains, he received a "commission of discovery" and the command of an expedition for that purpose. He made three marches, between March 1669 and September 1670. His first journey (Mar. 9–24, 1669), was from the head of the York River due west; he reached the top of the Blue Ridge Mountains, but did not descend their western slope. His second march (May–June 1670) was from the falls of the James River west and southwest, and through part of North Carolina; his third expedition left the falls of the Rappahannock in August 1670 and pushed westward to the mountains. Since there is no record of the visit of any white man to the upper Rappahannock after Capt. John Smith's explorations in 1608, and Smith may never have penetrated part of the region covered by his map, it is probable that Lederer entered territory never before visited by a white man. During this last expedition his companions became disheartened and deserted him. He ventured to continue his searches with only an Indian guide, who served him as an interpreter. His faithless companions did not expect him to survive and created prejudice against him by telling the people of Virginia that he had expended the public taxes of that year in his wanderings. Consequently, upon his return he was ill-treated by the inhabitants of Virginia and fled to Maryland to save his life. There he was naturalized in 1671 (*Archives of Maryland,* vol. II, 1884, pp. 282–83). He obtained a hearing from Sir William Talbot, a member of the Council, who found him a "modest ingenious person, and a pretty scholar," and determined to vindicate him by translating his account of his travels from Latin into English. Accordingly, *The Discoveries of John Lederer in Three Several Marches from Virginia, to the West of Carolina, and Other Parts of the Continent: Begun in March, 1669, and ended in September 1670, together with a General Map of the Whole Territory Which he Traversed,* was published in London in 1672. This book was the first scientific report upon the geology, botany, animals, and native tribes of the extensive district which it covered. Though Lederer appears to have reached only the "top of the Apalatæn

Mountains," he gives reasons for supposing that "they are certainly in a great errour, who imagine that the Continent of North *America* is but eight or ten days journey over from the *Atlantick* to the *Indian* Ocean." His account is generally accepted as descriptive of the Valley of Virginia, but his narrative seems apocryphal and his statements should be accepted with some reserve. The map that appeared in this volume is inaccurate, possibly because Lederer's instruments were carried off by his recreant companions.

[See *Bull. Fauquier Hist. Soc.*, Aug. 1921; *Va. Mag. of Hist. and Biog.*, Jan. 1901, April 1922; H. C. Groome, *Fauquier during the Proprietorship* (1927); Hermann Schuricht, *Hist. of the German Element in Va.*, I (1898), 40–41; H. A. Rattermann, *"Der Erste Erforscher des Alleghany Gebirges—Johannes Lederer,"* in *Der Deutsche Pionier*, Jan. 1877; F. L. Hawks, *Hist. of N. C.*, vol. II (1858); J. W. Wayland, *A Hist. of Rockingham County, Va.* (1912). Lederer's *Discoveries* was reprinted in 1891 and again in 1902, in very small editions.] F. W. S.

LE DUC, WILLIAM GATES (Mar. 29, 1823–Oct. 30, 1917), agriculturist, soldier, railroad promoter, and United States commissioner of agriculture, was born in Wilkesville, Gallia County, Ohio, the second son of Henry Savary and Mary (Stowell) Le Duc. His father's father was Henri Duc of Lyons, France, who came to America as a young officer in the army sent with Count D'Estaing to aid the colonies in the Revolution. About 1796, after stirring adventures in Guadeloupe, he came to Middletown, Conn., where he married Lucy, daughter of Col. John Sumner of the Colonial and Continental armies. Having acquired land near Gallipolis, Ohio, he moved thither with his family about 1812 and founded the settlement of Wilkesville. His son, in 1845, changed his name to Henry Savary Le Duc, believing that his father had left off the particle when he came to America because he thought the simple Duc more democratic. In order to attend school, William went to live in Lancaster, Ohio, where he was under the care of a great-uncle. He attended the Lancaster Academy and there had among his intimate companions William T. Sherman, John Sherman, and Thomas Ewing.

In 1844 he entered Kenyon College, Gambier, Ohio, graduating in 1848. He was afterward employed for about a year in introducing school books and law publications in the South and West. Meanwhile, he studied law and on Dec. 5, 1849, was admitted to the bar. He later spent several months in Boston and edited a book by J. Stanley Grimes [*q.v.*], entitled, *Etherology and the Phreno-philosophy of Mesmerism and Magic Eloquence* (1850). In July 1850 he moved to St. Paul, Minn., then a small village, where he opened a law office and a book and stationery store. Here, the following year, he brought his young bride, Mary Elizabeth Bronson, daughter of Rev. C. P. Bronson of Mount Vernon, Ohio, whom he had married on Mar. 25, 1851, and by whom he had four children. In connection with his book business he published the *Minnesota Yearbook* for 1851–53. He was active in the development of the region of which St. Paul was the center and in 1853 was appointed commissioner of Minnesota Territory at the exposition in New York, called the World's Fair. The display of products which he collected was largely influential in turning attention to Minnesota and the great opportunities it afforded settlers (see his article, "Minnesota at the Crystal Palace Exhibition, New York, 1853" in *Minnesota History Bulletin*, August 1916). In 1853 he secured the first charter for a railway in the territory and organized a company to build a railroad from St. Paul to Duluth. Mainly through his efforts that same year, the St. Paul Bridge Company was organized, which constructed the Wabasha Street Bridge, the first to be built over the Mississippi. Having acquired some land on the west side of the river, he laid out the town of West St. Paul. In 1856 he purchased a flour mill at Hastings, and was the first miller to manufacture and introduce upon the markets flour made from Minnesota spring wheat. Disposing of his St. Paul holdings in 1857, he moved to Hastings, which, except for the terms of his federal service and brief periods of travel, was his home during the remainder of his life.

In 1862 he entered the Union army as a captain in the quartermaster's department and was promoted to the rank of lieutenant-colonel, serving under McClellan, Hooker, Sherman, and Thomas. At the close of the war he was brevetted colonel and brigadier-general of volunteers. Returning to Hastings, he engaged in business and farming. He also projected and in part constructed the Hastings and Dakota Railroad, of which he was president until 1870. In July 1877 President Hayes appointed him United States commissioner of agriculture, which office he filled until June 30, 1881, performing its duties with conspicuous energy and ability. He established a tea farm at Summerville, S. C., to investigate the practicability of raising tea in the United States; he gave special attention to the production of sugar from sorghum and beets; and he secured a special appropriation for the investigation of animal diseases, which led to the establishment of the Bureau of Animal Industry. From 1890 to 1895 he was in Fayetteville, N. C., having been appointed by Secretary of the Treasury Windom as receiver of the national bank at that place.

He was a tall man, quick, active, and resourceful, and in his prime had great initiative and indomitable energy. He also had inventive ability (see "Genesis of the Typewriter," *Minnesota History Bulletin,* February 1916, in which he recounts his part in the development of the Remington typewriter). His personal papers and historical relics were presented to the Minnesota Historical Society, of which he was an active member for more than sixty-seven years. A paper by him on the organization and growth of the Historical Society is contained in its *Collections* (vol. IX, 1901). He died at Hastings in his ninety-fifth year.

[*Am. Ancestry,* vol. IV (1889); autobiography, typewritten copy in the U. S. Dept. of Agric. Lib.; G. S. Ives, "William Gates Le Duc," in *Minn. Hist. Bull.,* May 1919; W. H. C. Folsom, *Fifty Years in the Northwest* (1888); *Minn. Hist. Colls.,* vol. XIV (1912); D. S. Hall and R. I. Holcombe, *Hist. of the Minn. State Agric. Soc.* (1910); C. H. Greathouse, *Hist. Sketch of the U. S. Dept. of Agric.* (1898); *Who's Who in America,* 1916–17; T. M. Newson, *Pen Pictures of St. Paul* (1886); *Pioneer Press* (St. Paul), Oct. 31, 1917; *N. Y. Times,* Oct. 31, 1917.]

C. R. B.

LEDYARD, JOHN (1751–Jan. 10, 1789), explorer, was born in Groton, Conn., the son of John and Abigail (Hempstead) Ledyard and a nephew of William Ledyard [*q.v.*]. The father, a sea-captain, died at the age of thirty-five, and the mother remarried. The boy was then taken into the home of his paternal grandfather (also named John) at Hartford, where he attended grammar school. On the death of his grandfather he came under the guardianship of an uncle by marriage, Thomas Seymour, with whom for a time he studied law. In 1772, at the invitation of the Rev. Eleazar Wheelock [*q.v.*], the founder of Dartmouth College, he entered that institution with a view to becoming a missionary to the Indians; but though an apt student, he could not endure discipline, and in the following spring he returned to Hartford. Determined to see the world, he shipped as a sailor from New London for the Mediterranean. At Gibraltar he deserted and joined a British regiment, but was shortly afterward sent back to his vessel. Returning to New London, he went to New York, where he shipped for London. Here he presented himself to Capt. James Cook, then preparing for his third voyage, and as a corporal of marines sailed with the expedition that left the Thames on July 12, 1776. At Nootka Sound, which was reached in March 1778, he began to picture the vast possibilities of the northwestern fur trade and resolved to enter it at the first opportunity.

The return voyage, on which Cook was killed at the Hawaiian Islands, Feb. 14, 1779, brought him to London late in 1780. The American Revolution was still in progress, and refusing to serve against his countrymen, Ledyard remained in barracks for two years, and was then transferred to the North American station. Obtaining shore leave on reaching the Long Island coast in December 1782, he made himself known to his mother at Southold and then escaped to Hartford. After publishing his recollections of the voyage (*A Journal of Captain Cook's Last Voyage to the Pacific Ocean,* 1783), he went to New York and later to Philadelphia, trying to obtain aid for a sailing venture to the Northwest Coast. After a year's futile efforts he sailed for Spain in June 1784, and then went to France. Though he won the regard and friendly interest of Thomas Jefferson and Commodore John Paul Jones, and though success appeared certain a number of times, all his projects failed. He then proposed walking across Siberia, and in case he found a vessel that would take him to Nootka Sound, walking over the continent to Virginia. Jefferson approved the plan and sought a passport from the Empress Catherine, who refused it. Ledyard then went to London, where he at last found a vessel getting ready for a voyage to Nootka Sound. With funds supplied him by friends, he took passage in September 1786; but the vessel had hardly left the Thames before it was overtaken by a gunboat and brought back.

Reviving his Siberian project, he went to Hamburg, and by way of Norway, Sweden, and Lapland reached St. Petersburg. Catherine was absent, and he was permitted to go on. In September 1787, at Yakutsk, officials obstructed his progress and on Feb. 24, 1788, at Irkutsk, he was arrested by order of the Empress and brought back to the Polish boundary, where he was warned not to repeat the attempt. In London again at the beginning of May, "disappointed, ragged and penniless, but with a whole heart," he at once looked about for some new adventure. At the instance of Sir Joseph Banks he was engaged by the Association for Promoting the Discovery of the Interior Parts of Africa to explore the sources of the Niger. He left London at the end of July, visited Jefferson in Paris, telling the minister that his next journey would be from Kentucky to the Pacific, and then went on to Alexandria. At Cairo he arranged to accompany a caravan to the interior. Violent rage over delay in starting after the time of departure had been fixed brought on an illness which resulted in his death.

Ledyard was somewhat under six feet tall, of "rangy" and powerful build. His personality was attractive, even to those who could give him no higher appraisal than that of "the mad, romantic, dreaming Ledyard." Jefferson characterized him as a genius and earnestly sought to further his purposes. His dream of opening up the trade of the Pacific Northwest, which he followed with an unmatched singleness of purpose and which brought him only discouragement and disaster, came true for other men within less than a generation after his death.

[Jared Sparks, *The Life of John Ledyard* (1828); S. M. Schmucker, "John Ledyard," in *The Life of Dr. Elisha Kent Kane* (1858); *Proc. of the Asso. for Promoting the Discovery of the Interior Parts of Africa* (1810), I, 14–46; H. A. Tirrell, "Ledyard the Traveller," *Records and Papers of the New London County Hist. Soc.*, vol. III, Pt. II (1912); C. B. Moore, "John Ledyard, The Traveller," *N. Y. Geneal. and Biog. Record,* Jan. 1876; Henry Beston (Sheahan), "John Ledyard," in *The Book of Gallant Vagabonds* (1925); manuscript letter, Paine to Jefferson, June 18, 1789, Lib. of Cong.; *The Writings of Thomas Jefferson,* Memorial Ed. (1903–04), see Index.] W. J. G.

LEDYARD, WILLIAM (Dec. 6, 1738–Sept. 6, 1781), Revolutionary soldier, was born at Groton, Conn., a descendant of John Ledyard who sailed from Bristol, England, and settled in Connecticut. Ledyard's parents were John and Deborah (Youngs) Ledyard, and a nephew was the celebrated traveler John Ledyard [*q.v.*]. Practically nothing is known of William's early life. "Of fine form and good education for the times" is a description by N. H. Burnham (*post,* p. 32). He was married in January 1761 to Anne Williams of Stonington, by whom he had nine children. From the beginning of the Revolution he was a member of the committee of correspondence and of the military committee of his town. In 1776 he was made captain of artillery, and his command was extended to include the towns in the neighborhood. This part of the coast was exposed to British attacks, and had long been threatened. In the autumn of 1781 Benedict Arnold [*q.v.*], now a British general, led a raid into his native state, following a similar incursion into Virginia. He took New London, and dispatched Lieutenant-Colonel Eyre to capture Fort Griswold on Groton Heights, across the Thames River (Sept. 6, 1781). The fort was defended by Ledyard with a small body of militia, to a large degree youths, and poorly armed. The British commander, who had two battalions of regular infantry—800 men in all—demanded surrender, which Ledyard refused. Eyre then sent a second demand, stating that nc quarter would be granted if resistance was made. Ledyard again returned a spirited refusal, ordered his men to reserve fire, and inflicted a heavy loss. Eyre, who led one assaulting column, was mortally wounded; and Montgomery, who commanded the other column, was killed. Overwhelmed by numbers, Ledyard surrendered to Bromfield, who had succeeded to Eyre's place. A survivor of the conflict relates the event which followed: To Bromfield's demand: "Who commands this Fort?" Ledyard replied: "I did, but you do now," at the same moment tendering his sword (Hempstead, *post*). Ledyard was killed almost at once, apparently with his own sword, though the witnesses differ as to the British officer who was responsible for the deed. Ledyard's death was followed by a general massacre of the garrison, the odium of which has fallen upon Arnold, although he was not actually present. On the scene of the battle a monument was erected in 1830, and in 1854 Ledyard was honored by a smaller monument in the cemetery.

[C. B. Todd, "The Massacre at Fort Griswold" and J. A. Stevens, "The Ledyard Family," *Mag. of Am. Hist.,* Sept. 1881; J. A. Stevens, "The Family of Ledyard," *N. Y. Geneal. and Biog. Record,* Jan. 1876; narrative of Stephen Hempstead, a survivor of the battle, in *Missouri Republican* (St. Louis), Feb. 23, 1826; W. W. Harris, *The Battle of Groton Heights* (1870; rev. and enl. by Charles Allyn, 1882), containing narratives of Hempstead and others, but giving Ledyard's parents incorrectly; J. J. Copp, *Battle of Groton Heights* (1879); N. H. Burnham, *The Battle of Groton Heights* (1907); F. M. Caulkins, *Hist. of New London, Conn.* (1852); C. R. Stark, *Groton, Conn., 1705–1905* (1922); B. T. Marshall, *Modern Hist. of New London County* (1922).] E. K. A.

LEE, ALFRED (Sept. 9, 1807–Apr. 12, 1887), Protestant Episcopal bishop of Delaware, was born in Cambridge, Mass., and died in Wilmington, Del. His father, Benjamin Lee, was a native of Somersetshire, England, and had at one time been a midshipman in the British navy. His mother, Elizabeth (Leighton), also of English extraction, was connected with the family of William Pitt. Alfred graduated at Harvard College in 1827 and at once began the study of law. After admission to the bar he practised for two years in New London, Conn., and then entered the General Theological Seminary, New York. Graduating in 1837, he was ordered deacon on May 21, 1837, and made priest on June 12, 1838, by the Rt. Rev. Thomas Church Brownell. After a few months' service at Poquetanuck, Conn., he removed to Calvary Church, Rockdale, Pa. On Oct. 12, 1841, he was consecrated as the first bishop of Delaware in St. Paul's Chapel, New York City.

He at once removed to Wilmington, Del., where in October 1842 he became rector of St. Andrew's Church, remaining such throughout his life. It had long been the custom for bishops to be rectors of parishes, especially in the weaker dioceses, thereby securing their support in the absence of episcopal endowments; and Delaware was a weak diocese. Organized in 1786, it had no bishop until the consecration of Dr. Lee. There were in the diocese only four clergymen regularly conducting services of the Episcopal Church, and only 339 communicants. Bishop Lee was a pronounced Evangelical in his theological position and familiar with the Calvinistic theology of his school. He also had the fervor and zeal for souls likewise characteristic of Evangelicalism. Under his episcopal care new life was roused in all parts of the diocese. For a long time at least one new church was consecrated or an old one restored and opened almost every year. In 1863 he was assigned by the presiding bishop to exercise episcopal functions in Haiti, and was instrumental in establishing a mission there under the care of the American Church Missionary Society. He was also much interested in the Mexico mission, which had originated in the secession of some clergy from the Roman Catholic Church. In 1875 he was sent to Mexico to inquire into this movement and to perform episcopal duties. He confirmed over a hundred persons and ordained seven as priests. As a result of his visit the Mexican body was recognized as a foreign church under the care of the Protestant Episcopal Church (C. C. Tiffany, *History of the Protestant Episcopal Church in the United States of America,* 1895, pp. 519–20). Bishop Lee was regarded as a man of great scholarship and received honorary degrees from several institutions. His writings, however, are of the mildly edifying character common in his school of thought: *Life of the Apostle Peter in a Series of Practical Discourses* (1852); *A Life Hid in Christ with God* (1856), being a memoir of Susan Allibone; *Life of the Apostle John in a Series of Practical Discourses* (1857); *Eventful Nights in Bible History* (1886); and various sermons. He was, however, able to do more scholarly work as a member of the American committee which took part in preparing the revised version of the New Testament (1881). Here his conservative views, combined with a sound, if somewhat old-fashioned, scholarship in Greek and Hebrew, found a useful place. From May 31, 1884, to Apr. 12, 1887, he was the presiding bishop of the Protestant Episcopal Church. He married, in 1832, Julia White, daughter of Elihu White of New London, and was the father of eight children.

[Brief autobiog. sketch, privately printed; journal of Gen. Conventions of the P. E. Ch. and of the Del. Diocesan Conventions; Alfred Lee, *Memoir of Benjamin Lee* (1875); *Alfred Lee* (1888), a biography published by St. Andrew's Church, Wilmington; Heman Dyer, "Rt. Rev. Alfred Lee," in the *Churchman,* Apr. 23, 1887; *Living Ch. Ann.,* 1887; *Wilmington Daily Commercial,* Apr. 13, 1887.]

J. C. Ay—r.

LEE, ANN (Feb. 29, 1736–Sept. 8, 1784), founder of the Shakers in America, was born in Manchester, England. Though she is known in Shaker history as Ann Lee, her family name was probably Lees, a common surname in Lancashire at the time of her birth. Her father, John, was a blacksmith; she had five brothers and two sisters, and with them was sent to work early, never learning to read or write. She was employed first in a cotton factory, then as cook in the Manchester Infirmary, and later as a cutter of hatter's fur. In 1758 she joined a society called the Shaking Quakers, or Shakers, which had been founded in Manchester eleven years before as a result of the revivals conducted by the exiled Camisards. The form of worship centered about an open confession of sin, and the prophecies centered about the second appearance of Christ. On Jan. 5, 1762, according to the Manchester Cathedral register (Axon, *post*), Ann Lees was married to Abraham Standerin (known in Shaker history as Stanley or Standley). He was a blacksmith, by whom she had four children who died in infancy. She became obsessed with a morbid repugnance toward marriage and a conviction of the sin of sexual relations which caused her great mental suffering. In 1770, during an imprisonment for "profanation of the Sabbath," she received such an extraordinary illumination of "the mystery of iniquity, of the root and foundation of human depravity" that she was acknowledged by the society as their leader and thereafter called Ann the Word, or, more often, Mother Ann. She began to "speak with tongues" and to preach openly against marriage and sexual intercourse, and the authorities made several attempts to quiet her. In her later life she related these persecutions to her followers in elaborate detail, with emphasis on her miraculous escapes.

A vision, in 1774, directed her to go to America; and accordingly she and her husband, her brother, William Lee (or Lees), Nancy Lee, her niece, John Hocknell (whose generosity made the expedition possible), and a few others arrived in New York on Aug. 6. John Hocknell and William Lee went up the Hudson and secured a tract of land in Niskayuna, near Albany, where the village of Watervliet later stood. Mother Ann and her husband remained in New York, where she earned what she could by washing and ironing and he was employed in a blacksmith's shop. He later became ill and they were reduced to extreme poverty. When he recovered he renounced his "Shaker principles" and went off to live with another woman. In the summer of 1776 Ann joined the group near Albany. Here for three and a half years they lived together and worked on their buildings and held their religious meetings. Mother Ann continued to have visions and revelations concerning the conduct of the "Church." Her followers called themselves "the first witnesses of the Gospel of Christ's Second Appearing," and the church which was organized after her death was called "The United Society of Believers in Christ's Second Appearing," or "The Millennial Church." Mother Ann was herself regarded as this second appearance of Christ, Jesus having been the first, and both being necessary for the complete revelation of the Father-Mother God.

The group became known through the region, and because they preached against war and would not bear arms or take oaths, they were accused of pro-British sympathies and secret correspondence. In July 1780 "Ann Standerren" and the elders were arrested by the Albany County Commissioners for Detecting Conspiracies (*Minutes, post*), and imprisoned on charges of high treason. In December she was released, her brother, William Lees [*sic*], being one of the bondsmen for her good behavior. In the following year the religious revivals continued and the number of "Believers" was greatly increased. In May 1781 Mother Ann and some of the elders started on a tour through New England where there were already scattered groups of Shakers. They held meetings in many places and endured persecutions. Mother Ann's messages on this tour seem to have been more practical than prophetic. She encouraged simple honesty, frugality, and industry; urging her hearers to "put your hands to work, and give your hearts to God." She returned to Watervliet in July 1783 literally worn out, and died there in September of the following year. After her death the little that was known of her life and her own conversations and reminiscences were elaborated by her disciples, and their "testimonies" are full of "incidents" which constitute the framework of the largely legendary biography current among Shakers.

[W. E. A. Axon, *Lancashire Gleanings* (1883), pp. 79–107; Thomas Brown, *An Account of the People Called Shakers* (1812); *Testimonies of the Life, Character, Revelations and Doctrines of Mother Ann Lee* (collected by Rufus Bishop in 1812, revised by S. Y. Wells in 1816; second edition, revised by G. B. Avery, 1888); Calvin Green and S. Y. Wells, *A Summary View of the Millennial Church* (1823); B. S. Youngs, *The Testimony of Christ's Second Appearing* (1808; rev. 1810; 4th ed., 1856, with biography of Mother Ann appended); F. W. Evans, *Shakers: Compendium of the Origin*, etc. (1859); Charles Nordhoff, *The Communistic Societies of the U. S.* (1875); V. H. Paltsits, *Minutes of the Commissioners for Detecting and Defeating Conspiracies in the State of N. Y., Albany County Sessions, 1778–1781*, II (1909), 469–71, 504, 589, 592; Clara E. Sears, *Gleanings from Old Shaker Journals* (1916); J. P. MacLean, *A Bibliog. of Shaker Literature* (1905).]

H. W. S—r.

LEE, ARTHUR (Dec. 21, 1740–Dec. 12, 1792), diplomatist, was of the fourth generation of the Lees of Virginia, being the great-grandson of Richard Lee [*q.v.*], the first American immigrant, grandson of the second Richard and Lettice Corbin, and son of Thomas Lee, whose wife was Hannah Ludwell, daughter of Col. Philip Ludwell of "Green Spring." Born at "Stratford," the family seat in Westmoreland County, Va., built by his father, he was the eleventh child of his parents and the brother of Richard Henry, Francis Lightfoot, and William Lee [*qq.v.*]. The father having died when Arthur was only about ten years of age, the boy came under the guardianship of his eldest brother, by whom he was sent to Eton for his academic education. From Eton he passed to the University of Edinburgh, where he studied general science, polite literature, and medicine, and received in 1764 the degree of M.D. (*List of the Graduates in Medicine in the University of Edinburgh from MDCCV. to MDCCCLXVI.*, 1867, p. 8). After traveling a few months in Europe he returned to Virginia and began the practice of medicine in Williamsburg (1766). Shortly after his return to America he was elected a fellow of the Royal Society (May 29, 1766.) He did not, however, linger long at physic. America was just then deeply stirred by the Stamp Act agitation, and politics lured him with a stronger appeal. Accordingly, forsaking medicine for the law, the mounting block to politics, he returned to London in 1768, where he studied in Lincoln's Inn and the Middle Temple, subsequently establishing himself there in the practice of his new profession. His admission to the bar was in the spring of 1775, not in 1770, as usually stated (Jones, *post*, p. 123).

Whatever his other aptitudes and tastes, he soon discovered an eager pen. With the appearance of Dickinson's "Farmer's Letters," Lee set about writing a similar series, "The Monitor's Letters," designed, as he expressed it, to aid the "Farmer's Letters" in their operation "in alarming and informing" his countrymen. These, ten in number, were first printed in Rind's *Virginia Gazette* (Feb. 25–Apr. 28, 1768), at a time when Lee was in America. In London he found an alluring field for his controversial talents. At the beginning of 1769 the English political world was set agog by the "Junius Letters," and Lee, dipping his pen into the Junius bottle, proceeded to write a series of letters, some addressed to sundry British statesmen, others to the people of England, wherein, with a copious use of sarcasm and invective, he discussed American affairs, and signed himself "Junius Americanus." In some similar communications he used the signature "Raleigh." Though Jefferson, for one, had a poor opinion of the "Monitor's Letters" (P. L. Ford, *The Writings of Thomas Jefferson,* IX, 1898, p. 418), Lee's writings won him a considerable repute among political leaders in America, one consequence of which was that in 1770, mainly through the influence of Samuel Adams, he was chosen as agent of Massachusetts in London. The essay which probably deserves most consideration is *An Appeal to the Justice and Interests of the People of Great Britain,* ostensibly "By an Old Member of Parliament," published in 1774 and followed in 1775 by a *Second Appeal.*

In the meantime, Arthur Lee, together with his mercantile brother, William, plunged into London politics. In this activity he was the intimate associate as well as the political confrère of the notorious John Wilkes, for whom he conceived a great admiration. He procured the insertion in the famous Middlesex Petition of a resolution protesting against the obnoxious American measures, and the chief burden of much that he wrote was that the cause of Middlesex was the cause of Englishmen everywhere. During this period he nourished hopes that he might himself become a member of Parliament. In November 1775, he was asked by the committee of secret correspondence of the Continental Congress to become its confidential correspondent in London, and he made a characteristic beginning of his diplomatic career by casting suspicions upon some of the men who had appointed him. In October 1776, he was appointed (in place of Jefferson, who had declined) one of three commissioners, to negotiate a treaty with France and solicit aid. Joining his colleagues, Franklin and Deane, in Paris at the end of December, he found Deane, in France since July as the secret commercial agent of Congress, busily engaged in procuring supplies, and France not yet disposed to treat with the United States openly. Therefore, since he seemed not to be needed in Paris, with the advice of Franklin and Deane, he betook himself to Spain (February 1777) to see what he could do there. He was not permitted to proceed as far as Madrid, but he did succeed in obtaining through a commercial house substantial aid from the Spanish government. He next journeyed to Berlin (May to July 1777), where also he was refused recognition and succeeded only in having his papers filched.

Returned to Paris, he resumed making complaints against his colleagues. He even had the temerity at this time (Oct. 4, 1777) to suggest to Samuel Adams and Richard Henry Lee that he be made sole minister to France and that Franklin and Deane be sent to some less important corners of Europe. The chief controversy with Deane was whether or not the supplies which France was secretly furnishing the United States through Beaumarchais and his fictitious commercial house, Roderigue Hortalez & Company, were to be paid for. On the face of the evidence they were, but Lee, on the basis of conversations with Beaumarchais before Deane's coming, asserted that they were a gift and persistently pressed this contention upon Congress. Moreover, as he viewed Deane's numerous commercial transactions, his perfervid imagination saw many instances of guilt where there was at worst only error, and accusations of fraud and peculation, mounting in virulence with each increment and repetition, were poured into the ears of his friends in Congress. His distrust of Franklin, which had had earlier beginnings, deepened, now that Franklin usually supported Deane, and the charges against him became scarcely less severe than those against Deane. Deane, Beaumarchais, Franklin, and a crew of others, he declared, were plundering the public. "I am more and more satisfied," he wrote to his brother, Richard Henry, Sept. 12, 1778, "that the old doctor is concerned in the plunder, and that in time we shall collect the proofs" (*Life,* II, p. 148, in cipher). This was characteristic: accusations following close upon the heels of suspicion; proofs to be collected in time.

While these troubles were yet in their infancy, Congress, in May 1777, selected two more commissioners, William Lee and Ralph Izard. The former was appointed to the courts of Berlin and Vienna, the latter to the court of Tuscany, but they were destined to remain for the most part in Paris to confound wisdom and to add their grumblings to the general confusion. Arthur Lee was about the same time commissioned to the court of Spain, but he also remained in Paris. Congress had sown "militia diplomacy"; it reaped what might well be called guerrilla or sniping diplomacy. Despite, however, the bickerings among the representatives of the United States at the French capital, but thanks mainly to the success of arms at Saratoga, treaties of alliance and of amity and commerce were negotiated with France and signed by all three commissioners (Feb. 6, 1778). So far as Deane was concerned, this was nearly his last diplomatic act; for, largely in consequence of Lee's charges, he had been recalled (Dec. 8, 1777), and upon his return to America was harried for several months by Congress, then dismissed. In the midst of his ordeal, however, he turned upon his arch pursuer with counter charges, out of which came at least one significant development, namely, that Arthur Lee did not have the confidence of the French minister, Vergennes. As a consequence of all this Congress was split into two hostile factions, the supporters of Lee and the supporters of Deane. After mulling over these charges and counter charges through a good many months, Congress finally came to the solemn conviction that, whatever the truth, the "suspicions and animosities" which had arisen among the commissioners were "highly prejudicial to the honor and interests of these United States" (*Journals,* Apr. 15, 1779). Then came Arthur Lee's turn to be superseded (Sept. 27, 1779). William Lee and Ralph Izard had preceded him in dismissal. Franklin alone had successfully run the gauntlet.

Lee returned to America in September 1780, was elected to the Virginia House of Delegates in 1781, then to the Continental Congress, in which he served until 1784. But he was unhappy even in Congress, where, he declared, he could only lament what he could not prevent (letter to Samuel Adams, Apr. 21, 1782, *Letters of Members of the Continental Congress,* vol. VI, forthcoming), and where it was his fate to be frustrated in his favorite objects (Madison to Randolph, Oct. 8, 1782, *Ibid.*). Under the appointment of Congress he was one of the commissioners who negotiated the Indian treaties of Fort Stanwix (Oct. 22, 1784) and Fort McIntosh (Jan. 21, 1785). In July 1785, he was appointed by Congress to the treasury board and, despite Jefferson's prediction (*Writings,* IV, 1894, p. 53), held that office until the inauguration of the new government. He opposed the adoption of the Constitution. The few remaining years of his life were spent on his estate, "Lansdowne," Middlesex County, Va. He was never married.

[See R. H. Lee, *Life of Arthur Lee* (2 vols., 1829), containing selections from his correspondence (eulogistic and inaccurate); C. H. Lee, *A Vindication of Arthur Lee* (1894); E. J. Lee, *Lee of Va., 1642–1892* (1895); Francis Wharton, *The Revolutionary Diplomatic Correspondence of the U. S.* (1889), of which Vol. I contains a discussion of his character and career; E. A. Jones, *Am. Members of the Inns of Court* (1924); E. S. Kite, *Beaumarchais and the War of Am. Independence* (2 vols., 1918); and "The Deane Papers," *N. Y. Hist. Soc. Colls.,* Publication Fund Series, vols. XIX–XXIII (1887–91). Sparks's review of the *Life,* by R. H. Lee, in the *North Am. Rev.,* Apr. 1830, is especially useful. The chief collections of MSS., aside from the official correspondence in the Library of Congress, are those in the possession of the Harvard University Library, the American Philosophical Society, the University of Virginia, and the Virginia Historical Society.]

E. C. B.

LEE, CHARLES (1731–Oct. 2, 1782), soldier of fortune, Revolutionary general, was born at Dernhall, Cheshire, England, the son of John and Isabella (Bunbury) Lee. He went to school at Bury St. Edmunds and, later, in Switzerland. In 1747 he was ensign in his father's regiment (De Fonblanque, *post,* pp. 159–60), and, on May 2, 1751, was commissioned lieutenant in the 44th Regiment. His baptism of fire occurred in 1755, when the 44th accompanied the Braddock expedition into western Pennsylvania. After the retreat from Fort Duquesne, Lee was sent to the Mohawk Valley, N. Y., where in 1756 he purchased a captaincy for £900. There he was adopted into a Mohawk tribe under an alleged Indian name, "Ounewaterika," said to mean "boiling water," and married the daughter of a Seneca chief ("Lee Papers," *post,* I, 4–5). Lee was with the 44th during Abercromby's disastrous attack on Fort Ticonderoga in July 1758. Badly wounded, he was transported back to Albany, and thence went to Long Island. Here he got into an altercation with a surgeon, whom he whipped and who afterward tried to assassinate him. Rejoining his regiment, when the tide began to turn in favor of the British, Lee was present at the capture of Fort Niagara from the French and with Amherst at the capture of Montreal, Sept. 8, 1760. In the winter of 1760–61 he returned to England. Certain controversial pamphlets of this period are attributed to him, probably incorrectly (Sparks, *post,* ch. 1).

On Aug. 10, 1761, he was appointed major in the 103rd Regiment. The next year he accompanied the British expeditionary force to Portugal, where he became lieutenant-colonel and served brilliantly under Burgoyne in the campaign of Villa Velha (De Fonblanque, p. 50). Returning peace saw him once more in England, where the 103rd was disbanded and Lee put on half pay, in November 1763. About this time, seeing no future ahead in England, he considered a plan for establishing colonies in the Illinois country. Instead of concerning himself with that project, however, he went to Poland, then under Stanislaus Poniatowski. He reached Warsaw in March 1765, and soon was on intimate terms with the pro-Russian king. Going on an embassy to Constantinople in 1766, he almost froze to death when he was snowbound in the Balkans, and he escaped with his life during the Constantinople earthquake of May 23, 1766. By December he had returned to England; he had just been granted 20,000 acres in Florida. In 1767 and 1768 he remained in England with no particular employment save playing the races and criticizing the government. Because of this latter activity, he has been identified as the author of the *Letters of Junius,* but this is a hardly tenable theory. In 1769 a civil war broke out in Poland, precipitated by the Confederation of Bar against Stanislaus, and Lee rushed back to Warsaw to take sides with his friend. This time he was made "general and adjutant" ("Lee Papers," I, 87) in the Polish service, that is, in the pro-Russian faction. He accompanied the Russian armies against Turkey in the campaign of the winter of 1769–70, fell ill, was invalided back to Hungary, and recuperated on the Mediterranean. The summer of 1771 found him again in England, but the following winter he went to France. During all this time his writings were marked by a bitter hatred of the Tory party in England and a desire to be forever fighting for "liberty"—without any very clear idea of the meaning of the term.

He returned to America in 1773 and took up land in Berkeley County, Va. (now W. Va.), in 1775. To the pamphlet controversy preceding the American Revolution he contributed *Strictures on a Pamphlet, entitled, "A Friendly Address to All Reasonable Americans"* (1774), an attack upon the conciliatory efforts of Dr. Myles Cooper. When the war broke out between Great Britain and the colonies in 1775, he was almost violently on the patriot side. His military experience and capacity for self-advertisement helped him to insinuate himself into the councils of the Continental Congress, so that when, on June 22, 1775, he renounced his half pay in the British army, he had already (June 17, 1775) been appointed second major-general of the Continental Army. In accepting this appointment he insisted upon being compensated for whatever losses he might sustain through the confiscation of his English estates, as his new holdings in Berkeley County, Va., were not yet paid for.

In July he was at the American camp at Cambridge, Mass., and served during the siege of Boston. Early in 1776 he was ordered to New York to superintend the defense of that city, where he encountered some difficulty in dealing with the state officials, not yet accustomed to a federal authority. After ordering Lee to Canada, Congress countermanded the order, and, on Mar. 1, 1776, sent him off to oppose the British in the South. He reached Williamsburg, Va., Mar. 29, and remained there until May 12, organizing a cooperative effort by Virginia and North Carolina. On June 4 he reached Charleston, where Gov. John Rutledge put the South Carolina troops under his command ("Lee Papers," II, 57). Col. William Moultrie was already at work upon the defenses of the city, particularly upon the fort on Sullivan's Island. Lee did not look with favor upon this post, and spent most of his time arranging for the retreat of Moultrie's force, when the British should attack it. The assault on Fort Moultrie finally took place on June 28, 1776, while Lee was at Hedrals Point. The British failed on both land and sea, but credit for the American victory clearly belongs to Moultrie, as Lee generously admitted in his dispatches. The rest of the summer Lee spent supervising the defenses of South Carolina and Georgia.

Upon the retirement of the British from the southern area in the late summer of 1776, Lee was ordered back to rejoin the main army. In Philadelphia, on his way north (Oct. 7, 1776), he learned that Congress had generously advanced him $30,000 to pay for his Virginia plantation. This flattery, and the exaggerated reputation for his success in the Carolinas, increased his tendency to criticize his superiors on all occasions. He reached Washington's headquarters before the battle of White Plains. After that battle, Lee's division was posted at Philipsburg, N. Y. When it became apparent that the British general, Howe, intended to pursue Washington in his retreat across New Jersey, the latter sent Lee repeated and increasingly peremptory orders to join the main army. Lee was extremely dilatory in complying with these instructions, explaining that he preferred to hang on the flank of the British and harass them. This policy was consistent with his opinion that the Americans could not stand in a pitched battle against the British but that they could best them in guerrilla warfare. It is also consistent with the theory that Lee wished to play a lone hand and gain some brilliant individual success, the credit for which he would not have to share with the Commander-in-Chief. On Dec. 12 he reached Basking Ridge, N. J., whence he wrote his famous letter to Gates condemning Washington for the loss of Fort Washington and remarking "*entre nous,* a certain great man is most damnably deficient" ("Lee Papers," II, 348). His headquarters at Basking Ridge was four miles from his division, and only twenty miles from the British under Cornwallis. On the very next day, a detachment of Colonel Harcourt's British dragoons rushed his headquarters and took Lee prisoner in a manner most humiliating to him.

He was taken to New York, where General Howe had orders from Germain to return him to England for trial as a deserter from the British army. Fortunately for the British, Howe understood that Lee had actually resigned his half pay in the British army before joining the Americans, and that therefore retaliation would ensue if the orders from London were obeyed (W. C. Ford, *The Writings of George Washington,* V, 1890, p. 168). Lee was kept for a year in close and exasperating confinement. After a winter's imprisonment, he apparently became so intimate with Howe that he drew up a document giving the British information as to how to defeat the Americans. At present it is not known for whom this was prepared, or to whom it was given. It never came to light until 1858, when it was found among the papers of Henry Strachey, who had been with the Howes in their effort to conciliate America in 1776–77 (G. H. Moore, *post,* pp. 75 ff.). Historians have since drawn the conclusion that Lee was a traitor. The document is clearly in Lee's writing and is indorsed "Mr. Lee's Plan, 29th March 1777" (*Ibid.,* facsimile). At the same time Lee was sending insistent notes to Washington and to Congress requesting that a committee of Congress be sent to confer with him and the two Howes, with veiled hints that great things might be expected from such a conference. Congress and Washington wisely refused to accede to this suggestion. It is altogether possible that Lee, with his propensity for writing familiarly to his old friends in the British army, never saw this affair as treason. It is also possible that the "Plan" was a deliberate blind, intended to mislead Howe. It is, however, extremely difficult for the historian to deny that it was giving aid and comfort to the enemies of the United States.

In April 1778 Lee was exchanged, and in May went to York, Pa., where Congress was in session. Here he had the temerity to ask why he had not been promoted during his captivity, and to criticize the promotion of others in his absence ("Lee Papers," II, 392). On May 20, 1778, he rejoined the army at Valley Forge, just as it was setting out on the Monmouth campaign. When Washington was determined to attack the British army, retreating from Philadelphia, the work of beginning that attack should, by seniority, have fallen to Lee. He declined on the ground that he did not believe the Americans could stand up against the British regulars. Lafayette was then given the honor of leading the attack, whereupon Lee reconsidered and demanded the privilege, which the Marquis surrendered with extreme generosity and courtesy. The ensuing circumstances brought to an end Lee's career as a successful soldier of fortune. Wayne began the attack at Monmouth, and to his horror saw Lee's main body begin to retreat behind him without warning. Wayne had to fall back and the retreat of the Americans speedily took on the semblance of a rout, when Washington came up with Greene, Steuben, and the rest of the army. What actually passed between the Commander-in-Chief and the retreating Lee will probably never be known. Washington stopped the retreat, reformed the army, threw Greene, Stirling, and Wayne into the battle, and fought the British to a standstill until nightfall, when they decamped into the darkness, heading for their boats and New York (Stryker, *post*).

Without waiting for Washington's reprimand for this apparently cowardly retreat, Lee addressed an insulting letter to the Commander-in-Chief, demanding an apology for the words spoken in the heat of battle. Washington curtly refused to apologize. Demanding a court of inquiry, Lee immediately got a court martial, which sat at Brunswick from July 4 to Aug. 12, 1778. He was found guilty of disobedience of orders, misbehavior before the enemy, and disrespect to the Commander-in-Chief, and was then mildly sentenced to be suspended from the army for twelve months. He hung around the army until September, when he went to Philadelphia. Thence he wrote numerous quibbling letters to Congress, complaining of ill treatment. On Dec. 3, 1778, he published his "Vindication" (*Pennsylvania Packet,* Dec. 3, 1778; "Lee Papers," III, 255–69), which was so abusive of Washington that Col. John Laurens challenged Lee to a duel and wounded him, so that he could not take up another challenge from Anthony Wayne. By the following July Lee had retired to his estate in Virginia whence he wrote frequent and querulous letters to Congress, the newspapers, and all his friends. On Jan. 10, 1780, in consequence of an insulting letter to Congress, he was finally dismissed from the army. After living on in Virginia for two years more, he went to Philadelphia where, on Oct. 2, 1782, he died.

Lee is one of the most extraordinary and contradictory characters in American history. He had an exaggerated sense of his own ability and importance, and extraordinary luck in impressing them upon other people, until his capture by the British in 1776. His contemporaries agree that Rushbrooke's merciless caricature of him (G. H. Moore, *post*) gives a true idea of what he looked like. In anger he had little control over either his tongue or his pen. He so persistently interfered in matters which were not his business, by offering advice and criticism unasked, that one must marvel at the patience of his correspondents and particularly of his superiors. Men like John Adams and Benjamin Rush can rightly be blamed for encouraging his overweening ego. Yet British officers like Gage, Howe, and Burgoyne took his personal letters to them in all seriousness. As to whether his conduct at Monmouth was actual treason, planned ahead of time with the British commander, there may be two opinions. Clinton afterward said that Lee had to retreat. On the other hand, Washington said that Lee never should have accepted the command if he did not intend to fight; and there is ample evidence that Wayne, when he saw Lee retreating, twice sent frantic inquiries as to what to do and was never answered. It is equally clear that Lee was forgetful about sending orders, ignorant of the terrain of the battlefield, negligent in informing himself, and that he was almost crazed by the heat of June 28, 1778. But Lee had many redeeming qualities. He was extremely generous to his friends and considerate of his soldiers, and he had a genius for making loyal friends of important people.

He was buried in Christ Church graveyard in Philadelphia, despite his express desire that in death he be spared association with any church ("Lee Papers," IV, 31). His estate in Virginia was by his will divided among four loyal friends, and all his other property went to his sister in England.

[The papers left to Lee's friend, William Goddard of Baltimore, were published in 4 vols., as "The Lee Papers," *Colls. of the N. Y. Hist. Soc., for the Years 1871, 1872, 1873, 1874* (1872–75). The Lib. of Cong. has Lee's Orderly Book for 1776. Of biographies, the best is still Jared Sparks, in *Lives of Charles Lee and Joseph Reed* (1846); but see also Edward Langworthy, *Memoirs of the Life of the Late Charles Lee* (1792); and Sir Henry Bunbury, "Memoir of Charles Lee," in *The Correspondence of Sir Thomas Hanmer* (1838). All three of these have been printed in "The Lee Papers," as has Geo. H. Moore, *"Mr. Lee's Plan—Mar. 29, 1777," The Treason of Charles Lee, Major General* (1860), which considers the document found among the Strachey Papers. John Fiske, "Charles Lee," in *Essays Historical and Literary* (1902), vol. I, may also be mentioned. The best account of the end of Lee's military career is in W. S. Stryker, *The Battle of Monmouth* (1927), revised and edited by W. S. Myers. For the trial, see *Proc. of a General Court Martial . . . of Maj. Gen. Lee* (1778, 1864). The Junius question is discussed in John Almon, *The Letters of Junius* (2 vols., 1806); Thos. Girdlestone, *Reasons for Rejecting . . . the Presumptive Evidence of Mr. Almon* (1807), and *Facts Tending to Prove that Gen. Lee . . . was the Author of Junius* (1813). W. S. Baker has edited the MS. of Elias Boudinot, "Exchange of Major-General Charles Lee," *Pa. Mag. of Hist. and Biog.*, Apr. 1891. See also E. B. De Fonblanque, *Pol. and Mil. Episodes . . . Derived from the Life and Correspondence of the Right Hon. John Burgoyne* (1876); Wm. Moultrie, *Memoirs of the Am. Revolution*, etc. (2 vols., 1802); H. Lee, *Memoirs of the War in the Southern Department* (1812); Jas. Wilkinson, *Memoirs* (3 vols., 1816); John Drayton, *Memoirs of the Am. Revolution*, etc. (1821); *The Life, Public Services, Addresses and Letters of Elias Boudinot* (2 vols., 1896), ed. by J. J. Boudinot; *The Life and Letters of Lady Sarah Lennox* (2 vols., 1901), ed. by the Countess of Ilchester and Lord Stavordale; the writings of contemporary statesmen, and the various collections of sources for the Revolution and the Continental Congress.]

R. G. A—s.

LEE, CHARLES (1758–June 24, 1815), jurist, attorney-general, was the second son of Henry Lee and his wife Lucy Grymes, and the brother of "Light-Horse Harry" Lee and Richard Bland Lee [*qq.v.*]. He was descended from Richard Lee [*q.v.*], the emigrant ancestor of the family. In 1770 he entered the College of New Jersey where he was commended by President Witherspoon for his "application and genius." He received the degree of A.B. in 1775. In 1777 he was serving as "naval officer of the South Potomac" and apparently retained the office until 1789, when the Virginia office ended and he applied to Washington for retention as customhouse officer. His appointment as "collector of the port of Alexandria" was confirmed by the Senate in August 1789 and he served until 1793. His friendship for Washington was rooted in early attachments. He shared Washington's political outlook, gave him constant support, and aided in the struggle in Virginia for the ratification of the Constitution. At some time he studied law in Philadelphia, where he was admitted to the bar in June 1794 (J. H. Martin, *Martin's Bench and Bar of Philadelphia,* 1883). From 1793 to 1795 he was a member of the General Assembly of Virginia for Fairfax County. He vigorously supported Washington's policies and stanchly sought to stem the enthusiasm in Virginia for Genet and France and for Thomas Jefferson. On Nov. 19, 1795, Washington offered him the appointment to the office of attorney-general of the United States to succeed William Bradford. Lee accepted the appointment on Nov. 30 and held the office until the overthrow of the Federalists in 1801. He was persistent in his opposition to a conciliatory policy toward France, advised the recall of Monroe as minister to that country in 1796, and was sympathetic in his views with his close friend John Marshall.

President Adams sought in his final appointments to take care of Charles Lee among other Federalists and on Feb. 18, 1801, nominated him as judge of one of the new circuit courts. His confirmation on Mar. 3, 1801, placed him among the so-called "midnight judges." When Congress in 1802 repealed the Judiciary Act of the previous administration Lee retired to his home in Virginia. His political fortunes fell with the defeat of the Federalist party and his remaining years were spent in private law practice in the Virginia courts and before the federal courts, especially the Supreme Court of the United States, where his friend Marshall was presiding. He served in notable cases including the celebrated case of *Marbury* vs. *Madison.* He was also one of the defense lawyers in the trial of Aaron Burr in Richmond. In the impeachment of Judge Chase by the Republicans in 1805 he was one of the defense lawyers. Lee was twice married. His first wife was Anne, daughter of Richard Henry and Anne Lee whom he married at "Chantilly," Westmoreland County, Va., on Feb. 11, 1789. She bore him six children. His second wife was Margaret C. (Scott) Peyton, widow of Yelverton Peyton and daughter of the Rev. John and Elizabeth (Gordon) Scott. Of this marriage there were three children. He spent the latter years of his life at his stone house in Fauquier County, near Warrenton, where he died on June 24, 1815.

[The best sketch of Charles Lee is given in E. J. Lee, *Lee of Va., 1642–1892* (1895). See also: Gaillard Hunt, *Calendar of Applications and Recommendations for Office During the Presidency of Geo. Washington* (1901); Geo. Gibbs, *Memoirs of the Administration of Washington and John Adams* (1846), vol. II; Jared Sparks, *The Writings of Geo. Washington,* vol. IX (1835), and XI (1836); C. F. Adams, *The Works of John Adams,* vols. VIII and IX (1853–54); A. J. Beveridge, *The Life of John Marshall* (4 vols., 1916–19); *Daily Nat. Intelligencer,* June 29, 1815.] M. H. W.

LEE, CHARLES ALFRED (Mar. 3, 1801–Feb. 14, 1872), physician and scientist, was born at Salisbury, Conn., the son of Samuel Lee, a farmer, and Elizabeth (Brown) Lee. He was a descendant of John Lee of Essex, England, who emigrated to America in 1634. Intended for the ministry, he received a thorough education, preparing for college under his uncle, Elisha Lee of Sheffield, Mass., and at Lenox Academy. He entered Williams College in 1817 and received his degree in arts therefrom in 1822. His interest in the ministry having given way to an ambition for a medical career, he began to study under his brother-in-law, Dr. Luther Ticknor of Salisbury, and received his degree in medicine from Berkshire Medical Institution in 1826, having served incidentally as a pupil teacher in botany and anatomy. After a short sojourn in Salisbury he removed to New York City in 1827 to enter general practice. With Dr. James Stewart and others he founded the Northern Dispensary and for four years served as attending physician. In 1832 he was appointed physician to the Greenwich Cholera Hospital and in the same year physician to the New York Orphan Asylum where he taught hygiene to the personnel. He became a frequent contributor to periodical medical literature, writing on a great variety of subjects and reporting many unusual cases; and in 1835 he issued small popular treatises on physiology and geology. He helped establish the *New York Journal of Medicine and the Collateral Sciences,* in 1843, and edited it from 1846 to 1853. He also began the publication of American editions of well-known English medical works. The first of these, A. T. Thomson's *Conspectus of the Pharmacopœias of the London, Edinburgh and Dublin Colleges of Physicians,* with which he incorporated the United States' Pharmacopœia, appeared in 1843; and in the same year he issued his edition of Jonathan Pereira's *Treatise on Food and Diet.* This was followed in 1844 by J. A. Paris's *Pharmacologia* (rewritten in 1846), and in 1845 by an edition of W. A. Guy's *Principles of Forensic Medicine.* His major effort under this head, however, was his edition of James Copland's *Dictionary of Practical Medicine* in nine volumes (1834–59). To all of these works he added much valuable original matter.

While busily engaged in New York he is said to have declined the chair of materia medica in the University of the City of New York, but in 1844 he accepted the chair of pathology and materia medica in the Geneva Medical College and in 1847 had much to do with the admission of the first woman medical student, Elizabeth Blackwell [*q.v.*], to this institution. In 1846 he also joined the faculty of the Medical School of Maine as lecturer, later becoming professor of materia medica; in 1847 he was also a member of the faculty of the Starling Medical College, Ohio; and from 1848 to 1860, professor of pathology and materia medica at the University of Buffalo. He lectured at the Vermont Medical College and declined an offer to go to Louisville, Ky. In 1850 he decided to leave the metropolis for a residence in Peekskill and to divide his time among the smaller provincial schools. During his sojourn in these medical centers he was much in demand as a consultant and to avoid friction with local men required professional ethics of the highest type. At the outbreak of the Civil War he visited Europe for the Federal government in order to study hospital construction and administration, both military and civil, and brought back plans, models, and specifications. During this trip he wrote some forty letters to the *American Medical Times* of New York (June 14, 1862–Sept. 5, 1863; see also Dec. 5, 1863). On his return he served in the sanitary department of the army. He wrote no major work and his best-known effort is his *Catalogue of Medicinal Plants . . . in the State of New York* (1848). He wrote several papers on medico-legal subjects and insanity, contributed articles on geology and mineralogy to the *American Journal of Science and Arts,* and was a militant temperance advocate, publishing in 1871 *Remarks on Wines and Alcohol.* Although one of the committee of scientific men which exposed the imposture of the Fox sisters, he became eventually an enthusiastic spiritualist. He accumulated a private library of between 3,000 and 4,000 books and his herbarium contained 1,500 specimens. In 1828 he married Hester Anna Mildeberger of New York by whom he had nine children, only three of whom survived him.

[S. M. Lee, *John Lee of Farmington, Hartford County, Conn., and His Descendants* (1878); *N. Y. Medic. Jour.,* Apr. 1872; *Trans. Am. Medic. Asso.* (1881); *Boston Medic. and Surgic. Jour.,* July 3, 1850, Feb. 29, 1872; H. A. Kelly and W. L. Burrage, *Am. Medic. Biogs.* (1920); *N. Y. Times,* Feb. 15, 1872.] E. P.

LEE, ELIZA BUCKMINSTER (*c.* 1788–June 22, 1864), author, was born in Portsmouth, N. H., the daughter of the Rev. Joseph and Sarah (Stevens) Buckminster, both of whom were descended from Anne Bradstreet. Joseph Stevens Buckminster [*q.v.*] was her brother. Though brought up in a clergyman's family in which domestic duties were numerous and woman's position held to be subordinate, she acquired intellectual interests and considerable education from her father and brother. After her marriage in 1827 to Thomas Lee, a wealthy resident of Brookline, Mass., and a brother of Henry Lee, 1782–1867 [*q.v.*], she was able to pursue her studies and devote herself to literature. Her first work, *Sketches of a New England Village,* was published in 1838. This was followed in 1842 by her *Life of Jean Paul F. Richter,* a translation of his autobiography, to which she appended a biographical sketch. The work gave her a very considerable reputation. Her next most conspicuous work was *Memoirs of Rev. Joseph Buckminster, D.D., and of his Son, Rev. Joseph Stevens Buckminster* (1849); but she wrote much besides, including *Naomi; or Boston Two Hundred Years Ago* (1848); *Florence, the Parish Orphan* (1852); *Parthenia, or the Last Days of Paganism* (1858); and many translations from Richter, Auerbach, and other German authors, the popularity or prestige of which can be estimated from the fact that fifteen volumes of her works were included in a popular series of the seventies. The life of Richter owed some of its success to the vogue for him in particular and for German writers in general, introduced by Carlyle. A review in the *Eclectic Magazine* for November 1847 charges that it renders Richter's poetic language by dull prose, and displays such an elementary knowledge of German that the grammatical structure is not always given correctly. Carlyle's praise of her memoirs of her father and brother as revealing to him the highest aspect of New England character may also need to be discounted, as she was a disciple, or, at least, a follower of his. The fairest estimate would seem to be that she was not, according to present standards, either an accurate scholar or a writer of conspicuous creative ability or command over language. Her intellectual powers, however, were considerable, and though she had little aptitude for art, she had a strong sympathy for it, and is significant as an example of the way in which the New England intellect of her day was turning from the austerities and rigidities of Calvinism toward a more genial and tolerant philosophy.

[The details of Eliza Buckminster Lee's personal career have to be accumulated from widely scattered references. The date of her birth is established approximately by the records of Mount Auburn Cemetery. For printed references to her and to her works see: *New-Eng. Hist. and Geneal. Reg.,* Oct. 1854, Apr. 1855; *North Am. Rev.,* Oct. 1849; *Brownson's Quart. Rev.,* Oct. 1849; William Lee, *John Leigh of Agawam (Ipswich), Mass.* (1888); S. A. Allibone, *Critical Dict. of English Lit. and British and Am. Authors,* vol. III (1870).] S. G.

LEE, FITZHUGH (Nov. 19, 1835–Apr. 28, 1905), soldier, eldest of the six sons of Sydney Smith and Anna Maria (Mason) Lee, was born at "Clermont," Fairfax County, Va. His father, a naval officer in the United States and later in the Confederate service, was an elder brother of Gen. Robert E. Lee and the second son of "Light-Horse Harry" Lee by his second marriage, to Anne Hill Carter. His mother was a grand-daughter of the Revolutionary philosopher, George Mason, and a sister of Senator James M. Mason. After preliminary education in neighborhood private schools, Fitzhugh Lee entered West Point in 1852. He was distinguished more for comradeship and horsemanship than for scholarship and narrowly escaped dismissal for his pranks, but he was graduated forty-fifth in a class of forty-nine in 1856, and served as a cavalry instructor at Carlisle Barracks, Pa., until Jan. 1, 1858, when he was ordered to Texas as second lieutenant in the 2nd Cavalry. Dangerously wounded on May 19, 1859, in Indian fighting, he recovered in time to participate in another brush with the natives, June 16, 1860. Named assistant instructor in the department of tactics at West Point, he served there from Dec. 29, 1860, to May 3, 1861, then tendered his resignation (accepted May 21, 1861) and offered his services to Virginia. As first lieutenant in the regular Confederate army, he acted as a staff-officer to Ewell and to Joseph E. Johnston during the Manassas campaign and in August 1861 was made lieutenant-colonel of the 1st Virginia Cavalry. For his participation in the Peninsular operations and in Stuart's ride around McClellan, he was promoted brigadier-general on July 25, 1862. His delay in reaching the Rapidan on Aug. 17 was one factor in postponing the offensive against General Pope, and was censured in reports by Gen. "Jeb" Stuart, but if he was at fault, which is not altogether certain, he redeemed himself the next month when his admirable delaying-tactics, covering the withdrawal from South Mountain, gained for the main army a much-needed day in which to reconcentrate at Sharpsburg.

After the Dumfries and Occoquan raids of December 1862, the shortage of horses and the lack of forage threatened the disintegration of the Confederate cavalry, but Lee contrived to subsist his men and mounts on the upper Rappahannock. He was in direct command in the battle of Kelly's Ford, Mar. 17, 1863, where his handling of his small force in dealing with the largely superior column of Gen. W. W. Averell won great praise. During the Chancellorsville campaign, he led the only complete brigade of cavalry present with the main army and performed perhaps the greatest service of his military career in guarding Jackson's march on May 2 round the exposed right wing of Hooker's army. He it was who discovered that the right of the XI Corps was "in the air," and it was on the basis of his reconnaissance that Jackson extended Rodes's division to the left for the decisive attack. He participated creditably in the remaining operations of the Army of Northern Virginia during 1863 and on Sept. 3 was made major-general. During the operations of 1864 his stand at Spotsylvania Court House on May 8 made it possible for the I Corps to seize that strategic crossroads. He was ceaselessly engaged in exhausting combat, reconnaissance, and outpost duty with the Army of Northern Virginia until August. Then he was dispatched with his cavalry division to the Shenandoah Valley to support Gen. Jubal A. Early. On Sept. 19, in the desperate fighting at Winchester, where he had three horses shot under him, he was seriously wounded and incapacitated for duty until January 1865, when he assumed command of the cavalry on the north side of James River. After Wade Hampton was sent to North Carolina, Fitzhugh Lee became senior cavalry commander of the Army of Northern Virginia but did not operate as chief of the remnant of the cavalry corps until nearly the end of the siege of Petersburg. On Apr. 1, in his absence, his cavalry division was roughly handled at Five Forks, but during the retreat to Appomattox he kept the commanding general advised of the movements of the enemy and, when the army was surrounded and about to surrender on Apr. 9, he rode off with part of his troopers. Realizing, however, that resistance was useless, he surrendered Apr. 11 at Farmville.

While Fitzhugh Lee lacked the profound strategical sense of Forrest and made no such contributions as Stuart to the art of reconnaissance and the tactical employment of the mounted army, he was active in the field, a good tactician, hard-hitting, and not without skill in reconnaissance. He is generally ranked among the first dozen cavalry officers born in America. After spending a brief time in Richmond as a paroled prisoner of war, he went to Stafford County, where he engaged in farming. "I had been accustomed all my life," he subsequently said, "to draw corn from the quartermaster, and found it rather hard now to draw it from the obstinate soil, *but I did it!*" His historic name, his personal popularity, and his skill as a campaigner contributed to his election as governor of Virginia over John Sargent Wise by a vote of 152,544 to 136,510 in November 1885. His four-year term, though unmarked by any notable achievement, did much to secure the continued Democratic control of the state government.

Defeated for the nomination to the United States Senate in 1893, he was named consul-general to Havana, Apr. 13, 1896, which office he retained during the confused events preceding the outbreak of war in 1898. The tact and firmness which he then displayed made him a national figure, and his return to Washington on Apr. 12, 1898, took on something of the nature of a triumph. Commissioned major-general of volunteers on May 5, 1898, he was assigned the VII Army Corps, which was designed to be the chief combat-force in the occupation of Cuba. The capture of Santiago obviated the necessity of other operations, but he took his command to Cuba, established headquarters at Camp Columbia, near Havana, and was charged with the re-establishment of order. From Apr. 12, 1899, to Mar. 2, 1901, he was brigadier-general of volunteers under the act of Mar. 2, 1899, and for part of this time he commanded the Department of the Missouri. On Mar. 2, 1901, he was retired a brigadier-general. He then busied himself in planning for the Jamestown Exposition of 1907. He died in Washington and was buried in Hollywood cemetery, Richmond, Va. He had married, Apr. 19, 1871, Ellen Bernard Fowle, who with five children survived him. In physique, "Fitz" Lee, as he was always called, was about five feet ten inches in height, bearded, florid, heavy, and broad-shouldered, an admirable horseman. A facile writer, he published an address, "Chancellorsville" (*Southern Historical Society Papers,* December, 1879) and a biography, *General Lee* (1894). The latter is a standard work, though marred by many inaccuracies. His political abilities were, if anything, superior to those he displayed as a soldier, and he possessed much skill in public address. He is often confused with his first cousin, William Henry Fitzhugh Lee [*q.v.*], also a Confederate major-general of cavalry.

[The manuscript Letterbook of the superintendent of West Point contains the story of Fitz Lee's escapades as a cadet. A diverting account of some of his experiences in Texas appears in E. J. Lee, *Lee of Va., 1642–1892* (1895). G. W. Cullum, *Biog. Reg. of the Officers and Grads. of the U. S. Mil. Acad.* (3rd ed., 1891), gives his assignments in the Federal army prior to 1861. His scant correspondence and infrequent reports appear in the *War of the Rebellion: Official Records (Army).* His messages as governor of Virginia were published in the *Jour. of the House of Delegates of the State of Va.* and in the *Jour. of the Senate of the Commonwealth of Va.* Some of his dispatches as consul-general appear in *House Doc. 406,* 55 Cong., 2 Sess. Other sources include: *Who's Who in America,* 1903–05; *Confed. Mil. Hist.* (1899), III, 622–25; J. W. Jones, *Virginia's Next Gov., Gen Fitzhugh Lee* (1885); and the *Times-Dispatch* (Richmond), Apr. 29, 1905, Jan. 5, 1908. Lee left no unpublished military MSS., except for a few brief field-dispatches on the retreat to Appomattox. These are in the military papers of Gen. Robert E. Lee.] D. S. F.

LEE, FRANCIS LIGHTFOOT (Oct. 14, 1734–Jan. 11, 1797), revolutionist and statesman, was a member of the most talented group of brothers in Virginia history, which included Richard Henry, Arthur, and William Lee [*qq.v.*]. The son of Thomas and Hannah (Ludwell) Lee, he was born at "Stratford," Westmoreland County, Va. He did not attend college but received an excellent education at the hands of tutors. Leaving the family home in early life, he settled on an estate in Loudoun County which he inherited from his father. He was widely read and deeply interested in politics and served in the House of Burgesses from Loudoun County from 1758 to 1768. On his marriage to Rebecca Tayloe in the spring of 1769, he returned to the lower country, settling in Richmond County, on a plantation called "Menokin." He had already made somewhat of a reputation as a public man, and his marriage brought him many connections in Richmond County. He was almost immediately elected a burgess for that county and served in the crucial years immediately preceding the Revolution (1769–76). He was a man of far more political influence than is generally supposed. Much less widely known than his oratorical brother, Richard Henry Lee, he was hardly inferior to him in ability and was an even more ardent revolutionist. It is doubtful whether the coterie in Virginia that was bent on resisting the British government had in it a bolder spirit. He took part in every measure of defiance to the government: he signed the Westmoreland Association against the Stamp Act on Feb. 27, 1766; he was one of the members of the House of Burgesses who threw down the gauntlet to Great Britain on June 22, 1770; in 1773 he was one of the committee that undertook to form the Virginia committee of correspondence; he signed the call for the Virginia convention of August 1774, and was a member of that convention as well as of the convention of March 1775 in which the Virginia Revolution may be said to have begun. In the same year he was chosen a delegate to the Continental Congress, in which body he continued to sit until June 1779. He was one of the Signers of the Declaration of Independence, of which he heartily approved.

Lee was an influential and useful member of Congress. With farsighted vision he insisted on securing the free navigation of the Mississippi River for American citizens. He could have remained in the Continental Congress indefinitely if his longing for a quiet country life had not prevailed over such urgings of ambition as he had, which were few. On his return to Virginia, he sat for a time in the Virginia Senate and then retired. Unlike his brother Richard Henry, he was strongly in favor of the federal Constitution. After his retirement from public office he returned to "Menokin," where he died in the winter of 1797. He would have ranked as one of the leaders of the American Revolution if he had been a good speaker and had been self-seeking. But he was shy and inarticulate in public bodies and his excellent committee work remained unknown to the general public.

[E. J. Lee, *Lee of Va., 1642–1892* (1895); *Biog. Dir. Am. Cong.* (1928); J. C. Ballagh, *The Letters of Richard Henry Lee* (2 vols., 1911–14); E. C. Burnett, *Letters of Members of the Continental Cong.,* vols. I–IV (1921–28); "The Association in Williamsburg, in 1770," *Va. Hist. Reg.,* Jan. 1850; Jared Sparks, *The Writings of Geo. Washington,* vol. IX (1853); E. G. Swem and J. W. Williams, *A Reg. of the Gen. Assembly of Va., 1776–1918* (1918).] H. J. E.

LEE, GEORGE WASHINGTON CUSTIS (Sept. 16, 1832–Feb. 18, 1913), soldier and educator, eldest son of Gen. Robert Edward [*q.v.*]

and Mary Ann Randolph (Custis) Lee, was born at Fortress Monroe, Va. Receiving his early education in private schools of Virginia, he entered the Military Academy at West Point in 1850, from which he graduated at the head of his class in 1854. Upon graduation, he was assigned to service in the United States Army Corps of Engineers and performed work in river and harbor improvements in various sections of the country. At the outbreak of the Civil War he was on duty as assistant in the office of the chief engineer of the army at Washington. On May 2, 1861, he resigned his commission as first lieutenant in the army and offered his service to the Confederacy. His father made no effort to influence his son in his decision. "Custis," wrote the elder Lee to his wife, "must decide for himself and I shall respect his decision whatever it may be." Commissioned captain of engineers in the Confederate army, July 1, 1861, he was engaged in the construction of the fortifications of Richmond until his appointment, Aug. 31, 1861, as aide-de-camp on the staff of President Davis, with the rank of colonel of cavalry. His military ability was at once recognized by Jefferson Davis who often entrusted him with important missions. In September 1861, he was dispatched to Norfolk to examine the state of defense of that place; in October 1862, with the Federals threatening Wilmington, N. C., he was sent there to assist in the organization of the forces of resistance; and, in October 1863, his advice upon the reorganization of the Artillery Corps of the Army of Northern Virginia was sought by his father, General Lee. Although his active service on the battlefield was limited to the last months of the war, owing to the demand for his activities in other departments of the military service, his efficient and successful career won for him military advancement. He was promoted to the rank of brigadier-general, June 25, 1863, and later, on Oct. 21, 1864, to major-general.

Custis Lee longed for an active command, but President Davis was loath to part with him. "Our intercourse has been so pleasant," Davis wrote him in December 1864, "and your service so very useful to me in the relation of an Aid, that I should feel a two fold reluctance in parting from you, and should not hope to replace you by any one equally acceptable and beneficial to me. I have felt that your acquirements and natural endowments entitled you to a larger field and to better opportunities of fame than you have as a member of my staff. . . . For immediate usefulness it may well be doubted whether you are not as useful to the general service in the capacity of Aid to the Executive as you would be as Commander of a Division" (Rowland, *post,* VI, p. 431). During the last days of the Confederacy, Lee's brigade composed of departmental clerks and mechanics of Richmond, which he had previously organized for emergency purposes in the defense of Richmond, was attached to Ewell's corps and participated in the final retreat from Petersburg. Engaged at Sailor's Creek, it displayed "a gallantry never surpassed," and Lee was commended by his superior officer for his conduct in that sanguinary battle. He, with most of his command, was captured in this engagement. The war over, he became in October 1865 professor of military and civil engineering at the Virginia Military Institute, which position he occupied until he succeeded his father, Feb. 1, 1871, as president of Washington and Lee University. The adoption of the elective system of study, the establishment of endowed scholarships, and the increase of the endowment are achievements of his long administration of twenty-six years. He was also a generous benefactor of the institution, presenting, among his gifts, portraits of Washington and Lafayette by Peale, and heirlooms of the Custis family. Resigning July 1, 1897, he retired to "Ravensworth," an ancestral home, in Fairfax County, Va. He remained unmarried.

[*Who's Who in America,* 1912–13; H. L. Abbot, *Half Century Record of the Class at West Point 1850 to 1854* (1905); R. E. Lee, *Recollections and Letters of Gen. Robert E. Lee* (1904); G. W. Cullum, *Biog. Reg. of the Officers and Grads. of the U. S. Mil. Acad.* (3rd ed., 1891); E. J. Lee, *Lee of Va., 1642–1892* (1895); Dunbar Rowland, *Jefferson Davis, Constitutionalist, His Letters, Papers, and Speeches* (10 vols., 1923); *War of the Rebellion: Official Records (Army)*; *Confed. Veteran,* Apr. 1913; *Lexington Gazette,* Feb. 19, 1913; *Alexandria Gazette,* Feb. 18, 19, 1913.]

W. G. B.

LEE, HANNAH FARNHAM SAWYER (1780–Dec. 27, 1865), author, was born in Newburyport, Mass., where her baptism on Nov. 12, 1780, is recorded. Her father, Dr. Micajah Sawyer, was a well-known physician. On Jan. 20, 1807, she was married to George Gardner Lee of Boston, who had been for a time an officer in the United States navy. Her husband died in 1816 leaving her with three daughters, and she appears to have devoted herself to their upbringing till 1832, when, at the mature age of fifty-two, she began her literary career. Her first publication was an appreciation of Hannah Adams appended to the *Memoir of Hannah Adams* edited by Joseph Tuckerman. The authorship of this article was ascribed to "A Friend," and indeed none of her works was published under her own name. In 1835 she wrote a story, *Grace Seymour,* but though it was printed it was never distributed to the public, for practically the entire edition was destroyed by fire, and it was never republished. Her greatest success was achieved in 1837, when she published her *Three Experiments of Living.* This discussed living under, up to, and over one's income; and it went through thirty American and ten English editions, part of its popularity being probably due to the fact that the financial depression of 1837 made its subject timely. Taking advantage of the popularity of this work, she had bound up with some of its later editions enough of her other writings to make a fair-sized volume. These were "Elinor Fulton," "Contrast, or Modes of Education," "Rich Enough," and other rather short tract-like compositions designed to foster thrift and self-improvement. After this she began a series of educational works. In 1838 she published *Historical Sketches of Old Painters*; in 1839 *Rosanna, or Scenes in Boston,* and *The Life and Times of Martin Luther*; in 1841 *The Life and Times of Thomas Cranmer*; in 1843 *The Huguenots in France and America*; in 1844 *The Log Cabin; or, the World Before You*; in 1850 *Sketches and Stories from Life: for the Young*; in 1853 the *Memoir of Pierre Toussaint*; and in 1854 *Familiar Sketches of Sculpture and Sculptors.* These were her best-known works. None of them was very long, for she was not a voluminous writer. She seems to have outlived her fame, for no lengthy obituaries appeared at her death, and no biography or memoirs have been published; but from her first success to the early fifties she was widely read and frequently cited as an admirable and influential writer, although even in this period she was sometimes treated as superficial, as by a critic in the *New Englander* (February 1854) who dismissed her *Sketches of Sculpture* as a compilation that did not justify his notice.

[The fullest account of Mrs. Lee's career is in Sarah Josepha Hale, *Woman's Record, or Sketches of All Distinguished Women from "The Beginning" till A. D. 1850* (1853). See also the *New-Eng. Hist. and Geneal. Reg.*, Jan. 1851, Apr. 1866; Wm. Lee, *John Leigh of Agawam (Ipswich) Mass.* (1888); J. J. Currier, *Hist. of Newburyport, Mass., 1764–1909* (1909), vol. II.]

S. G.

LEE, HENRY (Jan. 29, 1756–Mar. 25, 1818), better known as "Light-Horse Harry" Lee, soldier and statesman, brother of Richard Bland and Charles Lee, 1758–1815 [*qq.v.*], was born at "Leesylvania" near Dumfries, Prince William County, Va., the son of Henry Lee, a cousin of the Lees of "Stratford," and a descendant of Richard Lee [*q.v.*]. His mother, Lucy Grymes, is claimed by tradition as one of Washington's boyhood loves. Lee graduated from the College of New Jersey in 1773 at the age of seventeen. He was preparing to go to England to study law, having been admitted to the Middle Temple, but the impending Revolution changed his plans and his career. In 1776 he was appointed a captain in Theodorick Bland's regiment of Virginia cavalry and in April 1777 his company joined Washington's army, which was weak in horse. Lee's soldierly qualities were recognized from the first and, young as he was, he was admitted to Washington's friendship and confidence. The relations between the two men continued to be intimate until death separated them. In January 1778, Lee was promoted major and put in command of a somewhat irregular force consisting of three troops of cavalry and three companies of infantry and known as "Lee's Legion." This force, on July 19, 1779, performed one of the most brilliant feats of the war by surprising the British post at Paulus Hook near New York, in which 160 of the enemy were captured almost without loss. It was comparable to Wayne's taking of Stony Point.

In 1780, Lee, now a lieutenant-colonel, was sent south to Greene, who was in great need of a competent cavalry commander. His subsequent story is the history of the Southern campaign. In the remarkable retreat across North Carolina to Virginia, in February 1781, Lee covered the rear of Greene's army, constantly skirmishing with Tarleton's British troopers, who were unable to prevail over the American cavalry. Turning suddenly aside from the main issue, Lee cut to pieces a force of Tories on the way to join Cornwallis, thereby greatly discouraging the British faction in the Carolinas. At Guilford Courthouse, Mar. 15, 1781, he fought brilliantly but failed to keep Greene informed of his position and after a hard-fought battle he was forced to retreat.

It was Lee who gave the advice to Greene that decided the latter to march south instead of following Cornwallis into Virginia. He continued his brilliant career by capturing several British forts, among them, Augusta, Ga., and he seems to have saved the drawn battle of Eutaw Springs, Sept. 8, 1781, from being an American defeat. It was his good fortune to be present at the siege of Yorktown and to witness the surrender of Cornwallis on Oct. 19, 1781.

Lee now came to the conclusion that the war was over and resigned his commission. A hero, one of the most notable Virginia soldiers, he won the hand of his cousin, Matilda Lee, heiress of "Stratford," whom he married early in 1782. By her he had several children, of whom a son, Henry Lee, 1787–1837 [*q.v.*], and a daughter survived. Turning to politics, he entered the

House of Delegates in 1785 and in the same year was sent to the Continental Congress, where he served, with one brief interruption, until 1788. He was an active member of the Virginia convention that ratified the United States Constitution in 1788 and voted for that measure. He was always a consistent Federalist and follower of Washington. In 1790, after the death of his wife, he thought of going to France for military service, as he was still young and still enamored of war. It was unfortunate that he did not do so, for he was unfitted for civil life. He gave up this plan in order to marry, on June 18, 1793, a second wife, Anne Hill Carter, of "Shirley." The fifth child of this marriage was Robert E. Lee [*q.v.*]. From 1792 to 1795 he served as governor of Virginia. While still governor, in 1794, he was chosen by Washington to command the army assembled to put down the Whiskey Rebellion in Pennsylvania. Lee managed to quell this uprising without the loss of life, and enhanced his prestige. In 1799 he entered Congress. The resolutions offered by John Marshall on the death of Washington were drawn by Lee and contained the description of Washington as "first in war, first in peace and first in the hearts of his countrymen" (*Annals of Congress,* 6 Cong., 1 Sess., col. 204). Lee repeated the phrase in his memorial oration in Philadelphia on Dec. 26, 1799.

Thus far Lee's life had been prosperous and happy; it was never again to be anything but sad and troubled. For some years he lived at "Stratford," harassed by debt and besieged by creditors. One of the most dashing and capable of soldiers, a fine orator, a learned and accomplished man of letters, Lee was wanting in all the qualities of a business man. His income was small and his expenditures were enormous, and he became heavily involved in land speculations. In 1808–09 he was imprisoned for debt and engaged himself in writing his *Memoirs of the War in the Southern Department of the United States,* published in two volumes in 1812. He left "Stratford" in 1811 to live in Alexandria, where his wife and second family would have suffered want but for Mrs. Lee's own means. He was always adventurous and whimsical. While in Baltimore, in July 1812, he attempted to aid his friend, Alexander C. Hanson, in defending the press of the *Federal Republican* against a mob which threatened violence. Lee and others were taken to jail. The following night the mob was admitted to the jail and in the riot which followed he received injuries from which he never recovered. (See *A Correct Account of the Conduct of the Baltimore Mob, by Gen. Henry Lee, One of the Sufferers,* 1814.) Handicapped now by ill health as well as by poverty, he succeeded, by the aid of the government, in reaching the West Indies, where he remained for several years, hoping for a cure. It was all in vain. Warned that death was approaching, he set sail for home but his strength gave out on the way. He was set ashore at Cumberland Island, Ga., and was tenderly cared for by the daughter of his old commander, Greene. There he died and was buried. In 1913 his remains were transferred to the Lee chapel of Washington and Lee University at Lexington, Va. Lee was not only one of the first but one of the best of American cavalry soldiers.

[Lee's *Memoirs* were republished by his son Henry Lee in 1827 and by his son Robert E. Lee in 1869. The latter edition contains a biographical sketch and letters. See also Thos. H. Boyd, *Light-Horse Harry Lee* (1931); C. B. Hartley, *Life of Maj.-Gen. Henry Lee* (1859); C. C. Jones, Jr., *Reminiscences of the Last Days, Death and Burial of Gen. Henry Lee* (1870); H. B. Grigsby, *The Hist. of the Va. Federal Convention of 1788* (2 vols., 1890–91); E. J. Lee, *Lee of Va., 1642–1892* (1895); *Daily Nat. Intelligencer* (Washington, D. C.), Apr. 8, 1818.] H. J. E.

LEE, HENRY (Feb. 4, 1782–Feb. 6, 1867), merchant and publicist, born in Beverly, Mass., was the ninth of twelve children of Joseph and Elizabeth (Cabot) Lee. Two older brothers were educated at Harvard College, but Henry after a course at Phillips Andover Academy, decided to go at once into the business in which the Cabots and the Lees had already attained prominence, the East India trade. On June 16, 1809, he married Mary Jackson, daughter of Jonathan Jackson and sister of James (1777–1867), Charles, and Patrick Tracy Jackson [*qq.v.*]. They had six children; Henry Lee Higginson [*q.v.*] was their grandson. Lee's partnership with his brother Joseph proved unsuccessful, and in 1811 he sailed for Calcutta. Being compelled by the War of 1812 to remain in India for several years, he utilized his time in study and in making acquaintances, which afterwards proved valuable, among the trading community. Upon his return to Boston he set up as a merchant trading to the East and West Indies, Europe, and South America. Temperamentally, however, he seems to have been a scholar rather than a business man, and overconfidence resulted more than once in serious losses. On each of these occasions, with the scrupulous honesty which characterized all his dealings, he paid all his creditors in full.

His interest in commerce went far beyond the limits of his own business, and he gave much thought to the tariff question on which opinion in Massachusetts was soon to be sharply divided. In 1820 the importing merchants and shipowners were still the dominant element in the business community and in politics. They bitterly opposed the demands of the Middle and Western states for higher import duties, foreseeing increased costs of ships and a declining volume of foreign trade. In the decade 1820–30, however, manufacturing made great strides in Massachusetts and a new group of factory owners arose, demanding protective duties. The woolen manufacturers, who were suffering rather severely from foreign competition, held meetings in Boston. Their demands were opposed by a group of merchants and traders, who chose Henry Lee to set forth their views. The pamphlet of nearly two hundred pages which he prepared, *Report of a Committee of the Citizens of Boston and Vicinity, Opposed to a Further Increase of Duties on Importations* (Boston, 1827), received wide circulation, being known as the "Boston Report." Drawing liberally on his wide acquaintance with both free-trade and protectionist literature, and with a vigorous and incisive style, the author made skilful use of the scanty statistical material then available.

The Tariff of 1828 was a triumph for the protectionists, the free-traders kept up the fight. In 1831, at the Free Trade Convention in Philadelphia, Lee worked in close association with Albert Gallatin [*q.v.*], and published *An Exposition of Evidence* (1832), a sort of statistical appendix, to accompany the latter's *Memorial of the Committee Appointed by the Free Trade Convention* (1832). As a result of these activities, Lee received in 1832 the eleven electoral votes of South Carolina for vice-president. His reputation as a student of economics and statistics spread to England, and he corresponded with McCulloch, Tooke, Newmarch, and others.

He retired from business in 1840, and devoted the remainder of his life mainly to writing and study. In 1850 he emerged from his retirement to wage an unsuccessful campaign for a seat in Congress. His unconquerable shyness made it almost impossible for him to take part in politics. The nobility and honesty of his character impressed all who knew him. To his intimates he revealed himself as an accomplished conversationalist, delighting them with his genial and gay spirit.

[J. T. Morse, Jr., *Memoir of Col. Henry Lee* (1905); H. A. Hill, in *Professional and Industrial Hist. of Suffolk County, Mass.* (1894), vol. II; section on "Other Lees" in William Lee, *John Leigh of Agawam (Ipswich), Mass., 1634–1671 and His Descendants of the Name of Lee* (1888); *Boston Daily Advertiser,* Feb. 7, 1867.] P. W. B.

LEE, HENRY (May 28, 1787–Jan. 30, 1837), soldier and author, was the son of Henry, "Light-Horse Harry," Lee [*q.v.*] and his first wife, Matilda (Lee) Lee. He was born at "Stratford," Westmoreland County, Va., some twenty years before the birth of his half-brother, Robert Edward Lee [*q.v.*]. He was graduated from the College of William and Mary in 1808. Though he had early displayed keen literary interests he entered upon a political and military career. From 1810 to 1813 he represented Westmoreland County in the Virginia House of Delegates. In April 1813 he was appointed major of the 36th Infantry. Attached to the staff of Gen. James Wilkinson and later to that of Gen. George Izard, he saw active service on the Canadian border. He was married in March 1817 to Anne, daughter of Daniel McCarty of Westmoreland County. He has been described by Henry A. Wise, a contemporary, as being "rather ugly in face" but "one of the most attractive men in conversation we ever listened to" (Wise, *post,* p. 99). From 1824 to 1826 he held a minor position in the Post Office Department and was employed as a political writer by Calhoun. Adams suspected him of disloyalty to his administration and about 1826 Lee definitely went over to the Jacksonian party. He was an active pamphleteer and writer for newspapers in Jackson's behalf. During the campaign of 1828 he lived at "The Hermitage" with the General and is credited with the literary form of Jackson's inaugural which he helped to write. As a reward for his services Jackson named him consul-general to Algiers with the others in the "batch of editors" to whom he gave recess appointments in 1829. The Senate in March 1830 failed to confirm these appointments, by a unanimous negative vote in Lee's case. While his campaign writings for Jackson were offensive to some, he was also opposed because of moral charges of a personal nature.

Lee had already journeyed to his post when news of the Senate's action reached him. He spent the remaining years of his life abroad, chiefly in Paris, and died in that city on Jan. 30, 1837. He had literary talent, though his writings were tedious and have proved ephemeral because of their controversial tone. In a notice of his work, the *Southern Literary Messenger* accused him of a spirit of captiousness. His first volume, *The Campaign of 1781 in the Carolinas* (Philadelphia, 1824), was intended "to expose and to frustrate the attempts of *William Johnson of South Carolina* in his *Sketches of the Life and Correspondence of General Greene,* to defame the late General Henry Lee" (p. 2). He again wrote a lengthy volume to defend his father, this time against what he deemed the aspersions cast upon him by Jefferson on the publication of that statesman's writings (*Observations on the Writings of Thomas Jefferson,* New York, 1832, Philadelphia, 1839). He admired Napoleon extravagantly. This he evidenced by a gift to Napoleon's mother of an autograph letter that George Washington had written his father, "Light-Horse Harry" Lee, and by writing a biography of Napoleon. This too was pitched on a controversial note, as he set out to defend Napoleon's name against Walter Scott's unfavorable treatment in the latter's *Life of Napoleon Bonaparte.* He planned a two-volume work on Napoleon. The first volume, *The Life of the Emperor Napoleon,* was published in 1835, but on Lee's death in Paris in 1837 it was republished with the added material he had prepared under the title: *The Life of Napoleon Bonaparte down to the Peace of Tolentino and the Close of his First Campaign in Italy.*

[The best sketch of Henry Lee is that in E. J. Lee, *Lee of Va., 1642–1892* (1895). See also: C. G. Bowers, *The Party Battles of the Jackson Period* (1922); H. A. Wise, *Seven Decades of the Union* (1872); Jas. Parton, *Life of Andrew Jackson* (1860); P. L. Ford, *The Writings of Thos. Jefferson,* vol. X (1899); *Letters and Other Writings of Jas. Madison* (1865), vols. III and IV; C. F. Adams, *Memoirs of John Quincy Adams,* vols. VI–IX (1875–76); J. S. Bassett, *Correspondence of Andrew Jackson,* vols. III–V (1928–31); *Southern Lit. Messenger,* Apr. 1835, p. 458; *Daily Nat. Intelligencer,* Mar. 14, 1837.] M. H. W.

LEE, JAMES MELVIN (May 16, 1878–Nov. 17, 1929), author, magazine editor, and for eighteen years director of the department of journalism of New York University, was born at Port Crane, N. Y., the son of James Newell Lee, a Methodist minister, and Emma (White) Lee. Graduating from Wyoming Seminary, Kingston, Pa., in 1896, he entered Wesleyan University, Middletown, Conn., where he received the degree of A.B. in 1900. At college he was largely self-supporting, and this fact led directly to the beginning of his writing career. Among his first articles for publication were several for newspapers on the means by which other students were earning their expenses—a series so successful that he later used the material in a book *How to be Self-Supporting at College,* published in 1903.

After his graduation from Wesleyan, he joined the news staff of the *Springfield Union* (Springfield, Mass.). In 1901 he became a teacher of English in Western Reserve Seminary, West Farmington, Ohio. The next year found him back in a newspaper office as circulation manager of the *Oneonta Star* (N. Y.). Beginning in 1905, magazine work engaged his attention. In succession he was circulation manager of *Outing,* editor of *Bohemian Magazine,* literary editor of the *Circle,* associate editor of *Leslie's Weekly,* and from 1909 to 1911, editor of *Judge.* While still with *Judge,* he became a pioneer in the teaching of journalism, being appointed a lecturer at New York University in 1910, and director of the department of journalism at that university in 1911. He held the latter position for the rest of his life.

During his association with New York University he was active in writing both books and articles, principally on topics dealing with journalism. He became an eager collector of early periodicals and of first editions in the field of American literature, especially works of Cooper and Poe. This pursuit made him a familiar figure at the bookshops near his office, in Washington Square, New York. With all this, however, he was no literary recluse. He liked people, and time and again was honored with offices in varied organizations. He spoke publicly as a champion of American journalism on many occasions. When others condemned newspapers for printing crime news and scandal, he pointed to the benefits of such publicity, adding: "It is the taste of the fish, not the fisherman, which denotes the kind of bait to be used" (*New York Times,* Dec. 1, 1925). Another saying credited to him is: "The newspaper and the cake of ice left on the back porch in the rays of the sun deteriorate at the same ratio, and when deterioration is complete you can't get much for either" (*Editor & Publisher,* Nov. 23, 1929). He called John Milton the "first copy reader," tracing the dates of his connection with *Mercurius Politicus* by the sudden improvement in its English and the later "reappearance of its former sloppy style." When the American press was stirred, in July 1926, by the cold-blooded murder of Don Mellett, youthful editor of the *Canton* (Ohio) *News,* who had attacked the vice ring of his city, Lee took the lead in establishing a fund to defray the expenses of a series of lectures on journalism in memory of the martyred editor. He also established a scholarship fund in memory of William Bradford, publisher of the first newspaper in New York. These were only two of nearly a score of such funds which he sponsored. One of his books, *History of American Journalism* (1917), has been widely used as a college reference book. Other books of his are: *Wordless Journalism in America* (1915), a book of cartoons; *Newspaper Ethics* (1915); *Instruction in Journalism in Institutions of Higher Education* (1918); *America's Oldest Daily Newspaper* (1918); *Opportunities in the Newspaper Business* (1919); *Business Writing* (1920), of which he was editor; and *Business Ethics* (1925). From 1922 until his death he was literary editor of *Editor & Publisher,* New York, conducting a weekly department in which he reviewed books and articles dealing with journalism. He edited for a time *Administration,* a business magazine, and the *Three-Em Dash,* the organ of the Newspaper Club of New York, in which he was one of the most active members. He also contributed a number of articles to the *Dictionary of American Biography.* In 1908 he married Helen Olga Wellner. They had one daughter.

[*Alumni Record of Wesleyan Univ.* (1921); *Who's Who in N. Y.,* 1924; *Who's Who in America,* 1928–29; *Independent,* Apr. 25, 1925; *Editor & Publisher,* Jan. 27, 1912, Apr. 6, 1929, Aug. 3, 1929, Nov. 23, 1929, and other issues; *N. Y. Times,* Nov. 18, 19, 1929.]

R. S. M.

LEE, JAMES WIDEMAN (Nov. 28, 1849–Oct. 4, 1919), minister, editor, author, son of Zachary J. and Emily H. (Wideman) Lee, was born at Rockbridge, Ga. In the hard times of Reconstruction he made his way, almost unaided, through Emory College, graduating in 1874; and on Dec. 26, 1875, he married Emma Eufaula Ledbetter. Having joined the North Georgia Conference of the Methodist Episcopal Church, South, in 1874, he was duly ordained and sent from place to place, according to the Methodist custom, until he reached Atlanta. Here he served the quadrennium limit first at Trinity Church and then at Park Street Church. Transferred to St. Louis in 1893, he remained there until his death save for another quadrennium (1905–09) at Trinity Church, Atlanta, and a year (1910) at Park Street Church. In St. Louis he was pastor of St. John's Church for three quadrenniums (1893–97, 1901–05, 1911–15), presiding elder of the St. Louis District (1898–1901, 1915–16), and chaplain of Barnes Hospital during his last four years. In each of his principal pastoral charges he secured the building of appropriate church auditoriums or parsonages or both; as presiding elder he raised money for the weaker churches of his district, and for the denomination's educational and benevolent enterprises, in satisfactory fashion. As a pastor he was much given to visiting and is said not only to have known every member of his church and Sunday school but also to have kept in touch with the members of past charges throughout the forty-four years of his ministry. As a preacher he was variously described by contemporaries as "eloquent and forceful," gifted with a "pungent colloquialism," of "voice high and notes a bit strident," but of "genuine spiritual insight and power." In 1892 he published *The Making of a Man,* which was at once translated into the Japanese tongue and later into the Chinese and the Korean. Three years later he edited *The Earthly Footprints of Christ and His Apostles,* containing photographs made under his personal direction in 1894. Through the enterprise of the publishers more than a million copies were sold. He was editor of three other publications (among them *The Self-Interpreting Bible* in four volumes, 1897) and author of eight, all of them save two being religious in character. His volume, *The Geography of Genius* (1915), was made up largely of travel notes arranged to illustrate his belief that "no places are of importance . . . except such as have been made significant by association with great people, great battles or great events of some kind" (Foreword). Most important of his writings was *The Religion of Science: The Faith of the Coming Man* (1912), in which he argued for the application of the scientific method to the phenomena of the Christian religion (not its dogma) in a series of essays deemed brilliant, illuminating, and satisfying by a great many, including prominent clergymen. A good deal of a philosopher and poet as well as a preacher, Lee was most noteworthy for the diversity of the people to whom his unmistakable friendliness and persistent optimism appealed. He was a speaker much sought for special occasions; and hundreds of people of all classes and in all regions voluntarily testified to his influence on them personally. His widow, three sons, and three daughters survived him.

[Biographical sketch by Lee's son, Ivy L. Lee, in *The Geography of Genius* (edition of 1920); letters and scrapbooks in private hands; *Who's Who in America,* 1918–19; Wm. Hyde and H. L. Conard, *Encyc. of the Hist. of St. Louis* (1899), vol. III; *Wesleyan Christian Advocate* (Atlanta), Oct. 31, 1919; *Christian Advocate* (Nashville), Oct. 17, 1919; *St. Louis Globe-Democrat,* Oct. 5, 1919; *St. Louis Post-Dispatch,* Oct. 4, 5, 1919.]

C. C. P.

LEE, JASON (June 28, 1803–Mar. 12, 1845), Methodist missionary, Oregon pioneer, a descendant of John Lee who settled in Farmington, Conn., in 1641, was the son of Daniel and Sarah (Whittaker) Lee. The father was a Revolutionary soldier. In 1798 the family moved from Massachusetts to a home in the neighborhood of Stanstead, Quebec, then considered a part of Vermont, where Jason was born. Experiencing a religious conversion in his twenty-third year, he three years afterward entered Wilbraham Academy, Mass., where he won the friendly interest of its president, the Rev. Wilbur Fisk. In 1830–32 he served as a minister to the Wesleyan Methodists in Stanstead and adjoining towns. In the latter year he attended the session of the New England Conference of the Methodist Episcopal Church, by which he was ordained deacon and later elder. About the same time the missionary society of this church decided to establish a mission in the Flathead country, and on June 14, 1833, Lee was chosen as its head. Accompanied by his nephew, the Rev. Daniel Lee, and three lay assistants, he left Independence, Mo., with Nathaniel J. Wyeth's second expedition, Apr. 28, 1834. On Sept. 15 the party arrived at Fort Vancouver, where they were welcomed by Dr. John McLoughlin, the chief factor of the Hudson's Bay Company.

For various reasons the Flathead project was abandoned, and on Oct. 6 four of the missionaries settled on the Willamette, ten miles northwest of the present Salem, Ore. In a short time the little colony was securely established. In the winter of 1836–37 Lee, in association with William A. Slacum, a purser in the navy, then on a tour of investigation of the northwest coast, drew up a petition for the establishment of a territorial government, which Slacum carried to Washington. In June 1837 an additional party, including Dr. Elijah White and his wife and Anna Maria Pittman, arrived from New York by sea. On July 16 Lee was married to Miss Pittman. New missions were established in the Clatsop country and at The Dalles, on the Columbia. On Mar. 26, 1838, Lee left on an overland journey to the East. At the Shawnee Mission, near Westport, Mo., in September, he was overtaken by a messenger with the information that his wife and infant son had died on June 26. He arrived in New York at the end of October, visited Washington, where he presented a settlers' petition for territorial organization, drawn up just before his departure, and during the next year addressed many meetings in behalf of his mission.

In July 1839 he married Lucy Thomson, of Barre, Vt., and on Oct. 9, with a party of fifty—the so-called Great Reinforcement—sailed from New York for the Columbia, arriving at its mouth on May 20, 1840. In the summer of the same year he had a disagreement with Dr. White, who left the mission and returned East. His work, in spite of adverse circumstances, went energetically on. By the end of the year, however, the character of his labors was undergoing a marked change. Though the mission at The Dalles had exerted a restraining influence on the thieving of the neighborhood Indians, the hope of Christianizing the savages of the Oregon country was coming to be recognized as futile. There followed a decline of missionary work and a concentration of efforts toward the material upbuilding of the settlements and the promoting of their political interests. In all these activities, as promoter, developer, business adviser, and constant advocate of the Americanization of the country, Lee took a leading part. On Feb. 7, 1841, he presided at the preliminary meeting for territorial organization, held at Champoeg; and though the movement lapsed for a time, he was influential in reviving it in the spring of 1843 and in bringing about the completion of a provisional government on July 5 of that year. He was also the chief mover in the fostering of education. As early as January 1841, he formed the plan that resulted, the following January, in the founding of Oregon Institute, later renamed Willamette University.

New problems decided him to return East for further aid. Sailing on Feb. 3, 1844, he learned at Honolulu that various criticisms of his conduct of the mission had caused the home office to supersede him in his post. He took ship for San Blas, crossed Mexico to Vera Cruz, and by way of New Orleans hurried to New York, where he arrived late in May. A conference of the Mission Board exonerated him of blame, but he was not restored to his post. In August his health failed. He returned to his native town, where he contracted a severe cold, from the effects of which, late in the winter, he died. A daughter survived him. His second wife had died in Oregon, Mar. 20, 1842. In 1906 his remains were taken to Oregon, and on June 15, with appropriate ceremonies, were reinterred at Salem. Lee's character has been variously appraised, and his influence in the settlement and acquisition of Oregon is a theme of endless controversy.

[Daniel Lee and J. H. Frost, *Ten Years in Oregon* (1844); Gustavus Hines, *Oregon* (1851); H. H. Bancroft, *Hist. of Oregon* (1890), vol. I; "Jason Lee Memorial Addresses," *Ore. Hist. Soc. Quart.*, Sept. 1906; "Diary of Rev. Jason Lee," *Ibid.*, June, Sept., Dec. 1916; A. Atwood, *The Conquerors* (n.d.); John Parsons, *Beside the Beautiful Willamette* (1924); H. W. Scott, *Hist. of the Oregon Country* (6 vols., 1924); C. H. Carey, *Hist. of Oregon* (1922); Leonard and S. F. Lee, *John Lee of Farmington, Hartford County, Conn., and His Descendants* (1897); Leonard Lee, *Supp. to John Lee*, etc. (1900); C. J. Brosnan, *Jason Lee, Prophet of the New Oregon* (1932); Daniel Lee, "Death of the Rev. Jason Lee," in *Christian Advocate* (N. Y.), Apr. 23, 1845.]

W. J. G.

LEE, JESSE (Mar. 12, 1758–Sept. 12, 1816), pioneer Methodist preacher, born in Virginia, revered as the apostle of Methodism in New England, and noted as the earliest historian of the Methodist movement in America, was the second son of Nathaniel and Elizabeth Lee. His father owned a farm of several hundred acres in Prince George County and enough slaves to cultivate it, was three times married, had twelve children, the last born when he was in his seventy-eighth year, and at his death, aged eighty-nine, left seventy-three grandchildren and sixty-six great-grandchildren. To these descendants Jesse made no contribution; he never married. His parents attended the Church of England, and though their own rector "was but a sorry preacher and of very questionable character," under the widely felt influence of Devereux Jarrett [*q.v.*] of Bath Parish, they were brought into a vital religious experience. Jesse, a boy of high emotional sensibility, was also converted. After the introduction of Methodism into Virginia the Lees joined a Methodist Society, and their home became a regular preaching place on one of the circuits. Here Jesse got his early preparation for the ministry. His secular education had been of the limited kind which neighboring schools afforded, but included attendance at a singing school where his natural gift for song was cultivated. In the latter part of 1777 he took charge of a widowed relative's farm in North Carolina. Zealously religious, he soon became a class-leader, exhorter, and finally a local preacher. Drafted into the army in 1780, he refused to bear arms because of conscientious scruples, but professed himself ready to perform any other duty assigned. Accordingly, until he was honorably discharged after three months' service, he was first a wagon driver and later sergeant of pioneers. Unofficially, he also did the work of a chaplain.

Although urged to become a traveling preacher he long hesitated, but in the latter part of 1782 put his fitness to the test by some circuit riding in Virginia and North Carolina. In 1783 he was admitted to the Virginia Conference on trial. For the next six years he labored with marked success in North Carolina, Virginia, and Maryland. Much to his regret, notice of the "Christmas Conference" held in Baltimore in 1784, at which the Methodist Episcopal Church in the United States was organized, did not reach him in time for him to attend. The February following, Bishop Asbury took him as a helper on a tour into South Carolina, which ended at Charleston. "I was comfortable in brother Lee's company," the Bishop notes in his journal under date of Feb. 22, 1785; and for many years thereafter, though they were not always in agreement, relations between the two were intimate.

While on this tour Lee met a man from New England and through conversation with him conceived the idea of carrying Methodism into that Congregational stronghold, but Asbury was not at the time favorable. Some four years later, however, Lee was appointed to the newly formed Stamford Circuit, Connecticut. Methodist preachers had visited New England before, but Lee went in to possess the land, and it was due to his faith and zeal, his tireless journeyings, and his evangelistic power that Methodism was everywhere planted in that unfriendly soil. Physically as well as spiritually he was well fitted for his mission. Over six feet tall, weighing more than 250 pounds, of genial countenance, he commanded attention everywhere. By his singing he could draw people about him, and by his fluent, forceful, colloquial preaching he could hold and convince them. He had the jovialness commonly attributed to fleshy persons, was somewhat of a joker, and in lively repartee was unequaled. His utterances had all the boldness of thorough-going conviction. "I did not give them velvet-mouth preaching," he said of a sermon on the loss of the soul and the torment of the damned, delivered in the meeting house at Newtown, Conn., "though I had a large velvet cushion under my hands." During the Conference year, May 1789 to October 1790, he not only labored in the principal towns of Connecticut with such effect that helpers from Maryland were sent him, but also traveled in Rhode Island, Massachusetts, Vermont, and New Hampshire. Up to 1790 he had refused ordination, but at the Conference held in New York in October of that year he was privately ordained deacon by Bishop Asbury, and the following day publicly ordained elder. He continued to labor in New England until 1797, serving as presiding elder of several districts, and carrying the conquest of Methodism as far north as Maine.

By this time the general superintendency of the work had become too onerous for even the indefatigable Asbury, upon whom, since Bishop Coke was out of the country much of the time, it largely fell. Asbury called Lee to his aid, and from September 1797 until the General Conference of 1800 he assisted Asbury as required, performing all the duties of a bishop except ordination. When at this General Conference another bishop was chosen, Lee, having been tied with Richard Whatcoat [*q.v.*] on the second ballot, was defeated on the third by four votes. Besides Whatcoat's fitness for the position, there were other reasons for this result. A few felt, or professed to feel, that the jovial Lee was not sufficiently dignified for the office. Someone started the rumor that he had forced his assistance on Asbury, and that the latter did not want him elected, a charge which Asbury denied. More effective probably in bringing about his defeat, was his independent attitude toward ecclesiastical rules and authorities, and his aggressiveness in the councils of the Church. As a youthful preacher, at the Conference in North Carolina, April 1785, he had vigorously differed with Bishop

Coke on the attitude the Methodist Church should take toward slave-holders and condemned the rules in force as ill-timed and likely to produce grave evils. Coke was so incensed that he objected to the passing of Lee's character. Lee also opposed the introduction of the "Council" into the organization of the church, and in a letter presented to its first meeting pointed out the errors of the plan. For his pains he received a reply almost insulting in tone. (See letter in L. M. Lee, *Life and Times of Rev. Jesse Lee, post.,* p. 282.) At that early date, he favored a delegated General Conference, and in 1792 submitted to Bishop Asbury a plan for such a body. Ezekiel Cooper [*q.v.*], who was associated with him in Massachusetts, wrote under date of Aug. 1, 1793, referring to Lee's policies in Lynn: "At General Conference, last November, in Baltimore, Brother Lee strove very hard to have several parts of the Discipline altered, and the bishop's power reduced, but he could not succeed. . . . Such parts of the Discipline as he favored in the General Conference . . . he was strenuous in and enforced, and required strict adherence; but such parts as he opposed in General Conference . . . he would not submit to. I told him it showed a stiff obstinacy. He wished everyone to bend to him, and would not bend to anyone, or even to the Conference." (G. A. Phoebus, *Beams of Light on Early Methodism in America,* 1887, p. 169.)

Lee accepted his defeat with good grace. He was invited to act as assistant to the bishops, but preferred to return to circuit work. After a long tour through New England he was stationed in New York until April 1801, when he was appointed presiding elder of the South District of Virginia. For the next fourteen years his labors were within the bounds of the Virginia Conference, except that in 1807 he traveled South on a roving commission as far as Savannah. In the summer of 1808 he made his last visit to New England where, while rejoicing in the great progress Methodism had made, he deplored various departures from the simplicity of early Methodism. Up to 1809 he had had no home of his own, but that year he bought a small farm near that of his father. During this period he also did some writing. His first publication was a memoir of his brother, *A Short Account of the Life and Death of the Rev. John Lee, a Methodist Minister in the United States of America* (1805). In 1810 he issued *A Short History of the Methodists in the United States of America,* the earliest written, and an invaluable compendium of facts. In 1814 he published two sermons. His *History* was criticized as lacking literary style and not sufficiently exalting Asbury; but the Bishop said of it: "I have seen Jesse Lee's History for the first time: it is better than I expected. He has not always presented me under the most favourable aspect: we are all liable to mistakes, and I am unmoved by his" (*Journal of Rev. Francis Asbury,* 1852, III, 340). In 1809, while at Baltimore superintending the publication of his book, Lee was elected chaplain of the House of Representatives, and was reëlected at the four succeeding sessions. In 1814 he was chosen chaplain of the Senate. He was criticized by some of his brethren and attacked in the Conference for holding such office on the ground that it was incompatible with his prior engagements as an itinerant Methodist. Without his consent he was transferred from the Virginia to the Baltimore Conference in 1815, and appointed to Fredericksburg. Rightly or wrongly, he considered the transfer a political move to prevent his election to the next General Conference. He refused to go to Fredericksburg and escaped censure from the Baltimore Conference on the apparently valid plea that Fredericksburg was not within its jurisdiction. In 1816 he was appointed to Annapolis, Md. While attending a camp meeting near Hillsborough in August of that year he was taken sick and died on Sept. 12, at the age of fifty-eight. He was buried in the old Methodist burying ground, Baltimore, but his body was moved with others in 1873 to Mount Olivet Cemetery. In the extent and importance of his labors for Methodism he perhaps deserves to rank next to Asbury.

[Lee left manuscript journals which were destroyed in the burning of the Methodist Book Room, New York, in 1836. Copious extracts are preserved in Minton Thrift's *Memoir of the Rev. Jesse Lee* (1823). See also L. M. Lee, *The Life and Times of the Rev. Jesse Lee* (1848); W. H. Meredith, *Jesse Lee, A Methodist Apostle* (1909); W. B. Sprague, *Annals Am. Pulpit,* vol. VII (1859); W. W. Bennett, *Memorials of Methodism in Virginia* (1871); M. H. Moore, *Sketches of the Pioneers of Methodism in North Carolina and Virginia* (1884); G. A. Crawford, *The Centennial of New England Methodism* (1891); Stephen Allen and W. H. Pilsbury, *History of Methodism in Maine* (1887); *The Methodist Magazine,* April 1822; *Methodist Quarterly Review,* January 1850; and standard histories of the M. E. Church.]

H. E. S.

LEE, JOHN DOYLE (Sept. 6, 1812–Mar. 23, 1877), Mormon elder, notorious for his part in the Mountain Meadows Massacre, was born in Kaskaskia, Randolph County, Ill. His father, Ralph Lee, was born in Virginia and according to the son "was of the family of Lees of Revolutionary fame" (*Mormonism Unveiled,* p. 36). At the age of eight he was left an orphan among relatives, and very early learned to shift for himself. He had little formal schooling. At nineteen he saw action in the Black Hawk War.

After his marriage on July 24, 1833, to Agathe Ann Woolsey, he settled in Fayette County, Ill. He had been reared a Catholic but had always shown an interest in various religions. Upon hearing of Mormonism from missionaries, he traveled to Missouri to investigate the new sect at first hand and remained there a convert. He was soon zealous in the new church and as a member of the Mormon military organization took part in several skirmishes with the Missourians. At Nauvoo, Ill., he rose rapidly in favor with the Mormon leaders, holding important municipal and ecclesiastical offices. He twice (1839 and 1841) served as missionary. He reports a number of prophetic dreams and visions which assisted him in his conversion of others. These "spiritual" phenomena suggest that he was neurotic, which supposition is confirmed by a kind of hysterio-epileptic attack during his last imprisonment (Whitney, *post,* II, p. 786). In 1843 he became a Mason. Like many other Mormons, he spent the spring of 1844 in near-by states supporting Joseph Smith's campaign for the presidency of the United States. After the Prophet's assassination, Lee returned to Nauvoo where he soon transferred his loyalty to Brigham Young.

In 1845–46 Lee accepted the Mormon practice of polygamy and added seven more wives to his household. He informs us that altogether he had eighteen wives who bore him sixty-four children. He refused to count as a wife one elderly woman—a mother-in-law—whom he married "for her soul's sake." Upon removing to Utah he was active in colonizing outlying sections and finally settled in southern Utah not far from the Mountain Meadows. He was a fanatical mystic about his religion. Like many other Mormons he was highly aroused during the summer of 1857 over the impending invasion of Utah by federal troops under Gen. Albert Sidney Johnston and over the rumors that a company of emigrants en route from Arkansas to California was robbing Mormon settlements. Early in September 1857 a band of Indians and Mormons treacherously massacred this company at Mountain Meadows. Doubtless Lee helped to plan and execute this atrocity. The first attempt (1859) to indict the leaders in the crime was unsuccessful. Finally in 1875 Lee and others were brought to trial. Lee's first trial ended in a disagreement of the mixed jury of eight Mormons and four non-Mormons. At the second trial (1876) Lee was found guilty of murder in the first degree and sentenced to be shot. After the supreme court of Utah had upheld the original judgment, he was executed on the spot where the massacre had taken place nearly twenty years before.

Certainly Lee alone was not guilty of planning and carrying out the massacre. In his *Mormonism Unveiled* (1877), which he wrote only after being sentenced to death, he throws all the blame upon local Mormon leaders: William H. Dame, Isaac C. Haight, John M. Higbee, and Philip Klingensmith. He tried to implicate Brigham Young, but this accusation has evidently no basis in fact. However, there is no denying that Lee served as a sacrifice to appease public clamor to punish those who committed the butchery. Lee sensed this and naturally his confessions are marked by extreme bitterness against those who formerly were his friends.

[In spite of its bias, Lee's *Mormonism Unveiled* (1877) is one of the best sources. W. A. Linn, *The Story of the Mormons* (1902), follows Lee's account. O. F. Whitney, *Hist. of Utah,* vols. I and II (1892–93), gives the official Mormon account. See also: H. H. Bancroft, *Hist. of Utah* (1890); M. R. Werner, *Brigham Young* (1925); "Report of the Massacre at Mountain Meadows and other Massacres in Utah," *Senate Executive Doc. 42,* 36 Cong., 1 Sess.; *Deseret Evening News* (Salt Lake City), Mar. 23, 24, 1877.] K. Y.

LEE, LUTHER (Nov. 30, 1800–Dec. 13, 1889), clergyman, abolitionist, was a leading figure in the anti-slavery movement within the Methodist Episcopal Church. Born in Schoharie, N. Y., of humble, illiterate parents, Samuel and Hannah (Williams) Lee, he received no schooling, and from the age of thirteen was dependent on his own resources. He had a vigorous, disputatious mind, however, and as occasion offered he spoke and preached at the little Methodist churches in his community. An elder brother taught him to read, and on July 31, 1825, he married a school-teacher, Mary Miller, who gave him whatever other formal education he received. In 1827, when he was admitted to the Genesee Conference, he was too ignorant to satisfy the examining committee, but he was approved because of his power as a revivalist. After an apprenticeship on frontier circuits in New York, he transferred to the Black River Conference in 1836, where he rapidly advanced to a position of leadership. He was a fighting reformer, a powerful debater by disposition and training, and the increasing anti-slavery agitation in the Church early caught his interest. The assassination of Elijah Lovejoy [*q.v.*] at Alton, Ill., late in 1837, moved him to declare himself an abolitionist.

Most Methodists of that day did not take kindly to the official abolition organizations. Believing them "important links in the great chain of operations of the Presbyterian and Congregational churches," Methodists organized societies of their own in order to "do their benevolent works in the name of their own denomination and proper character." Accordingly, Wesleyan anti-slavery societies were formed, in the promotion of which Lee engaged with consuming zeal. His efforts were so successful that in 1838 the American Anti-Slavery Society made him their agent in western New York. Describing slavery in language "expressive of the shrieking terrors of death, the gloom of rayless despair, and the glowing fires of hell" (*Autobiography, post,* p. 210), he met with much violence, which he fronted dauntlessly. In the fall of 1839 he was employed by the Massachusetts abolitionists. He now used all his influence to further the rising agitation for political anti-slavery organization, and in 1840 he took a leading part in founding the Liberty Party.

During these critical years Lee's services were frequently required to defend Methodist clergymen in church trials for participating in abolition activity. Through the board of bishops the Church was making a determined effort to thwart such activity among its ministers; but the dual nature of Methodist polity, with authority exercised both from above through the bishops, and from below through the Conferences, made a peaceful adjustment impossible wherever the Conferences protected the abolitionists. After years of increasing friction, many abolitionists withdrew, and in 1843 they organized the Wesleyan Methodist Connection of America, without an episcopacy and on an anti-slavery basis. At the first General Conference of the new denomination, in 1844, Lee was elected president. Delegates reported fifteen thousand communicants; but the denomination never grew larger. That same year Northern Methodists precipitated a division in the Church on the slavery issue, and there were no more secessions. Lee faithfully served his Church during the two following decades, as editor of its organ, the *True Wesleyan,* as pastor in New York state, Ohio, and Michigan, and as professor on the faculty of the Wesleyan Methodist school, Adrian College, Adrian, Mich. In 1867 he returned to the Methodist Episcopal Church and after ten more years' ministry in southern Michigan, he was superannuated, dying at the age of eighty-nine at Flint, Mich. He wrote *Universalism Examined and Refuted* (1836); *Ecclesiastical Manual, or Scriptural Church Government Stated and Defended* (1850); *Slavery Examined in the Light of the Bible* (1855); *Elements of Theology* (1856); *Natural Theology* (1866). Their importance is inconsiderable. In 1882 he published *Autobiography of the Rev. Luther Lee, D.D.*

[In addition to the above, see *Mass. Abolitionist,* 1839–1840; L. C. Matlack, *The Hist. of Am. Slavery and Methodism, from 1780 to 1849; and Hist. of the Wesleyan Meth. Connection of America* (1849); *Minutes of the Ann. Conferences of the M. E. Ch.* (1890).]

G. H. B.

LEE, RICHARD (d. 1664), statesman, was the emigrant ancestor of a noted family of Virginia. Among his descendants were Richard Henry Lee and his distinguished brothers, Henry, "Light-Horse Harry," Lee of Revolutionary fame, and Robert E. Lee [*qq.v.*]. He transmitted to his descendants, along with a goodly fortune, high standards of culture, morality, and a sense of public service. Of Lee's immediate parentage there is no definite information, but there is convincing evidence that he came of the Coton branch of the Shropshire Lees, an ancient and honorable English family. His coat of arms, which, carved in wood, long adorned the front door of old "Cobbs Hall," is registered in the Herald's office in London as that borne by "Colonel Richard Lee, Secretary of State in Virginia, *Anno* 1659." In legal documents he described himself as of "Stratford Laughton in the County of Essex Esquire." The name "Stratford" still remains in "Stratford Hall," birthplace of Richard Henry Lee and of Robert E. Lee. William Lee [*q.v.*] stated that his ancestor, Richard Lee, came to Virginia during the reign of Charles I, remained for a time, returned to England, and later made his home in Virginia. This seems true. In any event, Richard Lee emigrated in, or about, 1641 and settled in York County—in that part organized in 1651 as Gloucester County. A grant of a thousand acres of land to Richard Lee, gentleman, dated Aug. 10, 1642 (for bringing in settlers), states that it was due to him "for his own p'sonal Adventure, his wife Ann" (whose maiden name is not known), and for others. It is probable, however, that he did not live here, the "Paradise" estate, but at Gloucester Point.

About 1651 Lee removed to Northumberland County and settled on Dividing Creeks which afforded a good harbor opening into Chesapeake Bay. He was one of the first and most active pioneers of that region, acquiring tracts of land, raising large quantities of tobacco, and trading to England in ships in which he owned part interest. At one time or another he was clerk of the council, attorney-general of the colony, burgess, high sheriff of York County, councilor, and secretary of state. During the period of the Commonwealth he remained loyal to the King. A contemporary states that upon the death of

Charles I, Lee went to Europe, surrendered Sir William Berkeley's commission as governor of Virginia, and brought back a new commission from the exiled Charles II. It is said that he invited Charles to make his home in Virginia. After the subjugation of the colony, Lee acknowledged the supremacy of the Commonwealth and retained his influence in political affairs. In this he was not untrue to principle but acted in the best interests of the colony. After the Restoration he spent much of his time in England, and some of his children were educated in English universities, but he came home to die on his Dividing Creeks estate and was buried there at "Cobbs Hall." His will named eight surviving children. He has been described as "a man of good stature, comely visage, an enterprising genius, a sound head, vigorous spirit, and generous nature" (Lee, *post*, p. 245).

[The most useful work on Richard Lee and the Lee family is E. J. Lee, *Lee of Va., 1642–1892* (1895). See also: *New-Eng. Geneal. and Hist. Reg.*, Jan. 1890, Jan. 1892; and W. G. and M. N. Stanard, *The Colonial Va. Reg.* (1902). There are numerous references to Lee in the *Va. Mag. of Hist. and Biog.* and the *Wm. and Mary Coll. Quart. Hist. Mag.*] R. L. M—n.

LEE, RICHARD BLAND (Jan. 20, 1761–Mar. 12, 1827), statesman, brother of Henry, "Light-Horse Harry," and Charles Lee [*qq.v.*], was the son of Henry and Lucy (Grymes) Lee and a descendant of Richard Lee [*q.v.*]. He was born at the family homestead, "Leesylvania," Prince William County, Va. At an early age he moved to Loudoun County, where he owned an estate inherited from his father. He became a well-to-do and influential planter with wide connections. On June 19, 1794, he was married to Elizabeth Collins of Philadelphia, the daughter of a wealthy Quaker. A member of a prominent family and a planter with sufficient means and leisure for public affairs, Lee had entered politics while still very young and represented Loudoun County in the House of Delegates from 1784 until 1788, and again in 1796. Influenced no doubt by his brother, Henry Lee, and by his wife's family, he was an ardent Federalist in a state in which the Federalist party was always weak. As one of the few prominent members of that group in the Virginia Assembly of 1788, he opposed Patrick Henry's effort to call a new convention to reconsider the United States Constitution.

In 1789 he became a member of the first Congress under the Constitution. He was not a man of great force or ability, but it was his destiny to be one of the determining factors in an event of importance to the country. Hamilton was pressing his plan for the assumption of state debts by the federal government, but he lacked a majority in the House of Representatives. He succeeded in bringing over his rival, Jefferson, to favor the assumption scheme, however, and the two leaders held a conference in July 1789, to which Alexander White and Lee, both Virginia congressmen, were invited. Lee was undoubtedly selected for his Federalist leanings, though he seemed to be committed to vote against assumption. Lee and White agreed to change their attitude on assumption, while Hamilton, for his part, consented to the choice of the Potomac River as the seat of government. In this way Hamilton secured the necessary votes to put through his assumption bill and the District of Columbia came into existence. Richard Henry Lee wrote of this episode, "It was generally supposed that the Assumption part of our Bill would be rejected by the H. R. but Mess[r] R. B. Lee and White from our Country with Gale and Dan'l Carroll from Maryland, changing sides, the Assumption was agreed to" (*The Letters of Richard Henry Lee*, II, 535). Lee served in Congress until 1795, when he retired to his farm. In 1815 he moved to Washington. The following year he was appointed a commissioner of claims for property destroyed during the war, and from 1819 until his death he was judge of the Orphans' Court in the District of Columbia.

[See E. J. Lee, *Lee of Va., 1642–1892* (1895); J. C. Ballagh, *The Letters of Richard Henry Lee* (2 vols., 1911–14); *John P. Branch Hist. Papers of Randolph-Macon Coll.*, June 1903; *Biog. Dir. Am. Cong.* (1928); W. H. Bryan, *A Hist. of the Nat. Capital*, vol. II (1916); E. G. Swem and J. W. Williams, *A Reg. of the Gen. Assembly of Va., 1776–1918* (1918); P. L. Ford, *The Writings of Thos. Jefferson*, I (1892), 164; and *Daily Nat. Intelligencer* (Washington, D. C.), Mar. 13, 1827.] H. J. E.

LEE, RICHARD HENRY (Jan. 20, 1732–June 19, 1794), Revolutionary statesman, brother of Francis Lightfoot, William, and Arthur Lee [*qq.v.*], was the seventh of the eleven children of Thomas and Hannah (Ludwell) Lee and a descendant of Richard Lee [*q.v.*]. He was born at the family seat, "Stratford," in Westmoreland County, Va. Of his early life little is definitely known. He received his elementary instruction from private tutors and was sent to England to complete his education. Having finished his course at the academy at Wakefield, in Yorkshire, in 1751, he spent a few months in travel, then returned to Virginia, probably in 1752. He did not, it seems, plan a professional career, but he is said to have made a thorough study of the law and his letters reveal an acquaintance with outstanding works in history, government, and politics. Inasmuch as most of his ancestors had sat in the House of Burgesses or the council, or both, it is a natural inference that his aim from the first was a public career. His public service began in 1757, when he became a justice of the peace in his county, and in 1758 he entered the House of Burgesses. In the meantime, on Dec. 3, 1757, he had married Anne Aylett, daughter of William Aylett of Westmoreland County, and about this time he established his residence at "Chantilly," a neighboring estate to "Stratford."

It is related of Lee that in his earlier years in the House of Burgesses he took an inconspicuous, even a hesitant, part, but that once he had broken through the crust of deference to the older leaders he won the admiration of his friends and the respect of his opponents. His part in the activities of the House was one of increasing importance until he had attained a position of influence in its counsels. An aristocrat of the aristocrats, he steered from the beginning a democratic, or, perhaps more accurately, a progressive, course. One of his first speeches was in support of a measure designed to check the growth of slavery; he had a part, along with Patrick Henry, not yet a member of the House, in the matter of the so-called "Two-penny Act"; he was Henry's chief ally in the noted case of the speakership and the treasury; and he himself pushed the investigation of the treasury, winning thereby political enmities that vexed his course for a good many years. It was, however, his opposition to the Parliamentary plan of March 1764, to tax the colonies, that placed him at once in the forefront of the defenders of colonial rights. Immediately upon learning of the purpose of Parliament he declared, in a letter written to a friend in England (May 31, 1764), that "the free possession of property, the right to be governed by laws made by our representatives, and the illegality of taxation without consent" were "essential principles of the British constitution," and that colonial Britons had forfeited none of their rights and privileges, none of "the blessings of that free government of which they were members" (*The Letters of Richard Henry Lee,* I, 5–6).

When the House of Burgesses registered a protest against the proposed stamp duties, Lee was of the committee appointed on Nov. 14 to draw up an address to the King, a memorial to the Lords, and a remonstrance to the Commons, and he has been credited with the authorship of the first two of these papers. Although he was not present in the House of Burgesses when, in May 1765, Patrick Henry startled that assembly with his famous resolutions, he and Henry were in essential unison, and he shortly afterward reiterated his views in a published address to the people of Virginia. He is said to have led a "mob of gentlemen" to confront the appointed collector of stamps and compel him to promise not to serve in his official capacity. Then, in February 1766, he drew the citizens of his own county into an "association" binding themselves to import no British goods until the Stamp Act should be repealed. (See the *Virginia Historical Register,* January 1849.) This Westmoreland Association is chiefly of importance for the reason that it was the first of the numerous boycotting measures designed to bring the British government to repentance, as the Continental Association, itself promoted by Lee, was the most ambitious. It presently developed that, in November 1764, just when the House of Burgesses was uttering its protest, Lee had himself applied for appointment as collector. He was accordingly charged with inconsistency and rebuked unmercifully in the *Virginia Gazette;* but he explained that, after "reflecting seriously," he had withdrawn his application, and he pointed to his zealous works as proof of his thorough conversion.

Against the Townshend Acts he set his face even more firmly than he had done against the Stamp Act. They were "arbitrary, unjust, and destructive of that mutual beneficial connection which every good subject would wish to see preserved" (*Letters,* I, 27). The suspension of the legislature of New York, he wrote in March 1768, *"hangs like a flaming sword* over our heads and requires *by all means to be removed"* (*Ibid.*). A few months later he was urging, as a necessary means of uniting their counsels, that the several colonies set up committees for intercolonial correspondence (letter to Dickinson, July 25, 1768), an idea that was not however brought to fruition until 1773. In December 1768, his wife died, and in the following year he married Mrs. Anne Pinckard, widow of Thomas Pinckard and daughter of Col. Thomas Gaskins. During the relatively quiet period between 1768 and 1773 he engaged in shipping tobacco to his brother William in London. Yet he by no means forsook the political field, although he did, in the summer of 1770, meditate withdrawing from the popular assembly and seeking appointment as president of the council, which offered, he thought, the greater "means of doing good." Just what gave rise to this impulse it is not easy to determine. In May 1765 Patrick Henry had swept like a blazing comet across the political skies and made himself a popular idol, yet Lee was by no means eclipsed. As Henry had become the Demosthenes of Virginia, so Lee became the Cicero. He and Henry became congenial coworkers. Likewise, when Jefferson, a new luminary of liberalism, came to the House of Burgesses in 1769, Lee, Henry, and Jefferson, with a few other forward-looking men, pooled their ideas and their efforts. It was they who, in March 1773, originated the plan for intercolonial committees of correspondence, a measure which Lee declared ought to have been fixed upon from the beginning of the dispute "as leading to that union, and perfect understanding of each other, on which the political salvation of America so eminently depends" (*Letters,* I, 84); and it was the same group who, in May 1774, "cooked up," as Jefferson expressed it, a resolution to make the day when the port of Boston was to be closed a day of "Fasting, Humiliation, and Prayer." Lee himself had prepared a set of resolutions which included a declaration that the closing of the port of Boston was a "most violent and dangerous attempt to destroy the constitutional liberty and rights of all British America" (*Letters,* I, p. 116), and, what is of especial significance, a call for a general congress of the colonies to adopt means for securing these rights. A dissolution of the Assembly, in consequence of the fast-day resolution, prevented Lee from offering these propositions, but it did not prevent the Burgesses from gathering afterward and taking measures to the same end, including the summoning of a convention. Lee was of opinion that the action of the Burgesses was "much too feeble an opposition" to the "dangerous and alarming" despotism that was threatening. Nevertheless the past nine years had worked a great change in the minds of those elder statesmen who had long dominated the course of Virginia politics. They were at last being drawn from their long-time moorings in the quiet channels of conservatism and conciliation out into the current of revolution where Lee, Henry, and Jefferson were plying their radical oars.

Meanwhile, before the Virginia convention had assembled and voiced its demand for a general congress, Massachusetts had already sent forth the call, naming Philadelphia, September first, as the place and time. Of Virginia's seven delegates to the Congress, Peyton Randolph, speaker of the House of Burgesses and a conservative, was named first and Richard Henry Lee second. At Philadelphia Lee met with kindred spirits. John Adams pronounced him "a masterly man," and between Lee and Samuel Adams there began a lifelong friendship. As for remedies, Lee still believed that a non-importation, an enlarged form of his Westmoreland Association, would speedily and effectually accomplish the purpose, and in due time he moved it. The Continental Association, the first real step toward a federal union, was the result. The address to the King, as adopted by Congress, Lee thought was lacking in spirit.

In the Congress of 1775 Lee was active on many of the most important committees and was among the foremost proponents of strong measures. Lord North's conciliation offers, he warned, were insidious. How early he espoused the idea of independence cannot definitely be said, but in November 1775, he agreed with John Adams that it was time the colonies were adopting their own governments, and it was upon his suggestion that Adams drew up his *Thoughts on Government* (1776). Lee probably experienced no sudden change of heart, but it may have been Thomas Paine's influence that led him to join with George Wythe, in March 1776, in proposing a resolution that the King, instead of the ministry, was the "Author of our Miseries," a doctrine for which Congress was not quite ready. When presently he is discovered openly advocating independence, it is not independence as an end to be attained for its own sake that he emphasized, but rather as a necessary prerequisite to a foreign alliance. Although in this view Lee by no means stood alone, it was in no small measure in consequence of Lee's urgence that the Virginia convention, on May 15, adopted its resolutions in behalf of independence, foreign alliances, and a confederation, and it was altogether appropriate that he should be chosen to move those resolutions in Congress. By his pen they were redrawn in that compact form in which they appear in the journals of Congress (June 7, 1776).

With the presentation of the resolutions Lee's part in the Declaration of Independence, except for his subsequent signature to the finished document, was essentially ended. He had already planned to return to Virginia to take part in the formation of the new state government, and for that purpose he left Philadelphia June 13 (not on June 11, as has frequently been stated; see his *Letters,* I, 199, 201, 203). Accordingly he was not placed upon any one of the three committees to which the resolutions gave rise. Nevertheless it is to the confederation and foreign relations that the most significant phases of his career in Congress during the next two or three years appertain. In the formation of the Articles of Confederation he appears to have had but a minor part, yet no man in Congress was more concerned for the consummation of "this great bond of union" than he. When it became evident that no confederation was possible until Virginia had surrendered her claims to western lands he advocated the sacrifice and labored to that end. His connection with the problem of foreign relations became very soon anything but a happy one. Naturally, he became deeply involved in the controversy between his brother Arthur, and Silas Deane, and his vehement championship of his brother was largely instrumental in dividing Congress into two hostile factions and giving an unpleasant cast to the foreign relations of the United States for two years or more. During these years he added little to his reputation as a statesman, while his earlier buoyant hopes for the speedy triumph of the right, whether it were national or personal, were sadly dimmed. Nevertheless he continued for some time to labor zealously at his congressional tasks and in his country's cause. In May 1779, worn down in body and in spirit, he resigned his seat in Congress. In 1780 he was elected to the Virginia House of Delegates, where, strangely enough, he allied himself with the conservative forces. In 1784 he was again elected as a delegate to Congress, and by that body was chosen as its president for a year. Although handicapped by ill health and taxed by the business and the ceremonies of his office, the honor and distinction appear to have afforded him no small gratification.

Congress was at this time in a rather unstable situation. A movement essentially aimed at its dissolution had narrowly failed, and the wiser patriots, concerned for the salvation of the union, were seeking to strengthen the hands of Congress as an imperative necessity. Lee was alive to the fact that the Articles of Confederation were seriously defective, but he feared to give Congress the power of "both purse and sword." "The first maxim of a man who loves liberty," he declared, "should be never to grant to Rulers an atom of power that is not most clearly & indispensably necessary for the safety and well being of Society" (*Letters,* II, 343–44). He accordingly opposed the proposition to grant Congress a five-per-cent. impost. He was chosen as one of the delegates to the Constitutional Convention but declined on the ground that it was inconsistent that members of Congress should pass judgment in New York on their opinions in Philadelphia (*Letters,* II, 434). He did, however, while the Convention was sitting, have an important share in the creation of another great instrument of government, the Northwest Ordinance. When the Constitution was laid before Congress Lee led the opposition to it, and he was one of its most vigorous critics throughout the campaign for its adoption. His opposition was on several grounds, chief among them, that the Convention, called only to amend the Articles of Confederation, had exceeded its powers; that the Constitution lacked a bill of rights; that it was a "consolidated," rather than a federal, government, and therefore opened the way to despotism; and that the lower house was not sufficiently democratic. His arguments were set forth in a series of "Letters of the Federal Farmer" which became a sort of textbook for the opposition. His insistence was upon amendments before rather than after adoption. Through the instrumentality of his friend Patrick Henry, also an opponent of the Constitution, Lee was chosen one of Virginia's senators in the new government, and his chief concern in the Senate was to bring to fruition the amendments which he had advocated. Some of his propositions would probably now be regarded as chimerical, but the chief of them were embodied in the first ten amendments, and the verdict of time appears to have sustained their wisdom. In October 1792, broken in health, he resigned his senatorial seat and retired to "Chantilly," where he lingered a little more than two years.

[The *Memoir of the Life of Richard Henry Lee* (2 vols., 1825), by his grandson, R. H. Lee, is unsatisfactory. There are briefer biographies, as in Charles Campbell, *Hist. of the Colony and Ancient Dominion of Va.* (1860), but they are for the most part condensations from the *Memoir.* The present sketch is based primarily on *The Letters of Richard Henry Lee* (2 vols., 1911–14), edited by J. C. Ballagh, together with the *Journals of the House of Burgesses* and the *Journals of the Continental Cong.* Genealogical facts have been drawn mainly from E. J. Lee, *Lee of Va., 1642–1892* (1895), supplemented by items in the *Va. Mag. of Hist. and Biog.* Among the works that afford helpful contributions are C. R. Lingley, *The Transition in Va. from Colony to Commonwealth* (1910); H. J. Eckenrode, *The Revolution in Va.* (1916); E. C. Burnett, *Letters of Members of the Continental Cong.,* vols. I–V (1921–31), and the writings of John Adams, Samuel Adams, and Thomas Jefferson. For the Deane-Lee episode see "The Deane Papers," *N. Y. Hist. Soc. Colls.,* Publication Fund Series, vols. XIX–XXIII (1887–91). For his senatorial career see the *Annals of Cong.,* vols. I–III, and the *Jour. of Wm. Maclay* (1890, 1927), edited by E. S. Maclay. Characterizations of Lee's person and oratory are found in Wm. Wirt, *Sketches of the Life and Character of Patrick Henry* (1817 and later editions); and H. S. Randall, *Life of Jefferson* (1858), I, 102. Lee's "Letters of the Federal Farmer to the Republican," were in two series and were printed with the title, *Observations Leading to a Fair Examination of the System of Government Proposed by the Late Convention* (1787). The second series was published separately under the title: *An Additional Number of Letters from the Federal Farmer to the Republican* (1788); the first series was reprinted by P. L. Ford in *Pamphlets on the Constitution* (1888).]

E. C. B.

LEE, ROBERT EDWARD (Jan. 19, 1807–Oct. 12, 1870), soldier, the fifth child and third son of Henry, "Light-Horse Harry," Lee [*q.v.*] and Anne Hill (Carter) Lee, was born at "Stratford," Westmoreland County, Va. His father, a member of a famous Virginia family, a distinguished cavalry officer of the Revolution, and a former governor of the state, had married as his second wife a daughter of the wealthy and religious planter, Charles Carter of "Shirley." His brilliant political prospects were wrecked by a mania for speculation, and in 1811 he was forced to leave "Stratford," which belonged to Henry Lee [*q.v.*], a son by his first marriage. Moving to Alexandria, Va., which offered inexpensive educational facilities, the family lived modestly on the income from a trust estate left Mrs. Lee by her father. The fortunes of "Light-Horse Harry" continued to decline, and in 1813, having been badly injured in the Baltimore riot, he went to the West Indies. He died at Cumberland Island, Ga., on his way home, Mar. 25, 1818.

Diligent in his studies at the Alexandria schools and displaying marked aptitude for mathematics, Robert led a normal, outdoor life, but from boyhood he had the care of an ill mother. In 1824 the inspiration of his father's military career and the opportunity of procuring a professional education without draining the limited financial resources of the family led him to seek appointment to West Point. Entering in 1825, much more mature and better prepared than the average boy of his age, he distinguished himself alike by his scholarship and by his proficiency in military exercises, was adjutant of the corps, and was graduated number two in the class of 1829 without a demerit.

The seventeen years that followed his commission as brevet second lieutenant of engineers were such as might have been spent by any young officer of that service, who combined a fine presence with social graces, exemplary conduct, energy, and ability. After seventeen months of work on Fort Pulaski, Cockspur Island, Ga., he served as assistant engineer at Fort Monroe, Va., from May 1831 to November 1834. While stationed there, he married at "Arlington," June 30, 1831, Mary Ann Randolph Custis, only daughter of George Washington Parke Custis [*q.v.*], grandson of Martha Washington. Association with Custis and with the Washington traditions at "Arlington" made his father's old commander Lee's ideal, whom he seems consciously to have emulated in his bearing and in his conception of duty. His marriage was happy. Mrs. Lee was not a housekeeper, and by her tardiness habitually offended his sense of punctuality, but she was intelligent and appreciative, though strong and outspoken in her political likes and dislikes. A constant reader, she had a deeply religious nature. She held his love, without a suggestion of wavering, through nearly forty years of married life. She bore him seven children, George Washington Custis [*q.v.*], Mary, William H. Fitzhugh [*q.v.*], Agnes, Annie, Robert Edward, and Mildred, who were reared chiefly at "Arlington." Only William H. Fitzhugh and Robert left issue. The others died unmarried.

After leaving Fort Monroe, Lee was an assistant in the chief engineer's office in Washington during the years 1834–37, and in the summer of 1835 aided in running the Ohio-Michigan boundary line. His first important independent assignment came in July 1837, as superintending engineer for St. Louis harbor and the upper Mississippi and Missouri rivers. When this work, which he performed with much success, was suspended for lack of funds in October 1841, he was transferred to Fort Hamilton, New York harbor, where he remained, with one brief stay at headquarters in Washington (1844), until Aug. 19, 1846. Then he was sent, via Washington, to San Antonio, Tex., as assistant engineer to the army under Gen. John E. Wool. He followed Wool's futile marches until the column reached Buena Vista, and won much praise by a very bold reconnaissance in front of that place. Transferred then to the Vera Cruz expedition, he immediately captivated its commander, Gen. Winfield Scott, by his diligence and capacity, and had every opportunity of winning a name for himself. At Vera Cruz, he was charged with locating the heavy land-batteries. The strategy of Cerro Gordo was largely based on reconnaissance made by him. In the advance on Mexico City he distinguished himself by two crossings of the lava field between San Augustin and Padierna in the dark, and during the battle of Churubusco he conducted the column of General Shields to the left of Scott's line. His exhausting work in placing batteries in front of Chapultepec and a slight wound received in the battle of Sept. 13, 1847, forced him to retire from the field, but he rejoined Scott in Mexico City the next day and was promptly set to work preparing maps for future operations.

Lee had been made first lieutenant of engineers in 1836 and captain in 1838; when he returned to the United States in 1848 and was placed in charge of the construction of Fort Carroll, Baltimore harbor, he had been promoted for gallantry to the rank of brevet colonel. After three years and nine months at Fort Carroll (November 1848–August 1852), he was made superintendent at West Point, much against his wishes. His term there was distinguished by a number of improvements in the plant, by changes in the curriculum, and by close attention to the individual cadets, among whom were individuals as different in taste and sympathies as James Abbott McNeill Whistler, the artist, and "Jeb" Stuart, the Confederate trooper. The social life of the academy was pleasant, but Lee was glad, with the assistance of Jefferson Davis, secretary of war, to change from the staff to the line as lieutenant-colonel of the 2nd Cavalry in March 1855. The transfer hardly fulfilled his expectations. His long absences from home became increasingly burdensome as he grew older, and were rendered more tedious by repeated details for court-martial duty. In October 1857 his father-in-law died. He was named one of the executors and had to hasten home and procure a succession of furloughs to settle a large property under a confusing testament. Mrs. Lee, meantime, had developed chronic arthritis and was fast becoming an invalid, to her husband's great distress. These circumstances kept him from active duty and made 1857–59 a dark period in his life. At one time he contemplated resigning from the army. During the time his regiment was on frontier duty in Texas, Lee was actually with it only from March 1856 to October 1857, and from February 1860 to the same month of the next year. During the last period he was in command of the Department of Texas. Prior to 1861, he had never commanded more troops in the field than four squadrons of horse, and that number only for a forty-day scout in June-July 1856. Chancing to be in Washington at the time of the John Brown raid in 1859, he was sent to Harpers Ferry to put down the "insurrection." He did so with little waste of time and life.

During the later months of his second period of duty in Texas, the secession movement began. Lee had no sympathy with it. With him, a Whig, warmly devoted to the Union, the political and economic arguments for Southern independence did not weigh. He knew little of constitutional law, and the few slaves he had owned in earlier years had died or been manumitted. The question with him—a question he hoped he would never see brought to an issue—was simply whether his first allegiance was due his state or the Union. He answered it without mental debate: in case Virginia seceded, the traditions of his family and its long association with Virginia instinctively determined him to cast in his lot with her. He stated this repeatedly before he left Texas, and said at the same time that he regarded secession as revolution. It was not until the discussions of wartime camp-fires had acquainted him more fully with its constitutional basis that he accepted the doctrine of secession.

Recalled to Washington in February 1861, and placed by General Scott on waiting orders, probably with an eye to promoting him quickly in case of war, Lee watched the crisis approach, but his natural optimism led him to believe that some solution would be found before extremists, Northern and Southern, could destroy the Union. On Mar. 16, he was made colonel of the 1st Cavalry and accepted the commission without hesitation. On Mar. 15, the Confederate secretary of war wrote him offering him rank as brigadier-general in the Confederate States army, but if he ever received the letter, which shows plainly that he had not been consulted, he ignored it. Virginia, meantime, had called a constitutional convention to decide on secession. While waiting on the action of his state, Lee realized that, regardless of her decision, his conscience would not permit him to bear arms against the South. Therefore, when Francis P. Blair on Apr. 18, 1861, told him that he was authorized to offer him the field command of the United States army (Lee to Reverdy Johnson, Feb. 25, 1868, R. E. Lee, *Recollections and Letters of General Lee,* pp. 27–28), Lee declined the offer and stated his reasons for doing so. He then called on General Scott and recounted what had happened. Scott, his frank friend and admirer, told him that his position was anomalous and that he should either resign or be ready to accept any duty assigned him. Lee felt that this was true, but his affection for the army and the Union was so deep that he still hoped his honor would not compel him to dissociate himself from either. The next day he learned that the Virginia convention had voted in favor of secession. He had thereupon to decide whether he should resign immediately or await the action of the voters of the state on the ordinance of secession, which had to be submitted for their approval. The events of that single day, however, convinced him that war would not wait on a referendum. Accordingly, he submitted his resignation on Apr. 20, intending that it be effective immediately. As it was not accepted until his accounts had been checked in the routine manner, the formal date of resignation appears in official records as Apr. 25.

Lee had not communicated with the Virginia authorities, and had hoped that he would not have to participate in a war he deplored; but he considered that his sword was at the command of his native state, and when Virginia chose him as commander of her forces he accepted on Apr. 23 and threw all his energies into her defense.

After making an extraordinary record in fortifying the rivers and mobilizing the volunteers of the state, he was informally designated as military adviser to President Davis, with the rank of general (confirmed Aug. 31, 1861, to rank as of June 14, 1861). Dispatched on July 28 to the vicinity of Monterey, Va., he succeeded in halting a threatened invasion from western Virginia; but military jealousies, lack of supplies, bad weather, and over-elaborate strategy robbed him of larger results, and when he was recalled to serve again as the president's consultant his popular reputation had declined greatly. Despite some clamor against him, Davis's confidence in Lee was undiminished and he sent him, early in November, to organize the defenses of the South Atlantic seaboard. This work occupied Lee until March 1862, when he was summoned back to Richmond for a third time to assist the president, with the honorific but empty title of general in charge of military operations under the direction of the president.

The assignment was unpleasant, the duties were vague and the difficulties immense, but Lee steered a courageous course between President Davis and Gen. Joseph E. Johnston, both of them hypersensitive, and with the help of "Stonewall" Jackson [*q.v.*], then commanding in the Shenandoah Valley, he worked out a plan to keep the Federals in northern Virginia from reënforcing General McClellan, who was then preparing to besiege Richmond. Johnston having been wounded May 31, 1862, Lee was assigned next day to the command of the troops he promptly named "The Army of Northern Virginia." At this time, when his career as a field-commander really began, he was fifty-five years old, physically magnificent and in full vigor, five feet, ten and a half inches tall, weighing around 170 pounds, with powerful shoulders and chest, a large neck and well-moulded head, dark-brown eyes, a florid complexion, and hair that was rapidly turning gray. A short beard, which he had not worn until that spring, covered a powerful jaw, and thin, straight lips. He had never commanded in a battle. During the thirty-four months that followed he at no time had a force comparable in numbers, in artillery, or in equipment to the opposing armies. This is the fact that must constantly be remembered in any study of his campaigns. The odds against him were always three to two and sometimes three to one.

He inherited a crisis. McClellan, with nearly 100,000 men, was within seven miles of Richmond. Three separate forces were threatening Jackson in the Valley of Virginia. A large Federal army was on the Rappahannock, preparing to support McClellan. If McClellan were reenforced or permitted to bring his siege guns within range, Richmond would certainly fall. Lee hurriedly fortified the city and collected such troops as he could from the South. His problem was greatly simplified when Jackson, acting under the plan he and Lee had jointly formulated, defeated two Federal columns at Cross Keys and Port Republic, June 8–9. Lee brought Jackson's troops to Ashland, sixteen miles from Richmond, and, with the combined forces, took the offensive in what were destined to be the Seven Days' battles. At Mechanicsville on June 26, the slowness of a turning-movement that Lee entrusted to Jackson led A. P. Hill to a costly and futile attempt to storm Beaver Dam Creek; the next day at Gaines's Mill, Lee drove Fitz John Porter's corps from the north side of the Chickahominy River and forced McClellan to change his base to the James. The rearguard action at Savage Station on the 29th did little more than expedite and somewhat confuse the Federal retreat; on June 30 a mistake as to the line of the enemy's withdrawal and the non-arrival of two of the converging columns led to an indecisive battle at Frayser's Farm, where Lee had hoped to envelop and destroy McClellan; on July 1, at Malvern Hill, the inexperience of the staff prevented the massing of the whole army in a tangled terrain for a simultaneous attack on the strong Federal positions. Isolated attacks, though gallantly pressed, failed to dislodge McClellan, who withdrew that night unchallenged and took refuge under cover of his gunboats at Harrison's Landing. This campaign was the most important period in Lee's military education. Strategically sound in principle, though demanding too much of untrained officers, the campaign was tactically bad on the Southern side. It taught Lee the necessity of simpler methods and organization. It served its immediate purpose, however, in relieving the threat against Richmond, and it supplied a large part of his army with superior small-arms. Similarly it raised greatly the morale of the army and inspired confidence in Lee.

Quietly and quickly ridding himself of incompetent division commanders, Lee soon detached Jackson to the vicinity of Orange Court House to confront a new "Army of Virginia" under Maj.-Gen. John Pope. Lee had to watch both Pope and McClellan, not knowing which might strike first, but he carefully fed troops from the James to the Rapidan, and, at the first sure sign of the impending departure of McClellan to join Pope, he anticipated the actual Federal movement and soon confronted Pope with the greater part of his army. This was Lee's first display of skill in the difficult military art of troop-movement. Arriving at Gordonsville on Aug. 15, Lee determined on an immediate campaign of maneuver, in order to increase the distance between Pope and McClellan and to subsist his army in territory that otherwise would be occupied by the enemy. His initial plan of surprising Pope between the Rapidan and Rappahannock rivers was thwarted, but he crossed the Rapidan, shifted his line as far up the Rappahannock as possible, and then, boldly dividing his army, sent Jackson by roundabout roads to attack Pope's line of communication. Jackson chose to strike at Manassas Junction, Pope's advance base. Knowing that Jackson's move would force Pope to retreat at once, Lee followed Jackson's route with Longstreet's command and before noon on Aug. 29, when Jackson was fighting a defensive battle against part of the Union army, Lee concentrated his entire command in front of Pope. He encountered great unwillingness on the part of Maj.-Gen. James Longstreet [*q.v.*] to attack that afternoon, because Longstreet believed delay until the next morning would offer greater advantage. Lee held to the view that it was the duty of the commanding general to bring the forces together at the right moment on the chosen ground of action and to leave actual combat to the divisional and brigade commanders, and he usually contented himself with "suggestions" to competent officers. In this instance, he yielded to Longstreet's stubbornness and disclosed for the first time his one great weakness as field commander—his inability to work with unwilling tools. The general assault, thus delayed, was delivered on Aug. 30 and routed Pope in the battle of Second Manassas (Second Bull Run), but Aug. 31 was lost in reconcentrating the weary and scattered army, and a rainstorm at Chantilly (Ox Hill) on the afternoon of Sept. 1 kept Lee from overtaking his adversary.

Lee could not feed his army where it then stood. Neither could he attack the Washington fortifications, whither Pope had fled. A withdrawal would impair the morale of his army and raise that of the Federals. Accordingly, Lee determined to move into Maryland and to renew the campaign of maneuver there. Reaching Frederick on Sept. 7, he soon found that the Federals were not evacuating Harpers Ferry as he had anticipated they would be. His line of communications through the Shenandoah Valley lay close to that strongly garrisoned post, so he was forced to detach five divisions under Jackson to reduce it. After their departure, a false rumor of a Federal advance on Hagerstown led him to direct Longstreet thither. He did so the more readily as he now planned to destroy the Baltimore & Ohio and then to advance on Harrisburg and cut the other main railway line that linked East and West. While Longstreet was on the road to Hagerstown, McClellan suddenly undertook a swift westward advance on Frederick, having received a copy of Lee's general order that had been carelessly dropped by a courier or staff-officer. Lee was caught with his forces badly divided. Hurrying Longstreet back on Sept. 14 to support the rearguard under D. H. Hill, he vainly attempted to check McClellan on South Mountain (Boonsboro) that day. Finding this impossible, he ordered a retreat to Virginia, but learning that Harpers Ferry would certainly be captured by Jackson the next day, he retreated to Sharpsburg. He miscalculated the time required for the troop-movements, his only serious blunder in logistics, and on Sept. 17, the bloodiest single day of the war, the slow arrival of troops from Harpers Ferry nearly cost him a serious defeat in the battle of Sharpsburg (Antietam). He held his ground on the 18th and then returned to Virginia, hoping soon to reenter Maryland. Including the troops captured at Harpers Ferry, he had inflicted a loss of 27,000 on his adversary during the Maryland expedition, but he had lost 13,000 himself, and his army was so badly shaken by straggling that he had to forego a further offensive.

Lee at once reorganized the army into two corps under Longstreet and Jackson, refitted it and restored its morale, and awaited the next move of the Army of the Potomac, which was now placed under command of Maj.-Gen. A. E. Burnside. Nearly two months passed. Then, on Nov. 14, Lee interpreted certain Federal troop-movements as indicating that Burnside was marching toward Fredericksburg. Lee would have preferred to fight on the North Anna, where he could have followed up a victory, but he could not afford to sacrifice the supplies of the lower Rappahannock valley, so he followed Burnside, accepted battle at Fredericksburg and on Dec. 13 repulsed repeated Federal assaults with bloody losses. He could not pursue the enemy because the Union artillery on the north side of the Rappahannock dominated the plain.

Food was scarce and forage almost unprocurable during the winter that followed. Most of the cavalry had to be sent to the rear, and two divisions of Longstreet's corps were dispatched to the south side of the James to meet a threatened advance against the railroad leading southward from Richmond. Lee hoped for the speedy return of these troops, but Longstreet did not take the offensive and dispersed his troops so widely, while collecting supplies in eastern North Carolina, that he could not reconcentrate quickly on receipt of orders to rejoin Lee. The Army of Northern Virginia had, therefore, been reduced to 62,500 men when, on Apr. 29, a new Federal commander, Maj.-Gen. Joseph Hooker [*q.v.*], launched a well-planned offensive across the Rappahannock above and below Fredericksburg. Lee was just recovering at the time from a severe illness, but he did not hesitate. Reasoning that the main attack would be west of the town, he left 9,000 troops under Early at Fredericksburg, marched with the rest to meet Hooker and, on May 1, found his adversary withdrawing to a strong line around Chancellorsville. Lee decided to turn the Federal position from the west and directed Jackson to undertake this movement. Jackson early the next morning countered with a proposal to employ all his infantry, 28,000, with part of Stuart's cavalry, so as to roll up the whole right wing of the Federal army. Lee consented, and with 14,000 men faced the enemy's main force at Chancellorsville while Jackson marched beyond Hooker's right. Late in the day Jackson routed the XI Corps in one of the most spectacular operations of modern war. The next morning the two wings of the Army of Northern Virginia attacked the Federals, forced them into the country between Chancellorsville and the Rappahannock, and were about to deliver another assault when Lee was forced to detach troops to cope with Maj.-Gen. John Sedgwick, who had forced Early from the heights around Fredericksburg and was advancing on Lee's rear. Owing to the hesitant tactics of Maj.-Gen. Lafayette McLaws at Salem Church, it took Lee two days to dispose of Sedgwick and to reconcentrate in front of Hooker. When Lee prepared to attack again on the morning of May 6, he found that Hooker had retreated to the north bank of the Rappahannock. This, the battle of Chancellorsville, was the most brilliant of Lee's victories, but it was one of the greatest of Southern tragedies because it cost him the service of Jackson, who was wounded on May 2 and died May 10. Lee had worked in complete understanding with Jackson, whom he regarded as a perfect executive officer, and he never was able to replace him.

In the reorganization of the army that Jackson's death necessitated, Lee decided to increase the number of corps to three and to reduce their size, because he considered the old corps too large for one man to handle to the fullest advantage in a wooded country. Esteeming A. P. Hill the best division commander in the army, he named him to head the new III Corps, and for Jackson's II Corps he selected the latter's senior division commander, R. S. Ewell. This choice was dictated by sentiment, for Ewell had been associated with Jackson's most famous battles, but it placed one-third of the Army of Northern Virginia under an officer who had served only a few weeks with Lee and was unaccustomed to exercise the discretion that Lee always gave his corps commanders. The staff, of course, was reorganized at the same time, and many new officers were assigned to direct troops of whom they knew little. The result of all this was to create a new machinery of command for two-thirds of the army. Lee does not seem to have realized the dangers this change of command involved, but his decision to resume the offensive immediately and to carry the war into the enemy's country, before the new officers became familiar with their troops and their duties, must be accounted the major mistake of his entire career. It explains, more fully than anything else, the fatal lack of coördination at Gettysburg.

He was prompted to invade the North again for three reasons: first, to supply his army; secondly, to strengthen peace sentiment in the North by showing the futility of the effort to force the South into submission; and, thirdly, in the hope that he could compel Lincoln to detach troops from the far South and thereby relieve the pressure on Vicksburg. Leaving A. P. Hill with 20,000 to hold the line of the Rappahannock temporarily, he skilfully moved into the Shenandoah Valley and reëntered Maryland, with Harrisburg again his objective. On June 23 Stuart's fondness for raids around the enemy led him to exceed his orders and to separate the largest and most proficient part of the cavalry from the rest of the army at a time when Lee needed every mounted unit to watch Hooker, who was now between him and Stuart. Finding on June 28 that Hooker had crossed into Maryland on the 25th, Lee had to concentrate quickly his columns, which had been widely scattered for the collection of supplies. The advance of A. P. Hill discovered a force of unknown strength at Gettysburg on June 30. Ewell advanced promptly from the north to support him and the two, on July 1, won a stiff fight, capturing 5,000 men. Lee arrived during the afternoon and, in the language he usually employed in dealing with his corps commanders, suggested to Ewell that the advantage be pushed south of Gettysburg. In the absence of peremptory orders, Ewell delayed the attack and gave the Federals time in which to strengthen their forces on Cemetery Hill and

Culp's Hill. Lee's one chance of victory lay in striking before the Federals could concentrate all their force on the strong ground of Cemetery Ridge, but on the morning of July 2 he encountered an unexpected difficulty. Before the army had left Virginia, Longstreet had urged Lee to employ offensive strategy but defensive tactics in Pennsylvania, and he had persuaded himself that Lee had promised to do this. When he discovered that Lee was determined to attack Meade, who had now succeeded Hooker in command, Longstreet felt that Lee was courting ruin. All his pride of opinion asserted itself. He was chagrined and humiliated at the rejection of his plan, and if he did not deliberately delay in the hope of keeping Lee from what he believed would be a slaughter, he at least acted so slowly and unwillingly that Cemetery Ridge was heavily manned and its capture was almost impossible when the I Corps assaulted late in the afternoon of July 2. The movement was just successful enough to make a renewal of the attack the next morning a virtual necessity. Pickett's and Pettigrew's (Heth's) divisions charged with a valor worthy of the finest achievements of the army, but they were hurled back with dismal slaughter, and the battle was lost. Lee was forced to retreat the next day in order to reëstablish his line of communications. On the night of July 13–14 he crossed the Potomac to Virginia soil. Gettysburg was the great defeat of his military career. The caution of Ewell and the defective staff work on the two newly formed corps were responsible for some serious tactical blunders. The absence of Stuart's cavalry during the preliminaries of the battle, the strength of the Union position, and the obduracy of Longstreet explained the rest. Lee assumed full responsibility for all that had happened and sought to resign the command of the army. It was no mere gesture of humility, for however culpable Longstreet was for his behavior, Lee was to be blamed for not dealing effectively with that stubborn officer. Yet, for all of Longstreet's defects, Lee had no one in the army whom he felt justified in substituting for him. He was compelled to make the best of the personnel he had.

Despite his 20,000 casualties, Lee was anxious to resume the offensive after Gettysburg, but the detachment of two divisions of Longstreet's corps to Tennessee, the condition of the commissary, and the scarcity of replacements rendered this impossible. Only two abortive operations, one by him against Bristoe Station and one by Meade to Mine Run, occurred until May 4, 1864, when Grant crossed the Rapidan, headed for Richmond. Lee then had somewhat more than 60,000 men. Grant's force was almost precisely twice that. Grant's cavalry and artillery were better than they had ever been; the horses of the Army of Northern Virginia had been so close to starvation in the winter of 1863–64 that they could scarcely drag the guns or carry the men. The quartermasters' and commissary stores of the Army of the Potomac were ample and flawlessly organized; Lee's men had been subsisting on a daily ration of a pint of cornmeal and a quarter of a pound of bacon, and they had scarcely any equipment or supplies except their arms and ammunition. It was impossible from the outset, therefore, for Lee to assume the offensive against Grant on open ground where the artillery of the enemy could be used and the full Union strength be employed. He did not attempt to dispute the crossing of the Rapidan, but hurried forward to the Wilderness of Spotsylvania, in the hope of catching Grant on the move in that tangled terrain, the American counterpart of the Meuse-Argonne. On May 5 and 6 Lee repulsed Grant's attacks with heavy slaughter, and on the 6th was in the midst of a turning movement when the serious wounding of Longstreet threw the Confederate right into disorder. On May 7, Lee concluded that Grant was swinging southward, and by the dispatch of Longstreet's corps (now under R. H. Anderson) to Spotsylvania Court House, he blocked Grant's road to Richmond. Two weeks' fighting and maneuvering followed at Spotsylvania (May 8–21). Longstreet was *hors de combat.* A. P. Hill was ill and Ewell was scarcely able to keep the field. Lee had to give the closest attention to the tactical dispositions as well as to the strategy, but he constructed admirable field fortifications and beat off all Grant's assaults except that of May 12 on a salient in Ewell's front ("The Bloody Angle"). In that day's action Grant gained an early advantage because Lee, on mistaken reports from his scouts, had withdrawn the artillery supporting Edward Johnson's division; but a new line was drawn in rear of the salient and the enemy, on May 14, abandoned the captured position. Sensing on May 21 that Grant was starting another flank movement, Lee made a forced march to the North Anna and again confronted him when he arrived on May 23. The Army of Northern Virginia took up the strongest position it had yet occupied, diverted Grant's line of advance on Richmond, and effectively covered the Virginia Central railroad, though part of its track was temporarily torn up. Had Lee been able to strike either the Federal right, under Warren, or the left, under Hancock, immediately after the Union forces had crossed the river, he might have inflicted a severe defeat on one or the other of Grant's exposed wings; but after the Federals were entrenched, Lee's opportunity was lost. Moreover, he was stricken with a debilitating intestinal malady and before he recovered, Grant (May 27) had moved again by Lee's right, this time down the Pamunkey River. Lee marched swiftly, faced Grant on the Totopotomoy (May 28–30), and forced him to maneuver to the Confederate right for the fourth time. During the whole of this period, from the time he engaged Grant on May 4, Lee was constantly seeking an opportunity to catch Grant on the move, or to attack the Federals in detail, but he found no opening. At Cold Harbor, on June 3, Grant was repulsed with such heavy casualties that he abandoned his bludgeoning tactics. During the month that had then elapsed since Grant had crossed the Rapidan, his losses had been about 50,000, a number equal to approximately 90 per cent. of the strength of the infantry of Lee's army at the opening of the campaign. The record of Lee's losses, if ever filed, was destroyed in the evacuation of Richmond. The number was approximately half that of Grant's.

Beginning on the night of June 12–13, Grant withdrew from Cold Harbor, marched to Wilcox's Landing, and crossed the James River to destroy Lee's communications and to invest Richmond by way of Petersburg. Lee had anticipated such a move, but since the absence of his cavalry kept him from penetrating the screen Grant threw about the Army of the Potomac, and Beauregard on the south side of the river could not ascertain what part of Grant's army confronted him there, Lee was uncertain of the position of his adversary and therefore hesitated to uncover Richmond. He had been compelled to detach Breckinridge and later the II Corps (now Early's) to meet new threats in western Virginia and in the Shenandoah Valley, and for that reason, his ability to reënforce Beauregard was limited. He fed troops to the south side, however, as fast as he had assurance of a Federal concentration there and, with the help of Hoke's division, which Lee sent him promptly, Beauregard saved Petersburg. The investment of that city, which formally began on June 18, was essentially a campaign of attrition. With headquarters in or near the city, Lee had to defend a line of thirty miles, slowly lengthened to thirty-six. At the same time, he had to protect the railroads connecting Richmond with the South. He sent Early into Maryland in the hope that Grant would detach troops heavily to defend Washington, or else would be tempted to attack the strong lines in front of Petersburg. Early reached the outskirts of Washington but the diversion failed of its larger purpose. Lee's forces steadily declined through casualties and, after the winter began, through desertion, chiefly on the part of new conscripts. Every day brought starvation nearer; the exhaustion of the horse supply threatened to render the army immobile; Lee could only hold on by fortifying heavily and by using as a reserve the troops on the extreme right of the Petersburg front, where the lines of the opposing forces were not close together. The principal actions of the siege were the Crater, July 30, 1864, the battles of the Weldon railroad and Reams's Station, Aug. 19–25, 1864, and the capture of Fort Harrison, on the north side of the James, Sept. 29, 1864.

On Feb. 6, 1865, orders were issued designating Lee general-in-chief of all the Confederate armies, but the condition of his own command and the plight of operations elsewhere made it impossible for him to give more than a general strategic direction to the last-ditch battles of the exhausted Confederacy. In March the advance of Sherman's army into North Carolina made it certain that Lee would be overwhelmed if he remained at Petersburg. On the 25th he made a desperate attempt to divide the Federals by an assault on Fort Stedman, and when the repulse of this was followed by an extension of the Federal left and by a general assault on the Petersburg lines, he was forced to evacuate Petersburg and Richmond on the night of Apr. 2–3 and to begin a retreat toward the small army of Gen. Joseph E. Johnston in western North Carolina. Failure to receive supplies at Amelia Court House on Apr. 4 lost him a day and compelled him, when the Federals arrived in his front, to turn toward Lynchburg up the Southside railroad. On Apr. 6, his retreating line was struck at Sailor's Creek, and on the 9th, finding himself blocked by Sheridan, and almost surrounded at Appomattox Court House, he was forced to surrender to General Grant. Of the 35,000 troops with which he started from the Richmond-Petersburg line, only 7,800 remained with arms in their hands. When he appeared among his men after the surrender, mounted on his famous war horse, "Traveller," the veterans of the Army of Northern Virginia overwhelmed him with their regard and sympathy.

As a paroled prisoner of war, treated with great consideration by the Federal army, Lee returned to Richmond and remained there or in the vicinity until the autumn. He had no home, for "Arlington" had been sold in 1863 for nonpayment of taxes, but in September, having accepted the presidency of Washington College, he moved to Lexington, Va. He was profoundly interested in the education of the young men of the South, and, with the help of an enthusiastic faculty, he soon raised a discouraged college to a high level of scholarship and attendance, though it is not certain that all of the interesting educational innovations at the school originated with him. His supreme interest after the war was in restoring the economic, cultural, and political life of the South. Shunning all discussion of politics, and reading little about the war, though he at one time planned to write a history of the campaigns of his army, he set an example of obedience to civil authority. He applied for a pardon on June 13, 1865, and consistently urged his former soldiers to work hard, to keep the peace, and to accept the outcome of the war. Indicted for treason, he was never brought to trial. On his few lengthy journeys, especially on a tour of the South Atlantic seaboard for his health in the spring of 1870, he was welcomed with a measure of affection no other Southerner since Washington has received. His mail, which was immense, was crowded with offers of business proposals, all of which he rejected. In the midst of peaceful activities, he was stricken on Sept. 28 and died on Oct. 12, 1870, in Lexington, where he was buried. He probably had angina pectoris, and his final illness was due to some atherosclerotic process. The news of his death put every Southern community in mourning. Admiration for him, which had been almost universal in the South after 1862, found new expression in biographies, in monuments, and in countless memorial addresses. Washington College changed its name to Washington and Lee University in his honor. After sixty years, the affection and reverence of the South for him are, if anything, higher than in 1870. No American has ever had an influence on the people of the old Confederate states comparable to his. In all matters on which he expressed himself, he is still regarded as the final authority. In him the South still sees the embodiment of all its best ideals.

While Lee was distinguished as an educator, his place in American history is that of a notable Christian gentleman and a great soldier. He was confirmed in the Episcopal church in 1853, and the fundamentals of the Christian religion—humility, prayer, faith, and kindness—were his code of daily conduct. His equanimity was religious, rather than philosophical, and, though he was not a fatalist, he believed that God directed the daily affairs of man and ordered even man's adversities to his good. It was for this reason that he accepted defeat without repining. His unique relations with his soldiers, his affection for children, his dignified courtesy, and his love of animals are illustrated by a thousand anecdotes that are part of the spiritual treasury of Americans. His temper and patience seldom failed him. Self-control was second nature. His rare outbursts of wrath, usually attended by a reddening of the neck and a curious jerk of the head, were generally followed by some particularly gracious act to the object of his displeasure.

Both absolutely and in the light of the odds he faced in men and resources, Lee has been adjudged one of the greatest of modern soldiers and probably the most eminent American strategist. His achievements did not owe their brilliance to contrasted mediocrity, for most of his adversaries were able. Neither was he a great soldier because he had a great lieutenant in Jackson. Lee devised and Jackson executed. If Lee won fewer victories after Jackson's death it was not because he lacked strategical ability when acting alone but because his resources were diminished and because he found no successor to "Stonewall." His one great weakness was his inability to shape contrary minds to his purpose. Stubborn incompetents he courteously disregarded, but in dealing with Longstreet he thrice yielded to the latter's obstinacy and sought victory by assiduous pursuit of the second-best plan. Excessive consideration for the feelings of others explained this weakness. His strategical powers sprang from his extraordinary brain-power, his ability to put himself in the place of his opponents, his analysis of military intelligence, his masterful logistics, and his capacity for gauging accurately the offensive and defensive strength of given bodies of troops. These qualities and the long odds with which he had to contend in all his campaigns explain a daring that would have been rashness in a less capable leader. A desperate cause demanded desperate risks. His power to inspire confidence and to create morale was due to his record of victories, his inflexible justice, his attention to detail, his great aptitude for organization, his imperturbable presence in battle, his regard for his men, and the quality of his military material. He was less renowned as a tactician than as a strategist, because of his theory of the duties of a commanding general (outlined in the references to Second Manassas); but his facility in tactics increased steadily, especially in the employment of field fortification, which some consider his greatest contribution to the science of war. Where possible, he always reconnoitered in person, and with an unusual eye for terrain. He was wont to say that he had to see for himself. If he failed to follow up his successes, it was not for slowness or lack of dash but because the margin of superiority in combat was always so narrow that his army was usually exhausted after a victory.

Almost alone among the principal Confederate commanders he was consistently on good terms with the administration. Only on some three occasions, and these at times when President Davis was suffering to an unusual degree from the facial neuralgia that dogged him throughout the war, did he ever receive sharp messages from the chief executive. One of these he tore into bits; the others he ignored. The first reason for his success in dealing with as difficult a man as the Confederate President was his unfailing, deferential respect for constituted authority, a respect equaling that displayed by General Washington himself. The second reason was his willingness at all times to subordinate his operations to the general strategy of the administration and to explain his plans to the President. He knew Davis thoroughly, and in the urgent matter of reënforcements, which was always a subject of delicate and difficult correspondence, he usually got troops, if they were to be had, by stating frankly that if he did not receive them he might be compelled to retreat on Richmond. That never failed to arouse the President to action. Davis consulted him often regarding the enlistment and organization of the troops and about the strategy of campaigns on other fronts. Lee was prompt to answer and frank in his advice, but he was slow to impose his views on other commanders, especially on Gen. Joseph E. Johnston, whose capacities he perhaps over-valued. In nearly all his dispatches to the President, when operations elsewhere were under discussion, he explained that it was impossible to judge at a distance, when he did not know the special difficulties that had to be encountered. Consequently his influence on the "grand strategy" of the South was not great. To him, however, more than to any other military official, was due the enactment of the conscript laws.

[The major manuscript sources are as follows: Private papers, in the possession of the daughters of Capt. Robert E. Lee; engineering papers, Army Engineers' archives, Washington; educational papers, at West Point, and Washington and Lee University; military papers, War Department, Washington, and in the care of a committee of trustees for U. C. V., Richmond, Va.; field-telegrams on operations of June–Aug. 1864, Confederate Museum, Richmond, Va. His maps and military library are at the Virginia Military Institute, Lexington, Va. The greater part of his printed letters and dispatches appear in: *War of the Rebellion: Official Records (Army)*; *Lee's Dispatches* (1915); J. W. Jones, *Personal Reminiscences, Anecdotes and Letters of Gen. Robert E. Lee* (1874); J. W. Jones, *Life and Letters of Robert Edward Lee* (1906); and the invaluable *Recollections and Letters of General Robert E. Lee, by his son Capt. Robert E. Lee* (2nd ed., 1924). Other important books on his life or campaigns are: E. P. Alexander, *Military Memoirs of a Confederate* (1907); Gamaliel Bradford, *Lee the American* (1912); E. J. Lee, *Lee of Va., 1642–1892* (1895); A. L. Long, *Memoirs of Robert E. Lee* (1886); James Longstreet, *From Manassas to Appomattox* (1896); Sir Frederick Maurice, *Robert E. Lee, the Soldier* (1925); Sir Frederick Maurice, ed., *An Aide-de-Camp of Lee* (1927); Walter H. Taylor, *General Lee, His Campaigns in Virginia, 1861–65* (1906). To these may be added: *Memoirs of Lieut.-Gen. Scott* (1864); Jefferson Davis, *The Rise and Fall of the Confederate Government* (2 vols., 1881); *Battles and Leaders of the Civil War* (4 vols., 1887–88); Fitzhugh Lee, *General Lee* (1894); John Bigelow, Jr., *The Campaign of Chancellorsville* (1910). The best of the one-volume biographies, which number twenty or more, is H. A. White: *Robert E. Lee and the Southern Confederacy* (1897). The four-volume biography by the writer of this sketch will probably appear simultaneously with the publication of this work.]

D. S. F.

LEE, SAMUEL PHILLIPS (Feb. 13, 1812–June 5, 1897), naval officer, the son of Francis Lightfoot and Jane (Fitzgerald) Lee, was the grandson of Richard Henry Lee and the grandnephew of Francis Lightfoot Lee [*qq.v.*]. He was born at "Sully," Fairfax County, Va., and was appointed a midshipman in the United States navy on Nov. 22, 1825. After service on board the *Hornet* in the West Indies and on the *Delaware* and the *Java* in the Mediterranean, he was sent to the Pacific on the *Brandywine* but was later transferred to the *Vincennes* in 1834. From 1842 to 1855 he was chiefly employed in coast-survey duty. During the Mexican War he was in command of the coast-survey brig *Washington* and assisted in the capture of Tabasco on the east coast of Mexico. In 1851, in command of the *Dolphin,* he was sent to make deep-sea soundings, try currents, and search for shallow spots which had been reported by mariners. In performing this duty he cruised all over the Atlantic. His report was published by the direction of Congress and was of considerable assistance to Maury in his oceanographic work.

When news of the outbreak of the Civil War reached Lee, he was in charge of the *Vandalia* at the Cape of Good Hope, bound for the East Indies. He immediately returned without waiting for orders and was sent to the Charleston blockade. In 1862 he participated in the attack on New Orleans as commander of the *Oneida,* one of the three fast gunboats which were sent ahead to destroy the Confederate fleet above the forts. Lee drove off two rams that had attacked a Union ship, the *Varuna,* and received the surrender of Beverly Kennon, commander of the Confederate steamer *Governor Moore.* Later, in both passages of Vicksburg by the Union fleet under Farragut, the *Oneida* was second in line.

In September 1862, just after Lee had been made a captain, he was appointed an acting rear-admiral and ordered to command the North Atlantic blockading squadron off Virginia and North Carolina. He is credited with beginning the system of placing a cordon of ships far out at sea to intercept blockade runners who had escaped the ships nearer shore. As his territory included Wilmington, his prize money was considerable, and is estimated by Gideon Welles to have amounted to $150,000, the largest received by any officer. But in 1864, when the attack on Wilmington was contemplated, Welles displaced him because he did not consider him a fighting admiral or a man of prompt action. Lee was accordingly sent to command the Mississippi Squadron and did good work there on the Cumberland and Tennessee rivers in supporting Thomas against Hood and in preventing Hood from crossing the latter river at the most favorable point. After the war Lee served for a year as the head of the Signal Service, was made a rear-admiral in 1870, and commanded the North Atlantic Squadron from 1870 to 1872. He reached the retiring age in 1873 and spent the remaining years of his life in Washington, dying at Silver Spring, Md., of a stroke of paralysis. He was buried in Arlington. On Apr. 27, 1843, he had married Elizabeth, daughter of Francis P. Blair. A son (Francis Preston) Blair Lee, represented Maryland in the United States Senate from 1913 to 1917. Though never a popular hero, Lee seems to have been one of the most conscientious and efficient officers of his time.

[L. R. Hamersley, *The Records of Living Officers of the U. S. Navy and Marine Corps* (ed. 1890); Lee's *Report and Charts of the U. S. Brig Dolphin* (1854); *The Diary of Gideon Welles* (3 vols., 1911); *War of the Rebellion: Official Records (Navy)*; E. J. Lee, *Lee of Va., 1642–1892* (1895); R. M. Thompson and Richard Wainwright, *Confidential Correspondence of Gustavus Vasa Fox, Assistant Secretary of the Navy* (2 vols., 1918–19); letter from Lee to Senator J. R. Doolittle in *Southern Hist. Asso. Pubs.*, Mar. 1905; *Army and Navy Jour.*, June 12, 1897, *Evening Star* (Washington), June 7, 1897.] W. B. N.

LEE, STEPHEN DILL (Sept. 22, 1833–May 28, 1908), soldier and educator, at his appointment the youngest lieutenant-general in the Confederate army, was born at Charleston, S. C., the son of Thomas and Caroline (Allison) Lee, and a grandson of Thomas Lee [*q.v.*]. At seventeen he entered West Point, graduating in 1854 and being appointed second lieutenant in the 4th Artillery. After serving with his regiment on frontier duty in Texas, he was appointed first lieutenant in the fall of 1856 and during 1857 took part in the Seminole War as assistant adjutant-general of Florida. He was then appointed quartermaster of his regiment, continuing as such until the spring of 1861, during which time he saw frontier service in Kansas and Dakota. His sympathies being with the South, he resigned from the United States Army in February 1861.

He was immediately appointed captain in the South Carolina Volunteers, and later recommissioned in the Confederate army, where his rise was not only rapid but accompanied by an unbroken series of official commendations for heroic conduct, gallantry, and technical accomplishments. As aide-de-camp to Beauregard, commanding at Charleston, S. C., he was one of the officers appointed to treat with Major Anderson, commanding Fort Sumter, prior to and following its bombardment by Confederate forces in April 1861. Following the fall of Sumter, Lee performed staff duties pertaining to the defenses of Charleston, and was appointed major of artillery in November 1861. In 1862 he was present at the battles of Seven Pines, Savage's Station, Malvern Hill, second Manassas, and Sharpsburg, being made in turn lieutenant-colonel, colonel, and brigadier-general. Except for a short period following the Seven Days' battles, he held artillery commands with distinction, particularly at Sharpsburg. His short term of command of the 4th Virginia Cavalry in July brought favorable notice. Following his appointment as brigadier-general, he was sent by President Davis to Vicksburg, Miss., where he commanded in various capacities in minor engagements during the winter of 1862–63, and participated in the repulse of Sherman at Chickasaw Bayou in December. His heroic conduct at Champion Hills, May 16, 1863, was followed by a stiff defense against the Federal forces which pierced his lines in a determined assault on May 22, but were cleared from the redoubts before dark with the loss of many men and some colors. Following the fall of Vicksburg, Lee was soon exchanged, promoted major-general, and given command of the cavalry in Mississippi.

In February 1864, he assumed command of all cavalry west of Alabama, and in March, with a small force, harassed the flanks and rear of the large force of Sherman advancing on Meridian, Miss., but was unable to stop it. In June he was appointed lieutenant-general, which appointment was later reconsidered and confirmed as temporary. The one battle under his command occurred at Tupelo, Miss., July 14, where, with a mixed force of infantry and cavalry of about 6,000 men he fought a drawn battle with the superior forces of Gen. A. J. Smith, which resulted in Smith's being forced to withdraw to Memphis. When, within a few days, Hood was put at the head of the Army of Tennessee, Lee took command of his infantry corps, leading the assault, July 28, on Ezra Church, Ga. He commanded this corps through the operations around Atlanta, and in the advance on Nashville, being severely wounded at the latter place, but refusing to give up command of his corps until a rear-guard was formed and in action. For a day at this time his was the only organized corps, and the only one commended by Hood. On Feb. 9, 1865, Lee married Regina, daughter of James Thomas and Regina (Blewett) Harrison of Columbus, Miss. He assumed command of his corps and surrendered with Johnston at High Point, N. C., Apr. 26, being paroled May 1.

His civilian career following the war was distinguished. After twelve years as a planter he entered public life, 1878, as a senator in the Mississippi legislature. In 1880 he was appointed the first president of the Mississippi Agricultural and Mechanical College, serving as such until 1899, when he resigned to accept appointment by President McKinley as a member of the commission for organizing Vicksburg Military Park. He was a member of the Mississippi constitutional convention of 1890. At the time of his death he was commander-in-chief of the United Confederate Veterans, in which organization he had long been prominent. He was the author of important articles on the Civil War, which appeared chiefly in the *Publications* of the Mississippi Historical Association, and contributed "The South Since the War" to *The Confederate Military History* (1899), edited by C. A. Evans. He died at Vicksburg.

[*War of the Rebellion: Official Records* (*Navy*), vols. XII, XXIV–XXVI; *List of Staff Officers of the Confederate States Army* (1891); *Battles and Leaders of the Civil War* (1887–88), vols. I, III; M. F. Steele, *Am. Campaigns* (1909); *War of the Rebellion: Official Records* (*Army*), 1 ser., I, V, XI (pts. 1–3), XII (pts. 2–3), XVII (pts. 1–2), XIX (pts. 1–2), XXIV (pts. 1, 3), XXX (pt. 4), XXXI (pt. 1), XXXII (pts. 1–3); Dabney Lipscomb, "Gen. Stephen D. Lee; His Life, Character, and Service," in the *Pubs. of the Miss. Hist. Soc.*, vol. X (1909); Dunbar Rowland, *Hist. of Miss., the Heart of the South* (1925), vols. I, II; G. W. Cullum, *Biog. Reg. Officers and Grads. U. S. Mil. Acad.* (3rd ed., 1891), vol. II; *Commercial Appeal* (Memphis), May 29, 1908.] D. Y.

LEE, THOMAS (Dec. 1, 1769–Oct. 24, 1839), jurist and banker, was born in Charleston, S. C. His father was William Lee, a watchmaker, who as a captain in the South Carolina militia during the Revolution was exiled to St. Augustine in 1780 by the British. His mother was Anne, daughter of Jeremiah Theus [*q.v.*], the artist. Thomas attended the classical school of Thompson and Baldwin in Charleston, and after studying law under J. J. Pringle, was admitted to the bar about 1790. He made his first public appearance as an orator in 1789, at the Bastille celebration in Charleston; later he displayed a facility in French that enabled him to examine French witnesses without an interpreter. In 1791 he began his public service as associate justice or judge of the courts of sessions and of common pleas, and a few months later was elected solicitor for the southern circuit; in 1796 he was cashier of the lower house of the legislature, and in 1798, 1800, and 1802 he was its clerk; in 1804 he resigned as associate judge, but soon after was elected comptroller general, to which office he was repeatedly reëlected. He was presidential elector in 1816. He became president of the Bank of South Carolina in 1817, and six years later was appointed federal district judge for South Carolina; in both these offices he continued until his death. In politics Lee favored the principles of the Jeffersonian Republicans, but although he held public office for forty-five years, he showed too much independence ever to be rated a party man. During the nullification controversy he not only declined to contribute for the purchase of votes, but in a case involving the payment of duties under the tariff "in which it was intended to give a triumph to Nullification, by overriding the Act of Congress in the verdict of a jury" he "ruled out the defence, and thus defeated the project" (O'Neall, *post,* I, 85).

In 1817, when the pastor and certain members of the Congregational Church seceded and formed the Unitarian Church, he was chairman of the joint committee of ten that drew the articles of separation. He became a deacon, and one summer during the absence of the pastor he conducted the services. He was also identified with the rise of the temperance movement in Charleston, showing zeal without fanaticism. He was about to make a lecture tour in its interest through the upper districts of the state when he "closed his virtuous and useful life . . . after several days illness of country fever" (*Charleston Courier,* Oct. 25, 1839) and was buried in the Unitarian churchyard. The organizations with which he was identified voted formal mourning and published eulogistic tributes to his benevolence, business ability, oratorical powers, and judicial integrity (*Charleston Mercury,* Oct. 25, 28, 29, 1839). Lee is described as a man of "fine person, powerful voice, and elegant elocution" (O'Neall, *loc. cit*). He was married on Feb. 9, 1792, to Kezia, daughter of John Miles of Horse Savannah. He named her executrix of his will, suggesting that their five surviving sons dutifully counsel her. One of these sons, Thomas, became the father of Stephen Dill Lee [*q.v.*].

[Diary of Josiah Smith, Jr., 1780–81 (MS.), in S. C. Hist. Soc.; S. C. House Journals, 1791–1823; A. S. Salley, *Marriage Notices in S. C. Gazette* (1902); D. E. Huger Smith and A. S. Salley, Jr., *Register of St.*

Philip's Parish . . . Charleston, S. C. (1927); *S. C. Hist. and Geneal. Mag.*, July 1920, p. 122, July 1923; Caroline Gilman, *Record of Inscriptions in the Cemetery and Building of the Unitarian . . . Church, . . . Charleston, S. C.* (1860); J. B. O'Neall, *Biog. Sketches of the Bench and Bar of S. C.* (1859), vol. I; *Charleston Courier*, Oct. 25, 28, 29, 1839; Wills, 1839–45, Charleston; epitaphs.] A. K. G.

LEE, THOMAS SIM (Oct. 29, 1745–Nov. 9, 1819), governor of Maryland, the son of Thomas and Christiana (Sim) Lee, was born in Prince George's County, Md. He was the great-great-grandson of Richard Lee [*q.v.*] and the grandson of Philip Lee, who left Virginia to settle in Maryland in 1700. Thomas spent his early years on his father's estate and, on Oct. 27, 1771, married Mary Digges, the daughter of a wealthy Maryland landowner, a woman who was to earn distinction by her warm support of her husband's efforts in behalf of the Revolution and by mobilizing the women of Maryland for patriotic service. He began his political service in 1777 as a member of the provincial council, although he had seen military service as major of a battalion from his county. In November 1779, the legislature chose him to be governor. Unlike his predecessor, he entered upon his duties with little prestige, but his administration of difficult problems won him recognition as one of the Revolutionary leaders of his state. To his task, also, he brought unusually well-developed social talents, the exercise of which continued to add to his popularity throughout his life. When the Continental Army, weakened by hardships and desertions, was threatened with disintegration his first and most important care was furnishing troops and supplies to it. His encouragement enabled Maryland to respond to Washington's appeal for additional troops in 1780. Since such appeals for assistance were continuous throughout the remaining years of the war, his pen was constantly urging sacrifices in order to keep the state up to its requirements. As the trusted friend of Washington, he had information of the plan to trap Cornwallis at Yorktown so that, spurred by hope of victory, he strained every nerve to lend support. To him and to Maryland, it may be fairly claimed, was due much of the success of Greene, Williams, and Howard in the southern campaign.

Shortly after leaving the gubernatorial office in 1783, he was chosen a delegate to the Continental Congress, where he appeared during 1783 and 1784. Although he declined to serve in the federal convention of 1787, he consented to sit in the state convention which ratified the Constitution. In 1792, as presidential elector on the Federalist ticket, he voted for Washington for a second term. To him came the unusual honor of being recalled to the governorship after an interim of private life, when he was elected seventh governor of Maryland in 1792. In this period of service, the most important issues were the reorganization of the state militia and the aid of the federal government in crushing the Whiskey Insurrection in western Pennsylvania and Maryland. When he retired, in 1794, he established a winter home in Georgetown, near Washington, which he made a hospitable center for prominent Federalists. He declined two honors which his state would have thrust upon him: election to the United States Senate in 1794, and a third gubernatorial term, tendered him unanimously in 1798. He devoted the remainder of his life to improving his estate, "Needwood," a tract of fifteen hundred acres in Frederick County, on which he maintained two hundred slaves. Though a man of only respectable talents, his understanding and imagination rose to the challenge of a great crisis, while his social and friendly disposition won him respect and affection.

[H. E. Buchholz, *Governors of Md.* (1908); Folger McKinsey, *Hist. of Frederick County, Md.* (1910), vol. I; M. P. Andrews, *Tercentenary Hist. of Md.* (1925), vols. I, IV; J. T. Scharf, *Hist. of Md.* (1879), vol. II; E. J. Lee, *Lee of Va.* (1895); *Am. and Commercial Daily Advertiser* (Baltimore), Nov. 18, 1819.] E. L.

LEE, WILLIAM (Aug. 31, 1739–June 27, 1795), merchant, diplomat, a descendant of Richard Lee [*q.v.*], was the tenth child of Thomas Lee and his wife, Hannah Ludwell, and a brother of Richard Henry, Francis Lightfoot, and Arthur Lee [*qq.v.*]. He was born at the family seat, "Stratford," Westmoreland County, Va. Prior to 1766, when he was one of a group in Westmoreland County to adopt a vote of thanks to Lord Camden for his opposition to the Stamp Act and to subscribe for a portrait of that statesman, scarcely the vestige of a record exists concerning him. In 1768, accompanied by his brother Arthur, he went to London to engage in mercantile pursuits. There, Mar. 7, 1769, he was married to Hannah Philippa Ludwell, eldest daughter of Philip Ludwell of "Green Spring," and there, in 1770, we find him in partnership with the Dennys De Berdts (father and son) and Stephen Sayre [*q.v.*]. But he did not devote himself exclusively to business. Both he and his brother Arthur, as likewise Sayre, became deeply mersed in London politics, having thrown themselves enthusiastically into the movement of which John Wilkes was the leader. One outcome was that in 1773 William Lee and Sayre were elected sheriffs of London, and two years later Lee was chosen an alderman of the city, the only American who ever held that office.

Early in 1777 Lee was appointed by the secret committee of Congress to act jointly with Thomas Morris, sometime incumbent of the office, as commercial agent at Nantes, and in June he crossed over to France to enter upon his duties. At once he encountered a series of complications, not all of his own making, although he made some lively contributions of his own, chiefly the result of a distrust of two of the American commissioners, Franklin and Deane, a distrust sedulously fomented by Arthur Lee, the third commissioner. In short, William Lee and the commercial agency had become inextricably involved in the notorious Lee-Deane controversy. In the midst of this turmoil Congress, with characteristic ineptitude in foreign affairs, resolved to send representatives to other European courts, and in May 1777, chose William Lee to be commissioner to the courts of Berlin and Vienna. Neither of these courts was disposed to recognize the United States, and all of Lee's polite efforts through two years could not prevail upon them to change their minds. His one diplomatic accomplishment, though quite outside either of his assignments, was the negotiation with John De Neufville, an Amsterdam merchant, of a treaty of commerce between the United States and Holland. This proposed treaty, though never ratified by either party, possesses nevertheless an importance of its own (see the *American Historical Review,* April 1911, pp. 579ff.), in addition to having become the ostensible cause of war between England and Holland.

In June 1779, Lee and Izard were recalled, and in September following Arthur Lee was superseded. That William Lee's public career had been mostly a succession of failures is to be ascribed in part to defects of his own temperament, partly to circumstances beyond his control. The diplomatic missions would doubtless have proved abortive under any other person. For the next four years Lee remained abroad, making his residence at Brussels; but in September 1783, he returned to Virginia and retired to his estate at "Green Spring." His last years were saddened by almost total blindness.

[The principal printed sources for the life of Wm. Lee are: W. C. Ford, *Letters of Wm. Lee* (3 vols., 1891); Francis Wharton, *The Revolutionary Diplomatic Correspondence of the U. S.* (6 vols., 1889); "The Deane Papers," *N. Y. Hist. Soc. Colls.*, Publication Fund Series, vols. XIX–XXIII (1887–91); E. J. Lee, *Lee of Va., 1642–1892* (1895); and J. C. Ballagh, *The Letters of Richard Henry Lee* (2 vols., 1911–14). The principal manuscript sources are the Lee papers in the possession of the Virginia Historical Society, the University of Virginia, and the American Philosophical Society, and the Sparks MSS. at Harvard University.] E. C. B.

LEE, WILLIAM GRANVILLE (Nov. 29, 1859–Nov. 2, 1929), labor leader, was born in Laprairie, Ill., the son of James W. Lee and Sylvesta Jane (Tracy) Lee. His father's family settled in Washington County, Ind., about 1790, and his mother's family near Zanesville, Ohio, some five years later. Following a grammar-school education at Bowen, Ill., he assisted his father, a carpenter and contractor, for a time. Railroad service early attracted him, however, and after doing student work on the Chicago, Burlington & Quincy, he became brakeman, in 1879, on the Atchison, Topeka & Sante Fé at Emporia, Kan. Transferred shortly to the Raton-New Mexico Division, he was promoted late in 1880 to conductor on the run between Lajunta, Colo., and Las Vegas, which position he held until 1884, when he accepted the office of deputy recorder of deeds for Ford County, Kan. Returning to railroad service four years later, he became brakeman and switchman on the Wabash and subsequently on the Missouri Pacific. On June 25, 1890, he joined the Brotherhood of Railroad Trainmen at Sedalia, Mo. Early in 1891 he secured a position as brakeman, and later as freight conductor, with the Union Pacific out of Kansas City, and promptly organized there a new lodge, which he served as master, chairman of the local committee, and member of the general committee for the Union Pacific. He became first vice-president (first vice grand master) of the Brotherhood of Railroad Trainmen on Aug. 1, 1895, was promoted to president on Jan. 1, 1909, and held that office continuously until July 1, 1928, when he was transferred to the position of general secretary and treasurer. Until 1899 his headquarters were at Peoria, Ill., but for the last thirty years of his life they were at Cleveland, Ohio. Obliged to meet many changes in conditions and in legal regulations during his long period of leadership, especially during the war and post-war years, he proved himself a shrewd, far-seeing, and energetic business executive. Under his administration the organization grew steadily in membership and secured great material benefits through collective bargains and standardized wages, through the general introduction of safety appliances, and through legislation which finally reduced the hours of railway workers to eight a day. In 1920 Lee's wisdom and courage were severely tested by a series of unauthorized strikes, and he showed himself an uncompromising upholder of the sanctity of contracts by expelling more than one-sixth of the organization's membership; in 1921 he was credited with having done more than any other man to avert the threatened nation-wide strike of the railroad brotherhoods. His failure of reëlection to the presidency in 1928 was due primarily to his age and physical condition. In 1917 he was stricken with cancer, which recurred in 1923 and in 1927, perhaps as a result of his postponing a first operation in order to continue his fight for the Adamson law. Early in 1927, with his wife, Mary R. Rice, whom he had married in Chicago on Oct. 15, 1901, he sailed for a cruise on the Mediterranean. When he returned he was welcomed by a reception and dinner in New York. Later, his malady reappeared and he grew steadily worse until his death at his home in Lakewood, Cleveland. He was a Congregationalist, a Mason, and an anti-LaFollette Republican. His friendliness, sincerity, and undoubted integrity made him popular with opponents as well as with friends, and created public confidence in the Brotherhood of Railroad Trainmen as a great business organization ably and conservatively managed.

[Frequent references to Lee's work may be found in the file of *The Railroad Trainman,* and in the *N. Y. Times Index*; see also *Who's Who in America,* 1928–29; *Current Opinion,* May 1917, Sept. 1922. Information regarding certain facts has been furnished by his brother, J. C. Lee.] H. S. W.

LEE, WILLIAM HENRY FITZHUGH (May 31, 1837–Oct. 15, 1891), Confederate soldier and congressman from Virginia, familiarly termed "Rooney" Lee to distinguish him from his first cousin, Gen. Fitzhugh Lee [*q.v.*], was born at Arlington, Va. He was the second son of Gen. Robert Edward Lee [*q.v.*] and Mary Ann Randolph (Custis) Lee, the great-granddaughter of Martha Washington by her first marriage. He was educated at Harvard where, if one may believe his classmate, Henry Adams, he showed "the Virginian habit of command" but was far from being an intellectual. Even before he left in 1857, he was, in the official language of Gen. Winfield Scott, "dying to enter the army." On Scott's recommendation he was appointed second lieutenant in the 6th Infantry and served under Col. Albert Sidney Johnston in the Mormon campaign. In 1859 he resigned his commission and became a farmer on his historic estate, the "White House," near Richmond, Va.

Upon the outbreak of hostilities in 1861, Lee, an ardent adherent of the Confederacy, organized a picked cavalry company. In May he was successively appointed captain and major of cavalry and in the West Virginia campaign served as chief of cavalry for General Loring. In the winter of 1861–62 he was ordered to Fredericksburg and was commissioned lieutenant-colonel and, shortly, colonel, of the 9th Virginia Cavalry. He followed Stuart in all his subsequent campaigns from Yorktown to Richmond, riding with him in his first raid around McClellan's army. He fought at Second Manassas, and distinguishing himself in the rear-guard action at Turner's Pass, was unhorsed and left unconscious on the field. After making a brilliant record for bravery and leadership in Stuart's Chambersburg raid, in November 1862 he was appointed brigadier-general and commanded his brigade in the Chancellorsville, Fredericksburg, and Gettysburg campaigns. At Brandy Station, on June 9, 1863, he received a severe wound. Stuart, in his official report, deplored "the casualty which deprives us, for a short time only, it is hoped, of his valuable services." About two weeks later, while he was recuperating, he was captured and imprisoned. He was not exchanged until March 1864, when, at the age of twenty-seven, he was promoted major-general of cavalry. During the ensuing campaign of 1864, he opposed the Wilson raid in June and commanded the cavalry at Globe Tavern in August. He commanded the Confederate right at Five Forks, and during the last desperate fighting of the Appomattox campaign was second in command of the cavalry.

Had not Lee been the son of Robert E. Lee, who felt a modest hesitancy in promoting him, and had he not been so long imprisoned, his military ability probably would have won even greater recognition. He was not of the dashing type of cavalry officer, but he was a scientific fighter. Unfailingly cool, never playing for personal reputation, he held the perfect confidence and respect of his men. After the war he again became a farmer, was president of the Virginia State Agricultural Society, and served one term of four years (1875–79) in the state Senate. Elected three times to Congress, he served there from 1887 until his death in 1891. Six feet two inches in height and of powerful frame, he had pulled the stroke oar on the Harvard crew. Gen. Horace Porter, his classmate, told Lee's son that "Rooney Lee was the best oarsman I have ever seen, Fitz Lee the best horseman." But "Rooney" Lee was also a noted rider, and if possible was in the saddle every day. He was a courteous, genial gentleman and was regarded with affection by many Virginians. He was twice married: first, in 1859, to Charlotte Wickham; and in 1867 to Mary Tabb Bolling, who survived him. He died at "Ravensworth," near Alexandria, Va.

[R. E. Lee, *Recollections and Letters of Gen. Robert E. Lee* (1904); E. J. Lee, *Lee of Va., 1642–1892* (1895); *Confed. Mil. Hist.* (1899), III, 625–27; memorial addresses in Congress printed as *House Miscellaneous Doc. 320,* 52 Cong., 1 Sess.; *War of the Re-*

bellion: Official Records (Army); *Report of the Class of 1858 of Harvard Coll.* (1898); J. W. Thomason, *Jeb Stuart* (1930); the *Times-Dispatch* (Richmond), Oct. 16, 1891; information as to certain facts from members of the Lee family.] R. D. M.

LEE, WILLIAM LITTLE (Feb. 8, 1821–May 28, 1857), jurist, son of Stephen and Mary (Little) Lee, was born at Sandy Hill, Washington County, N. Y. He graduated at Norwich University in 1842, studied in the Harvard law school, and began the practice of law in Troy, N. Y. Indications of tuberculosis determined him to seek a more favorable climate, and in February 1846 he sailed from Newburyport in the brig *Henry* to begin life anew in the Oregon country. After rounding Cape Horn, the *Henry* touched at Honolulu on Oct. 12, 1846, after a tempestuous voyage, said to be the slowest on record, and was laid up for extensive repairs. The government of Hawaii had just passed from absolute despotism to limited monarchy, the first constitution having been granted in 1840, and the machinery of administration was being laboriously set up. There were as yet few residents competent to fill public office. It was only two years since the first lawyer had arrived in the kingdom, to be immediately appointed attorney-general, and he was still the only representative of his profession. Lee's legal training brought him to the notice of the authorities, and he made so favorable an impression that before the *Henry's* repairs were completed he was invited to remain in Hawaii as head of the judicial system. An act reorganizing the courts was to be considered at the next session of the legislature, and pending its passage Lee was appointed as one of the judges for the island of Oahu. In 1847 he became chief justice of the newly created superior court of law and equity, which for practical purposes was the highest court in the kingdom, although the old supreme court consisting of the king and certain chiefs continued a nominal existence until 1852. He was also appointed to the privy council, of which he at once became one of the most influential members. He took a leading part in the action of the council which resulted in the "Great Mahele" of 1848, whereby feudal tenures were abolished and individual ownership of land was established. On request of the legislature he drafted a penal code which was enacted in 1850 and is the basis of Hawaiian criminal laws to this day. In 1851 he was elected a member of the House of Representatives, a position not then forbidden to judges, and served as speaker. The new constitution adopted in 1852 was drafted by a commission of which he was the ruling spirit, and upon its adoption he was appointed chief justice of what was now the supreme court in name as well as fact. A great epidemic of smallpox swept the islands in 1853. Lee worked to exhaustion, assisting in the care of the sick, and his own health was never restored. That he might secure medical advice, he accepted appointment in 1855 as minister to the United States, but returned to Honolulu before his death. He was one of the little group of statesmen who were the real creators of the Hawaiian constitutional monarchy; few of them were so influential as he, and none other was so universally trusted. In 1849 he was married on shipboard in Honolulu harbor to Catherine E. Newton of Albany, N. Y., following a romantic courtship which had begun before he left Troy. After his death, she married Edward Livingston Youmans, editor of *Popular Science Monthly.*

[Article by T. M. Spaulding, in the *Honolulu Mercury,* Mar. 1930; obituaries in the *Polynesian* (Honolulu), May 30, 1857, and the *Pacific Commercial Advertiser* (Honolulu), June 11, 1857, the latter abridged in W. A. Ellis, *Norwich Univ., 1819–1911* (1911), II, 347; S. C. Damon's funeral sermon, published as *A Tribute to the Memory of Hon. William L. Lee* (1857); documents in the Hawaiian Archives in Honolulu.] T. M. S.

LEEDS, DANIEL (1652–Sept. 28, 1720), surveyor, almanac maker, author, was born in England, probably in Nottinghamshire, and emigrated to America with his father, Thomas, some time in the third quarter of the seventeenth century. The family may have settled first on Long Island; later they went to Shrewsbury, N. J. In 1677 Daniel Leeds removed from Shrewsbury to Burlington, and soon became a prominent figure in that town's development. He was appointed surveyor general of the Province of West Jersey in 1682, and was elected to the Assembly the same year. In 1702 he was appointed to Lord Cornbury's council, serving until 1708. As surveyor general, he made the first authorized map of Burlington, "The Streets and Lots of Land Laid in the Town of Burlington" (1696). He was also an almanac maker of note. His first almanac was issued in Philadelphia from the press of William Bradford, 1663–1752 [*q.v.*], under the title, *An Almanac for the Year of the Christian Account, 1687, Particularly Respecting the Meridian and Latitude of Burlington, but May Indifferently Serve All Places Adjacent.* The following year Bradford published a religious dissertation by Leeds entitled *The Temple of Wisdom for the Little World: In Two Parts,* etc. (1688). His second almanac, that for the year 1688, was suppressed by the Philadelphia Quarterly Meeting, because "in imitation of the Almanacs published in England, Daniel had added some light, foolish and unsavoury paragraphs, which gave great uneasiness and offence to Friends of Philadelphia" (Kite, *post,* p. 13). Bradford, the printer, was ordered by the Meeting to bring in all unsold copies of the offending almanac, and they were destroyed; although the Meeting, quite fairly, paid the printer for them.

Although he wrote a letter of apology to the Meeting after this episode, Leeds shortly withdrew from the Society of Friends, and consorted with Bradford and George Keith [*q.v.*], who had become opponents of Quakerism. Henceforth he wrote numerous pamphlets, rather recklessly accusing the founder of the Society, George Fox, of forgeries, and William Penn, of covering up the evidence of them. His pamphlets of this character, printed by Bradford, who removed to New York in 1693, include: *News of a Trumpet Sounding in the Wilderness* (1697); *A Trumpet Sounded out of the Wilderness of America* (1699); *The Rebuker Rebuked* (1703); *The Great Mistery of Fox-Craft Discovered* (1705), and *The Second Part of the Mystry of Fox-Craft* (1705). For his attacks upon the heads of Quakerdom, Leeds became a target for Quaker pamphlets. In 1700 Caleb Pusey published *Satan's Harbinger Encountered, His False News of a Trumpet Detected,* and in 1702, *Daniel Leeds Justly Rebuked for Abusing William Penn and his Foly and Fals-Hoods in His Two Printed Chalenges to Caleb Pusey.* The following year he appended "Remarks on Daniel Leeds Abusive Almanac for 1703" to his *Proteus Ecclesiasticus, or George Keith Varied in Fundamentals.* Pusey characterized Leeds as "a perverter of our Friends words," and a false citer in divers respects.

On the title-pages of his earliest almanacs Leeds described himself as a "Student of Agriculture." He passed the greater part of his life in Burlington, N. J., where he died. He was married four times: first, before he left England; second, Feb. 21, 1681, to Ann Stacy, who bore him a child and died; third, early in 1682, to Dorothy Young, who became the mother of several children; and fourth, sometime between 1700 and 1705, to a widow, Jane, *née* Revell. One of his sons, Titan Leeds (1699–1738), who computed the tables for the *American Almanac* from 1714 to 1746, is remembered as the victim of one of Benjamin Franklin's practical jokes. In his first almanac, 1733, "Poor Richard" predicted the death, "on Oct. 17, 1733, 3 hr. 29 m., P. M.," of "his good friend and fellow-student, Mr. Titan Leeds," and the next year, despite Leeds's published protest, insisted: "There is the strongest probability that my dear friend is no more," because "Mr. Leeds was too well bred to use any man so indecently and so scurrilously" as "Poor Richard" had been used in Leeds's protest. The controversy between them went on for several years. (See P. L. Ford, *"The Sayings of Poor Richard,"* 1890.) Another son of Daniel Leeds, Felix (1687–1744), was also an almanac maker, computing almanacs for the years 1727–30.

[While no complete collection of Leeds's almanacs and pamphlets is known to exist, there are copies of his Philadelphia almanacs for 1687, 1688, and 1693; and of his New York almanacs for 1694, 1699, 1705, 1711, and 1713 in public libraries in those cities. *The Second Part of the Mystry of Fox-Craft* was reprinted in the *Mag. of Hist., Extra No. 62* (1917), and *The Great Mistery of Fox-Craft,* in *Mag. of Hist., Extra No. 96* (1923). See also Clara Louise Humeston, *Leeds: A New Jersey Family* (1905); *Memoirs of the Hist. Soc. of Pa.,* I (1826), 105; Isaiah Thomas, *The Hist. of Printing in America* (2nd ed., 2 vols., 1874); Nathan Kite, "Antiquarian Researches," in *The Friend* (Phila.), Oct. 7, 1843; M. C. Tyler, *A Hist. of Am. Lit.* (1878), vol. II; E. M. Woodward and J. F. Hageman, *Hist. of Burlington and Mercer Counties, N. J.* (1883); Joseph Smith, *Descriptive Cat. of Friends' Books* (2 vols., 1867), and *Bibliotheca Anti-Quakeriana* (1873).]

J. J.

LEEDS, JOHN (May 18, 1705–March 1790), mathematician and astronomer, was born at Bay Hundred, Talbot County, Md. He was the only child of Edward and Ruth (Ball) Leeds, both Quakers. His family was of English origin, his great-grandfather, Timothy Leeds, having come to Virginia in 1607. John's grandfather, William, removed to Maryland about 1648. John Leeds was probably self-educated and seems to have spent his entire life in Talbot County. He married Rachel, daughter of William and Elizabeth Harrison, Feb. 14, 1726, at the Choptank Meeting House, Tred Avon Parish. They had three daughters, one of them the mother of John Leeds Bozman [*q.v.*], the historian. Leeds entered public office in 1734 as one of the commissioners and justices of the peace for Talbot County. In 1738 he became county clerk, an office which he held until 1777, when he either resigned or was removed because he refused to take the oath of allegiance to the new state government.

When in 1760 Lord Baltimore signed an agreement with Thomas and Richard Penn providing for a joint commission from Maryland and Pennsylvania to mark off the long-disputed boundary between the two colonies, Governor Sharpe named Leeds as surveyor or "assistant" to the Maryland group. In 1762 he was made a regular member of the commission. Fever and ague contracted while working in the swamps, lack of proper surveying instruments, and the frequent threat of Indian attacks discouraged the commissioners and decided them, in 1763, to employ Mason and Dixon, two professional surveyors, to run the line. They completed the survey in 1767, and the final report of the commission was made the next year. Leeds's account shows that he worked 177 days at a guinea a day. In the letters of Governor Sharpe to the Proprietor he is always referred to as "the best mathematician in the province."

In June 1769, "having no other instruments . . . but a pocket watch and a reflecting telescope about twenty inches long, of Sterrup's make," Leeds observed the transit of Venus, obtaining results important enough to be published in the *Philosophical Transactions . . . for the Year 1769* (1770) of the Royal Society of London. His article shows that he was a careful reader of that early scientific journal. From April to October 1766 he served as treasurer of the Eastern Shore, and in October was appointed a justice of the Provincial Court. Partly in recognition of his services on the boundary commission, he was also appointed naval officer of Pocomoke in the same month, and shortly afterward was made surveyor general of Maryland. All of these offices, along with his county clerkship, he appears to have occupied until his Loyalist tendencies forced him out. He was frequently threatened during the Revolution, but was never harmed. Sometime after the war he was again appointed surveyor general and continued in that office until his death in 1790 at Wade's Point. To the end of his life he believed that anarchy would sooner or later follow the separation from England.

[R. H. Spencer, *Thomas Family of Talbot County, Md., and Allied Families* (1914); Oswald Tilghman, *Hist. of Talbot County, Md.* (2 vols., 1915); *Easton Ledger*, Apr. 10, 1884; "Correspondence of Governor Horatio Sharpe," in *Archives of Md.*, vols. IX (1890) and XIV (1895); "The Calvert Papers," *Md. Hist. Soc. Fund Pubs.*, nos. 28, 34, 35 (1889, 1894, 1899); Maryland Commission Book, No. 82, Tred Avon Parish Records (transcripts), and Calvert Papers, Abstracts, vols. XVII and XXI, all MSS. in Md. Hist. Soc.]

M. E. F.

LEES, ANN [See LEE, ANN, 1736–1784].

LEESER, ISAAC (Dec. 12, 1806–Feb. 1, 1868), rabbi, editor, author, was born at Neuenkirchen, in the province of Westphalia, Prussia. His father, Uri, a merchant in comfortable circumstances, died when the boy was fourteen. His mother had died when he was eight, and he was brought up by his grandmother. He attended the Gymnasium of Münster, and besides the courses there, studied Bible and Talmud privately with Abraham Sutro, chief rabbi of Münster and Mark. Sutro was an ardent traditionalist and the author of a book, *Milhamot Adonai* ("The Wars of the Lord"), directed against the Jewish Reform Movement then beginning in Germany.

In 1824, Leeser emigrated to Richmond, Va., where an uncle, Zalma Rehine, desired to adopt him. Although he worked in his uncle's store, he was also, from the beginning, a volunteer teacher of the Jewish religion; and when but twenty-two years of age published two articles in the *Richmond Whig*, replying to an attack on the Jews which had appeared in the *London Quarterly Review*. These articles attracted the attention of Jews beyond Richmond, and in 1829 the oldest Jewish congregation in Philadelphia, Mikveh Israel, which at that time required the services of a minister, elected him to the post. Thereafter he was prodigiously active. He conducted the synagogue service; he preached; he taught privately, maintaining a Jewish free school in his own home until the Jewish community in Philadelphia created a Society for this purpose. He was the inspiring force in various charitable organizations in Philadelphia. He founded *The Occident and American Jewish Advocate*, and edited it from 1843 until his death; he wrote and translated many books of instruction for Jewish schools, among them *The Jews and the Mosaic Law* (1833), a *Hebrew Spelling Book* (1838), a *Catechism for Jewish Children* (n.d.), and a *Catechism for Younger Children* (1839). He edited and translated the Prayer Book for the Portuguese Jews (1837) and for the German Jews (1848); he translated the Bible into English (1853); he edited with Joseph Jaquett a complete Hebrew Bible; he translated into English a book of Jewish travels in Palestine and Joseph Schwartz's *Descriptive Geography and Brief Historical Sketch of Palestine*, and printed no less than ten volumes of his own sermons. These publications required the printing of many thousands of pages of Hebrew, and he saw the books through the press, incidentally making Philadelphia the center of Hebrew printing in America at that time. He traveled all over the country, but especially in the South and West, speaking in synagogues, organizing them, and dedicating them. The culmination of his career was the establishment of a Jewish college, Maimonides College, of whose faculty he was the head for the last year of his life.

He remained minister of Mikveh Israel Congregation until 1850, when he retired as a result of difficulties which had developed between him and the managers, principally due to his continued refusal to sign any form of contract. In 1857, a group formed a new congregation called Beth El Emeth, in order to give him a center from which to carry on his work. During this entire period he was the stanch advocate of traditional views and the protagonist of the traditional school of Jewish doctrine and practice. Although very popular, and more widely known in his time than any other Jewish minister in America, he had some unfortunate traits which impaired his influence. In the lively letters written by Rebecca Gratz [*q.v.*] it appears that he was very sensitive with regard to his appearance, and this sensitiveness increased after he had a severe attack of smallpox in 1834. His warm friend, Moses A. Dropsie [*q.v.*], wrote of him shortly after his death: "He had an indomitable will. He was impatient and impetuous, frank and outspoken, never learned the art of disguising his thoughts." He was a pioneer in the organization of Jewish life in America, there being no phase of it in which he did not create some organized effort. Many of his creations have lived, and those that have not have been replaced by stronger institutions planned along lines similar to those that he laid down.

[Henry Englander, "Isaac Leeser," in *Central Conf. of Am. Rabbis, Year-Book,* vol. XXVIII (1918); *The Occident,* Mar. 1868; Mayer Sulzberger, in *Jewish Encyc.*; H. S. Morais, *Eminent Israelites of the Nineteenth Century* (1880), and *The Jews of Philadelphia* (1894); Peter Wiernik, *Hist. of the Jews in America* (1931); M. A. Dropsie, *Panegyric on the Life, Character and Services of Isaac Leeser* (1868), published in the appendix to *The Occident,* vol. XXV (1868); *Letters of Rebecca Gratz* (1929), ed. by David Philipson; *Jewish Exponent,* Mar. 14, 1913, Feb. 8, 1918.]

C. A.

LEETE, WILLIAM (*c.* 1613–Apr. 16, 1683), colonial governor, was born at Dodington, Huntingtonshire, England, the son of John and Anna (Shute) Leete, formerly of Cambridge. He was educated as a lawyer and employed as registrar in the Bishop's Court at Cambridge. Here he witnessed the persecution of the Puritans and was so touched by their fortitude that he inquired into their faith and was converted. To escape persecution, he joined the Rev. Henry Whitfield's company which sailed for America in May 1639. Before leaving England, Leete had married Anna Payne, the daughter of the Rector of Southoe (1638). During the voyage (June 1) he, together with other colonists, signed a Plantation Covenant. Upon their arrival at New Haven, they purchased land from the Indians and founded a new town, later called Guilford. Leete was chosen one of the six trustees of this land and also one of the four who were to act as a temporary government. He was town secretary or clerk from 1639 until his resignation in 1662. He was also one of the "seven pillars" who organized the Guilford church in 1643. With the establishment of a church, Guilford entered the "Combination" at New Haven and sent Leete and Desborough to represent it there, and for several years thereafter he served as one of its deputies. He was advanced to the magistracy in 1651, an office which he continued to hold until his death. He was sent on various missions to the neighboring colonies and represented the New Haven Colony in the New England Confederation from 1655 to 1664. He was deputy governor of the New Haven Colony from 1658 to 1661 and governor from 1661 to 1664. As such, he connived at the escape of the regicides, Goffe and Whalley [*qq.v.*], who had sought refuge in the Colony. It was largely through his moderating influence that the New Haven Colony peaceably submitted, in 1664, to the Connecticut charter of 1662. As a reward, the Connecticut General Court chose Leete as one of its magistrates, and elected him assistant every year until 1669, when he was promoted to deputy governor of the Connecticut Colony. After serving seven years in that office and upon the death of Governor Winthrop, he was elected governor seven years in succession (1676–82) and was in office when he died. In addition, he frequently represented Connecticut in the New England Confederation, and was chosen president of the commissioners in 1673 and 1678. He died at Hartford and was buried in the cemetery of the First Church there. After the death of his first wife he was married to Sarah Rutherford, and after her death, to Mary Newman Street. He had a number of children, all by his first wife.

[Joseph Leete, *The Family of Leete* (2nd ed., renewed and enlarged, London, 1906); R. D. Smith, *Hist. of Guilford, Conn.* (1877); B. C. Steiner, *A Hist. of the Plantation of Menunkatuck* (1897); Leete's letters to John Winthrop, Jr., in *Mass. Hist. Soc. Colls.,* 4 ser. VII (1865); J. H. Trumbull, *The Public Records of the Colony of Connecticut, 1665–78* (1852); *Records of the Colony and Plantation of New Haven* (1857) and *Records of the Colony or Jurisdiction of New Haven* (1858); Ezra Stiles, *The Hist. of Three of the Judges of King Charles I* (1794); Cotton Mather, *Magnalia Christi Americana* (1702), bk. II, p. 29.]

J. H. R.

LEFEVERE, PETER PAUL (Apr. 30, 1804–Mar. 4, 1869), Roman Catholic missionary and bishop, was born in Roulers, Belgium, the son of Charles Lefevere, a farmer in easy circumstances, and his wife, Albertine-Angeline Muylle. He made his preliminary studies for the priesthood with the Lazarists in Paris, but before beginning his theological course, volunteered for service in the American missions. Destined for the diocese of St. Louis, he came to the United States in 1828, completed his studies in the diocesan seminary, and was ordained Nov. 20, 1831. Although stationed for a few months at New Madrid, Mo., his career began with his appointment to the Salt River mission in the fall of 1832. Making his headquarters in this tiny settlement in Ralls County, Mo., he ministered to the Catholic immigrant population of northeastern Missouri, southern Iowa, and western

Illinois. For some years he was the only priest on the Mississippi from St. Louis to Dubuque. Despite his utter poverty, and the appalling hardships encountered in the care of this untouched mission field, he knew no respite until his health became seriously impaired in 1840. In that year he returned to Belgium to recuperate, sailing from New York with his superior, Bishop Rosati, who was on his way to Rome. The prelate arrived while the Roman authorities were dealing with Bishop Rese's proffered resignation from the See of Detroit. They decided to appoint a coadjutor bishop to administer the diocese, and through the influence of Bishop Rosati, Father Lefevere was chosen. As titular bishop of Zela, and administrator of Detroit, he was consecrated in St. John's Church, Philadelphia, Nov. 21, 1841, by Bishop Francis Kenrick, assisted by Bishops England and Hughes.

When he entered upon his charge, he had seventeen priests, two parishes in Detroit, and sixteen more in the diocese. At his death there were eighty-eight priests, eleven parishes in the city, and 161 organized Catholic groups in the state. He was fitted to cope with this phenomenal expansion by his unlimited capacity for work, his firmness in governing, and his bent for order and discipline. The temporalities of the diocese, left in a precarious condition by his predecessor, were placed on a secure basis. He convened two diocesan synods to establish the polity which had been lacking. To supply his urgent need of priests, he became associated with Bishop Spalding of Louisville in the founding of the American College at Louvain. Its first three rectors were priests from the diocese of Detroit. In his efforts to build up a Catholic school system, he fostered the development of a diocesan community, the Sisters of the Immaculate Heart of Mary, and introduced into his diocese the Ladies of the Sacred Heart, the Sisters of Notre Dame, and the Christian Brothers. He conducted a vigorous but unsuccessful campaign in 1852–53 to obtain for his schools a proportionate share of the public funds devoted to education. To supply the lack of charitable institutions in Detroit, the Sisters of Charity were brought in, and with his help founded a hospital, an orphanage, and an asylum for the insane. He was deeply interested in the Indian population of his diocese, and strove to provide it with schools and missionaries. Personally, the Bishop was simple and unaffected in demeanor, frugal in his habits, austere in his mode of life. In protest against the drunkenness which he noticed in Detroit on his arrival, he publicly took the total-abstinence pledge. Every day at a fixed hour he could be found in his confessional. He died of erysipelas in St. Mary's Hospital in Detroit, and lies buried under the altar of the church of St. Peter and St. Paul, which he built and used as his cathedral.

[Sources include J. E. Rothensteiner, *Hist. of the Archdiocese of St. Louis* (2 vols., 1928); R. H. Clarke, *Lives of the Deceased Bishops . . . of the United States* (3 vols., 1888); *Cath. Encyc.*, IV, 759; *Detroit Free Press*, Mar. 5, 1869; other local newspaper references, and material in the diocesan archives. Lefevere's name is variously spelled in secondary accounts, but signatures in the diocesan archives testify that he himself used the spelling here given.] G. W. P.

LEFFEL, JAMES (Apr. 19, 1806–June 11, 1866), manufacturer, inventor, was born in Botetourt County, Va., and when nine months old was taken by his parents to the Ohio country, where they settled. During his childhood and youth he experienced all of the characteristic hardships borne by pioneer families, enjoying only an occasional bit of schooling. Early in life he displayed a natural bent for mechanics, particularly in metals, and shortly after coming of age, he left his home and settled in Springfield, Ohio, then but a hamlet, hoping to engage wholly in the work he most enjoyed. He first designed, built, and operated for a number of years a waterpower sawmill just outside of Springfield on the Mad River. Foreseeing the needs of the growing town, he established an iron foundry, the first in that vicinity. It was put into operation in January 1840, and within six years its business had grown to such proportions that Leffel was compelled to erect a second and larger one. For the first few years a general foundry business only was conducted. Believing that he could improve his waterwheel, he experimented for many years, patenting his various ideas as they were perfected. The first of these waterwheels was patented May 21, 1845, and so superior was it to the regular overshot or undershot wheel that in 1846, in company with one Richards, he established and operated by water power the first cotton-mill and machine-shop in Springfield. The business of manufacturing waterwheels, however, was not lucrative, and he turned his attention to designing other and more salable foundry products. He perfected, and on Dec. 10, 1850, patented a lever jack, and on Feb. 24, 1852, two types of cooking-stoves. Subsequently he reorganized his foundry business under the name of Leffel, Cook & Blakeney, for the manufacture of his lever jack, and his "Buckeye" and "Double Oven" stoves. He then returned to his waterwheel experiments and after devoting fully ten years to the work, finally perfected the double turbine wheel. This was patented Jan. 14, 1862 (patent reissued Oct.

11, 1864), and proved to be an important step in the development of the waterwheel. For the manufacture of this new product and of an improved lever jack of his own invention patented Nov. 15, 1864, he organized a stock company known as James Leffel & Company. Hardly was this business under way, however, when Leffel died without any of the reward which his products soon reaped. His chief interest outside of his business was the breeding of fine poultry and the exhibiting of his best specimens at county fairs. On July 4, 1830, he married Mary A. Croft of Ohio and at his death, in Springfield, he was survived by his widow and two sons.

[*Hist. of Clark County, Ohio* (1881); B. F. Prince, *A Standard Hist. of Springfield and Clark County, Ohio,* vol. I (1922); Patent Office records, 1850, 1852, 1864.] C. W. M.

LEFFERTS, GEORGE MOREWOOD (Feb. 24, 1846–Sept. 21, 1920), surgeon, laryngologist, was born in Brooklyn, the son of Marshall [*q.v.*] and Mary (Allen) Lefferts. In his fondness for discipline, his punctuality, his fastidiousness in personal attire, and other kindred qualities, he seems to have absorbed much of the military spirit of his father, who was colonel of New York's 7th Regiment at the time of the Civil War. Though he had a crippled leg, the son was naturally energetic and active, and became a proficient rider. He received his medical degree from the College of Physicians and Surgeons in 1870, and served as interne at Bellevue and St. Luke's. Attracted by the new specialty of laryngology, he then went abroad for study in the throat clinics of Europe. After attending clinics in London and Paris he went to Vienna, where he studied under two of the pioneers, Stoerk and Von Schrötter. So much was the former, Professor Karl Stoerk of the University of Vienna, impressed with his zeal and ability that he made him his chief of clinic, 1871–73, and at the completion of his term gave him a flattering certificate of service. This was a very unusual honor for a young alien.

Returning to New York in 1873, Lefferts began practice, specializing in diseases of the throat and nose. He was immediately appointed one of the laryngologists to Demilt Dispensary, sometimes styled the original school for postgraduate instruction in the United States, and in the same year was a cofounder of the New York Laryngological Society, later the Laryngological Section of the Academy of Medicine. In 1874 he was chiefly instrumental in establishing a throat clinic at the New York Eye and Ear Infirmary. In 1875, for the *New York Medical Journal,* he began an abstract department for laryngology and related subjects which was taken over in 1880 by the new *Archives of Laryngology,* which he had helped to found. In 1878 he became a cofounder of the American Laryngological Association, which he served as president in 1882.

Shortly after his return in 1873 from his European study, he began to teach his specialty at his alma mater, and in 1876 was made clinical professor there, retaining his chair until 1904, when he was given emeritus status. As a teacher he was unsurpassed and far in advance of his time. A man of large private means, he spared no expense in providing an abundance of wall charts, plates, models, and instruments. Himself a draftsman who excelled as a blackboard artist, he supervised the preparation of all exhibits. His lectures were scrupulously revised each year, and he circulated printed synopses of various kinds among his students. He was especially wedded to the idea of individual instruction, and divided his class into small groups. He is said to have disappointed his class but once in thirty years' service. His publications were few; his most pretentious work was *A Pharmacopœia for the Treatment of the Larynx, Pharynx and Nasal Passages* (2nd edition, revised and enlarged, 1884). He was married, June 11, 1891, to Annie Cuyler Van Vechten. In 1910 he gave up his extensive practice and retired to his estate at Katonah, N. Y. He died ten years later of angina pectoris.

[D. B. Delavan, *George Morewood Lefferts; A Sketch of His Life and Work* (1921), repr. in *Annals of Otology, Rhinology and Laryngology,* Mar. 1924; *Who's Who in America,* 1920–21; *Medic. Record,* Oct. 2, 1920; John Shrady, *The Coll. of Physicians and Surgeons, N. Y., . . . A Hist.* (n.d.), vol. I; *N. Y. Times,* Sept. 23, 1920; *Laryngoscope,* Aug. 1921.] E. P.

LEFFERTS, MARSHALL (Jan. 15, 1821–July 3, 1876), engineer, builder of telegraph lines, was born in Bedford, which later became a part of Brooklyn, N. Y., the son of Leffert and Amelia Ann (Cozine) Lefferts. His father was a descendant of Leffert Pieterse who came with his father, Pieter Janse Hoogwout (or Van Haughwout), from Holland to New Amsterdam in 1660 and settled on Long Island. The next generation adopted Lefferts as a surname. Marshall had only such schooling as was available to farmers' sons in that period, although living within the bounds of what eventually became Greater New York. At fifteen he was a clerk in a hardware store. For three years he was on the staff of engineers engaged in the survey of Brooklyn. He was also employed in laying out Greenwood Cemetery, but left engineering to enter an importing house, in which he soon became a partner.

Because his firm dealt extensively in zinc wire and other commodities used in the erection of telegraph lines, he interested himself in such operations and in 1849 was president of the New York & New England and the New York State telegraph companies, which constructed lines operating on the Bain system from New York City to Boston and Buffalo. After the consolidation of the Morse and Bain interests, however, he withdrew from line management for ten years and engaged in the manufacture of iron and in perfecting the process for galvanizing that metal. By 1860 he was back in telegraph construction work, planning lines for the automatic system, and was made electrical engineer for the American Telegraph Company. His work at this time was still largely experimental, for comparatively few scientific investigations had been made in this field since the invention of the magnetic telegraph. The practical men in charge of construction had to depend on their own resourcefulness for ways and means to achieve results. Most of the makeshift devices that Lefferts employed were of course superseded within a few years; his was the trail-blazing of the pioneer—often rough and incomplete, but necessary in its day. He was the first to introduce instruments for the detection of electric faults and the first to reduce resistance of relays to common standards. As executive manager for the American Telegraph Company he built up an efficient organization, his unfailing good humor helping to make him successful in dealing with subordinates.

The Civil War put a period to Lefferts' construction activities. He was colonel of the New York 7th Regiment, a unit that had unusual prestige. It attracted the notice of the whole country when its services were offered to the government at Washington in April 1861, since it was thought significant that a body of men including so many citizens of wealth and high social position in New York should rally to the support of the Union. The regiment's service was of short duration, however, and its colonel had little opportunity to prove his military prowess. After the war, on the merging of the American Telegraph Company with the Western Union, he was put in charge of a bureau for collecting and disseminating commercial news. In 1871 he resigned his connection with the Western Union and became president and general manager of the Gold & Stock Telegraph Company. For several years, also, he was consulting engineer of the Atlantic Cable Company. He died while on his way to Philadelphia with his comrades of the 7th Regiment Veteran Corps to take part in the observance of the centennial anniversary of the Declaration of Independence. His wife, Mary Allen, whom he married June 4, 1845, with five sons and two daughters, survived him. One of his sons was George Morewood Lefferts [*q.v.*].

[T. G. Bergen, *Geneal. of the Lefferts Family, 1650–1878* (1878); L. M. Haughwout, "The Lefferts-Haughwout Family," *N. Y. Geneal. and Biog. Record,* Jan. 1902; James Parton and others, *Sketches of Men of Progress* (1870–71); Emmons Clark, *Hist. of the Seventh Regiment of N. Y. 1806–1889* (1890); A. P. Eastlake, "The Great Monopoly," in *Lippincott's Mag.,* Oct. 1870; *Telegrapher,* July 8, 1876; *N. Y. Times,* July 4, 1876.] W. B. S.

LEFFLER, ISAAC (Nov. 25, 1788–Mar. 8, 1866), Virginia congressman, Iowa lawyer and legislator, brother of Shepherd Leffler [*q.v.*], was born on a plantation called "Silvia's Plain," in Washington County, Pa., where his grandfather, Jacob Leffler, had settled in 1774. He was the son of a second Jacob Leffler and Jane (Smith) Leffler. After studying law, he was admitted to the bar and entered upon the practice of his profession at Wheeling, Va. (now W. Va.). In 1817 he was elected to the Virginia legislature, and served during the years 1817–19, 1823–27, 1832–33. In 1827 he was elected as a member of the state board of public works. He was a representative of Virginia in the Twentieth Congress, 1827–29, but was an unsuccessful candidate for reëlection. In 1835, he removed to what is now Burlington, Iowa, but which was at that time a small settlement on the outskirts of the Territory of Michigan. Here on Apr. 15, 1835, he was admitted to the practice of law in the territorial courts. When the Territory of Michigan was divided in 1836, Isaac Leffler was elected to the legislature of the newly created Territory of Wisconsin. Reëlected for the following session, he was chosen speaker of the House. In 1836 he was the unsuccessful Whig candidate for the office of territorial delegate to Congress. He was among the first to see the importance of organizing the Iowa country into a separate territory, and on Sept. 16, 1837, was president of a meeting in Burlington at which resolutions were adopted calling for a convention to consider this subject. He also presided at the convention, which was held at Burlington Nov. 6–8, 1837, and was perhaps the most important convention in the Iowa country prior to the establishment of the Territory. In July 1838, the Territory of Iowa was created, and in 1841 Leffler was elected a member of the territorial House of Representatives to succeed his brother Shepherd, who had been elected to the territorial Council. Isaac Leffler had been recommended to President Tyler by Daniel Webster, then secretary of state, for appointment as one of the associate justices of Iowa Territory, but did not receive the appointment. In 1843, however, he was appointed by President Tyler as United States marshal for the district of Iowa, and served until removed by President Polk on Dec. 29, 1845. At this time he resumed the practice of law at Burlington; four years later he declined appointment as register of the land office at Stillwater, Mitchell County, Iowa. In 1852 President Fillmore appointed him receiver of public moneys for the Chariton Land District of Iowa, but the following year he was removed from the office by President Pierce. Leffler was married twice: to Rebecca Forman in November 1814, and after her death, to Lethenia Mitchell in 1832. He was a man of pleasing social qualities, amiable, kind, and hospitable. In personal appearance he is said to have resembled President John Tyler. He died at Chariton, Lucas County, Iowa, and was buried in Aspen Grove Cemetery, Burlington.

[*The Hist. of Des Moines County, Iowa* (1879); *Biog. Dir. Am. Cong.* (1928); *Iowa Jour. of Hist. and Politics,* Jan. 1908, July 1911, Oct. 1922; *The Wis. Almanac and Ann. Reg.,* 1857; E. H. Stiles, *Recollections and Sketches of Notable Lawyers and Public Men of Early Iowa* (1916); L. G. Tyler, *Encyc. of Va. Biog.* (1915), vol. II; H. E. Bromwell, "Leffler" (typescript, 1920), in Lib. of Cong.] B. E. M.

LEFFLER, SHEPHERD (Apr. 24, 1811–Sept. 7, 1879), Iowa legislator and congressman, son of Jacob and Jane (Smith) Leffler and brother of Isaac Leffler [*q.v.*], was born at "Silvia's Plain," Washington County, Pa., where his grandfather had settled a generation earlier. His early life was that of a farm boy. He attended Jefferson College at Canonsburg, Pa., graduating in 1833, studied law, and began the practice of his profession in Wheeling, Va. (now W. Va.). Deciding to seek his fortune in the West, he migrated in the spring of 1835 to what is now Burlington, Iowa. His father had preceded him to Burlington by a few weeks, and his brother Isaac also took up his residence at this place. The Leffler brothers soon became prominent in the affairs of Iowa Territory. In 1839 Shepherd Leffler was elected to the territorial House of Representatives, and in 1841, to the territorial Council; he served continuously in one house or the other of the legislature from 1839 till the admission of Iowa as a state in 1846. In public speeches and by private influence he resisted the removal of the capital from Burlington to Iowa City, but without success. He was selected as a delegate from Des Moines County to the first constitutional convention in Iowa, held at Iowa City in 1844. Although as presiding officer of this convention he was influential in the formation of the new constitution, when Congress altered the proposed constitution by changing the boundaries of the new state so that it would be cut off from the Missouri River on the west, Leffler and other prominent Democrats broke with the party leaders and joined the Whigs in opposing its adoption. Owing in no small measure to the opposition of this group, statehood on the terms offered by Congress was rejected by the voters. Leffler also served as a member of the convention of 1846, in which a constitution was framed with the boundaries of Iowa set forth as they are today. This constitution was approved by the people of Iowa and adopted by Congress. In the first state election, Leffler was chosen one of the first two Congressmen from Iowa. He was in Washington on Dec. 28, 1846, the day that the new state was admitted; and on the following day he took his oath of office. He represented Iowa in the Twenty-ninth, Thirtieth, and Thirty-first congresses, but was defeated for reëlection in 1850 by Bernhart Henn. Upon his retirement from office, Leffler engaged in agricultural pursuits near Burlington, in real-estate operations, and in the practice of law. In 1856 he made another unsuccessful campaign for Congress. Thereafter he withdrew as far as possible from the turmoil of political strife and practically abandoned his law practice, indulging his taste for the more quiet life of the farm. In 1875 he was persuaded to make the race for governor against Samuel J. Kirkwood [*q.v.*], who had served as chief executive of Iowa during the Civil War. Leffler made a remarkable campaign but was unable to overcome the Republican majority in the state. The remaining four years of his life he spent as a country squire, undisturbed by the trend of politics. He was a good neighbor and a man of great popularity in his community. Of impressive appearance and winning manners, he made many friends. In 1840 he had married Elizabeth Parrott, and their domestic life was very happy. He died in his sixty-ninth year and was buried in Aspen Grove Cemetery, Burlington.

[*Biog. Rev. of Des Moines County, Iowa* (1905); *Hist. of Des Moines County, Iowa, and Its People* (1915), I, 396; *Iowa Official Reg.,* 1929–30; E. H. Stiles, *Recollections and Sketches of Notable Lawyers and Public Men of Early Iowa* (1916); *Biog. and Hist. Cat. of Washington and Jefferson Coll.* (1902); H. E. Bromwell, *The Bromwell Geneal.* (copr. 1910), and "Leffler" (typescript, 1920), in Lib. of Cong.; *Biog. Dir. Am. Cong.* (1928); *Dubuque Herald* and *Burlington Hawk-Eye,* Sept. 9, 1879.] B. E. M.

LEFFMANN, HENRY (Sept. 9, 1847–Dec. 25, 1930), chemist, was born in Philadelphia, Pa. In speaking of his ancestors he once humorously said: "In these days of genetics and eugenics, it is worth while to show that a mongrel may have some merit" (LaWall, *post,* p. 113). His father, Henry Leffmann of Hamburg, Germany, was of Russian Jewish stock; his mother, Sarah Ann Paul of Doylestown, Bucks County, Pa., was a Hicksite Friend, of Welsh extraction. He was educated in the public schools, completing the four-year course at the Central High School in Philadelphia but failing to receive the degree because of illness in his last year. He was subsequently (1865) awarded the degree of A.M. (*honoris causa*). He graduated in medicine from the Jefferson Medical College in 1869, received the degree of Ph.D. from the Wagner Free Institute of Science in 1874, and that of D.D.S. from the Pennsylvania College of Dental Surgery in 1884.

Immediately after graduation from the Jefferson Medical College he began to teach chemistry there and at Central High School. He also taught toxicology in Jefferson Medical College for several years. Subsequently he became professor of chemistry in the Pennsylvania College of Dental Surgery, and in the Wagner Free Institute of Science. With the last-named institution he was actively connected for a half century. From 1888 to 1916 he occupied the chair of chemistry at the Woman's Medical College of Pennsylvania, becoming emeritus professor after his retirement from active work. At the time of his death he was lecturer on research in the Philadelphia College of Pharmacy and Science. He was an inspiring teacher, demanding industry, accuracy, and enthusiasm on the part of his students, imbuing them with the love of science and the hatred of sham, hypocrisy, and carelessness in research work. His humor, his personal charm, his encyclopedic memory, and his ability as a raconteur made him a brilliant conversationalist, and he was much in demand as a lecturer on various topics.

His contributions to chemical literature were extensive, comprising nearly five hundred papers, pamphlets, and books. *Elements of Chemistry,* issued in 1881, was followed a little later by a *Compend of Chemistry* (1882), which passed through five editions. Two books written in collaboration with William Beam, *The Examination of Water* (1889), and *Analysis of Milk and Milk Products* (1893), have gone through a number of editions; *Select Methods in Food Analysis* (1901), also in association with Beam, was favorably received and widely used. As a medical and scientific expert, testifying in courts, Leffmann was unsurpassed, and he was a master in the field of medical and legal jurisprudence. He held a number of official positions, serving as chemist to the coroner of Philadelphia, 1875–80; chemist to the coroner and the district attorney of Philadelphia, 1885–97; and in other capacities. He was port physician of Philadelphia from 1884 to 1887, and again in 1891–92. His delightful book, *Under the Yellow Flag* (1896), is the story of this phase of his work.

He was a member of many professional and scientific organizations, served as president of the Engineers' Club of Philadelphia for one term, and in 1930 was elected to honorary membership in the Franklin Institute "in recognition of valuable services to science and research, in teaching, as former Port Physician of the City of Philadelphia, and as a discriminating but good-tempered critic." For many years he was an active member of the Society of Ethical Culture of Philadelphia. Of special interest were the Sunday evening lectures which he gave from time to time. The first of these was on "Charles Dickens' Solution of the Problem of Poverty," and some of the others were: "Primitive Man and His Work"; "The Bible and Evolution"; "The Real Thomas Paine." The last mentioned was published in 1922. Other publications of Leffmann's, outside his professional field, were *About Dickens* (1908) and *The States-Rights Fetish* (1913). He was a many-sided humanitarian, "tolerant, friendly, familiar with art, music, literature, history, science, religion and ethics" (Griffith, *post,* p. 119). Death came to him on Christmas Day, in his eighty-fourth year, after a brief illness.

On Nov. 29, 1876, he had married Fannie Frank. They had no children. Leffmann lived quietly and economically, and his testamentary benefactions emphasize his interest in science. He left generous bequests to the Wagner Free Institute of Science, in which he had established, after the death of his wife, "The Fannie Frank Leffmann Memorial Lectureship" for lectures on scientific subjects and on subjects in American colonial history. He also left trust funds for the Jefferson Medical College and the Philadelphia College of Pharmacy and Science to be used for scientific research.

[*Outline Autobiography of Henry Leffmann of Phila., with a Reference Index of Contributions to Science and Literature* (1905); papers by C. H. LaWall, Ivor Griffith, S. Solis-Cohen, Martha Tracy, and others in *Am. Jour. Pharmacy,* Mar. 1931 (Leffmann Memorial Number); *Jour. Franklin Inst.,* Feb. 1931; *Who's Who in America,* 1930–31; *Phila. Inquirer,* Dec. 26, 1930; personal acquaintance.]
W. K.

LEFLORE, GREENWOOD (June 3, 1800–Aug. 31, 1865), Choctaw chieftain, Mississippi planter, was born near the present site of the old state capitol in Jackson, Miss. He was the son of Louis LaFleur, a French-Canadian who lived among the Choctaw Indians as agent and trader, and his wife Rebecca Cravat, who was of French and Indian blood. Later, Louis LaFleur kept an inn on the Natchez Trace. Major John Donly, who handled mail along the Trace, took Greenwood, when he was about twelve years old, to his home near Nashville, Tenn. There the boy attended school for some years, and won Rosa Donly as his wife. After her death he married Elizabeth Cody (or Coody), a Cherokee, the niece of Chief Ross. His third marriage was to Priscilla James Donly, a younger sister of his first wife. There were two children of the first marriage and one of the third. In his twenties he became a chief of the Choctaws and in this capacity so vigorously encouraged education, Christianity, and law-making that the white people of Mississippi began to fear that the tribe was becoming too firmly rooted in the state. As a remedial measure the legislature, in 1830, prohibited any chieftain from executing tribal laws. Leflore appealed to the government at Washington, which, to avoid trouble, opened negotiations for the westward removal of the Choctaws. By the treaty of Dancing Rabbit Creek (signed Sept. 15, 1830; proclaimed Feb. 24, 1831), the Choctaws sold all that remained of their Mississippi lands. Rewards were allotted to the chiefs, and 640 acres were provided for each head of a family electing to remain in Mississippi and become a citizen of the United States. The treaty displeased the Choctaws, and the federal agents unduly hurried their departure. Leflore's inability to detain them, in addition to his large responsibility for the ratification of the treaty, destroyed his influence over the tribe. He therefore separated from it, remained in Mississippi, and became a citizen of the United States. In 1841–44 he was a member of the Mississippi Senate.

His rise in the economic system of the white man was remarkable. Dwelling at first in a log cabin a few miles from the city that now bears his first name, he prospered so that in 1854 he moved into a stately mansion, "Malmaison," which he began to furnish by spending $10,000 for Louis XIV furniture for a single room. His domain came to comprise 15,000 acres in Mississippi, on which were 400 slaves, and he had a part interest in 60,000 acres in Texas. Becoming dissatisfied with the way his cotton was handled at the point where it was loaded on the Yazoo River boats, he built a small town, Point Leflore, and constructed a $75,000 turnpike to divert plantation business to his town. During the Civil War his various enterprises languished and his Texas lands were lost. He had deplored secession, and remained loyal to the Union until his death at the close of the war. In accordance with his last request, his body was wrapped in the flag of the United States and was buried near his home.

[See J. F. H. Claiborne, *Miss. as a Province, Territory and State* (1880); *Pubs. Miss. Hist. Soc.*, vol. VII (1903); Dunbar Rowland, *Miss.* (1907), vol. II; *Laws of Miss.*, 1830; Florence R. Ray, *Greenwood Leflore* (pamphlet, privately printed, 1927); Robt. Lowry and W. H. McCardle, *A Hist. of Miss.* (1891), pp. 450–52; *Trans. Ala. Hist. Soc.*, vol. III (1899); *Am. State Papers, Indian Affairs*, vol. II (1834); H. B. Cushman, *Hist. of the Choctaw* (1899), pp. 400–05. A number of Leflore's letters and papers are in the possession of his great-grand-daughter, Miss Florence R. Ray, Memphis, Tenn.]

C. S. S.

LEGARÉ, HUGH SWINTON (Jan. 2, 1797–June 20, 1843), lawyer, attorney-general under President Tyler, was born in Charleston, S. C., of Huguenot descent. His parents were Solomon Legaré and his wife Mary Swinton of South Carolina, daughter of Hugh and Susannah (Splatt) Swinton. Solomon Legaré died soon after his son's birth, and the entire care of the family rested upon his widow, a woman of rare nobility and strength of character. At the age of five the son was poisoned by an inoculation with smallpox, and after a severe and protracted illness recovered slowly, though with permanently crippled limbs. This infirmity cut him off from all boyish sports and centered his attention upon intellectual pursuits. It also produced, or at least intensified, a shrinking and highly sensitive disposition. After receiving his early education from his mother, he studied at several private schools, and then for eighteen months attended the high school which later became the College of Charleston, under Mitchell King, with whom he later studied law. He spent a year under Dr. Moses Waddel at Willington, and entered the sophomore class at South Carolina College when he was fourteen. Here he was a recluse, giving three years to hard study and wide reading. He was graduated in 1814 at the head of a large class. After three years' study of law, he went to Europe in 1818, and, after a brief stay in Paris to perfect his knowledge of French, proceeded to Edinburgh, where he studied Roman law under Irving and amused himself by studying natural philosophy, mathematics, and chemistry. He returned to South Carolina in 1820 and, taking charge of the family plantation on John's Island, which had been badly managed, began to raise sea-island cotton. In the same year he was elected to the lower house of the legislature and was reëlected the next year but defeated in 1822.

The plantation was now sufficiently restored to allow him to leave, and in 1821 he moved to Charleston, where he began to practise but with almost no success. In 1824 he was sent to the legislature from Charleston and, reëlected annually, served six years. When the *Southern Review* was established in 1828, he became associated with Stephen Elliott [*q.v.*] as editor. He was also its chief contributor until it suspended, in 1832, after running through eight volumes. He was later a contributor to the *New-York Review.*

During his legislative career, Legaré was a firm believer in state's rights and a bitter opponent of the protective system, but when the issue of nullification arose he joined the Union party and fought against Calhoun's "South Carolina Exposition" in 1828. In 1830 he was elected by his political opponents to succeed James L. Petigru as attorney-general of the state and at last had an opportunity to display his legal learning and power. Arguing a case before the Supreme Court of the United States, he attracted the favorable attention of Edward Livingston, then secretary of state, and by him was offered the post of chargé d'affaires in Belgium (1832). Legaré saw in this appointment a chance to escape from the clamor and, to him, unbearable heat of the nullification controversy and also an opportunity for further study of the civil law. Accepting gratefully, he spent four years in Europe where, with light official duties at Brussels, he was able not only to study Roman and civil law under Savigny, but to learn German and Dutch. He returned to America in 1836 and was at once elected to Congress, taking his seat at the special session of 1837, called to meet the financial crisis. He took an active part in the debates, with increasing reputation, but like his friend Preston opposed the independent treasury, and this lost him reëlection. He returned to his profession and quickly built up a large practice. Identifying himself with the Whig party, he was active in the campaign of 1840, being particularly interested in the success of John Tyler, his close personal friend. When Harrison's cabinet resigned, Tyler, in September 1841, made him attorney-general. He served with distinction. In the cabinet his wide learning and his knowledge of international law made him a valuable adviser. In the technical side of his position he was no less useful. He rendered 150 opinions on a wide variety of subjects and argued a number of cases before the Supreme Court (16 *Peters,* 174–578), where his legal learning attracted admiration. When Webster resigned as secretary of state, Tyler made Legaré secretary *ad interim.* His health was failing, however, and shock caused by the deaths of his mother and sister had weakened him seriously. He accompanied Tyler to the unveiling of the Bunker Hill monument, was attacked by a chronic disease which afflicted him, and died after an illness of four days.

Those who penetrated his shell of reserve found Legaré a man of great charm. His manner was gracious and he was noted as a conversationalist who, in spite of all his learning, lacked any touch of pedantry. Gifted with a superb voice, through determined effort he became an orator of power. He was inclined to vehemence, but there was in his smooth speech little of the artificiality characteristic of American oratory of that day.

[*Writings of Hugh Swinton Legaré* (2 vols., 1845–46), ed., with a memoir, by his sister, Mary S. L. Bullen; W. C. Preston, *Eulogy on Hugh Swinton Legaré* (1843); B. J. Ramage, in *Sewanee Rev.*, Jan., Apr. 1902, reviewed and corrected in *S. C. Hist. and Geneal. Mag.*, Apr., July 1902; *Official Opinions of the Attorneys General of the United States,* vol. IV (1852); *Jour. of the Legislature of S. C.*, 1820–21, 1824–30; L. G. Tyler, *The Letters and Times of the Tylers,* vol. II (1885); *Southern Lit. Messenger,* Sept. 1843; *Southern. Quart. Rev.*, Oct. 1843; *Daily Atlas* (Boston), June 21, 1843.]

J. G. deR. H.

LEGENDRE, CHARLES WILLIAM (Aug. 26, 1830–Sept. 1, 1899), soldier and diplomat, was the son of Jean François and Aricie Louise Marie Gertrude (Wable) LeGendre. Born at Ouillins, France, he was educated at the University of Paris. He married, Oct. 31, 1854, at Brussels, Clara Victoria Mulock, daughter of William and Marie Guilbert Mulock, residents of New York. He thereafter emigrated to the United States and became a naturalized citizen. He helped recruit the 51st New York Volunteer Infantry, and on Oct. 29, 1861, was commissioned a major of that regiment; on Sept. 20, 1862, he was promoted to lieutenant-colonel, and on Mar. 14, 1863, to colonel. At the capture of New Bern, N. C., Mar. 14, 1862, he was cited for displaying "most conspicuous courage until he fell wounded," a ball carrying away part of his jaw. In the second battle of the Wilderness, May 6, 1864, he was again severely wounded, a ball carrying away the bridge of his nose and his left eye. By reason of such disability he was honorably discharged, Oct. 4, 1864, and the brevet title of brigadier-general, for meritorious service, was given him to date from Mar. 13, 1865.

On July 13, 1866, he was appointed American consul at Amoy, China. His district included the island of Formosa, and in March 1867, the wreck of the American bark *Rover* on the southern coast of that island gave him an opportunity to render distinguished service. Fourteen members of the crew landed on the island but were massacred by the aborigines. LeGendre requested of the Chinese authorities that a search for possible survivors be made and that a more effective occupation and control of the shores of Formosa be established, but without success. Rear Admiral Bell, of the United States Navy, then conducted a punitive expedition against the aborigines, but it ended disastrously, since the landing party fell into an ambush and was forced to retire. This misadventure, however, did not deter General LeGendre from personally leading a small party across the island. He was successful in establishing relations with the most important tribes and concluded a convention for the future protection of shipwrecked mariners.

In November 1872, he arrived in Japan en route to the United States. The American minister introduced him to the Japanese authorities, who immediately recognized in him a possibly valuable assistant in their proposed negotiations with China and their expedition against Formosa, ostensibly to protest against the massacre of some of their shipwrecked seamen. LeGendre was offered the position of counselor to the proposed mission to China, with the prospect of further advancement in the Japanese service; and this offer he accepted, resigning as American consul on Dec. 19, 1872. The mission to Peking was not an entire success, but it encouraged the Japanese to undertake the expedition against Formosa. When, however, LeGendre arrived in China on his way to the island, he was arrested by the American consul at Amoy, but was later released on order of the Department of State at Washington. He continued in the Japanese service as foreign adviser until July 1875, and received the decoration of the second class of merit (Rising Sun), being the first among either foreigners or Japanese to be admitted into the Order after its institution by the Emperor of Japan. He resided in Japan until March 1890, when he was appointed vice-president of the Korean Home Office. Upon the resignation of Judge O. N. Denny, later in that year, LeGendre became adviser to the household department of the King of Korea, holding that position until his death by apoplexy at Seoul in 1899. His influence, in those days when intrigue was so prevalent between the two opposing groups of foreign powers, was always directed to peace; and his varied experience, together with the fact that his French birth and American citizenship inspired confidence, admirably fitted him for the position of adviser.

[*War of the Rebellion: Official Records (Army)*; files of the Adjutant-General's Office, War Dept., and Pension Office; *Foreign Relations of the U. S.*, 1873; Tyler Dennett, *Americans in Eastern Asia* (1922); *N. Y. Tribune*, Sept. 3, 1899.]

A. E. I.

LEGGETT, MORTIMER DORMER (Apr. 19, 1821–Jan. 6, 1896), Union soldier, lawyer, commissioner of patents, was born on his father's farm near Ithaca, N. Y., the son of Isaac and Mary (Strong) Leggett. When he was fifteen years old his parents moved to Montville, Geauga County, Ohio. Here Leggett helped his father clear the forests to obtain a farm, studied at night, and in 1839 entered Kirtland Teachers' School at Kirtland, Ohio, where he graduated at the head of his class. With the idea of practising law and specializing in medical jurisprudence, he then attended Western Reserve College and was admitted to the bar in 1844, supplementing his previous training by a special course at Willoughby Medical School. In 1846 he moved to Akron, Ohio. Having become deeply interested in the establishment of graded schools, he engaged with a group of others in behalf of this project. As a result of the agitation, the Akron School Law was enacted by the legislature in February 1847 and Leggett was employed by Akron as superintendent to execute its provisions (S. A. Lane, *Fifty Years and Over of Akron and Summit County*, 1892, pp. 122, 124). Three years later, 1849, he was called to Warren, Ohio, for a similar purpose, and it was here in 1850 that he began his law practice. In 1856 he became professor of law and pleading in the Ohio Law College at Poland, but in 1857 removed to Zanesville, Ohio, where he continued his law practice and served as superintendent of schools as well.

At the outbreak of the Civil War Leggett joined the staff of his friend Gen. George B. McClellan, and accompanied him into West Virginia, serving without pay. Later he was designated by Gov. William Dennison of Ohio to raise a regiment, and in forty days he enrolled 1,040 men in the 78th Ohio Volunteers and was commissioned colonel. The regiment joined Grant's western army and Leggett commanded it at Fort Donelson, Corinth, and Shiloh. For his gallantry he was commissioned a brigadier-general in 1862, and during that year commanded his brigade in the fighting along the Mississippi, having had much to do with the laying of the mines in the siege of Vicksburg. Subsequently, he commanded the 3rd Division in the XVII Army Corps under Gen. John A. Logan in Tennessee. In 1863 he was brevetted major-general and in the battle of Atlanta, his division took and held Bald Hill, the key to the whole position, and now known as Leggett's Hill. He marched with Sherman to the sea and up through the Carolinas; participated in the grand review in Washington; was promoted to the grade of major-general of volunteers, and resigned his commission Sept. 28, 1866.

Returning to Zanesville, he resumed the practice of law, and became connected with several manufacturing enterprises, all of which he gave up when President Grant appointed him commissioner of patents on Jan. 16, 1871. His capacity for organization here found expression. He continued effectively the work and policies of his predecessors; had a reclassification of patents made; established the office of third assistant examiner; and by other activities concerned with its internal affairs, distinctly advanced the work and standards of the Patent Office. Following his resignation on Nov. 1, 1874, he made his residence in Cleveland, Ohio, and engaged in the practice of patent law with his sons. In 1884 he organized and was the first president of the Brush Electric Company. After a struggle, this enterprise became highly successful and was finally absorbed by the General Electric Company. He was twice married: first, on July 9, 1844, to Marilla Wells of Montville, Ohio, who died in 1876; second, in 1879, to Weltha Post of Sandusky, Ohio, who with one daughter by his first wife survived him.

[*War of the Rebellion: Official Records (Army)*; *Mil. Order of the Loyal Legion of the U. S., Commandery of the State of Ohio, Circular No. 8, Series of 1896*; C. C. Reif, in *Jour. of the Patent Office Soc.*, July 1920; T. A. Leggett and A. Hatfield, Jr., *Early Settlers of West Farms, Westchester County, N. Y.* (t.p. 1913, Foreword, 1916); W. S. Robinson, *Hist. of the City of Cleveland* (1887); *Cleveland Weekly Leader and Herald*, Jan. 11, 1896.] C. W. M.

LEGGETT, WILLIAM (Apr. 30, 1801–May 29, 1839), journalist, descended from Gabriel Leggett, an emigrant from Essex, England, who settled in Westchester County, N. Y., about 1675, was born in New York City, son of Abraham Leggett, an officer in the Revolution, and his second wife, Catherine Wylie of New Rochelle. He attended Georgetown College for a time, but did not graduate, and in 1819 went with his parents to Illinois, where he lived a pioneer's life until his appointment as midshipman in the navy, Dec. 4, 1822. In May following, assigned to the *Cyane,* he sailed for the Mediterranean, but in 1825 he was court-martialed for a dueling affair with another midshipman at Port Mahon, was sent home, and on Apr. 17, 1826, threw up his commission. His faults were chiefly hot temper and a witty, unruly tongue—one offense was quoting passages of Shakespeare "of highly inflammatory, rancorous, and threatening import" against his captain, John Orde Creighton. His defense (Court Martial Records, Navy Department) is an able, entertaining document. He had published some youthful verse, *Leisure Hours at Sea* (1825), and now took up journalistic writing in New York. He published a second volume of poems, *Journals of the Ocean,* in 1826, and *Tales and Sketches, by a Country Schoolmaster* in 1829; contributed "The Blockhouse" to *Tales of Glauber Spa* in 1832; and wrote constantly for the *New-York Mirror* and other periodicals. In 1828 he married Almira, daughter of John Waring of New Rochelle, and in the same year established a weekly, the *Critic,* most of which he wrote himself and which lasted only ten months.

In 1829 he became part owner and assistant editor, under William Cullen Bryant, of the *Evening Post.* Whittier's poem, "To a Poetical Trio in New York" (Haverhill, *Iris,* Sept. 29, 1832), was an appeal to Bryant, Leggett, and James Lawson [*q.v.*], another New York editor, to give up vain political debates and devote themselves to the anti-slavery cause. From June 1834 to October 1835, during Bryant's absence abroad Leggett was chief editor. He was more fluent and more of a theorist than Bryant. Though at first he had disclaimed interest in politics, he now entered warmly into political issues, adopting strong Jacksonian principles. From opposing the United States Bank he advanced to denunciation of the state banks as the worst examples of chartered monopolies and special privilege. He advocated broad suffrage and free trade. Soon he had become the oracle of the radical Democrats whose extreme wing seceded to form the Equal Rights or Locofoco party in 1835. In that year, though not yet a thoroughgoing abolitionist, he hotly attacked the administration for excluding anti-slavery propaganda from the mails, and denounced the mobs that broke up abolitionist meetings in New York. His chief characteristics as a writer were energy and absolute independence; his chief defect was violence. Combative from his backwoods and naval antecedents, he was responsible for Bryant's attempt to horsewhip Sands, editor of the *Commercial,* and later challenged Sands to a duel. This was not fought, but he had a duel with an Englishman named Banks, treasurer of the Park Theatre. Convivial in tastes, he was prominent in New York social and literary life. His severe illness in the winter of 1835–36 hastened Bryant's return from Europe, and about October 1836, he left the *Evening Post.* From December of that year to September 1837, he edited the *Plaindealer,* in which, free from the restrictions imposed by his more conservative chief on the *Post,* he continued to attack political and economic abuses and to advocate free trade, direct taxation, and the right of workingmen to organize. He also advanced from the defense of the abolitionists' right of free speech to support of their attacks on slavery. The journal was influential in shaping Democratic policies, and was fairly successful till the failure of its publishers. During part of this time Leggett also edited a daily, the *Examiner.* "How he finds time to write so much," remarked Bryant, "I know not." In 1838 he nearly secured a Democratic nomination for Congress, but, having declared himself an abolitionist and refusing to modify his declaration, he was rejected for a less radical candidate. The next year Van Buren appointed him diplomatic agent to Guatemala, his friends hoping the climate might benefit his health, but he died before sailing for the post. Though Tammany, during his attacks on the administration in 1835, had abjured Leggett and disclaimed the *Post* as a party organ, the Tammany Young Men's General Committee erected the monument over his grave in Trinity (Episcopal) Church Cemetery, New Rochelle. Whittier refers to this episode in his poem, "Leggett's Monument." Theodore Sedgwick, Jr., his friend, published in two volumes *A Collection of the Political Writings of William Leggett* (1840), remarked upon at the time as the first American attempt to establish the standing of a writer on the basis of journalistic work.

[Biographical sketch by Bryant in *U. S. Mag. and Dem. Rev.,* July 1839, and poem, *Ibid.,* Nov. 1839; *Eve. Post* (editorial), June 3, 1839; *Morning Courier and N. Y. Enquirer* and *N. Y. Daily Express,* May 31, 1839; critical estimate in *U. S. Mag. and Dem. Rev.,* Jan. 1840; J. G. Wilson, *Bryant and His Friends* (1886); Parke Godwin, *A Biog. of Wm. Cullen Bryant* (2 vols., 1883), *passim*; C. I. Bushnell, *Crumbs for Antiquarians,* vol. II (1866); J. G. Whittier, *Old Portraits and Modern Sketches* (1850); Allan Nevins, *The Evening Post, A Century of Journalism* (1922); Wm. Trimble, "Diverging Tendencies in New York Democracy in the Period of the Locofocos," *Am. Hist. Rev.,* Apr. 1919; T. A. Leggett and A. Hatfield, Jr., *Early Settlers of West Farms, Westchester County, N. Y.* (t.p. 1913, Foreword, 1916).] A. W.

LEGLER, HENRY EDUARD (June 22, 1861–Sept. 13, 1917), librarian and author, the son of Henry and Raffaela (Messina) Legler, was a native of Palermo, Italy. His father was of Swiss-German blood and his mother Italian. Most of his early years were passed in Switzerland, whence the family emigrated to America soon after the Civil War. In 1873 they were domiciled at La Crosse, Wis., where Henry attended the public schools. In his seventeenth year, upon the death of his father, his formal education came to an end, and he began his literary career as a typesetter on the *Milwaukee Sentinel.* He soon rose to the position of reporter and later city editor and editorial writer. In 1888 he was sent to represent his paper at the Republican National Convention at Chicago. His report was so satisfactory that he was elected that year to represent the seventh district of Milwaukee in the state Assembly. This was his only political service; he was on the committee on state affairs, but due to youth and inexperience took little part in public discussion. On Sept. 4, 1890, he was married to Nettie M. Clark of Beloit, Wis.

In that same year he was chosen secretary of the school board of Milwaukee, a position he held till 1904. It was during this time that his scholarly interests began to develop. With a number of historically minded citizens of Milwaukee he founded the Parkman Club, and to its *Publications* contributed two historical essays: "Chevalier Henry de Tonty" (1896) and "A Moses of the Mormons" (1897), both of which are lasting contributions to historical lore. In 1898 he published a small volume, *Leading Events of Wisconsin History,* which has been much used in the state schools. An essay, *James Gates Percival* (1901), and an article on "Early Wisconsin Imprints" (in the *Proceedings* for 1903 of the State Historical Society of Wisconsin) completed his literary work during his residence in Milwaukee. He subsequently published a number of papers and pamphlets on historical and bibliographical topics.

In 1895 the Wisconsin legislature passed a bill creating a Free Library Commission, and in 1904 Legler was appointed secretary of the commission with headquarters at Madison. There he continued the policy of his predecessor in providing traveling libraries for remote and isolated communities; he also arranged for a legislative reference bureau and a training school for librarians, which later became the library school of the state university. During the five years of his administration (1904–09) Wisconsin's library policy became nationally famous. In 1909 he was appointed head of the Chicago Public Library system, where, during the eight years of his administration the library grew from 1,800,000 to 6,000,000 volumes, the branches from one to forty. Figures do not adequately represent his work in this position: he developed a staff of great ability and devotion, he aroused the reading habits of the community, he contributed to the upbuilding of every literary interest in the city, he made the library a factor in the lives of the people. The title of his volume published in 1912 by the Caxton Club is significant: *Of Much Love and Some Knowledge of Books.*

Personally Legler was very attractive. From his Sicilian mother he derived his love of beauty and his romantic disposition; but, on the other hand, he could be stern and practical. He was a loyal courageous friend, a passionate champion of humanity. He literally gave his life for his beliefs, for he died from overwork and too great devotion to the cause of learning.

[There is no adequate sketch of Legler's career; his successor Carl Roden wrote a brief biographical sketch for the Chicago Public Library *Book Bulletin*, Sept. 1917. See also *Who's Who in America*, 1916–17; *Chicago Daily Tribune*, Sept. 14, 1917.] L. P. K.

LEHMANN, FREDERICK WILLIAM (Feb. 28, 1853–Sept. 12, 1931), lawyer, was born in Prussia, to poor parents who emigrated to Cincinnati when he was about two. Sophia, his mother, soon died, and Frederick, the cobbler father, who married again, ruled with an iron hand. The boy ran away at eight and at ten left home permanently, never again seeing any of the family. Peddling newspapers and sleeping in vacant buildings, he spent the next seven years crossing the Middle West, working on farms, herding sheep, and getting an occasional term of school. At seventeen his earnestness was rewarded by Judge Epenetus Sears of Tabor, Iowa, who sent him to Tabor College. He received the degree of A.B. in 1873 and, after brief study in his benefactor's office, was admitted to the Iowa bar. Practising first in Tabor and Sidney, Iowa, and Nebraska City, he later settled in Des Moines. There he married Nora Stark, Dec. 23, 1879, became attorney for the Wabash Railroad, and was active in politics, being instrumental in the election of a Democratic governor, Horace Boies [*q.v.*], on an anti-prohibition platform. His railroad practice led him to remove to St. Louis in 1890. Here, serving some causes without charge, refusing others at any price, he soon had a reputation for fair dealing such as he had enjoyed in Iowa. In 1908 he was president of the American Bar Association.

Named solicitor-general by President Taft in 1910, he accepted the appointment through professional rather than political interest. Declaring the government in error when he thought it so, and often delighting the Supreme Court by his wit, he served for two years, handling the cases which established the government's right to tax corporation incomes. He then resigned to practise with his sons. In 1914, with Joseph Rucker Lamar [*q.v.*], he represented the United States at the conference sponsored by Argentina, Brazil, and Chile to mediate between the United States and Mexico. His most important cases in the course of private practice were those establishing the right of the Associated Press to news as property and securing for the Southwestern Bell Telephone Company the right to earn upon valuation determined by reproduction cost less depreciation. In 1918 he was general counsel for the United States Railway Wage Commission.

Republican one election, Democrat the next, Lehmann was politically independent from his college days, when he mounted the stump for Greeley. He believed in local self-government and considered prohibition a mistake. Frequently urged to seek office, he always refused, but in 1909 was appointed chairman of the Board of Freeholders which redrafted the St. Louis charter. An omnivorous reader with a remarkable memory, a collector of books and prints, a brilliant conversationalist, he was characterized by Rabbi Leon Harrison as "the best educated man in St. Louis." He was a founder of the art museum, president of the public library, a director of the Louisiana Purchase Exposition of 1904, and active in the Missouri Historical Society. Lehmann had a physique requiring what a cartoonist labeled "the widest banquet shirt front in St. Louis." He enjoyed public speaking, for which he was in frequent demand. His published addresses include: *John Marshall* (1901); *The Lawyer in American History* (1906); *Abraham Lincoln* (1908); *Conservatism in Legal Procedure* (1909); *Prohibition* (1910); and *The Law and the Newspaper* (1917). He was also the author of articles in *Missouri Historical Society Collections* (vol. IV, 1923), and in *Messages and Proclamations of the Governors of . . . Missouri* (vol. X, 1928). On May 10, 1932, Senator Glass had printed in the *Congressional Record* an opinion of Lehmann as solicitor-general, written twenty-one years before, which held national bank affiliates to be in violation of the law. He died of the infirmities of age, survived by his wife and three sons.

[Julius Klyman, in "Interesting St. Louisans," *St. Louis Post-Dispatch*, Feb. 2, 1930; *Who's Who in America*, 1930–31; *Who's Who in Jurisprudence*, 1925; S. G. Blythe, "Lehmann the Learned," in *Sat. Eve. Post*, Mar. 4, 1911 (in error about boyhood); W. B. Stevens, *Centennial Hist. of Mo.* (1921), vol. IV; G. S. Johns, in *St. Louis Post-Dispatch*, Sept. 13, 1931; F. H. Severance, "The Peace Conference at Niagara Falls," *Buffalo Hist. Soc. Pubs.*, vol. XVIII (1914); information from Lehmann's sons, Sears and John S. Lehmann.] I. D.

LEIB, MICHAEL (Jan. 8, 1760–Dec. 28, 1822), physician, congressman, senator, the son of Johann George Leib and Margaretha Dorothea Liebheit, was born in Philadelphia. His father, said to have been a native of Strasbourg, came to Philadelphia from Rotterdam in 1753 and served in the Philadelphia militia during the Revolution. Michael attended the common schools and studied medicine under Dr. Benjamin Rush. From Aug. 10, 1780, to the end of the war he was a surgeon in the Philadelphia militia. For the next fifteen years he was active in medical affairs, serving on the staffs of the Philadelphia Dispensary (1786–93), the Philadelphia Almshouse and Hospital (1788–90), and Bush Hill Hospital (1793). He was also a corporator of the College of Physicians of Philadelphia and a member of the Pennsylvania prison society. His activities in the Democratic Society and the German Republican Society and in the Assembly (1795–98), launched him on a political career. A rousing democratic speech of his in the legislature in 1796 moved Jefferson to predict a great future for him (*The Works of Thomas Jefferson,* edited by P. L. Ford, vol. VIII, 1904, p. 227). In 1798 he was elected to Congress. Here he distinguished himself (1799–1806) as a stanch, albeit violent, Jeffersonian. His motion to abolish the navy, subsequently withdrawn (1802), his fight for reforming the judiciary, for more liberal naturalization laws, and for reducing the marine corps, are typical of his democratic zeal. Not disposed to be "a duellist for national honor," he opposed (1806) the non-importation resolution of his colleague, Andrew Gregg [*q.v.*], convinced that the country would incur "more loss than profit by it" (*Annals of Congress,* 9 Cong., 1 Sess., p. 762). Leib collaborated with William Duane [*q.v.*] as political dictator of Philadelphia. For supporting Gov. Thomas McKean [*q.v.*] in 1799 he was rewarded with the post of physician to the Lazaretto Hospital (1800). His violence and avarice, however, soon wrecked the Republican party in Pennsylvania. Disappointed in McKean and exasperated by opposition to his candidacy for Congress in 1802 and 1804, he threw his influence with the radicals and against the Governor in 1805. The next year he resigned from Congress, reëntered the legislature (1806–08), determined to overthrow McKean, and as "the Magnus Apollo" of "the Catilinian faction" blocked the administration at every step and led the unsuccessful impeachment proceedings against the Governor. He was also a Democratic presidential elector (1808) and brigadier-general of militia (1807–11).

From 1809 to 1814 Leib was United States senator. He opposed Gallatin's taxation schemes and the recharter of the United States Bank (1811), demanded drastic measures against England (1810), but in 1812 tried to delay war, and was one of the "malcontents" whose tactics embarrassed the administration. On Feb. 14, 1814, he was appointed postmaster of Philadelphia, but hostile sentiment in Pennsylvania forced his removal early in 1815. His criticisms of Madison now became open denunciations. Speaking, May 13, 1816, before the St. Tammany Society, of which he formerly had been grand sachem, he asserted that the Republican party was controlled by men who had sacrificed the nation's prosperity to make war "a chess board for political gamblers to play upon" (*An Address to the St. Tammany Society,* 1816). Meanwhile his influence in state politics declined. As an old-school Democrat, he attacked the caucus nominating system, advocated a more virtuous democracy, and, curiously, by courting support from moderate Republicans and Federalists whom he earlier had abominated, was returned to the Assembly (1817–18) and to the state Senate (1818–21). From Nov. 15, 1822, to his death he was prothonotary of the district court for the city and county of Philadelphia. Keen in retort, but not a close reasoner, Leib "produced effect rather by the velocity of his missiles, than the weight of his metal" (C. F. and E. M. Richardson, *Charles Miner, a Pennsylvania Pioneer,* 1916, pp. 45–46). About 1808 he married Susan Kennedy. Two of his sons were physicians. He left an estate valued at $32,000.

[Sources, in addition to those cited above, include *Pa. Mag. of Hist. and Biog.,* Oct. 1925; Henry Adams, *The Life of Albert Gallatin* (1879); J. H. Peeling, "The Public Life of Thomas McKean, 1734–1817" (1929), typewritten Ph.D. thesis, Univ. of Chicago; J. T. Scharf and Thompson Westcott, *Hist. of Phila.* (3 vols., 1884); W. W. Harrison, *Harrison, Waples and Allied Families* (1910); *Poulson's Am. Daily Advertiser* (Phila.), Dec. 30, 1822.] J. H. P.

LEIDY, JOSEPH (Sept. 9, 1823–Apr. 29, 1891), naturalist, third of four children of Philip and Catherine (Mellick) Leidy, was born in Philadelphia. Both his parents were of German ancestry: his father, a grandson of John Jacob Leydig who came to Pennsylvania from Wittenberg in 1729; his mother, a member of a family long settled in New Jersey. She died when Joseph was but a year and a half old, and he was brought up by her sister Christiana, his stepmother. He was sent to a private classical academy kept by a Methodist clergyman, but did not distinguish himself in his studies, preferring to wander along the banks of the Wissahickon or the Schuylkill collecting plants and minerals. A talent for drawing evinced in his early teens led his father, a prosperous hatmaker, to take the boy from school at sixteen with a view to making a sign-painter of him. Joseph's scientific predilections, however, together with his stepmother's faith and ambition, at length turned him to the study of medicine and anatomy, and in 1844 he took the degree of M.D. at the University of Pennsylvania with a thesis on "The Comparative Anatomy of the Eye of Vertebrated Animals." After serving a short time as assistant in the chemical laboratory of the University he entered upon the practice of medicine, but two years later abandoned practice for teaching, and was elected demonstrator of anatomy at the Franklin Medical College. In 1848 he visited Europe in company with Dr. W. E. Horner [*q.v.*] of the University, and after his return began, in 1849, to give a course of lectures on physiology in the Medical Institute. With Prof. George B. Wood he visited Europe again in 1850 to collect specimens for use in Dr. Wood's courses, and upon returning, resumed his lectures at the Institute. When ill health compelled Dr. Horner to retire from teaching, Leidy, who had been serving as his prosector, was appointed his substitute, and upon Horner's death in 1853, his successor in the chair of anatomy at the University of Pennsylvania. This position he continued to hold until his death, thirty-eight years later, becoming recognized as the foremost American anatomist of his time. His publications in the field of human anatomy were few, but his *Elementary Treatise on Human Anatomy* (1861, 2nd edition 1889), has been characterized as "one of the best works ever offered to the medical profession on the subject" (Chapman, *post,* p. 359). During the Civil War he served as surgeon in the Satterlee United States Army General Hospital, and in this capacity performed some sixty autopsies reported in the *Medical and Surgical History of the War of the Rebellion* (1870–88). From 1870 to 1885 he was professor of natural history at Swarthmore College, and after 1884, in addition to being professor of anatomy, he was director of the department of biology at the University of Pennsylvania.

Distinguished as he was as an anatomist, he was scarcely less so in other fields of science. His initial publications, including papers on new species of fossil shells and the anatomy of the snail, appearing in 1845 when he was in his twenty-second year, brought him election to the Boston Society of Natural History and the Academy of Natural Sciences of Philadelphia, with the second of which he was ever after closely identified. His first noteworthy contribution to vertebrate paleontology was his paper "On the Fossil Horse of America" (*Proceedings of the Academy of Natural Sciences of Philadelphia,* September 1847) in which it was shown conclusively that the horse had lived and become extinct on the American continent long before its discovery by Columbus. In this line of work Leidy became a pioneer, and before O. C. Marsh and E. D. Cope [*qq.v.*] had begun their work he had shown, through fossil remains, the one-time presence in the western United States of the lion, tiger, camel, horse, rhinoceros, and other vertebrates long since extinct or found only in milder and distant climes. Notable publications on these subjects were *The Ancient Fauna of Nebraska* (Smithsonian Contributions to Knowledge, vol. VI, 1854) and his monograph of 1869, "On the Extinct Mammalia of Dakota and Nebraska" (*Journal of the Academy of Natural Sciences of Philadelphia,* vol. VII), which last is stated by Osborn (*post,* p. 339) to be "with the possible exception of Cope's *Tertiary Vertebrata,* the most important paleontological work which America has produced." Leidy was not merely a paleontologist, however; he was a naturalist in the full meaning of the word, and continued the foremost in his line until his death, although he largely discontinued his vertebrate work when the confining duties of the university prevented his participating and competing in a field where Cope and Marsh were rapidly becoming efficient. No subject seemed too large for him to grasp, none too small to excite his interest. The wide range which he covered and his handling of it cannot be better illustrated than by comparing the works mentioned above with his *Fresh Water Rhizopods of North America* (1879), Monograph XII of the Hayden Survey, in which are shown and described forty-eight quarto plates of microscopic forms, the drawings for which were from his own hand.

Parasitology had been a favorite study of Leidy's from very early in his career and was the subject of many of his most important papers. One of his early discoveries was the identity of a minute parasitic worm in pork with the dangerous *Trichina spiralis* sometimes occurring in the muscles of the human species (*Proceedings of the Academy of Natural Sciences of Philadelphia,* October 1846). His treatise on intestinal worms, in William Pepper's *System of Practical Medicine* (vol. II, 1885), was the first comprehensive work of its kind published in America, while his *Flora and Fauna within Living Animals* (Smithsonian Contributions, vol. V, 1853) is described as epoch-making. He was the first to suggest the probability that certain parasitic forms communicated from the other animals to man might be "one of the previously unrecognized causes of pernicious anæmia" ("Remarks on Parasites and Scorpions," in

Transactions of the College of Physicians of Philadelphia, 3 ser. VIII, 1886, p. 441).

Although an indefatigable worker, Leidy is stated to have been almost wholly devoid of all ambition but that of the collection of facts. He was not given to theory, and disliked controversy on any subject. "I am too busy to theorize or make money," he is quoted as saying. The honors which came to him were of a high order. In 1881 he was unanimously elected president of the Academy of Natural Sciences of Philadelphia, an office which he continued to hold until his death. In 1885 he was made president of the Wagner Free Institute of Science. He received the Walker prize of $1,000 from the Boston Society of Natural History in 1880, the Lyell medal from the Geological Society of London in 1884, the Cuvier medal from the Institute of France in 1888, and was an original member of the National Academy of Sciences.

In August 1864, he married Anna Harden of Louisville, Ky. They had no children, but adopted a little girl, the orphaned daughter of one of Leidy's colleagues. In 1889, broken in health from constant application, he made his last trip to Europe. Returning, he resumed his teaching and other duties, but his health continued to fail and he died in 1891, at the age of sixty-eight. "Among zoölogists he was the last to treat of the whole animal world from the protozoa to man, rendering in every branch contributions of permanent value" (Osborn, p. 339). His bibliography of over six hundred titles is a telling monument to his industry.

[Sources include: H. F. Osborn, in *Nat. Acad. Sci. Biog. Memoirs,* vol. VII (1913), with bibliography; "The Joseph Leidy Commemorative Meeting Held in Philadelphia, Dec. 6, 1923," in *Proc. Acad. Nat. Sci. of Phila.,* vol. LXXV (1924); *Researches in Helminthology and Parasitology by Joseph Leidy* (1904), ed. by his nephew, Joseph Leidy, Jr., with bibliography; H. C. Chapman, in *Proc. Acad. Nat. Sci. of Phila.* (1892); Persifor Frazer, in *Am. Geologist,* Jan. 1892; C. A. Pfender, in H. A. Kelly and W. L. Burrage, *Am. Medic. Biogs.* (1920), with additional references; John Eyerman, *A Cat. of the Palaeontological Pubs. of Joseph Leidy* (1891); *Phila. Inquirer,* Apr. 30, 1891. See also list of references in Max Meisel, *A Bibliog. of Am. Nat. Hist.,* I (1924), 204–05.] G. P. M.

LEIGH, BENJAMIN WATKINS (June 18, 1781–Feb. 2, 1849), lawyer and statesman, was born in Chesterfield County, Va. His father, Rev. William Leigh, after attending the College of William and Mary, studied theology in Edinburgh. Returning in 1772, he married Elizabeth Watkins, daughter of Benjamin Watkins and grand-daughter of Archibald Cary [*q.v.*], the two delegates from Chesterfield County to the Virginia Convention of 1776. The youthful minister was one of ten clergymen who protested against British taxation in 1774.

After receiving careful private tutelage and a course at William and Mary, Leigh began in 1802 the practice of law in Petersburg, and gained a reputation in his first case by securing the acquittal of a youth who in defense of his mother had killed his step-father. His first case in the Supreme Court of Appeals, likewise a *cause célèbre,* concerned his own admission to practice there. Having declined to take the oath against dueling required of attorneys, on the theory that they were officers of the court, he was at first denied admission; but later won over the court by a powerful argument prefaced with the statement that "he should have no doubt or apprehension which would preponderate with that tribunal, the love of justice or the pride of consistency" (*Leigh's Case,* 1 *Munford,* 468).

At the close of a brief service (1811–13) in the House of Delegates, he removed to Richmond. There he rapidly advanced in his profession and was repeatedly honored with public commissions. He supervised the preparation of the Code of 1819. In 1822 he represented Virginia in a controversy with Kentucky, whose advocate was Henry Clay, concerning lands granted as rewards for Revolutionary services. His fame reached its height in the notable Virginia convention of 1829–30, when he followed his forebears as the representative of the county of Chesterfield. In the conflict of interest between the eastern and western parts of the state, Leigh, as the representative of the wealthy, slave-holding, and conservative east, was a dominant figure; and while he was not the author of the compromise that settled the major problem, his trenchant service paved the way for its adoption. He was again a member of the House of Delegates in 1830–31. In 1833 Virginia sent him on a delicate mission to South Carolina, undertaken to secure her withdrawal of nullification—a service which had an ironic quality in its alignment of Leigh with President Jackson, whom he thoroughly disliked and distrusted.

In 1834 he was elected to the United States Senate to fill the vacancy occasioned by the resignation of W. C. Rives, who had refused to follow the instructions of the Virginia General Assembly to vote for the replacement of the government deposits in the Bank of the United States. Leigh vigorously advocated restoring the deposits, and President Jackson's protest against the resolution of censure drew from him an excoriating speech (Apr. 18, 1834). The sentiment of Virginia, however, was veering to Jackson, and Leigh was reëlected in 1835 by a majority of only two. On Feb. 20, 1836, the General Assembly, reversing its former position, instructed the Virginia senators to vote for Benton's expunging resolution. John Tyler declined and resigned, but Leigh, in a letter of noble dignity, refused either to comply or resign (*Letter from B. W. Leigh, Esq., to the General Assembly of Virginia,* 1836), and instead, on Apr. 4, 1836, made one of the greatest speeches of his career against the measure. While a member of the General Assembly in 1812 he had introduced resolutions sustaining the right of a state legislature to instruct senators, but expressly excepting a situation where the instructions required a violation of the Constitution or an act of moral turpitude. In his letter to the General Assembly, he recalled these exceptions and demonstrated that they controlled his action. The act was one of supreme courage. When on July 4, 1836, he resigned for personal reasons, he took pains to reaffirm his position. The General Assembly passed solemn resolutions of censure, which Leigh doubtless bore as unconcernedly as he had worn his honors.

He never again held public office, save, from 1829 to 1841, that of reporter of the Supreme Court of Appeals, then served by a bar of notable ability. There he was long a leader, and the court's decisions constitute the principal record of his life work. According to the lawyer's traditions, he "worked hard, lived well, and died poor." Contemporary testimony and his surviving writings and speeches reveal him as a master of the spoken and the written word. His family surroundings were distinctly intellectual. A brother, Judge William Leigh, friend and executor of John Randolph of Roanoke, was not his inferior in learning. He was thrice married: first to a cousin, Mary Selden Watkins; second, to Susan Colston, niece of Chief Justice Marshall; and third, to Julia Wickham, daughter of the eminent lawyer, John Wickham. He left numerous children.

While Leigh's services as codifier and reporter have somewhat prolonged his local reputation, even in Virginia he is to the rising generation but a name, and hardly a familiar one. An aristocrat in the best sense in a youthful and impatient democracy, of an intellectual reach far beyond most of those whose fame has outlived his own, he was forbidden, by the very clarity of his mental processes and the loftiness of his character, the compromises which the politician finds natural and the successful statesman inevitable. He chose what he believed the better way, and in maintaining his integrity, moral and intellectual, he counted as nothing the loss of present power or posthumous fame.

[See H. B. Grigsby, "The Virginia Convention of 1829–30," *Va. Hist. Reporter,* vol. 1, pt. 1 (1854); H. R. Pleasants, "Sketches of the Virginia Convention of 1829–30," *So. Lit. Messenger,* Mar. 1851; Wm. H. MacFarland, *An Address on the Life, Character, and Public Services of the Late Hon. Benjamin Watkins Leigh* (1851), published also in *So. Lit. Messenger,* Feb. 1851; Edwin James Smith, in *The John P. Branch Hist. Papers of Randolph-Macon Coll.,* June 1904, with valuable references to sources; J. B. Dunn, in *Lib. of So. Lit.,* vol. VII (1907); H. A. Wise, *Seven Decades of the Union* (1872); L. G. Tyler, *Letters and Times of the Tylers* (3 vols., 1884–96). Leigh's own letter, *Niles' National Reg.,* Dec. 11, 1841, repr., but with important comment omitted, in *Tyler's Quart. Hist. and Geneal. Mag.,* Oct. 1927, denies the story that Leigh might have received the vice-presidential nomination in 1839, which is told in G. F. Hoar's *Autobiography* (1903), II, 402. See also *Va. Hist. Reg.,* Apr. 1849; *Va. Mag. of Hist. and Biog.,* Apr. 1921, p. 156; Wm. Meade, *Old Churches, Ministers, and Families of Va.* (2 vols., 1857); death notice in *Niles' National Reg.,* Feb. 14, 1849. A number of his letters and speeches were printed.]

R. B. T.

LEIGHTON, WILLIAM (fl. 1825–1868), glass-maker, was the most notable member of a family of glass-makers. His father, Thomas Leighton (1786–1849), was born in Birmingham, England, became foreman, or "gaffer," of a glass-house in Dublin, and was holding a similar position at the Canongate Works in Edinburgh in 1825 when the New England Glass Company of Cambridge, Mass., contracted for his services as superintendent of its plant. Since glass-makers were forbidden to emigrate, he had to smuggle himself out of the country and was joined later by his wife Ann and their children. All seven of their sons entered the company's service: James as machinist, Oliver as cutter, the other five as blowers. John, the eldest, succeeded his father as gaffer. William learned every branch of the business and was specially interested in the chemistry of glass-manufacture. Experimenting constantly, he produced a great variety of colored glass and even made imitation jewels. In 1848 or 1849 he hit upon an original formula for ruby glass, which consisted of dropping the right number of twenty-dollar gold pieces into the mix. The resulting metal was a handsome rose-red, free from any suggestion of yellow, with a golden glint in some lights and an occasional tinge of magenta, and possessing its own characteristic weight and ring. It could stand comparison with the best European ruby glass and has always been prized. When the glass industry moved westward with the growth of the nation and the search for cheap fuel, Leighton went with it and in 1863 was taken into the firm of Hobbs, Brockunier & Company of Wheeling, W. Va. J. H. Hobbs, the senior member of the firm, was also a former employee of the New England Glass Company. Leighton now made several improvements in the technique of glass-manufacture, but his great stroke was the working out, in 1864, of a new formula for lime-flint glass. Hitherto it had been an inferior article and was little used. By substituting bicarbonate of soda for soda-ash in the batch and by determining the proportions of all the materials with greater care, he made a lime-flint glass equal in appearance to the old lead-flint, and distinguishable from it only by its weight and its lack of the resonant, metallic ring. The new glass could be manufactured for less than half the cost of the old, which it practically drove from the market. Leighton retired in 1868. He had been married, Mar. 8, 1829, to Mary Needham. His son William succeeded him as superintendent of the works of Hobbs, Brockunier & Company.

[*Vital Records of Cambridge, Mass., to the Year 1850* (2 vols., 1914–15); L. W. Watkins, *Cambridge Glass 1818–88* (1930); Deming Jarves, *Reminiscences of Glass-Making* (1865), pp. 95–96; Stephen Van Rensselaer, *Early Am. Bottles and Flasks* (Peterborough, N. H., 1926), p. 209; Jos. D. Weeks, "Report on the Manufacture of Glass," in *Report on the Manufactures of the U. S. at the Tenth Census* (1883).] G. H. G.

LEIPER, THOMAS (Dec. 15, 1745–July 6, 1825), merchant, was born at Strathaven, Lanark, Scotland, the son of Thomas and Helen (Hamilton) Leiper. He was educated in the schools of Glasgow and Edinburgh, for his parents wished him to become a minister of the Scottish Kirk. Such was not his desire, however, and in 1763, after the death of his father, he joined his brothers who had emigrated to America some years previously. Landing in Maryland in June 1763, he was first employed as a clerk in the store of John Semple at Port Tobacco. Later he went to Frederick County, and in 1765, to Philadelphia, where he entered the employ of his cousin, Gavin Hamilton, a tobacco exporter. In a few years he left his cousin and embarked in business for himself, becoming one of the leading wholesale and retail tobacco merchants of the city. He also built several large mills in Delaware County, Pa., for the manufacture of snuff and other tobacco products; and in 1780 he bought and operated stone quarries near his mills. Through the exercise of a high order of ability, energy, and business tact he soon accumulated a considerable fortune.

Some time before the Declaration of Independence he raised a fund for open resistance to the Crown, and when war was declared he contributed large sums to the cause. He was one of the original and most active members of the 1st Troop, Philadelphia City Cavalry (formed Nov. 17, 1774), taking part in the battles of Trenton, Princeton, Brandywine, and Germantown, and in several skirmishes. He was ranked as first sergeant until 1794, when he became second lieutenant, and then, treasurer of the troop. As such he carried the last subsidies of the French to the American army at Yorktown. After the war, he acted with the troop in quelling several civil riots in Philadelphia. One of the leading Democrats in Pennsylvania, he was in strong opposition to President Washington and the Federalists; later he acted as a major of the "Horse of the Legion" raised, largely at his expense, to oppose the "Black Cockade" forces of the friends of the Adams administration.

In his business affairs he was enterprising and progressive, adopting new machines and improvements in agricultural implements. He constructed, for example, in 1809, an experimental railroad in Philadelphia, on which vehicles were drawn by horses. After various experiments he became satisfied that the principle was sound, and in 1810 he built and equipped a tramway from his quarries on Crum Creek, Delaware County, Pa., to tide-water, a distance of three-quarters of a mile. This road continued in use until 1828, when it was superseded by a canal. He also subscribed largely to the stock of various turnpikes and canals in Pennsylvania, often without hope of any immediate return. He made it a rule never to accept offices of pay or profit; but, without ever seeking them, he was elected or appointed to many of trust and distinction. He was a presidential elector in 1808, and in 1825, a director of the Bank of Pennsylvania and the Bank of the United States; commissioner for the defense of the city in the War of 1812; a member and ultimately president (1801–05, 1808–10, 1812–14), of the Common Councils of the City of Philadelphia; one of the executive committee of the St. Andrew's Society; and one of the founders and first officers (1824) of the Franklin Institute in Philadelphia. On Nov. 3, 1778, he married Elizabeth Coultas Gray, and to them were born thirteen children. He died at his country estate, "Avondale," in Delaware County, Pa.

[Henry Simpson, *The Lives of Eminent Philadelphians now Deceased* (1859); J. T. Scharf and T. Westcott, *Hist. of Phila.* (1884), vol. I; E. P. Oberholtzer, *Phila., A Hist. of the City and Its People* (1912), vol. I; J. L. Wilson, *Book of the First Troop Phila. City Cavalry 1774–1914* (1915); L. B. Thomas, *The Thomas Book* (1896); A. Ritter, *Phila. and Her Merchants* (1860); *Aurora and Franklin Gazette* (Phila.), July 8, 1825.] J. H. F.

LEIPZIGER, HENRY MARCUS (Dec. 29, 1854–Dec. 1, 1917), educator and lecturer, was born in Manchester, England, the son of Marcus and Martha (Samuel) Leipziger. The family emigrated to the United States early in the boy's life and settled in New York City. He attended the public schools there, and entered the College of the City of New York, from which he received the degrees of A.B. and B.S. in 1873. He distinguished himself in history, literature, English composition, oratory, and debating. Entering the law school of Columbia College, he received the degree of LL.B. in 1875, and was admitted to the bar. He opened an office, but soon determined to return to teaching, a profession which he had been following in the evening schools of New York while pursuing his law studies.

He suffered a complete nervous breakdown in 1881 and from then until 1883 traveled widely and read extensively. In 1884 he persuaded a group of Jewish philanthropists to establish the Hebrew Technical Institute, of which he became the superintendent. In it he organized courses to train Jewish youths in the trades and crafts so as to fit them for special callings. The reputation which he won for this work led, in 1891, to his appointment as assistant superintendent of schools in New York City, a position which he held until 1896. During this period he laid the plans for a system of public lectures to be given evenings in different school centers, under the auspices of the board of education. That which was a small experiment at first soon grew into one of the largest organized lecture systems of the country, if not of the world. He himself used to call it "The People's University." Hundreds of lecturers were employed, thousands of lectures were given, and audiences numbering more than a million a year were in attendance. So heavy became the work that a special position of supervisor of public lectures was created, and this office Leipziger filled up to the day of his death. Thereafter the work gradually disintegrated, not primarily because of faulty foundations, but from various causes—evening extension courses in colleges and schools, and more particularly, the phonograph and the moving pictures. For twenty years, however, it had been one of the greatest forces for adult education in New York City, and as a result of it Leipziger became one of the best-known educators there.

Outside of his regular work he interested himself in various Hebrew charities, in libraries, and in historical societies. In personal appearance he was a most distinguished figure despite his medium stature and somewhat frail body. The best likeness of him in the form of an oil painting now hangs in the College of the City of New York.

[*Who's Who in America*, 1916–17; G. W. Harris, "Apostle of the Open Schoolhouse," in the *Independent* (N. Y.), Aug. 19, 1915; *City Coll. Quart.*, Mar. 1918; *N. Y. Times* and *Tribune*, Dec. 2, 1917.] J. S.

LEISHMAN, JOHN G. A. (Mar. 28, 1857–Mar. 27, 1924), steel-manufacturer, diplomat, was born in Pittsburgh, Pa. His father died when the boy was quite young, and in March 1865 his mother, whose health was poor, placed John and his sister Martha in the Protestant Orphan Asylum in Pittsburgh. Though Martha was soon given a foster home with a friend of the family, John remained in the Orphan Asylum until 1869, when a Miss E. Smith of Dunningsville, Washington County, applied for a boy "to take on trial." In the secretary's report book for that year the incident is recorded with the conclusion: "Resolved with his Mother's consent to give John Leishman." In September of that year, according to the same records, "his Mother came to Pittsburgh . . . in improved health and brought John to the City to work for himself." There is added the comment, "He is a bright good boy." His first job was that of office boy in the iron and steel works of Schoenberger & Company. Here he worked twelve years. The author of *The Romance of Steel* pictures him as "undersized," adding that "when he got his first job . . . he looked as if he had escaped from a kindergarten" (*post*, p. 149). He later rose to the position of "mud-clerk," with an office in a little shanty on the river bank, and the task of supervising the unloading of barges. Having accumulated a little money, he started a furnace of his own, but abandoned it after a time to form an iron and steel brokerage firm known as Leishman & Snyder. In this work he won the regard of Andrew Carnegie who employed the firm to obtain orders for him. Leishman dissolved the partnership in 1886, when, at the age of twenty-nine, he became vice-president of Carnegie Brothers, Limited. When this organization united with other interests in the formation of the Carnegie Steel Company, he was elected president.

In June 1897 President McKinley appointed him envoy extraordinary and minister plenipotentiary to Switzerland. He thereupon resigned from the steel company, and devoted the rest of his active life to public service in the diplomatic field. His next post was that of minister to Turkey, which he entered upon in 1900. Six years later he became the first ambassador to that country. During this time he had the opportunity to show his patience and tactfulness in the face of very trying circumstances. His principal task was to present to the Turkish government the demands of the United States for the same protection to American schools and American property that was accorded the schools and property of other nations. In April 1909 he was transferred to Rome as ambassador to Italy, and from 1911 to 1913 was in Berlin as ambassador to Germany. He died at Nice, France, on the eve of his sixty-seventh birthday. On Sept. 9, 1880, while still in the office of Schoenberger & Company, Leishman married Julia Crawford, daughter of Edward Crawford, a manufacturer. Of the three children born to them, one, Nancy, became the Duchess of Croy.

[*Palmer's Pictorial Pittsburgh and Prominent Pittsburghers* (1905); *Who's Who in America*, 1922–23; *Reg. of the Dept. of State, Oct. 15, 1912* (1912); *Foreign Relations of the U. S.*, 1897–1913; H. N. Casson, *The Romance of Steel* (1907); records of the Protestant Orphan Asylum of Pittsburgh; *Pittsburgh Post*, Feb. 20, June 10, 1897, Mar. 28, 1924.] A. I.

LEISLER, JACOB (1640–May 16, 1691), *de facto* lieutenant-governor of New York, was born in Frankfort, Germany, and baptized on Mar. 31, 1640. He was the son of a Calvinist pastor of Bockenheim, Jacob Victorius Leyssler, and his wife Susanna. In 1660 young Jacob came to New Amsterdam a penniless soldier in the Dutch West India Company. Three years later, Apr. 11, 1663, his marriage with Elsje Tymens, the rich widow of Pieter van der Veen, and a step-daughter of Govert Loockermans, connected him with leading Dutch families, among them the Bayards and Van Cortlandts, and provided him the capital to engage in the fur and tobacco, and later, in the wine, trade. He was soon numbered among the richest merchants of the colony. Until 1689 he played little part in the troubled affairs of New York. An arbitrator of various legal disputes, the mouthpiece of Suffolk country petitioners, a captain in the militia, and a deacon in the Dutch Reformed Church, he emerged from comparative obscurity only when, with Jacob Milborne, he attacked as a violation of ecclesiastical liberty the appointment to his church of the Anglican Dominie Nicholas van Rensselaer [*q.v.*]. In several suits brought against him he betrayed an unconsidered obstinacy of temper, while his own suit for a share of Govert Loockerman's estate changed the scorn with which his aristocratic kinsmen regarded his plebeian origin and his uncouthness of manner into bitter personal enmity.

Since Nicholas Bayard [*q.v.*] and Van Cortlandt were on the council, these personal feelings added a special vehemence to the course of the Revolution of 1689 in New York, caused there as elsewhere by fear of French invasion, suspicion of papists in the administration, and agitation for representative government. The overthrow at Boston of Sir Edmund Andros [*q.v.*], governor general of the Dominion of New England, of which New York was a part, left Lieutenant-Governor Francis Nicholson [*q.v.*] to continue alone at New York. It is uncertain what part Leisler played in instigating the first overt act against Nicholson, which was the seizure by his trainband of the fort at New York, but he soon emerged as leader of the various discontented elements, which numbered important Dutchmen and Englishmen as well as the mob. Nicholson fled the country in June, his council proved incapable of continuing the government, and Leisler on his own authority proclaimed William and Mary. In June a committee of safety representing his faction in six New York counties named him as captain of the fort, and in August, as commander-in-chief. In December he seized letters addressed to Nicholson or to "such as for the time being take care for Preserving the Peace and administring the laws," interpreted them as justifying his assumption of authority, and styled himself lieutenant-governor. He was, therefore, a revolutionary usurper, and was never sanctioned by the British government, which, in August 1689, selected a new governor, Sloughter, and authorized the raising of regular troops to restore order in New York. Nevertheless, during twenty months, Leisler filled the post of executive as well as the high feeling and disorder of the times permitted. Governing by military force, with his own supporters in administrative positions, he suppressed riots, constituted courts, struck a seal, signed commissions, collected taxes, and called an assembly composed of his partisans from a part of the province only. Albany recognized his authority early in 1690, largely because of Indian dangers, and his principal concern was thenceforth the French War, to which he devoted himself with vigor. His enthusiasm was responsible for the first attempt to create a military union of the colonies, though his quick temper, and that of his chief lieutenant and son-in-law, Milborne, contributed to the disastrous failure of the joint expedition which resulted.

Administrative difficulties delayed in England the sailing of Sloughter and the two companies of regulars. The latter, without Sloughter, arrived in January 1691, under Capt. Richard Ingoldesby, who, with no further authority than his own military commission and the knowledge that all the members of the new council were Leisler's enemies, demanded the surrender of the fort. Leisler refused, for acquiescence would have been an admission that his government had no shadow of legality. For nearly two months New York hovered on the brink of civil war, with Leisler's adherents in the fort, and Ingoldesby's, reinforced by militia from the countryside, in the town. Shots were exchanged on Mar. 17, and two of the king's soldiers were killed. Sloughter arrived two days later, proclaimed his commission, and again demanded the surrender. Reluctant to lose his power, Leisler hesitated too long, and so gave his enemies colorable grounds for bringing charges of treason against him. At his trial he refused to plead until the question of the legal basis of his authority was settled; he was condemned to death, and Sloughter was prevailed upon to sign the death-warrant. Both Leisler and Milborne were hanged. Leisler's career divided New York into two camps, and lent a peculiar passion to political controversies until well into the eighteenth century. In 1695 Parliament reversed his attainder and restored to his family confiscated property; in 1702 the New York Assembly voted an indemnity of £2,700 to his heirs.

[Berthold Fernow, *The Records of New Amsterdam* (1897); E. B. O'Callaghan, *Calendar of Hist. MSS. in the Office of the Secretary of State, Albany, N. Y., Pt. I, Dutch MSS.* (1865); E. R. Purple, *Geneal. Notes Relating to Lt. Gov. Jacob Leisler . . .* (1877); E. B. O'Callaghan, *Docs. Rel. to the Colonial Hist. of the State of N. Y.*, vol. III (1853); *Doc. Hist. of the State of N. Y.*, vol. II (1849); *Colls. of the N. Y. Hist. Soc.*, Pub. Fund Series, vol. I (1868); *Calendar of State Papers, Colonial, 1689–1692*; L. F. Stock, *Proc. and Debates of the British Parliaments Respecting North America*, vol. II (1927); C. M. Andrews, *Narratives of the Insurrections 1675–1690* (1915); A. B. Faust, *The German Element in the U. S.* (1927), violently pro-Leislerian; Mrs. Schuyler van Rensselaer, *Hist. of the City of N. Y.* (1909), sympathetic; H. L. Osgood, *The Am. Colonies in the Seventeenth Century*, vol. III (1907), tends to be hostile.] S. M. P.

LEITER, LEVI ZEIGLER (Nov. 2, 1834–June 9, 1904), merchant, was a descendant of James Van Leiter, a Dutch Calvinist who came from Amsterdam to Baltimore in 1760. In the village of Leitersburg on the tract which his ancestor had purchased from Lord Craven in Western Maryland, Levi Leiter was born, the son of Joseph and Anne (Zeigler) Leiter. He served his mercantile apprenticeship as clerk in the village store, until he was twenty years of age. Filled with the "Greeley spirit," he started West in 1854, worked for a year in the store of Peter Murray at Springfield, Ohio, and the following year arrived in Chicago, where he found employment as a clerk in the firm of Downs & Van Wyck. In 1856 he took a similar position with Cooley, Wadsworth & Company, wholesale dry-goods merchants. At the same time Marshall Field [*q.v.*] also joined the firm as a clerk and salesman and a strong friendship developed between the two young men. Later, both became partners in the concern.

Potter Palmer [*q.v.*] had already established himself as a dry-goods merchant on Lake Street, and, being desirous of retiring from this business, he interested Field and Leiter in the purchase of a controlling interest. Selling their interest in Cooley, Wadsworth & Company, to John V. Farwell [*q.v.*] in 1865, they established the firm of Field, Palmer & Leiter. At the end of two years Palmer withdrew. The others carried on the business for fourteen years, Field as merchant, Leiter as credit manager. The latter was a prodigious worker, with sound judgment and unquestioned integrity. He led the way in reducing the credit period for the purchase of goods at wholesale from four months to sixty days. Under Field's leadership, with a credit policy that greatly decreased losses, the firm prospered remarkably.

Leiter did not have Field's vision nor his boldness in projecting new plans. Furthermore, he had become interested in real estate, and in 1881 retired from the firm, already a very wealthy man. His good judgment and his faith in the future of Chicago induced him to risk his fortune on the city's continued growth, and as a result he greatly increased his already large fortune. To his credit it must be said that his success was in large part the consequence of his constructive leadership in aiding the recovery of the city from the consequences of the disastrous fire of 1871. As a director he induced the Liverpool & London & Globe Insurance Company to locate its office in the city and thus encouraged the return of other insurance companies. He had early given his support to the Chicago Art Institute, becoming its second president. In 1877 he took the lead in providing a new building for the Chicago Historical Society, which had suffered greatly in the fire. The founding of the Chicago Public Library had his financial support. As director of the Chicago Relief and Aid Society (1874–80), he was active in the work of philanthropy. He was a leader in his own group of business men and first president of the Chicago Commercial Club.

In October 1866 he married Mary Theresa Carver, daughter of Benjamin Carver of Chicago, by whom he had four children. One of them, Mary, married Lord Curzon, viceroy of India, and the family became socially prominent in England. Joseph, Leiter's one son, brought about the most dramatic episode in his father's life, when in 1897–98, he tried to "corner" the wheat market. The "corner" was unsuccessful and the older Leiter, who stood behind his son, is said to have lost $9,750,000. At the conclusion of this event, the Leiters withdrew from speculation and Levi busied himself with art, literature, the collection of Americana, and foreign travel. He lived in his latter years at Washington, where he collected a valuable library of early American history and literature.

[*Who's Who in America*, 1903–05; *Chicago Daily News*, June 9, 1904; *Chicago Daily Tribune*, June 10, 1904; *The Leiter Library, a Cat. of the Books and Maps Relating Principally to America, Collected by Levi Z. Leiter. With Collations and Bibliog. Notes by Hugh Alexander Morrison* (privately printed, Washington, 1907).] E. A. D.

LE JAU, FRANCIS (1665–Sept. 15, 1717), clergyman, teacher, first rector of the Goose Creek Anglican parish, South Carolina, was born in Angers, France, of Huguenot parents. Early in life he must have had educational advantages and cultural contacts, for he was master of at least six languages and displayed habitual inclination toward the fine arts. About 1685, probably under stress of persecution, he fled with others to England, where he embraced Anglicanism. He graduated from Trinity College, Dublin, receiving the degree of M.A. in 1693, and of B.D. in 1696; the degree of D.D. was conferred upon him, Jan. 24, 1700. Before 1700 he was canon in St. Paul's Cathedral, London, but though established in this influential parish, he decided in that year, because of ill health, to go to Antigua, West Indies, as a missionary. There he and his family lived nearly six years and laid the foundations for the social and moral uplift of 2,000 negro slaves who were under his immediate care. In 1706, after a brief return to the British Isles, he emigrated to Goose Creek, South Carolina, eighteen miles from Charles Town. At intervals, during the absence of the Commissary, he served St. Philip's Church, Charles Town. In addition to his regular work among the whites, he interested himself in the education of negroes and Indian slaves; and the work he did in their behalf constitutes an important chapter in the history of the province. Generations of them were taught to read and write when there was as yet no school in the parish. Despite long-continued resistance on the part of their owners, he established the family relation among the slaves, and composed ritual pledges adapted to their peculiar needs, to which they made public avowal at baptism, marriage, and reception into his church. He concerned himself, also, with their physical and social welfare, denouncing the brutal treatment accorded them, and publicly condemning the law that provided for physical mutilation of runaway slaves. He exposed cruel practices in letters to the British authorities and called upon them to put slavery upon a more humane basis.

Despite his wide learning Le Jau reflected some of the superstitions of his time. He found in cruelties practised on slaves the cause for epidemics of fever and smallpox, as well as of Indian wars; in the "dying of much cattle" he discerned a punishment of heaven for the laziness of the people. Until his death he defended the specifications of his creed and resisted all encroachments upon the Anglican liturgy. The luster of his pulpit, however, must have been a subject of frequent comment among visitors to Charles Town and Goose Creek. His letters contain references to large congregations, and indicate that it was common for the church building to be filled with white people, while negro slaves and Indians crowded the open windows and doorway.

Shortly before his death he was appointed to the pulpit of St. Philip's Church, Charles Town. Simultaneously he became Commissary of the Bishop of London. His appointment is dated July 31, 1717; but before this he had been attacked by a lingering illness, which caused a paralysis of his lower limbs and affected his speech. He died in poverty. His first marriage was with Jeanne Antoinette Huguenin, Apr. 13, 1690. She bore him four children and died Christmas day, 1700. Elizabeth Harrison, of Westminster, his second wife, bore him two children.

[The little that is obtainable about Le Jau's family is gleaned from the family record owned by the Rev. Francis Le Jau Frost, New Brighton, Staten Island, N. Y. The material pertaining to his life and work consists chiefly of letters in the archives of the Society for the Propagation of the Gospel in Foreign Parts, London, the Bodleian Library, Oxford, and Fulham Palace. There are transcripts of some of these in the Library of Congress and in the archives of the National Council of the Protestant Episcopal Church, New York City. See also Frederick Dalcho, *An Hist. Account of the Protestant Episcopal Ch. in S. C.* (1820); *Pubs. Huguenot Soc. of London*, VII (1893), 140, 142; C. P. Pascoe, *Two Hundred Years of the S. P. G.* (1901); *Alumni Dublinensis* (1924); A. H. Hirsch, *The Huguenots of Colonial S. C.* (1928), and in *Trans. of the Huguenot Soc. of S. C.*, No. 34 (1929); J. I. Waring, *St. James Ch., Goose Creek, S. C., a Sketch of the Parish from 1706 to 1909* (n.d.).] A. H. H.

LELAND, CHARLES GODFREY (Aug. 15, 1824–Mar. 20, 1903), writer, was born in Philadelphia, the eldest child of a commission merchant, Charles Leland, and his wife, Charlotte (Godfrey). On his father's side he was of Massachusetts, and on his mother's of Rhode Island stock. He received his early schooling at Jamaica Plain, Mass., and in Philadelphia, where Bronson Alcott was one of his teachers. At the age of nine Leland was already reading with the voracity of Macaulay. From 1841 to 1845 he attended the College of New Jersey, where "piety and mathematics rated extravagantly high in the course," but despite serious deficiencies in those subjects he not only graduated in due course but won the regard of his teachers, especially of Albert Baldwin Dod, of whom he has left a beautiful account in his *Memoirs* (1893). After graduating, he went to Germany, by way of Italy, and studied for two years at the universities of Heidelberg and Munich. By "incredible labour" he learned the German language, but learned it thoroughly, and meanwhile changed from an overgrown, delicate boy into a burly, genial giant of a man, with a beard like Charlemagne's and a Gargantuan appetite for food, drink, and tobacco. Germany he learned to love as he loved no other country but his own. In 1848 he migrated from the University of Munich to the Sorbonne in time to be a captain on the barricades for three days and to serve on a committee of Americans that congratulated the revolutionists on their successful coup.

Returning to Philadelphia, he studied law in the office of John Cadwalader, was called to the bar, but soon turned to journalism. For the next twenty-one years journalism and authorship, varied by forays into politics, war, and western exploration, were his vocation. In 1849 he began contributing articles on art to John Sartain's *Union Magazine.* A little later he became Rufus Griswold's assistant on P. T. Barnum's *Illustrated News* in New York. He next joined the staff of the Philadelphia *Evening Bulletin.* By this time the growing prosperity of his father made him only partially dependent on his writing, and on Jan. 17, 1856, he married Eliza Bella Fisher, daughter of Rodney Fisher of Philadelphia. Meanwhile he had published his first book, *Meister Karl's Sketch-Book* (1855), a volume of essays and sketches in the tradition established by Washington Irving but quite Lelandesque in style and flavor. He was also engaged at this time in translating Heine and in writing for various magazines. He was a master of literary journalism, always fluent, entertaining, good-humored, and well informed. He could acquit himself well on almost any subject, in prose or verse. From January to May 1857 he edited *Graham's Magazine* and contributed to the May number his famous "Hans Breitmann's Barty," the popularity of which has only been equaled by Bret Harte's "Heathen Chinee." He wrote other Breitmann ballads, which were published as pamphlets and were widely read both in America and England. They were finally collected in *The Breitmann Ballads* (London, 1871) and *Hans Breitmann's Ballads* (Cambridge, Mass., 1914). Many of them are merely humorous, but the best of them, in their wealth of parody and literary allusion, their rich humor, metrical skill, and poetic feeling, are unique creations of the comic spirit. Though Leland himself enjoyed them, he never realized that they are the best proof of his genius. In 1862 he became editor of the *Continental Monthly* in Boston, an organ of the Union cause and, according to his own story, coined the term *emancipation* as a substitute for the disreputable *abolition.* In 1863 he enlisted in a Philadelphia artillery company and saw, rather than participated in, the battle of Gettysburg. There followed a period of travel in Tennessee and the West and then, in 1866, he became managing editor of John W. Forney's Philadelphia *Press.*

His father having died, Leland gave up active newspaper work and went to Europe in 1869, settling finally in London, where he remained until 1879. By this time he had an international reputation as a humorist, poet, and essayist; he was socially one of the most agreeable of men; and in consequence he became very popular. He and Walter Besant founded the short-lived but famous Rabelais Club. Leland devoted himself to the study of gipsy lore and language and became a master of Romany, which he delighted in speaking. Becoming interested in the industrial arts, characteristically he began to think them of the utmost importance in education and returned to Philadelphia in order to introduce them into the public schools. He gave time and money without stint to the project, wrote a whole series of textbooks, and worked indefatigably. He achieved a certain measure of success, but in 1884, somewhat weary of the subject, he returned to London. During all these years he was publishing a number of books, the more important being: *The Music Lesson of Confucius* (1872); *The English Gipsies* (1873); *The Gypsies* (1882); *The Algonquin Legends* (1884); *A Dictionary of Slang* (1889, 1897), with Albert Barrere; *Etruscan-Roman Remains in Popular Tradition* (1892); *Memoirs* (1893); *Legends of Florence* (1895–96); and *The Unpublished Legends of Virgil* (1901). He prided himself especially on the discovery of Shelta, a dialect, of ancient descent, spoken by some Irish and Welsh gipsies. He had an extraordinary faculty for languages, and to the end of his life, was a student of anything mysterious or occult. During his later years he lived much in Florence and never ventured further north than Homburg, his favorite among the health resorts of Germany. He died in Florence and was buried in Laurel Hill Cemetery, Philadelphia.

[Leland MSS. in library of the Hist. Soc. of Pa. and of Princeton Univ.; C. G. Leland, *Memoirs* (1893); E. R. Pennell, *Charles Godfrey Leland* (1906), reviewed in the *Nation* (New York), Sept. 27, 1906, and the *Athenaeum* (London), Dec. 1, 1906; Joseph Jackson, *A Bibliog. of the Works of Charles Godfrey Leland* (1927), repr. from the *Pa. Mag.*, July 1925–Jan. 1927; Sherman Leland, *The Leland Mag.* (1850); A. W.

Smith, *Geneal. of the Fisher Family 1682–1896* (1896); *Pa. Mag.*, Apr. 1925; "American Humour," *British Quart. Rev.*, Oct. 1870; *Revue des Deux Mondes*, Aug. 15, 1872; *Academy*, Apr. 4, 1903; *Jour. Gypsy Lore Soc.*, vol. III, no. 3 (1924); *Who's Who in America*, 1899–1902; the *Press* (Phila.), Mar. 21, 1903.]

G. H. G.

LELAND, GEORGE ADAMS (Sept. 7, 1850–Mar. 17, 1924), physician, otologist, educator, was born in Boston, a son of Joseph Daniels and Mary Plimpton (Adams) Leland, and a descendant of Henry Leland who came to Massachusetts in 1652. He was educated at the Boston Latin School and at Amherst College, graduating with the degree of A.B. in 1874. At Amherst, which was the first American college to establish a department of physical education, he came under the influence of its first professor, Edward Hitchcock, 1828–1911 [*q.v.*], and acquired such an interest in the subject that after graduation he established a cash prize for excellence in gymnastics which was awarded annually for some forty years. Completing the course at the Harvard Medical School in 1877, he received the degree of M.D. in 1878, after eighteen months' service as interne in the Boston City Hospital. In July 1878, he married Alice Pierce Higgins of Boston. Recommended by President Seelye of Amherst to introduce a system of physical education into the schools of Japan, he took his bride to Tokio, where he remained until 1881, having charge of physical culture in the National Education Department, leading the classes in the normal schools and some in the preparatory department of the University, and thus training about one hundred young men to become teachers in all grades of the schools throughout the Empire. For this service he was awarded the Fourth Order of Merit of the Sacred Treasure of Japan. He was the author of works on Japanese anthropometry and on physical education and gymnastics (1881), published in Tokio in Japanese, as well as a volume on medical gymnastics published in Chinese.

In 1881 he went to Vienna, where he began the study of laryngology and otology with Von Schroetter and other well-known specialists, thence to Heidelberg and other German cities, returning to Boston in 1883. In 1885 he was appointed otologist to the Boston Dispensary. He was also assistant for diseases of the throat at the City Hospital Out Patient Department, with Drs. Hooper, De Blois, and Farlow. His most important appointment was as otologist to the City Hospital. This he retained throughout his life. He gave courses in otology and rhinology at the Boston Polyclinic, and was professor of laryngology at the Dartmouth Medical School from 1893 to 1914, when he became professor emeritus. His ideas upon physical development directed his attention to the need of free nasal respiration. His operations upon the deformed nasal septum were original, ingenious, and successful. They well deserved recognition. He was also expert in the treatment of tonsils. He was a fellow of the American Otological Society and of the American Laryngological Association, and in 1912 was president of the latter organization. He was also a member of the American Rhinological, Laryngological, and Otological Society; and of the New England Otological and Laryngological Society, of which he was president for two years. A man of rugged honesty, he was devoted to his profession, and though he had a keen sense of humor, had few outside interests. He died in Boston in his seventy-fourth year.

[J. W. Farlow, *George Adams Leland* (1924), repr. from *Trans. Am. Laryngol. Asso.*, vol. XLVI (1924); *Who's Who in America*, 1920–21; *Obit. Record Grads. and Non-Grads. Amherst Coll.*, 1924; *Amherst Coll. Biog. Record* (1927); Sherman Leland, *The Leland Mag., or a Geneal. Record of Henry Leland and His Descendants* (1850); *Jour. Am. Medic. Asso.*, Apr. 5, 1924; *Boston Transcript*, Mar. 17, 1924; personal acquaintance.]

D. B. D.

LELAND, JOHN (May 14, 1754–Jan. 14, 1841), Baptist clergyman, the son of James and Lucy (Warren) Leland and a descendant of Henry Leland who came to America in 1652, was born at Grafton, Mass. His early education was limited to the elementary training of the common schools. At eighteen, having received "a sign from God," he decided to forsake worldly pleasures and devote himself to the ministry. In 1774, he obtained a Baptist preacher's license, and two years later, with his bride Sarah Divine (or Devine), whom he married Sept. 30, 1776, he started for Virginia. There, after a temporary ministerial assignment at Mount Poney, he established himself at Orange. During his fourteen-year residence here, leading the Baptist forces, he played a prominent part in the disestablishment of the Episcopal Church and in the ratification of the Constitution. As an exponent of religious liberty, he was instrumental in the repeal of the incorporation act and began the successful fight to regain the glebe lands held by the clergy. While engaged in this work, he was nominated by the Baptists of Orange County as a delegate to the Virginia convention of 1788, to oppose the Constitution. Convinced by his opponent, James Madison, that the federal instrument would not interfere with religious freedom, he campaigned for his rival, who was consequently elected. On Aug. 8, 1789, at a meeting of the Baptist General Committee at Richmond, Leland proposed the abolition of slavery. Taking an active part in the revival of 1787, he was regarded as one of the most popular preachers in the "Old Dominion." His *Virginia Chronicle* (1790) added to his renown, since it became the basis of R. B. Semple's *History of the Rise and Progress of the Baptists in Virginia* (1810).

In 1791, Leland moved to Cheshire, Mass., where he resided for fifty years. In his native commonwealth, as well as in Connecticut, he fought diligently for the complete disestablishment of the Congregational Standing Order. As leader of the Connecticut Baptists, in his tract *Van Tromp* (1806), he suggested that a constitutional convention be called to adopt a new organic instrument providing for religious liberty. Twelve years later his suggestion was adopted. When a constitutional convention was held in his own state in 1820, Leland in his *Short Essays on Government,* published that year, proposed an amendment to separate church and state. In 1833, his hopes were realized with the final overthrow of the Congregational system in Massachusetts. An advocate of political as well as religious liberalism, he was at first a Jeffersonian Republican and later a Jacksonian Democrat. Enthusiastic over the election of Jefferson, in 1801 he traveled to Washington to present his hero with an enormous cheese, made by the women of Cheshire. For this incident he was dubbed the "Mammoth Priest." In 1811, he was elected on the Republican ticket to the Massachusetts legislature. Although engaged in these temporal pursuits, during his fifty-year abode in Massachusetts he took an active part in missionary work, in defending the Christian revelation against deism, and in composing popular hymns. In 1838 he published *Some Events in the Life of John Leland, Written by Himself.* When he was eighty-three, death claimed his wife, the mother of his nine children. Three years later he was buried by her side in the cemetery of Cheshire.

[L. F. Greene, *Writings of Elder John Leland* (1845), which contains Leland's autobiography, letters, and most important writings; H. M. Morais, "Life and Work of Elder John Leland" (master's thesis in the Faculty of Political Science, Columbia Univ., 1928); F. F. Petitcler, "Recollections of Elder John Leland," in Berkshire Hist. and Sci. Soc., *Berkshire Book,* 1892, I, pt. 2, 269–90; J. T. Smith, "Life and Times of Rev. John Leland," *Bapt. Quart.,* Apr. 1871; Sherman Leland, *The Leland Mag., or a Geneal. Record of Henry Leland and His Descendants* (1850); R. J. Purcell, *Conn. in Transition* (1918); W. B. Sprague, *Annals Am. Pulpit,* vol. VI (1856); *Boston Transcript,* Jan. 21, 1841.] H. M. M.

LEMKE, PETER HENRY (July 27, 1796–Nov. 29, 1882), Roman Catholic missionary, was born in Rhena, Mecklenburg, where his father was a magistrate. Privately tutored, he entered the Gymnasium at Schwerin in 1810, paying his own way by giving music lessons. Three years later, he joined the army of liberation and after campaigning against Napoleon and the Danes entered Paris in 1814. During the "Hundred Days" he was again in service and fought at Waterloo under Blücher. He then matriculated at the University of Rostock. Reacting against the riotous student life there and the rationalist philosophy which he encountered, he entered the Lutheran ministry, in 1819. While preaching at Dassow, he studied the writings of Luther and through Adler, a student at Ratisbon, and Melchior Diepenbrock, later cardinal of Breslau, he grew interested in the Roman Catholic Church, which he joined in 1824. On the completion of his theological studies, he was ordained, Apr. 11, 1826, and assigned to a curacy at Ratisbon, where he preached to the garrison, gave religious instructions in the state school, and served as Cardinal Diepenbrock's vicar general. In 1831, he was called as a private chaplain by Frederick Schlosser, a nephew of Goethe and a book collector, who maintained an estate near Heidelberg. Here Lemke busied himself with agriculture, riding, and lectures at the University. A robust man of action, he tired of this sinecure; and on learning of the demand for German priests in Pennsylvania, volunteered for the American missions and eventually took passage, landing in New York, Aug. 20, 1834. He hurried to present himself to Bishop F. P. Kenrick [*q.v.*] of Philadelphia, who assigned him to the German parish of Holy Trinity and tutored him in English. Finding that he had annoyed the trustees of Holy Trinity by a sermon on Luther, he asked to be transferred to the missions of Demetrius Augustine Gallitzin [*q.v.*]. Journeying on horseback through the woods from Munster to Loretto, he met the aged Gallitzin bundled up in a sleigh, on his way to a mass-station, and was appointed to a log chapel at Ebensburg (1834), from which he attended the countryside.

Like his superior, he became enthusiastic over colonization projects, and in 1837 he purchased land at Hart's Sleeping Place which he farmed in model fashion. Three years later, he founded Carrolltown, where he erected a rude chapel. Though injured in felling a tree in this year, he followed the trail to Loretto to attend the dying Gallitzin, whose place he filled for four years on Bishop Kenrick's insistence. He had hardly returned to his beloved settlement at Carrolltown when he set out for Germany, where he collected vestments, books, and money, even from Louis of Bavaria. Proud of his American citizenship, he refused all posts offered him by Cardinal Diepenbrock. In Munich, he inspired Dom Boniface Wimmer [*q.v.*] to lead a colony of Benedictines to Pennsylvania, thus bringing to a successful conclusion a project which he had outlined as early as 1835 in the pages of *Der Katholik* of Mainz. In 1846, he met Wimmer's party in New York, but to his disappointment, the Benedictine abbey was built at Beatty on the Sportsman's Hall Property instead of at Carrolltown. Later, however, Lemke's Carrolltown acreage was used for a priory. Thereafter, he attended churches at Reading and Philadelphia until 1851, when he joined the Benedictines.

Somewhat too settled in habits to accommodate himself to the discipline of a religious, Father Lemke departed for "bleeding Kansas" without his superior's permission (1855). As soon as difficulties with the Abbot were compromised he was assigned to a congregation at Doniphan by Bishop J. B. Minge. He then took up land near Atchison, where eventually there was established the Abbey of St. Benedict. After complete reconciliation, he returned to Pennsylvania (1858) and then toured Germany in the interest of American missions. During a sojourn in Vienna, he wrote his *Leben und Werken des Prinzen Demetrius Augustin Gallitzin* (Münster, 1861) in an effort to stimulate missionary zeal. Upon his return from Europe, he acted as pastor of St. Michael's Church at Elizabeth, N. J. (1861–71), where he established a Benedictine academy. In 1871, he built St. Henry's Church, which he served until his retirement, soon after the celebration of his golden jubilee in the priesthood. His last years were spent in the Carrolltown priory among his aged colonists. During this period he wrote for the *Northern Cambria News* a serial memoir of early days in Cambria County.

[See F. Kittell, *Souvenir of Loretto Centenary* (1899); A. A. Lambing, *Hist. of the Cath. Ch. in the Dioceses of Pittsburg and Allegheny* (1880), and memoir of Lemke in *Ave Maria,* Jan. 20–Feb. 24, 1883; *Cath. Encyc.*, IX, 146; *Sadlier's Cath. Directory,* 1883; sketch by L. F. Flick, in *Records Am. Cath. Hist. Soc.*, IX (1898), 129–92; Oswald Moosmüler, *Bonifaz Wimmer* (1891). Although Lemke's name is sometimes spelled Lemcke, according to Flick, *ante,* he himself always spelled it without the "c."] R. J. P.

LEMMON, JOHN GILL (Jan. 2, 1832–Nov. 24, 1908), botanist, was born at Lima, Mich., the son of William and Amila (Hudson) Lemmon. He attended the common schools and, for a time, the University of Michigan. Enlisting in the Union army in 1862, he was captured in 1864 and held in Andersonville Prison until the end of the war. In 1866, his health broken, he emigrated to Sierra Valley, California. Here, for a period of eight years, he wrote almost weekly letters to California newspapers, detailing in a fluent style his embittered recollections of the Civil War. Then one day a group of native herbs in the dooryard of his cabin attracted his attention and, recalling an early training in botany, he sent specimens of them to Asa Gray [*q.v.*]. Two of these were new species and one was named for him. He was of a highly enthusiastic temperament, and the incident changed the current of his life. His health partially restored by the new interest which meant to him undying fame, he eagerly set about the botanical exploration of wide untouched areas in California, Nevada, and finally Arizona, meanwhile keeping up for two decades a spirited correspondence with his botanical patron at Harvard. Highly successful in his herbarizings, he gratified his appetite for publicity by furnishing the newspaper public well-written articles on the wonders of California's vegetation and his own numerous discoveries at almost weekly intervals for a period of over twenty years. More than any other man of his time he acquainted the people of his adopted state with the existence of a science of botany.

Meantime he earned his living by keeping a small private school, and by reason of this occupation, assumed the title, professor. When Asa Gray came to California in 1876, Lemmon, ardent hero-worshiper, went to meet him, thrilled but with a secret fear that Gray would regard his professorship as irregular. The story of their meeting has been preserved: Gray, who was a little man, laid his hand with understanding kindness on the shoulder of the tall ungainly Lemmon and assured him that he was more of a professor than many of greater pretensions. Lemmon, glorified by the benediction, wore proudly to the end of his life the title thus confirmed by the great Harvard botanist.

In 1880 he married Sara Allen Plummer. He was gentle and she firm, but the two by their interests and instincts were admirably suited to each other; and they agreed to dedicate their lives to botanical science and to all altruistic movements. Their lack of money, however, tangled the skein of all their activities and efforts. Income derived from the collection and sale of botanical specimens proved insufficient for their needs, and Lemmon secured appointment to superintend California's exhibit in forestry and botany at the Cotton Centennial Exposition in New Orleans in 1884. He next promoted the movement to create a state board of forestry and was appointed its botanist in 1888. He made two reports on the forest trees of California,

"Pines of the Pacific Slope" (1888) and "Cone-bearers of California" (1890), in the biennial reports of the California State Board of Forestry. These volumes, the first attempt to undertake an account of the Pacific Coast forests from the standpoint of forestry, had high value and attracted world-wide attention. Though they are now forty years old, foresters of the present day recognize the similarity of Lemmon's canons of forest management to those of present-day practice. As botanist to the state board he served four years. California was still too backward to understand the need of scientific forestry, however, and the political causes which had set up the forestry board soon brought about its end. By way of popular education, Lemmon now issued a number of booklets and pamphlets on the trees, such as *Hand-book of West-American Cone-bearers* (1892) and *How to Tell the Trees; and Forest Endowment of the Pacific Slope* (1902), thus diffusing among the people a knowledge of the state's forests and helping to prepare public opinion for the established forestry policy which came after his death.

For the last twenty-eight years of his life he was a resident of Oakland, where he and his wife busied themselves with many civic and reform activities. He died in his seventy-seventh year, survived by the helpmeet who had energized his life. Mount Lemmon, a fine peak in the Tucson Range of Arizona, where he did valuable field work, was named for him.

[This sketch is based chiefly on MSS., including the abundant Lemmon correspondence. Exaggerated accounts of Lemmon and his wife have appeared in the ephemeral press. An obituary of Lemmon appeared in the *Examiner* (San Francisco), Nov. 25, 1908. The sketch by George Wharton James, in his *Heroes of California* (1910), is highly colored and somewhat exaggerated; it relates mainly to the field work of the Lemmons in Arizona. See also J. M. Guinn, *Hist. of the State of Cal. and Biog. Record of Oakland* (1907), vol. II.] W. L. J.

LEMOYNE, FRANCIS JULIUS (Sept. 4, 1798–Oct. 14, 1879), physician, abolitionist, advocate of cremation, was the son and grandson of Parisian physicians. His father, John Julius LeMoyne de Villiers, came to America with French colonists, among whom he practised his profession for four years at Gallipolis, Ohio. In 1797 he married Nancy McCully, lately arrived from Ireland, and they removed to Washington, Pa., where Francis Julius was born. After graduating at Washington College in 1815, he studied medicine first with his father and later at Jefferson Medical College in Philadelphia. Returning homeward across the Alleghanies in 1822, he encountered a great snowstorm. The party in the stagecoach were unable to find accommodation at the crowded taverns along the way and so all night pushed forward through intense cold. Reaching Pittsburgh, Francis procured a horse and rode on to Washington. Although he was of robust constitution, after this experience he suffered from chronic rheumatism that did not allow him a night's repose in bed through twenty-nine years.

In 1823 he married Madeleine Romaine Bureau, whom he met at his father's house, whither she had brought a sister from Gallipolis for medical treatment. They had three sons and five daughters. About the time of his marriage, LeMoyne's father in helping others became bankrupt, so that to the physical handicap of the young doctor was added a burden of debt. From friends he was able to borrow money and recover the fine homestead built by his father in 1813, which with its old garden is still a point of interest in Washington. By hard work and frugal living he succeeded in restoring the family fortune after several years. In the decade of the thirties he was an intrepid supporter of the anti-slavery movement, and an able debater in its cause, showing much physical courage in opposing the American Colonization Society, which he believed to be founded in the interests of slavery. He was the candidate of the Liberty Party for the vice-presidency of the United States in 1840, and the candidate of the Abolitionists for the governorship of Pennsylvania in 1841, 1844, and 1847. Later his house became one of the stations of the "Underground Railway," enabling slaves to reach freedom in the North.

When he was about fifty-five, the condition of his health made the active practice of medicine no longer possible for him, and he turned to scientific farming, introducing improved strains of sheep, cattle, and horses into the county. He donated $10,000 to the founding of a public library in his town, and for many years catalogued the books as they were acquired. Deeply concerned in the cause of education, he became in 1830 a trustee of Washington College (after 1865 Washington and Jefferson College) and in 1836, of the Washington Female Seminary at its founding. He gave the American Missionary Association $20,000 for the endowment and erection, on a bluff near Memphis, Tenn., of the LeMoyne Normal Institute for colored people, still a successful enterprise. Later he added $5,000 for its equipment. He established two professorships of $20,000 each at Washington and Jefferson College, one in agriculture and correlative branches (1872), the other in applied mathematics (1879). These donations were prompted by the conviction that for students not entering the learned professions more profit was to be derived from the physical sciences than from Latin and Greek.

About 1874, in France and Italy, there was a sudden rise of interest in favor of cremation as a means of disposing of the dead, and LeMoyne became its first prominent advocate in America. In 1876 he erected the first crematory in the United States, situated on his own property on a hill overlooking Washington, where it stands today. The first public cremation took place there on Dec. 6, 1876. It was that of a Bavarian nobleman, Baron Joseph Henry Louis de Palm who had come to America in 1862 and had died in New York. The event aroused much comment at the time. The body of LeMoyne himself was the third to be cremated, and up to the year 1900 there had been forty-one cremations in that place; since then none have occurred.

[*Commemorative Biographical Record of Washington County, Pa.* (1893); Alfred Creigh, *Hist. of Washington County, Pa.* (2nd ed., 1871); Boyd Crumrine, *Hist. of Washington County, Pa.* (1882); E. R. Forrest, *Hist. of Washington County, Pa.* (1926); *Phila. Record*, Oct. 15, 1879; information from LeMoyne's daughter, Mrs. George W. Reed of Washington, Pa.] E. M. W.

LE MOYNE, JEAN BAPTISTE [See BIENVILLE, JEAN BAPTISTE LE MOYNE, Sieur de, 1680–1768].

LE MOYNE, PIERRE [See IBERVILLE, PIERRE LE MOYNE, Sieur d', 1661–1706].

LE MOYNE, WILLIAM J. (Apr. 29, 1831–Nov. 6, 1905), actor, began his career in the theatre as a member of one of the numerous amateur dramatic clubs that flourished in Boston during the middle nineteenth century. He was born in that city, probably the son of Thomas and Elizabeth (Cody) Le Moyne, and after appearances with the Aurora Dramatic Club, of which he was a founder, at the Howard Athenæum and elsewhere in Boston, he went to Portland, Me., as a minor member of the company in which Catherine Norton Sinclair, the recently divorced wife of Edwin Forrest, was starring under the tutelage and with the support of George Vandenhoff. There he made his professional début, on May 10, 1852, as one of the officers in *The Lady of Lyons.* During that engagement he also played Friar Lawrence in *Romeo and Juliet,* Sir Oliver Surface in *The School for Scandal,* and Polydor in *Ingomar.* From that time onward he was continuously active in his profession for almost fifty years, with the exception of his period of service in the Union army during the Civil War. Going to Troy, N. Y., he joined the stock company under the management of George C. Howard, acting Deacon Parry in the first dramatic version of *Uncle Tom's Cabin.* He was for several seasons in Montreal, Philadelphia, Charleston, and Boston, being at the Howard Athenæum, Boston, in 1859–60 when that historic playhouse was under the management of Edward L. Davenport [*q.v.*]. In October 1861 he enlisted in Company B, 28th Massachusetts Regiment, being first lieutenant while Lawrence Barrett [*q.v.*] was captain, and succeeding Barrett when the latter resigned. He took part in the battles of James Island, second Bull Run, Chantilly, and South Mountain, where he was wounded. Permanently incapacitated for further service, he was honorably discharged. In after years he was wont to tell stories of picturesque and exciting incidents of his life as a soldier.

Returning to the stage upon his recovery, he began, after several seasons of desultory tours, an engagement with the stock company at Selwyn's Theatre in Boston which continued three successive seasons. Beginning in the fall of 1871, he was a member for two seasons of Augustin Daly's company at the Fifth Avenue Theatre in New York, his first part there being Burrit in *Divorce.* This rôle was followed by a number of others, which included Rocket Rural in *Old Heads and Young Hearts,* Moody in *The Provoked Husband,* Sir Harcourt Courtley in *London Assurance,* Simon in *Article 47,* Silky in *The Road to Ruin,* Dr. Caius in *Merry Wives of Windsor,* and Lord Durly in *Madeline Morel.* By the historian of that company, Edward A. Dithmar (*post*), he is described as "a natural humorist and a master of the art of make-up." He was at the Boston Museum for three seasons thereafter, and during this decade acquired a considerable fame on tour in a group of plays that gave him opportunity to interpret such divergent Dickens characters as Caleb Plummer, Captain Cuttle, Uriah Heep, Squeers, Fagin, and Dick Swiveller. From the beginning of the season of 1877–78 he was associated almost continuously for nearly twenty years with one or another of the leading New York stock companies, at the Union Square, Daly's, the Madison Square, and the Lyceum, the cast of practically every play given at the last mentioned theatre, during his ten years there, containing his name in an important rôle. He was the first Dick Phenyl in the United States in Pinero's comedy, *Sweet Lavender,* and among the many parts he acted at the Lyceum Theatre were Major Homer Q. Putnam in *The Wife,* Judge Knox in *The Charity Ball,* and Sir Joseph Darby in *The Case of Rebellious Susan.* The annual tours of the Lyceum company made his acting familiar to large numbers of playgoers in all the important cities of the United States. He supported Julia Marlowe in *Barbara Frietchie* in 1899–1900, but after a few other engagements was compelled to retire from the stage on account of ill health. William Winter (*post,* I, 286) says he was "an actor of rare talent and remarkable versatility. His impersonations of eccentric, humorous, peppery old gentlemen were among the finest and most amusing that our stage has known." He died at Inwood-on-Hudson, N. Y., where he had been living since his retirement. He was divorced from his first wife. His second wife was an actress, first known on the stage as Sarah Cowell, and after her marriage as Sarah Cowell Le Moyne, under which name she starred in *The Greatest Thing in the World* and other plays.

[J. B. Clapp and E. F. Edgett, *Players of the Present* (1899); W. F. Gilchrest, in F. E. McKay and C. E. L. Wingate, *Famous Am. Actors of Today* (1896); E. A. Dithmar, *Memories of Daly's Theatres* (privately printed, 1897); T. A. Brown, *A Hist. of the N. Y. Stage* (1903); Kate Ryan, *Old Boston Museum Days* (1915); J. F. Daly, *The Life of Augustin Daly* (1917); William Winter, *The Life of David Belasco* (1918), vol. I; Arthur Hornblow, *A Hist. of the Theatre in America* (1919); *N. Y. Dramatic Mirror*, Mar. 23, 1895, Nov. 11, 1905; *The Sun* (N. Y.), Aug. 31, 1902; *Boston Transcript*, Nov. 6, 1905; *N. Y. Tribune, N. Y. Times,* Nov. 7, 1905.] E. F. E.

LENEY, WILLIAM SATCHWELL (Jan. 16, 1769–Nov. 26, 1831), engraver, born in London of Scotch lineage, was the son of Alexander and Susanna Leney. As a youth he was articled to a clever, original artist, Peltro W. Tompkins, who held an appointment as historical engraver to Queen Charlotte and as drawing-master to the royal princesses. Tompkins executed considerable imaginative work as well as portraits of dignitaries, and young Leney, well-trained in the practice of both line and stipple engraving, "a smooth and dextrous worker" (Weitenkampf), followed his master into both fields. He was engraving over his own name for London publishers when he had little more than attained his majority. During his English career he executed numerous portraits, magazine illustrations, a series of small line plates portraying scenes from stage plays for John Bell's *British Theatre* (1791–97), and six large plates after Fuseli and others, for Boydell's Shakespeare. He also engraved a large plate of Rubens' "Descent from the Cross," of such merit that it won him a gold medal.

Leney was about thirty-six when, with his wife, Sarah (White) Leney, he left England for America, settling in New York. The directory for 1806–07 shows him established as an historical engraver in Greenwich Street, "near the Market." The New York of the opening century offered a promising field to a skilled engraver. America, beginning to take account of its assets in public men and natural beauty, was demanding portraits of the one and scenic "views" of the other, and developing an appetite for illustrated books and magazines. Leney engraved several large plates for Collins' Quarto Bible (1807), executed portrait plates for *Delaplaine's Repository* (1815) and the *Analectic Magazine,* and also a series of large plates of scenery, mostly in and about New York. Among his more important portraits are Trumbull's DeWitt Clinton, Stuart's Captain Lawrence and John Jay, West's Robert Fulton, Sully's Patrick Henry, Copley's John Adams, and Washington after Stuart and Houdon. His work commanded large prices for that early day, as is shown by entries in his account-book indicating that he received as much as $100 to $150 for engraving an octavo portrait. In 1812 he threw in his lot with William Rollinson [*q.v.*], banknote engraver, for whom he executed portrait vignettes. Rollinson's prospectus characterizes his partner as "the first artist in America and of very respectable rank in life." About 1820 Leney, with his wife and nine children, retired to a farm on the St. Lawrence at Longue Pointe, near Montreal, where he passed the rest of his life. For some years he continued to engrave, executing the first banknotes for the Bank of Montreal and a series of large views of Quebec and the Montreal region, which are now rare. He left numerous descendants in Canada.

[Frank Weitenkampf, *Am. Graphic Art* (1912); W. S. Baker, *The Engraved Portraits of Washington* (1880), and *Am. Engravers* (1875); *One Hundred Notable Engravers* (N. Y. Pub. Lib., 1928); D. M. Stauffer, *Am. Engravers* (1907), vol. I; G. C. Williamson, *Bryan's Dict. of Painters and Engravers,* vol. III (1927).] M. B. H.

L'ENFANT, PIERRE CHARLES (Aug. 2, 1754–June 14, 1825), soldier, engineer, was born in Paris. His father was Pierre L'Enfant, one of the "painters in ordinary to the King in his Manufacture of the Gobelins"; his mother was Marie Charlotte Leullier. Many of his father's paintings, battle scenes and landscapes, are preserved, several at the Musée de Versailles. The son apparently had received some instruction in engineering and architecture before his enthusiasm took him, at twenty-three, to fight for the independence of the United States. He served as a volunteer at his own expense, and spent his modest means freely in the enterprise. Accorded the brevet of lieutenant in the French colonial forces, he was promised by Silas Deane [*q.v.*] and later received, through resolutions of Congress, a commission as first lieutenant of engineers, with rank from Dec. 1, 1776. On Feb. 14,

1777, he sailed from L'Orient with Colonel du Coudray, a month ahead of Lafayette, and spent the winter at Valley Forge. On Feb. 18, 1778, he was commissioned captain of engineers, attached to the inspector-general, Steuben [*q.v.*]. A letter of his as published in translation in Rivington's *Gazette* contained some expressions which L'Enfant felt impelled to repudiate in a letter to Washington from White Plains, Sept. 4, 1778 (Library of Congress, Washington Papers, XXV, 337), leaving Washington's regard for his services unimpaired.

Seeing no prospect of action in the North he secured his transfer to the Southern army where he served under Laurens. In the assault on Savannah, Oct. 9, 1779, he was wounded while leading the advance guard of an American column. Still using a crutch when the enemy invested Charleston, he was made a prisoner in the capitulation of the city in May, and was not exchanged until January 1782. Returning to Philadelphia, he was promoted major by special resolution of Congress May 2, 1783, and on June 13 received a French pension of three hundred livres and was presented for a captaincy in the French provincial forces. In July and August he was with Steuben in his journey to secure the British evacuation of the posts on the northern frontier. Following leave to go to France, he was honorably retired from the American service in January 1784.

During the war his artistic abilities had been called into service on more than one occasion. In response to a request from Lafayette, Washington sat to L'Enfant for his portrait, an outline sketch only, which has not survived. At West Point is a sketch of the encampment of the Revolutionary army in the Highlands of the Hudson with an inscription by General Knox: "By Major L'Enfant, Engineer, 1780." Of his authorship there can be no doubt, but the date must be placed after his return to the North. He designed a pavilion for the fête given in Philadelphia July 15, 1782, by the French minister, to celebrate the birth of the Dauphin (*Pennsylvania Magazine,* vol. XXI, 1897, pp. 257 ff.).

He was one of the early members of the Society of the Cincinnati and, submitting by request a design for a medal, he proposed the wearing of an eagle instead. The eagle, which was adopted, and the diploma of the Society were both of his design (B. J. Lossing, *The Pictorial Field Book of the Revolution,* vol. II, 1852, p. 126 n.; L'Enfant's original drawings are in the archives of the Society in New York). He was asked to have these designs executed abroad, and late in 1783 sailed for France, charged by Washington with copies of the constitution of the Society and communications to the leading French officers.

Soon he showed the defects of his fine qualities of imagination and enthusiasm. He had undertaken to go at his own expense. "The reception which the Cincinnati met with," he wrote Hamilton, "soon induced me to appear in that country in a manner consistent with the dignity of the society of which I was regarded as the representative. . . . My abode at court produced expenses far beyond the sums I at first thought of" (Jusserand, *post,* p. 148). For the eagles ordered from Duval and Francastel, the large sum of 22,303 livres had to be carried on credit and was still unpaid three years later. Such financial difficulties caused L'Enfant to hasten back to New York, where he arrived Apr. 29, 1784. Fortunately the Society was appreciative of his efforts, and ultimately reimbursed him in part for his expenses.

Living in New York, he found occasional and increasing occupation for his talents. When in the autumn of 1787 Caffieri's monument to General Montgomery found its resting place under the portico of St. Paul's, facing Broadway, L'Enfant was asked to devise a means of concealing the rough stonework of the back which was visible from within through the great east window behind the altar. Accordingly, he designed the reredos still existing, a typical Louis XV composition of clouds and sunburst, with the tables of the Mosaic law. An altar rail was added in the same style, unique in America (Morgan Dix, *A History of the Parish of Trinity Church,* vol. II, 1901, pp. 141–42). The following July, he assisted in devising the pageantry of the procession in favor of New York's adopting the Constitution. At the banquet afterwards, the President and members of Congress sat under a dome of his design, surmounted by a figure of Fame proclaiming the new era. (A contemporary drawing and a description are given in the *New York Historical Society Quarterly Bulletin,* July 1925.) It was a fitting prelude to his next work, the first capitol of the young republic.

A large sum was subscribed to provide suitable accommodation for the new government in New York, its temporary seat, and L'Enfant was entrusted with the task of converting the old Jacobean City Hall at the head of Wall Street, on the site of the present Sub-Treasury, into Federal Hall. Here Congress met Mar. 4, 1789, and on the balcony, the railing of which is preserved by the New York Historical Society, Washington was inaugurated on Apr. 30. The building was indeed worthy of the occasion, both in form and symbolism. The House of Representatives, adorned with niches, occupied the rear portion of the lower story; the Senate chamber, over the foyer, had chimney pieces of American marble; the pilasters had American emblems; the thirteen metopes of the frieze without were each adorned with a star. The front, with a tall colonnaded loggia over a high basement, was illustrated in the *Massachusetts Magazine* (June 1789) and the *Columbia Magazine or Monthly Miscellany* (August 1789). It was the inspiration of James Hoban [*q.v.*] in the front of his South Carolina Capitol at Columbia. The cost, indeed, ran far beyond the funds subscribed, but the New Yorkers, hoping the handsome building would help them to retain the capital permanently, were reconciled; and, besides a handsome testimonial, they offered L'Enfant ten acres of land near Provost Lane. Feeling it less than his deserts, L'Enfant declined this gift. A decade later, when in financial distress, he made a request for payment in money instead, but again declined the $750 which was tendered.

L'Enfant now had his great opportunity, and proved himself worthy of it in imagination and prophetic foresight, if not in discretion. He was called on by Washington to survey the site and make the plan for the new Federal City. He stimulated Washington to enlarge the size of the area acquired to make it "proportioned to the greatness which . . . the Capitale of a powerfull Empire ought to manifest" (document in Kite, *post,* p. 47). For the site of the Capitol he urged the choice of Jenkins' Heights, which "stand as a pedestal waiting for a monument"; for the President's house, a lower eminence with a broad sweeping view southward toward the Potomac. He rejected the suggestion of a merely rectangular street plan, as "but a mean continance of some cool imagination, wanting a sense of the real grand and truly beautiful." "Having first determined," he writes, "some principal points to which I wished making the rest subordinate I next made the distribution regular with streets at right angle, *north-south* and *east-west,* but afterwards I opened others on various directions, as avenues to and from every principal places . . . menaging a reisprocity of sight." On these principles he produced by June 22 the essential features of his design. (See Memoir of June 22, 1791, printed in *Records of the Columbia Historical Society,* vol. II, 1899.) The more complete plan submitted to the President in August is preserved in the Library of Congress.

Although L'Enfant, in asking Jefferson for the plans of various European cities for reference (Apr. 4, 1791, see Kite, p. 42), emphasized that "it is my wish and shall be my endeavor to delineate on a new and original way the plan," and gives no hint which would diminish his own originality or arouse republican hostility, there can be no doubt that he was greatly influenced by the plan of what was then the French capital, Versailles (Fiske Kimball: "The Origin of the Plan of Washington, D. C.," *Architectural Review,* September 1918; Elbert Peets, "The Genealogy of L'Enfant's Washington," *Journal of the American Institute of Architects,* April-June 1927). The Capitol corresponds in position to the palace, the President's house to the Grand Trianon, the Mall to the *parc,* East Capitol Street, Pennsylvania and Maryland avenues on the east to the Avenues de Paris, de Sceaux, and de St. Cloud. On the west, Pennsylvania Avenue corresponds essentially with the Avenue de Trianon. L'Enfant was far, however, from forcing this analogy, and gave constant consideration to the nature of the ground.

Setting to work with the greatest energy, he cleared the principal sites and avenues, eager to establish their full extent at once, and even to begin the public buildings, plans for which he had not yet submitted. Difficulties soon arose through his unwillingness to submit to the authority of the Commissioners of the Federal District, or even to that of the President. He opposed the immediate sale of lots, withholding his plan at the sale itself even from members of Congress; and before the plan had been legally adopted or even completed on paper, forcibly tore down a house, previously begun by a powerful land-owner, which was found to lie within a street. To Washington's successive gentle "admonition," kindly "reprehension," and later reproof, he merely returned his own justifications and reasons. They might indeed have been convincing under other circumstances. Certainly it would have been desirable, abstractly, to postpone sales until the public itself, rather than speculators, should receive the increment of value on its lots; to push the work rapidly with a great force; to begin simultaneously the canals, wharves, bridges, aqueducts, the terracing and grading and quarrying operations, all of which he proposed to undertake in 1792 and some of which, without consultation, he had already begun before winter. It was natural, too, that the original proprietors, who later signed a testimonial to L'Enfant (Mar. 9, 1792), should be pleased with such a program of activity, which promised a rapid increase of value to their own lots. But this program left the Commissioners, the Secretary of State, and the President aghast, involving as it did more in the first year than the entire sum available for all the work, and necessitating an immediate borrowing of a million dollars, at a time when the hostility of many states made the whole Federal City project extremely precarious. Convinced of L'Enfant's genius, Washington and Jefferson exhausted every means of securing due subordination through official instructions and friendly private explanations, but L'Enfant was impervious to all. On Feb. 27 he was instructed that his services were at an end.

Among those interested in the Federal City who preserved their faith in L'Enfant were Hamilton and Robert Morris. Hamilton was the moving spirit in the Society for Establishing Useful Manufactures, which proposed to use the power of the falls of the Passaic, at Paterson, N. J. In July 1792, on Hamilton's recommendation, the Society employed L'Enfant at a salary of $1500 to lay out the "capital scene of manufactures." On Sept. 22 he laid before the directors "a plan of the town, which far exceeds anything of the kind yet seen in this country," and was pushing work on the first buildings and on the power canal. By 1793 it was evident that L'Enfant's plans and beginnings were over-sanguine, and he was at odds with the other executive officers of the corporation. In June he was even summarily suspended by some of the directors, but Hamilton intervened and L'Enfant continued at work with some measure of authority until September, when, having secured new employment, he accepted an honorable discharge. His expense accounts caused some demur, and in October he refused to give up certain plans. The differences between his employers' view of him and his own view of himself as an independent professional man were here as elsewhere, irreconcilable. (The whole affair is best covered by J. S. Davis, *Essays in the Earlier History of American Corporations,* 1917, I, 349–493.)

Morris and his associates, who were the principal speculators in lots in Washington, recognized in L'Enfant a man who could minister also to their tastes for elegance of life. John Nicholson, Morris's partner, employed him on his house on Ridge Avenue, reputed to have been built in 1791 at a cost of $50,000. Old views make it seem probable that L'Enfant's agency was confined to the interior. He also designed rooms for the Philadelphia Assembly. The project for a separate building proving abortive, a room was decorated at Oeller's Hotel—"most elegant, . . . with a handsome music gallery at one end . . . papered after the French taste, with the Pantheon figures in compartments . . ." (Wansey's *Excursion to the United States,* 1794, cited by T. W. Balch in *The Philadelphia Assemblies,* 1916, p. 100). His chief undertaking in Philadelphia, however, was Morris's famous house on Chestnut Street between Seventh and Eighth streets. It followed the style of L'Enfant's youth in Paris, untouched by the mounting classical tide of intervening years. Like the Hotel Moras (Biron), it had bowed pavilions at either end. A colonnade was to run between; the exterior, by L'Enfant's insistence, was to be faced with marble. In the fall of 1793 L'Enfant was actively at work, but his plans were so ambitious that the cost was multiplied by ten, and two years later Morris was begging that at least the west wing could be covered before winter (E. P. Oberholtzer, *Robert Morris,* 1903, pp. 298, 331). The financial embarrassments which crowded on Morris brought the work, little further advanced, to a standstill in 1797, and his complete bankruptcy in 1798 left promissory notes for large sums in L'Enfant's hands. The unfinished house, as depicted in Birch's well-known engraving, was set down as "Morris's Folly," and a larger share in his ruin was attributed to it than it deserved. Across the account of his property Morris wrote: "A much more magnificent house than I ever intended to have built." It was sold by the sheriff in 1797 and its ruins were demolished in 1801. There survive today only two bas-reliefs carved by the sculptor Jardella, one incorporated at the time in one of the Drayton tombs in South Carolina; the other, formerly at Harmonville, recently built into the house at "Olney," Harford County, Md.

The federal government, not averse to indicating that it still respected L'Enfant's abilities, on Apr. 3, 1794, appointed him temporary engineer at Fort Mifflin on Mud Island in the Delaware, charging him with the duty of strengthening the defenses. The fort had been first built by the British officer Montresor, and, until attacked from the rear, had made an excellent resistance against the British in their approach to Philadelphia. A plan designed by L'Enfant (now lost) was submitted to Congress by the Secretary of War, Dec. 19, 1794 (*American State Papers, Military Affairs,* vol. I, 1832, pp. 82–86), but little actual construction was done by L'Enfant, and we may assume that once more his proposals were too extensive for the means available at the time. After 1800 he appears chiefly as a claimant against the federal government, haunting the halls of Congress. His compensation for the work at Washington had not been fixed in advance. His claims for services ultimately rose to the fantastic amount of $95,500, as against the sum of $2,500 to $3,000 which Washington and the Commissioners had thought he would consider liberal. On two occasions Congress did vote certain grants to him which went to his creditors, leaving him still unsatisfied. That the administration remained well disposed was proved on two occasions: In 1812 he was tendered appointment as professor of civil and military engineering in the new Military Academy at West Point, but the entreaties of Monroe, then secretary of state, could not prevail on him to accept. The War of 1812 again brought him employment, in work on Fort Washington on the Potomac (*Ibid.*, pp. 587–88), but the old story of disappointed hopes and claims was here once more repeated.

Of his last years we have a picture in a letter of Thomas Digges, whose hospitable roof near Fort Washington furnished him a friendly asylum. "The old Major is still intimate with me—quiet, harmless and unoffending as usual—I fear from symptoms of broken shoes, rent pantaloons, out at elbows, &c &c that he is not well off—manifestly disturbed at his getting *the go by* . . . never facing toward the Fort, tho' frequently dipping into the eastern ravines and hills of the plantation—picking up fossils and periwinkles—early to bed and rising—working hard with his instruments on paper eight or ten hours every day as if to give full and complete surveys of his works &c . . ." (Library of Congress, L'Enfant-Digges-Morgan Papers, Oct. 26, 1816). He remained with the Digges family, removing finally to "Green Hill," the estate of William Dudley Digges in Prince George's County, where he laid out the grounds and gardens, and where he died June 14, 1825. His personal effects, a few surveying instruments, books, and maps, were valued at $45.

His aspect in somewhat earlier days, as reported from the recollections of W. W. Corcoran, was that of "a tall, erect man, fully six feet in height, finely proportioned, nose prominent, of military bearing, courtly air and polite manners, his figure usually enveloped in a long overcoat and surmounted by a bell-crowned hat—a man who would attract attention in any assembly" (*Records of the Columbia Historical Society,* II, 216).

L'Enfant was a hundred years ahead of his time. Through the decades of the nineteenth century the city of Washington was slowly growing up to his plan, and its wide dispersion over a large area prompted many a gibe at its chimerical designer. In the age of romanticism and formlessness, numerous and serious departures were made from it. The Mall was planted as an informal park, instead of a great *allée.* The Washington Monument was located neither quite on one of the chief axes, nor on the other. But a glorious resurrection awaited the design; and an apotheosis, its maker. The Park Commission of 1901 recognized all its merits, and recommended its restoration and extension. In letter and spirit it governs the development of the capital of today. L'Enfant's remains, disinterred from their unmarked grave, lay in state in the Capitol and were honored by the President and a great concourse (Apr. 28, 1909). They found a final resting place at Arlington, among the soldier dead, overlooking the city he had designed, and with its plan, his greatest title to fame, graved on the slab above.

[The chief manuscript sources are the L'Enfant-Digges-Morgan Papers, Washington Papers, Jefferson Papers, Hamilton Papers, and District of Columbia Papers from the Dept. of State, all in the MSS. Div., Lib. of Cong. The Taggart Papers in the same repository contain many clippings and transcripts regarding L'Enfant. The fullest publication of documents (some fully emended) pertaining to his connection with the Federal City is Elizabeth S. Kite, "L'Enfant and Washington," *Hist. Docs.: Institut Français de Washington,* cahier III (1929). This does not entirely supersede the earlier and more exact publication of documents in the *Records of the Columbia Hist. Soc.*, vols. II (1899), XI (1908), XIII (1910), and XVII (1914). The fullest and most judicious notice of his life is that of J. J. Jusserand in his *With Americans of Past and Present Days* (1916), reprinted as an introduction to "L'Enfant and Washington," cited above. Further details of his military career are given by Thomas Balch in *The French in America during the War of Independence,* vol. II (1895) and by A. B. Gardiner in *The Order of the Cincinnati in France* (1905). An obituary appeared in the *Daily National Intelligencer* (Washington), June 25, 1825.]

F. K.

LENKER, JOHN NICHOLAS (Nov. 28, 1858–May 16, 1929), Lutheran clergyman, historian, and translator, was born at Sunbury, Pa., the son of John Bobb and Mary Ann (Gearhart) Lenker. He attended Wittenberg College in Springfield, Ohio, where he received the degrees of A.B. and A.M. in 1879 and 1880, and in 1881 he received the candidate of theology degree from Hamma Divinity School in Springfield. The next year he spent in graduate study at the University of Leipzig, Germany. He was ordained in 1880 but did not enter the active ministry until two years later when he was called to Grand Island, Nebr. After four years there he was called to work for the Board of Church Extension of the General Synod of the Evangelical Lutheran Church in the United States and in eight years raised $400,000 for this cause. He then turned his attention to the virgin field of Pan-Lutheranism. During his student days in Germany he had traveled at his own expense in Denmark, Norway, Sweden, Finland, Russia, the Baltic Provinces, and in Austria and Germany. Everywhere he tried to arouse the churches to a "Lutheran consciousness," and everywhere he sought to persuade the churches in the older lands to take a conciliatory attitude toward the daughter churches in the "diaspora." To bridge the gap between the old and the new lands, Lenker joined Dr. Luthardt of Leipzig University and Pastor Medem of Magdeburg in publishing three pamphlets *Kirchliches Addressbuch fuer Auswanderer nach Nordamerika* (1882), *Blank Letters of Recommendation* (1882?), and *Dringende Bitte fuer Auswanderer* (1882). But the seeds of Pan-Lutheranism were most effectively sowed and disseminated in the epochal and prophetic Lutherans in All Lands Series.

In 1893 Lenker published a book, built largely of the materials that he had collected in his travels and from first-hand correspondence with leaders in various lands, which he called *Lutherans in All Lands.* The first edition of more than eight hundred pages was supplemented by other editions, the most notable being the supplemented edition of 1919. In 1901 the book appeared in German under the title *Die Lutherische Kirche der Welt.* A Lutherans in All Lands Company was formed at Grand Island, Nebr., and later at Minneapolis, Minn.; both of these were superseded by the Luther Press at Minneapolis. From these presses came the *Lutherans in All Lands Quarterly* and the *Northern Review,* both under the editorship of Lenker.

From 1900 to 1904 Lenker was at the Danish-American Lutheran institution, Trinity Seminary, Blair, Nebr., where he taught church history, Old Testament exegesis, Hebrew, and German. Again straining at the leash of routine, he set about to make another dream come true. Some years earlier he had resolved that he would issue a standard edition of Luther's works for the English-speaking people. The first volume, *Luther's Commentary on the First Twenty-two Psalms,* translated by Henry Cole, was issued in 1903. *Luther on the Creation* was published in 1904, supplemented in 1910 by a second volume: *Luther on Sin and the Flood. The Epistles of St. Peter and St. Jude* also appeared in 1904. Of "Luther's Church Postil Gospels," one volume appeared in 1904, two in 1905, one in 1906, and one in 1907. *Luther on Christian Education* was published in 1907. "Luther's Epistle Sermons" were published in three volumes (1908–09). These thirteen volumes were all issued from Lenker's two Minneapolis presses. At his death he had nine other volumes of Luther's works ready for the press. Lenker was president of the General Lutheran Missionary Conference; vice-president of the American Lutheran Mission for Russia; secretary of the American Lutheran Statistical Association; and founder of the students' missionary societies of Norway, Sweden, and Finland. On Sept. 18, 1919, he was married to Nora Cecelia Walsted of Christiania (Oslo), Norway. After 1904 he made his home in Minneapolis.

[See *Who's Who in America,* 1928–29; J. C. Jenssen (Roseland), *Am. Luth. Biogs.* (1890); *Luth. Church Herald,* June 11, 1929; the *Lutheran,* June 13, 1929; *Minneapolis Morning Tribune,* May 17, 1929. Information as to certain facts has been supplied by Lenker's friends and by Mrs. John Nicholas Lenker.]

J. M. R.

LENNON, JOHN BROWN (Oct. 12, 1850–Jan. 17, 1923), for twenty-seven years treasurer of the American Federation of Labor, was born in Lafayette County, Wis. When he was two years old his parents, John Alexander and Elizabeth Fletcher (Brown) Lennon, moved to Hannibal, Mo., where the boy attended the public schools. After his father entered the Union army in 1861, John, at the age of eleven, was obliged to assist his mother with the responsibility of their small farm. His father was a tailor by trade and after the war reopened his shop in Hannibal, where John served four years' apprenticeship. In 1869 he went West, settling in Denver, Colo., where he set himself up as merchant tailor. The next year he was joined by his parents and sisters, his father took charge of the shop, and young Lennon became a journeyman for various merchant tailors of Denver. On Apr. 5, 1871, he married Juna J. Allen of Hannibal.

Lennon was instrumental in organizing a Tailor's Union in Denver, of which he became secretary. Before the end of the convention year 1883, the Denver union became affiliated with the new national organization, the Journeyman Tailors' Union of America. The following year, while acting as president of his local union, Lennon was appointed as a delegate to the convention of the national union at Chicago. Here he was chosen national president, and in 1885 became one of the vice-presidents. Elected general secretary in 1887, he moved to New York, the seat of the national headquarters. At this time he also became first editor of *The Tailor,* the official journal of the organization. In 1896 the general office was removed to Bloomington, Ill., which was Lennon's home thenceforth until his death. He continued as general secretary until July 1910.

A delegate from the Tailors' Union to the convention of the American Federation of Labor for the first time in 1889, he was elected treasurer of the latter organization in 1890 and served continuously until 1917. As a member of the executive council he was closely associated with

Samuel Gompers [*q.v.*] and others prominent in the Labor Movement. In his later years he became well known as a public speaker, delivering numerous addresses upon the church and labor, and the anti-saloon movement before considerable gatherings in various parts of the country. He was a leader in organizing the forces arrayed against the liquor traffic and a member of the committee on social service of the Federal Council of Churches of Christ in America. In 1913 he was appointed by President Wilson as one of the three labor members representing the conservative traditions of the American Federation of Labor on the Commission on Industrial Relations, whose report was published in 1915. In 1917 he became a member of the board of mediators of the United States Department of Labor.

[*Who's Who in America,* 1922–23; *The Tailor,* Jan. 23, Feb. 5, 1923; P. U. Kellogg, in *Rev. of Revs.* (N. Y.), Sept. 1913; *Am. Federationist,* Mar. 1923; *N. Y. Times,* Jan. 19, 1923; *Daily Bulletin* (Bloomington, Ill.), Jan. 18, 1923.] J. R. C.

LENNOX, CHARLOTTE RAMSAY (1720–Jan. 4, 1804), novelist, dramatist, and translator, was born in New York, possibly in Albany where she spent most of her girlhood. Her father, James Ramsay, an army officer, is said (with no evidence) to have been lieutenant-governor of the province. Her childhood in New York was not happy, judging from a satire in her poems. At about the age of fifteen she was sent to England to be educated by a wealthy aunt, but on her arrival she found the lady incurably insane. Shortly after this her father died, leaving his widow and Charlotte unprovided for. At the age of twenty-seven she published her first book, *Poems on Several Occasions,* which was dedicated to Lady Isabella Finch, who probably had befriended the young woman. A year later (1748) she played in comedies at Richmond, where Garrick went to find some promising actors. Horace Walpole said that she was a "deplorable actress" (*Letters, post,* II, 126). On Oct. 6, 1747, she was married to Alexander Lennox who was in the printing shop of Strachan in Cornhill, and who was later employed in the Customs Office as tide-waiter. She had a daughter who died in 1802 and a son who was forced to leave the country, after committing an offense, and came to America. Her husband died about 1797, but for several years he had had nothing to do with his family.

Perhaps the most pleasant and valuable friendship in her life was with Samuel Johnson. He encouraged and advised her in her writing, introduced her to his friends and to other literary men who could help her, wrote favorable reviews of her books, quoted her in the *Dictionary,* and wrote dedications and other items for her. When her novel *Harriot Stuart* appeared he gave an all-night party to some twenty guests in celebration. His admiration seems to have aroused the jealousy of the other bluestockings in his circle. "Mrs. Thrale says that though her books are generally approved, nobody likes her" (*Diary and Letters of Madame D'Arblay,* I, 1842, p. 68). Johnson introduced her to Samuel Richardson and she likewise won his favor; she was a frequent visitor at his house and was admitted to his readings. In several places in her books she paid homage to these friends. Fielding also was an admirer and wrote enthusiastically of her work.

Mrs. Lennox's literary reputation depends chiefly upon her novels, a mixture of sentimental romance and the novel of manners combining in a strong feminine appeal. Her first, *The Life of Harriot Stuart* (1750), was in part autobiographical—an unorganized account of the heroine's misfortunes, adventures, and love affairs. Her most famous was *The Female Quixote, or the Adventures of Arabella* (1752), which burlesqued the old French romances of Scudéry in the story of a girl who formed her notions of life and love from such reading. A more exciting plot is in *The History of Henrietta* (1758), which she later dramatized. Her most sentimental and least effective work, *Sophia* (1762), was regretted even by her friendly critics. Her late novel, *Euphemia* (1790), written in old age, with feeble morality and delicate sensibility, was kindly reviewed and generally ignored. She was unsuccessful in her association with the theatre, both as an actress and as a dramatist. A poetic pastoral, *Philander* (1758), was not produced; nor was *Angelica, or Quixote in Petticoats* (1758), which was based on the theme of her novel, *The Female Quixote.* Garrick said that it too closely resembled Steele's *Tender Husband.* A hostile group hissed her best play, *The Sister* (1769), and it was withdrawn from Covent Garden after one performance. This comedy used the main theme of her novel *Henrietta,* and Burgoyne's *Heiress* is indebted to it for its best parts. At Garrick's suggestion she modernized *Eastward Hoe* under the title *Old City Manners* (1775), produced at the Theatre-Royal—introducing elegance at the expense of the vitality of the Elizabethan classic. Another division of her literary work is the translations from the French. These include *The Memoirs of M. de Bethune, Duke of Sully* (1756); *The Memoirs of the Countess of Berci* (1756), a romance nearly as absurd as those she burlesqued in *The Female Quixote; Memoirs for the History of Madame de Maintenon, and of the Last Age* (1757), translated from the French of Angliviel de la Baumelle; *The Greek Theatre of Father Brumoy* (1759), from the French of Pierre Brumoy, to which Dr. Johnson and others contributed; and *Meditations and Penitential Prayers Written by the Duchess de la Vallière* (1774). She wrote *Shakespear Illustrated* (1753) to show the sources of the plays, and generally condemned Shakespeare for a lack of originality, morality, and artistry, quoting much from Johnson, and following Rymer's lead. In 1760–61 she published *The Lady's Museum,* a periodical described by Nichols as "consisting of a Course of Female Education and variety of other Particulars for the Information and Amusement of the Ladies" (*Literary Anecdotes,* VIII, 1814, p. 497). Her books brought her very little income and her old age was "clouded by penury and sickness" (Nichols, *post,* III, p. 201). At the close of her life she received a pension from the Royal Literary Fund and was befriended by the Rt. Hon. George Rose and the Rev. William Beloe. She died on Jan. 4, 1804, at Dean's Yard, Westminster, and "was buried with the common soldiery in the further burying-ground of Broad Chapel" (*Ibid.*). Reynolds painted her portrait in 1761, of which an engraving by Bartolozzi was printed in Hardinge's *Shakespeare,* and one by Cooke accompanied the sketch of Mrs. Lennox in the *Lady's Monthly Museum* for June 1813.

[There is a biography of Charlotte Lennox in the *Dict. of Nat. Biog.* See also: John Nichols, *Lit. Anecdotes of the Eighteenth Century,* vol. III (1812), and *Illustrations of the Lit. Hist. of the Eighteenth Century,* vol. III (1818); G. B. Hill, *Boswell's Life of Johnson* (1887), vols. I–IV; Sir John Hawkins, *Life of Samuel Johnson* (1787); Peter Cunningham, *The Letters of Horace Walpole,* vol. II (1857); Austin Dobson, *Samuel Richardson* (1902), and *The Journal of a Voyage to Lisbon by Henry Fielding* (1892); *Gentleman's Mag.,* Dec. 1750, Mar. 1758, June 1762, Jan. 1804. Information as to certain facts was supplied by Miss Miriam R. Small, of Wells College, who is preparing a monograph of Mrs. Lennox for publication. On some points, however, the contributor's opinion differs from that of Miss Small.] R. W. B.

LENOX, JAMES (Aug. 19, 1800–Feb. 17, 1880), book-collector and philanthropist, was born at 59 Broadway, New York City, the third son of a family of nine children. His father, Robert, born in Kirkcudbright, Scotland, in 1759, had married Rachel Carmer in New York in 1783. He was a merchant, a heavy investor in New York City real estate, and when he died in 1839 was ranked as one of the five richest men of the city. From 1819 to 1826 he was vice-president of the Chamber of Commerce and served as president from the latter date until his death. He was a trustee of the College of New Jersey and according to Maclean (*post,* II, p. 308) "for many years all investments of College money were made under his direction." James Lenox received the degree of A.B. from Columbia College in 1818 and was admitted to the New York bar on Jan. 18, 1822. He took the usual European tours common to youths of his station, then settled down as partner in his father's business. Soon after his father's death he retired to give the rest of his life to the care of his investments, to the purchase of books and objects of art, and to an active but unobtrusive participation in the philanthropic life of the city.

Considering his Scotch-Presbyterian ancestry, it is not surprising that he collected Bibles. When he died he had brought together one of the great collections of the Bible in English. From Bibles his interest extended to works of the early printers, and for books printed in the fifteenth century his library ranked among the most important in the country at that time. It was for him that the first copy of the Gutenberg Bible was sent to the United States. Milton, Bunyan, the Roman Index Expurgatorius, and Shakespeare also appealed to him. His books soon came to fill the great house at 53 Fifth Avenue and to offer a serious problem, which he solved by giving books and objects of art to the Lenox Library, incorporated in 1870. To this corporation he gave also the entire block on Fifth Avenue between Seventieth and Seventy-first streets, and for it he erected a building designed by Richard Morris Hunt. He lived to see the collection opened to the public, with George Henry Moore its superintendent and Samuel Austin Allibone librarian. The library site was part of a thirty-acre tract originally owned by his father. With the opening of streets and the development of Central Park Lenox began to sell portions of the farm about 1864. The block between Seventieth and Seventy-first streets, and Madison and Park Avenues, he gave to the Presbyterian Hospital. He gave land also for the Presbyterian Home for Aged Women, land for churches and chapels, and continued his active part in the work of the "Old First" Presbyterian Church on Fifth Avenue opposite his home. In the last twelve years of his life it is estimated that he gave over three million dollars to charitable uses. The College of New Jersey received benefactions from him throughout his life.

Lenox has been characterized as "a man of few words and few intimate friends, but of varied information, much studious reading, extensive correspondence and many books. . . . He possessed an extraordinary aptitude for sticking to and finishing up any work he had in hand" (Stevens, *post,* pp. 2, 43). With John Carter Brown of Providence and George Brinley of Hartford he ranks as a pioneer in the field of American history. He published *Washington's Farewell Address to the People of the United States* (1850); *Nicolaus Syllacius De Insulis Meridiani atque Indici Maris Nuper Inventis* (1859), with a translation into English by the Rev. John Mulligan; *Shakespeare's Plays in Folio* (1861); *The Early Editions of King James' Bible in Folio* (1861); *Letter of Columbus to Luis de Santangel* (1864); and "Bibliographical Account of the Voyages of Columbus" (*Historical Magazine,* February 1861). Lenox died at 53 Fifth Avenue and was buried in the New York City Marble Cemetery on Second Street.

[The best account of Lenox as a book-collector is Henry Stevens, *Recollections of Mr. James Lenox of N. Y. and the Formation of his Lib.* (1886). See also D. B. Delavan, *Early Days of the Presbyterian Hospital in the City of N. Y.* (1926); John Maclean, *Hist. of the Coll. of N. J.* (2 vols., 1877); and the *N. Y. Times,* Feb. 19, 1880. For a sketch of his father see W. M. MacBean, *Biog. Reg. of Saint Andrew's Soc.* (1922), vol. I. The New York Public Library has also several collections of Lenox's letters and interleaved copies of such printed catalogues as Rich, Ternaux-Compans, and Lea Wilson, checked by him to show the progress of additions to his collections.] H. M. L.

LENTHALL, JOHN (Sept. 16, 1807–Apr. 11, 1882), naval architect, who was chiefly responsible for the wooden warships of the Union navy in the Civil War, was a native of the District of Columbia. His father, also John Lenthall, was an Englishman who while acting as Latrobe's superintendent in the building of the Capitol was killed on Sept. 19, 1808, by the fall of a vaulting in the north wing. His mother, Jane Lenthall, survived till 1852. The son is said to have learned shipbuilding from his father and from Samuel Humphreys. During several years of study in Europe he prepared drafts of 300 different ships in European navies. He entered the naval service on May 1, 1835, was appointed chief naval constructor in 1849, and chief of the bureau of construction in 1853, the first professional naval architect to occupy that post if the few months' occupancy by Samuel Hartt is excepted. Before entering this position he had served at the Portsmouth and Philadelphia navy yards. While at these places and in Washington from 1849 on, he was chiefly responsible for the design of the class of wooden, steam frigates represented by the *Merrimac* and including such ships as the *Wabash, Niagara, Roanoke, Colorado,* and *Minnesota.* They were recognized as the best ships of their kind before iron vessels appeared.

During the Civil War Lenthall remained as chief of the bureau of construction. Gideon Welles, who called him "honest John Lenthall," said of him: "He has not much pliability or affability, but, though attacked and denounced as corrupt and dishonest, I have never detected any obliquity or wrong in him. His sternness and uprightness disappointed the jobbers and the corrupt, and his unaffected manner has offended others" (Welles, *post,* I, p. 74). As a master of wooden shipbuilding, Lenthall was naturally a conservative regarding ironclads and the new monitors. Accordingly he seems to have let others, especially Fox and Stimers, go ahead with the building of light-draft monitors and iron gunboats without taking much interest in them, with the result that many of the ships built turned out to be deficient in some respects. Lenthall continued as head of his bureau till January 1871, although he had reached retiring age earlier. He continued to make his home in Washington and as late as 1881 was a member of an advisory board on new construction. Thus he had a hand in the building of the new navy that began at that time. He died suddenly in the Baltimore & Ohio railroad station in Washington as he was boarding a train for New York. A General Order from the secretary of the navy, W. H. Hunt, announced his death and commended his life and services. He was buried in Rock Creek Parish Cemetery, Washington, where his father, mother, and sister also lie.

[Besides the records of the Navy Department, the chief data about Lenthall can be secured from an obituary notice in the *Army and Navy Reg.,* Apr. 15, 1882. The General Order of Secretary Hunt is in the issue of Apr. 22. See also the *Diary of Gideon Welles* (3 vols., 1911), Latrobe's sketch of Lenthall's father in the *Nat. Intelligencer* (Washington), Sept. 23, 1808, and the *Washington Post,* Apr. 12, 1882. An interesting sidelight on Lenthall is found in R. P. Meade, *Life of Hiram Paulding* (1910), p. 237.] W. B. N.

LEONARD, CHARLES LESTER (Dec. 29, 1861–Sept. 22, 1913), physician, pioneer in the medical use of X-rays, came of old New England ancestry, being directly descended from John Leonard who settled in Springfield, Mass., in 1632. His parents were M. Hayden Leonard and Harriet E. (Moore) Leonard of Easthampton, Mass., where he was born. He graduated from the University of Pennsylvania in 1885 (A.B.), from Harvard in 1886 (A.B.), and from the Medical School of the University of Pennsylvania in 1889 (M.D.). He studied abroad from 1889 to 1892 and received the degree of master of arts from his Alma Mater in the latter year. After beginning his medical practice he inclined toward surgery and was connected with the surgical staff of the University Hospital, Philadelphia, mainly as anesthetist. He married Ruth Hodgson, by whom he had one daughter.

Leonard will always be remembered as one of the pioneer Roentgenologists of the United States. Possessed of a scientific and technical mind, he became intensely interested in the X-rays in 1896, very soon after their discovery and announcement by Roentgen ("Cases Illustrative of the Practical Application of the Roentgen Rays in Surgery," in collaboration with J. W. White and A. W. Goodspeed, *American Journal of the Medical Sciences,* August 1896). At the time, the X-rays were regarded as of service only in the detection of fractures and opaque foreign bodies such as bullets. Leonard was the first, in America, at least, to demonstrate the presence of stones in the kidney and other portions of the urinary tract by means of this agent (1898). This demonstration at once gave him world-wide publicity in the medical profession, especially among those beginning to specialize in this new branch of medicine. His ability to detect stones and his powers of observation and interpretation at that time were almost uncanny. He saw what others could not see, even when it was pointed out to them, and he was usually correct in his deductions. Throughout the early years of his experience he worked with small and what now seems most inefficient apparatus, but he was able to do more with little than almost any other man in his specialty. He was, indeed, a master of his art.

Leonard was a prolific writer, an untiring student, and a generous teacher of pleasing personality who was always ready to share his knowledge with his professional colleagues. In the thirteen years of his practice of Roentgenology he published forty-four articles on the diagnostic uses of X-rays and their application in the treatment of cancer and other conditions. He was an active member of the American Roentgen Ray Society and its president in 1904 and 1905, and was the founder of the Philadelphia Roentgen Ray Society. He was keenly interested in many other medical societies and a frequent contributor to their scientific programs. In 1902, he resigned from the University of Pennsylvania and engaged thereafter in the private practice of his specialty. As a result of excessive exposure to X-rays from the unprotected tubes of the early years and the frequent use of the fluoroscope to test the tubes and to demonstrate his hands to those interested, he soon developed the chronic skin affections which attacked the hands of so many of the early workers who knew nothing of the dangers of the rays. He refused surgical treatment until it was too late, largely because, like so many others then, he regarded the condition as harmless and likely to heal after protective measures were devised. In the latter years of his life he was a constant but uncomplaining sufferer, never allowing his affliction to interfere with his duties. Those who knew him well marveled at his fortitude. Some of the chronic ulcers on his hands eventually induced cancer, which spread to other parts of his body, and from which he died—a martyr. His last paper, "Radiography of the Stomach and Intestines," was a review of all the literature on the X-ray examination of the stomach and intestinal tract, up to 1913, prepared for the International Congress of Medicine, London, August 1913. Since he was unable to attend, it was read for him by a colleague, and was published in the *American Journal of Roentgenology,* November 1913, after his death.

[*Am. Jour. Roentgenology,* Nov. 1913, with bibliography; *Am. Jour. Roentgenology and Radium Therapy,* Aug. 1928; *Archives of the Roentgen Ray* (London), Sept. 1913; *Lancet* (London), Oct. 1913; H. A. Kelly and W. L. Burrage, *Am. Medic. Biogs.* (1920); *N. Y. Times,* Sept. 24, 1913; records of the Univ. of Pa.; personal recollections.] H. K. P.

LEONARD, DANIEL (May 18, 1740–June 27, 1829), lawyer, Loyalist, chief justice of Bermuda, was born in Norton, Mass., the son of Ephraim and Judith (Perkins) Leonard. Ephraim Leonard, an iron-monger, was fourth in descent from James, who with a brother came to America from Pontypool, Wales, and erected the first successful iron foundry at Saugus, Mass. In 1652 the Leonard brothers removed to Taunton, Mass., and set up their "bloomery" where bog ore was plentiful. For two hundred years Leonards were identified with the iron industry. During King Philip's War (1676) the family was immune from attack because they had supplied iron arrow-heads to appreciative Indians. The Leonards of New England belonged to the provincial aristocracy, and for more than a century the family dominated Southern Massachusetts socially and politically. John Adams was accustomed to refer to this region as the "Land of the Leonards." Brought up in what, for rural New England, was baronial style—in a spacious mansion with deer-park and family coach—Daniel had social prestige and was ranked second upon entering Harvard College with the class of 1760. At Commencement he delivered, in Latin, the salutatory address. Entering law practice at Taunton, he hung his shingle under that of Samuel White, speaker of the Massachusetts Assembly, whose daughter, Anna, he married in 1767. He succeeded his father-in-law as King's attorney for Bristol County in 1769 and was elected the following year to the General Court where at first he spoke with zeal in opposition to King George. As lieutenant-colonel of the 3rd Bristol County Regiment he was one of the Young Bloods of Massachusetts. Trumbull, in his satirical poem, "M'Fingal," refers to Leonard as one who would

> "Scrawl every moment he could spare
> From cards and barbers and the fair."

Governor Hutchinson, attracted by Leonard's ability and popularity, came to Taunton and, after a lengthy discussion under a pear tree (thereafter famous as the "Tory pear tree") persuaded Leonard to espouse the cause of the Crown and secured his appointment in 1774 as mandamus councilor. This so enraged his rebellious Whig neighbors that Leonard was subjected to indignities, his home at Taunton Green was fired upon, and he was forced to flee to Boston. Within British lines he was placed on the payroll as solicitor to customs commissioners. He then wrote a series of seventeen articles in defense of the Crown policies, published in the *Massachusetts Gazette* (1774–75) over the signature "Massachusettensis." To these, John Adams replied over the signature "Novanglus." Leonard's papers were published in England as the ablest exposition of Royal policy written in America.

When the Declaration of Independence was signed, Leonard was proscribed, his property confiscated, and he was forbidden to return on penalty of death. When British troops were dislodged from Boston he sailed away to Halifax and on to England, where he was admitted to the bar and, upon separation from the colonies, secured the post of chief justice of Bermuda, which he held from 1782 to 1806. He revisited Massachusetts in 1799 and again in 1808. About 1815 he returned to London to practise law and eventually became dean of English barristers, presiding at the quarterly dinners in the Inner Temple. Leonard's first wife died in 1768 on the birth of a daughter. In 1770 he was married to Sarah Hammock of Boston by whom he had two daughters and a son, Charles, who remained in America to inherit his grandfather's estate. His second wife died at sea on the way from England to Bermuda in 1806. In his ninetieth year, while living with his daughter Harriet, in London, Leonard died as the result of a pistol wound. The family insisted he was not of a temperament to commit suicide. He was buried in St. Pancras cemetery.

[See E. A. Jones, *The Loyalists of Mass.* (1930) and *Am. Members of the Inns of Court* (1924); Ralph Davol, *Two Men of Taunton* (1912); W. R. Deane, *A Geneal. Memoir of the Leonard Family* (1851); M. C. Tyler, *The Lit. Hist. of the Am. Revolution* (1897), vol. I; C. F. Adams, *The Works of John Adams* (10 vols., 1850–56); H. E. Egerton and D. P. Coke, *The Royal Commission on the Losses and Services of the Am. Loyalists, 1783–85* (1915); *Proc. Mass. Hist. Soc.*, 1 ser. XIII (1875), 2 ser. VI (1891); *Times* (London), June 30, 1829. The authorship of the "Massachusettensis" papers was questioned by John Adams, who attributed them to Jonathan Sewall. Leonard's authorship is confirmed in a letter by Gov. Hutchinson to Leonard from London, Apr. 8, 1776; in an affidavit by Ward Chipman, who testified in 1822 that he copied the letters for Leonard while a clerk in Leonard's Boston office; in a statement by Francis Baylies, a nephew of Leonard, in discussion with L. M. Sargent (see the *Boston Transcript*, Apr. 15, 18, 1851); and in an acknowledgment by Leonard himself in a reprint of the letters, London, 1821.]

R. D.

LEONARD, GEORGE (Nov. 23, 1742–Apr. 1, 1826), Loyalist, was born at Plymouth, Mass., the son of the Rev. Nathaniel and Priscilla (Rogers) Leonard, and the nephew of Major, later Colonel, George Leonard, a judge and member of the Council of the province. He was descended from James Leonard who emigrated from Pontypool, Wales, in the seventeenth century. His marriage to Sarah Thacher, a native of Boston, occurred on Oct. 14, 1765. During the blockade of Boston he served as a lieutenant of the Associated Loyalists, besides fitting out ten vessels to aid the British. In March 1776 he accompanied the Loyalists to Halifax and was not overlooked in the Banishment Act. In the spring of 1778 he was with the troops in Rhode Island. He left Newport to receive Burgoyne's army but was forced into Plymouth Harbor by bad weather. Soon he sailed for Boston with a fleet of provisions. As navy agent and contractor for the Associated Refugees in Rhode Island he furnished the vessels for their expeditions on Long Island Sound in 1779, being given £2,000 in advance. At Martha's Vineyard in September of the same year he had the tax collector seized by one of his naval officers and permitted the inhabitants to send a representative to Boston who obtained a suspension by the Assembly of the payment of taxes. He also destroyed eleven American vessels and exacted from the Islanders provisions and fuel for the garrison at Newport. With Col. Edward Winslow he warned the people of Nantucket that the renewal of their hostile activities would be punished.

At the end of 1780 Leonard was appointed one of eight directors of the recently revived Associated Loyalists, who thereafter carried on privateering operations from Manhattan, Long Island, and Staten Island. Resigning in September 1782, he was granted an allowance of £200 a year. In the following April he wrote from Brooklyn requesting a six months' advance of his annuity in order to remove to Nova Scotia with his family of fifteen persons, including servants. He was next named one of five agents to distribute lands at the mouth of the River St. John to the inpouring refugees. Remonstrances against these agents, including Leonard, who had drawn a large lot on the harbor, led them to submit voluntarily to a trial at Halifax before the governor and Council, who decided on Aug. 3, 1784, that they had been fair and impartial in their dealings. When Parr Town was incorporated in May 1785 as the city of St. John, Leonard was appointed by the governor of New Brunswick alderman and chamberlain.

In 1786 he was made superintendent of trade and fisheries for the coasts of the Maritime Provinces and neighboring islands. In this office he was energetic in suppressing illicit trade in Passamaquoddy Bay and asserting British rights to its islands. In 1790 he was appointed to the Council, in which he served thirty-six years. He labored for the education and conversion of the Indians to the Protestant faith and built the Indian Academy at Sussex Vale, where he lived. As senior councilor Leonard would have succeeded to the government on the death of Lieut.-Gov. George B. Smyth in April 1823, but he declined on account of his infirmities. He died on Apr. 1, 1826, surviving his wife scarcely two months. Both were buried at Sussex Vale, where their monument still stands.

[J. W. Lawrence, *The Judges of New Brunswick, and Their Times* (n.d.); W. O. Raymond, ed., *Winslow Papers, A.D. 1776–1826* (1901); Hist. MSS. Commission, *Report on Am. MSS. in the Royal Institution of Great Britain*, vols. II–IV (1906–09); Thos. Jones, *Hist. of N. Y. During the Revolutionary War* (1879), vol. II; J. H. Stark, *The Loyalists of Mass.* (1910); E. A. Jones, *The Loyalists of Mass.* (1930); W. R. Deane, *A Geneal. Memoir of the Leonard Family* (1851); *New-Eng. Hist. and Geneal. Reg.*, Oct. 1858; the *Quebec Gazette*, May 1, 1826.] W. H. S.

LEONARD, HARRY WARD (Feb. 8, 1861–Feb. 18, 1915), electrical engineer and inventor, was born at Cincinnati, Ohio, the son of Ezra George Leonard, a merchant, and Henrietta Dana (Ward). He was a descendant of Solomon Leonard, a native of Monmouthshire, England, who emigrated to Leyden, Holland, and thence, not long after 1630, to Massachusetts, where he lived successively at Plymouth, Duxbury, and Bridgewater. General Artemas Ward [*q.v.*] was an ancestor. Leonard attended grammar and high school at Cincinnati, and entered the Massachusetts Institute of Technology in 1879. He graduated in 1883 with the degree of electrical engineer, and the next year became associated with Thomas A. Edison as one of a staff of four employed by him to introduce the central-station system into the major cities of the country. When only twenty-six (1888), he became superintendent of the Western Electric Light Company at Chicago, and the next year was head of the firm of Leonard & Izard of that city, one of the first organizations in the United States to engage in central-station and electric-railway construction. In 1889 the firm was purchased by the Edison General Electric Company and Leonard became general manager for the United States and Canada of the light and power departments of the combined Edison interests. Resigning this position in 1894 he established a business of his own at Bronxville, N. Y., the Ward Leonard Electric Company, for the manufacture of electrical equipment, principally of his own invention. In 1889 he patented the first electric train-lighting system (patents 405895, 405896, 405897), the elements of which are in use today. He had this system in operation on two trains between Chicago and Milwaukee in 1888. The best-known of his inventions is the Ward Leonard system of motor control (patent 463802, Nov. 24, 1891, and many others), which provides a method of varying the speed of direct-current motors over a wide range without the use of a starting resistance, by applying a variable voltage to the motor armature. This system not only furnishes a very flexible and rapid control of heavy machinery, but also eliminates power loss in rheostats. It is estimated that fifteen percent. of the cost of rolling steel has been saved by replacing steam engines with electric motors equipped with the Ward Leonard system. An electric elevator-control device (patent 468100, Feb. 2, 1892) used by the Otis Elevator Company on the first electric elevators installed in the New York Athletic Club and the *Times* Building, New York City, the double-arm circuit breaker (patent 705102, July 22, 1902), a system of multiple voltage motor control (patent 478344, July 5, 1892), were important inventions of his and were incorporated by license rights in equipment manufactured by most of the leading electrical firms of the country. Other inventions of interest for which he was responsible are a system of regenerative braking for railroad trains and mine hoists, an incandescent-lamp socket, the "compound controller" for machine tool motors, and the four-speed-change gear that was used on several of the higher-priced automobiles. Leonard was interested also in the electric lighting and starting of automobiles, and designed one of the first of the simple and efficient systems of the modern type. He contributed many articles to the technical press, and papers and addresses of his appear in the *Transactions of the American Insti-*

tute of Electrical Engineers. He was a fellow, a vice-president (1893–95), and a manager (1890–93) of this Institute and received the John Scott Medal award of the Franklin Institute for his contributions to electrical development. He was president of the Inventor's Guild (1913–14), which was one of his hobbies, as was also the development of the village of Bronxville, N. Y., of which he was president. In 1895 he married Carolyn Good of New York; there were no children. He died suddenly while attending the annual dinner of the American Institute of Electrical Engineers in New York.

[*Ann. Report of the Commissioner of Patents*, 1889–1915; *Proc. Am. Inst. Electrical Engineers*, Mar. 1915 (vol. XXXIV); *Technology Rev.*, Apr. 1915; *Electrical Trades' Directory and Handbook* (London, 1899); Manning Leonard, *Memorial: Geneal., Hist. and Biog., of Solomon Leonard* (1896); *N. Y. Times*, Feb. 19, 28, 1915.] F. A. T.

LEONARD, HELEN LOUISE [See RUSSELL, LILLIAN, 1861–1922].

LEONARD, LEVI WASHBURN (June 1, 1790–Dec. 12, 1864), Unitarian clergyman, educator, the eldest of the three sons of Jacob and Mary (Swift) Leonard, was born in the South Parish of Bridgewater, Mass., where his family had been rooted for five generations. His father was a farmer and had been an ensign in the Revolution. He was a descendant of Solomon Leonard of Monmouthshire, England, who went to Holland, and thence, about 1633, came to America. Leonard graduated from Harvard College in 1815 and from the Divinity School in 1818, taught for two years in the Bridgewater Academy, and was ordained Sept. 6, 1820, as pastor of the First Congregational (Unitarian) Society of Dublin, N. H. There, in the shadow of Monadnock, he spent most of his active life, exerting over the whole town a strong, beneficent, and lasting influence. To a remarkable extent he molded the very character of the community. He organized its lyceum, established its library, superintended its schools, shaped the measures approved in its town meeting, and was the adored pastor of its principal church. He had a genius for the pastoral office and developed in his people a rare devotional spirit. Although, like so many of the Unitarian clergymen of his day, he was conservative in temper and chary of controversy, he could not hold the stanch Trinitarians of his parish, who withdrew amicably in 1827 and formed the Second Congregational Society. As an educator his influence was more than local. His plans for school buildings and his methods of teaching were widely copied; his textbooks were popular and long-lived. Besides two sermons, a tract, and a lecture, his publications, which were usually issued at Keene, N. H., include: *The Literary and Scientific Classbook* (1826); *Sequel to Easy Lessons* (1830); *Selections of Reading Lessons for Common Schools* (1830); *The North American Spelling Book* (1835); *Modes of Instruction in Common Schools* (1844); *Analysis of the Elementary Sounds of the English Language* (1848); and *The History of Dublin, N. H.* (1855). He was the chief compiler for the Cheshire Pastoral Association of *Christian Hymns* (1845). Among his interests were genealogy, mathematics, and entomology; in this last department he aided his classmate, Thaddeus William Harris [*q.v.*], who named *Hesperia Leonardus* for him. He was twice married: in 1830 to Elizabeth Morison Smith of Peterboro, N. H., who died in 1848; in 1851 to Elizabeth (Dow) Smith of Exeter, the widow of his first wife's brother. At her behest he moved to Exeter in 1853, but his congregation would not allow the pastoral connection to be dissolved. In 1855 William Frederick Bridge was installed as his colleague pastor, and Leonard continued to preach occasionally, as his failing health would permit. Meanwhile he edited for eight years the weekly *Exeter News-Letter.* He died in Exeter and was buried in Dublin.

[Manning Leonard, *Memorial: Geneal., Hist., and Biog. of Solomon Leonard* (1896); L. W. Leonard and S. A. Smith, *Geneal. of the Family of Wm. Smith of Peterborough, N. H.* (1852); L. W. Leonard and J. L. Seward, *Hist. of Dublin, N. H.* (1920); *New-Eng. Hist. and Geneal. Reg.*, July 1865; *Exeter News-Letter*, Jan. 2, 1865; *Gen. Cat. Harvard Divinity School*, 1910; S. A. Eliot, *Heralds of a Liberal Faith*, vol. III (1910).] G. H. G.

LEONARD, ROBERT JOSSELYN (Feb. 5, 1885–Feb. 9, 1929), educator, was born in San José, Cal., son of Joseph Howland and Ella Isabelle (Clark) Leonard. He was a descendant of James Leonard who came from Monmouthshire, England, in 1638, at the request of the Massachusetts Bay Colony, to survey the hills for iron; and settled in Taunton, Mass., where he set up an iron forge. Robert's father received the degree of M.D. at the University of Vermont (1861). Returning to his home in California, he lost everything in real-estate deals, retaining, however, his library, which included rarities like a complete file of the first San Francisco newspaper. After his death, Robert and his brother cared for their mother and sister. "Even so," he wrote later, "I have not known the 'pinch' of poverty, due to a well-educated, loving and helpful mother who never let us feel poor. We had a wealth of good books, left from more prosperous times, 'freedom of spirit' . . . and good companions." Following a year at the San José

High School, he entered the State Normal School in San José, from which he was graduated in 1904. Drawing and manual training engrossed him. Drawing he continued throughout his life; manual training gave him a lifelong interest in automobiles—his hobby; proficiency in manual arts gave him an opportunity to teach in Belmont School and later in Fresno. In after years he introduced industrial education into the Berkeley schools and into the Horace Mann School of Columbia University. From Columbia he received his academic degrees: B.S., 1912; A.M., 1914; Ph.D., 1923. On Aug. 13, 1912, he was married to Eugenie Ann Andruss of Seattle, Wash., by whom he had a daughter and a son.

In 1914 he was appointed to the chair of vocational education at the University of Indiana, the first such professorship ever established. That same year he analyzed the paper-box industry of New York City, making the first extensive occupational study with a view to determining the kind of education required for a specific industry. In 1915 he surveyed occupations in the state of Indiana and also in the cities of Hammond and Richmond. These studies resulted in his publishing several books: *An Investigation of the Paper Box Industry to Determine the Possibility of Vocational Training* (1915); *A Study of the People of Indiana and Their Occupations* (1915); *Some Facts Concerning the People, Industries and Schools of Hammond, Indiana* (1915); and *Report of the Richmond, Indiana, Survey for Vocational Education* (1916). In 1917–18 he was special agent of the Federal Board for Vocational Education; and as supervisor for the central states he traveled constantly, inaugurating and supervising schools for training teachers for the army, navy, and marine corps. This work was his contribution to the national defense.

From 1918 to 1923 at the University of California he was professor of education, director of the division of vocational education, acting dean of the school of education (1921–23), and University representative in educational relations (1921–23). In this last capacity he advised the president and regents on matters of policy in all parts of the institution and proposed a plan for the reorganization of the University. From 1923 to 1929 he was professor of education and director of the school of education in Teachers College, Columbia University, where he organized the first course in college administration. He directed surveys of the colleges of Maine, Florida, and the United Lutheran Church in America, as well as of many individual institutions. Believing profoundly in continuing education for all, he was one of the founders of the American Association for Adult Education, and during the last ten years of his life its object absorbed much of his interest. His addresses show that he was not in sympathy with much that is current in so-called progressive education, particularly in the elementary school, believing that it sugar-coated experience and cheapened real life values. A memorial volume containing some of his discourses, *An Outlook on Education,* was published in 1930. He was the author, also, with others, of *An Introductory Course on Part-time Education* (1920); *Data Sheets for Teachers' Course on Part-time Education* (1920); and *The Co-ordination of State Institutions for Higher Education Through Supplementary Curricula Boards* (1923). After a severe attack of influenza he returned to his work too soon, suffered a relapse, and in a delirium fell from the window of his apartment.

[*Who's Who in America,* 1928–29, which is incorrect in some details; unpublished notes by R. J. Leonard; information as to certain facts from his widow; *Industrial Educational Mag.,* Mar. 1929; *Kadelphian Rev.,* Mar. 1929; *Evening Star* (Washington, D. C.), Feb. 9, 1929; *N. Y. Times,* Feb. 10, 1929.] D. A. R.

LEONARD, STERLING ANDRUS (Apr. 23, 1888–May 15, 1931), educator, author, was born in National City, Cal., only child of Cyreno N., a dentist, and Eva (Andrus) Leonard, both of colonial New England stock. At his father's death his mother became a teacher in the public schools of Indianola, Iowa, where for a decade after his eighth year he attended school and college (Simpson), the relations between mother and son being particularly close, especially through their interest in great literature, from which they read aloud to each other. He received the degree of A.B. at the University of Michigan in 1908; that of M.A. in 1909, while an assistant in the English Department; and that of Ph.D. at Columbia in 1928, while on leave of absence from his professorship of English at Wisconsin, to which he was appointed in 1920. Previously, he had been experimenting pedagogically in the Milwaukee Normal School, in the Horace Mann School of New York, and, as exchange teacher, 1911–12, in the Gymnasium at Danzig, Germany, thus preparing himself for leadership in the National Council of the Teachers of English, of which he was president in 1926. At his untimely death he had already achieved much, while promising much more, by writing, by lecturing, and by training secondary-school teachers at his university. In 1913 he had married Minnetta F. Sammis of Terre Haute, Ind., a graduate of Teachers College, Columbia, who shared his educational ideals; and intimate association with their one child unquestionably stimulated his already shrewd and humane insight into the growth of mind and character and the objectives and methods of training them.

He was the author of *English Composition as a Social Problem* (1917); *Essential Principles of Teaching Reading and Literature* (1922); *General Language* (1925); and *The Doctrine of Correctness in English Usage, 1700–1800* (1928); and the editor of *Poems of the War and the Peace* (1920); Melville's *Typee* (1920); *Atlantic Book of Modern Plays* (1922); and, with W. W. Theisen, of a graded series of literature-readers, lively and fresh in substance. He left several almost completed manuscripts chiefly on English usage.

In an age of muddling transitions, ingenious fads, and noisy charlatanry in secondary education, Leonard was peculiarly serviceable by his sound scholarship, by his clear realization of life as changing in form and method while unchanging in essential values, by his scientific sense of observed and tested facts, by his resourceful and untiring energy, and by the fearless integrity of a cultured, witty, kindly, just, and lovable gentleman. He revealed the same balanced, alert, and genial radicalism in his active interest in social, economic, ethical, and political problems of the day.

A lover of good music and an excellent amateur with both violin and viola, he was for years an outstanding member of the Madison Civic Orchestra. He could swing a tennis racket. He loved to look at sunsets from a hill, to paddle a canoe through a forest stream, or to tack in the breezes of Lake Mendota. He did not play golf and belonged to no country club. He was of medium height, ruddy and round-faced with expression playing back and forth between quizzical and grave, wiry in frame, impetuous in gait, gesture, and speech, and fond of an evening of playful intellectual give-and-take with one or two or three friends on diverse themes, both within and outside his professional interests. He died, sinking numb with cold and exhaustion, in the late afternoon waters of Mendota, after clinging for an hour and a half to his over-turned sailing canoe, jesting to his companion, while the University crew rowed by with its launch in the sunny distance and the University life-saving station towered empty in plain sight across the waves a mile to the south.

[*Who's Who in America*, 1930–31; *Am. Speech*, June 1931; *Elementary Eng. Rev.*, June 1931; *Eng. Jour.*, Sept. 1931; *Capital Times* (Madison, Wis.), May 16, 1931; and, for a moving account of his drowning in Mendota, the letter by his rescued companion, Prof. I. A. Richards of Cambridge Univ., England, published in the *Capital Times*, July 17, 1931.] W. E. L.

LEONARD, WILLIAM ANDREW (July 15, 1848–Sept. 21, 1930), bishop of the Protestant Episcopal Church, was born at Southport, Conn., and died at Gambier, Ohio. His father was William Boardman Leonard, a banker, of Brooklyn, N. Y.; his mother, Louisa Dimon Bulkley. The Leonards were among the earliest settlers of Taunton, Mass., where they carried on the smelting of iron from local ores; the Bulkleys were descended from Peter Bulkeley [*q.v.*], a noted non-conformist divine who came to America in 1635 and founded Concord, Mass. William received his academic education at Phillips Academy, Andover, and at St. Stephen's College, Annandale, N. Y. During the Civil War he enlisted in the Union army, but, being under military age, was withdrawn by his father. He graduated at the Berkeley Divinity School in 1871, was ordained deacon of the Protestant Episcopal Church on May 31 of that year, and was advanced to the priesthood, July 21, 1872. In 1873 he married Sarah Louisa Sullivan, of Brooklyn, who died in 1916. He was assistant minister in Holy Trinity Church, Brooklyn, 1871–72, and rector of the Church of the Redeemer, Brooklyn, 1872–80. He founded the Brooklyn Free Library, and was chaplain of the 23rd Regiment, New York National Guard. From 1880 to 1889 he was rector of St. John's Church, Washington, where he became a near friend of many men of national prominence. He declined elections as bishop of Washington Territory, 1880, and as assistant bishop of Southern Ohio, 1889; but in the latter year accepted election as assistant bishop of Ohio, and was consecrated Oct. 12, 1889. Six days later, upon the resignation of Bishop Bedell, he became bishop of that diocese.

His most prominent achievements in Ohio were the building of the cathedral in Cleveland, which was consecrated in 1907, and the strengthening of Kenyon College and its divinity school, Bexley Hall, at Gambier, which institutions he found in a feeble condition financially and administratively. He was in charge of the Protestant Episcopal churches in Europe from 1897 to 1906, and was president of the Fifth Province of the Episcopal Church for ten years (1914–24). Upon the death of the presiding bishop, J. G. Murray, in October 1929, he became by seniority acting presiding bishop until the election of Bishop C. P. Anderson to that office in the following November; and again, upon the death of Bishop Anderson in January

1930, he became acting presiding bishop until the election of Bishop James De Wolf Perry in March following. For many years he was a trustee of Western Reserve University, Cleveland, and of Lake Erie College, Painesville, Ohio. Among his published works are: *Via Sacra* (1875); *History of the Christian Church* (1878), for Sunday Schools; *A Faithful Life* (1888); *New York Church Club Lectures* (1893); *Witness of the American Church to Pure Christianity* (1894); and a life of his grandfather, *Stephen Banks Leonard* (1909). He was devoutly religious, conservative in his views of theology and ritual, yet widely tolerant of differences of opinion and practice among his clergy; under him the diocese was singularly united and at peace. A man of great personal dignity, he was yet exceedingly genial and hospitable.

[L. E. Daniels, *William Andrew Leonard* (1930); G. F. Smythe, *A Hist. of the Diocese of Ohio Until the Year 1918* (1931); *Cleveland Plain Dealer*, Sept. 22, 1930; *Christian Century*, Oct. 1, 1930; *Who's Who in America*, 1930–31; letters and papers in Kenyon Coll. Lib.]

G. F. S.

LEONARD, ZENAS (Mar. 19, 1809–July 14, 1857), trapper, author, was born near Clearfield, Pa., the son of Abraham and Elizabeth (Armstrong) Leonard. His schooling, described by his publisher as "a common school education," appears to have been meager. He worked on his father's farm until the day he was twenty-one, when he announced his intention of striking out for himself. At Pittsburgh he found employment in the store of an uncle, remaining there several months. Determined to be a trapper in the Far West, he went to St. Louis, and in April 1831, as a clerk, left for the mountains with the party of Gantt and Blackwell. He was at the rendezvous in Pierre's Hole, Idaho, in the summer of 1832, and took part in the famous battle of July 18, of which he has left an account.

At the Green River rendezvous of 1833 he met Bonneville and was engaged as a member of Walker's California expedition. With this party, which after great privations and several bloody encounters with Indians, crossed the Utah and Nevada deserts and scaled the Sierras, and which was probably the first company of American whites to see the Yosemite Valley and the giant Merced sequoias, he reached the coast in November. Returning by a more southern route, and traversing what has since been known as Walker's Pass, the expedition reached Bonneville's camp on Bear River in July 1834. For another year Leonard remained in the mountains, trapping in various directions and undergoing many perilous experiences. In the summer of 1835 he returned with Bonneville and in the fall reached his old home. After a few months he returned to the West, settling in Sibley, Mo., on the site of Old Fort Osage, and engaging in the Indian and Santa Fé trade. He married Isabelle Harrelson, by whom he had two children. He died in Sibley.

It was in Clearfield that he wrote the account of his travels, which was published in part in the *Clearfield Republican*, and as a whole in book form under the title, *Narrative of the Adventures of Zenas Leonard* (1839). In 1904 it was republished, with an introduction and notes by W. F. Wagner, under the title, *Leonard's Narrative; Adventures of Zenas Leonard, Fur Trader and Trapper, 1831–1836*. Though, owing to the theft or loss of a part of his journal, Leonard is sometimes faulty as to incident and oftener faulty as to dates, his work is highly valued, and as a contemporary depiction of the daily life of the trapper is surpassed only by the *Journal . . . 1834–1843* (1914) of Osborne Russell. Of Leonard's personality little is known.

[*Leonard's Narrative: Adventures of Zenas Leonard* (1904), ed. by W. F. Wagner; Allen Glenn, *Hist. of Cass County, Mo.* (1917); information from F. C. Shoemaker, Columbia, Mo., and W. D. Leonard, Kansas City, Mo.]

W. J. G.

LE PAGE DU PRATZ, ANTOINE SIMON [See DUPRATZ, ANTOINE SIMON LE PAGE, fl. 1718–1758].

LE ROUX, BARTHOLOMEW (*c.* 1665–July 1713), New York gold and silversmith, is said to have been born in Amsterdam, Holland, between 1660 and 1665, the eldest son of Pierre and Jane Le Roux, who were of French Huguenot descent. The family emigrated to London, and the father became a naturalized English subject in 1681; the mother, in 1685/86 (*New York Genealogical and Biographical Record*, April 1919, pp. 151–53). Bartholomew evidently learned his trade from his father, who was a member of the Goldsmiths' Company of London. Young Le Roux emigrated to America some time prior to June 6, 1687, on which date he was made a freeman of the city of New York (*Collections of the New York Historical Society, Publication Fund Series*, vol. XVIII, 1886, p. 53). A year and a half later, Dec. 14, 1688, he married Gertrude Van Rollegom, the record describing him as "young man from London" (S. S. Purple, *Records of the Reformed Dutch Church, . . . Marriages*, 1890). They had eleven children; the eldest son, Charles [*q.v.*], became in after years the official silversmith of New York.

In 1689, at the outbreak of the rebellion led by

Jacob Leisler [*q.v.*], Le Roux was a member of the city militia company commanded by Capt. Gabriel Minvielle. He and his fellow soldiers supported Leisler by insisting that the whole company be on guard at the fort, in spite of regulations which permitted only half a company to be in arms at one time. Lieutenant-Governor Nicholson and Col. Nicholas Bayard, a member of the council, demanded an explanation for this action, and Le Roux, as spokesman for the company, declared that they feared an attack by Papists from Staten Island and Boston, and, as many of the soldiers already in the fort were Papists, they "thought themselves not secure to be so guarded" (E. B. O'Callaghan, *The Documentary History of the State of New York,* 8vo ed., vol. II, 1849, pp. 17–18). Le Roux disapproved of Leisler's subsequent political activities, however, for he seems to have taken no further part in the rebellion, and some years later when Governor Bellomont favored the Leisler faction and removed their opponents from office, Le Roux joined with Nicholas Bayard and several hundred other Protestants in an address of protest to William III.

As a silversmith he was a good craftsman and prospered, becoming well-known and trusted in the community. On Dec. 30, 1693, he purchased a house and lot at the corner of Broadway and Morris Street (Conveyances, XVIII, 268, in Hall of Records, New York City), and when he died he owned "Goods Chattels & Creditts In diverse places within this province" (Record of Wills, VII, 194–98, Hall of Records, New York). He was elected to several city offices—constable in 1691, collector in 1699, assessor in 1707, and assistant alderman in 1702–04 and 1708–13. He was often asked to be a sponsor at baptisms, a witness or executor of wills, and to make inventories of estates. He died in 1713, some time between July 10, when he made his will, and July 28, when the common council ordered the election of an assistant alderman "in the Room of Mr Bartholomew Le Roux deceased" (*Minutes, post,* III, 40). The School of Fine Arts, Yale University, owns a large two-handled bowl made by Le Roux, one of the most elaborate and ornate pieces in its collection.

[In addition to references given above, see: R. T. H. Halsey, *The Metropolitan Museum of Art: Cat. of an Exhibition of Silver Used in N. Y., N. J., and the South* (1911), pp. xx–xxi; *Minutes of the Common Council of the City of N. Y.* (1905), vols. I–III; E. B. O'Callaghan, *Docs. Relating to the Colonial Hist. of N. Y.*, vol. IV (1854); *Colls. of the N. Y. Hist. Soc., Pub. Fund Ser.*, vols. XXV, XXVI (1893–94); C. L. Avery, *Early Am. Silver* (copr. 1930).] A. E. P.

LE ROUX, CHARLES (December 1689–Mar. 22, 1745), engraver and silversmith, the eldest son of Bartholomew [*q.v.*] and Gertrude (Van Rollegom) Le Roux, was born in New York City and baptized there Dec. 22, 1689. He learned the gold and silversmith's trade from his father, and after the latter's death in 1713 he successfully carried on the business which the elder Le Roux had founded. In 1715 he married Catherine, daughter of Dr. Gerardus Beekman, and his connection with this well-known family added to his prestige and influence in the community. As a craftsman he excelled his father and for many years was the official silversmith of New York City. The records show that to him alone, from 1720 to 1743, was entrusted the making of the gold and silver boxes which enclosed the seal accompanying the engrossed freedom of the city granted by the common council for noteworthy service or to distinguished visitors. One of these boxes was presented to Andrew Hamilton [*q.v.*], the eminent Philadelphia lawyer who defended John Peter Zenger in the famous trial which established the freedom of the press (I. N. P. Stokes, *The Iconography of Manhattan Island, 1498–1909,* vol. IV, 1922, plate 33). Le Roux also engraved the plates for several of the series of bills of credit issued by the city and colony (*New York State Library . . . Calendar of Council Minutes, 1668–1783,* 1902, pp. 260–61), and in 1735, when there was a controversy between Mayor Richard and the common council as to the custody of the city seal, the goldsmith was directed to make and engrave a separate seal for the mayor's use, for which he received £5:9:3 (Stokes, *ante,* vol. IV, plate 31).

Like his father, Charles was also active in the civic and religious affairs of the city; and in the factional strife which prevailed during the administration of Governor Cosby he sided with the popular party. In 1734 he was chosen an assistant alderman on a ticket nominated by "an Interest opposite to the Governour's" (*New York Weekly Journal,* Oct. 7, 1734), and three years later, in a contested assembly election, he signed a petition protesting against the "Bare-faced Villany" of the sheriff in certifying the election of the candidate of the "court faction" (E. B. O'Callaghan, *The Documentary History of the State of New York,* 4to ed., vol. III, 1850, pp. 292–94). As a member of the common council from 1734 to 1739 his activities were extensive, including the auditing of the treasurer's accounts, investigating land titles, having lots surveyed, superintending repairs to the City Hall and to the fire engines, drafting new laws, and suppressing nuisances. He held the offices of church warden and deacon in the Reformed Dutch Church. In April 1738, he was captain of one of the city military companies, and on Aug. 15 of that year he was promoted to the rank of major (*Ibid.*, IV, 1851, pp. 139–40, 147). During the so-called Negro Plot of 1741–42 he was sworn as a member of the grand jury, and when one of his own negroes was accused of being a party to the conspiracy, he entered into a recognizance to have the slave transported (Daniel Horsmanden, *A Journal of the Proceedings in the Detection of the Conspiracy . . .*, 1744, pp. 137, 139, 150, 154).

[In addition to references given above, see: R. T. H. Halsey, *The Metropolitan Museum of Art: Cat. of an Exhibition of Silver Used in N. Y., N. J., and the South* (1911); *N. Y. Geneal. and Biog. Record*, Apr. 1919; *Minutes of the Common Council of the City of N. Y., 1675–1776* (8 vols., 1905), vols. III–V and index; *Colls. of the N. Y. Geneal. and Biog. Soc.*, vols. II, III (1901–02); *Colls. of the N. Y. Hist. Soc., Pub. Fund Ser.*, XLII (1910), 122; J. G. Wilson, *The Memorial Hist. of the City of N. Y.*, II (1892), 161–62; and *Ecclesiastical Records of the State of N. Y.*, vols. III, IV (1902).] A. E. P.

LÉRY, JOSEPH GASPARD CHAUSSEGROS de (July 20, 1721–Dec. 11, 1797), was an engineer of New France who made several journeys to the Great Lakes and the Mississippi Valley and laid out several forts in these regions. His father, Gaspard Chaussegros de Léry (1682–1756), a pupil of Vauban, was sent to Canada in 1716 to superintend its fortifications, and erected the defenses of Quebec and Montreal. He married Marie-Renée le Gardeur de Beauvais, of the Canadian *noblesse*. Their son Joseph entered Quebec Seminary at the age of ten and when only thirteen applied for the position of assistant engineer. He was then considered too young for such an office, but it was granted to him early in 1739. That same year he accompanied the expedition from Canada to Louisiana, which took part in the war against the Chickasaw Indians. With the Louisiana troops was the engineer Broutin, whom Léry assisted in reconnoitring the route to the Chickasaw villages. At the close of this campaign he was commissioned ensign and in 1743 went to Crown Point on Lake Champlain to complete the defenses of Fort Saint Frédéric. In 1748 he was commissioned first ensign and the following year was sent by the governor to Detroit to survey the route and to report on the fortifications. His account of this voyage is the first of the nine journals which he wrote that are still extant. In 1751 he was promoted to a lieutenancy and employed on forts in Acadia. The governor then sent him to France to explain the necessity of such posts, the existence of which had been declared by the English a violation of neutrality. After his return to Canada he married in 1753 Louise Martel de Brouague.

The journals of the years 1754–55 are the longest and most important of his diaries, for during those years he again visited Detroit, aided in erecting the forts along the Allegheny River, and made plans and sketches of routes, which he introduced into the text. In the French and Indian War he took part in the campaign against Oswego, was made captain in 1757, served in Montcalm's army, and was wounded on the Plains of Abraham. After the capitulation he and his wife visited France and England. In the latter country George III so admired Madame de Léry that he said to her: "Madame, if all the Canadian ladies are like you, I have truly made a conquest" (Lindsay, *post*, p. 373). In 1764 Léry returned to Canada, where in 1778 he was chosen a member of the legislative council of Quebec and in 1791 was member of the same council for Lower Canada. He died at Quebec and was buried in the Cathedral.

[The journals of Léry are published in *Rapport de l'Archiviste de La Province de Quebec* for 1926–29. There are nine, eight of which belong to the Quebec Archives; the ninth (1759), to the Canadian Archives, having been obtained from England. A translation of the journal of 1754–55, with a sketch by Col. Crawford Lindsay, is in the *Ohio Archæol. and Hist. Quart.*, Oct. 1908. The most complete account is in François Daniel, *Le Vicomte C. de Léry et sa famille* (1867). W. S. Wallace, *Dict. of Canadian Biog.* (1926), gives Léry's name as Joseph Gaspard (or Gaspard Joseph) and his father's name as Joseph Gaspard; sources also differ as to the spelling of the name of Léry's wife.] L. P. K.

LESCHI (d. Feb. 19, 1858), a Nisqualli chief, the son of a Nisqualli warrior and a Klikitat squaw, was born and lived within his father's tribe on the Nisqually River, in the present state of Washington. He joined the Indian uprising in 1855, became a chief, and commanded the forces west of the Cascades, while Kamaiakan [*q.v.*] led the resistance to the east of the mountains. Perhaps his chief exploit was the attack on the little village of Seattle, in January 1856, when he is said to have led a thousand warriors and to have been repulsed only with the aid of a ship in the harbor. After the failure of the outbreak he gave himself up to the army officer commanding in the Yakima country and received amnesty. Nevertheless Gov. Isaac I. Stevens [*q.v.*] did not relax his efforts to bring him to trial for murders committed during the uprising, and, by the promise of fifty blankets, bribed one of his own tribe to betray him to the civil authority. During his spectacular trial the rivalries and animosities of the frontier territory flamed. The influence of the United States army and the sympathy of the Hudson's Bay Company, as well as the interest of certain citizens, united to defend Leschi on the ground that he had not been present on the occasion in question and furthermore, that such acts were acts of war for which he could not be answerable to any civil authority. At the first trial, held immediately after his surrender in November 1856, the jury disagreed. After the court was moved to the capital at Olympia a second trial was held in March 1857 and a conviction was obtained. On appeal to the state supreme court Leschi was sentenced to be hanged on Jan. 22, 1858. When the arrest of the sheriff on a charge of selling liquor to the Indians prevented the execution on the day named, mass meetings of angry settlers protested against a further stay of sentence. A special session of the territorial supreme court ordered him to be resentenced and, before a possible pardon could be obtained from the federal capital, he was hanged according to the law.

[*Pioneer and Democrat* (Olympia, Wash. Territory), especially issues of Jan. 29, Feb. 5, 26, 1858; Ezra Meeker, *Pioneer Reminiscences of Puget Sound: The Tragedy of Leschi* (1905); C. A. Snowden, *Hist. of Wash.* (1909), vols. III and IV; H. H. Bancroft, *Hist. of Wash., Idaho, and Mont.* (1890); Hazard Stevens, *The Life of Isaac Ingalls Stevens* (2 vols., 1900).]

K. E. C.

LESLEY, J. PETER [See LESLEY, PETER, 1819–1903].

LESLEY, PETER (Sept. 17, 1819–June 1, 1903), geologist, third child but first son of Peter and Elizabeth Oswald (Allen) Lesley, was born in Philadelphia, Pa. The fourth Peter Lesley in direct succession, he was known at first as Peter Lesley, Jr., but disliking his first name, in early manhood transferred the "J" from Junior, and adopted the signature of J. P. Lesley. His grandfather, a cabinet maker, came to America from Aberdeenshire, Scotland, and, landing in Boston, walked thence to Philadelphia where he settled. A few years later he saw service in the Revolution. His son, Peter's father, was also a cabinet maker. Young Peter was a nervous, timid child, extremely near-sighted. At the age of six he was sent to a private school where he developed into a bright pupil, fond of his books. At fifteen he entered the University of Pennsylvania, graduating with the degree of A.B. in 1838, but with health so impaired that on the advice of his physicians he discontinued his studies and sought outdoor employment with the state geological survey. For this line of work he had shown no predilection, but he was appointed and made such creditable progress as to win special commendation from Henry Darwin Rogers [*q.v.*], the director.

For political reasons the survey was discontinued in 1841, and Lesley returned to his books, attending the Theological Seminary at Princeton, 1841–44. During his vacations, he continued to assist Rogers in editing the reports of the unfinished survey. In this work, particularly in the drawing of maps and sections, it is said he showed great skill. After being licensed as a preacher by the Philadelphia Presbytery in 1844, he sailed for a year in Europe, where he spent several months touring on foot, and several months studying at Halle. Returning to Philadelphia in May 1845, he took a position as colporteur for the American Tract Society, preaching and distributing tracts through the northern and central parts of Pennsylvania. This work taxed his strength too severely, however, and in 1846 he once more entered the service of Rogers, who was then located in Boston, aiding him as before in the preparation of his maps and sections. Late in 1847 he was called to act as pastor of a Congregational church at Milton, Mass. Here, Feb. 13, 1849, he married Susan Inches Lyman, daughter of Judge Joseph Lyman, a young woman whose religious affiliations were Unitarian. This step caused discord in Lesley's church, particularly since the young minister himself was quite liberal in his views, and in 1852 he formally abandoned pastoral work and turned once more to geology. The year before the Pennsylvania legislature had furnished funds for the completion of the state survey, on which he was again employed.

He subsequently surveyed coal and iron fields for various corporations in various parts of the country. His first book, *A Manual of Coal and Its Topography* (1856), confirmed his reputation as a geologist of the first rank. From 1856 to 1864 he served as secretary of the American Iron Association, and during this period published, in addition to several geological pamphlets, a volume of nearly eight hundred pages entitled *The Iron Manufacturer's Guide* (1859) which brought him no inconsiderable reputation. In 1859 he became professor of mining in the University of Pennsylvania, and with its growth became successively dean of the Science Department (1872) and dean of the newly established Towne Scientific School (1875), retiring, as professor emeritus, in 1883. In 1859 also he was made librarian and secretary of the American Philosophical Society, holding the former position until 1885 and the latter until 1887, when he became vice-president. In 1863 he was sent to Europe by the Pennsylvania Railroad to study rail manufacture and the Bessemer steel process. This year marked the beginning of the great petroleum excitement, which caused such a demand for his services as to bring about a nervous breakdown and forced him in 1866 to make another trip to Europe for rest and recreation.

Returning, two years later, he became in 1869 the editor of a weekly newspaper, *The United States Railroad and Mining Register,* which he conducted until the end of 1873.

In this year, in response to the clamor of the oil men, there was authorized a second geological survey of Pennsylvania, with Lesley as state geologist. He was at this time fifty-four years of age and at the height of his career. He continued as state geologist throughout the thirteen years of the survey's existence, or until 1887. From this organization there emanated the most remarkable series of reports ever published by any survey. Up to and including 1887, when all field work was discontinued, there were issued seventy-seven octavo volumes of text with thirty-three atlases and a Grand Atlas. These were followed in 1892 and 1895 by the three octavo volumes constituting the final report. The magnitude of the task was too great for Lesley's strength, and he again broke down in 1893—so completely, this time, that his summary and final reports were left for others to finish. Though for a time after this last breakdown his health caused his friends no great anxiety, he slowly weakened, and in 1903 he had a stroke of apoplexy, from which he died, in his eighty-fourth year. His wife and two daughters survived him.

The quantity of Lesley's work was enormous; that much of it was not of as high order as he could wish was not his fault, but that of a legislature crying for immediate benefits. He was a man of tall, lank, but commanding, figure, of an impressionable and emotional nature, endowed with tremendous nervous energy, aggressive and outspoken, an enthusiast and optimist, but at times lamentably melancholy. "His writings are full of expressions which for terseness and unpolished emphasis are unequalled" (Merrill, *post*). Nor were his writings limited to scientific subjects. He was a philologist of considerable repute; he wrote poetry; delivered a series of Lowell Lectures in 1865–66, published under the title, *Man's Origin and Destiny* (1868); under the pseudonym, John W. Allen, Jr., brought out a work of fiction, *Paul Dreifuss, His Holiday Abroad* (1882), a "photographically minute account of a holiday trip in the winter of 1881, 1882"; and contributed many articles to magazines and encyclopedias. As editor of the *Railroad and Mining Register* his paragraphs were well nigh numberless. He was an original member of the National Academy of Sciences, and a member or honorary member of many other scientific organizations.

[*Life and Letters of Peter and Susan Lesley* (2 vols., 1909), ed. by their daughter, Mary Lesley Ames, reprints as appendices the biographical notices from *Am. Geologist,* Sept. 1903; *Mines and Minerals,* July 1903; *Bull. Geol. Soc. of America,* vol. XV (1904); *Quart. Jour. Geol. Soc. of London,* May 14, 1904; *Proc. Am. Philosophical Soc.,* vol. XLV (1906); *Trans. Am. Inst. Mining Engineers,* vol. XXXIV (1904). See also W. M. Davis, in *Biog. Memoirs Nat. Acad. Sci.,* vol. VIII (1919); G. P. Merrill, *The First One Hundred Years of American Geology* (1924); *Phila. Inquirer,* June 3, 1903.]
G. P. M.

LESLIE, CHARLES ROBERT (Oct. 19, 1794–May 5, 1859), painter and author, was born in London, but his parents, Robert and Lydia (Baker) Leslie, were Americans, natives of Maryland, where their ancestors had settled early in the eighteenth century. In 1786 the family had moved to Philadelphia, where Robert Leslie established a clock and watch store. He found it expedient in 1793 to go to London for the purpose of buying goods for the establishment, taking his family with him. Thus both of his sons were born during the London sojourn. He already had three daughters, one of whom was Eliza Leslie [*q.v.*]. In the autumn of 1799 the family sailed for America from Gravesend in the American ship *Washington,* which, though a merchantman, was heavily armed, for France and the United States were at war. Only a few days after leaving England the *Washington* was attacked by a French man-of-war, *La Bellone.* After a brisk duel the latter was driven off, but the damage sustained by the American ship was so serious that her commander was forced to make for Lisbon, the nearest port, five hundred miles away, for repairs. On Mar. 31, 1800, the ship again put to sea, but it was forty-two days later when she finally dropped anchor at Philadelphia—nearly eight months from the time she left Gravesend.

Robert Leslie died a few years later, leaving so little property that his widow was obliged to open a boarding-house. Charles and his brother were sent to school at the University of Pennsylvania. In 1808, Charles was apprenticed to Bradford & Inskeep, booksellers. He now began to make sketches at every opportunity and haunted the theatre, making friends with the actors, drawing their portraits, and painting scenery. His likeness of George Frederick Cooke, the actor, made quite a hit, and convinced Bradford, his employer, that the youth's artistic talent was well worth cultivating. Consequently the boy was sent to London in 1811 to take up the serious study of painting. From the day of his arrival his choice of a vocation was justified and his career was successful almost from the start. He made a host of influential friends; worked assiduously in the school of the Royal Academy under Fuseli; sat at the feet of Benjamin West and Washington Allston; and roomed with Samuel F. B. Morse. His London life was interesting, and his autobiography is full of amusing anecdotes and genial personal gossip relating to such personages as Coleridge, Scott, Lamb, Irving, Sidney Smith, Wilkie, Landseer, Constable, Turner, Flaxman, and others equally eminent. But there is not a trace of egotism. Leslie's character was evidently modest and amiable in an exceptional degree.

After some early attempts at historical painting on a large scale, he wisely turned to anecdotic genre, a class of subjects far better adapted to his talents, in which for many years he had no superior. He took his motives from the works of Shakespeare, Sterne, Addison, Pope, Goldsmith, Fielding, and Smollett; he also illustrated many familiar scenes from the comedies of Molière, from *Don Quixote, Gil Blas,* and other works. His "Slender, Shallow and Anne Page," "Sir Roger de Coverley Going to Church," "May Day in the Time of Queen Elizabeth," and other early paintings of the sort established his reputation, and within a few years he was made an associate and then a member of the Royal Academy. In 1833 he accepted the appointment of teacher of drawing in the United States Military Academy at West Point, but after discharging the duties of the office for a few months he returned to England, where the rest of his life was passed. In 1847 he became professor of painting in the Royal Academy, and the substance of his lectures to the students during the four years that he held the office was published later under the title of *A Handbook for Young Painters* (1855). He wrote *Memoirs of the Life of John Constable, Esq., R.A.* (1843), and began a biography of Sir Joshua Reynolds which was completed by his literary executor, Tom Taylor (*Life and Times of Sir Joshua Reynolds,* 1865). Leslie's style is simple, clear, and pithy, and his writings form a valuable contribution to the literature of art. His biographer in the *Dictionary of National Biography* states that his principal defect as a painter was his use of color, which was at times harsh. The Pennsylvania Academy of the Fine Arts owns eleven of his early works, including his "Murder of Rutland by Lord Clifford," "Touchstone," "Audrey and William," "Olivia," and "Sophia Western." Leslie married Harriet Stone of London in 1825; he died in London at the age of sixty-five.

[Charles Robert Leslie, *Autobiog. Recollections* (1860), edited, with an essay on Leslie as an artist and selections from his correspondence, by Tom Taylor; Geo. Johnston, *Hist. of Cecil County, Md.* (1881); *Dict. Nat. Biog.*; Wm. Dunlap, *Hist. of the Rise and Progress of the Arts of Design in the U. S.* (3 vols., 1918); H. T. Tuckerman, *Book of the Artists* (1867); Samuel Isham, *Hist. of Am. Painting* (1905); P. G. Hamerton, article in *Fortnightly Rev.*, Jan. 1866; H. T. Tuckerman, article in *Christian Examiner,* Sept. 1860; R. C. Waterston, article in *North Am. Rev.*, Jan. 1861; *Living Age,* July 9, 1859, June 2, 1860; *Art Journal,* vol. XII (1860), LIV (1902); *Chambers's Jour.*, July 28, 1860; *Quart. Rev.* (London), Apr. 1860; *Temple Bar,* Mar. 1896; *Century Illustrated Monthly Mag.*, Dec. 1900.]

W. H. D.

LESLIE, ELIZA (Nov. 15, 1787–Jan. 1, 1858), author, sister of Charles Robert Leslie [*q.v.*], was born in Philadelphia, Pa., the daughter of Robert and Lydia (Baker) Leslie. Her great-grandfather, Robert Leslie, had emigrated from Scotland to the Maryland colony about 1745 and had bought a farm. Her grandparents and her parents were natives of Cecil County, Md. Soon after their marriage her parents removed to Philadelphia, where her father was a watchmaker. He seems to have been an unusual man, a self-taught mathematician and draftsman, a fair performer on the flute and violin, and enough of a scientist to be elected to the American Philosophical Society, where he was the friend of Thomas Jefferson and Benjamin Franklin. When Eliza was five, Robert Leslie took his family to England, where they remained over six years, while he was in the business of exporting clocks. A few years after their return to Philadelphia he died, leaving his family very poor; but, as Eliza Leslie said, they kept their difficulties to themselves, asked no assistance, and incurred no debts.

Eliza's education had been carried on chiefly at home, by reading and by private lessons in French and music, but she had had three months in a London school of needlework and had taken a course in the cooking school of Mrs. Goodfellow in Philadelphia. Recipes learned at this school she was in the habit of copying for friends, until one of her brothers suggested that it would save trouble to publish a book. This resulted in her first publication, *Seventy-Five Receipts for Pastry, Cakes, and Sweetmeats* (1837). Her only writing previous to this had been verses, with soldiers, sailors, and shepherds for heroes, which she herself estimated as foolish after seeing a real English shepherd. The publisher of the cook book urged her to write juvenile stories and she then began to publish the Mirror Series. Her literary success was now assured and cook books and stories continued to win for her popularity and a good income for the remainder of her life. Her story "Mrs. Washington Potts" won a prize from *Godey's Lady's Book* and three other prizes came to her from periodicals. She contributed frequently to the *Lady's Book* and *Graham's Magazine* and edited *The Gift,* an annual, and *The Violet,* a juvenile "souvenir."

Her only novel, *Amelia, or a Young Lady's Vicissitudes* (1848), was first published in the *Lady's Book.* Her other works include: *The American Girl's Book* (1831); *Pencil Sketches* (three series, 1833, 1835, 1837); *The Domestic Cookery Book* (1837), which went through thirty-eight editions by 1851; *Althea Vernon; or, The Embroidered Handkerchief* (1838); *The House-Book* (1840); *The Young Revolutionists* (1845), hero stories, chiefly of the American Revolution; *The Lady's Receipt Book* (1846); *The Dennings and Their Beaux* (1851); and *The Behaviour Book* (1853). As a story writer Eliza Leslie had an easy narrative style and a taste for satire, which was criticized by one contemporary reviewer as depriving her work of any "lasting attraction." Another critic considered her characters "perfect daguerreotypes of real life." Her contributions were said always to increase the circulation of periodicals. Her books on domestic economy were the most popular and brought in the largest financial returns. She lived for some years at the United States Hotel, Philadelphia, where she was visited by many of her own countrymen and travelers from abroad. She had a reputation for a remarkable memory, original ideas, and an unfailing supply of apt anecdote. During the last ten years of her life she was working on a biography of John Fitch, the inventor, who was a friend of her father. She died at Gloucester, N. J.

[Eliza Leslie's autobiography was published in John S. Hart, *Female Prose Writers of America* (1852). See also R. W. Griswold, *The Prose Writers of America* (1847); Sarah Josepha Hale, *Biog. of Distinguished Women* (ed. 1876); review of *Pencil Sketches in North Am. Rev.*, Oct. 1833; E. A. and G. L. Duyckinck, *Cyc. of Am. Lit.* (ed. 1875); *Godey's Lady's Book*, Apr. 1858; Geo. Johnston, *Hist. of Cecil County, Md.* (1881); *N. Y. Times*, Jan. 4, 1858.] S. G. B.

LESLIE, FRANK (Mar. 29, 1821–Jan. 10, 1880), wood-engraver, pioneer publisher of illustrated journals, born in Ipswich, England, was the son of Joseph Leslie and Mary Elliston Carter and was named Henry. His father, a glove-manufacturer, urged the boy to enter his business, but he preferred to carve wood and at the age of thirteen astonished his elders by making a wood-engraving of the coat-of-arms of the town of Ipswich (*Frank Leslie's Illustrated Newspaper*, Feb. 7, 1880). "Frank Leslie" was at first a pseudonym which he employed on sketches and engravings submitted surreptitiously to various publications. His work attracted the attention of the *Illustrated London News* and at twenty-one he was employed in that journal's engraving department. Firm in the belief that there was a wider field in the United States for his art he emigrated to New York in 1848. His name appears in the directory of the following year as "Leslie, F., engraver, 98 Broadway," although his name was not legally changed until 1857 (*Laws of the State of New York*, 1857, Chapter 205). In 1852 he was employed in Boston on *Gleason's Pictorial*, in which many of his full-page engravings appeared, but at the end of the year he returned to New York to become superintendent of the engraving department of a new publication, the *Illustrated News*, which was first issued on Jan. 1, 1853. The issue of July 30, 1853, carried a double-page engraving bearing Leslie's name and entitled "Inauguration Ceremonies of the Crystal Palace." An engraving of this size ordinarily required four months' time to complete, but through Leslie's ingenuity, this picture was completed in three days. After the drawing had been made, he had divided it into thirty-four blocks and had set as many engravers to work, thus accomplishing the feat. Using the same device subsequently in his own papers Leslie was able to picture events the day following their occurrence.

Before the end of 1853 the *Illustrated News* had merged with *Gleason's Pictorial* and Leslie had started the first publication of his own, *Frank Leslie's Ladies' Gazette of Paris, London, and New York Fashions*, first issued in January 1854. About a year later he bought out an unsuccessful publication, the *New York Journal*, which appeared under a new name, *Frank Leslie's New York Journal*, in January 1855. His next publication, *Frank Leslie's Illustrated Newspaper*, which was to give him enduring fame, was first issued on Dec. 15, 1855. In his initial editorial he declared that the earlier illustrated newspapers, such as *Gleason's Pictorial*, lacked "the artistic facilities for seizing promptly and illustrating the passing events of the day." Leslie had discovered how to succeed where others had failed. Beginning Aug. 15, 1857, he pleased the German-reading population by printing each weekly issue in German under the title *Illustrirte Zeitung*. *Frank Leslie's Monthly*, at first known as *Frank Leslie's New Family Magazine*, was started in September 1857, absorbing the earlier *Gazette of Fashion*.

During the Civil War Leslie's profits increased at a rapid rate. His artists were found wherever the campaigns were hottest. As his revenues increased, so did the number of his publications. They included the *Chimney Corner, Lady's Magazine, Lady's Journal, Boy's and Girl's Weekly, Sunday Magazine, Chatterbox, Pleasant Hours, Boys of America, Jolly Joker, Illustrated Almanac, Comic Almanac*, all bearing the name of Frank Leslie. It was his desire to provide "mental pabulum" for all classes of society. To one publication, the *Day's Doings,* "Illustrating Extraordinary Events of the Day, Police Reports, Important Trials, and Sporting News," he did not attach his name. When the *Times* editor called it "a most wicked and disgusting sheet" (*New York Times,* July 3, 1872), Leslie merely stated that he was indebted to the *Times* for the news items on which the pictures were based. Leslie greatly prized a gold medal presented to him by Napoleon III *"pour services rendus"* as a United States commissioner to the Exposition Universelle of 1867 at Paris. He also took great satisfaction, as a member of the New York state board of managers for the Centennial at Philadelphia, in producing a magnificently illustrated volume: *Frank Leslie's Historical Register of the United States Centennial Exposition, 1776* (1777). This was a distinct financial loss, however, and, coupled with colossal expenditures in connection with his estate "Interlaken," at Saratoga, and a pleasure trip to California, and with the general financial depression of 1877, brought him to bankruptcy. He left to his widow liabilities aggregating $300,000.

Until Frank Leslie was married a second time, July 13, 1874, to Mrs. Miriam Florence Squier [see Leslie, Miriam Florence Folline] his domestic life was particularly unhappy. By his first wife, whom he married in England, he had three sons. Litigation attending his divorce extended over several years. His death was undoubtedly hastened by additional litigation which he felt constrained to undertake against his two surviving sons in 1879 because they used the name "Frank Leslie" in connection with a journal they were publishing.

["Frank Leslie," in *Frank Leslie's Sunday Mag.,* Mar. 1880; *Frank Leslie's Illustrated Newspaper,* Jan. 24, 1880; obituaries in New York papers of Jan. 11, 1880, particularly the *World*; *Territorial Enterprise,* Extra (Virginia City, Nev.), July 14, 1878; *Harper's Weekly,* Jan. 31, 1880; Frederic Hudson, *Journalism in the U. S. from 1690 to 1872* (1873); A. B. Paine, *Th. Nast, His Period and Pictures* (1904); vital statistics, N. Y. City; court records, N. Y. county.]

A. E. P.

LESLIE, MIRIAM FLORENCE FOLLINE (*c.* 1836–Sept. 18, 1914), wife and successor of Frank Leslie [*q.v.*], daughter of Charles and Susan Danforth Follin, was born in New Orleans, La. She apparently changed the spelling of her last name. The date of her birth she successfully concealed. Her girlhood appears to be linked with New York City and she seems to have acquired a good education in the French, Spanish, and Italian languages. Her marriage to David Charles Peacock on Mar. 27, 1854, was annulled on Mar. 22, 1856. About two years later she was married to Ephraim George Squier [*q.v.*], diplomat and journalist, who during the early years of the Civil War was a member of Frank Leslie's editorial staff. It is probable that she was an assistant in the publisher's office in the late sixties. When *Frank Leslie's Lady's Journal* was issued on Nov. 18, 1871, it was "conducted by Miriam F. Squier." It was a weekly "Devoted to Fashion and Choice Literature," and each issue contained a leading article entitled "What New Yorkers are Wearing." With alternate numbers subscribers received a large colored fashion plate. The publisher, long estranged from his wife, became enamoured of his capable and comely editress who reciprocated his affection and divorced Squier, May 31, 1873 (*Superior Court Judgments,* New York County, vol. XXXV). Her married life with Leslie she spoke of as "her one happy matrimonial experience." She entertained lavishly both in the metropolis and at the Leslie Saratoga estate "Interlaken." She and Leslie took a trip across the continent in 1877 in sumptuous train accommodations and with a considerable retinue of friends and servants. In *California: A Pleasure Trip From Gotham to the Golden Gate* (1877) she wrote an account of the trip. Because of some uncomplimentary statements she made about Virginia City, Nev., both she and her husband were scored ruthlessly by the local news sheet, the *Territorial Enterprise,* Extra, July 14, 1878.

Days of adversity followed which culminated in her husband's death in 1880. She resolutely assumed the management of the business with its $300,000 deficit, knowing for a time what it meant to live "in a carpetless flat." A curious but undoubtedly advantageous move in 1882 was to have her name changed to Frank Leslie by court order. For fifteen years continuously she was her own manager and editor and was highly successful. This success she always claimed was due to her "ability to deal with and judge the value of news" (*New York Tribune,* May 20, 1895). Others said her charming and magnetic personality was a large factor. With ample income to retire she leased the business in 1895 to a syndicate for five years, but after three years she felt it necessary to occupy once again the editor's chair of *Frank Leslie's Popular Monthly* and resurrect the business. Her written works extended over several years and touched a variety of subjects. In 1871 she published *Travels in Central America,* from the French of Arthur Morelet. Later works included *Rents in Our Robes* (1888); *Beautiful Women of Twelve Epochs* (1890); *Are Men Gay Deceivers* (1893); and *A Social Mirage* (1899). On Oct.

4, 1891, Mrs. Leslie was married to the English art and dramatic critic, Wm. C. Kingsbury Wilde ("Willie" Wilde), a brother of Oscar Wilde, but a divorce followed two years later. After one of her many trips to France she returned in 1901 claiming to have succeeded to the title "Baroness de Bazus." An ardent feminist, she was a vice-president and generous benefactor of the Women's Press Club (*New York Tribune,* Nov. 29, 1903), and she willed the bulk of her fortune to the cause of woman's suffrage. She had no children.

[*Who's Who in America*, 1912–13; *Who's Who in N. Y. City and State* (1904); Rose Young, *The Record of the Leslie Woman Suffrage Commission, Inc., 1917–29* (1929); *Frank Leslie's Popular Monthly,* Nov. 1898; *Leslie's Illustrated Weekly Newspaper,* Oct. 1, 1914; *Daily Picayune* (New Orleans), July 31, 1898; *N. Y. Tribune,* May 22, 1894, May 20, 1895; Oct. 2, 1900, July 18, 1901; *N. Y. Times,* Sept. 19, 21, 1914; vital statistics, N. Y. City; court records, N. Y. County.] A. E. P.

LESQUEREUX, LEO (Nov. 18, 1806–Oct. 25, 1889), paleobotanist, son of V. Aimé and Marie Anne Lesquereux, was born in the village of Fleurier, in the canton of Neuchâtel, Switzerland. His ancestors were French Huguenots—victims of the edict of Nantes. His father was a manufacturer of watchsprings; his mother, a woman of education who aspired to see her son a minister in the Lutheran church and to this end persisted in attempting to make him a classical scholar. In this effort she failed. The boy could not and would not confine himself to his books, but early developed an almost uncontrollable enthusiasm for outdoor life and natural history. In one of his early mountain-climbing expeditions, when he was about ten years old, he fell from a high crag and was so badly injured that for days his life was despaired of, though he ultimately recovered with only the partial loss of hearing in one ear as a permanent result. When he was thirteen, at his mother's earnest solicitation he went to Neuchâtel to study, but though he did well in arithmetic and French, in Latin and Greek he failed.

By the age of nineteen, however, he was fitted for the University. Since his father was unable to bear the expense of maintaining him there, he accepted a position at Eisenach, Saxony, as professor of French, expecting to earn enough to pay his own expenses. Here he met Sophia von Wolffskeel von Reichenberg, the daughter of General von Wolffskeel, and despite the discrepancy in their respective stations, between Lesquereux and this young woman a mutual attachment developed which was ultimately allowed to culminate in marriage. Increasing deafness forced Lesquereux to give up teaching a year or two after his marriage. For a while he eked out a somewhat scanty living for his wife and children by engraving watchcases, and in time formed a partnership with his father in the manufacture of watchsprings. During his prolonged incapacity from a serious illness, his wife learned a branch of the trade and supported the family until his recovery.

Cut off almost completely from social intercourse by his deafness, he turned his attention back once more to nature, particularly to the mosses and lower forms of plant life, quickly mastering his subject and constituting himself a recognized authority. About this time, the Swiss government, in view of the increasing scarcity of fuel, offered a prize for the best essay on the formation and preservation of the peat bogs, which had become the chief source of supply. Lesquereux won the prize with his *Recherches sur les Tourbières du Jura* (1844). Furthermore, the essay brought him in touch with Jean Louis Rodolphe Agassiz [*q.v.*], Arnold Henry Guyot [*q.v.*], his former classmate, and other scientific men of the day. The episode proved a turning point in his career. The Swiss government next employed him to prepare a small textbook on peat for use in the schools, and created for his especial benefit the office of director of peat bogs. He was also—through the social influence of his wife, it is said—employed to report upon the peat bogs of Germany, Sweden, Denmark, and France. Unfortunately, while he was engaged in these congenial tasks the political revolutions of 1847–48 came about, and all employees of the existing government were ousted. Agassiz had gone to America in 1846, and Lesquereux and his friend Guyot followed, landing in Boston in September 1848. Lesquereux was at this time in his forty-second year, "stone deaf," and unable to speak English. Nevertheless he triumphed over his handicap by learning to read lip movements, and ultimately was able to carry on conversation with three persons at once, speak-in English, French, and German in turn, although it was necessary in such case that he be told in advance the language each individual was to speak. Since his own speaking knowledge of English was gained after he reached America, his vocalization was bad, as with deaf mutes in general.

His first scientific work in the United States was the classification of the plant collection made during the Agassiz expedition of 1848 to Lake Superior. Later he moved to Columbus, Ohio, where he became associated with the eminent cryptogamic botanist, William Starling Sullivant [*q.v.*], in his bryological work. He then turned to a systematic study of the coal plants and quickly became the recognized authority on matters relating to the entire Appalachian coal field, with the literature of which his name must be forever associated. His most valued single contribution is his "Description of the Coal Flora of the Carboniferous Formation in Pennsylvania and Throughout the United States" (*Second Geological Survey of Pennsylvania: Report of Progress, P.*, 3 vols. in 2, 1880–84), but he is to be credited also with the determinations of the coal plants for the Kentucky survey of 1860, the Illinois survey of 1866 and 1870, the Indiana survey of 1876 and 1884, as well as the Tertiary plants of the Hilgard survey of Mississippi and the Cretaceous and Tertiary plants of the Hayden survey of the Dakotas.

Lesquereux's deafness cut him off from all attendance on society meetings and he was known intimately to few. He had a very modest opinion of his own merits. He "was a devout Christian believer. . . . He extended his creed to take in all scientific discoveries, but he did not count any of its essentials disturbed thereby. He seems never to have been reached by the currents of modern thought which have overflowed the old foundations for so many" (Orton, *post*, p. 294). His friend and colleague, Peter Lesley, writes: "A homelier, a more beautiful face I never saw. The homeliness was in the flesh; the beauty was the varying expression of a perfectly lovely spirit. He was a little man with inexhaustible powers of life. His eyes were limpid; his smile heavenly; his gratitude for the smallest favors from men and his childlike confidence in the care of God, unbounded. Everybody trusted and loved him" (*post*, p. 210). He was honored by membership in the leading scientific societies of Europe and was the first member to be elected to the National Academy of Sciences after its organization. He died in Columbus, Ohio, in his eighty-third year.

[See autobiographical letter from Lesquereux in his posthumous monograph, *The Flora of the Dakota Group* (1891), also pub. as *Monographs of the U. S. Geol. Survey*, vol. XVII (1892); brief notice in *Am. Jour. Sci.*, Dec. 1889; memoir by Peter Lesley, based on material from Lesquereux himself, in *Biog. Memoirs Nat. Acad. Sci.*, vol. III (1895); memoir by Edward Orton, in *Am. Geologist*, May 1890; W. J. Youmans, *Pioneers of Science in America* (1896); *Pop. Sci. Mo.*, Apr. 1887; *Proc. Am. Philosophical Soc.*, vol. XXVIII (1890); C. R. Barnes, in *Botanical Gazette*, Jan. 1890; frequent references in M. L. Ames, *Life and Letters of Peter and Susan Lesley* (2 vols., 1909); *Cincinnati Commercial Gazette*, Oct. 26, 1889. J. C. Poggendorff, in *Biographisch-literarisches Handwörterbuch zur Geschichte der Exacten Wissenschaften* (1898), gives Lesquereux's name as Charles Leo, but he seems never to have used the Charles.] G. P. M.

LESTER, CHARLES EDWARDS (July 15, 1815–Jan. 29, 1890), author, was born at Griswold, Conn., of New England ancestry, son of Moses Lester and Sarah Woodbridge, a granddaughter of Jonathan Edwards. Following his schooldays in Connecticut he traveled in the Southwest, descending the Mississippi in the winter of 1834–35, and studied law at Natchez, Miss., under the Democratic leader, Robert J. Walker [*q.v.*], later secretary of the treasury under Polk. Lester, who, though an anti-slavery man, was always an ardent Democrat, afterward warmly acknowledged Walker's influence on his character and political views. He was admitted to the bar, but subsequently attended Auburn (N. Y.) Theological Seminary, 1835–36, and became a Presbyterian minister, holding several charges in northern New York. His interest in the anti-slavery movement appears in his book *Chains and Freedom* (1839), the life of a runaway slave. Compelled by ill health to leave the ministry, he visited England in 1840 as a delegate to the World Anti-Slavery Convention, held in Exeter Hall, London, where he met Campbell, Beatty, Dickens, and other British writers. His book *The Glory and the Shame of England* (2 vols., 1841), published upon his return, attracted much attention as an exposure of the hardships of British labor in factories and mines. To a defense by Peter Brown entitled *The Fame and Glory of England Vindicated* (1842), Lester replied in *The Condition and Fate of England* (1842). During Polk's administration he was consul at Genoa, 1842–47, an account of his service appearing in *My Consulship* (1853). His residence abroad gave opportunity for much study and writing, including translations from Machiavelli, Ceba, Alfieri, and Azeglio, all published in 1845. Following his return, he lived chiefly in the vicinity of New York, engaged in varied literary work, served as correspondent of the London *Times*, and was a prolific popular writer in biography, history, and allied fields. His *Life and Voyages of Americus Vespucius*, in collaboration with Andrew Foster, based partly on research in Italy and perhaps his best piece of investigation, was published in 1846 and passed through many editions, the last in 1903. Among his other books may be noted *Artists of America* (1846); *The Napoleonic Dynasty* (1852), with Edwin Williams; *Our First Hundred Years* (1874–75); *America's Advancement* (1876); and lives of Sam Houston (1855), Charles Sumner (1874), Tilden and Hendricks (1876), and Peter Cooper (1883). A complete list would number twenty-seven works, some in two volumes, and many of them republished. Though popular rather than erudite, and often compilations designed to meet demands of the hour, his books are generally clear and vigorous, showing genuine interest in the spread of knowledge and liberal ideas. During the Civil War he worked in Washington hospitals, recording his experiences in *The Light and Dark of the Rebellion* (1863). His wife, who survived him, was Ellen, daughter of Capt. Haley Brown of Sackett's Harbor, N. Y., whom he married Aug. 8, 1837. He had one child, Ellen Salisbury, who married Col. Sylvester Larned, and at whose home in Detroit Lester died of consumption after several years of increasing ill health. He was then engaged on a work to be called "The Great Explorers." In person he was of commanding presence, standing over six feet, possessed of unusual range of knowledge and gifts of conversation. During his long career he had known intimately Webster, Sumner, Frémont, Greeley, Tilden, the elder Bennett, and many other distinguished figures in public life.

[Sources include family material and Lester's writings; *Gen. Biog. Cat. of Auburn Theolog. Sem.* (1918); D. L. Phillips, *Griswold—A Hist.* (1929); *No. Am. Rev.*, Apr. 1846; *Detroit Free Press*, Jan. 30, 1890; *Sou. Quart. Rev.*, Jan. 1854; Lester in *Our First Hundred Years* quotes frequently from "My Life Note-Book, MS.," but this is not possessed by the family and if published has not been located.] A. W.

LESUEUR, CHARLES ALEXANDRE (Jan. 1, 1778–Dec. 12, 1846), artist, naturalist, distinguished in both France and the United States, was born at Le Havre, France, the son of Jean-Baptiste Denis Lesueur, an officer of the Admiralty, and his wife, Charlotte Geneviève Thieullent. He attended the Royal Military School at Beaumont-en-Auge from 1787 to 1796, and at eighteen was assigned to the dispatch boat *Le Hardi* for brief service in the English Channel. In his twenty-third year he secured through competitive examination a humble post with the scientific expedition sent out in 1800 by order of the First Consul to explore the coasts of Australia. His skill as an artist soon won him a place on the scientific staff, and with the young naturalist François Péron, his companion in the corvette *Géographe*, he formed an intimate friendship. The two remained with the expedition through hardships which decimated both scientific force and crew, and when they returned to France in 1804 brought to the Museum of Natural History at Paris a collection of more than 100,000 zoölogical specimens, including some 2,500 new species. A report by Cuvier credited Péron and Lesueur themselves with discovering more new species than all the other naturalists of the modern era up to their time. Lesueur collaborated at first with Péron and later with Louis Desaulx Freycinet, in preparing an account of the expedition, *Voyage de découvertes aux Terres Australes* (vols. I and II, 1807–16).

The death of Péron in 1810 and the final downfall of Napoleon in 1815 brought him sorrow and discouragement, and he welcomed the opportunity to become the traveling companion and coworker of William Maclure [*q.v.*], wealthy philanthropist and amateur geologist, with whom he left France in August 1815. After a survey of the West Indies in the winter of 1815–16, they reached New York May 10, 1816, proceeded thence to Philadelphia, and almost immediately set out on a tour of the interior. Their route took them through Delaware and a part of Maryland, to Mercersburg, Pa., across the mountains to Pittsburgh, north to Lake Erie, to Niagara Falls, thence across New York state past the Finger Lakes, and down the Mohawk Valley to Albany. They explored the shores of Lake George and Lake Champlain, went over into the Connecticut Valley, followed the river to the coast and the coast to Boston and Newburyport. Returning overland from Newburyport to Albany, they descended the Hudson by steamboat to Newburgh, and thence went by road to Philadelphia, arriving late in October. During the journey, while Maclure was making his geological observations, Lesueur sketched and painted, collected shells and fossils, and made notes for a work he hoped to produce on the fishes of North America.

In the following spring, after a brief field-trip into New Jersey, the period of his contract with Maclure expired, and for the next nine years he maintained himself in Philadelphia, by engraving and printing his own plates and by teaching drawing and painting. He was soon elected to membership in the American Philosophical Society and the Academy of Natural Sciences of Philadelphia, and was a frequent contributor to their publications. From 1817 to 1825 he was a curator of the Academy. In 1819 he worked for a time on the mapping of the northeast boundary between the United States and Canada; he visited Kentucky in 1821, and the upper Hudson in 1822 and 1823.

Maclure, meantime, had become interested in Robert Owen's projected community at New Harmony, Ind., and in 1825 Lesueur yielded to his persuasion and consented to join the venture. By the keel-boat *Philanthropist* from Pittsburgh, in which Thomas Say [*q.v.*], who became his close friend, Gerard Troost [*q.v.*], the mineralogist, Robert Owen, the founder, and his son, Robert Dale Owen [*q.v.*], were fellow passengers, he arrived in New Harmony in January 1826.

Here for twelve years he taught drawing in the community school, engraved plates for Say's important works on conchology and entomology, and produced several for his own *American Ichthyology,* which was abandoned after the publication of five plates in 1827. Traveling sometimes with Troost or Say, sometimes alone, from New Harmony as a base, he visited St. Louis in 1826, New Orleans repeatedly, Nashville, and the mountains of Tennessee, making notes, drawings, and sketches of the specimens he gathered, the geological formations he studied, the country itself, and the manners of the people.

In 1837 the gradual decline of the New Harmony community, his loneliness since the death of Say in 1834, and the warning that if he remained abroad his meager pension would cease, decided him to return to France, and for the next eight years he was in Paris, spending most of his time in the library or the museum, at work on his manuscripts and sketches. While here he also tried his hand at lithography. In 1845 he was called to Le Havre to become director of the newly founded Museum of Natural History there, and the last two years of his life were thus passed in his native city.

Lesueur was the first to study the fishes of the Great Lakes of North America. In addition to several papers on reptiles, crustaceans, and other subjects, he published twenty-nine papers on American fishes which are listed in Bashford Dean's bibliography (*post*). The most notable of all his American contributions is a monographic review of the family of suckers or *Catostomidae* (*Journal of the Academy of Natural Sciences of Philadelphia,* vol. I, 1817). He was one of the first in America of the school of systematic zoölogy which regards no fact as so unimportant that it need not be correctly ascertained and stated. "In showing his drawings," wrote a former pupil, "Lesueur generally offered a lens, that you might see every hair delineated." The same pupil, Prof. Richard Owen, also wrote (letter to D. S. J., Dec. 14, 1886), "In conversation with me, Agassiz once paid a high compliment to Lesueur's accomplishments in ichthyology, considering him then (as I inferred) the next best to himself in the United States."

[*Am. Jour. Sci. and Arts,* Sept. 1849; E. T. Hamy, *Les Voyages du Naturaliste Ch. Alex. Lesueur dans l'Amérique du Nord* (1904), and Mme. Adrien Loir, *Charles Alexandre Lesueur, Artiste et Savant Français* (1920), both based on Lesueur's MSS. and drawings in the Muséums d'Histoire Naturelle of Le Havre and Paris; D. S. Jordan, in *Pop. Sci. Mo.,* Feb. 1895; G. B. Lockwood, *The New Harmony Movement* (1905); Bashford Dean, *A Bibliog. of Fishes,* vol. II (1917); *Bull. Soc. Philomathique de Paris,* 8 ser. VIII (1896), pp. 15–33; G. B. Goode, in *Report of the U. S. Nat. Museum, 1897,* pt. II (1901); W. J. Youmans, *Pioneers of Science in America* (1896).] D. S. J.

LE SUEUR, PIERRE (*c.* 1657–*c.* 1705), explorer and trader, was one of the enterprising Frenchmen who opened up the Northwest and by his diplomacy with the Indians checked intertribal war and rapine. He was born in Artois, France, the son of Victor and Anne (Honneur) le Sueur. In 1679 or earlier he came to Canada as a servant or *donné* for the Jesuit missionaries. In this capacity he was sent to Sault Ste. Marie, where the lure of the fur trade tempted him to abandon the religious profession. As early as 1681 he was denounced as a *coureur de bois* and subjected to a fine; nevertheless he persisted in his adventures and by 1682 was among the Sioux Indians on the upper Mississippi. The early name for the Minnesota River —the St. Pierre—is believed to have been assigned in his honor.

Not much is known of Le Sueur's movements for six years after 1683; in 1689 he was with Perrot on the upper Mississippi, when possession of all Sioux territory was taken for France. The next year at Boucherville, Canada, Mar. 29, 1690, he married Marguerite Messier. When Duluth [*q.v.*] was recalled from the West, Le Sueur was sent in 1693 to negotiate with the Sioux and to persuade them to keep peace with the Chippewa. To further this end he built a fort on Madeline Island and in 1695 one at the end of the Brulé–St. Croix portage, Prairie Island, Mississippi River. Some time earlier he had built a fort on the west shore of Lake Pepin, opposite the mouth of Chippewa River. In 1695 he achieved his greatest diplomatic triumph: bringing to Canada a Sioux chief and his wife together with a Chippewa chief, so that the former might make an alliance with Governor Frontenac, and peace between the hereditary enemies might be publicly ratified.

Le Sueur next went to France to obtain permission to work a mine he thought he had discovered, but on the return voyage was captured by an English vessel off Newfoundland. Held prisoner for a time, he was released by the Peace of Ryswick, and made a second attempt to reach his mine, but before he succeeded his permit was confiscated and he was recalled. In 1700 he made a new effort to open his supposed mine; he joined Iberville [*q.v.*] in Louisiana and, going up the Mississippi in a sailing vessel, built Fort l'Huillier on a branch of the St. Pierre River, and left there a company to continue mining. The enterprise failed; the ore proved to be only colored earths, and Le Sueur's men abandoned the fort when attacked by hostile tribesmen. The site of this fort was marked in 1926 by the Minnesota Historical Society. In April 1702 Le Sueur returned to France to obtain new concessions. On his way back to Louisiana some years later he died on shipboard. His widow was living in Louisiana in May 1706.

[Little has been written on Le Sueur's career. The best outline is in *Bulletin des Recherches Historiques,* Mar. 1904; see also L. P. Kellogg, *The French Régime in Wis. and the Northwest* (1925), *passim*; W. W. Folwell, *A Hist. of Minn.,* I (1921), 38–42; his Mississippi voyage is narrated in Bénard de la Harpe, *Journal Historique de l'Établissement des Français à la Louisiane* (Paris, 1831), translated in J. G. Shea, *Early Voyages up and down the Mississippi* (1861). See also *Wis. Hist. Colls.,* XVI (1902), 177–93.] L. P. K.

LETCHER, JOHN (Mar. 29, 1813–Jan. 26, 1884), congressman and governor of Virginia, was born at Lexington, Rockbridge County, Va., the son of William Houston and Elizabeth (Davidson) Letcher and a great-grandson of Giles Letcher who emigrated to Virginia and settled in Goochland County. His father was first cousin to Gen. Sam Houston [*q.v.*]. He attended Washington College (later Washington and Lee University), graduating in 1833, and subsequently studied law. In 1839 he established himself in practice in Lexington and in the same year became editor of the *Valley Star,* a Democratic paper, recently established to promote the cause of Jacksonian Democracy in the Whig stronghold of Rockbridge County. From 1840 to 1844 he retired from his editorial duties to devote his time to law and politics, but from 1844 to 1850 he was again with the paper. In 1840, 1844, and 1848, he was active in the presidential campaigns, serving as a Democratic elector in 1848. He signed in 1847 the noted Ruffner pamphlet which advocated the abolition of slavery in that part of Virginia west of the Blue Ridge. He was a member of the state constitutional convention of 1850–51 and was a vigorous advocate of the white basis of representation in both houses of the legislature.

As a Democrat, he represented the eleventh Virginia district ("tenth legion of Democracy") in Congress from 1851 to 1859. A member of the committee on ways and means, he was a vigilant opponent of governmental extravagance, earning for himself the sobriquet of "Honest John Letcher, Watchdog of the Treasury." His views upon slavery had changed since 1847; in a public letter of 1858, he wrote: "At the time of the publication of that address [the Ruffner pamphlet] . . . I did regard slavery as a social and political evil. I did not regard it then or since as a moral evil for I was at that time, have been ever since, and am now the owner of slave property, by purchase, and, not by inheritance." Since 1851 he had convinced himself that his former views of the social and political evils of slavery were erroneous (*Valley Star,* July 15, 1858). In Congress he always upheld the rights of the South against Northern interference, though he never glorified slavery as an institution. Nominated by the Democratic party of Virginia, in 1859, for the governorship, he was elected by a small majority after a spirited campaign. His Whig opponents stigmatized him as an abolitionist; the *Lexington Gazette* referred to him as the candidate of the "free soil democracy of Virginia." In the presidential election of 1860, Letcher supported Stephen A. Douglas, and after the secession of the states of the lower South, he lent his support to the peace movement. He opposed the secession of Virginia until Lincoln called for troops to coerce the seceding states.

To the requisition upon Virginia for her quota of troops, Letcher replied to Secretary of War Cameron: "I have only to say that the militia of Virginia will not be furnished to the powers at Washington for any such use or purpose. . . . You have chosen to inaugurate civil war, and having done so we will meet it in a spirit as determined as the Administration has exhibited toward the South" (Munford, *post,* p. 282). As war governor he was a zealous supporter of the Confederacy and advocated the vigorous prosecution of the struggle until Southern independence should be won. At the close of the war he was confined for several months in the Old Capitol prison at Washington. Despite the fact that his private residence in Lexington was burned by Hunter's raiders in 1864, he advised the South to accept the results of the contest in good faith. Speaking to the cadets of the Virginia Military Institute, September 1866, he said: "Let the passions, the prejudices, and revengeful feelings . . . between the sections . . . be consigned, in solemn silence, to a common grave, there to sleep forever. . . . The past is gone and should be forgotten" (*Address . . . at the Virginia Military Institute,* 1866, pp. 11–12). After the war Letcher resumed his practice of law at Lexington and served two terms in the House of Delegates, 1875–76 and 1876–77. In early manhood, he had married Mary S. Holt of Augusta County, Va., and to them were born nine children.

[Oren F. Morton, *A Hist. of Rockbridge County* (1920); Beverley B. Munford, *Virginia's Attitude Toward Slavery and Secession* (1909); L. G. Tyler, *Hist. of Va.* (1924), vols. II and III; M. V. Smith, *Virginia . . . a Hist. of the Executives* (1893); S. R. Houston, *Brief Biog. Accounts of Many Members of the Houston Family* (1882), pp. 22, 47, 58–61; *Biog. Dir. Am. Cong.* (1928); *Valley Star,* July 15, 1858; *Lexington Gazette,* Mar. 10, 1859; *Richmond Dispatch,* Jan. 27, 1884.] W. G. B.

LETCHER, ROBERT PERKINS (Feb. 10, 1788–Jan. 24, 1861), Kentucky congressman, governor, was born in Goochland County, Va., the seventh of the twelve children of Stephen Giles and Betsey (Perkins) Letcher. His grandfather, Giles Letcher, was the first of the line in America. He was of Welsh descent, but at the time of his emigration the family was living in Ireland. About 1800 Stephen Giles Letcher moved his family to Kentucky, settling first near Harrodsburg and shortly afterward in Garrard County (M. B. Buford, *The Buford Family in America,* 1903, p. 116). The elder Letcher was a brick-maker and his sons worked with him in that trade. Robert Perkins attended the academy conducted by Joshua Fry, one of the most noted of the teachers of early Kentucky, and later studied law in the office of Humphrey Marshall. During the War of 1812 he saw a brief service as judge advocate in the regiment of Kentucky Mounted Volunteer Militia commanded by Lieut.-Col. James Allen (*Report of the Adjutant General of the State of Kentucky: Soldiers of the War of 1812,* 1891, p. 248). His term of enlistment came to an end in October 1812 and he did not reënlist. Instead of pursuing a military career he turned to politics and in 1813 was elected to represent Garrard County in the lower house of the state legislature. He was a representative in 1813, 1814, 1815, and 1817. In 1822 he was elected to Congress and was continuously reëlected till 1835. His influence in Congress was considerable, but it was due rather to his genial personality and to his intimacy with Henry Clay than to his own talents as a lawmaker. He had a prominent part in bringing about the Clay-Adams combination in the presidential election of 1825. Adams described him as a man of "moderate talents, good temper, playful wit, and shrewd sagacity" (C. F. Adams, *Memoirs of John Quincy Adams,* VIII, 1876, p. 336). In his last term in the House he was a member of the committee on foreign affairs.

Upon his return to Kentucky Letcher was elected to the state House of Representatives and continued to represent Garrard County in that body during 1836, 1837, and 1838. In December 1837 he was elected speaker of the House by a small majority and only after prolonged balloting. One year later he was unanimously reëlected to the same office. In 1840 he was elected governor of Kentucky on the Whig ticket. His chief service in this position consisted in halting, although he could not wholly stop, the ruinous policy of internal improvements on which the state was embarked. After the expiration of his term as governor in 1844, he remained a resident of Frankfort until August 1849 when he was appointed minister to Mexico. In this office he acquitted himself satisfactorily. Upon his return to Kentucky in 1852 he became again a candidate for Congress but was beaten by J. C. Breckinridge, his Democratic opponent. This was the end of his political career and thereafter he lived quietly in retirement until his death. Letcher was twice married: his first wife was Mary Oden Epps, his second, Charlotte Robertson who survived him. There were no children of either marriage.

[There is a sketch of Letcher in Alice E. Trabue, *A Corner in Celebrities* (1923), and one by Jennie C. Morton, in the *Reg. of Ky. State Hist. Soc.,* Jan. 1905. See also: Lewis and R. H. Collins, *Hist. of Ky.* (2 vols., 1874); *The Biog. Encyc. of Ky.* (1878); W. E. Connelley and E. M. Coulter, *Hist. of Ky.* (1922), vol. II; and the Kentucky legislative journals.] R. S. C.

LETCHWORTH, WILLIAM PRYOR (May 26, 1823–Dec. 1, 1910), philanthropist, was born in Brownville, N. Y., of Quaker ancestry, the son of Josiah and Ann (Hance) Letchworth and the great-grandson of John Letchworth who came to America from England in 1766. At the age of fifteen, after a common-school education, he began a business career, and ten years later was junior partner in the hardware firm of Pratt & Letchworth, Buffalo. He prospered and built up a comfortable fortune. In 1859 he purchased a large estate known as "Glen Iris," at Portage, N. Y. Rejected for the army during the Civil War, he allowed the New York volunteers to use his estate for a training camp. For some years history and archeology—especially the archeology of the Indians—were among his hobbies. In this connection he had the remains of Mary Jemison [*q.v.*], "the White Woman of the Genesee," removed in 1874 from the old Buffalo Creek Reservation to his estate. His collection of Indian antiquities eventually became the Genesee Valley Museum. He was an early member of the Buffalo Historical Society. He was also much interested in the fine arts and in 1871 was president of the Buffalo Academy of Fine Arts.

In 1869 he retired from business to devote himself to philanthropy. He refused to run for Congress as a Republican, although assured of election, but accepted a commissionership on the state board of charities. In this capacity his initial effort was directed toward removing normal children from the Erie County Poorhouse. After agitating the subject in the press, he succeeded by 1874 in having many of them interned temporarily in local asylums, and was largely instrumental in securing legislation (1875, 1876) prohibiting the confinement of normal children between the ages of three and sixteen in the state almshouses. This movement was later extended to promote the adoption of such children by private families, and became widely known as the Erie County System. In 1878 Letchworth was made president of the state board of charities.

With the problem of the dependent child on the way to solution, he now turned his attention to the delinquent child and the insane poor, and in 1880 began an extensive tour of Europe to study European methods of dealing with these problems. His copious findings on the second subject were published in 1889 under the title, *The Insane in Foreign Countries.* In 1883 he read a paper before the Tenth Annual National Conference of Charities and Corrections on the proper grouping of dependent and incorrigible children and was elected as president of the following conference (October 1884). In 1884, as a result of his efforts, manual training was introduced into the Western House of Refuge at Rochester, the name of the institution being changed to State Industrial School. In his work for the insane poor, also, he brought about several innovations. He pointed out some superiorities of European institutions, worked to secure state control of all insane persons and to establish farm colonies, and in 1886 aided in the addition of a new state insane asylum at Ogdensburg to the seven already established. In the early nineties he changed his objective from the insane to the epileptic, and in 1893, through his initiative, the tract of land known as Sonyea owned by the Shakers near Mount Morris was purchased by the state as a colony for epileptics. It was opened formally in 1896, as Craig Colony. In 1900 he published *Care and Treatment of Epileptics.* A stroke of apoplexy in 1903 made him an invalid for the rest of his life. When "Glen Iris" was threatened by the demands of electric power companies in 1906 he deeded the tract to the State of New York, and it was henceforth known as Letchworth Park. In 1909 the new Eastern New York State Custodial Asylum in Rockland County was renamed Letchworth Village. In addition to some sixty-five papers or reports on matters connected with charities and corrections, he published a *Sketch of the Life of Samuel F. Pratt* (1874), and issued an edition (1898) of James E. Seaver's *Narrative of the Life of Mary Jemison* with illustrations and supplementary material collected by himself.

[J. N. Larned, *The Life and Work of William Pryor Letchworth* (1912); Stephen Smith, *An Appreciation of the Life of William Pryor Letchworth* (1911); *Twelfth Ann. Report, 1907, of the Am. Scenic and Hist. Preservation Soc.* (1907); *Who's Who in America,* 1910–11; *Who's Who in N. Y.,* 1909; *N. Y. Times,* Dec. 3, 1910.] E. P.

LETTERMAN, JONATHAN (Dec. 11, 1824–Mar. 15, 1872), organizer of the field medical service of the Union Army in the Civil War, was born in Canonsburg, Washington County, Pa. His father was Jonathan Letterman, a physician, and his mother was a daughter of Craig Ritchie of Canonsburg. His early education, by a private tutor, was followed by a course in Jefferson College in his native town, from which he was graduated in 1845. He received his medical education at Jefferson Medical College, Philadelphia, where, in 1849, he received the degree of M.D. Immediately following his graduation he passed the examination before the United States Army examining board in New York and was appointed assistant surgeon.

During the following twelve years his service was largely on the western and southwestern frontiers, with troops engaged in intermittent warfare with Seminoles, Navajos, Apaches, and Utes. The ingenuity and the improvisations necessary in the treatment, care, and transportation of the wounded under the difficult conditions incident to such warfare was an excellent training for the larger problems which were to confront him later. At the outbreak of the Civil War in 1861 he was assigned to duty with the Army of the Potomac; in June 1862 he was promoted to major and surgeon and was appointed medical director of that army, then under the command of Major-General McClellan. In this position he displayed a remarkable degree of administrative ability. He completely reorganized the field medical service, created an effective mobile hospital organization, and instituted an ambulance service for the evacuation of battle casualties. This organization functioned so effectively at Chancellorsville and later at Antietam and Gettysburg that it was adopted for use throughout the Union army; in fact, the basic plan of field hospitalization and evacuation devised by Letterman has influenced that service in every modern army. He spent the latter part of the war as inspector of hospitals in the department of the Susquehanna. Resigning his army commission in December 1864, he took up his residence in San Francisco, Cal. In 1866 he published his *Medical Recollections of the Army of the Potomac.*

Letterman was married in October 1863 to Mary Lee, of Maryland, to whose home he came, worn from the fatigue of the battlefield of Antietam. Her sudden death in November 1867 was a crushing blow from which he never fully recovered. The consequent mental depression, coupled with a chronic intestinal trouble, kept him a semi-invalid until his death in his forty-eighth year. By a general order of the War Department, Nov. 13, 1911, the large military hospital in the Presidio of San Francisco was designated the Letterman General Hospital, in honor of the man who revolutionized the system of care of the wounded upon the battlefield.

[B. A. Clements, *Memoir of Jonathan Letterman* (1883), reprinted from *Jour. Military Service Inst.*, New York, Sept. 1883; J. T. Smith, "Review of Life and Work of Jonathan Letterman," *Johns Hopkins Hospital Bull.*, Aug. 1916; H. A. Kelly and W. L. Burrage, *Am. Medic. Biogs.* (1920); *Daily Morning Bull.* and *Daily Alta California* (San Francisco), Mar. 16, 1872.] J. M. P—n.

LEUPP, FRANCIS ELLINGTON (Jan. 2, 1849–Nov. 19, 1918), journalist, was born in New York City, the son of John P. and Emeline M. (Loop) Leupp. Graduating from Williams College in 1870 and from the Columbia Law School in 1872, he served under Bryant and Parke Godwin as assistant editor of the New York *Evening Post* till Bryant's death in 1878. After editing a memorial volume upon Bryant, in that same year he bought an interest in the Syracuse *Herald* and became its editor. In 1885 he removed to Washington to become a free-lance contributor to the *Evening Post,* and upon the death of its regular correspondent, E. B. Wright, in 1889, was placed in charge of its Washington bureau, representing at the same time the *Nation.* This post he held till 1904. From 1892 to 1895 he also edited *Good Government,* the official organ of the National Civil Service Reform League.

Leupp's chief reputation was made by his articles for the *Evening Post* and the *Nation,* which gave him for some years an almost unrivaled reputation among Washington correspondents for expertness, alertness, and honesty. A man of culture and breeding, he gained the confidence of leading public men, to whom he often supplied facts or advice of value. His habit was to make a daily round of the departments, Congress, and the White House. He gathered his material with great thoroughness, and he was painstaking in his verification of statements and in buttressing his opinions. Till the Venezuelan message brought a rupture of their close relations he was regarded as Cleveland's mouthpiece, often quoting him on public questions; and later he was intimate with Roosevelt, his book *The Man Roosevelt* (1904) being a record of their friendship. He particularly liked to write compressed, pungent sketches of public men, often spending six months on an essay. Frequently he expressed opinions at variance with those of the *Evening Post's* editorial page. As the years passed and his background of knowledge grew his articles became more philosophical and he dealt more fully with the play and counter-play of forces behind the scenes in Washington. Even after his retirement from the *Evening Post* he contributed occasionally to it and to the *Nation,* and his "National Miniatures" (1918) was a final compilation of *Nation* vignettes. He wrote also for the *Outlook,* and in the last week of 1911 published in it the most important interview which William Howard Taft gave out while president.

From early manhood Leupp took a keen interest in the Indians, visiting the reservations in New York state and mastering the literature upon Indian life. In 1886 he made an extended Western trip, visiting reservations as far as the Pacific Coast and spending several months with different tribes; and he repeated this excursion in 1889. He was frequently consulted by members of Congress on the Indian question. In 1895, during consideration of a treaty with the Utes for opening their land to settlement, Secretary Hoke Smith sent him to the Southern Ute reservation as confidential agent. In 1896–97 he was a member of the Board of Indian Commissioners and made repeated trips to visit Western tribes and schools and to talk with Indian chiefs. Roosevelt sent him in 1902 to investigate accusations against the officials in charge of the Kiowa, Comanche, and Apache Indians, and his report was printed as a public document (*Senate Document 26,* 58 Cong., 2 Sess.). His years as Indian Commissioner, 1905–09, witnessed much constructive work for Indian betterment. The aims and spirit of his labors are reflected in *The Indian and His Problem* (1910), which deals with the larger relations of the Indian to legislation and administration, and *In Red Man's Land* (1914), which treats of the Indian as an individual. On his retirement he devoted himself to general literary work. His habit of exploring little-known corners of the capital gave him materials for his *Walks About Washington* (1915). He had married Ada Lewis Murdock of New York City on Oct. 13, 1874, and on his death in Washington left three daughters and one son.

[*Who's Who in America,* 1918–19; "Washington Correspondents," the *Nation,* Nov. 30, 1918; *Evening Post* (N. Y.), *N. Y. Times,* Nov. 20, 1918.] A.N.

LEUTZE, EMANUEL (May 24, 1816–July 18, 1868), historical and portrait painter, was born at Gmünd, Württemberg; but his family moved to the United States soon after his birth and settled in Fredericksburg, Va. His father was "an honest but stern mechanic," whose prime motive in leaving his native land was political discontent. The family shortly moved from Virginia to Philadelphia, where Emanuel received his first instruction in drawing. His early work in painting, done at about twenty-one, consisted of portraits and figure-pieces. In 1840 his work gained for him the patronage and encouragement of Edward L. Carey and other influential Philadelphians, and he was thus enabled to go to Europe for further training in painting. He proceeded to Düsseldorf in 1841 and became a pupil of Karl Friedrich Lessing. His attention was now turned to historical painting, and his first serious essay in this line was "Columbus Before the Council of Salamanca," which was so well received by the authorities of the academy that at their instance it was bought by the Art Union of Düsseldorf. After this success he made a trip to the Swabian Alps, the Tyrol, and Italy. Returning to Düsseldorf, he married the daughter of a German officer and remained there for nearly twenty years. In 1859 he returned to the United States, where an important government commission and numerous private orders awaited him, and where he resided for the rest of his life, dividing his time between New York and Washington.

He had begun in Germany and continued in America a long series of large historical compositions, for the most part dealing with American subjects. The best-known and most important of these are his "Washington Crossing the Delaware," in the Metropolitan Museum of Art, New York, and "Westward the Course of Empire Takes its Way," on the wall of the west staircase of the House of Representatives in the Capitol at Washington. Among many other historical paintings may be mentioned "Washington at Monmouth," "The Landing of the Norsemen," "The Settlement of Maryland," "The Storming of Teocalli, Mexico," and "Cromwell and Milton," the last-named piece belonging to the Corcoran Gallery, Washington.

In common with most historical paintings, Leutze's work is labored, conventional, and in some cases stilted. The immense panel in the Capitol, illustrating the pioneering spirit and the conquering of the Far West, is a failure from the decorative point of view. Its color is dry and disagreeable. The painter had spared no pains, however, to make it veracious and spirited; he had traveled to the Far West to study the scenery and to Germany to consult Kaulbach on the best technical methods to employ in executing a mural painting. His effort to combine history and allegory in the one composition resulted in inevitable confusion, which was increased by the hard realism of the landscape setting, and the circumstance that the view embraced the Rocky Mountains on the one hand and the Pacific Ocean on the other. The method employed in the execution of the panel is interesting. The painting was done directly on the wall, on a thin layer of cement composed of crushed stone and lime. The watercolor was applied to this ground and fixed by a spray of water-glass solution. The artist received $20,000 for the work.

His most famous painting, "Washington Crossing the Delaware," has been extensively reproduced in school textbooks. The studies for the floating ice on the river, however, were made in the painter's Düsseldorf studio overlooking the Rhine. An ironical article in a newspaper referred to the work as "Washington Crossing the Rhine" (*St. Louis Globe-Democrat,* Mar. 3, 1918). The pose of Washington is undeniably theatrical. Moreover, to stand up in a small craft making its way through formidable ice floes would appear to be a needless invitation to disaster. The flag is an anachronism. Few modern historical pictures are more tumid and few have been more popular in this country. Among Leutze's portraits may be mentioned those of General Grant, Nathaniel Hawthorne, General Burnside, and the artist himself. The Hawthorne was painted in Washington in 1862 and now belongs to the Thomas B. Clarke collection. Leutze died in Washington.

[H. T. Tuckerman, *Book of the Artists* (1867); Samuel Isham, *Hist. of Am. Painting* (1905); Charles E. Fairman, *Art and Artists of the Capitol of the U. S. of America* (1927); Helen W. Henderson, *The Art Treasures of Washington* (1912); Lorinda M. Bryant, *Am. Pictures and their Painters* (1917); Charles H. Caffin, *The Story of Am. Painting* (1907); Jas. T. Fields, *Yesterdays with Authors* (1872); *Lit. Digest,* Mar. 16, 1918; *Mentor,* July 1926; *Lippincott's Mag.,* Nov. 1868; *Evening Star* (Washington), July 20, 1868.]

W. H. D.

LEVERETT, JOHN (1616–Mar. 16, 1679), governor of Massachusetts, was the son of Thomas and Anne (Fisher) Leverett and was baptized July 7, 1616, in St. Botolph's Parish, Boston, England. The family appears to have been of fair social rank and to have had some property. In 1629 Thomas received a grant of land on the Muscongus in New England, and in 1633 he emigrated with his wife and three children to Massachusetts. He had occupied various offices in old Boston, being alderman when he left. John became a freeman May 13, 1640. Sometime previous to that he had married Hannah Hudson who reached Boston with her parents in 1635. By her he had four children. She died in 1646 and in 1647 he married Sarah Sedgwick, who survived him and by whom he had fourteen children. He appears to have been prosperous and to have been engaged in foreign trade, for in 1646 it was noted that he and Edward Gibbons had lost a ship off Virginia valued at £2,000. He had also become interested in public affairs and soon after he became a freeman he was sent with Edward Hutchinson on a mission to the Indian chief Miantonomo. In 1644 he went to England and took part in the war, receiving a command in the Parliamentary army and gaining distinction. He had returned to Boston, Mass., by 1648, and from 1651 to 1653 he was a member of the General Court. In 1652 he was one of the commissioners sent to Maine to proclaim the settlements there subject to the jurisdiction of Massachusetts. He was also in 1651 one of the selectmen for the town of Boston. In 1653 he was appointed colonial agent in England and sailed sometime before 1655, remaining in London until 1662. On his return he was again elected to the General Court for the years 1663–65, being speaker of the House for a part of that time. From 1665 to 1670 he was a member of the Council, and from 1671 to 1673 deputy governor.

Leverett had always liked military life and in 1639 had joined the Ancient and Honorable Artillery Company of which he was a member for thirty-two years. In 1663 he was made major-general of all the Massachusetts forces and so remained until elected governor of the colony in 1673. He continued to be annually elected to the governorship until his death in 1679. His tenure as governor is noteworthy as including the period of King Philip's War, in which he rendered excellent service. It is also of importance as marking the beginning of the activities of Edward Randolph who was sent from England to enforce the laws of trade. Leverett refused to take the oath to administer them and had a long struggle with the royal official. Throughout his career he was constantly called upon for special services: he was one of the commissioners sent to confer with Stuyvesant at New York over the difficulties with the Dutch (1653); he led the force which expelled the French from the Penobscot (1654); and he was one of the four to whom was confided the custody of the colony charter in the troubled year 1664. It has always been claimed that he was knighted, though there is much confusion as to why and when (*Memoir, post,* pp. 81ff.). The date agreed upon by the family historians is 1676 and the reason, his services in the Indian War, though it seems odd that Charles II should thus honor the governor of the recalcitrant Massachusetts. It is said he never used the title, and in the long epitaph on his tomb he is described as "Esquire."

[Chas. E. Leverett, *A Memoir . . . of Sir John Leverett, Knt., Gov. of Mass., 1673–79* (1856); N. B. Shurtleff, *A Geneal. Memoir of the Family of Elder Thos. Leverett of Boston* (1850), and *Records of the Gov. and Company of the Mass. Bay in New Eng.* (5 vols., 1853–54); J. B. Moore, *Memoirs of Am. Govs.*, vol. I (1846); Samuel Waldo, *A Defense of the title of . . . John Leverett . . . to a Tract of Land in the Eastern Parts of the Province of the Mass. Bay, Commonly called Muscongus Lands* (1736); R. N. Tappan, "Edward Randolph," *Prince Soc. Pubs.*, vols. XXIV–XXVIII (1898–99); *Mass. Hist. Soc. Colls.*, 4 ser. II (1854).]

J. T. A.

LEVERETT, JOHN (Aug. 25, 1662–May 3, 1724), president of Harvard College, was the eldest son of Hudson Leverett, a disreputable attorney who was the eldest son of Gov. John Leverett [*q.v.*]. His mother was Sarah Peyton (or Payton). From the Boston Latin School John entered Harvard College, graduated A.B. in 1680, and A.M. in 1683. His student notebook includes selections from the Anacreontics of Cowley, a Latin salutatory oration to Governor Andros, and syllogistic disputations. In 1685 he was chosen fellow and tutor of the College, which during the next fifteen years (President Mather being an absentee) was governed and instructed largely by Leverett and William Brattle [*q.v.*]. These young men, while insisting on "Righteousness, Faith and Charity," were less concerned with religious forms or polity (Nathanael Appleton, funeral sermon, *A Great Man Fallen in Israel,* 1724, p. 30), than with preparing students for life. One pupil afterward declared that they had "made more Proselytes to the Church of England than any 2 men ever did that liv'd in America" (Henry Newman to Mr. Taylor, Mar. 29, 1714, S. P. C. K. MSS., London); and another spoke of the "enlarged catholic Spirit" cherished in him by Mr. Leverett (Ebenezer Turell, *The Life and Character of the Rev. Benjamin Colman,* 1749, p. 123). Hence the tutors were accused of subversive teaching. Leverett's support of his former pupil Benjamin Colman [*q.v.*] opened a breach between him and the Mathers; and in a shake-up of the college government, occurring in 1700, he was dropped out.

Leverett had already prepared for this eventuality by studying law, and by entering politics as representative from Cambridge, in 1696–97. One of his pupils complained of being obliged to recite "at five o'clock in the winter mornings that Mr. L. might seasonably attend the General Court at Boston" (Sibley, *post,* III, 183). In 1699 he was appointed justice of the peace (W. H. Whitmore, *The Massachusetts Civil List,*

1870, p. 138), and began practising as attorney (Samuel Sewall, *Diary,* I, 495); in 1700 he was chosen speaker of the House. Gov. Joseph Dudley [*q.v.*], an old friend, appointed him in 1702 judge of the superior court, and judge of probate for Middlesex County. Leverett was elected to the Provincial Council in 1706, as of Eastern Maine, where he had inherited a great land grant, the Muscongus Patent of 1630; in order to procure capital for settling this tract, he organized the Lincolnshire Company in 1719. Governor Dudley sent him on three missions: in 1704 to the Iroquois; down East in 1707 to rally the dispirited Port Royal expedition—a forlorn hope indeed; and to Governor Lovelace at New York in 1709. In the meantime Leverett's friends had recovered control of the Harvard Corporation, which on Oct. 28, 1707, elected him president, eight votes to five. This choice provoked a political commotion. Governor Dudley only obtained the customary legislative grant of £150 for the president's salary, by reviving the supposedly defunct College Charter of 1650, which flattered the legislature and eliminated from the Corporation those fellows opposed to Leverett. After the deal went through, he was inaugurated president Jan. 14, 1707/08.

Leverett was the first lawyer and judge to hold the Harvard presidency. Widely cultivated, comparatively broad-minded, and impressive in person, he governed the College "with great Sweetness and Candor . . . tempered with Convenient Severity" (S. Sewall, in Sibley, *post,* III, 191). Few alterations were made in the formal curriculum; but students were introduced to recent Anglican divinity, to Henry More's *Enchiridion Ethicum;* and were offered instruction in French. Colman wrote that after residing at Oxford and Cambridge he could assert that "no Place of Education can well boast a more free air than our little *College* may" (Turell, *op. cit.,* p. 123). Student life grew gayer, the first college club and periodical were started, and Commencements became uproarious. These tendencies raised a cry of idleness and extravagance against the students, in which young Benjamin Franklin joined (*New England Courant,* Nos. 41 and 44, 1722). Cotton Mather, who called Leverett the "pretended president," and the *"infamous drone"* (Quincy, I, 523–24, 343), accused the students of reading "plays, novels, empty and vicious pieces of poetry, and even Ovid's Epistles, which have a vile tendency to corrupt good manners" (Quincy, *post,* I, 559). Numbers increased so that Massachusetts Hall had to be built. President Leverett was elected in 1713 fellow of the Royal Society (Thomas Thomson, *History of the Royal Society,* 1812, p. xxxiii), to which Thomas Robie, one of the tutors, contributed astronomical and other scientific observations. Leverett was energetic in securing to the College former benefactions which had been neglected by his predecessors, and in procuring new ones: notably those of Thomas Hollis, whose professorship of divinity (1721) was kept free from religious tests by the determined stand of the president and fellows.

From 1713, when the College Corporation refused to appoint Governor Dudley's son to the vacant treasurership (Quincy, I, 206–07), Leverett had a clerico-political fight on his hands. Judge Sewall accused him of neglecting religious exercises (*Diary,* III, 202–03); Cotton Mather instigated an investigation of the College in 1723. The Corporation, in order to protect themselves, had coöpted liberal divines to vacancies in their fellowship, instead of following the ancient custom of admitting college tutors to the governing body. This gave the Mather and Dudley factions a popular political issue which they improved against the College, and only by subtle politics and the support of Governor Shute was Leverett able to prevent a complete shake-up. He died suddenly on May 3, 1724 (Samuel Sewall, *Diary,* III, 336–37). Benjamin Wadsworth succeeded to the presidency, and continued the liberal policy inaugurated by Leverett. "To his firmness, and that of his associates . . . the institution is probably in a great measure indebted for its religious freedom at this day" (Quincy, *post,* I, 324). Leverett married first, in 1697, the widow Margaret Berry, daughter of President Rogers (most of their children died young); and second, the widow Sarah (Crisp) Harris, who bore him no children but lived to have two more husbands.

[See J. L. Sibley, *Biog. Sketches of Grads. of Harvard Univ.,* III (1885), 180–98, where references to funeral sermons and other sources will be found; Josiah Quincy, *The Hist. of Harvard Univ.* (1840); Harvard Corporation Records, in *Colonial Soc. of Mass., Pubs.,* vols. XV and XVI (1925); *Diary of Samuel Sewall 1674–1729* (3 vols., 1878–82); *Journals* of the House of Representatives of Massachusetts, vols. I–VI; manuscript Commonplace book in Massachusetts Historical Society; Colman MSS., *Ibid.*; manuscript Diary (so-called, really his private record of Corporation meetings, 1707–23), in University Archives; a remnant of Leverett's personal papers in Vol. I of the Ewer MSS., New-England Historic Genealogical Society; Henry Newman's Letters in Archives of the Society for Propagation of Christian Knowledge, London. Leverett left no published works, and no portrait of him has been traced.]

S. E. M.

LEVERING, JOSEPH MORTIMER (Feb. 20, 1849–Apr. 4, 1908), Moravian bishop, historian, son of Lewis Alexander and Sophia (Hauser) Levering, was born in Hardin County, Tenn. On his father's side he was descended from a line of Moravian missionaries, settled in America during the eighteenth century. In 1852 his family moved to West Salem, Ill., and in 1856 to Olney, where he attended private school and prepared for college. In 1870 he entered the Moravian College and Theological Seminary at Bethlehem, Pa., where he distinguished himself for unusual ability, receiving both the arts and divinity degrees in 1874. After teaching for a few months at Nazareth Hall, Nazareth, Pa., he was ordained deacon (Dec. 20, 1874) and in January 1875 assumed the pastorate of the new congregation at Uhrichsville, Ohio. On May 21, 1876, he was ordained presbyter and three years later was called to the pastorate at Lakemills, Wis. He remained there until 1883 and then entered upon the pastorate of the church at Bethlehem, Pa., the largest congregation of his denomination in the United States. On Sept. 30, 1888, he was consecrated bishop at Bethlehem by Bishops A. A. Reinke and H. J. Van Vleck. In 1901 continued ill health forced him to retire temporarily from active work, but he devoted his leisure to an intensive study of the Moravians in America, and in 1903 published *A History of Bethlehem, Pennsylvania, 1741–1892,* in commemoration of the sesqui-centennial of the leading Moravian settlement in America. This huge volume of over eight hundred pages is far more than an ordinary town history. It is a cross-section of the whole story of the growth of the United States as revealed in the wealth of manuscript letters and reports of Moravian agents and missionaries preserved in the Archives of the Bethlehem church. It is especially strong in its revelation of the social and economic forces that were at work in the land. The author's distaste for the flimsy and trivial led him to avoid the pitfall that traps so many local historians—he included in the book no notices of individuals, as such, apart from the exposition of his theme. He prepared, also, many articles and papers for special occasions and anniversaries, most of them published in the proceedings of the Moravian Historical Society, of which, from 1895 to 1908, he was president. In 1903 he was elected president of the governing board of the Moravian Church, and in that capacity won distinction for his executive ability and tact. He died suddenly, Apr. 4, 1908. He was married, June 6, 1876, to Martha Augusta Whitesell of Bethlehem, who, with two daughters, survived him.

[Manuscript obituary, Moravian Archives, Bethlehem, Pa.; *Trans. Moravian Hist. Soc.*, vol. VIII (1909); John Levering, *Levering Family Hist. and Geneal.* (1897); *Bethlehem Daily Times,* Apr. 4, 1908; *Pub. Ledger* (Phila.), Apr. 5, 1908; *The Moravian,* Apr. 8, 1908.]

A. G. R.

LEVERMORE, CHARLES HERBERT (Oct 15, 1856–Oct. 20, 1927), educator and peace advocate, was born in Mansfield, Conn., the son of a Congregational clergyman, Rev. Aaron Russell Livermore, and his wife, Mary Gay (Skinner). His family in both branches was deep-rooted in the soil of his native state, his father being a direct descendant of John Livermore, who emigrated from Ipswich, England, to Boston and was one of the first proprietors of the town of Wethersfield, Conn.; and his mother, from Henry Wolcott, one of the first settlers in Hartford. Shortly after his graduation from college Charles adopted the early spelling of the family name. Educated as a boy at the Hopkins Grammar School, New Haven, he went to Yale, where he received the degree of A.B. in 1879. He then entered upon thirty years of teaching and study, serving as principal of Guilford Institute (1879–83), doing graduate work at Johns Hopkins University (1883–85), teaching history in the Hopkins Grammar School (1885–86), in the Massachusetts Institute of Technology (1888–93), and holding the position of principal in Adelphi Academy, Brooklyn, N. Y. (1893–96). He then became president of Adelphi College, Brooklyn, which he founded in 1896 and served until 1912.

His retirement from Adelphi, which was followed by a year of rest and recuperation in the South, marked his withdrawal from the field of education, and his definite entrance into activities in behalf of world peace, which became henceforth the work, almost the passion, of his life. For four years (1913–17) he was associated with the World Peace Foundation in Boston, during the last two, as acting director. In 1917 he became secretary of the New York Peace Society; in 1919, of the World Court and the League of Nations Union; and in 1922, of the American Association for International Co-operation. In 1923 he joined with other distinguished peace leaders in organizing the League of Nations Non-Partisan Association, which he served as vice-president until his death. During this period, after the establishment of the League of Nations, he prepared and published annually a complete survey of the work of the League for each current year, thorough, critical, and extremely useful. His learning, skill, devotion, and high statesmanship as a peace worker earned dramatic and distinguished recognition in 1924, when he won the American Peace Award of $50,000 offered by Edward W. Bok for "the best practicable plan by which the United States may co-operate with other nations to achieve and preserve the peace of the world." Several hundred thousand plans were submitted in this contest, of which 22,165 met the conditions and were considered by the judges. Levermore's plan emphasized the two "substantial provisions" that (1) the United States should adhere to the Permanent Court of International Justice, and (2) should extend its cooperation with the League of Nations, "without becoming a member of the League . . . as at present constituted." He received the prize from Hon. John W. Davis at a great mass meeting in Philadelphia, on Feb. 4, 1924. The enormous publicity which accompanied the granting of this award brought its winner fame and acclaim throughout the world. Invitations for articles and addresses were showered upon him; but a long-postponed dream of seeing Europe and studying peace in the area of war took him abroad, and he spent two years in England, France, Italy, and Switzerland, with visits to Athens, Constantinople, and North Africa. On his return, he went to California, in anticipation of a journey to the Orient, and stopped for a short stay in Berkeley. Here he died suddenly of arteriosclerosis of the brain. He was survived by his wife, Mettie Norton Tuttle, whom he married Sept. 4, 1884, two sons, and three daughters.

Zealous and thorough study made him a scholar of first-class attainment in many fields. Special knowledge of history and politics, coupled with utter devotion to his task, and a fine dignity and power of personality, constituted his equipment for success as a leader in the cause of peace. His publications disclose the avocations as well as the vocations of his life: *The Republic of New Haven* (1886); *Political History Since 1815* (1889, revised edition 1893), with D. R. Dewey; *The Academy Song Book* (1895); *The Students' Hymnal* (1911); *Forerunners and Competitors of the Pilgrims and Puritans* (2 vols., 1912), *The American Song Book* (1917); *Life of Samuel Train Dutton* (1922); and numerous magazine articles and reviews.

[W. E. Thwing, *The Livermore Family of America* (1902); *Yale Univ. Obit. Record*, 1928; F. W. Williams, *A Hist. of the Class of Seventy-nine, Yale College* (1906); *The Winning Plan Selected by the Jury of the Am. Peace Award* (1924); *N. Y. Times*, Feb. 4, 1924; *Who's Who in America*, 1926–27; *Boston Transcript*, Nov. 4, 1927; *San Francisco Examiner*, Oct. 21, 1927; *San Francisco Chronicle*, Oct. 22, 1927.]

J. H. H.

LEVIN, LEWIS CHARLES (Nov. 10, 1808–Mar. 14, 1860), lawyer, editor, congressman, was born in Charleston, S. C. He attended South Carolina College at Columbia until 1827 and about 1828 removed to Woodville, Miss., where he taught school and read law. After being wounded in a duel he left Woodville, became a "peripatetic law practitioner" in Maryland, Kentucky, and Louisiana, and in 1838 settled in Philadelphia where he was admitted to the bar. There he was first conspicuous as a temperance speaker and as editor of the *Temperance Advocate*. Next attracted to the Native-American movement, he took a prominent part in the formation of that party in Philadelphia (1843) and edited and published the *Sun*, a penny daily and Native-American organ. In the Philadelphia riots of 1844 he counseled moderation and respect for the property rights of Catholics, in order to maintain the honor of the party. In both the state convention at Harrisburg (Feb. 22, 1845) and the first Native-American national convention at Philadelphia (1845) he was untiring in his efforts to extend the party organization.

The high feeling against Catholics and the foreign-born crystallized by the riots of 1844 carried Levin into Congress where for three terms (1845–51) he preached nativism with almost fanatical zeal. Envisaging the country "on the very verge of overthrow by the impetuous force of invading foreigners" (Dec. 18, 1845), he pleaded for restricted immigration and stricter naturalization laws (*Congressional Globe*, 29 Cong., 1 Sess., App., pp. 46–50). Nativism seems to have been an obsession which colored his views on every question before the House. The Oregon struggle represented an attempt by England to implant feudalism on American soil. The sending of a chargé to Rome was "a proposition to unite this free Republic with absolute Rome" (*Ibid.*, 30 Cong., 1 Sess., App., p. 438). He would have none but native Americans serve in a proposed regiment of riflemen, and he opposed discontinuing the recruiting service because of the nation's internal enemies. He was a high-tariff advocate, a rabid expansionist, and as chairman of the committee on naval affairs labored indefatigably for the dry dock at Philadelphia. Although he was popular in his congressional district and supported by the Whigs for Congress in 1848, the disgruntled Native Americans took enough votes from the combined Whig-Native-American ticket in 1850 to defeat him. After leaving Congress he continued his law practice. Always loyal to nativism, in a broadside, *To the Americans of Pennsylvania* (1856), he urged the electorate to vote "a pure, unadulterated American Fillmore ticket," and to wash its hands of Black Republicanism, the instrument of the Pope. Before the next presidential campaign he was in his grave, a victim of insanity. A contemporary, not overly sympathetic, regarded Levin as "one of the most brilliant and unscrupulous orators" he had ever heard and doubted "whether during his day any person in either party of the State surpassed him on the hustings" (A. K. McClure, *Old Time Notes of Pennsylvania,* 1905, I, pp. 89, 90). He was married twice: first, to Anne Hays of Kentucky, and after her death to Julia Gist, a widow, of Philadelphia.

[Nothing is known of Levin's ancestry, though there is a reference to a Lewis Levin, Sr., in B. A. Elzas, *The Old Jewish Cemeteries at Charleston, S. C.* (1903). Family records were destroyed in the Charleston earthquake of 1886. See *Biog. Dir. Am. Cong.* (1928); H. S. Morais, *The Jews of Phila.* (1894); B. A. Elzas, *The Jews of S. C.* (1905); J. T. Scharf and Thompson Westcott, *Hist. of Phila.* (3 vols., 1884); *Niles' Nat. Reg.*, July 13, 1844; *Proc. of the Native Am. State Convention Held at Harrisburg, Pa., Feb. 22, 1845; Pub. Ledger* (Phila.), and *Phila. Daily News,* Mar. 15, 1860.] J. H. P.

LEVINS, THOMAS C. (Mar. 14, 1789–May 5, 1843), Roman Catholic priest, was born in ancient Drogheda, Ireland, the son of Patrick and Margaret Levins. He studied at the famous Jesuit institutions of Clongowes, Dublin, and Stonyhurst, Lancashire, England, a fact which in itself indicated that his family was comfortably circumstanced. Joining the Society of Jesus, he was apparently further trained on the Continent before being ordered to Georgetown College, Georgetown, D. C., where for three years he taught natural philosophy and mathematics (1822–25). Withdrawing from the Society, he accepted the invitation of Dr. John Power [*q.v.*] to enter the diocese of New York, where he served as an assistant at St. Peter's Church and as pastor of old St. Patrick's. A writer of ability with a Celtic taste for journalism, he associated himself with the newly founded *Truth Teller* and later (1833) became a joint editor with Rev. J. A. Schneller of the *New York Weekly Register and Catholic Diary,* a position which he held until the publication was merged with the Philadelphia *Catholic Herald* in 1836. Irreproachable in character but of a sour, critical disposition, he ran afoul of Bishop John Dubois [*q.v.*] who in 1834 suspended him for technical disobedience. Apparently a leader of the Irish faction, he resented a Frenchman as his ordinary. He was popular in the diocese, however, and with the trustees, who appointed him principal of the school and even threatened to cut off the bishop's income; but Dubois stood firmly for ecclesiastical discipline, and Levins as an orthodox priest soon severed his connections with the trustees and lived a model life as a lay Catholic. He now gave his attention to journalism, founding the ephemeral *Green Banner* and writing for the *Catholic Register.* Something of a mineralogist and an excellent mathematician when scientists were rare in New York, he acted twice on the board of examiners for West Point (see *Truth Teller,* Mar. 24, 1827) and was retained as an engineer on the Croton aqueduct. The plans for the high bridge are said to have been his work. Restored to his priestly office in 1841, he was assigned by Bishop John Hughes to the rectorship of St. John's Church, Albany, but owing to failing sight and threatened paralysis, he was unable to assume active duty. Levins was a versatile man and a capable controversialist, but his career was marred by his inability to fit into an organization.

[Archbishop Corrigan in U. S. Cath. Hist. Soc., *Hist. Records and Studies,* vol. II, pt. I, Oct. 1900; P. J. Foik, *Pioneer Cath. Journalism* (1930), in U. S. Cath. Hist. Soc. Monograph Ser., vol. XI; J. H. Smith, *The Cath. Ch. in N. Y.* (1905), vol. I; J. G. Shea, *Hist. of the Cath. Church in the U. S.,* vol. III (1890); *Freeman's Jour.,* May 6, 1843; *Cath. Herald,* May 11, 1843; *Cath. Mag.,* June 1843; *Metropolitan Cath. Directory* (1844); *N. Y. Tribune,* May 6, 1843.] R. J. P.

LEVY, JOSEPH LEONARD (Nov. 24, 1865–Apr. 26, 1917), rabbi, was born in London, England, the son of the Rev. Solomon and Elizabeth (Cohen) Levy. He received his Jewish training at Jews' College, London, and his secular education at the universities of London (B.A. with honors, 1884), and Bristol (1885–86). In Bristol on Dec. 26, 1888, he was married to Henrietta Platnauer. Two daughters were born to the union. At the early age of twenty he assumed his first clerical charge at Bristol. After four years, in 1889, he came to America, called by the Synagogue at Sacramento, Cal. From 1893 to 1901 he was associated with Joseph Krauskopf [*q.v.*] as rabbi of Temple Keneseth Israel of Philadelphia. From there he was called to Temple Rodeph Shalom of Pittsburgh in 1901, of which he was the rabbi for the rest of his life. Though orthodox in training and early inclination, in America he identified himself with reform Judaism, becoming one of its leaders. Gaining national fame as a preacher and orator, he attracted large congregations of both Jews and Christians. He frequently exchanged pulpits with preachers of Christian denominations, and in 1908 he introduced in Pittsburgh interdenominational services for Thanksgiving day.

Levy was a man of wide interests. He was a governor of the Hebrew Union College of Cincinnati, and a trustee of the University of Pittsburgh. He was especially active in spreading propaganda and in raising funds for the Department of Synagogue Extension of the Central

Conference of American Rabbis. As an earnest peace advocate, he was affiliated as founder, trustee, or officer, with several local, state, and world peace societies. He opposed the manufacture of military toys for children, and he advocated that Palestine be neutralized as the center of a world peace council empowered by an international force to prevent war. He aided in founding (1894), the Philadelphia Sterilized Milk, Ice and Coal Society and (1895) the Home of Delight Settlement, was a founder of the Pennsylvania Anti-Tuberculosis League, and a trustee of the Denver National Hospital for Consumptives. He took an active interest in the solution of the vice problem, urging the building of model tenement houses. He advocated pensions for widowed mothers, higher education for negroes, and the settlement of Jews in farming districts. In Pittsburgh he was active in virtually every public-welfare movement in the city. In the literary field, Levy was editor of the *Atlantic Coast Jewish Annual* (1896), editor (1901–05) and contributing editor (1905–10) of *The Jewish Criterion,* and author of *A Book of Prayer* (1902), *Questions for Our Consideration* (1898), *Nineteenth Century Prophets* (1907), *Founders of the Faiths* (1908), *Old Arrows from New Quivers* (1909), some sixteen volumes of sermons, and a number of prayer manuals and textbooks for Jewish religious schools. His special contribution to American Judaism was his success in correlating the Synagogue with the forces of social welfare.

[*Who's Who in America,* 1916–17; R. I. Coffee, article in *Central Conference of Am. Rabbis, Twenty-eighth Ann. Convention* (1917); the *Jewish Criterion* (Pittsburgh, Pa.), Apr. 27, May 5, 11, 1917; the *Reform Advocate* (Chicago), May 5, 1917; *Am. Jewish Year Book,* 1903–04.] D. deS. P.

LEVY, LOUIS EDWARD (Oct. 12, 1846–Feb. 16, 1919), photo-chemist, inventor, author, was born at Stenowitz, Bohemia, the son of Leopold and Wilhelmina (Fisher) Levy. When he was nine years old his parents emigrated to the United States and settled in Detroit, where he attended school. In 1861 he entered the employ of Louis Black & Company, opticians, and at the same time studied optics, the microscope, and surveying. He gained sufficient knowledge of the mariner's compass to correct the compasses of lake pilots. In 1866 he made observations in Detroit for the United States Meteorological Service and studied wet-plate photography to record his researches with the microscope. Photography fascinated him, and it was in this branch of science that he made his most notable achievements. At twenty-three he was given the management of the branch office of Louis Black & Company in Milwaukee. He continued his studies and experimented in methods of photo-engraving. In 1873 he accepted the invitation of David Bachrach, Jr., to use the facilities of the latter's photographic studio in Baltimore. The two worked together and invented a photo-chemical engraving process which they called the "levytype," and which they patented in January 1875. In the same year Levy organized the Levy Photo-Engraving Company in Baltimore and took into the business his brothers Max [*q.v.*] and Joseph. In 1877, believing that Philadelphia offered better opportunities for them, the brothers moved there and established the Levytype Company. Later Max and Joseph established similar plants in Chicago and Cincinnati.

About 1889 Max Levy returned to Philadelphia and worked with his brother Louis in an effort to develop better methods of half-tone reproduction. They invented the Levy half-tone screen—an etched glass grating—which they patented in Europe and America in 1893. For this invention they received the John Scott Legacy Medal. Louis Levy later invented an etching machine by which etchings could be produced by the application of a spray of acid forced upward against a horizontal metal plate by an air blast. For this invention he received the Elliott Cresson Medal of the Franklin Institute in 1899 and recognition from other sources. His last invention was a device for applying powdered resin to plates preparatory to the etching process. For this invention he received the Elliott Cresson Medal in 1907.

After the Levytype Company was established in Philadelphia a publishing department was added to the business. In 1887 Louis Levy purchased the *Evening Herald,* a Democratic daily which he published until July 1890, and the *Sunday Mercury.* He used these papers to demonstrate his inventions and to prove that his company could produce engravings of current events promptly. He was the author of several works, including *The Jewish Year* (1895); *The Jewish Refugees in the United States* (1895), and his own reminiscences, *Recollections of Forty Years: A Photo-Engraving Retrospect* (1912). Among the works which he edited are *The American Jew as Patriot, Soldier and Citizen* (1895), by Simon Wolf, and *Cuba and the Cubans* (1896), by Raimundo Cabrera. In his later years he gave much time to philanthropic work. He was one of the founders and for many years president of the Association for the Relief and Protection of Jewish Immigrants and served as president of the Jewish Community (Kehillah) in Philadelphia. He had married, on Jan. 9, 1881, Pauline Dalsheimer of Baltimore. She with two sons survived him.

[See *Specifications and Drawings of Patents issued from the U. S. Patent Office,* Jan. 1875, Feb. 1893, June 1899, Sept. 1905, Aug. 1906, May 1909; *Official Gazette of the U. S. Patent Office,* Apr. 27, Dec. 28, 1915; memoir of Levy in *Jour. of the Franklin Institute,* May 1919; *Who's Who in America,* 1918–19; *Photo-Engravers Bull.* (Chicago), Apr. 1926; *Jewish Exponent* (Phila.), Feb. 21, 1919; *Bull. of Photography* (Phila.), Mar. 5, 1919; and the *Press* (Phila.), Feb. 18, 1919. Information as to certain facts was supplied by Levy's sons; the author also had a long personal acquaintance with Levy.] S. H. H.

LEVY, MAX (Mar. 9, 1857–July 31, 1926), photo-engraver, inventor, was the son of Leopold and Wilhelmina (Fisher) Levy and was born in Detroit, Mich. At an early age he showed a distinct talent for drawing. During the course of his schooling in the Detroit public schools he decided to make architecture his life work and upon completing school in 1875 he entered an architect's office in Detroit. About this time his brother Louis [*q.v.*] patented a new photo-relief process which he called "levytype," for producing photo-relief plates for printing, and had established a successful photo-engraving business using the "levytype" process in Baltimore, Md. In need of assistance to carry it on, Louis induced his brothers Max and Joseph to join him, the former as draftsman and the latter as photographer. Max therefore gave up his architectural work and never returned to it. In the belief that Philadelphia offered a larger field of opportunity than Baltimore, the three brothers moved their photo-engraving plant to that city early in 1877. Success followed them and three years later Max and Joseph went to Chicago, Ill., and there opened the first photo-engraving enterprise in that city. A year or two later Max established Cincinnati's first photo-engraving plant and continued with the management of these two organizations for several years. About 1889 he returned to Philadelphia to work with his brother Louis on improvements in the process of half-tone reproduction. They concentrated their attention on making a perfect screen of lines used in the process between the camera and copy. Louis conceived the idea of etching the lines on glass and blackening the depressions and Max worked on the design and construction of the delicate machinery to make such screens absolutely accurate. After two years of tedious experimentation the screen was perfected in 1891 and patents were secured both in the United States and Europe in 1893. Max then gave up the photo-engraving business to engage in the manufacture of half-tone screens. His first place of business was established in Philadelphia but in 1902 he built a new plant in the suburb of Germantown.

Levy not only managed this business but also continued making improvements in his manufacturing methods, resulting in the production of screens of better quality. Before he died 25,000 were in use the world over. With his delicate machinery as many as four hundred perfect lines to the inch could be ruled and etched on glass, and diffraction gratings could be produced containing thousands of lines to the inch. In addition to making screens, Levy also manufactured photographic plate-holders and camera diaphragms of his own invention for photo-engravers' use. Although at the time of the World War Levy had retired, he engaged in work for the War Department and ruled the graticules used in the eyepieces of range-finders. He never gave up entirely his inventive work, and in 1917 patented the hemocytometer, a microscopic measuring machine used in blood-counting which has been adopted by the United States army and by many medical institutions. During his active career Levy wrote many articles for the technical press and trade journals and became widely known for his contributions to the advance of half-tone illustration. During the last ten or more years of his life he devoted much of his time to painting. For his contributions to half-tone illustration the Franklin Institute, Philadelphia, awarded him the John Scott Legacy Medal, and the Royal Cornwall Polytechnic Institute presented him with a silver medal. The Franklin Institute awarded him also the Edward Longstreth medal for his invention of the hemocytometer. Levy married Diana Franklin in Baltimore, Md., on Sept. 22, 1885, and at the time of his death in Allenhurst, N. J., he was survived by his widow and three sons.

[*Specifications and Drawings of Patents Issued from the U. S. Patent Office,* Feb. 1893, June 1894, Jan. 1895, Jan. 1896, Feb., Oct., 1897, May 1898, Aug. 1901, Dec. 1907, May 1909; *Official Gazette of the U. S. Patent Office,* Jan. 30, 1917, Oct. 8, 1918, Apr. 25, 1922; L. E. Levy, *Recollections of Forty Years: A Photo-Engraving Retrospect* (1912); F. E. Ives, *Autobiog. of an Amateur Inventor* (1928); *Who's Who in America,* 1926–27; *Jewish Exponent* (Phila.), Aug. 6, 1926; *Inland Printer* (Chicago), Sept. 1926; *Process Monthly* (London), Sept. 1926; *N. Y. Times,* Aug. 1, 1926.] C. W. M.

LEVY, URIAH PHILLIPS (Apr. 22, 1792–Mar. 22, 1862), sailor and patriot, born in Philadelphia, Pa., was the son of Michael and Rachel (Phillips) Levy. Between the ages of ten and twelve, Levy served, without his parents' consent, as a cabin boy on coasting vessels. In 1806 he began a four-year apprenticeship under John Coulter, Philadelphia merchant and shipowner, who placed Levy in the "best naval school" of Philadelphia for nine months during the 1808 embargo. Serving as first mate after his apprenticeship, Levy made enough money by October 1811 to become part owner of a schooner, the *George Washington,* of which he took command as master. The schooner was lost the following January through a mutiny off the Isle of May (*United States* vs. *Tully,* 28 *Fed.,* 226), and, war against England having been declared, Levy applied for a position in the United States navy. He was commissioned sailing master, Oct. 21, 1812, and served on harbor duty until the following June, when, as volunteer acting lieutenant, he joined the *Argus,* then about to transport the American minister to France. In August 1813, just before the *Argus'* encounter with the *Pelican,* Levy was transferred to a prize vessel, was captured, and spent sixteen months in England.

Returning to naval duty, for the next ten years his quarrelsome pride, his shipmates' contempt for his having risen from the ranks, and a prejudice against his Jewish ancestry involved him in a series of broils, most of them petty, but one of them culminating in a duel, fatal to his opponent. Six times court-martialed, he was twice dismissed from the service: the first time (1819) for contempt, but after nearly two years President Monroe's disapproval of the sentence reinstated him; the second time (1842) he was cashiered for the infliction of a bizarre punishment on a subordinate, but the sentence was commuted to twelve months' suspension by President Tyler. Levy's steady rise in rank during these years was evidence both of the pettiness of his squabbles and of his relentless energy, but his appointment as captain (1844) was followed by a decade of vain endeavor to obtain a command, his public service at this period being confined chiefly to an unofficial and indirect assistance in the abolition of flogging from the navy. In 1855 the newly created "Board of Fifteen" dropped him from the navy's rolls. He protested to Congress in a *Memorial* (New York, 1855), and defended himself before the Court of Inquiry in 1857, with the result that his rank was restored. He received a command, became flag officer of the Mediterranean Squadron in 1860, returned to his New York home, and died there. He had married rather late in life and was survived by his widow, Virginia Levy. Despite his sensitiveness, vanity, and occasional insubordination, he was a courageous and humane officer and a fervid patriot. His admiration for Jefferson led him to purchase "Monticello," which unforeseen litigation after his death prevented from becoming a public shrine (*Public Ownership of Monticello: Hearings Before the Committee on Rules of the House of Representatives . . . July 24, 1912*; 33 *N. Y. Reports,* 97; 40 *Barbour's Supreme Court Reports,* N. Y., 585); and at the outbreak of the Civil War he offered his fortune to President Lincoln for his country's use (Isaac Markens, "Lincoln and the Jews," *American Jewish Historical Society Publications,* 1909, no. 17, p. 158).

[Autobiographical data in Levy's *Defence . . . Before the Court of Inquiry, Held at Washington City, November and December, 1857* (1858); G. A. Townsend, *Monticello and Its Preservation* (1902); *Am. Jewish Hist. Soc. Pubs., passim*; *N. Y. Herald,* Mar. 26, 1862.]

J. C. W.

LEWELLING, HENDERSON [See LUELLING, HENDERSON, 1809–1878].

LEWELLING, LORENZO DOW (Dec. 21, 1846–Sept. 3, 1900), reformer, governor of Kansas, was born in Salem, Iowa, the youngest son of William and Cyrena (Wilson) Lewelling and a nephew of Henderson Luelling [*q.v.*], who retained the earlier spelling of the name. The family was originally Welsh. Lorenzo's grandfather moved from North Carolina to Indiana in 1825 and with his sons engaged in the nursery business there. When promising reports came to them of opportunities in Iowa several of the sons moved on and established themselves in Salem in the same business. William Lewelling became a minister in the Society of Friends, but he died when his son was only two years old, leaving a family of small children to be brought up by the widow and, after her death, by relatives. Young Lewelling worked for neighboring farmers and attended country school until he was sixteen. On the outbreak of the Civil War he attempted to enlist, but on account of his youth and their Quaker faith his relatives protested. He then engaged in several forms of non-military service in the Federal army, and after various experiences, returned to Iowa and entered Whittier College at Salem. Later he taught in the Iowa State Reform School for Boys. In 1870 he married Angie Cook, a school teacher, whom he had known in college. In 1873 they became the first superintendent and matron of the State Reform School for Girls, where they remained until the death of Mrs. Lewelling in 1885. During this period Lewelling became a member of the first board of the Iowa State Normal School at Cedar Falls, and later was president of the board. He also published for a time, beginning in 1880, the *Des Moines Capital,* an anti-administration paper in opposition to the Republican organization.

After his first wife's death he was married to Ida Bishop.

About 1887 Lewelling settled in Wichita, Kan., where he engaged in business. These were years in which the Populist movement was developing and Lewelling became known as a public speaker and as a reformer in politics. In 1892 he was the fusion candidate of the Democrats and Populists for governor and was elected, serving from 1893 to 1895. The Senate was controlled by the Populists, but in the lower house the vote was almost evenly divided. A legislative struggle resulted, two bodies were organized, each claiming to be the constitutional House of Representatives. In the course of this controversy open hostilities were narrowly avoided, and the Governor, to avert bloodshed, agreed to submit the decision to the supreme court, which decided in favor of the Republican House. Differences of opinion naturally developed in regard to the way in which the situation had been handled. An anti-administration group was formed, but Lewelling was renominated by the Populist party. The Democrats put a separate ticket in the field and the Republican candidate was elected. In 1896 and again in 1898 Lewelling was elected a member of the state Senate, and his death occurred while he was holding this office. He was a representative Quaker. He and his family were opposed to slavery and he taught in a school for negroes in Missouri after the close of the Civil War when it was necessary to have friends guard the door to protect him from the threatened assaults of the people of the neighborhood. His ancestry and life experience prepared him for his most striking rôle as the Populist governor of Kansas. Perhaps his Quaker aversion to the use of force led to his concessions in the legislative war, which featured his administration as governor.

[The principal sources of information are O. A. Garretson, "The Lewelling Family—Pioneers," in the *Iowa Jour. of Hist. and Pol.*, Oct. 1929; Clarence R. Aurner, *Hist. of Educ. in Iowa* (1920), vol. V; W. J. Costigan, "Lorenzo D. Lewelling," *Trans. Kan. State Hist. Soc.*, vol. VIII (1902); W. E. Connelley, *A Standard Hist. of Kan. and Kansans*, vol. II (1918); W. P. Harrington, *The Populist Party in Kan.* (n.d.) reprinted from the *Kan. State Hist. Soc. Colls.*, vol. XVI (1923–25); *Who's Who in America*, 1899–1900; *The Kan. Blue Book* (1899); B. F. Gue, *Hist. of Iowa* (1903), vol. IV; *Topeka Daily Capital*, Sept. 4, 1900; *Iowa State Reg.*, Sept. 5, 1900.] F. E. H.

LEWIS, ALFRED HENRY (*c.* 1858–Dec. 23, 1914), journalist, author, was born in Cleveland, Ohio, the son of Isaac J. Lewis, a carpenter, and his wife, Harriet Tracy. He was admitted to the bar as soon as he came of age, hung out his shingle, dabbled in politics while waiting for clients, and served as prosecuting attorney, 1880–81, in the city police court. Then with his family he went West, and for the next few years he was a hobo cowboy. He worked on the ranches of Senator S. W. Dorsey and Col. O. M. Oviatt in Meade County, Kan., in the Cimarron country, helped drive cattle to Dodge City and other shipping points, rode down into the Texas Panhandle, gained a little newspaper experience of a kind in New Mexico on the *Las Vegas Optic*, and wandered into southeastern Arizona. It was a happy, carefree period, but by 1885 he was living once more with his parents in Kansas City, Mo., and was trying to build up a law practice. Clients were few and far apart, and in his leisure he turned again to politics and journalism. About this time, too, he married Alice Ewing of Richfield, Ohio, who outlived him. One of his brothers was city editor of the *Kansas City Times*, and in 1890 Lewis contributed to it an imaginary interview with an old cattleman domiciled at the St. James' Hotel. The story was copied far and wide; Lewis had not received a dollar for it, but for his next "Old Cattleman" story he was paid $360. He joined the staff of the *Kansas City Star*, was sent to Washington the next year as correspondent of the *Chicago Times*, and when that paper died in 1894 became head of William Randolph Hearst's Washington bureau. His political articles were trenchant and partisan, often bitter; he was regarded as one of Hearst's ablest men. For the last sixteen or seventeen years of his life he lived in New York, devoting himself to writing magazine articles and fiction for the Hearst magazines, chiefly for the *Cosmopolitan*. From Dec. 19, 1898, to Nov. 12, 1900, he edited a weekly Democratic sheet, the *Verdict*, which was sponsored by O. H. P. Belmont. Most of his work was strictly ephemeral—fictionized biographies of John Paul Jones (1906), Andrew Jackson (1907), and Aaron Burr (1908); novels of political life such as *The Boss* (1903) and *The President* (1904); stories of the police and the underworld such as *Confessions of a Detective* (1906) and *The Apaches of New York* (1912). Of the eighteen books that he published in the last fifteen years of his activity, only his Wolfville stories of cowboy life are likely to be remembered. Of these there were, in all, six volumes: *Wolfville* (1897); *Sandburrs* (1900); *Wolfville Days* (1902); *Wolfville Nights* (1902); *Wolfville Folks* (1908); and *Faro Nell and her Friends* (1913). At the time of their publication they were immensely popular. They are all put into the mouth of the "Old Cattleman," a gentleman of infinite leisure, a tolerant philosophy, and a language all his own. Though containing little that is original, they belong to the best tradition of American humorous story-telling. Probably thousands of readers have been disappointed to find that Wolfville and its rival settlement of Red Dog are not on the map of Arizona, so real do they become in the discursive, drawling reminiscences of the "Old Cattleman." Lewis himself had many of the qualities of this, his chief character. He died in New York after a short illness.

[*Who's Who in America*, 1899–1915; *N. Y. Times*, Dec. 23, 24, 1914; *N. Y. Morning Telegraph*, Dec. 24, 25, 1914; *Kansas City Star*, Dec. 23, 1914; *Editor and Publisher*, Dec. 26, 1914; W. R. Coates, *A Hist. of Cuyahoga County and the City of Cleveland* (1924), vol. I; J. K. Winkler, *W. R. Hearst: An American Phenomenon* (1928); Cleveland and Kansas City directories.] G. H. G.

LEWIS, ANDREW (1720–Sept. 26, 1781), soldier, Revolutionary patriot, was born in Ireland. His parents, John and Margaret (Lynn) Lewis, came of Scotch-Irish or of Welsh stock, with a possible admixture of Huguenot blood. John Lewis killed his Irish landlord in self-defense and fled to America, finally settling in 1732 at "Bellefonte," near Staunton, Va. He was one of the first and most influential settlers in the Valley of Virginia. He fixed the location of Staunton, and aided in organizing Augusta County. Andrew and his wife, Elizabeth Givens, followed the retreating frontier and settled on the upper Roanoke River near the present site of Salem, Va. He was county lieutenant of Augusta, and justice of the peace and representative in the legislature from the county of Botetourt a few years after its creation. He was also a member of the Revolutionary colonial conventions of March and of December 1775. His life presents a chronicle of border warfare and of peaceful missions to Indian nations. Yet he found time to accumulate a considerable fortune which he bequeathed to his wife, five sons, a daughter, and three grandsons. He was upwards of six feet tall, agile, uncommonly strong, and possessed of a "reserved and distant deportment." He served in the Augusta militia and surrendered with Washington at Fort Necessity. He was in Braddock's army but was not present at its defeat. During General Forbes's campaign of 1758, Lewis was taken prisoner in Major Grant's unfortunate reconnaissance. He was later released and aided in making the Indian Treaty of Fort Stanwix (1768), one of the several important treaties which he helped to frame.

Lewis' chief claim to fame was his victory over the Indians in the battle of Point Pleasant, the outstanding event in Lord Dunmore's War. In 1774, when numerous Indian forays brought death and terror to the whole border country, Governor Dunmore of Virginia quickly organized two forces to attack the Indians northwest of the Ohio River. He placed Lewis in command of the force from the southwestern counties. Lewis' men left Camp Union (site of Lewisburg, W. Va.), and marched in nineteen days to Point Pleasant, just above the confluence of the Ohio and Kanawha rivers, a distance of 160 miles across the Alleghany Mountains. Here the army of more than 800 men was attacked at daybreak, Oct. 10, by an Indian force of about equal size. The ensuing battle was one of the fiercest and most bloody in the annals of Indian warfare. Lewis led his men with uncommon skill and courage. Eighty-one Virginians were killed and 140 wounded. About two hundred Indians were killed. The victory was the determining factor in this war, which brought far-reaching consequences. It gave peace with the Indians along the whole American frontier during the first three years of the Revolutionary War, practically nullified the Quebec Act of 1774, led to rapid westward expansion, and prepared the way for George Rogers Clark's great campaign of 1778–79. On Mar. 1, 1776, Congress commissioned Lewis brigadier-general, though Washington wished a higher command for him. He assumed command of the American forces stationed at Williamsburg. In July 1776 he drove Governor Dunmore from Gwynn's island. He resigned his commission in the Continental Army Apr. 15, 1777, but continued to serve his state in the military forces and in Gov. Thomas Jefferson's executive council until his death.

[The fullest account of Dunmore's War is Virgil A. Lewis, *Hist. of the Battle of Point Pleasant* (1909), which contains a useful bibliography. See also: Justin Winsor, *Narrative and Critical History of America*, vol. VI (1888); F. B. Heitman, *Hist. Reg. of Officers of the Continental Army* (1914); Louise P. Kellogg, *Frontier Advance on the Upper Ohio* (1916); *Va. Mag. of Hist. and Biog.*, July 1905, Apr. 1910, Oct. 1911, Apr. 1916; R. A. Brock, *The Official Records of Robt. Dinwiddie, Lieut.-Gov. of the Colony of Va.* (2 vols., 1883–84); Lyman Chalkley, *Chronicles of the Scotch-Irish Settlement in Va.* (3 vols., 1912–13); J. A. Waddell, *Annals of Augusta County, Va.* (ed. 1902); J. L. Peyton, *Hist. of Augusta County, Va.* (1882); *Orderly Book . . . of Gen. Andrew Lewis* (1860), ed. by Chas. Campbell; *Official Letters of the Govs. of Va.*, vol. II (1928), vol. III (1929).] R. L. M—n.

LEWIS, ARTHUR (Aug. 19, 1846–June 13, 1930), actor, manager, was born in the Hampstead section of London, the son of James Frederic and Françoise (Upward) Lewis, the latter of French birth and ancestry. He was the nephew of Sir George Lewis, an eminent solicitor, by whom he would have been trained for the legal profession but for the opposition of his father, who chose the physician's career for him. After studying in Edinburgh and London, he gladly renounced all thought of medicine for the stage, and on Dec. 27, 1868, acted his first rôle, a minor character in the Christmas pantomime of *Bluebeard* at the Drury Lane Theatre. He was so pleased at the opportunity to engage in congenial work that he exclaimed impetuously to a friend: "They are actually paying me for something I like to do."

Except for two brief intermissions, the rest of his life was passed on the stage, or in connection with the theatre in various capacities, although the testimony of his friends and associates bears witness to the fact that throughout his long life he was a man of more diverse interests than the average actor. During the Franco-Prussian War he left the stage temporarily to become a war correspondent, and in 1880 he interrupted his work in the theatre to visit the United States, unsuccessfully seeking rubies on the island of Santa Catalina. Returning to London, he became a member of Mary Anderson's company. He acted with her at intervals between 1882 and 1889 and accompanied her on her farewell tour of the United States, playing at the Lyceum Theatre in London and during her American engagements such characters as Mimos in *Pygmalion and Galatea,* De la Feste in *Comedy and Tragedy,* Benvolio in *Romeo and Juliet,* Lord Tinsel in *The Hunchback,* and Cleomenes in *The Winter's Tale.* For a time he was a manager, and had the direction of engagements and tours of Coquelin, Sarah Bernhardt, Mme. Rejane, and M. Antoine. Among the many parts he played in later years were the Marquis de Mirepoix in *Monsieur Beaucaire* (1902), Count Ivan Pavlovic in *Hawthorne of the U. S. A.* (1905), Mr. Viveash in *The Hypocrites* (1907), Huzar in *The Lily* (1911), Father Roubier in *The Garden of Allah* (1911), Mr. Justice Grimdyke, with Maude Adams, in *The Legend of Leonora* (1914), Dr. Stetson and Mr. Stapleton in *The Great Lover* (1915–16), and Dr. Dickinson in *The Camel's Back* (1923). His last rôle was that of Manuel in *A Hundred Years Old,* with Otis Skinner. In the autumn of 1929 illness compelled him to leave the stage, and he died the following year at the Home for Incurables in Bronx Borough, New York City.

In the course of an interview not long before his death, he said: "I have had the variety I was seeking in life. I never liked doctoring. That is a life that is too hard and confining for me, but I've always thought it ridiculous that I became an actor. I should never have done that, although I have enjoyed it thoroughly. What I should really have liked to be is a lawyer and a judge. Often, very often, I've played the part of a judge. I've worn the white curled wig and black gown of the English magistrates and felt very important and impressive. That's what we all like to feel, like someone who counts, isn't it?" (*Evening World,* New York, Dec. 27, 1928). Although he thus felt that he would have been happier in another walk of life, he was far from being a failure in the profession he served faithfully for nearly sixty years. He was survived by his widow, Essex Dane, actress and playwright.

[T. A. Brown, *A Hist. of the N. Y. Stage* (1903), vol. III; John Parker, *Who's Who in the Theatre,* 1925; *N. Y. Times* and *Sun* (N. Y.), June 14, 1930; *Billboard* (Cincinnati), June 21, 1930; personal information from Mrs. Lewis.] E. F. E.

LEWIS, CHARLES BERTRAND (Feb. 15, 1842–Aug. 21, 1924), humorist who wrote under the pseudonym "M. Quad," was born in Liverpool, Ohio, the son of a contractor and builder. His formal education included a course at the Michigan State Agricultural College, but like many other Middle Western writers of the period following the Civil War, Lewis gained his essential training in the composing rooms of small-town newspapers. He began to learn the printer's trade at the age of fourteen and served a thorough apprenticeship as journeyman printer and foreman on newspapers at Pontiac and Lansing, Mich. Some years as a private in the Union army further familiarized him with the rank-and-file American audience for which he was later to provide entertainment. After working for some time as a compositor on the *Lansing Jacksonian,* Lewis accepted the offer of a newspaper editorship in Jonesboro, Tenn., but while traveling on the Ohio River he was seriously injured by a boiler explosion during a steamboat race and spent many weeks recuperating in Cincinnati. He then returned to his old position at Lansing. Later, while in temporary charge of the paper, he printed a humorous account of the accident, entitled, "How It Feels to be Blown Up." This widely copied piece started him on his career as a professional "funny man."

In 1869 Lewis joined the staff of the *Detroit Free Press* as legislative reporter. Between sessions of the law-makers he wrote a variety of descriptive and humorous sketches which gained for his paper an enlarged circulation and a national renown. Similar work was being done by Robert J. Burdette of the *Burlington* (Iowa) *Daily Hawkeye* and James M. Bailey of the *Danbury* (Conn.) *News*; but the public demand for burlesque and verbal caricature was unlimited and was profitably exploited by a host of paragraphers. Among Lewis' most popular inventions was the negro organization known as the

Lime Kiln Club, presided over by a philosophic and pretentious negro called Brother Gardner. He also parodied Western journalism in imaginary items from the *Arizona Kicker* and developed a vein of domestic humor in describing the comic tribulations of the Bowser family. The production of these specialties soon became Lewis' main business, but he also found time to write several popular books on the Civil War besides a number of dime novels and plays. One of the plays, called *Yakie,* came on the stage in 1884. Lewis' profits as a commercial writer would seem to have been substantial. During the greater part of his twenty-two years on the *Free Press* he held a proprietary interest in the paper.

The last phase of Lewis' life added little or nothing to his reputation. In May 1891 he went to New York as a staff contributor on the *World* and the *Evening World,* for which he regularly wrote six columns of humor a week. Nearly all that he did, except for occasional magazine stories, was in continuation of the type of writing begun early in his career. During the last twelve years of his life he was crippled by rheumatism but persisted in his work to the end. His books, of which *Brother Gardner's Lime Kiln Club* (1882) and *The Life and Troubles of Mr. Bowser* (1902) are favorable examples, entitle him to a minor position in the school of Western humorists headed by Artemus Ward, Bill Nye, and Eugene Field. When he died in Brooklyn in his eighty-third year, he was the last representative of the group and his work was even then all but forgotten.

[*Who's Who in America,* 1920–21; *N. Y. Times, World* (N. Y.), Aug. 23, 1924; *Detroit Free Press,* Aug. 23, 24, 1924; *Lit. Digest,* July 29, 1922.]

G. F. W.

LEWIS, CHARLTON THOMAS (Feb. 25, 1834–May 26, 1904), classicist, editor, lawyer and publicist, was born in West Chester, Pa., the son of Joseph J. and Mary (Miner) Lewis and the grandson of Enoch Lewis and Charles Miner [*qq.v.*]. He was educated in West Chester and at Yale College, where he ranked high in the class of 1853, displaying special proficiency in the classics and in mathematics, and holding the office of class poet. A tabulation of his later occupations will suffice to show his extraordinary versatility. For a year after his graduation he studied law, the profession of his father. In 1854 he was admitted on trial, and in 1856 admitted into full connection by the Philadelphia Conference of the Methodist Episcopal Church, serving on the Newark circuit, in Wilmington, and in Philadelphia. In 1857–58 he was professor of languages in the Normal University of Illinois at Bloomington. From 1859 to 1862 he taught in Troy University, Troy, N. Y., first as professor of mathematics and later as professor of Greek; during 1862 he was also the acting president of the university. In the winter of 1862–63 he returned to the ministry of the Methodist Episcopal Church, at Cincinnati, but soon put this occupation aside to become deputy commissioner under his father, who had been made commissioner of internal revenue by President Lincoln. In 1864 he took up the practice of law in New York, and this was the chief occupation of the remainder of his life, with the exception of the years 1868–71, during which he was an editor of the New York *Evening Post.*

In all of his fields of endeavor Lewis was successful, and to most of them he made some permanent contribution. Among his published works were an English edition, in collaboration with M. R. Vincent, of *John Albert Bengel's Gnomon of the Greek Testament* (2 vols., 1860–62), and *A History of Germany, from the Earliest Times* (1874), founded on David Müller's *Geschichte des Deutschen Volkes* (1872). Other writings of his dealt with the law of insurance, in which he specialized and on which he was recognized as an authority. He was counsel to the Mutual Life Insurance Company of New York and in 1898–99 lectured on life insurance at Cornell, Harvard, and Columbia universities. His most important book was *Harper's Latin Dictionary,* prepared in collaboration with Charles Short, which was published in 1879 and fifty years later had not been superseded in its field. It was followed by *A Latin Dictionary for Schools* in 1889, and by *An Elementary Latin Dictionary* in 1891.

Lewis was active in politics and in other public affairs. In 1896 he was a delegate to the convention of Gold Democrats at Indianapolis, serving as a member of the committee on platform. During much of his life he was intensely interested in organized charities and in prison reform. He was president of the Prison Association of New York, 1893–1904, delegate of the United States to the International Prison Congress at Paris in 1895, and vice-president of the National Prison Association in 1897, and supplemented his personal efforts with pamphlets and articles. His work in this field, and his Latin dictionary, are the outstanding accomplishments of a career that was as unselfish as it was varied.

On July 25, 1861, he married Nancy D. McKeen of Brunswick, Me., who died Aug. 19, 1883. She was a grand-daughter of Joseph McKeen [*q.v.*], first president of Bowdoin College; one of her children was Charlton Miner Lewis (1866–1923), who as professor of English at Yale carried on the scholarly tradition of the family. Lewis' second wife, whom he married June 30, 1885, was Margaret P. Sherrard, of Michigan. He died at the age of seventy, in Morristown, N. J., which had been his home for a number of years.

[Records of the class of 1853 of Yale College, including *Yale College: Class of 1853* (1883) and *Supp. Hist. of the Yale Class of 1853* (1903), which contains bibliography of Lewis' writings; *Obit. Record Grads. Yale Univ.*, 1904; *Fifty-ninth Ann. Report of the Prison Asso. of N. Y., for the Year 1903* (1904); *Who's Who in America*, 1903–05; *Evening Post* (N. Y.), May 27, 1904; collection of newspaper articles in the possession of Mrs. Charlton Thomas Lewis, who has corrected and supplemented the information which they contain.]

A. E. C.

LEWIS, DIOCLESIAN (Mar. 3, 1823–May 21, 1886), temperance reformer and pioneer in physical culture, was born near Auburn, N. Y., the son of John C. and Delecta (Barbour) Lewis. His family, of Welsh descent, were farmers and home-builders. A younger brother, Loran L. Lewis, became a justice of the supreme court of New York and another brother, George Washington Lewis, a physician in Buffalo. Dio Lewis, as he was always called, left school at the age of twelve and, after a period of work and teaching, established a private school in Lower Sandusky (now Fremont), Ohio. After a year he returned to New York, studied medicine with a physician in Auburn, spent the year 1845–46 at the Harvard Medical School in Boston, and began practice, without a degree, in Port Byron, N. Y. In 1849 he was married to Helen Cecilia Clarke, daughter of Dr. Peter Clarke of New York, and began practice again in Buffalo. In this city he published the *Homœopathist,* a monthly magazine, and started gymnasium classes for women. He worked out a system of "free gymnastics," exercises to be performed without apparatus. Setting this idea aside temporarily, he embarked on a series of temperance lectures, based on the "Washingtonian movement" begun in 1840, and traveled throughout the South and later the Middle West and Canada. In 1851 he received an honorary degree of M.D. from the Homœopathic Hospital College, Cleveland, Ohio.

In 1860 he went to Boston, where he began to organize gymnasium classes. The work soon extended to private schools and to the hospitals in the vicinity of Boston. Lewis incorporated the Boston Normal Institute for Physical Education in 1861, with many prominent persons on the board of directors, and, during the next seven years, over four hundred men and women were graduated from his school. In 1862 he published his most important book, *New Gymnastics,* which had a large sale and served to make his name known in both the United States and Great Britain. From 1864 to 1868 he also conducted a sanitarium and gymnasium in Lexington, Mass., a large girls' school, with Theodore D. Weld [*q.v.*] as head-master, in the same town, and a private family hotel, the "Bellevue," in Boston.

After 1871 he again turned his attention to temperance reform and carried out an extensive program of lectures and campaigns throughout the country in aid of the Woman's Christian Temperance Union. In Boston and elsewhere he found considerable opposition to his views, for he always stoutly held that the cause of prohibition would never be advanced through legal methods but rather through a campaign of moral suasion. His appearance on the lecture platform is said to have been striking and dramatic. Quick of wit, pleasant and sympathetic, he usually won over his vast audiences. For a brief period before his death he again conducted a sanitarium near Boston; but in 1881 he removed to New York, giving up his practice and lecturing, although continuing his literary work. His publications, mostly books on gymnastics or health, were ephemeral in character.

[The best source of information is the laudatory *Biog. of Dio Lewis* (1891), by Mary F. Eastman. See also: H. A. Kelly and W. L. Burrage, *Am. Medic. Biogs.* (1920); *Boston Transcript,* May 21, 1886; *N. Y. Tribune,* May 22, 1886.]

H. R. V.

LEWIS, DIXON HALL (Aug. 10, 1802–Oct. 25, 1848), Alabama congressman and senator, was descended from Robert Lewis, a native of Brecon, Wales, who settled in what is now Gloucester County, Va., about 1635. The son of Francis Lewis and his wife, Mary Dixon (Hall), who was related to the Bolling and Randolph families of Virginia, Dixon Hall Lewis was born probably in Dinwiddie County, Va., but throughout most of his childhood lived in Hancock County, Ga. He attended the famous Mount Zion Academy conducted by Rev. Nathan S. S. Beman [*q.v.*], step-father of William Lowndes Yancey, and went thence to South Carolina College. Going to Alabama after his graduation in 1820 (LaBorde, *post,* p. 441), he studied law under Judge Henry Hitchcock in Cahawba, then the capital, and was admitted to the bar in 1823. Two years later he opened an office in Montgomery. Though he showed unusual capacity in his profession, the call of politics in the new state drew him to devote all his energies to government service. His political philosophy was largely influenced by his uncle, Bolling Hall, sometime representative in Congress from

Georgia, a supporter of William H. Crawford, and a member of the so-called "Georgia faction" in Alabama politics. Hall was an intimate of the leaders of the extreme state-rights viewpoint in Virginia and Georgia and he strongly indoctrinated his nephew with that political philosophy.

Lewis was elected to the lower house of the Alabama legislature in 1826 as an ardent advocate of state-rights principles, and during his service of three terms (1826–28) came to be recognized as the leader of the faction in the Democratic party in Alabama which was opposed to every tendency towards centralization. He was foremost in the organization of the State-Rights group. His outstanding career in the legislature earned for him an election to Congress in 1829, at the early age of twenty-seven, and he continued in Washington till his death in 1848. In Congress he soon became recognized as one of the chief supporters of the state-rights doctrines. He vigorously opposed, on constitutional grounds, the United States Bank, the high protective tariff, and internal improvements by the federal government. He served in the House from 1829 to 1844, became chairman of the committee on ways and means, and in 1839 lost the speakership by four votes in a bitter contest with the Benton faction (*Congressional Globe,* 26 Cong., 1 Sess., p. 56). When William R. D. King [*q.v.*], leader of the Union Democrats in Alabama, resigned from the Senate in 1844 to become minister to France, Lewis was appointed senator in his stead by Gov. Benjamin Fitzpatrick [*q.v.*], his wife's brother-in-law. At the regular election in 1847 he defeated King, again a candidate, and Arthur Francis Hopkins [*q.v.*], Whig leader, for the full term. In the Senate he continued to promote the principles he had advocated in the House. After a short time he was made chairman of the committee on finance and was instrumental in framing and passing the Walker Tariff of 1846. Though he seldom spoke in Congress, he was commonly considered one of the most influential men in party councils and was exceedingly popular.

He was married, Mar. 11, 1823, to Susan Elizabeth, daughter of Gen. John A. Elmore and sister of Franklin Harper Elmore [*q.v.*]. To them were born seven children. All his life Lewis was afflicted with excessive flesh and in his later years weighed 450 pounds. His huge bulk necessitated special arrangements on stage-coaches, in the legislative chambers, and in the halls of Congress. He died in New York, whither he had gone to address a free-trade organization, and was buried with civic honors in Greenwood Cemetery on Long Island.

[Yancey and Bolling Hall papers in the Dept. of Archives and Hist. of Ala.; T. P. Abernethy, *The Formative Period in Ala., 1815–1828* (1922); T. H. Jack, *Sectionalism and Party Politics in Ala., 1819–1842* (1919); T. M. Williams, *Dixon H. Lewis* (1910), in Ala. Polytechnic Inst. Hist. Studies, 4 ser.; W. Garrett, *Reminiscences of Public Men in Ala.* (1872); Willis Brewer, *Ala.: Her Hist.* (1872); T. M. Owen, *Hist. of Ala.* (1921), vol. IV; *Biog. Dir. Am. Cong.* (1928); "Calhoun as Seen by His Political Friends: Letters of Duff Green, Dixon H. Lewis, Richard K. Crallé, during the Period from 1831 to 1848," *Southern Hist. Asso. Pubs.*, vol. VII (1903); J. M. McAllister and L. B. Tandy, *Geneal. of the Lewis and Kindred Families* (1906); Maximilian LaBorde, *Hist. of the S. C. Coll.* (1859); newspaper files in Ala. Dept. of Archives and Hist.]

T. H. J.

LEWIS, EDMUND DARCH (Oct. 17, 1835–Aug. 12, 1910), landscape painter and collector, son of David and Camilla (Phillips) Lewis, was born in Philadelphia, Pa., where the family had been identified with the social and business life of the city since 1708, when Ellis Lewis, a native of Wales, came to America and settled in Kennett Township, Pa. David Lewis was a trustee of the University of Pennsylvania and an official of two Philadelphia insurance companies, but by temperament was a reader and a man of letters rather than a business man. From his mother's side of the family Edmund derived an artistic bent and a lifelong ardor for collecting. The Phillipses for generations had been collecting old china, furniture, curios, and prints; John Phillips, Edmund's uncle, left a collection of 40,000 prints to the Pennsylvania Academy of the Fine Arts.

Edmund Lewis had only a private school education. While still a youth he began the study of art under Paul Weber, with whom he remained for about five years. His success as a landscape painter was almost instantaneous; he soon became the favorite painter of Philadelphia, and although his facility and industry were phenomenal, the demand for his work exceeded the supply. Many exaggerated accounts have been given of his facility in turning out pictures. At one time it was stated that he painted his landscapes by the yard and cut them into strips of the desired size and shape. It is, however, true that he often duplicated his stock subjects. The result of this commercialization of his art was that in his later years the vogue for his work diminished sensibly. "Mr. Lewis," said a writer for the Philadelphia *Public Ledger,* "set a pace in pot-boiling such as the world of art had never before seen." He had a keen business sense and invested his savings so well that at the time of his death his estate amounted to about $300,000. Excepting a relatively small legacy from his father in 1895, this sum had been obtained entirely from the sale of his pictures.

His ruling passion, however, was his collection, on which he expended large amounts. He was a born collector, and his talent as a painter simply enabled him to satisfy this hobby. His residence, 30 South Twenty-second St., Philadelphia, consisted of two city houses thrown into one, with one room built especially for tapestries, and with a large ballroom constructed as an addition at the rear. This mansion became a veritable museum of period furniture, tapestries, old silver, porcelain and pottery, bric-a-brac and curios. Special rooms were devoted to exhibits of Empire furniture, Dresden china, Oriental art, and Colonial objects of household art. In the nineties many notable receptions and musicales were given by the owner, who was glad to share his enjoyment of his treasures with his friends. He died unmarried, and his collection, intact, passed into the hands of a nephew.

[An interesting account of Lewis' methods is given in a long article published by the Philadelphia *Public Ledger*, Aug. 28, 1910. Obituaries appeared in the *Public Ledger* and the *N. Y. Times*, Aug. 13, 1910, and a criticism in *Am. Art News*, Sept. 17, 1910. Most of the information in this sketch was supplied by Lewis' nephew, Clifford Lewis, Jr.] W. H. D.

LEWIS, ELLIS (May 16, 1798–Mar. 19, 1871), Pennsylvania jurist, was born at Lewisberry, Pa., the youngest of eight children of Maj. Eli and Pamela (Webster) Lewis. He was descended from Ellis Lewis, originally from Wales, who emigrated to Pennsylvania from Ireland in 1708. Though orphaned at the age of nine, he was well cared for by his brothers, sisters, and guardian, who gave attention to his early education. At twelve he was apprenticed for seven years to John Wyeth in Harrisburg to learn "the art and mystery of a Printer." There his work and the library facilities provided him an excellent chance to learn. After five years he tired of this life and ran away to New York City under an assumed name. In 1818 he returned to Pennsylvania to the town of Williamsport and engaged in the newspaper business, which brought him favorably before the public. In 1821 he began the study of law and was admitted to the bar the following year at the age of twenty-four. On Nov. 21, 1822, he was married to Josephine Wallis.

Lewis was a stanch Democrat throughout his career. In 1824 he was appointed deputy attorney-general of Lycoming and Tioga counties and in 1832 he was sent as a delegate to the state Democratic convention. His work showed his legal ability and judicial temperament, and in 1833 Governor Wolf appointed him attorney-general of the state. He retained at the same time his seat in the legislature, to which he had been elected previously, and was instrumental in abolishing imprisonment for debt, which did much to make him popular. After but a few months as attorney-general he succeeded to the office of president judge of the eighth judicial district. His opinion in the case of *Commonwealth* vs. *Armstrong* (reprinted in 1 *Pennsylvania Law Journal*, 1842, p. 393) against clerical interference with a parent's right to educate his child was published throughout the country. In 1843 he became president judge of the second district. In 1848 he published *An Abridgment of the Criminal Law of the United States.* Elected in 1851 to the supreme bench for the six-year term, he devoted himself to his duties with tremendous energy. In 1854 he automatically became chief justice. All his expositions were exact, direct, and luminous; and his technical mastery, his wide learning, and his conciliatory spirit had a great influence in the court's decisions. At the end of his term on Dec. 7, 1857, he retired to private life, after declining a unanimous renomination for the chief justiceship. It was said of him in the *Daily Pennsylvanian* (Mar. 27, 1857): "No man within our Commonwealth has had the judicial experience of the present Chief Justice, and no Judge has labored more zealously to free the docket of the Supreme Court of the accumulated litigation of ages. . . . We doubt much whether Judge Lewis has ever been equalled in industry on the Bench." His last years he spent in quiet retirement.

[B. A. Konkle, *The Life of Chief Justice Ellis Lewis, 1798–1871* (1907); *U. S. Mag. and Democratic Rev.* (N. Y.), Apr. 1847; Ellis Lewis, *Hist. of Eli Lewis and Family* (1925); the *Press* (Phila.), Mar. 21, 1871.] E. B. S.

LEWIS, ENOCH (Jan. 29, 1776–July 14, 1856), mathematician, educator, publicist, and editor, was born on a farm in Radnor, Pa., near Philadelphia, and spent almost the whole of his life within twenty miles of his birthplace. His parents, Evan and Jane (Meredith) Lewis, were descended from Welsh Friends who had settled the neighborhood nearly a century earlier; his paternal ancestor was another Evan Lewis who came from Pembrokeshire, South Wales, to Pennsylvania in 1682. Enoch, a serious-minded and precocious boy, rapidly exhausted the educational facilities of the Radnor school, of which he was himself made master at the age of fifteen. Thereafter he was almost entirely self-educated, feeling himself debarred, as a conscientious member of the Society of Friends, from attending the University of Pennsylvania, the only easily accessible institution of higher learning. Despite this handicap he became eminent in mathematics, a study for which he inherited an aptitude from his mother. From his fifteenth to his fifty-first year his chief occupation was teaching, in Philadelphia, in Westtown, or as head of his own school, which he opened in 1808 at New Garden, Pa., and later moved to Wilmington, Del. He combined or varied the scholastic life with farming and surveying, and for a time held the post of city regulator of Philadelphia.

Lewis began writing early in his career, and his literary activities increased as he grew older. He was the author of a large number of books, pamphlets, and articles on a wide variety of subjects. His textbooks on arithmetic, algebra, trigonometry, and grammar were the direct outcome of his profession. His devotion to the principles of his sect (which he defended in *A Vindication of the Society of Friends,* 1834) was responsible for the greater part of his published work. He wrote for the Society "Memoirs of the Life of William Penn" (*The Friends' Library,* vol. V, 1841), and nearly completed the first volume of a history of North America which was to emphasize the social and economic progress of the continent and to make plain the misery and folly of war. Although he sometimes dealt with purely doctrinal questions, his keenest interest was in moral and political issues, such as the abandonment of compulsory military service, the protection of the Indians, and the abolition of slavery. He believed that this last problem could best be solved by convincing the South that slavery was economically unsound, and to propagate this idea he founded in 1827 a monthly magazine, the *African Observer,* the failure of which after one year of life was due in part to its editor's moderation. In 1847, he founded, in Philadelphia, the *Friends' Review* (first issue, Sept. 4, 1847), a weekly journal which he edited until a few weeks before his death. In its pages he found an outlet for the expression of his views on all the wide range of subjects in which he was interested; he himself wrote most of the original material which it contained.

Lewis' mind was remarkable for its ingenuity and its lucidity; his character, for its consistency. If he convinced himself that a course of action was right he adopted it forthwith and held himself to it strictly, although with other people he was much more lenient. His personal efforts in behalf of the causes he supported were as persistent and as effective as his writings. He was twice married, first, on May 9, 1799, to Alice Jackson of New Garden, who died Dec. 13, 1813; second, in May 1815, to Lydia Jackson of Londongrove, Pa., a cousin of his first wife. Charlton Thomas Lewis [*q.v.*] was his grandson.

[The authoritative source for the facts of Lewis' life is the *Memoir of Enoch Lewis* (1882), by his son, Joseph J. Lewis, privately printed at West Chester, Pa. It contains no formal list of Lewis' writings, but many of them are mentioned in the text, pp. 77–100. See also J. S. Futhey and Gilbert Cope, *Hist. of Chester County, Pa.* (1881); *Friends' Intelligencer* (Phila.), 7th mo. 26, 1856; *Daily News* (Phila.), July 16, 1856.]

A. E. C.

LEWIS, ESTELLE ANNA BLANCHE ROBINSON (April 1824–Nov. 24, 1880), author, was the daughter of John N. Robinson and was born at her father's country home near Baltimore, Md. Her father, who died while his daughter was an infant, was a Cuban by birth, of Anglo-Spanish descent, a man of means, culture, and social prestige. His wife was the daughter of an officer in the American Revolution. Estelle was educated at Emma Willard's Female Seminary, Troy, N. Y., and remained a student throughout life. She became proficient in classical and modern languages and acquired some knowledge of the sciences and of law. While still in school she made translations from the *Æneid* into English verse and published stories in the *Family Magazine,* edited by Solomon Southwick, at Albany, N. Y. Soon after leaving school, she was married, in 1841, to Sylvanus D. Lewis, an attorney. They made their home in Brooklyn, N. Y., but were divorced about 1858 and after that Mrs. Lewis resided chiefly abroad.

Mrs. Lewis always devoted the greater part of her time to literary work. She contributed, under the name "Stella," poems, stories, translations, and articles on art, literature, and travel to the *Democratic Review,* the *American Review,* the *Spirit of the Nineteenth Century, Graham's Magazine, Godey's Lady's Book,* the *Home Journal,* and the *Literary World.* Public attention was first attracted to her poetry by the romantic poem, "The Ruins of Palenque," which appeared in the *New World.* In 1844 her first volume of poems, *Records of the Heart,* was published under the pen-name Sarah Anna Lewis. Included in her later works are *Child of the Sea and Other Poems* (1848); *Myths of the Minstrel* (1852); *Sappho; a Tragedy, in Five Acts* (1875); and *The King's Stratagem; or, the Pearl of Poland; a Tragedy in Five Acts* (1869). She was extravagently praised in her own time but the sincerity of some of the eulogy has since been called into question. It has been said that Poe, who was a friend of the Lewises, at a time of financial need accepted money from Sylvanus Lewis to revise and write flattering reviews of his wife's poetry. He is also said to have written the sketch of Mrs. Lewis which appeared in

Rufus Wilmot Guswold's *Female Poets of America.* Her best longer poems are generally conceded to be "Child of the Sea," a tale of sea adventure in the style of Byron, and *Sappho,* which, translated into modern Greek, was staged at Athens. Of her minor poems, perhaps the best are "Lament of La Vega in Captivity," "The Angel's Visit," and "The Forsaken." Her poetry is always somewhat stiff and over-regular in meter and rhyme, but it has emotional appeal. Her favorite type was the narrative poem of romance and heroic passion. Her last work was a sonnet series eulogizing Poe. She died in London, but her body was later removed to the United States for burial.

[See E. A. and G. L. Duyckinck, *Cyc. of Am. Lit.* (ed. 1875); Mary E. Phillips, *Edgar Allan Poe, The Man* (1926), vol. II; *Appletons' Ann. Cyc.*, 1881; Sarah Josepha Hale, *Biog. of Distinguished Women* (1876); *Pall Mall Gazette* (London), Nov. 25, 1880; *London Daily News,* Nov. 26, 1880. For Poe's criticisms, to be discounted, see *The Literati* (1850) and notices in the *U. S. Mag. and Democratic Rev.*, Aug. 1848, and *Southern Lit. Messenger,* Sept. 1848.] S. G. B.

LEWIS, EXUM PERCIVAL (Sept. 15, 1863–Nov. 17, 1926), physicist, educator, was born in Edgecombe County, N. C., the son of Henry Exum Lewis, a physician, and Emma (Haughton) Lewis. Educational facilities were meager in the rural community in which the Lewis family was settled. Privations that arose from the Civil War and the untimely death of his father when Lewis was only seven prevented his attending any elementary school whatever. His early education was obtained almost entirely by his own efforts, through reading and association with a country clergyman who gave him the freedom of his library. When he was yet a boy he went to West Chester, Pa., where he worked as a printer's apprentice. His service in this office stood him in good stead. No doubt it contributed greatly to his accuracy in spelling and his ability to read rapidly—habits that were valuable assets to him in the occupation he eventually adopted. His scientific training began a few years later when, as a young man, he accepted a position as clerk in the War Department, in Washington, D. C. While thus employed, he attended night classes at Columbian University (the present George Washington University) and received the degree of B.S. in 1888. Three years later he entered Johns Hopkins University as a graduate student in physics. There he came in contact with Professor H. A. Rowland [*q.v.*], the famous spectroscopist. Rowland was an inspiring teacher; his enthusiasm and idealism were a strong influence in Lewis' career, for he, too, adopted the study of spectroscopy as his life work.

In 1895, after receiving the degree of Ph.D. from Johns Hopkins, he went to the University of California as instructor in physics. Promotion to the grade of assistant professor came the following year, partly because a physicist was desired who could cooperate with the Lick Observatory in the field of astrophysics and spectroscopy. The period 1898–1900 Lewis spent abroad, as Whiting fellow, at the Physical Institute of the University of Berlin. He then returned to the University of California, where he became successively associate professor of physics (1902), professor (1908), and chairman of the department (1918); the last two positions he held until his death. In 1901 he was married to Louise Sheppard of San Francisco. They had two children—a son and a daughter. He was a member of expeditions to observe the eclipse of the sun in the South Seas, 1908, at Goldendale, Wash., June 1918, and at Ensenada, Lower California, in 1923. His chief studies in this connection were of the flash and the coronal spectrum. Although Lewis published no books, he was the author of papers on many diverse subjects, in the *Astrophysical Journal* and other scientific periodicals, and at the time of his death was working on the manuscript of a textbook of spectroscopy.

In the field of his major activity, his chief contributions related to the spectra of gases under various conditions of excitation, purity, etc. During his residence in Berlin he made the first systematic investigation of the influence of small quantities of a foreign substance on the character of the spectra of hydrogen, oxygen, and nitrogen. While he was engaged in studying the latter gas, he discovered a peculiar fluorescent afterglow that persists in the nitrogen discharge tube when a trace of oxygen or water vapor is present. Lord Rayleigh, inspired by these observations, discovered the chemical substance he termed "active nitrogen," which, he showed, was capable of exciting fluorescence in other vapors than oxygen or water. Lewis investigated the band spectra of many substances. He was a pioneer in the very difficult fields of infra-red and far ultra-violet spectroscopy. He studied the continuous spectrum of hydrogen in the Schuman region, its intensity and extent, and the conditions most favorable to its appearance. He measured the wave-lengths of several hundred new lines in the ultra-violet spectra of the rare gases krypton and xenon. Among his extensive researches in fields other than spectroscopy, were his investigations of ionization and electrical conductivity of gases. He devised a most ingenious method of determining the amplitude of sound waves by observation of illuminated ultra-microscopic particles set into forced vibration by the waves. He also studied various phenomena accompanying magnetic hysteresis.

Lewis was more than an able teacher. He possessed a rare ability to divest a complex subject of its difficulty. His lectures on spectroscopy were models of clarity. An idealist and a philosopher, he was distinguished by great simplicity of character and singleness of purpose. His devotion to the study of scientific truth made him uncompromising in dealing with civic or political questions. He was an early advocate of equal suffrage and was generous in support of projects for the improvement of political conditions.

[*Who's Who in America,* 1926–27; J. H. Moore, in *Pubs. Astron. Soc. of the Pacific,* Apr. 1927; E. E. Hall, in *Science,* May 6, 1927; *San Francisco Chronicle,* Nov. 18, 1926; informaton as to certain facts from Mrs. E. P. Lewis.] D. H. M.

LEWIS, FIELDING (July 7, 1725–*c.* Jan. 1, 1782), Revolutionary patriot, brother-in-law of George Washington, and builder of "Kenmore" at Fredericksburg, Va., was probably a descendant of Robert Lewis, a native of Brecon, Wales, who settled in what is now Gloucester County, Va., about 1635. Fielding's immediate forebears were cultivated, wealthy, and influential. He was the son of John Lewis, member of the Virginia Council, and of Frances, daughter of Henry Fielding, gentleman, of King and Queen County, Va.; his grandfather, John Lewis—also a Councillor—had married Elizabeth Warner, daughter of Col. Augustine Warner of "Warner Hall," in Gloucester County, and of Mildred Reade, his wife. In this way, it is said, there came into possession of the Lewis family the old mansion, "Warner Hall," in which Fielding was born.

His association with George Washington was long and intimate. On Oct. 18, 1746, he married Washington's cousin, Catherine Washington, by whom he had three children. After her death, he married, May 7, 1750, Washington's sister, Betty. There were eleven children of this union. The letters and diaries of Washington show that he was a frequent visitor at "Kenmore," and was much attached to the family there. It was after his marriage to Betty that Lewis built "Kenmore." The house is constructed of brick, with walls two feet thick. The woodwork in its spacious rooms is fashioned in exquisite detail. Washington was much interested in its building and aided in designing its interior decorations. During the Revolution he sent two Hessian artisans, captured at Trenton, to adorn the mansion with elaborately decorated mantels and ceilings. Lewis was also associated with Washington, in 1761, in the organization of the Dismal Swamp Company, formed to build a canal through that swamp and to drain its lands. Beginning in 1760, Lewis served for almost a decade as burgess from Spotsylvania County.

From the beginning of the struggle with Great Britain he was an ardent patriot. On June 1, 1774, he joined with a group of citizens of Fredericksburg, who adopted a resolution pledging themselves to concur in whatever the colonies should do respecting the "hostile invasions of the rights and liberties of the town of Boston." He was chosen a member of a committee to correspond with neighboring towns and counties. The Revolutionary county committee of Spotsylvania, of which Lewis was chairman, adopted, on May 9, 1775, resolutions thanking "Capt. Patrick Henry for the part which he played in the gunpowder affair." Ill health excluded Lewis from military service; but he spent his strength and fortune in the cause of liberty. In July 1775 the General Assembly decided to establish a factory at Fredericksburg for the making of small arms for the state troops, and appointed Lewis chief commissioner to superintend the undertaking. Early in 1776 operations were begun. Lewis remained in charge of the factory until 1781, when he was forced by sickness to resign. When necessary funds for this vital work could not be secured by the state, he advanced seven thousand pounds of his own money, thereby saving the enterprise. This generous action left him in very straitened circumstances at the end of his life. His death occurred sometime between Dec. 10, 1781, when he added a codicil to his will, and Jan. 17, 1782, when the will was probated.

[J. M. McAllister and L. B. Tandy, *Geneals. of the Lewis and Kindred Families* (1906); *William and Mary Coll. Quart. Hist. Mag.,* Apr. 1897, Jan., Apr., July, 1901, Oct. 1918, Jan., Apr. 1919; *Va. Mag. of Hist. and Biog.,* Jan. 1898, July 1922, July 1924; *Official Letters of the Governors of the State of Va.,* vol. II (1928); *Calendar of Va. State Papers,* vol. I (1875), ed. by W. P. Palmer; *The Diaries of George Washington, 1748–1799* (4 vols., 1925), ed. by J. C. Fitzpatrick; *Va. County Records—Spotsylvania County,* vol. I (1905), ed. by W. A. Crozier; V. M. Fleming, *The Story of Kenmore* (1924).] R. L. M—n.

LEWIS, FRANCIS (Mar. 21, 1713–Dec. 31, 1802), New York merchant and signer of the Declaration of Independence, was the only child of the Rev. Francis Lewis, rector of Llandaff, Glamorganshire, Wales, and Amy Pettingal of Caernarvon. Left an orphan at an early age, he spent his childhood and youth, under the care of his mother's relatives, in Wales and at Westminster School and in a mercantile house in

London. Thus soundly and prudently prepared he came to New York in 1738 and began a career in trade which was distinguished for activity and finally by success. He carried on business for a time in New York and Philadelphia, returned to England for two years, and made voyages between America and northern European ports in the course of which he twice suffered shipwreck. During this period of adventure he was captured by Indians in 1756 after the fall of Oswego, where he was present as friend of the English commander and as clothing contractor for the troops. He was sent to France for exchange and afterward received from the colonial government a grant of land in acknowledgment of his military services. He had married, on June 15, 1745, Elizabeth Annesley of New York. In 1765, having accumulated a considerable fortune and attained a position of influence in New York, he retired to Whitestone, Long Island, but in 1771 he returned to the city for a time to help establish his son, Francis, in business, even making a journey with him to England to form commercial connections there. After his return he was completely occupied with public affairs.

In the Revolutionary agitations in New York after 1774 his participation was continuous and occasionally conspicuous. In 1774 he was a delegate to the Provincial Convention and a member of the Committee of Fifty-one and the Committee of Sixty. In July of that year he was one of the eleven who resigned from the former in protest against what seemed excessive caution in opposing Parliamentary legislation. Throughout the exciting events of 1775 and 1776 he was active both in the proceedings of the Continental Congress and in the critically deliberate process of forming a government for the new state of New York. Increasingly identified with "continental" affairs, he was a delegate to Congress from May 1775 till November 1779 and served thereafter till July 1781 as one of the commissioners of the Board of Admiralty. He took no part in debate but was indefatigable in committee work. His long experience, orderly disposition, and practical sagacity made him a valued member of such semi-administrative bodies as the Marine, the Secret, and the Commercial committees, and finally of the Admiralty Board. He was frequently charged with duties in connection with the supply of the army and was a strong supporter of Washington at the time of the intrigues against his leadership.

With the rest of the New York delegation he was precluded by instructions from voting for the Declaration of Independence on July 4, 1776, but he was one of those whose signatures were appended to the document, probably on Aug. 2, 1776. A little more than a month later Lewis' house in Whitestone was destroyed by the British army and his wife was made prisoner. The rigorous conditions of her captivity during the months before she could be exchanged undermined her health and hastened her death (1779). The Revolution deprived Lewis of his home and, because of his expenditures in the cause, of most of his wealth. He lived in retirement with the families of his sons until his death in his ninetieth year.

[There is a sketch of Lewis by Robert Waln, Jr., in John Sanderson, *Biog. of the Signers to the Declaration of Independence*, vol. VI (1825). His career in Congress can be traced in the *Journals* and in E. C. Burnett, *Letters of Members of the Continental Cong.*, vols. I–V (1921–31). The account of him in Thos. Jones, *Hist. of N. Y. During the Revolutionary War* (2 vols., 1879), ed. by E. F. de Lancey, is hostile, while that in Julia Delafield, *Biogs. of Francis Lewis and Morgan Lewis* (2 vols., 1877), is strongly eulogistic. Some, though not all, of Jones's errors are corrected in the Editor's Note LIV. An inaccurate but vivid sketch is that in J. A. Scoville, *The Old Merchants of N. Y. City*, vol. III (1865). Notices of his death appeared in the N. Y. *Evening Post*, Jan. 3, 1803, and the *Spectator*, Jan. 5, 1803. The date of Lewis' birth and the names of his parents were supplied by one of his descendants.] C. W. S.

LEWIS, ISAAC NEWTON (Oct. 12, 1858–Nov. 9, 1931), soldier, inventor, son of James H. and Anne (Kendall) Lewis, was born in New Salem, Fayette County, Pa. In 1880 he was appointed from Kansas to the United States Military Academy, and upon his graduation in 1884 was commissioned second lieutenant in the 2nd Artillery. He was married, Oct. 21, 1886, to Mary, daughter of the Rev. Richard Wheatley of New York City, and had four children. He was promoted through the grades to colonel, which grade he reached Aug. 27, 1913, and on Sept. 20 of the same year he was retired from active service on account of disability incurred in line of duty. He graduated from the Torpedo School in 1886, and during the subsequent years of his service devoted himself to further technical study and experimentation. He was signally successful in perfecting and inventing a number of devices, notably the Lewis depression position finder (patent no. 447,335, Mar. 3, 1891), and the Lewis machine gun (patent no. 1,004,666, Oct. 3, 1911). He also invented a plotting and relocating system for seacoast batteries, a time-interval clock and bell system of signals for artillery fire control, a quick-firing field gun and mount, quick-reading mechanical verniers, an electric car lighting system (patent no. 504,681, Sept. 5, 1893), a windmill electric lighting system and a gas-propelled torpedo (patent no. 933,086, Sept. 7, 1909). During his service Lewis was entrusted with many important assignments, particularly along scientific lines in connection with artillery and ordnance. He served as a member of the board of regulation of coast artillery fire, New York Harbor (1894–98); recorder of the board of ordnance and fortification, Washington (1898–1902); instructor in electricity and power; director of the department of enlisted specialists; acting commandant of the Coast Artillery School at Fortress Monroe, Va.; commander of the post of Fortress Monroe and the Artillery District of the Chesapeake (1904–11). He also devised a system of fire control for San Francisco harbor, which he demonstrated in France, Germany, Austria, and Russia, and which the last-named country adopted. In 1900, under special instructions of the Secretary of War, he visited several European countries and made a study of their methods of manufacturing and supplying ordnance material. He was the originator of the modern corps organization of artillery which was adopted in 1902.

Immediately upon his retirement from active service he proceeded to Liège, Belgium, to build a factory for the development and manufacture of the Lewis machine gun in Europe, having failed to secure the approval of the War Department in Washington for the trial and development of the gun for the United States service. After the outbreak of the World War, he moved to England, and was connected with the Birmingham Small Arms Company. In 1916 tests were conducted in the United States for the purpose of selecting a machine gun for the United States service. The Lewis gun was submitted with others, and was rejected by the War Department board, because of the large number of malfunctions and stoppages during the firing test. Its rejection started a controversy, which raged for some time in the service and the press and finally reached a stage where open letters from high-ranking officers of the army were published. In order to settle the technical questions involved, a board was constituted, and the inspector-general of the army was ordered to investigate other aspects of the case. The findings of the board (see *New York Times,* Nov. 11, 1916), and of the inspector-general were approved by the Secretary of War, who ordered that further controversy on this subject cease (*Ibid.,* Dec. 18, 1916). After certain requirements had been complied with, the gun was accepted by the government and large numbers were used by the army in arming airplanes. Lewis remained in Europe throughout the war, in personal contact with the French, British, and Belgian field armies. Lewis guns were delivered to the Allies at the front at the rate of 3,500 complete gun units per week, and a total of over 100,000 guns were used by them. He was technical director of the Lewis Machine Gun Company of London; president of the Lewis Machine Gun Company and director of the Automatic Arms Company of Cleveland, Ohio; technical director and manager of the *Armes Automatique Lewis* of Belgium; and director of the *Société des Armes Lewis,* of Paris. Possessing a profound knowledge of mechanical and electrical engineering and thoroughly conversant with all phases of coast artillery construction and equipment, he earned an enviable reputation in his profession. At the close of his life his home was in Montclair, N. J.; his death occurred suddenly in a railroad station at Hoboken.

[G. W. Cullum, *Biog. Reg. Officers and Grads. U. S. Mil. Acad.* (3rd ed., 1891); record in the Adjutant General's Office, Washington; *Army Ordnance,* Dec.–Jan. 1931–32; *Specifications and Drawings of Patents Issued from the U. S. Patent Office,* Mar. 1891, Aug. 1892, Sept., Oct. 1893, Mar. 1894, Mar. 1898, Aug. 1902, Sept., Dec. 1909, Oct. 1911; *Official Gazette of the U. S. Patent Office,* Aug. 13, 1912, Aug. 18, 1914, June 15, 1915, Aug. 22 1916, Oct. 3, Dec. 26, 1922; *Who's Who in America,* 1930–31; C. H. Claudy, in *Sci. Am.,* Feb. 14, 1920; *Army and Navy Jour.,* Dec. 23, 1916, Jan. 6, June 30, 1917; *N. Y. Times,* July 1, 2, 1917, Nov. 10, 1931.] C. F. C.

LEWIS, JAMES (Oct. 5, 1837–Sept. 10, 1896), actor, whose real name was James Lewis Deming, was born in Troy, N. Y., the son of William Hoadley and Arabella (Benson) Deming. When he was seventeen years old and was employed as a clerk in a store in Troy, an actor who wished to look for a better engagement persuaded him to play a part in *The Writing on the Wall* for one night with the stock company at the Troy Museum. Although his part was a small one, he scored such a hit that he was offered an engagement for the remainder of the season, and this circumstance determined his choice of a career. From Troy he worked his way west and south, barnstorming, playing sometimes in tavern dining-rooms and even in churches. When the Civil War broke out he was playing in Montgomery, Ala., in a company in which John Wilkes Booth was leading man. He hastened to Savannah in time to catch the last steamer that sailed north before the blockade. Then came several seasons of "stock" in Rochester, Cleveland, and Pittsburgh, successively. In 1865 he was engaged as low comedian at the Olympic Theatre, in New York City. Here he acted in a great variety of farces and dramas. Later he was low comedian of the stock company at the Continental Theatre, Boston. During this engagement he was praised by the critics for his Dick Swiveller in *The Old Curiosity Shop.*

The popularity of burlesque at this time led Lewis into this field. His droll portrayals of the burlesque Lucretia Borgia, and Rebecca in *Ivanhoe* at the Waverly Theatre, New York, attracted the attention of the young Augustin Daly. Daly engaged Lewis for his stock company at the Fifth Avenue Theatre on West Twenty-fourth Street. Lewis first appeared there at the beginning of the third week of the Daly season, Sept. 6, 1869, as John Hibbs in *Dreams,* receiving very flattering notices from the press. He acted in many rôles, constantly gaining in artistic technique. His most notable success was as Bob Sackett in the five-act comedy *Saratoga* by Bronson Howard, which enjoyed a long run. In the second Fifth Avenue Theatre, at Broadway and Twenty-eighth Street, Lewis added still further to his reputation. It was here in *The Big Bonanza* (Feb. 17, 1875) that he and Mrs. George H. Gilbert [see Gilbert, Anne Hartley] had two of those parts which made the Daly Stock Company famous.

While Daly was in temporary retirement, Lewis, with Mrs. Gilbert, joined a company organized by Henry E. Abbey to play comedy in New York and on tour, but he rejoined the Daly company at Daly's Theatre, New York, in its second season, 1880–81, and continued as one of the shining lights of this organization of brilliant artists. With John Drew, Mrs. Gilbert, and Ada Rehan [*qq.v.*] he was one of the "Big Four" of the company, appearing several times with them in London and on the Continent and winning very favorable recognition from the critics. In old and modern comedy, especially in adaptations from the German, he excelled in the portrayal of comic old men. He was also very successful in his characterizations of blasé and worldly types. His outstanding characteristic as a comedian was his dryness, leading a Harvard professor to say, "Lewis is so dry he crackles." He died suddenly at West Hampton, Long Island. His first wife was a native of Cleveland, Ohio. His second wife, Medora Frances Herbert, whom he married on May 8, 1871, survived him.

[See J. F. Daly, *The Life of Augustin Daly* (1917); Wm. Winter, *Wallet of Time,* vol. I (1913); Laurence Hutton, *Curiosities of the Am. Stage* (1891) and *Plays and Players* (1875); Arthur Hornblow, *Hist. of the Theatre in America,* vol. II (1919); J. R. Towse, *Sixty Years of the Theatre* (1916); clippings on James Lewis in the Robinson Locke Collection in the N. Y. Pub. Lib.; *N. Y. Dramatic Mirror,* Sept. 19, 1896; *N. Y. Herald,* Sept. 7, 1869, Dec. 22, 1870; *N. Y. Tribune,* Dec. 22, 1870, Sept. 11, 1896; *Boston Herald,* Sept. 11, 1896; *N. Y. Times,* Sept. 11, 1896. Lewis was extremely reticent about his birth and family. A sketch of him in the *Troy Northern Budget,* Sept. 13, 1896, mentions his parents, and he appears in J. K. Deming, *A Geneal. of the Descendants of John Deming* (1904).]
L. H. F.

LEWIS, JOHN FRANCIS (Mar. 1, 1818–Sept. 2, 1895), Virginia Unionist and United States senator, was born near Port Republic, Rockingham County, Va., son of Gen. Samuel Hance and Nancy (Lewis) Lewis. Both parents were descended from John Lewis, an Irish immigrant "Who slew the Irish lord, settled Augusta County, Located the town of Staunton And furnished five sons to fight the battles of the American Revolution" (epitaph, printed in L. G. Tyler, *Encyclopedia of Virginia Biography,* 1915, V, 576). Lewis' formal education was meager. Management of the family plantation, along with some practice of law, was normally his chief occupation. In 1842 he married Serena Helen, daughter of Daniel Sheffey. Though both his father and his father-in-law were prominent public men and he himself professed ardent Whig sympathies, not until 1859 did he approach active politics. Having then expressed in the local newspaper his opposition to secession as a theory and as a policy, he was elected to the state convention of 1861. Here he offered no resolution, made no report, seems not even to have spoken; but he persistently voted against secession and ultimately refused to sign the ordinance. The coming of the Civil War prevented, it is said, his acceptance of President Lincoln's tender of the marshalship of western Virginia. During the war his rôle was that of a peaceful Unionist; it has been asserted, however, without recorded contradiction, that he also "manufactured large quantities of iron for the Confederacy, under special contracts with it" (A. F. Robertson, *Alexander Hugh Holmes Stuart,* 1925, p. 249). In 1865 he was a candidate for Congress against A. H. H. Stuart [*q.v.*], but was badly beaten. Lewis seems to have followed the lead of his friend John Minor Botts [*q.v.*] during the early part of the Reconstruction period (Botts, *The Great Rebellion,* 1866, p. 192), attending the various meetings which led to the formation of the Republican party in Virginia, appearing before the congressional investigating committee, endeavoring to build a strong and liberal party and to secure a place of prominence in it. Later he joined the combination with the Conservatives and was, in consequence, elected lieutenant-governor in 1869. The same combination (apparently much influenced by railroad and bond-holding interests) elected him to the federal Senate for the short term, John W. Johnston of the Southwest being the Conservative (Democratic) selection for the full term. In the Senate (January 1870–March 1875) he was chairman of the committee on the District of Columbia, but otherwise obtained no particular recognition. After the expiration of his term he was appointed marshal by President Grant, and served 1875–81. When the Republican-Readjuster combination was being effected, he was of much assistance and in consequence was again elected lieutenant-governor (1881). "There's Cameron, he's for the Democrats; and there's Lewis, he's for the negroes . . .," was the hostile comment of the *Richmond Dispatch* on the combination (June 4, 1881, p. 2, cited in Pearson, *post,* p. 139). In 1889 he broke with Gen. William Mahone [*q.v.*], head of the combination, and materially aided in his overthrow by working for a Straight-Out Republican movement. His last years were spent at "Lynwood," the family estate in Rockingham County, where he died of cancer after a long, brave fight. Three sons and four daughters survived him. The Democratic press noted that though his independence of thought and impulsiveness of action had often led him into disagreements with his friends and neighbors, these had never doubted his integrity, and even his political opponents credited him with robust, manly virtues.

[Obituaries and estimates appeared in the *Richmond Dispatch,* Sept. 3, and the *Rockingham Register,* Sept. 6, 1895. H. J. Eckenrode, *The Political Hist. of Va. during the Reconstruction* (1904), and C. C. Pearson, *Readjuster Movement in Va.* (1917), give the political background in detail.] C. C. P.

LEWIS, JOSEPH HORACE (Oct. 29, 1824–July 6, 1904), Confederate soldier, congressman, Kentucky jurist, was the son of John and Eliza Martz (Reed) Lewis. His father was a prominent and prosperous citizen of southern Barren County, Ky., and it was there, near Glasgow, that the younger Lewis was born. His early education was sufficient to secure him admission to Centre College which in the days before the Civil War was one of the leading educational institutions in the West. He was graduated from Centre in 1843, then began the study of law in the office of Judge C. C. Tompkins of Glasgow. He was admitted to the bar in 1845 and began the practice of law at Glasgow. His later career as a jurist and the high preferment he attained in that field would indicate, even if other testimony were lacking, that his law training was not insufficient nor his legal ability of a low order. For the time being, however, his law practice was subordinated to politics. In 1850 he was elected to the state House of Representatives. He was reëlected in 1851 and in 1853. The *Journals* of the House for these years do not indicate that he was active as a legislator.

Lewis found it necessary in the troubled years before the war to reconstruct his principles. He had been elected to the legislature as a Whig but upon the collapse of that party he transferred his loyalty to the Democratic party to which he afterward steadily adhered. He was the Democratic candidate for Congress in 1857 and again in 1861 but was defeated on both occasions. He was ardent in his Southern sympathies and in 1860 was active in his support of Breckinridge for the presidency. When war came it found him with his mind made up. Upon the establishment of Camp Dick Robinson he began recruiting in Kentucky for the Confederate army, and in September 1861 he was commissioned colonel of the 6th Regiment of Kentucky Infantry. He fought throughout the war and was frequently cited for his bravery in action, notably at Shiloh. In September 1863, as a result of his part in the battle of Chickamauga, he was made brigadier-general (Thompson, *post,* p. 391). With that rank he commanded the famous "Orphan Brigade" for the remainder of the war. He opposed Sherman in his march across Georgia and the Carolinas and surrendered with the Confederate forces at Washington Court House.

At the close of the war Lewis returned to Kentucky and resumed the practice of law at Glasgow. In the general reaction toward the Confederates in Kentucky he was elected to the state legislature in 1868. In 1870 he was elected to Congress to fill a vacancy and the next year was elected for a full term. After a few years spent in the practice of law he was elected circuit judge in 1880 but resigned in 1881 to seek election to a vacancy on the court of appeals. In 1882 he was reëlected for a term of eight years and in 1890 again elected for eight years (Z. F. Smith, *The History of Kentucky,* 1895, pp. 776, 778, and 817). It was these seventeen years of continuous service on the court of appeals (for four years of which he was chief-justice) that constituted the most valuable contribution made by Lewis to the state. His probity gave authority to his decisions and contributed no little to the high respect accorded to the court. Upon the expiration of his term in 1899 Lewis retired to his farm in Scott County and engaged in no further public activity beyond serving as chairman of the Goebel Reward Commission after 1900 (Louisville *Courier-Journal,* July 7, 1904). Lewis had married, on Nov. 29, 1845, Sarah H. Rogers of Glasgow, who died in 1858 leaving two children. After the war he was married to Cassandra (Flournoy) Johnson, widow of Jilson P. Johnson of Louisville.

[The best account of Lewis as a lawyer and as a legislator is given in H. Levin, *The Lawyers and Lawmakers of Ky.* (n.d.). Further sources include: E. P. Thompson, *Hist. of the Orphan Brigade* (1898); Lewis and Richard H. Collins, *Hist. of Ky.* (2 vols., 1874); *Biog. Cyc. of the Commonwealth of Ky.* (1896); *War of the Rebellion: Official Records (Army)*; and J. M. McAllister and L. B. Tandy, *Geneals. of the Lewis and Kindred Families* (1906), p. 60.] R. S. C.

LEWIS, LAWRENCE (June 20, 1856–Sept. 2, 1890), lawyer, author, was born in Philadelphia, the son of Robert Morton and Anna Elizabeth (Shippen) Lewis. Named for an uncle, he was known to his contemporaries as Lawrence Lewis, Jr. He was educated at Episcopal Academy and at the University of Pennsylvania, where he graduated in 1876 with the degree of A.B. and later secured the master's degree. After studying law in the office of William Henry Rawle, he was admitted to the bar in 1879, and was made a member and for a time secretary of the Law Academy of Philadelphia. In 1883 he married Dora Kelly. His earliest notable achievements were in the field of historical and legal literature. In 1880 he published *An Essay on Original Land Titles in Philadelphia,* which was awarded the Duponceau Prize Medal by the Law Academy. It was a product of genuine historical and legal scholarship. In 1881 he published another work showing remarkable powers of research and synthesis for so young a scholar—*The Constitution, Jurisdiction and Practice of the Courts of Pennsylvania in the Seventeenth Century* (reprinted from *Pennsylvania Magazine of History and Biography,* vol. V, no. 2). This was followed in 1882 by *A History of the Bank of North America,* a study prepared at the request of the president and the directors of the bank: a laudatory account from the Hamiltonian point of view, but valuable because of its portraits, facsimiles, letters, and list of subscribers and directors. He also published *Memoir of Edward Shippen, Chief Justice of Pennsylvania* (1883; reprinted from *Pennsylvania Magazine* for April 1883), and *A Brief Statement of the Origin, Nature, and History of the French Spoliation Claims* (n.d.). He annotated *The American and English Railroad Cases,* volumes X–XX (1883–85) and *American and English Corporation Cases,* volumes I–VIII (1884–85), edited *Weekly Notes of Cases,* 1879–90, and contributed to periodicals.

He early established himself as a practising attorney, winning his outstanding success as attorney for claimants under the Act of Congress of 1885 by which claims arising out of French actions prior to July 31, 1801, were to be adjudicated in the United States Court of Claims. As counsel for the defendant in the case of *Forepaugh* vs. *Delaware, Lackawanna & Western Railroad Company,* which involved the important new legal principle of limited liability of business associates, he secured a verdict validating contracts which limited the liability of the company. Because of his study of land titles and of legal procedure he was called upon to draft for the state a new law of escheats greatly simplifying complicated legal processes. His career was cut short by his death in a railroad accident near West Chester.

[See *Legal Intelligencer,* Sept. 12, 1890; *Meeting in Memory of Lawrence Lewis, Jr.* (Law Academy of Phila., 1890); *The Press* and *Public Ledger* (Phila.), Sept. 3, 1890. The various French spoliation cases in which Lewis was counsel may be studied in the appropriate volumes of the Court of Claims *Reports* and in the voluminous periodical literature of the time. See "French Spoliations," a bibliography, in *Boston Pub. Lib. Bull.,* Spring No., 1885.] W. B—n.

LEWIS, MERIWETHER (Aug. 18, 1774–Oct. 11, 1809), explorer and governor, was a native of that cradle of noted Americans, Albemarle County, Va., where he was a neighbor of the Jeffersons, Randolphs, and other prominent families. He was named for his mother, Lucy Meriwether, and was the eldest child of her marriage with her cousin, William Lewis. Both families were among the élite of their region; William Lewis, a cousin of Fielding Lewis [*q.v.*], served in the Continental Army and died soon after the surrender at Yorktown, leaving a considerable estate. Within a brief time his widow married John Marks, and when Meriwether was about ten years old the family removed with a large group of kinsfolk to upper Georgia, where they had plantations on the Broad River in the present Oglethorpe County. Here young Lewis grew up amid pleasant surroundings. Much of his time was spent in the open, and he became an expert hunter. He also took note of the fauna and flora of the vicinity and early showed both scientific and literary tastes. It is said that when told by his schoolmaster that the earth turned around he jumped high in the air and was disappointed that he came down in the same place, until it was proved to him that he moved with the moving earth. He also showed great presence of mind during danger; when a group of women and children, gathered about a bonfire, were frightened at an alarm supposed to be caused by Indians, it was Meriwether Lewis who dashed a bucket of water on the flames, leaving the group to grateful darkness (manuscript letter, Draper MSS., 15DD32 Wisconsin Historical Library).

At the age of thirteen Lewis returned to Virginia to study under the Rev. Matthew Maury, who grounded him well in Latin and also taught him mathematics and the rudiments of science. He continued his studies under private tutors for five years, planning to attend William and Mary College, but when he was eighteen years old his step-father died, his mother returned to the Virginia plantation, "Locust Hill," on Ivy Creek near Charlottesville, and Meriwether as the eldest son felt it his duty to remain at home and manage the estate. He also took great interest in the education of his brother, Reuben Lewis, and his young half-brother and sister, John and Mary Marks.

Lewis was twenty when the president called for troops to suppress the Whisky Rebellion; as a member of the local militia he went into camp first at Winchester, then across the mountains near Pittsburgh. There early in 1795 he wrote to his mother that he was "quite delighted with a soldier's life." In consequence, May 1, 1795, he enlisted in the regular army, being commissioned ensign in the 2nd Legion. That year he marched to Greenville, Ohio, where he attended the treaty made by Anthony Wayne [*q.v.*] with the northern Indians, which ended the wars in the Northwest Territory. During this campaign he was one of the subordinates of William Clark [*q.v.*], his future companion in exploring the West.

On Nov. 1, 1796, Lewis was transferred to the 1st Infantry and in 1799, commissioned lieutenant. During the last years of the eighteenth century he was stationed in turn at several cantonments. His honesty and industry were so noted that he was chosen paymaster for his regiment. In 1797 he obtained a furlough, visited his home, and later journeyed to Kentucky on business, for his own and the family estate (manuscript letters in Wisconsin Historical Library). Late in the summer of 1797 he was on active duty in command of a company at Fort Pickering, a newly erected fortification near the site of Memphis, built after the evacuation of that region by the Spanish. This fort was in Chickasaw Indian Territory and here Lewis learned the language and the customs of these Indians. Thence he was ordered to Detroit and was stationed at that outpost in 1801 when his friend and neighbor, Thomas Jefferson, was elected president.

In the first week after his election Jefferson wrote to Lewis, offering him the post of private secretary. The letter was couched in flattering terms. In selecting a secretary, said Jefferson, "I thought it important to respect not only his capacity to aid in the private concerns of the household, but also to contribute to the mass of information which it is interesting to the administration to acquire. Your knowledge of the Western country, of the Army and of all its interests and relations has rendered it desirable for public as well as private purposes that you should be engaged in that office." The salary would be only five hundred dollars, but Lewis would live in the executive mansion, and could retain his military rank. The letter concluded, "It has been solicited by several who will have no answer till I hear from you" (Jefferson Papers, Library of Congress).

Lewis received Jefferson's letter at Pittsburgh, en route from Detroit. He immediately accepted the offer it contained, and, acting on the President-Elect's suggestions, obtained leave of absence from his military superior, Gen. James Wilkinson. He was in Washington about the time of the inauguration, and shortly afterwards removed with the President to the White House. There he was expected to oversee the domestic arrangements, since Jefferson's daughters were both married and could stay with their father only occasionally. The establishment was served by eleven servants brought from Monticello; hospitality was lavish and democratic; Jefferson kept open house for diplomats, congressmen, and friends. Dinner was served at four o'clock and the table was surrounded by men of note, who often continued the conversation until midnight. Thomas Paine and Joel Barlow, Jefferson's former companions in Paris, were in Washington that winter, and the discussion and councils must have been a liberal education for the President's young friend and secretary. He was also employed in affairs of state. On Dec. 8, 1801, Jefferson sent Lewis to convey his annual message to the Senate, not wishing to appear and to read it in person as his predecessors had done.

During Lewis's two years at the White House, the matter of exploring for a land route to the Pacific Ocean was frequently discussed. It was a project which had occupied Jefferson's thought for twenty years, and Lewis had long cherished the wish to be chosen leader of such an expedition. In 1792 when but eighteen years of age he had importuned Jefferson, then secretary of state, to permit him to undertake the journey. It was deemed premature at that time, but the plan had never been abandoned by either Jefferson or Lewis. Now the time seemed ripe for carrying it into execution. On Jan. 18, 1803, Jefferson sent to Congress a private message concerning Indian trading houses; in it he discussed the advisability of learning something of the far western Indians, and proposed an appropriation for a journey of discovery. Lewis himself had made the estimate of the necessary expenses, and Congress quickly appropriated the $2,500 he desired.

Jefferson considered Lewis's qualifications for the leadership of such an expedition unsurpassed: "Of courage undaunted; possessing a firmness and perseverance of purpose which nothing but impossibilities could divert from its direction; careful as a father of those committed to his charge, yet steady in the maintenance of order and discipline; intimate with the Indian characters, customs, and principles; habituated to the hunting life; guarded by exact observations of the vegetables and animals of his own country against losing time in the description of objects already possessed; honest, disinterested, liberal, of sound understanding, and a fidelity to truth so scrupulous that whatever he should report would be as certain as seen by ourselves; with all these qualifications as if selected and implanted by nature in one body for this express purpose" (memoir by Jefferson in *History of the Expedition,* 1814). All he lacked, in Jefferson's opinion, was scientific knowledge—methods of taking latitude and longitude and the use of astronomical instruments. Jefferson therefore sent him to Philadelphia to study with the scientists there; afterwards, at Lancaster, Andrew Ellicott [*q.v.*] gave him advice on astronomy and map-making.

Jefferson had prepared instructions of a detailed nature for Lewis's conduct on the journey; these he sent him June 30, 1803, and with them his passports through French territory. Before his departure, however, news reached Washington of the purchase of Louisiana, which made it possible for the expedition to pass through territory belonging to the United States. At the instance of Jefferson, Lewis was to choose a companion officer; he offered the position to William Clark of Louisville, and the names and fame of Lewis and Clark are inseparably united.

The expedition mustered in Illinois, not far from the mouth of the Missouri; there during the winter of 1803–04 the men were enlisted and drilled. In the spring of 1804 Lewis assisted in the transfer at St. Louis of upper Louisiana to the United States, while Clark brought on the men and was joined by Lewis at St. Charles, Mo. The route was to follow the Missouri to its source. The chief difficulty apprehended was the enmity of some of the upper river tribes, especially the Sioux. A band of these Indians attempted to arrest the passage of the expedition, but the leaders' firmness and tact prevailed and they reached the Mandan villages in North Dakota late in the fall. There the men wintered and prepared for the further journey. Thence Lewis sent letters to his family and the President which were the last messages from him for eighteen months. As guides for the upper river a French-Canadian and his Shoshone wife, Sacajawea [*q.v.*], were taken from the Mandans, when, on Apr. 7, 1805, the voyage was resumed. By July they reached the falls, where a long portage was made; by August the explorers came to the end of navigation. Sacajawea here found relatives from whom horses were obtained to cross the divide. Arrived at the Columbia, the expedition built canoes and descended that river to the ocean. The continent had at last been crossed by means of its two great rivers.

Fort Clatsop was built, not far from Astoria, to house the party for the winter and the rainy seasons. Since no ships came to this port in the spring, it was determined to recross the continent by the route the party followed coming out. The explorers returned over another pass to the place where they had cached their canoes the previous autumn. Lewis determined to make a detour along Maria's River, which he had named on the outward journey for his cousin, Maria Wood. It appeared that this tributary went farther north than any other and might interlock with higher branches of the Columbia. On this stream he had a hostile encounter with a band of Indians, the only serious skirmish on the trip. Some days later he was accidentally wounded by one of his men, who mistook him for a deer. By the time they reached the Mandans Lewis was in bad condition, but with rest and care he made a quick recovery. The captains persuaded a Mandan chief to accompany them to St. Louis, where they arrived on Sept. 23, 1806, to the great joy of the entire nation, who had long given them up for lost.

The success of the expedition was due to the combined abilities of the two leaders, Lewis and Clark. Lewis, however, was the true chief, the ultimate authority on every question. His journals show that he was deeply impressed with his responsibility; they show also his intellectual ardor and scientific spirit, and his humane feeling for man and nature. The two chiefs at once began to plan for a published account of their adventures. In November 1806 they started for Washington. There Lewis resigned from the army and Jefferson appointed him governor of Louisiana, the territory embracing all the province north of the present state of that name.

On returning to St. Louis in the summer of 1807, he found much to do in pacifying factions and reconciling feuds. His services as governor were brief but useful. His even-handed justice, his humanity and honesty gave the province the administration it needed. He organized the militia, had the laws codified, and aided Clark, who had been appointed superintendent of Indian affairs, in negotiating with the Indians. In the summer of 1809 he learned with distress that because of some technicality some of the bills he had issued on the government had been repudiated. He decided to go to Washington to investigate, and left St. Louis intending to go by way of New Orleans and the ocean. At Chickasaw Bluffs (now Memphis), however, he changed his plan and went overland, striking the Natchez Trace at the crossing of the Tennessee below Muscle Shoals. He had with him two servants, a negro and a half-breed Spaniard. On the night of Oct. 11, at a rude inn in central Tennessee, he died. Jefferson later assumed it was by his own hand. His family and the people of the locality where his death occurred believed he was murdered, and the weight of evidence seems to be with this surmise. No money was found on his body and his watch was later recovered in New Orleans. In 1848 the state of Tennessee erected a monument to him, in the county which now bears his name, but his best monument is the Lewis and Clark expedition and the accounts thereof prepared by his own pen.

[The best brief biography of Lewis is that written by Jefferson for inclusion in the first edition of the *Hist. of the Expedition under the Command of Captains Lewis and Clark* (2 vols., Phila., 1814), prepared for the press by Nicholas Biddle and Paul Allen from material left by Lewis and lent by Clark. This account was published in London in 1814 under the title, *Travels to the Source of the Missouri River*. An edition was prepared by Elliott Coues (4 vols., 1893), and another by J. B. McMaster (3 vols., 1904). The first report of the expedition appeared as *Message from the President of the United States, Communicating Discoveries Made . . . by Captains Lewis and Clark . . . Feb. 19, 1806* (1806). The original journals remain in the Am. Phil. Soc., Philadelphia. R. G. Thwaites edited *Original Journals of the Lewis and Clark Expedition* (8 vols., 1904–05). An additional Lewis journal of his trip down the Ohio was edited by M. M. Quaife, in *Wis. Hist. Soc. Colls.*, vol. XXII (1916). G. R. Gilmer, *Sketches of Some of the First Settlers of Upper Georgia* (1855), describes the conditions of Lewis's boyhood. John Swain, in "The Natchez Trace," *Everybody's Mag.*, Sept. 1905, describes a visit to his grave in central Tennessee. On his government of Louisiana see Louis Houck, *A Hist. of Missouri* (1908), II, 408. For genealogy see W. T. Lewis, *Geneal. of the Lewis Family* (1893) and L. H. A. Minor, *The Meriwethers and their Connections* (1892).] L. P. K.

LEWIS, MORGAN (Oct. 16, 1754–Apr. 7, 1844), soldier, jurist, governor of New York, was the second son of Francis Lewis [*q.v.*] and Elizabeth Annesley, of New York. His early schooling was at home and in Elizabethtown, N. J., and he was graduated at the College of New Jersey (Princeton) in 1773. He was studying law at the time of the outbreak of the Revolution. After a summer of volunteer service in 1775 at Cambridge, Mass., and in New York, he was in the winter and spring of 1776, major in the 2nd Regiment of the "New York Line." From June 1776 till the end of the war he was deputy quartermaster-general for the New York Department and was chief of staff with Gates at Ticonderoga and at Saratoga. Resuming his legal studies at the close of the war he was admitted to the bar, and he also took his first steps in politics by successfully running for the Assembly in 1789–90 and in 1792. He had married, May 11, 1779, Gertrude, daughter of Robert R. and Margaret Beekman Livingston of Clermont. This alliance with the "Livingston interest," coupled with his honorable, if hardly brilliant, military record, practically set the conditions of his public career. For a considerable period he profited extensively at the hands of the Clinton-Livingston combination in the Anti-Federalist and Republican parties. He was attorney-general from November 1791 to Dec. 24, 1792, and third justice of the supreme court of New York from the latter date to Oct. 28, 1801, when he was promoted to the chief-justiceship. In the discharge of the duties of these offices his record was perhaps not especially distinguished, but certainly respectable.

In 1804 his nomination to the governorship by the Republicans (practically dictated by DeWitt Clinton) projected Lewis into quite a different scene. The exceptional situations both of the Federalists and of Aaron Burr enabled him, it is true, to win decisively over the latter after a campaign of unexampled virulence. But for vigorous exercise of a governor's power and the development and maintenance of party leadership, the sinuosities and the ruthlessness of New York politics at that period called for a disposition and for capacities which apparently Lewis did not possess. Clinton turned against him. Both factions, the Lewisites, or "Quids," and the Clintonians toyed with Federalist support, and each in turn captured the council of appointment and used its powers in savagely proscriptive fashion. As it proved, Lewis's tenderness for the Livingstons in patronage matters and his deposition of Clinton from the New York City mayoralty were acts of rashness; and the victory of Tompkins in the gubernatorial campaign of 1807 crowned Clinton's determination to subjugate the Livingston influence. As the War of 1812 approached Lewis was enabled to return to politics for terms in the state Senate and for a seat on the council of appointment. During the war he was quartermaster-general and in 1813 major-general in service on the Niagara frontier. In this campaign his age and, above all, the conditions of intrigue in the high command, forbade his winning distinction, and in 1814 he was in command of the region about New York City.

Whatever the extent or consequences of his errors or misfortunes in the field of party warfare, Lewis took an enlightened and frequently generous view of the duties and privileges of one in public station. During the war he advanced funds for the discharge of American prisoners of war and remitted rents on his estates for tenants who had rendered military service. His later years were filled with activities of a more or less public character. As landlord on the Livingston estates he took action characterized by enlightened foresight and to a large degree avoided the troubles of the anti-rent disturbances. He was a pillar of Masonry in the period of strong agitation against the order. He was also president of the New York Historical Society, 1832–36, president-general of the Society of the Cincinnati, 1839–44, and one of the founders of New York University. He died in his ninetieth year in New York City.

[Julia Delafield's *Biogs. of Francis Lewis and Morgan Lewis* (2 vols., 1877) gives much personal and family detail. See also: J. D. Hammond, *The Hist. of Pol. Parties in the State of N. Y.* (2 vols., 1842); D. S. Alexander, *A Pol. Hist. of the State of N. Y.*, vol. I (1906); Henry Adams, *Hist. of the U. S. of America During the Administration of James Madison*, vol. I (1891); J. S. Jenkins, *Lives of the Govs. of the State of N. Y.* (1851); *N. Y. Tribune*, Apr. 8, 9, 10, 1844.]
C. W. S.

LEWIS, ORLANDO FAULKLAND (Sept. 5, 1873–Feb. 24, 1922), social worker, penologist, and author, born at Boston, Mass., was the younger son of John Jay Lewis and Abbie Goodwin (Davis) Lewis. On his father's side, he was a descendant of George Lewis, who came from East Greenwich, England, to Plymouth, Mass., about 1630; on his mother's, of William Davis who, according to family tradition, emigrated to Massachusetts from Wales about 1635. His father was a Universalist minister, who, about 1890, gave up his pastorate for the lecture platform; his mother was a successful writer for children's magazines. Both were energetic and had many affiliations with religious, social, and civic undertakings.

Lewis was educated in the Boston schools but spent the last two years before entering college in Munich, Germany, where his brother was enrolled in the Royal Conservatory. In 1892 he matriculated at Tufts College, from which he received the degree of A.B. in 1895, and a master's degree after two years as a graduate student and instructor in modern languages. A brief period of foreign study in Munich and at the Sorbonne was followed by graduate work at the University of Pennsylvania, where, in 1900, he was granted a doctorate in Germanic languages. Five years of modern language teaching at the University of Maine did not give him the stimulus and the mental satisfaction which he craved. A summer course under the sociologist Charles R. Henderson [*q.v.*] at the University of Chicago interested him in the work of social betterment, and in 1905 he became superintendent of the Joint Application Bureau of the Charity Organization Society in New York City. Articles published by him subsequently show that he was profoundly interested at this time in the vagrant, in the child laborer, and in health problems. In 1908 he joined the faculty of the School of Philanthropy, and on Apr. 20 of the same year he married Edith Schieffelin Sabine, of New York City.

In 1910 he was elected general secretary of the Prison Association of New York, and in the work of aiding confined or released prisoners and their families and in the struggle for the application of modern penological principles, his sympathetic personality reached its full expression. Out of the studies to which this interest led him grew his most scholarly work: *The Development of American Prisons and Prison Customs, 1776–1845* (1922), unequaled by any other publication for the period it covers. From 1911 to 1918 he also issued a monthly journal, *The Delinquent.*

Excursions into the field of politics convinced him that he was temperamentally unfit to "play the game." Toward the end of his life he became aware of a talent which gave him, perhaps, as much pleasure as did his vocation, the writing of short stories. His products won immediate acceptance, and several found a place in anthologies of "best stories," among them "Alma Mater" and "The Get Away" (*O. Henry Memorial Award: Prize Stories of 1920* and *of 1921*).

[*Who's Who in America*, 1920–21; *N. Y. Times*, Feb. 25, 1922; E. R. Cass, in *The Seventy-Eighth Ann. Report of the Prison Asso. of N. Y. . . . 1922* (1923); H. S. Braucher, in *The Survey*, Mar. 4, 1922; *Lewisiana* (17 vols., 1887–1907), bk. XXIV; G. L. Davis, *Samuel Davis, of Oxford, Mass., and Joseph Davis, of Dudley, Mass., and Their Descendants* (1884).] T. S.

LEWIS, SAMUEL (Mar. 17, 1799–July 28, 1854), first state superintendent of common schools in Ohio and one of the most influential of the founders of the free public school system of that state, was born in Falmouth, Mass., son of Samuel Lewis, a sea-captain, and of Abigail (Tolman) Lewis. Unlike his contemporary, Horace Mann, whose career presents many interesting parallels, he was almost entirely self-educated, having left school at the age of ten. In 1813 his family, impoverished by losses at sea, removed to the neighborhood of Cincinnati, where, after working as farm-laborer, mail-carrier, and surveyor's assistant, he achieved a local reputation as a skilled carpenter. His keen and active mind sought a more intellectual occupation, however; and in 1819 he turned to the study of law, supporting himself and aiding his parents meanwhile by working in the office of the clerk of the court of common pleas. Here his ability, his indefatigable industry, and his uprightness of character won for him the favor and support of some of the leading citizens of Cincinnati. In 1822 he was admitted to the bar, where his devotion to the interests of his clients, together with the above-mentioned qualities, contributed to his marked success. During the following year he married Charlotte Goforth, daughter of Dr. William Goforth [*q.v.*], a well-known physician of Cincinnati.

Ever a champion of the weak and oppressed, he early became an advocate of a public system of education which should be "free to all, rich and poor, on equal terms" (*First Annual Report*, 1838, p. 8). His first successful stroke on behalf of this cause was made in 1826 when he advised and induced his friend and client, William Woodward, to establish the endowment which, through the agency of the magnificently housed and equipped Woodward High School, has exercised a beneficent cultural influence upon thousands of the youth of Cincinnati, poor as well as rich. The same purpose led Lewis to take an active part in the proceedings of the College of Teachers, a body organized in 1831 to promote the interests of education. In 1837, largely in consequence of an agitation inaugurated by this organization, the Ohio legislature created the office of state superintendent of common schools and appointed Lewis as the first incumbent. Impressed by the opportunities for public service which the position seemed to offer, he devoted himself to its duties with characteristic zeal and loftiness of purpose. To acquaint himself with the educational situation he traveled over twelve hundred miles, largely on horseback, visiting some sixty-five counties and over three hundred schools. Nearly all the recommendations of his first annual report, including a state school fund of $200,000, authority for districts to borrow money for schoolhouses and for city boards to establish schools of higher grade, and provision for evening schools, were enacted into law Apr. 7, 1838. This legislation proved, however, to be in advance of the public opinion of the time. Numerous memorials were presented urging its repeal and the abolition of the state superintendency. Lewis vigorously opposed this reactionary movement, but his health was already impaired by his strenuous labors, and in 1839 he resigned.

Soon after his return to private life he became actively interested in the anti-slavery movement. In 1841, in cooperation with Salmon P. Chase and others, he organized the Liberty Party, which nominated him for Congress in 1843 and 1848 and for the governorship in 1846, 1851, and 1853. His last campaign for the governorship greatly overtaxed his strength and helped to hasten his death, which occurred the following year.

[*Biog. of Samuel Lewis* (1857), by his son W. G. W. Lewis; J. W. Taylor, *A Manual of the Ohio School System* (1857); C. B. Galbreath, *Samuel Lewis, Ohio's Militant Educator and Reformer* (1904); *First, Second, and Third Annual Report of the Supt. of Common Schools . . . of Ohio* (1838–39); *Am. Jour. of Educ.*, Dec. 1858, Mar. 1859, p. 85; Sept. 1868, p. 793.]

L. F. A.

LEWIS, TAYLER (Mar. 27, 1802–May 11, 1877), Orientalist, was born in the village of Northumberland, Saratoga County, N. Y. His father, Samuel Lewis, had been an officer in the Revolutionary War; his mother, Sarah Van Valkenburg, was of Dutch descent; and he was named after her uncle, John Tayler, former lieutenant-governor of the state. He went to school in Northumberland and at Fort Miller, where the associations seem to have made a deep impression upon him, for he used to go back to the school and later to the school site year after year. He was prepared for college by Dr. Proudfit at Salem, N. Y., and entered Union College in 1816, graduating in the class of 1820. He studied in the law office of Judge S. A. Foote at Albany, was admitted to the Saratoga bar in 1825, and began to practise at Fort Miller. Here he joined the Dutch Reformed Church, was chosen to the consistory, and took up the study of Hebrew.

Dissatisfied with the law, he began to teach, as principal of the academy at Waterford (1833–35), then at Ogdensburg (1833–37), and in 1838 at Waterford again. A Phi Beta Kappa oration, "Faith, the Life of Science," which he delivered at Union College in 1838, aroused a good deal of attention, and that year he was appointed professor of Greek in the University of the City of New York. He now wrote and studied much; and his *Plato* ***contra*** *Atheos: Plato against the Atheists* (1845), may still be read with interest by Grecians. In 1850 he became professor of Greek at Union College, and later professor of Oriental languages and Biblical literature. He was a hard student and mastered (besides Latin and Greek) Syriac, Koptic, Arabic, and Chaldaic, and read widely in mathematics, music, astronomy, and history. He was also deeply interested in current events at an exciting time in the national history. A strong anti-slavery man, he contributed to the propaganda of the Civil War *State Rights: a Photograph from the Ruins of Ancient Greece* (1864). The chief interest of his life, however, was the study of religion, and his main purpose was to show that revelation and scientific knowledge are not merely consistent but interdependent. Among his more important publications are *The Six Days of Creation* (1855), *The Bible and Science, or the World Problem* (1856), and *The Divine Human in the Scriptures* (1860). He was a representative American student and contributed to the American edition of J. P. Lange's *Commentary on the Holy Scriptures* (1865–80) and was on the American board of the Committee for the Revision of the Old Testament. In 1833 he married Jane Keziah, daughter of Daniel Payn, by whom he had six children. He was of slight and fragile figure, which contrasted strikingly with the vigor of his controversial energy and the power of his scholarship. His portraits present a severe countenance, but those who remember him think of a very fine and gentle expression and beautiful silver hair. His students had a great affection for him, though in later years they took advantage of his deafness to say dreadful things in his classroom or when they met him on the campus.

[*Gen. Cat. of the Officers, Grads. and Students of Union Coll., 1795–1868* (1868); E. N. Potter, *Discourses Commemorative of Prof. Tayler Lewis, LL.D., L.H.D.* . . . (1878); Wm. Wells, "Tayler Lewis: In Memoriam," *Meth. Quart. Rev.*, Oct. 1878; Homer Gage, "Tayler Lewis," *Union Alumni Mo.*, Apr. 1930; A. V. V. Raymond, *Union Univ.* (1907), vol. II; "Univ. of the State of N. Y. Ninety-First Ann. Report of the Regents," *Docs. of the Assembly of the State of N. Y.*, 1878, no. 58; R. B. Welch, in *House Ex. Doc. No. 1, Pt. 5*, 45 Cong., 2 Sess.; *New Eng. Jour. of Educ.*, June 7, 1877; *N. Y. Tribune*, May 14, 1877.]

E. E. H.

LEWIS, WILLIAM (Feb. 2, 1751 o.s.–Aug. 16, 1819), lawyer, of Quaker stock, the son of Josiah Lewis and his wife, who was probably Martha Allen, was born on his father's farm near Edgemont, Chester (now Delaware) County, Pa. He attended a country school near his home and afterwards entered a seminary established by the Society of Friends at Willistown, Pa., where he made rapid progress. Although from early boyhood he wished to become a lawyer and was supported in this ambition by his father, his mother did not give her consent to the plan until his seventeenth year. He was then placed in the Friends' Public School in Philadelphia to receive instruction in Latin. In 1770 he commenced the study of law under Nicholas Waln of West Chester and Philadelphia. He was admitted to the bar in November 1773 and again in 1776, after the adoption of the state constitution, and became one of the leading Quaker lawyers of Pennsylvania. He attracted especial attention by his success as counsel for the defense in many of the treason cases which arose in Philadelphia during the Revolution and afterward. One of the most famous treason cases with which he was connected was that of the Northampton Insurgents in 1799, when he was one of the counsel for John Fries [*q.v.*], a defendant. In this case his client was pronounced guilty and sentenced to death, but was later pardoned by President Adams (see Francis Wharton, *State Trials of the United States during the Administration of Washington and Adams,* 1849, pp. 458–648; and *The Two Trials of John Fries,* 1800).

He was elected a member of the Pennsylvania legislature in 1787 and again in 1789, when he was also chosen a member of the state constitutional convention. On Oct. 6, 1789, he was appointed attorney of the United States for the district of Pennsylvania and on July 20, 1791, accepted appointment as judge of the federal district court for the eastern district of Pennsylvania, in which capacity he served until Apr. 11, 1792. He then returned to his more lucrative private practice, which he continued until two years before his death. In February 1794 he was employed as counsel by the petitioners against the election of Albert Gallatin to the United States Senate. In this capacity he addressed that body in the Senate chamber, the first time professional counsel had spoken from the Senate floor. In politics he was a thorough Federalist and was frequently consulted on legal matters by government officials. He was much interested in the abolition of slavery within the state of Pennsylvania and is credited with having been instrumental in securing the passage of the act of Mar. 1, 1780, "for the gradual abolition of slavery in Pennsylvania." Learned in the law, clear and logical in argument, he was admitted to be one of the leading lawyers of his generation. He sometimes procrastinated in preparing his cases, and then made use of many ingenious devices for gaining time. His annoying habit of studying his case while it was in progress and introducing new points when he had the closing argument led the court to make a general rule prohibiting new points by concluding counsel (Binney, *post*, p. 43). He was twice married: first to Rosanna Lort by whom he had three children, and second to Frances Durdin. He died in Philadelphia after a short illness.

[Wm. Primrose, "Biography of William Lewis" (written 1820), *Pa. Mag. of Hist. and Biog.*, Apr. 1896; J. S. Futhey and Gilbert Cope, *Hist. of Chester County, Pa.* (1881); Horace Binney, *The Leaders of the Old Bar of Philadelphia* (1859), repr. in *Pa. Mag.*, Apr. 1890; E. P. Oberholtzer, *Phila., A Hist. of the City and Its People* (n.d.), vol. I; J. T. Scharf and Thompson Westcott, *Hist. of Phila.* (1884), II, 1527–28; J. H. Martin, *Martin's Bench and Bar of Phila.* (1883); *Poulson's Am. Daily Advertiser*, Aug. 17, 19, 1819.]

J. H. F.

LEWIS, WILLIAM BERKELEY (1784–Nov. 12, 1866), planter, politician, was the son of John Lewis of Loudoun County, Va., whose wife was a Berkeley. At an early age he went to Nashville, Tenn., then a frontier village. The years of his youth are obscure, but his fortune was made when he eloped with the young daughter of William Terrell Lewis, a prominent planter and land speculator of the neighborhood. This marriage made him a brother-in-law of John H. Eaton [*q.v.*]. The bride, Margaret, and her husband were received into the home of James Jackson, a leading merchant of Nashville. The two Lewis families were not related by blood, nor was James Jackson related to Andrew Jackson, but the young couple was soon invited to "The Hermitage," where a life-long friendship between Lewis and the future President was cemented. The elder Lewis having died, his home, "Fairfield," near "The Hermitage," became the abode of the younger Lewises for the remainder of their lives.

During Jackson's Natchez campaign of 1812 and his Creek campaign of the next year, Lewis served as his quartermaster, and his efficient work during these trying times secured his place in the affections of the General. After the battle of New Orleans, Lewis was one of a small coterie of friends who recognized Jackson's availability for the presidency. The correspondence of 1816–17 between Jackson and Monroe, which later served a valuable political purpose, may not have been intended for such use, but it was Lewis who manipulated it and it was he who later capitalized it (Parton, *post*, II, 356–71), thus showing himself doubtless a man of keen foresight and consummate tact. When the time arrived, in 1821, for Jackson's presidential campaign to assume definite shape, it was Lewis, along with a few other Nashville friends, who busied himself in putting the cause before the people. His first wife having died, he had married Mrs. Adelaide Stokes Chambers, daughter of Gov. Montfort Stokes [*q.v.*] of North Carolina. The Monroe correspondence was now used to bring Stokes to Jackson's support. In such ways did the subtle Lewis work. When, during the campaign of 1828, charges were made concerning the legality of Jackson's marriage, Lewis was assigned the congenial task of investigating and reporting on the matter. His version was that adopted by Jackson's biographer, Parton, and by posterity. Upon Jackson's elevation to the presidency, Lewis became second auditor of the treasury, a resident of the White House, and a member of the "Kitchen Cabinet." He took a leading part in trying to conciliate the warring factions during the Eaton controversy, and on many other occasions acted as the personal agent of the President. He had early allied himself with the Van Buren forces and worked consistently to promote the cause of the New Yorker. He disagreed with Jackson on the spoils system and the bank question, but he never put himself in opposition to the President, and the two remained firm friends to the end.

After Jackson's retirement, Lewis retained his post as auditor. Van Buren, however, showed little gratitude for the faithful services rendered in his behalf, and Lewis had no influence with the new administration. In 1845 he retired to his home near Nashville in time to attend at the bedside of the dying Jackson. For the remainder of his days he lived in comparative seclusion, emerging, however, to furnish Parton with information which put numerous incidents concerning Jackson in the most favorable light. During the Civil War his sympathies were with the Union. He died shortly after its close, and lies in an unmarked grave in Mount Olivet cemetery at Nashville.

[J. T. Moore and A. P. Foster, *Tennessee, The Volunteer State* (1923); James Parton, *Life of Andrew Jackson* (1885); J. S. Bassett, *The Life of Andrew Jackson* (1911); and *Correspondence of Andrew Jackson* (vols. I–V, 1926–31); W. T. Lewis, *Geneal. of the Lewis Family* (1893); M. S. Asher, "Major William B. Lewis, of Fairfield," clipping from Nashville *American*, 1905, in book of clippings in State Lib., Nashville; *Republican Banner* (Nashville), Nov. 13, 1866.]

T. P. A.

LEWIS, WILLIAM DAVID (Sept. 22, 1792–Apr. 1, 1881), merchant, banker, was born at Christiana, New Castle County, Del., the son of Joel Lewis, who married a Miss Hughes. Both parents were Welsh Quakers. He attended Clermont Seminary and Lower Dublin Academy and at the age of seventeen was apprenticed to the house of Samuel Archer & Company, Philadelphia merchants in the East India and China trade. Four years later he was invited by his brother, John D. Lewis, who was a commission merchant in Russia, to join him at St. Petersburg. Unable to obtain passage because of the war between the United States and Great Britain, he called upon Henry Clay in Washington, procured an appointment as one of the private secretaries to the peace commission, and sailed from New York on the *John Adams* under a flag of truce (Feb. 27, 1814). At Gothenburg he left the commissioners and, continuing his journey, arrived at the Russian capital in the midst of the excitement aroused by the Allied triumphs over the Emperor Napoleon. He spent some months learning the Russian language, then entered his brother's employ, and lived in Russia until August 1824, during this period making two voyages to the United States for the house and a tour of western Europe. In Russia his genial personality and constant good humor won him many friends, including Count Nesselrode, the Tsar's Minister of Foreign Affairs, Platov, hetman of the Cossacks, the Nikolai Ivanovich Grech, editor of the *Syn Otechestva* (a weekly magazine), who introduced him into the literary group that met at the home of the poet Derzhavin. Much later, his metrical translation of Russian poems (*The Bokchesarian Fountain, by Alexander Pooshkeen, and other Poems by Various Authors,* privately printed, Philadelphia, 1849) was enthusiastically greeted by his friend Grech in the *Sievernaia Pchela* (St. Petersburg, July 18, 1851). In July 1817 Lewis was thrown into prison at the instance of John Leavitt Harris, United States consul at St. Petersburg, with whom he had a personal quarrel. He was soon released, and, returning to the United States in November 1819, was immediately challenged by Harris. Lewis promptly accepted and shot his opponent in the thigh when they met at Red Bank, on the Delaware. Shortly thereafter, Leavitt Harris, uncle of the duellist, who had also been consul at St. Petersburg, sued Lewis for slander, the latter having accused the elder Harris of corruption so gross that John Quincy Adams, secretary of state, characterized it as "unprincipled rapacity" (*Memoirs,* IV, 284). In St. Petersburg both parties sought documentary aid from the government of the Tsar, and after seven years of litigation, which involved Secretary Adams, President Monroe, and eminent legal counsel, a Philadelphia jury awarded Harris $100 (Feb. 15, 1827). On June 28, 1825, Lewis married Sarah Claypoole of Philadelphia and established himself as an importer and commission merchant in that city. He was for ten years cashier of the Girard Bank (1832–42) and helped finance a number of the early Pennsylvania railroads, including the New Castle & Frenchtown Railroad (1831–32), the Philadelphia, Germantown & Norristown Railroad, and the Philadelphia, Wilmington & Baltimore Railroad. He then became president of the Pennsylvania Academy of the Fine Arts, president of the Catawissa Railroad Company, and collector of customs for the Port of Philadelphia (1849–53). He was a life-long friend of Henry Clay, who procured confirmation by the Senate of his nomination to the collectorship in September 1850 after it had been blocked for months by Senator James Cooper of Pennsylvania. After he retired from business (about 1855) he lived on his estate near Florence, N. J., where he died in April 1881.

[Biog. memoirs of Lewis by J. W. Forney, in *Progress* (Phila.), Dec. 21, 1878, Apr. 9, 1881; *Memoirs of John Quincy Adams* (12 vols., 1874–77), ed. by C. F. Adams; *Writings of John Quincy Adams,* VI (1916), VII (1917), ed. by W. C. Ford; *Biog. Encyc. of Pa. of the Nineteenth Century* (1874); S. A. Allibone, *A Critical Dict. of Eng. Lit. and British and Am. Authors,* vol. II (1870); *The Charges against the Collector and Surveyor of the Port of Phila.; Reply of Chas. Gibbons to the Argument of David Paul Brown* (n.d.); W. D. Lewis, *A Brief Account of the Efforts of Senator Cooper of Pa. and Chas. Gibbons and their Associates* (1851); Rebecca I. Graff, *Geneal. of the Claypoole Family of Phila.* (1893); the *Press* (Phila.), *Phila. Inquirer,* and *Phila. Record,* all Apr. 2, 1881.]

F. E. R.

LEWIS, WILLIAM GASTON (Sept. 3, 1835–Jan. 7, 1901), soldier, engineer, was born at Rocky Mount, N. C., of Revolutionary stock, the son of Dr. John Wesley and Catharine Ann (Battle) Lewis, and the grandson of Exum and Ann (Harrison) Lewis. As a boy he attended Lovejoy's Military School at Raleigh and graduated from the University of North Carolina in the year 1855. Later he taught school at Chapel Hill, N. C., and in Jackson County, Fla. During 1857–58 he served as a government surveyor in Minnesota, and from 1858 to 1861 as assistant engineer on the Tarboro branch of the Wilmington & Weldon Railroad. The Civil War found him a member of the Edgecombe Guards, from which he received appointment as ensign and lieutenant in the newly organized 1st North Carolina Regiment, Apr. 21, 1861, and after creditable service in the battle of Big Bethel, he was promoted major of the 33rd North Carolina Infantry. For meritorious services at New Bern, he won additional promotion to lieutenant-colonel, 43rd North Carolina, and in June 1863 participated in Ewell's Shenandoah Valley campaign. He took part in the battle of Malvern Hill, and at Gettysburg received special commendation from his brigade commander. Subsequently he took part in the battles of Bristow Station, Mine Run, and in April 1864, in the capture of Plymouth, N. C. He was promoted to the colonelcy of his regiment, and at Drewry's Bluff, May 16, 1864, he received official praise from General Ransom for skilful construction of the outer works. For this he was promoted brigadier-general, June 2, 1864, as of May 31, 1864. As a brigade commander, Lewis was with Early in his engagements with Sheridan in the latter part of the year 1864, and in the battles around Petersburg (A. A. Humphreys, *The Virginia Campaign of '64 and '65*, 1883). He participated in the final retirement of the Confederate army westward, and at Farmville, Va., Apr. 7, 1865, was severely wounded and taken prisoner. It is of record that throughout the war, he took part in some thirty-seven battles and engagements (*Confederate Military History*, 1899, vol. IV, pp. 328–30).

After the close of the war, Lewis resumed practice as a civil engineer. He became agent of the state board for swamp lands, was state engineer for some thirteen years, was appointed chief engineer of the Albany & Raleigh Railroad in 1899, and was for an extended period chief of engineers of the North Carolina National Guard. He died suddenly of pneumonia at his home in Goldsboro, N. C., in his sixty-sixth year, and was survived by his widow, Martha E. (Pender) Lewis of Edgecombe County, N. C., to whom he had been married on Mar. 15, 1864. Two sons and four daughters also survived him. He was interred with military honors at Goldsboro.

[See Walter Clark, *Hist. of the Several Regiments and Battalions from N. C. in the Great War, 1861–'65* (1901); *Battles and Leaders of the Civil War* (4 vols., 1887–88); *War of the Rebellion: Official Records (Army)*; *Alumni Hist. of the Univ. of N. C.* (ed. 1924); W. J. Battle, *The Battle Book* (1930); *Charlotte Daily Observer*, Jan. 9, 1901; *Confed. Veteran*, Jan. 1901. There is a valuable sketch of Lewis in the possession of his son, Jas. S. Lewis, Rocky Mount, N. C.]

C. D. R.

LEWIS, WINSLOW (May 11, 1770–May 19, 1850), sailor, lighthouse builder, was born in Wellfleet, Mass., the son of Winslow and Mary (Knowles) Lewis and a descendant of Kenelm Winslow, brother of Gov. Edward Winslow of the Plymouth Colony. He married Elizabeth Greenough, Nov. 7, 1793, and after her death in 1842, married Martha S. Hurlburt, Nov. 22, 1843. There were no children by the second wife, and of those by the first, only Dr. Winslow Lewis of Boston survived him or left descendants. He was "bred to the sea," and had attained the rank of captain and made several voyages as a commander before retiring to engage in business in Boston. He left the sea before 1810, and in the War of 1812 he commanded the Boston Sea Fencibles, a volunteer organization of seamen. He was captured by the British in this war, but it was while he was on his way to inspect a lighthouse, and he was soon released on parole. He was a member of the first Common Council of the City of Boston in 1822; an alderman of the same city in 1829, 1830, 1835, and 1836; and a member of the lower house of the Massachusetts legislature from 1828 to 1833. He was president of the Boston Marine Society, a semi-official organization of shipmasters, from 1818 to 1820; and he was a member and officer of the Ancient and Honorable Artillery Company.

His chief business was as a contractor and builder, though he also manufactured rope and cotton duck; but his nautical experience probably led him to specialize in designing and building lighthouses and providing equipment for them. On June 8, 1810, he obtained a patent for a "lantern, reflecting and magnifying" for illuminating lighthouses, and in 1811 it was installed in Boston Light for trial. It proved satisfactory, and Secretary Gallatin contracted with him to put his lamps and reflectors in all the United States lighthouses, then forty-nine in number, Lewis giving a bond for $60,000 to save half the previous consumption of oil. When this work was completed in 1815, he entered into another agreement to supply all lighthouses with the best sperm oil for seven years, and to visit each of them annually and report its condition, "in consideration being allowed one-half the oil consumed under the old plan." On its expiration, this contract was renewed for one-third of the oil. He also built about a hundred structures for the lighthouse service. Some of these, like the beacon on Romer Shoal, New York Harbor, have been replaced; but others, like the beacon on Bowditch's Ridge in Salem (Mass.) Harbor, still stand (1933). On June 24, 1808, he had received a patent for a binnacle light and on Jan. 23, 1818, received another patent for lamps. In his lifetime he was charged with both fraud and incompetence, but rivalry for government contracts or for professional prestige seems to have been responsible for the accusations. Prior to 1852, the United States Lighthouse Service was undoubtedly badly organized and poorly equipped, but Lewis seems to have done a great deal to make it more effective and economical.

[The chief sources of information, not all of which is accurate, are the following publications: *New-Eng. Hist. and Geneal. Reg.*, Jan. 1863; O. A. Roberts, *Hist. of the Mil. Company of the Massachusetts, now Called The Ancient and Honorable Artillery Company*, vol. II (1897); David Melville, *An Exposé of the Facts Respectfully Submitted to the Govt. and Citizens of the U. S. Relating to the Conduct of Winslow Lewis of Boston* (Providence, 1819), copies in Mass. State House Lib. and Boston Athenæum; Winslow Lewis, *Review of the Report of I. W. P. Lewis on the State of the Light Houses on the Coast of Me. and Mass.*

Sent to the House of Representatives by the Hon. Walter Forward, Secretary of the Treasury, Feb. 24, 1842 (Boston, 1843), copy in Boston Athenæum; M. F. Willoughby, *Lighthouses of New England* (1929); Fitz-Henry Smith, Jr., *The Story of Boston Light* (1911); *A Digest of Patents . . .* (1840); *Boston Jour.*, May 20, 1850.] S. G.

LEXOW, CLARENCE (Sept. 16, 1852–Dec. 30, 1910), lawyer and politician, was born in Brooklyn, N. Y., a son of Rudolph and Caroline (King) Lexow. His father was editor of the *Belletristisches Journal*, a German-language periodical published in New York. For his secondary schooling Clarence attended the German-American Collegiate Institute of Brooklyn and at sixteen went with a brother to Germany, where both boys spent several years in study at the universities of Bonn and Jena. The father had counted on his training as a preparation for journalism, but the sons were attracted to the law as a profession. Returning to New York, Clarence Lexow was graduated from Columbia University Law School in 1874. He was admitted to the bar and practised in the city until 1881, when he removed to Nyack, Rockland County, N. Y., largely for reasons of health. After a time he began to take a modest part in up-state politics and rapidly developed into an organization Republican in the period of Thomas C. Platt's dominance. After an unsuccessful attempt to obtain a seat in Congress, he was chosen a state senator in 1893.

During his first term, the revelations of police corruption in the City of New York made by the Rev. Dr. Charles H. Parkhurst [*q.v.*] led the Chamber of Commerce to ask the legislature for an investigation. The leaders of the Republican majority in that body acceded to the demand, less with the intention of reforming conditions than with the view of exposing Tammany Hall's control of the ballot-box. Lexow moved for the appointment of a Senate special committee and was named as chairman. The matter seems to have been to him only a tactical move in partisan politics, though it may be set down to his credit that in a period marked for political hypocrisy he made no hollow profession of loftier aims. He and his committee were quite unprepared to deal with the mass of evidence of police extortion and blackmail that was marshaled by John W. Goff [*q.v.*] as counsel. Lexow and his colleagues, however, in the words of Dr. Parkhurst (*post*, p. 144), "in time became disciplined to a receptive attitude of mind." Police captains broke down and confessed their guilt on the witness stand; scores of indictments and dismissals from the force followed; a city administration pledged to reform was elected. Throughout the investigation, Lexow took only a perfunctory part. A leader of vision, with a similar opportunity, might have headed a triumphant crusade for civic decency. Failing that, he might at least have secured for himself an independent position as a legislator. Lexow did neither the one thing nor the other. Although his name was long a reminder of one of the most dramatic episodes in New York municipal history, the man himself never rose above the confines of narrow partisanship. In his report as committee chairman the outstanding feature was a recommendation for a bi-partisan board of police commissioners. This suggestion was opposed by the enlightened public opinion of the city and was rejected in later legislation.

As head of the Senate committee on cities Lexow had charge of the Greater New York charter, enacted in 1897. His own account of that law, as it appears in *The Autobiography of Thomas Collier Platt* (1910), gives the major part of the credit for the measure to Platt. For two years Lexow had been recognized as one of the group of senators who could be depended on to block reform bills at Platt's behest (*New-York Tribune*, Apr. 3, 1895). He was the author of a report on trusts and unlawful combinations and in 1898 his service in the Senate ended. He was chairman of the New York Republican convention of 1895, and a presidential elector in 1900. The remainder of his life was devoted to his law practice. He was survived by his wife, Katherine M. Ferris, whom he had married Feb. 3, 1881, together with a son and two daughters.

[*Who's Who in America*, 1910–11; E. L. Murlin, *An Illustrated Legislative Manual: The N. Y. Red Book*, 1898; E. B. Andrews, *The U. S. in Our Own Time* (1903); J. D. Townsend, *N. Y. in Bondage* (1901); C. H. Parkhurst, *My Forty Years in N. Y.* (1923); obituaries in N. Y. papers, notably *The Sun*, Dec. 31, 1910.] W. B. S.

LEYNER, JOHN GEORGE (Aug. 26, 1860–Aug. 5, 1920), inventor, manufacturer, the second white male child born in Colorado, was born on his father's ranch in Left Hand Creek Canyon, Boulder County. He was the eldest son of Peter A. Leyner, of German birth, and Maria A. Dock, of Dutch ancestry, who as bride and groom "went West" by ox-team from Des Moines, Iowa. His education was limited to that afforded by the public school in his district. Until he was nineteen years old he remained on his father's ranch, always more interested in machinery than in tilling the soil. After engaging for four years, 1879–83, in threshing grain for the farmers in his neighborhood and working for two more as engineer, first for a mining and milling company in Jackson, and then for a flour-milling company in Canfield, Colo., he established in 1886 a machine shop and foundry in Longmont, Colo. After a year or two, however, he sold this business and purchased an interest in a machine shop in Denver, of which he later acquired full ownership. The experience gained in repairing mining machinery here gave Leyner an insight into the mechanical needs of the mining industry and the opportunity to exercise his inventive talents. Accordingly he devised many improvements in the machinery then used, and in 1893 perfected a compressed air rock-drilling machine of the piston type in which the drilling steel is attached to and oscillates with the piston. In an endeavor to improve on this first machine he developed a means of supporting the drill loosely in the rock-drilling engine in position to be struck by a rapidly oscillating piston of light weight. After nine years of constant effort the new engine was perfected and patented June 13, 1899 (patent no. 626,761). It was far superior to any rock-drilling machine then made, for it not only increased by 100 per cent. the number of blows struck by the piston but also reduced the weight of the latter from sixty to sixteen pounds. Not content with this achievement, Leyner next devised the hollow drill, through which he forced air and water to the bottom of the drill hole to expel the rock cuttings while drilling. The resulting Water Leyner Rock Drill or "jackhammer," as it is popularly called, was adopted the world over, and in 1902, to supply the demand, Leyner organized the J. George Leyner Engineering Works Company and erected an extensive manufacturing plant at Littleton, Colo. Continuing his inventive work, he perfected, after seven years of effort, a drill-sharpening machine incorporating many radical improvements. He secured patent 917,777 for this invention, engaged in its manufacture, and was soon handling 80 per cent. of the drill-sharpening business of the world. He also made many novel improvements in the air compressor, for the most important of which he received patent no. 938,004, dated Oct. 26, 1909. All of his patented machines and other mining machinery were manufactured in his plant at Littleton until 1911, when he disposed of the entire establishment to the Ingersoll-Rand Company of New York. Instead of retiring, he began working in 1913 on a farm tractor of the caterpillar type. Receiving a patent for this device on Jan. 29, 1918, he organized a manufacturing company and had constructed two experimental machines when he was injured in an automobile accident and died, at Littleton. He was married twice: first, in 1883 to Fanny Batterson; and after her death, to Lina M. Brooks, on June 3, 1912. His widow survived him.

[*Specifications and Drawings of Patents Issued from the U. S. Patent Office,* May, Nov. 1893, June–Sept. 1896, July 1897, May, Aug., Sept. 1898, June 1899, June 1900, Sept. 1902, Sept. 1903, Apr. 1904, Feb., Aug., Nov. 1905, Mar. 1906, Feb., Apr., Dec. 1907, July, Oct. 1908, Mar., May, Aug., Oct. 1909, May 1910, Aug. 1911, May 1912; *Official Gazette of the U. S. Patent Office,* Oct. 1, 1912, Apr. 8, June 17, Sept. 9, Nov. 11, Dec. 23, 1913, May 12, Aug. 4, 1914, Jan. 12, 1915, Jan. 29, 1918; W. B. Kaempffert, *A Popular Hist. of Am. Invention* (1924); *Rocky Mt. News* (Denver), Aug. 6, 1920; data furnished by Ingersoll-Rand Company, N. Y., and J. Ditson, Littleton, Colo.]

C. W. M.

LEYPOLDT, FREDERICK (Nov. 17, 1835–Mar. 31, 1884), publisher, bibliographer, was born in Stuttgart, Germany, the son of Michael Friedrich and Christiane Magdalene (Deihle) Leypoldt. He was originally named Jakob Friedrich Ferdinand, but after he came to America was known as Frederick Leypoldt. Of a literary inclination and reluctant to follow his father's trade, he left his native land in 1854, and eventually became a naturalized citizen of the United States. In New York he obtained employment in the foreign bookstore of F. W. Christern, who in 1859 helped him to establish in Philadelphia a bookstore dealing in books in all languages. This store, with its reading-room of foreign periodicals and its circulating library, became a literary center. While the Civil War prevented the importation of books, Leypoldt extended his interests to publishing. His initial venture, *The Ice-Maiden* by Hans Christian Andersen, translated by Fanny Fuller, appeared in 1863 and was followed by other publications, at first translations, later textbooks for the study of modern languages. He opened a branch office in New York in 1864, soon giving up the bookstore to concentrate his interest on the New York office. In 1865 Henry Holt [*q.v.*], afterward his lifelong friend, joined him in business; and in January 1866 the firm of Leypoldt & Holt was formed. It continued the policy of publishing translations and textbooks, of which Leypoldt wrote several under the anagram, L. Pylodet. On Sept. 27, 1867, he married Augusta Harriet Garrigue, who survived him thirty-five years.

In 1868 he relinquished the publishing side of the business and began his career as a bibliographer by taking charge of the firm's *Literary Bulletin, a Monthly Record of Current Literature.* This bulletin formed the beginning of a series of publications of varying titles which, after absorbing by purchase from George W. Childs [*q.v.*] the *American Literary Gazette and Publishers' Circular,* became, in January 1873, *The Publishers' Weekly.* Leypoldt was sole editor and publisher from 1871 until Jan. 5, 1879; Richard Rogers Bowker then became proprietor, but Leypoldt was again editor and publisher from July 5, 1879, until his death. Many features of the present *Publishers' Weekly* owe their origin to him. In 1880 he established the monthly *Literary News,* which, after his death, was edited by his widow until its cessation in 1904.

As early as 1862 he felt the lack of trade bibliographies, and in the *Publishers' Weekly* he endeavored to provide current lists. No annual catalogue had been published in America since 1856. In the issue of his *Literary Bulletin* for January 1869 appeared the forerunner of his effort to supply the lack. Beginning in 1870, he issued a series of three such annuals: *The American Catalogue of Books for 1869* (1870), *The Trade Circular Annual for 1871 including The American Catalogue of Books Published in the United States during 1870* (1871), and *The Annual American Catalogue, 1871* (1872), the last prefaced by the statement that the work was to be discontinued because of "great obstacles and discouragements." The following year (1873), however, *The Uniform Trade List Annual* anticipated in form by the appendix to his second annual catalogue, and by similar publications by Howard Challen, made its first appearance. It consisted of catalogues of 101 publishers bound in alphabetical order. This project for the book trade was so successful that the idea was adopted in other countries and the American publication, under the revised title, *The Publishers' Trade List Annual,* has continued without interruption.

Work on *The American Catalogue,* under consideration since 1872, the culmination of the series of book-trade aids designed by Leypoldt, was begun in 1876. The compilation of this list of books in print July 1, 1876, proved so costly an undertaking that Leypoldt was obliged to make a financial arrangement with A. C. Armstrong, under whose imprint the volumes were issued in 1880 and 1881. Leypoldt was one of the founders of the *Library Journal* in 1876, and its publisher until his death. When in June 1880 the *Journal,* then published at a loss, was about to discontinue, he personally assumed the responsibility for its continuance. He was interested in the founding of the American Library Association in 1876, and published several library aids for others, compiling and issuing *A Reading Diary of Modern Fiction* (1881) and, with Lynds E. Jones, *The Books of All Time* (1882). In 1879 he undertook the publication of the *Index Medicus,* which, though it brought him a financial loss, proved so valuable that it was continued until the end of his life and afterward. In June 1927 it combined with the *Quarterly Cumulative Index* to form the *Quarterly Cumulative Index Medicus.* With his high ideals and scholarly standards Leypoldt made an important contribution to American bibliography. He died of cerebral fever in the spring of 1884.

[R. R. Bowker, "Frederick Leypoldt," *Publishers' Weekly,* Memorial Number, Apr. 5, 1884; A. Growoll, *Book-trade Bibliog. in the U. S. in the XIXth Century* (1898); R. R. Bowker, "Augusta H. Leypoldt, 1849–1919," *Publishers' Weekly,* June 14, 1919; *Am. Bookseller,* Apr. 15, 1884; S. S. Green, *The Public Library Movement in the U. S., 1853–1893* (1913); *N. Y. Tribune,* Apr. 1, 1884, N. Y. *Evening Post,* Mar. 31, 1884, *N. Y. Times,* Apr. 1 1884; personal communications from R. R. Bowker, Marian A. (Leypoldt) Osborne, Henry Holt & Company.] A. S. P.

L'HALLE, CONSTANTIN de (d. June 6, 1706), Recollect priest, was an early chaplain at Detroit. He is said to have been of distinguished family, but nothing is known of his life before his arrival, June 1, 1696, in Canada. For the next five years he served as parish priest in several localities. He was for a time at Longueuil and in November 1701 signed the register at Batiscan. Meanwhile Antoine de la Mothe, Sieur Cadillac [*q.v.*], had founded under a grant from the King a new colony on the strait that lies between Lake Erie and Lake St. Clair. Cadillac, who had served some time previously as commandant at Mackinac, had a strong dislike for the Jesuit missionaries and chose that his new colony of Detroit should be served only by Recollects. At just what time Father Constantin became chaplain for the garrison is not definitely established, because the earliest records of the parish church of Ste. Anne, Detroit, were destroyed by fire; he is said to have accompanied Cadillac to Detroit in June 1701 but his signature on the register at Batiscan shows that he was in Canada in November of that year. The first entry on the Ste. Anne parish record is by Father Constantin, the baptism in 1703 of Cadillac's daughter. From then on the records of this mother church of the Northwest are extant.

Father Constantin is said to have promoted the interests of religion in the infant colony. Cadillac wrote that he was well satisfied with him (*Michigan Pioneer and Historical Collections,* vol. XXXIII, 1904, p. 150). Although his mission was for Europeans, he often ministered to the neighboring Indians, many of whom had been baptized by the Jesuits at Mackinac. In 1706, however, a revolt broke out among the Ottawa, led by the renegade known as Le Pesant. The Indians rushed through the town, found the missionary in his garden, seized and bound him. He was loosed by a friendly Indian, and sent towards the fort, but the rebels, seeing him escaping, shot and killed him. He was found to have received several knife and gunshot wounds. His body was buried beneath the church of Ste. Anne; it has been several times removed; the first time, in 1723, it was identified by the vestments. Although he was not a martyr in the strict sense of the word, Father Constantin's sad fate and untimely death have kept his memory alive. His handwriting in the earliest records of the parish shows him to have been a man of refinement and culture.

[See J. G. Shea, *Hist. of the Cath. Ch. in the U. S.*, vol. I (1886); *Mich. Pioneer and Hist. Colls.*, especially the volume mentioned above, containing the Cadillac papers; Silas Farmer, *The Hist. of Detroit and Mich.* (1884); *Am. Cath Hist. Researches*, vol. XIII (1896); A. C. Laut, *Cadillac* (1931). The form of Father Constantin's name given above is taken from a signature. Several secondary accounts give Nicolas Bénoit Constantin de L'Halle as his full name.] L. P. K.

L'HALLE, NICOLAS BÉNOIT CONSTANTIN de [See L'HALLE, CONSTANTIN DE, d. 1706].

L'HOMMEDIEU, EZRA (Aug. 30, 1734–Sept. 27, 1811), lawyer, legislator, agriculturist, was born at Southold, Long Island, the son of Benjamin L'Hommedieu and his wife, Martha Bourne, daughter of Ezra Bourne of Sandwich, Mass. His grandfather, Benjamin L'Hommedieu, a French Huguenot (born at La Rochelle), came to America about 1686, settled at Southold in 1690, and died there in 1748 at the age of ninety-two. Graduating from Yale in 1754, Ezra studied law and was admitted to the bar, but he appears to have occupied himself chiefly in administering his own affairs. In 1765 he married Charity Floyd, sister of William Floyd [*q.v.*] and of the wife of Gen. Nathaniel Woodhull [*q.v.*]. It has been said that in politics he consistently furthered Floyd's interests in preference to his own.

From 1775 until his death L'Hommedieu was continuously in public service, his local, state, and national services often overlapping, since there was no "self-denying ordinance" to forbid. He was a member of all the New York provincial congresses, and accordingly was one of the framers of the constitution of 1777, then a member of the Assembly until 1783, and thereafter until 1809 (excepting the year 1792–93) of the state Senate. Twice (1784, 1799) he served on that curious New York body, the council of appointment, and again in the interpretative constitutional convention of 1801. Meanwhile he had been sent for four successive terms (1779–83) as a delegate to the Continental Congress, and once more in 1788. In January 1784 he became clerk of Suffolk County, an office which he held, except for one year (March 1810–March 1811), for the remainder of his life.

As a legislator, whether in the Assembly or Senate of his state or in Congress, his career is marked by an active though unobtrusive participation in proceedings, particularly in the important labors of committees, whose reports he often drew. In Congress, whilst closely coöperating with his colleagues in all matters affecting his own state, as was customary in the New York delegation, on other questions he showed an independent mind, not always following the lead of his persuasive colleague, Duane, or of that other dominating character, Robert R. Livingston. Faithful to his instructions, he nevertheless did not hesitate to point out to his own government what he conceived to be errors of counsel. His letters to Governor Clinton are a valuable source of information upon proceedings in Congress. As in Congress he consistently supported measures looking toward governmental efficiency, so in the Constitutional period he was a Federalist.

L'Hommedieu's chief title to fame is as the principal author of the University of the State of New York as reconstituted in 1787. Tradition has ascribed the fatherhood of the institution to Hamilton, but legislative records seem to show conclusively that it was the measure fathered by L'Hommedieu, leader of the "country party," rather than that proposed by Hamilton, sponsor for the Columbia College group, that constitutes the foundation of the university, although the Hamiltonian party eventually succeeded in effecting important modifications of L'Hommedieu's plan. He was a regent of the university from its first establishment in 1784 until his death. In his later years he interested himself largely in agricultural experiments and wrote numerous papers upon agricultural subjects for the Transactions of the New York Society for the Promotion of Agriculture, Arts, and Manufactures, of which he was for a number of years vice-president. His wife having died in 1785, in 1803 he married Mary Catharine, daughter of Nicoll Havens of Shelter Island. His death occurred at the family seat at Southold, and his monument stands near the Founders' Monument in the Presbyterian cemetery.

[Consult C. B. Moore, "Biography of Ezra L'Hommedieu," *N. Y. Geneal. and Biog. Record*, Jan. 1871; E. Whitaker, "The Founders of Southold," *Ibid.*, July 1895; "Salmon Records," *Ibid.*, Oct. 1916–July 1918; B. F. Thompson, *Hist. of L. I.* (1839); E. Whitaker,

History of Southold, L. I. (1881); R. H. Gabriel, *The Evolution of L. I.* (1921); *Southold Town Records*, vol. II (1884); C. Z. Lincoln, *The Constitutional Hist. of N. Y.* (1906), vol. I; Sidney Sherwood, "University of the State of N. Y.: Origin, History, and Present Organization," *Regents' Bull.*, no. 11 (1893), reprinted in U. S. Bureau of Educ., *Circular of Information*, no. 3 (1900); *Pub. Papers of Geo. Clinton* (10 vols., 1899–1914); *Journals of the Provincial Cong. . . . of N. Y.* (2 vols., 1842); *Journals of the Continental Cong.*; and F. B. Dexter, *Biog. Sketches of the Grads. of Yale Coll.*, vol. II (1896). The date of L'Hommedieu's death, given in this sketch, is taken from his tombstone.] E. C. B.

LIBBEY, EDWARD DRUMMOND (Apr. 17, 1854–Nov. 13, 1925), glass-manufacturer, philanthropist, patron of art, was born at Chelsea, Mass., the son of William L. and Julia (Miller) Libbey. He received his education in Boston and later attended lectures at Boston University. In 1874 he entered the factory of the New England Glass Company, East Cambridge, Mass., of which his father was general manager, and worked in all branches of it to learn every detail in the manufacture and marketing of glass. In 1883, upon the death of his father, who had bought the business some years before, he became sole proprietor. In 1886, a strike by the workmen for higher wages, which conditions could not justify, made it necessary to close the plant permanently.

Libbey then went to Toledo, Ohio, attracted by the ample supply of natural gas and good glass sand, and in 1888 began operations there under the name of the Libbey Glass Company. In 1893 he erected a building at the World's Columbian Exposition, Chicago, in which he operated a demonstration glass plant throughout the period of the fair. Becoming interested in the development of automatic machinery for the manufacture of table tumblers, the invention of Michael J. Owens [*q.v.*], he organized the Toledo Glass Company (1894) and in the plant which was constructed for it carried on the manufacture of table tumblers until 1899, when the plant was acquired by the American Lamp Chimney Company of which Libbey was president. This company was soon consolidated with the Macbeth-Evans Glass Company of Pittsburgh, Pa., and the Toledo plant operated as a branch factory.

In 1899 Owens developed a machine for blowing bottles, perhaps the most revolutionary contribution to the glass industry since the invention of the blowing iron. In 1903, the machine having been perfected, Libbey organized and became president of the Owens Bottle Machine Company (reorganized in 1919 as the Owens Bottle Company), which took an exclusive license from the Toledo Glass Company for the manufacture in the United States of the bottle machine and all kinds of bottles. The Owens European Bottle Machine Company was organized in 1905. In 1912 Libbey purchased for the Toledo Glass Company the Colburn patents for the manufacture of sheet glass, and after the process had been further developed by Owens and the original inventor, he organized and became president in 1916 of the Libbey-Owens Sheet Glass Company, which purchased these patents and embarked upon the manufacture of sheet and plate glass, at Charleston, W. Va.

Libbey was intensely interested in civic, philanthropic, and educational work. He served on the Toledo board of education and, as its president, began a notable building program. For many years he supplied scholarships through which the teachers of the public schools could continue their higher education, and by his will provided for the perpetual maintenance of a scholarship fund. He was also a member of the City Plan Commission. In company with other citizens, he organized, in 1901, the Toledo Museum of Art, of which he was president until his death. In his first annual report, 1902, he advocated a policy of education as well as conservation, foreseeing for the institution a future in which it should take its place as an educational factor along with the public schools, colleges, and universities. He made possible the erection of the first unit of the museum building, opened in 1912, and later gave an addition, dedicated in 1926, which more than doubled its size. He made frequent trips abroad and with his wife Florence (Scott) Libbey, whom he had married in 1890, formed a collection of paintings, including work of Holbein, Hals, Rembrandt, Velasquez, De Hoog, Van Cleef, Reynolds, Gainsborough, and Raeburn, which he gave to the Toledo Museum. He also presented to the Museum a collection of Egyptian antiquities and a unique collection of glass, and by bequest left it the bulk of his estate, providing funds for additions to its building, for the maintenance and operation of the Museum and its educational program, and for the acquisition of works of art for its permanent collections. In 1922, in recognition of his services to industry, commerce, and art, King Albert conferred upon him the Belgian Order of the Crown with the rank of Commander.

[Harvey Scribner, *Memoirs of Lucas County and the City of Toledo* (1910), vol. II; J. M. Killits, *Toledo and Lucas County, Ohio* (1923), vol. III and supp., *Hist. of Toledo* (1923); N. O. Winter, *A Hist. of Northwest Ohio* (1917), vol. III; *Who's Who in America*, 1924–25; T. F. MacManus, *A Century of Glass Manufacture* (1918), published by Libbey Glass Company; *System*, June 1919; A. E. Fowle, *Flat Glass*

(1924); *The Glass Container*, Dec. 1925; *Museum News* (Toledo), Mar. 1926; Libbey's will; newspaper articles, Nov. and Dec. 1925, esp. *Toledo News Bee*, Nov. 13–15, 17, 20, 1925, and *The Sun* (N. Y.), Nov. 18, 1925, editorial.] B–M. G.

LICK, JAMES (Aug. 21, 1796–Oct. 1, 1876), philanthropist, born of German ancestry in Fredericksburg, Lebanon County, Pa., was the eldest son of John and Sarah (Long) Lick. His grandfather, William Lick (Lük), had served as a soldier in the war of the Revolution, and at the time of his death in 1819 had reached the age of 104. Shortly before this event, possibly as early as the autumn of 1817, the grandson, after snatches of an elementary education and a short apprenticeship as a carpenter and joiner, went to Baltimore, where for a year or more he worked as a piano-maker in the employ of Joseph Hiskey. In 1820 he went to South America, and lived there for seventeen years, first in Buenos Aires, later in Valparaiso and Lima. He came back to the United States once, probably in 1832, and considered for a time remaining in Philadelphia or New York. He seems to have been engaged in piano and organ making during these years, but apparently had other interests and derived a very considerable income from them, for when he arrived in San Francisco, Cal., on the eve of the discovery of gold, he brought with him a large sum of money, which in later years was estimated at $30,000. He commenced at once the purchase of real estate in San Francisco, the greatest amount of his acquisitions being made in the year 1848. His property came to include large holdings in the Santa Clara Valley, smaller amounts on the shores of Lake Tahoe, in Virginia City, Nev., and on the "Isla de Santa Catalina," off the coast of southern California. Near San José he built a flour mill at great cost. In this venture and in others he revealed extreme eccentricity in his choice of materials, in his treatment of workmen, and in the objects of his interest. In San Francisco at the corner of Montgomery and Sutter streets he built a hotel which bore his name. Here he spent his later years.

As his fortune grew he seems to have given more and more thought to its disposal. In 1874 he prepared an elaborate deed in trust, naming a board of seven trustees who were to carry out his plans. The program was changed a year later and again shortly before his death. The chief beneficiaries were to be the Society of California Pioneers, of which he was president at the time, and the California Academy of Sciences, but the bequest which came to be of greatest significance was that providing $700,000 for "a powerful telescope, superior to and more powerful than any telescope ever yet made." It is not definitely known just when Lick fixed upon this idea. It is clear that it was modified by others before it took final form. He left more than a third of a million dollars to various charities in San Francisco and San José. Not a religious man, and for a time actively interested in the memory of Thomas Paine, he had at one time elaborate plans for perpetuating in this world the name of his family and his own name in particular. These took the form of monuments to be erected in San Francisco. In the final deed of trust, $20,000 was set aside for the monument and commemorative tablets at his birthplace. This sum and $150,000 left to John H. Lick (born to Barbara Snavely, in Fredericksburg, in 1818), whom he had recognized as his son, together with some small bequests, were all that he reserved for his family from a fortune well above three million. He never married.

On the occasion of his funeral in San Francisco the editor of the *Daily Evening Bulletin* wrote: "So long as San Francisco and the state of California shall endure the name of James Lick will be associated with them" (*Bulletin*, Oct. 2, 1876). Horatio Stebbins [*q.v.*], who preached the funeral sermon, summed up the life of this "man of property" as "without romantic incident or exploit," and anticipated the biographer in saying that his benefactions would "encircle the name of our citizen with a quiet, steady lustre of beneficence" (*Ibid.*, Oct. 4, 1876). The Lick Observatory, built upon Mount Hamilton, Santa Clara County (thirteen miles east of San José), was completed and placed in the hands of the regents of the University of California in June 1888. Eighteen months earlier, on Jan. 9, 1887, the body of James Lick had been brought from the Masonic cemetery in San Francisco and placed in the pier which now supports the great telescope.

[Sources include: *Cal. Mail Bag* (San Francisco), Aug. 1874; *Daily Evening Bulletin* (San Francisco), Oct. 2, 3, 4, 1876; S. C. Upham, *Notes of a Voyage to Cal. via Cape Horn, together with Scenes in El Dorado in the Years 1849–50* (1878); E. T. Sawyer, *Hist. of Santa Clara County, Cal.* (1922); H. S. Foote, *Pen Pictures from the Garden of the World or Santa Clara County, Cal.* (1888); E. S. Holden, *A Brief Account of the Lick Observatory* (1894); *Quart. of the Soc. of Cal. Pioneers*, June 30, 1924. The director of the Lick Observatory gives date of birth as Aug. 25; the date here given was obtained from the baptismal records of St. John's Lutheran Church, Fredericksburg, Lebanon County, Pa., through the aid of a "half-nephew" of James Lick.] E. E. R.

LIEB, JOHN WILLIAM (Feb. 12, 1860–Nov. 1, 1929), mechanical engineer, son of John William and Christina (Zens) Lieb, was born in Newark, N. J. His father, a native of Württemberg, Germany, had emigrated to the United States in 1846, and was an especially skilled mechanical craftsman and inventor. At the age of sixteen, after attending Newark Academy and Stevens High School, Hoboken, young Lieb entered Stevens Institute of Technology, from which he graduated with the degree of M.E. in 1880. For six months after leaving the Institute, he worked as a draftsman for the Brush Electric Company, Cleveland, Ohio; then, in January 1881, he obtained similar employment in the engineering department of the newly organized Edison Electric Light Company in New York. Here he assisted in making plans for the dynamos and other electrical equipment of a proposed central electric lighting plant; but, before the year closed, he was transferred to the Edison Machine Works in New York, where the equipment was being prepared, to assist Thomas A. Edison in the experimental researches involved. No central lighting plants existed at that time, so that the work of Edison and Lieb was of a pioneering character. When the plant, called the Pearl Street Station, was put into regular operation in New York on Sept. 4, 1882, under the auspices of the Edison Electric Illuminating Company, Lieb was made electrician in charge. Two months later he was selected by Edison to go to Milan, Italy, as his representative in connection with the design, installation, and operation of the Edison underground electrical system for the Italian Edison Company. Lieb remained in Italy for the succeeding twelve years: serving, first, as chief electrician of the Milan Edison Station; then, as chief engineer; and finally, as other electrical stations were erected and the activities of the Italian Edison Company expanded, as manager and technical director, not only of the power plants, but also of the manufacture of incandescent lamps, dynamos, and other electrical equipment. The Milan station began regular service early in 1883, and was, at that time, the largest and most successful electric light and power station in Europe. Under Lieb's direction some of the earliest experiments were undertaken at Milan, in the parallel operation of large direct-driven alternators, in the operation of large synchronous motors, and in the long-distance transmission of high-tension alternating current by underground cables. In 1893, he installed, also, an electric trolley car system in Milan, which was one of the earliest in Italy. Returning to the United States in 1894, he was made assistant to the vice-president of the Edison Electric Illuminating Company. Later he was made vice-president and general manager, serving in this capacity until the company's reorganization as the New York Edison Company in 1901. Subsequently, he became successively associate general manager, vice-president and general manager, and finally, senior vice-president, which position he held at the time of his death. In this last capacity he was in general charge of the installation and operation of the company's power plants and of the transmission systems, and directed all research and development work. He served in a like capacity for all of the affiliated electric companies in the metropolitan area. From 1900 until his death he was president of the Electrical Testing Laboratories in New York, which organization, through his influence and direction, made many important contributions in the electrical field. He was a member and officer of many technical and scientific societies both in the United States and Europe, a lecturer on engineering, industrial, and economic subjects in many of the leading universities and technical schools of the United States, and a contributor to the transactions of professional and learned societies. His work was recognized the world over and he was signally honored both at home and abroad, being made a Grand Officer of the Royal Society of the Crown of Italy, an *ufficiale* of the order of St. Maurizio e Lazzaro, and an officer of the Legion of Honor. The American Institute of Electrical Engineers in 1924 awarded him the Edison Medal for his work in connection with "the development and operation of electric central stations for illumination and power." During the World War he was chairman of the National Committee on Gas and Electric Service; adviser to the Federal, New York State, and New York City Fuel Administrations; and chairman of the Joint Fuel Committee of the National Public Utility Association.

As a recreation, he engaged for many years in a critical study of the manuscripts of Leonardo da Vinci, investigating and translating sketches and texts covering his researches and observations, particularly in natural science and engineering. He possessed one of the largest libraries of Vinciana in existence, was a corresponding member of the Raccolta Vinciana of Milan, Italy, and published "Leonardo da Vinci —Natural Philosopher and Engineer" (*Journal of the Franklin Institute,* June, July 1921). On July 29, 1886, he married Minnie F. Engler of New York City, who with two daughters and a son survived him at the time of his death in New York.

[*Jour. Am. Inst. of Electrical Engineers,* Dec. 1929; F. D. Furman, *Morton Memorial: A Hist. of the*

Stevens Institute of Technology (1905); *Who's Who in America,* 1928–29; obituary sketch printed and circulated by the Edison Pioneers; *Trans. Am. Soc. Civil Engineers,* vol. XCIV (1930); *Mechanical Engineering,* Dec. 1929; *Electrical World,* Nov. 9, 1929; *N. Y. Times,* Nov. 2, 1929.] C. W. M.

LIEBER, FRANCIS (Mar. 18, 1800–Oct. 2, 1872), political scientist, educator, was born in Berlin, Germany, the tenth child of Friedrich Wilhelm Lieber in a family of nine sons and three daughters. His boyhood was spent amid the turmoils of the Napoleonic conquest when family and friends were charged with patriotic emotions. His elder brothers enlisted in the war of 1813, but Francis had to wait impatiently till 1815 upon the return of the emperor from Elba. With two brothers he joined the army under Blücher and fought through the campaign of Waterloo, receiving at the battle of Namur wounds which nearly cost him his life. As a schoolboy he was somewhat wayward and inattentive to formal instruction, but possessed of an ardent desire to become famous in some way.

About 1811 he had come under the influence of Friedrich Ludwig Jahn, the great German teacher and founder of societies for the cultivation of gymnastics and patriotism, and for eight years as pupil and companion was closely associated with him in awakening the youth of the Fatherland. After Waterloo Lieber resumed his studies, but the governmental reaction which ensued had a serious effect upon the young men who followed the teachings of Jahn. In 1819 he was arrested as a dangerous character and when released after four months was forbidden to study at any university except Jena, a decree which ended any hope of advancement in his native province. At Jena he received the degree of Ph.D. in 1820, but was immediately ordered away and spent the following year in the study of surveying at Halle and Dresden. Just then the war of liberation in Greece broke out and roused the enthusiasm of the oppressed German liberals. Lieber at once enlisted and, making his way with difficulty to Marseilles, sailed for Greece in January 1822, with a mixed crowd of foreign recruits. The experiences of these enthusiasts were bitter. Refused food and shelter, robbed by bandits, and finding only cowardice and incapacity among the supposed Greek patriots, they were soon disillusioned and Lieber with much difficulty made his way back to Italy. Eventually he reached Rome and in his ragged and penniless condition approached the German ambassador, Niebuhr. His intelligence as well as his misfortunes made such an impression that he was taken in as a tutor to the ambassador's son and for a year enjoyed the society and the inspiration of the great historian of Rome while in the midst of the art and antiquities of the ancient capital. At Niebuhr's suggestion he wrote his first book, *Tagebuch Meines Aufenhaltes in Griechenland* (Leipzig, 1823), which was published also in Dutch as *De Duitsche Anacharsis* (1823). In his *Reminiscences of an Intercourse with Mr. Niebuhr the Historian* (1835), Lieber refers to this period as the most instructive of his life. Following Niebuhr's resignation, Lieber returned to Berlin in the summer of 1823 and sought a revocation of the order which prevented him from study or preferment in Prussia. After much difficulty this was obtained with a small subsidy now needed because his father, an iron merchant, had lost his fortune and could no longer assist. He pursued mathematics at Berlin and Halle until August 1824, when the government in its fear of liberal conspiracies arrested a group of young men, including Lieber, and placed them in prison in Köpenick. Detained ostensibly only as a witness, he was threatened by the police with life imprisonment because he would neither give evidence nor confess, but after six months he was released on the petition of Niebuhr and returned to Berlin to find livelihood difficult. A request for a government position, even with Niebuhr's recommendation, came to nought, and Lieber in 1826 made his way secretly to England.

A year of uncertainty occupied with teaching languages, writing for German periodicals, and less congenial tasks, ended with a call to Boston, Mass., where he landed in June 1827, to take charge of a gymnasium and swimming school. Here he acquired influential friends and continued literary work, though with meager returns, until he hit upon a plan for an encyclopædia modeled after Brockhaus' *Conversations Lexikon.* This was the foundation of the *Encyclopædia Americana* (13 vols., 1829–33), and the work found immediate acceptance. Many distinguished Americans contributed to its pages and Lieber made acquaintances which were mutually helpful throughout his career. He married upon her arrival in New York Sept. 21, 1829, Matilda Oppenheimer, to whom he had been a tutor in England, and returned with her to Boston. To facilitate his literary work he moved to Philadelphia in 1834 and among other activities prepared the elaborate constitution and regulations of Girard College (*A Constitution and Plan of Education for Girard College . . . with an Introductory Report,* 1834). His growing reputation led to his election in 1835 to the chair of history and political economy in South Carolina College (now University of South

Carolina). In the latter subject he was the successor of Thomas Cooper [*q.v.*]. Remaining there twenty-one years, he gained a great reputation as a teacher but had difficulties as a disciplinarian and was viewed with some suspicion because of his sympathy for the abolitionists, though he owned slaves while in the state. His resignation was thought to have been due to his disappointment at his failure to be elected president in 1855. (E. L. Green, *A History of the University of South Carolina,* 1916, pp. 60–61).

Although he complained of the distance from his former friends and regarded himself as an exile, this period was decidedly fruitful, for in the course of it Lieber produced the works which eventually made him famous. These were his *Manual of Political Ethics* (2 vols., 1838–39), *Legal and Political Hermeneutics* (1839), and *On Civil Liberty and Self-Government* (2 vols., 1853). Numerous shorter essays and a wide correspondence with public men on both sides of the Atlantic contributed further to a marked influence upon American thought. The object of his *Political Ethics* is indicated by a sub-title which he once proposed, namely, "the Citizen considered with regard to his Moral Obligations arising from his Participation in Government" (Perry, *post,* p. 106), and the solution lay in the repeated injunction "no right without its duties, no duty without its rights" (*Ibid.,* p. 416). The work is a theory of the State, but includes many practical topics of extra-constitutional character, such as public opinion, parties, obligation to vote, influence in voting, friendship in politics, newspaper publicity, and the respective duties of representatives, judges, advocates, and officeholders. He reversed the usual order by discussing the natural rights of man, not as a creature in a primitive state, but in his present highly civilized condition. Viewing the State as founded upon the relation of right he coined the term "a jural society" (*Manual of Political Ethics,* p. 171), a condition not based on contract, but aboriginal with man. Sovereignty to him is an attribute of society expressed through public opinion, law, and power, definitions which Lieber claimed to be the first to employ. In general his system endeavors to reconcile the differences between the philosophical idealists and the historical school which taught that whatever is is right. His many personal experiences with governments came to the assistance of his learning. The *Hermeneutics* was intended as a chapter of his *Political Ethics,* but became so extended that it was published separately. His distinction between interpretation and construction had great influence among legal writers of his day. The first is "the art of finding out the true sense of any form of words" (*Legal and Political Hermeneutics,* p. 23) in the sense which the author intended to convey, while construction is the drawing of conclusions respecting subjects that lie outside the direct expression of the text. Constitutions should be construed closely, he holds, since their words have been carefully weighed. The treatise received high commendation from Chancellor Kent, Henry Clay, Rufus Choate, and others. *On Civil Liberty and Self-Government* is the best known of Lieber's works, as it was widely read and adopted as a college textbook. He discusses historically the various elements of freedom in their relation to law and government and defines liberty as the protection or check against undue interference, either from individuals, from masses, or from government. His treatment of Anglican liberty was new, dealing with the elements and actual amount of guaranteed freedom rather than the terms of the constitution. Originality lay also in his valuation of social institutions as invincible protectors of political liberty. In these volumes Lieber presented the first systematic works on political science that appeared in America. Political writing had been voluminous, but the contents had been confined to concrete legal or political controversy with no complete philosophy of the State. Later writers have observed that he falls into some confusion of state with government, and that his learned but diffuse illustrations obscure his argument, but he retains credit as a notable pioneer with wide influence in more than one generation. Along with theoretical studies Lieber maintained a lifelong interest in the special field of penal law. In 1833 he translated with notes Beaumont and De Tocqueville, *On the Penitentiary System in the United States.* His own views were published in 1838 in *A Popular Essay on Subjects of Penal Law,* containing forty-one rules based on the fundamental principles of "mild laws, firm judges, calm punishments" (*Miscellaneous Writings,* II, 471). In 1848 he prepared a report later published as a document by the legislature of New York and reprinted by him as "Abuse of the Pardoning Power," as an appendix to *On Civil Liberty.* Some of his suggestions for reform were embodied in later state constitutions.

In 1857 he was appointed to a chair in Columbia College, New York, from which he was transferred in 1865 to the law school, where he remained for the rest of his life. His personal characteristics doubtless contributed to his reputation and influence. He was of medium stature with refined features, somewhat stout in body, but muscular and abounding in energy, and his physical vigor permitted him to work long hours at his desk. His cheerful disposition, ready conversational powers and sprightly wit, coupled with extensive learning, made him a delightful companion to young or old. Possessed of deep religious sentiment he worshipped as a liberal Episcopalian, though with dislike for the then new theories of Darwin. At Columbia he became more than ever a prominent figure among political philosophers and extended his attention into international relations. After the outbreak of the Civil War he was much consulted by the Union government. Among other papers and opinions he wrote *Guerrilla Parties Considered with Reference to the Laws and Usages of War* (1862), and *A Code for the Government of Armies* (1863), which was issued by the War Department in revised form as *Instructions for the Government of Armies in the Field, General Orders No. 100.* No work of this kind was in existence at that time in any language. It was accepted as standard by writers on military law, was adopted by Germany in the conflict of 1870, and has continued to be the basis of international understanding on the conduct of war. Lieber was also the first to propose an unofficial congress of political savants to codify the existing rules of international law, a project recognized soon after his death by the founders of the Institut de Droit International. The public services of his later life included a government appointment as keeper of the Confederate records captured during the war, and another in 1870 as umpire to the Mexican Claims Commission. With this last he was occupied at the time of his death.

The children of Francis and Matilda Lieber included a daughter who died in infancy and three sons: Oscar Montgomery, who became a prominent geologist in the South and died of wounds received while in the Confederate army; Hamilton, who volunteered in the Union army, lost an arm at Fort Donelson, and subsequently filled various military positions; Guido Norman, who fought in the Federal infantry and eventually became judge advocate-general of the United States.

[The most important sources of information are: T. S. Perry, ed., *The Life and Letters of Francis Lieber* (1882); Lewis R. Harley, *Francis Lieber: His Life and Pol. Philosophy* (1899); Daniel C. Gilman, ed., *Reminiscences, Addresses, and Essays by Francis Lieber . . . Being Vol I of His Miscellaneous Writings*; *Contributions to Pol. Science, . . . by Francis Lieber . . . Being Vol. II of His Miscellaneous Writings* (1881), the latter containing a bibliography; Elihu Root, "Francis Lieber," *Am. Jour. of International Law,* July 1913, giving an estimate of Lieber's contributions to international law, which may be compared with a similar tribute by Bluntschli in *Miscellaneous Writings,* vol. II; C. S. Phinney, *Francis Lieber's Influence on American Thought and Some of His Unpublished Letters* (1918). At the Johns Hopkins University a collection of his manuscripts consisting of lectures, annotated copies of his works, legal opinions, is displayed with similar relics of his colleagues Bluntschli and Laboulaye in memory of their "international cloverleaf." For an account of this, see *Bluntschli, Lieber, and Laboulaye* (privately printed, 1884). In the Huntington Library, San Marino, Cal., a large body of MSS. includes his diaries, many letters from prominent men, and material connected with the *Encyclopædia Americana.*]

J. M. V.

LIEBLING, EMIL (Apr. 12, 1851–Jan. 20, 1914), pianist, teacher, and composer, the second son of Jacob and Henriette (Mosler) Liebling, was born in Pless, Germany. His brothers Max, Saul, and Georg also became well-known musicians. Their father was a church singer and he gave all of his children their first musical training. Emil emigrated to America in 1867 at the age of sixteen and taught first in and about Covington, Ky., and later in Cincinnati, Ohio. He was fond of relating his early experiences in Kentucky, where, after buying a saddle-horse, he rode horseback across the country, stopping at every house in which he heard a piano or learned of there being one. After introducing himself as a pianist, he would offer to play and he generally emerged with one or more pupils to add to his growing class. In 1872 he settled in Chicago as a private teacher but soon returned to Germany to study. He first went to Berlin where he was a student of Kullak and Ehrlich in piano and of Dorn in composition. From Berlin he went to Vienna to study piano with Dachs, and finally he became a student of Liszt at Weimar. During his entire stay abroad, he taught part of the time, first in the Kullak Conservatory at Berlin, later in Vienna and Weimar, evidently earning his own way.

He did not confine his study to music but acquired a large literary knowledge and became a proficient linguist. During his sojourn in Europe he enjoyed the friendship of Sherwood, Von Sternberg, and Moszkowski, the first two of whom later became prominent in America. He returned to America in 1876 and immediately won recognition as a pianist and composer. While he was considered an especially fine Bach player, he was equally brilliant as an interpreter of Liszt, Chopin, Beethoven, and Schumann. In 1877 he appeared as soloist with the Theodore Thomas Orchestra and he made many successful appearances with the violinist August Wilhelmj, both as soloist and accompanist. He was greater as a pianist than as a composer; many of his compositions were fashioned on the popular order of his period. Among the best are the following: "Gavotte Moderne," *opus* 11, "Florence Valse," *opus* 12, "Feu Follet," *opus* 17, "Albumblatt," *opus* 18, "Cradle Song," *opus* 23, and "Menuetto Scherzoso," *opus* 28. With W. S. B. Mathews he compiled the *Pronouncing and Defining Dictionary of Music* (1896) and he edited the last volume, "Essentials of Music" (1910), of *The American History and Encyclopedia of Music* (12 vols., 1908–10). He also contributed many articles to musical magazines. An outstanding personal characteristic was his generosity, and many an indigent student and fellow musician received help from him. He was married to Mrs. Florence Jones who survived him by a few years.

[See W. S. B. Mathews, *The Great in Music* (1900); G. L. Howe and W. S. B. Mathews, *A Hundred Years of Music in America* (1889); Albert Payne, *Celebrated Pianists of the Past and Present* (Am. ed., 1894); *Who's Who in America*, 1912–13; and obituaries in the *Musical Courier*, Jan. 28, 1914, and in the *Chicago Daily Tribune*, Jan. 21, 1914. Information as to certain facts was supplied by Liebling's nephew, Leonard Liebling, editor of the *Musical Courier*, and from his friend, Mr. D. A. Clippinger.] F. L. G. C.

LIGHTBURN, JOSEPH ANDREW JACKSON (Sept. 21, 1824–May 17, 1901), soldier, Baptist preacher, son of Benjamin and Rebecca (Fell) Lightburn, came of backwoods stock, his Scotch grandfather having migrated in 1774 to the transmontane region on the Youghiogheny River near West Newton, Westmoreland County, Pa. Here Joseph was born and spent his earlier years, and at Mount Pleasant, in the same county, he obtained the rudiments of an education. In 1840 he removed to western Virginia with his father, who in 1841 acquired 600 acres of land on Broad Run in Lewis County. He helped his father build an overshot grist mill on the West Fork of the Monongahela River near the boyhood home of Thomas Jackson, later famous as "Stonewall," against whom, in 1842, Joseph Lightburn competed unsuccessfully for a cadetship at West Point. Near his home he gained such further education as was provided by the schools of the period, and attended the local Broad Run Baptist Church. In 1846, during the Mexican War, he enlisted in the regular army and was assigned to the recruiting service. He remained in the army as a non-commissioned officer till 1851, then returned to milling and farming. In October 1855 he married his stepsister, Harriet Ellen Whittlesey. Her father, Stephen Whittlesey, a graduate of Williams College, had been a Baptist minister. Her widowed mother, Nancy Anne Whittlesey, had become the second wife of Benjamin Lightburn in 1852. To Joseph and Harriet Lightburn were born five children.

In 1861, Lightburn, a stanch Union man, was selected as delegate to the Wheeling conventions of May 13 and June 11 which established the "Reorganized Government of Virginia"—a step toward the formation of the separate state of West Virginia. On Aug. 14, 1861, he received from Gov. Francis H. Pierpont [*q.v.*] a commission as colonel of the 4th Regiment of Virginia (West Virginia) Volunteers (Union forces) and participated in the battles of Charleston and Gauley Bridge. Placed in general command of the forces in the Kanawha Valley on Aug. 17, 1862, following the transfer of General Cox to Washington, he conducted a successful retreat down the Kanawha to Point Pleasant before the superior force of General Loring. Early in 1863 he was ordered to the Mississippi near Vicksburg, and attached to the Army of the Tennessee under General Grant. In March he was promoted to be brigadier-general and in May assumed command of a brigade in F. P. Blair's division, XV Army Corps. His command led the first assault on Vicksburg and subsequently participated in engagements at Jackson, Chickamauga, and Missionary Ridge, and in Sherman's advance on Atlanta. After recovering from a gunshot wound in the head, which he received in August 1864, he was transferred to the Shenandoah Valley, where he participated in several engagements. He was a warm friend of Gen. Lew Wallace.

In 1867 he represented Lewis County in the legislature of West Virginia. Before the war he had served irregularly as a Baptist minister, and in 1868 was ordained by the Broad Run Baptist Association. He became a leader of his denomination in the state and continued in active service until his death. He was a man of fine physique and striking military bearing, and as a preacher was strong and effective.

[R. B. Cook, *Lewis County in the Civil War* (1924); T. F. Lang, *Loyal W. Va. from 1861 to 1865* (1895); E. C. Smith, *A Hist. of Lewis County, W. Va.* (1920); C. B. Whittelsey, *Geneal. of the Whittelsey-Whittlesey Family* (1898); *War of the Rebellion: Official Records (Army)*, esp. 1 ser. XIX (pts. 1, 2), XXIV (pt. 2), XXV (pts. 2, 3), XXXVIII (pts. 3, 5), XLIII (pt. 2), XLVI (pt. 2); *Exponent Telegram* (Clarksburg, W. Va.), Mar. 4, 1928, Nov. 11, 1928.] J. M. C.

LIGON, THOMAS WATKINS (May 1, 1810–Jan. 12, 1881), congressman, governor of Maryland, was born on a farm in Prince Edward County, Va., the son of Thomas D. Ligon and his wife, Martha, daughter of Thomas Watkins, a Revolutionary officer. His father died while young Thomas was still a boy and his mother was married again, to Jack Vaughan of Prince Edward County, by whom she had six children. Thomas was educated at Hampden-Sydney Col lege (where he graduated in 1830), at the University of Virginia, and at the Yale Law School (1831–32). He passed the examination for the bar in his native state but felt obliged to turn elsewhere for an opportunity to practise law. His choice fell on Baltimore, whither he repaired in 1833. In 1840 he married Sallie Dorsey and established his residence permanently near Ellicott City, although he maintained his office in Baltimore. After the death of his first wife he married her sister, Mary.

Immediately after his arrival in Baltimore he entered heartily into politics, vigorously sustaining the Jacksonian policies. In 1843 he became the Democratic candidate for the Maryland House of Delegates and was elected. The following year he was a successful candidate for Congress, where he served two terms (1845–49), being invariably arrayed with the strict constructionists. Winning the Democratic nomination for governor of Maryland in 1853, he was elected by a small majority. During his entire administration he was involved in a bitter struggle with the Know-Nothing party, which dominated both houses of the Assembly. During this period the Baltimore elections were characterized by open street fights around the markets and Monument square: awls became weapons and policemen remained mere spectators of violence. Although Governor Ligon undoubtedly realized how bitterly his antagonists would defend themselves, he opened an attack in his annual message of 1856 on "the formation and encouragement of secret political societies" (*Message of the Executive of Maryland, to the General Assembly,* 1856, p. 28). Fire drew fire: a special committee on the message produced a partisan report which was largely an attack on the governor for his "ill-timed and undeserved discourtesy" (Appendix to *Journal of the Proceedings of the House of Delegates of the State of Maryland, January Session,* 1856). Ligon's determination to interpose the militia to preserve order in Baltimore during the election of 1857 brought him to the verge of an open conflict with the mayor. The Governor yielded when a citizens' committee secured precautionary measures from the mayor, but he showed battle to the end by boldly devoting eleven pages of his last annual message to a discussion of "lawlessness in Baltimore." By giving his address to the newspapers before presenting it to the Assembly he further antagonized that august body, which at first refused to accept his communication.

Kindly and courteous, but reserved and simple, Ligon failed to awaken the personal enthusiasm which rallies followers in a battle, but although he retired under apparent defeat, his struggle encouraged a reform movement which bore fruit within less than three years. He spent the remainder of his long life quietly at his beautiful residence, "Chatham," where he died at the age of seventy. He was buried in the old family plot near his dwelling with the unostentatiousness which marked his entire life. though his body has since been removed to St. John's Cemetery, Ellicott City.

[H. E. Buchholz, *Governors of Md.* (1908); J. T. Scharf, *Hist. of Md.* (1879), vol. III; L. F. Schmeckebier, "History of the Know Nothing Party in Maryland," in *Johns Hopkins Univ. Studies in Hist. and Pol. Sci.*, ser. XVII, nos. 4–5 (Apr.–May 1899); Baltimore *Sun* and *Baltimore American,* 1854–60; M. P. Andrews, *Hist. of Md.* (1929); F. N. Watkins, *A Cat. of the Descendants of Thomas Watkins of Chickahomony, Va.* (1852); obituaries in the *Sun* and *Baltimore American,* Jan. 13, 1881.] E. L.

LILIENTHAL, MAX (Oct. 16, 1815–Apr. 5, 1882), rabbi, was born in Munich, Bavaria, the son of Loew Seligmann and Dina (Lichtenstein) Lilienthal. The father was one of the leading members of the small Jewish community of the Bavarian capital. Max Lilienthal was among the few young Jews of his generation who matriculated in the University of Munich. He graduated in 1837, receiving the degree of doctor of philosophy. His brilliant showing in his final examination attracted the attention of government officials and he was offered a position in the diplomatic service, which he declined when he found that to hold a government appointment he would be obliged to accept Christianity.

While waiting for an opening elsewhere he continued his studies in the royal library of Munich, and contributed a series of bibliographical notices of the Hebrew manuscripts in its possession to the literary supplement of *Die Allgemeine Zeitung des Judenthums.* As a contributor he came into close relation with the editor, Dr. Ludwig Philippson, the best-known rabbi in Europe, who was at that time in correspondence with Uwaroff, the minister of education of the Russian Empire. A plan was afoot to modernize the Jewish schools in Russia, and a beginning was to be made in Riga, where a new school was to be established. When Uwaroff applied to Philippson to recommend a superintendent for this new school, Philippson suggested Lilienthal, who accepted the appointment. He remained in Russia five years, but the governmental attempt to establish modern schools failed, notably when it appeared that this policy was a part of a proselytizing plan. Disheartened and disillusioned, Lilienthal left Russia, determined to seek asylum in a free land. He stopped en route at his birthplace to marry his fiancée,

Babette Nettre. With his bride he landed at New York in November 1845.

Lilienthal was the first rabbi with a European reputation to settle in the United States. Shortly after his arrival he was elected chief rabbi of three congregations in New York. He established also a day school for boys which attracted the attention of fathers not only in New York but also in other parts of the country. Among them were some Jewish residents of Cincinnati, Ohio, who urged the selection of Lilienthal for the vacant pulpit of the Bene Israel Congregation of that city. He was elected to the post, preached his inaugural sermon on July 14, 1855, and soon became one of the leading citizens of Cincinnati. He served as a member of the board of education, 1860–69; he was elected a member of the union board of high schools in 1861 and of the board of directors of the University of Cincinnati in 1872, holding the latter place until his death. The keynote of his activity was his intense Americanism. He contested with all his power every attempt of sectarian religionists to encroach upon the American principle of the separation of church and state. He opposed in burning words the attempt to introduce Bible reading into the public schools. This Cincinnati "Bible in the Schools" case, which was argued before the courts in 1870 (*Cincinnati Board of Education* vs. *John D. Minor, 23 Ohio, 211*), became a *cause célèbre* in the educational annals of the country.

Lilienthal took an active part in the establishment of the Union of American Hebrew Congregations in 1873 and the foundation of the Hebrew Union College at Cincinnati in 1875. He served as associate editor of the *American Israelite,* to which he contributed articles on "My Travels in Russia" (1854–56), and as editor of the first Jewish juvenile weekly published in the United States, the *Sabbath School Visitor.* He published a volume of German poems, *Frühling, Freiheit und Liebe,* in 1857, and in that same year, a *Synopsis of the History of the Israelites from the time of Alexander the Macedonian to the Present Age* (Cincinnati, 1857). He organized the Rabbinical Literary Association in 1879 and was elected its first president. He edited two volumes of the quarterly journal issued by this organization, the *Hebrew Review,* which ceased publication after his death.

Possibly his greatest service lay in the promotion of good will between Christians and Jews. He was the first rabbi to preach frequently from Christian pulpits. He was a real ambassador of religious amity. The closing years of his life were saddened by the virulent outburst of anti-Semitism in Germany and by the anti-Jewish persecutions in Russia, but even these inhumanities could not quench his optimistic hope of the coming of the better day of human brotherhood and universal peace. Indeed, this was the leading motif of his activity.

[David Philipson, *Max Lilienthal, American Rabbi* (1915), and memoir in *Central Conf. of Am. Rabbis, Yearbook,* vol. XXV (1915); Sophie Lilienthal, *The Lilienthal Family Record* (privately printed, San Francisco, 1930); R. J. Wunderbar, *Geschichte der Juden in den Provinzen Liv-und Kurland* (1853); Pauline Wengeroff, *Memoiren einer Grossmutter* (Berlin, 1908), I, 118–37; Leon Scheinhaus, *"Ein deutscher Pionier,"* in *Allgemeine Zeitung des Judenthums,* Aug. 25, 1911; J. S. Raisin, *The Haskalah Movement in Russia* (1913); *Jewish Encyc.* (ed. of 1925), vol. VIII; *Cincinnati Enquirer,* Apr. 6, 7, 8, 10, 1882.] D. P.

LINCECUM, GIDEON (Apr. 22, 1793–Nov. 28, 1874), frontier physician, naturalist, son of Hezekiah and Sally (Hickman) Lincecum, was born in Hancock County, Ga., and died near Long Point, Washington County, Tex. He was a grandson of Gideon, born in France, who came to America with his father, Paschal, and settled in Maryland. The boy's early years were spent in restless wanderings with his family through Georgia and western South Carolina, and up to the time he was fourteen years old he had obtained only five months' formal schooling. For eight months during the War of 1812 he served as a volunteer Georgia militiaman. On Oct. 25, 1814, he married, near Eatonsville, Ga., Sarah Bryan, daughter of Robert Bryan. After some years spent in the private study of medicine, and an experience in teaching in Georgia, he became a merchant at the frontier settlement of Columbus, Miss. In 1821 he was appointed by the Mississippi legislature commissioner to organize Monroe County. After the region had become settled, he was for several years an Indian trader in the Choctaw country of central Mississippi, and became familiar with the languages and legends of the Choctaw and Chickasaw tribes, which knowledge he used later in his "Life of Apushimataha" (*Mississippi Historical Society Publications,* vol. IX, 1906) and "Choctaw Traditions about Their Settlement in Mississippi and the Origin of Their Mounds" (*Ibid.,* vol. VIII, 1904). Becoming a physician (in the frontier manner of getting a stock of drugs and hanging out a shingle), he practised medicine with unusual success in the towns of Cotton Gin Port and Columbus from 1830 to 1848. In the latter year he went to Texas, where he settled at Long Point, on a tract of land that he had chosen while exploring Texas thirteen years before.

Lincecum was a true frontiersman, impatient of inaction and restraint. Passionately fond of nature from his boyhood, he improved his leisure hours during his first fourteen years in Texas in making a series of extensive studies of the agricultural or mound-building ants, which were published in the *Journal of the Proceedings of the Linnean Society; Zoology,* vol. VI (London, 1852); and later in the *Proceedings of the Academy of Natural Sciences of Philadelphia,* second series, vol. X (1866). Because of Lincecum's unfortunate tendency to personalize animal behavior, his conclusions, although sponsored by Charles Darwin, met with incredulity on the part of savants such as Forel; but his observations have been verified in the main by later workers (see H. C. McCook, *The Natural History of the Agricultural Ant of Texas,* 1879, pp. 12–13; W. M. Wheeler, *Ants . . .,* 1913, pp. 286–90). He maintained a wide correspondence with naturalists in Europe and America, and sent rich collections from Texas and Mexico to the Smithsonian Institution, the Academy of Natural Sciences of Philadelphia, and the Jardin des Plantes of Paris. He was gifted with an acute, independent, and observant mind, but being self-taught and isolated from other workers, he at first lacked the precision of the trained naturalist—a defect that he later largely overcame by diligence and persistence in observation. In addition to the works already mentioned, his publications include papers on natural-history subjects, chiefly insects, and his posthumously printed "Autobiography."

["Autobiography," *Miss. Hist. Soc. Pubs.,* vol. VIII (1904); *Southwest Rev.,* Autumn, 1929; *Dallas Daily Herald,* Dec. 12, 1874; original materials in the possession of S. W. Geiser, and in the archives of the University of Texas Library.] S. W. G.

LINCOLN, ABRAHAM (Feb. 12, 1809–Apr. 15, 1865), sixteenth president of the United States, was, to use his own words, born "in the most humble walks of life" (*Works,* I, 8). His birthplace was a log-cabin about three miles south of Hodgen's mill on what was known as the "Sinking Spring Farm" in Hardin (now Larue) County, Ky. Lincoln himself could trace his line no farther back than to certain ancestors in Berks County, Pa., whom he vaguely described as Quakers; but research has disclosed a lineage reaching back to Samuel Lincoln who came from Hingham, England, and settled in Hingham, Mass., in 1637. On the Lincoln side the descent was as follows: Samuel Lincoln (d. 1690); Mordecai Lincoln of Hingham and Scituate, Mass. (d. 1727); Mordecai Lincoln of Berks County, Pa. (d. 1736); John Lincoln of Berks County, Pa., and Rockingham County, Va. (d. 1788); Abraham Lincoln of Rockingham County, Va., and later of Kentucky; Thomas Lincoln, father of the President. The merging of the Lincolns with the migratory streams of pioneer America is illustrated by the progeny of John Lincoln mentioned above—"Virginia John" as he was called. Of his five sons, whose names were reminiscent of ancient Israel, Jacob alone remained in Virginia, while Abraham, Isaac, John, and Thomas removed to Kentucky, eastern Tennessee, or Ohio. Abraham Lincoln, grandfather of the President, emigrated from Rockingham County, Va., to Green River, Lincoln County, Ky., about 1782; but was killed about 1786 by Indians while opening a farm in the forest (Beveridge, *post,* I, 11, note 2).

Thomas Lincoln (1778–1851) was large, powerful, and compactly built. According to his distinguished son, he was "a wandering laboring-boy," and "grew up literally without education" (*Works,* VI, 25), and in mature life was barely able to write his name. Born in Rockingham County, Va., he went with his father to Lincoln County, Ky., roved about for some years, married and settled in Elizabethtown, Hardin County, after which he pursued the occupations of carpenter and farmer, changing his residence frequently, making nothing of his poorly chosen farms, avoiding contacts with "society" in town, and bequeathing little besides life itself to his son. Thomas' first wife, Nancy Hanks, was the mother of Abraham. According to the best available authority, she was the natural child of Lucy Hanks; and her paternity is unknown, the date of her birth being a matter of conjecture. Some years after the birth of Nancy, Lucy Hanks married Henry Sparrow in Mercer County, Ky.; and Nancy was reared by her aunt, Betsy Hanks (Mrs. Thomas Sparrow). Though many tender eulogies of Lincoln's mother have been written, there is little reliable evidence concerning her. She seems to have been superior to the general Hanks level in intellectual vigor, and was described as spiritually inclined, affectionate, amiable, cool, and heroic (Herndon and Weik, *post,* I, 10). Whatever her natural endowments, she was "absolutely illiterate" (Beveridge, I, 16) and was throughout life identified with lowly people. Her marriage to Thomas Lincoln occurred on June 12, 1806, the backwoods ceremony being performed in the cabin of a friend in Washington County, Ky., by Jesse Head, a Methodist parson. On the Hanks side the ancestry of Lincoln is beclouded in a maze of misinformation; and much of the data presented by earlier biographers on this subject must be rejected, including unreliable accounts of a mythical Nancy Shipley Hanks, sometimes erroneously mentioned as Lincoln's maternal grandmother, and of various alleged Hankses whose real name was Hawks. According to W. E. Barton (*Lineage of Lincoln,* pp. 186, 210), the parents of Lincoln's grandmother, Lucy, were Joseph and Ann (Lee) Hanks of Hampshire County, Va., and Nelson County, Ky.; and one finds Hankses in the seventeenth and eighteenth centuries living on the Rappahannock as close neighbors of various Lees with whom at times they intermarried. It is only by conjecture as to several links, however, that Barton argues a connection between Lincoln's line and that of Robert E. Lee (*Ibid.,* pp. 208–11).

Without following all the migrations of "Thomas the unstable," it may be noted that during the years of Abraham's early boyhood the family lived in a picturesque spot on Knob Creek about eight miles from his birthplace—a spot of natural beauty, of peace and grandeur, in a region of rocky cliffs, noble trees, and clear streams. Throughout life Lincoln carried fresh recollections of his Kentucky home—of the backwoods school where he was taught to read, write, and "cipher to the rule of three," of fishing and hunting adventures, of boyish escapades, of the old stone house on Nolin Creek where the young people gathered for dances, and of the mill to which as a child he carried the family grist. When the boy was seven the family was again on the move, this time for the Indiana woods. With their sorry stock of household goods they "packed through" to the Ohio River, ferried across, and followed a newly blazed trail to the home in the brush which Thomas had selected. This home, in which the Lincolns were at first but squatters, was located in the Pigeon Creek neighborhood in what is now Spencer County, Ind. The first winter they had not even a cabin —merely a rude shelter of poles, brush, and leaves enclosed on three sides and called a "half-faced camp." Their cabin, when Thomas got round to building it, had at first neither floor, door, nor window; and the family fare was a matter of game animals, honey, birds, nuts, and wild fruit. The family of Thomas and Nancy Lincoln, with their two children, Sarah and Abraham, was soon joined by Nancy's foster parents, Betsy and Thomas Sparrow, with the colorful Dennis Hanks, who was as essential a part of this backwoods picture as "that Darne Little half face camp," as Dennis called it, which the Sparrows used after the Lincolns had discarded it. Tragedy soon descended upon Pigeon Creek. Thomas Sparrow and Betsy his wife were stricken with what the settlers called the "milk sick," and were laid away in coffins fashioned by Thomas Lincoln. To these and other sufferers Nancy Lincoln had generously ministered. She soon fell ill, lingered without medical help for a week, and died (October 1818) with words of pious admonition for her children. In life and death her brief story was that of the American pioneer woman.

Thomas Lincoln soon found another wife in Sarah (Bush) Johnston of Elizabethtown, Ky., widow of Daniel Johnston, who came with her three children to the Indiana cabin; and with the addition in 1823 of John Hanks there were nine persons in this narrow abode. The household equipment was now improved; and the stepmother became an important factor in the boy's rearing. From the Weik manuscripts—memories of Lincoln's early associates recorded after many years—we may reconstruct, through Beveridge's pages, a fairly definite picture of Lincoln as an easy-going backwoods youth who did his stint of hard labor on the homestead, performed odd jobs for neighbors, shunned the vociferous camp-meetings of the time, avoided membership in the church, and used his leisure for self-improvement by the reading of a few good books. The Bible, *Robinson Crusoe, Pilgrim's Progress,* Aesop's *Fables,* William Grimshaw's *History of the United States,* the *Kentucky Preceptor,* Weems's *Life of Washington,* and various other biographies and books of verse were the principal works known to have been used by Lincoln at this period. As to formal schooling, there was very little. While living in the Knob Creek home in Kentucky, Abraham and his sister Sarah had attended country schools for some weeks; now in Indiana he sat for brief periods under several schoolmasters (Andrew Crawford, Azel W. Dorsey, and William Sweeney by name) to whose log schools he had to walk long distances; but, in all, his attendance at school did not exceed one year. Out of school his vigor for reading and study was probably less a matter of ambition than of healthy intellectual interest. It was his stepmother who told the familiar story of his ciphering on boards which he shaved off with a drawing-knife to prepare for fresh efforts. His readiness to walk many miles for books is well attested, as is also his fondness for speech-making and for mimicking the preachers and orators who penetrated to the rough creekside. He somehow grew up without the frontier vices, avoiding liquor and being wholly free from dissoluteness and profanity. Though avoiding girls, he was uncommonly sociable; and the nearby country store at Gentryville held for him an unfailing fascination. The river attracted him powerfully and entered largely into his early life. He earned a few dollars by rowing passengers from the shore to passing steamers; and in the year 1828 he made the trip from Gentry's landing on the Ohio to New Orleans. Though stirred with the ambition to become "a steamboat man," he returned to the monotony of Pigeon Creek, where his father had a claim upon his labor. As the boy emerged from his teens he was tall, powerful, muscular, ungainly, tender toward animals, a recounter of robust stories, mighty with the axe, and not without a certain latent poetry in his nature. His relations with his father seem not to have been happy, and he welcomed the day when he could shift for himself.

In the year of Abraham's coming of age (1830) the Lincolns were again on the move. Having sold his Indiana holdings, Thomas set out with his family to Macon County, Ill., whither John Hanks had preceded them. With ox-drawn wagons they trekked through forest and prairie, crossed the Wabash, and settled on the Sangamon River not far from Decatur. At first Abraham remained with the family, helping to build the new cabin, splitting fence rails, planting corn, and assisting in the rough tasks of the following winter. In the service of one Denton Offutt he assisted in building and navigating a flatboat from a point on the Sangamon River near Springfield to New Orleans; but the story that "the iron entered his soul" on seeing the New Orleans slave auction, and that he vowed if he ever had a chance to "hit that thing" he would "hit it hard," is untrustworthy (Beveridge, I, 107). Returning from the southern mart on a steamer, Lincoln, then only a drifter, selected as his home the village of New Salem, about twenty miles northwest of Springfield—a remote hamlet set high on a bluff overlooking the Sangamon.

Here he spent six picturesque and formative years (1831–37), working in the store of Denton Offutt till it "petered out"; managing a mill; conducting a store with W. F. Berry, who died leaving a heavy debt ($1,100) all of which Lincoln finally paid; splitting rails and doing odd jobs to earn a scant living; acting as village postmaster; traversing the county as deputy surveyor; and all the while reading law, studying grammar, widening his acquaintance, following the trends of national politics, and laying the foundations for a wide personal influence. It was during this period that he served in the Black Hawk War, being unanimously elected captain by the men of his company. Another gauge to measure his stature is the devotion of the "Clary Grove Boys"—stalwart rowdies to whom hero worship was as natural as swearing, drinking, and fighting. This tribute to Lincoln's manhood, which came in spite of his freedom from the vices of the gang, seems to have been in part a recognition of his prowess in competitive sport, especially wrestling, and in part a pure matter of personal attachment.

In 1834 Lincoln was chosen to the state legislature; and he served during four successive terms (1834–41), first at Vandalia, the old capital, and later at Springfield. It was a frontier legislature, but its party maneuvers were spirited, and it offered Lincoln his first political training. Being a Clay Whig in a Democratic body, he belonged to the minority; but he became Whig floor leader and directed the fortunes of his party in the lower house, receiving in several sessions the full party vote for the speakership. On national issues, which were necessarily of concern to him as a prominent party worker, he acted as a regular Whig, supporting the Bank of the United States, opposing the leading measures of Jackson and Van Buren, and attacking the independent treasury. He studiously avoided association with abolitionists, but he did not want this attitude construed as positive support of slavery. Consequently, when the legislature in 1837 passed resolutions severely condemning abolition societies, Lincoln and his colleague Dan Stone from Sangamon County entered a protest, asserting that slavery was "founded on both injustice and bad policy, but that the promulgation of abolition doctrines tends rather to increase than abate its evils" (*Works,* I, 52).

In 1837 Lincoln left New Salem, which was soon thereafter abandoned, later to be rebuilt as a memorial to him, and made his home in Springfield. So poor was he at this time that his surveying instruments had been attached to pay a debt; he rode into town on a borrowed horse carrying his possessions in two saddle-bags, and was glad to make arrangements with friends for free lodging and board. He was now a practising lawyer, having been licensed as an attorney Sept. 9, 1836; and he formed a partnership with J. T. Stuart, a man of influential family, able in the law, and prominent in Whig circles. While in New Salem, Lincoln had paid court to Ann Rutledge whose father kept the rude inn where he boarded. Though the girl's attractions and tragic death have inspired an extravagant amount of sentimental fiction, actual evidence on the matter is scant. She was engaged to a man named John McNamar, but his long absence suggested desertion. Her engagement to Lincoln seems to have been conditional upon honorable release from her absent lover. That Ann preferred Lincoln in case her lover should return and renew his suit seems doubtful; and on both sides there were reasons for deferring marriage. With matters in this unsettled state, Ann died of "brain fever," Aug. 25, 1835. Lincoln's proposal to Mary Owens, whom he met through the kindness of her sister at New Salem, need not be treated here; nor is there room to analyze the confused testimony that surrounds his troubled courtship of Mary Todd.

Herndon's sensational story of Lincoln's failure to appear at his wedding, said to have been set for Jan. 1, 1841, has produced a mass of contradictory discussion. In the best treatment of the subject (Sandburg and Angle, *Mary Lincoln, Wife and Widow,* 1932, pp. 40–60, 174–185, 330), the conclusion is reached that there was no defaulting bridegroom at a wedding, but that some violent emotional disturbance did occur; indeed, no one can read Lincoln's correspondence of the period without being impressed with his excessive morbidity. After a series of breaks and reconciliations, complicated by Mary's rumored flirtations with other men, the disturbed lovers were finally brought together; and they were married in some haste on Nov. 4, 1842. As to the degree of happiness that attended their married life it is equally difficult to reach a fully rounded conclusion (see Lincoln, Mary Todd). On Lincoln's side there was indifference to domestic niceties and a certain untidiness and lack of dignity that grated upon the sensibilities of a proudly reared woman; on the other hand, the domestic atmosphere was not improved by Mary's bursts of temper. Their first son, Robert Todd [*q.v.*], was born Aug. 1, 1843; he alone grew to manhood. The other children were: Edward Baker (Mar. 10, 1846–Feb. 1, 1850), William Wallace (Dec. 21, 1850–Feb. 20, 1862), and Thomas or "Tad" (Apr. 4, 1853–July 15, 1871).

In the years 1847–49 Lincoln served one term in Congress, where he had the distinction of being the only Whig from Illinois. His election with more than 1,500 majority over the doughty backwoods preacher, Peter Cartwright, was a significant personal triumph, for Cartwright was himself a man of great popularity. In his undistinguished career as congressman the matters most worthy of comment are those which pertain to the Mexican War and to slavery. Lincoln had not opposed the war while campaigning as a candidate; but when his party sought political advantage by denouncing the conflict as a Democratic war unjustly begun by Polk, Lincoln joined aggressively in this party attack. He voted (Jan. 3, 1848) that the war was "unnecessarily . . . begun by the President"; and on Dec. 22, 1847, he introduced his "spot resolutions" (*Congressional Globe,* 30 Cong., 1 Sess., p. 64), which were so worded as to imply that the "spot" on which had occurred the shedding of American blood, which Polk had interpreted as Mexican aggression, was in fact an unoffending settlement of Mexican people, outside American jurisdiction, against which an American force had been unnecessarily sent contrary to General Taylor's advice. On Jan. 12, 1848, he made a striking speech on his resolutions—a Whig speech in which he subjected the President's evidence to cold analysis, accused him of befogging the issue, and questioned the purposes of the administration as to the duration of the war and the terms of peace (*Ibid.,* pp. 154–56). In this speech Lincoln made a declaration which hardly comported with his later declarations against Southern secession; for he asserted the right of "any people," or of "a majority of any portion of such people," to "shake off the existing government, and form a new one" (*Works,* I, 338–39). Though Lincoln had voted to grant supplies to sustain the war, and though his antiwar speech made but slight impression generally, he had deeply offended the people of his state. His attitude was denounced in Illinois as unpatriotic; he was described as a "second Benedict Arnold," and was accused of having plead the cause of the enemy (Beveridge, I, 432). On various occasions Lincoln voted for the Wilmot proviso; and on Jan. 10, 1849, he read a proposal to abolish slavery in the national capital (*Congressional Globe,* 30 Cong., 2 Sess., p. 212). It is characteristic of his conservatism that he proposed such abolition only in case three conditions should be met: emancipation was to be gradual; compensation was to be made to slaveholders; and the proposed act was not to go into force unless approved by the citizens of the District at a special election.

Lincoln did not move among the great in Washington, nor did he rise above the obscurity of the average congressman. He amused a small circle by his camaraderie and droll stories, but the more brilliant social life of the capital was closed to him. Vigorous anti-slavery men were not his associates, but he formed a real friendship with Alexander H. Stephens of Georgia. Party affairs took much of his energy. He spent weary hours addressing documents to voters; wrote numerous letters; served as the Illinois member of the Whig national committee; delivered a rollicking speech against Cass which was essentially a campaign document (July 27, 1848, *Works,* II, 59–88); and participated in the Whig convention at Philadelphia in 1848, laboring hard for the inexperienced Zachary Taylor and against his former hero, Henry Clay. In the campaign of 1848 his services on the stump were not eagerly sought, least of all in Illinois; but he visited Massachusetts, speaking at Worcester, Chelsea, Dedham, Cambridge, Lowell, and Boston. One misses in these speeches the resonant tone of Lincoln's later declarations. Antislavery as he was at heart, he counseled against voting for the Free-Soil candidate, Van Buren, since such action would help to elect Cass. Though the Whigs were nationally successful in this election, Lincoln had the humiliation of seeing his party lose his own district, where the defeat of S. T. Logan for Congress might be interpreted as a repudiation of Lincoln's record by his neighbors. With a sense of futility he bade goodbye to Washington; and, while the thunders of the mid-century slavery crisis were shaking the country, he renounced politics, returned to the obscurity of Springfield, and sadly resumed his law practice.

As a lawyer Lincoln rose to front rank in his own state. He was associated with capable partners—at first John Todd Stuart, then Stephen T. Logan, and finally William H. Herndon. His practice was important and extensive in the state supreme court and also in the federal courts. After Illinois was divided into two federal judicial districts, Lincoln attended the sessions of the United States courts in Chicago with increasing frequency. In his circuit practice, where cases had to be quickly whipped into shape, he was not more than ordinarily successful; but in the higher courts, where careful study served to bring into play the sureness of his matured judgments, his record was outstanding (Paul M. Angle, in *Lincoln Centennial Association Papers,* 1928, esp. pp. 38–41). It is true that Lincoln is chiefly remembered as a luminous figure among the circuit-riding lawyers who traveled the judicial circuit presided over by Judge David Davis. He thoroughly enjoyed this picturesque life, jogging over the prairies in his rickety buggy, meeting the country folk on their own level, and joining the happy migratory life of judge and attorneys as they lodged two in a bed and eight in a room, swapped stories, and made the taverns resound with hilarity. During court week the lawyers were in demand for political speeches, and Lincoln's popularity was enhanced by his aptness on these occasions. It was here that his humor and story telling showed at their best; and to the stories themselves must be added the wizardry of Lincoln's quaint manner and the charm of his smile. Some of the specific cases of this circuit-riding phase have received undue emphasis, such as the Wright case in which Lincoln represented the widow of a Revolutionary soldier and recovered an exorbitant fee which a grasping pension agent had charged, and that of "Duff" Armstrong whom Lincoln successfully defended on a murder charge, making use of an almanac to refute testimony as to moonlight on the night of the murder. The human interest of these smaller cases has served to obscure the really important litigation with which Lincoln was connected. His services were enlisted in determining such important matters as the right of a county to tax the Illinois Central Railroad (17 *Illinois,* 291–99), the right to bridge a navigable stream (the *Effie Afton* case, Beveridge, I, 598–605), and the protection of the McCormick Reaper Company against infringement of its patents (*Ibid.,* I, 575–83). In this McCormick case, which was tried before a federal court at Cincinnati, Lincoln suppressed his feelings when snubbed by eastern attorneys; and later as president he appointed one of these lawyers, Stanton, to his cabinet. A study of his whole legal career shows that he was more than a country lawyer; and to those factors which gave him fair success in the rural county seats—his common sense, his shrewdness, his effectiveness before a jury, his strong invective, and his reputation for honesty—one must add further qualities that mark the outstanding attorney: a searching thoroughness of investigation (Beveridge, I, 573–74), a familiarity with pertinent judicial doctrines, and a knack of so stating a legal question as to brush away its technicalities and get at the core of the controversy. There are instances of his declining to receive excessive fees, refusing questionable cases, and even withdrawing from a case on discovering during the trial that his client's cause was unjust. In fragmentary notes for a law lecture he stated his conception of professional standards (*Works,* II, 140–43). A successful lawyer, he said, must stress diligence, attend promptly to the preparation of documents, and cultivate extemporaneous speaking as the "lawyer's avenue to the public." He should discourage litigation and choose honesty above professional success. "Work, work, work," he said, "is the main thing" (*Ibid.,* VI, 59).

The Lincoln of the prairies was a man of marked individuality. Standing six feet four, with uncommon length of arms and legs, his figure loomed in any crowd, while the rugged face bespoke a pioneer origin and an early life of toil and poverty. In a head not over large each feature was rough and prominent. In contrast to the round, full-cheeked Douglas, Lincoln's face showed deep hollows and heavy shadows. The craggy brow, tousled hair, drooping eyelids, melancholy gray eyes, large nose and chin, heavy lips, and sunken, wrinkled cheeks produced an effect not easily forgotten. A wide variety of qualities is revealed in his portraits, which give the impression of a character whose depth is not readily sounded—a personality in which conflicting hereditary strains were peculiarly blended. Those who have described him from life dwell upon the contrast between the seeming listlessness of the face in repose and the warmth of the countenance when animated with conversation or public speech. The trappings of the man intensified the effect of crudeness. In a day of grandiloquent male adornment Lincoln's habiliments departed as far from the Godey fashion plate as did his mid-western speech from the sophisticated accent of the East. The battered stovepipe hat stuffed with papers, the rusty ill-fitting coat, the ready-made trousers too short for the legs, the unpolished boots, the soiled stock at the neck, the circular cloak in winter or linen duster in summer, the bulging umbrella and hard-used carpet-bag, gave an entirely unpremeditated effect of oddity, the man's appearance being apparently of no more concern to him than the food which he seemed to eat without tasting.

Few men could match Lincoln as a stump-speaker. Beginning with apparent diffidence he gained composure and assurance as he proceeded, speaking with freedom, naturalness, and convincing power. In impassioned periods the gaunt figure, despite the sunken chest, became "splendid and imposing" (Herndon and Weik, II, 77); and in the directness of his intense passages the tall form seemed to gain in height. His mind had that tenacity and steadfastness of logic that goes with slowness in forming conclusions. There is a clarity and compactness in his writings which is in pleasing contrast to the verbosity so common in his day. Never descending to triteness or banality, his papers show careful composition and abound in epigrams and pithy phrases. This power of written and spoken utterance must be reckoned high among his qualities as a statesman. His political philosophy revealed a democratic liberalism closely resembling the creed of Thomas Jefferson. Anglo-Saxon principles of civil liberty were fundamental in his thinking (A. C. Cole, in *Journal of the Illinois State Historical Society*, Oct. 1926–Jan. 1927, pp. 102–14); he advocated the broadening of political rights, even favoring woman suffrage far ahead of his time; and the leveling doctrines of the Declaration of Independence became a kind of religion with him. Laborers and the less favored classes generally found in him an earnest champion. Though never identifying himself with any ecclesiastical denomination, he was not lacking in the religious sense; and in his public papers he expressed with sincerity the spiritual aspirations of his people.

In the agitation that swept the country with the repeal of the Missouri Compromise Lincoln emerged from political inactivity and launched upon the larger career which occupied the coming years. From 1854 on there appeared a new tone in his speeches, a notable earnestness combined with adroitness in narrowing the contest to one phase of the slavery question, thus making it a suitable party issue. In a speech at Springfield, Oct. 4, 1854, repeated at Peoria on Oct. 16 (*Works*, II, 190–262), Lincoln answered Douglas, who had spoken in the same hall the previous day. His reasoned appeals to the Declaration of Independence, his sarcasm, his searching questions, and his shrewdness in avoiding pitfalls, indicated that he had now struck his stride as a leader. Still calling himself a Whig, though events were drawing him toward the new Republican party, he worked hard for the senatorship from Illinois in 1855; but, after successive ballots in the legislature indicated his dwindling strength, he aided the cause of the Anti-Nebraska fusionists against the Democrats by throwing his support to Trumbull.

The next year Lincoln became definitely identified with the new party; and at the Republican state convention at Bloomington he delivered, on May 29, 1856, what some have called his greatest speech (*Works*, II, 308 note). In a time of high excitement over the Kansas struggle, when radicals were trying to capture the Republican party, Lincoln's task was to make a fighting speech which would have enough boldness to inspire the crusading abolitionists and yet so define the issue as to keep the support of moderates. Herndon exhausted his adjectives in describing the speech and declared that on that occasion his partner was seven feet tall. Lincoln soon became active in the new party, attending every meeting he could reach, speaking frequently, managing the details of party machinery, and carrying on an extensive correspondence with voters. He was now the leading Republican as he had been the leading Whig of Illinois. At the time of Frémont's nomination for the presidency at Philadelphia in 1856 he received 110 votes for the vice-presidential nomination; and in this way his name was widely advertised in the North. He campaigned for Frémont in this election, though McLean had been his choice; but he had only partial success in winning Whig support for the Republican cause.

Successfully seeking the Republican senatorial nomination in 1858, Lincoln delivered a carefully prepared speech on June 16 before the state Republican convention at Springfield. "A house divided against itself cannot stand," said he. "I believe this government cannot endure permanently, half slave and half free. I do not expect the Union to be dissolved—I do not expect the house to fall—but I do expect it will cease to be divided. It will become all one thing, or all the other" (*Works,* III, 2). In this speech, as elsewhere, Lincoln denounced the Dred Scott decision of 1857 as part of a pro-slavery conspiracy which, unless thwarted, would one day legalize slavery even in the free states. In the campaign with Douglas for the senatorship, Lincoln at first trailed his opponent, speaking at Chicago on July 10 just after his antagonist had spoken at the same place, and repeating the performance at Bloomington and elsewhere. On July 24, 1858, he challenged Douglas [*q.v.*] to a series of debates; and the acceptance of the challenge gave Lincoln the advantage of being matched against the outstanding leader of the Democratic party. Beginning at Ottawa, Aug. 21, reaching an early climax at Freeport, Aug. 27, and closing at Alton on Oct. 15, the seven "joint debates" were but the most striking incident of a long duel between Lincoln and Douglas. It was indeed a memorable contest. The emotion of cheering crowds, the clack and rattle of western campaigning, the sporting spectacle of contestants facing each other in successive forensic rounds, the physical disparity between the candidates, the contrast between Douglas' private railroad car and the crowded coach or freight caboose in which Lincoln, not without an eye to political effect, lumbered into town to be fetched to his lodging in a hay-wagon—these features lent a picturesque interest to a contest in which the importance of the stakes far exceeded the realization of participants or spectators. Each candidate showed respect for the other, and the discussions were conducted on a high plane, albeit with a deadly earnestness. In the speeches there were few elements that were new. Lincoln shrewdly capitalized the growing split in the Democratic ranks; he denounced Douglas' indifference as to the right or wrong of slavery; and he used with telling effect the inconsistency between "popular sovereignty" and the doctrine of the Dred Scott decision, both of which Douglas favored. At Freeport, by a question as to whether the people of a territory could exclude slavery, he forced Douglas to compromise himself as presidential candidate in 1860 by taking a position which offended the South, though gaining votes for the senatorial contest in Illinois.

Once and again in the debates Lincoln disavowed abolitionist doctrines and stressed the conservative note. He did not advocate the unconditional repeal of fugitive-slave laws nor oppose the admission of states in which slavery might be established by constitutions honestly adopted. Negro citizenship did not receive his indorsement, nor did he urge political or social equality for the races. His advocacy of abolition in the District of Columbia was again qualified by those safeguarding conditions which he had previously proposed as congressman. With the politician's eye for vote-getting and for uniting the incongruous elements of his nascent party, he avoided the language of the anti-slavery crusader and narrowed the issue to the clear-cut doctrine of freedom in the territories. The effectiveness of his campaign was shown in the election returns. His party carried districts containing a larger population than those carried by the Democrats, but inequitable apportionment gave Douglas a majority in the legislature, insuring his election. The contest lifted Lincoln into national prominence; and in 1859 he made many speeches in Ohio, Indiana, Iowa, Wisconsin, and Kansas, impressing his ideas upon the people of important doubtful states.

His name was now being mentioned for the presidency, and it was as a presidential possibility that he delivered on Feb. 27, 1860, his Cooper Institute speech in New York (*Works,* V, 293–328). This was a notable formulation of the issues on which the new party could do battle. Exclusion of slavery from the territories as the doctrine of the fathers was the keynote of the address, which was delivered in Lincoln's best style and with a dignity in keeping with the occasion. Decrying the efforts to discredit the Republican party by identifying it with the radicalism of John Brown or the abusiveness of Helper's *Impending Crisis,* he spoke for an attitude of understanding and friendliness toward the Southern people. He urged his party to "yield to them if . . . we possibly can," doing "nothing through passion and ill temper"; and he denounced efforts to destroy the Union.

Lincoln was named in state convention as the choice of Illinois Republicans for the presidency; and a combination of factors led to his success in the national convention at Chicago. Seward was considered too radical and was injured by the powerful opposition of Greeley. Other candidates had weak points; Bates could not carry the Germans; Chase could not muster his own state.

The moderate element was growing in the new party, and in certain "battle-ground states"—Illinois, Indiana, Pennsylvania, and New Jersey, which had supported Buchanan in 1856—it was vitally important to nominate a conservative candidate. Lincoln had steadily counseled moderation; he had avoided connection with the Know-Nothings, had pleased the Germans by his opposition to measures directed against foreigners, and had made himself highly acceptable as a second choice in case Seward could not be named. In short, Lincoln was so free from radicalism, so careful to avoid offense, and yet withal so skilful in inspiring enthusiasts that he proved to be precisely the type of candidate to which a convention turns after the luminous stars of the pre-convention canvass have proved unavailable. The atmosphere of the wigwam at Chicago was favorable to the "rail splitter," opposition within the state having been skilfully sidetracked. O. H. Browning, for instance, who favored Bates because of his strength with the old Whigs, was a member of the Illinois delegation pledged to Lincoln; and he labored loyally for him at the convention. David Davis, in charge of the Lincoln forces at Chicago, worked tirelessly and did his part well, though his bargaining in cabinet positions was contrary to Lincoln's instructions. With 465 delegates present and 233 necessary to a choice, the first ballot stood: Seward 173½, Lincoln 102, Cameron 50½, Chase 49, Bates 48, the rest scattered. On the second ballot Cameron's name was withdrawn to Lincoln's advantage, Seward receiving 184½ votes, Lincoln 181, Chase 42½, Bates 35. On the third ballot the change of four Ohio votes during the count precipitated a stampede to Lincoln, who became the convention's choice amid scenes of wild excitement.

In the fury of the ensuing campaign, with the Democratic party split between North and South and disunion threatened in case of Republican success, Lincoln remained quietly at Springfield. He conferred with leaders, received delegations, wrote letters, and prepared a short autobiography for campaign purposes; but he avoided political speeches. While the people of the South were expecting the worst from him, he did but little to reassure them. In the election of Nov. 6, 1860, he was chosen president by pluralities in enough states to give him a considerable electoral majority; but as regards the whole popular vote he was a minority president. There were ten Southern states in which not a single popular vote had been cast for him; and, strangely enough, his own county in Illinois voted against him. Lincoln carried every Northern free state except New Jersey. His vote in New England was nearly three times that of Douglas; elsewhere in the East his vote stood to that of Douglas as 7 to 4; in the Western states the contest was closer, the ratio being 8 to 7. Lincoln's total in the popular vote was 1,866,452 as compared to 1,376,957 for Douglas, 849,781 for Breckinridge, and 588,879 for Bell (Edward Stanwood, *A History of the Presidency,* 1924, I, 297). The electoral vote stood: Lincoln 180, Breckinridge 72, Bell 39, Douglas 12.

In the critical interval between his election and his inauguration Lincoln continued his policy of silence, making no speeches and avoiding public statements as to his policy. While events were moving rapidly in the lower South and disunion was consummated by the formation of a Southern Confederacy without hindrance from Washington, the President-Elect, though never doubting that the government possessed the authority to maintain itself, remained passive and quiet at Springfield. Matters of patronage, cabinet making, the preparation of his inaugural address, conferences, and correspondence occupied his attention. He found time for a trip to Coles County where he visited his aged stepmother, directing that the grave of his father be suitably marked, and for one to Chicago to meet Hannibal Hamlin, Nov. 21–26, 1860. To the measures of compromise proposed in Congress he gave scant encouragement. The Crittenden proposal to avert disunion was shattered by Lincoln's inflexible refusal to countenance the territorial extension of slavery. He requested General Scott to be ready to "hold or retake" the forts in the South as the case might require; and he did little to allay Southern fears as to his policy. He assured John A. Gilmer of North Carolina (Dec. 15, 1860, *Works,* VI, 81) that he would not discriminate against the South in appointments and that the only substantial difference between the Southern people and himself was in the matter of slavery extension. To another Southerner, Samuel Haycraft, he wrote that the "good people of the South" would find in him "no cause to complain" (Nov. 13, 1860, *Ibid.,* VI, 69–70). These and other similar letters, however, were confidential, and the pacific nature of his intentions was not appreciated. The pliable Seward, during these days, was more prominent as Republican spokesman than the President-Elect. A survey of the Southern press in this crisis shows a division of sentiment between those who recognized Lincoln's election as legal and would await an "overt act" before embarking upon disunion and those who asserted that abolition had swept the North and that the "cause of the South" had no future except by separation. (See D. L. Dumond, *Southern Editorials on Secession,* 1931, esp. pp. 221–223, 304–06; see also A. C. Cole in *American Historical Review,* July 1931, pp. 740–67.) It was not long before the men who held the latter view seized the reins in the lower South; and fast-moving events made theirs the controlling policy for the South in general. (Much light is thrown on Lincoln as president-elect by the colorful letters of Henry Villard to the *New York Herald,* November 1860 to February 1861). In the matter of cabinet making the inclusion of Seward, Chase, and Bates was a recognition of rivals, while Welles was chosen as a New Englander and a former Democrat who had turned Republican. Lincoln had wished to include some representative of the South (as distinguished from the border states) and had approached John A. Gilmer of North Carolina on this subject, but his efforts to this end proved unsuccessful. Bargains in the nominating convention were kept by the appointment of Caleb B. Smith of Indiana and Simon Cameron of Pennsylvania.

On Feb. 11, 1861, with words of restrained emotion, Lincoln left Springfield for Washington. His speeches en route did little to reassure the skeptical East, but they made it clear that the government would resist secession. The effect of these speeches in the South was distinctly unfavorable (D. L. Dumond, *The Secession Movement,* 1931, pp. 258–60). Newspapers carried full accounts of the journey, and unfortunate publicity was given to trivial incidents, as when Lincoln, whose chin was now marred by a new-grown beard, publicly kissed a little girl for whom he inquired as his train stopped at her town, and explained that the facial adornment had been assumed at her request. His secret night ride to Washington, occasioned by detective reports of assassination plots, was a humiliation to his friends and a subject of ridicule by his opponents. In a conciliatory inaugural address Lincoln again disclaimed any intention to interfere with slavery in the states, counseled observance of all federal laws (not excepting the Fugitive-slave Law), and plead earnestly for the preservation of the Union, which he declared to be perpetual (*Works,* VI, 169–85). Denouncing secession as anarchy he announced that the national power would be used to "hold, occupy, and possess" (he did not say "repossess") federal "property and places." Declaring that "physically speaking, we cannot separate," he asked his countrymen "one and all" to "think calmly," pledging that the government would not assail them, and closed with a poetic reminder of those "mystic chords of memory" which he hoped would yet "swell the chorus of the Union."

Inexperienced as he was in the management of great affairs, untrained in executive functions requiring vigorous action, the new President found himself borne down by a cruel pressure of miscellaneous duties, overwhelmed by a horde of office seekers, and embarrassed by unfamiliar social exactions, while through it all the Sumter crisis, involving the momentous issue of civil war, was pressing for a solution. With the eyes of the nation on the fort at Charleston as a test of the new administration, with Major Anderson reporting that in a few weeks the garrison must surrender unless provisioned, and with informal negotiations in progress between Union leaders and Southern commissioners concerning the relation of the Washington government to the Confederacy, events were pushing the new executive to a decision. Meanwhile his very position as leader was at stake. Seward had begun by supposing that he would be premier, and had fatuously proposed a startling program of foreign aggression as a means of reuniting the country. Lincoln's answer to his secretary left no doubt as to who was president, but his words left no sting. If a certain thing must be done, said he simply, "I must do it" (*Works,* VI, 237). As to Sumter, Lincoln took advice but made his own decision, not, however, without a certain laxness in his control of the situation which unfortunately gave Southern leaders the impression of bad faith; for Seward, without Lincoln's authority, had made virtual promises which the administration could not keep. Lincoln asked his cabinet to submit written advice as to provisioning Sumter. Only two members, Chase hesitatingly and Blair emphatically, favored it. Seward, Cameron, Welles, Smith, and Bates counseled evacuation, though some of the secretaries later changed their positions. Having already committed himself to the general policy of holding federal property, and feeling that evacuation would be tantamount to surrender, Lincoln ultimately decided to provision the fort. Yet Seward assured the Confederate commissioners that the fort would be evacuated; and Lincoln himself was willing to evacuate it if by this means the secession of Virginia could be averted. "A State for a fort," he is reported to have said, "is no bad business" (*Annual Report of the American Historical Association for the Year 1915,* 1917, p. 211). Late in March he sent Ward H. Lamon [*q.v.*] to Charleston, primarily to investigate and report; but Lamon unfortunately gave Anderson, Beauregard, and Governor Pickens the impression that the garrison would be withdrawn (*War of the Rebellion: Official Records,* ser. I, vol. I, 1880, pp. 222, 230, 237, 294). In all this there was considerable muddling, though without bad faith on Lincoln's part; and the confusion was increased by a bungling of orders due to Seward's interference with arrangements made by Lincoln and Welles, as a result of which the Sumter expedition was crippled by the detachment of the powerful *Powhatan.* The pacific attitude of the President was manifest in the purpose of the expedition (to convey food to the garrison and to land reënforcements only in case of attack), and also in the care which he took to notify the governor of South Carolina of his action, thus removing the element of hostile surprise.

Diverse interpretations have been placed upon Lincoln's action, and the whole subject has occasioned a flood of controversy. There are many threads to the story; and to the perplexities of conflicting evidence must be added the difficulties of reading thoughts and assessing motives in a field where violent misunderstandings were inevitable. Under the onslaught of opposing forces, with the border states and upper South on the brink of secession and the war clouds gathering, Lincoln himself seems to have vacillated, to have pondered evacuation, meanwhile testing its possible consequences and even giving hints that such a course was under consideration without committing himself to it (a process to which statesmen must often resort), and in the end to have concluded that, in view of the uncertainty of compensating benefits accruing to the cause of union, the fort should not be surrendered. As the exhaustion of supplies made some change inevitable, the closest approximation to the preservation of the status quo was what Lincoln decided to do—to feed the garrison without aggressively strengthening it.

When the war came, Lincoln met the issue with a series of purely executive measures, for Congress was not convened until July 1861. He treated the conflict as a huge "insurrection"; and before Congress, on July 13, 1861, recognized a state of war, he had summoned the militia, proclaimed a blockade, expanded the regular army beyond the legal limit, suspended the *habeas corpus* privilege, directed governmental expenditures in advance of congressional appropriation, and in cooperation with his cabinet and the state governments had launched a multifold series of military measures. In a masterly message to Congress on July 4, 1861, he explained his Sumter policy, recounted the steps that led to war, stated the issue as between separation and union, commented on the world significance of the struggle, and appealed for ratification of previous acts as well as for future cooperation (*Works,* VI, 297–325). This legislative ratification of the president's irregular acts was soon given (*United States Statutes at Large,* XII, 326); and the Supreme Court added its sanction by deciding in the Prize Cases (67 *U. S.,* 635–99), though not without vigorous dissent, that executive proclamations were adequate for the inauguration of maritime war.

As the war progressed, Lincoln extended his executive powers until, man of peace that he was, he was called a dictator. In dealing with disloyal activities—a serious problem because of pro-Southern activity in the North—he urged no special laws against treason, he but slightly used such laws as existed, and he had no system of nation-wide prosecutions; but, under his suspension of the *habeas corpus* privilege, thousands of persons were arrested on suspicion, after which, usually without trial, they were kept in prison for a time and then released. In this his purpose was precautionary and preventive, not punitive or vindictive. When confronted with anti-war or anti-administration agitation in speech or press, Lincoln usually showed toleration; and throughout the war "Copperhead" meetings were common and opposition newspapers persisted in their attacks upon the President and his party. The case of C. L. Vallandigham [*q.v.*], arrested for an anti-war speech of May 1, 1863, by order of General Burnside, was a familiar theme of denunciation by Lincoln's opponents; but the facts show leniency and tact in him rather than severity. He and all the cabinet regretted the arrest; and when a military commission condemned the agitator to imprisonment during the war, Lincoln commuted the sentence to banishment within the Confederate lines. Later, when Vallandigham escaped from the South and conducted a violent agitation in Ohio, Lincoln left him unmolested. There were, it is true, instances of newspaper suppression, as in the case of the *Chicago Times* in June 1863 (in which case Burnside's suspension order was promptly revoked); but in general Lincoln advised military restraint and counseled the suppression of assemblies or newspapers only when they were working "palpable injury" to the military (*Works,* IX, 148).

Looking broadly at his administration, one is impressed with the many difficulties that beset Lincoln's path. He had a rival for the presidency (Chase) in his cabinet. Within his own party the "Jacobins," a group which seemed at times a cabal of congressional leaders but which became the dominant element, tried his patience with their radicalism, their defiant opposition, and their interference in the conduct of the war. Abolition demands required his utmost tact; for the outcries of such men as Wendell Phillips reached at times an almost hysterical pitch. Always he had the activities of anti-war leaders to deal with. Though bringing Democrats within his cabinet and appointing many of them to civil and military positions, he was unable to carry through his "all parties program"; and he found it necessary to function as leader of one party, the Republican or "Union" party. Scheming men imposed on his generosity and a constant stream of people clamored at his doors. He had the defeatists to deal with—men who demanded peace first and union afterward; while he had the equally hard problem of keeping the Union cause clear of abuse, so that victory, when achieved, would not itself become a curse. The maladjustment of governmental activities, state and federal, military and civil, made his tasks needlessly hard; while the profiteering, plunder, and graft that came in the wake of war wounded his honest soul. A group of senators, partisans of Chase [*q.v.*], descended upon him in December 1862, demanding the removal of Seward and threatening to take important matters of policy out of his hands. Though inwardly suffering bitter distress (*Diary of O. H. Browning,* I, 601), Lincoln received the intriguing senators with calm, rode the storm by shrewd steering, kept both Seward and Chase in his cabinet, silenced his critics, and reassured the public. Often he faced a hostile and meddling Congress, and at times he seemed almost deserted. Favoring a war policy with as little of vengeance as possible, always remembering that the people of the South were to be respected, he encountered the opposition of the vindictive element which ultimately seized the Republican party and overthrew his policy in reconstruction days. It is in his reaction to these difficult circumstances that we find the measure of Lincoln's qualities as president: his unaffected kindness, his poise, his humor, his largeness of soul, his fairness toward opponents, his refusal to get angry, his steadiness, his ability to maintain that well-tempered morale which is so indispensable in a desperate war. There was also the notable trait of selflessness; for if Lincoln suffered when his pride was pierced, such was the temper of his self-control (which must not be misunderstood as mere humility) that no outward reaction of irascibility, peevishness, or ungenerous conduct resulted.

In his cabinet Lincoln found an ill-assorted group. Welles inwardly denounced Seward; Bates distrusted Stanton, Seward, and Chase; Stanton and Seward were uncongenial; and Chase, though never actually disloyal to Lincoln, was a constant source of discord. Yet Lincoln, lax as he was in administrative methods, maintained an attitude of cooperation in his official family. Such changes as occurred in his cabinet were of a sort to strengthen the President's position, the vigorous Stanton displacing the incompetent Cameron, Chase being shrewdly kept in the cabinet until after the renomination of Lincoln when he gave way to the more pliable Fessenden, Speed and Dennison serving as acceptable substitutes for Bates and Blair.

In the military phases of his task Lincoln was sorely beset. Governmental organization for war purposes was ill suited to the emergency and seemed at times formless. Some of the state governors embarrassed him by over-activity that trenched upon the duties of the secretary of war; others caused trouble by sheer recalcitrancy. Military efficiency was subordinated to personal ambition; there was a superfluity of political generals; and there was confusion and experimentation in the central control of the army. Troops when brought into the field were often unreliable; "some of the brigadier-generals," wrote Halleck (*Works of Lincoln,* VII, 77), were "entirely ignorant of their duties and unfit for any command." The war machine suffered from an ill-advised system of conscription, from undue state control of military matters, from widespread desertion and "bounty jumping," and from harmful newspaper activity, which betrayed military secrets, discredited the government, defamed generals, fomented antagonism among officers, and weakened the morale of soldier and citizen. Congressional interference was evident in the Committee on the Conduct of the War (W. W. Pierson, in *American Historical Review,* April 1918, pp. 550–76), which investigated Union disasters, held protracted conferences with the President, and considered themselves "a sort of Aulic Council clothed with authority to supervise the plans of commanders in the field, to make military suggestions, and to dictate military appointments" (*Ibid.,* p. 566, citing W. H. Hurlbert, *General McClellan and the Conduct of the War,* 1864, p. 160). That Lincoln listened patiently to the committee and yet never permitted them to take the wheel from his hand, is evidence at once of his tact and his shrewdness.

With his burning sense of the issues at stake and his pathetic eagerness for one battle to end it all, Lincoln was subjected to repeated humiliation in the defeat of Union arms. His reaction to defeat is illustrated in his memorandum of

July 23, 1861, following the first Bull Run, in which he outlined a comprehensive plan for pushing the blockade, drilling the forces, discharging "three-months men" who would not reënlist, bringing forward new volunteer units, protecting Washington against attack, and formulating a joint forward movement in the West (*Works,* VI, 331–32). The pressure of military duties upon Lincoln was more than any president of a republic should bear. He pored over books on strategy; scanned the military map; prepared orders for the army; gave counsel concerning such details as the acquisition of horses and the price of guns; outlined plans of campaign, not forgetting, however, the hazard of binding a distant commander to specific lines and operations; directed the allocation of supplies; attended war councils; and devoted constant attention to military appointments. He assumed a special degree of military responsibility at the time of McClellan's illness in January 1862; and he had to make those repeated calls for troops which intensified the depression of the country. In his experimentation with men he expressed a whimsical wish for a "school of events"—mimic situations in which men might be tried (F. B. Carpenter, *Six Months at the White House,* p. 225); and he even contemplated taking the field himself (*Diary of O. H. Browning,* I, 523).

Kindness and forbearance, mingled at times with fatherly admonition, characterized his attitude toward his generals. When Frémont issued impossible orders in the West without consulting the President, Lincoln sent him a word of "caution, and not of censure," directed that certain orders be "modified," sent Blair from his cabinet for a friendly conference, and finally removed the General only when his insubordinate conduct left no alternative. Lincoln's search for a winning general is a painful story. McClellan snubbed him, differed with him as to plans, wrote complaining letters, and fell short in the business of fighting. Lincoln ignored the snubs with the remark that it were better "not to be making points of . . . personal dignity" (*Letters of John Hay and Extracts from Diary,* I, 53); and on the retirement of Scott in November 1861 he made McClellan general-in-chief of all the armies. The President's plans, beset as he was by boards, senators, councils, military "experts," and clamoring editors, proved hopelessly at variance with McClellan's performance. In January 1862 the perplexed President issued a peremptory "war order" directing a "general movement of all the land and naval forces of the United States against the insurgent forces" for Feb. 22 (*Works,* VII, 89). This order was ignored, and Lincoln acquiesced in McClellan's oblique movement against Richmond via the peninsula. At the outset of the peninsular campaign, however, Lincoln relieved McClellan of supreme command; and he modified the latter's plan for the concentration of Union forces against Richmond by retaining McDowell's corps near Washington, while he also decreased McClellan's importance by reorganizing the army under corps commanders. McClellan's ineffectiveness caused Lincoln to put Pope in command of a separate Army of Virginia; but on Pope's failure at the second battle of Bull Run the President dropped him and ordered a reconsolidation of forces under McClellan, who was thus given a new opportunity. Then came McClellan's failure to pursue Lee after Antietam, upon which Lincoln finally removed him from command. The failure of McClellan's successors—of Burnside at Fredericksburg and Hooker at Chancellorsville—added to Lincoln's perplexity and tended to discredit his ability in military matters; while Meade's success at Gettysburg was marred by another failure to pursue and crush Lee's army, and even under Grant, whom Lincoln brought to the East in 1864, there were months of sanguinary fighting with hope deferred. Lincoln's blunders in military matters, which are not to be denied, were largely attributable to political pressure or to unsatisfactory human material, and were partly offset by constructive factors such as his guarding of Washington, his attention to the western phases of the war, and his final support of Grant in the face of bitter criticism.

Cautious in his dealings with Congress, Lincoln seldom seized the initiative in the framing of legislation. He went his own way by a remarkable assumption of executive authority; and on the few occasions when he sought to direct important legislation he was usually unsuccessful. The congressional election of 1862 was unfavorable to him; and elements out of sympathy with Lincoln were often dominant in Congress, which sought to curb the president's power of arrest, passed measures which he disapproved, and came to an *impasse* with him as to reconstruction. Though the reconstruction issue is a notable exception, Lincoln usually yielded when Congress enacted measures distasteful to him, as in the case of the West Virginia bill and the second confiscation act. Moderates were disappointed in this pliancy, which they described as "going over to the radicals"; yet the radicals themselves were far from capturing Lincoln, and at the time of his death in office an open break such as that which occurred under Johnson seemed probable.

Though the issuing of the Emancipation Proclamation is the most memorable of Lincoln's acts, the stereotyped picture of the emancipator suddenly striking the shackles from millions of slaves by a stroke of the pen is unhistorical. Lincoln's policy touching slavery was a matter of slow development. Throughout the struggle he held that Congress did not have the power to abolish slavery in the South; and in keeping with his "border-state policy" he resisted for many months the clamors of abolitionists. When Union generals, notably Frémont in Missouri and Hunter in the lower South, attempted emancipation by military edict, Lincoln overruled them; and he said to a religious group: "I do not want to issue a document that . . . must . . . be inoperative, like the Pope's bull against the comet" (*Works,* VIII, 30). Answering Greeley's anti-slavery appeal on Aug. 22, 1862, he wrote, though with the proclamation already in his drawer, that his "paramount object" was to "save the Union," and was not "either to save or to destroy slavery" (*Ibid.,* VIII, 16). It was found, however, that war over a vastly extended front with a slave-holding power forced the government either to take steps toward emancipation or to become both its own enemy and a promoter of slavery. By July 1862, therefore, Congress had, at least on paper, provided as much as the Emancipation Proclamation involved, by freeing slaves coming within Union military lines, emancipating slave-soldiers, and decreeing liberation generally as to all "rebel-owned" slaves in the sweeping though ineffectual confiscation act of July 17, 1862. In addition, Congress had by this time prohibited slavery in the territories and in the District of Columbia.

Meanwhile, from Lincoln's pondering of the slavery problem there had emerged a plan of constructive statesmanship. Recognizing state authority in the premises, mindful of Southern property rights, and moved by the conviction that the North ought equitably to share the financial burden of emancipation, since it must share the guilt of slavery, Lincoln had urged Congress to launch a scheme of gradual emancipation by voluntary action of the states, with federal compensation to slave-holders. This plan, however, as well as the scheme of deportation and colonization in Africa, had broken down; and in July 1862 Lincoln reached the decision to issue his edict of liberation. By this time the increasing radicalism of the war mind, the indifference of the border states to his compensation scheme, and the realization that foreign sympathy could not be obtained for a government which "sought to put down the rebellion with the left hand, while supporting slavery with the right hand" (Chase Manuscripts, Library of Congress, vol. LXII, no. 1989) had done their work. On July 22, 1862, Lincoln summoned his cabinet and read aloud the first draft of the Emancipation Proclamation. His decision was now made; he was not asking advice "about the main matter." Rather he was announcing his course and taking counsel about incidental questions pertaining to its execution. Accepting Seward's suggestion that the measure would gain force if issued on the morrow of victory, he waited until Lee had been fought off at Antietam and gave out his preliminary proclamation on Sept. 22, 1862 (*Works,* VIII, 36–41). In this edict he gave warning that on Jan. 1, 1863, all slaves in rebellious districts would be made free; but the proclamation was far from an abolition document, for the President emphasized the restoration of the Union as the object of the war, and pledged further efforts to provide compensation to slave-holders. By common usage, the term "Emancipation Proclamation" applies to the edict of Jan. 1, 1863, that of Sept. 22, 1862, being but a warning. The Proclamation of Jan. 1, 1863, contained no general declaration against slavery as an evil (*Ibid.,* VIII, 161–64). The Union slave states were naturally not affected; and important districts of the South (the whole state of Tennessee as well as portions of Virginia and Louisiana) were excluded from the terms of the proclamation. The most curious fact about the whole matter was that the proclamation applied only to regions under Confederate control; and Lincoln was denounced for freeing slaves only on paper in districts where his power could not extend. It is hard to put in a word the actual effect of the Proclamation. Preservation of slavery in non-rebellious districts was clearly implied; and if the Southern states had done all Lincoln asked in September 1862, thus obviating the necessity of the final proclamation, there was nothing in the preliminary document to prevent the war from ending with slavery still maintained. Yet the President's stroke at slavery did somehow change the character of the war; and its moral effect was great, albeit somewhat offset by the displeasure of those who opposed a "war to free the negroes." Military emancipation extended as the armies advanced in the South; but as to the legal potency of the Proclamation Lincoln himself had grave doubts. Effective liberation, in fact, came through state action in the border states and more notably through the anti-slavery amendment to the Constitution. Perhaps the chief importance of the Proclamation was in paving the way for these final measures. Lincoln's part in the whole matter was necessarily central. It was he who determined the time, circumstances, and manner of the proclamation; and it was his conviction that, had it been issued six months earlier, public sentiment would not have sustained it (F. B. Carpenter, *Six Months at the White House,* p. 77).

In spite of serious complications with France and Great Britain, Lincoln gave little direct attention to foreign affairs. He brushed aside Seward's bellicose foreign program of Apr. 1, 1861; and he materially assisted in the preservation of peace by softening Seward's instructions of May 21, 1861, to Charles Francis Adams on the general question of Great Britain's attitude toward the war and by directing that Adams treat the whole dispatch as confidential. In the *Trent* affair the influence of Sumner, Seward, and Bright contributed powerfully toward peace with Great Britain, the threads being in Seward's hands; but Lincoln's moderation, though at first he seems to have supposed that Mason and Slidell ought not to be released (Frederic Bancroft, *The Life of W. H. Seward,* 1900, II, 234), was an important factor. His restraint in international dealings is shown by a "paper" which he prepared, advocating that the *Trent* case be arbitrated (*Diary of O. H. Browning,* I, 517). On such questions as the French proposal for mediation, French intervention in Mexico, and the protests against British aid in the building and equipment of Confederate warships, the course of the administration was successfully directed by Seward, to whom Lincoln wisely delegated foreign affairs with the minimum of presidential interference.

While preserving the dignity of his high position, Lincoln's manners as president were unconventional and his habits irregular. Often his meals, when carried upstairs, would be left untouched for hours. He took no regular exercise, his chief relaxation being found in the summer evenings at the Soldiers' Home. During the first week of the battle of the Wilderness, says Carpenter (*Six Months at the White House,* p. 30), he "scarcely slept at all"; and the black rings under his eyes bespoke the strain under which he labored. In his last year his friends all noted his mental weariness; as he expressed it, the remedy "seemed never to reach the *tired* spot" (*Ibid.,* p. 217). Despite this strain there was always a readiness to shake hands with a casual visitor and to receive the humblest citizen or soldier. In reviewing the death penalty for desertion or sleeping on sentinel duty, he eagerly sought excuses for clemency; yet his mercy was not mere weakness, and at times he did confirm the death sentence. He read the newspapers but little, for news reached him through more direct channels. Day and night his familiar form was seen in the telegraph office of the War Department across from the White House. In humorous stories and the repetition of favorite literary passages he found mental relaxation. The poem "Oh Why Should the Spirit of Mortal Be Proud" had a peculiar fascination for him, and his familiarity with Shakespeare was often a matter of surprise. Laughter was an absolute need of his harassed mind and he habitually thought in terms of parable, his anecdotes usually having a backwoods flavor and a tang of the pioneer West. His enjoyment of rough jest is shown in his fondness for such humorists as Nasby and Artemus Ward; his matter-of-fact secretaries had to endure a chapter from Ward as a preface to his reading of the Emancipation Proclamation in cabinet meeting. The melancholy of the earlier Lincoln deepened under the pressure of war. Not alone did the nation's woes bear heavily upon him, but the death of his son Willie in February 1862, following nightly vigils at the bedside, added a personal bereavement which would have come nigh to prostration but for the pressure of public duties.

Though a ready speech-maker, Lincoln as president made very few public addresses, the chief examples being his inaugurals, his Gettysburg address, and his last speech, Apr. 11, 1865, which dealt with reconstruction (*Works,* XI, 84–92). In lieu of the "White House publicity" of later presidents, he made use of the art of correspondence. When answering criticism or appealing to the people, he would prepare a careful letter which, while addressed to an individual or delegation, would be intended for the nation's ear. When a meeting of citizens protested against the arrest of an agitator, Lincoln wrote an elaborate letter (to E. Corning and others, June 12, 1863) explaining his policy of arbitrary arrests and pointing out the inability of the courts to deal with rebellion. Referring to the death penalty for desertion he asked, "Must I shoot a simple-minded soldier boy who deserts, while I must not touch a hair of a wily agitator who induces him to desert?" (*Works,* VIII, 308). Writing to Cuthbert Bullitt, July 28, 1862, he raised the question whether Southern unionists should be "merely passengers . . . to be carried snug and dry throughout the storm, and safely landed right side up" (*Ibid.,* VII, 296). On finding it impossible to attend a meeting of "unconditional Union men," at Springfield, Ill., he wrote an important letter to J. C. Conkling (*Works,* IX, 95–102) in which he defended the Emancipation Proclamation as a measure for saving the Union. In this letter he paid tribute to the men of Antietam, Murfreesboro, and Gettysburg, not forgetting "Uncle Sam's web-feet," for whose noble work "at all the watery margins" he expressed deep thanks. Of like importance were his letter to Greeley on the slavery question (Aug. 22, 1862), to Raymond of the *Times* regarding compensated emancipation, to Governor Seymour concerning the opposition of New York to the conscription law, and to Mrs. Bixby, whom he beautifully consoled for the loss of her sons in battle. On Nov. 19, 1863, in dedicating a soldiers' cemetery at Gettysburg, Lincoln lifted the nation's thoughts from the hatreds and imminent horrors of war in a brief address which is recognized as his most famous speech (*Works,* IX, 209–10). In his few simple words of dedication the factor of enmity toward the South was notably lacking; and the prevailing note was Lincoln's central idea of the broad significance of the Civil War as a vindication of popular rule.

The story of the campaign and election of 1864 has never been fully told. In an atmosphere of national depression and war-weariness, with prominent men denouncing the "imbecility" of the administration at Washington, with victory deferred after three years of terrible losses, with financial credit at low ebb, and with defeatists demanding peace on the ground that the war was a failure, the President faced the hazard of a popular election. Though the presidential boom of Salmon P. Chase [*q.v.*], to which Lincoln closed his ears, soon collapsed, Frémont accepted nomination from an anti-Lincoln group; and the Democrats ominously gathered their forces while at the same time postponing their nomination until August. Such Republicans as Greeley, H. W. Davis, Beecher, Bryant, Whitelaw Reid, and many others, were minded to drop Lincoln; but Republican managers set an early date for the party convention (June 7), Lincoln meanwhile keeping Chase in the cabinet, and there was little difficulty in obtaining the President's renomination when the convention met at Baltimore. The renomination was in fact unanimous; but in the months that followed, the military outlook became still gloomier; and when McClellan was nominated by the Democrats in August on a peace platform his strength seemed truly formidable. At this juncture a surprising movement developed—nothing less than an effort to supplant Lincoln with a "more vigorous leader" and force his withdrawal (New York *Sun,* June 30, 1889, p. 3). A plan was laid for a convention to meet at Cincinnati, Ohio, on Sept. 28 "to concentrate the union strength on some one candidate, who commands the confidence of the country, even by a new nomination if necessary" (*Ibid.*). At this time Greeley wrote that Lincoln was "already beaten," and that only "another ticket" could save the party from "utter overthrow." As late as Aug. 25, H. W. Davis wrote: "My letters from Maryland say Lincoln can do nothing there, even where the Union party is most vigorous, and everybody is looking for a new candidate from somewhere." These extracts will serve to suggest the active opposition to Lincoln within his own party, which was due to such factors as the lack of Union success in battle, the conservatism of Lincoln, his leniency toward the South which ran counter to the radical plan of reconstruction, his call of July 18, 1864, for 500,000 volunteers, and the feeling that the President under Seward's influence was an opportunist and compromiser rather than a vigorous executive. The real strength of the anti-Lincoln movement is difficult to gauge because a favorable turn in the administration's fortunes occurred in September with the fall of Atlanta and Republican electoral successes in Vermont and Maine, after which, for the sake of party harmony, various anti-Lincoln men such as Wade and Greeley gave him their support. With this turn of the tide the demand for Lincoln's withdrawal lost its point and the Cincinnati convention was never held. Efforts were put forth to include certain states of the Confederacy in the election, and the President carried Louisiana and Tennessee where reorganized "loyal" governments had been set up; but the votes of these states, being unnecessary, were not recognized by Congress in the electoral count. Thus only the Union states were counted; and all of them except Kentucky, Delaware, and New Jersey gave Lincoln their electoral vote. This electoral sweep, together with Lincoln's popular majority of more than 400,000 over McClellan, gave the election somewhat the appearance of a Lincoln landslide; there were, however, powerful McClellan minorities in Illinois, Indiana, Ohio, New York, and Pennsylvania. (H. M. Dudley, "The Election of 1864," *Mississippi Valley Historical Review,* March 1932.) In the event of McClellan's election Lincoln had resolved "to so cooperate with the President-elect as to save the Union between the election and the inauguration." As his secretaries record, it was the President's intention to "talk matters over" with McClellan and say to him: "Now let us together, you with your influence and I with all the executive power of the Government, try to save the country." At the time when this patriotic resolve to cooperate with a victorious opponent was made (Aug. 23, 1864), the President considered his own defeat "exceedingly probable" (Nicolay and Hay, *Lincoln,* IX, 251–52).

At his second inauguration, Mar. 4, 1865, Lincoln made no effort to review the events of his administration, but delivered a brief address which, for loftiness of tone, ranks among his greatest state papers (*Works,* XI, 44–47). Breathing a spirit of friendliness toward the enemy, he refused to blame the South for the war, and counseled his countrymen to "judge not, that we be not judged." "With malice toward none; with charity for all," he concluded, "let us strive on to finish the work we are in; to bind up the nation's wounds; . . . to do all which may achieve and cherish a just and lasting peace. . . ." There were few Northern leaders who manifested as fair an understanding of the Southern people as Lincoln (A. C. Cole, in *Lincoln Centennial Association Papers,* 1928, pp. 47–78); and he devoted careful thought and labor to the restoration of the Southern states to the Union. In his proclamation of Dec. 8, 1863, he pardoned (with certain exceptions) those Confederates who would swear allegiance to the Union; and he vigorously promoted the organization of "loyal" governments in the Southern states, requiring that they abolish slavery, and standing ready to welcome them into the Union though the loyal nucleus be no more than ten per cent. of the voters of 1860. When Congress, on July 2, 1864, passed the Wade-Davis bill providing a severe plan that would hinder reconstruction, Lincoln applied the "pocket" veto, and announced his reasons in a "proclamation" of July 8 (*Works,* X, 152–54), upon which the authors of the bill, with an eye to the President's embarrassment in the campaign for reëlection, severely attacked him in an address to the people known as the Wade-Davis manifesto. The details of Lincoln's further efforts toward reconstruction are too elaborate to be recounted here. His scheme was carried through to his own satisfaction in Tennessee, Louisiana, Arkansas, and Virginia; but Congress never recognized any of these "Lincoln governments" of the South.

As to peace negotiations with the Confederacy, Lincoln insisted upon reunion and the abolition of slavery, but manifested a generous disposition on collateral issues. This was his attitude in connection with the peace efforts of Horace Greeley [*q.v.*] in 1864; and the same moderate attitude was manifested in connection with Blair's mission to Richmond (see Blair, Francis Preston, 1791–1876) and in the Hampton Roads Conference of February 1865. In this conference Lincoln, in company with Seward, conferred on board a warship with three Confederate commissioners (J. A. Campbell, A. H. Stephens, and R. M. T. Hunter); and accounts agree that, while the President again insisted upon reunion and emancipation, he showed willingness to use the pardoning power freely in the South, to allow self-government to the returning states, and even to recommend liberal compensation to slave-holders. On the fall of Richmond Lincoln visited the Confederate capital, where he walked the streets unmolested, and advised with Southern leaders, notably J. A. Campbell. He expressed a desire to permit the "rebel" legislature of Virginia to return and reorganize the state; but this purpose, as well as his other plans for the South, was defeated.

He gave the closest attention to the final military phase of the war, visiting the army and remaining with Grant at City Point from Mar. 24 until Apr. 9, except for his two-day visit to Richmond on the 4th and 5th. His return to Washington coincided with Lee's surrender, an event which gave added significance to the President's last speech, which was a statesmanlike paper read to a cheering crowd at the White House on the night of Apr. 11. Returning to the subject of reconstruction, he appealed to a divided North to let the South come back to the Union. Casting theories aside, he said: "We all agree that the seceded States . . . are out of their proper practical relation with the Union, and that the . . . object of the government . . . is to again get them into that proper practical relation" (*Works,* XI, 88). "Concede," he said, "that the new government of Louisiana is . . . as the egg is to the fowl, we shall sooner have the fowl by hatching the egg than by smashing it" (*Ibid.,* XI, 91). On the last day of Lincoln's life the subject of reconstruction was discussed at length in cabinet meeting; and a project was considered which resembled the plan later announced by President Johnson on May 29, 1865 (40 Cong., 1 sess., *Report of Committees of the House of Representatives,* no. 7, pp. 78–79). Again Lincoln expressed the wish that all vindictiveness be laid aside and that the Southern people be leniently treated (F. W. Seward, *Reminiscences,* 1916, p. 254). With opposition growing within his own party and threatening the ruin of his generous plans had he lived, he was removed by assassination, which silenced criticism and conferred the martyr's crown. At Ford's Theatre on the night of Apr. 14, 1865, he was shot by John Wilkes Booth [*q.v.*]. After lying unconscious through the night he died the following morning. The state rites over, the funeral train moved west with frequent stops; and amid fulminations of vindictive oratory, with people and soldiers mourning their beloved Chief, the body was laid to rest at Springfield.

The early crystallization of the enduring Lincoln tradition was illustrated by Stanton's comment, "Now he belongs to the ages." That he was among the "consummate masters of statecraft" may be disputed, but such was the impression he left that this distinction has been accorded him. In the shortest list of American liberal leaders he takes eminent place: liberalism with him was no garment; it was of the fiber of his mind. His hold upon the affections of his own people has not been due merely to the fact that he, a backwoods lad, rose to the highest office in the land. It is doubtful whether any other leader of the North could have matched him in dramatizing the war to the popular mind, in shaping language to his purpose, in smoothing personal difficulties by a magnanimous touch or a tactful gesture, in avoiding domestic and international complications, in courageously persisting in the face of almost unendurable discouragements, in maintaining war morale while refusing to harbor personal malice against the South. Not inappropriately, he has become a symbol both of American democracy and the Union.

[For bibliographies, see Daniel Fish, *Lincoln Bibliography* (1906), also in *Complete Works,* XI, 135–380; Jos. B. Oakleaf, *Lincoln Bibliography* (1925); W. E. Barton, "The Lincoln of the Biographers," *Trans. Ill. State Hist. Soc. for the Year 1929* (1929), pp. 58–116. The most important edition of the writings and speeches is J. G. Nicolay and John Hay, *Complete Works of Abraham Lincoln* (Gettysburg ed., 12 vols., 1905), and it is to this edition that the foregoing references are made. Additional writings are to be found in G. A. Tracy, *Uncollected Letters of Abraham Lincoln* (1917); *Lincoln Letters, Hitherto Unpublished, in the Library of Brown Univ. and other Providence Libraries* (1929); P. M. Angle, *New Letters and Papers of Lincoln* (1930). The best edition of the Lincoln-Douglas debates is that of E. E. Sparks in *Colls. of the Ill. State Hist. Lib.,* vol. III (1908). Of manuscript collections the most important are the Weik MSS. (preserved by J. W. Weik, collaborator with Herndon), and the voluminous Lincoln papers deposited in the Lib. of Cong., but withheld from investigators for many years. Certain alleged Lincoln documents have proved to be forgeries, such as the letters to Senator Crittenden, Dec. 22, 1859, and to A. H. Stephens, Jan. 19, 1860 (see W. C. Ford in *Mass. Hist. Soc. Proc.,* May 1928), the letter to an Italiar named Melloni, alleged to have been written in 1853 (*N. Y. Times,* Nov. 20, 23, 24, 1931, May 8, 1932), and the fantastic collection of Lincoln and Ann Rutledge letters published in the *Atlantic Monthly,* Dec. 1928–Feb. 1929 (see P. M. Angle, "The Minor Collection: A Criticism," *Ibid.,* Apr. 1929). Autobiographical portions of Lincoln's utterances have been collected in *An Autobiography of Abraham Lincoln* (1926), by N. W. Stephenson.

Campaign biographies were issued by J. L. Scripps, J. H. Barrett, and J. Q. Howard in 1860, and by H. J. Raymond, W. M. Thayer, and J. H. Barrett again in 1864. After Lincoln's death there appeared a number of biographies by men who had known him more or less closely. Ward H. Lamon [*q.v.*] brought out *The Life of Abraham Lincoln from his Birth to his Inauguration as President* (1872). This work, which gives a realistic and partly unfavorable picture of Lincoln, was written not by Lamon but by Chauncey F. Black. Isaac N. Arnold of Chicago, from years of association with Lincoln, published studies in 1866 and 1869, and *The Life of Abraham Lincoln* (1885). J. G. Holland, *Life of Abraham Lincoln* (1866), though produced too soon to permit of historical perspective, was a work of merit, compiled with discrimination and attractively written. In 1889 appeared *Herndon's Lincoln: The True Story of a Great Life,* by W. H. Herndon and J. W. Weik, which should be used in the edition of P. M. Angle (1930). With all its limitations, this biography is a classic. It presents Lincoln without the halo, giving a view of the every-day life of the man with a wealth of anecdote and a power of portrayal which has caused it to be extensively used by later biographers. Herndon substituted "for Lincoln's aureole the battered tall hat, with valuable papers stuck in its lining, which he had long contemplated with reverent irritation" (Charnwood, *Abraham Lincoln* p. 102). It is, however, the Lincoln of the prairies whom Herndon and Weik present; their account of the presidency is wholly inadequate. Many years later Weik returned over the same trail and published *The Real Lincoln* (1922), reaffirming certain disputed statements in the Herndon work and adding minor details. The monumental work by Lincoln's secretaries, J. G. Nicolay and John Hay, *Abraham Lincoln: A History* (10 vols., 1890), inaugurated a new era of Lincoln historiography. It is a voluminous history as well as a biography, for the authors attempted to include everything. Approved by Robert Lincoln, it possesses both the advantages and the defects of an authorized biography. From their daily contact with the President, Nicolay and Hay had an inside acquaintance with his administration; and they made use of a vast range of material, including papers which have been used by no other writers. Their uniform tendency, however, to treat everything from the point of view of Lincoln, their unsympathetic attitude toward his opponents, and their partiality for the Republican party, made it impossible for them to produce the definitive biography.

Since Nicolay and Hay, the Lincoln bibliography has reached tremendous dimensions, and a full list would comprise thousands of items. The activity of collectors and dealers in Lincolniana has magnified the importance of every trivial item; and the yearly output of Lincoln addresses and articles, tinctured with the political or social predilections of the authors, is of staggering proportions. Only a few outstanding titles can be mentioned here. At the forefront of recent biographies is Albert J. Beveridge, *Abraham Lincoln, 1809–1858* (2 vols., 1928). This great work is not as readable as certain other biographies, for the author has presented his material as he found it with the minimum of literary coloring; its high value derives from its soundness and thoroughness of historical investigation. Ida M. Tarbell, *The Life of Abraham Lincoln* (2 vols., 1900), is based on material collected by the author in the service of *McClure's Mag.,* and was first published serially in that periodical in 1895–96. It has merit as a popular "life," but some of its statements, *e.g.,* those concerning the parentage of Nancy Hanks, have been disproved. *Abraham Lincoln* (1917), by Lord Charnwood, is an excellent one-volume biography. Though he conducted but little original research and used easily available published sources, Charnwood has produced a well-proportioned narrative which gains much by being addressed to an English audience. Another short biography of high merit is *Lincoln: An Account of His Personal Life,* etc. (1924), by N. W. Stephenson. With rare literary artistry Stephenson treats the "emergence" of Lincoln's character from its earlier hesitancies into the "final Lincoln," whom he places among the "consummate masters of statecraft." W. E. Barton has been tireless in his researches and has produced a great many books on Lincoln, among which are: *Life of Abraham Lincoln* (2 vols., 1925); *The Pa-*

ternity of Abraham Lincoln (1920); *The Soul of Abraham Lincoln* (1920); *The Women Lincoln Loved* (1927); *The Lineage of Lincoln* (1929); *Lincoln at Gettysburg* (1930). Carl Sandburg, *Abraham Lincoln: The Prairie Years* (2 vols., 1926), though attempting no elaborate documentation or critical evaluation of sources, is extraordinarily vivid and has a remarkable pictorial quality in its portrayal of the rough American pioneer life out of which Lincoln came. Emil Ludwig, *Lincoln* (1930), translated from the German by Eden and Cedar Paul, though of slight importance as a historical contribution, is dramatic and readable, conforming to the new biographical vogue. Edgar Lee Masters, *Lincoln the Man* (1931) is almost alone in its devastating treatment. The following biographies should also be mentioned: Carl Schurz, *Abraham Lincoln* (1891); E. P. Oberholtzer, *Abraham Lincoln* (1904); J. T. Morse, *Abraham Lincoln* (2 vols., 1893); J. G. Nicolay, *A Short Life of Abraham Lincoln* (1902).

Certain works of reminiscence give special emphasis to Lincoln, such as: H. C. Whitney, *Life on the Circuit with Lincoln* (1892); U. F. Linder, *Reminiscences of the Early Bench and Bar of Illinois* (1879); A. K. McClure, *Abraham Lincoln and Men of War-Times* (1892); H. B. Rankin, *Intimate Character Sketches of Abraham Lincoln* (1924); A. T. Rice, ed., *Reminiscences of Abraham Lincoln by Distinguished Men of His Time* (1886); Joshua F. Speed, *Reminiscences of Abraham Lincoln* (1884); James Speed, *James Speed; A Personality* (1914); and W. O. Stoddard, *Inside the White House in War Times* (1890). The following diaries are of special note: *Letters of John Hay and Extracts from Diary* (3 vols., p.p., 1908, with omissions and with personal names reduced to initials); *Diary of Gideon Welles,* ed. by J. T. Morse, Jr. (3 vols., 1911), a voluminous and valuable record for the presidency containing many devastating statements concerning members of Lincoln's cabinet (critically analyzed, especially as to Welles's numerous emendations, by H. K. Beale in *Am. Hist. Rev.*, Apr. 1925, pp. 547–52); "Diary and Correspondence of Salmon P. Chase" (*Annual Report of the Am. Hist. Asso. for the Year 1902*, vol. II, 1903); "The Diary of Edward Bates," ed. by H. K. Beale, *Annual Report of the Am. Hist. Asso. for the Year 1930*, vol. IV (1932); *The Diary of Orville Hickman Browning,* ed. by T. C. Pease and J. G. Randall (3 vols. 1927–33, in the *Ill. Hist. Colls.*). Various problems of Lincoln's presidency are treated by J. G. Randall in *Constitutional Problems Under Lincoln* (1926).

The following are special studies of particular phases of Lincoln's career: C. F. Adams, "President Lincoln's Offer to Garibaldi," *Mass. Hist. Soc. Proc.*, 3rd ser., vol. I (1908), pp. 319–25; P. M. Angle, "Abraham Lincoln: Circuit Lawyer," *Lincoln Cent. Asso. Papers . . . 1928* (1928); D. H. Bates, *Lincoln in the Telegraph Office* (1907); F. B. Carpenter, *Six Months at the White House with Abraham Lincoln: The Story of a Picture* (1866); A. C. Cole, *Lincoln's "House Divided" Speech* (1923), "Lincoln and the American Tradition of Civil Liberty," in *Jour. Ill. State Hist. Soc.*, Oct. 1926–Jan. 1927, pp. 102–14, "Abraham Lincoln and the South," in *Lincoln Cent. Asso. Papers . . . 1928* (1928), "President Lincoln and the Illinois Radical Republicans," in *Miss. Valley Hist. Rev.*, March 1918, pp. 417–36, and "Lincoln's Election an Immediate Menace to Slavery in the States?", *Amer. Hist. Rev.*, July 1931, pp. 740–67; W. E. Dodd, *Lincoln or Lee* (1928); D. K. Dodge, *Abraham Lincoln, Master of Words* (1924); J. T. Dorris, "President Lincoln's Clemency," *Jour. Ill. State Hist. Soc.*, Jan. 1928, pp. 547–68; John Eaton, *Grant, Lincoln and the Freedmen* (1907); C. R. Fish, "Lincoln and the Patronage," *Am. Hist. Rev.*, Oct. 1902, pp. 53–69, and "Lincoln and Catholicism," *Ibid.*, July 1924, pp. 723–24 (a rebuke to those who by spurious quotations have falsified Lincoln's attitude toward the Catholics); F. I. Herriott, "Memories of the Chicago Convention of 1860," *Annals of Iowa,* Oct. 1920, and "The Conference in the Deutsches Haus, Chicago, May 14–15, 1860," *Trans. Ill. State Hist. Soc. . . . 1928* (1928); Frederick T. Hill, *Lincoln the Lawyer* (1906); Caroline Hanks Hitchcock, *Nancy Hanks: The Story of Abraham Lincoln's Mother* (1899), an unreliable work, unfortunately followed by certain biographers; E. C. Kirkland, *The Peacemakers of 1864* (1927); J. H. Lea and J. R. Hutchinson, *The Ancestry of Abraham Lincoln* (1909), useful as to the English Lincolns but unreliable as to the American line; M. D. Learned, *Abraham Lincoln, An American Migration* (1909), useful in proving that the origin of the Lincoln family was English, not German, and in tracing the movements of the Lincolns as a "typical American migration"; Waldo Lincoln, *History of the Lincoln Family* (1923), a valuable genealogical contribution; C. H. McCarthy, *Lincoln's Plan of Reconstruction* (1901); J. B. McMaster, *A Hist. of the People of the U. S. during Lincoln's Administration* (1927); Charles Moore, compiler, *Lincoln's Gettysburg Address and Second Inaugural* (1927); Mary L. Miles, "The Fatal First of January, 1841," *Jour. Ill. State Hist. Soc.*, Apr. 1927, pp. 13–48; Rexford Newcomb, *In the Lincoln Country* (1928); C. O. Paullin, "President Lincoln and the Navy," *Am. Hist. Rev.*, Jan. 1909, pp. 284–303, and "Abraham Lincoln in Congress, 1847–1849," *Jour. Ill. State Hist. Soc.*, Apr.–July 1921, pp. 85–89; J. G. Randall, "Lincoln in the Rôle of Dictator," *So. Atl. Quar.*, July 1929, and "Lincoln's Task and Wilson's," *Ibid.*, Oct. 1930; P. O. Ray, *The Convention that Nominated Lincoln* (1916); J. F. Rhodes, "Lincoln in Some Phases of the Civil War," *Harvard Graduates' Mag.*, Sept. 1915, pp. 1–19; J. T. Richards, *Abraham Lincoln, the Lawyer-Statesman* (1916); Don C. Seitz, *Lincoln the Politician* (1931); Albert Shaw, *Abraham Lincoln* (2 vols., 1929), a "cartoon history" with hundreds of contemporary drawings; J. W. Starr, Jr., *Lincoln & the Railroads* (1927); N. W. Stephenson, "Lincoln and the Progress of Nationality in the North," *Annual Report of the Am. Hist. Asso. for the Year 1919*, vol. I (1923), pp. 353–63; Ida M. Tarbell, *In the Footsteps of the Lincolns* (1924), a somewhat inaccurate book; W. H. Townsend, *Lincoln the Litigant* (1925), and *Lincoln and His Wife's Home Town* (1929); L. A. Warren, *Lincoln's Parentage and Childhood* (1926), a most valuable and scholarly work. For references on the assassination, see Booth, John Wilkes.]

J. G. R.

LINCOLN, BENJAMIN (Jan. 24, 1733–May 9, 1810), Revolutionary soldier, was the descendant of a simple yeoman family which had lived in Hingham, Mass., since the settlement of that town, where he himself was born. His father, Benjamin, a maltster and farmer who had accumulated a modest property, was an officer in the local militia and represented his town in the General Court. He married Elizabeth Thaxter, widow of Capt. John Norton, and she became the mother of the younger Benjamin. The boy received only a common-school education at Hingham, but he had a good mind and wrote English well, as his numerous letters and dispatches show. On Jan. 15, 1756, he married Mary Cushing, daughter of Elijah and Elizabeth (Barker) Cushing, of Pembroke, Mass. They lived together over fifty-four years and had six sons and five daughters. In 1757 Lincoln was chosen town clerk, and in 1762, justice of the peace. He had apparently settled down to the life of a moderately prosperous small-town farmer, when with the increasing excitement over the political difficulties between the colonies and the mother country he began to take a more prominent part in public affairs. He was a member of the legislature in 1772 and 1773, and during the next two years sat in the Provincial Congress. He was elected secretary of that body and a member of the committee on supplies, and for a short time in 1775, during the absence of Joseph Warren, he acted as its president.

His military career had begun some years before. In July 1755 he had been made adjutant of the 3rd Regiment of Suffolk County; he was commissioned major in June 1763, and lieutenant-colonel in January 1772. In February 1776 he was appointed brigadier-general by the Council and became known to Washington. Promoted to third major-general the following May, he was given command, Aug. 2, 1776, of the Massachusetts troops stationed near Boston and in September was chosen to command the militia regiments raised to reinforce the army at New York. He took part in the operations in that section and won Washington's good opinion.

On Feb. 19, 1777, he was appointed major-general in the Continental service, and the next summer was ordered to command the militia in Vermont. Here his common sense and knowledge of local conditions were of great assistance to Stark, whom he aided by reinforcements in the defense of Bennington. Operating on Burgoyne's flank, he prepared the way for the victory at Saratoga by breaking the enemy's line of communication with Canada. During the last fighting against Burgoyne he was severely wounded in the leg, and returned to Hingham, where he remained for some ten months. In August 1778 he was declared fit for duty and rejoined Washington. Because of a controversy over seniority occasioned by the promotion of Benedict Arnold [*q.v.*], Lincoln had considered resigning, but was prevailed upon not to do so, and on Sept. 25, 1778, he was appointed to the command of the American army in the Southern department.

After being detained ten days at Philadelphia by Congress, he finally reached Charleston, S. C., on Dec. 4. He had gathered laurels in his northern campaign and much was expected of him in the South. He had, however, the usual troubles of the Revolutionary commander with undisciplined troops and short-time patriots, and although he was able to force Prevost to let go his hold on Charleston, he could not turn the enemy out of Savannah. D'Estaing, with the French fleet, attempted to cooperate with him in the Savannah River, but the operation was a failure and D'Estaing sailed away. This left the sea open to Clinton at New York, who sailed for South Carolina with 7,000 troops. He landed at a short distance from Charleston, marched his troops overland, and attacked the city. Lincoln, instead of retreating into the back country, shut himself up in the town and in May 1779 was captured with his whole army by Clinton. In extenuation of his blunder it must be said that the civil authorities had strongly objected to the evacuation of the town and a considerable part of Lincoln's force was made up of Carolina militiamen who might not have followed him had he abandoned the city. He was granted unusually good terms by the British, but his surrender was a severe blow to the American cause. When the news was received in the North the task of retrieving the Southern situation was given to Horatio Gates [*q.v.*].

Lincoln was paroled and allowed to proceed north, but there were delays and he did not reach Philadelphia until July. He asked for a court of inquiry to investigate his conduct at Charleston, but the court was never held and no charges were ever pressed. Returning to his home at Hingham, he anxiously awaited exchange so that he might join the army again. In November he was formally exchanged for the British general, Phillips. During the winter he remained in Massachusetts raising recruits and supplies, but the following summer he was once more in the field, operating under Washington in the neighborhood of New York. Commanding the troops which at the end of August 1781 marched southward to join in the Yorktown campaign, he took part in that last fighting of the war. On Oct. 30, 1781, he was made secretary of war by Congress, an office which he held until his resignation just two years later, after the signing of the Treaty of Peace.

Lincoln now returned to his farm at Hingham. It was many years before he could realize upon the certificates of pay which he had received for his service, and in the meantime he engaged in speculation in wild lands in Maine, a venture which nearly brought him to financial ruin. He made frequent trips to the Province and in 1784 and 1786 was one of the Massachusetts commissioners to treat with the Penobscot Indians concerning land purchases. About Jan. 1, 1787, he was appointed to lead the state troops to suppress Shays's Rebellion. The legislature had planned to raise some five thousand men but had provided no money for expenses, and Lincoln personally raised about twenty thousand dollars among some citizens of Boston to finance the campaign. He then marched to Worcester, where trouble was expected at the next session of the court, but no violence occurred, and he went on to the assistance of General Shepherd who was defending the federal arsenal at Springfield. Within a month the two insurgent forces under Day and Shays had been dispersed. On the night of Feb. 2, Lincoln made his famous night march through a terrible snow storm to Petersham, where he captured 150 men, the remnant of Shays's band, and brought the rebellion to an end. He now proved his statesmanship by urging the legislature to be lenient with the rebels, making an example of a few ringleaders only, but his advice was not accepted.

In 1788 he was chosen a member of the convention to consider the new Federal Constitution, and worked for its ratification. That same year he ran for the office of lieutenant-governor and, when no candidate received the majority necessary to a choice, was elected by the legislature. Defeated the next year, he was appointed to the federal office of collector of the port of Boston, a post accompanied by a salary which was most welcome in his now straitened circumstances. In 1789, also, he was one of the federal commissioners appointed to treat with the Creek Indians on the borders of the Southern states, and four years later (1793), was a member of a similar commission to negotiate with the Indians north of the Ohio. In this connection he kept a journal, published in the *Collections of the Massachusetts Historical Society* (3 ser. V) in 1836. His "Observations on the Climate, Soil, and Value of the Eastern Counties, in the District of Maine: Written in the Year 1789" appeared in the same *Collections* (1 ser.) in 1795. He retired from the collectorship at Boston Mar. 1, 1809, and died the following year.

[The longest account of Lincoln is that by Francis Bowen, in Jared Sparks, *The Lib. of Am. Biog.*, 2 ser. XIII (1847). There is some material in the *Hist. of the Town of Hingham* (1893), vol. III; a number of references to him appear in *Am. Hist. Asso. Report for 1896*, vol. I, *passim*; see also *Mass. Hist. Soc. Colls.*, 2 ser. III (1846), 233–55; letters regarding the Burgoyne campaign in *New-Eng. Hist. and Geneal. Reg.*, Oct. 1920; F. S. Drake, *Memorials of the Soc. of the Cincinnati of Mass.* (1873). Citations of certain manuscript and other material relating to his part in Shays's Rebellion are given by J. T. Adams, *New England in the Republic* (1926), pp. 159–63, notes. A. J. Bowden, *Fifty-five Letters of George Washington to Benjamin Lincoln, 1777–1799* (1907), a calendar, and *N. Y. Pub. Lib., Calendar of the Emmet Coll. of MSS., etc., Relating to Am. Hist.* (1900), also point the way to manuscript material. *Year Book, 1897, City of Charleston, S. C.* (n.d.), contains documents on the siege of Charleston. An obituary appeared in the *Columbian Centinel* (Boston), May 12, 1810.] J. T. A.

LINCOLN, ENOCH (Dec. 28, 1788–Oct. 8, 1829), lawyer and politician, fourth son of Levi [*q.v.*] and Martha (Waldo) Lincoln, and brother of the younger Levi [*q.v.*], was born at Worcester, Mass. He attended Harvard College for a short time but left without taking a degree. Having studied law in Worcester, he was admitted to the bar in 1811 and began practising at Salem, but moved, in 1812, to Fryeburg in the District of Maine, still a part of Massachusetts. Fryeburg was then a center of considerable importance and he spent five years in practice there, moving to Paris, Me., in 1819. He was assistant United States district attorney, 1815–18. Although a young lawyer of promise, he soon devoted most of his time and energy to politics, his affiliations being with the Jeffersonian Republicans. On Mar. 16, 1818, he was elected to the federal House of Representatives to serve the unexpired term of Albion K. Parris [*q.v.*], recently appointed to the federal bench, and took his seat in the second session of the Fifteenth Congress, Nov. 16, 1818. He was reëlected to the four following Congresses, his total service covering the period 1818–26. Maine had, in the meantime, 1820, been admitted to the Union as a separate state. He rarely spoke and his congressional career was without special distinction.

Resigning from the House in 1826, he was elected governor of Maine that same year, and was reëlected in 1827 and 1828. He was a popular and successful executive and encountered little opposition. His messages to the legislature, which show considerable literary ability, dealt with problems of the new state, then essentially a frontier community. The fact that the dispute with Great Britain over the Northeastern Boundary was becoming serious probably accounts for his emphasis on the need of protection for the state's long maritime and inland frontiers. He insisted on the validity of Maine's title to the entire area in dispute and stated emphatically his belief that the federal government had no right, without the consent of a state, to cede the property of that state. The portions of his messages dealing with the boundary question are important items in the documentary history of that protracted diplomatic controversy, which remained unsettled long after his death. He had been influential in the selection of Augusta as the state capital and his death occurred in that place a few days after he had participated in the ceremonies attending the laying of the cornerstone of a new academy for young women. His health had been failing for some time and he had declined another nomination, hoping to devote himself to literary work in Scarborough, where he had lately established a residence. He never married. He had several avocations which throw considerable light on his character and temperament. In 1816 he published a poem, *The Village* (printed by Edward Little & Company, Portland), evidently based on his observation of life in Fryeburg. More important was his interest in Indian languages and tribal institutions in Maine, which led him to carry on investigations there and in neighboring British territory. This study naturally brought him into contact with the earlier history of the white settlements in Maine. From his unfinished work in this connection, two studies were afterwards printed, "Remarks on the Indian Languages" and "Some Account of the Catholic Missions in Maine" (*Collections of the Maine Historical Society*, 1 ser., vol. I, 1831; 2nd ed., annotated, 1865, pp. 412–17 and 428–46, respectively).

[William Lincoln, *Hist. of Worcester, Mass.* (1837); Waldo Lincoln, *Hist. of the Lincoln Family* (1923); E. H. Elwell, "Enoch Lincoln," *Colls. Me. Hist. Soc.*, 2 ser., vol. I (1890); *Me. Hist. and Geneal. Recorder*, vol. III, no. 3 (1886); "The Late Governor of Maine," in *The Yankee and Boston Literary Gazette*, Nov. 1829; L. C. Hatch, *Maine, A Hist.* (1919); *Kennebec Jour.* (Augusta), Oct. 9, 16, 1829; MSS. in the Am. Antiq. Soc.] W. A. R.

LINCOLN, JOHN LARKIN (Feb. 23, 1817–Oct. 17, 1891), university professor, Latinist, author, teacher, was born in Boston, Mass. He was of English stock, sixth in descent from Stephen Lincoln, husbandman, who emigrated from Windham, England, in the seventeenth century. His maternal great-grandfather, Samuel Larkin, also came from England in the seventeenth century. He was himself the son of Ensign and Sophia Oliver (Larkin) Lincoln. His father, printer and publisher in Boston, was a man of strong religious convictions and similar convictions his son always held. Trained for four years in the Boston Latin School young Lincoln was ready for college at thirteen but, "to fill in the time," remained at school, graduating as valedictorian and entering Brown University at fifteen. He was graduated with honors from Brown in 1836 and for one year was tutor in Columbian College, Washington, D. C. During the years 1837–39 he studied at Newton Theological Institution but nevertheless chose a collegiate career. After acting as tutor in Greek at Brown for two years, he spent three years in Europe, where he studied philology and theology at the universities of Halle and Berlin (1841–43). Among his distinguished classical teachers were Bernhardy and Böckh. He spent the year 1843–44 in travel and study, mainly in Geneva and Rome. Returning to Brown University he was for one year assistant professor, then in 1845 he was made full professor of the Latin language and literature. In 1857, and again in 1887, he refreshed and increased his equipment by travel and study in Greece, Germany, and Italy. He had married, in 1846, Laura E. Pearce of Providence.

From 1859 to 1867 the University granted Lincoln part-time absence to conduct a school for young women. He was a born teacher. He twice refused to leave his life work for a college presidency elsewhere. He made his teaching of Latin a medium for the appreciation of beauty in all literatures and was "quick to feel and to point out the deeper philosophical ethical lesson" in a given text. His unfailing wit and humor relieved his indefatigable demands for exactitude in scholarship and he was one of the best-loved men on the teaching staff. Significant evidence of this affection was the gift of $100,000—at that time a large sum—collected by grateful graduates and friends in order that Lincoln "whether teaching or not," might always receive his full salary. His human interest in student life is also reflected in the name, "Lincoln Field," given to the old athletic grounds.

Lincoln's published works include *Titus Livius: Selections from the First Five Books, Together with the Twenty-first and Twenty-second Books Entire* (1847, 1871); *The Works of Horace* (1851, 1882); and *Selections from the Poems of Ovid* (1882, 1884). He also contributed many articles to the *North American Review*, the *Christian Review*, the *Baptist Quarterly*, and *Bibliotheca Sacra*. The clarity of his commentaries gave perspective to the study of Latin by many thousands of American students outside of Brown University. From his numerous essays some of the more characteristic on classical subjects are reprinted in the memorial volume published in 1894. He was an early member of the American Philological Association. There is an admirable portrait of Lincoln by Herbert Herkomer at Brown University. It reveals a face of spiritual beauty, intellectual vigor, and human kindliness.

[Wm. E. Lincoln, *In Memoriam: John Larkin Lincoln* (1894); W. C. Bronson, *The Hist. of Brown Univ., 1764–1914* (1914); *Hist. Cat. of Brown Univ., 1764–1904* (1905); obituary and editorial in the *Providence Daily Jour.*, Oct. 17, 1891.] F. G. A.

LINCOLN, LEVI (May 15, 1749–Apr. 14, 1820), lawyer and politician, was born at Hingham, Mass., the son of Enoch and Rachel (Fearing) Lincoln. His father was the great-grandson of Samuel Lincoln who emigrated from England to the Colonies in 1637 and settled at Hingham. Levi was apprenticed to a blacksmith in his youth, but when friends discovered the boy's ability and fondness for study, they persuaded his father to permit him to continue his education. Having graduated from Harvard College in 1772, he began the study of law in Newburyport, continuing it later in Northampton. At the outbreak of the

Revolution he performed a brief tour of duty with the militia. He began the practice of law in Worcester, and maintained a residence there throughout the remainder of his life. He immediately became prominent in local affairs, holding various civil offices during the remainder of the war and serving as judge of probate from 1777 to 1781. In 1779 he was elected to the convention which drew up the first state constitution and two years later declined an election to the Continental Congress. His services during these years gave him a share in the important work of establishing the civil institutions of the new state.

In the meantime his legal practice had been growing rapidly and he had become widely known as a successful trial lawyer. In 1781, together with several eminent members of the Massachusetts bar, he shared in one of the most famous litigations in the history of the state, although its importance was not fully realized until later years. Three cases came before the courts, *Quork* (spelling varies) *Walker* vs. *Nathaniel Jenison, Nathaniel Jenison* vs. *John Caldwell and Seth Caldwell,* and *The Commonwealth* vs. *Nathaniel Jenison,* which involved the question of the right to hold a negro in slavery in view of the Bill of Rights in the constitution of 1780. Lincoln, and Caleb Strong [*q.v.*], who afterwards was one of his bitter political opponents, appeared as counsel for the Caldwells, and argued against the legality of slavery in Massachusetts. The decision of the supreme court, upholding their contentions, was afterwards regarded as a landmark in the long struggle against slavery. (For details of these cases see Emory Washburn, "The Extinction of Slavery in Massachusetts," *Collections of the Massachusetts Historical Society,* 4 ser. IV, 1858, pp. 337–44.)

In the gradual development of the Republican-Federalist alignment, Lincoln became a leader of the former party in Massachusetts, despite the fact that members of his profession and social class were generally Federalists. He served a term in the state House of Representatives and another in the Senate, 1796–97, and in 1800, after a bitter campaign involving, under the existing law which required a majority, three special elections, he was chosen, Dec. 19, to serve the remainder of the unexpired term of Dwight Foster, resigned, in the Sixth Congress. In the meantime, Nov. 3, he had also been elected a member of the Seventh Congress; but before he could take his seat in the latter he was appointed attorney-general of the United States by President Jefferson. For some months he also acted as secretary of state, pending James Madison's arrival in Washington. He served creditably as attorney-general from Mar. 5, 1801, to Dec. 31, 1804, but the office at this time offered no particular opportunities for distinction. Meantime, he was active in party politics and was the object of a vast amount of abuse by Federalist newspapers, clergymen, and campaign orators. He did not tamely submit and in his *Letters to the People, by a Farmer* (Salem, 1802) he assailed the political activity of the clergy. "The blow," records Rev. William Bentley, "is serious, & the more the Clergy & their friends attempt to defend themselves, the more severe are the strokes upon them. This subject never was so freely handled in New England & never did the Clergy suffer a more serious diminution of their influence & of their power" (*Diary,* II, 1907, p. 407). Jefferson's letters show that Lincoln was firmly established in the President's confidence and entrusted with important responsibilities in the Republican "regeneration" of New England, including distribution of the patronage by which that process was expedited (P. L. Ford, *The Writings of Thomas Jefferson,* VIII, 1897).

Lincoln gave up his federal post, greatly to President Jefferson's regret and soon resumed his political activity in Massachusetts, being elected to the Governor's Council in 1806, and lieutenant-governor in 1807 and 1808, when the Republicans succeeded in getting control of the governorship for the first time. He served as governor following the death in office of James Sullivan, but was an unsuccessful candidate in 1809, when the reaction caused by the Embargo gave the state to the Federalists. He served two terms on the Governor's Council, 1810–12, and in the latter year was offered a place on the United States Supreme Court by President Madison. Justice Cushing, a stalwart Federalist, had recently died, an event described by Jefferson as "another circumstance of congratulation," inasmuch as it offered opportunity to establish a Republican majority in that tribunal. Jefferson's letters to Madison describe Lincoln as an eminently desirable appointee because of his legal attainments, equal to those of any other New England Republican, his integrity, political firmness, and unimpeachable character (P. L. Ford, *Ibid.,* IX, 1898, pp. 282–84, *passim*). Lincoln declined, however, for his eyesight was failing rapidly. He spent his remaining years on his farm in Worcester. A life-long friend of one of his sons many years later described "this home, so like an English manor in its dignity and hospitality and the variety and extent of its occupations, so like a New England farm in the homeliness of its daily employments" (Alonzo Hill, *Memorial Address on Levi Lincoln, Jr.*, 1868). It is probably not a mere coincidence that from it two of his sons, Levi and Enoch [*qq.v.*], went forth to distinguished political careers. He had married, Nov. 23, 1781, at Lancaster, Mass., Martha, daughter of Daniel and Rebecca (Salisbury) Waldo, by whom he had nine children.

[William Lincoln, *Hist. of Worcester, Mass.* (1837); Waldo Lincoln, *Hist. of the Lincoln Family* (1923); C. F. Aldrich, "The Bench and Bar," in D. H. Hurd, *Hist. of Worcester County* (1889), vol. I; *National Aegis* (Worcester), Apr. 19, 26, 1820; letters of Levi Lincoln, Sr., in the possession of the Mass. Hist. Soc. and Am. Antiquarian Soc.] W. A. R.

LINCOLN, LEVI (Oct. 25, 1782–May 29, 1868), lawyer and politician, eldest son of Levi [*q.v.*] and Martha (Waldo) Lincoln, was born and spent his life, except when absent on public service, in Worcester, Mass. He graduated from Harvard College in 1802, was admitted to the bar in 1805, and began practice in his native town. A Jeffersonian Republican by inheritance and belief, he was soon active in politics. It was in this field, rather than at the bar, that he was destined to achieve distinction. In 1812 he was elected to the Massachusetts Senate, beginning a public career which lasted for about thirty-five years. Between 1814 and 1822 he served several terms in the state House of Representatives, opposing there the policy of Gov. Caleb Strong during the second war with Great Britain, and especially the state's participation in the Hartford Convention in 1814. With the subsidence of party acrimony after the war, his influence grew, and he served as speaker during his last term, although the House majority was nominally Federalist.

In 1820–21, as a member of the state constitutional convention, he delivered speeches on elections (*Journal of Debates and Proceedings*, 1821, pp. 265–66) and on the judiciary (*Ibid.*, p. 216) which show that he was still a Jeffersonian, but he soon began to move toward the National Republican position and in 1824 supported John Quincy Adams for the presidency. Meantime, he had seen service as lieutenant-governor (1823) and, briefly, as a member of the Massachusetts supreme court. In 1825 he was elected to the governorship, the first incumbent of that position, as he stated in his message to the legislature, June 2, 1825, "whose whole experience is more recent than the adoption of the Frame of Government which he is called to participate in administering" (*New England Palladium & Commercial Advertiser*, Boston, June 3, 1825). In many respects a new era was beginning in Massachusetts history, and party activity was temporarily quiescent. Lincoln was reëlected annually until 1834, with a measure of unanimity never attained by his successors in office.

Like other members of the family, he had notable executive capacity, though perhaps his greatest service as governor was his appointment, in 1830, of Lemuel Shaw [*q.v.*] as chief justice of the state supreme court, in defiance of the precedent which called for the promotion of the senior associate justice. Rev. Alonzo Hill declared, after Lincoln's decease, that, unlike his father, he was "no classical scholar nor profound metaphysician," no great reader, but a man of sound common sense, "whose gifts were eminently practical" (*Memorial Address on Levi Lincoln, Jr.*, 1868). An examination of his semi-annual messages to the legislature confirms the truth of this estimate. Among the problems discussed were such eminently practical matters as a topographical survey of the state, an investigation of its geological resources, improvement in the administration of justice by elimination of obsolete common law provisions, amelioration of the laws of debt and insolvency, and proper methods of assuring the medical profession an adequate supply of anatomical material. His comments on the problem of penitentiary administration constitute an interesting contribution to the history of American penology. In his first message he urged that the corporation laws be amended in order to limit the liability of shareholders for corporate debts, and, reverting to the same subject on Jan. 6, 1830, he showed that, as a consequence of existing business depression, the principle of holding shareholders liable to the full extent of their property, had "brought irretrievable ruin to individuals" and had fatally impaired "that confidence in property, upon which alone, credit can be obtained." He was insistent that the state assume broader educational functions and in 1826 urged the establishment of "a Seminary of practical Arts and Sciences." He likewise emphasized the need of better professional training for teachers. His later messages as governor contained numerous disquisitions on the nature of the Union, provoked by the South Carolina nullification movement. "Opposition, by force, to the laws of the General Government, is Rebellion, from which the only escape is in Revolution," he declared on Jan. 8, 1833 (*Boston Daily Advertiser & Patriot*, Jan. 9, 1833).

He could, apparently, have had an indefinite tenure of the governorship but gave up the post in order to enter national politics. On Feb. 17,

1834, he began service in the House of Representatives in place of John Davis [*q.v.*], who had resigned to succeed Lincoln as governor. He was elected to the three succeeding Congresses, his service extending from Feb. 17, 1834, to his resignation on Mar. 16, 1841. He was a constant participant in debate but hardly an outstanding figure in Washington. Following his withdrawal from Congress, he served as collector of the Port of Boston, 1841–43, until removed by President Tyler. He also served two more terms in the state Senate, 1844–45, the last one as president of that body. He then retired to his home in Worcester, where he spent the rest of his life. He had always been active in local affairs and his name appears in a wide variety of social and business activities in that community. He served as mayor of Worcester in 1848, after its incorporation that year as a city. He was one of the founders of the American Antiquarian Society. His interest in educational matters is indicated by his long service on the governing boards of Leicester Academy and Harvard University. He was an enthusiastic promoter of agricultural improvement and a successful practical farmer; a number of his addresses on agricultural topics were printed. In person he is described as erect and dignified in carriage, retaining the manners of the first part of the century, and being regarded by neighbors and associates as "a gentleman of the old school." He married, Sept. 6, 1807, Penelope Winslow, daughter of William and Mary (Chandler) Sever, by whom he had eight children.

[Waldo Lincoln, *Hist. of the Lincoln Family* (1923); *A Memorial of Levi Lincoln the Gov. of Mass. from 1825–34* (privately printed, Boston, 1868); D. H. Hurd, *Hist. of Worcester County, Mass.* (1889); Emory Washburn, in *Proc. Mass. Hist. Soc.*, vol. XI (1871); *Proc. Am. Antiq. Soc.* (1868); MSS. in Am. Antiq. Soc. including "Life, Services and Character of Hon. Levi Lincoln of Worcester, Mass.," by Charles Hudson; Joseph Palmer, in *Boston Daily Advertiser*, supplement to issue of July 15, 1868; *Worcester Daily Spy*, May 30, June 3, 1868; *Worcester Palladium*, June 3, 1868.]
W. A. R.

LINCOLN, MARY JOHNSON BAILEY (July 8, 1844–Dec. 2, 1921), teacher, author of the "Boston Cook Book," was born in South Attleboro, Mass., the daughter of a Congregational minister, Rev. John Milton Bailey and his wife Sarah Morgan Johnson Bailey. After the death of her father in her seventh year, the mother and three children had little for support beyond their own earnings; and they moved to Norton so that the two daughters might have the benefit of Wheaton Female Seminary (later Wheaton College). After her graduation from Wheaton in 1864, Mary taught a country school in Vermont for one term and then married David A. Lincoln of Norton on June 21, 1865. Some years later business reverses made it desirable that she should be an earner as well as her husband. At about this time, 1879, the Boston Cooking School was being organized, and through the aid of her elder sister, who as a kindergarten teacher had been associated with some of its founders, she was invited to assume direction of it. After a few lessons in fancy cookery from Miss Sweeney, who had been a pupil of Pierre Blot, a famous French teacher of cookery of the sixties in New York and Boston, and after observing Maria Parloa's methods, Mrs. Lincoln agreed to undertake this new work. From 1879 to 1885, as the first principal of this novel school, she shaped its general plan and indirectly shaped the course of much later work in domestic science in grade and normal schools. After her resignation from the Boston Cooking School she was busy with lectures before schools, clubs, and some of the leading food fairs.

Mrs. Lincoln's Boston Cook Book, published in 1884, grew out of her experience as housekeeper and teacher. It marked a change in culinary literature, for most of the earlier works lacked the orderly plan which the application of school-room methods had given to this work. In 1885 Mrs. Lincoln published the *Peerless Cookbook,* followed in 1886 by *Carving and Serving* and in 1887 by the *Boston School Kitchen Textbook* (1887), which was the model for many later editions. *What to Have for Luncheon* was published in 1904. For ten years (1894–1904) Mrs. Lincoln was culinary editor of the *American Kitchen Magazine* and her department "From Day to Day" was read by thousands of housekeepers and teachers. She combined in rare fashion the direct methods of the teacher with her long experiences as housekeeper. Understanding the needs of home women, she used words they could quickly grasp. Thus she accomplished more in her period than more scientifically trained women have done in a later day, in attracting attention to household science.

[Mary J. B. Lincoln, "How I Was Led to Teach Cookery," the *New Eng. Kitchen*, May 1894; *Who's Who in America*, 1920–21; *N. Y. Herald*, Dec. 4, 1921; *Evening Post* (N. Y.), Dec. 5, 1921; personal acquaintance.]
A. B.

LINCOLN, MARY TODD (Dec. 13, 1818–July 16, 1882), wife of Abraham Lincoln, was born in Lexington, Ky., of distinguished ancestry and was reared amid genteel surroundings. Her great-grandfather, Gen. Andrew Porter, was prominent in the Revolution; her great-uncle, John Todd, accompanied George Rogers Clark, serving as county lieutenant of

Illinois; and her grandfather, Levi Todd, participated in the battle of Blue Licks, served as major-general of militia, and lived in a proud estate called "Ellerslie" close by the home of Henry Clay. Her parents, Robert S. and Eliza (Parker) Todd, had six children that survived infancy; by a second marriage to Betsy Humphreys her father had eight others that reached maturity. Of the six Todd-Parker children four are said to have had "abnormal personalities" (Evans, *post,* p. 51). Lexington was a cultural center and distinguished guests entered the Todd home. Mary was carefully educated at an academy kept by Dr. John Ward and in the select school of Mme. Mentelle where she learned French and was instructed in the social graces. In 1837 she visited Springfield, Ill.; and two years later she made the Illinois capital her home, living with her sister, Mrs. Ninian W. Edwards, daughter-in-law of Gov. Ninian Edwards. Favored by the prominence of the Edwards home, and aided by her own accomplishments, she became a belle in the fashionable society of Springfield; and her acquaintance among people of political importance was extensive. Her engagement to Lincoln and the discredited story of the defaulting bridegroom have been treated above (see Lincoln, Abraham). One of the factors in the renewal of the interrupted courtship was Mary's complicity in the Lincoln-Shields duel, an affair in which Lincoln assumed blame for certain newspaper skits which she wrote in ridicule of Shields. On Nov. 4, 1842, the pair were married after hasty preparations, and Springfield remained their home until 1861. Despite Lincoln's awkwardness they moved in the best of local society; but in their own home there was a limited hospitality. Unfavorable things were said of their domestic life, and even her friends admitted that Mary's temperament was difficult; while her background and outlook differed markedly from those of her husband, toward whose family she was unsympathetic. Within the limitations of her unstable and tempestuous temperament, however, she was a devoted wife and mother. Her reputation has suffered much from the Ann Rutledge legend and from the ungracious writings of Herndon; but it is hard to believe that the Lincoln home was as thoroughly unhappy as Herndon has pictured it. Lincoln's home letters show an affectionate regard for his wife and a playful delight in their four boys.

During the presidency of her husband, Mrs. Lincoln, in what Stoddard called her "somewhat authoritative" way, gave special attention to levees and other social affairs. A Southern lady in the White House, she was subjected to criticism, much of which was gossip and malicious slander; certainly the imputations of disloyalty were unfounded. Even the touches of social gayety with which she relieved the strain of wartime anxiety were criticized as inappropriate. She suffered during the war by reason of divisions in her own family (her sister's husband, Ben. H. Helm, being a Confederate general), and by the crushing bereavement of her son Willie's death. From the terrible moment when her husband was assassinated at her side, troubles multiplied upon her head. The death of "Tad" in 1871 left only one of her four sons. A certain mental instability now became more pronounced; she was adjudged insane and spent some months in a private sanitarium at Batavia, Ill. (1875), after which, on second trial, she was declared to be sane and again capable of managing her estate. In 1870 Congress tardily granted her an annual pension of $3,000. This was increased in 1882 to $5,000, at which time an additional gift of $15,000 was voted. After some years of foreign travel she spent her last clouded days in the home of Mrs. Edwards at Springfield, where she died of paralysis, July 16, 1882.

A short, plump brunette, Mrs. Lincoln had a certain formal beauty and was described as vivacious and apt in conversation. Accounts of her extravagance combined with penuriousness, her interference in politics, her irritable temper, and her concealment of expenditures from her husband are too numerous and authoritative to be ignored; but on the other side of the picture one finds kindlier testimony such as that of W. O. Stoddard who found her, in spite of varying moods, an agreeable mistress in the White House and a ministering friend to soldiers in Washington hospitals.

[A. J. Beveridge, *Abraham Lincoln, 1809–1858* (2 vols., 1928); W. E. Barton, *Life of Abraham Lincoln* (2 vols., 1925); Katherine Helm, *The True Story of Mary, Wife of Lincoln* (1928), based on diaries, letters, and recollections of Mrs. Ben H. Helm; Honoré W. Morrow, *Mary Todd Lincoln* (1928), a novelist's book, of little historical value; Elizabeth H. Keckley, *Behind the Scenes, or Thirty Years a Slave and Four Years in the White House* (1868), intimate, revealing comment by Mrs. Lincoln's colored seamstress; Gamaliel Bradford, *Wives* (1925), a well considered portrait; W. O. Stoddard, *Inside the White House in War Times* (1890); W. H. Townsend, *Lincoln and His Wife's Home Town* (1929); W. A. Evans, *Mrs. Abraham Lincoln: A Study of Her Personality and Her Influence on Lincoln* (1932), a full-length treatment, from the medical and scientific viewpoints; Carl Sandburg and P. M. Angle, *Mary Lincoln, Wife and Widow* (1932), especially significant for its documentary study of the Lincoln-Todd courtship and wedding.]

J. G. R.

LINCOLN, ROBERT TODD (Aug. 1, 1843–July 26, 1926), secretary of war and minister to England, devoted most of his life to private and personal affairs, and sedulously avoided the appearance of capitalizing the reputation of his father. He was the eldest and the only surviving child of Abraham and Mary (Todd) Lincoln and was born in Springfield, Ill. During his boyhood his father rose from insignificance to national importance, and every effort was made to give to Robert the educational advantages that Abraham was conscious of having missed. He attended the Springfield schools, and then Phillips Exeter Academy in New Hampshire. He was sent on to Harvard in the fall of 1859, carrying to the president a note of introduction from Stephen A. Douglas, which characterized him as the son of his friend, "with whom I have lately been canvassing the State of Illinois" (J. S. Currey, *Chicago: Its History and Its Builders,* 1912, II, p. 82). He was kept in college while his associates entered the army, for his father, as he wrote to Grant, did not "wish to put him in the ranks" (*New York Times,* July 27, 1926). After graduating in 1864 he spent four months in the Harvard Law School but left when he was given an appointment on the staff of General Grant. He was married on Sept. 24, 1868, to Mary, the daughter of Senator James Harlan of Iowa (Johnson Brigham, *James Harlan,* 1913, p. 238). Of the three children of this marriage, two daughters survived him.

On leaving the army Lincoln studied law in Chicago and was admitted to the bar in 1867. He gained profitable clients among the railroad and corporate interests, and his name appears as a charter member of the Chicago Bar Association (1874). He was often mentioned by political leaders, who were not averse to profiting by his name, but he generally kept aloof. He went to the state Republican convention, however, in 1880, at the head of a Grant delegation from Chicago, and was in close sympathy with the effort of Senator Logan to procure a third term for Grant. Logan repaid him, when he had himself accepted defeat and had switched his allegiance to Garfield, by inducing Garfield to summon Lincoln to the War Department. Lincoln became secretary of war without enthusiasm and had an uneventful term of office, with the army dominated by his father's old generals, and with the Grant retirement bill as the most important controversial matter save for the perennial case of Gen. Fitz-John Porter. His management of the relief of the Greely Expedition evoked a public criticism from his subordinate, the chief signal officer, Gen. W. B. Hazen [*q.v.*]. He felt impelled to support Arthur for renomination in 1884, to the disappointment of Logan. He resumed the practice of law in 1885 but was recalled to public service in 1889 by President Harrison who sent him to London as minister. Here the name did him good service, and he withstood the charms of British society so well as to earn the encomium of Theodore Roosevelt, who characterized "all of our ministers to England [as] pro-British except Bob Lincoln" (M. A. DeW. Howe, *James Ford Rhodes,* 1929, p. 121). He continued, however, to keep his name out of the papers and gained none of the distinction as spokesman for the people of the United States that has come to many of the ministers at the Court of St. James's.

For nearly twenty years after his return from England, Lincoln continued in his work as counsel for great business interests, and in his semi-seclusion upon which he would permit no intrusion. Among his chief clients was the Pullman Company; and when the founder of this company, George M. Pullman, died in 1897, he became first its acting executive and then its president. After the Pullman strike of 1894, and the use of the injunction in connection with this, it became common for radicals to compare adversely his apparent lack of interest in the common man and his father's humanity in the emancipation of the slaves, but he paid no attention to the criticisms. In 1911 he was forced to resign the presidency on account of his health though he retained a connection with the company as chairman of the board of directors. In 1912 he moved to Washington, D. C. He remained almost unknown as he advanced in years. He had acquired a summer home, "Hildene," at Manchester, N. H., and there he found seclusion and the golf that he thought kept him alive. He was interested in astronomy and found pleasure in the solution of algebraic problems. His father's papers, which Hay and Nicolay had worked over in the eighties, remained in his possession until near the end of his life when he deposited them in the Library of Congress to be sealed for twenty-one years after his death.

[*Harvard Coll. Class of 1864: Secretary's Report,* no. 8 (1914); the *Harvard Grads.' Mag.*, Sept. 1926; *Ill. State Hist. Lib. Pub.*, no. 11 (1906); *Lit. Digest,* Aug. 14, 1926; *Rev. of Revs.*, Sept. 1926; *Outlook,* Aug. 4, 1926; *N. Y. Herald-Tribune* and *N. Y. Times,* Sept. 27, 1926.] F. L. P.

LINCOLN, RUFUS PRATT (Apr. 27, 1840–Nov. 27, 1900), physician, laryngologist, and intranasal surgeon, was born at Belchertown, Mass., the son of Rufus S. and Lydia (Baggs) Lincoln. He studied at Williston Seminary, Easthampton, Mass., and at Phillips Exeter Academy, from which he graduated in 1858. He then entered Amherst College, where he received the degree of A.B. in 1862. Following his graduation, he enlisted in the 37th Massachusetts Volunteers as second lieutenant and was promoted to a captaincy after two months. He served through the Civil War, was in many battles, and was twice wounded. He rose to the rank of colonel and toward the close of the war was made inspector-general of the VI Corps, Army of the Potomac.

As soon as he was mustered out of the army he began the study of medicine, attending the College of Physicians and Surgeons, New York, for one year and Harvard Medical School for two more years, and received from the latter institution in 1868 his medical degree. Settling in New York, he formed a partnership with the well-known surgeon Willard Parker [*q.v.*], but was soon attracted to the then new specialty of laryngology, which included intranasal surgery. He leased the house which had been presented to Gen. George B. McClellan, where for thirty-two years, without interruption, he was entirely occupied with the duties of a practice which was enormous. His career was almost unique, since patients came to him solely because of his merit. He acquired no prestige from post-graduate study in Europe, he declined to associate himself with any college faculty, hospital, or clinic, and he did little writing. In the belief of good judges he stood at the head of his special field, an estimate which seems to be borne out by the fact that his opinion was sought by Morell-Mackenzie in the case of Emperor Frederick of Germany. He was distinguished especially for his technic in the removal of retronasal growths by means of the electric snare, and here he seems to have had no peers or successors. These formations are semi-malignant and, in theory at least, should be extirpated by a bloody and mutilating intervention; but Lincoln succeeded in removing many of them by the bloodless and painless method. One of his earliest patients with this trouble is said to have been General Judson Kilpatrick, and the renown of his cure had much to do with Lincoln's early vogue as an intranasal surgeon. Of the few papers contributed by Lincoln to medical literature the majority were devoted to the removal of retronasal growths. He was a cofounder and past president of the New York Laryngological Society —later the Laryngological Section of the Academy of Medicine—and was also a past president of the American Laryngological Association. In 1869 he married Caroline C. Tyler; his only son, Rufus Tyler Lincoln, died of appendicitis at the age of sixteen. Lincoln's own death was premature, for he was stricken in the midst of apparent health with appendicitis. At the operation Dr. Charles B. McBurney [*q.v.*] found an anomalous congenital formation which made it impossible to locate the appendix, so that after much effort it was finally necessary to abandon the operation, and the patient succumbed to exhaustion; at an autopsy the suppurating organ was found in an inaccessible position.

[The date of birth is that given in *Amherst Coll. Biog. Record of the Graduates and Non-Graduates* (1927); T. F. Harrington, *The Harvard Medic. School* (1905), vol. III, gives Apr. 27, 1841 and some other sources give Apr. 17, 1841. See also *Boston Medic. and Surgic. Jour.*, Dec. 6, 1900; *Medic. Record*, Dec. 8, 1900; *N. Y. Medic. Jour.*, Dec. 1, 1900; H. A. Kelly and W. L. Burrage, *Am. Medic. Biogs.* (1920); *N. Y. Times*, Nov. 28, 1900; personal knowledge.] E. P.

LIND, JOHN (Mar. 25, 1854–Sept. 18, 1930), lawyer, congressman, governor, diplomat, was born in Kånna, Småland, Sweden, the son of Gustav and Catherine (Jonason) Lind. His family came to the United States in 1867 and settled in Goodhue County, Minn., and Lind remained a resident of that state throughout his life. He attended the schools of his native and adopted countries and became sufficiently proficient in the use of English to teach in a district school in Sibley County in 1872–73, after which he set himself to the task of studying law. He was admitted to the bar in 1877, and while he was gaining experience as a lawyer he served for two years as superintendent of schools in Brown County and for four years as receiver of the United States land office at Tracy, Lyon County. His election to Congress in 1886 marked the inception of three successive terms as a Republican (1887–93) and one as a Democrat (1903–05). He had already won a reputation for simplicity of manner and directness of speech and as a legislator showed a disposition to belittle extreme partisanship and to shy at blind party loyalty. Although regarded as a "good" Republican during his first three terms, he was a believer in the free coinage of silver, tempering his course, however, with a statement on the floor of the House that something ought to be yielded to expediency and that the Sherman Silver Purchase Act for the time being was an effective substitute (*Congressional Record*, 51 Cong., 1 Sess., p. 5696).

In 1896 he was the gubernatorial candidate of the Silver Republicans, Democrats, and Populists but was defeated. In 1898, speaking as the nominee of the Democrats and their allies, he undoubtedly gave an accurate statement of his political faith when he said: "I have not been a Populist, and I cannot say that I have become a Populist. To be frank with you, my friends, I will say to you that I don't know that I have any party. Perhaps it might be said of me that I am a political orphan" (*Minneapolis Tribune,* Oct. 11, 1898). As governor (1899–1901) Lind was the first to interrupt the succession of Republican incumbents since 1859. He remained until his death a leader and oracle of independent and progressive thought. He was an admirer of William Jennings Bryan, and he gave support to the foreign and domestic policies of Woodrow Wilson. In 1924, however, he deserted the Democratic party in favor of the Progressive candidate, Robert M. LaFollette, and in 1928 he refused to support Alfred E. Smith. In 1910 he declined the Democratic nomination for the governorship.

During the first days of August 1913, the country was surprised at the appointment of Lind to be the personal representative of President Wilson in Mexico. The object of his mission was to help effect the peaceful overthrow of Huerta and the return of stable government (Baker, *post,* p. 267). He remained in Mexico for several months but was unable to accomplish the object of his mission. From the beginning of December 1913 he consistently advocated the recognition of Carranza and after his return was active and influential in his favor. Probably his greatest contribution was his influence upon progressive legislation affecting his state—in railroad regulation, taxation, legal reform, and public education. During the interim in his political career he served in the Spanish-American War. The pension which he received from this service formed the basis of a trust fund to be used to aid crippled students at the University of Minnesota, an act prompted, perhaps, by the fact that he had lost his left hand in his youth. Physically he was unmistakably Swedish, tall, wiry, sandy-haired, and blue-eyed. He possessed the industry, initiative, bent for controversy, and facility of expression of his race, but he was intensely American and in the heat of political campaigns made no appeal to racial or nationalistic prejudice. In his declining years he interested himself in ancient Scandinavian history, but he never identified himself with the activities of the Swedish-Americans as a group. His liberal point of view in religion and his defection from orthodox Republicanism explains the lukewarm, not to say hostile, attitude of the Swedish-American clergy toward him. Lind married, on Sept. 1, 1879, Alice A. Shepard of Mankato, Minn.

[W. W. Folwell, *A Hist. of Minn.*, vol. III (1926), has a chapter on "Lind and his Times, 1899–1901," with ample citations. Ray S. Baker, *Woodrow Wilson: Life and Letters,* vol. IV (1931), is the best printed source for Lind's mission to Mexico. Other sources include: A. E. Strand, *A Hist. of the Swedish-Americans in Minn.* (1910), vol. I; J. H. Baker, *Lives of the Govs. of Minn.* (1908); Edith L. O'Shaughnessy, *A Diplomat's Wife in Mexico* (1916); *Minneapolis Tribune,* Sept. 19, 1930. The author of this sketch made use of Lind's papers, some of which are in the possession of the Minn. Hist. Soc.] G. M. S.

LINDABURY, RICHARD VLIET (Oct. 13, 1850–July 15, 1925), lawyer, was born on a farm near Peapack, Somerset County, N. J. His father, Jacob H. Lindabury, was of English descent while his mother, Mary Ann Vliet, was of Holland-Dutch parentage. His boyhood was spent in farm work and in rather irregular attendance at the district school. An apt pupil, he enlisted the interest of his teacher and through him of the local pastor of the Dutch Reformed Church with the result that the latter secured permission to teach the boy in preparation for Rutgers College and ultimately for the ministry. Thus some three years largely devoted to the evening study of Greek and Latin ensued. A serious illness which made the boy an invalid for two years prevented the consummation of these plans. In 1870, however, young Lindabury was offered the opportunity to take up the study of law in the office of Alvah A. Clark, of Somerville, N. J., a relative, and a former member of Congress. Supporting himself by teaching a local school he was able to be admitted to the bar in 1874 and opened an office in Bound Brook. In 1878 he moved to Elizabeth where he made his first and last effort to enter politics by seeking the post of city attorney, an effort which was unsuccessful.

For several years Lindabury engaged in general practice. He was counsel for the Anti-Race-Track Gambling League and made speeches widely against gambling. Though a Democrat he opposed his party in this situation since he believed they had been corrupted by the gambling interests. In 1892 he defended the Singer Manufacturing Company against the payment of a tax from which the company claimed it was immune under its charter. Losing the case in the lower court he retained Joseph H. Choate to aid him on appeal and won the case in the court of errors and appeals. The next year the state's effort to collect the tax was renewed and again, with Choate's aid, he won a decision. This began his career as a corporation lawyer. His next important case was his defense of the American Tobacco Company against an action brought by the state of New Jersey to dissolve it as an illegal combination in restraint of trade. Choate, as counsel for the tobacco company, retained Lindabury as associate counsel and allowed him to handle the case on appeal. He won a significant victory which firmly established his reputation and brought him all the business he could manage.

In 1896 Lindabury moved his office to Newark where he remained for the rest of his life. After two years alone he became senior partner of the firm of Lindabury, Depue & Faulks. His practice was tremendous in scope and lucrative in character. After his death one of the leaders of the bar said of him: "No other American lawyer ever represented and counseled so large an aggregate of capital investment as Lindabury represented and counseled" (Guthrie, *post,* p. 48). In 1905 he represented the Metropolitan and Prudential Life Insurance companies in the Armstrong investigation in New York. He headed the distinguished group of lawyers which defended the United States Steel Corporation against the dissolution suit brought against it by the federal government in 1911 and won a decisive victory in the Supreme Court's decision in 1920 (251 *U. S.*, 417). In 1912 and 1913 he appeared for J. P. Morgan and other financial interests before the Pujo committee in Congress which was investigating the so-called "money trust." Besides those mentioned he had as clients such business interests as the Standard Oil Company of New Jersey, the Central Railroad of New Jersey, the International Harvester Company, the United States Rubber Company, Bethlehem Steel Company, American Sugar Refining Company, the Pennsylvania Railroad Company, and many others.

Lindabury could never be persuaded to enter politics although he was many times sought by the leaders of his party for public office. Nor would he accept judicial appointment though this was twice tendered him. He was, however, a member of the New Jersey Palisades Interstate Park Board and a trustee of Stevens Institute of Technology. He retained an interest in farming and lived on a six-hundred-acre farm at Bernardsville, which he called "Meadowbrook" and which he operated on a paying basis. He was a tall handsome man, fond of riding and outdoor life. On July 8, 1892, he was married to Lillian (Van Saun) Dinger, who had one daughter and by whom he had a son and a daughter. He died from apoplexy after a fall from his horse.

[Wm. D. Guthrie, "Richard V. Lindabury," *Am. Bar Asso. Jour.*, Jan. 1926; *Who's Who in America*, 1924–25; *N. J. Law Jour.*, Sept. 1925; the *Jour. of Commerce* (N. Y.) and *N. Y. Times*, July 16, 1925.] R. E. C.

LINDBERG, CONRAD EMIL (June 9, 1852–Aug. 2, 1930), Lutheran clergyman, was born in Jönköping, Sweden, where he received his early schooling in the Gymnasium. At eighteen he began to preach, and in 1871, with the aid of friends, he came to the United States to study at Augustana College and Theological Seminary, then located at Paxton, Ill. In two years he completed the theological course, but being too young to be ordained he continued his studies at Mount Airy Lutheran Theological Seminary, Philadelphia, where he remained until 1876. In 1874 he was ordained to the Lutheran ministry by the Augustana Synod, and while under its charge he also managed to study at the University of Pennsylvania. In 1879 he was called to the Gustavus Adolphus Church in New York City, where for eleven years he served as pastor and as president of the New York Conference of the Augustana Synod. In 1890 he was called to be professor of systematic theology at the Augustana College and Theological Seminary, which had been removed to Rock Island, Ill. From 1901 to 1910 he was vice-president, and from 1920 until his death, dean of the institution. He was also vice-president of the Augustana Synod (1899–1907), and a member of the Augustana Synod Home and Foreign Mission Board (1899–1913). In 1901 he was made Knight of the Royal Order of the North Star by the King of Sweden and in 1924, Commander of the Royal Order of Vasa.

He was a diligent student throughout his whole life, and the fact that he was a bachelor rendered it possible for him to adhere closely to a fixed schedule of devotions and study; his whole life, as well as his theology, was pervaded by a spirit of deep mysticism and reverence. Although at different times, he taught in practically every theological field, his chief work was done in dogmatics and apologetics. In 1898 he published *Encheiridion I Dogmatik Jämte Dogmhistoriska Anmärkninger.* This was later expanded into a larger book, *Christian Dogmatics and Notes on the History of Dogma,* which in 1922 was issued in an English translation by Rev. C. E. Hoffsten. It was adopted as a textbook in Lutheran theological seminaries both in America and Europe, and attained a position of established authority. In 1928 a revised edition appeared.

In the field of apologetics, he wrote *Apologetics, or a System of Christian Evidence* (1917, 1926). Unlike Lutheran theologians who have come to America in their maturity, Lindberg apparently had no fear of issuing his works in the English language. Besides these major productions, he also wrote a number of smaller books, and articles and reviews in church magazines. He was chief editor of the *Augustana Theological Quarterly* from 1900 to 1902, and after his retirement from the editorship, due to other pressing duties, he still continued to contribute to the publication. He died just as he had finished his last book, *Beacon Lights of Prophecy in the Latter Days,* issued posthumously in 1930.

[*Augustana Alumni Reg.* (1924); *Who's Who in America,* 1930–31; *Tidskrift: Augustana Theological Quarterly,* vol. X, no. 1; *Lutheran Companion,* Aug. 16, 1927; *Augustana,* vol. LXXV, no. 33 (1930); *Lutheran Church Herald,* Aug. 26, 1930; J. C. Jensson (Roseland), *Am. Lutheran Biogs.* (copr. 1890).] J. M. R.

LINDBERGH, CHARLES AUGUSTUS (Jan. 20, 1859–May 24, 1924), congressman and leader in the Non-Partisan League, was born in Stockholm, Sweden, the son of August and Louise (Carline) Lindbergh. His parents emigrated to the United States in 1859 and settled on a farm near Melrose, Stearns County, Minn. The son, after some preliminary education, attended the law school of the University of Michigan and graduated in 1883. He began the practice of law in Little Falls, Minn., where he made his home for the remainder of his life. In 1906 he was elected as a Republican to Congress and served for five successive terms (1907–17). In 1916 he was defeated by Frank B. Kellogg in the primary election for United States senator. Two years later, as a Progressive Republican with Non-Partisan League indorsement, he was defeated for the governorship of Minnesota. He entered the primary for the same office on the Farmer-Labor ticket in 1924, but his death occurred before the election.

The name Lindbergh did not have the ring in Minnesota in 1917–18 that it had ten years later when his only son, of the same name, electrified the world by his transatlantic flight. The elder Lindbergh was of the type to whom statues are erected only after the lapse of many years. Starting his congressional career as a Rooseveltian, when the West was infatuated with progressive policies that brought Republican "insurgency" against "standpat" leadership, Lindbergh was always in the first rank of "reformers." His praise for Roosevelt's attacks on the methods of big business, following the panic of 1907; his vote against the Payne-Aldrich tariff; his vote to declare the office of speaker vacant, despite the unwillingness of some of the leaders of the revolt against "Cannonism" to go to that length; his commendation of the moral influence of Wilson in framing the Underwood tariff, including the income tax provision; his espousal of rural credits and postal savings banks; his resolution which inspired the Pujo investigation of the "money trust"; his advocacy of the repeal of the canal tolls exemption; his indorsement of Wilson's Mexican policy; his statement that the Socialists' view of war was correct; and his denunciation of "war propaganda—dollar plutocracy versus patriotic America" and a "nation muzzled by false national honor"—all reacted favorably upon his constituency and the people of his state. It was not long after the United States declared war on Germany, however, that his prophecy (Mar. 1, 1917) was strikingly fulfilled: "The man who reasons and exercises good sense to-day may be hung in effigy tomorrow by the jingoes" (*Congressional Record,* 64 Cong., 2 Sess., App. p. 701).

Lindbergh's interest in financial reform prompted his volume entitled *Banking and Currency and the Money Trust,* published in 1913. In July 1917 he published *Why is Your Country at War, and What Happens to you After the War,* purporting to analyze the causes of the war. The book was used against him in the following year, when his candidacy threatened to plunge the Republican party down to defeat by the Non-Partisan League. The press vilified him, his meetings were broken up, and he was threatened with violence. His defeat was hailed as a victory for "loyalty." His appointment to the War Industries Board was greeted with such a storm of protest that Lindbergh resigned in order not to obstruct the cooperation of certain elements in the prosecution of the war. His last work was *The Economic Pinch* (1923), which explained further his social and economic ideas. Although he was generous, honest, and a champion of the common people, he had few personal friends. After his death his name gained increased respect. Lindbergh married, soon after he settled in Little Falls, Mary Lafond. After her death he married Evangeline Lodge Land, who became the mother of Charles Augustus Lindbergh, Jr.

[Lynn and Dora B. Haines, *The Lindberghs* (1931); *Biog. Dir. Am. Cong.* (1928); Margaret S. Ernst, "Lindbergh's 'Bolshevik' Father," the *Nation,* June 15, 1927; *Lit. Digest,* June 11, 1927; the *Minneapolis Tribune* and *N. Y. Times,* May 25, 1924.] G. M. S.

LINDE, CHRISTIAN (Feb. 19, 1817–Nov. 24, 1887), pioneer Wisconsin physician, was born on the family estate near Copenhagen, Denmark. He was of a noble Danish family and his full name was Christian Lemvigh Paul Lövenörn de Linde-Freidenreich. He was educated in the Royal University of Copenhagen, from which he graduated in 1837. After his graduation, while working in the hospitals of the Danish capital, he became involved in the political troubles that were disturbing all Europe and in 1842 he emigrated to America. He chose the vicinity of Oshkosh, Wis., where there was good hunting, as the place to establish a landed estate and live the life of a country gentleman. In a new community, where medical knowledge was at a premium, he was called upon to treat neighboring settlers and Indians, among whom he quickly established a wide reputation as a healer. Many local traditions are current regarding his early professional work among the Indians of the Fox River valley. Possessed of great physical strength and courage, qualities strongly appealing to the Indian mind, he was highly regarded as a mighty hunter and medicine man. In adopting him into their life and confidence they gave him the name of Muckwa (White Bear), a tribute to his size and blonde complexion. A campaign of vaccination which he was compelled to institute against a smallpox outbreak put to a severe test the Indians' confidence and the doctor's tact and ingenuity. Insistent demands for his professional services compelled him to give up his country home and to settle for practice, first in Green Bay, then in Fond du Lac, and finally in Oshkosh, where he made his home for the remainder of his life. He was the pioneer surgeon of that section of the state, a skilful operator, of sound judgment and original ideas. He is credited with having discovered the value of animal tendons for surgical suture material and with having first applied them to the treatment of wounds. Specialization in medicine was hardly known in the pioneer community in which he lived and he was always a busy general practitioner. He was a member of county, state, and national medical societies, serving as president of the Winnebago County society and vice-president of the Wisconsin organization. His writings, mainly on surgical subjects, were presented before meetings of these societies. In addition to his medical attainments, he was a classical scholar and a linguist, able to converse in seven languages, though he never achieved any great mastery of the English tongue. Exposure incident to country practice in the inclement winters of Wisconsin made him a chronic sufferer from bronchitis, which caused his death, in Oshkosh. He was married three times: to Sarah Dickinson in 1843, to Sarah Davis in 1852, and to Mrs. Huldah Henning Volner in 1858. A son, Fred, issue of the first marriage, studied medicine, and until his death in 1880, was associated with his father in practice. Two daughters survived him.

[H. A. Kelly and W. L. Burrage, *Am. Medic. Biogs.* (1920); *The U. S. Biog. Dict.*, Wis. Vol. (1877); R. J. Harney, *Hist. of Winnebago County, Wis.* (1880); *Wis. State Jour.* (Madison), Nov. 25, 1887; information from the family.]

J. M. P—n.

LINDENKOHL, ADOLPH (Mar. 6, 1833–June 22, 1904), cartographer, oceanographer, was born at Niederkaufungen, Hesse Cassel, Germany, fifth of the nine children of George C. F. Lindenkohl and Anna Elizabeth (Krug). At Cassel he received the thorough education of the Realschule and later of the Polytechnische Schule, graduating from the latter in 1852. That same year he came to the United States with an elder sister and engaged in teaching in private schools, first in York, Pa., and then in Washington, D. C. In 1854 he joined the United States Coast and Geodetic Survey as cartographic draftsman, and here he labored for practically half a century, rising step by step to the position of senior cartographic draftsman. He became a citizen of the United States in 1857, and at different times during the Civil War was assigned to duty with the army, serving as a topographer on the defenses of Baltimore, and assisting in a topographic survey of the Potomac River and in the compilation of cartographic data for the department of West Virginia. In 1872 he married Pauline Praeger of Baltimore; three boys and three girls were born to them between the years 1873 and 1883.

Lindenkohl's official duties were wholly of a technical nature, connected with the production of hydrographic charts; and his charts published by the Coast and Geodetic Survey are notable examples of high technique in engraving, etching, and lithography. His map of New York City and environs, printed privately in New York City in 1860 and engraved by his brother, Henry Lindenkohl, is an outstanding example of cartographic art of that day. Being possessed of a scientific bent of mind, he went behind the data shown on the charts and related them to the broader fields of scientific inquiry. He mastered the mathematical principles of projections and became recognized as a leading authority on the subject. He made the first transverse polyconic map of the United States; he pointed out the advantages of the transverse polyconic projection for reducing scale error for mapping regions of considerable extension in longitude; and he directed attention to the advantages of the transverse mercator projection in the solution of certain cartographic problems. In the field of oceanography, the submarine channel of the Hudson River, which can be followed clearly on a hydrographic chart for a number of miles out into the open sea, was a problem that early engaged his attention. In the *Report,* 1884, of the Coast and Geodetic Survey, and in the *American Journal of Science,* June 1885, he presents a careful study of this channel, tracing its connection with the geological features of the adjacent coastal region, and concluding that it was brought about by glacial action. Other papers, which appeared in the annual reports of the Coast and Geodetic Survey, in *Petermann's Mitteilungen,* and in various other journals, dealt with the Gulf Stream, the circulation in the Gulf of Mexico, and with the temperature and salinity of the North Pacific Ocean. He was not a prolific writer, but each of his publications is a carefully prepared paper, informed by broad scholarship. These papers stimulated interest and encouraged discussion in the field of oceanography, which at that time counted but few active workers in this country.

[*Bull. Philosophical Soc. of Washington,* Aug. 1905; *Proc. Washington Acad. of Sci.,* vol. X (1908); *Evening Star* (Washington, D. C.), June 23, 1904; Coast and Geodetic Survey records; family records.]

H. A. M—r.

LINDERMAN, HENRY RICHARD (Dec. 26, 1825–Jan. 27, 1879), director of the mint, was born in Lehman township, Pike County, Pa., son of Dr. John Jordan and Rachel (Brodhead) Linderman. After studying medicine with his father, and also probably in New York City, he practised for several years in Pennsylvania. In 1853 he was made chief clerk in the mint at Philadelphia, and served in that capacity for twelve years, resigning to enter private business. On Mar. 4, 1867, President Johnson appointed him director of the Philadelphia mint, where he remained for two years. Removed by President Grant in April 1869, he was thereafter associated with various governmental activities for which his experience and ability fitted him. In 1869–70 he assisted Comptroller John Jay Knox [*q.v.*] in drafting the coinage act of 1873. Among other provisions of this important measure was one combining the mint and assay offices into a bureau administered as a unit of the Treasury Department. In 1872 Secretary Boutwell authorized Linderman to conduct an examination of the Western mints. When the coinage act took effect, on Apr. 1, 1873, President Grant appointed him the first director of the Bureau of the Mint.

On Nov. 19, 1872, Linderman made a detailed report to the secretary of the treasury, urging certain monetary changes. One of these was the establishment of a true par of exchange with Great Britain, to replace the inaccurate technical par which dated from colonial times; accordingly, an act was passed, effective Jan. 1, 1874, which correctly expressed the relation between the legal moneys of the two countries. In the same report he had proposed the coinage of a silver "trade dollar" of 420 grains, designed to supersede the popular Mexican silver dollar in Oriental trade, but not to be used as a medium of domestic exchange. This anomalous coin had a short and unhappy history. Authorization for its coinage was included in the act of Feb. 12, 1873; its limited legal-tender status was revoked and power to suspend coinage given in 1876; finally, in 1887, the right to coin it was repealed. One writer says of this fiscal experiment, "Its creation was a misfortune, its existence a failure, and its retirement a necessity" (Watson, *post,* p. 207). In general, however, Linderman had sound ideas on questions of coinage. His annual reports are full of valuable information ably presented, especially that of 1876, which contains a "Review of the Several Propositions for the Coinage of Legal Tender Silver Dollars under a Double Standard." In 1877 he published his *Money and Legal Tender in the United States,* a concise and accurate handbook since superseded by more extensive treatments, to which the agitation about silver gave a timely significance. "As to merely technical matters . . . ," a reviewer declared, "nothing could be more lucid and methodical" (*The Nation,* Jan. 10, 1878, p. 30).

Because of criticism of its management, Linderman conducted an exhaustive investigation into the San Francisco mint, making a report of his findings, dated October 1877. Less than a year later the Bureau of the Mint itself was under fire, and specific charges of misconduct in office were made against Linderman by a congressional sub-committee. These were categorically denied by him (*New York Tribune,* June 17, 18, 1878). The anxiety caused by these investigations, after the strenuous work of the year before, proved too much for his health; he was not on duty after November, and his death followed in January. No conclusive report on the investigations exists, but there is no question as to Linderman's personal integrity. He was an exceptionally able director of the mint at a period when efficient conduct of the office was particularly difficult.

[*The Biog. Encyc. of Pa. of the Nineteenth Century* (1874); *Frank Leslie's Illustrated Newspaper,* Nov. 20, 1875; J. P. Watson, *The Bureau of the Mint. Its Hist., Activities and Organization* (1926); *Ann. Reports of the Director of the Mint,* 1867, 1868, 1873–78; information from the Bureau of the Mint, Treasury Department; *Evening Star* (Washington, D. C.), *N. Y. Tribune,* Jan. 28, 1879; D. K. Watson, *Hist. of Am. Coinage* (1899); A. B. Hepburn, *Hist. of Coinage and Currency in the U. S.* (1903).]

L. P. B.

LINDHEIMER, FERDINAND JACOB (May 21, 1801–Dec. 2, 1879), botanist, was born in Frankfurt-am-Main, Germany, and died in New Braunfels, Comal County, Tex. He was the son of a well-to-do merchant of Frankfurt, Johan H. Lindheimer. He attended the universities of Wiesbaden and Bonn, but left the latter without a degree in 1827. He taught in Georg Bunsen's *Erziehungsanstalt* in Frankfurt until the institute was closed by the government in the spring of 1834, because of revolutionary activities. He then accompanied Bunsen and another colleague to America and lived for a few months in the famous German "Latin-farmer" community at Belleville, St. Clair County, Ill. In the fall of 1834, with five companions, he went to Mexico by way of New Orleans, but after a sojourn of sixteen months he returned to New Orleans to enlist in the ranks of the Texans in their war for independence (*Aufsätze, post,* pp. 78–144). After the war he tried farming near Houston, but he was unsuccessful. Then, encouraged by his old university friend and fellow-student, George Engelmann [*q.v.*], he undertook the systematic collection of botanical specimens in Texas. He succeeded in interesting Asa Gray of Harvard College in this work, and for nine years made most extensive collections of Texan plants. These were described in the work entitled *"Plantæ Lindheimerianæ,"* published in Volumes V (October 1845) and VI (no. 1, 1850) of the *Boston Journal of Natural History.* He was a man of unusual will, determination, and devotion to science. Completely fearless, he spent months at a time in the wilderness, without seeing a white man. The Indians came to look upon him with a deep reverence as a great medicine man (*Aufsätze,* pp. 63–78).

In 1846, at San Antonio, Lindheimer had married Eleonore Reinarz, the daughter of a recently arrived immigrant from Aachen. She was of great assistance to him in the preparation of his specimens. In 1847 he took part in the "Darmstädter Kolonie," or the "Communistic colony of Bettina," occupying a tract of land between the Llano and the San Saba rivers. The colony lasted but little more than six months. In 1852 he became editor of the *Neu Braunfelser Zeitung,* which he conducted for eighteen years. The paper was nominally Democratic, but independent. During the fifties Lindheimer opposed the German agitation for abolition and himself supported the Southern cause during the Civil War. Aside from wielding a political influence through his paper, he published in it and in the *Neu Yorker Staats-Zeitung* valuable scientific, philosophical, and historical essays. An appreciative former student, Gustav Passavant, collected and published a number of these in 1879, at Frankfurt, under the title, *Aufsätze und Abhandlungen von Ferdinand Lindheimer in Texas.* Lindheimer also conducted a free private school and served as superintendent of public instruction in the county and as justice of the peace. He is described as quiet and deliberate, and temperate in his habits. He was a freethinker in his opinions, but he never antagonized religious institutions and he valued nothing more than freedom and independence.

[*Allgemeine Deutsche Biog.,* Band XVIII (1883); Ferdinand Roemer, *Texas* (1849); R. L. Biesele, *The Hist. of the German Settlements in Tex., 1831–61* (1930); *Der Deutsche Pionier,* Jan. 1880; C. H. Winkler, "The Botany of Tex.," *Bull. of the Univ. of Tex.,* no. 18 (1915); J. W. Blankinship, "Plantæ Lindheimerianæ, Part III," *Mo. Botanical Garden, Eighteenth Ann. Report* (1907); files of the *Neu Braunfelser Zeitung*; S. W. Geiser, "Ferdinand Jacob Lindheimer," *Southwest Rev.,* Winter 1930.]

S. W. G.

LINDLEY, CURTIS HOLBROOK (Dec. 14, 1850–Nov. 20, 1920), lawyer, jurist, was born in Marysville, Cal., a descendant of John Lindley, an early settler in Guilford, Conn. Charles Lindley, his father, who studied at the Yale Law School, went to California in 1849, with his wife, Ann Eliza Downey, a native of Newtown, Conn. In 1865–66 young Lindley attended the Eagleswood Military Academy at Perth Amboy, N. J., and at the age of sixteen enlisted in the regular army. His father secured his release before the full term of his enlistment and he returned to study. He attended the San Francisco High School, 1868–70, and spent the next two years at the University of California. Military instruction in the University was organized at this time, and Lindley became ranking captain of the cadets and the first commissioned officer. Meanwhile, when he was seventeen, he started out with companions on a prospecting expedition in Nevada. He ran a stationary engine on the Comstock Lode and just before practising law was stationary engineer at the Union Works. He firmly believed that every lawyer should take some sort of an engineering course, and himself studied mining engineering to aid him in the practice of mining law.

He was admitted to practise in May 1872 and within a short time was appointed secretary of the California Code Commission, of which his father was a member. On June 19, 1872, he was married to Elizabeth Mendenhall. He practised law in Stockton, being appointed to fill a vacancy as superior judge of Amador County. Failing of election to the same office, he moved to San Francisco, forming, in 1890, a partnership with Henry Eickhoff. While on the bench in Amador County, Lindley had occasion to decide several mining cases. He began to specialize in this branch of the law and ultimately published a treatise on the subject (*A Treatise on the Amer-*

ican Law Relating to Mines and Mineral Lands, 1897). His work, familiarly known as "Lindley on Mines" quickly took rank as the leading text on the subject and became recognized as the most authoritative text on mining law in the United States. It gives evidence of painstaking research and philosophic insight far beyond that of the average legal textbook. Rossiter W. Raymond, the eminent mining engineer, refers to the three-volume third edition as "truly an imposing *magnum opus.*"

Before the war Lindley had delivered lectures on mining law at the Leland Stanford, Jr., University and at the University of California. Among his Stanford students was Herbert Hoover, and from that contact a lasting friendship was formed. Upon Hoover's appointment as head of the Food Administration, he called Lindley to Washington as a "dollar-a-year" man to assist in organizing its legal department. Standing out from the infinite detail and perplexing problems of this organization which had sprung up on a moment's notice was the creation of the United States Grain Corporation. Lindley carefully drafted a proposed charter for this corporation and submitted it to President Wilson as a "tentative draft." It was a matter of pride to him that the President penned out the words "tentative draft," and, without delay, signed the proclamation making the charter effective. Despite the fact that his special field was mining law, he was able to turn at once to problems of commercial and constitutional law, and to matters concerning which there were no precedents, but his judgments proved eminently sound. Finding the climate of Washington a severe drain upon his vitality, Lindley returned to California to build up his health and his practice. He died, as he had so often expressed a wish to die, "in the harness," being stricken, an hour after the conclusion of a most trying mining case, with the illness that resulted in his death five days later.

[See *Who's Who in America,* 1920–21; W. E. Colby, "Curtis Holbrook Lindley, 1850–1920," *Cal. Law Rev.,* Jan. 1921; the *Engineering and Mining Jour.,* Apr. 18, 1914; *Econ. Geology,* Sept. 1914; J. M. Lindly, *The Hist. of the Lindley-Lindsley-Linsley Families in America,* vol. I (1930), vol. II (1924); *San Francisco Chronicle,* Nov. 22, 1920. Information as to certain facts was supplied by Lindley's son, Curtis Lindley.]

W. E. C.

LINDLEY, JACOB (June 13, 1774–Jan. 29, 1857), a leader among the founders of Ohio University, was born in the Blockhouse or Lindley Fort near the site of Prosperity Town, in Washington County, Pa., the seventh son of Demas Lindley. At the age of eighteen he was sent to an academy in Canonsburg, Pa., which subsequently became Jefferson College. A few years later he entered the College of New Jersey, having traveled the entire distance from the Monongahela River by the "ride and tie" method in company with James Carnahan, destined to become the ninth president of that institution. In 1800 he graduated, married Hannah Dickey, and was licensed to preach by the Washington County Presbytery. In 1803 he settled as pastor of the church at Waterford, Ohio. Two years later he was appointed trustee of the, as yet, nonexistent Ohio University. Unlike some of his fellow appointees he took from the first an active interest in the affairs of the prospective institution. On Apr. 2, 1806, he was made member of a committee "to contract with some person or persons for building a house in the town of Athens for the purpose of an academy on the credit of rents that will hereafter become due" (from the two townships of land granted to the University). On the completion of this building Lindley was appointed to a committee "to report a plan for opening and conducting an academy and providing a preceptor." A few days later he was himself elected preceptor and entered upon his duties in the spring of the same year, 1808. For the first four years he was the sole instructor in the only department of the University then existing, the preparatory department.

By 1822 the institution was in a position financially to make possible the provision for instruction of college grade. A college faculty was organized in which Lindley was assigned to the chair of mental and moral philosophy and belles-lettres. Two years later, in 1824, he was transferred to the chair of mathematics, which position he held until 1826. With his scholastic duties he apparently combined those of pastor of a Presbyterian church established there in 1809 largely through his influence. Although there is no evidence that he possessed unusual talent as teacher, administrator, or scholar, he seems nevertheless to have been the moving spirit in inaugurating the activities of the first university to be founded on a grant made by the federal government. In 1828 he took charge of a church at Walnut Hills, near Cincinnati, but in 1829 he removed to Grave Creek in Virginia and shortly afterward to Pennsylvania. After he had left the state, the legislature appointed Thomas Bryce to his seat on the board of trustees of the university. Lindley contested the action (1836) and won his suit, but he resigned from the board two years later upon removing to the South. Finally he returned to Connellsville, Pa., where he died at the residence of his son, Dr. Lutellus Lindley, in 1857. At the solicitation of his daughters and some other young mothers Lindley published at Uniontown, Pa., in 1846, a little treatise on the training of children entitled *Infant Philosophy.* The work is characterized chiefly by the importance it attaches to the education of children while still very young, below three years of age, and by its vigorous attack on Locke's *"tabula rasa"* theory.

[In preparing this sketch, the author made use of an unpublished biographical sketch of Lindley by Emma C. McVay, a grand-niece. Printed sources include: C. M. Walker, *Hist. of Athens County, Ohio* (1869); W. E. Peters, *Legal Hist. of the Ohio Univ.* (1910); C. W. Super, *A Pioneer Coll. and Its Background* (1924); C. L. Martzolff, *Ohio Univ.* (1910); *Gen. Cat. of Ohio Univ.*, 1804–57.] L. F. A.

LINDSAY, NICHOLAS VACHEL (Nov. 10, 1879–Dec. 5, 1931), poet, known as Vachel Lindsay, was born in Springfield, Ill. His paternal ancestry was Kentuckian, his maternal Virginian, and on both sides it was Scotch. His father, Vachel Thomas Lindsay, one of the pioneer settlers in the Springfield region, was a physician; his mother, Catharine (Frazee) Lindsay, possessed some literary talent and was an ardent member of the Christian Church. Their son early developed the combined interest in religion, poetry, and art, which was to dominate his entire life. After graduation from the local high school in 1897, he attended Hiram College in Ohio for three years with the thought of entering the ministry. This aim was then abandoned for the study of art, pursued under difficulties, while working in Marshall Field's wholesale department, at the Chicago Art Institute night school, 1900–03, and later continued at the New York School of Art, 1904–05, where he worked under William M. Chase and Robert Henri, also lecturing on art at the West Side Y. M. C. A. in the winter of 1905–06. Meanwhile, beginning at the age of eighteen, he had written a few intermittent poems, and, in the spring of 1906, being without funds and unable to obtain work, he started on his famous walking trip through the South, distributing a poem, "The Tree of Laughing Bells," in exchange for bed and board (Lindsay, *A Handy Guide for Beggars, . . . Being Sundry Explorations Made . . . in Florida, Georgia, North Carolina, Tennessee, Kentucky, New Jersey, and Pennsylvania,* 1916). After further Y. M. C. A. lecturing in New York City, he drifted back to Illinois in 1908, where in the course of the winter he appeared on Y. M. C. A. programs at Springfield and during the next two years stumped the state on behalf of the Anti-Saloon League. In the spring of 1912 he attempted to repeat his Southern adventure on a walking trip to the Pacific Coast, but he found the Western ranchmen less hospitable to the claims of poetry and his journey came to a sudden end in New Mexico (Lindsay, *Adventures while Preaching the Gospel of Beauty,* 1914).

His first volume of poetry, *General William Booth Enters into Heaven and Other Poems* (1913), attracted little attention, but its successor, *The Congo and Other Poems* (1914), met with wide popular acclaim. The title-poem started a whole school of literature devoted to the negro; its striking originality of conception, its imaginative reach, and its infectious, insistent rhythms ensure its literary immortality. In it Lindsay created a new poetic music of ragtime and echolalia, a blend of speech and song, clattering but impassioned, that well expressed the hurtling energy of America. His new technique was exercised with almost equal felicity in "A Negro Sermon: Simon Legree" and "John Brown," while in the more conventional verse of "The Eagle that is Forgotten" (in honor of Altgeld) and of "Abraham Lincoln Walks at Midnight" he achieved high dignity and prophetic power. His unusual temperament, that of a revivalist preacher poetically inspired, and devoted to the political liberalism of the West, enabled him for a time to realize in his poetry a Messianic quality that responded to the hopes of the hour. The lyrical impact of his style, united with its whimsicality and colloquial phrasing, seemed to infuse a new note of aspiration into everyday existence. His remarkable chanting of his own verses was in these first years an unforgettable experience for his auditors, and he became in the popular mind a romantic modern analogue of the medieval troubadour. (Thirty phonograph records of his chantings, not made, unfortunately, until late in his career, are in the possession of the library of Barnard College.)

Unquestionably, Lindsay's influence counted greatly in the contemporary revival of American poetry. But his genius early began to show signs of exhaustion. *The Chinese Nightingale and Other Poems* (1917) was notably uneven, and *The Golden Whales of California and Other Rhymes* (1920) was, for the most part, labored and artificial. When he was invited in 1920 to recite his poems at Oxford University—the first American poet to be so honored—Lindsay's creative work was already definitely over; the season of British lionizing that followed marked the high point of his public recognition which henceforth steadily declined. Essentially intuitive, and almost totally devoid of critical ability—his prose works, *The Art of the Moving Picture*

(1915) and *The Golden Book of Springfield* (1920) show the extravagance of his generous enthusiasms—he became in his later years a formalized echo of himself. As his creative power lessened, his manner grew steadily more pompous and hieratic. Of his later volumes, *Going-to-the-Sun* (1923) is chiefly interesting because of its bizarre illustrations by the author; *Going-to-the-Stars* (1926) and *The Candle in the Cabin* (1926) are both quite negligible; while *The Litany of Washington Street* (1929), a prose collection of orations on an imaginary highway stretching from California to India, though better than the later poetry, expresses little more than a vague emotional idealism. His personal eccentricities, such as his habit of dining publicly with a number of huge dolls set up at his table, continued to attract local attention wherever he sojourned, but in the literary world at large he had already become a legend rather than a living reality long before his death. He was married on May 19, 1925, to Elizabeth Conner of Spokane, Wash., where he resided for a time, but his last days were spent in his native town of Springfield. They were ended, suddenly and unexpectedly, by heart failure on Dec. 5, 1931. There were two children, a son and a daughter.

[There are good obituaries in the *N. Y. Herald-Tribune,* Dec. 6, 1931, *Boston Evening Transcript,* Dec. 5, 1931, and the *Ill. State Register* (Springfield), Dec. 5, 6, 1931; there are interesting personal reminiscences in Stephen Graham, *Tramping with a Poet in the Rockies* (1922), and Christopher Morley, *Ex Libris Carissimis* (1932), pp. 90–98. An excellent biographical-critical sketch by Louis Untermeyer is prefixed to the selections in his anthology, *Modern American Poetry* (3rd ed., 1925). A. E. Trombly, *Vachel Lindsay, Adventurer* (1929), contains a bibliography. For various estimates see Edward Davison, *Some Modern Poets* (1928); Alfred Kreymborg, *Our Singing Strength* (1929), pp. 368–78; Edgar Lee Masters, "Vachel Lindsay," *Bookman,* Oct. 1926; "A Letter from Vachel Lindsay," *Ibid.,* Mar. 1932; H. M. Robinson, "The Ordeal of Vachel Lindsay: A Critical Reconstruction," *Ibid.,* Apr. 1932; Ludwig Lewisohn, *Expression in America* (1932), pp. 569–74; Stephen Graham, "Vachel Lindsay," *Spectator* (London), Jan. 23, 1932; Hazleton Spencer, "The Life and Death of a Bard," *Am. Mercury,* Apr. 1932.] E. S. B.

LINDSAY, VACHEL [See LINDSAY, NICHOLAS VACHEL, 1879–1931].

LINDSAY, WILLIAM (Sept. 4, 1835–Oct. 15, 1909), jurist and senator, was born near Lexington, Va., the son of Andrew and Sallie (Davidson) Lindsay, and the grandson of James Lindsay, who emigrated from Scotland and settled in Rockbridge County, Va., before 1795. He attended the common schools and the high school at Lexington and then began to study law with Judge John W. Brockenborough. In 1854 he moved to Clinton, Ky., where he continued reading law with Judge Edward Crossland while he taught school, was admitted to the bar in 1858, and began to build up a successful practice. At the outbreak of the Civil War, with a group of Kentuckians, he enlisted as a private in the Confederate service, became lieutenant of Company B, 22nd Tennessee Infantry, and, on Feb. 23, 1862, captain of the company. After the battles of Belmont and Shiloh, his company was transferred to the 3rd Kentucky Regiment, in which he was captain of Company M, but soon resigned to become assistant quartermaster of the 7th Kentucky Infantry in Preston's brigade of Breckinridge's division. Having taken part in the battles around Vicksburg, his regiment was mounted in 1864 and acted with Forrest's cavalry under Abraham Buford. After the surrender of General Taylor, he was paroled at Columbus, Miss., in May 1865 and resumed practice at Clinton, Ky., where, the year before, he had married Swann Semple, who died in 1867. The next year he married her sister, Hattie Semple.

Lindsay was a member of the Kentucky Senate from 1867 to 1870. In 1870 he was elected to the court of appeals, of which he became chief justice in 1876. He soon established a reputation as a clear and able jurist, and his opinions were widely quoted as authoritative. His opinion in *Douglass* vs. *Cline* (75 *Ky.,* 608–10) established a precedent in regard to the nature of mortgages and the extent of judicial discretion in appointing receivers. His opinion denying the right to try an extradited person for an offense not named in the extradition proceedings (*Commonwealth* vs. *Hawes,* 76 *Ky.,* 697–98), the first decision of the kind, was upheld by the United States Supreme Court and was called "very able" by Justice Samuel Freeman Miller (*U. S.* vs. *Rauscher,* 119 *U. S.,* 428). Having declined reëlection, in 1878 he retired from the bench and soon built up a lucrative practice in Frankfort. In 1883 he married as his third wife, Eleanor Holmes. He was again a member of the state Senate from 1889 to 1893; in the latter year he was chosen to fill a vacancy in the national Senate and, in 1894, to serve a full term. At Washington he was a friend and supporter of Cleveland. In 1896 he indorsed the sound-money Democrats and supported their ticket by speeches. Not seeking reëlection, he established a law firm in New York City, the firm of Lindsay, Kremer, Kalish, and Palmer. He was also a trustee of the Carnegie Institution and commissioner of the Columbian Exposition and of the Louisiana Purchase Exposition. His last years were spent in Frankfort, Ky.

[*The Biog. Encyc. of Ky.* (1878); *Biog. Cyc. of the Commonwealth of Ky.* (1896); H. Levin, *The Lawyers* and *Lawmakers of Ky.* (1897); *Rept. of the Adj.-Gen. of the State of Ky. Confederate Ky. Volunteers, War 1861–65*, vol. I (1915); *War of the Rebellion: Official Records (Army)*, ser. I, III (1881); *Who's Who in America*, 1908–09; *Green Bag*, July 1897, Sept. 1900; M. I. Lindsay, *The Lindsays of America* (1889), pp. 243–45; *The Courier-Journal* (Louisville), Oct. 16, 1909, Aug. 21, 1896.] W. C. M.

LINDSEY, WILLIAM (Aug. 12, 1858–Nov. 25, 1922), manufacturer, author, playwright, was born in Fall River, Mass., the son of William and Maria (Lovell) Lindsey. After completing his education in the public schools of Fall River, he was employed or engaged there in a number of businesses, for the most part connected with or dependent upon cotton manufacturing. In 1886 he moved to Boston and became a salesman for establishments dealing in textile products. He was to those who knew him intimately at this time a rather unusual person, for though he possessed both aptitude and enthusiasm for business, he also displayed literary tastes and ambitions not usually associated with ability in practical affairs. He accumulated a considerable and choice collection of books for a man of his means, and he tried his hand at authorship, publishing a book of poems, *The Apples of Istakhar*, in 1895, and a collection of short stories dealing with athletics, *Cinder Path Tales*, in 1896. But he did not neglect money making. In 1899 he succeeded in securing the adoption by the British government of a fabric belt for carrying ammunition, and he established factories in England, France, and Germany to supply the demand created by the outbreak of the Boer War. In 1904 he retired and returned to Boston to live on the considerable fortune thus created, which was to be increased by the World War.

His circumstances now permitted him to devote himself more completely to literature, and in 1909 he published in London and Boston *The Severed Mantle*, a romance of medieval Provence. This was followed in 1915 by *The Red Wine of Roussillon*, a blank-verse drama having Southern France in the Middle Ages for its setting. Under the title of *Seremonda*, it was performed in New York from Jan. 1 to Feb. 10, 1917, and afterward in Boston and Chicago, with Julia Arthur in the title rôle. Although the *New York Times* review of *Seremonda* dismissed the play as the work of an uninspired amateur, it probably brought him more public notice than any of his other works, despite the fact that in England there had been some spontaneous appreciation of his Provençal romance by persons sharing his enthusiasm for the place and period it depicted. His next work was a novel having the region of the Adirondacks for its setting. Called *The Backsliders*, it appeared in 1922, followed in 1923 by a posthumous volume, *The Curtain of Forgetfulness*, a sonnet sequence. In general, his literary works reflect books more than they do life.

In 1915 one of Lindsey's daughters, who was on her way to England with her husband immediately after their marriage, lost her life in the sinking of the *Lusitania*. As a memorial to her, her parents erected a chapel adjoining Emmanuel Church in Boston which has come to be recognized as a structure of architectural and artistic distinction. Lindsey either conceived or approved of practically everything in this building, showing he had a genuine instinct for refinement. He died in Boston, his wife, Annie Hawthorne Sheen, whom he had married on Dec. 16, 1884, and a son and daughter surviving him.

[See *Who's Who in America*, 1922–23; Elwood Worcester, *Life's Adventure* (1932); *Boston Transcript*, Nov. 25, 1922; *Fall River Globe*, Nov. 27, 1922. For reviews of *Seremonda*, see the *N. Y. Times*, Jan. 2, 14, 1917.] S. G.

LINDSLEY, JOHN BERRIEN (Oct. 24, 1822–Dec. 7, 1897), physician, clergyman, educator, was born at Princeton, N. J., the son of Rev. Philip Lindsley [*q.v.*], professor in the College of New Jersey, and Margaret, daughter of Nathaniel Lawrence, attorney-general of New York. He was named for his mother's grandfather, John Berrien, a Huguenot, chief justice of the province of New Jersey. Having been the pupil of his father, who had become president of the University of Nashville, he graduated from that institution in 1839, and then took two years of further work there. He studied medicine in Louisville and Philadelphia, and received the degree of M.D. at the University of Pennsylvania in 1843. Turning to theological study, he was ordained in 1846 by the Presbytery of Nashville. During the next two years he served churches near that city, and also ministered to colored people, under appointment from the Presbyterian Board of Domestic Missions. Another important part of his education was acquired in his close association with the eminent geologist Gerard Troost [*q.v.*], begun in college and continued till Troost's death in 1850.

His principal interest, medical education, developed in 1849. Having spent a winter in studying facilities for such education in other institutions, he organized, in 1850, the medical department of the University of Nashville, the first school of its kind south of the Ohio River. He was its dean for six years at the end of which time there were four hundred students, and professor of chemistry and pharmacy for twenty-three years. Becoming chancellor of the University in 1855, he brought about the merger of the collegiate department, which had been closed since 1850, with the Western Military Institute, and the adoption of a military organization. In this form the college flourished till 1861. During the Civil War he cared vigilantly for the university's interests, the medical department continuing while the college was closed. The Confederate hospitals in Nashville, one of which occupied the university buildings, were in his charge till the Federal occupation in 1862. After the war he was again dean of the medical school for four years. In 1867 he organized Montgomery Bell Academy as a preparatory school. His proposal that the college be made a school for teachers in connection with the Peabody Education Fund was realized in 1875, when the Peabody Normal College was opened, in the university buildings. He resigned his chancellorship in 1870, but taught in the medical school till 1873. In this year he took part in the organization of the Tennessee College of Pharmacy, in which later he was professor of materia medica.

His energy, public spirit, and power of leadership impelled him to activity in many social concerns. He devoted himself especially to public health, serving through four cholera epidemics in Nashville, and from 1876 to 1880 occupying the position of health officer, in which capacity he brought about important improvements in sanitation. During these years he was also secretary of the state board of health. As a member of the board of education of Nashville (1856–60) he had much to do with the establishment of a school system of high rank. In 1866 he was superintendent of schools, and at a critical time effectively defended them against political attacks. He was secretary of the state board of education from 1875 to 1887. His pamphlet, *Our Ruin: Its Cause and Cure* (1868), provoked a movement which resulted in a change of officials in Nashville in 1869. A pamphlet, *On Prison Discipline and Penal Legislation* (1874), was widely circulated. He was a member of many medical and learned societies and organizations for social progress. After he had been a minister of the Presbyterian Church in the United States of America for twenty-four years, in 1870 he joined the Cumberland Presbyterian Church, because he considered its theological spirit more liberal; subsequently he made important contributions to the history of this denomination. His writings were chiefly articles, pamphlets, and reports. For many years he collected materials for a history of his state, and in 1886 published *The Military Annals of Tennessee, Confederate, Series I*. He was married, Feb. 9, 1857, to Sarah, daughter of Jacob McGavock of Nashville, and grand-daughter of Felix Grundy [*q.v.*]; they had six children. His death occurred in Nashville.

[J. M. Lindly, *The Hist. of the Lindley-Lindsley-Linsley Families in America*, vol. II (1924); *Ann. Report of Am. Hist. Asso. for the Year 1889* and *1892*, for bibliog. of Lindsley's publications; W. W. Clayton, *Hist. of Davidson County, Tenn.* (1880); I. A. Watson, *Physicians and Surgeons of America* (1896); records of Univ. of Nashville; *Minutes Gen. Assembly Presbyt. Ch. U. S. A., passim*; *Nashville American*, Dec. 8, 1897; information from a daughter, Louise L. Lindsley.] R. H. N.

LINDSLEY, PHILIP (Dec. 21, 1786–May 25, 1855), educator, Presbyterian clergyman, was a descendant of Francis Linley, who was in New Haven, Conn., as early as 1645, and settled in New Jersey in 1666. The Lindsleys (the name was variously spelled) were important supporters of the American cause during the Revolution and were strongly attached to Presbyterianism. Philip was born near Morristown, N. J., the son of Isaac and Phebe (Condict) Lindsley. At thirteen he entered the school of Robert Finley [*q.v.*] at Basking Ridge and in 1802 was admitted to the junior class of the College of New Jersey, from which he graduated in 1804. After teaching in Morristown and in Finley's school, he returned to the college in 1807 as tutor and to study theology under President Samuel Stanhope Smith [*q.v.*], who deeply influenced him. On Apr. 24, 1810, he was licensed to preach by the Presbytery of New Brunswick. During the next two years he preached for a time at Newton, Long Island, and later continued his theological studies under Rev. Matthew La Rue Perrine. Appointed senior tutor at Princeton in 1812, the next year he became professor of languages, and later also librarian. In June of 1817 he was ordained by the Presbytery of New Brunswick, and that year became vice-president of the College. After a year's service as acting president, in 1823, he declined an election to the presidency. During his Princeton teaching he declined also the presidencies of Transylvania University in Kentucky, Ohio University, and Cumberland College at Nashville. In 1824, however, he yielded to the importunities of Cumberland College, which had just been chartered as the University of Nashville.

He gave up a secure place in the East to take charge of a struggling school in Tennessee, because he saw the possibilities of the Southwest, and its educational needs appealed to him. "Throughout the immense valley of the lower Mississippi, containing at least a million of inhabitants," he wrote in a circular letter to his friends, "there exists not a single college"

(*Works,* III, 25). At his ceremonious inauguration in January 1825, he already held the largest conceptions for the future. "Provision should be made," he said, "for instruction in all the sciences and in every department of philosophy and literature" (*An Address, Delivered . . . at the Inauguration of the President of Cumberland College,* 1825, p. 34), and he soon announced a splendid scheme of buildings. His hope of aid from the state government was short-lived, and since he planned an institution which should be positively religious, but not denominational, he could not seek church support; private gifts were disappointing; yet after twelve years he proclaimed undiminished ambitions for the University. Neither impossibly magnificent ideals nor difficulties, however, kept him from working effectively toward what was practicable, an undergraduate college. To the building up of this he devoted himself steadfastly for a quarter of a century, refusing six academic presidencies and the provostship of the University of Pennsylvania. He gathered an able faculty and a growing body of students, and brought into being a strong and useful institution, the foundation of the educational eminence of Nashville.

Meanwhile he was a powerful educational missionary. His baccalaureate addresses were widely circulated in the state. In these and other speeches and in many newspaper articles he preached the value of education, particularly higher education, and the need of colleges and schools. His effect on public opinion appeared in the fact that by 1848 there were twenty colleges in Tennessee. He was a man of wide reading—in history, literature, contemporary politics, theology, church affairs, and social reform. Though he had not been active in ecclesiastical matters, his work in education brought him in 1834 the moderatorship of the Presbyterian General Assembly. In 1850 he resigned his office as president to become professor in New Albany Theological Seminary at New Albany, Ind. There he spent his last five years, resigning his professorship in 1853. He died at Nashville, whither he had gone to attend the General Assembly. He was married in October 1813 to Margaret Elizabeth, daughter of Nathaniel Lawrence, attorney-general of New York; and on Apr. 19, 1849, to Mrs. Mary Ann (Silliman) Ayers, a niece of Benjamin Silliman [*q.v.*]. One of his sons, John Berrien Lindsley [*q.v.*], was also head of the University of Nashville. Lindsley's publications were chiefly addresses on educational subjects and sermons; his complete *Works* in three volumes, edited by L. J. Halsey, were issued in 1866.

[L. J. Halsey, introduction and supplementary biographical sketch in *Works of Philip Lindsley* (1866); J. M. Lindly, *The Hist. of the Lindley-Lindsley-Linsley Families in America,* vol. I (1930); *Gen. Cat. of the Coll. of N. J., 1746–1896* (1896); John MacLean, *Hist. of the Coll. of N. J.* (1877), vol. II; W. B. Sprague, *Annals Am. Pulpit,* vol. IV (1859); *Am. Jour. of Educ.,* Sept. 1859; W. W. Clayton, *Hist. of Davidson County, Tenn.* (1880); *Nashville Union and American,* May 26, 1855.]

R. H. N.

LINING, JOHN (1708–Sept. 21, 1760), physician, pioneer physiologist, experimenter in electricity, came to Charles-Town in the Province of South Carolina when he was twenty-two years old. He brought with him from Scotland an excellent training in medicine and a scientific zeal that only intensive research could satisfy. His attention was first directed to those epidemic diseases, "which," he wrote, "as regularly return at their stated Seasons, as a good Clock strikes Twelve when the Sun is in the Meridian" (*Philosophical Transactions of the Royal Society of London,* vol. XLII, 1743, p. 492). He had many occasions to treat yellow fever, particularly during the epidemics of 1732 and 1748. During the latter year, especially, he made a thorough study of this disease, and sent to Europe the earliest account, from America, of its symptoms and pathology. This description was in the form of a letter to Dr. Robert Whytt, professor of medicine at the University of Edinburgh. It was published in an Edinburgh medical journal in 1753 and reprinted many years later both separately and as a supplement to Colin Chisolm's *An Essay on the Malignant Pestilential Fever* (1799).

The warm weather of South Carolina, contrasted with the rugged climate of the Scotland of his boyhood, particularly impressed the young physician and led him to study the effects of climatic conditions upon his own metabolism. This celebrated experiment, which extended over one year, was reported in the *Philosophical Transactions of the Royal Society of London* (vols. XLII and XLIII) in 1743 and 1745. Each day he noted the temperature, using Fahrenheit's newly devised thermometer, and recorded the humidity, the extent of cloudiness, the amount of rainfall, and the force of the wind. These observations were the first published records of the weather in America. At the same time he recorded his weight both morning and night, his pulse rate, the daily intake of food and water, and the weight of his excretions. This experiment yielded important data on the variations in the amount of the so-called insensible perspiration under different conditions of temperature and extended the observations made by the illustrious Sanctorius many years before. While Lining's results are now mainly of historical interest, the plan of his experiment and the faithful performing of the tedious measurements still arouse admiration.

Lining extended his meteorological observations over several years, and his accounts of Charleston weather were published in communications to the secretary of the Royal Society in 1754 (*Philosophical Transactions,* vol. XLVIII, pt. 1). He corresponded with Benjamin Franklin and upon one occasion asked the Philadelphia sage how he had arrived at the "out-of-the-way notion" of the identity of lightning and electricity. Franklin answered with a detailed account of the reasons that had led him to perform his famous kite experiment. Lining repeated Franklin's experiment, and he, too, soon gained a not inconsiderable renown as an investigator of electricity. A London inquirer sought information from him about the possible danger to the observer in conducting such investigations. His reply, published in the *Philosophical Transactions of the Royal Society* (vol. XLVIII, pt. 2) in 1755, in which he emphasized the necessity of proper grounding and insulation of the apparatus, was very practical and quite indicative of his skill. He died in 1760. In 1739, according to data obtained by Dr. Robert Wilson, he had married Sarah Hill of Hillsboro, N. C., but left no children. Contemporary writers referred to him as "the celebrated Dr. Lining" or "the ingenious Dr. Lining." Today he holds a secure position in the history of science as a distinguished member of that group of intellectual Americans who played a leading part in the early development of science and medicine in this country.

[David Ramsay, *The Hist. of S. C.,* vol. II (1808); F. C. Bing, "John Lining, an Early American Scientist," in *Scientific Monthly,* Mar. 1928; Robert Wilson, in H. A. Kelly and W. L. Burrage, *Am. Medic. Biogs.* (1920); letter from Benjamin Franklin to John Lining in Jared Sparks, *The Works of Benjamin Franklin,* V (1837), 347–55.] F. C. B.

LINN, JOHN BLAIR (Mar. 14, 1777–Aug. 30, 1804), poet, clergyman, was born in Shippensburg, Pa., of an ancestry distinguished for learning and piety. His grandfather and great-grandfather emigrated from the north of Ireland to Chester County, Pa., in 1732. His father, William Linn, was an eminent Presbyterian clergyman, and his mother, Rebecca, was the daughter of the Rev. John Blair, whose brother and son were likewise clergymen. When John was nine years old, the family removed to New York City, and in 1795 he graduated from Columbia College. While still an undergraduate, he wrote both verse and prose, some of which he collected and published in two volumes: *Miscellaneous Works, Prose and Poetical; By a Young Gentleman of New-York* (1795) and *The Poetical Wanderer* (1796). After his graduation, he began the study of law under the direction of Alexander Hamilton, who was a friend of his father, and who had recently resigned as Secretary of the Treasury and resumed his legal practice in New York. While he was a law student he wrote at least two plays, neither of which is extant. One of these, *Bourville Castle, or the Gallic Orphan,* was first presented at the John Street Theatre, New York, Jan. 16, 1797. Charles Brockden Brown and William Dunlap [*qq.v.*] "corrected the manuscript and wrote out the parts for the performers" (William Dunlap, *post,* p. 157). "Its success," says Brown, "was such as had been sufficient to have fixed the literary destiny of some minds" (*Valerian, post,* p. viii).

Linn, however, soon abandoned both the writing of plays and the study of law to prepare himself for the ministry. He studied theology in Schenectady under the Rev. Dirick Romeyn and while there wrote prose and verse for Schenectady newspapers. He received a license to preach from the classis of Albany in 1798, and soon afterwards accepted a call from the First Presbyterian Church of Philadelphia. In 1799 he married Hester Bailey, daughter of Col. John Bailey, of Poughkeepsie, N. Y. Of the three sons that were born to them the two youngest survived their father. In Philadelphia, despite ill health and heavy parochial duties, he wrote much and planned much that he was unable to write. His first volume after he entered the ministry was *The Death of George Washington: a Poem in Imitation of the Manner of Ossian* (1800). Next appeared *The Powers of Genius* (1801, 1802; London, 1804), a long poem reminiscent of Shenstone and Akenside. In 1802 came *A Discourse Occasioned by the Death of the Reverend Jong Ewing.* In the summer of 1802 Linn was overcome by the heat, and during the two remaining years of his life he never recovered his health. In 1803, however, he published in Philadelphia two letters written in reply to Unitarian tracts by Dr. Joseph Priestley. At the time of his death he was writing a narrative poem which was published in imperfect form in 1805 under the title *Valerian, a Narrative Poem, Intended, in Part, to Describe the Early Persecutions of Christians, and Rapidly to Illustrate the Influence of Christianity on the Manners of Nations.*

Charles Brockden Brown, who in 1804 married Linn's sister, Elizabeth, and who wrote for *Valerian* a biographical sketch of the author, praised his ability as a preacher: "It is well known, that few persons in America, though assisted by age and experience, have ever attained so great a popularity as he acquired before his twenty-third year." Brown's less laudatory judgment of his poetry is indubitably correct: "All his performances . . . candour compels us to consider as preludes to future exertions, and indications of future excellence" (*Valerian,* p. xxi).

[William Dunlap, *A Hist. of the Am. Theatre* (1832); B. F. French, *Biographia Americana* (1825); W. B. Sprague, *Annals Am. Pulpit,* vol. IV (1858); Henry Simpson, *The Lives of Eminent Philadelphians Now Deceased* (1859); Linn's manuscript letters in the collection of the Hist. Soc. of Pa.; *Poulson's Am. Daily Advertiser,* Sept. 1, 1804.] N. E. M.

LINN, LEWIS FIELDS (Nov. 5, 1795–Oct. 3, 1843), physician, senator, was born near Louisville, the grandson of Col. William Linn, a Kentucky pioneer and one of the favorite officers of George Rogers Clark; the son of Asahel Linn and Nancy Ann Hunter, who was the widow of Israel Dodge and the mother of Henry Dodge [*q.v.*]. Left an orphan at the age of twelve and equipped only with the meager educational advantages of the frontier, he decided to study medicine. Despite interruptions caused by ill health and by participation in the War of 1812 as the "surgeon" attached to Dodge's troops, Linn completed his professional training at Philadelphia in 1816. Removing to Sainte Genevieve, Mo., he commenced immediately the arduous life of a frontier physician; he loved his profession and soon had an extensive practice in southeastern Missouri. He was an authority on Asiatic cholera and rendered inestimable professional services in combating that desolating scourge through two epidemics. A man of fine presence and bearing, with a personal charm and professional skill that won for him many devoted friends, Linn was urged frequently to run for Congress. Although interested in public affairs and in the Democratic party, he refused to abandon his professional obligations except for one term during the late twenties in the state Senate. In 1833 he became a commissioner to settle French land claims, and, upon the death of Alexander Buckner, Governor Dunklin appointed him to the United States Senate, many Whigs urging his selection as the most preferable Democrat. He entered the Senate as an ardent admirer of Jackson, "the hero of his heart's warmest admiration."

Linn's ten years of service, 1833–43, fall naturally into two divisions. During the first few sessions he was primarily a representative of his section, pressing with marked success numerous private claims of his constituents, keeping in active touch with an incredible number of them, instituting public surveys of the iron and lead resources, and assisting the infant glass industry of Missouri. He rarely addressed the Senate, but his invariable friendliness toward his colleagues and his moderation of speech and action, in a day of intense partisanship, brought him the almost universal esteem of his associates. "He had political opponents in the Senate, but not one enemy" (*Congressional Globe,* 28 Cong., 1 Sess., p. 29). He had none of the arrogance and pomposity of his colleague, Benton; they were a strangely mated but effective pair. Linn was a strong political and personal supporter of the measures of the second Jackson administration and an able exponent of the self-conscious Jacksonian Democracy (*Letter to Constituents,* 1840). He maintained his position in Missouri, being easily reëlected in 1837 and in 1843, with practically no opposition from the Whigs. During Van Buren's administration Linn became a leader in the revival at Washington of interest in Oregon. Benton long had been a vehement advocate of extension to the Pacific; Linn shared his views, indorsed by the economic interests of Missouri, that the Oregon territory must be "saved" from the English (Benton, *post,* II, pp. 468ff.).

Following the Slacum report of December 1837, Linn, chairman of the committee on territories, began persistently to press the issue. He introduced in 1838 a bill to "reoccupy" the territory and to establish a government with military protection. For five years he continued to urge upon an indifferent Senate the protection of American interests there, and in every session of several congresses he sponsored without success legislation providing for the occupation and settlement of Oregon, against the "daring designs of England." In the early forties, two powerful economic factors, free land and the lure of trade, forced new interest. Following a prolonged and spirited debate Linn's Oregon Bill, with its governmental, military defense, and liberal land-grant policies, passed the Senate on Feb. 28, 1843, by a vote of twenty-four to twenty-two (*Congressional Globe,* 27 Cong., 3 Sess., App., *passim*). His effort on this occasion was the final act of his public life as he died suddenly in Missouri in October 1843. His wife, Elizabeth A. Relfe, whom he married in 1818, survived him. He was a representative product of the new West, a sincere exponent of Manifest Destiny, and a devoted friend of the adventurous and aggressive frontier.

[The *Cong. Globe,* 25 Cong., 2 and 3 Sess., 26 Cong., 1 Sess., 27 Cong., 3 Sess., and *Senate Executive Doc.* 470, 25 Cong., 2 Sess., are valuable. E. Linn and N. Sargent, *Life and Pub. Services of Dr. Lewis F. Linn*

(1857) is useful, but laudatory and uncritical. J. M. Greenwood, *Lewis Fields Linn* (1900), and W. F. Switzler, *The Father of Ore.* (1899), contain much information. The Oregon issue is treated in T. H. Benton, *Thirty Years' View* (2 vols., 1854–56), in W. I. Marshall, *Acquisition of Ore.* (2 vols., 1911), and in Cardinal Goodwin, *The Trans-Mississippi West* (1922). The *St. Louis New Era*, Oct. 11, 12, 1843, reflects significant contemporary opinion, and J. H. Linn, *A Funeral Discourse on the Life and Character of the Hon. Lewis Field* [sic] *Linn* (1844), gives a good account of Linn's charitable work in connection with his medical activities.]
T. S. B.

LINN, WILLIAM ALEXANDER (Sept. 4, 1846–Feb. 23, 1917), newspaper editor, author, son of Dr. Alexander and Julia (Vibbert) Linn, was born at Deckertown, now Sussex, N. J. After preparatory schooling at Deckertown and Andover, Mass., he entered Yale College, where he became an editor of the *Yale Literary Magazine* and graduated in 1868 as class poet. He next joined the staff of Horace Greeley as a reporter and served the *New York Tribune* for three years, then became city editor of the *Evening Post* of William Cullen Bryant in 1871. From July 1872 to May 1873 he edited the *Morning Whig,* Troy, N. Y., but it was not successful financially and he returned to the *Evening Post.* He was made news editor in 1883, after the accession to the editorship of Edwin Lawrence Godkin [*q.v.*], and managing editor in 1891. His worth as a first-rate news editor and as a journalist of the highest professional standards became speedily apparent. The *Evening Post* of this period never sought popular favor, but because of the brilliancy of the editorial page of Godkin and the complete reliability and trustworthiness of the news columns under Linn, was considered almost unique in the journalism of that time.

Eager as he was for news promptness, Linn never permitted his news sense to interfere with the kindliness and consideration which should be foremost in the calendar of a journalist who is also a gentleman. Nevertheless, he shared to the full Godkin's capacity for wrath at injustice. "Fiery in rebuke and cutting in contempt," as the *Evening Post* described him at the time of his death (Feb. 24, 1917, p. 7), he was also tender-hearted, thoroughly just, of an impeccable intellectual honesty, and possessed of unusual executive power. As a master of the details of his profession he was unexcelled. His highest journalistic achievement was his refusal after the election of 1884 to accept the returns from New York State disseminated by the Associated Press, with their insistence that Blaine was elected. The returns extended over several days because of the difficulty of getting news from remote counties. In the *Evening Post's* first issue the day after the election, Linn insisted that Cleveland had "probably" won and set himself to the task of obtaining from every disputed county a separate, trustworthy report. The result was that the *Evening Post* announced on the second day: "Cleveland President—New York Gives Him Her Vote," although the Associated Press (not to be confused with the existing organization of that name) still insisted on the third day that Blaine had carried New York by 1,000 votes.

After retiring from the *Evening Post* in 1900, because of ill-health, Linn gave considerable time to independent writing. His most ambitious literary work, *The Story of the Mormons* (1902), a volume of 637 pages, was the first to make use of the extensive Helen Gould collection of materials on the Mormon Church. It was admittedly the most authoritative treatment until recent years. A biography, *Horace Greeley* (1903), was less successful. *Rob and His Gun* (1902), four valuable historical monographs published in the *Papers and Proceedings of the Bergen County Historical Society* (1905, 1908, 1915, 1917), and numerous articles on the building-and-loan movement are among the products of his pen. For many years he was a resident of Hackensack, N. J., where he was a founder of the Johnson Public Library, the Historical Society, the Hackensack Mutual Building and Loan Association (a pioneer enterprise over which he presided thirty years with remarkable efficiency and success), and the Peoples National Bank, of which he was president for a dozen years. He was county collector (1915–17), and a member of the Palisades Park Commission, which created the New York and New Jersey Interstate Park. On Jan. 31, 1871, he married Margaret A. Martin, who died in 1897. They had no children.

[*The Evening Post Hundredth Anniversary, Nov. 16, 1801–1901* (1902); Allan Nevins, *The Evening Post: A Century of Journalism* (1922); *Papers and Proc. Bergen County Hist. Soc., 1916–17,* no. 12 (1917); *Who's Who in America,* 1916–17; H. P. Wright, *Hist. of the Class of 1868, Yale Coll.* (1914); *Obit. Record Grads. Yale Univ.,* 1917; *Evening Post* (N. Y.), Feb. 24, 1917.]
O. G. V.

LINTNER, JOSEPH ALBERT (Feb. 8, 1822–May 5, 1898), entomologist, was born in Schoharie, N. Y., the son of Rev. George Ames Lintner and his wife, Maria Wagner. He graduated from Schoharie Academy in 1837, then entered business in New York City, continuing his studies in the Mercantile Library and contributing occasional scientific articles to the *New York Tribune.* In 1848 he returned to Schoharie, where he remained in business until 1860, when he moved to Utica and was there for some years as a manufacturer of woolens. During this business career he continued his scientific studies. He began collecting insects in 1853, and published his first article in 1862. In 1856 he married Frances C. Hutchinson of Utica. In 1868 he abandoned his business to become assistant in zoölogy in the State Museum. He was placed in charge of the entomological department in 1874 and in 1880 was appointed state entomologist. For the last thirty-six years of his life he was occupied almost solely in work with insects. He published over nine hundred separate articles, and, in addition to these, thirteen annual reports and four numbers of a pamphlet entitled *Entomological Contributions* (1872–79). He wrote extensively for the agricultural press, especially for the *Country Gentleman,* and for twenty-five years was the entomological editor of this journal. His articles were always of a practical character. His annual reports were prepared with extreme care and were models of their kind. His style was simple, dignified and concise, and his treatment of his topics was extremely thorough. The regents of the University of the State of New York awarded him the degree of Ph.D. He was president of the Association of Economic Entomologists in 1892, and was a member of many American scientific societies. His chief claim to distinction rests in his thirteen annual reports, which are worthy successors to the reports of his predecessor, Asa Fitch [*q.v.*]. He died in Rome, Italy.

[*N. Y. State Museum Bulletin,* May 1899; *Entomological News,* June 1898, with portrait; *N. Y. Tribune,* May 7, 1898.] L. O. H.

LINTON, WILLIAM JAMES (Dec. 7, 1812–Dec. 29, 1897), wood-engraver, political reformer, poet, and printer, was born in London, the grandson of an Aberdeen ship-carpenter who had settled in London as a builder. From him, says Linton, "I perhaps inherited some tendency to radicalism" (*Memories,* 1895, p. 16). He was educated under Dr. Burford at Stratford, was apprenticed in 1828 to George Wilmot Bonner, wood-engraver, and later worked for John Orrin Smith, whose partner he became in 1842. About this time he did much engraving for the *Illustrated London News.* Meanwhile he espoused the cause of personal liberty, going into the Chartist movement, and, says Richard Garnett, "beyond it in professing himself a republican" (*post*). In close contact with Henry Hetherington, he edited the *Odd Fellow* (April 1841–August 1842), opposed the "laws then gagging the press," became deeply interested in the plans of Mazzini, was the friend of Italian and Polish reformers, and was concerned in the publication of the *National* (1839), the *Leader* (1850), the *English Republic* (1851–55) and the *Northern Tribune* (1854). He engaged also in purely literary activities, was intimate with the group of R. H. Horne, succeeded Douglas Jerrold as editor of the *Illuminated Magazine* (1845), and wrote a *Life of Paine* (1839), *To the Future* (1848), *The Plaint of Freedom* (1852), and *Claribel and Other Poems* (1865). In addition, he established his reputation as a wood-engraver, doing notable work for the Moxon Tennyson (1857) and Milton's *L'Allegro* (1859). He married, about 1836, a sister of Thomas Wade, the poet; after her death, another sister (d. 1855); and in 1858, Eliza Lynn, the novelist. The last marriage was ended by amicable separation. "In 1866," he wrote, "I had little occupation in England. . . . So in November of that year I crossed the ocean to New York" (*Memories,* pp. 204, 205).

Here he taught wood-engraving at the Cooper Union (1868–70) and worked for Frank Leslie's *Illustrated News.* Among American books illustrated with his engravings, many after his own designs, were Whittier's *Snow-Bound* (1868); J. G. Holland's *Katrina* (1869); Longfellow's *Building of the Ship* (1870), and *Edwin Booth in Twelve Dramatic Characters* (1872), both from drawings by W. J. Hennessy; W. C. Bryant's *Thanatopsis* (1878) and *The Flood of Years* (1878). The last-named included his "most ambitious pieces of imaginative work" (Parkes, "Wood-Engravings," *post,* p. 178), and occasioned his own poetical *Interpretations* of the designs, printed by him in three copies. He also contributed to other books and to *Scribner's* and *The Century.* He became an academician of the National Academy of Design in 1882 and received an honorary A.M. degree from Yale in 1891. His engravings have distinction, and show that firmness and honesty which he himself called "the first qualification of an engraver." He was an adherent of the "white line," and believed that the engraver should draw with the graver and be an interpreting artist. About 1877 there arose the "new school" of American wood-engravers, finding first vigorous expression in the blocks by Frederick Juengling [*q.v.*] after James E. Kelly. The work of this school showed some vagaries, especially a sometimes slavish devotion to the rendering of details in texture. Linton's warning against a tendency to give substance rather than spirit was denounced. Thereupon he wrote *Some Practical Hints on Wood-Engraving for the Instruction of Reviewers and the Public* (1879) and *The History of Wood-Engraving in America* (1882). In the latter indispensable reference book, commenting critically on the "new school," he ends: "Notwithstanding all my censures, the revival of wood-engraving is in their hands. They will outgrow their mistakes." In 1884 he also published *Wood-Engraving: A Manual of Instruction.*

Linton removed, probably in the early seventies, to Hamden, near New Haven, Conn., established the Appledore Press, and from 1878 on issued books, pamphlets, and leaflets in limited editions. The two most noteworthy were *The Golden Apples of Hesperus: Poems not in the Collections* (1882)—"the whole of it, drawing, engraving, composition, and printing the work of my own hands"—and *Masters of Wood-Engraving.* The latter was printed, in three copies, to serve as a model for the London publication of 1889. Other products of this press were *Translations* (1881); *Rare Poems of the Sixteenth and Seventeenth Centuries* (5 copies, 1882), later issued in trade editions in Boston and London; *In Dispraise of a Woman—Catullus with Variations* (1886), and *Love Lore* (1887), a collection of his own poems. He also edited *The Poetry of America, 1776–1876* (London, 1878) and, with R. H. Stoddard, *English Verse* (1883, 5 vols.), and wrote *The Flower and the Star* (1868), with illustrations drawn and engraved by himself; *Poems and Translations* (London, 1889); *European Republicans* (1892); *The Life of John Greenleaf Whittier* (London, 1893); and *Memories* (1895), first issued as *Threescore and Ten Years* (1894). His last publication was *Darwin's Probabilities: A Review of his Descent of Man* (1896). He was aggressively vigorous in asserting his beliefs, "amiable and helpful, full of kind actions and generous enthusiasms" (Garnett, *post*); "obstinate and affectionate, and intolerant of interference" (Parkes, *op. cit.*, p. 176). He died in New Haven, at the house of Thomas W. Mather, who had married his daughter Margaret in February 1875.

[Examples of Linton's work are in the British Museum, the Victoria and Albert Museum, the New York Public Library, and Yale University; the large collection in the last-named institution includes books by Linton, letters, manuscripts, and drawings. An idea of his enormous production in wood-engraving is given in Kineton Parkes, "The Wood-Engravings of W. J. Linton," in *Bookman's Jour. and Print Collector,* July 8, 1921, and his work on wood, as well as his relations to the "new school" of American wood-engravers, is discussed by S. R. Koehler, in *Vervielfältigende Kunst der Gegenwart,* vol. I (Vienna, 1887) and in Frank Weitenkampf, *American Graphic Art* (1924); the Appledore publications are described by Howard Mansfield, from copies in his own possession, in the *Gazette of the Grolier Club,* no. 2, November 1921, by A. H. Bullen in *The Library,* February 1889, and by Kineton Parkes in *Bookman's Jour.,* Aug. 12, 1921; his place at Hamden is minutely described by Linton himself in "An Artist's Habitat," in *Lippincott's Monthly Mag.,* May 1895; see also his *Memories*; G. S. Layard, *Mrs. Lynn Linton, Her Life, Letters, and Opinions* (1901); sketch by Richard Garnett in Supplement (1901) to *Dict. Nat. Biog.*; *Report . . . of the Century Asso. for the Year 1897* (1898); *N. Y. Times, Evening Post* (N. Y.), Dec. 30, 1897.]

F. W.

LIPPARD, GEORGE (Apr. 10, 1822–Feb. 9, 1854), novelist, founder of the Brotherhood of the Union, the son of Daniel B. Lippard, once county treasurer of Philadelphia, and of Jemima Ford, was born on his father's farm in West Nantmeal township, Chester County, Pa. When he was two years old his parents removed to Philadelphia, where his father opened a grocery and later became a constable. George was sent to a public school, where he developed so rapidly that at fourteen he attracted the attention of members of his church and was sent to the Classical Academy, Rhinebeck, N. Y., to prepare for college, and eventually for the ministry of the Methodist Church. It is said (Elliott, *post,* p. 14) that "in disgust at the contradiction between theory and practice" of Christianity which he observed, he left his studies, determined to renounce the sacred calling. He then spent four years reading law, but abandoned that profession also, as not according with his ideas of human justice. Toward the close of the year 1841 he was given a place on the staff of the *Spirit of the Times,* an energetic, even sensational, Democratic daily then published in Philadelphia. He began his journalistic career by reporting police-court hearings in an original, sympathetic, and humorous way which attracted readers and resulted in an increase in the circulation of the paper. He then wrote for its columns a series of sketches under the general title, "Our Talisman," which in character were not unlike some of the "Sketches by Boz." When Dickens visited Philadelphia in 1842, Lippard wrote an impression of the historic "levee" held in the novelist's honor. Soon afterward, he produced a series called "Bread Crust Papers," in which Henry B. Hirst [*q.v.*] was satirized as "Henry Bread Crust" and Thomas Dunn English [*q.v.*], as "Thomas Done Brown," a title Poe later saw fit to revive.

Lippard worked so industriously that his health began to fail, and he retired from journalism determined to become an author. For his first story, "Philippe de Agramont," which appeared in the *Saturday Evening Post,* July 9, 1842, the young author received fifteen dollars. A more lengthy romance, "Herbert Tracy; or, the Legend of the Black Rangers," was begun in the same weekly, Oct. 22, 1842. At the beginning of 1843, Lippard became connected with *The Citizen Soldier,* a new weekly, to which he contributed "The

Battle Day of Germantown," "The Ladye Annabel," and "Adrian, the Neophyte," all immediately republished in pamphlet form. Early in 1844 he began *The Monks of Monk Hall,* published in ten semi-monthly parts. This story, subsequently called *The Quaker City,* was an exposé of vice in Philadelphia, and upon being reprinted with additions (1845) had an enormous sale throughout the United States, was reprinted in England, and translated into German. Lippard dramatized it, and in December 1844 it was announced for representation in the Chestnut Street Theatre, Philadelphia, but was withdrawn by order of the mayor, who feared a mob would destroy the playhouse. The play, much altered for the worse, was performed at the Chatham Theatre, New York, in January 1845. Lippard wrote another play, *Coro, the Priest Robber,* which was not printed; but the story appears in the posthumous volume, *Legends of Florence* (1864).

In 1844 he began his career as a lecturer, his subjects being what he termed "legends" of the Revolution. During one of these lectures he defended *The Quaker City* against the charge of immorality. By this time it had reached a sale of 4,000 copies, and the author's popularity was very great. He was engaged by the *Saturday Courier* of Philadelphia to contribute to its pages a series of "Legends of the Revolution," and before the series was completed that weekly's circulation had increased from 30,000 to 70,000 copies. The "Legends" were copied by newspapers all over the United States. His lectures, usually upon Revolutionary characters and incidents, became so popular that he was invited to speak in many parts of the country, and became as widely known for his platform appearances as for his romances.

Meantime, books were coming from his pen in rapid succession: in 1846 he published *The Nazarene* and *Blanche of Brandywine*; in 1847, *Legends of Mexico* and *Washington and His Generals: or, Legends of the Revolution*; in 1848, *Paul Ardenheim* and *Bel of Prairie Eden.* During this year he contributed articles to *The Nineteenth Century,* a quarterly. In 1849 he published a weekly, *The Quaker City,* which contained few contributions that he did not write. In 1850 appeared *Washington and His Men—Second Series of Legends of the Revolution*; and in 1851, *Adonai, the Pilgrim of Eternity* and one number only of *The White Banner,* launched as a quarterly, which he wrote entirely himself. These were followed by *Mysteries of the Pulpit* (1852), *The Man with the Mask* (1852), *The Empire City* (1853); *New York: Its Upper-Ten and Lower Million* (1854); and *Eleanor; or, Slave Catching in Philadelphia* (1854). For several years before his death he was a regular contributor to the *Sunday Mercury* and *Scott's Weekly* of Philadelphia, in which some of his later romances and essays originally appeared.

Disgusted with all conventions of his time, Lippard originated a philosophy and a religion of his own. On May 14, 1847, he married Rose Newman by the simple ceremony of taking her hand, the event occurring upon a high rock (Mom Rinker's Rock) of the romantic Wissahickon. In 1850 he organized the Brotherhood of the Union, of which he constituted himself the "Supreme Washington," or head. This organization was an effort to carry into effect his idea of a brotherhood of man, and at the time of his death there were circles, or lodges, of the order in twenty-three states. He was an enemy of capital and, in his own undisciplined manner, had developed a Marxian theory while Karl Marx was still an unknown schoolboy. As a novelist he was ignored by the recognized American critics. He wrote hurriedly and almost constantly, and declared he appealed to the worker and not to the literary man. There are many poetical passages in his novels, however, and he really became the poet of the proletariat. After the death of his wife in 1851 he traveled a great deal in the interest of the Brotherhood of the Union, and lived for a while in Cleveland. In 1853 he returned to Philadelphia, where he died of consumption the following year. His grave in Odd Fellows Cemetery there is marked by a symbolic monument of granite, erected in 1886 by the Brotherhood he founded, now known as the Brotherhood of America.

[Lippard's autobiography appeared in the *Saturday Courier,* Jan. 15, 1848; a sketch and critique by C. C. Burr is prefixed to *Washington and His Generals* (1847), and a sketch by J. B. Elliott to the reprint (1894) of Lippard's lecture, *Thomas Paine: Author-Soldier of the Revolution.* See also E. W. C. Greene, in *Sunday Mercury* (Phila.), Feb. 12, 1854; *The Life and Choice Writings of George Lippard* (1855); E. P. Oberholtzer, *The Lit. Hist. of Phila.* (1906); *Daily News* (Phila.), Feb. 10, 1854; *Official Souvenir Fiftieth Annual Session Supreme Council, Brotherhood of the Union* (Phila., 1900); *The Brotherhood,* Dec. 1900. Further material for a biography and bibliography of Lippard has been gathered by the author of this sketch, who contributed "A Bibliography of the Works of George Lippard" to the *Pa. Mag. of Hist. and Biog.,* Apr.–Oct. 1930.] J. J.

LIPPINCOTT, JAMES STARR (Apr. 12, 1819–Mar. 17, 1885), horticulturist and meteorologist, was born in Philadelphia, Pa. He was the son of John and Sarah West (Starr) Lippincott, and a lineal descendant of Richard Lippincott, who had emigrated from Devonshire, England, and about 1665 moved from New England to Shrewsbury, N. J. James attended Haverford

College, Haverford, Pa., in 1834–35. He began his career as a teacher, but later changed to farming, first establishing himself at Cole's Landing near Haddonfield, N. J. Soon, however, he became interested in the science rather than the practice of farming and in 1868 removed to Haddonfield where he continued to study and write on agricultural subjects. While living on the farm, he invented a "vapor index" for measuring the humidity of the air. He kept meteorological instruments outside of his Haddonfield house, and took accurate records of the weather and climate. He tabulated and reduced observations made by Benjamin Sheppard near Greenwich, Cumberland County, N. J., from March 1856 to June 1861, for the Smithsonian Institution, and was its observer at Cole's Landing from 1864 to 1866, and from 1869 to 1870 at Haddonfield. He visited Europe twice, once, in 1850, as a delegate to the World's Peace Congress in Frankfort, Germany. On these trips he made extensive observations which he recorded in letters to his friends and to the press.

His literary activities were directed to the collection of a large and select library, containing rare books on a wide variety of subjects, and to writing on genealogical, biographical, and agricultural matters. He did much work on Lippincott's *Universal Pronouncing Dictionary of Biography and Mythology* (1870) and wrote a series of papers which were published in the *Reports of the Commissioners of Agriculture:* "Climatology of American Grape Vines," 1862; "Geography of Plants," 1863; "Market Products of West New Jersey," 1865; "Observations on Atmospheric Humidity," 1865; "The Fruit Regions of the Northern United States and Their Local Climates," 1866. He contributed various shorter articles to *The Gardener's Monthly and Historical Advertiser,* later, *the Gardener's Monthly and Horticulturist,* and other agricultural periodicals. He was much interested in the Society of Friends, of which he was a member, and he prepared an index to forty volumes of their journal, *The Friend.* He compiled also a catalogue of the books belonging to the library of the four Monthly Meetings of Friends of Philadelphia (1853). At the time of his death he had collected a great deal of genealogical data relating to both the Lippincott and Starr families, a considerable portion of which was published later. He was a man of wide learning and a kindly critic, able to give constructive assistance on nearly all subjects. He was married twice: first, in 1857, to Susan Haworth Ecroyd, of Muncy, Pa.; and, in 1861, to Anne E. Sheppard. He had no children by either marriage. His death occurred at Greenwich, Cumberland County, N. J.

[*The Lippincotts in England and America* (1909), ed. from his genealogical papers; Chas. Lippincott, *A Geneal. Tree of the Lippincott Family* (1880); *Biog. Cat. of the Matriculates of Haverford Coll. . . . 1833–1922* (1922); *Ann. Reports of the Board of Regents of the Smithsonian Institution,* 1863, 1868–72; G. R. Prowell, *The Hist. of Camden County, N. J.* (1886); *The Friend,* Apr. 4, 1885; information from George P. Lippincott, Jr., Marlton, N. J.] W. B. M—k.

LIPPINCOTT, JOSHUA BALLINGER (Mar. 18, 1813–Jan. 5, 1886), publisher, the only child of Jacob and Sarah (Ballinger) Lippincott, was born in Juliustown, Burlington County, N. J. He was descended from Richard Lippincott who moved from New England to Shrewsbury, N. J., about 1665. After receiving a common-school education he went to Philadelphia between 1827 and 1830 and entered the employ of Clarke, the bookseller. He applied himself to this business and mastered its details sufficiently so that when his employer became financially embarrassed and the stock was purchased by creditors, he was continued in sole charge of the business although he was but eighteen years of age. He remained in this position until 1836 when he began business on his own account at Clarke's old location under the name of J. B. Lippincott & Company. At first he published principally Bibles and prayer books, then religious works. He was ambitious to place himself at the head of the Philadelphia book trade, and with this end in view, in 1849 he bought the firm of Grigg, Elliot, & Company, which was then the largest and most prosperous publishing house in the city. His firm was reorganized, Jan. 1, 1850, and became Lippincott, Grambo & Company. In 1851, while on a trip to Europe, he laid the foundations for the extensive book-importing business in which his firm later engaged. On June 30, 1855, with the retirement of Grambo, the firm resumed the name J. B. Lippincott & Company and Lippincott became the acknowledged head of the publishing business in Philadelphia. In 1865 he again visited Europe and entered into business relations with nearly all the leading publishing houses in London. His foreign business increased and in 1876 he established a London agency.

In 1855 Lippincott published the first edition of *Lippincott's Pronouncing Gazetteer,* under the editorship of Joseph Thomas and Thomas Baldwin, which was accepted as a standard reference and went through several editions. In the sixties he took over the publication of Prescott's histories. In 1870, having delegated Thomas to head a companion work to the *Gazetteer,* he published in two volumes the *Universal Pronouncing Dictionary of Biography and Mythol-*

ogy. In 1870 and 1871 he published the second and third volumes of Samuel Austin Allibone's *Critical Dictionary of English Literature and British and American Authors.* He also published successive editions of the *Dispensatory of the United States,* some of Bulwer's novels, Worcester's dictionaries, and numerous other works of reference. Not confining himself to the printing of books, he put out the *North American Medico-Chirurgical Review,* edited by Samuel D. Gross, which was suspended after the outbreak of the Civil War, established *Lippincott's Magazine* in 1868, and in 1870 began the publication of the *Medical Times.*

Lippincott's eminence as a business man led him into many connections. In 1854 he was elected a director of the Farmers' & Mechanics' Bank of Philadelphia, in 1861 a member of the board of managers of the Philadelphia Savings Fund Society, and in 1862 a director of the Pennsylvania Company for Insurance on Lives and Granting Annuities. In 1874 he was chosen a member of the board of trustees of Jefferson Medical College, and in 1876 he was elected to the board of trustees of the University of Pennsylvania. Besides these positions, most of which he held until his death, he was for many years a member of the board of directors of the Philadelphia & Reading Railroad Company. He was a lover of animals and for some time was president of the Society for the Prevention of Cruelty to Animals. He was also a generous donor to the department of veterinary medicine of the University of Pennsylvania, of which he was regarded as one of the founders. In February 1885 he incorporated his firm as the J. B. Lippincott Publishing Company and retired from business because of ill health. He had married Josephine Craige on Oct. 16, 1845, and they had four children. He died in Philadelphia, leaving an estate valued at several million dollars.

[*Joshua B. Lippincott: A Memorial Sketch* (1888); J. T. Scharf and Thompson Westcott, *Hist. of Phila., 1609–1884* (1884), vol. III; Geo. Morgan, *The City of Firsts* (1926); Henry Hall, *America's Successful Men of Affairs,* vol. II (1896); J. L. Chamberlain, ed., *Universities and Their Sons: Univ. of Pa.,* vol. I (1901); Chas. Lippincott, *A Geneal. Tree of the Lippincott Family* (1880); the *Pennsylvanian* (Phila.), Oct. 20, 1845; *Publishers' Weekly,* Jan. 9, 1886.] J. H. F.

LIPPINCOTT, SARA JANE CLARKE (Sept. 23, 1823–Apr. 20, 1904), author, better known as "Grace Greenwood," was the youngest daughter and one of eleven children of Dr. Thaddeus and Deborah Clarke and was born in Pompey, Onondaga County, N. Y. Dr. Clarke, a physician of some prominence, was born in Lebanon, Conn., of Puritan ancestry. His wife, of Huguenot descent, came from Brooklyn, Conn. Sara Jane's childhood was passed in Pompey, in the neighboring town of Fabius, and chiefly in Rochester, N. Y., where she was educated in public and private schools. In 1842 the family removed to New Brighton, Pa., near Pittsburgh. Here, in 1844, she began her prose writing under the pseudonym "Grace Greenwood" in some articles contributed to the *New Mirror.* She had in her girlhood published some verse under her own name. Several volumes of prose and verse appeared during her years at New Brighton: *Greenwood Leaves; a Collection of Sketches and Letters* (1850); *History of My Pets* (1850); *Poems* (1851); *Greenwood Leaves: Second Series* (1852); and *Recollections of My Childhood, and Other Stories* (1852). After spending fifteen months in Europe, 1852–53, she published *Haps and Mishaps of a Tour in Europe* (1854), which was unfavorably reviewed in the London *Athenæum,* Nov. 18, 1854.

In October 1853 Sara Jane Clarke was married to Leander K. Lippincott of Philadelphia and with him undertook the editorship of the *Little Pilgrim,* a juvenile monthly. From this time her writing was continuous and included contributions to *Hearth and Home,* the *Atlantic Monthly, Harper's New Monthly Magazine,* the *New York Independent,* the *New York Times,* the *New York Tribune,* and the English magazines *Household Words* and *All the Year Round.* She was one of the earliest women in the United States to become a regular newspaper correspondent and her letters from Washington and Europe, which she often visited, to leading New York, Chicago, and California papers were very popular. Her place of residence was sometimes Philadelphia, sometimes Washington, sometimes New York City. During this period her writings included *Merrie England: Travels, Descriptions, Tales, and Historical Sketches* (1855); *A Forest Tragedy and Other Tales* (1856); *Bonnie Scotland: Tales of Her History, Heroes, and Poets* (1861); *Stories and Sights of France and Italy* (1867); *New Life in New Lands: Notes of Travel* (1873); *Heads and Tails: Studies and Stories of Pets* (1875); and *Queen Victoria: Her Girlhood and Womanhood* (1883), published also in London.

During the Civil War Mrs. Lippincott visited many camps and hospitals, talking and reading to the soldiers. President Lincoln spoke of her as "Grace Greenwood the patriot." She was actively interested, though not a vigorous propagandist, in all movements for the advancement of women. A contemporary critic, John S. Hart, said of Mrs. Lippincott that her life was so full of pleasant social relations, variety, and excitement that she was never able to concentrate on any important work but contented herself with "light critiques, and lighter letters." It is probable, however, that her popularity was greater because of the lightness of her work, and her style does not indicate capacity for more serious productions. Her most representative and best-liked volumes are *Greenwood Leaves* and *Haps and Mishaps of a Tour in Europe.* Her best poems are probably "Ariadne," a stiff classical imitation, and "Darkened Hours," a conventional lament over unattained ambition. Neither her prose nor her poetry is much read today. Mrs. Lippincott was the mother of one daughter in whose home in New Rochelle, N. Y., she spent the last four years of her life.

[*Who's Who in America,* 1903–05; Frances E. Willard and Mary A. Livermore, *A Woman of the Century* (1893); E. P. Oberholtzer, *The Lit. Hist. of Phila.* (1906); J. S. Hart, *The Female Prose Writers of America* (ed. 1855); Stanley Waterloo and J. W. Hanson, Jr., *Famous Am. Men and Women* (1895); R. W. Griswold, *The Female Poets of America* (1849); Chas. Lippincott, *A Geneal. Tree of the Lippincott Family* (1880); obituaries in the *N. Y. Times,* and the *N. Y. Daily Tribune,* Apr. 21, 1904.] S. G. B.

LIPPITT, HENRY (Oct. 9, 1818–June 5, 1891), manufacturer, governor of Rhode Island, was a member of a family long associated with industrial interests. His first American ancestor was John Lippitt who settled in Rhode Island in 1638. John's great-grandsons, Charles and Christopher, organized in 1809 one of the pioneer cotton-mills of the state. Warren, son of Charles, followed the sea for a time and rose to the rank of captain, but later in life he became a cotton merchant in Providence and Savannah. He married Eliza Seamans and their son Henry was born in Providence. The boy was educated at the academy at Kingston, R. I., and shortly after his graduation began his business career. He first worked as a clerk, and then as a bookkeeper, for merchants in Warren and Providence, entering into a partnership in a commission business in 1838. In 1848 with his father and brother he became part owner of a cotton mill, the first of those with which he was later to be connected. The Tiffany Mill at Danielson, Conn., and in Rhode Island the Coddington Mill at Newport, the Social and Harrison Mills and the Globe Mill at Woonsocket, and the Manville Mills at Lincoln, came successively under Lippitt's control between 1848 and 1862. His position as a leader in the manufacturing world naturally drew him into other important connections also. He was president of two of its banks, and of corporations controlling its leading hotel and its opera house. With others he organized the Providence Board of Trade, acting as its presiding officer for three years.

As a young man, Lippitt was one of those who organized the Providence Marine Corps of Artillery in 1840. He eventually became lieutenant-colonel of this company and in the Dorr War of 1842 took an active part against Dorr and his party. During the Civil War he served on a commission for enrolling and drafting men under the call for soldiers in 1862. In 1875 he ran for the governorship of the state. Upon the failure of any of the candidates to obtain a majority of the votes the election was carried to the General Assembly, where Lippitt was elected. He retained the office for a second year, having been chosen in the same manner. He proved a competent executive. Lippitt had married, in 1845, Mary Ann Balch of Providence. They had eleven children, one of whom, Charles Warren, later became governor.

[*Biog. Cyc. of Representative Men of R. I.* (1881); T. W. Bicknell, *The Hist. of the State of R. I. and Providence Plantations* (1920), vol. III; *Proc. of the R. I. Hist. Soc., 1891–92* (1892); *Providence Daily Jour.,* June 5, 1891.] E. R. B.

LIPSCOMB, ABNER SMITH (Feb. 10, 1789–Dec. 8, 1856), lawyer, jurist, was born in Abbeville District, S. C. His parents, Elizabeth Chiles and Joel Lipscomb, were both natives of Virginia. His father early removed to South Carolina and there bore a part in the American Revolution. During his boyhood young Lipscomb attended the rural schools of Abbeville District, which were then extremely poor. Later he studied law in the office of John C. Calhoun and was admitted to the bar in 1811. He moved west and settled at St. Stephens on the Tombigbee River, in what was then the Mississippi Territory, afterward a part of Alabama. Here he rose rapidly in his profession and in 1819, at the age of thirty, was appointed one of the circuit judges, who, sitting *in banc,* constituted the supreme court. Four years later he became chief justice of the supreme court, a position he held for twelve years. His opinions are to be found in the first ten volumes of the *Alabama Reports.*

In 1835 he resigned from the supreme court and opened a law office in Mobile. Three years later, upon the unsolicited nomination of his party, he became a candidate and was elected to the legislature as a Democrat in a district overwhelmingly Whig in sentiment. As a member of the legislature and chairman of the judiciary committee he did much to simplify the system of pleading and practice in use in the state. The next year, resigning his seat in the legislature, he once more heeded the call of the frontier and removed to Texas where he speedily acquired a large law practice. He had resolved to stay out of public life, for which he had undoubted talent but little taste, but within a year after his arrival he had allowed President Mirabeau B. Lamar to persuade him to accept the office of secretary of state of the young Republic of Texas. In this capacity he became a warm advocate of annexation and as a member of the Convention of 1845 introduced the resolutions accepting the terms of annexation proposed by the United States. He also had a conspicuous part in framing the constitution for the new state, and to him have been attributed the provisions for homestead exemption and marital rights which have won admiration from statesmen in other lands. After annexation, the new governor, J. Pinckney Henderson, appointed him a justice of the supreme court. This position he filled most acceptably until his death in 1856, having twice been elected to the office by popular vote. His opinions, which are to be found in the first seventeen volumes of the *Texas Reports,* were usually short and to the point, and were generally couched in the forceful language of the frontier. Law books were almost non-existent, both in Alabama and in Texas, and the opinions of the courts were largely the product of the logic and sense of justice of the judges who composed them. Nearly half of the opinions handed down by the supreme court of Texas from 1845 to 1856, including most of those dealing with questions of procedure, were written by Lipscomb. Thus it was that he had a conspicuous part in laying the foundations of the jurisprudence of two important Southern states. He was twice married: on Apr. 13, 1813, to Elizabeth Gaines, the daughter of a planter of St. Stephens, Ala., who died in 1841; and on May 10, 1843, to Mary P. Bullock, daughter of Dr. Thomas Hunt, of Austin, Tex., who survived him.

[J. D. Lynch, *The Bench and Bar of Tex.* (1885); 17 *Tex. Reports,* iii–vi; 19 *Tex. Reports,* iii–ix; H. S. Thrall, *A Pictorial Hist. of Tex.* (1879); W. A. Garrett, *Reminiscences of Pub. Men in Ala.* (1872); *State Gazette* (Austin), Dec. 13, 1856; *Dallas Morning News,* Sept. 1, 1929, Feature Section, p. 3.] C. S. P.

LIPSCOMB, ANDREW ADGATE (Sept. 16, 1816–Nov. 23, 1890), minister, college president, son of William Corrie and Phoebe (Adgate) Lipscomb, was born in Georgetown, D. C., and died in Athens, Ga. His father, who had withdrawn from the Methodist Episcopal Church because it seemed to him autocratic, was a minister in the Methodist Protestant Church. At eighteen, the son followed the father into that ministry and preached subsequently in several places—in Baltimore and Washington, and in Alexandria, the girlhood home of his mother. In 1839 he published a small *Life of Rev. Charles W. Jacobs,* a fellow denominationalist. At about that time also he married Henrietta Blanche Richardson of Baltimore, and in 1840, or soon afterward, he went to preach in Montgomery, Ala. There he was ordained a Methodist Episcopal minister. He soon resigned his pastorate to found a school called the Metropolitan Institute for Young Ladies. In 1844 he won second prize in a contest promulgated by the American Protestant Society in New York in an attempt to show the menace of Romanism to America. This thesis, published as *Our Country, its Danger and its Duty* (1844), was republished ten years later. In 1845 his interest in psychology, which later caused him to write at length on Hamlet, led him to deliver before the University of Alabama an address on the "Morbid Exhibitions of the Human Mind." The next year in his *Social Spirit of Christianity,* he noted and approved the rising disposition to consider religion as more social than individual. In 1853, probably as the result of a recent trip, he published in Mobile a pamphlet called *Impressions of Northern Society upon a Southerner.* The following year he published *Studies in the Forty Days Between Christ's Resurrection and Ascension,* and later he wrote *Studies Supplementary to the Studies in the Forty Days.* About 1855 he left Montgomery to become president of the Female College at Tuskegee. His wife died soon afterward, and he subsequently married a former Alabama student of his, Susan Dowdell.

In 1860 the chancellorship of the University of Georgia, at Athens, became vacant, and Lipscomb was advanced as a candidate. Elected, he assumed the office and retained it till the death of his son in 1874, when he resigned. He was considered an innovator in his day because of his substitution of moral suasion for force as a means of discipline, and the affectionate veneration in which he was held contributed to the success of his administration. After a brief interval he went to Vanderbilt University to teach esthetics, but after a few years he resigned on account of his health and went back to Athens to live in retirement. There he continued to contribute to religious periodicals; published a booklet, *Lessons from the Life of St. Peter* (1882); and wrote sermons and hymns and many lectures on Shakespeare. But the main interest of his life was always teaching.

[M. L. Rutherford, *The South in Hist. and Lit.* (1907); A. L. Hull, *A Hist. Sketch of the Univ. of Ga.* (1894); E. M. Coulter, *College Life in the Old South* (1928); *Atlanta Constitution,* Nov. 24, 25, 1890.]

J. D. W.

LISA, MANUEL (Sept. 8, 1772–Aug. 12, 1820), fur trader, was born at New Orleans, the son of Christopher de Lisa, a native of Murcia in Spain, who came to America about the time the Spanish took possession of Louisiana, and of María Ignacia Rodríguez, a native of St. Augustine, Florida. Probably not later than 1790, Manuel Lisa went to St. Louis, where during the next ten years he became well established in the fur trade. The Spanish government awarded him a patent entitling him to a monopoly of trade with the Osage Indians. About 1806 he formed relations with a group of St. Louis traders, and on Apr. 19, 1807, headed an expedition of forty-two men up the Missouri River with the purpose of erecting trading posts and forts where furs might be stored and exchanged and from which watch might be kept upon the Indians. On Nov. 21 he placed a trading house at the mouth of the Big Horn River and during the following spring built near it a fort which he called Fort Raymond in honor of his son. This post, later known as Fort Manuel, was the first structure of its kind on the upper Missouri. Upon his return in the summer of 1808 he joined with Andrew Henry, Pierre Chouteau [*qq.v.*], and others in forming the Missouri Fur Company, of which William Clark [*q.v.*], who with Meriwether Lewis had ascended the Missouri in 1804, was to be resident agent at St. Louis. In June 1809, the company sent forth from St. Louis its first expedition, 350 men, half of them Americans and half French Canadians and Creoles, with Lisa as one of the leaders. About twelve miles above the mouth of the Big Knife River, in what is now North Dakota, they erected Fort Lisa. It had been Lisa's intention to proceed to the Three Forks of the Missouri, but he sent Pierre Ménard [*q.v.*] and Andrew Henry instead, and in October 1809 himself returned to St. Louis. In the spring of 1811 he led a search party of twenty-five men, sent out from St. Louis to look for Henry and his command. The trip of 1811 is famous in Missouri River annals for a race between the barge of the Lisa party and a flotilla belonging to the John Jacob Astor interests which was on its way to the Columbia River under the command of Wilson Price Hunt [*q.v.*]. Hunt had about three weeks' start of Lisa, but, on the second of June, was overtaken by the latter, just beyond the mouth of the Niobrara River. Here the two expeditions fraternized, and, when the Astorians, through Lisa's help, had secured horses from the Arikara and Mandan Indians, took their departure overland. Lisa, together with Andrew Henry, who had arrived at the Niobrara, returned to St. Louis in October. In the summer of 1814 he was appointed by William Clark, now governor of Missouri Territory, to the post of sub-agent for the Indian tribes on the Missouri above the mouth of the Kansas River.

Lisa's travels on the Missouri took him vast distances. Between 1807 and his death he made twelve or thirteen trips, performing some 26,000 miles of river travel. His trade was profitable, amounting sometimes to as much as $35,000 in one season. He was three times married. His first wife was Mary (or Polly) Charles, by whom he had three children, all of whom died when young. While his first wife was still living he married, in 1814, Mitain, an Omaha woman, daughter of one of the leading families of the Omaha tribe. By Mitain he had two children, who survived him. In 1819, on his last trip up the Missouri, he took with him his third bride, who had been Mrs. Mary (Hempstead) Keeney; she was a daughter of Stephen Hempstead, a prominent figure in the early history of St. Louis. They spent the winter at Fort Lisa, a post erected in 1812 a few miles above the site of the present Omaha. At this post Lisa entertained members of the famous expedition led by Maj. Stephen H. Long [*q.v.*] into the region beyond the Missouri. He died at St. Louis in the following summer, and was buried in Bellefontaine Cemetery, where a shaft marks his grave.

[H. M. Chittenden, *The Am. Fur Trade of the Far West* (1902) vol. I; W. B. Douglas, "Manuel Lisa," in *Mo. Hist. Soc. Colls.*, vol. III, nos. 3, 4 (1911); Kathryn M. French, in *S. Dak. Hist. Colls.*, vol. IV (1908); G. F. Robeson, in *Palimpsest* (Iowa City), Jan. 1925; F. L. Billon, *Annals of St. Louis in Its Territorial Days* (1888); *Missouri Gazette & Public Advertiser* (St. Louis), Aug. 16, 1820.] I. B. R.

LIST, GEORG FRIEDRICH (Aug. 6, 1789–Nov. 30, 1846), economist, journalist, was born in the free imperial city of Reutlingen in Württemberg, Germany, the youngest child of a prosperous tanner, Johannes List. His mother's family name was Schäfer. He attended the local Latin school and in 1806 entered the public service of Württemberg, rising to the rank of ministerial undersecretary. Having rounded out his education by extensive reading and study at the University of Tübingen, he was appointed professor of administration and politics there, during the ministry of his friend Von Wangenheim (1817). When the succeeding reactionary government took exception to his affiliation with the *Handelsverein*, an association of merchants seeking the abolition of internal duties, List resigned his professorship, became secretary of the association and editor of its journal, and as such took a leading part in the movement which culminated in the German Customs Union (*Zollverein*).

During his professorship he married Catherine Neidhard, a beautiful young widow, daughter of Professor Seybold.

In 1819 he was elected to the Diet of Württemberg from Reutlingen, but his liberal ideas and his advocacy of economic reforms (aid to industry, equitable taxes, and a budget system) incurred the enmity of the bureaucratic government. He was indicted for sedition and sentenced to ten months' imprisonment. Eluding arrest by flight, he spent the four years following in exile. In Paris he met Lafayette, who invited him to accompany him on his proposed visit to America. During a visit to England in 1823 he made his first acquaintance with railroads. On the advice of friends, he returned to Württemberg in May 1824, but was arrested and taken to the fortress Asperg. In the following January he was released on condition that he leave the country. Finding his further stay on the Continent impossible, he emigrated, with his wife and four children, to the United States, arriving in New York June 10, 1825.

Having accepted the invitation of Lafayette—with whom and his son, Georges, he kept up a life-long friendship—to accompany him on his tour of the Atlantic states, List met many of the leading men in American public life. After a temporary sojourn on a farm near Harrisburg, he moved to Reading, Pa., in 1826. There he became editor of the *Readinger Adler,* a German-American weekly founded in 1796. His versatility, his intimate knowledge of international affairs, and the patriotic spirit which animated his writings soon made the *Adler* one of the most influential papers in Pennsylvania. It was popularly styled "the Berks County Bible." During the presidential campaign of 1828 List's influence among Pennsylvania Germans had much to do with swinging Pennsylvania to Andrew Jackson.

His interest in economics, and especially in questions of commercial policy, brought him into close contact with Charles Jared Ingersoll, Pierre Du Ponceau, Mathew Carey [*qq.v.*], Redwood Fisher, and other leaders of the Pennsylvania Society for the Encouragement of Manufactures and the Mechanic Arts, which was then the center of the protectionist movement; and List soon became one of its foremost literary exponents. His *Outlines of American Political Economy* (1827), *Observations on the Report of the Committee of Ways and Means* (1828), address, *On the Boston Report, and Particularly on Its Principles Respecting the Landed Interest of Pennsylvania,* delivered in 1828 before the Pennsylvania legislature, and his controversy with Gov. W. B. Giles [*q.v.*] of Virginia made him known throughout the country as one of the ablest advocates of the "American System." As a tribute to his effective work, the Pennsylvania Society gave a banquet in his honor at Philadelphia, Nov. 3, 1827, and requested him to write under its auspices a college textbook on political economy. The presidency of Lafayette College was offered to him about the same time. List, however, turned his attention to business projects. These included the development of rich anthracite deposits which he had discovered near Tamaqua, and the building of a railroad from that point to Port Clinton. In 1828 he organized the Little Schuylkill Navigation, Railroad & Coal Company, the progenitor of the modern Reading System, and successfully initiated the building of its line, which was opened to traffic in 1831.

In the same year, as an executive agent of the Department of State, he went to Europe, where he planned to introduce Pennsylvania anthracite. Having become naturalized, he was appointed United States consul at Hamburg by President Jackson in 1831, and, failing of confirmation by the Senate, was given the consulate at Baden. From 1834 to 1837 he was United States consul at Leipzig and from 1843 to 1845 at Stuttgart. After his return to Europe he divided his energies mainly between literary work and the promotion of a German railway system. In pursuance of a long-cherished plan he founded, jointly with Rotteck and Welcker, the *Staats-Lexikon* in 1835, to which he contributed several noteworthy articles on American institutions, including railway transportation. In furtherance of the latter he founded the *Eisenbahn-Journal* (1835), and with indomitable energy and in the face of obstacles of all kinds successfully championed the building of a railroad from Leipzig to Dresden. His epochal brochure, *Über ein sächsisches Eisenbahn-System,* appeared in 1833.

Continued persecutions by Metternich and his agents caused him to leave Germany once more, in 1837, and he spent the next three years in research and literary work in Paris. There he wrote a prize essay, *Système naturel d'économie politique* (1837), on the most feasible method of changing from protection to free trade, which was adjudged an *"ouvrage remarquable"* by the French Academy. Returning to Germany in 1840, he again took up his studies on commercial policy, and in 1841 published his *opus magnum,* under the title, *Das Nationale System der Politischen Ökonomie.* In the *Zollvereinsblatt* (1843–46) he founded an organ through which he created a popular interest in questions of political economy and helped to lay the economic foundation of modern Germany as brought about later by Bismarck. He was for many years a leading contributor to the *Augsburger Allgemeine Zeitung*.

On a visit to Austria and Hungary in 1844 as a missionary of protection to domestic industry, he met a cordial welcome; but a visit to England in 1846, where he hoped to prepare the way for a commercial alliance between Great Britain and Germany, proved a disappointment; and he returned to his home in Augsburg broken in health and spirits. He sought relief in a journey to the Tyrol, where, in a moment of despondency, he ended his life.

List was one of the leading economists of the nineteenth century. His theory of productive forces, of the economic importance of nations as against the individualism and cosmopolitanism of Adam Smith, and his application of the historical method fructified and advanced the study of economics. His *National System* (translated into French in 1851; into English, 1856), while in the main a defense of protectionism, upholds it not as an end unto itself but rather as a temporary means of nursing infant industries, his ultimate goal being universal free trade. In American tariff history he was, next to Alexander Hamilton, the most constructive among the early advocates of protection.

[The two best German biographies of List are Ludwig Häusser's *Friedrich List's gesammelte Schriften* (3 vols., 1850–51), and Karl Jentsch's *Friedrich List* (1901). Margaret E. Hirst, *Life of Friedrich List* (1909), contains selections from his writings, including his *Outlines of American Political Economy.* The most recent noteworthy biography is K. A. Meissinger, *Friedrich List der tragische Deutsche* (1930). Walter von Molo, *Ein Deutscher ohne Deutschland* (1931), is a historical novel based on List's career. His life in the United States is discussed by William Notz in *Weltwirtschaftliches Archiv*, Kiel, April and July 1925, and in the *Am. Econ. Rev.*, June 1926. The 8th German edition (Stuttgart, 1925) of his *Das Nationale System der politischen Okonomie* contains a historical and critical introduction by K. Th. Eheberg and an elaborate bibliography by Max Hoeltzel. A new English edition of the *National System,* with an introduction by J. S. Nicholson, appeared in 1904. The Friedrich List-Gesellschaft, E. V., Stuttgart, in cooperation with the German Academy, is publishing a complete critical edition of List's works: *Friedrich List, Schriften-Reden-Briefe* (9 vols., Berlin, 1927–33), of which vol. II, *Friedrich List: Grundlinien einer politischen Okonomie und andere Beiträge der amerikanischen Zeit, 1825–1832, herausgegeben von William Notz* (1931), contains his American writings.] W. N.

LISTEMANN, BERNHARD (Aug. 28, 1841–Feb. 11, 1917), violinist, conductor, educator, was born at Schlotheim, Thuringia, Germany, the son of Wilhelm and Henrietta Listemann. His father was a merchant. Bernhard, who early showed exceptional musical ability, had instruction at the Leipzig Conservatory from Ferdinand David and at Vienna from Joseph Joachim and Henry Vieuxtemps. With his brother Fritz, also a violinist, he went on one occasion to Weimar to give a recital when both were so poor as to seek out necessarily the cheapest lodging house. Bernhard was fortunate in attracting the attention of Franz Liszt who gave him a private hearing and aided him in obtaining engagements. From 1858 to 1867 Listemann was concert master at the residence of the Prince of Schwarzburg-Rudolstadt. In the latter year he came with his brother Fritz to the United States. He spent a year in New York and then joined the orchestra of the Harvard Musical Association in Boston. Finding that "the programs were very conservative in character and reflected . . . the conservatism of the patrons of the concerts," he presently secured employment as concert master of the Theodore Thomas Orchestra during the seasons from 1871 to 1874. Both he and Thomas were enthusiastic pioneers in introducing Wagner to American audiences. Listemann had previously, while briefly revisiting Germany, married, July 25, 1870, Sophie Sungershausen.

In 1875 Listemann founded the Boston Philharmonic Club which gave many concerts, local and national. From this nucleus grew the Boston Philharmonic Orchestra, which, without financial guaranty, engaged famous artists and presented notable programs. In 1880 Listemann produced for the first time in Boston both the "Faust" and the "Dante" of Abbe Liszt. When, a year later, the Boston Symphony Orchestra, founded by Maj. Henry L. Higginson [*q.v.*], gave its first concert with Georg Henschel as conductor, Listemann was concert master. His musicianship contributed toward the initial successes of the orchestra, but he remained with it only four seasons. He is described by the Symphony's historian, M. A. DeWolfe Howe, as "a very superior artist in his way," but "a man of too much impulsive initiative to follow any one's beat implicitly." He was one of several musicians who left the Symphony when Wilhelm Gericke began his first conductorship; "whether they were dismissed for musical or disciplinary reasons, the public knew only that they were gone" (Howe, *post*, p. 71).

Listemann remained for a time in Boston where he taught, served as conductor of the Boston Amateur Orchestral Club and directed a string quartet. He accepted in 1893 an offer to head the violin department of the Chicago Musical College, founded by Florenz Ziegfeld, Sr. The rest of his career was that of a successful instructor and performer at Chicago. He had hundreds of pupils; among the most distinguished were Francis Macmillan and Benjamin

Cutter. His quartet was active down to the period of the World War and he often appeared as a soloist. His death was caused by heart disease. Surviving him were his widow, four sons, and a daughter. Among his professional publications was his *Method of Modern Violin Playing,* brought out by Oliver Ditson & Company in 1869.

[For references to Listemann's achievements with the Boston Philharmonic see *Dwight's Jour. of Music,* Aug. 16, Oct. 11, Nov. 8, Dec. 6, Dec. 20, 1879. Brief but revealing characterizations appear in M. A. DeW. Howe, *The Boston Symphony Orchestra* (rev. ed., 1931). See also: the *Musician,* July 1908; *Musical America,* Feb. 17, 1917; the *Boston Transcript* and the *Chicago Tribune,* Feb. 12, 1917. A manuscript by Listemann's widow, prepared for the author of this sketch in 1929, is now in the library of the New England Conservatory of Music.] F. W. C.

LITCHFIELD, ELECTUS BACKUS (Feb. 15, 1813–May 12, 1889), railroad builder, was born in Delphi Falls, N. Y., to which place his parents, Elisha and Percy (Tiffany) Litchfield had removed in 1812 from Connecticut. Both families were of early Massachusetts stock. The father served at Sacketts Harbor during the War of 1812 under Gen. Electus Backus, for whom the son was named. He afterward became prominent in local and state politics, serving five terms in the state Assembly and two in Congress. Electus began business as a merchant in Cazenovia but in 1844 moved to New York City where for ten years he conducted a wholesale grocery business. His younger brothers, E. Darwin Litchfield and Edwin C. Litchfield, soon followed him to the metropolis, and through Edwin, who, as a member of the law firm of Litchfield & Tracy, handled much legal work for railroads, all the brothers were drawn into the railroad business.

The state of Michigan in 1846 sold its uncompleted Michigan Southern railroad to a firm in which the engineer, John B. Jervis, and Edwin Litchfield were the leading members. By uniting it with the Northern Indiana Railroad and completing the construction on both lines they secured by May 1852 a through route from Lake Erie to Chicago. Meanwhile Electus was treasurer, and later president, of the Toledo & Cleveland, a portion of which the Litchfields built. They constructed also a Toledo-Detroit line, the Air Line from Toledo to Elkhart, Ind., and minor branches, all of which formed a well-knit system. They allied themselves with the Chicago & Rock Island, then building west to the Mississippi, of which Jervis was president and Elisha C. Litchfield, another brother, a director. They were interested in the construction of the Terre Haute & Alton, and Litchfield, Ill., on this line was named for them. East of Cleveland an understanding was reached with the new roads along the south shore of the lake to Buffalo, thence across New York state, and with the Hudson River Railroad, which resulted in connecting interests from New York to Chicago. The meager facts available do not reveal any one author of this remarkable network of interests, the most impressive before the Civil War, but the Litchfields contributed much to bring it within the realm of possibility, and would have profited immensely had not the panic of 1857 broken it up for a time. Caught with interests too far extended, they could not hold their control in the reorganizations.

For several years afterward Electus Litchfield busied himself with building the Fifth Avenue and Atlantic Avenue street railways, the Coney Island Plank Road, and other enterprises in Brooklyn, of which city, after 1846, he was a leading resident. With his brother Edwin he developed the old Cortelyou farm which they had purchased south of the expanding city. Needing money after the panic he successfully urged the city to buy a large part of this area for park purposes, and to this combination of self-interest and vision Brooklyn owes her famous Prospect Park. Much later he purchased and renovated the Brooklyn, Bath & West End Railroad which did much to develop West Brooklyn and the New Utrecht sections. Meanwhile, in 1862, E. B. Litchfield & Company contracted with the St. Paul & Pacific to build their lines in Minnesota, taking stock and bonds in pay. Financial difficulties soon landed the road in Litchfield's hands, and to complete enough construction to obtain the appertaining land grants he organized the "First Division of the St. Paul & Pacific Railroad," sold bonds in Holland to finance the work, and finished the main line west to Breckenridge and the branch north to St. Cloud. Litchfield, Minn., received its name at this time. In 1870 the Litchfields sold to the Northern Pacific, then booming under Jay Cooke's control, but when that road collapsed in 1873 the stock came back to them. They attempted a reorganization in 1875, but failed, and in 1879 sold their remaining holdings to James J. Hill [*q.v.*] who made their lines the nucleus of his Great Northern system. Curiously, it was E. B. Litchfield's son, W. B. Litchfield, and a half-brother, E. S. Litchfield, who had helped Hill to a start when in 1867 they became silent partners with him in his warehouse business on the St. Paul levee.

During most of this time the Litchfields had been bankers, brokers, and agents for railroad loans in New York City and had been interested in various minor undertakings. Electus married Hannah Maria Breed, daughter of Elias Breed of Norwich, N. Y., in 1836. Five children were born to them. He was a man of ingratiating personality and of vision, but his enterprises were characterized by the extravagant financing of boom periods.

[See W. W. Folwell, *A Hist. of Minn.* (1926), III, 441–61; J. G. Pyle, *Life of Jas. J. Hill* (2 vols., 1917); Abner Morse, "Geneal. of the Descendants of Lawrence Litchfield," *New-Eng. Hist. and Geneal. Reg.*, Apr., July 1855; N. O. Tiffany, *The Tiffanys of America* (1901); *Railroad Gazette* (N. Y.), May 17, 1899; and annual reports of the railroads concerned. Information as to certain facts was supplied for this sketch by Litchfield's grandsons, Electus D. and Percy Litchfield of New York City.] O. W. H.

LITTELL, ELIAKIM (Jan. 2, 1797–May 17, 1870), editor and publisher, was born at Burlington, N. J., grandson of a Revolutionary officer, Eliakim Littell, for whom he was named, and son of Stephen and Susan (Gardner) Littell. He attended a grammar school at Haddonfield, N. J., but his formal education was limited. By reading the works of standard authors, however, he acquired a sound literary judgment. After serving an apprenticeship in a bookstore he ventured into publishing. Soon he began editing reprint periodicals of a high literary and intellectual quality and to this work practically his whole life was given. His first periodical was the *Philadelphia Register and National Recorder,* a sixteen-page weekly, of which he was editor and joint publisher, the first number appearing on Jan. 2, 1819. In July following, it became the *National Recorder.* It consisted at first largely of American newspaper reprint, interspersed with a little original copy, but on July 7, 1821, it was renamed the *Saturday Magazine,* and consisted thereafter "principally of selections from the most celebrated British reviews, magazines, and scientific journals." The size was increased to twenty-four pages. A year later it became a ninety-six-page monthly, as the *Museum of Foreign Literature and Science* and was edited for more than a year by Robert Walsh [*q.v.*], who combined this work with his duties as editor of the Philadelphia *National Gazette.* After Walsh's departure, Littell assumed editorial responsibility, except during 1835, with the occasional assistance of his brother, Dr. Squier Littell [*q.v.*]. The *Museum* began to experiment with illustrations in 1826 and soon made them a regular feature. In 1843 it was united with the *American Eclectic* as the *Eclectic Museum of Foreign Literature, Science, and Art,* published in New York and Philadelphia, with John Holmes Agnew as editor.

In 1844 Littell sold out his interest in the *Eclectic Museum* and went to Boston, where in April this "indefatigable caterer for the public mind" founded *Littell's Living Age,* consisting mainly of reprints from the British press. The *Museum* had had a circulation of 2,000, but under Littell the *Living Age* reached 5,000—a respectable figure for the time. His chief successes were with magazines which he himself both edited and published. The *Journal of Foreign Medical Science and Literature,* which he began to publish in 1824 as the continuation of an earlier journal, soon merged with the *American Medical Recorder.* The *Religious Magazine and Spirit of the Foreign Theological Journals,* founded in 1828 with the Rev. George Weller as editor, survived only four volumes before it was discontinued—"very much liked but did not pay." In 1855 Littell founded still another periodical, the *Panorama of Life and Literature,* a 144-page monthly, which he announced as "not so comprehensive in its scope; so redundant in its fulness, or so complete in all its parts" as the *Living Age.* He continued in active direction of his business until his death, which occurred at his home in Brookline, Mass.

He was remarkable for his business acumen, wide reading in ancient and modern literature, a somewhat irascible temper, and a clever pen. His editorial duties did not prevent his occasional production of graceful prose and verse, and he was a sprightly correspondent. He is especially significant for his service in bringing foreign thought to the attention of Americans during the early development of the national culture. During his lifetime, no cultivated American home was complete without at least one of his publications. He took a lively interest in national affairs and was a stanch supporter of the Union during the Civil War, contributing particularly to the discussion of financial questions. On Feb. 12, 1828, he married Mary Frazee Smith, by whom he had six children, two of whom died in infancy. His son, Robert Smith Littell, succeeded him as editor of the *Living Age.*

[Family records and the files of Littell's various periodicals; John Littell, *Family Records: or Geneals. of the First Settlers of Passaic Valley* (1852); G. T. Little, *The Descendants of George Little* (1882); S. A. Allibone, *A Critical Dict. of English Literature and British and Am. Authors* (1870), vol. II; Algernon Tassin, *The Mag. in America* (1916); A. H. Smyth, *The Phila. Mags. and Their Contributors, 1741–1850* (1892); F. L. Mott, *A Hist. of Am. Mags., 1741–1850* (1930); *Littell's Living Age*, June 18, 1870; *New-England Hist. and Geneal. Reg.*, Apr. 1875; *Memorial Biogs. of the New-England Historic Geneal. Soc.*, vol. VI (1905).] J. B.

LITTELL, SQUIER (Dec. 9, 1803–July 4, 1886), physician, was born in Burlington, N. J., the son of Stephen and Susan (Gardner) Littell. Losing both parents very early in his childhood, he was adopted by his uncle Squier Littell of Butler, Ohio, and received his early education in schools near Lebanon, Ohio. Association with his uncle, who had a large practice, inspired him to study medicine, and after a period of apprenticeship at home he went to Philadelphia in 1821 and continued his studies under the guidance of Joseph Parrish. He matriculated at the medical school of the University of Pennsylvania and received the degree of M.D. in 1824, his graduating thesis being entitled "Theory of Inflammation." Lured by youthful love of adventure and the prospect of a medical appointment there, he went to South America. On arriving in Buenos Aires he was amazed at the degree of learning possessed by the medical men, and though he missed the appointment he sought, he became by examination a licentiate of the Academy of Medicine. Four months' effort convinced him that Buenos Aires was not a suitable field for him and he embarked on a journey toward the United States, rounding the Horn and stopping at Valparaiso, Lima, and other Pacific ports. Thinking that Guayaquil, Ecuador, offered opportunities for one of his calling, he sojourned there for a while; but ultimately he continued his trip to Philadelphia by way of the Isthmus of Panama and Cartagena.

In Philadelphia he renewed his former acquaintances and contacts and engaged in general practice. He had long nourished an ambition to teach anatomy, but an impediment in his speech discouraged him. In Philadelphia his success was progressive, and about 1834 he married Mary Graff Emlin, daughter of Caleb Emlin, by whom he had one son and one daughter. His wife died shortly after the birth of the second child. His medical activities for a long while were of a general character, but with the development of especial skill in ophthalmic surgery he came to be prominently identified with that specialty. When Wills Hospital, founded for the treatment of the lame, the halt, and the blind, was organized in 1834, he became one of its first surgeons. He served in this capacity for some thirty years, thus aiding materially in creating the reputation that has made the ophthalmic work of the hospital internationally famous. He was elected a fellow of the College of Physicians in 1836 and later became one of its councilors. It is an interesting fact that, despite his skill as an ophthalmic surgeon, he learned the use of the ophthalmoscope late in life and with some difficulty.

His literary efforts were many and varied. He edited the *Monthly Journal of Foreign Medicine* (January 1828–June 1829), and he contributed over many years articles to various medical journals, particularly on ophthalmological subjects. From time to time he assisted his brother, Eliakim Littell [*q.v.*], in the editing of the *Museum of Foreign Literature and Science.* In 1837 he wrote *A Manual of Diseases of the Eye* which was favorably received abroad, although it was one of the earliest American books on this subject. He was active in all the organizations with which he was affiliated and wrote many memoirs of distinguished members of the College of Physicians of Philadelphia. He was also active in the affairs of the Episcopal Church and from January 1839 to May 1841 edited *The Banner of the Cross,* one of the most influential of the church papers of that period. He also wrote poetry and arranged no less than twelve metrical translations of the medieval hymn *"Dies Irae."* He succumbed at the age of eighty-three to what would now be designated as cardio-renal disease, his death occurring at Bay Head, N. J.

[John Littell, *Family Records, or the Geneals. of the First Settlers of Passaic Valley* (1852); T. H. Shastid, in C. A. Wood, *The Am. Encyc. of Ophthalmology,* vol. X (1917); H. A. Kelly and W. L. Burrage, *Am. Medic. Biogs.* (1920); A. D. Hall, in *Trans. Coll. of Physicians of Phila.,* vol. IX (1887); *Phila. Press,* July 7, 1886.]

L. W. F.

LITTELL, WILLIAM (1768–Sept. 26, 1824), lawyer and author, was a native of New Jersey, but removed with his father when very young to the western part of Pennsylvania, where he remained, "it is believed," until he emigrated to Kentucky about the year 1801. In "early life" he studied "Physics and Divinity." (*The Argus of Western America,* Frankfort, Ky., Sept. 29, 1824.) These facts, given in his obituary, represent all that seems to be known of the first thirty years of his life. Whatever career he may have had as a divine was probably limited to Pennsylvania, but he practised medicine for a short time at Mount Sterling, Ky. (Statement of Col. William Sudduth in Shane MSS., 12CC64, State Historical Society of Wisconsin.) He gave up medicine for law and it is a matter of record that Transylvania conferred the degree of LL.D. upon him in 1810 (Robert and Johanna Peter, *Transylvania University,* Filson Club Publications No. 11, 1896, pp. 90, 125).

In 1805, presumably while engaged in the practice of law at Frankfort, he contracted with the state to publish the *Statute Law of Kentucky.* This work appeared in five volumes, 1809–19. In 1806, however, before the first volume appeared, he published three books at Frankfort. The first was styled *Epistles of William, Surnamed Littell, to the People of the Realm of Ken-*

tucky and consisted largely of satirical essays dealing with the prominent men of his time, the second was *A Narrative of the Settlement of Kentucky,* and the third the well-known and meritorious *Political Transactions in and Concerning Kentucky.* From these adventures in politics and history he turned to the writing of law books, beginning in 1808 with his *Principles of Law and Equity.* There ensued a period of six years while he practised law and devoted himself to the compilation of his *Statute Law,* but in 1814 he had a relapse into frivolity with the publication of his *Festoons of Fancy, Consisting of Compositions Amatory, Sentimental and Humorous in Verse and Prose.* In 1822 he issued, in association with Jacob Swigert, *A Digest of the Statute Law of Kentucky,* in two volumes; and, in 1823–24, *Reports of Cases at Common Law and in Chancery, Decided by the Court of Appeals of the Commonwealth of Kentucky.* In 1824 his last book appeared, *Cases Selected from the Decisions of the Court of Appeals of Kentucky Not Hitherto Reported.* Littell's fame rests on his work as a compiler of law books. His *Epistles* was of such a character as to bring him into disrepute and to give him a reputation for flippancy and scurrility that he never succeeded in living down.

He was twice married; first, on Jan. 22, 1816, to Martha Irwin McCracken, daughter of William Irwin of Fayette County and widow of Capt. Virgil McCracken of Woodford County (Fayette County Marriage Records, vol. I, p. 58). They had one son, William, who died Aug. 30, 1824 (*Western Statesman,* Sept. 1, 1824). After the death of his first wife, Littell married, Dec. 9, 1823, Eliza P. Hickman, widow of Capt. Paschal Hickman of Franklin County (Franklin County Deed Book L, pp. 71–73), who, with a son, survived him. According to the tax lists he died possessed of some five thousand acres of land, but he was heavily in debt—probably as a penalty of authorship—and the General Assembly at its next session provided that his lands should be sold by a special official instead of at a forced sale (*Session Acts,* 1824–25, ch. 91, pp. 98–99). A Kentucky historian writing from material no longer available characterizes him as a man of bad morals, of great eccentricity, and of no particular ability except as a land lawyer (Lewis and Richard H. Collins, *History of Kentucky,* 1874, I, 412). The evidence is too scanty to allow a judgment as to his legal abilities, but is overwhelming as to his eccentricities. He had a reputation for immorality; his will hints at domestic unhappiness. The fact that he named a prominent Episcopal minister as one of the two guardians of his sons indicates that he was not without respect for the clergy and the preface to his *Statute Law* indicates his religious belief.

[Littell's will is recorded in Franklin County Will Book, no. 2, p. 1; his *Political Transactions* has been republished as Filson Club Pubs., No. 31 (1926); a poem, "Rapture," from his *Festoons* is included in F. P. Dickey, *Blades o' Bluegrass* (Louisville, 1892), p. 287.]
R. S. C.

LITTLE, CHARLES COFFIN (July 25, 1799–Aug. 9, 1869), publisher, was born in Kennebunk, Me., the son of David and Sarah (Chase) Little and a descendant of George Little who came to Newbury, Mass., in 1640. He left Maine as a youth and secured employment in a Boston shipping house, but in 1821, when the small bookstore of Carter, Hilliard & Company advertised for a clerk, he obtained the position. In 1827 the firm was reorganized as Hilliard, Gray & Company, with Little as a member, and in 1837 he became its senior partner. His chief associate thenceforth was James Brown, 1800–1855 [*q.v.*], formerly an employee of Hilliard. After being known as Charles C. Little & Company for a time, the firm adopted the title of Little & Brown, which in 1847 was changed to Little, Brown & Company.

The business had been greatly increased during Little's connection with it as employee and junior partner, and it continued to grow in importance after he became its head. His particular responsibility was the supervision of the legal publications of the firm, and in a few years his house became the foremost in America in this field. In 1843 and again in 1846 it issued *A Catalogue of Law Books Published and For Sale by Charles C. Little and James Brown,* and though this list included many imported English works, the number of the firm's own publications was large. Little continued as the principal partner and general manager of the business throughout his life. At his death, the house retained its leadership in the publishing of legal works and was prominent among American publishers of books of a general nature.

Little was active as a capitalist, and to some extent in public affairs. He was selectman of Cambridge in 1836 and 1841, in the lower house of the Massachusetts legislature in 1836 and 1837, and was for many years president of a Cambridge bank, besides being an active director of a gas company and a street railroad. Since he employed a considerable part of his personal fortune in the erection of buildings that did much to introduce a more convenient type of structure for both residential and business purposes, his influence on the economic and material development of his community was widely recognized. The day after his death the "booksellers of Boston" held a special meeting in recognition of his services as a publisher and as a citizen.

Little was married on Jan. 1, 1829, to Sarah Anne Hilliard, daughter of his partner, William Hilliard, and sister of Francis Hilliard [*q.v.*]. After her death on Aug. 29, 1848, he was married, Jan. 18, 1854, to Abby, daughter of Henry Wheaton of Providence, R. I. He left four sons and one daughter, all by the first marriage.

[G. T. Little, *The Descendants of George Little* (1882); *Books from Beacon Hill* (1927), pub. by Little, Brown & Co.; L. R. Paige, *Hist. of Cambridge* (1877); *New-Eng. Hist. and Geneal. Reg.*, Oct. 1869; *Proc. Am. Antiquarian Soc.*, vol. LIII (1869); *Boston Transcript*, Aug. 9, 1869; *Boston Post* and *Boston Traveler*, Aug. 10, 1869; *Boston Daily Advertiser*, Aug. 11, 1869; *Cambridge Press*, Aug. 14, 1869.]
S. G.

LITTLE, CHARLES JOSEPH (Sept. 21, 1840–Mar. 11, 1911), theologian, was born in Philadelphia, Pa., the son of Thomas Rowell and Ann (Zimmermann) Little. On his father's side he was descended from George Little who came from England to Massachusetts in 1640. Though in his boyhood his health was frail, he spent his days in manual work and studied at night by lamp and candle light. He had a double endowment in American and German opportunities in his home and in time became a linguist of unusual skill in Greek, Latin, Italian, and French. When he was twenty-one he graduated from the University of Pennsylvania, and in 1862 was admitted to the Philadelphia Conference of the Methodist Episcopal Church. He served pastorates at Newark, Del., Saint James and Spring Garden Street, Philadelphia; Springfield, Pa., and Chestnut Hill, Philadelphia. His exceptional abilities were soon recognized and he was called from the pastorate into the educational field, becoming teacher of mathematics in Dickinson Seminary in 1867. He studied in Europe, 1869–72, and in the latter year married Anna Marina Elizabeth Bahn, daughter of Dr. Carl Bahn. Returning to the United States, he spent two years in the pastorate of Christ Church, Philadelphia, and then became professor of philosophy and history in Dickinson College. In 1885 he was made professor of logic and history in Syracuse University, and in 1891 was elected to the chair of church history in Garrett Biblical Institute. He became president of the Institute in 1895 and held that position to the day of his death.

Little believed in a thoroughgoing theological education in the old-time essentials. His administration covered the years of transition in higher criticism, and while the battle raged most fiercely he was steady as a rock, holding fast to old truths and welcoming all new light. He was a member of the General Conferences of the Methodist Episcopal Church in 1888, 1892, 1896, 1900, 1904, and 1908. He was a man of power and influence in his church, and in every community of which he became a part, and an orator of great impressiveness upon special occasions. As a delegate to the Methodist Centennial Conference at Baltimore in 1884 he made one of the notable addresses, and at the British Wesleyan Conference in 1900 he delivered the Fernley Lecture, *Christianity and the Nineteenth Century* (1900). It was a strong presentation of the value and permanence of an experimental religion, maintaining itself against all the reactions of rationalism.

He appeared to be an inexhaustible fountain of information, giving the impression of encyclopaedic knowledge available at a moment's notice. Some of his greatest efforts seemed to be the product of immediate inspiration. He was extraordinarily versatile and a remarkable conversationalist; his phenomenal memory seemed to retain all he had read. He had a temperamental aversion to the publishing of books. The conditions of the Fernley lectureship necessitated the publication of that lecture, but *The Angel in the Flame* (1904), a series of sermons preached in First Church, Evanston, was published only at the solicitation of the Methodist Book Concern. These sermons, while they illustrate Little's power of clear thinking and vivid expression, hardly show him at his best. A volume entitled *Biographical and Literary Studies* (1916), brought out some five years after his death, is more representative of his finest work. The papers and addresses here gathered together suggest the wide range of his interests and his grasp on many subjects, literary, historical, and religious. The memorial volume of 1912 (*post*) contains eight of his addresses and essays.

[*In Memoriam, Charles Joseph Little* (1912), ed. by C. M. Stuart; *Who's Who in America*, 1910–11; Matthew Simpson, *Cyc. of Methodism* (1882); histories of Northwestern University and Garrett Biblical Institute; G. T. Little, *The Descendants of George Little* (1882); obituaries of Anna (Bahn) Little, in *Christian Advocate* (N. Y.) Nov. 24, 1904, and *Minutes of the Rock River Conference*, 1905; *Northwestern Christian Advocate*, Mar. 15, 1911; *Christian Advocate* (N. Y.), Mar. 16, 1911; *Chicago Tribune*, Mar. 12, 1911; *Journals* of the General Conferences named above.]
D. A. H.

LITTLE, GEORGE (Apr. 15, 1754–July 22, 1809), naval officer, was born in Marshfield, Mass., the son of Lemuel and Penelope (Eames or Ames) Little. He was descended from Thomas Little who emigrated to Plymouth from Devonshire, England, in 1630, and from Lieut. William Fobes, second in command in King

Philip's war. Nothing is known of Little's first service in the American Revolution beyond the information that he landed at Bristol, R. I., on Mar. 7, 1778, after a period of confinement on board the British prisonship *Lord Sandwich* at Newport. Later in that year he served in the Massachusetts navy, successively, as second lieutenant of the brigantine *Active* and master of the brigantine *Hazard.* On May 3, 1779, he was commissioned first lieutenant, and as first officer on the *Hazard* participated in the unfortunate Penobscot expedition. He was first lieutenant on the state ship *Protector* when on June 9, 1780, that vessel captured the British privateer *Admiral Duff,* thirty-two guns, in one of the severest naval engagements of the Revolution. In the following year when the *Protector* surrendered to his Majesty's ships *Roebuck* and *Medea* he was taken prisoner and was for a time confined in Mill Prison, England. Bribing a sentry, he, with several other American officers, made his escape, crossed the channel to France, and with the aid of Franklin returned to Massachusetts. In 1782 he was promoted to a captaincy, given command of the sloop *Winthrop,* and ordered on a cruise along the Eastern Coast. He had the good fortune to capture nearly the whole of the armed British force at Penobscot, thereby retrieving somewhat the naval honor of his state, lost in the Penobscot expedition of 1779. A voyage that he made in the *Winthrop* during the winter of 1782–83 was the last cruise in the war of the Massachusetts navy.

After his discharge on June 23, 1783, Little returned to Marshfield where he owned a farm. From Mar. 4, 1799, he served by appointment of President Adams as captain in the new federal navy, then undergoing expansion on account of the naval war with France. His part in this desultory conflict was, with the exception of Commodore Truxtun [*q.v.*], exceeded by no other officer. He was appropriately given command of the frigate *Boston,* a gift of the Bostonians to the federal government. On July 24 he put to sea under orders to proceed to Cape François and to cruise off the northern coast of Santo Domingo for the protection of American trade. In December while in company with the *General Greene* he captured the Danish brig *Flying Fish.* Notwithstanding the fact that the taking of this prize was plainly authorized by the orders of the Navy Department, the Supreme Court which finally passed upon the case held Little liable for damages. In 1800, the last year of the war, Little captured several ships, including the *Deux Anges,* a letter of marque of twenty guns, and the *Berceau,* a naval vessel of twenty-four guns, next to the largest prize made by the Americans. It was taken after a severe action, as the *Berceau,* although inferior to the *Boston,* made a strong resistance. With the arrival of the two vessels in Boston in November 1800, Little's active part in the war came to an end. Under Jefferson the navy was greatly reduced and Little was discharged from the service on Oct. 20, 1801. He died suddenly in Weymouth, Mass., at the age of fifty-five. On June 24, 1779, he was married to Rachel Rogers (1758–1838) of Marshfield. Their son Edward Preble Little, who was named for Commodore Preble and was a midshipman on the *Boston,* was a member of the United States House of Representatives, 1852–53.

[*Mass. Soldiers and Sailors of the Revolutionary War,* IX (1902), 868; L. S. Richards, *Hist. of Marshfield,* vol. II (1905); C. O. Paullin, *The Navy of the Am. Revolution* (1906); G. W. Allen, *Our Naval War with France* (1909); *Mass. Hist. Soc. Proc.,* vol. XX (1884); *New-England Palladium* (Boston), July 28, 1809.]

C. O. P.

LITTLE CROW V (*c.* 1803–July 3, 1863), Indian chief, was the son of Little Crow IV. The name Little Crow, Chetan-wakan-mani, "the sacred pigeon-hawk that comes walking," was held in succession by several chiefs of the Kapoja band of Mdewakanton Sioux, in southeastern Minnesota. The Little Crow who appears in Pike's journal (1805–06) and who signed the treaty ceding the ground on which Fort Snelling was built, is generally accounted the third of the dynasty. Wabasha [*q.v.*], the head chief, told Pike that Little Crow III was "the man of most sense in their nation." He appears frequently in the accounts of travelers of the time and always with praise. In 1824 he visited Washington. He was succeeded by Little Crow IV, known also as Big Thunder and Big Eagle. The accounts of his life are hopelessly conflicting. It is agreed that he died of an accidentally self-inflicted wound, but the dates given are widely divergent. Gen. H. H. Sibley, who was present at the death of the chief, says that he died in 1834, and that he was a good and wise man who taught his people agriculture and as an example to them worked in his own fields. On his deathbed he called in his eldest son and after reproving the young man for his evil ways and telling him that another son, recently killed by the Chippewas, had been intended for the succession, reluctantly gave him the chieftainship.

Little Crow V, according to Sibley, paid little heed to his father's reproof. He was a drunkard and a confirmed liar, with few redeeming qualities. He signed the treaty of Mendota, Aug. 5, 1851, by which the Mdewakanton Sioux ceded most of their lands and withdrew to the upper

Minnesota River, but he afterward used this treaty as an argument for stirring up antagonism to the whites. A persuasive orator, he was chiefly responsible for the outbreak which followed eleven years later. On Aug. 18, 1862, incensed because of the non-arrival of the annuities provided for in the treaty and deluded by the belief that because of the Civil War no soldiers would be available for the defense of the settlements, the Sioux rose in revolt. Along a stretch of the frontier for more than two hundred miles they pillaged and burned the farm houses and villages and with an unparalleled ferocity tortured and massacred the inhabitants, nearly a thousand of whom are estimated to have perished. Little Crow commanded the force which unsuccessfully attacked Fort Ridgely, Aug. 20–22, and also the force which was routed by General Sibley at Wood Lake, Sept. 23. After this decisive action he fled to his kinfolk farther west, but in the following year, with a young son, again ventured into the devastated territory, to which many of the settlers had returned. On the evening of July 3, while prowling about a farm near Hutchinson, McLeod County, he was shot and killed.

Despite his dissoluteness, Little Crow V was a man of energy and determination. He possessed, however, no military talents, and he held power solely through his oratorical abilities. Though he is said to have had twenty-two children, the issue of six wives, the dynasty ended with his death.

[Cyrus Thomas, *Handbook of Am. Indians,* vol. I (1907); H. H. Sibley, "Reminiscences of the Early Days of Minn.," *Minn. Hist. Soc. Colls.,* vol. III (1880); W. W. Folwell, *Hist. of Minn.* (4 vols., 1921–30); Elliott Coues, *The Expeditions of Zebulon Montgomery Pike* (3 vols., 1895); H. R. Schoolcraft, *Summary Narrative of an Exploratory Expedition . . . in 1820* (1855).]

W. J. G.

LITTLE TURTLE (*c.* 1752–July 14, 1812), Miami chief, whose Indian name was Michikinikwa, was born in a Miami village on Eel River, twenty miles northwest of Fort Wayne, Ind. His father was a Miami chief and his mother is said to have been a Mahican. Of his early life little is known. He was on good terms with the British and rendered some service to them in the American Revolution. He took part in the massacre of De La Balme's forces, at Aboite River, in 1780. In the troublous years that followed, when the early Ohio settlements were being made, Little Turtle grew no more friendly toward Americans. His skill in war and his oratorical powers made him one of the most important chiefs in the old Northwest. With great military shrewdness he acted as one of the principal leaders of the Indians at the defeat of Harmar, in 1790, and of St. Clair, in 1791. In the autumn of 1792 he commanded the Indian forces in a skirmish with a company of Kentuckians. When General Anthony Wayne marched his troops into the Northwest, Little Turtle led the attack on Fort Recovery in 1794 and sought British aid against the Americans, but, later, counseled peace. His advice was not taken by the other chiefs, who were elated over their former successes; he lost his leadership in council and was not in command at Fallen Timbers. He signed the Treaty of Greenville in 1795 and many subsequent treaties with the United States. When William Henry Harrison [*q.v.*] undertook the rapid acquisition of title to Indian lands, Little Turtle was granted a special annuity by the United States (Indian Office Letter Book, A, pp. 144, 205, 233) and, with his son-in-law, William Wells, was sent to obtain Indian support for the cession; but his activities failed to satisfy Harrison. Nevertheless, in 1805 his annuity was increased by fifty dollars and he was given a negro slave (*American State Papers, post,* p. 702).

He visited the cities of the United States several times and became a popular Indian hero to the Americans. He met the French philosopher, Volney, who questioned him about the native races, and he received gifts from the great Kościuszko. In 1801 he delivered, before a committee of Friends in Baltimore, a speech against the introduction of whiskey into the Indian country (*Memorial of Evan Thomas, and others, a Committee Appointed for Indian Affairs by the Yearly Meeting . . . 1802,* 1802, pp. 5–10). The United States built him a house at his village. He adopted some American ways and acquired a white man's disease, gout. Among his own people his prestige declined sharply, but he is credited with keeping the Miami from joining the confederacy of Tecumseh. A frequent visitor at Fort Wayne, he received medical attention from the army surgeon and died there shortly after the beginning of the second war with England.

[C. M. Young, *Little Turtle* (1917); C. F. Chasseboeuf, Comte de Volney, *Tableau du Climat et du Sol des États-Unis* (1803), vol. II; "Governors Messages and Letters. Messages and Letters of Wm. H. Harrison," *Ind. Hist. Colls.* (2 vols., 1922); *Am. State Papers, Indian Affairs,* vol. I (1832); E. D. Mansfield, *Personal Memories* (1879); J. P. Dunn, *True Indian Stories* (1908).]

W. B—r.

LITTLEFIELD, GEORGE WASHINGTON (June 21, 1842–Nov. 10, 1920), cowman, banker, and patron of higher education, was born in Panola County, Miss., the child of Fleming and Mildred M. (Satterwhite) Littlefield. His father, a cotton planter, emigrated to Texas to settle in Gonzales County in 1850. Three years later he died and left the problems of an extensive plantation and two hundred slaves to the management of his capable wife. In August 1861 George W. Littlefield enlisted in Company I of the 8th Texas Cavalry, known to fame as Terry's Texas Rangers, and served until the Civil War was almost over. As a lieutenant he fought at Shiloh, where his company lost one-third of its men; as a captain he experienced heavy fighting under Bragg. He fought at Chickamauga and at the battle of Lookout Mountain. During a furlough, Jan. 14, 1863, he married Alice P. Tiller of Houston, Tex. Late in December 1863, while he held the brevet rank of major, he suffered a severe wound; and several months afterward was mustered from service and returned to Texas apparently a hopeless invalid.

His health improved, however, while he was managing a family plantation and operating a small country store, and when the floods of the San Marcos and Guadalupe rivers destroyed the local crops in 1871, he retrieved the family fortune by driving a herd of Texas cattle over the trail to Abilene, Kan. Seeing the possibilities of driving cattle from the over-crowded ranges of Texas to the markets of the Middle West, he formed a mercantile and trail-driving partnership which lasted seven years and proved very profitable. In 1877 he established a cattle ranch on the free, open ranges of the Panhandle near Tascosa which in 1881 he sold to a Scotch company for $253,000. Another ranch which he located on the Pecos River in New Mexico in 1882 soon ranged 40,000 head of cattle and spread the fame of Littlefield's LFD brand the length of the West. In 1883 he moved from Gonzales to Austin, where in 1890 he organized the American National Bank. Its growth was rapid, and he served as its president until his death. The great bronze doors of its present building, embossed with herds of LFD cattle, still suggest the basis of its origin. In time murals were painted upon the walls depicting the work of handling approximately 70,000 cattle upon 450,000 acres in the Littlefield name.

In 1912 Littlefield's attention was attracted to the need of a great depository of Southern historical source material, and two years later he established the Littlefield Fund for Southern History at the University of Texas, an endowment which he later enlarged to $125,000, the income from which was to be used "for the full and impartial study of the South and its part in American History." The interest thus encouraged led him to make further gifts and bequests: $225,000 for the purchase of the Wrenn Library, $350,000 for the Alice Littlefield Dormitory, $250,000 for an entrance to the University commemorating great Southern statesmen, $500,000 to apply on the construction of a main building, besides other generous donations.

Littlefield had the traditional characteristics of the Western man in that he was easily approached and generous hearted. He was of heavy, medium stature, while his ruddy complexion suggested the man of the open rather than the office. He was a strong supporter of the Democratic party, a Mason, and an adherent of the Southern Presbyterian Church. At his death in his seventy-ninth year he was survived by his wife, but he left no children.

[E. C. Barker, "Southern History in the South," *Nation* (N. Y.), July 2, 1914; letters from E. C. Barker suggesting a Southern History fund, and replies in decision by Geo. W. Littlefield, 1912–14, in the Archives of the Univ. of Texas; L. E. Daniell, *Types of Successful Men of Texas* (1890); J. M. Hunter, *The Trail Drivers of Texas*, vol. II (1923); *The Alcalde* (Austin), X, 1513; *Who's Who in America*, 1918–19; *Austin American*, Jan. 6, 1918; *Dallas Morning News*, Nov. 11, 1920.]

J. E. H.

LITTLEJOHN, ABRAM NEWKIRK (Dec. 13, 1824–Aug. 3, 1901), Protestant Episcopal bishop of Long Island, was born in Florida, Montgomery County, N. Y., where his maternal grandfather, Abram Newkirk, was among the early settlers of the region. Soon after his birth his parents, John and Eleanor (Newkirk) Littlejohn, removed to Johnstown, N. Y. After graduating with high standing from Union College in 1845, he studied privately for the ministry of the Episcopal Church and was ordained deacon Mar. 19, 1848, by Bishop William Heathcote DeLancey of Western New York. After a brief ministry in St. Ann's Church, Amsterdam, N. Y., he removed to St. Andrew's Church, Meriden, Conn., and was ordained to the priesthood by Bishop Thomas C. Brownell in Christ Church, Hartford, June 12, 1849. In 1850–51 he was in charge of Christ Church, Springfield, Mass., and then became rector of St. Paul's Church, New Haven, Conn., where his successful ministry brought him into prominence. He served as lecturer in pastoral theology at the Berkeley Divinity School during most of his rectorship at St. Paul's. In 1858 he was elected president of Geneva (now Hobart) College, Geneva, N. Y., but declined the office. He was called in 1860 to the Church of the Holy Trinity, Brooklyn, N. Y., where both as a preacher and pastor he attained notable success. When, in 1868, two new dioceses, those of Central New York and Long Island, were created in the state of New York, he had the honor of being elected simultaneously by both to the office of bishop.

He chose Long Island, and was consecrated to the episcopate in his own church on Jan. 27, 1869.

Bishop Littlejohn was one of the earliest members of the American episcopate to press for the erection of a cathedral. He interested Alexander T. Stewart [*q.v.*], the New York merchant, and his wife, and through their donations the Cathedral Church of the Incarnation was erected at Garden City, Long Island, in 1885. After Stewart's death his widow gave a large sum for the endowment of the work, and the Cathedral Schools, St. Paul's for boys and St. Mary's for girls, were erected on the same foundation. Littlejohn was in charge of the American Episcopal churches in Europe from 1874 to 1885. He officiated at the consecration of the American Church of St. Paul at Rome and was instrumental in establishing the present Church of the Holy Trinity in Paris. In the field of literature he attained a considerable reputation and contributed articles on literary, philosophical, and religious topics to American and English reviews. He was invited in 1880 by the University of Cambridge, England, to deliver a course of lectures, which were afterward published under the title, *Individualism: Its Growth and Tendencies, with Some Suggestions as to the Remedy for Its Evils* (1881); and in 1884 he delivered the Paddock Lectures at the General Theological Seminary, published that year as *The Christian Ministry at the Close of the Nineteenth Century*. He was married to Jane Armstrong, in June 1851, and had two daughters. He died suddenly, in his seventy-seventh year, while visiting in Williamstown, Mass.

[W. S. Perry, *The Episcopate in America* (1895); F. S. Lowndes, *Bishops of the Day* (1897); *Lloyd's Clerical Directory*, 1898; *Am. Church Almanac*, 1902; *Churchman*, *Church Standard*, and *Living Church*, all of Aug. 10, 1901; *N. Y. Tribune*, Aug. 4, 1901; information from Mrs. Harry Hart, Pelham, N. Y., and from the vital records of New Haven, Conn.] G. L. R.

LITTLEPAGE, LEWIS (Dec. 19, 1762–July 19, 1802), soldier of fortune, born in Hanover County, Va., was the son of Col. James Littlepage by his second wife, Elizabeth Lewis. His paternal ancestors had been settled in Virginia since 1660. In 1778 he entered the College of William and Mary, but, eager for a diplomatic career, in which ambition his uncle and guardian, Col. Benjamin Lewis, supported him, he was accepted as a protégé, after solicitation, by John Jay [*q.v.*], recently appointed minister to Spain. He sailed for Bordeaux late in 1779, remained many months in Nantes learning French, and arrived at Madrid in November 1780, when Jay took him into his family. By petty intrigues with William Carmichael, Jay's secretary, and Henry Brockholst Livingston, Jay's brother-in-law, he contributed to dissensions in the Jay household. Meanwhile Jay advanced him numerous sums of money, amounting to more than a thousand dollars. In June 1781, despite the pointed advice of Jay, he turned from diplomacy to war and joined the staff of the Duc de Crillon. Jay refused to advance him further moneys, whereupon the posts were filled with insulting letters from the youthful warrior. To these Jay replied in patient, conciliatory spirit. At the siege of Port Mahon Littlepage was wounded. Jay demanded in March 1782 that he return to Madrid; he replied that his "military Quixotism is not yet abated" and joined the Duc de Crillon in the disastrous siege of Gibraltar. He was on a floating battery which was blown up, but he escaped and won a reputation for gallantry and the praises of the King of Spain. At Gibraltar he formed a friendship with Lafayette and the Prince of Nassau.

In the fall of 1783 he was in Paris, where he attempted to secure the appointment to carry the definitive treaty of peace to Congress. His failure he unjustly attributed to the machinations of Jay, from whom he was now completely estranged. In December 1783 he accompanied the Prince of Nassau to Constantinople; the following year, at the Diet of Grodno, he met Stanislaus Augustus, King of Poland, and agreed, when once he had settled his affairs in the United States, to enter his service.

He arrived in Virginia in July 1785; in November he went to New York to secure from Congress a letter of recommendation to the King of Poland. He transmitted to Jay, then secretary for foreign affairs, letters from various European worthies. When Congress adjourned on Dec. 2 without having considered his petition, Littlepage suspected another of Jay's machinations. Jay meanwhile began suit to collect the moneys due him. Littlepage, encouraged by the French minister, prepared a vituperative attack upon Jay which was published in the *New York Daily Advertiser* for Dec. 6, 7, and 10. Littlepage had been given money by the State of Virginia to settle accounts with Houdon; this money he deposited as a bond to settle the debt, and sailed for France. Jay, to contradict "this Young Man's Ebullitions," early in 1786, published a lengthy pamphlet, *Letters, Being the Whole of the Correspondence between the Hon. John Jay, Esquire and Mr. Lewis Littlepage,* later republished with additional material. Littlepage, from Warsaw, replied with his *Answer to a Pamphlet . . .* (1786), which did little more than confirm his vituperative abilities.

On Mar. 2, 1786, he became chamberlain to the King of Poland and during the next several years negotiated a successful treaty with the Empress of Russia and another with the court of Spain. He traveled in Italy and was employed as a secret envoy to the French court. He participated, in 1788, in the naval victory over the Turks at Oczacow and from 1792 to 1794 he fought against the Russian invasion of Poland. When in February 1798 his friend King Stanislaus died, the Emperor of Russia paid him almost £10,000 sterling promised him by Stanislaus. He remained in Warsaw until early in 1801 when he went to Hamburg. Here his life and fortune were threatened by numerous plots; and he became involved in difficulties with England and France. Wearied by European intrigues, he returned to Virginia. His health had been shattered by the active life of court and camp, and he died in Fredericksburg at the age of thirty-nine. In accordance with his request, his papers were destroyed by his executors.

[Jay's pamphlet, collated with the original letters, is an exact printing of the correspondence between Jay and Littlepage while they were in Spain; H. E. Hayden's *Va. Geneals.* (1891; repr. 1931), pp. 395–420, contains a valuable and sympathetic sketch, with important letters to and from Littlepage; see also the *New York Daily Advertiser* (*ante*); William Jay, *Life of John Jay* (1833), I, 204–29; and *Va. Herald* (Fredericksburg), July 20, 1802.] F. M.

LIVERMORE, ABIEL ABBOT (Oct. 30, 1811–Nov. 28, 1892), Unitarian clergyman, author, president of the Meadville Theological School, was a descendant of John Livermore who in 1634 came to Watertown, Mass., from Ipswich, England. He was the grandson of the Rev. Jonathan Livermore, pastor of the Congregational Church in Wilton, N. H., and son of Jonathan Livermore, a Wilton farmer of high repute, who married Abigail Abbot, daughter of Maj. Abiel Abbot, a Revolutionary patriot. The son Abiel, after early years of farm employment and district schooling, was for six months, at the age of fifteen, a student in an academy in Chelmsford, Mass., and thereafter in Phillips Exeter Academy until in 1830 he was admitted to the sophomore class of Harvard College. In Harvard he roomed with Francis Bowen, the later philosopher, was active in college societies, supported himself by tutoring boys for college entrance, and won high standing for scholarship.

After theological study (1833–36) in the Cambridge Divinity School, he was ordained, Nov. 2, 1836, as pastor of the Congregational Church in Keene, N. H. During this congenial pastorate he was a community leader in the promotion of culture. He served on the school committee, was a trustee of Cheshire Academy, founded a flourishing book and periodical club, stimulated interest in foreign literature, and edited a *Social Gazette* for the publication of the literary efforts of local young people. In 1841 he published a commentary on Matthew's Gospel which in three years had four editions and was reissued in Belfast, Ireland. By 1844 the work covered four Gospels and the Book of Acts, and in this form was republished in London, 1846. In 1854 he added a volume on Romans, and in 1881 two more on the rest of the New Testament. The work afforded a moderate liberal interpretation on principles learned in the Cambridge school. At this time he shared in the anti-slavery movement and successfully competed for a prize of five hundred dollars offered by the American Peace Society by a work entitled *The War with Mexico Reviewed* (1850). This historical discussion shows a mastery of many original sources and skilfully exhibits the social psychology of the country in that period.

Seeking a milder climate Livermore accepted a call to the Unitarian Church in Cincinnati, serving there from May 26, 1850, to July 6, 1856. To this troubled church he brought stability by his tolerant, inclusive, fraternal spirit, his talent for organization, and the sustained high thinking and literary charm of his preaching. To unite and increase the liberal churches he organized in 1852 the Western Unitarian Conference, serving it as corresponding secretary. The publication of his elevated *Discourses* in 1854 and articles in the *North American Review* (July 1855) and the *Christian Examiner* (January 1856) made him widely known and led to an appointment as editor of the *Christian Inquirer,* necessitating a removal to New York in July 1856. Aiding in the organization of a Unitarian Church in Yonkers, N. Y. (1857), he became its settled pastor in June 1859. In addition to these two offices he served as non-resident lecturer for brief annual periods in the Theological School of Meadville, Pa., and in 1863 relinquished other duties to become the president of that institution.

Conservative as he was by temperament, his new administrative career showed open-minded hospitality to new policies and progressive thought. In 1864 the school was opened to women students. In the autumn of that year he gave twelve lectures in the Lowell Institute in Boston upon Christianity as related to an environment of general religious development and in the following he gave in Meadville a course on comparative religion, sharing with Bouvier of Geneva and James Freeman Clarke of Harvard the distinction of first introducing the subject into the academic curriculum. He made some adjustment of his Biblical teaching to the modern critical views of Kuenen and in his course in ethics dealt with modern social problems. From 1881 there was a rapid development of courses in practical and theoretical sociology in the curriculum. While president he published *Lectures to Young Men on Their Moral Dangers and Duties* (1864), completed his New Testament commentary (1881), collaborated with Sewall Putnam in a *History of the Town of Wilton* (1888), and wrote varied articles for the *Unitarian Review* (1874–91). On May 17, 1838, he married his cousin Elizabeth Dorcas Abbot of Windham, N. H., a woman of poetic gift, author of a novel, *Zoe, or the Octaroon's Triumph.* She died Sept. 13, 1879. On June 18, 1883, he married Mary A. (Keating) Moore of Meadville who survived him. He had no children. Resigning his presidency in 1890 he retired to the ancient hillside home in Wilton and there he died. An oil portrait of Livermore is preserved in the Meadville School, now situated in Chicago.

[For biographical details see: W. E. Thwing, *The Livermore Family of America* (1902); S. G. Griffin, *Hist. of the Town of Keene* (1904); G. A. Thayer, *The First Cong. Ch. of Cincinnati: A Hist. Sketch* (1917), and the *Hist. of the Town of Wilton* (1888), mentioned above. For characterizations see: F. A. Christie, *Makers of the Meadville Theol. School* (1927); F. L. Phalen, "Abiel Abbot Livermore," in *Heralds of a Liberal Faith* (1910), vol. III, ed. by S. A. Eliot; and J. H. Morison, article in the *Christian Reg.*, Dec. 2, 1892. Livermore's diary for the years 1836–48, with notes by J. H. Wilson, is in the possession of the N. H. Hist. Soc., Concord, N. H. That for earlier and later years is in the possession of the Rev. John Henry Wilson, Littleton, Mass.] F. A. C.

LIVERMORE, ARTHUR (July 29, 1766–July 1, 1853), chief justice of New Hampshire, congressman, third son of Judge Samuel Livermore, 1732–1803 [*q.v.*], and Jane, daughter of the Rev. Arthur Browne of Portsmouth, was born in Londonderry (now Derry), N. H. His early education was begun at a school in Portsmouth and was continued after 1775 at Holderness by his father and by Dr. John Porter. He was sent when about fifteen to a school in Concord, and here he later studied law in the office of his brother, Edward St. Loe Livermore [*q.v.*]. Admitted to the bar in 1791, he practised in Concord till 1793, and then in Chester. Already he was showing signs of both the ability and the fiery temper which distinguished him in later life, for besides building up a practice, he was elected a representative to the legislature (1794–95), was commissioned solicitor of Rockingham County (1796–98), and gave a thrashing to the notorious "Lord" Timothy Dexter [*q.v.*], then living in Chester. In 1798 he was appointed a judge of the superior court of New Hampshire, and in 1809 he was made chief justice. When the courts were reorganized in 1813 he was appointed associate justice of the supreme court. This court, however, was dissolved in 1816, and Livermore, for a time, exchanged the bench for the floor of Congress, to which he was three times elected a representative, in 1816, 1818, and 1822. In 1820 he was elected to the Senate of New Hampshire, and in 1822 he was made judge of probate in Grafton County, but he resigned the next year. At the expiration of his third term in Congress, in 1825, he returned to the bench as chief justice of the New Hampshire court of common pleas, but in 1832 this court was abolished, and he retired from public life, after thirty-eight years of continuous service. He had married, on Mar. 27, 1810, Louisa Bliss, daughter of Joseph Bliss of Haverhill, N. H. There were eight children, six of whom were sons.

Livermore was an able member of the state legislature and of Congress, where he was known as a strong opponent of the extension of slavery in general, and of the Missouri Compromise in particular. Despite this attitude, he numbered prominent Southerners among his friends, even including John Randolph of Roanoke. He was not a great speaker, but he effectively employed his sarcastic wit. As a judge he was guided by honesty and common sense rather than by precedents, and he refused to allow the discussion of technicalities to obscure justice. He was never a rich man, but he was always generous. Soon after his father's death (1803), he purchased from his elder brother the family estate at Holderness. Here there was always hospitality for the poor. Obliged to sell the Holderness property, he retired in 1832 to a small farm, "Craigie Burn," in the neighboring township of Campton, where he spent the last twenty years of his life. He lies buried in the old churchyard at Holderness.

[The most interesting biographical material is contained in unsigned manuscript notes now known to be by Livermore's son, Arthur, and preserved in the library of the N. H. Hist. Soc. at Concord. These are partially reproduced in an address by E. S. Stearns, printed in the *Proc. Grafton and Coos County Bar Asso.*, vol. II (1893). Additional material is found in letters from Arthur Livermore, Jr., in *Ibid.*, vol. III (1897). The manuscript copies of the records of Trinity Church, Holderness, now in the library of the N. H. Hist. Soc., are of some value. See also: *Annals of Cong.*, 1817–21, 1823–25; C. H. Bell, *The Bench and Bar of N. H.* (1894); W. E. Thwing, *The Livermore Family of America* (1902); E. S. Stackpole, *Hist. of N. H.* (1916), vol. II; and the *Portsmouth Jour. of Lit. and Pol.*, July 9, 1853. Two portraits are reproduced in the *Proc. Grafton and Coos County Bar Asso.*, II, 434, 439, and a copy of one of these hangs in the court-room in the State Library at Concord.] E. V. M.

LIVERMORE, EDWARD ST. LOE (Apr. 5, 1762–Sept. 15, 1832), lawyer, congressman, was born in Portsmouth, N. H., the eldest son of Samuel Livermore, 1732–1803 [*q.v.*] and Jane Browne. His early youth was passed during the critical years preceding the American war for independence. His father, who held the office of King's attorney for New Hampshire, withdrew with his family from Portsmouth to Londonderry (now Derry) and later (1775) to Holderness, then a frontier settlement with no roads and little communication with the world. As there was no school, Edward, now thirteen, and his younger brothers, George and Arthur [*q.v.*], were taught by their parents and by Dr. John Porter and his wife, who had accompanied the Livermore family to Holderness. Porter was a Harvard graduate and his wife a woman of culture, and Edward and his brothers were given the foundation of a classical education. This seems to have been the only academic training he had, but it was sufficient to give him the polished speech, which later distinguished him, and to prepare him for the study of law. The latter he pursued in the office of Chief Justice Theophilus Parsons, at Newburyport, Mass., and at the age of twenty-one he began to practise in Concord, N. H. A few years later he returned to his birthplace, Portsmouth, where he soon entered public life.

In 1791 Livermore was elected to the convention (of which his father was president) assembled to revise the constitution of New Hampshire and he served on several important committees. He was also appointed during this period solicitor of Rockingham County (1791–93) and United States district attorney in New Hampshire, 1794–97. He resigned the latter office when the governor made him judge of the superior court, and a year later he resigned this position also because of its meager salary of only eight hundred dollars. On Sept. 20, 1798, President Adams appointed him naval officer for the port of Portsmouth, but Jefferson removed him in 1802 for party reasons. Livermore appears after this as an ardent Federalist. Having moved to Newburyport, Mass., he was elected (1807) to represent Essex County in Congress, where he served for four years, proving himself an able speaker and a strong opponent of measures favored by Jefferson and Madison, especially the Embargo, against which he spoke frequently and forcefully. In 1811 he took up his residence in Boston. Here he became prominent as a sharp critic of the War of 1812. In 1815 he removed with his family to Zanesville, Ohio, then considered "the West," where he expected to settle, but he soon returned to New England and purchased a farm near the confluence of the Concord and the Merrimac rivers, in that part of Tewksbury, Mass., which was later included in Lowell. Here he died, at the age of seventy. He was buried in Boston in the Old Granary Burying-ground. Livermore was twice married: on Aug. 7, 1784, to Mehitable, daughter of Robert Harris of Concord, by whom he had five children; and on May 2, 1799, to Sarah, daughter of William Stackpole of Boston, by whom he had seven children. Samuel Livermore, 1786–1833 [*q.v.*], a son by the first marriage, distinguished himself in the law; Harriet Livermore, a daughter by the first marriage, became well known as an evangelist. Quick of temper, proud, impatient of contradiction, and intellectually keen, he was respected and admired, but he did not attain the popularity or prominence of his father.

[See C. H. Bell, *The Bench and Bar of N. H.* (1894); E. S. Stackpole, *Hist. of N. H.* (1916); W. E. Thwing, *The Livermore Family of America* (1902), which reproduces a portrait; the memoir by C. L. A. Read in *Contributions of the Old Residents' Hist. Asso. of Lowell, Mass.*, vol. II (1883); and the obituary in the *Boston Daily Advertiser & Patriot*, Sept. 21, 1832. There are personal references to him in some manuscript notes furnished by his nephew, Arthur, to E. S. Stearns, and now in the library of the N. H. Hist. Soc. at Concord. *The N. H. Provincial and State Papers*, vols. X (1877) and XXII (1893), and the *Annals of Cong.*, 1807–11, contain the official record of his public service and his speeches in Congress.] E. V. M.

LIVERMORE, GEORGE (July 10, 1809–Aug. 30, 1865), antiquarian, was the son of Deacon Nathaniel and Elizabeth (Gleason) Livermore and a descendant of John Livermore who emigrated to Massachusetts from Ipswich, England, in 1634. Born in Cambridge, Mass., he attended public and private schools in the town until he was fourteen years old and then went to work in a store kept by his brothers. College was denied him because of his frail constitution. In 1834 he entered the shoe and leather business and four years later he became a wool merchant, but his great interest was in books and reading. Biblical works were his specialty, and as his collection of Bibles and related material grew, be became recognized as an authority in that field. In 1845 he traveled abroad and met, among other distinguished men, Dibdin, the bibliographer, and the poëts Rogers and Wordsworth. Upon landing at Liverpool, and again upon leaving England, he visited the grave of William Roscoe, for whose achievements and character he had great admiration. In 1849 he wrote a series of eight articles for the *Cambridge Chronicle* (Apr. 5–May 24), signed "The Antiquary," reprinted in a thin volume entitled *The Origin, History, and Character of the New-England Primer* (1849) which attracted considerable attention. He was elected a member of the American Antiquarian Society and of the Massachusetts Historical Society in the autumn of that year. At Commencement in 1850 Harvard conferred upon him the honorary degree of master of arts. In 1855 he became a member of the American Academy of Arts and Sciences and was the treasurer of that institution at the time of his death.

When the Civil War broke out Livermore threw himself whole-heartedly into the cause of the Union. The question whether the government should accept colored troops evoked from him a work of over two hundred pages entitled *An Historical Research Respecting the Opinions of the Founders of the Republic, on Negroes as Slaves, as Citizens, and as Soldiers* (1862). His thesis was that the leaders of the American Revolution regarded negroes as men capable of bearing arms and of being citizens, and that the same attitude should prevail in the current crisis. President Lincoln consulted the book when preparing the Emancipation Proclamation and later gave Livermore the pen with which he signed that document. Livermore survived the Civil War, but the excitement of Lee's surrender and the shock of Lincoln's death were more than his delicate constitution could bear. He died less than six months after these events occurred and was survived by his wife, Elizabeth Cunningham (Odiorne) Livermore, and three sons. Although his nature was sensitive, intense, and sometimes intolerant, his outstanding qualities were simplicity, modesty, and conscientiousness. As an antiquarian and scholar he was remarkable for his accuracy.

[The *Memoir of Geo. Livermore* (1869), by Chas. Deane, is the best account, but good side-lights are thrown on his career by the tributes of contemporaries in the *Proc. Mass. Hist. Soc.*, vol. VIII (1866); *Boston Daily Advertiser*, Sept. 2, 1865; H. C. Badger, *The Consecrated Life* (1865); and E. E. Hale, *The Pub. Duty of a Private Citizen* (1865). For genealogical details see W. E. Thwing, *The Livermore Family of America* (1902).] L. S. M.

LIVERMORE, MARY ASHTON RICE (Dec. 19, 1820–May 23, 1905), reformer, suffragist, author, was the fourth child of Timothy and Zebiah Vose Glover (Ashton) Rice. Her father was descended from Edmund Rice, who came to Massachusetts in 1638; her mother's father was born in London. In her parents' Boston home on Salem Street, not far from the Old North Church, Mary Rice passed most of her childhood. Here she was indoctrinated with the tenets of Calvinistic religion and with high ethical standards, while she received the education provided for girls by the public and private schools of Boston. Her New England schooling was once interrupted, when her father, infected with the western fever of the thirties, moved to a frontier section of New York state, only to return to Boston two years later, convinced that pioneer farming had few attractions.

Mary, having completed the work of the Hancock Grammar School at fourteen, entered the Female Seminary of Charlestown, where, before the end of her first year, she was teaching as well as studying. After graduation, she remained here as an instructor in French and Latin until an opportunity came to teach on a Virginia plantation. From this experience she later drew the picture of plantation life which is to be found in her *Story of my Life*. After her return to Massachusetts, while teaching at Duxbury, she met and married (May 1845) the Rev. Daniel Parker Livermore, of the Universalist Church. They lived together fifty-four years, until the death of Livermore on July 5, 1899. The first pastorate served by the young couple after their marriage was at Fall River, where they were indefatigable in their labors with reading and study groups, one of which was made up of factory operatives. Here Mary Livermore's first published work, a temperance story, was written. The next post, at Stafford, Conn., was resigned because of Daniel Livermore's advocacy of the temperance cause, in opposition to the majority of his congregation. After serving pastorates in Weymouth and Malden, Mass., they started for Kansas in 1857, but abandoned their intention to settle there and remained in Chicago. Here Daniel Livermore became editor and proprietor of a church periodical, the *New Covenant,* which he conducted from 1857 to 1869, his wife serving as associate editor. At the same time she cared for her two children, took a lively interest in local charities, and did much miscellaneous writing. She was the only woman to report the convention which nominated Lincoln.

With the outbreak of the Civil War, she devoted her extraordinary energy to the work of the Northwestern Branch of the United States Sanitary Commission. Up to this time she had given scant attention to the extension of the suffrage to women, believing that desirable social reforms could be accomplished by other methods than the vote. Her war experience seems to have convinced her that woman's suffrage would be the most direct route to the curtailing of the liquor traffic, improvements in public education, and the alleviation of many problems of poverty; and at the close of hostilities she directed all her efforts to the enfranchisement of women. At the first woman's suffrage convention in Chicago she delivered the opening address, and was elected president of the Illinois Woman's Suffrage

Association. In 1869 she established *The Agitator,* a paper devoted to the cause. A few months later, *The Agitator* was merged with the *Woman's Journal,* just established in Boston, and she undertook the editorship of the new periodical. The family then moved from Chicago, and for the remainder of her life she lived in Melrose, Mass.

In 1872 she gave up her editorial work to devote her time to public lecturing, and for the last twenty-five years of the century she was a well-known platform speaker, on social questions and topics of history, biography, politics, and education. The lecture she most frequently delivered was probably, "What Shall We Do with Our Daughters?" a plea for the higher education and the professional training of women. The two subjects in which she was most interested and in which her influence was most largely felt were the education of women and the cause of temperance. For ten years she was president of the Massachusetts Women's Christian Temperance Union; she was also president of the Massachusetts Woman's Suffrage Association, and was connected with the Women's Educational and Industrial Union and the National Conference of Charities and Corrections. Notable among her later publications are her two autobiographical volumes, *My Story of the War: A Woman's Narrative of Four Years Personal Experience* (1888) and *The Story of My Life, or, The Sunshine and Shadow of Seventy Years* (1897). In 1893 her name appeared, with that of Frances E. Willard [*q.v.*], as joint editor of *A Woman of the Century,* a compilation of biographical sketches, which went through a number of editions, under other titles. Throughout her life her vigor rarely failed, and she spoke from a public platform after she had passed her eighty-third birthday.

[Works mentioned above; *Arena,* Aug. 1892; Lilian Whiting, *Women Who Have Ennobled Life* (1915); E. S. Phelps, in *Our Famous Women* (1884); Mrs. J. A. Logan, *The Part Taken by Women in Am. Hist.* (1912); E. L. Didier, in *The Chautauquan,* July 1906; E. C. Stanton, S. B. Anthony, and M. J. Gage, *Hist. of Woman Suffrage* (6 vols., 1881–1922); W. E. Thwing, *The Livermore Family of America* (1902); *Woman's Jour.,* May 27, June 10, 1905; *Outlook,* June 3, 1905; *Boston Transcript,* May 23, 1905.] E. D.

LIVERMORE, SAMUEL (May 25, 1732–May 18, 1803), jurist, congressman, senator, was the third son and fourth child of Deacon Samuel Livermore and Hannah Brown, daughter of Deacon William Brown of Waltham, Mass. The Livermore family in America descended from John Livermore (Leathermore or Lithermore), a potter by trade, who left England in 1634 and was admitted the following year as freeman in Watertown, Mass. His descendants became people of substance and of importance. His great-grandson, Deacon Samuel, inherited from an uncle a farm in the township of Waltham, where he took up his residence and held various offices. Here his son Samuel was born. Nothing is known of the boy's early education, but at eighteen he was teaching in Chelsea, Mass., and at nineteen he entered the College of New Jersey (later Princeton), where he expected to fit himself for the ministry. He took his degree in one year, after which he returned to his teaching, at the same time studying law in the office of Edmund Trowbridge. At the age of twenty-four he was admitted to the bar and began to practise in Waltham, but he soon moved to Portsmouth, N. H., where he established his reputation as an energetic and fearless lawyer. He also became the warm friend of the royal agent, Governor Wentworth.

When trouble was brewing between the colony and the mother country, Livermore withdrew from Portsmouth to the Scotch-Irish settlement of Londonderry (now Derry), N. H. He was elected to represent the township in the General Assembly of 1768–70 but was recalled to Portsmouth in 1769 when Wentworth appointed him judge-advocate in the Admiralty court, and attorney-general. Five years later, however, he returned to Londonderry, and the next year (1775) he pushed farther still into the wilds to Holderness, at that time accessible only in winter, when vehicles could travel over the snow. Here he made his home, acquiring by grant and purchase more than two-thirds of the whole township, over which he practically ruled as "squire," building a dignified residence, a church, and a gristmill, and personally superintending both farm and mill when the break with England prevented the fulfilment of his duties as King's attorney-general. Despite his apparent withdrawal from the Revolutionary conflict, popular confidence in him led to his election in 1776 as attorney-general, and from this time almost until his death he held office under the state practically continuously, sometimes, indeed, filling two offices at once.

In 1779 he was elected by the General Court as commissioner to the Continental Congress to represent the interests of the state in the controversy over the "New Hampshire Grants" on the west side of the Connecticut River. His services as commissioner led to his being chosen again as a representative to Congress in 1785, 1789, and in 1791. At the end of the last term (1793), he was elected to the United States Senate, and at the end of the six-year term, he was reëlected for another six years but resigned in 1801 because of failing health. Twice he was chosen president of the Senate, *pro tempore,* and as such signed the address to the President on the death of Washington. Meantime, he had also been holding other state offices, the most important being that of chief justice of the superior court (1782–90). Thus he did not at first resign when elected to Congress, for there was then no law requiring it. When the Constitution of the United States was being debated, and the vote of New Hampshire hung in the balance, Livermore as a member of the convention of 1788 did great service in bringing about ratification, thus securing the ninth state and ensuring the acceptance of the Constitution. In 1791 he was president of the New Hampshire constitutional convention.

On Sept. 23, 1759, Livermore married Jane, daughter of the Rev. Arthur Browne of Portsmouth, the first minister of the Church of England to settle in New Hampshire. There were five children, the eldest of whom died in infancy. Of his surviving sons, Edward St. Loe and Arthur [*qq.v.*] both became distinguished lawyers, and George Williamson (1764–1805) held for many years the office of clerk of the court and register of deeds at Holderness. Few more picturesque or important figures than Samuel Livermore are found in early New Hampshire history. Homely and sometimes harsh of speech, he possessed a frankness and kindness of heart which atoned for his brusqueness, while his honesty and common sense as a judge made amends for his contempt for precedents and for his sometimes inconsistent decisions. He died at his home in Holderness and was buried there in the cemetery of Trinity Church.

[A part of Livermore's journal, telling of his journey to college in 1751, is quoted in a manuscript sketch of him (140 pp., undated) by his grandson, in the library of the N. H. Hist. Soc. at Concord. This manuscript also contains copies of letters and other memoranda. The journal has been printed in part in *Putnam's Mag.,* June 1857, pp. 631–35. *The N. H. Provincial and State Papers,* vols. VII, VIII, X, XXII (1873–1893), contain the records of his activities in the state, and the *Jours. of Cong.* and *Annals of Cong.* give his congressional service. A good sketch of his life by C. R. Corning may be found in the *Proc. Grafton and Coos County Bar Asso.,* vol. I (1888), and there are also sketches in C. H. Bell, *The Bench and Bar of N. H.* (1894); E. S. Stackpole, *Hist. of N. H.* (1916), vol. II; and the *N. H. Hist. Soc. Colls.,* vol. V (1837). More of his personality is given in the chapter devoted to him by Geo. Hodges in *Holderness* (1907). For the family genealogy, see Henry Bond, *Geneals. of the Families and Descendants of the Early Settlers of Watertown, Mass.* (1855), and W. E. Thwing, *The Livermore Family of America* (1902). See also F. M. Colby, "Holderness and the Livermores," *Granite Monthly,* Feb. 1881. A copy of a portrait by Trumbull hangs in the courtroom in the State Library at Concord and is reproduced in the *Proc. of the Grafton and Coos County Bar Asso.,* vol. II, and by Hodges, who also reproduces a portrait of Mrs. Livermore, attributed to Copley.]

E. V. M.

LIVERMORE, SAMUEL (Aug. 26, 1786–July 11, 1833), lawyer and legal writer, was born in Concord, N. H., the son of Edward St. Loe Livermore [*q.v.*], by his first wife, Mehitable Harris. He graduated from Harvard College in 1804, studied law, and was admitted to the Essex County bar. After his admission to the bar he moved to Boston, where he practised law for several years. During the War of 1812 he served as a volunteer on board the *Chesapeake* and was wounded in the engagement with the *Shannon.* After the war he moved to Baltimore and with others assisted Alexander C. Hanson [*q.v.*] in the publication of the *Federal Republican.* From Baltimore he moved to New Orleans, where his name appears in the city directory for 1822. Within a few years he had achieved distinction as a lawyer.

In 1811 Livermore published in Boston *A Treatise on the Law Relative to Principals, Agents, Factors, Auctioneers, and Brokers,* the first American work of its kind (Charles Warren, *A History of the American Bar,* 1911, p. 337). A second edition of this work in two volumes, entitled *A Treatise on the Law of Principal and Agent: and of Sales by Auction,* was published in Baltimore in 1818. In 1828 he published in New Orleans *Dissertations on the Questions which Arise from the Contrariety of the Positive Laws of Different States and Nations,* the first American work on the conflict of laws. The book has been described as "a forceful but belated attempt to reinstate the statutory theory of the mediaeval commentators" (J. H. Beale, *post,* part 1, par. 38, p. 49). His doctrines, however, "could not be applied in a country where both commercial and social intercourse between all parts of it are constant and continuous." Livermore influenced Story and other American lawyers by calling attention to the works of medieval authors. He presented to the Harvard Law School his collection of medieval works, containing 400 volumes and including the writers of the sixteenth, seventeenth, and eighteenth centuries on the conflict of laws. This collection "formed the basis of the large apparatus which Story's bibliography describes" (*Ibid.*). Livermore died at Florence, Ala., while he was on his way from New Orleans to New England to visit his relatives.

[For biographical data see W. E. Thwing, *The Livermore Family of America* (1902); W. T. Davis, *Bench and Bar of the Commonwealth of Mass.* (1895), vol. I; *Quinquennial Cat. of the Officers and Grads. of Harvard Univ.* (1915); and the *Florence* (Ala.) *Gazette,* July 12, 1833. For his legal writings consult J. G. Marvin, *Legal Bibliog.* (1847), and J. H. Beale, *A Treatise on the Conflict of Laws, or Private Internat. Law,* vol. I, pt. 1 (1916). References to his gift of books to the Harvard Law School appear in *The Centennial Hist. of the Harvard Law School* (1918).] M. J. W.

LIVINGSTON, EDWARD (May 28, 1764–May 23, 1836), statesman, was born at "Clermont," Columbia County, N. Y., the youngest son of Robert R. Livingston the elder [*q.v.*] and Margaret Beekman. His eldest brother was the distinguished Chancellor Robert R. Livingston [*q.v.*], and his sisters, by their marriages, added notable names to the family connection. Upon the death of his father in 1775, Edward Livingston was sent to school in Albany but he soon transferred to the school of Dominie Doll at Esopus (now Kingston) where he prepared for the College of New Jersey (Princeton), entering the junior class in 1779. He subsequently declared that at college he had been an indifferent scholar, learning only so much as was absolutely necessary to obtain his degree, which was granted in 1781. But he was already proficient in languages and his interest in philosophy and poetry was sufficient to attract the attention of John Jay. From Princeton he returned to "Clermont" to spend a year in the study of French under a Mr. Tetard and German under a refugee minister to whom his mother had given shelter. In 1782 he began the study of law at Albany in the office of John Lansing [*q.v.*] where he found as fellow students Alexander Hamilton, Aaron Burr, and James Kent. The removal of the British troops from New York City in November 1783 permitted the Livingston family to reoccupy their town house and there Edward continued his studies until his admission to the bar in January 1785. Moving freely in the society of New York, he acquired the title of "Beau Ned" on account of his habits of dress. While engaged in the practice of law he married, on Apr. 10, 1788, Mary, eldest daughter of Charles McEvers, a New York merchant. Three children were born to them before Mrs. Livingston contracted scarlet fever and died, Mar. 13, 1801.

The political career of Edward Livingston began with his election to Congress in 1794. The Livingstons had joined with the Schuylers in the movement for the ratification of the Constitution. They were, however, overlooked by Washington in the distribution of patronage and, almost in a body, they went over to the Clintons and the party of Thomas Jefferson. Taking his seat in the House of Representatives on Dec. 7, 1795, Edward Livingston moved on Dec. 15 to revise the penal code of the United States, which he said was in general too sanguinary and very badly proportioned. Nothing came of this effort in behalf of what was already a pet measure with him, but in March 1796 he secured the enactment of a measure for the relief of American seamen who were impressed or abandoned destitute on foreign shores. In the same month the House was called upon for appropriations to carry out Jay's treaty of 1794 with England. Although the treaty had been ratified, it was still opposed by the Republicans, and Livingston introduced a resolution calling for all the papers from the President, except those which any existing negotiation might render improper to be disclosed (*Annals of Congress,* 4 Cong., 1 Sess., p. 426). Representing the Republican stronghold of New York City, Livingston was reëlected in 1796 and again in 1798. He was, therefore, a member of the House of Representatives in 1801 when the failure of the electoral college to choose a president threw the election into that body. In the ensuing contest between Aaron Burr and Thomas Jefferson, there were rumors, not entirely groundless, that Livingston was favorable to the candidacy of Burr (Hunt, *post,* p. 86; D. S. Alexander, *Political History of The State of New York,* 1906, I, 103; Edward Livingston Manuscripts). The two men came from the same social class in New York and were personal friends. Nevertheless, Livingston was one of the six New York members who voted consistently for Jefferson, although it was believed he did so without enthusiasm.

Livingston had refused to run again for Congress in 1800 but the success of the Republicans in the election led to his appointment as United States attorney for the District of New York. Almost simultaneously he was appointed mayor of New York, a post estimated to be worth $10,000 a year. He collected and published *Judicial Opinions Delivered in the Mayor's Court of the City of New York in the Year 1802* (1803). While carrying the burden of both offices, he fell a victim to the yellow fever which raged in New York during the summer of 1803. He recovered to find that during his illness one of his agents, in the collection of custom house bonds sent him by the Treasury, had absconded with the funds. Livingston immediately resigned his offices and turned over his property to trustees to be sold in payment of his debts. "I can show, however, upwards of $100,000 in property at a very moderate valuation above my debts," he wrote his sister, Mrs. Montgomery, Aug. 24, 1803. "I shall with the close of this year begin the world anew and have serious thoughts of doing so at New Orleans" (Edward Livingston Manuscripts). Without waiting for an adjustment of his accounts, he voluntarily confessed judgment in favor of the United States for $100,000 although the sum actually due turned out to be $43,666.21. In December he started for New Orleans, arriving there in the middle of February. Immediately he began the practice of the law, appearing in thirty-five cases during the spring of 1804 and receiving payments chiefly in the form of land. That he was desperately in need of money soon became apparent. His brother, who had been left in charge of his affairs in New York, found that Livingston's private debts amounted to $195,000. This sum, added to the debt due the United States, exceeded the value of his property. When all his property had been sold, he still owed $18,000 on his private debts as well as the debt due the government.

Determination to pay his debts soon brought him into difficulties. Among his creditors was Aaron Burr [*q.v.*], who had embarked upon his famous "conspiracy." Burr, on July 26, 1806, transferred his debt to Dr. Justus E. Bollman [*q.v.*], who presented a draft upon Livingston in New Orleans. Payment had scarcely been made when General Wilkinson [*q.v.*], who had originally been a confederate of Burr but who had betrayed him and was energetically striving to bring him to punishment, accused Livingston in open court of connection with the "conspiracy" (Hunt, pp. 126–33; account by Livingston in Edward Livingston Manuscripts). The only ground of this accusation was the payment of the draft to Dr. Bollman. Livingston had just cleared himself of the calumny when the famous Batture controversy brought him into conflict with President Jefferson. Certain alluvial lands at New Orleans had passed by descent to John Gravier who, in 1803, fenced a portion of them which had long been used by the people for the anchorage of their ships. Gravier brought suit against the city to confirm his title and engaged Livingston as his attorney. When judgment for the plaintiff was secured in 1807, Livingston received half the property as his fee. Livingston believed he was now within immediate reach of great wealth, for he observed that the improvement of the property would provide wharfage and warehousing facilities for the growing city. But the improvements were hindered by popular disturbances and the grand jury declared the work a nuisance. Appeal to Governor Claiborne led to the reference of the matter to Washington. But Jefferson was angry because Livingston in his conduct of the office of United States attorney had given ground for criticism of his party and its appointments. The Attorney-General ruled against Livingston and the United States marshal was directed to dispossess him on the ground that the land belonged to the United States as sovereign of the soil. The dispossession was carried out in contravention of an injunction from the territorial court, whereupon Livingston brought an action against the marshal in the United States court at New Orleans to recover damages, according to the forms of the civil law, for his expulsion and a restoration to possession, and, a little later, an action for damages against Thomas Jefferson. Meanwhile, he published pamphlets upon the subject and made the halls of Congress ring with his complaints, but all his labors were without fruit, so far as the action of any branch of the government was concerned. (The documents in the case are collected in *American State Papers, Public Lands,* vol. II, 1834.)

Since coming to New Orleans, Livingston had been separated from his children. One son had died in 1802 and the daughter and remaining son had been confided to the care of relatives. On June 3, 1805, Livingston married Madame Louise Moreau de Lassy, widow of a French officer and the daughter of Jean D'Avezac de Castera, a rich planter of Santo Domingo, who with her mother had been forced to flee during the negro insurrection on the island. She was the sister of Auguste D'Avezac [*q.v.*]. To Livingston and his wife a daughter was born in October 1806, who proved to be the only one of his children to live to maturity. In January 1809, Livingston, accompanied by his wife and daughter, went to Washington where he remained to fight for his Batture property while they proceeded to "Clermont." While pressing his claims before Congress, he was encouraged by the news that title to the property had been denied the city of New Orleans. At the same time the suit against the marshal was pending in the court at New Orleans and thither Livingston returned. In 1813 the news that his daughter Julia was dying of consumption obliged him once more to take the long journey to New York. He arrived to hear that she had been buried the day before he landed.

The outbreak of war with Great Britain in 1812 afforded Livingston an opportunity to reduce his debt to the United States by supplying live-oak to the government for the construction of frigates. The autumn of 1814 saw the war carried into Louisiana. Livingston, who had been the friend of Andrew Jackson since they had served together in Congress, asked an appointment as aide-de-camp. This Jackson refused in kindly fashion, but requested Livingston to give him information about the country. As chairman of the committee on public defense, Livingston not only organized the people of Louisiana to resist the British but also brought to his support the brothers Laffite (see Laffite, Jean). At the battle of New Orleans, he served Jackson as aide-de-camp, military secretary, interpreter, and confidential adviser upon all subjects. He not only drafted the various orders and proclamations of the General but also undertook the negotiations with the British for the exchange of prisoners. Before leaving New Orleans, General Jackson sat for his miniature, painted on ivory, which he presented to Livingston. (Hunt, ch. x; Jackson to Livingston, Sept. 30, 1814, and Oct. 23, 1814, Livingston to Mrs. Montgomery, Jan. 20, 1815, Edward Livingston Manuscripts.)

The close of the war left Livingston free to struggle again with his debts. His project to sell timber to the government was no longer feasible and he returned to his law practice. In 1820 he was elected a member of the Louisiana legislature and the following year was commissioned to revise the penal law of the state. His early interest in penal legislation had increased as he studied the writings of Bentham, which came to him in the French of Dumont in 1802. "Although strongly impressed with the defects of our actual system of penal law," Livingston wrote to Bentham, "yet the perusal of your works first gave method to my ideas, and taught me to consider legislation as a science governed by certain principles" (*Works of Jeremy Bentham*, 1843, XI, 51). The task of compiling the penal law of Louisiana was almost completed when the results of his labors were destroyed by fire. The work had to be done again, and in 1825 the finished code was presented to the legislature. It was divided into a Code of Crimes and Punishments, a Code of Procedure, a Code of Evidence, and a Code of Reform and Prison Discipline, besides a Book of Definitions. The machinery proposed for the working of the system included a house of detention, a penitentiary, a house of refuge and industry, and a school of reform; all under the superintendence and conduct of one board of inspectors. Every part of the work evinces the most elaborate attention to the preservation of a complete unity of design and aims at the prevention rather than the avenging of crime. Although it was not adopted, the publication of the code brought Livingston immediate and wide fame. (It can be most conveniently consulted in *The Complete Works of Edward Livingston on Criminal Jurisprudence*, 2 vols., 1873.) He was chosen foreign associate of the Institute of France and was later described by Sir Henry Maine as "the first legal genius of modern times" (*Cambridge Essays, Contributed by Members of the University, 1856,* n.d., p. 17).

Meantime, Livingston was unanimously chosen in July 1822 to represent the New Orleans district in Congress. He was afterward twice reelected, and gave as his chief reason for desiring to remain in the House of Representatives the hope that he might adapt his penal code to the use of the United States. In 1826 he paid his long-standing debt to the government, which, with accumulated interest, amounted to $100,014.89. The means of discharging the debt was afforded by a court decision which gave him title to a portion of the Batture property, although the larger part continued in dispute. Released from financial worry, he became less interested in Louisiana, where he had always regarded himself as in exile. He was attentive to the interests of his constituents but failed to visit his district and spent much of his time in New York. Popular favor deserted him and he was defeated for reëlection in 1828 but was immediately chosen by the legislature to represent Louisiana in the United States Senate. Livingston entered the Senate at the same time that Andrew Jackson became president. The two men had continued firm friends; Livingston had voted for Jackson in the contested election of 1824 and worked for his election in 1828. The President wished to employ his friend in the administration, and Livingston would have accepted the post of minister to France. His private affairs, however, were not in condition to permit him to depart at once and Jackson was obliged to make another appointment. Livingston presented to the Senate his *System of Penal Laws for the United States of America* (1828), but no action was taken on it. He continued in the Senate, firmly attached to the party of Jackson, until the spring of 1831, when he was appointed secretary of state.

In 1828 his sister, Mrs. Montgomery, died, bequeathing to him the bulk of her fortune, including her home at "Montgomery Place." He was therefore able to maintain a large establishment and "his manner of living and of entertaining guests was not excelled, if equalled, at Washington" (Hunt, p. 365). At the same time, he had not sought the office and would have preferred the cultivation of roses at "Montgomery Place." Among the more important matters which came before him as secretary of state was a treaty with France whereby the government of that country agreed to pay the claims of United States citizens for spoliations suffered under the Berlin and Milan decrees. He also drafted in 1832 the celebrated proclamation to the nullifiers of South Carolina. On May 29, 1833, he resigned as secretary of state to become minister to France. As secretary of the legation Jackson appointed Thomas P. Barton, who had married the daughter and only surviving child of Livingston.

The appointment of Livingston to the French mission was made in an effort to bring about the payment of the claims of American citizens for spoliations during the Napoleonic wars which the French government had admitted in the treaty of July 4, 1831. The agreement was to pay twenty-five million francs in six yearly instalments, but no payments had been made, the Chamber of Deputies having failed to make the necessary appropriations. Although Livingston was courteously received in France, a year of negotiations failed to secure action. Jackson became thoroughly angry, and in his message of December 1834 suggested that Congress authorize reprisals upon French property in case no provision should be made for the payment of the debt at the next session of the Chamber of Deputies. This suggestion produced great public excitement in France but, through further pressure from Livingston, the Chamber of Deputies, in April 1835, determined to appropriate the money. At the same time it was provided that payment should not be made until satisfactory explanations were given of the terms used in the presidential message. Livingston felt that he could no longer remain at his post and, with a conciliatory message to the French government, he handed over the business of his office to Barton as chargé d'affaires and returned home. Retiring to "Montgomery Place" in the late summer of 1835, he found that public opinion in the United States approved of his conduct in France. In January 1836, he visited Washington to argue a case before the Supreme Court. While there he counseled the President on the pending negotiations with France, which were soon to be brought to a favorable conclusion through the friendly mediation of England. This visit to Washington was Livingston's last absence from his family. He passed the remainder of the winter in New York, and early in the spring was once more at "Montgomery Place." Taken suddenly and violently ill with bilious colic on May 21, he died two days later and was buried in the family vault at "Clermont." Later, his remains were removed to the tomb of his second wife at Rhinebeck, N. Y.

"The pursuit of honest fame, the desire to serve your country," were once extolled as virtues by Edward Livingston in a letter to his young son (Hunt, p. 236). In reality they were his own ideals. Utterly lacking in ability to manage his own financial affairs, he possessed great power as a lawyer and a statesman. His services to mankind were remarked in the many tributes paid to his memory. The common council of the city of New York declared that he had been "a leader in every enterprise calculated to improve or adorn society" (Hunt, p. 433). In his oration delivered before the Academy of the Institute of France, François Mignet, the historian, said: "By the death of Mr. Livingston, America has lost her most powerful intellect, the Academy one of its most illustrious members, and Humanity one of her most zealous benefactors" (*Ibid.*, p. 434).

[The MSS. of Edward Livingston are privately owned; they include about 2,500 letters and documents. Among printed sources, the following may be cited: C. H. Hunt, *Life of Edward Livingston* (1864); E. B. Livingston, *The Livingstons of Livingston Manor* (1910); H. D. Gilpin, "Biog. Notice of Edward Livingston," in *Trans. of the Hist. and Lit. Committee of the Am. Philosophical Soc.*, vol. III, part 1 (1843); C. H. Peck, "Edward Livingston," in *The Conservative Review*, June 1900; Carleton Hunt, "Life and Services of Edward Livingston," in *Proc. of the La. Bar Asso., May 9, 1903* (1903); S. Lewis, *Strictures on Dr. Livingston's System of Penal Laws* (1825), and *Remarks on the Hon. Edward Livingston's Introductory Report to His System of Penal Law* (1831); "Two Letters of Chancellor Kent," *Am. Law Review*, Apr. 1878, pp. 479–90; Eugene Smith, "Edward Livingston and the La. Codes," *Columbia Law Review*, Jan. 1902, pp. 25–36; E. H. Moore, "The Livingston Code," *Jour. of the Am. Inst. of Criminal Law and Criminology*, Nov. 1928, pp. 344–63, with an excellent bibliography; Francis Rawle, "Edward Livingston," and E. I. McCormac, "Louis McLane" and "John Forsyth," in S. F. Bemis, ed., *The Am. Secretaries of State and Their Diplomacy*, vol. IV (1928).]

W. S. C.

LIVINGSTON, HENRY BROCKHOLST (Nov. 25, 1757–Mar. 18, 1823), jurist, was born in New York City. His father was William Livingston [*q.v.*], a governor of New Jersey, and his mother was Susanna French. He graduated from the College of New Jersey (Princeton) in 1774, James Madison being a fellow student. At the outbreak of the war he entered the Continental Army with a captain's commission. He served as aide, with the rank of major, to Gen. Philip Schuyler, and also to General St. Clair. He took part in the siege of Ticonderoga, and was a member of Benedict Arnold's staff during the Saratoga campaign and at the surrender of Burgoyne. He later returned to Schuyler and left the service with the rank of lieutenant-colonel. In 1779 he went to Spain as private secretary to John Jay, his brother-in-law, who was sent as minister to that country. On his return voyage in 1782 he was captured by the British, taken to New York, and imprisoned there until the arrival of Sir Guy Carleton who released him on parole. Barred from further military activity he went to Albany and studied law under Peter Yates and in 1783 was admitted to the bar. He returned to New York in that year, after its evacuation by the British, and began the practice of his profession. At this time he abandoned his first name and was thereafter known merely as Brockholst Livingston. He rapidly rose to a position of prominence at the bar. He developed a violent antagonism to Federalism under the new constitution and cast in his lot with Jefferson's party. In spite of his close relationship with Jay he bitterly opposed the Jay Treaty, being present at the riot at which Hamilton was wounded by a stone, and also at the burning of Jay in effigy.

In 1802 Livingston was appointed a judge of the supreme court of New York, on which James Kent was one of his colleagues. His appointment to the Supreme Court of the United States was seriously considered by Jefferson in 1804, and he was strongly recommended by Albert Gallatin, secretary of the treasury, but the appointment went to William Johnson [*q.v.*]. On Nov. 10, 1806, however, upon the death of Justice William Paterson, Jefferson nominated Livingston to the Supreme Court and the appointment was confirmed in December of that year. He took his seat at the ensuing February term. Owing to the practice of Chief Justice Marshall of writing most of the opinions of the court himself, especially in cases of importance, it is not easy to identify the individual contributions or views of the associate justices in the early period. During the seventeen years that Livingston sat on the Supreme Court he wrote the opinion of the majority in only thirty-eight cases. Not one of these involved any constitutional problem; they dealt rather with questions of maritime and commercial law in which he was deeply interested and highly trained. He dissented in eight cases and either wrote or joined in six concurring opinions. He is said to have been in great doubt as to the proper decision in the Dartmouth College Case, after hearing the arguments, but was won over to Marshall's position, partly through his respect for the expressed opinion of Kent. His decisions on the circuit court were more noteworthy than those on the Supreme Court. In 1808 he clarified the law of treason by holding that resistance, even violent resistance, to the Embargo acts could not be held to be treason if the intention of the accused was private gain (1 *Paine's Circuit Court Reports,* 265). In 1810 he attracted notice by an opinion on the circuit court indicating his belief in the constitutionality of the Embargo acts, a point upon which the Supreme Court never squarely passed. In 1817 he held, also in the circuit court, that the power of Congress to enact bankruptcy laws was not exclusive and that the bankruptcy law of New York was valid (1 *Paine's Circuit Court Reports,* 79).

Livingston died in Washington in his sixty-sixth year. He was married three times: to Catharine Keteltas, to Ann Ludlow, and to Catharine (Seaman) Kortright. He had a keen interest in history and was chosen one of the vice-presidents of the New York Historical Society when it was founded in 1805. He also helped in the organization of the public school system of New York. Justice Joseph Story, describing him in 1808, wrote: "Livingston has a fine Roman face; an aquiline nose, high forehead, bald head, and projecting chin, indicate deep research, strength, and quickness of mind. I have no hesitation in pronouncing him a very able and independent Judge. He evidently thinks with great solidity and seizes on the strong points of argument. He is luminous, decisive, earnest and impressive on the bench. In private society he is accessible and easy, and enjoys with great good humor the vivacities, if I may coin a word, of the wit and moralist" (W. W. Story, *Life and Letters of Joseph Story,* 1851, I, p. 167).

[See Alden Chester, *Courts and Lawyers of N. Y.* (1925), vol. III; E. B. Livingston, *The Livingstons of Livingston Manor* (1910); Charles Warren, *The Supreme Court in U. S. Hist.* (1922), vol. I; D. S. Alexander, *A Pol. Hist. of the State of N. Y.*, vol. I (1906); H. L. Carson, *The Supreme Court of the U. S.* (1891); *Daily Nat. Intelligencer* (Washington, D. C.), Mar. 19, 1823. Livingston's opinions on the Supreme Court can be found in 4 *Cranch* (U. S.) to 8 *Wheaton* (U. S.). His circuit court opinions appear mainly in *Paine's Circuit Court Reports* (2 vols., 1810–23).] R. E. C.

LIVINGSTON, JAMES (Mar. 27, 1747–Nov. 29, 1832), Revolutionary soldier, was probably born in Montreal, where his father, John Livingston, the grand-nephew of Robert Livingston [*q.v.*], had settled soon after his marriage to Catryna Ten Broeck. At the outbreak of the American Revolution his parents returned to Saratoga County, N. Y., while Livingston, with two of his brothers, joined the invading army of Gen. Richard Montgomery, their kinsman by marriage. In 1775 Livingston raised and commanded a regiment of Canadian refugees. During the siege of St. John's, Quebec, he led 300 of his Canadians, supported by fifty Americans under Maj. John Brown, 1744–1780 [*q.v.*], against Fort Chambly, which he captured with eighty prisoners and important stores of munitions and foodstuffs. His possession of this fort materially reduced the strength of the defenses of St. John's, and his prisoners provided a useful threat of retaliation to any measure that the British might take against such prisoners as Ethan Allen and his comrades. At the close of the unsuccessful siege of Quebec he found himself without a command, but, on Jan. 8, 1776, the Continental Congress commissioned him colonel and shortly afterwards he was in command of an additional battalion of the New York line. He served under Benedict Arnold [*q.v.*] on the expedition to relieve Fort Stanwix and fought in both battles of Saratoga. In 1780, he was in command at Stony Point and Verplanck's Point when the *Vulture* brought André up the Hudson to arrange with Arnold for the betrayal of West Point. Suspicious of the circumstances, he fired on the British vessel, caused her to drop down the river instead of waiting for André, and thus prevented the safe return of André to the British lines. When his regiment was reduced in 1781, he resigned from the army.

Under the act of 1784 he became a member of the first board of regents of the University of the State of New York and continued to be a member after the reorganization of 1787. In 1786 and 1787 he was a member of the New York Assembly from Montgomery County, and he sat in that body again from 1789 to 1791. He died at Schuylerville in Saratoga County. He married, probably about 1771, Elizabeth Simpson of Montreal. They had nine children; of these the first was Elizabeth, the mother of Gerrit Smith [*q.v.*], and the sixth was Margaret, the wife of Daniel Cady and the mother of Elizabeth Cady Stanton [*qq.v.*].

[Most authorities give Nov. 29 as date of death although *Daily Albany Argus,* Dec. 8, 1832, gives Nov. 20; see John Schuyler, *Institution of the Soc. of the Cincinnati* (1886), pp. 251–53; J. H. Smith, *Our Struggle for the Fourteenth Colony* (2 vols., 1907); E. A. Werner, *Civil List and Constitutional Hist. . . . of N. Y.* (1889); Peter Force, *Am. Archives,* 4 ser., IV (1843), col. 1636; E. B. Livingston, *The Livingstons of Livingston Manor* (1910); E. Ten B. Runk, *The Ten Broeck Genealogy* (1897).] K. E. C.

LIVINGSTON, JOHN HENRY (May 30, 1746–Jan. 20, 1825), Dutch Reformed clergyman, educator, was born near Poughkeepsie, N. Y., the son of Henry and Susanna (Conklin) Livingston. His father, Henry, was the son of Gilbert, a younger son of Robert Livingston [*q.v.*], first lord of Livingston Manor. John Henry was taught at home by his parents and by a private tutor, then studied under Rev. Chauncey Graham at Fishkill and Rev. Nathaniel Taylor at New Milford, Conn. Ready for Yale at twelve years of age, he was graduated there in 1762 and began the study of law at Poughkeepsie. After two years, his health impaired, he gave himself to personal reflections, came to a positive religious experience, and felt himself called to the Christian ministry. His family was of the Dutch Reformed Church and the circumstance of the church at the time appealed to him. The English language was just finding place in its pulpits, a movement was afoot for the education of ministers in America, and independence from the rule of the church in Holland was increasing; controversy on these matters divided the church into two parties.

Going to Holland to study theology, as was then the custom, he remained there from 1766 to 1770. He was examined by the Classis of Amsterdam, June, 1769, was licensed, and in April 1770, was ordained; he passed a vigorous examination at the University of Utrecht, May 16, 1770, and received the degree of doctor of theology. His distinction in family, education, and personal gifts was such that a call was sent to him by the church in New York to be one of its ministers, to preach chiefly in English, occasionally in Dutch. Accepting, he served this charge for forty years. On Nov. 26, 1775, he married his second cousin, Sarah, daughter of Philip Livingston [*q.v.*]. She died Dec. 29, 1814. They had one child.

Upon returning to New York Livingston became almost immediately an effectual influence in the church at large. Though so young, he set forth a plan of union, brought from Holland, which in about two years united the two opposing factions. The American party had secured from George III, in 1766, the charter for Queen's College, at New Brunswick, N. J., where in 1771 work was commenced. In 1774 the faculty at Utrecht recommended Livingston for the office of president and professor of theology, but because of the war no appointment was made. The British occupied New York, and Livingston, a Patriot, left the city. Until the close of hostilities he was in the Hudson River country, serving successively the churches of Kingston, Albany, Livingston Manor, and the two charges of Poughkeepsie and Red Hook. In 1783 he resumed his ministry in New York. The following year the General Synod of the Dutch Reformed Church elected him its professor of theology, establishing by this appointment the first theological seminary in the United States. Thenceforth he held the professorship in addition to his pastorate. He taught his students in New York and at times at Flatbush, Long Island. During this period he was also very active in the further organizing of the united church. He prepared its *Psalm Book* (1789), *The Psalms of David, with Hymns and Spiritual Songs . . . For the Use of the Reformed Dutch Church in North America* (1796), and also *The Constitution of the Reformed Dutch Church, in the United States of America,* accepted by the Synod in 1792 and published in 1793, a compilation of the church's law, worship, and doctrinal standards. He was zealous in communication with other church bodies in America and in the Old World, and zealous in the cause of foreign missions.

In 1810 he was chosen president of Queen's College (now Rutgers University), with the understanding that his duties in this office would be only formal, that his professorship of theology would continue and be his chief concern. He brought to New Brunswick his five theological students of that time. The college continued small and without adequate resources, and after a time its classes were omitted for some years. The theological classes continued, however, and other professors were associated with Livingston. After fifteen years in his new home and his twofold office, active to the end, he died in his sleep, at the age of seventy-nine.

Livingston published a number of sermons and addresses, including: *Oratio Inauguralis de Veritate Religionis Christianae* (1785); *The Glory of the Redeemer* (1799); *An Address Delivered at the Commencement Held at Queen's College in New-Jersey, Sept. 25, 1810* (1810); *A Funeral Service, or Meditations Adapted to Funeral Addresses* (1812); and *A Dissertation on the Marriage of a Man with his Sister-in-law* (1816). He had a fine physical presence; he was tall, of dignified bearing, and impressive public address. With high attainments in the classics and in theology and unusual spiritual qualities he combined a practical understanding of church affairs. He was the accepted leader who guided the Dutch Reformed Church, now the Reformed Church in America, to its complete and independent American organization.

[Alexander Gunn, *Memoirs of the Rev. John Henry Livingston* (1856); W. B. Sprague, *Annals Am. Pulpit*, vol. IX (1869); E. T. Corwin, *A Manual of the Ref. Ch. in America* (3rd ed., 1879); F. B. Dexter, *Biog. Sketches Grads. Yale Coll.* vol. II (1896); D. D. Demarest, *Hist. and Characteristics of the Ref. Prot. Dutch Church* (4th ed., 1889); W. H. S. Demarest, *A Hist. of Rutgers College* (1924); *Centennial of the Theol. Sem. of the Ref. Ch. in America* (1885); *Eccl. Records, State of N. Y.*, vol. VI (1905); *The Acts and Proc. of the Gen. Synod of the Ref. Prot. Ch. in North America*, vol. I (1859); C. C. Cuyler, *A Sermon Occasioned by the Death of the Rev. John H. Livingston* (1825); N. J. Marsellus, *A Sermon . . . on . . . the Death of the Rev. John H. Livingston* (1825); John De Witt, *The Path of the Just as the Shining Light; a Funeral Discourse* (1825).] W. H. S. D.

LIVINGSTON, JOHN WILLIAM (May 22, 1804–Sept. 10, 1885), naval officer, the son of Eliza (Livingston) and William Turk, a surgeon in the United States navy, was born in New York City. In 1843, by act of the New York legislature, he and his wife, Mary A. (Livingston) Turk, changed their name to Livingston. Livingston, then John William Turk, was appointed a midshipman on Mar. 4, 1823. In his early years of service he was on the *Ontario*, *Delaware*, and *Constitution* in the Mediterranean, and on the *Constellation* during the later years of the campaign against pirates in the West Indies. After being promoted to a lieutenancy in 1832, he cruised in the Pacific in the *Dolphin* and the *Fairchild* and returned to the United States in the frigate *Columbia*. On the voyage the *Columbia* proceeded to Muckie in the northern part of Sumatra, and, on New Year's Day of 1839, bombarded the village in punishment for outrages committed upon American ships and seamen trading for pepper on that coast. The *Columbia* then proceeded to China and the Sandwich Islands and home around Cape Horn.

During the Mexican War Livingston was executive officer of the *Congress* on the west coast of Mexico, and took part in several attacks on Mexican towns, especially Mazatlán, where he commanded the artillery division. Later he served in the East India Squadron. When he became a commander, in 1855, he was given the *St. Louis* on the coast of Africa, where he served from 1856 to 1858. Early in the Civil War he was in command of the steamer *Penguin* operating on the blockade of Wilmington and Hampton Roads and, later, of the steamer *Bienville*. He commanded the sailing frigate *Cumberland* but had left her, on account of sickness, before she was sunk by the *Merrimac*. After the recapture of the Norfolk navy yard in May 1862, he was made its commandant. From this duty he was detached in 1864 and sent to command the naval station at Mound City, Ill. In 1861 he had been commissioned captain and, in 1862, commodore. Although he held no other important post and had been retired in 1866 he was promoted rear admiral in 1868. He died in New York City.

[Files of the Bureau of Navigation in Washington; L. R. Hamersly, *The Records of Living Officers of the U. S. Navy*, 4th ed. (1890); *War of the Rebellion: Official Records* (*Navy*), esp. ser. 1, IV, V, VI, XXVII (1896–1917); for cruise of the *Columbia*, F. W. Taylor, *The Flagship* (1840), vol. I, esp. pp. 364, 387; for capture of Mazatlán, *U. S. Naval Institute Proc.*, May–June, 1915, pp. 894–95; *Jour. of the Assembly of the State of N. Y. . . . 1843* (1843), p. 155; *Army and Navy Jour.*, Sept. 12, 1885; *N. Y. Tribune*, Sept. 11, 1885.] W. B. N.

LIVINGSTON, PETER VAN BRUGH (October 1710–Dec. 28, 1792), merchant, brother of Philip and William Livingston [*qq.v.*], was born at Albany, N. Y., and baptized Nov. 3, 1710. He was a grandson of Robert Livingston [*q.v.*], and the son of Philip Livingston, second lord of the manor, and of Catharine (Van Brugh). Most of his boyhood was spent in Albany, where his father served as secretary of Indian affairs during the latter years of Robert Livingston's life. He was educated at Yale, graduating in the class of 1731. Shortly after receiving his degree, he settled in New York City, and joined the mercantile interests of the little port. On Nov. 3, 1739, he married Mary Alexander, daughter of James Alexander [*q.v.*], a member of the council and surveyor-general of New Jersey, and sister of William [*q.v.*], who later married Livingston's sister Sarah. His business ventures prospered sufficiently to enable him to build a mansion in the Dutch tradition on Princess Street. During the French wars he accumulated a small fortune from government contracts for supplying various military expeditions. His privateering enterprises were likewise fortunate and profitable. Having formed a business arrangement with his brother-in-law, Alexander, he secured through his partner a commission from Governor Shirley to supply the army which was being equipped for an assault on Fort Niagara in 1755. The profits from this contract were partially dissipated during a protracted suit in chancery between Alexander and Livingston over the precise terms of their agreement. In his extensive mercantile operations Livingston was judged, even by his political foes, to belong to that group known as "fair traders and honest men" (Jones, *post,* II, 321). He found time during the busiest years of his career to serve from 1748 to 1761 as a trustee of the College of New Jersey, later Princeton. After the death of his first wife, in 1767, he married Elizabeth, widow of William Ricketts.

In provincial politics he was generally found on the side of the popular party, which was strongly Presbyterian in its religious preferences. For a time he was an able lieutenant in carrying out the plans of the Whig triumvirate consisting of his brother William, John Morin Scott, and William Smith, Jr. [*qq.v.*]. He heartily indorsed the merchants' memorials in 1763 and 1764 against Grenville's projects to raise a revenue in America and he seems to have been less alarmed than his wealthy colleagues by the high-handed tactics of the mechanics and small shopkeepers in the year of the Stamp Act. At any rate, in 1774 he took his stand with the radical wing of the Whig faction. A member of the Committee of Fifty-One, organized to choose delegates to the First Continental Congress, he protested against the attempt of the conservative merchants to dominate the committee and resigned in company with such radicals as Alexander MacDougall and Isaac Sears in order to give point to his protest. When John Adams stopped in New York on his way to the First Continental Congress he dined with Livingston and found him "an old man, extremely staunch in the cause, and very sensible," who was not afraid of the extremists in New England. "He has been in trade," wrote Adams, "is rich, and now lives upon his income" (*The Works of John Adams,* vol. II, 1850, pp. 348, 351).

Livingston was a member of the Committee of Sixty organized in November 1774 to enforce the "Association" entered into by the Continental Congress and to assume such governmental powers as seemed necessary in the emergency. In this group the radicals had a clear majority, which they used to create the Committee of One Hundred, an extra-legal body charged with the responsibility for provincial affairs until the opening of the first provincial congress in 1775; Livingston was a member of this committee and was sent to the provincial congress, which promptly named him its presiding officer. In the summer of 1775 he was designated treasurer, but withdrew in August on the plea of ill-health and thereafter took no active part in provincial affairs. "With a continual slow fever," he wrote, "a reluctance to food, and a constant vigilance or want of sleep, I find myself reduced to the necessity of taking some measures to preserve life" (*American Archives,* 4 ser. III, 559). That the measures were efficacious is evident from the fact that he lived to be eighty-two, the last sixteen years of his life, if one may judge by the absence of his name from the public records, being spent in retirement. He died at Elizabethtown, N. J.

[E. B. Livingston, *The Livingstons of Livingston Manor* (1910); F. B. Dexter, *Biog. Sketches Grads. Yale Coll.,* vol. I (1885); E. B. O'Callaghan, *Docs. Relative to the Colonial History of the State of N. Y.,* vol. VI (1855); Peter Force, *Am. Archives,* 4 ser. III–V (1840–44), 5 ser. I–III (1848–53); C. L. Becker, *The Hist. of Political Parties in the Province of N. Y.* (1909); Wm. Smith, *The Hist. of the Late Province of N. Y.* (2 vols., 1829); Thomas Jones, *Hist. of N. Y. during the Revolutionary War* (2 vols., 1879), ed. by E. F. de Lancey; *New-Jersey Journal* (Elizabethtown), Jan. 2, 1793.]

J. A. K.

LIVINGSTON, PHILIP (Jan. 15, 1716–June 12, 1778), merchant, signer of the Declaration of Independence, gave generously of his time and money to a wide variety of philanthropic enterprises. Born at Albany, fifth son of Philip and Catharine (Van Brugh) Livingston, he was reared in the well-nigh princely style affected by his father, the second lord of the manor. He was awarded the degree of A.B. at Yale in 1737, thus entering the select company of less than a score in the province who had received collegiate training. He established himself as an importer in New York City and like his elder brother, Peter Van Brugh Livingston [*q.v.*], became closely identified with the commercial progress of the seaport. Understanding the devious ways of trade during the French wars, he realized handsomely upon his ventures, especially his privateering expeditions. Having married Christina, daughter of Col. Dirck Ten Broeck of Albany, on Apr. 14, 1740, he established his family in a comfortable town house on Duke Street and maintained a beautiful country seat on Brooklyn Heights, overlooking the harbor into which his ships brought his increasing wealth. In 1755 Sir Charles Hardy, then governor of the province, wrote: "Among the considerable merchants in this city no one is more esteemed for energy, promptness and public spirit than Philip Livingston" (Livingston, *post,* p. 170).

Livingston's subsequent career marked him as unique in his concern over civic affairs. He early deplored the province's lack of a collegiate establishment and was one of the first to advocate the founding of King's College, now Columbia. Though the Episcopalian control of the institution was not to his liking, he contributed to its support. Indeed, for his day there was a remarkable catholicity about his benefactions. Anglicans as well as the Presbyterians with whom he worshipped received his bounty. In 1746 he set aside a sum for the establishment at Yale of a professorship of divinity which still bears his name. He bore a hand in the building of the stone meeting house in John Street which housed the first Methodist society in America. Every sort of public enterprise was apt to arouse his enthusiasm. Recognizing the increased taste for good reading within the province, he helped to organize the New York Society Library in 1754 along the lines outlined by Benjamin Franklin and his colleagues in Philadelphia. About the same time he assumed the presidency (1756–57) of the newly established St. Andrew's Society, the earliest benevolent institution in New York City. With Leonard Lispenard, John Cruger, and others, in 1768 he collaborated in the organization of the New York Chamber of Commerce. When the New York Hospital was incorporated in 1771 he became a member of the first board of governors.

His civic interests gradually led him into politics, his apprenticeship being served in the board of aldermen, where he sat for nine years after 1754 as representative for the East Ward. In the developing struggle between the De Lanceys and the Livingstons, he supported the family whose name he bore, but his partisanship was never as intense as that of his younger brother, William [*q.v.*]. In his view the Whig faction, or popular party, was essentially a protest against the political ascendancy of certain groups whom he did not like and a means of voicing in dignified fashion his belief that the province should enjoy a large measure of local autonomy. His religious nonconformity undoubtedly helped him to see the errors of the Anglican supporters of the De Lanceys. When the Livingstons achieved their first important victory, in the election of 1758, Philip was swept into the Assembly on a wave of anti-De Lancey votes. During his service in the lower house he was a determined foe of the financial policy brought forward by Grenville and other imperial administrators. In 1764 he helped phrase the address of the Assembly to Lieutenant-Governor Colden [*q.v.*], calling upon him to join in an endeavor to secure that "great badge of English liberty," the right of His Majesty's subjects everywhere to be taxed only with their own consent. When the Stamp Act became a reality, Livingston frowned upon the rioting of the "Sons of Liberty," but joined in the more dignified protests of lawyers and merchants. He was a member of the New York delegation which attended the Stamp Act Congress, spending most of his time apparently in consultation with the committee which drafted the protest to the House of Lords.

As the rift between the "Sons of Liberty" and the aristocratic leaders of the popular party widened, Livingston was inclined to favor a truce with the De Lanceys, that factional quarrels might be forgotten in the common cause of merchants and gentry against Parliamentary interference. He was elected to the Assembly for the third time in 1768 and on Oct. 27 was chosen speaker of the House. When the governor dissolved the Assembly in January 1769, Livingston hoped to win the support of moderate men in both the De Lancey and Livingston factions. Failing in this conciliatory gesture, he was defeated in New York City. Thereupon his nephew, Peter R. Livingston, withdrew and allowed him to be returned from the manor. The majority in the Assembly, refusing to recognize his right to sit for a "pocket borough" in which he did not reside, declared his seat vacant. Undismayed by this turn of events, he remained active in politics, emerging as one of the forceful but conservative leaders of the opposition to the "Intolerable Acts." In 1774 he served on the Committee of Fifty-One which named the New York delegates to the First Continental Congress and he was one of the five selected to attend the sessions at Philadelphia. At the moment he was in a distinctly conservative mood, weighing carefully the cost to colonial merchants of any disruption of normal trade with Great Britain. John Adams found him disinclined to listen to radical proposals. "Philip Livingston," he wrote, "is a great, rough rapid mortal. There is no holding any conversation with him. He blusters away; says if England should turn us adrift, we should instantly go to civil wars among ourselves" (*Works, post,* II, 351). Livingston became a member of the Committee of Sixty to enforce the terms of the "Association" and was placed on the Committee of One Hundred to carry forward provincial affairs until the meeting of the first provincial congress in 1775. He and his cousin, the second Robert R. Livingston [*q.v.*], were members both of the New York congress and the Second Continental Congress. They apparently had an arrangement whereby one would be in New York while the other was attending sessions in Philadelphia. It thus happened that Philip was in New York when the vote on Richard Henry Lee's historic resolution was taken, but he signed the Declaration of Independence in August 1776. He cannot, however, be regarded as one who forced an affirmative answer when the question of independence was raised.

Both in New York and in Philadelphia he rendered conscientious service on important committees. For his province he sat upon the committee "for the hearing and trial of disaffected persons of equivocal character." In the Continental Congress he was in turn a member of the Committee on Indian Affairs, the Treasury Board, the Marine Committee, the Committee on Commerce, and the board of commissioners to inspect the army under the command of Washington. His duties in Continental affairs were constantly interrupted by the demands of the province. In 1777 he was chosen by the convention of the state of New York as one of the senators from the southern district in the upper house of the new legislature. He attended the first meetings of this body and then, despite ill health and the protests of his family, he returned to the Continental Congress, then sitting at York, Pa. There he continued in the public service until his death in June 1778.

Philip Livingston's career as philanthropist and statesman was an interesting contrast to that of his acquisitive grandfather, Robert [*q.v.*], the founder of the family in America. He gave generously of his private fortune, pledging his personal credit without hope of future profit to maintain confidence in the Continental Congress. Honored by his generation for probity and ability, he was too dignified in bearing to win popularity and too austere in temper to arouse warm personal friendships. His intimate associates found behind his austerity and somewhat forbidding manner an affectionate disposition and a kindliness which constantly responded to urgent public appeals.

[E. B. Livingston, *The Livingstons of Livingston Manor* (1910); C. L. Becker, *The Hist. of Political Parties in the Province of N. Y.* (1909); Thomas Jones, *Hist. of N. Y. during the Revolutionary War* (2 vols., 1879), ed. by E. F. de Lancey; Martha J. Lamb, *Hist. of the City of N. Y.* (2 vols., 1877–81); Theodore Sedgwick, Jr., *A Memoir of the Life of William Livingston* (1833); *The Works of John Adams,* ed. by C. F. Adams, vol. II (1850); *Am. Archives,* 4 ser. III–V (1840–44), 5 ser. I–III (1848–53); *Journal of the Provincial Congress . . . of N. Y.* (1842); *Journal of the Votes and Proc. of the General Assembly of the Province of N. Y.* (1766); F. B. Dexter, *Biog. Sketches Grads. Yale Coll.,* vol. I (1885); John Sanderson, *Biog. of the Signers to the Declaration of Independence,* vol. III (1823).]

J. A. K.

LIVINGSTON, ROBERT (Dec. 13, 1654–Oct. 1, 1728), first lord of the manor of Livingston in New York, was born at Ancrum, Roxburghshire, Scotland, the son of John Livingston, a vigorous preacher of the Scottish church, and Janet Fleming, daughter of an Edinburgh merchant. His father belonged to a younger branch of the Livingstons of Callendar, who as earls of Linlithgow were important courtiers at Holyrood. When his son was nine years old, to avoid the displeasure of the episcopal party in Scotland after the Stuart restoration, Rev. John Livingston took his family to Rotterdam, where he became pastor of a Presbyterian congregation. Robert's boyhood was spent among the Scottish refugees whose children easily adopted the speech, manners, and customs of their Dutch neighbors. In April 1673, one year after his father's death, he sailed for New England, but his ultimate destination was the frontier village of Albany, where he appeared in 1674, the year that the province of New York was returned to the British by the Treaty of Westminster. The following year the young Scot, who was equally fluent in Dutch and English, was appointed town clerk of Albany and secretary of the board of commissioners for Indian affairs. He soon transformed the latter office from a mere clerkship to a position of control and direction; his reports and recommendations on Indian relations were of great importance to the successive governors of the province, with whom he came, consequently, to have considerable influence.

Both this influence and the knowledge of the Indian trade gained in his official position helped him to advance his larger plans to acquire wealth and standing in the community. Within five years of his coming to Albany he had purchased the Indian claims to choice tracts along the Hudson and had married (July 9, 1679) Alida Van Rensselaer, widow of Domine Nicholas Van Rensselaer and sister of Peter Schuyler [*qq.v.*]. This marriage brought him social connection with two of the most important families in the province, aristocratic landholders who expected and received favors from the Proprietor and the Crown. In 1686, by reason of his friendship with Governor Dongan, he secured a patent erecting his landholdings into the manor and lordship of Livingston. As later confirmed by a charter of George I, the manor consisted of more than 160,000 acres in the present counties of Dutchess and Columbia. This princely domain was made possible by income from public office carefully invested, by profits from governmental contracts, by interest on large sums advanced to the governor in anticipation of the collection of the provincial taxes, and by many pounds sterling drawn from private trade with the Indians and the French.

Though a supporter of the Stuarts, Livingston discreetly acknowledged the result of the Revolution of 1688 in England, but vigorously repudiated Jacob Leisler [*q.v.*] and his followers in New York. The aftermath of his opposition to the Leislerians was a series of attempts on the part of his political foes to deprive him of his offices and estates. Twice within ten years he visited England to defend his interests. On his first mission, in 1694–95, he made the acquaintance of the Earl of Bellomont [*q.v.*], to whom he recommended Capt. William Kidd [*q.v.*] as a suitable commander of a privateer to be fitted out against the pirates preying on British commerce. He returned to the colony as secretary of Indian affairs for life. Prior to the failure of the privateering venture through Kidd's treachery in turning pirate himself, Bellomont and Livingston were close friends, and when the former became governor he showered the Albany official with favors and summoned him to the Council. After Bellomont's death in 1701 Livingston's enemies persuaded the Assembly to sequestrate his estates. Again he sought help in England, remaining until 1705, when he returned to the province armed with a royal commission confirming him in all his offices and property. The provincial governors now turned to him for advice. Lord Cornbury [*q.v.*] leaned upon him heavily and Gov. Robert Hunter [*q.v.*] used his extensive knowledge of the fur trade and frontier conditions. The latter rewarded him with valuable contracts, notably in connection with the supply of provisions to the Palatine refugees, who were settled on land purchased from Livingston.

From 1709 to 1711 he was sent to the provincial Assembly from the Albany district, and five years later his manor returned him as its representative. Elected speaker in 1718, he displayed a marked tendency to support the Assembly in its frequent quarrels with the governor, a tendency which in his descendants took the form of more serious political nonconformity. Retiring from office in 1725 because of ill health, he died three years later. He left the manor to his son Philip, who in 1721 had become his deputy as secretary for Indian affairs and succeeded him in that office and on the Council. A younger son, Robert, received 13,000 acres at "Clermont."

To the end of his days Livingston persisted in his efforts to draw a considerable income from public office. Governor Fletcher wrote of him in 1696: "He has made a considerable fortune . . ., never disbursing six pence but with the expectation of twelve pence, his beginning being a little Book keeper, he has screwed himself into one of the most considerable estates in the province . . . he had rather be called knave Livingston then poor Livingston" (*Documents, post,* IV, 251), while in a moment of anger over army contracts Bellomont charged that he had "pinched an estate out of the poor soldiers' bellies" (*Ibid.,* IV, 720). In him was a curious mixture of the steadfast courage of the Covenanter and the grasping shrewdness of the trader. His success in winning the support of the British government for his private ventures marked him as a courtier and diplomat of no mean ability. In some measure that success was probably due to his genial presence and courtly manner, which easily won him friends who quickly discerned his intelligence and resourcefulness.

[E. B. O'Callaghan, *Docs. Relative to the Colonial Hist. of the State of N. Y.*, vols. III–V (1853–55), and *The Doc. Hist. of the State of N. Y.*, vols. I–III, 8vo. ed. (1849–50); Wm. Smith, *The Hist. of the Late Province of N. Y.* (2 vols., 1829); E. B. Livingston, *The Livingstons of Livingston Manor* (1910); W. L. Fleming, "The Public Career of Robert Livingston," a scholarly article in *N. Y. Geneal. and Biog. Record,* July–Oct., 1901; Peter Wraxall, *An Abridgement of the Indian Affairs . . . Transacted in the Colony of N. Y., from the Year 1678 to the Year 1751* (1915), ed. by C. H. McIlwain.] J. A. K.

LIVINGSTON, ROBERT R. (August 1718–Dec. 9, 1775), jurist, Revolutionary patriot, baptized Aug. 30, 1718, was the only son of Robert Livingston of "Clermont," who was a younger son of Robert [*q.v.*], first lord of Livingston Manor in New York; his mother, Margaret Howarden, was of English ancestry. In accordance with a custom common in New York families at that time, he was known as Robert R., to distinguish him, as Robert son of Robert, from other Roberts in the family. On Dec. 8, 1742, he married Margaret Beekman, only daughter of Col. Henry Beekman of Rhinebeck and his wife, Janet Livingston, who was a daughter of Robert Livingston (nephew of the first lord) and of Margaretta Schuyler. His wife's rich inheritance, added to "Clermont," made him one of the greatest landholders of the province. Of his four sons, two, Robert R. and Edward [*qq.v.*], took conspicuous part in public life, while four of his five daughters made notable marriages, bringing into the family connection Gen. Richard Montgomery, Freeborn Garrettson, the Methodist preacher, Morgan Lewis, later governor of the state, and John Armstrong, 1758–1843, soldier, diplomat, and secretary of war.

Livingston applied himself early to legal studies and devoted himself all his life to the law and politics. In 1756 he was recommended to the Board of Trade by Governor Hardy to fill a vacancy in the Council, but was not appointed. From 1758 to 1768 he served as member of the Assembly from Dutchess County and in 1762 promoted a compromise whereby a loan was made to Parliament to pay bounties for volunteers requisitioned by Sir Jeffery Amherst. He was appointed judge of the Admiralty court in 1759 and in January 1763 was made puisne judge of the supreme court of the Colony. The acceptance at this time by Livingston and the other judges of commissions on tenure of the King's will marked the cessation of a bitter struggle over the independence of the judiciary. When in 1764 the question arose of the right to appeal from the courts to the governor and Council, Livingston, being one of the judges who refused to allow appeal, became one of the leading antagonists of Lieutenant-Governor Cadwallader Colden [*q.v.*] in his effort to establish that right, and Colden, in letters to the Lords of Trade and to the Earl of Halifax (Jan. 22, 23, 1765), sought his removal from the bench, but without success.

Livingston was chairman of the New York committee of correspondence appointed to concert measures with the other colonies in opposition to the execution of the Stamp Act, and was one of the earliest promoters of the movement which culminated in the Stamp Act Congress. As a member of that body his most important service was the drafting of the address to the King, but he was also a leader in debate. He proposed a series of resolves which embodied a plan of confederation providing a permanent congress to assign to each colony a quota to be raised for imperial purposes by each colony in its own way. Although these resolves were couched in mild language, they referred to the possibility that "the wish to retain" the Mother Country might be weakened. Ten years later, writing to his son in the Continental Congress, Livingston displayed similar views: he still opposed independence, favoring conciliation, yet recognized that conditions might in time require more aggressive tactics.

In 1768 he lost his seat in the Assembly. The following year, when his cousin Philip [*q.v.*], elected from Livingston Manor, was refused admittance, Robert R. Livingston was chosen in his stead. The now conservative Assembly, however, anticipating his election, had passed a resolution that henceforth no judge should be allowed to take a seat. He was therefore rejected, but continued the struggle, and when he finally relinquished his claim in favor of Philip's nephew, Peter R. Livingston, who became a member in February 1774, he had been five times elected by the manor and as many times rejected by the Assembly. In April 1768 he had been named for the Council a second time, by Governor Moore, but his previous political activity made his appointment out of the question. In 1767 and again in 1773 he was one of the commissioners to settle the New York–Massachusetts boundary, which the Livingston lands adjoined. Amiable, admired by a wide circle of personal friends, social in disposition, he had a career illustrative of many phases of the conditions and conflicts of pre-Revolutionary New York. Though an Anglican and a great landholder, he was a leader of the "Whig" interest: in imperial problems he was ready to go as far as necessary to assure the colonies' economic welfare; little influenced by the philosophy of revolution, he was opposed to going further merely for the sake of principle.

[Published material includes: E. B. Livingston, *The Livingstons of Livingston Manor* (1910); T. S. Clarkson, *A Biog. Hist. of Clermont* (1869); A. M. Keys, *Cadwallader Colden* (1906); C. L. Becker, *The Hist. of Political Parties in the Province of N. Y. 1760–76* (1909); E. B. O'Callaghan, *Docs. Relative to the Colonial Hist. of the State of N. Y.*, vols. VII, VIII (1856–57); *Journal . . . of the Gen. Assembly of the Colony of N. Y.*, vol. II (1766); *Journal of the First Congress of the American Colonies in Opposition to the Tyrannical Acts of the British Parliament* (1845), ed. by Lewis Cruger; *The Address of Mr. Justice Livingston to the House of Assembly of N. Y. in Support of his Right to a Seat* (1769). Manuscript material is found in the Olin Collection, Bancroft Transcripts, and William Smith Papers in N. Y. Pub. Lib.; John Ross Delafield, Johnston Redmond, and L. W. Smith collections in private hands; and in the MSS. Div., Lib. of Cong.]

R. C. H.

LIVINGSTON, ROBERT R. (Nov. 27, 1746–Feb. 26, 1813), chancellor of New York, statesman, diplomat, farmer, experimenter, was born in New York City, the third child and eldest son of Judge Robert R. Livingston [*q.v.*] and Margaret Beekman his wife. He was a brother of Edward Livingston [*q.v.*]. Many were his relatives in public life, notably, the Revolutionary leaders Philip, William, and Peter Van

Brugh Livingston [*qq.v.*], his cousins, and John Armstrong, Richard Montgomery, and Morgan Lewis [*qq.v.*], his brothers-in-law. Much of his significance as an historical figure is due to the unofficial and largely unchronicled influence he wielded after becoming the most important member of the family group. His formal education was acquired at King's College, where he graduated with the class of 1765. At the college Commencement in Trinity Church he delivered a speech (as did each of his classmates) which was reported by the uniformly appreciative *New York Mercury* (May 27, 1765) as "a spirited Oration in Praise of Liberty. . . The graceful young speaker, animated with his noble subject, gave the highest satisfaction." When he left college he studied law, as his father and grandfather had done, at first in the office of his cousin, William Livingston, then with William Smith, Jr., the colonial judge. Admitted to the bar in 1770, he practised for a time in partnership with John Jay. On Sept. 9, 1770, he married Mary, daughter of John Stevens and sister of John Stevens, the inventor [*q.v.*]. Of this marriage two daughters were born. In 1773 he received his first political office, the only one he held under the Crown, recorder of the City of New York, by virtue of which he presided over certain criminal trials. In 1775, his revolutionary sympathies having made him no longer acceptable, he was replaced.

In the same year he was elected delegate to the Continental Congress, in which he served during 1775–76, 1779–81, and 1784–85. The best-known but least important of his activities during his first period of service in this body was his membership in the committee of five appointed to draft a declaration of independence. Probably the chief motive of his appointment was a politic attempt to gain for the idea of independence the support of the hesitating province of New York. His personal opinion was that independence was inevitable and necessary, but at that time inexpedient, and in debate he was, according to Jefferson, one of the chief speakers for a postponement of the issue. When independence was considered on July 2 every colony voted affirmatively except New York, whose delegation was excused from voting because it was not authorized to do so by the New York convention. On the 9th a newly elected convention declared for independence. On July 15 Livingston left for New York to take a seat in that body, and was therefore absent when the signing of the engrossed copy of the Declaration began on Aug. 2. Thus it happened that, although a member of the drafting committee, he neither voted for nor signed the Declaration of Independence.

Far more important, although not spectacular, was his other work in Congress. He served on the committees to draft an address to the people of Great Britain, to confer with the New York convention regarding the defense of the Hudson, to confer with Washington and Schuyler on military affairs, to investigate the powder supply; on the committee of ways and means, and as the representative of New York on the committee to draw up a plan of confederation. During his second period of attendance on Congress (1779–81) he was even busier. He was an active member of committees on financial affairs, supplies, legal organization, foreign affairs, military problems, and special correspondence. In the dispatch book of Congress, listing committees, reports, and commitments, his name often appears three or four times on a page, increasing steadily in frequency until 1781. Few other members were more indefatigable or more in demand as committee members, and probably no one else showed a greater versatility in the variety of work in which he engaged. Notable in this activity was his membership on committees for establishing a court of appeals, drafting commissions for its judges, and preparing their instructions. Early in 1780 he was nominated as judge of this court, but he apparently declined to be considered for the position (Burnett, *post,* V, 12). He wrote many reports, of which perhaps the most important was that adopted by Congress, Dec. 14, 1779, describing the financial exigencies of the general government and recommending methods of meeting them. In August of the following year he was added to the ways and means committee and later was one of those with whom Robert Morris corresponded on financial matters.

On Jan. 10, 1781, Congress by resolve established a department of foreign affairs; on Aug. 10, Livingston, then enjoying at "Clermont" a brief respite from public affairs, was elected secretary of this department, having at different times been nominated by both Lloyd and Varnum. Various other leaders and local favorites had been nominated, but only Arthur Lee made a real attempt to secure the office. Livingston was the candidate most acceptable to France, and Luzerne claimed that he influenced the election in his behalf. The most important of Livingston's diplomatic correspondence while secretary related to the negotiations of peace with Great Britain. He approved the instructions to the American commissioners at Paris, directing them to act with the knowledge and concurrence of France, and did not share Jay's suspicions, which were intensified by Marbois' famous letter recommending that the United States be excluded from the fisheries. This was, he held, the unauthorized expression of a subordinate, not that of the French court whose interests, in his opinion, coincided with those of the United States. He deplored the secret article relating to the Florida boundary and communicated it to Luzerne, with explanations designed to prevent a sense of injury on the part of France. When the treaty was submitted by the commissioners, he approved it as a whole, but reprimanded them for their manner of negotiating without the full concurrence of France, eliciting a defense of their conduct in which even Franklin joined. During the negotiations he sent quantities of ammunition for the diplomatic battle: arguments for extended boundaries, for fishing rights, and against the repatriation of Loyalists; discussions of Western territories and West Indian trade; and warnings that the boundary of Florida, if held by Spain, should be definitely specified. He recommended minor improvements in the provisional treaty which were incorporated in the definitive treaty.

He ended the practice, which had been followed by countries that had not recognized American independence, of treating with Franklin at Paris through the agency of France instead of directly as the representative of a free nation. He limited his dealings with Rendon, the unofficial Spanish agent in the United States, because the latter was without full credentials; and he approved Jay's dignified course at Madrid, recommending that Jay, when Aranda wished to treat in 1782, repay the latter for Spain's previous hauteur "with all the delays we can interpose" (to Jay, Dec. 30, 1782, Wharton, *post,* IV, 176). He advocated the appointment of Americans only to diplomatic and consular posts, opposing accordingly Adams' proposal to appoint R. F. W. Dumas as chargé d'affaires, and his policy was subsequently adopted by Congress. Strongly adverse to Congress' unfortunate practice of sending diplomats to many European courts, he expedited the recall of Francis Dana from Russia and prevented the establishment of diplomatic agents in Lisbon and in Brussels.

The establishment of the department of foreign affairs marked an advance in the development of American executive machinery. The enterprising, painstaking, and systematic, but not unimaginative way in which Livingston proceeded in the securing of quarters and assistants, the filing of correspondence and reports, and the establishing of routine practices did much to combat the vagueness of the methods of Congress. He kept the military leaders informed of political developments; sent to the state governments circular letters, foreign-news dispatches, and information as to the bearing of state activity on the foreign prestige and obligations of the Republic; and made digests of European news for the information of Congress. He resigned, on Dec. 2, 1782, because of the inadequacy of his salary, which, he reported, was $3,000 a year less than the expenses of the office. His resignation may also have been due in part to the inconsistent and, according to Madison, "frequently improper" actions of Congress. He was twice induced by Congress to prolong his stay, first until Jan. 1, 1783, and thereafter until May. It was June when he finally left for "Clermont." Unfortunately the office thereafter became for a time practically non-existent and a large part of Livingston's work of organization was undone. The noteworthy events of his third period of attendance upon Congress (1784–85) were his motion to appoint a minister to Great Britain, the adoption of which created the post to which Adams was elected in 1785; his membership on the committee to define such duties of the court of appeals as related to matters referred to it by the secretary for foreign affairs; his candidacy, never resulting in election, for the posts of minister to Great Britain, Spain, and the Netherlands; and his activity on several committees.

Far from being engrossed in federal concerns, Livingston was deeply involved in the public affairs of his state. He was a leader in the successive Revolutionary organizations that replaced the imperial governmental machinery: the New York congress and committee of safety of 1776; the council of safety of 1777; and the commission to carry on the government during the interval between the adoption of a state constitution and the time when it began to function. After the war he was a member of the commission to govern New York following the British evacuation, and of the commissions to fix on a boundary with Massachusetts in 1784, and with Vermont in 1790. In 1811 he was on the first canal commission, which projected plans that were later realized in the Erie Canal. More important was his membership on the committee to draft the first New York constitution, drawn up in 1777. His principal contribution to this instrument was the council of revision, consisting of the governor, the chancellor and the justices of the supreme court, which should exercise the veto power.

Although he is usually identified by the title,

"Chancellor," "the one undisputed fact in his Chancellorship is that he held the position from 1777 to 1801" (James Brown Scott, *post*), for there were no chancery reports in his time. He drew up "Rules in Chancery" to guide the court, but Chancellor Kent later wrote that there was not a single dictum of his predecessors to guide him. According to Chancellor Jones, this court "never boasted a more prompt, more able or more faithful officer" (*Albany Law Journal*, Apr. 9, 1881, quoting J. W. Francis), and Jefferson described him as "one of the ablest of American lawyers." Noteworthy among his opinions in the records of the council of revision are those opposing the confiscation and alienation laws directed against the Loyalists, laws granting special powers to the magistracy (lest the freedom of the citizenry be endangered), special taxes, the paper money bill of 1786, and the bill of 1785 to abolish slavery in New York. By virtue of his office as chancellor he administered the oath to President Washington in 1789.

In the New York ratifying convention he not only led the influential Livingston factions in support of the federal Constitution but was also one of the most frequent speakers. He proposed and carried a resolution that only after the whole of the Constitution had been considered, each part in turn, should any vote be put on any clause or amendment, thus preventing the possible rejection of the whole by an adverse vote on the most criticized part, and forestalling attempts at obstruction by multiplying amendments. Excepting Hamilton, possibly no individual at this time contributed more toward the success of Federalism in New York. Nevertheless, in the distribution of patronage Livingston was entirely overlooked by the new government. Carrying with him the numerous family group, he became a Republican some time before 1791, when he successfully supported Burr for Philip Schuyler's place in the United States Senate. He disagreed with Hamilton's financial plans, especially the plan for funding the debt. Washington's offer, in 1794, of the ministry to France, in succession to Morris, seemed an afterthought and was declined. He became one of the leading opponents of Jay's treaty, publishing against it, as "Cato," *Examination of the Treaty of Amity, Commerce, and Navigation, Between the United States and Great Britain* (1795). In the first election for governor he had received an unsolicited nominal vote. In 1795 he ran for the office, but was defeated by Jay. In 1800 Jefferson offered him the secretaryship of the navy, which he declined, but early the following year he accepted the appointment as minister to France.

In October 1801, a year after the treaty of San Ildefonso, he sailed with two principal objectives: first, to prevent the rumored retrocession of Louisiana to France, and if too late for that, to acquire West Florida for the United States; second, to negotiate for the payment of American claims arising from French spoliations. Soon suspecting, in spite of the repeated denials of French officials, that the delivery of Louisiana to France had already been made, he decided that it would be fruitless to raise objections to this at Paris (to Madison, Jan. 13, 1802, *American State Papers, Foreign Relations*, II, 1832, p. 513). Nevertheless, he sought through Rufus King in London to induce Great Britain, during the peace negotiations at Amiens, to put obstacles in the way of the cession (to King, Mar. 10, 1802, *Ibid.*, II, 515). In his representations to the French court Livingston was met by Talleyrand with a policy of silence and inattention; and he finally sent a strong note of remonstrance to that minister, who was obliged to make a verbal apology and, through Marbois, a written explanation (Livingston to Madison, Nov. 2, 1802, State Department Archives). Subsequently, Livingston repeatedly assured his friends that his treatment was better than that of other diplomatic representatives in Paris.

Of his policy in the negotiations leading to the Louisiana purchase he has left his own account: "I had long forseen that the possession of the East bank of the Mississippi . . . would be insufficient. . . . I therefore (though without powers) . . . endeavored to satisfy the people in power here, that . . . it was proper to give us all the country above the Arkansas. . . . In March I ventured upon what was here considered as a bold and hazardous measure a direct and forcible address to him [Napoleon] personally on the subject of our claims upon which having received from him a positive assurance that they should be fully and promptly paid, I began to look forward to this as a means of accomplishing my other object because I was sure he could not, . . . in case of a war, . . . find any other means of discharging it" (Livingston to Mitchell, July 13, 1803, Columbia University Library, "Letters to Clinton, Miscellaneous 34"). Livingston took advantage of the excitement in the United States following the closing of the Mississippi by transmitting to Talleyrand as soon as he received it (Apr. 8, 1803), Senator James Ross's resolution for an armed expedition against New Orleans (*American State Papers, Foreign Relations*, II, 552), with a note expressing his expectation that the threat would be fulfilled. When Napoleon, foreseeing the difficulty of retaining Louisiana during the impending war with Great Britain, suddenly offered to sell the whole, Livingston after waiting in order to act concurrently with Monroe, who was on his way to join him, seized the opportunity; and after some profitable haggling over the price, sixty million francs and payment of the spoliation claims by the United States was agreed upon (May 2, antedated to Apr. 30). This was, according to Henry Adams, "the greatest diplomatic success recorded in American history" (*History of the United States,* II, 48). "From this day," said Livingston as he signed the treaty, "the United States take their place among the powers of the first rank" (E. B. Livingston, *post,* p. 372). He believed that the treaty would "forever exclude us from the politics of this stormy quarter of the globe" (to Madison, June 3, 1803, *American State Papers, Foreign Relations,* II, 563).

Talleyrand refused to say whether West Florida was included in the purchase, in spite of repeated questions and even threats. Although Livingston previously held that Florida was not so included, shortly after the treaty was signed he formulated the theory that the treaty of retrocession, based on the original session of 1762, indicated that West Florida was a part of the purchase. This theory later became the basis of American policy. Another qualification of his success lay in the faults of the claims convention which later caused Livingston much bitterness. As a minister, Livingston displayed great pertinacity and the courage to undertake firm measures, as well as capacity to overcome the handicaps of deafness and imperfect command of French. While often deploring the lack of instructions, he did not hesitate to act boldly without them. By the French he was regarded as a "most importunate" negotiator and some of his arguments seemed "almost menacing." He hated a quarrel but, even more, he hated degrading submission which never prevents one. Tact also he showed, as, for example, when on his arrival he allayed the fears that he was a "violent democrat" and "on every occasion . . . carefully avoided entering into any party matters" (Livingston to Janet Montgomery, May 9, 1802, John Ross Delafield Manuscripts).

Livingston resigned in the autumn of 1804. He was given a cordial leave-taking by Napoleon, and after a visit to London and several months' travel with his family in Europe he returned to "Clermont," where he lived the rest of his life in political retirement. He devoted his leisure to a wide range of intellectual interests and hobbies. He had designed and built near "Clermont" a beautiful house which he embellished with the many fine things he brought from France—books, paintings, furniture, silver, Gobelin tapestries. Much of his time he occupied with the study of agriculture, corresponding with Washington, Jefferson, and his friends abroad in the interest of scientific methods. He was a pioneer in the importation of Merino sheep and in the use of gypsum as fertilizer. He was one of the organizers, in 1791, of a society subsequently called the Society for the Promotion of Useful Arts, served as president from 1791 to his death, and contributed to its publications. (There is "An Eulogium" upon him in the *Transactions,* vol. III, 1814.) His scientific curiosity expressed itself also in his interest in paleontology.

He had been associated with the attempts in steam navigation of Fitch, Morey, Stevens, and Nicholas Roosevelt, and in 1798 had undertaken the construction of a steamboat. His aid, which was technical as well as financial, made possible the experiment of Robert Fulton [*q.v.*] on the Seine and later the success of the *Clermont* on the Hudson. "It is doubtful whether Fulton would have done anything in steam navigation . . . had it not been for the arrival [of Livingston] in France . . ." (H. W. Dickinson, *Robert Fulton, Engineer and Artist,* 1913, p. 134). From the beginning, he sought exclusive rights in steam navigation. His great political influence enabled him to secure the grant of a New York monopoly in 1798 (on conditions, however, which his boat failed to fulfill), the renewal of this monopoly in 1803 in his and Fulton's joint interest, and supplementary laws in 1808 and 1811. The monopoly was popularly felt to be onerous, New Jersey, Connecticut, and Ohio all passing retaliatory laws relating to navigation on interjacent waters, but Livingston turned his earnings back into the business, and the money from the monopoly was partly responsible for the rapidity with which the steamboat was developed (*Ibid.,* p. 267). The difficulty of maintaining the monopoly was great, and in the consequent litigation and pamphlet warfare Livingston was personally very active, visiting the Assembly to urge legislation, outlining argument for counsel, and maintaining the right of the state to erect a monopoly in a correspondence with his brother-in-law and rival, John Stevens [*q.v.*]. Undaunted by competition, the partners extended their operations to the Mississippi, and petitioned the legislature of Virginia for a monopoly on the James River. Legal conflict over the New York monopoly continued after Livingston's death and was ended only by the decision in the case of *Gibbons* vs. *Ogden.*

Livingston was founder and first president of the American Academy of Fine Arts, and trustee of the New York Society Library. As a versatile intellectual luminary, a jurist, and a political leader, he occupied a higher place in the esteem of his contemporaries than it has been his lot to retain in the memory of his countrymen.

[Date of death here given is from E. B. Livingston, *post,* and *Albany Argus,* Mar. 2, 1813; the *Albany Reg.,* and the N. Y. *Evening Post,* Mar. 2, and other papers, give Feb. 25. Good biographical sketches are M. L. Bonham, Jr., "Robert Livingston," in S. F. Bemis, ed., *The Am. Secretaries of State and Their Diplomacy,* vol. I (1927); E. B. Livingston, *The Livingstons of Livingston Manor* (1910); J. L. Delafield, "Chancellor Robert R. Livingston of New York and His Family," in *Sixteenth Annual Report, 1911, of the Am. Scenic and Historic Preservation Soc.* (1911). Other sketches of some value are Frederic DePeyster, *A Biog. Sketch of Robert R. Livingston* (1876); James Brown Scott, in *Great Am. Lawyers,* ed. by W. D. Lewis, vol. I (1907), and John Bassett Moore, "Robert R. Livingston and the La. Purchase," *Columbia Univ. Quart.,* June 1904; D. S. Alexander, "Robert R. Livingston, the Author of the La. Purchase," in *Proc. N. Y. State Hist. Asso., the Seventh Ann. Meeting* (1906). Also to be consulted are Theodore Sedgwick, Jr., *A Memoir of the Life of William Livingston* (1833); C. H. Hunt, *Life of Edward Livingston* (1864); T. S. Clarkson, *A Biog. Hist. of Clermont* (1869); Henry Adams, *Hist. of the U. S.* (9 vols., 1889–90); D. S. Alexander, *A Pol. Hist. of the State of N. Y.,* vol. I (1906); J. D. Hammond, *The Hist. of Pol. Parties in the State of New-York,* vol. I (1842); C. E. Hill, "James Madison," in S. F. Bemis, ed., *The Am. Secretaries of State and Their Diplomacy,* vol. III (1927). Much of the information available in printed form is in published collections of documents: W. C. Ford and Gaillard Hunt, *Jours. of the Continental Cong.* (27 vols., 1904–28); E. C. Burnett, *Letters of Members of the Continental Cong.,* vols. I–V (1921–31); Jonathan Elliot, *The Debates in the Several State Conventions, on the Adoption of the Federal Constitution,* vol. II (1836); Peter Force, *Am. Archives* (9 vols., 1837–53); Francis Wharton, *The Revolutionary Dipl. Correspondence of the U. S.* (6 vols., 1889); *Am. State Papers, Foreign Relations,* vol. II (1832); "State Papers and Correspondence bearing on the Purchase of La.," *House Doc. 431,* 57 Cong., 2 Sess.; A. B. Street, *The Council of Revision of the State of N. Y.* (1859).

The manuscript sources are scattered among public repositories, family archives, and private collections. The Lib. of Cong. has the papers of the Continental Congress, including letters of Livingston and the committee for foreign affairs, and pertinent material in the papers of Livingston's contemporaries and in the British transcripts. The N. Y. Public Lib. has a box of Livingston papers and pertinent material in the Emmett, Olin, and Bancroft papers; the Department of State has Livingston's official correspondence while minister; the N. Y. Hist. Soc. has his minutes of the debates in the ratifying convention, his account books, and other material; the Columbia Univ. Library, the Pa. Hist. Soc., the Huntington Library, the Mass. Hist. Soc., each has from a few to several dozen Livingston papers.]

R. C. H.

LIVINGSTON, WILLIAM (November 1723–July 25, 1790), lawyer, first governor of the state of New Jersey, grandson of Robert and brother of Philip and Peter Van Brugh Livingston [*qq.v.*], was in many ways the ablest of the sons of Philip and Catharine (Van Brugh) Livingston. He was born at Albany (baptized Dec. 8, 1723), and spent his childhood there under the indulgent care of his maternal grandmother, Sarah Van Brugh. At the age of fourteen he lived for a year with a missionary among the friendly Mohawks, an experience which his family felt would be valuable if the lad turned his attention later to the fur trade or the possibilities of land speculation on the frontier. The following year he was sent to New Haven to follow the path chosen by his three elder brothers. He graduated from Yale in the class of 1741. While in college he decided that law had a larger claim than mercantile affairs upon his interest. Accordingly, he avoided his brothers' counting-houses in New York City and entered the law office of James Alexander [*q.v.*], who had been a vigorous champion of the freedom of the press in connection with the Zenger trial. Under such preceptors as Alexander and William Smith, 1697–1769 [*q.v.*], both veteran advocates of Whiggish tendencies, Livingston became confirmed in political views distinctly liberal for his generation. His intimate associates among the younger men were John Morin Scott [*q.v.*], William Peartree Smith, and William Smith, Jr. [*q.v.*], the historian, with whom he prepared a digest of the provincial laws (1752, 1762). Around these three gathered a group of sturdy Calvinists who courageously objected to the dominant position of the Anglican gentry and their allies in provincial politics. About 1745, before he had completed his legal studies, Livingston married Susanna French, the daughter of a wealthy New Jersey landholder. Henry Brockholst Livingston [*q.v.*] was their son; their daughter Susanna married John Cleves Symmes [*q.v.*], their daughter Sarah became the wife of John Jay [*q.v.*].

From the day of his admission to the bar in 1748 Livingston was a leader among those of assured position who liked to be known as supporters of the popular cause. Petulant and impatient of restraint, he soon aroused the resentment of the conservatives by his sweeping criticism of established institutions. Always more facile in writing than in speech, he delighted to compose satirical verse and witty broadsides which earned him a greater reputation as a censor than as a satirist. A young lady of his acquaintance, alluding to his tall, slender, and graceless figure, named him the "whipping-post."

In 1751 the controversy over the establishment of a college in the province became a focal point in his developing political philosophy. Although anxious to promote a collegiate foundation, he protested against the plan to place the institution in the hands of a board of trustees dominated by the Episcopalians and refused to serve as a representative of the Presbyterians on the board. To him the proposal appeared as the first step toward establishing the Anglican Church in New York and giving it general supervision of educational matters. His views were ably presented in the *Independent Reflector,* a weekly which his friends inaugurated in 1752 "to oppose superstition, bigotry, priestcraft, tyranny, servitude, public mismanagement and dishonesty in office" and to teach the "inestimable value of liberty." On the question of the college he took the stand that the institution should be non-sectarian and catholic, that it should be established not by royal charter but by act of the Assembly, and that the trustees and faculty should be subject to no religious or political tests. Though he failed to prevent the chartering of King's College by George II, his efforts were responsible for the diversion of half of the "college fund" to the building of a jail and pest house.

His contributions to the *Independent Reflector* and the "Watch Tower" column in the *New York Mercury* violently attacked the movement to establish an Anglican episcopacy in America and accused the faction, headed by Lieutenant-Governor James De Lancey [*q.v.*], of favoring the union of church and state. His appeals on this issue aroused the nonconformists and strengthened the liberal party, which was rapidly becoming a Livingston faction in provincial politics. The first important victory of the Livingstons at the polls resulted in driving the De Lanceys from their control of the Assembly in 1758. William Livingston was accorded a position of leadership not only in the councils of the party but also in its tactics in the legislative body. He was determined in his opposition to Parliamentary interference in provincial affairs. Convinced of the desirability of provincial home rule, he was equally persuaded of the necessity of the wealthy liberals continuing to rule at home. As the issues raised by Grenville's tax program reached a crisis, the unity of the Livingston forces was seriously threatened, for the patrician elements in the party were troubled by the violent reaction of the plebeian groups to the Stamp Act. Livingston labored hard to reconcile the "Sons of Liberty" and other radicals to the moderate leadership which his family represented, but the masses were dissatisfied with the temporizing Whigs. Even the attack on the Anglicans, which he renewed in his *Letter to the Right Reverend Father in God, John, Lord Bishop of Landaff* (1768), no longer aroused the voters. In the election of 1769 the De Lanceys won a decisive victory and secured a majority in the Assembly. William Livingston's power was gone for the moment. In disappointment he penned *A Soliloquy* (1770), purporting to be a meditation of Lieutenant-Governor Colden, which beneath a thin veneer of satire was an unsparing invective against the provincial representatives of British authority.

Never entirely happy in his legal work and temporarily dispirited by the turn of his political fortunes, Livingston determined to retire to his country estate near Elizabethtown, N. J. Years earlier, in his *Philosophic Solitude* (1747), he had ventured to reveal in verse his longing for the quiet of the countryside. In May 1772 he laid out pretentious grounds, planted an extensive orchard, and erected a mansion known as "Liberty Hall." There he began life anew as a gentleman farmer, but he did not find solitude. The removal to New Jersey was merely a prelude to a career more illustrious than the one just finished in New York politics. Becoming a member of the Essex County Committee of Correspondence, he quickly rose to a position of leadership and was one of the province's delegates to the First Continental Congress. There he served on the committee with his son-in-law, John Jay, and Richard Henry Lee [*qq.v.*] to draft an address to the people of British America. He was returned as a deputy to the Second Continental Congress, serving until June 5, 1776, when he assumed command of the New Jersey militia. It was a responsibility extremely irksome to him, yet he discharged his duties with his usual conscientiousness until the legislature under the new constitution elected him first governor of the state. For the next fourteen years he bore the responsibilities of the governorship during the extraordinary conditions of war and reconstruction. The multitudinous duties, civil and military, the threats of the enemy, and the disloyalty of friends harassed his nervous and excitable temper but failed to overcome his spirited support of the patriot cause. Rivington's *Royal Gazette* dubbed him the "Don Quixote of the Jerseys."

His boundless energy was an incalculable asset during the gloomiest period of the war. When peace came his messages to the legislature dealt discriminatingly and comprehensively with the problems of reconstruction. He opposed the cheapening of the currency by unrestricted issues of paper money, counseled moderation in dealing with the Loyalists and their property, and looked forward to the day when the question of slavery would be settled on the basis of gradual emancipation. As authority slipped out of the hands of Congress, he called for a revision of the Articles of Confederation, in which he was privileged to participate at the Federal Convention of 1787. Though he was not conspicuous in debate, he ably supported the New Jersey plan and worked for a compromise that would mean success. His influence was largely responsible for the alacrity and unanimity with which the state convention ratified the Constitution. Two years later, while he was resting at Elizabethtown, his years of public service came to an end.

Though his life was spent in the excitement of political strife and affairs of state, he longed for the quieter routine of the farmer. After his removal to New Jersey he managed to devote some time to experiments in gardening, becoming an active member of the Philadelphia Society for the Promotion of Agriculture. It was his pleasure to show his friends his vegetables at "Liberty Hall." Among his intimates and in an ever-widening circle of acquaintances he was honored for his high moral courage and his fine sense of social responsibility. The confidential agents of the French government reported to Paris that he was a man who preferred the public good to personal popularity. No better estimate in brief compass remains in the writings of his colleagues than the sketch penned by William Pierce in 1787 (Farrand, *post,* III, 90). "Governor Livingston," wrote the Georgian, "is confessedly a man of the first rate talents, but he appears to me rather to indulge a sportiveness of wit than a strength of thinking. He is, however, equal to anything, from the extensiveness of his education and genius. His writings teem with satyr and a neatness of style. But he is no Orator, and seems little acquainted with the guiles of policy."

[A body of papers of William Livingston, containing many letters and extensive records of his legal practice, was presented to the Mass. Hist. Soc. by Charles L. Nichols in 1922, and some additional MSS. were given to the society in 1923. Theodore Sedgwick, Jr.'s *A Memoir of the Life of William Livingston* (1833), was written from materials in possession of Livingston's descendants, but contains numerous inaccuracies. C. H. Levermore, "The Whigs of Colonial New York," in *Am. Hist. Rev.*, Jan. 1896, is valuable, and there are important references in C. L. Becker, *The Hist. of Political Parties in the Province of N. Y.* (1909) and E. B. Livingston, *The Livingstons of Livingston Manor* (1910). See also Max Farrand, *The Records of the Federal Convention of 1787* (1911); L. Q. C. Elmer, in *Colls. N. J. Hist. Soc.*, vol. VII (1872); F. B. Dexter, *Biog. Sketches Grads. Yale Coll.*, vol. I (1885); and M. C. Tyler, *The Lit. Hist. of the Am. Rev.* (1897), esp. II, 17–20.] J. A. K.

LIVINGSTONE, WILLIAM (Jan. 21, 1844–Oct. 17, 1925), lake carrier, newspaper owner, banker, was born at Dundas, Ontario. His parents, William Livingstone, a ship's carpenter, and Helen (Stevenson) Livingstone, moved to Detroit while he was a child. Here he completed a common-school education, learned the machinist's trade, and began his career with the lake merchant marine, a career which lasted more than sixty years and included all grades of service and all types of shipping. "Sailor Bill," as he was known, mastered each step of ship operation and carrier management. In 1864 he was in partnership with Robert Downie as ship chandler and general merchant. Two years later, in June 1866, he married his partner's daughter, Susan. He owned a line of tugs which assisted sailing freighters between Lake Erie and Lake Huron. Later, as general manager of the Percheron Steam Navigation Company and of the Michigan Navigation Company, he was responsible for the construction of the steamships *Palmer* and *Livingstone,* 297 feet in length. These, the largest ships then on the Great Lakes, were too large, his associates felt, to be practical, yet Livingstone lived to see 600 feet a common length for freighters.

A Republican in politics, he early became a party leader. He served for many years as chairman of the Republican State Central Committee. He represented his district in the Michigan legislature in 1875, was collector of revenue for the port of Detroit under President Arthur, and chairman of the Michigan delegation to the National Convention in 1896. In 1892, with Senator Thomas W. Palmer, he purchased the defunct *Detroit Journal.* This paper he made a respected organ of the Republican party and a financial success. He was proud of his capabilities as a newspaper writer and later wrote and printed privately *Livingstone's History of the Republican Party* (1900), in two volumes. In 1884 he helped organize the Dime Savings Bank (now the Bank of Michigan), which he served as vice-president, 1884–1900, and as president from 1900 to his death. He was president of the American Bankers Association and of the Detroit Clearing House Association.

Throughout his career he was a force among the lake carriers. It was he who saw the possibilities of consolidating into a single body the voluntary associations of shippers. From its incorporation in 1902 until his death he was president of the Lake Carriers' Association. In this capacity he was influential in getting the federal government to construct the Davis and Sabin locks at Sault Ste. Marie and the Livingstone Channel in the Detroit River. As president of the Lake Carriers' Association he personally took charge of the relief work during the memorable storms of 1917, and succeeded in freeing many ships and in saving immense sums in ships and cargoes.

Active in social and philanthropic circles, he was a member of more than one hundred clubs and societies and possessed a host of friends among owners, seamen, statesmen, and politicians. From all walks of life men came to seek his counsel, and although both stern and busy, he was always ready to aid and advise the sailor, the captain, or the bank employee who asked his help. Tall, lean, broad-shouldered, "straight as an arrow," he was a figure to be remembered. Untiring physically, mentally alert, efficient and self-sufficient, he overcame all odds and made a success of each activity. Yet the thing in which he took most pride was his license testifying to his fitness as a pilot for ships of all tonnage. Death came to him suddenly one afternoon, while he was at work in the office of the Lake Carriers' Association. A lighthouse designed by Giza Maroti and completed in 1930 was erected at the east end of Belle Isle by the Lake Carriers' Association and other friends as a memorial to his life and work.

[*Livingstone's Hist of the Republican Party* (2 vols., 1900); *Cyc. of Mich.* (2nd ed., 1900); *Mich. Biogs.* (1924), vol. II; *Early Hist. of Mich. with Biogs.* (1888); *Am. Mag.*, Jan. 1923; *Ann. Report of the Lake Carriers' Asso.*, 1902–25; esp. that for 1925; *Who's Who in America*, 1924–25; G. N. Fuller, *Historic Mich.* (1928), III, 397; A. N. Marquis, *The Book of Detroiters* (1914); *N. Y. Times*, Oct. 18, 1925.] J. J. S.

LLOYD, ALFRED HENRY (Jan. 3, 1864–May 11, 1927), philosopher, was born in Montclair, N. J., the son of Henry H. and Anna (Badger) Lloyd. The death of Henry Lloyd in 1868 left his widow and five children in financial difficulties, from which they were temporarily saved by the assistance of her father, Daniel Badger. Upon his death in 1874, the family sank to the brink of penury. Alfred and his twin brother, Arthur, were sent to their uncle, Myrom Lloyd, principal of a school in Westfield, Mass. Later the twins attended high school in Andover, Mass., whither their mother had removed, and still later they completed their preparatory work at St. Johnsbury Academy. At this time Alfred intended to enter the Congregational ministry and a friend offered to pay his expenses through Dartmouth if he would pledge himself to do so, but the lad refused to mortgage his right to change his mind. Instead, he virtually worked his own way through Harvard by means of tutoring and scholarships. Elected president of the college Young Men's Christian Association, he resigned because of the organization's refusal to admit Unitarians. This experience, and similar ones, revealing the narrowness of many devout Christians, along with a growing interest in philosophy, finally dissuaded him from entering the ministry. He graduated from Harvard in 1886, and after a year of teaching at Phillips Academy, Andover, he returned to the college for graduate work in philosophy. In 1889 he gained the Walker Fellowship, which took him abroad for two years of study at Göttingen, Berlin, and Heidelberg. He became instructor in the department of philosophy under John Dewey at the University of Michigan in 1891. Here he remained for the rest of his life, as assistant professor from 1894 until 1899, associate professor until 1906, and full professor thereafter. In 1915 he became dean of the graduate school, and on the death of President Marion L. Burton [*q.v.*] in February 1925 he was made acting president, in which capacity he served during the trying period that preceded the coming of President Clarence C. Little in October 1925. His sound judgment, unfailing tact, and irenic disposition caused him to be pushed inevitably into the administrative work for which he was so well fitted. Nevertheless this work equally inevitably deflected him from his even more important productive work as a philosopher. In his early books, *Citizenship and Salvation* (1897), *Dynamic Idealism* (1898), and *Philosophy of History* (1899) he laid the foundations of an activist idealism, which in many respects foreshadowed the famous *filosofia del atto* of Croce and Gentile, although Lloyd's method was at once more cursory and more objective than that of either of the great Italians. He concerned himself almost entirely with the implications of relationship, in which he found proof of the activity, intelligibility, and ultimate intelligence of the universe. His highly original dialectic of the categories, influenced but not governed by Hegel, brought time, space, and causality into a thorough-going dynamic monism. With a Spinoza-like aloofness and high serenity, from the vantage-point of reason he accepted the necessary involution of evil with good and found no need to take refuge in mere faith. *The Will to Doubt*, which he published in 1907, may be taken as an impersonal answer to William James's *The Will to Believe*, but, though much more profound, it never obtained a fraction of the influence of that far-reaching essay. Both Lloyd's thought and terminology were too original to be easily grasped, his reasoning was difficult to follow, and his fondness for paradox often rendered him obscure. His one easily understood work was the least important, *Leadership and Progress* (1922), a study of the post-war psychology from the standpoint of a political liberal. He was married, Dec. 28, 1892, to Margaret E. Crocker of Springfield, Mass.

[*Jour. of Philosophy*, Mar. 1, 1928; *Philosophical Rev.*, Nov. 1927; *Mich. Alumnus*, May 21, Dec. 24, 1927; *Science*, July 1, 1927; *Who's Who in America*, 1926–27; *Detroit News*, May 11, 1927; personal acquaintance.] E. S. B.

LLOYD, DAVID (*c.* 1656–Apr. 6, 1731 o.s.), lawyer, politician, chief justice of Pennsylvania, was born in the parish of Manafon, Montgomeryshire, Wales. Nothing is known about his family, but he was probably a relative of Thomas Lloyd [*q.v.*]. They came from the same county in Wales, and Thomas, in his will, refers to David as his kinsman. He may have lived for a time at Cirencester in Gloucestershire, for it was there that he married his first wife. He studied law and on Apr. 24, 1686, received a commission from William Penn as attorney-general of Pennsylvania. He and his family arrived in Philadelphia on July 11 and he was shortly afterward appointed clerk of the county court, clerk of the provincial court, and deputy master of the rolls. He was closely associated with Thomas Lloyd, who was at that time master of the rolls, in his controversy with deputy-governor Blackwell. For refusing the demand of the provincial council to produce the court records, he was removed from the clerkship of the provincial court on Feb. 25, 1689, but the post was apparently restored after Blackwell's recall (*Minutes of the Provincial Council of Pennsylvania*, 1838 edition, I, pp. 202, 347). He served in the Assembly as a representative from Chester County, where he had landed interests, 1693–95, and began his long intermittent career as speaker of the Assembly in 1694. He was a member of the provincial council from Chester in 1695–96 and again from 1698 to 1700.

In 1698, Lloyd became involved in a quarrel with Robert Quarry, the judge of the newly created court of vice-admiralty. He was accused of advising the magistrates to take goods by force out of the King's warehouse at Newcastle and of otherwise resisting the enforcement of the acts of trade and navigation. On one occasion, when the marshal of the court produced his commission, Lloyd held it aloft and pointing to the picture of his Majesty which adorned it, is said to have exclaimed: "Here is a fine baby, a pretty baby, but we are not to be frightened with babies" (Root, *post*, p. 100). As a result of Quarry's complaints, Lloyd was rebuked by Penn, removed from his post as attorney-general, and suspended from the council in 1700.

This was the turning point of Lloyd's career. He became an almost lifelong enemy of Penn and of James Logan [*q.v.*], secretary of the province and the chief representative of the proprietary interests in Pennsylvania. His first reaction was to join forces with Quarry, who appointed him deputy judge and advocate to the admiralty. But this was only a passing phase. He was elected to the Assembly from Philadelphia County in 1703 and almost immediately became the recognized leader of the democratic or anti-proprietary party. He was reëlected annually from either the county or the city of Philadelphia until 1710 and was speaker in 1704–05 and from 1706 to 1709. During these years he was constantly in conflict, not only with Logan, but also with the deputy governors, John Evans [*q.v.*] and Charles Gookin. As an orthodox Quaker, he advocated the right of affirmation for jurors and witnesses and opposed the appropriation of public funds for military purposes. Supplies were to be voted only on condition that they "should not be dipt in blood." As a democrat, he insisted upon constitutional reform, upon the right of the Assembly to meet and adjourn at its own pleasure, and upon the popular control of the judiciary. He was the author of the famous remonstrance or list of grievances sent to William Penn in 1704 and the prime mover in the attempt to impeach Logan in 1707. The people finally became tired of the eternal bickering and Lloyd and nearly all of his partisans were defeated in 1710. He soon regained his popularity, however, and was reëlected to the Assembly, but not to the speakership, in the following year. He removed from Philadelphia to Chester, in 1711, and represented Chester County in the Assembly in the years 1712–14, 1715–18, 1723–24, and 1725–29. He was again chosen speaker for the sessions 1714–15, 1723–24, and 1725–29. He was recorder of the city court of Philadelphia from 1702 to 1708 and chief justice of the province from 1717 until his death, which occurred at Chester on Apr. 6, 1731.

It is difficult to analyze Lloyd's character and assess the value of his work because the records of the time were written almost entirely by his enemies. According to their view, his ethical standards as a lawyer were questionable and he was vindictive and unscrupulous as a politician. He is said to have ante-dated the remonstrance that was sent to Penn in 1704 and to have signed it as speaker, although the Assembly had adjourned. James Logan says that he was a man "of a sound judgment, and a good lawyer, but extremely pertinacious and somewhat revengeful" (Penn and Logan Correspondence, vol. I, p. 18). Proud and other early historians of Pennsylvania followed this lead and Lloyd was long regarded as a quarrelsome demagogue. He has been rehabilitated, however, in recent years, and the tendency now is to represent him as a pioneer in the fight for democratic principles in America. He helped to organize the forces of popular opinion which resulted in the issue of Markham's "Frame of Government" in 1696 and Penn's "Charter of Privileges" in 1701 and it is believed that the abolition of the legislative powers of the council was due to his influence. He steadily resisted the efforts of the governor and council to control the judiciary and to encroach upon the functions of the Assembly. Members of the Society of Friends are grateful to him for the struggle that he made to secure the right of affirmation and to oppose the establishment of a military force. He was probably also responsible for the vigorous protests against the slave trade that came so frequently from the Chester Monthly Meeting between 1711 and 1731. He was the greatest lawyer of colonial Pennsylvania and he probably exerted the greatest single influence on the character of its early legislation. Although he was obstinate and vindictive during the active period of his life, he mellowed in his later years, signed an affectionate and loyal tribute to the memory of Penn, and was even known to cooperate with Logan. Lloyd was married twice. His first wife, whose name was Sarah, lived at Cirencester in Gloucestershire, England. His second wife was Grace Growden, daughter of Joseph Growden of Bucks County, Pa. They were married in 1697 and she was still living at the time of his death.

[The traditional view of Lloyd's life and work is based on the Penn MSS. in the Hist. Soc. of Pa. and the "Correspondence Between Wm. Penn and Jas. Logan," in the *Memoirs of the Hist. Soc. of Pa.*, vols. IX and X (1870–72). There is also considerable source material in the *Minutes of the Provincial Council of Pa.*, vols. I and II (1838). For a favorable account, see Isaac Sharpless, *Pol. Leaders of Provincial Pa.* (1919), and Frank M. Eastman, *Courts and Lawyers of Pa.* (1922), vol. I. For the controversy with Robert Quarry, see W. T. Root, *The Relations of Pa. with the British Govt., 1696–1765* (1912). See also: Robert Proud, *The Hist. of Pa., 1681–1742* (2 vols., 1797–98); Lawrence Lewis, Jr., "The Courts of Pa. in the Seventeenth Century," *Pa. Mag. of Hist. and Biog.*, vol. V, no. 2 (1881); John H. Martin, *Martin's Bench and Bar of Phila.* (1883); W. R. Shepherd, *Hist. of Proprietary Govt. in Pa.* (1896); and C. H. Browning, *Welsh Settlement of Pa.* (1912). Lloyd himself published two small treatises, *A Vindication of the Legislative Powers* (1725), and *A Defense of the Legislative Constitution of the Province of Pa.* (1728). An answer to the *Vindication*, written by Logan (1725), is reprinted in the *Pa. Mag. of Hist. and Biog.*, Oct. 1914. The inscription on Lloyd's tombstone in the Friends' Burial Ground in Chester states that he was seventy-five years old at the time of his death. A book by B. A. Konkle, "David Lloyd and the First Half-Century of Pa.," is now in preparation.]

W. R. S.

LLOYD, EDWARD (Nov. 15, 1744–July 8, 1796), Maryland official, was designated "the Patriot" because of his eminent services during the Revolutionary period, in order to distinguish him from others of the family succession. He was the eldest son of Edward Lloyd, III, and Ann (Rousby) Lloyd and was descended from an Edward Lloyd who emigrated to Lower Norfolk, Va., in 1623 and later moved to Maryland. Edward Lloyd, 1779–1834 [*q.v.*], was his son. Nothing definite is known of his formal training but he acquired a library of over a thousand volumes of luxurious editions. His public service, which began with his election in 1771 as burgess for Talbot County, continued under provincial, state, and federal governments until his death. He was elected because of his acknowledged hostility to Gov. Robert Eden's proclamation, fixing fees of certain officers in opposition to legislative desires. He naturally joined in a remonstrance to the governor, protesting against the usurpation of legislative prerogative. The election of 1773 returned him to his seat, which he held till the overthrow of the colonial government.

Lloyd was made a member of the Committee of Correspondence for Talbot County to attend a gathering of similar committees at Annapolis in June 1774. This body created the responsible Council of Safety, of which Lloyd was made a member, charged with executive control during legislative adjournment. It also authorized an election of delegates to a convention to be held at Annapolis. Although Lloyd was not originally returned to this body, he took his seat in January 1776 after the expulsion of one of the members. He was returned to the lower house at the first election held under the new state constitution and there elected early in 1777, by joint legislative ballot, to the executive council, a post to which he was twice successively reëlected. In November 1779, when the Assembly balloted for governor, Lloyd was defeated by Thomas Sim Lee [*q.v.*]. After one more year of service in the lower house, he was chosen in 1781 by the state electoral college senator for the Eastern Shore, winning reëlection at the end of his five-year term and again in 1791, though he did not live to complete his third term. He had already rendered national service by acting as one of the two Maryland delegates in the Congress of the Confederation during 1783–84, participating in the vote on the peace treaty with Great Britain. As a delegate from Talbot County in the state convention, he voted for the ratification of the new federal Constitution.

After his marriage on Nov. 19, 1767, to Elizabeth Tayloe of Virginia, Lloyd had settled down to the management of his vast landed estate. He lived a life of splendor and of lavish hospitality, ordering luxuries prodigally from London—clothes, wines, plate, coaches, a pleasure-boat—and maintaining a large deer-park for his guests' pleasure. As a member of the Maryland Jockey Club he kept and raced pedigreed horses. He prided himself on being one of the largest wheat growers in America. The burning and looting of "Wye House" late in the war has usually been ascribed to a military expedition from the British fleet, but may well have been the act of a predatory band. The despoiled owner lost no time in erecting an imposing mansion near the original site and also erected a town house in Annapolis for his greater comfort during legislative sessions. In view of his monetary interests his public activities may be regarded as indicating real public spirit.

[See Oswald Tilghman, *Hist. of Talbot County, Md., 1661–1861* (2 vols., 1915); Christopher Johnston, "Lloyd Family," *Md. Hist. Mag.*, Dec. 1912; Rebecca L. P. Shippen, "The Lloyds of 'Wye House,' Talbot County, Md.," *Md. Original Research Soc. of Baltimore, Bulletin*, June 1906; *Archives of Md.*, vols. XI (1892), XVI (1897), XXI (1901); *Proc. of the Conventions of the Province of Md. Held at . . . Annapolis in 1774, 1775, and 1776* (1836); legislative journals. The date of birth is taken from Lloyd's tombstone.]

E. L.

LLOYD, EDWARD (July 22, 1779–June 2, 1834), congressman, governor of Maryland, was born at "Wye House," the only son of Edward Lloyd, 1744–1796 [*q.v.*], and Elizabeth (Tayloe) Lloyd. His formal training, gained from tutors, was supplemented by his contact with the political thinkers who were constant guests at his father's home. Probably owing to his family connections, he entered public service young and was sent as a delegate to the state legislature in 1800 when he had barely reached his majority. His chief service during this period was the promotion of the constitutional amendment providing for the removal of the property qualification from the franchise, an action which undoubtedly increased his popularity with the mass of his constituents. From the state Assembly he passed to the national House of Representatives in 1806 to fill a vacancy in the Ninth Congress. He was reëlected to the Tenth Congress, but his congressional career was terminated abruptly by his election by the legislature (June 1809) to the governorship, left vacant by the resignation of Governor Wright. This unexpired term ended the following November, but Lloyd was twice reëlected for one-year terms. Republicanism scored a significant victory under his benevolent direction: the free ballot act repealed the last remaining property qualification—that for holding office. The two parties were so evenly balanced in Maryland at that time that though the Republicans controlled the executive post, the Federalists regained the speakership in the House with resulting friction between administrative and legislative branches.

Lloyd left the governorship in 1811 to enter the state Senate, where he heartily supported President Madison in his attitude toward England, and where he served until his resignation in January 1815. When another turn of the political wheel restored the Republicans to power toward the close of the second decade of the century, Lloyd was sent to the United States Senate. Reëlected in 1825, he found himself obliged, owing to constant attacks of gout, to resign in January 1826, and to retire temporarily to private life. He was drawn forth for a final service in the Maryland Senate for the period 1826–31, part of the time as its presiding officer. Lloyd had married on Nov. 30, 1797, Sally Scott Murray, the daughter of an Annapolis physician. He died at Annapolis in his fifty-fifth year and was buried in the family burying-ground at "Wye." He lived the life of the typical Maryland gentleman, characterized by a genuine enthusiasm for agricultural interests, by munificent private hospitality, and by humanitarian interests. In the midst of luxurious surroundings he moved with simplicity and dignity of manner, while his advocacy of democratic legislation attested his devotion to patriotic principles.

[Oswald Tilghman, *Hist. of Talbot County, Md., 1661–1861* (2 vols., 1915); Christopher Johnston, "Lloyd Family," *Md. Hist. Mag.*, Dec. 1912; Rebecca L. P. Shippen, "The Lloyds of 'Wye House,' Talbot County, Md.," *Md. Original Research Soc. of Baltimore, Bulletin*, June 1906; H. E. Buchholz, *Governors of Md. from the Revolution to the Year 1908* (1908); M. P. Andrews, *Tercentenary Hist. of Md.* (1925), vol. I; *The Biog. Cyc. of Representative Men of Md. and the District of Columbia* (1879); *Republican Star* (Easton), June 21, 1803; *Baltimore Patriot and Mercantile Advertiser*, June 3, 1834; *Baltimore Republican*, June 4, 1834; *Easton Gazette*, June 7, 1834; legislative journals.]

E. L.

LLOYD, HENRY DEMAREST (May 1, 1847–Sept. 28, 1903), journalist, author, born in New York City, was the eldest child of Aaron and Maria Christie Demarest Lloyd. He inherited from both sides of the family a long pioneer and dissenting tradition and was brought up by his father, a penurious minister of the Dutch Reformed Church, in a rigidly Calvinistic atmosphere against which in later life he definitely reacted. He was granted the degree of A.M. from Columbia College in 1869 and in the same year was admitted to the New York bar. Three years of youthful reform activity followed. In 1871 with the Young Men's Municipal Reform Association he contributed to the defeat of Tammany Hall. In 1872, in accordance with his enthusiastic free-trade principles, he vigorously opposed Greeley's nomination at the Liberal Republican Convention. Disappointed in politics, he turned to journalism, accepted a position with the *Chicago Tribune,* and settled in Chicago where, in 1873, he married Jessie Bross, the daughter of William Bross, formerly lieutenant-governor of Illinois.

As financial editor and editorial writer, he familiarized himself with the growing trust and labor movements and started, if one excepts his college oration against monopoly, the campaign that was his life. In 1881 his "Story of a Great Monopoly" so vividly exposed the methods of the railroads and the Standard Oil Company that the *Atlantic Monthly* (March 1881), in which Howells had had the courage to publish it, ran to seven editions. With this article he became the first, as he remained perhaps the greatest, of the new "muck-rakers." He perceived the dangers of the rising monopolies and became the untiring champion of the independent competitor, the consumer, and the worker. In succeeding articles he attacked the classical political economy, with its reliance upon competition, the abuses of grain speculation, the financial machinations and rebate practices of the railroads, and monopoly in all its guises.

In 1885 he decided to devote his whole time to public welfare. He left the *Tribune,* and, in the course of a European trip, made invigorating contacts with English leaders in politics and industry. He returned with renewed interest in problems of labor which was rapidly intensified by succeeding events. The current depression was accompanied by increasing industrial unrest which culminated in the Haymarket "massacre" of 1886. In defiance of the dominant opinion of the time, Lloyd, who had no sympathy with anarchism or violence, espoused the cause of the convicted anarchists and assisted in having two death sentences commuted. This experience of legal oppression was complemented by his investigation of industrial oppression in the Spring Valley coal strike. His first book, *A Strike of Millionaires against Miners* (1890), was a characteristically dramatic plea for industrial justice. He continued this direct interest in the industrial conflict by acting in 1893 as an unofficial organizer of the Milwaukee street-car workers and by defending Debs for his conduct of the Pullman Strike of 1894. All this contributed to the writing of his most important book, *Wealth against Commonwealth* (1894), five hundred pages of denunciation of monopolies, especially the Standard Oil Company, distilled from the records of court and legislative inquiries. It was widely read but stimulated no such uprising of an informed public as his faith in democracy had led him to expect.

The growth of the National People's party temporarily restored his hopes of an independent political party, and after playing an influential rôle in its conventions, he reluctantly accepted its nomination for Congress in 1894 but was, of course, overwhelmingly defeated in his corporation-controlled Chicago district. Two years later, the narrowing of the platform to the remonetization of silver, which he regarded as necessary but not sufficient, and the absorption of the party by the Democrats, so disappointed him that he withdrew from active participation in national political life. He continued, however, to play an active and frequently official rôle in the progressive politics of his home suburban village, Winnetka. He did not formally join the Socialist party until 1903, but he meanwhile supported the Socialists because they alone seemed to have a program designed to achieve the abolition of monopolistic power and the emancipation of the working class. His democratic idealism led him independently to the advocacy of "Social Democracy" and to occasional support of a communistic or cooperative experiment.

These interests hungered for an outlet more constructive than mere denunciation. After elaborating his semi-religious philosophy in the "Manuscript of 1896" and other essays, published in *Man, the Social Creator* (1906), he spent the years 1897–1901 in travel for the purpose of observing social experiments. From England he brought back the message of labor copartnership (*Labour Copartnership,* 1898; *Newest England,* 1900) and from New Zealand, a profound enthusiasm for compulsory arbitration of industrial disputes (*A Country without Strikes,* 1900), an enthusiasm that to his deep regret failed to convert the American Federation of Labor. His last trip was to Switzerland to study the initiative and referendum (*A Sovereign People,* 1907). During the long anthracite strike of 1902, Lloyd was active in attacking the operators' policy and in promoting relief work. When the owners finally agreed to arbitrate he was the principal associate of Mitchell and Darrow in presenting the miners' case. Before recovering from this strain, he entered in 1903 an equally exhausting campaign for the municipal ownership of street railways in Chicago, at the height of which he died.

[Caro Lloyd's *Henry Demarest Lloyd* (1912), a laudatory but reliable biography by his sister, contains a full bibliography of his writings. Shorter notices appear in the *Winnetka Town Meeting: Memorial Meeting in Honor of Henry Demarest Lloyd* (1903); *Chi-*

cago Daily Tribune, Sept. 29, 1903; *Chicago Daily News,* Sept. 28, 1903; *Arena,* December 1903. Lloyd's more important addresses and articles have been reprinted in *Men, the Workers* (1909); *Mazzini and Other Essays* (1910); and *Lords of Industry* (1910).]

W. J. C.

LLOYD, JAMES (Mar. 24, 1728–Mar. 14, 1810), pioneer obstetrician and surgeon, was born at Oyster Bay, Long Island, the youngest of ten children of Henry and Rebecca (Nelson) Lloyd. His grandfather, James Lloyd, emigrated to Boston, Mass., about 1670 from Somersetshire, England, and became an important colonial merchant. His father, who had a large estate on Long Island, N. Y., was also a Boston merchant. After a preliminary education in a private school at New Haven, Conn., young Lloyd was apprenticed in medicine for five years to Dr. William Clark, one of the leading practitioners of Boston. He then went to England and spent two years in London, listening to lectures on midwifery by the first "man-midwife," William Smellie, attending the demonstrations of the leading London surgeon of the time, William Cheselden, then at the height of his career, acting as a "dresser" at Guy's Hospital, and meeting and perhaps working with two young men, the brothers William and John Hunter, who were destined to revolutionize obstetrics and surgery even more completely than Smellie and Cheselden. Both were great influences in Lloyd's life, then and later.

Lloyd returned in 1752 to Boston, where he began the practice of surgery. Success came rapidly and completely; his practice became extensive and he was considered in consultation "one of the most useful and intelligent physicians in the State" (Gardiner, *post,* p. 17). He introduced the new methods of surgery to New England and was the first physician to practise midwifery in America, thus taking obstetrics away from the hands of midwives and putting it upon a scientific basis. He made no contributions to medical literature; he was eminently a practitioner, not a scholar, although he had many pupils. His handsome home was the center of fashionable Boston; his garden was noted, for he was somewhat of a practical as well as a scientific horticulturist; he was fond of sports; he numbered among his intimate friends, as well as patients, General Howe and Lord Percy. When war came, greatly to his credit, he remained in Boston as a physician; his only important medical contemporary, Silvester Gardiner [*q.v.*], retired to Halifax. He rendered good service to both the remaining English, after the evacuation, and to the Americans; and Gen. Israel Putnam is said to have made his home with him on entering the town. He was, however, greatly shaken by the war; many of his more well-to-do patients had left Boston, his Long-Island estate, inherited from his father, had been partially destroyed by the British troops, who had cut down his woodland; and he was somewhat broken in health. He made a half-hearted attempt to obtain compensation for the loss of his woodland and even went to London (1789) for the purpose. His claim was refused, unless he would become a British subject; this he steadfastly refused to do and, with his self-respect unimpaired, he returned home the same year empty-handed. He lived through the reconstruction period after the Revolution, although life must have lost much of its zest. His wife, Sarah Corwin, died in 1797. When Dr. Benjamin Waterhouse [*q.v.*] began vaccination for smallpox in Boston in 1800, by the Jennerian method, Lloyd saw the significance of the discovery and became an ardent advocate of it. After a long illness, Lloyd died at the age of eighty-two. A son, James Lloyd, became United States senator from Massachusetts.

[J. S. J. Gardiner, *Sermon . . . on the Decease of Dr. Jas. Lloyd* (1810); Jas. Thacher, *Am. Med. Biog.* (1828), pp. 359–76; Lorenzo Sabine, *Biog. Sketches of Loyalists of the Am. Revolution* (2 vols., 1864), II, 23; S. A. Green, *Hist. of Medicine in Mass.* (1881); Ephraim Eliot, "Account of the Physicians of Boston," *Proc. Mass. Hist. Soc.,* vol. VII (1864); *New Eng. Jour. Medicine and Surgery,* Apr. 1813; *Am. Ancestry,* vol. III (1893); W. L. Burrage, *Hist. Mass. Medic. Soc.* (1923); Lawrence Park, *Gilbert Stuart* (1926), vol. I; *Boston Gazette,* Mar. 15, 1810.]

H. R. V.

LLOYD, MARSHALL BURNS (Mar. 10, 1858–Aug. 10, 1927), inventor, manufacturer, was born in St. Paul, Minn., the son of John and Margaret (Conmee) Lloyd. His father was an Englishman who had emigrated to Canada in 1832 and in the early fifties had settled in St. Paul with his bride. While Lloyd was still an infant, however, his parents returned to Canada to live and settled on a farm at Meaford on Georgian Bay. Here young Lloyd obtained a bit of an education and at the age of fourteen went to work in the village store. Possessing unusual initiative and aggressiveness he soon gave up this work to sell fish, catching his own fish and peddling them from door to door. At sixteen he went alone to Toronto and for two years worked in a grocery store and also peddled soap. At eighteen he became a rural mail-carrier on the sixty-five-mile route between Port Arthur and Pidgeon River, and while so engaged he joined the rush of settlers and real-estate speculators to Winnipeg. For a living he worked as a waiter, and by shrewd purchases of land with his meager savings he accumulated several thousand dollars within a few months. With this fund he went to North Dakota, bought a farm at Grafton, and brought to it his parents and brothers and sisters. He soon discovered that he did not like farming and went alone again to St. Thomas, N. Dak., where he engaged in the insurance business. While thus employed he patented a weighing scale for the use of farmers and undertook to manufacture the article in St. Thomas. Shortly after getting under way, however, the factory was completely destroyed by fire and Lloyd lost everything. In the hope of securing financial aid to rebuild his plant he went to Minneapolis, Minn., but was not successful. In order to live he became a shoe salesman and in his spare time worked on other inventions.

After more than ten years Lloyd was eventually rewarded when the C. O. White Manufacturing Company of Minneapolis gave him an interest in the company in exchange for the right to use a machine he had patented for weaving wire door and table mats. He then patented a machine for weaving wire spring mattresses. With this invention he was able to buy out the White Company in 1900 and to found the Lloyd Manufacturing Company. The success of his woven-wire bed spring was immediate and he sold manufacturing rights not only to American industrialists but also to manufacturers in Europe, Australia, New Zealand, and South Africa. Following this venture he perfected a machine to make wire wheels for baby carriages and began their manufacture first in Minneapolis and then in Menominee, Mich., where his plant was permanently established. His next successful invention was the machinery for manufacturing thin tubing out of ribbons of steel of any width, and the machinery to weave wicker-ware of other than flat surfaces. He changed the time-honored method of weaving, and instead of attaching the weft or warp to the frame of the article desired, he found a way of weaving the wicker independently of the frame and attaching it afterward. He then devised a loom to weave wicker in the new way. This machine, capable of weaving wicker-ware more exactly and in one-thirtieth of the time required by the expert hand-weaver, revolutionized the wicker-manufacturing industry.

In addition to his activities in the several manufacturing companies which he founded, Lloyd, a few years before his death, successfully organized a community cooperative department store and theatre in Menominee. He was also mayor of Menominee for two terms from 1913 to 1917. He was married three times but there were no children from any of the marriages. His third wife, Mrs. Henriette Hammer Pollen of Orange, N. J., whom he married on Apr. 11, 1922, survived him at the time of his death in Menominee.

[*Who's Who in America*, 1926–27; *Ann. Report of the Commissioner of Patents*, 1888 and years following; *Menominee Herald-Leader*, Aug. 10, 1927; information as to certain facts from the Lloyd Manufacturing Company.] C. W. M.

LLOYD, THOMAS (Apr. 17, 1640 o.s.–Sept. 10, 1694 o.s.), physician, deputy governor of Pennsylvania, was the son of Charles Lloyd of Dolobran, Meifod parish, Montgomeryshire, Wales, and Elizabeth Stanley of neighboring Shropshire. He was born at Dolobran and was educated at Jesus College, Oxford; he is probably the Thomas Lloyd who graduated in January 1661/62. After leaving college, he studied medicine and managed the estate of his brother Charles, who had been imprisoned as a Quaker. He also joined the Society of Friends and was interned at Welshpool near Dolobran from 1665 until 1672, but was allowed considerable freedom to practise his profession. He arrived in Philadelphia Aug. 20, 1683, was appointed master of the rolls in December, and was elected to the provincial council early in 1684. The council acted as chief executive of the province from Penn's departure to England in August 1684 until it was replaced by an executive commission of five members in February 1688. Lloyd was president of the council during this period and was the most influential member of the executive commission which served until the arrival of deputy-governor John Blackwell in December 1688. He also received a commission from Penn (August 1684) as keeper of the great seal of the province. The appointment of Blackwell, who was not a Quaker, was displeasing to Lloyd and he refused to affix the great seal to certain commissions which Blackwell had prepared. His attitude was insolent and the legality of his conduct was doubtful, but he had popular support and, in spite of Blackwell's opposition, was reëlected to the council in 1689. The quarrel lasted for more than a year and was finally settled by the proprietor himself, who removed Blackwell and restored the council's executive powers. Lloyd was again chosen president of the council and served in that capacity until March 1691, when Pennsylvania was temporarily separated from the three lower counties on the Delaware. He was then appointed deputy governor of the province, while William Markham [*q.v.*] was made deputy governor of the lower counties. When Pennsylvania became a royal province, Governor Fletcher requested Lloyd to remain in office as deputy or lieutenant governor, but he refused and was superseded by Markham in April 1693. He died in Philadelphia.

Lloyd married Mary Jones of Welshpool, Montgomeryshire, Wales, Nov. 9, 1665. They had a large family. After the death of his first wife he was married, possibly in 1684, to Patience Story (née Gardiner), the widow of Robert Story of New York. The dominating factors of his career were his love of democracy and his loyalty to the principles of the Society of Friends. His controversy with Blackwell involved the right of the executive to organize the judiciary and to interfere with the legislative branch of the government. He and his Quaker friends were also offended by Blackwell's efforts to establish a militia force for the defense of the province against the French and the Indians. His orthodoxy was likewise reflected in his opposition to George Keith [*q.v.*] and the so-called Christian Quakers. He was the ablest and most popular political leader in Pennsylvania from 1684 to 1693, a worthy predecessor of his "kinsman" David Lloyd [*q.v.*].

[For a sympathetic account of Lloyd's political career see Isaac Sharpless, *Pol. Leaders of Provincial Pa.* (1919), pp. 55–83. The controversy with George Keith is discussed in Rufus M. Jones, *The Quakers in the Am. Colonies* (1911), pp. 437–58. See also W. R. Shepherd, *Hist. of Proprietary Govt. in Pa.* (1896); C. H. Browning, *Welsh Settlement of Pa.* (1912); Robert Proud, *The Hist. of Pa., 1681–1742,* vol. I (1797); Mrs. R. H. Lloyd, *The Pedigree of the Lloyds of Dolobran* (p.p. 1877); C. P. Smith, *Lineage of the Lloyd and Carpenter Family* (1870), sometimes inaccurate; and T. A. Glenn, *Geneal. Notes Relating to the Families of Lloyd, Pemberton, Hutchinson, Hudson, and Parke* (1898). There is considerable source material in the *Minutes of the Provincial Council of Pa.,* vol. I (1838). Two pamphlets written by Lloyd himself in 1682 have been published: *An Epistle to my Dear and Well Beloved Friends of Dolobran* (1788) and *A Letter to John Eccles and Wife* (1805).] W. R. S.

LOCHMAN, JOHN GEORGE (Dec. 2, 1773–July 10, 1826), Lutheran clergyman, was born in Philadelphia, the son of Nicolaus and Anna Maria (Schneider) Lochman. As a catechumen he impressed J. H. C. Helmuth [*q.v.*], who urged the boy's parents to stint themselves if necessary in order to educate their son for the ministry. Upon his graduation in 1789 from the University of Pennsylvania Lochman took up the study of theology under Helmuth's direction, supporting himself meanwhile by teaching, was licensed by the Ministerium of Pennsylvania at Reading in 1794, and was ordained at Hanover in 1800. He was married twice: on Sept. 7, 1795, to Mary Magdalena Grotz of Philadelphia, who died, leaving him with two children; and on June 3, 1799, to Susan Hoffman of Philadelphia, who bore him thirteen children and outlived him by fifteen years. One of his sons, Augustus Hoffman Lochman (1802–1891), was a prominent clergyman of the next generation. Lochman was a man of solid though probably not extensive attainments, humane and charitable in disposition, modest and dignified in manner, industrious and wise in the discharge of his duties. As pastor at Lebanon 1794–1815 and at Harrisburg 1815–26, he was respected and even venerated by his parishioners. His theological opinions were distinctly Lutheran though not rigidly orthodox; like his preceptor Helmuth he saw little value in precise theological definitions and had a warm appreciation for the work of other denominations. He was the author of *Haupt-Inhalt der Christlichen Lehre* (Lebanon, 1808); *A Valedictory Sermon Preached at Lebanon* (1815); *An Inaugural Sermon Preached at Harrisburg* (Harrisburg, 1815); *The History, Doctrine, and Discipline of the Evangelical Lutheran Church* (1818); *Principles of the Christian Religion, in Questions and Answers, Designed for the Instruction of Youth in Evangelical Churches* (1822; 4th ed., 1834); and *Hinterlassene Predigten* (1828). He trained about thirty candidates for the ministry. One of his greatest services to the Church was his share in the formation of the General Synod, which was designed to bind all the Lutheran congregations of the United States into a general organization for the administration of common enterprises and the maintenance of educational and doctrinal standards. As president in 1818 of the Ministerium of Pennsylvania he took the leading part in the negotiations with the Lutherans of the South and West, and when the General Synod was organized at Frederick, Md., Oct. 21–23, 1821, he was chosen president. But among the rural congregations of the Ministerium of Pennsylvania opposition to the General Synod was stubborn and united; and Lochman had the bitter disappointment of seeing the Ministerium deny the General Synod its support. Five years later, as a result probably of overwork, he suffered an apoplectic stroke. After months of invalidism he died at Harrisburg while the bells of his church were tolling for the deaths of Jefferson and Adams.

[C. A. Hay, *Memoirs of Rev. Jacob Goering, Rev. Geo. Lochman, D.D., and Rev. Benj. Kurtz, D.D., LL.D.* (1887); *Univ. of Pa. Biog. Cat. Matriculates of the Coll., 1749–1893* (1894); D. M. Gilbert, *Services Commemorative of the 100th Anniversary of Zion Evangelical Luth. Ch., Harrisburg, Pa., Nov. 10–11, 1895* (1896); T. E. Schmauk, *Old Salem in Lebanon* (1898); G. F. Krotel, "The Gen. Synod and the Pa. Synod: A Few Chapters of History," *Luth. and Missionary,* Nov. 9, 16, 23, 1865; *Documentary Hist. of the Evangelical Luth. Ministerium of Pa., . . . 1748 to 1821* (1898); Lochman's diary (Luth. Hist. Soc., Gettysburg, Pa.); W. B. Sprague, *Annals Am. Pulpit,* vol.

IX (1869); *Pa. Intelligencer* (Harrisburg), July 14, 1826.] G. H. G.

LOCKE, DAVID ROSS (Sept. 20, 1833–Feb. 15, 1888), journalist and political satirist, who, under the pseudonym of Petroleum V. Nasby, achieved fame during the Civil War, was born at Vestal, Broome County, near Binghamton, N. Y., the son of Nathaniel Reed and Hester (Ross) Locke. His grandfather, John, had been a minute man in the Revolution; his father, a soldier in the War of 1812; while his mother, daughter of Dr. William Ross, was a granddaughter of Joshua Mersereau, who in various capacities saw service during the Revolution.

David's academic education ended when he was ten years old, and he went directly into newspaper work, from which he was never afterwards dissociated. After a fourteen-mile walk he presented himself at the office of the Cortland *Democrat* and made overtures for a job. He was a little too short to have full command of a typecase at the time, but was, nevertheless, apprenticed for a period of seven years. The *Democrat* was a vigorous political organ. Locke was connected with it until he reached the age of seventeen, when he became an itinerant printer and was employed successively in a number of cities of the North and South.

In 1852 he formed a partnership with a young man by the name of James G. Robinson. Together they founded at Plymouth, Richland County, Ohio, the *Plymouth Advertiser*. There he married Martha H. Bodine, who bore him three sons. Though the newspaper prospered after a fashion, Locke left it and, seeking better opportunities, was located afterwards in various Ohio towns. He was editor of the *Jeffersonian* at Findlay when he wrote the first letter signed with the name of Petroleum V. Nasby. It bore the date of Mar. 21, 1861. Locke had followed his father in his opposition to slavery, and his travels through the South had served to deepen the conviction that it was an evil for which the best remedy was extermination. His newspaper experience had sharpened his conviction to a cutting edge. The device to which he resorted in his newspaper attacks was a common and popular one. His creation, Petroleum V. Nasby, for whom Thomas Nast later created a pictorial embodiment, was an overdrawn but effective caricature of the Copperhead. Locke made Nasby in the image of an illiterate, hypocritical, cowardly, loafing, lying, dissolute country preacher, whose orthographical atrocities were fashioned after the style of his predecessor, Artemus Ward. Nasby sponsors slavery and the Democratic party, and thus condemns them; he is not only foolish but corrupt, the necessary inference being that the Copperheads and the Democrats were as foolish in their opinions and as corrupt in their practices; and his "advenchers" were always so invented as to make the Democratic or Southern side of an argument appear ludicrously inept. The letters were marked by a rich humor, aggressive maliciousness, skilful caricature, sustained resourcefulness, and a merciless insistence. They brought Locke fame and a fortune. In 1865 he took editorial charge of the *Toledo Blade* and in a few years owned a controlling interest in it. In 1871 he went to New York as managing editor of the *Evening Mail*, but later returned to Ohio. He continued the Nasby letters in the *Blade* almost until the time of his death, the last one appearing Dec. 26, 1887. Under his editorship the paper attained immense popularity. During his later years he espoused the cause of prohibition and carried on a campaign against the liquor traffic under the flaunting banner line, "Pulverize the Rum Power." Abraham Lincoln was one of Locke's most unreserved admirers, and on more than one occasion he was known to hold up business of state in order to read his visitors a few of the Nasby letters. Lincoln, and later Grant, offered Locke political opportunities, but he declined them all. The only office he ever aspired to was that of alderman from the third ward in Toledo, and it was with considerable difficulty that he secured his election to this post. He held the office when he died in 1888.

Beginning with *The Nasby Papers* (1864), numerous collections of the letters appeared in book form. Locke wrote other published works, including *The Morals of Abou Ben Adhem* (1875) and *The Demagogue* (1891), a political novel, and he was a popular lecturer, but the letters alone constitute the fame which he achieved and which died with him. He was the most powerful political satirist of his day and country. "Wat posterity will say, I don't know; neither do I care," said Nasby. ". . . It's this generashen I'm going for." The succeeding generation has treated him accordingly.

[Robert Ford, *Am. Humourists, Recent and Living* (1897); *The Nasby Letters* (1893); G. L. Faxon, *The Hist. of the Faxon Family* (1880); H. L. Mersereau, "Mersereau Family Geneal.," in *N. Y. Geneal. and Biog. Record*, Oct. 1896, Jan. 1897; A. B. Paine, *Th. Nast, His Period and His Pictures* (1904); J. B. Pond, *Eccentricities of Genius, Memories of Famous Men and Women of the Platform and Stage* (1900); H. P. Smith, *Hist. of Broome County, N. Y.* (1885), and *Hist. of Cortland County, N. Y.* (1885); J. M. Killits, *Toledo and Lucas County, Ohio 1623–1923* (1923); *Toledo Blade*, Feb. 15, 1888; *N. Y. Herald*, Feb. 16, 1888; clippings and information furnished by relatives.]

J. A. E.

LOCKE, JOHN (Feb. 19, 1792–July 10, 1856), physician, scientist, inventor, was born at Lempster, N. H., the son of Samuel Barron Locke and his first wife, Hannah Russell. He was descended from William Locke who emigrated to Massachusetts from England in 1635, settling first at Charlestown, and then at Woburn. For the first few years of his life Locke lived in a number of places but in 1796 his father settled on a large tract near Bethel, Me., and in connection with his home and farm, built saw and grist mills, a Methodist meeting house, and other establishments. In time the settlement came to be known as Locke's Mills. Here young Locke received his early schooling which was augmented by the books of his father's large library. He became intensely interested in botany, learned as much as he could locally, and then by working in the mills and by teaching school earned enough money to attend intermittently an academy at Bridgeport, Conn. The smattering of additional knowledge of the natural sciences he received only made him more desirous for an education, but his father opposed his ambitions. In the summer of 1815, following a bitter religious quarrel with his father, Locke left home and worked his way to Yale College. There he attended Silliman's lectures on chemistry and for a while was an assistant in his laboratory. Then from 1816 to 1818 he studied medicine under several doctors in Keene, N. H., and at the same time continued his studies in botany, delivering lectures on the subject in various schools and colleges of New England.

In the autumn of 1818 Locke received an appointment of assistant surgeon in the United States navy and was assigned to the frigate *Macedonian* under special order to explore the Columbia River. A storm wrecked the ship, however, and the expedition was abandoned. Locke then went to Boston, where he wrote and published in 1819 his *Outlines of Botany*. It contained over two hundred illustrations, all drawn and engraved by himself. In the same year he obtained the degree of M.D. at Yale. For a time then he was curator of botany at Harvard College, but in 1821 he seized the opportunity of getting away from New England, which he felt was dominated by religious intolerance, and accepted a teaching position in a girls' school in Lexington, Ky. After a year he resigned this position and went to Cincinnati, Ohio, and established there the Cincinnati Female Academy which he conducted until 1835. He then was appointed professor of chemistry and pharmacy in the Medical College of Ohio in Cincinnati and very successfully occupied this chair for eighteen years, resigning in 1853, just three years before his death. By far the most productive years of his life were those from 1835 onward. In this period his interests and his researches gradually changed from the natural to the physical sciences and it was in the latter field that he did his foremost work.

Between 1835 and 1840 he engaged in some private geologic and paleontologic studies, publishing the results in scientific journals. These studies included observations on the characteristics of certain species of fossil trilobites and on the occurrence of certain unusual ore deposits. Locke was employed, too, for geological survey work by both the state of Ohio and the federal government. One of his subsequent reports on the mineral lands of Iowa, Illinois, and Wisconsin was published by Congress in 1840 (*House Executive Document 239,* 26 Cong., 1 Sess.) and republished in enlarged form in 1844 (*Senate Document 407,* 28 Cong., 1 Sess.). After 1840 his attention was directed to the study of terrestrial magnetism and electricity. He contributed over fifteen papers on these and allied subjects to the *American Journal of Science and Arts,* to the *Transactions* of the American Philosophical Society, and to the *Smithsonian Contributions to Knowledge.* He also lectured both in the United States and in England, using for illustration scientific apparatus of his own and his son's design and construction. He invented several valuable instruments including a surveyor's compass, level, an orrery, and his so-called electromagnetic chronograph (see the *American Journal of Science and Arts,* September 1849). This instrument, devised between 1844 and 1848, at the request of the United States Coast Survey, completely changed the art of determining longitudes, for it recorded on a time scale, automatically printed by a clock, the occurrence of an event to within one one-hundredth of a second. Furthermore it could be connected with the nation's telegraph system so that an observer of an astronomical event anywhere, by the simple depression of a key, could record the time of the event as indicated by the clock to which the instrument was attached. Locke's instruments and system were installed in the Naval Observatory, Washington, in 1848, with wonderful results, and for his invention Congress awarded him $10,000 in February 1849. Locke married Mary Morris of Newark, N. J., on Oct. 25, 1825, in Cincinnati, and at the time of his death there, was survived by his widow and a number of children.

[G. M. Roe, *Cincinnati: The Queen City of the West* (1895); J. G. Locke, *Book of the Lockes* (1853); M. B. Wright, *An Address on the Life and Character of the Late Prof. John Locke* (1857); E. H. Knight, *Knight's*

Am. Mech. Dict. (3 vols., 1874–76); *Am. Jour. of Sci.*, 2 ser. VIII (1849); *Cincinnati Daily Enquirer,* July 11, 1856; Patent Office records.] C. W. M.

LOCKE, MATTHEW (1730–Sept. 7, 1801), Revolutionary soldier and congressman, son of John and Elizabeth Locke, went from Pennsylvania to piedmont North Carolina about 1752 and settled near the present city of Salisbury, Rowan County. In 1749 he was married to Mary Elizabeth Brandon, and in later life to Mrs. Elizabeth Gostelowe of Philadelphia. Before the Revolution he achieved local prominence as justice of the peace, vestryman, and member of the House of Commons, 1770–71, and 1773–75. In the Regulator disturbance he was a moderate, apparently preserving the confidence of both parties; in January 1771 he favored the legislative regulation of official fees and in the following March was a representative of the county officials on a joint committee for the final determination of disputed cases involving fees, arising between the Regulators and the county officials, one of whom (Francis Locke) was his brother.

He was active in the patriot cause before and during the Revolution, as an agent and member of the Rowan Committee of Safety (1774–76) in its execution of the resolves of the Continental and Provincial congresses and its discipline of Loyalists; as a delegate to the Third (August 1775), Fourth (April 1776), and Fifth (November 1776) Provincial congresses; as paymaster, brigadier-general, and auditor for the district of Salisbury; and as a member of the state House of Commons (1777–81, 1783–84, and 1789–92) and of the Senate (1781–82, and 1784). His stubborn hostility to the adoption of the federal Constitution is shown by his votes in the Hillsborough Convention of 1788 and in the Fayetteville Convention of the next year, and by his selection in 1788 as a North Carolina delegate to a projected second federal convention. Numerous important committee assignments attest his influence in the colonial and state political bodies of which he was a member.

From 1793 to 1799 Locke represented the Salisbury district in the national House of Representatives. So far as the records show, he never participated in the debates of Congress and he usually cast a negative vote. Rural, provincial, uneducated, religious, with little knowledge of statecraft and international relations, he was an extreme Jeffersonian Republican who believed that the best government is the one which governs least and most economically. He was hostile to the Federalist policies of the administrations of Washington and Adams and was one of the twelve radical Republicans in the House who voted against the complimentary reply to Washington's message of Dec. 7, 1796 (*Annals of Congress,* 4 Cong., 2 Sess., cols. 1667–68). His opposition to the popular measures for national defense in the spring of 1798, when war with France was impending, brought about his crushing defeat in August (3,131 votes to 231) by Archibald Henderson [*q.v.*] of Salisbury. "The Election of Mr. Henderson is very honourable to him and his Constituents," wrote President Adams (Wagstaff, *post,* I, p. 161). But the Federalist excesses of 1798 and the passing of the French crisis strengthened Republicanism in North Carolina; and Locke, though defeated by Henderson in the congressional election of 1800, polled a larger vote than in 1798 and was mentioned as a senatorial candidate in the Republican General Assembly of 1800 (*North-Carolina Mercury and Salisbury Advertiser,* Aug. 21, 1800).

At the opening of the Revolution, he was operating a wagon line between points in piedmont North Carolina and Charleston, S. C., but agriculture was his chief occupation. He acquired considerable landholdings in Rowan and Iredell counties and in Tennessee, and was the sixth largest slaveholder in his county in 1790. He was a trustee of Salisbury Academy, incorporated in 1784. His common sense, character, and faithfulness to the will of his rural constituents kept him in public life almost steadily for thirty years. On Sept. 7, 1801, at his home near Salisbury, he "breathed his last, a firm and fixed Republican."

[*Colonial Records of N. C.* (10 vols., 1886–90); *State Records of N. C.* (16 vols., 1895–1905); A. L. Fries, ed., *Records of the Moravians in N. C.* (4 vols., 1922–30); H. M. Wagstaff, ed., *The Papers of John Steele* (2 vols., 1924); *Annals of Cong.*, 1793–99; *Raleigh Reg. and N.-C. State Gazette*, Oct. 13, 1801; *N.-C. Jour.* (Halifax), Sept. 10, 1798; Rowan County Wills, in N. C. Hist. Commission, Raleigh; Jethro Rumple, *A Hist. of Rowan County, N. C.* (rev. ed., 1916); J. H. Wheeler, *Reminiscences and Memoirs of N. C. and Eminent North Carolinians* (1884); W. E. Dodd, *The Life of Nathaniel Macon* (1903); George McCorkle, "Sketch of Col. Francis Locke," in *N. C. Booklet*, July 1910.] A. R. N.

LOCKE, RICHARD ADAMS (Sept. 22, 1800–Feb. 16, 1871), journalist, was born in England, at East Brent, Somersetshire. Some works of biography have given New York as his birthplace. In his early career in America, realizing the prejudice which then existed against British writers, he did not emphasize the fact that he was not a native American. He was not, as Edgar Allan Poe wrote of him, a lineal descendant of John Locke. The descent was collateral, through the philosopher's uncle, Louis

Locke. Their common ancestor first mentioned in the written pedigree was John Locke, sheriff of London in 1460. The father of Richard Adams Locke was Richard Locke of Highbridge House, Burnham, and of East Brent, Somersetshire, a land surveyor entered as "gentleman" in the College of Arms pedigree; the grant of arms to the Lockes was made by Queen Mary in 1555 (*An Account of the Locke Family, East Brent,* 1792). His mother was Anne Adams of East Brent. He married Esther Bowering of East Brent, probably in 1826.

After leaving Cambridge University Locke started the London *Republican,* an organ of democracy. This and his second literary venture, the *Cornucopia,* were failures. In 1832 he emigrated to New York City with his wife and infant daughter Adelaide and became a reporter on the *Courier and Enquirer.* In the summer of 1835 he joined the *Sun,* then a struggling penny paper, at a salary of twelve dollars a week. He was taken on by the founder of the paper, Benjamin H. Day [*q.v.*], and not, as Edgar Allan Poe says (*post,* p. 120), by Moses Yale Beach, the second owner. In August 1835 Locke wrote for the *Sun* the celebrated "Moon Hoax," which purported to reveal the discovery, by Sir John Herschel with his new telescope at the Cape of Good Hope, of men and animals on the moon. The revelations pretended to be reprinted from the Edinburgh *Journal of Science,* although that periodical was then defunct. Locke peopled the moon with winged humans and invented a variety of animals, including biped beavers from whose houses smoke issued. The hoax was so well written and so sprinkled with astronomical terms as to deceive most of the *Sun's* readers. A delegation came from Yale College to ask to see the original *Journal of Science.* The hoax increased the *Sun's* circulation to more than nineteen thousand, the largest of any daily of that time. The articles were reprinted in pamphlet form in Paris, London, Edinburgh, and Glasgow. Poe wrote that, having found the hoax anticipative of all the main points of his own "Hans Phaall," he let that tale remain unfinished. It has been suggested—Augustus De Morgan took it for granted in his *Budget of Paradoxes* (1872)—that the hoax was the work of Jean Nicolas Nicollet, French astronomer who, like Locke, came to America in 1832. There is no real evidence to support the suggestion. Locke resigned from the *Sun* in the autumn of 1836 and, with Joseph Price, started the *New Era,* a penny daily. In this he attempted to duplicate the success of the "Moon Hoax" with "The Lost Manuscript of Mungo Park," a fabrication which purported to tell hitherto unrelated adventures of the Scottish explorer. The public, knowing Locke, was not again deceived. When the *New Era* failed Locke became an editorial writer on the *Brooklyn Daily Eagle.* Later he was employed in the New York custom house. He died at his home on Staten Island at the age of seventy years. He is thus described by his friend Poe (*post,* p. 127): "Like most men of *true* imagination, Mr. Locke is a seemingly paradoxical compound of coolness and excitability. He is about five feet seven inches in height, symmetrically formed; there is an air of distinction about his whole person—the *air noble* of genius. His face is strongly pitted by the smallpox and, perhaps from the same cause, there is a marked obliquity in the eyes; a certain calm, clear *luminousness,* however, about these latter amply compensates for the defect, and the forehead is truly beautiful in its intellectuality. I am acquainted with no person possessing so fine a forehead as Mr. Locke."

[F. M. O'Brien, *The Story of The Sun* (1918); Edgar Allan Poe, *The Literati* (1850); Frederic Hudson, *Journalism in the U. S. from 1690 to 1872* (1873); *N. Y. Herald,* Feb. 18, 1871; information as to certain facts from Locke's grand-daughter, Mrs. F. Winthrop White, New Brighton, Staten Island, N. Y.] F. M. O.

LOCKHART, CHARLES (Aug. 2, 1818–Jan. 26, 1905), pioneer oil producer, refiner, and one of the early promoters of the Standard Oil Trust, was born at Cairn Heads, Wigtownshire, Scotland. His father, John, and his mother, Sarah (Walker)—the latter a daughter of a noted linen manufacturer in Sorbie—brought their seven children to the United States in 1836. In Scotland Charles had received an elementary education, and, while working for an uncle, a rudimentary business training. During the first nineteen years after his arrival he was in Pittsburgh as errand boy and later clerk for James McCully, a wholesale grocer and dealer in produce and flour, beginning at a wage of seventy-five cents a week and working fourteen hours a day. In 1855, however, he and William Frew, a fellow clerk, were taken into partnership under the firm name of James McCully & Company and during the Civil War the concern enjoyed unusual prosperity.

Lockhart's first interest in oil was awakened in 1852 upon meeting one Isaac Huff, who had come to Pittsburgh with three barrels of oil that had been taken out of his salt well near Tarentum, Pa. The latter could find no purchaser for this then little-used product, but Lockhart agreed, as a speculation, to take all that was produced during a period of five years at 31¼ cents per gallon. He then made a fortunate bargain to sell this oil to Samuel M. Kier [*q.v.*] during the same period at twice the amount. In the following year he bought the well, which was one of the first in the state, and assumed active direction. In 1859, the year oil was discovered in Titusville, Lockhart and four associates organized a firm under the name of Phillips, Frew & Company, and leased the land on Oil Creek. The first well yielded forty-five barrels a day. In 1860, filling a couple of gallon oyster cans, one with crude and the other with distilled oil (refining was not yet generally practised), he took them to England, and lighted the first petroleum lamp. Upon the basis of these samples he was able to build up a considerable export trade in oil. Lockhart and Frew soon bought out their partners' interests and built the Brilliant refinery, the first important refinery erected. This was followed by the building of the Atlantic refinery in Philadelphia. He was prominent in the rapidly extending activities of the Standard Oil Company. In 1872 he became a stockholder in the South Improvement Company, and in 1874, at a meeting with John D. Rockefeller, William G. Warden, and Henry M. Flagler [*q.v.*], he helped to lay the foundation of the Standard Oil Trust, transferring his refineries to the Standard Oil Company and taking stock in return. He had agreed to absorb as rapidly as possible the other refineries in the neighborhood of Pittsburgh, and in 1874 he became president of a newly organized concern, called the Standard Oil Company of Pittsburgh, which began to lease or buy these refineries. In 1879, at the instigation of the Petroleum Producers' Union, he was indicted with other officials of the Standard Oil group, on the charge of conspiracy to effect various illegal ends (Tarbell, *post*, I, 239, 393ff.). A compromise was achieved the following year, however, and the case did not come to trial (*Ibid.*, I, ch. viii and p. 401). When the Standard Oil Trust was incorporated he became one of its directors, and at its dissolution in 1892 he became president of the Atlantic Refining Company.

He was also engaged in the manufacture of saws, axes, shovels, iron and steel, and locomotives, and had timber, farming, and gold mining interests in Colorado and Idaho. He was also among the founders of the American and Red Star steamship lines. He retired from active direction of his interests in 1900 and died five years later. In his will he gave generously of his fortune to the four leading hospitals of Pittsburgh and to various welfare organizations. In June 1862 he married Jane Walker, by whom he had five children.

[Erasmus Wilson, *Standard Hist. of Pittsburg, Pa.* (1898); I. M. Tarbell, *The Hist. of the Standard Oil Company* (2 vols., 1904); *Biog. Rev.*, vol. XXIV (1897); *Pittsburg Post, Pittsburg Dispatch*, and *Pittsburg Press*, Jan. 27, 1905.] A. I.

LOCKREY, SARAH HUNT (Apr. 21, 1863–Nov. 8, 1929), surgeon, suffragist, was born in Philadelphia, Pa., the daughter of Charles and Martha Jane Wisner Lockrey. Her father had been left an orphan at the age of six when all the others of his immediate family died during a yellow fever epidemic in Philadelphia. He was cared for by a neighbor, learned the carpenter's trade, and became a successful business man. Her mother's ancestors were Scotch Covenanters. She graduated from the Girls' Normal School and began teaching at the age of seventeen. Although a shy girl who preferred books to other companions, she early showed the conscientiousness that later made her a courageous leader. In her longing to be of service to others she was active in religious organizations and wished to be a missionary, but finally she turned to medicine as a career. While a medical student she taught in the night schools of Philadelphia and tutored in physiology. She graduated from the Woman's Medical College of Pennsylvania in 1888 and then served as an interne at the Woman's Hospital. With the rapid growth of her practice she became a specialist in abdominal surgery. In 1895 she was appointed assistant to Dr. A. E. Broomall at the Woman's Hospital and later became chief of the gynecological staff, soon after which the West Philadelphia Hospital for Women made her a visiting chief on its surgical staff. These positions, which she held until her death, gave her constant opportunity to exercise her skill as a surgeon. She was consultant to the Elwyn school for the feeble-minded and for over twenty-five years physician to the Methodist Episcopal Deaconess Home, where she was instrumental in starting a daily clinic.

Notwithstanding her very active professional life, Dr. Lockrey always found time for church work. For a number of years she served on the board of the Methodist Collegiate Institute, a school for girls, and was president of the board of trustees of the Thirteenth Street Methodist Episcopal Church, an unusual position for a woman to hold at that time. In 1921 she became a Presbyterian. One of her keenest interests was the advancement of women. Years before woman's suffrage became popular she worked and sacrificed to bring about the political equality of women. She gave generously of her time and money, took part in pageants and parades, and developed ability as a public speaker. Dr. Anna Howard Shaw found in her a faithful and active supporter. Later she worked with Mrs. Lawrence Lewis and Alice Paul, went frequently to Washington, and was among the delegates who presented the subject to President Wilson and to members of Congress shortly before the passage of the Nineteenth Amendment. Finally she was one of those imprisoned for suffrage activities. With a number of others, mostly professional women, she received a jail sentence in August 1918 for taking part in the Lafayette Square meeting in Washington, but the sentence was remitted.

[*Jour. Am. Medic. Asso.*, Dec. 7, 1929; *Medic. Woman's Jour.*, Dec. 1929; *Weekly Roster and Medic. Digest*, Nov. 23, 1929; the *Pa. Medic. Jour.*, Dec. 1929; *Bull. of the Medic. Women's Nat. Asso.*, Jan. 1930; *Equal Rights*, Nov. 16, 1929; *Pub. Ledger* (Phila.), Nov. 9, 1929; information as to certain facts from Dr. Lockrey's associate, Dr. Miriam M. Butt.] A. L. L.

LOCKWOOD, BELVA ANN BENNETT (Oct. 24, 1830–May 19, 1917), teacher, lecturer, lawyer, suffragist, daughter of Lewis Johnson and Hannah (Green) Bennett, was born in Royalton, Niagara County, N. Y. She was educated in the public schools there, and in the Genesee Wesleyan Seminary. In 1848, at the age of eighteen, she married a farmer, Uriah H. McNall, and was left a widow at twenty-four with one child. After her husband's death she taught at Royalton, but finding that she received only half the salary granted to men she went to Genesee College for further training, graduating (A.M.) in 1857. She taught at Lockport, at the Gainesville Seminary, and was principal of the McNall Seminary in Oswego, N. Y. After the Civil War she moved to Washington, D. C., and there began the study of law. On Mar. 11, 1868, she was married to Dr. Ezekiel Lockwood, a dentist and claim agent, who died in 1877. She graduated from the National University Law School in 1873 at the age of forty-three and was admitted to the Washington bar. In her practice she specialized in cases of claims against the government. She was the first woman admitted to practice before the Supreme Court of the United States, and she began to plead before this court at the age of forty-nine. Her activities centered about a life-long struggle for women's rights, and she made her law office in her own house the meeting place for national leaders in the struggle to improve conditions for women. In her capacity as lawyer she helped to secure for the women of the District of Columbia equal property rights and equal guardianship of children. She also prepared an amendment to the statehood bill granting suffrage to women in Oklahoma, Arizona, and New Mexico. For eight years she lectured successfully and was prominent both nationally and internationally in promoting women's rights, temperance, peace, and arbitration. She was the first woman candidate for president of the United States, receiving twice, in 1884 and 1888, the nomination of the National Equal Rights party of the Pacific Coast ("How I Ran for the Presidency," *National Magazine,* March 1903). In 1884 she contested the election of Cleveland in the electoral college. She was a delegate from the State Department to the International Congress of Charities, Correction, and Philanthropy in Geneva in 1886 and a delegate to the Universal Peace Congress in Paris in 1889. In 1892 she was made a member of the International Peace Bureau in Berne and was secretary of the American Branch of the Bureau. She was also one of the nominating committee for the Nobel Peace Prize. A few of her papers on peace and arbitration have been published. A life-size oil portrait of her was unveiled by the women of the District of Columbia in 1913 and is now in the gallery of the National Museum. She is on the state honor roll of New York of the National League of Women Voters. She was a vigorous, persistent, aggressive personality, and she fought incessantly for fifty years for women's rights, using all the legal weapons at her command. An eloquent advocate, she made some of the most effective speeches heard in the long suffrage campaign.

[*Who's Who in America,* 1916–17; Frances E. Willard and Mary A. Livermore, *A Woman of the Century* (1893); the *Lit. Digest*, June 16, 1917; the *Woman Citizen*, June 2, 1917; the *Suffragist*, May 26, 1917; *Case and Comment*, Aug. 1917; the *Evening Star* (Washington), May 19, 1917; *N. Y. Times*, May 20, 1917.] F. F. P.

LOCKWOOD, JAMES BOOTH (Oct. 9, 1852–Apr. 9, 1884), army officer and Arctic explorer, was descended from Richard Lockwood, who settled on the Eastern Shore of Maryland about the beginning of the eighteenth century. The son of Henry Hayes Lockwood, artillerist and brigadier-general of volunteers during the Civil War, and Anna (Booth) Lockwood of Delaware, he was born at Annapolis, Md., where his father was serving as professor in the Naval Academy. After attending a private school at Bethlehem, Pa., and St. John's College, Annapolis, he entered the army in 1873, as second lieutenant, 23rd United States Infantry. He served with his regiment at various posts in the Trans-Mississippi region until he volunteered in June 1881 for duty with the Lady Franklin Bay Arctic Expedition, under the command of Lieut. A. W. Greely. During the autumn of 1881 he made scientific observations at the headquarters, Lady Franklin Bay, Grant Land, and was engaged in preliminary field work for future explorations. In March 1882 he crossed Kennedy Channel to Greenland, visited the observatory and grave of Charles F. Hall [*q.v.*], examined caches, and explored the various routes in northwest Greenland to the Polar Ocean which might be used for future travel. This journey of ten days, covering a distance of 135 miles, was made in temperatures seventy-four degrees below freezing, without injuries of any kind.

On Apr. 3, 1882, Lockwood started again, under orders charging him with "the full control and arrangement of the most important sledging and geographical work of this expedition, the exploration of the northeastern coast of Greenland . . . [and] the extension of knowledge regarding lands in the Polar circle" (*Report, post,* I, 182–83). Supported by a man-drawn-sledge party to Cape Bryant, he left that point with a dog sledge, accompanied by Sergeant D. L. Brainard and Christiansen, the Eskimo, and, traveling entirely over the ice-floes of the Arctic Ocean, after incredible efforts and great suffering, reached his farthest, Lockwood Island, 83° 24′ N., 40° 46′ W., on May 13. From a mountain top his vision reached Cape Washington, nine miles south of the northernmost land of the world. This expedition, also, returned without injury, although the journey out and back involved travel of 1,070 statute miles, in average temperatures below zero for sixty days and at times eighty-one degrees below freezing. The journey gained the honors of the highest north, held continuously by England for three centuries. It proved that extreme north Greenland was a mountainous, glacier-covered region; the 124 miles of new coast was indented by eight inlets of unknown depth; the main ice of the Arctic Ocean was marked by a tidal crack, sometimes a hundred feet wide, through which a sounding of 840 feet failed to reach bottom.

An attempt to surpass this northing in 1883 was prevented by Lockwood's finding extensive open water at Black Horn Cliffs, Greenland, which his orders forbade his passing. This trip failing, he was ordered to attempt the crossing of Grant Land to the western ocean, whose indistinct limits had been seen from Mount Arthur by Greely in 1882, crossing from the head of Archer Fiord. With Brainard, Christiansen, and a dog team, Lockwood started on Apr. 25, 1883, and on May 15, after an extraordinarily difficult journey overland, discovered and camped in a great inlet of the western ocean (Greely Fiord), in 80° 48.5′ N., 78° 26′ W., making in his two trips one-eighth the way around the world north of the eightieth degree. The divide between the two oceans was 2,600 feet, and from a mountain over 4,400 feet high Lockwood discovered the remarkable configuration of Grant Land. It is an ice-free, vegetation-covered region, bounded on the north by the mountains discovered by Greely in 1882, and by similar mountain peaks to the south, which were fronted for a hundred miles by an unbroken glacial front varying from 140 to 200 feet in perpendicular height. Greely Fiord was about sixty miles long, and from ten to fifteen miles broad. One mountain was called Fossil from the great quantities of fossils found there—petrified wood, shells, and fish. Seals were seen in Greely Fiord and much game abounded in the country, and the extended trip was only possible because game supplied food after the rations gave out.

Following his return to headquarters, Lockwood was ordered, June 1, 1883, to take over the duties of naturalist of the expedition, and he prepared an inventory of the specimens collected. During the boat retreat, beginning in August, and the starvation winter at Cape Sabine, 1883–84, he distinguished himself by his manly attitude, and when the crossing of Smith Sound was considered, asked that in his weak state he be left behind so as not to lessen any other comrade's chance of life. He died at Cape Sabine some two months before the survivors of the party were rescued.

[F. A. Holden and E. D. Lockwood, *Descendants of Robert Lockwood* (1889); Charles Lanman, *Farthest North; or, The Life and Explorations of Lieut. James Booth Lockwood, of the Greely Arctic Expedition* (1885); A. W. Greely, *Three Years of Arctic Service: An Account of the Lady Franklin Bay Expedition of 1881–84* (2 vols., 1886), and *International Polar Expedition: Report of the Proc. of the U. S. Expedition to Lady Franklin Bay, Grinnell Land* (2 vols., 1888), which contains Lockwood's journal (App. No. 122, in vol. I).]

A. W. G.

LOCKWOOD, RALPH INGERSOLL (July 8, 1798–Apr. 12, 1858?), lawyer, author, was born at Greenwich, Conn., the son of Stephen and Sarah (Ingersoll) Lockwood. Although members of the family held no positions of national importance, it was, nevertheless, a distinguished one. Robert, the founder of the family in America, emigrated from England about 1630 and settled first in Watertown, Mass., and later in Fairfield, Conn. During Colonial and Revolutionary times, many of his descendants held military offices, and by the year 1834 eleven had graduated from Yale College. Ralph was the fourth of a family of eight children. In March 1821, his parents moved to Mount Pleasant, now Ossining, Westchester County, N. Y., where the father purchased a farm of 100 acres.

Ralph and two younger brothers, Albert and

Munson, studied law and became members of the bar. Albert and Munson practised in Westchester County—Albert eventually becoming county judge—but Ralph moved to New York City and there practised for the remainder of his life. His wit and eloquence attracted attention, and he soon became one of the well-known lawyers of the city. When he was twenty-seven years old he published a vigorous analysis of the problems confronting Congress in the enactment of a national bankruptcy act (*Essay on a National Bankrupt Law,* 1825) in which he discussed the mooted question as to whether the benefits of the law should be extended to all classes or confined solely to the trading class, himself advocating a middle course. In December 1838, he was elected a member of the New York Law Library, later the New York Law Institute. He was severely critical of what he termed "the faults and absurdities of the English common law." His interest lay in the field of equity and he became, in time, one of the leading chancery lawyers of the state. Reverence for the courts he did not regard as a duty and his attacks upon the decisions of the court of chancery were distinguished for their vigor and fearlessness. In addition to his capabilities as a lawyer he had a natural interest in literature and was an excellent French scholar. He visited France upon two occasions and for a number of years acted as counsel for the leading French citizens of New York City. In 1848 he published *Analytical and Practical Synopsis of All the Cases Argued and Reversed, in Law and Equity, in the Court for the Correction of Errors, of New York, 1799 to 1847*; he also edited the American edition of J. E. Bright's *A Treatise on the Law of Husband and Wife* (2 vols., 1850).

Lockwood was the author of two novels, *Rosine Laval* (1833) and *The Insurgents* (2 vols., 1835). Both were published anonymously, *Rosine Laval* appeared under the pseudonym, "Mr. Smith." He had long cherished an ambition to write fiction, and when forced to leave New York temporarily to escape a plague of the cholera he found himself with sufficient leisure to gratify it. In thirty minutes the plot was conceived and in six weeks *Rosine Laval* was finished. A nervous breakdown, induced by overwork, gave him the leisure to write *The Insurgents,* which was completed in three months. Neither of the two, from the literary point of view, is valuable and only in the most exhaustive histories of American literature is it possible to find any mention of them. *Rosine Laval* was intended to be a light novel, but its humor is of a past generation, and the swoonings and the harrowing death, which seemed to the author necessary occurrences before the love problem could be resolved, are unconvincing. *The Insurgents,* a novel of Shays's Rebellion, was a more serious undertaking. The same faults which mar *Rosine Laval* are present, however, and reveal that Lockwood, whatever his accomplishments as a lawyer, was not possessed of marked aptitude for the writing of fiction. In the preface to his first novel he wrote that he had for several years threatened to fall seriously in love and to marry, but when he died he was still a bachelor.

[F. A. Holden and E. D. Lockwood, *Descendants of Robert Lockwood, Colonial and Revolutionary Hist. of the Lockwood Family in America* (1889), which gives date of death as Apr. 12, 1858, and also as 1855; information from J. F. Conillon, Librarian, N. Y. Law Institute; biog. material in his works.] H. Ca—s.

LOCKWOOD, ROBERT WILTON (Sept. 12, 1861–Mar. 20, 1914), painter, known as Wilton Lockwood, was born at Wilton, Conn., a town for which he was named by his parents, John Lewis and Emily Waldon (Middlebrook) Lockwood. He was descended from Robert Lockwood who emigrated to Massachusetts in 1630 and ultimately settled in Fairfield, Conn. His mother died in 1865 and the father removed the household to New York, but the boy showed distaste for city life and was sent to the home of his aunts at Rowayton, Conn. He worked on their farm and attended school in winter. Later he was employed in a New York broker's office where his ability to draw attracted some attention and led to his introduction to John La Farge [*q.v.*], at whose studio he had instruction. He also attended classes at the Art Students' League of New York, whence he went to Paris to draw at Julian's under Benjamin Constant. He returned to New York, painted several portraits, and, with the money thus earned, resumed his studies at Munich, a city which Frank Duveneck had made popular with American art students. He lived also for several years at Paris where his style matured and his personality, that of a tall, rufous American, of courteous bearing and sharp repartee, made him a marked figure among artists. A group of his portraits at the New Salon in 1895 won special encomia. He married at London, England, in 1892, Ethel Whiton of Boston.

Returning to the United States in 1896 the Lockwoods settled in Boston. Whether this was a wise choice of location for an artist of Lockwood's talent and temperament is debatable. Working quietly at his Boylston Street studio in the winter, and in the summer at South Orleans, Cape Cod, he lived a life outwardly uneventful but always actively creative. His portraiture was penetrating, searching, and psychologically profound, some of his likenesses being almost uncanny in revealing a personality. Among his notable sitters were John La Farge, the canvas now at the Boston Museum of Fine Arts; Grover Cleveland, for Princeton University; Justice Oliver Wendell Holmes, for the Massachusetts Bar Association; President Francis A. Walker, of the Massachusetts Institute of Technology, for the St. Botolph Club; and Otto Roth, violinist, a work awarded the Temple Gold Medal at the Pennsylvania Academy of the Fine Arts in 1898. Other portraits won for Lockwood silver medals at Paris in 1900, Buffalo in 1901, and St. Louis in 1904.

Lockwood's flower paintings grew out of his enthusiastic gardening. As a peony grower he was nationally known and won several prizes for his flowers. His paintings were exquisitely subtle and still quite objective apparitions of the choicest blooms at his Cape Cod home. They were painted against a thinly toned background, usually on the reverse side of a primed canvas. Some of these are owned by the Metropolitan and Worcester Art museums, and the Corcoran Gallery of Art in Washington. After the artist's death, the St. Botolph Club, Boston, of which he was long a member, held a memorial exhibition of his works. The catalogue's foreword, by a brother painter, acclaimed him as "one of the ablest artists Boston has ever had—perhaps the most subtle and sensitive."

[See especially the biographical sketch by Charles Hovey Pepper in the memorial exhibition catalogue, Dec. 19, 1914. The *Boston Evening Transcript* and *Boston Herald,* Mar. 21, 1914, printed long obituaries by William H. Downes and F. W. Coburn. Other sources include: T. R. Sullivan, article in *Scribner's,* Feb. 1898; Samuel Isham and Royal Cortissoz, *The Hist. of Am. Painting* (1927); *The Artists' Year Book,* 1905–06; *Time and the Hour,* Mar. 5, 1898; F. A. Holden and E. D. Lockwood, *Descendants of Robert Lockwood: Colonial and Revolutionary Hist. of the Lockwood Family in America* (1889); L. F. Middlebrook, *Reg. of the Middlebrook Family* (1909).] F. W. C.

LOCKWOOD, SAMUEL DRAKE (Aug. 2, 1789–Apr. 23, 1874), jurist, was born in Poundridge, N. Y., the son of Joseph and Mary (Drake) Lockwood, and a descendant of Robert Lockwood who emigrated to Watertown, Mass., in 1630 and later settled in Fairfield, Conn. His schooling was very scanty. From 1803 to 1811 he lived and studied law with an uncle, Francis Drake, in Waterford, N. Y. Licensed in February 1811, he practised in Batavia, Sempronius, and Auburn until he started for Illinois in October 1818. Meanwhile he had evinced unusual maturity. He served as sergeant major (1808) and paymaster (1811) of a militia regiment, as a justice of the peace and master in chancery (1812 only), became a trustee of his church (Presbyterian, 1812), and participated in organizing (1815) New York's first Bible society. He carried to the West commendatory letters that assured him immediate recognition. Like other ambitious settlers in the new state, he was a candidate for political office. On Feb. 6, 1821, he was elected by the legislature attorney-general. Next an unsuccessful candidate for election to the United States Senate, in the autumn of 1822, he was appointed, before that ambition was disappointed, secretary of state (Dec. 28, 1822), thereupon resigning the attorney-generalship; only to resign the secretaryship when confirmed (Jan. 28, 1823) receiver of the Edwardsville land-office. He remained for some years somewhat ambitious and influential in politics. In the passionate struggle in the years 1822–24 over the calling of a constitutional convention (to make Illinois a slave state), he was active and powerful in behalf of the anti-slavery cause, which he aided, particularly, by editing one anti-convention newspaper and contributing to others. The next legislature elected him an associate justice of the state supreme court (commissioned Jan. 19, 1825), which office he filled with exceeding success and honor until Dec. 4, 1848, when a new constitution, framed by a convention in which he was an active delegate, went into effect, making the judges elective by the people. He did not seek popular indorsement.

Through his twenty-four years of service, Lockwood bore the heaviest burden in the labors of the court. His, also, was the greatest individual contribution to the notable revision of the Illinois statutes prepared in the years 1826–29 by the judges and the legislature. He was an excellent and a learned lawyer; a judge characterized by intelligence, urbanity, and social wisdom; a kindly man, of pure character, somewhat austere in his unbending rectitude, of marked modesty, yet equally of marked energy and determination. His reputation in the state was notable, and his influence continually exercised for good causes. At various times and in various capacities he was active in fostering public education, and in promoting measures for the care of mental and physical defectives. He was a charter trustee of each of the state institutions established for the care of the insane, deaf mutes, and blind. From 1851 until his death he was a legislative trustee of the land-department of the Illinois Central Railroad. Originally a Whig, he acted after 1855 with the Republican party. On Oct. 3, 1826, he married Mary Virginia Stith Nash of St. Louis. The last years of his life he spent in Batavia, Ill., where he died.

[See Wm. Coffin, *Life and Times of Hon. Samuel D. Lockwood* (1889); *The Biog. Encyc. of Ill. of the Nineteenth Cent.* (1875); J. M. Palmer, *The Bench and Bar of Ill.* (1899), vol. I; Thos. Ford, *A Hist. of Ill.* (1854); T. C. Pease, "The Frontier State, 1818–48," *The Centennial Hist. of Ill.*, vol. II (1918); F. A. Holden and E. D. Lockwood, *Descendants of Robt. Lockwood: Colonial and Revolutionary Hist. of the Lockwood Family in America* (1889); F. W. Scott, "Newspapers and Periodicals of Ill., 1814–79," *Ill. State Hist. Lib. Colls.*, vol. VI (1910); *Trans. Ill. State Hist. Soc. . . . 1903* (1904), pp. 213–14; *Chicago Legal News*, Apr. 20, 1889; *Chicago Tribune*, Apr. 25, 1874. Lockwood's opinions, so far as they survive, appear in 1–9 *Illinois Reports*.] F. S. P.

LOCKWOOD, WILTON [See LOCKWOOD, ROBERT WILTON, 1861–1914].

LOCY, WILLIAM ALBERT (Sept. 14, 1857–Oct. 9, 1924), zoologist, teacher, historian of the development of biological science, came of Dutch ancestry, his forefathers having emigrated from Holland in 1651. Born at Troy, Mich., son of Lorenzo Dow and Sarah (Kingsbury) Locy, he grew up in a home that provided education in music, science, and the humanities. His father was a dentist. Having received the degree of B.S. from the University of Michigan in 1881, he continued his studies in biology there during 1881–82 and received the degree of M.S. in 1884. During 1884–85, under a fellowship at Harvard University, he completed a noteworthy embryological investigation on the development of *Agelena naevia* (a spider), in the laboratory of Prof. Edward Laurens Mark. The year 1891 he spent at the University of Berlin. Under an honorary fellowship at the University of Chicago in 1894, he prosecuted studies upon the structure and development of the vertebrate head, in the laboratories of Prof. Charles O. Whitman, producing a thesis on this subject which was accepted for the degree of Ph.D. in 1895 (*Journal of Morphology*, May 1895). For several summers he was occupied in research at the Marine Biological Laboratories at Woods Hole, Mass.

After an experience of three years' teaching in secondary schools, in 1887 he became professor of biology in Lake Forest University, Illinois, his title being changed in 1889 to professor of animal morphology. While at Lake Forest he also served one year as professor of physiology at the Rush Medical College, Chicago. In January 1896 he went to Northwestern University, Evanston, Ill., as professor of zoology and director of the zoological laboratories, in which capacity he remained for twenty-eight years. During this time fifty-four advanced degrees were given by the university for work done under his direction and supervision.

He produced no less than fifty-six scientific papers, some of which are regarded as landmarks in their fields. "His study of the embryonic neuromeres of the fore and mid-brain of fishes stands in the fore-front of investigation on neural metamerism"; while "his study of the *nervus terminalis* (accessory cranial nerve) in Elasmobranchs . . . was so thorough as to dominate and become the standard for all later investigations" (Crew and Lillie, *post*, p. 492). Other highly valued papers concern the embryonic development of elasmobranchs (sharks), and the derivation of the pineal eye.

During the later years of his career he gave his attention more and more to developing a general interest in the early history of the sciences of biology and medicine, and his devotion to this field of research is marked by a series of brief, valuable, historical, non-technical papers; among them, *Malpighi, Swammerdam and Leeuwenhoek* (1901); "Service of Zoology to Intellectual Progress" (*Popular Science*, October 1909); "Earliest Printed Illustrations of Natural History" (*Scientific Monthly*, September 1921); "Wilhelm Hofmeister" (*Ibid.*, October 1924). In 1911 appeared a more extended paper upon "Anatomical Illustrations Before Vesalius" covering forty-four pages, with twenty-three figures, and appearing in the Whitman memorial number of the *Journal of Morphology* (December 1911). The final outcome of his zeal in the study of the historical development of biology took the form of three books: *Biology and Its Makers* (1908, 3rd ed. 1915, German ed., Jena, 1915); *The Main Currents of Zoology* (1918); and, his last work, completed a few days before his death, *Growth of Biology* (1925). He was editor in charge of zoological articles for the *New American Supplement to the Encyclopaedia Britannica* (5 vols., 1897), writing several of them himself; and he held a membership in many scientific societies. On June 26, 1883, he married Ellen Eastman, daughter of Dr. Joseph and Nancy McAllister Eastman of Flint, Mich., by whom he had two sons.

[Henry Crew and F. R. Lillie, "William A. Locy, 1857–1924," *Science*, Nov. 28, 1924; F. H. Garrison, "William A. Locy, In Memoriam," *Annals of Medic. Hist.*, June 1925; C. E. Tharaldsen, "William A. Locy, Zoologist and Historian of Biological Science," *Scientific Mo.*, Nov. 1925; J. McK. Cattell and D. R. Brimhall, *Am. Men of Science* (3rd ed., 1921); *Who's Who in America*, 1924–25; *Chicago Daily Tribune*, Oct. 11, 1924.] C. B. A.

LODGE, GEORGE CABOT (Oct. 10, 1873–Aug. 21, 1909), poet, was born at Boston, Mass., the son of Henry Cabot Lodge [*q.v.*] and Anna Cabot Mills (Davis) Lodge. His childhood was spent in his father's home on the windy peninsula of Nahant; and as he grew older he became the protégé of that charmed circle which included Henry Adams, Edith Wharton, Sturgis Bigelow, John Hay, Cecil Spring-Rice, and Theodore Roosevelt. At the age of eighteen he entered Harvard. In college he passed four studious and thoughtful years, read Leconte de Lisle, Renan, Schopenhauer, and the Upanishads, and developed a mood of poetic pessimism which sat oddly upon his perfect health and joyous vitality. The winter of 1895–96 was spent with his friend Joseph Trumbull Stickney at the Sorbonne in Paris, observing the humors of the Boulevards and reading the Italian and Greek poets. The next year at the University of Berlin he mastered the German language, frequented the productions of classic drama, took courses in philosophy, and digested the initiation into esoteric Buddhism which he had received the previous summer at Tuckanuck from his life-long mentor Dr. Bigelow. In the autumn of 1897 he settled in Washington as his father's secretary. His first volume *The Song of the Wave, and Other Poems* was published in the spring of 1898. Here, along with echoes of Whitman, Browning, Swinburne, Leconte de Lisle, and Leopardi, were found his characteristic elevation of thought and sonorous melody of verse, culminating in the fine sonnet "To Silence" beginning:

> "Lord of the deserts 'twixt a million spheres."

The year 1898 brought the Spanish-American War, a vivid episode in his life. As ensign on the *Dixie,* under his uncle, Capt. Charles H. Davis [*q.v.*], he commanded a gun crew, fought two minor engagements, was of the landing party that demanded the surrender of Ponce, Porto Rico, and with his own hands raised the American flag over the city hall. Theodore Roosevelt states: "He made an admirable officer, training his men with unwearied care and handling them with cool readiness under fire" (*post,* pp. xiv, xv). After the war Lodge resumed his duties as secretary of a Senate committee, yet, as always, reading omnivorously and writing copiously. Several novels and plays were written and destroyed, but his sonnets began to meet a welcome from the editors of *Scribner's,* the *Century,* and the *Atlantic Monthly.* On Aug. 18, 1900, he married Matilda Elizabeth Frelinghuysen Davis, by whom he had two sons and a daughter. After a winter in Paris the remaining eight years of his life were passed at Washington, with summers at Tuckanuck, in domestic happiness, numerous friendships, vigorous open-air life by day, and, unfortunately for his health, constant poetic composition far into the night. He died of heart failure following an attack of ptomaine poisoning, at Tuckanuck.

The brief years of Lodge's poetic activity produced a remarkable body of published work. Following *The Song of the Wave* in 1898 came *Poems (1899–1902)* in 1902, *Cain, a Drama* in 1904, *The Great Adventure,* inspired by the death of Trumbull Stickney, in 1905, and *Herakles* in 1908. *The Soul's Inheritance, and Other Poems* appeared in 1909 after his death. In 1911 his *Poems and Dramas* were published in two volumes with an introduction by Theodore Roosevelt, companioned by a third containing an intimate and perceptive biography by Henry Adams. Lodge was a sound scholar in the fields of philosophy, and of classic and contemporary literature. His early work was academic, a little rhetorical, more than a little metaphysical, but with each succeeding volume he came nearer to the poignant realities of modern life. He fell, however, upon a barren time in English poetry, and died before the first stirrings of the poetic renaissance which preceded the Great War. During his lifetime both the production of poetry and public interest in it were at lowest ebb. Outside of the circle of his friends he had small appreciation while living and has found few readers since his death. Yet his two poetic dramas, *Cain,* presenting the eternal foe of compromise, and *Herakles,* the vicarious savior of mankind, do not suffer in comparison with any others in American literature. A half-dozen of his sonnets belong with the best in our language.

[*The Life of George Cabot Lodge* (1911), published anonymously but written by Henry Adams; Edith Wharton, "George Cabot Lodge," in *Scribner's Mag.,* Feb. 1910; Theodore Roosevelt, introduction to *Poems and Dramas of George Cabot Lodge* (1911); *Living Age,* May 17, 1913; *Who's Who in America,* 1908–09; *Washington Times,* and *Evening Star* (Washington), Aug. 23, 1909; personal acquaintance.]

F. G.

LODGE, HENRY CABOT (May 12, 1850–Nov. 9, 1924), senator, author, was born in Boston. He was the only son of John Ellerton Lodge, a prosperous merchant and owner of swift clipper-ships engaged in commerce with China. His mother was Anna Cabot, grand-daughter of George Cabot [*q.v.*], the Federalist sage. After an early education in E. S. Dixwell's Latin School, Boston, he entered Harvard College and graduated in 1871 near the middle of his class without having distinguished himself either in his studies or in any of the outside activities. Immediately after graduation Lodge married his cousin, Anna Cabot Davis, daughter of Rear Admiral Charles H. Davis [*q.v.*], and went to Europe for a year, spending most of the time in Rome. He had, as he later wrote, "no definite plan; no taste, no aptitude, no mastering passion" so far as the choice of a life career was concerned. Returning to Boston in 1872 without having formed any definite plans for the future, he decided to study law as a presumably useful preparation for whatever vocation he might ultimately enter. Accordingly, he spent the next two years at the Harvard Law School, from which he graduated in 1874, again without any special distinction, and in April 1875 he was admitted to the Boston bar.

Meanwhile, Henry Adams, his former teacher of history at Harvard, offered Lodge the assistant editorship of the *North American Review* and this opportunity was eagerly accepted (1873–76). All thought of following the active practice of law was forthwith cast aside, and for the next few years Lodge devoted himself with great zest to various literary pursuits. In addition to routine editorial work he wrote articles for various periodicals and at the same time completed his work for the first degree of Ph.D. (1876) ever obtained in political science at Harvard. His thesis was published as "The Anglo-Saxon Land-Law," in *Essays in Anglo-Saxon Law* (1876). In the following year appeared his *Life and Letters of George Cabot,* still the standard biography of his great-grandfather. Lectures given by Lodge at Harvard (1876–79) formed the substance of his book, *A Short History of the English Colonies in America* (1881). His most notable historical work is represented by his contributions to the American Statesman Series, edited by his cousin, John T. Morse, Jr.: *Alexander Hamilton* (1882), *Daniel Webster* (1882), and *George Washington* (2 vols., 1888). These readable biographies, however, are colored by his political predilections, and as time went on his writings were marred by increasing partisanship. Books of less consequence in the field of history are his *Historical and Political Essays* (1892), and *The Story of the Revolution* (2 vols., 1898). In the course of his career he published several collections of essays and speeches.

Lodge's interest in history inspired him to an initial participation in public affairs, and the thrust of his ancestry also impelled him to take some part in the politics of his own neighborhood. His first venture into the arena of partisanship was made in 1879 when he became a candidate for the Massachusetts House of Representatives from the district which included the town of Nahant, near Boston, where he maintained his legal residence. This district being strongly Republican, he was elected. In the following year, shortly after his thirtieth birthday, he went as a delegate to the Republican National Convention which nominated Garfield for the presidency. He was reëlected to the lower branch of the state legislature in the same autumn; but in 1881 he sought promotion to the state Senate and failed. Turning to national politics, he then tried to secure the Republican nomination for Congress from his district in 1882, but here again he was unsuccessful. Lodge was much discouraged by these two reverses, but a chance to regain self-confidence came in 1883 when he was chosen to manage the Republican campaign for governor against the redoubtable Gen. Benjamin F. Butler. In this fight Lodge displayed political generalship of a high order, and an adroitness which surprised even his own friends. His candidate won, and the prestige which came to the campaign manager from the victory enabled Lodge to get himself chosen as delegate-at-large to the Republican National Convention which nominated Blaine in 1884. Along with Theodore Roosevelt at that convention he worked strenuously against the selection of Blaine, but unlike most of his own intimates Lodge did not desert the ranks of Republican regulars. He not only supported the national ticket in the campaign but put himself forward as the regular Republican candidate for Congress in his own district. By reason of the Mugwump defection he was badly defeated, but by staying regular he placed himself in line for another nomination in 1886, and was then elected to Congress by a narrow margin.

Although Lodge was not yet thirty-seven years of age when he entered Congress he soon became known to the entire membership because he took the floor often and effectively. The clarity with which he presented his arguments gained attention and made him one of the notable figures in the House, even before his first term was finished. The most conspicuous measure with which he closely associated himself during his career in the House was the so-called "Force Bill," which aimed to establish federal supervision over all polling places at national elections, and thus to prevent the exclusion of colored voters in the Southern states. The debates on this bill stirred up a vast amount of sectional bitterness, much of which recoiled on Lodge as the reputed author of the proposal. In his own district, however, his attitude proved to be a political asset of direct value, and he had no difficulty in securing reëlection by increased majorities in 1888 and 1890. He served six years in the House (1887–1893). Besides stirring up the South he ran foul of the practical politicians in all parts of the country by his championship of civil-service reform. His sturdy defense of the civil-service laws was of the utmost value to the cause at a critical juncture. Moreover, it was on his recommendation that Theodore Roosevelt became a member of the national Civil Service Commission and proceeded to make the system function.

From the time of his first venture into politics Lodge nurtured an ambition to become a senator from Massachusetts. In January 1893 the two chambers of the legislature agreed upon him as a successor to Senator Dawes, who declined to be a candidate for reëlection. To the end of his life, his hold on his seat in the Senate was never seriously in doubt save on one occasion: in January 1911, during the Progressive upheaval, he was reëlected by the Massachusetts legislature by a majority of only six votes. During his career of thirty-seven years in the House and Senate Lodge had to do with the framing of many important measures. He helped to draft the Sherman Anti-Trust Law of 1890, the Pure Food and Drugs Law, and several tariff measures, especially the one of 1909. On tariff matters he proved himself a thorough-going protectionist at all times. He was in the forefront of the fight against free silver during the years 1894 to 1900. He was a consistent strong-navy man, viewed all proposals for compulsory international arbitration or disarmament with suspicion, approved the Venezuela message of 1895, supported the acquisition of the Philippines, and abetted Roosevelt's successful intrigue in Panama. He voted against the proposal for direct election of senators, opposed woman suffrage, voted against the adoption of the Eighteenth Amendment, and helped to pass the soldiers' bonus measure over President Coolidge's veto.

Lodge always regarded the field of international affairs as his sphere of special competence. He read widely on this subject and his speeches in the Senate disclosed a thorough familiarity with international law and precedents. He was restrained by no ingrowing conscience in dealing with the rights or claims of countries other than his own. Roosevelt set a high value on Lodge's judgment on international matters of every sort and during the years 1901–09 the latter became one of the President's closest advisers in this field of executive policy. He was selected as one of the American representatives on the Alaskan Boundary Commission of 1903, despite the fact that the commission was required to be made up of "impartial jurists." Lodge was neither impartial nor a jurist. His mind was thoroughly made up and closed before he started for London on this mission. Lodge soon found a place on the Foreign Relations Committee, and helped draft the resolutions which led to the war with Spain; he reported the Hay-Pauncefote treaty as well as the Alaskan Boundary agreement with Great Britain. But it was not until late in his senatorial career that the rule of seniority gave him the chairmanship. Almost immediately thereafter he was thrown into the thick of the most important controversy which the Senate had waged in more than a half century. His leadership of the fight against the ratification of the Peace Treaty and the Covenant made him in 1919 a national figure and the acknowledged leader of those who desired to keep the United States out of the League of Nations.

Before the peace conference began, Lodge had expressed himself as favorable to the imposition of harsh terms and a heavy indemnity on Germany, and as opposed to the coupling of the League of Nations, which in principle he approved, with the treaty of peace (*Congressional Record,* 65 Cong., 2 Sess., pp. 9392–93, Aug. 23, 1918; memorandum to White, Dec. 2, 1918, Allan Nevins, *Henry White: Thirty Years of American Diplomacy,* 1930, pp. 352–55). Convinced that his own ideas rather than Wilson's represented American opinion, he even suggested that Henry White [*q.v.*] show to certain leaders of the Allies his (Lodge's) memorandum, and thus strengthen the hands of those opposed to Wilson. This White did not do. In the course of the negotiations, however, certain of Lodge's speeches, widely quoted in the European press, served to make his hostility to Wilson's plans well known. The differences between the two men were not composed by the White House dinner, after Wilson's first return, and in March 1919 Lodge submitted in the Senate a resolution signed by himself and thirty-six other Republican senators which set forth their objections to the combination of the Treaty and the Covenant in a single document. Under the rules of the Senate this resolution could not be formally received, but it served notice that more than one-third of the senators were not prepared to accept the Covenant in the form proposed. In July 1919 the Treaty and Covenant, now somewhat modified, were officially transmitted to the Senate in their final form. After prolonged deliberation the Foreign Relations Committee, through Lodge as its chairman, reported them with a series of reservations. After a lengthy debate these were adopted by a majority vote; but in the end the two documents (with the reservations added) were rejected, chiefly by the votes of Democratic senators at the behest of Wilson, to whom the reservations were objectionable. Much of the bitterness that was engendered might have been avoided if both sides to the controversy had disclosed a spirit of compromise at an earlier stage. Lodge's action gained for him at the time warm admiration and bitter resentment in about equal measure. His own account of the controversy may be seen in his posthumously published book, *The Senate and the League of Nations* (1925).

In the presidential election of 1920 the issue of the entry of the United States into the League of Nations became an outstanding one and the result was regarded by Lodge as a complete vindication of his course. He was one of those who had been chiefly responsible for the nomination of Harding, and with the latter's election Lodge's influence in the field of foreign relations became greater than it had been at any previous time, even in Roosevelt's day. With the inauguration of President Harding in 1921, negotiations for a separate treaty with Germany were begun and this treaty in due course received ratification. Lodge was now the senior member of the Senate, titular leader of the Republican majority there, and chairman of the Foreign Relations Committee. He served as one of the four American Representatives at the Washington Conference of 1921. His leadership was also demonstrated by the action of the Senate on the World Court reservations a little later. During the next year or two, however, failing health impaired his work. In the end it became necessary for him to undergo a severe surgical operation from which he never fully recovered. He died at the Charlesgate Hospital in Cambridge on Nov. 9, 1924. A son, George Cabot Lodge [*q.v.*], had died in 1909; his other children, a daughter and a son, survived him.

Lodge was unquestionably a man of acute intellect, a wide reader with a retentive memory, and was endowed with literary skill of a high order. A diligent worker, he was in addition an adept in the art of getting others to work for him. As a practical politician he was equal to the best, nor was he always scrupulous in his choice of the means, provided they served the end. Conservative in temperament, he revered the ancient landmarks in government, and was rarely receptive to reform proposals of any sort. His diction was distinguished and his eloquence persuasive, especially when he put himself forward as the valiant defender of American rights, claims, or aspirations, as he so often did. Lodge was loyal to his friends, but ruthlessly vindictive toward those whom he disliked or opposed. His breadth of view was frequently warped by personal grudges. He was not always frank and sometimes took refuge in sophistry. Hence even those who admired him greatly often did so with reservations.

[Lodge's autobiographical volume, *Early Memories* (1913), does not deal with his political career. William Lawrence, *Henry Cabot Lodge* (1925), is an intimate biographical sketch. C. S. Groves, *Henry Cabot Lodge, the Statesman* (1925), deals more fully with political activities. See also *Mass. Hist. Soc. Proc.*, vol. LVIII (1925), pp. 99–110, 324–76; *Memorial Addresses Delivered in the Senate and House of Representatives . . . in Memory of Henry Cabot Lodge* (1925); *Eleventh Report of the Class of 1871 of Harvard Coll.* (1921); *Who's Who in America*, 1924–25; and articles or notices in the following: *Outlook*, Nov. 19, Dec. 10, 1924; *Nation*, Nov. 19, 1924, Nov. 4, 1925; *Living Age*, Dec. 20, 1924; *Literary Digest*, Nov. 29, 1924, Nov. 7, 1925; *Boston Evening Transcript*, Nov. 10, 1924; *N. Y. Times*, Nov. 10, 11, 16, 1924.] W. B. M—o.

LOEB, JACQUES (Apr. 7, 1859–Feb. 11, 1924), physiologist, the son of Benedict and Barbara (Isay) Loeb, was born at Mayen in the Rhine province. His parents died in his youth. He attended the Askanisches Gymnasium in Berlin, the universities of Berlin, Munich, and Strassburg, receiving a medical degree in 1884 and passing the *Staatsexamen* in 1885. He returned to Berlin and in 1886 went to Würzburg as assistant to Fick. Two years later he became assistant to Goltz in Strassburg. The winters of 1889–90 and 1890–91 he spent at Naples, carrying on experiments in heteromorphosis. In 1891 he accepted a position at Bryn Mawr and a year later went to the University of Chicago. He remained until 1902 when he accepted a call to the University of California. In 1910 he became a member of the Rockefeller Institute for Medical Research and remained there until his death. He was married, in October 1890, to Anne L. Leonard.

Loeb's original bent was toward philosophy but he was not satisfied with metaphysics: rather he demanded that the great questions of philosophy be put to experimental test. One of the most fundamental of these questions which had a special fascination for him was the freedom of the will. Could this be tested experimentally? In the universities of Berlin and Munich, and in the laboratory of Goltz at Strassburg, he found no answer though Goltz was then experimenting on the brains of dogs by a method which at first seemed promising. At last from Julius von Sachs, the famous botanist of Würzburg, he obtained a clue. Sachs controlled the behavior of plants with great precision on the assumption that plants are simple machines. Loeb tried similar experiments on animals and found that in many cases they reacted with the same machine-like regularity as plants. He called such reactions tropisms. Before the age of thirty he published the "tropism theory" which was destined to make him famous.

An illustration of his method of thought is apparent in the study of the behavior of certain caterpillars which emerge from the ground in spring and climb up trees to the tips of the branches where the opening buds furnish food. What leads them to do this, in some cases before the buds have started to open? The current answer was: A marvellous instinct which directs them to their food without any apparent cause and which is inherited from generation to generation. Not satisfied with this explanation, Loeb made the following experiment. He placed some of the caterpillars in a test-tube in a darkened room and directed the closed end toward the light. The caterpillars crawled to this end and there remained. Food was then pushed along the tube until it almost touched them but, as Loeb expressed it, they were slaves to the light, just as plants are; they could not turn around to take the food which was beside them and they starved to death within easy reach of it. The reason for their climbing trees was now clear: they were attracted by the light and the only assumption needed in regard to heredity was that they inherited some substance which made them sensitive to the light. To this extent they were mechanisms, completely under the control of the experimenter.

Thus at the outset of his career Loeb concluded that certain instincts may be resolved into tropisms. He subsequently developed these ideas. Eventually he was able, by adding carbonic acid to water, to produce in an aquatic animal, ordinarily indifferent to the light, a reaction drawing it irresistibly toward a source of illumination. This led him to question whether certain psychological problems might be placed upon a physicochemical basis. If behavior might be changed by the addition of an acid why not by the secretions of a gland? "Might not this idea be applied to attraction between the sexes, which may involve a change from a selfish to an altruistic attitude? And why limit the consideration to glandular products? Since Pawlow [the Russian physiologist] and his pupils have produced a salivary secretion in dogs by means of optical or auditory signals it no longer appears strange that what we call an idea should bring about chemical changes in the body" (*Journal of General Physiology,* vol. VIII, Sept. 15, 1928, p. xxiii).

Relating these considerations to the nature of ethics, Loeb stated his theory in the following terms: "If our existence is based on the play of blind forces and only a matter of chance; if we ourselves are only chemical mechanisms—how can there be an ethics for us? The answer is, that our instincts are the root of our ethics and that the instincts are just as hereditary as is the form of our body. We eat, drink, and reproduce not because mankind has reached an agreement that this is desirable, but because, machine-like, we are compelled to do so. We are active, because we are compelled to be so by processes in our central nervous system; and as long as human beings are not economic slaves the instinct of successful work or of workmanship determines the direction of their action. The mother loves and cares for her children, not because metaphysicians had the idea that this was desirable, but because the instinct of taking care of the young is inherited just as distinctly as the morphological characters of the female body. We seek and enjoy the fellowship of human beings because hereditary conditions compel us to do so. We struggle for justice and truth since we are instinctively compelled to see our fellow beings happy. Economic, social, and political conditions, or ignorance and superstition, may warp and inhibit the inherited instincts and thus create a civilization with a faulty or low development of ethics. Individual mutants may arise in which one or the other desirable instinct is lost, just as individual mutants without pigment may arise in animals; and the offspring of such mutants may, if numerous enough, lower the ethical status of a community. Not only is the mechanistic conception of life compatible with ethics: it seems the only conception of life which can lead to an understanding of the source of ethics" (*The Mechanistic Conception of Life,* p. 31).

Loeb believed that a fixed idea may produce a sort of tropism to which the mind mechanically responds without any such process as deliberate choice and this may happen over and over again until deliberate choice is almost or quite impossible. He even believed that much which appears to be deliberate choice is really largely mechanical and that in ordinary human actions there is far less freedom of the will than would appear at first sight. When he first announced his ideas in the nineties they created a sensation. They came at a time when the trend toward anthropomorphic thinking was very strong and they had a marked influence upon philosophy, psychology, sociology, and kindred disciplines.

But Loeb was not content merely to influence the will of the animal; he wished also to control the entire process of life, the whole course of development from beginning to end, and his experiments in these directions led to some brilliant discoveries. Development usually commences with the fertilization of the egg. This was regarded as the most mysterious of life processes. The way in which Loeb set to work to solve the mystery is characteristic. He reasoned that the sperm carries into the egg something which starts its development. In an effort to discover whether he could introduce this substance without using sperm, he subjected the egg to treatment of the most varied sort and discovered a number of methods, both chemical and physical, of starting development without the aid of sperm. He found that in some cases these parthenogenetic animals, as they are called, could be raised to full and normal maturity. He also found means of bringing about fertilization between different species and of thus producing hybrids not occurring in nature. From this beginning he found means of controlling generation in such a way as to produce at will all sorts of things not ordinarily found in nature, such as Siamese twins and triplets, and two-headed animals. He believed that in this way he could lay the foundation for a theory of development.

From this standpoint he studied regeneration, a field which attracted him because it was so long a stronghold of mysticism. It had often been assumed that when a missing part of the organism is replaced, there must be a "directive force" which ensures that the regenerated part shall be exactly what is needed to complete the organism. Loeb found that this is not always so; under some conditions a hydroid instead of regenerating a lost stolon produces a polyp "so that we have an animal terminating at both ends of its body in a head." Such cases are difficult to explain on the basis of a "directive force" which operates to supply the needs of the animal; they are less difficult to explain if it is assumed that the formation of organs is due to the accumulation of specific substances (as had been postulated in the case of plants) at the place where the organ in question is to be formed. Such an accumulation of substances can be controlled to a certain extent by the experimenter.

Loeb went on to examine from a mechanistic approach the equally important question of adaptation. He found that many characteristics of the organism which are regarded as adaptive may be explained on a mechanistic basis. The reactions of animals to light depend on a photochemical substance which may arise without reference to adaptation. It is not necessary to suppose that heliotropism can arise only in response to a need or under the guidance of a "directive force." Loeb emphasized the fact that in many cases what are called "adaptations" arose without any "directive force" before they could possibly have been useful. Where adaptations really exist they can often be explained on a physicochemical basis so that the assumption of a directive force is not necessary.

The process of death, which in higher animals terminates development after a longer or shorter interval, had a great fascination for Loeb. He made experiments which showed that in certain animals death could be postponed by keeping the temperature sufficiently low. He also called attention to the fact that by means of his method of artificial parthenogenesis the life of the egg can be indefinitely prolonged. His brother Leo Loeb, by means of transplantation and tissue culture, had succeeded in doing the same thing for the ordinary cells of the body.

Back of his desire to control life processes was his profound belief that the ills of mankind are largely due to ignorance and superstition and that if some of the mysteries of biology could be cleared up the greatest possible good to mankind would result. His own words were: "What progress humanity has made, not only in physical welfare but also in the conquest of superstition and hatred, and in the formation of a correct view of life, it owes directly or indirectly to mechanistic science" (*Yale Review,* July 1915, p. 785). He believed that the development of scientific knowledge could lead to a philosophy free from mysticism by which the human being could achieve a lasting harmony with itself and its environment. Such a goal he believed could be reached only by research, which would eventually reveal altruism as an innate property of human nature, just as the tropisms and instincts are inherent in lower organisms. To establish such a conception he exerted his utmost effort. The great driving force of his life lay not only in a powerful intellectual urge, but also in profound emotion. He spared no effort in his attempt to reduce life processes to mechanism. It may be added that he was often rewarded with startling success.

In making his experiments Loeb believed that the only satisfactory method was to follow the procedure of the exact sciences and to try to express all the observed phenomena by equations containing no arbitrary constants. He followed the progress of physics and chemistry with the closest attention and seized upon all that could be made useful in solving his own problems. Thus he made extensive use of the dissociation theory of Arrhenius which led him to discover artificial parthenogenesis and the action of balanced solutions, that is, solutions like blood and sea water, in which a salt, which is toxic by itself, serves as an antidote to other toxic salts so that when mixed in proper proportions a non-toxic mixture is obtained. So also he found in the principle of the Donnan equilibrium a clue to unraveling certain puzzling features in the behavior of colloids, the study of which is so important for biology. He was actively engaged in this work when, during a visit to Bermuda, he was overtaken by death.

Loeb was above all an idealist. Protected by academic life, and by a devoted wife, he lived largely in a world of ideals which dominated his life. He embodied Pasteur's profession of faith before the Academy, in the words now graven on his tomb: "Heureux celui qui porte en soi un dieu, un idéal de beauté, et qui lui obéit." He possessed the austerity which goes naturally with high ideals, and the temper of the aristocrat, but he had also a tender heart which responded to the sorrows of all who suffered and a sympathy for the masses who struggle against oppression, whether economic or spiritual. His temperament was that of an artist, running the gamut of the creative imagination, its brooding depression, its rare exaltation. He could not remain on the level of mediocrity. The outstanding feature of his intellectual equipment was his creative faculty. But fortunately his imagination was associated with a keen critical sense. The more audacious the conception, the more rigorously he tested it: he repeated his experiments over and over again. Few of his observations of fact had subsequently to be modified. He published only a small part of his experimental work, and few of his many ideas found their way into print. He would often think aloud in the course of a lecture, making and discarding one hypothesis after another. Ideas came to him so rapidly that often he did not know which to follow, but when he had singled one out he was not satisfied until he had thoroughly tested it. To him research was a happy adventure, however much it involved what might be called drudgery. He selected problems on the basis of their importance, and his mind gloried in difficult problems. It was always alert, poised to turn easily in any direction.

He had supreme confidence in the cause to which he consecrated his life: a conviction that mechanism could explain the most baffling mysteries. It almost approached a dogma. It was a militant faith which grew firmer with each new discovery, and if a philosophy be judged by its fruits, his convictions justified themselves. The emotional character of his thought, in conversation, was sometimes bewildering to more phlegmatic natures. A visitor to his laboratory was quite likely to leave in a somewhat breathless state. The rapidity with which he evolved, examined, and rejected ideas was astonishing. But the conceptions that survived were thought through and worked over under an emotional stress which is often evident in his writing. This emotional urge seemed to be capable of lifting him above personal considerations to levels of complete objectivity. And this seemed to him the true scientific attitude. Inspired by a militant idealism, he revolutionized more than one field of thought and made contributions which constitute an epoch in the progress of biology.

Aside from his numerous papers, Loeb published the following books: *Der Heliotropismus der Tiere und seine Übereinstimmung mit dem Heliotropismus der Pflanzen* (1890); *Untersuchungen zur physiologischen Morphologie der Tiere,* Volume I, *Über Heteromorphose,* Volume II, *"Organbildung und Wachstum"* (1891–92); *Comparative Physiology of the Brain and Comparative Psychology* (1900); *Studies in General Physiology* (1905), containing reprints of several papers previously published; *The Dynamics of Living Matter* (1906); *Untersuchungen über künstliche Parthenogenese und das Wesen des Befruchtungsvorgangs* (1906); *The Mechanistic Conception of Life* (1912); *Artificial Parthenogenesis and Fertilization* (1913); *The Organism as a Whole* (1916); *Forced Movements, Tropisms, and Animal Conduct* (1918); *Proteins and the Theory of Colloidal Behavior* (1922); and *Regeneration* (1924). He also founded and edited, in collaboration with W. J. V. Osterhout, the *Journal of General Physiology,* and in collaboration with Osterhout and T. H. Morgan, edited the Monographs on Experimental Biology.

[A biographical sketch by W. J. V. Osterhout, with a complete bibliography, printed in the *Jour. of Gen. Physiol.,* vol. VIII, Sept. 15, 1928, was reprinted in the *Nat. Acad. Sci. Biog. Memoirs,* vol. XIII (1930). See also: R. L. Duffus, "Jacques Loeb: Mechanist," *Century Mag.,* July 1924; Simon Flexner, "Jacques Loeb and His Period," *Science,* Oct. 14, 1927; T. B. Robertson, "The Life and Work of a Mechanistic Philosopher, Jacques Loeb," *Science Progress* (London), July 1926; P. H. DeKruif, "Jacques Loeb, the Mechanist," *Harper's Mag.,* Jan. 1923; *Science,* May 16, 1924; *N. Y. Times,* Feb. 13, 14, 24, 1924.]

W. J. V. O.

LOEB, LOUIS (Nov. 7, 1866–July 12, 1909), painter and illustrator, was born in Cleveland, Ohio. His parents were Alexander and Sarah (Ehrman) Loeb. At the age of thirteen he found employment in a lithographing establishment where he obtained his first instruction in drawing. He then went to New York and entered the Art Students' League, of which he was later to become the president. The next logical step was Paris, where he was a pupil of J. L. Gérôme. He soon began to send his works to the exhibitions, but the first official recognition he received was an honorable mention at the Salon of 1895, when he was almost thirty, for his "Dreamer" and a portrait. In 1897 he received the third-class medal of the Salon for his "Woman with Poppies" and "Fireflies." The former canvas was subsequently shown at the Society of American Artists' exhibition and at the Pennsylvania Academy. It was also in the nineties that he began to come before the public as an illustrator for magazines and books. He illustrated for the *Century* Mark Twain's "Pudd'nhead Wilson" (beginning November 1893); John Fox's "Cumberland Vendetta" (beginning June 1894); Langdon E. Mitchell's "Lucinda" (May 1895); Francis Marion Crawford's "Via Crucis" (beginning November 1898); two or three papers by Thomas A. Janvier; and many other single pieces or series.

After his return to America in 1896 he took a studio in New York where the rest of his life was passed. He was made an associate of the National Academy of Design in 1901 and became an academician in 1906. He was a member of the Society of American Artists, the Society of Illustrators, the Architectural League of New York; and he conducted antique and life classes in the Art Students' League. Between 1901 and 1906 he received eight medals for his paintings and drawings. His "Temple of the Winds" was acquired by the Metropolitan Museum, New York, and "The Siren" (1904) became the property of the National Gallery of Art, Washington. The former, a characteristic classical theme, is the most widely known of his pictures. Isham found his paintings academic, and a little oversweet; but that criticism does not apply to his black-and-white works. Interesting testimony as to his practice is supplied by William A. Coffin, who states that Loeb never placed his works before the public until he believed he had expressed in them the last word he was capable of in thought and execution. None of his illustrations give the measure of his imaginative power quite so well as the drawings he made to accompany Thomas A. Janvier's paper on "The Comédie Française at Orange," in the *Century* for June 1895. The event was of singular artistic interest. The leading actors of the Théâtre Français presented *Œdipus* and *Antigone* in the majestic Roman theatre at Orange. Loeb's nocturnal motives, especially his "Mademoiselle Bréval Singing the 'Hymn to Pallas Athene'" and his "Entrance of the Upper Tier," are uncommonly impressive in their light-and-shade effects, and have something of grandeur and mystery which one does not often meet with in illustrations. Loeb's brief but brilliant career came to an untimely end at Canterbury, N. H., in 1909.

[*Century*, Nov. 1909; *Bookman*, Feb. 1900; *Outlook*, Aug. 14, 1909; *Harper's Monthly Mag.*, June 1907; *Harper's Weekly*, July 31, 1909; *Am. Art Ann.*, 1909–10; Samuel Isham, *Hist. of Am. Painting* (1905); the *Am. Hebrew*, July 16, 1909; *N. Y. Times*, July 14, 1909.] W. H. D.

LOEB, MORRIS (May 23, 1863–Oct. 8, 1912), chemist, son of Solomon and Betty (Gallenberg) Loeb, was born at Cincinnati, Ohio. While he was still a lad, his parents moved to New York, where his father cooperated in establishing the banking firm of Kuhn, Loeb & Company. After extended study at Julius Sachs's school, he entered Harvard University in 1879. Early in his course his interest in chemistry was awakened by Charles L. Jackson and stimulated by other teachers. At his graduation in 1882 he received honorable mention in this subject, and *magna cum laude* for his general work. He continued his study of chemistry in Germany under the foremost teachers, including A. W. von Hofmann, and received the degree of Ph.D. at the University of Berlin in 1887. Anticipating the significance of the new field called physical chemistry, he studied this branch first at Heidelberg and later at Leipzig under Ostwald and Nernst. Upon his return to the United States in the fall of 1888, he declined the inviting career of a banker and adopted chemistry as his life work. After spending a year as an assistant in the private laboratory of Wolcott Gibbs [*q.v.*] at Newport, R. I., he went to Clark University, Worcester, Mass., as a docent in physical chemistry, and thereby became one of the American pioneers in this branch. In 1891 he was elected professor of chemistry in New York University, where he remained until 1906, having served as director of the laboratory during the eleven years preceding his resignation.

Being naturally sympathetic and generous, he really severed his formal connection with the University in order to devote himself unreservedly to the needs of charitable and scientific organizations. This service, which was continued throughout the remainder of his life, was not restricted to his own race, indeed it was limited only by his resources, time, and strength. One of his major interests was the Chemists' Club of New York. Of this he was a founder and patron, and its successful establishment as a meeting place of American chemists, its growth as a center of chemical interests, and its permanency as a depository of chemical literature and memorabilia are due in largest measure to his wise counsel, executive service, and generous gifts. He contributed liberally to the building fund, was personally interested in the construction of the building, and in his will left all his holdings of stock to the Chemists' Building Company for cancellation. In 1908 he was appointed on the committee to visit the chemical laboratory of Harvard University. He met his responsibilities with faithfulness and generosity. His early interest in chemistry at Harvard, deepened by years of study and research, soon found expression in a gift of $50,000 (jointly with his brother James) to the fund for founding the Wolcott Gibbs Memorial Laboratory for research in physical and inorganic chemistry. He was a founder and promoter of the Association of Harvard Chemists.

During the twenty-five or more years of his activity as a chemist, he published about thirty articles, including essays, lectures, and research papers, in foreign and domestic journals. The earlier contributions are on organic chemistry; many, from 1888 onward, are on physical chemistry (especially on the determination of molecular weights); and several, scattered through the entire period, relate to various aspects of chemical education and similar interests. Three of his early scientific papers, which were found in manuscript form after his death, were condensed and edited by Theodore W. Richards because they were the first presentation of physical chemistry in America; in this condensed form they are included under the title "Fundamental Ideas of Physical Chemistry" in *The Scientific Work of Morris Loeb* (1913). He also wrote a *Laboratory Manual Prepared for Students in Elementary Inorganic Chemistry at New York University* (1900). Although prepared for his students at New York University, the book was so clear and concise that it found its way into other institutions. An unusually helpful feature of this book was a set of laboratory maxims at the end; two reflect the methods of the author, *viz.*, "Note-books have good memories; jottings on loose paper are useful when you can find them," and "An unrecorded experiment was never begun." He was a member of the American Chemical Society and other important chemical organizations, and was an enthusiastic worker in these societies and in the meetings sponsored by them, a notable example being the Eighth International Congress of Applied Chemistry held in New York, 1912. At this congress he read a significant paper on "Studies in the Speed of Reductions" (published in *The Scientific Work of Morris Loeb*). From 1911 until his death he was a member of the New York City Board of Education. On Apr. 3, 1895, he married Eda Kuhn who shared his manifold interests. His death occurred in New York; among his bequests was a fund of $500,000 to be used eventually by Harvard University for the furtherance of the science of chemistry and physics.

[T. W. Richards, *The Scientific Work of Morris Loeb* (1913), includes a chronological list of his papers and a brief biog.; see also *Morris Loeb, 1863–1912, Memorial Vol.* (1913), privately printed for the Chemists' Club; *Jour. of Industrial and Engineering Chemistry*, Nov. 1912; *Science*, Nov. 15, 1912; *Am. Hebrew*, Oct. 11, 18, 1912; *Survey*, Oct. 26, 1912; *Harvard Graduates' Mag.*, Dec. 1912; *Who's Who in America*, 1912–13; *N. Y. Times*, Oct. 9, 1912.] L. C. N.

LOEB, SOPHIE IRENE SIMON (July 4, 1876–Jan. 18, 1929), social worker, journalist, author, is credited with having secured more constructive welfare legislation than any other woman in America. She was born in Rovno, Russia, in a Jewish home. The eldest child of Samuel and Mary (Carey) Simon, she was descended from generations of rabbis and scholars. Brought to the United States by her parents at the age of six, she grew up in McKeesport, Pa. When she was sixteen her father, a watchmaker and jeweler, died, leaving his widow practically penniless. Her mother's bitter struggle to keep the home together and educate six children fixed Sophie's determination from girlhood to do something to help the widowed mothers and fatherless children of America. After graduation from high school she taught, devoting her leisure to social work. At twenty she married Anselm Loeb, of Pittsburgh. The union proved an unhappy one, and on recovering her legal freedom she called herself "Miss Loeb." For some years she supported herself in Pittsburgh by teaching china painting and by newspaper writing.

In 1910, unknown, and without means, she removed to New York to launch a crusade for legislation providing aid for mothers with dependent children. As a reporter on the *Evening World*, she sought assignments in the slums in order to get facts at firsthand, and wrote a series of compelling "human-interest stories." From the platform, too, she plead the case for subsidized mother-care as against orphanage care. Within a year she had the backing of influential people and was making headway with her first bill at Albany. Three years of work, "educating legislators," secured the appointment in 1913 of a commission for the relief of widowed mothers. As a member of this commission she went abroad to study conditions in the six European countries most advanced in child-conservation, and later rendered an exhaustive report. She headed the hard-fought campaign which secured in 1915 the passage of the initial mothers' pension act in accordance with which the New York Child Welfare Board was appointed with Miss Loeb as president. During her seven years' tenure of this unsalaried post, appropriations for mothers' aid rose from $100,000 to over $5,000,000, largely through her unremitting fight to liberalize the application of the law. Other crusades for housing relief, model tenements, cheaper milk, cheaper gas, public baths, play streets, maternity care, school centers, and safer movie-theatres, she carried through by newspaper publicity plus direct legislative campaigning. Single-handed she waged a fight for low taxi fares and bonded drivers. In 1917 she settled a strike of taxi drivers in seven hours. During wartime coal shortage she stimulated Congressional inquiry, spending six months among the miners to ascertain facts. In 1920 she served on the commission appointed by Gov. Alfred E. Smith to codify the child-welfare laws of the state. In 1924, as first president of the Child Welfare Committee of America, founded largely through her determination, she carried her campaign to the nation, addressing many of the state legislatures. She toured Palestine in 1925, interviewing dignitaries—Arab, Jewish, and Christian, and embodied the results in a series of articles, afterward put into book form. In 1926 the International Child Welfare Congress at Geneva indorsed her anti-orphanage resolution. The League of Nations, 1927, solicited her aid as adviser on Child Welfare, requesting a report on blind children in America, which she completed. Beside her regular work for the *World*, carried on for eighteen years, she wrote syndicate articles, plays, and moving-picture features of humanitarian interest. Among her several books are *Epigrams of Eve* (1913), *Everyman's Child* (1920), and *Palestine Awake* (1926).

She was a little woman, endowed with tremendous driving power, courage, and tenacity of purpose. For herself she wanted nothing, least of all concessions to the fact that she was a woman. She organized her work like a man of affairs, fought in the open, and took hard knocks with impersonal unconcern. In quickness of mind and a certain intolerance of slower thinking, she was wholly feminine. When she died in New York, a thousand people attended her funeral.

[N. Y. *Evening World*, Jan. 19, 1929; *World* (N. Y.), Jan. 19, 22, 1929; *N. Y. Times*, Jan. 19, 21, 1929; *National Mag.*, Dec. 1923; *Survey*, Feb. 15, 1929; *Jewish Tribune*, Jan. 25, 1929; *Am. Hebrew*, Jan. 25, 1929; *Woman's Jour.*, Feb. 1929; *Who's Who in N. Y.*, 1924; *Who's Who in America*, 1924–25; information as to certain facts from a brother, A. M. Simon, McKeesport, Pa.] M. B. H.

LOEW, MARCUS (May 7, 1870–Sept. 5, 1927), theatre owner and motion-picture producer, was born on New York's East Side. His parents, Herman L. and Ida (Lewinstein) Loew, were Austrian Jews who had recently emigrated from Vienna. The family was in humble circumstances and the boy's formal schooling ended at about his tenth year. Even at that early age he was employed by a map-coloring firm and later, with another boy, started a job-printing business and issued a weekly paper. When this venture proved unprofitable, he found employment with a fur company and at eighteen was in business on his own account. There followed six or seven years of ups and downs, including bankruptcy succeeded by a full discharge of obligations to which he could not have been legally held. In 1895 he made an investment that opened to him the gate to prosperity and by the turn of the century he was well established, with a portion of his capital invested in New York apartment houses. His real-estate investments led incidentally to his acquaintance with David Warfield, the actor, and the two men, by the merest chance, had their attention directed to the profitable business being done in New York by the so-called penny arcades, or peep shows. They joined Adolph Zukor in promoting that form of popular amusement but after a time withdrew from partnership with him and in 1904 formed a company of their own with a capital of $100,000.

The moving picture was just beginning to give some promise of its power to entertain the public. Loew and Warfield were among the first to sense its possibilities. At Cincinnati they made their first serious effort to "bring the movies to the arcades." Then they opened picture houses—usually remodeled stores—in New York. These were soon as great money-makers as the penny arcades had been. In Brooklyn Loew took over a real playhouse and by the time the film producers had turned out actual photoplays he was ready to show them to his public, at the same time presenting vaudeville features to offer variety. That was a program which quickly appealed to popular audiences and within a few years Loew was operating scores of small theatres in New York and other cities. At his death in 1927 there were about three hundred amusement places under his control. Until 1920 Loew had no part in the production of film plays, but in that year he bought the Metro Film Corporation and in 1924 the Goldwyn Pictures and the Louis B. Mayer Company. Loew's Incorporated, with about a hundred subsidiary companies, was capitalized at $100,000,000, with 10,000 stockholders.

His brilliant success as a showman was ascribed by Loew himself largely to good fortune.

His associates found him a genial and witty companion, whose early experiences had left him not unwilling to make ventures. By some he was credited with a genuine esthetic sense. His mistakes, from a business standpoint, were remarkably few, considering the magnitude of his operations. In 1894 he married Caroline Rosenheim. She with twin sons, Arthur and David, survived him.

[C. D. Fox and M. L. Silver, *Who's Who on the Screen*, 1920; *Lit. Digest*, Sept. 24, 1927; Will Irwin, *The House that Shadows Built* (1928); B. B. Hampton, *A Hist. of the Movies* (1931); Terry Ramsaye, "Little Journeys to the Homes of Famous Film Magnates," *Photoplay Mag.*, Aug. 1927; the *Am. Hebrew*, Sept. 16, 1927; *N. Y. Times*, Sept. 6, 1927.] W. B. S.

LOEWENTHAL, ISIDOR (*c.* 1827–Apr. 27, 1864), Presbyterian missionary, the son of Jewish parents, was born in Posen, Prussia (now Poznan, Poland). He received at home and at school the early education of the orthodox Jewish boy, chiefly in the Hebrew language, literature, and religion. Later he attended a gymnasium where he studied with great success classical literature, modern languages, science, philosophy, and music. After graduation at seventeen from the gymnasium, he engaged for a time in clerical service in a mercantile house, continuing his studies meanwhile with a view to entering one of the German universities. He shared the liberal political opinions of a growing number of young men of his day and associated with certain of them in their agitation for governmental reform. He published anonymously in the summer of 1846 a poem adverse to the State. His authorship thereof was soon detected by the police, and he chose to flee from Posen to escape arrest. He secured at Hamburg passage on an English ship bound for America and landed at New York in the fall of the year. Finding no other employment, he took to peddling "notions" throughout the countryside about Philadelphia. Chance took him to the home of the Rev. S. M. Gayley, a minister of Wilmington, Del., who saw in the peddler a man of extraordinary qualities. Through the good offices of this clergyman and his son in Lafayette College, Loewenthal secured a post on the college faculty. Beginning in January 1847, he taught Hebrew and German, and pursued courses toward a degree. He was tutor in Latin, also, during the year 1847–48. He received from Lafayette College in 1848 the degree of B.A., and later that of M.A. In the spring of 1847 his mind turned favorably toward Christianity. In the autumn he professed conversion, was baptized by the Rev. Mr. Gayley, and was received into membership in the Rockland, N. J., Presbyterian Church, of which Gayley was then the minister. After spending the years 1848–50 as a teacher of languages in the collegiate school at Mount Holly, Pa., he entered Princeton Theological Seminary. He distinguished himself as a theological student. Articles of his were published in the *Biblical Repository*, and at graduation in 1851 he read a paper on "India as a Field of Missions." He served during 1854–55 as a tutor in Princeton College. On Apr. 18, 1855, he was ordained by the Presbytery of New York, and in the following August he sailed from New York for a missionary career in India under the auspices of his Church. His first year in India was spent in language study at Rawal Pindi. Thereafter he worked at Peshawar among the Afghans in particular.

Although frequently in danger both to property and life, in this turbulent northwestern region, he gave diligent and effective attention to evangelism and translation. He preached in Pashtu, Persian, and Urdu, and knew other tongues, also, including Arabic. He made at least one tour in Kashmir and familiarized himself with Kashmiri. By the spring of 1863 he had completed and published (in Great Britain) a Pashtu version of the New Testament. Before his untimely death he had nearly finished a Pashtu dictionary. He died at the age of thirty-eight—shot in his own garden after midnight by his watchman who may have mistaken him for a robber. He left certain unpublished manuscripts, including Pashtu translations of portions of the Hebrew Old Testament. He had contributed articles to British and American periodicals, including the *Foreign Missionary* magazine of his own Board.

[See the *Twenty-Third Ann. Report of the Lodiana Mission* (1857); the *Foreign Missionary*, July, Oct. 1863, Feb., Sept. 1864; J. C. Lowrie, *A Manual of the Foreign Missions of the Presbyt. Ch.* (1868); B. H. Badley, *Indian Missionary Directory and Memorial Vol.* (Lucknow, 1876); *Missionary Review of the World*, Aug. 1891; Wm. Rankin, *Memorials of Foreign Missionaries of the Presbyt. Ch.* (1895); H. H. Holcomb, *Men of Might in India Missions* (1901); the *Jewish Era*, Apr. 1902; *Encyc. of Missions* (1904); and E. M. Wherry, *Our Missions in India* (1926).] J. C. Ar—r.

LOGAN, BENJAMIN (*c.* 1743–Dec. 11, 1802), Kentucky pioneer, was born in Augusta County, Va., whither his parents, David and Jane Logan, had come from West Pennsborough Township, Cumberland County, Pa., in 1740. The Logan family, originally of Scotch stock, had settled in northern Ireland and emigrated from that country to Pennsylvania early in the eighteenth century. Benjamin, the eldest of six children, was left by the death of his father in 1757 the head of the family. Under the Virginia law of primogeniture he was sole heir of the estate, which seems to have been of respectable proportions. In 1764 he accompanied Bouquet's expedition with the rank of sergeant. Upon his return he and his brother John removed to the Holston region where Benjamin bought a farm and, in 1773 or 1774, married Ann Montgomery. He held the rank of lieutenant in a company of Virginia militia which accompanied the Governor in Dunmore's War against the Ohio Indians in 1774 (R. G. Thwaites and L. P. Kellogg, *Documentary History of Dunmore's War, 1774*, 1905, p. 82, note). His importance in Western history began in 1775 when with other frontiersmen of southwest Virginia he joined Richard Henderson who was going out to settle his Transylvania colony. Logan established a fort within the limits of the present Stanford and called it St. Asaph's. The coming of the Revolution brought incessant Indian warfare to Kentucky and gave Logan many opportunities to show his worth. His chief service in the war was as a leader of the retaliatory expeditions against the Indians in Ohio after their invasions of Kentucky in 1778, 1780, and 1782. In 1781 he was appointed county lieutenant of Lincoln County and as such was the ranking militia officer of the district. He was also a member of the Virginia General Assembly from Lincoln County for three terms, 1781–82, and 1785–87. Throughout the Revolution he was the most influential and the most trusted of the Kentucky leaders.

With the transition from war to peace in Kentucky Logan failed to hold his dominant position. His education had been so imperfect as probably to be a handicap to him even on the frontier, and he was temperamentally more a man of action than a politician. Yet he represented his county in the various conventions which marked the "struggle for autonomy" in Kentucky, he was a member of the convention (1792) which made the first constitution of Kentucky, and he was a member of the electoral college which made Isaac Shelby the first governor of the state. He was a presidential elector in 1792 and a member of the electoral college which chose the first Senate of the Kentucky legislature. During these years his military exploits were few, although in 1788 he led the Kentucky troops in the expedition against the Indians of the Northwest. In 1790 Washington appointed him a member of the Board of War in the West and Governor Shelby subsequently made him brigadier-general of state militia. In 1793 and 1794 he represented Lincoln County in the Kentucky House of Representatives, and in 1795 he was elected a representative from Shelby County, to which place he had removed. In 1796 he was a candidate for governor, receiving a plurality of votes on the first ballot of the electoral college but being beaten on the second by James Garrard. His death in 1802 was the result of apoplexy; he was buried near the present Shelbyville, Ky. He had eight children, one of whom, William Logan, later was United States senator from Kentucky. Logan was of giant physique and was renowned throughout the West for his great strength and courage. He had more worldly wisdom than was usual with frontiersmen and at his death possessed one of the largest estates in Kentucky.

[J. A. Waddell, *Annals of Augusta County, Va.*, vol. II (1888); Lewis and R. H. Collins, *Hist. of Ky.* (1874); W. H. Egle, *Notes and Queries, Ann. Vol., 1900* (1901), p. 209; Lyman Chalkley, *Chronicles of the Scotch-Irish Settlement in Va.* (3 vols., 1912); T. M. Green, *Hist. Families of Ky.* (1889); L. D. V. Harper, *Colonial Men and Times; Containing the Jour. of Col. Daniel Trabue* (1916); B. T. Conkwright, "A Sketch of the Life and Times of Gen. Benj. Logan," *Reg. of the Ky. State Hist. Soc.*, May 1916; J. A. McClung, *Sketches of Western Adventure* (1832); C. C. Graham, "Pioneer Life," *Louisville Monthly Mag.*, vol. I (1879).]

R. S. C.

LOGAN, CORNELIUS AMBROSE (Aug. 24, 1832–Jan. 30, 1899), physician, politician, was born at Deerfield, Mass., the son of Cornelius Ambrosius [*q.v.*] and Eliza (Akeley) Logan. His father was a distinguished actor and theatrical manager. Olive Logan [*q.v.*] was his sister. The home of the family after 1840 was Cincinnati, Ohio. Logan was educated at Auburn Academy and later entered the medical profession. In 1854 he was married to Zoe Shaw. For a time he was medical superintendent of St. John's Hospital, Cincinnati, but in February 1857 he emigrated to Leavenworth, Kan. During the Civil War he was commissioned (June 29, 1864) surgeon of the first regiment of Kansas state militia. After the war he was active in the medical profession. As botanist of the state geological corps in charge of sanitary relations he made a study published under the title: *Report on Sanitary Relations of the State of Kansas* (1866). When the Kansas State Medical Society (chartered 1859) was reorganized in 1866 he was elected its first president and, for several years thereafter, served on one or more of its committees. His presidential address, delivered Apr. 3, 1867, sounded the keynote of his medical activity in the state: first, the strengthening of the medical society; second, the raising of the standards of the profession and the eliminating of quacks; third, the establishing of regular medical instruction at the state university. In June 1867, in association with Tiffin Sinks, M.D., he established the *Leavenworth Medical Herald*, a monthly magazine, and conducted the editorial section until April 1871. He published a book, *Physics of the Infectious Diseases* (1878), and wrote several articles for professional periodicals. No great scientific attainments and no important scientific discoveries can be attributed to him. Kansas was a frontier community and its greatest need was the establishment of stabilized institutions, and in medicine as in politics, the elimination of incompetents and impostors who were particularly numerous as a result of some two decades of disorder.

The lure of politics eventually drew Logan into the two contests for United States senatorships in 1873, but he was defeated in the first contest, and in consequence of the exigencies of both local and national politics, he was removed from the second by his appointment as envoy extraordinary and minister plenipotentiary to Chile. The Senate confirmed the appointment Mar. 17, 1873, and he held the position until 1877. During 1874 he arbitrated differences between Chile and Peru, arising out of the alliance of 1865, and also handled early stages of the Tacna dispute. In 1879 he was appointed from Illinois, to which state he had removed from Kansas, to the post of minister resident to the Central American states and was confirmed by the Senate Apr. 1. This position was held until 1882 when he was transferred to his former post in Chile, the new appointment being confirmed Mar. 15. The outstanding problem of this second Chile mission was the Tacna-Arica controversy. Aside from his political and professional activities he was a devoted Odd Fellow. He held high offices in the Grand Lodge of Kansas and during his residence in Chile established the order there. Subsequent to his return to the United States in 1885 Logan became the literary executor of his cousin, Gen. John A. Logan of Illinois. In this capacity he published the latter's book: *The Volunteer Soldier of America* (1887), together with a biographical memoir. Later he removed to California where after a long illness he died in Los Angeles at the home of his daughter, Celia Logan Waterous.

[There is no biography of Logan and such sketches as appear in encyclopedias are inaccurate. The library of the Kansas State Historical Society (Topeka) has a limited amount of manuscript and printed material pertaining to the Kansas phase of Logan's career. Such diplomatic correspondence as is in print is contained in *The Papers Relating to the Foreign Relations of the U. S.*, 1874, 1875, 1883. W. R. Sherman, *The Diplomatic and Commercial Relations of the U. S. and Chile, 1820–1914* (1926), gives a bare skeleton of a part of the period of Logan's diplomatic career. See also: H. A. Kelly and W. L. Burrage, *Am. Medic. Biogs.* (1920); D. W. Wilder, *The Annals of Kan., 1541–1885* (1886); memoir in *Jour. of Proc. of the Seventy-Fifth Ann. Communication of the Sovereign Grand Lodge, I.O.O.F.*, 1899; *Evening Standard* (Leavenworth, Kan.), Jan. 31, 1899. Available information seems to indicate that Logan was named *Cornelius Ambrosius* but later adopted the simpler form for the middle name.]

J. C. M.

LOGAN, CORNELIUS AMBROSIUS (May 4, 1806–Feb. 22, 1853), actor, dramatist, manager, was of Irish parentage, the son of a farmer who was killed by British troops while working on his farm near Baltimore, Sept. 12, 1814. He was one of a large family of children, and during his boyhood and early youth he sang as a church choir boy, began to study for the priesthood at St. Mary's College, worked in a shipping house, and made several voyages across the Atlantic as sailor and supercargo. Reaching New York on one of his return trips, he abandoned the sea and engaged in newspaper work there. Removing to Philadelphia, he began his connection with the theatre which continued for the rest of his life. One of his earliest appearances as an actor was made at the Tivoli Garden, Philadelphia, in July 1825, as Bertram in Maturin's tragedy of that name, and he afterward acted at the Walnut Street Theatre and other playhouses in that city. The records of the New York stage reveal him at the Bowery Theatre in 1826, announced as "a new actor from Philadelphia," and playing Smith in *The Road to Ruin,* Claudio in *Much Ado About Nothing,* and Trip in *The School for Scandal.* Moving from Philadelphia to Pittsburgh with his family, he became manager of the theatre there and later embarked on a wandering career that carried him through the central West, encountering the precarious hazards of theatrical fortune by traveling with his company, baggage, scenery, and properties, by canal-boat, steamboat, and wagon.

Despite his labors as manager and writer of plays, Logan never gave up acting, and his name is frequently found on the playbills of Cincinnati, where he lived for some years, and in the records of many other cities. He acted Sir Peter Teazle in *The School for Scandal* and Peter Simpson in *Simpson & Co.* so often that he was called Peter Logan in private life by many who supposed that it was his real name. At one time he managed a theatre in Albany, and on May 24, 1849, he returned to New York, after an absence of many years, and at Burton's Chambers Street Theatre took the part of Aminadab Slocum in his own play, *Chloroform, or New York a Hundred Years Hence.* It was played for eight successive nights, a remarkable run in those days. As an actor, he is reported by one who saw him many times to be full of an innate and quiet humor that was in no degree dependent upon physical action or facial grimace. He was one of the earliest dramatists to capitalize Yankee eccentricities for comedy purposes, among his numerous plays being *Yankee Land, or the Foundling of the Apple Orchard, The Wag of Maine,* and *The Vermont Wool Dealer,* a farce in one act popularized by Dan Marble. His daughter Celia declares that he was the author of *The People's Lawyer,* famous for its central character of Solon Shingle, and that Dr. Joseph Stevens Jones, to whom its authorship is accredited, merely revised it. His three daughters, all of considerable prominence on the stage, were Eliza, Celia, and Olive [*q.v.*], and his son, Cornelius Ambrose Logan [*q.v.*], was well known in the triple capacity of physician, journalist, and author. He died suddenly of apoplexy near Marietta, Ohio, while on a steamboat, accompanied by his daughter Eliza, on his way from Cincinnati to Pittsburgh. His wife, Eliza (Akeley) Logan, survived him.

[J. N. Ireland, *Records of the N. Y. Stage* (2 vols., 1866–67); H. P. Phelps, *Players of a Century* (1880); T. A. Brown, *A Hist. of the N. Y. Stage* (1903), vol. III; Arthur Hornblow, *A Hist. of the Theatre in America* (1919), vol. II; A. H. Quinn, *A Hist. of the Am. Drama from the Beginning to the Civil War* (1923); Montrose J. Moses, *The Am. Dramatist* (1925); G. C. D. Odell, *Annals of the N. Y. Stage,* vol. III (1928); J. T. Scharf, *Hist. of Baltimore City and County* (1881); *Cincinnati Daily Enquirer,* Feb. 25, 1853; article by Celia Logan in an unidentified newspaper, embodying personal reminiscences by James Rees; records of the Cemetery of Spring Grove, Cincinnati, Ohio.] E. F. E.

LOGAN, DEBORAH NORRIS (Oct. 19, 1761–Feb. 2, 1839), historian, was the daughter of Charles and Mary (Parker) Norris and a grand-daughter of Isaac Norris [*q.v.*], chief justice of Pennsylvania. As "saucy Debby Norris" she attended the school of Anthony Benezet [*q.v.*], who found that her sense of fun could be restrained only by her sense of honor. Though female education was then held of little importance, she continued her studies at home through self-imposed courses of reading and formed lasting habits of literary work. Her father's "palatial" residence, then in the outskirts of Philadelphia, on Chestnut Street near Fifth, and her grandfather's at Fairhill, were both centers of hospitality in which the girl received social training and formed a wide acquaintance with the leaders of the time. On Sept. 6, 1781, she became the wife of George Logan [*q.v.*]; of their three children—all sons—one survived her. Through nearly forty years of happy marriage she was devoted to her husband and his interests. He trusted her judgment fully, and gave her unlimited control of his property during his absence from the country in 1798. After his death she prepared a *Memoir of Dr. George Logan of Stenton,* which was published by her great-grand-daughter in 1899.

In all the relations of life her contemporaries credit her with exemplary conduct and great personal charm. Her extensive family connections gave her a close acquaintance with the leading men of the place and time; her beauty, ability, and goodness attracted to "Stenton" eminent Philadelphians and the most distinguished visitors to the city. To her clear memory and graphic description in the memoir of her husband we owe some of the most vivid accounts of the Revolutionary and early Republican city. When John F. Watson was writing his *Annals of Philadelphia* (1830) he found her a source of invaluable information. Her greatest service to history, however, was in recognizing the value of the family papers at "Stenton." In spite of the current lack of interest in colonial history, she preserved them for posterity. Large quantities of these papers were stored in the garrets, mouldy, worm-eaten, and tattered, literally perishing from neglect. Beginning in 1814, she deciphered, copied, and annotated thousands of pages that eventually constituted eleven quarto manuscript volumes. These were given to the American Philosophical Society and were later published by the Historical Society of Pennsylvania ("Correspondence between William Penn and James Logan," being vols. IX and X of its *Memoirs,* 1870–72). Deborah Logan survived her husband nearly eighteen years. She was buried in the little family cemetery at "Stenton."

[Sarah Butler Wister and Agnes Irwin, *Worthy Women of Our First Century* (1877); Deborah Norris Logan, *The Norris House* (1867); *Sally Wister's Journal* (1902), ed. by A. C. Myers; *Poulson's Am. Daily Advertiser,* Feb. 4, 1839.] A. L. L.

LOGAN, GEORGE (Sept. 9, 1753–Apr. 9, 1821), physician, United States senator, was the son of William and Hannah (Emlen) Logan. He was born at "Stenton," the home established near Germantown, Pa., by his grandfather, James Logan [*q.v.*], in 1728. His father was a wealthy merchant in Philadelphia until 1751, when he inherited "Stenton"; subsequently he devoted himself to the cultivation of its 500 acres. A strict Quaker and a leader of the conscientious objectors to war, he was a loyal supporter of the Penn family, whom he represented in America after 1741. George was sent to school in England for a time and then continued his studies under Robert Proud [*q.v.*]. In spite of the boy's predilection for medicine, his father apprenticed him to a Philadelphia merchant. In the counting-house, however, he had time to read much from the fine collection of medical books that had come to the library at "Stenton" through the death of Dr. William Logan of Bristol, England, a brother of James Logan. At the end of his apprenticeship, he was able to turn to medicine as a profession, went to England, and lived for some months in the home of Dr. Simms, in Essex, compounding prescriptions and studying pharmacy. He entered the University of Edinburgh, and after graduating in medicine in 1779, traveled in England and on the Continent, spending some time in Paris studying anatomy and enjoying a close friendship with Benjamin Franklin that continued until the latter's death.

When Logan returned to Philadelphia in 1780 his parents and brother were dead and his inheritance was seriously impaired by the war. Except for "Stenton," which had escaped destruction, there remained to him only "wasted estates and piles of utterly depreciated paper currency" (*Memoir, post,* p. 41). Reluctantly abandoning the idea of practising medicine, he moved to "Stenton" soon after his marriage, Sept. 6, 1781, to Deborah Norris [see Deborah Norris Logan], and applied himself enthusiastically to the study of improved methods of farming. He was elected a member of the American Philosophical Society in 1793, and was a founder of the Philadelphia Society for the Promotion of Agriculture.

In 1785 he was elected to the Pennsylvania Assembly, and during three successive years was reëlected. A friend of Jefferson, who often visited him, he became a Republican and as such was elected to the legislature in 1795, 1796, and 1799. While there he advocated the encouragement of agriculture, domestic manufacture, and popular education. Like his father a devoted friend to peace, he determined to bring about a better understanding with France in order to avert the war that threatened in 1798. In spite of bitter opposition from the Federalists to his generous project—opposition that even caused him to be put under surveillance—he sold some land to pay his expenses and, equipped with a letter of introduction from Jefferson, sailed for Hamburg. There, through the influence of Lafayette, who was living in exile nearby, he obtained papers from the French legation which permitted him to enter France. Reaching Paris, Aug. 7, soon after the departure of Elbridge Gerry [*q.v.*], the last of the American commissioners, he endeavored to impress Talleyrand with the disastrous effect that the recent French policy had had upon public opinion in the United States. Treated with respect by Talleyrand and with cordiality by Merlin, head of the Directory, he eventually secured the release of imprisoned American seamen, had the pleasure of seeing the embargo raised on American ships, and was given assurances that a minister from the United States would be favorably received. His mission was the object of much hostile criticism; upon his return to America he was accorded icy contempt by Washington, while on Jan. 30, 1799, Congress passed the so-called "Logan Act" (1 *Statutes at Large,* 613), forbidding a private citizen to undertake diplomatic negotiations without official sanction. President Adams was more friendly, however, and Logan's unofficial messages from Talleyrand, though anticipated by a communication through William Vans Murray [*q.v.*], United States minister to the Netherlands, doubtless helped to modify the general bitterness toward France.

Popular approval of Logan was shown, meanwhile, by his appointment, and later election, to the United States Senate in 1801 after the resignation of Peter Muhlenberg [*q.v.*]. He served until 1807, when he declined reëlection. Despite the "Logan Act" of 1799, he went to England in 1810 in an unsuccessful attempt to prevent the war of 1812. During his visit he received much social consideration and established pleasant relations with Englishmen interested in agriculture and negro emancipation. His last years were spent quietly at "Stenton," where he died and was buried. Much in his life suggests the influence of Franklin. That he habitually wore homespun to encourage domestic manufacture indicates his sincerity and disinterestedness. His courage was undaunted by bitter political rancor; his humane spirit was often ahead of his time. He was one of the few strict Quakers who have sat in the United States Senate.

[*Memoir of Dr. George Logan of Stenton by his Widow, Deborah Norris Logan: With Selections from his Correspondence* (1899), ed. by his great-granddaughter, Frances A. Logan; J. W. Jordan, *Colonial Families of Phila.* (1911), vol. I; J. F. Watson, *Annals of Phila.,* enlarged by W. P. Hazard (3 vols., 1898); *The Quid Mirror* (1806); P. L. Ford, *The Writings of Thomas Jefferson,* vol. VII (1896); C. F. Adams, *The Works of John Adams,* vols. VIII, IX (1853–54); J. S. Bassett, *The Federalist System* (1906); "Correspondence between William Penn and James Logan," vol. I, being *Memoirs of the Hist. Soc. of Pa.,* vol. IX (1870); Charles Warren, *Memorandum on the Hist. and Scope of the Laws Prohibiting Correspondence with a Foreign Govt.* (1915); *Nat. Gazette and Lit. Reg.* (Phila.), Apr. 10, 1821; Logan Papers and Norris Papers (MSS.), Hist. Soc. of Pa.]

A. L. L.

LOGAN, JAMES (Oct. 20, 1674–Oct. 31, 1751), colonial statesman and scholar, founder of a prominent Pennsylvania family, was of Scottish ancestry on both sides. His father, Patrick Logan of East Lothian, was a master of arts of the University of Edinburgh and a clergyman in the Established Church until his conversion to Quakerism in 1671; his mother, Isabel (Hume), came of a noble family connected with the lairds of Dundas. His father was master of a Latin school in Lurgan, County Armagh, Ireland, when James was born, and later was master of a school in Bristol, England, where his eldest son, William (1686–1757), became a distinguished physician. James, the second son, early showed a scholarly aptitude. Before he was thirteen he had received from his father a creditable knowledge of Greek, Latin, and Hebrew, and at nineteen, upon his father's return to Ireland, he was left in charge of the school at Bristol. James continued his studies until 1697. He then wished to go to Jamaica, but since his mother opposed this desire, he engaged in the shipping trade between Dublin and Bristol. At about this time he made the acquaintance of William Penn, who was impressed with the young man's ability and learning. He became Penn's secretary in 1699, and was his confidential adviser and friend and the counselor of his sons and grandsons, for half a century.

In September 1699 he sailed with Penn on the *Canterbury* for Pennsylvania. The persistent anecdote survives that on the voyage the ship was attacked by pirates; Logan took a spirited part in the defense of the ship, while Penn, the pacifist, retired below. On being reproved by Penn for resorting to arms, Logan retorted: "I being thy servant, why did thee not order me to come down?" (A. H. Smyth, *The Writings of Benjamin Franklin,* vol. I, 1905, pp. 366–67). Though the legend may be apocryphal, question and answer are characteristic of the attitudes and policies of the two men. Logan, who later declared that he was not a "strict professor," believed defensive war justifiable. In 1741 he suggested that Friends who could not conscientiously vote for measures of defense should refrain from seeking election to the legislature (*To Robert Jordan and Others,* 1741, reprinted in *Pennsylvania Magazine of History and Biography,* vol. VI, no. 4, 1882).

His career of fifty-two years in Pennsylvania was one of increasing responsibility and honor. Penn made him secretary of the Province and clerk of the Provincial Council, in which capacities he served from 1701 to 1717. When the Proprietor returned to England, he made Logan commissioner of property and receiver general, an office which involved issuing titles to lands, collecting quit rents, and the general supervision of the Penn family interests in the colony. On Apr. 21, 1702, Logan was made a voting member of the Council, and on the arrival of Governor Evans (Feb. 8, 1703/4) a fully qualified member, which he remained until his retirement on May 29, 1747. He became in time president and senior member of the Council, and, as such, was chief executive of the Province from Aug. 4, 1736, to June 1, 1738 (after the retirement of Governor Gordon), during which interval the "Border War" between Maryland and Pennsylvania took place. He was elected to the board of aldermen of Philadelphia on Oct. 17, 1717, and mayor of the city on Oct. 2, 1722.

In politics Logan represented the Proprietary party, made up mostly of wealthy Philadelphia Quakers and supporters of the Penn family, all with strong aristocratic interests. Opposed to this faction was the democratic party led by David Lloyd [*q.v.*], speaker of the Assembly, a member of the Society of Friends, but opposed to the increase or even to the maintenance of the proprietary authority. Lloyd's support came from the country Friends and from the people of small means. It was inevitable that Logan and Lloyd should come into conflict. Technical charges of usurpation of authority were lodged against the Secretary. These were drawn up as articles and first presented to the Council in February 1706/7, but were defeated by adjournment. When they were revived in September 1709 Logan carried the case to England, and upon his return in March 1711/12, completely vindicated, all impeachment proceedings were dropped.

Logan's judicial career began with his appointment, Aug. 25, 1726, by Governor Gordon, as one of the justices of Philadelphia County. On Sept. 2, 1727, he was re-commissioned and made a judge of the court of common pleas, and on Aug. 25, 1731, he was appointed chief justice of the supreme court, to succeed his old enemy David Lloyd, who had recently died. This post he held until Aug. 9, 1739. His *Charge Delivered from the Bench to the Grand Inquest . . . 1736* (Philadelphia, 1736; London, 1737) dealt with the duties of man in society, a subject upon which he began a treatise which was apparently never completed.

Apart from his official duties, he made a fortune in land investment and in trade with the Indians. He was a voracious reader and collected a library of over three thousand books which he left to the city of Philadelphia. He corresponded with many of the eminent men of his time. On Dec. 9, 1714, he married, at the Friends' Meeting House in Philadelphia, Sarah Read, the daughter of Charles Read, a prominent merchant. By this marriage he had five children. James, his eldest son, became the first librarian of the Loganian Library, which was formed into the Library Company of Philadelphia in 1792. Logan was also at one time a suitor for the hand of the beautiful Anne Shippen, who eventually married Thomas Story.

Logan established a family seat at "Stenton," an estate of 500 acres near Germantown, where he is recorded as living in "princely style" and keeping open house. He was always successful in his relations with the Indians, and the accounts of the ceremonial visits of delegations of Indians to "Stenton," and of the hospitality they enjoyed there give a pleasant picture of a phase of pioneer America which disappeared all too quickly. After his retirement from the Council in 1747, he spent most of his time at his estate, and devoted himself to study. Natural science was his absorbing interest and botany his special field. He was a friend of John Bartram [*q.v.*] and a correspondent of Peter Collinson, and his botanical investigations received recognition from Linnæus, who named the *Loganiaceae* for him, an order with thirty genera and over three hundred species. His most important scientific work was a series of "Experiments Concerning the Impregnation of the Seeds of Plants," the results of which he reported to his friend Peter Collinson in London and to the Royal Society (1736; see Charles Hutton and others, *Philosophical Transactions . . . Abridged,* 1809, VII, 669). His conclusions he later published in a Latin treatise, *Experimenta et Meletemata de Plantarum Generatione* (Leyden, 1739). Translated into English by Dr. John Fothergill, the celebrated Quaker physician, it was published in London in 1747. Other papers contributed by Logan to the Royal Society of London include "An Account of Mr. T. Godfrey's Improvement of Davis' Quadrant" (*Philosophical Transactions, Abridged,* VII, 669); "Some Thoughts on the Sun and Moon, When Near the Horizon Appearing Larger than When Near the Zenith" (*Ibid.,* VIII, 112); "Concerning the Crooked or Angular Appearance of the Streaks or Darts of Lightning in Thunderstorms" (*Ibid.,* VIII, 68). He also published two translations: *Cato's Moral Distiches, Englished in Couplets* (1735), and *M. T. Cicero's Cato Major; or His Discourse of Old Age* (1744), the latter said by Charles Evans (*American Bibliography,* II, 1904, p. 258) to be generally considered the best specimen of printing from Franklin's press.

Portraits of Logan reveal a man of aristocratic bearing and commanding presence. He has been described as "scholarly and genial among his friends, but harsh and unfair in his judgment of his enemies" (R. M. Jones, *The Quakers in the American Colonies,* 1911, p. 483). In his politics, his manner of life, and his tastes, he represented the artistocracy of the intellect, the antithesis of the democracy that was soon to be dominant.

[Logan Papers (45 vols.), Logan Letter Books (7 vols.), Deborah Logan's Selections (5 vols.), all in Hist. Soc. of Pa.; "Correspondence between William Penn and James Logan," ed. by Edward Armstrong, in *Memoirs of the Hist. Soc. of Pa.,* vols. IX, X (1870–72); Norman Penney, *The Correspondence of James Logan and Thomas Story* (copr. 1927); A. C. Myers, *Immigration of the Irish Quakers into Pa., 1682–1750* (1902), containing, pp. 238–40, an autobiog. sketch of Logan; Wilson Armistead, *Memoirs of James Logan* (1851); Irma Jane Cooper, *The Life and Public Services of James Logan* (1921); Isaac Sharpless, *Political Leaders of Provincial Pa.* (1919); Wm. Darlington, *Memorials of John Bartram and Humphry Marshall* (1849); J. W. Harshberger, *The Botanists of Phila.* (1899); R. H. Fox, *Dr. John Fothergill and His Friends* (1919); J. F. Watson, *Annals of Phila.* (2 vols., 1830), enlarged, etc., by W. P. Hazard (3 vols., 1898); J. W. Jordan, *Colonial Families of Phila.* (1911), vol. I.]

M. P. S.

LOGAN, JAMES (*c.* 1725–1780), a Mingo leader and orator, sometimes called John Logan, the son of Shikellamy [*q.v.*], was probably born at Shamokin, now Sunbury, Pa. He was named Tahgahjute, but rather early in life he began to be called Logan, probably in honor of the secretary of Pennsylvania, James Logan [*q.v.*]. His elder brother, John Shikellamy, or Taghneghdoarus, after their father's death, became sachem of the Iroquois and their agent at Shamokin, while James Logan, "the lame Son of Shick Calamys" (*Minutes of the Provincial Council, post,* VI, p. 35), continued to maintain a close and serviceable association with the Pennsylvania authorities. Probably it was this James Logan who became conspicuous in the Ohio country in the decade between 1770 and 1780, though in the accounts of him dating from that period there occurs no reference to his lameness, and in a document of the time, not now extant in its original form, his name seems to have been signed for him as "Capt. John Logan."

Though he does not appear in contemporary records as chief or sachem, he occupied a position of prominence among the Mingo bands on the Ohio and Scioto rivers, and, after the Yellow Creek massacre of April 1774 in which certain members of his family were slaughtered, he was the leader of small detachments engaged in retaliatory forays against the settlements. Though far from being the cause of Dunmore's War, as sometimes asserted, this cruel massacre certainly provided the occasion for its outbreak. It was also the incident that changed to hatred Logan's friendship for the colonists and set him upon the path of vengeance. He was more successful in his campaign than were Cornstalk [*q.v.*] and his warriors, and when, in November 1774 after the battle of Point Pleasant, the defeated Indians gathered at Chillicothe to make a treaty, Logan refused to become reconciled even though he was said to have taken already some thirty scalps in his private quarrel. His reply to John Gibson [*q.v.*], who had been sent by Dunmore to obtain his presence at the making of the treaty, was that "morsel of eloquence" which was read at the conference, was copied in many colonial newspapers and was later made famous through Jefferson's use of it in his *Notes, on the State of Virginia* (especially the edition of 1800, Appendix 4). The exactness with which his speech was repeated at the conference must always be open to question, and, in spite of the credence given the charge by Jefferson, the truth of his accusation that Michael Cresap [*q.v.*] was the leader of the Yellow Creek massacre has been successfully challenged by later historians.

During the Revolution, Logan employed himself successfully in bringing in scalps and prisoners to the British at Detroit. As time went on, be became increasingly the ferocious and drunken savage, in pitiable contrast to the intelligent, capable, and friendly Indian of his earlier days. The testimony as to the manner of his death is conflicting, but it seems clear that he was killed by a nephew or cousin, probably in retaliation for a deed committed by him in a drunken rage.

[Brantz Mayer, *Tah-gah-jute; or Logan and Cresap* (1867); F. B. Sawvel, *Logan the Mingo* (copr. 1921), with some confusion of the deeds of Logan and his brother John Shikellamy; J. J. Jacob, *A Biog. Sketch of the Life of the Late Capt. Michael Cresap* (1826); Samuel Kercheval, *A Hist. of the Valley of Va.*, 4th ed. (1925); *Minutes of the Provincial Council of Pa.*, vol. VI (1851) pp. 35, 119, 216, vol. VII (1851), pp. 47, 51–52; *Pa. Archives*, ser. 1, vol. II (1853), pp. 23–24, 33–37, vol. IV (1853), p. 525.] L. C. W.

LOGAN, JAMES HARVEY (Dec. 8, 1841–July 16, 1928), jurist, horticulturist, was the son of Samuel McCampbell and Mary Elizabeth (McMurty) Logan, both of Scotch ancestry and both natives of Kentucky. He was born near Rockville, Ind., the seventh of eight children. After graduating from Waveland Collegiate Institute in 1860 he taught school for a year at Independence, Mo., then started West as driver of an ox team for the Overland Telegraph Company. By the fall of 1861 he had made his way to California, where for a year he lived with his uncle, a physician, at Los Gatos. In December 1863 he commenced to read law at San Jose, in the office of C. T. Ryland, and in 1865 was admitted to the bar. Three years later he moved to Santa Cruz, where he became deputy district-attorney almost immediately, served from 1870 to 1880 as district attorney, and for the next twelve years was a judge of the superior court in Santa Cruz County. In 1892 he retired from office because of failing health.

Although he was comfortably successful in his profession, it was through his avocation that Logan attained his special distinction. In 1880 he started an experimental fruit and vegetable garden at his home in Santa Cruz. He was interested in producing a cross between the Texas Early blackberry and the wild California blackberry (*Rubus Vitifolius*) and planted a row of the wild berry bushes between a row of the Texas Early and one of Red Antwerp raspberries. By 1881 he had secured several hundred seedlings of the blackberry. When the fruit came, he found he had made a successful cross between the blackberries, producing a new variety which he named the Mammoth. Furthermore, he discovered one plant which resembled a raspberry more than a blackberry, and when the fruit ripened he found that it had a flavor and character all its own. This fruit, since known as the loganberry, he described as a true hybrid, believing it a cross between the Red Antwerp raspberry and the wild blackberry. He gave it to Professor Wickson of the University of California for free distribution. It is now extensively cultivated (by propagating cuttings) from British Columbia to California, and forms the basis of a substantial industry in canning and preparing fruit juice for the market. In 1916 evidence was reported tending to disprove the belief that the loganberry is a hybrid and to show that it is a true species (*Journal of Heredity,* November 1916), but in 1923 Judge Logan delivered an address reasserting his conviction that it is a hybrid (*Seventeenth Biennial Report of the Board of Horticulture of the State of Oregon,* 1923). He died at his home in Oakland, Cal., survived by his second wife, Mary Elizabeth Couson, whom he married Aug. 1, 1910, and by their daughter.

[Autobiographical material in R. D. Hunt, *California and Californians* (1926), V, 141ff.; *New Internat. Year Book,* 1928; *Literary Digest,* Nov. 25, 1916; *Country Life in America,* Sept. 1916; *San Francisco Chronicle,* July 17, 1928.] M. P. S.

LOGAN, JOHN ALEXANDER (Feb. 9, 1826–Dec. 26, 1886), Union soldier, United States senator, was born on a farm in Jackson County, Ill. His father, Dr. John Logan, was of Scotch descent, an immigrant from the north of Ireland who settled first in Maryland, then in Missouri, and finally in Jackson County, Ill., near the present Murphysboro. His second wife, Elizabeth Jenkins, also of Scotch ancestry, was the mother of his eleven children. John, the eldest, received a broken education which included some study of law. After service as a lieutenant in the Mexican War, he continued his legal studies under his uncle, Lieut.-Gov. Alexander M. Jenkins, began practice, served in local offices and in the Illinois legislature, and married, on Nov. 27, 1855, Mary Simmerson Cunningham, the daughter of a comrade in the war. In 1858 he was elected to Congress from the eleventh Illinois district, as an anti-Lecompton Democrat.

Logan's spread-eagle oratory and contentious spirit, together with the abundant black hair that suggested Indian ancestry, made him a noticeable spokesman of the "Egyptian" counties constituting his district. He was sent to the Charleston convention of 1860 as a Douglas supporter, and was again elected to Congress that autumn. At intervals for the rest of his life he was forced to repel the calumny of having been at heart a Southern sympathizer; but he was able to bring to his vindication the testimony of Lucius Q. C. Lamar and the words of his numerous Union speeches in Congress (*Congressional Record,* 49 Cong., Special Session of the Senate, pp. 132, 330, Mar. 30, Apr. 19, 1881). When his Democratic associates from the South went home in the winter of 1861, he repeatedly avowed his determination to stand by the Union. In the spring he seized a musket and marched with a Michigan regiment to the battle of Bull Run; and when the special war session came to an end he hurried back to "Egypt" and raised the 31st Illinois Regiment, of which he was at once made colonel.

His military career was distinguished. He took his regiment into early action, had a horse shot under him at Belmont, was twice wounded, was made a brigadier-general after Fort Donelson, and a major-general after Vicksburg. In the fighting around Atlanta he commanded the XV Corps of the Army of the Tennessee; and upon the death of McPherson, July 22, 1864, he took command of that army. It was a matter of deep chagrin to him, and to his Illinois supporters, that, upon the recommendation of Sherman, Lincoln relieved him of this command. Logan believed that the discrimination against him was due to the West Point prejudice against a volunteer; but the fact was that Sherman mistrusted Logan's active political interests, which often took him from the field, and furthermore, as he later explained, although he considered Logan "perfect in combat," the latter "entertained and expressed a species of contempt" for the laborious preparations in logistics that a commander, to be successful, must carry on (*Report of the Proceedings of the 19th Annual Meeting, Society of the Army of the Tennessee,* 1887, p. 57).

Logan declined a permanent commission in the regular army and was discharged in 1865. He helped organize the Society of the Army of the Tennessee and the Grand Army of the Republic, of which he was three times president (*Proceedings of the First to Tenth Meetings . . . of the National Encampment, Grand Army of the Republic,* 1877, pp. 23, 29, 74); and he went back to Congress as a Republican, elected in 1866 as representative-at-large from Illinois. The Democratic counties of his old district now gave him a substantial majority as a Republican. He was reëlected in 1868 and 1870, and in 1871 was chosen senator from Illinois. He lost this seat in 1877, because of a coalition of Democrats and independents that gave it to David Davis [*q.v.*]; but he obtained the other seat by ousting R. J. Oglesby in 1879; and was chosen for a third term after a prolonged deadlock in 1885 (D. W. Lusk, *History of the Contest for U. S. Senator before the 34th General Assembly of Illinois,* 1885).

In the Senate Logan was a stalwart Republican who associated himself with all matters of veteran relief. His dislike for West Point and its graduates was never far beneath the surface. He clung to his job, for he had no other means of support; and when his defeat in 1877 threw him into poverty his wife was bitter because President Hayes did not provide him with an appointment (*Reminiscences of a Soldier's Wife,* p. 360). He was naturally a worker for the nomination of Grant in 1880, making every effort to establish the right of the Illinois convention to name the district delegates and to bind them to the unit rule; but he accepted Garfield and organized the western canvass. In 1884 he had some local support for the presidency, but was obliged to take the second place on the Republican ticket. He fought a vigorous campaign, knowing it to be a losing one, and in the outcome derived his mortification less from Cleveland's victory than from that of Hendricks, whom he believed to have been disloyal. The last months of his life were devoted to the compilation of his war book, *The Great Conspiracy: Its Origin and History* (1886), which is unimportant save as an expression of his views, and to the preparation of a ponderous manuscript published after his death under the title: *The Volunteer Soldier of America, With Memoir of the Author and Military Reminiscences from General Logan's Private Journal* (1887).

Logan was described as "clearly the most eminent and distinguished of the volunteer soldiers" of the Civil War (*Diary and Letters of Rutherford Birchard Hayes,* vol. IV, 1925, p. 302). He had conceived the idea of Memorial Day and inaugurated it on May 30, 1868; his last public utterance was a plea for every disabled "Union soldier who served in the army and has an honorable discharge" and for "Every Union soldier over sixty-two years old" (*Chicago Tribune,* Nov. 20, 1886). He died in Washington, D. C., survived by two children, and by his wife, whose intelligence and charm had always been valuable assets in his campaigns.

[G. F. Dawson, *Life and Services of Gen. John A. Logan as Soldier and Statesman* (1887), a revamped campaign biography, provided the basis for most of the material of the elaborate obituary in the *Chicago Tribune*, Dec. 27, 1886. Mary S. C. Logan, *Reminiscences of a Soldier's Wife; an Autobiog.* (1913), is affectionate and personal. Memorial addresses in Congress were printed as *Sen. Misc. Doc. No. 93*, 49 Cong., 2 Sess. See also: *Hist. of Jackson County, Ill.* (1878); *War of the Rebellion: Official Records (Army)*; *Memoirs of Gen. Wm. T. Sherman* (2 vols., 1875); J. G. Blaine, *Twenty Years of Cong.* (2 vols., 1884–86); *Personal Memoirs of U. S. Grant* (2 vols., 1885–86); *Autobiog. of Oliver Otis Howard* (2 vols., 1907).] F. L. P.

LOGAN, OLIVE (Apr. 22, 1839–Apr. 27, 1909), actress, journalist, lecturer, author, was the daughter of Cornelius Ambrosius [*q.v.*] and Eliza (Akeley) Logan. Cornelius Ambrose Logan [*q.v.*] was her brother. She was born in Elmira, N. Y., and when a little child was taken by her parents to Cincinnati, where she attended school. As the daughter of an actor, dramatist, and manager, she became interested in the stage at an early age, making her début in Philadelphia at the Arch Street Theatre, Aug. 19, 1854, under the management of John Drew and William Wheatley, as Mrs. Bobtail in *Bobtail and Wagtail.* Her stage appearances, however, were confined wholly to her younger years; the greater part of her professional life was actively spent in the writing of plays, books, newspaper articles, and in lecturing on woman's rights and other social and political subjects. She appears to have attempted the acting of a male character when she was less than eighteen years of age, for Joseph Norton Ireland (*post,* p. 653) notes that she appeared at the Broadway Theatre, Feb. 21, 1857, as one of the two Antipholi in *A Comedy of Errors,* with the brothers Placide as the two Dromios. She was also, according to the same authority, at the new Broadway Theatre in 1865, being described as a "valuable coadjutress" of Mr. Chanfrau in *Sam.* T. Allston Brown says that after having spent several years in France and England, she reappeared at Wallack's Theatre, New York, in 1864 in a play of her own composition called *Eveleen,* and that then, after a starring tour in the West and South she "reappeared in the New York boards at the Broadway Theatre under the management of her brother in law, George Wood, in November, 1865, in the play called 'Sam,' and for nearly one hundred consecutive nights played the same role to large and admiring audiences" (*post,* pp. 222 and 225).

By 1868 she had retired as an actress. Her record as a writer of plays comprises also *Surf, or Summer Scenes at Long Branch,* a comedy in five acts travestying fashionable life at a seaside resort, produced by Augustin Daly at his Fifth Avenue Theatre, New York, Jan. 12, 1870; *Newport,* produced at Daly's Theatre, New York, Sept. 17, 1879; and a dramatization of Wilkie Collins' novel, *Armadale.* Among her books are *Photographs of Paris Life* (1862), written under the pen name of "Chroniqueuse"; *Apropos of Women and Theatres* (1869); *Before the Footlights and Behind the Scenes* (1870); *The Mimic World* (1871); and *They Met by Chance* (1873), a society novel. None of them is of more than temporary interest. She was a woman of alert mind, a forceful personality, but she was erratic and had little ability to turn her talents in the direction of permanent success in the theatre, in literature, or in any profession. She was married three times: in 1857 to Henry A. De Lille (or Delille), from whom she was divorced in 1865; about 1872 to William Wirt Sikes [*q.v.*], a member of the American consular service at Cardiff, Wales, who died in 1883; and third to James O'Neill (not the famous actor of that name), who was some twenty years her junior. She and her last husband were known as Mr. and Mrs. James O'Neill Logan. Her last years were spent in poverty and were clouded by insanity, and she died in Banstead, England, while an inmate of an asylum.

[See J. N. Ireland, *Records of the N. Y. Stage,* vol. II (1867); T. Allston Brown, *Hist. of the Am. Stage* (1870); E. A. Dithmar, *Memories of Daly's Theatres* (1897); Wm. Winter, *The Wallet of Time* (1913), vol. I; J. F. Daly, *The Life of Augustin Daly* (1917); the *Sun* (N. Y.), Apr. 11, 1906, Feb. 26, Apr. 29, 1909; *Telegram* (N. Y.), and *N. Y. Tribune,* Apr. 11, 1906; *Chicago Chronicle,* Apr. 15, 1906. The date of birth is taken from *Who's Who in America,* 1899–1900.] E. F. E.

LOGAN, STEPHEN TRIGG (Feb. 24, 1800–July 17, 1880), jurist, law partner of Lincoln, son of David and Mary (Trigg) Logan, was born in Franklin County, Ky., of Scotch-Irish and English ancestry. Much of the history of pioneer Kentucky may be read in the chronicles of his family. His grandfather, Col. John Logan, represented a Kentucky county in the legislature of Virginia and served in the Kentucky constitutional convention of 1799; his great-uncle, Gen. Benjamin Logan [*q.v.*], established a fort in Lincoln County in 1776 and took prominent part in the Indian wars of the Boone period. Stephen Trigg, his maternal grandfather, moved from Virginia to Kentucky in 1779 and was killed in 1782 in the battle of Blue Licks. The first thirty-two years of Logan's life were spent in Kentucky. He was educated at Frankfort, admitted to the bar before attaining his majority, served as deputy in the circuit clerk's office of Barren County, held the office of commonwealth's attorney of the Glasgow circuit, and practised law in Barren and adjoining counties until 1832. He then moved to Illinois, lived for a time on a farm in Sangamon County, gave up agriculture for the law, and made his home in Springfield. He soon became one of the foremost lawyers of the state. Elected in 1835 by the legislature as judge of the first judicial circuit of Illinois, he held this office until 1837, when he resigned to resume his law practice. He served in the state legislature for four terms (1842–48, 1854–56), and he was a prominent member of the Illinois constitutional convention of 1847, where he urged strict economy and opposed debt repudiation. Indorsing the obligations of a friend, he had become insolvent; but through personal thrift he paid all of his vicarious debt.

In 1841 he formed a partnership with Abraham Lincoln and for a time these two men, together with E. D. Baker, formed a group known as the "Springfield junto," their word being locally decisive as to the nomination of candidates in Whig conventions (A. J. Beveridge, *Abraham Lincoln,* 1928, I, p. 302). Lincoln owed much to his senior partner, for it was during the period of this partnership that Lincoln's serious practice of the law began. After the dissolution of the partnership late in 1844—a dissolution which has sometimes been attributed to political rivalry between the partners, though the evidence on this matter is insufficient—the two men remained warm friends. In 1848 Logan was the Whig candidate to succeed Lincoln in Congress; but, suffering from the unpopularity of Lincoln's attitude toward the Mexican War, he was defeated. In 1860 he served as a member of the Republican convention which nominated Lincoln, and in February 1861 he was one of the representatives of Illinois in the Peace Convention which assembled in Washington at the call of Virginia to avert the Civil War. In this convention he delivered a notable speech, striving hard to effect a compromise which might reunite the North and South. From this time, having acquired considerable means, he lived in comfortable retirement. He died in his Springfield home, July 17, 1880.

On June 25, 1823, Logan was married to America T. Bush of Glasgow, Ky. There were four sons and four daughters, of whom David (1824–1874) became prominent in Oregon politics, Mary (1831–1874) married Milton Hay of Springfield, and Sally (1834–1892) became the second wife of Ward Hill Lamon [*q.v.*]. Logan was small, thin and wiry, with an intellectual face surmounted by thick, reddish curling hair. "Though of ample means," says a contemporary (*Memoirs of Gustave Koerner,* 1909, I, pp. 478–79), "occupying a very fine residence surrounded by a large and beautiful park, his clothes were shabby. . . . I never saw him wear a necktie. He wore an old fur cap in winter and a fifty-cent straw hat in summer, baggy trousers, and a coat to match. Thick, coarse, brogan shoes covered his feet." It has been said that Lincoln once sought Logan's appointment as federal judge, at that time regarding him "as the most thorough and accomplished lawyer he had ever known" (*Memorials, post,* p. 61).

[See *Memorials of the Life and Character of Stephen T. Logan* (1882); *Encyc. of Biog. of Ill.,* vol. I (1892); *Chicago Legal News,* July 24, 1880; J. M. Palmer, *The Bench and Bar of Ill.* (1899), vol. I; J. G. Nicolay and John Hay, *Abraham Lincoln* (10 vols., 1890); A. J. Beveridge, *Abraham Lincoln* (2 vols., 1928); P. M. Angle, ed., *Herndon's Life of Lincoln* (1930) and *New Letters and Papers of Lincoln* (1930). As stated by Beveridge on the authority of Logan Hay (*op. cit.,* I, p. 446, note), Logan destroyed all the letters he had received from Lincoln.]

J. G. R.

LOGAN, THOMAS MULDRUP (July 31, 1808–Feb. 13, 1876), sanitarian and climatologist, was born in Charleston, S. C., son of Dr. George Logan, a navy surgeon, and Margaret White (Polk), a native of Delaware. The Logans, according to family tradition, were descended from Col. George Logan, scion of a Scottish noble family, who came from Aberdeen to Charleston in 1690. Thomas attended Charleston College and subsequently began the study of medicine with his father. He was graduated from the Medical College of South Carolina in 1828, commenced practice in Charleston, and after a year of study in London and Paris (1832–33), was appointed lecturer on materia medica and therapeutics in the Charleston school. While here he collaborated with Dr. Thomas L. Ogier in the preparation of two volumes of a *Compendium of Operative Surgery* which appeared in 1834 and 1836. He moved in 1843 to New Orleans, where he joined the medical staff of the Charity Hospital, transferring to the staff of the Luzenberg Hospital in 1847. Moving to California in 1850, he took up his residence in Sacramento, where he spent the remainder of his career.

For the next quarter century his name was identified with every movement for the physical, mental, and moral improvement of the community in which he had settled. He interested himself in climatic and hygienic conditions and during his first three years in the new state he contributed a series of articles on these subjects to Southern medical journals. He was an observer at Sacramento for the Smithsonian Institution for a number of years. To the *Annual Report* of the Institution for 1854 and 1855 he furnished articles upon climatology and meteorology of the Pacific coast region. Among his other writings worthy of note are the "History of Medicine in California" (*California State Medical Journal,* 1858); "Report on the Medical Topography, Meteorology, Endemics and Epidemics of California" (*Transactions of the Third Session of the Medical Society of the State of California,* 1858); "Report on the Medical Topography and Epidemics of California" (*Transactions of the American Medical Association,* vol. XII, 1859); "Mushrooms and Their Poisonings" (*Pacific Medical and Surgical Journal,* April 1868); and "Mortality in California" (*Transactions of the Medical Society of the State of California,* 1870–71). He was elected president of the State Medical Society in 1870, and in 1872, at its Philadelphia meeting, was chosen president of the American Medical Association. At the St. Louis meeting in the following year his presidential address was a scholarly paper on medical education and state medicine. When in 1870 the California State Board of Health was authorized, Logan became its permanent secretary. In this capacity he was especially interested in the improvement of school hygiene. His studies of the epidemiology of the state are particularly complete. He was an active advocate of a national board of health and he prepared a bill which was introduced into Congress with that end in view, but was not acted upon (*Second Biennial Report of the State Board of Health of California,* 1873). Though he is most widely remembered for his public health work, Logan was a competent practitioner and had a devoted following in his home city. He spent the summer of 1867 visiting the medical centers of England, France, and Germany. He was president of the Agassiz Institute of Sacramento and meteorologist of the State Agricultural Society of California. He was an honorary member of the Imperial Botanical and Zoological Society of Vienna. He died in Sacramento of pneumonia.

Logan married Susan, daughter of Judge John S. Richardson of Charleston, S. C. She died in 1864, and in the following year he married Mary A. Greely of Hudson, N. H. A son of his first marriage became a physician practising in Alabama; Gen. T. M. Logan [*q.v.*] was a nephew.

[*Charleston Medic. Jour. and Rev.,* Apr. 1876; *Western Lancet* (San Francisco), Feb. 1876; *Trans. of the Medic. Soc. of the State of Cal.,* 2 ser., VI (1876); J. M. Toner, in *Trans. Am. Medic. Asso.,* vol. XXIX (1878); H. A. Kelly and W. L. Burrage, *Am. Medic. Biogs.* (1920); G. W. Logan, *A Record of the Logan Family of Charleston, S. C.* (1874; new ed., enl., by L. L. Morrill, 1923); *Sacramento Union,* Feb. 14, 1876.]

J. M. P—n.

LOGAN, THOMAS MULDRUP (Nov. 3, 1840–Aug. 11, 1914), Confederate general and capitalist, was born in Charleston, S. C., the tenth child of Judge George William and Anna D'Oyley (Glover) Logan and a nephew of Dr. Thomas Muldrup Logan [*q.v.*]. He was graduated from the South Carolina College in 1860, first in his class. The following year he served as a volunteer at Fort Sumter and then, aiding in the organization of Company A, Hampton Legion, was elected first lieutenant. After First Manassas (Bull Run) he was promoted captain. In spite of a wound received at Gaines's Mill in June 1862, he commanded his company at Second Manassas the following August. For "great bravery" at Sharpsburg (Antietam) in September, he was officially cited and promoted major. He then served in the campaigns of Micah Jenkins' brigade, particularly distinguishing himself in reconnaissance duty. In 1864, he was severely wounded. His daring leadership was rewarded by further promotions which in February 1865 culminated in his appointment as brigadier-general, the youngest then in the army. This promotion had been indorsed by Lee (Logan and Morrill, *post,* p. 55) as "the best appointment that can be made for this brigade" (M. C. Butler's). Transferred to Johnston's army, Logan led its last charge of the war, at Bentonville, N. C., in March 1865. When Johnston went to Sherman to surrender, Logan, "a slight, fair-haired boy," accompanied him; his youthful appearance made it difficult for Sherman to believe that he commanded a brigade.

A month after the surrender, Logan borrowed five dollars from a friend and on May 25, 1865, married Kate Virginia Cox, daughter of Judge James H. Cox of Chesterfield County, Va. He successfully managed a local coal mine and its railroad for a few years, and then practised law in and near Richmond. Shortly before 1878 he started upon his career of railroad organization by beginning to purchase the stock of the Richmond & Danville Railroad. In this venture he saw profit for himself after long waiting, but he was more concerned with the development of a great railroad, which would aid the growth of Richmond. In 1878 he organized a Richmond syndicate to buy the pool of the Richmond & Danville controlled by the Pennsylvania Railroad. This syndicate quietly purchased at a low price the Pennsylvania pool, and, securing a broad charter for a new corporation, the Richmond & West Point Terminal Company, built the Georgia Pacific from Birmingham to the Mississippi and bought several other Southern railroads. In less than two years the Terminal Company increased its trackage from 300 to over 2,000 miles. When Richmond & Danville and Terminal stocks were succumbing to a bear attack in Wall Street, Logan threw in $1,500,000 of his own money to protect them. About two years later he was aided by John D. Rockefeller in purchasing and disposing of the controlling share of these stocks, and made a profit of approximately $1,500,000. In 1894, the railway system which he had organized was given its present name, the Southern Railway.

About 1890 Logan bought control of the Seattle, Lake Shore & Eastern Railroad, which he soon sold at a large profit to the Northern Pacific. From about 1888 until his death, as president of the Gray National Telautograph Company, he worked despite great discouragement to adapt a new invention, the telautograph, to the market. He spent a fortune in the development of the machine; but only after his death did it prove its great usefulness. Logan was chairman of the Virginia Democratic Executive Committee in 1879 and of the Virginia Gold Democrat Party in 1896. He was an old-fashioned Southern host, a lover of good literature, an influential speaker and writer. A skilful though daring promoter, he carried into business the same capacity he showed on the battlefield. Although he probably lost several fortunes, after each disaster he returned to his enterprises with renewed courage. He died in New York City.

[Information obtained from W. P. de Saussure and other Richmond business associates of Logan; G. W. Logan and Lily Logan Morrill, *A Record of the Logan Family of Charleston, S. C.* (1923); *Richmond News-Leader,* Jan. 11, 1929; *War of the Rebellion, Official Records (Army)*; *Confed. Mil. Hist.* (1899), vol. V; *Who's Who in America,* 1914–15; M. J. Verdery, in *News and Courier* (Charleston), May 10, 1899; *Times-Dispatch* (Richmond) and *N. Y. Times,* Aug. 12, 1914.]

R. D. M.

LOGUEN, JERMAIN WESLEY (*c.* 1813–Sept. 30, 1872), bishop of the African Methodist Episcopal Zion Church, was born near Manscoe's Creek in Davidson County, Tenn., the natural son of a white resident, David Logue, and a slave mother, Cherry, who had been kidnapped in Ohio. The story of the experiences of Cherry and her family forms one of the blackest pictures of the slavery system. Growing up without schooling, with many hardships and few glimpses of the sunnier aspects of life, Jermain long planned to break away from slavery, but determined never to buy his freedom. Although his first attempt at escape failed, the sale of his sister aroused anew his resolution. The account of his flight through Kentucky and southern Indiana (*c.* 1834–35), antecedent to the organization of the Underground Railroad, shows that the preliminary surveys for that system had been made and that a few lines already ran through the homes of Quakers as unerringly as railroads run through the large towns and cities. Jermain crossed from Detroit to Canada, making his way to Hamilton, Ont., in search of work. Writing to Frederick Douglass in May 1856 (see *The Rev. J. W. Loguen,* p. 339), he refers to this episode as "twenty-one years ago—the very winter I left my chains in Tennessee" and to himself as "a boy twenty-one years of age (as near as I know my age)." This statement furnishes the best available guide to the chronology of his early life.

In Canada, he learned to read, while by hard farm labor and thrift, in the face of great discouragement, he made a start towards competency. After two years as porter in a hotel at Rochester, N. Y., he was able to study at Oneida Institute, Whitesboro, where he received the only schooling he had. He then opened a school for colored children in Utica, and later one in Syracuse. At Busti, N. Y., in November 1840 he married Caroline Storum, a woman with some negro blood. Settling in Syracuse shortly afterward, he became one of the local managers of the Underground Railroad. He subsequently became an elder in the African Methodist Episcopal Zion Church, with successive pastorates (1843–50) in Bath, Ithaca, Syracuse, and Troy. He was presiding elder of the last-named district. He had begun to call himself Loguen, and through the persuasion of his Methodist friends he adopted Wesley as his middle name.

As a speaker against slavery he aroused much interest. Citizens of Cortland, N. Y., raised a fund to purchase his mother, but her master, Manasseth Logue, a brother of David, refused to sell her unless Jermain would buy his freedom also. His liberty imperiled by the Fugitive-slave Act of 1850, he left Troy and returned to the comparative safety of Syracuse, where his home again became an important station of the Underground Railroad. During the decade before the Civil War, he was a central figure in the activities of that organization, especially such as centered around his Peterboro neighbor, Gerrit Smith [*q.v.*]. In various ways he assisted some fifteen hundred fugitives. Indicted for participation in the "Jerry rescue" case (1851), he sought temporary refuge in Canada. Just before John Brown's raid on Harpers Ferry, Loguen went again into Ontario with John Brown, Jr., in behalf of the League of Liberty and possibly also to further plans of the elder Brown. In 1864, Loguen declined election as a bishop of his denomination, but accepted in 1868, and was assigned to the Fifth District (Alleghany and Kentucky conferences). After two years he was transferred to the Second District (Genesee, Philadelphia, and Baltimore conferences). In 1872 he was reëlected bishop and appointed to take charge of mission work on the Pacific Coast, but he died at Saratoga Springs, N. Y., before he could go to his field.

[The main source of information is *The Rev. J. W. Loguen, as a Slave and as a Freeman, a Narrative of Real Life* (t.p. 1859, but the book contains letters dated 1860); although it is written in the third person, its detailed information indicates autobiography. A manuscript note by a Syracuse genealogist in a copy at the Syracuse Pub. Lib. states that Loguen died in his sixty-third year, which would place his birth *c.* 1810. See also W. H. Siebert, *The Underground Railroad* (1898); J. W. Hood, *One Hundred Years of the African Meth. Episc. Zion Ch.* (1895); death notice in *N. Y. Tribune*, Oct. 1, 1872.] W. H. A.

LOMAX, JOHN TAYLOE (Jan. 19, 1781–Oct. 1, 1862), jurist and teacher of law, was born on his father's plantation, "Port Tobago," Caroline County, Va., the fourth of eleven children of Thomas and Anne Corbin (Tayloe) Lomax. With both Dissenter and Cavalier ancestry, a descendant of John Lomax who came from England to Jamestown, Va., about 1700, he was by birth and breeding a member of the Tidewater aristocracy. Graduating in 1797 from St. John's College, Annapolis, he studied law and began practice in Fredericksburg. In 1805 he married Charlotte Belson Thornton, a member of a prominent Northumberland County family. From about 1810 to 1818 he practised in Richmond County and during the War of 1812 served as a militia officer for the lower counties of the Northern Neck. Returning to Fredericksburg, he attained eminence at the bar. Meanwhile the University of Virginia had been established, but, largely owing to the inadequate salary, a suitable professor of law had not been secured. After receiving a number of disheartening refusals the Board of Visitors in 1826 offered the place to Lomax. He accepted and became the first professor of law in the University.

Fervent and faithful in the study of the law, he taught its principles with a high sense of moral responsibility. To him a law school was something more than a trade school in which to gain the means of livelihood. During 1827–28, under the unique Jeffersonian system, unchanged until 1904, Lomax was chairman of the faculty and, incidentally, the only native American among its members. In 1830, however, the General Assembly unanimously elected him associate judge of the circuit superior court of law and chancery, a position carrying a higher salary. Unfortunate investments had swept away the Lomax holdings during his father's later years, so for the sake of his family he regretfully resigned his professorship. He was assigned to the fifth judicial circuit, comprising his native Caroline and neighboring counties, and once more made his home in Fredericksburg, where he remained until his death. In 1848 he was appointed to a temporary court established to relieve the overburdened supreme court of appeals. In drafting the constitution of 1851, the convention set the age limit for judges at seventy; Lomax, then seventy, thus faced disqualification. On request of the bar of his circuit, however, the clause was eliminated and, judicial office becoming elective under this constitution, he returned to his post without opposition. He was the author of a *Digest of the Laws Respecting Real Property* (3 vols., 1839) and *A Treatise on the Law of Executors and Administrators* (2 vols., 1841). For many years he conducted a private law school in Fredericksburg and continued to influence legal education in Virginia. After twenty-seven years of faithful service on the bench the aged jurist resigned in 1857, despite a contrary plea from the bar. Although politically inactive, he was a student of public affairs and the gathering war clouds appalled him. When Virginia seceded, however, he followed his state. He died a few weeks before the defeat of Burnside at Fredericksburg.

Judge Lomax was stately and impressive in appearance, but with a simplicity of manner and a benevolence of face which endeared him to all. Although an Episcopalian since middle life he was too broad for strict sectarianism. A calm scholar rather than a dynamic teacher, he was a careful and analytical judge whose sense of right was instinctive.

[E. L. Lomax, *Geneal. of the Va. Family of Lomax* (1913); Joseph Lomax, *Geneal. and Hist. Sketches of the Lomax Family* (1894); P. A. Bruce, *Hist. of the Univ. of Va., 1819–1919* (1920–21), vols. II, III; L. L. Lewis (a grandson), in *Va. Law Reg.*, May 1896; E. W. P. Lomax, in *Green Bag*, Sept. 1897.] T. S. C.

LOMAX, LUNSFORD LINDSAY (Nov. 4, 1835–May 28, 1913), Confederate soldier, nephew of John Tayloe Lomax [*q.v.*], was the son of Mann Page Lomax of Virginia, major of ordnance in the United States Army, and of Elizabeth Virginia Lindsay, a descendant of Capt. William Lindsay of Light-Horse Harry Lee's cavalry in the Revolutionary army. Born at Newport, R. I., he was educated in the schools of Richmond and Norfolk, Va., and appointed to the Military Academy at West Point in 1852.

He was graduated in 1856 with his lifelong friend, Fitzhugh Lee [*q.v.*], and as second lieutenant of cavalry did frontier duty in Kansas and Nebraska. He was serving as first lieutenant when Virginia seceded, and on Apr. 25, 1861, he resigned his commission and was appointed captain in the state forces of Virginia, serving first as assistant adjutant-general on the staff of Gen. Joseph E. Johnston. Later he was transferred to the Confederate Army as inspector-general on the staff of brigadier-general McCulloch in Van Dorn's army. After McCulloch's death he served as inspector-general with the rank of lieutenant-colonel on Van Dorn's staff until October 1862, when he was made inspector-general of the army in East Tennessee. He took part in battles in Arkansas, Mississippi, Louisiana, and Tennessee, and in 1863 was called to the eastern campaign as colonel of the 11th Virginia Cavalry. He participated in the raid into West Virginia with Jones's brigade, and in the campaign culminating in the battle of Gettysburg. On July 23, 1863, he was promoted brigadier-general, and his brigade was one of the principal factors in Fitz Lee's operations from Culpeper through the Wilderness campaign and the fighting around Richmond. On Aug. 10, 1864, he was made major-general and fought in the Valley campaign of Gen. Jubal A. Early. He was captured at the battle of Woodstock by a cavalry company but overcame his captors and escaped in a few hours. On Mar. 29, 1865, he was put in entire command of the Valley District of the Army of Northern Virginia. After the fall of Richmond he removed his troops to Lynchburg and when General Lee surrendered he tried to effect a juncture with General Echols in order to continue the struggle, but he finally surrendered his division with Johnston at Greensboro.

Immediately after the close of the Civil War Lomax bought a place near Warrenton, Va., and settled down to farming. He remained here until his election in 1885 to the presidency of the Virginia Agricultural and Mechanical College (now Virginia Polytechnic Institute), at Blacksburg. In 1899 he resigned this position and moved to Washington, where he took up the compilation, begun in 1880, of the Civil War records, published by the War Department under the title, *War of the Rebellion: Official Records of the Union and Confederate Armies.* He was engaged in this task until it was completed and then (1905) was appointed one of the commissioners of the military park at Gettysburg. To this work he gave enthusiastic service until his death, which took place at Washington. He was married, Feb. 20, 1873, to Elizabeth Winter, daughter of Dr. Alban S. Payne and cousin of Gen. William H. Payne. Distinguished in manner and known for his great physical and mental vigor, he enjoyed the esteem and close friendship of leading men in both the Union and Confederate armies, and won the affection of those associated with him in his college work.

[The best sketch of Lomax is in *Forty-fifth Ann. Reunion, Asso. Grads. U. S. Mil. Acad.* (1914); family history is found in Joseph Lomax, *Geneal. and Hist. Sketches of the Lomax Family* (1894) and E. L. Lomax, *Geneal. of the Va. Family of Lomax* (1913); an interesting estimate of Lomax written to Gen. Stanley, U. S. A., by L. J. Perry, U. S. A., is in the possession of Mrs. Lomax. See also *Who's Who in America*, 1912–13; *War of the Rebellion: Official Records (Army)*; *Confed. Veteran* (Nashville), Sept. 1913; *Washington Post*, May 29, 1913. The sketch in *Confed. Mil. Hist.* (1899), vol. III, is notably inaccurate.]

J. E. W.

LONDON, JACK (Jan. 12, 1876–Nov. 22, 1916), writer, was born in San Francisco, Cal., the only child of John and Flora (Wellman) London. On both sides he came of nomadic pioneer stock. John London, of whose eleven children by a first marriage only the two youngest lived with him, was neither well-to-do nor destitute. He did many kinds of work, chiefly truck-gardening, first on one side and then the other of San Francisco Bay. Jack attended what schools were available, finally graduating from grammar school in Oakland. Before that time, financial troubles had forced John London to give up farming and to settle on the Oakland waterfront. Thereafter his poverty grew increasingly acute. Jack delivered newspapers, worked on an ice wagon, and set up pins in a bowling alley. For a year after graduation he worked in a cannery. During these years he read voraciously in the public library, chiefly books of romance, travel, and adventure.

The Oakland waterfront was a disreputable neighborhood. Jack London had a skiff which he sailed in the Estuary and on the bay and he knew the region intimately. When fourteen, he caroused with a runaway sailor and a harpooner on an opium-smuggling yacht. Already he had formed his lifelong passion for the sea, and wished to be a sailor. When fifteen, he bought the sloop *Razzle Dazzle* and turned oyster pirate. He won the title, Prince of the Oyster Pirates, chiefly by taking with him the girl called the Queen of the Oyster Pirates. For a year or so he sailed San Francisco Bay, robbing oyster beds, living a lawless, reckless life, full of danger and hard drinking. For a little while he joined the fish patrol as deputy. For a few weeks he was a hobo. Then he returned to the Oakland waterfront and spent most of his time loafing in saloons until he signed up, Jan. 12, 1893, on the *Sophie Suther-*

land, a sealer, as able-bodied seaman and boat-puller. After he had established his position on board by one fierce fight, he enjoyed the voyage, with its riotous visits to Japan before and after the seal hunt off the Siberian coast.

On his return to Oakland in the fall of 1893, he decided to settle down. He won a newspaper prize with an account of a typhoon near Japan, and did some other writing, a little of which appeared in a local paper. He worked in a jute mill, stoked a furnace; but as always rebelled against such monotonous labor. In the spring of 1894, an army of the unemployed, similar to Coxey's, appeared in Oakland. Jack London decided to join it, but arrived after it had been sent off to Sacramento. He followed and became a tramp, making his way eastward until at Council Bluffs, Iowa, he overtook Kelly's Army, only to leave it as soon as it reached Hannibal, Mo. As a hobo he roamed over the eastern part of the United States. In Niagara Falls he was arrested and sent to the Erie County penitentiary for thirty days. As soon as released, he worked his way back to Oakland, resolved to make a complete change in his manner of life.

For a year he attended high school, working as school janitor and doing odd jobs. In the high-school paper he published some of his experiences on the road. He read eagerly, being interested especially in sociology and popular science. Herbert Spencer influenced him definitely. He became a socialist and made soapbox speeches, for which he was arrested and gained some notoriety. He decided to go to college at once; after three months of unaided cramming he passed his entrance examinations, and in August 1896 entered the University of California at Berkeley. In January 1897 he left the university and took to writing, but sold none of his work. Forced to earn money, he got a job in the laundry of Belmont Academy, south of San Francisco. In the summer of 1897 he joined the gold rush to the Klondike, sailing July 25 and arriving in August at Dyea. He and his partners packed over Chilkoot Pass, made boats, and navigated rivers and lakes until on Oct. 9 they stopped for the winter on the Yukon near the Stewart River. When spring came, London was so ill with scurvy that he was forced to leave for the outside. He voyaged down the Yukon to St. Michael. Thence he worked his way as stoker to British Columbia and traveled steerage from there on. Before reaching home, he learned that his father had died.

Unable to get a job of any sort, he returned to writing and worked furiously. Early in December 1898 the *Overland Monthly* accepted a story of the Yukon, "To the Man on Trail," for five dollars. Later the editors offered to take all similar work at seven dollars and a half a story, and during 1899 London published eight stories in the magazine. Finding great difficulty in collecting the small sums due him from this and other periodicals, he was close at times to desperation. But when the *Atlantic Monthly* accepted "An Odyssey of the North" in July 1899 (published in January 1900) and Houghton Mifflin took the collected stories, *The Son of the Wolf* (published in 1900), he had arrived. During the five years 1899–1903 he averaged yearly two dozen contributions to periodicals—short stories, serials, juveniles, essays, articles, verses, newspaper hackwork. During the same years he published eight volumes, of which five—two novels and three collections of stories—dealt with the Klondike. The second of these novels, commonly thought his best book, brought him enormous and world-wide popularity: *The Call of the Wild,* a story of a dog who, taken to Alaska, reverts to type and runs with a wolf pack.

Meanwhile, with success, his private life had altered. From his high-school days until after his return from the Yukon, he had been in love with a girl whom he portrays as Ruth in *Martin Eden.* But on Apr. 7, 1900, he was married to Elizabeth Maddern. By this marriage he had two daughters, Joan and Bess, born in 1901 and 1902. Before this time he had made many acquaintances among Bohemians and socialists. In the fall of 1899 he met Anna Strunsky, and the two wrote each other long letters of intellectual discussion. In the summer of 1902 he went to London and spent several weeks in the slums of the East End, writing up his experiences in *The People of the Abyss* (1903). After a short visit to the Continent, he returned to California. Although he then wrote *The Call of the Wild* and became famous, this was a time of extreme depression and sense of futility, to which he later referred as "the long sickness." Perhaps domestic troubles were partly responsible; he separated from his wife in the summer of 1903. In January 1904 he set off for the Russo-Japanese War as war correspondent for the *San Francisco Examiner,* but he returned in June. At once he was sued for divorce. The final decree was granted Nov. 18, 1905. The next day, in Chicago, he married Charmian Kittredge. He was on a lecture tour at the time; having fulfilled his engagements and made a visit to the Caribbean, he established his home at Glen Ellen, Sonoma County, Cal., where he lived until his death.

In April 1907, he and Mrs. London set forth to sail around the world in a forty-five-foot yacht, the *Snark*. After visiting Honolulu, they cruised among the islands of the southern Pacific. Every one on board was extremely ill, with fever and other maladies. Jack London himself was stricken with a severe disease which he called "Biblical leprosy" and which he attributed to the tropic sunlight. Upon reaching Australia he was sick for six months. He abandoned the voyage and returned to California by way of Ecuador, getting home in July 1909. Thenceforth his chief interest was his ranch. He planned, and in part achieved, a magnificent patriarchal estate. The burning in August 1913 of his huge stone house, still unfinished, was a great blow to him. During his last years he took great pleasure in driving a coach with four horses, and in sailing his yawl, the *Roamer,* on inland bays and rivers. In 1912, returning from New York, he took passage round the Horn in a sailing vessel. In 1914 he went to Vera Cruz, Mexico, as war-correspondent. Toward the end of his life he made several pleasure trips to Honolulu. These years were clouded by a growing depression and lassitude. He was constantly ill with uremia and was warned to alter his diet and habits. He did not care enough for life, however, to follow this advice. On the morning of Nov. 22, 1916, he was found unconscious and died that evening.

In sixteen years Jack London published forty-three volumes and by 1933 seven more had been issued posthumously. Besides fiction, he produced volumes of socialistic and miscellaneous essays. Several of his books are directly autobiographical: *John Barleycorn* (1913) tells the story of his life with special reference to alcohol; *The Road* (1907) relates his experiences as a tramp; *The Cruise of the Snark* (1911) has to do with his voyage across the Pacific. *Martin Eden* (1909) is a semi-autobiographical novel dealing with the time when he was beginning to write. The rest of his fiction for the most part is mined direct from first-hand experience. Most important are the dozen or so volumes of short stories and novels laid in the Far North. Of less consequence are those laid in the South Seas. Among his sea stories the chief is *The Sea Wolf* (1904), for which he drew upon his adventures in the sealer, *Sophie Sutherland,* in 1893. Less intimately connected with his own life are his two novels of prize-fighting, *The Game* (1905) and *The Abysmal Brute* (1913), and his phantasies of the remote past and future.

Almost all his writing, whether it deals with the future, the past, prize-fighters, sailors, dogs, gold-seekers, Indians, tramps, or the proletariat, has to do with one motif—the primitive, and above all reversion to savagery. His insistence is constant upon the importance of brute force. Civilized beings are "mollycoddles" to be destroyed or regenerated through conflict with a savage environment. The title of one of his books, *The Strength of the Strong* (1914), announces his favorite theme. His first popularity he gained because the brutality in his stories shocked and thrilled his readers and because his highly colored and sometimes violent style excited them. He is still read as a master of swift and vivid action and adventure. In his art his chief debt is to Kipling. His European vogue he owes not only to his "Americanism" (in the tradition of Cooper, Harte, and Mark Twain) but also to his socialism. For all the prevalence of the "abysmal brute" in Jack London's writing, he himself was a man of abnormal sensitiveness both physical and emotional. His own life, it is true, was affected by his cult of the primitive, yet he must not be confounded with the tough, hardened supermen he portrays. He was generous and sympathetic; he accepted conventional duties for the most part, and supported many dependents. His extraordinarily keen feelings and intense sensibilities were his most striking traits. Everything about him, when he was at his best, from his lively blue eyes and brown curly hair to the quick play of his muscles, bespoke a man alert, ardent, and alive.

[Besides London's own works mentioned above, the principal source of information is Charmian K. London, *The Book of Jack London* (2 vols., 1921, with a bibliography), though it is vague, confused, and not wholly reliable. Some further information is contained in Rose Wilder Lane's journalistic and untrustworthy "Life and Jack London," *Sunset* (San Francisco) Oct. 1917–May 1918. For his life in the South Seas, see also Charmian K. London, *The Log of the Snark* (1915) and *Our Hawaii* (1917); and Martin E. Johnson, *Through the South Seas with Jack London* (1913). Georgia L. Bamford, *The Mystery of Jack London* (1931) was banned (see *Publishers' Weekly*, Dec. 12, 1931) because the author used copyrighted material without authorization. The *Overland Monthly* (San Francisco) contains many reminiscences and impressions of London, including those of Ninetta Eames, May 1900, and those in the London memorial number, May 1917 (see especially G. W. James, "A Study of Jack London in his Prime," pp. 361–99). For other recollections and criticism, see: H. M. Bland, article in the *Craftsman*, Feb. 1906; and C. H. Grattan, article in *Bookman*, Feb. 1929. The best critical study is by F. L. Pattee in *Sidelights on Am. Lit.* (1922), pp. 98–160. For the Russian view of London, see L. S. Friedland, article in *Dial,* Jan. 25, 1917. For the French view, see Régis Michaud, *Mystiques et Réalistes Anglo-saxons* (1918); E. Sainte-Marie Perrin, article in *Revue des Deux Mondes*, Sept. 1, 1922. For the German, see Frank Thiess, article in *Die Neue Rundschau*, Nov. 1927; Edgar Stern-Rubarth, article in *Deutsche Rundschau,* July 1927.] T. K. W.

LONDON, MEYER (Dec. 29, 1871–June 6, 1926), socialist and labor leader, was born in the Russian-Polish province of Suwalki, but in his boyhood moved with his family to Zenkov in the province of Poltava. His mother, Rebecca Berson, came from a family of learned rabbis. His father, Ephraim London, was trained in Talmudic studies, but early became a free-thinker and social radical. He emigrated to New York in 1888, and the family followed in 1891. Meyer, the eldest of five sons, gave private lessons, worked in a library, studied law at night, and was admitted to the bar in 1898. His practice never became lucrative. He would not deal with clients whom he did not respect nor refuse his services to those who were unable to pay.

In 1896 the Socialist Labor party nominated him for the New York Assembly. Opposing the leadership of Daniel DeLeon [*q.v.*], he went over in 1897 to the Social Democratic party, newly organized by Eugene V. Debs [*q.v.*] and Victor L. Berger, and through the realignments of 1899 to 1901 he became one of the founders of the Socialist Party of America. In 1914 he was elected to Congress from the Ninth (later the Twelfth) district, and in spite of Democratic-Republican fusion was reëlected in 1916 and 1920 and only narrowly defeated in 1918. A gerrymander in 1921 made further election in that district impossible. During his three terms in Congress London advocated measures against lynching, better salaries for government employees, abolition of injunctions in labor disputes, prohibition of child labor, unemployment insurance, old-age pensions, maternity allowances, and nationalization of coal mines, and opposed the Fordney tariff, restriction of immigration, the property qualification for voting in Puerto Rico, intervention in Mexico, and increases of army and navy. He urged strict neutrality in the World War, and when the crisis came he voted against the declaration of war and the conscription and espionage laws and threw himself into a fight against profiteering and for defense of civil liberties. Savagely denounced for his lack of "war patriotism" and at the same time attacked by those extremists in his own party who later became Communists, he stedfastly followed what he thought the right course.

London was as active in the trade-union field as in politics. No man did more for the development of unions in the "needle trades." He served them as legal counsel, as adviser in matters of union policy, as spokesman in negotiations with employers, and as inspiring speaker in time of strike. His influence was felt in every clothing center in North America and, though strongest among the Jewish workers, it affected the whole labor movement. He sharply criticized the nonpolitical and, as he deemed it, too conservative policy of the American Federation of Labor, yet his services were warmly acknowledged by Samuel Gompers and other Federation leaders. Besides the unions, he had much to do with the building up of the Workmen's Circle, a great mutual-benefit society with educational features.

London was wholeheartedly American, but he could not be indifferent either to his native land or to his race. In 1916 he wrote: "I deem it a duty of the Jew everywhere to remain a Jew as long as in any corner of the world the Jew is being discriminated against" (quoted by Rogoff, *post,* p. 118). It is fair to say, however, that only a sense of loyalty to those suffering under racial discrimination kept London from being in effect an assimilationist. He valued Jewish cultural tradition, but wished to see it become an element of the general culture. He strenuously combated Antisemitism and at the same time worked hard for the relief of Jewish sufferers. That he was respected by his opponents was shown by his election as chairman of the Jewish Relief Committee and by the large part he was able to play in getting the factions to work together in the Jewish Congress.

He always took a lively interest in the struggle against Tsarism and rendered invaluable services to the *Bund* and other Russian revolutionary organizations. The revolution in February 1917 filled him with hope, and he held that if the United States and the Entente Powers had dealt reasonably with the provisional government and the Russian people the Bolshevist *coup* in October could have been averted, the democratic uprising in Germany hastened, and the war brought to an earlier close. While strongly condemning Bolshevism or Communism in theory and practice, he as vigorously denounced the Allies' policy of intervention and blockade, both on general principles of humanity and because it rallied the Russian masses to the support of the Bolshevist régime. He died in the height of his powers, being fatally injured by a taxicab while crossing a New York street. His body lies in the Workmen's Circle plot of Mount Carmel cemetery, where memorial exercises are held annually. He was survived by his wife, Anna Rosenson, whom he married in 1899, and by their only child, a daughter.

Meyer London was of slight build and small stature, with thin features and bright blue eyes. His movements were quick and restless, and his face commonly wore a somewhat sardonic expression, which easily broke into a quizzical smile or hardened into grim resoluteness. His speeches in Congress were argumentative, with flashes of wit but with no attempt at oratorical grace. He spoke best in labor mass-meetings and conventions, especially when he had to meet opposition. On such occasions he made free use of a quaint folk-humor and his climaxes were often highly poetic. He was an unresting rather than a tireless worker. Saddened by the suffering he saw about him, often deeply hurt by hostile reactions for which his too impulsive frankness might be in part responsible, wearied by labors beyond his physical strength, he had fits of black melancholy, from which he emerged to throw himself into action with reckless abandon. He died poorer in worldly goods than many a mechanic, rich only in the love of the masses, which first found full expression at his grave.

[Harry Rogoff has written a life of London entitled *An East Side Epic* (1930). Materials for a much fuller biography are scattered through the files of Socialist, Labor, and Jewish periodicals (especially the *Arbeiter Zeitung, Jewish Daily Forward, N. Y. Call,* and *People and Worker*) from 1896 to 1926 and through the records of the 64th, 65th, and 67th Congresses. Character sketches appeared in the *Nation* (N. Y.) and the *Outlook,* June 23, 1926, and obituaries in all the New York papers. The present article is based partly on personal acquaintance with London, partly on information supplied by his widow and his brothers.] A. L.

LONESOME CHARLEY [See REYNOLDS, CHARLES ALEXANDER, *c.* 1842–1876].

LONG, ARMISTEAD LINDSAY (Sept. 3, 1825–Apr. 29, 1891), military secretary and biographer of Gen. Robert E. Lee, was born in Campbell County, Va. His father, Col. Armistead Long, was a son of Armistead Long of Loudoun County, Va., and Elizabeth, daughter of Col. Burgess Ball; his mother was Calista Cralle of Campbell County. Long was graduated from West Point in 1850 and appointed brevet second lieutenant of artillery. After serving at Fort Moultrie and on the frontier, he was promoted first lieutenant in 1854 and stationed chiefly in Indian Territory, Kansas, and Nebraska until 1860. Shortly before the outbreak of the Civil War, he was in garrison at Augusta Arsenal, Ga., but in February 1861 was transferred to duty in the defenses of Washington, and on May 20, was appointed aide-de-camp to Gen. Edwin Vose Sumner, whose daughter, Mary Heron, he had married the year before. Because of the influence of his father-in-law as well as his own military ability, Long had much to hope for by remaining in the old army. Nevertheless, on June 10, 1861, he resigned his commission and offered his services to the Confederacy.

Following a short service in West Virginia, he was ordered, in the fall of 1861, to report to Gen. Robert E. Lee in South Carolina. He arrived in Charleston on the eve of the great fire and that night he and Lee fled together from a burning hotel, each clasping a baby in his arms. Thus Long was introduced to an intimate companionship with his chief which continued throughout the war. Shortly afterward, when Lee became commander of the Army of Northern Virginia, Long was appointed his military secretary with the rank of colonel, and served in that capacity until September 1863. Lee had chosen Long, whom he loved and trusted, for the most responsible position upon his staff. In September 1863 Long was promoted brigadier-general of artillery and during the subsequent Virginia campaigns he handled his guns with skill and vigor.

After the war he was appointed chief engineer of a Virginia canal company, but in 1870 he became totally blind as the result of exposure during his campaigns. While laboring under this disability, using a slate prepared for the blind, he wrote his *Memoirs of Robert E. Lee, His Military and Personal History* (1886). This volume contains the most intimate of the accounts of General Lee during the Civil War. Although the author was naturally influenced in his judgments by his close association with Lee, his book gives no evidence of narrow partisanship. The information obtained from personal recollections and from his careful wartime diary he substantiated by information and documents from other individuals who had been in Lee's confidence. In all, the work is one of the most valuable source books for the history of Lee and of the Civil War, and is a memorial to Long's courage and biographical skill. Prior to its publication he had contributed two articles, "Seacoast Defences of South Carolina and Georgia" and "General Early's Valley Campaign," to the *Southern Historical Society Papers* (vols. I, II, 1876, and vol. III, 1877, respectively). The latter article he revised in Volume XVIII (1890) of the same *Papers.* He died in Charlottesville, Va., where a few years after he had become blind his wife had been appointed postmistress by President Grant.

[A. L. Long, *Memoirs of Robert E. Lee*; information as to certain facts from Long's daughter, Mrs. Robert A. Brown; *Confed. Mil. Hist.* (1899), vol. III; *War of the Rebellion: Official Records (Army)*; G. W. Cullum, *Biog. Reg. Officers and Grads. U. S. Mil. Acad.* (3rd ed., 1891), vol. II; *Twenty-second Ann. Reunion Asso. Grads. U. S. Mil. Acad.* (1891); *Richmond Dispatch,* Apr. 30, 1891.] R. D. M.

LONG, CHARLES CHAILLÉ [See CHAILLÉ-LONG, CHARLES, 1842–1917].

LONG, CRAWFORD WILLIAMSON (Nov. 1, 1815–June 16, 1878), anæsthetist and surgeon, the son of James Long, a cultivated Southerner, by his wife Elizabeth Ware, was born in Danielsville, Ga. His grandfather, Capt. Samuel Long, a Scotch-Irish Presbyterian born in the province of Ulster, settled in Pennsylvania about 1761 and later fought in the War of the Revolution. Crawford Long, who as a boy was studious, entered Franklin College (now the University of Georgia) at the early age of fourteen and was graduated in 1835, second in his class. After a year of teaching in the academy which his father had founded at Danielsville, he began to read medicine, first under a preceptor, later at Transylvania University, Lexington, Ky., and finally, in 1838, at the University of Pennsylvania, where in 1839 he received his medical degree. He then spent eighteen months in New York, where he gained the reputation of being a skilful surgeon. In 1841, owing to family difficulties, he was forced to return to Georgia and began to practise in the isolated village of Jefferson, Jackson County, where he obtained the clientele of his old preceptor, Dr. Grant. During idle moments and during horseback rides in the country necessitated by his rural practice Long read widely in general literature, developing a particular fondness for Shakespeare and Dickens. On Aug. 11, 1842, he married Caroline Swain, niece of Governor David Lowry Swain [*q.v.*] of North Carolina.

In the early forties the exhilarating effect of laughing gas was a subject much under discussion, and wandering charlatans gave demonstrations of its action to voluntary subjects [see G. Q. Colton]. In January 1842, after witnessing such a demonstration, several of Long's friends induced him to permit them to have a "nitrous oxide frolic" in his room. Unfortunately no nitrous oxide was available, but Long offered a substitute. Telling of the incident later, he said: "I informed them . . . that I had a medicine (sulphuric ether) which would produce equally exhilarating effects; that I had inhaled it myself, and considered it as safe as the nitrous oxide gas" (*Southern Medical and Surgical Journal,* December 1849). The young men inhaled the volatile gas and became hilarious, and many received more or less severe bruises. Long made the shrewd observation that the bruises were unaccompanied by pain; from this observation he inferred that ether must have the power of producing insensibility, and he decided to test it in his surgical practice. A few months later (Mar. 30, 1842) he administered sulphuric ether to a patient, James Venable, who, when completely anæsthetized, had removed from the back of his neck a small cystic tumor. This patient later testified that he experienced no pain, and a second operation, involving the removal of another similar tumor from the same man's neck, was performed by Long on June 6, 1842. On July 3, 1842, he amputated the toe of a negro boy named Jack and on Sept. 9, 1843, he removed an encysted tumor from the head of Mrs. Mary Vincent. A fifth operation, the amputation of a finger, was carried out Jan. 8, 1845. Three other operations were performed before September 1846, making a total of eight. His experience with ether was not published, however, until December 1849, when, as a result of the controversy that had arisen over the claims of W. T. G. Morton [*q.v.*], Long described his first five operations in a short paper contributed to the *Southern Medical and Surgical Journal,* under the title, "An Account of the First Use of Sulphuric Ether by Inhalation as an Anæsthetic in Surgical Operations" (see also *Transactions of the Medical Association of Georgia,* April 1853). His apologia for his delay in publication may best be given in his own words: "I was anxious before making my publication, to try etherization in a sufficient number of cases to fully satisfy my mind that anæsthesia was produced by the ether, and was not the effect of the imagination, or owing to any peculiar insusceptibility to pain in the person experimented on . . . I determined to wait . . . and see whether any surgeon would present a claim to having used ether by inhalation in surgical operations prior to the time it was used by me." His claim was issued in modest terms, but, as Dr. W. H. Welch has remarked, "Long is necessarily deprived of the larger honor which would have been his due had he not delayed publication of experiments with ether until several years after the universal acceptance of surgical anæsthesia. . . . We need not . . . withhold from Dr. Long the credit of independent and prior experiment and discovery, but we cannot assign to him any influence upon the historical development of our knowledge of surgical anæsthesia or any share in its introduction to the world at large" (*post,* p. 9). He was ever modest in urging his claims, but in the year before his death, Dr. J. Marion Sims [*q.v.*] published in the *Virginia Medical Monthly* (May 1877) a paper recalling Long's statement made in 1849 and declared him to be the "first discoverer of anæsthesia."

In 1850 Long removed to Athens, Ga., where he immediately acquired a large surgical practice. In June 1878 he died in that city after a long and useful career as surgeon and general practitioner. An obelisk, given by Dr. L. G. Hardman, was erected at Athens in 1910 to the memory of the anæsthetist.

[Biographies and appreciations include H. H. Carlton, in *Trans. Medic. Asso. of Ga.,* vol. XXXII (1881); F. R. Packard, in *Alumni Reg.* (Phila.), Oct. 1902, portr.; L. B. Grandy, in *Va. Medic. Mo.,* Oct. 1893; L. H. Jones, in *Trans. Medic. Asso. of Ga.,* 1899. A critical discussion of Long's claim, with full quotations from important original documents, is given by H. H. Young, in *Bull. Johns Hopkins Hospital,* Aug.-Sept. 1897. See also W. H. Welch, *A Consideration of the Introduction of Surgical Anæsthesia* (n.d.), Ether Day address, Boston, 1908; R. M. Hodges, *A Narrative of Events Connected with the Introduction of Sulphuric Ether into Surgical Use* (1891); D. W. Buxton, in *Proc. Royal Soc. of Medicine* (London), vol. V, pt. 1, Section of Anæsthetics, Dec. 1911. The most exhaustive authority is *Crawford W. Long* (1928), a biography by his daughter, Frances Long Taylor, who has supplied certain additional information for this sketch.]

J. F. F.

LONG, JAMES (*c.* 1793–Apr. 8, 1822), military adventurer in Texas, was born in North(?) Carolina (*Lamar Papers,* I, 47), some time between Oct. 10, 1792, and Apr. 8, 1793, and as a child moved with his father to Rutherford, Tenn. Early failure as a merchant led him to complete his education and study medicine. During the War of 1812 he served as a doctor in Carroll's brigade, and saw action at New Orleans in 1815. Later that year he married Jane Wilkinson, niece of Gen. James Wilkinson [*q.v.*], and resigned from the army. In 1817, after attempts at medicine and farming, he became a merchant at Natchez, Miss.

Two years later his fellow townsmen, aroused by the treaty of Feb. 22, 1819, chose him to lead an expedition intended to open Texas to American settlement. He gathered three hundred men, mostly ruffians, and proceeded to Nacogdoches, where a republic was formed with Long as president of the supreme council and commander-in-chief. He declared independence, June 23, 1819 (*Niles' Weekly Register,* Sept. 11, 1819, pp. 31–32), and thereafter made provision for easy land sales and land bounties to soldiers and settlers. On Aug. 14 Eli Harris began to issue the weekly *Texas Republican,* the first Texas newspaper. Long intended an early march against Bexar, but because of the non-arrival of expected supplies he was compelled to send most of his force in four trading parties to the Trinity and Brazos rivers. About Oct. 10 culmination of negotiations with Jean Laffite [*q.v.*] took Long to Galveston, which he declared a port of entry. Laffite, as governor, was commissioned to outfit privateers. Meanwhile, the Spanish, having protested Long's presence to the United States, dispatched Perez from Bexar with several hundred troops to expel him. Perez routed Long's outlying parties, devastated east Texas, and drove Long's men on the lower Trinity to Bolivar Point. Long, forced across the Sabine, returned with provisions after the departure of Perez. Having issued a proclamation ordering his forces to gather at Bolivar, he coasted to New Orleans, where he enlisted Ben Milam and John Austin, and spent two months gathering supplies and men. In June Long, again at Bolivar, decided that the republican cause would benefit by a new leader, and tendered the presidency to E. W. Ripley, who accepted but never assumed office. Long now proposed to free Texas by capturing La Bahia and Bexar, but his supporters required him to remain at Bolivar to await immigration, which his presence was expected to induce. About October 1820, Long and Ripley entered into alliance with Jose Trespalacios, a Mexican revolutionist, who secured formal recognition from juntas in Mexico (*Lamar Papers,* II, 93; *Niles' Weekly Register,* June 2, 1821, pp. 223–24), thus giving the enterprise the same status as movements in the interior. Trespalacios assumed command late in 1820, but little occurred until September 1821, when Iturbide's successes made action imperative. Trespalacios and Milam sailed for Mexico, and Long undertook a friendly visit to Bexar. Through misinformation acquired en route he was led to attack and capture La Bahia Oct. 4. When Perez arrived from Bexar Long refused terms but was soon forced to surrender with his fifty-two men. They were sent from Bexar to Monterey, and Long was allowed to proceed to Mexico City in March 1822. There he found Trespalacios in high favor, and was himself well received. Nevertheless, he became offended by Iturbide's monarchism, and shortly determined to settle his affairs and quit the country; but on Apr. 8 he was shot and killed by a sentry, ostensibly because of a misunderstanding concerning his passport. H. H. Bancroft (*History of the North Mexican States and Texas,* 1889, II, 51) contends that Long struck the sentry. Lamar (*Lamar Papers,* II, 119) and Milam (J. H. Brown, *History of Texas,* vol. I, 1892, p. 81) both claim that Long's death was an assassination, but Lamar holds Iturbide responsible, while Milam charges Trespalacios. The three theories are about equally tenable.

Long, though hot-headed and rather impractical, was extremely tenacious in the pursuit of his ideal, an Americanized Texas. His career may be regarded as an honest but ill-considered attempt to achieve by military force what the Austins were even then undertaking by peaceful colonization.

[*The Papers of Mirabeau Buonaparte Lamar,* here cited as *Lamar Papers,* esp. vols. I (1921), 30–53, and II (1922), 51–134, are the best source of material. Lamar gathered considerable information for a life of Long and completed part of the projected work. Portions of his account of Long's early life and activities through 1819 were first published in H. S. Foote, *Tex. and the Texans* (1841), I, 192–217. These are reprinted in *Lamar Papers,* vol. II, together with the body of Lamar's sketch and a conclusion compiled by the editors from Lamar's notes. The *Lamar Papers,* vol. I, contain also translations of several documents on the La

Bahia incident. Important references to Long's activitives are to be found in *Niles' Weekly Reg.*, vols. XVI–XXII (1819–22). *Quart. of the Tex. State Hist. Asso.*, Oct. 1902, Jan. 1904, and *Southwestern Hist. Quart.*, Jan. 1913, July 1932, contain essential articles on the *Texas Republican.* Long's activities in Texas as a factor in negotiations concerning the ratification of the treaty of Feb. 22, 1819, may be traced in *Am. State Papers, For. Rel.*, IV (1834), 664–84. Most of the standard histories of Texas, esp. H. K. Yoakum, are inaccurate and inadequate in their treatment of Long after 1819. The detailed account in A. H. Abney, *Life and Adventures of L. D. Lafferty* (1875) is fictitious. The period given above for Long's birth is deduced from *Lamar Papers,* I, 48, II, 123: the date of his death, from *Lamar Papers,* II, 118, 121, and *The Austin Papers,* pt. I (1924), pp. 498, 505. Among guides showing the location of manuscript material, the most important is H. E. Bolton, *Guide to Materials for the Hist. of the U. S. in the Principal Archives of Mexico* (1913).] B. F. L.

LONG, JOHN DAVIS (Oct. 27, 1838–Aug. 28, 1915), governor of Massachusetts, congressman, secretary of the navy, was born in the village of Buckfield, Me. His father, Zadoc, was descended from Miles Long who went to Plymouth, Mass., from North Carolina about 1770; his mother, Julia Temple (Davis) Long, was a descendant of Dolor Davis who came to Massachusetts from Kent, England, in 1634. Two influences shaped Long's boyhood, the village and his father. Without the village he would not have had his cheerful and tolerant philosophy, his shrewd but kindly understanding of human nature, and his dreams and poems of pleasant meadows and sunny blue skies. Without his father he would have had neither the ambition nor the discipline necessary for reaching the goals he attained. He was never satisfied with his schooling. His preparatory education at Buckfield and in the Academy of nearby Hebron, Me., seemed inadequate. In spite of a high scholastic rating, he considered his years at Harvard College (1853–57) both an educational failure and an unhappy personal experience. Likewise he believed that his legal training, picked up in law offices and during a term in the Harvard Law School, had left him poorly grounded in fundamentals and permanently handicapped. His real education must have been gained from his own insatiable eagerness for self-improvement. Typical is his translation into English blank verse of Vergil's *Æneid* (1879) during the winter he was serving as lieutenant-governor in order to increase his own vocabulary.

After leaving Harvard he taught for two years in the Academy at Westford, Mass., but to Boston and to the law he was driven inevitably by what he called a desire to express "the consciousness of power" within him (*Journal, post,* pp. 117–18). In 1863 he wrote in his journal (*Ibid.*, p. 129): "Can such a man [as I] *succeed, get rich, acquire a reputation?*" The answer was triply in the affirmative. He was admitted to the bar in 1861 and after a year in Buckfield, returned to Boston, where he built up a lucrative practice. During his steady advance in his profession his home life was pleasant. He lived in the attractive village of Hingham, close enough to Boston for daily visits. On Sept. 13, 1870, he married Mary Woodward Glover of Hingham. She died in 1882 after bearing her husband two daughters, and on May 22, 1886, he married Agnes Peirce of North Attleboro, who bore him a son.

In politics Long was honest and something of a peacemaker rather than venturesome. If he desired reform it never led him either to leave his party or to prod it into traveling at an uncomfortable pace. After 1871, in which year he accepted a Democratic nomination for the legislature and ran (unsuccessfully) as an independent, he was steadfastly associated with the Republican party, accepting Blaine in 1884 and denouncing Roosevelt in 1912. He was elected to the legislature in 1875, held the speakership in 1876 and 1877, and rapidly ascended the ladder of party service until he reached the governorship, which he occupied for three annual terms, 1880, 1881, and 1882. His office was run efficiently and honestly, but it was in the main a routine administration. From 1883 to 1889 he sat in Congress, his committees—Shipping, Commerce, and Appropriations—indicating his main interests. Perhaps his most important speeches during this period of service were those on the whiskey tax, Mar. 25, 1884; on interstate commerce, Dec. 3, 1884; on silver coinage, Mar. 27, 1885; and on the French spoliation claims, Aug. 4, 1888. Some of his addresses were published under the title, *After-dinner and Other Speeches* (1895).

In 1897 William McKinley appointed him secretary of the navy. He was too wise to endeavor to master the intricacies of his department. "My plan," he wrote (*Journal,* p. 157), "is to leave all such [technical] matters to the bureau chiefs . . . limiting myself to the general direction of affairs . . . especially personal matters." Here his tactful manner did much to remove friction and to promote cooperation within the department. Again he opined that the cabinet officer "does not so much represent the Department before the people as he represents the people in the Department" (*Ibid.*, p. 195). The untarnished record of the navy in the war with Spain must in part be accredited to the secretary. He was closely associated with McKinley, was conservative and calm in judgment, and gave his department loyal support. Involved in the unhappy Sampson-Schley controversy, he conducted himself in a wholly creditable manner. He retired from the cabinet in 1902.

Much of his later life was devoted to writing, chiefly on naval affairs. He published a number of articles and books on the navy and the Spanish-American War, by far the most important of which is *The New American Navy* (2 vols., 1903). Some of his poems appeared in a little volume entitled *At the Fireside* (1905). In 1888 he had edited a campaign history, *The Republican Party, Its History, Principles, and Policies,* and, with others, he edited *The American Business Encyclopædia and Legal Adviser* (5 vols., 1913). To the *Proceedings of the Massachusetts Historical Society* (vol. XLII, 1909), he contributed "Reminiscences of My Seventy Years' Education." He also found time to advocate a number of reforms, including prohibition, woman's suffrage, world peace, and the abolition of the death penalty. He died in Hingham, Aug. 28, 1915.

[Long's journal from 1848 to 1915, filling twenty volumes in manuscript, has been made the basis of Lawrence Shaw Mayo's *America of Yesterday, as Reflected in the Journal of John Davis Long* (copr. 1923). See also tributes by J. F. Rhodes and W. R. Thayer, in *Proc. Mass. Hist. Soc.,* vol. XLIX (1916); W. R. Castle, Jr., in *Harv. Grads. Mag.,* June 1917; *Hist. of the Town of Hingham, Mass.* (1893), vol. III; Alfred Cole and Charles F. Whitman, *A Hist. of Buckfield, Oxford County, Me.* (1915); *Boston Transcript,* Aug. 30, 1915.] P. H. B.

LONG, JOHN HARPER (Dec. 26, 1856–June 14, 1918), chemist, was born near Steubenville, Ohio, the son of John and Elizabeth (Harper) Long, both of Protestant Irish ancestry. Left an orphan at an early age, he made his home with an uncle in Olathe, Kan., and in 1877 graduated from the University of Kansas with the degree of B.S. An interest in chemistry fostered by the able and enthusiastic teaching of George E. Patrick, then a recent graduate of Cornell, led him to continue his studies in that science (1877–80) at the universities of Würzburg, Breslau, and Tübingen. At Tübingen, where he was a student of Lothar Meyer, he was granted the degree of D.Sc. in 1879. After serving as assistant, 1880–81, to W. O. Atwater [*q.v.*] of Wesleyan University, a pioneer in agricultural and food chemistry in the United States, he was appointed in 1881 to the professorship of chemistry in the Liberal Arts department of Northwestern University, and the next year was transferred to the chair of chemistry in the Medical School, a position which he held until his death in 1918. During its existence he taught also in the School of Pharmacy, of which he was dean from 1913 to 1917. He was married, Aug. 24, 1885, to Catherine Stoneman of Cedar Rapids, Iowa, by whom he had five children.

He was a fellow and vice-president of the American Association for the Advancement of Science, a member of the revision committee of the United States Pharmacopoeia, a member of the council on pharmacy and chemistry of the American Medical Association, president, 1903–04, of the American Chemical Society, and first president of the Institute of Medicine of Chicago. For a number of years he was consulting chemist for the State Board of Health of Illinois and the Sanitary District of Chicago, and it was largely his work in this capacity, confirmed by thousands of analyses on the oxidation of sewage by running streams, that led to the decision of the Supreme Court (Feb. 19, 1906) for the defendants in the case of *Missouri* vs. *Illinois and the Sanitary District of Chicago* (200 *U. S.,* 496), a question of sewage disposal which directly affected the future of Chicago. As a member of the Remsen "Referee Board" of consulting scientific experts appointed by the Department of Agriculture, he directed long and painstaking investigations, carried out in the Northwestern laboratories, on the influence of sodium benzoate, of copper, and of alum on the health of man (*United States Department of Agriculture Reports,* 88, 94, 97 and *Bulletin 103,* 1904–14). This work was of very great benefit in the later administration of the Food and Drugs Act.

A pioneer in the chemical phase of medical education, he found the existing texts inadequate and in an endeavor to supply the need, wrote a series of books which played an important rôle in his educational service: *Elements of General Chemistry* (1898), *A Text-book of Elementary Analytical Chemistry* (1898); *A Text-book of Urine Analysis* (1900); *Laboratory Manual of Elementary Chemical Physiology and Urine Analysis* (1894); *The Optical Rotating Power of Organic Substances* (1902), translated from the German of H. H. Landolt; *A Text-book of Physiological Chemistry* (1905). His research papers and reports in chemistry and biochemistry, numbering 109 titles, are listed in the memorial volume (Gault, *post*) and in the "Proceedings" of the American Chemical Society for 1919. His most important papers (1913–18) related to the action of digestive ferments, with special reference to those of the pancreas.

Long was a man of pronounced personality, a hard fighter for his convictions, but a fast friend, genial, and with a keen sense of humor. His interests were many-sided, and that characteristic, coupled with his capacity for work, enabled him to achieve great success in many lines. Modest and unassuming, he was a hater of cant, pretension, and slovenly work. As a scientific man he was rigidly accurate and dependable, and his conclusions were based upon all the evidence that could be brought to bear on the problem under investigation. He was conservative, but with that best kind of conservatism that is ready to accept new views when they become matters of fact and not mere speculation.

[F. B. Dains, in "Proc. Am. Chem. Soc., 1919," published as an appendix to the *Jour. Am. Chem. Soc.*, vol. XLI (Jan.–June, 1919); *John Harper Long, 1856–1918 . . . A Tribute from His Colleagues* (n.d.), ed. by Robert Gault; *Who's Who in America*, 1918–19; *Chicago Tribune*, June 15, 1918.] F. B. D.

LONG, JOHN LUTHER (Jan. 1, 1861–Oct. 31, 1927), author, dramatist, was born at Hanover, Pa. He was admitted to the bar in Philadelphia, Oct. 29, 1881, and became a practising lawyer, but his bent was toward literature, and he wrote many short stories. One of these, "Madame Butterfly," published in the *Century Magazine* for January 1898 and later that year in a collection, attracted much attention. A little tale of the deserted Japanese wife of an American naval officer, it was touching in its simple tragedy and caught with seeming authenticity the Oriental atmosphere. As a matter of fact, the author had never been in Japan. His story and atmosphere were based on the observation of his sister, Mrs. Irwin Correll, the wife of a missionary. The details were carefully verified from her experience. More than one American actress sought the dramatic rights to this story, among them Maude Adams, but Long disposed of them to David Belasco, because Belasco proposed himself to dramatize the tale. He did so, and the play was produced as an after-piece to a comedy, at the Herald Square Theatre, New York, Mar. 5, 1900, with Blanche Bates as the little Japanese wife. The dramatization was entirely the work of Belasco, but he used much of the original dialogue, and had Long's assistance in the creation of atmosphere. The production was an immediate success, but the stage life of the play was soon to be indefinitely prolonged, because Puccini, the Italian composer, chose it for the libretto of what time has proved his most popular opera, *Madame Butterfly*. First produced in Milan, without success, it was sung in English translation in America at the Garden Theatre, New York, Nov. 12, 1906, and highly acclaimed. Since then it has gone into the repertory of every opera house, and the pathetic, wistful story of little Butterfly is known all over the civilized world, and seems likely to perpetuate Long's name for many years to come.

This collaboration with Belasco led to further work together, in which Long contributed the actual scenarios and dialogue of two plays, which were then worked over by the two men, and resulted in two dramas of distinction, marking, with *Madame Butterfly,* the best of Long's production. The plays were *The Darling of the Gods,* a romantic Japanese melodrama, produced in Washington, Nov. 20, 1902, with Blanche Bates and George Arliss in leading rôles, and *Adrea,* a tragedy of the late Roman Empire, produced in Washington, Dec. 26, 1904, with Mrs. Leslie Carter in the title part. The former play was the more successful on the stage, perhaps because of its exotic color, its thrilling situations, a certain strain of romantic mysticism, and superb acting. The latter play, however, had much tragic dignity, and represented on Long's part a prodigious amount of careful historical research (see his letters to Belasco, in William Winter, *post,* pp. 135–38).

These three plays represented the peak of Long's achievement in the theatre, or, indeed, in literature. He was not, by himself, a successful dramatist, but needed the technical skill of a collaborator in sympathy with his romantic conceptions to give them stage form. With E. C. Carpenter he wrote *The Dragon Fly* (produced in Philadelphia, 1905), and alone he wrote *Dolce* (produced by Mrs. Fiske in Philadelphia and then in New York in 1906), *Kassa* (produced in New York, Jan. 23, 1909, with Mrs. Leslie Carter in the leading rôle), and finally *Crowns* (produced at the Provincetown Theatre, Nov. 11, 1922). None of these plays was a success, nor exhibited the striking quality of romantic imagination Belasco had enabled his friend to release into the theatre.

Long's published prose works included *Madame Butterfly, Purple Eyes,* etc. (1898), *Miss Cherry-Blossom of Tôkyô* (1895), *The Fox-Woman* (1900), *The Prince of Illusion* (1901), *Naughty Nan* (1902), *Billy-Boy* (1906), *The Way of the Gods* (1906), *Felice* (1908), *Baby Grand* (1912), and *War, or What Happens When One Loves One's Enemy* (1913). He also wrote the text for several cantatas, and tried his hand at two opera librettos. With the passage of time, however, all these works have been largely forgotten, save only the story of *Madame Butterfly,* on which his fame will undoubtedly rest. He was married to Mary J. Sprenkle, and lived quietly in Philadelphia until his death, reticently avoiding the publicity which generally comes to successful writers.

[Wm. Winter, *The Life of David Belasco* (2 vols., 1918); *Who's Who in America*, 1926–27; *Green Room Book* (1909); J. H. Martin, *Martin's Bench and Bar of Phila.* (1883); obituaries in *N. Y. Herald Tribune,*

Nov. 1, 1927; *Evening Pub. Ledger* (Phila.), Oct. 31, 1927; *Phila. Record*, Nov. 1, 1927.] W. P. E.

LONG, STEPHEN HARRIMAN (Dec. 30, 1784–Sept. 4, 1864), explorer and engineer, was born in Hopkinton, N. H., the son of Moses and Lucy (Harriman) Long. He graduated from Dartmouth College in 1809, and in 1814, following a period of teaching, he entered the army as a second lieutenant of engineers. After serving for two years as assistant professor of mathematics at West Point, he was transferred to the topographical engineers with the brevet rank of major and continued with this branch of the service throughout the remainder of his life. He was made major in 1838, and in 1861 became chief of the corps and colonel. In 1817 the War Department sent him West to examine the portages of the Fox and Wisconsin rivers and to explore the upper Mississippi. His account of this expedition appears under the title, "Voyage in a Six-oared Skiff to the Falls of St. Anthony in 1817" (*Collections of the Minnesota Historical Society*, vol. II, pt. I, 1860). Returning, a skilled explorer, he was assigned by Secretary Calhoun in 1819 to command the expedition to the Rocky Mountains. After selecting an encampment for his party, he returned to Philadelphia to spend the winter of 1819–20 with his bride, Martha Hodgkins, whom he had married on Mar. 3, 1819. Rejoining the expedition the following spring, he pushed westward along the Platte and South Platte, reaching the Rockies in July 1820 and discovering the lofty peak which bears his name. He did not penetrate the Front range but turned south to the vicinity of Colorado Springs, and headed east by way of the Arkansas and its tributaries, exploring a considerable section of the southwestern country, about which only vague and inaccurate geographical ideas had hitherto prevailed. A vivid narrative of the journey is given by Edwin James [*q.v.*] in *Account of an Expedition from Pittsburgh to the Rocky Mountains, Performed in the Years 1819 and '20* (2 vols. and atlas, 1822–23). In 1823 Long was assigned to examine the sources of the St. Peter's (Minnesota) River and the northern boundary of the United States to the Great Lakes. W. H. Keating [*q.v.*], who accompanied the party, prepared the *Narrative of an Expedition to the Source of the St. Peter's River, Lake Winnepeek, Lake of the Woods . . . Performed in the Year 1823* (2 vols., 1824).

From this time on, railroad routes supplanted Indian trails in Long's interest and activities. In 1827 he was assigned by the War Department to act as consulting engineer for the Baltimore & Ohio Railroad Company, and in association with Jonathan Knight [*q.v.*] he selected the route of the road. He later was president of its board of engineers. Continued friction with the management of the company led to his withdrawal from all official connection in 1830, but only after he had made a reputation as an authority in the new field of railway engineering (S. H. Long and W. G. McNeill, *Narrative of the Proceedings of the Board of Engineers of the Baltimore & Ohio Rail Road Company,* 1830). In connection with his theory of grades and curvatures, which appeared first in *Report of the Engineers, on the Reconnoissance and Surveys Made in Reference to the Baltimore and Ohio Railroad* (1828), and was afterward embodied in his *Rail Road Manual* (1829), he developed tables which obviated the need of all computations in the field. In 1834 he made a preliminary survey of possible railway routes between points in Georgia and Tennessee, which was followed by a period as chief engineer of the Atlantic & Great Western Railroad, 1837–40. Subsequently, he served as a consulting engineer for a number of railroad companies when not engaged in active military service. An outgrowth of this experience was his interest in bridge construction, on which he published a thin pamphlet in 1830 (*Description of the Jackson Bridge, Together with Directions to Builders of Wooden or Frame Bridges*). Six years later he obtained a patent on his method of bracing and counterbracing wooden bridges (*Description of Colonel Long's Bridges, Together with a Series of Directions to Bridge Builders,* 1836). A number of bridges in New England and elsewhere were constructed in accordance with his specifications. On duty at the mouth of the Mississippi River at the outbreak of the Civil War, he was called to Washington and advanced to the rank of colonel, retiring in 1863, and dying on Sept. 4 of the following year in Alton, Ill. His wife survived him; they had four sons and a daughter.

[C. C. Lord, *Life and Times in Hopkinton, N. H.* (1890); G. T. Chapman, *Sketches of the Alumni of Dartmouth Coll.* (1867); R. G. Thwaites, *Early Western Travels,* vol. XIV (1905), preface; H. M. Chittenden, *The Am. Fur Trade of the Far West* (1902); Edward Hungerford, *The Story of the Baltimore & Ohio Railroad* (1928), vol. I; W. T. Norton, *Centennial Hist. of Madison County, Ill., and Its People* (1912), vol. I; F. B. Heitman, *Hist. Reg. of the U. S. Army* (1890); *Minn. Hist. Bull.*, Nov. 1923.]

H. C. D.

LONGACRE, JAMES BARTON (Aug. 11, 1794–Jan. 1, 1869), line and stipple engraver, was born in Delaware County, Pa., the son of Peter Longacre and a descendant of early Swedish settlers. John F. Watson, the annalist of Philadelphia, discovered the talents of the boy and took him into his family as an apprentice in his bookstore. Later he placed Longacre with

George Murray, an engraver in Philadelphia, to learn the art of engraving, for which he displayed talent. He remained in Murray's establishment until in 1819 he set up in business for himself. He already was regarded as one of the best engravers in the country, and during his last years with his old employers, Murray, Draper, Fairman & Company, he had been engaged to engrave the portraits of Washington, Jefferson, and Hancock, on the facsimile of the Declaration of Independence published by John Binns in Philadelphia in 1820. This plate, thirty-five by twenty-five inches in size, was the largest engraving that had been made in the United States up to that time. John Vallance executed the other engraving on the plate. The finished production, which was the first correct facsimile of the document ever made, cost the publisher $9,000.

Soon after he had established himself in business, Longacre was commissioned to engrave many of the portraits for John Sanderson's *Biography of the Signers to the Declaration of Independence,* publication of which was begun in 1820. In 1826 he engraved some of the portraits of actors which accompanied the Lopez & Wemyss edition of the *Acting American Theatre.* His chief work as an engraver may be said to rest with the ambitious series of volumes, the first of its kind ever attempted in this country, known as *The National Portrait Gallery of Distinguished Americans.* In this publication he was associated with James Herring, of New York. It was a difficult undertaking, but between 1834 and 1839 four octavo volumes were published. Longacre engraved a number of the portraits, and some of the engravings were made from portraits he had painted from life. The *Portrait Gallery* was reissued several times and constitutes the engraver's principal claim to fame. His other work included engraved plates for annuals and illustrations for many of the juveniles issued by the American Sunday School Union in Philadelphia. He succeeded David Edwin [*q.v.*] as the best stipple engraver in the country, although he had developed an entirely different technique.

On Sept. 16, 1844, Longacre became chief engraver of the United States Mint, having succeeded Christian Gobrecht [*q.v.*]. During his occupancy of the office, he designed and engraved the first double-eagle, in 1849, the first three-dollar gold piece, in 1854, and the gold dollar struck at that time. He was also engaged in remodeling the coinage of the Republic of Chile, a work which he completed within two years of his death. Longacre died in Philadelphia on Jan. 1, 1869. Four days later a memorial meeting, attended by all the employees of the Mint, was held and honor was paid him through eulogies on his character and skill. In 1928 he was represented in the exhibition of one hundred notable American engravers held in the New York Public Library.

[Wm. Dunlap, *A Hist. of the Rise and Progress of the Arts of Design in the U. S.* (1834), vol. II; W. S. Baker, *Am. Engravers and Their Works* (1875); David McN. Stauffer, *Am. Engravers upon Copper and Steel* (1907); *Recollections of the Life of John Binns* (1854); F. C. Wemyss, *Twenty-Six Years of the Life of an Actor and Manager* (1847); J. T. Scharf and Thompson Westcott, *Hist. of Phila.* (1884), vol. II; *Hist. of the Longacre-Longaker-Longenecker Family* (n.d.), p. 75; excerpts from Longacre's diary for the year 1825 in the *Pa. Mag. of Hist. and Biog.*, Apr. 1905; G. G. Evans, *Illustrated Hist. of the U. S. Mint* (rev. ed., 1888); *Pub. Ledger* (Phila.), Jan. 5, 1869.]

J. J.

LONGFELLOW, ERNEST WADSWORTH (Nov. 23, 1845–Nov. 24, 1921), painter, was a son of Henry Wadsworth Longfellow [*q.v.*], and Frances (Appleton) Longfellow. His early surroundings, productive of frustrations and a sense of inferiority, may have been disadvantageous to him. He once wrote: "Any one who has had the misfortune to be the son of an illustrious parent knows how hard it is to be taken seriously by people" (*Random Memories,* p. v). His autobiography, witty, informing, opinionated, not always good-natured or charitable, is a document to interest psychologists. He was born at the Craigie House, Cambridge, whence his father walked to his modern language classes at Harvard. "The Castle-Builder" describes him as "a gentle boy, with soft and silken locks." His formal education began at a dame school facing the Washington Elm and was continued at Ambrose Wellington's school, Cambridge, and the Dixwell School, Boston. Not being proficient in languages, as his father notably was, but displaying good scholarship in mathematics, Ernest tried vainly for a West Point appointment. He was temperamentally inclined to it, and, contrary to the elder Longfellow's pacifist views, he had a life-long interest in military science. He entered the Lawrence Scientific School at Harvard College during the Civil War, in which he hoped to serve, but the conflict ended just before he was graduated in engineering in 1865.

When the Union armies were disbanded, engineers were numerous and Longfellow, perhaps mistakenly, felt that competition might be too keen in the profession for which he had been trained. Having seen much of art in his parents' home and elsewhere, and having shown ability in mechanical drawing, he decided to become an artist. With his uncle, the Rev. Samuel Longfellow, he went to London, then proceeded to Paris, where he studied with Ernest Hébert, who found his draftsmanship good. Bohemianism never appealed to him and he had few Latin Quarter contacts. Returning to Boston, he opened in 1866 a studio in the Studio Building, Tremont Street, where he had as neighbors George Inness, Appleton Brown, and B. C. Porter. In the same year he inherited a fortune from the estate of his mother, who was burned to death in 1861. In May 1868 he was married to Harriet Spelman, the daughter of Israel Spelman, and the following summer they went abroad. In Paris Longfellow studied with Leon Bonnat and in Rome, through G. P. A. Healy, painter of his father's portrait, he became one of Abbe Liszt's friends. Some years later (1876–78) he returned to France. This time he sought out Thomas Couture, whose work he had admired and from whom he received valuable instruction. In 1879 he was elected a vice-president of the Boston Art Club. In that year he painted the portrait of his father which hangs at Bowdoin College. An earlier portrait, for which he had less regard, hangs at Craigie House.

As the years passed Longfellow and his wife usually spent winters in New York or abroad and summers at Magnolia, Mass. Possessed of ample means he had little incentive to commercialize his work. While his painting was always well drawn and intelligently thought out, it has generally been thought cold and unsympathetic. He was also disadvantaged as an artist by feeling that in matters of art his own time was out of joint; a bitter tone toward his professional contemporaries often appears in his memoirs. He died at the Hotel Touraine, Boston, after a long illness, and was buried from the Craigie House. His will, which left his collection of paintings and $200,000 to the Boston Museum of Fine Arts, and the major part of his estate to his widow, specifically disinherited his nephews, H. W. L. Dana and Allston Dana, because of "their socialistic and pacifist tendencies."

[*Random Memories* (1922) is Longfellow's informal autobiography. For a just if somewhat severe evaluation of his art works see Harley Perkins' review of the Longfellow Memorial Exhibition, Museum of Fine Arts, published in the *Boston Evening Transcript*, Jan. 17, 1923. C. H. Hawes described the Longfellow collection in the *Museum of Fine Arts Bulletin*, Dec. 1923. See also: Clara E. Clement and Laurence Hutton, *Artists of the Nineteenth Century and Their Works* (1879), vol. II; *Am. Art News*, Dec. 3, 1921; and the *Boston Herald*, Nov. 25, 1921.] F. W. C.

LONGFELLOW, HENRY WADSWORTH (Feb. 27, 1807–Mar. 24, 1882), poet, was born in Portland, Me. His first known ancestor was Edward Longfellow, a man of property in Yorkshire early in the seventeenth century, whose grandson, William, settled in Newbury, Mass., about 1676, and married Ann Sewall, a sister of Judge Samuel Sewall [*q.v.*]. Their grandson Stephen took two degrees at Harvard, and became teacher, town clerk, and clerk of the courts in Portland, Me. His son Stephen was a Massachusetts legislator and judge of the court of common pleas. The judge's son Stephen [*q.v.*], the poet's father, a Harvard graduate, was a distinguished lawyer in Portland, member of Congress, trustee of Bowdoin College, and president of the Maine Historical Society. The poet's maternal grandfather, Peleg Wadsworth [*q.v.*], was descended from Christopher Wadsworth, Englishman, who settled in Duxbury, Mass., before 1632. Peleg, a Harvard graduate, a general in the Revolution, and member of Congress, married Elizabeth Bartlett of Plymouth; and through these grandparents the poet had descent from at least four of the Pilgrims, including John Alden, Priscilla Mullens, and Elder Brewster. His mother, Zilpah, a nervous invalid, was an intense lover of music, poetry, and nature.

Henry, the second child, was educated chiefly in private schools. He began to write early, the *Gazette of Maine*, Portland, publishing a poem by him on Nov. 17, 1820. (He denied that he wrote the doggerel about Mr. Finney and his turnip.) Entering Bowdoin College as a sophomore, he graduated in 1825, fourth in a class of thirty-nine; Hawthorne was a classmate, but they were not intimate. While in college Longfellow had many poems accepted by the magazines; and by his senior year he had set his heart on a literary career, writing to his father, "I most eagerly aspire after future eminence in literature." He planned to study at Harvard and then attach himself to a magazine; but soon after graduation he was offered a projected professorship of modern languages at Bowdoin, on condition that he study abroad, and therefore spent the years 1826–29 in France, Spain, Italy, and Germany. From 1829 to 1835 he was professor and librarian at Bowdoin, also preparing textbooks and contributing essays and sketches to the magazines. He married, Sept. 14, 1831, Mary Storer Potter of Portland, a beautiful and cultivated woman.

In 1835 Longfellow accepted the professorship of modern languages and belles-lettres at Harvard, and went abroad for a year to improve his knowledge of German and the Scandinavian tongues. In spite of the sudden death of his wife at Rotterdam in that year, he held to his course and made an extensive study of German literature before returning to America in 1836. At Cambridge, where he lodged in the Craigie House, Washington's former headquarters, his life settled into a pleasant routine. His college duties were heavy, for he had to prepare three lectures a week, besides supervising four native teachers and often taking the classes himself. But he went much into society, a jaunty figure immaculately clad; and he made many friends, the closest being Professor Cornelius C. Felton, Charles Sumner, George S. Hillard [*qq.v.*], and Henry R. Cleveland, who with the poet formed "The Five of Clubs," dubbed by outsiders "The Mutual Admiration Society." After 1837 his relations with Hawthorne were increasingly friendly; and at this time, as always, he kept up by letter his intimacy with George W. Greene [*q.v.*] of Rhode Island, whom he had met in Italy in 1828. During 1837–40 he contributed five articles to the *North American Review;* and in 1839 published *Hyperion,* a romance, and *Voices of the Night,* his first book of verse. The spring and summer of 1842 he spent mostly at Marienberg, a water-cure on the Rhine; but he formed a lifelong friendship with the German poet Ferdinand Freiligrath, visited Dickens and other men of letters in England, and wrote *Poems on Slavery* (1842) during the voyage home.

On July 13, 1843, he married Frances Elizabeth Appleton, the original of the heroine of *Hyperion,* whom he had met in Switzerland in 1836. She was now a woman of twenty-six, "of stately presence, of cultivated intellect, and deep, though reserved feeling" (Samuel Longfellow, *Life, post,* II, 1, 2). Her father, a Boston merchant, bought the Craigie House for the pair as a wedding present. The poet's life now flowed on for many years with full and placid tide. Six children were born to him, among them Ernest Wadsworth Longfellow [*q.v.*]. Lowell and Agassiz became his intimate friends. In the summer he found congenial society at Nahant, where he and his brother-in-law, Thomas Gold Appleton [*q.v.*], finally bought a cottage. In 1854 he resigned his professorship, which had grown increasingly irksome; and his life thereafter had more unity and peace—until tragedy suddenly engulfed him. On July 9, 1861, Mrs. Longfellow was sealing up packages of her daughters' curls; a match set fire to her dress, and, in spite of her husband's efforts to put out the flames, by which he also was badly burned, she died the next day. How deep was his wound is shown by the few words wrung from him after some weeks: "How can I live any longer!" is the second entry in his journal, on Sept. 12, after a long gap. In a letter to George W. Curtis on Sept. 28, he says that although "to the eyes of others, outwardly calm" he is "inwardly bleeding to death." The persistence of his grief is revealed by "The Cross of Snow," written eighteen years afterwards. Next to the care of his children he found most solace in daily labor to complete his translation of Dante's *Divine Comedy.* While the work was slowly going through the press, in 1865, Lowell and Charles Eliot Norton aided in the last revision. "Every Wednesday evening," wrote Norton, "Mr. Lowell and I met in Mr. Longfellow's study to listen while he read a canto of his translation from the proof-sheet. We paused over every doubtful passage, discussed the various readings, considered the true meaning of obscure words and phrases, sought for the most exact equivalent of Dante's expression, objected, criticised, praised, with a freedom that was made perfect by Mr. Longfellow's absolute sweetness, simplicity, and modesty. . . . Almost always one or two guests would come in at ten o'clock, when the work ended, and sit down with us to a supper, with which the evening closed. Mr. Longfellow had a special charm as a host, the charm of social grace and humor" (*First Annual Report of the Dante Society,* May 16, 1882, p. 22).

In the poet's remaining years honors were heaped upon him. During a tour of Europe with his family, in 1868–69, he received the degree of LL.D. from Cambridge, and that of D.C.L. from Oxford; breakfasted or lunched with Gladstone, the Duke of Argyll, and other notables; was given a private audience by the Queen; visited Tennyson on the Isle of Wight; and met scholars and artists in Italy, including Liszt, who soon after set to music the introduction to *The Golden Legend.* To the Craigie House came distinguished visitors year after year—Froude, Trollope, Kingsley, Dean Stanley, Lord and Lady Dufferin, Salvini, Ole Bull, the Emperor of Brazil, and many others. He was more and more lonely, however; Hawthorne and Felton had died before his European tour; Agassiz and Sumner died in 1874; Lowell went abroad; Greene became feeble and depressed; yet Longfellow kept at work with calm cheerfulness. The summers he spent at Nahant, except for a week's visit each year with his sister in the old Portland home. On his seventy-second birthday the children of Cambridge gave him an arm-chair made of wood from the chestnut tree of "The Village Blacksmith." His next birthday was celebrated in the public schools of Cincinnati, and the following year many schools throughout the country observed the day. During the last three months of 1881 he was confined to his room by vertigo followed by nervous prostration, and never fully recovered. On Mar. 18, 1882, four schoolboys called, and he showed them the house with his usual courtesy. That afternoon he became ill, peritonitis developed, and six days later he died. He was buried at Mount Auburn. On Mar. 2, 1884, a bust of him was unveiled in Poets' Corner, Westminster Abbey.

Longfellow's gentleness, sweetness, and purity have always received due emphasis. Lord Ronald Gower's eulogy in 1878 is typical: "There is a kind of halo of goodness about him, a benignity in his expression which one associates with St. John at Patmos" (*My Reminiscence,* vol. II, 1883, p. 265). Other essential aspects of his personality have often been ignored, however. "Injustice in any shape he could not brook," said his sister of him as a boy; and he proved it as a young man when he hotly refused to accept an instructorship at Bowdoin instead of the promised professorship, and the corporation yielded to the indignant stripling. The sterner side of his nature showed itself at his Boston club one day: "Felt vexed at seeing plover on the table at this season, and proclaimed aloud my disgust at seeing the game-laws thus violated." The comments in his journal and letters are often severe. "The smokers turned my study into a village tavern with cigars and politics, much to my annoyance." "My ways of thinking are so different from those of most of the Bostonians that there is not much satisfaction in talking with them. —— himself is an exception. He has a liberal, catholic mind, and does not speak as if he were the pope." "The American character seems often wanting in many of the more generous and lofty traits which ennoble humanity." "The fugitive slave is surrendered to his master . . . Dirty work for a country that is so loud about freedom as ours!" This critical edge he may have got from his father; from his mother he inherited nervous sensibility verging on disease. In boyhood he begged to have cotton put in his ears on Fourth of July, to deaden the sound of the cannon; his illness in 1842 was disorder of the nerves; in middle life he was sometimes "half crazed" with neuralgia; a medical examination in 1867 found his "bell-wires . . . out of order"; nervous prostration preceded the end. This sensibility caused restlessness, fretfulness, and depression. "I pray a benediction on drudgery. It . . . takes the fever out of my blood and keeps me from moping too much." "I know not in what littlenesses the days speed by; but mostly in attending to everybody's business but my own, and in doing everything but what I most want to do. It frets my life out." Abnormal excitement appears in some entries. "It [Niagara] drives me frantic with excitement. . . . My nerves shake like a bridge of wire." More often his nervous delicacy gave delight. "It is raining, raining with a soft and pleasant sound. I cannot read, I cannot write, . . . but dream only." "Like delicious perfume, like far-off music, like remembered pictures, came floating before me amid college classes, as through parting clouds, bright glimpses and visions of Tyrolean lakes." "I have still floating through my brain that crowd of fair, slender girls, waving, like lilies on their stems, to the music as to a wind." He had a marked fondness for good dinners, choice wines, and fine clothes. An English traveler who met him at a reception in 1850 pictures him as "dressed very fashionably . . . almost too much so, a blue frock coat of Parisian cut, a handsome waistcoat, faultless pantaloons, and primrose-colored 'kids' set off his compact figure, which was not a moment still; for like a butterfly glancing from flower to flower, he was tripping from one lady to another, admired and courted by all" (quoted by Higginson, *post,* p. 279, from *The Home Circle,* London, October 1850). He had not yet begun to be St. John.

This artistic sensibility affected his modes of composition. He worked steadily, so far as moods allowed; but he could not twang off a lyric at will or mechanically grind out a long poem. "I was often excited, I knew not why; and wrote with peace in my heart and not without tears in my eyes, 'The Reaper and the Flowers, a Psalm of Death.' I have had an idea of this kind in my mind for a long time, without finding any expression for it in words. This morning it seemed to crystallize at once, without any effort of my own." "Why do no songs flit through my brain, as of old? It is a consolation to think that they come when least expected."

Longfellow's popularity in his later years was great, both at home and abroad. "No other poet has anything like your vogue," Hawthorne wrote from England in 1855. In London 10,000 copies of *The Courtship of Miles Standish* were sold the first day. Before 1900 his poems had been translated into German, Dutch, Swedish, Danish, French, Italian, Portuguese, Spanish, Polish, Bohemian, Hungarian, and Russian. In German thirty-three different translations had appeared, including eight of *Evangeline* and five of *Hiawatha*; in French, nine, including four of *Evangeline*; in Italian, twelve. The prices he received for poems show the growth of his fame: fifteen dollars for "The Village Blacksmith" in

1840; \$3,000 for "The Hanging of the Crane" in 1874. Poe was hostile, but most American men of letters praised the new poet warmly. Bryant wrote of his "exquisite music" and "creative power." Motley found himself "more and more fascinated with Evangeline" and the hexameters "'musical as is Apollo's lute.'" Hawthorne wrote, "I take vast satisfaction in your poetry, and take very little in most other men's." Prescott thought the "Skeleton in Armor" and "The Wreck of the Hesperus" the best imaginative poems since "The Ancient Mariner." European criticism was also very favorable. Professor Philarete Chasles, of the College of France, wrote in 1851: "Longfellow seems to us to occupy the first place among the poets of his country" (*Études sur la littérature et les mœurs des Anglo-Américains au XIXe siècle,* 1851, p. 299). *Blackwood's Edinburgh Magazine* said in February 1852: "In respect of melody, feeling, pathos, and that exquisite simplicity of expression which is the criterion of a genuine poet, Mr. Longfellow need not shun comparison with any living writer." The London *Spectator* (June 20, 1868) spoke of "the sweet and limpid purity, . . . and the thoroughly original conception and treatment, of his later poems, especially that which will doubtless live as long as the English language, 'Hiawatha.'"

Longfellow's writings belong to the Romantic Movement in its milder phases: they have nothing of the Storm-and-Stress mood, except in *Hyperion,* and nothing of Byron's or Shelley's spirit of revolt. He was a Victorian only in his moderation and decorum, which were a part of his Puritan heritage: social reforms, except the abolition of slavery, did not much interest him; and his Unitarian faith combined with his unspeculative nature to save him alike from the theological struggles of Tennyson, Arnold, and Clough, and from the paganism of Swinburne and Morris. His first prose model was Irving, soon succeeded by the florid German school. His poetic style may have owed its purity to Bryant, whose nature poems he imitated in youth, but it also has something of Goldsmith's soft grace and Keats's sensuous beauty. In his nature poetry as a whole he is more like Keats than Bryant or Wordsworth; but Wordsworth may have quickened his sympathy with children and with common men and women. "The Ancient Mariner" clearly influenced his ballads of the sea. From the Finnish *Kalevala* he got the metre of *Hiawatha*; and his use of hexameters, an innovation in American verse, was doubtless due to their success in German narrative poems. The strongest single foreign influence was that of Goethe and the German romantic lyrists. Most of the prose works had only a passing value, but *Outre-Mer* and *Hyperion* are still worth reading for their pictures of European life in the early nineteenth century. The poems did a threefold service to American readers: they brought a sense of the beauty in nature and the lives of common people; they gave some feeling for Old-World culture; they handled American themes, especially Indian legends and colonial history, more broadly and attractively than had been done before in verse.

Didacticism is the charge most often brought against Longfellow's poetry. If this means merely that his purpose was to teach, he might well be content to stand with Dante, Spenser, and Milton. The true criticism is that his method is sometimes bald preaching, as in "A Psalm of Life," and sometimes silly symbolism, as in "Excelsior"; that at other times he pins a moral to incident or portrait which needs none, as in "The Village Blacksmith"; and that in general his way of presenting truth lacks the imagination, passion, and power of the great poets. But it is also true that most of his didactic poems are pleasing in form, and that the larger part of his poetry is not didactic at all but depicts various aspects of life for their own sake. His nature poems, such as "An April Day" or "Amalfi," are often purely sensuous; and those on the sea give with rare felicity a sense of its magic and its terror. His ballads are astir with spirited incident. In the delightful poems on children he anticipated Swinburne. His sketches of individuals show vivid appreciation of a wide range of human types—men of action, like the hero in "Victor Galbraith" or "Kambalu"; men of science, like Agassiz; poets, like Dante and Chaucer; ecclesiastics good and bad, like those in *The Golden Legend* and "The Monk of Casal-Maggiore"; women, like Evangeline, Priscilla, and the heroic mother in "Judas Maccabaeus." His sympathy with the joys and sorrows of "the common lot" is genuine and deep, as in "The Bridge" and "The Goblet of Life." The love scenes in *The Spanish Student, Evangeline,* and "The Courtship of Miles Standish" have delicate beauty although they lack warmth; and "Stars of the Summer Night," in the first named, is one of the best serenades in English. The joys of wine and social drinking are sung jollily in "King Witlaf's Drinking Horn" and with a connoisseur's discrimination in "Catawba Wine."

As interpreter of the Old World to the New, Longfellow still has no rival among American poets. Even now there is cultural charm in "Nuremberg," "The Belfry of Bruges," "Monte

Cassino," "Castles in Spain," and the translations from German, French, and Spanish. The spirit of the Northland and the Vikings lives in "The Saga of King Olaf." Much of the Middle Ages is in *The Golden Legend,* where, said Ruskin, the poet "entered more closely into the temper of the Monk, for good and for evil, than ever yet theological writer or historian" (*Modern Painters,* 1862, IV, 359). The translation of *The Divine Comedy,* although its line-for-line exactness sacrifices some lucidity and ease, first revealed Dante to numberless readers, and is still one of the great versions.

Longfellow's approach even to American life was through his library. The poems on slavery, although sincere enough, seem "literary" and slight for so terrible a theme. He knew the Indian almost wholly from books; but the more significant fact is that in the legends as recorded by Schoolcraft and others he rejected the darker and more primitive elements, making Hiawatha too much like a Christian gentleman—as Tennyson had begun to make King Arthur; yet "Hiawatha" paints delightfully the poetic phases of the Indian imagination, which are as real as Indian cruelty or treachery. *Evangeline* smells not only of the library but also of a "diorama" of the Mississippi that came to Boston while he was writing the poem; but the first part sketches beautifully the peaceful life of Acadia, with the heroine as its perfect center, and in the second part the interest is sustained largely by the broad pictures of Western scenery, although the poet had seen neither Acadia nor the West. "The Courtship of Miles Standish" conveys a neglected truth by its playful emphasis on the lighter side of the Pilgrims' doings; the grimmer aspects of Puritanism are painted black enough, though without dramatic power, in "John Endicott" and "Giles Corey of the Salem Farms." It is unnecessary to insist upon the truth and vividness of the pictures of American life in Longfellow's popular short poems. Admirable also are the less-known sonnets and poems on his friends, all representative American figures and drawn with the sure touch of the poet's maturity.

The later poems in general have more merit than is commonly recognized. They lack the freshness and easy sweetness of the earlier works; but the thought is broader and maturer, the style often has more distinction and strength. The most ambitious of these, *The Divine Tragedy,* is not a success either by itself or linked with *The Golden Legend* and *The New England Tragedies* in an attempt to depict the development of Christianity. "The Hanging of the Crane" and "The Masque of Pandora" are also inferior. But no one knows Longfellow fully who is not familiar with the sonnets, some of which are among the best of the century; with "Morituri Salutamus," less buoyant than "Rabbi Ben Ezra" and less venturesome than "Ulysses," but more truthful than either in its statement of the mingled weakness and strength of old age; and with "Michael Angelo," in which the elderly poet and scholar moves thoughtfully in high regions of Italian art and character. Longfellow's fame will never again be what it was in his own century; but it remains to be seen whether, by the pure style and gracious humanity of his best poems, he will not outlast louder men, in popular favor.

The principal works published in book form during his lifetime appeared as follows: *Outre-Mer* (1835); *Hyperion* (1839); *Voices of the Night* (1839); *Ballads and Other Poems* (dated 1842, issued late in 1841); *Poems on Slavery* (1842); *The Spanish Student, a Play in Three Acts* (1843); *Poems* (1845); *The Belfry of Bruges and Other Poems* (dated 1846, issued in December 1845); *Evangeline* (1847); *Kavanagh, a Tale* (1849); *The Seaside and the Fireside* (dated 1850, issued in December 1849); *The Golden Legend* (1851); *The Song of Hiawatha* (1855); *Prose Works* (1857); *The Courtship of Miles Standish, and Other Poems* (1858); *The New England Tragedy* (1860); *Tales of a Wayside Inn* (1863); *The Divine Comedy of Dante Alighieri* (3 vols., 1865–67); *Flower-de-Luce* (title-page dated 1867, published in November 1866); *The New England Tragedies* (1868); *The Divine Tragedy* (1871); *Christus, a Mystery* (*The Divine Tragedy, The Golden Legend, The New England Tragedies,* 3 vols., 1872); *Three Books of Song* (1872); *Aftermath* (1873); *The Hanging of the Crane* (1874); *The Masque of Pandora, and Other Poems* (1875); *Kéramos and Other Poems* (1878); *Ultima Thule* (1880); *In the Harbor: Ultima Thule, Part II* (1882). The posthumous volume, *Michael Angelo,* appeared in 1883. A "complete" edition, *The Writings of Henry Wadsworth Longfellow,* in eleven volumes, was published in 1886.

[Two useful bibliographies are L. S. Livingston, *A Bibliography of the First Editions in Book Form of the Writings of Henry Wadsworth Longfellow* (p.p. 1908), and bibliog. by H. W. L. Dana, in *The Cambridge Hist. of Am. Lit.,* II (1918), 425–36. The most important biography is *Life of Henry Wadsworth Longfellow with Extracts from his Journals and Correspondence* (3 vols., 1886–87), by his brother, Samuel Longfellow [*q.v.*]. See also T. W. Higginson, *Henry Wadsworth Longfellow* (1902); "New Longfellow Letters," *Harper's Mo. Mag.,* Apr. 1903; E. S. Robertson, *Life of Henry Wadsworth Longfellow* (1887); G. R. Carpenter, *Henry Wadsworth Longfellow* (1901); G. L. Austin, *Henry Wadsworth Longfellow: His Life, His*

Works, His Friendships (1883), containing the early poems not republished in *Voices of the Night*; E. W. Longfellow, *Random Memories* (1922); Annie Fields, *Authors and Friends* (1896); E. Montégut, "Oeuvres de H. W. Longfellow," *Revue des Deux Mondes*, Oct. 15, 1849; F. Kratz, *Das deutsche Element in den Werken H. W. Longfellows* (2 vols., Wasserburg, 1901–02); A. Johnson, "The Relation of Longfellow to Scandinavian Literature," *Am. Scandinavian Rev.*, Jan. 1915; R. H. Stoddard, ed., *The Works of Edgar Allan Poe* (1884), vol. VI; J. R. Lowell, in *Atlantic Mo.*, Jan. 1859; O. W. Holmes, in *Ibid.*, June 1882; G. E. Woodberry in *Harper's Mo. Mag.*, Feb. 1903; T. B. Aldrich in *Atlantic Mo.*, Mar. 1907; P. E. More, *Shelburne Essays*, 5 ser. (1908); W. D. Howells, in *No. Am. Rev.*, Mar. 1907; Bliss Perry, in *Atlantic Mo.*, Mar. 1907; W. P. Trent, in *The Cambridge Hist. of Am. Lit.*, vol. II (1918); W. H. O. Smeaton, *Longfellow and his Poetry* (1919); H. S. Gorman, *A Victorian American: Henry Wadsworth Longfellow* (1926).] W. C. B.

LONGFELLOW, SAMUEL (June 18, 1819–Oct. 3, 1892), teacher, clergyman, poet, philosopher, was the youngest son of Stephen [*q.v.*] and Zilpah (Wadsworth) Longfellow and was born in Portland, Me. His early boyhood was made happy by the enjoyment of imaginative literature and by his rare sensitiveness to the beauty of his seashore home where he rambled, botanizing and sketching. From the classes of the Portland Academy he went to Harvard College, where (1835–39) he stood high in studies and enjoyed many intimate friendships. In 1839–40 he taught in a family school at Elkridge, Md., then returned to Cambridge, where he acted as college proctor, cultivated his love of music, and tutored young boys for college entrance. For the latter task he had unusual aptitude through his remarkable understanding and affection for the young and his power to kindle their moral aims.

Entering the Harvard Divinity School in 1842, he shared with a gifted group of students including Samuel Johnson, O. B. Frothingham, and T. W. Higginson an enthusiasm for the new thought of "Transcendentalism" as taught by Convers Francis, preached by Theodore Parker, read in the pages of Cousin, Emerson, Carlyle. Delicate health, a lifelong recurrence, made him spend the next year in Horta, Fayal, as tutor to the children of the American consul, Charles Dabney. Returning to the Divinity School in 1844 he clarified his ardent theistic conviction—essentially like Parker's though held with more philosophical precision—and in his freedom from dogma was satisfied with a reverential love of Jesus as "a living human friend . . . whose life is to be interpreted by our own deepest, holiest experience" (*Samuel Longfellow: Memoir and Letters*, p. 60). Before graduation he collaborated with Samuel Johnson in *A Book of Hymns, for Public and Private Devotion* (1846, 1848), which gave prominence to the new hymnody of Whittier, H. B. Stowe, Jones Very, and Theodore Parker.

On grounds of health he at first declined a settled pastorate but after temporary engagements in West Cambridge, Mass., and Washington, D. C., he was ordained to the Unitarian ministry in Fall River, Mass., Feb. 16, 1848. His spiritual discourse, his beautiful voice, together with the charm that made the children gather round him, won him high esteem, but discouraged by what he deemed inadequate success he withdrew, June 18, 1851, and spent a year in England and France as companion and tutor of a young student. Suspicion of his religious views, then deemed radical, delayed parochial appointment and he thought of serving as chaplain in prisons or reform schools, but in April 1853 he was summoned by the Second Unitarian Church in Brooklyn, N. Y., where his nature and talent came to full expression. He exalted the act of worship in the church, initiated a vesper service with more music and a meditative talk, and introduced in the Sunday School a manual of worship and a children's sermon. His *Vespers* (1859) contains his own beautiful vesper hymns. With equal stress on the social service of the church he sought to organize his parish for the study of social problems and to diffuse a love of art and literature. Another decline in health and some protest against his utterances concerning slavery led to his resignation in June 1860. After two years of extensive travel in Europe he returned to Cambridge, preaching (1867–68) to the congregation gathered by Theodore Parker, traveling abroad again in 1865 and 1868, writing powerful theological essays for the *Radical* edited by Sidney H. Morse. Once more he was a settled pastor, serving the Unitarian church in Germantown, Pa., from January 1878 to the summer of 1882 when he sought leisure for writing in Cambridge. He published in 1886 a two-volume biography of his brother, *Life of Henry Wadsworth Longfellow*, and in the following year he published a sequel, *Final Memorials of Henry Wadsworth Longfellow.* On Oct. 3, 1892, he died in Portland, Me.

Of the group ill named Transcendentalists he was the clearest and most methodic in thought and will be remembered for his discriminating argument and for the devout fervor and beauty of his hymns. A gentle and serene spirit, a man of social charm, he gave and received abundant love. In addition to the works already mentioned he published a book of poems, *Thalatta: A Book for the Seaside* (1853), in collaboration with T. W. Higginson; *A Book of Hymns and*

Tunes (1860, 1876); and *Hymns of the Spirit* (1864), with Samuel Johnson. A final collection, *Hymns and Verses,* was edited and published by Edith Longfellow in 1894.

[See Joseph May, *Samuel Longfellow: Essays and Sermons* (1894) and *Samuel Longfellow: Memoir and Letters* (1894); O. B. Frothingham, *Transcendentalism in New England: A Hist.* (1876); O. F. Adams, "Samuel Longfellow," *New Eng. Mag.*, Oct. 1894; J. W. Chadwick, "Samuel Longfellow," in S. A. Eliot, *Heralds of a Liberal Faith* (1910), vol. III; H. W. Foote, "The Anonymous Hymns of Samuel Longfellow," *Harvard Theol. Rev.*, Oct. 1917; J. H. Allen, *Sequel to "Our Liberal Movement"* (1897); *Christian Reg.*, Oct. 6, 13, 1892; *Daily Eastern Argus* (Portland), Oct. 4, 1892.] F. A. C.

LONGFELLOW, STEPHEN (Mar. 23, 1776–Aug. 3, 1849), lawyer, congressman from Maine, fourth of the name, was born on his father's farm in Gorham, Me., whither his parents, Stephen and Patience (Young) Longfellow had fled on the destruction of Falmouth (now Portland) by the British in October 1775. His great-great-grandfather, William Longfellow, had settled in Newbury, Mass., about 1676. It is not surprising that he chose the law for his profession, since his grandfather, a graduate of Harvard College in 1742, was register of probate and clerk of the judicial court for York County, and his father, judge of the court of common pleas. Stephen entered Harvard in 1794, graduating in 1798, having been elected to Phi Beta Kappa. He immediately commenced the study of law with Salmon Chase of Portland, who had the most extensive practice of any lawyer in the county. On being admitted to the bar in 1801, he established himself in Portland, which with a population of 3,800 was already served by seven lawyers. By 1807 he had won recognition as one of the leading lawyers in the District of Maine. The volumes of Massachusetts and Maine reports show that he was engaged in a considerable number and a wide range of cases.

Longfellow was a representative in the Massachusetts General Court in 1814 and 1815, and, being a stanch Federalist, was chosen a delegate to the Hartford Convention in 1814. In 1816 he actively opposed measures then being taken for the separation of Maine from Massachusetts. The same year, as a presidential elector, he, along with others from Massachusetts, threw his vote to Rufus King. He represented Maine in the Eighteenth Congress (1823–25), where he opposed the great expenditures on internal improvements then under consideration. In 1826 he represented Portland in the state legislature. From 1811 to 1817 he was an overseer, and from 1817 to 1836, a trustee of Bowdoin College. He served as president of the Maine Historical Society in 1834. An attack of epilepsy in 1822 so weakened his constitution that he was forced gradually to relinquish a good part of his law practice. As a lawyer he was direct and forceful, depending not at all upon brilliant rhetoric or abstract arguments. At the same time he never forgot courtesy nor did he lose his wonted suavity of manner. He married, on Jan. 1, 1804, Zilpah, the daughter of Peleg Wadsworth [*q.v.*]. They had four daughters and four sons. Of the latter Henry Wadsworth and Samuel [*qq.v.*] are the best known.

[The sketch of Longfellow in Wm. Willis, *A Hist. of the Law, the Courts, and the Lawyers of Me.* (1863), is reprinted from the *Me. Hist. Soc. Colls.*, 1 ser., V (1857). See also Wm. Willis, ed., *Jours. of the Rev. Thos. Smith and the Rev. Samuel Deane* (1849), p. 384 note; S. E. Titcomb, *Early New England People* (1882); *Portland Daily Advertiser,* Aug. 6, 1849. The Me. Hist. Soc. owns two small collections of Longfellow papers.] R. E. M.

LONGFELLOW, WILLIAM PITT PREBLE (Oct. 25, 1836–Aug. 3, 1913), architect, author, grandson of Stephen Longfellow [*q.v.*], was a son of Stephen and Marianne (Preble) Longfellow and a nephew of Henry Wadsworth Longfellow [*q.v.*]. He was born at Portland, Me. After graduating from Harvard College in 1855, he continued his studies in the Lawrence Scientific School at Harvard, winning the degree of S.B. in 1859. He then joined the staff of Edward Cabot, the Boston architect. In 1868–69 he served as secretary of the Boston Society of Architecture, making many pleasant and valuable professional contacts. For the following three years he was an assistant architect of the United States Treasury Department and took an active part in designing and constructing the Boston Post Office. Later, for one year, 1881–82, he served as adjunct professor of architectural design at the Massachusetts Institute of Technology. He had married in Boston, on May 26, 1870, Susan Emily Daniell, and for many years he and his wife had a residence adjacent to the Craigie House in Cambridge, in which his uncle lived. When school children of Cambridge planned to surprise the aging poet on his seventy-second birthday with a chair made from wood of the spreading chestnut tree over the familiar village smithy, Longfellow the architect was selected to design the chair.

Longfellow was of a reserved disposition, a clever amateur musician and a serious student of literature. His contributions to the progress of his profession were solid, not showy or spectacular. He was for a time director of the newly opened school of drawing and painting at the Boston Museum of Fine Arts; of the museum itself he became a trustee. He was the first editor of the *American Architect* during the years in which it was published in Boston. In 1893 he served on the jury of award of the architectural section of the World's Columbian Exposition. Increasingly in his later years he gave practically his whole time to writing on architectural subjects. Among his published works were *Abstract of Lectures on Perspective* (1889); *A Cyclopaedia of Works of Architecture in Italy, Greece and the Levant* (1895); *The Column and the Arch* (1899); and *Applied Perspective* (1901). His musical compositions, particularly his settings for some of Tennyson's poems, were creditable. He and his wife were accustomed to spend their summers on the Maine coast with his bachelor cousin, Alexander Wadsworth Longfellow, also an architect. His death occurred at East Gloucester, Mass., during a brief visit at the summer art colony. He left no children.

[There is a manuscript biographical note in the records of the School of the Boston Museum of Fine Arts. For printed sources see *Who's Who in America*, 1912–13; the *Am. Architect*, Aug. 13, 1913; *Boston Evening Transcript*, Aug. 4, 1913.] F. W. C.

LONGLEY, ALCANDER (Mar. 31, 1832–Apr. 17, 1918), publisher and social reformer, was born in Oxford, Ohio. Between 1843 and 1846 his father, Abner Longley, a Universalist minister, was interested in a Fourierist phalanx at Clermont, Ohio, and the son early adopted Fourier's ideas. In 1852 he was connected with the North American Phalanx in Monmouth County, N. J., but left the Community, about 1854, to return to Cincinnati to be married. Shortly afterward, he joined his four brothers in establishing, at Cincinnati, a printing firm that specialized in reform literature. One of its publications, *The Type of the Times,* was partly in phonetic spelling. On his own account, Longley began in 1857 the publication of a small monthly, *The Phalansterian Record.* Although the firm of brothers seems to have been dissolved by 1860, he remained in Cincinnati as a printer and, in 1862, was a postoffice clerk there. His first attempts at organizing Utopian colonies were along the lines of producers' cooperation, but, after two or three short-lived ventures, he abandoned cooperation for communism. In 1867 he and his family became probationary members of Icaria, the colony founded by Étienne Cabet in Iowa. Delighted as he was with the altruistic spirit of the Icarians, he, nevertheless, withdrew after a few months.

In January 1868, he began the publication in St. Louis of *The Communist,* devoted to the propagation of his own program of social reform and to communistic activities all over the country. At first it consisted of only four pages, and, although advertised as a monthly, it appeared somewhat irregularly. In 1885 he changed the name to *The Altruist,* under which name he continued it until May 1917. For almost fifty years, in the face of all sorts of difficulties and discouragements, he persisted in issuing his paper and in proceeding with designs for the organization of ideal communities. In the years 1868 to 1885 he made no less than five attempts to establish a communistic society in various parts of Missouri, but each failed within a comparatively short time. The weakness common to all his experiments was lack of capital. Immediately after the disruption of one colony he began his projects for another, and, as late as 1909, was planning still another communistic group at Sulphur Springs, Mo. A printer of the older type, who was typesetter, compositor, and pressman as well as editor, he worked at his trade, during the intervals between experiments, in the composing rooms of one or another of the St. Louis newspapers.

His program of social reform had nothing of the religious element characteristic of many American communistic experiments. He was an ardent believer in the equal rights and responsibilities of women. On marriage and the relations of the sexes his ideas were liberal but not radical. Under a capitalistic system he found that marriage was despotism, but he had no sympathy with the promiscuity of the Perfectionists or the celibacy of the Shakers. His colonists were to be "free and independent in the enjoyment of their affections and in the control of their own persons" (*Communist,* Jan. 1868, p. 3). Misinterpretation of this statement led him to state explicitly that he contemplated no innovation in sex relations that would be contrary to existing laws (*Ibid.,* Feb. 1868, p. 16). He became interested in the political means for the improvement of society and was an active member of the Socialist Labor party in St. Louis. In 1880 he brought together many of his theories on social reform in a book called *Communism: the Right Way and the Best Way for All to Live.* He also arranged, in 1878, a phonetic figure musical system, in which figures denoted the length of sound while the staff designated only the pitch, and he published *The Phonetic Songster and Simple Phonography* (n.d.).

He was married three times. On Nov. 19, 1854, he married Zelie Mottier, the daughter of John E. Mottier, a well-to-do grape grower of Cincinnati. Devoted to the ideals of communism, he used his wife's money for his various colonies, to feed the poor, and to help the unfortunate, even when it meant deprivation for his wife and their three children. At last, after about twenty years, she took the children and left him. His second wife, Genevieve, died, in 1891, soon after their marriage. About 1901 he married Susan Ella Jones of Paris, Ky., who was burned to death, on Jan. 11, 1907, in spite of his heroic attempts to save her from the flames of an exploded lamp. He died in Chicago at the home of his daughter.

[Information obtained from his daughter, Mrs. Justine M. Thrift of Washington, D. C.; from pamphlets, leaflets, and clippings in the St. Louis Public Library as well as from a relative through the courtesy of Irving Dilliard of St. Louis; from letters of Longley to the Oneida Community and clippings in the Oneida *Circular* scrapbook supplied by Mrs. S. R. Leonard of Oneida, N. Y. Published material includes *St. Louis Post-Dispatch,* Sept. 26, 1909; *Circular* (Oneida Community), June 14, 21, 1869; *Williams' Cincinnati Directory . . . 1862* (copr. 1862); Albert Shaw, *Icaria* (1884); W. A. Hinds, *Am. Communities,* revised ed. (1902), esp. pp. 351, 388; J. H. Noyes, *Hist. of Am. Socialisms* (1870); F. A. Bushee, "Communistic Societies in the U. S.," *Pol. Sci. Quart.,* Dec. 1905. Papers and letters are in the possession of his granddaughter, Mrs. Walter J. Cook, Colmar Manor, Brentwood Post Office, Md.] P. W. B.

LONGSTREET, AUGUSTUS BALDWIN (Sept. 22, 1790–July 9, 1870), jurist, author, educator, was born in Augusta, Ga., and died in Oxford, Miss. His parents, William [*q.v.*] and Hannah (Randolph) Longstreet, of Dutch and French-English ancestry, migrated to Georgia from New Jersey about 1785. Until he was fifteen, he was dilatory in his studies, but after that time, inspired by the zeal of his friend George McDuffie, he was more faithful. From 1808 to 1810 he attended the academy of Dr. Moses Waddel [*q.v.*] in Willington, S. C., and in 1811, following the example of his friend John C. Calhoun, he entered Yale College. He finished his course there in 1813, and, still following Calhoun, entered the Litchfield (Conn.) Law School. Returning to Georgia late in 1814, he was married after about two years to Frances Eliza Parke, of Greensboro, where he had taken up his residence. She was wealthy and he was poor, but he was already a capable lawyer and he had to a phenomenal degree the gift of attracting friends and keeping them. He was in the state legislature in 1821, and from 1822 to 1825 was a judge of the superior court. In 1824, he offered himself for election to Congress, but soon afterward the death of his eldest child caused him to abandon all political ambition, and to turn from his hitherto skeptical attitude in religion to the devout Methodism of his neighbors.

He returned to Augusta to live in 1827, and there wrote a series of sketches called "Georgia Scenes," begun anonymously for the Milledgeville (Ga.) *Southern Recorder,* but soon transferred to his own paper, the Augusta *State Rights Sentinel.* These humorous, often crudely realistic compositions, dealing with life in Georgia as he knew it, were at once widely popular. The author silenced his misgivings relative to their frivolity by reminding himself of how valuable they would become as a source of history. In addition they are significant as being among the earliest manifestations in America of the type of literature which later produced such characters as Tennessee's Partner, Uncle Remus, and Huckleberry Finn. Longstreet first published the *Georgia Scenes* in book form (still anonymously) in Augusta in 1835, but in 1840 the firm of Harper & Brothers in New York gave them introduction under the author's name to a national body of readers which proved enthusiastic and persistent. They were frequently imitated, but scarcely equaled even by Longstreet himself, who in the same vein wrote many other stories and sketches, and also a novel, *Master William Mitten* (1864).

Literature was in Longstreet's mind always chiefly a means of diversion. His real interests were politics and religion. In his fervent advocacy of nullification as the proper course for the state of Georgia he established and edited a newspaper, the *State Rights Sentinel* (Augusta, 1834–36), but with the collapse of his hopes in this regard he felt himself driven for refuge to something that he could believe more dependable than democracy. In 1838 he became a Methodist minister, and in that capacity, with conspicuously good results, he presided (1839–48) over Emory College, newly founded in Oxford, Ga. In 1844 he went to New York to take part in the General Conference of his Church at which the denomination, after debating the propriety of slave-ownership among its bishops, divided into two branches. The disagreement centered about Bishop Andrew, of Oxford, and Longstreet took active part in the discussion through both speech and writing, publishing, in 1845, *Letters on the Epistle of Paul to Philemon, or the Connection of Apostolic Christianity with Slavery,* and two years later, *A Voice from the South* (1847). During 1849, he was president of Centenary College in Jackson, La., and from 1849 to 1856 of the University of Mississippi. Here his administration was successful, but his continued political activities, as evidenced primarily by his *Letters from President Longstreet to the Know-Nothing Preachers of the Methodist Church South* (1855), published by the Democratic State Central Committee, occasioned so much opposition that he determined to withdraw from public life.

He had barely retired with his family to his near-by plantation when he was invited (1857) to become president of the University of South Carolina. The opportunity was more than he could resist. The executive's position there was at that time most difficult, but he soon established his mastery. He was a vigorous proponent of secession, but when he saw war actually upon him—and, what was worse, upon his students—he had no longer any courage in his belief, and went about appealing frantically on all sides that something be done at once to hold off the terrible destroyer. From then on till the war's end he was a strenuous but sadly dismayed patriot. In 1865 he settled down again in Mississippi and wrote extensively to prove that the South had always been right and the North always wrong. His happiest companionship in his extreme age was with his son-in-law, L. Q. C. Lamar [*q.v.*]. As an author his distinction is more one of date than of quality; as a public character he possibly effected as much harm as he did good; but in everything he did he was sincere and throughout his life was animated by high motives.

[J. D. Wade, *Augustus Baldwin Longstreet* (1924), with a full bibliography; Edward Mayes, *Geneal. of the Family of Longstreet* (1893); O. P. Fitzgerald, *Judge Longstreet; a Life Sketch* (1891); F. B. Dexter, *Biog. Sketches Grads. Yale Coll.*, vol. VI (1912); *XIX Century* (Charleston), Feb., Aug., Oct. 1870.]

J. D. W.

LONGSTREET, JAMES (Jan. 8, 1821–Jan. 2, 1904), soldier, the son of James and Mary Anna (Dent) Longstreet and the nephew of Augustus Baldwin Longstreet [*q.v.*], was born of New Jersey stock in Edgefield District, S. C., but removed in early childhood to the vicinity of Augusta, Ga., where his father farmed until he died in 1833. The widow then resided at Somerville, Morgan County, Ala., from which state James Longstreet was admitted to West Point in 1838. He attended the academy with McDowell, Sherman, Halleck, Thomas, and Grant, and was graduated fifty-fourth in a class of sixty-two in July 1842. Brevetted second lieutenant of the 4th Infantry, he served at Jefferson Barracks, Mo., Natchitoches, La., and then with the 8th Infantry at St. Augustine, Fla. In the Mexican War, he was with Zachary Taylor until after the battle of Monterey and with Scott during the expedition to Mexico City. Wounded at Chapultepec and brevetted major, he continued in the army and in 1861 was a major (as of July 19, 1858) in the paymaster's department. Following his resignation (effective June 1, 1861) to join the Confederacy, he sought commission in the same department because, as he said, he had abandoned his aspirations for military glory; but his good reputation and rank in the "old army" won him commission as a Confederate brigadier-general, June 17, 1861.

Longstreet's admirable employment of his troops at First Manassas (Bull Run) and his skill in organization brought him promotion to the grade of major-general, Oct. 17, 1861, with command of a division under Joseph E. Johnston. He was with Johnston at Yorktown in the spring of 1862 and conducted the rearguard action at Williamsburg, May 5, 1862, when he enhanced his prestige; but at Seven Pines, May 31, his tardiness in taking position and his singular misinterpretation of his orders were material factors in the Confederate failure. During the Seven Days' Battles around Richmond (June 25–July 1, 1862), after Gen. Robert E. Lee assumed direction of the army, Longstreet moved promptly, did his full share of the fighting, and won Lee's entire confidence. Recent criticism of his action at Frayser's Farm, June 30, and in the pursuit of McClellan, July 2, is hardly justified by the evidence.

After the Seven Days, Lee placed more than half his infantry under Longstreet and on Aug. 13 sent him to reënforce "Stonewall" Jackson, who was near Orange Court House, confronting a new Federal army under Maj.-Gen. John Pope. In the first stage of the campaign of Second Manassas, which now opened, Longstreet was slow in crossing the Rapidan, but he later conducted with much skill his part of the difficult shift up the Rappahannock River, and on the morning of Aug. 29 he brought his troops into position on the right of Jackson, who had completed his famous march to Manassas Junction and had then stood on the defensive near Groveton to await reënforcements. Lee was anxious for Longstreet to assume the offensive that day, but Longstreet, always cautious and deliberate in attack, made repeated excuses for not doing so, and did not enter the action till Aug. 30, when the Federals were quickly routed. Examined in detail, Longstreet's reasons for not attacking on the 29th are certainly defensible and may be valid, but his general attitude showed for the first time that though he was vigorous and effective when his judgment approved the plans of his superior, he was slow to yield his own opinions and equally slow to move when he thought his commander's course was wrong. This was to become the greatest defect of his military character.

Longstreet did not indorse the expedition into Maryland in September 1862, but he fought well at Sharpsburg (Antietam) and was made lieutenant-general, Oct. 11, 1862, on Lee's recommendation. His various divisions were organized as the I Corps with which, on Dec. 13, 1862, he bore the brunt of the defensive fight at Fredericksburg. On Feb. 17, 1863, he followed Pickett's and Hood's division to southeastern Virginia to guard the roads to Richmond from the south and east. In this so-called "Suffolk campaign," he exercised his first semi-independent command, but without substantial achievement of any sort. Although his force equaled that of the Federals, he failed to seize the initiative and was content to employ his troops in collecting supplies from eastern North Carolina. Lee diplomatically urged him either to fight or to rejoin the Army of Northern Virginia, but at a distance from Longstreet and without precise knowledge of his difficulties, Lee refrained from giving him peremptory orders. The result was that Longstreet neither fought nor returned. The absence of two of his divisions from Charlottesville was the chief reason Lee could not follow up the victory won at Chancellorsville, May 2–3.

After the death of "Stonewall" Jackson, May 10, 1863, Longstreet was Lee's most distinguished lieutenant and seems to have taken it upon himself to be Lee's mentor. He advised that the campaign into Pennsylvania, which Lee was then planning, should be offensive in strategy but defensive in tactics, and in some way he got the mistaken idea that Lee made him a promise to this effect. The consequence was that, when Longstreet at the head of his corps joined Lee in front of Gettysburg on July 1, 1863, and learned that Lee intended to attack Meade, he was disappointed, perhaps disgruntled, and certainly filled with misgivings of failure. The story of Gettysburg, as it concerns the I Corps, is the story of Longstreet's slow, reluctant, and despairing acquiescence in orders he believed would bring disaster. He delayed action on July 2 till it was too late to execute Lee's plan to storm Cemetery Ridge before it was fully manned, and by that delay he made the attack of July 3 almost a military necessity. The disadvantages which convinced Longstreet that it was dangerous for Lee to assume the offensive were heightened by Longstreet's tardiness and lack of confidence (see Lee, Robert Edward).

Gettysburg virtually concluded Longstreet's service with the Army of Northern Virginia during the period of its major offensive operations. He was dispatched to Georgia in September 1863 and did admirably at Chickamauga, but he was not successful in front of Knoxville, Tenn., in November, and later, isolated in eastern Tennessee, was so close to despair that he contemplated resignation. Aroused, however, by the danger of a Federal invasion of Georgia, he proposed several plans for an offensive in Tennessee and Kentucky. None of these was considered practicable by President Davis. Brought back to Virginia with his troops in April 1864 and stationed near Gordonsville by Lee, Longstreet arrived on the field on the morning of May 6 in time to rally Hill's corps in the second day's battle of the Wilderness. He at once organized an excellent counter-stroke, in the execution of which he was wounded. He returned to duty in November, participated in the later phases of the defense of Richmond and still had the remnant of his corps in good order when it was surrendered with the rest of the army at Appomattox on Apr. 9.

After the war, Longstreet became head of an insurance company and prospered for a time as a cotton factor in New Orleans, but he joined the Republican party, was ostracized in consequence, and turned to political office for a living. From 1869 till his death at Gainesville, Ga., he held a series of Federal appointments—surveyor of customs at New Orleans, postmaster of Gainesville, minister resident to Turkey, United States marshal for Georgia, and United States railroad commissioner. He was twice married: first, on Mar. 8, 1848, to Maria Louise Garland of Lynchburg, Va., who died Dec. 29, 1889; second, on Sept. 8, 1897, to Helen (or Ellen) Dortch, who survived him. In person he was slightly below middle height, broad-shouldered and somewhat heavy in his prime, and during the war was afflicted with a partial deafness that sometimes made him appear taciturn.

Longstreet's espousal of the Republican faith made him unpopular in the South and probably caused some post-bellum Southern writers to do him less than justice. The claims he made in his military autobiography, *From Manassas to Appomattox* (1896), and in his earlier contributions to *The Annals of the War* (1879) and *Battles and Leaders of the Civil War* (4 vols., 1887–88), aggravated the feeling against him. Despite these criticisms, his place in American military history is not difficult to fix. Essentially a combat officer, he did not possess the qualities necessary to successful independent command, and his skill in strategy was not great. His marching was apt to be slow and he was too much prone to maneuver and await attack; but once battle was joined, he displayed a cheerful composure, a tactical understanding, and a skill in handling his troops that made him an almost ideal corps commander.

[The first two chapters of Longstreet, *From Manassas to Appomattox* (1896), contain an autobiographical review, somewhat inaccurate as to dates, of his life prior to the Civil War. G. W. Cullum, *Biog. Reg. of the Officers and Grads. of the U. S. Mil. Acad.* (3 ed., 1891), contains all his assignments to duty prior to his resignation from the U. S. Army and an outline of his civil career after the war. He was painstaking in the preparation of his reports of battles, all of which appear in the *War of the Rebellion: Official Records (Army)*. Much of his correspondence is published there also. His military correspondence during the last months of the war, not published in the *Official Records,* is in Lee's military papers. No biography of Longstreet has been printed, and the sketches in *Confed. Mil. Hist.* (1899), I, 660–63, and in similar works are perfunctory. His wife, Helen D. Longstreet, published *Lee and Longstreet at High Tide* (1904). For the Gettysburg controversy, see J. W. Jones, "The Starting of the Longstreet-Gettysburg Controversy," *Richmond Dispatch,* Feb. 16, 1896; Dunbar Rowland, *Jefferson Davis, Constitutionalist, . . .,* 1923, vol. IX, 531. See also Edward Mayes, *Genealogy of the Family of Longstreet* (1893); *Who's Who in America,* 1903–05; *Atlanta Constitution,* Jan. 3, 1904.] D. S. F.

LONGSTREET, WILLIAM (Oct. 6, 1759–Sept. 1, 1814), inventor, was born near Allentown, Monmouth County, N. J., the son of Stoffel and Abigail (Wooley) Longstreet, and a descendant of Dirck S. Langestraet who emigrated from the Netherlands to New Netherland in 1657. William was educated in the country school near his home and early showed a marked mechanical skill. About 1780, either through a book which he secured or through local discussions of the work being done by Oliver Evans and John Fitch [*qq.v.*] in nearby communities, he became greatly interested in the steam engine. It is possible that he attempted the construction of an engine at this time, but the public ridicule to which he was subjected deterred him from working very seriously on such a project. After his marriage to Hannah Randolph of Allentown, N. J., in 1783, and the establishing of his own home in Augusta, Ga., he applied himself earnestly to the construction of a steam engine. With the financial aid of one Isaac Briggs, he had made such good progress by 1788 that on their petition, the General Assembly of Georgia, Feb. 1, 1788, passed an act securing to "Isaac Briggs and William Longstreet, for a term of fourteen years, the sole and exclusive privilege of using a newly constructed steam engine invented by them." With this protection Longstreet proceeded to build engines and apply them to useful work. He had already patented in Georgia the so-called "breast roller" of cotton gins, which was operated by horsepower and was of incalculable value to the growers of sea-island cotton. He then undertook the construction of steam-operated gins, but because of lack of money he completed only a few. They were built and put into operation in Augusta but were almost immediately destroyed by fire. Commenting on this occurrence, the *Augusta Herald,* Dec. 23, 1801, concludes, "This accident seems to have been particularly unfortunate as the ingenious proprietor of the works had, we understand, the day before completed a new boiler which had, on trial, been found to equal his utmost expectations, and enabled him with a single gin and with a trifling expense of fuel, to give from 800 to 1000 weight of clean cotton per day." Longstreet also designed a portable steam sawmill, a number of which he erected and operated in various parts of Georgia; one of these, near St. Mary's, was destroyed by the British in 1812. His third application of steam power was to propel a boat. As early as 1790 he solicited, by letter, the aid of Gov. Edward Telfair in raising funds for such a purpose. The letter was published in the Savannah and Augusta newspapers but without avail. Sixteen years later, however, Longstreet succeeded in building a small steamboat which ran on the Savannah River against the current at the rate of five miles an hour. No record exists of the design of boat or engine, nor of the method of propulsion. He died in Augusta, Ga., and was survived by his wife and six children. Augustus Baldwin Longstreet [*q.v.*] was his son.

[T. G. Bergen, *Reg. in Alphabetical Order of the Early Settlers of Kings County, Long Island, N. Y.* (1881); Edward Mayes, *Geneal. of the Family of Longstreet* (1893); C. C. Jones, Jr., *Memorial Hist. of Augusta, Ga.* (1890); G. H. Preble, *A Chronological Hist. of the Origin and Development of Steam Navigation* (1883).] C. W. M.

LONGWORTH, NICHOLAS (Jan. 16, 1782–Feb. 10, 1863), horticulturist, was born in Newark, N. J., of a Loyalist family whose property was confiscated during the Revolution. His parents were Thomas and Apphia (Vanderpoel) Longworth, and his uncle was David Longworth, the publisher of the early directories of New York City. His great-grandson was Nicholas Longworth [*q.v.*], the speaker of the House of Representatives. For a time he was a clerk in his elder brother's store in South Carolina but, returning to Newark because of his health, he began the study of law. About 1803 he moved to Cincinnati, a log village of eight hundred inhabitants, and continued his law studies in Judge Jacob Burnet's office. He married, in 1807, Susan Connor, widowed daughter of Silas Howell, by whom he had four children. The fee for his first case, the defense of an alleged horsethief, was two second-hand copper stills which he traded for 33 acres, later valued at $2,000,000. He offered $5,000, on time, for Judge Burnet's cow-pasture, was reproved for his foolhardiness, but saw his acquisition reach a valuation of $1,500,000. His practice of accepting land for fees soon involved him in extensive real-estate dealings. In 1850 he paid, next to William Backhouse Astor, the highest taxes on realty in the United States. He was patron of the sculptors, Hiram Powers and Shobal Vail Clevenger [*qq.v.*] and the donor of the site of the Cincinnati observatory. He seldom gave away money, but he offered the unemployed work in his stone-quarry on the Ohio and often deeded widows half the property their husbands had leased. A Whig and an attendant of the Presbyterian Church, he had little respect for politicians or preachers. He was active in the Cincinnati Horticultural Society and was, for some time, president of the Pioneer Association of Cincinnati.

Lawyer, millionaire, patron of the arts, he is one of the ablest horticulturists America has produced. By his experiments he succeeded in making the growing of grapes a commercial success. He imported thousands of European grapes but was unsuccessful until he obtained the native Catawba from John Adlum. In 1828 he produced marketable wine, retired from the law, and devoted himself to grape-culture and wine-manufacture. He had extensive vineyards and two large winehouses near Cincinnati. His sparkling Catawba and Isabella wines took many state agricultural society prizes, and a gift of wine to Longfellow inspired the poem, "Catawba Wine." The part he played in the cultivation of strawberries was equally interesting. Of the gardeners about Cincinnati, only Abergust, a German from Philadelphia, raised strawberries profitably. One day Abergust's son, sauntering through Longworth's strawberry patch, remarked that the crop would be poor as nearly all the plants were male. With this clue, Longworth soon discovered that, virtually, staminate and pistillate plants must be interplanted for successful culture. He informed Cincinnati's market growers, who soon took a leading position in strawberry production, published his discovery, and, when met with scepticism, precipitated, in 1842, the "Strawberry War," which he triumphantly waged against the foremost horticulturists of his time (*Horticultural Review*, June 1854, pp. 288–89). Longworth denied the value of hermaphrodite strawberries but, later, introduced one, the Longworth Prolific, found by a tenant. He also introduced the Ohio Everbearing Black Raspberry. He wrote numerous articles, which appeared in horticultural periodicals and, in 1846, published *A Letter from N. Longworth . . . on the Cultivation of the Grape, and Manufacture of Wine, also, on the Character and Habits of the Strawberry Plant* (1846). He wrote the "Appendix Containing Directions for the Cultivation of the Strawberry" for the 1852 edition of Robert Buchanan's *The Culture of the Grape.*

[L. H. Bailey, *Cyc. of Am. Horticulture*, vol. II (1900); Charles Cist, *Sketches and Statistics of Cincinnati* (1851); C. F. Goss, *Cincinnati, the Queen City* (1912), vol. IV; L. H. Bailey, *Sketch of the Evolution of our Native Fruits* (1898); S. W. Fletcher, *The Strawberry in North America* (1917); *Mag. of Horticulture*, Apr. 1903; *Ohio Arch. and Hist. Quart.*, Jan. 1923, p. 20; *Archives of State of N. J.*, ser. 2, vol. I (1901); G. B. Vanderpoel, *Geneal. of the Vanderpoel Family* (1912); *Cincinnati Daily Commercial*, Feb. 11, 1863; *World* (N. Y.), Feb. 11, 1863, Feb. 25, 1895.]

H. D. H.

LONGWORTH, NICHOLAS (Nov. 5, 1869–Apr. 9, 1931), speaker of the House of Representatives, was born at Cincinnati, Ohio, the son of Nicholas and Susan (Walker) Longworth and the great-grandson of Nicholas Longworth [*q.v.*]. His father, his grandfather, and his great-grandfather were men of wealth, prominent in the business and cultural life of Cincinnati. Graduated at Harvard (B.A.) in 1891, he entered the Harvard Law School in 1892 but received his LL.B. degree from the Law School of Cincinnati College in 1894. Election to the Cincinnati board of education, in 1898, brought him into politics. He attracted the eye of George B. Cox [*q.v.*], the Republican boss of the city and, with his backing, won a seat in the state House from 1899 to 1901 and in the state Senate from 1901 to 1903. He then served in Congress, for the first Ohio district, from 1903 to 1913 and, again, from 1915 to his death in 1931. From 1923 to 1925 he was Republican floor leader of the House and was elected speaker of the Sixty-ninth, Seventieth, and Seventy-first congresses. As a young man of thirty-four he set resolutely to work to study the machinery of the House and to master the intricate details of parliamentary procedure. On his first committee, that for Foreign Affairs, he helped initiate legislation to provide buildings for embassies and legations abroad. In the Sixtieth Congress, he was placed on the ways and means committee, where, as a strong believer in the protective tariff, he came to exercise a commanding influence on tariff matters and, as chairman of the sub-committee on chemicals, paints, and oils, was one of the leaders in framing these important schedules in the 1922 tariff act.

When Frederick H. Gillett became a senator, in 1925, Longworth was elected speaker. A firm believer in responsible party government, he laid down three requisites for the efficient working of the House, strong leadership, adherence to a system of rules that permits a majority to function when necessary, and cooperation. Though a partisan Republican, he never tried to ride rough shod over the Democrats and the western radicals. So strong an impression did his fairness make on his colleagues, that, when he was reëlected speaker in 1927, Finis J. Garrett, the minority leader, told the House that the fitness he had already shown inspired entire confidence in the rectitude of his future administration of the great office. In spite of his party loyalty, he, at times, opposed a Republican president. He left the speaker's dais to take the floor in opposition to the naval program of Coolidge and helped to push the soldiers' loan bill through the House over the opposition of Hoover.

On Feb. 17, 1906, he married, at the White House, Alice Lee Roosevelt. The wedding was one of the most brilliant in the history of the capital. His rise to prominence, however, could be attributed neither to the accident of his birth nor to his marriage to the daughter of Theodore Roosevelt. In 1912, when Roosevelt broke with Taft, Longworth refused to follow. He supported Taft and was defeated that year for Congress.

Longworth will not rank as a great speaker, yet his place will be an honored one. He defended the prerogatives of the House and sought to enhance its prestige against the Senate; in a notable decision from the chair, he insisted that, in their comments on individual senators, House members observe the courtesies laid down in Jefferson's Manual, even though the presiding officer of the Senate had ruled that senators were free to indulge in personalities about members of the House (*Congressional Record,* 71 Cong., 2 Sess., pp. 8453–56). As a tactful mediator, he helped adjust many a dispute. He was a musician of real distinction, democratic in his social contacts, and possessed withal a geniality that won the hearts even of political opponents. He, his wife, and their little daughter, Paulina, enjoyed a position of importance in American life. He will be remembered as much for his personality as for his abilities as a presiding officer and parliamentarian.

[Sources of information include: *Cong. Record,* 72 Cong., 1 Sess., pp. 11171–78, 413–14; C. F. Goss, *Cincinnati, the Queen City* (1912), vol. IV; Harvard College Class of 1891, *Secretary's Report,* nos. IV, VI (1906–16?); *Scribner's,* Mar. 1928; *Review of Reviews* (N. Y.), Aug. 1926, Apr. 1925; *Am. Mercury*; Sept. 1931; *New York Times,* Apr. 10, 1931, Feb. 12, 1928; *New York Herald Tribune,* Apr. 10, 1931; *The Times* (London), Apr. 10, 1931. As this sketch goes to press publication is announced of *The Making of Nicholas Longworth* (1933), by his sister, Clara Longworth de Chambrun.] O. M., Jr.

LONGYEAR, JOHN MUNROE (Apr. 15, 1850–May 28, 1922), capitalist, was born in Lansing, Mich., the son of Harriet (Munroe) and John Wesley Longyear, a congressman and jurist of some distinction. He was educated in the Lansing public schools, in the preparatory departments of Olivet College at Olivet, Mich., and of Georgetown College at Washington, D. C., and in Cazenovia Seminary at Cazenovia, N. Y. Forced by ill health, he sought outdoor employment and scaled and shipped lumber in the Saginaw Valley. In the spring of 1873 he joined an expedition into the Upper Peninsula of Michigan to examine and report on the widely scattered state mineral reserve lands. The steamer *Rocket* landed the party at Marquette, then with a population of about three thousand in an almost unbroken wilderness. The explorations proved so interesting to him that he decided to spend the next five years in an extensive study of the timber, water power, and mineral resources of the Upper Peninsula. He acquired an extraordinary knowledge of the country's resources, which helped him to become, in later years, the trusted agent and associate of capitalists.

The first large concern to appoint him its agent, in 1878, was the Lake Superior Ship Canal, Railway & Iron Company, now the Keweenaw Land Association, whose extensive holdings he continued to direct until his death. However, it is the opening and development of the Menominee and Gogebic iron ranges for which Longyear is best known. His magnetic survey of these regions in 1880 and 1881 led to unusual success in the development of iron and iron ore. By 1912 the Gogebic range was producing three million tons annually. In 1885 he investigated the possibility of valuable deposits in the Mesaba district of Minnesota and brought back findings that resulted in contracts made with the Wright & Davis Lumber Company, Ex-Governor Pillsbury, James J. Hill, and the United States Steel Corporation. In addition to all this he had a share in exploring and developing a high-grade bituminous coal deposit at Longyear City, on the Arctic island of Spitzbergen, which he continued to hold even after Norwegian bankers bought out all other interests during the World War. He also maintained an unflagging interest in the "Longyear Process" for utilizing low-grade ores, which is still in the course of development.

Among his many connections, he was president of a bank, president of a button company in Detroit, and joint owner of a score of large property holdings controlling some three million acres. He was also active in public affairs, a leader in the Michigan taxpayers' association, mayor of Marquette in 1890–91, and patron of education. He was a member of the board of control of the Michigan College of Mines for twenty-four years and was also a member of the corporation of the Massachusetts Institute of Technology. Among numerous contributions were gifts to hospitals, colleges, libraries, and high schools. In 1919 he helped establish a printing plant for the blind in Los Angeles, which became the printing department of the Braille Institute of America. For many years he was president of the Marquette County Historical Society and a member of many other organizations. He and his wife, Mary Hawley (Beecher) Longyear, whom he married on Jan. 4, 1879, founded the Zion Research Foundation of Brookline, Mass., and also presented to the Church of Christ, Scientist, in Boston, the park which separates it from Huntington Avenue.

[A large part of the material for this sketch was furnished by a daughter, Mrs. Carroll Paul, from the papers of the Longyear Estate, and from Longyear's own unpublished reminiscences; Mrs. Paul is the authority for the spelling of the middle name; see also papers of the Marquette County Historical Society; *Memorial Record of the Northern Peninsula of Mich.* (1895); A. L. Sawyer, *A Hist. of the Northern Peninsula of Mich.* (1911) vols. I, II; N. H. Dole, *America in Spitsbergen; the Romance of an Arctic Coal-mine* (1922) largely from material supplied by Longyear; *Mich. Hist. Mag.*, nos. 2–3 (1922); *A Biog. Sketch of J. Robert Atkinson* (copr. 1932) reprinted from *Cal. and Californians*, ed. by R. D. Hunt (1932); *Early Hist. of Mich. with Biographies*, comp. by S. D. Bingham (1888) for father's career; *Boston Transcript*, May 29, 1922.] H. L. G.

LOOMIS, ARPHAXED (Apr. 9, 1798–Sept. 15, 1885), law reformer and congressman from New York, was born in Winchester, Litchfield County, Conn., a son of Thaddeus and Lois (Griswold) Loomis and a descendant of Joseph Loomis, who emigrated from England to Windsor, Conn., about 1639. His family removed, while he was a small boy, to Salisbury in Herkimer County, N. Y. Until he was about fourteen he worked on his father's farm and then became a district school teacher. By teaching in the winter and going to the academy at Fairfield, Conn., in the summer, he managed to acquire a good basic education. In 1818 he began to read law and was admitted to the bar in 1822, when he established himself in practice at Sacketts Harbor. He removed to Little Falls in 1825, where he lived for the rest of his life. On Oct. 5, 1831, he married Anne P. Todd, daughter of Stephen Todd of Salisbury.

In 1828 he became surrogate of Herkimer County and served until 1836; from 1835 to 1840 he was first judge of the county. Elected to Congress as a Democrat in 1837, he served in that body until 1839. He was elected to the state Assembly for the sessions of 1841 and 1842, where he became chairman of the judiciary committee and prepared a bill designed to improve the administration of justice. Gifted with the ability to speak well in public, he became widely known for his support of measures in behalf of law reform and was chosen to sit in the constitutional convention of 1846, where he took a prominent part in the proceedings, particularly in relation to the judiciary article. The constitution provided for the appointment by the legislature of a commission on practice and pleadings. The three commissioners appointed were Loomis, Nicholas Hill, Jr., and David Graham [*q.v.*]. Hill was not in harmony with the other two members and resigned. When David Dudley Field [*q.v.*] was appointed in his place, the commission was united in desiring an entire revision in the system of pleading and practice instead of various attempts at amendment. It rendered to the legislature six reports, in all, which remain a distinct contribution to the history of codification. The Code of Civil Procedure drawn up by it was duly enacted and went into effect July 1, 1848, but the commission continued until Dec. 31, 1849, the date of its final report.

Loomis was again a member of the state Assembly in 1853 and was a delegate to the state nominating conventions of 1861 and 1863. Afflicted with a progressive deafness, he retired more and more completely but exerted himself from time to time, nevertheless, to oppose such measures as the suspension of the writ of *habeas corpus* during the Civil War. In 1879 he published his own account of his activities for law reform in a pamphlet, *Historic Sketch of the New York System of Law Reform in Practice and Pleadings.* His reputation has been overshadowed by the fame of his co-worker, David Dudley Field; yet he rendered service of real importance and lasting value. His claim to a share in the credit for the work of the committee of 1848 has been set forth by John T. Fitzpatrick: "The Code of Procedure, as amended in 1849, is commonly referred to as the Field Code, from the common belief that David Dudley Field drafted the greater part. Field never denied this, but Arphaxed Loomis, one of the commissioners, presents a very good case to show that the work was jointly that of all three commissioners, none having a preponderating part" (*Law Library Journal,* Oct. 1924, p. 15).

[S. Croswell and R. Sutton, *Debates and Proc. in the N. Y. State Convention, for the Revision on the Constitution* (1846); W. G. Bishop and W. H. Attree, *Rept. of the Debates and Proc. of the Convention for the Revision of the Constitution of the State of N. Y.*,

1846 (1846); *Jour. of the Convention of the State of N. Y. . . . 1846* (1846); E. A. Werner, *Civil List and Constitutional Hist. of the Colony and State of N. Y.* (1889); *Memorial Proc. of the Herkimer County Bar, with a Few Obit. Notices on Death of Hon. Arphaxed Loomis* (1885); David McAdam and others, *Hist. of the Bench and Bar of N. Y.*, vol. I (1897); G. A. Hardin and F. H. Willard, *Hist. of Herkimer County, N. Y.* (1893); D. A. Alexander, *A Pol. Hist. of the State of N. Y.*, vols. II, III (1906–09); *Biog. Dir. of the Am. Cong.* (1928); E. S. Loomis, *Descendants of Joseph Loomis* (1908).] A. S. M.

LOOMIS, CHARLES BATTELL (Sept. 16, 1861–Sept. 23, 1911), humorist, was born in Brooklyn, N. Y., son of Charles Battell and Mary (Worthington) Loomis, and brother of Harvey Worthington Loomis the composer. He was a descendant of Joseph Loomis of Braintree, Essex, England, who emigrated to Boston, Mass., in 1638 and by 1640 was living in Windsor, Conn. Charles attended the Brooklyn Polytechnic Institute, without graduating, and from 1879 to 1891 was engaged in clerical work chiefly in Brooklyn. On Feb. 14, 1888, he married Mary Charlotte Fullerton of Brooklyn, by whom he had two sons and a daughter. The illness of his eldest child led him in 1891 to leave the city and settle in the Battelle family home, Torringford, Conn., where his great-grandfather had lived. Having already contributed jokes and light verse to *Puck* and other periodicals, he soon found writing more profitable than chicken-farming, and turned definitely to it as a career. After 1899 the family usually spent the winters at Leonia or some other Jersey suburb, but each spring returned to Torringford. It was from the people around him—Connecticut Yankees, suburbanites, and some city folk—that Loomis drew the kindly, whimsical, everyday characters of his sketches. With a remarkable voice and irresistibly humorous manner—he was by general testimony one of the homeliest and most lovable of men—he also took up public reading, and by the late nineties his success in this field began to keep pace with his reputation as a writer. In 1905 he accompanied Jerome K. Jerome on a platform tour through the United States, and subsequently went with Jerome to England. With his audiences Loomis was always very effective, his funereal aspect, skill in impersonation, and quick but never caustic wit adding to his work a quality which in print is hardly conveyed. "His writings," remarks Jerome (*My Life and Times,* 1926, p. 254), as scattered through the magazines, "were mildly amusing, but that was all . . . until . . . he read them, when at once they became the most humorous stories in American literature. He made no gestures; his face, but for the eyes, might have been carved out of wood; his genius was in his marvelous voice." As a member of the Salmagundi and Authors clubs of New York he was loved for his modesty and warm friendliness. He was in constant demand as an entertainer, possessing both as a reader and after-dinner speaker an unusual ability to sense the spirit of an audience and draw it to him with his first effort. His earliest published book was a collection of light verse, *Just Rhymes* (1899). His prose contributions to magazines were published from time to time in some fifteen volumes, the best of which, perhaps, are his *Cheerful Americans* (1903) and *A Holiday Touch* (1908). *A Bath in an English Tub* (1907) followed his stay in England, and *Just Irish* (1909) was the outcome of his visit to Ireland the next year. Death came at a hospital in Hartford, Conn., from cancer of the stomach, from which he had suffered for nine months. During this time he was writing some of his best work, a series of Irish fairy tales for the *Saturday Evening Post,* never collected in book form. It was as a platform humorist that Loomis won his chief title to fame. As such, in the view of Ellis Parker Butler (letter to A. F. Loomis), he was "the most important in his period, and far and away the funniest . . . the last of the great platform humorists and the link between the speaking and reading humorist and the printed humorist that later usurped public favor."

[Elias and E. S. Loomis, *Descendants of Joseph Loomis in America* (1908); *The Bookman,* May 1912; *Who's Who in America,* 1910–11; *Hartford Daily Courant,* Sept. 25, 1911; family sources.] A. W.

LOOMIS, DWIGHT (July 27, 1821–Sept. 17, 1903), jurist and congressman from Connecticut, a descendant of Joseph Loomis of Braintree, England, who settled in the Connecticut colony, at Windsor, about 1639, and the second son of Mary (Pinneo) and Elam Loomis, a prosperous farmer, was born in the small town of Columbia, in Tolland County, Conn. He received a common-school education and attended the academies at Monson, Mass., and at Amherst, Mass. For a short time thereafter he taught in the Connecticut towns of Andover, Columbia, Lebanon, and Hebron. In 1844 he began to read law with John H. Brockway of Ellington and, in 1846, entered the law department of Yale College. The next year he was admitted to the bar and began practice in Rockville. In 1851 he was a member of the lower house of the state legislature. Five years later he was a delegate to the Philadelphia convention that nominated Frémont as Republican candidate for the presidency. In 1857 he was a member of the state Senate. From 1859 to 1863 he was a representative in Congress. During his first session, on June 16, 1860, he made a long speech, in which he upheld the rights of the House of Representatives against a supposed attempt on the part of the President to influence legislation. He was moved by such a strong feeling of animosity to Buchanan that, in closing his address, he remarked that, were the administration to collapse, a fitting funeral sermon might be preached on the theme—"With rapture we delight to see the cuss removed" (*Cong. Globe,* 36 Cong., 1 Sess., App., pp. 429–31). In advocating his favorite principles, opposition to a strong executive, economy in public expenditures, and the desirability of a high tariff, he was restating the policies held by most Connecticut politicians of the first half of the nineteenth century, and in supporting the Union against secession, he was guided, for the most part, by motives of local or state interest.

In 1864 he became judge of the superior court of Connecticut, was reëlected in 1872, but did not finish his second term, for, in 1875, he was elected associate judge of the supreme court of errors, on which he continued to serve with distinction until he reached the age of retirement in 1891.

After he left the bench he moved to Hartford, where he devoted himself to various professional pursuits; from 1891 to 1893 he was an instructor in the Yale Law School; in 1895 he edited, with J. Gilbert Calhoun, *The Judicial and Civil History of Connecticut*; he acted as arbitrator in such disputes as those between the state, Yale University, and Storrs Agricultural College; and he served as a member of the state board of mediation and arbitration. Most of his attention, however, he gave to his duties as state referee, to which position the General Assembly appointed him in 1891. He was returning home from a hearing at Torrington, when he died suddenly near Waterbury. In November 1848 he married Mary E. Bill, who died in 1864 and, in May 1866, he married Jane E. Kendall.

[*Biog. Encyc. of Conn. and R. I.* (1881); *Conn. Reports,* vol. LXXVI (1904); *Encyc. of Conn. Biog.* (1919), vol. VI; *Representative Men of Conn.,* ed. by W. F. Moore (1894); J. R. Cole, *Hist. of Tolland County, Conn.* (1888); *Roll of State Officers and Members of Gen. Assembly of Conn. from 1776 to 1881* (1881); E. S. Loomis, *Descendants of Joseph Loomis* (1908); *Hartford Courant,* Sept. 18, 1903.]

J. M. M.

LOOMIS, ELIAS (Aug. 7, 1811–Aug. 15, 1889), mathematician and astronomer, was one of six children of Rev. Hubbel Loomis of Willington, Conn., and his wife, Jerusha Burt of Longmeadow, Mass. The father was a Baptist clergyman and a descendant of Joseph Loomis who emigrated from England to Massachusetts in 1638 and two years later was in Windsor, Conn. As a young man Hubbel Loomis attended Union College for a time, and in 1812 Yale University conferred upon him the honorary degree of master of arts. Soon after the death of his wife in 1829, he joined the pioneers in what was then known as the West, settling in Illinois. Here he became vice-president of the state antislavery society and was one of the prime movers in establishing Shurtleff College. Before leaving New England he had personally attended to the preliminary education of Elias, his eldest son, who was admitted to Yale College at the age of fourteen and graduated in 1830.

After a year of teaching mathematics in Mount Hope Academy, near Baltimore, Elias entered Andover Theological Seminary in 1831, but two years later, receiving a call to his alma mater, abandoned his intention to become a minister and returned to Yale, where he taught Latin, mathematics, and natural philosophy. Here he found the opportunity to pursue further some work in astronomy in which he had been interested while in college. He devoted much attention to the study of the variations of the magnetic needle and with Professor Alexander C. Twining [*q.v.*] of West Point carried on a series of important observations (1834) to determine the altitude of shooting stars. With Professor Denison Olmsted [*q.v.*], he rediscovered Halley's Comet on its return to perihelion (1835) and again computed its orbit. In 1836 he was appointed to the professorship of mathematics and natural philosophy at Western Reserve College, then at Hudson, Ohio, and went abroad for further study in Paris (1836–37) under the direction of Arago, Biot, and others. There and in London he purchased the apparatus needed for the professorship awaiting him, and particularly the outfit for a small observatory. Returning to America in 1837, he assumed his duties at Western Reserve, where he remained until 1844.

From 1844 to 1860, except for one year (1848) at Princeton, he was professor of mathematics and natural philosophy in the University of the City of New York. Thence he went to Yale, succeeding Denison Olmsted, and there he remained until his death in 1889. In 1873 he was made a member of the National Academy of Sciences. He contributed to various scientific journals, notably the *American Journal of Science,* in which he published a series of papers on the aurora borealis (November 1859–September 1861) and a series of twenty-three papers with the general title "Contributions to Meteorology" (July 1874–April 1889). It was through his textbooks, however, that he exerted his greatest influence. These included works on natural philosophy, astronomy, meteorology, analytic geometry, and the calculus, besides other and more elementary subjects. From their sale he derived a comfortable fortune. His books were translated into Chinese and Arabic, and did much to make western mathematics known in the Orient. As a teacher he was possessed of unusual ability; Chief Justice Waite said of him, "If I have been successful in life, I owe that success to the influence of tutor Loomis more than to any other cause whatsoever" (Newton, *post*, p. 29). In his will he left $300,000 to Yale, the largest single donation received by his alma mater up to that time.

Loomis was interested in the history of his family and compiled a genealogy, *The Descendants of Joseph Loomis, Who Came from Braintree, England, in the Year 1638, and Settled in Windsor, Connecticut, in 1639,* first published in 1870, which went through three editions in his lifetime and was again revised in 1908. He was married, May 18, 1840, to Julia Elmore Upson, of Tallmadge, Ohio, who died in 1854. They had two sons, Francis Engelsby and Henry Bradford Loomis, each of whom established a scientific fellowship at Yale.

[*The Descendants of Joseph Loomis* (1908), revised by E. S. Loomis; H. A. Newton, *Elias Loomis, LL.D. . . . Memorial Address Delivered in Osborn Hall, Apr. 11, 1890* (1890), repr. in *Am. Jour. Sci.*, June 1890; *Obit. Record Grads. Yale Univ.* (1890); J. L. Chamberlain, *N. Y. Univ. . . . with Biog. Sketches* (1901–03); *Morning Journal and Courier* (New Haven), Aug. 16, 1889.] D. E. S.

LOOMIS, ELMER HOWARD (May 24, 1861–Jan. 22, 1931), physicist, was born in Vermillion, Oswego County, N. Y., the son of Hiram Warren and Adaline Sabra (Sayles) Loomis. He was a descendant of Joseph Loomis of Braintree, Essex, England, who came to Massachusetts in 1638 and later settled in Windsor, Conn. Hiram Loomis was engaged in the insurance business, and was at one time a member of the New York legislature. He removed to Mexico, Oswego County, while Elmer was still young. The boy was prepared for college in an academy of that town, and in 1883 was graduated from Madison University (now Colgate). He taught physics and chemistry for seven years in Colgate Academy, Hamilton, N. Y., and while there, July 23, 1885, married Mary E. Bennett of Mexico. By this marriage he had two children who died in infancy, and a son, who survived him. In 1904 his wife died, and on Oct. 12, 1911, he married Grace Eaton Woods of Rochester, N. Y.

In 1890 he went to Germany for study. He began his work at the University of Göttingen and later transferred to the University of Strassburg, where he received, in 1893, the degree of doctor of philosophy. His dissertation, *"Ueber ein exacteres Verfahren bei der Bestimmung von Gefrierpunktserniedrigungen"* (*Annalen der Physik und Chemie*, Neue Folge, Band LI, no. 3, 1894), dealt with the lowering of the freezing points of solutions, and presented a critical study of the difficulties involved in making exact determinations of these important quantities, and with various improvements in the methods of observation. It was honored with a *summa cum laude*. On his return to America, he became in 1894 instructor in physics at Princeton University, and was later assistant professor and professor. He continued for some years to publish papers on the same general subject as that of his dissertation, in which he presented a great collection of measurements that were carried to the highest degree of exactitude which the nature of the problem permitted. In particular he proved that non-electrolytes in solution obey Raoult's law with great precision, and he made what may be considered a final determination of Raoult's constant. These papers appeared in the *Annalen der Physik* and the *Physical Review* (1896–1901). He was a fellow of the American Association for the Advancement of Science, and of the American Physical Society. In 1929 he retired from his professorship.

He was a man of strong philanthropic instincts, serving for years as a member of the Princeton board of health, and as a director of the New Jersey Sanitarium for Tuberculosis. His sympathy went out to the poor and the unfortunate, and he was always ready with labor and thought to contribute to their welfare. He amused himself in the later years of his life by collecting antique furniture, and he became an adept as a collector and restorer. His other hobby was the planting of shrubs and trees. Many of the streets of Princeton are lined with the trees which he planted.

[Elias and E. S. Loomis, *Descendants of Joseph Loomis in America* (1908); *Who's Who in America,* 1930–31; *Princeton Alumni Weekly,* Jan. 30, 1931; *Princeton Herald,* Jan. 23, 1931; *N. Y. Times*, Jan. 23, 1931; information as to certain facts from family, and personal acquaintance.] W. F. M.

LOOMIS, MAHLON (July 21, 1826–Oct. 13, 1886), dentist, experimenter, pioneer in wireless telegraphy, was descended from Joseph Loomis, who came from England to Massachusetts in 1638 and later settled in Windsor, Conn. His father was Prof. Nathan Loomis, associated with Benjamin Peirce of Harvard in founding the *American Ephemeris and Nautical Almanac*; his mother was Waitie Jenks (Barber) Loomis. He was born in Oppenheim, N. Y., moved to Virginia with the family in the forties, and in 1848 went to Cleveland, Ohio, where he studied dentistry and taught school for a time. After a period as a traveling dentist he practised successively in Earlville, N. Y., Cambridgeport, Mass., and Philadelphia. On May 2, 1854, he patented a mineral-plate (kaolin) process for making artificial teeth, for which he also received a patent in England. He was married, May 28, 1856, to Achsah Ashley.

About 1860, he turned his attention to electricity. One of his early experiments was the forcing of growth of plants by buried metal plates connected to batteries. At about the same time he became interested in the electrical charges which could be obtained from the upper air by means of kites carrying metal wires. At first, he planned to use this natural source of electricity to replace batteries, and actually did so on a telegraph line four hundred miles long. From this experiment, by one step after another, he was led to the discovery that a kite wire sent aloft in one region would affect the flow of electricity to ground in another kite wire some distance away. In 1868 in the presence of members of Congress and eminent scientists, he carried on two-way "wireless" communication for a distance of eighteen miles between two mountain peaks in Virginia. From one peak, he sent up a kite and wire, connecting this to ground through a galvanometer. At once the galvanometer deflected, showing a steady passage of current to ground from the charged air stratum above. He then set up a similar outfit from a peak eighteen miles away. When ready to "send," he touched this second kite wire to ground; by this action he tapped the "aerial battery" and reduced the voltage of the entire charged stratum of air above, thus lessening the voltage available at the distant air-wire, and hence causing the galvanometer needle there to move to a smaller deflection. This change in deflection was a true telegraphic signal; Loomis had succeeded for the first time in "sending signals to a distance without wires." He interested a group of Boston capitalists in his discovery, only to lose their support in the "Black Friday" panic of 1869. Two years later, the promise of Chicago bankers to aid him likewise came to naught, owing to the great Chicago fire. In 1870 a bill incorporating the Loomis Aerial Telegraph Company was introduced into Congress; it passed the House in May 1872 and the Senate in January 1873, and was signed by President Grant, but it failed to provide the appropriation of $50,000 for which Loomis had hoped. Thereafter, he was unable to find anywhere the financial backing he needed for his experiments. He died in 1886 at Terre Alta, W. Va., heartbroken by what he deemed his failure.

Of Loomis' inventiveness there is no question. His brain teemed with ideas. Some were not altogether practical, such as replacing batteries by atmospheric electricity; some were eminently practical. His notebooks, in the Manuscripts Division of the Library of Congress, are filled with cryptic references and suggestions; on the other hand, he actually carried out many of his experiments, and his records of these are clear and eloquent. It was not until twenty-seven years after his experiment of 1868, however, that Marconi used this same air-wire in true Hertzian-wave communication, the modern "radio." Although Loomis produced sparks when he touched his kite wire to ground, and hence sent out electric waves, he had no means of detecting them. Had Branly brought out his coherer or Fessenden his electrolytic detector prior to Loomis' experiment, it would have been a simple matter to use one of these instruments instead of the galvanometer, and Loomis instead of Marconi might have been known as the father of radio. As it is, his distinction is, that of the long line of those who carried on experiments in wireless telegraphy, using the aerial, he was the first.

[Elias and E. S. Loomis, *Descendants of Joseph Loomis in America* (rev. ed., 1908); *Cong. Globe,* 41 Cong., 2 Sess., p. 5439, 42 Cong., 2 Sess., pp. 3667–70, 3687–88, 3 Sess., pp. 604–05, 631–32; Mary Texanna Loomis, *Radio Theory and Operating* (1925); E. S. Loomis, *Dr. Mahlon Loomis and Wireless Telegraphy* (1914); *The Candlestick* (Springfield, Mass.), Dec. 1910; W. J. Rhees, article in *Evening Star* (Washington), Nov. 18, 1899; "An American Pioneer in Wireless," (Baltimore) *Sun,* Sept. 7, 1930; Robert Marriott, "How Radio Grew Up," *Radio Broadcast,* Dec. 1925.]

G. H. C.

LOOP, HENRY AUGUSTUS (Sept. 9, 1831–Oct. 20, 1895), portrait and figure painter, was born at Hillsdale, N. Y. He was the son of George H. and Angelica M. (Downing) Loop and a descendant of Gerlach Leupp who emigrated to America from the Netherlands. He received his early education in a school for boys at Great Barrington, Mass. At the age of nineteen he went to New York City and began the study of his art under Henry Peters Gray, with whom he remained for about a year. About 1857 he went to Paris and continued his studies under Thomas Couture. Later he made independent preparations for his life work in the galleries of Rome, Venice, Florence, and other Italian cities. On his return to New York he was made a member of the National Academy of Design in 1861. In 1865 he married Jennette Shepherd Harrison of New Haven, Conn. (1840–1909), one of his most talented pupils. She became an accomplished portraitist and an associate of the National Academy. They had three daughters, one of whom, Edith, also became a portrait painter.

From about 1860 Loop was one of the most regular exhibitors in the annual exhibitions of the National Academy of Design for some thirty years. His genre and mythological subjects, though doubtless somewhat academic in conception and execution, were marked by grace, refinement, and a pleasant vein of sentiment, and were consequently popular. Among the most interesting of these performances were his "Undine" (1863), which was warmly praised by the critics of the time; his "Aphrodite," which was bought by Collis P. Huntington after being shown at the Centennial Exposition of 1876 in Philadelphia; his "Italian Minstrel," which appeared in the Paris Salon of 1868; and "Love's Crown," which was given to the Metropolitan Museum of Art, New York, in 1898, by his wife. This last-named piece represents a female figure clad in loose, flowing white draperies, and crowned with a wreath of flowers. Loop also found steady employment as a portrait painter, and among his sitters were Bishop Gregory T. Bedell of Ohio, Anson Phelps Stokes, J. M. Ward, Russell Sage, Hon. William G. Choate, Worthington Whittredge, and other well-known men. The artist went abroad again in 1867 for the purpose of visiting the principal Continental art centers and was away from home for a year and a half. With this exception his professional life was passed in New York, where for many years he had a studio on Madison Avenue. He was a member of the Artists' Fund Society and the Century Club. He died at Lake George in his sixty-fifth year.

[Sources include: Clara E. Clement and Laurence Hutton, *Artists of the Nineteenth Century and Their Works* (1879), vol. II; the *Art Jour.*, May 1876; *Evening Post* (N. Y.), June 3, 1863, Oct. 21, 1895. Information as to certain facts was supplied for this sketch by Loop's daughter, Miss Edith Loop.]

W. H. D.

LOOS, CHARLES LOUIS (Dec. 23, 1823–Feb. 27, 1912), clergyman of the Disciples of Christ, editor, college president, was born at Woerth-sur-Sauer, Lower Alsace. His father, Jacques George Loos, was French and had been a lancer in Napoleon's army; his mother, Katharina P. Kull, was German. The boy had thus the opportunity to learn two languages and, perhaps, varying political opinions; he adopted, however, his father's patriotic and religious views to the extent of favoring France and attending the Lutheran Church. Admiring Napoleon, the lad became, in opposition to the Bourbonists, a Republican, and afterward related how he helped in 1830 to sing the *Marseillaise* through the streets of his native town.

At the age of four he went to the academy in Woerth and continued his schooling there until the family emigrated to the United States in 1834, settling on a farm near Canton, Ohio. For the next few years he spent his time in farming, in acquiring an education in a new environment, and in pondering matters of religion. He was confirmed in the Lutheran Church in 1837, but the next year, having become convinced that the views of the Disciples of Christ were most satisfying, he joined that body and retained membership therein until his death. At sixteen he was teaching school; at seventeen he served as a lay minister in the church he had just espoused. Ambitious to advance in teaching and preaching, he entered Bethany College, Bethany, Va. (now West Virginia), in 1842. After graduation in 1846, he spent the following years as instructor in the preparatory department of the college, and in 1848 married Rosetta Erina Kerr. The year 1849 found him a preacher in Wellsburg, Va.; from 1850 to 1856 he held a pastorate in Somerset, Pa.; and for one year he served a congregation in Cincinnati (1856–57). Ministerial duties did not absorb all his energies: in Somerset he headed a Collegiate Institute from 1853 to 1856, and also founded and edited in 1851 *The Disciple,* a magazine which survived two years. When he moved to Cincinnati he became assistant editor of *The Christian Age.* Dividing his loyalties between church and school, Loos nevertheless preferred the latter, and from 1857 his occupation was largely educational. In that year he became president of Eureka College, Illinois, and in 1858 he accepted a call to the professorship of ancient languages at his alma mater. Here he remained until 1880, assisting in the editing of *The Millennial Harbinger* from 1865 to 1871 and widening his reputation as a classical scholar whose desire was to make scholarship an aid to piety. In 1880 this reputation resulted in an offer of the presidency of Kentucky University (now Transylvania College) and in that year he moved to Lexington to assume this position. For seventeen years he performed his duties with wisdom and tact, and after his resignation in 1897 he remained in the institution as professor of Greek.

The closing decade of his life found him respected as a personal friend of Alexander Campbell [*q.v.*] and as a scholar thoroughly familiar with his church's history and proficient in Hebrew, Latin, French, German, and Italian, as well as in Greek. Prominent in days of bitter controversy, he nevertheless pursued a career singularly free from disputes and antagonisms, a fact easily credited by one who examines the gentle features revealed in his photographs. He wrote no books, but his contributions to church papers exerted no little influence. He was concerned over the proper execution of the sacrament of baptism; he championed the rights of colored members of his church; he resented alleged efforts of the French Catholic Church to interfere in education. He is buried in the Lexington cemetery.

[W. T. Moore, *A Comprehensive Hist. of the Disciples of Christ* (1909); J. T. Brown, *Churches of Christ* (1904); *Biog. Cyc. of the Commonwealth of Ky.* (1896); A. W. Fortune, *The Disciples in Ky.* (1932); *Who's Who in America*, 1910–11; *Courier-Journal* (Louisville, Ky.), Feb. 28, 1912; files of *The Crimson* (Ky. Univ.); Charles Louis Loos's scrapbook, in library of Transylvania Coll.; information from acquaintances.] G. C. K.

LOPEZ, AARON (1731–May 28, 1782), colonial merchant, was the son of Diego Jose Lopez; his mother was also "of the Lopez family." He was born in Portugal. On Oct. 13, 1752, he arrived in Newport, R. I., with his wife, who was the daughter of his half-sister Elizabeth, his daughter, and younger brother. An older half-brother named Moses had been residing in Newport since the middle forties. In Portugal the three Lopez brothers had lived openly as Christians but secretly as Jews. Aaron and his wife had been named Edward and Anna, but on coming to America they adopted Jewish names and were remarried according to Jewish ceremony. Apparently Aaron Lopez' beginnings as a merchant were exceedingly meager, for even by the period of the Seven Years' War he does not appear to have been at all active. It seems that he at first started, as did so many other merchants of the day, by buying, selling, and exchanging only in Newport and Providence. In 1756 he was in regular correspondence with Henry Lloyd of Boston. At this time, however, his chief interest was the spermaceti candle business in which he and Jacob Roderique Rivera were among the pioneers. By 1761 there were so many competitors in this whale-oil industry that the New England firms formed the United Company of Spermaceti Candlers and arranged price agreements.

Previous to 1765 the Lopez shipping was mostly coastwise, and the invoices usually listed boxes of candles. After 1765 Lopez attempted, in addition to his small business with London, to enter the Bristol trade on a large scale, a venture which proved most disappointing. Far more successful was his later search for new markets in the West Indies. His first factor, Abraham Pereira Mendes, was incompetent, but Mendes' successor, Capt. Benjamin Wright, gradually built up a lucrative trade. Markets in the Caribbean were poor until about 1770 when at last Lopez realized a number of profitable ventures and had so extended his commerce that his vessels could have been seen riding the bounding main to Jamaica, Hispaniola, Surinam, Honduras, Newfoundland, England, Holland, Spain, Portugal, Africa, the Azores and Canaries. The debt to his Bristol correspondent, Henry Cruger, Jr., in 1767 was £10,514 sterling, but by 1773 this enormous liability appears to have been practically erased. Lopez had learned the necessity of a multiform commerce, and by the seventies he had found prosperity. The years 1773 and 1774 had seen a tremendous increase in his shipping, but these were the last golden years for both the house of Lopez and the town of Newport. He was still pushing his trade in the West Indies, in Europe, Africa, and America. Indeed, he had even joined Francis Rotch of New Bedford in dispatching a fleet of thirteen whalers to the Falkland Islands. It may be said conservatively that by 1775 he had a complete or part ownership in over thirty vessels.

When the violence of the American Revolution finally broke, Lopez moved from Newport to Leicester, Mass. The war not only brought an abrupt end to his business ventures but left his accounts in utter chaos. In May 1782, while on a journey to Rhode Island with his wife and family, he stopped to water his horse at Scott's Pond near Providence and was accidentally drowned. The tragedy was a blow to his friends throughout the commercial world. Although in 1761 he was refused citizenship in Newport and was forced to go to Massachusetts for it, at the outbreak of the American Revolution no man in Newport was more highly respected. On his death, Ezra Stiles, pastor of the Second Congregational Church and later president of Yale College, recorded: "On the 28th of May died that amiable, benevolent, most hospitable & very respectable Gentleman, Mr. Aaron Lopez Merchant. . . . He was a Jew by Nation, was a Merchant of the first Eminence; for Honor & Extent of Commerce probably surpassed by no Mercht in America: He did Business with the greatest Ease & Clearness—always carried about with him a Sweetness of Behav. a calm Urbanity an agreeable & unaffected Politeness of manners. Without a single Enemy & the most universally beloved by an extensive Acquaintance of any man I ever knew. His beneficience to his famy [family] connexions, to his Nation, & to all the

World is almost without a Parallel" (*post,* p. 24). Lopez' first wife, who took the name Abigail, died in 1762, the mother of seven children. His second wife, Sarah Rivera, the daughter of Jacob Roderique Rivera, survived him and moved to New York. She was the mother of ten children, eight of whom lived to maturity.

[See the *Biog. Cyc. of R. I.* (1881); M. J. Kohler, "The Lopez and Rivera Families of Newport," *Am. Jewish Hist. Soc. Pubs.*, no. 2 (1894), and scattered references to Lopez in *Ibid.*, no. 27 (1920); Leon Huhner, "A Merchant Prince of Colonial New England," *Jewish Comment,* May 26, June 2, 1905; F. B. Dexter, *The Lit. Diary of Ezra Stiles, D.D., LL.D.*, vol. III (1901). Many Lopez letter books, ledgers, day books, shipping books, sailors' books, etc., are in the possession of the Newport Hist. Soc. A few Lopez manuscripts are in the Wetmore Collection of the Mass. Hist. Soc. Some of these have been printed in "Commerce of R. I.," *Mass. Hist. Soc. Colls.*, 7 ser. IX and X (1914–15). For a detailed account of the commerce of Lopez see the doctoral thesis at Brown University by B. M. Bigelow on "The Commerce Between Rhode Island and the West Indies Before the American Revolution."]
B. M. B.

LORAS, JEAN MATHIAS PIERRE (Aug. 30, 1792–Feb. 19, 1858), Roman Catholic prelate, was the tenth child of Jean Mathias and Étiennette (Michalet) Loras. Born at Lyons just as the Revolution in France was rushing toward its climax, he was but an infant held in his mother's arms when she pleaded with the tyrant Couthon for the life of her husband, a wealthy merchant and councilor of Lyons. Loras, however, was in the very first group to be guillotined in the Square des Terreaux. Young Jean Mathias received his early education at the hands of priests who sought the hospitality of his mother's home. In an old Carthusian house nearby he commenced his priestly studies. As a lad, he had visited the exiled and imprisoned Pius VI at Valence. In 1807 he entered the seminary of L'Argentière (Hautes-Alpes) and was ordained a priest in the Cathedral of Lyons by the Cardinal-Archbishop in 1817. He was immediately appointed president of the Petit Seminaire of Meximieux; and in 1824 he was promoted to the important office of superior of the seminary of L'Argentière. Having resigned in 1827 to act as pastoral missioner in the Lyons archdiocese, he met Bishop Michael Portier of Mobile, Ala., and decided in 1829 to accompany him to America. For seven years he labored in Alabama as pastor of the Cathedral of Mobile, superior of the newly founded Spring Hill College, and vicar-general of the young diocese.

Chosen in 1837 for the newly created bishopric of Dubuque (then in Wisconsin Territory) he was consecrated on Dec. 10 of the same year by Bishop Portier in the cathedral at Mobile. He did not arrive in Dubuque until Apr. 19, 1839, having spent the intervening months in France seeking priests and funds for his American missions. His new diocese reached from the northern boundary of Missouri to the Canadian line and westward from the Mississippi River to the Missouri River. One priest he found in all that expanse—Father Samuel Charles Mazzuchelli [*q.v.*], the versatile and illustrious Dominican missioner—30,000 Indians, and a few widely scattered white settlements. Believing that the rich soil of the upper Mississippi Valley could be transformed into an agricultural empire, he strove sturdily and steadily to draw the Catholic immigrants from the crowded cities of the Atlantic seaboard. He himself went about among the immigrants of his wide diocese, by canoe and steamboat, in stage-coach and on foot, ministering and organizing. With the strategic eye of a general he picked church sites in new villages even before the arrival of Catholics; he organized schools; he evangelized the Indians; he brought in teaching and nursing sisterhoods; he induced a Trappist order of monks to erect a monastery near Dubuque; and he founded a college—a short-lived project but crowned with success while it endured. Offered an archbishopric in France by influential relatives if he would return to that country, he refused it emphatically; and roused by remarks of some French bishops, he wrote: "We have no martyrs of blood in the United States but many of charity."

He also participated actively in many public and civic movements. A firm total abstainer, he appealed to the Catholics to uphold temperance by voting for the Iowa Liquor Law of 1855. In May 1846 he and Bishop John Hughes [*q.v.*] of New York called on James Buchanan, then secretary of state, and succeeded in having President Polk appoint chaplains to serve the Catholic soldiers during the Mexican War.

[Louis de Cailly, *Memoirs of Bishop Loras, First Bishop of Dubuque, Iowa, and of Members of his Family from 1792 to 1858* (1897); J. F. Kempker, *Hist. of the Cath. Ch. in Iowa* (1887); published letters of Loras in *Acta et Dicta* (1907–08, 1916–18); John Ireland, in *The Cath. World,* Sept.–Oct., 1898; unpublished documents and letters in the archdiocesan archives of Dubuque and St. Louis.]
M. M. H.

LORD, ASA DEARBORN (June 17, 1816–Mar. 7, 1875), educational leader, was born at Madrid, N. Y. His father, Asa Lord, died when the boy was two years old, and his early education was directed by his mother, Lucretia (Dearborn) Lord, a woman of marked intelligence and an experienced teacher. After attending the district school he became a teacher at the age of seventeen. His further professional preparation he acquired while pursuing a course of study in the academy at Potsdam, N. Y. In 1837 he taught a private school at Willoughby, Ohio, and entered the sophomore class of Western Reserve College in 1838. The following year he was chosen as head of the Western Reserve Teachers' Seminary in the neighboring village of Kirtland, a position which he held for eight years. On July 21, 1842, he married Elizabeth W. Russell, who, herself, had a remarkable career, first, in helping her husband in his work for the blind and, after his death, as superintendent at Batavia, in his place, and as assistant dean at Oberlin College. While still principal of the seminary he attended lectures in the medical department of the neighboring Willoughby University. Though he obtained a diploma in 1846, he never entered upon regular practice.

At about the same time, influenced largely, it seems, by Henry Barnard, who visited Ohio in 1843 and again in 1846, he engaged in a variety of educational activities. In 1845 he gave instruction in what is usually considered the first teachers' institute held in Ohio, though he had, in 1843, organized and conducted a similar institution at Kirtland. During 1846 he began the publication of the *Ohio School Journal,* which he continued to publish until 1849, when it was combined with *The School Friend.* In 1847 he was appointed superintendent of schools at Columbus, Ohio, an office created largely through the influence of Henry Barnard and the first of its kind in the Middle West. In the process of classifying the pupils he was led to organize the first public high school in Columbus and one of the first in the state. While continuing to publish *The Ohio School Journal,* he also published *The Public School Advocate,* primarily in the interest of good understanding between the school board and the patrons of the public schools. Convinced, as was Barnard, of the importance of the interchange of ideas among teachers, he promoted the organization of the Ohio State Teachers' Association in 1847 and, from the first, took a leading part in its activities. When, in 1852, the association established, as its organ, *The Ohio Journal of Education* that became, in 1860, *The Ohio Educational Monthly,* he was elected its resident editor and served until 1855. In 1854 he resigned, temporarily, his superintendency in order to act as agent of the association. He resumed his work as superintendent in 1855, but the following year, became head of the Ohio Institution for the Education of the Blind. In this field of educational activity, to which he devoted the remainder of his life, he paid especial attention to training in the practical arts. Already qualified as a physician, he took up the study of theology and, in 1863, was licensed to preach by the Presbytery of Franklin. In 1868 he was called to be head of the new state school for the blind at Batavia, N. Y., where he died.

[The unpublished reminiscences of Lord by his daughter, Mrs. H. F. Tarbox of Batavia, N. Y.; Lord's address—"Twenty-five Years in the Schools of Ohio," delivered before the Ohio State Teachers' Association at Cleveland on July 1, 1863, of which an abridgment is published in the *Ohio Educational Monthly,* Sept. 1863; J. J. Burns, *Educational Hist. of Ohio* (1905); J. W. Taylor, *A Manual of the Ohio School System* (1857): *Am. Journal of Education,* Dec. 1866, Mar. 1859, June 1859, Sept. 1865.] L. F. A.

LORD, DANIEL (Sept. 23, 1795–Mar. 4, 1868), lawyer, was born in Stonington, Conn., the only child of Daniel and Phebe (Crary) Lord. His father, a physician of ability but scholarly rather than practical, removed in 1797 to New York City, where he rendered devoted service in the yellow-fever epidemic of 1798, incidentally gathered data relating to that disease that, later, proved to be of great value, and soon thereafter abandoned his profession to become a druggist with a store in his house on Water Street. The boy, associating mostly with adults, matured early and enjoyed school, where he acquired, especially, a love of French that was a pleasure and resource to him all his life. In 1811 he entered Yale College as a Sophomore and graduated in 1814, second in his class. Having already decided on his profession, he spent a year at the law school in Litchfield, Conn., then entered the office of George Griffin, an eminent lawyer, and was called to the bar in October 1817. On May 16, 1818, he married Susan, the second daughter of Lockwood de Forest.

He spent a few years of discouragement in faithful application and thorough research, then his progress was rapid, and he attained a position of first rank in his generation. His absorption in the law was such that he declined all offers of public office and devoted himself wholly to his profession until two or three years before his death. One of his first important cases, that of *Aymar and Aymar* vs. *Astor* (6 *Cowen,* 266), led to a business connection with John Jacob Astor that was of great advantage to the young lawyer. Another early case, *Grover* vs. *Wakeman* (11 *Wendell,* 187), became a leading case on voluntary assignments in trust, and his victory made him a favorite lawyer for influential business men. He successfully conducted trials, involving large interests, that grew out of the fire of 1835 and of the panic of 1837, and he was intrusted with the case of *The Attorney General ex rel Marselus* vs. *The Minister and Elders of the Dutch Reformed Protestant Church of New York* (36 *N. Y.*, 452). Among the famous cases argued by him were *A. N. Lawrence and Others* vs. *The Trustees of the Leake and Watts Orphan House* (2 *Denio*, 577), both the John Mason will case (1 *Barbour*, 436) and the contest over the will of Anson G. Phelps (28 *Barbour*, 121, 23 *N. Y.*, 69), and *Charles Barnard and Others* vs. *Joseph Adams and Others* (10 *Howard*, 269) on general average. The Methodist Church case (*Bascom* vs. *Lane, Federal Cases,* case no. 1089), brilliantly argued, was followed by the *People of New York on the Relation of the Bank of Commerce* vs. *the Commissioners on Taxes for the City and County of New York* (2 *Black*, 620), and a series of prize cases, notably *The Schooner Crenshaw* (2 *Black*, 635).

From 1833 until his death he was an active member of the Brick Presbyterian Church. Among other addresses, he delivered July 30, 1851, the Phi Beta Kappa oration at Yale *On the Extra-Professional Influence of the Pulpit and the Bar* (1851). In 1861 he published a pamphlet on *The Legal Effect of the Secession Troubles on the Commercial Relations of the Country.*

[*Memorial of Daniel Lord* (1869); L. B. Proctor, *The Bench and Bar of N. Y.* (1870); F. B. Dexter, *Biog. Sketches of the Grads. of Yale College,* vol. VI (1912); E. J. de Forest, *A Walloon Family in America* (1914), vol. II; *N. Y. Tribune,* Mar. 6, 1868.]

A. S. M.

LORD, DAVID NEVINS (Mar. 4, 1792–July 14, 1880), merchant and theologian, was born at Franklin, Conn., the youngest but one of the sixteen children of Nathan and Mary (Nevins) Lord. At fifteen he went to work in New York, where a brother was established in business. After four years of city life he was advised by his physician to change his occupation and he returned to the country. Here he indulged a taste for studious pursuits and eventually entered Yale College, from which he graduated in 1817. With a view to entering the ministry he studied theology, but the loss of his voice and recurring ill health closed that calling to him, and in 1823 he again settled in New York, this time as an importer of dry goods. His business prospered until the great fire of 1835, in which he lost heavily; and the financial panic of 1837 played even greater havoc with his fortunes. Later an inheritance from his brother, Rufus, restored them temporarily, but soon this, too, was swept away.

In spite of the disasters in his career, Lord seems to have been a fairly skilful and sagacious business man; but it is hardly to be doubted that his inclinations and ambitions lay in another direction. His theological researches were never given up. He followed a daily program of study in Biblical prophecy, interpretation, and symbolism. In 1848 appeared the first number of a quarterly review entitled *Theological and Literary Journal,* of which Lord was editor. In the thirteen years of this periodical's existence most of its articles were written by the editor and his brother, Eleazar [*q.v.*], one of the early presidents of the Erie Railroad. Both men were tremendously concerned with the meaning of scriptural prophecy, and it was not unusual to give seventy-five pages of the *Journal* to a book review or original article on that subject. David also made excursions into geology and questioned the scientific theory of stratification. Even the Darwinian hypothesis did not escape his challenge. Had he lived fifty years later he would undoubtedly have been classified as a Fundamentalist. The *Journal* expired in the first year of the Civil War, but its editor lived on to 1880. Among his published works are: *The Characteristics and Laws of Figurative Language* (1854); *Geognosy; or, The Facts and Principles of Geology Against Theories* (1855); *The Coming and Reign of Christ* (1858); *Visions of Paradise* (1867). In 1824 he married Eliza J. Lyon; there were no children.

[*Obit. Record Grads. Yale Coll.,* 1881, pp. 8–9; *N. Y. Tribune,* July 18, 1880.]

W. B. S.

LORD, ELEAZAR (Sept. 9, 1788–June 3, 1871), preacher, railway president, author, son of Nathan and Mary (Nevins) Lord, was born at Franklin, Conn. He received his early education in the district school, and at the age of sixteen left home to become a clerk at Norwich. In 1808 he began to prepare for college, studying with Rev. Andrew Lee, pastor of the Congregational church at Hanover (now Lisbon). In 1810 he entered Andover Theological Seminary, two years later he was licensed to preach by the Haverhill Association, and after supplying various pulpits for a year, he entered the College of New Jersey (Princeton) to complete his studies for ordination. Within a few months, however, serious eye trouble compelled him to give up his chosen calling, and he went to New York City, where three brothers were already established as merchants.

After travel in Europe, 1817–18, he commenced a notable business career. He was the founder and first president, 1821–34, of the Manhattan Fire Insurance Company, and first president (1833) of the New York and Erie Railroad

Company, which he served again as president in 1839–41 and 1844–45. Although his policy of locating the road in the Susquehanna Valley and his insistence on the six-foot gauge have been severely criticized, he is credited with having "tided the New York and Erie Railroad Company over some of its darkest days" (Mott, *post,* p. 460).

He early showed ability as a political lobbyist and in 1819, 1820, and 1823–24 visited Washington as a representative of the merchants of New York City to promote the then new idea of a high protective tariff. He published a book in 1829 entitled *Principles of Currency and Banking,* in which he advocated the "Free Banking System" later established in New York and other states. This was reprinted, with additions, under the title, *Credit, Currency, and Banking* (1834) and was followed by other publications in the same field. His *Six Letters on the Necessity and Practicability of a National Currency* (1862) attracted the attention of W. H. Seward, and Lord was summoned to the Capital to advise on the national fiscal policies, but it does not appear that he played any prominent part in the active measures by which the "Free Banking System" was actually established.

His interest in religious work was life-long. In 1815 he called the meeting which resulted in the formation of the New York Sunday School Union Society, which he served as secretary, 1818–26, and president, 1826–36. He devoted much time to organizing Sunday Schools and editing lesson material. He was also a charter member and active leader in the American Home Missionary Society; was its first secretary, and wrote its first report. He was a founder and a member of the council (1831–34) of the University of the City of New York, and a founder of Auburn Theological Seminary (1820). In addition to his other activities he gave such time as he could spare to writing. His earliest notable book was *A Compendious History of the Principal Protestant Missions to the Heathen* (1813). In 1825 he edited *Lempriére's Universal Biography* in two volumes, and, with his brother David Nevins Lord [*q.v.*] contributed to it some eight hundred sketches of American subjects. At the age of forty-eight he retired from many of his business pursuits and thenceforth, at Piermont, N. Y., overlooking the Hudson, devoted a large part of his time to literary work. Among the books he published during this period are: *Geological Cosmogony; or, an Examination of the Geological Theory of the Antiquity of the Earth* (1843); *The Epoch of Creation* (1851); *The Messiah: in Moses and the Prophets* (1853); *Symbolic Prophecy* (1854); *A Historical Review of the New York and Erie Railroad* (1855); *Plenary Inspiration of the Holy Scriptures* (1857); *The Prophetic Office of Christ* (1859), and an *Analysis of the Book of Isaiah* (1861). He also contributed frequently to the *Theological and Literary Journal* edited by his brother David.

On July 12, 1824, he married Elizabeth, only daughter of Jeremiah H. Pierson of Ramapo, N. Y., and to them seven children were born. She died in 1833, and two years later, Dec. 31, 1835, he married Ruth, daughter of Deacon Eben Thompson, of East Windsor, Conn. He died at his home at Piermont.

[E. H. Mott, *Between the Ocean and the Lakes: A History of the Erie* (1899); unpublished biography of Eleazar Lord by his son; unpublished "Autobiography of Eleazar Lord, LL.D." in the handwriting of his son-in-law, Wm. H. Whiton, in the possession of his great-grandson, Henry D. Whiton, Esq., New York; obituary in *N. Y. Tribune,* June 6, 1871.]

H. A. M—n.

LORD, HENRY CURWEN (Apr. 17, 1866–Sept. 15, 1925), astronomer, was born in Cincinnati, Ohio, the son of Henry Clark and Eliza Burnet (Wright) Lord. His grandfather, Rev. Nathan Lord [*q.v.*], was president of Dartmouth College from 1828 to 1863, and his father, a prominent citizen of Cincinnati and at one time a railroad president. Henry studied at Ohio State University (1884–87), and then entered the University of Wisconsin, from which he graduated in 1889. At the latter institution he took part, as assistant, in the work of the Washburn Observatory.

After graduation he engaged for a short time in electrical work, but in 1891 he joined the faculty of Ohio State University, as assistant in mathematics and astronomy. On leave of absence in 1893, he was astronomer for the Alaskan Boundary Survey. He was promoted through the various ranks to a professorship in astronomy (1900). In the meantime, 1895, he had become director of the observatory which Emerson McMillin built and equipped. In connection with this enterprise, Lord was sent East to visit observatories and instrument makers. The building and complete equipment for instruction were the first considerations, but there were sufficient funds to warrant a 12½-inch equatorial and a spectroscope for research. The spectroscope was designed by Lord, following the best features of the Lick and Potsdam instruments, and was built by him, as well as most of the other accessory apparatus, largely to minimize expense, but also, apparently, because of a fondness for mechanical work, in which he was skilled.

As a line of research he took up the measurement of the radical velocities of stars, feeling his way along in this new field as others were doing. He published careful and specific directions for focussing a telescope accurately on the slit of a spectroscope (*Astrophysical Journal*, May 1897), and a derivation of Scheiner's formula for the curvature of spectral lines (*Ibid.*, May 1897). In 1897 he adopted a suggestion of Keeler's and had a compound correcting lens made for use with the visual objective to flatten the color curve (*Ibid.*, August 1897). In 1898 he made his first detailed report on the radical velocities of stars (*Ibid.*, August 1898). His observing program was necessarily limited to the brighter stars because the telescope was small and the observatory was "located within the limits of a city of 150,000 population, where soft coal is used extensively." The preliminary probable error of 2 km. sec. was satisfactorily small. Distressed at his inability to photograph the faint iron lines in stars of type I, he developed a graphical comparison of the effects on the efficiency of spectroscopes resulting from the variation of any one of the several elements that enter into their optical design (*Ibid.*, April 1899). The final results of ten years of work on radical velocities was published in 1905 (*Ibid.*, May 1905) when he had decided to give up this line of research "in view of the optical giants at work in this branch of research today, and in further consideration of the fact that our sky . . . is yearly getting worse." In May 1900 he observed with the United States Naval Observatory eclipse expedition, using his spectroscope on a 4-inch telescope, and obtaining one of the early successful photographs of the flash spectrum. This he measured completely, discussing the identifications of the lines and the elevations to which the various gases rise in the sun's atmosphere (*Ibid.*, March 1901). He also published some observations of double stars (*Astronomical Journal*, Apr. 27, 1920). His optical studies included the testing of various kinds of glass for prisms; the statement and proof of a relation which must be satisfied in order that a symmetrical photographic doublet of four separated thin lenses may be free from the errors of achromatism and astigmatism (*Astrophysical Journal*, October 1913); and the formulation for the illumination of the field of a photographic doublet (*Monthly Notices of the Royal Astronomical Society*, Jan. 14, 1916).

He was the author of *The Elements of Geodetic Astronomy for Civil Engineers* (1904). This he printed himself on a hand printing-press. In 1898 he married Edith Lelia Hudson of Middleport, Ohio, by whom he had one child, a daughter.

[R. G. Thwaites, *The Univ. of Wis.* (1900); Alexis Cope, *Hist. of the Ohio State Univ.*, vol. I (1920); *Thirtieth Ann. Report of the Board of Trustees of the Ohio State Univ.* (1900); *Monthly Notices of the Royal Astronomical Soc.*, Feb. 12, 1926; *Who's Who in America*, 1924–25; *Ohio State Jour.* (Columbus), Sept. 16, 1925.]

R. S. D.

LORD, HERBERT MAYHEW (Dec. 6, 1859–June 2, 1930), financial administrator, was born at Rockland, Me., the son of Sabin and Abbie (Swett) Lord. He was a descendant of Nathan Lord of Kent, England, who settled in Kittery, Me., about the middle of the seventeenth century. Following a common-school education, he worked his way through Colby College, Waterville, Me., receiving the degree of A.B. in 1884. On leaving college his first work was that of teacher, but he soon entered newspaper work, writing editorials for papers at Rockland, Me., Denver, Col., and Cardiff, Tenn. His real career began in 1894, when he was appointed clerk of the committee on ways and means of the House of Representatives. This position he held until the outbreak of the Spanish-American War in 1898, when he resigned in order to offer his services to the War Department. These services were accepted and on May 17, 1898, he was appointed major and paymaster of volunteers, in which capacity he served until honorably discharged in order to accept appointment as captain and paymaster in the regular army, Feb. 5, 1901. He was promoted until he reached the rank of brigadier-general, July 15, 1919. Upon the entrance of the United States into the World War he was made assistant to Major-General Goethals, with the title of director of finance. In this capacity he supervised the disbursement of more than $24,000,000,000. In recognition of the ability with which he handled the many difficult and complicated problems connected with the financing of the war he was awarded the Distinguished Service Medal. Upon the reorganization of the army, July 1, 1920, he was made chief of finance and as such headed the newly created finance section of the War Department.

On June 30, 1922, he was retired from active service, and on July 1, he succeeded Gen. Charles G. Dawes as director of the budget, an office created by the Budget and Accounting Act of June 10, 1921. This position he filled until May 31, 1929, when he retired. About a year later he died at his residence in Washington, D. C. On Sept. 9, 1885, he married at Thomaston, Me., Annie Stuart, daughter of Shubael and Martha (Haskell) Waldo. He had three children, one of whom died in infancy. His religious affiliations were with the Christian Science Church; in politics he was a Republican.

Lord, undoubtedly, was one of the ablest financial administrators ever connected with the United States government. As director of finance of the War Department his responsibilities were heavy and were performed with great ability. As director of the budget, he had great responsibilities, not only in respect to the handling of the current work of his office, but in determining, during the early years of the bureau's history, the principles and procedures to be followed. Though compelled to oppose the demands of the spending services of the government for money, he did it in a way to elicit universal respect for his courage, his fairness, and his skill in meeting conflicting considerations.

[C. C. Lord, *A Hist. of the Descendants of Nathan Lord of Ancient Kittery, Me.* (1912); *Third Gen. Cat. of Colby Coll.* (1909); *Army and Navy Jour.*, June 7, 1930; *Who's Who in America*, 1930–31; *Evening Star* (Washington, D. C.), June 2, 1930; *N. Y. Times*, June 3, 1930; information as to certain facts from a son, Maj. Kenneth P. Lord.] W. F. W.

LORD, JOHN (Dec. 27, 1810–Dec. 15, 1894), historical lecturer, was born in Portsmouth, N. H., the son of John Perkins and Sophia (Ladd) Lord. He was a descendant of Nathan Lord of Kent, England, who settled in Kittery, Me., about the middle of the seventeenth century. For the first ten years of his life his home was in Portsmouth, where he attended a Lancasterian School and was whipped, he says, at least once a day, until his "hand became as hard as a sailor's." In 1820 his father failed in business and moved to South Berwick, Me., in the academy of which town John prepared for college, without proving, however, a promising scholar. His uncle, Nathan Lord [*q.v.*], was president of Dartmouth College, and in 1829 he entered that institution, graduating in 1833 with an awakened interest in history and literature. Without feeling any particular call to the ministry apparently, he entered Andover Theological Seminary, from which he graduated in 1837. During these years of his education he contributed to his support by teaching school in various places, and while at Andover he had the temerity to undertake a lecture tour in New York State, his subject being the Dark Ages.

After he finished his course at Andover, his uncle, William Ladd [*q.v.*], president of the American Peace Society, offered him a position as agent for that organization. In this capacity he traveled, preached, and lectured for a year or more, his labors being brought to an end by a letter from his uncle, who stated that he did not wish longer to invest capital in unproductive property. A brief period of pastoral work was equally unsatisfactory in its outcome. After serving on trial as minister of the Congregational Church, New Marlboro, Mass., he was called to be its settled pastor. The call was not unanimous, however, for some were doubtful of his orthodoxy. An ecclesiastical council decided that it was inexpedient to ordain him. For a time he supplied the pulpit of the Second Presbyterian Church, Utica, N. Y.; but he soon decided that he was unfitted for the ministry and resolved to become an historical lecturer.

From 1840 to 1843 he lectured with encouraging success, chiefly in New England. In the latter year he went abroad, where he remained three years, lecturing acceptably in England and Scotland, gathering material in the British Museum, and in May 1846, at a country church near Brixton, marrying Mary Porter, an English woman, by whom he had a son and a daughter. He was now well launched on a career which he followed for many years, achieving considerable popularity and fortune. From 1852 to 1854 he was again in Europe. Upon his return he chose Stamford, Conn., as his permanent residence, later acquiring there six acres of land and building a home. In his lectures, as a rule, he portrayed history by grouping its events around a series of striking personalities. He made no pretense of originality, appropriating to his use the results of the best scholarship available. His characterizations were vivid and he spoke with fervor and conviction, his delivery being marked by numerous eccentricities. A professor of rhetoric once told him that "he succeeded by neglecting all rhetorical rules, and that if he had followed them he would have been a failure" (Twombly, *post*, pp. 217, 218). During his lifetime he delivered some six thousand lectures on many different topics. His books were popular and widely read, some of them being used as textbooks in schools and colleges. Among them are *A Modern History from the Time of Luther to the Fall of Napoleon* (1849); *The Old Roman World* (1867); *Ancient States and Empires* (1869); *The Life of Emma Willard* (1873); *Points of History for Schools and Colleges* (1881). Probably his best-known publication, however, largely a rewriting of his lectures and other works, is *Beacon Lights of History* (8 vols., 1884–96). His first wife died in 1860 and in 1864 he married Louisa Tucker, an English woman, whom he first met in Paris. Two years later she also died. Lord's death occurred in Stamford.

[C. C. Lord, *A Hist. of the Descendants of Nathan Lord of Ancient Kittery, Me.* (1912); G. T. Chapman. *Sketches of the Alumni of Dartmouth Coll.* (1867); *Andover Theological Seminary—Necrology, 1894–95* (1895); A. S. Twombly, "The Life of John Lord," in *Beacon Lights of Hist.*, vol. VIII (1896), based in part on Lord's manuscript "Reminiscences of Fifty Years"; *Boston Transcript*, Dec. 15, 1894.] H. E. S.

LORD, NATHAN (Nov. 28, 1792–Sept. 9, 1870), Congregational clergyman and college president, was born at South Berwick, Me., the son of John and Mehitabel (Perkins) Lord and a descendant of Nathan Lord of Kent, England, who settled in Kittery, Me., about 1652. He was educated at the local academy and at Bowdoin College, where he graduated in 1809. After two years as a teacher at Phillips Exeter Academy, he began the study of theology, completing his work in the seminary at Andover in 1815. In May 1816 he was ordained pastor of the Congregational Church at Amherst, N. H., and on July 24 of the same year he married Elizabeth King Leland of Saco, Me. His pastorate lasted twelve years and he was considered one of the ablest and most successful ministers in the state. Certain liberals, however, withdrew from membership in his church and formed a separate congregation.

In 1821 he was elected a trustee of Dartmouth College and in 1828, president. At this time conditions there were far from satisfactory, since the institution was still feeling the effects of its contest with the state in respect to its charter (1816–19). The new president assumed the task of rehabilitation with notable success and great improvements were soon in evidence; but his administration as a whole can hardly be considered noteworthy for financial or other material progress. He was not a pioneer in educational policy, although one innovation, the abolition of honors and prizes, introduced in 1830, attracted some attention—mostly unfavorable. He was an able executive and disciplinarian, however, and like his contemporary Mark Hopkins [*q.v.*] at Williams, a great teacher, whose character exercised a deep influence on students and associates. For many years he conducted courses in theology and ethics.

Intellectually, he represented a school which was rapidly passing, and his views on the great question of the day—slavery—eventually cost him his position. He had at first supported the Liberty Party, but soon after the Mexican War, an event which drove many other New Englanders into the anti-slavery movement, he became a decided supporter of slavery as an institution. His thesis was simple and logical. Slavery was sanctioned by the Bible, it was therefore divinely ordained and not to be questioned on political, humanitarian, or economic grounds. He had no sympathy with "a philosophy which makes happiness the end of living," or with "the sentiment and romance which had infected the descendants of the Puritans." His views on the question are well stated in *Letter of Inquiry to Ministers of all Denominations on Slavery* (1854), *A Northern Presbyter's Second Letter . . .* (1855), and in *A Letter to J. M. Conrad, Esq., on Slavery* (1859). The last-named first appeared in the *Richmond Daily Whig*, Richmond, Va., and denounced the recent raid at Harpers Ferry. *A True Picture of Abolition* (1863) subjected him to widespread censure, and in July 1863, the trustees, while refusing to remove him from office, expressed such disapproval that he felt obliged to resign. In a dignified statement he defended his views and denied the right of the board to impose any religious, political, or ethical test not authorized by the charter. In spite of the intensity of his views, however, he had what many men of his type have lacked, a genuine sense of humor and a large measure of tolerance and kindliness. Furthermore, he was fond of outdoor life, had athletic tastes and good health, and whatever he may have thought of ultimate human destiny, he enjoyed association with his fellows.

After retirement he spent his last years in Hanover, his friends having provided an annuity in recognition of his long and scantily remunerated services. His last publication, a letter to the alumni on the occasion of the college centennial in 1869, continues to emphasize his opposition to the current philosophy which stressed "the ability, not the weakness of man; his dignity, and not his sinfulness and shame; his rights, and not his duties; and the reorganization of society upon the basis of universal freedom, equality and fraternity."

[Many of his addresses, sermons, and papers were published in pamphlet form and the library of Dartmouth College has, it is believed, a complete collection of manuscript material dealing with his administration. See also C. C. Lord, *A Hist. of the Descendants of Nathan Lord of Ancient Kittery, Me.* (1912); J. K. Lord, *Hist. of Dartmouth Coll.* (1913); *Proc. N. H. Hist. Soc.*, vol. IV (1906); D. F. Secomb, *Hist. of the Town of Amherst, N. H.* (1883).] W. A. R.

LORD, OTIS PHILLIPS (July 11, 1812–Mar. 13, 1884), jurist and legislator, the second son of Nathaniel and Eunice (Kimball) Lord, was born in Ipswich, Mass., where his ancestor, Robert Lord, had settled when he emigrated from Ipswich, England, in 1631. In the early years of his education Otis was taught by his father; he was prepared for college in the grammar school of Ipswich and, in 1832, was graduated from Amherst College. The next year he began to read law with Judge Oliver B. Morris of Springfield, then entered the Harvard Law School, and received the degree of LL.B. in 1836. He was admitted to the Essex County bar and practised in Ipswich, where he married Elizabeth Wise Farley on Oct. 9, 1843. In November of the next year he moved to Salem. The Whigs sent him to the lower house of the legislature for 1847 and 1848 and, the next year, to the Senate. So stanch was his party loyalty that he supported Webster even after the Seventh-of-March speech. In 1852 and 1853 he was again in the House, contending unsuccessfully for the speakership. When, in 1853, a constitutional convention was called to consolidate the recent alliance of Free Soilers and Democrats, he offered an obstinate resistance, as a leader of the Whig minority. The proposed constitution called for a popularization in the frame of government: judicial tenure was to be for ten years instead of life; juries were to determine the law as well as the facts; appointive offices were to become elective; voting was to be secret; and the payment of a poll tax was no longer to be a prerequisite. He spoke vehemently against these innovations (*Official Report, post,* especially I, 573–81; III, 187–88, 460–61, 510–11). A reaction set in; the constitution was rejected, and his prestige was enhanced by his "masterly exposition of the blunders, incongruities and iniquities of the rejected constitution" (*Boston Transcript,* Mar. 14, 1884). In 1854 he again sat in the House and became speaker in the last Whig legislature. After the decline of the Whigs he became a man without a party. He refused to support Frémont and, on Oct. 8, 1856, made a speech against him in Faneuil Hall (*Frémont's "Principles" Exposed,* 1856). In 1858 he was nominated for Congress by an independent group of old-line Whigs but was defeated. Two years later he lost as a Constitutional Unionist. In 1868 he declined the Democratic nomination.

In the meantime he became a leader at the bar. He was celebrated for his "thorough knowledge of the law and an impulsive force and vigor not always under rigid restraint" (*Proceedings of the Bar, post*). As a cross-examiner he proceeded, as he once said, "somewhat energetically." In 1859 he accepted appointment to the superior court and proved to be an able *nisi prius* judge. In 1875 he became an associate judge on the supreme bench of the commonwealth, where he sat until, in 1882, protracted illness obliged him to resign. It was a moot question whether in this case it was a step upward from bar to bench. "The tone of his mind was forensic rather than judicial. . . . His learning was not extensive, and his temperament was always too impatient for much research, but he could recognize a distinction or detect a fallacy at a glance" (137 *Mass. Reports,* 593). "Whether his views were right or wrong, he saw them clearly and strongly; and such was his power of forcible expression, that there was at times danger that he might make the worse appear the better reason"; but he had the candor frequently "to yield his willing assent to a result which he had in the outset vigorously resisted" (*Ibid.,* 596).

[*Proc. of the Bar of the Commonwealth and of the Supreme Judicial Court . . . on the Death of Otis Phillips Lord* (1884); *Obit. Record of Grads. of Amherst College for . . . 1884* (1884); W. L. Montague, *Biog. Record of the Alumni of Amherst College* (1883); Asahel Huntington, *Memorial Address before the Essex Institute* (1872) reprinted from the *Hist. Colls. of the Essex Institute,* vol. II (1872); James Schouler, "The Mass. Convention of 1853," *Proc. of the Mass. Hist. Soc.,* ser. 2, vol. XVIII (1905); *Official Report of the Debates and Proc. in the State Convention Assembled May 4th, 1853 to Revise and Amend the Constitution of the Commonwealth of Mass.,* 3 vols. (1853); C. F. Adams, *Richard Henry Dana* (1890), vol. I; *Boston Transcript,* Mar. 14, 1884.] C. F.

LORD, WILLIAM PAINE (July 1, 1839–Feb. 17, 1911), Oregon jurist and governor, was born in Dover, Del., the son of Edward and Elizabeth Paine Lord. He was educated in the schools of Dover and by private tutors, graduated from Fairfield College, New York, in 1860, studied law, and, at the outbreak of the Civil War, enlisted in the Union army, in which he rose to the rank of major. At the close of the war he entered the law school at Albany, from which he graduated in 1866, and was admitted to practice of law in New York. Military life, however, had a stronger appeal so he again joined the army, as a second lieutenant, with stations successively at Fort Alcatraz, near San Francisco, Fort Steilacoom, Washington, and, for four months, in Alaska. In the fall of 1868 he resigned his commission to take up the practice of law in Salem, the capital city of Oregon, where he served, in turn, as city attorney, state senator in 1878, justice of the state supreme court from 1880 to 1894, and governor from 1895 to 1899. He was married to Juliette Montague of Baltimore, Md., on Jan. 14, 1880.

His eight years as associate justice and his six years as chief justice of the supreme court were the most notable of his career. He made a reputation as one of the judges who have most influenced the jurisprudence of the state. The state bar association selected him, in 1914, as the greatest of Oregon's chief justices, and designated his picture for the frontispiece in the forty-second volume of *Corpus Juris* (1927). His judicial opinions, when read today, seem characterized by clearness of statement, close reasoning, convincing argument, and a humanitarian point of view, and he seems to have been less influenced by technicalities than other judges of his generation. His election as governor on the Republican ticket against Nathan Pierce, the candidate of the People's Party, was due in great measure to his personal reputation and popularity. As governor he recommended a policy of retrenchment and economy, the taxation of "all property liable to taxation," the self-support of the penitentiary, a school law "simple in its provisions and inexpensive in its arrangements," and such support of the state university as should lift it to "a plane where it may compete with similar institutions in other states" (*The Journal of the Senate . . . of Oregon . . . 1895,* 1895, pp. 57, 58 and *Ibid. . . . 1897,* 1898, App., pp. 25, 29). He condemned the practice of creating numerous administrative boards, as dividing executive responsibility and as increasing salaries of the governor and other state officers in violation of the limitations fixed by the constitution. The legislative assembly of 1895, however, spent most of the session in controversy over the election of a United States Senator and gave little attention to legislation, while that of 1897, known as "the hold-up" session, failed to organize because of the conflict over the senatorship. In 1899 he was appointed minister to the Argentine Republic, a position which he held until 1902, when he returned to Oregon to resume the practice of law. His last important public service was to compile and annotate *Lord's Oregon Laws* (3 vols., 1910).

[J. C. Moreland, *Governors of Oregon* (1913); Elwood Evans and others, *Hist. of the Pacific Northwest* (1889), vol. II; F. E. Hodgkin and J. J. Galvin, *Pen Pictures of Representative Men of Ore.* (1882); *Biennial Rept. of the Secretary of State of . . . Oregon . . . 1897–98* (1899); *San Francisco Call,* Feb. 18, 1911; *Daily Oregon Statesman* (Salem), Feb. 18, 1911.]
R. C. C.

LORD, WILLIAM WILBERFORCE (Oct. 28, 1819–Apr. 22, 1907), poet, clergyman, was born in Madison County, N. Y., the son of John Way and Sarah Bryant (Chase) Lord. After attending the Geneseo high school he entered the now defunct University of Western New York and graduated in 1837. There is reason to believe that the next four years were spent as a seaman on the Pacific in search of health (R. W. Griswold, *Poets and Poetry of America,* 1850, p. 467). He entered the Auburn Theological Seminary in 1841 but transferred to the Princeton Seminary for his senior year. In 1845–46 he held a Boudinot fellowship at the College of New Jersey (now Princeton), and for a short time thereafter he taught mental and moral science at Amherst. In 1848 he took orders as deacon in the Episcopal Church, and two years later he was ordained priest. After holding a few minor posts in the South, including one at Baltimore where he served bravely in a deadly epidemic of cholera, he was made, in 1854, rector of Christ Church, Vicksburg, Miss.

In 1845 he had brought out a small volume, *Poems,* which Wordsworth praised in a letter to the author, but which Poe savagely attacked (*Broadway Journal,* May 24, 1845, p. 328). In the main the poems show, to use Poe's mildest phrase, "a very ordinary species of talent," but at least one of them, "On the Defeat of a Great Man," has found numerous admirers and is included with several others by Lord in Edmund C. Stedman's *An American Anthology* (1900). His later volumes were *Christ in Hades* (1851), an epic notable chiefly for its Miltonic echoes; and *André* (1856), an unacted tragedy, written in uninspired blank verse and showing but little dramatic sense.

When the Civil War broke out, Lord continued as rector of Christ Church and became chaplain of the 1st Mississippi Brigade. Throughout the siege of Vicksburg he worked tirelessly in his double capacity of chaplain and pastor. During the siege all his possessions were destroyed, including his library, which was reputed to be the largest and most scholarly private collection in the Southwest. When Vicksburg fell, Grant urged upon him a passport to St. Louis, where he would be free from danger. Far from accepting it, he pushed still further into the Confederacy in the pursuit of his calling. Shortly after the conclusion of the war, he assumed the rectorate of St. Paul's Church, Charleston, S. C. In 1871 he was back in Vicksburg, where he founded the Church of the Holy Trinity. In 1876 he was called to Christ Church, Cooperstown, N. Y., and there he served until his retirement from the ministry about 1883. At his death, which occurred in New York City, he was survived by his wife (formerly Margaret Stockton, whom he married Feb. 19, 1851), a son, and a daughter.

[*Gen. Biog. Cat. of Auburn Theological Seminary* (1918); *Princeton Theological Seminary Bull. Necrological Report,* Aug. 1908; *The Albany Ch. Record,* May 1907, p. 349; *The Church Almanac* and its successor, *The Am. Church Almanac,* 1850–1908; W. W. Lord, Jr., "A Child at the Siege of Vicksburg," *Harper's Mag.,* Dec. 1908, and "In the Path of Sherman," *Harper's Mag.,* Feb. 1910; *N. Y. Tribune* and *Sun* (N. Y.), Apr. 23, 1907.]
O. S. C.

LORILLARD, PIERRE (Oct. 13, 1833–July 7, 1901), merchant, sportsman, and breeder of race horses, was born in New York City, the son of Peter and Catherine (Griswold) Lorillard.

His family, originally of German stock, had been engaged for two generations in the manufacture of tobacco and snuff. In his youth Pierre distinguished himself in various sports—notably in shooting and yachting. As the owner of the schooner *Vesta* and the steam yacht *Radha* he made Newport a yachting center. Later he became a road driver of trotting horses in the days of Bonner and Vanderbilt. Taking up the breeding of trotters, he sent from his stables five or six peers of the road in their day. In 1873 he bought 1,200 acres of land at Jobstown, N. J., and established a famous stock farm known as "Rancocas." From there he began in 1878 to ship horses to run the principal English races. His Parole won the Newmarket Handicap, the City and Suburban Stakes, the Great Metropolitan Stakes, the Great Cheshire Stakes, and the Epsom Gold Cup. In 1879 he sent over Iroquois, winner of the Derby in 1881 and one of the greatest racers ever bred in America. Pontiac and several other horses from the "Rancocas" stables made heavy winnings at home and abroad. Lorillard became a "plunger" in betting. In 1898 he formed a partnership with Lord William Beresford on the English turf.

Since 1812 Lorillard's family had owned a tract of 7,000 acres in Orange County, N. Y. Pierre bought up the interests of the other heirs in this property, acquiring a clear title to the entire tract. His purpose was to establish a shooting and fishing club and to that end he enclosed 5,000 acres in wire fence eight feet high. Thus a game preserve was formed, containing deer, pheasants, and a trout hatchery (the lake on the domain had been stocked with black bass as early as 1860). The club was organized, the name Tuxedo Park adopted, and a clubhouse built. The plans were expanded to include a residential park, developed in accordance with the best engineering practice of the day, with modern roads, sewer and water systems. After his father's death Lorillard had bought the interests of his four brothers in the tobacco industry and had been unusually successful in expanding the business. His income from that source was exceptionally large. For the last six years of his life he lived abroad most of the time, a sufferer from Bright's disease, but he died in New York. He shared with the French Republic the cost of the Charnay archeological expeditions to Central America and Yucatan and for this benefaction he was admitted to the Legion of Honor. He had married, in 1858, Emily Taylor of New York. She with a son and two daughters survived him.

[Russel Headley, *The Hist. of Orange County, N. Y.* (1908), pp. 401–03; *Race Horses and Racing: Recollections of Frank Gray Griswold* (1925); W. S. Vosburgh, *"Cherry and Black": The Career of Mr. Pierre Lorillard on the Turf* (1916); *N. Y. Geneal. and Biog. Record*, Apr. 1877, p. 89; *Turf, Field and Farm*, July 12, 1901; *Tobacco* (N. Y.), July 12, 1901; *Sun* (N. Y.), July 8, 1901.]

W. B. S.

LORIMER, GEORGE CLAUDE (June 4, 1838–Sept. 7, 1904), Baptist clergyman, was born and received his early schooling in Edinburgh, Scotland. While he was still a child, his father died and his mother married W. H. Joseph, a theatrical manager. As a result, the boy's impressionable years were passed in the atmosphere of the theatre, and at the age of seventeen he became a professional actor and emigrated to the United States. While playing at Louisville, Ky., he had a religious experience which led him to abandon the stage for the ministry. After a period of study at Georgetown College, Kentucky, he was called to a church in Harrodsburg, Ky., where he was ordained in 1859. Pastorates at Paducah, the Walnut Street Baptist Church, Louisville, the First Baptist Church, Albany, N. Y., and the Shawmut Avenue Church, Boston, followed.

In 1873 he began the first of two pastorates at Tremont Temple, Boston, the scene of his real life-work. They were separated by a period of twelve years, however, which were spent in Chicago with the First Baptist Church (1879–81) which he freed from serious financial straits, and with the Immanuel Baptist Church (1881–91) where, under his leadership, the membership increased from 170 to 1,100. His health was impaired by his arduous and successful efforts to raise $400,000 to meet the conditions of a Rockefeller gift to that church, and returning East he began his second pastorate at Tremont Temple. Here he soon had the largest congregations in Boston and despite three disastrous fires the great institution flourished and grew. During this period he formed the habit of preaching every summer in London. In 1900 he declined the presidency of Columbian University, Washington, D. C., but in 1901 accepted a call to the Madison Avenue Baptist Church, New York City, with which he was connected until the time of his death at Aix-les-Bains, France, where he had gone for his health. On Feb. 26, 1859, he had married Arabelle D. Burford.

Lorimer was a man of magnetic personality, and an enthusiasm that was infectious. He was a popular preacher, but his discourses were carefully prepared and filled with the fruits of wide reading. His sermons, committed to memory at a single reading, were delivered in a voice of remarkable sweetness, compass, and power. He published a number of books, which deal chiefly with Christianity in relation to modern thought and social conditions. Among the more important are *Isms Old and New* (1881); *Jesus the World's Savior* (1883); *The People's Bible History* (1896); *Christianity and the Social State* (1898); *Christianity in the Nineteenth Century* (1900); the Lowell Lectures, Boston, delivered in 1900.

[William Cathcart, *The Baptist Encyc.* (1881); W. B. Burford, *Burford Geneal.* (1914); *The Watchman*, Boston, Sept. 15, 1904; *Outlook*, Sept. 17, 1904; *Boston Daily Globe*, Sept. 9, 1904.] G. H. E—g.

LORIMIER, PIERRE LOUIS (March 1748–June 26, 1812), Indian trader, interpreter, Spanish commandant, founder of Cape Girardeau, Mo., was a native of Lachine, Canada, and is said to have been of noble blood. He accompanied his father in 1769 to the Miami River, and was established at a place called Pickawillany. Here he had a post known as "Loramie's" in what is now Shelby County, Ohio. He traded with various tribes of Indians and exercised great influence over them. He was an agent and interpreter for the British and his post became a rendezvous for them during the Revolutionary War. In 1778 during one of his raids he captured Daniel Boone. Raids by the Shawnee and Delaware Indians under Lorimier caused George Rogers Clark to attempt their extermination, and in 1782 he destroyed the post. Lorimier lost his stores, barely saving his life, and fled to Wapakoneta, Auglaize County, Ohio. In 1787 he was driven by his creditors to Spanish territory, where he settled near the present town of St. Mary's, Mo., and traded with the Indians in partnership with the commandant of Ste. Genevieve. Many Indians from the vicinity of his old post, who had been cowed by the Americans, were coaxed by Lorimier to his new home. They were welcomed by the Spaniards, who relied upon them for protection from the Osages and conferred upon them large tracts of land. Lorimier was appointed agent of Indian affairs and established their village at Apple Creek. He chose for himself the present site of Cape Girardeau, and in 1808 laid out this town from his own land grants. He was appointed captain of the militia and Spanish commandant of that district. After the Louisiana Purchase he was appointed by the United States government to be one of the judges of the court of common pleas. His Spanish land titles were rejected by the first board of land commissioners and were not confirmed until long after his death. Cape Girardeau did not emerge until 1840 from the cloud thus cast upon these grants.

Lorimier was called upon by the lieutenant-governors of Upper Louisiana to serve as interpreter to the chiefs of the several Indian nations and as conciliator. On many critical occasions he made perilous voyages, and through persuasion and gifts, kept peace and tranquillity in the country. He was given many concessions of land by the Spanish, and license to trade on the St. François, White, and Arkansas rivers. His first grant was for six thousand arpens, and his petition in 1799 for thirty thousand arpens was granted before the American occupation. In 1796 the first Americans came to his district and stimulated by his favor and encouragement others followed. His district became inhabited by the most intelligent farmers. Lorimier himself could neither read nor write but was undoubtedly a man of great natural ability. He spoke French, English, and several Indian languages with fluency. He had a beautiful signature and appended it to documents only after they had been read to him many times. He was a firm, brave, and successful commander, feared and respected by the Indians. His reputation for justice, both as an official and as a man, became firmly established. All his personal debts, even those made in gambling, were fully paid. He was twice married. His first wife was a half-breed of Shawnee and French blood named Charlotte Pemanpieh Bougainville. They had several children of whom one son was graduated from West Point. His second wife was Marie Berthiaume, also a half-breed Shawnee. He was a well-formed, handsome man, fond of dress and display. His profusion of hair was arranged in a long plait, fastened with ribbons, which he used as a whip for his horse while riding.

[Sources include Louis Houck, *The Spanish Régime in Mo.* (1909), vol. II, containing a transcript of Lorimier's journal for the years 1793–95; the same author's *Memorial Sketches of Pioneers* (1915) and *Hist. of Mo.* (1908), vol. II; F. A. Rozier, *Rozier's Hist. of the Early Settlement of the Miss. Valley* (1890); *Hist. of Southeast Mo.* (1888); *Jour. of Capt. Wm. Trent* (1871), ed. by A. T. Goodman; *The John Askin Papers*, vol. I (1928), ed. by M. M. Quaife; L. J. Kenny, "Geo. Rogers Clark in Ohio," *Ill. Cath. Hist. Rev.*, Jan. 1928; Census of St. Louis and Ste. Genevieve, 1787; original petitions for concession of land; Lorimier's will, dated Oct. 20, 1788; Ste. Genevieve archives. The last items are in the possession of the Mo. Hist. Soc.] S. M. D.

LORING, CHARLES HARDING (Dec. 26, 1828–Feb. 5, 1907), naval officer, was born in Boston, Mass., the son of William Price and Elizabeth (Harding) Loring. He was a descendant of Deacon Thomas Loring of Axminster, Devonshire, England, who emigrated to America in 1634 and settled at Hingham, Mass. Charles received his early education in the public schools of his native city. Later, since technical schools were not established at that time, he became a machine-shop apprentice and thus began his career on a practical basis. On Feb. 26, 1851, he formally entered the navy by a competitive examination, in which he stood first in a group of fourteen.

During the next decade, he laid the foundation for his subsequent career, passing through the various naval grades and becoming chief engineer on Mar. 25, 1861. Among his assignments had been that of assistant to the engineer-in-chief, and as such he had had charge of the experimental work, particularly the testing of steam-engineering devices. The outbreak of the Civil War found him in active service, and he was first made fleet engineer of the North Atlantic station; later, he became general inspector of all the iron-clad steamers that were being constructed west of the Alleghanies, his duties including supervision over the famous "monitors."

After the Civil War, the question of supplanting simple with compound engines arose. In 1872 Loring and Charles H. Baker were appointed a board to consider this subject, and after an exhaustive study, they recommended the use of compound engines (*Report of the Secretary of the Navy,* 1873, pp. 120 ff.). For several years, Loring conducted thorough investigations in various phases of engineering details and the recommendations in his published reports have become standard engineering practice the world over. (See especially *Report of the Secretary of the Navy,* 1874, pp. 105 ff.) In 1881 he was a member of the "First Naval Advisory Board," significant because it brought about the abandonment of the old wooden naval ships and started work on the modern steel fighting ships. President Arthur in 1884 appointed Loring engineer-in-chief with the rank of rear admiral. The following year, he came into conflict with departmental politics and resigned this office. Thereafter he served on important experimental boards and contributed much to their researches up to his retirement from the navy on Dec. 26, 1890. During the Spanish-American War, he was recalled to active service and made inspector of engineering work in New York City.

He was well known throughout the engineering world and was president of the Engineers' Club of New York, and of the American Society of Mechanical Engineers (1891–92), the highest honor which his profession could offer him. In 1852 he married Ruth Malbon of Hingham, Mass., and they had one daughter. His death occurred at Hackettstown, N. J.

[C. H. Pope and K. P. Loring, *Loring Geneal.* (1917); *Jour. Am. Soc. Naval Engineers,* Feb. 1907; *Trans. Am. Soc. Mech. Engrs.,* vol. XXIX (1907); *Official Records of the Union and Confederate Navies in the War of the Rebellion*; L. R. Hamersly, *The Records of Living Officers of the U. S. Navy and Marine Corps* (5th ed., 1894); *Reg. of the Commissioned and Warrant Officers of the Navy of the U. S. and of the Marine Corps* (1907); *Army and Navy Reg.,* Feb. 9, 1907; *Army and Navy Jour.,* Feb. 9, 1907; *Who's Who in America,* 1906–07; *Brooklyn Daily Eagle,* Feb. 6, 1907.]

A. R. B.

LORING, CHARLES MORGRIDGE (Nov. 13, 1832–Mar. 18, 1922), national figure in civic betterment work, was born in Portland, Me., the son of Horace and Sarah (Willey) Loring and a descendant of Thomas Loring who emigrated to Hingham, Mass., in 1634. After his school days several trips to the West Indies in his father's vessels convinced him that this was not the calling he should follow and he set his face toward the West. After four years in a Chicago wholesale house he went to the little town of Minneapolis, Minn., in 1860, hoping the climate would be more suitable to his never too robust health. As merchant, miller, and dealer in real estate, he acquired what then passed for a considerable fortune. Merely as a successful business man he was not to be distinguished from others who utilized the opportunities of a new country. From the first, however, he exhibited a lively and intelligent interest in the civic problems of a community unhampered by fixed traditions. Politics as such did not attract him, although he held a minor office or two in his earlier years; his attention was drawn to the possibilities of enhancing the beauty and increasing the healthfulness of his city. He was active in the state horticultural society and in the forestry association, over each of which he was president for a time. In them his activities were only incidental to his major avocation—seeing that Minneapolis was provided with parks, playgrounds, and the like, laid out and equipped with consideration for future growth.

In 1864 Loring made his first definite move toward this goal when he persuaded a citizen to donate a small tract of land for a park. For years he struggled to secure the cooperation of a citizenry reluctant to spend money for anything that seemed to have no immediate practical utility. He saw them neglect many opportunities to acquire land cheaply for park purposes. Not until 1880 was any real step taken in the direction he desired to go; then a small sum appropriated by the city council permitted the improvement of a few acres donated several years before, and he not only supervised the laying out of paths and the planting of trees, but did much of the work with his own hands. In 1883 the state legislature, against the protest of the city council, created a board of park commissioners for Minneapolis and named Loring a member. Made president, he served in this capacity until 1890 when he failed of reëlection owing to a Democratic landslide. Elected again in 1892 he served a year and then resigned since the board contemplated purchasing land in which he had an interest. He was commissioner again from 1903 to 1906.

Whether or not on the board he labored incessantly for, and gave freely of his own means to, the cause, and before his death had the satisfaction of seeing Minneapolis equipped with a comprehensive system of parks, parkways, and playgrounds which form some of the principal attractions of the city. By his addresses, newspaper contributions, and ready advice he aroused dormant civic pride in many towns of the state. In Riverside, Cal., where he spent his winters from the early eighties until near the close of his life, he stimulated the same kind of betterments that he had in Minneapolis and it was through his efforts that Mount Rubidoux was made a scenic park and one of the first bird sanctuaries of the country, while the planting of thousands of trees about it was the direct result of his endeavors. Having become nationally known, he was consulted by people from all over the country and through the American Park and Outdoor Art Association, of which he was president in 1899 and 1900, he spread his gospel. While the whole Minneapolis park system was the outgrowth of his work and planning for the future, certain features peculiarly owed their origin to him. One of the last projects to receive his impress was the Victory Memorial Drive in the Grand Rounds which took form in accordance with his suggestions and to which he not only donated money to plant some six hundred trees dedicated to victims of the World War, but left a sum to provide for maintenance of the memorial. In his honor Central Park was renamed Loring Park. Loring was twice married: in 1855 to Emily Smith Crossman, who died in 1894, and on Nov. 28, 1895, to Florence Barton. He died at Minneapolis.

[Warren Upham and R. B. Dunlap, "Minn. Biogs.," *Minn. Hist. Soc. Colls.*, vol. XIV (1912); M. D. Shutter and J. S. McLain, *Progressive Men of Minn.* (1897); W. W. Folwell, *Hist. of Minn.*, vol. IV (1930); C. H. Pope and K. P. Loring, *Loring Geneal.* (1917); C. M. Loring, "Hist. of the Parks and Pub. Grounds of Minneapolis," *Minn. Hist. Soc. Colls.*, vol. XV (1915); *Minneapolis Tribune*, Mar. 19, 1922; birth record, Portland, Me.] L. B. S.

LORING, EDWARD GREELY (Sept. 28, 1837–Apr. 23, 1888), ophthalmologist, who devised the first practical ophthalmoscope, was born in Boston, Mass., the second son of Judge Edward Greely and Harriet (Boott) Loring. He passed his boyhood in Boston and in Winthrop, where his father had a summer home, and there he acquired a fondness for boating which he retained through life. He prepared for college at the Boston Latin School and entered Harvard in 1857. At the end of his sophomore year, he went to Florence, Italy, and began the study of medicine. He spent three years between the clinics of Florence and Pisa, coming under the individual instruction of Dr. Grysanovski and, in anatomy, of Dr. Duranti of Pisa. Returning to Boston in 1862 he entered Harvard Medical School and received the degree of M.D. in 1864, taking the Boylston Prize on graduating with an essay on "The Causes of Exudation in Inflammation." He then became associated with Dr. Henry Willard Williams, Boston's pioneer ophthalmologist, as ophthalmic externe at the Boston City Hospital, and also followed the clinics at the Massachusetts Charitable Eye and Ear Infirmary. After a year of this training, he married, Jan. 3, 1866, Chevalita Jarves, a daughter of James Jackson Jarves [*q.v.*], and moved to Baltimore to begin practice. In another year he went to New York and became a partner of the noted ophthalmologist, Cornelius Rea Agnew. After six years he set up practice by himself and had a good and remunerative clientele. In 1883 his wife died and in 1886 he was married to Helen Swift, a niece of Judge Rapallo. He had no children by either marriage. On Apr. 23, 1888, when returning from the Hudson River, where he had superintended the fitting out of a yacht, he fell dead. A post mortem disclosed that the cause of death was coronary occlusion.

Loring had served as surgeon to the Brooklyn Eye and Ear Hospital, was one of the original staff of the Manhattan Eye and Ear Hospital and, at the time of his death, was surgeon to the New York Eye and Ear Infirmary. His greatest contribution to medicine was his improvement of the ophthalmoscope, an instrument for looking into the eye. The first ophthalmoscope, invented in 1847 by an English mathematician, Charles Babbage, consisted of a small plane mirror from the central portion of which the silvering had been removed. Through this hole the physician's eye looked into the eye of the patient, a light placed beside the patient's head being reflected by the mirror into the patient's eye. This was a rough affair, did not allow for varying refraction of the media of different eyes, and was hard to manipulate. Helmholtz in 1851 independently invented another ophthalmoscope, but Loring made the first practical instrument by gathering many little lenses on the edge of a disc behind the mirror that could be rotated by the forefinger to bring the lens best suited to the refraction of the eye under examination before the physician's eye (*Transactions of the American Ophthalmological Society,* 1869, pp. 47–51). He brought out an improved form in 1874 which he demonstrated to the fifth international ophthalmological congress in New York two years later. His ophthalmoscope, though modified by many oculists, was in general use until, with the development of electric lighting, a small incandescent bulb was placed in the instrument and the eye ground illuminated by direct light. Loring wrote many papers on subjects connected with diseases of the eye. His *magnum opus* was his book entitled: *A Text Book on Ophthalmoscopy,* the first volume of which was published in 1886. The second volume, partially finished at his death, appeared in 1891, edited by his brother, Dr. Francis Boott Loring of Washington, D. C. Loring did much by his writings and by the perfection of the ophthalmoscope to place American ophthalmology on an equal footing with the best practice of the world.

[*Trans. Am. Ophthalmol. Soc.,* vol. V (1890), containing bibliography; *Am. Encyc. of Ophthalmol.,* vol. X (1917); *Hist. of the Boston City Hospital* (1906); *Boston Medic. and Surgic. Jour.,* May 3, 1888; J. J. Walsh, *Hist. of the Medic. Soc. of the State of N. Y.* (1907); *Medic. Record* (N. Y.), Apr. 28, 1888; C. H. Pope and K. P. Loring, *Loring Geneal.* (1917); *N. Y. Times,* Apr. 25, 1888.] W. L. B.

LORING, ELLIS GRAY (Apr. 14, 1803–May 24, 1858), lawyer and anti-slavery advocate, was born in Boston, Mass., the only son of James Tyng Loring, an apothecary, who died in 1805, and Relief (Faxon) Cookson Loring. He was descended from Thomas Loring who emigrated to America in 1634 and settled in Hingham, Mass. From the Latin School, where he was distinguished for scholarship, and where he made Emerson's friendship, he went to Harvard College. He was a member of the class of 1823, attaining membership in Phi Beta Kappa, but he left in May 1823, when members of his class were dismissed for resistance to college discipline. Later he studied law and in 1827 he began a successful career at the bar. Troubled by the existence of slavery, he was "one of the little band who assembled, on the evening of January 1st, 1831, . . . to consider the expediency of organizing a New England Anti-Slavery Society" (the *Liberator,* June 4, 1858, p. 91). These twelve zealots were of divided counsel. Loring favored "gradualism" as opposed to Garrison's "immediateism." The constitution called for "immediate freedom," and Loring withheld his signature. But by January 1833 he was holding office in the society.

There were many aspects to Loring's support of the abolition movement. Unlike Garrison, he had social prominence to lose: the movement cost him many clients and the friendly intercourse of leading Boston families. He gave decisive financial support, without which the *Liberator* could not have continued. On Oct. 29, 1827, he had married Louisa Gilman and together they made their home a center for anti-slavery workers, to whom other doors were closed. Here Harriet Martineau visited and observed the movement at close range. Loring opened his house to fugitive slaves as well and was perhaps the first lawyer to take a colored boy into his office to train him for the bar. More widely known abolitionists, as Dr. Channing, drew strength from his counsel. From his hand Wendell Phillips received his first anti-slavery pamphlet. Though he shrank from speaking in public, Loring could on occasion argue to good purpose, notably in the hearing before the legislative committee considering Gov. Edward Everett's suggestion that the abolitionists be repressed.

In anti-slavery as in other matters, Loring was of liberal but moderate views. He opposed third-party sentiment in the American Anti-Slavery Society and also Phillips' view that abolition must be sought either in blood or over the ruins of the church and the Union. In *An Address to the Abolitionists of Massachusetts on the Subject of Political Action,* printed about 1838, he sketched the tactics by which agitation should be conducted: by petitioning legislative bodies, by interrogating candidates publicly, and by using the suffrage. In his profession he was rather a chamber counsel than an advocate. His best-known argument was for the slave Med, brought to Massachusetts by her mistress (*Commonwealth* vs. *Thomas Aves,* 35 *Mass.,* 193). On *habeas corpus* proceedings Loring won against Benjamin R. Curtis. The case established the principle that a slave brought voluntarily by his owner into Massachusetts could not be removed from the state against his will. Justice Story wrote: "I have rarely seen so thorough and exact arguments as those made by Mr. B. R. Curtis, and yourself. They exhibit learning, research, and ability, of which any man may be proud" (W. W. Story, *Life and Letters of Joseph Story,* 1851, II, 235). In his petition for the pardon of Abner Kneeland, convicted of blasphemy, he made a splendid defense of free speech. For some years prior to his death he had withdrawn from public observation, being content that others should assume prominence in the movement he had helped to launch. He has sometimes been confused with his distant kinsman, Edward Greely Loring, United States commissioner, who was attacked by the abolitionists for the rendition of Burns, a fugitive slave.

[W. P. and F. J. Garrison, *Wm. Lloyd Garrison, 1805–1875* (4 vols., 1885–89), vols. I–III; A. H. Grimké, *Wm. Lloyd Garrison* (1891); Lindsay Swift, *Wm. Lloyd Garrison* (1911); W. H. Channing, *The Life of Wm. Ellery Channing, D.D.* (1880); Henry Wilson, *Hist. of the Rise and Fall of the Slave Power in America*, vol. I (1872); C. H. Pope and K. P. Loring, *Loring Geneal.* (1917); the *Liberator*, May 28, June 4, 18, 1858; *Boston Transcript*, May 25, 1858.]

C. F.

LORING, FREDERICK WADSWORTH (Dec. 12, 1848–Nov. 5, 1871), author, journalist, was born in Boston, Mass., the first of three sons of David Loring, a cabinet maker, and Mary Hall Stodder, a native New Englander. The first Loring in America was Deacon Thomas Loring who came from Devonshire, England, and joined the Hingham colony in Massachusetts in 1634. Under the guidance of his mother, Frederick read and absorbed English literature and was well versed in Shakespeare at the age of seven. Though she died when he was eleven years old, she left an indelible mark upon her devoted son who inherited her sympathetic sensitiveness and intelligence. He was sent to Phillips Academy at Andover, Mass., and entered Harvard in 1866. Here he abhorred the exact sciences and used his pen to extravagance in ridiculing mathematical formulas. Only his unusual promise kept him within the pale. After the death of his friend Prof. Elbridge J. Cutler, which was the second great grief of his life, he was befriended by James Russell Lowell. He was a regular contributor to the *Harvard Advocate* and while at college showed a passion for the drama. He made friends of actors and dramatists. Miss Mazie Mitchel, dramatist, permitted him to revise an act of her play and had the play produced. During these years also, to assist a friend, he wrote *Wild Rose*, which was produced with success in Boston by George Selwyn.

After his graduation in 1870, Loring became assistant editor of the Boston *Saturday Evening Gazette*. Later he was connected with the *Boston Daily Advertiser* and *Every Saturday*, "a journal of choice reading." Meanwhile he contributed short stories as well as short poems to the *Atlantic Monthly*, New York *Independent*, New York *World*, and *Appletons' Journal*. A serial story, "Two College Friends," which appeared in *Old and New* (April, July 1871), was published in book form later in 1871. His best-known poem, "In the Church Yard at Fredericksburg," first appeared in the *Atlantic Monthly* for September 1870. *The Boston Dip, and Other Verses* was published a year later. The publisher's advertisement quotes the *New York Tribune* as saying the poems were noticeable as "celebrating young love with a tenderness, flavored with a certain cool humor which might have been done by Thackeray in that fresh, earnest, enthusiastic stage of his literary career which he depicts in Arthur Pendennis."

In 1871 Loring was sent with the Wheeler Expedition as correspondent for *Appletons' Journal*. His reports, written always in a light and humorous vein, were interesting. Apparently safe from the many dangers he had experienced Loring took the Wickenburg and La Paz (Arizona) stage on his way home. The stage was attacked by Apaches and he was one of those killed.

[C. H. Pope and K. P. Loring, *Loring Geneal.* (1917); *Triennial Report of the Secretary of the Class of 1870 of Harvard Coll.* (1873); H. H. Bancroft, *Hist. of the Pacific States of North America*, vol. XII (1888), "Arizona and New Mexico"; T. E. Farish, *Hist. of Ariz.*, vol. VIII (1918); *Appletons' Jour.*, Dec. 9, 1871; the *Weekly Ariz. Miner*, Nov. 11, 1871; *Boston Daily Advertiser*, Nov. 14, 16, 1871; information from the Division of Vital Statistics for the state of Mass.]

F. W. S.

LORING, GEORGE BAILEY (Nov. 8, 1817–Sept. 14, 1891), physician, agriculturist, political leader, was born at North Andover, Mass., the son of Bailey and Sally Pickman Osgood Loring and a descendant of Thomas Loring who emigrated to Hingham, Mass., in 1634. He attended Franklin Academy at North Andover and graduated from Harvard College in 1838, a classmate of James Russell Lowell. Four years later the Harvard Medical School awarded him the degree of M.D. After a few months of practice in his ancestral village he became a surgeon at the Marine Hospital at Chelsea, Mass. During his seven years of service in that institution he made an impression sufficient to win an appointment as commissioner to revise the marine hospital system of the United States. He left the hospital, however, in 1850, removed in 1851 to Salem, Mass., and thereafter devoted himself to agriculture and politics. He developed a stock farm which became widely known as "Loring Manor." He speedily made himself sufficiently useful in the Democratic party to receive the postmastership of Salem from the Pierce administration and held the office from 1853 to 1857. After this first step he skilfully made his two new interests play complementary rôles in furthering his personal advancement.

In 1856 Loring attended the National Democratic Convention as a member of the Massachusetts delegation. After 1861 he allied himself with the War Democrats. In a Fourth of July oration at Salem in 1862 he rejoiced that "all our desire is manifested in the Flag which we still call our own, and from which no star has been stricken by hand of ours." After this speech he steadily developed into a popular orator. His tall robust figure, his handsome face, and his dignified manner made him a notable figure at public gatherings. His oratory, as over-decorated as a Victorian interior, pleased the New England taste of his day. He never championed unpopular causes, and his orations—which he was careful to have printed—reflected the religious and political conservatism of his times. In 1864, chafing, perhaps, under the disadvantages of being a Northern Democrat in the changed situation brought about by the war, he publicly renounced his allegiance to his old party and became a Republican. The change of standards proved almost immediately advantageous. He served in 1866–67 as a member of the Massachusetts House of Representatives. He was chairman of the Republican state committee (1869–76) and was a delegate to the national conventions of that party in 1868, 1872, and 1876. He was president of the state Senate from 1873 to 1876 and representative in Congress for the next four years. When his constituency recalled him from Washington in the election of 1880, President Garfield saved his political fortunes by selecting him in 1881 for commissioner of agriculture, a post which he held until the inauguration of Cleveland.

Garfield's choice was excellent. Loring was sincerely interested in agriculture and was an intelligent leader in the contemporary efforts to improve husbandry, taking care, however, that his activities should aid in making him conspicuous. From 1860 to 1877 he represented the Essex Agricultural Society on the Massachusetts Board of Agriculture and served on the same board by appointment of the governor in the years 1888–90. In this capacity he did much to further the interests of the recently established Massachusetts Agricultural College and lectured on stock-farming in that institution from 1869 to 1872. In 1864 he founded the New England Agricultural Society and served as its president until 1889. He published in 1876 *The Farm-Yard Club of Jotham,* a curious volume intended to popularize discussions of agricultural subjects. The book is in part a loose narrative characterized by a somewhat sugary sentimentality and gives a romanticized picture of the rural life that Loring knew. The story is constantly interrupted by sensible essays on many aspects of husbandry presented in the guise of papers read before the Farm-Yard Club. Late in life Loring disclosed even more intimately than in the volume of 1876 his attitude toward agriculture. He remarked of his former friend, Ralph Waldo Emerson: "His aesthetic love of nature, which made him rejoice in a bare hillside with stumps and briars . . . was in me a practical reality, which moved me as it did him, but with the addition of a farmer's consideration of the value of the scenes he loved. Nature to him meant God; to me it meant also the rule God gave man over the fowls of the air and the beasts of the field" (*A Year in Portugal,* p. 160). Such an outlook helps to explain why Loring, like his good friend Louis Agassiz, rejected Darwinism with "scorn and contempt."

In his latter years Loring's mind ranged over a variety of subjects. He wrote, among other things, *A Vindication of General Samuel Holden Parsons against Charges of Treasonable Correspondence During the Revolutionary War* (1888). In 1889–90 he tried his hand at diplomacy when he served as minister to Portugal under appointment by President Benjamin Harrison. His rambling travelogue, *A Year in Portugal,* was published in the year of his death, 1891. He died on Sept. 14 from heart disease following an acute attack of dysentery. He was twice married: on Nov. 6, 1851, to Mary Toppan Pickman, who died in 1878; and on June 10, 1880, to Anna (Smith) Hildreth, the widow of Charles H. Hildreth.

[L. H. Bailey, *Cyc. of Agric.*, vol. IV (1909); *Biog. Dir. Am. Cong.* (1928); C. H. Pope and K. P. Loring, *Loring Geneal.* (1917); the *Critic*, Sept. 19, 1891; *Boston Transcript*, Sept. 14, 1891; *N. Y. Times*, Sept. 15, 1891.]

R. H. G.

LORING, JOSHUA (Aug. 3, 1716–October 1781), naval officer, Loyalist, was born in Boston, the son of Joshua and Hannah (Jackson) Loring and the descendant of Thomas and Jane (Newton) Loring, who emigrated from Axminster, Devonshire, England, to Dorchester, Mass., about 1634 and, later, settled in Hingham, Mass. In his youth he learned the tanner's trade, being apprenticed to James Mears of Roxbury. About 1740 he married Mary Curtis, daughter of Samuel Curtis of Roxbury. When continual warfare between England and France made privateering attractive to many New Englanders, he became commander of a brigantine privateer, which was captured by two French men-of-war in August 1744. The next few months he spent as a prisoner in the Fortress of Louisburg. The outbreak of the French and Indian War again found him in the naval service. On Dec. 19, 1757, he was commissioned captain in the British navy. In 1759 he commanded naval operations on Lakes George and Champlain and, the next year, on Lake Ontario, and he is now usually referred to as Commodore Loring. He was severely wounded in 1760. He participated in the capture of Quebec by General Wolfe and the subsequent conquest of Canada by General Amherst. At the close of the war he retired on half pay and settled down at Jamaica Plain, Roxbury. Joshua Loring was one of the five commissioners of revenue and became a member of General Gage's council by a writ of mandamus. He was sworn in on Aug. 8, 1774. Gage's appointees were immediately subjected to the greatest pressure to induce them to resign. Writing under date of Aug. 30, John Andrews said, "Late in the evening a member waited upon Commodore Loring, and in a friendly way advis'd him to follow the example of his *townsman* (Isaac Winslow who had already resigned). He desir'd time to consider of it. They granted it, but acquainted him, if he did not comply, he must expect to be waited upon by a larger number, actuated by a different spirit. His principal apprehension was that he should lose his *half pay*" (*Proceedings of Massachusetts Historical Society,* ser. 1, vol. VIII, 1866, p. 349).

Loring is said to have deemed the cause of his countrymen just, but he did not believe it could succeed. On the morning of the battle of Lexington, he left his home and rode into the British lines of Boston, remarking to a neighbor, "I have always eaten the king's bread, and always intend to" (Drake, *post,* p. 417). On Mar. 30, 1775, the Provincial Congress of Massachusetts denounced Loring and other irreconcilables as implacable enemies of their country. On Oct. 16, 1778, he was proscribed and banished by act of the General Court. His home at Roxbury was, for a while, the headquarters of General Nathanael Greene, and then a hospital for American soldiers. The passage of the confiscation act in 1779 made his property the possession of the state, for whose benefit it was eventually sold. Upon the evacuation of Boston, he went to England and was the recipient of a pension from the crown until his decease at Highgate. In 1789 his widow died at Englesfield, Berkshire County, England, where their son, Joshua Loring [*q.v.*], had settled after the Revolution.

[J. H. Stark, *The Loyalists of Mass.* (1910); E. A. Jones, *The Loyalists of Mass.* (1930); F. S. Drake, *The Town of Roxbury* (1878); Lorenzo Sabine, *Biog. Sketches of the Loyalists* (1864), vol. II; Justin Winsor, *The Memorial Hist. of Boston,* vols. II, III (1881); *Proc. Mass. Hist. Soc.* ser. 1, vol. VIII, ser. 2, vol. X (1866–96); *Colls. Mass. Hist. Soc.* ser. 4, vol. IX (1871); *Pubs. of the Colonial Soc. of Mass.,* vol. XVII (1915); *Letters and Diary of John Rowe,* ed. by A. R. Cunningham (1903); C. H. Pope and K. P. Loring, *Loring Geneal.* (1917).]

J. G. V–D.

LORING, JOSHUA (Nov. 1, 1744–August 1789), Loyalist, was born at Hingham, Mass., the son of Mary (Curtis) and Joshua Loring [*q.v.*]. As a young man he served with the army; on July 11, 1761, he was commissioned ensign, became lieutenant on Aug. 1, 1765, and retired in 1768. For his military services he was granted 20,000 acres of land in New Hampshire. In 1769 he was appointed permanent high sheriff of Massachusetts and married, on Oct. 19 of the same year, Elizabeth Lloyd of Boston. He became a pew-holder in King's Chapel and a citizen of importance. He signed a protest against the solemn league and covenant issued by the committee of safety, and he was one of the one hundred and twenty-three who affixed their names to an address approving the course of Governor Hutchinson and presented it to him on the eve of his departure for England in 1774. He signed a similar address to General Gage the next year. One of the last official acts of Gage was to sign a proclamation of Oct. 7, 1775, appointing him sole vendue-master and auctioneer. When General Howe evacuated Boston, in March 1776, Loring went with the royal army to Halifax, and early the next year was appointed commissary of prisoners in the British army.

In the conduct of this office he made himself detested by the Whig leaders, who charged him with excessive cruelty in his treatment of prisoners. Ethan Allen complained of his murder of two thousand prisoners. Others affirmed that he charged for supplies furnished to prisoners long after they were dead, so that he must be "feeding the dead and starving the living" (Frank Moore, *Diary of the American Revolution,* 1860, vol. II, 210). Elias Boudinot, who occupied a corresponding position in the American army, accused him of neglect and ill-treatment, although he admitted that the situation had been very much worse before Loring became commissary. On Aug. 16, 1777, Boudinot sent to Washington Loring's memorandum denying these charges and pointing out the lack of interest in Congress for the welfare of those colonials who had been taken prisoner (Boudinot papers, *post*). The truth is not easy to discover. War is grim and conditions in the best military prisons are always bad enough. It is probable, too, that partisan feeling was responsible for some exaggeration. The letters of General Gold Selleck Silliman testify that Loring treated him with "complaisance, kindness, and friendship" (Thomas Jones, *post,* II, 425).

Banished from Massachusetts, he spent the last years of his life in Berkshire, England. One of his sons, Sir John Wentworth Loring, became a Vice Admiral in the British Navy and another son, Henry Lloyd Loring, was archdeacon of Calcutta.

[Transcripts of Elias Boudinot papers and the Washington papers in the Lib. of Cong.; J. H. Stark, *The Loyalists of Mass.* (1910); Lorenzo Sabine, *Biog. Sketches of the Loyalists* (1864), vol. II; E. A. Jones, *The Loyalists of Mass.* (1930); Thomas Jones, *Hist. of N. Y. during the Rev. War* (2 vols., 1879); F. S. Drake, *The Town of Roxbury* (1878); Peter Force, *Am. Archives,* ser. 4, vol. III (1840), col. 984; *Letters and Diary of John Rowe,* ed. by A. R. Cunningham (1903); H. W. Foote, *Annals of King's Chapel,* vol. II (1896); C. H. Pope and K. P. Loring, *Loring Geneal.* (1917).]

J. G. V–D.

LORING, WILLIAM WING (Dec. 4, 1818–Dec. 30, 1886), a soldier who fought under three flags, was descended from Thomas Loring who emigrated to America in 1634 and settled in Hingham, Mass. His father, Reuben Loring, a native of Hingham, moved to Wilmington, N. C., and there married Hannah Kenan. William was born in Wilmington but at an early age moved with his parents to Florida, where as a youth he fought with the 2nd Florida Volunteers against the Seminoles in engagements at Wahoo Swamp, Withahoochee, and Alachua, and at nineteen years of age, won for himself a second lieutenancy. He prepared for college at Alexandria, Va., attended Georgetown College, studied law, returned to Florida as a member of the state bar, and was elected to the state legislature for three years. He was appointed captain, Mounted Rifles, May 27, 1846, and major, Feb. 16, 1847, accompanying General Scott's expedition to Mexico and participating in the campaign from Vera Cruz to the capture of the city of Mexico (T. F. Rodenbough, *From Everglade to Cañon with the Second Dragoons,* 1875, pp. 140–41). He commanded his regiment at Contreras and led the fighting at Chapultepec where he lost an arm. For these acts of gallantry he was brevetted lieutenant-colonel, Aug. 20, 1847, and colonel, Sept. 13, 1847. He was promoted lieutenant-colonel in the regular army, Mar. 15, 1848, and the following year crossed the continent with his regiment in the van of the army of gold-seekers. After a march of some twenty-five hundred miles, he assumed command of the military department of Oregon, 1849–51. During the five years following he was stationed with his regiment in Texas, being promoted colonel, Dec. 30, 1856, and engaging hostile Indians in several skirmishes in New Mexico, 1856–58. In the latter year he marched his command into Utah, taking part during the years 1858–59 in the so-called Mormon War under Gen. Albert Sidney Johnston (T. F. Rodenbough, *The Army of the United States,* 1896, pp. 200–01). Granted leave of absence thereafter, he spent a year traveling in Europe, Egypt, and the Holy Land, studying foreign armies. Returning to the United States, he commanded the Department of New Mexico during the years 1860–61, and although he was opposed to secession, he approved of state rights and resigned from the army on May 13, 1861, to join the Confederacy.

His ability as a military commander was promptly recognized by his appointment as brigadier-general on May 20, 1861. He was given a command in West Virginia but in December 1861 his army was included in Gen. "Stonewall" Jackson's command. He took part in Jackson's Valley campaign in 1862 but after a violent controversy with Jackson [see biography of Thomas Jonathan Jackson] he was detached and placed in command of the army in southwestern Virginia. Meanwhile he had been promoted major-general, February 1862. Late in 1862 he was transferred to the Southwest where he participated in engagements at Grenada, Miss., and Champion Hills (F. V. Greene, *The Mississippi,* 1882, pp. 100 ff., and *Personal Memoirs of U. S. Grant,* vol. I, 1885, p. 435). Thereafter he served as a corps commander in Georgia, Mississippi, and Tennessee, and was active in the battles of Franklin and Nashville, where he was second in command to Gen. John B. Hood (J. D. Cox, *The March to the Sea,* 1882, pp. 88–125). His last Civil War service was under Gen. Joseph E. Johnston in the Carolinas, where, in April 1865, he surrendered to Sherman.

For a time he engaged in banking in New York City but in 1869, in company with certain other officers of the late Confederacy, Loring entered the military service of the Khedive of Egypt with the rank of brigadier-general, first acting as inspector-general, and later, in the year 1870, assuming command of the defenses of the city of Alexandria and of all Egyptian coast defenses. In the years 1875–76 he took part in the Egyptian expedition against Abyssinia and participated in the important battle of Kaya-Khor. Promoted to the grade of general of division, he was elevated by the Khedive to the dignity of a Pasha, and decorated with the Egyptian orders of the Osmanli and of the Medjidie. In the year 1879, in company with other American officers, he was mustered out of the Khedive's service and returned to the United States, residing for a time in Florida and later making his home in New York City. He contributed articles to magazines and to the press and in 1884 published a book: *A Confederate Soldier in Egypt,* which gives an entertaining narrative of his ten years' service under the Khedive. He died in New York City in his sixty-eighth year of an acute heart attack. At the time of his death he had in preparation an autobiography, "Fifty Years a Soldier." He never married.

[In addition to sources cited see: F. B. Heitman, *Hist. Reg. and Dict. of the U. S. Army* (1903), vol. I; *Battles and Leaders of the Civil War* (4 vols., 1887–88); *War of the Rebellion: Official Records (Army)*; *Confed. Mil. Hist.* (1899), vol. XI; J. M. Morgan, *Recollections of a Rebel Reefer* (1917); C. H. Pope and K. P. Loring, *Loring Geneal.* (1917); *N. Y. Herald* and *World* (N. Y.), Dec. 31, 1886. The genealogy gives Loring's middle name as *Wallace.*] C. D. R.

LOSKIEL, GEORGE HENRY (Nov. 7, 1740–Feb. 23, 1814), bishop of the Renewed Unitas Fratrum or Moravian Church, was born at Angermuende, Courland, Russia, the son of John Christian Loskiel, a Lutheran preacher. He studied theology at Halle and on Dec. 26, 1759, while he was still a student, joined the Moravian Church. On leaving the university he taught and filled various pastoral charges. He was married to Maria Magdalena Barlach of Volmer, Livonia, on June 27, 1771. In 1782 he was appointed superintendent of the mission in Livonia and agent for the Church in Russia. He occupied himself also for ten years, 1791–1801, with administrative and financial matters in connection with mission affairs. He was consecrated bishop on Mar. 14, 1802, and sailed almost immediately for the United States to take charge of the work in North America in place of John G. Cunow.

He reached the Moravian headquarters, Bethlehem, Pa., at a critical time in the history of the Moravian Church on the continent. The original establishments had been founded in 1742 on land purchased by funds advanced from the estate of Count Zinzendorf. The business depression of 1750, following the Treaty of Aix-la-Chapelle, had thrown Zinzendorf's affairs into bankruptcy and receivers had been appointed. At that time investments in the New World were looked upon with little favor, for France and England were on the brink of another war. As a consequence, in 1750 the entire establishment of the Moravian Church in the English colonies had been ordered to shift for itself in the belief that the investment was lost. This attitude on the part of the European authorities at Herrnhut continued until after the Revolution when, affairs in Europe having been rehabilitated, the receivers were discharged and the estate became a sustaining fund for the world-wide mission operations of the Church. By that time circumstances had altered the fortunes and possibilities of the Bethlehem group. The property had advanced in value, and the attention of the Herrnhut authorities was now riveted upon reëstablishing a connection that had been broken for a generation. It was too late, however, for such a backward movement, and Cunow, whom Loskiel replaced, had found himself in a generation that knew not the old times. On all sides he had been met with refusal when he proposed a return to the old paternalism and European control. As a consequence he gave up his task, and the suave and diplomatic Loskiel took his place.

For ten years this shrewd and clever scholar labored to bring about a compromise whereby the European and American interests might be separated. There was, on the part of the Bethlehem group, no denial of either the debt or the obligation to pay interest. Upon the basis of this acknowledgment, Loskiel proceeded to effect the desired result. From Pennsylvania to North Carolina, he jogged from station to station; and it is solely to his credit that at the conference of 1810 a scheme of adjustment was adopted, and that from it there emerged a successful plan of separation. There is no doubt that the anxieties incident to his strenuous efforts shortened his life. Although he was relieved of his duties in May 1811, the state of his health and the outbreak of war with England prevented his return to Europe, and he died at Bethlehem in 1814. His was a work that, necessarily, was performed without trumpets and drums. Hence history has often omitted his name from the list of those who have contributed to the creation of the American national spirit. Nevertheless he was the first of the Moravian bishops to visualize and strive for a new spirit of nationalization and to bring about, in those early days, a process of Americanization. He was the author of *Geschichte der Mission der Evangelischen Brueder unter den Indianern in Nordamerika* (1789), translated into English as *History of the Mission of the United Brethren among the Indians in North America* (London, 1794); and a devotional book, *Etwas für' Herz* (*c.* 1791).

[Bethlehem Diary, 1801–14, *Gemein Nachrichten,* 1802–12, and Loskiel's diary of his journeys, all MSS. in Bethlehem Archives; J. M. Levering, *Hist. of Bethlehem* (1892); E. W. Cröger, *Geschichte der Erneuerten Brüderkirche,* vol. III (1854); J. M. Hark, Introduction to *Extempore on a Wagon; A Metrical Narrative of a Journey from Bethlehem, Pa., to the Indian Town of Goshen, Ohio, in the Autumn of 1803* (1887).] A. G. R.

LOSSING, BENSON JOHN (Feb. 12, 1813–June 3, 1891), wood-engraver, author, editor, son of John and Miriam (Dorland) Lossing, was born at Beekman, Dutchess County, N. Y. The family name descended from Pietre Pieterse Lassingh, a Dutch settler who came to Albany about 1658. John Lossing, a small farmer, died when his son was an infant, and the boy's mother died when he was about twelve years old. Attendance at the district schools for three years gave him the only formal education he was to receive. At thirteen he was apprenticed to a watchmaker at Poughkeepsie and his early life was hard. In spite of many obstacles, however, he found time for reading and study, especially in the field of history. When he was twenty-two years old he became a joint editor and proprietor of the *Poughkeepsie Telegraph,* the official Democratic newspaper of Dutchess County; later he was joint editor of a literary fortnightly called the *Poughkeepsie Casket.* From J. A. Adams, who drew illustrations for his periodical, he learned the art of engraving on wood. In 1838 he moved to New York City, where he established himself as a wood-engraver. From June 1839 to May 1841 he edited and illustrated the weekly *Family Magazine* for J. S. Redfield. In his leisure moments he wrote an *Outline History of the Fine Arts,* which appeared in 1840 as No. 103 of Harpers' Family Library.

In 1848 Lossing conceived the idea of writing a narrative sketchbook treating of scenes and objects associated with the American Revolution. Harper & Brothers advanced funds to enable him to carry out the project, which ultimately took the form of the *Pictorial Field Book of the Revolution,* in two large octavo volumes. In gathering material for this work the author traveled more than eight thousand miles in the United States and Canada, occasionally returning home with sketches from which he made drawings on the block for the engraver. The preparation of the book consumed about five years. It was published in parts, 1850–52, and gave Lossing a wide reputation. For the next thirty-five years he was a prolific writer and editor of books mostly on popular subjects in American history. His historical and biographical works comprise more than forty titles, including: *Our Countrymen, or Brief Memoirs of Eminent Americans* (1855); *The Hudson, from the Wilderness to the Sea* (*Art-Journal,* London, Jan. 1, 1860–Dec. 1, 1861; issued in book form in 1866); *The Life and Times of Philip Schuyler* (2 vols., 1860–73); *Pictorial Field-Book of the War of 1812* (1868); *Pictorial History of the Civil War* (3 vols., 1866–68, later editions entitled *Pictorial Field-Book . . .*); *Our Country* (2 vols., published in parts, 1876–78); *A Biography of James A. Garfield* (1882); *History of New York City* (1884); *The Empire State* (1887). Among his many enterprises the *American Historical Record and Repertory of Notes and Queries,* a magazine which he edited in the years 1872–74, deserves mention. One of his best pieces of work was *A Memorial of Alexander Anderson, M.D., the First Engraver on Wood in America* (1872), a paper he read in 1870 before the New York Historical Society.

Although to the appraising eye of the twentieth century Lossing appears to have been primarily a successful popularizer of American history, his *Pictorial Field Book of the American Revolution* still commands respect. It was an original idea well executed, and the antiquarian of today turns to it for details which cannot be found elsewhere. Lossing was married first, June 18, 1833, to Alice, daughter of Thomas Barritt; she died in 1855, and on Nov. 18, 1856, he married Helen, daughter of Nehemiah Sweet. He made his home at "The Ridge," Dover Plains, N. Y., near the Connecticut boundary.

[G. W. Willis, in *Appletons' Jour.,* July 20, 1872, portr.; Nathaniel Paine, in *Proc. Worcester Soc. of Antiquity, 1891* (1892), with a list of Lossing's works; *Proc. Am. Antiq. Soc.,* n.s., VII (1891); F. L. Mott, *A Hist. of Am. Mags.* (1930); *Am. Ancestry,* vol. III (1888); C. E. Fitch, *Encyc. of Biog. of N. Y.,* vol. II (1916); J. H. Smith, *Hist. of Duchess County, N. Y.* (1882); *N. Y. Daily Tribune,* June 4, 1891.]

L. S. M.

LOTHROP, ALICE LOUISE HIGGINS (May 28, 1870–Sept. 2, 1920), social worker, was born in Boston. The daughter of Albert H. and Adelaide A. (Everson) Higgins, she was descended from Richard Higgins of Plymouth, a founder of Eastham, Mass. She was educated in local private schools and at twenty-eight entered the service of the Associated Charities as a worker in training. Her rare qualifications for social service were at once manifest, and when in 1900 she was entrusted with the secretaryship of a Charities district, she showed such qualities of leadership, such grasp of community problems that after but two years' experience, supplemented by a summer course at the New York School of Philanthropy, she was called to headquarters as general secretary. Upon her marriage, in 1913, to a Boston business man, William H. Lothrop, she resigned the secretaryship and was made a director of the society for life.

Alice Higgins was a breathing refutation of the old charge that organized charity is necessarily mechanized, formal, heartless. She was, as Dr. Samuel M. Crothers said, "not only a clear intelligence, but a great soul" (*The Family,* December 1920, p. 2). She interpreted family cases in terms of community needs, yet never lost sight of the individual. To the efficiency and sound judgment of the born executive and the swift-moving, original mind that pierced beyond conditions to underlying causes she added quick sympathies, perennial freshness of interest, buoyancy, and a stimulating faith in other people. For ten years she may be said to have animated the Associated Charities. Her influence went far beyond the society; for in practice as in her sixteen years (1904–20) of teaching in the Boston School of Social Work, she upheld her belief that interrelated social agencies should strengthen one another. Her support meant much to the medical-social group which began work in 1905 at the Massachusetts General Hospital under the leadership of Dr. Richard C. Cabot, and she did much to spread the modern medical-social viewpoint among Boston workers. She helped to shape important social legislation, including the provision for state inspection of charitable corporations and the Massachusetts mothers' aid law; she served on the Massachusetts Child Labor Commission, on tuberculosis boards, and in the Civic League. She was active in founding the American Association for Organizing Family Social Work, largely for the sake of the Boston society, some of whose directors could see no point in studying methods pursued in other places. Said she, "No movement so provincialized could live" (*Ibid.*, p. 16). She remained chairman of the executive and administration committees of the American Association from 1914 to her death.

In 1906, while the ruins of San Francisco still smoked, she entered on her first signal service in disaster relief. She spent some nine weeks in San Francisco, where, in cooperation with Lee Frankel and Oscar K. Cushing she organized rehabilitation practice which served as a model in later disasters. After the fires at Chelsea (1908) and Salem (1914), and the explosion at Halifax (1917), she showed herself an expert. It was she who after the Halifax explosion dispatched with the Red Cross contingent eye-surgeons whose prompt aid saved the sight of many gashed by flying glass. Her connection with the Red Cross began in 1916, when she developed plans for the Emergency Relief Unit of the Boston chapter. When America entered the war, she was the first division director of civilian relief to be appointed. She had to break new ground, and much that was vital in the success of Home Service to soldiers' families was due to her initiative. Dr. Crothers used to say, "We always knew where to find Mrs. Lothrop. It was where the need was greatest, the issue most vital" (*Ibid.*, p. 2). She died at her home in Newtonville.

[K. C. Higgins, *Richard Higgins and His Descendants* (1918), and *Supp.* (1924); *Boston Transcript*, Sept. 3, 11, 1920; *Survey*, Sept. 15, 1920; Memorial number of *The Family* (organ Am. Asso. for Organizing Family Social Work), Dec. 1920.] M. B. H.

LOTHROP, AMY [See WARNER, ANNA BARTLETT, 1827–1915].

LOTHROP, DANIEL (Aug. 11, 1831–Mar. 18, 1892), publisher, was born in Rochester, N. H., the son of Daniel and Sophia (Horne) Lothrop. Both his parents were of American descent for several generations; his father, descended from Mark Lothrop who was in Salem, Mass., in 1643, also numbered John and Priscilla Alden among his ancestors. Daniel was given a classical education to prepare him for college, but at fourteen was diverted to a business career when an elder brother asked him to take charge of his drug store while its owner studied medicine. The youthful manager found the Rochester store so profitable that in 1848 he opened others in Newmarket and Laconia. In 1850 he bought out a book store in Dover, N. H. Soon he introduced the sale of books into his drug stores and later made some small experiments in publishing. In 1856 he went West and established a drug store and a bank in St. Peter, Minn., which was then the capital of the Territory; but the transfer of the seat of government to St. Paul and the panic of 1857 caused the failure of both ventures.

After a period of inactivity, he returned East, and in 1868 established a publishing business in Boston. He had carefully matured his plans and determined that his policy should be to cater to the needs of Sunday-schools and to specialize in juvenile literature. He met with such success in this undertaking that, notwithstanding severe losses incurred in the famous Boston fire of 1872, he expanded his business in 1874 and again in 1887. He sought to choose the material he published for its interest as well as for its informative and edifying qualities, and though his Sunday-school books had the inevitable moral note, they usually contained things that appealed to the children themselves rather than the more solemn matter that their elders thought they ought to have. In addition to publishing works of such well-known writers as Edward Everett Hale, Thomas Nelson Page, and Margaret Sidney, he founded several popular juvenile periodicals, the best-known of which was *Wide Awake,* established in 1875 with Mary Mapes Dodge [*q.v.*] as a prominent contributor. The publishing house of D. Lothrop & Company became a leader in the field in which it specialized, and had a considerable influence on juvenile literature in America.

A prominent figure in the business life of Boston, Lothrop also took great interest in good government, and in 1880 founded the American Institute of Civics, an organization designed to spread a knowledge of politics and an interest in government. He married, first, on July 25, 1860, Ellen Morrill of Dover, N. H., who died in 1880; and, second, on Oct. 4, 1881, Harriett Mulford Stone, who wrote under the name of Margaret Sidney [see Lothrop, Harriett Mulford Stone]. He had one daughter by the second marriage.

[E. B. Huntington, *A Geneal. Memoir of the Lo-Lathrop Family* (1884); E. E. Hale, in *Lend a Hand*, Oct. 1892; J. N. McClintock, in *Bay State Monthly*, Dec. 1884; *Publishers' Weekly*, Mar. 26, 1892; *Boston Daily Advertiser, Boston Herald, Boston Transcript*, Mar. 19, 1892; *Boston Globe*, Mar. 20, 1892.]

S. G.

LOTHROP, GEORGE VAN NESS (Aug. 8, 1817–July 12, 1897), lawyer, minister to Russia, was born at Easton, Bristol County, Mass. His ancestor, Mark Lothrop, came to Massachusetts in 1643, settling first in Salem and then in Bridgewater. Howard Lothrop, father of George, served in both branches of the Massachusetts legislature and as member of the governor's council; his wife, George's mother, was Sally Williams, daughter of Edward Williams of Easton. George owed his middle name to his father's friend, C. P. Van Ness, at one time governor of Vermont. His early years were spent on his father's farm. He acquired his preparatory education at the Wrentham Academy and in a private school at Taunton. In 1834 he became a freshman at Amherst and in 1835 entered the sophomore class at Brown, where he graduated in 1838. Immediately after his graduation he went to Harvard to study law under Joseph Story and Simon Greenleaf. One year later, however, impaired health compelled him to give up his studies, and he removed to Prairie Ronde, Kalamazoo County, Mich., where his brother, Edwin H. Lothrop, was living on a farm. Here he practised farming with marked success. Outdoor life soon restored his health, and, after having studied law for a short time in Detroit, he was admitted to the bar (1843) and entered practice with D. Bethune Duffield, whose partner he presently became.

During his forty-odd years of practice before the Michigan supreme court he secured the invalidation of several laws as unconstitutional. Among these measures were an act providing for taking the vote of soldiers in the field (13 *Mich.*, 127) and acts authorizing municipalities to aid in the building of railroads (20 *Mich.*, 452 and 23 *Mich.*, 499). He practised also in the federal courts, interesting himself especially in Admiralty law. In 1848 he became attorney-general of Michigan, but resigned three years later. In 1853 he accepted a position as recorder of Detroit. He was a Democrat, and in 1860 was a delegate to the convention at Charleston. From 1879 to 1896 he was president of the Detroit Bar Association. He was general solicitor for the Michigan Central Railroad for twenty-five years. In Detroit he acquired valuable property and in various parts of eastern Michigan he owned extensive farms. His real-estate holdings were valued at about $2,000,000 (*Sunday News-Tribune*, Detroit, July 28, 1895).

In May 1885 he was appointed minister to Russia by President Cleveland, who had met him at Buffalo the previous year and had been struck by his fine appearance and apparent ability. While he was stationed at St. Petersburg one of his daughters was married to a Russian baron. Returning to Michigan in 1888 on account of his health, he spent his last nine years in peaceful retirement at Detroit, where he died. On May 13, 1847, he had married Almira Strong, daughter of Gen. Oliver Strong of Rochester, N. Y. Of seven children born to them, two sons and two daughters survived their father. Lothrop was a man of irreproachable manners, modest, dignified, courteous, affable, a master of correct English, a painstaking scholar; for many years he was called the "leader of the Michigan bar."

[C. A. Kent, in W. D. Lewis, *Great American Lawyers*, VII (1909), 163–99; E. B. Huntington, *A Geneal. Memoir of the Lo-Lathrop Family* (1884); *Illustrated Detroit* (1891); G. I. Reed, *Bench and Bar of Mich.* (1897); Fred. Carlisle, *Wayne County Hist. and Pioneer Soc.: Chronography* (1890); Brown Univ. necrology in *Providence Daily Journal*, June 15, 1898; *Sunday News-Tribune* (Detroit), July 28, 1895, Apr. 4, 1897, and *Evening News* (Detroit), July 12, 1897.]

A. H.

LOTHROP, HARRIETT MULFORD STONE (June 22, 1844–Aug. 2, 1924), widely known under the pen name Margaret Sidney as a writer of books for children, was born in New Haven, Conn., the daughter of Sidney Mason and Harriett (Mulford) Stone. Her father was one of the earliest professional architects of that city, and her mother, the daughter of a prominent merchant. Harriett graduated from the Grove Hall School, New Haven, and early showed talent for writing both fiction and verse. Contributions to *Wide Awake*, begun in 1878, attracted attention, and in 1880 there appeared serially in that magazine a story which, published subsequently in book form, has given delight to thousands of youthful readers, *Five Little Peppers and How They Grew* (1881). For years it was one of the books for children in greatest demand. It was followed by a number of other somewhat less popular but widely read tales dealing with the fortunes of the Pepper family, together with many more narratives of interest to boys and girls. Their author had the gift of writing simply and naturally, of making very real the homely, everyday life of ordinary people, both on its serious and its amusing side, and an understanding of the mental operations of young and old which make her characters attractively human. Occasionally the didactic motive distorts the portrayals a little, but in general it does not much diminish the pleasurable impression of reality which one receives. The kindly, affectionate spirit in which the stories are written also contributes much to their charm. Among them may be noted *So As By Fire* (1881); *The Pettibone Name, a New England Story* (1882); *Hester and Other New England Stories* (1886); *A New Departure for Girls* (1886); *Dilly and the Captain* (1887); *How Tom and Dorothy Made and Kept a Christian Home* (1888); *Rob, a Story for Boys* (1891); *A Little Maid of Concord Town* (1898); *The Judges' Cave* (1900); *Sally, Mrs. Tubbs* (1903); *A Little Maid of Boston Town* (1910).

One of those whose interest was aroused by Miss Stone's earlier writings was Daniel Lothrop [*q.v.*], head of the publishing house of D. Lothrop & Company, and on Oct. 4, 1881, she became his second wife. The firm which he controlled specialized in juvenile literature, especially in the kind suitable for Sunday-school libraries, and the numerous books written by Mrs. Lothrop did much to give it success. She also contributed to young people's magazines and wrote verse for children which was popular. In 1883 the Lothrops purchased "Wayside," Hawthorne's old home at Concord, which they made their residence until Daniel Lothrop's death in 1892. Later Mrs. Lothrop acquired the nearby estate of Ephraim Wales Bull [*q.v.*], restored "Grapevine Cottage," and dedicated it as a memorial to its former owner, the propagator of the Concord grape. She was descended from colonial stock, and was active in patriotic societies. She founded the Old Concord Chapter, Daughters of the American Revolution, and in 1895 formed the Old North Bridge Society, Children of the American Revolution, the beginning of a national organization of which she was president until 1901, and honorary president until her death, when it had a membership of over 22,000. During the latter part of her life she spent her summers in Concord, and her winters at her home at Stanford University, Cal. She died at San Francisco in her eighty-first year.

[*Daughters of the Am. Revolution Mag.*, Sept. 1924; *Children of the Am. Revolution*, Sept. 1924; *Who's Who in America*, 1924–25; J. L. Swayne, *The Story of Concord Told by Concord Writers* (1906); G. B. Bartlett, *Concord, Historic, Literary and Picturesque* (15th ed., 1895); *Book News*, Oct. 1892; *Publishers' Weekly*, Aug. 9, 1924; *Boston Transcript*, *San Francisco Chronicle*, Aug. 4, 1924.] H. E. S.

LOTHROPP, JOHN (1584–Nov. 8, 1653), clergyman, minister at Scituate and Barnstable in the Colony of New Plymouth, was the son of Thomas and Mary Lothropp (variously spelled) of Cherry Burton and Etton, Yorkshire. He was baptized at Etton Dec. 20, 1584. He matriculated at Queen's College, Cambridge, and received the degrees of bachelor of arts in 1606 and master of arts in 1609. After preaching at Bennington, Hertfordshire, and at Cheriton and Egerton, Kent, he renounced his orders because he could no longer conform to the ceremonies of the Church of England. He united with a congregation of non-conformists and separatists which met in and about London in 1624, and succeeded Henry Jacob as pastor of the group in 1625. This congregation was tracked down at the house of Humphrey Barnett, a brewer's clerk, in Blackfriars, Apr. 29, 1632, by Tomlinson, a pursuivant of Bishop Laud, and Lothropp and two-thirds of his congregation were arrested. He appeared before the Court of High Commission May 3 and May 8 and was committed to prison, where he remained for two years. During his imprisonment his wife died. Her name is unknown, but he married her prior to 1614, and she bore him eight children. He was liberated Apr. 24, 1634, on a bond to absent himself from all private conventicles and to appear before the Court of High Commission in Trinity Term (*Calendar of State Papers, Domestic Series, 1633–34*, 1863, p. 583). At the invitation of the settlers of Scituate in the Colony of New Plymouth to become their pastor (*Calendar of State Papers, Colonial Series, America and the West Indies, 1574–1660,* 1860, p. 194), and accompanied by some thirty followers, he fled to New England, where Winthrop recorded his arrival at Boston in the *Griffin*, Sept. 18, 1634. He proceeded immediately to Scituate, arriving there Sept. 27 and preaching twice on the following day. On condition that a church should be organized at Scituate, the church at Plymouth on Nov. 23 dismissed its members living at the former place. A church was gathered there Jan. 8, 1634/35, and Lothropp was chosen first pastor and ordained Jan. 19. Services were held in homes until a meeting-house was completed and dedicated in 1636. Soon after his arrival at Scituate, Lothropp took as his second wife a widow, Ann (surname unknown), by whom he had six children. He was admitted freeman of the Colony of New Plymouth June 7, 1637. With other freemen of Scituate he complained to the Court of Assistants of the Colony of scarcity of land at Scituate, Jan. 1, 1637/38, and he wrote to Governor Prence, Sept. 28, 1638, and again Feb. 18, 1638/39, asking for the grant of a new site. The Colony granted the group Seppekann or Rochester Jan. 22, 1638/39, but this tract proved unacceptable and Lothropp and more than half of his congregation removed to Barnstable, Oct. 11, 1639. A church was gathered there Oct. 31, 1639, and services held in dwelling houses until a meeting-house was erected in 1646. There Lothropp served as pastor until his death at the age of sixty-nine.

[J. and J. A. Venn, *Alumni Cantabrigienses,* pt. I, vol. III (1924), p. 104; *Reports of Cases in the Courts of Star Chamber and High Commission* (Camden Soc., 1886), ed. by S. R. Gardiner; E. B. Huntington, *A Geneal. Memoir of the Lo-Lathrop Family* (1884); *Winthrop's Journal* (2 vols., 1908), ed. by J. K. Hosmer; "Scituate and Barnstable Church Records," *New-Eng. Hist. and Geneal. Reg.,* July 1855, Jan. 1856; *Records of the Colony of New Plymouth in New England,* vols. I and III (1855), and vol. XII (1861); Samuel Deane, *Hist. of Scituate, Mass.* (1831); H. H. Pratt, *The Early Planters of Scituate* (1929); *Geneal. Notes of Barnstable Families,* vol. II (1890), rev. and completed by C. F. Swift; Nathaniel Morton, *New Englands Memoriall* (1669; 6th ed., with notes, 1855); Daniel Neal, *The Hist. of the Puritans* (first ed., 4 vols., 1732–38; 3 vols., 1837); Champlin Burrage, *The Early English Dissenters in the Light of Recent Research* (2 vols., 1912); John Lathrop, "Biog. of Rev. John Lothropp," *Mass. Hist. Soc. Colls.,* 2 ser. I (1814); W. B. Sprague, *Annals Am. Pulpit,* vol. I (1857); sketch by Alexander Gordon, in *Dict. Nat. Biog.*]

I. M. C.

LOTTA [See Crabtree, Charlotte, 1847–1924].

LOUCKS, HENRY LANGFORD (May 24, 1846–Dec. 29, 1928), agrarian politician, was the son of William J. Loucks (or Lux), of Luxemburg-German ancestry, and his wife, Anna York, born in Pennsylvania of Irish parents, who had gone soon after their marriage to Hull, across the Ottawa River from Ottawa, Canada. Here William Loucks engaged in general merchandising and here Henry was born. He was educated in the Canadian common schools. After reaching manhood, he engaged in mercantile pursuits in Canada, Michigan, and Missouri, and in 1884 settled upon a government homestead in Deuel County, Dakota Territory.

His settlement in Dakota came as the great boom was subsiding and the reaction was setting in. Economically the situation was difficult at the best; markets were distant, rates high, and prices low. Loucks, who possessed great vitality and public spirit, at once took up the cause of the farmers in a movement for the legal regulation of transportation rates, the prohibition of usury, and the exclusion of middlemen in marketing and purchasing. He became the leader and president of the Territorial and soon of the National Farmers' Alliance and assisted in organizing a number of cooperative business ventures, including fire and hail insurance and merchandising. He also established the *Dakota Ruralist* as the exponent of his economic views and published it for nearly a score of years.

At first, he and his associates, who generally affiliated with the Republican party, hoped to accomplish their objectives through the existing parties, but in 1890, at a joint convention of the Knights of Labor and the state Farmers' Alliance, of which he was then president, Loucks was named as candidate for governor. He was defeated, but succeeded in consolidating a large section of the farmers into a separate political party (at first known as the Independent, later identified with the People's or Populist party) that for a number of years was an important factor in affairs. He had an influential part in directing the fusion of Populists and Democrats which resulted in the election of James H. Kyle [*q.v.*] to the United States Senate in 1891. The following year he was president of the national convention of the People's party held in Omaha, and in November 1892 he was elected president of the National Farmers' Alliance and Industrial Union. He threw himself into the fight for the adoption of the initiative and referendum in South Dakota in 1898 and its success was conceded to have resulted from his efforts and finesse. From early in his career he devoted much energy to the promotion of temperance, and attained more than provincial reputation for his labors in that cause. In all his work for temperance and economic reform he was notable for kindly spirit, fairness to his opponents, and moderate temper. He was an acute debater, ingenious in method, and utterly imperturbable before violent attack. He published several works, the titles of which indicate the direction of his thought: *The New Monetary System* (1893); *Government Ownership of Railroads and Telegraphs* (1894); and *The Great Conspiracy of the House of Morgan and How to Defeat It* (1916).

In Canada, May 2, 1878, he married Florence McCraney, of an Irish family, and they became the parents of seven children. His death occurred at Clearlake, S. Dak., in his eighty-third year.

[Letters from Loucks's family and files of the *S. Dak. Ruralist,* 1888–1900, in Archives S. Dak. Dept. of Hist.; J. D. Hicks, *The Populist Revolt: A Hist. of the Farmers' Alliance and the People's Party* (1931); F. E. Haynes, *Third Party Movements Since the Civil War* (1916); F. G. Blood, *Hand Book and Hist. of the National Farmers' Alliance and Industrial Union* (1893); *Memorial and Biog. Record . . . S. Dak.* (1898); *Nation* (N. Y.), June 12, 1890; *National Economist* (Washington, D. C.), July 19, 1890; *N. Y. Times,* Dec. 30, 1928.] D.R.

LOUDON, SAMUEL (*c.* 1727–Feb. 24, 1813), merchant, printer, and publisher, was born probably in Ireland of Scotch-Irish ancestry and emigrated to America some time before 1753. In October of that year he was proprietor of a store opposite the Old Slip Market in New York City, where his stock in trade included speaking trumpets, pots and kettles, powder and shot, and "a parcel of ready-made coats and breeches, in the newest fashion" (*New York Mercury,* Oct. 8, 1753). Four years later he had changed his location to Hunter's Quay and was calling himself a ship-chandler (*Ibid.,* Sept. 19, 1757). His correspondence with Philip Schuyler of Albany during the years 1769–74 shows that he was one of several who had invested money in the "Saratoga patent" in upper New York, seeking a profit by dividing it into lots and selling to Scotch immigrants. Another of his ventures, undertaken in 1771, is disclosed by an advertisement of "A Book Store just Opened" (*New York Mercury,* Dec. 23, 1771), with which he later combined "Samuel Loudon's Circulating Library" (Jan. 1, 1774).

Soon after the outbreak of the Revolution he began, Jan. 4, 1776, the publication of *The New York Packet and the American Advertiser,* a weekly newspaper. Stanch patriot though he was, he fell into disfavor with the radical Committee of Mechanics in the city when, in March, he started to issue *The Deceiver Unmasked; or Loyalty and Interest United,* written anonymously as an answer to Paine's *Common Sense.* He was warned not to publish the pamphlet and promised to proceed no further with it at that time. Nevertheless, on Mar. 19 his printing office was invaded and 1,500 impressions carried away and burned. (A pamphlet preserved in the New York Historical Society bears the inscription "This copy was saved.") Always a keen observer of his balance sheet, he bitterly bewailed this misfortune which, he said, represented a £75 loss. In an open letter "To the Public" (*New York Packet,* Apr. 11, 1776) he strongly avowed his patriotism and resented the affront to the freedom of the press at a time when the question of independence was still a debatable matter. The following week (Apr. 18, 1776) he advertised as "necessary at the present time for all families who have the good of their country at heart" a pamphlet, *Essays upon the Making of Salt-Petre and Gun-Powder,* just published by order of the Committee of Safety of the Colony.

The arrival of the British forces at New York necessitated the suspension of the *Packet* (Aug. 29, 1776) and the removal of Loudon's numerous family to a place of safety. After a brief period as a merchant in Norwich, Conn., he opened a store and printery at Fishkill, N. Y., and resumed publication of the *Packet,* Jan. 16, 1777. Regularity of issue was at times interrupted by shortage of paper, but he kept the news sheet going during the remainder of the Revolution. Furthermore, he was state printer and for a time postmaster at Fishkill. In the former capacity he printed the first constitution of the State of New York (1777), and also several issues of state paper money. The British gone, he moved back to New York City, reopened his printery, resumed publication of the *Packet* as a biweekly, and started again his bookshop and circulating library. Because of alleged sharp practice in connection with the issue of another batch of paper money for the state (1786), a rival newspaper editor said of him:

> "To good and evil equal bent,
> He's both a Devil and a Saint"
> (Shepard Kollock [*q.v.*], quoted by Wall, *post.*)

In 1786 he printed *Laws of the State of New York,* in one volume, also Noah Webster's short-lived periodical, the *American Magazine.* In 1792 the *Packet* became the *Diary or Loudon's Register.* By this time the founder's son Samuel was prominently connected with the paper.

Loudon was an elder in the Scotch Presbyterian Church, a member of the St. Andrew's Society, and an honorary member of the Society of the Cincinnati. He was twice married: first, Jan. 24, 1756, to Sarah Oakes, and second (before 1768), to Lydia Griswold, sister of Gov. Matthew Griswold of Connecticut. He had five sons and three daughters. He died near Middletown Point, N. J., in his eighty-sixth year.

[A. J. Wall, in *N. Y. Hist. Soc. Quart. Bull.,* Oct. 1922; "Loudon's Diary," in W. W. Pasko's *Old New York,* Nov. 1889; Isaiah Thomas, *The Hist. of Printing in America* (1810), vol. II; C. R. Hildeburn, *Sketches of Printers and Printing in Colonial N. Y.* (1895); M. E. Perkins, *Old Houses of the Antient Town of Norwich, 1660–1800* (1895); E. E. and E. M. Salisbury, *Family Hists. and Geneals.* (1892), II, 52; J. W. Francis, *Old New York* (ed. of 1866); files of *N. Y. Packet,* 1776–83, and of *The Diary,* 1792–95, also *N. Y. Gazetteer,* Jan. and Feb. 1786; letters of Loudon among the Schuyler Papers in N. Y. Pub. Lib., in Peck Lib., Norwich, Conn., in N. Y. Hist. Soc., and in private hands; *Jours. of the Provincial Cong. . . . of N. Y.* (2 vols., 1842); *N. Y. Gazette and General Advertiser,* Mar. 2, 1813.] A. E. P.

LOUDOUN, JOHN CAMPBELL, Fourth Earl of (May 5, 1705–Apr. 27, 1782), British commander-in-chief in North America, was the son of Hugh, third earl, of Loudoun Castle, Galston, Ayrshire, and of his wife Margaret, only daughter of John Dalrymple, first Earl of Stair. Choosing to follow the military profession, he entered the Scots Greys as cornet in 1727, and by 1739 had become captain, with the army rank of lieutenant-colonel, in the 3rd Foot Guards. His interests were not confined to the army, however. Having succeeded to the title in 1731, he was elected in 1734 as a Scottish representative peer, and shared in the Scottish patronage by getting, in 1741, the governorship of Stirling Castle. In Ayrshire he improved his own estates by systematic and scientific planting, and encouraged the building of roads and bridges. The Royal Society elected him fellow in 1738. In 1743 he saw service in Flanders and after Dettingen became aide-de-camp to George II. Loyal to the king, as his family had ever been, he played an important part in the Jacobite rebellion of 1745, acting as adjutant-general to Sir John Cope, commanding later in the north of Scotland where the Young Pretender eluded him, and raising as colonel a regiment of Highlanders. This regiment was cut to pieces at Preston Pans; recruited again, it relieved Fort Augustus and was later reduced. In 1749 Loudoun became colonel of the 30th Regiment and in 1755 major-general.

A believer in the necessity of stern disciplinary measures to preserve colonial dependence on the royal prerogative, Loudoun readily accepted, in January 1756, the post of commander-in-chief of all forces in North America, offered him by the Duke of Cumberland with the approval of Fox and Halifax. At the same time he was appointed governor-general of Virginia, a sinecure post, and colonel-in-chief of the new Royal American Regiment. Administrative entanglements in London delayed his arrival at New York until July 23. There his candor and affability, his readiness to accept wise suggestions, his incessant attention to infinite detail (which was to undermine his health), and his direct methods of dealing, provoked favorable comment, at first, from such different men as Franklin and Hutchinson. His tasks were two: to mold the British army in North America into an efficient fighting unit, and to unite jealous and divided colonies in support of the war. Without the aid of an adequate staff, he organized the transportation, supply, and ranging services to function without direct colonial support. He took the preliminary steps in training the raw recruits of the army for wilderness warfare. Such work constituted his greatest achievement and gives him a place among the conquerors of Canada. In his relations with the colonies Loudoun was less successful. The British ministry had intended them to furnish, not only provincial troops, but recruits, funds, and quarters for the regular army. Loudoun's blunt insistence on his authority, accompanied often with deliberate outbursts of temper, led many colonial assemblies to fear military government, while Massachusetts almost refused him support. His campaigns were completely unsuccessful. Montcalm took Forts Oswego and William Henry in successive summers, and his own projected invasion of Canada by way of Louisbourg and the St. Lawrence failed. None of these disasters was wholly his fault, for he was a good soldier, if no genius. In December 1757 Pitt determined on his recall, less because he had not accomplished visible results than because Pitt refused to continue longer the extensive political and military authority he possessed.

Second in command of the British expedition to Portugal in 1762, Loudoun, after Tyrawley's resignation in June, acted as commander of British troops in the Peninsula until the following spring, and aided in turning back a Franco-Spanish invasion. There, as in America, he irritated the somewhat dilatory civil ministers by his tactless insistence upon conditions he deemed essential for the health of his troops. Lieutenant-general in 1758, governor of Edinburgh Castle in 1763, he became general in 1770, and colonel of the Scots Guards. He died unmarried at Loudoun Castle, and was succeeded by his cousin. Peter Wraxall in 1756 described him as "short, strong made & seems disposed & fit for Action," his countenance "full of Candor, his Eyes Sprightly & good Humoured."

[Original materials for Loudoun's American career are in the Loudoun Papers in the Henry E. Huntington Library, San Marino, Cal., in the Amherst, Chatham and various state papers in the Public Record Office, in the Newcastle, Bouquet, and Hardwicke Papers in the British Museum, in the Cumberland Papers in the Royal Archives, and in printed collections of colonial documents and correspondence for the period. Recent accounts of his command are by C. T. Atkinson, in *The Cambridge Hist. of the British Empire*, vol. VI, "Canada and Newfoundland" (1930); and by S. M. Pargellis, *Lord Loudoun in North America* (1933). A good general history is J. S. Corbett, *England in the Seven Years' War* (2 vols., 1907).] S. M. P.

LOUGHRIDGE, ROBERT McGILL (Dec. 24, 1809–July 8, 1900), missionary and educator among the Creek Indians, came of Scotch-Irish people in South Carolina. He was born at Laurensville, S. C., but in his childhood, with his parents, James and Deborah Ann (McGill)

Loughridge, moved to the Alabama country. He was taught by the Rev. John H. Gray, with whom he afterward studied theology, and in the Mesopotamia Academy until he went to Ohio to attend Miami University, where he graduated in 1837. He entered the Princeton Theological Seminary, but, after one year there, he returned home to Eutaw, Ala., on account of his father's death. While he was teaching school and continuing his theological studies near their former territory, he became concerned for the Creeks who, deprived of their lands in Alabama and Georgia and moved to what is now Oklahoma, remained resentful and intractable. In 1836 the missionaries, who had worked among them for a few years with small success, had all left the country because of their opposition.

Nevertheless five years later Loughridge went there to find a place for work, armed with letters to the chiefs from the Presbyterian board of foreign missions and from the war department. On Apr. 9, 1841, he was licensed to preach. On Oct. 15 of the next year he was ordained by the Presbytery of Tuscaloosa, Ala., and in December, with his bride, Olivia (Hills) Loughridge, to whom he had been married on the sixth of the month, left Alabama to settle among the Creeks. He gained a grudging admittance and built a school at Coweta. There, in June 1843, he began teaching and preaching. Four years later the situation was greatly changed. The mission was prospering, and its founder was publicly called by a Creek chief "their friend Loughridge" (*Foreign Missionary Chronicle,* Aug. 1847, p. 243). In 1847 the Creek Council made an agreement with the Presbyterian board for joint support of the original school, now become a boarding-school, and of another one, to be established. This was opened in 1850, as a manual labor boarding-school at Tallahassee, and to it, especially, he devoted himself. Under his direction the mission continued to flourish. In 1855 he reported twelve missionaries at work, and the same year began, with *The Gospel According to Matthew,* the publication of his translations of the Gospels. By 1861 several hundred Creek men and women had received elementary and industrial education. Two churches had been organized and two Indian ministers trained. Schoolbooks and literature for religious instruction had been published in Muskokee, the principal Creek dialect. As early as 1845 he had published the first edition of *Muskokee Hymns,* based on the earlier work of John Fleming [*q.v.*] and the next year had published his *Translation of the Introduction to the Shorter Catechism.* He had acquired a commanding influence among the Indians. Yet, at the outbreak of the Civil War, white men hostile to the mission were able to instigate the Indians to expel the missionaries.

From that time until 1880 he was minister of Presbyterian churches in several places in eastern Texas, among them Lagrange, Goliad, and Marlin. In 1881, he returned to his mission, which had been revived in 1866. From 1883 to 1885 he had charge of the Tallahassee school in a new building provided, at Wealaka, by the Creek council. Then he gave himself to preaching among the Indians and to completing his *English and Muskokee Dictionary,* which was published in collaboration with David M. Hodge in 1890. At the age of seventy-nine he had ended his work for the Creeks, in whose progress toward civilization he had played a great part. In 1888 he became minister of the Presbyterian church in Tulsa and in 1889 moved to Red Fork, I. T. For three years he had charge of both these churches. In 1892 he went to Waco, Tex., where he ministered to churches in the neighborhood until he was eighty-six years old and where he died. In September 1845 his first wife died and, on Dec. 4, 1846, he married, in Conway, Mass., Mary Avery, who died Jan. 20, 1850. On Oct. 15, 1853, he took as his third wife Harriet Johnson.

[*Necrological Report Presented to the Alumni Asso. of Princeton Theol. Sem. . . . 1901* (1901); information from the Rev. R. H. Lamb, Tulsa, Okla.; *Foreign Missionary Chronicle,* esp. Mar., July, Aug. 1847; *Foreign Missionary,* Feb. 1854; *Annual Reports of the Board of Foreign Missions of the Presbyt. Church* for 1850, 1855, 1867, 1881, 1883, 1885; *Minutes of the General Assembly of the Presbyt. Church of the U. S.* (1863–80); *Minutes of the General Assembly of the Presbyt. Church in the U. S. of America,* n.s., vols. XI–XV (1888–92).]

R. H. N.

LOUNSBURY, THOMAS RAYNESFORD (Jan. 1, 1838–Apr. 9, 1915), author and philologist, was born in Ovid, N. Y., the son of the Rev. Thomas and Mary Janette (Woodward) Lounsbury. He prepared for college in Ovid and entered Yale in the class of 1859. As an undergraduate he won prizes in English composition, debating, and public speaking, was elected to Phi Beta Kappa, and was one of the editors of the *Yale Literary Magazine.* A few months at home convinced him that life in a farming community was neither "mentally stimulating nor pecuniarily profitable," and he moved to New York City where he occupied himself writing for Appleton's *New American Cyclopædia.* On Aug. 9, 1862, he joined the Union army as first lieutenant of Company C in the 126th New York Regiment. His first adventures in the field terminated ingloriously at Harpers Ferry, where he was surrendered with nine thousand other men to General Jackson, by what he characterized as "an imbecility so hopelessly imbecile, as almost to reach the sublime in that department" (*Yale College Class of 1859: Decennial Record,* 1870, p. 64). He was exchanged in November and was on active service in Virginia until the close of the Gettysburg campaign. His impressions of Virginia in war time are recorded in a paper written in 1864 and subsequently published under the title, "In the Defenses of Washington" (*Yale Review,* April 1913). His regiment suffered heavily in the battle of Gettysburg, and he was one of seven officers who escaped uninjured. In August 1863 he was detailed to Elmira, N. Y., as adjutant-general of the draft rendezvous; and here he remained until mustered out of service in June 1865.

He taught Latin and Greek for some months in Lespinasse's French Institute on Washington Heights, New York, and was tutor in a private family at Milburn, N. J., for two years. During this period he pursued a rigorous course of reading and study, with particular attention to Anglo-Saxon and early English. In January 1870 he returned to Yale as instructor in English in the Sheffield Scientific School, and in the following year he married Jane D. Folwell, daughter of Gen. Thomas J. Folwell of Kendaia, N. Y. In 1871 he was made professor of English in the Sheffield Scientific School, and he continued to hold this chair until 1906. He was librarian of the Scientific School from 1873 to 1896, its representative on the university council from 1900 until the year of his retirement, and for many years a member of the standing committee in charge of the university library.

In teaching English literature in a scientific school, Lounsbury was more happily situated than might at first appear. Sheffield was still a new enterprise when he joined the faculty, and he had more freedom to deal imaginatively with a subject still under some suspicion than he would have had in an institution bound by the old academic traditions. He broke away from the formal teaching of rhetoric, took his students straight to the texts of the poets and prose writers, and taught them to recognize in literature the record of a life as real as their own. The principal interests of most of his students lay naturally in other directions, but he succeeded in making literature a permanent interest with a surprisingly large number of them. He brought to his classroom the hard common sense, the firm regard for fact, and the unshakable sense of values that distinguished his own scholarship; and the first object of his teaching was to assure himself that his pupils knew what they were talking about. That he did not flatter himself that he had been invariably successful one may infer from a passage in his life of Cooper. "We need not feel any distrust," he says, in speaking of Cooper's education, "of his declaration, that little learning of any kind found its way into his head. Least of all will he be inclined to doubt it whom extended experience in the class-room has taught to view with profoundest respect the infinite capability of the human mind to resist the introduction of knowledge" (*James Fenimore Cooper,* p. 7). Evidence that he was able to view with the same sardonic amusement the teacher's inevitable failure to hold the attention of his pupils at all times and seasons is to be found in the oft-told tale that he once exhorted a class, growing unusually restless toward the end of the hour, to bear with him a little longer, for he had a few more pearls to cast.

As a scholar, Lounsbury was recognized in Europe and America as one of the most eminent masters of his subject. He was one of the fifteen original members of the American Academy of Arts and Letters, and in 1896 he was made fellow of the American Academy of Arts and Sciences. His first book, an edition of Chaucer's *Parlament of Foules* (1877), was followed by a *History of the English Language* (1879, 1894, 1907), and *James Fenimore Cooper* (1882). His *Studies in Chaucer,* published in three volumes in 1892, was one of the most important works in the field to appear in the nineteenth century and remains one of the great classics of Chaucerian scholarship. Three volumes upon Shakespeare, grouped under the title *Shakespearean Wars* were published between 1901 and 1906. An increasing interest in questions of spelling, pronunciation, and usage manifested itself in a number of articles in the magazines, which were subsequently collected in book form under the titles *The Standard of Pronunciation in English* (1904), *The Standard of Usage in English* (1908), and *English Spelling and Spelling Reform* (1909). In April 1907 he was elected president of the Simplified Spelling Board. Four lectures delivered at the University of Virginia were published in 1911 under the title *The Early Literary Career of Robert Browning*; and *The Yale Book of American Verse,* an unusual anthology with a striking preface, appeared in 1912. His last work was left unfinished at his death and was published in the autumn of 1915 by Wilbur L. Cross, with the title *The Life and Times of Tennyson from 1809 to 1850.*

Lounsbury's style is pungent, forthright, and voluble. His books are entirely free from the affectation and arrogance of pedantry, and although they are sometimes too diffuse, their vitality is unfailing. Lounsbury taught and wrote and lived with an honest vigor that left upon all who met him an indelible impression of the man beneath the scholar. "His appearance was by no means academic," says Barrett Wendell; "rather his burly vigor bespoke the old soldier. . . . A tall man and a large, sandy-haired and bearded, with heavy-lidded eyes which troubled him in his later years, he might have looked ponderous, if he had been less alert" (*Proceedings of the American Academy of Arts and Sciences, post,* p. 833). Many hours, in the latter part of his life, were spent in a darkened room, and much of his writing was done in the evening without a light. His accurate and well-stored memory was of great service to him in these years. He once addressed a class of undergraduates, after his retirement, entertaining them for an hour with a running commentary upon Chaucer's *Nonne Preestes Tale.* The text was before him on the desk, and at the close of the hour, the instructor in the course asked him if he had been able to see it without difficulty. Lounsbury explained that he had not been able to see it at all but had not wanted the boys to know he was reciting the poem from memory. A simple and unpretentious manliness was the essence of his nature. He loved sport and he loved good talk. He was overtaken by death in the midst of a conversation with a friend, and collapsed in his chair with a half-smoked cigar between his fingers.

[Barrett Wendell, in *Proc. of the Am. Acad. of Arts and Sciences,* Sept. 1918; Brander Matthews, in *Proc. of the Am. Acad. of Arts and Letters,* no. IX (1916); R. H. Chittenden, *Hist. of the Sheffield Scientific School of Yale Univ.* (1928), vol. I; *Obit. Record of Yale Grads. 1914–15* (1915); *Yale College, Class of 1859: Decennial Record* (1870); *Hist. of the Class of 1859* (1914); *Yale Alumni Weekly,* Apr. 30, 1915; *N. Y. Times,* Apr. 10, 1915.] R. D. F.

LOVE, ALFRED HENRY (Sept. 7, 1830–June 29, 1913), radical pacifist, son of William Henry and Rachel (Evans) Love, was born and spent his life in Philadelphia, Pa. As a high-school student he showed a bent for journalism, which later found expression in the periodicals which he edited. His marriage to Susan Henry Brown in January 1853 brought him into affiliation with the Society of Friends, although he did not at once become a formal member of a meeting. From 1853 until his death he was a package woolen commission merchant. When the Civil War came, many Quakers and almost all the members of peace organizations compromised with their principles and accepted the struggle. Unable to make this adjustment, Love defended his position in *An Appeal in Vindication of Peace Principles* (Philadelphia, 1862). To support the war seemed to him both unchristian and inhuman, and he pointed to the danger of "becoming absorbed in the enthusiasm of the hour" and of floating along "on the swelling tide, forgetful that popular movements always should be watched, often even doubted." Though an active and thoroughgoing friend of the negro, Love did not believe that any great good could be achieved for him through war, which, he maintained, would not be a death-blow to "Slavery in its widest sense." He refused to sell his goods for army use, and his business suffered. In 1863 he was drafted, but he refused to serve or to procure a substitute. William Lloyd Garrison, the high-priest of non-resistance, having accepted the war, wrote to Love that he believed money could be paid in lieu of service "without any compromise of the peace or non-resistance principle" (manuscript "Anti-Slavery Letters Written by William Lloyd Garrison, 1861–65," vol. VI, Boston Public Library), but Love thought otherwise and maintained his position.

Since the American Peace Society had justified the Civil War, a handful of non-resistants felt the need for a new and thoroughly radical peace organization. Love assumed the leadership of this movement (*Address before the Peace Convention Held in Boston, Mar. 14 and 15, 1866*) which resulted in the formation of the Universal Peace Society, later the Universal Peace Union. Its platform was expressed in its motto, "Remove the causes and remove the customs of war! Live the conditions and promulgate the principles of peace." Until his death Love was president of the organization and responsible for its periodical. The society maintained close relations with European peace groups and came to number some ten thousand American adherents. It worked for a reconciliation between North and South, for a more humanitarian treatment of the Indian, for the rights of women, and for the abolition of capital punishment. It also labored for the peaceful adjustment of disputes, local as well as international. In the eighties Love became a pioneer in popularizing the idea of the arbitration of disputes between capital and labor, his own services as a mediator in strikes attesting his faith in the efficacy of pacific principles.

Love was not unknown to congressmen, secretaries of state, and presidents from Lincoln to Wilson. He urged party conventions and presidents-elect to mention international arbitration in their platforms and messages. He instigated delegations and petitions praying for the outlawry of war by constitutional amendment, for the negotiation of permanent treaties of arbitration, and for an international court. He was an uncompromising opponent of militarism in all its forms. Again and again he wrote vigorously if naïvely to the secretary of state and to foreign governments suggesting peaceful means for preventing a threatening war. His letters and cables on the eve of the Spanish-American war aroused such indignation among certain patriots that he was burned in effigy. His uncompromising pacifism seemed, in the opinion of certain moderate friends of the cause, to injure the peace movement by making it appear unpractical. As the cause became more realistic and scientific Love's work, which he carried on courageously against great odds, appeared to some of the new leaders sentimental and ineffective. Yet his service in keeping alive the high standard of pacifism in the dark, discouraging days during and after the Civil War, and in forcing the question upon skeptical politicians and an indifferent people, gives him a secure though minor place in the history of American idealism. Love's wife, two sons and a daughter, survived him.

[The above sketch is based largely on material in the periodicals which Love edited: *Bond of Peace, Voice of Peace,* and *The Peacemaker,* published in Philadelphia. Consult also: *Who's Who in America,* 1912–13; *A Brief Synopsis of Work Proposed, Aided, and Accomplished by the Universal Peace Union* (1912); the *Advocate of Peace,* Nov. 1913; *Friends' Intelligencer,* July 26, 1913; *Phila. Inquirer* and *Pub. Ledger* (Phila.), June 30, 1913. The "Miscellaneous Letters" in the Department of State contain many letters from Love.]

M. E. C.

LOVE, EMANUEL KING (July 27, 1850–Apr. 24, 1900), Baptist clergyman, was born in slavery near Marion, Perry County, Ala., the son of Cumby Jarrett Love and Maria Antoinette Love, both of African blood. His early life was one of hard work on a farm, but he was ambitious to learn and studied nights by torch light. Obtaining admission to Lincoln University in Marion in 1871, he remained only part of the year, but mastered most of the restricted curriculum. The following year he entered Augusta Institute, Augusta, Ga., where he led all his classes and graduated in 1877. During this period he was ordained to the Baptist ministry at Augusta, Dec. 12, 1875. For a time he had charge of his church at Marion and did some teaching at Augusta Institute and in negro public schools of Georgia. From 1877 to 1879 he was a missionary for the state of Georgia under joint appointment of the American Baptist Home Mission Society and the Georgia Mission Board, both organizations of white Baptists. On Oct. 30, 1879, he married Josephine Carter Leeks, and that year became pastor of the First African Baptist Church at Thomasville, Ga., which throve under his leadership. For about four years, 1881–85, he was supervisor of Sunday-school mission work among the negroes of Georgia, under an appointment of the American Baptist Publication Society of Philadelphia. His most distinctive work and greatest influence came in his pastorate of the First African Baptist Church of Savannah, which he served from Oct. 1, 1885, until his death. This was probably the largest Baptist church in the world and the oldest negro Baptist church in the United States. He not only increased its membership, but broadened the scope of its work. In 1888 he published *History of the First African Baptist Church, from Its Organization, January 20th, 1788, to July 1st, 1888.* He was one of the organizers of the Baptist Foreign Mission Convention, of which he was president in 1889–91 and 1893, while at the time of his death he was president of the Georgia Negro Baptist Convention and editor of its organ, *The Baptist Truth,* which he had founded. He was especially interested in securing for the negro an education which would provide adequate leaders in church, state, and industry. When the Georgia State Industrial College was established, he was largely responsible for its location in Savannah and formulated the plan for raising the necessary money. He was among the prime movers in the founding of Central City College, which opened in 1899. Selma University, Selma, Ala., conferred upon him the degree of doctor of divinity in 1888. He was a man of native eloquence, with an ability to secure cooperation from whites as well as from members of his own race.

[Love's book, mentioned above; E. R. Carter, *Biog. Sketches of Our Pulpit* (n.d.); A. W. Pegues, *Our Baptist Ministers and Schools* (1892); W. J. Simmons, *Men of Mark* (1887); *Morning News* (Savannah), Apr. 25, 1900; information as to certain facts from a brother, Philip E. Love, M.D.]

W. H. A.

LOVE, ROBERTUS DONNELL (Jan. 6, 1867–May 7, 1930), journalist and author, was the second son among five children of the Rev. Dr. Thomas Shelby and Nancy Eveline (McFarland) Love. His grandfather, William Calhoun Love, was a Cumberland Presbyterian minister in eastern Tennessee and his father, taken as a child into Kentucky, was ordained in the same denomination, after which he assumed a charge at Irondale, in the Missouri Ozark foothills. Near this place Robertus was born on a rocky farm. His first literary effort was an "obituary poem" on a neighborhood girl, written at the age of fourteen. The next year his father was called to another pastorate and the family moved to Louisiana, Mo. Thereafter throughout the period of his schooling at McCune College, then situated at Louisiana, his favorite pastime was to lie outstretched on a bluff overlooking the Mississippi, with books of poetry ordered by mail from the East. He received the degree of A.B. in 1884 and after further study at Lincoln University, Illinois, he returned to Louisiana, Mo., to become at nineteen local editor of the Louisiana *Press,* with wages of five dollars a week. Ten months later he was city editor of the *Daily Journal,* Wichita, Kan., and his forty-three years of itinerant journalism had begun.

His career included virtually every duty connected with the writing side of newspapers, and took him into cities of varying sizes, scattered from coast to coast. He was editor of the *Press,* at Asbury Park, N. J., 1892–95; coast correspondent of the New York *Sun,* 1895; and founder of the *Asbury Park Daily Star,* 1896. He also established *Seashore Life* at Asbury Park, the first of several periodicals of which he was, as he said, "both founder and funeral director." From 1896 to 1899 he was managing editor of the *Day,* New London, Conn.; and he was reporter on the *St. Louis Post-Dispatch,* 1900–03. An early assignment on the *Post-Dispatch* was the Galveston hurricane (September 1900). When Mark Twain made his last visit to Missouri in 1902, Love accompanied him, and was fondly introduced as "my son." Another warm friendship he enjoyed was with Joaquin Miller. He had charge of press bureaus at the Louisiana Purchase, Lewis and Clark, and Jamestown expositions, in 1905 was editorial writer on the Portland *Oregonian* and columnist for the *Los Angeles Times*; and from 1906 to 1911 wrote and edited material for the American Press Association's "boiler plate." He returned to the *St. Louis Post-Dispatch* as feature writer, 1911–13; then wrote "Rhymes Along the Road" for the *St. Louis Republic,* 1913–16. He went to Oklahoma as Sunday editor of the Tulsa *Democrat,* 1917–18, and editor of the Ardmore *Ardmoreite,* 1918–20. After a period in Kansas City, Mo., 1921, on the editorial staff of the *Kansas City Post,* he returned to St. Louis where he was Sunday magazine writer, 1922–25, and literary editor, 1925–26, of the *Post-Dispatch*; then Sunday magazine writer, *St. Louis Globe-Democrat,* 1926–28, and literary editor thereafter until his death.

Love's topical newspaper verse found its way into many a Mississippi Valley scrapbook and his rhymes about the Ozarks attracted attention to the beauties of that then little appreciated region. He was the author of two books, *Poems All the Way from Pike* (1904), homely pieces on the Missouri meerschaum, old spellers, and the like, and *The Rise and Fall of Jesse James* (1926), first printed in the *Post-Dispatch.* This latter work, a running story of Missouri banditry, resulted from a life-long interest in Middle-western outlaws. Picturing Jesse James as a product of his times, it was one of the first full-length studies of American desperadoes. The *Springfield Republican* (July 18, 1926) described it as "an admirable piece of research in the lighter style."

At thirty-four, Dec. 31, 1901, Love married Catherine Heck of Ruma, Ill., who was unable to walk for the last seventeen years of her life. She died in 1926, the union childless. Love's yearning to break away from journalism and devote himself entirely to other writing went unrealized. He died of pneumonia following an operation and was buried in Oak Grove Cemetery, near St. Louis, leaving unpublished "The Joy-Log of a Journalist," a ramblingly repertorial autobiography, befitting his roving and light-hearted life.

[Unpublished MS. of "The Joy-Log of a Journalist" in possession of Love's brother, Dr. William H. Love of St. Louis, who also supplied information; *Who's Who in America,* 1928–29; obituaries in the *St. Louis Post-Dispatch,* May 7, 1930, and the *St. Louis Globe-Democrat,* May 8; *Mo. Hist. Rev.,* July 1930; W. A. Kelsoe, *St. Louis Reference Record* (1928); *N. Y. Times,* June 6, 1926; *Saturday Review,* July 17, Sept. 11, 1926; *Book Review Digest,* 1926.] I. D.

LOVEJOY, ASA LAWRENCE (Mar. 14, 1808–Sept 10, 1882), lawyer, companion of Marcus Whitman on his famous ride, founder of Portland, Ore., was the third son of Dr. Samuel Lovejoy and Betsey (Lawrence) Lovejoy, a sister of Abbott Lawrence [*q.v.*]. He was born and spent his boyhood in Groton, Mass. At sixteen he began work with a Boston mercantile house. Later he attended school again and then studied law. After his admission to the bar he moved to Sparta, Mo. (1840) and began the practice of law. In the spring of 1842 he joined Dr. Elijah White, United States Indian agent, on his way to Oregon, and was one of three men who recorded the experiences and discoveries of the trip. Dr. Marcus Whitman, head of the mission at Waiilatpu, where the party stopped in October 1842, persuaded Lovejoy to return with him to the states. Together the two men started on their arduous ride in November. Whitman finally reached Missouri in February by the southern route through Santa Fé, Mexico. Lovejoy stayed at Bent's Fort on the headwaters of the Arkansas River until the following July, when he joined Whitman and the emigrant train and returned to Oregon, settling at Oregon City. In this train he met Elizabeth McGary whom he married in 1845.

Lovejoy began the practice of law but took

an active part in public affairs. In 1844 he was chosen one of the eight members of the legislative committee of the provisional government, which remodeled the organic laws drawn up the year before. During the same year he held the office of attorney-general. In 1845 he was defeated as candidate for governor against George Abernethy but was elected mayor of Oregon City. Running against Abernethy again in 1847, he lost the election by only sixteen votes. In 1846 and again in 1848 he was sent to the provisional legislature. After the Whitman massacre, Lovejoy together with Jesse Applegate and Governor Abernethy pledged their personal credit to the Hudson's Bay Company for supplies to carry on war against the Indians. Lovejoy served as adjutant-general during the war. He was elected supreme judge in 1848 and held that position until the establishment of the territorial government in 1849. He was speaker of the House in the first territorial legislature, a member of the council in 1851–52, postal agent in 1853, and delegate to the lower house in 1854 and again in 1856. As one of the members of the convention of 1857, he took an active part in shaping the state constitution.

Lovejoy is remembered in Oregon as one of the founders of the city of Portland. He was a stockholder in the People's Transportation Company, which was organized in 1862, to promote a project for a portage at Oregon City. He was also a member of the Oregon City Woolen Manufacturing Company, which was incorporated in 1863, and a director of the Oregon Telegraph Company. He was interested in railroads and in 1847 acted as chairman of a public meeting called to memorialize Congress on the construction of a transcontinental line. Later he became one of the directors of the east-side Oregon Central Railway Company, which completed the first railroad through the Willamette Valley. In 1873 he moved to Portland where he remained until his death.

[*Hist. of the Pacific Northwest* (1889), vol. II; Jos. Gaston, *Portland, Ore.: Its Hist. and Its Builders* (1911), vol. I; H. W. Scott, *Hist. of the Ore. Country* (6 vols., 1924), especially vol. II; letters of Lovejoy describing the Whitman ride in W. H. Gray, *A Hist. of Ore.* (1870); O. W. Nixon, *How Marcus Whitman Saved Ore.* (1895); C. E. Lovejoy, *The Lovejoy Geneal.* (1930); H. H. Bancroft, *Hist. of Ore.*, vol. II (1888); *Morning Oregonian*, Sept. 11, 1882.]

R. C. C.

LOVEJOY, ELIJAH PARISH (Nov. 9, 1802–Nov. 7, 1837), the "martyr abolitionist," was born at Albion, Me., the son of a clergyman, Rev. Daniel Lovejoy, and Elizabeth (Pattee) Lovejoy, both of old New England stock. He graduated from Waterville (now Colby) College in 1826, taught school until May 1827, then emigrated to St. Louis, Mo., where he again taught school and for a short time edited a Whig newspaper. Determining to follow his father into the ministry he returned to the East in 1832 to attend the seminary at Princeton. He was licensed to preach by the Philadelphia Presbytery in April 1833 and went back to St. Louis as editor of the Presbyterian weekly for the far West, the *St. Louis Observer*. On Mar. 4, 1835, he married Celia Ann French, the daughter of a nearby planter. His editorial career began peacefully enough, but a spirit like his could not be peaceful long. Fired by the "expanding benevolence" that inspired his church in the early thirties, he enlisted his paper in the Presbyterian war against slavery, intemperance, and "popery." The border-states movement for the gradual abolition of slavery, so nearly successful in Kentucky and Virginia, had not extended to Missouri; and St. Louis, river port for the lower South, would hear no discussion of the subject. Protests multiplied, and rather than moderate his tone, in 1836 Lovejoy moved to Alton, Ill., twenty-five miles up the river.

At that time Alton was the most prosperous city in Illinois. Emigrants from New England and the Eastern states made up its population; and the doctrine Lovejoy had preached in St. Louis, the evil of slavery and its gradual emancipation, was their own as well. Abolitionism, as the doctrine of immediate emancipation then was called, Lovejoy had denounced in the strongest terms. But even as he left St. Louis for Alton his views were changing. At the next General Assembly, which he attended shortly before he moved to Alton (July 1836), the equivocating course of that body toward abolition petitions so angered him that with his own indignant pen he wrote the protest which the abolitionists published to the church. An abolitionist by conviction and sympathy, if not by affiliation, he returned to edit the *Alton Observer*.

At the outset he encountered misfortune. His press arrived from St. Louis on a Sabbath morning and Lovejoy's Sabbatarian convictions compelled him to leave it unguarded on the wharf. Some time during Sunday night it was dumped into the river. But the good citizens of Alton called a public meeting, unanimously condemned the outrage and—carefully expressing their disapproval of abolitionism—pledged the money for a new press. On his part Lovejoy expressed his gratitude and promised to edit his paper in the interest of the church alone. That promise he could not keep. Week by week his abolitionism crept into the columns of the *Observer* reports of his local anti-slavery society; his abolition resolutions to the Presbyterian Synod; his correspondence with a score of fearless agitators here and there in the state; and even accounts of the progress of the cause in the nation. Finally, July 4, 1837, he printed a call for a meeting of the anti-slavery host at Alton to form a state auxiliary to the American Anti-Slavery Society; and after numerous delays the state society was organized on the 26th of October. Alton citizens were outraged. Mobs destroyed the *Observer* press again and yet again; but each time the Ohio Anti-Slavery Society sent another. Lovejoy wrote defiantly: "These mobs will cease as soon as some of the mobites are hung up by the neck, and not before. . . . Mercy no less than Justice calls for a summary execution of some of the wretches as an example to the rest."

After the founding of the state society the press was destroyed again, but news soon arrived that another press from Ohio was on the way. Lovejoy's friends caught his defiant spirit. Sixty young abolitionists from towns nearby assembled with arms in their hands, determined that this press should not go the way of the others. At a public meeting leading citizens implored Lovejoy to leave, but he replied that he was ready for martyrdom. The press arrived on Nov. 7 and was placed in a warehouse under guard. Merchants closed their stores and the whole city waited in dread for the night. An armed mob gathered in the darkness and stormed the warehouse, but the guard fought them back. Some of the mob tried to set the warehouse on fire, and Lovejoy, rushing out to prevent it, was shot dead.

[The chief source for Lovejoy's biography is the *Memoir of the Rev. Elijah P. Lovejoy* (1838), by Joseph C. and Owen Lovejoy. One of the armed band, Henry Tanner, reported the trials of the rioters, *The Alton Trials* (1838). His other later accounts are largely based on the *Memoir*. Edward Beecher's *Narrative of the Riots at Alton* (1838) is an honest but prejudiced account. Similar in the contrary direction is the account in Thos. Ford, *A Hist. of Ill.* (1854). Essential to an understanding of the story as part of the national anti-slavery agitation are the *Alton Observer*, 1836–37, the *Philanthropist*, 1836–38, and the *N. Y. Evangelist*, 1835–38. For Lovejoy's ancestry see C. E. Lovejoy, *The Lovejoy Geneal.* (1930).] G. H. B.

LOVEJOY, OWEN (Jan. 6, 1811–Mar. 25, 1864), abolitionist and statesman, brother of Elijah Parish Lovejoy [*q.v.*], was born at Albion, Me., the son of the Rev. Daniel and Elizabeth (Pattee) Lovejoy. He attended Bowdoin College from 1830 to 1833, but did not graduate, and after studying at law and teaching school, he journeyed in 1836 to Alton, Ill., to prepare for the ministry under his brother. Elijah Lovejoy had just begun active abolition propaganda and Owen speedily enlisted in the anti-slavery cause. In the growing excitement in Alton he stood steadfastly by his brother, and on the final tragic night after Elijah had been killed, Owen knelt beside his body and vowed "never to forsake the cause that had been sprinkled with his brother's blood." After completing his theological studies, he served as minister of the Congregational church at Princeton, Ill., for seventeen years. In January 1843 he married a widow, Eunice (Storrs) Dunham, who bore him seven children. He was a popular and devoted minister, but persistently kept his vow, never losing an opportunity to testify to the wrong of slavery. During the decade from 1840 to 1850 he spoke fearlessly for the cause wherever he could find a hearing, despite the Illinois state law prohibiting abolition meetings. Frequently he encountered violence, but his unflinching boldness and the memorable name he bore saved him from injury. His colleague in the Illinois agitation, Ichabod Codding, was an abler orator, but Lovejoy, more than any other man, advanced abolition sentiment in the state.

During the next decade, Lovejoy became increasingly influential; and in 1854, when the Republican organization began, he was elected to the state legislature to lead the forces of freedom. In Illinois the new party embraced anti-foreign "Know-Nothings" and Germans representing the hundred thousand foreign-born in Illinois, disgruntled Democrats and their enemies—old-line Whigs, and, feared by all, the Abolitionists. Lovejoy believed that only one man in Illinois could discipline this "rag-tag and bob-tail gang" into party organization, and that man was Abraham Lincoln. He urged Lincoln to lead the new movement, but Lincoln replied that the time was not yet ripe. He even tried to force Lincoln's hand by placing his name at the head of the state central committee for the Republican party. However, when Lincoln came to the Bloomington convention in 1856, it was Lovejoy who compelled the radicals to relinquish their abolition program and to accept Lincoln's conservative leadership. The same year Lovejoy was elected to Congress. There and in the Republican conventions at Pittsburgh and Philadelphia he was a radical leader; but in Illinois he was still Lincoln's henchman. When Lincoln stood for the Senate, Lovejoy put all his influence at his disposal. It was a dangerous gift. If Lincoln's opponents could "make Lincoln hang on Lovejoy's coat tails for Republican strength," the semblance of a bargain with Lovejoy would "choke Lincoln to death." Only Lovejoy's self-effacement prevented this catastrophe. Though he stumped the state in Lincoln's interest, he suffered Lincoln's repudiation of abolitionism gladly. While his contest with Douglas was lost, Lincoln thereby captured radical support, without losing his name for conservatism, for the presidential contest two years later.

In Congress Lovejoy assailed slavery and the South with a violence equaled only by Thaddeus Stevens and Sumner; but when Lincoln came to Washington, Lovejoy once more became his loyal supporter. To William Lloyd Garrison's attacks on Lincoln in 1862 he made fierce rejoinder, and to Thaddeus Stevens' proposals to treat the defeated South as a conquered province, he replied in the spirit of Lincoln's magnanimous reconstruction program. To him fell the honor of proposing the bill by which slavery in all the territories of the United States was abolished forever. He heard at last the Emancipation Proclamation, and died the next year. Lincoln wrote (J. G. Nicolay and John Hay, *Abraham Lincoln: Complete Works,* 1894, II, p. 527): "My personal acquaintance with him . . . has been one of increasing respect and esteem, ending, with his life, in no less than affection on my part. . . . To the day of his death, it would scarcely wrong any other to say he was my most generous friend."

[See the *Liberator,* 1862–63; the *Nat. Anti-Slavery Standard,* 1840–58; the *Philanthropist,* 1836–42; Albert J. Beveridge, *Abraham Lincoln* (1928); J. C. and Owen Lovejoy, *Memoir of the Rev. Elijah P. Lovejoy* (1838); T. C. Smith, *The Liberty and Free Soil Parties in the Northwest* (1897); C. E. Lovejoy, *The Lovejoy Geneal.* (1930); *Addresses on the Death of Hon. Owen Lovejoy, Delivered in the Senate and House of Representatives, on Monday, Mar. 28, 1864* (1864); *Cong. Globe,* 35 Cong., 1 Sess., pp. 752–54, 36 Cong., 1 Sess., App., pp. 202–07, 37 Cong., 2 Sess., p. 194; *N. Y. Tribune, Daily Ill. State Jour.* (Springfield), Mar. 28, 1864.] G. H. B.

LOVELACE, FRANCIS (*c.* 1621–1675), second English governor of New York, was eighth in descent from John Lovelace, who founded Lovelace Place at Bethersden, Kent, in 1367. His father was Sir William (1584–1627) of Bethersden and Woolwich, son of Sir William, the elder, and Elizabeth Aucher. The family was only remotely related to the Lords Lovelace of Hurley. Francis' father was knighted by James I, on Sept. 20, 1609, and about 1610 married Anne, daughter of Sir William Barne, of Woolwich, and Anne Sandys, daughter of Edwin Sandys, archbishop of York in Elizabeth's reign, and sister of Sir Edwin Sandys of the Virginia Company and George Sandys the poet. The Barne and Sandys families were actively concerned in Virginia's colonization. In 1627 Francis' father was killed at the siege of the Burse, or the Groll, in Holland, and his mother died about 1633. They had five sons and three daughters, of whom Richard (1618–1658), poet and Cavalier, was the eldest, and Francis, the third son. Both were bachelors. Two brothers, Thomas and Dudley, were in New York with their governor-brother. The eldest daughter, Anne, wife of the Rev. John Gorsuch, emigrated to Virginia with seven younger children about 1650.

Lovelace's immediate forebears were Royalists supporting the Stuarts. He himself served as a colonel for Charles I in the civil wars, and was active in Wales, where he was governor of Carmarthen Castle until it capitulated to Parliamentary forces in 1645. The death of his brother William in that siege was lamented in a poem written by Richard Lovelace, in *Lucasta.* For a while Francis and his brothers Richard and Dudley served Louis XIV on the Continent. In 1650, Francis seems to have gone to Virginia for two years, probably to accompany and aid his sister, Anne Gorsuch. After December 1652 he was an exile on the Continent with Charles II and his retinue; but in 1658 he was back in England aiding the Royalist cause. On Aug. 5, 1659, he was arrested and imprisoned in the Tower of London, but he was freed upon the Commonwealth's collapse. He is mentioned by Pepys in his *Diary,* as being in London on Dec. 16, 1662, and perhaps was then employed in the Admiralty. On May 14, 1667, he is referred to as "appointed Governor of New York," in an English warrant to the Ordnance (*Calendar of State Papers, Colonial Series, America and West Indies 1661–68,* no. 1480, p. 466), and the earliest reference to his appointment appears in a newsletter as of Apr. 12, 1667. While waiting to go to America he was, on June 13, 1667, commissioned as lieutenant-colonel in a regiment raised by Col. Sir Walter Vane, with the Duke of York's approval. The evidences all point to his selection as governor as a reward for his royalist services and because he had been before in English-America.

The treaty of Breda was proclaimed in New York in 1668. Lovelace arrived in March and for several months was familiarized by Gov. Richard Nicolls with the administration. Lovelace had been instructed to continue unabated the policies of government that were in operation. About the middle of August 1668, he assumed full control. It was a time of epidemic diseases and deaths were numerous. He took hold of the situation with concern. He instituted regular sessions of his executive council on Sept. 2, 1668, and its minutes, to July 11,

1673, were the first regular English council minutes recorded in New York. Since their publication in 1910 (see bibliography) it can no longer be justly charged that Lovelace was arbitrary or incompetent. He was a conscientious man, and in tolerance was the equal of his predecessor, from whom he had inherited unfulfilled promises, unsettled problems, and precedents in administration which the Duke of York required to be continued. This made him cautious rather than phlegmatic in what he undertook. Yet, in his five years in office, he transacted much business by himself, with his councilors, in the high court of assizes, or by commissions appointed by him and under his control. He not only watched over his vast territory, but entered into every phase of its needs and difficulties. His administration was harassed, internally and externally, by Indian troubles, boundary disputes, an insurrection in the Delaware country, a rebellion in New Jersey, and the incompatibilities of a mixed population of Dutch, English, Swedish, and other nationalities. He interested himself in better ferriage, roads, and transportation by land and water; and the regulation of trade and extension of commerce. He instituted the first merchants' exchange and the first haven master of the port. He promoted shipbuilding and himself owned a fine ship, *The Good Fame of New York.* He extended settlements and laid out new villages and townships, and by purchase for the Duke freed Staten Island from Indian control. He was tolerant toward religious sects, even to Quakers. He was interested in Indian missions and, though unsuccessful, made the first attempt to introduce the art of printing into the middle British colonies. He furthered the strengthening of fortifications and the raising of foot companies and troops of horse, keeping them in training. The drift whale, as well as sport fisheries, engaged his attention. His intercolonial activities, especially with New England, are outstanding, for he instituted the first continuous post road between New York and Boston, under a postmaster. It was while on a visit to Connecticut to promote this laudable object, that his vigilance lapsed, and he lost New York to a Dutch naval squadron, July 30–Aug. 9, 1673. Had he been at his fort and used all the meager resources he had, the capitulation could not have been prevented. The defenses of New York were not capable of withstanding an attack of a Dutch naval expedition, already encouraged by former triumphs. By the loss of New York Lovelace was impoverished and degraded. All his property was stripped from him, first by the Dutch, then by his countrymen, some for debts to the Duke of York, others for unpaid property or mortgages, or other private debts in New York. Litigation over these debts continued many years. While traveling in the Mediterranean, in 1674, he was captured by Turks, taken to Algiers, and there stripped of his jewels and several hundred pounds. On being ransomed he returned to England, where he was pursued by the vindictiveness of the Duke of York, who claimed a debt of seven thousand pounds and was irritated by the loss of his proprietary province. In January 1675 he was imprisoned in the Tower, but he was released in April on security, on account of being "dangerously ill of a dropsy." Meanwhile he had been under examination, for the loss of New York, by a committee appointed by the King. His last months were spent in retirement at Woodstock, near Oxford, where he probably died in the latter part of 1675, as letters of administration were issued to his brother Dudley on Dec. 22 of that year. This administration was still unsettled in 1686, when Dudley died.

[The best account is J. H. Pleasants, "Francis Lovelace, Gov. of N. Y.," *N. Y. Geneal. and Biog. Record,* July 1920, which includes sketches of the brothers Thos. and Dudley Lovelace. The plantations of the Lovelaces on Staten Island are discussed by E. C. Delavan in "Col. Francis Lovelace and His Plantation on Staten Island," *Proc. Nat. Sci. Asso. of Staten Island,* Mar. 10, 1900, reprinted separately in 1902. See also: A J. Pearman, "The Kentish Family of Lovelace," *Archæologia Cantina,* vol. X (1876); Elizabeth Doremus, *Lovelace Chart* (n.d.); J. R. Brodhead, *Hist. of the State of N. Y.,* vol. II (1871); I. N. P. Stokes, *The Iconography of Manhattan Island,* vol. IV (1922); *Minutes of the Executive Council of the Province of N. Y.: Administration of Francis Lovelace, 1668–1673* (2 vols., 1910), ed. by V. H. Paltsits, with collateral and illustrative documents; E. B. O'Callaghan, ed., *Docs. Relative to the Colonial Hist. of the State of N. Y.,* vol. II (1858), vol. III (1853); Berthold Fernow, ed., *Docs. Relating to the Colonial Hist. of the State of N. Y.,* vol. XIII (1881), vol. XIV (1883), and *The Records of New Amsterdam* (1897), vols. VI and VII; "The Interment of Wm. Lovelace," *Am. Hist. Rev.,* Apr. 1904; *Calendar of State Papers, Colonial Ser., America and West Indies, 1661–68* (1880), *1669–74* (1889), *1675–76* (1893); *Calendar of State Papers, Domestic Ser., . . . 1673 . . . 1675* (1904); "The MSS. of H. S. Le Fleming, Esq., of Rydal Hall" (1890), *Hist. MSS. Commission: Twelfth Report,* App., pt. 7.]

V. H. P.

LOVELAND, WILLIAM AUSTIN HAMILTON (May 30, 1826–Dec. 17, 1894), pioneer Colorado merchant and railroad promoter, was born in Chatham, Mass. His parents, Leonard and Elizabeth (Eldridge) Loveland moved to Illinois in 1837, settling first in Alton and then in Brighton. The boy received as good an education as the district afforded. After attending the common schools, he was sent first to McKendree College and then to Shurtleff College, in Alton, but owing to ill health he did not complete his formal training. In 1847 he was lured from home to serve as wagonmaster in the Mexican War. Wounded, he returned to Illinois, but he had tasted the joy of adventure and in 1849 went to California. He mined in Grass Valley, traveled to Central America, and, in 1851, once more went home. A few years of mercantile life ended in another venture westward. In the spring of 1859 tales spread of rich finds of gold at Pike's Peak. Loveland sold out, packed a wagon-train with goods, crossed the plains, and reached Denver in June, at the time when everyone was hurrying to the newly discovered mines in the valley of Clear Creek. He promptly left Denver to open a store in Golden, a town at the foothill entrance to the mines. His wanderings were over; he settled down to become a prosperous merchant, a political leader, a builder of railroads, and one of the leading men of his generation in Colorado.

Loveland was always a keen man of business. He owned the largest general merchandise store in Golden, held mining properties in the nearby mountains, and invested in real estate. In 1878 he purchased the Denver *Rocky Mountain News,* a political as well as a business investment, and held it until 1886. In later life he was president of an ore reduction company and organizer of an electric railway between Denver and Golden. In politics he was a leader in the Democratic party. He was a member of the council of the territorial legislature from 1862 to 1870, and president of the abortive constitutional convention of 1865. Largely owing to his influence, Golden was the seat of the territorial government from 1862 to the end of 1867. Thereafter he was not so successful. He was Democratic candidate for the United States Senate in 1876 and 1879, and for governor in 1878, but he failed of election.

The spectacular struggle of his life was for railroad connections with the eastern states. Both Denver and Golden hoped to become the railroad center of the state. Loveland promoted the Colorado Central & Pacific Railroad Company which was to effect a connection between the Kansas Pacific and the Union Pacific, through Golden. Before that road was completed, Denver was connected with the Union Pacific at Cheyenne, and Golden lost in the race. In the late seventies the Colorado Central was absorbed by the Union Pacific. In December 1894 Loveland contracted pneumonia and died in Lakeside, a suburb of Denver. He was survived by his second wife, Maranda Ann Montgomery, whom he had married in Alton on Aug. 25, 1856. His first wife, Philena Shaw, whom he married in Brighton, Ill., on May 13, 1852, died in 1854. Loveland's name is commemorated in that of a small town on the railroad which had been his pride.

[There is an unsatisfactory account of Loveland's life, taken by dictation from him July 24, 1886, in the Bancroft Library. For printed sources see Frank Hall, *History of Colorado* (4 vols., 1889–95) containing scattered references and a biographical sketch in vol. IV; J. B. and George Loveland, *Geneal. of the Loveland Family,* vol. II (1894), containing a sketch by Loveland's son; *Rocky Mountain News* and *Denver Republican,* Dec. 18, 1894.] J. F. W.

LOVELL, JAMES (Oct. 31, 1737–July 14, 1814), school-master, politician, second son of John [*q.v.*] and Abigail Lovell, was born in Boston. He received his early training in the South Grammar School, of which his father was master, graduated from Harvard in 1756, took a post-graduate course the following year, then became usher in his father's school, a position which he held acceptably for eighteen years. Such was his scholarship that he delivered an oration in Latin in the chapel of Harvard College, Feb. 19, 1760, at the funeral of Henry Flynt, a long-time tutor in the college. On Nov. 24 of that year he married Mary Middleton, daughter of Alexander Middleton, a native of Scotland, and settled down to a life of uneventful usefulness as a trainer of young Bostonians. Ten years later he was chosen as the first orator to commemorate the Boston Massacre. The oration which he delivered (Apr. 2, 1771) placed him amongst the stanchest opponents of British measures respecting the colonies. The South Grammar School was closed by the British military authorities in April 1775, and following the battle of Bunker Hill James was arrested for spying and giving intelligence to the rebels and in 1776 was sent as a prisoner to Halifax. It happened that his father took up his residence in Halifax at about the same time, as a Loyalist refugee. After some delay, owing to the fact that some of Lovell's "billets," as he called them, fell into the hands of General Howe, an exchange was effected in the autumn of 1776, and Lovell returned to Boston "to the no small joy of the inhabitants" of that city.

Within a few days of his landing he was chosen as a delegate to the Continental Congress, taking his seat Feb. 4, 1777, at Baltimore. From the first Lovell took an active part in the proceedings of Congress, distinguishing himself at once for industry and zeal. Investigation of the conduct of Schuyler and conferences with Gates enhanced his conception of the prowess of the latter general, and partiality for Gates, which, after Saratoga, attained a degree of perfervid devotion, led him straight into the ranks of the critics of Washington. What part he may have had in the actual formation of the plot known as the Conway Cabal is not definitely known, but that he fomented it with all the power that was in him, is sufficiently evidenced by his letters to Gates and other intimate correspondents. Lovell surpassed all his colleagues in his vocabulary of sneers and sarcasm directed at Washington yet, like many another, in 1789 he could profess a pious devotion to the "demi-god"—and beseech him for an appointment to office.

Lovell's early appointment to the committee on foreign applications must have had no small share in shaping his subsequent course. Congress was besieged by a horde of French officers seeking commissions, and Lovell was one of the few members who knew French. "These Frenchmen have used me up quite," he wrote in June 1777, and his mood had not changed, when, a month later, he met Lafayette and sought vainly to chill the ardor of that young enthusiast. But the most far-reaching consequence of this episode was the distrust, mounting to fierce hostility, engendered in a large group in Congress toward Silas Deane [*q.v.*] who was in a measure responsible for the coming of the Frenchmen. The anti-Deane party, of which Lovell was one of the most rabid, were not able to destroy Franklin, but they succeeded in hounding the life out of poor Deane. As a member of the committee for foreign affairs, to which he was appointed May 26, 1777, Lovell probably achieved his greatest distinction, whether for better or for worse. The committee was neglected by Congress, and for months at a time Lovell was all that was left of it. Members came and members went, but Lovell stayed on, never once in five years so much as visiting his wife and children. Diligent to a fault, he kept his seat all day in Congress, then spent long hours at night "quill-driving," as he expressed it. Marbois described Lovell as "Homme de capacité, souple, insinuant . . . laborieux, intelligent," but little conversant with foreign affairs. Lovell, nevertheless, sought in the autumn of 1779 to be placed where he might catch Franklin's mantle when it should fall. He had already done what he could to loosen it. He was not a diplomat, though he was liberally gifted in intrigue and loved mystery and mystification. A useful member of Congress in many ways, serving on innumerable committees, sometimes taking high ground, he nevertheless vitiated his career by his intense partisanship.

For reasons that do not wholly appear Lovell quitted Congress in April 1782, apparently chagrined over the failure of so many of his cherished ambitions. He became receiver of continental taxes in Boston, then (in 1788) collector of customs for the state of Massachusetts, and on Aug. 3, 1789, was appointed naval officer for the district of Boston and Charlestown. This office he held for the remainder of his life. He died while visiting relatives at Windham, Me. His eldest son, also named James, made a creditable record as an officer in the Revolution and lived till 1850; his grandson, Joseph Lovell [*q.v.*], rose to be surgeon-general of the United States; and his great-grandson, Mansfield Lovell [*q.v.*], became a Confederate general.

[*Mass. Hist. Soc. Colls.*, 2 ser., I (1814), 3 ser., III (1833), 4 ser., IV (1858); *Colonial Soc. of Mass. Pubs.*, vol. XV (1925); *Essex Inst. Hist. Colls.*, July, Oct. 1876; Peter Force, *Am. Archives*, 4 ser. (6 vols., 1837–46), 5 ser. (3 vols., 1848–53); J. S. Loring, *The Hundred Boston Orators* (1852); Francis Wharton, *Revolutionary Diplomatic Correspondence of the U. S.* (1889), vols. I–IV; S. A. Drake, *Old Landmarks and Historic Personages of Boston* (1873); E. C. Burnett, *Letters of Members of the Continental Cong.* (1921–); *Cat. of the Boston Pub. Latin School* (1886); *Columbian Centinel* (Boston), July 20, 1814; *Boston Gazette* and *Independent Chronicle* (Boston), July 21, 1814; Boston town records and records of births and marriages.]

E. C. B.

LOVELL, JOHN (Apr. 1, 1710–1778), schoolmaster, was born in Boston, Mass., the son of John and Priscilla (Gardiner) Lovell. Graduated from Harvard College in 1728, he was appointed an usher of the South Grammar or Latin School in Boston in the following year. In 1734 he became master of the school and continued to serve in that capacity until Apr. 19, 1775. Among the boys who came under his tutelage were Samuel Adams, Samuel Langdon, James Bowdoin, Robert Treat Paine, Andrew Oliver, John Lowell, John Hancock, Thomas Brattle, Jeremy Belknap, Francis Dana, Henry Knox, William Phillips, William Eustis, Christopher Gore, and Harrison Gray Otis. By his contributions to the *Weekly Rehearsal* (1731–35) Lovell won at least a local reputation as "a pleasing and elegant writer," and at the first annual town meeting held in Faneuil Hall, Mar. 14, 1742/43, he delivered a funeral oration upon Peter Faneuil, the donor. Toward the end of the address he exclaimed, "May Liberty always spread its joyful wings over this place!" But in another breath he added, "And may Loyalty to a King, under whom we enjoy this liberty, ever remain our character!" True to his invocation Lovell chose the British side in the American Revolution and left Boston with many other Loyalists and the British army in March 1776. He died at Halifax, Nova Scotia, in 1778. His son, James Lovell [*q.v.*], stanchly American, was carried to Nova Scotia in 1776 as a British prisoner but was exchanged in the fall and returned to Boston.

John Lovell was a severe teacher, but socially a humorous and agreeable companion. He was a member of a French Club, at the meetings of which "the whole conversation was to be in French" (*Diary and Letters of Thomas Hutchinson,* 1883, I, p. 47), and of the Fire Club (*Letters and Diary of John Rowe,* 1903, p. 36). Various members in the *Pietas et Gratulatio Collegii Cantabrigiensis apud Novanglos* (1761) are attributed to Lovell's pen, and he was also the author of "The Seasons, an Interlocutory Exercise at the South Latin School." By his contemporaries he was considered an excellent classical scholar and also a sound critic. A record of Lovell's intention to marry Abigail Green was filed in Boston on Apr. 10, 1735.

[J. S. Loring, *The Hundred Boston Orators* (1852), contains a good biographical sketch including specimens of Lovell's verse. H. F. Jenks's "Hist. Sketch" in the *Cat. of the Boston Pub. Latin School* (1886) is excellent and devotes a number of pages to Lovell, but should be supplemented by Robert F. Seybolt's "Schoolmasters of Colonial Boston," *Colonial Soc. of Mass. Pubs.,* XXVII (1930), 130–56, which lists many useful references to Lovell and his son James. See also Justin Winsor, *Memorial Hist. of Boston,* II (1881), 264–65; S. E. Morison, *Harrison Gray Otis* (1913), vol. I; and records of Boston births and marriages. Lovell's oration on Peter Faneuil was printed in 1743 and was reprinted in Caleb Hopkins Snow, *A Hist. of Boston* (1825), pp. 235–37. A portrait of Lovell by Nathaniel Smybert, a former pupil, is reproduced in Winsor's *Memorial Hist. of Boston* (1881), II, p. 401. The original is in the possession of Harvard University.]

L. S. M.

LOVELL, JOHN EPY (Apr. 23, 1795–May 3, 1892), educator, was born in Colne, Lancashire, England, the eldest child of John and Elizabeth (Epy) Lovell. His parents sent him to a private boarding-school at St. Ives, where in five years' time he finished at the head of his class. As tutor at the age of sixteen in the family of the Duke of Bedford he made the acquaintance of Joseph Lancaster, originator of the famous Lancasterian system of instruction, whereby a single teacher could instruct many by using the older pupils as teachers of the younger. This acquaintance was decisive for Lovell's further career. Through Lancaster's influence he shortly became principal of a Lancasterian school at Burr Rose, England, but after some years decided to try his fortune with the system in the United States. After attempts to establish himself in Philadelphia and in Baltimore, he finally started a school in New Haven, Conn., in 1822, which was immediately successful. In 1827, however, a rift in the community's support led him to accept an appointment to teach elocution in the Mount Pleasant Classical Institute at Amherst, Mass. The New Haven school languished during his absence and in three years he was recalled. For the next quarter century this school, under his control, was the pride of the town and Lovell's personal popularity was unbounded. In fact, so successful was he that New Haven clung to the Lancasterian system long after other cities were adopting the more modern plan of graded schools. He published *Introductory Arithmetic* (1827) and *Rhetorical Dialogues* (1839). In 1857 he tendered his resignation to the New Haven Board of Education, assigning the burden of his textbook writing as the cause. The next few years he spent in completing a series of school readers, *Lovell's Progressive Reader* (5 vols., 1855–59), and in doing some private tutoring. Later he made his home with his daughter, and when she moved to Waterbury, Conn., about 1882, he accompanied her. Some time after 1890 he moved with her to Milwaukee, Wis., where he died.

Lovell's place in American educational history is almost identical with that of the Lancasterian system of instruction. His influence was never national in scope. Some of his books were known outside Connecticut, but it is doubtful if his reputation as a teacher extended thus far. He recognized his debt to Lancaster by dedicating to him his first publication, *Introductory Arithmetic,* and when, late in life, Lancaster was in want, Lovell was active in raising funds for him. Lovell's own peculiar success with the Lancasterian mode of instruction seems to have resided in his ability to infuse a highly mechanical system of instruction with the warmth of personal magnetism. Regarding his application of the system he wrote at length for the *Connecticut Common School Journal* (June 1840). His forte was elocution, and among his pupils were Henry Ward Beecher and Edwin Booth. It was in this field that he wrote his most successful book, *The United States Speaker* (1833).

One child survived his first wife, Harriet Fletcher, who died in 1835. Two children were born to him by his second wife, Minerva Camp, whom he married Mar. 29, 1845.

[*New Haven Daily Palladium, New Haven Evening Register,* and *New Haven Leader,* May 4, 1892; *Memories, Reminiscences, etc., in Verse of the Old Lancasterian School* (New Haven, 1897); information from Lovell's scrapbook in possession of his grandson, George Blakeman Lovell.]

J. S. B.

LOVELL, JOSEPH (Dec. 22, 1788–Oct. 17, 1836), surgeon-general of the army from 1818 to 1836, was born in Boston, Mass., the son of James S. and Deborah (Gorham) Lovell and the grandson of James Lovell [*q.v.*]. His early education was obtained from Boston schools, after which he entered Harvard College, graduating in 1807. He at once began the study of medicine under Dr. Ingalls of Boston, and was graduated from Harvard Medical School in 1811, in the first class to receive the M.D. degree. Prior to that time only the degree of M.B. had been awarded. On May 15, 1812, he entered the army as surgeon of the 9th Infantry. He was but twenty-four years old, but he was much better educated than most medical men of his day. He was soon put in charge of the general hospital at Burlington, Vt., which became known as a model. On June 30, 1814, he was appointed hospital surgeon and the next month he established a general hospital for 1,100 patients at Williamsville, N. Y. All of his work was of a quality to excite the admiration of his superiors and he won praise from Generals Wilkinson, Scott, and Brown. After the establishment of peace, Lovell continued in the service as hospital surgeon. In 1817, as chief medical officer of the Northern Department, he submitted to General Brown a paper discussing the causes of disease in the army. Naturally, in the total lack of any knowledge of bacteriology, the diseases were generally attributed to meteorological conditions, to insufficient clothing, and to insufficient or spoiled food. But Lovell also discussed medical administration, and he did it in such a way that this report, together with his excellent record, resulted in his appointment as surgeon-general in 1818 when the army was reorganized and a medical department established. He was at the time but thirty years old. He continued in office until his death. He did much to establish the new corps in public and official esteem. At one time Secretary of War Eaton advised Congress that "the Surgeon General of the Army might be dispensed with," but Lovell obtained permission to write a reply to be forwarded to Congress and as a result obtained a long-sought increase in his corps, instead of a reduction.

Immediately upon becoming surgeon-general, Lovell ordered all medical officers to submit quarterly reports of weather and of the incidence, prevalence, and causes of disease. From the medical reports were later compiled departmental reports of the greatest historical value. The weather reports form the historical beginning of the present Weather Bureau. He also rendered a positive service to the army and the country in continually inviting attention to the great evils of the alcoholism of that day, and in bringing about, as he did in greater measure than any other single man, the abolition of the rum ration. Finally he will be remembered for the encouragement and official assistance which he gave to William Beaumont [*q.v.*], in promoting the latter's study of gastric physiology. After the Black Hawk War Lovell obtained another small increase in the size of his corps and he was seeking yet a third at the time of his death, which occurred on Oct. 17, 1836. Harvey E. Brown wrote of him (*post*, p. 157): "In all his relations, whether as christian philanthropist, profound scholar, skilful surgeon, experienced officer or true-hearted gentleman, he was one of whom the Medical Staff may always be proud and the memory of whose good life is written on every page of its history." Lovell survived his wife, Margaret (Mansfield) Lovell, and left a family of eleven children, one of whom was Mansfield Lovell [*q.v.*].

[H. E. Brown, *The Medic. Dept. of the U. S. Army* (1873); J. E. Pilcher, "Joseph Lovell, Surgeon General of the U. S. Army, 1818–1836," *Jour. Asso. Mil. Surgeons*, May 1904, and reprinted in Pilcher's *Surgeon Gens. of the U. S. Army* (1905); James Mann, *Medic. Sketches of the Campaigns of 1812, 13, 14* (1816); T. F. Harrington, *The Harvard Medic. School: A Hist.* (1905), vol. II; J. S. Myer, *Life and Letters of Dr. Wm. Beaumont* (1912); biography of Lovell's son in *Fifteenth Ann. Reunion, Asso. Grads. U. S. Mil. Acad.*, 1884; *Nat. Intelligencer* (Washington, D. C.), Oct. 19, 1836.]

P. M. A.

LOVELL, MANSFIELD (Oct. 20, 1822–June 1, 1884), soldier and civil engineer, was born in Washington, D. C., the son of Dr. Joseph Lovell [*q.v.*], surgeon-general of the army, 1818–36, and his wife, Margaret (Mansfield) Lovell. Having received an ordinary school education, he entered West Point at sixteen, graduating in 1842 and being commissioned second lieutenant, 4th Artillery. His army service was unremarkable prior to the Mexican War, during which he was commissioned first lieutenant in February 1847, brevetted captain for gallantry at Chapultepec in September, and was twice wounded. After the war he saw garrison service on the frontiers and in New York. In 1849 he married Emily, daughter of Col. Joseph Plympton. Resigning from the army in 1854, he secured employment in Cooper & Hewitt's Iron Works, Trenton, N. J. He became superintendent of street improvements, New York, in April 1858, and deputy street-commissioner in November, serving as such until his resignation in September 1861, to join the Confederate army. During the two years previous he had kept in touch with things military by teaching the old City Guard, a select organization, how to handle the guns of Fort Hamilton. That he was favorably remembered as a soldier is evidenced by a letter from Joseph E. Johnston to Jefferson Davis, recommending him as a possible division commander a month before he resigned his New York position. On Oct. 7, 1861, he was appointed a major-general in the Confederate army, and ordered to assume command at New Orleans. Before proceeding there, and afterwards, he protested against the divided command of land and sea forces. His garrison was none too large to withstand an attack, and in spite of strenuous efforts throughout the winter of 1861–62 to improve the defenses, he was hampered by requisition of the field armies for troops and guns. When Farragut appeared with his fleet in April 1862, Lovell had but 3,000 ninety-day men, not half of whom possessed muskets. For ten days he stood off the superior Federal fleet, but on Apr. 23 it passed the city, and he judged evacuation necessary to save the city from bombardment by naval guns. He withdrew his forces and all state and government property up the Mississippi, and prepared to defend Beauregard's rear against attack from the river. These dispositions were approved by Robert E. Lee; but Lovell was not entrusted with important command again until the battle of Corinth (Miss.), Oct. 3–4, when he commanded the I Corps and attacked on the Confederate right the first day. After the Confederate defeat, at Coffeeville on Oct. 5, he commanded the rearguard so skilfully as to draw praise from his opponent, Rosecrans.

Feeling had arisen regarding the loss of New Orleans, and in December 1862, Lovell was relieved of command. He took up the matter with the War Department (see *Correspondence between the War Department and General Lovell Relating to the Defences of New Orleans,* 1863), and secured the appointment of a military court of inquiry, which finally published its findings in November 1863, absolving him of blame for the loss of New Orleans, but mildly censuring him for minor faults incident to the evacuation (*Proceedings of the Inquiry Relating to the Fall of New Orleans,* 1864). No bitterness appears in the correspondence of this trying time, but the endeavors of his friends to obtain further commands for him failed. In a final effort to demonstrate his ability he served under Joseph E. Johnston as a volunteer staff officer in the summer of 1864.

Following the war, he returned to New York, and later, after a disastrous venture into rice-planting on the Savannah River, he took up civil engineering and surveying there, and was assistant engineer under Gen. John Newton in removing East River obstructions at Hell Gate. Lovell was courageous, and a good soldier, with a clear grasp of strategy, but it was his great misfortune to lose New Orleans through governmental ineptitude after he had repeatedly warned that it could not be held without unified command and the presence of ample garrison and sufficient long-range guns.

[G. W. Cullum, *Biog. Reg. Officers and Grads. U. S. Mil. Acad.* (3rd ed., 1891); G. W. Smith, in *15th Ann. Reunion Asso. Grads. U. S. Mil. Acad.* (1884); *War of the Rebellion: Official Records (Army)*, 1 ser.; *Battles and Leaders of the Civil War* (4 vols., 1887–88), esp. vol. II; M. J. Wright, *Gen. Officers of the Confed. Army* (1911); *War of the Rebellion: Official Records (Navy)*, 1 ser.; M. F. Steele, *Am. Campaigns* (1909); *Confed. Mil. Hist.* (1899), vol. X; *N. Y. Herald,* June 2, 1884.]

D. Y.

LOVERING, JOSEPH (Dec. 25, 1813–Jan. 18, 1892), for fifty years Hollis Professor of Mathematics and Natural Philosophy in Harvard College, was born in Charlestown, Mass., the son of Robert and Elizabeth (Simonds) Lovering. The Rev. James Walker [*q.v.*], afterward president of Harvard, aided him in various ways to fit himself for college. He graduated from Harvard as the fourth scholar in his class, in 1833. While a student in the Harvard Divinity School, he was also an assistant teacher of mathematics in the college, and in the year 1835–36 for a time conducted morning and evening prayers in the college chapel. These temporary engagements led to his appointment as lecturer in natural philosophy and in 1838 he was appointed to the Hollis professorship. The same qualities, mental, moral, and physical, that would have made him an impressive preacher made him, for his time, a much respected professor of natural science, and with respect a considerable measure of affection was mingled. At the same time, people were likely to smile when they mentioned him, for some of his rather infrequent remarks were witty and some of his unchanging ways were odd. He was highly praised by eminent men as a lecturer, stating the facts and laws of science with lucidity and grave oratorical effect, illustrating them by carefully prepared experiments. In the classroom, on the other hand, he seems to have followed in its most extreme form the then prevailing habit of setting for his students definite lessons to be learned and recited in the exact words of the textbook.

Despite the limitations of his experimental work, Lovering wrote a paper "On a New Method of Measuring the Velocity of Electricity" (*Proceedings of the American Association for the Advancement of Science,* vol. XXIV, 1876), describing a procedure which apparently he had devised. The method he employed gave no information of importance, but as evidence of the will of an old-fashioned teacher, in his sixty-second year, to break ground in what was for him a novel field of experimental research, it is of considerable importance. He also wrote various essays on scientific subjects, many notices of deceased scientific men, a number of addresses which he made as president (1880–92) of the American Academy of Arts and Sciences, and discussions of natural physical phenomena such as the aurora borealis and other atmospheric happenings. He produced, it appears, no books, but he did much editorial work, especially for the *Proceedings* of the American Association for the Advancement of Science of which he was permanent secretary from 1854 to 1873 and president for the year 1873. He was frugal in his way of life and not disposed to follow changing fashions. One of his pithy sayings, which had a peculiar pungency for his younger colleagues, was substantially this: "The reason why the undulatory theory of light is now universally accepted is that the people who formerly held the corpuscular theory are all dead." He married in 1844 Sarah Gray Hawes of Boston, and of this marriage came two sons and two daughters. Retiring in 1888, he lived till Jan. 18, 1892.

[B. O. Peirce, memoir in *Nat. Acad. Sci., Biog. Memoirs,* vol. VI (1909), with bibliography; *Memorials of the Class of 1833 of Harvard Coll.* (1883); *Proc. Am. Acad. Arts and Sci.,* n.s., XIX (1893); *Popular Sci. Monthly,* Sept. 1889; T. B. Wyman, *The Geneals. and Estates of Charlestown* (1879), vol. II; *Boston Transcript,* Jan. 19, 1892.] E. H. H.

LOVETT, ROBERT WILLIAMSON (Nov. 18, 1859–July 2, 1924), orthopedic surgeon, was born in Beverly, Mass., the only child of John Dyson and Mary Elizabeth (Williamson) Lovett, his ancestry running back through mariners and merchants to early colonial days. His boyhood seems to have been somewhat restricted because of a natural parental solicitude for the last male of his line. The woolen business in which his father was engaged brought the family to Boston winters and the lad was prepared for college at two famous old schools, Chauncy Hall and Noble's. He received the degree of A.B. from Harvard College in 1881 and that of M.D. from the Harvard Medical School in 1885. After gaining surgical experience from an eighteen months' internship at the Boston City Hospital and from a four months' service at the New York Orthopædic Hospital, he began to practise in Boston. In 1895 he married Elizabeth Moorfield Storey, eldest daughter of Moorfield Storey [*q.v.*].

Becoming connected with the out-patient department of the City Hospital he was at length appointed visiting surgeon. Early interest in crippled children became a controlling passion, which slowly drew him away from general surgery, until in 1899 he resigned from the City Hospital. Thereafter the Boston Children's Hospital became his main clinic. The breadth of view which long surgical training had given him was now focused upon orthopedic surgery. He held many accessory appointments, was made chief surgeon of the Massachusetts Hospital School at Canton, and until his death was the guiding spirit in the development of the New England Peabody Home for Crippled Children. In 1912 he became head of the department of orthopedic surgery at the Boston Children's Hospital and succeeded Edward Hickling Bradford [*q.v.*] as the John Ball and Buckminster Brown Professor of Orthopædic Surgery at the Harvard Medical School.

A charter member of the American Orthopædic Association and of the Boston Surgical Society, he was elected to the presidency of both. He organized the Harvard Infantile Paralysis Commission and became its chairman in 1916. The states of New York, Vermont, and Massachusetts sought his aid in their fights against the ravages of this disease. Holding the commission of major during the World War, he was in charge of the training of medical officers in military orthopedic surgery. He was a fellow of the American Academy of Arts and Sciences, and of the American College of Surgeons, a member of the Société Internationale de Chirurgie, and honorary or corresponding member of British, French, and Italian orthopedic associations. His contributions to medical literature were voluminous. Among his more important monographs are *Diseases of the Hip Joint* (1891), *Lateral Curvature of the Spine and Round Shoulders* (1907), *The Treatment of Infantile Paralysis* (1916). He was co-author with Edward H. Bradford of the leading early textbook in his special field, *A Treatise on Orthopedic Surgery* (1890), and his crowning work, prepared in cooperation with his friend Sir Robert Jones, *Orthopedic Surgery,* appeared in 1923.

Wise counsellor of the Harvard Medical School, controlling spirit of the Boston Children's Hospital, eminent practitioner, subtle in approach, rarely polemic, quick of wit, often merry, this tall, spare aristocrat of medicine compelled men and women to work for him and with him and retained their loyalty. The controlling purpose of his life was to make contributions to his specialty which would outlive him. For this he successfully labored with an intensity which never dulled his intellect but proved his physical undoing. He was taken ill on a journey to England and died in Liverpool at the house of Sir Robert Jones. His wife and a daughter survived him.

[Sir Robert Jones in *British Medic. Jour.,* July 12, 1924; Harvey Cushing, in *Boston Medic. and Surgic. Jour.,* Aug. 14, 1924; R. B. Osgood, in *Jour. of Bone and Joint Surgery,* Oct. 1924; *Harvard Grads. Mag.,* Sept. 1924; *Boston Transcript, N. Y. Times,* July 3, 1924; information from widow and friends.] R. B. O.

LOVEWELL, JOHN (Oct. 14, 1691–May 8, 1725), Indian fighter, was born in that part of Dunstable, Mass., now lying within Nashua, N. H. He was the son of Anna (Hassell) and John Lovewell, who served under Captain Benjamin Church in the "Great Swamp Fight" of 1675. In 1724 he was the owner of a two-hundred-acre farm at Dunstable and had a wife, Hannah, and two children. When the town was attacked, his brother-in-law, Josiah Farwell, was one of the few who escaped out of the pursuing company, which was ambushed by the Indians. Soon afterward, Lovewell and others petitioned the Massachusetts government for a commission "to range . . . the woods . . . in order to kill and destroy their enemy Indians" (Fox, *post,* p. 110). The General Court granted two and a half shillings a day with a bounty for every male Indian scalp. After managing, with a force of thirty recruits, to kill one Indian and capture a boy on Dec. 10, 1724, he was able to raise a company of eighty-seven men for a second expedition. Taking a course along the Merrimac, past Lake Winnepesaukee and nearly to the White Mountains, they found a warm trail and, on Feb. 20, 1725, surprised and killed ten sleeping Indians. On Mar. 10 the company marched in triumph through the streets of Boston. He raised a third expedition with some difficulty because of the planting season and, advancing with forty-six men into the stronghold of the Pequawkets, on the site of Fryeburg, Me., he showed himself more daring than prudent. At Lake Ossipee he built a small fort and garrisoned it. With his force reduced to thirty-four, on May 8, he crossed the Saco just above where it enters what is now called Lovewell's Pond. Decoyed by an Indian, the company was ambushed by a band of Pequawkets, and, in the first fire of the enemy, he and several others were killed. The remainder of the force fought stubbornly throughout the day. At evening the Indians withdrew leaving the fallen bodies untouched.

Lovewell and his company were the subjects of balladry even before the full truth of the fight was known. The earliest version of the song was advertised under the title "The Voluntier's March" in the *New England Courant* for May 31, 1725, and, though no known copy has been preserved, is probably the same ballad as "Lovewell's Fight," which appeared in the February 1824 issue of *Collections, Historical and Miscellaneous,* edited by John Farmer and J. B. Moore, and followed closely the account of the battle in Franklin's paper of May 24, 1725. The second known version, also called "Lovewell's Fight," was printed by Farmer and Moore in their issue for March 1824 and has usually been attributed to Thomas Cogswell Upham [*q.v.*], who was at that time a minister at Rochester, N. H.

[Frederic Kidder, *The Expeditions of Capt. John Lovewell* (1865) and *The Adventures of Capt. Lovewell* (1853), reprinted from the *New-England Hist. and Geneal. Register,* Jan. 1853; C. J. Fox, *Hist. of the Old Township of Dunstable* (1846); Francis Parkman, *A Half-Century of Conflict* (1892), vol. I; Thomas Symmes, *Lovewell Lamented* (1725) and *The Original Account of Capt. John Lovewell's "Great Fight,"* ed. by Nathaniel Bouton (1861); E. S. Stearns, *Early Generations of the Founders of Old Dunstable* (1911); *Hist. Sketches of Dunstable, Mass. Bi-Centennial Oration* (1873); G. L. Kittredge, "The Ballad of Lovewell's Fight" in *Biog. Essays; a Tribute to Wilberforce Eames* (1924); R. P. Gray, *Songs and Ballads of the Maine Lumberjacks* (1924).] A. I. D.

LOW, ABIEL ABBOT (Feb. 7, 1811–Jan. 7, 1893), merchant in the China trade, was born in Salem, Mass., one of a family of twelve children of Seth and Mary (Porter) Low. His ancestors had been natives of Massachusetts, the founder of the American line, Thomas Low, having settled in Massachusetts Bay in the first half of the seventeenth century. Low was educated in the public schools and at an early age became a clerk in the house of Joseph Howard & Company, engaged in the South American trade. In 1829 his father removed from Salem to Brooklyn, N. Y., and established himself as an importer of drugs and India wares, and the son worked in his employ for several years. In 1833, at the invitation of a relative, Low sailed to Canton, China, and became a clerk in the mercantile house of Russell & Company, the largest American firm in China. He soon acquired a thorough knowledge of the intricacies of foreign trade and in 1837 was admitted to the firm. Three years later, desirous of returning home, he engaged in a joint enterprise with a Chinese merchant which remitted both parties a handsome profit and enabled Low to enter into business in New York on his own account, thus laying the foundations of A. A. Low & Brothers. Low's firm very soon gained a prominent position in the trade in China tea and Japanese silk. Celebrated among their fleet of clipper ships were *The Houqua,* launched in 1844 and named after the Chinese mandarin who had engaged with Low in the joint enterprise, the speedy *Samuel Russell,* which gained a reputation for outstripping its rivals with ease, and *The Contest* and *Jacob Bell,* both destroyed by Confederate privateers, recovery for which was effected before the Joint High Commission at Geneva. Low's economic interests extended beyond the flourishing import business which his firm conducted. He actively participated in financing the first Atlantic cable and, together with Collis P. Huntington and others, was associated with the building of the Chesapeake & Ohio Railroad through West Virginia to the Ohio River and in the founding of Newport News, Va., and Huntington, W. Va.

Though an unusually powerful and eloquent speaker, and well equipped for public life, Low seems to have felt no desire to enter politics, in which field his father, in a modest way, and his son, Seth Low [*q.v.*], more spectacularly engaged. He by no means, however, held himself aloof from civic affairs. During the Civil War he was president of the Union Defence Committee of New York and of other war financing bodies. As president of the New York Chamber of Commerce from 1863 until his resignation in 1866, he voiced the hostility of New York business men to Great Britain's rôle in relation to the Confederate commerce destroyers (J. B. Bishop, *A Chronicle of One Hundred & Fifty Years—The Chamber of Commerce of the State of New York, 1768–1918,* 1918, p. 82). On his return to New York in 1867 from a voyage around the world he urged a policy of government subsidies for the American merchant marine (*Entertainment Given to Mr. A. A. Low by Members of the Chamber of Commerce . . . Oct. 8, 1867,* 1867, p. 26). Despite the conciliatory attitude which his son Seth demonstrated throughout his life in dealing with the labor problem, he himself was hostile to labor combinations (*Address by A. A. Low . . . May 3, 1866,* 1866, p. 9). After the Civil War he gave vigorous expression to the demands of the New York merchants for a resumption of specie payments (*Centennial Celebration of the Chamber of Commerce of the State of New York, Apr. 6th, 1868,* 1868, pp. 21–30). One of his last important public services was in rendering a report as commissioner of charities of Kings County on the bearing of the growth of urban population and unsanitary conditions on the increase of pauperism: Low was married on Mar. 16, 1841, to Ellen Almira, daughter of Josiah Dow of Brooklyn. Following her death, he married, on Feb. 25, 1851, his brother William Henry's widow, Anne, daughter of Mott Bedell. He was a Unitarian in religion and an exceptionally liberal patron of education and welfare work. He died in Brooklyn.

[See Benjamin R. C. Low, *Seth Low* (1925); W. G. Low, *Some Recollections for His Children and Grandchildren* (1909); A. L. Moffat, "Low Geneal.: The Descendants of Seth Low and Mary Porter" (1932), a copy of which is in the Lib. of Cong.; *Tribute of the Chamber of Commerce of the State of N.-Y. to the Memory of Abiel Abbot Low* (1893); *Brooklyn Daily Eagle,* Jan. 7, 1893.] R. B. M.

LOW, FREDERICK FERDINAND (June 30, 1828–July 21, 1894), governor, diplomat, banker, was born in that part of Frankfort which later became Winterport, Me. His father was a small farmer in the Penobscot Valley; the common school provided his education. At fifteen he was apprenticed to the East India firm of Russell, Sturgis & Company, Boston, and during the next five years he learned much about California and the Far East, where the firm operated. He also broadened his education by diligent attendance at the lectures given by the most distinguished men of the time at Faneuil Hall and the Lowell Institute. The expiration of his apprenticeship coincided with the amazing news from California in 1849. On Feb. 22 he embarked for the Isthmus of Panama, and after the usual hardships and delay, passed through the Golden Gate on the steamer *Panama* on June 4, 1849. He at once struck out for the mines and panned some gold on the south fork of the American River, but when the winter rains began he returned to San Francisco. Then began a successful business career as a merchant, first in San Francisco, then in the autumn of 1850 in partnership with his brother in Marysville, where he married Mollie Creed. In March 1854 he brought about a merger of almost all the inland steamship lines on the bay and the Sacramento River. This was followed by the establishment of a banking business in Marysville.

In 1861 he was nominated as a Union Republican for representative-at-large in Congress after the census of 1860 disclosed that California would be entitled to a third member. It was not until June 3, 1862, the day after a special act was approved granting the additional seat, that he was sworn into office. During the remainder of the session, until Mar. 3, 1863, he took little active part, but manifested his interest in revenue and banking bills and in California land titles. On retiring from Congress, he was persuaded by Secretary Chase to accept the post of collector of the port of San Francisco, but this position was soon terminated by his election as ninth governor of California. He was the first to serve for a four-year term (Dec. 10, 1863–Dec. 8, 1867). As governor he was respected for his sound judgment and fearlessness, and much credit is due him for the later founding of the University of California and for the preservation, from land grabbers, of the site of San Francisco's Golden Gate Park. He vetoed many objectionable bills and withheld his assent to others, and he pleaded for justice to the Chinese immigrants.

In December 1869 Low was appointed minister to China. During his four years in Peking (1870–74) the major incidents were the Tientsin massacre (1870), the attempt of the United States to secure a treaty with Korea, which resulted in naval operations in May 1871, and the long controversy over the audience question, which was partially won by the foreign representative in 1873. As minister, Low won the esteem of Chinese and foreigners alike. On returning to San Francisco he accepted the position of joint manager of the Anglo-California Bank (1874–91), the second in size on the Pacific Coast, and was also interested in many other business enterprises. He died there on July 21, 1894. While he could hardly be considered a remarkable political leader or diplomat, he held the respect of his contemporaries because of his good sense, honesty, courage, and friendliness.

[The best memoir of Low is that by E. T. Sheppard, to which is appended a biographical sketch compiled from the Low papers in the Bancroft Lib., in the *Univ. of Cal. Chronicle,* Apr. 1917. For his administration as governor see T. H. Hittell, *Hist. of Cal.,* vol. IV (1897); for his messages as governor see the *Journals* of the California Senate and Assembly, 1863–67. For his career as diplomat see Tyler Dennett, *Americans in Eastern Asia* (1922); and *Foreign Relations of the U. S.,* 1870–74. For an obituary, see the *San Francisco Chronicle,* July 22, 1894.] P. J. T.

LOW, ISAAC (Apr. 13, 1735–July 25, 1791), New York merchant, member of the First Continental Congress, Loyalist, was born at Raritan Landing, near New Brunswick, N. J., the son of Cornelius, Jr., and Johanna (Gouverneur) Low, and a descendant of German, Dutch, and French settlers in New York in the seventeenth century. He moved to New York, built up a sizable fortune as a merchant, possessed wide commercial connections, and was financially interested in a slitting mill (P. Curtenius to Boston Committee of Correspondence, Aug. 26, 1774, Boston Committee of Correspondence Papers, New York Public Library, II, 381–85). He was married, on July 17, 1760, to Margarita, daughter of Cornelius Cuyler, mayor of Albany. In the pre-Revolutionary conflict he was an active Whig and was long to head merchants' committees in their efforts to obtain trade concessions from Parliament. He was a delegate to the Stamp Act Congress of 1765 and was chosen in 1768 to head a committee of inspection to enforce the non-importation agreement (C. L. Becker, *The History of Political Parties in the Province of New York, 1760–76,* 1909, p. 75). On the eve of the Revolution his liberal attitude brought down upon his head the condemnation of the more fanatical conservatives who held him to be "a person unbounded in ambition, . . . extremely opinionated," whose principles of government were "inclined to the republican system" (Jones, *post,* I, p. 35). Low served as chairman of the Committee of Fifty-one and was one of the five who drafted the proposals for a general congress to deal with non-importation.

As Low was essentially a moderate, his adherence to the cause of outright independence was doubted by shrewd observers. As early as 1773, he had, with Jacob Walton, opposed forcible resistance to the landing of the tea (Peter Force, *American Archives,* 4 ser., I, 1837, p. 254 note), and in the summer of 1774, John Adams, on his way to the First Continental Congress, was a breakfast guest at Low's elegant mansion on Dock Street. While favorably impressed by Low's "rich furniture for the tea table" and his beautiful wife, Adams was frankly skeptical. "Mr Low, the chairman of the Committee of Fifty-one," his *Diary* records, "they say, will profess attachment to the cause of liberty, but his sincerity is doubted" (C. F. Adams, *The Works of John Adams,* II, 1850, p. 350). Subsequent events proved the accuracy of this prediction. Elected a delegate from New York to the First Continental Congress (Force, *op. cit.,* pp. 305–30), he pursued a moderate course, was hostile to independence, and opposed the prohibition of all exports to the West Indies. Lee's demand for a bold front was met by an expression of fear on Low's part that Parliament might not yield and that therefore it would be wise "to provide ourselves with a retreat or a resource" (E. C. Burnett, *Letters of Members of the Continental Congress,* I, 1921, p. 64). Nevertheless, with the other conservative delegates from New York, he signed the Association.

In the end Low threw his own influence against independence. After the outbreak of hostilities in April 1775, he declined membership in the Provincial Convention of Apr. 20–22, and thus deliberately rendered himself ineligible for election to the Second Continental Congress. On sober second thought he accepted the chairmanship of the Committee of Sixty of Apr. 26, 1775, which called for an emergency Committee of One Hundred, which he again headed. In this capacity he sought to guide the action of the Provincial Congress which began its sessions in May. When the British took possession of New York, Low, unlike his brother Nicholas [*q.v.*], who embraced the colonial cause, remained and continued to give loyal support to the authorities. Chosen in 1775 president of the New York Chamber of Commerce, of which he was one of the founders, Low called a meeting of that body in 1779, which, attended by the Loyalist wing, expressed sympathy with the British cause (J. B. Bishop, *A Chronicle of One Hundred and Fifty Years: The Chamber of Commerce of . . . New York,* 1918, p. 29). Previous to the evacuation he was appointed by Sir Guy Carleton one of the board of commissioners for the settlement of debts due the Loyalists. He was named in an act of attainder of the state of New York of Oct. 22, 1779, and his property, including a tract of land in Tryon County, was confiscated. In 1783 he moved to England, where he died in Cowes, Isle of Wight, July 25, 1791. His only son, Isaac, became a commissary-general in the British army.

[See Lorenzo Sabine, *Biog. Sketches of Loyalists of the Am. Revolution* (ed. 1864), vol. II; M. J. Lamb, *Hist. of the City of N. Y.*, vol. I (1877); W. C. Abbott, *N. Y. in the Am. Revolution* (1929); *Biog. Dir. Am. Cong.* (1928); M. C. Nicoll, *The Earliest Cuylers in Holland and America and Some of Their Descendants* (1912); Thos. Jones, *Hist. of N. Y. During the Revolutionary War* (2 vols., 1879). The date of death is taken from the *Biog. Dir. Am. Cong.*] R. B. M.

LOW, JOHN GARDNER (Jan. 10, 1835–Nov. 10, 1907), potter and painter, was a son of John and Hannah Gardner Low, of Chelsea, Mass. The father, a surveyor, and a prominent citizen, encouraged John to study art, of which he himself was a connoisseur. The younger Low accordingly was sent, in 1858, to Paris where he had three years at the ateliers of Thomas Couture and Constant Troyon. According to tradition he was somewhat wild as a student but he acquired a sound professional technique. His interest in pottery is said to have been aroused during his stay in France, but he returned to the United States purposing to be a painter and he engaged for several years in scenic and other decorative work. In 1866 Alexander William Robertson started at Chelsea, where clay is abundant, a pottery for manufacture of artistic wares. At this plant Low served an apprenticeship, learning all he could about glazing and firing, and conducting experiments of his own. About 1877, in partnership with his father, Low inaugurated a manufactory under the style of the Low Art Tile Works. Picturesquely situated under Powderhorn Hill the plant exemplified in architecture, fixtures, and output its founder's conception of a combination of utility and beauty. Some of Low's processes in tile making were original, as when by use of a specially devised screw he pressed upon unburnt clay leaves, grasses, ferns, and laces, which left their impress on the finished product. The works employed as head designer Arthur Osborne, an artist, whose creative ingenuity was similar to Low's. Later Low's son, John F. Low, entered the firm.

A kiln of tiles was first successfully fired at the Low Works in May 1879. In September following an exhibit of the tiles sent to the Cincinnati Industrial Exposition won a silver medal. In 1880 Low tiles were entered in competition with the well-established English potters at the Crewe, Stoke-upon-Trent, Exposition, held under royal auspices. Award of the gold medal to the American entrant created a veritable sensation in the Five Towns, and the occurrence naturally had wide publicity in the American press. Other prizes and medals followed. In 1882 by invitation an exhibit of Low tiles and plastic sketches was held at the rooms of the Fine Art Society, London. It was visited and commended by members of the royal family, by Sir Frederick Leighton, and by many other members of the Royal Academy.

The output of the Low Tile Works was extensive for about twenty years. It included, besides tiles and plastic sketches (the latter being ceramic portraits, figure compositions, and landscapes in low relief), such objects as paperweights, inkstands, clock cases, candlesticks, and especially, tiling for soda fountains. In time, however, the activities of the Low Tile Works gradually lessened. In the last ten years of his life John G. Low resumed his painting in which his attainments were respectable. He was temperamentally an intense, positive man, but he was also constructive and public-spirited. He was long a member of the Chelsea park commission, and he held offices in the Allston and Paint and Clay clubs of Boston. In religion he was a Unitarian. He died after a brief illness and his remains were cremated for deposition at Mt. Auburn Cemetery.

[*J. and J. G. Low Art Tile* (1881); *Plastic Sketches of J. G. and J. F. Low* (1887); E. A. Barber, *The Pottery and Porcelain of the U. S.* (1909); *Art. Jour.* (London), Aug. 1882; *Am. Pottery and Glassware Reporter,* Sept. 9, 1880; *Vital Records of Chelsea, Mass., to the Year 1850* (1916); *Boston Transcript,* Sept. 3, 1880, Nov. 11, 1907; *Boston Herald,* Nov. 11, 1907; *Chelsea Citizen,* Nov. 16, 1907.] F. W. C.

LOW, JULIETTE GORDON (Oct. 31, 1860–Jan. 17, 1927), founder of the Girl Scouts in America, was of Scotch descent, the daughter of Gen. William Washington Gordon and Eleanor (Kinzie) Gordon. Through her mother she was descended from John Kinzie [*q.v*]. She received her education in private schools in Staunton and Edgehill, Va., and in New York City. After her marriage on Dec. 21, 1886, to William Low of Wellesbourne House, Warwickshire, England, she divided her time between England, Scotland, and America, maintaining homes in all three countries. Through her friendship with

Sir Robert Baden-Powell, founder of the Boy Scouts, and his sister, founder of the Girl Guides in England, she became interested in the Scout movement. She organized her first group of Girl Guides in the valley of Glenlyon in Scotland. In that region girls left home at an early age in order to earn their living. Mrs. Low taught them to support themselves at home, in addition to teaching them camp lore. It was the following year, on Mar. 9, 1912, that she organized the first troop of Girl Guides in America in her home in Savannah, Ga. The organization gained favor rapidly, national headquarters were opened in Washington, D. C., and the name was changed to the Girl Scouts, as being more appropriate in America. Soon after the organization was established, the headquarters were moved to New York City. Mrs. Low gave unceasingly of her time and energy and private means to furthering the interests of the organization, and though handicapped by deafness, she interviewed people in many parts of the country in its behalf. Upon her retirement from the office of president, the national convention of the Girl Scouts gave her the title of Founder, and her birthday was made Scouts Founder's Day. From the first meeting, attended by eight leaders and eighteen girls, the organization, at the time of her death, had grown to one of more than 140,000 members with troops in every state in the Union.

Mrs. Low was a woman of broad culture and wide interests. She won her causes by her vitality, her disarming sense of humor, and her infallible charm. Though without formal training in art, she had a keen interest in the subject and was one of the organizers of the Savannah Art Club which she served as vice-president. She modeled several small figures which were cast in porcelain, one of them being the figure of her mother, said to have been the first white child born in Chicago, and which Mrs. Low presented to that city. The wrought-iron gates in the park in Gordonston, a suburb of Savannah, were also her handiwork and were presented by her in memory of her mother and father. Her last work was a bust of her grandfather, Gen. William Washington Gordon, the founder of the Central of Georgia Railway and the mayor of Savannah from 1832 to 1834. This was a gift to the city of Savannah, and although it arrived from England only a few days before her death, when she was very ill she completed the plans for its presentation.

[Anne Hyde Choate and Helen Ferris, *Juliette Low and the Girl Scouts* (1928); *Juliette Low: Founder of the Girl Scouts* (Savannah, Ga., 1927), a memorial; *Am. Girl*, Mar. 1927; *Savannah Morning News*, Jan. 18, 19, and 24, 1927; *Savannah Press*, Jan. 18, 1927.]

B. R.

LOW, NICHOLAS (Mar. 30, 1739–Nov. 15, 1826), New York merchant, land speculator, and legislator, was born near New Brunswick, N. J., the son of Cornelius, Jr., and Johanna (Gouverneur) Low. As a young man he was a clerk in the establishment of Hayman Levy, prominent New York pre-Revolutionary merchant, who assisted him in going into business on his own account. Low attained considerable prominence as a member of the important mercantile firm of Low & Wallace. He was likewise interested in finance and industry. In 1784 he was one of the committee appointed to receive subscriptions for stock of the Bank of New York and was elected a director in 1785 (H. W. Domett, *A History of the Bank of New York, 1784–1884,* 1884, pp. 9, 18, 28, 132). He was also a director of the branch of the Bank of the United States, and was associated in the enterprise known as the Society for Establishing Useful Manufactures at Paterson, N. J. (Low to Elisha Boudinot, Sept. 2, 1793, New York Public Library). Unlike his brother, Isaac [*q.v.*], who joined the Loyalist ranks at the outbreak of the Revolution, Nicholas espoused the cause of independence. He was elected to the Assembly and was a Federalist member of the state convention which met at Poughkeepsie in 1788 and adopted the federal Constitution.

In later life his chief interest was in the rôle of proprietor and land speculator. His real-estate transactions in New York City were conducted on an extensive scale and he was one of the city's most highly assessed property owners (J. G. Wilson, *The Memorial History of the City of New-York,* III, 1893, p. 151). He possessed extensive tracts of land in St. Lawrence, Jefferson, and Lewis counties in New York state. As an active Federalist he strongly supported the project for the Black River Canal and for a connection between Lake Champlain and the St. Lawrence (D. R. Fox, *The Decline of Aristocracy in the Politics of New York,* 1918, p. 156). He introduced extensive developments on his western New York lands, building a hotel and cotton factory in Ballston about 1810, and giving much attention to the settlement of his tracts, which included the sites of Adams, Watertown, and Lowville. In the summer of 1814, at seventy-five, he joined the "New York Hussars" to defend New York from possible bombardment by the British. He died in New York City at the age of eighty-seven. He had married, late in life, Alice Fleming, a widow, by whom he had three children.

[Low's real-estate transactions in New York City can be estimated from *Minutes of the Common Council of the City of New York, 1784–1831* (19 vols., 1917). His upstate land speculations are developed in F. B. Hough, *A Hist. of St. Lawrence and Franklin Counties* (1853), *Hist. of Lewis County, N. Y.* (ed., 1883), and *A Hist. of Jefferson County* (1854). The N. Y. Pub. Lib. has the land book, No. 2, of Nicholas Low relating to lands in New York City, Ballston Spa, Township No. 2 (Watertown), Township No. 7 (Adams), and Township No. 11 (Lowville), 1794–1862. A large collection of ancient deeds of the Nicholas Low estate, covering, in addition to these regions, Montgomery and Washington counties, as well as New York, is in the possession of Ruland & Benjamin, real-estate brokers, of New York City.] R. B. M.

LOW, SETH (Jan. 18, 1850–Sept. 17, 1916), merchant, college president, youngest child of Abiel Abbot Low [*q.v.*] by his first wife, Ellen Almira (Dow) Low, was named after his paternal grandfather, who had left Massachusetts, where the Lows had dwelt from the seventeenth century, and moved to Brooklyn in 1829, setting himself up as a merchant. In his youth Low enjoyed the advantages of extensive travel, was educated in a private school, and completed his secondary studies at the Brooklyn Polytechnic Institute. He entered Columbia College with the class of 1870, earning the encomium of President Barnard, as "the first scholar in college and the most manly young fellow we have had here in many a year" (B. R. C. Low, *Seth Low,* p. 41). Reared in a home on Brooklyn Heights overlooking the New York harbor, he early acquired an enthusiasm for maritime trade evoked by the sight of his father's famous clipper ships. At the end of his senior year at Columbia, yielding to his father's wishes, he terminated a year's study of law and entered the establishment of A. A. Low & Brothers. He was employed in his father's warehouse from 1870 to 1875 and became a member of the firm a year later, supervising importations of raw silk from China, Japan, and France. On the retirement of the senior members four years later he succeeded with other junior partners to the business which was finally liquidated in 1887. On Dec. 9, 1880, he married Anne Wroe Scollay Curtis of Boston, the daughter of Justice Benjamin R. Curtis [*q.v.*] of the United States Supreme Court.

Low's efforts in behalf of civic reform were first enlisted in charitable work. In 1878 he organized and became the first president of the Bureau of Charities of Brooklyn. He first attained political prominence as president of a Republican Campaign Club organized in Brooklyn in 1880 to promote the election of Garfield and Arthur. The club, reorganized under the title of "The Young Republican Club," addressed itself to municipal reform and advocated the complete separation of local and national politics. The mayoralty contest of 1881, the first under Brooklyn's new charter, was warmly contested. The Republican party was divided in allegiance between two contestants, Gen. Benjamin F. Tracy and Ripley Ropes. The former, in the interest of party unity, suggested that both candidates withdraw in favor of Low, who was then nominated and elected mayor of Brooklyn by a fair majority. He was renominated in the autumn of 1883 and reëlected by a close margin of votes in a hotly contested campaign against the Democratic nominee, Joseph C. Hendrix. A feature of his administration was the introduction of the merit system in the municipal service of Brooklyn, a reduction of the city debt, and a complete reform of the public-school system (*Fourth Annual Message of Hon. Seth Low, Mayor of Brooklyn,* 1885; *World,* New York, Sept. 2, 1897). Low, ever a stanch friend of civil service, stood for the separation of local and national politics and refused to use the patronage of the city for any party in the presidential campaign or in any other election. In refusing to support the candidacy of James G. Blaine in 1884, he maintained: "I am not a Republican mayor, as you say I am. I am Mayor of the whole people of Brooklyn" (*Seth Low,* p. 53). Casting his vote for Cleveland, Low never again received the whole-hearted support of the Republican organization.

In 1889, shortly after his retirement from active business, Low received a call to the presidency of Columbia College. He was not quite forty years of age when he accepted the office. His selection was symbolic of a new day, when the university administrator would not be a clergyman nor a professional scholar, but a broad-visioned executive. It was in the latter capacity that he was to render notable service to Columbia. At the beginning of his administration, which covered the years 1890–1901, he centralized graduate organization and established the University Council. Graduate and professional instruction was reorganized and widened considerably in scope. Teachers' College, Barnard, and the College of Physicians and Surgeons, among other institutions, were brought into association with the university. The most forward-looking step taken through his initiative was the purchase of the new site on Morningside Heights in 1892. Low made himself responsible for a library building on the new site which he contributed as a memorial to his father. In addition he established a number of trust funds for the encouragement of study and research (*A History of Columbia University, 1754–1904,* 1904, pp. 154–71).

Low's activities as president of Columbia did not preclude his participation in public affairs during this decade. He served on the board of the Rapid Transit Commission and assisted in drafting the charter for Greater New York. He was frequently selected to act as arbiter in labor disputes and aided generously in relief work, especially during the cholera epidemic of 1893. In 1899 he went as a delegate to the first Hague Conference. In 1897 he was nominated by the Citizens' Union for the first mayor of Greater New York. As in his vigorous Brooklyn campaigns, his keynote was the complete separation of municipal and national politics (*Seth Low's Great Speech at Cooper Union, Oct. 6, 1897,* 1897, pp. 3, 8). The failure of the Republican party to support him, coupled with the death of Henry George toward the end of the campaign, brought about his defeat by Robert Van Wyck of Tammany Hall. Low ran second, 50,000 votes ahead of Benjamin F. Tracy, Republican. In 1901, however, he was elected to the mayoralty of New York by a large majority on a reaction of public sentiment against the Tammany régime. His administration was distinguished as a brief era of civic reform. Patronage was checked and the civil service was developed. Through his efforts the first subway to Brooklyn and the Pennsylvania tunnel to Long Island were planned and the electrification of the New York Central within the city limits was effected. Notwithstanding this excellent record, he failed of reëlection in 1903.

From leadership in civic affairs Low turned to the farmer's cooperative movement, laying out a home and farm at Bedford Hills in Westchester County, N. Y., and organizing the Bedford Farmers' Cooperative Association. He firmly believed that the two major problems which America must solve were the negro and labor. In 1905 he became a member of the board of trustees of the Tuskegee Institute and two years later was elected chairman of the board, a position which he held until his death. During this period he actively cooperated with Booker T. Washington. In the last decade of his life, he devoted much of his time to securing more harmonious relations between capital and labor. In 1907 he became president of the National Civic Federation, and in the autumn of 1914 he was appointed by President Wilson a member of the Colorado Coal Commission for the investigation of labor difficulties in that state. In 1914, after a long membership in the New York Chamber of Commerce, he was elected president of that body. His service to the organization was as notable as that of his father as its president during the Civil War. His administration is associated with the organization of a committee on problems of shipments, the organization at Washington of the Bureau of War Risk Insurance, and with the movement for the rehabilitation of American shipping. His last important public service was rendered as chairman of the committee on cities of the New York constitutional convention of 1915, a position to which he was justly entitled. He had gained international recognition as an advocate of municipal self-government and executive responsibility, ideas which he elaborated upon at Lord Bryce's invitation in a chapter which he wrote for the first edition of *The American Commonwealth,* and in his *Addresses and Papers on Municipal Government* (1891).

In later years Low was portly in physical appearance; in manner, kindly and benevolent, but in public somewhat shy and reserved. He possessed a talent for merging himself in a cause and an unfailing acumen in the selection of experts. He was universally respected as the pattern of the scholar in politics. In religion he was an active Episcopalian. His death occurred at his home in Bedford Hills after a lingering illness.

[Benjamin R. C. Low, *Seth Low* (1925); *Columbia Alumni News,* Oct. 20, 1916; *Board of Estimate and Apportionment and Board of Aldermen: Joint Session in Memory of Honorable Seth Low . . . Sept. 25, 1916* (1916); A. L. Moffat, "Low Geneal.: The Descendants of Seth Low and Mary Porter" (1932), a copy of which is in the Lib. of Cong.; and the New York press of Sept. 18, 1916.]

R. B. M.

LOWE, CHARLES (Nov. 18, 1828–June 20, 1874), Unitarian clergyman, was born in Portsmouth, N. H., the son of John and Sarah Ann (Simes) Lowe. As a boy he attended Phillips Academy in Exeter, N. H., where his father had become manager of a cotton-mill. Entering Harvard College as a sophomore he graduated as salutatorian of the class of 1847. For a year he read law with Amos Tuck [*q.v.*] in Exeter, then he began the study of theology under the direction of the Rev. Andrew P. Peabody [*q.v.*] of Portsmouth, completing the course in the Harvard Divinity School (1849–51) while he served as tutor in the college of arts. In the spring of 1851 he became the colleague of the Rev. John Weiss in the Unitarian church of New Bedford, Mass., but two years later a serious malady of the lungs made him seek health in extensive travel in Western Europe and the Turkish Empire. After a winter semester, 1854–55, in the University of Halle under the theologians Erdmann and Tholuck he became in September 1855 the pastor of the North Church in Salem, Mass., but after nearly two years of ministry he was again obliged to resign. On Sept. 16, 1857, he was married to Martha A. Perry, daughter of Justus and Hannah (Wood) Perry of Keene, N. H., and settled on a farm near Salem. In February 1859, his health improved, he became pastor of the Unitarian church in Somerville, Mass., and during the Civil War he added to his pastoral care temporary service as army chaplain in 1863, as chairman of the Army Committee of the American Unitarian Association in 1864, and in behalf of the Freedmen's Aid Society in 1865. His sagacity and success in these activities led to another responsibility, a leadership in the effort to organize the autonomous, loosely related Unitarian congregations into a National Conference (April 1865) which would be composed of devout conservatives, who cherished recognition of Christ as a superhuman being, and younger innovators, some of whom were disinclined even to the name Christian since for them it necessarily implied the inherited system of authoritative dogma. In this difficult situation Lowe, now transferred from his parish to the office of executive secretary of the American Unitarian Association, served as a catalyst. His calm courage and frankness, his catholicity of mind, and his sweetness of spirit won divergent parties to unity. After six years of remarkably efficient administration he was too ill to continue the work and in 1871 again traveled abroad for his health. Returning in May 1873 he declined the pastorate of the First Church of Cambridge, and the presidency of Antioch College, but undertook the editorship of the *Unitarian Review and Religious Magazine,* planned to succeed the older *Monthly Religious Magazine.* A few months after he had taken over the work he sought the sea air of Swampscot, May 30, 1874, but immediately suffered the beginning of hemorrhages from which he died on June 20.

[Martha Perry Lowe, *Memoir of Chas. Lowe* (1884); *Memorial to Chas. Lowe* (1874), reprinted, with additions, from the *Unitarian Rev. and Religious Mag.,* July, Aug. 1874; S. A. Eliot, ed., *Heralds of a Liberal Faith* (1910), vol. III; the *Christian Reg.* (Boston), June 27, July 4, 1874; *Boston Transcript,* June 22, 1874.]
F. A. C.

LOWE, RALPH PHILLIPS (Nov. 27, 1805–Dec. 22, 1883), governor and chief justice of Iowa, was the son of Jacob Derrick and Martha (Per-Lee) Lowe, who conducted a tavern in Warren County, Ohio, where the boy early heard great issues discussed by Henry Clay and other distinguished guests. He worked on the farm and acquired enough preparation by 1825 to enter Miami University, from which he graduated in 1829. Estranged from his father on account of his refusal to farm, he made his way to Ashville, Ala., where he taught school, read law, was admitted to the bar, and began to practise. After five years he returned to Ohio to open a law office in Dayton. In 1837 he married Phoebe Carleton and three years later removed to a farm near Bloomington, now Muscatine, Iowa. He quickly became active in public affairs and served in the constitutional convention of 1844. Defeated the following year as the Whig candidate for territorial delegate, he devoted himself to building up a successful practice, served as district attorney and, from 1852 to 1857, was judge of the first district. When, in 1858, he became the first governor under the constitution of 1857, he faced a serious situation. With no banking system of her own, Iowa was overrun with wildcat currency from neighboring states and was still experiencing the disastrous effects of the panic of 1857. She was deeply stirred, too, by the slavery issue. In cooperation with the able Seventh General Assembly, his administration put the new constitution into effect, established a banking system, enacted ample revenue laws, rescued the school lands and funds from fraud and waste, encouraged railway construction, created the state agricultural college, and placed the township and county government on a sounder basis. These measures together with good crops and good prices, in 1860, restored state prosperity. Yet when the time came for the nominating convention in June 1859 Samuel J. Kirkwood [*q.v.*] had so far established himself as the leader of the antislavery sentiment in Iowa that there was a general desire to make him the next governor. Lowe's record and character undoubtedly entitled him to a renomination, but he was not as popular as Kirkwood. His tolerance, gentleness, and dignity gave the appearance of weakness to what was, in reality, a sturdy, fearless character. In the interest of party harmony he reluctantly consented to go to the supreme bench while Kirkwood became governor.

He served on the bench until 1868, acting as chief justice in 1860 and from 1866–68. As a judge he was broad-minded, sympathetic, and intellectually honest. Being neither deeply read in the law nor thoroughly convinced of the efficacy of the law as a general rule of action he regarded equity as a higher law and rendered decisions that seemed to him just, even if not in strict accord with the technicalities of the law. When he left the bench he was interested in Iowa's "Five Per Cent Claim." He spent some years trying to collect about $800,000, in accordance with the agreement of the federal government to pay the states five per cent. of the proceeds of land sales in return for five years' exemption from state taxation on land sold by the government. In order to prosecute the claim more advantageously he moved to Washington, where he died without knowing that the Supreme Court had already decided against his suit. He was a member of the Presbyterian church and deeply interested in such phases of religious thought as the interpretation of Biblical prophecies and the question of the lost tribes of Israel. His faith in human beings continued to be strong throughout a varied and active life. A colleague wrote of him, that he "was a most credulous man, taking every man to be honest and true until convinced otherwise" (*Annals of Iowa,* Oct. 1893, p. 211).

[B. F. Shambaugh, *Hist. of the Constitutions of Iowa* (1902); E. H. Stiles, *Recollections and Sketches of Notable Lawyers and Public Men of Early Iowa* (1916); *Iowa Hist. Record,* Oct. 1891; *Annals of Iowa,* Oct. 1900; *Gen. Cat. of the Grads. and Former Students of Miami Univ.* (1910?); *Iowa State Register,* Dec. 23, 1883; *Washington Post,* Dec. 25, 1883.]

C. E. P.

LOWE, THADDEUS SOBIESKI COULINCOURT (Aug. 20, 1832–Jan. 16, 1913), aeronaut, meteorologist, and inventor, was born at Jefferson Mills, N. H., now known as Riverton, the son of Clovis and Alpha (Green) Lowe. As early as 1856 he became interested in ballooning as a means of investigating upper-air currents, and in 1858 he made his initial voyage, from Ottawa, Canada, in connection with the celebration of the laying of the first Atlantic cable. The following year he built an airship, named the *City of New York.* As the result of an ascension made in Philadelphia, June 1860, Prof. Joseph Henry [*q.v.*] of the Smithsonian Institution became interested in Lowe's experiments and furnished him with certain instruments. He himself invented a device for getting latitude and longitude quickly without a horizon, which he miscalled an altimeter. On Apr. 20, 1861, he left Cincinnati, Ohio, in a balloon and after traveling some nine hundred miles in nine hours, landed near Pea Ridge, close to the boundary between North and South Carolina. He was regarded as a Yankee spy, arrested, and was in some danger of mob violence; but a gentleman who had witnessed an ascent made by Lowe at Charleston, S. C., the previous year, identified him and vouched for him as a scientific investigator not connected with military matters. Lowe maintained that he was thus the first prisoner taken in the Civil War. He tells of his experiences in a chapter in *Navigating the Air* (published by the Aero Club of America, 1907). This voyage was made purely in the interest of science. Lowe believed that aloft there were strong winds blowing from west to east and that advantage might be taken of their presence to carry a balloon from America to Europe. To satisfy Professor Henry, a test was made with a smaller balloon than the one intended for transoceanic purposes. Coal gas was used to inflate, and the trip as a whole was successful. The balloon moved west in the lower levels at the start, to the great delight of the doubters; but at a height of 7,000 feet, a reverse current carried it eastward. The average height was 16,000 feet and the greatest 23,000 feet.

Soon after the outbreak of the Civil War, Lowe went to Washington with a view to interesting the authorities in the use of balloons for observation purposes. On June 6, 1861, Secretary of War Cameron asked Professor Henry to report on the matter. On June 18, Lowe made an ascent, during which he sent to President Lincoln the first telegraph message from a balloon in air. On June 21, Henry reported to Secretary Cameron (*Official Records,* 3 ser. I, 283–84) that balloons would probably be of military value. Lowe was made chief of the aeronautic section and rendered valuable service to the Army of the Potomac from the battle of Bull Run to that of Gettysburg. He was the first in the country to take photographs from a balloon. For his services he was elected an honorary member of the Loyal Legion.

After the war, Lowe became interested in the manufacture of artificial ice and as early as 1866 had constructed a plant for this purpose. He is credited with making the first artificial ice for commercial purposes in the United States. The New York *Sun* (Dec. 21, 1868) described his equipment of a refrigerated steamer for the transportation of perishable meats, vegetables, and fruits from Galveston to New York. A shipment of fresh beef from Texas to New Orleans arrived there Dec. 10, 1868, on the steamer *Agnes,* in good condition, looking as if freshly slaughtered although killed five days earlier. A company was formed to transport perishable goods in refrigerating devices; but the company failed, leaving Lowe in debt.

Later he made several improvements in the manufacture of gas and coke. By building regenerative metallurgical furnaces (1869–72) he succeeded in producing gas and fuel. In 1873–75 he invented and built water-gas apparatus; and in 1897 he constructed the New Lowe Coke Oven system for producing gas and coke, the latter known as anthracite coke, and used in smelting furnaces. The grade of coke produced equaled the best European product. From 1891 to 1894, while he was living in California, he became widely known because of his construction of an inclined railway at Rubio Canyon on Echo Mountain. The peak near the well-known Mount Wilson was named Mount Lowe, and he equipped and maintained an observatory on the summit. On Feb. 14, 1855, he married Leontine A. Gachon of Paris, by whom he had three sons. He died at Pasadena.

[T. S. C. Lowe, *The Air-Ship City of N. Y.* (1859) and "Observation Balloons in the Battle of Fair Oaks," *Rev. of Revs.* (N. Y.), Feb. 1911; *War of the Rebellion: Official Records (Army)*; W. J. Rhees, "Reminiscences of Ballooning in the Civil War," *The Chautauquan*, June 1898; *Jour. of the Franklin Institute*, Feb. 1887; J. S. Brainard, in *The Californian Illus. Mag.*, Aug. 1892; G. W. James, in the *Arena*, Oct. 1907; editorial in the *Arena*, Nov. 1907; *A Biog. Album of Prominent Pennsylvanians* (3 ser., 1890); *Who's Who in America*, 1910–11; *N. Y. Herald*, Sept. 29, 1859; *Daily National Intelligencer* (Washington, D. C.), June 20, 1861; *Los Angeles Times*, Jan. 17, 1913; *Scientific American*, Jan. 25, 1913.] A. M.

LOWELL, AMY (Feb. 9, 1874–May 12, 1925), poet and critic, the daughter of Augustus Lowell and Katharine Bigelow (Lawrence) Lowell, was born in Brookline, Mass., in the house in which she died. She was, as she said, "of thoroughgoing New England stock," and her forebears were men of positive character, a trait which she inherited. Her first American ancestor, Perceval Lowell (or Lowle), a merchant of Bristol and member of a family of Somerset gentry, came to Newbury, Mass., in 1639. His descendant, John Lowell, 1743–1802 [*q.v.*], was a member of the Provincial Congress which defied the authority of the Crown, and later a member of the Federal Congress. His son, in turn, John Lowell, 1769–1840 [*q.v.*], who called himself on occasion "the Boston Rebel," opposed the War of 1812, and affirmed England's right to impress American seamen. His son, John Amory, Amy Lowell's paternal grandfather, a cousin of James Russell Lowell, was a pioneer in the development of the cotton industry in New England, and with him was associated her maternal grandfather, Abbott Lawrence [*q.v.*], at one time minister to the Court of St. James's. Her father followed in his father's footsteps. She grew up, accordingly, in a family where the sense of tradition was strong, and in an atmosphere of comparative affluence.

She was the youngest of five children, of whom Percival Lowell [*q.v.*], the astronomer, and Abbott Lawrence Lowell, president of Harvard University, were the eldest. When eight years old she was taken to Europe for six months, "traveling at a fearful rate of speed" over England and the Continent. The overstimulation of her brain resulted in serious illness; her nights for months afterwards "were made horrible by visions of the iron virgin" of Nürnberg; and it was many years before she ceased to be afraid in the dark. Of a trip to California when she was nine the two details which stuck in her memory were "the lassoing of a horse in a corral, and the wild dash in a coach along the steep roads of the Yosemite." Except for these journeys her early life was spent entirely between Boston and Brookline. "Living at home in those days," she wrote, "was very simple. I was devoted to animals, and as we kept horses, cows and dogs, I had plenty of opportunity to gratify these tastes." Under an old family coachman, a one-time Newmarket jockey, she "learned to ride and drive in a fearless manner, to which training," she remarked, "I attribute a great many useful things." Her love of animals (which at one time extended to seven huge and notorious English sheepdogs) never left her, and it was rivaled by her affection for the immediate surroundings of her home. For three generations the men of her family had been lovers and planters of gardens. The garden of her poems had been planned entirely by her father, and in it still bloomed azaleas brought from France and given to "the Boston Rebel" for his greenhouse. Almost every detail of her home and every influence upon her childhood found expression later in her poems.

Her formal education was gained entirely in private schools. To her mother, however, who was an accomplished musician and linguist, she owed, as she said, far more than to her other teachers, especially her thorough grounding in French. In 1895, when she was twenty-one, her mother died; in 1896 she spent six months on the Continent; and in the winter of 1897 went up the Nile in a dahabiyeh. The overstrain of traveling once more brought on a nervous breakdown, and the winter of 1898–99 was spent on a fruit ranch in California, and the following summer in Devonshire. In 1900 her father died; she purchased the family place ("Sevenels") in Brookline; and at once identified herself with the municipal and educational interests of the town, and with the movement for better libraries through the state. But "about 1902," to use her own words, "I discovered that poetry . . . was my natural mode of expression. And from that moment I began to devote myself to it seriously, studying as hard as possible, and endeavoring to perfect myself in the art." There were trips to Europe again in 1905 (including Constantinople and Greece), in 1913, and in 1914 (when she was caught by the outbreak of the Great War); but from 1902 until her death the supreme interest of her life was her art.

She followed, however, the Horatian maxim, for eight years elapsed before her first published poem appeared (*Atlantic Monthly,* August 1910), and her first book, *A Dome of Many-Coloured Glass* (1912), was not published until two years later. Meantime, in 1911, she had translated Alfred de Musset's *Caprice,* and had taken the leading part herself at an amateur performance in Boston. During her visit to England in 1913 she met Ezra Pound; became associated with the Imagists, then just crystallizing into a school; and contributed to the first Imagist anthology, *Des Imagistes* (1914). On her return she made the authorized translation of Edmond Rostand's *Pierrot qui pleure et Pierrot qui rit,* given in Boston as an opera in February 1915. From her visit to England in 1914 she brought back the manuscript of *Some Imagist Poets,* an anthology of which three numbers were issued (1915, 1916, and 1917), the first with a Preface, not written by her, which defined the tenets of the group, and which she later elaborated in *Tendencies in Modern American Poetry* (below, pp. 239–48). In 1914 her second volume, *Sword Blades and Poppy Seed,* was published, and in it are to be found her first poems in *vers libre,* or, as she preferred to call it, "unrhymed cadence," the principles of which she defined in the Preface, and later in two noteworthy articles (*North American Review,* January 1917; *Dial,* January 17, 1918). The same volume also contained her first experiments in so-called "polyphonic prose," elucidated later in the Preface to *Can Grande's Castle.* Both the new techniques owed their suggestion to her intimate acquaintance with contemporary French poetry, and in 1915 appeared *Six French Poets: Studies in Contemporary Literature.* A third volume of verse, *Men, Women, and Ghosts* (1916), included, together with poems in the conventional meters, further experiments in the two new forms. *Tendencies in Modern American Poetry* (1917), a series of critical studies of six contemporary American poets, was followed in 1918 by *Can Grande's Castle,* a collection of four long pieces wholly in "polyphonic prose," of which the last, "The Bronze Horses," remains the most notable example. During these half-dozen years she was one of the storm-centers of an active controversy on both sides of the Atlantic over the new forms of verse. *Pictures of the Floating World* (1919), containing some of her most beautiful work, showed markedly the influence of her studies in Chinese and Japanese poetry; while in *Legends* (1921) she retold, using all the varieties of technique at her command, a dozen "Tales of Peoples which [she had] loved," drawn from Peru, Yucatan, the North American Indians, China, Europe, England, and her own New England. In *Fir-Flower Tablets: Poems Translated from the Chinese* (1921) her interest in China reached its culmination. She collaborated in the enterprise with Mrs. Florence Ayscough, whose literal translations she turned into unrhymed English verse, preserving so far as possible the spirit of the originals. In 1922 she published anonymously *A Critical Fable* (later acknowledged), a spirited skit in rhymed couplets, in which she let herself go in a series of lively sketches of her fellow poets, and included a racy and vivid characterization of herself. This *jeu d'esprit,* however, was largely relaxation from a more arduous undertaking. In 1921 she had been invited to deliver a commemorative address at Yale University on the one hundredth anniversary of the death of Keats. Out of this grew her most important critical performance, *John Keats* (1925), which occupied almost without cessation the last four years of her life. It frankly essays to interpret Keats as "a new generation of poets and critics" saw him, and it owes its distinctive quality as a biography to the fact that in it one poet has relived, almost from day to day, another poet's life.

From 1915 until her death in 1925 she lectured and read from time to time, with a verve and brilliancy peculiarly her own, before audiences at Harvard, Yale, Columbia, and other universities, and before societies and clubs the country over. During the same period she expounded with skill and defended with vigor, in various periodicals, her own poetic creed and her technique. On the eve of a visit to England, during which she was to have lectured at Oxford, Cambridge, Eton, Edinburgh, and elsewhere, she was stricken with paralysis, and died without recovering consciousness. For many years she had endured unintermitted physical discomfort and often acute pain, and her achievements represent the triumph of an indomitable will. The legend that her death was hastened by hostile criticism of *John Keats* is as baseless as, in view of her militant character, it is absurd. At the time of her death three volumes of poems were in preparation. They were posthumously published—*What's O'Clock* in 1925, *East Wind* in 1926, *Ballads for Sale* in 1927—under the oversight of Mrs. Harold Russell, her literary executor and the "A. D. R." to whom, in *John Keats,* were dedicated all her poems. *Poetry and Poets: Essays* was published in 1930.

During the later years of her life Amy Lowell was the most striking figure in contemporary American letters. Like every one who, without shunning publicity, prefers his own road to the beaten track, she stirred the general myth-making faculty. Her serene independence of conventional opinion, which found its popular symbol in her frank addiction to cigars; her Elizabethan outspokenness; her choice of the hours from dark to dawn for work, and of the daylight hours for sleep; her insistence upon the elaborate paraphernalia which accompanied her travels; her Olympian detachment from all demands of punctuality—traits such as these inevitably kept her more or less picturesquely in the public eye. What the public eye, however, often failed to see was the vivid and powerful personality which dominated handicaps and resolved apparent inconsistencies. She had not the gift of physical beauty, except as spirit and intelligence animated every expression of a keen and finely modeled face. Grace of form had also been denied her, but her presence, on occasion, could be regal. She could be arrogant, even domineering; yet open-mindedness, willingness to learn, and generosity were among her most deeply ingrained qualities. Her insurgencies, when all is said, were intellectual; the bedrock was conservative. And in her paradoxes lay half the richness of her character. She was a brilliant and provocative talker, but her talk was seldom a monologue. She loved best the give and take between contending minds, and her flashing wit and quickness of repartee and often crisp finality of statement will always be associated with the great book-walled room in which she met her friends. Her mind was endlessly acquisitive; she had the instinct, though not the training, of a scholar; and her more ambitious poems and *John Keats* were the fruits of ardent and indefatigable study. In the end it was her eagerness of spirit which outran her bodily strength.

Her poems number more than six hundred and fifty titles, in eleven volumes. Collectively, they exhibit extraordinary catholicity of interests; an almost unrivaled command of the vocabulary of sensuous impressions; a "firm belief that poetry should not try to teach"; a corresponding emphasis on finished craftsmanship; and a passion for adventures in technique. In "unrhymed cadence" she perfected a new and (in skilled hands) effective instrument. "Polyphonic prose," on the other hand, proved too alien a visitant to domiciliate itself. She suffers, as she recognized herself (*A Critical Fable,* pp. 46–50), from her profusion. Her blaze of colors tends to draw attention from her thought and feeling; her "hurricaning" (as she called it), from her clarity and restraint. The final appraisal of her contribution belongs to later times, but in her best work she has left securely a body of verse of distinction and beauty.

[This biography is based upon Miss Lowell's autobiographical memoranda, written about 1917; upon information contributed by Mrs. Harold Russell; and upon the writer's personal knowledge. See also D. R. Lowell, *The Hist. Geneal. of the Lowells of America* (1899); *Who's Who in America,* 1924–25; Winifred Bryher, *Amy Lowell, a Critical Appreciation* (1918); *The Dial,* Nov. 2, 1918; *North Am. Rev.,* Mar. 1925; *Revue Anglo-Americaine,* Aug. 1925, Apr. 1929; *Saturday Rev. of Literature,* Oct. 3, 1925; *New Republic,* Nov. 18, 1925; *Bookman,* Mar. 1926; *Scribner's Mag.,* Sept. 1927; *Modern Language Notes,* Mar. 1928. The authorized biography, by S. Foster Damon, is in course of preparation.]

J. L. L.

LOWELL, EDWARD JACKSON (Oct. 18, 1845–May 11, 1894), historian, son of Francis Cabot and Mary Lowell (Gardner) Lowell, was born in Boston, Mass., where his father was actively engaged in business for more than fifty years. His paternal grandfather, Francis Cabot Lowell [*q.v.*], was a son of the second wife, and his maternal grandmother, Rebecca (Lowell) Gardner, a daughter of the third wife of Judge John Lowell, 1743–1802 [*q.v.*]. His uncle, John Lowell, 1799–1836 [*q.v.*], was the founder of the Lowell Institute. When he was nine years old Lowell was taken abroad by his father and placed in Sillig's school at Bellerive near Vevey, Switzerland. Later he attended the Latin school of E. S. Dixwell in Boston and entered Harvard College in 1863. While an undergraduate he wrote a good deal of verse, and he was Class Odist at Commencement, 1867. In January 1868 he married Mary Wolcott Goodrich, daughter of Samuel Griswold Goodrich [*q.v.*], who is best remembered by his pen name, Peter Parley. Lowell spent a year or two in business, and then studied law. Admitted to the bar in 1872, he opened an office in connection with Brooks Adams [*q.v.*], but after his wife's death in 1874 he gave up his practice and devoted himself to his three children and to study. In June 1877 he married Elizabeth Gilbert Jones, daughter of George Jones [*q.v.*], who was one of the founders and for many years the manager of the *New York Times.*

Going abroad in the summer of 1879, Lowell spent a number of years in Europe, where he became interested in the history of the German mercenaries used by Great Britain in America during the Revolution. In German archives he collected documents which enabled him to write to the *New York Times* in 1880–81 a series of letters on this subject. These were developed into a volume entitled *The Hessians and the Other German Auxiliaries of Great Britain in the Revolutionary War,* which appeared in 1884.

Shortly after it was published the author was elected a member of the Massachusetts Historical Society and of the American Academy of Arts and Sciences. In 1888 he contributed to Justin Winsor's *Narrative and Critical History of America* the chapter on "The United States of America, 1775–1782: Their Political Struggles and Relations with Europe." He had considered preparing a biography of Lafayette, but changed his plan, deciding instead to study conditions in France just before the French Revolution. He approached the subject without theory or prejudice and with a comprehensive interest. The book was published in 1892 under the title *The Eve of the French Revolution.* In it the author made clear his conviction that the great upheaval was due not to lack of prosperity among the French people but to France's consciousness "that her government did not correspond to her degree of civilization." He later undertook a study of the influence of the French Revolution in other countries, which was unfinished at his death.

For a number of years Lowell was treasurer of the American School of Classical Studies at Athens. In the winter of 1893 he visited the Mediterranean, then returned to America. A few months later he died, at Cotuit, Mass., his summer residence. His "strong social instincts and quick and comprehensive sympathy made him beloved by his contemporaries" (A. L. Lowell, *post*). In conversation he had a happy gift of aphorism which lent additional charm to his remarks. Guy Lowell [*q.v.*] was his son.

[Memoir by A. Lawrence Lowell, in *Proc. Mass. Hist. Soc.*, 2 ser., IX (1895); memoir by H. W. Haynes, in *Proc. Am. Acad. Arts and Sci.*, n.s., XXII (1895), with a list of Lowell's published writings; *Harvard Coll. Class of 1867, Secretary's Report No. 10* (1897); *Harvard Grads. Mag.*, Sept. 1894; D. R. Lowell, *The Hist. Geneal. of the Lowells of America* (1899); *Boston Transcript*, May 12, 15, 1894.] L. S. M.

LOWELL, FRANCIS CABOT (Apr. 7, 1775–Aug. 10, 1817), textile manufacturer, was born at Newburyport, Mass., the son of Judge John Lowell, 1743–1802 [*q.v.*], and his second wife, Susanna (Cabot) Lowell, and a half-brother of John Lowell, 1769–1840 [*q.v.*]. In 1776 his father moved to Boston and here Francis received his education, entering Harvard in 1789 at the age of fourteen. For lighting a bonfire in the college yard during his senior year he was "rusticated" to Bridgewater where he continued his studies under Rev. Zedekiah Sanger, but graduated with his class in 1793. In college he excelled in mathematics, an aptitude which in later years served him well and provoked the admiration of the great mathematician, Nathaniel Bowditch.

After leaving Harvard Lowell engaged successfully in importing and exporting in company with his uncle, William Cabot, until 1810, when ill health induced him to make a prolonged journey to the British Isles. This trip to England was fraught with great significance for the future of American industry. Impressed by the importance of manufacturing as a source of national wealth, he closely studied the textile machinery which he saw in Lancashire, and upon his return to America in 1812, determined to establish a cotton factory. The almost total cessation of commerce owing to the War of 1812 left him free to devote his entire time to this project. Interesting his brother-in-law, Patrick Tracy Jackson [*q.v.*], in the scheme, he formed the Boston Manufacturing Company, purchased land at Waltham, and busied himself during the winter of 1812–13 in designing and constructing with the aid of a mechanical genius, Paul Moody [*q.v.*], spinning machinery and a practical power loom. With little to aid him except recollections of observations in Europe and imperfect drawings, Lowell not only designed an excellent power loom but contributed such improvements to textile machinery as the double speeder and the method of spinning the thread directly through the quill. "I well recollect," said a leading stockholder, Nathan Appleton [*q.v.*], who had been invited by Lowell to view his new power loom, "the state of admiration and satisfaction with which we sat by the hour, watching the beautiful movement of the new and wonderful machine, destined as it evidently was, to change the character of all textile industry" (Appleton, *post,* p. 9). Another year was to pass before the factory was in complete operation, but when all the machinery was functioning the plant at Waltham was believed to be the first mill in the world which combined all the operations of converting raw cotton into finished cloth. "Although Messrs. Jackson and Moody," says Appleton, "were men of unsurpassed talent and energy in their way, it was Mr. Lowell who was the informing soul, which gave direction and form to the whole proceeding" (*Ibid.*, p. 15). Of a humanitarian turn of mind, Lowell was also interested in proper living conditions for his employees and his efforts at his Waltham mills had a salutary influence on the development of the New England textile industry.

Scarcely were the wheels turning in the new mill before the war with England came to an end, and the infant industry seemed destined to be submerged in a flood of cheap foreign goods. Lowell with others repaired to Washington, where he was influential in convincing Lowndes and Calhoun of the wisdom of incorporating in the tariff of 1816 a substantial duty on cotton cloth. The full realization of his plans he did not live to see. In ill health for some years, he died in Boston at the early age of forty-two. He had married, Oct. 31, 1798, Hannah Jackson (Feb. 3, 1776–May 10, 1815), daughter of Jonathan and Hannah (Tracy) Jackson, of Newburyport, who bore him three sons and a daughter. One of the sons, John, 1799–1836 [*q.v.*], was the founder of the Lowell Institute, while among his descendants through his other children were John, 1824–1897, Edward Jackson, Percival, Amy, and Guy Lowell [*qq.v.*].

[Nathan Appleton, *Introduction of the Power Loom, and Origin of Lowell* (1858), is the most authoritative source, while almost all that is known of the man is collected in a speech by his descendant F. C. Lowell, in *Exercises at the Seventy-Fifth Anniversary of the Incorporation of the Town of Lowell* (1901). See also Alfred Gilman, "Francis Cabot Lowell," in *Contributions of the Old Residents' Hist. Asso., Lowell, Mass.*, I (1879), 73–86; F. W. Coburn, *Hist. of Lowell and Its People* (1920), vol. III; D. R. Lowell, *The Hist. Geneal. of the Lowells of America* (1899); *Illus. Hist. of Lowell and Vicinity* (1897); *New-Eng. Palladium & Commercial Register* (Boston), Aug. 12, 1817.]

H. U. F.

LOWELL, GUY (Aug. 6, 1870–Feb. 4, 1927), architect, was born in Boston, of an old Boston family, the son of Edward Jackson Lowell [*q.v.*] and Mary (Goodrich) Lowell. He received his early schooling in Dresden and Paris, was prepared for college at Noble's School in Boston, and graduated with the degree of A.B. from Harvard in 1892. He next entered the department of architecture at the Massachusetts Institute of Technology, then flourishing under the leadership of the brilliant Frenchman, Despradelle, and followed a two-year course leading to the degree of B.S. in 1894. Feeling the need of European training, he sailed for France in 1895 and entered the Atelier Pascal of the École des Beaux-Arts in Paris. He received his diploma from the École in 1899 and almost immediately returned to America to practise. Meantime, in April 1898, he had married Henrietta Sargent of Brookline, Mass., daughter of Charles Sprague Sargent [*q.v.*].

In Paris, Lowell followed the regular course of the Beaux-Arts. His designs had the exuberance and the frequent lack of restraint so often observed in students' work in France. More important, he absorbed the logic and, above all, the inherent grasp of planning which is the especial glory of French architecture and the most useful asset in French architectural education. From the beginning of his practice in America, however, he showed that he was to abandon the flashy and exuberant detail that he had learned in Paris and would return to the conservatism and refinement which has marked American architecture at its best. In America, he had immediate success. His social position and connections gave him unusual opportunities which his unusual gifts and thorough training enabled him to capitalize. That his success was largely due to his own ability, however, was proved by the fact that he in no wise feared competition with the most brilliant of his contemporaries. His work was extremely variegated. At Harvard he built Emerson Hall, the New Lecture Hall, and the President's House. He was the leading spirit of the architectural expression of Phillips Academy, Andover, Mass., where he designed many buildings and created one of the most inspiring ensembles in American scholastic work. His hand is seen in the Carrie Memorial Tower at Brown, in buildings at Simmons College, Boston, and at the State Normal School, Bridgewater, Mass. His designs for private residences —many of them of the most elaborate sort—are to be found in Massachusetts, in Maine, and on Long Island. At Piping Rock he designed one of the most attractive and simplest of country clubs, using a modified Dutch Colonial style indigenous to the district. His most notable single work was the New York County Court House, for which in 1913 he furnished the winning design, distinguished by its ingenuity of plan. The detail was severely classical and Lowell, to the end of his career, remained a confirmed classicist. Other public buildings which came from his office were the Museum of Fine Arts, Boston; the Cumberland County Court House, Portland, Me.; and the New Hampshire Historical Society, Concord, N. H.

His interest extended to landscape architecture and he designed not only gardens in connection with estates, but city gardens as well. Although his inspiration came undoubtedly from his studies in Italy, his work was never imitative nor offensively archeological. In the field of landscape architecture he published *American Gardens* (1902), *Smaller Italian Villas and Farmhouses* (1916), and *More Small Italian Villas and Farmhouses* (1920). His style was charming in its informality. He was an enthusiastic amateur photographer and largely illustrated his books with his own photographs. For a number of years he lectured on landscape architecture in the Massachusetts Institute of Technology.

During the World War he entered the American Red Cross with the rank of major and served principally in Italy. There his skill, tact, courage, and gift for organization enabled him to accomplish much, and his outspoken friendship for Italy gave courage to a country which received far less attention and sympathy in America than did the better-known and better-understood allies, Great Britain and France. For this service he was awarded the Italian War Cross, with two citations, the silver medal for valor, the Order of Mauritius and Lazarus, and the Order of the Crown of Italy.

He was a lover of music, painting, and sculpture, and had more than an amateur's knowledge of these arts. After the death of his cousin, Percival Lowell [*q.v.*], he was the sole trustee of the Lowell Observatory at Flagstaff, Ariz., and the responsibility gave him a new hobby—the grinding of lenses for telescopes. He was an enthusiastic yachtsman and participated in the international races at Kiel. His death occurred suddenly, at Madeira, while he was on a vacation with his wife. His body was cremated in Italy, and the ashes brought to the United States for burial.

[A. S. Pier, "Guy Lowell," in *Harvard Grads. Mag.*, June 1927; *Harvard Coll. Class of 1892, Necrology*, Report X, pt. II (1927); D. R. Lowell, *The Hist. Geneal. of the Lowells of America* (1899); *Who's Who in America*, 1926–27; *Am. Architect*, Feb. 20, 1927; *Arch. Record*, Apr. 1927; *Architecture and Building*, Mar. 1927; *Architecture*, Apr. 1927; *Bull. Boston Soc. of Architects*, Feb. 1927; *N. Y. Times*, Feb. 5, 1927.]

G. H. E—l.

LOWELL, JAMES RUSSELL (Feb. 22, 1819–Aug. 12, 1891), author, teacher, public servant, foremost American man of letters in his time, was born and died in the same house, "Elmwood," in Cambridge, Mass. His father, the Rev. Charles Lowell, for more than forty years minister of the West Church (Unitarian), Boston, was descended from Perceval Lowell (or Lowle) who emigrated in 1639 from England to settle at Newbury in the Massachusetts colony. Immediately back of Charles Lowell in descent were two John Lowells, graduates, like himself, of Harvard College, of which his father, Judge John Lowell, 1743–1802 [*q.v.*], was a fellow. From Harriet Brackett Spence, daughter of Keith and Mary (Traill) Spence of Portsmouth, N. H., the wife of the Rev. Charles Lowell, their poetic son received a sharply different strain of inheritance. Her forebears on both sides had come from the Orkney Islands; she herself, brought up in the Episcopal Church, in which one of her sons, Robert Traill Spence Lowell [*q.v.*], became a clergyman, was of a mystical strain, with a reputed gift of second sight and a contagious love of old ballads, proper to one not impossibly related to the hero of the ballad of Sir Patrick Spens. The spirit of this mother was, indeed, so sensitive that in her final years it fell into a disorder that called forth her son's poem, "The Darkened Mind," ending with the sorrowful lines:

> "Not so much of thee is left among us
> As the hum outliving the hushed bell."

Through Lowell's boyhood and younger manhood, however, her influence played a vital part in the forming of the poet, even as the paternal strain fortified the future publicist.

After preparation at the classical school of Mr. William Wells in Cambridge he entered Harvard College. As an undergraduate he took his prescribed duties with a lightness that could meet only with disapproval from academic authorities. Promiscuous reading in the college library was not then encouraged, but without it he could hardly have formed those lasting friendships with books described in his paper on Landor. "It was," he wrote, "the merest browsing, no doubt, as Johnson called it, but how delightful it was! All the more, I fear, because it added the stolen sweetness of truancy to that of study, for I should have been buckling to my allotted task of the day. I do not regret that diversion of time to other than legitimate expenses, yet shall I not gravely warn my grandsons to beware of doing the like?" (*Latest Literary Essays*, p. 54). This tendency might have been overlooked, but at the end of his senior year came a concrete offense which could not escape punishment. In T. W. Higginson's *Old Cambridge* (1899, p. 157) and Ferris Greenslet's *James Russell Lowell* (p. 23) may be found good evidence for believing that Lowell's personal celebration of his election as class poet sent him to chapel one afternoon when he might better have gone to his room, for at the beginning of the service he rose in his place and bowed, with smiles, to left and right, as if in acknowledgment of the honor his classmates had paid him. On the ground of "continued neglect of his college duties" the faculty promptly rusticated him to the care and instruction of the Rev. Barzillai Frost in the neighboring town of Concord until "the Saturday before Commencement." Thus he was prevented from reading his own class poem, a young conservative's fling, both jaunty and grave, at causes and persons soon to enlist his sympathies. Here he is even found decrying:

> "those who roar and rave
> O'er the exaggerated tortures of the slave."

The poem is not included in his published works, but, filling thirty-nine generous pages of what has now become a rare pamphlet (*Class Poem*, 1838), it may be read as a truly promising and prophetic performance for the youth of nineteen who received his bachelor's degree with the Harvard class of 1838.

The few years of "finding himself" that followed immediately upon his leaving college were far from placid. He began the study of law, and, in spite of many uncertainties about its continuance, graduated at the Harvard Law School in 1840. An unhappy youthful love affair had made its contribution to the unsettled state of his mind. In 1866 he recalled this distressful time: "I remember in '39 putting a cocked pistol to my forehead—and being afraid to pull the trigger, of which I was heartily ashamed, and am still whenever I think of it" (*Letters,* II, 136).

It was not until he met and became engaged in marriage to Maria White, the gifted and beautiful sister of a classmate in Watertown, immediately adjoining Cambridge, that his future began to clarify itself. His prospects of self-support were so meager that their marriage had to be deferred for more than four years. Before it occurred (on Dec. 26, 1844) Lowell made his public beginnings as poet, editor, critic, and reformer. In poetry this period marked the appearance of *A Year's Life* (1841) and *Poems* (1844). The second volume contained several anti-slavery poems. Now Maria White was a devotee not only of poetry but of anti-slavery sentiments, and the happy "Band" of young people who became Lowell's intimates through his association with her was eagerly devoted to the reforms of the day, among which abolitionism ranked high. Thus the young conservative became something of a radical before he was twenty-five. As a critic of literature he printed his first book, *Conversations on Some of the Old Poets* (1845), the preface of which was dated one week before his marriage. Much of this volume had already appeared serially in the *Boston Miscellany,* edited by Nathan Hale, even as many poems in the two previous volumes had been printed first in periodicals. Though Lowell declared in later life, "I am a book-man" (see address on "The Place of the Independent in Politics," 1888, *Literary and Political Addresses,* p. 235), he might have said with equal truth, "I am a magazine man," for both as editor and as contributor he touched the periodicals of his time at an extraordinary number of points.

His first appearance as an editor was in connection with *The Pioneer: A Literary and Critical Magazine,* produced in the months of January, February, and March 1843, by Lowell and his friend Robert Carter as editors and proprietors. Whether through lack of support or through a failure of Lowell's eyesight which drove him to New York for treatment by a specialist, the venture was short-lived; but the three issues, containing contributions from Poe, Hawthorne, Whittier, and others whose names have endured, testify to Lowell's instincts and capacities as an editor. In an introduction to the first issue, setting forth the aims of *The Pioneer,* he wrote in a vein that seems contemporaneous today, even while it was prophetic of what was to befall Lowell himself: "We hear men speak of the restless spirit of the age, as if our day were peculiar in this regard. But it has always been the same . . . still the new spirit yearns and struggles and expects great things; still the Old shakes its head, ominous of universal anarchy; still the world rolls calmly on, and the youth grown old shakes its wise head at the next era."

Before completing this process himself Lowell was to live through some years of relative radicalism. Brought into the anti-slavery movement by his ardent young wife's enthusiasm for the cause and never himself counted one of its more violent advocates, he nevertheless identified himself completely with it by serving in Philadelphia for a few months immediately after his marriage as an editorial writer for the *Pennsylvania Freeman,* by continuing, on his return to Cambridge early in the summer of 1845, to write, in prose and verse, against slavery, and, within a year, by forming a connection with a New York publication, *The National Anti-Slavery Standard,* of which, two years later, in 1848, he became "corresponding editor."

Not in this quarter only did the sympathy and influence of Lowell's wife prevail with him. Her interest in reform was matched by her devotion to poetry, in which, besides the gift of appreciation, she possessed a graceful lyric faculty of her own. Their idyllic life together seemed fulfilled in the birth of their first child, Blanche, who died (in March 1847) when an infant of less than fifteen months, but lived on in lines among the best known of Lowell's shorter poems: "She Came and Went," "The Changeling," and "The First Snow-fall." A second daughter, Mabel, who survived him, was born in September 1847. A daughter, Rose, born in 1849, lived but a few months. A son, Walter, born in December 1850, died in Rome in April 1852. Before the end of the next year (Oct. 27, 1853) Mrs. Lowell, deeply affected by these losses, herself died. In 1855 a slender volume, *The Poems of Maria Lowell,* "privately printed" in Cambridge and thus offered rather to friends than to the general public, bore witness to Lowell's appreciation of his wife's poetic gift.

The year 1848, called by one of Lowell's biographers (Ferris Greenslet) his *annus mirabilis,* certainly justified that name, for during its course, besides a volume of *Poems by James Russell Lowell, Second Series,* he published *A Fable for Critics,* the first volume of *The Biglow Papers,* and *The Vision of Sir Launfal.* To his claims for consideration as a poet and critic, this output added the claims of a humorist and political satirist. Thus at twenty-nine he had made his challenge in all the fields of production in which his ultimate place among American writers must be determined. With regard to his poetry, there would be less dissent today from an opinion of Margaret Fuller's than there was either when she expressed it some three years before the *Fable for Critics* appeared or in the later decades of the nineteenth century. "His interest in the moral questions of the day," she declared, "has supplied the want of vitality in himself; his great facility at versification has enabled him to fill the ear with a copious stream of pleasant sound. But his verse is stereotyped; his thought sounds no depth, and posterity will not remember him" (*Papers on Literature and Art,* pt. II, 1846, p. 132). If posterity does not forget Margaret Fuller, it may be in part because Lowell included in his *Fable* such lines about an unmistakable "Miranda" as the following:

> "She always keeps asking if I don't observe a
> Particular likeness 'twixt her and Minerva."

As a humorist and satirist Lowell can hardly be considered apart from his qualities as a critic and political observer. In the *Fable for Critics* humor and criticism are more frankly and plentifully blended than anywhere else in his writings. The critical estimates of his contemporaries among American writers have in general proved surprisingly near to the verdicts of posterity. When he wrote about himself:

> "The top of the hill he will ne'er come nigh reaching
> Till he learns the distinction 'twixt singing and preaching,"

he forestalled what others may still say about a considerable portion of his poetic work. Nearly twenty years later he wrote in a letter to Norton (Aug. 28, 1865), "I shall never be a poet till I get out of the pulpit, and New England was all meeting-house when I was growing up" (*Letters,* II, 105). Nowhere more clearly than in the *Fable for Critics,* from its ingeniously rhymed title-page through its seventy-four pages of text in the first edition, does Lowell exhibit his facility in the twisting of words into all the shapes demanded by punning and verse-making. He was indeed an incorrigible punster in prose as well as verse. Even in a serious book review he was capable of applying to certain Shakespearian commentators "the quadrisyllabic name of the brother of Agis, King of Sparta"—in which it took a Felton to recognize Eudamidas ("White's Shakespeare," *Atlantic Monthly,* February 1859, p. 244). This, for all its elaboration, has a neatness that justifies it—which cannot be said for all of Lowell's verbal pranks. Some of his ineptitudes became apparent even to Lowell after their first commission and were removed from later printings. Witness, for example, in the course of so serious and admirable a poem as "The Cathedral" (*Atlantic Monthly,* January 1870, p. 4), the miserable interchange with an Englishman at Chartres:

> "'Esker vous ate a nabitang?' he asked;
> 'I never ate one; are they good?' asked I."

Such things are incredible, but there they are in the spontaneity of Lowell's first printing, subject to all such discount as the spirit of a period of ponderous jocosity will warrant, yet certainly dimming the luster to which he had so many valid claims as a wit and, in the eighteenth-century meaning of the term, a man of taste.

As the *Fable for Critics* illustrates, from several angles, one aspect of Lowell, so do *The Biglow Papers,* of which the first series appeared in the same year, 1848. Lowell's preoccupation with words is here displayed through the medium of dialect. Proud of his intimacy with the finer shades of the Yankee vernacular—"I reckon myself a good taster of dialects," he once wrote—he carried to an extreme of phonetic exactness his reproductions of the peculiarities of New England speech. To this somewhat elaborate vehicle of his humor another was added in the academic utterances of the Rev. Homer Wilbur, whose list of degrees in an imaginary college catalogue is one of Lowell's triumphs of fooling. Through the mingled prose and verse of this clergyman, the rustic Hosea Biglow, and other mouthpieces, Lowell delivered himself, in the first series of *Biglow Papers,* of trenchantly telling criticism of the national government in the conduct of the Mexican War, especially in relation to the possible extension of slavery. These articles, appearing in the periodical press before their assemblage between covers, produced a palpable effect upon public opinion and first gave to Lowell the place he was henceforth to occupy as a patriotic observer of political affairs whose opinions about them must be reckoned with. Nearly twenty years later the same medium of *Biglow Papers* stood ready to convey his sentiments on the Civil War—sentiments in which a distrust and dislike of England held a surprisingly large place for one who was to become one of the most acceptable of American ministers to Great Britain. Out of all the writings of James Russell Lowell, the two series of *Biglow Papers,* joining wit, highly skilful writing, and a passionate devotion to liberty and country, may be regarded as his most distinctive contribution to the literature of his time.

Between 1848 and 1853, the year of his wife's death, Lowell spent fifteen months (July 1851–October 1852) in Europe, ripening his powers by observation and study. The death of Mrs. Lowell a year after his return was a desolating blow, yet before and after it fell he busied himself with writing for magazines and with much intercourse with friends. It is significant that between 1849, when he brought out a two-volume edition of his *Poems,* and 1864, when his *Fireside Travels,* a volume of essays, appeared, he made no addition to the list of his published books. The decade ending in 1864 was nevertheless of great moment in his career. Early in its course, and immediately after his delivery (January 1855) of a series of Lowell Institute lectures in Boston on the English poets, he was appointed, in succession to Longfellow, Smith Professor of the French and Spanish Languages and Literatures, and professor of belles-lettres in Harvard College; and in 1857 he became editor of the *Atlantic Monthly,* of which the first number was issued in November of that year. In his teaching position the scholarly interests which he had long pursued as an amateur became professional interests, with the large by-product of critical writing which he was henceforth to produce. Through his editorship—four years with the *Atlantic Monthly* (1857–61), followed for several years beginning in January 1864 by an association with Charles Eliot Norton [*q.v.*] in the conduct of the *North American Review*—he not only found an outlet for his vigorous thinking on political matters and his appreciations of contemporary letters, but exerted a powerful influence in the direction of public thought and taste.

On Lowell's appointment to the Harvard professorship he went, alone, to Europe (June 1855–August 1856) for studies, especially in Germany and Italy, which should augment his qualifications for the teaching of European letters. He had left his only daughter, Mabel, in Cambridge at the home of his brother-in-law, Dr. Estes Howe, in charge of a governess, Frances Dunlap, whose admirable qualities of mind and character led to the fortunate repair of Lowell's shattered domestic structure through his marriage with her in September 1857. This was at the beginning of his second year of college teaching, in which he continued without interruption for sixteen years. After two years' intermission (August 1872–July 1874) he took it up for four years more. Nominally he held the Smith Professorship from 1855 to 1886, when he became professor emeritus for the remaining six years of his life. In Barrett Wendell's *Stelligeri* (1893, pp. 205–17) a sketch of Lowell as a teacher of Dante to a small class in a college lecture-room or, still more personally, in his own study at "Elmwood," shows forth the informal method of the sympathetic, stimulating instruction which made him one of the most memorable influences with many college generations at Cambridge.

Through his identification with the infant *Atlantic Monthly* Lowell bore a leading part in a highly significant episode in the history of American letters. The remarkable group of writers in and about Boston at the middle of the nineteenth century—Emerson, Hawthorne, Whittier, Holmes, Longfellow, and others, who had flowered simultaneously with the Unitarian reaction from the extreme Calvinism of earlier New England—was really the fortuitous springing up of a band of neighbors of diverse gifts yet with much in common. The *Atlantic,* standing for liberal thought and speech on matters of politics, religion, and letters, provided them with a single mouthpiece and afforded that sense of solidarity which contributes to the formation of a "school." Lowell proved himself an admirable editor, not merely in such larger matters of *Atlantic* policy as his insistence upon securing contributions from Holmes as a "condition precedent" to his accepting the editorship, but in the minutiæ of editing, even with respect to emendations in poems by Emerson and Whittier. He gave evidence, moreover, by his own striking contributions in prose and verse to the pages of his magazine, that he should be counted also among its best contributors.

Lowell laid down his editorship of the *Atlantic* just about the time the Civil War was beginning, and began his association with the *North American Review* when, in January 1864, it was nearing its end. During the war, however, the *Atlantic* published several political papers from his pen, besides the second series of *Biglow Papers.* From 1864 till late in 1866 he contributed to the *North American Review* a series of vigorous prose papers, afterwards assembled with earlier articles, and one later, in his *Political Essays* (1888). To Lowell's passion for freedom there was allied, in all his feeling about the war and its consequences, the poignancy of the deaths of three beloved nephews at the front. No wonder that his writings about the issues of the times, whether in prose or in verse, glowed with a special fervor. No wonder that when it fell to him to produce the "Ode Recited at the Harvard Commemoration, July 21, 1865," in honor of the sons of his college who had given their lives in the war, he produced the poem which, by common agreement, represents him at his best.

The occasion itself was memorable. Phillips Brooks, then a young clergyman settled in Philadelphia, made a prayer which seemed to eclipse all other utterances of a day on which scholars and soldiers held the center of the stage. Lowell's Ode, written at white heat on the very eve of the celebration, after many fears that it would not "come," suffered grave disadvantages: it was delivered under a strain of weariness from presiding at a Phi Beta Kappa meeting on the day before, and from much sacrifice of sleep for a final copying of the lines; and it lacked the noble strophe relating to Lincoln, which was added after the poem was read. Like Lincoln's Gettysburg Address, it seems to have fallen far short of recognition as an outstanding event of the day: indeed, in two Boston newspapers of the next morning no mention of it is found in the long accounts of the exercises. New York papers did better. From the time of its reaching the general public with its Lincoln strophe, in the *Atlantic Monthly* for September 1865, it took the place which it has held ever since, in the front rank of poems proceeding from the war and preeminent in its expression of Lowell's exalted spirit of patriotism.

Closely related to Lowell's work as a teacher in Harvard College stands the changed proportion of critical to creative writing as he grew older. A volume of poems, *Under the Willows* (1869), and a single poem, *The Cathedral* (1870), followed, to be sure, upon his *Fireside Travels*; but in 1870 also appeared another volume of essays, *Among My Books*; in 1871 still another, *My Study Windows*; and in 1876, *Among My Books,* second series. Literary criticism was the substance of all these volumes. The topics, such as Dryden, Dante, Shakespeare, and other poets, English and American, were topics with which he dealt in the classroom. They lent themselves well to treatment also for such periodicals as the *Atlantic* and the *North American Review,* and to assemblage in book form when they sufficed for a new volume.

As a critic Lowell was highly rated in his day, but with the passing of the years his stature has diminished. In *The Romantic Revolution in America* (1927), V. L. Parrington has found him an exemplar of Bostonian Victorianism (p. 436), of the united dignity and conscience of English liberalism and Cambridge Brahminism (p. 472), and has defined him as "a bookish amateur in letters, loitering over old volumes for the pleasure of finding apt phrases and verbal curiosities" (p. 461). An English student of his writings, John M. Robertson, calls him "a man primarily endowed with a great gift of copious literary expatiation, highly 'impressionistic,' and only under pressure of challenge analytic" (*North American Review,* February 1919, p. 256). W. C. Brownell, in his *American Prose Masters* (1909), alluding to Lowell's cleverness and personal charm, remarks: "Nothing is more envied in the living. Nothing finds prompter interment with their bones" (p. 277); and says of his critical work in general that it "will excel more in finding new beauties in the actual than in discovering new requirements in the ideal" (pp. 300–01). The upshot of Professor Norman Foerster's penetrating study of Lowell in his *American Criticism* (1928) is that he fell short of realizing his ambitions, "partly because his native force was inadequate, and partly because he was sucked into the current of his times" (p. 156). Nevertheless, every critic must acknowledge the breadth and alertness of his reading, the gusto and common sense that pervaded his prose writings, the exuberance of fancy and expression, the flow of humorous extravagance which he would have done well at times to check, the ardor, even the passion, of his feeling for his native land and its traditional ideals. To these qualities may be attributed his influence upon his contemporaries and the generation following.

The books that Lowell was still to write did not materially affect his place in American literature. Prose was decidedly to predominate over poetry. After 1876 two volumes of verse were published during his lifetime: *Three Memorial Poems* (1877), and *Heartsease and Rue* (1888); after his death appeared *Last Poems of James Russell Lowell* (1895). In prose—omitting pamphlets included also in collected writings—were *Democracy and Other Addresses* (1887), *Political Essays* (1888), and, after his death, *Latest Literary Essays and Addresses* (1891), *The Old English Dramatists* (1892), *Letters of James Russell Lowell* (2 vols., 1893), edited by Charles Eliot Norton, and *New Letters of James Russell Lowell* (1932), edited by M. A. De Wolfe Howe. Other posthumous publications were reprints or rescues of fugitive writings which had not seemed to him worthy of preservation.

As the literary and political essays included

in his earlier volumes had reflected his life as an editor and professor, so the later essays bore a recognizable relation to his later interests as a public servant. These began when, in 1876, he went as a delegate to the Republican National Convention, to bear his part in the defeat of Blaine and the selection of Hayes as a nominee for the presidency. Serving as a member of the Electoral College, after refusing solicitations to run for Congress, he adhered to Hayes, in the election contest with Tilden, on the clear ground that Hayes was the candidate he was chosen to support. For such party service men less qualified than Lowell for a diplomatic post have received their reward. His came in the spring of 1877, in the form of an invitation to assume the post of United States minister to Spain. His saying, "I should like to see a play of Calderon," accounted in part for the acceptance of this offer, but for nearly three years in Madrid—from the summer of 1877 to the spring of 1880—he enacted the rôle of minister with much credit to himself and his country, adapting himself well to the formalities of a ceremonious court, appreciating and appreciated by the cultivated society of Madrid, extending his knowledge of the Spanish language and literature, seizing a summer opportunity for visiting Turkey and Greece, yet sorely harassed in the third year of his mission by the serious illness of his wife. When he received notice in January 1880 that the President had nominated him minister to the Court of St. James's, his equipment for service there had greatly improved since he left home, and his immediate perception that his wife's health would probably be much the better for the change gave added reason for accepting the post.

Of Lowell in England, Henry James wrote characteristically that "some of his more fanatical friends are not to be deterred from regarding his career as in the last analysis a tribute to the dominion of style," and that "the true reward of an English style was to be sent to England" (*Essays in London and Elsewhere,* 1893, pp. 45, 55). The reward would have seemed more fitting if in earlier years Lowell's antagonism to England and the English had not been so pronounced. During the Civil War, beyond expressing himself frankly as he did in the "Jonathan to John" verses in the *Biglow Papers,* he found it nearly impossible to write to a single English correspondent. In his essay on "New England Two Centuries Ago" (*North American Review,* January 1865), he alluded to our "English cousins (as they are fond of calling themselves when they are afraid we may do them a mischief)"; and "On a Certain Condescension in Foreigners" (*Atlantic Monthly,* January 1869) contains the remark, "Not a Bull of them all but is persuaded he bears Europa upon his back." When Lowell and the English came to know each other, the war was fifteen years in the past and there was as much inclination to forgive on the one side as to forget on the other. Lowell indeed performed a notable mission of good will, besides conducting to the satisfaction of all but certain Irish-Americans the delicate relations growing out of Fenian disturbances and carrying on the general work of the London legation. At private and public dinner tables, as on ceremonial and other occasions—such as his assuming the presidency of the Birmingham and Midland Institute (Oct. 6, 1884), when he delivered one of the best of his addresses, "Democracy"—his gift of informal and formal speech kept him in constant demand. In England, as in America, his friendships with the most interesting men and women of his time played a vital part in his life. In London, as in Madrid, his wife's health was a cause of grave anxiety, and on Feb. 19, 1885, she died. A few months later the newly elected President Cleveland appointed Edward J. Phelps to succeed Lowell in London, and in June 1885 he returned to private life, mainly in America. In his six remaining summers there were four visits to England, where his many associations caused him to feel greatly at home. It was really at home, however, at "Elmwood," on Aug. 12, 1891, that he died, in his seventy-third year.

From Lowell's writings in general his personality is clearly to be deduced—ardent, affectionate, whimsical, deeply serious. In the *Letters* edited by his friend Charles Eliot Norton his characteristics are revealed perhaps most clearly and consistently. If what seems a consciously "literary" quality in the letters causes a suspicion that ultimate publication was not wholly absent from Lowell's mind, such a suspicion may be dismissed. He was himself conscious of a tendency to write as if for more than a single reader. "It is a bad thing for one's correspondents, I find," he wrote to his daughter in 1869, "that one has been lecturing these dozen years" (*Letters,* II, 215). His letters indeed seem to have been much like his talk, in which he sparkled, perhaps as brightly as his Saturday Club colleague, Dr. Holmes, though with a superiority over that friend in the capacity of listener. One of his pet topics was the detection of a Jewish strain in unexpected quarters, and "to say the truth," wrote Sir Leslie Stephen, "this was the only subject upon which I could conceive Lowell approaching within measurable distance of boring" (Lowell's *Letters,* III, 336). His occasional speeches, like his *vers d'occasion,* abounded in felicities. In more serious speeches, of which his address (Nov. 8, 1886) at the 250th anniversary of the founding of Harvard University is an admirable example, he gave impressive utterance to his ripened wisdom.

Professor Norman Foerster, in an appraisal of Lowell (*American Criticism,* p. 150), states that he "stood forth among his contemporaries because of his accomplished versatility rather than because of high attainment." Lowell himself, in his essay on Carlyle, wrote that "real fame depends rather on the sum of an author's powers than on any brilliancy of special parts" (*My Study Windows,* p. 58). In special parts Lowell was abundantly brilliant, but the parts were so many and diverse—all of his writings being capable of separate or loosely connected magazine publication—that the effect of his work in its totality is inevitably diffused, and suffers in comparison with that of writers, perhaps of more limited abilities, who employed them with greater concentration. His *Biglow Papers,* a few of his poems, a few of his essays, seem forty years after his death to be compacted of the stuff of permanence. The great body of his work today offers its reward chiefly to the student of Lowell's time and of Lowell as an eminent figure of that period.

[The first important edition of Lowell's collected works was *The Writings of James Russell Lowell,* Riverside Edition (10 vols., 1890), to which vols. XI and XII, *Latest Literary Essays and Addresses* and *The Old English Dramatists,* ed. by C. E. Norton, were added in 1891 and 1892; the most comprehensive collection is *The Complete Writings of James Russell Lowell,* Elmwood Edition (16 vols., 1904), which includes the letters, ed. by Norton, in 3 vols. Citations in the foregoing article, except where otherwise indicated, are of the Elmwood Edition. Noteworthy collections of fugitive writings are *Lectures on English Poets* (printed for the Rowfant Club, Cleveland, 1897), being the Lowell Inst. Lectures of 1855, repr. from the *Boston Daily Advertiser*; *The Anti-Slavery Papers of James Russell Lowell* (2 vols., 1902), repr. from the *Pa. Freeman* and the *Nat. Anti-Slavery Standard*; and *Impressions of Spain* (1899), comp. from the Diplomatic Correspondence by J. B. Gilder, with introduction by A. A. Adee. Bibliographies include: L. S. Livingston, *A Bibliog. of the First Editions in Book Form of the Writings of James Russell Lowell* (1914); G. W. Cooke, *A Bibliog. of James Russell Lowell* (1906); and that comp. by Irita Van Doren for *The Cambridge Hist. of Am. Lit.,* II (1918), 544 ff. The main sources of biographical material are *Letters of James Russell Lowell* (2 vols., 1894), ed. by C. E. Norton and *New Letters of James Russell Lowell* (1932), ed. by M. A. DeWolfe Howe. The *Papers Relating to the Foreign Relations of the U. S.,* 1877–85, contain the record of his diplomatic career. See also H. E. Scudder, *James Russell Lowell* (2 vols. 1901); Ferris Greenslet, *James Russell Lowell* (1905); E. E. Hale, *James Russell Lowell and His Friends* (1899); E. E. Hale, Jr., *James Russell Lowell* (1899); A. L. Lowell, memoir in *Proc. Mass. Hist. Soc.,* 2 ser. XI (1897); G. W. Curtis, *James Russell Lowell, An Address* (1892); A. H. Thorndike, "Lowell," in *The Cambridge Hist. of Am. Lit.,* vol. II (1918); J. J. Reilly, *James Russell Lowell as a Critic* (1915); E. W. Emerson, *The Early Years of the Saturday Club* (1918); D. R. Lowell, *The Hist. Geneal. of the Lowells of America* (1899); *Letters of John Holmes to James Russell Lowell and Others* (1917), ed. by W. R. Thayer; W. D. Howells, *Literary Friends and Acquaintance* (1900).] M. A. DeW. H.

LOWELL, JOHN (June 17, 1743–May 6, 1802), legislator, jurist, born at Newburyport, Mass., was the only son of the Rev. John and Sarah (Champney) Lowell. His father, pastor of the First Religious Society of Newburyport, was descended from Perceval Lowell (or Lowle), who emigrated from Bristol, England, to Newbury in 1639. John, after graduating from Harvard in 1760, studied law in the office of Oxenbridge Thacher, in Boston, and was admitted to the Massachusetts bar. Returning to his native town, he early took part in public affairs. In 1767 he was chosen to draft a report upon a letter from the selectmen of Boston concerning plans for resistance to obnoxious acts of Parliament. He was a selectman of Newburyport in 1771, 1772, 1774, and 1776; in April of the last-mentioned year he was delegate to a county convention called to prepare plans for a more equal representation of voters in the General Court, and in the following month he represented Newburyport in the Provincial Congress and was apparently a major in the militia.

In 1777 he moved to Boston and in 1778 represented that town in the General Court. In 1779–80 he was a delegate to the state constitutional convention. It has frequently been asserted, on the basis of a letter from his son, Rev. Charles Lowell, to Charles E. Stevens in 1856, that he was responsible for introducing into the declaration of rights the words "free and equal," which the courts later decided excluded slavery from the state. Since, however, the declaration was adopted practically as drafted by John Adams, and the phrase in question was similar to phrases used previously in the Virginia and Pennsylvania declarations, Lowell was probably not its author. He was decidedly in favor of abolishing slavery, however, and showed his sympathy with the negro on several occasions. (Deane, *post.*)

He was a member of the Continental Congress in 1782 and 1783, and in the former year was appointed one of three judges to hear appeals in Admiralty cases. In 1784 he was made a member of the Harvard Corporation, and served, with great benefit to the college, until his death. In 1784 also he was a member of the commission appointed to settle the boundary dispute between Massachusetts and New York. In 1789 he became a United States judge for the district of Massachusetts and in 1801 was appointed chief judge of the First Circuit (Maine, Massachusetts, New Hampshire, and Rhode Island) under the new organization of the United States courts. He was for many years president of the Massachusetts Agricultural Society, and contributed greatly to the establishment of the Botanic Garden at Cambridge. He was also one of the founders of the American Academy of Arts and Sciences (1780), and an occasional writer in verse and prose. Several distinguished men, one of whom was Harrison Gray Otis, began their legal careers in his office.

One of the most upright, capable, public-spirited, and cultured citizens of his state in his time, Lowell was the worthy progenitor of a notable family. By his first marriage (Jan. 3, 1767), to Sarah, sister of Stephen Higginson [*q.v.*], he was the father of two daughters and a son, John, 1769–1840 [*q.v.*]. His second wife, Susanna Cabot of Salem, whom he married May 31, 1774, bore him a daughter and a son, Francis Cabot Lowell [*q.v.*], for whom the city of Lowell is named. After her death he married, third, Rebecca (Russell) Tyng, widow of James Tyng of Dunstable and daughter of James and Katharine (Graves) Russell of Charlestown. Of this union there were three daughters and a son, Charles, who became the father of James Russell and Robert T. S. Lowell [*qq.v.*]. Judge Lowell died in Roxbury toward the close of his fifty-ninth year.

[Emory Washburn, *Sketches of the Judicial Hist. of Mass.* (1840); J. J. Currier, *"Ould Newbury"* (1896) and *Hist. of Newburyport, Mass.* (2 vols., 1906–09); Josiah Quincy, *The Hist. of Harvard Univ.* (1840), vol. II; D. R. Lowell, *The Hist. Geneal. of the Lowells of America* (1899); Charles Deane, "Judge Lowell and the Massachusetts Declaration of Rights," *Proc. Mass. Hist. Soc.*, XIII (1875), 299–304, and XIV (1876), 108–09.]

J. T. A.

LOWELL, JOHN (Oct. 6, 1769–Mar. 12, 1840), lawyer, political writer, was born in Newburyport, Mass., the son of Judge John Lowell, 1743–1802 [*q.v.*], and his first wife, Sarah (Higginson) Lowell. He was a half-brother of Francis Cabot Lowell [*q.v.*]. Entering Harvard in 1783, he graduated in 1786, and in 1789 was admitted to the bar. Brilliant and enthusiastic, he soon acquired a wide and lucrative practice. On June 8, 1793, he married Rebecca Amory. He ably represented Boston in the Massachusetts legislature from 1798 to 1800 (Lodge, *post,* p. 298). His active professional career ended in 1803, when, his health broken through overwork, he went abroad for a three-year rest. Already he had amassed a sufficient fortune to retire for the remainder of his life.

After his return to Massachusetts in 1806 he took an active part in the political controversies of the day, writing vigorous pamphlets and letters to the press, generally supporting the Federalist point of view, and opposing the Embargo, Madison, the "French alliance," and the War of 1812. An expression in one of his papers gained him the sobriquet of "the little Rebel" or "the Boston Rebel." He opposed the Hartford Convention because "it would not go far enough" (Pickering Papers, XXX, 325). Though he was consequently and with some justification (Lodge, *post,* pp. 128–29) regarded as a secessionist, he denied the allegation. His *Review of a Treatise on Expatriation by George Hay Esquire* (1814) is said to have been influential in persuading the government not to retaliate for the death of three British deserters captured in the Chesapeake affair (Greenwood, *post,* pp. 16–17). Henry Adams (*post,* VIII, 5) refers to him as "literary representative" of Timothy Pickering [*q.v.*], and their correspondence indicates that Pickering often dictated Lowell's political views (see particularly Pickering Papers, XV, 64 and XXX, 325). Because of his failure to sign his writings and his distaste for publicity it is difficult to estimate his importance. Unquestionably influential in New England, his pamphlets seem to have been generally unknown elsewhere (Pickering Papers, XXXVIII, 114).

From 1810 to 1822 he was a member of the Harvard Corporation; from 1823 to 1827, an Overseer. He was a founder of the Massachusetts General Hospital and the Provident Institution for Savings, as well as an early and influential member of the Boston Athenæum, Massachusetts Agricultural Society, Massachusetts Historical Society, and American Antiquarian Society. After his retirement he quietly gave both money and legal services to those in need. His religious articles were widely read; his contributions to the current controversy about the constitutions of the Massachusetts Congregational churches were considered valuable. His writing, clear, forceful, and carefully argued, was praised by such men as Edward Everett, John Jay, and John Marshall. He was a scientific farmer and cattle-breeder, a competent botanist, and a frequent contributor to the *New England Farmer.* On his Roxbury farm he had some of the finest greenhouses in the country, the first to be built on truly scientific principles. He loved farming, and "wanted only to be known as the 'Norfolk Farmer'" (D. R. Lowell, *post,* p. 58). The following titles are representative, among his many pamphlets: *Mr. Madison's War* (by a New England Farmer), issued in 1812; *Are You a Christian or a Calvinist?* (by a Layman), 1815; *An Address Delivered Before the Massachusetts Agricultural Society* (1818).

Through his son John Amory Lowell he was the grandfather of John Lowell, 1824–1897 [*q.v.*] and the great-grandfather of Percival [*q.v.*], Amy [*q.v.*], and Abbott Lawrence Lowell.

[F. W. P. Greenwood, *A Sermon on the Death of John Lowell, LL.D.* (1840); Pickering Papers (MSS.), in Mass. Hist. Soc.; John Amory Lowell, "Memoir of John Lowell," *Proc. Mass. Hist. Soc., 1835–55,* 1 ser. II (1880); *Proc. Mass. Hist. Soc.,* 2 ser. XII (1899), 114; Edward Everett, *A Memoir of Mr. John Lowell, Jun.* (1840); D. R. Lowell, *The Hist. Geneal. of the Lowells of America* (1899); Theophilus Parsons, *Memoir of Theophilus Parsons* (1859); F. S. Drake, *The Town of Roxbury* (1878); H. C. Lodge, *Life and Letters of George Cabot* (1877); Henry Adams, *Hist. of the U. S.,* vol. VIII (1891); and *Documents Relating to New England Federalism* (1877); S. E. Morison, *Life and Letters of Harrison Gray Otis* (2 vols., 1913).] G. S. J.

LOWELL, JOHN (May 11, 1799–Mar. 4, 1836), founder of the Lowell Institute, was born in Boston. His father, Francis Cabot Lowell [*q.v.*], was the pioneer of cotton manufacturing in the United States; his mother, Hannah (Jackson) Lowell, was the daughter of the wealthy and locally esteemed Jonathan Jackson. Such aristocratic parentage brought wealth and social prominence to the son. His preparatory education was gained in the schools of Boston and Edinburgh, Scotland. He entered Harvard College in 1813, but the ill health which seems to have pursued so many youthful collegians of those days compelled his withdrawal two years later. Then came long voyages to India, partly for recuperation, partly for instruction in a phase of his father's business. In 1817 he returned to Boston and there began his business career. He gave little more attention to his affairs, however, than was necessary. His main interests were intellectual. He read widely and wisely, and rapidly acquired a large and well-selected library. Public affairs also attracted his attention; he sat in the city council and in the state legislature. Here again, however, his interests were more philosophical than practical. John Lowell was an observer of life far more than an active participant in it.

The peaceful and conventional course of his life was rudely shattered when successive deaths in the years 1830 and 1831 deprived him of his wife, Georgina Margaret (Amory) Lowell, whom he had married in 1825, and the two children, both daughters, who had been born of this happy union. A settled existence in Boston henceforth became distasteful to him and he spent the remainder of his short life in travel. He died in Bombay, India, before he was thirty-seven.

The endowment of Lowell Institute is provided for in a will which Lowell drew up in 1832 and in a codicil added in 1835. New England, he observed, was a "sterile and unproductive land." Its prosperity depended on the moral qualities, the intelligence, and the information of its inhabitants. Motivated by this idea, he sought to provide free or practically free lectures of the highest type in all branches of human knowledge. He bequeathed half of his estate, amounting to approximately $250,000, for the establishment of a trust, and made intelligent stipulations for its administration and increase.

Lowell combined two dominant tendencies of the New England educational movement of his day: the "higher lecture for the average citizen," and provision for adult education. The Institute was so liberally endowed, and the trust has been so skilfully administered, that the best work of the world's leading scholars has been made accessible to Boston audiences and, through publication of the lectures, to a much larger reading public. In a sense also the Institute has been a patron of learning, since its liberal stipends have served as an encouragement to those who have been called to its lecture platform. In all respects the Lowell Institute stands as a foundation-stone in the cultural life of New England and as a happy monument to him who placed it there.

[The chief source of information is Edward Everett's excellent *Memoir of Mr. John Lowell, Jun.* (1840). See also Harriette Knight Smith, *The History of the Lowell Inst.* (1898); D. R. Lowell, *The Hist. Geneal. of the Lowells of America* (1899); Justin Winsor, *Memorial Hist. of Boston,* vol. IV (1881).] P. H. B.

LOWELL, JOHN (Oct. 18, 1824–May 14, 1897), jurist, was born in Boston. His father, John Amory Lowell, was the son of John Lowell, 1769–1840 [*q.v.*]; his mother, Susan Cabot (Lowell), was the daughter of Francis Cabot Lowell [*q.v.*]. From private schools he went to Harvard, graduating from the college with distinction in 1843 and from the law school in 1845. After studying in the office of Charles G. Loring, he was admitted to the Boston bar in 1846. Directly afterwards he spent a year abroad. His early practice, in association with his brother-in-law, William Sohier, chiefly concerned trust estates. He began practice alone in 1857. The panic and his family mill connections brought him into much litigation which made him a lifelong expert in insolvency law. In 1853 he married Lucy Buckminster Emerson of Boston, daughter of George B. Emerson [*q.v.*] and his first wife, Olivia Buckminster, who was of New Hampshire stock. They had three sons and four daughters. In 1858 Lowell purchased a large farm at Chestnut Hill where he lived the rest of his life. Though he was a small man, not especially robust, his constant activity in walking about his land, planning its development, kept him free from any illness until shortly before his death. The beautiful grounds, with the pond, woods, and wild flowers, were by his tacit consent almost common property. From 1856 to 1860 he edited the *Monthly Law Reporter* (volumes XIX–XXII), assisted the last two years by S. M. Quincey. An article adversely criticizing the Dred Scott decision, by Lowell and Horace Gray, was published in the *Law Reporter,* June 1857, and reprinted as a pamphlet with the title, *A Legal Review of the Case of Dred Scott* (1857).

In March 1865, President Lincoln appointed Lowell United States district judge for Massachusetts. Many of his most interesting opinions deal with marine controversies. These show a strong sense of practical situations and emergencies. "They smell of the sea; you can almost smell the tar, almost hear the wind rustling through the rigging" (*Proceedings of the Bench and Bar, post,* p. 23). The enactment in 1867 of a national Bankruptcy Act, after an interval of twenty years, gave him the opportunity to display his mastery of that field. His promotion in 1878 to be circuit judge for the first circuit transferred his work to the common law and patents. He disliked patent cases at first, but soon handled them with sound common sense and an acute perception of mechanical facts.

In his judicial opinions Lowell cited few cases. His wide knowledge of precedents took shape chiefly in a clear and orderly statement of principles. Every proposition was ultimately tested for its practical working value. He realized keenly the human factors of a case, and had a remarkable instinct for perceiving on which side real justice lay. One of the bar of his court said: "He would not, unless the law and the evidence compelled him, do what he thought was a practical injustice. And it seldom happened that he found himself so compelled. He had a marvellous talent for escaping from that difficulty" (*Ibid.,* p. 45). Consequently, some called him a wayward judge, independent to the verge of wilfulness in establishing justice. When he resigned his office in 1884, the merchants of Boston took the unusual course of giving him a public dinner in recognition of his able solution of commercial questions. They requested him to prepare a new bankruptcy act, that of 1867 having been repealed. His draft was printed but not adopted. He also wrote *A Treatise on the Law of Bankruptcy* (2 vols., 1899), which was completed after his death by his son, James A. Lowell, and is still useful, although much of the author's knowledge was superseded by the Act of 1898.

After his retirement Lowell had a large practice. He did not quite cease to be a judge, for he was frequently selected as arbitrator or referee in important controversies. On the bench his uniform courtesy had often relieved a young practitioner of all embarrassment and aided him in the proper presentation of his case, and in later life his learning and experience were always at the service of younger members of the bar. He was an Overseer of Harvard, and had long service on the board of the Massachusetts General Hospital. In 1896 he became chairman of the commission to revise the Massachusetts tax laws.

He was a delightful conversationalist, who walked up and down as he talked. His fund of humor never failed even on the bench. A man of very strong likes and dislikes, he was consciously on guard to prevent their affecting his judicial action.

[*Judgments Delivered in the Courts of the U. S. for the Dist. of Mass.* (2 vols., 1872–77); *Proc. of the Bench and Bar of the Circuit Court of the U. S., Dist. of Mass., upon the Decease of Hon. John Lowell* (1897); T. K. Lothrop, in *Proc. Am. Acad. Arts and Sci.,* vol. XXXV (1900), and *Proc. Mass. Hist. Soc.,* 2 ser. XI (1897); D. R. Lowell, *The Hist. Geneal. of the Lowells of America* (1899); *Later Years of the Saturday Club* (1927), ed. by M. A. DeW. Howe; *Boston Transcript,* May 14, 1897. Judge Lowell's portrait hangs in the U. S. District Courtroom in Boston.]

Z. C., Jr.

LOWELL, JOSEPHINE SHAW (Dec. 16, 1843–Oct. 12, 1905), philanthropist and reformer, was born in West Roxbury, Mass., to a family of wealth and high traditions. Her father, Francis George Shaw, was esteemed for his learning, his integrity, and his wise administration of the fortune inherited from his merchant father, Robert Gould Shaw, of Boston. Her mother, a cousin of her father, was Sarah Blake Sturgis, daughter of Nathaniel Russell Sturgis, also a Boston merchant. When Josephine was three years old the family moved to Staten Island, which remained her home until 1874, when a New York residence became the center of her manifold activities. In 1851 her father took his family abroad and until she was twelve she was in school at Paris or Rome. A year in Miss Gibson's school, New York, and another in a Boston school completed her formal training, from which she probably gained less than from her association with her parents and the group of friends which they drew to the home. After 1856, when he married her sister Anna, George William Curtis [*q.v.*] was a member of the household, and Josephine frequented his library and was much influenced by him. Her diary, kept for a few months after the outbreak of the

Civil War, gives an excellent idea of her intellectual development and her qualities of character at this time, while it also describes the mingled feelings of the Northern group to which she belonged, as the war news came from day to day (Stewart, *post,* pp. 10–37). The war brought her the greatest sorrows of her life. On July 19, 1863, her brilliant young brother, Robert Gould Shaw, was killed at Fort Wagner, and on Oct. 19, 1864, less than a year after her marriage (Oct. 31, 1863), she lost her husband, Col. Charles Russell Lowell, a nephew of James Russell Lowell [*q.v.*]. Six weeks after his death a daughter, Carlotta Russell, was born to the young widow.

With the close of the war she interested herself in the Freedmen's Association, in local hospitals of New York, and in the work of the State Charities Aid Association. In connection with the last named she prepared a report on the methods, the scope, and the results of the administration of the poor law in West Chester County, with special attention to the old problem of the "sturdy beggar." The competence displayed in this report attracted the attention of Gov. Samuel J. Tilden, who in 1876 made her a member of the State Board of Charities, the first woman to be appointed to that board. During her thirteen years of service, she was concerned with the housing and reform of vagrants, and the care of delinquent women, the mental defectives, and the insane. Her reports on these and kindred topics, based on a wealth of information and a thorough familiarity with the history of poor law administration, were models of clarity and cogency. In 1889, convinced that the most effective attack on the problem of poverty was to be made by adjusting the difficulties between capital and labor, she resigned from the State Board to devote more of her energy to the improvement of industrial conditions.

Her most enduring monument, however, is the Charity Organization Society, which she founded and to which she gave unremitting service for twenty-three years. She was also one of the organizers of the Consumer's League and an active worker for civil service reform, municipal lodging houses, and many other good causes. Reports and addresses on such subjects constitute the bulk of her published work. Over forty of these have been printed, all characterized by insight and vigor. Of her other publications, the most important perhaps are *Public Relief and Private Charity* (1884) and *Industrial Arbitration and Conciliation: Some Chapters from the Industrial History of the Past Thirty Years* (1893). Her achievements are attributable to a rare combination of courageous idealism and practical common sense. Her judgment as to ways and means was never that of a fanatic but rather that of a sagacious person, who was willing to wait for results but never lost sight of the ultimate goal.

[W. R. Stewart, *The Philanthropic Work of Josephine Shaw Lowell* (1911) contains biog. sketch, extracts from reports, and list of writings; see also *Charities and the Commons,* Dec. 2, 1905, Jan. 27, 1906; E. W. Emerson, *Life and Letters of Charles Russell Lowell* (1907); *Outlook,* Oct. 21, 1905.] E. D.

LOWELL, PERCIVAL (Mar. 13, 1855–Nov. 12, 1916), astronomer, business man, and gifted writer, brother of Amy Lowell [*q.v.*], was born in Boston, Mass. His father was Augustus Lowell, a brother of John Lowell, 1824–1897 [*q.v.*]; his mother, Katharine Bigelow (Lawrence), was the daughter of Abbott Lawrence [*q.v.*], United States minister to Great Britain in 1851. Lowell prepared for college at Noble's School and graduated from Harvard in 1876, distinguishing himself particularly in mathematics. After a year of travel in Europe and the East he returned to Boston. He rapidly became a force in the business world, taking an active part in the development of cotton-mills, trust, and electric companies.

The years 1883 to 1893 were spent in travel and writing in the Far East, chiefly in Japan. Soon after his arrival in Tokyo he was appointed counselor and foreign secretary to the special mission from Korea to the United States; and at the conclusion of this mission he went to Korea as the guest of the government. His travels there are described in *Chöson—The Land of the Morning Calm* (1885). His *Soul of the Far East,* published in 1888, shows a remarkable insight into the Oriental mind. Lafcadio Hearn, in recommending this book to a friend, wrote: "Please don't skip one solitary line of it and don't delay reading it,—because something, much! is going to go out of it into your heart and life and stay there!" (letter in G. M. Gould, *Concerning Lafcadio Hearn,* 1908, p. 116). Lowell's *Noto,* a delightful account of his rambles in Japan, appeared in 1891, and his interest in the strange rites of Shintoism, awakened by a trip up the sacred mountain of Ontaki, resulted in *Occult Japan,* published in 1895.

With all his other interests and activities he retained a keen taste for mathematics and astronomy. In a letter to Hector MacPherson he said that his interest in the latter study dated "from 1870, when I used to look at Mars with as keen an interest as now." In 1877 he spent many hours on his father's roof gazing at Mars with a 2-inch telescope, and his enthusiasm was fired anew in that year by Schiaparelli's announcement of the discovery of fine markings on Mars which the Italian astronomer called *Canali.* It was not until the early nineties, however, that Lowell's many-sided interests allowed him to devote his main energies and fortune to astronomy. Schiaparelli's eye-sight had failed and Lowell determined to carry on the work. Realizing that the first essential in planetary observation is good "seeing," he first investigated, with an admirable curb on his impatience, the steadiness and cloudlessness of the atmosphere in various parts of the world. "A large instrument in poor air," he said, "will not begin to show what a smaller one in good air will. When this is recognized . . . it will become the fashion to put up observatories where they may see rather than be seen" (*Mars,* p. v). His final choice as the site for his observatory was the mesa three hundred feet above the town of Flagstaff, Ariz., at an altitude of 7,200 feet, "far from the smoke of men." Isolation in an undeveloped country necessitated the gathering not only of a staff of observers, but also mechanics and carpenters to build the instruments, domes, machine shop, and houses, and laborers to build roads, cut the winter's supply of wood, and milk the cows. Lowell's own picturesque, rambling house, which he called the "Baronial Mansion," was built on the edge of the mesa where he could look through and over the age-old pines of the Conconino Forest, across a plain, to the San Francisco Peaks. "The Peaks this morning are white-laced from yesterday's storm, a white mantilla over their heads and shoulders," he wrote on one occasion (Leonard, *post,* p. 70).

Observation was begun on "Mars Hill" in 1894 with an 18-inch refractor. This was replaced two years later with a 24-inch. Since then, a 40-inch reflector and many smaller instruments and accessories have been added. Visual, photographic, and micrometric observations of Mars and their careful discussion are prominent in the three volumes of the *Annals of the Lowell Observatory,* vol. I (1898), vol. II (1900), vol. III (1905), and in many of the *Bulletins,* started in 1903. What Lowell saw was, in his own words, "over a geography not unakin to the Earth's . . . a mesh of lines and dots like a lady's veil." The gradually increasing conspicuousness of the markings in lower latitudes as the "wave of quickening" spread from the shrinking polar cap, the spectroscopic evidence of water-vapor, the color changes in the blue-green areas, all strengthened his conviction that Mars is the abode of intelligent life. Interest at the Observatory, however, was not long confined to Mars. Mercury, Venus, and all the other planets as well as their satellites were subjected to the same careful study and measurement. Some of the most reliable values for diameter, oblateness, and rotation periods of planets and satellites were derived at the Lowell Observatory. New divisions in Saturn's rings were seen. Lowell was quite justified in stating in one of his lectures that the study of the solar system "is chiefly carried on at the present time by the observatory which I represent." It was not long, either, before members of the staff carried the campaign far out beyond the solar system, in the spectroscopic study of clusters and nebulae. Lowell himself contributed researches on the development of the solar system, the structure of Saturn's rings, and the problem of a trans-Neptunian planet. The discovery of Planet X in January 1930 was the direct result of his mathematical prediction.

His passionate interest in the planets embraced also the earth. "The planet Mars was the only rival to his botanical love. Study of the trees was his chief delight in his tramps afield." His letters are full of delightful records, such as: "May 13. Holly and Potentilla canadensis near the mullein patch. Radishes big enough to eat, *and eaten*" (Leonard, p. 76). There are also references to "Paint Brush Point," "Arrowhead Hills," and "Holly Ravine."

Lowell believed ardently that the results of scientific research should be made accessible to all, by voice and pen. He was a brilliant lecturer and his books on astronomical subjects are delightful reading. Among these are *Mars* (1895); *The Solar System* (1903); *Mars and Its Canals* (1906); *Mars as the Abode of Life* (1908); *The Evolution of Worlds* (1909); *The Genesis of the Planets* (1916). He was appointed non-resident professor of astronomy at the Massachusetts Institute of Technology in 1902. He received medals from the astronomical societies of France and Mexico and honorary membership in the Royal Astronomical Society of Canada. In 1908 he married Constance Savage Keith, of Boston. He died in his sixty-second year and was buried on Mars Hill, close beside the 24-inch telescope with which the work he started is being carried forward through his endowment.

[Louise Leonard, *Percival Lowell—An Afterglow* (1921); Hector MacPherson, "Percival Lowell, an Appreciation," *Observatory,* Jan. 1917; *Percival Lowell* (1917), pub. by the Lowell Observatory; R. G. Aitken, in *Pubs. Astronomical Soc. of the Pacific,* XXVIII (1916), 266–68; A. Fowler, in *Nature,* Nov. 23, 1916; *Popular Astronomy,* Apr. 1917; G. R. Agassiz, in *Proc. Am. Acad. Arts and Sci.,* vol. LII (1917); D. R. Lowell, *The Hist. Geneal. of the Lowells of America*

(1899); *Harvard College, the Class of 1876* (1926); *Ariz. Republican* (Phoenix), and *N. Y. Times*, Nov. 14, 1916.] R. S. D.

LOWELL, ROBERT TRAILL SPENCE (Oct. 8, 1816–Sept. 12, 1891), Protestant Episcopal clergyman and author, was born in Boston, Mass. He was the son of Rev. Charles Lowell, a distinguished Unitarian clergyman, minister of the West Church, and of Harriet Brackett Spence. The fifth in a family of six children, he was the older brother by three years of James Russell Lowell [*q.v.*]. He began his education at the Round Hill School in Northampton, Mass., an institution founded by Joseph Green Cogswell [*q.v.*], who had been a tutor at Harvard and also librarian of the college, and was thus favorably known to the Lowell family. Cogswell seems to have made a profound impression on his young pupil, who years later dedicated to him a book of poems with "love and reverence." From Round Hill, Robert went to Harvard, where he graduated in 1833. He then went through a full course of medicine but, without taking a degree, abandoned his medical pursuits to go into business with his eldest brother. Three years later, however, he decided to enter the ministry of the Protestant Episcopal Church, in which his mother had been reared, and went to Schenectady, N. Y., to study for holy orders under Dr. Alonzo Potter, who had been rector of St. Paul's Church in Boston.

On the invitation of Bishop A. G. Spencer, young Lowell went in 1842 to Bermuda, where he was ordained deacon, and the next year (1843) was ordained priest and appointed domestic chaplain to the Bishop. Later he was transferred at his own request to Newfoundland, where he took a missionary post at Bay Roberts as representative of the English Society for the Propagation of the Gospel. On a trip home in 1845, he married, on Oct. 28, Mary Ann (Marianna) Duane, of Duanesburg, N. Y., by whom he had seven children. Shortly after his return to Newfoundland, he encountered a famine in which he suffered with his parishioners, and, broken in health, returned in 1847 to America after receiving the thanks of the Colonial Secretary. By appointment of Bishop G. W. Doane, he began a mission in a poor quarter of Newark, N. J., where he reëstablished and rebuilt a neglected church. In 1859 he became rector of Christ Church, Duanesburg, N. Y. In 1868 he was appointed professor of belles-lettres in Racine College, Wisconsin, but declined. After ten years' work among the farming people of Duanesburg, he accepted in 1869 the headmastership of St. Mark's School, Southboro, Mass. In 1873 he was made professor of Latin language and literature in Union College, Schenectady, N. Y., and remained in this position until 1879. He died on Sept. 12, 1891, just a month after the death of his more famous brother.

Robert Lowell was a delicate, sensitive, strangely rarefied soul. In his missionary experiences, at home and abroad, he displayed something of that robust quality which was characteristic of his family, but he had mystic elements which were all his own. The literary gift of the Lowells he shared; he wrote with facility and occasional distinction. Several of his books were the product of his varied personal experiences. Thus, *The New Priest in Conception Bay*, a story which appeared in 1858, contained vivid pictures of Newfoundland. This book, an excellent piece of work, was published by Phillips, Sampson & Company just as the senior partner died and the firm went into bankruptcy. It thus had a poor start, and though republished years later never enjoyed the popularity and fame it merited. A book for boys, *Antony Brade, a Story of a School* (1874), grew out of Lowell's experiences as headmaster of St. Mark's. His life at Schenectady suggested *A Story or Two from an Old Dutch Town* (1878). He published also *Fresh Hearts that Failed Three Thousand Years Ago, with Other Things* (1860), a volume of *Poems* (1864), and occasional verses, short stories, sermons, and addresses. His best-known poem, the spirited "Relief of Lucknow," appeared in the *Atlantic Monthly* (February 1858) under his brother's editorship.

[D. R. Lowell, *The Hist. Geneal. of the Lowells of America* (1899); *Memorials of the Class of 1833 of Harvard College* (1883); H. C. Scudder, *James Russell Lowell, A Biog.* (2 vols., 1901); *Appletons' Ann. Cyc. of 1891* (1892); *The Churchman*, Sept. 19, 1891; *Boston Transcript*, Sept. 14, 1891.] J. H. H.

LOWERY, WOODBURY (Feb. 17, 1853–Apr. 11, 1906), lawyer, annotator and editor of law books, historian, collector of maps, was the only son of Archibald H. Lowery, merchant, and Frances Anstriss Woodbury, daughter of Levi Woodbury [*q.v.*]. Born in New York City, he spent several years with his parents in Europe, gaining an unusual cultural and linguistic equipment. He graduated from Harvard in 1875 and continued there two years more in the chemical laboratory, receiving in 1876 the degree of M.A. His thesis "On Parabrombenzyl Compounds" appears in the *Proceedings of the American Academy of Arts and Sciences* (n.s. vol. IX, 1877). Meanwhile, his parents had removed (1873) to Washington, D. C., where the young chemist now went seeking a place in the Smithsonian Institution or the Department of Agriculture. Failing in this he studied law at Columbian University (LL.B., 1880, LL.M., 1881), was admitted to the bar in 1881, and entered the firm of Baldwin, Hopkins & Peyton. Early in his practice, he took up legal editorial work and gave to it most of his time for fifteen years. His publications in this field include: *Patents, Copyright, and Trade-Marks* (1886), edited in collaboration with W. D. Baldwin, which is Volume XXV of Myer's *Federal Decisions*; volumes IV–XX of *Brodix's American and English Patent Cases* (1887–92); *Interference Proceedings in the United States Patent Office* (1891); and *Index-Digest to the Decisions of the Supreme Court of the United States in Patent Causes* (1897).

Following the example of his uncle, Charles Levi Woodbury, who from deliberate choice had remained a bachelor, he did not marry, finding the close companionship of his parents and his only sister Virginia all that his quiet, studious nature seemed to need. But now, in the space of a few months, his home circle was obliterated. His mother died in June 1895; in August his sister married, and went with her husband, José Brunetti, Duke de Arcos, to his post of Spanish minister to Mexico; his father died in April 1896. Lowery now abandoned the law and gave the remainder of his life, ten years, to historical work. On the advice of his uncle he chose for his field a synthetic treatment of Spain's policy in her North American possessions—the reasons for her preliminary success, her later apathy, her final decadence. He collected and studied indefatigably all printed sources. The Duke de Arcos aided in opening to him archives hitherto inaccessible. He traveled widely, spending many months in research in the archives and libraries of Mexico, Madrid, Seville, London, Paris, and Rome.

In 1901 appeared the first volume of the work which preserves his name: *The Spanish Settlements Within the Present Limits of the United States, 1513–61*; the second volume, devoted to Florida, 1562–74, was published in 1905. Authoritative criticism declares this work to combine in a rare degree accuracy of statement with charm of literary style. He was encouraged to make extensive notes for more volumes—never to appear. After a sudden illness of a few days, he died at Taormina, Sicily, Apr. 11, 1906. He left to the Library of Congress his manuscripts, such of his books as it might select, his 300 early maps, with an elaborate descriptive list of them which the Library published in 1912 as *The Lowery Collection*. In his memory his sister and her husband established at Harvard a fund of $20,000 in aid of historical research.

[A sketch by Lowery's sister, in P. L. Phillips, *The Lowery Collection*, with portrait, is the chief authority. See also the class records for the Harvard University class of 1875; *Harvard Grads.' Mag.*, June 1906; *Washington Post*, Apr. 15, 1906.] F. W. A.

LOWNDES, LLOYD (Feb. 21, 1845–Jan. 8, 1905), governor of Maryland, was a member of a family which had been conspicuous in social and political affairs of Maryland from the days when his great-grandfather, Christopher Lowndes, emigrated from Cheshire, England, to settle at Bladensburg. Through Richard Lowndes, of Bostock House in Cheshire, he seems to have been related to the family of Rawlins Lowndes [*q.v.*], and he was the great-grandson of Edward Lloyd, governor of Maryland [*q.v.*]. He was born in Clarksburg, Va. (now W. Va.), where his father, Lloyd Lowndes, a successful merchant with large farming and lumbering interests, was living with his wife, Maria Elizabeth (Moore) Lowndes. After preparatory training at the Clarksburg academy the lad entered Washington College in Pennsylvania but transferred for the last two years to Allegheny College, graduating in 1865. He graduated from the law school of the University of Pennsylvania, two years later, and settled at Cumberland, in which city his father had opened a store. However, he was soon taking a prominent part in politics, and, shortly after his marriage, on Dec. 2, 1869, to his cousin, Elizabeth Tasker Lowndes, he abandoned law for the more congenial fields of finance and mining. He was also identified with the agricultural interests of his section. He acquired a controlling interest in many financial, mining, and milling enterprises throughout the state and, by virtue of such business experience, was able to contribute by his counsel to the stability and soundness of the state finances. His warm heart, gracious manner, and frank kindliness made him a charming companion and, with the means afforded by his wealth, made him the esteemed benefactor of many public and private undertakings. He was a member of the Emmanuel Episcopal Church of Cumberland, which he served as vestryman and faithful representative to the diocesan conventions for twenty years.

His first political venture was as Republican candidate for Congress in the Grant-Greeley campaign of 1872, in which he demonstrated his popularity by defeating his Democratic opponent with a reversal of about 3,200 votes. The youngest member in Congress, he proved by committee service that he was a worker rather than a talker and demonstrated his independence in defying his party by opposing the Civil Rights Bill. The large negro constituency in his district deserted him when he came up for reëlection, and his defeat silenced his political ambitions for over two decades, though he continued to influence Republican policies throughout the state. In 1895, however, at the solicitation of friends of both parties, he accepted the Republican nomination for governor and was the first Republican elected in thirty years. He administered the affairs of the state in a manner which elicited warm commendation from both parties, and, in spite of an unsympathetic legislature, he fulfilled his campaign pledges for reform. Especially notable were the creation of a state geological survey, a new charter for Baltimore city, and an excellent election law, drafted by the reform league, which greatly improved the conduct of Maryland elections. His nice sense of honor forbade his permitting his name to be considered for United States senator at either of the two legislative elections that occurred during his term, though he secretly cherished ambitions for the office. He failed of reëlection in 1899, partly because friendly Democrats felt that a change was imperative for the good of Baltimore. After his retirement, he continued to be intimate with national party leaders and to be the strongest figure of his party in the state. At the time of his sudden death he was regarded as the probable candidate for governor in 1908.

[Manuscript Letters in the possession of the family are still unavailable; date of death was taken from a copy of the death certificate in the files of the Congressional Joint Committee on Printing; for published sources see H. E. Buchholz, *Governors of Md.* (1908); J. T. Scharf, *Hist. of Western Md.* (1882), vol. II, esp. pp. 1448–50; J. W. Thomas and T. J. C. Williams, *Hist. of Allegany County, Md.*, 1923, vol. I; *Baltimore American*, Jan. 9, 1905; *Sun* (Baltimore), Jan. 9, 10, 1905; *Daily News* (Cumberland), Jan. 9, 1905; *News* (Frederick, Md.), Jan. 9, 1905.] E. L.

LOWNDES, RAWLINS (January 1721–Aug. 24, 1800), president of South Carolina and leader in opposing the adoption of the federal Constitution, was born in St. Kitts, British West Indies. He was the grandson of Charles Lowndes who was probably a younger brother of Richard Lowndes of Cheshire, England, an ancestor of Lloyd Lowndes [*q.v.*]. He was the son of Charles Lowndes who emigrated, first, to St. Kitts, where he married Ruth, the daughter of Henry Rawlins, an influential planter. In 1730, on account of financial difficulties, the family went to Charleston, S. C., where the father died when Rawlins was about fourteen years old. The widow returned to St. Kitts, leaving her son in the care of Robert Hall, provost-marshal of the colony, whose careful guidance and extensive library served admirably for his education at law. The youth did not reach his majority before his guardian died, in 1740, but nevertheless he was allowed to fill Hall's position temporarily and later was permanently appointed provost-marshal. In 1754 he resigned this position to practise law. In 1749 he had been elected to the legislature from St. Paul's Parish, and from 1751 until the Revolution he almost continuously represented St. Bartholomew's in that body, becoming speaker of the lower house, from 1763 to 1765, and, again, from 1772 to 1775. In 1770 he was chairman of a committee that reported a plan to establish eight free schools for the newly settled districts as well as to found a provincial college (Commons House Journal, Mar. 1, 1770). He made the motion, passed unanimously, to erect a statute of William Pitt in Charleston as a memorial to his efforts to obtain the repeal of the Stamp Act. In 1766 he was appointed associate judge of the court of common pleas and, in that capacity, espoused provincial and popular rights. He refused to enforce the use of stamp paper, defied the chief justice on the bench (Council Journal, Feb. 3, 1772), and, in a *habeas corpus* case of 1773, denied the right of the royal council to act as an upper house of assembly (McCrady, *Royal Government, post,* pp. 717–21). Not long afterward he was removed from the bench (Commons House Journal, Oct. 24, 1773).

As a conservative in temperament and conviction he opposed rebellion or separation from the Mother Country and deplored the trend of events after the break. Yet he continued to be bound by his devotion to his province and to the rights of her representative government. When the provincial congress was considering the appointment of delegates to the First Continental Congress, he favored sending delegates with strictly limited powers, who should be allowed to support only measures to obtain the repeal of Parliament's oppressive acts and the redress of grievances. In this way he hoped to place his colony in opposition to the more radical northern colonies, particularly in New England, which favored independence. When the South Carolina convention discussed granting money to continue the "American Association," he advised caution, and upheld the right of Parliament to legislate for the colonies. St. Bartholomew's sent him to both the provincial congresses of 1775, from which he was chosen a member of the Council of Safety, where he opposed the confiscation of the property of Loyalists leaving the colony. He was one of the committee of eleven selected to form a new constitution for the colony, although he was unfavorable to the idea, and, after the new government was established in 1776, was made a member of the legislative council. When, in 1778, radical changes were proposed in the constitution, the church, and the legislature, he opposed them vigorously, yet he accepted the presidency of the colony when John Rutledge vetoed the measures and resigned. His position weighed heavily upon him, the colony was threatened with a British attack, and he had personal griefs to occupy his attention. His health was affected, he had lost one son, and another was so seriously ill that he later died. Moreover dissatisfaction with his administration broke out in open strife. He asked Christopher Gadsden [*q.v.*], the vice-president, to act for him but with characteristic vigor continued his own activities by proposing strong measures to thwart the attack, which, however, did not occur during his administration. He declined reelection in 1779 and was the last president of South Carolina, for his successor took the title of governor. When the British captured Charleston in 1779 and overran the state, he quietly abandoned the struggle, retired to his plantation, and seems to have accepted British protection, though this is a matter of dispute.

After the end of the war he represented Charleston in the legislature. In the committee of the whole he opposed the ratification of the Constitution, though his constituents favored it, basing his opposition on the failure of that document adequately to guard the rights of minorities, on the excessive power given the Senate, and on the limitation of slave trade to twenty years. He closed his objections with the statement that he wished no other epitaph than, "Here lies the man that opposed the constitution, because it was ruinous to the liberty of America" (Jonathan Elliot, *The Debates of the Several State Conventions of the Adoption of the Federal Constitution,* 2 ed., vol. IV, 1836, p. 298). This was his last public appearance, for, though he was elected to the constitutional convention, he did not serve. He was married, on Aug. 15, 1748, to Amarinthia Elliott of Rantoules, Stone River, who died in January 1750. The following year, on Dec. 23, he celebrated his marriage to Mary Cartwright of Charleston, who bore him four daughters and three sons. Bereaved of his second wife in 1770, he married, in January 1773, Sarah Jones of Georgia, a girl of sixteen, whose third and youngest child was William Lowndes [*q.v.*].

[Journals of the Commons House and of the Council of S. C., through the courtesy of Prof. Robert L. Meriwether, Columbia, S. C.; a few letters in the Lib. of Cong.; G. B. Chase, *Lowndes of S. C.* (1876); Mrs. St. Julien Ravenel, *Life and Times of Wm. Lowndes* (1901); W. R. Smith, *S. C. as a Royal Province* (1903); Edward McCrady, *The Hist. of S. C. under the Royal Government* (1899) and *The Hist. of S. C. in the Revolution* (1901); F. A. Porcher, "Christopher Gadsden," *S. C. Hist. Soc. Colls.*, vol. IV (1887); *S. C. Hist. and Geneal. Mag.*, July 1901, Oct. 1902, Apr. 1903, Apr. 1906, Jan. 1911, Jan. 1914, July 1915, Apr. 1920, July 1926.] H. B–C.

LOWNDES, WILLIAM (Feb. 11, 1782–Oct. 27, 1822), congressman from South Carolina, was the son of Rawlins Lowndes [*q.v.*], who was prominent in the affairs of the province and state. When something over fifty years old Rawlins Lowndes married, as his third wife, Sarah, the sixteen-year-old daughter of Col. Charles Jones, of Georgia. Their third child was born at the Horseshoe Plantation in the parish of St. Bartholomew, Colleton County, S. C., and was christened William Jones, but he never used in any form his second baptismal name. In his seventh year he was placed in school in England and, while there, contracted an inflammatory rheumatism that weakened his health all through his life. Returning to South Carolina after three years, he studied in private schools, being especially interested in Latin, Greek, and French. He was early marked for his clear, luminous style of writing and speaking. On Sept. 16, 1802, he married Elizabeth, daughter of Thomas Pinckney [*q.v.*]. He practised law for a few years but soon gave this up for love of his plantation.

He identified himself with the Republican party, though his wife remained a strong Federalist, and, from 1806 to 1810, he served in the General Assembly. He was in close touch with Joseph Alston, Daniel Huger, Langdon Cheves, and John C. Calhoun. The original draft of the act of 1809 to amend the state system of representation in behalf of the upper country is in his handwriting. Strongly opposing the Embargo and Non-Intercourse policy of Jefferson, he was elected to the Twelfth Congress in 1810 along with Cheves and Calhoun, and these, with David R. Williams and others, formed the nucleus of a war party. In this Congress he served on the committee for commerce and manufactures and on that for military affairs and, in the Thirteenth Congress, as chairman of the committee on naval affairs. He had served, in 1807, as captain of a military company and regretted, in later life, that he had not given himself to a military career. He spoke in behalf of every motion to increase the military and naval strength of the country, and his service on the naval committee added to his reputation. In 1815 he was appointed chairman of the committee on ways and means and served for three years. He supported the creation of the second Bank of the United States, and he reported and, along with Calhoun, advocated the tariff of 1816, avowedly for protection. He was offered the position of secretary of war but declined. He was the author of the sinking fund act, under the operation of which the national debt was paid off in fourteen years. He supported Forsythe's bill of 1817 against privateering and in the next year supported the right of the executive to a free hand in investigating affairs in the South American republics. His speech of Jan. 30, 1819, expressing disapprobation of Andrew Jackson's course in the Seminole War is a fair sample of his style (*Annals of Congress,* 15 Cong., 2 Sess., cols. 912–22). He argued closely, without heat or passion, stated first the position of his opponent so fairly that John Randolph once said, "He has done that once too often; he can never answer that" (Ravenel, *post,* pp. 239–40), and then won his argument by logical statement. In this year, 1819, as chairman of a special committee on coinage, he submitted a classic report on the relative value of coins of different nations in relation to our own (*Annals of Congress,* 15 Cong., 2 Sess., cols. 788–96). The summer of 1819 he spent in European travel in a vain attempt to build up his failing health. In the Sixteenth Congress, 1819, he was appointed chairman of the Committee on Foreign Affairs, and in 1820 was the candidate of his party for speaker of the House. The debate on the Missouri question was the last important public work in which he was engaged. He spoke briefly in the beginning, as one of the conference committee, in favor of the compromise under which Missouri was allowed to make her own constitution. When Missouri offered her constitution at the next session, he was chairman of a committee of three to report on its acceptance. This report took the ground that Missouri was already a state, and he supported it by a speech so calm and dispassionate as to win approval from both sections in the midst of a frenzied debate. After this effort, his health compelled him to entrust the handling of the Missouri question to Clay.

In 1822 he was offered the mission to France but was compelled to decline this, as he had previously declined appointments to Turkey and to Russia. In December 1821, he had been nominated by the South Carolina legislature for the presidency. In this connection he made the statement, often quoted since, "The Presidency is not an office to be either solicited or declined" (Ravenel, *post,* p. 226). On May 8, 1822, he resigned his seat in Congress and again tried the effect of a sea voyage for his health. When six days out from Philadelphia he died and was buried at sea. Of striking height, over six feet six, he was unusually slender and loose-limbed. Grave and dignified in bearing, he won such a position of leadership in the House that Henry Clay in his old age said, "I think the wisest man I ever knew was William Lowndes" (Ravenel, *post,* p. 239). He considered his part as one of the "War Hawks" in bringing on the "Second War for Independence" his greatest achievement.

[The most valuable of the Lowndes papers were destroyed in the Charleston fire of 1861; Mrs. St. Julien Ravenel's *Life and Times of William Lowndes* (1901) is the fullest account extant, dealing mostly with the personal side of his life; G. B. Chase's *Lowndes of South Carolina* (1876) is genealogical but contains a valuable sketch based on a life by Major Rawlins Lowndes, of which the manuscript was lost before publication; see also *Memoirs of John Quincy Adams,* ed. by C. F. Adams, vols. IV, V, VII, VIII (1875–76), and Mrs. St. Julien Ravenel, *Charleston* (1906).]

J. E. W.

LOWREY, MARK PERRIN (Dec. 30, 1828–Feb. 27, 1885), Baptist clergyman, Confederate soldier, educator, was born in McNairy County, Tenn., the ninth in a family of eleven children. His father, Adam Lowrey, who was born in Ireland, and his mother, Margaret Doss, of English descent, were of good stock but uneducated. When Mark was but a few years of age his father contracted cholera while on a trip to New Orleans, and died. Living in a comparatively newly settled country, his mother widowed and impoverished, he had practically no educational advantages. When he was fifteen he moved with his mother to the village of Farmington in Tishomingo County, Miss. Enlisting in the 2nd Mississippi Regiment, he went to Mexico in 1847, though his organization did not arrive in time to see active service in the Mexican War. Two years later he married Sarah Holmes, daughter of Isham Holmes, a farmer living near Rienzi, Miss. For several years he earned his livelihood as a brick-mason, but at the age of twenty-four he decided to enter the ministry. He was ordained by the Farmington Baptist Church in 1853 and until the outbreak of the Civil War held pastorates, served as missionary, and improved his education as best he could. It is said that he frequently boarded the district school teacher in order to learn from him at night.

Entering the Confederate army, he served for a while in the fall of 1861, as colonel of the 4th Regiment of sixty-day volunteers. The regiment suffered much from sickness and at the end of their term of enlistment the men were mustered out. In 1862 Lowrey raised and organized the 32nd Mississippi Regiment, of which he was elected colonel. He was wounded in the arm in the battle of Perryville, served with great distinction at the battle of Chickamauga, and was promoted to brigadier-general Oct. 4, 1863. He commanded a brigade in Hardee's corps, and later a division, until his resignation from the army, Mar. 14, 1865.

At the conclusion of hostilities he returned to Mississippi, where he served for a while as state missionary and did much to reorganize and revive churches that had suffered from the war. In 1873 he founded Blue Mountain Female Institute (later Blue Mountain College). This institution he served as president and as professor of history and moral science until his death. It exercised considerable influence in the field of education for women in Mississippi, and continued under the control of the Lowrey family until 1920, when it was taken over by the Mississippi Baptist Convention. From 1872 to 1876 Lowrey was a member of the board of trustees of the University of Mississippi. His prominence and influence in the Baptist denomination in his state are attested by the fact that he was president of the Mississippi Baptist Convention from 1868 to 1877. He fell dead in the railway station at Middleton, Tenn.

[MSS. in Am. Antiquarian Soc., Worcester, Mass.; *Southern Hist. Soc. Papers*, vol. XVI (1888); Dunbar Rowland, *Mississippi* (1907), vols. II, III; C. A. Evans, *Confed. Mil. Hist.* (1899), vols. VII, VIII; *War of the Rebellion: Official Records (Army)*; J. L. Boyd, *A Popular Hist. of the Baptists in Miss.* (1930); L. S. Foster, *Miss. Baptist Preachers* (1895); *Commercial Appeal* (Memphis, Tenn.), Feb. 12, 1906; I. A. Buck, *Cleburne and His Command* (1908).] C. J.

LOWRIE, JAMES WALTER (Sept. 16, 1856–Jan. 26, 1930), missionary to China, was born in Shanghai and died in Paotingfu. Missionary interests surrounded his boyhood. His grandfather, Hon. Walter Lowrie [*q.v.*], who had emigrated from Scotland about 1792, was the first secretary of the Board of Foreign Missions of the Presbyterian Church in the United States of America. One uncle, John Cameron Lowrie, had been a missionary to India; and another uncle, Walter Mason Lowrie, a missionary to China, had been killed in 1847 by pirates near Ningpo. His father, Reuben Post Lowrie, was a missionary stationed in Shanghai when the boy was born, and died there in 1860 when James Walter was less than four years old. After the father's death, his mother, Amelia Palmer (Tuttle) Lowrie, returned to the United States with her daughter and son. The boy studied at the Lawrenceville, N. J., high school and at Princeton University, receiving the degree of B.A. there in 1876 and that of M.A. in 1879. For three years (1877–80), he taught at Madison, N. J., and then entered Princeton Theological Seminary. The impulse towards missionary life had been his by inheritance; but quietly and characteristically he waited until he was convinced of his "call." On June 3, 1883, the year of his graduation from the Seminary, he was ordained by the Presbytery of New York and appointed a missionary of the Presbyterian Board to China.

For eight years he was stationed at Peking, laying the foundations for his unusual command of the Chinese language and taking an increasingly active part in mission work. A short interval (1892–93) in the United States ensued, during which he served as stated supply for a church in Longmont, Col. Returning to China, he became one of the founders of the mission station at Paotingfu. The next six years were an active and happy period. His evangelistic efforts were fruitful; and, always an intense home lover though he never married, he had his mother with him at Paotingfu, and his sister and her husband, Dr. B. C. Atterbury, were also members of the mission. While he was absent from the station in 1900 for the purpose of escorting to the coast his mother, who was returning for a time to America, the Boxer massacres occurred at Paotingfu. In after years his thankfulness for their escape was obviously tinged with regret that he had not been with his fellow Christians during those days. He at once plunged into the work nearest at hand. Joining the Allies at Tientsin, he accompanied them to Peking immediately after the relief of the beleaguered legations; and from Peking he was sent, as guide and interpreter, with the allied detachment which was dispatched to Paotingfu. The first intention of the allied officers was to raze that city as punishment for the massacres, and it was only Lowrie's courageous and incessant pleas that prevented its destruction. This unexpected example of Christian magnanimity profoundly impressed the Chinese, and their gratitude became a factor in the subsequent success of mission work in that place of the martyrs.

Honors began to come to him. In 1903 the Chinese Imperial Government made him a Mandarin of the fourth degree. In 1910 he was chosen as the first chairman of the China Council, the executive body on the field of the seven China missions of the Presbyterian Church in the United States of America. His headquarters were in Shanghai, but his duties led him far afield. His work was modestly and quietly done, but was effective in constructive and unifying results. Equally effective was his personal influence. A man of social graces and warm sympathies, he was the favorite guest in a multitude of homes. During his later years ill health and failing eyesight limited his activities; and he was deeply troubled by those whom he feared to be destroying the true foundations of Christianity. In 1925 he became honorary chairman of the China Council, and four years later he left Shanghai to spend his last days in Paotingfu. His death occurred after only a few months, however, and he was buried in the Paotingfu cemetery beside the grave of his mother.

[*Necrological Report of Princeton Theological Sem.*, 1930; *Who's Who in America*, 1918–19; W. T. Ellis, "Some Missionaries I Know," *Outlook*, Apr. 17, 1909; *China Council Bull.*, Feb. 5, 1930; records of the Board of Foreign Missions of the Presbyterian Church in the U. S. A.; *Chinese Recorder*, Mar. 1930; *N. Y. Times*, Jan. 29, 1930.] H. Cl—s.

LOWRIE, WALTER (Dec. 10, 1784–Dec. 14, 1868), United States senator, missionary secretary, the son of John and Catherine (Cameron) Lowrie, was born in Edinburgh, Scotland. About 1792 his family came to Huntington County, Pa., and a few years later settled in Butler (then part of Allegheny) County. John Lowrie was an enterprising farmer, a stanch Presbyterian, and influential in his community. Walter was reared on the farm. He attended a subscription school and began to study the classics under Rev. John McPherrin with a view to entering the ministry. Despite his fervent desire to preach the Gospel, unforeseen obstacles made him change his plans, and in 1807 he went to Butler to teach school. There, attracted by the opportunities of public life, he was successively a clerk, member of the board of commissioners, and justice of the peace. He also opened a store in partnership with his brother. On Jan. 14, 1808, he married Amelia McPherrin, the daughter of his preceptor. In 1811–12 he served in the state House of Representatives and in 1812 was elected state senator as a Democrat, holding his seat until his resignation in 1819 to enter the United States Senate. His maiden effort in the Senate was a speech (Jan. 20, 1820) on the Missouri question in which he boldly announced that "if the alternative be . . . a dissolution of this Union, or the extension of slavery over this whole Western country, I, for one, will choose the former" (*Annals of Congress*, 16 Cong., 1 Sess., pp. 201–09). As a member of the committee on public lands, he opposed a revision of the land policy which would place it upon a cash rather than a credit basis, and otherwise championed the cause of land purchasers and Western settlers. He was also on the committees on roads and canals, accounts, finance, and Indian affairs. He was an ardent temperance advocate, and a founder of the congressional prayer meeting. After one term as senator he was secretary of the Senate from 1825 until 1836.

In 1836 Lowrie was elected corresponding secretary of the Western Foreign Missionary Society, which a year later became the Board of Foreign Missions of the Presbyterian Church. Under his guidance, 1836–68, the organization grew from obscurity to a great missionary enterprise. He later declared that the sacrifices and self-denial involved in the post were the charms by which the office secured its incumbent. Invariably in close touch with all phases of the work, he corresponded extensively with missionaries abroad, solicited contributions for the cause, personally supervised the sending of household provisions and farm implements to the Indians, and frequently visited the Indian missions in the West. Three of his sons were foreign missionaries. James Walter Lowrie [*q.v.*] was his grandson. His first wife, by whom he had eight children, died in 1832, and two years later he married Mary K. Childs. He died in New York City.

[Lowrie edited his son's memoirs, *Memoirs of the Rev. Walter M. Lowrie, Missionary to China* (1849), which appeared in several editions and contains valuable material. John D. Wells, "The Hon. Walter Lowrie," in *The Record of the Presbyt. Ch. in the U. S. A.*, Apr. 1869, portrays his activities with the Board of Foreign Missions. See also J. A. McKee, *20th Century Hist. of Butler and Butler County, Pa.* (1909); *Hist. of Butler County, Pa.* (1895), ed. by R. C. Brown; *Ann. Reports of the Board of Foreign Missions of the Presbyt. Ch. in the U. S. A.*, 1838–68; *Presbyt. Mag.*, Mar. 1855; *Biog. Dir. Am. Cong.* (1928); *The Centennial of the Western Foreign Missionary Society* (1931), ed. by J. A. Kelso; *N. Y. Times*, Dec. 15, 1868.] J. H. P.

LOWRY, HIRAM HARRISON (May 29, 1843–Jan. 13, 1924), for more than fifty years a missionary in China, was born on a farm near Zanesville, Ohio, the son of Hiram and Margaret (Speare) Lowry. In 1862 and 1863 he was in the Union army—for fourteen months in active service and then for several months in military hospitals as a patient. Entering Ohio Wesleyan University in 1864, he graduated from that institution in 1867 and during his senior year, Feb. 28, 1867, was married to Parthenia Nicholson. That same year he was ordained to the ministry of the Methodist Episcopal Church and, with his bride, sailed for China to join the mission of his Church at Foochow. In the spring of 1869 he was transferred to Peking. Here, together with L. N. Wheeler, he founded the Methodist mission in North China. Upon the retirement of Wheeler because of illness in 1873, Lowry became superintendent of the North China mission and served in this position for twenty years. During his tenure of office the mission expanded steadily in staff, in institutions, and in territory covered. It was a period when Protestant missions in China were growing rapidly, and when churches in Europe and America were augmenting their efforts abroad. Lowry proved to be an able, broad-minded, unselfish, and diligent administrator. He traveled extensively throughout the region which his colleagues were attempting to occupy and helped them meet the obstacles of their pioneer enterprises, including the acquisition of property in the face of local prejudice and opposition. During much of the time he was also the head of the school for the training of Chinese preachers, an institution which later became the Wiley College of Theology of Peking University.

By 1893 the North China mission had been so enlarged that it was erected into a Conference, and, accordingly, the office of superintendent passed. Lowry was, however, almost immediately made the head of Peking University, which had been begun by his mission. From December 1893 to June 1894 he was acting president and thereafter, president. He held the office during the years when education of a Western type was becoming popular in China, and he helped the institution to take advantage of the situation. In time—with the hearty cooperation of Lowry—the University, later to be known as Yenching, was reorganized to include the higher educational work of several of the Protestant denominations. After this federation was accomplished, Lowry, in 1918, became president emeritus. He served as acting president for a year longer, however, and was the head of Peking Academy, a secondary school of his mission, until his formal retirement from active life in 1922. For years he had struggled against ill health, but he lived to be well past eighty years of age. He died in Peking.

[*Ann. Reports* of the Missionary Soc. of the M. E. Ch. (after 1907, the Board of Foreign Missions of the M. E. Ch.); *Official Minutes, No. China Conference of the M. E. Ch.*, esp. for 1924, which contains biog. sketch; *China Christian Advocate*, Mar. 1924; *China and Methodism* (1906); *Christian Advocate* (N. Y.), Jan. 24, 1924; *Who's Who in America*, 1922–23.]

K. S. L.

LOWRY, ROBERT (Mar. 10, 1830–Jan. 19, 1910), lawyer, Confederate soldier, governor of Mississippi, was born in Chesterfield District, S. C., the son of Robert and Jemimah (Rushing) Lowry, both of Scotch-Irish extraction. The family moved to Tennessee about 1833 and to Tishomingo County, Miss., in 1840. Robert's educational advantages were limited. In 1846 he went to Raleigh, Miss., to live with his uncle, Judge James Lowry, with whom he engaged in mercantile enterprises first at Raleigh and later at Brandon. On Sept. 9, 1849, he married Maria M. Gammage, of Jasper County, Miss. From about 1854 to 1859 he was in Arkansas, during which period he read law. Upon his return to Mississippi he practised law as a partner of Judge A. G. Mayers.

When the Civil War began he enlisted as a private in the Rankin Grays, but in August 1861 was elected a major of the 6th Mississippi Regiment, which was being organized at Grenada. He was twice wounded at the battle of Shiloh and in 1862 was commissioned colonel. He served with Gen. Joseph E. Johnston during the Vicksburg campaign. On the death of his superior officer, Brigadier-General John Adams, he was placed in command of the brigade and was commissioned brigadier-general, Feb. 4, 1865; he was with Gen. Joseph E. Johnston when he surrendered to Sherman on Apr. 26, 1865.

Returning to Mississippi, he served as state senator in 1865–66, and with Giles M. Hillyer was appointed by Gov. B. G. Humphreys on a commission, authorized by the legislature, to visit Washington and request President Johnson to release Jefferson Davis. In 1869 he was the Democratic candidate for the office of attorney-general but was not elected. In the campaign which resulted in the overthrow of the Carpetbag government in 1876, he took an active part. In 1881 the adherents of Gov. J. M. Stone and Ethelbert Barksdale caused a deadlock in the state Democratic convention and Lowry was nominated as a compromise candidate for governor. The following campaign, which was the last in which the Republican party (under the name of Independent Party) put forward candidates for state offices in Mississippi, resulted in a victory for Lowry. He was renominated in 1885 and elected without opposition. During his term of office the local-option law was passed, the Industrial Institute and College for women at Columbus was established, and appropriations for public schools were increased. After retiring from the governorship he practised law at Jackson, Miss. In 1891, in collaboration with William H. McCardle, he published *A History of Mississippi*. He was a candidate for the unexpired term of United States Senator E. C. Walthall, who died in 1898, but failed of election. For seven years prior to his death he was state commander of the United Confederate Veterans. He died in Jackson and was buried in Brandon.

[*Official and Statistical Reg. of the State of Miss. Centennial Edition* (1917); Dunbar Rowland, *Encyc. of Miss. Hist.* (1902), and *Mississippi* (1907); Lowry and McCardle, *A Hist. of Miss.* (1891); *Confed. Mil. Hist.* (1899), vol. VII; *Who's Who in America*, 1908–09, which is the authority for years of birth and marriage; *Confed. Veteran*, Apr. 1910; *Vicksburg Herald*, Jan. 20, 21, 1910.]

C. J.

LOWRY, THOMAS (Feb. 27, 1843–Feb. 4, 1909), capitalist, was the son of Samuel R. Lowry, who emigrated from Ireland to Pennsylvania, married Rachel Bullock and, about 1834, settled in Illinois. Thomas was born in Logan County and reared under frontier conditions. He attended country schools and, after a journey through the West, began to read law, was admitted to the Illinois bar, and then settled in Minneapolis in 1867. Blessed with a likable personality, he had established a paying practice within two years and was becoming interested in business, especially in real estate. On Dec. 14, 1870, he married Beatrice Goodrich, who bore him a son and two daughters. Though the panic of 1873 affected him seriously, he not only extricated himself from the effects of the depression but was generally conceded to have been a large factor in helping Minneapolis weather the storm. Gradually his business interests so completely occupied his attention that he gave up the practice of law. In 1875 in order to salvage his land holdings he bought, with eastern financial aid, an interest in the Minneapolis Street Railway Company, a new corporation, abandoned because of the panic. Two years later he controlled a majority of its stock. During the next decade, getting little support at home and relying upon New York capital, he struggled with his traction company, which he would gladly have sold could he have found a purchaser (letter of Pliny Bartlett, *Minneapolis Journal,* Apr. 18, 1889). He began to acquire control of the St. Paul street railways in 1882 and 1883 and, in 1891, consolidated the systems of both cities in a holding company, the Twin City Rapid Transit Company, capitalized at more than twice the stock value of the two systems. During the period of consolidation the railways were electrified and the most serious labor disturbances of his career took place. In April 1889 the lines were paralyzed in a strike caused by a wage cut and by the requirement that operatives sign an "iron clad" agreement not to join a union. Public sympathy was with the strikers and futile efforts were made to induce Lowry to arbitrate; but he showed his understanding of human nature by keeping still until acts of violence alienated public support from the strikers, who gradually capitulated.

By 1890, having accumulated a comfortable fortune, he decided to retire from business and celebrated the event by a trip around the world. On his return he found he had been elected president of the Minneapolis, St. Paul and Sault Sainte Marie Railway, which he had helped to promote. Abandoning the idea of retirement, he not only continued his direct interest in the traction company and in the railroad, but engaged in numerous other activities. He helped found the North American Telegraph Company and the Minneapolis General Electric Company, was vice-president of a bank, and carried on his real-estate operations. At the same time he was active in several lines of civic endeavor, giving time and money to the public library, to parks, and to the church work of the Universalists. In 1901 he showed a lively interest for the first time in political matters by becoming a candidate for United States senator after the death of Cushman K. Davis. His defeat in the legislature offended him, and he never thereafter consented to be a candidate for any office. By 1905 his vigorous constitution had begun to show unmistakable signs of weakening. He spent the last years of his life in a vain search for health through the various resorts of the Southwest, and in writing *Personal Reminiscences of Abraham Lincoln* (1910), which is thirty-one pages of random notes.

[Isaac Atwater, *Hist. of the City of Minneapolis* (1893); *Hist. of Minneapolis,* ed. by M. D. Shutter (1923), vol. II; H. B. Hudson, *A Half Century of Minneapolis* (1908); *Compendium of Hist. and Biog. of Minneapolis,* ed. by R. I. Holcombe and W. H. Bingham (1914); *Hist. of Minneapolis, ed. by Isaac Atwater and Hennepin County, ed. by Col. J. H. Stevens* (1895); Eva Gay, *A Tale of the Twin Cities* (1889); H. K. Webster, "Lords of Our Streets," *Am. Illustrated Mag.,* Sept. 1905; *Minneapolis Jour.,* Apr. 18, 1889, Feb. 4, 1909.]

L. B. S.

LOY, MATTHIAS (Mar. 17, 1828–Jan. 26, 1915), Lutheran clergyman, was born in Cumberland County, Pa., of German parentage, the fourth of the seven children of Matthias and Christina (Reaver) Loy. After a bleak, poverty-pinched boyhood he was apprenticed in 1847 to the printing firm of Baab & Hummel at Harrisburg, was treated well by his masters, read several of the English classics, learned the rudiments of Latin and Greek at the Harrisburg Academy, was confirmed by the Rev. Charles William Schaeffer [*q.v.*], and began to think of a ministerial career. In 1847 he went west for his health and at Circleville, Ohio, was persuaded by the Rev. J. Roof to become a beneficiary student in the seminary (later part of Capital University) of the Joint Synod of Ohio at Columbus, where he had Christian Spielmann and Wilhelm Friedrich Lehmann as his teachers. He was influenced strongly by the writings of C. F. W. Walther [*q.v.*] and by several friends among the clergy of the Missouri Synod. His only pastorate was at Delaware, Ohio, 1849–65. On Dec. 25, 1853, he married Mary Willey of Delaware, who with five of their seven children survived him. Frail of body and often ill, Loy had a strong mind and a great capacity for work. As president of the Joint Synod 1860–78 and

1880–94, editor of the *Lutheran Standard* 1864–91, professor of theology in Capital University, 1865–1902, and president of the University, 1881–90, he dominated the Synod, which grew during his lifetime into an organization of national scope. He was a zealous student of the Lutheran confessions but had little knowledge of Biblical criticism or appreciation of its implications. He was a truculent controversialist, never forgetting that the Church Visible is also the Church Militant, and never giving his opponents time to forget it. In 1867 he refused to let the Joint Synod become a member of the General Council of the Evangelical Lutheran Church in North America and framed the questions about the "four points"—chiliasm, altar fellowship, pulpit fellowship, membership in secret societies—that afflicted so sorely the spokesmen of the General Council. In 1871, however, he carried the Joint Synod into the Synodical Conference. Ten years later he rejected Walther's doctrine of predestination, founded and edited the *Columbus Theological Magazine* (1881–88) to combat it, and of course withdrew the Joint Synod from the Synodical Conference. He was the author of twenty published hymns and of *The Doctrine of Justification* (1869; 1882); *Essay on the Ministerial Office* (1870); *Sermons on the Gospels* (1888); *Christian Prayer* (1890); *Story of My Life* (3rd ed., 1905); *The Augsburg Confession* (1908); *The Sermon on the Mount* (1909); and *Sermons on the Epistles* (1910). He shows to best advantage in his sermons, which are simple in language, earnest, and deeply felt. In 1902 an attack of angina pectoris compelled him to retire, but for eight years more he continued to write and to take pleasure in his garden, before softening of the brain set in. He died at his home in Columbus.

[Matthias Loy, *Story of My Life* (3rd ed., 1905); J. Julian, *A Dict. of Hymnology* (rev. ed., 1907); T. E. Schmauk, "Dr. Loy's Life and Its Bearings on the Lutheran Church in This Land," *Luth. Ch. Rev.*, Jan. 1907; P. A. Peter and Wm. Schmidt, *Geschichte der Allgemeinen Evang.-Lutherischen Synode von Ohio und anderen Staaten* (1908); G. W. Mechling, *Hist. Ev. Luth. District Synod of Ohio* (1911); C. V. Sheatsley, *Hist. Ev. Luth. Joint Synod of Ohio and Other States* (1919); *Who's Who in America*, 1914–15; *Lutherische Kirchenzeitung*, Feb. 6, 20, Mar. 6, 1915.]

G. H. G.

LOYD, SAMUEL (Jan. 31, 1841–Apr. 10, 1911), better known as Sam Loyd, composer of chess problems and puzzles, was born in Philadelphia, the son of Isaac Smith and Elizabeth (Singer) Loyd. The family moved in 1844 to New York, where Loyd attended the public schools until he was about seventeen. He studied to be an engineer; held a steam and mechanical engineer's license in New York, and is said to have had an editorial connection with the *Sanitary Engineer*. At one time he owned a printing office in Elizabeth, N. J., and at other times engaged in a variety of business enterprises.

As a youth, with his two elder brothers he frequented a chess club on University Place and there became acquainted with Miron H. Hazeltine, long chess editor of the *New York Clipper*. At that time the exploits of Paul Charles Morphy [*q.v.*] were causing a widespread interest in chess in America which resulted in the establishment of chess columns in many newspapers and journals. Loyd began composing chess problems in 1855, won first place in numerous contests, and as early as 1858 was recognized in Germany as the leading American problem composer. In 1860, the *Chess Monthly*, edited by Morphy and D. W. Fiske [*q.v.*], engaged him as problem editor. Fiske and Loyd collaborated in a form of literary anecdote resting upon some ingenious chess problem. These stories and problems have often been reprinted and the problems, which were Loyd's part, are recognized as the work of a genius. Another type of problem cultivated by Loyd places the chessmen upon the board to make a letter or numeral. Later Loyd himself wrote sketches and made problems or puzzles to fit the conditions. In chess problems he always defended the thesis, now generally accepted, that the position must be a possible one in play. To *American Chess-Nuts* (1868), edited by E. B. Cook, W. R. Henry, and C. A. Gilbery, he contributed many problems, and in 1878 he published *Chess Strategy*, a collection consisting mainly of his own work, in which the rather difficult classification of problems is attempted.

Loyd was abroad in 1867, participating, without notable success, as a player in the International Chess Tournament. In problem tournaments his greatest achievement was at the Centennial Exposition of 1876, when his various entries won first and second prize, as well as numerous minor prizes. In 1870 he married Addie J. Coombs of Utica, N. Y. About this time he originated a puzzle called "The Trick Donkeys," which sold literally in millions of copies. Later he developed "Pigs in Clover" and the 14-15 puzzle, both widely popular in Europe and America. The game "Parchesi" is also his invention. In 1896 he collaborated with his son Sam in a puzzle called "Get Off the Earth" or "The Disappearing Chinaman." About this time some newspapers and magazines began to introduce Sam Loyd puzzle columns, edited by father and son, who collaborated in the invention of the puzzles featured. The Loyd puzzles display remarkable ingenuity, particularly in the application of simple algebraic devices or old mathematical puzzles in such new garb as to conceal the source. The story devices applied by Fiske and Loyd to chess problems were developed with puzzles by the Loyds. Until his death in 1911, Loyd continued to make puzzle columns and advertising devices employing puzzles his source of livelihood.

[A. C. White, *Sam Loyd and His Chess Problems* (Leeds, 1913), and "Reminiscences of Sam Loyd's Family," *The Problem* (Pittsburgh), Mar. 28, 1914; W. P. Eaton, in *Delineator*, Apr. 1911; *Woman's Home Companion*, June 1911; *Am. Chess Bull.*, May, June 1911; *Sci. American*, Apr. 22, 1911; *Am. Mag.*, May 1911; *N. Y. Daily Tribune*, *N. Y. Times*, *Times-Democrat* (New Orleans), Apr. 12, 1911; *Brooklyn Daily Eagle*, Apr. 11, 12, 1911; information from Sam Loyd of Brooklyn.] L. C. K.

LOZIER, CLEMENCE SOPHIA HARNED (Dec. 11, 1813–Apr. 26, 1888), homeopathic physician, feminist, was born at Plainfield, N. J., the daughter of David and Hannah (Walker) Harned. She studied at the Plainfield Academy, and at the age of sixteen was married to Abraham Witton Lozier, an architect and builder of New York City. Not long afterward his health failed, and she opened a school for girls which she conducted for eleven years. Through a brother, who was a physician, she became interested in the study of medicine, and after the death of her husband she entered, in 1849, the Rochester Eclectic Medical College. Later she attended the Syracuse Medical College, from which she graduated in 1853. She at once settled in New York City and in 1860 began to teach physiology and hygiene to a class of girl students in her own home. This class became the nucleus of the New York Medical College and Hospital for Women, a homeopathic institution which was formally established in 1863. After the conclusion of the Civil War she toured Europe to investigate hospital construction and administration and upon her return in 1867 reorganized her school and hospital, taking the title of dean and professor of gynecology and obstetrics. She was aided in her work by her daughter-in-law, Charlotte (Denman), first wife of A. W. Lozier, Jr., and after her death, by his second wife, Jeanne M. Lozier, both graduates of the medical school. A niece, Dr. Anna Manning Comfort, was also a valued lieutenant. The school and hospital, although small, flourished for many years, until with other minor institutions they were merged with the New York Homeopathic Medical College. Although Dr. Lozier is said to have performed a number of major operations, she wrote but little on medical subjects. One small pamphlet, *Childbirth Made Easy*, appeared in 1870. As a feminist, she was interested in most of the movements intended to improve the economic and social status of women. She was for five years president of the National Woman's Suffrage Association and was active in the New York City Suffrage League, the New York Sorosis, the Woman's Christian Temperance Union, of which she was a past president, and the National Working Women's League. She died of angina pectoris in her seventy-fifth year.

[*In Memoriam, Mrs. Charlotte Denman Lozier* (1870); *Eminent Women of the Age* (1868); H. A. Kelly and W. L. Burrage, *Am. Medic. Biogs.* (1920); *Evening Post* (N. Y.), Apr. 27, 1888.] E. P.

LUBBOCK, FRANCIS RICHARD (Oct. 16, 1815–June 22, 1905), governor of Texas, Confederate soldier, second child and eldest son of Dr. Henry T. W. and Susan Ann (Saltus) Lubbock, was born in Beaufort, S. C. His ancestors on both sides were of English stock and prominent as planters, ship-owners, and merchants. The boy was educated in private schools until he was fourteen, when his father's death forced him to take a clerkship in Charleston. He later removed to Hamburg, S. C., and in 1834 went to New Orleans where he opened a drugstore. On Feb. 5, 1835, he married Adele Baron, a member of a French Creole family of New Orleans. In December 1836, he emigated to Texas and opened a store, first in Velasco and later in Houston. In 1837 he became a clerk of the Texas Congress and was appointed comptroller of the Republic by President Houston, serving one year. He was again appointed comptroller in 1841, but resigned to look after the ranch he had acquired near Houston. For sixteen years he was district clerk of Harris County. Elected lieutenant-governor by the Democrats in 1857, he was defeated by Edward Clark in 1859, when Sam Houston was successful as the head of an independent ticket. Lubbock was a delegate to the Charleston convention of his party in 1860, and supported secession. In the summer of 1861 he defeated Edward Clark for the governorship.

At the beginning of his administration the treasury was empty, Texas bonds were unsalable, and the wild Indians were hostile. Lubbock exerted himself to strengthen the defenses and increase the resources of the state. At his suggestion the legislature raised a mounted regiment for frontier defense and in the spring of 1862 created a military board, composed of the governor, comptroller, and treasurer, to provide means for the defense of the state. The board sought to raise funds by selling a part of the United States "indemnity bonds" acquired through the sale of the Santa Fé region in 1850, and by the exportation of cotton through Mexico. It also established a state foundry and a percussion-cap factory, and contracted with private firms for the manufacture of arms for state troops, but these operations were only moderately successful. Lubbock had better success in developing a cloth and shoe factory at the state penitentiary. He supported the war measures of the Confederate government, maintained cordial relations with the military authorities, and endeavored by proclamations and public addresses to keep up the spirits of the people. At the close of his term he was commissioned colonel in the Confederate army, and served on the staff of General Magruder and then on that of General John A. Wharton in the campaign against Banks in Louisiana. In the summer of 1864 President Davis called him to Richmond as adviser on trans-Mississippi affairs. He was captured with Davis in May 1865, and was imprisoned for several months in Fort Delaware (*Southern Historical Society Papers,* March 1878).

After his release he returned to Texas, opened commission houses in Houston and Galveston, turned to ranching again, and lost everything in a beef-packery venture. He next became tax collector of Galveston. In 1878 he was elected state treasurer and held this office until he voluntarily retired in 1891. After the death of his first wife he married, in December 1883, Mrs. Sarah E. (Black) Porter; and twenty years later, on Aug. 12, 1903, he married Lue Scott. His *Six Decades in Texas, or Memoirs of Francis Richard Lubbock,* edited by C. W. Raines, was published in 1900. Though he was not possessed of extraordinary ability, he won and held public confidence. His last years were spent in Austin, where the bent form of the vivacious little old man, dressed on all important occasions in Confederate gray, was a familiar and popular figure.

[Lubbock's *Six Decades* (1900); *War of the Rebellion: Official Records (Army)*; war-time files of Texas newspapers, especially the *Houston Telegraph*; *Southwestern Hist. Quart.*, Apr. 1924; *Confed. Mil. Hist.* (1899), I, 733–34; *Who's Who in America*, 1903–05; *Dallas Morning News*, June 23, 1905.] C. W. R.

LUBIN, DAVID (June 10, 1849–Jan. 1, 1919), agriculturist, was born at Klodowa in Russian Poland, the son of Simon and Rachel (Holtz) Lubin. His father died in David's early infancy. His mother, who was left with six children, married again. About 1853 the family, after passing unharmed through a pogrom, fled to England and, in 1855, emigrated to the United States. David's boyhood was spent in the Ghetto of New York City and his formal education was that of the public grammar school. His mother, a resolute, high-tempered, energetic, and deeply religious woman, trained him so thoroughly in faith and morals that her influence persisted throughout his life. The boy learned the trade of goldsmith and jeweler. Going west at sixteen, he knocked about San Francisco and in 1868 was a member of a party of gold-hunters in Arizona. Returning east without having found gold, he met with failure as a traveling salesman. In 1874 he opened a small dry-goods store in Sacramento, Cal., in partnership with his half-brother, Harris Weinstock. Two principles, complete truth in the representation of articles for sale and a fixed price, dominated the enterprise. The idea of a fixed price was new in California. The principles, together with sound management, made the business an outstanding success. A mail-order department speedily grew into the largest mail-order undertaking on the Pacific Coast. In 1884, now prosperous, he fulfilled a promise to his mother by taking her on a pilgrimage to Palestine. In the Holy Land, he later remarked, "I was vividly reminded of the mission of my people" (Agresti, *post,* p. 71). He became a militant reformer, a minor Hebrew prophet. His passion "to render service in ways in which Israel is to serve" was directed by a restless and inquiring mind. He read much of economics, political science, and history, and was influenced particularly by Herbert Spencer and John Stuart Mill. His own ideal was abstract justice.

From his mercantile venture Lubin branched into fruit-growing in California. He promptly discovered that the policies of the railroads worked to the disadvantage of the small grower and to the undue profit of certain Eastern middle-men and he became one of the leaders of an agrarian revolt which caused the railroads to modify their practices and which eventuated in the organization of the fruit-growers. Soon he advanced from a provincial to a national point of view. He was a protectionist because he feared the results for America of competition with the low-paid labor of Europe. He argued that since the tariff could not protect the farmer, who was primarily an exporter, the system of protection worked an injustice to the agricultural group. By means of lectures and pamphlets he began an agitation for "equalization of protection." His proposal was to offset the protection afforded to manufacturers and industrial laborers by granting the producers of the staples a bounty on exports in the form of a government subsidy to reduce the cost of ocean carriage from shipping points to the foreign import markets. He won a following, but the dominant protectionists publicly sneered at the "crank" while privately one of their number tried to silence him by persuading him to accept a consulship. The country was not ready to carry the principle of protection to its logical limit.

In 1896 the intense and often irascible reformer parted from his first wife, Louisa Lyons, whom he had married in 1875, under circumstances which caused his physician to order a trip to Europe to ward off a breakdown. The journey caused Lubin to transfer the emphasis of his thought from the American husbandman to the farming classes of the world. Attending the International Agricultural Congress of 1896 at Budapest, he sketched in an address the rough outlines of a project that was to absorb his energies for the rest of his life. Convinced now that justice to the American farmer was impossible without justice to the husbandmen of the world, he proposed an International Institute of Agriculture in which could be pooled and made available that information concerning crops and other agricultural matters which would enable the husbandmen of any country to fight intelligently for their own interests. During the next twelve years he talked, wrote letters and pamphlets, and traveled widely seeking to win adherents to his plan. After a snub by the United States Department of Agriculture he laid his case before the governments of Europe. Great Britain and France ignored him, for his proposal seemed almost absurd in a day of intense nationalism. Victor Emanuel of Italy, however, was persuaded. Italian initiative resulted in the establishment in 1910 of the International Institute of Agriculture, the creation of a treaty ratified by forty-six nations. Lubin remained for the rest of his life the United States delegate to the permanent committee of the Institute. Success did not change his mood. He consciously tried to personify Israel fighting for mankind. "But there is a higher service . . . and that is for the United States of the World. And I am happy to be an humble soldier and private in that army" (Agresti, *post*, p. 1). He died of influenza in Rome on Jan. 1, 1919. He had married, in 1897, Florence Platnauer. He was survived by his second wife and by eight children, three sons and five daughters.

[Signora Olivia Rosetti Agresti, a woman of marked ability who was familiar with European society, assisted Lubin in his long and difficult task of securing co-operation from European governments. Her book, *David Lubin* (1922), is the only important study. For other printed sources see R. D. Hunt, *Cal. and Californians* (1926), vol. IV; *Lit. Digest*, Feb. 8, 1919; *Outlook*, Jan. 15, 1919; *Am. Rev. of Revs.*, June 1919; *Overland Monthly*, Aug. 1919; *Sacramento Union*, *San Francisco Chronicle*, Jan. 3, 1919. Information as to certain facts was supplied for this sketch by Lubin's son, Simon J. Lubin, Sacramento, Cal.] R. H. G.

LUCAS, ANTHONY FRANCIS (Sept. 9, 1855–Sept. 2, 1921), geologist, engineer, was born in Spalato, Dalmatia, Austria, the son of a ship-builder and ship-owner, Capt. Francis Stephen Luchich, and his wife, Giovanna Giovanizio, of Montenegrin descent. When Anthony was six years old his family removed to Trieste, Austria, where he received his primary education. At the age of twenty he graduated from the Polytechnic Institute, Gratz, and then entered the Naval Academy of Fiume and Pola from which he graduated in 1878. The following year he came to the United States to visit an uncle residing in Saginaw, Mich., and became so much interested in the lumber industry that he resigned from the Austrian navy, followed his uncle's example and changed his name to Lucas, and applied for American citizenship. His final naturalization papers were granted May 9, 1885. From 1879 to 1893 he engaged first in lumbering and then, as a consulting mechanical and mining engineer, with offices and residence in Washington, D. C., in mining activities in the West. In 1893 he accepted a position as mining engineer for a salt-mining company at Petit Anse, La. During his three years' service with this organization he became much interested in the occasional mounds of low elevation occurring in the Gulf Coastal Plain areas of Louisiana and Texas, and in 1896 he began privately the serious study of these so-called domes. In the course of this work, which involved prospecting with a diamond drill, he located a number of great deposits of rock salt and also studied the seepages of petroleum and sulphur from other domes. He came to the conclusion that these elevated areas were geological structures *per se*, distinct from the surrounding sedimentary deposits with which the elevation was encircled, and that the areas showing seepages on the surface were in reality natural reservoirs of petroleum. On the basis of this theory, he selected an elevated area known as Big Hill, now Spindletop, near Beaumont, Tex., leased 220 of its 300 acres, and then sought financial aid to undertake drilling for oil. Because of his unusual theory, for which there was no proof in any of the oil fields then existing in the world, Lucas could secure the aid of only the J. M. Guffey Petroleum Company of Pittsburgh, Pa., and that only by relinquishing the larger part of his interest in the undertaking. Operations were begun on Oct. 27, 1900, using a crude form of hydraulic rotary drill. After successfully overcoming discouraging difficulties with quicksand by devising a check valve (which he failed to patent) he struck oil at a depth of 1,139 feet on Jan. 10, 1901. Within twenty-four hours petroleum was gushing from the well at the rate of nearly a hundred thousand barrels a day—the largest oil well, by far, ever completed in the United States. The Lucas Gusher on Spindletop started a new era in the oil industry, but while Lucas, as the discoverer, became famous the world over, his own financial reward was negligible. He continued with the J. M. Guffey Petroleum Company for about a year and then in 1902 undertook petroleum exploration in Mexico for the Mexican Eagle Oil Company, Limited. In 1905 he returned to Washington, D. C., and resumed his consulting practice, which he continued until his death. He was a member of the American Institute of Mining Engineers, the Franklin Institute, and the American Electrochemical Society, and of the Engineers' Club, New York, and the Cosmos Club, Washington. On Sept. 22, 1887, he married Carolina Weed Fitzgerald, who with a son survived him.

[*Trans. Am. Inst. Mining and Metallurgical Engrs.*, vol. LXV (1921); R. S. McBeth, *Pioneering the Gulf Coast; A Story of the Life and Accomplishments of Capt. Anthony F. Lucas* (1918); *Who's Who in America*, 1920–21; *Mining and Scientific Press*, Sept. 17, 1921; *Evening Star* (Washington, D. C.), Sept. 2, 1921.] C. W. M.

LUCAS, DANIEL BEDINGER (Mar. 16, 1836–July 28, 1909), jurist, author, "poet of the Shenandoah Valley," was born at "Rion Hall," near Charles Town, Va. (now W. Va.). He came of a family of distinguished soldiers. The first Lucas of which there is record, Robert, came from England and settled in Pennsylvania in 1679. Edward, a son of this Robert, moved on to the Shenandoah Valley of Virginia and settled near Shepherdstown; his grandson, William, built on one of the most beautiful spots of the Valley, "Rion Hall," where his son Daniel was born. The boy's mother, Virginia Bedinger, was a daughter of Daniel Bedinger, collector of the Port of Norfolk during John Adams' administration, a man of considerable poetic talent. Because of an injury to his spine during infancy, which kept him from more active amusements, Daniel spent much time in his father's excellent library, forming a taste for good literature and a desire to write poetry. After some schooling under private tutors in the home of Braxton Davenport at Charles Town he went to the University of Virginia where he excelled in oratory. Completing his course in 1854, he attended the law school of Judge John W. Brockenbrough at Lexington, Va., where he graduated with honors. In 1859 he began practising law at Charles Town but moved the next year to Richmond. At the beginning of the Civil War he joined the staff of Gen. Henry A. Wise and took part in the Kanawha Valley Campaign; physical disability kept him from active service during the last years of the war. Toward the end of the war he courageously ran the blockade to help defend his classmate, John Yates Beall [*q.v.*], accused in New York of being a spy. Unable to return south he stayed in Canada where upon the surrender of Lee he published his best-known poem, *The Land Where We Were Dreaming*. The war over he returned to Charles Town. Barred from the practice of his profession by the test oath, he turned to literature and became co-editor of the Baltimore *Southern Metropolis*, in which magazine he published some of his poems. The same year he married Lena Tucker Brooke, grand-niece of Gov. Robert Brooke of Virginia.

In 1871 Lucas reëntered his profession and shortly became one of the most distinguished practitioners before the courts of West Virginia. A stanch Democrat of the Jeffersonian school he took a prominent part in the politics of the state. He was Democratic presidential elector in 1872 and 1876; elector at large on the Cleveland ticket in 1884; was elected to the legislature in 1884 and 1886; and was a member of the supreme court of appeals from 1889 to 1893, serving as president from Nov. 8, 1890, to Jan. 1, 1893. Because of ill health he was comparatively inactive during the last ten years of his life, spending the time quietly on his estate with his wife and only child, Virginia, who like her father was a contributor to several magazines. Lucas' volumes of poetry include, besides the first, *The Wreath of Eglantine* (1869), written in collaboration with his sister, and *Ballads and Madrigals* (1884). A collected edition of his poems, edited by Charles W. Kent and Lucas' daughter, was published in Boston in 1913 under the title *The Land Where We Were Dreaming*. His plays, three in number, are in blank verse. *The Maid of Northumberland* was published in 1884. *Hildebrand* and *Kate McDonald* were published posthumously in the *Dramatic Works of Daniel Bedinger Lucas* (1913). All three have to do with the Civil War in America, *The Maid of Northumberland* being perhaps the first play written in America on this subject. In two of the plays the author makes use of his blockade-running experiences at the time of the John Yates Beall trial. They are full of Shakespearian echoes, contain some excellent speeches, and some good descriptions of nature, but on the whole, Lucas the dramatist is inferior to Lucas the writer of lyrics. His poems are of different kinds—nature poems, love poems, narrative poems, poems of sentiment, poems dealing with the South and the war, and poems written for special occasions. They show the influence of Keats, Tennyson, and Poe. His prose works include *The Memoir of John Yates Beall* (1865), and *Nicaragua, War of the Filibusters* (1896). At the time of his death he was writing a life of Lincoln.

[*Who's Who in America*, 1908–09; J. E. Norris, *Hist. of the Lower Shenandoah Valley* (1890); G. W. Atkinson and A. F. Gibbens, *Prominent Men of W. Va.* (1890); G. W. Atkinson, *Bench and Bar of W. Va.* (1919); *Lib. of Southern Lit.*, vol. VII (1909); Lucy F. Bittinger, *Bittinger and Bedinger Families* (1904); *Univ. of Va., Its Hist., Influence, Equipment, and Characteristics* (1904), vol. I.] F. M. S.

LUCAS, ELIZA [See PINCKNEY, ELIZA LUCAS, 1722–1793].

LUCAS, FREDERIC AUGUSTUS (Mar. 25, 1852–Feb. 9, 1929), naturalist, museum administrator, was born at Plymouth, Mass., the son of Augustus Henry and Eliza (Oliver) Lucas. The first eighteen years of his life were spent in his native town, where he received a common-school education and where his inherent fondness for natural history was given opportunity for expression. He writes that as a boy he was only second-rate at the ordinary boyish sports but that he did possess a more than average mechanical ability and skill at handling tools.

At the end of his second long voyage in a clipper ship, of which his father was captain, he found himself, at eighteen, confronted with the problem of what to do in life. He had a strong desire to become a taxidermist and collector of birds, and through Prof. J. W. P. Jenks of Pierce Academy, at Middleboro, Mass., a taxidermist of considerable ability, he became acquainted with the museum of that institution. Soon he secured a position in the Natural Science Establishment of Prof. Henry A. Ward [*q.v.*] at Rochester, N. Y., and for eleven years, 1871 to 1882, he was a member of that famous organization. There he had as laboratory associates men who were later to become leaders in various branches of natural-history work. There also he had ample opportunity for the development of his mechanical ability along many lines, although he specialized in the preparation and mounting of skeletons. In this work he developed such a high technique that in 1882 he was called to the United States National Museum in Washington as osteologist. Under the influence of Dr. George Brown Goode [*q.v.*] he developed so rapidly and so broadly that in 1902 he was simultaneously curator of comparative anatomy, acting curator of fossil vertebrates, in charge of biological exhibits, and in charge of the children's room. In 1904 he was called to Brooklyn as curator-in-chief of the Museum of the Brooklyn Institute of Arts and Sciences.

Here he found a museum in a somewhat chaotic state, with the exhibits unbalanced and a general lack of coordination. He gave his attention particularly to the natural-history department, and when he resigned the mark of his genius was left in the exhibition halls. His idea of a natural-history museum was that it should not be merely a collection of curious objects from various parts of the world but a teaching institution with the specimens cautiously selected, carefully installed, and instructively labeled. This idea he carried out first in the National Museum, then in Brooklyn, and finally in the great American Museum of Natural History in New York, to which he was called as director in 1911 and where he remained until his death. His influence on the museums of America was great and lasting.

As a field naturalist, he was given but few opportunities. There are only three major expeditions to his credit, but each one was carried out successfully. The first was to Funk Island for remains of the Great Auk, the second to the Pribilof Islands as a member of the Fur Seal Commission, and the last to a whaling station in Newfoundland for the great sulphur-bottom whale. His published writings, both technical and popular, comprise some 365, and the wide range of subjects covered indicates the breadth of his interest and activities. Probably his best-known works are two small volumes, *Animals of the Past* (1901) and *Animals before Man in America* (1902), and the articles contributed to Johnson's *Universal Cyclopædia*. On Feb. 13, 1884, he married Annie J. Edgar, by whom he had two daughters.

[T. S. Palmer, in *The Auk*, Apr. 1929; C. H. Townsend, in *Science*, Apr. 26, 1929; R. C. Murphy, in *Natural Hist.*, Mar.–Apr. 1929; *Who's Who in America*, 1926–27; *N. Y. Times*, Feb. 10, 1929; autobiography and bibliography entitled "Fifty Years of Museum Work," to be published (1933) by the Am. Museum of Natural Hist.] W. G.

LUCAS, JAMES H. (Nov. 12, 1800–Nov. 9, 1873), banker, capitalist, railroad president, was born at Pittsburgh, the fifth son of John Baptiste Charles Lucas [*q.v.*] and Anne (Sebin), who came to America from Normandy in 1784. Appointed territorial judge and commissioner of land claims of upper Louisiana Territory in 1805, John Lucas moved with his large family to St. Louis, then "an untamed and unprogressive trading town." He commenced immediately to purchase large tracts of land in, and adjacent to, the town and to lay the foundation for a great fortune. The boy received his early education there under unsatisfactory conditions and was sent to St. Thomas' College, Kentucky, in 1814, and later, to Jefferson College, Pennsylvania. He then studied law under the direction of family friends in Poughkeepsie, N. Y., and in Litchfield, Conn., but with no desire to follow that profession. In 1823 he moved to Arkansas Territory, where he remained for thirteen years and had a varied experience. He was, successively, a school-teacher, a merchant, county clerk, a plantation owner, a lawyer, a probate judge, and a militia officer. Here, in May 1832, he married Mary Emilie Desruisseaux, a native of Cahokia, Ill., by whom he had numerous children. Upon his father's request, his four brothers having died, he returned to St. Louis in 1837 to assume the management of the family properties. By this time the "Lucas estate" comprised vast holdings in the city, together with plantations in several counties. With the economic transformation of St. Louis and its firm establishment as a commercial and industrial center, there came a phenomenal rise in land prices and in the value of the estate. The wealth thus acquired enabled Lucas to sponsor numerous enterprises. He early realized the vital need for better transportation facilities in the West, and with other wealthy and public-spirited men of the city he was instrumental in the organization of the Pacific Railroad in 1849, the first and most important line built in Missouri. He donated large sums for its construction, served as a director and twice as president, and assisted it in the recurrent financial crises which beset early railroad ventures. He founded the private banking house of Lucas, Simonds & Company, organized the St. Louis Gas Company, and was a director and large stock holder in a score of corporations. His interests extended to California, but the St. Louis property was the corner-stone. He was not content, however, merely to accumulate money, but was a generous patron of enterprises of an educational, cultural, and religious character. In politics he was a stanch Whig, and twice ran for office, serving one term, 1844–48, in the state Senate, and being defeated for the office of mayor of St. Louis in 1847. He was an effective exponent of the conservative business interests of his city. The grave conditions in Western finance occasioned by the panic of 1857 were successfully met by him, despite considerable losses; but the outbreak of the Civil War precipitated a crisis in the governmental and economic situation in Missouri. Lucas, in common with many business men, supported the Bell-Everett ticket, and in 1861 was opposed both to secession and to coercion of the South. He labored for compromise, and when that failed, steadily and resolutely supported the Union cause. During the critical and uncertain decade following the war, he was chiefly concerned with the economic restoration of St. Louis and in the administration of his estate. Following a long period of ill health he died a few days before the completion of his seventy-third year.

[J. T. Scharf, *Hist. of St. Louis* (1883); L. U. Reavis, *St. Louis: the Future Great City* (1875); *Mo. Hist. Soc. Colls.*, vol III, no. 3 (1911); R. E. Riegel, *Story of the Western Railroads* (1926) and "Trans-Mississippi Railroads during the Fifties," *Miss. Valley Hist. Rev.*, Sept. 1923; H. L. Conard, *Encyc. of the Hist. of Mo.*, vol. IV (1901); *St. Louis Democrat* and *St. Louis Republican*, Nov. 10, 1873.] T. S. B.

LUCAS, JOHN BAPTISTE CHARLES (Aug. 14, 1758–Aug. 29, 1842), congressman, jurist, was born in the ancient town of Pont-Audemer on the river Brille, in Normandy, France. His father was Robert Édouard Lucas, *procureur du roi*; his mother before her marriage was a Mademoiselle de l'Arche. He attended the Honfleur and Paris law schools, and in 1782 graduated from the law department of the University of Caen. For the next two years he practised law in his native town, and sometime during this period he married Anne Sebin.

In 1784 he emigrated to the United States and settled on a farm on the Monongahela River, a short distance above Pittsburgh, Pa. Here, in addition to agricultural pursuits, he devoted his time to the acquisition of the English language and to familiarizing himself with the history, constitution, and laws of his adopted country. During these early years in Pennsylvania he seems to have made some trading voyages down the Ohio and Mississippi rivers to New Madrid, in what was to become the state of Missouri. He soon gained the confidence of his neighbors and was elected to the Pennsylvania House of Representatives, where he served from 1792 to 1798. During the year 1794 he was also a judge of the court of common pleas in his district. He was elected to Congress as a Democrat from the Allegheny district, to succeed Albert Gallatin, and served from Mar. 4, 1803, until 1805, when, having been appointed United States judge for the northern district of Louisiana by President Jefferson, he resigned and removed to St. Louis. He served in this capacity until 1820 and was also a member of the commission for the adjustment of land titles in the territory from 1805 until its dissolution in 1812. At one time he was acting governor of Missouri Territory, and when the first state legislature met he was a candidate for the United States Senate.

It is probable that service on the commission for the adjustment of land titles directed the attention of Judge Lucas to the acquisition of real estate. When he came to St. Louis it was a small French frontier village, but he foresaw its future and possessed himself of all the land he could obtain. As a result he left to his heirs a large estate. Some time after the death of his wife, in 1811, he built a small stone house on what is now the corner of Seventh and Market streets, and here he made his home until his death.

He has been described as small in stature, and as a man of honor and of untiring industry. He was eccentric and irritable and frequently exhibited these defects while on the bench. His administration of the laws was excellent, for he understood the old French and Spanish titles as well as any man in the territory. During his later years he was very melancholy, due in large part to the fact that several of his sons met violent deaths. One of them, Charles, was killed in a duel with Col. Thomas Hart Benton [*q.v.*] in 1817. A surviving son, James H. Lucas [*q.v.*], was prominent in the commercial development of Missouri.

[*Biog. Dir. Am. Cong.* (1928); J. T. Scharf, *Hist. of St. Louis City and County,* vol. II (1883); F. L. Billon, *Annals of St. Louis in Its Territorial Days: from 1804 to 1821* (1888); W. B. Davis and D. S. Durrie, *An Illustrated Hist. of St. Louis* (1876); W. V. N. Bay, *Reminiscences of the Bench and Bar of Mo.* (1878); William Hyde and H. L. Conard, *Encyc. of the Hist. of St. Louis* (1899), vol. III; obituary in *St. Louis Daily New Era,* Aug. 30, 1842.] M. J. W.

LUCAS, JONATHAN (1754–Apr. 1, 1821), millwright, was born in Cumberland, England, the son of John and Ann (Noble) Lucas. His mechanical genius is said to have been inherited from his mother's family, who were mill-owners in Whitehaven. On May 22, 1774, he married Mary Cooke; and the christenings of their five children are on record in St. Mary's Church, Egremont. After the death of his first wife, between 1783 and 1786, he married Ann Ashburn, of Whitehaven. About 1790, he came to Charleston, S. C., where he attracted attention by setting up a small windmill on the gable of a wooden store in King Street, where he lived. A passing rice-planter, learning that the maker of the mill was in needy circumstances and desired work, took him to Santee. There the system of flooding rice fields by action of the tide was coming into general use; but a large crop was considered a dubious blessing because of the difficulty of removing husks from the grain. Much was pounded out by hand in wooden mortars with pestles, a slave's task being from a bushel to a bushel and a half a day. Crude mills turned by animals were in use: the pecker machine, which moved its pestle like the stroke of a woodpecker, and the cogmill, whose upright pestles were driven by a horizontal cog wheel. These could clean from three to six barrels a day. Lucas set up a new type of pounding-mill, probably at first moved by wind; but he is remembered for his water-mill, driven by a very large undershot water-wheel. He built the first on Peach Island Plantation for J. Bowman, who as late as 1810 owed him £1,500. For Andrew Johnston, on Millbrook Plantation, he built the first of his tide mills, which operated automatically with every ebb tide, day and night. In 1793, he built for Henry Laurens on Mepkin Plantation, Cooper River, an improved tide mill, with rolling screens, elevators, and packers. After the rice was threshed from the straw, it was lifted by the elevators (buckets on an endless belt) to a rolling screen in which it was freed of sand, and was then poured into a hopper above the millstones. A wind fan having blown away chaff, the milled rice passed into mortars where pestles weighing some two hundred pounds struck the grain from thirty to forty times a minute. It then went through a rolling screen to remove the flour, and after a winnowing fan had blown off the remainder of the chaff, the clean grain was placed in six-hundred-pound barrels by the packer. Three persons could manage such a mill, and, on a favorable tide, beat from sixteen to twenty barrels.

Assisted by his son, Lucas installed his mills throughout the rice region, some early ones being on the reserves of Mrs. Middleton, Gen. Peter Horry, and Col. Wm. Alston of Santee. He prospered, and in 1793 he bought at auction a plantation on Shem Creek in Christ Church Parish. There he made his home and built a combined rice and saw mill, called Greenwich Mills. Later, in partnership with two carpenters, he bought a large lot in Charleston, where afterwards the rice mills centered. In 1803 he acquired five lots in Mount Pleasant, and in 1804 he purchased fifty acres on Shute's Folly in Charleston harbor, where he is said to have built a windmill. In 1817 either he or his son Jonathan [*q.v.*] built in Charleston the first steam rice mill; but in all essentials the later rice mills adhered to his plans, and the rice industry owed as much to him as the cotton industry to Eli Whitney. On the afternoon of Apr. 2, 1821, his funeral was held at the residence of his son in Charleston, and he was buried in St. Paul's churchyard.

[John Drayton, *A View of S. C.* (1802); R. F. W. Allston, *A Memoir of the Introduction and Plantinr of Rice in S. C.* (1843); *Year Book, City of Charleston,* 1883. *Charleston Courier,* Apr. 2, 1821; *Charleston Mercury,* June 17, 1851; *Southern Cabinet of Agriculture, Horticulture, Rural and Domestic Economy* (Charleston, 1840); Charleston Mesne Conveyance Records; family records; epitaph.] A. K. G.

LUCAS, JONATHAN (1775–Dec. 29, 1832), millwright and inventor, was born in England and christened in St. Mary's Church, Egremont, Cumberland, Feb. 26, 1775. His parents were Jonathan [*q.v.*] and Mary (Cooke) Lucas, both of Cumberland. As a lad of about fifteen years he came to South Carolina with his father, whom he assisted in building rice mills. In 1798 he bought a large tidewater lot in Cannonborough, Charleston, where he banked a mill pond and built a rice mill that attracted a considerable toll business. On July 18, 1799, he married Sarah Lydia Simons, daughter of Benjamin Simons of the Grove Plantation in Christ Church Parish. In 1801, on Middleburg Plantation, Cooper River, inherited by his wife from her father, he built a toll rice mill. On July 12, 1808, he patented a new type of machine for removing the husks from rice without pounding by pestles. This machine consisted of two vertical conical cylinders, turning in opposite directions, one within the other, the inner cylinder having a much higher velocity than the outer. The outer cylinder was faced with sheet iron punched like a grater; the inner was sometimes similarly faced, sometimes covered with fluted cork or other soft wood, and sometimes had sand or another scouring substance cemented to the surface. The rice passed into the space between the cylinders, which were usually about a half inch apart, though the inner cylinder might be moved up or down at will. From the cylinders it went to the rolling screen where the flour was sifted off, and finally it was polished by the brushing machine.

The South Carolinians preferred to keep the rice-pounding mills of the elder Lucas, but the new machine was a great success in England, which, with a duty of four dollars a tierce on clean rice, became a depot for heavy shipments of paddy or rough rice. In 1822, Jonathan Lucas the younger, at the invitation of the British government, returned to England; and in 1827, he and his son-in-law, Henry Ewbank, doing business in Mincing Lane, London, received a British patent for his invention. Rice-cleaning mills were eventually established at London, Liverpool, Copenhagen, Bremen, Amsterdam, Bordeaux, and Lisbon; and Jonathan Lucas amassed a large fortune.

At Hatcham Grove, his residence in Surrey, he became ill on Christmas morning, 1832, and a few days later died of what was called an effusion of blood to the head. On Jan. 5, 1833, his body was placed in a vault in Camberwell Church, London. By his will, dated Oct. 7, 1831, but not recorded in Charleston until 1836, he appointed his sons-in-law as trustees to manage his plantations, negroes, and trading and other partnerships in Great Britain, America, or elsewhere, making provision for his adult and minor children and bequeathing to his widow all his real and personal property in South Carolina.

[Family papers in possession of T. S. Lucas, Society Hill, S. C., including records copied from St. Mary's Church, Egremont, and letter from Elizabeth Lucas, Dec. 1832; Charleston Mesne Conveyance Records; H. L. Ellsworth, *A Digest of Patents Issued by the U. S. from 1790 to Jan. 1, 1839* (1840); *S. C. Hist. and Geneal. Mag.,* Jan. 1917, Oct. 1924; R. F. W. Allston, *A Memoir of the Introduction and Planting of Rice in S. C.* (1843); *Year Book City of Charleston, S. C., 1883*; *Charleston Courier,* May 28, 1827.] A. K. G.

LUCAS, ROBERT (Apr. 1, 1781–Feb. 7, 1853), governor of Ohio and territorial governor of Iowa, was born at Shepherdstown, Va. (now W. Va.), the son of Susannah (Barnes) and William Lucas, a Revolutionary soldier of some wealth. His early education was obtained largely from a private tutor, who instructed him especially in mathematics and surveying. When he was about twenty, he moved with his parents to the valley of the Scioto in the Northwest Territory, and in the new state of Ohio he became surveyor for Scioto County, justice of the peace, and an officer in the militia, in which he reached the grade of major-general. On Apr. 4, 1810, he married Elizabeth Brown, who died in 1812. In the War of 1812, after helping to organize a battalion of volunteers from his brigade of Ohio militia, he acted as a detached officer in the disastrous campaign of General Hull. During this time he kept a daily journal that has been published as *The Robert Lucas Journal of the War of 1812* (edited by J. C. Parish, 1906, reprinted from *Iowa Journal of History and Politics,* July 1906). State politics engrossed his attention in the period following the war. He had been a member of the lower house in 1808 and 1809. In 1814 he was elected to the state Senate. On Mar. 7, 1816, he married Friendly Ashley Sumner and, about that time, moved to the newly organized Pike County, where he opened a general store at Piketon. He continued to represent his district in the state Senate until 1822 and, again, from 1824 to 1828 and from 1829 to 1830. In the session of 1831 and 1832 he served once more in the lower house. As a stanch supporter of Jacksonian politics he had become well known in Ohio and in 1830 was nominated for the governorship of the state. He was defeated but, two years later, was again nominated and was elected. During the presidential campaign of this year he attended the first national convention of the Democratic party and was given the honor of acting as its temporary and permanent chairman.

He served for two terms as governor of Ohio. His most notable service was the vigorous part he took in the acute controversy over the boundary line between the state of Ohio and the territory of Michigan, which led to the "Toledo War." After two years of retirement he was appointed, in 1838, by Van Buren as governor and superintendent of Indian affairs for the newly created territory of Iowa. He was fifty-seven years old, full of experience, intense in his convictions, and positive in his methods. The early part of his governorship was stormy because of the hostility of an ambitious young secretary of the territory and the opposition of a youthful and spirited territorial legislature that chafed at the limitations imposed by the absolute veto power of the governor. Again he found himself involved in a boundary dispute, the line between the state of Missouri and the territory of Iowa being at issue. In 1841 Harrison appointed John Chambers, a Whig, as governor of the territory, and Lucas retired to private life. His most conspicuous public service in the dozen years of life still left him was his participation in the convention of 1844 to form a constitution for the state of Iowa. His messages and proclamations and his public and private correspondence show him to have been a man of practical common sense and of seasoned wisdom in political matters, and, though stern and unbending in his policies, he was the type of executive greatly needed by the territory of Iowa in its initial period. He spent his last years for the most part on his farm near Iowa City, Iowa, and devoted much energy to the causes of temperance and public education, and to the encouragement of railroad projects. He was an ardent worker in the Methodist Church and spent a good deal of time writing religious hymns and verses. Although he had been a life-long Democrat he refused to vote for Franklin Pierce, and cast his ballot in the last year of his life for the Whig ticket.

[Collection of Letters and Papers of Lucas in the Lib. of the State Hist. Soc. of Iowa; *Executive Jour. of Iowa, 1838–41*, ed. by B. F. Shambaugh (1906); "Documents Relating to Governor Lucas," *Iowa Hist. Record*, April 1900; J. C. Parish, *Robert Lucas* (1907); Frederick Lloyd, "Robert Lucas," *Annals of Iowa*, Jan., Apr., July 1870; N. W. Evans, *A Hist. of Scioto County* (1903); T. S. Parvin, "The Quarrel between Gov. Lucas and Sec. Conway," *Annals of Iowa*, July–Oct. 1895.]

J. C. P.

LUCE, STEPHEN BLEECKER (Mar. 25, 1827–July 28, 1917), naval officer, was born in Albany, N. Y., the son of Vinal and Charlotte (Bleecker) Luce, who traced their ancestry back to English and Dutch colonists. His paternal ancestor, Henry Luce, is said to have settled on Martha's Vineyard in the last quarter of the seventeenth century. When Stephen was about eight years old the family moved to Washington, D. C. On Oct. 19, 1841, at the age of fourteen, he was appointed a midshipman as from the state of New York. He learned the rudiments of seamanship on the *North Carolina*, the *Congress*, and the *Columbus*. In March 1848 he was ordered to the Naval Academy, and in the following year, promoted to the rank of passed midshipman, he was ordered to sea again on the *Vandalia* and cruised in the Pacific until October 1852. After shore duty at Washington, during which he assisted in astronomical work, he joined the *Vixen*, May 1853, and the following year was ordered to the Coast Survey. Promoted to master and lieutenant in 1855, he was on the *Jamestown* until February 1860, cruising for much of the time along the Mosquito Coast. In March he was assigned to the Naval Academy as assistant to the commandant. Meanwhile, Dec. 7, 1854, he married Eliza Henley, a grandniece of Martha Washington. They had one son and two daughters.

Shortly before the firing on Fort Sumter, Luce was detailed to the *Wabash* as a watch officer, but his cruise was cut short by his detachment, at the urgent request of the superintendent of the Naval Academy, to become head of its department of seamanship. The Naval Academy, at that time, was at Newport, R. I., having been moved there because of the proximity of Annapolis to the war zone. In 1862 Luce was promoted to the rank of lieutenant commander. His tour of duty at the Academy marks the beginning of work which led to the publication of his book, *Seamanship* (1863). This supplied a great lack in text-books and became the standard treatise on the subject, passing through many editions. In October 1863 he was ordered to command the monitor *Nantucket*; later he took over command of the *Pontiac*; and in 1865, he was ordered to cooperate with General Sherman in the capture of Charleston. He next became commandant of midshipmen at Annapolis under the leadership of Admiral Porter, and on July 25, 1866, was promoted to the grade of commander. In 1869 he was detached, and until 1884 he was with the European Squadron (1869–72), on shore duty (1872–75), in command of the flag ship *Hartford* (1875–77), of the training ship, *Minnesota* (1877–81), and of all apprentice ships (1881–84).

Luce was a "lean, wiry man of medium height, with thin features between iron gray sidewhiskers, a prominent hawk-like nose, thin lips and determined chin, and . . . piercing gray eyes" (J. M. Ellicott, in *United States Naval Institute Proceedings,* October 1924, p. 1616). He was good-humored, witty, shrewd, and, above all, inspiring. In the years following the Civil War, when the navy was in a deplorable condition, he believed in its future, and, determined, persistent, and unselfish, did as much perhaps as any one person to upbuild it. While his activities were varied, he directed his energies principally to raising the efficiency of the personnel. In 1873 he read a paper at the Naval Academy, entitled, "The Meaning of Our Navy and Merchant Marine," which appeared as the first paper in the initial number of the *United States Naval Institute Proceedings.* In this and subsequent publications he plead for a better training of seamen, both for the navy and for the merchant marine. Many of his suggestions were later adopted. During the periods when he was in command of training ships he put into operation numerous original methods, the success of which proved their value.

Appreciating as did few naval men of his day the great importance of tactics and strategy, he labored, in the face of no little opposition, to secure better training facilities for officers. It was his own practice, when opportunity offered, to put ships through the most intense and exacting tactical maneuvers, often to the extreme annoyance of their officers. Convinced of the need of officers being versed in naval methods he long advocated, though at first meeting not only indifference but ridicule, the establishment of an institution where they might pursue advanced studies. The army had schools for this purpose, but the navy's need of them had not been recognized. Finally, however, on May 30, 1884, Secretary Chandler appointed a board to make a report on the whole proposition of "post graduate" work for naval officers. Its report resulted in a general order dated Oct. 6, 1884, establishing the Naval War College, with Luce, who had received the rank of commodore Nov. 25, 1881, as the first president. The College was opened in Newport, R. I., and it was not long before Luce had secured as lecturer on tactics and naval history Capt. A. T. Mahan [*q.v.*], who also became a molding influence in the development of the institution. At first the college received poor support, both financially and professionally. Time proved its value, however, and eventually, together with technical war-game studies, it provided officers with instruction in history, foreign policy, international law, and higher command. Similar naval institutions in England, Japan, Germany, and France were patterned after Luce's ideas. The value of what he did for the education of officers is incalculable; as Admiral Fiske succinctly stated in the *Naval Institute Proceedings* (*post,* p. 1936), he "taught the navy to think." The building at the Naval Academy housing the department of seamanship was named in his honor.

In 1886 Luce was commissioned rear admiral and three years later was retired. He was the naval editor of Johnson's *Universal Cyclopaedia* and of Funk and Wagnall's *Standard Dictionary.* He also compiled a book of naval songs. He was a prolific writer, most of his articles appearing in the *Naval Institute Proceedings* and the *North American Review.* Professional reports of boards on which he served appeared in the reports of the Secretary of the Navy. From 1901 to 1910 he was on special duty at the War College. He died at Newport in his ninety-first year.

[B. R. Fiske, in *U. S. Naval Inst. Proc.,* vol. XLIII, no. 175 (Sept. 1917) and C. S. Alden, in *Ibid.,* vol. L, no. 262 (Dec. 1924); Albert Gleaves, *Life and Letters of Rear Admiral Stephen B. Luce* (1925); C. F. Goodrich, *In Memoriam: Stephen Bleecker Luce* (1919); *Who's Who in America,* 1916–17; L. R. Hamersly, *The Records of Living Officers of the U. S. Navy and Marine Corps* (6th ed., 1898); *Official Records of the Union and Confederate Navies in the War of the Rebellion*; obituaries in *Army and Navy Jour.* and *Army and Navy Reg.,* Aug. 4, 1917; *N. Y. Times,* July 29, 1917.]
A. R. B.

LUDELING, JOHN THEODORE (Jan. 27, 1827–Jan. 21, 1891), jurist, son of John and Françoise Lorette (de Salnavo) Ludeling, was born in New Orleans, but moved when a boy to Monroe, La. His mother was from Santo Domingo. Her father, a coffee planter, and most of his family were massacred in 1801 during the rebellion of the blacks under the leadership of Toussaint L'Ouverture. The future Mrs. Ludeling, then three years of age, escaped with her grandmother and reached a vessel which brought them to New Orleans. Here she was brought up by her grandmother, and here she married John Ludeling, an emigrant from France. After his death she married Bernard Hemken, and settled in Monroe. On July 18, 1839, when he was twelve years of age, John enrolled, as a Roman Catholic, in St. Louis University, St. Louis, Mo., which at that time drew more than half of its students from Louisiana. He attended until 1843, but neither he nor his brother, who enrolled at the same time, remained to complete the work for the bachelor's degree, which then required six years. His name appears in a very small roster of students of excellent conduct, and again in a long roll of diligent students, but he seems to have won no premiums for scholarship. While at the university both brothers were known by the name of their stepfather, Hemken, but John, at least, later took back the family name of Ludeling.

After leaving St. Louis University, he returned to Monroe, studied law in the office of Isaiah Garrett, was admitted to the Louisiana bar, and married Maria Copley, daughter of Enoch Copley. He early took the side of the North in the sectional controversy, joined the Republican party soon after its organization, and, although two brothers served in the army of the Confederacy, he remained a Union man. The Republican governor, H. C. Warmoth, appointed him chief justice of Louisiana, and he held the office from Nov. 1, 1868, to Jan. 9, 1877, through the bitter years of reconstruction. When he retired from the bench he returned to Monroe and associated himself with Talbot Stillman, and the connection continued until his death.

Ludeling was a man of indomitable courage and unshakable integrity, and was charitable in ways not published to the world. He was an able and successful lawyer, and he was also successful financially. He was instrumental in building the Vicksburg, Shreveport & Pacific Railroad, and served as its first president. It has been said that the Ludeling court was one of the best that Louisiana ever had. It failed to receive local credit, however, because it was Republican and in office during reconstruction days. Ludeling died at Killeden Plantation, his country home near Monroe. His funeral was conducted by Western Star Lodge No. 24, F. & A. M., and he was buried in the old City Cemetery, Monroe.

[Information from John T. L. Hubbard, attorney-at-law, Bridgeport, Conn.; Rev. Laurence J. Kenney, S.J., of St. Louis University; E. G. Courtney, Monroe, La., secretary of Western Star Lodge No. 24, F. & A. M.; and Judge Rufus E. Foster of New Orleans; H. P. Dart, "The History of the Supreme Court of Louisiana" and W. K. Dart, "The Justices of the Supreme Court," in 133 *La. Reports*, repr. in *La. Hist. Quart.*, Jan. 1921; L. C. Quintero in *Green Bag*, Mar. 1891; Wm. F. Fanning, *Memorial Volume of the Diamond Jubilee of St. Louis Univ.* (1904); *Times-Democrat* and *Daily Picayune* (New Orleans), Jan. 23, 28, 1891.]

M. J. W.

LUDLOW, DANIEL (Aug. 2, 1750–Sept. 26, 1814), merchant and banker, eldest child of Gabriel Ludlow by his second wife, Elizabeth (Crommelin), was born in New York City, where for over fifty years the Ludlows had been prominent merchants and distinguished citizens. He was a descendant of Gabriel Ludlow, grand-nephew of Roger Ludlow [*q.v.*] and member of a Somerset family, who emigrated to New York in 1694. At the age of fifteen the boy was sent to Holland to enter the counting-house of the great Amsterdam firm of Crommelin & Zoon, which had been founded by his maternal grandfather, Charles Crommelin. Here he learned the banking business and acquired a knowledge of the French, German, and Dutch languages. Returning to New York after four or five years, he joined his father as a general merchant and upon the latter's death in 1773 continued the business under his own name. After the Revolution, during which he remained loyal to the British Crown, Ludlow, with Edward Goold as partner, conducted a general importing business at 47 Wall St. This partnership was dissolved about 1790, and thereafter until 1808 Ludlow and his nephew, Gulian, under the firm name of Daniel Ludlow & Company, carried on the enterprise and built up the largest mercantile and importing trade in the city. In 1799 he was active in the organization of the Manhattan Company and was chosen its first president. This company was formed ostensibly to supply New York "with pure and wholesome water"; but apparently its real object was to establish a bank, since an inconspicuous clause in the charter permitted surplus funds to be used in any "monied transactions and operations" not inconsistent with state or national laws (*Laws of New York*, 1799, ch. LXXXIV). Though there were many complaints about the water supply, the Bank of the Manhattan Company, established on Sept. 1, 1799, at 40 Wall St., prospered under Ludlow's leadership and remains today one of New York's greatest financial institutions. The succeeding years were busy ones for the merchant banker, for in addition to his other activities he was appointed navy agent in 1801 and later he became a leading director of the Harlem Bridge Company.

Ludlow was also prominent socially. He had a summer home at Barretto's Point on the East River, whither he often conveyed guests in his four-in-hand equipage. An avenue and square in that locality, now part of the Borough of the Bronx, still retain the family name. Both at his country seat and at his large marble house at 54–56 Broadway he dispensed hospitality, keeping six or eight places set at table for unexpected guests. The unsettled trade conditions in Europe, culminating in the Berlin and Milan decrees, brought Daniel Ludlow & Company to bankruptcy, however, and in 1808 Ludlow was forced to sell both his city home and his country estate. As a matter of policy he resigned as president of the Manhattan Company, and shortly afterward moved to Skaneateles, N. Y., where he was an honored resident until his death. He was twice married: first, Oct. 4, 1773, to Arabella Duncan, who died in 1803; and later, to a Mrs. Van Horne. George Duncan and Gabriel George Ludlow [*qq.v.*] were his half-brothers.

[*N. Y. Geneal. and Biog. Record,* Jan., Apr. 1919; *New-Eng Hist. and Geneal. Reg.,* Apr. 1888; E. N. Leslie, *Skaneateles: Hist. of its Earliest Settlement and Reminiscences of Later Times* (1902); J. A. Scoville, *The Old Merchants of N. Y.,* 3 ser. (1865); J. G. Wilson, *The Memorial Hist. of the City of N. Y.,* vols. II–IV (1892–93); J. A. Stevens, *Colonial N. Y. Sketches Biog. and Hist, 1768–1784* (1867); N. Y. City directories; *Minutes of the Common Council of the City of N. Y. 1784–1831* (1917), vol. I; death notice in *Evening Post* (N. Y.), Oct. 6, 1814.] A. E. P.

LUDLOW, FITZ HUGH (Sept. 11, 1836–Sept. 12, 1870), writer, was born in New York City, son of Rev. Henry G. and Abby (Wills) Ludlow. His father, a prominent abolitionist, was minister of the Spring Street Presbyterian Church, New York, from 1828 to 1837, and for many years pastor of a Presbyterian church at Poughkeepsie. After a bookish boyhood, studying largely at home under his father's guidance, Fitz Hugh Ludlow entered the junior class of the college of New Jersey (1854), but after the burning of Nassau Hall transferred to Union College, where he graduated in 1856. By classmates he is described as brilliant in conversation, genial, generous to a fault, of active physique, with finely chiseled features and most expressive eyes. One of his poems written at Union is still the college song. Before entering college he had become addicted to the narcotic hashish, and in December of his graduation year published "The Apocalypse of Hasheesh" in *Putnam's Magazine.* Parts of this article were incorporated into a volume, *The Hasheesh Eater* (1857), his most remarkable work. It was strongly influenced by DeQuincey, but showed original powers of imagination and style. The rest of his life was an almost constant struggle against hashish. He taught a year at Watertown, N. Y., then studied law in New York City under William Curtis Noyes. Though admitted to the bar in 1859, he never practised, and even during his studies was engaged largely in writing. In June 1859 he married Rosalie H. Osborne.

He was subsequently on the staff of the *World* and the *Commercial Advertiser,* and in 1861 contributed a serial, "The Primpenny Family," to *Vanity Fair,* edited by Charles Farrar Browne. During these and the following years he also furnished dramatic, art, and music criticism for the *Evening Post* and *Home Journal,* and wrote for Harper's publications; contributing to the *Monthly,* up to 1870, two poems and twenty or more tales, clever but hardly memorable; to the *Weekly* (Jan. 14–Apr. 14, 1860), a continued story, "The New Partner in Clingham and Co., Bankers"; and to *Harper's Bazar* (May 30–Aug. 22, 1868), "The Household Angel," pronounced by a contemporary "a real work of genius amidst the usually rather vapid temperance literature" (*Harper's Bazar,* Nov. 12, 1870).

Ludlow and his wife were members of the literary circle of the Bayard Taylors, Stedmans, and Stoddards (Lilian W. Aldrich, *Crowding Memories,* 1920, p. 18). Stedman wrote of him: "He has talent enough for anything, and a *heart* as noble as native sunshine can make it" (*Life and Letters of Edmund Clarence Stedman,* 1910, I, 259). For his health, in 1863, he traveled overland to California, describing his journey in articles for the *Atlantic Monthly* which were later included in *The Heart of the Continent* (1870). His "Through-Tickets to San Francisco: A Prophecy," in the *Atlantic* for November 1864, correctly outlined the route of the first Pacific railway. In the West he met Mark Twain, who speaks appreciatively of Ludlow's favorable criticism. In 1864 he dramatized *Cinderella* for the New York Sanitary Fair, and coached the child performers. Two of his best stories were included in *Little Brother; and Other Genre-Pictures* (1867), which was republished in 1881. A vivid and powerful treatise on the effects of opium, "What Shall They Do to be Saved?", was published in *Harper's Monthly,* August 1867.

Ludlow's first marriage ended unhappily, and in December 1867 he was married again, to Maria O. Milliken, widow of Judge Milliken of Augusta, Me. Accompanied by his wife and his sister, he went to Switzerland, June 1870, in a final effort to recover his health, but died at Geneva in September of that year. His body was brought home to Poughkeepsie a year later for burial. Contemporary memoirs testify to the tragedy of Ludlow's life, in which a brilliant intellect and a character noble in many ways were ruined by a habit that broke down moral and physical strength.

[Article by F. B. Carpenter in N. Y. *Mail,* Dec. 1871 (clipping); *Poughkeepsie News,* Jan. 12, 1872; *Atlantic Monthly,* July 1870; *Harper's New Monthly Magazine,* Dec. 1870; material collected in the Union College library; L. J. Bragman, "A Minor De Quincey," *Medical Journal and Record,* Jan. 7, 1925; information from Hugh Sebastian, Esq., Ann Arbor, Mich., whose dissertation, "A Biographical and Critical Study of Fitz Hugh Ludlow," is in the Univ. of Chicago Library.] A. W.

LUDLOW, GABRIEL GEORGE (Apr. 16, 1736–Feb. 12, 1808), Loyalist and president of

New Brunswick, was descended from Gabriel Ludlow, born at Castle Cary, Somerset County, England, who arrived in New York on Nov. 24, 1694, became a successful merchant, built and owned vessels engaged in the coasting trade, and obtained a royal patent for 4,000 acres on the west bank of the Hudson in what is now Orange County, then known as the Rockland Tappan tract. His son Gabriel married Frances Duncan and became the father of George Duncan Ludlow [*q.v.*], and of Gabriel George Ludlow. By his second marriage he was the father of Daniel Ludlow [*q.v.*]. On Sept. 3, 1760, Gabriel George (the subject of this sketch) married Ann Ver Planck and established himself at Hyde Park near Hempstead, Long Island, on an estate of 144 acres, which he valued at two thousand pounds sterling in his claim for damages before the Loyalist commissioners at Saint John in 1787. He was governor of King's College, colonel of militia, and justice of the peace in Queens County. During the Revolution he commanded the third battalion of De Lancey's Long Island brigade of loyal Americans, in which he held a colonel's commission at the close of the war. At various times his battalion was stationed at Brookhaven, Lloyd's Neck, and Flatbush on Long Island. He was included in the act of attainder passed by the legislature of New York on Oct. 22, 1779. His property was confiscated and sold for the benefit of the state.

In 1783, before the evacuation of New York by the British armies, he sailed for England. After a short residence there, he was given a grant of land at Carleton in the newly created province of New Brunswick. The royal instructions to Lieut.-Gov. Thomas Carleton named him a member of the first council of the province. He was sworn in on Nov. 22, 1784, and held the position until his death. He was also a member of the first city council of Saint John, was the first mayor of Saint John from 1785 to 1795, and was the first judge of the Vice-Admiralty Court from 1787 to 1803. After Carleton embarked for England in 1803, as senior member of the council, he administered the government of New Brunswick until his death, under the title of President of His Majesty's Council and Commander-in-Chief of the Province.

[Thomas Moffat Diary and a few letters of Samuel Culper in Lib. of Cong.; *Second Report of the Bureau of Archives for the Province of Ontario*, ed. by Alexander Fraser (2 pts., 1905); *Winslow Papers*, ed. by W. O. Raymond (1901); W. O. Raymond, "Loyalists in Arms," in *New Brunswick Hist. Soc. Colls.* no. 5 (1904) and "A Sketch of the Life and Administration of Gen. Thomas Carleton," *Ibid.*, no. 6 (1905); W. S. Gordon, *Gabriel Ludlow and his Descendants* (1919); Thomas Jones, *Hist. of N. Y. during the Revolutionary War* (2 vols., 1879); J. W. Lawrence, *Foot-Prints* (1883), pp. 8–12; Henry Onderdonk, *The Annals of Hempstead* (1878); *The Orderly Book of the Three Battalions of Loyalists Commanded by Brig.-Gen. Oliver DeLancey* (1917); *The Judges of New Brunswick*, ed. by A. A. Stockton (1907), esp. p. 3; James Hannay, *Hist. of New Brunswick* (1909), vol. I; Lorenzo Sabine, *Biog. Sketches of the Loyalists* (1864), vol. II, incomplete and inaccurate.]

J. G. V–D.

LUDLOW, GEORGE DUNCAN (1734–Nov. 13, 1808), jurist, was the son of Gabriel and Frances (Duncan) Ludlow. At first an apothecary, he abandoned this venture, retired to his estate near Hempstead, Long Island, adjoining that of his brother Gabriel George Ludlow [*q.v.*], and studied law, in which profession he met with immediate success. In 1768 he became a member of the governor's council in the colony of New York. The next year, he was named by Governor Colden as one of the four justices of the supreme court of the colony. When, in 1778, the chief justiceship became vacant, he was disappointed at not receiving the vacant post and resigned. In order to appease the angry jurist, whose many friends were influential, the governor gave him the positions of master of rolls and of superintendent of police for Long Island, which together were of much greater pecuniary value than the chief justiceship. Like his brother Gabriel George Ludlow and his half-brother Daniel Ludlow [*q.v.*], he was a Loyalist during the Revolutionary troubles. He signed the address to General Howe upon his occupation of New York City and supported the administration of Gov. James Robertson. He barely escaped from the colonials who broke into his house and, in 1779, was attainted by the New York legislature and lost all his property by confiscation. On June 19, 1783, he sailed for England.

He was appointed by the Crown as the first chief justice of the new province of New Brunswick and became a member of the governor's council. He took his oath of office in the fall of 1784 and continued on the supreme bench until his death. He was not popular with all classes. James Glenie, a radical reformer elected to the lower house in 1791, described him as "the ignorant, strutting Chief Justice" (Hannay, *post*, I, 213). A disagreement of the court in a slave case of 1800 was anything but satisfactory. The chief justice believed that, as there was nothing contrary to slavery in the laws of the province, slaves might be held, and one other judge concurred. The remaining two judges held that as slaves could not be owned in England, slavery could have no legal existence in New Brunswick. Although his opinion was sustained by the King in council, he received much abuse for his decision of 1805 that there were no exclusive private fishing rights in navigable waters. In March 1808 he suffered a paralytic stroke, and he died at "Spring Hill," his estate of 1500 acres near Fredericton. He was survived by his widow Frances (Duncan) Ludlow, his cousin, whom he had married on Apr. 22, 1758, and by a son and two daughters.

[*The Judges of New Brunswick*, ed. by A. A. Stockton (1907); W. S. Gordon, *Gabriel Ludlow and his Descendants* (1919); W. O. Raymond, "Loyalists in Arms," *New Brunswick Hist. Soc. Colls.*, no. 5 (1904) and "A Sketch of the Life and Administration of Gen. Thomas Carleton," *Ibid.*, no. 6 (1905); Thomas Jones, *Hist. of N. Y. during the Revolutionary War* (2 vols., 1879); James Hannay, *Hist. of New Brunswick* (1909), vol. I; *Winslow Papers*, ed. by W. O. Raymond (1901); "Colden Papers," *N. Y. Hist. Soc. Colls.*, vol. X (1877); *New York during the American Revolution . . . from the MSS. now in the Possession of the Mercantile Lib. Asso. of New York City* (1861); Lorenzo Sabine, *Biog. Sketches of the Loyalists* (1864), vol. II, incomplete and inaccurate.] J. G. V–D.

LUDLOW, NOAH MILLER (July 3, 1795–Jan. 9, 1886), actor, theatrical manager, author, was born in New York City, the son of John and Phebe (Dunham) Ludlow, and a descendant of Gabriel Ludlow who emigrated to New York in 1694. At an early age the boy was placed in a mercantile house. During the summer of 1813, after the death of his father, he went to live at his brother's home in Albany. He was irresistibly attracted to the stage and in Albany he became acquainted with some actors and was soon playing small parts. In the spring of 1815 he was engaged as a member of Samuel Drake's company, who were to travel to Kentucky, giving performances at towns along the way. By the middle of August 1815, they had reached Pittsburgh where they played until about the middle of November. Traveling by flat-boat down the Ohio River from Pittsburgh to what is now Maysville, Ky., thence by wagon, they arrived at Frankfort, after many thrilling experiences, and opened their season there in early December. After a barn-storming tour through Kentucky to Nashville, Tenn., Ludlow married there on Sept. 1, 1817, Mary (Maury) Squires (or Squire). He had left the Drake company in June of that year and had formed a partnership with two fellow actors. They took with them such members of their troupe as cared to go, and opened in New Orleans on Dec. 24, 1817. These were the first performances given in English in New Orleans by a professional company, according to Ludlow's autobiography.

For several years Ludlow traveled in the South, sometimes managing his own company, but more often acting under the management of others. In many towns in which he appeared, no professional performances had ever been given. On June 29, 1826, he made his début in New York as Young Wilding in a one-night performance of *The Liar* at the Chatham Theatre. He reappeared in New York at a benefit at the Park Theatre on July 15, 1828, and in the fall of the same year his own company played at the Chatham. After this, he presented his company in Mobile, Louisville, Cincinnati, and St. Louis. In the fall of 1835 he formed a partnership with Sol Smith [*q.v.*] which lasted till 1853. During this partnership, Ludlow assisted in the management of theatres in Mobile, St. Louis, Cincinnati, and New Orelans, where the local stock companies supported as visiting stars at frequent intervals the famous actors of the day. Ludlow himself occasionally found time during this period to act. Some of his best-known parts were Rolando in *The Honeymoon,* Young Marlowe in *She Stoops to Conquer,* Scamper in *The Promissory Note,* and Doctor Pangloss in *The Heir at Law.* From 1853 until his death he lived in retirement in St. Louis, occasionally appearing at benefit performances and engaging in literary work. His book, *Dramatic Life as I Found It* (1880), is well known. He also compiled *A Genealogical History of the Ludlow Family* (1884) and wrote a "sketch or tale," "Manatua, or the Spirit of the Glen." As a player he is said to have been "unquestionably a general actor of considerable merit" (Ireland, *post,* p. 614). As a manager, with his partner, Sol Smith, he blazed the trail of the drama in what was then almost a wilderness.

[In addition to Ludlow's books mentioned in the text, see: W. G. B. Carson, *The Theatre on the Frontier* (1932); J. N. Ireland, *Records of the N. Y. Stage,* vol. I (1866); Mary C. Crawford, *Romance of the Am. Theatre* (1925); G. C. D. Odell, *Annals of the N. Y. Stage,* vol. III (1928); *Daily Picayune* (New Orleans), Dec. 3–10, 1846; *Mo. Republican* (St. Louis) and *St. Louis Globe-Democrat,* Jan. 10, 1886. The name of Ludlow's wife is spelled differently in the *Dramatic Life* and the genealogy.] L. H. F.

LUDLOW, ROGER (fl. 1590–1664), colonial lawmaker, was baptized at Dinton, Wiltshire, England, Mar. 7, 1590, the son of Thomas and Jane (Pyle) Ludlow. The family, which was typical of the west country gentry, had first risen to prominence under Henry VIII. Of Roger's early life we know little beyond that he entered Balliol College, Oxford, in 1610, and two years later was admitted to the Inner Temple for the study of law. At the meeting of the General Court of the Massachusetts Bay Company held in London, Feb. 10, 1630, he was elected an Assistant of the company; and on Mar. 20 sailed from Plymouth on the *Mary and John,* known as "Mr. Ludlow's ship," arriving at Massachusetts Bay on May 30, where he became one of the founders of Dorchester and took an active part in the early government of the colony. In 1634 he was elected deputy-governor. The following year he threw in his lot with the colonists who were making settlements along the Connecticut River, and at Windsor, on Apr. 26, 1636, presided, under a commission from Massachusetts, over the first court held in Connecticut. He is credited with having drafted the Fundamental Orders adopted by the colony in January 1638/39 which, embodied with some additions and changes in the Charter of 1662, remained the basis of Connecticut government until 1818. In 1646 the General Court requested him "to take some paynes in drawing forth a body of Lawes for the gouernment of this Coñon welth"; the result was "Ludlow's Code" or "The Code of 1650," the first gathering together and codification of the Connecticut laws which had been enacted previous to that date.

Meanwhile, as a direct result of the Pequot war, and probably as part of a well-planned policy of expansion against the Dutch, Ludlow had, in 1639, planted a settlement at Fairfield, whither he removed and from which town he was annually elected for the next fifteen years either as magistrate or deputy-governor, and during the years 1651–53 as commissioner of the United Colonies of New England. In 1654, owing either to irritation at the refusal of the colonies to back up his proposed expedition against the Dutch at Manhattan or because of a tempting offer from the Cromwellian government for his services at home, he suddenly returned to England, and in the autumn of that year we find him in Dublin as a member of a distinguished commission for the hearing and determination of claims in and to forfeited lands in Ireland, which was then undergoing the rigors of the Cromwellian Settlement. This office, together with others of high honor, he held until the collapse of the Commonwealth in 1660. That he continued to reside in Dublin until 1664 (when he was seventy-four years of age) is evident from various documents. When or where he died is not known. His wife, Mary Ludlow, died in Dublin in 1664.

That Ludlow was of quick temper and blunt speech is amply attested; that these qualities seriously affected his career may be doubted—despite the statements of those early biographers who knew nothing of his life subsequent to 1654. That he was honest, capable, and public-spirited to a high degree is obvious from the esteem in which he was held by his contemporaries. His return to England may be interpreted in the same light as that of the Mathers and many another who, from 1642 to 1659, left America to serve the Commonwealth in England, coming back later to reap fame in America; only Ludlow did his great work before he left and he did not, so far as is known, return.

[See H. F. Waters, *Geneal. Gleanings in England* (2 vols., 1901); J. M. Taylor, *Roger Ludlow, the Colonial Lawmaker* (1900); Elizabeth H. Schenck, *The Hist. of Fairfield*, vol. I (1889); R. C. Winthrop, *Life and Letters of John Winthrop* (2 vols., 1864–67); John Winthrop, *The Hist. of New England* (2 vols., 1853), ed. by Jas. Savage; H. R. Stiles, *The Hist. and Geneals. of Ancient Windsor, Conn.* (rev. ed., 1892); N. B. Shurtleff, *Records of the Gov. and Company of the Mass. Bay* (5 vols., 1853–54); Robt. Dunlop, *Ireland Under the Commonwealth* (2 vols., 1913); Jos. Foster, *Alumni Oxonienses*, Early Series; C. H. Firth, *The Memoirs of Edmund Ludlow* (2 vols., 1894); J. H. Trumbull, *The Pub. Records of the Colony of Conn.*, vol. I (1850); W. A. Beers, "Roger Ludlowe," *Mag. of Am. Hist.*, Apr. 1882. In Taylor, *op. cit.*, Ludlow's signature appears with a final *e*, but this sketch has followed the spelling more commonly used.] R. V. C.

LUDLOW, THOMAS WILLIAM (June 14, 1795–July 17, 1878), lawyer and financier, was born in New York City, the second son of Thomas Ludlow, a well-known architect. Both his father and his mother (Mary Ludlow, a first cousin of her husband) were members of an old and prosperous New York family, whose founder, Gabriel Ludlow, had emigrated to the city in 1694 from Somerset, England. The family was strongly Episcopalian, and Thomas William was a faithful and generous supporter of his church throughout his life. A precocious boy, at the age of sixteen he graduated in the class of 1811 from Columbia College, of which he was later trustee (1833–36). Thereafter, he studied law in the office of Martin Wilkins, a leader of the bar of that day, a study interrupted by a short service in the New York militia during the War of 1812. Quite as important in the formation of his character and his mind was his constant association at home and among family friends with the best that the city offered socially and intellectually. He early acquired a taste for archeology and became an enthusiastic numismatist.

Ludlow devoted himself to the general practice of law for but a short time. He soon became counsel for a number of wealthy corporations, among others the important Dutch banking house of Crommelin & Company, whose American representative he was. This work, the settlement of many large estates, and the management of his own extensive property filled all his time. His legal activities were increasingly subordinated to his operations as a financier. One of his earliest enterprises was the promotion of the New York Life Insurance and Trust Company, of which he was a trustee from its organization (1830) until his death. For long years he was a member of its committee on investments and in later life was one of its vice-presidents. He was also a founder of the New York Life Insurance Company (1845). For some years he was a trustee and, at the time of his death, vice-president of the National City Bank of New York. Like many other financiers of his day he took a lively interest in the development of railroads as promising fields for the investment of capital. In 1849 he helped to incorporate and to finance the Panama Railroad Company; he became its first president and was for some years one of its directors. Before it was completed he and two of his associates in the enterprise, J. W. Alsop and William H. Aspinwall [*q.v.*], shared with others in the promotion of the Illinois Central Railroad. He was also connected at an early date with the Harlem Railroad. His interest in all these enterprises appears to have been limited to their financial operations.

Aristocrat that he was, Ludlow was none the less a Jacksonian Democrat. Though on intimate terms with the leaders of his party, he refused to share in the conflicts of the political arena. He declined all political offices but, when his friend, President Van Buren, needed an able and trustworthy representative to place treasury notes in Europe during the depression of 1837–39, Ludlow cheerfully accepted the commission, which he carried out successfully. To the majority of New Yorkers of the ante-bellum period he was quite as much a social leader as a financier. His urbanity and charm, his high family connections, and his wealth placed him in the highest rank of New York society. In the pages of Philip Hone one frequently sees him dining with the élite of the city and on occasions entertaining admirably at his country home near Yonkers. His wife, Frances W. Morris, whom he married in 1828, died ten years before him. They had no children but adopted a son who was a namesake and distant relative of Ludlow. He died at Yonkers.

[A manuscript sketch of his life by W. S. Gordon has apparently served as a basis for later accounts, especially that which appears in W. K. Ackerman, *Hist. Sketch of the Ill. Central Railroad* (1890); see also *The Diary of Philip Hone* (1889), ed. by Bayard Tuckerman; *N. Y. Tribune*, July 19, 1878.] P. D. E.

LUDLOW, WILLIAM (Nov. 27, 1843–Aug. 30, 1901), soldier, engineer, was the son of Gen. William Handy Ludlow, who distinguished himself in the Civil War, and Frances Louise Nicoll, of Islip, Long Island, a descendant of the royal secretary of New York after its transfer from the Dutch. Born at Islip on the original Nicoll patent, the second child of a family of six children, William Ludlow received his early education at Burlington Academy, New Jersey, and the University of the City of New York (later New York University). In 1860 he entered the Military Academy at West Point, from which he graduated four years later. Plunged into the Civil War as chief engineer, XX Army Corps, he won the brevet of captain for gallant services in the battle of Peach Tree Creek, July 20, 1864. After participation in the siege and capture of Atlanta, and in General Sherman's campaigns, he was brevetted major, Dec. 21, 1864, for meritorious services in the Georgia campaign, and lieutenant-colonel, Mar. 13, 1865, for services in the Carolinas—a brilliant record for an officer less than a year out of the Military Academy. He was commissioned captain of engineers, Mar. 7, 1867, and became assistant to the chief of engineers until Nov. 10, 1872. During these years he was stationed at Staten Island and Charleston, S. C. From 1872 until May 1876 he served as chief engineer, Department of Dakota. During this period he made valuable surveys of the Yellowstone National Park (1873 and 1875), and of the Black Hills country (1874). His prophecy (report of Mar. 1, 1876) that the National Park would some day be thronged with visitors from all parts of the world has approached fulfilment.

Ludlow was on duty in Philadelphia from 1876 to 1882 in connection with river and harbor work, then served as engineer secretary of the Light House Board at Washington until March 1883, and was chief engineer of the Philadelphia water department from 1883 to 1886. In the last-named duty he reorganized and rejuvenated the city water system, which had fallen into a deplorable state of inefficiency. He was promoted major of engineers, June 30, 1882. On Apr. 1, 1886, he was appointed by the President engineer commissioner of the District of Columbia and was responsible for many improvements in the capital city. He was on several engineering duties from 1883 to 1893 and was military attaché at London from 1893 to 1896. He made a thorough inspection of the deep-water canals of Suez, Kiel, Corinth, and of those in Holland, and served from April to November 1895 as chairman of the Nicaragua Canal Board. He was promoted lieutenant-colonel of engineers, Aug. 13, 1895, and on Feb. 23, 1897, was placed in charge of river and harbor improvements in New York Harbor. His recommendations that the East River channel be deepened have since been carried out.

With the outbreak of war with Spain, Ludlow

was appointed brigadier-general of volunteers, May 4, 1898, accompanied Shafter's V Corps to Santiago-de-Cuba, and commanded the 1st Brigade in the attack on El Caney and in the subsequent investment of the city of Santiago. For meritorious services in this campaign he received written commendation from both Generals Shafter and Lawton (official reports, War Department). On Sept. 7, 1898, he was commissioned major-general of volunteers, and on Dec. 13, following, was made military governor of Havana. On Jan. 21, 1900, he was commissioned brigadier-general in the regular army. In discontinuing the Department of Havana, May 1, 1900, the secretary of war expressed high appreciation of Ludlow's services while governor, in the maintenance of order, the administration of the city government, and in greatly improved sanitary conditions in Havana. Early in 1900, he became president of the Army War College Board, and during the summer of that year, inspected the French and German military systems and methods of training. This duty completed, he was ordered, April–May 1901, to active duty in the Philippines, then in a state of insurrection; was on sick leave of absence until Aug. 30 of that year; and on that date, his constitution weakened by arduous labor, much of it in the tropics, he died at his daughter's home, Convent Station, N. J. In the year 1866 Ludlow had been married to Genevieve Almira Sprigg, of St. Louis, who with a daughter and two grandsons survived him. He was interred at Islip with military honors, from Trinity Church, New York; later his ashes were removed to Arlington Cemetery. A brave soldier, he achieved notable success as engineer, governor, and commander.

[For biographical data see G. W. Cullum, *Biog. Reg. . . . U. S. Mil. Acad.*, vols. III (1891), IV (1901), and V (1910); sketch by W. M. Black in *Thirty-third Ann. Reunion, Asso. Grads. U. S. Mil. Acad.* (1902); E. H. Nicoll, *The Descendants of John Nicoll of Islip, England* (1894); *N. Y. Times*, Aug. 31, 1901. The librarian of the U. S. Mil. Acad. has compiled a complete bibliography of Ludlow's writings which includes the reports of his western surveys and his reports as military governor of Havana.] C. D. R.

LUDLOWE, ROGER [See LUDLOW, ROGER, fl. 1590–1664].

LUDWELL, PHILIP (fl. 1660–1704), colonial governor of Carolina, was the son of Thomas and Jane (Cottington) Ludwell, of Bruton, Somerset, England. According to Bishop Meade (*post*), he belonged to "an old and honorable family . . . the original of them many ages since coming from Germany." He emigrated to Virginia about 1660, acquired two estates, "Rich Neck" and "Green Spring," in James City County, and gave Bruton Parish its name. After serving as deputy for his brother, Thomas, who was secretary of the colony, he was made a member of the Governor's Council in March 1674/75. Later he held the office of secretary for a short time. During Sir William Berkeley's administration as governor, Ludwell was one of those who petitioned for the pardon of Nathaniel Bacon [*q.v.*], leader of the popular uprising known as Bacon's Rebellion, but when the disturbances were renewed, Ludwell espoused the cause of Berkeley and went with twenty-six armed men who captured Giles Bland and others implicated in the revolt. Because of his activities in this connection he was considered "rash and fiery" by the Lords of Trade and Plantations and deprived of his seat in the Council in 1679, but was reinstated the following year. In 1686–87 he led the resistance to levies made by the corrupt and unpopular governor, Lord Howard of Effingham. In consequence, charged with having "rudely and boldly disputed the King's authority," he was suspended from the Council and then dismissed. Though elected to the House of Burgesses in 1688, as a suspended councillor he was not permitted to take his seat. The following year he was sent to England to present the Burgesses' charges against Howard, and obtained a series of instructions to the governor which were favorable to the colony.

On Dec. 5, 1689, the Lords Proprietors of the Province of Carolina elected Ludwell "Governor of that part of our province . . . that lyes North and East of Cape Feare" (*Records,* I, 362). His commission gave him power to appoint a deputy governor; and he appointed two in succession, Thomas Jarvis and John Harvey, himself spending most of his time in Virginia. His immediate predecessor in office, Seth Sothell, had been guilty of every manner of abuse, public and private, but, although he was instructed to inquire into these abuses, Ludwell seems to have given little time to such investigation. On Nov. 2, 1691, his commission was altered to make him governor of the entire province of Carolina, and in 1692 he was given the hereditary title of cacique. While Ludwell was governor, Col. John Gibbs (said to be a cousin of the Duke of Albemarle) put forth a proclamation claiming the governorship and denouncing the incumbent as a "Rascal, imposter & usurp^r" and offering to do battle personally "as long as my Eye-lidds shall wagg" in any part of the King's Dominions, with "any of the boldest Heroe [*sic*] living in this or the next County" who should uphold Ludwell's title (*Records,* I, 363). Little attention was paid to the verbal vaporings of Gibbs; but when he seized two magistrates who were holding court, the Carolina colonists chased him back to Virginia.

According to F. L. Hawks, the historian of North Carolina, "Ludwell understood the character and prejudices of the people thoroughly; and, as he was possessed of good sense and proper feeling, he had address enough, by harmlessly humoring their prejudices, gradually to restore a state of comparative peace, without the surrender of any important principle" (*post,* II, 494). In 1694, however, the Proprietors recalled his commission, and he ultimately returned to England. He was twice married: first to Lucy Higginson, relict of Maj. Lewis Burwell and of Col. William Bernard, and second, to the widow of Governor Berkeley (Frances Culpeper), whose first husband, Samuel Stephens, had been governor of Albemarle in Carolina. Among the descendants of Philip Ludwell by his first marriage was Hannah Ludwell who married Thomas Lee and became the mother of Richard Henry, Francis Lightfoot, Arthur, and William Lee [*qq.v.*]. Ludwell died in England sometime after 1704, possibly after 1707. He was buried at Stratford-le-Bow.

[H. R. McIlwaine, *Minutes of the Council and Gen. Court of Colonial Va.* (1924); *Journals of the House of Burgesses of Va., 1659/60–1693* (1914); *The Colonial Records of N. C.,* vol. I (1886), ed. by W. L. Saunders; *Calendar of State Papers, Col. Ser., America and West Indies, 1677–80* (1896) and *1685–88* (1899); William Meade, *Old Churches, Ministers, and Families of Va.* (1857), II, 138–39; F. L. Hawks, *Hist. of N. C.,* II (1858), 492–95; Edward McCrady, *The Hist. of S. C. under the Proprietary Govt.* (1897); S. A. Ashe, *Hist. of N. C.* (1908), vol. I; *Va. Mag. of Hist. and Biog.,* Oct. 1893; E. J. Lee, *Lee of Va.* (1895).]

M. DeL. H.

LUDWICK, CHRISTOPHER (Oct. 17, 1720–June 17, 1801), superintendent of bakers in the Continental Army, philanthropist, was born at Giessen, in Hesse, formerly Hesse-Darmstadt, Germany, and was taught the trade of baker by his father. When he was fourteen he was sent to a free school and given the rudiments of an education. Being naturally of an adventurous disposition, at seventeen he enlisted as a soldier, fought against the Turks (1737 to 1740), and later took part in the seventeen weeks' siege of Prague. After the surrender, in 1741, he enlisted in the army of the King of Prussia, and shortly afterward, peace having been declared, was discharged and went to London. There he signed up as baker on an East Indiaman, and after three and a half years spent in India, returned to London in 1745. He visited his native town, where he learned that his father had died and left him his entire estate. It consisted principally of a freehold, which young Ludwick converted into money—five hundred guilders. Back to London he hastened, his pockets filled; and when he reached his last shilling, once more he went to sea, this time as a common sailor. For the succeeding seven years (1745–52), he made voyages to the West Indies and to European ports. Desiring to quit the sea, he invested £25 in ready-made English clothing and in 1753 embarked for Philadelphia. Having sold the clothing there for four times its cost, he went back to London, where he spent nine months learning to bake gingerbread and make confectionery.

The following year he returned to Philadelphia, taking with him implements for the bakery which he soon started in Laetitia Court of that city. In 1755 he married Mrs. Catharine England, a widow. His business prospered, and he became a respected figure in the neighborhood, being alluded to as "The Governor of Laetitia Court." Frugal as well as industrious, at the time of the Revolution he was the possessor of nine houses, a farm in Germantown, and £3,500, Pennsylvania currency, at interest. He actively supported the war, on one occasion subscribing £200 for firearms, and in the summer of 1776 volunteering in the flying camp and refusing to draw either pay or rations. Upon his request, Congress gave him permission to visit the Hessian camp on Staten Island, disguised as a deserter. Once among the mercenaries, he reminded them that they were slaves, and invited them to follow him to Philadelphia, where they could live in comfort and in freedom. Hundreds of desertions followed, and the deserters were placed in Ludwick's charge by Congress, which voted him money for the purpose. His loyalty, integrity, and business ability were so highly regarded that on May 3, 1777, Congress, by a resolution, appointed him superintendent of bakers and director of baking in the Continental Army. He was everywhere known in the army and was permitted almost as much freedom as the Commander-in-Chief himself. Washington was very fond of him, addressed him as "old gentleman," and called him "my honest friend." He was frequently in private conference with Washington and often dined with him when large companies were present. He was always referred to as the Baker General, and was familiarly called "General," although his title was superintendent.

When the war was ended, Ludwick returned to find that his home in Germantown had been plundered by the British, and that he had scarcely any ready cash; but he would neither borrow money nor buy on credit. In 1785 Washington wrote what might be termed a certificate of character for him, attesting his patriotism and other virtues. His first wife died in 1795, and in 1798 he married Mrs. Sophia Binder. His private donations were large for one of his means. During the yellow-fever epidemic in Philadelphia, in 1797, he volunteered his services to bake bread for the stricken. In addition to bequeathing substantial sums to churches and various charities in Philadelphia, he left the residue of his estate to his executors to be used in providing free education for poor children; the entire fund to be given to such free schools as should be established before the lapse of five years after his death. He was buried in the yard of Trinity Lutheran Church, Germantown, Philadelphia.

[Benjamin Rush, *An Account of the Life and Character of Christopher Ludwick* (1831), which originally appeared in *Poulson's Am. Daily Advertiser* (Phila.), June 30, 1801; Henry Simpson, *The Lives of Eminent Philadelphians now Deceased* (1859); *Pa. Archives*, 1 ser. V (1853); J. F. Watson, *Annals of Phila. and Pa. in the Olden Time* (2nd ed., 1844), vol. II; *Jour. of the Continental Cong.*, vols. VII (1907), VIII (1907), X (1908), XIII (1909), XIX (1912); *Papers of the Continental Cong.*, No. 41, V, folios 175 and 230, No. 136, I, folio 113; *Poulson's Am. Daily Advertiser*, June 19, 1801.]

J. J.

LUELLING, HENDERSON (Apr. 23, 1809–Dec. 28, 1878), nurseryman, was born in Randolph County, N. C., of a Welsh family which had been in America for a number of generations. His father was Meshach Luelling, and his mother, whose family name was Brookshire, was of English extraction. Both the parents were Quakers. The elder Luelling was a physician, but combined the practice of his profession with the nursery business. The family moved to Greensboro, Ind., in 1825, and on Dec. 30, 1830, Henderson Luelling was married to Elizabeth Presnell, who had lived near his old home in North Carolina.

In 1837, he and his brother John went to Salem, Iowa, and started a nursery. Here he remained ten years, making numerous journeys to the East in search of the best varieties of fruit for his stock. Accounts of the Lewis and Clark expedition stirred in him a desire to see the Western country, and with the news of the beginnings of settlements in the Willamette Valley of Oregon, he conceived the idea of transporting across the plains by ox-team a small nursery stock, sufficient to start him in business there. He set about preparing for the adventure, and after much discouragement and delay he began the journey Apr. 17, 1847. With him were his wife and eight children, the eldest about thirteen; the youngest, named Oregon Columbia, was born shortly before they started. A friend, William Meek, accompanied the family. The nursery stock, consisting of 800 to 1,000 young trees and shrubs, was planted in two long boxes, containing about a foot of soil, built to fit a wagon-bed. Racks were constructed about the cargo to prevent the trees being eaten by the cattle. The wagon was drawn by four yoke of oxen.

The journey across the two thousand miles of wilderness was one of hardships and hazards. The party with which the Luellings traveled was a small one, and on one occasion an Indian attack was averted only by the fact that one of the wagons was laden with living trees, which the Indians regarded as under the special care of the Great Spirit. The trees were tended and watered with the utmost care, and about half of the total number ultimately survived. At The Dalles the nursery stock was taken from the boxes, wrapped in bundles and transported down the Columbia by flatboat to a point opposite Fort Vancouver. Here the party remained for some time, while Luelling was seeking a place for his nursery. He chose a point near the present site of Milwaukee, a few miles south of Portland. It was already late in November, but the trees and shrubs were planted as soon as the ground could be cleared for them. They included apples, pears, quinces, plums, cherries, grapes, and the common berry-bushes, and were the first grafted fruit stock that had ever come to the Pacific Coast. The varieties had been selected with the greatest care. Luelling and Meek formed a partnership and the nursery throve. The settlers, of whom there were scarcely more than 5,000 in the whole Oregon country, eagerly purchased every tree offered for sale. In 1850, Seth Luelling, a brother of Henderson, arrived and joined in the enterprise.

A spirit of restlessness, however, increased perhaps by private misfortune, especially the death of his wife and his eldest daughter, who had married William Meek, soon started Luelling on a new venture. In 1854 he moved a part of his nursery stock to a point near Oakland, Cal., and began again. Here he prospered even more than in Oregon, and within five years he had accumulated a considerable fortune. Not content, a new adventure, the nature of which seems not to be recorded, took him, with two of his sons and their families, to Honduras, in a vessel purchased and equipped by himself. This venture ended disastrously, and he returned to California to engage again in the nursery business. He never regained what he had lost, and seems to have lived rather quietly for the remainder of his days, making his home in California. He died in San José, and was interred in Mountain View cemetery, Oakland. He was an uncle of Lorenzo Dow Lewelling [*q.v.*].

[J. R. Cardwell, *Brief Hist. of Early Horticulture in Ore.* (1906), and *Proc. of the Am. Pomological Soc.* (1913); S. A. Clarke, *Pioneer Days of Oregon Hist.* (1905), vol. II; Joseph Gaston, *The Centennial Hist. of Ore.* (1912), vol. I; H. K. Hines, *Illustrated Hist. of the State of Ore.* (1893); *Iowa Jour. of Hist. and Politics*, Oct. 1929; *Oakland Tribune*, Mar. 5, 1916; *Eighth Biennial Report of the Board of Horticulture of the State of Ore.* (1905); *Trans. of the Seventh Ann. Re-Union of the Oregon Pioneer Asso., 1879* (1880); *Trans. Ore. State Horticultural Soc.* (1910); H. W. Scott, *Hist. of Oregon* (1924), vol. III; *The Call* (San Francisco), Dec. 30, 1878.] M. E. P.

LUFBERY, RAOUL GERVAIS VICTOR (Mar. 21, 1885–May 19, 1918), aviator, greatest American ace in the World War, was born in Clermont, department of Oise, France. His father, Edward, was a United States citizen, born in New York; his mother, Annette Vessières, was French. The latter died when Raoul was young, his father married again and went to the United States, and the child, with two brothers, was brought up by his grandmother. As a youth he worked in a chocolate factory at Blois and in a factory at Clermont-Ferrand. When he was about nineteen he started out to see the world and thereafter lived a roving life. He made his way to Algiers, then visited Tunis, Egypt, Turkey, the Balkans, and Germany, supporting himself by whatever work he was able to secure. In Constantinople he was a waiter in a restaurant; in Hamburg he found employment with a steamship company. In 1906 he appeared in Wallingford, Conn., where his father had established himself, but the latter, his second wife having died, had left his family there and gone to France. For two years Raoul worked in the silver shops of the town, and then set out for new adventures. Cuba was his first destination; later he was a baker in New Orleans and a hotel waiter in San Francisco. In the last-named place he enlisted in the United States Army and was sent to the Philippines. His term of service over, he went to Japan, from there to China, and finally to India, where for a time he was a ticket collector in the Bombay Railroad station. During all his wanderings he had never been more than a week out of work.

In Calcutta he met Marc Pourpe, a French aviator who was giving exhibition flights, and became his mechanic. The two were in France to secure a new machine when the World War began. Pourpe enlisted in the air service and Lufbery in the Foreign Legion, but he was shortly permitted to transfer to aviation and served as Pourpe's mechanic. When the latter was killed, December 1914, Lufbery determined to become a pilot. He was sent to the aviation school at Chartres and after further training saw service as a pilot in the Voisin Bombardment Squadron 106. On May 24, 1916, having qualified as a *pilote de chasse,* he joined the *Escadrille Lafayette*. Fearless, and handling his plane with superb mastery and ease, he was soon cordially acknowledged by his comrades to be the best of them all. There was no love of the spectacular or heroic in him, only keen zest for flying and simple devotion to his work. "Above all the pilots who found themselves at Verdun," said his commanding officer, Captain Georges Thenault, "was Lufbery 'without fear and without reproach.' . . . His Spad was always the highest and every day he won new victories. He seemed to hardly care about having them confirmed. Calmly he reigned as sovereign lord in his chosen element and beat down his foes to accomplish his duty and not for the sake of glory" (*The Story of the LaFayette Escadrille,* 1921, translated by Walter Duranty, p. 152). While with the Escadrille he was officially credited with seventeen victories, though he undoubtedly brought down twice that number of planes, was awarded the *Croix de Guerre,* the *Médaille Militaire,* and the Military Medal (British), and was promoted to adjutant and decorated with the Legion of Honor.

On Jan. 10, 1918, he was commissioned major in the air service of the United States Army. On Jan. 28, he joined the 95th Aero Squadron, and was relieved a week later to go to the front at Villeneuve (Marne) to prepare the way for the 94th Squadron of the First Pursuit Group. The squadron arrived in March, but because machine guns were lacking could do no fighting. In April it began patrol duty in the Toul sector. On May 19 Lufbery went in pursuit of a German plane which had come over the lines. In the combat which ensued Lufbery's plane burst into flames and he jumped from a height of more than two thousand feet. His body was found in the garden of a house in the little town of Maron and was buried in the American Cemetery, Sebastopol Barracks. On July 4, 1928, it was removed to the Lafayette Escadrille Memorial at Villeneuve, near Paris.

[War Department Records; J. N. Hall and C. B. Nordhoff, *The Lafayette Flying Corps*, vol. I (1920); L. La Tourette Driggs, *Heroes of Aviation* (1918); P. A. Rockwell, *Am. Fighters in the Foreign Legion, 1914–18* (1930); *Hartford Courant*, May 21, 1918; *Hartford Times*, May 20, 1918.] H. E. S.

LUKENS, REBECCA WEBB PENNOCK (Jan 6, 1794–Dec. 10, 1854), iron manufacturer, was born in Coatesville, Pa., the daughter of Isaac and Martha (Webb) Pennock. Her father was the founder of the Brandywine Rolling

Mill, the first mill in the United States for the manufacture of boiler plate. Rebecca received the education customarily accorded to young ladies of her time and in 1813 was married to Charles Lloyd Lukens, a physician, to whom she bore three children. After the death of her father, her husband assumed the management of the iron works, and when he died in 1825, in fulfilment of his wish she succeeded him as manager, thus becoming the first woman in the United States to engage in the iron industry. Employing a superintendent to direct the works and handle the employees, she herself assumed full control and management of the commercial end of the business. Among the difficulties confronting her was the problem of transportation. Her finished product had to be hauled by teams thirty-eight miles to Philadelphia or twenty-six to Wilmington, while her coal was carried from Columbia, a distance of more than forty miles. Her exceptional ability in marketing her product enabled her to enlarge the business. The boiler plates made in her plant became famous among engineers, and several shipments were made to England, where they were used in the building of some of the earliest locomotives. She died in Coatesville, Pa., leaving the business to be carried on by two sons-in-law, Abraham Gibbons and Dr. Charles Huston [*q.v.*]. Upon her death the name of the iron works was changed to Lukens Mills in her honor, and in 1890 the business was incorporated as the Lukens Steel Company.

[J. B. Pearse, *A Concise Hist. of the Iron Manufacture of the Am. Colonies up to the Revolution and of Pa. until the Present Time* (1876); J. M. Swank, *Hist. of the Manufacture of Iron in All Ages* (1884); Gilbert Cope and H. G. Ashmead, *Hist. Homes and Institutions and Geneal. and Personal Memoirs of Chester and Delaware Counties, Pa.* (1904), vol. I; G. P. Donehoo, *Pennsylvania: A Hist.* (1926), vol. VIII; J. W. Jordan, *Colonial Families of Phila.* (1911), vol. I; *Lukens Steel Company* (5th ed., 1924), a handbook; *The Friend,* Fourth Month 28, 1855; date of birth supplied from family Bible by C. L. Huston, Esq., Coatesville, Pa.]

J. H. F.

LULL, EDWARD PHELPS (Feb. 20, 1836–Mar. 5, 1887), naval officer, was born at Windsor, Vt., the youngest of the six children of Martin Lull. When Edward was nine his widowed mother moved to Milwaukee, Wis. After a brief schooling, he was apprenticed to learn printing, a calling that he abandoned when on Oct. 7, 1851, he entered the navy, through the favor of a former governor of Wisconsin. On graduating from the Naval Academy in June 1855, he was warranted midshipman and ordered to the *Congress* of the Mediterranean Squadron. In April 1858 he joined the *Colorado*; and later in that year the *Roanoke,* a few months before he was warranted master. His studious habits led to his appointment in September 1860 as assistant professor of ethics and English at Annapolis, to the duties of which position were shortly added those of teacher of fencing, as he was an excellent swordsman. He was promoted lieutenant from Oct. 30, 1860. Desiring active duties he was on May 23, 1861, ordered to the *Roanoke* and on that vessel took part in the engagement at Hatteras Inlet. In September, against his own wishes and at the request of the superintendent of the academy, he returned to that institution as assistant to the commandant of midshipmen in charge of the *Constitution* and later was promoted commandant. On July 16, 1862, he was commissioned lieutenant commander and in June 1863 he took part as commander of the *John Adams* in the search off the Atlantic Coast for the privateer *Tacony.* In December he became executive officer of the *Brooklyn* and in that capacity participated in the battle of Mobile Bay. He remained in active service until the end of the war, commanding the captured ironclad *Tennessee,* the *Seminole* when she was blockading Galveston, and for a time the third division of the Mississippi Squadron.

After a period of service with the *Swatara* of the West India Squadron, Lull from 1866 to 1869 was attached to the Naval Academy, first as an instructor in mathematics, and later in Spanish. Following his promotion to the grade of commander on June 10, 1870, he had a varied experience as an explorer and surveyor. In 1870–71 he was in charge of the *Guard* of the Darien Surveying Expedition. In 1872–73 he commanded the Nicaragua Exploring Expedition and received the thanks of the department for the energetic manner in which he performed a laborious task. After serving on the Interoceanic Ship Canal Commission, and commanding the Panama Surveying Expedition, he was from 1875 to 1880 hydrographic inspector in the Coast and Geodetic Survey and was frequently employed in active surveying duties. When he left the survey he was highly commended by the superintendent. In 1880–81 he commanded the *Wachusett* of the Pacific Squadron and received the thanks of the department for his efficient services. On Oct. 1, 1881, he was promoted captain. In the following year he visited Nicaragua in the interest of the Provisional Interoceanic Canal Society and on his return was made equipment officer of the Boston Navy Yard. His last duty was as commandant of the navy yard at Pensacola.

The results of Lull's survey of Nicaragua were published in 1874 (*Senate Executive Document*

57, 43 Cong., 1 Sess., pp. 33–143); and those of his survey of Panama in 1879 (*Senate Executive Document 75,* 45 Cong., 3 Sess., pp. 7–52). He was the author of a *History of the United States Navy-Yard at Gosport, Va.* (1874), and joint-author of *Methods and Results: Table of Depths for Harbors on the Coasts of the United States* (1883). About 1863 Lull was married to Elizabeth F. Burton. His second wife, Emma Gillingham Terry, to whom he was married on Nov. 5, 1873, was a sister of Commodore Edward Terry.

[Record of Officers, Bureau of Navigation, 1846–88; H. V. Eddy, *The Lull Book* (1926); Stephen Terry, *Notes of Terry Families* (1887); *War of the Rebellion: Official Records (Navy),* 1 ser. XXI, XXII, XXVII; *Army and Navy Jour.,* Mar. 12, 1887; *N. Y. Tribune,* Mar. 7, 1887; information as to certain facts from R. S. Lull.]
C. O. P.

LUMBROZO, JACOB (fl. 1656–1665), physician, planter, and merchant, was born in Lisbon of Portuguese-Jewish ancestry. His family removed from Portugal to Holland during his lifetime and he had a sister in the latter country with whom he corresponded. He emigrated from Holland to Maryland in 1656 and at once began the practice of medicine, being one of the first Jews to settle in that colony, and the first physician to practise there. The court records for 1657 and 1658 show that he obtained judgments for the payment of debts owed to him. In 1658 he had trouble with his fellow colonists on account of his religious views. Charged with blasphemy, he declared that he had only answered from the point of view of a Jew the questions put to him, and had said nothing scoffingly (*Archives of Maryland,* XLI, 203). He was ordered held for the next court. The penalty if he were convicted was death and the confiscation of goods; but he was released under a general amnesty, proclaimed by Lieut.-Gov. Josias Fendall [*q.v.*] in honor of the proclamation of Richard Cromwell as Protector (*Ibid.,* p. 258). He was not subjected to any further annoyance, because he was recognized as an asset to the colony and probably because the fanatical element among the colonists lost the ascendancy. For the next five years little is known of him. During 1663 he served as a juror and on Sept. 10 of that year letters of denization were issued to him along with certain privileges which allowed him to take up land and become a planter. About this time he married a woman, Elizabeth by name, who had come to the colony in 1662, and who is believed to have been a Christian. He had for some time been engaged in commerce as well as agriculture, is known to have traded extensively with London merchants, and in 1665 was commissioned to trade with the Indians. After 1663 he signed his name John. He was living as late as Sept. 24, 1665, but died before May 31, 1666. A son, John Lumbrozo, was born posthumously in June. The widow soon remarried and the son may have taken the name of his step-father, for the name Lumbrozo disappears abruptly and permanently from the records of the colony.

[*The Jewish Encyc.,* vol. VIII; *Pubs. Am. Jewish Hist. Soc.,* no. 1 (1893), no. 2 (1894); *Archives of Md.,* vols. II (1885), XLI (1922), XLIX (1932).]
E. P.

LUMMIS, CHARLES FLETCHER (Mar. 1, 1859–Nov. 25, 1928), author, editor, was born at Lynn, Mass., the son of Henry and Harriet (Fowler) Lummis. His early education was received largely at home, his father being a minister and teacher. He studied at Harvard from 1877 to 1881, but did not receive his degree until 1906. From 1882 to 1884 he was editor of the *Scioto Gazette,* at Chillicothe, Ohio. In September of the latter year he started from Cincinnati on a walking trip to Los Angeles "for recreation and observation," arriving at his destination on Feb. 1, 1885, after covering a distance of 3,507 miles. In a cañon in Arizona on this trip he broke his arm but after setting the bone himself and binding it up in a rude sling he continued on his way. The day after his arrival at the end of his journey he entered the employ of the Los Angeles *Times* and served as city editor from 1885 to 1887. Overwork brought on paralysis, and in January 1888, with one arm hanging limp, he went to New Mexico to recuperate and for long periods lived among the Pueblo Indians in their villages, learning their customs, languages, folk lore, and folk songs, much of which material he incorporated later in books of history, fiction, essay, and verse. By 1891 he had recovered fully from his illness. In 1892, associated with Adolph Bandelier [*q.v.*], he took part in a two years' ethnological and historical expedition to Peru and Bolivia. Upon his return to Los Angeles in 1894, he founded and assumed the editorship of *Land of Sunshine,* a magazine devoted to the life and history of the Far West, continued later under the title *Out West.*

The decade of the nineties was a period of productive writing. In 1891 appeared *A New Mexico David* and in the following year *A Tramp Across the Continent,* describing his walking trip of 1884–85. In the same year he published *Some Strange Corners of Our Country.* In 1893 appeared the two books by which he is perhaps most widely known: *The Land of Poco Tiempo,* descriptive of the Southwest and its people, and *The Spanish Pioneers,* a historical account of the conquistadores and priests who played a conspicuous part in the fifteenth and sixteen centuries. Before the end of the century he had published *The Man Who Married the Moon* (1894), Pueblo folk tales; *The Gold Fish of Gran Chimú* (1896); *The King of the Broncos* (1897); *The Enchanted Burro* (1897); and *The Awakening of a Nation: Mexico of Today* (1898). In 1905 he became librarian of the Los Angeles Public Library serving until 1910 and building up in this period a fine collection of Southwest material. In 1911 he was stricken with blindness which was complete for many months but from which he fully recovered. One of his greatest achievements was the founding and building of the Southwest Museum in Los Angeles, an institution fostering the historical, archeological, and ethnological interests of the Southwest. To this work he gave much of his time and energy in his later years. He was the founder of The Landmarks Club and through many years was indefatigable in his efforts to preserve the Spanish missions and other historical relics of California and the neighboring states. He also interested himself in the songs of the Southwest and made phonographic records of more than five hundred early Spanish songs of the region and more than four hundred Indian songs in many languages. *Spanish Songs of Old California* (2 vols., 1923–28) and *Mesa, Cañon and Pueblo* (1925) reflect his ethnological and literary interests in these years.

The early Spanish and Mexican inhabitants and the native population of the region provide the personal content of most of Lummis' literary products. But he occasionally wrote on other phases of life, as for example *My Friend Will* (1911) which is a stimulating account of the psychological battle which he fought against paralysis and of his subsequent recovery. His first book was a collection of verses published in 1879 on real bark, bearing the title *Birch Bark Poems,* and the last book which appeared in his lifetime was a poetical volume entitled *A Broncho Pegasus* (1928). *Flowers of Our Lost Romance* was accepted by the publishers before his death but did not appear until 1929. His style was stirring and colorful, full of imagery and original and well-turned phrases. Although a pioneer in the study of the Southwest, he was a journalist rather than a scholar and he was more successful in his prose descriptions of strange people and places than he was in the field of verse or in that of history or archeology. Without doubt his greatest contribution was the service he rendered in arousing interest in the non-American inhabitants and the half-known regions of the Southwest by his writings and lectures and by his organization and development of the Southwest Museum. He was married three times; to Mary Dorothea Roads, Apr. 16, 1880, to Eva Douglas, Mar. 27, 1891, and to Gertrude Redit, May 9, 1915.

[The main facts of his life are outlined by Lummis in *Who's Who in America,* and in a biographical record filled out and filed at the Los Angeles Public Library. Further autobiographical material is to be found in his writings. See also: Ben Field, article in *Overland Monthly and Out West Mag.,* July 1929; *Nation,* Dec. 12, 1928; *Harvard Coll. Class of 1881: Fiftieth Anniversary* (1931); *Harvard Grads.' Mag.,* Mar. 1929; Los Angeles *Times,* Nov. 26, 1928.] J. C. P.

LUMPKIN, JOSEPH HENRY (Dec. 23, 1799–June 4, 1867), first chief justice of the supreme court of Georgia, was born on a plantation in Oglethorpe County, Ga., the seventh son of John and Lucy (Hopson) Lumpkin. His parents were among the numerous Virginians who had gone to middle Georgia immediately after the Revolutionary War. John Lumpkin prospered and had numerous progeny. His second son, Wilson Lumpkin [*q.v.*], became governor of Georgia. In his formative years Joseph had access to what was regarded as an unusual library and was thrown with the foremost men of the state, who were his father's frequent guests. At fifteen he entered Franklin College (later the University of Georgia) and when that institution was temporarily closed he went to the College of New Jersey, where he was graduated with honors in 1819. Returning to Georgia he studied law in the office of Thomas W. Cobb and upon his admission to the bar in 1820, entered the practice at Lexington, later moving to Athens where he made his home for the rest of his life. In February 1821 he was married to Callender C. Greve, a native of Edinburgh, Scotland. Many of his descendants attained prominence; two, Samuel and Joseph Henry Lumpkin II, became justices of the supreme court over which their grandfather was the first to preside.

Lumpkin was a successful practitioner from the beginning. His arguments were well reasoned and reflected scholarship and wide reading, but his forte was eloquence. His impressive figure, handsome features, and the resonant qualities of his clear and melodious voice added no little to the effectiveness of his utterances. He never sought public office and, with the exception of serving two terms in the state legislature (1824 and 1825) and assisting in framing the Georgia Penal Code in 1833, devoted his time to his profession until called to the bench. In 1844, his health having become somewhat impaired, he took a year's vacation in Europe. During his absence the General Assembly, heeding at last the constitutional mandate of 1835, passed the legislation necessary to establish a supreme court. Lumpkin was unanimously elected one of the justices, and his associates—Hiram Warner and Eugenius A. Nisbet—made him their chief. He presided over the court for more than a score of years and died in office. Soon after he was made chief justice a school of law was added to the University of Georgia and given his name. Here he lectured until the outbreak of the Civil War. He gave much thought to social and economic problems and in 1852 published a treatise, *The Industrial Regeneration of the South,* in which he urged the encouragement of manufacturing, primarily to give employment to the "poor whites" whose condition he deplored. (See *The South in the Building of the Nation,* vol. VII, 1909, p. 179.) In 1860 he was elected chancellor of the University of Georgia but declined to serve. He had also declined, a few years before, a position on the federal court of claims tendered him by President Pierce.

The task which confronted the first chief justice and his associates was made difficult by the fact that for more than seventy years the people of Georgia had tenaciously clung to a system of jurisprudence unique in English-speaking countries. Each judge of the superior (circuit) courts, bound neither by the decisions of his predecessors or his colleagues—and not always by his own—was the final arbiter of all litigation in his circuit. The people were not only satisfied with this form of judicature, they were aggressively antagonistic to courts of review that lived by correcting the errors of others and adhering to their own. Therefore, for the supreme court to survive, its judges were under the necessity not only of promulgating principles that would harmonize and make uniform the administration of law throughout the commonwealth; they also had to pronounce judgments the inherent justice of which would be apparent. That the first justices met these requirements to the satisfaction of the people is attested by an act of the legislature of 1858 which declared the decisions of the supreme court to be the law of the state having the same force and effect as acts of the General Assembly. Lumpkin had strong convictions against the tendency of courts to permit technical rules of practice to defeat justice. The scientific application of legal principles meant less to him than deciding a case on its merits. Nevertheless, a number of his decisions became widely followed precedents. His opinions were delivered orally and delighted his hearers. Many of them as later—sometimes carelessly and hastily—reduced to writing are worthy of his reputation. But a large proportion of the more than two thousand that bear his name, in the judgment of so competent a critic as Chief Justice Bleckley, "afford no just ideal of his wonderful gifts. . . . Those who never saw and heard him cannot be made to realize what a great master he was."

[See memorial in 36 *Ga. Reports,* 1–42; sketch by Bernard Suttler in W. J. Northen, *Men of Mark in Ga.,* vol. II (1910); J. R. Lamar, "Hist. of the Establishment of the Supreme Court of Ga.," *Report of the Twenty-Fourth Ann. Session of the Ga. Bar Asso.* (1907); Walter McElreath, *A Treatise on the Constitution of Ga.* (1912); L. L. Cody, *The Lumpkin Family of Ga.* (1928); *Daily Intelligencer* (Atlanta, Ga.), June 6, 1867. Lumpkin's opinions are contained in volumes 1–35 *Ga. Reports.*] B. F.

LUMPKIN, WILSON (Jan. 14, 1783–Dec. 28, 1870), Georgia statesman, son of John and Lucy (Hopson) Lumpkin, was born in Pittsylvania County, Va., second of eleven children. In 1784 when Wilson was an infant, the family moved to the Georgia frontier, where they became pioneers on Long Creek, in what became Oglethorpe County. Wilson was educated in the common schools of the county. He supplemented this scanty education by wide reading in history and public law during five years (1799–1804) while he assisted his father as clerk of superior court, worked on the farm, taught school, and studied law. In 1804, at the age of twenty-one, he was admitted to the bar and began practice at Athens, Ga. In the same year he was elected to the lower house of the Georgia legislature, where he served for the greater part of the next ten years. In 1814 he was elected to Congress but was defeated for reëlection in 1816. He then took up residence in Morgan County, west of Oglethorpe, where he intended to farm, but in the same year (1818) he was appointed a commissioner to run the lines of lands recently ceded by the Creek Indians to the state of Georgia. He began at this time that long and intimate connection with Indian problems in Georgia, in which field he rendered his most distinctive service. In 1819 he again went to the legislature, but he retired in 1821 to accept another appointment as Indian commissioner.

He was elected to Congress in 1826, serving through two terms (1827–31). Although reelected for a third term in 1831, he resigned from Congress to run for the governorship and was successful. At this time the chief public question in Georgia was the removal of the Creek and Cherokee Indians from the state. In Congress, Lumpkin supported the vigorous governors, George M. Troup and John Forsyth, in their controversies with the federal government over Indian removals. As governor of Georgia for two terms (1831–35) Lumpkin was chiefly preoccupied with the problem of removing the Cherokees, settled by favorable treaty in 1835. In handling the Cherokee situation he maintained the vigorous state-rights attitude of his predecessors. In 1836 he was appointed Cherokee commissioner and was serving in this capacity when elected in November 1837 to fill the unexpired term of John P. King in the United States Senate. Retiring from the Senate in 1841 he devoted two years to the task of rehabilitating the affairs of the state railroad, the Western & Atlantic, then under construction, in which he had long taken interest. The southern terminus of this road (now Atlanta) was for a time called Marthasville, in honor of Governor Lumpkin's daughter. In 1843 he retired to his plantation, where he continued for years to exercise large public influence through his correspondence and friends. In the developing sectional controversy, 1845–60, he maintained extreme state-rights views. When secession came, his advanced age precluded participation in public affairs, but his sympathies were with secession and the Southern Confederacy. He died at Athens, Ga., in his eighty-eighth year. He had married, on Nov. 20, 1800, Elizabeth Walker, who bore him five sons and three daughters. She died in 1819 and on Jan. 1, 1821, he was married to Annis Hopkins, by whom he had four children. The Lumpkin family was distinguished for its jurists, among them being the brother of Wilson, Joseph Henry Lumpkin [*q.v.*], chief justice of the supreme court of Georgia.

[Lumpkin left a voluminous manuscript captioned "The Removal of the Cherokee Indians from Georgia," but in effect an autobiography, containing letters, speeches, and public papers, covering his entire career. In 1907 this was privately printed in 2 vols. by Wymberly De Renne. Other sources include: G. G. Smith, *The Story of Ga. People: 1732–1860* (1900); R. H. Shryock, *Ga. and the Union in 1850* (1926); J. F. Jameson, "Correspondence of John C. Calhoun," *Ann. Report of the Am. Hist. Asso. for the Year 1899* (1900), vol. II; U. B. Phillips, "Ga. and State Rights," *Ann. Report of the Am. Hist. Asso. for the Year 1901* (1902), vol. II; L. L. Cody, *The Lumpkin Family of Ga.* (1928); W. J. Northen, *Men of Mark in Ga.*, vol. II (1910).]

H. J. P., Jr.

LUNA Y ARELLANO, TRISTAN de (fl. 1530–1561), Spanish explorer, son of Don Carlos de Luna y Arellano, came from Castile to New Spain in 1530 or 1531 and served as captain and *maestre de campo* under Francisco Coronado on his New Mexico expedition, accompanying that leader on part of his Quivira journey. In 1548 he suppressed for viceroy Mendoza a dangerous Indian outbreak in Oaxaca. His wife was Isabel de Rojas, widow successively of Juan Velázquez and Francisco Maldonado, "first conquerors." Their *encomiendas* were inherited by her children, and Luna hypothecated the properties to finance his Florida expedition. In December 1557 Philip II, fearful that the French would advance from their holdings in Newfoundland into his northern frontier, revoked previous orders forbidding the conquest of Florida and commanded its occupation. The viceroy, Luis de Velasco, chose his friend Luna as governor and captain-general of Florida and the Punta de Santa Elena (Port Royal). The task was to select a base on the Gulf, advance to an intermediate province, Coosa in Alabama, and thence press on and fortify the Punta to protect the north coast, assure the Bahama Channel freedom from pirates, and serve as a mission center from which to proselyte among the Indians.

The expedition, costing 300,000 *pesos* of the King's money and all Luna's fortune, comprised 500 soldiers and 1,000 colonists and servants. It sailed from San Juan de Ulúa on June 11, 1559, and, after a stormy voyage, reached Ochuse or Pensacola Bay, previously selected by Guido de Las Bazares, on Aug. 14. On Aug. 19 a terrific wind destroyed nearly all the ships and provisions, sealing the doom of the enterprise. Compelled to live off the country, Luna moved to Nanipacana on the Alabama River, sending a party under Mateo del Sauz to Coosa, fabulously opulent according to Soto's accounts. When the governor tried to lead his starving followers to Coosa his captains voted to return to the Gulf coast. At Ochuse Luna again tried, upon the suggestion received from Sauz, to reach Coosa; but his officers challenged his authority and judgment, averring that he, long a sick man, had lost his wits. Reports from them and the Dominican friars with the party led Velasco to relieve Luna by sending as governor Angel de Villafañe. An attempt under Luna's nephew Martin Doz and Diego Biedma to reach Santa Elena by sea failed because of storms; a second effort, under Villafañe himself, actually reached the region desired, but storm again wrecked the ships, driving the leader to Havana.

After being relieved on Apr. 8, 1561, Luna left Ochuse for Spain to petition the King to decide the suit his officers had brought for the purpose of defeating his commands, and to petition for reimbursement and restoration of his governorship. He was unsuccessful in this; nor did he inherit from his brother Pedro the title of mariscal of Castile; Pedro briefly outlived him, and the inheritance went to Carlos; Tristán died in poverty in Mexico city. His children, Carlos de Arellano and Juana de Ávalos, married into the Mendoza-Velasco family; their descendants, being members of the noble families of the counts of Santiago Calimaya and of the Valle de Orizaba, served in many important colonial offices.

[The best Spanish accounts of Luna in Florida are in Andrés González de Barcia, *Ensayo Cronológico para la Historia General de la Florida* (1723) and Agustin Dávila Padilla, *Historia de la Fundación y Discurso de la Provincia de Santiago de México* (1596). There are a few pages by J. G. Shea, in Justin Winsor's *Narrative and Critical Hist. of America,* vol. II (1886). See also Ricardo Ortega y Pérez Gallardo, *Historia Geneal. de las Familias mas Antiguas de Mexico* (1908), vol. II; Woodbury Lowery, *The Spanish Settlements Within the Present Limits of the U. S., 1513–61* (1901), and *The Luna Papers* (2 vols., 1928), edited and translated by H. I. Priestley.] H. I. P.

LUNDIE, JOHN (Dec. 14, 1857–Feb. 9, 1931), engineer, inventor, son of James and Anne (Honeyman) Lundie, was born in Arbroath, Scotland. After graduation from the Dundee high school in 1873, he served for four years as a pupil in the office of the harbor engineer of the Port of Dundee, where he obtained some excellent training in civil engineering. Entering the University of Edinburgh, he graduated in 1880 with the degree of bachelor of science, having been first prize man in mathematical physics.

He then came to the United States and for four years was engaged upon railroad work in Oregon and Washington, including the building of Table Rock Tunnel, of which he was in charge. Going to Chicago, he engaged in private practice and later entered the employ of the city. In this capacity he made the preliminary survey of the Chicago Drainage Canal and designed several bridges. In 1890 he became engineer in Chicago for the King Bridge Company of Cleveland. This position he held for four years, during which time he erected numerous structures, including steelwork for some of the buildings of the Columbian Exposition. He then returned to private practice, during the course of which he laid out the first low-level drainage system for Chicago and was connected with water-supply projects for other places. While engaged upon work at Memphis, Tenn., he developed a method of determination of the yield of artesian wells. As a result of investigations regarding the use of electricity for the suburban travel of the Illinois Central Railroad came one of his principal achievements. After an entire year of research he enunciated the principle of "rapid acceleration" and the advisability of utilizing a high percentage of weight upon the driving wheels. From this work he prepared a thesis, "The Economics of Electric Train Movement," which he presented to the University of Edinburgh, from which he received the degree of doctor of science in 1902. This thesis also established the Lundie formula for train resistance.

In 1898 he was called to New York City in connection with some heavy traction problems, and soon afterward began practice there. About this time he reported upon power handling of freight for the Central of Georgia Railroad and in the course of his investigation designed the first combined electric hoist and tractor, since called a telpher. He also designed and patented (Patent No. 687,569, Nov. 26, 1901) the Lundie Ventilated Rheostat, now in extensive use. In addition to a wide consultation practice upon railroad electrification problems in the United States, he was called to London to advise regarding the Metropolitan Underground system; and to Canada, on important electric railway work. In 1904 he reported to the General Electric Company upon water-power development and the use of electric power on the Isthmus of Panama, and at the same time directed the affairs of the Panama-American Corporation. In 1913 he designed and patented the Lundie Tie Plate (Patent No. 1,065,696, June 24, 1913), and later, a duplex rail anchor. Thereafter these inventions and their applications took much of his time and energy, requiring eventually the formation of the Lundie Engineering Corporation, of which he was president. He was now able to give more personal time to research and technical work, in which his greatest interest lay. In 1921 he became technical adviser to the United Central America Corporation. Although not in the best of health during the latter part of his life, he remained active in business up to the time of his death, which occurred in New York City. In 1906 he married Iona Oakley Gorham, who died in 1925; and in 1929, Mrs. Alice Eddy Snowden, widow of Dr. Albert A. Snowden.

[*Trans. Am. Soc. Civil Engineers,* vol. XCV (1931); *Specifications and Drawings of Patents Issued from the U. S. Patent Office,* Nov. 1901; *Official Gazette of the U. S. Patent Office,* June 24, 1913; *Who's Who in America,* 1930–31; *Engineering News-Record,* Feb. 12, 1931; *N. Y. Times,* Feb. 10, 1931.] H. K. B.

LUNDIN, CARL AXEL ROBERT (Jan. 13, 1851–Nov. 28, 1915), optician and mechanician, was born at Venersborg, Sweden, third of the eleven children of Carl Fredrik and Ulrika Henrietta (Anderson) Lundin. During his childhood the family moved to Falun, where he was educated at the high school. He early showed an interest in things mechanical and in drawing, and after his course at Falun he served an apprenticeship of seven years at Stockholm as an instrument maker. Subsequently he went to Christiania, where he was employed by the instrument maker Olsen, his work being principally on chronometers. In Christiania he met Hilda Marie Hansen, his future wife, who was indirectly responsible for his later contact with the already famous firm of Alvan Clark & Sons, Cambridgeport, Mass., makers of telescopes. She came to America in October 1872 as governess in the family of the Norwegian consul at Boston and within less than a year he followed. Landing at New York in August 1873, he went immediately to Boston and soon found employment in nearby Newton as a skilled mechanic in work on fire-alarm apparatus. In a short time his unusual skill was brought to the attention of the Clarks and in November 1874 he became their chief instrument maker. With them and their successors he saw continuous service until his death forty-one years later. His ability and good judgment, combined with extreme patience and modesty, immediately won for him the closest confidential relations with each member of the firm. Finding himself now established in congenial surroundings, he married in April 1875, and began his residence at Cambridge. Here were born his two children, a daughter and a son.

From his earliest associations with the firm he was interested in its optical work and since he showed himself unusually gifted, Alvan Clark [*q.v.*] personally instructed him—and him alone —in the methods by which this talented family had attained success in making their famous telescope lenses. Though continuing his contact with the mechanical work, he was soon devoting so much of his attention to optical matters that, shortly, skill superior to his in this line was not to be found. With time his responsibilities increased until the failing health of Alvan G. Clark [*q.v.*], the last surviving member of the original firm, brought to him complete responsibility for all undertakings bearing the name of Clark. He did important work on the 30-inch lens for the Pulkovo Observatory in Russia, at that time the largest lens in existence, which was installed by him personally under special decree of the Russian government in 1883. The Clarks followed this lens with two others, each in turn of record-breaking dimensions, the 36-inch lens for the Lick Observatory (1887) and the 40-inch lens for the Yerkes Observatory (1896), in the production of which he took an important part and was specially designated to complete the latter in case Clark should be unable to finish the task. He completed the 24-inch lens for the Lowell Observatory (1895). He made the 16-inch lens for the University of Cincinnati (1904), the 18-inch for Amherst College (1905), and many smaller lenses, mirrors and optical parts. During these experiences he had devised and applied several important optical tests. Definite plans for large lenses were being delayed at the time of his death because optical glass could not then be obtained from Europe. In 1876 he received a medal from the authorities in charge of the Centennial Exhibition for the excellence of his "flats"; and in 1893, a diploma from the Columbian Exposition for excellence in the optical parts of engineering instruments. He was a fellow of the American Association for the Advancement of Science and a charter member of the Astronomical and Astrophysical Society of America (later, the American Astronomical Society). In 1905 he received from Amherst College the honorary degree of master of arts as "scientific expert in cutting and fashioning glasses of great telescopes."

With his patience and skill was combined an extreme sensitiveness. He was deeply disturbed by extravagance of any kind. Though modest in the expression of opinion, he held firmly to conclusions which had resulted from a rich experience. His solution of a problem was direct and through the application of simple devices. Instrumental astronomy in America is in debt to him for his generosity in placing his experience at the service of others—a generosity limited only by his being "unwilling to waste time on a poor telescope."

[*Nature,* Jan. 6, 1916; *The Observatory,* Feb. 1916; *Science,* Aug. 4, 1905, Dec. 17, 1915; *Popular Astronomy,* Jan. 1916; *Guide to Nature,* Jan. 1916; *Boston Transcript, Journal, Post, Herald,* and *Globe,* Nov. 29, 1915; family documents and personal acquaintance.]

J. M. P—r.

LUNDY, BENJAMIN (Jan. 4, 1789–Aug. 22, 1839), abolitionist, was born in Sussex County, N. J., the only child of Joseph and Eliza (Shotwell) Lundy, both Quakers. His great-grandfather, Richard Lundy, son of Richard Lundy who came from Devonshire to Philadelphia in 1682, was a Quaker minister and established several Friends' meetings in Pennsylvania and New Jersey. Benjamin Lundy received only elementary education, and the strenuous physical labor he undertook in youth is said to have injured his hearing. In 1808 he went to Wheeling, Va., to learn the saddler's trade, and there first came into contact with slavery, witnessing coffles of negroes passing through the town in the inter-state slave trade. In 1815, at St. Clairsville, Ohio, to which place he had removed, he organized an anti-slavery group known as "The Union Humane Society," and in January 1816 issued a circular letter urging the formation of anti-slavery societies with common name and constitutions, with machinery for correspondence and cooperative effort, and with general conventions for determining policies. In this suggestion may be seen the germ of the later national anti-slavery societies. He began soon to contribute to *The Philanthropist,* published by Charles Osborn at Mount Pleasant, Ohio, in which slavery was discussed, and eventually accepted Osborn's invitation to join him in the publication of the paper. This necessitated closing his saddlery, which had been financially profitable; accordingly, he loaded his stock of goods on a flatboat and took it to St. Louis, arriving there in the fall of 1819 at the time when the Missouri slavery question was everywhere under discussion. Lundy at once associated himself with the anti-slavery forces and contributed articles to the newspapers. During his absence from Ohio, Osborn sold *The Philanthropist,* and when Lundy returned to Mount Pleasant he began publication, January 1821, of a new paper, *The Genius of Universal Emancipation.* After but a few issues it was removed to Greenville, Tenn., where it was published until the summer of 1824, when Lundy removed it to Baltimore.

During the next decade he became deeply interested in the question of colonization of freed negroes, as a possible solution for the national problem. He spent much time trying to find suitable places for such colonies, journeying to Hayti in 1825 and again in 1829, to the Canadian province of Upper Canada in 1832, and to Texas three times, 1830–31, 1833–34, and 1834–35. While he was absent on his first visit to Hayti, his wife, Esther Lewis, whom he had married in 1815, died at Baltimore. In January 1827 he was assaulted by Austin Woolfolk, a Baltimore slave-dealer, as a result of critical comments in the columns of *The Genius* upon Woolfolk's business. In 1828 Lundy went on a six months' lecturing trip through the Northern states, in the course of which he met William Lloyd Garrison and sought his help in the publication of *The Genius.* Garrison at first declined, but in 1829 joined Lundy at Baltimore and became associate editor. His vitriolic pen quickly involved the paper in lawsuits, however, and he and Lundy separated; while growing opposition in Baltimore led to the removal of the paper to Washington. During 1830–31, when Lundy was absent from home to obtain subscribers, he carried part of his equipment with him and had the paper printed in local shops wherever he happened to be. Publication became more and more irregular until finally, toward the end of 1835, *The Genius* ceased to appear.

In the following August, Lundy began the publication in Philadelphia of *The National Enquirer and Constitutional Advocate of Universal Liberty,* the chief purpose of which seems to have been to expose what the editor regarded as slaveholders' plots to wrest Texas from Mexico. At this time he was in close touch with John Quincy Adams and doubtless supplied Adams with much of the information concerning the Texas situation which he used so effectively in his speeches in Congress. In 1836 Lundy also published his pamphlet, *The War in Texas,* which presented arguments against the annexation of Texas and was one of the most vigorous of the writings to appear in that controversy. He continued to publish *The National Enquirer* at Philadelphia until March 1838 when it was taken over by John G. Whittier and its name changed to *The Pennsylvania Freeman.* In May of that year Lundy lost all his papers and journals when a Philadelphia mob destroyed "Pennsylvania Hall," and in the following summer he left for Illinois where his family resided. There he associated himself with the local anti-slavery societies and reëstablished *The Genius,* twelve issues of which appeared before his death, after a brief illness, in August 1839. Though dated from Hennepin, the Illinois numbers of *The Genius* were printed at Lowell, Ill. Lundy was buried in a Friends' graveyard on Clear Creek, in Putnam County.

Cheerful in temperament, gentle and mild in manner, a keen observer of men and nature, as his writings show, he was ready to adapt himself to whatever conditions he encountered. He was a pioneer in the organization of anti-slavery societies and in the publication of an anti-slavery newspaper, and was the most active figure in the whole movement during the twenties, while his enlistment of Garrison brought to the abolitionist cause its chief figure in the later period.

[*The Life, Travels and Opinions of Benjamin Lundy* (1847), comp. by Thomas Earle "under the direction and on behalf of his children"; W. C. Armstrong, *The Lundy Family and Their Descendants of Whatsoever Surname* (1902); files of *The Genius of Universal Emancipation*; W. P. and F. J. Garrison, *Wm. Lloyd Garrison* (4 vols., 1885–89); G. A. Lawrence, "Benjamin Lundy—Pioneer of Freedom," in *Jour. Ill. State Hist. Soc.,* July 1913; "The Diary of Benjamin Lundy Written during His Journey through Upper Canada, January 1832," repr. from *The Genius,* with notes by Fred Landon, in *Ontario Hist. Soc., Papers and Records,* vol. XIX (1922); Fred Landon, "Benjamin Lundy, Abolitionist," in *Dalhousie Rev.,* July 1927.]

F. L.

LUNT, GEORGE (Dec. 31, 1803–May 16, 1885), author and journalist, son of Abel Lunt, a sea-captain, and Phoebe (Tilton) Lunt, was born at Newburyport, Mass., where his ancestor, Henry Lunt, had settled in 1635. He attended Phillips Academy at Exeter, N. H., and was graduated from Harvard College in 1824. While a student at Harvard he kept a district school at Groton, Mass.; later he was for several years the principal of the high school in his native town. After studying law in the office of Asa W. Wildes of Newburyport he was admitted to the bar in 1831. In the preceding year he had represented the town in the General Court. In 1835 and 1836 he was a member of the state Senate; in 1837 and 1841 he was in the lower house; and in 1847 was again elected representative, to fill the unexpired term of Caleb Cushing [*q.v.*], resigned. He removed to Boston in 1848, and the following year was appointed United States attorney for the district of Massachusetts, as a reward for his activity in the Whig convention that nominated Gen. Zachary Taylor for the presidency. Lunt held this office until 1853, when he resumed private practice. During this period of his life he appears to have enjoyed a considerable reputation as an orator and he made speeches on various occasions. Upon the dissolution of the Whig party he became a Democrat, and in 1857 assumed the editorship of the *Boston Daily Courier,* the leading Democratic newspaper in the city. In this capacity, dreading hostilities and the disruption of the Union, he opposed such policies as would tend to estrange the South, and thus during the years immediately preceding the war gained for himself the name of being a defender of "slavery and its attendant evils" (Hurd, *post,* p. xli). He continued in the editorship until 1863, when he retired and devoted his leisure to literature.

As early as 1826 he had published a volume of verse entitled *The Grave of Byron, with Other Poems.* This was followed by *Poems* (1839); *The Age of Gold, and Other Poems* (1843); *The Dove and the Eagle* (1851); *Lyric Poems, Sonnets and Miscellanies* (1854); *Julia: a Poem* (1855); and finally *Poems* (1884). His work included some translations from Vergil and Horace; it is filled with classical allusions and marked by dignity and a certain grace. In prose he produced *Eastford; or Household Sketches* (1855); *Three Eras of New England, and Other Addresses* (1857); *The Union* (1860); a pamphlet entitled *Review of McClellan's Campaigns as Commander of the Army of the Potomac* (1863); *The Origin of the Late War* (1866); and *Old New England Traits* (1873), as well as magazine articles and editorials. The last-named book gives a picture of Newburyport in the old days and incidentally throws not a little light on Lunt's childhood. In January 1877 he contributed "Recollections of Thackeray" to *Harper's Magazine.* During his later years he spent much time at Scituate, Mass. He became interested in the improvement of Scituate harbor, and it is said that the work done on it by the federal government in the eighties and likewise the establishment of a life-saving station at the Third Cliff are attributable largely to his efforts and influence. As advocate or adversary of any cause he was independent and unyielding, but always honorable. His manner was a happy combination of simplicity and dignity. In religious matters he was an ardent Episcopalian. He was married three times: on Oct. 25, 1834, to Sarah Miles Greenwood of Newburyport; on Dec. 4, 1845, to Emily Ashton, then residing in Newburyport; and in 1864 to Adeline Parsons of Boston, sister of Thomas William Parsons [*q.v.*].

[*Boston Daily Courier,* May 24, 1885; *Boston Daily Advertiser,* May 18, 1885; *Boston Morning Journal,* May 19, 1885; Newburyport *Herald,* May 19, 1885; *Turner's Public Spirit* (Ayer, Mass.), May 23, 1885; D. H. Hurd, *Hist. of Essex County, Mass.* (1888), vol. I; J. J. Currier, *Hist. of Newburyport,* II (1909), 281, 513; *Old Scituate* (1921); T. S. Lunt, *A Hist. of the Lunt Family in America* (1914).] L. S. M.

LUNT, ORRINGTON (Dec. 24, 1815–Apr. 5, 1897), philanthropist, was born at Bowdoinham, Me., the son of William Webb Lunt, for some time a member of the state legislature, and his wife, Ann Matilda Sumner. He was descended from Henry Lunt, who emigrated from England and settled at Newburyport, Mass., in 1635. Orrington Lunt entered his father's store in his fourteenth year, became a partner when he was twenty-one, and was made clerk and treasurer of the town at twenty-two. His reputation for stability and integrity was established at this early day. On Jan. 16, 1842, he married Cornelia A. Gray, who became the mother of his four children. In this same year he moved to Chicago to seek a fortune. He engaged in business in a small way, but it was a time of financial depression and he found it difficult to get a start. In 1845 he began to buy wheat and in November he sold all the wheat he had accumulated in two storehouses and a large elevator. The transaction was so profitable that he was led to buy largely and rather recklessly, and in a year lost all he had made. He later said that he had learned two things by this experience: not to buy on speculation and not to go outside Chicago for his market; and he thought this wisdom had been cheaply bought. He soon reëstablished himself, and thenceforth had a permanent standing in the business world. He helped to project the Galena & Chicago Union Railroad, the first built from Chicago, which ran its cars from Chicago to Des Plaines in 1849; he was for two years its vice-president, and served as a director until the road was consolidated with the Chicago & Northwestern. In 1862, because his health was poor, he gave up active business life, and in 1865 he went abroad for two years with his family, traveling extensively in Europe and Asia.

A devout Methodist, Lunt had joined the Clark Street Church in Chicago as soon as he arrived in that city and he was identified with all the Methodist enterprises in the next generation. He had a pleasing countenance and in his later years a patriarchal appearance, and he was always characterized by a beautiful and benign disposition. He had a singing voice in his youth which maintained its sweetness even in old age. A shrewd and honest business man, he was much sought for as treasurer of important funds. When the Chicago fire threatened his offices he removed the valuable papers belonging to the institutions with which he was connected before he took care of his own. He was a trustee of the Chicago Young Men's Christian Association, president of the Chicago Bible Society, a member of the Committee of Safety and Finance during the Civil War, secretary and treasurer of the board of trustees of Northwestern University and also of Garrett Biblical Institute for many years.

Lunt and his friend and fellow trustee, John Evans [*q.v.*], were appointed on a committee to choose a site for the projected Northwestern University, but it was Lunt alone who waded through the swamp which lay between the road and the lake shore and discovered the ridges and hardwood groves along the lake which marked the site of the present university campus. The trustees purchased 379 acres at seventy dollars an acre. The city of Evanston, which they wished to call Luntville or Orrington, but which was finally named after John Evans, grew up about the university; Lunt moved his residence to Evanston in 1874 and was a foremost citizen until the day of his death. Orrington Avenue and the Orrington Lunt Library Building on the Northwestern campus preserve his name.

[*Biog. Sketches of the Leading Men of Chicago* (1876); A. D. Field, *Worthies and Workers of the Rock River Conference* (1896); A. H. Wilde, *Northwestern Univ., a Hist.* (4 vols., 1905); J. S. Currey, *Chicago: Its Hist. and Its Builders* (1912), vol. IV; T. S. Lunt, *Lunt: A Hist. of the Lunt Family in America* (1914); E. F. Ward, *The Story of Northwestern Univ.* (1924); *Chicago Daily Tribune* and *Chicago Times-Herald*, Apr. 6, 1897.] D. A. H.

LURTON, HORACE HARMON (Feb. 26, 1844–July 12, 1914), jurist, the son of Sarah Ann (Harmon) and Lycurgus L. Lurton, a practising physician who later became a clergyman in the Protestant Episcopal Church, was born at Newport, Ky. His early education was with private teachers and, in 1859, he entered the old University of Chicago. His collegiate course was interrupted by the Civil War and never completed, but by constant study and discriminating reading he became a man of learning and broad culture. In 1861, at the age of seventeen, he enlisted in the 5th (afterwards the 35th) Tennessee Infantry Regiment of the Confederate States Army and served as sergeant major until discharged in 1862 for physical disability. A few weeks later he enlisted in a Kentucky Regiment, was taken prisoner upon the surrender of Fort Donelson, confined at Camp Chase, from which he escaped in April 1862, and at once enlisted under Gen. John Morgan. During that general's raid into Ohio, he was captured and held a prisoner until early in 1865, when his mother appealed to Lincoln to parole him on account of his serious illness. After the war he graduated, in 1867, from the law school of Cumberland University at Lebanon, Tenn., where in September of the same year he married Mary Frances Owen, who bore him two sons and two daughters. He settled at Clarksville, Tenn., and practised law there until 1886, except that from 1875 to 1878 he served as a chancellor. He soon became known as a profound and successful lawyer. Strong in his convictions and a natural leader, he possessed unusual political sagacity, and, though he himself was never a candidate for any except judicial office, his counsel was always valued by his party and by his friends. From 1898 to 1910 he was professor in the law school of Vanderbilt University and, for the last five years of that time, he was dean of the law school. He was, for many years, a vestryman in the Trinity Episcopal Church of Clarksville.

In August 1886 he was elected as one of the justices of the supreme court of Tennessee and began a judicial career that ended only with his death. In January 1893 he succeeded to the chief-justiceship. Several months later, Cleveland appointed him United States circuit judge to succeed Howell E. Jackson whom Harrison had promoted to the supreme bench. He thus became a member of the circuit court of appeals for the sixth circuit, of which William Howard Taft was the presiding judge. After Taft resigned to become governor-general of the Philippines, Lurton was the presiding judge. During these years on the bench he became a close friend of Taft, who was so much impressed with his legal and judicial ability that, in December 1909, he offered him the appointment as associate justice of the United States Supreme Court. Such an appointment by a Republican president of a southern Democrat caused some surprise. Moreover, Lurton was sixty-six years old, a more advanced age than that at which any other justice had ever been appointed, but he was strong and vigorous and came to the Supreme Court with a longer experience on the federal bench than most of his predecessors. As a judge, his opinions were clear and accurate, as in the cases of the *City of Omaha* vs. *Omaha Water Company* (218 *U. S.*, 191–205) and *United States* vs. *Baltimore and Ohio Railroad Company* (231 *U. S.*, 280–98). He was devoted to the Constitution and to the established rules of law. Although he was aware of the changing conditions in modern life and thought, which demanded certain adjustments of governmental machinery, he had little sympathy with those who wished such adjustments to come by way of judicial interpretation. In 1911 he published an essay (*North American Review,* Jan. 1911) in which he expressed his faith in Montesquieu's system of divided powers and his belief that the opposite tendency led to "a substitution of government of men for a government of law" (p. 12). He was a member of the committee to revise the federal equity rules. In order to study the course of English experience he went to England in the vacation of 1911 and carried on some correspondence with the Lord Chancellor. The edition of *The New Federal Equity Rules* edited by James Love Hopkins (1913) was dedicated to him in recognition of this work. In December 1913 he was forced by ill health to absent himself from the court, but after a vacation in Florida he returned to his place in April 1914 and sat to the end of the session, when he sought rest at Atlantic City, where he died.

[U. S. Circuit Court of Appeals for the Sixth Circuit, *In Memory of Horace Harmon Lurton* (1914); J. T. Moore, *Tenn. the Volunteer State* (1923), vol. II; 237 *U. S. Reports*; *Who's Who in America,* 1914–15; *Outlook,* Jan. 1, 1910, July 25, 1914; *Current Literature,* Mar. 1910; *New York Times,* July 13, 14, 16, 1914; *Nashville Tennessean and the Nashville American,* July 13, 1914; *Evening Star* (Washington, D. C.), July 13, 1914.] W. L. F.

LUSK, WILLIAM THOMPSON (May 23, 1838–June 12, 1897), obstetrician, was born at Norwich, Conn., the son of Sylvester Graham and Elizabeth Freeman (Adams) Lusk. His father was a great-grandson of John Lusk who emigrated from Scotland to Wethersfield, Conn., in 1788. After preliminary schooling under Rev. Albert Spooner in Norwich, at Charles Anthon's classical school in New York City, and at Russell's Military Academy, New Haven, he entered Yale College in 1855. Before the close of his freshman year, however, he was compelled to give up his studies because of an eye affection. After a brief experience in business he went to Geneva, Switzerland, to consult a famous oculist, and received such encouragement in regard to his condition that he resumed his studies, entering upon a medical course at Heidelberg in 1858. After two years there he spent a third year at the University of Berlin. Returning to America at the outbreak of the Civil War, he enlisted in the 79th New York Infantry Highlanders as a private and fought in a number of battles, including first Bull Run, Antietam, and Fredericksburg. He was several times commended for gallantry in action. During the draft riots in New York City he was a captain. In September 1863 he retired to the inactive list and the following winter entered Bellevue Hospital Medical College, graduating at the head of his class in 1864. After eighteen months of post-graduate study under Sir James Y. Simpson of Edinburgh and Karl Braun of Vienna, he undertook general practice at Bridgeport, Conn., for one year. In 1866 he accepted the offer of a junior partnership with Benjamin Fordyce Barker [*q.v.*] which lasted until 1873. During this period he was professor of physiology and microscopic anatomy at Long Island College Hospital, 1868–71; delivered a course of lectures in physiology at Harvard, 1870; and jointly with Dr. J. B. Hunter, edited the *New York Medical Journal,* 1871–73. In 1871 he accepted the professorship of obstetrics, diseases of women, diseases of infancy, and clinical midwifery at Bellevue Hospital Medical College, to succeed George T. Elliot, deceased. This chair he retained until his death. From 1889 he was president of the faculty, and in 1894 he was president of the American Gynecological Society. Among his numerous hospital appointments were those of gynecologist to Bellevue and St. Vincent's, obstetrical surgeon to Bellevue and the Emergency Hospital, consulting obstetrician to the Lying-In and Maternity hospitals and, earlier in his career, visiting physician to the Nursery and Child's Hospital and to the Charity Hospital. He contributed freely to periodical literature and at the International Medical Congress in 1876 read a paper upholding the germ origin of puerperal fever, which at that time had very few supporters (*Transactions of the International Medical Congress of Philadelphia, 1876,* 1877). Succeeding Fordyce Barker as the fashionable obstetrician of the day, he had a large private practice.

Lusk is known chiefly for his classic work, *The Science and Art of Midwifery,* which first appeared in 1882 and went through eleven printings in thirteen years. The author's familiarity with the German language and literature, old and recent, gave to the book all the authority and thoroughness of a German monograph. Considered the most learned textbook of the day in English, it was translated into French, Italian, Spanish, and Arabic. It could have survived the author's death had not his heirs always refused consent to any alteration of the original text in the interest of revision. Lusk was married twice: on May 4, 1864, to Mary Hartwell Chittenden, and in 1876 to Matilda (Myer) Thorn. Four of the five children of his first marriage survived him, the two sons attaining distinction in medicine and medical education, while a daughter of the second marriage married a well-known professor of gynecology.

[*War Letters of Wm. Thompson Lusk* (1911); sketch by a son, Graham Lusk, in H. A. Kelly and W. L. Burrage, *Am. Medic. Biogs.* (1920); *N. Y. Jour. Gynaecol. and Obstetrics*, Feb. 1892; *Am. Jour. Obstetrics*, July 1897; *British Gynaecol. Jour.*, Aug. 1897; *Medic. Record* (N. Y.), June 19, 1897; *Medic. News*, June 19, 1897; *N. Y. Medic. Jour.*, June 19, 1897; *Trans. Am. Gynecol. Soc.*, vol. XXIII (1898); *Trans. N. Y. Acad. of Medicine, 1896–1901* (1903); *Am. Gynecol. and Obstetrical Jour.*, Dec. 1907; *Medic. Pickwick*, July 1915; *Album Am. Gynecol. Soc.*, 1918; F. A. Virkus, *The Abridged Compendium of Am. Geneal.*, vol. I (1925); *N. Y. Tribune*, June 13, 1897.] E. P.

LUTHER, SETH (fl. 1817–1846), carpenter and pioneer advocate of labor reforms, was born toward the end of the eighteenth century, probably in Providence, R. I. His ancestors may have been the Welsh Luthers who settled in Rhode Island about 1650, and founded there the first Baptist church in America. Of formal education he had but little. "For myself," he wrote, "I had no advantages but those of a common school, and that of a far inferior kind to those of the present day. . . . I am indebted for *what little I do know* to newspapers and books, and to a constant habit of observation" (*Address on . . . Avarice*, p. 38). In 1817 he made a trip down the Ohio River from Pittsburgh to Cincinnati. His travels took him "in and about 14 of the United States, including a visit to the frontiers of Upper Canada and East Florida" (*Ibid.*). Upon his return from his journeys he went to work as a carpenter, in Providence or Boston, or one of the mill towns that were growing so fast just before 1830. According to his own account, he lived for years "among Cotton mills, worked in them, traveled among them" (*Address to the Working-men*, p. 35).

He espoused the workingman's cause wholeheartedly. From the West he had brought back the democratic spirit of the frontier, and the class distinctions of New England irritated him. "You cannot raise one part of the community above another," he wrote, "unless you stand on the bodies of the poor" (*Avarice*, p. 42). His first pamphlet, *An Address to the Working-men of New England* (1832, 3rd ed., 1836), based on speeches in a half-dozen towns and cities, was an attack on the abuses of the factory system. The author cited instances of children who worked twelve to fifteen hours per day and of their physical maltreatment; quoted factory regulations showing paternalistic control exercised by employers, and asserted that "the whole system of labor in New England, more *especially in cotton mills*, is a cruel system of exaction on the bodies and minds of the producing classes, destroying the energies of both" (p. 28). His conclusion may be questioned, since his temperament was not that of an impartial observer; nevertheless, although political leaders frowned upon the proposals of Luther and his fellow agitators and the newspapers gave them no support, the best educated and the most intelligent element of the community were sympathetic, and in 1842 Massachusetts enacted the first American child-labor law. In 1833 Luther published *An Address on the Right of Free Suffrage* (Sabin, *post*), and in 1834 *An Address on the Origin and Progress of Avarice*. The latter was a denunciation of political and religious as well as economic oppression. At its conclusion the author laid down the following program of reform: Universal equal education by means of manual labor schools supported at the public expense; abolition of all licensed monopolies; abolition of capital punishment and of imprisonment for debt; the entire revision or total abolition of the militia system; a less expensive system for the administration of justice; equal taxation for property; and an effective mechanic's lien law. His deadly sincerity, forceful language, grim humor, and biting sarcasm made his pamphlets valuable weapons in the labor movement. The General Trades Convention in Boston in 1834 selected him as one of its secretaries and a year later he helped draft a manifesto known as the *Boston Circular*, in favor of the ten-hour day, which, reprinted in Philadelphia, is said to have inspired a general strike. In 1835 he addressed the National Trades Union Convention upon the condition of women and children in cotton mills. The last mention which has been found of him is a record of his participation in a ten-hour convention in Manchester, N. H., in 1846.

[J. R. Commons and others, *A Doc. Hist. of Am. Industrial Soc.*, vols. VI, VIII (1910), X (1911), and *Hist. of Labour in the U. S.* (2 vols., 1918); R. T. Ely, *The Labor Movement in America* (1886); Edith Abbott, "A Study of the Early History of Child Labor in America," *Am. Jour. Sociology*, July 1908; S. M. Kingsbury, *Labor Laws and Their Enforcement* (1911); Joseph Sabin, *A Dictionary of Books Relating to America*, vol. X (1878).] P. W. B.

LUTKIN, PETER CHRISTIAN (Mar. 27, 1858–Dec. 27, 1931), educator, composer, and conductor, was born in Thompsonville, Racine County, Wis., the youngest of six children of Peter Christian and Hannah Susanna Define (Olivarius) Lutkin. Both parents were born in Denmark. The father was interested in the violin as an amateur, but Peter was the only one of his children to display musical ability. Before the family moved to Chicago in 1869, the father was engaged in the wholesale grocery business in Racine, from which district he was elected to the Wisconsin legislature. The sudden death of both parents in 1871 threw the boy on his own resources. He obtained his education in the public schools of Chicago and in the choir school of the Episcopal Cathedral, where in 1869 he became alto soloist of the pioneer boy choir of the midwest. At the age of fourteen he became organist at the Cathedral, though as yet technically untrained, holding this position till 1881. In the meantime he began the study of piano with Mrs. Regina Watson, organ with Clarence Eddy, and theory with Frederick Grant Gleason. From 1879 to 1881 he was instructor of piano at Northwestern University in Evanston. For the next two years he was in Berlin studying organ with Haupt, piano with Raif, and theory with Bargiel (mostly at the *Hochschule für Musik*), winning a scholarship in the *Königliche Meisterschule für Composition* in October 1882. He also studied piano in the Leschetizky Piano School in Vienna (1883) and with Moszkowski in Paris (1884).

Returning to Chicago, Lutkin became organist and choirmaster at St. Clement's (1884–91) and at St. James's (1891–96). From 1888 to 1895 he was director of the theory department of the American Conservatory of Music. Meanwhile, in 1891, when the department of music of Northwestern University was organized, he was appointed professor of music and in 1897 became dean of the School of Music upon its organization. The development of this school into one of the important musical institutions of the country was one of the main achievements of his life. He became dean emeritus in 1928 but continued active as a teacher until a few weeks before his death. He was conductor of the Evanston Musical Club (1894–1919) and the Ravenswood Musical Club (1896–1904). In 1906 he founded the noted a cappella choir of the University, an organization which, of all his major activities, probably lay closest to his heart and for which he wrote most of his compositions for unaccompanied voices. These choral units made it possible for him to establish, with the financial aid of influential citizens, the Chicago North Shore Festival Association in 1908, of which he was the choral conductor until 1930. The first festival took place in May 1909. These annual festivals, among the best of their kind, exerted a large influence in developing the musical interests of Chicago.

Lutkin was one of the founders of the American Guild of Organists (1896) and was twice president of the Music Teachers National Association (1911–12 and 1919–20). His special interest from early manhood was in church music and until his death he kept the headship of the department of church and choral music of the School of Music, writing and editing many pamphlets on various phases of church music. He was also special lecturer on church music in the Western Theological Seminary (Chicago) and the Garrett Biblical Institute (Evanston), one of his lecture courses in the former being published as *Music in the Church* (1910). As a composer he wrote little outside the field of church music and part-songs. His best work displays a good understanding of contrapuntal writing and characteristic choral effects, particularly with unaccompanied voices. Among his best compositions may be listed the following: *Te Deum,* "Peace" (first given at the North Shore Festival, 1919), Communion Service in C, *Te Deum* No. 2 in B-flat, *Magnificat* and *Nunc Dimittis* in B-flat, and several anthems—"Christians, Awake," "Fairest Lord Jesus," and "What Christ Said." Lutkin died at Evanston in his seventy-fourth year. He was a man of simple, dignified bearing, of striking sincerity and kindliness, and with a delightful sense of humor. He was survived by his wife, Nancy Lelah Carman, whom he had married on Oct. 27, 1885, and by a son, Harris Carman Lutkin.

[*Who's Who in America,* 1930–31; article by Carl Beecher in *Northwestern Univ. Alumni News,* Feb. 1932; the *Diapason,* Apr. 1, 1930; Jan. 1, Feb. 1, Apr. 1, 1932; *Chicago Tribune,* Dec. 28, 1931; information as to certain facts from Mrs. Peter C. Lutkin.]

R. G. C—e.

LYALL, JAMES (Sept. 13, 1836–Aug. 23, 1901), inventor, manufacturer, was born in Auchterardar, Perth, Scotland, the son of Charles and Mary (Cooper) Lyall. When he was three years old his parents came to the United States and settled in New York City. Here Lyall was educated in the public schools and then went to work in his father's shop, making and mounting Jacquard looms. On the outbreak of the Civil War he enlisted in the 12th New York Infantry and served for a short time in the defense of the national capital. In 1863, while still in the service, he prepared a new substance for enameling cloth, and the government awarded him a large contract to supply enameled haversacks and knapsacks. Following the completion of this work, he and his brother William founded the firm of J. & W. Lyall, for the manufacture of looms and other cotton-making machinery. On Aug. 11, 1868, he obtained the basic patent on his positive-motion loom. This loom he further perfected with two additional inventions, patented July 4, 1871, and Dec. 10, 1872. Its special feature lies in the fact that the shuttle is not thrown as a projectile through the wedge-shaped space between the two sets of warp threads, but is positively dragged back and forth by an endless belt attached to the shuttle carriage, running first in one direction and then in the other. While this invention did not eliminate the flying-shuttle loom, it revolutionized the manufacture of cotton goods throughout the world; for it abolished the use of picking sticks, permitted great widths of fabric to be woven, and made it possible to unite several looms into one machine and weave a number of fabrics simultaneously.

Besides attending to the enormous business resulting from this invention, Lyall found time to make other improvements in textile machinery, including a new take-up motion for looms, patented in 1875 and 1877, and a cap press for compressing cotton on the shuttles. In the eighties he established mills for manufacturing cotton and jute goods. These included the Chelsea Jute Mills, New York; the Planet Cotton Mills, Brooklyn; the United States Corset Company, New York, which manufactured the first machine-made corsets in the world; and the Brighton Mills, established in New York and later moved to Passaic, N. J. He also patented, in 1888 and 1889, two improvements in the manufacture of jute binder twine. Between 1893 and 1896 he obtained five patents for a new kind of woven fabric for pneumatic tires and fire hose. Its peculiarity lay in the fact that both warp and filling threads were of the same length, thus overcoming the squirming tendency of hose or tires consisting of fabric woven with threads of unequal length. Finally, in 1897, he invented a "tubular wheel tire," the cotton fabric of which was made with a large number of warp threads and very few filling threads per inch. In 1869 the American Institute of New York awarded him a gold medal of honor for his positive-motion loom; and for subsequent inventions, a bronze medal in 1871 and a silver medal in 1873. He was married on Sept. 8, 1864, to Margaret Telford of Meredith Hollow, near Delphi, N. Y., and at the time of his sudden death in New York City he was survived by his widow and five children.

[*Textile World*, Sept. 1901; *Wool and Cotton Reporter*, Aug. 29, 1901; E. W. Byrn, *The Progress of Invention in the Nineteenth Century* (1900); *Who's Who in America*, 1901–02; *House Ex. Doc. No. 52*, 40 Cong., 3 Sess.; *Specifications and Drawings of Patents Issued from the U. S. Patent Office*, July 1871, Dec. 1872, Dec. 1875, June 1877, Jan. 1888, Aug. 1889, Sept., Oct. 1893, Mar., June 1896, Feb. 1897; *N. Y. Tribune*, Aug. 24, 1901.]

C. W. M.

LYDSTON, GEORGE FRANK (Mar. 3, 1857–Mar. 14, 1923), physician, was the son of George N. and Lucy A. Lydston, both descended from Scotch-English ancestors who had early emigrated to New England. As a recently married couple they went to California during the gold excitement of 1849 and there in Jacksonville, a mining village in Tuolumne County, their son was born. Following a childhood in these primitive surroundings he was sent to private schools, first in California and later in New York. His medical courses were taken at Bellevue Hospital Medical School in New York, where he graduated in 1879. After a year's service as interne in the New York Charity Hospital he was appointed resident surgeon to the State Immigrant Hospital at Ward's Island. He resigned this latter position in 1881 and moved to Chicago to practise his profession. The year following his arrival he joined the faculty of the recently organized College of Physicians and Surgeons.

For over twenty years he conducted courses in genito-urinary surgery and venereal diseases at that school, for nine years as lecturer, then as head of the department. His teaching was marked by that originality and independence of thought which characterized his whole career. He was always interested in the business management of medical practice. During his Chicago career he built up a large and select clientele and was said to have had the most lucrative practice of his time. From the time of his graduation Lydston was a prolific writer upon widely varying topics. Beginning in 1880 he contributed over one hundred articles to medical periodicals, mostly relating to his specialty. In addition he was the author of *Surgical Diseases of the Genito-Urinary Tract* (1899, 1904), *Diseases of Society* (1904), a work upon the problems of vice and crime, and *Impotence and Sterility* (1917). Of fiction, he wrote *Over the Hookah* (1896) and *Poker Jim* (1908). *Panama and the Sierras,* written in 1900, is a book of travel. He also wrote a play, *The Blood of the Fathers* (1912). He was especially interested in criminology and was a friend of Lombroso. For many years he was professor of criminal anthropology at the Kent College of Law. Many of his later contributions to medical literature were devoted to the possibilities of securing rejuvenation by gland transplantation.

Lydston was a man of aggressive personality and was frequently involved in controversy. He had a keen and satirical humor to which he gave full vent with tongue and pen. For years he acted the part of the bad boy of the medical profession, hitting right and left among the organized fraternity. He was in perpetual feud with the American Medical Association. Physically he was tall and powerfully built. He practised boxing and was interested in all athletics. He was surgeon of 2nd Illinois Infantry before and during the Spanish-American War. In his later years he spent much of his time in California, and in Los Angeles, he died of pneumonia. He was married to Josie M. Cottier of Chicago in that city in 1884.

[R. F. Stone, *Biog. of Eminent Am. Physicians and Surgeons* (1894); *Jour. Am. Medic. Asso.*, Mar. 17, 1923; *Am. Jour. of Clinical Medicine*, Apr. 1923; *Los Angeles Times*, Mar. 15, 1923; personal acquaintance.]

J. M. P—n.

LYMAN, ALBERT JOSIAH (Dec. 24, 1845–Aug. 22, 1915), Congregational clergyman, author, was born in Williston, Vt., the first child and only son of Josiah and Mary L. (Bingham) Lyman. The family sprang from early colonial stock, the earliest progenitor in this country being Richard Lyman of High Ongar, Essex, who crossed the Atlantic in 1631 in the same ship, the *Lion,* which brought John Eliot, the famous apostle to the Indians, and the wife and the eldest son of Gov. John Winthrop. Josiah Lyman, a graduate of Williams College and a licensed preacher, was teaching school at Williston when his son was born. A few years later he removed with his family to Lenox, Mass. Albert early showed an aptitude for literary and scholarly pursuits, and he became a district school teacher at fifteen years of age; but his interests turned him to the ministry, and after a period of study in Williston Seminary, Easthampton, Mass., where he was graduated in 1863, he was licensed to preach. He determined, however, to obtain a thorough education. To this end he spent a year (1865–66) at the Chicago Theological Seminary, attended the Union Theological Seminary in New York, where he was graduated in 1868, was a resident licentiate at the Yale Theological School (1868–69), and on Sept. 7, 1870, was regularly ordained to the Congregational ministry in connection with his settlement as minister of the First Congregational Church of Milford, Conn.

In a long career of forty-five years, Lyman served only two parishes—the Milford church (1869–73), and the South Congregational Church, Brooklyn (1874–1915). "For the best of reasons," says a distinguished associate, "might the South Church be called Dr. Lyman's, for it was his. For more than forty years he gave it all the wealth of his intellect and his heart." An active man, in a busy pastorate, he entered deeply and widely into the life of his city. He was an intimate friend of Henry Ward Beecher and of Richard S. Storrs, and succeeded the latter as president of the Brooklyn Academy of Arts and Sciences. In his religious views he represented the liberal wing of Orthodoxy, but he was never interested primarily in theological thought, and contributed little of importance to its development. It was his practical ability, attractive personality, and utter loyalty to his denomination which early lifted him to that position of leadership in American Congregationalism which he held through many years. Exceptional grace as a preacher made him a popular guest in college pulpits. He gave important courses of lectures at Hartford Theological Seminary, Bangor Theological Seminary, and Auburn Theological Seminary. He frequently preached and lectured abroad, in Scotland and in Switzerland; but his heart was always in his parish. Handsome in person, of warm sympathies, possessed of a genius for friendship, he was unrivaled in pastoral power. He was a lover of nature, and an indefatigable mountain climber, having the ascent of Mont Blanc to his credit. His published works, mostly volumes of sermons and lectures, are: *Preaching in the New Age* (1902), *A Plain Man's Working View of Biblical Inspiration* (1907), *The Christian Pastor in the New Age* (1909), *Underneath Are the Everlasting Arms* (1910), *The Three Greatest Maxims in the World* (1911), *The Mystery of Jesus* (posthumous, 1916). He was twice married: on June 1, 1870, to Ella Stevens, of Brooklyn, who died in 1893; and on June 26, 1902, to Elizabeth Hills, of Philadelphia.

[E. A. Lyman, *A Sketch of the Record of the Descendants of Daniel Lyman and Sally Clapp of Easthampton, Mass.* (1923); Lyman Coleman, *Geneal. of the Lyman Family in Great Britain and America* (1872); *A Service in Memory of the Reverend Albert Josiah Lyman, D.D.* (1915); *The Congregationalist*, Sept. 2, 1915; *The Congreg. Year Book* (1915); *Brooklyn Daily Eagle*, Jan. 13, 1899, Aug. 23, 1915; papers and records in possession of Dr. Lyman's family.]

J. H. H.

LYMAN, BENJAMIN SMITH (Dec. 11, 1835–Aug. 30, 1920), geologist, mining engineer, was the son of Samuel Fowler and Almira (Smith) Lyman and was born in Northampton, Mass. He was descended from Richard Lyman who emigrated to America in 1631, settling first in Charlestown, Mass., and later in Hartford, Conn. In his native city he prepared for college and entered Harvard University with the class of 1855. During the first year after graduating he tried his hand at school-teaching and the mercantile business but his greatest interest, he soon discovered, was in neither of these occupations but in geology. In 1856, therefore, he became an associate of Peter Lesley [*q.v.*], his uncle by marriage, and spent two field seasons in topographical and geological survey work in eastern Pennsylvania. During the intervening winter he taught school in Philadelphia. In 1858 he joined the Iowa State Geological Survey as assistant geologist but resigned within a year and went abroad for further study in his profession. From 1859 to 1861 he attended the Imperial School of Mines in Paris, France, and during 1861 and 1862 he attended the Royal Academy of Mines at Freiberg, Germany. Returning to the United States late in 1862 he established his residence in Philadelphia and opened an office as a consulting mining engineer. From 1863 to 1865 his principal work was that of surveying coal lands in and around Cape Breton, Nova Scotia, and also in gold mining in California; between 1865 and 1870 he undertook general geological and topographical work in many sections of the United States. In 1870 he was appointed mining engineer in the public-works department of the government of India and devoted that year to studying and preparing a report on the Punjab oil lands.

Upon returning to the United States in 1871 Lyman carried on his private practice until 1873 when he was made general geologist and mining engineer for the Japanese government. During the succeeding seven years in Japan he made both topographical and geological surveys of the major part of the Japanese Empire, the results of which were published in governmental reports. In the course of this work he discovered many of the coal and other mineral deposits of Japan and upon the completion of the survey he was prevailed upon to remain in Japan to assist in the development of several of these deposits. He returned to the United States early in the eighties and settled for a time in his boyhood home in Massachusetts. In 1887 he again took up his residence in Philadelphia and became assistant geologist for the state of Pennsylvania and served in this capacity until 1895. Thereafter he was privately engaged in geological researches not only in the United States but in Europe, India, China, and the Philippines as well. He was the author of 150 papers on geological subjects and wrote on a number of other subjects. Many of his articles were published in the *Transactions* of the American Institute of Mining Engineers and in the *Proceedings* of the American Philosophical Society and of the American Association for the Advancement of Science. His first professional paper was *Bourinot Coal Claims and Lands, Cape Breton* (1865). His other published writings include: *General Report on the Punjab Oil Lands* (1870); *Geological Survey of Japan* (1878); and *Against Adopting the Metric System* (1897). In 1864 Lyman became an advocate of vegetarianism and in 1917 published *Vegetarian Diet and Dishes* which has enjoyed a wide circulation. He held but one political office during his long career, namely, that of common councilman for Northampton, Mass., in 1885–86. He was a member of twenty-three technical and scientific societies, a fellow of the American Association for the Advancement of Science, and an honorary member of the Mining Institute of Japan. He died unmarried in Philadelphia and was buried in Northampton.

[*Who's Who in America,* 1920–21; *Report of the Secretary of the Class of 1855, Harvard Coll.* (1865); *Apocrypha Concerning the Class of 1855 of Harvard Coll.* (1880); Lyman Coleman, *Geneal. of the Lyman Family in Great Britain and America* (1872); M. L. Ames, *Life and Letters of Peter and Susan Lesley* (2 vols., 1909); G. P. Merrill, *The First One Hundred Years of Am. Geology* (1924); *Science,* Sept. 10, 1920; *Engineering and Mining Jour.,* Sept. 11, 1920; *Pub. Ledger* (Phila.), and *N. Y. Times,* Aug. 31, 1920.]

C. W. M.

LYMAN, CHESTER SMITH (Jan. 13, 1814–Jan. 29, 1890), astronomer and physicist, was born at Manchester, Conn., the son of Chester and Mary (Smith) Lyman. His father was a farmer and descendant of Richard Lyman who came to America from England in 1631. Chester attended the district common-school at Manchester, performed the farm boy's usual routine of chores, and spent a large part of his playtime in his father's tool shop. Before he was thirteen he had made several of the simple astronomical instruments that he found described in James Ferguson's *Astronomy.* When he was sixteen he decided to enter the ministry and taught the district school at Manchester two winters (1830–32) to obtain funds to prepare for college. He then attended the Ellington Academy for twelve months and entered Yale University in 1833. At Yale he took several prizes in composition and translation, was an originator and an editor of the *Yale Literary Magazine,* and was assistant to the professor of natural philosophy. This last position gave him the opportunity to use the observatory, where he spent most of his leisure. Upon graduation (1837) he became superintendent of the Ellington Academy. In September 1839 he entered

Union Theological Seminary and the next year returned to Yale to attend the theological school. In February 1843 he became pastor of the First Church (Congregational) at New Britain, Conn., from which position he resigned in 1845 because of ill health. He then traveled for his health and in the next five years was successively missionary, school teacher, and surveyor in Hawaii, and surveyor and gold digger in California. The journal he kept during his travels (published as *Around the Horn to the Sandwich Islands and California, 1845–50,* 1924) and the letters that he wrote to the *American Journal of Science and Arts* (September 1848 to January 1850) are detailed accounts of his travels and work, as well as interesting records of life in those places at that time. The letter published in the issue of September 1848 is said to be the first credible account of the discovery of gold in California to be received in the East and was widely copied by the press. His name appears on the first list of trustees for the proposed College of California (S. H. Willey, *A History of the College of California,* 1887, p. 5).

Lyman returned to New Haven in April 1850 and on June 20 of the same year was married to Delia Williams Wood. He was then employed for some time in preparing definitions of scientific words for an edition of Webster's *Dictionary.* In 1859 he became professor of industrial mechanics and physics in the Sheffield Scientific School at Yale. In 1871 the professorship was modified to include only physics and astronomy and after 1884 included only astronomy. While at Yale, Lyman invented the first combined transit and zenith instrument for determining latitude by Talcott's method (*American Journal of Science and Arts,* July 1860); an apparatus for demonstrating the theory of wave motion (*Ibid.,* May 1868); a pendulum apparatus for describing Lissajon's acoustic curves; and improvements in clock pendulums and escapements. The wave motion apparatus was patented and manufactured by Ritchie & Son of Boston and was widely sold to schools and colleges. In astronomy, Lyman was actively interested in the Yale Observatory, of which he was a manager, and there in 1866 he made the first satisfactory observation of Venus as a delicate ring of light when very near the sun in inferior conjunction (Agnes M. Clerke, *A Popular History of Astronomy During the Nineteenth Century,* 2nd ed., 1887, p. 302). He was a vice-president of the American Association for the Advancement of Science (1874) and president of the Connecticut Academy of Arts and Science (1859–77). He died at New Haven.

[*Record of the Class of 1837 in Yale Univ.* (7th ed., 1887); J. L. Chamberlain, *Universities and Their Sons,* vol. III (1899); Lyman Coleman, *Geneal. of the Lyman Family in Great Britain and America* (1872); *Am. Jour. of Sci. and Arts,* Mar. 1890; *Sidereal Messenger,* Nov. 1890; *Popular Sci. Monthly,* Nov. 1887; *Morning Jour. and Courier* (New Haven), Jan. 30, 1890.] F. A. T.

LYMAN, JOSEPH BARDWELL (Oct. 6 1829–Jan. 28, 1872), agriculturist, was born at Chester, Mass., the son of Timothy and Experience (Bardwell) Lyman and a descendant of Richard Lyman who emigrated to New England in 1631. After graduating from Yale in the class of 1850 he taught school for three years, first in Cromwell, Conn., then in Mississippi. In June 1853 he went to Nashville, Tenn., where, until he moved to New Orleans early in 1855, he studied law and again taught school. In 1856 he graduated from the law department of the University of Louisiana and for the next five years practised law in New Orleans. On July 14, 1858, he was married to Laura Elizabeth Baker. Upon the outbreak of the Civil War he enlisted as a private in the 1st Louisiana Cavalry. Taken prisoner at Loudon, Tenn., in September 1863, he was sent to the military prison at Louisville, Ky., from which he was released later in the month upon taking the oath of allegiance to the United States. He spent some months in Massachusetts, farming part of the time, then moved to New York City in 1864 to engage in journalism. In 1865 he published *Resources of the Pacific States.* His various writings brought him to the attention of the New York press and in 1867 he became agricultural editor of the New York *World.* From December 1868 to August 1869 he was also managing editor of *Hearth and Home.* In 1868 he had published some of his observations on Southern husbandry in *Cotton Culture,* and in 1869, in collaboration with his wife, he published *The Philosophy of Housekeeping.* In the latter year he became agricultural editor of the *New York Weekly Tribune.* The nationwide circulation, particularly among farmers, of this paper gave him an opportunity to exercise considerable influence on agricultural development.

In New York City Lyman was a member of the American Institute, a group of agricultural experts who met periodically to discuss questions of all sorts coming from farmers from all over the nation. These discussions he summarized in clear and simple language for his *Tribune* readers. He was conscientious and diligent rather than brilliant, and he gave as patient attention to letters requesting the most elementary information as to those dealing with the most interesting of contemporary questions. He constantly impressed upon American farmers the necessity of sustaining home manufactures, of diversifying their products, and of supporting every movement by which the power of association could be employed for the public good. Much of his time during 1871 he spent in supervising the building of a house at Richmond Hill, Long Island. He had barely moved his family into the new home when he died of smallpox on Jan. 28, 1872, and was buried the same day. He left six children.

[*Biog. Record of the Class of 1850 of Yale Coll.* (1877); *Obit. Record of Grads. of Yale Coll.* (1872); A. B. Booth, *Records of La. Confed. Soldiers and La. Confed. Commands* (3 vols. in 4, 1920); *Thirty-second Ann. Report of the Am. Inst. of the City of N. Y.* (1872); Lyman Coleman, *Geneal. of the Lyman Family in Great Britain and America* (1872); the *Cultivator and Country Gentleman*, Feb. 8, 1872; *N. Y. Tribune*, Jan. 29, 1872.]

R. H. G.

LYMAN, PHINEAS (1715–Sept. 10, 1774), provincial general, was born near Durham, Conn., the second son of Noah and Elizabeth Lyman and a descendant of Richard Lyman who emigrated to America in 1631. Renouncing the weaver's trade he had learned, Phineas prepared for and entered Yale, graduated in 1738, was elected tutor, and began to study law. In 1742 he resigned his tutorship, in October married Eleanor, only daughter of Col. Timothy Dwight of Northampton, and moved to Suffield, where he became prominent at the bar, in the local militia, and in town government. Through his efforts Suffield, in 1749, joined Connecticut, and he represented the town as deputy in the colonial Assembly until 1752, then acted as assistant until 1759. During the Seven Years' War, in which Lyman, as commanding officer of the Connecticut troops, served eight campaigns, and won the reputation of being the ablest and most trustworthy provincial general in the northern colonies, he succeeded in gaining the approval of his British superiors at the same time that he aided, through his high political position, in maintaining the independence of his colony. His military career contains few brilliant feats, but dull work conscientiously done. In 1755, as major-general and second in command of the Lake George expedition, he shared with Johnson the honors of defeating the French under Dieskau. In 1756 he associated with the moderates in the provincial-regular dispute over military rank; as commander of the garrison at Fort Edward, which he had laid out as Fort Lyman the previous year, he followed the suggestions and orders of his superiors in matters of camp discipline and sanitation. In 1757 he was with Webb, and in 1758 he was leading one column at the lower end of Lake George when Lord Howe [*q.v.*], leading another, was killed. He accompanied Amherst the following year against Crown Point, and later commanded at Ticonderoga. There, over the construction work that his provincial troops were engaged upon, he conducted with Amherst a close, friendly correspondence that shows him to have been earnest, responsible, grateful for favors and flattery, and proud of his trust. In 1760, after serving at Montreal, he commanded the construction work at Fort Ontario. He was again in New York the next year and in 1762, arrayed in "the finest Coat ever seen at New York," he sailed to join Albemarle at Havana as commander of all the provincial troops on that expedition.

In the third and last period of his life Lyman became known as one of the chief projectors of western colonies. Having Amherst's support, he first hoped to settle discharged provincial soldiers on lands east of Lake Champlain; but after 1763, when he went to England as agent for his own company of "Military Adventurers," and for the remaining subscribers to Samuel Hazard's colonization scheme of 1755, he planned a series of colonies along the Mississippi, and especially a large one of his own at the mouth of the Ohio. The unfavorable attitude of the ministry to western colonization, and the uncertainty of British politics prevented any of his various schemes from succeeding, although in 1770 he obtained 20,000 acres near Natchez. In 1772 he returned home, with a pension, but broken in health and disappointed. He served two further terms as deputy, and when the inclusion of Dartmouth in the ministry seemed to promise favorable action on his last petition for a new colony, "Georgiana," he reorganized the Adventurers, and left for the west. A change of policy defeated this project, too, and he obtained only squatters' rights. Soon after his arrival at Natchez, he died, leaving his wife and surviving children to continue his ill fortune.

[Lyman Coleman, *Geneal. of the Lyman Family in Great Britain and America* (1872); Wm. Fowler, *Hist. of Durham, Conn.* (1866); H. S. Sheldon, *Documentary Hist. of Suffield* (1879); Timothy Dwight, *Travels in New Eng. and N. Y.* (1823), I, 271–81, III, 349–58; *Commissary Wilson's Orderly Book . . . 1759* (1857), ed. by J. W. DePeyster; *Gen. Orders of 1757, Issued by the Earl of Loudoun and Phineas Lyman* (1899), ed. by W. C. Ford; C. J. Hoadly, *The Pub. Records of the Colony of Conn.*, vols. IX–XIV (1876–87); "The Wolcott Papers," *Conn. Hist. Soc. Colls.*, vol. XVI (1916); "The Fitch Papers," *Ibid.*, vols. VII and XVIII (1918–20); C. W. Alvord, *The Miss. Valley in British Politics* (2 vols., 1917); C. W. Alvord and C. E. Carter, "The New Régime, 1765–67," *Ill. State Hist. Lib. Colls.*, vol. XI (1916); F. B. Dexter, *Biog. Sketches of the Grads. of Yale Coll.*, vol. I (1885), and *The Lit. Diary of Ezra Stiles* (3 vols., 1901); *Acts of the Privy Council of England, Colonial Ser. . . . 1766–83* (1912).]

S. M. P.

LYMAN, THEODORE (Feb. 20, 1792–July 18, 1849), author, mayor, philanthropist, father of Theodore Lyman, 1833–1897 [*q.v.*], was born in Boston, Mass., a descendant of Richard Lyman who emigrated to New England in 1631. He was the second son of Theodore Lyman, a wealthy merchant, and the latter's second wife, Lydia Williams, niece of Timothy Pickering. The boy prepared for college at Phillips Exeter Academy and graduated from Harvard in 1810. Believing that he would pursue a career in letters, he spent the years until 1819 chiefly in study and travel, establishing European contacts, and accumulating a library. His first published efforts, two small books and several articles of travel and description, grew out of these years. He returned to Boston in 1819 and two years later married Mary Elizabeth Henderson of New York. In 1823 he published *A Short Account of the Hartford Convention* and in 1826 *The Diplomacy of the United States,* enlarged and republished in two volumes in 1828.

Lyman's political activities, which began almost immediately upon his return to Boston, were greatly affected by his inheritance and social position. His father had been of the Essex Junto, the family was related to Pickering, and the elder Lyman's intimate friend, Harrison Gray Otis, was still a candidate for office. Consequently Lyman was inescapably bound to that small group of die-hard Federalists who were vainly endeavoring to prevent the disintegration of the party. From 1820 to 1825 he sat in the state legislature in steadfast opposition to the Republicans. In 1823 he actively supported Otis in the latter's unsuccessful campaign for governor. In 1824 he fought against the elevation of John Quincy Adams to the presidency. Gradually he emerged as the leader of a silk-stocking group in uncompromising opposition to the Adams wing of the Republican party. This enmity, the disappearance of Federalism as a party, and the hope that Calhoun would come to control the movement, influenced Lyman to throw his support to Jackson in the election of 1828. Jackson was already receiving in Massachusetts the support of a popular and democratic following built up by Henshaw, and with this faction Lyman brought his aristocrats into a union that had little in common except hostility to Adams. The Lyman group worked heroically in the canvass. They established in August 1828 a newspaper, the *Jackson Republican* (merged in December 1828 with the *Evening Bulletin*). In the course of the campaign Lyman wrote an editorial (Oct. 29, 1828) which so infuriated Webster as to result in a suit of criminal libel. The trial was celebrated, but the jury could not agree on a verdict and the case was later dropped.

After the election of Jackson, Lyman continued in active support of him, but the patronage went to the Henshaw faction and Lyman grew lukewarm. The disaffection of Calhoun and Jackson's attack on the Bank completed the alienation, and Lyman in course of time became a Whig. But the currents remained confused. In 1831 Lyman ran for mayor of Boston with the support of anti-Jacksonian elements. He was defeated. Two years later he ran again, supported by Henshaw and the (Jacksonian) *Boston Post* although he was far from being a Jacksonian at this time, and triumphed over the National-Republican and Anti-Masonic candidates. He ran again in 1834 and was reëlected, thus serving as mayor throughout 1834 and 1835. His administration was able but undistinguished. The one noteworthy event was the mobbing of Garrison. Lyman's conduct during this riot was bitterly assailed by abolitionists, but it seems now that he acted with courage and discretion.

The later years of Lyman's life were devoted to philanthropy. There was in Boston a Farm School, a private charity intended to rescue morally exposed children. Lyman was called to the board of managers of this school and was thus introduced to the problem of reformatory schools. Consequently when the Massachusetts legislature appropriated in 1846 the sum of $10,000 for the purpose of establishing at Westborough a state-owned reformatory for juvenile offenders, Lyman greeted the venture with the greatest satisfaction. The amount appropriated, however, seemed to him inadequate, and he therefore acted promptly to insure the institution ample funds for a successful start. Between the founding date and his death in 1849 Lyman gave the school $22,500 and in his will there was a further bequest for $50,000. This financial aid was the vital factor in establishing the school on a strong foundation of usefulness. Lyman also bequeathed $10,000 to the Boston Farm School and a like sum to the Horticultural Society of Boston.

[Contemporary newspapers are important for Lyman's political career. Other sources include: *Memorial Biogs. of the New-Eng. Historic Geneal. Soc.*, vol. I (1880); J. H. Benton, Jr., *A Notable Libel Case: The Criminal Prosecution of Theodore Lyman, Jr., by Daniel Webster* (1904); *Proc. Mass. Hist. Soc.*, vol. XIX (1882); Lyman Coleman, *Geneal. of the Lyman Family in Great Britain and America* (1872); W. P. and F. J. Garrison, *Wm. Lloyd Garrison, 1805–1879,* vol. II (1885); Theodore Lyman, III, *Papers Relating to the Garrison Mob* (1870); A. B. Darling, *Pol. Changes in Mass., 1824–48* (1925); *Ann. Reports of the Trustees of the State Reform School at Westborough,* 1848–52; *Reports of the Boston Asylum and Farm School,* 1835,

1836, 1839, 1845, 1847, 1852; *Am. Jour. of Educ.*, Mar. 1861; *Boston Daily Atlas*, July 19, 1849.] P. H. B.

LYMAN, THEODORE (Aug. 23, 1833–Sept. 9, 1897), zoölogist, was born in Waltham, Mass., the son of Theodore Lyman, 1792–1849 [*q.v.*], a man of broad culture and varied interests, and Mary Elizabeth Henderson. He was reared in a home of affluence and culture and in his early youth was instructed by private tutors. In 1855 he was graduated from Harvard College, and at the time of his graduation he stood fourth in his class. He was attractive in physical appearance, of great personal charm, with a keen intelligence and sense of humor. During the years immediately following his graduation he worked under the tutelage of Louis Agassiz in the Lawrence Scientific School, joined an expedition of scientific research in Florida waters, took the degree of B.S. in 1858, and began the publication of papers on Ophiurans. In 1859 he was elected one of the original trustees of the Museum of Comparative Zoölogy, and somewhat later treasurer. "His rare common sense," wrote George R. Agassiz, "acted as a balance wheel in its somewhat hectic development" (S. E. Morison, *Development of Harvard University, 1869–1929*, 1929, p. 405). For the next score of years he wrote numerous articles on the Ophiuridae, which appeared in the publications of learned societies, and he came to be recognized as an authority on the subject.

From 1861 to 1863 Lyman was abroad in the pursuit of his scientific work and securing collections for the Museum. The outbreak of the Civil War did not seem to stir him greatly. He was opposed to the abolitionists and did not vote for Lincoln in 1860. The progress of the war, however, awakened his interests and a letter from General Meade whose acquaintance he had made on the Florida research expedition, inviting him to be a member of his staff, offered him an opportunity for service in the Unionist cause. He was commissioned as volunteer member of the staff of Governor Andrew, serving without pay, and in the autumn of 1863 joined Meade's headquarters with the rank of lieutenant-colonel. As personal aide-de-camp of the General he served bravely and efficiently at the battles of the Wilderness, Spotsylvania, and Cold Harbor. He was present at the siege of Petersburg and at the surrender of Lee at Appomattox. His letters to his wife covering this period (*Meade's Headquarters, 1863–65: Letters of Col. Theodore Lyman from the Wilderness to Appomattox*, 1922, selected and edited by George R. Agassiz) furnish valuable information on these campaigns. Upon his return to civil life he read before the Military Historical Society of Massachusetts of which he was a member numerous papers on phases of these operations.

In 1866 Lyman became chairman of the newly established Fisheries Commission of Massachusetts and in 1884 president of the American Fish Cultural Association. He was elected Overseer of Harvard College in 1868. Founder of the Reform Club, he was elected to Congress in 1882 on the issue of civil-service reform on an independent ticket, but he failed of reëlection largely because of the disappearance of the reform issue, and because of the beginning of the malady which was to make him a helpless invalid for the last dozen years of his life. He died at his summer home in Nahant. He had married, on Nov. 28, 1856, Elizabeth Russell, daughter of George Robbert Russell, a successful merchant of Dorchester, Mass. Besides numerous articles written for scientific societies, he contributed a short biography of his father to the *Memorial Biographies of the New-England Historic Genealogical Society* (vol. I, 1880) and published *Papers Relating to the Garrison Mob* (1870) in vindication of the action of his father who was mayor of Boston at the time of the riots.

[Henry P. Bowditch, memoir in *Nat. Acad. Sci., Biog. Memoirs*, vol. V (1905), with bibliography; C. F. Adams, memoir in *Proc. Mass. Hist. Soc.*, 2 ser. XX (1906); remarks occasioned by Lyman's death in *Ibid.*, 2 ser. XII (1899); M. A. DeWolfe Howe, *Later Years of the Saturday Club* (1927); *Boston Transcript*, Sept. 10, 1897.] H. M. V.

LYNCH, ANNA CHARLOTTE [See BOTTA, ANNA CHARLOTTE LYNCH, 1815–1891].

LYNCH, CHARLES (1736–Oct. 29, 1796), soldier, planter, and justice of the peace after whom the term "Lynch Law" appears to have been named, was born at "Chestnut Hill," his father's estate near the present site of Lynchburg, Va. He was the eldest son of Charles Lynch, a Virginia burgess who had emigrated from the north of Ireland as an indentured servant, and who had married Sarah, daughter of Christopher Clark the indenter. The early death of his father left whatever intermediate education Lynch received in the hands of his Quaker mother, but nothing is known specifically of his life until 1755, when, on Jan. 12, he married Anna Terrell (spelled variously). Settling on his patrimonial lands in the newly formed Bedford County, Lynch rapidly became a man of wealth and importance. He took the oath of office as justice of the peace in 1766. The following year he was "disowned" by the Quakers "for taking solemn oaths" (J. P. P. Bell, *Our Quaker Friends of Ye Olden Time*, 1905, p. 147). In 1769 he became a member of the House of Burgesses, continuing as such until the Revolution. He signed the Williamsburg protests of 1769 and 1774 against English taxation, served in the Virginia constitutional convention of 1776, and was a member of the Virginia House of Delegates until January 1778. Already a member of the Burgesses' committee of trade, Lynch played an important part in the mobilization of the state's resources for war. On Feb. 24, 1778, he was recommended for the office of colonel of militia; and in 1781 he was dispatched by Governor Jefferson to the assistance of General Greene in North Carolina (H. R. McIlwaine, *Official Letters of the Governors . . . of Virginia*, II, 1928, *passim*). With his volunteer regiment, he participated in the battle of Guilford Court House and continued with Greene until the surrender of Cornwallis at Yorktown, after which he resumed his duties as justice of the peace. He later served inconspicuously in the Virginia Senate between May 1784 and December 1789.

The disrupted state of the courts in Bedford County during the Revolution early led to the formation of an extra-legal court "to punish lawlessness of every kind" (J. E. Cutler, *Lynch-Law,* 1905, p. 27). With Lynch as the presiding justice, convictions by this court were frequent and were followed by summary whippings. In 1780 when Cornwallis' success seemed probable, a Loyalist conspiracy was discovered in Bedford County; and, as the General Court had been dispersed, Lynch's impromptu court tried and sentenced the conspirators. Two years later Lynch and his companions were exonorated by the Assembly, on the ground that their acts, though not "strictly warranted by law," were "justifiable from the imminence of the danger" (W. W. Hening, *The Statutes at Large . . . of Virginia,* XI, 1823, p. 135). Though remembered now chiefly on account of the connotation of the term "Lynch Law," Charles Lynch, a man of considerable public spirit and broad-mindedness, was of at least minor importance in the economic development of Virginia. He died at his estate on the Staunton River, leaving three sons. The city of Lynchburg was named for his younger brother, John.

[J. T. McAllister, *Va. Militia in the Revolutionary War* (1913); T. W. Page, "The Real Judge Lynch," *Atlantic Monthly,* Dec. 1901; H. C. Featherston, "The Origin and Hist. of Lynch Law," *Green Bag,* Mar. 1900; E. G. Swem and J. W. Williams, "A Reg. of the Gen. Assembly of Va.," *Fourteenth Ann. Report of the . . . Va. State Lib., 1916–17* (1917); Margaret C. A. Cabell, *Sketches and Recollections of Lynchburg* (1858); R. H. Early, *Campbell Chronicles and Family Sketches* (1927).]

J. C. W.

LYNCH, JAMES DANIEL (Jan. 6, 1836–July 19, 1903), Confederate soldier, author, was born in Boydton, Mecklenburg County, Va., the scion of a family well known in the early history of Virginia. He was prepared for college in an academy near his home, and in 1855 entered the University of North Carolina, where he remained for three years. In 1860 he moved to Mississippi and became instructor in Greek and Latin in the Franklin Academy at Columbus. In February of the following year he was married to Hettie M. Cochran of West Point, Miss., and the same year, upon the outbreak of the Civil War, he volunteered his services to the Confederacy. After serving as a private for a year, during which time he took part in the Shiloh campaign, he returned to Columbus and organized a company of cavalry, of which he was elected captain, and returned to the front. On June 30, 1864, while leading a charge at Lafayette, Ga., he was severely wounded. He was subsequently captured in a skirmish near Rome, Ga., but managed to make his escape by jumping from a moving freight car at night. During the closing months of the war he was connected with the Niter and Mining Department of the Confederacy and was stationed at Selma, Ala.

After the war Lynch engaged for several years in farming near West Point, Miss., then took up the practice of law at Columbus. He was soon forced to abandon the practice of law, however, owing to an impairment of his hearing, brought on by the wound received during the war. He accordingly turned to the profession of letters for a living. In 1879 he published a volume entitled *Kemper County Vindicated, and a Peep at Radical Rule in Mississippi*; and this was followed in 1881 by *The Bench and Bar of Mississippi,* a volume of biographical sketches of prominent jurists in his adopted state. In 1884 he moved to Texas, making his home at Austin for several years. There he collected the materials for the most important of his prose works, *The Bench and Bar of Texas* (1885). He also published at various times a number of poems. The best known of them are "The Clock of Destiny," "The Siege of the Alamo," and "Columbia Saluting the Nations," the last of which was selected by the World's Columbian Commission in 1893 as America's salutation to the visiting nations at the World's Fair in Chicago. Lynch spent his declining years at Sulphur Springs, Tex., and there prepared for the press two volumes: "The Industrial History of Texas" and "A History of the Territory Indians," neither of which has been published. He was a gentleman of the old school, kindly, chivalrous, unpretentious, but impulsive. He died at Sulphur Springs, Tex., and is buried there.

[The chief authority on the life of Lynch is Dabney Lipscomb, "James D. Lynch of Miss., Poet Laureate of the World's Columbian Exposition," *Miss. Hist. Soc. Pubs.*, vol. III (1900). The author used also a scrapbook, compiled by Lynch's wife, now in the possession of their daughter, Mrs. J. O. Creighton, Austin, Tex.]
K. C.

LYNCH, JAMES MATHEW (Jan. 11, 1867–July 16, 1930), labor leader, was born at Manlius, N. Y., the son of James and Sarah (Caulfield) Lynch. He attended the Manlius public school until his seventeenth year, when he became a "printer's devil" in the office of the Syracuse *Evening Herald.* In August 1887, at the end of his apprenticeship, he joined the Syracuse Typographical Union, of which he soon afterward became secretary, later vice-president, and in 1889 he was elected to the presidency, an office in which he served for two terms. He also served for seven terms as president of the Syracuse Central Trades and Labor Assembly. In November 1898, on his election as first vice-president of the International Typographical Union, he moved to Indianapolis. On June 28 of the following year he married Letitia C. McVey, of Syracuse. In 1900 he was elected to the presidency of the I.T.U. and was reëlected for each of the six following biennial terms. His administration was marked by great energy and exceptional executive ability. Under his leadership the union won for its members the eight-hour day (1906–08), established an old-age pension system, enlarged and improved the Union Printers' Home at Colorado Springs, provided for the better education of apprentices, virtually doubled its membership, and greatly strengthened its financial position.

In 1913 Lynch was appointed by Governor Sulzer commissioner of labor of New York, but the Senate rejected the nomination. A few months later he was reappointed, this time by Governor Glynn, and the nomination was confirmed. On Jan. 8, 1914, he resigned the presidency of the I.T.U. He then returned to Syracuse, where he established his home, though his official duties for the next seven years kept him for the greater part of his time in Albany. In 1915, when the Department of Labor was merged in the Industrial Commission, he was appointed by Governor Whitman one of the five members of the new body, and in 1919 he was reappointed by Governor Smith. In 1916 he was an unsuccessful candidate, on the Democratic ticket, for the place of delegate at large to the state constitutional convention. At the opening of Governor Miller's administration, in 1921, the commission was reorganized and he was legislated out of office. During this period he exerted himself actively in behalf of a rigorous enforcement of the labor laws and gave particular attention to the condition of women wage-earners and to the movements for health insurance and old-age pensions. On leaving office he became president of the American Life Society, a mutual insurance company, but after a year's service became dissatisfied and resigned. In 1924 he was again elected president of the I.T.U., but was defeated in 1926. In June 1929 he was appointed by Governor Roosevelt a member of the Old Age Security Commission, which drew up the old-age pension bill later enacted. From some time in 1927 he had been ill, and in the fall of 1928 suffered an attack of heart disease. He continued at work, however, until toward the end of June 1930, when he was taken to St. Joseph's Hospital, in Syracuse, where three weeks later he died. His wife, six sons, and three daughters survived him. He was buried in the Catholic Cemetery at Fayetteville.

Lynch was a large man, and his bulky figure, with his round, bald head and jovial, bespectacled face, was a familiar sight at many labor and social-reform gatherings. He traveled extensively, was a member of many fraternities, and was widely known. Though genial and expansive in manner, he had a good share of pugnacity and when defending a cause which he had at heart was a doughty antagonist. His services as a public speaker were eagerly sought, for though not an orator he talked with clearness and force and with a thorough understanding of his subject. He wrote many articles for the press, and during his last year edited a Syracuse labor paper, the *Advocate.* His social philosophy was that of a conservative trade-unionist, and he was influential in the councils of the American Federation of Labor. Though active in forwarding social legislation, he was not interested in general schemes of social reconstruction or in projects for independent political action. He was generally recognized as one of the ablest of the labor executives and of the public officials intrusted with the care of the wage-earners' interests.

[*Who's Who in America*, 1922–23; files of the *Typographical Jour.* (Indianapolis), especially the issue of Aug. 1930, containing articles by M. P. Woods and Frances Perkins; *Am. Labor Legislation Rev.*, Sept. 1930; *Inland Printer* (Chicago), Aug. 1930; *N. Y. Times*, July 17, 1930; various controversial pamphlets issued by printers' organizations in 1924 and 1926; information from Jerry R. Connolly, Syracuse, N. Y.; recollections of the writer.]
W. J. G.

LYNCH, PATRICK NEESON (Mar. 10, 1817–Feb. 26, 1882), Roman Catholic bishop of Charleston, S. C., was born at Clones, Ireland. At the age of one he emigrated with his parents, Conlan Peter and Eleanor McMahon Lynch, to

Cheraw, S. C. Manifesting a desire to study for the priesthood, he was sent to the College of the Propaganda, in Rome, later received the degree of doctor of divinity, and was ordained on Apr. 5, 1840, by the Cardinal Prefect. He became successively rector of St. Mary's Church, Charleston (1845), rector of the Cathedral (1847), and vicar-general (1850). Upon the death of the Rt. Rev. Ignatius Reynolds, he was consecrated bishop, at Charleston, by the Most Rev. F. P. Kenrick (Mar. 14, 1858). His episcopal ring, a gift, had once been worn by Cardinal Ximenes. He proved not only a successful administrator but also a forceful preacher and writer who had profited by experience gained as professor of theology and editor of the *United States Catholic Miscellany*. The coming of Ursuline Sisters, invited to establish an academy in the diocese, aroused much non-Catholic opposition. This slowly disappeared, however, and Lynch reported favorably upon conditions when he attended the ninth council of the province of Baltimore in 1858. At the opening of the Civil War he was ministering to ten thousand Catholics. But a disastrous fire which swept Charleston on Dec. 11, 1861, destroyed the Cathedral, the bishop's residence, and other ecclesiastical structures, causing a loss of $180,000. Undaunted, the bishop erected temporary chapels and found time to intervene in behalf of Federal prisoners sent south from the battlefields of the war.

During 1863, Lynch went to Rome bearing a letter from Jefferson Davis expressing the desire of the Confederacy for peace. Pius IX replied, Dec. 3, 1863, by saying: "May it please God at the same time to make the other peoples of America and their rulers, reflecting seriously how terrible is civil war, and what calamities it engenders, listen to the inspirations of a calmer spirit, and adopt resolutely the part of peace." This was widely taken to imply an indorsement of the Confederacy. The Holy See promptly denied such intention, however, pointing to the fact that it had no diplomatic relations with the Confederacy. Shortly afterward, Sherman's army marched into the Carolinas, and much remaining Catholic property was destroyed. When peace had been signed, Lynch, still abroad, petitioned Secretary of State Seward for permission to return, pleading his kindness to Federal prisoners. The request was granted, Jan. 12, 1866, and the Bishop arrived to find his diocese in ruins and his scattered priests discouraged. He therefore visited many cities in the North for the purpose of collecting alms and was so successful in this as well as so instrumental in promoting better feeling between North and South that he was widely termed "ambassador of good will." His imposing figure (he was more than six feet in height) and his eloquence enforced respect. Once again he went to Rome, attending in 1869 the Vatican Council where he upheld the dogma of papal infallibility. He died in Charleston and is buried there.

[Diocesan archives, Charleston; J. G. Shea, *Hist. of the Cath. Ch. in the U. S.*, vol. IV (1892); F. X. Reuss, *Biog. Cyc. of the Cath. Hierarchy in the U. S.* (1898); J. H. O'Donnell, *The Cath. Hierarchy of the U. S., 1790–1922* (1922); Elizabeth Lynch, *The Lynch Record* (1925); the *News and Courier* (Charleston), Feb. 27, 1882; the *Irish-American* (N. Y.), Mar. 11, 1882; Lynch's middle name is sometimes spelled *Nieson* or *Niesen*. The spelling given in this sketch follows Shea, *op. cit.*]

G. N. S.

LYNCH, ROBERT CLYDE (Sept. 8, 1880–May 12, 1931), physician, was born in Carson City, Nev., the only child of William Mercer Lynch and Minerva Ann Maitlen, the former of English-Bohemian, the latter of English descent. When the son was three years old, the family moved to New Orleans, La., the father, who was an assayer, having been transferred from the Carson City to the New Orleans Mint. The family so completely adapted itself to the strange but sympathetic environment that the son always felt himself to be a native of the city. He was educated at McDonogh School, Number 9, at the Warren Easton Boys' High School, and at the Tulane University of Louisiana, receiving from the latter, on Apr. 29, 1903, the degree of M.D., with special honors. Immediately after graduation he proceeded to Natchitoches, La., where he began the practice of medicine under almost frontier conditions, being sometimes compelled to spend the whole day in the saddle in order to make the rounds of his patients. Before he left this community he had so far overcome difficulties as to have succeeded in organizing a little hospital, the staff consisting of himself and one nurse.

Upon his return to New Orleans, in January 1906, he began intensive preparation for his specialty at the local Eye, Ear, Nose, and Throat Hospital. In August of that year he was married to Amanda Cecile Genin, a member of an old French Louisiana family. From September 1906 until April 1907 he rounded out his special training in Europe, under the direction of distinguished specialists in London, Paris, Vienna, and Freiburg. For three years he practised independently, then he became associated with Dr. A. W. De Roaldes, at that time surgeon-in-charge of the Eye, Ear, Nose, and Throat Hospital. After the death of his senior, Lynch was appointed to his position at the hospital. In 1924 he was made acting surgeon-in-chief and in

1930, surgeon-in-chief. In these capacities he proved himself an unusually able administrator. During this period and until his death, he was also consultant in otolaryngology at the Touro Infirmary. For the period of the Great War, he served as a contract surgeon, in the capacity of medical examiner in the aviation corps.

In 1911 Lynch was appointed to the faculty of the post-graduate school of medicine of Tulane University. From this date until the time of his death he served his university in various capacities as professor of rhinology and otolaryngology, in both the undergraduate and graduate schools of medicine, as well as on various administrative committees which directed advanced study in the medical sciences. Here, too, he won respect for his administrative talent and for his high ideals of medical education. In his specialty he won particular distinction for his improvement of suspension laryngoscopy, for his outstanding contributions to operative treatment of cancer of the larynx, and for his development of the radical frontal sinus operation, now known as the "Lynch operation." He was the first to make successful moving pictures of the larynx and the vocal cords. Some twenty-five articles dealing with his contributions he published in medical journals. In 1924 he was president of the American Bronchoscopic Society and at the time of his death he was chairman of the otolaryngological section of the American Academy of Ophthalmology and Otolaryngology. He was admired as a great surgeon, demonstrator, and teacher, and was loved for his personal qualities. He died, in the prime of life, from injuries received in an automobile accident, near Richmond, Ky.

[The article is based upon information from Lynch's widow, Mrs. Amanda Genin Lynch, and upon the records of Tulane University. For printed sources see: obituary and bibliography of Lynch's writings in *Laryngoscope*, May 1931; *Times Picayune* (New Orleans), and *New Orleans States*, May 13, 1931.] M. ten H.

LYNCH, THOMAS (1727–December 1776), planter and member of the Continental Congress, was a member of the third generation of the family in America. Jonack Lynch, his grandfather, emigrated from Ireland to South Carolina shortly after the first settlement of that colony. His youngest son, Thomas, discovered a method of cultivating rice on the alluvial lands periodically flooded by the tides. He took out grants for large tracts of tidal areas on the North and South Santee rivers and laid the basis of a fortune which he bequeathed to his son. Thomas Lynch, son of Thomas Lynch by his second wife, Sabina Vanderhorst, was born in St. James Parish, Berkeley County, S. C. He gave early promise of interest in public affairs, and for several terms was the representative of the Parish of of St. James, Santee, in the House of Commons of the provincial Assembly (1751–57, 1761–63, 1765, 1768, 1772). He was an ardent advocate of resistance to the encroachments of Crown and Parliament. With Christopher Gadsden and John Rutledge [*qq.v.*] he represented South Carolina in the Stamp Act Congress (1765) which convened in New York City. Denying the jurisdiction of Parliament, Lynch opposed sending any remonstrance to that body. Subsequently, however, he was chairman of the committee which drafted a petition to the House of Commons. He was a member of the General Committee (1769–74) and of the First and Second Continental congresses (1774–76). Silas Deane, in a letter to his wife, described Lynch as he appeared in Congress: "He wears the manufacture of this country, is plain, sensible, above ceremony, and carries with him more force in his very appearance than most powdered folks in their conversation. He wears his hair strait, his clothes in the plainest order, and is highly esteemed" (Burnett, *post,* I, 18). Since he favored non-importation as the measure best calculated to bring the British government to terms, the merchant group opposed his candidacy for Congress, but he was one of the delegates selected by a popular convention in Charleston, and the selection was subsequently ratified by the provincial congress. In the early part of 1776, a stroke of paralysis incapacitated him from further participation in public affairs. He recovered sufficiently to attempt to make his way homeward in company with his son, but at Annapolis, Md., a second stroke ended his life. He was buried in St. Anne's Churchyard, Annapolis.

Thomas Lynch was married, probably on Sept. 5, 1745, to Elizabeth Allston, and in March 1755 he was married a second time, to Hannah Motte, daughter of the treasurer of South Carolina. He had one son, Thomas [*q.v.*], and three daughters, one of whom, Elizabeth, became the mother of James Hamilton [*q.v.*] of Nullification fame. Lynch's widow subsequently married Brigadier-General William Moultrie [*q.v.*].

[Josiah Quincy, *Memoir of the Life of Josiah Quincy, Jun.* (1825), pp. 108, 112–13; E. C. Burnett, *Letters of Members of the Continental Cong.*, vol. I (1921); A. S. Salley, Jr., *Marriage Notices in the S. C. Gazette and Its Successors* (1902) and *Marriage Notices in the S–C. and Am. General Gazette* (1914); *S. C. Hist. and Geneal. Mag.*, July 1916; references in bibliog. of Thomas Lynch, Jr.] J. G. V–D.

LYNCH, THOMAS (Aug. 5, 1749–1779), signer of the Declaration of Independence, only son of Thomas [*q.v.*] and Elizabeth (Allston) Lynch, was born in Prince George's Parish, Winyaw, S. C. He received a good academic education at the Indigo Society School, Georgetown, then went to England where he completed his education at Eton and Cambridge and studied law at the Middle Temple (1764–72). In 1772, he returned to South Carolina. Having acquired a distaste for the law, he persuaded his father to permit him to abandon that profession. This task was easier because his father had formed the design of introducing him to public life. To promote this object, he presented him with Peach Tree plantation in St. James Parish on the North Santee. The young man now married Elizabeth Shubrick (May 14, 1772) and settled down as a planter. Being the only son of a wealthy and influential father, he was elected to many important civil offices. He was a member of the first and second provincial congresses (1774–76), of the constitutional committee for South Carolina (1776), the first state General Assembly (1776), and the Second Continental Congress (1776–77). On June 12, 1775, the provincial congress elected him one of the captains in the 1st South Carolina Regiment. He accepted the command, somewhat in opposition to the wishes of his father, who offered to use his influence to obtain him a military appointment of higher rank. In July he went into North Carolina to recruit his company. During this service he contracted bilious fever which made him a partial invalid for the remainder of his life.

On Mar. 23, 1776, the General Assembly of South Carolina, organized under the constitution which young Lynch had cooperated in drafting, elected him to the Continental Congress as a sixth delegate in order that he might care for his father, whose health had given way. His own health was too feeble to permit continued activity in public concerns, but he was present and voting when the Declaration of Independence was adopted and shortly afterward affixed his signature to that document. He did not remain long in Congress, for his health began to decline with alarming rapidity. The elder Lynch had experienced a temporary recovery and his physicians hoped he might live to reach Carolina. Father and son began the journey homeward by easy stages, but the father died on the way. The younger Lynch reached his native state, but in a physical condition which did not promise a long continuance of his own life. After more than two years of illness, with the hope of possibly regaining health, he and his wife took passage for the West Indies toward the close of 1779, expecting to board a vessel there for the south of France. The ship on which they sailed was never heard of again and it is probable that all on board were lost.

[A. S. Salley, Jr., *Delegates to the Continental Cong. from S. C. 1774–89, with Sketches of the Four who signed the Declaration of Independence* (Bull. 9, S. C. Hist. Commission, 1927); John Sanderson, *Biog. of the Signers to the Declaration of Independence*, vol. V (1824); E. A. Jones, *Am. Members of the Inns of Court* (1924); *Biog. Dir. Am. Cong.* (1928); A. S. Salley, Jr., *Marriage Notices in the S. C. Gazette and Its Successors 1732–1781* (1902), *Marriage Notices in the S–C. and Am. General Gazette* (1914), *Marriage Notices in S. C. Gazette and Country Journal (1765–1775)* and in the *Charleston Gazette* (1904); "Journal of Mrs. Ann Manigault, 1754–1781," in *S. C. Hist. and Geneal. Mag.*, vol. XX (1919); *S. C. Hist. and Geneal. Mag.*, Jan. 1927.]

J. G. V–D.

LYNCH, WILLIAM FRANCIS (Apr. 1, 1801–Oct. 17, 1865), naval officer, was born in Norfolk, Va. In his *Naval Life; or, Observations Afloat and on Shore,* published in 1851, which is partly autobiographical, he states that he was early left motherless, that his father was occupied with care of property, and that he welcomed eagerly his appointment as midshipman (Jan. 26, 1819). His first cruise was in the *Congress* to Brazil, thence to China, and around the world. Next he was in the *Shark* on the African coast, then for two years under Porter hunting pirates in the West Indies. He was made lieutenant on May 17, 1828, and commander, Sept. 5, 1849. Following service in the Gulf during the Mexican War, Lynch, who was both an earnest Christian and a lover of adventure, planned the exploring expedition to the River Jordan and the Dead Sea with which his name was afterward chiefly associated. With official support, he left New York in the storeship *Supply,* and after a steamer trip from Smyrna to Constantinople for a firman from the Porte, finally disembarked, Apr. 1, 1848, at Acre. Thence, with the five officers and nine seamen of his party, he proceeded to the Sea of Galilee, dragging overland his two large metal boats, one of iron and one of copper, for navigation of the Jordan. The trip down river to the Dead Sea he made in eight days, Apr. 10–18, accompanied by a caravan on shore, and encountering very real dangers and hardships from the innumerable rapids and hostile Arab tribes. After three weeks of sounding, sketching, and scientific study, the party returned overland through Palestine, and was back in New York at the close of 1848. Though there had been earlier expeditions, Lynch's was the most successfully executed and most productive of scientific results. His *Official Report of the United States Expedition to Explore the Dead Sea and the River Jordan* was published by the Naval Observatory in 1852, and his more popu-

Lynde

lar *Narrative of the United States Expedition to the River Jordan and the Dead Sea* (1849) went through several editions. In 1851 he published his *Naval Life,* before-mentioned, a curious medley of tales, descriptions, and sea experiences. In 1853 he was on the west African coast, reconnoitering for another exploring expedition there (see his report in the *Report of the Secretary of the Navy* for 1852, pp. 329–89), which was not carried out. He was promoted to captain, Apr. 2, 1856.

When the Civil War came his sympathies were with the South, and he was made captain, first in the Virginia, and later (June 10, 1861) in the Confederate navy. He commanded the Aquia Creek batteries on the Potomac, May 30 and June 1, 1861, during their bombardment by Union gunboats; and thereafter, in charge of North Carolina naval defenses, commanded the nine small gunboats that opposed the Union expedition against Roanoke Island. Hopelessly inferior, his "mosquito flotilla" lost two boats in the action of Feb. 6, 1862, and the next day retreated to Elizabeth City, where on the 10th they were completely destroyed by Northern vessels. Capt. W. H. Parker, who served in this campaign, tells of spending the evening before the Roanoke Island battle talking with Lynch of books and reading. "He was," says Parker, "a cultivated man and a most agreeable talker . . . I never served under a man who showed more regard for the comfort of his officers and men" (*Recollections of a Naval Officer, 1841–1865,* 1883, p. 228). Lynch was in charge of naval forces around Vicksburg from March to October 1862, and then until September 1864 was in command of ships in North Carolina waters, including the *North Carolina* and the ironclad *Raleigh.* The latter crossed the Wilmington bar on May 7, 1864, and drove off the blockaders, but went aground and was irreparably damaged on her return. Lynch also commanded at Smithville, N. C., during the attacks on Fort Fisher. He died in Baltimore six months after the war ended. His wife, according to J. F. Cooper (*Lives of Distinguished Naval Officers,* 1846, p. 145), was Virginia, daughter of Commodore John Shaw. According to the same writer, he had two children.

[In addition to references in the text, see J. T. Scharf, *Hist. of the Confederate States Navy* (1887), biog. sketch, p. 277; *War of the Rebellion: Official Records (Navy)*; J. C. Thom, "The American Navy and the Dead Sea," *U. S. Naval Inst. Proc.,* Sept. 1926; *Baltimore Weekly Sun,* Oct. 21, 1865.] A. W.

LYNDE, BENJAMIN (Oct. 5, 1700–Oct. 5, 1781), jurist, was born in Salem, Mass., the son of Benjamin and Mary (Browne) Lynde. He was a descendant of Simon Lynde of London who emigrated to New England in 1650. The elder Benjamin was a lawyer and served as chief justice of the superior court of the province of Massachusetts. The son graduated from Harvard in 1718 and received the degree of A.M. in 1721. After studying law for a brief period in the office of his uncle, Samuel Browne, he accepted the post of naval officer at Salem. Political differences with Gov. William Burnet [*q.v.*] led to his resignation in 1729. He was active in local affairs, being repeatedly elected moderator of town meeting and town treasurer, and representing Salem in the General Court from 1728 to 1731. On May 25, 1737, he was chosen by the General Court a member of the Council, and, barring a brief period, served continuously thereon for over a quarter of a century. In the same year he was appointed an agent to adjust the boundary dispute between New Hampshire and Massachusetts, and in 1739, to determine the boundary between Rhode Island and Massachusetts. Meanwhile, he had launched upon a judicial career, for on June 28, 1734, he was appointed special judge of the inferior court of common pleas for Suffolk County, and on Oct. 5, 1739, was made one of the standing judges of the same court for Essex County. The death of his father in 1745 created a vacancy on the bench of the superior court, and he was appointed, Jan. 24, 1746, associate justice. In 1766 the propriety of having judges serve as councillors was questioned by the House of Representatives, ostensibly on the ground that membership in the council hampered their administration of justice, but really because the House desired to place at the Council board members more friendly to the popular interest. Lynde was reluctant to be drawn into the controversy and on May 28 his resignation from the Council was announced.

The most noteworthy incidents in his career as a justice of the superior court were two. He was on the bench when the legality of the writs of assistance was argued in 1761; and in 1770, when Thomas Hutchinson [*q.v.*], the chief justice, was obliged to occupy the executive chair, on the departure to England of Gov. Francis Bernard [*q.v.*], Lynde presided over the trial of the British soldiers involved in the Boston Massacre. The latter duty demanded great firmness and courage, since the mob was crying for vengeance upon the red-coats. Hutchinson accuses Lynde of timidity in the face of the popular clamor, alleging that Lynde twice offered his resignation in order to avoid trying the cases (J. K. Hosmer, *The Life of Thomas Hutchinson,* 1896, p. 196). A portion of Lynde's charge to the jury has been preserved (*Diaries, post,* pp. 228–30), and attests his thorough knowledge of the law and his earnest desire to deal justly with the defendants. Upon Hutchinson's appointment to the governorship and "as the result of strong political and other influences" (*New-England Historical and Genealogical Register,* October 1886, p. 349), Lynde was commissioned, Mar. 21, 1771, chief justice of the superior court. His tenure was brief. On Jan. 15, 1772, owing to a dispute regarding payment of judges' salaries by the Crown, and because he felt too old to ride the circuit, he resigned, accepting the less onerous post of judge of probate for Essex County, his last public office.

On Nov. 1, 1731, Lynde was married to Mary (Bowles), widow of Capt. Walter Goodridge and a descendant of John Eliot. He was the owner of considerable real estate, including part of Thompson's Island in Boston harbor, a mansion in Salem, and a fine summer residence near Castle Hill, which he built in 1748 and where he dispensed generous hospitality. Among his many public benefactions were the gift of a fire engine to his native town and a set of English statute books to the state. On one occasion he devoted his salary as town treasurer to the advancement of education. He was an active member of a society to obtain employment for poor people in Boston, and a ruling elder of the First Church, Salem. A diligent scholar, he was keenly interested in the genealogy of his family and the history of his section. His death occurred at Salem from the effects of the kick of a horse.

[Lynde's legislative and judicial career may be studied in the manuscript legislative journals of the General Court and the manuscript records of the superior court, Boston. Consult also Emory Washburn, *Sketches of the Judicial Hist. of Mass.* (1840); *Hist. Colls. of the Essex Institute,* Aug. 1861; *The Diaries of Benj. Lynde and of Benjamin Lynde, Jr.* (1880), ed. by F. E. Oliver; W. T. Davis, *Hist. of the Judiciary of Mass.* (1900).]

E. E. C.

LYNDE, FRANCIS (Nov. 12, 1856–May 16, 1930), novelist, was born in Lewiston, N. Y., the son of William Tilly and Elizabeth (Need) Lynde. Though both of his parents were born in Canada, his father at Whitby and his mother in Montreal, the family had come from the United States. The immigrant ancestor on his father's side was Deacon Thomas Lynde, a member of the Massachusetts Bay Colony, who settled in New England in 1634. When Francis was four years old his parents moved to Kansas City, Mo., where he spent his boyhood and attended the public schools. At the age of fifteen, he returned to the East and endeavored by work in the cotton-mill at Suncook, N. H., to earn money for an advanced education. Discouraged by the severe toil and long hours, he found employment in a railroad machine-shop as a machinist's helper, won advancement, and went to California in 1876, becoming master mechanic in the shop of the Southern Pacific Railroad at Tulare by the time he was twenty-one. Subsequently, he was appointed chief clerk to the general-passenger agent of the Union Pacific Railroad, and thereafter held various executive appointments in Western roads. At the age of thirty-five he was traveling-passenger agent for the Union Pacific with headquarters in New Orleans.

Here he made the acquaintance of Maurice Thompson [*q.v.*], to whom he confided his earnest desire to become a writer. Encouraged by the successful author to make a trial, he sent a story to the *Century Magazine,* and when it was rejected set himself the task of learning how to write successful fiction, using his constant travels as a source of material. His first article to be accepted dealt with the process of manufacturing artificial ice. He composed it in the writing-room of a hotel in Baton Rouge and sent it to the *Youth's Companion.* Continuing to write, in 1893 he felt justified in giving up his position with the railroad company and devoting his whole time to literary work.

In 1891 he had moved to Chattanooga, Tenn. To secure solitude for his writing, he purchased a part of the Craven Farm on Lookout Mountain, the scene of severe fighting in the Civil War. There he constructed, chiefly with his own hands, a comfortable stone dwelling which he called "Wideview," and which remained his home until his death. In this congenial environment he wrote diligently, producing a large number of magazine articles, short stories, and books. The first of his novels of American life, "A Question of Courage," was published in *Lippincott's Magazine* in 1894. Of some thirty-five novels the most popular have been, perhaps, those that like *David Vallory* (1919) and *The Wreckers* (1920) were based upon his railroad experience in the West. Others were tales of pioneer adventure and five were specifically stories for boys. Among the best of his later books were *Blind Man's Buff* (1928) and *Young Blood* (1929). In 1926, his work was recognized by the degree of Litt.D. from the University of the South at Sewanee.

Lynde was twice married: first, in 1874, to Marietta Williams, who bore him two sons; and second, Jan. 17, 1888, to Mary Antoinette Stickle of Denver, Colo. Of this union there were four children, of whom two daughters, with their mother, survived him. He was a member of the Protestant Episcopal Church and for a number of years was lay reader in charge of a mission at St. Elmo near his home. He is described as straight and slender, auburn-haired, fond of walking, and skilful with his hands. His death occurred at "Wideview" after an illness, and he was buried in Forest Hills Cemetery, Chattanooga.

[E. Y. Chapin, "Literary Figures of Chattanooga," *Chattanooga News,* Apr. 9, 1930, and sketch in *Lib. of Southern Lit.* vol. XVII (1923); *Who's Who in America,* 1930–31, containing a list of Lynde's books; *Chattanooga News,* May 16, 1930; *Chattanooga Daily Times,* May 17, 1930; unpublished personal reminiscences by Mrs. Francis Lynde.] J. C. F.

LYNDS, ELAM (1784–Jan. 8, 1855), prison administrator, was born in Litchfield, Conn. While he was still an infant, his parents moved to Troy, N. Y., where he learned the hatter's trade. In 1808 his name appeared among the lieutenants of Lieut.-Col. Adam Yates's regiment from Rensselaer County and by 1812 he had risen to major's rank as aide-de-camp of the commander of the 8th Infantry Division. He entered the federal service Apr. 30, 1813, as captain in the 29th Infantry and was honorably discharged June 15, 1815. When the Auburn state prison was established in 1817, he became its principal keeper and four years later he succeeded to the agentship of the prison, only to be forced out in 1825 because of certain scandals arising from his severe disciplinary methods. His executive ability, however, caused him to be placed that same year in charge of the construction and management of the new Mount Pleasant state prison—now Sing Sing. After four years, during which he employed only prison labor, the institution was completed. In 1838, he was again called to Auburn, and once more he aroused such public indignation by his disciplinary measures that he was compelled to resign in 1839 under circumstances which included a grand jury indictment. This episode did not deter the board of inspectors of Sing Sing from engaging him a few years later (1843) as principal keeper, but his experience in that position was short-lived, for in 1844 he was removed on charges of cruelty and misappropriation of state property. Apparently he held no other public office until his death in South Brooklyn a decade later.

Lynds is regarded by some penologists as the creator of the so-called Auburn system, with its solitary confinement of prisoners during the night, its labor in silence in the common workshops during the day, and its lockstep. It is certain that the order and system which impressed the visitor to his prisons were the product of the mailed fist. He was a great believer in the lash, which he considered the least harmful and the most efficient of all disciplinary means, and he so inculcated this belief into his staff that their excesses, which on at least two occasions hastened the death of a prisoner, caused him the loss of his positions. The interview with him which G. A. de Beaumont and Alexis de Tocqueville published in 1833 (*Du système pénitentiaire aux États-Unis* ..., Paris, 1833, pp. 336–41) pictures him as a man of undoubted courage, an autocrat who brooked no interference from political superiors, whose philosophy of punishment was as rigid as his backbone. All prisoners were to him cowards, who should be "tamed" and bent to submission. The interviewers reported as characteristic a story they had heard at Sing Sing. When Lynds learned that a certain prisoner had threatened to kill him, he called that individual into his bedroom, made him shave him, and sent him away saying, "I knew you wanted to kill me, but I despised you too much to believe that you would ever have the courage to do it. Alone and unarmed, I am still stronger than all of you."

[Brief biographical note, with rare portrait, in F. G. Pettigrove, "The State Prisons of the United States under Separate and Congregate Systems," in vol. II, pp. 27–67, of C. R. Henderson, *Correction and Prevention* (1910); Henry Hall, *The Hist. of Auburn* (1869); John Luckey, *Life in Sing Sing State Prison, as Seen in a Twelve Years' Chaplaincy* (1860); *A Letter from John W. Edmonds, One of the Inspectors of the State Prison at Sing Sing to General Aaron Ward, in Regard to the Removal of Captain Lynds as Principal Keeper of That Prison* (1844); *Actes du Congrès pénitentiaire international de Rome, Novembre 1885,* vol. III, pt. II (1888), pp. 275–77; *Mil. Minutes of the Council of Appointment of the State of N. Y., 1783–1821* (1901), II, 993, 1364; F. B. Heitman, *Hist. Reg. and Dict. U. S. Army* (1903), vol. I; *N. Y. Times,* Jan. 9, 1855.] T. S.

LYON, CALEB (Dec. 8, 1821–Sept. 7, 1875), politician, art and literary connoisseur, son of Caleb and Mary (duPont) Lyon, was born at Lyonsdale, Lewis County, N. Y. His father's family had lived in New England for six generations; his mother was the daughter of Major Jean Pierre duPont, nephew and aide of General Montcalm. Caleb received an excellent education at the regular public school of Lyonsdale, a boys' school in Montreal, and Norwich University, Northfield, Vt., where he graduated in 1841. He entered politics at an early age. On Jan. 20, 1847, he was nominated and on Feb. 15 confirmed, as United States consul at Shanghai (*Journal of the Executive Proceedings of the Senate of the United States of America, 1845–48,* 1887, pp. 182, 184, 194), but he never reached China, and resigned his position within a year. He did get as far from home as California, however, and there served as an assistant secretary of the constitutional convention of 1849. In accordance with the wish of the real designer, Maj.

Robert Selden Garnett, Lyon was credited with designing the State Seal of California, adopted by the convention in 1849 (*Governmental Roster . . . State and County Governments of California*, 1889, pp. 191–94).

He soon returned to New York, where he was elected to the state Assembly for the session of 1851, but he did not take an active part in its proceedings. In November 1852, he was elected to the Thirty-third Congress as an independent supported by the Whigs. While there he showed a marked interest in the debates. His most important speeches were on naval and territorial questions. He advocated an increase in the navy, and urged larger subsidies for American shipping lines to enable them to compete with the British as carriers of the mails. He opposed the abrogating of the Missouri Compromise in 1854 and the sanctioning of polygamy in Utah. His congressional speeches were filled with literary quotations, historical and classical allusions, statistics, innumerable adjectives, and witty personal remarks that called forth frequent laughter.

At the close of this Congress, he retired to private life until he was appointed (Feb. 26, 1864) second territorial governor of Idaho, which office he held until April 1866. The one act of his administration that seemed important to the people was the moving of the capital from Lewiston to Boise, but there were others of a more beneficial character that caused less comment. A polished misfit in a country of mining camps, he amazed, amused, and antagonized the people of Idaho by his "weird and fantastic" official utterances, and by his insistence on cleanliness and formal dress. As superintendent of Indian affairs in the Territory, he failed to account satisfactorily for about $50,000 of an appropriation, but he died before the congressional investigation of the matter took place.

The last years of his life were spent in retirement at Rossville, Staten Island, and at the time of his death he was preparing a book on the ceramics of the Revolutionary period. His own collection of pottery contained many valuable pieces from Europe and Asia, and a good-sized group of American pieces of historical interest. His wife, Anna, whom he had married about 1842, survived him until 1881.

[*Lyon Memorial*, vol. I (1905); *Biog. Dir. Am. Cong.* (1928); J. R. Browne, *Report of the Debates of the Convention of California on the Formation of the State Constitution* (1850); H. T. French, *Hist. of Idaho* (3 vols., 1914); W. A. Goulder, *Reminiscences* (1909); J. H. Hawley, *Hist. of Idaho* (1920), vol. I; F. B. Hough, *Hist. of Lewis County, N. Y.* (1883); W. J. McConnell, *Early Hist. of Idaho* (1913); *Catalogue of the "Governor Caleb Lyon Collection of Oriental and Occidental Ceramics" . . . to be Sold at Auction* (1876); Green-Wood Cemetery Records, lot 2244, sec. 94, authority for date of birth; *N. Y. Times*, Sept. 9, 1875.]

M. L. B.

LYON, FRANCIS STROTHER (Feb. 25, 1800–Dec. 31, 1882), Alabama congressman, bank-commissioner, was born in Stokes County, N. C., where his father, James Lyon, a Virginian by birth, owned a large tobacco plantation. His mother was Behetheland (Gaines) Lyon, daughter of James Gaines, a Revolutionary soldier and member of the North Carolina convention which ratified the Constitution of the United States. Francis Strother Lyon was educated in the schools of North Carolina and when he was seventeen years old left the state to make his home with his mother's brother, George Strother Gaines [*q.v.*], Indian agent at St. Stephens, Ala. Lyon's handwriting, which was remarkable for its neatness and legibility, procured him employment as clerk in the bank at St. Stephens and before long he was clerk of the court as well. He read law and was admitted to the bar in 1821. A year later he became secretary of the state Senate and held that position for eight years. On Mar. 4, 1824, he married Sarah Serena Glover. In 1833 he was elected state senator, served three years, and in 1835 was elected to Congress as a Whig. He represented the Mobile district in the Twenty-fourth and Twenty-fifth congresses and then resumed his law practice.

Lyon was a popular lawyer. He often sacrificed a fee to settle disputes between neighbors out of court. Whenever he appeared before a jury, although he was not an eloquent pleader, he was acknowledged to be a dangerous opponent. His hair, which had turned white early in life, gave him an appearance of venerable kindliness which predisposed the jury in his favor. Added to this was his skill in cross-examination, which he conducted with such suave courtesy and careful politeness that his opponents' witnesses often became his own before they were aware of it. Although he was one of the busiest lawyers in Alabama and managed several large plantations and other interests, he always found time for public service and, in a day when good dogs and guns were a necessary part of every man's life, possessed the best in the state.

His greatest public service was rendered in connection with the liquidation of the Bank of the State of Alabama. This institution had been organized as a bank of issue in 1823. From the beginning it was poorly managed. By 1844 it had become hopelessly involved and the state refused to renew its charter. Liquidation was a long and difficult process. Lyon was appointed member of a commission created to close up the affairs of the bank and in 1847 was made sole commissioner with extraordinary powers to collect debts, take up depreciated state bonds, ascertain assets, adjust, extend, renew or exchange securities in such ways as would best serve the interests of the state. He was also to conduct all litigation arising from the liquidation of the bank and to arrange for the payment of the interest and the principal of the public debt. Rarely has a state entrusted such large powers to one man. By shrewd management and untiring vigilance he saved Alabama from bankruptcy and many of the bank's creditors from ruin.

Although Lyon had been elected to Congress by the Whigs, as he came to accept the necessity of secession he drifted into the Yancey wing of the Democratic party. He was chairman of the state Democratic committee in 1860 and a delegate to the Charleston convention. Elected to the Provisional Congress of the Confederacy, he declined to serve, but was elected to the first Congress of the Confederate States and served throughout the Civil War. Most of his fortune was lost through heavy subscriptions to the cotton loan. Throughout the Reconstruction period he was a vigorous supporter of the rights of the state against the national government and he took an active part in the constitutional convention of 1875 which drafted the constitution designed to restore white supremacy. This was his last important public service. He died at Demopolis, Ala., in his eighty-third year.

[J. M. L. Curry, *Hon. Francis Strother Lyon as Commissioner and Trustee of Ala.* (printed in 1889 for private circulation), is the best account but somewhat rare; see also T. M. Owen, *Hist. of Ala. and Dict. of Ala. Biog.* (1921), vol. IV; *Biog. Dir. Am. Cong.* (1928); and obituary in *Daily Register* (Mobile), Jan. 2, 1883. J. G. Baldwin has an interesting character sketch in *The Flush Times of Ala. and Miss.* (1853) but strangely enough writes of Lyon as "Honorable Francis Strother."] H. F.

LYON, HARRIS MERTON (Dec. 22, 1883–June 2, 1916), author, was born at Santa Fé, N. Mex. His mother was Mary (Merton) Lyon, successively a cook in a railroad hotel, a "bawler out" for a loan shark, a private detective, and an insurance agent; his father, apparently, he never knew. In spite of the severity of the mother's struggle for existence, she managed to put her son through a Texas high school and to send him to the University of Missouri, where, supporting himself by casual employment and some newspaper writing, he graduated in 1905. His college years appear to have been happy. Having a good linguistic sense, he worked hard at Latin and fairly reveled in modern French literature, especially in the work of the symbolists and naturalists. He enjoyed hunting and various field sports, entered into correspondence with William Marion Reedy [*q.v.*], and for a short time was theatrical reporter on the Houston, Tex., *Post*. As was inevitable with a young man seething with literary ambition, he quickly made his way to New York, where, in the spring of 1906, he was doing minor assignments for the *Broadway Magazine* when Theodore Dreiser became its editor. Under Lyon's rough, surly exterior Dreiser discerned an honest, sensitive mind and an unusual talent for writing; and as soon as he could he put Lyon on the staff of the magazine. He remained with the *Broadway* through two reorganizations and modifications of its name, and, when it became *Hampton's Magazine* in 1909, was made dramatic critic and a director of the concern. The owner sent him to Europe to interview Dr. Frederick A. Cook at Copenhagen and to visit Paris and gave him other opportunities. For a few years, during which he married and bought a farm in Winsted, Conn., he lived in a hectic, uncertain prosperity, was somewhat bemused by the rush and glitter of metropolitan life, lived beyond his income, and overestimated his security and influence. With the suspension of *Hampton's Magazine* in 1912 this prosperity came to an abrupt end, and the remaining four years of his life were marked by poverty, the bitterness of frustrated ambition, and the rapid progress of a fatal disease of the kidneys. Though he continued to write with furious energy, the market for his stories had vanished. To *Reedy's Mirror* in 1914–15 he contributed, probably without pay, an excellent series of essays under the general title, "From an Old Farmhouse," and he also did some work for a motion-picture company on the Pacific coast. His place in American literature depends on two volumes of short stories, *Sardonics* (1908) and *Graphics* (1913). The first was dedicated, significantly enough, to the memory of "the Norman master," and the second to Joseph Conrad. They were issued by obscure publishing houses and received little notice, but they contain some of the best short stories ever written by an American. In sharpness of observation, in deft, sympathetic characterization, and in the concentration and poetic quality of his language Lyon displayed literary power of a high order. At the time of his death he was practically forgotten, and he has been neglected since; but among his fellow writers he has always been admired.

[*Who's Who in America*, 1910–11; *N. Y. Times*, June 4, 1916; editorial comment, *Reedy's Mirror*, June 9, 1916; Alexander Harvey, "Harris Merton Lyon," *Ibid.*, June 23, 1916; Carl Sandburg, "No Regrets," *Ibid.*, Aug. 4, 1916; Theodore Dreiser, "De Maupassant, Junior," *Twelve Men* (1919); portrait, *Bookman*, Mar. 1909, p. 6.] G. H. G.

LYON, JAMES (July 1, 1735–Oct. 12, 1794), psalmodist, Presbyterian minister, was born in Newark, N. J., the son of Zopher and Mary Lyon, and a descendant of Henry Lyon who emigrated to America in 1649 and settled first in Milford, Conn., and then in Newark. His father died in 1744. On July 18, 1750, by order of the court of Essex County, he was given as guardians Isaac Lyon and John Crane. He attended the college of New Jersey (later Princeton) and was mentioned as the composer of the music for the class ode, presented at the graduation exercises in 1759. In May 1760 he was in Philadelphia taking subscriptions for a projected collection of hymn tunes, probably printed in 1761, which came out under the title *Urania.* It is likely that it was he who brought out in 1763, through William Dunlap in Philadelphia, *The Lawfulness, Excellency and Advantages of Instrumental Musick in the Public Worship of God,* an exposition urging Presbyterians to relax their hostility to instrumental music. Having been licensed to preach, he was ordained by the synod of New Brunswick in 1764 and the next year was settled at Halifax, N. S. There and at Onslow, N. S., he supported himself with difficulty. Finally in 1771 he went in search of a better parish. In Boston he met a member of the committee charged with getting a preacher for the newly founded town of Machias, Me., and in the spring of 1772 he accepted a call to that place with a salary of £84 and £100 as a settlement.

Lyon preached at Machias (except for two intermissions, 1773 and 1783–85) until he died. He was an ardent supporter of the Revolution and in 1775 he outlined in a communication to General Washington plans for the conquest of Nova Scotia with whose places and people he was well acquainted. This elicited a "polite reply" in which the feasibility of the project was not denied. During three years of the Revolution Lyon received no salary but later he was awarded £1,000 in back pay. To eke out an income he operated for a time a salt distillery on Salt Island near Machiasport. His health began to fail in 1793 and he died in the following year. At Machias he retained his interest in music, but his fame rests chiefly upon *Urania,* which must have been conceived while he was in college. Its purpose was to "Spread the Art of Psalmody, in its Perfection, thro' our American Colonies" (*Pennsylvania Journal,* May 22, 1760). It was reported that the first edition had "ruined the publisher," but this was evidently malicious for in 1767 the work went into a second edition. As a composer Lyon possessed respectable but not extraordinary technical accomplishments. His best piece is the "Hymn to Friendship" which contains some fairly beautiful passages to prove that the writer had innate musical ability. He may have written music during his Machias pastorate, but so far as is known no music of that period survives. He was twice married: on Feb. 18, 1768, to Martha Holden of Cape May, West Jersey, and on Nov. 24, 1793, to Sarah Skillen, in Boston.

[O. G. T. Sonneck, *Francis Hopkinson . . . and James Lyon, Patriot, Preacher, Psalmodist, 1735–1794* (1905); F. J. Metcalf, *Am. Writers and Compilers of Sacred Music* (1925); G. W. Drisko, *Narrative of the Town of Machias* (1904); Geo. Hood, *A Hist. of Music in New Eng.* (1846); *Lyon Memorial,* vol. II (1907); *Columbian Centinel* (Boston), Nov. 15, 1794.]

F. W. C.

LYON, JAMES BENJAMIN (Apr. 21, 1821–Apr. 16, 1909), manufacturer of pressed glass, was born at Pennsylvania Furnace, Pa., the son of John and Margaret (Stewart) Lyon. His grandfather had come to Pennsylvania from Enniskillen, Ireland, in 1763. James entered Jefferson College, Canonsburg, Pa., in 1837, but left without graduating. In 1841 he began working for his father in the iron works of Lyon, Shorb & Company. Six years later he obtained a position with a bank at Hollidaysburg, Pa., but gave it up when he found that his health suffered from indoor work.

On Jan. 1, 1849, under the name of Wallace, Lyon & Company, he started the manufacture of glass. Three months later fire destroyed the entire plant, but he put it into operation again, and in 1851 bought his partner's interest, incorporating the business as James B. Lyon & Company, with William B. David and Alexander P. Lyon as his associates. In 1852 he purchased the old O'Hara glassworks and increased its furnace capacity threefold. Although when he entered the industry, as he himself said, he "did not even know what glass was made of," he obtained a knowledge of the chemistry of the subject from a Boston chemist, and being of a practical and inventive turn of mind, developed a number of new methods and processes, which he refused to patent. He also introduced into glass-making the use of natural gas as a fuel.

Although pressed glass had been made in America since 1827, Lyon was the first to make it the chief output of his factory. He originated most of his beautiful patterns himself, and produced work fully equal in merit to the more famous Sandwich glass manufactured on Cape Cod. Indeed, the founder of the Sandwich plant, Deming Jarves [*q.v.*], wrote of the product of Lyon's firm: "To such a degree of delicacy and fineness have they carried their manufacture that only experts in the trade can distinguish between their straw stem wines, and other light and beautiful articles made in moulds, and those blown by the most skilled workmen" (*post,* p. 94). In 1867 Lyon was chosen by the National Flint Glass Manufacturers' Association to represent the United States at the Paris Exposition, where his products were awarded a diploma and a bronze medal.

He was interested in education and was one of the incorporators of the Pittsburgh Female College, now the Pennsylvania College for Women. He was also the leading spirit in the organization of the Pittsburgh School of Design. On Oct. 3, 1850, he married Anna Margaret Lyon, a third cousin, and they had three daughters and four sons. In 1893 he sold his business to the United States Glass Company, of which he became treasurer. He retired in 1904 and died, following an attack of pneumonia, at the age of eighty-eight.

[Deming Jarves, *Reminiscences of Glass-Making* (2nd ed., 1865); *Lyon Memorial,* vol. III (1907); R. M. Knittle, *Early Am. Glass* (1927); *Mag. of Western Hist.,* Feb. 1886; *Nat. Glass Budget,* Apr. 24, 1909; *Pittsburgh Dispatch,* Apr. 16, 1909; *Pittsburgh Post,* Apr. 17, 1909.] A. I.

LYON, MARY (Feb. 28, 1797–Mar. 5, 1849), educator, was born in Buckland, Mass., the sixth of eight children. She had in her veins good old New England blood; among her ancestors were Lieut. Samuel Smith, who sailed for the new world in the *Elizabeth* in 1634, and Rev. Henry Smith, who came from England a few years later. Her father, Aaron Lyon, was a man beloved in the community, a good neighbor, and devoted to his home and children. His death when his daughter Mary was less than seven years old left the mother, Jemima (Shepard) Lyon, with the responsibility of a large family and slender means with which to meet it.

It was a merry, light-hearted young girl, however, who grew up among the hills, in many ways not different from other girls, but outstripping them all in the quickness of her mind and by her passion for learning. Her education was mainly in the academies at Ashfield and Amherst, terms interrupted by periods of teaching. Her extraordinary mental quickness and her zeal for study are shown in the familiar story of her mastery of the English grammar in four days and of the Latin in three. It is not surprising that she was not satisfied with the terms in the Ashfield and Amherst academies and that in 1821 she was eager to go to the seminary at Byfield, which the Rev. Joseph Emerson [*q.v.*] had made famous by his championship of education for women. She was then twenty-four and in those days it was a thing unheard of for a woman so old to go to school. But she went, and the two terms there gave her a new inspiration for learning, not for acquirement simply, but for service. Thirteen years of teaching followed, three in the academy at Ashfield, of which she was associate principal, and ten with Zilpah Grant at Londonderry, N. H., and Ipswich, Mass.

During these thirteen years, Mary Lyon became more and more impressed with the importance of establishing a seminary for women which should not be dependent "upon the health or life of a particular teacher, but, like our colleges, be a permanent blessing to our children and to our children's children." At first, it was her hope and that of Zilpah Grant that the seminary at Ipswich might be put on a permanent basis, but when she saw that this hope was not likely to be realized, she began to think of a new project, in a different field.

On Sept. 6, 1834, a few gentlemen met with her in Ipswich, "to devise ways and means for founding a permanent female seminary, upon a plan embracing Miss Lyon's favorite views and principles." These "views and principles" had grown more definite, during the months of deliberation, and among them was the hope that the seminary would be "like our colleges, so valuable that the rich will be glad to avail themselves of its benefits, and so economical that people in very moderate circumstances may be equally and as fully accommodated." This interest in the girls of moderate means became a vital part of her plan. "Indeed," she wrote, "it is for this class principally, who are the bone and sinew and the glory of our nation, that we have engaged in this undertaking."

The months between Sept. 6, 1834, and Nov. 8, 1837, were a critical period in the history of the higher education of women. With indomitable spirit Mary Lyon faced indifference and antagonism, difficult to comprehend in this later day. In the effort to raise the amount necessary to establish the seminary, she was indefatigable; but although she was the mainspring of all the effort, she kept herself in the background as much as possible, "pushing forward a few gentlemen of independence and repute who would yet do what she wanted them to do," a task truly requiring "a nice diplomacy." On Oct. 7, 1836, she wrote: "I have indeed lived to see the time when a body of gentlemen have ventured to lay the corner stone of an edifice which will cost about $15,000, and will be an institution for the education of females. Surely the Lord hath remembered our low estate. This will be an era in female education."

On Nov. 8, 1837, Mount Holyoke Seminary was opened, at South Hadley, Mass. In order to bring the opportunities of the school within the range of girls of moderate means, each student had assigned to her some definite household task, but there was no attempt to teach housework. "However important this part of a woman's education," the founder insisted, "a literary institution is not the place to secure it." There was no preparatory department; the course of study covered three years—junior, middle, and senior—with a curriculum based on that followed at Amherst College.

The brief span of Mary Lyon's life after the opening of Mount Holyoke is difficult to realize, so much was accomplished in the twelve years before her death. The growth of the seminary in numbers, as well as in strength and popularity, was steady; the second year four hundred applicants were turned away for lack of room. The main building, accommodating eighty students, was completed and a south wing added. Landscape architects proving too costly, the students brought from home plants and shrubbery, the beginning of the lovely seminary gardens. The original curriculum, including mathematics, English, science, philosophy, and Latin, was expanded by the addition of the modern languages and music, with the hope that Greek and Hebrew and more music might come in the future. The regular instructors were women, their courses supplemented by lectures from the faculties of Williams and Amherst.

Mount Holyoke's claim to priority in the higher education of women is based not only on the curriculum but also on the fact that it was the first institution "where the buildings and grounds, the library and apparatus" were "pledged as permanent contributions to the cause of female education," the permanency of the institution being an essential part of the plan. Mary Lyon's contribution to educational theory is better appreciated today than in her own age. She believed in physical as well as intellectual and spiritual training; in adding music, English, and the sciences to the curriculum; in concentrating attention upon a few subjects. Her contribution to the education of women was threefold: first, the opening to them of the highest educational opportunities; second, the conviction that these opportunities should be used as a preparation for service; third, the conception of such education as the development of all the powers of the individual.

[*The New-England Hist. and Geneal. Reg.*, Apr. 1849; *The Power of Christian Benevolence, Illustrated in the Life and Labors of Mary Lyon* (1851), comp. by Edward Hitchcock; S. D. L. Stow, *Hist. of Mount Holyoke Seminary, South Hadley, Mass., during its First Half Century, 1837–87* (1887); *Lyon Memorial*, vol. I (1905); Beth Bradford Gilchrist, *The Life of Mary Lyon* (1910); Thomas Woody, *A Hist. of Women's Education in the U. S.* (2 vols., 1929); unpublished letters and diaries in the possession of Mount Holyoke College.]

M. E. W.

LYON, MATTHEW (July 14, 1750–Aug. 1, 1822), soldier, politician, pioneer, and entrepreneur, was born in County Wicklow, Ireland, and emigrated to America in 1765. He is known to have worked out the cost of his passage by three years' service to Jabez Bacon of Woodbury, Conn., and Hugh Hannah of Litchfield. About 1771 he married a Miss Hosford of Litchfield, niece of Ethan Allen. Removing to Vermont in 1774, he purchased lands at Wallingford, and resided there for three years. A born forester and pioneer, possessing natural qualities of leadership, he was soon prominent in the turbulent border country of Lake Champlain. He took part in the incessant Hampshire Grants dispute and the early organization for revolutionary action, followed Ethan Allen at Ticonderoga, and served as adjutant of a Vermont regiment under Montgomery in the early stages of the Canadian campaign. In 1776 he was again in service as a lieutenant near the Canadian border, when the indiscipline of his command, characteristic of the Revolutionary army, led to his being cashiered by General Gates. That this action was probably unjustified was evidenced by his reinstatement and distinguished service during St. Clair's retirement in 1777 and the subsequent operations around Saratoga.

He resigned from the army after Burgoyne's surrender and thenceforth took a prominent place in the civil and military affairs of Vermont, being promoted to the rank of colonel in the militia, serving as secretary to the governor and Council, and representing Arlington in the legislature. He was probably in touch with the leaders of the Haldimand intrigue although not a principal in that affair. His share in the operations of the council of public safety and those of the court of confiscation is not clear. In 1785 he was impeached for failure to deliver the records of the latter body, although proceedings were soon dropped, apparently through fear of unpleasant disclosures. His first wife died in 1782 and a year later he married Mrs. Beulah (Chittenden) Galusha, a daughter of Gov. Thomas Chittenden. In 1783 he moved to Fair Haven and became the leading business man of the locality, opening ironworks, manufacturing paper from basswood, establishing a printing-press, and getting out ship-timber for the Lake Champlain-Montreal trade. When the great party struggle of the next decade began he was in an established position. "I had wealth, high political standing, an established character and powerful connections attached to me by long riveted confidence, as well as matrimonial affinity, to throw in the scale" (McLaughlin, *post,* p. 500). This statement is important in view of Federalist slanders creating the impression that Lyon was an ignorant, uncouth demagogue of the frontier.

Following the admission of Vermont to the Union, Lyon was an unsuccessful candidate for both the federal Senate and House, but he was elected to the latter body in 1797. New England had as yet furnished few Republicans to Congress and the Vermont member was immediately an object of unfriendly curiosity, heightened by his vigorous objections to the current practice of waiting on the president with a reply to the annual message (*Annals of Congress,* 5 Cong., 1 Sess., col. 234). He was mercilessly lampooned by Cobbett (*Porcupine's Works,* 1801, VI, 16–17, 168–71) and the whole Federalist press was soon in action. On Jan. 30, 1798, he spat in the face of Roger Griswold [*q.v.*] when the latter made an insulting reference to his military record, and, on Feb. 15, Griswold assaulted him with a cane. These, the first and probably the most famous personal encounters on the floor of the House, with the subsequent investigations, serve to enliven the dreary pages of the *Annals* for several weeks. Lyon escaped expulsion but endured an incredible amount of scurrility and abuse, the whole affair showing in unequaled fashion the intense bitterness of party spirit at the time.

He was now a marked man and the newspapers were carefully watched for material that would render him liable to prosecution under the Sedition Act, which he had manfully opposed on the floor. Actionable matter was discovered in a letter of his, published in the unfriendly *Vermont Journal* on July 31, 1798. Prosecution followed and on Oct. 9, 1798, Lyon was sentenced to serve four months in jail at Vergennes and to pay a fine of one thousand dollars. (The report of the trial is in *The Debates and Proceedings of the Congress . . .,* 16 Cong., 2 Sess., pp. 478–86, Dec. 1820.) This stupid prosecution, of doubtful legality, combined with grave suspicion of jury-packing, had the natural result. Lyon was reëlected by an overwhelming majority and on release enjoyed a triumphal progress to Philadelphia. In 1840 a bill was passed, refunding the fine to his heirs (*Congressional Globe,* 26 Cong., 1 Sess., pp. 410–14, 478). During his second term he continued a vigorous opposition to the Adams administration, resisted the tampering of agents of Burr during the presidential contest in the House, and, on the withdrawal of his colleague Lewis R. Morris, cast the decisive vote of Vermont for the election of Thomas Jefferson. Then followed his famous letter to "Citizen John Adams" (McLaughlin, pp. 397–406) which is a valuable index to the sentiment of the day, although history has revised the contemporary estimates of both men.

Lyon had already decided to move West and after a preliminary journey went with a considerable colony of relatives and associates to Eddyville, Ky., in 1801. There his career was in many respects a repetition of that in Vermont. Eddyville became a prosperous business center and Lyon was soon a political power in Kentucky, serving a legislative term in 1802 and being elected for a further period of congressional service extending from 1803 to 1811. These years served to bring out Lyon's best qualities as a vigorous speaker and debater, who displayed elements of statesmanship sufficient to refute the earlier slanders. In fact, his repeated clashes with John Randolph on the Yazoo question and his vigorous denunciation of the Embargo and the foreign policies of President Madison brought him into friendly relations with some of his old enemies. He became a friend and correspondent of Josiah Quincy [*q.v.*], and took advantage of the fact to urge the Massachusetts leader not to endanger the Union in the critical days of 1814. In his speeches in Congress Lyon's ingrained love of democracy constantly crops out. He denounced the tyranny of the House rules, the speaker's appointment of committees, the centralizing tendencies to which the Jeffersonians had resorted, the arbitrary government of the western territories, the growth of executive prerogative, and the congressional caucus. He argued for the protection of infant industries with a vigor worthy of Henry Clay, even suggesting the possibility of using slave labor in the industrial development of the South and West (*Annals of Congress,* 11 Cong., 1 Sess., cols. 122–26, 163, 183, 185; 11 Cong., 2 Sess., cols. 1900–03).

His vigorous opposition to the policies leading to the War of 1812, together with neglect of his "fences" in an attempt to recoup heavy losses incurred by the Embargo, led to his defeat for election to the 12th Congress. His business suffered during the war and on Jan. 16, 1817, he wrote: "I am reduced to dependence on my children" (McLaughlin, p. 496). He was always on good terms with President Monroe, who soon found a federal office for him, and in 1820 Lyon went to Arkansas as factor to the Cherokee Nation. He was soon in politics, being defeated as congressional delegate in the first territorial election but succeeding in the second; he died at Spadra Bluff, Ark., before taking his seat. In his seventy-third year he had performed a three-thousand-mile journey on a flatboat to New Orleans and return. A vigorous blast of his against the extravagance and degeneracy of the times in general and of Washington society in particular was posthumously published in *Niles' Weekly Register,* Dec. 7, 1822; this was a typical utterance of the Republican stalwart of 1798. In many ways his career was symbolic of national progress and "this national growth which I almost idolize," as he once put it in the course of debate. He was typical both of the northern frontiersmen and "the men of the Western waters," but with a shrewd business ability which, uninterrupted by politics, might well have made him an early American merchant prince. The loss of his autobiography, said to have been destroyed by mice in a Kentucky garret, undoubtedly deprived the country of an entertaining and valuable historical document.

[J. F. McLaughlin, *Matthew Lyon: The Hampden of Congress* (1900), though eulogistic, is valuable for certain aspects of Lyon's career and contains some important correspondence and reminiscences. See also *Records of the Council of Safety and Governor and Council of the State of Vt.,* vols. I–III (1873–75), with a biographical sketch of Lyon, vol. I, pp. 123–28; *State Papers of Vt. Volume Three. Jours. and Proc. of the Gen. Assembly* . . . (4 vols., 1924–29); Pliny H. White, *The Life & Services of Matthew Lyon* (1858); A. N. Adams, *A Hist. of the Town of Fair Haven, Vt.* (1870); R. H. and Lewis Collins, *Hist. of Ky.* (1874), II, 491–92; Elizabeth A. Roe, *Aunt Leanna, or Early Scenes in Ky.* (1885), a tale by Lyon's daughter which has some sketches of the family life.] W. A. R.

LYON, NATHANIEL (July 14, 1818–Aug. 10, 1861), soldier, son of Amasa and Keziah (Knowlton) Lyon, was born at Ashford, Conn. His father was a descendant of William Lyon who settled in Roxbury, Mass., in 1635; his mother was a niece of Thomas Knowlton [*q.v.*]. At Ashford, Lyon received a common-school education and a Puritan upbringing. He entered the United States Military Academy and graduated in June 1841, being commissioned second lieutenant of infantry, and assigned to the 2nd Regiment, which was already fighting the Seminoles in Florida. He was next ordered to the quiet post of Sacketts Harbor on Lake Ontario. While here he became deeply interested in national politics, and unbosomed himself by writing (1844) that the sending of troops to the Texas frontier bore the earmarks of "madness and folly." Nevertheless, two years later he was ably doing his bit at Vera Cruz, Cerro Gordo, and Mexico. He was commissioned first lieutenant during this campaign and captain in 1851. For several years he was on frontier duty in California. Between 1854 and early 1861 he was stationed, most of the time, in "Bleeding Kansas."

Impressed with his experiences in Kansas, and Washington, D. C. (during a leave of absence), Lyon wrote a series of political articles (1860–61) for the *Manhattan* (Kan.) *Express,* wherein he bitterly condemned Douglas, called President Buchanan a "blue-eyed old hypocrite," and praised Lincoln and the Republican party. He felt that no state could withdraw from the Union short of revolution, and that in case of attempted secession "discreet measures of coercion" should be used. Nevertheless, he was opposed to disturbing slavery where it already existed, and even approved the enforcement, "in good faith," of the Fugitive-slave Law. After his death some of his papers were gathered into a volume, *The Last Political Writings of Gen. Nathaniel Lyon* (1861).

The most critical epoch in his career opened when he was assigned (Feb. 6, 1861) to the St. Louis Arsenal. Here he was not only efficiently alert in all military matters, but was in constant conference with Francis Preston Blair, Jr. [*q.v.*] and other Republican leaders. After Lyon had questioned the zeal of his superior officer, Gen. W. S. Harney [*q.v.*], and had threatened to throw the Arsenal ordnance officer into the Mississippi if he weakened toward the Southerners, and after Blair had exerted pressure at Washington, Lyon was made a brigadier-general and placed in supreme command (May 1861) of the Union forces in St. Louis. Among his important acts immediately thereafter were the seizure of Camp Jackson and the arming of volunteers. On June 12, Sterling Price and Gov. Claiborne F. Jackson [*q.v.*], in a final effort at compromise, met Blair and Lyon for a conference at the Planters' Hotel. Although it was expected that Blair would lead the discussion for the Union, it was Lyon who took control. Proving himself a master of the issues involved, he dominated the entire four-hour conference. His final conclusion was, "This means war."

The next day he sent Colonel Franz Sigel with a small force directly into southwest Missouri, while he, with some two thousand regulars, pushed up the Missouri River, took Jefferson City June 15, and captured Boonville two days later. The state forces retreated to southwest Missouri and Lyon turned in pursuit, reaching Springfield July 13. After fruitless efforts to obtain reënforcements he decided (Aug. 9) to attack the main forces of the enemy, camped ten miles southwest on Wilson's Creek. The combined effective state and Confederate troops in this battle totaled slightly over ten thousand, while Lyon's regulars and others numbered 5,400. At night Lyon sent Sigel with 1,200 men to attack, early the next morning, the enemy's extreme right wing, while he, with 4,200 troops, fell upon the rear of their left. Initially successful, Sigel was later surprised and routed, and thus a probable Union victory was turned into defeat. After about five hours of courageous and able fighting Lyon was killed at the head of his troops. The entire North mourned his death and he immediately became a national hero and martyr. In spite of the defeat at Wilson's Creek, his brilliant work had done much to hold Missouri for the Union. The volunteer private soldiers did not like him because, among other things, "he had no compliments or kind words for anybody, and talked to his soldiers as he did to a mule." Nevertheless, they had that respect for him which all soldiers feel toward an officer who understands his business.

[James Peckam, *Gen. Nathaniel Lyon and Mo. in 1861* (1866) and Ashbel Woodward, *Life of Gen. Nathaniel Lyon* (1862), are eulogistic. Other sources are: "The Diary of Private Ironquill," in N. L. Prentis, *Kan. Miscellanies* (1889); *Springfield* (Mo.) *Leader*, Sept. 29, 1928; *War of the Rebellion: Official Records* (*Army*), 1 ser., vol. I; *Report of the Joint Committee on the Conduct of the War*, pt. 3 (1863); T. L. Snead, *The Fight for Mo.* (1888); W. E. Smith, "The Blairs and Fremont," *Mo. Hist. Rev.*, Jan. 1929; *The Lyon Monumental Asso.* (1871), comp. by E. H. E. Jameson; W. F. Switzler, *Switzler's Illus. Hist. of Mo.* (1879); J. G. Nicolay and John Hay, *Abraham Lincoln* (10 vols., 1890); R. J. Rombauer, *The Union Cause in St. Louis in 1861* (1909); Allan Nevins, *Frémont* (1928); L. U. Reavis, *The Life and Mil. Services of Gen. Wm. Selby Harney* (1878); Galusha Anderson, *The Story of a Border City During the Civil War* (1908); G. W. Anderson, *Life and Character of Gen. Nathaniel Lyon* (1863), an address; files of St. Louis newspapers, Feb.–July 1861, and esp. *Daily Mo. Democrat*, Aug. 14, 1861; *Lyon Memorial*, vol. I (1905); G. W. Cullum, *Biog. Reg. Officers and Grads. U. S. Mil. Acad.* (3rd ed., 1891), vol. II.] H. E. N.

LYON, THEODATUS TIMOTHY (Jan. 23, 1813–Feb. 6, 1900), pomologist, was born at Lima, N. Y., the son of Timothy and Mary (Davis) Lyon and a descendant of Richard Lyon who settled in Fairfield, Conn., in 1649. His father, a millwright, architect, and farmer, removed from New York state to Plymouth, Mich., in 1828, when the boy was in his sixteenth year. The son had attended the village school in Lima and in the West had the varied experiences of frontier life. For a time he carried the mail to outlying points on horseback. In 1834 he returned to Lima, attended school for a summer, then taught at Conesus, 1834–35, and at Penfield, 1835–36. He went west again to Plymouth in 1836 and engaged in milling, farming, and fruit-growing. Two years later he was married to Marilla, daughter of William S. Gregory of Plymouth. He was active in pioneer railroad construction and for several years was president of two of the roads which eventually became a portion of the Pere Marquette Railway system. About 1844 he established a nursery, collecting varieties of trees from surrounding orchards. He soon learned that the local varietal nomenclature was badly confused. He became interested in the study of fruit varieties and assembled a large collection of apples. He made intensive study of their identity and nomenclature, publishing from time to time articles in the *Michigan Farmer* and other periodicals of the region. The accuracy of his published descriptions interested Charles Downing who was then engaged in the revision and enlargement of *The Fruits and Fruit Trees of America* which his deceased brother, Andrew Jackson Downing, had first published in 1845. Through the correspondence which developed with Downing and other pomologists of that epoch, as well as through his published articles, he soon came to be regarded as "the most critical and accurate of American pomologists" (Bailey, *post*, p. 1586).

In 1874, when the development of the then new "fruit belt" of western Michigan was in progress, he removed to South Haven, where he spent the remainder of his life. He took charge of a nursery there, which, though not financially successful, constituted an important factor in the rapid development of the orcharding of the region because of the accuracy and honesty of varietal description and the trueness to name of the stock grown and sold for planting. Lyon's particular interest in the study and appraisal of fruit varieties was such that he consistently devoted more time and energy to it than to the development of a nursery business. In 1876 he was elected president of the Michigan Pomological Society (after 1880 the Michigan Horticultural Society) and served actively until 1893, when he became honorary president. His "History of Michigan Horticulture" was published in the *Seventeenth Annual Report of the ... State Horticultural Society* (1887). In 1889 the collection of fruit varieties which he had assembled on his own property at South Haven was taken over by the state board of agriculture as the nucleus of the South Haven substation of the Michigan Experiment Station. He was in charge of this station from 1889 until his death, issuing frequent published reports for the guidance of the fruit growers of the state. As chairman of the committee on revision of catalogue of fruits of the American Pomological Society from 1889 to 1897, he initiated and developed as an agent of the division of pomology of the United States Department of Agriculture, the card catalogue of fruits which later, as further enlarged by W. H. Ragan, became the basic fruit-variety reference list of the Department. Lyon was one of the most eminent of the self-taught pomologists of the nineteenth century and deserves recognition for his efforts at clarifying pomological nomenclature and for his insistence upon the accurate description and honest appraisal of varieties of fruits.

[L. H. Bailey, *Standard Cyc. of Horticulture*, vol. III (1915); C. W. Garfield, "Theodatus Timothy Lyon," *Hist. Colls., Colls. and Researches . . Mich. Pioneer and Hist. Soc.*, vol. XXIX (1901), and memorial address in *Thirtieth Ann. Report . . . of the State Horticultural Soc. of Mich.* (1901); *Lynn Memorial*, vol. II (1907); *Detroit Free Press*, *Detroit Jour.*, Feb. 7, 1900; personal acquaintance.] W. A. T.

LYON, WILLIAM PENN (Oct. 28, 1822–Apr. 4, 1913), legislator, jurist, was born of Quaker parents at Chatham, Columbia County, N. Y. His father, Isaac Lyon, was descended from Thomas Lyon who was born in England about 1621 and died in Connecticut. His mother, Eunice (Coffin) Lyon, was descended from Tristram and Dionis Coffin, English Quakers who emigrated to America in 1642 and settled in Nantucket. William was the third child in a family of ten children. The father conducted a small country store for some years but suffering financial reverses moved with his family to the town of Hudson (later Lyons), Walworth County, Wis., in 1841. William grew up in a community in which the Quaker tradition was predominant. He attended a district and select school, but his formal education, meager as it was, he supplemented by extensive reading. Under the guidance of his mother, who seems to have been a woman of great wisdom and unusual foresight, he began the study of law by reading Blackstone's *Commentaries,* Cowan's *Treatise,* and Chitty's *Pleading*. He studied in the law offices of Judge George Gale and Judge Charles M. Baker and was admitted to the bar of Walworth County in the spring of 1846. He was at once elected a justice of the peace and later town clerk. His income was sixty dollars for the first year. On Nov. 18, 1847, he was married to Adelia Caroline Duncombe, daughter of Dr. E. E. Duncombe of St. Thomas, Ontario. He later practised law at Burlington and Racine, served as district attorney of Racine County, 1855–58, and was a member of the Assembly as well as its speaker for two terms, 1859–60.

In September 1861 he entered military service as captain of Company K, 8th (Eagle) Regiment of Wisconsin Volunteers. In 1862 he was commissioned colonel in the 13th Wisconsin. He saw much hard service, participated in many battles and engagements, and served throughout his enlistment with credit and distinction. Shortly after his discharge he was breveted a brigadier-general of the United States volunteers to date from Oct. 26, 1865. In the spring of 1865, while he was still in the service, he was elected judge of the first judicial circuit, then second in importance to the fourth circuit, which included Milwaukee County. Upon his return to Racine, he entered upon his duties as circuit judge and five years later (1871) he was appointed justice of the supreme court to fill the unexpired term of Byron Paine. He was elected to the same office in 1871, 1877, and 1883, and served until his voluntary retirement on Jan. 1, 1894. For the last two years he was by virtue of seniority, chief justice. Although at the time of his retirement Lyon had passed three score and ten years, he was two years later called to serve as a member of the state board of control, governing penal and charitable institutions, and served in that capacity for seven years. Upon his retirement his services were commended by Gov. Robert M. LaFollette. He passed his declining years with his son and daughter at Edenvale, Cal., where he died in the ninety-first year of his age. A perusal of his career leaves one with a distinct impression that he lacked almost entirely the dramatic instinct. It never occurred to him to set the stage, or in any way seek to win public acclaim. He was modest, of a gentle but firm spirit. Perhaps no public man in the history of the state had fewer enemies or was more generally beloved and respected.

[Clara Lyon Hayes, *Wm. Penn Lyon* (1926), reprinted from the *Wis. Mag. of Hist.*, Sept. 1925–July 1926; Adelia C. Lyon, *Reminiscences of the Civil War* (1907), compiled from Lyon's correspondence and other papers; 154 *Wis. Reports*, xxviii–xl; P. M. Reed, *The Bench and Bar of Wis.* (1882); J. R. Berryman, *Hist. of the Bench and Bar of Wis.* (2 vols., 1898); J. B. Winslow, *The Story of a Great Court* (1912); *Lyon Memorial*, vol. III (1907); *Mag. of Western Hist.*, Apr. 1887; the *Wis. State Jour.* (Madison), Apr. 4, 5, 1913.] M. B. R.

LYONS, PETER (1734/35–July 30, 1809), Virginia jurist of Irish ancestry, was presumably born in County Cork to John and Catherine (Power) Lyons. Nothing is known of his schooling: the supposition that he attended Trinity College, Dublin, is erroneous. According to family tradition he was persuaded by his maternal uncle, James Power, of King William County, Va., to emigrate to America. It is known that he studied law under Power and was licensed to practise in the county courts of Virginia on Feb. 5, 1756. Succeeding to the profitable practice of his uncle, he rose rapidly in his profession; and having moved to Hanover County, he attained there "an unrivalled reputation for legal learning" (William Wirt, *Sketches of* *the Life and Character of Patrick Henry,* 1817, p. 16). He was plaintiff's attorney in the celebrated "Parsons' Cause" when the Rev. James Maury brought suit for the recovery of the part of his salary lost through the "two penny act" of 1758. Lyons, arguing the nullity of an act which had never received the royal sanction, won the case on a demurrer. A jury was chosen to assess the damages, and Patrick Henry, having become counsel for the defense when the case was already lost, so far succeeded in stirring the latent prejudices of the jury that damages of one penny were awarded.

Daniel Call states that "in the contest with Great Britain" Lyons "took part with the colonies, and was a friend to the revolution" (4 Call, *Va. Reports,* xix), but he seems to have seen no active service. In 1779 he was appointed judge of the general court of Virginia, and in the same year, by virtue of this position, became a judge of the court of appeals. He was one of the first five judges in the reorganized court of December 1788 and on the death of Edmund Pendleton in 1803 became its second president. Among the most important cases argued during his connection with the court was one limiting the independent pardoning powers of the lower house, and another, as a result of which the church lost its glebe lands. Though Lyons continued as president of the court until his death, ill health prevented his active connection with it after 1807.

The portrait of Lyons by Thomas Sully in the supreme court room at Richmond shows a man past middle age, of clear, rounded features and benevolent appearance. He was not a brilliant man but was a close student of the law and enjoyed a reputation for unvarying impartiality. He was twice married, first to his cousin, Mary (Catherine?) Power, and secondly to Judith Bassett. He died at "Studley," his home in Hanover County.

[David J. Mays, "Peter Lyons," *Proc. Thirty-Seventh Ann. Meeting: The Va. State Bar Asso.,* 1926, pp. 418–26, is the best account of Lyons' life and contains full bibliographical information. Some letters of Lyons to his grand-daughter, of little biographical value, are printed in *Tyler's Quart. Hist. and Geneal. Mag.,* Jan. 1927. Call's sketch (cited above) gains in authority what it lacks in length and perspective.] J. C. W.

LYSTER, HENRY FRANCIS LE HUNTE (Nov. 8, 1837–Oct. 3, 1894), physician, was born at Sander's Court, County Wexford, Ireland, to the Rev. William N. and Ellen Emily (Cooper) Lyster. The father, an Episcopal clergyman, graduate of Trinity College, Dublin, had already been to America, where in 1833 he built St. Peter's Church at Tecumseh, Mich., the first church of his denomination in Michigan. He brought his family to America in 1838. The son received his preliminary education in private schools in and about Detroit, graduated in arts at the University of Michigan in 1858 and in medicine from the medical college of the university in 1860. At the outbreak of the Civil War he was commissioned assistant surgeon of the 2nd Michigan Volunteer Infantry, subsequently becoming surgeon of the 5th Michigan. He served in the Army of the Potomac from the battle of Bull Run to Appomattox, mainly as an operating surgeon. He was at one time acting medical director of the III Army Corps.

Returning to Detroit at the close of the war he quickly became one of the leading physicians and surgeons of the state. In 1868 he was appointed lecturer on surgery in the University of Michigan which position he filled for two years. From 1888 to 1890 he was professor of theory and practice of medicine and clinical medicine at the same school. The travel involved in going from Detroit to Ann Arbor compelled him to give up his teaching connection with the university. He was one of the founders and served as president of the faculty of Michigan College of Medicine. After its fusion in 1885 with the Detroit Medical College, when the Detroit College of Medicine was formed, he served as professor of the practice of medicine and of clinical diseases of the chest until 1893. At different times he was connected editorially with the *Peninsular Journal of Medicine* and the *Detroit Clinic.* His professional writings appear in these journals and in the *Transactions of the State Medical Society.* He was appointed in 1873 a member of the original State Board of Health and served eighteen years, taking particular interest in the protection of water supplies. His genius for organization gave him a prominent part in the founding of the Detroit Academy of Medicine, the Wayne County Medical Society, and the Michigan State Medical Society. For years he was medical director of the Michigan Life Insurance Company.

Though he came out of the Civil War with an unusual surgical experience and a reputation as a skilful operator, he continued to the end as a family practitioner, a conscientious attendant upon whatever patient called upon his skill and counsel. This exacting service took its toll of his health and his last years were marked by invalidism from pernicious anemia from which he died. Throughout his career he was in the forefront of every movement in his city and state that had to do with the physical or moral welfare of the community. In his chosen vocation he was an example of the honor and generosity which mark the ideal man of medicine. He was always a student and in his later years his fund of learning and his gift for logical expression made him one of the most accomplished public speakers in Detroit. Personally he was tall and of spare build, with dark hair and clear blue eyes. He was married in Washington, D. C., on Jan. 30, 1867, to Winifred Lee Brent, daughter of Capt. Thomas Lee Brent of Stafford County, Va. His wife and five children survived him.

[H. A. Kelly and W. L. Burrage, *Am. Medic. Biogs.* (1920); *Trans. Mich. State Medic. Soc.*, vol. XIX (1895); B. A. Hinsdale, *Hist. of the Univ. of Mich.* (1906); *Cyc. of Mich.: Hist. and Biog.* (1900); *Detroit Tribune*, Oct. 5, 1894; information as to certain facts from Lyster's son, Col. Wm. Lyster, U. S. A.]

J. M. P—n.

LYTLE, WILLIAM HAINES (Nov. 2, 1826–Sept. 20, 1863), soldier, poet, was born in Cincinnati, Ohio. He was descended from a family distinguished for its martial spirit. His great-grandfather, William, a captain in the French and Indian War and a colonel in the Revolution, moved from Cumberland County, Pa., to Kentucky in 1779. His son, William, generally called General, settled in Ohio. Robert, the father of William Haines Lytle, was for many years an influential political leader, a representative to Congress from the Cincinnati district, and, during President Jackson's administration, surveyor-general, an office which his father had once held. From his mother, Elizabeth (Haines), William probably inherited his poetic strain. When sixteen years old he graduated from Cincinnati College. His military predilections made him desirous of entering West Point, but his family urged him to select law as a profession. Accordingly, he entered the law office of his uncle, E. S. Haines, where he remained for five years. Upon the outbreak of the Mexican War, he deserted his books and entered the service as first lieutenant of the 2nd Ohio Infantry. For ten months he was in active service, and at the close of hostilities had attained the rank of captain. At the conclusion of the war he began practising law as a member of the firm of Haines, Todd & Lytle. In 1852 and again in 1854 he was elected to the state legislature on the Democratic ticket. During part of this time he was speaker of the House. He was an unsuccessful candidate for lieutenant-governor in 1857 and the same year Gov. Salmon P. Chase appointed him major-general in command of the first division of the Ohio Militia.

The period of Lytle's greatest literary activity was during the years between the Mexican and Civil wars; and although his military record during the latter conflict was distinguished, his national fame rests upon his poetical writings. His best known poem, the lyric "Anthony and Cleopatra," is a "passionate glorification of love and war" (Randall and Ryan, *post*, V, 72). Its publication in the *Cincinnati Commercial*, July 29, 1858, brought the author instant recognition. It has long remained a popular favorite because of its "melody, dramatic vividness, and bold imagery." Among his other poems are, "Popocatepetl," "Jacqueline," "Macdonald's Drummer," "Volunteers," "Farewell," and "Sweet May Moon." A collection, *Poems of William Haines Lytle*, was published in 1894, and reprinted in 1912.

Upon the outbreak of the Civil War Lytle organized and established Camp Harrison at Cincinnati. In June 1861 he was appointed colonel of the 10th Ohio Infantry. He was twice severely wounded, first at Carnifex Ferry, Sept. 10, 1861; and later, at Perryville, Oct. 8, 1862, on which occasion he was left upon the field for dead. Recovering from his wound, he was paroled and permitted to return home. His gallantry at Perryville won for him the congratulations of Secretary Stanton, and, upon his exchange, Lytle was promoted to the rank of brigadier-general. On the second day of the battle of Chickamauga, he was severely wounded while leading a charge and died shortly afterwards. His funeral in Cincinnati, Oct. 22, 1863, was one of the most impressive of the war and reflected the high esteem in which he was held by friend and foe.

[E. O. Randall and D. J. Ryan, *Hist. of Ohio* (1912), vol. V; memoir by W. H. Venable in *Poems of William Haines Lytle* (1894, 1912); W. H. Venable, *Beginnings of Literary Culture in the Ohio Valley* (1891); Emerson Venable, *Poets of Ohio* (1909); *The Biog. Cyc. and Portrait Gallery . . . of the State of Ohio*, vol. I (1883); Whitelaw Reid, *Ohio in the War* (1868); *Cincinnati Daily Commercial*, Oct. 23, 1863.] R. C. M.

LYTTELTON, WILLIAM HENRY (Dec. 24, 1724–Sept. 14, 1808), colonial governor, author, was the sixth son of Sir Thomas Lyttelton, bart., and Christian Temple, daughter of Sir Richard Temple, bart., of Stowe, Buckinghamshire. After attending Eton College and Saint Mary Hall, Oxford, he was called to the bar at the Middle Temple in 1748 and represented the borough of Bewdley, Worcestershire, in Parliament from December of that year until February 1755, when he was appointed governor of South Carolina.

Arriving in Charleston in 1756, he found awaiting him the task of arranging for the care of the unfortunate Acadians who had been deposited there, over one thousand strong. Some of these people he settled in the town, binding them out or placing them in suitable occupations.

Others he scattered over the province with any families who were willing to receive them as bond servants. The principal problem that confronted him as governor, however, was presented in 1759 as a result of Cherokee raids on the frontier. In that year he held a conference with the Cherokee chiefs, who seem to have desired peace; but contrary to the advice of his more experienced lieutenant-governor, William Bull [*q.v.*], he planned a punitive expedition against the tribe, broke off the conference, and detained the chiefs who had attended under the pledge of safe conduct, forcing them to accompany his army on its march to Fort Prince George. There, in a second conference with the Cherokees, it was agreed that these chiefs should be held as hostages until the Indians responsible for the murders on the frontier were surrendered. Unfortunately for Lyttelton's plans, smallpox broke out in his army, which gradually dispersed, leaving him practically alone except for the garrison at the fort. Under these circumstances he returned to Charleston in January 1760. After his departure the Indians, who had been greatly enraged by what they deemed his treachery in detaining their chiefs, killed the commander and some of his men and attacked the fort. In revenge the garrison turned on the Indian hostages and murdered them. The result was renewed Indian war and further ravages on the frontier.

The full force of this catastrophe was not felt by Lyttelton, for in April he sailed for Jamaica to assume the governorship, then considered the choicest of colonial appointments. Here he came into conflict with the Council and Assembly for interfering with their commitments of offenders. His action was bitterly denounced by the Assembly in July 1766 and Lyttelton himself represented as a tyrant (Edwards, *post,* II, 347–53; Bridges, *post,* II, 105–09). In October of that year he was appointed ambassador to Portugal. Returning home in 1771, he lived an active life and received many honors, being raised first to the peerage of Ireland and subsequently to that of Great Britain, as Lord Lyttelton, baron of Frankley. He wrote "An Historical Account of the Constitution of Jamaica," which was prefixed to the new edition of *The Laws of Jamaica* issued in 1792, and in 1793 was published as an appendix to Bryan Edwards' *History, Civil and Commercial, of the British Colonies in the West Indies* (I, 250–60). In 1803, he printed *Trifles in Verse* for private circulation. He was married June 2, 1761, to Mary, eldest daughter of James Macartney of County Longford, and on Feb. 19, 1774, to Carolina, daughter of John Bristow of Quiddenham, Norfolk. He had two sons, one by each marriage. He died at Hagley in 1808.

[Sketch by J. M. Rigg, in *Dict. Nat. Biog.*, with bibliography; Maud Wyndham, *Chronicles of the Eighteenth Century, Founded on the Correspondence of Sir Thomas Lyttelton and His Family* (2 vols., 1924); Edward McCrady, *The Hist. of S. C. under the Royal Govt.* (1889); Alexander Hewat, *An Hist. Account of the Rise and Progress of the Colonies of S. C. and Ga.* (2 vols., 1779); David Ramsay, *The Hist. of S. C.* (2 vols., 1809); W. R. Smith, *S. C. as a Royal Province* (1903); Edwards, *ante*; G. W. Bridges, *The Annals of Jamaica,* vol. II (1828); *Gentleman's Mag.* (London), June 1761, Oct. 1766, Feb. 1774, Sept. 1808.]

H. B–C.

MAAS, ANTHONY J. (Aug. 23, 1858–Feb. 20, 1927), Roman Catholic priest and educator, son of John and Elizabeth (Peetz) Maas, was born at Bainkhausen, Westphalia. He attended private schools at Hellefeld and Stockum (1869–74) in preparation for the gymnasium of Arnsberg, where he studied until about 1877, when he emigrated to the United States. He immediately sought entrance into the Society of Jesus; and after satisfying the scrutiny of the superior of the mission, Charles Charaux, he was admitted to the novitiate at West Park, N. Y., Apr. 9, 1877. At Frederick, Md., he continued the study of the classics and Hebrew before taking the philosophical course (1880–83) at the College of the Sacred Heart, Woodstock, Md. After a year's teaching of Latin and Greek to scholastics, he returned to Woodstock for theology (1884–88). He was ordained in 1887. A tried man of marked ability, he was assigned to an instructorship in scripture (1891–1902) and Hebrew (1885–1902) and to the custodianship of the rich library at Woodstock (1888–1902). These labors were interrupted in 1893, when he was ordered to Ignatius Loyola's own Manresa in Spain for the third year of his novitiate, or tertianship. In 1894, with intensified zeal, he returned to his chair at Woodstock.

Here he remained as prefect of studies (1897–1905) and as rector and consultor of the province after 1907, save for a leave of absence (1905–07) during which he was an editor of the *Messenger of the Sacred Heart.* In June 1910 he was delegate to the congregation of procurators at Rome. Two years later, under the rule of obedience (Oct. 4, 1912), he was appointed provincial of the Maryland-New York province with direction over 872 priests, scholastics, and lay brothers as well as authority over a dozen universities and colleges and a number of other institutions belonging to the Society. During his tenure of six years, he proved a benevolent ruler who was far more stern with himself than with his men; and the Society of Jesus prospered accordingly. As ex-provincial, from 1918 until his death he was instructor of tertians at St. Andrews-on-the-Hudson, except for a term in Rome (1923), where he aided in the revision of the *Institute* of the Society.

Through his publications, Maas had an influence which reached beyond the confines of his society. He contributed essays to the *American Catholic Quarterly Review,* to *America,* and to the *Ecclesiastical Review,* in which he edited the department of scripture; he was the author of about a hundred sketches and articles in the *Catholic Encyclopedia,* and wrote several books, including *The Life of Our Lord Jesus Christ* (1891), *Enchiridion ad Sacrarum Disciplinarum Cultores* (1892), *A Day in the Temple* (1892), *Christ in Type and Prophecy* (2 vols., 1893–96), and a *Commentary on the Gospel of St. Matthew* (1898).

[*Am. Cath. Who's Who* (1911); *Who's Who in America,* 1926–27; annual Catholic directories; *The Cath. Encyc. and Its Makers* (1917); *N. Y. Times,* Feb. 21, 1927; and material furnished from the Woodstock archives.] R. J. P.

MABERY, CHARLES FREDERIC (Jan. 13, 1850–June 26, 1927), chemist, son of Henry and Elizabeth A. (Bennett) Mabery, was born at New Gloucester, Me., and died at Portland, Me. His early education was received in the public schools of Gorham, Me., and in Kent's Hill Academy. After graduation from the academy he taught for five years in schools of his native state. In 1873 he studied chemistry in the summer school of Harvard University and in the fall enrolled in the same institution for intensive study in chemistry under Josiah P. Cooke [*q.v.*]. Three years later he graduated from the Lawrence Scientific School with the degree of B.S. Continuing at Harvard as a graduate student, he received the degree of Sc. D. in 1881. During this time and also for two additional years he was an assistant in chemistry and supervised the work in chemistry in the Harvard Summer School. On Nov. 19, 1872, he married Frances A. Lewis of Gorham, Me.; they had one child, who died in infancy. He was appointed instructor in chemistry at the Case School of Applied Science, Cleveland, Ohio, in 1883, and the next year he became professor, retaining this rank until he retired in 1911.

After his retirement he continued investigations which he had long been carrying on. They dealt principally with petroleum, though he did considerable original work in organic chemistry, water analysis, and electric smelting. He published nearly sixty papers on petroleum chiefly in the *Proceedings of the American Academy of Arts and Sciences, American Journal of Science, American Chemical Journal, Journal of the American Chemical Institute,* and *Journal of Industrial and Engineering Chemistry.* His work on petroleum includes both theoretical studies of the geo-chemical evidence of the origin of petroleum and its relation to coal and asphalts, and practical investigations of lubrication and lubricants. About twenty-five papers deal with the composition of petroleum from the principal oil fields of the world. This comprehensive work, especially the analytical testing, was conducted with much skill and sagacity and as a result he became an authority on petroleum, particularly on questions concerning the proportion of sulfur and the identification of hydrocarbons in different oils. In electro-chemistry he published seven papers (some jointly with the Cowles brothers). One was "On the Electric Furnace and the Reduction of the Oxides of Boron, Silicon, Aluminum and Other Metals by Carbon" (*Proceedings of the American Association for the Advancement of Science, 1885,* pp. 136–40). Others dealt with various products from the electric furnace. All gave information on its construction and application at a time when such knowledge was helpful in solving initial problems in electric smelting. His four papers on water chemistry were a definite contribution to the vexatious question of municipal water supply. The fifteen papers on organic chemistry, which were published from 1877 to 1884, deal mainly with certain organic acids, *e.g.,* uric, propionic, and acrylic, and their halogen substitution products. Throughout his career he was deeply interested in chemical education, and he delivered twelve public addresses devoted to methods and problems of teaching chemistry.

[Information from Case School of Applied Science, Cleveland, Ohio; *Who's Who in America,* 1926–27; *Harvard Coll.: The Class of 1876: Tenth Report, June 1926* (1926); *Industrial and Engineering Chemistry,* news ed., July 10, 1927; *Portland Press Herald,* June 27, 1927.] L. C. N.

MABIE, HAMILTON WRIGHT (Dec. 13, 1845–Dec. 31, 1916), editor, critic, and in his earlier years a lawyer, was born in Coldspring, N. Y., near West Point, the son of Levi J. Mabie, a business man engaged in the lumber, and later in the boot and shoe, industry, and his wife Sarah (Colwell) Mabie. He came of mingled Scotch and English blood on his mother's side and of French Huguenot on his father's. The American progenitor of the family was Sergeant Gaspard Mabille, who was driven from his estate at Névy, in Anjou, after the St. Bartholomew's Day Massacre. The name was Americanized to Mabie within a few generations after

Sergeant Mabille settled in New York state. Hamilton Mabie grew up in Coldspring, Buffalo, and Brooklyn, where his parents lived at various times during his youth. Prepared for college by a private tutor, he was ready for entrance at sixteen but, being held back a year on account of his youth, he occupied the interval reading law in the office of a Brooklyn attorney. During his four years at Williams College, where he was a member of the class of 1867, he occupied his leisure chiefly in reading. After graduating he returned to the law, received the degree of LL.B. from Columbia in 1869, and was admitted to the New York bar in the same year. For eight years he practised with fair success, though with no great enthusiasm; later he admitted that he read more poetry than law. After his marriage on Oct. 11, 1876, to Jeannette Trivett, daughter of the Rev. Robert Trivett, of Poughkeepsie, he began to think more definitely of a career in letters and in time determined to gratify his literary tastes while retaining his law practice.

Through Edward Eggleston, then at the height of his fame, Mabie in 1879 became a member of the staff of the *Christian Union,* renamed in 1893 the *Outlook,* and thus began his lifelong association with Lyman Abbott. He never joined another staff, though he was for a time contributing editor of the *Ladies' Home Journal* and helped to edit the Library of the World's Best Literature. He began his work for the *Christian Union* as editor of a department of church news, but he revealed critical talent and was soon made literary editor. Gradually he also began to read manuscripts and write editorials. In 1884 he became associate editor, a post which he occupied with the *Christian Union* and from 1893 until his death with the *Outlook.* He had already begun to write stories for children, and his series of *Norse Stories Retold from the Eddas,* originally published in the *Christian Union,* appeared in book form in 1882. In 1888 he moved to Summit, N. J., where a great deal of his journalistic work was done. During the years that followed, he poured forth books in rapid succession, including *My Study Fire* (1890); *Essays in Literary Interpretation* (1892); *Nature and Culture* (1896); *Books and Culture* (1896); *The Life of the Spirit* (1899); *William Shakespeare: Poet, Dramatist, and Man* (1900); *Works and Days* (1902); *Introductions to Notable Poems* (1909); *American Ideals, Character and Life* (1913); and *Japan To-Day and To-Morrow* (1914), the two last an outcome of his Carnegie lectureship in Japan in 1912–13. In this difficult task of explaining the intellectual and spiritual phases of American life to Orientals, he was admirably successful. Among his most charming books were the series of *Myths* (1905), *Legends* (1906), *Heroes* (1906), and *Heroines that Every Child Should Know* (1908).

In 1915 Mabie suffered a sharp recurrence of writer's cramp which had occasionally afflicted him, and he was forced to dictate. In December he was stricken with dilatation of the heart at the University Club in Philadelphia and was never again able to resume active work. He died a year later, of pneumonia developing from cardiac asthma, and was buried in the Sleepy Hollow Cemetery at Tarrytown. Both in his personal life and in his criticism, he was remarkable for a peculiar gentleness and serenity. On this his college mates, his editorial associates, and his friends alike commented. He was influential, through his writings and his lectures, in fostering the development of literary culture in the United States, but he did not personally look forward to a truly national literature "until we have certain fundamental ideas universally held, and a deep and rich national experience in which every man in every section of the country shares" (*Bookman,* New York, December 1895). He was actively interested in education and social betterment and served various organizations. He was first secretary of the National Institute of Arts and Letters and a member of the American Academy of Arts and Letters. A special room in Williams College Library perpetuates his memory.

[The chief authority for Mabie's life is Edwin W. Morse, *The Life and Letters of Hamilton W. Mabie* (1920). There are several articles in periodicals, including an obituary by Lyman Abbott in the *Outlook,* Jan. 10, 1917, and a review of Morse's book in *Ibid.,* Nov. 17, 1920. Report of the 35th Anniversary of the Class of 1867, Williams College, contains a sketch and there are articles in the *Williams Alumni Rev.,* Jan., Apr. 1917. Mabie summarized his own critical views in an interview in the *Bookman* (New York), Dec. 1895, written by James MacArthur. An interpretive editorial in the *Springfield Republican,* Jan. 2, 1917, was probably written by his friend Solomon Bulkley Griffin. Some authorities give Mabie's birth date as Dec. 13, 1846. The date given in this sketch is correct according to Mrs. Hamilton W. Mabie.] J. B.

McAFEE, JOHN ARMSTRONG (Dec. 12, 1831–June 12, 1890), educator, clergyman, was the eldest of nine children of Joseph and Priscilla (Armstrong) McAfee, who on their wedding trip had emigrated from Kentucky to Marion County, Mo. Joseph was descended from one of three McAfee brothers who joined other pioneers in establishing the first permanent settlement near Harrodsburg, Ky. Until of age, McAfee worked on his father's farm and obtained most of his education by his own efforts. The day's work done, he often lay studying before an open fire which supplied his light. Few books were available, and his self-tuition included little more than classical and American history and elementary science. His schooling began when, at twenty-one, he left home, hiring a substitute for the farm. After seven years' study, interrupted by several periods of school-teaching and other activities for self-support, he was graduated from Westminster College in Fulton, Mo., in 1859. At once he entered upon the educational career which continued until his death. After teaching at Ashley, Mo., from 1867 to 1870, he was successively connected with Pardee College at Louisiana, Mo., 1867–70, and with Highland College at Highland, Kan., 1870–75. In these colleges he was interested in plans for offering students means of self-help. In 1875 he cooperated with Col. George S. Park in founding Park College, which he served as president until his death. Here he offered an education to all worthy young persons of small or no financial resources.

This self-help plan, which remained the outstanding mark of Park College for many years after McAfee's death, was less to train artisans than to reduce student expense and to inspire service. McAfee's leading emphasis was on intellectual and spiritual discipline in preparation for religious leadership. He sought to develop the character resources of the growing West. He also fostered preparation for missionary service; of Park College graduates a notably large number have become foreign missionaries. Though he attended no theological school, McAfee was early ordained a Presbyterian minister and later received the honorary degree of D.D. from Westminster College, Mo. He married, Aug. 23, 1859, Anna W. Bailey. Of their five sons and one daughter, each for some years shared in the teaching or administrative work of Park College. As a preacher, McAfee was ardent and positive; as an educator, a determined classicist and advocate of traditional views; as an administrator, he was essentially practical.

[The author used an unpublished biographical manuscript, written by Jos. E. McAfee. For printed materials see the latter's memoir, "My Father," in the *Bull. of Park Coll.*, Jan. 1926; Neander M. Woods, *The Woods-McAfee Memorial* (1905); Theodore Roosevelt, *The Winning of the West*, vols. I and II (1889); C. A. Phillips, *A Hist. of Educ. in Mo.* (1911); *Presbyt. Jour.*, June 26, 1890.] P. P. F.

McAFEE, ROBERT BRECKINRIDGE (Feb. 18, 1784–Mar. 12, 1849), Kentucky politician and historian, was born in the Salt River settlement in what is now Mercer County, Ky. He was of Scotch-Irish stock, a grandson of James McAfee who came to Pennsylvania in 1739 and later moved to western Virginia; his parents, Robert and Anne (McCoun) McAfee, were among the earliest settlers in Kentucky. His father had explored that region in 1773 and 1774, and had been sergeant-at-arms of the Transylvania Convention in 1775. Beginning at the age of five, young Robert attended various local schools and was evidently a proficient pupil. During 1795–97 he was a student in Transylvania Seminary. In 1798 he became aroused over the Alien and Sedition Acts and determined to become a politician. For a year he was an usher at Mahan's School, Danville, but in 1800 he began the study of law under John Breckinridge, 1760–1806 [*q.v.*], one of his guardians and the Jeffersonian leader in Kentucky. After being admitted to the bar in 1801 (too young, he decided), he had to borrow money to buy law books, and his practice (in Franklin County) was so small that he paid his debts by surveying land. He took part in local politics, becoming a leading member of the "Republican Society" and a captain of militia. He continued to read much, in philosophy, theology, and rhetoric. He wrote both poetry and prose, and some of his historical articles and other pieces were published in newspapers. In 1807 his growing practice enabled him to marry Mary Cardwell.

During the War of 1812, he volunteered as a private, was later second lieutenant, and in 1813 organized a mounted company in R. M. Johnson's regiment, which reinforced Harrison at Fort Meigs and took an important part in the battle of the Thames. There McAfee was wounded. In 1816 he published a *History of the Late War in the Western Country* (reprinted 1919), based on his own journal and on the correspondence of Harrison, Shelby, and other participants. The larger and more valuable part of the book is devoted to the operations in Indiana and on the Lakes. He endeavored to be fair, he said, but in his Preface confessed to "a natural attachment to his country and hostility to her enemies according to their deserts."

Resuming legal practice, he rose in politics to be a member of the state House of Representatives (1819) and state senator (1821). Supporting the relief of debtors and the new and more popular court of appeals, he was in 1824 elected lieutenant-governor by the Relief, or New Court, party. In 1825, the lower house passed a bill to abolish the new court, but the measure was defeated for the time by McAfee's deciding vote in the Senate. Later, as a member of the lower house (1830–33), he opposed reckless expenditures for internal improvements. He was a member of the first National Democratic Convention (1832), and the following year President Jackson appointed him chargé at Bogotá, New Granada (1833–37). He was later state senator (1841) and president of the board of visitors of the United States Military Academy (1842). After living in retirement for some years, he died on his farm in Mercer County.

[McAfee MSS. in the Ky. State Hist. Soc., including "History of the Rise and Progress of the First Settlements on Salt River" (*Reg. Ky. State Hist. Soc.*, Jan.–July 1931), "The Life and Times of Robert B. McAfee" (*Ibid.*, Jan.–Sept. 1927), and "The McAfee Papers" (*Ibid.*, Jan.–Sept. 1928); M. C. Weaks, *Calendar of the Ky. Papers of the Draper Collection of MSS.* (Pubs. State Hist. Soc. of Wis., Calendar Ser., vol. II, 1925); W. E. Connelley and E. M. Coulter, *Hist. of Ky.* (1922), vol. II; Lewis and R. H. Collins, *Hist. of Ky.* (2 vols., 1874); *The Biog. Encyc. of Ky.* (1878); N. M. Woods, *The Woods-McAfee Memorial* (1905); *Ky. Yeoman* (Frankfort), Mar. 22, 1849.] W. C. M.

MACALESTER, CHARLES (Apr. 5, 1765–Aug. 29, 1832), merchant, son of Charles and Isabella (MacQuarrie) Macalester, was born at Campbeltown, Argyllshire, Scotland. He attended the schools of his native town, receiving a thorough grounding in the fundamentals, but at an early age went to sea as a foremast hand. Before he was twenty-one he came to America, settling in Philadelphia, and was naturalized in 1786, soon after reaching his majority. He continued to follow the sea, however, and for the next eighteen years commanded merchant vessels sailing from the port of Philadelphia. Usually he also acted as supercargo and in this capacity achieved a considerable reputation as a trader. With an increase in his fortune, he became owner of the vessel in which he sailed, and in the course of time, one of the leading merchant traders of his day. In the late years of the century, when privateers were seriously hindering commerce, he armed one of his vessels, the *George Barclay*, with twenty guns and manned it with a hundred seamen, and, thus equipped, made voyages with a rapidity and safety which further enhanced his reputation. Shortly after 1800, he designed a vessel, the *Fanny*, which was constructed for him by one of the ablest of the Philadelphia ship-builders, and proved to be the fastest merchant vessel of the day. Her first voyage, from Philadelphia to Cowes in the Isle of Wight, was accomplished in seventeen days, which was then a record.

In 1804 Macalester retired from the sea but continued in the shipping trade, with headquarters in Philadelphia. His vessels sailed to China, India, and the Dutch East Indies, as well as to European ports. In 1825 he planned to retire from all business, but was persuaded to accept the presidency of the Insurance Company of the State of Pennsylvania, which was then in financial difficulties. In two years he had restored the organization to a profitable basis, but he continued as president until he died. He was also a director of the Bank of North America. A loyal Presbyterian, he was a founder of the Mariner's Church of Philadelphia and of the Marine Bible Society. He was a promoter and vice-president (1813–25) of the St. Andrew's Society. By his wife, Ann Sampson, he had a number of children, among them Charles Macalester [*q.v.*].

[Henry Simpson, *The Lives of Eminent Philadelphians Now Deceased* (1859); S. N. Winslow, *Biogs. of Successful Phila. Merchants* (1864); *An Hist. Cat. of the St. Andrew's Soc. of Phila. with Biog. Sketches of Deceased Members, 1749–1907* (1907); C. H. Browning, *Americans of Royal Descent* (1891); *Poulson's Am. Daily Advertiser* (Phila.), Aug. 31, Sept. 4, 1832.] J. H. F.

MACALESTER, CHARLES (Feb. 17, 1798–Dec. 9, 1873), financier, was born in Philadelphia, Pa., the son of Charles [*q.v.*] and Ann (Sampson) Macalester. His father was a prosperous merchant and ship-owner. The boy received a good education, at Grey and Wylie's School in Philadelphia, and during the War of 1812 entered his father's business. In 1821 he moved to Cincinnati, Ohio, where he engaged in a mercantile venture of his own. Returning to Philadelphia some years later, he soon became prominent in commercial circles there and in 1834, 1835, and 1837 was appointed a government director of the second Bank of the United States. In 1835 he became a member of the firm of Gaw, Macalester & Company, bankers. Various political appointments were tendered him at different times, all of which he declined, preferring the independence of private life. In 1842 he visited England and there became acquainted with the American banker, George Peabody of London. He served for years as Peabody's agent and correspondent in Philadelphia and later as one of the trustees of the Peabody Education Fund.

Through shrewd purchase of real estate in Philadelphia and western cities, particularly Chicago, he accumulated a large fortune, of which he gave liberally to various charities. Chief among the objects of his philanthropy, perhaps, was the Philadelphia Presbyterian Hospital, of which he was one of the founders. In 1873 he gave a piece of property in Minneapolis, Minn., for the establishment of an institution of higher learning which the trustees named Macalester College. He was a director of the Fidelity Insurance, Trust & Safe Deposit Company, and of other corporations, was a manager of and contributor to the Philadelphia Orthopaedic Hospital, and president of the St. Andrew's Society from 1864 until the year of his death. He was twice married: first, in 1824, at

Cincinnati, to Eliza Ann Lytle, and second, in 1841, to Susan Bradford Wallace. There were two children by the first marriage. In 1849 he retired from business and occupied himself with his private affairs and various trusts and executorships. He died suddenly from heart disease in Philadelphia.

[*In Memoriam—Charles Macalester* (privately printed, 1873); *Jour. of the Exec. Proc. of the Senate, 1829–37* (1887); Henry Hall, *America's Successful Men of Affairs*, vol. II (1896); C. H. Browning, *Americans of Royal Descent* (1891); *An Hist. Cat. of the St. Andrew's Soc. of Phila.* (1907); J. L. M. Curry, *A Brief Sketch of George Peabody and a Hist. of the Peabody Educ. Fund* (1898); H. D. Funk, *A Hist. of Macalester Coll.* (1910); *Press* and *Public Ledger* (both of Phila.), Dec. 10, 1873.] J. H. F.

MACALISTER, JAMES (Apr. 26, 1840–Dec. 11, 1913), educator, was born in Glasgow, Scotland, son of John and Agnes Robertson MacAlister. In early childhood he lost his father and, with his widowed mother and two older sisters, went to live with his paternal grandfather, a man of strong character, an elder in the Presbyterian Church, engaged in business in Glasgow. After the grandfather's death the family emigrated to Wisconsin in 1850. James MacAlister's early schooling was obtained in Scotland; his three years of college training at Brown University, where he graduated in 1856. After leaving college he taught school in Milwaukee, Wis. Here, also, after graduation from the Albany Law School in 1864, he practised law. On June 24, 1866, he was married to Helen Lucretia Brayton. His success as a student of public affairs and as a speaker led to his absorption in the cause of education. In 1873 he was appointed superintendent of the public schools of Milwaukee. Thereafter he devoted himself to education.

When Philadelphia sought to reorganize its public-school system it chose as leader the notably successful Milwaukee superintendent. In 1883 he undertook the task of introducing progressive ideas into what was then a very conservative community. The contagious enthusiasm and skilful address which had won Milwaukee enlisted the interest of Philadelphia. He frequently lectured on modern education. Addressing the Modern Language Association at the University of Pennsylvania in 1887 he proposed that the writings of Dante, Cervantes, Shakespeare, and Goethe be added to a curriculum which had hitherto recognized only the ancient classics. He developed a program of industrial training in the schools. One of the earliest educational monographs issued by the New York College for the Training of Teachers under the editorship of Nicholas Murray Butler (vol. III, no. 2, March 1890) was by MacAlister: "Manual Training in the Public Schools of Philadelphia." When he resigned in 1890, the Philadelphia *Press* declared that he had transformed the schools through his "energy, tact, industry, enthusiasm, ability, and unflexible pertinacity."

He resigned to become president of the newly established Drexel Institute of Art, Science, and Industry. The main building was dedicated Dec. 17, 1891, in the presence of Thomas A. Edison, Andrew Carnegie, J. Pierpont Morgan, and many educational and public officials, by Chauncey M. Depew. The first classes were held in 1892. A happy association with Anthony J. Drexel and his friend George W. Childs was ended by the death of Drexel in 1893 and that of Childs shortly after. The well-founded movement went on under MacAlister's guidance with the help of other friends. In addition to the courses which included among others the then undeveloped fields of electrical engineering, business, domestic economy, and library science, a powerful influence was exerted among students and the general public by the museum of industrial art, the picture gallery, and the organ recitals and other concerts. The success of the institution drew visitors from all over the world. The founder of the Armour Institute, Chicago, consulted MacAlister, as did the founder of Pratt Institute. He enjoyed friendships at home and abroad based upon a common enthusiasm for practical education, literature, and the fine arts. While the Drexel Institute building was being erected he studied technical education in Europe. He frequently visited London and Edinburgh, always returning with delight to Philadelphia or to his summer cottage in Rhode Island. His wife, who died in 1898, shared his joy in a hospitable home. One who gave himself so completely to students, colleagues, friends, and the public found little time for writing. He lectured at Drexel Institute, Johns Hopkins, the Harvard Summer School, and at many educational association meetings. He was an Officier d'Académie Français, trustee of the University of Pennsylvania (1885–97), and a member of the Committee of Fifty for the Investigation of the Liquor Problem (1897–1900). In 1913 his health had declined so seriously that he resigned in June. He was then made president emeritus of Drexel Institute. On his way to Bermuda in December he died of heart failure at sea.

[*Who's Who in America*, 1912–13; *Hist. Cat. of Brown Univ., 1764–1914*; R. B. Beath, *Hist. Cat. of the St. Andrew's Soc. of Phila.*, vol. II (1913); *Pub. Ledger* (Phila.), Dec. 13, 1913; publications of the Drexel Institute; information as to certain facts from MacAlister's daughter, Miss MacAlister.] D. A. R.

McALLISTER, CHARLES ALBERT (May 29, 1867–Jan. 6, 1932), marine engineer, shipping official, was one of the outstanding advocates of the merchant-marine revival after the World War. He was born in Dorchester, N. J., the son of William and Abigail Ann Shute McAllister. His father, a ship-builder, had emigrated from Scotland and later established a shipyard on City Island in the Bronx, New York City. There Charles first became acquainted with naval architecture. To study marine engineering, he attended Cornell University where he received the degree of mechanical engineer in 1887. He spent the next five years as a draftsman, at first with the Cramp yards in Philadelphia and then with the navy. He helped to design the boilers for the *Oregon* and for other vessels of the new navy. For the next quarter century he was an engineer officer in the Revenue-Cutter Service. Appointed second assistant engineer on June 30, 1892, he was promoted to first assistant engineer on June 6, 1895. During the Spanish-American War he served in the navy as engineer officer on the *Pennsylvania* in the Pacific. On Apr. 13, 1902, he became chief engineer of the Revenue-Cutter Service where he exerted great influence. He is credited with suggesting the legislation approved on Jan. 28, 1915, combining the Revenue-Cutter Service and the Life-Saving Service into a single organization known as the Coast Guard. On Mar. 9, 1916, he became engineer-in-chief of the new service with a rank equivalent to that of commander in the navy and served in that capacity until his resignation on July 12, 1919.

He left the service to become vice-president of the American Bureau of Shipping at the instance of his friend, Stevenson Taylor, whom he succeeded as president upon the latter's death in 1926. Before McAllister's death the organization was registering ninety per cent. of the American merchant marine eligible for classification. In his new capacity, McAllister took a leading part in the agitation for governmental support of the American merchant marine. The Bureau brought him into contact with all the principal ship-builders and ship-owners, while his years at Washington had given him exceptional contacts with legislators, officials, and journalists. He made almost weekly trips from New York to Washington, testified at congressional merchant-marine hearings, and did much to facilitate the passage of the Jones-White Merchant Marine Act of 1928. His last efforts were to secure an appropriation of $125,000,000 to build a hundred new fast steamships for the merchant marine. He served with distinction as a delegate to the International Conference on Safety of Life at Sea in London in 1929 and, as chairman of the Shipping Board's committee on fuel conservation, was active in introducing the use of pulverized coal for economy. He was the author of two books on marine engineering and wrote numerous popular and technical articles on the merchant marine. McAllister was married to Adelaide Kenyon of Chicago on Mar. 6, 1907. He died at his home on Park Avenue in New York City.

[The principal source is the memorial number of the *Bull. of the Am. Bureau of Shipping*, Mar.–Apr., 1932, containing obituary notices, resolutions and personal messages. See also: *Who's Who in America*, 1930–31; *Jour. Am. Soc. Naval Engineers*, Feb. 1932; *Marine Engineering and Shipping Age*, Feb. 1932; *Marine Rev.*, Feb. 1932; *Cornell Alumni News*, Jan. 21, 1932; *N. Y. Times*, Jan. 7, 1932.] R. G. A—n.

McALLISTER, HALL (Feb. 9, 1826–Dec. 1, 1888), lawyer, son of Matthew Hall [*q.v.*] and Louisa Charlotte (Cutler) McAllister, was born in Savannah, Ga. He was named for his father but seems to have dropped the first name, Matthew, after he left college. In May 1846, he entered Yale College with the class of 1849 but withdrew during his sophomore year, in July 1847, studied law in Savannah, was admitted to the bar, probably in January 1849, and soon afterward sailed for California with his cousin, Samuel Ward. He arrived in San Francisco on June 4, 1849, in company with W. M. Gwin and Joseph Hooker [*qq.v.*], and he immediately engaged in law practice. In September he became second lieutenant of the California Guards, a military company organized to assist in the maintenance of law and order. Upon the arrival, in 1850, of his father and brother, Samuel Ward McAllister [*q.v.*], the three McAllisters formed a law partnership that continued until Ward's withdrawal and the father's elevation to the bench. As assistant to Horace Hawes, in 1850, he was active in apprehending and bringing to trial and conviction, before the unofficial court that had been set up, a band of desperate characters first known as the Hounds and later as the Regulators. The organization and methods of the vigilance committee the next year, however, seem not to have enlisted his approval or co-operation.

His courtly manners and popular personality, his character, and intellectual abilities soon brought him a large and lucrative law practice. He seems to have eschewed politics throughout most of his career. In 1860, however, he was one of sixty-five signers of an address to California Democrats declaring their support of the Breckinridge ticket. He did not confine his talents to any particular kind of legal practice. One of his best-known cases was the defense of Adolph Spreckels for shooting M. H. de Young, the owner of the *San Francisco Chronicle.* He was most at home before a jury, where his sense of humor often led him to inject into his arguments doggerel of his own composition. When trying a case, he habitually took down the testimony of witnesses himself, in spite of the fact that the court stenographer was doing this at the same time. Although not remarkable as a speaker, he had a convincing way with a jury, growing out of the thorough preparation and mastery of his cases. His name constantly appears in the seventy-odd volumes of California's supreme court reports published during his lifetime, beginning with the case of *Payne* vs. *The Pacific Mail Steamship Co.* in the first volume. Resolutions adopted by the bar association of San Francisco shortly after his death declared that he had tried more cases, won more verdicts, and received larger fees than any other California lawyer of the period (*Morning Call,* San Francisco, Mar. 24, 1889). Two of his most important victories were the judgments, for the plaintiff, in *Charles Lux et al.* vs. *James B. Haggin et al.* (69 *Cal.* 255–454), which involved irrigation projects and riparian rights in California and, for the defendant, in *Ellen M. Colton* vs. *Leland Stanford et al.* (82 *Cal.* 351–412), which involved the relations of trustee and beneficiary. This was his last great case. The actual trial lasted for many months in the lower courts, and his argument required seventeen days for delivery. Two years after his death, the California supreme court sustained his victory in the trial court.

In the summer of 1888 he became ill and went to Europe for several months in the hope of recovery. Returning in November, he died a month later of a brain tumor, at his country estate "Miramonte" in Ross Valley, near San Rafael, and was buried from Trinity Episcopal Church in San Francisco. He was survived by his wife, Louisa Clemence (Hermann) McAllister, the daughter of Samuel Hermann of San Francisco, and by four children, three daughters and a son. McAllister street in San Francisco was named in his honor and his bronze statue stands near the city hall.

[O. T. Shuck, *Bench and Bar in Cal.* (1888) and *Hist. of the Bench and Bar in Cal.* (1901), pp. 417–21; J. C. Bates, *Hist. of the Bench and Bar in Cal.* (1912); Z. S. Eldredge, *Hist. of Cal.* (copr. 1915), vol. III; T. H. Hittell, *Hist. of Cal.,* vols. II, III, IV (1885–97); H. H. Bancroft, *Popular Tribunals* (2 vols. 1887); M. F. Williams, *Hist. of the San Francisco Committee of Vigilance of 1851* (1921); *An Account of the Meetings of the Class of 1849 of Yale College . . . 1852* (1852); Ward McAllister, *Society as I Have Found It* (copr. 1890); M. C. McAllister, *Descendants of Archibald McAllister* (1898); W. J. Davis, *Hist. of Political Conventions in Cal.* (1893); *Morning Call* (San Francisco), June 24, 1885, Dec. 2, 4, 8, 1888, Mar. 24, 1889; *San Francisco Chronicle,* Dec. 2, 8, 1888.] P. O. R.

MCALLISTER, MATTHEW HALL (Nov. 26, 1800–Dec. 19, 1865), jurist, was born at Savannah, Ga., the great-grandson of Archibald McAlister, who emigrated from Scotland before 1730, acquired a large tract of land in the Cumberland Valley, owned a gristmill and a smith shop, and was one of the organizers of the First Presbyterian Church of Carlisle, Pa. His father, Matthew McAllister, a graduate of the College of New Jersey in the class of 1779, was a lawyer of some eminence whom Washington appointed district attorney for the southern district of Georgia. His mother was Hannah (Gibbons) McAllister, a sister of William Gibbons of Georgia [*q.v.*]. In June 1817 the son entered his father's college, where he did not distinguish himself academically and left college in October 1818. He prepared himself for the law and was admitted to the bar about 1820. For twenty-nine years thereafter he practised his profession in Savannah with great success. He was married to Louisa Charlotte Cutler of New York City, grand-daughter of Esther (Marion) Mitchell, the sister of Gen. Francis Marion and the aunt of Julia Ward Howe [*qq.v.*]. In 1827 he was appointed United States district attorney for the southern district of Georgia. His first noteworthy activity in politics came in 1832, when he appeared as an outstanding defender of the Union under the constitution and the opponent of nullification. From 1834 to 1837, he served in the Georgia Senate, in which he was a prominent and influential member. He was instrumental in bringing about the establishment, in 1846, of the Georgia supreme court for the correction of errors. Until 1840 he seems to have been identified with the National Republicans and, later, with the Whig party; but, after the nomination of Harrison for the presidency, he bolted that party and appealed to other state-rights Whigs to join the Democratic party. On July 4 of that year he made an *Address to the Democratic-Republican Convention of Georgia* (1840) which set forth his principles with a good deal of clarity. Although a coastal rice planter and a member of the most exclusive social aristocracy in the state, he soon became one of the three or four Democratic leaders in Georgia. In 1845 he ran for governor but was defeated by a close vote. During this campaign, he was denounced by opponents as an "aristocrat who has no sympathy with the people," and as belonging to "that class in Savannah known as the 'Swelled Heads' who think the up-country people no better than brutes" (Shryock, *post,* p. 115). He was several times elected mayor of Savannah and, in that office, acquired some reputation as a protector of the colored people. In 1848 he was a delegate-at-large to the Democratic National Convention at Baltimore, supported the nomination of Lewis Cass, and campaigned in Tennessee for the Cass ticket. Early in 1850 the state legislature elected him one of the state's two delegates-at-large to the Nashville convention, but he declined the honor. Later that year, he moved with his family to California and practised law with his two sons Hall and Ward [*qq.v.*] in San Francisco. In 1853 he returned to Georgia during a legislative deadlock over the election of a United States senator. There he was nominated for the senatorship by his friends and received 93 out of 111 votes necessary to a choice.

In 1855 Pierce appointed him to be the first United States circuit judge in California. The character and variety of his judicial decisions is apparent from the volume of *Reports of Cases in the Circuit Court of the United States for the District of Columbia* (1859) reported by his son, Cutler McAllister. In those years he rendered many important decisions affecting the title to lands in California acquired under Mexican grants, notably, *United States* vs. *Andres Castillero,* in which the decision of his court was sustained by the United States Supreme Court (23 *Howard,* 469). Owing to impaired health, he resigned from the bench in 1862. Three years later he died in San Francisco, being survived by his wife, a daughter, and five sons. He was buried from the Episcopal Church of the Advent. His death evoked eulogies from the bench and bar of more than ordinary earnestness and impressiveness.

[Information from the secretary of Princeton University; O. T. Shuck, *Representative and Leading Men of the Pacific* (1870) and *Hist. of the Bench and Bar in Cal.* (1901); R. H. Shryock, *Ga. and the Union* (1926); *Federal Cases,* vol. XXX (1897), p. 1383; Ward McAllister, *Society as I Have Found It* (copr. 1890); M. C. McAllister, *Descendants of Archibald McAllister* (1898); State of Ga. Department of Archives and Hist., *Georgia's Official Register, 1927* (1927); L. E. Richards and M. H. Elliott, *Julia Ward Howe* (1915), vol. I; *Daily American Flag* (San Francisco), Dec. 20, 25, 1865.] P. O. R.

McALLISTER, SAMUEL WARD (Dec. 1827–Jan. 31, 1895), New York society leader, son of Louisa Charlotte (Cutler) and Matthew Hall McAllister [*q.v.*], was born in Savannah, Ga. His father, at one time an officer of the Georgia Hussars and, afterward, a leader of the Savannah bar and federal circuit judge in California, was famous for his hospitality and entertained many of the reigning wits and beauties of his day. When Ward, as he was usually called, was about twenty he visited New York, where he spent some time under the social patronage of a maiden relative, who introduced him into the fashionable circles of the city. After her death, he returned to Savannah and passed his bar examination. In 1850 he and his father joined his brother, Hall McAllister [*q.v.*], at San Francisco in order to establish a law firm. By 1852 he had made a comfortable fortune and in the autumn of that year returned to New York. The next year he married Sarah T. Gibbons, the daughter of a Georgia millionaire then living in Madison, N. J. They had one daughter and two sons. He bought "Bayside Farm," near Newport, R. I., and began his career as a society man. He initiated his campaign with several years' residence abroad, where he everywhere managed to form distinguished social connections and perfected himself in the arts of the finished host. On his return to the United States, he spent his winters in New York and Savannah but made Newport his home for nine months of the year. Always restless and feverishly active, he began at once to convert the sleepy old town of Newport into the gilt-edged, multi-colored scene he loved. The modest country picnic under his practised hand became a *fête champêtre* with music, floral decorations, dancing, banqueting, and exquisitely iced champagne. Beginning thus with successes at Newport he had, by the late sixties, made himself the arbiter of the New York social world and, as such, maintained his position with a diplomatic skill worthy of a higher aim. Yet, in his own belief, a social career was an end sufficient in itself because Society, as he saw it, tended to elevate and refine life and to stimulate all the higher arts that satisfy esthetic wants. His chief triumphs in the New York social world were the organization of the "Patriarchs" and the choosing of the "Four Hundred." As a protest against the powers of exclusion held by a few very rich men, in 1872, he banded together the oldest New York families, whose approval of any social aspirant should be final. The heads of the families so honored were called "Patriarchs," and they gave subscription balls for which regular invitations became a warranty of social position. The "Four Hundred" was a group of more casual origin. Mrs. William Astor, in planning her ball of Feb. 1, 1892, found that the ballroom would not accommodate all those upon her list. He undertook to cut the list and afterward boasted in the Union Club that there were "only about four hundred people in New York Society." The phrase was given publicity and the whirlwind of controversy that followed made it an idiom of the language. In 1890 he brought out his book, *Society as I Have Found It,* a curious mélange of reminiscence, good dining, servant management, and social etiquette and diplomacy. His many vanities and affectations laid him open, at times, to extravagant ridicule. Yet even those whom his militant individualism annoyed acknowledged his charm of manner and his amiability and freedom from malice, throughout a life devoted to maintaining the balance of his little throne in a glittering world that "smiles and smiling kills."

[Ward McAllister, *Society as I Have Found It* (copr. 1890); F. T. Martin, *Things I Remember* (1913); M. C. McAllister, *Descendants of Archibald McAllister* (1898); *N. Y. Times,* Feb. 2, 16, 1892, abstracted in I. N. P. Stokes, *Iconography of Manhattan Island,* vol. V (1926), pp. 2008–09; *N. Y. Tribune,* Feb. 1, 1895; *New York Times,* Feb. 1, 1895.]

E. M. H.

McALPINE, WILLIAM JARVIS (Apr. 30, 1812–Feb. 16, 1890), civil engineer, was born in New York City, the eldest son of John and Elizabeth (Jarvis) McAlpine. His paternal grandfather, Donald McAlpine, was an officer in the famous "Black Watch"; his mother was a granddaughter of Abraham Jarvis [*q.v.*], second Protestant Episcopal bishop of Connecticut. John McAlpine, who was a millwright and mechanical engineer with a large practice, desired his son to enter the engineering profession with a view to carrying on his own business. Accordingly, after completing his elementary education at private academies in Newburgh and Rome, N. Y., William, then fifteen, was apprenticed to John B. Jervis [*q.v.*], a civil engineer.

He served under Jervis as pupil, assistant, and resident engineer for eight years, showing remarkable aptitude and developing rapidly. In 1836, he succeeded his preceptor as chief engineer of the eastern division of the Erie Canal. After several years' service in this capacity, he became chief engineer of the government dry dock in Brooklyn. This was a project of the first magnitude, and, because the foundations had to be laid on a deep layer of quicksand, forty feet below tide level, one of extraordinary difficulty. McAlpine handled the construction in a masterly manner, and by the successful completion of the work definitely established himself as one of the leading engineers of his time. As state engineer and railway commissioner of New York from 1852 to 1857, he made studies on comparative costs of rail and water transportation which achieved international recognition. He served as chief engineer of the Erie Railroad 1856–57, of the Chicago & Galena (later Northwestern), 1857, and of the Ohio & Mississippi, 1861–64; and as consulting engineer to many others. He prepared plans and reports on water supply systems for Chicago (1851–54), Brooklyn (1852), Buffalo (1868), Montreal (1869), Philadelphia (1874 and 1884), San Francisco (1879), New York (1882), Toronto (1886), and many smaller cities. As chief engineer of the Third Avenue drawbridge over the Harlem River, New York (1860–61), he did pioneer work on the design and sinking of the caissons for the piers. Later he acted either as chief engineer or consulting engineer for a number of the greatest bridge projects of the time, including the Eads bridge over the Mississippi at St. Louis (1865), the Clifton suspension bridge at Niagara (1868), and the Washington bridge over the Harlem in New York City (1885–88). He was superintendent of construction of the New York State Capitol at Albany in 1873, a project of great magnitude and difficulty; and later, as engineer of parks for New York City, he built the famous boulevard, Riverside Drive. At the time of his death he was actively engaged upon plans for the "Arcade Railway"—a project for providing an underground rapid transit system for New York City and also second level streets under some of the congested thoroughfares. The scheme was one of remarkable ingenuity and in many respects far ahead of its time, but opposition of abutting property owners and legal and financial difficulties forced its abandonment.

McAlpine enjoyed wide professional recognition in England and Continental Europe, where he was consulted on many important projects, including the Manchester Ship Canal, a proposed railway to India, and improvement of the navigation of the Danube River near the "Iron Gate." He was the first and for many years the only American honored by membership in the British Institution of Civil Engineers, and was elected president of the American Society of Civil Engineers, 1870, and honorary member, 1889.

McAlpine was a prolific writer on technical subjects. Besides reports upon the various projects with which he was connected, he contributed to the *Transactions of the American Society of Civil Engineers* a number of original papers (perhaps the most important being "The Foundations of the New Capitol at Albany, N. Y.," in vol. II, 1874) and many detailed discussions. Possibly his most notable contribution to technical literature was his paper on "The Supporting Power of Piles," published in the *Minutes of Proceedings of the Institution of Civil Engineers* (vol. XXVII, London, 1868), which won him the Telford Medal. He also published in book form a work entitled *Modern Engineering* (1874).

McAlpine was one of the last great general practitioners of civil engineering, and was the recognized dean of the profession when he died. He was married on Feb. 24, 1841, at Watervliet, N. Y., to Sarah Elizabeth Learned (*Daily Albany Argus*, Feb. 26, 1841). His death occurred at New Brighton, Staten Island.

[*Proc. Am. Soc. Civil Engineers*, vol. XVIII (1892); *Minutes of Proc. of the Inst. of Civil Engineers* (London), vol. C (1890); *Engineering News*, Feb. 22, Mar. 8, 1890; *Engineering and Building Record* (N. Y.), Feb. 22, 1890; *Engineering and Mining Jour.* (N. Y.), Feb. 22, 1890; *Engineering* (London), Mar. 7, 1890; *N. Y. Tribune*, Feb. 18, 1890; personal acquaintance.]

J. I. P.

McANALLY, DAVID RICE (Feb. 17, 1810–July 11, 1895), Methodist clergyman, educator, journalist, was born in Grainger County, Tenn. Like his father, Charles, local preacher, sheriff, surveyor, who weighed 360 pounds and was married twice, the son was above the average in size and the husband of two wives. His mother was Elizabeth, daughter of the Rev. Rice Moore; and his wives were Maria Thompson and Julia Reeves. His early education, which was scanty, was received in a country school and in a private academy. Admitted on trial to the Holston Conference of the Methodist Episcopal Church in 1829, for fourteen years he served charges in Tennessee, North Carolina, and Virginia. In spite of the fact that he himself had not been privileged to go to college, he was elected in 1843 to the presidency of the East Tennessee Female Institute, and as administrator and by the publication of tracts and newspaper articles he served in that position effectively. His interest included not only the denominational institution of which he was head, but the common-school system as well; and for a number of years he was connected with Horace Mann [*q.v.*] and other prominent educational leaders in an effort to improve it. In 1851 he was chosen editor of the *St. Louis Christian Advocate*, and the next year he was chairman of the convention which founded Central College, Fayette, Mo., and cooperated with Enoch M. Marvin [*q.v.*] and others in raising what was then considered a good endowment for such an institution.

He continued as editor of the *Advocate*, with slight intermissions until his death. As a journalist, two aims seem to have been in his mind: first, through the arrangement and presentation of news of the week to acquaint his readers with the march of events; and second, by editorial exposition to ground those same readers in "sound doctrine." When the Civil War broke out, he strove diligently to allay excitement. In a series of editorials during April and May 1861, under such titles as "The Times," "The Duty of Christian Men," "The Time for Prayer," he warned his people of "the magnitude of the rebellion" and the "unprecedented unanimity of the South." His advice to the men of Missouri was to remain at home, cultivate friendly relations, and pray for a restoration of peace. Unfortunately, his straightforward account of the events of the conflict led to his arrest as an enemy of the Federal government, and for months he lay in the Myrtle Street Military Prison in St. Louis.

In addition to his editorial work, he wrote the following books: *Life and Times of Rev. William Patton* (1858); *The Life and Times of Rev. Samuel Patton* (1859); *The Life and Labors of Rev. E. M. Marvin* (1878); a biography of Mrs. Laura Ramsey; and *History of Methodism in Missouri* (1881). He was not a scholar, but his intimate touch with men and public affairs over a long period enabled him to present first-hand information. His primary interest was in the Church, and to that he gave greatest space; but in some of the volumes there are chapters devoted to an interpretation of the life and thought of the period. Sixty-six years a preacher, five times a delegate to the General Conference, more than forty years editor, "probably no man had more to do with fixing the ideals and customs of Missouri" than did he.

[*Christian Advocate* (Nashville), July 18, 1895; *Minutes of the Ann. Conferences of the M. E. Church, South* (1895); R. N. Price, *Holston Methodism*, vol. III (1908); M. L. Gray and W. M. Baker, *The Centennial Vol. of Mo. Methodism* (1907); J. B. McFerrin, *Hist. of Methodism in Tenn.* (3 vols., 1869–73); W. M. Leftwich, *Martyrdom in Mo.*, vol. I (1870); W. S. Woodward, *Annals of Mo. Methodism* (1893); Wm. Hyde and H. L. Conard, *Encyc. of the Hist. of St. Louis* (1899), vol. III; *Knoxville Daily Jour.*, July 13, 1895; *St. Louis Republic*, July 12, 1895.]

R. W. G.

McARTHUR, DUNCAN (Jan. 14, 1772–Apr. 28, 1839), congressman and governor of Ohio, was born in Dutchess County, N. Y., the son of John and Margaret (Campbell) McArthur, natives of the Scotch Highlands. His mother died when he was very young, and in 1780 his father, who was poverty-stricken, moved to the neighborhood of Pittsburgh. McArthur somehow learned to read and write, but his youth was spent in farming or as a driver of transalleghany pack-trains. In 1790 he enrolled for service against the Indians and took part in Harmar's campaign and in other expeditions. During the winter of 1792–93 he was a salt-boiler at the licks near Maysville, Ky. In the spring he joined a surveying party under Nathaniel Massie, which penetrated the Scioto valley to the region of Chillicothe. When the Indians in the region became excited, he served two years observing their movements as a ranger. In March 1795, he was again associated with Massie and learned surveying. In

February 1796 he married Nancy McDonald and settled with her on a farm near the recently founded village of Chillicothe. He rapidly amassed property by shrewd buying and locating of Virginia land warrants that were issued to Revolutionary soldiers. Unquestionably he could drive a hard bargain, and his enemies charged that he was unscrupulous. His subsequent life was embittered by constant litigation over land titles. By 1804 he was considered the wealthiest land holder in the Scioto valley. In that year he was elected to the Ohio House of Representatives. The next year he was elected to the state Senate, where he served eight consecutive terms, and in the session for 1809–10 he was the speaker.

In 1806 he was elected a colonel of the militia. In February 1808 he became a major-general, and he held this rank in the spring of 1812, when the Ohio militia marched for Detroit. Upon the reorganization of the Ohio volunteers, he was elected colonel of one of the three militia regiments under Hull's command. He took a noteworthy part in the campaign. On arriving at Detroit he urged Hull to attack Malden immediately, led a raid that penetrated some thirty miles into Canada, and was acting as an escort for a supply train at the time of Hull's surrender, when his troops were included in the terms of Hull's capitulation. He was later a principal witness at Hull's court martial. He returned to Chillicothe from Detroit with reputation unimpaired and was elected to Congress in the autumn of 1812. He did not qualify, however, and on Apr. 5, 1813, shortly after he had been informed of the exchange of the prisoners taken at Detroit, he resigned to undertake active service in the regular army, to which he had been appointed brigadier-general in March. His first activity was to raise volunteers for the assistance of Harrison, who was in danger from Proctor. He then undertook the defense of Fort Meigs. During the campaign that ended at the battle of the Thames he was stationed at Detroit. Following that battle he was placed in command of the troops at Sacketts Harbor on Lake Ontario. He criticized Harrison because of his inactivity during the winter of 1814 and his correspondence with the Secretary of War and with General Cass has been severely criticized (Goebel, *post*, p. 194). On Harrison's resignation in May 1814, he succeeded to the command of the army in the Northwest. Save for one spectacular raid in Upper Canada, nothing important was achieved in his period of command.

Following the war he served as a member of several commissions for treaty-making with the Indians. He was frequently a member of the state legislature, in the lower house for three sessions, 1815–16, 1817–18 when he was speaker, and 1826–27, and in the upper house for three sessions, 1821–22, 1822–23, and 1829–30. He made himself unpopular by supporting the United States Bank when it was bitterly attacked by the legislature in 1817. In 1822 he was elected to Congress, where he served inconspicuously. In 1830 he was elected governor by a narrow margin over Robert Lucas, a Jackson man. In 1832 he chose to run for Congress rather than for reelection as governor but was defeated by a single vote by William Allen, who later married his daughter, Effie. In 1830 he met with a serious accident from which he did not fully recover. He died at his home "Fruit Hill" near Chillicothe.

[McArthur Papers in Lib. of Cong.; some letters in Ohio State Lib.; files of the Cong. Joint Committee on Printing; John McDonald, *Biog. Sketches of General Nathaniel Massie, General Duncan McArthur* (1838); L. S. Evans, *A Standard Hist. of Ross County, Ohio* (1917), vol. I; *Hist. of Ross and Highland Counties, Ohio* (1880); W. A. Taylor, *Ohio Statesmen and Hundred Year Book* (1892); D. B. Goebel, *W. H. Harrison* (1926); F. P. Weisenburger, *Ohio Politics during the Jacksonian Period* (1929); "The Bounty Lands of the Am. Revolution in Ohio," a typewritten dissertation by W. T. Hutchinson in the Lib. of the Univ. of Chicago.]

W. T. U.

McARTHUR, JOHN (May 13, 1823–Jan. 8, 1890), architect, known as John McArthur, Jr., was born in Bladenock, Wigtownshire, Scotland. He is said to have come to America in his childhood, perhaps in the care of his uncle, John McArthur. He was subsequently apprenticed to this uncle, who was a carpenter in Philadelphia. Being of a studious habit and earnestly desiring a knowledge of architecture, he devoted his evenings to acquiring instruction in drawing and design at the period when the Franklin Institute afforded opportunity through a course of lectures by Thomas U. Walter [*q.v.*]. It is said that McArthur declined his uncle's offer of means to obtain a liberal school education because he preferred to pursue his technical studies in the special field to which he aspired. As apprentice and later as foreman and superintendent of works he gained practical experience and promotion when such progressive advancement was highly regarded as the path to master craftsmanship. The influences under which he acquired the principles of design developed a classical taste which, joined with strict regard for utility and fitness, thereafter marked his architectural accomplishments.

In his twenty-sixth year (1848) while serving as superintendent of works with his uncle, he won, in competition with established architects, the first premium for a design of a new building for the House of Refuge at Philadelphia. He subsequently served as architect for the successive enlargement of the institution during his lifetime. Thus established in his profession, he planned numerous important public and private buildings, including the once famous Continental, Girard, and LaPierre hotels, Dr. David Jayne's granite business block and his marble residence, the Public Ledger Building, and George W. Childs's mansion, besides buildings for Lafayette College at Easton, the State Asylum for Insane at Danville, Pa., and others. During the Civil War he was employed by the United States government in the erection of hospitals and was architect of the naval hospitals at Philadelphia, Annapolis, and Mare Island. He twice declined the office of supervising architect of the United States Treasury Department, but superintended the erection of the post office at Philadelphia.

Judged by the standard of popular taste and architectural practice during the period of his career, his work exhibited sound construction and in design compared favorably with that of his contemporaries. It is claimed that his crowning achievement was the Philadelphia City Hall or Public Buildings, for which competitive designs were submitted in 1869. Although the structure has not escaped criticism, this criticism has been due primarily to the controversy its location involved and to the prolonged period of construction which brought it into conflict with changing fashions in design, and with the higher buildings which now surround it. It was at the time one of the two largest public buildings in the United States and was considered unique for its originality and the merit of its sculptural work and adornment. In his personal and professional career McArthur has been described as a worthy successor of Latrobe, Mills, Strickland, Haviland, and Walter [*qq.v.*], self-trained architects who were famed in their day. He died at Philadelphia, survived by his wife, Matilda (Prevost) McArthur, by two sons and two daughters.

[Joseph Jackson, *Early Phila. Architects and Engineers* (1923); Charles Morris, *Makers of Phila.* (1894); *The City Hall, Phila.: Architecture, Sculpture and Hist.* (1897); *The Twenty-first Ann. Report of the House of Refuge of Phila.* (1849), and later reports; *The Biog. Encyc. of Pa. of the Nineteenth Century* (1874); obituary in *Public Ledger* (Phila.), Jan. 9, 1890.]

H. W. S—s.

McARTHUR, JOHN (Nov. 17, 1826–May 15, 1906), manufacturer and soldier, born at Erskine, Scotland, was expected by his parents, John and Isabella (Neilson) McArthur, to fulfill the bright promise of his parish school days and enter the Presbyterian ministry. He preferred his father's smithy, however, and one year after his marriage in 1848 to his neighbor, Christina Cuthbertson, he emigrated to America, joining his brother-in-law, Carlile Mason, in Chicago. After McArthur had gained a little capital by several years' work for a Chicago boiler-maker, he became Mason's partner (1854–58) in the ownership of the successful Excelsior Iron Works, "making steam boilers, engines, and iron work of every description." From 1858 to 1861 McArthur conducted the business alone.

During these years he rose from 3rd lieutenant to captain of the Chicago Highland Guards, and in May 1861 he was at Cairo, as colonel of the 12th Illinois Infantry. Drilling, Kentucky reconnaissances, and railway patrol filled the rest of the year, and by its close he commanded the 1st Brigade of the 2nd Division. From Fort Henry (February 1862) until the war ended, his troops were frequently on special duty. Grant found the tall, brawny, tight-lipped Scot both "zealous and efficient," a plain man who won his superiors' confidence and his soldiers' love. "Meritorious service" at Donelson made him a brigadier-general (Mar. 21, 1862), and at Shiloh, although wounded, he commanded his division after Gen. W. H. L. Wallace was killed. He effectively led the 6th Division, Army of the Tennessee, through the hard fighting around Corinth and Iuka. In the Vicksburg campaign, under General McPherson, his men were often detached for emergency service to McClernand's, F. P. Blair's, or Sherman's command. Grant requested his promotion, but McArthur had no political influence at Washington and his advance to higher rank was retarded.

From the early autumn of 1863 to Aug. 1, 1864, he was post commander of Vicksburg. For two months thereafter he protected Sherman's line of communication about Marietta, Ga., and was then ordered to Missouri to oppose General Price. In December, he was rushed to Nashville and here, on the 16th, his military career reached its climax. Not unwillingly yielding to his impatient troops, and with only the silent sanction of his superior, Major-General A. J. Smith, he charged the opposing heights, crushed Hood's left wing, and turned the battle of Nashville into a Confederate rout. On Thomas' recommendation, McArthur was brevetted major-general. Thereafter, until he was mustered out, Aug. 24, 1865, he served under Major-General E. R. S. Canby in the Alabama campaign and was stationed at Selma during the summer.

For twenty years after the war, McArthur suffered a series of reverses. Efforts to revive his foundry business failed. The Chicago Fire darkened his term as commissioner of public works (1866-72), and while he was postmaster of Chicago (1873-77), $73,000 of post-office funds disappeared in a bank crash. Bowing to a court decision, he used most of his fortune to make good this loss. Another of his ventures, the Chicago and Vert Island (Lake Superior) Stone Company, succumbed to two successive ship disasters in the early eighties. About 1885 he retired from business, but continued to take an active interest in the Presbyterian Church, the St. Andrew's Society, the Grand Army of the Republic, and the Loyal Legion. He died of paralysis and was buried in Rose Hill Cemetery, Chicago. He was the father of seven children. In 1919, a bust of General McArthur was unveiled on the Vicksburg battle-ground.

[Interview with a son, J. N. McArthur, Chicago, who possesses a MS. by J. N. Warrington entitled "McArthur Genealogical Tables and Family Record"; Chicago Directories, 1850 ff.; G. L. Paddock, "The Beginnings of an Illinois Volunteer Regiment in 1861," in *Military Essays and Recollections* (comp. in 1894 by Ill. Commandery, Mil. Order of the Loyal Legion of the U. S.), II, 258 ff.; *Mil. Order of the Loyal Legion . . . Commandery of the State of Ill., Circular No. 22*, series of 1906; *Who's Who in America*, 1906-07; T. B. Van Horne, *Life of Maj. Gen. George H. Thomas* (1882), pp. 324 ff.; *War of the Rebellion: Official Records (Army)*; *Sunday Times-Herald* (Chicago), Feb. 17, 1901; *Chicago Chronicle*, Oct. 6, 1903; *National Tribune* (Washington), July 8, 1906, and Oct. 26, 1916; *Chicago Daily News*, Aug. 26, 1906; *Chicago Tribune*, Oct. 16, 1919; *British-American* (Chicago), Sept. 27, 1919, and Chicago newspapers of the period May 15-26, 1906.] W. T. H.

MACARTHUR, ROBERT STUART (July 31, 1841-Feb. 23, 1923), Baptist clergyman, editor, author, was born at Dalesville, Quebec, the eleventh child of Archibald and Margaret (Stuart) MacArthur. His parents had left the Highlands of Scotland in quest of religious freedom. His father was a stanch Covenanter; his mother, a devoted Baptist. After preparatory studies at the Canadian Literary Institute at Woodstock, Ontario, MacArthur went to Rochester, N. Y. He graduated from the University of Rochester in 1867 and from the Rochester Theological Seminary in 1870. In due time he became an American citizen. Ordained to the Baptist ministry in New York City in 1870, he served as pastor of the Calvary Baptist Church there for forty-one years. During his pastorate the membership increased from 200 to 2,300, a beautiful edifice was erected, and large contributions were made to benevolence. MacArthur was an eloquent speaker and was in constant demand as a preacher and lecturer. His preaching was exegetical and evangelical, marked by style and adornment, copious allusion, and spiritual discernment. His sermon, "What think ye of Christ," was translated into nine languages. His two volumes entitled *Quick Truths in Quaint Texts* (1895, 1907) have been the sources for many a sermon. Though conservative in his theological point of view, he was able to present his ideas in a way that appealed to the modern mind. Throughout a five-decade preaching career, he missed preaching only one Sunday on account of illness. He made it a rule to visit every member of his church every year. This pastoral service was the laboratory of his pulpit ability.

MacArthur was an enthusiastic Baptist and promoted the interests of that denomination in three continents. He was a correspondent of various Baptist periodicals, editor for a time of the *Baptist Quarterly Review* and the *Christian Inquirer*, and was the author of more than a score of popular homiletical books. From 1881 to 1913 he acted as trustee of the New York Baptist Union for Ministerial Education. In 1911 he left his New York City pastorate when he was unanimously elected president of the Baptist World Alliance. In this capacity he visited Russia to secure the Czar's permission to erect a Baptist theological seminary at St. Petersburg, but the outbreak of the World War cancelled the provisional imperial consent. He also attended the centennial of Baptist missions in Burma. The growth of the ritual of worship in the Baptist Church is due in part to his promotion of a rather stately and formal service in his own church and the publication of addresses and books concerned with liturgy. His homiletical works include *The Attractive Christ and Other Sermons* (1898) and *The Old Book and the Old Faith* (1900). MacArthur was married, on Aug. 4, 1870, to Mary Elizabeth Fox, the daughter of the Rev. Norman Fox, for some years a member of the New York legislature. He died at Daytona Beach, Fla., within an hour after he was stricken with acute indigestion.

[*Who's Who in America*, 1922-23; *Annuals of the Northern Bapt. Convention*, 1907-23; Annual Sessions of the Baptist Congress, 1882, 1885, 1892, 1901; the *Baptist*, Mar. 10, 1923; the *Watchman-Examiner*, Mar. 1, 1923; *N. Y. Times*, Feb. 25, 1923.] C. H. M.

MCARTHUR, WILLIAM POPE (Apr. 2, 1814-Dec. 23, 1850), hydrographer, naval officer, was born at Ste. Genevieve, Mo., the son of John and Mary (Linn) McArthur. Appointed midshipman in the United States navy (Feb. 11, 1832) at the request of his uncle, Dr. Lewis Fields Linn [*q.v.*], later United States senator from Missouri, he spent several years in the South Pacific station and then attended the naval school at Norfolk. He commanded one of the vessels in the expedition to the Everglades during the second Seminole War (1837-38) but was severely wounded and sent to the naval hospital at Norfolk, where the energetic convalescent courted and married on May 3, 1838, Mary Stone Young, daughter of the hospital superintendent. In 1840 he was ordered to the brig *Consort,* which had been detailed to the United States Coast Survey, and during the next year he participated in the survey of the Gulf coast and was promoted to lieutenant (1841). Continuing in the Coast Survey, he was appointed by Alexander Dallas Bache [*q.v.*] in the autumn of 1848 to the command of the hydrographic party sent to make the first survey of the Pacific Coast. Arriving at Panama, McArthur found the isthmus overrun with lawless Americans and at once became the head of an effective vigilance committee. He then took command of the *Humboldt,* which lay at the island of Taboga without a captain and overloaded with emigrants, and sailed her to California. There he selected Mare Island as the most suitable location for a navy yard and sailed northward along the coast in the schooner *Ewing.* His pioneer work on the West coast, including a preliminary survey and a successful reconnaissance of the coast from Monterey to the Columbia River, was carried out in spite of mutiny, desertion, and McArthur's recurring attack of malignant fever. The results of the survey were published in 1851 by the United States Coast Survey (*Notices of the Western Coast of the United States*). McArthur died from an acute attack of dysentery as the *Oregon* was entering Panama Harbor on the return voyage.

[See *Senate Executive Doc. 1,* 30 Cong., 2 Sess.; *Senate Executive Doc. 5,* 31 Cong., 1 Sess.; *House Executive Doc. 12,* 31 Cong., 2 Sess.; and Lewis A. McArthur, "The Pacific Coast Survey of 1849 and 1850," *Quart. of the Oregon Hist. Soc.,* Sept. 1915. For the memorial meeting of the U. S. Coast Survey, see the *Daily Nat. Intelligencer* (Washington, D. C.), Jan. 10, 1851, and App. No. 40 of *Senate Executive Doc. 3,* 32 Cong., 1 Sess.] F. E. R.

MACAULEY, EDWARD YORKE [See McCauley, Edward Yorke, 1827–1894].

McAULEY, JEREMIAH (*c.* 1839–Sept. 18, 1884), reformed criminal, "apostle to the lost," was born in Ireland. His father was a counterfeiter who found it expedient to leave for parts unknown while Jerry, as he was always called, was an infant. He was brought up by a Roman Catholic grandmother whose head he frequently made a target for missiles as she knelt in prayer, for which impudence, upon arising, she was accustomed to curse him vigorously. He never went to school, was harshly treated, and grew up in idleness and mischief. When thirteen years of age he was sent to New York, where he made his home with a married sister until, confident that he could live by his own wits, he took lodgings on Water Street. Here, in association with other criminals he became a river thief, boarding vessels at night and stealing whatever he could take away. At nineteen he was arrested for highway robbery, and, though innocent of the charge, was convicted and sentenced to Sing Sing for a term of fifteen years and six months. A Sunday morning talk given by a reformed criminal, Orville Gardner, better known as "Awful" Gardner, started him on the road to conversion. In 1864, having served more than seven years of his sentence, he was pardoned, and left prison determined to lead a sober and righteous life; but temptation was too strong for him and he reverted to evil ways. With others he began buying stolen goods of sailors; then, compelling them to join the army through fear of arrest, collected the bounty. After the war he was engaged in river thieving and in disposing of stolen and smuggled goods. It was profitable business, but he spent all his gains in riotous living. His conscience was never quiet, however, and through the influence of Water Street mission workers he was again, and this time permanently, converted.

Having secured honest employment, he was one day sitting at his work when, he says, "I had a trance or vision . . . and it seemed as if I was working for the Lord down in the Fourth Ward. I had a house and people were coming in. There was a bath, and as they came in I washed and cleansed them outside, and the Lord cleansed them inside." He interested others in the realization of his dream, a little money was raised, and on Oct. 8, 1872, he opened a mission at 316 Water Street. For nearly ten years, often persecuted by the vicious and not always supported by the police, he ministered to the fallen. His wife, Maria, who also had been rescued from a life of degradation, was his devoted colaborer. Scores were converted, and knowledge of the mission was carried by sailors and others to distant quarters of the world. It was incorporated as the McAuley Water Street Mission in 1876, and a three-story brick building erected for its work. In 1882 McAuley founded the Cremorne Mission on West Thirty-second street, which he conducted until his death. He also began in June 1883 the publication of a journal, *Jerry McAuley's Newspaper,* which contained accounts of mission meetings and testimonies of converts. An autobiographical sketch dictated by him, entitled *Transformed, or the History of a River Thief,* appeared in 1876, and was widely circulated. During his later years he suffered from consumption, which was the cause of his comparatively early death. He was buried in Woodlawn Cemetery.

[*Jerry McAuley, His Life and Work* (1885), ed. by R. M. Offord, with introduction by S. Irenæus Prime; 5th ed. (1907) entitled *Jerry McAuley, An Apostle to the Lost,* with additions; S. H. Hadley, *Down in Water Street* (1902); Helen Campbell, *The Problem of the Poor* (1882); *N. Y. Observer,* Sept. 25, 1884; *N. Y. Times, N. Y. Tribune,* Sept. 19, 22, 1884.] H. E. S.

McAULEY, THOMAS (Apr. 21, 1778–May 11, 1862), Presbyterian clergyman, educator, was born in Ireland, possibly at Coleraine, the son of Thomas A. and Eliza J. (Warden) McAuley. During a debate in the General Assembly of 1837 he stated that he had been a missionary on the frontier as early as 1799 (E. H. Gillett, *History of the Presbyterian Church in the United States of America,* 1864, II, 505). Except for this hint, his early life is altogether obscure. His missionary activity seems to have preceded his entrance to college, for he graduated from Union, Schenectady, N. Y., in 1804, having given his residence at the time of his enrolment as Salem, N. Y. He remained at the college for some years, serving as tutor (1805–06), lecturer in mathematics and natural philosophy (1806–14), and professor of these subjects (1814–22). In 1819 he was ordained by the Presbytery of Albany and in 1822 became pastor of the Rutgers Street Church, New York City. A warm-hearted Irishman whose conversation was full of racy humor, a fluent and ardent preacher, and a faithful pastor, he was popular personally and successful in his ministry. He took an active part in the affairs of the denomination and was moderator of the General Assembly in 1826. In 1827 he was elected president of Transylvania University, Kentucky, but declined (Robert Peter, *Transylvania University,* 1896, p. 156), accepting, however, a call to the Tenth Presbyterian Church, Philadelphia. Here he served until 1833 when he returned to New York and took charge of the Murray Street Church, which later moved to Eighth Street.

Unlike most Presbyterian ministers of his race, McAuley aligned himself with the new-school party, and was one of its leaders in the memorable General Assembly of 1837 at which the old-school adherents took action which resulted in a division of the Church. He was also present at the convention held in Auburn, N. Y., that same year, when the Auburn Declaration "stating the 'true doctrines' of the new-school men over against the 'errors' charged on them in the old-school memorial" was drawn up. Two years earlier he had taken part in the founding of Union Theological Seminary, originally known as the New York Theological Seminary, and his name heads the list of the original directors elected Nov. 9, 1835. He was subsequently chosen the first president of the institution, and professor of pastoral theology and church government. He rendered valuable service for four years, resigning in 1840. In 1845 he also resigned his pastorate, and his later life was spent in retirement. The degree of LL.D. was conferred upon him by Dublin University.

[*A Gen. Cat. of the Officers, Grads. and Students of Union Coll., 1795–1868* (1868); *Gen. Cat. of Union Theolog. Sem.* (1919); E. F. Hatfield, *The Early Annals of Union Theolog. Sem.* (1876); G. L. Prentiss, *The Union Theolog. Sem. . . . Hist. and Biog. Sketches of Its First Fifty Years* (1889); S. J. Baird, *A Hist. of the New School* (1868); *N. Y. Times,* May 13, 1862; information from James Brewster, Librarian of Union Coll.] H. E. S.

McBRYDE, JOHN McLAREN (Jan. 1, 1841–Mar. 20, 1923), agriculturist, college president, the son of John and Susan (McLaren) McBryde, Scotch immigrants who came to America about 1820, was born in Abbeville, S. C. His father, a prosperous cotton factor and merchant, gave his son the best education the South then afforded. Prepared in the village academy, he was admitted to the sophomore class of the South Carolina College, where, inspired by the lectures of John and Joseph Leconte [*qq.v.*], he developed a love of science that determined his life work. From Columbia he went to the University of Virginia in 1859, and left there in January 1861 to become a soldier of the Confederacy. Joining a volunteer company from Abbeville, he was stationed first on Morris Island. Mustered out, he volunteered for service in Virginia, and was with Beauregard at the first battle of Manassas. In 1862 he served with the cavalry on James Island, and thence, stricken with typhus fever, was invalided home. Unfit for military service, he entered the Treasury Department at Richmond and at the age of twenty-two was appointed chief of a division of the War Tax Office. He married Cora Bolton, daughter of James and Maria (Harrison) Bolton of Richmond, on Nov. 18, 1863. To this union six children were born.

At the close of the war he began farming near Charlottesville, Va., where through reading and private study he learned to apply scientific methods to agriculture. His enthusiasm and gift for leadership soon drew others to him and he organized farmers' clubs, before which he presented the results of his studies and experience. Through his addresses and articles in the newspapers he became well known as an agriculturist and in 1879 was called to the chair of agriculture in the University of Tennessee. His first report, published in 1880, marks an epoch in the history of scientific agriculture in the South.

In 1882 he accepted a chair in the South Carolina College, just then beginning to recover from the horrors of the war. Soon afterward, he was elected president and in that capacity reorganized the College and expanded it into a university along modern lines. As the director of experiment stations in different sections of the state he supervised the planting and fertilization of cotton and other crops. His experiments and reports gave an impetus to the revival of agriculture in South Carolina and had a lasting influence on methods of farming throughout the South. Though offered the directorship of the Agricultural Experiment Station in Texas and the presidency of the University of Tennessee, he chose to remain in the service of his native state.

Unfortunately, however, during the political disturbances in South Carolina in the nineties the University was reduced to a college and the agricultural department, in which his heart was engaged, was removed to Clemson. Therefore, when offered the presidency of the Virginia Agricultural and Mechanical College and Polytechnic Institute, at Blacksburg, he accepted, and in September 1891 took charge of a moribund school with a faculty of ten instructors and a student body of less than a hundred. In sixteen years he created a high-grade polytechnic institute with sixty teachers and more than seven hundred students. He had numerous flattering offers, including the assistant secretaryship of agriculture under Cleveland (1893) and the first presidency of the University of Virginia, but refused to leave his post. As a member of the board of directors of Sweet Briar Institute he organized the new school on a broad basis and outlined its policy. In June 1907 having tendered his resignation, he was made president emeritus of the Virginia Polytechnic Institute and granted the degree of Doctor of Science. In 1912 the University of South Carolina awarded him the McMaster Medal in recognition of his distinguished services to the state. He died in New Orleans.

Few other college executives in the South have rendered longer and more faithful service or have contributed to the cause of education along so many different lines. Six feet tall, erect, with keen gray eyes and kindly smile; calm, dignified, courteous towards high and low alike; gentle yet firm, McBryde had a charm of manner that captivated every one. He was an accomplished musician, a fine horseman, a keen sportsman, and an elegant gentleman of the old school. He inspired both faculty and students with confidence and enthusiasm and developed an *esprit de corps* that contributed to the healthy, permanent growth of every institution with which he was connected.

[*Bull. Univ. S. C.*, no. 31 (July 1912), pt. II; *Bull. Va. Polytechnic Inst.*, Jan. 1908; *Who's Who in America*, 1922–23; *Men of Mark in Va.*, vol. III (1907), portr.; D. C. MacBryde, *MacBryde (McBryde—Macbride) of Auchinnie Parish . . . Wigton, Galloway, Scotland* (1931); MSS. in possession of the author and the family; *Times Picayune* (New Orleans), Mar. 21, 1923.] C. W. D.

McBURNEY, CHARLES (Feb. 17, 1845–Nov. 7, 1913), surgeon, was born in Roxbury, Mass., the son of Charles and Rosine (Horton) McBurney. His father, an immigrant from the North of Ireland, was of Scotch extraction; his mother came from Bangor, Me., and was of old native stock. Their son was named Charles Heber, but after graduation from college apparently never used his middle name. He received his preliminary education at the Roxbury Latin School and at private institutions, graduated (A.B.) from Harvard in 1866, and was granted the doctor's degree in medicine at the College of Physicians and Surgeons, New York, in 1870. For the next eighteen months he was an interne at Bellevue Hospital, then followed postgraduate studies in Vienna, Paris, and London, giving special attention to surgery. On his return, he settled in New York and began his surgical career as assistant demonstrator (1873–74) and demonstrator (1875–80) of anatomy at the College of Physicians and Surgeons, under the ægis of the well-known surgeon Henry B. Sands. In 1874, he became junior associate in private practice of Dr. George A. Peters. This relationship continued until the retirement of Peters ten years later.

McBurney's first important hospital appointment was that of visiting surgeon at St. Luke's in 1875. This he retained until 1888 when he resigned to become visiting surgeon at Roosevelt Hospital. In the meantime (1882–88) he had served in the same capacity at Bellevue Hospital. He was made instructor in operative surgery at the College of Physicians and Surgeons in 1880, promoted to professor of surgery in 1889, and in 1892 became professor of clinical surgery. In 1907 he resigned and was made professor emeritus.

Late in the eighties of the nineteenth century antiseptic surgery had developed to such an extent that it became practicable to operate with safety in the abdominal cavity. McBurney had the merit of being one of a small group who led in both the diagnosis and the treatment of appendicitis. In the *New York Medical Journal* for Dec. 21, 1889, he published a paper entitled "Experience with Operative Interference in Cases of Disease of the Vermiform Appendix," in which he first described his diagnostic tender pressure point known thereafter throughout the world as "McBurney's point." His other gift to surgery, "McBurney's incision," a later development (1894), was characterized by his mode of exposing the appendix without cross section of the fibers of the abdominal muscles. In 1892, with money donated to Roosevelt Hospital by William J. Syms, McBurney planned and carried out the construction of an elaborate private operating pavilion which became one of the novel medical institutions of the city. He contributed "Surgical Treatment of Appendicitis" to F. S. Dennis' *System of Surgery* (vol. IV, 1896), and for *The International Text-book of Surgery* (2 vols., 1899), edited by J. C. Warren and A. P. Gould, he wrote "Technic of Aseptic Surgery" and "Surgery of the Vermiform Appendix." For about ten years after 1897 he was occupied with his extensive private practice and his work at Roosevelt, but in 1907 his health failed and he retired to his country seat at Stockbridge, Mass., where for several years he was an invalid. In June 1913 his wife died, and five months later his death occurred at the home of a sister in Brookline, Mass. According to his friends, McBurney was not of a scientific bent of mind; he was not classed as a brilliant operator, and he wrote little; yet he was regarded as one of the world's great surgeons. His interests outside his profession were limited to sports—shooting, fishing, and golf, of which he was an early devotee. He was married on Oct. 8, 1874, to Margaret Willoughby Weston. Two sons and a daughter survived him.

[*The Thirteenth Secretary's Report of the Class of 1866 of Harvard College* (1916); *The College of Physicians and Surgeons, a Hist.* (n.d.) ed. by John Shrady; H. A. Kelly and W. L. Burrage, *Am. Medic. Biogs.* (1920); *An Account of Bellevue Hosp. with a Cat. of the Medic. and Surgic. Staff, 1736–1894* (1893), ed. by R. J. Carlisle; *Medic. Jour. and Record*, Feb. 20, 1924; *Surgery, Gynecol. and Obstetrics*, Mar. 1923; *N. Y. Medic. Jour.*, Nov. 15, 1913; *Medic. Record*, Nov. 15, 1913; *Jour. Am. Medic. Asso.*, Nov. 15, 1913; *Boston Medic. and Surgic. Jour.*, Nov. 20, 1913; *Lancet*, Nov. 22, 1913; *N. Y. Times*, Nov. 8, 1913.] E. P.

McBURNEY, ROBERT ROSS (Mar. 31, 1837–Dec. 27, 1898), Young Men's Christian Association secretary, was born of Scotch-Irish parentage at Castle-Blayney, Ulster, Ireland. His father, a prominent anti-Catholic leader, was a physician and surgeon: his mother, *née* Ross, was an ardent Methodist and the first of Dr. McBurney's three wives. She died when Robert was six years old. Early religious training gave him a relish for church singing and hymnody and a zest for Christian service. He came to America in his eighteenth year (1854), a poor immigrant, and found employment as a clerk in a hat-establishment, which position he held until the business failed at the beginning of the Civil War.

McBurney early interested himself in religious work for young men and boys in New York City, becoming, in 1856, a leader of noon prayer-meetings at the North Dutch Church on Fulton Street. In 1852 an organization similar to the Young Men's Christian Association founded in London by George Williams in 1844 was organized in New York City, and after it had passed through a decade of volunteer leadership, McBurney was elected in 1862 as its employed officer at a salary of five dollars a week. He had a genius for friendship as well as sagacity and high intelligence, and succeeded in enlisting many prominent New Yorkers in the work of the Association. Leaving it for a brief period in business in 1864, he was called back in April of the following year.

After attending his first International Convention in Philadelphia, in 1865, McBurney realized the extent of the work of the Young Men's Christian Association throughout the United States and Europe, and the scope and variety of its activities. A survey was made of the needs of young men in New York and, as a result, a building was erected at a cost of $487,000, with adequate equipment for games, gymnasium, library, and meeting rooms, and with a central control which made the secretaryship an important office. The erection of this building, with its unified activities, marked an epoch in Young Men's Christian Association history. By the year 1868 there were five hundred Associations in the United States, all looking increasingly for leadership to the New York branch. Here for twenty-five years McBurney's study, "The Tower Room," heard every tale of human joy and tragedy, and in it he laid the plans which have been creative in the life of the Association.

From 1887 to 1898 McBurney was metropolitan secretary in New York City. Owing to his energy the railroad branch was established in 1887; the Bowery building purchased, athletic grounds and a boat house leased, and the Harlem building completed in 1888; the French branch opened, and student work organized in 1889; the Mott Haven railroad rooms and the Washington Heights branch opened in 1891; the Madison Avenue railroad building in 1893; the Lexington Avenue student building in 1894; the West Side building in 1896; and the East Side building partially erected in 1896.

The membership had grown in thirty-six years from 151 to 8,328, with a daily attendance of 5,670.

McBurney's outstanding contributions to the Association movement were the conviction that the work should be carried forward by young men for young men; the creation of a varied program, including games, gymnasium, libraries, education, trade classes, as well as evangelism; the development of specialized foreign work; the organization of the International Convention; the development of national supervisory agencies of help and counsel; training for leadership; the creation of the physical directorship; assistance in the founding of the training school for Young Men's Christian Association workers at Springfield, Mass., but greatest of all, the creation and development of the general secretaryship. The formative influence exercised by him upon the subsequent development of the Association in North America and throughout the world was profound, exceeding that of any other man. He was never married, and died at Clifton Springs, N. Y.

[L. L. Doggett, *Life of Robert R. McBurney* (1925) and *Hist. of the Young Men's Christian Assos.* (cop. 1922); R. C. Morse, *Hist. of the North Am. Young Men's Christian Assos.* (cop. 1913), and *My Life with Young Men* (1918); *Robert R. McBurney: A Memorial* (cop. 1899), ed. by R. C. Morse; *N. Y. Times*, Dec. 28, 1898.]
G. S.

McCABE, CHARLES CARDWELL (Oct. 11, 1836–Dec. 19, 1906), Methodist Episcopal bishop, popularly known as Chaplain McCabe because of his Civil War services, was born in Athens, Ohio, the son of Robert McCabe, whose grandfather, Owen, came to Pennsylvania from County Tyrone, Ireland, and whose father, Robert, in 1813 migrated to Ohio. Charles's mother, Sarah, daughter of Cuthbert Cardwell Robinson, was brought by her parents to the United States in 1822 from Kildwick, Yorkshire, England. She was a woman of literary tastes and an occasional contributor to the *Ladies' Repository*. From her Charles got his good looks and poetical imagination; from his father's family he derived his singing ability and persuasive eloquence. Both parents were devout Methodists. When he was about fifteen the family moved to Chillicothe, Ohio and then to Burlington, Iowa. For a short time he took charge of a farm in Mount Pleasant, belonging to his father, and then became clerk in a store at Cedar Rapids. He early displayed the characteristics which later gave him popularity and power, personal magnetism, bold initiative, glowing optimism, unfailing good humor, capacity for leadership, ability as a speaker, and a rich barytone voice which he could use in song with great effect. Since he was also evangelically religious, people were sure he was called to the ministry, and with a view to fitting himself for this work, in 1854 he entered the preparatory department of Ohio Wesleyan University. He never graduated, however, though later the college made him an alumnus of the class of 1860. He had an acquisitive mind and read widely, but he was not a student; he was a person of feeling and action rather than of thought; his natural gifts determined his career. For days he would be away from college assisting at revival meetings. His health soon broke down and his schooling ceased. For two years he was principal of the high school in Ironton, Ohio. Here, July 6, 1860, he married Rebecca Peters. In 1860 he joined the Ohio Conference of the Methodist Church.

While at his first appointment, Putnam, now a part of Zanesville, Ohio, he became chaplain of the 122nd Regiment of Ohio Volunteers, and that he might perform all the functions of a clergyman, he was ordained elder, Sept. 7, 1862. His work in connection with the war made him nationally known. On June 16, 1863, while remaining behind at Winchester to care for the wounded on the field, he was taken prisoner. For four months his optimism and song made him the life of Libby Prison. His experiences there he afterward told over and over again throughout the country in his famous lecture, "The Bright Side of Life in Libby Prison." He was broken by fever when freed by exchange of prisoners, but upon his recovery entered the service of the Christian Commission for which by his eloquence and song he raised large sums of money. His singing did much to popularize the "Battle Hymn of the Republic."

So great was his ability to persuade people to give that it destined him to be a money-raiser and promoter for much of the remainder of his life. After the war he was pastor at Portsmouth, Ohio, and agent for Ohio Wesleyan University, for which he secured $87,000. For sixteen years (1868–84) he was assistant corresponding secretary of the Board of Church Extension, and was largely responsible for its remarkable success. In this capacity he wrote to Robert Ingersoll his famous reply to the latter's assertion that churches were dying out all over the land: "We are building more than one Methodist church for every day in the year and propose to make it two a day!" In 1884 the General Conference elected him corresponding secretary of the Missionary Society. He at once sounded the slogan, "A Million for Missions." The goal was reached, and a new one set. Perhaps the most popular of American Methodists, in 1896 he was elected bishop. In December 1902, he became chancellor of the American University, Washington, D. C. Strenuously active almost to the close of his career, he died in New York of cerebral hemorrhage soon after completing his seventieth year, and was buried in Rose Hill Cemetery, near Chicago.

[F. M. Bristol, *The Life of Chaplain McCabe* (1908); *Christian Advocate* (N. Y.), Dec. 27, 1906; *Zion's Herald*, Dec. 26, 1906; *Phila. Inquirer*, Dec. 20, 1906; Julia Ward Howe, *Reminiscences* (1899); Florence H. Hall, *The Story of the Battle Hymn of the Republic* (1916).] H. E. S.

McCABE, JOHN COLLINS (Nov. 12, 1810–Feb. 26, 1875), Episcopal clergyman and antiquarian, was born in Richmond, Va., of substantial Scottish and Irish descent, son of William and Jane (Collins) McCabe, and grandson of James McCabe who distinguished himself under Montgomery at the storming of Quebec. Denied the opportunity of much formal schooling, he largely educated himself, developing his youthful talent for speaking by active attendance upon a Richmond debating society and writing copiously for the newspapers and local magazines. He originally intended to prepare for the bar and read law for about a year, but the press of domestic circumstances altering his plans he entered the Farmer's Bank of Richmond, where he remained for a number of years. On Oct. 28, 1848, he was ordained to the priesthood of the Episcopal church by Bishop William Meade, having taken deacon's orders two years earlier. From his first parish, Isle of Wight County, where he was rector of the old brick church near Smithfield, he was called to historic St. John's in Hampton. During his pastorate here he served as chairman of the state yellow-fever committee when the plague ravaged Norfolk and its environs. From 1856 to 1859 he was rector of the Church of the Ascension in Baltimore, and then of St. Anne's Parish, Anne Arundel County, Md., until 1861, when he gave up his charge, "ran the blockade," and joined the Confederate army as chaplain of the 32nd Virginia Regiment. In 1862 he was transferred from field service to become chaplain-general to the Confederate military prisons of Libby and Castle Thunder in Richmond, remaining in this office until the close of the war and winning the affection of the Federal prisoners by his many kindnesses to them. Afterward he had charges at Bladensburg, Md., and Middletown, Del., before settling in Chambersburg, Pa., where he died.

During his lifetime McCabe enjoyed considerable local reputation as a man of letters, and is said to have commanded a high price for his writings, although his only publication in book form was the juvenile collection of periodical pieces and verses called *Scraps* (1835). He was a frequent contributor to the *Southern Literary Messenger* while Poe and, later, John R. Thompson were its editors. Poe not only gave him literary advice and encouragement, but was himself apparently attracted by McCabe's individuality, genial manners, and lofty character, for their professional relations rapidly developed into intimacy. He also lectured on literary or historical subjects, delivered numerous memorial addresses, wrote for the newspapers and the church journals, and composed occasional lyrics, several of which possess real merit; but the bulk of this work was ephemeral and perhaps his chief service to posterity grew out of his antiquarian interests, opportunity for the indulgence of which was supplied by his pastorates in tidewater Virginia. A recognized authority on the colonial beginnings and subsequent growth of the church in his native state, he made abstracts from the parish registers for an "Early History of the Church in Virginia" and published in the *Church Review* sketches of many of the parishes embodying the results of his scholarly genealogical and historical investigations, ultimately transferring his manuscript to Bishop Meade for use in writing the latter's *Old Churches, Ministers and Families of Virginia* (2 vols., 1857). McCabe was twice married: first, to Emily Hardaway and, second, Aug. 7, 1838, to Eliza Sophia Gordon Taylor, widow of John Rutledge Smith of South Carolina. William Gordon McCabe [*q.v.*] was a son of the second marriage.

[Lyon G. Tyler, *Men of Mark in Va.* (1907), III, 233–34; Armistead C. Gordon, *Memories and Memorials of Wm. Gordon McCabe* (1925), I, 14–27, and *passim*; *Public Opinion* (Chambersburg, Pa.), Mar. 2, 1875.] A. C. G., Jr.

McCABE, WILLIAM GORDON (Aug. 4, 1841–June 1, 1920), schoolmaster and author, was born in Richmond, Va., of distinguished stock, son of the Rev. John Collins McCabe [*q.v.*] and Eliza Sophia Gordon Taylor. After graduating (1858) with highest honors from Hampton Academy, he was for a time tutor in the Selden family of "Westover" before entering the University of Virginia in the autumn of 1860. Here his time was short, for on the day that Virginia seceded he left the University for Harpers Ferry with a student company, and until Johnston's surrender, after Appomattox, remained a soldier of the Confederacy, rising, throughout a succession of major campaigns, from private to captain of artillery, and by his courage, gallantry, and determination winning the admiring affection of his men and of his battalion commander Pegram. In October 1865 he opened the University School at Petersburg, Va., and continued it there for thirty years before removing it to Richmond. From its founding it maintained a reputation for the highest standards of scholarship; and there were few who ever left its doors without having gained from association with the bright-eyed, fiery-souled little headmaster a love of truth and a noble code of living. An inspiring leader and a gifted administrator, McCabe was also known, partly through the textbooks which he edited, as a brilliant Latinist. When in 1901 he closed the school and retired, it was with a fame as a teacher second to none in America; he had previously declined professorships in several leading colleges or universities, and when the movement for an executive head for the University of Virginia was inaugurated, which was not put into effect until several years later, a majority of the Board of Visitors favored his election as its first president. During his school period he continued the writing career which he had begun while in his teens with contributions to the *Southern Literary Messenger,* and achieved enviable distinction as editor and author. His poems, mostly written in war time, have found a place in various anthologies; the foremost English and American magazines published his essays on literary and military topics; he edited sundry works; he composed historical and biographical papers, including many for the publications of the Virginia Historical Society, of which he was long president; and he was an eloquent and charming orator, his frequent occasional addresses—many of them championing the cause of his beloved Confederacy—compounding the same wit and solid information and sureness of touch that lent grace and point to his writings. Over and above the offices which he held, however, above his honorary degrees, his illustrious friendships, and above his scholastic achievements, it was the personal human side of McCabe "that was his most meaning and attractive possession" (A. C. Gordon, *Virginian Portraits,* 1924, p. 121). He had a genius for friendship, and wherever he went, into whatever company, he was a welcome guest. His extensive travels and wide experience, his knowledge of what was best in books and in people, his gift as a story-teller, combined with his courtesy, sincerity, and generous sympathy, his warm heart and intellectual independence, to make him a typical example of the cultured old-school Virginian. He married, Apr. 12, 1867, Jane Pleasants Harrison Osborne; she died in 1912, and he married, second, Mar. 16, 1915, the daughter of his boyhood schoolmaster, Gillie Armistead Cary.

[Armistead C. Gordon, *Memories and Memorials of Wm. Gordon McCabe* (2 vols., 1925); L. G. Tyler, ed., *Men of Mark in Va.* (1909), vol. III; P. A. Bruce, *Hist. of the Univ. of Va.* (5 vols., 1920–22); obituary notices in the Richmond, Va., newspapers.] A. C. G., Jr.

McCAFFREY, JOHN (Sept. 6, 1806–Sept. 26, 1881), Catholic educator and theologian, was born at Emmitsburg, Md., and rarely wandered from there during a long lifetime. At the age of thirteen, he entered the preparatory department of Mount St. Mary's College at Emmitsburg and progressed through the college and seminary. A deacon in 1831, he refused in a spirit of humility to undertake the duties of priesthood until 1838 when he was ordained by Archbishop Eccleston. As a teacher in the preparatory school, as a prefect of discipline, as professor of moral theology in the seminary, as vice-president, as pastor of the neighboring church, as rector from March 1838 until his resignation in August 1872, as professor of Latin literature, and as a member of the governing council until his death, McCaffrey served the Mount with the unswerving loyalty of one whose heart and soul were entwined with the fortunes of the institution. At that time Mount St. Mary's was one of the two leading Catholic seminaries, and a nursery of innumerable priests and no small proportion of the hierarchy. Upon all these ecclesiastics, McCaffrey left a definite impression. He was a sound theologian, who spoke with an old-fashioned exactness of rhetoric save when in ordinary conversation he fell with a degree of pride into the Maryland vernacular. He was also a classical enthusiast, and an encyclopedic source of information concerning men and events in the history of the Church in America. A courtly figure, deeply religious but somewhat Puritanical, he was accorded the right to rule, and rule he did with a stern and unyielding discipline. He might well maintain that "I am the college" for he governed quite free from the nominal responsibility to the various archbishops of Baltimore.

McCaffrey had no episcopal ambitions, though few vacant sees were filled from 1840 to 1860 for which his name was not on the list of nominees. He refused actual appointments to the bishoprics of Savannah and Charleston, and probably to Natchez, as he declared: "Here I am fully as useful as if I held a crozier." As early as 1853 he had been honored by the hierarchy when his predecessor in the rectorship, Archbishop Purcell, laid the corner-stone of McCaffrey Hall. In 1860 he attracted attention when he petitioned the Maryland legislature to forbid the sale of liquor to minors. A Southerner and state-rights advocate, he was a devotee of Calhoun and an open sympathizer with the South during the war as were several members of the faculty and a majority of the students to the annoyance of such outstanding alumni as the unionist bishops Hughes, Purcell, and McCloskey. He was a link between John Carroll and later times, but his contribution was as intangible as that of the usual great teacher, for aside from an occasional sermon or lecture he published little—a eulogy of Charles Carroll, an oration in commemoration of the landing of the "Pilgrims of Maryland," a discourse on Bishop Bruté, a sketch of Bishop Dubois, an essay on classical education, and *A Catechism of Christian Doctrine* (1865) which was widely used in elementary classes in Christian doctrine. His merits were extolled by Bishop F. S. Chatard at the obsequies over which Archbishops Gibbons and Corrigan presided as his remains were interred in the college cemetery near those of his priest-brother, Thomas McCaffrey.

[E. F. X. McSweeny, *The Story of the Mountain* (2 vols., 1911); *Sadliers' Cath. Directory* (1882), p. 63; sketch by Bishop Richard Gilmour in *Cath. Universe* (Cleveland), Oct. 6, 1881; obituaries in the *Sun* (Baltimore), Sept. 27, 30, and *N. Y. Freeman's Jour. and Cath. Reg.*, Oct. 8, 1881.] R. J. P.

McCAINE, ALEXANDER (*c.* 1768–June 1, 1856), clergyman, controversialist, leader in founding the Methodist Protestant Church, was a native of Ireland. When about twenty years of age he came to the United States, landing at Charleston, S. C. Soon, under the preaching of a Methodist missionary, he professed conversion and determined to enter the Methodist ministry. Bishop Asbury became acquainted with him and was favorably impressed with his training and gifts. He was admitted on trial to the Methodist Conference, meeting at Charleston in 1797, and two years later was received into full membership. His early preaching circuits were in the Carolinas and Virginia. In 1806 he withdrew from the active ministry to educate his children. On the death of his wife in 1815, at Bishop Asbury's solicitation, he reëntered the active ministry, but again withdrew in 1821 and became the head of a flourishing boys' school in Baltimore. Though not a member of the General Conference of 1820, he was elected secretary of that body, a recognition of his ability and training.

At this period an attempt was being made on the part of some to introduce into the government of the Methodist Episcopal Church a larger degree of democracy, by securing lay representation in the Conferences and the election, rather than the appointment, of presiding elders. Those advocating these changes were called "Reformers" and they were particularly active in the vicinity of Baltimore, Nicholas Snethen and Alexander McCaine being the two most prominent leaders. McCaine offered strong arguments in favor of reform, ably setting forth his views in *The History and Mystery of Methodist Episcopacy* (1827); *A Defence of the Truth* (1829); and *Letters on the Organization and Early History of the Methodist Episcopal Church* (1850), published originally in the Boston *Olive Branch.* The reformers established a paper called *Mutual Rights* (1824), to which McCaine frequently contributed. His contention was that the Methodist Episcopal organization never had the sanction of John Wesley, and that episcopacy had been "foisted upon the Methodist societies." When the General Conference of 1828 refused to pass reform legislation, numerous churches split over the issue and in 1830 a convention of reformers was held in Baltimore and there organized the Methodist Protestant Church, which in four years had a membership of 26,387. In this new branch of Methodism McCaine was active as a writer and critic until the end of his life. During his latter years he lived with his children in South Carolina and Georgia, his eldest son being a physician at Lott's, S. C. He died at the home of his daughter, Mrs. James M. Brett, in Augusta, Ga.

Soon after the formation of the Methodist Protestant Church slavery became an issue of prime importance. Its General Conference in 1842 refused to legislate on the subject and recommended that each Conference make its own regulations. Numerous objections were raised to this proposal and some withdrew from the Church, but McCaine, among others, became an active advocate of slavery and wrote a pamphlet in its defense, entitled, *Slavery Defended from the Scripture Against the Attacks of the Abolitionists* (1842). In 1843–44 he carried on a controversy on the same subject in the *Western Recorder.* He was a striking figure, with majestic head and clearly cut features. As a preacher he was endowed with great native eloquence. He despised shams, was impetuous in his defense of what he thought was the truth, and was bold to bluntness in dealing with personalities, a characteristic which often laid him open to criticism.

[E. J. Drinkhouse, *Hist. of Meth. Reform and Meth. Protestant Church* (1899); T. H. Colhouer, *Sketches of the Founders of the Methodist Protestant Church* (1880); A. H. Bassett, *A Concise Hist. of the Meth. Protestant Church from its Origin, with Biographical Sketches* (1877); *The Meth. Mag. and Quart. Rev.*, Jan., Apr., July 1830; *Daily Constitutionalist* (Augusta, Ga.), June 3, 1856.] W. W. S.

McCALEB, THEODORE HOWARD (Feb. 10, 1810–Apr. 29, 1864), jurist and educator, third son of David and Matilda (Farrar) Mc-

Caleb, was born in Pendleton District, S. C. His great-grandfather, William McCaleb (or McKillip, as the name was originally spelled), after taking part in the battle of Culloden, 1746, in behalf of "Bonnie Prince Charlie," fled to Ireland for refuge and in 1747 emigrated to South Carolina. His grandfather, William McCaleb, served as captain in the American Revolutionary army, was a member of the South Carolina convention that ratified the federal constitution, and in 1797 moved to the Spanish province of West Florida and settled in the Natchez district. His father, David McCaleb, was high sheriff of Pendleton District, S. C., and moved to Mississippi Territory in 1802. Theodore McCaleb was educated by private tutors at "Cold Springs Plantation," Claiborne County, Miss., and at Phillips Exeter Academy and Yale College. He is said to have withdrawn from Yale before completing his work there and to have begun to study for the ministry. But after pursuing theological studies for a year, he decided to become a lawyer and began to study law in 1830 in the office of Rufus Choate in Salem, Mass. In 1832 he moved to New Orleans and succeeded to the large law practice which his older brother, Thomas, who died in that year, had built up during the fourteen years he had resided there. Among his clients was the eccentric John McDonough of New Orleans.

In 1841, when he was only thirty-one years old, he was appointed judge of the United States District of Louisiana by President Tyler. In 1846 Congress passed an act dividing Louisiana into two districts and making his court the one for eastern Louisiana, presumably to get rid of him because of his stanch Whig politics; but if that was the case, President Polk rose above partisanship and appointed him to succeed himself. He remained in this office until January 1861, when, notwithstanding his Union sentiments, he decided to throw in his lot with the Confederacy on the secession of Louisiana from the Union. Meanwhile he had launched upon an academic career. He was one of the original members of the law-school faculty of the University of Louisiana, now Tulane University, and served as professor of admiralty and international law from 1847 to 1864. He also served as president of the collegiate faculty from 1850 to 1862. He was a distinguished linguist and even understood several Indian dialects. At one time he is said to have welcomed the Choctaw chief, Billy Bowlegs, to New Orleans in behalf of the mayor of that city in the chief's own language. He was famed for his oratory, his most noted addresses being those delivered on the occasions of the dedication of the Lyceum at New Orleans, the death of his friend, Henry Clay, the unveiling of the Clay monument in Canal Street in New Orleans, and the death of S. S. Prentiss. He was a most liberal entertainer and was host to many foreigners of distinction, including Thackeray, Macready, Châteaubriand, and De Tocqueville. He was married to Agnes Bullitt, daughter of William and Octavia (Pannell) Bullitt of New Orleans, in 1832. They had five daughters and one son. He died and was buried at "Hermitage Plantation," Mississippi, which had been bequeathed to him by his uncle, Jonathan McCaleb.

[This sketch is based upon brief biographical sketches in Thos. M'Caleb, *The La. Book* (1894); *Biog. and Hist. Memoirs of La.* (1892), vol. II; *La. Sunday Rev.* (New Orleans), Dec. 23, 1894; J. S. Whitaker, *Sketches of Life and Character in La., . . . Principally from the Bench and Bar* (1847); and upon data supplied by the authorities of Phillips Exeter Academy, Yale Univ., and Tulane Univ., and by Dr. James F. McCaleb of "Byrnmore Plantation," Carlisle, Miss., who has in his possession numerous documents pertaining to the McCaleb family.] E. M. V.

McCALL, EDWARD RUTLEDGE (Aug. 6, 1790–July 31, 1853), naval officer, was born at Beaufort, S. C., the son of Hext and Elizabeth (Pickering) McCall. On losing his father at an early age, he was placed under the care of a guardian, who, when the boy showed a preference for a seafaring life, directed his studies in preparation for that calling. Appointed a midshipman on Jan. 1, 1808, McCall, after a period of duty at the Charleston naval station, was ordered to the *Hornet,* on which vessel he in 1811 became acting master. Early in that year he joined the *Enterprise,* and at the outbreak of the War of 1812 was serving on her as acting lieutenant. On her successful engagement with the *Boxer,* off the coast of Maine on Sept. 5, 1813, he was next in rank under Lieut. William Burrows [*q.v.*], her commander, and when early in the action Burrows fell mortally wounded, McCall took command and brought the prize into Portland. Recognition of McCall's share in the victory came from the residents of Charleston, S. C., who gave him a sword, and from the South Carolina legislature which appropriated money for the purchase of one. On Jan. 6, 1814, Congress expressed its appreciation of his gallantry by voting him a gold medal. In the previous year the Senate had confirmed his appointment to a lieutenancy.

After serving on the *Ontario,* McCall in the years 1815–17 made a cruise on the *Java* of the Mediterranean Squadron. On his return home he did duty at navy yards and shore stations at Charleston, Baltimore, Philadelphia, and elsewhere, and once, following his promotion as a master-commandant in 1825, he went to sea. This was in 1830–31 as commander of the *Peacock* of the West India Squadron. In March 1835 he was commissioned captain and thereafter he was on waiting orders until his death, which occurred at his residence in Bordentown. N. J. He had married Harriett McKnights of that city.

[Record of Officers, Bureau of Navigation, 1815–53; T. Wyatt, *Memoirs of the Generals, Commodores, and Other Commanders Who Distinguished Themselves in the Am. Army and Navy during the Wars of the Revolution and 1812* (1848), pp. 257–60. Theodore Roosevelt, *The Naval War of 1812* (1882); *Charleston* (S. C.) *Courier*, Aug. 10, 1853; information from Mr. D. E. Huger Smith, Charleston, S. C.] C. O. P.

McCALL, JOHN AUGUSTINE (Mar. 2, 1849–Feb. 18, 1906), insurance official, was born at Albany, N. Y., a son of John A. and Katherine (MacCormack) McCall. His parents were of Irish descent. Compelled in early life to support himself, he found work with an Albany agency of the Connecticut Mutual Life Company and at twenty-one obtained a clerkship in the New York state department of insurance, where he won rapid advancement, becoming in 1876 deputy superintendent and examiner of fire, life, and accident companies doing business in the state. In that capacity he attracted attention by the energy and thoroughness with which he exposed the illegal practices of insurance officials. Insurance men of good standing and the business community generally were so favorably impressed by young McCall's activities and methods that in 1883 his appointment as superintendent was urged upon Gov. Grover Cleveland by men of both political parties. When the nomination was made and unanimously confirmed, Cleveland was heartily commended by the press. By this time McCall's knowledge of the insurance field and of insurance problems had been widely advertised. It was not to be expected that the state could long retain his services. Among the life insurance companies of New York City the Equitable was the first to offer him an attractive bid. It created a comptrollership for him and in 1885 he resigned his state office and went to the metropolis to accept double the salary that the state had paid him. Seven years' service as comptroller of the Equitable seems to have enhanced his reputation and popularity among insurance men. He was described at that time as a man of magnetic, vigorous personality, affable and kindly in all the relations of life.

In 1892 the New York Life Insurance Company, ranking in prestige with the Equitable and the Mutual Life, was falling behind its rivals in the race for business as a result of internal dissensions. New blood was needed and the trustees' choice of an executive to succeed William H. Beers was McCall. The business record of the New York Life under McCall's administration seemed indeed to justify the faith of the trustees in calling him to the presidency. The company's business increased amazingly within a few years. The whole organization developed new life. In the twelve years ending in 1904 the income from all sources more than tripled, while the company's investments at the close of that period (nearing $325,000,000) were more than one hundred and thirty per cent. greater than at the beginning. This prosperity was in great part due to McCall's initiative and energy. But in spite of this brilliant showing, the year 1905 opened ominously. The disclosure of serious disagreements among the Equitable's officers was followed by rumors of unsound conditions in the "Big Three" companies and a public demand for an investigation, which was met by the appointment of the so-called Armstrong committee of the New York legislature and the retention of Charles Evans Hughes as chief counsel. Called as witnesses before this committee McCall himself and Vice-President George W. Perkins testified as to the use of the company's funds in political campaigns and in lobbying. When the New York Life's trustees declined to take the responsibility for these irregularities, McCall resigned the presidency and voluntarily obligated himself to make good $235,000 that had been advanced to Andrew Hamilton of Albany. To do this he had to transfer to the company his life insurance and a costly residence at Elberon, N. J. Within a few months he died of cancer of the liver. He was survived by his wife, Mary (Horan) McCall, whom he had married at Albany in 1870, and by two daughters and five sons.

[Obituaries in the New York newspapers of Feb. 19, 1906; M. C. Harrison, *N. Y. State's Prominent and Progressive Men*, vol. I (1900); *Testimony taken before the Joint Committee of the Senate and Assembly . . . of N. Y., to Investigate . . . Life Insurance Companies* (1906), vols. II and III; B. J. Hendrick, *The Story of Life Insurance* (1907); J. M. Hudnut, *Hist. of the N. Y. Life Insurance Company, 1895–1905* (1906); L. F. Abbott, *The Story of Nylic* (1930), pp. 149–51, 178–88; H. S. Beardsley, "The Despotism of Combined Millions," the *Era Mag.*, Nov. 1904, Oct. 1905.] W. B. S.

McCALL, SAMUEL WALKER (Feb. 28, 1851–Nov. 4, 1923), congressman and governor of Massachusetts, was born in East Providence, Pa., the sixth of the eleven children of Henry and Mary Ann (Elliott) McCall. Two years after he was born, his parents removed to Mount Carroll in northern Illinois. His father was able to take with him eight or nine thousand dollars in gold, which he invested in land and in the manufacture of plows and farming tools. When the panic of 1857 brought financial reverses, the family moved to a farm near the town and again prospered. From the public schools the boy went to Mount Carroll Seminary, then in 1867 to New Hampton Literary and Biblical Institution at New Hampton, N. H., and three years later to Dartmouth College, where he graduated in the class of 1874 with high rank. He began the study of law in Nashua, N. H., went a year later to Worcester, Mass., where he was admitted to practice in 1875, and then opened an office in Boston. At Lyndon, Vt., May 23, 1881, he married Ella Esther Thompson, who had been a fellow student at New Hampton and was the daughter of Sumner Shaw Thompson, a railroad builder and manager. The newly married couple made their home in Winchester, a suburb of Boston, where they reared their five children. In 1887 his district elected him to the General Court. In his first session he introduced the act that practically ended imprisonment for debt in Massachusetts by abolishing the system of fees and giving jurisdiction to an established court in poor debtor cases. In 1888 he bought an interest in the *Boston Daily Advertiser* and became its editor-in-chief for two years. Reëlected to the state legislature that year he became chairman of the judiciary committee and took a leading part in the effort of the legislature to force the supreme court to give its opinion of certain questions on laws relating to public schools. He served two years as a ballot law commissioner and returned to the House for the session of 1892, where he obtained the passage of an act designed to regulate the use of money at elections.

In the autumn of 1892 he was elected to Congress, where his course so commended him to his constituents that he was easily reëlected nine times, thus rounding out an even twenty years of congressional service. Fortunately for him, he represented a district that thought more of independence of judgment than of party regularity, for, although in general loyal to the broad principles of the Republican party, he did not hesitate to take a bold stand in opposition to such policies as his judgment could not approve. He supported the measures in favor of the gold standard and advocated civil-service reform, but he disapproved of the annexation of the Philippines, urged moderation in fixing tariff rates, and opposed rigid control of the railroads, fearing that such a measure as the Hepburn Act concentrated too much power in the federal government and opened the way to public ownership. He did not speak often, but when he did take the floor he commanded the attention and respect of the House by the force of his argument and the scholarly nature of its presentation. Both in and out of the House his discussion of such constitutional questions as arose was masterly. A firm believer in the established order and a convinced individualist, he opposed any development that he thought paternalistic. He regretted the aggrandizement of the central government at the expense of state and local prerogatives and, in the height of Roosevelt's popularity, he pointed out the dangers of executive encroachment. In 1902 he took the occasion of the centennial celebration at Dartmouth to discuss Daniel Webster's theories on the struggle of liberty against executive power (*Daniel Webster,* 1902). His retirement from the House, although his district would have been glad to have him stay indefinitely, may have been due to a well-warranted ambition to go to the Senate, and presumably the same consideration played some part in his declining to become president of Dartmouth College. He was a candidate for the Senate in the election of 1913, and he had strong support but in the end failed of a majority. Esteem for him, however, brought him back to the political arena the following year, as the nominee for governor. He could not, on the first trial, defeat the popular Democratic incumbent but succeeded in the following year and served as chief executive from 1916 to 1918 inclusive. As Republican governor in the war period he supported Wilson, and he advocated the ratification of the Versailles Treaty. The exceptional feature of his administration was the constitutional convention he led in obtaining, the first in more than sixty years. His public service ended with the dedication of the Lincoln Memorial at Washington in 1922, for which he was largely responsible and to which he had given much care as a member of the commission that had it in charge.

Throughout his busy life he found time for study and writing. His *Thaddeus Stevens* (1898) and *The Life of Thomas Brackett Reed* (1914), both of which appeared in the American Statesmen Series, are good examples of his readable style. Lectures at Columbia and at Yale were printed as *The Business of Congress* (1911) and *The Liberty of Citizenship* (1915). Various addresses on other than official topics have been published, and in the year before his death appeared his final volume, *The Patriotism of the American Jew.*

[L. B. Evans, *Samuel W. McCall* (1916); *Proc. Mass. Hist. Soc.*, vol. LVII (1924); C. H. Thompson, *A Geneal. of Descendants of John Thomson* (1890); *Boston Transcript,* Nov. 5, 1923; *New York Times,* Nov. 5, 6, 7, Dec. 3, 1923.] R.L.

McCALLA, BOWMAN HENDRY (June 19, 1844–May 6, 1910), naval officer, was descended from John M'Calla who emigrated from Scotland in 1747, having received from the Crown a grant of land in Northumberland County, Pa.; his grandfather, Auley M'Calla, commanded a regiment of New Jersey militia in the Revolution. Bowman was born in Camden, N. J., the son of Auley and Mary Duffield (Hendry) McCalla. His parents died when he was a boy, and he was cared for by older sisters. At thirteen he was placed in Nazareth Hall, the Moravian boarding school at Nazareth, Pa. On the breaking out of the Civil War he wanted to join the army, but being thwarted in this desire because of his youth, he turned his attention to the navy and entered the Naval Academy on Nov. 30, 1861. Three years later he was graduated, fourth in a class of thirty-four. His first assignment was to the steam sloop *Susquehanna* of the Brazil Squadron. Later orders sent him to various ships of the South Atlantic, South Pacific, and European Squadrons, and then to shore duty at the Naval Academy. Meanwhile he had been commissioned lieutenant, Mar. 12, 1868, and lieutenant commander, Mar. 26, 1869. On Mar. 3, 1875, he was married to Elizabeth Hazard Sargent, daughter of Gen. Horace Binney Sargent of Boston. McCalla was made commander on Nov. 3, 1884. His first command was the *Enterprise* on the European Station (1887–90). He was known for his "advanced ideas" on naval administration, but in sharp contrast with his later success he seems at this time not to have been happy in carrying out his policies. At the end of the cruise several charges were brought against him. That of striking with the back of his sword an unruly sailor resulted in his being tried by court martial and convicted. The sentence was suspension for three years and loss of numbers. The next year (1891), however, the Secretary of the Navy returned him to duty; and a few years later, when he had been advanced seven numbers for heroic and distinguished services during the Spanish-American War, he fully recovered what he had lost.

His conspicuous service in the navy began with the Spanish-American War. For nearly a year he had been commanding the cruiser *Marblehead.* In this vessel he directed the gallant affair of cutting the cables off Cienfuegos, Cuba. Later he had charge of landing the first battalion of marines at Guantanamo, and led the forces that drove back the Spaniards. Continuing in command, he superintended the landing of great quantities of supplies, made an enviable reputation for sanitation, and also won the confidence of the Cubans. On Aug. 10, 1898, he was promoted to the rank of captain. In the Philippine insurrection he took part in the restoration of order. He received the surrender of the provinces of Cagayan and Isabela, northern Luzon (December 1899), and turned them over to the army. He was then commanding officer of the *Newark,* and as such did important work the following year in China. When the American and other legations in Peking reported that they were threatened by the Boxers, McCalla in Tientsin took the initiative in urging the officers of the several powers to go to Peking and post additional guards. On their return, when train service was interrupted and the naval officers and consuls could agree on no plan of action, it was McCalla who proposed, even if the troops of other nations remained behind, to set out for Peking. An allied expedition was organized and made the attempt, but on reaching Lang-fang, forty miles from Peking, was obliged to turn back. In the fighting against heavy odds that followed, McCalla, commanding the American force, had the honor of leading the van and in course of the operations was wounded three times. For his efficient service and gallantry he was highly commended by Sir Edward Seymour, R. N., commanding the expeditionary forces. McCalla's last command was the Mare Island Navy Yard. He had been promoted, Oct. 11, 1903, to the rank of rear admiral, and was retired in 1906 for age. He died at Santa Barbara, Cal.

[Admiral McCalla left in manuscript "Memoirs of a Naval Career," which is in the possession of his son-in-law, Capt. Dudley Knox, Washington, D. C. For published material see *Army and Navy Register,* May 7, 1910; *Report of the Secretary of the Navy* (1900); L. R. Hamersly, *The Records of Living Officers of the U. S. Navy and Marine Corps* (7th ed., 1902); J. D. Long, *The New American Navy* (2 vols., 1903); *Who's Who in America,* 1910–11; *Los Angeles Times,* May 7, 1910.]

C. S. A.

McCALLA, WILLIAM LATTA (Nov. 25, 1788–Oct. 12, 1859), Presbyterian clergyman, controversialist, was born in Jessamine County, Ky., near Lexington, the son of Dr. Andrew and Martha (More) McCalla. He was a descendant of James McCalla, who was in Pennsylvania as early as 1732, and a grandson of William, who was a captain in the Revolutionary War. Andrew McCalla, a physician, was noted for his good works and was one of the projectors of Fayette Hospital, later the Eastern Lunatic Asylum (Lewis and R. H. Collins, *History of Kentucky,* 1874, II, 195). William received his early education chiefly at home. Various accounts of his career say that he graduated from Transylvania University, but the records of the institution do not corroborate this statement. He studied theology privately. In 1813 he was examined by the West Lexington Presbytery but his licensure was delayed. A strong supporter of the War of 1812, he became involved in an altercation with Rev. James Blythe, who held different political views. McCalla arraigned him before his presbytery on various charges, among them that Blythe had threatened to oppose the licensure of such a firebrand as himself. The case was referred to the Synod, and Blythe, having made some acknowledgments, was acquitted. (See *Case of McCalla Against Blythe, Tried Before the Synod of Kentucky in September, 1814*, 1814.) Soon afterward, apparently, McCalla went to Ohio, for he was commissioned chaplain in the army from that state, Apr. 29, 1816, and served until Apr. 14, 1818 (F. B. Heitman, *Historical Register and Dictionary of the United States Army*, vol. I, 1903, p. 653). In 1819 he was settled over a Presbyterian church in Augusta, Ky., where he remained until 1823.

For the next twenty years his ministry was in or near Philadelphia, during which time he became one of the most conspicuous figures in the Presbyterian body. He was pastor of the Eighth, or Scots' Church (1824–35). On Apr. 20, 1836 he assumed charge of the Fourth Church, but dissension arose because of his uncompromising preaching and strict construction of the constitution of the Church, and he and his friends withdrew and were recognized as the Assembly Church, with which he remained, except for a period of travel, until 1842. From Apr. 16, 1850, to May 31, 1854, he was pastor of the Union Church. Intervening years were spent in travel and in serving several small Pennsylvania churches. Tall and of commanding presence, gifted with fluency of speech, he was an effective preacher and debater. He had Scotch-Irish tenacity and pugnaciousness, and a bitter tongue which kept him in a turmoil all his life. Philadelphia was a hotbed of theological disturbance, and McCalla, a militant leader of the old-school party. He also waged vigorous warfare with those outside his denomination. He debated the subject of eternal punishment with Abner Kneeland [*q.v.*]; on two occasions he argued publicly with Alexander Campbell [*q.v.*] over modes of baptism; and on these and other theological questions he had vigorous controversies with opponents of less prominence. A number of these debates are preserved in printed form. He also published: *A Correct Narrative of the Trial of the Rev. Albert Barnes* (1835); *Review of Dr. Boardman's Address Against Kossuth* (1852); and *An Argument for Cleansing the Sanctuary, . . . Being in Opposition to the Prevailing System of Allowing Ungodly and Irresponsible Trustees to Manage Church Property, and Non-communicants to Vote at Church Elections* (1853). Of adventurous disposition, he spent some time roughing it in Texas, and recorded his experiences in *Adventures in Texas, Chiefly in the Spring and Summer of 1840* (1841), a curious miscellany of narrative, broad humor, religious sentiment, and defense of the morals of the Texans, along with several appendices, including a manual of procedure for church tribunals.

His last years were spent in the South, where he preached in St. Louis, doing missionary work among the boatmen and slaves, and on plantations in Mississippi and Louisiana. He died and was buried in the latter state, apparently near what was then known as Bayou Bidal Church. His wife, whom he married Mar. 30, 1813, was Martha Ann, daughter of Gen. Samuel Finley of Chillicothe, Ohio.

[*The Presbyt. Hist. Almanac . . . for 1861* (n.d.); Alfred Nevin, *Encyc. of the Presbyt. Ch. in the U. S. A.* (1884), *Hist. of the Presbytery of Phila.* (1888); Robert Davidson, *Hist. of the Presbyt. Ch. in the State of Ky.* (1847); E. H. Gillett, *Hist. of the Presbyt. Ch. in the U. S. A.* (1864); W. P. White and W. H. Scott, *The Presbyt. Ch. in Phila.* (1895); T. L. Montgomery, *Encyc. of Pa. Biog.*, XIV (1923), 246–47.] H. E. S.

McCALLUM, DANIEL CRAIG (Jan. 21, 1815–Dec. 27, 1878), engineer, military director of railroads during the Civil War, was the son of a Scottish tailor. Born in Johnston, Renfrewshire, Scotland, he came as a boy with his parents to Rochester, N. Y., where after an elementary education he became a carpenter and builder, and eventually an architect and engineer. Settling for a time in Lundy's Lane, N. Y., he married Mary McCann. In the year 1851 he originated and patented a form of bridge described in *McCallum's Inflexible Arched Truss Bridge Explained and Illustrated* (1859). This invention in time brought him a large revenue, and thereafter, he specialized more or less in bridge construction. About 1852 he moved to New York and associated himself with Samuel Roberts, constructing engineer of High Bridge over the Harlem River; in 1855–56 he was general superintendent of the New York & Erie Railway. During 1858–59, as president of the McCallum Bridge Company, he devoted most of his time to railway bridges, especially in the West and as far south as the Panama Railroad; and for a while he acted as consulting engineer for the Atlantic & Great Western Railway.

Less than a year after the outbreak of the Civil War, Secretary Stanton appointed him military director and superintendent of railroads in the

United States (Feb. 11, 1862), with extraordinary war powers to seize and operate all railroads and equipment necessary for the successful prosecution of the war. He was commissioned colonel and given the position of aide-de-camp on the staff of the commander-in-chief. Beginning with a single Virginia railway about seven miles in length, his administrative control was extended until it embraced 2,105 miles of railroad as far south as the Division of the Mississippi; his construction corps, which was gradually expanded from 300 to 10,000 men, built or rebuilt some 641 miles of railroad and twenty-six miles of bridges; 419 locomotives and 633 cars were under his management; and expenditures for labor, materials, and upkeep reached a total of nearly $40,000,000. His most important achievement in this period was probably the supplying of General Sherman's army, during the Atlanta campaign, with rations, forage, and munitions. He transported supplies for 100,000 men and 60,000 animals from a supply base 360 miles distant, over a single-track railroad which was constantly subject to destructive raids by an energetic enemy. On Sept. 24, 1864, McCallum was brevetted brigadier-general, and on Mar. 13, 1865, major-general, for meritorious services during the war. His report, "United States Military Railroads," appeared in 1866 as part of *House Executive Document No. 1* (39 Cong., 1 Sess.). After the close of hostilities McCallum was for a time inspector of the Union Pacific Railroad, but eventually retired to private life and with his wife and three sons made his home in Brooklyn, N. Y. He died after a year of ill health, and was buried in Mount Hope Cemetery, Rochester, N. Y. A large, powerfully built man, with a strict disciplinary temperament, McCallum was of a cheerful and genial disposition and wrote poetry as a diversion. A volume of his verse, *The Water-Mill and Other Poems,* was published in 1870.

[*N. Y. Times, N. Y. Herald,* Dec. 28, 1878; *Sun* (N. Y.), Dec. 29, 1878; McCallum's writings mentioned above; *War of the Rebellion: Official Records (Army)*; C. R. Fish, "The Northern Railroads, April, 1861," *Am. Hist. Rev.,* July 1917, with additional references; F. B. Heitman, *Hist. Reg. U. S. Army* (1890); for bridge patent, *Sen. Ex. Doc. 118,* 32 Cong., 1 Sess.]

C. D. R.

MACCAMERON, ROBERT (Jan. 14, 1866–Dec. 29, 1912), figure and portrait painter, was born in Chicago, Ill., the son of Hattie and Thomas MacCameron, who had been residents of Long Island. When their son was barely a year old, the parents moved to Necedah, Wis. The artist's childhood and early manhood were spent there, surrounded by wild forest in which he played with Indian children, learning to be a woodsman and an expert rifle shot. Although his father was moderately well off, the locality offered little in the way of formal education, and in his later years MacCameron used to say that he never had more than one year of schooling. He acquired, however, a magnificent physique from working in the woods. At the age of fourteen he commanded a man's wage—$2.50 a day and board—as a lumberjack. Chance acquaintance with a French drawing teacher awakened his interest in art and gave him an opportunity to develop his talent. He saved his wages until he was able to go to Chicago, where he studied art at the Young Men's Christian Association.

Successful in making a living as an illustrator in Chicago and later in New York, he went to London at the age of twenty-two and obtained employment with a publication called *The Boy's Own.* His commercial success here enabled him to move on to Paris, where his ability soon won him entrance to the École des Beaux Arts. Here he studied under Jean Léon Gérôme, and after Gérôme's death, was helped along by Collin and James McNeill Whistler. His life in Paris was not easy, however; he achieved some recognition, but little money, and was often on the verge of starvation. In July 1902, he married Louise Van Voorhis of Rochester, N. Y. A son was born in 1904 and a daughter in 1906. Fortunately, things took a turn for the better with him at this time. In 1904 he received his first public recognition in the form of honorable mention at the Salon des Artistes Français. In 1906 he won the third-class medal, at the Salon, with a picture called *"Les Habitués."* The following year he painted *"Groupe d'Amis,"* popularly known as "The Absinthe Drinkers," which was purchased by the Corcoran Gallery of Washington, D. C. It was not a pleasant picture, but was thought to be technically excellent, showing a rich and luminous color scheme. "The Last Supper," painted in 1900, was an attempt to dramatize the spiritual significance of a religious theme.

MacCameron was always interested in the poor and destitute, claiming that his "peasant background," the product of his childhood in a small western town, gave him a sympathy with the common man which most artists could not feel. He was anxious that his painting have social influence. In "The People of the Abyss," named after Jack London's novel, he attempted to portray the mystical aspect of human squalor and suffering. "MacCameron was at his best," wrote a critic some years after his death, "when his brush, incisive and remorseless as a knife at a clinic, laid bare the misery and hopelessness of that portion of humanity which heredity or misfortune had submerged and deadened and deformed" (*American Art News,* Apr. 26, 1924). According to the same critic, "The Undercurrent," "Waiting for the Doctor," and "Don Quixote" were notable among his pictures. During his last years MacCameron made his success in portraiture. After long residence abroad he returned to America in 1912 (as a chevalier of the Legion of Honor and a royal knight of La Mancha), to paint the portraits of the wealthy Goelet family. He died suddenly in New York of heart disease, in December of that year. A memorial exhibit of his work was held in New York in 1913.

[Sources of information include C. H. Caffin, "Some New American Painters in Paris," *Harper's Mag.,* Jan. 1909; *Who's Who in America,* 1912–13; *Am. Art Annual,* vol. X (1913); Briggs Davenport, "The Making of a Salon Picture," *Harper's Weekly,* Feb. 8, 1913; *Am. Art News,* Jan. 4, 18, 1913, Apr. 26, 1924; N. Y. *Evening Sun,* Nov. 24, 1912; *N. Y. Times,* Dec. 30, 1912, and Jan. 5, 1913; *Atlanta Constitution,* June 1, 1924. Several accounts of MacCameron, including the obituaries in New York papers, give his name as Robert Lee MacCameron, but the middle name does not appear in *Who's Who in America* or in the catalogues of the Nat. Acad. of Design, of which he was an associate.] R. H.

McCANN, ALFRED WATTERSON (Jan. 9, 1879–Jan. 19, 1931), journalist, pure-food crusader, was born in Pittsburgh, Pa., the son of Michael McCann, a printer and engraver of Irish birth, and Maria Watterson, whose ancestors had come to Pennsylvania in 1762. During his youth he suffered from an ailment that he believed was remedied by proper diet. This experience marked the beginning of his life-interest in food. After attending Mount St. Mary's College, Emmitsburg, Md., he was graduated from Pittsburg College of the Holy Ghost (now Duquesne University) in 1899, remained there as an instructor in English, mathematics, and elocution, and studied nutrition in his spare time. He was soon engaged to write advertisements for various food concerns, including Francis H. Leggett & Company. In 1912, when Harvey W. Wiley [*q.v.*] resigned from the government service, McCann became impatient of pure-food reform through federal action and turned to newspaper propaganda, outlining his program in a full-page article, "The Pure Food Movement," in the New York *Globe* for Oct. 24, 1912. He was able to arouse public interest by his bitter personalities, his unearthing of startling news, and his torrent of catchy phrases. During the next ten years he wrote for the *Globe* series after series of sensational articles against manufacturers who used coal tar dyes, bleaches, inert fillers, and injurious preservatives, and against public officials who condoned such abuses. The *Globe* provided him with a laboratory and stood behind him in the ensuing law suits. He took part in many inquiries such as that into the food at Ellis Island (September 1913), the milk supply of New York City (1919), and the egg supply (1921). In 1913 he published *Vital Questions and Answers Concerning 15,000,000 Physically Defective Children* and *Starving America.* In 1917 he produced a war emergency food book, *Thirty Cent Bread,* which urged the advantages of using cornmeal, of dehydrating instead of canning fruits and vegetables, and of killing off grain-consuming steers. These suggestions were the basis of an article in the *Forum* (October 1917) severely criticizing the United States Food Administration. He insisted continually on the value of the mineral salts in food in *This Famishing World* (1918; revised as *The Science of Eating,* 1919) and in *The Science of Keeping Young* (1926). After publishing a violent anti-evolution book, *God—or Gorilla* (1922), he received the degree of LL.D. from Fordham University. His *Greatest of Men—Washington* (1927) was a laudatory volume written to inspire young people. He wrote for the New York *Evening Mail* after the *Globe* suspended publication in 1923, and established the Alfred W. McCann Laboratories, Inc., in New York, whence issued a stream of indorsements of special brands of everything from chickens to cigars. In 1928 he began to broadcast food talks over the radio. He died of a heart attack Jan. 19, 1931, just after an hour of broadcasting. His wife, Mary Carmody, whom he married in 1905, and four of their five children survived him.

[*Pittsburg Coll. of the Holy Ghost,* 1901–02 (catalogue); *Who's Who in America,* 1930–31; letter from John B. Harvey, registrar of Duquesne Univ., Pittsburgh, June 23, 1931; *N. Y. Times,* Aug. 31–Sept. 13, 1913, July 3, 1925, Jan. 20, 21, 23, 27, 1931; portrait in *World's Work,* Oct. 1923; H. T. Finck, *Girth Control* (1923).] M. W. G.

McCANN, WILLIAM PENN (May 4, 1830–Jan. 15, 1906), naval officer, was born in Paris, Ky., the son of James Harvey and Jane R. (Lowrey) McCann. From the latter's mother, Nancy Penn, he derived his middle name. The McCann family had come originally from near Wigtown in Scotland, where the name was spelled McKeand. William entered the navy as a midshipman in 1848 and served on the *Raritan* both in the Gulf of Mexico and in the South Pacific. Then, after nine months of instruction at Annapolis, he went again to the Pacific for three years on the *Independence.* He was promoted to passed midshipman, June 15, 1854, and to lieutenant, Sept. 16, 1855.

When the Civil War broke out, McCann, who

had taken part in the Paraguay expedition on the *Sabine,* was at Vera Cruz on the same ship. He went in this vessel to the relief of Fort Pickens and to the Charleston blockade, where the *Sabine* rescued the crew of the *Governor* of the Port Royal expedition. He was made lieutenant commander, July 16, 1862, and during that year was on the York and James rivers in the thick of the Peninsular campaign as executive, and frequently as commander of the *Maratanza.* She fought at Malvern Hill and also captured the *Teaser,* on which were the Confederate plans for the defense of Richmond. The next year McCann commanded the *Hunchback* in the attack on New Bern, N. C., and Washington, N. C. In November 1863, he received command of the fast 5-gun propeller *Kennebec* and served thirteen months off Mobile. His assistance in the destruction of the *Ivanhoe* under the guns of Fort Morgan secured him the favorable notice of Farragut. In the battle of Mobile Bay the *Kennebec* was lashed to the *Monongahela,* and was at close quarters with the *Tennessee,* for the latter scraped across the *Kennebec's* bow, set her on fire with a shell, and otherwise severely punished her.

After the Civil War McCann did duty at the Naval Academy, was promoted to commander, July 25, 1866, commanded the *Tallapoosa,* and held navy-yard and inspection posts till he was made a captain, Sept. 21, 1876, and was sent to command the *Lackawanna* in the North Pacific. On Jan. 26, 1887, he attained the rank of commodore. He had charge of the naval forces in Chile in 1891 and secured the surrender of the *Itata,* a ship that attempted to bring arms from the United States to the insurgents. When the insurgents refused him the use of the American cable, McCann had it cut several miles off shore. He retired in 1892. His death occurred at his home in New Rochelle, N. Y., and he was buried at Arlington. He was married in New York City, Jan. 31, 1867, to Mary Elizabeth Vulte. Schley, who was on the *Baltimore* with him in Chile, refers to him as "much beloved for his sterling qualities of heart and head" (*Forty-five Years Under the Flag,* 1904, p. 214).

[The Navy Department has the logs of the ships on which McCann served, his official dispatches, the record of his assignments, and a sketch he made of the battle of Mobile Bay. The best account of the *Itata* affair is by Osgood Hardy in the *Hispanic-American Hist. Rev.,* May 1922. See also, *Official Records of the Union and Confederate Navies in the War of the Rebellion*; L. R. Hamersly, *The Records of Living Officers of the U. S. Navy and Marine Corps* (7th ed., 1902); *Army and Navy Jour.,* Feb. 9, 1867, record of marriage; Jan. 20, 27, 1906; *Who's Who in America,* 1906–07; N. Y. *Sun,* Jan. 16, 1906.]

W. B. N.

McCARREN, PATRICK HENRY (June 18, 1847–Oct. 23, 1909), politician, was born in East Cambridge, Mass., the son of Owen and Mary (McCosker) McCarren. Both parents were born in County Tyrone, Ireland. They removed from East Cambridge to Williamsburgh, now a part of Brooklyn, N. Y., where young McCarren attended school until he was seventeen. He then learned the cooper's trade and worked in sugar refineries along the waterfront. He made friends easily, became a natural leader in the district, and at the age of twenty-one was made a member of the Democratic general committee of Kings County. Hugh McLaughlin [*q.v.*], Brooklyn Democratic boss since 1857, recognizing his value, had him nominated and elected to the state Assembly in 1881. He was twice reëlected, and in 1889 was advanced to the state Senate, of which, except for the years 1894–95, he remained a member until his death. In that body his influence was felt in the committee room, and he is reported to have expressed the opinion that it was "only once a century that a vote was changed by argument on the floor" (*Brooklyn Eagle,* Oct. 23, 1909). In 1897 he served on the Lexow committee to investigate the trusts and his minority report dissenting from that of the majority with respect to the American Sugar Refining Company gave him a reputation as the friend of trusts in a period when they were distinctly unpopular. He was chairman of the committee which managed the campaign of Van Wyck against Roosevelt for governor in 1898, and, though the shouting was all on the colorful Colonel's side, McCarren's remarkable marshaling of the opposition forces made the race exceedingly close. Having first served as one of McLaughlin's ablest lieutenants, McCarren overthrew the veteran Brooklyn leader of forty-six years' standing when, in 1903, he defied orders by supporting McClellan for mayor and carried Brooklyn for his candidate. He thus allied himself temporarily with boss Charles F. Murphy [*q.v.*] of Tammany, but almost immediately declared that the Brooklyn Democracy would maintain its independence. During the remainder of his life he fought desperately and successfully to keep Murphy from securing control of Brooklyn. Frequently, McCarren held the balance of power between Tammany and the upstate democracy, and he used it in 1904 to support Parker rather than Hearst for the presidential nomination, and again in 1906 when he threw the Brooklyn vote to Hughes as against Hearst for governor, thereby furnishing the margin by which the former was elected. Almost immediately, however, he plunged into a spectacular legislative campaign against Hughes's reform program and came close to wrecking it.

Few men were more bitterly attacked in the New York press by innuendo and caricature than McCarren; yet men who believed him an evil influence in public life liked him personally. His genius for tactical management was unquestioned and many stories are told of how he escaped from tight corners when he seemed defeated. A little over six feet in height, spare, and slightly stooped, with an unusually long head, and a habitual grim expression on his face, he was a figure of which cartoonists made the most. The loss of his wife, Kate Hogan, and their five children seemed to have imparted a fatalistic turn to his philosophy. He solaced himself by wide reading; by the study of law—he was admitted to the bar after he was forty-three years old; by indulgence in various forms of gambling, notably the race-track, of which he was passionately fond; and by politics, which also he seemed to have enjoyed chiefly for the game's sake.

[R. B. Smith, ed., *Hist. of the State of N. Y.* (1922), vol. IV; scrapbooks of the Hughes Administration, compiled by Hughes's secretary, R. H. Fuller (190 vols.; in N. Y. Public Library); *Brooklyn Daily Eagle,* Oct. 23, 1909; *N. Y. Times,* Oct. 23, 1909; information from David Hogan, nephew and former secretary of McCarren, and from Mrs. Anastasia McCarthy, a niece.] O. W. H.

McCARROLL, JAMES (Aug. 3, 1814–Apr. 10, 1892), journalist, poet, dramatist, inventor, was born at Lanesboro, County Longford, Ireland. Emigrating to Canada at the age of seventeen, he settled in or near Toronto and almost at once began writing for the newspapers and magazines. By 1845 he had become editor and proprietor of the *Peterborough Chronicle,* and an active force in local politics. For his skill in influencing public opinion, he was rewarded by sinecures in the Customs service at Coburg and Niagara in the years 1849 and 1851 respectively, and in 1854 by appointment to the surveyorship of the port of Toronto. In the meantime he had settled at Coburg where in addition to his other activities he taught music. He was an accomplished flutist and upon occasion went on tour. In the course of these travels he met most of the celebrities in the concert field. It was at this time that his reputation as a technician and composer won him the post of music critic for the *Toronto Leader* and the *Toronto Colonist.* He contributed also to the Quebec *Morning Chronicle.* In view of his other interests, his literary output must have been considerable. Very little of his work appeared in book form, however, and of these writings the best are the *Terry Finnegan Letters* (1864), a series of humorous sketches done in the Irish dialect. Typical examples of his work in the drama are *The Adventures of a Night* (1865) and *Almost a Tragedy, A Comedy* (1874), both of them patterned upon the well-made play of the Scribe-Dumas school. At the same time, McCarroll was writing a great deal of verse in the whimsical, sentimental, highly imaged style of Clarence Mangan and Tom Moore. An occasional poem he sent to Oliver Wendell Holmes for criticism, but no collected edition appeared until 1889 (*Madeline and Other Poems*) and by that time McCarroll, after a few years of journalistic gypsying in northern New York state, had permanently settled in New York City. Here he became associated with *The People's Cyclopedia of Universal Knowledge* and *The American Cyclopædia,* and latterly he served on the editorial staff of *Humanity and Health* and contributed articles of a scientific character to *Belford's Magazine.* Linked with his talents for music and letters was an interest and ingenuity about mechanical things. At the time of his death he was negotiating the sale of patents upon his inventions: an improved elevator and a fire-proof wire gauze, but before the sales were closed he was seized with pneumonia and died after a short illness of nine days. He was very much a man of his own time. His associates knew him as a choice and merry spirit and a true Irish gentleman of the old school.

[*Belford's Monthly,* June 1892; prefatory sketch by C. L. Hildreth in *Madeline and Other Poems*; *Specifications and Drawings of Patents Issued from the U. S. Patent Office,* Mar., May 1882, Apr. 1883, Dec. 1884; *N. Y. Tribune,* Apr. 11, 1892.] E. M. H.

McCARTEE, DIVIE BETHUNE (Jan. 13, 1820–July 17, 1900), medical missionary, educator, diplomat, was born in Philadelphia, the eldest of the ten children of Robert and Jessie (Bethune) McCartee, both of Scotch descent, though the Bethunes were originally French Huguenots. His mother was a sister of George W. Bethune [*q.v.*], and had some reputation as a poet. Divie spent his childhood in New York, where from 1822 to 1836 his father was pastor of the Irish Presbyterian Church. From early childhood he read widely, gaining much knowledge of law and theology from his father's library. In 1829 a course of popular lectures aroused in him an enthusiasm for science, to which he devoted his spare time thereafter. Prepared in private schools, he entered Columbia when only fourteen, but, disliking the classical course, left after the junior year to study medicine in the University of Pennsylvania. He graduated in 1840 and did post-graduate work while seeking appointment as a missionary. Designated to China by the Presbyterian Board in 1843, he arrived in Hong Kong early in the following year. While awaiting a vessel to the north he taught a few weeks in the Morrison School, having as one of his pupils Yung Wing, who was destined to be the first Chinese graduate of an American college.

Reaching Ningpo in June 1844, he founded a hospital and aided his colleagues in starting schools and evangelistic work. In 1853 he married Joanna M. Knight. To his other activities he added consular duties until a regular consulate was established in 1857. When the Taiping rebels were overrunning Eastern China, and it seemed necessary to secure their pledge not to molest Americans or their property, Flag Officer Stribling, in 1861, requested McCartee to accompany him to Nanking on this errand. Owing in no small part to McCartee's command of Chinese, the mission was successful. The same year, on account of his health, he went to Japan for a vacation, and later, to Chefoo to live. From 1862 to 1865 he served as vice-consul there. Returning to Ningpo in 1865, he might have remained permanently but for opposition by colleagues to some of his plans, which led to his transfer (1872) to Shanghai and, shortly thereafter, to his resignation from the mission to join the consular staff in Shanghai as interpreter and assessor in the mixed court.

Soon after this, when the Japanese government liberated certain coolies on their way to virtual slavery in the Peruvian ship *Maria Luz,* en route from Macao to Peru, McCartee suggested to the Nanking viceroy an embassy to thank Japan and repatriate the unfortunates. He was invited to accompany this embassy as a secretary and acquitted himself with distinction. Through Dr. Guido Verbeck's recommendation, he was detained in Tokyo to become professor of law and science in the Imperial University and joint curator of the botanical gardens. He was in this congenial position during five crucial years of Japan's metamorphosis and won Japanese confidence. He returned to his old consular position in 1877, but soon reappeared in Tokyo as secretary to the new permanent Chinese legation. In the strain between the two countries over the Loochoo Islands, in 1879, he was able from researches into Japanese—having by that time mastered the Japanese language also—to enlighten General Grant, whom China had invited to mediate; also to confute the more radical Japanese propaganda by a series of articles entitled *"Audi Alteram Partem."* Furthermore, he suggested a compromise, the division of the islands; but first Japan and then China refused to accept it. His relations with both sides helped to avert a break during the crisis. After his term was ended, he spent some time in America and Hawaii. From 1885 to 1887 he was counselor to the Japanese legation in Washington. He was then reappointed by the Presbyterian Board and sent to Tokyo, where he engaged in executive and literary duties until a few months before his death, which occurred at San Francisco.

[*A Missionary Pioneer in the Far East* (1922), ed. by Robert E. Speer, contains McCartee's memoirs. See also David Murray, "Divie Bethune McCartee," *N. Y. Observer,* July 17, 1902; H. W. Rankin, "A Short Study in Heredity: Influence of Ancestry upon the Life of Dr. D. B. McCartee," *Ibid.,* Oct. 30, 1902; *Missionary Review of the World,* Apr. 1906; *San Francisco Chronicle,* July 20, 1900; State Dept. Archives.]

W. J. H.

McCARTHY, CHARLES (June 29, 1873–Mar. 26, 1921), political scientist and publicist, was born in Brockton, Mass. His mother, Katherine O'Shea, of scanty education but strong mentality, had been a domestic servant in Brockton, when she married John McCarthy, an engine-tender in a shoe-factory, a man of some self-education and, like his wife, a native of Ireland and an ardent Fenian. She maintained a lodging and boarding house, patronized by young Irish and English shoe-workers of various shades of political and sociological belief. Charles sold newspapers, ushered in a theatre, and worked on docks and coasting vessels. At nineteen, having succeeded in entering Brown University, he supported himself by working as a stage carpenter and scene-shifter. Although of meager build and weighing under 135 pounds, he quickly won a distinguished place in inter-collegiate football. After receiving, in 1896, the degree of Ph.B. from Brown, he spent a year at the University of Georgia. In 1899 he made his way to the University of Wisconsin and became a graduate student in political science. In 1901 he obtained the Ph.D. degree and married Louise Howard Schreiber, of Madison, who bore him one daughter. The next year his thesis *The Anti-Masonic Party* (1903) won the Justin Winsor prize of the American Historical Association.

The field of his activities, in the two decades that followed, presents an approximate cross-section of the liberal sociological and economic thinking that was being translated into political action and legislation. With his magnetic vitality, vivid speech, and ready pen he generally was able to enlist an influential following and to maintain the interest of a wide public. He organized in the State House at Madison, for the use of legislators, the first official reference library and bill-drafting bureau in the United States, which he served as director until his death. From 1905 to 1917, he conducted seminar courses on legislation in the university. In 1912 he published *The Wisconsin Idea,* which, in spite of the faults of hasty preparation and too great emphasis on German influence, was a valuable attempt to describe the development of the state. *An Elementary Civics* (1916) written with Flora Swan and Jennie McMullin was designed as a textbook for the training of pupils in the upper grammar grades. Throughout his career he extended the scope of his teaching by addresses and by numerous magazine articles. He collected material and made contacts with legislators and writers, which helped him to influence the adoption of progressive legislation in Wisconsin and elsewhere. By adapting methods of the "correspondence schools" he brought about the creation of a new type of state university extension service for carrying instruction into remote rural homes. With the help of John R. Commons and others, he effected the establishment of part-time education for youths, of continuation schools for adults, and of special schools for apprentices, still the most advanced system in America of education for workers. He was an early national exponent of farmers' cooperation for purchasing and marketing; he influenced the growth of the state system for regulating rates, service, and practices of railroads and public utilities, wherein Wisconsin was then the pioneer among the states; and he actively advocated such steps in municipal government as budget reform and the commission form of administration. He was among the first, in writings and addresses, to undertake to organize public support for special training for public service in schools and universities. Throughout these activities he maintained a dynamic touch with contemporary legislative problems everywhere, being in personal contact with successive American presidents, with national party leaders, through whom he pushed new legislative ideas into party platforms, and also with foreign statesmen and publicists, by whom he was frequently consulted. In 1914 and 1915 he served as the first director of the United States Commission on Industrial Relations, appointed by President Wilson. After the United States entered the World War, he rendered important service to his state in the administration of the draft law and to the nation as an assistant in the food administration. In 1918 he campaigned unsuccessfully in the Democratic primaries for nomination for United States senator. After about three years of failing health he died in Prescott, Ariz.

[Personal acquaintance; memoranda and letters in McCarthy's files; Horace Plunkett, "McCarthy of Wis.," *Nineteenth Century,* June 1915; *New Republic,* Apr. 27, 1921; *Yale Review,* Nov. 1907; *Irish Homestead,* Apr. 9, 1921; *American School,* May 1921; *Wis. Lib. Bulletin,* Apr.–May, 1921; *Wis. State Journal* (Madison), Mar. 27, 1921.]

L. B. W.

McCARTNEY, WASHINGTON (Aug. 24, 1812–July 15, 1856), educator, mathematician, lawyer, born in Westmoreland County, Pa., was early left an orphan, dependent upon his own resources. After attending the common-schools until he reached the age of eighteeen, he entered Jefferson College at Canonsburg, Pa., from which he graduated with high honors in the class of 1834. In 1835 he became professor of mathematics in Lafayette College, Easton, Pa., but after a year was recalled to Jefferson as professor of mathematics and modern languages, resuming his chair at Lafayette, however, in 1837. Here, for most of the time until 1846, he taught mathematics, natural philosophy, and astronomy. On Apr. 18, 1839, he was married to Mary E. Maxwell of Easton. In 1843 he resigned his professorship to practise law, but resumed his connection with the college the following year. In 1844 he published *The Principles of the Differential and Integral Calculus,* which was widely used as a textbook. Because the trustees of Lafayette would not increase his salary from $600 to $800 a year, he relinquished his professorship again in 1846, although the students protested vigorously and offered to make good the difference themselves. From 1847 to 1852 he was a trustee of the college, and professor of mental and moral philosophy from 1849 to 1852.

These academic distinctions were attained outside of McCartney's chosen career, which was in the legal profession. Having studied law while teaching, he was admitted to the bar in 1838. From 1846 to 1848 he was deputy attorney-general for Northampton County. His bent for educational activities led him in 1844 to open a law school, in which, he announced, he would offer both the usual legal subjects and "an ample course in history," "the whole being designed to furnish a liberal system of legal instruction" (Easton *Democrat and Argus,* Sept. 10, 1846). McCartney's *Origin and Progress of the United States,* a textbook, or series of lectures, on United States history, was published in 1847. The school was so successful that in 1854 it was incorporated by the legislature as The Union Law School, but being a one-man institution it expired with its founder. In 1851 McCartney was elected president judge of the third judicial district of Pennsylvania.

Besides his work as teacher, lawyer, and judge, he engaged in many other activities. He delivered public lectures on such general topics as "How to Read a Book" as well as on the subjects of his special studies, and he was active in the formation of the Easton Lyceum in 1842. As an industrious member of the school board and an enthusiast for free education he was influential in the establishment of the Easton High School. At the time of his death a local editor wrote: "Perhaps no man in the borough had a closer relation to all its vital interests. . . . Without aspiring to leadership in anything, he was ever designing schemes to benefit his fellowmen" (Easton *Daily Express,* July 17, 1856). Living before the age of specialization, McCartney explored most of the fields of knowledge that then interested the scholarly mind. He was described as a learned theologian and as an accomplished linguist who, after mastering the common ancient and modern languages, took up the study of Russian. When he died, at the age of forty-four, he left unpublished a work on evidence and papers on other legal subjects and on logic, rhetoric, optics, and various mathematical topics.

[F. B. Copp, *Biog. Sketches of Some of Easton's Prominent Citizens* (1879); *The Biog. Encyc. of Pa.* (1874); S. J. Coffin, *Record of the Men of Lafayette* (1879); D. B. Skillman, *The Biog. of a Coll.: Being the Hist. of the First Century of the Life of Lafayette Coll.* (1932); Joseph Smith, *Hist. of Jefferson Coll.* (1857); J. F. Stonecipher, *Biog. Cat. of Lafayette Coll.* (1913).]

D. L. M.

McCAULEY, CHARLES STEWART (Feb. 3, 1793–May 21, 1869), naval officer, was born in Philadelphia, the son of John and Sarah (Stewart) McCauley and the nephew of Commodore Charles Stewart [*q.v.*], under whom he first served after receiving his appointment as midshipman in January 1809. During the War of 1812 he took part in a gunboat attack on the *Narcissus* in Hampton Roads and in the defense of Craney Island, and served in the *Jefferson* on Lake Ontario. He was made acting lieutenant in September 1813, and lieutenant in December 1814. After the war he saw much service in the Mediterranean, in the *Constellation* and the *United States.* In 1822 he obtained a furlough to make a voyage to the East Indies. After his return to the navy in 1825 he filled several minor positions at shore stations and in 1826–29 was attached to the *Boston* of the Brazil Squadron. In March 1831 he was made a master commandant and three years later commanded the *St. Louis* of the West India Squadron. His first important sea duty after reaching the grade of captain, December 1839, was performed in 1841–44 as the commander of the *Delaware,* 74 guns, of the Brazil Squadron. From 1846 to 1849 he was commandant of the Washington navy-yard; and from 1850 to 1853, commander-in-chief of the Pacific Squadron, whose cruising grounds at that time extended from the west coast of the two Americas to the 180th meridian. In 1855 as temporary commander of the home squadron, McCauley performed his most notable, as well as his last, sea service. This was the delicate mission of guarding American interests in Cuban waters, where a Spanish frigate had caused alarm by asserting the right of visitation and search. His successful efforts were commended by President Pierce.

On July 25, 1860, McCauley was made commandant of the Norfolk navy-yard, a position which, in the spring of the following year, entailed much responsibility. After the secession of Virginia, when the yard was threatened by the Confederates, he ordered its guns spiked and its ships scuttled and abandoned it without making a defense. This disaster ended his professional career. In 1862 he was retired with the rank of captain and in 1867 he was promoted commodore on the retired list. A select committee of the Senate that inquired into his conduct at the Norfolk yard reported that it was highly censurable. Feeling that his honor had been wounded and his professional reputation tarnished unjustly by the government, he fell into a melancholy that probably hastened his death, which occurred at his residence in Washington, D. C. On Oct. 25, 1831, he was married in Washington to Leila E. Dickens. Edward Yorke McCauley [*q.v.*] was his nephew.

[Record of Officers, Bureau of Navigation, 1809–71; *Army and Navy Jour.,* May 29, 1869; *Senate Report No. 37,* 37 Cong., 2 Sess.; *Official Records of the Union and Confederate Navies in the War of the Rebellion,* 1 ser.; *Diary of Gideon Welles* (1911), vol. I; *Sunday Morning Chronicle* (Washington), May 23, 1869.]

C. O. P.

MACCAULEY, CLAY (May 8, 1843–Nov. 15, 1925), Unitarian clergyman, missionary, publicist, was born in Chambersburg, Pa., the son of Isaac H. and Elizabeth (Maxwell) MacCauley. Descended from Scotch-Irish ancestors, he early decided to join the Presbyterian ministry, and at fourteen began his studies by reading aloud from books on science, theology, and philosophy to a blind pastor who repaid him with lessons in the classics. At sixteen he entered the sophomore class at Dickinson College, but after hearing Lincoln speak at Harrisburg withdrew from college to enlist. This enlistment was canceled because the lad was still a minor, and MacCauley transferred to the College of New Jersey (Princeton). He enlisted again in 1862, suffered a wound in the knee at Fredericksburg, was promoted to a second lieutenancy in February 1863, was captured by "Stonewall" Jackson, and, on his twentieth birthday, was committed to Libby Prison. He was paroled home, reëntered the college at Princeton, and after graduating in 1864 joined the United States Christian Commission, in which he served until the conclusion of the Civil War.

He then enrolled at Western Theological Seminary, Allegheny, Pa., and, on the removal of his parents to Illinois, transferred to the Presbyterian Theological Seminary of the Northwest (later McCormick), from which he was graduated in 1867. The following month he married Annie Cleveland Deane, daughter of Dr. Josiah and Annie (Everett) Deane of Bangor, Me., and as a licentiate of the Old School Presbytery of Chicago, began his first charge, at Morrison, Ill. His liberal views, however, aroused opposition to his ordination which caused him to refuse a call to continue in the Morrison pastorate and led to the revocation of his license to preach. In 1868, at the urgent suggestion of Charles Carroll Everett and Robert Collyer [*qq.v.*], he entered the Unitarian ministry. After serving charges in Detroit, Rochester, and Waltham, Mass., he resigned in 1873 to study philosophy and theology at Heidelberg and Leipzig. He returned to America in 1875, and from 1877 to 1880 was pastor of the First Unitarian (now All Souls') Church, Washington, D. C. Resigning this charge because of ill health, he was commissioned by the United States Bureau of American Ethnology to study the Indian tribes east of the Mississippi. His report on "The Seminole Indians of Florida" was published in the Bureau's *Fifth Annual Report, 1883–84* (1887). He also deposited in the Bureau's archives an extensive list of Seminole words and phrases and an analysis of the Seminole verb construction. After visits to the south of Europe and the American Northwest, he settled in Minnesota, where from 1883 to 1889 he gave his time to preaching, writing, and lecturing. During part of this period (1885–86) he was pastor in St. Paul, and during part, was editor of the Minneapolis *Commercial Bulletin.*

After the death of his wife, in April 1887, he applied for foreign-missionary service, and from 1889 until his retirement in 1920 was a member or director of the Unitarian mission in Japan. His furlough years, a brief intermission from 1901 to 1904, and the period from his retirement until his death, from abscess of the stomach, at Berkeley, Cal., were all spent in lecturing and in writing for the promotion of better relations between the United States and Japan. In addition to his missionary work in Tokyo, he edited the Japanese Unitarian magazine, *Shūkyo* ("Religion") from 1890 to 1895, and, during much of his residence in Japan was correspondent for the *Boston Transcript.* He was vice president and acting president of the Asiatic Society of Japan, 1910–16; vice president of the International Press Association, a Tokyo journalists' club, 1915–16; president of the American Peace Society of Japan, 1916–19. He was twice decorated by the Emperor, being awarded the Order of the Rising Sun in 1909, and the Order of the Sacred Treasure in 1918, and in 1920 he received the Red Cross Service badge.

Throughout his career MacCauley was a prolific writer. In addition to lectures, sermons, and contributions to periodicals, he published a number of books, including *Christianity in History* (1891), issued in both English and Japanese; *An Introductory Course in Japanese* (1896; 2nd ed., 1906); *Thought and Fact for Today* (1911), issued in both English and Japanese; and *The Faith of the Incarnation* (1913). In 1897 he contributed an article on Japanese literature to the *Library of the World's Best Literature,* edited by Charles Dudley Warner, and in 1899 he published, with an introduction, a translation of the Japanese classic *Hyaku-nin-issiu,* or "Single Songs of a Hundred Poets" (*Transactions of the Asiatic Society of Japan,* vol. XXVII, pt. 4, December 1899). From the days of his post-graduate study in Germany he had been influenced by the philosophy of Krause, and his last considerable publication was a pamphlet, *Karl Christian Friedrich Krause: Heroic Pioneer for Thought and Life, A Memorial Record,* issued in the spring of 1925. Two volumes, the autobiographical *Memories and Memorials* (1914) and *Looking Before and After: Some War Time Essays* (1919), contain reprintings of a number of fugitive articles.

[*Who's Who in America,* 1924–25; *Japan Advertiser* (Tokyo), Dec. 8, 1925; *Boston Transcript,* Nov. 17, 1925; *Christian Register,* Nov. 26, Dec. 10, 1925; portrait in *Trans-Pacific* (Tokyo), Dec. 12, 1925.]

H. E. W.

McCAULEY, EDWARD YORKE (Nov. 2, 1827–Sept. 14, 1894), naval officer, Egyptologist, nephew of Charles Stewart McCauley [*q.v.*], was born in Philadelphia, Pa., but spent his boyhood in Tripoli, where his father, Daniel Smith McCauley, a former naval lieutenant, was United States consul. His mother, Sarah (Yorke) McCauley, died in 1830. By 1840 Edward could speak five languages and had navigated his father's yacht from Tripoli to Malta. Appointed a midshipman in 1841, he cruised in the Mediterranean in the *Fairfield* till 1845, when he was ordered to the new naval school at Annapolis. During the Mexican War he served on the coast of Africa, and then returned to Annapolis till sent to the Mediterranean in the *Constitution* in 1849. From 1852 to 1855 he served on the *Powhatan* in the Orient, and he was with M. C. Perry [*q.v.*] on his second visit to Japan, when the treaty was signed. In 1858, as a lieutenant on the *Niagara,* he assisted in laying the Atlantic cable. Ill health, however, and perhaps his marriage, Jan. 28, 1858, to Josephine McIlvaine Berkeley of Virginia, caused him to resign and enter business in St. Paul, Minn.

With the outbreak of the Civil War he volunteered (May 1861), and subsequently spent nearly two years on the west coast of Florida, between Tampa and Appalachicola, where, in spite of an attack of yellow fever, his zeal was said by the squadron commander to have made his ship, the ferry boat *Fort Henry,* "the terror of the coast for fifty miles." His chief exploit was a launch expedition (armed only with howitzers and rifles) to capture vessels at Bayport, where he attacked enemy rifle pits and a small battery with considerable damage to the enemy and the burning of one vessel. He was commissioned lieutenant commander July 16, 1862. In 1863 he was sent to the Bahamas in the *Tioga* in a vain search for the *Florida.* During the last year of the war he commanded the *Benton* on the Mississippi, and operated between Grand Gulf and Natchez to prevent illegal movement of cotton and the escape of Confederate leaders to Texas. After the Civil War McCauley served as fleet captain in the North Atlantic Squadron, at the Portsmouth and Boston navy yards, as head of the department of French at the Naval Academy, as commander of the *Lackawanna* in the Pacific, and finally as superintendent of the Naval Asylum, Philadelphia. Having been promoted commander (1866), captain (1872), and commodore (1881), he was made a rear admiral in March 1885 and retired in 1887.

The environment of his early life had given him a keen interest in the languages and thought of the peoples of the Levant, and in his later days he made an especial study of Egypt, where his father had served as consul in the forties. Elected to the American Philosophical Society, Philadelphia, in 1881, he presented, that year, as his first contribution to its *Proceedings,* "A Manual for the Use of Students in Egyptology" (vol. XX, published in 1883). Some two years later he published a dictionary of Egyptian hieroglyphics (*Transactions of the American Philosophical Society,* n.s., vol. XVI, pt. 1, 1883). He died at his summer home, "The Mist," on Canonicut Island, Narragansett Bay, after a painful illness, bravely borne.

[Official papers and letter books in possession of the Navy Dept.; Persifor Frazer, in *Proc. Am. Philosophical Soc.,* vol. XXXIV (1895); L. R. Hamersly, *The Records of Living Officers of the U. S. Navy and Marine Corps* (4th ed., 1890); *Official Records of the Union and Confederate Navies,* I ser., II, XVII, XXVI; John Mullaly, *The Laying of the Cable, or the Ocean Telegraph* (1858); *Army and Navy Jour.,* Sept. 22, 1894; *The Press* (Phila.), Sept. 15, 1894. Throughout most of his active career McCauley spelled his name as given above, but toward the end of his life began to write it Macauley.]

W. B. N.

McCAULEY, MARY LUDWIG HAYS (Oct. 13, 1754–Jan. 22, 1832), Revolutionary heroine, better known as Molly Pitcher, was the daughter of John George Ludwig Hass (or Has), who apparently dropped his last name some time after coming to America. One of the sturdy German peasants who emigrated from the Palatinate in 1730 (I. D. Rupp, *A Collection of Thirty Thousand Names of German . . . Immigrants in Pennsylvania,* 1856, p. 16), he acquired a small dairy farm near Trenton, N. J., where Mary was born. In 1769 she went, as a servant in the family of Dr. William Irvine, to Carlisle, Pa. There she married John Caspar Hays, on July 24, 1769 (*Pennsylvania Archives,* 2 ser. II, 133). On Dec. 1, 1775, her husband enlisted in the 1st Pennsylvania Regiment of Artillery, served one year, and in January 1777 joined the 7th Pennsylvania Regiment (*Ibid.,* X, 614, XI, 176). Molly Hays remained for some time in Carlisle, then returned to her parents' home to help them, and to be near her husband. At the battle of Monmouth, June 28, 1778, John Hays was detailed to the artillery. It was a terrifically hot day, and Molly, who was on the field, went back and forth from a well, carrying water to the exhausted and wounded. This won for her the sobriquet of "Molly Pitcher." Her husband fell, overcome by the heat. Molly stepped into his place beside his cannon, and filled it ably and heroically for the rest of the battle. After the war she and her husband returned to Carlisle. Some years after the death of John Hays in 1789, she married George McCauley, a union which proved unhappy. Molly obtained a livelihood by scrubbing, caring for children, and similar tasks. The General Assembly of Pennsylvania took notice of her services during the Revolution, passing on Feb. 21, 1822, "An act for the relief of Molly M'Kolly" which directed that she be paid forty dollars immediately and an annuity of the same amount (*Acts of the General Assembly of the Commonwealth of Pennsylvania,* 1821–22, p. 32). Molly was described by contemporaries as a short, thick-set woman, of rather rough appearance and brusque manner, but industrious and kindly. Her grave was marked in 1876 and in 1916 by monuments, and she is also depicted on the monument commemorating the battle of Monmouth.

[The accounts of Molly Pitcher's life are varied and conflicting. Several of them are summarized in W. S. Stryker, *The Battle of Monmouth* (1927), ed. by W. S. Myers, but Stryker's own account has errors in dates. J. B. Landis, "An Investigation into the American Tradition of a Woman Known as 'Molly Pitcher,'" in *Jour. Am. Hist.*, vol. V (1911), no. 1, p. 83, attempts to clear up the confusion. Other good accounts are: E. W. Biddle, *Hist. Address at the Unveiling of Molly Pitcher Monument* (1916), and J. A. Murray, *Contributions to the Local History of Carlisle, Pa.*, no. 2 (1902), which quotes obituaries from Carlisle papers of January 1832.]
V. R.

McCAUSLAND, JOHN (Sept. 13, 1836–Jan. 22, 1927), Confederate soldier, was the son of John McCausland, an emigrant from Tyrone County, Ireland, who became a successful merchant in Lynchburg, Va., married Harriet Kyle, the daughter of an old friend, and moved to St. Louis, Mo., where his son was born. After receiving his preparatory education at Point Pleasant, Mason County, Va. (now W. Va.), the boy entered the Virginia Military Institute and graduated there in 1857, first in a class of twenty-three. He studied at the University of Virginia the next year and then returned to his alma mater as assistant professor of mathematics. He was present with the detachment of cadets at the execution of John Brown at Charles Town. Upon the secession of Virginia he was sent by Robert E. Lee to the Kanawha Valley to organize a regiment of volunteers for the Confederacy. Commissioned colonel of the 36th Virginia Regiment, he was assigned to the division of John B. Floyd and was stationed in western Virginia until his command joined, in the latter part of 1861, the army of Albert Sidney Johnston in Kentucky. Commanding a brigade of Virginians at the siege of Fort Donelson, he displayed daring courage, and, before the surrender, escaped with his brigade. From April 1862 to June 1864 his brigade was a part of the department of West Virginia and engaged in several battles in southwestern and western Virginia. The chief duties of this Confederate force were to protect the Virginia and Tennessee Railroad and the saltpeter works at Saltville from Federal raids and, by constantly harassing the enemy, to detain a large body of Federals in western Virginia.

Promoted to brigadier-general on May 24, 1864, and given command of a brigade of cavalry, he opposed Hunter's army in the Valley of Virginia during the summer of 1864. Confronted by superior forces, he delayed Hunter's advance upon Lynchburg until the arrival of Early's army, despatched by Lee to hold this strategic place. In recognition of his services the citizens of Lynchburg presented him with a golden sword and memorialized him as the savior of Lynchburg. In Early's counter offensive in the Valley of Virginia his brigade played a conspicuous part; his brilliant attack upon the flank of Lew Wallace's position at Monocacy resulted in the rout of the enemy; and he led his soldiers into the outskirts of Washington, D. C. On July 30, 1864, in retaliation for the destruction of property by Hunter's army in the Valley, he burned Chambersburg, Pa., under specific orders from Early, and after the refusal of its citizens to pay a levy of $100,000 in gold. Participating in the subsequent engagements in the Valley between the forces of Early and Sheridan, he finally joined Lee's army and took part in the retreat to Appomattox, where he and his brigade, refusing to surrender, cut their way through the Federal lines to safety.

After the war, on account of bitter feeling against him in West Virginia, he spent two years in Europe and Mexico, but returned to Mason County, W. Va., to spend the remainder of his life. He acquired a tract of about 6,000 acres, which he drained and developed. He was survived by one daughter and three sons.

[*War of the Rebellion: Official Records* (*Army*), esp. 1 ser., vol. XXXVII, pts. 1, 2; *Confederate Military Hist.*, ed. by C. A. Evans (1899), vols. II, III; J. A. Early, *A Memoir of the Last Year of the War of Independence* (1866); M. P. Shawkey, *West Va.* (1928), vol. V; *Nation*, Feb. 9, 1927; *News* (Lynchburg), Jan. 25, 1927; *Wheeling Register*, Jan. 24, 1927.]
W. G. B.

McCAW, JAMES BROWN (July 12, 1823–Aug. 13, 1906), physician, editor, teacher, and Confederate medical officer, was born at Richmond, Va. He was a descendant of James McCaw, a Scotch surgeon who emigrated from Wigtownshire, Scotland, to Virginia in 1771 and settled near Norfolk. His son, James Drew, was a pupil of Benjamin Bell of Edinburgh and graduated from the medical school of Edinburgh University. Returning to Richmond he practised there until his death. Dr. William Reid McCaw, son of the last-named and also a Richmond practitioner, married Ann Ludwell Brown and was the father of James Brown McCaw. Having received his premedical education from Richmond Academy, James studied medicine in the University of the City of New York, where he was a pupil of Valentine Mott. He graduated in 1843, returned to Richmond, and soon became a leader in his profession. He was a founder and charter member of the Medical Society of Virginia, and a member and once president of the Richmond Academy of Medicine. From April 1853 to December 1855 he was an editor of the *Virginia Medical and Surgical Journal.* The name of the publication was then changed to *Virginia Medical Journal,* and McCaw was co-editor from January 1856 to December 1859. In

1858 he became professor of chemistry in the Medical College of Virginia.

His military service began with his enlistment in a cavalry troop, in which he was serving when Gen. Joseph Johnston asked for hospitalization for 9,000 men of his army. Surgeon-General Samuel P. Moore, who had but 2,500 beds at his disposal, went to see McCaw and they selected the site and name of Chimborazo Hospital. Early in 1862 it was opened. Eventually there were 150 wards, each 100 x 30 feet. Five large hospitals, or divisions, each consisting of thirty wards, were organized. A surgeon with forty or fifty assistant surgeons had charge of each, and all were under the supervision of McCaw. In addition to the buildings for wards, there were 100 Sibley tents for convalescents, and such service buildings as ice houses and Russian baths. Chimborazo was the largest hospital of the Civil War, the next largest being Lincoln Hospital in Washington. Seventy-six thousand patients were treated there. In view of the poverty of the Confederacy in subsistence, clothing, and medicines, and of what was generally accomplished by the practice of the day, the results achieved at Chimborazo were considered good. In 1864 McCaw became editor of the *Confederate States Medical Journal,* the only medical periodical published under the Confederacy, fourteen numbers of which were issued.

After the war McCaw resumed private practice, teaching, and writing. He took up again his work as a professor of chemistry in the Medical College of Virginia, and in 1868 became professor of the practice of medicine, which position he held until 1883. He was also dean of the college for twelve years and later president of the board of visitors. In April 1871 he became one of the editors of the *Virginia Clinical Record,* of which three volumes were published. In 1845 he married Delia Patteson; nine children were born to them, three of whom entered the medical profession. McCaw was a man of striking presence and forceful but genial personality. He was fond of music and was for many years president of the Mozart Society of Richmond. He died at Richmond.

[F. H. Garrison, "Dr. James Brown McCaw," *The Old Dominion Jour. of Medicine and Surgery,* Aug. 1906; J. R. Gildersleeve, "Hist. of Chimborazo Hospital, Richmond, Va., and Its Medical Officers during 1861–1865," *Va. Medic. Semimonthly,* July 8, 1904; *Ibid.,* Aug. 24, 1906; *British Medic. Jour.,* Sept. 8, 1906; H. A. Kelly and W. L. Burrage, *American Medic. Biogs.* (1920); *Times-Dispatch* (Richmond), Aug. 14, 1906.]
P. M. A.

McCAWLEY, CHARLES GRYMES (Jan. 29, 1827–Oct. 13, 1891), soldier, of Scotch-Irish ancestry, was born in Philadelphia. His father was Capt. James McCawley, United States Marine Corps, son of a leading merchant of Philadelphia who emigrated from Ulster County, Ireland, in the eighteenth century; his mother was Mary Eliza Holt, of Norfolk, Va., whose father was mayor of that city for some years. Young McCawley attended school in Abington, Montgomery County, Pa., and later, at the Moravian school, Nazareth. After the death of his father in 1839, he entered business in New Orleans with his uncle, William McCawley; attended night school; and on Mar. 3, 1847, received appointment as second lieutenant in the Marine Corps.

He sailed immediately for Vera Cruz, joined Scott's army, and participated in the storming of the castle of Chapultepec and capture of the city of Mexico. For gallantry in battle, he was brevetted first lieutenant, Sept. 13, 1847. From 1848 to 1861, he served at sea and at various stations, being promoted first lieutenant, Jan. 2, 1855, and captain, July 26, 1861. After the beginning of the Civil War, he joined the battalion of marines at Bay Point, S. C. In May 1862, he commanded the detachment of marines which hoisted the national colors over the Norfolk navy-yard, and in August of the same year he saw service with the South Atlantic Squadron, landing at Morris Island, S. C., and taking part in the bombardment and occupation of Fort Wagner and Fort Gregg. In the night attack on Fort Sumter by the naval forces under Rear Admiral J. A. Dahlgren, Sept. 8, 1863, Captain McCawley's command of marines, which had volunteered for the hazardous duty, cooperated in a gallant but unsuccessful boat-maneuver, losing nearly one-third of its number in killed, wounded, and missing (*Official Records of the Union and Confederate Navies in the War of the Rebellion,* 1 ser. XIV, 622–23). For gallant and meritorious services in this action, McCawley received the brevet of major. He was promoted major, June 10, 1864, and lieutenant-colonel, Dec. 5, 1867. In June 1871 he was ordered to command the Marine Barracks at Washington, and to superintend recruiting. Five years later, Nov. 1, 1876, he was made colonel-commandant of the Marine Corps. His retirement from active service, by operation of law, occurred Jan. 29, 1891, and the following March, a stroke of paralysis led to his last illness and death, at Rosemont, Pa., where he had sought to regain his health. He was buried in the old churchyard at Abington, Pa.

McCawley was married in St. John's Church, Washington, March 1863, to Elizabeth Colegate (d. 1867), daughter of James Colegate, and grand-daughter of Rev. James Laurie, who emigrated from Scotland in 1800. He was married a second time, in 1870, to Elise Alden Henderson of Philadelphia, a niece of Admiral James Alden, United States Navy, who survived him, as did also two sons by his first marriage.

[L. R. Hamersly, *The Records of Living Officers of the U. S. Navy and Marine Corps* (4th ed., 1890); *Mil. Order of the Loyal Legion of the U. S. Commandery of the State of Pa., Circ. No. 18,* series of 1891; M. A. Aldrich, *Hist. of the U. S. Marine Corps* (1875); R. S. Collum, *Services of the Marines During the Civil War* (1886); *Public Ledger* (Phila.), Oct. 15, 1891.]
C. D. R.

McCAY, CHARLES FRANCIS (Mar. 8, 1810–Mar. 13, 1889), mathematician, actuary, brother of Henry Kent McCay, was born at Danville, Pa., the son of Robert and Sarah (Read) McCay and great-grandson of Donald McCay who came to the United States in 1758 from the Isle of Skye. He attended Jefferson College and was graduated in 1829. For a year, 1832–33, he taught mathematics, natural philosophy, and astronomy at Lafayette College, Easton, Pa., then for twenty years, 1833–53, he was at the University of Georgia at Athens. He was the author of a text on differential and integral calculus and was noted for the vigor, originality, and "modernism" of his teaching. His retirement from the University of Georgia was occasioned by a "disagreement" which he and the brothers John and Joseph L. Le Conte had with the then chancellor of the university, Alonzo Church [*q.v.*]. From 1848 to 1855 he served as actuary of the life department of the Southern Mutual Insurance Company of Athens, Ga. His connection with that company ceased when its life business was transferred to the Southern Mutual Life Insurance Company of Columbia, S. C., in 1855. While in Athens, he also acted as agent for the Mutual Life Insurance Company of New York (1846–53).

In December 1853 McCay was elected professor of mathematics at South Carolina College (later the University of South Carolina) at Columbia. In 1855 he became president. His career there was stormy, but despite some of his eccentricities, he was regarded as one of the most remarkable men on the faculty at the time. In 1859 he proposed a bill for the Georgia legislature which was passed and signed by the Governor, making effective for valuation purposes in Georgia his Southern Mutual Mortality Table. This was said to have been the first adoption of a life-insurance valuation table by any of the states. His connection with South Carolina College ceased in 1857 and he later entered the insurance business in Augusta, Ga. There he was also cashier, then president, of a bank. He accumulated a modest fortune and in 1869 he gave $1,000 to the University of Georgia for a collection of books on the Civil War.

On Dec. 18, 1848, McCay established an agreement with the Girard Trust Company of Philadelphia, whereby an original sum of $337.35, with additional contributions to $2,000, was to be invested and its proceeds reinvested until the amount should equal the state debt of Pennsylvania, at which time the fund was to be used to extinguish the debt. About 1906 his children heard about the trust accidentally, and instituted suit to test the validity of the "elaborate and somewhat fantastic scheme, impossible of accomplishment." Judge J. B. McPherson in the United States Circuit Court (Eastern District of Pennsylvania) rendered an opinion in the case, directing the payment of $21,000 to the McCay heirs, on the ground that the trust violated the Pennsylvania statute against perpetuities (171 *Fed. Reporter,* 161). On appeal, the decision was affirmed (179 *Fed. Reporter,* 446). On Aug. 5, 1879, the board of trustees of the University of Georgia signified their willingness to accept from McCay the sum of seven thousand dollars in bonds, which sum by successive reinvestment would by 1970 amount to about $1,000,000 and then be used to pay the salaries of the faculty. The fund is now valued at more than one hundred thousand dollars. The trustees' committee said in 1880: "After all our arguments and persuasions, the donor could not be induced to change his purpose!"

McCay removed from Augusta to Baltimore in 1869. In 1886 he suggested to President Garrett of the Baltimore & Ohio Railroad the formation of the Employees Relief Association of which he became actuary, serving without pay through the remainder of his lifetime. He was also actuary of the relief fund for the clergy of the Southern Presbyterian Church, and of the Maryland Insurance Department from its formation in 1871 until his death. He acted as consulting actuary to a number of life insurance companies at various times between 1848 and 1889, achieving the high regard of insurance officials in this country and abroad. In 1875 he passed upon the validity of the mortality statistics of the Mutual Life Insurance Company of New York for the period 1843–73. He prepared what is believed to have been the first "select and ultimate" table of life-insurance mortality in the United States (1887). This table was based upon the combined experience of the Mutual Life (New York), Mutual Benefit Life (Newark), and Connecticut Mutual Life (Hartford) insurance companies. McCay was married, on

Aug. 11, 1840, to Narcissa Harvey Williams, the daughter of William and Rebecca Harvey Williams of Georgia. He died in Baltimore in 1889.

[E. L. Green, *A Hist. of the Univ. of S. C.* (1916); Maximilian La Borde, *Hist. of the S. C. Coll.* (rev. ed., 1874); E. M. Coulter, *College Life in the Old South* (1928); *Hunt's Merchants' Mag.*, Jan. 1850, Apr., May, July 1860, Feb. 1861; *The Internat. Insurance Encyc.*, vol. I (1910), somewhat inaccurate; the *Spectator*, June 23, 1887; *Weekly Underwriter*, Mar. 16, 1889; *Baltimore American*, Mar. 14, 1889; *Baltimore Underwriter*, Mar. 20, 1889; *Pittsburgh Dispatch*, July 2, 1906; *Macon Telegraph*, Oct. 30, 1907; *Atlanta Constitution*, Feb. 17, 1929; personal communications.]

E. W. K.

McCAY, HENRY KENT (Jan. 8, 1820–July 30, 1886), Confederate soldier and jurist, was born in Northumberland County, Pa., the son of Robert and Sarah (Read) McCay. His name was pronounced McCoy. He received an elementary education in Pennsylvania and in 1839 was graduated from the College of New Jersey. Soon afterward he removed to Georgia, where his elder brother, Charles Francis McCay [*q.v.*] was a member of the faculty of the University of Georgia. He taught school at Lexington in Oglethorpe County for two years, studied law in the office of Joseph Henry Lumpkin [*q.v.*], and was admitted to practice in 1842. In the same year he married Catherine Hanson and removed to Americus in southwest Georgia. There he formed a partnership with George H. Dudley, which lasted for seven years. Then he became a law partner of Willis A. Hawkins. Like himself these two partners later became associate justices of the state supreme court. His first appearance in politics appears to have been as a member of the state Democratic convention of 1860, which split on the question of indorsing the action of those members of the Georgia delegation who had seceded from the recent Charleston national convention. He was among the minority that declined so to indorse the seceders and refused to recognize the pending Richmond convention called by the bolters from the Charleston convention. This action seems to place him on the conservative side of the issues that were leading to war. On the outbreak of the Civil War he entered the army: On June 15, 1861, he became second lieutenant of Company A in the 12th Georgia Regiment, was wounded at Alleghany, Va., in December, and was promoted to be captain and assistant quartermaster the next February. He resigned, but late in the war he was in command of a brigade of state troops at the defense of Atlanta.

On the reconstruction issues he took the unpopular course and joined the Republican party. He has been classified, by a contemporary, as belonging in the small group of honest Georgians who thought the best interests of the state would be served by cooperation with Congress (Avery, *post*, p. 375). As a member of the constitutional convention of 1868 he has been given credit for some of the best features of the new constitution. On the coming into power of the Republican régime with Rufus B. Bullock as governor, he was appointed associate justice of the state supreme court. He served for seven years, resigned in 1875, and resumed the practice of law in Atlanta. On Aug. 4, 1882, he was appointed judge of the district court of the United States for the northern district of Georgia. He died in office.

[Letter from his grandniece, Mrs. Mark Sullivan, Washington, D. C.; I. W. Avery, *The Hist. of the State of Ga.* (1881); *Men of Mark in Ga.*, ed. by W. J. Northen, vol. III (1911); H. W. Thomas, *Hist. of the Doles-Cook Brigade* (1903); *War of the Rebellion: Official Records (Army)*, 1 ser., vol. V; *Atlanta Constitution*, July 31, Aug. 1, 2, 1886.]

R. P. B.

McCLAIN, EMLIN (Nov. 26, 1851–May 25, 1915), lawyer and teacher, was born in Salem, Columbiana County, Ohio. His father, William McClain, and his mother, Rebecca (Harris) McClain, were natives of Pennsylvania, and Quakers, the former of Scotch-Irish and the latter of English descent. Emlin entered the State University of Iowa in 1867, completing both the scientific and classical courses in four years, in addition to studying music and indulging in amateur theatricals. He then did graduate work for a year in the classics and German. He thus earned the degree of Ph.B. in 1871 and that of A.B. in 1872. Entering the University law school, he completed the course there with honors and the degree of LL.B. in 1873. He began practice in Des Moines, but neither trial work nor a two-year view of politics in Washington (1875–77), where he served as secretary to a United States senator and as clerk of a Senate committee, interested him, and in 1881 he returned to the University as a professor of law. There he remained until 1901, becoming vice-chancellor of the law department in 1887, and chancellor in 1890. While acquiring an exceptionally wide reputation as a teacher, he also retained close touch with practitioners. From 1889 onward he was active in the American Bar Association, serving as a member of its section on legal education and of its committees on classification of the law and on uniform state laws. In various years he was one of Iowa's commissioners on uniform state laws and came to be recognized as the leading authority on the statutory law of the state. In 1894 he took a prominent part in reviving the defunct state bar association.

It was not surprising, therefore, that he was

twice elected a justice of the supreme court, serving for twelve years (1901–13), and as chief justice in 1906 and 1912. As a judge he profited by the exceptional knowledge of legal principles and their history, the training in legal analysis, and the warning against extreme technicality which he had acquired in years of teaching; but his general attitude toward law remained conservative. He was neither a reformer nor a blind adherent to precedent. As one of his colleagues said, "his best work was done in cases involving the application of old principles to new conditions"; on the other hand, "he believed that justice, as administered by the courts, was not morality, and that justice under the law was all to which any man was entitled" (*Proceedings, post,* p. 63). While on the bench he continued to lecture in the Law College; and upon leaving the court he accepted a professorship in Stanford University, returning to Iowa, however, in 1914 to serve as dean.

He was a man of prodigious industry. He published *Annotated Statutes of Iowa* (2 vols., 1880, with a supplement in 1884), which by statute of 1882 was given the authority of an official compilation in all courts of Iowa as evidence of law; *A Digest of the Decisions of the Supreme Court of Iowa* (2 vols., 1887, with later supplements) and *McClain's New Iowa Digest* (4 vols., dated 1908–09 but all issued in 1909), the former prepared by him alone, the latter merely edited by him; *Annotated Code and Statutes of the State of Iowa* (2 vols., 1888; 2nd ed., rev., 1889, with a supplement in 1892), which was treated by courts and legislature as authoritative; *Outlines of Criminal Law and Procedure* (1883; 2nd ed. 1892); *A Selection of Cases on the Law of Carriers* (1893; subsequent editions of altered content and titles, 1894, 1896, 1914); *A Treatise on the Criminal Law* (2 vols., 1897), his most ambitious textbook; *A Selection of Cases on Constitutional Law* (1900; 2nd ed. 1909); *Constitutional Law in the United States* (1905; 2nd ed. 1910); monographic articles in the fields of carriers, insurance, and constitutional law for several legal encyclopedias; and about twoscore miscellaneous articles, addresses, and syllabi of legal courses. His editions of the statutes supplanted the official edition of 1873 and served as official until the Code of 1897 was prepared by a commission of which he was a member. His fellows largely deferred to his judgment and knowledge; his arrangement and system of annotation were adopted; his prior annotations were purchased and embodied in the work; and he continued them in official supplements.

His mind was systematic, independent, and highly intelligent. Its fullness in the field of law is attested by his writings. He was also interested throughout life in history and problems of government, and had catholic tastes in literature. His sincerity, modesty, tolerance, and warm-heartedness constituted a gift for friendship which, coupled with his wide intellectual interests, led him, despite his professional industry, into an active social life. Though he remained a Quaker, he supported the local Congregational Church. On Feb. 19, 1879, he married Ellen Griffiths of Des Moines, and was survived by two sons and one daughter.

[H. E. Deemer, "Emlin McClain; 1851–1915," in *Proc. of the Twenty-first Ann. Session of the Iowa State Bar Asso.* (1915); Jacob Van der Zee, "Emlin McClain," in *Iowa Law Bulletin,* Nov. 1915, pp. 157–79, and Eugene Wambaugh, "Emlin McClain: a Great Teacher of Law," *Ibid.,* pp. 180–82; *Am. Law School Rev.,* Nov. 1915; *Who's Who in America,* 1914–15; *Register and Leader* (Des Moines), May 26, 1915.]

F. S. P.

McCLELLAN, GEORGE (Dec. 23, 1796–May 9, 1847), anatomist, surgeon, and founder of the Jefferson Medical College, Philadelphia, was born in Woodstock, Conn., the son of James and Eunice (Eldredge) McClellan. He came of Scottish ancestry. He received his early education at the Woodstock Academy, of which his father was principal, and in 1812 he went to Yale where he graduated in 1816. He entered the office of Dr. Thomas Hubbard of Pomfret, Conn., but after a year moved to Philadelphia where he became a pupil of John Syng Dorsey and entered the medical school of the University of Pennsylvania. He was a brilliant student and received the appointment of resident student in the hospital of the Philadelphia Almshouse. Here he showed great zeal in performing autopsies and in operating on the cadavers. He graduated in medicine in 1819, his thesis being entitled "Surgical Anatomy of Arteries." He began practice at once and soon acquired an enviable reputation, particularly in surgery. Not content with practice alone, he began also to teach. In those days private schools in medicine were in fashion, and from them the teachers were often chosen for chairs in the regular colleges. In 1821 he founded an institution for diseases of the eye and ear, which continued for four years. He also taught anatomy and surgery, for the former having a private dissecting room. In a few years he had the most successful private school in Philadelphia.

Having developed a large private following, he began to plan for the establishment of a new medical school. The proposal to found such an institution was not popular with the University of Pennsylvania and every effort was made to block the project. But McClellan was a fighter and did not give up although he was subjected to abuse and ostracized by part of the Philadelphia profession. The bitterness of this controversy affected him for the rest of his life. The influence of the University was sufficiently strong to block all attempts to secure an independent charter for the proposed new school from the legislature, but McClellan found a way to solve the difficulty by having the trustees of Jefferson College at Canonsburg, Pa., establish a medical department in Philadelphia, hence the name Jefferson Medical College. The college was opened in 1825 but when the time came for the granting of degrees in 1826, the legal difficulties had not been completely overcome. Driving to Harrisburg, a distance of one hundred miles, in less than twenty-four hours, he secured the authority giving the new institution power to grant the degree in medicine. In 1838 the medical department of the college was given a separate charter and continued as an independent institution. McClellan served as professor of surgery in the college from its beginning until 1839, and as professor of anatomy from 1827 to 1830. Students were attracted to the institution and by 1836 the enrolment had reached 360, but dissensions developed and in 1839 the trustees dissolved the faculty. There is some evidence that McClellan was given an opportunity to apply for reappointment but apparently he took no notice of it. He promptly engaged in the establishment of the "Medical Department of Pennsylvania College" in connection with Pennsylvania (later Gettysburg) College at Gettysburg. The school had fair success and continued until the Civil War.

One of McClellan's achievements of consequence was his establishment of a clinic with the opening of the Jefferson Medical College. He had conducted a clinic of his own and apparently referred these patients to the college clinic. Though naturally the facilities were meager his early attempt to bring medical students into contact with patients is notable. As a surgeon he had the reputation of being a bold and skilful operator. The operation for the removal of the parotid gland, which he did a number of times, was especially noteworthy. He was keen, ambitious, energetic, and always interesting, but his impulsive disposition excited opposition and enmity. His projected work on surgery, *Principles and Practice of Surgery,* which he did not live to complete, was published by his son in 1848. As a teacher he was brilliant rather than thoughtful, and notoriously unsystematic. Gross said that he "lacked judgment, talked too much, and made everybody his confidant" (*Autobiography,* II, p. 251). McClellan was married in 1820 to Elizabeth Brinton. He died suddenly in his fifty-first year. Gen. George B. McClellan [*q.v.*] was his son, and George McClellan, 1849–1913 [*q.v.*], his grandson.

[S. G. Morton, article in *Summary of the Trans. of the Coll. of Physicians of Phila.,* vol. II (1849); W. Darrach, *Memoir of Geo. McClellan* (1847); G. M. Gould, *The Jefferson Medic. Coll.: A Hist.* (1904), vol. I; S. D. Gross, *Lives of Eminent Am. Physicians and Surgeons of the Nineteenth Century* (1861), and *Autobiography* (2 vols., 1887); C. W. Bowen, *The Hist. of Woodstock, Conn.* (1926–32), vols. I and IV; *Pa. Inquirer and Nat. Gazette* (Phila.), May 10, 1847.]

T. M.

McCLELLAN, GEORGE (Oct. 29, 1849–Mar. 29, 1913), anatomist and physician, was born in Philadelphia, Pa., the son of Dr. John H. B. McClellan, an anatomist and surgeon, and the grandson of Dr. George McClellan, 1796–1847 [*q.v.*], for whom he was named. His mother was Maria Eldredge. He attended school in Philadelphia and later took the arts course at the University of Pennsylvania, graduating in 1869. In 1870 he was graduated from the Jefferson Medical College and began practice, devoting himself particularly to anatomy and surgery. Two years later he went abroad for a year, working with Hyrtl of Vienna. His fondness for anatomy had been evident in his student days and the influence of Hyrtl determined him to specialize in that branch of medical science. His methods and approach to anatomical problems were those of his preceptor. On his return to Philadelphia in 1873 he resumed practice and soon began to give private courses in anatomy and surgery. He was appointed to the staff of the Philadelphia and Howard hospitals, and in 1881 he founded the Pennsylvania School of Anatomy and Surgery in which he taught with great success until 1898. Interested in the study of anatomy as related to art, he was appointed professor of artistic anatomy at the Pennsylvania Academy of the Fine Arts, where he taught from 1890 till his death in 1913. In 1906 he was appointed professor of applied anatomy in the Jefferson Medical College, which position he also held with distinguished success until his death.

McClellan's monumental work, *Regional Anatomy,* published in two volumes in 1891 and 1892, went through four editions in the United States and was translated into French. The illustrations were remarkable in that they were made from photographs which he had taken and had colored himself. Another notable work, *Anatomy in Relation to Art* (1900), grew out of his work in anatomy in the Academy of the Fine Arts. His unusual ability in illustrating his lectures by drawings on the blackboard contributed greatly to his powers as a teacher. This talent, and his skill and facility as a dissector, made a lasting impression upon his students. He taught anatomy both as a science and as a subject which the medical student should be able to use. The recognition of his standing by the appointment to a professorial chair in his own college came late. No one ever questioned that it was well deserved. By nature he was tenacious and somewhat dour, with an impetuous temper. Probably only a few really knew him intimately and much of what seemed a stern outlook on life served to cover a sensitive nature. His death occurred in March 1913, from a rare condition, thrombosis of the abdominal aorta. He was survived by his wife, Harriett (Hare) McClellan, whom he had married in 1873.

[J. C. Da Costa, memoir in *Trans. Coll. of Physicians of Phila.*, 3 ser. XXXVI (1914); H. A. Kelly and W. L. Burrage, *Am. Medic. Biogs.* (1920); the *Independent*, May 29, 1913; *Pub. Ledger* (Phila.), Mar. 30, 1913.]

T. M.

McCLELLAN, GEORGE BRINTON (Dec. 3, 1826–Oct. 29, 1885), soldier, was born in Philadelphia, the third child and second son of Dr. George McClellan, 1796–1847 [*q.v.*] and Elizabeth (Brinton) McClellan. The family had come from Scotland to New England early in the eighteenth century. His great-grandfather, Samuel McClellan, served through the Revolutionary War with the Connecticut militia, and reached the grade of brigadier-general. In the Civil War, several members of the family were in service. His younger brother, Arthur, was one of his aides-de-camp; a first cousin, Carswell McClellan, was on the staff of General Humphreys; another first cousin, Henry Brainerd McClellan [*q.v.*], was chief of staff to the Confederate generals Stuart and Hampton, and wrote a biography of Stuart.

McClellan attended preparatory schools in Philadelphia, and entered the University of Pennsylvania in 1840, but left there upon appointment as cadet at West Point in 1842. He graduated in 1846, as No. 2 in his class, and was assigned to the Engineers. Joining a company of sappers and miners that was being organized at West Point for service in Mexico, he assisted in training it, and went with it to Matamoros. In January 1847 the company formed part of the column that marched from the Rio Grande to Tampico, and was charged with the road and bridge construction. It then became a part of General Scott's command, landed with the first troops at Vera Cruz, and served throughout his campaign. McClellan at once attracted attention, and was often mentioned in dispatches. He received the brevet rank of first lieutenant for service at Contreras and Churubusco, and of captain for Chapultepec. (*The Mexican War Diary of George B. McClellan,* edited by W. S. Myers, was published in 1917.) He returned with his company to West Point in 1848, and for three years served there as assistant instructor in practical military engineering. During this time, he translated the French regulations on the bayonet exercise and adapted them to use in the American service; his regulations were tested in the company, and in 1852 were adopted for the army. He also became an active member of a group of officers formed for the study of military history.

In the summer of 1851 he was relieved from duty at West Point and assigned as assistant engineer for the construction of Fort Delaware. In March of the next year, however, he went with the expedition of Capt. R. B. Marcy to explore the sources of the Red River, in Arkansas (*Senate Executive Document No. 54,* 32 Cong., 2 Sess.). This duty was completed in July. He acted as chief engineer on the staff of Gen. Persifor F. Smith until October, and then took up river and harbor work in Texas. The next spring he was placed in command of an expedition to survey a route for a railway across the Cascade Mountains, which occupied him until the end of the year. His route did not ultimately prove the best; but Jefferson Davis, then secretary of war, was so much pleased with his work that he directed him to continue his study of railways, and report on the practicability of construction on the line selected (*House Executive Document No. 129,* 33 Cong., 1 Sess.; *Senate Executive Document No. 78,* 33 Cong., 2 Sess.). This study being completed, Davis sent him to report upon Samana Bay, in Santo Domingo, as a possible naval station (*House Executive Document No. 43,* 41 Cong., 3 Sess.).

An increase in the regular army was made in 1855, and McClellan was appointed a captain in one of the new regiments of cavalry, resigning his commission as first lieutenant of engineers. He never joined his regiment, for in April 1855 he was detailed as a member of a board of officers to study the European military systems. The board spent a year in Europe, visiting most of the principal countries as well as the theatre of operations in the Crimea. McClellan was to observe particularly the engineers and cavalry, as well as to make a special study of the Russian army at large. The board arrived too late to see much of active operations in the Crimea, but was able to make a very complete study of the siege of Sevastopol. McClellan's reports are most excellent (*Senate Executive Document No. 1,* 35 Cong., Special Sess.). In submitting them, he made numerous recommendations for improvements in the American service; notably, he proposed a new type of saddle, modeled on the lines of the Hungarian. This was adopted. Alterations in the McClellan saddle have been few and slight, and the specifications of 1929 reverted very nearly to his original design. In January 1857 he resigned his commission to become chief engineer of the Illinois Central Railroad. The next year he was made vice-president, in charge of operations in Illinois; and in 1860 he became president of the Ohio & Mississippi Railroad, with his residence in Cincinnati.

At the outbreak of the Civil War his services were sought by both New York and Pennsylvania. He started for Harrisburg to consult with Governor Curtin, but stopped in Columbus to inform Governor Dennison as to conditions in Cincinnati. Here he was tendered appointment as major-general of Ohio Volunteers, with command of all the Ohio forces, militia and volunteer. He accepted, a special act was hastily passed by the legislature, empowering the Governor to appoint to this office one who was not an officer of the militia, and he entered upon his duties the same day, Apr. 23, 1861.

By reason of the rioting in Baltimore, mail connection with Washington was uncertain, and states in the Ohio and Mississippi valleys had to act largely on their own initiative. The work of organizing, equipping, and training the troops fell chiefly upon McClellan, under state authority only. On May 13, however, he received appointment (dated May 3) as a major-general in the regular army, and was placed in command of the Department of the Ohio, including the states of Ohio, Indiana, and Illinois, and later certain portions of western Pennsylvania and Virginia. During this period Grant called upon him, to ask for employment on his staff or with troops. McClellan happened to be absent, and before his return Grant had been offered an Illinois regiment; so the interesting experiment, McClellan in command with Grant as chief of staff, was never tried.

McClellan's refusal to support the neutrality of Kentucky, when called upon by Simon B. Buckner [*q.v.*] to do so, had great influence in keeping that state in the Union. Western Virginia was chiefly Unionist in sentiment. To control this territory for the South, troops from eastern Virginia occupied Grafton, the junction point of the two branches of the Baltimore & Ohio Railroad. McClellan sent troops, which regained possession of the railways. This action led to further concentrations of troops on both sides and to the campaign of Rich Mountain, in which McClellan personally commanded, and by means of which that region was cleared of Confederate troops and kept in the Union.

This success, just before McDowell's defeat at Bull Run, led to McClellan's appointment to command the Division of the Potomac, which included McDowell's department south of the river and Mansfield's in the city of Washington. He reached Washington on July 26, and found the troops in utter confusion. He plunged into his work with great energy, soon brought his command under discipline, and began reorganization and training. Spirit at once improved, and the army gained rapidly, both in strength and in efficiency. In a few months the troops became tired of inactivity and were anxious to take the offensive. McClellan, however, overestimating the strength of the enemy and underrating his own condition, refused to move. Meanwhile, his relations with General Scott became more and more strained. In November, Scott retired and McClellan became general-in-chief in his stead; this led to further delay, while he studied his enlarged problems.

The President began to exhibit impatience. Not only did he feel that the army was strong enough for a move, but the financial situation, with the increasingly unfavorable rate of exchange, convinced him that some military risk was preferable to certain bankruptcy. McClellan's plan was, not to move frontally upon the Confederate force at Manassas, and thence upon Richmond, but to transport his army by water to the lower Rappahannock or to Fortress Monroe, and advance on Richmond from the east. To this Lincoln demurred, fearing that Washington would not be sufficiently protected. Finally, on Jan. 27, 1862, the President issued his General War Order No. 1, prescribing an advance of all the armies on Feb. 22, and on the 31st his Special War Order No. 1, requiring that the move of the Army of the Potomac should be upon Manassas (*Official Records, Army,* 1 Ser., V, 41). This brought matters to a head. McClellan again urged his own plan, and Lincoln consented to a move by way of Fortress Monroe, but reluctantly and doubtfully, imposing conditions in regard to the security of Washington. The Confederate force at Manassas was withdrawn to the Rappahannock early in March, somewhat relieving this anxiety. A few days later the Army of the Potomac began embarking at Alexandria. McClellan, having taken the field with it, was relieved as general-in-chief and left only that army, reporting, as did the other independent commanders, direct to the secretary of war. Jackson's activity in the Shenandoah Valley now caused renewed alarm, and McDowell's corps and other troops intended for the expedition were held back for the defense of Washington.

Advancing from Fortress Monroe, McClellan encountered the Confederates at Yorktown and approached the lines there by regular siege operations, which delayed him for a month. He then moved up the Peninsula toward Richmond. Upon his urgent representations that he was outnumbered, McDowell's corps was ordered to march by way of Fredericksburg to join him; but Jackson's renewed activity caused these orders to be countermanded. Finally, over McDowell's protest, the corps was withdrawn from the Army of the Potomac and constituted a separate command. On the Chickahominy there was another long delay. Heavy rains had set in; the streams were up, and the roads almost impassable. The first troops to cross had heavy fighting at Seven Pines and Fair Oaks on May 31 and June 1; a position almost at the gates of Richmond was occupied and entrenched, and work was begun on bridges to bring the rest of the army across. Meanwhile, lingering hopes of McDowell's arrival made McClellan reluctant to relinquish his hold on the left bank of the river, where he expected to effect the junction.

Instead of McDowell, Jackson came. Having drawn as many Union troops as possible to the Valley, he had secretly moved his own force out by rail, and come down to join the army at Richmond. Upon his approach, on June 26, Lee launched a powerful attack upon the part of McClellan's army on the left bank of the river, and defeated it at Gaines's Mill. The bridges, just finished and ready to take that wing to the right bank for an attack upon Richmond, had to be used to bring supports across, the other way; and then, the immediate emergency having been met, to take them all back to the right bank, not now for an advance, but for a flank march to the James. The Confederate pursuit was finally checked at Malvern Hill on July 1, ending the Seven Days' Battles, and the army established itself at Harrison's Landing. McClellan, in his dispatches, attributed his reverses to lack of support from Washington, and insisted, as he had throughout the campaign, that he was outnumbered. He still contemplated a further offensive, south of the James, but he demanded for it a greater reinforcement than the President—or Halleck, who became general-in-chief late in July—was willing to provide. Finally, on Aug. 3, the Army of the Potomac was ordered withdrawn. McClellan established his headquarters at Alexandria. His troops, as they arrived, were detached from him and assigned to General Pope's Army of Virginia.

After Pope's defeat at Manassas, McClellan was again called upon to reorganize the army and prepare the defense of Washington. Orders from General Halleck to this effect reached him on Sept. 1; the next morning the President called upon him in Washington and personally requested him to undertake the task. He immediately rode out to meet Pope, took over the command from him, and went on to join the retreating troops, who received him with enthusiasm. Their spirits rose, and they forgot their defeat. Lee did not pursue in the direction of Washington, but moved toward the upper crossings of the Potomac. McClellan assembled the incoming troops at Rockville and Leesburg, assuming personal command for an advance, although his orders were simply to provide for the defense of Washington. Pending further information of the enemy, he directed his right upon Frederick, and kept his left on the Potomac. On the morning of Sept. 13 he learned, through a copy of one of Lee's orders which fell into his hands, that the Confederates were much scattered. He moved to take advantage of this, but too slowly; Lee succeeded in concentrating, and was able to avoid destruction in the battles of South Mountain and the Antietam. After these battles, McClellan did not press, and Lee accomplished the withdrawal of his army across the Potomac. McClellan did not follow until late in October. Early in the month he had been ordered by Lincoln to give battle, and on Oct. 13 he was asked by the President: "Are you not overcautious when you assume that you cannot do what the enemy is constantly doing?" (*Official Records,* 1 Ser., Vol. XIX, Pt. I, pp. 11, 13). At Warrenton, on Nov. 7, he received an order to turn over his command to General Burnside and to proceed to Trenton, N. J., to await orders. He was never again employed in the field. In 1863 he prepared a report covering his period of command of the Army of the Potomac (published as *House Executive Document No. 15,* 38 Cong., 1 Sess.).

In 1864 he was nominated as the Democratic candidate for the presidency. The country seemed weary of the war, and the leaders of the Democratic party thought they could see an opportunity to win on a platform calling for immediate cessation of hostilities. McClellan seemed the logical candidate. He could be represented as a victim of the injustice of the administration—a general who had accomplished much and would have accomplished more if he had been fairly treated. He accepted the nomination, although it placed him in a most embarrassing position; he had always stood for vigorous prosecution of the war, and had recently reaffirmed this attitude in an oration at West Point. In his letter of acceptance he tried to harmonize the inconsistency, but without conspicuous success. On election day he resigned his commission in the army. The returns showed that he had carried only New Jersey, Delaware, and Kentucky, with 21 electoral votes against Lincoln's 212.

The next three years he spent abroad. Upon his return he was placed in charge of construction of a new type of steam war-vessel, designed by Edwin A. Stevens of Hoboken, and being built with money left for that purpose in his will. The funds were exhausted before the ship was completed, and the project was abandoned in 1869. He was invited to become president of the University of California in 1868, and of Union College in 1869, but declined both offers. In 1870 he was appointed chief engineer of the New York City Department of Docks, but resigned in 1872. In 1871 he declined appointment as comptroller of the city. From January 1878 to January 1881 he served as governor of New Jersey. He was married in 1860 to Ellen Mary Marcy, and had two children, a daughter and a son. His wife was the daughter of his old commander in the Red River exploring expedition, Randolph B. Marcy [*q.v.*], who served later as his chief of staff. He died of heart trouble, at Orange, N. J., Oct. 29, 1885.

McClellan was slightly under the middle height, but very squarely and powerfully built, with exceptional strength and endurance. His features were regular and pleasing, his hair and moustache red. His tastes were quiet and scholarly. An excellent linguist, he knew and used all the principal languages of western Europe, ancient and modern. Not only did he always keep up military study, but he was well informed in current literature, particularly that dealing with archeological research and exploration. He spent much time abroad, chiefly in Switzerland, and interested himself in mountain climbing.

As a soldier, he fell barely short of conspicuous success. He took the best of care of his men and had the happy faculty of inspiring confidence and loyalty. His knowledge and comprehension of military affairs was great, and he was able to select from foreign systems features that were appropriate to the American service, and adapt them to its requirements. His ideas of organization, strategy, and tactics were clear and sound. But he was never satisfied with what he had, nor willing to make the best of an imperfect tool. He could always see wherein he might make improvements, given time; and he took the time, at the expense of losing his opportunities. He could not be content with a plan that took into account all apparent factors, and trust to the inspiration of the moment to take care of the unforeseen; his plan must be complete. His reasoning powers carried him up to contact with the enemy; at that moment, when an independent will entered the problem, he became hesitating. Knowing accurately his own numbers, and knowing also the weaknesses and defects of his own force, he allowed for these and discounted the numbers. For the enemy's strength, he accepted too readily the estimates of his intelligence service, directed by Allan Pinkerton [*q.v.*], and these estimates were usually too high. Further, not knowing the enemy's troubles, he failed to make the discounts. Hence he always believed himself outnumbered, when in fact he always had the superior force.

While he had seen much field service, he had never held even the smallest command in war, until he conducted the operations in West Virginia as a major-general. Except for the campaign in Mexico, his only knowledge of warfare was gained at Sevastopol, and the siege technique observed there controlled his action in the Peninsula. In the Antietam campaign he showed that he was beginning to learn to attack. Under a good teacher—had there been such a teacher—he might have mastered the lesson. He probably came to the supreme command too early. In his *Own Story* he hints that such was the case. But at the time, possibly through a half recognition of his deficiencies, he expressed the utmost confidence, and always took the attitude that his superiors, through ignorance or jealousy, were not properly supporting him. Thus his successes were only half successes; at the same time, his failures were not disasters. Lee, who should have known, set him down as the best commander who ever faced him (R. E. Lee, Jr., *Recollections and Letters of General Robert E. Lee*, 1924, p. 416). But Lee saw the deficiencies, too; he once remarked, half seriously, when he learned that Burnside had taken command, that he regretted to part with McClellan, "for we always understood each other so well. I fear they may continue to make these changes until they find someone I don't understand" (*Battles and Leaders*, III, 70).

[*McClellan's Own Story* (1887) is a poorly constructed book and unsatisfactory in that it assumes the defensive throughout. Everything printed about him during or soon after the war is partisan. John G. Barnard, *The Peninsular Campaign and Its Antecedents* (1864), is a military analysis, sharply critical of McClellan. An excellent example of contemporary defenses of him is G. S. Hillard, *Life and Campaigns of George B. McClellan* (1864). Later and more dispassionate writings are P. S. Michie, *General McClellan* (1901), and Francis W. Palfrey, *The Antietam and Fredericksburg* (1882). See also G. W. Cullum, *Biog. Register of the Officers and Grads. of the U. S. Mil.*

Acad. (3 ed., 1891); *War of the Rebellion: Official Records (Army)*; "Report of the Joint Committee on the Conduct of the War," *Senate Report No. 108*, 37 Cong., 3 Sess.; memoir by Gen. W. B. Franklin in *Seventeenth Annual Reunion of the Asso. of the Grads. of the U. S. Mil. Acad.* (1886); J. G. Nicolay and John Hay, *Abraham Lincoln* (10 vols., 1890); Emory Upton, *The Mil. Policy of the U. S.* (1904); *Battles and Leaders of the Civil War* (4 vols., 1887–88); G. C. Gorham, *Life and Public Services of Edwin M. Stanton* (2 vols., 1899); *Diary of Gideon Welles* (1911), vol. I; J. H. Stine, *Hist. of the Army of the Potomac* (1892); G. T. Curtis, "McClellan's Last Service to the Republic," *North American Rev.*, Apr., May 1880; *Army and Navy Journal*, Oct. 31, Nov. 7, 14, 1885. Col. John R. Meigs Taylor, of Washington, has furnished recollections of conversations with his grandfather General Meigs, which have thrown light upon some of McClellan's relations with the administration.] O. L. S., Jr.

McCLELLAN, HENRY BRAINERD (Oct. 17, 1840–Oct. 1, 1904), Confederate soldier, educator, was born in Philadelphia, Pa., of distinguished Scotch-Irish and English ancestry. His parents were Dr. Samuel McClellan and Margaret Carswell (Ely), both of Connecticut families. His great-grandfather, Gen. Samuel McClellan, commanded the 5th Brigade, Connecticut Militia, in the Revolutionary War; his maternal grandfather, Rev. Ezra Stiles Ely, moved to Philadelphia and donated part of the land for Jefferson Medical College, of which Dr. Samuel McClellan and his brother, Dr. George McClellan, 1796–1847 [*q.v.*], were the founders.

Henry McClellan was graduated from Williams College in August 1858 when not yet eighteen years old. He had already determined to enter the ministry, but since he was so young his family decided that he should teach for a few years. Consequently, for the next two and a half years he tutored in a private family in Cumberland County, Va., and here, under the influence of older persons, acquired a firm belief in state's rights. Only a short time before his death he laughingly declared that he was still a rebel, reconstructed but absolutely unrepentant. In 1861 he entered the Confederate army as a private in the 3rd Virginia Cavalry. He was handicapped not only by his lack of military training but by his Northern birth and affiliations. Three of his brothers served in the Federal army, while his first cousin, Gen. George B. McClellan [*q.v.*], was twice commander of the Army of the Potomac. Despite these obstacles he rose in two years, at the age of twenty-three, to the position of assistant adjutant-general and chief of staff of the cavalry of the Army of Northern Virginia. In 1862–63 he was adjutant of the 3rd Virginia Cavalry and from 1863 to the end of the war he served, with the rank of major, as assistant adjutant-general and chief of staff, first to Gen. J. E. B. Stuart and then to Wade Hampton.

Some important items regarding McClellan's military career may be gleaned from the *Official Records.* In his report of the engagement at Kelly's Ford, Va., Mar. 17, 1863, Fitzhugh Lee "particularly commended" him for his gallantry (*Official Records,* 1 ser. XXV, pt. 1, p. 62). Reporting the engagement at Fleetwood, June 9, 1863, Stuart wrote that McClellan "displayed the same zeal, gallantry, and efficiency which has on every battlefield, in the camp, or on the march, so distinguished him as to cause his selection for his present post" (*Ibid.*, XXVII, pt. 2, p. 685). Again, after the Bristoe (Va.) campaign in October 1863, Stuart reported McClellan as having been at his side "night and day" and that he was "greatly indebted" to McClellan "for the clearness with which orders and dispatches were transmitted" (*Ibid.*, XXIX, pt. 1, p. 453). After Stuart was wounded at Yellow Tavern, McClellan went to the bedside of his dying chief, who gave him his bay horse as a final evidence of his esteem. Two days later, May 14, 1864, McClellan was assigned to duty at Lee's headquarters and, on Aug. 11, 1864, was made assistant adjutant-general and chief of staff under Wade Hampton. He served under Hampton in his subsequent campaigns, including that with Johnston's army in the Carolinas. McClellan was notified that his commission as lieutenant-colonel had been issued, but since he did not receive it until after Lee's surrender, he modestly disclaimed the rank.

After the close of the war, he resided for some years in Cumberland County, Va. In 1870 he became principal of Sayre Female Institute, Lexington, Ky., which he conducted successfully until shortly before his death. He was the author of *The Life and Campaigns of Major-General J. E. B. Stuart* (1885), still the standard biography. In preparing this work he was aided by former high officers in the Union army, by Stuart's family, and by surviving Confederate associates. It contains much valuable source material, including in the appendix the personal war records of the officers and men in several Virginia cavalry regiments; it has been translated into German and is used as a source book by students of cavalry tactics and Civil War history. McClellan was married on Dec. 31, 1863, to Catherine Macon Matthews of Cumberland County, Va., and was survived by several children.

[H. B. McClellan, *The Life and Campaigns of Gen. J. E. B. Stuart* (1885); *War of the Rebellion, Official Records (Army)*; *Who's Who in America*, 1903–05; Cleveland Abbe and J. G. Nichols, *Abbe-Abbey Geneal.* (1916); M. S. Beach, *The Ely Ancestry* (1902); information from Miss Margaret E. McClellan, Lexington, Ky.] R. D. M.

McCLELLAN, ROBERT (1770–Nov. 22, 1815), scout, Indian trader, was born near Mercersburg, Pa., the son of a pioneer farmer, also named Robert. He had little schooling, but he became an expert woodsman and hunter. His first employment was that of a pack-horseman in the transport of goods. In 1790, at Fort Gower, on the Ohio, he joined the army as a spy, or ranger, and in the following year went to Fort Washington (Cincinnati) and later to Fort Hamilton, where he again found work as a pack-horseman. On the arrival of Wayne's army he was engaged as a scout, serving throughout the campaign of 1794–95 and distinguishing himself by a series of daring exploits which won for him the rank of lieutenant. In the summer of 1799 he journeyed south and at New Orleans was stricken with yellow fever. On his recovery he went to Philadelphia, where on account of wounds suffered in Wayne's campaign he was awarded a small pension and where for a time he was employed in the quartermaster's department. Sent to the Illinois country on official business in 1801, he shortly afterward resigned and entered the Indian trade.

In 1807 McClellan and Ramsay Crooks led an expedition toward the upper Missouri. On meeting Ensign Pryor's party returning from its defeat by the Arikaras they turned back to a point near Old Council Bluffs and established a trading post. They again started upstream in 1809 but were halted by a Sioux tribe and compelled to erect another establishment for trade. On the retirement of Crooks from the partnership early the following year, McClellan continued alone, but on being robbed by the Sioux he became disheartened and started for St. Louis. At the mouth of the Nodaway he found Crooks in the winter camp of Hunt's Astoria party and at once joined the Pacific Fur Company. He accompanied the expedition the following spring, arriving in Astoria, ragged, ill, and emaciated, in January 1812. In March he withdrew from the company, and in June started eastward with Stuart's party, which reached St. Louis, after extreme hardships and privations, Apr. 30, 1813. A month later he was imprisoned for debt. In January 1814, with a stock of goods furnished by a friend, he opened a store in Cape Girardeau, Mo., but ill health compelled his return to St. Louis the following summer. He found a home on the farm of Abraham Gallatin, and it was probably there that he died. He was buried on Gen. William Clark's farm, where his tombstone was unearthed in 1875. Though of slight physique, McClellan was in his prime a man of great strength and agility, and pioneer annals credit him, while a scout in Wayne's army, with many amazing athletic feats. His courage is well attested by the inscription on his tombstone, thought to have been written by Clark: "Brave, honest and sincere; an intrepid warrior, whose services deserve perpetual remembrance."

[See: Jas. McBride, *Pioneer Biog.* (1871), vol. II; Stella M. Drumm, "More About Astorians," *Quart. of the Ore. Hist. Soc.*, Dec. 1923; Washington Irving, *Astoria* (1836); H. M. Chittenden, *The Am. Fur Trade of the Far West* (1902); John Bradbury, *Travels in the Interior of America* (1817, 2nd ed. 1819); H. M. Brackenridge, *Views of La., Together with a Jour. of a Voyage up the Mo. River in 1811* (1814); J. L. Finafrock, "Robt. McClellan," *The Kittochtinny Hist. Soc. . . . Papers*, vol. IX (1923). By Irving the name of McClellan is erroneously spelled M'Lellan, and by Chittenden, McLellan.] W. J. G.

McCLELLAND, ROBERT (Aug. 1, 1807–Aug. 30, 1880), congressman, governor of Michigan, secretary of the interior, was born at Greencastle, Pa., the son of Dr. John McClellan (*sic*) and Eleanor Bell McCulloh. He graduated from Dickinson College in 1829 and was admitted to the bar at Chambersburg in 1831. After practising for a year in Pittsburgh he migrated to Monroe, Mich., in 1833, where four years later he married Sarah E. Sabine of Williamstown, Mass. Michigan was about to become a state and McClelland was active in organizing the new government and the Democratic party. He served in the constitutional convention of 1835 and in the legislature, 1838–43; in the last-named year he went to Congress, to which he was twice reelected. At Washington he was interested in commerce and foreign affairs, and enjoyed the friendship of Wilmot and of Lewis Cass. He was in close association with the former and supported the "Proviso" to his later embarrassment. He became Cass's chief Michigan lieutenant and aided him considerably in his presidential campaign in 1848.

McClelland retired from Congress in 1849 and after participating in the constitutional convention of 1850 was twice elected governor (1850, 1852). During this period he labored to heal the party schism of 1848 by abandoning his support of the Wilmot Proviso and successfully urging the Michigan Democracy to indorse the compromise measures of 1850. His success in Michigan, his activities at the national Democratic convention of 1852, and especially his close association with Cass, attracted attention outside of Michigan, and when President-Elect Pierce sought a representative man from the Cass faction for his cabinet he invited McClelland to become secretary of the interior.

McClelland found his four-year-old department badly organized and set himself to produce order. His four bureaus, land, Indian, pension, and patent, were scattered over Washington and their work was behindhand. He instituted new regulations requiring more effort from his clerks, classified them under a recently enacted law, and in due time was able to report a coherent and efficient service. He struggled to reduce the corruption and waste that clung persistently to the land, Indian, and pension bureaus and his strictness improved conditions in these respects without adding, however, to the popularity of the Pierce administration. He urged that pensions be given only to the indigent. The Indians he favored placing upon reservations, as quickly as possible, so that they might be taught the arts of civilization. Money payments to them should be stopped, he argued, and their annuities settled in goods. As to the public lands, he was at first much interested in grants to the states to be used for railroad purposes and favored a Pacific railroad constructed by the aid of land subsidies from the federal government, but as the railroad interests became more importunate and brought to bear upon Congress what the Pierce administration considered improper pressure, he withdrew his support from projects for this form of aid. The land system itself he thought needed no improvement, and like the dominant element in his party he opposed homestead legislation. None of his major recommendations was adopted by Congress, however; the value of his service to his department lay in his ability to produce system, order, and honesty. As a member of Pierce's cabinet he belonged with Marcy and Guthrie to the more conservative wing and joined the former in advising the President to follow a neutral policy in Kansas.

In 1857 McClelland returned to Michigan, settling down in Detroit to twenty-three years of legal practice. He returned to public service briefly in 1867 as a member of the Michigan constitutional convention. In personality he was always plain and unprepossessing; his manners were somewhat brusque and forbidding; and he was regular and painstaking in his mode of life to an extent which in his later years became proverbial among his neighbors.

[A brief manuscript biography is in the possession of McClelland's grandson, R. McClelland Brady, Santa Barbara, Cal.; a few of his papers are in the Lib. of Cong., his family have a few, and a number of the letters he received from Cass are in the Burton Coll., Detroit Pub. Lib. See also Alfred Nevin, *Men of Mark of Cumberland Valley, Pa.* (1876); *Am. Biog. Hist. of Eminent and Self-Made Men . . . Mich. Vol.* (1878); *Pioneer Colls.—Report of the Pioneer Soc. of the State of Mich.*, IV (1883), 454–57; *Evening News* (Detroit), Aug. 30, 31, 1880; *Detroit Free Press*, Sept. 1, 1880.] R. F. N.

McCLERNAND, JOHN ALEXANDER (May 30, 1812–Sept. 20, 1900), congressman and Union soldier, the son of John A. and Fatima McClernand, was born near Hardinsburg, Ky., and moved to Illinois when a small boy. His father died probably in 1816 and John, the only child, attended village school at Shawneetown, helped support his mother, and read law in a local office. He was admitted to the bar in 1832, but the Black Hawk War, Mississippi River trading, and the editorship of the *Gallatin Democrat and Illinois Advertiser* temporarily diverted him from his profession. As an assemblyman between 1836 and 1843, his political acumen and expansive eloquence, fortified with many allusions to the classics, quickly gained him prominence. Ever a stanch Jacksonian, he hated Abolitionists and supported sound money and extensive internal improvements. He married Sarah Dunlap of Jacksonville, on Nov. 7, 1843, and removed to that town eight years later. In Congress from 1843 to 1851 and from 1859 to 1861, although courting war with foreign powers for territorial gain, he urged conciliation and the popular sovereignty panacea during crises over slavery extension. He figured prominently in the tumultuous speakership contests of the first sessions of the Thirty-first and the Thirty-sixth congresses and shared in framing the compromise measures of 1850. He broke with Douglas in 1854, but they worked together for peace and the Union six years later. His wife having died he married his sister-in-law, Minerva Dunlap, probably on Dec. 30, 1862.

Following the first battle of Bull Run he proposed a resolution in the House to spend men and money without stint to restore the Union, and when the resolution was adopted he, himself, already a colonel of militia, left Congress to accept a brigadier-general's commission. While post commander at Cairo on reconnaissance in Kentucky and at Belmont, his vigor and bravery won Grant's approval; but at Fort Henry, despite orders, he failed to block the Confederate retreat and, after the fall of Fort Donelson, angered his superior by virtually crediting the victory to his own division, the 1st. Nevertheless, he was a major-general after Mar. 21, 1862, outranked in the West by Halleck and Grant alone. Ambitious and untactful, he resented dictation, disliked West Pointers, and never forgot his political fences in Illinois. He wrote of his decisive rôle at Shiloh to Lincoln and to Halleck, criticizing Grant's strategy and protesting assignments to duty inconsistent with his rank. He sought to supplant McClellan in the East, and, warning Lincoln that a closed Mississippi meant dangerous discontent in the upper valley, was authorized in October 1862 to raise a large force in the Northwest for a river expedition against Vicksburg. At Sherman's suggestion and unauthorized by Grant, he and his thirty thousand, with Porter's ironclads, reduced Arkansas Post on Jan. 11, 1863, and thereby gained the congratulations of Lincoln and Governor Yates of Illinois. Grant tartly ordered him to return to Millikens Bend and, over his protest, dissolved the Mississippi River expedition and assigned him to command the XIII Corps. For three months he supervised the making of roads, levees, and canals on the peninsula opposite Vicksburg. Although Charles Dana, war department observer in the field, repeatedly advised Stanton to remove him, he led the advance across the Mississippi at the end of April 1863. Grant charged him with tardiness at Grand Gulf and Champion Hills and with half of the heavy losses before Vicksburg on May 22. When he, without Grant's authorization, furnished the press with a congratulatory order, extolling his men as the heroes of the campaign, Grant, eagerly supported by Sherman and McPherson, ordered him to Illinois on June 18, 1863. Here, ever popular, and unbroken in spirit, he rallied the people to a renewed support of the war, and Governor Yates besought Lincoln on the eve of Gettysburg to give him the eastern command. When the President refused to call a court of inquiry, McClernand warned him that he would publish a severe indictment of Grant (*War of the Rebellion: Official Records, post,* 1 ser., XXIV, pt. 1, pp. 169–86). In early February 1864 he regained command of the XIII Corps, then scattered from New Orleans to the Rio Grande. For three months he contended with bad weather and water, shifting sands, an elusive enemy, a dwindling corps, and his own thwarted ambition. Hardly had he left his headquarters on Matagorda Island in late April to participate in the Red River expedition, than acute sickness forced him to return to Illinois. He resigned his commission on Nov. 30, 1864.

He served as circuit judge of the Sangamon district from 1870 to 1873, as a member of the state Democratic central committee, as chairman of the National Democratic Convention in 1876, and on the Utah commission under Cleveland. He died of dysentery in Springfield, where he had lived since some time before the Civil War. He was survived by his wife and four children.

[A few letters in the Chicago Hist. Soc. Lib. and in the McCormick Hist. Asso. Lib. in Chicago; *Ill. State Jour.* (Springfield), Oct. 19–Nov. 16, 1859, Aug. 8, Oct. 10, 31, 1860, Apr. 24, June 5, Aug. 7, Oct. 2, 1861, May 21, Aug. 6, Sept. 3, 10, Oct. 8, Nov. 19, 26, Dec. 31, 1862, Mar. 18, July 1, 1863, Feb. 3, 1864; *Ill. Weekly State Jour.* (Springfield), Dec. 31, 1862; J. M. Palmer, *The Bench and Bar of Ill.* (1899), vol. I; *Hist. of Sangamon County, Ill.* (1881); T. C. Pease, *Illinois Election Returns* (1923); *Jour. of the Ill. State Hist. Soc.*, Oct. 1923–Jan. 1924, Jan. 1929; *War of the Rebellion: Official Records (Army)*, 1 ser., III, VII, X, pts. 1, 2, XVI, pt. 2, XVII, pts. 1, 2, XXII, pt. 2, XXIV, pts. 1, 3, XXXIV, pts. 1–3, LI, pt. 1, LII, pt. 1; *Battles and Leaders of the Civil War* (1887), vols. I, III; John Fiske, *The Mississippi Valley in the Civil War* (1900); *Personal Memoirs of U. S. Grant* (1885), vol. I; *Memoirs of Gen. W. T. Sherman*, 2nd ed. (1886), vol. I; *Ill. State Register* (Springfield), Feb. 24, 1843, Nov. 10, 1843, Sept. 20, 1900.] W. T. H.

McCLINTOCK, EMORY (Sept. 19, 1840–July 10, 1916), mathematician, actuary, was born at Carlisle, Pa., the son of the Rev. John M'Clintock [*q.v.*], a clergyman and educator, and Caroline Augusta Wakeman, a descendant of John Wakeman, treasurer of the New Haven Colony, 1655–59. At the age of fourteen he entered Dickinson College, leaving in 1856 to enter Yale. A year later he transferred to Columbia where he was graduated with high honors in 1859, being at once appointed to a tutorship in mathematics. A year later he went to Paris for the purpose of studying chemistry, spending the following year at Göttingen. From 1863 to 1866 he served as vice-consul at Bradford, England, and in the latter year he took a position with a banking firm in Paris. He continued his interest in mathematics, and particularly in the special field of actuarial science. He returned to America in 1868 to accept an appointment as actuary in the Asbury Life Insurance Company of New York. In 1871 he was called to a similar position with the Northwestern Life Insurance Company of Milwaukee, remaining there for eighteen years. In 1889 he became actuary of the Mutual Life Insurance Company of New York and continued with the organization in this capacity until 1911, when he became consulting actuary. Meantime (1905) he became a member of the board of trustees and one of the vice-presidents.

In the general reorganization of the American life-insurance companies in 1905–06 McClintock's grasp of the insurance problem was at once manifest, and his recommendations did much to reëstablish the position of these American companies in the United States. He was for many years the recognized leader in actuarial circles in this country, being one of the founders of the Actuarial Society of America (1889) and later (1895) its president. He was also a fellow of the Institute of Actuaries of Great Britain (1874), a corresponding member of the Institut des Actuaires Français, and of the Association d'Actuaires Belges, and a member of the permanent committee of the International Congress of Actuaries. In the domain of pure mathematics he was hardly less interested. He was one of the founders of the New York Mathematical Society, its second president (1891), and one of the leaders in transforming this organization into the American Mathematical Society (1894), and in establishing its *Bulletin* and *Transactions.* To both of these periodicals he contributed numerous articles. In his articles on the calculus of enlargement in the *American Journal of Mathematics* (June 1879, January 1895) he attempted to coördinate in a new way certain special fields of mathematics. For his work in actuarial science and in pure mathematics he received several honorary doctorates and was elected an honorary fellow of the American Academy of Arts and Sciences. McClintock's first wife was Zoe Darlington, of Yorkshire, England, by whom he had one son, Maj. John McClintock, for a time military attaché in the legation at Vienna. His second wife was Isabella Bishop of New Brunswick, N. J.

[T. S. Fiske, article in the *Bull. of the Am. Math. Soc.,* May 1917, with bibliography; Wm. A. Hutcheson, article in the *Trans. Actuarial Soc. of America,* vol. XVII, 1916, and discussion of article in *Ibid.,* vol. XVIII, 1917; *Weekly Underwriter,* July 15, 1916; *N. Y. Times,* July 12, 19, 1916.] D. E. S.

M'CLINTOCK, JOHN (Oct. 27, 1814–Mar. 4, 1870), Methodist Episcopal clergyman, educator, and editor, was the son of John and Martha (M'Mackin) M'Clintock, both of whom were born in County Tyrone, Ireland. The younger John was a native of Philadelphia, where his father carried on a retail dry-goods business. He received his early schooling under Samuel B. Wylie [*q.v.*], also an Irishman, and a noted classicist. When he was fourteen years old he became a clerk in his father's store, and two years later, bookkeeper in the Methodist Book Concern, New York. While here he was converted, and began to consider entering the ministry. In 1832 he enrolled as a freshman at the University of Pennsylvania and completed the required course in three years. During the latter part of it he had preached regularly, and in April 1835 had been admitted on trial to the Philadelphia Conference of the Methodist Episcopal Church and appointed to Jersey City. His health broke down in 1836, and he was obliged to relinquish his charge. Thereafter he suffered from a recurrent throat trouble, and was never physically strong.

Turning now to the educational field, he accepted an assistant professorship of mathematics at Dickinson College, Carlisle, Pa., and in 1837 was made full professor. He remained with this institution for twelve years, being transferred to the chair of classical languages in 1840. While there he published some widely used textbooks, *A First Book in Latin* (1846) and *A First Book in Greek* (1848), both in collaboration with George R. Crooks [*q.v.*]. They were followed by *A Second Book in Greek* (1850), and *A Second Book in Latin* (1853). With Charles E. Blumenthal he prepared a translation of Neander's *Das Leben Jesu Christi,* issued in 1848 under the title, *The Life of Jesus Christ in Its Historical Connexion and Development.* Improvement in his health enabled him to preach more frequently, and on Apr. 19, 1840, he was ordained elder by Bishop Elijah Hedding [*q.v.*]. When in 1847 two slave-owners from Maryland came to Carlisle to recover some runaway slaves, M'Clintock endeavored to see that the legal rights of the latter were respected. Before the matter was settled, a riot occurred and he and a number of negroes were arrested on the charge of instigating it. Excitement ran high and the feeling against him was strong, but a jury acquitted him.

In 1848 he resigned his professorship and became editor of the *Methodist Quarterly Review,* to which office the General Conference of that year elected him. For this position he was now well fitted. Having an acquisitive mind and a studious disposition, he had become "the most universally accomplished man American Methodism had produced" (J. M. Buckley, *A History of Methodists in the United States,* 1896, American Church History Series, V, 528). During the eight years he conducted the *Review* he made it a scholarly exponent of the best Christian thought, and under him it became, for the first time, self-supporting. Twice in this period he went abroad for the benefit of his health. In 1851 he was elected president of Wesleyan University, and in 1855, president of Troy University, both of which honors he declined. He published in 1855 *The Temporal Power of the Pope,* an exposition of the Ultramontane theory of the relation of church and state. Two years before, with Dr. James Strong [*q.v.*], he had begun the now well-known *Cyclopædia of Biblical, Theological, and Ecclesiastical Literature,* upon which ambitious undertaking he spent much time for the rest of his life. Three volumes only were published before his death, the first in 1867.

His connection with the *Review* terminated in 1856 and with Bishop Matthew Simpson [*q.v.*] he went abroad as delegate to the British Wesleyan Conference, and the conference of the Evangelical Alliance at Berlin. Upon his return he became pastor of St. Paul's Church, New York, where he soon ranked among the ablest preachers of the city. In 1860 he was appointed pastor of the American Chapel, Paris. During the Civil War, by speeches, writings, and personal contacts, he was a potent influence in removing misapprehensions abroad, and through the *Methodist,* of which he was a corresponding editor, in disseminating correct information at home. It is reported that President Lincoln declared him fitted for the position of minister to France (Buckley, p. 528). He again became pastor of St. Paul's Church, New York, in 1864, but ill health soon compelled him to resign. From 1864 to 1866, as chairman of a committee appointed by the General Conference, he was busily engaged in putting into operation an elaborate scheme for the celebration of the centenary of American Methodism. In accordance with the desire of Daniel Drew [*q.v.*], in 1867 he became the first president of Drew Theological Seminary, but less than three years later death brought his career to a close. His publications included *Sketches of Eminent Methodist Ministers* (1854), and *History of the Council of Trent, from the French of L. F. Bungener* (1855). After his death *Living Words: or Unwritten Sermons Reported Phonographically* (1871), and *Lectures . . . on Theological Encyclopaedia and Methodology* (1873), appeared. He was married first, in 1837, to Caroline A. Wakeman; Emory McClintock [*q.v.*] was their son. In October 1851, he married Catharine W. Emory, widow of his friend, Rev. Robert Emory.

[G. R. Crooks, *Life and Letters of Rev. John M'Clintock, D.D., LL.D.* (1876); E. S. Tipple, *Drew Theological Seminary, 1867–1917* (1917); C. F. Himes, *A Sketch of Dickinson College* (1879); F. L. Mott, *A Hist. of Am. Magazines, 1741–1850* (1930); *Methodist Review,* July 1894, Nov. 1917; *Methodist,* Mar. 12, 1870; *N. Y. Times,* Mar. 5, 1870.] H. E. S.

McCLINTOCK, OLIVER (Oct. 20, 1839–Oct. 10, 1922), merchant and political reformer, was born in Pittsburgh, Pa., the eldest of seven children of Washington and Eliza (Thompson) McClintock. He was a descendant of Scotch ancestors who came to Pennsylvania from Ireland in 1740. His grandfather engaged in Conestoga wagon freighting between Philadelphia and Pittsburgh and ran a blacksmith shop and ferry at Fort Pitt. Washington McClintock entered the business of his father-in-law, Samuel Thompson, who manufactured uniforms in the War of 1812 and established a carpet and drygoods store in Pittsburgh. In 1844 the firm became W. McClintock & Company. Oliver received a good education in local academies and graduated from Yale in 1861. He served as a corporal in the 15th Pennsylvania Emergency Militia during Lee's invasions, and was also a member of the subsistence committee which fed 500,000 Federal troops as they passed through Pittsburgh. He was taken into his father's business in 1862, but shortly established a separate store, which merged with the parent company in 1864 as Oliver McClintock & Company. His brothers, and later two of his sons, were admitted to the firm, which attained a position of leadership in the mercantile life of the city and was finally dissolved on Apr. 1, 1914, after 106 years of activity by three generations.

McClintock was a prime mover in many civic enterprises. He was an elder of the Presbyterian Church, first president of the Pittsburgh Young Men's Christian Association (1866), a trustee and president of the board of Western Theological Seminary and of Pennsylvania College for Women. In 1883 he and his brother-in-law, Albert H. Childs, founded Shadyside Academy; and his sons were members of its first graduating class. He was long an official of the Chamber of Commerce and at his death was its oldest member. When the city government collapsed during the railroad-strike riots of 1877, McClintock acted for two weeks on the Emergency Public Safety Committee authorized by a mass meeting. He was a founder and director of the Civic Club of Allegheny County, and was active in such national and state bodies as the American Civic Association, National Civil Service Reform League, National Municipal League, Ballot Reform Association, and Indian Rights Association of Pennsylvania.

In the 1880's and '90's Pittsburgh was in the grip of a political ring led by Christopher L. Magee [*q.v.*], which distributed long franchises to utilities, let bids for public works at exorbitant prices, and generally battened on public moneys under cover of legal forms. A small group of citizens, inspired by McClintock and David D. Bruce, had for years vainly fought the public-works corruption in and out of court. In 1895 they aroused enough public sentiment to organize a Citizens' Municipal League, and campaigned to beat the ring in the election of February 1896. McClintock was a member of the executive committee of five, which nominated for mayor George W. Guthrie [*q.v.*], an able Democratic lawyer. The Magee machine was hampered by a factional fight with the state boss, Senator Matthew S. Quay [*q.v.*], and Guthrie actually won a majority; but he was fraudulently counted out and denied a recount by the courts. In 1902 McClintock again led a Citizens' Party, which partially broke the hold of the Magee ring. In 1906 the independents succeeded in electing Guthrie mayor, and a great exposé of councilmanic iniquity followed. McClintock secured in 1907 the passage of a state civil-service law for second-class cities (Pittsburgh, Scranton). In 1910 the veteran reformer threw his influence into the fight for a new city charter which replaced the corrupt and inefficient two-chambered council, elected by wards, with a small council of nine, elected at large on a non-partisan ballot. McClintock himself never sought public office. His tireless efforts for good government were attended by ridicule, threats, and boycotts of other business men. He said that he met his greatest discouragement in the cowardice and civic apathy of prosperous citizens. He attributed his reforming zeal to a hatred of autocracy inherited from his Revolutionary and Scotch-Irish ancestors. Lincoln Steffens, writing in *McClure's Magazine* in 1903, said of him: "This single citizen's long, brave fight is one of the finest stories in the history of municipal government."

McClintock was married, June 7, 1866, to Clara Courtney Childs of Pittsburgh. He had three sons and three daughters, all of whom survived him.

[G. I. Reed, *Century Cyc. of Hist. and Biog. of Pa.* (1904), vol. II; J. N. Boucher, *A Century and a Half of Pittsburgh and Her People* (1908), vol. I; G. T. Fleming, *Hist. of Pittsburgh and Environs* (1922), vol. IV; Lincoln Steffens, "Pittsburg: A City Ashamed," *McClure's Magazine*, May 1903; *Yale Univ. Obit. Record*, 1923; *Who's Who in America*, 1922–23; *Pittsburgh Post, Pittsburg Dispatch*, Oct. 11, 1922; notes of family.]

K. M. G.

McCLOSKEY, JOHN (Mar. 10, 1810–Oct. 10, 1885), Roman Catholic prelate, first American cardinal, was the son of Patrick and Elizabeth (Harron) McCloskey, recent immigrants from County Derry, Ireland. He was born in Brooklyn, N. Y., where his father was a clerk in the firm of H. P. Pierrepont and Company. Receiving his first lessons from an English actress, the boy learned to speak with a precision and perfect enunciation of which in later life he was proud. In New York, he attended Thomas Brady's classical school and St. Patrick's Church, where he attracted the attention of Rev. John Power, Pierre Malou, S. J., and the philanthropic merchant, Cornelius Heeney, who on the death of McCloskey's father became the boy's guardian. Entering Mount St. Mary's College, Emmitsburg, Md., in 1821, he completed both the preparatory and collegiate courses, graduating in 1828. After spending a year on his mother's Westchester farm, he returned as a seminarian to Mount St. Mary's where he came into contact with such influential ecclesiastics as Dubois, Bruté, Hughes, and Purcell, and was recognized as a cultured gentleman rather than an ascetic or a scholar.

Ordained by Bishop Dubois at old St. Patrick's (Jan. 12, 1834), he was selected as an assistant at the cathedral and chaplain at Bellevue Hospital, and later received an appointment in the new seminary at Nyack. When this institution was burned, McCloskey was permitted to attend the Gregorian University at Rome (1835–37), where he made influential friends. Well traveled, fluent in French and Italian, and conversant with the mind of the Church, he returned to New York as rector of St. Joseph's Church in Greenwich. By prudent forbearance, he won the hostile trustees who would have closed the church doors upon him. In 1841, he was given additional duties as a teaching rector of St. John's College, Fordham. Two years later, on the application of Bishop John Hughes [*q.v.*] for a coadjutor, he was recommended by the bishops in a provincial council at Baltimore to Pope Gregory XVI, who forthwith named him titular bishop of Axiern with the right of succession to New York.

On Mar. 10, 1844, he was consecrated at St. Patrick's, Mott Street. While retaining his pastorate, he was chiefly engaged in visitations, ironing out difficulties in various parishes, toning down the opposition of certain pastors to Bishop Hughes, and winning over the aristocratic Catholics, whose ways he understood. While not openly involved in the nativist troubles or the school controversy, he was a conservative, dependable counselor upon whom the more virile Hughes learned to rely. The two bishops were decided opposites in character, yet they worked in perfect harmony. With the growth of the New York diocese, Buffalo and Albany were created separate sees, and McCloskey was given charge of the latter (May 21, 1847).

Though he took no part in politics, he was on intimate terms with Horatio Seymour, Erastus Corning, Rufus King, Thurlow Weed, and the Van Rensselaers. No doubt his work merited promotion, yet when he was elevated by Pius IX to the archbishopric of New York on the death of Hughes in 1864, there was a prevalent feeling that he had made use of consequential friends in Rome. Not until 1902 was it known that he had written to Cardinal Reisach beseeching that he, as physically frail, be spared the possible appointment and that M. J. Spalding or John Timon [*qq.v.*] be honored. His installation (Aug. 27, 1864) pleased the war administration in Washington, however, as well as the clergy and prominent laity of the archdiocese, who were relieved that the strenuous days of Hughes were over. Hence, he commenced his administration under the happiest auspices, although he always gracefully insisted that he was but reaping the fruits of his predecessor's labor. He retained the old council of priests, and there was no noticeable break with the past save in the method of conducting affairs. In 1866, he attended the Second Plenary Council of Baltimore, where he preached the opening sermon. In agreement with its deliberations, he silenced the Fenians by a letter of admonition read from all diocesan pulpits (Mar. 2, 1866), in which he counseled against wild schemes of freeing Ireland and invading Canada. Renewing work on St. Patrick's Cathedral, which had been discontinued during the war, he was so successful in collections and in obtaining furnishings during his frequent European journeys that the cathedral was ready for dedication on May 25, 1879. Compromising old administrative differences with the religious, he gave equal encouragement to Paulists, Franciscans, Dominicans, Augustinians, and Jesuits, as well as to the various communities of nuns. Deeply interested in eleemosynary institutions, he wheedled liberal donations for them from the increasingly large class of prosperous Catholics. In the Vatican Council, he considered the declaration of infallibility inexpedient, since the papacy was generally recognized as having the authority involved, but on the final ballot (July 18, 1870) he voted in the affirmative. For his hesitancy he was criticized by the ultramontane James A. McMaster [*q.v.*] of the *Freeman's Journal.* None the less, he gained rather than lost influence in Rome.

Pius IX preconized McCloskey in the same public consistory (Mar. 15, 1875) in which Archbishop Manning of Westminster was elevated to the cardinalate. There was almost universal approval in the United States, for even in non-Catholic circles national vanity was gratified that an American citizen had become a prince of the Church. McCloskey had made few enemies and had always worn his honors becomingly. Dignified in manner, benignant, confiding, and easily accessible, he held both the love and the respect of his priests and people. The investiture (Apr. 27) was a brilliant function. Three years later he journeyed to Rome, but was too late for the conclave which elected Pope Leo XIII, from whom he formally received the ring and red hat. In 1880 his work was lightened by the appointment of Bishop M. A. Corrigan [*q.v.*] as coadjutor; though until his golden jubilee (1884), he actively managed his great diocese himself. His last year was spent in quiet retirement at St. Vincent's-on-the-Hudson. His obsequies at St. Patrick's Cathedral (Oct. 25, 1885), presided over by Cardinal Gibbons, bore a national character.

[J. M. Farley, *The Life of John Cardinal McCloskey* (1918), *Hist. of St. Patrick's Cathedral* (1908), and notes on McCloskey's life in U. S. Cath. Hist. Soc., *Hist. Records and Studies,* vols. I, II (1900–01), and in *Cath. Encyc.,* IX (1910), 485; J. J. Walsh, *Our Am. Cardinals* (1926); R. H. Clarke, *Lives of the Deceased Bishops of the Cath. Ch. in the U. S.,* vol. III (1888); J. T. Smith, *The Cath. Ch. in N. Y.* (1905), vol. I; Louis Teste, *Préface au Conclave* (1877); Catholic Directories; *Celebration of the 50th Anniversary or Golden Jubilee of . . . Cardinal McCloskey* (1884); James Gibbons, *Funeral Oration on His Eminence John Cardinal McCloskey* (1885); M. A. Corrigan, *Words Spoken at the Month's Mind of his Eminence Cardinal McCloskey* (1885); J. G. Shea, *The Hierarchy of the Cath. Ch. in the U. S.* (1886); *N. Y. Times, N. Y. Tribune,* Oct. 10, 1885; *Donahoe's Mag.,* Jan. 1886; *N. Y. Freeman's Jour.,* May 7, Aug. 13, 1864.] R. J. P.

McCLOSKEY, WILLIAM GEORGE (Nov. 10, 1823–Sept. 17, 1909), Roman Catholic prelate, was born in Brooklyn, N. Y., where he received his early schooling. His father, George, was a dairy farmer and long trustee of St. James's Church. In 1835, the boy was enrolled in Mount St. Mary's College, Emmitsburg, Md. Later he studied law in New York prior to his entrance into the seminary at Mount St. Mary's, where he served as a prefect and teacher and received his master's degree. Ordained by Archbishop Hughes, Oct. 6, 1852, he was assigned as an assistant to his brother George, pastor of the Church of the Nativity, New York. A year later he was recalled to Emmitsburg as a teacher of Latin, scripture, and moral theology. In 1857 he was promoted to the directorship of the seminary, and in that capacity became known in clerical circles as a man of distinguished appearance and some administrative ability. Two years later, when the American College in Rome was established, the American hierarchy submitted a list of fifteen candidates for the rectorship, from which the cardinals of the Sacred College of the Propaganda, with the assent of the Holy Father, selected McCloskey (Dec. 1, 1859). The selection was well received and McCloskey proved an excellent rector. Under his guidance the enrolment of students increased greatly, indicating that he had the confidence of the American bishops who furnished the seminarians. Tact was essential in the Civil War days, when the students separated into northern and southern factions. Then too there were financial difficulties as the war economies dwarfed diocesan allocations. Nevertheless, the institution was in a flourishing condition when McCloskey resigned to accept the bishopric of Louisville, left vacant by the death of Bishop Peter J. Lavialle.

Consecrated by Cardinal Count August de Reisach of Munich in the college chapel (May 24, 1868), McCloskey is said to have been the first American so consecrated in Rome. For forty-one years he ruled the Louisville diocese which, during that time, saw an increase of from eighty to 200 priests and from sixty-four to about 165 churches, of which a large number had schools attached. He introduced into the diocese the Passionists, the Benedictines, the Priests of the Congregation of the Resurrection who managed St. Mary's College, and the Brothers of Mary, as well as the Sisters of Mercy and the Franciscan Sisters for elementary schools and academies. As early as 1869 he established Preston Park Seminary, over which his brother George (died, 1890) later presided as rector. In no work was he more concerned than in the charitable and reformatory institutions of the Sisters of the Poor and of the Good Shepherd. This interest led him to translate from the Italian a *Life of St. Mary Magdalen* (1900). He won a place of influence as a figure in the Vatican Council and in the Plenary Council of Baltimore (1884), as an active proponent of Catholic education, and as the oldest member of the hierarchy at the time of his death. With a pontifical requiem mass by Archbishop Moeller [*q.v.*] and a eulogy by Bishop Denis O'Donaghue, at the Cathedral of the Assumption, he was buried in the cemetery of the Sisters of Charity at Nazareth, Ky.

[*Cath. Encyc.*, IX (1910), 388; E. F. X. McSweeny, *The Story of the Mountain* (2 vols., 1911); J. G. Shea, *The Hierarchy of the Cath. Ch. in the U. S.* (1886); H. A. Brann, *Hist. of the Am. College of the Roman Cath. Ch. of the U. S., Rome, Italy* (1910); *N. Y. Freeman's Journal*, Jan. 7, Mar. 3, 1860; obituaries in *The Record* (diocesan organ) and *Louisville Courier-Journal*, Sept. 17, 18, 1909.] R. J. P.

McCLURE, ALEXANDER KELLY (Jan. 9, 1828–June 6, 1909), editor, lawyer, legislator, son of Alexander and Isabella (Anderson) McClure, was born in Sherman's Valley, Perry County, Pa., of Scotch-Irish descent. He was reared on his father's farm, educated at home, and at the age of fifteen was apprenticed to a tanner. At the same time he learned the printing trade in the office of the *Perry County Freeman*, where he absorbed Whig political principles. In the late forties he edited and published the *Juniata Sentinel* at Mifflintown. In 1849 he was commissioned colonel on the staff of Governor Johnson, and in the following year he was appointed deputy United States marshal for Juniata County. In 1852 he became part owner of the *Franklin Repository*, published in Chambersburg, and shortly afterward he secured full control. Under his direction it became one of the influential newspapers in the state. After failing of election as the Whig candidate for auditor-general in 1853, he turned his attention to law. He was admitted to the bar in 1856 but continued to devote most of his time to the *Repository*. He took particular interest in the organization of the Republican party and was a member of the state convention that met in Pittsburgh in the summer of 1855. In 1860 he was a member of the Pennsylvania delegation to the Republican National Convention which was committed to Simon Cameron for the presidency. When it became evident that two-thirds of the delegates from the other states were in favor of William H. Seward, Curtin and McClure succeeded in switching the Pennsylvania vote from Cameron to Lincoln. McClure was elected chairman of the Republican state committee and in this office perfected a complete political organization in every city, county, township, and precinct in the state. Following a campaign of unprecedented aggressiveness Andrew G. Curtin was elected governor and later Lincoln swept the state by a large majority.

After a term in the state House of Representatives in 1858, McClure was elected in 1859 to the state Senate. There he was spokesman for Pennsylvania's war governor, and as chairman of the Senate committee on military affairs he was active in support of both state and federal governments for the preservation of the Union. In 1865 he was again in the House of Representatives. At the request of President Lincoln, he accepted a commission as assistant adjutant-general of the army and placed seventeen regiments in the field. In 1868 he became a resident of Philadelphia. He opened a law office and immediately became active in civic affairs. He was a delegate-at-large to the Republican National Convention that nominated General Grant in 1868. Differing with the dominant Republican leadership in 1872 he became chairman of the Pennsylvania delegation to the Liberal Republican national convention which nominated Horace Greeley for the presidency. He gave further evidence of political independence by running as a Citizen's candidate, with Democratic indorsement, for the state Senate in the West Philadelphia district, and after a bitter contest was sworn in. In 1874 he was the Citizen's-Democratic candidate for mayor of Philadelphia, making his canvass upon charges of gross corruption in the city administration, but he was defeated. In response to a demand for a newspaper to support the independent forces in Philadelphia, McClure in conjunction with Frank McLaughin on Mar. 13, 1875, established the *Times* which became a well-known newspaper in the country. McClure was a man of impressive appearance and was in demand as a speaker on public occasions. He was twice married, first to Matilda S. Gray, on Feb. 10, 1852; and second to Cora M. Gratz, on Mar. 19, 1879. His later years were largely devoted to literary work, his books including *Three Thousand Miles through the Rocky Mountains* (1869); *The South: Its Industrial, Financial and Political Condition* (1886); *Abraham Lincoln and Men of War Times* (1892); *Our Presidents and How We Make Them* (1900); *To the Pacific and Mexico* (1901); *Col. Alexander K. McClure's Recollections of a Half Century* (1902); and *Old Time Notes of Pennsylvania* (2 vols., 1905). He edited *Famous American Statesmen and Orators* (6 vols., 1902).

[In addition to McClure's books see: *Encyc. of Contemporary Biog. of Pa.* (1893), vol. III; H. H. Hain, *Hist. of Perry County, Pa.* (1922); *Who's Who in America*, 1908–09; J. A. McClure, *The McClure Family* (1914); the *Press* (Phila.), June 7, 1909.] L. C. P.

McCLURE, ALEXANDER WILSON (May 8, 1808–September 1865), clergyman, editor, author, was born in Boston, Mass., the youngest son of Thomas and Mary (Wilson) McClure. His maternal great-grandfather was the Rev. John Morehead, the first Presbyterian minister of Boston. He prepared for college at the Latin School, spent two years at Yale, and then transferred to Amherst where he graduated in 1827. After his graduation at Andover Seminary in 1830 he began to preach at the First Congregational Church at Malden, Mass., but was not ordained till Dec. 19, 1832. His pastorate continued till 1843 when he resigned on account of failing health. When he went to Malden, the church was weak and on the point of dissolution, but under his wise and courageous leadership it revived and he left it in a flourishing condition. Going as acting pastor to a Presbyterian church in St. Augustine, Fla., he accomplished a remarkable evangelistic work among the soldiers garrisoned there. In 1847 he returned to Boston and edited the *Christian Observatory* till 1850, at the same time acting as assistant editor of the *Puritan Recorder*. He also again served his old church in Malden from 1848 to 1851. At the close of the latter year he became pastor of the Dutch Reformed church on Grand Street in Jersey City, N. J., remaining a member of that denomination for the rest of his life.

In 1855 he became secretary of the American and Foreign Christian Union, an organization for carrying on Protestant work in Europe and other countries. In the first year of his secretaryship he served as pastor of the chapel in Rome maintained by this society, and it was largely through his efforts that the Paris chapel, an evangelical and unsectarian place of worship for American residents, was established. During his secretaryship he was also the editor of the monthly magazine, the *Christian World*, and other publications of the Union. At the end of 1857 he retired on account of ill health and died at Canonsburg, Pa., after several years of inactivity. In addition to numerous religious and theological articles in various periodicals, McClure was the author of *The Life Boat; an Allegory*, a tract of wide circulation; *Lectures on Ultra-Universalism* (1832); *Lives of the Chief Fathers of New England* (1846), of which Volume I was "The Life of John Cotton" and Volume II "The Lives of John Wilson, John Norton and John Davenport"; and *The Translators Revived* (1853), consisting of biographical sketches of the translators of the King James version of the Bible. He was also a joint author of *The Bi-Centennial Book of Malden* (1850).

McClure accomplished a vast amount of work in spite of frail health. He was a man of wide and varied knowledge, a brilliant writer and preacher, formidable in debate and outspoken against what he considered to be evil. He had abounding wit, a deeply religious nature, and his life was rich in numerous friendships. In theology he was thoroughly evangelical and deeply attached to the standards of the Dutch Reformed Church. But he worked in sympathetic cooperation with all other evangelical denominations, regarding them as equally members of the Church of Christ. He married Mary Brewster Gould of Southampton, Mass., by whom he had eight children.

[*Christian World*, Nov. 1865, p. 349; *Biog. Record of the Alumni of Amherst Coll. During its first Half Century, 1821–71* (1883); *Boston Recorder*, Nov. 10, 1865; E. T. Corwin, *A Manual of the Reformed Church in America, 1628–1878* (3d ed., 1879), p. 373; Jacob Abbott, *The Corner-Stone* (1834), pp. 320–31; J. A. McClure, *The McClure Family* (1914). The date of McClure's death is given in the Amherst *Biog. Record*, cited above, as Sept. 17, 1865. Other sources give Sept. 20.] F. T. P.

McCLURE, GEORGE (*c.* 1770–Aug. 16, 1851), soldier, was born near Londonderry, Ireland, son of Finla McClure, and a descendant of Scotch immigrants to Ireland. He relates that from his fourth to his fifteenth year he attended school under "cruel and tyrannical" pedagogues; that he then learned the carpenter's trade; and that at the age of twenty he emigrated to America (McMaster, *post*). He landed at Baltimore, and after working as a carpenter there and at Chambersburg, Pa., about 1793 went to Bath, Steuben County, N. Y., in a region which was then just being opened to settlement. Here he soon became a merchant. He studied the Seneca dialect in order to trade more successfully in furs; he erected a distillery, a flour mill, and a mill for making woolen yarn; he speculated in land; he built boats for lake and river traffic and conducted cargoes of flour, lumber, and cattle down the Susquehanna to Baltimore, or to Columbia, Pa., and thence overland to Philadelphia. On Aug. 20, 1795, he married Eleanor Bole of Derry, Pa., and after her death, Sarah Welles (1808). He held various civil offices and rose in the militia to the rank of brigadier-general (*Military Minutes of the Council of Appointment of the State of New York,* vol. I, 1901, pp. 411, 651, 843).

In the fall of 1812 his brigade was called into service by Gen. Alexander Smyth [*q.v.*], and McClure was one of a group of militia officers who protested in writing against Smyth's dilatory tactics. In the fall of 1813, when the expedition against Montreal under Gen. James Wilkinson [*q.v.*] was in preparation, McClure was ordered again to the Niagara frontier to command a detachment of militia and to defend the frontier in the absence of the regular troops. He established his headquarters at Fort George, on the Canadian side of the Niagara River at its mouth, and indulged a propensity for the writing of bombastic proclamations. When Wilkinson definitely abandoned the campaign against Montreal (Nov. 13), the British turned their attention to the Niagara. Meanwhile, the terms of enlistment of McClure's volunteer troops were expiring; the War Department inexcusably neglected to reënforce him; and by Dec. 10 he had only 100 men at Fort George to face 500 advancing British. Upon the advice of a council of his officers he determined to abandon the fort; and the nearby village of Newark, once the capital of Upper Canada, was given to the flames. The reason advanced by McClure for this wanton act of destruction was that it would deprive the enemy of winter quarters; he also appealed to a letter from Secretary of War John Armstrong, which had authorized the officer commanding at Fort George to destroy the village if necessary for the defense of the fort. This letter did not cover McClure's act, and in view of the fact that all the barracks, as well as tents for 1,500 men, were left standing, his plea that he was destroying winter quarters was without merit. That the burning of Newark was generally disapproved on the American side is indicated by the hostile reception accorded McClure in Buffalo. His popularity must have been still less after Dec. 30, when the British burned Buffalo and Black Rock in retaliation for the destruction of Newark. McClure returned to his home in Bath and did not again appear on the Niagara frontier. His conduct at Newark was disavowed by his superior officer, General Wilkinson, in a letter to Sir George Prevost. That his popularity at home did not suffer seriously is indicated by his appointment as sheriff of Steuben County in 1815 and his three elections as representative of the county in the legislature. About 1834 he removed to Elgin, Ill., where he died. Politically, he is described as having been "a staunch free-soiler, a radical temperance man, and a firm believer in the future glory of the United States" (McMaster, *post,* p. 113).

[M. F. Roberts, *Hist. Gazetteer of Steuben County, N. Y.* (1891); G. H. McMaster, *Hist. of the Settlement of Steuben County, N. Y.* (1853), containing a brief autobiog. narrative of McClure's early life; Ernest Cruikshank, *The Documentary Hist. of the Campaigns upon the Niagara Frontier in 1812–14* (9 vols., 1896–1908); L. L. Babcock, "The War of 1812 on the Niagara Frontier," *Buffalo Hist. Soc. Pubs.*, vol. XXIX (1927); Henry Adams, *Hist. of the U. S. of America,* vol. VII (1891).] J. W. P.

McCLURG, ALEXANDER CALDWELL (Sept. 9, 1832–Apr. 15, 1901), bookseller, publisher, Union soldier, a first cousin of Joseph W. McClurg [*q.v.*], was the son of Alexander and Sarah (Trevor) McClurg. His paternal grandfather, Joseph, of Scotch-Irish descent, was involved in the Irish troubles of 1798 and fled to the United States, settling in Pittsburgh, whither his family followed him. Here he established what was probably the first iron foundry in that place, his son Alexander being associated with him in this and other business ventures. At the time of Alexander Caldwell's birth his parents were living in Philadelphia. When he was eight years old they returned to Pittsburgh, where he received his early education. At seventeen he entered Miami University, Oxford, Ohio, graduating from that institution four years later. Returning home, he entered the law office of Walter H. Lowrie, then chief justice of the Pennsylvania supreme court, but deserted the law after one year because of failing health and of declining interest in the legal profession. In 1859 he went to Chicago and became a clerk in the house of S. C. Griggs & Company, then the largest bookstore in the West.

At the commencement of the Civil War he enlisted as a private in a company recruited in Chicago which, however, was disbanded because the state quota was full. In 1862, with two others, he organized the Crosby Guards, mustered into the service, Aug. 27, 1862, as Company H of the 88th Illinois Volunteer Infantry. A few days later, much to his surprise, he was unanimously elected to the captaincy of his company, notwithstanding his complete inexperience and his small physical stature. At a second election, necessitated because of faulty procedure in the first, his selection was confirmed, again unanimously. His regiment received its baptism of fire at the battle of Perryville, Ky., Oct. 8, 1862. McClurg's conduct in the field, and his marked executive ability, brought him to the notice of his corps commander, Gen. Alexander McDowell McCook, who, in May 1863, detailed him as acting assistant adjutant-general of the corps. In August 1864 he was assigned to General Baird's division as assistant adjutant-general and chief of staff. Soon afterward, he was invited by General Sheridan, then commanding a division in the same corps, to join his staff, but declined. When Sheridan went to the Army of the Potomac he renewed the invitation but McClurg again declined it. He served through the Chickamauga and Chattanooga campaigns with great distinction, being frequently mentioned in dispatches and winning recognition as one of the ablest staff officers in the western army. Gen. J. C. Davis recommended his promotion to the rank of lieutenant-colonel for especial gallantry at the battle of Jonesboro, and made him chief of his staff. Continuing in this position, he participated in the campaigns of Sherman's army from Atlanta to the sea, ending in the battle of Bentonville, N. C., Mar. 19, 1865. His account of this engagement, in the *Atlantic Monthly* (September 1882), entitled "The Last Chance of the Confederacy," is regarded as a notable military narrative. He was mustered out in Chicago, Sept. 9, 1865, with the brevet rank of colonel, afterwards raised to brigadier-general, and despite the fact that Sherman, Thomas, and other officers urged him to enter the regular army, he returned to his former occupation in Chicago.

In April 1866 he purchased an interest in the firm of S. C. Griggs & Company. A disastrous fire, two years later, wiped out his capital, but the creditors were paid in full and the firm reëstablished itself in a new location on State Street, where three important book-dealers occupied adjoining premises, locally known as Booksellers' Row. Here the great fire of 1871 interrupted the thriving business. In the reorganization that followed, S. C. Griggs sold his interest to his partners and in 1886 McClurg became the principal owner. In 1880 the firm began publication of the *Dial* (Chicago). The Old English Book Department, a project originated by McClurg in 1877, developed into an important specialty, in part by reason of the interesting group of bibliophiles who foregathered there and whose lucubrations Eugene Field [*q.v.*] celebrated and imaginatively expanded as the proceedings of the "Saints and Sinners" corner in the "Sharps and Flats" of the Chicago *Morning News*. A third fire, in 1899, led the senior partner, long a confirmed invalid and frequently absent in search of health, to contemplate withdrawal from active business; but devotion to his firm, and a characteristic concern for the welfare of his large staff, prevailed over his inclination. His health continued to fail, however, and his death, of Bright's disease, occurred Apr. 15, 1901, at St. Augustine, Fla.

He was married, Apr. 17, 1877, to Eleanor, daughter of Judge Nelson Knox Wheeler of New York City. Two sons were born to them. McClurg was a booklover and reader as well as a bookseller, and, withal, a lively hater of the cheap and trashy, both in the contents and the makeup of books. A fluent and entertaining writer, he contributed numerous addresses to the proceedings of the many organizations to which he belonged and several articles to the magazines. A portion of his manuscript memoirs, left uncompleted at his death, was published under the title, "The American Volunteer Soldier," in Mabel McIlvane's *Reminiscences of Chicago During the Civil War* (1914). It presents a vivid account of his enlistment and early army experiences.

[*A Sketch of the Origin and Hist. of the House of A. C. McClurg & Co.* (privately printed); *Hist. of Allegheny County, Pa.* (1889), pt. II, pp. 295–96; A. T. Andreas, *Hist. of Chicago*, vol. III (1886); John Moses and Joseph Kirkland, *Hist. of Chicago* (1895); *Memorials of Deceased Companions . . . Commandery of . . . Ill., Mil. Order of the Loyal Legion of the U. S.* (1901); *Soc. of the Army of the Cumberland, Thirtieth Reunion* (1901); *War of the Rebellion, Official Records (Army)*; *Who's Who in America*, 1899–1900; Newton Bateman and others, *Hist. Encyc. of Ill. and Hist. of Morgan County* (1906); *Dial* (Chicago), May 1, 1901; *Chicago Daily Tribune*, Apr. 16, 1901; personal acquaintance.] C. B. R.

McCLURG, JAMES (*c.* 1746–July 9, 1823), physician, officer of the Revolution and delegate to the Philadelphia convention of 1787, was born near Hampton in Elizabeth City County, Va. His father, Dr. Walter McClurg, was superintendent of the Hampton Small Pox Hospital, which was probably one of the first hospitals of its kind in America. After thorough preparation James was sent to the College of William and Mary and graduated in 1762 with an unusually excellent scholastic record. He then studied medicine at the University of Edinburgh, graduating M.D. in 1770. His inaugural essay at Edinburgh, "De Calore," gave him an admirable reputation among his scientific friends. He devoted several years to post-graduate medical studies in Paris and London and while in London published his *Experiments upon the Human Bile and Reflections on the Biliary Secretions* (1772), which aroused for its author considerable notice and was reckoned a valuable contribution to the science of medicine, being translated into several languages. He returned to Virginia in 1773 but seems to have had no prominent part in the preliminary controversies of the Revolution. During the war he was active as a surgeon in the Virginia militia and is referred to frequently in the official records as physician-general and director of hospitals for the state. On May 22, 1779, he was married to Elizabeth Selden, daughter of Cary Selden. In the same year he was appointed professor of anatomy and medicine at the College of William and Mary but in 1783 the chair was discontinued and it is uncertain whether he did any teaching. By the latter year he had probably removed to Richmond, where he made his home for the rest of his life. He was ranked as one of the most eminent physicians in the state, was president of the state medical society in 1820 and 1821, and was honored by the dedication of Volume I of the *Philadelphia Journal of Medical and Physical Sciences* for 1820.

McClurg's political career may be said to have begun in 1782–83 when Madison advocated, but did not bring about, his appointment to succeed Livingston as secretary of foreign affairs for the United States. In 1787, after Patrick Henry and Richard Henry Lee had declined to serve in the Philadelphia Convention, McClurg was selected to complete the Virginia delegation. His activities in the Convention centered in the advocacy of a life tenure for the executive and a federal negative on state laws. The McClurg motion for life tenure for the executive received the votes of four of the ten states then represented, though part of its support was probably due to the hope that provision for a stronger executive might be made through the medium of compromise. McClurg insisted that the executive be kept as far from legislative control as possible and his efforts to make the executive independent of its rival branch undoubtedly were rewarded in the provisions for the administrative branch in the completed constitution. His only political services of consequence after the federal convention were rendered as a member of the executive council for Virginia during the early years of Washington's administration. According to Madison McClurg's talents were of the highest order but he was modest and unaccustomed to exert them. Possibly his interest in his profession precluded any pronounced ambition toward a political career.

[See J. B. McCaw, *A Memoir of Jas. McClurg, M.D.* (1854); H. A. Kelly and W. L. Burrage, *Am. Medic. Biogs.* (1920); Jas. Thacher, *Am. Medic. Biog.* (1828), vol. I; W. C. Blanton, *Medicine in Va. in the Eighteenth Century* (1931); Max Farrand, *The Records of the Fed. Convention* (3 vols., 1911); H. D. Gilpin, *The Papers of Jas. Madison* (3 vols., 1842); W. P. Palmer and Sherwin McRae, *Calendar of Va. State Papers*, vols. I, V, and VI (1875–86); "McClurg Descent," *Wm. and Mary Coll. Quart.*, Jan. 1893; *Richmond Enquirer*, July 11, 1823; auditor's account book for Virginia during the Revolution.] F. H. H.

MCCLURG, JOSEPH WASHINGTON (Feb. 22, 1818–Dec. 2, 1900), congressman, governor of Missouri, a first cousin of A. C. McClurg [*q.v.*], was born in St. Louis County, Mo. His grandfather, Joseph, came to the United States from Ireland as a refugee in 1798, his family, including Joseph Washington McClurg's father, also named Joseph, following later. The second Joseph married Mary Brotherton, a native of St. Louis County, Mo. Their son, orphaned at an early age, was reared by relatives in Pittsburgh, Pa. He attended school in Xenia, Ohio, and for two years (1833–35) was a student at Miami University, Oxford, Ohio. He then taught for a year or more in Louisiana and Mississippi; later he was admitted to the bar in Texas and practised law there. From 1841 to 1844 he was deputy sheriff of St. Louis County, having married in the former year Mary C. Johnson. In 1849 he was living in Hazelwood, Mo., at which time he joined the California gold seekers, in charge of a caravan of twenty-four ox teams. Back in Missouri again in 1852, McClurg, with two partners, established a large wholesale and retail mercantile business at Linn Creek, which was increasingly prosperous.

Upon the outbreak of the Civil War he immediately took a strong stand for the Union. He organized, equipped (at considerable financial loss), and commanded a home-guard unit, called the Osage Regiment of Missouri Volunteers. Later, he became colonel of the 8th Cavalry, Missouri Militia, but resigned this position in 1862 when he was elected to Congress, in which he served practically three full terms. Though opposed to slavery in principle, he did not liberate the slaves which his wife had inherited until shortly before Lincoln's Emancipation Proclamation. Of great significance for his future political career was the fact that in the House he became an ardent disciple of Thaddeus Stevens [*q.v.*], the bell-wether of radicalism. Moreover, his bitter attacks upon his congressional colleague, Francis P. Blair [*q.v.*], a leading conservative Unionist, endeared him to the hearts of all Missouri radicals. In 1868 McClurg resigned his seat in the House to run for governor of Missouri on the Radical Republican ticket.

Because of the military and strictly partisan enforcement of the noted test oath and registry law, enacted by the legislature in 1865–66, McClurg was elected by a majority of nearly 20,000. During the campaign, at the polls, and throughout his administration, the spirit and the principles of Thaddeus Stevens and the carpetbaggers were logically and proudly set forth in the public utterances and policies of McClurg and his advisers. Their aim was not only to disfranchise the "rebels," but also so to control the election machinery as to render the loyal Union Democrats and the Liberal Republicans powerless. The *St. Louis Dispatch,* in an admittedly partisan broadside (July 17, 1868), asserted that "McClurg is the embodiment of all that is narrow, bigoted, revengeful, and ignorant in the Radical party." If he was ignorant, it was only in the sense that he did not comprehend the shortsightedness of the radical policies. He was, in fact, less a leader than a follower. Such radicals as Charles D. Drake [*q.v.*] and others long since forgotten really dominated the party of which McClurg was the nominal head. The controversies relating to negro and white suffrage claimed the major share of his attention during the two years he was in office. With the test oath and the registry law on the shelf in 1870, he was overwhelmingly defeated for the governorship. The memory of the proscriptions which he sponsored was largely responsible for the fact that Missouri remained in the Democratic column for over thirty years.

After his term as governor he lived at Linn Creek and engaged in various business enterprises. In 1885 he moved to Lebanon, where he lived until his death, except for the years 1889 to 1893, when he was register of the Federal Land Office at Springfield.

[*Gen. Cat. of the Grads. and Former Students of Miami Univ., 1809–1909* (n.d.); G. G. Avery and F. C. Shoemaker, *The Messages and Proclamations of The Governors . . . of Mo.,* vol. IV (1924); T. S. Barclay, "The Liberal Republican Movement in Mo.," *Mo. Hist. Rev.,* Oct. 1925–Oct. 19, 1926; *Pictorial and Geneal. Record of Greene County, Mo.* (1893); *Hist. of Laclede and Camden Counties, Mo.* (1889); *Kansas City Times,* Sept. 4, 1870; *St. Louis Dispatch,* July 17, 1868; *St. Joseph Herald,* Dec. 10, 1869; *Columbia Statesman,* July 24, 1868; *N. Y. Times,* Apr. 24, 1872; *Booneville Weekly Eagle,* May 21, 1870; *Mo. Democrat,* Oct. 1, 1869; *Jefferson City Peoples' Tribune,* Sept. 7, 1870; *St. Louis Globe-Democrat* and *St. Louis Republic,* Dec. 3, 1900; *Booneville Weekly Advertiser,* Dec. 21, 1900.]

H. E. N.

McCOMAS, LOUIS EMORY (Oct. 28, 1846–Nov. 10, 1907), Maryland congressman, senator, jurist, was born near Williamsport, Md., the second child of Frederick C. and Catharine (Angle) McComas. The family was of Scotch-Irish origin, the founder of the American line having settled in Harford County, Md., early in the eighteenth century. McComas' paternal grandfather, Zaccheus, fought in the War of 1812 and subsequently entered the Methodist ministry, holding charges in Baltimore and Williamsport. His maternal grandfather, Henry Angle, of Pennsylvania origin, was a prosperous Washington County farmer. After an unsuccessful attempt at storekeeping in Springfield, Ill., his parents returned to Maryland where the father engaged first in agriculture and then in the hardware business. Louis McComas received his elementary education in Williamsport, after which he attended St. James College in Maryland and Dickinson College in Pennsylvania, graduating from Dickinson with high honors in 1866. He then began to read law in an office at Cambridge, Md., completed his studies under Judge R. H. Alvey of Hagerstown, was admitted to the bar in 1868, and practised law in the latter city until 1892. On Sept. 23, 1875, he married Leah Humrichouse of Baltimore. To them two daughters were born.

McComas' political career opened with his unsuccessful candidacy as a Republican for a seat in the Forty-fifth Congress. Entering the lists again some years later, he was chosen representative in the Forty-eighth Congress and served four terms, 1883–91, retiring following his defeat for reëlection to the Fifty-second Congress. During these years he developed into an able parliamentarian. His membership on the committee on coinage, weights, and measures and on those on appropriations and ways and means gave him a keen insight into currency and credit problems and several of his speeches on those subjects were used as campaign documents. Through his efforts, Antietam battlefield was placed under governmental control. He is also said to have framed the effective section of the contract labor law ("An act to prohibit the importation and migration of foreigners and aliens under contract or agreement to perform labor in the United States, its Territories, and the District of Columbia") passed in the Second Session of the Forty-eighth Congress. He gained national attention by procuring the passage of a private pension bill over President Cleveland's veto.

In 1892 McComas attended the Republican Convention in Minneapolis as delegate-at-large from Maryland and, being named secretary of the Republican National Committee, served in that capacity during the presidential campaign of 1892. In November of the same year President Harrison appointed him associate justice of the supreme court of the District of Columbia, which position he held until 1899 when he was elected senator from Maryland. During his six years in the upper chamber, he served as chairman of the committee on education and labor and as a member of various other committees. He played a prominent part in drawing up the organic laws of Puerto Rico and the Philippines, was an active supporter of civil-service reform, favored anti-trust legislation, made the Naval Academy his special charge, and took an active interest in the beautification of Washington. In 1900 and 1904 he again represented Maryland as delegate-at-large at the Republican conventions. From 1897 to 1901 he was lecturer on the law of contracts and evidence at the Georgetown University Law School and thereafter lecturer on international law and American foreign relations. For a quarter of a century he served as a trustee of Dickinson College.

McComas retired from the Senate in March 1905 and in July was appointed justice of the court of appeals of the District of Columbia by President Roosevelt. In July 1907, some years after his first wife's death, he married Mrs. Hebe Harrison Muir, the widow of Judge Upton Muir of Kentucky. He was stricken with pneumonia while on his way to Europe with his bride, returned home in feeble health after some weeks in an English hospital, and died of heart failure a month later. Affable and obliging, though possessed of marked judicial dignity, McComas was greatly admired and respected by his constituents, colleagues, and students.

[J. T. Scharf, *Hist. of Western Md.* (1882), vol. II; T. J. C. Williams, *A Hist. of Wash. County, Md.* (1906), vol. II; *Biog. Dir. Am. Cong.* (1928); *Who's Who in America*, 1906–07; the *Evening Star* (Washington), Nov. 11, 1907; the *Sun* (Baltimore), Nov. 11, 1907; Dickinson Coll. records; Georgetown Univ. records; private information.] L. J. R.

MCCOMB, JOHN (Oct. 17, 1763–May 25, 1853), architect, was the son of John and Mary (Davis) McComb. His father, son of James who came to America from Scotland, via North Ireland, in 1732, was born in Princeton, N. J. After his marriage, Apr. 27, 1761, he resided in New York, acting as architect and builder. His best-known work included the Brick Church, 1767, the North Dutch Church, 1769, and the New York Hospital, of which the cornerstone was laid in 1773. Upon the outbreak of the Revolution he took his family to Princeton, where he was made quartermaster in the Continental Army in 1777. He returned to New York in 1783 and was made a City Surveyor on Mar. 16, 1784. He was also influential in the founding of the General Society of Mechanics and Tradesmen in 1785. On his death in New York City, in 1811, he left three children, John and Isaac, both architects, and Elizabeth, who was an amateur artist of some skill.

The younger John was born in New York. He seems to have received the greater part of his culture and professional knowledge from his father, whose assistant he became in 1783. At some time prior to 1790 he made an extended tour of Europe and in that year began his independent career with an engagement to design the façade of Government House in New York (McComb MSS.). From that time on he became one of the busiest of the New York builders and architects. Among his public buildings were three lighthouses, the Montauk (1795) and the Eaton's Neck Light (drawings dated 1798), both still in use, and the Cape Henry Lighthouse (1791), now a national monument to the landing of Captain John Smith. Castle Garden in the Battery, New York, was designed and built by him (Account Books in New York Historical Society). On Oct. 4, 1802, the competition for the New York City Hall was decided by the award of a premium to the design submitted by McComb and Joseph F. Mangin [*q.v.*]. After some conferences and the curtailing of the original drawings, McComb was appointed architect to superintend the construction, and he was in sole charge of the detailing and execution of the design until its completion in 1812. During this period he also designed the New York Free School House (1808), the Hubert Street Fort (1808), Washington Hall, home of the Washington Benevolent Association (1809–12), and subsequently used as a hotel and assembly rooms, Queens Building, Rutgers College (cornerstone laid Apr. 27, 1809), the building of the Society of Mechanics and Tradesmen on Park Place (1802–03), and Alexander Hall of Princeton Theological Seminary (1815).

His most important church was St. John's Chapel on Varick Street (cornerstone laid Sept. 1, 1803), which he did in partnership with his brother Isaac. He was also the architect of the Cedar Street Presbyterian Church (1807), the Murray Street Presbyterian Church (1811–12), and the very beautiful Bleecker Street Presbyterian Church (1825). In 1822, he altered the interior and designed and built a new spire for the Brick Presbyterian Church, originally built by his father. Of his numerous houses, that for John Coles, on Whitehall Street, deserves mention for its size. "The Grange," designed for Alexander Hamilton, still stands in a new location as the rectory for St. Luke's Church, Convent Avenue and 141st Street, New York City. In 1817, on the resignation of B. H. Latrobe [*q.v.*] as architect of the United States Capitol, he was mentioned for the post, and on Dec. 5, 1817, his friend the elder James Renwick [*q.v.*] wrote him from Washington to find out, unofficially, if he would accept it (E. S. Bulfinch, *The Life and Letters of Charles Bulfinch*, p. 207;

Glen Brown, *History of the United States Capitol,* 1900–02, I, 55; Collingwood papers).

McComb was married, Dec. 15, 1792, to Elizabeth, daughter of James Embree Glean. By this marriage he had two children, a son and a daughter. His wife died June 3, 1817, and on June 24, 1821, he married Mrs. Rebecca Rockwell, a widow, who survived him. He was street commissioner of New York City from 1813 to 1821. On Dec. 31, 1816, he was made an Academician of the American Academy of Fine Arts, and in 1818, president of the General Society of Mechanics and Tradesmen. He was a trustee of the Brick Presbyterian Church, 1816–25, and deacon from 1827 until his death. His carefully kept account books reveal alike his generosity and his painstaking attention to detail. In general, his architectural work shows excellent taste, careful study, a refined sense of detail, and well illustrates the persistence of American Colonial tradition, with strong British influence, into the nineteenth century. The French character of the New York City Hall is so exceptional that it is probably to be accounted for by the connection of Joseph François Mangin with its original design.

[Manuscript biography by a great-grand-daughter, Mrs. Helen A. Collingwood, and notes of the family (copies in N. Y. Hist. Soc. and N. Y. City Hall); drawings and papers in the possession of Mrs. Collingwood; McComb Papers and Drawings and Ebenezer Stevens Papers, N. Y. Hist. Soc.; I. N. P. Stokes, *The Iconography of Manhattan Island* (6 vols., 1915–28); *Minutes of the Common Council of the City of N. Y.* (1917), vols. VII–XII; W. H. S. Demarest, *A Hist. of Rutgers Coll.* (1924); Morgan Dix, *A Hist. of the Parish of Trinity Ch. . . . N. Y.*, vol. II (1901); Thomas Earle and C. T. Congdon, *Annals of the Gen. Soc. of Mechanics and Tradesmen of the City of N. Y., 1785–1880* (1882); *National Advocate* (N. Y.), June 4, 1817, June 30, 1821; *N. Y. Herald,* May 27, 1853.] T. F. H.

McCONNEL, JOHN LUDLUM (Nov. 11, 1826–Jan. 17, 1862), author, was born in what was then Morgan but is now Scott County, Ill., the son of Murray and Mary Mapes McConnel. His father was a self-made pioneer lawyer who served in both branches of the state legislature and in the Black Hawk War, and was appointed by President Pierce one of the auditors of the United States Treasury, a post which he held for about five years. The eldest son John studied law under his father and at the Transylvania law school, from which he was graduated in 1843 in a class of twenty-nine. He enlisted for service in the war with Mexico and before leaving the rendezvous of his company at Alton, Ill., he was made first lieutenant. After the battle of Buena Vista, where he was wounded, he became captain in the 1st Illinois Volunteers. Returning to Jacksonville, he took over his father's practice, but he was as much interested in creative writing as in his professed deity, the law. His first works were melodramatic novels. *Grahame: or Youth and Manhood* (1850) is an improbable tale which leaves the modern reader quite out of sympathy with any of the characters or situations. *Talbot and Vernon* (1850), a tale of love intrigue and the war in Mexico, with some excellent descriptions of that region and of court scenes in the West, and *The Glenns: A Family History* (1851), interesting for the author's pictures of the Southwest and the turbulent society of frontier Texas, throw valuable light on the social history of the period. *Western Characters: or Types of Border Life in the Western States* (1853) is a valuable descriptive volume which portrays the picturesque figures of the frontier. At the time of his premature death in 1862 he was engaged in a study to be entitled "History of Early Exploration in America," treating especially the work of the early Roman Catholic missionaries. Shortly after his return from Mexico in 1847, McConnel was married to Eliza Deniston of Pittsburgh. She, with two children, survived him.

[G. M. McConnel, "Some Reminiscences of My Father, Murray McConnel," *Jour. of the Ill. State Hist. Soc.*, Apr. 1925; Newton Bateman and others, *Hist. Encyc. of Ill. and Hist. of Morgan County* (1906); C. M. Eames, *Hist. Morgan and Classic Jacksonville* (1885); *Daily Ill. State Jour.* (Springfield), Jan. 28, 1862; family records.] D. A. D.

McCOOK, ALEXANDER McDOWELL (April. 22, 1831–June 12, 1903), soldier, came of a Scotch-Irish family known as "the fighting McCooks" from the fact that his father with eight sons and the five sons of his uncle saw distinguished service in the Union forces during the Civil War. His paternal grandfather, George McCook, emigrated from Ireland about 1780 and settled in Canonsburg, Pa., whence he subsequently moved to Carroll County, Ohio. Daniel and John, in the second generation, also settled in Ohio and here, in Columbiana County, Alexander was born to Daniel and Martha (Latimer) McCook. He was the fifth of nine sons, of whom one died in infancy. He graduated from the United States Military Academy in 1852, thirtieth in a class of forty-seven members, and was commissioned lieutenant in the 3rd Infantry. After service at frontier posts and field duty against hostile Utes and Apaches, in 1858–61 he was assistant instructor in infantry tactics at West Point. The day that President Lincoln called for volunteers, he was commissioned colonel, 1st Ohio Volunteers, and in the action at Vienna, Va., on June 17, and at Bull Run, July 21, 1861, was commended for coolness and good conduct.

He commanded a brigade in Kentucky until

January 1862, and a division in the Army of the Ohio until the end of June of that year, and distinguished himself at Corinth, Nashville, and Shiloh, receiving the brevets of lieutenant-colonel and of colonel. Promotion to the grade of major-general of volunteers followed, July 17, 1862, and during the operations of the Army of the Ohio in northern Alabama, Tennessee, and Kentucky, McCook commanded the I Army Corps at Nashville and in the battle of Perryville, Ky. (Oct. 8, 1862). For distinguished service in the latter engagement, he was brevetted brigadier-general, United States Army. After the organization of the Army of the Cumberland, he commanded the XIV and later the XX Corps with distinction, serving in the battle of Stone River, the advance on Tullahoma, and the battle of Chickamauga. He received blame for the disaster to the Union forces at Chickamauga and was relieved from command, Oct. 6, 1863, but a court of inquiry, convened at his request, exonerated him from responsibility. He was on duty with the defenses of Washington until October 1864, commanded the District of Eastern Arkansas until May 1865, and served with a joint committee of Congress, investigating Indian affairs, until October of the same year. For gallant and meritorious services in the field throughout the war he received the brevet of major-general, United States Army, Mar. 13, 1865.

In post-war army reorganization, McCook was appointed lieutenant-colonel, 26th Infantry, at the age of thirty-seven years, and again saw arduous frontier service. In 1874–75 he was acting inspector-general and from 1875 to 1881, aide-de-camp to Gen. William T. Sherman. He was promoted colonel, 6th Infantry, Dec. 15, 1880, and after protracted duty in the West and a period in command of the Infantry and Cavalry School at Fort Leavenworth, Kan., was promoted brigadier-general (1890) and major-general (1894). He was retired from active service for age, Apr. 22, 1895. In May 1896 he represented the United States at the coronation of Nicholas II as Czar of Russia, and in September 1898 was a member of the commission appointed to investigate the conduct of the War with Spain. He died at Dayton, Ohio. McCook was twice married: on Jan. 23, 1863, to Kate Phillips of Dayton, Ohio, who died in 1881, and on Oct. 8, 1885, to Annie Colt of Milwaukee, who survived him, as did three daughters by his first marriage.

[J. H. Wilson, biographical sketch in *Thirty-fifth Ann. Reunion, Asso. Grads. U. S. Mil. Acad.* (1904); J. H. Woodward, *Gen. A. McD. McCook at Stone River* (1892); *Battles and Leaders of the Civil War* (4 vols., 1887–88); *Personal Memoirs of U. S. Grant* (2 vols., 1885–86); *Personal Memoirs of P. H. Sheridan* (2 vols., 1888); *War of the Rebellion: Official Records (Army)*; Whitelaw Reid, *Ohio in the War* (1868), I, 806–09, severely critical of McCook's work at Perryville, Stone River, and Chickamauga; Henry Howe, "The Fighting McCooks," in *The Scotch-Irish in America, Proc. and Addresses of the Sixth Cong.* (1894); G. W. Cullum, *Biog. Reg. U. S. Mil. Acad.* (3rd ed., 1891); *Who's Who in America*, 1901–02; *Army and Navy Jour.*, June 20, 1903; *Ohio State Jour.* (Columbus), June 13, 1903.] C. D. R.

McCOOK, ANSON GEORGE (Oct. 10, 1835–Dec. 30, 1917), Union soldier, congressman, publisher, was born in Steubenville, Ohio, a first cousin of Alexander McDowell McCook [*q.v.*] and the second son of Dr. John McCook, a native of Canonsburg, Pa., and of Catharine Julia (Sheldon) of Hartford, Conn. He was brought up in the town of Lisbon (then New Lisbon), Ohio. At the age of fifteen he left school and went to Pittsburgh where he was employed in a drugstore. After two years in Pittsburgh he taught school at a little crossroads town near Lisbon and worked as transitman on a local railway. When news of the discovery of gold in California reached the Middle West, he went overland to the coast with a party taking cattle across the plains. For the next five years he lived as a miner and businessman in California and Nevada. Upon his return to Ohio in 1859 he read law in the office of his cousin, George W. McCook of Steubenville, law partner of Edwin M. Stanton. The following year he was admitted to the bar.

McCook belonged to the famous "fighting McCooks" of Ohio. He, with his father and four brothers, was at that time a War Democrat, and upon the outbreak of the Civil War the five sons, among whom were Edward M., Henry C., and John James McCook [*qq.v.*], entered the military or naval service of the United States. Anson George organized a company of infantry at Steubenville and on Apr. 17, 1861, was commissioned captain in the 2nd Ohio Volunteers. He rose successively through the grades of major, lieutenant-colonel, and colonel of the same regiment, and when it was mustered out he became colonel of the 194th Ohio Volunteers. In March 1865 he was brevetted brigadier-general of volunteers "for meritorious services." During the war he took part in many engagements, including the battles of Bull Run, Perryville, Stone River, Chattanooga, Lookout Mountain, Missionary Ridge, Kenesaw Mountain, and Atlanta. He was also in the Shenandoah campaign which preceded the surrender of Lee at Appomattox.

Upon his honorable discharge at the close of the war he returned to Steubenville, where from 1866 to 1872 he was assessor of internal revenue. In 1873 he moved to New York and was admitted to practice in the courts of that state. Political honors soon came to him in his new domicile, and in 1876, 1878, and 1880 he was elected to the national House of Representatives from the eighth congressional district of New York. His congressional record was creditable but not outstanding. In 1884 he was chosen secretary of the United States Senate, a position which he retained until August 1893. Two years later he was appointed chamberlain of the City of New York by Mayor William L. Strong and served until the expiration of the latter's term of office in 1897.

When he removed from Ohio to New York, McCook became interested in the *Daily Register* (later the *New York Law Journal*) and was for many years its editor. He was also president of the New York Law Publishing Company and a member of many organizations. In May 1886 he married Hettie B. McCook, a daughter of his cousin and law preceptor. A son and a daughter were born to them. McCook died at the age of eighty-three at his home in New York.

[*N. Y. Times*, Dec. 31, 1917; *N. Y. Law Jour.*, Jan. 2, 1918; *Who's Who in America*, 1916–17; Whitelaw Reid, *Ohio in the War* (1868), I, 974; *War of the Rebellion: Official Records (Army)*, 1 ser., XX, XXIII, XXX–XXXII, XXXVIII, XXXIX, XLVI, LII; *Biog. Dir. Am. Cong.* (1928); Henry Howe, "The Fighting McCooks," in *The Scotch-Irish in America, Proc. and Addresses of the Sixth Cong.* (1894).] H. J. C.

McCOOK, EDWARD MOODY (June 15, 1833–Sept. 9, 1909), Union soldier, minister to Hawaii, governor of Colorado Territory, was born at Steubenville, Ohio, of a family which gave many famous soldiers to the Civil War. A brother of Anson George, Henry Christopher, and John James, and a first cousin of Alexander McDowell McCook [*qq.v.*], he was the eldest son of Dr. John McCook, a physician, and Catharine Julia (Sheldon). Educated in public schools at Steubenville, he went to Minnesota when he was sixteen, and in the gold rush of the year 1849 went on to Colorado, where he practised law. In 1859, he represented his district in the legislature of Kansas Territory, and when Kansas became a state he was a leader in the organization of the Territory of Colorado. Upon the fall of Sumter, he joined the Kansas Legion in Washington, and in recognition of his success in carrying dispatches to General Scott through unfriendly Maryland lines, was appointed a lieutenant of cavalry. During the southern campaigns of 1862–63 he made a brilliant record, being brevetted first lieutenant for gallant services at Shiloh, captain for services at Perryville, Ky., major for his conduct at Chickamauga, and lieutenant-colonel for cavalry operations in East Tennessee. He was appointed brigadier-general of volunteers, Apr. 27, 1864, and commanded the cavalry of the Army of the Cumberland. His most brilliant exploit of the war was performed during the Atlanta campaign when he prevented the reinforcement of General Hood, then shut up in Atlanta. Sweeping with his cavalry in the rear of the city, he destroyed the Confederate transportation trains, cut railroads leading south, captured many prisoners, and finally made his way back to rejoin the main Union army at Marietta, Ga. At the close of the war he received the brevets of brigadier-general, United States Army, and major-general of volunteers in recognition of his record.

After the close of hostilities he acted as military governor of Florida, until June 1865. On May 9, 1866, he resigned his military commission, and until 1869 was United States minister to Hawaii. During his term in this office he negotiated a treaty of commercial reciprocity. In 1869 President Grant appointed him governor of the Territory of Colorado. As governor, he organized a school system, encouraged the building of railroads, secured the opening up of vast mineral and agricultural lands by the transfer of the troublesome Ute Indians to Utah, and was instrumental in the building of water-works for the city of Denver. He was unpopular in Colorado, where he was regarded as an office-seeker trading upon his military reputation; enemies charged him with participation in Indian frauds. At the request of the people of the territory Grant did not reappoint him in 1873, but in January 1874, after McCook had declined the office of postmaster general, the President renominated him for the governorship, and six months later the appointment was ratified by one vote. Early the next year he resigned.

After his retirement from public life, McCook had financial interests in many great enterprises in Colorado and the West, and at one time he was the largest real-estate owner and tax-payer in the Territory. Later, his investments extended to European telephone syndicates and to rich mines in Mexico. He was an early advocate of woman's suffrage. McCook was married twice: first, in 1865 to Mary Thompson of Peoria, Ill., grand-daughter of Charles Thompson, secretary of the Continental Congress, and after her death, which occurred in 1874, to Mary McKenna of Colorado. He died of Bright's disease in Chicago and was buried at Steubenville, Ohio.

[*Who's Who in America*, 1908–09; Henry Howe, "The Fighting McCooks," in *The Scotch-Irish in America, Proc. and Addresses of the Sixth Cong.* (1894); H. M. Cist, *The Army of the Cumberland* (1882) and J. D. Cox, *Atlanta* and *The March to the Sea* (both 1882), in Campaigns of the Civil War, vols. VII, IX, X; *Battles and Leaders of the Civil War*, vols. III,

IV (1888); *Mil. Order of the Loyal Legion of the U. S., Commandery of D. C., War Papers, 29* (1898); Frank Hall, *Hist. of the State of Col.*, vols. I, II (1889–90); *Daily Rocky Mountain News* (Denver), for 1874, esp. June 20; *Rocky Mountain News* and *Denver Republican*, Sept. 10, 1909; *Inter Ocean* (Chicago), Sept. 10, 1909.] C. D. R.

McCOOK, HENRY CHRISTOPHER (July 3, 1837–Oct. 31, 1911), Presbyterian clergyman, naturalist, third son of Dr. John McCook and Catharine Julia (Sheldon), was born at New Lisbon, Ohio. His father was of Scotch-Irish and his mother of New England descent. A brother of Anson George, Edward Moody, and John James, and a first cousin of Alexander McDowell McCook [*qq.v.*], he belonged to that branch of the family which gave rise in the army to the expression "the fighting McCooks." He received the degree of A.B. in 1859 from Jefferson College, Canonsburg, Pa. Although attracted to the law at first, he changed to theology and studied at the Western Theological Seminary, Pittsburgh, in 1860–63. He was ordained to the Presbyterian ministry in Steubenville, Ohio, in 1861, but in July of that year, the Civil War having begun, he resigned his charge (the Presbyterian Church at Clinton, DeWitt County, Ill.), and volunteered. He raised two companies and part of a third, and served as first lieutenant in the 41st Illinois Volunteers and later as chaplain of that regiment, 1861–62. In 1863–64 he preached at Clinton, Ill., and from 1864 to 1869 was engaged in city mission work in St. Louis. In 1870 he became the pastor of the Tabernacle Presbyterian Church in Philadelphia, and remained in this post until 1902, when he resigned on account of ill health. During the Spanish-American War he was very active in hospital and relief work.

McCook was primarily a clergyman, but he was also an ardent naturalist. In 1873 he began to study spiders; later he became interested in ants, and all through his active life, from 1876 to 1909, he published from time to time technical papers of much value, the majority of them relating to either spiders or ants. He also wrote many semi-popular papers and several books. One of the best-known of his books was *Tenants of an Old Farm: Leaves from the Note Book of a Naturalist* (1885). His last popular work was entitled *Ant Communities and How they are Governed, a Study in Natural Civics* (1909). Most of his more technical papers were published in the *Proceedings* of the Academy of Natural Sciences of Philadelphia and the *Transactions* of the American Entomological Society. Two articles, "Mound-Making Ants of the Alleghanies, Their Architecture and Habits" (*Transactions of the American Entomological Society,* November 1877) and *The Natural History of the Agricultural Ant of Texas* (1879), brought him prominently to the attention of the entomological world. A later paper entitled *The Honey Ants of the Garden of the Gods and the Occident Ants of the American Plains* (1882), based on original field observations, made during a visit to the West, was widely read. This and his earlier papers showed him to be a keen observer, and his publications continue to be highly regarded.

His most notable work was a large, three-volume quarto called *American Spiders and Their Spinning Work: A Natural History of the Orb-Weaving Spiders of the United States with Special Regard to Their Industry and Habits.* The first volume, issued in 1889, relates to "Snares and Nests"; the second (1890), to "Motherhood and Babyhood, Life and Death"; and the third volume (1893) is composed of "Biological Notes, Descriptions of Species." The work is admirably illustrated, containing 853 text figures and forty colored lithographic plates of 913 figures. It was printed privately in an edition of 250 copies. McCook's published bibliography contains 101 titles. Of these writings eleven are verses and hymns, two are tracts, sixty are scientific papers, and the rest include addresses, sermons, teaching outlines, and stories. Among his non-scientific writings are *The Latimers—A Tale of the Western Whiskey Insurrection* (1897), *The Flag at Cedar Creek—A Ballad for the War of the Union* (1907), *Lincoln and His Veterans, a Centenary Ode* (1909), *Quaker Ben—A Tale of Colonial Pennsylvania in the Days of Thomas Penn* (1911), and *Prisca of Patmos—A Tale of the Time of Saint John* (1911). He married in 1860 Emma C. Herter, who died in 1897. In 1899 he married Mrs. Eleanor D. S. Abbey.

[P. P. Calvert, bibliographical account, in *Entomological News*, Dec. 1911; *Jour. Presbyt. Hist. Soc.*, McCook Memorial Number, Dec. 1911; *Ohio Archaeol. and Hist. Soc. Pubs.*, vol. VI (1900); *Press* (Phila.), Nov. 1, 1911.] L. O. H.

McCOOK, JOHN JAMES (Feb. 2, 1843–Jan. 9, 1927), Protestant Episcopal clergyman, educator, was born in New Lisbon, Ohio, fifth and youngest son of John, a physician, and Catharine Julia (Sheldon) McCook, and brother of Edward Moody, Anson George, and Henry Christopher [*qq.v.*], and Roderick S. McCook. Alexander McDowell McCook [*q.v.*] was his first cousin. He attended Jefferson (now Washington and Jefferson) College, 1858–60. At the outbreak of the Civil War he was reading law in Steubenville, Ohio. His four brothers and an uncle, Daniel McCook, with his eight sons, enlisted in the service of the Union and made a record that gave them the name of "the fighting McCooks." As a lad of eighteen, John James helped to organize a company which was mustered into the 1st Regiment of Virginia Volunteers. He rose from private to be second lieutenant, served throughout McClellan's West Virginia campaign, and was later attached to McClellan's headquarters as acting assistant-quartermaster. Declining a permanent staff appointment, he entered Trinity College, Hartford, Conn., from which he was graduated in 1863. He studied a few months in the College of Physicians and Surgeons in New York and then transferred to the Berkeley Divinity School, graduating in 1866. In that year he was admitted to deacon's orders in the Protestant Episcopal Church and, on June 7, married Eliza Sheldon Butler of Hartford. After a year in St. John's Church, East Hartford, he was ordained priest (1867) and became rector of St. John's Church, Detroit, Mich., but returned in 1868 to the church in East Hartford which he served thenceforth until his death in 1927. In 1883 he began forty years of teaching as instructor of Latin in Trinity College. In 1886 he was made professor of modern languages. At different times he taught German, French, Italian, and Spanish, finally specializing in German.

Though voluntarily carrying more than the usual quantity of class work and active in building up his East Hartford church and a summer congregation in Niantic, he took vigorous part in civic affairs. In 1890 he was chairman of a "Committee to Confer with the Selectmen in the Matter of Outdoor Alms in the Town of Hartford." The *Report* submitted in 1891 led to a reform of abuses. In the years following, McCook started a movement to establish a state reformatory for youthful delinquents and in 1895 was appointed chairman of the first commission of the Connecticut Reformatory. After agitating for some time against the prevalent bribing of voters, he became in 1901 chairman of a nonpartisan committee which, with the cooperation of the two major political parties, succeeded in putting a stop to the practice in Hartford. In 1901, also, he was elected a member of the high-school committee of Hartford, on which he served until 1915, the last two years as chairman.

In his civic activities he always sought exact knowledge, especially of a statistical character, and thus found matter for a number of publications. His most considerable contribution is the *Report of the Special Committee on Outdoor Alms* (1891), referred to above, of which he was the author although his name does not appear on the title page. The report is broader than the title indicates, since indoor relief is also considered and the Appendix contains material on methods followed in other places. At the time of issue it was the most informing American publication on official poor-relief. From 1892 to 1901 he published articles on venal voting, tramps, the saloon, and pauperism, in the *Forum,* the *Independent, Charities Review,* and *Journal of Social Science.* The most entertaining of these papers are the "Leaves from the Diary of a Tramp" which appeared in the *Independent* at intervals between Nov. 21, 1901, and June 26, 1902. All his papers are well-written and interesting because of their concrete detail, but his writings do not reveal the dynamic personality of the man and the deep impression which he made on those who knew him personally.

[Henry Howe, "The Fighting McCooks," in *The Scotch-Irish in America, Proc. and Addresses of the Sixth Cong.* (1894); *Who's Who in America,* 1926–27; *Trinity College Bulletin—Necrology,* 1926–27; *Hartford Courant* and *Hartford Times,* Jan. 10, 1927; *Trinity Tripod,* Jan. 14, 1927.] G. A. K.

McCORD, DAVID JAMES (January 1797–May 12, 1855), editor and agitator, was born in St. Matthew's Parish, S. C., the son of Russell and Hannah (Turquand) McCord. His grandfather, John McCord, emigrated from Ireland and about 1750 acquired lands and the ferry on the Congaree known afterwards by his name. David McCord left the South Carolina College in his senior year (1813–14). He studied law and was admitted to the bar in Columbia in 1818. With his partner, H. J. Nott [*q.v.*], he began a series of reports on cases in the state courts (*Reports of Cases . . . in the Constitutional Court,* 2 vols., 1820–21), and, after the dissolution of the partnership in 1821, he continued the series (*Reports of Cases . . . in the Constitutional Court,* I, II, 1822–23; *Reports of Cases in the Court of Appeals,* III, IV, 1826–30; *Chancery Cases,* I, II, 1827–29). In 1822 he became the partner of W. C. Preston. His editorship of the *Columbia Telescope* began in 1823, at the time that Dr. Thomas Cooper [*q.v.*] was leading the agitation of the tariff question in South Carolina. McCord agreed with him; the *Telescope* became the most violent of all the nullification papers, and the editor himself one of an influential group of state leaders in Columbia. In 1832 he was elected to the House of Representatives. After their victory in 1833 the nullifiers determined to clinch their doctrine of state sovereignty by forcing the oath of allegiance upon all state officers. This harsh business, from which the chief leaders shrank, he took in hand, and one of his distinguished opponents afterwards declared him "about the bitterest politician" with whom he had been acquainted (O'Neall, *post,* II, 510). His service in the legislature continued until 1837, when he was elected president of the Columbia branch of the Bank of the State (*Miller's Planters' and Merchants' Almanac,* 1837–41). He lost his position in 1841 because of his support of the Whig party in the preceding year. The death of Dr. Cooper in 1839, after he had edited five volumes of the *Statutes at Large of South Carolina* (1836–39), resulted in McCord's assignment to the task, and the remaining five volumes, including an elaborate index, were completed in three years more.

At various other times he served as intendant of Columbia, as trustee for the South Carolina College, and as trustee for the new state hospital for the insane. A year after the death of his first wife, Emmeline Wagner of Charleston, he married on May 2, 1840, Louisa Susanna Cheves, the gifted daughter of Langdon Cheves [*qq.v.*]. "Lang Syne," her plantation in St. Matthew's Parish, became their home, although they later built a house in Columbia, where they resided for a part of each year. He also owned cottonland in Alabama, which he sold before his death. During this period of his life his unchanged political and economic principles found expression in a number of able articles or reviews in the *Southern Quarterly Review* (Apr. and Oct. 1846—reviews of Polk's message and Calhoun's report; initialed reviews, Oct. 1847, Apr. and Jan. 1850). Hot-tempered, impulsive, but frank, cheerful, and a lover of good company, he lacked neither friends nor enemies. He was small but well built and, refusing all challenges, met insults instantly with fist or cane.

[Notes and copies of a few letters in the possession of Mrs. John Bennett, Charleston, and David McCord Wright, Savannah; McCord's will in the Richland County Courthouse; J. B. O'Neall, *Biog. Sketches of the Bench and Bar of S. C.* (1859), vol. II; M. LaBorde, *Hist. of the S. C. College* (1859), pp. 451, 286; J. M. Fraser, "Louisa C. McCord," *Bulletin of the Univ. of S. C.*, no. 91 (1920); Dumas Malone, *The Public Life of Thomas Cooper* (1926); J. P. Carson, *Life, Letters, and Speeches of James Louis Petigru* (1920); E. J. Scott, *Random Recollections* (1884), pp. 56–57.]

R. L. M—r.

McCORD, LOUISA SUSANNA CHEVES (Dec. 3, 1810–Nov. 23, 1879), woman writer of the ante-bellum South, was born in Charleston, S. C., the daughter of Langdon Cheves [*q.v.*] and Mary Elizabeth (Dulles) Cheves. Her ancestors were of Scotch, Irish, and Huguenot extraction and represented the best element in South Carolina society. Her father gave her the education usual to girls of her day, sending her to Grimshaw's School in Philadelphia, and later employing M. and Mme. Picot, French émigrés, to instruct her in languages before her presentation to Philadelphia and Washington society. He further allowed and encouraged her to study mathematics and other unusual branches under the tutor instructing her brothers. But the greatest educational influence she received was the society of her father and his eminent friends, and at an early age she became interested in questions pertaining to her state and to the South. In 1840 she was married to David James McCord [*q.v.*], a distinguished lawyer. They lived at "Lang Syne," her plantation near Fort Motte, S. C., and here she spent her busiest and most fruitful years. The care of the plantation and its several hundred negroes took most of her time, but she found leisure for translating and writing political and economic reviews and essays and poetry.

In 1855 her husband died, and for two years she sought solace in traveling through Europe. Upon her return she settled in Columbia, S. C., and lived there nearly all of her remaining years. During the Civil War her means, time, and sympathy were devoted to the cause that her state had espoused. In 1861 she became president of the Soldier's Relief Association and in the same year president of the Lady's Clothing Association, in which capacity, from her own funds, she armed and clothed the company under her son, Capt. Langdon Cheves McCord. Upon the death of her son at the battle of Second Manassas, she devoted herself to nursing, feeding, and clothing the soldiers in the military hospital housed in the dormitories of the South Carolina College in Columbia. After the Civil War, her family broken, her means diminished, and her dreams shattered, she retired to Charleston, dying there in November 1879. She was buried in Magnolia Cemetery.

Although her heroic labors during the Civil War overshadow the rest of her achievements, her writings are notable contributions to Southern literature. In 1848 she published a translation from Fréderic Bastiat's *Sophismes Économiques.* It influenced all of her subsequent political thinking. Her essays, contributed to various Southern journals, polemic, satiric, and always clear and coherent, were conservative, proslavery, and pro-Southern. Her ideal was a South with Southern culture, classic learning, and with economic independence based upon slavery and cotton. Her attitude toward slavery was that of the aristocratic Southern planter, an attitude expressed in the statement: "Christian slavery, in its full development, free from the fretting annoyance and galling bitterness of abolition interference, is the brightest sunbeam which Omniscience has destined for his [the negro's] existence" (the *Southern Quarterly Review,* January 1853, p. 120). *My Dreams,* her only volume of poetry, does not exhibit the vigorous style or maturity of thought of her essays. *Caius Gracchus,* a five-act blank-verse drama based upon the death of Gracchus, contains many of the poet's personal convictions but never rises above the average of the type of closet drama in vogue in the Victorian period.

[In addition to Mrs. McCord's writings see Jessie M. Fraser, *Louisa C. McCord* (1920), which is Bull. of the Univ. of S. C., no. 91; G. A. Wauchope, *The Writers of S. C.* (1910); Mary T. Tardy, *The Living Female Writers of the South* (1872); *Lib. of Southern Lit.*, vol. VIII (1907); W. P. Trent, *Wm. Gilmore Simms* (1892); *News and Courier* (Charleston), Nov. 27, 1879.]
R. D. B.

McCORMACK, JOSEPH NATHANIEL (Nov. 9, 1847–May 4, 1922), physician and sanitarian, was born on a farm near Howard's Mill, Nelson County, Ky. His father, Thomas McCormack, was a native of County Fermanagh, Ireland. His mother, Elizabeth Brown, was of a Pennsylvania family which migrated to Kentucky. He attended the local schools until the age of thirteen, after which he worked on the farm and in a store operated by his father. In 1868 he matriculated in the medical department of the Miami University at Cincinnati, which gave him the degree of M.D. in 1870. He was valedictorian of his class and delivered a thesis upon the physical and mental equality of man and woman. After an interneship in the Cincinnati General Hospital he returned to his father's home in Nelson County, Ky., for practice. In 1875 he moved to Bowling Green.

Here, during an epidemic of yellow fever in 1878–79, he attracted the attention of Gov. Luke P. Blackburn [*q.v.*], himself a physician, with the result that McCormack was appointed to the State Board of Health shortly after its formation in 1879. He had been a general practitioner with a leaning toward surgery, in which branch he was quite expert. The new appointment, however, focused his interest on the problems of public health, particularly those of the rural districts of his native state. When he was appointed secretary of the state board in 1883, he found it necessary to abandon his private practice. During the thirty years of his tenure of this office he was responsible for many noteworthy reforms. In the legislature of 1882 he caused the introduction of the state's first medical practice act, which failed of passage until the session of 1888. He drafted the state's first sanitary code and was a potent influence in its enactment into law. He followed this achievement with a state-wide campaign of education upon sanitary measures which led to a much-needed reorganization of the Kentucky State Medical Society and of its constituent county societies. The success of these activities gave McCormack a national reputation in public-health work. In 1892 he was made a member of the International Quarantine Commission. He was a member of the National Conference of State Boards of Health (1888–94) and of the National Conference of State Licensing and Examining Boards (1899).

His most notable service to the medical profession as a whole was his chairmanship (1899–1913) of the committee on organization of the American Medical Association. His ability as an organizer was recognized by the president, Dr. Charles A. L. Reed of Cincinnati, who found the organization in dire straits from an unworkable constitution and internal dissension. McCormack and his colleagues after a year's work brought in a draft of a new constitution and a plan for the rehabilitation of the society. These were presented at the St. Paul meeting in 1901 and adopted after a prolonged debate. It then became McCormack's function to put through the committee's plan by bringing all eligibles into the society and making them subscribers to its journal. To further these purposes he journeyed from state to state and even from county to county. It is said that he delivered his address, "The New Gospel of Health and Long Life," in a majority of the counties of the United States. As a result, the membership of the society was greatly increased, the subscriptions to the journal multiplied sixfold, and the erection of a permanent home for the association in Chicago was made possible. He was a member of the House of Delegates of the Association (1902–07) and of its Council of Health and Public Instruction (1910–13). He resigned from the Association work in 1913 and from the Kentucky state board the same year, but was retained as state sanitary inspector. In the meantime he had been instrumental in the erection and equipment of a model office and laboratory building in Louisville for the State Board of Health. In this building hangs an oil portrait of him, a gift of the medical profession of the state.

He died in Louisville, his home after 1913, from a cerebral hemorrhage. An ardent advocate of cremation, he directed that such disposal be made of his body. Physically he was above medium height, slight of build in his younger years but taking on more weight in later life. He was notably courteous and dignified, with a gift of persuasion in any cause that he advocated. Many honors came to him. He was made president of the state medical society in 1884 and was elected a member of the state legislature in 1912. In 1888 he received the personal thanks of President Cleveland for his work in the cholera epidemic. He was married in Bowling Green, to Corinne Crenshaw of Glasgow, Ky., on Sept. 14, 1871. A son, Dr. A. T. McCormack, succeeded him on the state board when he resigned in 1913.

[*Ky. Medic. Jour.* (Bowling Green), Jan. 1923, contains a symposium upon the life and work of McCormack by L. S. McMurtry, D. M. Griffith, J. C. W. Beckham, A. T. McCormack, and others; and prints his address on "The New Gospel of Health and Long Life." See also *Jour. Am. Medic. Asso.*, May 13, 1922, portrait; H. A. Kelly in H. A. Kelly and W. L. Burrage, *Dict. Am. Medic. Biog.* (1928); *Courier-Journal* (Louisville), May 5, 1922.] J. M. P—n.

McCORMICK, CYRUS HALL (Feb. 15, 1809–May 13, 1884), inventor, manufacturer, and philanthropist, the eldest son of Robert [*q.v.*] and Mary Ann (Hall) McCormick, was born on "Walnut Grove" farm, Rockbridge County, Va., and died in Chicago. His formal education was limited, and it was not until he was twenty-two that his latent inventive ability became fully evident. In the spring of 1831 he invented and took out a patent for a hillside plow of original design. As the harvest of that year approached his father again attempted to perfect a reaping machine, an idea upon which he had been engaged spasmodically for twenty years. Following his father's final abandonment of the problem, Cyrus decided to undertake its solution. Avoiding Robert McCormick's mistakes, he constructed a crude machine, designed upon entirely different principles, and tried it upon ripe wheat at "Walnut Grove." Encouraged by the result, he built another implement with added parts and in the latter part of July gave a successful public trial on late oats in the field of John Steele. The seven fundamental principles contained in this reaper, the divider, reel, straight reciprocating knife, fingers or guards, platform, main wheel and gearing, and the front-side draft traction, together with their peculiar combination, have proved essential to reaping machinery down to the present day.

In 1832 McCormick introduced improvements and exhibited his machine on several farms near Lexington. It attracted the attention of the editor of the *Lexington Union,* whose commendation (Sept. 14, 21, 28, 1833) was echoed in Edmund Ruffin's *Farmers' Register* (October 1833), and thence in several New York periodicals. During the same year McCormick invented and patented a self-sharpening horizontal plow. In April 1834 the *Mechanics' Magazine* of New York City, published notice of a reaper invented by Obed Hussey [*q.v.*] in 1833. This caused McCormick to warn Hussey of the priority of his own invention (*Ibid.,* May 1834); and on June 21, 1834, he took out a patent. Not sufficiently satisfied that his machine was capable of meeting all the varied conditions of harvest, he decided against placing it on the market. Although he spent some time perfecting his reaper and giving exhibitions during the next few years, he was mainly engaged in the business of making iron. The panic of 1837 and other handicaps spelled the doom of the Cotopaxi iron furnace, leaving him and his father greatly in debt. McCormick now turned seriously to the exploitation of his reaper, and after making further improvements began its commercial manufacture. Early construction took place chiefly at "Walnut Grove" but he sold rights to build the reaper in various sections of the state beginning with 1843. He awoke to the possibilities of sale throughout the country in 1844 and, after a trip through the North and West, arranged for manufacture at Brockport, N. Y., Cincinnati, and other western points. His licensees, less careful than the workers at "Walnut Grove," turned out machines made of inferior materials, poorly assembled. To save the good reputation of his reaper, McCormick resolved to concentrate all manufacture in one place, under his own direction. With clear vision, in 1847, he erected his factory in Chicago, then an insignificant lakeport, and closed other manufacturing contracts as quickly as possible. By 1850 he had succeeded in building up a national business.

Obed Hussey was his first rival. Beginning with 1843 the two men were frequently competitors in the fields and elsewhere, each winning his share of public favor. The fact that McCormick's machine was better designed for reaping and Hussey's for mowing was not appreciated in the early years. Hussey's belated recognition of this fact came too late to maintain him in competition. Eventually his invention became the basis of the modern mower. McCormick had succeeded in convincing the public of the value of his reaper by the time his original patent expired in 1848. The basic principles of his implement now became public property and, although he was partially protected by patents for improvements taken out in 1845 and 1847, a flood of competition ensued. In 1847 McCormick and Hussey were the only manufacturers in the business. By 1850 there were at least thirty rivals and by 1860 over a hundred. Unable to cope with the situation, Hussey sold his patents in 1858 and retired. McCormick in this crisis showed himself so resourceful and fought with such courage that he retained his place as the pioneer inventor and manufacturer of reaping machines. He continued to improve his reaper up to the time of his death. A mowing attachment was added in the fifties. In the sixties and later, McCormick machines were foremost in presenting such developments as the automatic self-raking device, the hand-binding harvester, the wire-binder, and the twine-binder. After 1860 McCormick gave little time to actual invention, but employed skilled mechanics and engineers to make improvements. He also bought new and promising inventions, for which he was always seeking. In an effort to obtain the benefit of his unexpired patents, McCormick's rivals employed skilful patent lawyers to combat reissues, to find fault in the loose wording of specifications, and thus to secure advantages to which they were not entitled. Political influence was brought to bear upon the Patent Office and Congress. The press was resorted to in an effort to prejudice public opinion. When all else failed, patents were frequently infringed. McCormick battled to the last in defense of his rights and for this reason was constantly in litigation. Eminent lawyers, such as William H. Seward, Abraham Lincoln, Edwin M. Stanton, Reverdy Johnson, Judah P. Benjamin, and Roscoe Conkling, were engaged as counsel for or against him. McCormick outfought and outlasted two generations and lived to lead a third. As soon as his reaper was well established in his own country he seized the opportunity offered by the first great world's fair in London, in 1851, to introduce it into Europe. His brilliant success in the field, before an international jury and under most unfavorable circumstances, made him world-famous overnight. The London *Times* (Aug. 12, Sept. 27, 1851) announced that the machine, if it fulfilled its promise, was worth the whole cost of the exhibition; and McCormick was awarded the Council Medal. Although other manufacturers quickly followed him abroad, he continued to win the major prizes at subsequent world fairs at Paris, London, Hamburg, Lille, Vienna, Philadelphia, and Melbourne between 1855 and 1880. The French, particularly appreciative of his services, made him a chevalier and later an officer of the Legion of Honor and in 1879 elected him a member of the French Academy of Sciences as having done more for agriculture than any other living man. In spite of this recognition, Europe was slow to adopt the new labor-saving machines; McCormick received little financial return for his effort abroad, but he did lay the foundation for the foreign business enjoyed by his successors.

McCormick's invention and development of the reaper constitute his chief title to fame. With the advent of the reaper, for the first time the farmer felt secure about his crops. They could be cut whenever they were ready, in a much shorter time than heretofore, with less labor, less cost, and a greater yield. Since the machine could not operate well in fields strewn with rocks, stumps, and other obstructions, agriculturists soon began to clear their lands and put them in better shape for cultivation. The reaper facilitated the rapid settlement of vacant lands by a large emigrant population moving westward. Labor released from the fields by its use helped to build up urban and industrial enterprises. The success of the machine greatly stimulated the invention and adoption of other improved agricultural implements. The reaper also proved an important factor in the Civil War, since it enabled the North to maintain a large force at the front, to feed both them and the civilian population, and in addition to export large quantities of grain to Europe. The income from this trade tended to relieve the tremendous financial strain upon the government. McCormick was not only a pioneer in the invention and evolution of reaping machinery, but also in the creation of modern business methods. He was among the first to introduce the use of field trials, guarantees and testimonials in advertising, cash and deferred payments for merchandise, and to promote the invention and use in his factory of labor-saving machinery designed to insure mass production. A man of vision, great force of character, and boundless energy, he possessed the unusual combination of inventive ability and practicality. More than most men, he was able to convert his creative ideas into reality.

On Jan. 26, 1858, McCormick married Nancy Maria, daughter of Melzar Fowler of Jefferson County, N. Y. Seven children were born to them. Mrs. McCormick, who possessed a practical mind, keen perception, and rare charm, proved an efficient aid to her husband in his career. McCormick, by nature deeply religious, was keenly interested in the Presbyterian church. Attracted by the views of Nathan L. Rice, he induced him to assume the pastorate of his church and later made him editor of the *Presbyterian Expositor,* a religious paper which McCormick acquired (1860) to aid in bringing about a peaceful solution of the difficulties between the North and the South. In 1859 he endowed four professorships in the Presbyterian Theological Seminary of the Northwest, which in 1886 was named McCormick Theological Seminary. The *Expositor* was discontinued at the outbreak of the Civil War, but in 1872 McCormick bought the *Interior* (later known as the *Continent*) and, installing W. C. Gray as editor, made it the leading Presbyterian paper in the West. Following the War, McCormick consistently advocated the reunion of the Presbyterian church in the North and South. He joined the Democratic party in Virginia in the forties, and after 1857 took an active part in its councils until his death. He understood both sections and was deeply disturbed by the rising conflict over the question of slavery. Coincident with the acquisition of the *Expositor,* he bought the *Chicago Times* in 1860, and published it for a year in the hope of influencing the Democratic Party toward a peace policy. He used his influence for Douglas at Baltimore, and later for Breckinridge, and during the War supported the peace efforts of Greeley. McCormick was abroad from 1862 to 1864. Upon his return in the fall of 1864 he ran for Congress on the Democratic ticket against John Wentworth, but was defeated. He served as chairman of the Democratic state central committee in Illinois in 1872 and 1876. McCormick was a director of the Union Pacific prior to the Crédit Mobilier scandals; he displayed much interest in the expansion of the railroads and in the Nicaragua Canal; he made large investments in gold, silver, and copper mines. An advocate of free trade, he was one of the organizers of the Mississippi Valley Society which aimed to promote trade relations between England and the Mississippi Valley. In an endeavor to reestablish the institutions of the South after the War, in 1866 he made gifts to the Union Theological Seminary at Hampden-Sidney, Va., and to Washington College at Lexington, Va. As late as 1880 he served as president of the Virginia Society in Chicago.

[R. G. Thwaites, *Cyrus Hall McCormick and the Reaper* (1909); H. N. Casson, *Cyrus Hall McCormick, His Life and Work* (1909); W. T. Hutchinson, *Cyrus Hall McCormick: Seed-Time, 1809–1856* (1930); L. J. McCormick, *Family Record and Biography* (1896); Edward Stabler, *A Brief Narrative of the Invention of Reaping Machines* (1854); M. F. Miller, *The Evolution of Reaping Machines* (1902); Cyrus McCormick, *The Century of the Reaper* (1931); R. B. Swift, "Who Invented the Reaper?" in *Implement Age,* Apr. 15, 1897; L. J. Halsey, *A Hist. of the McCormick Theol. Seminary . . .* (1893); contemporary agricultural and scientific periodicals, proceedings of agricultural organizations, newspapers, reports of World Fairs, court records, McCormick family papers, and records of McCormick Reaper companies in Lib. of McCormick Hist. Asso., Chicago, Ill.] H. A. K.

McCORMICK, JOSEPH MEDILL (May 16, 1877–Feb. 25, 1925), journalist, United States senator, was born in Chicago, Ill., the son of Robert Sanderson McCormick [*q.v.*], diplomat, and Katharine Van Etta Medill, the daughter of the editor of the *Chicago Daily Tribune,* Joseph Medill [*q.v.*]. Brought up under the influence of his maternal grandfather, Medill McCormick imbibed at an early age an aggressive Americanism, though as a result of several years abroad he acquired a competent knowledge of foreign languages and learned to appreciate European points of view. After attending preparatory school at Groton, Mass., he became a student at Yale, and upon his graduation in 1900 returned to Chicago where he entered upon his career as newspaper editor and publisher. Beginning as police reporter for the *Tribune* at a salary of three dollars a week, he served in various capacities until by 1908 all departments of the paper were under his management. With the outbreak of revolt in the Philippines in 1901, he was sent to the seat of the disturbance as a special correspondent for the paper, and after participating in the Samar campaign he traveled about the Far East for several months. During this period he also became associated with Charles A. Otis in the ownership of the *Cleveland Leader* and the *Cleveland News.*

Actively entering into politics in 1908, McCormick became an ardent follower of Theodore Roosevelt, and in the Progressive revolt of 1912, served as a member of the National Campaign Committee, having complete charge of the Western headquarters of the Progressive party and using all the resources of the *Chicago Tribune.* Much against his will, he was elected during the same campaign to the lower house of the Illinois state legislature and in 1914 was reëlected. At this time he led the remaining Progressive recalcitrants back into the Republican party, for in the face of threatening war in Europe he believed that party harmony should prevail. In 1916 he was elected congressman at large from Illinois and served in the Sixty-fifth Congress until 1919, when he took his seat in the Senate. He had definitely imperialistic leanings, although he rejected the extreme position of the *Tribune,* then under the control of his brother. Throughout his senatorial career he was a bitter opponent of the League of Nations and the Versailles Treaty. He stood squarely in his opposition to any entangling alliance, although in 1923 as a member of the committee on foreign relations he admitted the value of a World Court. In domestic affairs he sponsored the McCormick-Good bill, providing for the creation of the Bureau of the Budget, which was vetoed by President Wilson in June 1920, but passed in virtually the same form in the next session and became law in June 1921. He also encouraged the proposed "Great Lakes to Gulf waterway" and favored the child-labor amendment. One of his last acts in the Senate was his effort toward securing the ratification of the Isle of Pines treaty.

In the Republican primary campaign of 1924, McCormick was defeated by Charles S. Deneen. He died in Washington, D. C., on Feb. 25, 1925, only a few days before his term of office was over. He was a vivid person, ambitious and hard-working, and eager for a real knowledge of the matters with which he dealt. In 1917, while still a member of the House of Representatives, he journeyed to the Western front, and again in 1920 and 1924 he was in Europe seeking additional knowledge on the foreign situation. He was survived by his wife, Ruth Hanna, the daughter of Marcus Alonzo Hanna [*q.v.*], whom he had married on June 10, 1903.

[*Who's Who in America*, 1924–25; *Yale Univ.: Obit. Record of Grads. Deceased During the Year Ending July 1, 1925* (1925); *Current Opinion*, Dec. 1916; the *Independent*, Nov. 22, 1924; the *Nation*, Mar. 11, 1925; L. J. McCormick, *Family Record and Biog.* (1896); *Cong. Record*, 68 Cong., 2 Sess., pp. 5087–89; obituaries in the Chicago newspapers, Feb. 25–27, 1925; *Chicago Tribune* clipping department.] T. E. S.

McCORMICK, LEANDER JAMES (Feb. 8, 1819–Feb. 20, 1900), manufacturer, philanthropist, the son of Robert [*q.v.*] and Mary Ann (Hall) McCormick, was born on "Walnut Grove" farm, Rockbridge County, Va., and died in Chicago. He was educated in an old-field school and also received instruction from private tutors. As a boy he manifested much interest in mechanics and when he grew older aided his father and his brother Cyrus Hall McCormick [*q.v.*] in the construction of reapers in the blacksmith shop at "Walnut Grove." Cyrus engaged Leander to sell, set up, and repair reapers in Virginia in the early forties, and in 1847 brought him to Cincinnati to superintend the manufacture of a hundred reapers at the foundry of A. C. Brown. In 1849 Leander moved to Chicago, where he took charge of the manufacturing division of the McCormick factory, under contract on a salary basis, for one year. From 1850 to 1859 he held the same position on salary. In the latter year Cyrus McCormick gave a share of the profits of the reaper business to Leander and also to another brother, William S. McCormick. This gift was confirmed by contract and the name of the firm was changed from C. H. McCormick to C. H. McCormick & Brothers. Under this arrangement Leander continued to supervise the manufacturing department. Upon the expiration of the contract in 1864 it was renewed for a further period. The death of William in 1865 necessitated a change in the firm, and it was known as C. H. McCormick & Brother from 1866 to 1874, when it became C. H. and L. J. McCormick. In 1879 Leander was made vice-president of the McCormick Harvesting Machine Company. He retired from active participation in the reaper business in 1881 and ten years later sold out his interest to his nephew, Cyrus H. McCormick.

Leander McCormick introduced a number of minor improvements in the McCormick machines, took out several patents jointly with employees of the engineering division, and was a factor in helping to build up the successful business so closely connected with the name of the family. Because of differences in temperament and opinion, relations between him and Cyrus McCormick were strained long before he retired from the family business; in his *Memorial of Robert McCormick* (1885) he sought to gain for his father, rather than his brother, credit for the invention of the reaper. (For the entire controversy, see Hutchinson, *post*, ch. v.) From 1891 to 1900 he devoted his attention to extensive real-estate holdings acquired in the course of his long residence in Chicago. Being much interested in art, he assembled a notable collection of paintings at his home. In 1874 he gave to the University of Virginia a refractor telescope, built by Alvan Clark [*q.v.*]. This gift was followed by another, of $18,000, for an observatory, which was named for the donor. In 1896, after years of research, he published a McCormick genealogy under the title, *Family Record and Biography.* On Oct. 22, 1845, he married Henrietta Maria, daughter of John Hamilton of Rockbridge County, Va. Four children were born of this union.

[W. T. Hutchinson, *Cyrus Hall McCormick: Seed-Time, 1809–1856* (1930); *Who's Who in America*, 1899–1900; *Daily Inter Ocean* (Chicago), Feb. 21, 1900; *Farm Implement News* (Chicago), Feb. 22, 1900; *Alumni Bulletin of the Univ. of Va.*, May 1900; Collections of the McCormick Hist. Asso. Lib., Chicago; references cited in bibliography of Cyrus Hall McCormick.] H. A. K.

McCORMICK, MEDILL [See McCORMICK, JOSEPH MEDILL, 1877–1925].

McCORMICK, RICHARD CUNNINGHAM (May 23, 1832–June 2, 1901), journalist, politician, business man, was born in New York City, the eldest of the seven children of Richard Cunningham and Sarah Matilda (Decker) McCormick. He was of Scotch-Irish ancestry, a descendant of Hugh McCormick who emigrated from Londonderry to Dauphin County, Pa., before 1735. His father, a liberally educated man and for many years a journalist, gave him a classical education in the private schools of the city with a view to his entering Columbia College. His health, however, was not particularly good, and the family decided that it would be better for him to travel. He spent most of 1854 and 1855 in Europe and Asia. He was in the Crimea during the war and while there acted as correspondent for the *Morning Courier and New York Enquirer* and other New York journals. Later he published accounts of his travels and experiences in the Crimea under the titles *A Visit to the Camp before Sevastopol* (1855), and *St. Paul's to St. Sophia* (1860). Soon after his return to America he became editor of the *Young Men's Magazine,* holding the position from 1857 to 1859. During the same period he contributed to various periodicals and lectured frequently. In 1861–62 he was in Washington and with the Army of the Potomac as correspondent for the New York *Evening Post* and the *Commercial Advertiser.* His description of the battle of Bull Run was considered one of the best journalistic accounts printed.

On returning from Europe, McCormick had enthusiastically entered the movement for the formation of the Republican party. His antislavery opinions and the interest he had shown in 1856 secured him a prominent part in the campaign of 1860, when he became a member of the Republican state committee. During this campaign his friendship with both Lincoln and Seward began. In 1862 he was the defeated Republican nominee for the first congressional district of New York. Shortly after he was appointed chief clerk of the Department of Agriculture. In March 1863 he was appointed secretary of the newly organized Arizona Territory, an office which he held until Apr. 10, 1866, when he was appointed governor. In 1869 he was elected territorial delegate to Congress and held the office through three successive terms, but he declined renomination in 1874.

When he went to Arizona he took with him a small printing outfit and started the *Arizona Weekly Miner,* a publication supposed by some to have been devoted to furthering his own political ambitions (Farish, *post,* III, p. 46). Whatever these were, his ambitions for Arizona were intelligently and earnestly put before the government and the people. During his terms as secretary and governor, he was continually active in urging the construction of roads and railroads in order to improve communication between Arizona and New Mexico and California, the development of agriculture along with mining, the development of an educational system, and the intelligent treatment of both the friendly and hostile Indians in the territory. While in Congress, he spoke convincingly in favor of sharp and immediate punishment of the unnecessarily brutal Indians, such as the Apaches, and of the advisability of paying the friendly tribes on the reservations for work actually done instead of pauperizing them by gifts outright. He also advocated more government roads and surveys for the territory, restriction of wanton killing of the buffalo, conservation of the forests, and the development of irrigation. In 1876 he was appointed commissioner to the Centennial Exposition in Philadelphia. The following year he was offered the mission to Brazil and in 1879 that to Mexico, both of which he declined. In 1878 he was appointed commissioner general for the United States to the Paris Exposition. At the Exposition he was made a commander of the Legion of Honor. On returning to America, he retired from public life and entered business in New York, but resided at Jamaica, Long Island, where he served as president of the board of education and later as president of the local board of managers of the State Normal and Training School. He became interested in several western mining enterprises. From Apr. 12, 1892, until his death he was a trustee of the Citizens' Savings Bank of New York. In 1886 he ran for Congress but was defeated by the Democratic candidate. In 1894 he ran again and was elected, but refused renomination on account of ill health. He died in Jamaica a few hours after he had suffered a stroke of apoplexy. He was twice married: on Oct. 1, 1865, to Margaret G. Hunt, of Rahway, N. J., who died in 1867; and on Nov. 11, 1873, to Elizabeth Thurman of Columbus, Ohio.

[T. E. Farish, *Hist. of Ariz.* (8 vols., 1915–18); H. H. Bancroft, *Hist. of Ariz. and N. M.* (1889); S. R. De Long, *The Hist. of Ariz.* (1905); R. E. Sloan, *Hist. of Ariz.* (1930), vol. I; *Biog. Dir. Am. Cong.* (1928); L. J. McCormick, *Family Record and Biog.* (1896); *Ariz. Weekly Miner,* 1864–69; *Young Men's Mag.,* 1857–59; the *Evening Post* (N. Y.), July 22–24, 1861; *Brooklyn Daily Eagle,* June 3, 1901.] M. L. B.

McCORMICK, ROBERT (June 8, 1780–July 4, 1846), inventor, the youngest son of Robert and Martha (Sanderson) McCormick, was born and died at "Walnut Grove," Rockbridge County, Va. He was the grandson of Thomas McCormick who emigrated from Ulster in 1734 and settled first in Lancaster County and later in Cumberland County, Pa., where he made a name for himself as a weaver and an Indian fighter. The elder Robert McCormick settled in Juniata County, Pa., in 1755. In July 1779 he moved to the Valley of Virginia and purchased a tract of land lying partly in Rockbridge and partly in Augusta County, which he called "Walnut Grove." Later he fought in the Revolution. His son Robert was educated in a private school in the neighborhood and instructed at home in the strictest tenets of the "Seceder" branch of the Presbyterian church. On Feb. 11, 1808, he married Mary Ann Hall, daughter of Patrick Hall, who was also of Scotch-Irish descent. McCormick, who was medium in height, slight in physique, quiet and reserved in manner, and dreamy, displayed a wide range of interest. Mary Ann Hall was tall and robust, vivacious, possessed of great energy, and extremely practical. Both were deeply religious and noted in the community for integrity of character.

Although interested in music and astronomy, McCormick chiefly distinguished himself by the invention of a number of agricultural implements, designed to lighten the labor of the husbandman. In 1830 and 1831 he invented and took out patents on a hempbrake, gristmill, and a hydraulic machine. About this time he also invented a blacksmith bellows. In 1834 he produced a threshing machine. Although he built a number of his various machines in the blacksmith shop at "Walnut Grove" and sold them to the farmers and planters in the vicinity, his inventions never became commercially valuable. He was interested in too many devices and lacked the patience and perseverance to develop any of them to the point of practicality. Most important perhaps were his attempts to devise a power implement for reaping grain, extending intermittently over more than twenty years. His first reaping machine is said to have been produced as early as 1809 and in the course of years he experimented with several different types of apparatus. The most ingenious of these was a machine, completed in 1831, which consisted of a number of sickles projecting horizontally from a wooden bar. On top of the bar were placed an equal number of vertical cylinders with long spikes. In action the cylinders were designed to revolve, the spikes thrusting the grain across the edges of the sickles. The continued revolutions of the cylinders, aided by a series of leather bands studded with nails, discharged the severed grain to one side in swath. This implement cut straight grain fairly well but proved useless where the stalks were inclined or fallen and the discharging apparatus threw the grain to one side in a tangled mass. Discouraged, McCormick thereupon abandoned the problem.

If he accomplished nothing else, however, his efforts served as the inspiration for one of the world's great inventions, the reaper, devised that same year by his son, Cyrus Hall McCormick [*q.v.*]. In 1836 Robert and Cyrus built an iron furnace which they called Cotopaxi. Following the panic of 1837 the enterprise failed and threw Robert heavily into debt. In this crisis Cyrus McCormick turned to his reaper and Robert McCormick began to manufacture it on a contract basis. By 1845 he had won back his financial independence. The next year he caught a severe cold which resulted in his death a few months later. Among his children were William S. and Leander James McCormick [*q.v.*], both of whom were associated with their elder brother in the development of the reaper.

[The best printed source is W. T. Hutchinson, *Cyrus Hall McCormick: Seed-Time, 1809–1856* (1930). L. J. McCormick, *Memorial of Robert McCormick* (1885), and R. H. McCormick and J. H. Shields, *Robert McCormick, Inventor* (1910), seek to credit the invention of the reaper to Robert rather than his eldest son. See also L. J. McCormick, *Family Record and Biography* (1896); and references cited under Cyrus Hall McCormick. The Collections of the McCormick Hist. Asso. Library, Chicago, contain much material.] H. A. K.

McCORMICK, ROBERT SANDERSON (July 26, 1849–Apr. 16, 1919), diplomat, was born in Rockbridge County, Va., the eldest son of William Sanderson and Mary Ann (Grigsby) McCormick, and grandson of Robert [*q.v.*] and Mary Ann (Hall) McCormick. His father (1815–1865) inherited the paternal homestead in 1846 but three years later moved to Chicago and joined his two brothers, Cyrus Hall and Leander J. McCormick [*qq.v.*], in the manufacture of reaping machines. Robert S. McCormick was educated at the preparatory department of the University of Chicago and at the University of Virginia. He inherited from his father not only a liberal fortune but much of his attractive personality and sound business ability. He early decided on a diplomatic career, but not until April 1889 did he obtain the appointment of second secretary of legation at London under Minister Robert T. Lincoln, which position he held for two years. On Feb. 18, 1892, he was appointed resident commissioner in London for the World's Columbian Exposition at Chicago in 1893. He had a difficult task to overcome the indifference and prejudice against participation that existed at that time in England, arising out of the ill feeling engendered by the McKinley tariff. McCormick's public addresses in various parts of the country, particularly that in London before the Society of Arts giving a scholarly review of British trade developments and an analysis of existing trade relations between the two countries, undoubtedly led to the success of his mission. After returning to Chicago from London he served for several years on the Public Library board. He was an ardent collector of books and specialized in Napoleonic biographies and etchings.

On Mar. 7, 1901, President McKinley appointed him minister to Austria, and on May 27, 1902, when the post was raised to an embassy, McCormick became the first American ambassador to Austria-Hungary. On Sept. 26, 1902, President Roosevelt appointed him ambassador to Russia. While there he aided in gaining entrance to Russia for the Associated Press which made possible a lifting of the veil that had hidden events in Russia from the rest of the world. He also succeeded in obtaining from the Russian government recognition of passports granted by the United States to its Jewish citizens. During the Russo-Japanese War he handled the interests of Japan in Russia, and for this the Japanese government decorated him with the first class of the Order of the Rising Sun; while in recognition of his services to Russia during the War the Emperor Nicholas conferred on him the Order of St. Alexander Nevsky. On Mar. 8, 1905, McCormick was promoted to the ambassadorship of France. This change was welcome to him as he had spent much of his earlier life in Paris and had a wide acquaintance there. The Russian climate having undermined his health, he was compelled to resign and left his post on Mar. 2, 1907. The French government as a mark of appreciation of his services conferred on him the grand cordon of the Legion of Honor. He died at his home in Chicago on Apr. 16, 1919, from pneumonia. He was married on June 8, 1876, to Katharine Van Etta Medill, daughter of Joseph Medill [*q.v.*]. They had two sons, Joseph Medill McCormick [*q.v.*], who became United States senator for Illinois, and Robert Rutherford McCormick.

[*Who's Who in America*, 1918–19; L. J. McCormick, *Family Record and Biog.* (1896); the *Chicago Tribune* and *N. Y. Times*, Apr. 17, 1919; records in the appointment section of the Department of State.] A. E. I.

McCORMICK, SAMUEL BLACK (May 6, 1858–Apr. 18, 1928), Presbyterian clergyman, educator, was born in a rural district of Westmoreland County, Pa. His father, James Irwin McCormick, a classical scholar and well-known physician, was a grandson of John McCormick who came to America from Ireland in 1788; his mother, Rachel Long (Black), was a granddaughter of George Long, a captain in the Revolutionary War. Prepared by his father he entered Washington and Jefferson College and graduated with highest honors in 1880. During the next two years he taught Greek at his alma mater, served as an instructor in nearby Canonsburg Academy, and studied law. He was admitted to the Allegheny County bar in 1882 and on Sept. 29 of that year married Ida May Steep of Washington, Pa. Two sons and two daughters were born of this union.

In 1883 he removed to Denver, Colo., where he engaged in the practice of the law for four years, but, finding the legal profession an inadequate field for the realization of his aspirations, he decided to give his life to the Christian ministry. Returning to Pennsylvania, he entered the Western Theological Seminary in Allegheny from which he was graduated in 1890, meanwhile serving intermittently as an instructor in the Western University of Pennsylvania. Ordained (1890) by the Presbytery of Allegheny, he began his active ministry in the Central Presbyterian Church of that city. After four years he was called to the First Presbyterian Church of Omaha, Nebr., which he served three years. In 1897 he accepted the presidency of Coe College, Cedar Rapids, Iowa, where for seven years he grappled with problems of endowment, curriculum enrichment, faculty building, and the awakening of community interest in the rapidly growing institution.

His success in college administration earned for him an invitation to the chancellorship of the Western University of Pennsylvania, a dormant old college in Allegheny with a small group of recently affiliated professional schools in Pittsburgh. Intense loyalty to his native state made his acceptance inevitable. Here for sixteen years (1904–20) he wrought out his enduring monument, a modern university. He organized an educational program based on the obligations of the institution to the community; he purchased a new campus in the civic center of Pittsburgh and constructed modern buildings thereon; he secured appropriations from the state legislature for buildings and for maintenance; he had the name of the institution changed to University of Pittsburgh (1908) in order to win greater local interest and support and to characterize more accurately its field of service; he raised the scholastic standards, coordinated and integrated the constituent schools, secured the endowment of the Mellon Institute of Industrial Research, and created schools of education and economics and a summer session. In 1920 he was retired from active service with the title of chancellor emeritus. With an undiminished interest in public affairs he continued to write, speak and preach until, after a brief illness from pneumonia, he died at his home in Coraopolis Heights near Pittsburgh.

McCormick was a man of strong friendships and intense loyalties. While small of stature, he had tremendous energy and an active imagination. Neither his labors nor his reputation were limited to the field of his professional duties. He was a member of the committee of the General

Assembly of the Presbyterian Church for the revision of the confession of faith; and a director of the Carnegie Foundation for the Advancement of Teaching, of the Western Theological Seminary, and of the Pittsburgh Chamber of Commerce.

[*Who's Who in America*, 1899–1927; *Reports of the Chancellor of the University of Pittsburgh*, esp. 1910–20; *The Pitt Weekly*, Apr. 1928; *The Carnegie Foundation for the Advancement of Teaching, Twenty-third Ann. Report* (1928); *Univ. of Pittsburgh Bull.*; *The Celebration of the One Hundred and Twenty-fifth Anniversary* (1912); *Biog. and Hist. Cat. of Washington and Jefferson Coll.* (1902); *A Century and a Half of Pittsburg and Her People* (1908), vol. III, ed. by J. W. Jordan; *Pittsburgh Record*, June 1928; *Pittsburgh Post-Gazette*, Apr. 19, 1928.] W. G. C.

McCORMICK, STEPHEN (Aug. 26, 1784–Aug. 28, 1875), inventor and manufacturer, was born at Auburn, in Fauquier County, Va., the son of John and Elizabeth (Morgan) McCormick and a kinsman of Robert McCormick [*q.v.*]. His paternal ancestors emigrated from Ulster, Ireland, to Pennsylvania and thence moved to Virginia. He did not take kindly to his father's suggestion that he study law but sought a more congenial occupation in inventive activities. One of his first enterprises was to improve the shape of the nether millstone on a water-power gristmill, thereby increasing its productivity. He next became interested in the development of a practical iron plow and by 1816 had invented, manufactured, and put into use a cast-iron plow, superior to that invented earlier by Charles Newbold. He took out his first patent Feb. 3, 1819, and followed it with subsequent patents on January 28, 1826, and December 1, 1837. His plow, made of detachable parts, consisted of an especially designed cast-iron mould board to the bottom of which was fastened an adjustable wrought-iron point. In practice, this implement decreased the draft, deepened the furrow, and pulverized the soil more thoroughly. The introduction of the principles of replacement and standardization of parts made the iron plow a practical invention and also aided in the development of manufacturing processes. When Lafayette visited the United States in 1824, McCormick presented him with one of his plows. Lafayette lent it to the Royal Central Agricultural Society of France which on May 17, 1826, highly commended its principles.

At first McCormick manufactured his plows in small numbers on the farm at Auburn and marketed them in the vicinity. Coincident with the grant of his second patent in 1826, he began an active campaign to introduce his plow into Virginia and other Southern states. He designed some twelve types intended to cover the needs of every variety of plowing. Still maintaining the factory at Auburn, he established factories at Leesburg and Alexandria, Va. The product from these factories was sold directly to consumers or through the agency of the firm of McCormick & Minor in Richmond. Supplementing his personal activities, McCormick arranged for the construction of his plows with several Virginia iron furnaces on a license fee basis. Other iron furnaces of the state began to pirate his invention as early as 1827, manufacturing and selling his plow on an extensive scale in violation of his patent rights. He also had to contend with a claim of infringement of his patent by another inventor, Gideon Davis, who sued him but eventually compromised the case out of court.

McCormick's plows were manufactured chiefly between 1826 and 1850, when they were widely used in Virginia and to a less degree in other Southern states. The production figures available show that five thousand and forty were made and sold at the furnaces of William Weaver and Jordan & Irvine between 1827 and 1839, and that as many or more were made by a dozen other Virginia iron furnaces in the same period. McCormick wrote in 1830 that Benjamin Blackford, a Virginia iron manufacturer, was paying him annually between $1,200 and $2,000 in license fees, the royalty on each plow usually being seventy-five cents or less. McCormick's most widely known contemporary was Jethro Wood of New York, who took out a patent for his cast-iron plow some seven months later than McCormick's patent of the same year, and subsequently built and sold his plows in the Northern states. With Wood, McCormick shares the honor of the introduction of the cast-iron plow into the United States. McCormick married Sarah Barnett of Fauquier County in February 1807. She died in 1814, leaving three children, and on Feb. 29, 1816, he married Elizabeth M. Benson of Stafford County, Va., by whom he had nine children. He was a devoted "Old School" Presbyterian and a stanch Democrat. In character he was said to have been honest, candid, and fearless. Retiring from business in his later years, he died at the age of ninety-one and was buried on his old farm at Auburn.

[L. J. McCormick, *Family Record and Biog.* (1896); H. L. Ellsworth, *A Digest of Patents Issued by the U. S.* (1840); the *Am. Farmer* (Baltimore), July 28, Nov. 10, 1826, Oct. 24, Nov. 7, 1828; *Farmers' Reg.* (Shellbanks, Va.), Oct. 1834; *Farmers' Reg.* (Petersburg, Va.), Feb. 1836; *New Eng. Farmer* (Boston), Jan. 20, 1826, and correspondence and records in the Colls. of the McCormick Hist. Asso., Chicago, Ill.] H. A. K.

McCOSH, ANDREW JAMES (Mar. 15, 1858–Dec. 2, 1908), surgeon, was born at Belfast,

Ireland, son of Rev. James McCosh [*q.v.*], then professor of logic and metaphysics at Queen's College, and Isabella Guthrie, the daughter of Dr. Alexander Guthrie of Edinburgh. In 1868, following his call to the presidency of the College of New Jersey, James McCosh moved his family to Princeton. Andrew was educated at the local schools and at the college, where he was graduated in 1877. He was athletic, played on the football team for three of his undergraduate years, and developed a superb physique. In 1880 he received the degree of M.D. from the College of Physicians and Surgeons, New York, and after serving an interneship for eighteen months at the Chambers Street Hospital, where he had unusual facilities for studying casualties, he spent some time in Vienna under the renowned surgeon Billroth. Returning to the metropolis he entered practice in 1883 as junior associate of T. Gaillard Thomas, a gynecologist, with whom he remained for eleven years. By all precedent he should himself have become known as a gynecologist, but he refused to limit his surgical activity in any way and while he was a master of gynecological surgery he remained in his affiliations and practice a general surgeon. In 1887 he was made an attending surgeon to the Presbyterian Hospital, a position he retained until his death; he was at the same time one of the professors of surgery at the New York Polyclinic, from its inception until 1895, and he was also professor of clinical surgery at the College of Physicians and Surgeons. In 1903 he was made president of the medical board of the Presbyterian Hospital. His premature death resulted from an injury received in a runaway accident.

As a surgeon McCosh had few equals, and while he published no major work on surgery he wrote papers which covered every department of major surgery—abdominal, gynecological, urological, thoracic, and neurological. The records of the Presbyterian Hospital show that during the twenty-one years of his surgical connection with that institution he had operated sixteen hundred times for appendicitis alone. His papers on peritonitis, one of which was read before an International Congress at Brussels, attracted unusual attention. He collaborated with M. Allen Starr, the neurologist and a classmate, in a work entitled *A Contribution to the Localisation of the Muscular Sense* (1894). For many years he spent his summers abroad for the joint purpose of taking a vacation and of keeping in touch with European surgery. At a late period in his career he began the custom of holding monthly sessions at his office for the benefit of his junior hospital associates. His interests outside of the profession were limited largely to philanthropic and sociological activities. He never married.

[*N. Y. Medic. Jour.*, Dec. 5, 1908; *Medic. Record*, Dec. 5, 1908; C. A. McWilliams, "Master Surgeons of America," *Surgery, Gynecology, and Obstetrics*, June 1923; H. A. Kelly and W. L. Burrage, *Am. Medic. Biogs.* (1920); H. F. Osborn, *Fifty Years of Princeton '77* (1927); *Princeton Alumni Weekly*, Dec. 9, 16, 1908; *N. Y. Tribune*, Dec. 3, 1908.] E. P.

McCOSH, JAMES (Apr. 1, 1811–Nov. 16, 1894), college president, was born within a mile of the river Doon, about ten miles from its mouth on the bay of Ayr, the region which had passed through stirring scenes in the days of Wallace. He was the son of Andrew and Jean (Carson) McCosh. At the early age of thirteen he entered Glasgow University. After a notable record there he finished his academic career at Edinburgh University, receiving the degree of master of arts in March 1833. The following year he became a licensed preacher of the Established Church of Scotland and was successful in his pastorates at the Abbey Chapel, Arbroath; and, later, at Brechin. While he was at Brechin the historic controversies arose in the Established Church of Scotland between the conservatives and the more liberally inclined. McCosh courageously allied himself with his colleagues who protested against the intolerable burdens and restrictions placed upon them by the technical demands of the state. This group, committed to the logic of their convictions, left the Established Church in a body, facing the total loss of all of their emoluments and without financial resources or assurance of support. The result was the establishment of the Free Church of Scotland. This action of McCosh was characteristic of his whole life, the following of his convictions in scorn of results. It was a noble company of patriots and churchmen, of which he was a member, led by the great Thomas Chalmers, the most conspicuous preacher, scholar, and philanthropist in Scotland.

At the University of Edinburgh McCosh had come under the influence of the philosophy and personality of William Hamilton, who stimulated his interest in philosophical studies. With a singular independence of thought, however, young McCosh soon began to react in opposition to the many negations of Hamilton and to find himself in closer sympathy with the Intuitionism of Reid and the Scottish school. In the intuitive powers of the human mind as expressed in the fundamental principles of that school, he became, at length, a firm believer. In 1843 John Stuart Mill's *System of Logic* appeared. To McCosh it seemed to evolve a view of nature that excluded the supernatural from the course of the world. Mill's philosophy and its growing influence called forth McCosh's first book, *The Method of the Divine Government, Physical and Moral* (1850). This brought him into public notice at once in the philosophical world and eventually led, through Lord Clarendon, to his appointment to the chair of logic and metaphysics in Queen's College, Belfast.

The sixteen years at Belfast (1852–68) mark a most productive period of McCosh's work. During it he published *Typical Forms and Special Ends in Creation* (1855), in collaboration with George Dickie; *The Intuitions of the Mind Inductively Investigated* (1860); *The Supernatural in Relation to the Natural* (1862); and *An Examination of Mr. J. S. Mill's Philosophy; Being a Defence of Fundamental Truth* (1866). His *Intuitions* presented the fundamental doctrines of the Scottish school, namely, that there are certain constitutional principles in the human mind which determine the form of its experience, and at the same time guarantee the objective authority of its fundamental beliefs. He maintained that our intuitions have their beginning in simple cognition, where they take on singular and concrete forms, and then pass into the realm of our higher judgments and beliefs, where they become universal and necessary principles. He did not, however, rest their authority alone, or even mainly, on experience, but appealed to certain marks by which they become accredited, namely, self-evidence, necessity, and catholicity. With him self-evidence held the main and unique place. He affirmed, moreover, that the intuitive principles bear intrinsic evidence which substantiates their claims, and that they are the chief grounds on which the negations of Kant and Hamilton are to be refuted and a positive philosophy constructed. Hamilton's *Lectures on Metaphysics and Logic* called forth, in 1865, Mill's *An Examination of Sir William Hamilton's Philosophy.* McCosh attacked vigorously Mill's position, his sensational psychology, his empirical logic, his utilitarian ethics, his negative metaphysics, and his skeptical attitude towards religion. The *Examination of Mr. J. S. Mill's Philosophy; Being a Defence of Fundamental Truth* is one of the most convincing statements concerning the principles of the Intuitional philosophy in opposition to pure Empiricism.

McCosh's reputation was extending rapidly in Ireland, Scotland, and England, and echoes of it reached American shores. In 1868 President John Maclean, of the College of New Jersey, Princeton, resigned. McCosh was immediately suggested as his successor, and the board of trustees unanimously called him to assume the office, exactly one hundred years after the calling of his fellow countryman, John Witherspoon [*q.v.*], from Edinburgh to the same position. During his labors at Princeton McCosh continued to publish many works, among which the most important were *The Laws of Discursive Thought, Being a Text-book of Formal Logic* (1870); *Christianity and Positivism* (1871); *The Scottish Philosophy, Biographical, Expository, Critical, from Hutcheson to Hamilton* (1875); *Realistic Philosophy Defended in a Philosophic Series* (2 vols., 1887); a two-volume work, *Psychology* (1886, 1887); and another metaphysical treatise entitled *First and Fundamental Truths* (1889), the latter being in large measure a revised edition of his *Intuitions.*

Throughout all his philosophical writings, McCosh led up to his philosophy of religion, in which he presented the fundamental arguments for theism and expressed his belief in the divine origin and government of the world. One of his most conspicuous contributions to philosophical and theological discussions during his early years at Princeton was in connection with the subject of evolution. Although brought up in the conservative theology of Scotland, he had an open and ever-deepening mind. In the early seventies he stood out almost alone among the ministers of the United States, in defense of the doctrine of evolution. No one would have been more astonished and perplexed by the trial in Tennessee in which William Jennings Bryan figured, than McCosh would have been. In an age when the discussion was just starting, he insisted that the doctrine of evolution was not directly, or by implication, a denial of God; but that the program of evolution magnified the wonder and mystery of the process of creation.

When McCosh became president of the College of New Jersey it was at low ebb. After the Civil War, few students came from the South, formerly the chief recruiting ground; the attendance was small and the financial affairs of the institution were in a most critical state. The new president proved an able administrator, and his twenty years in office constitute a memorable period in the history of the college. His plans were well conceived and the power of his personality commanded enthusiastic support at all times. Eminent and well-qualified instructors were added to the faculty; a wisely balanced system of elective studies and of graduate work was instituted; schools of science, philosophy, and art were organized; fellowships and other means for stimulating research were provided; additions to scientific equipment were made; and buildings, the beauty and effective arrangement of which revolutionized the appearance of the campus, were erected.

As a teacher, also, McCosh had rare gifts. In his classes in psychology and the history of philosophy he succeeded in awakening in the students a unique interest in the subjects taught, and discussions there stimulated were carried on outside of the classroom. From time to time he held meetings in his library, to which he invited men of distinction in various philosophical fields to read papers and to lead in discussion. Admission into this inner circle was regarded by all the students as a highly prized privilege.

Throughout his life at Princeton McCosh was most ably aided, and at critical moments guided, by his wife, Isabella Guthrie McCosh, whom he had married on Sept. 29, 1845. She was a daughter of Alexander Guthrie, an eminent physician known throughout the length and breadth of Scotland, and a brother of the distinguished Rev. Thomas Guthrie, who had been intimately associated with McCosh in opposition to the Established Church of Scotland. A woman of personal charm, unusual mental capacity, and a heart overflowing with sympathy for all who needed help, she carried on labors of goodwill and mercy among the students and in the community. There was never a student ill but she immediately heard of it and would herself go to his room with comfort and encouragement. She took upon herself the function of a visiting nurse and, naturally, was beloved by all of the student body. To honor her memory an infirmary bearing her name was erected upon the college campus in 1892. A son, Andrew James McCosh [*q.v.*], was a distinguished surgeon.

McCosh resigned as president and was made emeritus in 1888, his death occurring at Princeton six years later. That the present and future of the college rest upon the foundations which he laid is being increasingly recognized as time brings a fuller understanding of the value of his labors.

[W. M. Sloane, *The Life of James McCosh* (1896), contains autobiog. material and complete bibliog. of McCosh's writings; see also the *Nation*, Oct. 8, 1896; *Princeton Coll. Bull.*, Feb., June 1895; F. L. Patton, "James McCosh: a Baccalaureate Sermon," in *Presbyt. and Reformed Rev.*, Oct. 1895; sketch in F. B. Lee, *Geneal. and Memorial Hist. of the State of N. J.* (1910), vol. I, reprinted in *Memorial Cyc. of N. J.*, vol. I (1915); *Disruption Worthies* (1881); M. A. DeW. Howe, *Classic Shades* (1928); *N. Y. Times*, *N. Y. Tribune*, Nov. 17, 1894.] J. G. H.

McCOY, ELIJAH (Mar. 27, 1843–Oct. 10, 1929), negro inventor, was born in Canada, the son of George and Mildred (Goins) McCoy, both natives of Kentucky. He seems to have engaged in mechanical work at an early age and soon developed inventive talent, which he applied almost exclusively to the field of automatic lubrication of machinery. About 1870, at which time he was a resident of Ypsilanti, Mich., he began experimenting with lubricators for steam engines, and after two years of labor, June 23, 1872, he received patent No. 129,843. Probably he had an experimental machine-shop of his own, and as each of his ideas was perfected he made a partial or total assignment of his rights to the invention, thereby obtaining sufficient money to continue with his work. Thus his first patent was assigned outright to William and S. C. Hamlin of Ypsilanti; his second he retained for himself; while his third and fourth, granted May 27, 1873, and Jan. 20, 1874, respectively, were assigned to S. M. McCutchen and E. P. Allen, also of Ypsilanti. Between 1872 and 1876 McCoy obtained six patents for lubricators and one for an ironing table, the latter on May 12, 1874. For a period of six years thereafter his inventive work apparently ceased. Meanwhile, he moved to Detroit, and there from 1882 to 1926 he continued his activities. During this period forty-four patents were granted him, all but eight of which pertained to lubricating devices. McCoy is regarded as the pioneer in devising means for steadily supplying oil to machinery in intermittent drops from a cup, thus obviating the necessity of stopping a machine to oil it. His lubricating cup was in use for years on stationary engines and locomotives of the great railways of the West, on the engines of steamships on the Great Lakes, on transatlantic liners, and on the machinery of many factories. Other patents which he secured included those for the following devices: steam dome for locomotives, June 16, 1885; scaffold support, June 4, 1907; valve and plug-cock, June 30, 1914; vehicle wheel tire, Oct. 2, 1923; and a rubber heel, Nov. 10, 1925. About 1920 he organized the Elijah McCoy Manufacturing Company in Detroit and assigned to his company an improved airbrake lubricator, which he patented that year. Some time after 1926 his health began to fail He was apparently alone in the world, his wife having died, and in 1928 he was committed to the Eloise Infirmary, Eloise, Mich., where he died about a year later. He was buried in Detroit.

[B. T. Washington, *The Story of the Negro* (1909), vol. II; *Jour. of Negro Hist.*, Jan. 1917; Patent Office Records; H. E. Baker, *The Colored Inventor* (1913); D. W. Culp, *Twentieth Century Negro Literature* (1902); *Negro Year Book . . . 1921–22* (1922); vital record, Eloise Infirmary, Eloise, Mich.] C. W. M.

McCOY, ISAAC (June 13, 1784–June 21, 1846), Indian agent and missionary, was born near Uniontown in Fayette County, Pa. His father, William McCoy, was a clergyman and his mother a devout Christian woman, who early instilled in her son those religious principles that were later to shape his life. About 1790 he removed with his parents to Kentucky, where he received a limited education in the public schools. His conversion occurred in his seventeenth year, and in 1803 he married Christiana Polke, a young woman with religious convictions and missionary spirit, who bore him thirteen children and remained throughout his life his devoted fellow worker. In 1804 the young couple removed to Vincennes, Ind., and the following year to Clark County, Ind. Here McCoy was licensed by the Baptist Church to preach, and a little later he was ordained as pastor of Maria Creek Church. He remained for eight years making some short missionary tours but in 1817 was appointed missionary to the Indians in the valley of the Wabash. He labored for many years among the western Indians and in 1828 was appointed as member of a commission to arrange for the removal of the Ottawa and the Miami westward. Becoming convinced that the welfare of the Indians demanded their removal from the influence of the whites, he began agitation for a plan to remove the Indians east of the Mississippi to the region beyond that river and to form an Indian state. In 1827 he published *Remarks on the Practicability of Indian Reform* to set forth his ideas of the situation. Having visited Washington and obtained approval of his plans from John C. Calhoun, secretary of war, he accepted in 1830 an appointment as surveyor and agent to assist the Indians in their migration westward. Acting in this capacity, he aided the Indians in selecting new reservations in the West, surveyed their boundaries, and helped them to remove to their new homes. Assisted by his sons, Dr. Rice McCoy and John Calvin McCoy, he surveyed or had surveyed most of the Indian reservations in Kansas and the Cherokee Outlet in Oklahoma. He visited the present state of Oklahoma several times and lived for a time with his family at Union Mission in the Cherokee country.

In spite of his labors as missionary, surveyor, and United States Indian agent, he found time to write a *History of Baptist Indian Missions,* published in 1840, and numerous pamphlets on Indian affairs including several numbers of the *Annual Register of Indian Affairs within the Indian Territory,* which he published from 1835 to 1838. His plans for an Indian state never materialized, though he went so far as to survey a tract of land near the Ottawa Mission in Kansas as a site for the capital of the proposed Indian government. In 1842 he became first corresponding secretary and general agent of the Indian mission association at Louisville, Ky., where he died.

[Diary and correspondence in 38 vols. in possession of the Kan. Hist. Soc.; letters in Congregational House Lib. in Boston; W. N. Wyeth, *Isaac McCoy* (1895); *Kan. State Hist. Soc. Colls.*, vols. II, IV, IX, X, XII, XVI (1881–1925); A. H. Abel, "The Hist. of Events Resulting in Indian Consolidation West of the Mississippi," *Am. Hist. Asso. Rept. . . . 1906*, vol. I (1908); J. B. Thoburn, *A Standard Hist. of Okla.* (1916), vol. I; L. B. Hill, *A Hist. of the State of Okla.* (1908), vol. I.]

E. E. D.

McCOY, JOSEPH GEATING (Dec. 21, 1837–Oct. 19, 1915), pioneer cattleman, was born in Sangamon County, Ill., the son of David McCoy, a Virginian who moved to Illinois in 1815, and Mary (Kirkpatrick) McCoy of Kentucky. He went to the district school and, from 1857 to 1858, to the academical department of Knox College. On Oct. 22, 1861, he married Sarah Epler of Pleasantplains, Ill., and the same year entered the cattle business. In 1867 he left the prosperous farm in Illinois and went west with the hope of getting beef from the southwest to the northern and eastern markets, where there was a great scarcity. He found in Texas vast herds of cattle, which had been increasing for many years. Cut off from the markets, they were of so little value as to be neglected and permitted to roam the plains at will. Notwithstanding the failures of others, he moved swiftly toward success. He favored the plan of driving the cattle to some shipping point, but the railroads would take no part in his seemingly impracticable scheme. He was ridiculed, and some persons even thought him crazy. He chose for his shipping-point Abilene, Kan., on the Kansas Pacific Railway and bought the whole town site with about 480 acres for $2,400. There he built a three-story hotel and constructed his own stockyards. He hired surveyors, laid out and marked a trail across the prairies from Abilene to Corpus Christi, Tex., and arranged facilities for pasture and water. By advertising and by personal contact he persuaded ranchers to drive their herds to Abilene. The first drive passed over this trail in September 1867, and by the end of the year 35,000 cattle reached Abilene and were shipped east. Following that year a very great movement of live stock took place. Ten millions of cattle are said to have reached the market over this trail. Notwithstanding lack of faith in the project, the Kansas Pacific Railway agreed to give him one-eighth of the freight on each car of cattle shipped. After the second year the sum of $200,000 was due him on this account. The company repudiated the contract on the ground that it was improvidently made, since such large shipments had not been anticipated. He surrendered his contract on a promise of another one, but the company never kept its promise. He sued for the amount due him, which he collected several years later, but the failure to receive the new contract cost him dearly. He served as mayor of Abilene and received many commissions from the federal government. His report on the live-stock industry, as director of that branch of the 11th U. S. Census, attracted large capital to meet production in the grazing regions.

Rival interests finally diverted the trade from Abilene, but he followed the industry. He established the cattle drives to Cottonwood Falls, to Wichita, and helped open the famous Chisholm Trail. He went to Wichita in May 1872. In 1881, operating from Wichita, he served as agent for the Cherokee Nation in collecting their land revenues. He lived for a time in Oklahoma, where he took part in political conventions. A stanch Democrat, he was nominated for Congress in 1890 but failed of election. With a reputation for honesty and character, he was probably, for a generation, the best-known man in southern Kansas. He was the author of *Historic Sketches of the Cattle Trade* (1874) and was the original for the character thinly disguised as Joe McCoyne in Emerson Hough's *North of 36* (1923). He was well known in Kansas City, where he lived for a time and where he died. He was survived by one son and two daughters.

[Letter from his daughter, Dr. Florence L. McCoy, Wichita, Kan.; autobiog. material in *Historic Sketches of the Cattle Trade* (1874); *Kansas Mag.* (Wichita), Dec. 1909; *Portrait and Biog. Album of Sedgwick County, Kan.* (1888); *Parsons' Memorial and Hist. Lib. Mag.*, ed. by Mrs. Augustus Wilson (1885); S. O. Henry, *Conquering our Great Am. Plains* (copr. 1930); *Chronicles of Okla.*, Sept. 1929; *Kan. City Star*, Dec. 3, 1911; *Kan. City Jour.*, Oct. 20, 1915.] S. M. D.

MACCRACKEN, HENRY MITCHELL (Sept. 28, 1840–Dec. 24, 1918), Presbyterian clergyman, educator, was born at Oxford, Ohio, the eldest son of the Rev. John Steele and Eliza Hawkins (Dougherty) Welch MacCracken. His great-grandfather, Henry MacCracken of Sunbury, Pa., fought in the Revolution, and was killed by Indians in 1780. On his mother's side, he was descended from the English Col. Charles Hawkins, who was killed at the siege of Gibraltar in 1704. John Steele MacCracken was a minister of the Reformed Presbyterian Church, and his wife had established and conducted for several years in Oxford a female seminary, which was the forerunner of the Oxford College for Women, later merged in Miami University.

In 1857 Henry graduated from Miami. Following his graduation, he was principal of an academy in Cedarville and superintendent of schools in South Charleston, Ohio. In his twenty-first year, along with his teaching of the classics in the local high school, he began the study of theology in the seminary of the United Presbyterian Church, Xenia. After two years here he spent a year in Princeton Theological Seminary. On Nov. 7, 1863, he was ordained and became pastor of the Westminster Church, Columbus, Ohio. In 1867–68 he was in Europe, where he devoted a portion of the time to study in the universities of Tübingen and Berlin. Upon his return, he assumed the pastorate of the First Presbyterian Church, Toledo, which he served until 1881. On July 2, 1872, he married Catherine Almira Hubbard, daughter of the Rev. Thomas Swan Hubbard, of Rochester, Vt., by whom he had four children. His chief literary work during this period was *The Lives of the Leaders of Our Church Universal* (3 vols., 1879), a translation of Ferdinand Piper's *Die Zeugen der Wahrheit*, with the lives of American religious leaders added.

The year 1881 marks his definite turn from pastoral to educational activity. In that year he became chancellor of the Western University of Pennsylvania, at Pittsburgh, and professor of philosophy. During his three years as head of this institution he accomplished its removal from the heart of Pittsburgh to Allegheny, where it was to remain until its return to a new site in Pittsburgh. In 1884 he went to the University of the City of New York (now New York University) as professor of philosophy. A year later, he was made vice-chancellor, and from that time on the actual administration of the institution was in his hands. On the resignation of Dr. John Hall in 1891, MacCracken succeeded him as chancellor.

In the twenty-five years that it was under his direction, the University experienced a complete transformation. The University College, with the school of engineering, was removed to University Heights. On the old site at Washington Square a ten-story structure was erected, the upper floors to be used by certain University divisions; the remainder to be rented for business use, thereby producing an income for educational purposes. A graduate school and school of pedagogy and commerce were established. The loosely related Medical College was brought under direct control of the university council and given new strength and vitality by union with the Bellevue Hospital Medical College. The School of Law was likewise brought under full University control. The ambulatory encircling the main group of buildings at University Heights was designated as the Hall of Fame for

Great Americans, and a plan was elaborated by which this was to be made a shrine of patriotic remembrance. These advances were made only with the greatest difficulty, and brought into full play the dominant elements of the Chancellor's character, his active and creative imagination, his courage and tenacity of purpose, and his resourcefulness in finding ways to ends deliberately chosen.

On the completion of his seventieth year, in 1910, he resigned the chancellorship, and received from the University the designation of chancellor emeritus. He continued to the end of his life his membership in the university council, with special service as committeeman of the Hall of Fame. In the year following his retirement he made a tour of the world, the immediate fruit of which was an address on *Urgent Eastern Questions* published in 1913.

His interest in religious activities continued, with occasional preaching, to the end of his life. He was not an active participant in the doctrinal dissensions of the time, though by no means indifferent to them. For years he was an active member of the American Institute of Christian Philosophy, founded by Dr. Charles F. Deems. He became its president in 1900, and brought it into close working relations with New York University. His most important contribution to the Institute's proceedings, "Kant and Lotze," published in *Christian Thought* (November, December 1885), gives some indication of his philosophical position. He was also associated with Howard Crosby and Charles H. Parkhurst in the Society for the Prevention of Crime. His annual reports and occasional addresses give a general view of his thought and work, particularly "A Metropolitan University," in *The Christian at Work* (May 5, 11, 1892), and his state convocation address of 1904, *University Problems in the Metropolis*. His death, after a brief illness, occurred at Orlando, Fla.

[J. L. Chamberlain, *Universities and Their Sons: N. Y. Univ.* (1901); *Henry Mitchell MacCracken: In Memoriam* (1923); T. F. Jones, *N. Y. Univ. 1832–1932* (1933); *Who's Who in America*, 1916–17; *N. Y. Times*, Dec. 25, 1918.]

E. E. B.

VOLUME VI, PART 2

McCRADY - MILLINGTON

(VOLUME XII OF THE ORIGINAL EDITION)

CROSS REFERENCES FROM THIS VOLUME ARE MADE TO THE VOLUME NUMBERS OF THE ORIGINAL EDITION.

CONTRIBUTORS
VOLUME VI, PART 2

Charles G. Abbot	C. G. A.	Ruth Lee Briscoe	R. L. B.
Mather A. Abbott	M. A. A.	Jean Lambert Brockway	J. L. B.
Thomas P. Abernethy	T. P. A.	Robert Preston Brooks	R. P. B—s.
Evelyn Abraham	E. A.	Van Wyck Brooks	V. W. B.
Adeline Adams	A. A.	L. Parmly Brown	L. P. B.
James Truslow Adams	J. T. A.	Oswald E. Brown	O. E. B.
Nelson F. Adkins	N. F. A.	Carleton L. Brownson	C. L. B.
Cyrus Adler	C. A.	John S. Brubacher	J. S. B.
Robert Greenhalgh Albion	R. G. A.	Kathleen Bruce	K. B.
William F. Albright	W. F. A.	Robert Bruce	R. B.
Carroll S. Alden	C. S. A.	G. MacLaren Brydon	G. M. B.
Freeman H. Allen	F. H. A.	Paul H. Buck	P. H. B.
Gardner W. Allen	G. W. A.	F. Lauriston Bullard	F. L. B.
John Clark Archer	J. C. A.	William Mill Butler	W. M. B.
Edward C. Armstrong	E. C. A.	Isabel M. Calder	I. M. C.
Charles F. Arrowood	C. F. A.	Robert G. Caldwell	R. G. C—l.
Percy M. Ashburn	P. M. A.	Harry J. Carman	H. J. C.
Clifford W. Ashley	C. W. A.	William S. Carpenter	W. S. C.
Horace B. Baker	H. B. B.	Louise Fontaine Catterall	L. F. C.
Ray Palmer Baker	R. P. B—r.	Zechariah Chafee, Jr.	Z. C., Jr.
Hayes Baker-Crothers	H. B-C.	Arney R. Childs	A. R. C.
William W. Ball	W. W. B.	Russell H. Chittenden	R. H. C.
Thomas S. Barclay	T. S. B.	O. P. Chitwood	O. P. C.
Claribel R. Barnett	C. R. B.	Hubert Lyman Clark	H. L. C.
Adriaan J. Barnouw	A. J. B.	Robert Glass Cleland	R. G. C—d.
Harold K. Barrows	H. K. B.	Oral Sumner Coad	O. S. C.
Robert Duncan Bass	R. D. B.	Frederick W. Coburn	F. W. C.
Ernest Sutherland Bates	E. S. B.	Rudolph I. Coffee	R. I. C.
G. Philip Bauer	G. P. B.	Fannie L. Gwinner Cole	F. L. G. C.
Albert C. Baugh	A. C. B.	Christopher B. Coleman	C. B. C.
William G. Bean	W. G. B.	Henry T. Colestock	H. T. C.
Mary R. Beard	M. R. B.	John R. Commons	J. R. C.
Elbert J. Benton	E. J. B.	Royal Cortissoz	R. C.
Percy W. Bidwell	P. W. B.	Edward S. Corwin	E. S. C.
Theodore C. Blegen	T. C. B.	Robert Spencer Cotterill	R. S. C.
Ernest Ludlow Bogart	E. L. B.	George S. Cottman	G. S. C.
Robert W. Bolwell	R. W. B.	E. Merton Coulter	E. M. C.
Leonard Napoleon Boston	L. N. B.	Isaac J. Cox	I. J. C.
Archibald L. Bouton	A. L. B.	Owen C. Coy	O. C. C.
Witt Bowden	W. B—n.	Katharine Elizabeth Crane	K. E. C.
Sarah G. Bowerman	S. G. B.	Verner W. Crane	V. W. C.
Walter Russell Bowie	W. R. B.	Frederic R. Crownfield	F. R. C.
F. E. Bowman	F. E. B.	Edward E. Curtis	E. E. C.
Julian P. Boyd	J. P. B.	Virginius Dabney	V. D.
William L. Boyden	W. L. B.	Stuart Daggett	S. D.
William Joseph Bradley	W. J. B.	Edward E. Dale	E. E. D.
William Bridgwater	W. B—r.	Charles B. Davenport	C. B. D.
John E. Briggs	J. E. B.	Donald Davidson	D. D.
Lyman J. Briggs	L. J. B.	Henry C. Davis	H. C. D.

Contributors

Richard E. Day . . . . R. E. D.
Edward S. Delaplaine . . . . E. S. D.
D. Bryson Delavan . . . . . D. B. D.
William H. S. Demarest . . . W. H. S. D.
Everett N. Dick . . . . E. N. D.
Irving Dilliard . . . . I. D.
Lee Wilson Dodd . . . . . . L. W. D.
Leonidas Dodson . . . . L. D.
Dorothy Anne Dondore . . . D. A. D.
William Howe Downes . . . . W. H. D.
Stella M. Drumm. . . . . . . S. M. D.
Raymond S. Dugan . . . . . . R. S. D.
Lionel C. Durel . . . . L. C. D.
Frank L. Dyer . . . . F. L. D.
Edward Dwight Eaton . . . . E. D. E.
Walter Prichard Eaton . . . W. P. E.
Edwin Francis Edgett . . . . E. F. E.
Joseph D. Eggleston . . . . . J. D. E.
Katharine S. Eisenhart . . . K. S. E.
L. Ethan Ellis . . . . L. E. E.
Milton Ellis . . . . M. E.
John Erskine . . . . J. E.
Paul D. Evans . . . . P. D. E.
Charles Fairman . . . . C. F.
Paul Patton Faris . . . . . . P. P. F.
Hallie Farmer . . . . H. F.
Harold U. Faulkner . . . . . H. U. F.
George Haws Feltus . . . . . G. H. F.
Gustav J. Fiebeger . . . . . G. J. F.
Edward Fitch . . . . E. F.
William Foster . . . . W. F.
John H. Frederick . . . . . . J. H. F.
John C. French . . . . J. C. F.
Claude M. Fuess . . . . C. M. F.
George W. Fuller . . . . . . G. W. F.
Joseph V. Fuller . . . . . . J. V. F.
John F. Fulton . . . . J. F. F.
Franklin DeR. Furman . . . . F. DeR. F.
Charles B. Galbreath . . . . C. B. G.
W. Freeman Galpin . . . . . W. F. G.
Herbert P. Gambrell . . . . H. P. G.
William A. Ganoe . . . . . . W. A. G.
Lee Garby . . . . L. G.
Richard Cecil Garlick, Jr. . . R. C. G., Jr.
Curtis W. Garrison . . . . . C. W. G.
George Harvey Genzmer . . . G. H. G.
W. J. Ghent . . . . W. J. G.
Robert W. Goodloe . . . . . R. W. G.
Armistead Churchill Gordon, Jr. . . . . A. C. G., Jr.
Dorothy Grafly . . . . D. G.
Walter Granger . . . . W. G.
Ruth Shepard Granniss . . . R. S. G.
John N. Greely . . . . J. N. G.
Edwin L. Green . . . . E. L. G.
Ernest S. Griffith . . . . . . E. S. G.
Ernest Gruening . . . . E. G.
Le Roy R. Hafen . . . . L. R. H.
Marguerite Bartlett Hamer . M. B. H—r.
Philip M. Hamer . . . . P. M. H.
J. G. deR. Hamilton . . . . . J. G. deR. H.
Talbot Faulkner Hamlin . . T. F. H.
Lloyd C. M. Hare . . . . . . L. C. M. H.
Alvin F. Harlow . . . . A. F. H.
George M. Harper . . . . . . G. M. H.
John W. Harshberger . . . . J. W. H.
Edward Hart . . . . E. H.
Freeman H. Hart . . . . . . F. H. H.
Mary Bronson Hartt . . . . M. B. H—t.
Daniel C. Haskell . . . . . . D. C. H.
Frank Wilson Cheney Hersey F. W. C. H.
John L. Hervey . . . . J. L. H.
Rufus P. Hibbard . . . . . . R. P. H.
Granville Hicks . . . . G. H.
John Donald Hicks . . . . . J. D. H.
Helen Hill . . . . H. H.
Edward M. Hinton . . . . . . E. M. H.
M. M. Hoffman . . . . M. M. H.
Oliver W. Holmes . . . . . . O. W. H.
A. Van Doren Honeyman . . . A. V-D. H.
Walter Hough . . . . W. H.
William I. Hull . . . . W. I. H.
Augustus E. Ingram . . . . . A. E. I.
Asher Isaacs . . . . A. I.
Joseph Jackson . . . . J. J.
M. C. James . . . . M. C. J.
Charles F. Jenkins . . . . . . C. F. J.
T. Cary Johnson, Jr. . . . . . T. C. J., Jr.
Theodore F. Jones . . . . . . T. F. J.
James R. Joy . . . . J. R. J.
Louis C. Karpinski . . . . . . L. C. K.
Louise Phelps Kellogg . . . . L. P. K.
Rayner W. Kelsey . . . . . . R. W. K.
Benjamin B. Kendrick . . . . B. B. K.
John Kieran . . . . J. K.
Fiske Kimball . . . . F. K.
James Gore King, Jr. . . . . . J. G. K., Jr.
Max J. Kohler . . . . M. J. K.
Alois F. Kovarik . . . . A. F. K.
Kenneth S. Latourette . . . K. S. L.
Charles H. LaWall . . . . . C. H. L—l.
H. Barrett Learned . . . . . H. B. L—d.
Harvey B. Lemon . . . . . . H. B. L—n.
William R. Leonard . . . . . W. R. L.
Allen F. Lesser . . . . A. F. L.
William S. Lewis . . . . W. S. L.
William E. Lingelbach . . . . W. E. L.
Ralph G. Lounsbury . . . . . R. G. L.
Selden Gale Lowrie . . . . . S. G. L.
William T. Lyle . . . . W. T. L.
Charles H. Lyttle . . . . . . C. H. L—e.
Eugene I. McCormac . . . . . E. I. McC.
Nelson Glenn McCrea . . . . N. G. M.
Joseph McFarland . . . . . . J. M.
Walter M. McFarland . . . . W. M. M.
W. J. McGlothlin . . . . . . W. J. M.

Contributors

Reginald C. McGrane . . . . R. C. M.
Douglas C. McMurtrie . . . D. C. M.
John H. T. McPherson . . . J. H. T. M.
M. D'Arcy Magee . . . . . . M. D. M.
James C. Malin . . . . J. C. M.
W. C. Mallalieu . . . . W. C. M.
Dumas Malone . . . . D. M.
Kemp Malone . . . . K. M.
H. A. Marmer . . . . H. A. M.
Frederick H. Martens . . . . F. H. M.
Frank Jewett Mather, Jr. . . F. J. M., Jr.
Shailer Mathews . . . . . . S. M.
Lawrence S. Mayo . . . . . . L. S. M.
Robert Douthat Meade . . . R. D. M.
Newton D. Mereness . . . . . N. D. M.
Robert L. Meriwether . . . . R. L. M—r.
George P. Merrill . . . . . . G. P. M.
Gerrit S. Miller . . . . . . G. S. M.
Edwin Mims, Jr. . . . . E. M., Jr.
Harvey C. Minnich . . . . . H. C. M.
Samuel Chiles Mitchell . . . S. C. M.
Carl W. Mitman . . . . C. W. M.
Fulmer Mood . . . . F. M.
Robert E. Moody . . . . . . R. E. M.
Albert B. Moore . . . . . . A. B. M.
Charles Moore . . . . C. M.
Samuel Eliot Morison . . . . S. E. M.
Richard L. Morton . . . . . R. L. M—n.
Kenneth B. Murdock . . . . K. B. M.
H. Edward Nettles . . . . . H. E. N.
Lyman C. Newell . . . . . . L. C. N.
A. R. Newsome . . . . A. R. N.
Jeannette P. Nichols . . . . J. P. N.
Robert Hastings Nichols . . R. H. N.
Roy F. Nichols . . . . R. F. N.
John Scholte Nollen . . . . J. S. N.
Walter B. Norris . . . . . . W. B. N.
Alexander D. Noyes . . . . . A. D. N.
George C. D. Odell . . . . . G. C. D. O.
Herman Oliphant . . . . . . H. O.
Louis A. Olney . . . . L. A. O.
Vincent O'Sullivan . . . . . V. O.
Frank Lawrence Owsley . . . F. L. O.
Francis R. Packard . . . . . F. R. P.
Victor H. Paltsits . . . . . V. H. P.
John I. Parcel . . . . J. I. P.
Stanley M. Pargellis. . . . . S. M. P.
Henry B. Parkes . . . . H. B. P.
Francis Parkman . . . . F. P.
Julius H. Parmelee . . . . . J. H. P—e.
S. Howard Patterson . . . . S. H. P.
James W. Patton . . . . J. W. P—n.
Charles O. Paullin . . . . . C. O. P.
Frederic Logan Paxson . . . F. L. P.
Charles E. Payne . . . . . . C. E. P.
Haywood J. Pearce, Jr. . . . . H. J. P., Jr.
C. C. Pearson . . . . C. C. P.
Henry G. Pearson . . . . . . H. G. P.
James H. Peeling . . . . . . J. H. P—g.
James M. Phalen . . . . . . J. M. P.
Francis S. Philbrick . . . . F. S. P.
Paul Chrisler Phillips . . . P. C. P.
David deSola Pool . . . . . . D. deS. P.
Julius W. Pratt . . . . J. W. P—t.
Edward Preble . . . . E. P.
Richard J. Purcell . . . . . R. J. P.
Lowell Joseph Ragatz . . . . L. J. R.
Charles W. Ramsdell . . . . . C. W. R.
Harrison Randolph . . . . . H. R.
P. O. Ray . . . . P. O. R.
Thomas T. Read . . . . T. T. R.
Charles Dudley Rhodes . . . C. D. R.
George L. Ridgeway . . . . . G. L. R.
Robert E. Riegel. . . . . . . R. E. R.
Donald A. Roberts . . . . . D. A. R—s.
David A. Robertson . . . . . D. A. R—n.
Burr A. Robinson . . . . . . B. A. R.
Doane Robinson . . . . D. R.
William A. Robinson . . . . . W. A. R.
William M. Robinson, Jr. . . . W. M. R., Jr.
William Rosenau . . . . . . W. R.
A. S. W. Rosenbach . . . . . . A. S. W. R.
Lois K. M. Rosenberry . . . . L. K. M. R.
Victor Rosewater . . . . . . V. R.
Frank Edward Ross . . . . . F. E. R.
George Y. Rusk . . . . G. Y. R.
John A. Ryan . . . . J. A. R.
George H. Ryden . . . . . . G. H. R.
Joseph Schafer . . . . J. S.
Louis Bernard Schmidt . . . . L. B. S—t.
Charles Schuchert . . . . . C. S.
Frederic C. Sears . . . . . . F. C. S.
Benjamin F. Shambaugh . . . B. F. S.
Bertha M. H. Shambaugh . . . B. M. H. S.
William Bristol Shaw . . . . W. B. S.
Guy Emery Shipler . . . . . G. E. S.
Lester B. Shippee . . . . . . L. B. S—e.
Enoch W. Sikes . . . . E. W. S.
Kenneth C. M. Sills . . . . . K. C. M. S.
Francis Butler Simkins . . . F. B. S.
David Eugene Smith . . . . . D. E. S.
Marion Parris Smith . . . . . M. P. S.
William E. Smith . . . . W. E. S.
William Roy Smith . . . . . . W. R. S.
George Franklin Smythe . . . G. F. S.
George A. Soper . . . . G. A. S.
James P. C. Southall . . . . . J. P. C. S.
Oliver L. Spaulding, Jr. . . . O. L. S., Jr.
Harris Elwood Starr . . . . H. E. S.
Bertha Monica Stearns . . . B. M. S.
George M. Stephenson . . . . G. M. S.
Witmer Stone . . . . W. S.
Tracy E. Strevey . . . . . . T. E. S.
R. H. Sudds . . . . R. H. S.
Fletcher Harper Swift . . . F. H. S.
Charles S. Sydnor . . . . . . C. S. S.

Contributors

David Y. Thomas	D. Y. T.
Milton Halsey Thomas . . .	M. H. T.
C. Mildred Thompson	C. M. T.
Ernest Trice Thompson . . .	E. T. T.
Irving L. Thomson	I. L. T.
Edward Larocque Tinker . .	E. L. T.
Richard F. F. Tyner	R. F. F. T.
William T. Utter	W. T. U.
John R. Vance	J. R. V.
John G. Van Deusen	J. G. V–D.
Irene Van Fossen	I. V–F.
Bertha Van Hoosen	B. V–H.
Francis Preston Venable . .	F. P. V.
Henry R. Viets	H. R. V.
Eugene M. Violette	E. M. V.
Albert T. Volwiler	A. T. V.
James Elliott Walmsley . . .	J. E. W.
W. Randall Waterman	W. R. W.
Mabel L. Webber	M. L. W.
Frank Weitenkampf	F. W.
F. Estelle Wells	F. E. W.
Allan Westcott	A. W.
Joseph L. Wheeler	J. L. W.
Arthur P. Whitaker	A. P. W.
Melvin J. White	M. J. W.
Harry Emerson Wildes	H. E. W.
Allen Sinclair Will	A. S. W.
James F. Willard	J. F. W.
Mary Wilhelmine Williams .	M. W. W.
Walter Williams	W. W.
Louis B. Wilson	L. B. W.
Helen Sumner Woodbury . . .	H. S. W.
Maude H. Woodfin	M. H. W.
C. P. Wright	C. P. W.
Helen Wright	H. W.
Walter L. Wright, Jr.	W. L. W., Jr.
Robert Sterling Yard	R. S. Y.
Donovan Yeuell	D. Y.
Harold Zink	H. Z.

DICTIONARY OF

AMERICAN BIOGRAPHY

McCrady — Millington

McCRADY, EDWARD (Apr. 8, 1833–Nov. 1, 1903), lawyer, Confederate officer, historian, was born at Charleston, S. C., the second son of Edward and Louisa Rebecca (Lane) McCrady and a great-grandson of Edward McCrady who emigrated from the north of Ireland about the middle of the eighteenth century. On Feb. 24, 1863, he was married to Mary Fraser Davie. They had no children. He was graduated in 1853 from the College of Charleston, read law in his father's office, and was admitted to the bar in 1855. In his profession—as, indeed, in his later avocation of history—he seems to have made his way by energy and persistence rather than by the possession of exceptional talents. During the Civil War he achieved a creditable record in the Confederate service, rising from captain to lieutenant-colonel in the Virginia campaigns, 1861–62. Severely wounded at Second Manassas, he fought again at Fredericksburg but was injured by an accident early in 1863, and in March 1864 he was detailed to command a camp of instruction at Madison, Fla. His military concerns, which colored his writings, continued after the war; in 1882 he was appointed major-general in the South Carolina militia. Through the agency of the Survivors' Association he began to collect the state military records in the late conflict, his first service to South Carolina history. These collections were the foundation of the South Carolina war records.

McCrady's interest in writing history developed late in an active career. During Reconstruction he built up a legal reputation in the political trials and in bank and railroad cases. After working for Wade Hampton's election (1876) he launched the movement to disfranchise the negro without resort to open fraud and intimidation and drafted the "Eight Ballot Box Law" of 1882. Between 1880 and 1890 he sat for Charleston County in the South Carolina House of Representatives. He had already published a number of pamphlets on public questions when his first historical essay appeared in 1883. *Education in South Carolina Prior to and During the Revolution* (reprinted in the *Collections of the South Carolina Historical Society,* vol. IV, 1887) was a spirited reply to a passage in McMaster. It set the tone of much of McCrady's later writing—a tone of aggressive state-loyalty, justified in some measure by the neglect of Southern history on the part of American historians. In 1889 he was invited to supply the volume on South Carolina in the American Commonwealth Series. Although he later withdrew from the engagement, this was the genesis of his detailed narrative of South Carolina through the War of Independence. Completed in thirteen years, it was a remarkable *tour de force* for an amateur whose studies of local history had hitherto been desultory, and who until a few years before his death did all his literary work after office hours.

In 1897 appeared the first volume, *The History of South Carolina under the Proprietary Government, 1670–1719.* It met a favorable reception even in those professional journals which called attention to its too exclusively chronological arrangement, its concentration on political annals, neglect of manuscript sources, and pedestrian style. Though McCrady developed in skill, he never quite overcame these faults. In his first volume he had leaned heavily upon his able predecessor, W. J. Rivers; in the next, *The History of South Carolina under the Royal Gov-*

ernment, 1719–76 (1899) he followed the earlier chroniciers, Alexander Hewat and David Ramsay, but less slavishly, and drew upon the colonial gazettes as well as other contemporary printed sources. But he always slighted the state archives and preferred calendars to the voluminous transcripts from the Public Record Office. Consequently he revealed little consciousness of the place of the province in the empire, or of its frontier rôle in the international struggles, which he treated only episodically. In this volume there were a number of chapters devoted to economic and social conditions, but these were somewhat antiquarian, and too little correlated with the political themes. Toward the approaching Revolution he adopted Lecky's views rather than Bancroft's: he was eminently fair to the Loyalists, so numerous in South Carolina. His patriotic bias, indeed, was not continental but Carolinian. This stood out strongly in *The History of South Carolina in the Revolution, 1775–80* (1901), and especially in its sequel (1902), a work of the same title covering the years 1780–83. But despite his failings, he wrote one of the best narrative histories which exist for any of the original commonwealths. Recognition came locally in his election to the presidency of the South Carolina Historical Society (1899), and nationally when he was chosen in 1902 second vice-president of the American Historical Association.

[Memoirs of McCrady were written by A. S. Salley, Jr., for the *S. C. Hist. and Geneal. Mag.*, Jan. 1904, and by the historian's brother, Louis deB. McCrady, for the Charleston *Year Book* of 1904 (reprinted, 1905), with bibliography. See also: *Who's Who in America*, 1901–02; *Proc. Mass. Hist. Soc.*, 2 ser. XVIII (1905); *News and Courier* (Charleston), Nov. 2, 1903. Reviews of McCrady's works appeared in the *Am. Hist. Rev.*, Apr. 1898, Jan. 1900, Oct. 1901, Apr. 1903, and in the *Nation*, June 2, 1898, Jan. 11, 1900, Jan. 30, 1902, Apr. 16, 23, 1903. Information for this sketch was supplied by the late Joseph W. Barnwell of Charleston, S. C.] V. W. C.

McCRARY, GEORGE WASHINGTON (Aug. 29, 1835–June 23, 1890), jurist and congressman, was born near Evansville, Ind., the son of a hard-working farmer, James McCrary, and a religious mother, Matilda (Forest) McCrary. In 1837 the family settled in what is now Van Buren County, Iowa, where the Indians were still roaming and settlers were widely scattered. Hard drudgery with brief intervals at school and academy marked the boy's early life. Nevertheless he obtained a good training and at eighteen was teaching a country school. He studied law in Keokuk with John W. Rankin and Samuel F. Miller, the latter of whom became a justice of the United States Supreme Court in 1862, at which time McCrary entered partnership with Rankin. In the meantime he was admitted to the bar in 1856, began practice in Keokuk, and the next year was married to Helen Gelatt and was elected state representative. From 1861 to 1865 he was state senator, serving as chairman of the committees on Indian affairs and on the judiciary. At thirty-three he began eight years of active congressional services, from 1869 to 1877. His experience as chairman of the committee on elections, which he became in the Forty-second Congress, enabled him to publish in 1875, *A Treatise on the American Law of Elections*, which went through four editions. He also acted on the committee of investigation for the Crédit Mobilier scandal, where his presence helped "guarantee that the inquiry would not result in a whitewashing report" (J. F. Rhodes, *History of the United States*, vol. VII, 1906, p. 2). As chairman of the committee on canals and railroads in the Forty-third Congress he reported a bill to regulate commerce among the states that would have created a commission to make a schedule of rates for each road. After a memorable debate it passed the House but died in the Senate. It became, however, a basis for later legislation. In the Hayes-Tilden election controversy his wisdom and moderation helped avert a grave crisis. In the creation of the Electoral Commission, Rhodes says that he was "prominent in sympathetic co-operation" (*Ibid.*, p. 256). Before that body, as one of Hayes' counselors, Garfield wrote that he made "a very powerful argument . . . making his points with great clearness and force" (T. C. Smith, *The Life and Letters of James Abram Garfield*, 1925, vol. I, p. 634).

Upon the inauguration of Hayes he became secretary of war and was in full sympathy with Hayes's reform of the civil service and with his more generous attitude toward the South. By the President's orders he withdrew the support of federal troops from the remaining Carpet-bag governments in South Carolina and Louisiana. In the railway strike of 1877 the new secretary used the federal troops, and, during Mexican disturbances, he ordered the troops to pursue marauding Mexicans across the Mexican border. The latter act resulted in American recognition of the Diaz government. The war department also began in this administration the publication of the *War of the Rebellion: Official Records*. In December 1879, he resigned from the cabinet to become federal judge of the Eighth Judicial Circuit. He had a judicial mind and his opinions were clear, sound, and comprehensive. During his years on the bench he reported and published the cases tried before his court (*Mc-*

Crary's Reports, 5 vols., 1881–84). After five years he left the bench, moved to Kansas City, Mo., and acted as general-counsel for the Atchison, Topeka & Sante Fé Railroad for the rest of his life. He had an unusually well-balanced nature, singularly devoid of weakness or pretension. While his interests were chiefly intellectual he was an excellent story teller and an ardent trout-fisher. In faith he was a Unitarian. An original Frémont Republican he was always a stanch party supporter, but his opponents conceded that he honestly tried to subordinate partisan to public interests.

[Pioneer Lawmakers Assoc. of Iowa, *Reunions of 1890 and 1892* (1890–93); B. F. Gue, *Hist. of Iowa*, (copr. 1903), vols. I, III, IV; E. H. Stiles, *Recollections and Sketches of Notable Lawyers and Public Men of Early Iowa* (1916); C. R. Williams, *The Life of Rutherford B. Hayes* (2 vols., 1914).] C. E. P.

McCREARY, JAMES BENNETT (July 8, 1838–Oct. 8, 1918), governor of Kentucky, representative, and senator, was born in Madison County, Ky., the son of Sabrina D. (Bennett) and E. R. McCreary, a physician. He was educated in the common schools, at Centre College, from which he graduated (A.B.) in 1857, and in the law department of Cumberland University, where he received the degree of LL.B. in 1859. Admitted to the bar in 1859, he practised in Richmond, Ky. During the Civil War he enlisted in the 7th (later the 11th) Kentucky Cavalry, C.S.A., and was commissioned major on Sept. 10, 1862. Under General John H. Morgan, his regiment took a prominent part in the battle of Hartsville, Tenn. He raided Monticello, Ky., and Burkesville, Ky., and rendered distinguished service in the battle of Greasy Creek. On July 4, 1863, he was commissioned lieutenant-colonel. Captured at Cheshire, Ohio, during Morgan's raid, he was sent to the Ohio penitentiary and then to Morris Island, near Charleston, S. C. Later he was exchanged and, after a short furlough, took command of a battalion in Virginia under Gen. J. C. Breckinridge. Resuming practice at Richmond, Ky., he was married on June 12, 1867, to Katherine Hughes of Lexington. He joined the conservative Democrats, was chosen a delegate to the national convention in 1868, was a member of the Kentucky House of Representatives from 1869 to 1875, and speaker from 1871 to 1875. He favored the much-discussed charter of the Cincinnati Southern Railroad, and his election as speaker facilitated its passage. Then he won the gubernatorial nomination over the popular Gen. John Stuart Williams and defeated the Republican candidate, John M. Harlan. As governor from 1875 to 1879 he devoted himself to suppressing mountain feuds and establishing an independent agricultural college, a normal school, a health board, and an agricultural department. Beginning in 1884, he was six times elected to Congress, usually with little or no opposition. In the House, he served on the coinage and foreign affairs committees and was also interested in the tariff. He introduced the bill authorizing the first Pan-American conference. As a delegate to the International Monetary Cónference at Brussels in 1892 (*Report of the Commissioners on Behalf of the U. S., and Journal of the Sessions of Nov. 22, 1892 to Dec. 17, 1892,* 1893) he favored international bimetallism and opposed the Rothschild silver-purchase plan. After the failure of the conference, he favored the repeal of the silver-purchase act and allied himself with the Sound-Money Democrats, who supported him for the Senate in 1896. But the Silver Democrats prevented even his nomination for the House. In 1900 he was made state chairman and was delegate to the four national conventions from 1900 to 1912. In 1902 he was elected to the Senate but was defeated in 1908 and 1914. In the Senate he served on the committees for foreign affairs, for immigration, and for military affairs. In 1911 he easily won the gubernatorial nomination and election on a platform of progress and county option. To fulfill his platform he recommended county option, a longer school term, cheaper textbooks, campaigns against tuberculosis and illiteracy, departments of banking, public roads, fish and game, and forests, workmen's compensation, restriction of campaign funds, and direct primaries. These recommendations, except the last three, were heeded by the legislature. He spent his last years in Richmond, Ky., where he died. He was survived by his one son.

[Misc. Military Papers, 1875–77, in MSS. of Governors' Papers in Ky. State Hist. Soc.; H. Levin, *The Lawyers and Lawmakers of Ky.* (1897); *The Biog. Enc. of Ky.* (1878); J. J. McAfee, *Ky. Politicians* (1886); W. E. Connelley and E. M. Coulter, *Hist. of Ky.* (1922), vol. II; *Bulletin of the Pan American Union*, Oct. 1918; *Biog. Directory of Am. Cong.* (1928); *Who's Who in America*, 1916–17; *War of the Rebellion: Official Records (Army)*, ser. 2, vol. VIII; *Report of the Adjutant-General of the State of Ky.*, vol. II (1919), esp. pp. 96–99; *Courier-Journal* (Louisville), Oct. 9, 1918; *Evening Post* (Louisville), Oct. 8, 9, 1918.] W. C. M.

McCREERY, CHARLES (June 13, 1785–Aug. 27, 1826), pioneer Kentucky physician, was born near Winchester, Clark County, Ky., to Robert and Mary (McClanahan) McCreery, both of Scotch-Irish descent, who had moved to Kentucky from Maryland. After such an education as he could obtain in the local schools he studied medicine under Dr. Goodlet of Bardstown and in 1810 he settled in Hartford, Ohio County, for the practice of his profession. The remainder of his life was spent in this community where he covered an area of several counties, mostly on horseback. He built up a large practice among a clientele that was devoted to him. No distance was too long nor pains too great for him to respond to a call. From the beginning of his career he had a bent for surgery. In 1813, his third year of practice, at the age of twenty-seven, he performed the operation upon which rests his greatest claim to remembrance. It involved the complete extirpation of the clavicle, the first operation of its kind performed in the United States. The patient, a boy of fourteen, had been suffering for a long time from a tubercular infection of the right collar bone. Not only was the condition relieved, but the loss of the clavicle did not seriously impair the function of the corresponding arm. It was not until a similar operation performed by Valentine Mott of New York in 1828 attracted country-wide attention that the brilliant surgical feat of McCreery was made generally known. The technique of Mott was practically the same as that of McCreery and the operation still follows much the same procedure. (McCreery's case is reported by James H. Johnson in the *New Orleans Medical and Surgical Journal,* January 1850.)

In the midst of an exacting practice McCreery found time for lectures to his own students, and to those of others. He was a ready speaker and a good instructor. By diligent reading he developed from a meagerly educated youth to a scholarly man. He is described as being a tall, well-formed, handsome man with dark hair and fine dark eyes. He married in 1811 Ann Wayman Crowe of Hartford whose parents were from Maryland. They had seven children. McCreery died at the early age of forty-one of cardiac dropsy at West Point, Ky. He is buried at Hartford.

[See the *Am. Practitioner and News* (Louisville), July 1, 1901; H. A. Kelly and W. L. Burrage, *Am. Medic. Biogs.* (1920).] J. M. P.

McCREERY, JAMES WORK (July 13, 1849–Feb. 20, 1923), lawyer, legislator, authority on irrigation law, came of Scotch-Irish ancestry. His grandfather, William McCreery, emigrated to America in 1793 from County Donegal, Ireland. James was born in Indiana County, Pa., the son of William G. and Mary (Work) McCreery, and was reared on his father's farm. He attended public school and graduated from the State Normal School at Indiana in 1877. After teaching for a time he took up the study of law in the offices of Judge Silas M. Clark and George Shiras, Jr., in Pittsburgh and was admitted to the Pennsylvania bar in 1880. Feeling that the West afforded good opportunities for a legal career, he went to Colorado in 1881 and settled in Greeley. The country was agricultural, the farming was done on irrigated lands, and the young lawyer's chief practice had to do with water rights. Many phases of irrigation law had not as yet received definite formulation and McCreery came to be an important influence in working out and establishing sound principles of law regarding the new questions that arose. He became an authority in this branch of law, writing several papers on the subject and lecturing on irrigation law at the University of Colorado (1905–23). He also contributed the section on "Irrigation and Water Rights" to Volume VI of *Modern American Law,* edited by E. A. Gilmore and W. C. Wermuth. His specialized practice, devoted to water-rights cases, brought him before the courts of several western states and before the Supreme Court of the United States.

McCreery was active in political life and was twice elected to the state Senate on the Republican ticket (1888 and 1896). During his eight years in the legislature, he was a leader in matters relating to farm interests, finance, and especially to water rights. He was the author and the chief force in effecting the enactment of the bill which created the State Normal School (later the State Teachers' College of Colorado) at Greeley. From 1891 to 1897 he was on the board of trustees of this institution and served for four years (1893–97) as president of the board. In 1907–08 he was president of the Colorado Bar Association. In addition to his legal practice he developed and operated large farming properties east of Greeley. During the World War he worked effectively for the various welfare organizations and for the conservation of resources. He had married, on Aug. 27, 1883, Mary M. Arbuckle of Greeley. They had four children. Until a few months before his death he remained active in his law practice. Temperamentally, he was an advocate rather than a judge; his inherited persistency made him loath to yield a point. By nature conservative, he was not a champion of pure democracy but emphasized the constitutional safeguards to the rights of minorities and to individual liberty.

[*Portrait and Biog. Record of the State of Colo.* (1899); J. C. Smiley, *Semi-Centennial Hist. of the State of Colo.* (1913), vol. II; W. F. Stone, *Hist. of Colo.,* vol. II (1918); J. H. Baker and L. R. Hafen, *Hist. of Colo.* (1927), vol. V; *Report Colo. Bar Asso.:*

Twenty-Sixth Ann. Meeting (1923); Greeley *Tribune and Republican*, Feb. 20, 1923; Denver *Post*, Feb. 21, 1923; information from relatives and associates of McCreery.] L. R. H.

McCULLAGH, JOSEPH BURBRIDGE (November 1842–Dec. 31, 1896), journalist, was born in Dublin, Ireland, one of the sixteen children of John and Sarah (Burbridge) McCullagh. At eleven he left home and worked his way to New York on a sailing vessel. Little is known of the next five years except that for a time he worked as an apprentice in the printing office of the *New York Freeman's Journal*. In 1858 he moved to St. Louis and became a compositor in the office of the *St. Louis Christian Advocate*. The next year he obtained a position on the local staff of the *St. Louis Democrat*, and his proficiency in stenography gained for him an assignment to report the proceedings of the State General Assembly during the session of 1859–60. Accepting an offer at an increased salary he left the *Democrat* early in 1860 to become a reporter for the *Cincinnati Daily Gazette*, but at the outbreak of the Civil War he entered the Union army as a lieutenant in the Benton Cadets, Gen. John C. Frémont's body guard. After Frémont's retirement he became war correspondent for the *Gazette*. He fought at Fort Donelson where he was one of the first men who volunteered to go on board the gunboat *St. Louis*, the first boat to pass the fire of the Fort. When the *Gazette* refused to publish his report of the first day's fighting at Shiloh, discrediting the conduct of the Union forces, he resigned his position but was immediately taken on by the *Cincinnati Commercial* at twice the salary he had been receiving. His war correspondence was widely popular and gained for him as a writer a reputation for fairness and reliability.

After the capture of Vicksburg he left the army in 1863 to become Washington correspondent of the *Commercial*, and for several years he was also the Senate reporter for the New York Associated Press. He made special use of the interview and gained added fame by his interviews with Alexander H. Stephens and with President Andrew Johnson in 1867–68. Writing over the name of "Mack" he proved popular with public officials and with the public. President Johnson often called on him to talk with him and to "give out" interviews. In 1868 he resigned as Washington correspondent for the *Commercial* to become managing editor of the *Cincinnati Enquirer*, a position held for some months. He then went to Chicago with a brother, John W. McCullagh, to take charge of the *Chicago Republican*. His personality was beginning to be felt when the fire of 1871 swept Chicago and destroyed his paper, his library, and his small fortune. Undaunted he went to St. Louis and became editor of the *Democrat*, the first newspaper on which he had been employed. After the founding of the *St. Louis Daily Globe* he edited the new paper from 1873 to 1875 when the two papers were combined as the *St. Louis Globe-Democrat*, of which he was editor until his death. As an editor he possessed a biting wit and frequently engaged in controversy through the columns of the *Globe-Democrat*. His newspaper was strongly Republican in a state largely Democratic, but his readers were of all political parties, brought to the paper by the brightness of its editorial page and the comprehensiveness of its news service. McCullagh was killed by falling out of his bedroom window during an illness. He had never married.

[Walter B. Stevens, "Joseph B. McCullagh," *Mo. Hist. Rev.*, Oct. 1930, and "The New Journalism in Mo.," *Ibid.*, Apr. 1923–July 1925; H. L. Conard, *Encyc. of the Hist. of Mo.* (1901), vol. IV; J. T. Scharf, *Hist. of St. Louis City and County* (1883), vol. I; *St. Louis Globe-Democrat*, Jan. 1, 1897; personal recollections.] W. W.

McCULLOCH, BEN (Nov. 11, 1811–Mar. 7, 1862), Texas and Confederate soldier, was born in Rutherford County, Tenn., an elder son in a family of six sons and six daughters. His parents were Maj. Alexander McCulloch, an aide-de-camp to Gen. James Coffee in the Creek War and War of 1812, and Frances LeNoir of Virginia. In 1820 the family moved to Alabama, and in 1830, when Ben was nineteen, they moved to Dyersburg, a village in western Tennessee some twenty miles from the Mississippi. Here a cabin was built and a clearing made in the forest. Two years later, after a visit to Missouri, Ben joined his younger brother Henry in the business of cutting cypress logs and floating their rafts in the spring to a market at Natchez or New Orleans. The McCulloch family lived only thirty miles from that of the celebrated David Crockett [*q.v.*] and, after the fashion of the woods, they regarded one another as neighbors. So when "Davy" Crockett went to Texas to meet a glorious death at the Alamo, he was soon followed by his young friend, Ben McCulloch, and shortly after by Henry and other members of the family. Ben McCulloch went in time to see service at the battle of San Jacinto, where he was in charge of one of the two little cannons called the "Twin Sisters," which were the only pieces of artillery in Houston's army.

After the battle, McCulloch returned to Tennessee to study surveying under his father but was back in Texas before the opening of the

Texas land office in February 1838. The young surveyor established himself at the frontier town of Gonzales. Unmarried and unencumbered with a family, he relieved the tedium of his professional duties by exploits against the Indians. His resourceful activity during the great Comanche raid of August 1840 especially added to his growing reputation. Of medium height and slender, with quiet manners, he was not the type which one associates with heroic deeds on the frontier. On horseback and leading a band of Texas rangers, however, he was the idol of his men and one of the most popular figures in Texas. At the outbreak of the Mexican War, he organized a company of mounted men which rendered effective and daring service to Taylor's army in the campaigns of Monterey and Buena Vista. His exploits caught the attention of the newspaper correspondents, and the reports of George Wilkins Kendall in the New Orleans *Picayune* had soon made the fame of McCulloch's rangers familiar through the South. McCulloch emerged from the war a major. He returned to surveying and devoted his spare time to reading of the campaigns of the great captains of history.

In 1849 he joined in the gold rush to California, where he became for a time sheriff of Sacramento. He does not appear to have made his fortune and in 1852 he was again in Texas. In March 1853 he was appointed by President Pierce marshal for the coast district of Texas, a position which he continued to hold by reappointment of President Buchanan until his resignation in the spring of 1859. In 1858 he was sent as one of two commissioners to conciliate the Mormons in Utah, a task which he seems to have performed with reasonable success. In February 1861, with the rank of colonel, he was in command of the Texas troops which received the surrender of General Twiggs at San Antonio. He was subsequently commissioned brigadier-general in the Confederate army and was assigned to the command of the troops in Arkansas. Later, under General Price in Missouri, he had the chief command of the Confederates at the battle of Wilson's Creek (Aug. 10, 1861) and won an important victory. In the spring of 1862, under the command of General Van Dorn, he led his brigade against Union troops at Elkhorn Tavern, and at the opening of that engagement, while reconnoitering the Federal lines, rode into a party of sharp-shooters and was fatally wounded in the breast.

[V. M. Rose, *The Life and Services of Gen. Ben McCulloch* (1888); S. C. Reid, Jr., *The Scouting Expeditions of McCulloch's Tex. Rangers* (1847); C. A. Evans, ed., *Confed. Mil. Hist.* (1899), vol. XI; *War of the Rebellion: Official Records (Army)*, 1 ser. III, pp. 104–07, and VIII, pp. 283–301; H. H. Bancroft, *Hist. of Utah, 1540–1886* (1889), p. 531.]

R. G. C—l.

McCULLOCH, HUGH (Dec. 7, 1808–May 24, 1895), comptroller of the currency, secretary of the treasury, was born at Kennebunk, Me., to which place his parents had moved from Kennebunkport in 1802. A grandson of Adam McCulloch who came to Maine from Scotland about 1766, he was the son of Hugh and Abigail (Perkins) McCulloch. His father was a ship-builder and West India merchant. Hugh entered Bowdoin College, but left during his sophomore year. In 1863 Bowdoin gave him the honorary degree of A.M., and in subsequent catalogues he was listed among the graduates of 1829 (information from office of Alumni Secretary, Bowdoin College). After leaving college he taught school, studied law in Boston, and was admitted to the bar in 1832. In 1833 he moved to Fort Wayne, Ind., where he began the practice of law and in 1838 married Susan Mann. In 1835 he was appointed cashier and manager of the Fort Wayne branch of the State Bank of Indiana, a position which he accepted with some hesitation because he possessed "no practical knowledge" of banking. Until 1856 he managed the Fort Wayne branch, and then, until 1863, the State Bank itself, of which he had been made president. The bank weathered the panic of 1837, though not without suspending specie payments; but in the panic of 1857 it was the only state bank in the country, except the Chemical at New York and isolated Kentucky institutions, to avoid such suspension.

McCulloch's larger field of achievement opened to him unexpectedly, as a result of the high repute won through his Indiana career. He visited Washington in 1862 to oppose, on behalf of the old state banks, the projected national banking legislation. When the law had been enacted, in March 1863, he was asked by the secretary of the treasury, Salmon P. Chase [*q.v.*], to launch the new system himself as comptroller of the currency. After some hesitation he consented, and in his arduous task he was completely successful, largely because of his influence with the existing state banks. With the Secretary, whom he greatly respected, he seems to have had but one dispute: he disapproved positively Chase's plan of requiring numerical titles for all state banks rechartered as national institutions. The Comptroller insisted that compulsory relinquishment of well-known titles or "trade names" such as Bank of Commerce or Chemical Bank, in exchange for designation as Tenth or Twentieth National, would seriously impede the acceptance of national charters, and the Secretary had eventually to yield through visible force of circumstances.

McCulloch remained in charge of the national banking system until March 1865. Chase had resigned the Treasury portfolio in 1864 to become chief justice of the Supreme Court; W. P. Fessenden [*q.v.*], his successor, withdrew at the beginning of Lincoln's second term; and Lincoln thereupon offered the place to McCulloch, who thus succeeded to the administration of the Treasury virtually at the moment when the Civil War ended. He was confronted immediately with the question of what to do with the government's war-time issues of paper money, irredeemable in gold. Of this, $450,000,000 was in existence, and its value in gold had ranged early in 1865 from 42¾ cents per dollar in January to 77⅞ cents in May, when the war was definitely over.

In his official declarations, the new Secretary at once recommended retirement of the United States notes and return to the gold standard. In his first report to Congress he took the advanced ground that authority for the government "to issue obligations for a circulating medium as money, and to make these obligations a legal tender," could be found "only in the unwritten law" which warrants assumption in war-time of powers ordinarily withheld and that, since the "present legal tender acts were war measures," he believed that "they ought not to remain in force one day longer than shall be necessary to enable the people to prepare for a return to the constitutional currency" ("Report of the Secretary of the Treasury . . . 1865," *House Executive Document No. 3,* 39 Cong., 1 Sess., pp. 3, 4). He referred to the abnormally high prices, reduction of which was imperative, and declared that "there is more danger to be apprehended from the inability of government to reduce its circulation rapidly enough, than from a too rapid reduction of it." He did not believe "that return to specie payments will bring prices back to the standards of former years," but held that "the longer contraction is deferred, the greater must the fall eventually be and the more serious its consequences" (*Ibid.,* p. 12).

McCulloch's clear and cogent reasoning in this report won him a pledge from the House of Representatives, in a resolution adopted by a handsome majority, for cooperation in his program, "with a view to as early a resumption of specie payments as the business interests will permit" (*Congressional Globe,* 39 Cong., 1 Sess., p. 75), but the bill authorizing issue of bonds for early and progressive retirement of the United States notes failed to get a majority. Congress in 1866 authorized the retirement of only $10,000,000 in the first six months under the law and $4,000,000 per month thereafter. Two years later it revoked even these powers. Resumption was destined not to be actually achieved until eleven or twelve years afterward.

Although failing in his primary purpose, McCulloch continued to conduct the Treasury until March 1869. The policy of regular and large-scale reduction of the funded public debt, the task of readjusting the public revenue and carefully re-introducing federal taxation in the South, occupied all his energies. The Secretary was as bold when occasion warranted as he was habitually cautious. He did not hesitate, for instance, to purchase United States bonds on the market with Treasury funds, in order to support the price when panic was threatened in Wall Street on the news of Lincoln's assassination. With President Andrew Johnson he was able to maintain cordial relations; though he criticized severely Johnson's ill-judged public speeches. Indeed McCulloch described Johnson as one who "in intellectual force had few superiors" (*Men and Measures,* p. 406) and held that his official attitude on public questions of the day was justified by the event and by subsequent Supreme Court decisions.

After his retirement from the Treasury in 1869, McCulloch was for several years a partner in the London banking house of Jay Cooke, McCulloch & Company. The firm survived the failure in 1873 of the affiliated American house of Jay Cooke & Company, continued to meet all payments, and was in due course reorganized under the title McCulloch & Company. McCulloch made one brief reappearance in public life when, in October 1884, at the age of seventy-six, he was asked by President Arthur to resume the office of secretary of the treasury to succeed W. Q. Gresham [*q.v.*], resigned. He held the post until the end of the Arthur administration in the ensuing March. In this brief time he had little opportunity for constructive effort; his chief contribution was the warning, in his "Annual Report . . . on the State of the Finances," in December 1884, of what was happening to the currency. As a result of the compulsory Silver Coinage Act of 1878, he wrote, "It is evident . . . that silver certificates are taking the place of gold, and later a panic or an adverse current of exchange might compel the use in ordinary payments by the Treasury of the gold held for redemption of the United States notes, or the use of silver or silver certificates in payment of its gold obligations" (*House Executive Document No. 2,* 48 Cong., 2 Sess., p. xxxi). The first conditional prediction actually came true in 1894; fulfilment of the second was narrowly averted.

In his last years McCulloch lived in retirement in the neighborhood of Washington, D. C. In 1888 he published *Men and Measures of Half a Century,* containing reminiscences of his early Western career and his official experiences, together with personal impressions of American life and opinions concerning public questions of the period. He died at "Holly Hill," Prince George's County, Md., survived by two sons and two daughters.

[*Men and Measures of Half a Century* and a review in the *Nation* (N. Y.), Mar. 7, 1889; annual reports of the Secretary of the Treasury, 1865–68; E. P. Oberholtzer, *Jay Cooke, Financier of the Civil War* (2 vols., 1907); William Henry Smith, *Hist. of the Cabinet of the U. S.* (1925); E. E. Bourne, *Hist. of Wells and Kennebunk* (1875); Charles Bradbury, *Hist. of Kennebunk Port* (1837); *A Biog Hist. of Eminent and Self-made Men of the State of Ind.* (1880), vol. II; obituary in *Evening Star* (Washington), May 24, 1895.]

A. D. N.

McCULLOCH, OSCAR CARLETON (July 2, 1843–Dec. 10, 1891), Congregational clergyman, son of Carleton B. and Harriet (Pettibone) McCulloch, was born at Fremont, Ohio. After a common-school education, he entered the occupation of his father, that of a drug-salesman. Soon he was covering most of the West for a Chicago firm at a high salary. In 1867, however, although twenty-four years old, he entered the Chicago Theological Seminary, from which he graduated in 1870. Ordained at Sheboygan, Wis., on Oct. 19, 1870, he was pastor of the Congregational church there until 1877. He was then called to Plymouth Church, Indianapolis, Ind., with which he was connected for the remainder of his life. He had unusual executive and business ability, and gave himself tirelessly to the work of organization. As a result his sermons were usually prepared on Saturday evening, or even Sunday morning, and were chiefly straightforward talks, reflecting wide reading, contact with diverse classes of people, and much knowledge of human character. In a few years he had succeeded in building a great institutional church, dedicated Jan. 27, 1884. He discarded the confession of faith as a requirement for admission, and the membership became a group of "friends associated for Christian work and worship." As one of its departments he established Plymouth Institute, in connection with which lecture courses were given; classes conducted in various subjects, including manual training, with work benches in the neighboring high school; and a saving and loan association operated. To aid in worship and services of song, he compiled *Hymns of Faith and Hope* (1884).

His genius for organization was exercised not only through his church, but also in behalf of the charitable needs of the city and state. Practically all the philanthropical enterprises in Indianapolis for a generation were his creations—the Charity Organization Society (1878–79), the Friendly Inn, with its woodyard (1880), Children's Aid Society (1881), Flower Mission Training School for Nurses (1882), Dime Savings and Loan Association (1885–87), free baths (1885), district nursing (1885), and the Summer Mission for Sick Children (1890). He was prominent in the National Conference of Charities and Correction and was its president at the Indianapolis meeting in 1891. His paper on the "Tribe of Ishmael" (*Proceedings,* 1888), read at the Buffalo meeting, July 1888, embodied more than eight years' investigation of six generations of a degenerate inheritance, involving 1,692 individuals and 250 families with intensive studies of thirty. In cooperation with others, he drafted and, in 1889, secured the passage of a law creating the Board of State Charities, of which he was appointed a member; also a law providing for a Board of Children's Guardians for Center Township, Indianapolis (later extended to all counties of the state), to take charge of children of vicious or incompetent parents.

He was married, first, Sept. 8, 1870, to Agnes Buel of Chicago, by whom he had two sons; she died Aug. 31, 1874, and May 8, 1878, he married Alice Barteau of Appleton, Wis., by whom he had three daughters. He died of Hodgkin's disease after a lingering illness and was buried in Crown Hill Cemetery, Indianapolis. In 1892 his widow published *The Open Door,* containing some of his sermons and a biographical sketch.

[In addition to the above, see J. P. Dunn, *Indiana and Indianans* (1919), vol. II; "Plymouth Church," *Ind. Quart. Mag. of Hist.,* Sept. 1911; *Proc. of the Nat. Conference of Charities and Correction,* 1892; *Congregational Year Book,* 1892; *The Advance,* Dec. 17, 1891; *Indianapolis Sentinel,* Dec. 11, 1891; McCulloch file, Indiana Board of State Charities.]

C. B. C.

McCULLOUGH, ERNEST (May 22, 1867–Oct. 1, 1931), structural engineer, editor, author, and soldier, was born on Staten Island, N. Y., the son of James and Caroline (McBlain) McCullough. His formal education was obtained in the high school of Wyandotte (now Kansas City), Kan., the Institute of Technology in Chicago, Ill. (1884–85), and the Van der Naillen

School of Practical Engineering in San Francisco, where he took courses in engineering and architecture. Upon graduation, in 1887, he engaged in municipal engineering work in San Francisco until 1898. During this period he acted as consulting engineer of the Merchants' Association, served as chief engineer for the Midwinter Exposition, built the Sutro Baths, and for three years was editor of *Engineer and Contractor.* Removing to Lewiston, Idaho, he continued his municipal work there, as city engineer and in private practice. In 1903 he became chief engineer of the Municipal Engineering & Construction Company, in Chicago. During his two years in this position he had charge of putting in one-half mile of reinforced concrete storm conduit, being one of the first American engineers to do reinforced-concrete work. As a specialist in reinforced concrete and structural steel, he acquired a large practice. More than sixteen miles of sewers were constructed by him in St. Louis, Mo., and he superintended the establishment of water purification plants for the Union Stock Yards in Chicago. For a time he served as city engineer of Cedar Rapids, Iowa. From February 1916 to March 1917 he was in charge of the fireproof construction bureau of the Portland Cement Association, being one of the first experts employed by that organization. He was one of a committee of three engaged by the city of Chicago to prepare regulations for concrete flat-slab design. Owing largely to his initiative and aggressiveness, moreover, the state of Illinois, July 5, 1915, passed a law for the licensing of structural engineers. In 1909 while in Chicago, McCullough was editor of *Engineering-Contracting* (later, *Engineering and Contracting*), and in 1910 associate editor of *Railway Age Gazette* (later *Railway Age*). He also taught night classes in engineering at the Young Men's Christian Association College and at Lewis Institute, where he was well liked by his students, for he shared with them the "short cuts" he had learned from long and varied experience.

In June 1917, after a few months' connection with the Stone & Webster Corporation of Boston, Mass., he began service in the World War, going to France as acting chief engineer of the American Red Cross. Later, he entered the chemical warfare service, in which branch he attained the rank of lieutenant-colonel. He was gassed at the battle of Cambrai in 1917. Returning to the United States in August 1919, he became assistant commandant of the Lakehurst Proving Grounds and director of the School for Officers of the Chemical Warfare Service.

McCullough resigned from the army in July 1920. After being connected for a short time with the Semet-Solvay Company, Syracuse, N. Y., as structural engineer, he became, in 1921, associate editor of *The American Architect and the Architectural Review.* In 1923 and 1924 he was associated with the construction firm of Dwight P. Robinson & Company, Incorporated, in New York. He then went to London, and for two years was chief structural engineer for Vickers and International Combustion, Limited. Returning to New York City in 1925, he became an editor of *Building Age* (later *American Builder and Building Age*), and served as such until 1928, the last year as editor-in-chief. He resigned to engage in writing and in practice as a consultant.

McCullough was the author of numerous books, among the best known of which are: *Engineering Work in Towns and Small Cities* (1906, 1908); *Reinforced Concrete* (1908); *Engineering as a Vocation* (1911); *Practical Surveying* (1915, 1921); *Practical Structural Design* (1917, 1921, 1926); *How to Spend Your Money* (1931). He was likewise a frequent contributor to magazines on engineering and economic topics. For his paper on "The Structural Engineer in America" (*Structural Engineer,* March 1925) he received in 1925 the medal of the Institution of Structural Engineers, London. He was twice married: first, in 1891, to Elizabeth Townsend Seymour of Troy, N. Y., who died in 1918, survived by their four children; second, in 1919, at Tours, France, to Thérèse Claquin.

[*Who's Who in America,* 1930–31; *Who's Who in Engineering,* 1931; *Trans. Am. Soc. Civil Engineers,* vol. XCVI (1932); *N. Y. Times,* Oct. 2, 1931; letters from a son, Capt. G. S. McCullough, and from a friend, B. F. Affleck, president of the Universal Cement Co.] B. A. R.

McCULLOUGH, JOHN (Nov. 14, 1832–Nov. 8, 1885), actor, made his way in the world and on the stage through his own individual efforts, aided by an innate talent for his profession. He was born of peasant parentage in a little village not far from Coleraine, Londonderry, near the northeast coast of Ireland. His father, James McCullough, was a poor farmer, and his mother, Mary, left at her death in 1844 a family including also three daughters and her husband. John McCullough emigrated to the United States in the spring of 1847 some weeks after one of his sisters had made the trip. He went to Philadelphia, where resided a cousin, with whom he obtained employment as a chairmaker. His father, with his two other sisters, followed soon afterward. At the age of fifteen he could neither read nor write, but he soon overcame that handicap, and within a few years by reading and study, by practical experience as an amateur with a Philadelphia dramatic club, and by taking lessons with a teacher, he found himself well equipped in body and mind for the profession he followed almost uninterruptedly for twenty-seven years. He made his first professional appearance on Aug. 15, 1857, as Thomas in *The Belle's Stratagem* at the Arch Street Theatre, Philadelphia. His advance was slow but always forward and was the undeniable result of close study and hard work. He remained in Philadelphia until the summer of 1860, and was then engaged by Edward L. Davenport for the company at the Howard Athenæum in Boston, acting there through the season of 1860–61. Again in Philadelphia, he reached the turning point in his career when he was chosen by Edwin Forrest to act second parts with him. He first acted with Forrest while on tour with him in Boston in October 1861, as Pythias to the star's Damon in John Banim's famous play. He was soon, as Forrest's leading man, playing Laertes, Macduff, Iago, Edgar, Richmond, Icilius, and Titus, also seconding him in those dramas that were Forrest's personal property, *Metamora, The Gladiator, Jack Cade,* and *The Broker of Bogota.*

After traveling with Forrest for several seasons, McCullough spent two years at McGuire's Theatre in San Francisco then entered a partnership with Lawrence Barrett at the California Theatre which continued until November 1870. He remained in San Francisco as sole manager of the theatre until a heavy financial loss in 1875 compelled his permanent abandonment of theatre management. In 1873 he had begun a series of tours over the country, and for season after season he was everywhere received with a continuous favor that did not abate until his compulsory retirement on account of illness. Frequent engagements in New York added to his reputation not merely as Forrest's successor in robust characters, but also through his own merits. In 1881 he played a brief engagement in London. At the height of his career he was one of the most eminent and popular actors of his day. The word noble was frequently, and justly, applied to his characterizations. He found in the tragedies of Shakespeare, in the classic plays of our language such as *Virginius, Richelieu,* and *Damon and Pythias,* and also in the melodramas first made famous by Forrest, a fitting and expressive means for the denotement of a dramatic skill that was always effective even though it fell short of inspiration and genius. Like Forrest, he was imposing in stature, forceful in voice and action, and although he lacked the finer powers that gave spiritual significance to the interpretations of other actors, he was in many ways the real embodiment of a long line of theatrical figures. William Winter has said (*Brief Chronicles,* part 2, p. 215): "He played many parts, but the parts in which he was best—in which his nature was liberated and his triumph supreme—were distinctly those which rest upon the basis of the genial human heart and proceed in the realm of the affections. He displayed artistic resources, intellectual intention, and sometimes a subtle professional skill in such characters as Hamlet and Richelieu; but he never was in sympathy with them, and he did not make them his own. He was an heroic actor."

The last days of McCullough were pathetic. After vainly seeking renewed health in Germany, he returned to the stage for a brief period, his final mental and physical breakdown occurring at McVicker's Theatre in Chicago, Sept. 29, 1884, during a performance of *The Gladiator.* The audience, not realizing the cause of his failure to go on with his part, broke out into laughter, and when he was helped before the curtain by two members of his company, he said: "Ladies and gentlemen, you are the worst mannered audience I ever saw. If you had suffered tonight as I have, you would never have done this. Good night." He never acted again. After a while he was placed by friends in a sanitarium, remaining there from June 27 to Oct. 25, 1885, being removed thence to his home in Philadelphia, where he died two weeks later. He was married on Apr. 8, 1849, to Letitia McClain (or McClane) who survived him. They had two sons, James and William F. Johnson McCullough. In 1888 an ornate monument was erected with elaborate ceremonies in Mount Moriah Cemetery, Philadelphia.

[William Winter, *Brief Chronicles,* part 2 (1889); Susie C. Clark, *John McCullough as Man, Actor and Spirit* (1905); *In Memory of John McCullough* (1889); Percy MacKaye, *Epoch: The Life of Steele MacKaye* (1927), vol. I; John R. Towse, *Sixty Years of the Theatre* (1916); *Daily Inter Ocean* (Chicago), Nov. 9–11, 1885; *Boston Transcript, N. Y. Tribune, N. Y. Times,* Nov. 9, 1885.] E. F. E.

McCULLOUGH, JOHN GRIFFITH (Sept. 16, 1835–May 29, 1915), lawyer, attorney general of California, governor of Vermont, railroad president, was born in Newark, Del., of Scotch and Welsh ancestry, the son of Alexander and Rebecca (Griffith) McCullough. At the age of seven he was left an orphan. He graduated with honors from Delaware College (University of Delaware), in 1855 and for the next three years studied law at the University of Pennsylvania, receiving the degree of LL.B. in 1858. A complete failure of health drove him to California. Here, at Mariposa, in the foothills, he opened a law office. Political honors came quickly in the early days of California, and in 1861 the newcomer was elected to the legislature by a coalition of Republicans and Union Democrats. The following year he was sent to the state Senate. By this time the Union men had control of the state government. Several Republicans aspired to the United States Senate, among them Trenor W. Park [*q.v.*], a Vermonter who had come to San Francisco and made a considerable fortune at the bar and by wise investments. McCullough supported Park, and in the caucus just before the election exposed the attempt of a rival to buy off one of Park's adherents. This incident led to recriminations, and eventually the legislature chose a war Democrat. In 1863 McCullough was elected attorney general and served one term of four years. While in office he represented the state in some 250 cases, his experience in enforcing ill-considered statutes leading him in one of his reports to declare that "too much legislation is one of the curses of the country." He urged revision and codification, provided the legislature would employ competent legal talent; he criticized the code of criminal procedure and especially the rule making inadmissible the testimony of Asiatics; he urged a conservative policy in grants to railroads. Defeated for reëlection along with the entire ticket, for the next five years he had a lucrative practice in San Francisco.

By 1863 Park had returned to Bennington, Vt., and here, Aug. 30, 1871, McCullough was married to his daughter, Eliza. Shortly thereafter, Park became president of the Panama Railroad, and in 1875 McCullough, having moved to Bennington, became the vice-president. Upon Park's death in 1883, with the support of Ferdinand de Lesseps, whose company now controlled the road, McCullough was made president and served as such until 1888. In the meantime he was elected to the directorates of other roads, among them the New York, Lake Erie & Western. Of the executive committee of its board he was made chairman in 1888. "The company was bankrupt *de facto*" (not an unusual experience for the Erie), and only by the "tact and resourcefulness" of the new régime was it kept out of the bankruptcy court (Mott, *post,* p. 273). Finally in 1893 it was unable to renew its floating debt of nine millions, and to preclude attachments and the sacrifice of collaterals a friendly suit was brought and President John King and McCullough were appointed co-receivers. After some disagreement among the various interests, a reorganization was effected late in 1895. It has been called "the best that had ever been applied to the rehabilitation of Erie's affairs" (Daggett, *post,* pp. 72–73). For some years thereafter the road was prosperous. McCullough was also interested in the Central Vermont and the Bennington & Rutland railroads, serving as president of the latter from 1883 to 1900.

During all this time he took a part in politics. As a delegate to the Republican national convention of 1880 he favored the nomination of Senator George F. Edmunds for the presidency, and in the conventions of 1888 and 1900, as a delegate-at-large, he supported the successful candidates from the start. He was a member of the Vermont Senate in 1898 and for a time hoped to head the state ticket. In matters of national policy he favored active competition for world markets and a "broader reciprocity" in the tariff; the growing friendliness with England met his hearty approval; he was mistrustful of the strain which the acquisition of the Philippines put upon American political institutions. In 1902 he entered upon what proved a lively scramble for the office of governor. Since 1852 Vermont had had prohibition; those favoring it and those opposed were about evenly balanced. In the pre-convention canvass Percival W. Clement, one of McCullough's rivals for the nomination, made an attack on prohibition. The convention adopted a plank calling for a referendum, and nominated McCullough for governor. Clement bolted his party, charging the Republicans with insincerity. McCullough received only a plurality of the votes, but was chosen by the legislature. The next year a license–local option referendum was carried by a narrow margin. In his messages as governor McCullough advocated a primary election law, the development of roads without federal aid, and the conservation of the esthetic and economic values of forests and rivers. After the expiration of his term he continued his railroad and banking connections until his death, which occurred in New York City.

[T. H. Hittell, *Hist. of Cal.*, vol. IV (1897); W. H. Crockett, *Vermont: The Green Mountain State,* vol. IV (1921); E. H. Mott, *Between the Ocean and the Lakes: the Story of Erie* (1899); Stuart Daggett, *Railroad Reorganization* (1908); *National Mag.* (N. Y.), Mar. 1892; *Proc. Vt. Hist. Soc., 1915–16* (1918); *Who's Who in America,* 1914–15; *N. Y. Times,* May 30, 1915.] C. F.

McCURDY, RICHARD ALDRICH (Jan. 29, 1835–Mar. 6, 1916), insurance official, was born in New York City, a son of Robert H. and Gertrude Mercer (Lee) McCurdy. His father, a leading drygoods importer in his day, was descended from John McCurdy who emigrated from County Antrim, Ireland, in 1745 and became a merchant in New York City. The son grew up in New York, enjoying many advantages. At twenty-one he was graduated from Harvard Law School and at once entered practice in his native city. Such interest in his profession as he may have had at first seems to have yielded to the demands of a business career. His father was director of the Mutual Life Insurance Company and in 1860 Richard was appointed counsel for the organization. After serving five years in that capacity he was asked to fill a vacancy in the office of vice-president. Thereafter administrative matters absorbed his energies and he never returned to law practice. From the time he was thirty until he was seventy his activities were completely centered in the affairs of the insurance company. In the first half of this period his rôle, so far as the public knew, was subordinate; he was supposed to be acquiring a knowledge and grasp of details. After his election as president, in 1885, he gradually emerged as a dominant, even autocratic personality. His administration was marked by unparalleled gains in business and resources: huge reserve funds were credited to the company, and statisticians busied themselves with the computations of the Mutual Life's assets.

Meanwhile, rumor-mongers were equally busy circulating reports that the policy-holders' money had been squandered by the executives. Finally came the investigation of the New York life-insurance companies by the Armstrong committee of the state legislature in 1905–06, in the course of which Charles Evans Hughes as counsel elicited from testimony given by McCurdy himself, by his son John, and by other officers of the Mutual Life, many sensational facts for which no satisfactory explanation was forthcoming. It remained for a committee appointed by the company's trustees to verify the most damaging of the disclosures and to complete the "house-cleaning." It was found that McCurdy, having taken office as president at a salary of $30,000, had received repeated increases until by 1905 his yearly stipend was $150,000, while a group of relatives also on the company's payroll brought the total, in salaries and commissions, annually paid out to the family, to more than $500,000. Large contributions had been made to political campaign and legislative corruption funds, while policy dividends had decreased. The trustees concluded that McCurdy and officers intimately associated with him were in debt to the company in the sum of $8,000,000 and brought suit to recover that amount. McCurdy had at first offered to take a cut in salary to $75,000 and then resigned. The suit was withdrawn, however, McCurdy paying $815,000 as a refund—$750,000 in cash. He escaped criminal prosecution. During the years 1906–07 he lived in France but returned in 1908 to Morristown, N. J., where in his years of large income he had built a house supposed to have cost $1,000,000. There he died in his eighty-second year. He had outlived his wife, Sarah Ellen Little of Boston, Mass., and was survived by two daughters and a son.

[*Testimony Taken Before the Joint Committee of the Senate and Assembly of the State of N. Y. to Investigate . . . Life Insurance Companies* (10 vols., 1905–06); B. J. Hendrick, *The Story of Life Insurance* (1907); H. S. Beardsley, "The Despotism of Combined Millions," *Era Mag.*, Nov. 1904, Oct. 1905; *Campaign and Other Contributions Made by Life Insurance Companies Doing Business in Tenn.* (1906); G. T. Little, *Descendants of Geo. Little* (1882), p. 209; *Nation* (N. Y.), Oct. 26, 1905; the *Eastern Underwriter*, Mar. 10, 1916; *Weekly Underwriter*, Mar. 11, 1916; *World* (N. Y.), and *N. Y. Times*, Mar. 7, 1916.] W. B. S.

McCUTCHEON, GEORGE BARR (July 26, 1866–Oct. 23, 1928), novelist, eldest of three sons of John Barr and Clara (Glick) McCutcheon, was born in Tippecanoe County, near Lafayette, Ind. His father, descended from Scotch ancestors who settled in Virginia and Kentucky, was a drover with literary tastes, which evinced themselves in the authorship of a play, produced by a cast of his neighbors. George's childhood was spent at farm chores and study at a country school. He taught himself to draw and then taught his brother John, who became a cartoonist. At the age of eight he wrote his first tale of adventure, "Panther Jim," which was never finished. When the McCutcheon family moved into Lafayette, the boys had a better school and continued their writing and drawing in secret, often by candlelight in the cellar. They were also athletic and played football and lacrosse. In 1882–83 George was a student at Purdue University at Lafayette, where his chums were his brother John and George Ade. He reported Purdue news for the *Lafayette Journal* and before long left college and took a regular reporter's post on the paper at six dollars a week. In 1893 he went to the *Lafayette Daily Courier* as city editor and remained until 1901.

McCutcheon's first published short story was "The Ante-Mortem Condition of George Ramor," which appeared in the *National Magazine*, October 1896. His letters in dialect, "Waddleton Mail," had previously had newspaper publication. In spare moments at the editorial office he wrote a romance, *Pootoo's Gods*, which at first sold poorly, but later, under the new title *Nedra* (1905), became a season's success. *Graustark*

(1901), written in the same way and sold for $500, brought McCutcheon his first fame and is said to have cleared over $250,000 for publishers and theatrical producers. The publishers later voluntarily paid him royalties. This tale of a mythical Balkan country, whose name was a combination of the German words *grau* and *stark,* with its capital Edelweiss and its Princess Yetive, actually deceived many readers who wrote to ask McCutcheon for the best route to Graustark. His next romances were *Castle Craneycrow* (1902), *Brewster's Millions* (1902), and *The Sherrods* (1903). To test the sales value of his name he published *Brewster's Millions* under the pseudonym Richard Greaves. It became a best seller when *The Sherrods* had only moderate sales. His other romances, many of them Graustark tales, include: *The Day of the Dog* (1904), a story in which a dog is the villain; *Beverly of Graustark* (1904); *Jane Cable* (1906); *The Daughter of Anderson Crow* (1907); *Mary Midthorne* (1911), a realistic Indiana story and his own favorite work; *The Hollow of Her Hand* (1912); *A Fool and His Money* (1913); *The Prince of Graustark* (1914); *Sherry* (1919); *Anderson Crow, Detective* (1920); *West Wind Drift* (1920); *East of the Setting Sun* (1924); *The Inn of the Hawk and Raven* (1927); and *The Merivales* (1929).

McCutcheon wrote with zest and lived for the time in his own romances. For *Graustark* he prepared a complete geographical and genealogical plan. He wrote only one draft, with pencil, from an elaborate outline, and produced about a thousand words a day. He worked best in the afternoon, but he frequently wrote in the evenings. Though his success was in the realm of romance, he much preferred realism. With an output of almost two books a year, he published much that was hasty and slight. Even at his best, he can hardly be called a great romanticist, but he furnished wholesome, not too extravagant, romances to a public weary of extreme realism and materialism. One editorial at the time of his death said that he supplied innocent happiness for "many college boys, kitchen maids, and daughters of millionaires" (*New York Times,* Oct. 24, 1928). On Sept. 26, 1904, he was married to Mrs. Marie Van Antwerp Fay. They made their home in New York City. He died suddenly, at a luncheon of the Dutch Treat Club at the Hotel Martinique, and his ashes were buried in Lafayette, Ind.

[*Who's Who in America,* 1928–29; Arnold Patrick, "Getting into Six Figures: George Barr McCutcheon," *Bookman,* May 1925; A. B. Maurice, "The History of their Books: Concerning George Barr McCutcheon," *Bookman,* Jan. 1929; John T. and G. B. McCutcheon, "Brothers Under the Pen," *Collier's,* Apr. 11, 1925; "Buying a Ticket to Graustark," *Lit. Digest,* Nov. 17, 1928; *Indianapolis Star,* Oct. 24, 1928; *N. Y. Times,* Oct. 24, 25, Nov. 15, 1928.] S. G. B.

MCDANIEL, HENRY DICKERSON (Sept. 4, 1836–July 25, 1926), lawyer, Confederate soldier, governor of Georgia, industrialist, was born in Monroe, Ga., at the home of his mother's parents. His father, Ira Oliver McDaniel, a native South Carolinian of Virginian ancestry, had come to Georgia as an instructor at Mercer University, then located at Penfield, in Green County, and had married Rebecca J. Walker, member of an important Georgia family. About 1850 the McDaniels removed to Atlanta, at that time a small town at the meeting point of three principal railway systems of the state. There Ira McDaniel became a merchant and a leading citizen. After passing through the schools of Atlanta, Henry enrolled as a student in Mercer University, which by that time had been removed to Macon. After his graduation, in 1856, he settled in Monroe and began the practice of law. He was the youngest member of the secession convention of 1861. Though opposing secession, when hostilities began he joined the army as a lieutenant and during the next two years was promoted to major. He commanded Anderson's brigade on the third day at Gettysburg, and on the retreat through Maryland was wounded and captured. He was sent to a military hospital for five months, and from December 1863 to July 28, 1865, was imprisoned on Johnson's Island, Lake Erie.

On the close of the war he returned to Monroe, resumed his law practice, and was a member of the constitutional convention of 1865. During the next seven years he was prevented by political disability from taking any overt part in the political life of the state, but there is reason to believe that he wielded large influence in a quiet way. Bitterly opposed to the reconstruction policies and to the control of the state government by those who furthered them, he labored indefatigably for the restoration of home rule and for the material rehabilitation of Georgia. On the passage of the General Amnesty Act he was elected to the lower house of the General Assembly (1872) and became acting chairman of the finance committee, which at that time included the ways and means and appropriations committees. In 1874 he became a member of the state Senate, and was twice reëlected. In that body he was chairman of the finance committee and of the judiciary committee. On the death of Gov. Alexander H. Stephens (1883), McDaniel was chosen governor to fill the unexpired term and was reëlected in 1884. In this office he displayed financial ability of a high order and managed the affairs of Georgia with conspicuous success. The state bonded debt was reduced by a million dollars, and the tax rate was lower than at any time since 1865.

McDaniel was much interested in railroads. He was the author of the act of 1874, providing for the taxation of railroads in the same manner as other property, and was co-author of the act of 1879 creating the state railroad commission. For forty years he was a director of the Georgia Railroad and Banking Company. A memorial presented to the board on the occasion of his death attributed the success of the corporation largely to his wise leadership. He was also director of several other banking and railroad corporations, and of manufacturing enterprises. Always noted for his sound judgment in business matters, through careful management and wise investment he amassed a considerable fortune.

Not the least of McDaniel's public services were those rendered during his thirty-eight years as a member of the board of trustees of the University of Georgia. For twenty-four years he was chairman of the board. To the management of university affairs he brought the same ability that had characterized his public and business career, and it was during his chairmanship of the board that the modern expansion of the university began. On Dec. 20, 1865, he married Hester C. Felker, daughter of Stephen Felker, of Monroe, Ga., by whom he had two children. He died at his home in Monroe.

[W. J. Northen, *Men of Mark in Ga.*, vol. IV (1908); *Biog. Souvenir of the States of Ga. and Fla.* (1889); P. W. Meldrim, "Memorial of Henry D. McDaniel," *Report of the Forty-fourth Ann. Session of the Ga. Bar Asso.* (1927); *Who's Who in America*, 1926–27; L. L. Knight, *Ga.'s Bi-Centennial Memoirs and Memories* (1923), vol. II; *Atlanta Constitution*, July 26, 1926; information from a son, Sanders McDaniel.] R. P. B—s.

McDILL, JAMES WILSON (Mar. 4, 1834–Feb. 28, 1894), representative, senator, and member of the Interstate Commerce Commission, the son of Frances (Wilson) and John McDill, who was a graduate of Miami University and a United Presbyterian minister, was born in Monroe, Ohio. He was taken by his parents to Hanover, Ind., where his father died in 1840. He attended the preparatory department of Hanover College in 1844 and 1845. In that year his mother went back to Ohio to live at South Salem with her father, the Rev. Robert G. Wilson, who had been a Presbyterian minister at Chillicothe and president of Ohio University at Athens. Here the boy profited by the teaching of his grandfather and attended Salem Academy. In 1853 he graduated from Miami University. After a year of teaching in Jefferson Academy at Kossuth, Des Moines County, Iowa, he studied law in the office of Samuel Galloway [*q.v.*] at Columbus, Ohio, and was admitted to the bar in 1856. The next year he began practice in Afton, Iowa, and, in August 1857, was married to Narcissa Fullenwider. They had five children. He went to Iowa when pioneer conditions still prevailed and when Eastern settlers led by James Grimes were turning the state from Democracy to Republicanism on the slavery issue. In this movement, as friend and admirer of Grimes, he played his part and has left a vivid picture of the period and its leaders in "The Making of Iowa," which was published in the *Iowa Historical Record* for October 1891. He became judge of Union County and during the war held minor federal offices in Washington, D. C. Returning to Iowa in 1866, he practised law in Afton, which remained his home until his removal to Creston in 1885. After presiding over the circuit and district courts he was a member of Congress from 1873 to 1877, where he did useful service on the committees on the Pacific railroad and on public lands.

Declining a third term he hoped to return to the practice of law, but a new factor in Iowa politics soon brought him into public service again. Ever since their construction the railroads had been regulated only by the common law. Their officials regarded them "from a purely proprietary standpoint" (*Report, post,* II, p. 944), and grave abuses had developed. Impelled by the Grange and similar organizations, Iowa in 1874 had passed a law fixing a maximum tariff and forbidding discriminations. The law was sustained by the courts, but it lacked provision for effective enforcement. In consequence there was substituted in 1878 a board of railroad commissioners empowered to supervise the roads, investigate all alleged violations of state laws, and modify unreasonable charges. Governor Gear desired a strong commission and appointed McDill one of the Board. After filling out Samuel J. Kirkwood's unexpired term in the Senate, which extended to Mar. 4, 1883, he was reappointed to the railroad commission for another three years. In 1885 a committee, with Shelby M. Cullom [*q.v.*] as chairman, was appointed in the United States Senate to investigate the regulation of freight and passenger transportation. As an Iowa commissioner, McDill testified that the chief objection to the Iowa method of regulation was that the commission lacked power to enforce its decisions. He maintained that the only method by which there could be any intelligent and sufficient control would be through a federal commission authorized to lower rates when too high, while the right of appeal to the courts was reserved to the railroads only after they had complied with the orders of the commission (*Ibid.*, II, pp. 948–50). The result of this investigation was the creation of the Interstate Commerce Commission, to which McDill was appointed in 1892 by President Harrison. He died at Creston, while serving in this capacity. As a man he was unpretentious, deliberate in thought and action. As a lawyer he was regarded as a safe counselor, who always tried his cases on law and evidence. On the bench he was fair and approachable though not lacking in dignity. He exercised great care in considering cases and measures and had the confidence of his associates.

["Report on Interstate Commerce, with Testimony, and Establishment Recommended," *Sen. Rept. 46*, 49 Cong., 1 Sess. (1886), pt. II; E. H. Stiles, *Recollections and Sketches of Notable Lawyers and Public Men of Early Iowa* (1916); B. F. Gue, *Hist. of Iowa* (copr. 1903), vols. II, III, IV; *Biog. and Hist. Record of Ringgold and Union Counties, Iowa* (1887); L. S. Evans, *A Standard Hist. of Ross County, Ohio* (1917), vol. I; *Illustrated Centennial Sketches, Map and Directory of Union County, Iowa* (1876); A. M. Antrobus, *Hist. of Des Moines County, Iowa* (1915), vol. II, p. 534; *General Cat. of the Grads. and Former Students of Miami Univ.* (1910?); *Iowa State Register* (Des Moines), Mar. 1, 1894; information from McDill's daughter, Mrs. Elmer Bradford, Watkins, Colo.] C. E. P.

McDONALD, CHARLES JAMES (July 9, 1793–Dec. 16, 1860), jurist, governor of Georgia, was born in Charleston, S. C., the son of Charles and Mary (Glas) Burn McDonald. The elder McDonald had emigrated from Scotland in 1761 and about 1794 he took his family to Georgia and settled in Hancock County. The son was sent to South Carolina College (now the University of South Carolina) and was graduated in 1816. After studying law for a short time under Joel Crawford, an eminent Georgia lawyer, he was admitted to the bar in 1817 and began practice in Milledgeville, Ga. In a few years he entered upon a career of public service and held office successively as solicitor-general (1822–25) and judge (1825–30) of the Flint circuit; as a member of the General Assembly of Georgia (1830, 1834–37); as governor (1839–43); and as justice of the supreme court of the state (1855–59). His terms as governor occurred during a period of economic distress following the crisis of 1837. The state in 1828 had set up a bank of issue known as the Central Bank, entirely state-owned, and for a number of years Georgia enjoyed the enviable situation of being able to dispense with state taxation, the profits of the bank being more than sufficient to meet the state's obligations, which at that time were small. The "general tax" usually collected was remitted to the counties for their support. With the coming of economic difficulties in the late thirties, the bank's profits were inadequate to finance the state, but the legislature could not be induced to resort to taxation. Instead, the bank was required to borrow money to meet the legislative appropriations. The capital stock of the bank was in this way consumed and when McDonald came into office a $300,000 obligation of the bank had been protested for non-payment. It became McDonald's duty to devise means for rehabilitating the state financially. He finally prevailed upon the legislature to resume its taxing function and the general tax was reënacted in 1841 for the first time in six years. The legislature also empowered the Governor to issue $1,000,000 of state bonds for the redemption of state bank notes. In this way the state's credit was restored.

In national politics McDonald was a Democrat of the strict-construction school. He was an advocate of secession in 1850 and went as the leader of the Georgia delegation to the Nashville Convention where he was vice-president of the first session and president of the second session. Along with Rhett, Barnwell, and Colquitt, he attempted to commit the convention to extreme action. Unionists considered it of prime importance that Georgia should set the example to other Southern states of acquiescing in Clay's compromise measures. Toombs, Stephens, and Cobb organized a Constitutional Union party on that issue with Cobb as the gubernatorial candidate. McDonald was nominated by the opposing group, which took the name Southern Rights party. Its platform denounced Clay's compromise measures and specifically upheld the sovereign right of secession. In the election McDonald was overwhelmingly defeated, carrying only twenty-one of the ninety-five counties. In 1819 McDonald had married Anne Franklin, of Macon, Ga., by whom he had five children. After her death he was married to Mrs. Ruffin, of Virginia. Some time after his term as governor he removed to Marietta, Ga., and there he died.

[See R. H. Shryock, *Ga. and the Union in 1850* (1926); St. George L. Sioussat, "Tenn., the Compromise of 1850, and the Nashville Convention," *Miss. Valley Hist. Rev.*, Dec. 1915; R. P. Brooks, "Howell Cobb and the Crisis of 1850," *Ibid.*, Dec. 1917; U. B. Phillips, "Ga. and State Rights," *Ann. Report of the Am. Hist. Asso. for the Year 1901* (1902), vol. II, and "The Correspondence of Robert Toombs, Alexander H. Stephens, and Howell Cobb," *Ibid.* for the year 1911 (1913), vol. II; and W. J. Northen, *Men of Mark in Ga.*, vol. II (1910). The facts bearing on lineage and the dates used in this sketch were taken from the family Bible of Mrs. Mary Ann Atkinson, eldest daughter of McDonald.] R. P. B—s.

MACDONALD, JAMES WILSON ALEXANDER (Aug. 25, 1824–Aug. 14, 1908), a sculptor often signing his works Wilson MacDonald, was born in Steubenville, Ohio, the son of Isaac MacDonald. In childhood he showed an aptitude for art by drawing caricatures, but he was without advantages for art study. At sixteen he saw for the first time a plaster bust of Washington and resolved to become a sculptor. His father wished him to be a blacksmith. The outcome was that he ran away to St. Louis, Mo., where he worked by day in a publishing house and at night studied art, encouraged and instructed by the painter Alfred Waugh. Within eleven years he became the senior partner in the publishing firm. Meanwhile he was pursuing art as well as business. At twenty-one he modeled his first bust in clay, a likeness of a business associate. He studied anatomy in St. Louis and is said to have had a year's study in New York in 1849. Five years later, having given up business, he became well known as a sculptor through his bust of Thomas H. Benton, senator from Missouri. This work was studied from life and was said to have been the first portrait-bust cut from marble west of the Mississippi. His early attempts in ideal figures were his "Italia" and "Joan of Arc." Later came "La Somnambula," a life-size marble figure.

After the Civil War, MacDonald settled permanently in New York City. Among his portrait-busts are those of the jurist Charles O'Conor, ordered by the New York bar and presented to the supreme court of the state (now in the Appellate Court Building, New York City); of Thurlow Weed, of the poet Bryant, "Prince" John van Buren, and James T. Brady, the last a posthumous work. His heroic bronze bust of Brig.-Gen. Winfield Scott Hancock, given to the city in 1891, is in Hancock Square. In New York's Central Park, near the head of the Mall, is his heroic seated bronze statue of the American poet and wit, Fitz-Greene Halleck, placed in 1877. It does not suffer greatly in comparison with the adjacent contemporary but more monumental effigies of Robert Burns and Sir Walter Scott, by Sir John Steell, but it is distinctly inferior to two neighboring works by J. Q. A. Ward, the "Indian Hunter" and the "William Shakespeare." It is fair to consider these five works together, since all were made in practically the same decade. Other important productions by MacDonald are bronze statues—the "Edward Bates," Forest Park, St. Louis, the "General Custer," West Point, N. Y., and the "General Nathaniel Lyon." Committees on monumental projects have valued his sculpture for its realistic correctness. Besides sculpturing, he painted a few portraits and landscapes, wrote art criticism, and lectured on anatomy. Several accounts state that he possessed the original model of the Houdon bust of Washington, and that he received many orders for bronze copies. Expert criticism has rejected the attribution to Houdon of MacDonald's model, and the matter remains controversial (C. H. Hart and Edward Biddle, *Memoirs of the Life and Works of Jean Antoine Houdon,* 1911, p. 224). MacDonald died at Yonkers, N. Y.

[H. T. Tuckerman, *Book of the Artists* (1867); Clara E. Clement Waters and Laurence Hutton, *Artists of the Nineteenth Century and Their Works* (1879); *Cat. of the Works of Art Belonging to the City of N. Y.* (1909); *Biog. Sketches of Am. Artists* (1924), pub. by the Mich. State Lib.; Edna Marie Clark, *Ohio Art and Artists* (1932); *Am. Art News,* Sept. 12, 1908; *N. Y. Herald,* Aug. 15, 1908.]

A. A.

McDONALD, JOHN BARTHOLOMEW (Nov. 7, 1844–Mar. 17, 1911), contractor and railway builder, was born in Fermoy, County Cork, Ireland, the son of Bartholomew and Mary McDonald. In 1847 his parents emigrated to America and settled on the West side in New York City. From small beginnings the elder McDonald built up a successful contracting business, and with the *flair* for politics that characterized so many Irish immigrants he became an active worker in Tammany Hall and eventually attained a position of considerable influence, serving as a member of the Board of Aldermen for many years. John McDonald received a common-school education in the New York public schools and at eighteen started his business career as a clerk in the office of the register of deeds, a position obtained through his father's influence. In the same manner he obtained somewhat later a position as time-keeper on the construction of the dam at Boyd's Corners, a part of the Croton water-supply project. He rose from this position to inspector on the construction of the Vanderbilt tunnels of the New York Central and Hudson River railroads located above Forty-second Street. He was a keen observer and made the most of his experience on the two construction projects. When still in his early twenties, he resigned his position as inspector to make his first venture in contracting on a small subcontract of the New York Central's improvements at Ninety-sixth Street. In this undertaking he had the benefit of his father's financial backing and business experience, and he completed his contract with marked success.

Shortly afterward his father died and McDonald took over his contracting business. While this was a well-established and prosperous business, it was limited in scope, and the younger

McDonald had both the ambition and the technical qualifications for success in a larger field. This was the great period of railway expansion in the United States and Canada, and into this field he threw his entire energy, rising during the two decades following 1870 to a position in the front rank of railroad constructors. Among the important projects on which he was engaged during this period were: the line of the West Shore Railroad from Weehawken to Buffalo; the Potomac Valley Railroad; the Illinois Central from Elgin, Ill., to Dodgeville, Wis.; the Trenton cut-off of the Pennsylvania Railroad; and the Baltimore & Ohio from Baltimore to Philadelphia. He also executed subcontracts on the Boston, Hoosac Tunnel, & Western Railway, the Georgian Bay branch of the Canadian Pacific Railway, and the Delaware, Lackawanna & Western line from Binghamton to Buffalo. His most remarkable achievement and the one which gained him a national reputation was the Baltimore belt-line railroad—a project to connect the Baltimore & Ohio lines by a tunnel, some two miles long, through the heart of the city of Baltimore. This was a most difficult and expensive piece of work, involving a contract in excess of $8,000,000. The plan was originated and promoted by McDonald (who had taken residence in Baltimore), and the construction was successfully carried out by him (1890–94) through the firm of Ryan & McDonald.

Between 1890 and 1900 McDonald became identified with several important business ventures in addition to his large contracting business. He was president of the Eastern Ohio Railroad, 1894–95; of the Maryland Bolt and Nut Company; and of the South Baltimore Car Works. In 1900 he was the successful bidder on the New York subway project ($35,000,000) and entered upon the final achievement of his career as a constructor. He was vice-president of the Interborough Rapid Transit Construction Company, especially organized by August Belmont to finance the work, and he took personal charge of the construction from start to finish, and though the project was one of the most difficult in the history of engineering construction, it was completed well within the time limit. He also built the Jerome Park Reservoir in New York City, which, at the time of its completion, was the largest artificial reservoir in the world. With W. J. Oliver of Knoxville, Tenn., he prepared a bid for the construction of the Panama Canal before it was decided that the United States government should handle the work directly.

McDonald was married in 1869 to Georgeann Strang, by whom he had a son, born 1870, and a daughter, born 1878. From the late nineties until his death he resided in New York City. He was a quiet, unassuming man, of retiring habit and disposition, and his personality was little known to the world. He was a born executive with a talent for mastering and handling details, however intricate and diverse, which was little short of genius. He died shortly after completing the New York subway—"burned out," in a manner, by the prolonged and strenuous exactions of the project. He was buried from St. Patrick's Cathedral with all the pomp and circumstance befitting the passing of a great public figure, and as the funeral service began, the power on all subways in the city was turned off for two minutes as a tribute of respect to the man whose skill and energy had been so largely responsible for their completion.

[*Who's Who in America*, 1910–11; *Engineering News*, Mar. 23, 1911; *Iron Age*, Mar. 23, 1911; J. C. Frost, *The Strang Geneal.* (1915), p. 86; *Evening Post* (N. Y.), Mar. 17, 20, 1911; articles relating to railway and tunnel construction in various technical journals, 1890 to 1910.]
J. I. P.

McDONALD, JOSEPH EWING (Aug. 29, 1819–June 21, 1891), Indiana lawyer and politician, was born in Butler County, Ohio, of Scotch and Huguenot ancestry. His father, John McDonald, died while Joseph was an infant, and his mother, Eleanor (Piatt) McDonald, was soon married to John Kerr, who removed with his family in 1826 to Montgomery County, Ind. There young Joseph worked on his step-father's farm, attended school, and when he was twelve years of age began a term of apprenticeship to a saddler. He learned his trade well, but his ambitions led him to attend first Wabash College, Crawfordsville, Ind., then Asbury College (now De Pauw University), at Greencastle, where he was graduated in 1840. After leaving college he read law and in 1843 was admitted to the bar. In 1845 he moved to Crawfordsville. He showed early his talent for politics. He was twice nominated and elected by the Democrats prosecuting attorney for the LaFayette circuit, and in 1848 he was elected to Congress from the eighth district, which was normally Whig. He thus sat in the Congress made famous by its adoption of the compromise measures of 1850, and he was later gratified to recall that he had joined with Clay, Webster, Cass, and "a whole band of conservative men" in their efforts to forestall sectional strife (Foulke, *post*, I, p. 338). In 1856 and again in 1858 he was the successful Democratic candidate for attorney-general of Indiana. His widening law practice led him to move to Indianapolis in 1859.

During the Civil War McDonald stood loyally by the Democratic party. He was a caustic and consistent critic of the Lincoln administration, and of the Morton administration in Indiana. He believed that the war might and should have been avoided, and he was "utterly opposed" to making it an anti-slavery crusade. He branded the methods used by Morton to thwart the will of the Democratic majority in the legislature as revolutionary and indefensible. These views he stated freely and fearlessly during the stormy campaign of 1864 when, as Democratic candidate for governor, he met Morton, the Republican candidate, in joint debate. McDonald always counseled obedience to law, however, and he never stooped to the extreme methods of the peace-at-any-price men. Morton was reëlected, but by a smaller majority than he had received in the preceding election. It was to the credit of both men that they were able to hold their turbulent adherents in leash during the campaign, and to maintain their friendship and respect for each other.

After 1874 McDonald came again to the front in Indiana politics. He was chairman that year of the Democratic state committee and did much toward reorganizing the party for the successful campaign that followed. In 1875 he was sent to the United States Senate, where, much to the distress of some of his Democratic colleagues, he warmly advocated hard-money measures and a protective tariff. He served on the Senate judiciary committee, and more spectacularly on a special committee to investigate the frauds in the Southern states that occasioned the Hayes-Tilden election dispute. His argument before the electoral commission in defense of the Democratic position demonstrated his ability as a constitutional lawyer. In 1881, however, he was succeeded in the Senate by a Republican, Benjamin Harrison, and soon afterward dropped out of politics. McDonald was three times married: on Dec. 25, 1844, to Nancy Ruth Buell, who died in 1872; on Sept. 15, 1874, to Araminta W. Vance, who died in 1875; and on Jan. 12, 1880, to Mrs. Josephine F. Bernard, who survived him. He was the father of four children. His strong features, his unmistakable talent as an orator, his courageous championing of the causes in which he believed, and his humble beginnings —he was sometimes called "Old Saddle-Bags"— made him deservedly popular with the people. Even his political adversaries admired him. He died in Indianapolis.

[See: *A Biog. Hist. of Eminent and Self-Made Men . . . of Ind.* (1880), vol. II; *Biog. Dir. Am. Cong.* (1928); *Proc. of the Electoral Commission . . . Relative to the Count of Electoral Votes Cast Dec. 6, 1876* (1877); J. A. Woodburn, "Party Politics in Ind. During the Civil War," *Ann. Report of the Am. Hist. Asso. for the Year 1902* (1903), vol. I; W. D. Foulke, *Life of Oliver P. Morton* (2 vols., 1899); *Appletons' Ann. Cyc.*, 1891; the *Indianapolis Jour.*, June 22, 1891.]

J. D. H.

MACDONALD, RANALD (Feb. 3, 1824–Aug. 26, 1894), adventurer, early teacher of English to the Japanese, was born of an Indian mother, Princess Sunday, at the old Hudson's Bay Company post, Fort George (formerly Astoria), where his father, Archibald McDonald (*sic*), was a chief trader in the company's service. After some home schooling of a kind he was sent in 1834 across the Rocky Mountains to the Red River Missionary School at Fort Garry (now Winnipeg, Canada), where he spent five years. He was there apprenticed as a bank clerk to Edward Ermatinger, an early banker of St. Thomas, Ontario.

Tiring of the tedium of bank book-keeping, in 1841, at the age of seventeen, he threw down his pen, vacated his bank stool, and ran away to sea. After seven years of adventure, he carried out a long-cherished and carefully planned purpose to push his way into Japan, from whose shores all foreigners were at the time rigorously excluded. He reached the Japan Sea on the American whaler, *Plymouth*. Leaving ship in a boat prepared for the purpose, he capsized it when near shore and entered the country under the guise of a shipwrecked sailor. His strategy availed him little, for he was confined in a bamboo prison cage during most of his stay in the Flowery Kingdom. The awakening interest of the Japanese in world affairs caused the Japanese officials secretly to utilize MacDonald as a teacher of English to government interpreters. A few years later some of his pupils were the Japanese interpreters in the negotiations between Commodore Perry and the Mikado's representatives that resulted in the treaty of 1854 between the United States and Japan.

In 1849 MacDonald with a number of other shipwrecked American sailors was rescued from further imprisonment in Japan and taken to Macao, China, by Commodore James Glynn of the American sloop-of-war, *Preble*. Later wanderings and adventures took him to the Australian gold fields, and into British Columbia during the Cariboo "gold rush" of the sixties, where with his brother he ran a supply store for prospectors at Douglas, Harrison Lake, and a ferry across Fraser River to Lilloet. Finally, in his declining years, he settled on a homestead adjoining the site of the old trading post, Fort Colville, Stevens County, Wash. He died near Toroda P. O., Ferry County, Wash., poor and unknown; his remains were buried in an unmarked grave in an old Indian cemetery on Kettle River in that neighborhood. He never married, and the social prejudice against his mixed blood, together with his secret resentment thereof, probably prevented him from taking his proper position in the world. His Japan exploit marks him as one of the adventurous spirits of his century.

[W. S. Lewis and Naojiro Murakami, *Ranald MacDonald . . . 1824–1894* (1923) contains MacDonald's account of his Japan adventure; E. M. Dye, *McDonald of Oregon* (1906) is an historical romance based upon MacDonald's life. See also, Richard Hildreth, *Japan as It Was and Is* (1855); W. E. Griffis, *The Japanese Nation in Evolution* (1907) and *America in the East* (1899); *Senate Exec. Doc. 59*, 32 Cong., 1 Sess.; *China Mail* (Hong Kong), May 31, 1849; E. R. Custer, "An Out-of-the-Way Outing," *Harper's Weekly*, July 18, 1891; *Morning Oregonian* (Portland), Feb. 12, 1891; *Spokesman-Review* (Spokane, Wash.), Aug. 31, 1894).]

W. S. L.

MCDONOGH, JOHN (Dec. 29, 1779–Oct. 26, 1850), merchant and philanthropist, was born in Baltimore, Md., the son of John and Elizabeth (Wilkins) McDonogh. He was of Scotch-Irish stock, descended from ancestors who settled in York County, Pa., early in the eighteenth century. His father moved from that region to Baltimore several years before the son's birth. At an early age the boy was placed with the house of William Taylor, a Baltimore merchant who had an extensive trade with Europe, the West Indies, and Spanish America. At the age of twenty-one he was sent by Taylor to New Orleans to act as his agent in receiving consignments, and he continued in this capacity for several years, at length beginning business also on his own account. With the rapid expansion of trade at this port, influenced in 1803 by the purchase of Louisiana, he became eminently successful. About this time he began to transfer his capital into West Florida and Louisiana lands, and in 1806 he retired from mercantile business to attend to his properties. His holdings were gradually increased until they grew to enormous proportions. Though private affairs absorbed him principally he was, in 1806, elected director in the Louisiana State Bank. Like most of his fellow citizens, he took part in Jackson's defense of New Orleans against the British and was enrolled in a volunteer corps called Beale's Rifles. In 1818 he was an unsuccessful candidate for the United States Senate.

McDonogh's active participation in the social life of New Orleans came to an end in 1817 with his removal to one of his plantations across the river. Tradition represented this withdrawal from society as a dramatic seclusion from the pleasures of the world because of unfortunate affairs of the heart. This is probably untrue. The increasing detail of business connected with his estates made the change natural. He was a self-contained man and gradually his retirement deepened until, in the popular imagination, he became the miser millionaire, eccentric, parsimonious, and unsociable. Contrary to the general opinion of the day, however, he was a benevolent man, and his thoughts were wrapped up in various philanthropic enterprises. One, a scheme for the emancipation of his slaves, was most unique and practical. To prevent a "desecration" of the Sabbath he gave his slaves one-half of Saturday to labor for themselves and to enable them to purchase little necessities which their master did not supply. From this he was led to calculate how long it would take a slave to purchase his entire working time if he had his half-Saturdays as a start and devoted every day he added to his freedom to working for his total liberty. Calling his slaves together he laid before them a plan for their emancipation. They accepted it, and the contract was completed in fifteen years as McDonogh had planned. In June 1842, about eighty were sent to Liberia on a ship provided by the American Colonization Society. McDonogh was no abolitionist; on the contrary he purchased more slaves when these departed. He disliked to see human bondage but did not think the two races could live happily together. In his later years he matured a splendid but visionary plan for the education of the youth of New Orleans and Baltimore, based on his large properties which he felt he held as trustee for this one great purpose of his life. Unfortunately the lands were overvalued, but enough was saved after the depreciation caused by the Civil War to found schools in New Orleans and an industrial school near Baltimore which bears his name.

[William Allan's *Life and Work of John McDonogh* (1886), is an excellent biography, based on all available papers and other sources. *Some Interesting Papers of John McDonogh* (1898), edited by J. T. Edwards, contains the well-known letter on African colonization which appeared in full in the *African Repository and Colonial Jour.*, Feb. 1843. See also: D. M. Benham, *A Useful Life* (1899); J. S. Kendall, *Hist. of New Orleans* (1922), II, 643–44; Baltimore and New Orleans newspapers for several weeks following McDonogh's death.]

C. W. G.

MACDONOUGH, THOMAS (Dec. 31, 1783–Nov. 10, 1825), naval officer, was born at The Trap (now Macdonough), Del., sixth of the ten children of Maj. Thomas McDonough (*sic*), a physician, and of Mary (Vance) McDonough. His grandfather, James, who was of the Protestant faith, had emigrated from County Kildare, Ireland, to America about 1730. On Feb. 5, 1800, Thomas entered the navy as a midshipman, and that year made his first cruise in the West Indies against the French. He next participated in the war with Tripoli, first on the *Constellation* and later on the *Philadelphia.* When the last-named ship captured the Moorish vessel *Mirboka,* he was ordered to the prize as second officer. Later he joined the *Enterprise,* Capt. Stephen Decatur [*q.v.*], and took part in the two daring exploits of that officer, the burning of the captured *Philadelphia* and an attack on the Tripolitan gunboats. In 1805 he was made first lieutenant of the *Enterprise* and two years later filled the same office on the *Syren,* on which vessel he returned to America. In January 1807, he received a permanent appointment as lieutenant.

He was ordered to Middletown, Conn., in October 1806, to assist Capt. Isaac Hull [*q.v.*] in the construction of some gunboats. This proved to him an exceedingly important tour of duty, although it lasted only three months, for in Middletown he found a new home among new friends, joined the Episcopal church, and on Dec. 12, 1812, married Lucy Ann Shaler after six years of courtship. As first lieutenant of the *Wasp* he spent the years 1807–08 in a voyage to England and in cruises along the Atlantic coast enforcing the Embargo. Since the navy at this time offered little chance for advancement, he requested and obtained a furlough, in 1810, in order to make a voyage to the East Indies. He sailed from New York in command of the brig *Gulliver,* bound for Liverpool and Calcutta, and returned home with a cargo of mixed merchandise. A second venture of a similar character as commander of the ship *Jeannette* was interrupted early in 1812 by the passage of the Non-Intercourse Act.

On the outbreak of the War of 1812 Macdonough applied for active duty and was ordered to Washington to join the *Constellation* as first lieutenant. Finding this vessel not ready for sea, he sought and obtained command of the naval station at Portland, Me. A few weeks later he was ordered to take command of the fleet on Lake Champlain, and early in October arrived at the scene of his new duties. Here he was confronted with the task of fitting out a small fleet and maintaining a superiority in naval force over the enemy. He worked at a great disadvantage, since armament, naval stores, artisans, and seamen had to be moved from the seacoast to the lake. By the time he was ready for operations, the season was too far advanced to undertake them and he went into winter quarters at Shelburne, Vt. Soon after the cruising season of 1813 opened, he lost two of his vessels through the bad judgment of one of his officers, and the balance of naval power shifted to the enemy. September arrived before he could assemble another fleet and contest the possession of the lake. As he sailed down the lake, the British retreated into Canadian waters and a decision was postponed until the coming year.

The season of 1814 opened with naval superiority on the side of Macdonough. By energetic efforts he had built or otherwise obtained a fleet of thirteen small vessels, of which his flagship *Saratoga,* 26 guns, was the largest and most powerful. By September the British commander, Commodore George Downie, had regained the naval advantage, chiefly by the construction of the *Confiance,* 37 guns. A formidable British army cooperating with the navy had advanced to the vicinity of Plattsburg. Its further movements awaited the destruction or capture of the American fleet, confidently expected. Outclassed in a contest in open water, Macdonough made his dispositions in an advantageous position in Plattsburg Bay, with his vessels riding at anchor, and awaited the arrival of the enemy. The action began about 9 A.M. on Sept. 11. After a sanguinary and indecisive fight of an hour and a half, in which both sides suffered severely, Macdonough wound his ship, a maneuver that he had anticipated and prepared for, and brought to bear on the *Confiance* an uninjured broadside. The enemy was too much damaged to make a similar maneuver, and was forced to surrender. The American loss was fifty-seven; the British, more than a hundred.

The battle of Plattsburg was one of the most decisive engagements ever fought by the American navy. Before it took place the British planned to make the Great Lakes British waters. Macdonough's victory caused the enemy's army to retreat into Canada and left the government of Great Britain no ground upon which to claim territorial adjustments at Ghent (Mahan, *post,* 355–57, 381–82). Macdonough's action has been cited as an illustration of foresight and accurate reasoning in preparation for battle and of undaunted perseverance, gallantry, and skill in fighting (J. H. Ward, *A Manual of Naval Tactics,* 1859, p. 108). For his great services he received many honors, including the thanks of Congress, and promotion (Nov. 18) to a captaincy, with rank from Sept. 11, the date of the battle. Previously, on July 24, 1813, he had attained the rank of master-commandant.

After serving as commandant of the Portsmouth (N. H.) navy-yard for three years, he took command in 1818 of the frigate *Guerriere* and convoyed to Russia the newly appointed American minister, G. W. Campbell. Thence he joined the Mediterranean Squadron. Differences with his commander over a question of precedence respecting a court martial led to his return home. In 1820 he was assigned to the command of the *Ohio,* 74 guns, under construction at New York, and four years later once more visited the Mediterranean, this time as the commander of the squadron. His health, which had been seriously impaired in the War of 1812, now rapidly declined, and, moved by a longing to see his native land, he gave up his command and sailed for home on the merchantman *Edwin.* He died at sea some six hundred miles from the American coast. His body was received in New York City with military honors and after a funeral service there was conveyed to its last resting place in Middletown, Conn. In person, Macdonough was tall and slender. If one may judge from the pleasing portrait of him (*c.* 1816) by Gilbert Stuart, his disposition was amiable and generous. His son, Charles S. Macdonough, died in 1871, a captain on the retired list of the navy.

[Record of Officers, Bureau of Navigation, 1798–1825; Rodney Macdonough (a grandson), memoir in *Papers of the Hist. Soc. of Del.,* no. XVIII (1897), *Life of Commodore Thomas Macdonough* (1909), and *The Macdonough-Hackstaff Ancestry* (1904); A. T. Mahan, *Sea Power in Its Relations to the War of 1812* (1905, 1919); J. F. Cooper, *Hist. of the Navy of the U. S. A.* (1839); *Am. State Papers, Naval Affairs,* vol. I (1834); N. Y. *Spectator,* Nov. 25, Dec. 2, 1825; *Commercial Advertiser,* Dec. 1, 1825.] C. O. P.

McDOUGAL, DAVID STOCKTON (Sept. 27, 1809–Aug. 7, 1882), naval officer, was born in Chillicothe, Ohio. His father, Dr. John McDougal, born in Dumbarton, Scotland, was a member of the Ohio legislature from 1813 to 1815; his mother, Margaret Stockton, was a descendant of Robert Stockton of Lancaster County, Pa. In later life David discarded his middle name. He entered the navy as a midshipman in 1828, was promoted through the various grades, and was made rear admiral, Sept. 27, 1873. He served first on the *Natchez* in the West India Squadron (1829–31), and while at Pensacola he is said to have gained reputation for heroism by rescuing a sailor from waters infested with sharks. Various assignments to shore and sea duty followed, and the Mexican War found him a lieutenant on the *Mississippi* at the capture of Vera Cruz.

Soon after the Civil War began, he was given command of the *Wyoming,* a wooden screw sloop, the former commander of which had been dismissed for disloyalty. Following a cruise to South America, the ship was sent to the Far East to seek Confederate privateers, especially the *Alabama.* On this duty McDougal cruised about the China Sea and the Straits of Sunda till 1864, but, although at one time the *Alabama* was only twenty-five miles away, she learned of his presence and escaped. The chief incident of the cruise occurred in Japan on July 16, 1863. McDougal had been informed in Yokohama that an American steamer, the *Pembroke,* had been fired on by Choshu clansmen in the Straits of Shimonoseki, in obedience to a decree of the Emperor that foreigners should be excluded from Japan—a decree which the friendlier Shogun at Tokyo had refused to promulgate. In retaliation for this violation of treaty promises, the *Wyoming,* single-handed, attacked the entire Japanese force at Shimonoseki, consisting of land batteries and three armed vessels—in all about forty guns—and by clever maneuvering and rapid firing was able to destroy the ships and do much damage to the batteries. The engagement was at close range and lasted for an hour, after which the *Wyoming* withdrew with a loss of four killed and seven wounded. McDougal's action without orders was approved by Seward and Lincoln, and, with a later attack by an international fleet, secured better protection for foreigners.

After bringing the *Wyoming* back to Philadelphia in 1864, McDougal was sent to Mare Island as commandant, but by 1868 he was at sea on the Pacific in the *Powhatan.* From 1870 to 1872 he commanded the South Pacific Squadron. His last days were spent in the vicinity of San Francisco, where he died. His wife, whom he married in 1833, was Caroline Sterrett of New York City.

[Records of the Navy Department; name of wife and date of marriage from a grand-daughter, Mrs. Ralph Rainsford; L. R. Hamersly, *The Records of Living Officers of the U. S. Navy and Marine Corps* (3rd ed., 1878); *Official Records of the Union and Confederate Navies in the Civil War,* 1 ser., vols. I, II, III; P. J. Treat, *Diplomatic Relations Between the U. S. and Japan, 1853–1895* (1932), vol. I; Tyler Dennett, *Americans in Eastern Asia* (1922); *Army and Navy Jour.,* Aug. 12, 1882; *Daily Examiner* (San Francisco), Aug. 8, 1882.] W. B. N.

McDOUGALL, ALEXANDER (July or August 1732–June 9, 1786), Revolutionary agitator, soldier, son of Ronald and Elizabeth MacDougal (*sic*), was born in the parish of Kildalton, Islay, Inner Hebrides, the second of five children. He accompanied his parents to America when, in 1738, they came over with the first party of Lachlan Campbell's colonists to establish a settlement near Fort Edward, N. Y. (*Historical Magazine,* October 1861, p. 302). The project failed to materialize and Ronald MacDougal settled in New York City as a milkman. The son early evinced a fondness for the sea, and during the years 1756–63 commanded the privateers *Tyger* and *Barrington.* Having accumulated a competence, he returned to New York, where he became a merchant and "gave himself to hard Study & made very singular Advancem[ts] in the Cultivation of his Mind" (Stokes, *post*, VI, 31).

He came into prominence in 1769 as the author of a broadside addressed "to the Betrayed Inhabitants of the City and Colony of New York," issued Dec. 16, which violently attacked the General Assembly (reprinted by O'Callaghan, *post*). The broadside was declared libelous, and he was arrested Feb. 8, 1770, on the testimony of the printer. He remained in jail until after his indictment in April, refusing to give bail. "The Arm of Power could not perhaps, have fallen on a Subject more fearless of its Menaces" was the self-confident conclusion to his defense, issued from prison (*New York Journal*, Feb. 15, 1770). He was looked upon by supporters and opponents as the "Wilkes of America." So numerous were the visits of his partisans that he was obliged to appoint visiting hours. William Smith, historian of New York, wrote of him: "[He] possesses great presence of mind, is methodical & connected in the Arrangement of his Ideas, writes well speaks (tho' with some small Impediment) yet with tolerable Ease—Has great Fire & Vehemence without Hurry and Precipitation" (Stokes, VI, 31). Because of the death of the principal witness, the case was never tried, but in December McDougall was summoned by the General Assembly for questioning concerning the authorship of the broadside. On his refusal to answer, he was committed for contempt and was kept in confinement until March 1771.

He was one of the most prominent of the radical leaders as an accelerator of public opinion during 1774–75 in the New York Committee of Fifty-one and in the first and second Provincial congresses. He presided over the famous mass meeting in the "Fields," July 6, 1774. In 1775 he was appointed colonel of the first New York regiment and was later made a Continental brigadier-general (1776) and major-general (1777). He participated in the battles of White Plains and Germantown, but rendered his most important military service in the Highlands of the Hudson, where he was stationed the greater part of the war, much of the time as commanding officer. Washington wrote him in 1778: "The vast importance of it [control of the Hudson] has determined me to confide it in you" (W. C. Ford, *The Writings of George Washington*, vol. VI, 1890, p. 429). On the discovery of Arnold's treason, Washington placed McDougall in command of West Point. In 1781 he declined appointment as minister of marine. In 1782 a quarrel with General Heath led to his arrest and court-martialing for insubordination. In the winter of 1782–83 he headed the delegation sent by the officers of the army to confer with the Continental Congress upon questions of pay.

He represented New York in the Continental Congress, 1781–82 and 1784–85, and served as state senator, 1783–86. He was one of the organizers and the first president of the Bank of New York. Another indication of the increasingly conservative attitude of his later years was his service as president of the New York State Society of the Cincinnati from its organization until his death. By his first wife he had two sons and one daughter. Both sons died without issue; the daughter, Elizabeth, became the wife of John Laurance [*q.v.*]. In 1767 he was married to Hannah Bostwick, who survived him.

[Birth record from manuscript register, New Register House, Edinburgh. Other material from McDougall MSS. (N. Y. Hist. Soc.); a few McDougall letters and William Smith's diary (MS.), in N. Y. Pub. Lib.; C. L. Becker, *The Hist. of Political Parties in the Province of N. Y.* (1909). I. N. Phelps Stokes, *The Iconography of Manhattan Island*, vols. IV–V (1922–28); *Public Papers of George Clinton* (10 vols., 1899–1914); E. B. O'Callaghan, *The Doc. Hist. of the State of N. Y.*, 4to ed., III (1850), 317–21; "Heath Papers," *Mass. Hist. Soc. Colls.*, 5 ser. IV (1878) and 7 ser. IV, V (1904–05); C. S. Hall, *Life and Letters of Samuel Holden Parsons* (1905); James Thacher, *A Mil. Jour. during the Am. Rev.* (1823); H. W. Domett, *A Hist. of the Bank of N. Y.* (1884); obituary in *Daily Advertiser* (N. Y.), June 12, 1786.]

D. C. H.

McDOUGALL, ALEXANDER (Mar. 16, 1845–May 23, 1923), inventor, ship-builder, eldest child of Dougald and Ellen (McDougall) McDougall, was born in Port Ellen on the Island of Islay, just off the southwest coast of Scotland. His father was a carpenter and storekeeper in very poor circumstances, and as his family increased it became necessary for him to seek employment elsewhere. Accordingly, when Alexander was seven years old, his parents moved to Glasgow and two years later, in 1854, the family emigrated to Canada. They settled at Nottawa, a Scotch community near Collingwood at the southern end of Georgian Bay, Ont. Here the boy continued his common-school education, begun in Scotland; but within a few months, upon the death of his father in a grist-mill accident, he went to work as a farm hand. After several years he became a blacksmith's apprentice but at the age of sixteen ran away, to ship as deck hand on a Lake vessel bound for Chicago, Ill. For twenty-one years he sailed the Great Lakes. He became a second mate at the age of eighteen and at twenty-five was made captain of the *Thomas A. Scott*, one of the finest ships then on the Lakes. Until 1871 he made his home in Nottawa, but in that year established his mother and sisters in

Duluth, Minn. He continued a resident of this city until his death.

When he was twenty-six years old he helped to build for the Anchor Line the three passenger ships, *China, Japan,* and *India,* which were for years the "queens" of the Great Lakes. This experience spurred him on to develop his radical design for a freight ship which came to be known as the whaleback. He patented the basic design in 1881. In that year he gave up navigation and took charge of stevedoring for ship owners at a number of lake ports, meanwhile endeavoring to interest capital in his whaleback steamship. His efforts resulted after seven years in the organization of the American Steel Barge Company (1888), and in the construction of the first whaleback, in the company yard at Duluth. Seven vessels were launched from this yard and forty from that at Superior, Wis., established in 1891. These ships were used principally for transporting iron ores, grain, and coal. Although within a generation they became obsolete, they revolutionized the architecture of Great-Lakes freighters.

In 1892 McDougall built the first steel-ship yard in the Pacific Northwest and founded the city of Everett, Wash. Five years later he sold his interest in the American Steel Barge Company, and in 1899 organized the Collingwood Shipbuilding Company at Collingwood, Ont. Later he acquired control of the Kingston Shipbuilding Company at Kingston, Ont. In 1899, also, he organized the St. Louis Steel Barge Company of St. Louis, Mo., which built three vessels suitable for the navigation of the lower Mississippi River. While managing these several widely scattered enterprises, he patented, between 1888 and 1900, forty inventions pertaining chiefly to ship construction and equipment, ore and grain loading apparatus, and dredging machinery. From 1900 to 1903 he was one of the prime movers in establishing the Great Northern hydro-electric power plant at Duluth, and during the four years following gave much attention to perfecting and patenting a successful process for washing and cleaning the sand iron ores of the western Mesabi Range. During the last few years of his life (1920–22) he was plaintiff in one of the largest suits for damages ever filed in the federal courts—a claim against the Oliver Iron Mining Company, a subsidiary of the United States Steel Corporation, for $40,000,000 for alleged infringement of his ore-washing patents (Case No. 6061). The court gave an opinion in favor of the defendant, which was later affirmed by the United States circuit court of appeals, eighth circuit. During the World War, as president of the McDougall-Duluth Ship Building Company, he directed the work of constructing a large fleet of freighters and steamers for both Lake and ocean service, and just prior to his death he had completed and opened the McDougall Terminal at Duluth. Even toward the end of his career he continued his inventive work. With his son he invented a sea-going canal boat in 1914; he also devised a variety of mining machinery, apparatus for destroying submarines, improved ship's equipment, and a peat fuel machine which was patented a few months before his death. He married Emmeline Ross of Toronto, Canada, in January 1878, and at the time of his death in Duluth was survived by a son and a daughter.

[W. B. Kaempffert, *A Popular Hist. of Am. Invention* (1924), vol. I; *Who's Who in America,* 1922–23; *Riverside Review* (McDougall-Duluth Co.), Apr. 1918; Walter Van Brunt, *Duluth and St. Louis County, Minn.* (1921), vol. I, *Duluth Herald,* May 23, 1923; *N. Y. Times,* May 24, 1923; Patent Office records.]

C. W. M.

McDOUGALL, FRANCES HARRIET [See Green, Frances Harriet Whipple, 1805–1878].

McDOWELL, CHARLES (*c.* 1743–Mar. 31, 1815), Revolutionary soldier, was born in Winchester, Va., the son of Joseph McDowell and Margaret O'Neal or O'Neil. Joseph McDowell is said to have been a grandson of Ephraim McDowell, who emigrated from Ireland to America (1735) at the age of sixty-two. With his family, Ephraim settled first in Pennsylvania, then in 1737 migrated to the Valley of Virginia. Joseph, the father of Charles, moved to Quaker Meadows (near Morganton), Burke County, N. C. After the outbreak of the Revolution Charles McDowell was named captain and in April 1776 was commissioned lieutenant-colonel of a militia regiment. He was never attached to the regular Continental armies, but in the backwater region of the South, continually subject to attack from hostile Indians and zealous Loyalists, he rendered valuable aid to the patriot cause as commander of one of the rear-guards of the Revolution. He occupied himself with the repression and destruction of Loyalists and took part in the successful expedition of Brigadier-General Griffith Rutherford against the Cherokees (1776). In 1780 Patrick Ferguson, major, 71st Highlanders, invaded the Carolinas with a large army of Loyalists. McDowell promptly sent word over the mountains to Col. Isaac Shelby [*q.v.*] asking immediate aid. Even with Shelby's force, McDowell's army was too small to deal with Ferguson and so the mountaineers began guerrilla warfare. They hung upon the flanks of the Loyalist army and destroyed small groups coming to join Ferguson. It was a warfare in which Shelby's restless activity brought immediate result. Three times he was detached from McDowell's army for hasty sallies. Finally, McDowell sent him to disperse a Loyalist encampment at Musgrove's Mill. He circled Ferguson's camp, which intervened, and routed the Loyalist forces. An express from Gov. Richard Caswell informed McDowell of the defeat of Gates at Camden and the mountaineers withdrew to the frontier and dispersed. A few weeks later Ferguson sent word by a paroled prisoner that he would lay waste the entire countryside if submission were refused. McDowell and Shelby at once sent out an alarm and the "backwater men" assembled again in September 1780. McDowell was in command of the military district, but the colonels feared his slowness and elected Col. William Campbell [*q.v.*] commander. McDowell, leaving his brother Joseph [*q.v.*] in charge of his regiment, went to obtain a general officer for the command from General Gates. Although the battle of King's Mountain (Oct. 7, 1780) was fought in McDowell's absence, it was his and Shelby's initiative that brought the forces together and made possible the first Continental victory in the South after Gates's defeat, a victory which prevented lukewarm patriots from becoming Loyalists and helped to stem the flow of recruits to the British armies. McDowell was commissioned brigadier-general by the North Carolina legislature and placed in command of an expedition sent against the Cherokees (1782). He sat in the North Carolina Senate in 1778 and from 1782 to 1788. Toward the close of the war he married Grace or Grizel (Greenlee) Bowman, widow of Capt. John Bowman.

[*The Colonial Records of N. C.* (10 vols., 1886–90) and *The State Records of N. C.* (20 vols., 1895–1914); David Schenck, *N. C., 1780–'81* (1889); Isaac Shelby, *Battle of King's Mountain, To the Public* (1823); *American Review*, Dec. 1848; L. C. Draper, *King's Mountain and Its Heroes* (1881); J. H. Wheeler, *Hist. Sketches of N. C.* (1851); J. R. Gilmore, *The Rear-Guard of the Revolution* (1886); J. H. McDowell, *Hist. of the McDowells and Connections* (1918); T. M. Green, *Hist. Families of Ky.* (1889); *N. C. Booklet*, July 1904; S. A. Ashe, *Biog. Hist. of N. C.*, vol. VII (1908).]

F. E. R.

MACDOWELL, EDWARD ALEXANDER (Dec. 18, 1861–Jan. 23, 1908), distinguished American composer, was born in New York City, the son of Thomas and Frances (Knapp) MacDowell and the grandson of Alexander MacDowell, born in Belfast of Scotch parents, who emigrated to New York early in the nineteenth century. His father was a business man with an aptitude for painting. His mother had no talents in art, but was high-spirited, witty, and ambitious. Thomas MacDowell was a Quaker. His wife was not. Blest with remarkable parents, Edward McDowell escaped the misunderstandings and the lack of sympathy which often shadow the early years of genius. He spent his boyhood in a home rich in culture and affection. Though he was a sensitive and imaginative child, he had his share of fun and mischief, and with his brother Walter, three years his senior, he exercised all the instincts which belong to normal and happy children. When he began his piano studies he showed the usual reluctance to practise. On one occasion the family were astonished at the noises he was making, and discovered at the piano not Edward but Walter, whom Edward had hired to do his practising for him, at two cents an hour, while he read a story book. His first piano teacher was a friend of his father's, Juan Buitrago, a native of Colombia. Buitrago brought the talented boy to the attention of Teresa Carreño, who became his next teacher. He seems to have studied at about the same time with Paul Desvernine. Since all these teachers were of the Latin tradition, it is not surprising that when he was later taken abroad to study, it was to France rather than to Germany. He went to the public schools, and after his tenth year, when his father removed to East Nineteenth Street, near Third Avenue, close to Gramercy Park, he attended a French school, the *Institution Elie Charlier*, on East Twenty-fourth Street. Coming home from this school one day he exhibited to his astonished Quaker father a revolver which he had won in a public contest at a local shooting gallery.

McDowell's education became exactly what it should have been for his art. He spoke the modern languages and knew more about the ancient ones than most college graduates. He was widely read in literature and history, and he had a passion for ideas. Few artists have been more in touch with the philosophical and political currents of their times, as well as with the artistic. His dreams for American music and for music in American education in his day seemed impractical. But he had no opportunity to know the educational system in America, the obligations or the traditions of faculties and curricula, and to his innocence of such matters may be ascribed some of his disappointment later at Columbia University. His early teachers were impressed more by his versatility than by his excellence in any one direction. Though he disliked practising, he liked to play and he liked to compose. He also liked to draw, and there are portraits of his father and of himself, reproduced in Abbie Farwell Brown's *The Boyhood of Edward Mac-*

Dowell, which show convincing talent. It is no disparagement of his achievements in music to say that all his life he gave the impression of greater powers than he ever fully developed.

In April 1876 his mother took him to Paris, where he passed his examinations for the Conservatoire, and studied the piano with Marmontel and theory and composition with Savard. He also took private lessons in French. Some of his drawings came to the attention of Carolus Duran, who offered free instruction if he would give up music for painting, but Marmontel persuaded him without much difficulty to continue in the art of his first choice. His stay in France influenced him deeply, but his temperament was not at home with French music. Later on he cared little for Debussy, a fellow student at the Conservatoire, or for César Franck, and one cannot imagine him enthusiastic about D'Indy, or Ravel. At the end of three years in Paris he followed his natural bent and turned to Germany. After nearly a year at Wiesbaden (1878–79), where he studied composition with Louis Ehlert, he entered the Frankfort Conservatory, attracted by the brilliant pianist Carl Heymann, then at the height of his tragically brief career. Joachim Raff, the director of the Conservatory, took charge of MacDowell's studies in composition, and with Heymann gave him prompt recognition and encouragement. When Heymann retired because of failing health in 1881, he suggested the young American, barely twenty, as his successor, and Raff seconded the nomination. Though the faculty refused to make the appointment, on the ground that the candidate was as yet unproved, the confidence which these two master musicians showed in him gave MacDowell a place of respect in the musical world. He began to take private pupils, among them Marian Nevins, whom he later married. Appointed head piano teacher at the Darmstadt Conservatory in 1881, he continued to live in Frankfort, giving his private lessons, and commuting to Darmstadt. Most of his composing at this period he did on the train. This program soon proved too great a tax on his strength, and he resigned the Darmstadt post.

In 1882, at Raff's suggestion, he called upon Liszt at Weimar, with the manuscript of his first concerto, in A-minor (*opus* 15). This work, afterward revised, had been improvised in little more than a fortnight, though the themes had been gathered in advance. MacDowell arrived on Liszt's doorstep in such a condition of nervousness and self-distrust that he could not ring the bell. One wonders now why he had not gone directly to that doorstep when he began his European studies. Liszt received him with characteristic generosity, told one of his pupils, Eugen d'Albert, to play the orchestral part on the second piano, and listened to the concerto with approval. Immediately after this visit he recommended MacDowell's First Modern Suite (*opus* 10) for the program of the nineteenth annual convention of the Allgemeiner Deutscher Musik-Verein, at Zürich, July 1882. MacDowell himself played the Suite with success, on July 11. He still thought he was primarily a pianist, and set little value on his compositions. Some of the German critics objected to his playing the Suite with the notes before him. Years later he explained to Henry T. Finck that until his appearance before the Musik-Verein he had not considered his notes worth memorizing (*Century Magazine,* January 1897, p. 451). In 1883 Breitkopf & Härtel brought out this Suite, together with the Second Modern Suite (*opus* 14). Nothing of MacDowell's had previously been published, and this beginning he owed to Liszt.

For the next two years he devoted himself seriously to composition, chiefly in orchestral forms, seizing the opportunity to hear his experiments rehearsed by the local orchestras of Baden-Baden and Wiesbaden. To this period belong the five songs of *opus* 11 and *opus* 12, the Prélude and Fugue (*opus* 13), the "Serenata" for piano (*opus* 16), the "Two Fantastic Pieces" (*opus* 17), the "Barcarolle" and "Humoresque" (*opus* 18), and "Forest Idyls" (*opus* 18). In June 1884, he returned to America to marry Miss Nevins. After their wedding, July 21, at Waterford, Conn., they went to London and Paris, and settled in Wiesbaden for the winter of 1885–86, to complete, among other things, his second concerto, in D-minor (*opus* 23), and his symphonic poem, "Hamlet and Ophelia" (*opus* 22). Later he bought a small cottage outside of Wiesbaden, near the forest, and settled down for one of the happiest periods of his life, storing up inspiration for much that he composed later, as well as for the orchestral works, the piano pieces, and the songs which belong to this fertile time—among them the symphonic poems "Lancelot and Elaine" (*opus* 25), "Lamia" (*opus* 29), "The Saracens," and "The Lovely Alda" (*opus* 30); the six songs, "From an Old Garden" (*opus* 26), Four Compositions for Piano (*opus* 24), and the "Romance" for cello and orchestra (*opus* 35). It was the devotion and sympathy of his wife which provided MacDowell with this ideal opportunity to develop his genius.

In September 1888 he gave up his Wiesbaden cottage and sailed for Boston. The growth of his reputation, the success of his works at home as well as in Europe, made this step natural, but with it the tragic chapters of his life began. Some of his admirers regret for his sake that he did not stay in Europe, others lament that in his youth musical conditions in America were such that for even these few years he had to expatriate himself. Undoubtedly he missed some of the contacts with national life which are helpful to creative art. The deep emotions of his early manhood were bound up with Europe, with a tradition and an atmosphere not to be found on this side the ocean. Perhaps he was always looking for it here, wistfully and tragically. He gave the impression, against his will, of being a visitant in his own land, trying to establish himself in alien conditions. His interest in America was genuine and deep, reaching far beyond the field of music, but it is doubtful whether he knew how close he was to his country, how ready it was to welcome him, how instinctively it looked to him to be its spokesman in his art. On the other hand, the Europe he loved was a dream country, suggested by the great poets and artists and by ancient monuments, by folk-lore, by enchanting forests. Had he remained abroad he would probably not have been happy. He was by temperament energetic and surprisingly active, needing the society of his fellows as well as creative solitude. He came a little late for Europe and a little early for America.

In Boston the MacDowells lived first in Mt. Vernon Street, then at 13 West Cedar Street, then at 38 Chestnut Street. For eight busy and successful years he composed, taught his pupils, gave frequent performances and recitals. On Nov. 19, 1888, he appeared with the Kneisel Quartet in Chickering Hall, Boston, playing the Prelude, the Intermezzo, and the Presto from his First Piano Suite, and the piano part in Goldmark's B-flat Quintet. On Mar. 5, 1889, he played his Second Concerto for the first time in public at Chickering Hall, New York, Theodore Thomas conducting. A few weeks later he repeated the same concerto in Boston, under Gericke, and in July he made a flying trip to France to play the same work in an American concert at the Paris Exposition, with Frank Van der Stucken conducting. The critics acclaimed him at once as the leading American pianist and composer. During these years he wrote, among other works, the First Suite for Orchestra (*opus* 42), the Second, or Indian, Suite (*opus* 48), "Eight Songs" (*opus* 47), the Sonata Eroica (*opus* 50), the Sonata Tragica (*opus* 45), and the popular "Woodland Sketches" (*opus* 51). The performance of his larger compositions by the American and European orchestras became frequent. No American musician before him had achieved, or perhaps deserved, such recognition.

In 1896 MacDowell accepted a call to the recently established professorship of music at Columbia University. The intention of the endowment was "to elevate the standard of musical instruction in the United States, and to afford the most favorable opportunity for acquiring instruction of the highest order." McDowell took these words at their face value, not knowing that universities, like other institutions, must interpret their trusts in terms of their general policy. He assumed that he was to train musicians, just as his colleagues might be training historians or mathematicians. By January 1904 he found out his mistake, and resigned. Much has been said and written about this episode in MacDowell's life. (For an intelligent discussion see John Tasker Howard, *Our American Music.*) The tragedy was one of misunderstanding, a conflict not of personalities but of educational ideals. MacDowell threw himself into his work with enthusiasm and extreme conscientiousness. His name attracted large classes, of whom only a few were prepared for the kind of instruction he could give. He organized an excellent orchestra, he gathered a male chorus to sing serious music, perhaps the earliest attempt to interest a college glee club in art, he composed six Columbia Songs (published in 1901 but afterward withdrawn), as an experiment in the improvement of undergraduate music, he held departmental concerts and tried to make music function in the academic community. When his work became too much even for his devotion, he had an assistant for his classes, Leonard McWhood, and a conductor for the orchestra, Gustav Hinrichs. But the students in his classes received no academic credit for music courses. Music in those days was an "extra."

MacDowell also learned to his disappointment that the best musical talent rarely goes to college, nor does the best talent, with some exceptions, in painting and sculpture. He tried to persuade his colleagues to open the academic doors to the arts. "I have tried," he wrote, "to impress the 'powers that be' with the necessity of allowing no student to enter the university without some knowledge of the fine arts. Such knowledge may be very general, and not technical. This would force upon the preparatory school the admission of fine arts to its curriculum . . . I proposed that music be taken out of the faculty of philosophy, and architecture out of the School of Mines, and with Belles Lettres form a faculty of fine arts, to complete which, painting and sculpture would be indispensable. Owing to my inability to persuade rich men of New York into endowing a chair of painting and sculpture, the scheme, though approved by the 'powers that be,' was not realized" (New York *Evening Post,* Feb. 10, 1904, p. 9, quoted by Howard, *post,* p. 400). His resignation was a sad blow for his Columbia students, even for many who were not in his classes but who knew instinctively that he had stood in the community for something ideal. He was in some respects a great teacher, certainly a great musician and a scholar, as his lectures, published after his death, indicate. Given a student who was already well prepared, with something of the professional attitude toward the arts, MacDowell was one of the most stimulating of lecturers. But many of the pupils in his Columbia classes, though charmed by his personality and impressed with his genius, did not know what he was talking about, and their distress bewildered him. If part of the teacher's mission is to diagnose ignorance, MacDowell was not a teacher at all. Perhaps he failed to recognize some talent because it did not take the forms he was accustomed to in European conservatories.

During his Columbia years he lived in Eighty-eighth Street, near Riverside Drive, then at the Majestic Hotel, then at Ninety-sixth Street and Central Park West. For two seasons he conducted the Mendelssohn Glee Club, he gave occasional performances, he taught private pupils, and he composed—though this was chiefly during the vacations. His schedule was enough to crush a giant. But he was a singularly healthy figure, above medium height, who walked vigorously, dressed usually in brown or grey tweeds, with heavy brown shoes—an out-of-doors person, strongly Nordic. His blue eyes were alternately merry and dreamy. When he spoke, his listeners were caught by the quiet beauty of his voice and by the exquisiteness of his speech. It was not apparent that he was killing himself by overwork. To this period belong his Norse Sonata (*opus* 57) and his Keltic Sonata (*opus* 59), many of his finest songs and part songs, and a suite for stringed orchestra which he left unfinished. That he was able to accomplish so much in these years of teaching, he owed to his wife's foresight in securing, in 1896, the little farm at Peterboro, N. H., which became his happiest refuge and home. There, in a log cabin, at a distance from the main house, he spent his summers composing. After his resignation from Columbia he resumed his private teaching. In 1905 his health began to break. A nervous collapse was succeeded by an obscure brain trouble which proved incurable. He died Jan. 23, 1908, at his New York home in the Westminster Hotel, Irving Place, in the neighborhood where his boyhood had been passed. After the funeral at St. George's Church, he was buried at Peterboro, on a favorite hilltop. As a tribute to his memory his widow developed the farm into a large and beautiful estate, incorporated as a memorial to the composer, and equipped with studios for the use of poets, musicians, painters, and sculptors.

MacDowell's music is highly original and extremely colorful. The popularity of some of his small things, such as "To a Wild Rose," or the song, "Thy Beaming Eyes," threatened for a while to obscure his large qualities, but in time competent musicians showed increasing respect for the orchestral works, for the greater piano pieces, the sonatas particularly, and the second concerto, and for the best of the songs. In all his work the quality is lyrical, a quality revealed in his poems written for his songs (*Verses,* 1903, 1908), as well as in his music. He once said that he would never compose an opera, since the form always seemed to him unreal. His temperament was for song, not for drama. Though his work is harmonically rich, he deliberately turned away from the extreme experiments of the music of his day. He understood them and could say illuminating things about them, but he believed that art progresses by developing national and racial impulses, by developing hints supplied by the folk, rather than by imposing on the folk a new idiom intellectually arrived at. Even in the popular rhythms of dance music he recognized a significant development. Whatever the course of American music, he will remain one of its first great figures.

[See Lawrence Gilman, *Edward MacDowell: A Study* (1909), containing a bibliography of MacDowell's works; Wm. H. Humiston, *Little Biogs.: MacDowell* (1921); Abbie Farwell Brown, *The Boyhood of Edward MacDowell* (1924); O. G. T. Sonneck, *Cat. of First Editions of Edward MacDowell* (1917), and *Suum Cuique: Essays in Music* (1916); J. F. Porte, *Edward MacDowell* (1922); R. W. Brown, *Lonely Americans* (1929); J. T. Howard, *Our Am. Music* (1930); Paul Rosenfeld, *An Hour with Am. Music* (1929); Jas. G. Huneker, *Unicorns* (1917), ch. II; Hamlin Garland, *Roadside Meetings* (1930); T. P. Currier, "Edward MacDowell as I Knew Him," *Musical Quart.,* Jan. 1915; H. F. Gilbert, "Personal Recollections of Edward MacDowell," *New Music Rev.,* Nov. 1912; the *Musician,* Mar. 1908; New York newspapers at the time of MacDowell's death. MacDowell's *Critical and Historical Essays* (1912) is a volume of lectures delivered at Columbia University. Some of his letters and papers, not yet available to investigators, are in the music division of the Library of Congress.]

J. E.

McDOWELL, EPHRAIM (Nov. 11, 1771–June 25, 1830), physician, pioneer in abdominal surgery, was born in Rockbridge County, Va., the son of Samuel and Mary (McClung) McDowell. He was the ninth of eleven children.

His father, a veteran of the French and Indian War and a colonel in the Revolution, went to Kentucky in 1784, taking his family with him. He was a prominent man in the history of Kentucky, where he presided over the first organized court and also over the convention which framed the constitution of the state. The family settled in Danville, and Ephraim received his premedical education at the seminary of Worley and James, located first at Georgetown and afterward at Bardstown. Soon after leaving that school he went to Staunton, Va., and entered the office of Dr. Alexander Humphreys as a medical student. In 1793–94, he attended lectures at the medical school of the University of Edinburgh, where his preceptor had graduated, and at the same time took a course with John Bell, a brilliant private teacher.

He returned to America in 1795 without having secured a degree, but with a broadened understanding of the medicine of that day and particularly of anatomy and surgery. He settled in Danville, and established a reputation as the best surgeon west of Philadelphia. In 1802 he married Sarah Shelby, daughter of Gov. Isaac Shelby [*q.v.*]. Six children were born to this union. McDowell is said to have had an excellent library; he was always a student and, with the young men studying in his office, carried on dissections during each winter. It is to his credit that he cautioned his students against too free a use of medicines and gave it as his opinion that the employment of medical drugs was more of a curse than a blessing to the human race. This was his doctrine at a time when Benjamin Rush [*q.v.*], the leader of American medicine, was teaching the opposite principle.

McDowell was not a writer and did not even keep notes on his cases. He published but two papers, in an obscure journal (*Eclectic Repertory and Analytical Review*, April 1817, October 1819), which together described inadequately the first five cases upon which he performed ovariotomy. Recognition of his work was consequently slow in coming, and his reports attracted practically no attention until one contained in a letter addressed to John Bell of Edinburgh, but never received by him, was published by John Lizars in the *Edinburgh Medical and Surgical Journal* for October 1824, seven years after it was written. A similar report sent to Philip Syng Physick in Philadelphia was never acknowledged, if received, and never published.

Nevertheless McDowell was doing bold surgery. In a letter dated Jan. 2, 1829, to Robert Thompson, a student of medicine in Philadelphia, he described vividly the circumstances under which he performed his first operation for diseased ovaria. "I was sent for in 1809," he wrote, "to deliver a Mrs. Crawford near Greentown of twins; as the two attending physicians supposed. Upon examination per vaginam I soon ascertained that she was not pregnant; but had a large tumor in the Abdomen which moved easily from side to side. I told the Lady I could do her no good and candidly stated to her her deplorable situation; Informed her that John Bell Hunter Hey and A Wood four of the first and most eminent Surgeons in England and Scotland had uniformly declared in their Lectures that such was the danger of Peritoneal Inflammation, that opening the abdomen to extract the tumour was inevitable death. But notwithstanding this, if she thought herself prepared to die, I would take the lump from her if she could come to Danville; She came in a few days after my return home and in six days I opened her side and extracted one of the ovaria which from its diseased and enlarged state weighed upwards of twenty pounds; The Intestines, as soon as an opening was made ran out upon the table remained out about thirty minutes and, being upon Christmas day they became so cold that I thought proper to bathe them in tepid water previous to my replacing them; I then returned them stitched up the wound and she was perfectly well in twenty-five days." (The letter is published in full by J. N. McCormack, *post*, pp. 20–33, and in the *Military Surgeon*, April 1928.) At the date of this writing McDowell had performed ovariotomy twelve times, with but one death, and he had repeatedly performed radical operative cures for non-strangulated hernia. This last fact was unknown to Samuel D. Gross [*q.v.*], whose excellent sketches of McDowell are the most reliable and accurate to be found. Gross states that McDowell performed at least thirty-two operations for stone in the bladder, without a death. He used the lateral perineal incision. One patient upon whom he successfully operated for both stone and hernia was James K. Polk, afterwards president of the United States.

McDowell was a large man, vigorous and athletic, as he needed to be to withstand the hardships of the long journeys he took on horseback. He did much professional work for charity, but from those who could pay them he demanded fees large for that day. He was a religious man, and assigned as a reason for his preference for operating on Sundays his desire for the prayers of the congregation. He helped to found and gave the ground for the Episcopal Church in Danville, and was one of the founders and first trustees of Centre College. In June 1830, he was seized with an acute attack of illness marked by violent pain and nausea at the outset, then fever; and his death occurred on June 25. His disease at the time was referred to as inflammatory fever, but it is an interesting speculation, and not improbable, that the founder of abdominal surgery died of appendicitis. In 1879 a monument to him was erected in Danville, and McDowell and his wife were buried beside it.

[*Some of the Medic. Pioneers of Ky.* (1917), ed. by J. N. McCormack, pub. as supp. to vol. XV, *Ky. Medic. Jour.*; Mary Young Ridenbaugh, *Biog. of Ephraim McDowell, M.D.* (1890); August Schachner, *Ephraim McDowell* (1921); S. C. Swartzel, in *Lancet-Clinic*, Dec. 25, 1909; L. S. McMurtry, in *Surgery, Gynecol. and Obstetrics*, Feb. 1923; S. D. Gross, "Origin of Ovariotomy," in *Trans. Ky. Medic. Soc., 1852* (1853), *Lives of Eminent American Physicians and Surgeons of the Nineteenth Century* (1861), and *Memorial Oration in Honor of Ephraim McDowell* (1879); H. A. Kelly and W. L. Burrage, *Am. Medic. Biogs.* (1920), with additional references.] P. M. A.

McDOWELL, IRVIN (Oct. 15, 1818–May 4, 1885), soldier, was born at Columbus, Ohio, the son of Abram Irvin McDowell, and Eliza Selden Lord, his wife. The family was Scotch-Irish; its founder in America, Ephraim McDowell, came to Pennsylvania in 1735 and later migrated to the Valley of Virginia, whence his descendants crossed the mountains into Kentucky. Irvin McDowell received his early education in France, at the Collège de Troyes. Returning home, he was appointed a cadet at the Military Academy in 1834, and graduated in 1838, as No. 23 in a class of forty-five. Assigned to the 1st Artillery as brevet second lieutenant, he became second lieutenant almost immediately (July 7, 1838), upon the occurrence of a vacancy in his regiment. His first service was on the Canadian frontier, from Niagara to Maine, in connection with the border disturbances then in progress. In 1841, however, he was brought back to the Military Academy as a tactical officer, and served in that capacity and as adjutant until the outbreak of the Mexican War. Meanwhile (Oct. 7, 1842) he had been promoted first lieutenant. On Oct. 6, 1845, he was detailed as aide-de-camp to General Wool, and served with that officer's command throughout the war and in the Army of Occupation, most of the time acting as his adjutant general. For his services at the battle of Buena Vista he was made captain by brevet, and on May 13, 1847, was transferred with that rank to the Adjutant General's Department. He returned to the United States in 1848, and until 1861 served at headquarters of the Army and of various territorial departments, except for the year 1859, which he spent on leave in Europe. He was promoted major in 1856.

At the outbreak of the Civil War he was serving in Washington. Through General Scott, who had known him since his graduation and thought highly of him, he became acquainted with the leaders of the new administration, and particularly with Secretary Chase, whose confidence and esteem he immediately won. On May 14, 1861, he was promoted brigadier-general and assigned to duty with the forces assembling in Washington under the command of Gen. J. K. F. Mansfield. As these troops were transferred across the Potomac, it became necessary to organize those south of the river into a separate command, later known as the Army of the Potomac; and McDowell received this assignment, together with command of the Department of Northeastern Virginia. Although neither he nor most other officers concerned considered the army in any condition to operate in the field, both the political and the military situation seemed to demand a move to dislodge the Confederate forces at Manassas Junction, where the rail line from the West joined that from the South—for at that time the direct railway from Washington to Richmond did not exist. He was therefore required to undertake the brief campaign which ended in the disastrous battle of Bull Run (First Manassas), a campaign of which it has been well said that "although foredoomed to failure, yet it came within inches of success" (Johnston, *post*, p. 269).

He was now superseded by McClellan in command of the army, but remained with it as a division commander. In March 1862 he was made major-general of volunteers, and assigned to command the I Corps, Army of the Potomac. When McClellan moved to Fort Monroe to open his Peninsular campaign, this corps was retained, against the judgment of both generals, for the direct defense of Washington; it was later separated from McClellan's command entirely, and designated as the Army of the Rappahannock, McDowell retaining command of the troops and of the territorial Department of the Rappahannock. When, after the Peninsular campaign, most of McClellan's troops were transferred to General Pope's new Army of Virginia, McDowell's force became the III Corps of that army. At the second battle of Bull Run (Second Manassas), McDowell's conduct was severely criticized, and he was relieved of his command. He at once applied for an inquiry, and was ultimately exonerated, but was never afterward employed in the field. In 1864 he was assigned to territorial command in San Francisco; in 1868 he was transferred to the Department of the East, and in 1872 to that of the South. In that year he was promoted major-general in the regular army.

In 1876 he returned to San Francisco, where he remained until his retirement in 1882. He then took up his residence in that city, and interested himself in local affairs, serving as park commissioner until his death in 1885. In this capacity he planned the park improvement of the Presidio reservation, and laid out its roads overlooking the Golden Gate. He was buried on the reservation. He was married in 1849 to Helen Burden, of Troy, N. Y., and had four children, three of whom, a son and two daughters, survived him.

Although able, energetic, and devoted to his profession, McDowell was always unfortunate as a field commander. His previous service, while most creditable, had been entirely as a staff officer; until he took over the Army of the Potomac he had never held a command of his own, not even the smallest. In the preparation of his plans for Bull Run, he seemed instinctively to assume the position of a staff officer or second in command to General Scott, not that of the commander of an army; and in their execution he perhaps deferred too much to the views of his subordinates, and accepted situations instead of controlling them. But to control the situation that existed at that time would have required a most exceptional man, and no such man was found until much later in the war.

In person, McDowell was squarely and powerfully built. His manner was frank and agreeable. An appreciation of him by Secretary Chase exists, written Sept. 4, 1862, just after the second battle of Manassas. According to this estimate he was loyal, brave, truthful, and capable; a good disciplinarian. Contrary to the usual customs of the time, he used neither alcohol nor tobacco. He was serious and earnest, never sought popularity, and had no political aims. In official relations, his manner was purely military; he seemed to disregard individuals, and did not as a rule arouse warm personal sentiment in officers or men.

[Personal and family information is taken chiefly from a letter to the writer from Mrs. Maud Appleton McDowell, a daughter-in-law, and from W. H. Russell, *My Diary North and South* (1863). An outline of McDowell's military career is found in G. W. Cullum, *Biog. Reg. Officers and Grads. U. S. Mil. Acad.* (3rd ed., 1891); his reports and dispatches appear in *War of the Rebellion: Official Records (Army)*; analyses of his action in command in R. M. Johnston, *Bull Run: Its Strategy and Tactics* (1913), J. B. Fry, *McDowell and Tyler in the Campaign of Bull Run* (1884), Thomas Worthington, *A Correct Hist. of Pope, McDowell and FitzJohn Porter at the Second Battle of Bull Run* (1880), and in his own *Statement . . . before the Court of Inquiry* (1863). See also memoir by G. W. Cullum in *Sixteenth Ann. Reunion, Asso. Grads. U. S. Mil. Acad.* (1885); T. M. Green, *Hist. Families of Ky.* (1889); "Report of the Joint Committee on the Conduct of the War," *Senate Report No. 108*, 37 Cong., 3 Sess.; *Battles and Leaders of the Civil War* (4 vols., 1887–88); *Daily Alta California* (San Francisco), May 5, 1885.]

O. L. S., Jr.

McDOWELL, JAMES (Oct. 13, 1795–Aug. 24, 1851), governor of Virginia, congressman, was of Scotch-Irish ancestry. His father, Col. James McDowell, was the great-grandson of Ephraim McDowell who, coming from Ulster, was a pioneer settler of Rockbridge County, Va., in 1738. His mother, Sarah Preston, was the grand-daughter of John Preston, who that same year emigrated from Londonderry to Augusta County, Va. His sister, Elizabeth, was the wife of Thomas H. Benton [*q.v.*]. In the character of James McDowell the pioneer spirit and the Presbyterian faith were dominant, though he had no taste for agricultural pursuits. Born at the ancestral home, "Cherry Grove," Rockbridge County, he was educated in private schools, attended Washington College (now Washington and Lee University) for one year, and in 1813 was sent to Yale. After a year here, he entered the College of New Jersey and graduated in 1816, delivering the Latin salutatory for his class. He was considered the most talented writer in college and had early developed a gift for public speaking, which led him into the study of law. On Sept. 7, 1818, he was married to his cousin, Susanna Smith Preston, grand-daughter of Gen. William Campbell [*q.v.*] and Elizabeth Henry, sister of Patrick Henry [*q.v.*]. At this time his father burdened him with the gift of two thousand acres of land near Lexington, Ky., where he tried to give himself to the farm as well as to the law, with the result that he soon abandoned both. Returning to Virginia, he established himself at "Colalto," an estate about a mile from Lexington.

Following the course of the Virginia gentleman of the day, he entered the legislature in 1830, and was concerned with local matters, mostly road building, until the Nat Turner Insurrection of 1831. When the legislature was asked by Gov. John Floyd [*q.v.*], McDowell's uncle, to turn its deliberations "to the melancholy subject which has filled the country with affliction" (Miller, *post*, p. 81), McDowell prepared and delivered one of his greatest speeches (*Speech of James M'Dowell, Jr., . . . on the Slave Question*, 2nd ed., 1832). He maintained that slavery was a cause of national dissension, that separation could not be peaceful, and that the separate existence of the slave states would be disastrous to their own welfare. He also advocated, in this session, a state-controlled canal connecting the tide-water of the James with the Ohio River. In 1832, owing to a division in the ranks of the Jackson Democrats, McDowell was defeated for the United States Senate by John Tyler. He strongly opposed Nullification and stated in 1833 that the doctrine "that each state had the right 'peaceably to secede' is wholly unwarranted by the Constitution" (Miller, *post,* p. 115). He canvassed southwestern Virginia in the interests of Van Buren's election as president, but in 1838 was defeated for reëlection to the legislature. His address at the College of New Jersey in 1838 (*Address Delivered before the Alumni Association of the College of New Jersey,* 1839) was ranked by many with Patrick Henry's orations.

In 1842 he was elected governor and served for the three-year term beginning Jan. 1, 1843. During his administration he gave himself largely to the problems of internal improvement, especially the James River and Kanawha Canal. He anticipated later developments by thirty years in recommending that the canal be abandoned above Lynchburg and a railroad be built at once to the Ohio. A few weeks after the expiration of his term as governor, his brother-in-law, William Taylor, died, and McDowell was elected in his place as representative in the Twenty-ninth Congress; he also served through the Thirtieth and Thirty-first congresses (1846–51). He supported the bill to create a lieutenant-general for the prosecution of the Mexican War, with the understanding that his brother-in-law, Thomas H. Benton, would receive the appointment. This act probably contributed to his defeat for the Senate in 1847 by a combination of Whigs and Calhoun Democrats. The remaining four years of his congressional service were marked by failing health, but three of his speeches during this period are considered among his best—his memorial tribute to John Quincy Adams (*Congressional Globe,* 30 Cong., 1 Sess., p. 386), and two speeches on the Wilmot Proviso, Feb. 23, 1849, and Sept. 3, 1850 (*Ibid.,* 2 Sess., Appendix, pp. 212–19 and 31 Cong., 1 Sess., Appendix, pp. 1678–85). In speaking against the Proviso, he reconciled his position with that which he had taken in 1831 by the argument that Virginia had the right to abolish slavery within the limits of the state, but that Congress in adopting the proposed act would create the very conditions which he had tried to avert in Virginia. His death occurred at his home near Lexington and he was buried in the Presbyterian Cemetery. He had ten children, three sons and seven daughters. A sidelight on his character is the fact that he was the first governor of Virginia to ban wine at official entertainments.

[His speech of 1849 on the Wilmot Proviso is reviewed in *Southern Literary Messenger,* May 1849; that on the slave question is discussed in *Richmond Whig,* Jan. 23, 1832; Henry Wilson, *Hist. of the Rise and Fall of the Slave Power* (3 vols., 1872–77) gives many details of McDowell's speeches, especially in vol. I, p. 205, and vol. II, pp. 194–97; see also, S. C. P. Miller, "James McDowell," *Washington and Lee Univ., Lexington, Va., Hist. Papers,* no. 5 (1895); D. X. Junkin, *The Christian Statesman: A Discourse Occasioned by the Death of the Hon. James McDowell* (1851); *Richmond Enquirer,* Aug. 29, 1851.]

J. E. W.

McDOWELL, JOHN (Feb. 11, 1751–Dec. 22, 1820), lawyer and educator, was born in Peters Township, Cumberland, now Franklin, County, Pa., the second of the twelve children of William and Mary (Maxwell) McDowell. His grandfather, William, born in Ireland, had emigrated to America about 1715 and settled in Chester County, Pa. The second William was a man of standing in his community, a justice of the peace and a Presbyterian elder. With other families of the neighborhood, the McDowells were several times driven from their home during the French and Indian wars, and on one occasion their dwelling was burned. John seems to have received a good elementary education and when he was seventeen years old he entered the College of Philadelphia, from which he graduated in 1771, being assigned the part of English orator on the Commencement program. Before his graduation he had served as tutor and in this capacity he continued his connection with the college until 1782. He joined Capt. Samuel Patton's company as a private in 1777, but was not rugged enough to undergo the hardships of army life. A rather frail constitution, in fact, was more or less a factor in his whole career.

Going to Cambridge, Dorchester County, Md., in 1782, he taught, took up the study of law, and was admitted to the bar. He was successful as a practitioner and had some of the prominent people of the state as his clients. Teaching still attracted him, however, and on Aug. 11, 1789, at a meeting of the visitors and governors of St. John's College, soon to be opened at Annapolis, he appeared and accepted the professorship of mathematics, which had been tendered him on the 14th of May preceding. The institution began to give instruction in November, with McDowell acting as principal. The original plan to bring over some one from England to head the college failed, and on May 14, 1790, McDowell was formally elected principal. He served in this capacity for the next sixteen years, during which time the institution drew students from at least eight of the states, not a few of whom later became nationally prominent. In 1806 the Maryland legislature withdrew its support, and the board of visitors and governors voted that the principal and faculty "be discontinued." They were offered reappointment, however, but McDowell declined to serve longer. He was made a member of the board but soon resigned owing to his connection with the University of Pennsylvania, where in 1806 he became professor of natural philosophy, and the following year, provost. In 1810 ill health caused him to relinquish both these offices. Returning to Maryland in 1815, he was again offered the principalship of St. John's College. This he declined, but he accepted an election to the board of visitors and governors and seems at times to have acted as principal. He is described as "a man of fine presence, and of pleasing and winning address, combining in a remarkable degree great firmness and dignity of character with an almost feminine gentleness" (*Commemoration of the One Hundredth Anniversary of St. John's College,* 1890, p. 88). He never married, and the last two years of his life were spent in Peters Township, Pa., with a sister, Margaret, widow of Matthias Maris. Here he died and was buried. That he was a man of sagacity and frugality is indicated by the fact that he left an estate of $40,000. His Latin and Greek books, and his books on mathematics and natural philosophy, he bequeathed to the University of Pennsylvania.

[In addition to source cited above, see *Gen. Alumni Cat. of the Univ. of Pa.* (1917); *The Alumni Reg., Univ. of Pa.,* Oct. 1903; *Old Mercersburg* (1912); *Biog. Annals of Franklin County, Pa.* (1905); W. B. Norris, *Annapolis: Its Colonial and Naval Story* (1925); *The Kittochtinny Hist. Soc. . . . Papers . . . 1901–03* (1904).] H. E. S.

MCDOWELL, JOHN (Sept. 10, 1780–Feb. 13, 1863), Presbyterian clergyman, was born in Bedminster, Somerset County, N. J. He was the son of Matthew and Elizabeth (Anderson) McDowell, whose parents were of Scotch descent and had migrated to America from the north of Ireland. His schooling was more or less interrupted by work on his father's farm, but he secured sufficient preparation at a classical school, conducted by Rev. William Boyd about two miles from the McDowell home, to enable him in 1799 to enter the junior class of the College of New Jersey. After graduating with honors in 1801, he studied theology, first, under Rev. H. W. Hunt of Newton, N. J., and later, under Rev. John Woodhull of Freehold. He was licensed to preach by the Presbytery of New Brunswick, at Basking Ridge, Apr. 25, 1804, and was ordained by the Presbytery of New York and installed pastor of the Presbyterian Church in Elizabethtown, N. J., on Dec. 26 of the same year. On Feb. 5, 1805, he married Henrietta, daughter of Shepard Kollock [*q.v.*]. Although called to a number of important churches elsewhere, he remained in Elizabethtown for more than twenty-eight years, during which time his church had large growth, and from its membership the Second Presbyterian Church was formed. In 1833 he took charge of the newly organized Central Church, Philadelphia. Resigning in 1845, he became pastor of the Spring Garden Church, constituted by some of his former parishioners. The duties of this office he performed until he was past eighty, when a colleague was called.

A practical mind, executive ability, exactitude, methodical industry, and a thorough acquaintance with Presbyterian procedure, made him a valuable member of church boards, and of the General Assembly. The latter body he served as clerk, trustee, and, in 1820, as moderator. During the controversy which resulted in the division of 1837, he did not approve of the extreme measures taken by the conservatives, but after the division was effected he loyally supported the Old School branch of the church. He was an enthusiastic promoter of education, religious and secular. Early in his first pastorate he formed a class for the study of the Bible and church history, and in 1814 his congregation united with the Methodists and Episcopalians in establishing the first Sunday school in Elizabethtown. He published, probably the next year, a system of Bible questions, a fourth edition of which, 1820, bears the title, *Questions on the Bible for the Use of Schools,* said to have been the earliest work of its kind in this country. It circulated to the extent of 250,000 copies before being superseded by publications of the American Sunday School Union. He also issued in 1838 *Bible Class Manual: or, a System of Theology in the Order of the Westminster Shorter Catechism, Adapted to Bible Classes.* He was a member of the Presbyterian General Assembly in 1812, which determined to establish a theological seminary at Princeton, and was chosen one of the first directors. Two years later he became a trustee of the College of New Jersey, and in 1822, a trustee of the Seminary. These positions he held until his death, serving as secretary of the Seminary Board from 1824 to 1860. On several different occasions, notably in 1818 when he visited the Southern states, he solicited funds for the Seminary, and once he made a tour in the interests of the College. His most ambitious publication was *Theology, in a Series of Sermons in the Order of the Westminster Shorter Catechism* (2 vols., 1825–26). In 1828 he declined an appointment by the General Assembly as professor of ecclesiastical history and church government in Western (Allegheny) Theological Seminary, and in 1831 accepted the chair of church history and polity in Union Seminary, Va., but later withdrew his acceptance. On Dec. 31, 1854, he preached a sermon, published under the title, *Fifty Years a Pastor: a Semi-Centenary Discourse Delivered in the Spring Garden Presbyterian Church* (1855), which contains much biographical material. Several of his sermons were printed separately; two appear in *The New Jersey Preacher* (1813), and three in the *American National Preacher* (vol. V, no. 6, 1830; and vol. XI, no. 8, 1837).

[W. B. Sprague, *Memoirs of the Rev. John McDowell, D.D., and the Rev. Wm. A. McDowell, D.D.* (1864); *Gen. Cat. of Princeton Univ., 1746–1906* (1908); *The Presbyt. Hist. Almanac,* 1864; *N. Y. Observer,* Feb. 26, 1863; *The Presbyterian* (Phila.), Feb. 21, 28, 1863; *Phila. Inquirer,* Feb. 17, 1863.]
H. E. S.

McDOWELL, JOSEPH (Feb. 15, 1756–Aug. 11, 1801), Revolutionary soldier, congressman, was born at Winchester, Va., the son of Joseph McDowell and Margaret O'Neal or O'Neil and the brother of Charles McDowell [*q.v.*]. His father settled at Quaker Meadows (near Morganton), Burke County, N. C., where Joseph's youth was spent. After the outbreak of the Revolution he was attached to Charles McDowell's militia regiment and accompanied his brother on the Rutherford expedition against the Cherokees (1776). He took part in the numerous battles in North Carolina against the Loyalists—including Ramsour's Mill (June 20, 1780), the Pacolet River skirmish, and Musgrove's Mill. When the "backwater men" assembled in September 1780 to oppose the Loyalist invasion of Maj. Patrick Ferguson of the 71st Highlanders, McDowell was major in his brother's regiment. During the absence of Charles McDowell on a mission to General Gates, Joseph commanded the McDowell regiment in the battle of King's Mountain, Oct. 7, 1780 (Isaac Shelby, *Battle of King's Mountain, To the Public,* 1823). At the battle of Cowpens (Jan. 17, 1781) he commanded a detachment of 190 mounted riflemen from Burke County. In the same year he was active in attacking the Cherokees and later commanded the McDowell regiment during his brother's expedition against the Cherokees (1782). He was a member of the North Carolina House of Commons (1785–88), of the North Carolina Senate (1791–95), and of the North Carolina conventions of 1788 and 1789 that met to consider ratification of the Federal Constitution. He opposed ratification because the Constitution lacked a bill of rights. A leader of the Democratic-Republicans in western North Carolina, he was elected to the Fifth Congress (1797–99), where he joined other Democratic-Republicans in opposing the Alien and Sedition acts. He is usually said to have been a member of the Third Congress (1793–95), but the *Biographical Directory of the American Congress* (1928) credits the term to his cousin Joseph, known as "Pleasant Gardens Joe." The descendants of the latter insist that it was he who commanded the McDowell militia at King's Mountain, but the claim is disproved by the testimony of other officers. "Quaker Meadows Joe" married Margaret Moffett of Virginia, by whom he had six daughters and two sons, one of whom was Joseph Jefferson McDowell, member of Congress from Ohio.

[*The Colonial Records of N. C.* (10 vols., 1886–90) and *The State Records of N. C.* (20 vols., 1895–1914); David Schenck, *N. C., 1780–'81* (1889); J. W. Moore, *Hist. of N. C.* (2 vols., 1880); J. H. Wheeler, *Hist. Sketches of N. C.* (1851); *Proc. and Debates of the Convention of N. C.* (Hillsborough, N. C., 1788); L. C. Draper, *King's Mountain and Its Heroes* (1881); T. M. Green, *Hist. Families of Ky.* (1889); J. H. McDowell, *Hist. of the McDowells and Connections* (1918); *N. C. Booklet,* July 1904; S. A. Ashe, *Biog. Hist. of N. C.*, vol. VII (1908).]
F. E. R.

MacDOWELL, KATHERINE SHERWOOD BONNER (Feb. 26, 1849–July 22, 1883), short-story writer and novelist under the pen name Sherwood Bonner, was born in Holly Springs, Miss. Her father, Dr. Charles Bonner, early in life came from Ireland to Pennsylvania, where he studied medicine, and then moved to Mississippi, where he married Mary Wilson of Holly Springs. Katherine grew up with her younger brother and sister under the devoted care of a negro mammy whose superstitious lore and lovable personality are reflected in many stories. Her father supervised her early reading, and later she attended a private school in Holly Springs, leaving at the age of fourteen for six months at a fashionable boarding school in Montgomery, Ala. The Civil War left a deep impression on her mind. The siege of Vicksburg and Port Hudson, the passage of Johnston's army through Holly Springs, and nearby raids and skirmishes were the outstanding events of her life in 1863. Her attitude, revealed in her later writings, was one of love for the South, hatred of slavery, and admiration for the intellectual standards of the North. Her first story was published in 1864 in the *Massachusetts Ploughman,* whose editor, Nahum Capen, saw the promise of her pen and became her friend and adviser. In 1871 she married Edward MacDowell of Holly Springs, by whom she had a daughter, but her high-strung temperament and literary ambitions were incompatible with domestic routine, and not long after the birth of her child she separated from her husband.

Leaving her daughter with a relative, she went

to Boston, where she served at first as secretary to Nahum Capen. Through him she became acquainted with important literary figures. Longfellow engaged her as an amanuensis and encouraged her in her writing. Under this stimulation she contributed articles, letters, and verses to the Boston *Times, Memphis Avalanche,* and other papers. From 1875 on, her stories of Southern life and character appeared in periodicals; most of them were later collected in two volumes, *Dialect Tales* (1883) and *Suwanee River Tales* (1884). These stories place her in the midst of the local-colorist movement which was part of the drift toward realism in her generation. She made a tour of Europe in 1876, spending most of her time in Italy. Her novel *Like unto Like,* dedicated to Longfellow, appeared in 1878 and was favorably received. This story with its background of the Civil War and the reconstruction era is autobiographical in nature and is of value for the interpretation of her character and her marital experience. She returned to Holly Springs to nurse her father and brother who died of yellow fever in August 1878; then once more threw herself into the writing of short stories and produced several dialect tales of Tennessee mountain life and of the "Egypt" district of Illinois. Her work shows a further increase in realism during this period, making use of gloomy scenes from her experience with the yellow fever and vivid details of Mississippi life. The intensity and frankness of "The Volcanic Interlude," published in *Lippincott's Magazine* in April 1880, caused many readers to cancel their subscriptions. Under the strain of absorbing work her health began to give way. In 1882 she was urged to have an operation for cancer, but refused. She worked with undiminished energy into the spring of 1883 and then, accompanied by her friend Sophia Kirk, returned to Holly Springs, where she died.

[Monograph by Dorothy L. Gilligan, "Life and Works of Sherwood Bonner" (MS.), in George Washington University library; accounts by friends: A. L. Bondurant, in *Pubs. Miss. Hist. Soc.*, vol. II (1899) and Sophia Kirk in preface to *Suwanee River Tales* (1884); B. M. Drake, article in *Southern Writers,* vol. II (1903); *Appletons' Ann. Cyc.*, 1884; M. L. Rutherford, *The South in Hist. and Lit.* (1907); *Harper's Weekly,* Aug. 11, 1883.]

R. W. B.

McDUFFIE, GEORGE (Aug. 10, 1790–Mar. 11, 1851), representative and senator, was probably born in Columbia County, Ga. There is some doubt as to the date and the place of his birth. His parents were John and Jane McDuffie, both natives of Scotland who came to Georgia after the Revolution and settled in the pinelands about thirty miles from Augusta. The father was a man of fine mind and character but very poor, and the boy began life with no prospect of education beyond that offered by an old-field school. At the age of twelve he was a clerk in a country store and, two years later, obtained a similar place in Augusta, where he boarded with his employer, James Calhoun, who, seeing the boy's capacity, in 1810 persuaded William Calhoun, a brother, to take him to live with him while attending Moses Waddell's school at Willington, which was close by. There McDuffie remained for a year and then entered the junior class at South Carolina College, where he was graduated in 1813 with a reputation as a debater and orator. He was admitted to the bar a year later and began practice at Pendleton, S. C. In 1815 he moved to Edgefield and became the partner of Eldred Simkins, who had a large practice. McDuffie was soon elected to the lower house of the legislature and served two terms. In 1818 Simkins succeeded to Calhoun's seat in Congress and, after a second term, retired in favor of McDuffie, who remained in the House from 1821 until 1834, when he resigned to become governor of South Carolina. Returning to the bar after two terms as governor, he at once built up a large practice. In 1842 he succeeded William C. Preston in the Senate. He resigned in August 1846 and returned to private life. About 1829 he moved to "Cherry Hill," a plantation in the Sumter District, S. C., near the Savannah River and there ended his days. Although he came from poverty and obscurity, he won admission into exclusive South Carolina society. He married in 1829 Mary Rebecca, the daughter of Col. Richard Singleton, who died on Sept. 14, 1830. Their only child married the younger Wade Hampton, 1818–1902 [*q.v.*].

McDuffie entered Congress a strong nationalist. In the same year he wrote as a newspaper article a "Defence of a Liberal Construction of the Powers of Congress," directed against state sovereignty and strict construction, which, amusingly enough in the light of later events, James Hamilton, Jr., had reprinted in pamphlet form with laudatory comment (1821). In discussing the right of a state to judge of its own powers, McDuffie said, "No climax of political heresies can be imagined, in which this might not fairly claim the most prominent place" (see Magoon, *post,* 246). But his nationalism did not long endure. He was attacking the tariff in a short time, opposing internal improvements with almost equal vehemence in 1825, advocating a prohibitory tax on Northern goods in 1828, and in 1831 declaring that a Union made by the majority was a foul monster whose deformity could be worshiped only by those worthy of their chains. In

1830, while fulminating against the protective tariff, he developed what was known as the "forty-bale" theory. Holding that the tariff affected cotton growers particularly and that it subtracted from their profits by forcing them to sell their produce in exchange for a reduced purchasing power, he argued that the producer and not the consumer paid the duty on imports, and that, as a result, the Southern planters gave to the government, or to Northern manufacturers, forty out of every hundred bales of cotton they produced (*Register of Debates in Cong.,* 21 Cong., 1 Sess., 1830, pp. 842–62). Like most of his contemporaries in South Carolina, he was utterly unable to perceive how far slavery was an economic handicap to the South.

He favored nullification, although he was inclined to regard it, if not a revolutionary remedy, at least one outside of the Constitution. Nor would he agree that it was a peaceful one but believed that secession would probably follow it, a prospect that aroused no terrors in his soul. His speech of May 19, 1831, at Charleston is frequently said to have brought Calhoun to open advocacy of nullification. He was a delegate to the nullification convention in 1832 and wrote the address to the people of the other states in which, after severe condemnation of the protective tariff, he warned them that secession might follow and declared that, if the federal government employed force, South Carolina would rather be "the cemetery of freemen, than the habitation of slaves" (*Journal of the Convention of the People of S. C. . . . 1833,* 1833, p. 78). He was disappointed at the success of the compromise and frankly scornful of the nullification of the Force Bill in 1833, which he thought an empty and impotent gesture.

In Congress he quickly acquired reputation as a ready, eloquent, and sensational debater, and the news that he intended speaking rarely failed to fill the galleries. His speeches, usually extemporaneous, were always delivered as if he were in a frenzy of passion. They were characterized by their noise and fury, extravagance of phrase, and denunciatory quality, though on occasions he could also be persuasive. His voice was fine and powerful, his memory unfailing, his face expressive, his fluency never failed, and always he "pounded the air with his fists." All of this was in striking contrast to his normal manner, for he was ordinarily quiet and reserved, almost to taciturnity, with a somber cast to his thought, which made a smile almost a stranger to his face. John Quincy Adams said he had a "gloomy churlishness" (*post,* vol. IX, p. 119) in his character. The explanation of this characteristic probably lies in his physical condition. He was a confirmed dyspeptic. During the session of Congress of 1821–22 he became involved in a quarrel with William Cumming of Georgia growing out of the Calhoun-Crawford rivalry for the presidency. After they had extensively abused each other in the press, Cumming challenged McDuffie and came to Washington for the duel, which occurred after the close of the session. McDuffie suffered a permanent injury to the spine and was never again a well man. His health grew steadily worse, and he suffered from severe fits of depression, which finally amounted to attacks of melancholia. He also grew increasingly irritable, during his last years was a pitiable wreck, and finally died insane. The Cumming duel was not his only affair of the kind. In fact, Cumming again challenged him, but the duel was never fought. At the same session McDuffie had a quarrel with James M. Wayne of Georgia, later associate justice of the United States Supreme Court, which led to a challenge, but the matter was adjusted. During the Twentieth Congress he challenged Thomas Metcalfe of Kentucky, who chose rifles as the weapons for the encounter. James Hamilton, Jr., McDuffie's second, horrified at this breach of the code, refused to let his friend appear and later made it known that McDuffie, as a result of his wound, could not fire a rifle. McDuffie also challenged Joseph Vance, of Ohio, who declined to meet him.

In Congress McDuffie became the most radical of the opponents of the protective tariff. He was venomous in his hatred of the Adams administration, and in the first session of the Nineteenth Congress he made furious charges of a corrupt bargain between Adams and Clay and proposed an amendment to the Constitution providing for a more direct election of president in order to prevent a recurrence of such a thing. During the Adams administration he was chairman of the ways and means committee. He had supported Jackson strongly in 1821 in the Florida matter and from 1825 to 1829 was an enthusiastic advocate of his election as president, and it was confidently expected in 1829 that he would be in the cabinet. But his support was soon lost. He broke with Jackson on the questions of nullification and the bank. McDuffie was as enthusiastic in his support of the bank as he was of nullification, and in 1832 he presented to the House the bank's memorial for recharter. During his brief senatorial career he favored the annexation of Texas, although as governor of South Carolina he had opposed it, and introduced a resolution for it. He opposed the occupation of Oregon as impracticable, declaring that never, even in the sanguine dreams of youth, had he conceived of having under the same government people who lived 3,000 miles apart (*Congressional Globe*, 27 Cong., 3 Sess., p. 200). After the expiration of his term as governor he lost influence in South Carolina, as Calhoun gained it. Up to that time he was in high popular favor and genuinely beloved. He was a little above medium height with a large, spare figure. He had prominent, striking features, brilliant and deep-set blue eyes, and black hair. Always he was grim-looking with the "fierce earnestness" of passionate conviction. His temperament was nervous, he was easily moved emotionally, and his motives seem not to have been selfish. He was as frank as he was bold, clear-headed, and strikingly consistent for a politician. He relaxed somewhat with his intimates and, when in good health, enjoyed cards, checkers, and backgammon.

[Some letters in Lib. of Cong.; family records and MSS. in private hands; *Trinity Archive*, Sept. 1892; *Memoirs of John Quincy Adams*, ed. by C. F. Adams, vols. V–IX (1875–76); J. B. O'Neall, *Biog. Sketches of the Bench and Bar*, 1859, vol. II; E. L. Magoon, *Living Orators in America* (1849); B. F. Perry, *Reminiscences of Public Men* (1883); *Hist. of S. C.*, ed. by Yates Snowden (1920), vol. II; C. S. Boucher, *The Nullification Controversy in S. C.* (copr. 1916); D. F. Houston, *A Critical Study of Nullification in S. C.* (1896), pp. 35–49; *Charleston Daily Courier*, Mar. 13, 1851.]
J. G. deR. H.

McELRATH, THOMAS (May 1, 1807–June 6, 1888), publisher, partner of Horace Greeley in the publication of the *New York Tribune*, was born at Williamsport, Pa. After an early apprenticeship on the *Harrisburg Chronicle*, he pushed on to Philadelphia, finding employment in a book-printing establishment. He later returned to Williamsport and studied law. Equipped now for a struggle with fortune, he went to New York City, where he was employed as proof-reader and head salesman by the Methodist Book Concern, and subsequently he engaged on his own account in the publication of school books and religious works. In 1828 he was admitted to the bar, formed a partnership with William Bloomfield and Charles P. Daly, and entered upon a lucrative practice. In 1833 he was married to Elizabeth Price of New York City. His ability and attractive personal qualities brought him advancement. Elected as a Whig to the New York Assembly, he won attention by a minority report on the petition for removing the state capital from Albany to Utica, his report closing with a recommendation to transfer the seat of government to New York. During the same session he presented for the judiciary committee an adverse report on a petition for the abolishment of capital punishment. He was also among those who protested against the action of Congress in resolving to table without debate, printing, or reference, all petitions affecting slavery.

In 1841 McElrath became business manager of the *New York Tribune*, then in its uncertain infancy. On July 31 Horace Greeley made this terse announcement over his name: "The principal Editorial charge of the paper will still rest with the subscriber; while the entire business management of the concern henceforth devolves upon his partner." McElrath declared "his hearty concurrence in the principles, Political and Moral" on which the *Tribune* had been conducted. Surveying this combination of sanctum and counting-room, James Parton, in his life of Greeley, exclaimed: "Oh! that every Greeley could find his McElrath! and blessed is the McElrath that finds his Greeley!" (*post*, p. 162). Although the business manager did not share every enthusiasm of his partner's flaming pen, the steady course of the *Tribune* as a publishing concern insured a constant enlargement of its influence and prosperity. When muscular men of the "bloody sixth" ward, in resentment of plain language, swore to wreck the *Tribune* building, McElrath did his share to put the office in a state of defense. When he withdrew from the *Tribune* in 1857, to become corresponding secretary of the American Institute, the paper had risen to a position of social and political leadership.

McElrath had numerous official trusts. He was a master of chancery for New York City in 1840; state director of the Bank of America in 1841; New York alderman in 1845–46; appraiser-general of the New York district in 1861, by appointment of President Lincoln; custom-house officer in 1866; United States commissioner to the Paris Exposition in 1867; commissioner to the Vienna Exposition in 1873 and superintendent of American exhibitions; general executive officer of the New York state commission at the Centennial Exposition in Philadelphia in 1876; and commissioner of the World's Fair in New York in 1884. In 1864 he had resumed the post of publisher of the *Tribune* and was associated with Greeley in the publication of works issued by the firm. He himself was the author of a standard work of reference, *A Dictionary of Words and Phrases Used in Commerce* (1871).

[James Parton, *The Life of Horace Greeley* (1889); Frederic Hudson, *Journalism in the U. S. from 1690 to 1872* (1873); J. C. Derby, *Fifty Years Among Authors, Books, and Publishers* (1884); *N. Y. Tribune*, June 7, 1888.]
R. E. D.

McELROY, JOHN (May 14, 1782–Sept. 12, 1877), priest and missionary, was born in Enniskillen, County Fermanagh, Ireland. where as a barefooted boy, carrying his daily ration of turf, he obtained a scant education in a hedge-school. A gigantic fellow, wiry, and red faced, he spoke with the nasal twang of Ulster and committed treason with the Presbyterian United Irishmen. Like many of his associates who were "on the run after the troubles," McElroy found relief in emigration to America and took passage on a flax ship returning to Baltimore (1803). Within a year he was in business in the port of Georgetown, D. C., but he soon experienced a religious call and joined the partially restored Society of Jesus as a lay brother (1806). At Georgetown College he served as a buyer and bookkeeper for a number of years until Father Grassi, who recognized his natural cleverness and fine qualities, urged him to study for the priesthood and assisted him by patient tutoring in preparation for his theological studies. It was as a seminarian that he witnessed from the college windows the wanton burning of Washington with all the pent-up hatred of an Irish rebel. Although tempted to enlist, he remained in the cloister and was finally ordained by Archbishop Leonard Neale (May 21, 1817) whom strangely enough he prepared for death within a month. For a few years he remained at the college and attended nearby stations in Maryland and Virginia, when on the petition of Roger B. Taney and others, he was stationed as pastor at Frederick, Md. (1822–46). In this capacity he built a church at Liberty (1828), a new church of St. John at Frederick, an orphanage under the Sisters of Charity (1824), and established the first local free school which attracted Protestant children to such an extent that the ministers became exercised. In 1829 he founded St. John's Literary Institute or College which at one time rivaled Georgetown. Despite the lack of a thorough education, Father McElroy was winning fame as a forceful preacher and a retreat-master who gave missions throughout Virginia, Maryland, and Pennsylvania. In 1842 he was invited by Bishop Hughes to preach at the latter's diocesan synod, and he also conducted the first clerical retreat in the Boston diocese. In 1846, probably at the suggestion of Hughes who was called upon by the government for chaplains for the Mexican War, McElroy and Anthony Rey were commissioned chaplains. McElroy served in Taylor's army with considerable success. He won the soldiers' favor and became a living argument to the Mexicans that the war was not being waged against their Catholic religion.

After the war, McElroy was assigned to St. Mary's Church in north Boston by Bishop Fitzpatrick, who found its congregation factious. As the first Jesuit pastor in Boston, he virtually made St. Mary's a city church. In 1853 he bought the old jail lands for a college, but when the city council learned the purpose of the purchase it imposed impossible restrictions upon the property. After vexatious litigations, he purchased another site where the Church of the Immaculate Conception (1859) and Boston College (1860) were erected. As rector of the largest Catholic church he became an influential leader in Boston despite his age. A patron of the Sisters of Notre Dame, whom he introduced into the diocese (1849), he assisted them in their establishment at Lowell (1852), and in the foundation of an academy in Boston. In 1854 he gave the first retreat for the Hartford diocesan clergy. Archbishop Hughes called him to his death bed. At ordinations, episcopal consecrations, cornerstone ceremonies, and at anniversaries, he was a favorite preacher partly because of his almost legendary prestige, his favor with Irish-American bishops, his reputed refusal of three bishoprics, and, toward the end, as the world's oldest Jesuit both in point of years and of service in the Society. Sightless, he retired to Frederick, Md., where he finally succumbed to death, the victim of an accident in which he had broken several ribs.

[*Woodstock Letters,* vols. III (1874), V (1876), VI (1877), and X (1880); *Records of the Am. Cath. Hist. Soc. of Philadelphia,* vols. VI (1895), VIII (1897), XII (1901), and XXII (1911); Wm. Byrne, ed., *Hist. of the Cath. Ch. in the New Eng. States* (2 vols., 1899); J. G. Shea, *Hist. of the Cath. Ch. in the U. S.,* vols. III and IV (1890–92); *Sadliers' Cath. Directory,* 1878; *N. Y. Freeman's Jour.,* Sept. 22, 1877.] R. J. P.

McELROY, JOHN (Aug. 25, 1846–Oct. 12, 1929), soldier and editor, was born in Greenup County, Ky., the son of Robert McElroy, a builder of blast furnaces, and Mary (Henderson) McElroy, both of Scotch-Irish ancestry. He was given his mother's maiden name as a middle name but, throughout his career, he was known as John McElroy. His formal schooling was fragmentary. In 1855 his father died, his mother remarried, and young John, leaving home, went to St. Louis, where he became a printer's devil at the age of ten. Aided by sympathetic journeymen printers, he succeeded in setting the type for popular songs and sold the sheets on the streets of St. Louis. Later he moved to Chicago, where he enlisted in McClernand's body-guards after the outbreak of the Civil War. On Mar. 29, 1863, he enlisted in Company L of the 16th Illinois Cavalry and served through the various enlisted grades in that organization. On Jan. 3, 1864, after he had been appointed sergeant-major, he was captured by the Confederates at Jonesville, Va.

He spent more than a year in various Confederate prisons, chiefly at Andersonville, which had been established the previous November. His story of this camp, *Andersonville* (1879), is remarkable for its force and, aside from the compelling nature of its narrative, is a noteworthy document from a historical as well as a literary standpoint.

At the close of the Civil War, after release from Andersonville, he went to Ottawa, Ohio, where he studied pharmacy in a drugstore and in February 1866 married Elsie Pomeroy, the daughter of the owner. They had two children, a son and a daughter. Moving to Chicago in 1868, he became a reporter on the *Inter Ocean* and later became an editorial writer. His private reading was enormous, and his memory was of the photographic kind that imprints entire pages indelibly upon the mind. In 1874 he was called to Toledo, Ohio, by D. R. Locke (Petroleum V. Nasby), to be an editor of the *Toledo Blade*. He filled this post with distinction for ten years. Then he became an editor of the *National Tribune* of Washington and, upon the death of George Lemmon, editor and publisher. He continued to be active in this position until his death. Perhaps his most important literary contribution was his book, *Andersonville,* although Champ Clark was said to have considered the *Struggle for Missouri* (1909) the finest history of that state ever written. His writings were numerous, including the *History of Slavery in the United States* (1896), and the well-remembered "Si Klegg" series, among the most popular of which were *Si Klegg, his Development from a Raw Recruit to a Veteran* (1897) and *Further Haps and Mishaps to Si Klegg and Shorty* (1898). He also wrote numerous pamphlets and monographs. He became a national figure by his efforts to obtain aid for veterans of the Civil War, and his pocket and pen were unfailingly at their service. In 1901 he was senior vice-commander-in-chief of the Grand Army of the Republic, was many times commander of the Kit Carson post of that organization, was three times commander of the Department of the Potomac, and was a member of the legislative committee of the Grand Army of the Republic for fifteen years. He was a charter member of the Press Club in Washington and a member of the Board of Trade. Some years after the death of his first wife he married, on May 16, 1925, Isabel (Worrell) Ball, a member of the staff of his own newspaper, who attained some distinction as a newspaper writer and interested herself in many patriotic organizations and projects, especially in the details of the history and etiquette of the flag as a national emblem.

[Private papers of McElroy in the possession of his son, K. P. McElroy, Washington, D. C.; *Who's Who in America, 1928–29*; *Report of the Adjutant General of the State of Ill.*, vol. VIII (1867), p. 512; *Evening Star* (Washington), Oct. 12, 1929; *National Tribune* (Washington), Oct. 17, 1929.]

D. Y.

McELWAIN, WILLIAM HOWE (Feb. 11, 1867–Jan. 10, 1908), shoe-manufacturer, was born in Charlestown, Mass., the son of John Allen McElwain, a Baptist minister, and Susan Gilbert McElwain. Leaving high school at the age of sixteen, he obtained employment with George H. Burt, a shoe-manufacturer, as office boy and order clerk, at a salary of $100 a year. In the course of the next eleven years he acquired a thorough knowledge of the business in all its details; he also perceived the changes that must be made in the manufacture and the distribution of shoes to meet the changed conditions created by the use of new machinery and constantly increasing competition. Severing his connection with Burt, he borrowed $9,000, to which he added $1,500 of his own savings, and started a shoe factory at Bridgewater, Mass., in October 1894. At the end of nine months he bought out his partner. His purpose was to make a man's shoe, retailing for two dollars, that would have the attractive qualities of higher priced shoes and that could be manufactured profitably by the methods of quantity production. He had worked out for himself principles of scientific management, and he applied these principles to the manufacture and the distribution of his product. Thus he perfected the technique of quantity production at the moment when it was necessary to meet the new demand.

As a result of his boldness in putting his conclusions into effect, his business went ahead by leaps and bounds. Within five years he had established himself as a successful shoe-manufacturer; from 1902 to 1906 he built several new factories in Manchester, N. H.; for the year ending May 31, 1908, the production reached 5,716,955 pairs of shoes, the largest output of any shoe factory in the United States. This volume was attained by what McElwain called the "sheet system," which, based upon a searching analysis of every operation, consisted of a time schedule which controlled strictly the work of the factory. The application of scientific methods in the field of production was followed by a study of the methods by which jobbers placed their orders, as a result of which seasonal employment was eliminated and the cost of manufacture reduced; and by the establishment of a labor department to determine with accuracy the piece rate for each operation. Working in a period when the principles of scientific management as formulated by

F. W. Taylor were but little known, McElwain, without knowledge of Taylor's work, created a model large-scale industrial organization based on those principles. The intensity of his labors for thirteen years in building up and perfecting his business precluded his giving very much attention to anything else. He died suddenly at the age of forty, following an operation for appendicitis, and was survived by his wife, Helen (Merriam) McElwain, and four children.

[H. G. Pearson, *Wm. Howe McElwain* (1917); L. D. Brandeis, *Business: A Profession* (1925); *Shoe and Leather Reporter*, Jan. 16, 1908; *Boot and Shoe Recorder*, Jan. 15, 1908; *Shoe and Leather Facts*, Feb. 1908; *Boston Transcript*, Jan. 10, 1908.] H. G. P.

McENERY, SAMUEL DOUGLAS (May 28, 1837–June 28, 1910), jurist, governor of Louisiana, United States senator, the son of Henry O'Neil and Caroline H. (Douglas) McEnery, was born in Monroe, Ouachita Parish, La. His father, originally from Ireland, emigrated to Virginia when quite young, and after living there for some years, removed to Louisiana in 1835 and settled in Monroe, where he became a planter and for eight years was register of the Land Office. His knowledge of land matters enabled him to give valuable information regarding locations for settlement to immigrants from other states, and in this way he contributed greatly to the settlement of northern Louisiana. Samuel attended the public schools of Monroe, Spring Hill College in Mobile, Ala., the United States Naval Academy, the University of Virginia, and in 1859 graduated from the State and National Law School at Poughkeepsie, N. Y. For a year following his graduation he practised law at Marysville, Mo. Soon after the outbreak of the Civil War he entered the Confederate service as a member of a Louisiana volunteer company known as the Pelican Grays. In 1862 he was commissioned a lieutenant under General Magruder in Virginia. Later he was placed in charge of an instruction camp at Trenton, La., and here it seems he was when the war ended.

After the war McEnery returned to Monroe, was admitted to the Louisiana bar in 1866, and began to practise his profession, but while he was successful as a lawyer, the bar proved only a stepping-stone to his political career. A democrat in politics, he was in 1879 nominated by that party for the office of lieutenant-governor on a ticket with L. A. Wiltz for governor. They were elected and upon the death of Wiltz in October 1881, McEnery succeeded him as governor. He was reëlected governor in 1884 but four years later was defeated for the office by Francis T. Nicholls, who appointed him an associate justice of the state supreme court for the term of twelve years. In 1892, during the struggle for the recharter of the Louisiana Lottery, he was the candidate of the lottery wing of the Democratic party for governor but was defeated by the anti-lottery candidate. On May 28, 1896, he was elected to the United States Senate for the term beginning Mar. 4, 1897, to succeed N. C. Blanchard, and by reëlection served until his death in 1910.

McEnery was a well-proportioned man, with a ruddy face and keen blue eyes. He walked with a slight stoop or forward bend of neck and head. During his later years he was troubled by deafness. His legal opinions are said to indicate an impatience with detail but a thorough knowledge of principles; his messages and papers while governor, repressed and condensed to the point of dryness, are not marked by the literary distinction which takes such matters out of the ordinary. His greatest gift, perhaps, was his ability to handle men. He kept no diary and left no reminiscences. After a brief illness he died in New Orleans, where he was buried in Metairie Cemetery. He had married, on June 27, 1878, Elizabeth Phillips of Monroe, La.

[*Biog. Dir. Am. Cong.* (1928); *Who's Who in America*, 1910–11; 127 *La. Reports*, xxvii–xxix; Alcée Fortier, *Louisiana* (1914), vol. II; *Biog. and Hist. Memoirs of La.* (1892), vol. II; *Biog. Sketches of Louisiana's Governors from D'Iberville to McEnery, By a Louisianaise* (1885); *Senate Doc. 871*, 61 Cong., 3 Sess.; New Orleans newspapers for June 29, 1910; information as to certain facts from McEnery's niece, Mrs. Henry Baumgarten, New Orleans, La.] M. J. W.

McENTEE, JERVIS (July 14, 1828–Jan. 27, 1891), landscape painter, born at Rondout, N. Y., the eldest child of James S. and Sarah Jane (Goetcheus) McEntee, came of Irish and Huguenot stock. His father, an engineer, had charge of the construction of the Delaware & Hudson canal and the terminal docks at Rondout. Jervis McEntee received his early education at Clinton Institute, Clinton, N. Y., and soon after leaving this school he became (1850–51) a pupil of Frederick E. Church in New York City. In 1854 he married Gertrude, daughter of the Rev. Thomas Jefferson Sawyer. For three or four years he engaged in business at Rondout, but without much success, and in 1858, at the age of thirty, he definitely turned to art and opened a studio in the metropolis. In 1859, with his friend Sanford R. Gifford [*q.v.*], he went to Europe, visited all the leading art galleries, and sketched from nature in Italy and Switzerland. In 1861 his "Melancholy Days" was bought by James A. Suydam, N. A., who left it to the National Academy. McEntee was elected an Academician the same year.

As a rule he spent his summers and autumns at Rondout, whence he made frequent painting excursions to the nearby Catskills. A place especially endeared to him was Lanesville, where many of his best studies were made. He soon became noted for his winter and autumn scenes, which were his best productions and have a marked poetic character. Tuckerman found in his landscapes "a subtle feeling, a latent sentiment, and a delicate touch . . . rarely found even among the most skilful scenic limners" (*post*, p. 545); but Isham, less lenient, wrote that he "had no thorough training, and his works sometimes show the lack of it" (*post*, p. 245). It is perhaps just to say that he shared the technical weaknesses as well as the engaging personal qualities of the men of the Hudson River school. Their work, in spite of its lack of substance and depth, has a historic significance. In the eyes of their compatriots, at least, it was peculiarly winning because of its native ingenuousness.

McEntee had many warm friends and ardent patrons in the New York of the late nineteenth century. At the Paris Exposition of 1867 he exhibited two landscapes. At the Centennial Exposition, Philadelphia, 1876, he was represented by eight pictures. He exhibited also at the Royal Academy, London, 1872, and at the Paris Exposition of 1878. His "Eastern Sunset Sky" was in the Thomas B. Clarke collection, and his "November Days" was in the J. Taylor Johnston collection. The "Autumn Landscape with Figures," from the Borden collection, is in the Metropolitan Museum of Art, New York. A work of dramatic interest, outside the customary range of his subjects, was "The Danger Signal." In a driving snow-storm a passenger train has been brought to a sudden stop by a red lantern swung by a track-walker in the foreground. The snow lies in drifts on the track, and the glare of the locomotive headlight illuminates the wintry scene with strong effect. McEntee died at his old homestead at Rondout, at the age of sixty-two. He left no children. His wife had died some twelve years before him.

[The *Kingston* (N. Y.) *Daily Freeman*, Jan. 27, 1891; H. T. Tuckerman, *Book of the Artists* (1867); Samuel Isham, *The Hist. of Am. Painting* (1905); *Bull. of the Metropolitan Museum, N. Y.*, Apr. 1913; *Internat. Exhibition, 1876: Official Cat.*, Part II; *Cat. of the Thos. B. Clarke Coll. of Am. Pictures* (1891); Sadakichi Hartmann, *A Hist. of Am. Art* (1902), vol. I; G. W. Sheldon, *Am. Painters* (1881); *N. Y. Times*, Jan. 28, 1891.] W. H. D.

McFARLAND, JOHN THOMAS (Jan. 2, 1851–Dec. 22, 1913), Methodist Episcopal minister and educator, was born at Mount Vernon, Ind. His parents were Sylvanas and Elizabeth (Ginn) McFarland, pioneer settlers, who later moved to the prairies of Iowa, where he spent his boyhood on a farm. His father was of a deeply religious nature, and the son used to tell of his own conversion, when a college junior, after an earnest conversation with his parent in an old farm wagon on a country road. He studied at Iowa Wesleyan University, but received the degree of A.B. at Simpson College, Indianola, Iowa, in 1873. In that year he was ordained as a Methodist minister and began to serve a rural Iowa charge. Ambitious, however, for thorough ministerial preparation, he soon entered Boston University School of Theology, graduating in 1878. He had already married, in 1873, Mary Burt, of Mount Pleasant, Iowa, a college mate. They had two sons and a daughter. For years he devoted himself to the round of pastoral duty—in Iowa till 1880, and in Peoria, Ill., from 1880 to 1882. During the latter year he was called to Iowa Wesleyan University as vice-president, succeeding in 1884 to the presidency, which he held until 1891. The institution was limited in resources, but he somewhat enlarged its physical equipment and liberalized and strengthened its cultural courses. Subsequently he served as pastor of three large churches—Grace Church, Jacksonville, Ill. (1891–96), New York Avenue Church, Brooklyn, N. Y. (1897–99), and the First Church, Topeka, Kan. (1899–1904).

Always a keen student of philosophy and educational theory, he had success in applying the principles derived from these to the training of the young people of his churches. In 1904, he was elected editor of the Sunday-school literature of the Methodist Episcopal Church. He inherited an elaborate system of Biblical and religious lesson periodicals, which had wide circulation but which reflected the scholarship as well as the pedagogical theories and methods of a former generation. With patience and courage he devoted himself to the task of reforming the lesson material in such a way as to bring it into harmony with the advances in pedagogy, archeology, and Biblical criticism. As signs of new life in the periodicals began to appear, the editor became the object of bitter attacks from conservatives in his own denomination who accused him of "putting poison in the milk." He persevered in his course, however, with serene confidence in its essential rectitude. At the General Conference of 1912 an attempt was made by the conservative ministers and laymen to censure him, and, if possible, to prevent his reëlection as editor. His dignified speech in defense of his course is one of the high points in his career (see *Daily Christian Advocate*, Minneapolis, Minn., May 23, 1912) and is a landmark in the history of the development of progressive thinking in the denomination. The result was his complete vindication and reëlection. Eventually the strain of incessant labor, coupled with the hostility of his enemies, wore him down. His health gave way; partial paralysis set in; yet he toiled at his task, and gave to the churches the first complete system of lessons scientifically adapted to the needs and capacities of the developing mind of childhood, adolescence, youth, and maturity. Other Protestant churches acknowledged his leadership and adopted or imitated the system which he had worked out. After the summer of 1913 he continued to work, though some of his bodily powers were seriously impaired, and in December at Maplewood, N. J., he died.

His writings were largely fugitive editorials in Sunday-school periodicals, but some of the convictions for which he stood he embodied in *Preservation vs. the Rescue of the Child* (1906), and in *The Book and the Child* (1907). The vein of genuine poetry that lay deep in his fine nature found occasional expression in verse, a volume of which, *Poems,* was published in 1914. The spiritual yearnings of his nature are seen in his *Etchings of the Master* (1909). He was one of the editors of *The Encyclopedia of Sunday Schools and Religious Education* (3 vols., 1915).

[Memoir of McFarland by L. H. Murlin, in the *Jour. of the Twenty-seventh Delegated General Conference of the M. E. Ch.,* 1916; *M. E. Ch. Official Record, Kan. Conference,* 1914; *Who's Who in America,* 1912–13; *Christian Advocate* (N. Y.), Dec. 25, 1913; *Northwestern Christian Advocate* (Chicago), Dec. 31, 1913; *N. Y. Tribune,* Dec. 23, 1913.] J. R. J.

McFARLAND, SAMUEL GAMBLE (Dec. 11, 1830–Apr. 25, 1897), a Presbyterian clergyman who served in Siam first as a missionary and later in the educational department of the Siamese government, was born in Washington County, Pa., the son of William and Mary (McKenahan) McFarland and the grandson of Samuel McFarland who emigrated from the North of Ireland to Pennsylvania about 1793. He graduated from Washington (now Washington and Jefferson) College in 1857 with the degree of A.B., studied theology in the Western Theological Seminary, Pittsburgh, 1857–60, and was ordained by the Presbytery of Washington (Pa.) and commissioned for Siam in April 1860. On the 3rd of May following he married Jane E. Hays, daughter of John Hays of Canonsburg, Pa. To this union four children were born.

McFarland reached Bangkok Sept. 15, 1860. After a year of language study he was assigned, together with Rev. Daniel McGilvary [*q.v.*], to open at Petchaburi the first station outside the capital. It fell to his lot to construct the early buildings for the mission, in fulfillment of which task he found it necessary not only to draw plans but to supervise the brick-making and lumber mill and to direct the workmen item by item in the process of construction. When funds failed for the school building he appealed to the Siamese who were sympathetic with the work and in response received half the required amount from the king and the balance from princes and nobles. The first Siamese to be licensed to the gospel ministry was trained by him. McFarland became a thorough scholar in the Siamese language, mastering both the idiom and the pronunciation so that in its oral use he was as proficient as an educated native. His versatility is further shown in the publication (1876) of a Siamese hymnbook, the first to include tunes. In this undertaking it was necessary for him to teach the translator each separate tune to enable him to provide the correct meter; he then supervised the making of the plates in the United States, and finally printed the book at Petchaburi on a wooden press which he himself had made.

His acquaintance with the language and his achievement in his school work commended him to King Chulalongkorn, who was then purposing to initiate the work of education by the government. As the first step in the realization of his plan, he appointed McFarland, in 1878, principal of the proposed royal school for princes and sons of nobles. To accept this appointment McFarland resigned his commission as missionary. His new task involved the laying out of a curriculum together with a standard of grades and examinations, the enlistment of a faculty and provision for future training of teachers, and the adaptation and translation of suitable textbooks. All this had to be accomplished despite the opposition of a conservative council which was imbued with reactionism against the progressive policies of the king. He succeeded, however, by the exercise of tact and a sympathetic understanding of his co-workers, who at the same time had confidence in his wisdom. Sharing the king's vision of a future national system of education, in developing the royal school he laid the foundations for the system of universal compulsory education which was eventually established. On account of broken health, however, he was obliged to resign, in 1896, before the scheme was completed. He died in Canonsburg, Pa., the following year.

The literary work accredited to him includes *An English-Siamese Dictionary* (1865), which went through a number of editions; the hymnbook previously mentioned; translations into Siamese of the Pentateuch, the Minor Prophets, the Westminster Shorter Catechism, and a Bible textbook; together with original works, written in Siamese, on Church history, Christian evidences, botany, geology, bookkeeping; and numerous sermons and tracts.

[*Biog. and Hist. Cat. of Washington and Jefferson Coll.* (1889); *Commemorative Biog. Record of Washington County, Pa.* (1893); J. F. McFarland, *20th Century Hist. of the City of Washington and Washington County, Pa.* (1910); Daniel McGilvary, *A Half Century Among the Siamese and the Lāo* (1912); G. B. McFarland, *Hist. Sketch of Protestant Missions in Siam 1828–1928* (1928); S. S. Gilson, "Thirty-six Years in Siam," *Presbyterian Banner* (Pittsburgh), Feb. 17, 1897; *Pittsburgh Post and Pittsburg Press,* Apr. 27, 1897; biographical notes by McFarland's son, George B. McFarland, M.D., in Presbyterian Foreign Missions Library, New York.] G. H. F.

McFARLAND, THOMAS BARD (Apr. 19, 1828–Sept. 16, 1908), California jurist, was born in the Cumberland Valley, near Mercersburg, Pa., the son of John and Eliza (Parker) McFarland. His paternal ancestry was Scotch-Irish, his maternal English. Little is known of his education until his graduation in 1846 from Marshall College at Mercersburg (now Franklin and Marshall College at Lancaster). He then moved to Chambersburg and began the study of law under the tutelage of Robert M. Bard, a relative as well as a distinguished lawyer. He was admitted to the bar in 1849 and immediately made plans to join one of the numerous caravans then making its way across the plains to the Pacific Coast. He reached California in September 1850, and influenced by the success of others, staked for himself a small claim in the gold region. This venture proved so successful that he followed mining for a period of three years in Eldorado, Placer, Nevada, and Yuba counties, before beginning the practice of law in Nevada City in 1853. In 1856 he served as a member of the California General Assembly. On Nov. 20, 1861, at Nevada City, he was married to Susie Briggs, a native of New York. In the same year, 1861, he was elected to the judgeship of the fourteenth judicial district, at that time consisting of Nevada County. Two years later, his term having ended prematurely because of changes in the constitution, he was reëlected to the judgeship and given an enlarged judicial district including both Nevada and Placer counties. He served the full term of six years in this capacity, resuming private practice in 1870 in Sacramento. From 1874 to 1878 he served as the register of the United States Land Office in that city, though he accepted the appointment with reluctance and resigned within two months after his reappointment for a second term. During his residence in Sacramento he was also a member of the board of education.

McFarland served as a member of the convention which in 1878–79 formulated the constitution of the state of California, but he consistently opposed numerous provisions of the constitution itself and the adoption of that instrument by the people. Considering the influences active in the convention, which to many of that day seemed exceedingly radical, it is not hard to understand his opposition. In December 1882 he was appointed by Governor Perkins judge of the superior court of Sacramento County, and in 1884 he was elected by a large majority to succeed himself. Nominated in 1886 by the State Republican Convention, he was elected justice of the supreme court of California in the same year. He served in this capacity twenty-two years, having been reëlected in 1898 for a second term, which was cut short by his death in 1908. As a young man McFarland had been an ardent Whig, but with the election of Lincoln he had transferred his allegiance to the Republican party. This he served with intense loyalty for the remainder of his life. He was regarded as a man of scholarly attainments in his profession, of high personal integrity, kindly and genial, with an enormous capacity for work. He was a member of the board of trustees of Stanford University, for which he had been chosen by Senator Stanford, from the foundation of the University until his death. He died at his home in San Francisco at eighty years of age.

[*Who's Who in America,* 1908–09; O. T. Shuck, *Hist. of the Bench and Bar of Cal.* (rev. ed., 1901); *The Bay of San Francisco . . . A Hist.* (1892), vol. I; *Cal. Blue Book,* 1907; 154 *Cal. Reports,* 807–09; G. O. Seilhamer, *The Bard Family* (1908); *San Francisco Chronicle,* Sept. 16, 17, 1908.] R. G. C—d.

MACFARLANE, CHARLES WILLIAM (Nov. 5, 1850–May 15, 1931), engineer, builder, economist, was born in Philadelphia, Pa., of Scotch ancestry, the youngest son of David and Catherine (Macfarlane) Macfarlane. After preparatory work in the Philadelphia Central High School, he attended Lafayette College for a year, then transferred to Lehigh University, from which institution he received the degree of civil engineer in 1876. He remained at Lehigh University for postgraduate work in analytical chemistry, later entering the employment of a Philadelphia manufacturing concern, William Sellers & Company. His first two years were spent at manual labor in the shops, after which apprenticeship he served as superintendent of the foundry department for seven years. During these days he spent his evenings in study and writing, particularly on *Canons of Criticism* (1885). Eventually he entered business for himself. His operations were chiefly confined to the building of residences in West Philadelphia; he was his own architect, supervisor of building operations, and business manager. When he had attained a small fortune he decided to retire from business and to devote his time to intellectual pursuits and in 1888–89 he engaged in graduate study at the University of Pennsylvania, emphasizing philosophy, history, and economics. He then continued his studies in Germany, receiving the degree of Ph.D. at Freiburg, Baden, in 1893. The remainder of his life was spent in study and writing.

During his collegiate years at Bethlehem, Macfarlane made the acquaintance of Kathleen Selfridge, a gifted singer, whom he married on Mar. 8, 1883. He and his wife spent most of their lives in Philadelphia, but long visits were made to Europe, especially to France. He died in Philadelphia after years of failing health. His chief theoretical work in economics was *Value and Distribution,* published in 1899 and republished in 1911. It was an exposition of the Austrian School, attempting a reconciliation of this new approach with the older one of the British classical economists. His best-known work in applied economics was *The Economic Basis of an Enduring Peace* (1918) which was chiefly devoted to a discussion of the distribution of the coal lands of Germany, France, and Belgium. His other works include: *Pennsylvania Paper Currency* (1896); *The Three Primary Laws of Social Evolution* (1902); *The Place of Philosophy and Economics in the Curriculum of a Modern University* (1913); *Economic Interpretation of Early Roman History* (1915); *Les Défenses du Sanglier* (1915); and numerous small essays. In 1893 he published *The Ultimate Standard of Value,* translated from the German of the Austrian economist, Eugen Böhm von Bawerk. Several of his monographs on economic subjects were published by the American Economic Association and the American Academy of Political and Social Science. The later years of his life he devoted to the collection of material for an economic history of Rome. Unable to finish the work, he directed that his library and source material be given to Lehigh University with the understanding that this project be brought to completion. He also endowed at that institution chairs of philosophy and economics. In February 1931, a few months before his death, several of his works were collected by his wife and published under the title *Science and Literature.*

[See the Foreword by Isaac Pennypacker in *Science and Lit.*; *Who's Who in America,* 1926–27; *Jour. of Commerce* (Phila.), May 23, 1931; *Lehigh Alumni Bull.,* Oct. 1931; *N. Y. Times, Pub. Ledger* (Phila.), May 17, 1931. There is some doubt about the date of Macfarlane's birth. The date given here appears on his tombstone and is believed by his widow to be correct.]

S. H. P.

MACFARLANE, ROBERT (Apr. 23, 1815–Dec. 20, 1883), dyer, writer on scientific subjects, was born in Rutherglen, near Glasgow, Scotland. His educational advantages in youth were limited. He learned the art of dyeing at his father's works in Paisley; but, dissatisfied with the prospect of advancement in his native country, he emigrated at the age of twenty to America and in 1840 he settled in the city of Albany, N. Y. The scientific cast of his mind declared itself gradually and in 1846, with Joel Munsell, he began the publication of the *Mechanics' Mirror.* To this periodical he contributed a series of scientific papers which brought him a reputation as an expositor of mechanical principles and opened a larger field to him. Called in 1848 to the editorial chair of the *Scientific American,* in New York City, he devoted seventeen years to the journal, becoming a recognized authority on mechanical devices and kindred subjects. He was also an acceptable lecturer in the field. In 1851 he published a *History of Propellers and Steam Navigation with Biographical Sketches of the Early Inventors,* which ran into several editions. In the preface to this work, he stated his leading design in its preparation: "The arrangement and description of many devices which have been invented to propel vessels, in order to prevent many ingenious men from wasting their time, talents and money on such projects."

Macfarlane's connection with the *Scientific American* embraced a period of the Civil War in which the attention of the country was fixed on the machinery of marine warfare, in particular on the competing types of armored vessels; and his journal was among the stoutest champions of effective naval construction. Threatened with failure of eyesight, he resigned his editorship, and, returning to Albany, purchased a dyeing establishment. He had not lost his interest in the industry and in 1860 had published *A Practical Treatise on Dyeing and Calico-Printing.* During his years in America his remembrance of Scotland and the fascination of Scottish history and romance had kept their hold on his mind. His birthplace was not remote from the ancient possessions of the clan Macfarlane. He returned twice to his native land, and there found employment for his pen in sketches of travel, which appeared, under the name "Rutherglen," in the *Scottish American Journal.* If Scottish antiquities and scenery appealed to him, hardly less did the story of Scottish emigration to America. In Albany he was active in the St. Andrew's Society, serving at one time as its president, and was president of the Burns Club. Late in life he removed to Brooklyn, where he died. His wife was Anna Garth Macfarlane.

[A. J. Parker, *Landmarks of Albany County, N. Y.* (1897), pt. 3; G. R. Howell and others, *Bi-Centennial Hist. of Albany: Hist. of the County of Albany* (1886); Mrs. C. M. Little, *Hist. of the Clan MacFarlane* (1893), pp. 227–30; Peter Ross, *The Scot in America* (1896); *Sci. American,* Jan. 5, 1884; *Albany Evening Jour.,* Dec. 20, 1883; *Brooklyn Daily Eagle,* Dec. 21, 1883.] R. E. D.

McFAUL, JAMES AUGUSTINE (June 6, 1850–June 16, 1917), Roman Catholic prelate, son of James and Mary (Heffernan) McFaul, was born in the village of Larne, County Antrim, Ireland. At the age of six months, he was brought to New York by his parents, who soon afterward settled permanently at Bound Brook, N. J. As a child, he attended the local schools of Weston and Millstone, journeying to New Brunswick or Raritan for mass and religious instruction under Benedictine missionaries. Through the influence of the Benedictines, he was sent to St. Vincent's College, Beatty, Pa., and later completed his classical education at St. Francis Xavier College, New York. Having studied theology at Seton Hall College, South Orange, N. J., he was ordained, May 26, 1877, by Archbishop Corrigan [*q.v.*]. He served as curate at Paterson, Orange, St. Patrick's Church in Jersey City, St. Peter's Church in New Brunswick, and finally at St. Mary's Church, Trenton, where he was under the distinguished Vicar General, Anthony Smith. St. Mary's Church was selected as a cathedral by Bishop M. J. O'Farrell, when, in 1881, he was named first bishop of the newly created diocese of Trenton. Hence the young assistant and secretary came into intimate contact with his ordinary, who appreciated his zeal and mental equipment. In 1884 McFaul was promoted to the rectorship of the Star of the Sea Church at Long Branch, where he paid off a heavy mortgage and built St. Michael's Church in the neighboring town of Elberon. Called back as pastor of the cathedral in 1890, he acted as the bishop's secretary and chancellor, and in 1892 became vicar general. On Bishop O'Farrell's death, he served as administrator and was soon appointed to the see, being consecrated by Archbishop Corrigan on Oct. 18, 1894.

Bishop McFaul proved a capable leader who gained the whole-hearted support of his priests and people. During his rule the diocese advanced rapidly, the number of priests, teaching and nursing sisters, and churches and chapels greatly increasing. About twenty-five parochial schools were erected, largely because of his insistence on Catholic education. In addition to five academies, he gave unstinted patronage to Mount St. Mary's College, Plainfield, which cared for the higher education of women. Interested in the newer immigrant groups, he exerted himself to provide churches for the Poles and Hungarians and especially for the Italians, who presented a discouraging problem. Deeply concerned in social welfare work, he gave close attention to two hospitals, to Morris Hall (the home for the aged at Lawrenceville), and to St. Michael's Orphan Asylum and Industrial School at Hopewell. His interests, however, were not bounded by his diocese.

An active friend of Irish societies and the Home-Rule movement, he served as the arbiter of differences between two factions of the Ancient Order of Hibernians, welding them together into a united fraternal society (1897–98). He was equally successful in organizing the American Federation of the Catholic Societies with a total membership of about 2,000,000, though his inspiration failed to make this organization as effective in Catholic social and civic action as might have been anticipated. Liberal in spirit, he took an active part in municipal and state reforms, supported labor, and served on the state tuberculosis commission. As a Catholic controversialist and lecturer, he was able and courageous, but popular in tone. An energetic, self-denying man, he labored to the end despite a year of ill health. In 1916, *Pastoral Letters, Addresses, and Other Writings of the Rt. Rev. James A. McFaul,* edited by J. J. Powers, was published.

[W. T. Leahy, *The Cath. Ch. of the Diocese of Trenton* (1907); J. M. Flynn, *The Cath. Ch. in N. J.* (1904); J. H. Fox, *A Century of Catholicity in Trenton, N. J.* (1907); T. F. McGrath, *Hist. of the Ancient Order of Hibernians* (1898); annual Cath. directories; *Am. Cath. Who's Who,* 1911; *Who's Who in America,* 1916–17; *Daily State Gazette* (Trenton, N. J.), May 24, June 18–22, 1917; *N. Y. Times,* June 17, 1917; *Messenger of the Sacred Heart,* Apr. 1910; *Ill. Cath. Hist. Rev.* (later *Mid-America*), 1927–29.] R. J. P.

McFERRIN, JOHN BERRY (June 15, 1807–May 10, 1887), Methodist clergyman, was born in Rutherford County, Tenn., and throughout his entire life was a citizen of that state. Emigrating to America from Ireland about 1750, the McFerrins were a family of fighters. The grandfather of John served during the American Revolution; his father, James, saw service under General Jackson in the War of 1812, and attained the rank of colonel in the Indian wars; through his mother, Jane Campbell Berry, he was directly related to the Col. William Campbell [*q.v.*] of King's Mountain celebrity. Their militant characteristics John McFerrin manifested throughout his long career as a leader in the affairs of his denomination. Never was he more at home than when under the fire of criticism or questions on the floor of public assemblies. Of large frame, heavy features, standing square on his feet, he was a typical son of the West. Although of Presbyterian stock, with his father he was converted under the preaching of a Methodist circuit rider and, also with his father, entered the Methodist ministry. He was never enrolled in an institution of higher learning, being of that group of pioneers who felt that a call to preach did not mean a call to go to school to get ready to preach.

In 1825 he was admitted to the Tennessee Conference on trial and spent two years as a circuit rider. Ordained deacon in 1827, he was appointed missionary to the Cherokee Indians in the territory where Chattanooga and Fort Oglethorpe now stand. He was ordained elder in 1829, and was a stationed preacher and presiding elder until 1840, when he became editor of the *Southwestern Christian Advocate,* Nashville. This paper he conducted with ability for eighteen years. In the meantime the Methodist Church divided over the question of slavery and McFerrin, who had been a delegate to the General Conference of 1844, was also a delegate to the Louisville Convention of 1845 at which the Methodist Episcopal Church, South, was organized. In 1858 he reluctantly relinquished his editorship to take charge, as book agent, of the publishing interests of his denomination, continuing in this office until 1866, though during the Civil War he also had charge of all the Methodist missionary work in the Army of the Tennessee. At the General Conference of 1866 he was elected secretary of the board of domestic missions; four years later the domestic and foreign boards were consolidated, and McFerrin directed the work of both until 1878. During his term of service he cleared away a depressing indebtedness, yet, because he lacked the faculties and sympathies necessary for successful missionary propagation, this period gave him less satisfaction than others in his long official career. The nine years from 1878 to 1887, when he again served as book agent, proved the climax of his labors. As a result of the war and bad management, the Methodist publishing house was in an almost hopeless struggle with debt. Shaping a plan of bond sales similar to that in use at the time by the federal government, he raised within a remarkably short time $350,000, and before his death saw every obligation met, every bond refunded, and the publishing house flourishing again. His business ability is indicated by the fact that he owned real estate and bank stock, and was at one time president of a street railway company.

In the midst of his many activities he found time to write *History of Methodism in Tennessee* (1869–73), a three-volume work which gives a first-hand account of life in Tennessee during the first quarter of the nineteenth century. He was twice married: first, in 1833, to Almyra Avery Probart; second, in 1855, to Cynthia Tennessee McGavock. The second wife and four children survived his death.

[O. P. Fitzgerald, *John B. McFerrin* (1888); *Christian Advocate* (Nashville), May 14, 21, 28, 1887; *General Minutes of the Methodist Episcopal Church, South* (1887); S. A. Steel, *Eminent Men I Met Along the Sunny Road* (1925).] R. W. G.

MACGAHAN, JANUARIUS ALOYSIUS (June 12, 1844–June 9, 1878), war correspondent, son of James and Esther (Dempsey) MacGahan, both of Irish descent, was born in Perry County, Ohio, on a small farm near the home of his cousin, Philip Sheridan [*q.v.*]. During his boyhood his father died, but the widowed mother managed to keep her children in school for some years, and after a period in St. Louis as a bookkeeper MacGahan resolved to go abroad to improve his general education and to continue his study of law. He lived in Brussels, in Paris, and in Germany, acquiring several languages, and on the outbreak of the Franco-Prussian War he obtained, partly through the influence of General Sheridan, an appointment as a special correspondent for the *New York Herald.* At once his adventurous disposition and his facility as a vivid descriptive writer with an eye for drama, manifested themselves. He had found his vocation. He followed the campaign of General Bourbaki, returned to Paris in time to witness the opening of the Commune, was imprisoned by the Versailles troops, and released through the efforts of the American minister. In the course of the next eight years he saw service in places widely distant from each other. During a summer in the Crimea he became a favorite with the Czar's court and conceived a warm liking for Russia. He "covered" the Caucasus expedition of General Sherman (1872) and the sittings of the Alabama Claims tribunal at Geneva.

There followed his ride into the desert of Central Asia (1873), which, according to Eugene Schuyler [*q.v.*], American secretary of legation at St. Petersburg, was "spoken of everywhere ... as by far the most wonderful thing that ever had been done there" (Schuyler, *Turkistan,* 1885, I, 66). He defied the Russian embargo on newspaper men to find the expedition sent out under General Kauffmann to reduce the Khanate of Khiva. Cossacks pursued him almost a thousand miles. After twenty-nine days, with two attendants who could not understand his language, sometimes forced to wade to his knees in sand and several times "lost," he reached the camp. As an American he was allowed to stay; as a *molodyetz,* a hero, he instantly became popular. With the army he remained through the campaign against Khiva and the war with the Turkomans. At Khiva he met General Skobelev and they became affectionate friends. Later in the same year he reported the *Virginius* complications in Cuba; after that, the Carlist campaign in the Pyrenees (1874); and then, the expedition to the Arctic of the barque *Pandora* (1875) promoted by the younger James Gordon Bennett [*q.v.*].

Back in London, he found the Eastern Question the absorbing subject of the day. Rumors of the *bashi-bazouk* massacres in Bulgaria filtered through Europe. The opportunity for MacGahan's greatest service came when the *Daily News* sent him to make an independent investigation and write the exact truth. His Bulgarian letters of July and August 1876 wrought a great change in British sentiment and did much to produce the political reaction which made war inevitable between Russia and Turkey. Since that war gave Bulgaria her independence, he came to be known in that country as "the Liberator." For his London paper he followed the campaign, much of the time as a comrade of Skobelev, rendering distinguished service even when almost fully disabled. After the fall of Plevna, he went to Constantinople to nurse Francis Vinton Greene [*q.v.*] through typhoid, only himself to fall a victim to typhus. The burial was at Pera, with Skobelev as a mourner. In 1884, on the initiative of the General Assembly of his native state, his body was brought to America on a United States cruiser. A monument now marks his grave near New Lexington, to which the Bulgarian envoys at Washington make ceremonial visits at times.

At Yalta, MacGahan had met Barbara Nicholavna Elagin, of an ancient Russian family, whom he married in Paris in 1872. They had one son. MacGahan was very popular among his fellow correspondents and with army officers, who respected him both for his personal qualities and his professional abilities. His most important writings appeared in book form as follows: *Campaigning on the Oxus and the Fall of Khiva* (1874); *Under the Northern Lights* (1876), on the cruise of the *Pandora*; *The Turkish Atrocities in Bulgaria* (1876), and articles in *War Correspondence of the Daily News* (2 vols., London, 1877–78).

[Archibald Forbes, *Souvenirs of Some Continents* (1885); F. L. Bullard, *Famous War Correspondents* (1914); *Ohio Archaeol. and Hist. Quart.*, Apr.–July 1912; *N. Y. Herald,* June 11, 1878; *Daily News* (London), June 11, 12, 1878; references in the works of Frederick Boyle, Frederic Villiers, Frank Millet, and Gen. F. V. Greene; documentary material furnished by the family.]

F. L. B.

McGARVEY, JOHN WILLIAM (Mar. 1, 1829–Oct. 6, 1911), minister of the Disciples of Christ, educator, and writer, was born in Hopkinsville, Ky., where his father, John, a native of Ireland, conducted a small dry-goods business. His mother, whose maiden name was Sallie Ann Thomson, born near Georgetown, Ky., was of Virginia stock. After her husband's death in 1833, she married Dr. G. F. Saltonstall, and when John was about ten years old the family moved to Tremont, Tazewell County, Ill. Here he received a good preparatory training, and in 1847 entered Bethany College, graduating in 1850 with high rank as a classical scholar. Going to Fayette, Mo., where his family was then living, he conducted a boys' school for about a year. In September 1851 he was ordained by the Fayette church of the Disciples, and afterwards preached for that and neighboring churches, until, in February 1853, he accepted a call to Dover, Lafayette County, Mo. On Mar. 23, he married Ottie F. Hix of Fayette.

During the next nine years he became widely known throughout Missouri as a man of scholarly tastes, interested in education, alive with missionary zeal, and keen for theological controversy. He secured funds to establish a school in Dover and conducted it for a time, made preaching tours, and debated publicly with representatives of other denominations. At the time of the Civil War he was one of the ministers of his order who signed the circular "Concerning the Duties of Christians in this Conflict," which declared that Christians ought not to go to war. In 1862 he was called to Lexington, Ky.; and the following year he published *A Commentary on Acts of Apostles with a Revised Version of the Text.* Several other commentaries by him appeared later. In 1865 he was made professor of sacred history in the College of the Bible affiliated with Kentucky University, but for a number of years still carried on his pastoral work. His insistence upon larger support for the College brought him into conflict with President J. B. Bowman [*q.v.*] of the University and in 1873 he was dismissed. Two years later he was reinstated. Finally, in 1877, the College of the Bible became an independent institution, with McGarvey as professor, although it used the University classrooms and ultimately erected buildings on the University campus. From 1895 until his death McGarvey was president of the College.

Over a long period he was one of the most

prominent of the Disciples. His influence was thrown entirely on the side of conservatism. In the earlier part of his career he strenuously combated all modern methods and organization in church work. He was one of those who established (1868) and edited the *Apostolic Times,* designed to oppose the more liberal Isaac Errett [*q.v.*], editor of the *Christian Standard.* Later his guns were trained chiefly on the higher criticism. Through a department in the *Christian Standard,* which he began to edit in 1890, he familiarized the Disciples with the views of the critics, and fought them with both argument and ridicule. He published *Evidences of Christianity* in two volumes (1886, 1891), of which the first discusses the integrity of the New Testament text and the genuineness of the New Testament books, while the second treats of the credibility and inspiration of the New Testament; *Jesus and Jonah* (1896); *The Authorship of the Book of Deuteronomy, with its Bearing on the Higher Criticism of the Pentateuch* (1902); *The Standard Bible Commentary* (4 vols., 1905–08), with P. Y. Pendleton; *Short Essays in Biblical Criticism* (1910). In 1879 he made a tour of Egypt and Palestine, one of the results of which was *Lands of the Bible* (1881), which had a considerable circulation. He also published *Sermons, Delivered in Louisville, Kentucky, June–September 1893* (1894), and was for half a century a constant contributor to periodicals. His death occurred in Lexington in his eighty-third year.

[W. T. Moore, *The Living Pulpit of the Christian Church* (1869); J. T. Brown, *Churches of Christ* (1904); Errett Gates, *The Disciples of Christ* (1905); M. M. Davis, *How the Disciples Began and Grew* (1915); A. W. Fortune, *The Disciples in Ky.* (1932); *Who's Who in America,* 1910–11; *Christian Standard,* Oct. 14, 21, 1911; *Evening Post* (Louisville), Oct. 7, 1911; *Courier-Journal* (Louisville), Oct. 8, 1911.]

H. E. S.

McGEE, WILLIAM JOHN (Apr. 17, 1853–Sept. 4, 1912), geologist, anthropologist, and hydrologist, was born in a log-cabin near Farley, Iowa, the fourth of nine children of James and Martha Ann (Anderson) McGee. His father was a native of Antrim, Ireland, who came to America in 1831; his mother, born in Kentucky, was also of Scotch-Irish descent. The boy spent the first years of his life on a farm. His mind early took its bent toward science and he studied by himself, with some assistance from an elder brother who had attended Cornell College. The habit of self-help led him into studies far beyond anything to be furnished on the frontier in the sixties. His formative years saw him striving for knowledge and material support. He tried blacksmithing and studied surveying. Becoming greatly interested in the structure of the earth, he made surveys of the geology of Iowa which he reported in the *American Journal of Science* (1878–82). During these investigations, mounds and other traces of former inhabitants of the prairies also came under his observation. The work he carried on independently attracted the attention of the United States Geological Survey, and in 1883, at the age of thirty, he was invited by Maj. J. W. Powell [*q.v.*] to become a member of that force. Soon he was given charge of the branch of the survey dealing with the geology of the Atlantic Coastal Plain, and during the years 1883–94 he conducted important studies of this area. His geological publications include more than a hundred papers, notable among them being: "The Geology of the Head of Chesapeake Bay" (*Seventh Annual Report of the United States Geological Survey . . . 1885–'86,* 1888); "Three Formations of the Middle Atlantic Slope" (*American Journal of Science,* February, April, May, June 1888); "The Pleistocene History of Northeastern Iowa" (*Eleventh Annual Report, United States Geological Survey . . . 1889–'90,* pt. 1, 1891); "The Lafayette Formation" (*Twelfth Annual Report . . . 1890–'91,* pt. 1, 1891); "The Gulf of Mexico as a Measure of Isostasy" (*American Journal of Science,* September 1892). In 1888–91 he edited the *Bulletin* of the Geological Society of America.

McGee's official connection with anthropology began with his transfer in 1893 to the post of ethnologist in charge, in the Bureau of American Ethnology, of which his chief, Major Powell, was director. Bringing to the new work a genius for essential classification and the ability to inspire his younger helpers and colleagues, he gave the Bureau an impetus which was felt for years. His anthropological writings include some thirty titles. Noteworthy among the papers which he published in the *Annual Reports* of the Bureau were: "The Siouan Indians" (*Fifteenth . . . 1893–'94,* 1897); "Primitive Trephining in Peru" (*Sixteenth . . . 1894–'95,* 1897); "The Seri Indians" (*Seventeenth . . . 1895–'96,* 1898, pt. I); and "Primitive Numbers" (*Nineteenth . . . 1897–'98,* pt. I, 1900). During Powell's last illness he assumed the administrative work, and at the time of Powell's death in 1902 was serving as acting director.

The following year he resigned and took charge of the anthropological and historical exhibit at the Louisiana Purchase Exposition in St. Louis. He was subsequently appointed by President Roosevelt to the Inland Waterways Commission, and by the Secretary of Agriculture to take charge of the study of the water resources of the United States, an investigation begun in his surveys of Iowa. A report on this subject ("Wells and Subsoil Water," *Department of Agriculture Bulletin No. 92,* 1913) was his last contribution to science. His death, from cancer, occurred in his sixtieth year.

In 1888 he was married to Anita Newcomb, daughter of Simon Newcomb [*q.v.*] the astronomer. His wife survived him. Throughout his mature life he was known even to his friends by the initials only of his given names, and always signed himself W J McGee, without periods. Facile in expressing the stores of his mind, he delivered unnumbered addresses and discussions. Approachable, benevolent, willing to impart and to learn, he filled an important place in the scientific life of his time.

[F. H. Knowlton, in *Bull. Geol. Soc. of America,* Mar. 1913; F. W. Hodge, in *Am. Anthropologist,* Oct.–Dec. 1912; *The McGee Memorial Meeting of the Washington Academy of Sciences . . . Dec. 5, 1913* (1916); *Who's Who in America,* 1910–11; Emma R. McGee, *Life of W. J. McGee* (1915), which is eulogistic and does not treat of his scientific work; *Evening Star* (Washington), Sept. 4, 1912; personal recollections.]

W. H.

McGHEE, CHARLES McCLUNG (Jan. 23, 1828–May 5, 1907), financier, was born in Monroe County, Tenn. He was the fifth and youngest child of Betsy Jones (McClung) McGhee, the daughter of Charles McClung, and John McGhee, the grandson of Irish emigrants who had settled in Lancaster County, Pa. From his father he inherited a large estate in lands and slaves. In 1846 he graduated from East Tennessee University, which is now the University of Tennessee. On June 10, 1847, he was married to his cousin, the daughter of Hugh A. M. White of Knoxville, Isabella McNutt White, whose only child died shortly after her own death on May 13, 1848. On Apr. 14, 1857, he was married to his first wife's sister, Cornelia Humes White. They had five children. During the Civil War he served as colonel in the commissary department of the Confederate army. The war over, he devoted his energies to the financial rehabilitation of his section. He served his alma mater for a number of years, from 1869 to 1884, in the several offices of trustee, treasurer, and secretary and treasurer. He helped to maintain the institution on the meager revenue furnished by the state, which was financially so embarrassed that, instead of paying interest on its bonds held by the university, it issued depreciated warrants. He succeeded in marketing these advantageously by virtue of his financial connections as president of the People's Bank of Knoxville. He further served his university and his city as a member of the Tennessee legislature in the session of 1871–72. Finding the representatives from western Tennessee opposed to the giving of state support to the university in the eastern section, he placated them by a resolution that resulted in the granting of free transportation by the railroads to state students on their way to and from Knoxville. This effort seems the more commendable when it is noted that he already had a controlling interest in Tennessee railroads.

When the railroads (for the financing of which the state had gone heavily into debt) proved unprofitable, were thrown into receiverships, and advertised for sale, he and his business friends enlisted the financial support of such northern capitalists as Thomas A. Scott of Pennsylvania and obtained the formation of the Southern Railway Security Company. The various roads running out of Knoxville were consolidated into the East Tennessee, Virginia & Georgia Railroad, of which he became one of the directors. They purchased the state's interest in certain delinquent roads and acquired the Knoxville & Ohio, the Memphis & Charleston, and the Rogersville and Jefferson railroads. The South was joined by one more railway when a road to Macon, Ga., was built and consolidated. The Alabama & Chattanooga Railroad, too, became another link in the great southern combination. The Atlantic, Mississippi & Ohio Railroad (Norfolk and Western) was added and equipped with a highly ornamented train of red coaches. From the end of the Civil War until his death he was concerned with every railroad that affected the life of East Tennessee. Until his retirement about ten years before his death he was active in the organizations, reorganizations, receiverships, and changes in control of the network of railroads that, completely bankrupt, passed to the J. P. Morgan interests in 1894 and were rehabilitated under the control of the Southern Railway Company. In spite of the collapse in the financial structure of the railroads, in these years he amassed a fortune, from which he endowed many Knoxville enterprises, notably the Lawson-McGhee Library.

[W. T. Hale and D. L. Merritt, *A Hist. of Tenn.* (1913), vols. III, V; John Allison, *Notable Men of Tenn.* (1905), vol. I; Henry Hall, *America's Successful Men of Affairs,* vol. I (1895); *War of the Rebellion: Official Records (Army),* 2 ser., vol. I; *University of Tenn. Record,* July 1898; H. V. and H. W. Poor, *Manual of the Railroads of the U. S.* (1877–96), esp. 1886 and 1894; Stuart Daggett, *Railroad Reorganization* (1908); *Jour. House of Representatives of . . . Tenn.,* 37 Gen. Assembly, 1 Sess. (1871), joint resolution no. 119, p. 363. Wm. McClung, *The McClung Geneal.* (1904), pp. 36–37; *Journal and Tribune* (Knoxville), May 6, 1907.]

M. B. H—r.

McGIFFIN, PHILO NORTON (Dec. 13, 1860–Feb. 11, 1897), naval officer, was born in Washington, Pa. His great-grandfather, who came from Scotland, fought in the Revolution. His father, Col. Norton McGiffin, served in the Mexican and Civil wars. His mother was Sarah Houston (Quail). After preliminary schooling in Washington, Pa., where he attended the Washington and Jefferson Academy, Philo McGiffin entered the United States Naval Academy in his seventeenth year. Here he distinguished himself not so much in scholarship as by the many escapades in which he was involved. He spent several months on the station ship *Santee* in punishment, and took five years to complete the four-year Academy course. On graduation in 1882 he was assigned to duty in the *Hartford,* the flagship of the Pacific Squadron. Two years later he was examined for the grade of past midshipman. It was a time when commissions in the service could be granted only as vacancies occurred. Thus, with many of his classmates, instead of being promoted, he was given an honorable discharge with a year's pay. He is said to have long treasured the hope that Congress might reinstate the naval cadets who had been denied commissions, but such an act was never passed.

In the spring of 1885 the Tongking affair in China induced him to go to the East. Applying in person to the viceroy Li Hung-Chang, he was given a commission in the Chinese navy. Upon the conclusion of peace with France, he was made professor of seamanship and gunnery at the Naval College in Tien-tsin. When four Chinese ironclads were ordered in England, he was sent to superintend their construction. Serving for ten years as naval constructor and during the same time as profesor of gunnery and seamanship, he taught most of the Chinese officers that were destined to serve in the Sino-Japanese War.

On the beginning of hostilities McGiffin was the executive and second in command on board the *Chen Yuen,* a seven-thousand-ton battleship, the sister ship of the *Ting Yuen,* flagship of Admiral Ting. In the decisive naval engagement fought off the Yalu River, Sept. 17, 1894, the two Chinese battleships withstood the main Japanese squadron until the Japanese steamed away. "It was due to the *Chen Yuen's* skillful manœuvers that the Chinese flagship did not suffer more," wrote a Japanese (*United States Naval Institute Proceedings,* XX, 812). The Chinese captain of this ship having failed utterly in the crisis, everything devolved on McGiffin. Although the *Chen Yuen* was miserably equipped with ammunition and was on fire eight different times, he carried her through to safety. He was so severely wounded and burned, however, that he was left a physical and mental wreck. Resigning from the Chinese service he returned to America. For two years he lived in New York City, suffering in the extreme. In a state of intense nervous prostration, a victim of hallucinations, he was cared for by a life-long friend, Col. Robert M. Thompson, and sent to the Post Graduate Hospital. For a while he seemed much improved; then, eluding his attendants, he secured his revolvers and committed suicide. He was absolutely fearless, and when given the opportunity excelled in action; but he seems to have been impelled not so much by a spirit of patriotism or self-sacrifice as by a love of adventure. Richard Harding Davis, a boyhood friend, gave him a proper characterization by including him in his *Real Soldiers of Fortune* (1906).

[Davis, *Real Soldiers of Fortune*; Park Benjamin, in *Army and Navy Jour.,* Feb. 20, 1897; McGiffin's article, "The Battle of Yalu, Personal Recollections by the Commander of the Chinese Ironclad *Chen Yuen,*" *Century Magazine,* Aug. 1895; *U. S. Naval Inst. Proc.,* XX (1894), 803–18, and XXI (1895), 479–521; letter from Alumni Secretary, Washington and Jefferson College; *Evening Post* (N. Y.), Feb. 11, 1897; the *Sun* (N. Y.), Feb. 12, 1897.] C. S. A.

McGILL, JOHN (Nov. 4, 1809–Jan. 14, 1872), Roman Catholic prelate, son of James and Lavenia (Dougherty) McGill, was born in Philadelphia, where his father, an immigrant from County Derry (1788), was engaged in business. About 1819 the McGills moved westward, finally settling in Bardstown, Ky. Here John completed his elementary schooling and in 1828 graduated from St. Joseph's College. Having read law under Gov. Charles A. Wickliffe [*q.v.*], he was admitted to the bar and practised with success in New Orleans and in Bardstown. Dissatisfied in this profession, he studied theology at the neighboring St. Thomas Seminary and under the Sulpicians at St. Mary's, Baltimore. Ordained at Bardstown by Bishop David [*q.v.*], June 13, 1835, he was assigned to St. Peter's Church, Lexington, Ky., and later as an assistant to Dr. I. A. Reynolds of St. Louis' Church, Louisville, whom he succeeded as pastor when the latter was named to the See of Charleston. An assistant editor of *The Catholic Advocate* under Dr. M. J. Spalding [*q.v.*], whom he also served as vicar general, he won reputation as a somewhat aggressive controversialist. To a local disputation, he contributed a brochure on the origin of the Church of England and a translation of J. M. V. Audin's *History of the Life, Works, and Doctrines of John Calvin* (1845). On Oct. 10, 1850, he was named bishop of Richmond, Va., and a month later consecrated at Bardstown by Archbishop P. R. Kenrick [*q.v.*].

Bishop McGill found Richmond an impoverished diocese with only eight priests. Within ten years, however, he paid the bulk of the diocesan debt, built several churches, established a number of missions, assigned St. Mary's German Church in Richmond to the Benedictines, founded schools at Richmond, Norfolk, Petersburg, and Harpers Ferry, erected a hospital at Norfolk, and neutralized the evil effects of the Know-Nothing agitation by his judicious carriage and a series of letters in refutation of charges made by Robert Ridgway in nativist papers. The Civil War threw all into chaos. A strong Southern sympathizer, the Bishop urged enlistments, especially in the Emmett and Montgomery Guards, furnished chaplains for the Confederate forces, ministered personally at Libby Prison, and detailed Sisters of Mercy and of Charity as military nurses. Unable to visit the churches of the diocese, he utilized his time in writing *The True Church, Indicated to the Inquirer* (1862) and *Our Faith, the Victory: or a Comprehensive View of the Principal Doctrines of the Christian Religion* (1865), which in revised form appeared in several editions. In the latter work he was inclined to view the war as a punishment for the treatment of slaves and hoped "that by the present convulsions, his providence is preparing for them at least, a recognition of those rights as immortal beings, which are required for the observance of the paramount laws of God."

On Lee's surrender, Bishop McGill visited his war-torn diocese and entered upon the arduous labor of reconstruction: churches were rebuilt and scattered congregations mobilized; academies were established by the Visitation nuns, Sisters of Charity, and Sisters of Notre Dame; and orphan asylums were provided. At the Second Plenary Council of Baltimore he depicted to the assembled bishops the needs of the Church in the South and pled for its support. In 1867 he visited Rome for the second time in the interest of the diocese, and two years later attended the Vatican Council, at which he preached a public discourse. His active career was then practically at an end, though as an invalid, dying of a cancer, he lived on bravely for several years.

[F. J. Magri, *The Cath. Ch. in the City and Diocese of Richmond* (1906); R. H. Clarke, *Lives of the Deceased Bishops of the Cath. Ch. in the U. S.*, vol. III (1888); J. G. Shea, *Hist. of the Cath. Ch. in the U. S.*, vol. IV (1892); B. J. Webb, *The Centenary of Catholicity in Ky.* (1884); *U. S. Cath. Mag.*, July 1845; *The Metropolitan Cath. Almanac*, 1851, pp. 120 f.; *Sadliers' Cath. Directory*, 1873, p. 39; *Richmond Daily Enquirer*, Jan. 16, 1872; *Freeman's Journal*, (N. Y.), Sept. 29, 1855.]

R. J. P.

McGILLIVRAY, ALEXANDER (*c.* 1759–Feb. 17, 1793), Creek chief, belonged to the Wind clan of the Upper Creek Indians, among whom descent was traced on the maternal side. His mother is said to have been Sehoy Marchand, a French-Indian halfbreed (Pickett, *post*, I, 32); his father was Lachlan McGillivray, a prominent trader and politician of Georgia. Probably until the age of fourteen, Alexander lived with the Indians at his father's trading post on the Tallapoosa River. He was then taken to Charleston and Savannah, where he is said to have worked in a counting-house and to have spent his spare time reading history. Upon the outbreak of the American Revolution the McGillivrays became Loyalists and their property was confiscated. Father and son each returned to his childhood home, Lachlan to Scotland and Alexander to the Creek country, where he spent the rest of his life. During the Revolution he served as a British agent among the Southern Indians, sent out war parties against the American frontier, and formed a connection with the Loyalist traders, Panton, Leslie & Company. After the Revolution, this connection was of great value to both parties, for each advanced the other's interests with the Spanish government, which had acquired the Floridas in 1783. At the same time, McGillivray seems to have been genuinely devoted to the welfare of his people. His immediate purpose was to form a confederation of the Southern Indians and, with the aid of Spain or perhaps Great Britain, compel the Americans to restore the Indian line as it existed in 1773; in other words, to evacuate a large part of Georgia, Tennessee, and Kentucky. Since he also sought the cooperation of the Northern Indians, he may be regarded as the prototype of Tecumseh, whose mother was a Creek woman of McGillivray's generation.

From 1784 to his death in 1793, McGillivray touched the life of the Old Southwest at many of its most important points, and his career possessed international significance. He was courted by merchants, land speculators, and filibusters and by the governments of Georgia, the United States, and Spain. In June 1784 the Spanish governor, Esteban Rodríguez Miró [*q.v.*], concluded a treaty with the Creek Indians at Pensacola, and through the aid of Panton, Leslie & Company, McGillivray was appointed Spanish commissary to enforce Spain's monopoly of trade with the Creeks. His salary was fifty dollars a month. In the following year he rewarded the Loyalist traders by helping them to obtain Spain's permission to establish a branch at Pensacola. In 1786 he first precipitated a war with the American frontiersmen and then forced the reluctant Spaniards to provide him with munitions with which to prosecute it. One of the causes of the war was his resentment at the confiscation of his family's property by Georgia. It was waged for the purpose of annihilating American competition in the southern Indian trade and driving back the American frontier within the line of 1773. In 1785 he had opposed Georgia's effort to establish Bourbon County on the Mississippi, and his war parties now harried the outlying settlements from Georgia to Cumberland. His power was probably at its height in 1787, when his warriors' attacks almost succeeded in destroying the stations on the Cumberland River; when men under his orders murdered a Georgia agent in the midst of the friendly Chickasaws; and when he himself was visited by the agent of Congress, James White, to whom he is said to have expressed the wish that the Creek towns might be organized as a state and admitted into the Union.

Two sources of his strength were Spanish aid and the weakness of the United States government. At the end of 1787 the cautious Spaniards stopped furnishing him with munitions; and, although his intrigue with the adventurer William Augustus Bowles [*q.v.*] frightened them into renewing the practice in 1789, mutual confidence was never restored. In the latter year a stronger government was established in the United States. President Washington immediately gave his attention to Creek relations and the dangerous designs of the Yazoo land speculators, who were bidding for McGillivray's support. After one abortive effort at peace, when David Humphreys, Benjamin Lincoln, and Cyrus Griffin [*qq.v.*] were sent to negotiate a treaty with the Creek nation, Col. Marinus Willett persuaded McGillivray to come to New York, where a pension of $1,200 to him obtained a treaty (Aug. 7, 1790) satisfactory to the United States but contrary to the Creek treaty of 1784 with Spain. Returning to the Indian country, McGillivray was induced by the resentment of the Indians, the return of the hostile Bowles, the arguments of William Panton [*q.v.*], and the increase of his Spanish pension to $2,000 and ultimately to $3,500, to sign a convention (July 6, 1792) with Governor Carondelet [*q.v.*] repudiating the Treaty of New York. During the progress of further negotiations for the formation of a confederation of the Southern Indians in alliance with Spain against the United States, McGillivray died at Pensacola of a complication of "gout in the stomach" and pneumonia. He is said to have been buried with Masonic honors in the garden of William Panton at Pensacola.

McGillivray was not a warrior and almost never took part in the incessant fighting on the southern frontier. His chief interests were diplomacy, trade, and planting. Far better educated than most of the leading American frontiersmen of his day, he wrote clearly and forcefully in both his private and public correspondence. Although closely associated with Panton, Leslie & Company and financially dependent upon them, he was not a member of the company. He had three plantations and about sixty slaves, engaged extensively in stock raising, set a good table, lived well, and was never out of debt. He was a heavy drinker and frequently suffered from blinding headaches. He had two wives at least and his involved estate was left to his two children, Alexander and Elizabeth, who later brought suit to recover it from the executors, William Panton and John Forbes, 1769–1823 [*q.v.*]. McGillivray was a relative of John Weatherford, another well known halfbreed, and a nephew of the Creek chief, Red Shoes.

[*Am. State Papers, Indian Affairs,* vol. I (1832); A. J. Pickett, *Hist. of Ala.* (2 vols., 1851); John Pope, *A Tour through the Southern and Western Territories of the U. S.* (1792); A. P. Whitaker, *The Spanish-American Frontier* (1927) and two articles, "Alexander McGillivray, 1783–1789," in which the date of his birth is discussed, and "Alexander McGillivray, 1789–1793," *N. C. Hist. Rev.,* Apr. and July 1928, both giving copious references to manuscript and printed sources.]

A. P. W.

McGILVARY, DANIEL (May 16, 1828–Aug. 22, 1911), missionary in Siam, was born in Moore County, N. C., son of Malcolm McGilvary and his wife, Catharine McIver. He received his academic education in the private academy of Rev. William Bingham at Hillsboro, from which he graduated in 1849. He served as principal of a new academy at Pittsboro for four years, then entered Princeton Theological Seminary, where he graduated in 1856. After a brief pastorate at Carthage, in his native state, he was appointed to the Siam mission of the Presbyterian Church, and was ordained, Dec. 11, 1857, by the Presbytery of Orange, N. C. He reached Bangkok in June of the following year. On Dec. 6, 1860, he married Sophia Royce Bradley, eldest daughter of Rev. Dan Beach Bradley, pioneer medical missionary in Siam. To this union were born two sons and three daughters.

In 1861, with Rev. Samuel G. McFarland [*q.v.*], he was appointed to open a new station at Petchaburi. There he came into contact with a colony of Lao war captives and discovered that their language varied but slightly from the Siamese, although they used a different written character. Finding that these people were more willing to receive his message than the Siamese, he made an exploratory trip into the Lao States and thereupon decided to establish a mission among them. With the consent of the Prince of

Chieng-mai, the Siamese government issued the necessary passports. McGilvary and his family reached Chieng-mai in the winter of 1867, and were joined the following year by the Rev. Jonathan Wilson and his family. Thus these two men became the founders of the mission to the Lao. In token of goodwill the Prince donated land for a permanent establishment.

McGilvary was a man of clear vision, quick intuition, candor, and honor; furthermore, he had courage to the point of daring. When on the occasion of the first Christian marriage ceremony the family patriarch refused to consent to the new form unless the customary "spirit-fee" should be paid to him, McGilvary was quick to perceive that acquiescence would not only appear to condone spirit worship in the eyes of the people but would set a precedent for future demands. Accordingly, when the Prince, fearing to oppose custom, excused himself from interference on the pretext that only the King of Siam could regulate religious matters, McGilvary promptly took him at his word and made an appeal to the King for religious freedom on behalf of the native Christians. In response, the Royal Commissioner resident at Chieng-mai received instructions from Bangkok to issue in the King's name an "edict of religious toleration" (Oct. 8, 1878). The turning of this crisis by the statesmanship of McGilvary proved to be all but the last step in the passing of the feudal power of the Prince of Chieng-mai. When the reigning prince died no successor was appointed and the Lao provinces were brought fully under the Siamese government.

Undeniably McGilvary had a love of adventure. He early made several elephant tours through the provinces to learn the state of affairs. In 1884 he gave his services as interpreter for Holt S. Hallett, who was prospecting for a British rail route from Maulmain into southwest China. Subsequently he made an annual tour through various parts of the region covered by the upper watershed of the Menam and the central watershed of the Mekong. He was among the first to investigate the several aboriginal tribes in the mountains of that region. Through these tours he came to know personally all the provincial governors and to be on friendly terms with many of the village chiefs. He was more widely acquainted with the geography, ethnography, and travel routes than any other Westerner up to his time and than most of the government officials of that day.

Of his fifty-three years in Siam, McGilvary spent forty-three among the Lao, coming to be known as "the Apostle to the Lao." On several occasions he received expressions of royal favor for his labors. Toward the end of his life he prepared his autobiography, *A Half Century among the Siamese and the Lāo,* which was published in 1912, the year after his death. In the Preface to this book McGilvary's superior officer, Dr. A. J. Brown, summarized his achievements in the following words: "He laid the foundations of the medical work, introducing quinine and vaccination among a people scourged by malaria and smallpox, a work which has now developed into five hospitals and a leper asylum. He began educational work, which is now represented by eight boarding schools and twenty-two elementary schools. He was the evangelist who won the first converts, founded the first church, and had a prominent part in founding twenty other churches." He died in Chieng-mai in his eighty-fourth year.

[McGilvary's autobiography, mentioned above; H. S. Hallett, *A Thousand Miles on an Elephant in the Shan States* (1890); Lilian J. Curtis, *The Laos of North Siam* (1903); G. B. McFarland, *Hist. Sketch of Protestant Missions in Siam* (1928); *Princeton Theol. Sem. Bull.; Necrological Report,* Aug. 1912; *Minutes of the Gen. Assembly of the Presbyterian Church in the U. S. A.* (1912); *Assembly Herald,* Oct. 1911.] G. H. F.

McGIVNEY, MICHAEL JOSEPH (Aug. 12, 1852–Aug. 14, 1890), Roman Catholic priest, a founder of the Knights of Columbus, was the eldest of the thirteen children born to Patrick and Mary (Lynch) McGivney. On completion of his elementary education in the parochial and public schools of his native town, Waterbury, Conn., he worked in the spoon factory of Holmes, Booth & Haydens. On discerning a religious vocation in their son, his parents, though recent immigrants from Ireland, managed to send him to the college of St. Hyacinth in Canada, a preparatory institution, and then to Niagara University at Niagara Falls, where he was graduated in 1873. That autumn, he enrolled as a theological student in St. Mary's Seminary, Baltimore, where on Dec. 22, 1877, he was ordained by Archbishop Gibbons. Early in the following year, he was assigned by Bishop Thomas Galberry [*q.v.*] as an assistant to Father P. A. Murphy of St. Mary's Church, New Haven, Conn. An energetic, zealous priest, he organized a parochial total-abstinence society and unstintingly gave his time to sodalities and to a social organization known as the Red Knights, which, after the Civil War, had grown out of the Sarsfield Guard, an Irish military unit. Since the Red Knights died a natural death and Catholics were not permitted to join the various attractive secret societies, Father McGivney grew interested in the establishment of an acceptable

Catholic fraternal order which would bring men together in mutually helpful association. As a result of a series of meetings at the parochial house commencing Jan. 16, 1882, he and nine lay associates established the Knights of Columbus, a fraternal insurance society of a semi-secret character, which was chartered by the State of Connecticut Mar. 29, 1882. McGivney assisted in composing the ritual, and as an advocate of total abstinence insisted that members of the order must be recognized practical Catholics who were in no way directly connected with the liquor traffic. Through his good offices the order was approved by Bishop Lawrence S. McMahon of Hartford, and soon spread its local councils throughout the diocese, though its extension beyond the state of Connecticut, in the face of clerical suspicion, was slow until it was approved by the papal delegate. As national chaplain and a member of the supreme council, McGivney remained the inspiring force in the society until his death in Thomaston, Conn., where for six years he had been pastor of St. Thomas' Church. His inspiration was continued through two brothers, Monsignor P. J. and Father John J. McGivney, who in turn succeeded him in the national chaplaincy of the order, which at its high tide during the World War approached a million members.

[M. F. Egan and J. B. Kennedy, *The Knights of Columbus in Peace and War* (2 vols., 1920), vol. I; *Souvenir of Twentieth Anniversary, Sheridan Council, K. of C., Waterbury, Conn.* (1905), ed. by C. Maloney; information furnished from the files of the Knights of Columbus and by Rev. J. J. McGivney; New Haven *Daily Morning Journal and Courier*, Aug. 15, 19, 1890.]

R. J. P.

McGLYNN, EDWARD (Sept. 27, 1837–Jan. 7, 1900), Catholic priest, social reformer, was born in New York of Irish parents, Peter and Sarah McGlynn, and educated in the public schools of his native city. At the age of thirteen he was sent by Bishop Hughes to the Urban College of the Propaganda, Rome, and there he was ordained priest, Mar. 24, 1860. Immediately after ordination he became assistant to Rev. Thomas Farrell at St. Joseph's Church, Sixth Avenue, New York.

Inasmuch as Father Farrell had been an ardent opponent of slavery and left five thousand dollars in his will for a colored Catholic church, he probably was in large measure responsible for the charitable and humanitarian views and practices for which his young assistant became and remained conspicuous. In 1866 McGlynn was appointed pastor of St. Stephen's parish, one of the most populous in New York. Here he worked with great energy and zeal, not only in the various fields of parochial activity, but on behalf of every worthy public cause. After a time he began to feel that life was made a burden "by the never-ending procession of men, women and little children coming to my door begging, not so much for alms as employment." "I began to ask myself," he wrote, "'Is there no remedy?' . . . I began to study a little political economy, to ask, 'what is God's law as to the maintenance of his family down here below?'" (Malone, *post,* p. 4).

He thought that he had found the answer in the teachings of Henry George, 1839–1897 [*q.v.*]. With his accustomed fervor, energy, and eloquence he expounded the Single-Tax doctrine as the universal and fundamental remedy for poverty. In the year 1886 he took an active part in the campaign of Henry George for the office of mayor of New York. This brought him into open conflict with Archbishop Corrigan.

About four years previously, Cardinal Simeoni, prefect of the Congregation of the Propaganda, had directed the authorities of the Archdiocese to compel McGlynn to retract his views on the land question. Cardinal McCloskey [*q.v.*], at that time the head of the Archdiocese, merely required McGlynn to refrain from defending these views in public. After the death of Cardinal McCloskey, McGlynn considered himself free again to advocate the Single-Tax doctrine. On Sept. 29, 1886, Archbishop Corrigan [*q.v.*] forbade him to speak on behalf of Henry George's candidacy at a scheduled public meeting. McGlynn replied that to break this engagement would be imprudent, but promised to refrain from addressing any later meeting during the political campaign. The Archbishop immediately suspended him from the exercise of his priestly functions for a period of two weeks. Toward the end of November a second temporary suspension was imposed. On Jan. 14, 1887, Archbishop Corrigan removed McGlynn from the pastorate of St. Stephen's. Two days later a cablegram arrived from Cardinal Simeoni commanding McGlynn to retract publicly his land theory and to come immediately to Rome. On Feb. 18 Cardinal Gibbons [*q.v.*], who was then in Rome, sent word that McGlynn ought to go to Rome as soon as possible. On Mar. 11 Dr. Burtsell, as McGlynn's canonical advocate, cabled a reply that his client would do so on certain conditions. At the same time he wrote a long letter to Cardinal Gibbons explaining fully the canonical situation from McGlynn's viewpoint. For reasons which seemed good, Cardinal Gibbons did not present either the cablegram or the letter to the Roman authorities, contenting himself with an oral statement of their contents. Failing to receive any written reply from McGlynn, the Pope ordered him to come to Rome within forty days under penalty of excommunication. Holding that he had been guilty of no contumacy, and unaware that the reply made on his behalf by Dr. Burtsell had never reached the Holy Father, McGlynn, on the score of health, refused to obey the order, and the excommunication became effective July 4, 1887. For more than five years following this censure he defended the Single-Tax doctrine at the Sunday afternoon meetings of the Anti-Poverty Society, of which he was the first president. He lived at the home of his widowed sister in Brooklyn.

In December 1892, upon the assurance of four professors at the Catholic University that McGlynn's Single-Tax views were not contrary to Catholic teaching, Msgr. Satolli, the Papal Ablegate in the United States reinstated him in the ministry. On Christmas Day 1892 McGlynn said mass for the first time since his excommunication in 1887. The following June he visited Rome and was cordially received in private audience by the Holy Father. In his description of this event shortly afterwards, McGlynn reported that the Pope had said to him, "But surely you admit the right of property," and that he had answered in the affirmative as regards "the products of individual industry." Apparently the Pope was satisfied with this answer.

In January 1894, McGlynn became pastor of St. Mary's at Newburgh, N. Y., where he died Jan. 7, 1900. In the years following his restoration to his priestly functions he frequently spoke at Single-Tax meetings and made it quite clear that he had not been required by the Pope to retract his view on the land question. His funeral occasioned widespread expressions of sorrow and appreciation in all walks of life, both within and without the Catholic Church.

[Some of the details contained in the foregoing sketch were taken from a long letter written by Bishop Moore of St. Augustine, Fla., to Cardinal Manning in November 1887. The principal printed sources concerning McGlynn are: the daily papers of New York City from 1886 to 1900; the *Cath. Encyc.*, XI (1911), 24, 25; John Talbot Smith, *Hist. of the Cath. Ch. in N. Y.* (1905), II, 420–23, 432–36; S. L. Malone, *Dr. Edward McGlynn* (1918); and Arthur Preuss, *The Fundamental Fallacy of Socialism* (1908). See also *N. Y. Freeman's Jour.*, Apr. 9, May 7, 1887; *N. Y. Times*, Jan. 8, 1900.]

J. A. R.

McGOVERN, JOHN (Feb. 18, 1850–Dec. 17, 1917), journalist and author, was born in Troy, N. Y., the eldest of three children of James and Marion (Carter) McGovern. In 1854, when his father and sister died of cholera, his mother took him to Ligonier, Ind., where she died four years later. The boy then lived with Judson Palmiter, a printer, in Ligonier, where he attended school and worked during the summer months on the farm of his uncle, Henry Carter, at Lima, Ind. In 1862 when Palmiter moved to Kendallville, Ind., to publish the *Noble County Journal*, McGovern began his journalistic career by working in the printing office. Under the kindly influence of Palmiter he developed an appreciation of music and poetry which colored his later life. He worked as a printer in Sturgis, Mich., in 1866, returning the following year to Kendallville, and thence going to Kalamazoo to join the staff of the *Michigan Telegraph*. In 1868 he moved to Chicago, became a typesetter on the *Chicago Tribune*, and gradually advanced to proof-reader, telegraph editor, and night editor. In these years he began to write poetry, some of which was published in the *Tribune*. In 1877 he was married to Kate C. Van Arsdale of Philadelphia, who bore him two sons and a daughter. For two years (July 1884–July 1886) he was associate editor and for a few weeks (July–October 1886) sole editor of the *Current*, a literary magazine, which printed poems, essays, and editorials by him, and from 1887 to 1889 he was chief editorial writer for the *Chicago Herald*.

Encouraged by his growing literary experience, he gave up newspaper work to devote his time to literature. His writings fall into several categories; all show his understanding of public taste in easy reading, sensational matter, and moral emphasis. Four published novels and two still in manuscript, two volumes of poetry, along with other lyrics printed in newspapers, and nearly twenty volumes of moral and literary essays and miscellaneous writings make up the bulk of his work. Numerous philosophic and moral essays still remain unpublished, also several dramas and manuscripts of personal experiences. McGovern was always confident of his literary powers and wrote with the conviction that posterity would value his unpublished works more than his contemporaries did his printed volumes. The manuscripts were preserved by his daughter, Mary Harriet McGovern, whom he made his literary executrix. His novel, *David Lockwin; The People's Idol* (1892), is of interest because McGovern accused the British novelist, Gilbert Parker, of taking its plot for his novel, *The Right of Way* (*Chicago Evening Post*, May 23, 1902, May 24, 1903). In 1899 McGovern served as literary expert for Samuel Eberley Gross in his plagiarism case against Edmund Rostand, and studied texts of *Cyrano de Bergerac* and the *Merchant Prince of Cornville* for similarities. His testimony and evidence won the case for Gross (May 21, 1902). After 1902 he became an occasional lecturer on literary and biographical subjects. He was a genial person, was referred to as the "grand old man" of the Chicago Press Club, where he gave many lectures, and was the leading spirit of the Old Printers Club. The last two years of his life were dark with sickness. He died in Chicago.

[Andrew F. Leiser, "The Life and Writings of John McGovern" (1930), an unpublished thesis at the library of George Washington University; *Who's Who in America*, 1916–17; *Chicago Tribune*, May 21, 1902, Dec. 18, 19, 1917; *Chicago Herald*, Dec. 18, 1917.]

R. W. B.

McGOWAN, SAMUEL (Oct. 9, 1819–Aug. 9, 1897), jurist and Confederate soldier, was born in the Crosshill section of Laurens District, S. C., the son of William and Jeannie (McWilliams) McGowan, Irish Presbyterians who in 1801 emigrated to South Carolina from Ireland. His father became a prosperous farmer, able to fulfil the ambition to send his sons to college. The younger McGowan attended the school of Thomas Lewis Lesly and was graduated from the South Carolina College in 1841. He then went to Abbeville, where he studied law under T. C. Perrin and was admitted to the bar in 1842. This son of Irish emigrants possessed personal qualities that made possible his rise to positions of distinction. Although not brilliant, he was studious and ambitious and endowed with a fund of simple humor. He was powerful in body, commanding in personal appearance, and possessed of a degree of physical courage and sense of civic duty that won admiration. His rise in the somewhat exclusive social and professional circles of Abbeville was facilitated by his conduct in an affair of honor. He reprimanded John Cuningham, an experienced duelist, for slurring remarks about a young woman, accepted Cuningham's challenge, and was slightly wounded in the duel that followed at Sandbar Ferry, S. C. He became the partner of Perrin and was soon recognized as a popular politician and eloquent advocate. He was elected a major-general of militia and for thirteen years before 1865 represented Abbeville District in the state House of Representatives. He married Susan Caroline, the daughter of David L. Wardlaw, a distinguished judge of Abbeville. They had seven children.

His civil career was interrupted by military services. In 1846 he entered the famous Palmetto Regiment as a private in the Mexican War, rose to the rank of staff captain, and was complimented for gallantry in action near Mexico city. In 1861, as commander of a South Carolina brigade, he assisted in the capture of Fort Sumter. In 1862 he became colonel of the 14th South Carolina Volunteers, which was attached to Maxcy Gregg's famous brigade. When in 1863 Gregg was killed, he was made commander of the brigade. He served in that capacity until the surrender at Appomattox. In many of the bloodiest battles in Virginia he displayed extraordinary bravery. He was wounded at least four times. After the Civil War he resumed the practice of law at Abbeville as the partner of William H. Parker. He was a member of the state constitutional convention of 1865 and was elected to Congress in the same year, but he was denied a seat by the Republican majority. He was a leader in the struggle to redeem South Carolina from Republican rule in 1876. In 1878 he was again elected to the legislature, and a year later he was made an associate justice of the state supreme court, where he won a high reputation as a jurist. In 1893 he was defeated for reëlection through the influence of Ben Tillman, the Democratic boss of the state, whom he had antagonized by casting the deciding vote in a supreme-court decision declaring the proposed liquor dispensary unconstitutional. He died at his home in Abbeville and after services in Trinity Episcopal Church was buried in upper Long Cane Cemetery in that town.

[*Cyc. of Eminent and Representative Men of the Carolinas* (1892), I; C. A. Evans, *Confederate Military Hist.* (1899), vol. V; *Hist. of S. C.*, ed. by Yates Snowden (1920), vol. II; J. E. J. Caldwell, *The Hist. of a Brigade of South Carolinians, Known First as "Gregg's" and Subsequently as "McGowan's Brigade"* (1866); *South Carolina Reports*, esp. speeches made before the supreme court at his death, in vol. LI; F. B. Simkins, *The Tillman Movement in S. C.* (copr. 1926); *Proceedings of the Reunion of the McGowan Family Held at Liberty Springs Church* (1915); J. G. Wardlaw, *Geneal. of the Wardlaw Family* (1929), p. 87; U. R. Brooks, *S. C. Bench and Bar*, vol. I (1908), quoting the *News and Courier* (Charleston), Aug. 10, 1897.]

F. B. S.

McGRATH, JAMES (June 26, 1835–Jan. 12, 1898), Roman Catholic priest, was born in Holy Cross, County Tipperary, Ireland, and received his early training in the local schools and in the University of Dublin. While a student at the University, he was professed in the Oblates of Mary Immaculate at Inchicor (1855), and the following year was sent to Canada, where he completed his theological studies at the University of Ottawa. Ordained in 1859, he was assigned to a curacy in St. Patrick's Church, Ottawa, for three years and was then transferred to the Texan missions. In 1864, he returned to Ottawa, where he built the Church of the Immaculate Conception. Subsequently, while attached to the Holy Angels' Apostolic School of Buffalo, he preached missions throughout New York and New England, winning recognition as a preacher in both French and English. In 1870 he was appointed pastor at St. John's Church, Lowell, Mass., and there erected the Church of the Immaculate Conception (1872), one of the largest in the archdiocese of Boston. One of the first New England priests to introduce parochial education, he organized a school under the Canadian Grey Nuns of the Cross (1880).

In the belief that Canadian control was preventing the normal growth of his community in the United States, McGrath successfully urged the creation of an American province of the Oblate Fathers. In 1883 he was elected first provincial, with authority over the community's churches and monasteries in Lowell, Buffalo, and Plattsburg, as well as in Texas and Mexico. During his administration of ten years, the Sacred Heart house was opened in Lowell, and monasteries were founded in Eagle Pass and Rio Grande, Tex. In 1883 a novitiate was established at Tewksbury, Mass., to which in 1888 was added a juniorate for recruiting novices. Three years later, the Provincial transferred the juniorate to Buffalo. On the completion of his term, Father McGrath returned to Buffalo where he was superior of the Holy Angels' Church and Apostolic School, until his sudden death of heart failure in the Albany railway station while on his way to a chapter meeting in Lowell.

[*Albany Argus*, Jan. 13, 1898; *Buffalo Courier*, Jan. 13–16, 1898; material contributed from the community archives at the Tewksbury Novitiate; annual Catholic directories.]

R. J. P.

McGRAW, JOHN HARTE (Oct. 4, 1850–June 23, 1910), governor of Washington, was born in Penobscot County, Me., soon after the arrival from Ireland of his parents, Daniel and Catherine (Harte) McGraw. His father was drowned about two years later. His mother remarried, and he left home at the age of fourteen. Earning his living as a clerk in a general merchandise store, he became manager at seventeen, and at twenty-one he and a brother opened a grocery store. They failed in the panic of 1873. He decided to go west and reached San Francisco by ship on July 10, 1876, drove a horse-car a few months, and then sailed for Seattle arriving on Dec. 28. After working as a clerk in the Occidental Hotel, he went into the hotel business with a partner. He was left stranded again when their place, the American House, burned in 1878, and he joined the police force of four men. Fearlessness and ability won his election as city marshal from 1879 to 1882 and as sheriff of King County for two terms. During the Anti-Chinese riots in 1886 he became unpopular by performing his duty, and he lost his office at the next election. He had studied law while sheriff, and after his defeat he became a member of the law firm of Greene, Hanford & McGraw. He was admitted to the bar in 1886. In 1888 he accepted election as sheriff in vindication of his previous actions. He was elected president of the First National Bank of Seattle before the completion of this term and retained the position until 1897. He was elected governor of Washington in 1892, and his four-year term, falling in a time of financial depression, was a stormy period of railway and mining strikes and of riotous conditions in Tacoma and elsewhere attending the march of Coxey's Army. He went alone into mining districts to reason with the strike leaders. The legislature was extravagant, and he vetoed many appropriation bills and defeated a raid on the capitol building fund. During these years he neglected his private affairs, and at the end of his term he was left bankrupt.

In 1897 he borrowed money to go to Alaska, and he returned in two years with enough gold to pay all his debts. Though active in Republican politics, he refused further political honors. His private fortunes improved steadily, and he devoted much time to public enterprises, notably the Lake Washington canal and the Alaska-Yukon-Pacific Exposition. He was greatly interested in the University of Washington and in Whitman College, of which he was an overseer. While still a policeman, he gave books to the new library of the university. He was president of the Seattle Chamber of Commerce from 1905 to 1909 and was the first president of the associated chambers of commerce of the Pacific Coast. On Oct. 12, 1874, he married May L. Kelley of Bancroft, Me. He was survived by a son and daughter.

[Seattle Chamber of Commerce, *In Memoriam John Harte McGraw* (1911); Elwood Evans, *Hist. of the Pacific Northwest* (1889), vol. II; C. A. Snowden, *Hist. of Washington*, vol. V (1911); Clarence B. Bagley, *Hist. of Seattle* (1916), vol. II; E. S. Meany, *Governors of Washington* (1915); *Seattle Daily Times*, June 24, 1910.]

G. W. F.

McGREADY, JAMES (*c.* 1758–February 1817), pioneer Presbyterian preacher, and revivalist, was born in western Pennsylvania of Scotch-Irish parents. In his early childhood they moved South and he spent the greater part of his boyhood in Guilford County, N. C. There was a quality about him as a youth which convinced a visiting uncle that he ought to be educated for the Christian ministry. Accordingly he accompanied his uncle to Pennsylvania to prepare for the work of a preacher. He began his study in the autumn of 1785 in a Latin school conducted by Rev. Joseph Smith at Upper Buffalo, Pa., and completed his literary and theological education at Canonsburg, Pa., under Rev. John McMillan, and on Aug. 13, 1788, was licensed to preach by the Presbytery of Redstone, Pa. Soon he decided to move to North Carolina, and on the way spent some deeply significant days at Hampden-Sidney College in Virginia, with Dr. John Blair Smith [*q.v.*], who at the time was the leading spirit in a great revival of religion. It was here that McGready was first deeply impressed with the value of evangelistic preaching and felt the kindling of revival zeal in himself.

Settling in North Carolina, he preached with such effect that he soon brought about a religious awakening "in which ten or twelve young men were brought into the fold, all of whom became ministers of the gospel" (Beard, *post,* p. 9). One of these was Barton W. Stone [*q.v.*]. About 1790 McGready became pastor of a church in Orange County. Possessed of great physical stamina and a voice which won for him the title Boanerges, he was so vehement in his denunciation of sin and hypocrisy that the community was divided into two factions: his ardent supporters and his blood-thirsty enemies. "A letter was written to him in *blood,* requiring him to leave the country at the peril of his life" (*Ibid.*). Partly because of this hostility and partly for the sake of following the migration of his North Carolina converts, he went to Kentucky in 1796, and there took charge of the three small congregations of Gaspar, Red, and Muddy rivers in Logan County. Here he soon induced his people to sign the following covenant: "We bind ourselves to observe the third Saturday of each month, for one year, as a day of fasting and prayer for the conversion of sinners in Logan County and throughout the world. We also engage to spend one half hour every Saturday evening, beginning at the setting of the sun and one half hour every Sabbath morning from the rising of the sun, pleading with God to revive his work" (*Ibid.,* p. 11). With this covenant as a background, at each of McGready's three churches, in connection with sacramental services, remarkable revivals broke out in 1797, 1798, and 1799. These were the forerunners of the Great Revival of 1800. Although many were converted during these three preceding years, yet all that work, McGready wrote later, was "but like a few scattering drops before a mighty rain, when compared with the overflowing floods of salvation . . . poured out like a mighty river" in the year 1800 (*New-York Missionary Magazine,* April 1803, p. 154). Beginning in Logan County, Ky., the revival swept over the western and southern states, affecting all the denominations on the frontier. It was marked by the highest degree of religious excitement, accompanied by violent physical demonstrations, trances, and visions. In connection with it the camp meeting originated, families coming to meeting places in wagons from miles around and camping out together for several days as they took part in the revival exercises. McGready wrote "A Short Narrative of the Revival of Religion in Logan County in the State of Kentucky, and the Adjacent Settlements in the State of Tennessee, from May 1797 until September 1800," which was published serially, February–June 1803, in the *New-York Missionary Magazine.*

One of the consequences of the Great Revival was the organization of the Cumberland Presbyterian Church, which separated from the older Presbyterian body on two issues: the denial that a classical education is prerequisite to ministerial ordination, and renunciation of the fatalism in the Westminster standards. McGready allied himself with the Cumberland Presbytery in its policy regarding licensing preachers who do not have classical training, but finally (1809) refused to go with them in their renunciation of the strict Calvinism of the Westminster Confession. After a period of discipline and silence he was restored to the orthodox Transylvania Presbytery. In 1811, he was sent as a pioneer preacher to found churches in southern Indiana. In the fall of 1816, at a camp meeting near Evansville, Ind., he preached with such effectiveness that he exclaimed, "I this day feel the same holy fire that filled my soul sixteen years ago, during the glorious revival of 1800" (Beard, p. 14). Just a few months later, February 1817, he died at his home in Henderson County, Ky. According to his biographer, Beard (*post*), he was married about 1790, but the name of his wife is not recorded. A number of years after his death there appeared *The Posthumous Works of the Reverend and Pious M'Gready* (2 vols., 1831–33), edited by James Smith.

[Richard Beard, *Brief Biog. Sketches of Some of the Early Ministers of the Cumberland Presbyt. Ch.* (1867); T. C. Blake, *The Old Log House* (1878); E. H. Gillett, *Hist. of the Presbyt. Ch. in the U. S. A.* (2 vols., 1864); W. B. Sprague, *Annals Am. Pulpit,* III (1859), 278; B. W. McDonnold, *Hist. of the Cumberland Presbyt. Ch.* (1888); R. V. Foster, "A Sketch of the History of the Cumberland Presbyterian Church," *Am. Church Hist.,* vol. XI (1894); Joseph Smith, *Old Redstone; or, Hist. Sketches of Western Presbyterianism* (1854); Robert Davidson, *Hist. of the Presbyt. Ch. in the State of Ky.* (1847); C. C. Cleveland, *The Great Revival in the West, 1797–1805* (1916).]
O. E. B.

McGROARTY, SUSAN [See JULIA, SISTER, 1827–1901].

McGUFFEY, WILLIAM HOLMES (Sept. 23, 1800–May 4, 1873), educator, compiler of school-readers, was born near Claysville in Washington County, Pa. He came from Scotch-Irish stock; his grandfather, William McGuffey, emigrated from Scotland to America in 1774 and settled in Pennsylvania; his father, Alexander, became an Indian fighter, served under both St. Clair and Anthony Wayne, and in 1794 married Anna Holmes. When the "Connecticut Reserve" was opened in Ohio in 1802, the young couple with their son settled near Youngstown. On this pioneer homestead, William Holmes McGuffey spent sixteen years. His mother gave him instruction in the rudiments, and he attended the intermittent sessions of the rural schools. In his teens his parents sent him to take private lessons in Latin from the pastor of the Presbyterian Church at Youngstown. His striking capacity to memorize marked him as a prodigy; he committed to memory entire books of the Bible, and much other literature. In 1818 he entered the Old Stone Academy of Darlington, Pa., under the Rev. Thomas Hughes, and thence proceeded to Washington College, from which he graduated with honors in 1826. Between his periods of college attendance, he taught school, chiefly in Kentucky.

On Mar. 29, 1826, he was elected by the Board of Trustees to the position of professor of languages in Miami University, Oxford, Ohio. In the following year he married Harriet Spinning of Dayton, to which union two daughters and three sons were born. He was licensed to preach in the Presbyterian church in 1829, but never held a regular ministerial appointment; while in Oxford, however, he preached every Sunday at Darrtown, four miles distant. He always spoke extemporaneously and in later life often said that he had preached three thousand sermons and had never written one of them. In 1832 he became head of the department of mental philosophy and philology at Miami and four years later (1836), was called to the presidency of Cincinnati College. During this period his fame as a lecturer on moral and Biblical subjects spread rapidly; with Samuel Lewis [*q.v.*] and others he took part in organizing the College of Teachers, an association formed to promote the interests of education; and with Lewis he labored to secure the passage of the law under which the common schools of Ohio were first organized. On Sept. 17, 1839, he was elected president of Ohio University at Athens, Ohio, and served until the institution closed its doors in 1843. He then returned to Cincinnati to become a professor in Woodward College. Here he remained until his election as professor of moral philosophy in the University of Virginia, July 1845, a post which he held for the rest of his life, teaching until within a few weeks of his death. He soon became ranking professor and was widely remembered and quoted. In Virginia as in Ohio he was an earnest advocate of a public-school system. His wife died in 1853 and in 1857 he married Laura Howard, daughter of Dean Henry Howard of the University. One daughter, who died at the age of four, was born of this second marriage. Through the lean years of the Civil War and Reconstruction he was noted for his philanthropy and generosity among the poor and the negroes.

Despite his long career as a college and university professor, McGuffey is most widely known for his *Eclectic Readers* for elementary schools. While he was professor at Miami University he began, at the solicitation of the Cincinnati publishers, Truman & Smith, to compile the series of schoolbooks which have made his name a household word. The First and Second Readers were published in 1836, the Third and Fourth in 1837. These books—with the Fifth, added in 1844, the *Eclectic Spelling Book,* added in 1846 by McGuffey's brother, Alexander Hamilton McGuffey, and a Sixth, added in 1857—went through edition after edition, were revised and enlarged, and reached the fabulous sale of 122,000,000 copies. Even the simplest lessons, although containing obvious, sometimes explicit, morals, were designed to win the pupil's interest, and the more advanced selections included well-chosen extracts from the greatest English writers. The *Readers* served to introduce thousands of boys and girls to the treasures of literature. Their influence, moral and cultural, upon the children in the thirty-seven states in which they were used contributed much to the shaping of the American mind in the nineteenth century.

[H. H. Vail, *A Hist. of the McGuffey Readers* (1910); H. C. Minnich, *Wm. Holmes McGuffey and the Peerless Pioneer McGuffey Readers* (1928); M. Tope, *A Biog. of Wm. Holmes McGuffey* (1929); Mark Sullivan, *Our Times,* vol. II (1927); P. A. Bruce, *Hist. of the Univ. of Va., 1819–1919* (5 vols., 1920–22); *Ohio Archæol. and Hist. Quart.,* Apr. 1927; Daniel Read, in *Addresses and Jour. of Proc. Nat. Educ. Asso.,* 1873; *Daily Dispatch* (Richmond), May 6, 1873.]

H. C. M.

McGUIRE, CHARLES BONAVENTURE (Dec. 16, 1768–July 17, 1833), Franciscan friar, was born of a gentle family in Dungannon, County Tyrone, Ireland, the name of which is often given as Maguire. Charles obtained his rudimentary education from a refugee master in a "hedge-school." Forced by the penal laws to flee the land, he was educated in a French or Belgian college and at Louvain. Ordained a Franciscan friar, he served in the Low Countries until proscribed by the French Revolutionists. Dragged to the guillotine, he was rescued by a cooper, who was instantly cut to pieces by the infuriated mob, while McGuire made his escape. Thereafter he dwelt in Rome until the arrival of Napoleon's soldiers. Again escaping, he traveled over the Continent making observations and conducting confidential work for his order and, presumably, for the papacy. Commissioned by the king of Bohemia to perform a religious office for a member of the royal family then in Brussels, he was on hand to attend the wounded from Waterloo and to collect battle relics, which he preserved. An adventurous friar, he sought service in the American missions, for which he was warmly recommended to Archbishop Maréchal [*q.v.*], by Cardinal Litta. Arriving in Pennsylvania in 1817, he was assigned to the Western missions, to Sportsman's Hall or Latrobe, and in 1820 to the pastorate of the diminutive church of St. Patrick's in Pittsburgh.

Aided by Col. James O'Hara, one of the founders of the Pittsburgh glass industry, and the donations of the increasing number of German artisans and Irish laborers, Father McGuire enlarged the church. Within a few years, 1829, he laid the corner-stone of St. Paul's Church on Grant Hill, which, when completed by his successor, was one of the largest in America. A year earlier, he was named superior of the Poor Clare nuns, who opened a convent and academy in the town of Allegheny. Catholicism in Western Pennsylvania found a worthy expositor in this simple religious, whom Bishop Fenwick [*q.v.*], of Cincinnati, was anxious to have named bishop of a proposed see in Indiana in 1823 (J. H. Lamott, *History of the Archdiocese of Cincinnati,* 1921, p. 55). His fluent use of several languages, intimate knowledge of Europe, cosmopolitan character, commanding appearance, ready wit, and urbanity added to the prestige of the uneducated Catholic minority and made him a social favorite in Pittsburgh. Without episcopal ambition, he remained a pastor to his death. Buried in a vault in St. Paul's his remains were later moved to St. Mary's cemetery.

[A. A. Lambing, *Hist. of the Cath. Ch. in the Dioceses of Pittsburg and Allegheny* (1880); *Records of the Am. Cath. Hist. Soc.*, vol. III (1891); *The Am. Cath. Hist. Researches*, Oct. 1894; *N. Y. Weekly Register*, Apr. 19, 1834; *The Jesuit*, Aug. 10, 1833, reprinting obit. in *Pittsburg Manufacturer*; *U. S. Cath. Almanac*, 1834.]

R. J. P.

McGUIRE, HUNTER HOLMES (Oct. 11, 1835–Sept. 19, 1900), surgeon, was born in Winchester, Va., the son of a physician and surgeon, Dr. Hugh Holmes McGuire, and of Ann Eliza (Moss) McGuire. He was a descendant of Edward McGuire of County Kerry, Ireland, who settled in Virginia in 1747. Hunter McGuire received his premedical education at Winchester Academy and later studied at the Winchester Medical College, from which he received his diploma in 1855. The year following, he matriculated at both the University of Pennsylvania and Jefferson Medical College, Philadelphia, but was forced to return home because of an attack of rheumatism. In 1857 he was elected professor of anatomy in the College at Winchester, but he resigned the position after one session and went once more to Philadelphia, where he established a quiz class and pursued further studies. John Brown's raid gave rise to such intense sectional feeling in 1859 as to lead to a mass meeting of Southern medical students in Philadelphia and a resolution that they go South. McGuire was the leading spirit in this movement and assumed the expenses of such of the three hundred students as could not pay their own way to Richmond. He resumed studies there and acquired a second medical degree. He then went to New Orleans, where he established a quiz class in connection with the medical department of the University of Louisiana.

When Virginia seceded from the Union, he volunteered as a private soldier and marched to Harpers Ferry. He was soon commissioned as a medical officer, and in May 1861 he was made medical director of the Army of the Shenandoah, then under command of "Stonewall" Jackson. Later, when Jackson organized the First Virginia Brigade, he asked that McGuire be made its surgeon. Thereafter he served as chief surgeon of Jackson's commands until the latter's death. He was also his personal physician. Subsequently he was surgeon of the II Army Corps, under General Ewell, medical director of the Army of Northern Virginia under General Ewell, and medical director of the Army of the Valley of Virginia, under General Jubal Early. It is said that he organized the "Reserve Corps Hospitals of the Confederacy" and that he perfected the "Ambulance Corps." The latter consisted of a detail of four men from each company to assist the wounded from the field to hospitals in the rear. The men wore conspicuous badges, and no other soldiers were permitted to leave the ranks during battle for the purpose of rendering aid. Just what constituted the "Reserve Corps Hospitals of the Confederacy" does not appear from any available records. McGuire was always active in securing the release of captured Union medical officers, and when he was himself captured by General Sheridan's troops in March 1865, he was at once paroled and in two weeks released.

In 1865 he was elected professor of surgery in the Virginia Medical College, and served as such until 1878, when he resigned; in 1880 he was made professor emeritus. He was actively connected with the establishment at Richmond in

1893 of the College of Physicians and Surgeons, later named the University College of Medicine, and was its president and professor of surgery at the time of his death. He also organized St. Luke's Home for the Sick, with a training school for nurses. He wrote a great variety of articles, mostly upon surgical matters, but also upon such subjects as "Nervous Troubles Following Organic Urethral Stricture" (*Virginia Medical Monthly,* October 1890), "Sexual Crimes among the Southern Negroes, Scientifically Considered" (*Ibid.,* May 1893), "Cases of Tuberculosis Cured by Cancrum Oris" (*Kansas City Medical Record,* April 1897), "The Treatment of Acute Exudative Nephritis Following Infectious Diseases" (*Bi-monthly Bulletin of the University College of Medicine,* March 1898). He also contributed to John Ashhurst's *International Encyclopædia of Surgery* (6 vols., 1881–86), to William Pepper's *System of Practical Medicine* (5 vols., 1885–86), and to the American Edition of Timothy Holmes's *System of Surgery, Theoretical and Practical* (3 vols., 1881–82).

Always an ardent Southerner, when in his later life his attention was called to the "efforts of Northern writers and their friends to pervert the world's judgment and secure a world verdict in their favor," he at once undertook a campaign which resulted in the appointment of a committee to examine the school histories in use in Virginia, in the reorganization of the Virginia School Board, and in the condemnation of offending books. His account of the death of his own good friend, "Stonewall" Jackson (*American Medical Weekly,* Jan. 6, 1883), is touching and beautiful in its simplicity and in the pictures which it evokes so vividly. In 1866 he married Mary Stuart, by whom he had nine children. His death, after six months of invalidism, resulted from cerebral embolism. Always an outstanding and honored figure in his community, McGuire was also the recipient of many honors from his professional fellows. In Capitol Square, Richmond, a bronze statue of heroic size, which is a remarkable likeness, perpetuates his memory.

[W. G. Stanard, *The McGuire Family in Va.* (1926); H. A. Kelly and W. L. Burrage, *Am. Medic. Biogs.* (1920); *The Clinic Bull.,* Sept.–Oct. 1910; *Revue de Chirurgie,* Nov. 1900; *British Medic. Jour.,* Sept. 29, 1900; *Medic. News,* Sept. 29, 1900; *Va. Medic. Monthly,* Oct. 1877; *Richmond and Louisville Medic. Jour.,* Oct. 1877; *Dublin Jour. of Medic. Science,* Nov. 1, 1900; *New England Medic. Monthly,* Jan. 1885; *Trans. of the Thirty-first Ann. Session of the Medic. Soc. of Va., 1900* (1901); *Trans. of the Southern Surgic. and Gynecological Asso., 1902* (1903); *Annals of Gynecology and Pediatry,* Nov. 1900; *Pacific Medic. Jour.,* Nov. 1900; *Jour. Am. Medic. Asso.,* Sept. 29, 1900; *Boston Medic. and Surgic. Jour.,* Sept. 27, 1900; *N. Y. Medic. Jour.,* Sept. 22, 1900; *Medic. Record,* Sept. 22, 1900; *Surgery, Gynecology and Obstetrics,* Jan. 1923; the *Times* (Richmond), Sept. 20, 1900.] P. M. A.

McGUIRE, JOSEPH DEAKINS (Nov. 26, 1842–Sept. 6, 1916), anthropologist, was born in Washington, D. C., the son of James C. and Margaret (Deakins) McGuire. After studying at Georgetown College, he entered the College of New Jersey in 1859, but left at the opening of the Civil War with the intention of enlisting in the army. On account of his youth, however, his family sent him abroad to complete his education. After studying languages and scientific farming in France and Germany for two years, he returned to the United States and settled at Ellicott City, Md. Having prepared himself for the practice of law, he was admitted to the bar in 1876. From 1884 to 1900 he held the office of state's attorney for Howard County. In 1901 Princeton University conferred upon him the honorary degree of A.M. and at the same time awarded him the degree of A.B. as of the class of 1863.

Stone implements and other archeological relics scattered over his estate at Ellicott City attracted his interest, and for years he collected these, amassing a large number of objects now in the Smithsonian Institution. At times his explorations were carried on further afield. Moving to Washington in 1900, he occupied his time in investigations conducted at the Smithsonian, where he was appointed honorary collaborator. The study of aboriginal technology was then being pursued and McGuire applied himself to some of the problems involved. He was the first white man to shape a stone axe with stone tools and to carve in stone by aboriginal methods. As a result of his studies and experiments, he published "Materials, Apparatus, and Processes of the Aboriginal Lapidary" (*Anthropologist,* April 1892); "The Development of Sculpture" (*Ibid.,* October 1894); "On the Evolution of the Art of Working Stone" (*Ibid.,* July 1893); "The Stone Hammer and Its Various Uses" (*Ibid.,* October 1891); and "A Study of the Primitive Methods of Drilling" (*Report of the United States National Museum* for 1894). Following explorations in Maine, he published "Ethnological and Archeological Notes on Moosehead Lake, Maine" (*American Anthropologist,* October–December 1908). Ethnological papers of his which attracted much attention were: "Ethnology in the Jesuit Relations" (*Ibid.,* April–June 1901), and "Pipes and Smoking Customs of the American Aborigines" (*Report of the United States National Museum* for 1897). These papers, written by McGuire in his mature years, are considered valuable contributions to anthropological science, because of their empirical character and the light they throw on the fundamental shaping arts of primitive man. His trained legal mind was an asset in his scientific work, bringing to it acumen and judgment in weighing facts, and habits of keen observation. His compeers in science considered him an earnest, fair-minded worker with the saving grace of humor. On Dec. 19, 1866, he married Anna Chapman of Staunton, Va.

[*Princeton, Sixty-three: Fortieth Year Book of the Members of the Class of 1863* (1904); *Am. Anthropologist,* July–Sept. 1916; *Who's Who in America,* 1916–17; *Evening Star* (Washington), Sept. 7, 1916; personal recollections.] W. H.

MACHEBEUF, JOSEPH PROJECTUS (Aug. 11, 1812–July 10, 1889), Roman Catholic prelate, son of Michael Anthony and Gilberte (Plauc) Machebeuf, was born at Riom, in the heart of Auvergne, France. Since his family was in comfortable circumstances, he was privileged to attend a private school, a Christian Brothers' college, and the old Oratorian College of Riom, which had become secularized. In 1831 he entered the Sulpician Seminary of Montferrand, where his theological studies were interrupted by forced vacations in the Volvic Mountains for the preservation of his health. Ordained on Dec. 21, 1836, Abbé Machebeuf was named curate at Cendre, where he was inspired with missionary zeal by Dr. J. M. Odin and Bishop B. J. Flaget [*qq.v.*], traveling through their native France in the interest of American missions. Along with Abbé J. B. Lamy [*q.v.*], he accepted the call of Bishop John Purcell and accompanied him and Bishop Flaget to Cincinnati in 1839. Though only slightly acquainted with German and English, he was immediately sent to Tiffin, which served as a mission center for northern Ohio and was being settled by Germans with a sprinkling of Irish and French. In 1841 he was assigned to Lower Sandusky (Fremont), and Sandusky City, where he built three churches, made extensive visitations to railroad camps, and labored for temperance among hard-drinking navvies. He journeyed to Montreal and Quebec soliciting financial aid, and on behalf of Bishop Purcell went back to France and Rome seeking helpers and bringing back in 1844 a colony of Ursuline nuns and the first American group of sisters of Notre Dame de Namur. In 1849 Father Pierre-Jean De Smet [*q.v.*], learning of Machebeuf's disinterested missionary zeal, visited him in the hope of obtaining his services for the Rocky Mountain missions; but while he longed for a wider field, he hesitated to go unless Father Lamy would accompany him, for on leaving France they had pledged themselves to remain together. The desire for a frontier field was soon answered, for in 1850 Lamy was appointed vicar apostolic of New Mexico and Machebeuf went with him to Santa Fé.

He learned Spanish and the Mexicans turned out in mass to meet the itinerant *señor vicario* when he visited the scattered stations with his muleteam. At Albuquerque in 1852, he replaced the popular but irregular José Gallegos, later a delegate to Congress, and quieted a tumultuous congregation by sheer personal courage. As vicar general, he administered the vicariate during Mgr. Lamy's absence, and in 1856 journeyed to France for additional priests. As pastor of the adobe cathedral of Sante Fé he ministered to 5,000 souls and yet found time to attend missions at Arroyo Hondo and Taos, where with Kit Carson's aid he put down an uprising caused by a Mexican priest who did not relish the new American jurisdiction. Sent to care for Arizona, he barely escaped assassination, but neither Indians nor desperadoes could deter one who boasted the Auvergne motto *Latsin pas.* At Tucson he erected a rude chapel and undertook the preservation of the historic mission of San Xavier del Bac.

Since the newly developing region of Colorado could not be cared for from Santa Fé, Lamy sent him in 1860 to Denver along with Father John B. Raverdy. Soon his strange wagon loaded with supplies, cooking utensils, bedding, and books was known in all gulches, boom towns, mining camps, and army posts of Colorado and Utah. It was a desperate field for a lone missionary, yet he was everywhere, even fraternizing with Brigham Young and his elders in Salt Lake City. Alive to the future of Colorado and Denver, he bought church sites when land values were low, though he invested little in mining properties. On small plots of land, at a time when few men looked beyond gold diggings, he demonstrated that Colorado valleys were suitable for agriculture. Within a few years he built churches, in Denver, Central City, and Golden City, besides establishing a dozen chapels and stations in mining towns and the new agricultural villages. Under his direction the Sisters of Charity erected hospitals in Denver and Pueblo, the Sisters of Loretto founded St. Mary's Academy in Denver and a school in Pueblo, and the Sisters of St. Joseph erected a school at Central City.

In 1868 when Colorado and Utah were made a vicariate, Machebeuf was named vicar apostolic with the title of Bishop of Epiphania. Consecrated in Cincinnati by Archbishop Purcell, Aug. 16, 1868, he traveled through the East visiting the chief seminaries in a vain effort to obtain volunteers. A year later he sought aid in France from the Propagation of the Faith and finally obtained three French missionaries and an Irish priest for his distant diocese. A boom in Colorado was followed by hard times. Rumors reached the East and even Rome that Machebeuf was insolvent, although the only danger lay in frightened creditors driving him to the wall by forcing property sales at auction prices. Going to Rome he offered to resign, but his resignation was refused. Instead, he was made a bishop (1887), and his friend, Nicholas C. Matz, was named coadjutor with the right of succession. Meanwhile a holding company had been established, some properties were sold, and in time the financial tangle was straightened out, leaving a surplus besides some of the finest church sites in the state. Active to the end despite injuries received in mountain wrecks, he journeyed to Washington for the foundation of the Catholic University in 1888, the year the Jesuits removed their college from Morrison to Denver and his dearest friend, Archbishop Lamy, died. Within a year, after an illness of a few days, Machebeuf, too, passed away.

[W. J. Howlett, *Life of the Rt. Rev. Joseph P. Machebeuf* (1908); *Cath. Ency*c., vol. IV (1908); J. G. Shea, *Hist. of the Cath. Ch. in the U. S.*, vol. IV (1892), *The Hierarchy of the Cath. Ch. in the U. S.* (1886); R. H. Clarke, *Hist. of the Cath. Ch. in the U. S. with Biog. Sketches of the Living Bishops*, vol. II (1890); Sadliers' *Cath. Directory for 1890* (1890); *Denver Republican*, July 10, 11, 1889.] R. J. P.

McHENRY, JAMES (Nov. 16, 1753–May 3, 1816), Revolutionary soldier, secretary of war, son of Daniel and Agnes McHenry, was born in Ballymena, County Antrim, Ireland, and received his classical education in Dublin. In 1771, he joined the immigrant crowds who left Ulster for Philadelphia; and on his insistence, the remainder of the family emigrated the following year. His father and his brother John established a profitable importing business in Baltimore and built up a considerable estate, to which ultimately (in 1790) James fell heir. He attended the Newark Academy, Delaware (1772), where he displayed a weakness for poetry, and then studied medicine in Philadelphia under Dr. Benjamin Rush.

An ardent patriot because of his pronounced hostility to England, he hurried to Cambridge in 1775 to volunteer for military service. In January 1776, he was assigned to the medical staff of the military hospital in Cambridge, where he won recognition from the Continental Congress and assurance of advancement. On Aug. 10, he was named surgeon of Col. Robert Magaw's 5th Pennsylvania Battalion. Captured at the fall of Fort Washington in November, he was paroled Jan. 27, 1777, and remained in Philadelphia and Baltimore until a complete exchange was arranged, Mar. 5, 1778. For a short time, apparently, he acted as "Senior Surgeon of the Flying Hospital, Valley Forge," and on May 15 was appointed secretary to Washington. With this appointment, according to one of his biographers (Steiner, *post*, p. 17), he abandoned the practice of medicine for the rest of his life. Winning the confidence of Washington for ability and prudence, McHenry was transferred to Lafayette's staff in August 1780. Ever afterward he gloried in his association with Lafayette, and some years later contributed an account of the French general's services to Dr. William Gordon [*q.v.*], for use in his *History of the Rise, Progress and Establishment of the Independence of the United States of America* (1788). With characteristic loyalty he urged Washington to aid Lafayette when the latter was a prisoner at Olmütz. Commissioned a major, May 30, 1781, McHenry continued in active service until he was elected to the Maryland Senate (September 1781), where he sat for five years.

In May 1783, he was appointed to Congress and through later elections and reëlections served until 1786. During this period he wrote (1784) three articles, published five years later under the general title, "Observations Relative to a Commercial Treaty with Great Britain," in Mathew Carey's *American Museum* (April, May, June 1789). A Maryland delegate to the Convention of 1787, which drafted the federal Constitution, he attended from May 28 to June 1, when the illness of his brother recalled him to Baltimore, and was again in attendance from Aug. 6 until the convention adjourned. He was a conscientious worker, but for one of such varied training and experience added little to the debates. He kept a private record of the proceedings of the Convention, however, which is one of the valuable sources for its history (*American Historical Review*, April 1906; Max Farrand, *The Records of the Federal Convention of 1787*, 1911). A stout Federalist, he campaigned for state adoption of the Constitution and served as a member of Maryland's ratifying convention. Subsequently, in a warm contest, he defeated Samuel Chase for a seat in the Assembly, in which he sat until 1791, when he entered the state Senate for a period of five years. As an intimate associate of the President-Elect, he was named to the Maryland commission which formally welcomed Washington on his journey to New York for the inauguration in April 1789.

In January 1796, fourth choice for the post, he was offered the secretaryship of war, to succeed Timothy Pickering [*q.v.*], who had become secretary of state. As a member of the cabinet, he won the President's esteem and apparently considerable influence in the distribution of patronage. He retained his portfolio into Adams' administration. Like his colleague Pickering, he regarded Hamilton as his political leader and on all major matters of policy reflected Hamilton's opinions. Consequently, with the increasing difficulty of the question of war with France, his relations with President Adams [*q.v.*] became more and more strained. When Hamilton, Pinckney, and Knox were appointed generals, under Washington, to provide for the event of war, Adams suspected McHenry of machinations in Hamilton's favor; later he believed McHenry guilty of intriguing against his reëlection, but this McHenry denied. In May 1800, on Adams' demand, he resigned from the cabinet. His troubles were not over, however, for the Republicans violently assailed his administration of the department of war. Yet a congressional committee (Apr. 29, 1802), reported against undertaking an investigation of his expenditure of funds. Keenly sensitive to criticism, McHenry prepared an elaborate defense which was read from the floor of the House on Dec. 28, 1802, and privately printed under the title, *A Letter to the Honourable Speaker of the House of Representatives of the United States,* early in 1803.

Thereafter, he lived in retirement on his pleasant estate at Fayetteville, near Baltimore, with his wife, Margaret Allison Caldwell, whom he had married Jan. 8, 1784. As a Federalist, he was opposed to the War of 1812; though his son John volunteered in the defense of Fort McHenry (named for McHenry during his secretaryship) and of Baltimore. Of other activities he had but few. He served as president of the first Bible society founded in Baltimore (1813), and published a Baltimore directory (1807). A brochure, *The Three Patriots* (1811), dealing with Jefferson, Madison, and Monroe, has been attributed to him, though not conclusively (Steiner, p. 572). Without marked ability as an orator, a legislator, a surgeon, or a soldier, he was a high-minded gentleman, a conservative politician, and an associate of great men in stirring days. He died in his sixty-third year. Of his children, only two, a son and a daughter, survived him.

[B. C. Steiner, *The Life and Correspondence of James McHenry* (1907); F. J. Brown, *A Sketch of the Life of Dr. James McHenry* (1877); *Biog. Dir. Am. Cong.* (1928); *Pubs. Southern Hist. Asso.,* Sept., Nov. 1905, Jan., Mar. 1906, Jan. 1907; James McHenry Papers, MSS. Div., Lib. of Cong.] R. J. P.

McHENRY, JAMES (Dec. 20, 1785–July 21, 1845), poet, novelist, was born at Larne, County Antrim, Ireland, where he studied first for the Presbyterian ministry, but being disinclined to the pulpit because he was a hunchback he became a student of medicine at Belfast and later at Glasgow. Sensitive and deeply impressionable, he turned to poetry and wrote many lyrics to celebrate the valley of the Larne and the blue Scottish hills. For some years after his certification he practised medicine in his native town of Larne and Belfast; but in 1817, with his wife and infant son, he emigrated to the United States, living in Baltimore, Butler County, Pa., and in Pittsburgh until 1824 when he settled in Philadelphia. In that city for eighteen years he was prominent as a physician, merchant, political leader, magazine editor, poet, and critic. With the assistance of his wife he established and kept a draper's shop near his home at 36 Second Street: in addition to this he very soon met with some success in professional and literary circles.

As early as 1822, while in Pittsburgh, he had brought out a volume of miscellaneous verse, *The Pleasures of Friendship,* and a year later his first exclusively American work, *Waltham,* a poetic legend of Revolutionary days. About the same time, his first novel, written under the pseudonym of Solomon Secondsight, was published in London. *The Wilderness; or The Youthful Days of Washington* (1823), is an account of the adventures of Protestant Ulstermen in America during the Revolutionary days of the West. In 1824 McHenry began his brief career as an editor when he founded the *American Monthly Magazine* as a Philadelphia rival of the *North American Review.* This magazine, devoted to criticism, essays, poetry, and social satire, failed within its first year for reasons principally financial. He had already published his second novel, *The Spectre of the Forest* (1823), to be followed in 1824 by *O'Halloran, or the Insurgent Chief,* and in 1825 by *The Hearts of Steel,* an Irish historical tale. In 1827 he undertook to launch his sole venture in the dramatic field, *The Usurper,* a tragedy of Druidical times in blank verse and interesting as having been the first attempt to place Irish legendary history upon the American stage. *The Usurper* appeared at the Chestnut Street Theatre Dec. 26, 1827, but was received without enthusiasm. McHenry now turned again to novel writing, producing American historical tales of which *The Betrothed of Wyoming* (1830) and *Meredith, or the Mystery of Meschianza* (1831) are types.

In the meantime the success of his earliest and perhaps his best work, *The Pleasures of Friendship,* which had reached a seventh edition in 1836, led McHenry, whose views upon poetry were highly conservative, to attack Wordsworth, Scott, Byron, and other romanticists of their respective schools in the most unmeasured terms. As leading poetry reviewer for the *American*

Quarterly Review, he was led by his bias into extravagances so effectively rebutted by writers for *Blackwood's Edinburgh Magazine* and the *Athenæum* as to discredit him as a critic. He now turned once more to prose fiction and verse. Ambitious like Pope, to whom he has been not very happily likened, he attempted an epic and in 1839 published *Antediluvians, or the World Destroyed,* a blank verse chronicle of the Flood. It was scathingly reviewed in *Blackwood's* (July 1839). Undoubtedly he was at his best with the Irish lyric. For all his many talents, his sole contribution to American letters was his portraiture of the Ulster Irishman who in conduct, beliefs, and religious tenets resembles the lowland Scot. In 1843 he was appointed to the consulate in Londonderry. He assumed his duties and after two years in office died in his native town of Larne.

[E. P. Oberholtzer, *The Lit. Hist. of Phila.* (1906); F. L. Mott, *A Hist. of Am. Mags., 1741–1850* (1930); F. C. Wemyss, *Twenty Six Years of the Life of an Actor and Manager* (1847); A. H. Quinn, *A Hist. of the Am. Drama from the Beginning to the Civil War* (1923); the *Knickerbocker,* July 1834, Apr. 1859; *Pub. Ledger* (Phila.), Aug. 12, 1845.] E. M. H.

MCILVAINE, CHARLES PETTIT (Jan. 18, 1799–Mar. 13, 1873), Protestant Episcopal bishop, son of Joseph and Maria (Reed) McIlvaine, was descended on his father's side from the McIlvaines of Ayrshire, Scotland; his mother's family was of English origin. Joseph McIlvaine, a lawyer by profession, was from 1823 until his death in 1826 a member of the United States Senate. Charles was born at Burlington, N. J.; he studied at the Burlington Academy, graduated with high honors from the College of New Jersey at Princeton in 1816, and subsequently pursued theological studies there and in private. Ordered deacon on July 4, 1820, he at once took charge of Christ Church, Georgetown, D. C., where he remained until 1824. He was ordained priest Mar. 20, 1823. On Oct. 8, 1822, he married Emily, daughter of William Coxe [*q.v.*], whom he had known in childhood. At Georgetown his preaching attracted the attention of many leading statesmen in Washington, and in the year 1821–22 he served as chaplain of the Senate. In January 1825 he was appointed chaplain and professor of geography, history, and ethics at West Point, where he remained until December 1827. Here he instituted revivals of religion that profoundly affected many officers and cadets—something unusual at the Military Academy, and not altogether pleasing to those in authority.

McIlvaine's theology was of the most evangelical school and he received calls to several churches of that type, while on the other hand he incurred the strong opposition of some prominent high-churchmen. He was rector of St. Ann's, Brooklyn, N. Y., from December 1827 until 1833, and was also for part of the same time professor of the evidences of Christianity at the University of the City of New York. In the winter of 1831–32 he delivered a series of lectures which were published under the title, *The Evidences of Christianity in Their External Division* (1832).

Elected bishop of Ohio in 1831, he was consecrated to that office Oct. 31, 1832, and the next year moved to Gambier, Ohio, the seat of Kenyon College and its divinity school, of which institutions he became president *ex officio.* As bishop he was incessant in his labors, incurring cheerfully the hardships involved in traveling over miserable roads in primitive conveyances. Never robust, he often sought rest by visits to Europe, especially to England. Both at home and in England he was recognized as a leader of the evangelical cause in the war on the tractarian doctrines. His activity in this connection brought him into unhappy controversies in Ohio, although he had the steadfast support of a strong majority of his diocese. In controversy he was strenuous but without asperity. In the administration of affairs he was decided and imperative. He ruled the institutions at Gambier with a strong hand, and by obtaining money for them at several times rescued them from bankruptcy and secured the erection of many buildings. In 1846 he moved to Clifton, near Cincinnati, which was thereafter his home.

In 1861 when British opinion was greatly inflamed because of the *Trent* affair, he visited England at the request of President Lincoln and exerted himself, particularly among the higher clergy, to make friends for the United States. He was most cordially received and his efforts were in a considerable degree successful. On a subsequent visit to England he was presented to the Queen at her request, and was shown marked attentions by the Prince of Wales. He died in March 1873, at Florence, Italy, to which place he had gone in search of health. His body was taken to England, where a funeral service was held in Westminster Abbey, and was then brought to America and buried at Clifton, Ohio.

In addition to his *Evidences of Christianity,* McIlvaine published many books and pamphlets, the majority of them in exposition and defense of evangelical doctrines, the most important being *Oxford Divinity Compared with That of the Romish and Anglican Churches* (1841). Although a decided Episcopalian, he was on friendly terms with evangelical Christians of all denominations, and was a member of many interdenominational societies. He was tall, stately, handsome, of impressive appearance. His manners were reserved, and he was thought by many to be "cold," yet he was of a very affectionate and sympathetic nature, and was greatly loved by all who knew him well. He was famous as an eloquent and effective preacher. His opinions when once formed seldom changed. His religious faith, clear and unwavering, was the sustaining and controlling power in his life.

[William Carus, *Memorial of the Right Rev. Charles Pettit McIlvaine* (London, 1882); G. F. Smythe, *A Hist. of the Diocese of Ohio* (1931); McIlvaine papers, including letters, journals, memoranda, etc., in the library of Kenyon College, Gambier, Ohio; letters at Trinity Cathedral, Cleveland; annual journals of the Diocese of Ohio, esp. *Jour. of the Fifty-sixth Ann. Conv. . . .* (1873); N. N. Hill, *Hist. of Knox County, Ohio* (1881); Harriet Weed, *The Life of Thurlow Weed* (1884), vol. I; *Cincinnati Commercial*, Mar. 15, 1873.] G. F. S.

McILWAINE, RICHARD (May 28, 1834–Aug. 10, 1913), Presbyterian clergyman, college president, was the son of Archibald Graham and Martha (Dunn) McIlwaine, of Petersburg, Va. He entered Petersburg Classical Institute at the age of ten, and in January 1850 enrolled in Hampden-Sydney College, where he was an honor graduate with the degree of A.B. in 1853. He studied law at the University of Virginia, 1853–55; was enrolled at Union Theological Seminary, Hampden-Sydney, 1855–57, and in 1857–58 studied in the Free Church College, Edinburgh, Scotland. On May 14, 1857, he married Elizabeth, daughter of Clement Carrington Read of Farmville, Va. From 1858 to 1861 he was pastor of the Presbyterian Church at Amelia Court House, Va. At the outbreak of the Civil War he became lieutenant and chaplain of the 44th Virginia Volunteers, continuing in this capacity until 1862, when precarious health caused him to retire from active service. Returning to Farmville, Va., he became volunteer chaplain of the army hospital located there, and was pastor until 1870. From September 1870 till 1872 he was pastor of the First Presbyterian Church of Lynchburg, Va.; from 1872 to 1882 he was coördinate secretary of the Executive Committee of Foreign Missions and the Executive Committee of Home Missions of the Southern Presbyterian body (Presbyterian Church in the United States). In 1882–83 he was sole secretary of the latter committee. These positions he filled with signal ability, greatly stimulating interest in mission work.

From 1883 to 1904, he was president of Hampden-Sydney College and filled also the chair of moral philosophy and Bible studies. His administration was one of sustained vigor. The curriculum was broadened; the endowment was enlarged; the faculty was increased. He had marked gifts as a teacher. In 1901, without seeking the position, and without opposition, he was elected by the citizens of Prince Edward County as a member of the state constitutional convention, and became chairman of the committee of that body on education and public instruction. In this capacity he was instrumental in the establishment of a central Board of Education with large powers, under which the public-school system of the state has made its greatest progress. He retired from the presidency of Hampden-Sydney College in 1904 and thereafter lived in Richmond, Va., until his death. He was buried at Petersburg. McIlwaine was a prolific writer for church and secular papers. Many of his sermons and addresses were collected in a volume, *Addresses and Papers Bearing Chiefly on Education* (1908). He also published an autobiography, *Memories of Three Score Years and Ten* (1908), and several biographical sketches in the Hampden-Sydney *Kaleidoscope*, a student publication.

[McIlwaine's *Memories*; Hampden-Sydney *Kaleidoscope*, 1895, 1907; L. G. Tyler, *Men of Mark in Va.* (1909), V, 282; *Who's Who in America*, 1912–13; *Times-Dispatch* (Richmond, Va.), Aug. 11, 12, 1913; personal acquaintance.] J. D. E.

McINTIRE, SAMUEL (January 1757–Feb. 6, 1811), architect, wood-carver, who was to fix the characteristic aspect of his native town of Salem, Mass., was the son of Joseph McIntire, a housewright, and his wife, Sarah (Ruck). He was baptized on Jan. 16, 1757. In his father's shop he learned the family trade with his brothers, Joseph and Angier, before the death of the elder McIntire in 1776. At twenty-one, in 1778, he married Elizabeth Field.

Already, apparently, he had a skill and inspired a confidence beyond his years, for his was the major share in the design of the great house built by Jerathmeel Peirce on land bought in 1779. In general scheme it did not differ from a number of fine houses built in Massachusetts before the Revolution—four-square, three stories in height, with tall pilasters at the corners; but it did differ from all but a very few buildings by cultivated amateurs such as Peter Harrison and John Smibert in its more literate adherence to academic profiles and proportions in the pilasters and other classical details, and thus in its total effect. This was one of great solidity and dignity, not a little enhanced by the formality of its stable court and elaborate fence. The details come from a work long familiar to the colonial carpenters, Batty Langley's *City and Country Builder's and Workman's Treasury of Designs,* first published in 1740, but they are followed with unusually literal faithfulness. The young designer clearly was beginning to know his books, and had taught himself to draw better than any of his predecessors among the builder-architects.

The success of the Peirce house brought him the patronage, which was to be lifelong, of the greatest of Salem merchants at that time, Elias Hasket Derby [*q.v.*], and of his wife, Elizabeth Crowninshield, whose love of display was responsible for a series of commissions. The first was for a great house near the Derby wharf, begun in 1780, on which work was abandoned in 1783. In its plan it had little that was unusual except a screen of columns parting the front hall from the stairs, a feature new to New England; its façade, however, was remarkable for a portico of four Ionic columns opposite the ground story, with a Palladian window and a great lunette marking the center of the two stories above. For the Derbys also the house on Washington Street built about 1764 by Benjamin Pickman was enlarged and remodeled about 1790 on a design by McIntire very similar to that of the Peirce house, but with pilasters Ionic instead of Doric.

It is probably safe to infer from the accounts that Samuel McIntire designed the fine house built by Francis Boardman on Salem Common in 1782–89. This house, likewise three stories and four-square, had quoins at the corners instead of pilasters, a charming small porch of the Roman-Doric order, and a bold staircase with columns for balusters. Many Salem porches and doorways recall the Doric boldness and simplicity of these features in the Peirce and Boardman houses. In the Forrester house, finished after 1791, there is a unique specimen of McIntire's early carving, the rich adornment of the parlor chimneypiece.

McIntire's skill was meanwhile laid under contribution for public and semi-public buildings. The earliest was the Assembly House or "Concert Hall" as built in its first form about 1782. It was succeeded in 1792 by Washington Hall, also from McIntire's drawings. In 1785 he provided the design for the Salem Court House, demolished in 1839. One of the first of the governmental edifices built in New England after the Revolution, it was in its early days one of the most ambitious. A Doric portico below, Ionic pilasters above, adorned the front; a tall cupola in three stages rose over the center.

These successes emboldened McIntire to submit in 1792 a competitive design for the Federal Capitol—one by no means unworthy of consideration among the majority of those received (F. Kimball, in *Journal of the American Institute of Architects,* March 1920). It showed a noble palace with a great central frontispiece of six tall Corinthian columns above a high basement, itself fronted along the wings by Doric colonnades. The suggestion came, obviously, from a plate of James Gibbs, published as Plate 41 in his *Book of Architecture* (1728), a work from which James Hoban [*q.v.*] derived his winning front for the President's House. This plan for the Capitol, his most ambitious attempt, closed the early period of McIntire's work.

A new sun had meanwhile risen in New England architecture; a new style had been revealed in the first designs of Charles Bulfinch [*q.v.*]. McIntire was quick to recognize and study the new fashion. By 1793 he was following it in his own practice. Several of his works in the new manner date from that year. The Nathan Read house, long destroyed, was typical of many to follow. Although it preserved the plan and the shape of the earlier great houses, their massive dignity gave way in it to more refined elegance. The tall pilasters and corner quoins disappeared. The cornice, the balusters above, were thinner and more delicate, as were the columns of the porch, here a reduced echo of the large semicircular portico of Bulfinch's Barrell house. Within, the mid-Georgian detail of fireplace and doorway, with their heavy architraves, was replaced by slender Adam forms, reeded or paneled pilasters, with capitals and friezes delicately enriched. The ornaments cast in composition, characteristic of the style abroad and used in Bulfinch's work and many of McIntire's later houses, were evidently not available for this one, and the native craftsman was stimulated to supply the lack by his own carvings. They included not only fine Corinthian capitals, but baskets of fruit, horns of plenty, and sprays of grape, motives which became typical of McIntire's decorative work.

A house of exceptional qualities, in which Bulfinch's innovations in planning had an influence, was the Theodore Lyman house in Waltham, the only building outside the Salem vicinity from McIntire's designs. The land was bought in March 1793, and by 1798 Mr. Lyman's "elegant seat," with its beautiful grounds in the landscape style, was an object of admiration to travelers. The front was adorned in the upper story with pairs of small Ionic pilasters; below, with rustic blocks about the openings. The hall, ending in a screen of columns, led into an oval drawing room projecting toward the garden as in the

Barrell house. Wings to left and right for kitchens and ball room, connected by lower passages, gave the house something of the air of the Maryland houses of the period. The Assembly House in Salem, remodeled as a private dwelling at this time, was given a similar front of Ionic pilasters.

Mrs. Derby, although she had occupied the remodeled Pickman house for but three or four years, could not be left behind by the change of fashion. Great preparations were made, and local talent was not alone considered. Bulfinch himself was called on for a set of drawings, and others were got even from New York. Features of Bulfinch's design and of his Barrell and Russell houses were then combined in the final plans drawn by McIntire and executed in 1795–98. (F. Kimball, in *Essex Institute Historical Collections,* vol. LX, 1924, pp. 273–92.) A vista from the entrance on the north ran through the central stair-hall with curved ends, and through an oval drawing-room which formed the center of a suite along the southern garden front. Over the central bow toward the garden rose a majestic curved portico. The front in general followed Bulfinch's sketch, itself based on the Provost's House in Dublin, and thus was a distant descendant of Burlington's famous house for General Wade in London. To left and right were formal outbuildings; a summer house in the form of a temple adorned the landscape garden which ran down to a terrace toward the water. All told, the Mansion—by which name it was distinguished among other houses of the Derbys—seemed to contemporaries "more like a palace than the dwelling of an American merchant." In the decoration of the interior there was the greatest lavishness. For every room McIntire carved capitals, medallions, roses, draperies, cabling on beads. The single chimneypiece which survives shows an almost overladen richness, its columns wreathed in sprays of laurel. In the oval room the stucco worker Daniel Raynerd executed a sumptuous Adam ceiling. The owners had but a few months to inhabit and enjoy the house, for Mrs. Derby's death on Apr. 19, 1799, was closely followed by that of her husband, Sept. 8. In 1815, "the convenience of the spot for other buildings brought a sentence of destruction," wrote the Salem diarist William Bentley, "& before the world it was destroyed from its foundations" (*Diary, post,* IV, 362).

On the death of the great merchant, those of his children who had not received one of the fine existing houses as part of their inheritance began to build in feverish rivalry. Thus by 1800 Elizabeth Derby, who had married Capt. Nathaniel West, built "Oak Hill" from McIntire's designs on her tract in Peabody. The richness of decoration rivaled even that of her father's mansion, Samuel McIntire's carvings being supplemented in 1813, after his death, by further ornaments executed by his son. The interior has now lost its principal features, three of the principal rooms being installed in the Museum of Fine Arts, Boston. The third son, Ezekiel Hersey Derby, secured plans for his house on Essex Street from Bulfinch, but the execution of the carved detail was left to McIntire. The mantels were enriched with figural ornament; the great semicircular stair hall, with carved archways and a stucco ceiling. Degraded to business uses, the house has now been stripped of its decorations, the principal ones being incorporated in the Pennsylvania Museum of Art (*Pennsylvania Museum Bulletin,* April 1930, pp. 11–17). Anstis Derby, who had married Benjamin Pickman, Jr., contented herself with adding a new porch, a new bow, and new mantel-pieces to the fine old Pickman house on Essex Street. Meanwhile many other clients were coming to McIntire for their houses, among them Benjamin Carpenter in 1796 (the house now much remodeled), Samuel Cook about 1804, and John Gardner, 1804–05. The Cook and Gardner houses are among the finest of the architect's works still preserved. The great parlor of the Peirce house, remodeled for the wedding of Sally Peirce to George Nichols in 1801, is rightly considered one of McIntire's masterpieces in the Adam manner.

He was also commissioned to do work for several churches during these middle years. In 1796 he replaced the old steeple of the North Meeting House with a plain octagonal cupola. In 1804 the South Church was begun from his designs. The steeple had three stages above the tower, one square and two octagonal, with a tall spire above—certainly one of the most graceful in New England. The tower rested on a broad porch fronted by four Ionic pilasters with festooned capitals. The church was gutted by fire in 1903 and demolished. The Branch Church, built in 1804–05, was removed to Beverly and rebuilt in 1867. In the emulation among the churches even the old Tabernacle had to have a new steeple, which was built in 1805. McIntire was now well recognized as a local celebrity, whom the Town Clerk was to describe at his death as "The Architect of Salem." Thus when the Common was leveled and fenced as Washington Square in 1802 he was called on to design the several gateways—the principal one a little wooden triumphal arch adorned with sculpture and crowned by an eagle. Hamilton Hall, to which the Salem Assemblies were transferred about 1805, was a very admirable and dignified solution of the problem: the great hall above with a row of five Palladian windows under simple brick arches.

The houses of his last years, from 1805 to 1811, are all of brick. For Benjamin March Woodbridge he designed and ornamented the fine square mansion still standing (1933) on Bridge Street; for the Recorder of Deeds, in 1807, a house of which only a single mantelpiece, carved with an eagle, survives. The Gideon Tucker house (1809) was closely similar to the Gardner house opposite; the Joseph Felt house, with a square Doric porch to the street, was one of the architect's last works. In all this group, and especially the two latest, there was an increasing note of austerity, as the growing classicism of the time laid its restraint on the craftsman's facile hand. With the growth of trade and of communication certain newer and larger tasks were imposed upon him—hotels and business buildings of a larger scale. The Archer (Franklin) Building in Salem (1809–10) was perhaps his most extensive undertaking. The treatment was sober, of admirable proportion, depending only on the skilful grouping of the openings in the brick walls and on a rich balustrade at the eaves. There were McIntire carvings in many houses not otherwise known to be his: particularly the Joseph Hosmer house, the David P. Waters house, and the Clifford Crowninshield house. His carving was lavished not only on interior woodwork but on furniture. Some scores of pieces showing his handiwork survive—sofas, chairs, tables of various sorts, beds and their canopies, mirror frames, and chests of drawers—preserved by Salem families, by certain museums (the Essex Institute, Boston Museum of Fine Arts, Yale University, Metropolitan Museum, Pennsylvania Museum) and by a very few private collectors. They show all his characteristic motives of ornament: eagles, baskets and dishes of fruit, urns, rosettes, festoons of drapery and of husks, horns of plenty, sprays of grape and of laurel, executed with a brilliance which has never been surpassed in America (F. Kimball, in *Antiques,* November 1930–March 1931; corrected, *Ibid.,* January 1932, and M. M. Swan, *Ibid.,* November, December 1931).

Although McIntire's achievements in sculpture cannot compare in intrinsic value with those in architecture and furniture carving, he has in this field the merit of a pioneer. Little enough had been done in sculpture anywhere in America, less by native talent. In New England, John and Simeon Skillin of Boston carved in 1793 four figures for the Derby summer house and garden. McIntire, who had perhaps already carved some of his famous eagles, was stimulated to take up figural sculpture, both in relief and in the round, all executed in wood. In 1798 he made a bust of John Winthrop, which the Rev. William Bentley exhibited in the East Church. In 1802, for the Common gates, he carved several bas-reliefs, now preserved by the Essex Institute, among them a profile medallion of Washington (F. Kimball, in *Art in America,* December 1923). The figure of a Canton merchant, clothed, in the Peabody Museum, has head and hands carved by McIntire in 1801; and a small ship's figurehead there, holding a medallion portrait, is believed to be his work (*Old-Time New England,* October 1921, p. 67). His eagles in the round adorned the Pickman (Derby) house, the Common gateway, the Peirce house, and other buildings. Eagles in relief formed part of the external ornament of the Custom House and Hamilton Hall, and of the interior decoration of the Registry of Deeds and a number of private houses, all executed after 1805.

When McIntire died of congestion of the lungs, after rescuing a child from drowning, William Bentley wrote in his diary: "This day Salem was deprived of one of the most ingenious men it had in it. Samuel McIntire, *aet.* 54, in Summer St.... By attention he soon gained a superiority to all of his occupation . . . indeed all the improvements of Salem for nearly thirty years past have been done under his eye. In Sculpture he had no rival in New England. . . . To the best of my abilities I encouraged him in this branch. In music he had a good taste, & tho' not presuming to be an original composer, he was among our best Judges & most able performers. All the Instruments we use he could understand & was the best person to be employed in correcting any defects, or repairing them. He had a fine person, a majestic appearance, calm countenance, great self command & amiable temper. He was welcome but never intruded" (*Diary,* IV, 6). No likeness of his features is known.

He was survived by his wife, and by his son Samuel Field McIntire (1780–1819), who carried on the work in carving until his own death, and whose works have often been confused with his father's (F. Kimball, in *Antiques,* February 1933). Samuel's brother Joseph (1748–1825) and the latter's son Joseph, Jr., were carvers as well as carpenters, and continued the business until the death of the last of the line after 1850, when the contents of his shop—still including some of the characteristic eagles—were sold. No architectural designs drawn by these successors are known, however, and none of them approached in distinction the founder of the house.

[Many of McIntire's drawings and bills, as well as his carving-tools and certain of his carvings, are preserved by the Essex Institute in Salem, which also has an extensive archive of photographic negatives and prints of his work. These form the primary basis of Fiske Kimball's "Mr. Samuel McIntire, Carver, The Architect of Salem," in preparation. Some of them are reproduced (partly with incorrect captions) in Frank Cousins and P. M. Riley, *The Woodcarver of Salem* (1916). A paper on McIntire is also to be found in W. A. Dyer, *Early American Craftsmen* (1915). *The Diary of William Bentley, D.D., 1784-1819* (4 vols., 1905–14), contains many references to McIntire and his works and forms an important source. Obituaries appeared in the *Salem Gazette*, Feb. 8, 12, 1811, and *Essex Register*, Feb. 9, 1811. J. B. Felt's *Annals of Salem* (2nd ed., 2 vols., 1845–49), H. W. Belknap, *Artists and Craftsmen of Essex County, Mass.* (1927), and many papers in the *Essex Inst. Hist. Colls.* and in the *Essex Antiquarian* contain allusions to him of documentary value.] F. K.

McINTOSH, JOHN BAILLIE (June 6, 1829–June 29, 1888), Union soldier, was born in Florida, the son of Col. James Simmons McIntosh, United States Army, and the brother of James McQueen McIntosh, later a brigadier-general in the Confederate army. His mother, Eliza (Matthews) Shumate McIntosh, was the daughter of James Matthews of Brooklyn, N. Y. The last of an illustrious fighting family, John entered the navy during the Mexican War and served aboard the U. S. S. *Saratoga* as a midshipman. Upon his return home after the war, he learned of his father's death in Mexico as the result of wounds received in the battle of Molino del Rey. He thereupon resigned from the navy and went to live with an uncle at New Brunswick, N. J. Here, in 1850, he married Amelia Stout. One child, a daughter, was born to this union. For the next decade McIntosh engaged in business with his father-in-law.

When the Civil War began, he declared for the preservation of the Union and applied for a commission in the Regular Army, notwithstanding the many family and social influences tending to enlist his sympathies with the South. He considered as a blot on his family honor the resignation from the Federal service of his brother, who had been educated at West Point and now took up arms against the government.

In June 1861, he entered the Federal service as a second lieutenant of cavalry. Serving in the Shenandoah Valley in 1861 and later with the Army of the Potomac, he at once drew the attention of his commanders and was frequently commended in orders. In July 1862 he was assigned temporarily to the command of the 95th Pennsylvania Volunteers, whose colonel had been killed. For gallant and meritorious services at White Oak Swamp (August 1862) he was brevetted major; he participated in the battles of South Mountain and Antietam, and in November 1862 was appointed colonel of the 3rd Pennsylvania Cavalry. When the Union cavalry was reorganized by Gen. Alfred Pleasanton in the spring of 1863, McIntosh was given the command of a brigade, with which he distinguished himself at Kelly's Ford (March 1863). He fought at Chancellorsville and played a significant rôle in the cavalry fighting of the Gettysburg campaign, demonstrating that as a brigade commander he had no superior (letter of General W. W. Averell, War Department files). While recuperating from a fall from a horse, he was placed in charge of the Cavalry Depot in Washington. Returning to the command of his brigade in May 1864, he took part in the great cavalry operations of that year, ending with the battle of Winchester, where he received wounds necessitating the amputation of his right leg. He received in succession every brevet grade from major to major-general for bold, valiant, and gallant action under fire.

After the war, he was commissioned a lieutenant colonel in the Regular Army upon the special recommendation of General Grant. He commanded the 42nd Infantry 1866–67, was deputy governor and governor of the Soldier's Home at Washington 1867–68, and superintendent of Indian affairs in California, 1869–70. He was retired in 1870 with the rank of brigadier-general, and made his residence in New Brunswick, N. J., where he took an active interest in public affairs. McIntosh was a born fighter, a strict disciplinarian, a dashing leader, and a polished gentleman. He represents the highest type of volunteer soldier.

[Navy records; War Dept. records; Pension Office records; *War of the Rebellion, Official Records (Army)*; J. G. B. Bulloch, *A Hist. and Geneal. of the Family of Baillie of Dunain . . . with a Short Sketch of the Family of McIntosh . . .* (1898); L. R. Hamersly, *Records of Living Officers of the U. S. Army* (1884); F. B. Heitman, *Hist. Reg. U. S. Army* (1890); *Army and Navy Jour.* and *Army and Navy Reg.*, July 7, 1888; *N. Y. Herald*, July 1, 1888.] J. R. V.

McINTOSH, LACHLAN (Mar. 17, 1725–Feb. 20, 1806), Revolutionary soldier, born at Raits in Badenoch, Scotland, was the son of John Mohr and Marjory (Fraser) McIntosh, who came to Georgia with other Highlanders in 1736 and settled at Inverness (later Darien). In 1748 Lachlan moved from bankrupt Georgia to Charleston, S. C. (*Georgia Historical Quarterly*, September 1919), where he is said to have worked as a clerk in a counting-house and to have lived with Henry Laurens.

Little is known of his life before July 1775, when he appeared at Savannah as a member for the Parish of St. Andrew of the Provincial Congress. On Jan. 7, 1776, he was appointed colonel of a battalion of Georgia troops. This force was later increased and incorporated in the Continental Army, and McIntosh was appointed brigadier-general as of Sept. 16, 1776. The efforts of Button Gwinnett [*q.v.*] to bring the Continental troops under local control, and an investigation of the failure of a military expedition into Florida in 1777 which vindicated the civil authority at the expense of the military, together with personal differences and the bitter factional disputes of the Georgia patriots, led to a duel (May 16, 1777), between the two men in which both were wounded, Gwinnett mortally. Though acquitted when brought to trial, McIntosh suffered from the hostility of Gwinnett's friends. Alleging this as his reason, George Walton, Georgia delegate in Congress, obtained McIntosh's transfer to Washington's headquarters (*Letters of Members of the Continental Congress,* vol. II, 1923, p. 439). After a winter at Valley Forge, he was appointed in May 1778 to command the Western department, with headquarters at Fort Pitt. His plans for an expedition to Detroit and an attack on the Northern Indians were not carried out; his subordinates, Daniel Brodhead and George Morgan [*qq.v.*], complained of his conduct; Gouverneur Morris described him to Washington as "one of those who excel in the Regularity of still Life from the Possession of an indolent uniformity of soul" (Kellogg, *post,* 252–53); and on Mar. 5, 1779, Washington directed him to turn over the command to Brodhead. On May 18 he was ordered south again by Congress, and commanded the 1st and 5th South Carolina regiments in the disastrous attack on Savannah (October 1779). Taken prisoner by the British at the capture of Charleston (May 12, 1780), he was exchanged for General O'Hara under an agreement dated Feb. 9, 1782. In the meantime his enemies in Georgia, led by George Walton, had induced Congress to suspend him from active service by a resolve of Feb. 15, 1780. The resolve was repealed on July 16, 1781, and he was brevetted major-general Sept. 30, 1783; but his final vindication was delayed until Feb. 24, 1784, when a committee of Congress, of which James Monroe was a member, quoted with approval a resolution of the Georgia Assembly charging Walton with forgery, and praised McIntosh for his Revolutionary services.

When he returned to Georgia in 1783 he was, according to his own statement, "incredibly poor." He took little part in public life thereafter, devoting much of his time to the management of his deceased brother George's estate. He was a charter member of the Society of the Cincinnati of Georgia (1784); was elected a delegate to Congress on Feb. 23, 1784, but apparently never attended its sessions; was twice appointed a commissioner to adjust the boundary dispute between Georgia and South Carolina; and was one of the four commissioners of Congress to treat with the Southern Indians (1785–86). In 1791 he was a member of the committee that welcomed President Washington at Savannah. He married Sarah Threadcraft. His death occurred in Savannah and he was buried in the Colonial Cemetery there.

[*Jours. of the Continental Cong.*, Feb. 11, 15, June 23, Sept. 25, 1780, July 16, 1781; *Calendar of the Correspondence of George Washington . . . with the Officers* (4 vols., 1915), see Index; Jared Sparks, ed., *Writings of George Washington,* V (1834), 361–62, 382; W. B. Stevens, *Hist. of Ga.* (2 vols., 1847–59); C. C. Jones, *Hist. of Ga.* (2 vols., 1883); L. P. Kellogg, *Frontier Advance on the Upper Ohio* (1916); J. G. B. Bulloch, *A Hist. and Geneal. of the Family of Baillie of Dunain . . . with a short Sketch of the Family of McIntosh . . .* (1898); *Charleston Courier,* Feb. 26, 1806.] A. P. W.

McINTOSH, WILLIAM (*c.* 1775–May 1, 1825), Creek Indian chief, brigadier-general of the United States Army, was born in the Coweta country, Creek Nation, on the east bank of the Chattahoochee River, in the present limits of Carroll County, Ga. His father was William McIntosh, captain in the British army, and agent to the Creek Indians; his mother, a full-blooded Indian woman of unknown name. The sister of his father, Catherine, became the mother of George M. Troup [*q.v.*], and with the career of his cousin that of the Indian chief was closely intertwined. He emerges from obscurity as leader of the Lower Creeks, friendly to the Americans in the War of 1812, in which the Upper Creeks sided with the British. As a reward for notable service in this war he was commissioned brigadier-general in the United States Army, and served with Jackson in the campaigns against the Seminoles, 1817–18 (*Historical Collections of Georgia, post,* pp. 170–73).

After the Indian wars McIntosh was known as the friend of the white man and of Georgia. Troup became governor in 1823 and endeavored to secure the removal of the Creek and Cherokee Indians still occupying choice lands in the western part of the state. The Upper Creeks or "Red Sticks," resident in Alabama and long hostile to the whites, were determined to make no cession of tribal lands. The Lower Creeks, on the Georgia side of the river, influenced by McIntosh, were disposed to conclude treaties of cession. McIntosh was proscribed by the hostile faction of Creeks, and expelled from the Cherokee council as a renegade (he had married a Cherokee wife). After the failure of treaty negotiations at Broken Arrow, Ala., Dec. 1, 1824, United States commissioners arranged a council at Indian Springs, Ga., Feb. 7, 1825. Here the Upper Creeks continued to oppose any cession and succeeded in breaking up the council. On Feb. 12, however, the McIntosh party signed a treaty of cession. Its fairness was at least doubtful, and McIntosh's disinterestedness was called in question. The Upper Creeks, supported by the United States agent, Crowell, protested the treaty; but eventually its provisions went into effect. The vengeance of the Upper Creeks was not long delayed. McIntosh's house on the east bank of the Chattahoochee River was surrounded during the night of Apr. 30, and set on fire, and in the ensuing mêlée McIntosh was slain. In person he is described as "tall, finely formed and of graceful and commanding manner." He had much of the polish of the gentleman. In his life and death he illustrates the not infrequent tragedy of the American half-breed Indian. He had several Indian wives, and left Indian progeny.

[*Am. State Papers. Indian Affairs,* vols. I, II (1832–34), contain the documents bearing on McIntosh's public career; the best secondary account is E. J. Harden, *The Life of George M. Troup* (1859); other sources are: George White, *Statistics of the State of Ga.* (1849), and *Hist. Colls. of Ga.* (1854); A. J. Pickett, *Hist. of Ala.* (2 vols., 1851); U. B. Phillips, *Ga. and State Rights* (1902); J. G. B. Bulloch, *A Hist. and Geneal. of the Family of Baillie of Dunain . . . with a Short Sketch of the Family of McIntosh* . . . (1898).] H. J. P., Jr.

McIVER, CHARLES DUNCAN (Sept. 27, 1860–Sept. 17, 1906), Southern educator, the son of Matthew Henry and Sarah (Harrington) McIver, was born on a farm in Moore County, N. C. He was of Scotch Presbyterian descent, and as a youth lived amidst the austere surroundings which characterized the poverty-stricken era of reconstruction in the South. In 1881 he graduated from the University of North Carolina, and after a few years of teaching in private and public schools decided to make education his life work. At this time in North Carolina, as in the South generally, the idea that higher education, or even elementary education, should be at public expense found little acceptance. Except at the University, which each year received a few thousand dollars from the state treasury, such higher education as was afforded was paid for either by the churches or privately, and even this was wholly inadequate both in quality and quantity. McIver saw that wider opportunities for higher education would be distinctly advantageous to the state, and, despite the depleted condition of the state treasury, he urgently recommended that a system affording such opportunities, supported largely by taxation, be inaugurated. Inasmuch as the University of North Carolina already constituted a skeleton for the widening of the advantages open to men, he turned his attention to the establishment of a similar institution for women. Since the greater part of elementary and high school teaching is done by women, he argued, it is the part of wisdom for the commonwealth to provide advantages that will better fit women to fulfil the function of teaching or the equally important function of motherhood. In arriving at these views he was aided largely by his wife, Lula (Martin) McIver, herself a teacher, to whom he was married in 1885 and by whom he had five children.

Having been appointed by the Teachers' Assembly of North Carolina chairman of a committee to appear before the legislature in 1889 and urge the adoption of a bill for the establishment of a training school for teachers, he argued eloquently for its approval. Although the measure did not pass, his earnestness reduced the opposition from a huge to a very scant majority. In that year the state board of education transferred its appropriation from the short-term summer normal schools to a system of county institutes, and appointed McIver and Edwin A. Alderman co-conductors. They at once commenced a remarkable campaign. Beginning in September 1889, McIver appeared in virtually every county in the state, and almost every town and hamlet, urging the dual causes of universal public education for all children in the state and the higher education of women. In 1891 a bill was again presented to the legislature for the establishment of a college for women and this time it passed with little opposition. At the initial meeting of the board of directors of the newly formed North Carolina State Normal and Industrial College (later North Carolina College for Women), located at Greensboro, McIver was elected president.

Despite numerous tempting offers of more remunerative employment in the business and educational world, he continued in this position for the remainder of his life. During the fourteen years of his presidency he built the college upon such firm foundations that it has become one of the outstanding women's colleges in the South. This achievement, however, was by no means the sum of his accomplishments. Assisted by a few kindred spirits, he gave unstintedly of his time and energy to the further awakening of North Carolina from the lethargy into which it had fallen at the close of the Civil War. As a prime mover in the organization of the Conference for Education in the South, as secretary of the Southern Education Board, and as a public-spirited citizen, he carried on his crusade throughout the South for the extension of educational facilities. Although he died in the prime of life, he lived to see his section well on the way toward that educational renaissance which has been notable in recent years. He had well earned the tribute, "educational statesman," which was universally bestowed upon him after his untimely death.

[Information derived from associates of McIver and particularly his widow; *Charles Duncan McIver* (1906), privately printed; *Program of Exercises for N. C. Day —McIver Memorial Day* (1906), compiled by R. D. W. Connor; *Report of the Commissioner of Education* (1908); B. J. Hendrick, *The Life and Letters of Walter H. Page* (1924), vol. I; *Charlotte Daily Observer*, Sept. 18, 1906.] B. B. K.

McKAY, DONALD (Sept. 4, 1810–Sept. 20, 1880), naval architect and master ship-builder, was born on a farm on the east side of Jordan River in Shelburne County, Nova Scotia, second of sixteen children (W. L. Kean, *The Genealogy of Hugh McKay,* 1895, p. 6) of Hugh and Ann (McPherson) McKay. His paternal grandfather, for whom he was named, was a Scottish army officer who took up the farm among United Empire Loyalists in 1783. Equipped only with a common-school education, Donald emigrated in 1827 to New York where he was apprenticed as a ship-carpenter to Isaac Webb. When his indenture was up and he became a free-lance shipwright, his talents were noticed and encouraged by the leading New York ship-builders. Jacob Bell [*q.v.*] sent him to Wiscasset, Me., in 1839 to finish a vessel; he then found employment at Newburyport, Mass., where in 1841 he formed a partnership with William Currier as master ship-builder. There he quickly made a reputation by building two New York packet ships, and after forming a new partnership, with William Pickett, was chosen in 1844 to design and build the *Joshua Bates* for the Boston-Liverpool line. The owner, Enoch Train, induced McKay to come to Boston, and aided him in establishing a shipyard at East Boston.

Here, for five years, he concentrated his attention on packet ships. On Dec. 7, 1850, he launched the *Stag Hound* (1,534 tons), his first clipper ship; and on Apr. 15, 1851, the *Flying Cloud* (1,783 tons), which made San Francisco in less than ninety days from New York, a passage but twice equaled, once by herself. Three other great clippers left his yard that year. In 1852 he built the *Sovereign of the Seas* (2,421 tons) on his own account, since no one would order so great a vessel, and placed her in command of his brother Lauchlan (1811–1895), who was a practical builder as well as master mariner. After two remarkable voyages the *Sovereign of the Seas* was sold to British purchasers, and gave her builder an international reputation. In the same year he built the clippers *Westward Ho!* and *Bald Eagle.* In 1853, with amazing courage, Donald McKay built on his own account the *Great Republic,* registering $4,555\frac{2}{3}$ tons, $334\frac{1}{2}$ feet long (Boston Vessel Registry, MS., 1853, no. 457), with a 120-foot yard arm and a main skysail truck over 200 feet above her deck. Although burned before going to sea, the *Great Republic* as razeed and rebuilt was the pride of the American merchant marine. The *Empress of the Seas, Star of Empire, Chariot of Fame,* and *Romance of the Seas* were also of that year. In 1854–55 McKay again surpassed himself with six clipper ships built for the Liverpool-Australia trade, two of which, the *James Baines* (2,515 tons) and *Lightning* (2,084 tons), hold world records for speed under sail. The *Baines* made the fastest transatlantic port-to-port passage, twelve days six hours Boston to Liverpool, and the round-the-world record of 134 days; at times she attained a speed of twenty-one knots. The *Lightning* made the greatest day's run in the annals of sail, 436 nautical miles. In fact ten out of twelve recorded days' runs of 400 miles and upward were made by McKay's ships.

McKay designed all these and many other vessels, superintended every detail of their construction, and invented several labor-saving devices. A man of indefatigable industry, a skilful draftsman and a practical builder, he had an innate sense of beauty and proportion, and intuitive perception of both how and what to build. A characteristic declaration was, "I never yet built a vessel that came up to my own ideal; I saw something in each ship which I desired to improve" (*Boston Daily Advertiser,* Oct. 29, 1864). At prime of life he was a fine figure of a man, with strong features, and dark hair curling back from a high forehead. He loved music and played the violin. His character won the affection of his employés and the respect of his competitors; in the Boston of Webster and Everett he was one of the most prominent citizens. In religion he was a Methodist. His two wives did much for his career: Albenia Martha Boole (m. 1833, d. 1848), a ship-builder's daughter, assisted his education; Mary Cressy Litchfield (m. 1849, d. 1923) acted as his adviser and secretary in business matters, and named his famous clippers. He had fifteen children, most of whom survived him.

By 1855 the day of extreme clipper ships was over, and McKay turned to a more economical type, but the panic of 1857 left his yard vacant. Having obtained a contract to furnish 500 loads of ship timber to the British Admiralty, he spent over a year (1859–60) in Europe, where his reputation gave him access to the leading government dockyards. He watched the construction of the new ironclads, and assisted at armor tests, which convinced him that the United States navy was obsolete, and made him a vigorous advocate of steam screw ironclads of the largest class. These views, coming from the supreme master builder of wooden sailing ships, made a deep impression. In March–April 1861, he proposed to build an ironclad corvette of 2,390 tons displacement, mounting twelve 9-inch guns in casemates (J. P. Baxter 3rd, *post*, pp. 239–40). These and other plans were not accepted, largely for want of funds, and as McKay obtained no orders, he returned to England in July 1861 and remained until April 1863, again doing business with the Admiralty. After his return to America he equipped his yard to produce iron ships and marine and locomotive engines, and in 1864–65 built at considerable financial loss the monitor *Nausett* and three other naval vessels for the government; in 1866–69 he built a few steamers and sailing ships, of which the last, the *Glory of the Seas* (2,102 tons), although a loss to her builder, proved a fast and profitable vessel, and lasted until 1923. Although in 1869 he sold his shipyard, he built elsewhere for the government the wooden sloops-of-war *Adams* and *Essex* in 1874–75 (Bradlee, *post*, pp. 317–18). Being threatened with tuberculosis he retired in 1877 to a country estate at Hamilton, Mass., where, with characteristic energy, he endeavored by scientific farming to recoup health and fortune. Both suffered, and on Sept. 20, 1880, he died.

[The only biography is Richard C. McKay, *Some Famous Sailing Ships and Their Builder Donald McKay* (1928), with list of vessels; the best brief account is the introduction to John Robinson and G. F. Dow, *The Sailing Ships of New England*, ser. 2 (1924), which is in part based on information in F. B. C. Bradlee, "The Ship 'Great Republic' and Donald McKay, Her Builder," published in *Hist. Colls. of the Essex Inst.*, vol. LXIII (1927) and separately. A. H. Clark, *The Clipper Ship Era* (1911), gives a personal impression, the background, and an account of McKay's ships, which may be supplemented by O. T. Howe and F. C. Matthews, *American Clipper Ships* (2 vols., 1926–27), and C. C. Cutler, *Greyhounds of the Sea* (1930). McKay's letters on naval policy are printed in the Boston *Commercial Bulletin*, Nov. 17 and Dec. 1, 1860, Mar. 16, 1861, and *Boston Daily Advertiser*, Oct. 29, 1864. Letters from and about him are in the Navy Department Archives, the Welles Papers, Lib. of Cong., and the Admiralty papers in the Public Record Office, London. His relation to naval policy is described in J. P. Baxter 3rd, *Introduction of the Ironclad Warship* (1933), and "Report of the Joint Committee on the Conduct of the War" (*Sen. Doc. No. 142*, 38 Cong., 2 Sess.), vol. III, pt. 2. A prospectus of a work by Donald McKay on naval architecture was issued in 1859, but the book was never written; his brother Lauchlan published *The Practical Ship-Builder* in 1839.]

S. E. M.

McKAY, GORDON (May 4, 1821–Oct. 19, 1903), industrialist, inventor, was born in Pittsfield, Mass., the son of Samuel Michel and Catherine Gordon (Dexter) McKay. His father, the son of Samuel Mackay, a captain in the British army and afterwards professor of French in Williams College (1795–99), was a cotton manufacturer, amateur farmer, and a politician of some prominence in the western part of Massachusetts; his mother, the daughter of Samuel Dexter [*q.v.*] of Boston, an eminent lawyer who in 1800 served as secretary of war and afterwards as secretary of the treasury. McKay was a delicate youth and what little schooling he had was directed toward an outdoor occupation. He studied engineering and for eight years, beginning when he was sixteen, he worked with the engineer corps of the Boston & Albany Railroad and of the Erie Canal. At the age of twenty-four he returned to Pittsfield and established a machine shop for the repair of paper and cotton mill machinery. This he operated profitably for seven years and then, in 1852, accepted the position of treasurer and general manager of the Lawrence Machine Shop at Lawrence, Mass. In 1859 he became interested in the machine recently invented by Lyman R. Blake [*q.v.*] for sewing the soles of shoes to the uppers. McKay bought the patent, paying Blake $70,000 for it, $8,000 in cash and $62,000 to be paid from future profits. He then set to work to improve the machine so that it would stitch the soles around the toes and heels. With the great material assistance of R. H. Matthies, an expert machinist, the attempt succeeded after several years of effort, and on May 6, 1862, McKay obtained a patent (No. 35,165) for a "process of sewing soles of boots and shoes." He immediately organized the McKay Association to manufacture the machine, and since the Civil War was creating a demand for army shoes, he experienced little difficulty in securing the necessary capital. Within a few months he was filling a government contract for 25,000 pairs of army shoes in his two factories at Rayham and Farmington, N. H., and was also manufacturing his shoe machine for other firms. The machines were not sold outright but leased to other manufacturers on a royalty basis. By the end of 1862 McKay was drawing royalties from over sixty shoe factories in the East and Middle West, and by 1876 he was receiving more than a half million dollars annually in royalties. During this time he not only directed the business of his association and worked out the details for manufacturing the machine, but also kept in close touch with the experimental work for the further perfection and application of shoe machinery. He was the joint patentee with Blake for five patents on sewing-machine improvements in 1864, and in 1865 on a machine for manufacturing shoes with turned soles. In 1874 he and Blake fought to secure the extension of the latter's patent, and upon the winning of this battle he paid Blake a large sum of money for the reassignment of the patent to the McKay Association. Meanwhile, the welt-shoe sewing machine controlled by Charles Goodyear, 1833–1896 [*q.v.*], was coming to the fore, and by 1876 the McKay and Goodyear interests were in bitter competition and for four years constantly involved in litigation. In 1880, however, they joined forces, McKay turning over his turned-shoe machinery patents to Goodyear, who, in turn, assigned his rights in welt-and-turned-shoe machinery to McKay. McKay then confined his attention to the development and manufacture of machinery for making the heavier grades of shoes, but fifteen years later, 1895, he sold all of his interests to the Goodyear Company. McKay was also interested in the perfection of machines for nailing and pegging soles on shoes, in improvements in metallic fastenings for shoes, and in machinery for the manufacture of the stouter grades of boots and shoes. In the course of his life he was the patentee or joint patentee of more than forty inventions, which brought him wealth estimated at $40,000,000.

Following his retirement in 1895, he lived quietly in Cambridge and Newport, devoting his time to philanthropic work. His benefactions were many. He established the McKay Institute at Kingston, R. I., for the education of colored boys, and he bequeathed a trust fund of $4,000,000 to Harvard University for the establishment of a department of applied science, with the condition that it should not be used until the last annuitant of the McKay estate died. It is estimated that by that time the fund will amount to about $20,000,000. He was twice married: first, in 1845, to Agnes Jenkins, of Pittsfield, Mass., from whom he was divorced several years later; second, in 1878, to Marian Treat of Longwood, Mass., which marriage likewise terminated in a divorce (1890). He died in Newport, R. I., after a year's illness, and was buried in Pittsfield.

[W. B. Kaempffert, *A Popular Hist. of Am. Invention* (2 vols., 1924); O. P. Dexter, *Dexter Geneal., 1642–1904* (1904); Hennen Jennings, *The McKay Endowment and Applied Science at Harvard* (1918); J. D. Van Slyck, *Representatives of New England* (1879); J. E. A. Smith, *Hist. of Pittsfield*, vol. II (1876); *Sewing Machine Advance*, Feb. 1904; *Sewing Machine Times*, Oct. 25, 1903; *Shoe and Leather Reporter*, Oct. 22, 1903; *Springfield Daily Republican*, Oct. 20, 1903; Patent Office records.] C. W. M.

MACKAY, JAMES (1759?–Mar. 16, 1822), explorer, was born in the Parish of Kildonan, County of Sutherland, Scotland, the son of George and Elizabeth (McDonald) Mackay. He came of a family that produced many distinguished men. He was well educated, spoke French and Spanish fluently, and was a surveyor by profession. About 1776 he emigrated to Canada, where he joined a fur-trading expedition. He was employed by the British to explore the region of the upper lakes and the far West, hoping to open communication with the South Sea. After some years in this perilous occupation, which carried him as far as the Rocky Mountains, he went to Spanish Louisiana to partake of the privileges extended by the Spanish government to foreign settlers. Although a Scotchman, he grew rapidly in favor with the Spanish government. In 1795 Baron de Carondelet appointed him director of the third expedition sent by the Spanish commercial company to explore the vast country on both sides of the Missouri River and across the continent to the Pacific Ocean and, incidentally, to construct forts for the protection of the Spanish trade. In August 1795, with thirty-three men, he started from St. Louis on this enterprise which cost the Spanish government 104,000 pesos. Thus engaged for two years, he brought about peace among the Indian tribes and between them and the Spanish, took possession of a British fort at the Mandan village, prepared a map of the region explored, and furnished the Spanish government with a journal of the expedition (journal printed in Houck, *Spanish Régime, post,* II, pp. 181–94). Lewis and Clark made use of Mackay's map on their famous expedition to the Pacific Ocean.

In 1797 Mackay was appointed deputy surveyor by Antoine Soulard, the Spanish surveyor-general. As a reward for his services he was made captain of the militia and commandant of San Andres, a settlement on the south bank of the Missouri River, in St. Louis County, to which many Americans were attracted. He was given thirty thousand arpens of land, but this property became a burden to him, as only a small part was productive. On May 20, 1799, Governor Manuel Gayoso de Lemos, at New Orleans, wrote to him and commended him for opening roads and establishing good regulations of military and civil police. He promised him great things in the future through Lieutenant-Governor Delassus and the Court. Mackay remained commandant until the transfer of Upper Louisiana to the United States in 1804, when he was appointed one of the judges of the Court of Quarter Sessions. Delassus's comments on his subordinates to the United States authorities described him as "an officer of knowledge, zealous and punctual . . . a recommendable officer with many good qualities" (F. L. Billon, *Annals of St. Louis,* vol. I, 1886, p. 367). In 1816 he was a member of the legislature of Missouri Territory from St. Louis County and served as major of militia. He was married to Isabella, daughter of John Long, on Feb. 24, 1800, at St. Charles.

[Mackay Papers and Documents from Spain in possession of the Mo. Hist. Soc.; *House Exec. Doc. 59,* 24 Cong., 1 Sess. (1836?), pp. 31–37; Louis Houck, *A Hist. of Mo.* (1908), vols. II, III and *The Spanish Régime in Mo.* (2 vols., 1909); *Mo. Hist. Soc. Colls.,* vol. IV (1912), pp. 20–21; *Am. Hist. Assoc. Report 1908,* vol. I (1909); *Miss. Valley Hist. Review,* Mar. 1924, Mar.); *St. Louis Enquirer,* Mar. 23, 1822.]

S. M. D.

McKAY, JAMES IVER (July 17, 1792–Sept. 14, 1853), congressman, was born in Bladen County, N. C., the son of John and Mary (Salter) McKay and the grandson of Bladen Iver McKay who emigrated from Scotland to North Carolina about 1780. His only academic training, of which there is authentic record, was received at the Raleigh Academy, but he bore every evidence of a liberal education. He studied law and was admitted to the bar and in 1815 was elected state senator. Serving four consecutive terms, he was again elected in 1822, 1826, 1829, and 1830. On Mar. 6, 1817, he was appointed federal district attorney for North Carolina. Elected to Congress, he served from 1831 until 1849, when he declined reëlection.

His congressional career was distinguished. His voice was harsh and unpleasant, but, fluent though terse in speech, and convincing because of the wealth of his carefully prepared information, he was regarded as one of the most influential debaters in the House. Public honesty and economy became his passion, and, as an untiring and profane enemy of claim agents and extravagant members, he won the reputation of being an "Old Money Bags," to whose eyes a dollar seemed as big as a cart-wheel. While chairman of the ways and means committee he would not allow the appointment of a clerk and did all the work himself. Yet in spite of economical notions he favored military preparations and obtained the establishment of Fort Caswell on the Cape Fear and the arsenal at Fayetteville. He was chairman of the committee on ways and means from 1843 to 1847 and was the author of the tariff bill of 1843 that failed to pass Congress. His report on the tariff in 1844 was an important state paper, and in 1846 he introduced the Walker tariff bill, which he had helped prepare.

He rarely smiled and had the reputation of great severity, but he was warm-hearted, charitable, personally generous, and exceedingly popular. He was much interested in the welfare of his constituents and is said to have spent more than his salary every year of his congressional service in buying government publications, chiefly concerning agriculture, and in distributing them in his district. He inherited property and amassed more. On Dec. 3, 1818, he married Eliza Ann Harvey the daughter of Travis and Sarah (Robeson) Harvey, a woman of wealth, who died in 1847. They had one son who died in infancy. By his will McKay provided that his valuable plantation, "Belfont," should become a county home and experimental farm for Bladen. His negroes, numbering between two and three hundred, were freed and sent to Liberia. He died suddenly at Goldsboro and was buried at "Belfont."

[Some McKay Papers in the possession of the Univ. of N. C.; files of the Congressional Joint Committee on Printing; S. A. Ashe, *Biog. Hist. of N. C.,* vol. IV (1906); James Sprunt, *Chronicles of the Cape Fear River* (1914); *Memoirs of John Quincy Adams,* ed. by C. F. Adams, vols. IX-XII (1876–77); *The Diary of James K. Polk* (1910), vols. I, IV; *Daily Journal* (Wilmington, N. C.), Sept. 15, 1853; date of marriage and other information from McKay's grand-niece.]

J. G. deR. H.

MACKAY, JOHN WILLIAM (Nov. 28, 1831–July 20, 1902), miner, capitalist, was born in Dublin, Ireland, one of four children. Desperately poor, his family emigrated to America in 1840. For a short time after their arrival, Mackay attended a public school, but the death of his father ended his formal education, and he became an apprentice in the office of the New York ship-builder, William H. Webb [*q.v.*]. In 1851 he determined to try his fortune in the mines of California and reached the west coast by way of New Orleans and the Isthmus of Panama. For the next seven years, with indifferent success, he worked as a drift and placer miner in various California mines, then went to Virginia City, Nev., where, as a timber man at six dollars a day, he developed expert knowledge and facility in timbering mines.

Having accumulated much practical experience and a small amount of money, he struck out for himself. His first venture at the Esmeralda, Aurora, was a failure, but the Petaluma mill which he built with J. M. Walker at Gold Hill, Nev., turned out profitably. In 1864 Walker and Mackay joined their resources with those of James C. Flood and William S. O'Brien, saloon keepers of San Francisco, and in 1868 the group was joined by James G. Fair [*q.v.*], later United States senator from Nevada. Some time later Walker retired, selling his interest to Mackay. It was the belief of Fair and Mackay that the old workings of the Comstock Lode would reveal a considerable amount of low-grade ore which might be profitably utilized with up-to-date machinery. Following this theory they obtained control in 1865 of the Hale and Norcross Mine, from which they made profits of half a million. The profits were immediately sunk into nearby mines, one of which was the Virginia Consolidated. Here, in 1873, they struck the "Big Bonanza," from which more than a hundred million dollars in gold and silver was taken. Mackay, who at this time had a two-fifths interest in the concern, became a millionaire almost over night. To the end of his life he retained a controlling interest in several of the Comstock ventures and for many years reaped from them a large income. Of all those who sought their fortunes in the western mines, Mackay achieved the most spectacular success.

He acquired important real estate holdings in San Francisco and elsewhere in the West, became a director of the Southern Pacific, and with Flood and Fair organized the Bank of Nevada, San Francisco (from which he withdrew in 1887), but his interests, as time went on, became less concerned with the region from which he had drawn his fortune. In 1867 he had married, at Virginia City, Marie Louise (Hungerford) Bryant, widow of Dr. William C. Bryant and daughter of Col. Daniel E. Hungerford of New Orleans; they had two sons. In 1874 the Mackays took up their residence in San Francisco, and in 1876 moved to New York, but they spent most of their remaining years in Europe, and maintained palatial establishments in London and Paris. The activities of few other millionaires of Mackay's day were more constantly chronicled by the public press. The marriage of his step-daughter to Prince Ferdinand Colonna, and later her divorce; a spectacular attempt to assassinate him in San Francisco in 1895 by an unwise speculator who blamed him for his misfortunes; the lurid reports of the vast sums spent by his wife for jewelry and of their extravagant living, all kept his private life before the public.

More than all this, however, his spectacular battle during the eighties to break the telegraph and cable monopoly built up by Jay Gould [*q.v.*] commanded the attention and admiration of the entire business world. With James Gordon Bennett [*q.v.*], against an almost universal opinion that it would never succeed, he founded the Commercial Cable Company in 1883 and in the following year laid two submarine cables to Europe. A bitter eighteen months' struggle ensued between the strongly entrenched Gould monopoly and the new lines, but the latter won, and in 1886 Mackay organized the Postal Telegraph Cable Company and commenced the construction of telegraph lines to fight the Gould–Western-Union monopoly on land. This was the great constructive work of his career. As a third step in the building of his Postal Telegraph–Commercial Cable system, he planned the laying of a cable across the Pacific and was engaged in this project when he died, in London, in July 1902.

"Of all the bonanza millionaires," said a San Francisco dispatch, "Mackay was the only one who could be called popular" (New York *Sun*, July 21, 1902). As a practical miner, he worked with his hands long after he was rich, and was well liked by his workmen, who looked upon him as an honest and fair employer. In personal appearance, he was tall, slender, well-knit, and active, with a rapid gait, a gentle, measured voice, but a prompt and hearty address (*New York Times*, July 21, 1902). His presence made him distinguished in any gathering. Although he mixed freely with his friends, he shunned interviews and detested publicity. The Prince of Wales is reported to have described him as "the most unassuming American I ever met" (New York *Sun*, July 22, 1902). He twice refused the Republican nomination for senator from Nevada. In religion he was a Roman Catholic.

[James Burnley, *Millionaires and Kings of Enterprise* (1901), inaccurate; S. P. Davis, *The Hist. of Nevada* (1913), vol. I; H. H. Bancroft, *Hist. of Nevada, Colorado, and Wyoming* (1890); J. J. Powell, *Nevada: the Land of Silver* (1876); C. H. Shinn, *The Story of the Mine* (1896), ch. xvi; Don C. Seitz, *The James Gordon Bennetts* (1928); *Who's Who in America*, 1901–02; *The Times* (London), July 21, 1902; *N. Y. Times*, July 21, 22, and *Sun* (N. Y.), July 21–23, 1902.]

H. U. F.

MACKAYE, JAMES MORRISON STEELE (June 6, 1842–Feb. 25, 1894), dramatist, actor, and inventor, better known as Steele MacKaye, was born in Buffalo, N. Y., the son of James Morrison McKay (as the name was then spelled) and Emily Steele. His father was a legal associate of Millard Fillmore and a friend of many of the leading men of the day. The son, in his youth, had as playmates Winslow Homer and William and Henry James. At sixteen he entered the École des Beaux-Arts in Paris, with "unlimited funds at his disposal," and perhaps thereby failed to learn the use and value of money; at any rate, he had an obvious disregard for it in later life. In Paris he worked especially with Troyon. In 1859 he returned to America. His father now lived in New York, a friend of many artists as well as public men. The Civil War soon broke in on American life, Steele joined the 7th Regiment, and made his first stage appearance as Hamlet in a regimental performance in 1862. At this period William James declared he was "effervescing with inco-ordinated romantic ideas of every description." After the war, his incoördination led him into many fields in an attempt to find himself. He was a painter and an art dealer; he invented "photo-sculpture" and launched a company to commercialize it. In 1869 his father set him adrift financially, so he went to Paris, where he met Delsarte and became his enthusiastic disciple. To spread the Delsartian philosophy of expression, he returned to America to give lectures, one of them at Harvard in 1871, and to try to establish a school.

On Jan. 8, 1872, MacKaye made his début in New York as an actor, in *Monaldi,* supported by his pupils, and in a theatre rented and reconstructed by himself. The next autumn he studied acting in France and acted Hamlet in Paris in French that year, and in London in English the following spring—the first American to play the rôle in England. A year of acting and play-writing followed, and then he returned to America, opening a "school of expression" at 46 East Tenth Street, lecturing, and trying to get a foothold on the American stage for himself and his plays. His *Rose Michel,* an adaptation of the French play by Ernest Blum, was produced in 1875, in sets designed by himself. *Won at Last* was acted at Wallack's, Dec. 10, 1877, with a notable cast and much success. Finally he succeeded in having a small theatre on West Twenty-fourth Street, N. Y., rebuilt in accordance with his ideas, and it opened as the Madison Square Theatre in 1879, one of the earliest of American "intimate" playhouses. During his occupancy MacKaye invented for it a double, or elevator stage (anticipating German inventions by a generation), artificial ventilation, and overhead and indirect lighting of the scene. Here, in 1880, his play *Hazel Kirke* was presented and ran for more than a year—a phenomenal run at the time. The play was acted everywhere, for two decades, and should have made him a large fortune, had he not been so childlike and improvident in all business matters that he signed contracts which gave most of the profits of both inventions and plays to others. Forced from the control of this theatre, he built the Lyceum Theatre on Fourth Avenue, and established there the first dramatic school in America (later the American Academy of Dramatic Art). This school influenced many future players and was an important development in the American theatre.

MacKaye continued to write plays, invent mechanical and electric stage devices (he was the first to light a New York theatre entirely by electricity—the Lyceum, in 1884), to preach the gospel of the social value of drama and the educational value of its study, and to fight against constant debt. When the Chicago World's Fair came, he dreamed his biggest dream, rallied capital to his support, and began the erection, outside the Fair grounds, of a vast auditorium, with a still vaster stage, called a Spectatorium, wherein was to be enacted a gigantic scenic spectacle of his devising, called *The World Finder* —a tale of Columbus. Financial disaster prevented the completion of this scheme, and MacKaye's end was hastened by his frantic work and worry. He did, however, live long enough to see the scheme realized in a large working model, so that a few audiences in Chicago were able to vision what had been his conception. This conception included a vast cyclorama background, a flexible proscenium, which was instantly adjustable to the size of the picture desired, and scenic and light effects, such as dawn, sunset, moonlight, clouds, at that time revolutionary in depth and illusion but later in common use. MacKaye died of complete nervous exhaustion at Timpas, Colo., while he was on his way to California. He was the author of more than twenty plays, seven of them in collaboration with others, but only *Hazel Kirke* is remembered. Many were spectacular in nature and foreshadowed the so-called "crowd movies" of today. MacKaye was tall, dark, slender, and oddly resembled, in face, Edgar Allan Poe. He was intensely dynamic, worked sometimes for twenty hours on a stretch, was indifferent to food and creature comforts (including money), idealistic to the point sometimes of fanaticism (so it seemed to those working with him), and a bit lacking in the humor which makes for corrective self-criticism. On June 30, 1862, he was married to Jennie Spring but was later divorced. On June 6, 1865, he was married to Mary Keith Medbery, of Portsmouth, N. H., a descendant of Roger Williams. One of their sons, Percy MacKaye, later became well known as a dramatist.

[Percy MacKaye, *Epoch: The Life of Steele MacKaye* (2 vols., 1927); Wm. Winter, *The Life of David Belasco* (1918), vol. I; I. F. Marcosson and Daniel Frohman, *Chas. Frohman, Manager and Man* (1916); *Chicago Daily Tribune,* Feb. 26, 1894.] W. P. E.

MACKAYE, STEELE [See MACKAYE, JAMES MORRISON STEELE, 1842–1894].

McKEAN, JOSEPH BORDEN (July 28, 1764–Sept. 3, 1826), jurist, son of Thomas [*q.v.*], signer of the Declaration of Independence, and Mary (Borden) McKean, was born in New Castle, Del. He graduated from the University of Pennsylvania in 1782, studied law, and was admitted to the Philadelphia bar in 1785. His marriage, Apr. 13, 1786, to Hannah, daughter of Col. Samuel Miles, increased the opportunities for legal preferment he already enjoyed as son of the chief justice of Pennsylvania. For some years, in addition to his law practice, he was active in the militia. In 1799 he and fellow officers of the 1st City Troop became involved in a suit for assault for administering a sound beating to William Duane [*q.v.*], because his *Aurora and General Advertiser* had printed an article impeaching the conduct of the troop in the Fries Rebellion. The case dragged on until 1809 when the defendants were acquitted. Although the incident disturbed Republican harmony, having occurred when McKean's father was running for governor, Duane nevertheless supported the elder McKean with undiminished enthusiasm. He never forgot the episode, however, and it remained to plague the McKeans.

From May 10, 1800, to July 22, 1808, Joseph was attorney-general of Pennsylvania, previously having been register of wills of Philadelphia. The Governor was bitterly assailed for appointing his son, whom many regarded as inferior to other Philadelphia lawyers. Despite the assertions of his enemies to the contrary, he was a lawyer of parts, but his aristocratic bearing and domineering manner did not help party harmony. He scorned the attacks of the Jacobins on the judiciary, and incurred their animosity by refusing legal aid in the impeachment trial of the three supreme-court judges (1805). He was an active promoter of the moderate Republican-Federalist coalition which elected his father governor in 1805. In some quarters his influence over his father's administration was regarded as tantamount to domination (*Norristown Register,* quoted in the *Aurora,* May 18, 1805). He was ambitious to be chief justice, and his father would have appointed him in 1806, had reasons of expediency not forbidden his doing so (McKean Papers, III, 104). After 1808, in which year he resumed his law practice, he had little prospect for political office, for he was out of favor with the state administration. He was likewise *persona non grata* to President Madison, because in a legal opinion (1803) he had upheld the contention of the Marquis de Casa Yrujo, his brother-in-law, that Spain was not responsible for damages inflicted by the French on American citizens in Spanish waters. On Mar. 27, 1817, however, Gov. Simon Snyder, a former enemy, appointed him associate judge of the district court for the city and county of Philadelphia, of which he was named president judge Oct. 1, 1818. His commission as associate judge was renewed Mar. 17, 1821. Reappointed president judge on Mar. 21, 1825, he held this post until his death. He was a trustee of the University of Pennsylvania (1794–1826), a member of the Pennsylvania Academy of the Fine Arts, the American Philosophical Society, the Philadelphia Law Association, and the State Fencibles, a military company organized in 1813. On his father's death (1817) he came into possession of the family mansion at Third and Pine Streets, where he died.

[The McKean Papers in the Hist. Soc. of Pa., Philadelphia, contain source material; see also Roberdeau Buchanan, *Geneal. of the McKean Family of Pa.* (1890); *Pa. Mag. of Hist. and Biog.,* Jan. 1925; J. H. Martin, *Martin's Bench and Bar of Phila.* (1883); J. H. Peeling, "The Public Life of Thomas McKean, 1734–1817" (1929), doctor's thesis (MS.), Univ. of Chicago; J. T. Scharf and Thompson Westcott, *Hist. of Phila.* (1884), vols. I, II; *Poulson's Am. Daily Advertiser,* Sept. 4, 5, 1826.] J. H. P—g.

McKEAN, SAMUEL (Apr. 7, 1787–Dec. 14, 1841), congressman, senator, son of James and Jane (Scott) McKean, was born in Huntingdon County, Pa., of Scotch ancestry, the eighth of ten children. James McKean, a native of Cecil County, Md., moved to Pennsylvania about 1774, served with Washington's army in the Revolution, and later settled near Elmira, N. Y. Finding his land title fraudulent, about 1791 he took up a tract of land on Sugar Creek near Burlington, Pa. Samuel's opportunities for education were meager until he was sixteen. At that age he visited an uncle in Maryland who gave him a thorough education. At his uncle's death, falling heir to part of the estate, he established himself as a merchant in Burlington and did a flourishing business. In 1814 he was elected county commissioner of Bradford County, and, with other Republicans, founded the *Bradford Gazette,* published at Towanda, to further his political fortunes. From 1815 to 1819 he was in the state legislature. In 1822 he was elected to Congress where (1823–29) he was identified with the group favoring high tariff and internal improvements. In 1829 he was a strong contender for the nomination for governor in Pennsylvania. Elected state senator the same year, he resigned almost immediately to become secretary of the commonwealth. While secretary (1829–33) he drafted a bill providing for the taxation of all property for free school purposes, which subsequently became a law. He was a presidential elector on the Jackson ticket in 1832.

In 1833, assisted by his opposition to constitutional and national conventions, he was elected United States senator after a long and bitter struggle. As senator, although opposed to Van Buren and the "kitchen cabinet" and steering a middle course on the question of the deposits, he was an enemy of the United States Bank and generally supported Jackson. He voted against the resolutions (1834) declaring the Treasurer's reasons for removing the deposits unsatisfactory and censuring the president, because they were "exclusively censorious," but he denounced the subsequent expunging of the censure as unconstitutional (*Niles' Weekly Register,* Feb. 25, 1837). While sanctioning the removal of the deposits, nevertheless, he voted to restore them because of "sheer expediency" and to satisfy his constituents (*Register of Debates in Congress,* 23 Cong., 1 Sess., p. 1895). He disapproved of anti-slavery agitation and on Jan. 6, 1838, presented two resolutions: that Congress possessed no power to abolish slavery in the states where it existed; and that it was inexpedient to legislate on slavery in the District of Columbia (*Congressional Globe,* 25 Cong., 2 Sess., p. 80). He was chairman of the committee on contingent expenses and was a member of the committees on militia, public lands, pensions, commerce, roads and canals, and agriculture. In 1839 severe neuralgia in the head caused him to become an opium addict, and in a delirium suffered as a consequence he cut his throat with a razor. He never fully recovered from the wound. He was an adroit politician and a power in local politics for many years. Van Buren regarded him as "an honest, but exceedingly prejudiced man" (Fitzpatrick, *post,* p. 763). He was a major-general of militia. He died at West Burlington, Pa., survived by his wife, Julia McDowell, whom he had married on Jan. 7, 1812.

[David Craft, *Hist. of Bradford County, Pa.* (1878); C. F. Heverly, *Hist. of the Towandas, 1776–1886* (1886); Cornelius McKean, *McKean Geneals.* (1902); *Biog. Dir. Am. Cong.* (1928); J. C. Fitzpatrick, "The Autobiog. of Martin Van Buren," *Ann. Report of the Am. Hist. Asso. for the Year 1918* (1920), vol. II; *Daily Nat. Intelligencer* (Washington, D. C.), Dec. 23, 1841; *Niles' Weekly Reg.,* Jan. 17, 1824, Nov. 9, Dec. 21, 1833.]

J. H. P—g.

McKEAN, THOMAS (Mar. 19, 1734–June 24, 1817), statesman, second son of William and Letitia (Finney) McKean, was of the fourth generation from William McKean of Argyllshire, Scotland, who emigrated to Londonderry, Ireland, about 1674. Coming to Pennsylvania with his mother at an early age (*c.* 1725), William, the father of Thomas, lived on a farm in Chester County and later became a tavern keeper. His wife, Letitia Finney, belonged to a wealthy and prominent family of Scotch-Irish settlers in Pennsylvania. Thomas was born in New London Township, Chester County. After spending seven years at Rev. Francis Allison's academy, New London, he went to New Castle, Del., to study law with his cousin, David Finney. His connections there soon put him on the road to success as a lawyer and politician. First a prothonotary's clerk, in 1752 he was appointed deputy prothonotary and recorder for the probate of wills for New Castle County. He was admitted to the bar in the Lower Counties at twenty, and within the next decade acquired a wide practice in Delaware, Pennsylvania, and New Jersey.

The same period saw many of his ambitions for a political life realized. He was appointed deputy attorney-general in 1756; was clerk of the Delaware Assembly, 1757–59; and in 1762 began the first of seventeen years' successive service in the latter body. A leader of the country party, he assisted in compiling the provincial laws in 1762 and was a trustee of the New Castle County loan office, 1764–72. He was an uncompromising foe of the Stamp Act, was among the most radical delegates to the Stamp Act Congress, and as justice of the court of common pleas and quarter sessions (1765) ordered business to proceed as usual on unstamped paper. He was also chief notary and tabellion officer in 1765, collector of the port of New Castle in 1771, and speaker of the Assembly, 1772–73. His marriage on July 21, 1763, to Mary, eldest daughter of Joseph and Elizabeth Borden of Bordentown, N. J., further widened his legal and political connections. After her death in 1773, he married Sarah Armitage of New Castle, Sept. 3, 1774, and in the fall of that year established a home in Philadelphia.

The widening breach between the American colonies and the mother country in 1774 offered McKean a political opportunity which he was quick to grasp. He led the movement in Delaware for a colonial congress and, excepting the period between December 1776 and January 1778, represented that colony in the Continental Congress continuously until 1783. Prior to July 4, 1776, he was on five standing committees (secret, qualifications, prisoners, claims, and treasury), and on more than thirty others. At first hopeful for reconciliation, he became early in 1776 an ardent advocate of separation. As chairman of the Philadelphia committee of observation he played a conspicuous part in engineering the popular movement in Pennsylvania for a new state government and for independence. In Delaware he effected the repudiation of the Crown and support for independence by his personal appearance in the Assembly. In Congress he voted for Lee's resolution for independence (July 1). His vote being tied with that of his colleague George Read [*q.v.*], he dispatched an express for Cæsar Rodney [*q.v.*], third Delaware delegate, who arrived in time (July 2) to vote for the resolution. McKean seems to have been the first man to challenge the later popular impression that the Declaration of Independence was signed on July 4. Finding that his name did not appear as a signer in the early printed journals of the Congress, he asserted in a letter to Alexander J. Dallas (Sept. 26, 1796; McKean Papers, III, 10), what the corrected Journals and contemporary letters have since substantiated, that no one signed on July 4. The exact date of his signing is not known. Although he later insisted it was in 1776, it is almost certain that it was after Jan. 18, 1777. That it was as late as 1781, as some writers aver, is doubtful.

During July and August 1776, McKean, as colonel, commanded a battalion of Philadelphia associators at Perth Amboy, N. J., but saw no action. He then participated (Aug. 27–Sept. 21) in framing Delaware's first constitution, the authorship of which tradition ascribes to him, relying on his statement made years later to Cæsar A. Rodney (Sept. 22, 1813; Burnett, *post,* I, 535). Although his influence in the convention was considerable, the *Proceedings* of that body indicate that the constitution was not solely his work. In the fall of 1776, failing, through conservative opposition, of reëlection to the Congress, he transferred his exertions to the Assembly, was elected speaker shortly thereafter, and in that capacity became acting president of Delaware for two months in 1777 (Sept. 22–*c.* Nov. 17).

During all this time his major interests had been gravitating toward Philadelphia, and on July 28, 1777, he was commissioned chief justice of Pennsylvania. Nevertheless, he remained active in Delaware politics, and for the next six years (1777–83) held office in both states, enjoying the anomalous position of being assemblyman, acting president, or congressman for one state and chief justice of another. In Congress (1778–83) he supported the Articles of Confederation, favored a federal court of appeals, attacked administrative inefficiency and corruption, decried the dangers of military and financial dictatorships, and was close to the Adams-Lee faction. From July 10 to Nov. 5, 1781, he was president of Congress, despite the protests of his Pennsylvania enemies who were eager to force him to relinquish either the presidency or his judicial position.

Decidedly less liberal after independence had been declared, McKean opposed the radical Pennsylvania constitution of 1776, although he accepted the chief justiceship of the supreme court under it and served for twenty-two years, being convinced that failure to support the new government would endanger the American cause. As a Federalist, he was active in securing ratification of the Federal Constitution in the Pennsylvania convention of 1787. Comparing the arguments of the opposition to "the feeble noise occasioned by the working of small beer," he pronounced the frame of government "the best the world has yet seen" (J. B. McMaster and F. D. Stone, *Pennsylvania and the Federal Constitution,* 1888, pp. 378–79). In the Pennsylvania constitutional convention (1789–90), he manifested his belief in government by the few to an even greater extent, and at the same time was the author of a clause providing education for the poor at state expense.

As chief justice (1777–99) his frequent conservative decisions and his struggle for judicial sanctity and against the encroachments of the military on the civil authority brought numerous conflicts with the Assembly, council, or military authorities. He upheld the proprietors in their property rights (1779), interpreted the law of libel rigorously, sanctioned the doctrine that courts can punish for contempt (*Respublica* vs. *Oswald,* 1788, 1 *Dallas,* 319), and in 1798 created a sensation by appearing as witness against William Cobbett and later sitting as judge in the same case. Although somewhat harsh and domineering, his decisions were unmistakably to the point and reflected honesty and a high sense of justice. McKean also rode the circuit and, from its establishment in 1780, was a judge of the Pennsylvania court of errors and appeals.

After 1792 Federalist foreign policy forced him into the ranks of the Jeffersonians. His friendship for France and his aversion for England made him a favorite of the Republicans, and in 1799 they nominated him for governor. A strong candidate because of his prestige and moderate republicanism, he defeated James Ross, Federalist, after a bitter campaign, his victory entailing a revolution in state politics. As governor he removed his political enemies from office, giving their places to his Republican friends, thereby winning the appellation of "the father of political proscription" and fastening the spoils system on Pennsylvania. He adhered to the principle of giving "a preference to real republicans or whigs, having equal talents and integrity, and to a friend before an Enemy . . . for it is not right to put a dagger in the hands of an assassin" (McKean to Jefferson, Jan. 10, 1801; McKean Papers, III, 46). He warmly espoused Jefferson's election (1800), and later urged on the

President, with some success, a policy of removing Federalists from office.

In 1802 McKean was reëlected by more than 30,000 majority. Personal and factional jealousies, however, soon threatened Republican harmony. William Duane [*q.v.*] whose *Aurora and General Advertiser* had rendered invaluable service in the campaign of 1799, found the state administration disinclined to heed his advice. Chafing at his failure to control the executive in appointments and other matters, he started a movement through the *Aurora's* columns late in 1802 to shunt McKean into the vice-presidency, but this design failed, for the latter could not be moved to relinquish his responsibilities and influence in Pennsylvania. Revolts by friends of the administration against Duane's dictatorship over the party in Philadelphia added further irritation. Moreover, McKean, a consistent advocate of a strong executive and an independent judiciary, was the chief means of frustrating the attacks made by the radical Republicans on the executive's prerogatives, and on judges, lawyers, and judicial practices. He repeatedly vetoed bills extending the jurisdiction of justices of the peace and other "giddy innovations," opposed attempts to impeach three supreme-court judges (1804–05), and refused to sanction pleas for a convention to revise the constitution. Violent schism now disrupted party ranks. The radicals, under Duane's leadership, determined to achieve their ends by shelving the governor, and in 1805 nominated Simon Snyder [*q.v.*], farmer and arch-Jacobin, attacking relentlessly lawyers, judges, courts, and all semblances of aristocracy. Friends of the constitution, denominated Constitutionalists—moderate Republicans and Federalists alike, the former styled Quids by the radicals—united, and elected McKean by 5,000 majority, thus preserving the constitution.

Construing his reëlection as a vindication, the governor now drove from office his Republican enemies, giving their places to his more recent Federalist supporters. The *Aurora* accused him of nepotism, and on Jan. 15, 1806, published the names of twelve relatives appointed to office, under the title, "The Royal Family," dubbing Joseph [*q.v.*], the Governor's eldest son, "heir apparent." Libel suits were instituted against his more violent opponents, and the Assembly was urged to fix more drastic penalties for the punishment of libel. His enemies in the legislature (1806–07) retorted with impeachment proceedings, charging him with having violated the constitution by avoiding a sheriff's election in Philadelphia, assuming unwarranted judicial authority, abusing his power of appointment and removal, stamping his name on state papers, and using his influence improperly to discontinue two court actions involving his son (*Report of the Committee Appointed to Enquire into the Official Conduct of the Governor of Pennsylvania,* 1807). The charges were based on trivialities or absurdities, magnified into high crimes and misdemeanors through spite. By clever strategy, however, the coalition behind the administration secured a general postponement of them (Jan. 27, 1808), and the Governor completed his term in comparative quiet.

Although active in promoting education and internal and other improvements, Governor McKean's main achievement lay in restraining the excesses of the Pennsylvania Jacobins. Throughout his gubernatorial career he was a veritable storm center in state politics. Cold in manner, energetic, independent, proud and vain, too tactless for a practical politician, he had a personality which readily aroused antagonisms. Yet he possessed many admiring friends, and even his enemies in their cooler moments admitted his ability, candor, and honesty. After his retirement he lived in Philadelphia, his tall, stately figure being a familiar sight in the city. These sunset days were spent in reading, writing, and reminiscing, and in following with watchful eye the trend of current affairs. He had six children by his first wife and five by his second, of whom only four, with his second wife, survived him. His will disposed of a considerable estate consisting of stocks, bonds, and large tracts of land in Pennsylvania. He compiled *The Acts of the General Assembly of Pennsylvania* (2 vols., 1782) and collaborated with Edmund Physick in *A Calm Appeal to the People of the State of Delaware* (1793), a plea for a fair settlement of the proprietary interests. Another volume, James Wilson and Thomas McKean, *Commentaries on the Constitution of the United States of America* (1792), contains his speeches in the Pennsylvania convention of 1787.

[McKean's correspondence and papers, including an incomplete autobiographical sketch begun in his eightieth year, are in the library of the Hist. Soc. of Pa. Some of his judicial decisions appear in A. J. Dallas, *Pa. Reports* (4 vols., 1797–1807). Other sources include E. C. Burnett, *Letters of Members of the Continental Congress* (1921–); *Journals of the Continental Cong.*; *Proc. of the Convention of the Delaware State . . . 1776* (1776, repr. 1927); "Governor McKean's Papers," *Pa. Archives,* 4 ser. IV (1900); Roberdeau Buchanan, *Geneal. of the McKean Family of Pa., with a Biog. of the Hon. Thomas McKean* (1890); *Poulson's Am. Daily Advertiser,* June 26, 1817; J. H. Peeling, "The Public Life of Thomas McKean, 1734–1817" (1929), doctor's thesis (MS.) at Univ. of Chicago.] J. H. P—g.

McKEAN, WILLIAM WISTER (Sept. 19, 1800–Apr. 22, 1865), naval officer, was the son of Judge Joseph Borden McKean [*q.v.*] and grandson of Thomas McKean [*q.v.*], the signer of the Declaration of Independence; his mother was Hannah (Miles). Born in Philadelphia, he became a midshipman on Nov. 30, 1814, and was promoted lieutenant (1825), commander (1841), captain (1855), and commodore (1862). He made his first cruise in the *Java* under O. H. Perry to the Mediterranean. For the most of the time between 1822 and 1824 he was in the West Indies fighting pirates, first on the *Alligator* and then on the *Terrier*. Later, he served on the *Warren* in the Mediterranean and on the *Natchez* off South America. In 1843–44 he was in charge of the Naval Asylum, Philadelphia, then the chief place for the instruction of midshipmen. When George Bancroft [*q.v.*] proposed the establishment of a regular naval school, McKean and his first cousin, Franklin Buchanan [*q.v.*], were on the board that recommended locating it at Annapolis. During the Mexican War he commanded the *Dale* on the west coast till invalided home; but in 1852 he assumed command of the *Raritan*. By 1860 he had secured the finest ship in the navy, the *Niagara*, and in that year carried the Japanese embassy back home. Returning to Boston in April 1861, he had his first news of the Civil War, and promptly refitted his ship, eliminating Southerners by exacting a new oath of allegiance, and sailed to blockade off Charleston, where, on May 12, he made his first capture. In October of the same year he was in charge of the Gulf blockading squadron and occupied the Head of the Passes of the Mississippi. In November he took part in the attack on Pensacola, but by the next June ill health had forced him to relinquish his command, and his naval career was practically over. He died at his home, "The Moorings," near Binghamton, N. Y., and was buried in Spring Forest Cemetery. On Aug. 25, 1824, he had married Davis Rosa Clark, who survived him. They had twelve children, one of whom became an officer in the navy and another in the Marine Corps. In addition to his other sterling qualities he was noted for his piety. When an able chaplain on the *Niagara* stirred up a great revival of religion, he was strongly seconded by McKean. Commodore Schley, who served under him on the same ship, called him "noble old Captain McKean" (*post*, p. 11).

[McKean's naval records and dispatches, as well as some of his letter-books, are in the custody of the Navy Department. See also Roberdeau Buchanan, *Geneal. of the McKean Family of Pa.* (1890); G. W. Allen, *Our Navy and the Barbary Corsairs* (1905), and *Our Navy and the West Indian Pirates* (1929); C. L. Lewis, *Admiral Franklin Buchanan* (1929); W. S. Schley, *Forty-Five Years Under the Flag* (1904); *Official Records of the Union and Confederate Navies in the Civil War*, 1 ser. IV, V; *Army and Navy Jour.*, May 6, 1865; *Daily National Intelligencer* (Washington, D. C.), Apr. 25, 1865.] W. B. N.

McKEE, JOHN (1771–Aug. 12, 1832), Indian agent and congressman, was the son of John (or James) and Esther (Houston) McKee and the cousin of Sam Houston and John Letcher [*qq.v.*]. He was born in Rockbridge County, Va., and attended Liberty Hall Academy, now Washington and Lee University. In 1792 he was appointed by Gov. William Blount of Tennessee as a commissioner to the Cherokee in order to agree on the line designated by the treaty of Holston and, with the other two commissioners, reported that, when the Cherokee did not appear, the line had been measured according to instructions. The next year he was appointed by Blount to try to conciliate the Cherokee and was sent to accompany a deputation of five Chickasaw to visit the president at Philadelphia. In 1794 he was appointed temporary agent of the Cherokee. He signed the treaties of December 1801 and of November 1805 with the Choctaw and appears on the official roll sent to Congress on Feb. 17, 1802, as agent to that tribe. During the Creek War he was active in persuading the other tribes to remain at peace with the United States and in 1814 led an expedition of six or seven hundred Choctaw and Chickasaw to the Black Warrior River. After the war he bent his energies toward the final removal of the Five Civilized Tribes to reservations beyond the Mississippi. He helped to negotiate the treaty of October 1816 with the Choctaw, but in 1818 he was on a commission that failed in its attempt to win their consent to removal. He was one of the first settlers in Tuscaloosa County, where he had charge of the land office. In 1823, as an ardent admirer of Andrew Jackson, he was sent to represent the Tuscaloosa district in Congress. There he spoke but rarely, and after three successive terms he retired. He was a member of the commission to settle the boundary between Kentucky and Tennessee. In 1830 he was one of the commissioners to negotiate the treaty of Dancing Rabbit Creek, whereby the Choctaw ceded their claim to all their eastern lands except such small parcels as might be granted to individual Indians who would undertake to accept allotment and citizenship rather than emigrate across the Mississippi. He died at his plantation home, "Hill of Howth," which he had built about 1818 near Boligee, Ala. He was said to have been legally married to an Indian wife, and he provided that after his death his friend and heir, William P. Gould, should make a quarterly payment in gold to his half-breed son.

[Some papers and diary in possession of J. McKee Gould, Boligee, Ala.; date of death from the diary of Wm. P. Gould; files of the Congressional Joint Committee on Printing; files of the Indian Office; *Am. State Papers: Indian Affairs* (2 vols., 1832–34); *Biog. Dir. Am. Cong.* (1928); *Trans. Ala. Hist. Soc.*, vol. III (1899); A. H. Abel, "The Hist. of Events Resulting in Indian Consolidation West of the Mississippi," *Am. Hist. Asso. Report . . . 1906*, vol. I (1908); W. R. Smith, *Reminiscences of a Long Life* (copr. 1889); S. R. Houston, *Brief Biog. Accounts of the Houston Family* (1882), pp. 46–47.] K. E. C.

McKEEN, JOSEPH (Oct. 15, 1757–July 15, 1807), Congregational clergyman, first president of Bowdoin College, was born in Londonderry, N. H., of Scotch ancestry. His grandfather, James, came to America from County Antrim, Ireland, in 1718 and was one of the founders of Londonderry. He brought with him his son, John, who later married his first cousin Mary McKeen. Their son, Joseph, was prepared for college under Rev. Simon Williams of Windham, N. H., and graduated from Dartmouth in the class of 1774 with first honors. For the next eight years he taught school in his native town, undisturbed by the turmoil of the Revolutionary War, except for a brief period when he was in military service under General Sullivan. By nature a student, he proceeded to Cambridge in 1782 and studied natural philosophy, mathematics, and astronomy under Prof. Samuel Williams of Harvard. Later he was tutored in theology by his old teacher, Simon Williams, and licensed to preach by the Londonderry Presbytery. After a short time as assistant at Phillips Academy, Andover, and some practice in preaching at Boston, he was called to the First Congregational Church at Beverly, Mass., as successor to Rev. Joseph Willard, who had been chosen president of Harvard. Here, in May 1785, he was ordained and remained for seventeen years, becoming one of the most eminent divines of New England. He was reputed to have been "not quite orthodox in the opinion of some of his parishioners, nor so liberal in his theological views as others would have liked. But he was candid, upright, prudent and conciliatory" (Hatch, *post*, p. 15)—qualities not always found in college presidents, but traits so harmoniously combined in him as to commend him to the authorities of Bowdoin when they were looking for someone to preside over that infant college.

Though his administration was brief, lasting only five years (1802–07), he won the regard of students, officers, and the public. He laid broad and sound foundations. With a wise boldness he insisted on making the requirements for admission equal to those of Harvard; he argued for a reasonably broad curriculum; he was a stout advocate of liberal education. In his very excellent inaugural address he stated that "literary institutions are founded and endowed for the common good, and not for the private advantage of those who resort to them for education"; and "that every man who has been aided by a public institution to acquire an education, and to qualify himself for usefulness, is under peculiar obligations to exert his talents for the public good." As a teacher he broke away from the older formal methods of his time, using models in mathematics and illustrations from actual life in moral philosophy. He brought to Bowdoin several excellent teachers, among them Parker Cleaveland [*q.v.*], and gave the new-born college worthy standards of scholarship. His promising career was cut short by a most painful illness, dropsical in nature, which ended in his death at Brunswick in his fiftieth year.

In appearance the first president of Bowdoin College was tall, of robust frame, and athletic vigor. He was a man of sound judgment, cool decision, kindly spirit, moral and religious fervor combined with a love of science, and notable tolerance. His scientific attainments gave him membership in the American Academy of Arts and Sciences, to the publications of which he made occasional contributions. In 1785 he married Alice Anderson, by whom he had three sons and two daughters.

[Nehemiah Cleaveland, *Hist. of Bowdoin Coll.* (1882); G. T. Little, "Hist. Sketch of Bowdoin Coll.," in *Gen. Cat. Bowdoin Coll. 1794–1894* (1894); L. C. Hatch, *The Hist. of Bowdoin Coll.* (1927); G. H. Wheeler, *Hist. of Brunswick, Topsham, and Harpswell, Me.* (1878); G. T. Chapman, *Sketches of the Alumni* of Dartmouth Coll. (1867); E. L. Parker, *The Hist. of Londonderry* (1851); *The Repertory* (Boston), July 24, 1807; W. B. Sprague, *Annals Am. Pulpit*, vol. II (1857).] K. C. M. S.

MACKELLAR, PATRICK (1717–Oct. 22, 1778), British military engineer, was born in Scotland, probably in Argyllshire. After entering the ordnance service in 1735 he acted for seven years, the last three at Minorca, as a clerk. From 1742, when he was commissioned as engineer extraordinary, to 1754, he remained at Minorca, attaining in 1751 the rank of engineer in ordinary. Selected as engineer *en second* under James G. Montrésor [*q.v.*] for service in America, he accompanied Braddock's expedition to its defeat at the Monongahela in 1755. His two detailed maps of that battle-field, which delineate accurately the position of the troops at the important stages of the attack, show him to have been a cool, self-possessed observer, better fitted temperamentally than any of his colleagues for the direction of siege operations under fire. He was rated the most competent engineer in

America as early as 1756, when he was sent to Oswego to strengthen the works there. His journal of the summer's proceedings—the most elaborate British account extant—clears him from any responsibility for the disaster of August, when Montcalm stormed the place in four days, and took the captured garrison, among them Mackellar, to Canada. At Quebec the engineer was able to make observations on the fortifications, embodied in a report to the ordnance board, that were invaluable two years later. After being exchanged in England in 1757, and after repairing batteries in the north of Scotland, he returned to America, a sub-director and major, but in the capacity of engineer *en second* under J. H. Bastide, in Amherst's expedition against Louisbourg. When Bastide was wounded, Mackellar assumed charge of siege operations. The following year he served as chief engineer under Wolfe at Quebec, and is credited with having dissuaded his commander from attempting a frontal attack on the citadel from the lower town. He remained in Canada under General Murray, and in 1760 was wounded at the battle of Sillery. Late in 1760, as chief engineer at Halifax, he organized a training school for engineers. He was Monckton's chief engineer in 1762 in the admirably planned and executed capture of Martinique. The next year, a lieutenant-colonel, he acted as Albemarle's chief engineer at the siege of Havana, where he directed elaborate approaches against Morro Castle. Wounded, he returned to England, and published a journal of the siege. In 1763, as chief engineer, he returned to the scene of his early labors at Minorca, where he remained in active service until his death. In 1777 he became director and colonel.

[A. G. Doughty, *The Siege of Quebec*, contains a journal of the siege, attributed to Mackellar; his report of 1757 on Quebec is printed as an appendix to the Champlain Society edition of Capt. John Knox's *Hist. Jour. of the Campaigns in North America* (1916), ed. by A. G. Doughty; a map of Sillery is in *Report Concerning Canadian Archives for the Year 1905*, vol. I, pt. 4; his maps of Braddock's field are in the Public Record Office; his journal and map of Oswego, in the Royal Archives at Windsor. See also R. H. Vetch in *Dict. of Nat. Biog.*; Whitworth Porter, *Hist. of the Corps of Royal Engineers* (1889).] S. M. P.

MACKELLAR, THOMAS (Aug. 12, 1812–Dec. 29, 1899), printer, type-founder, and poet, was born in New York City, the son of Archibald and Harriet (Andrews) MacKellar. His father, who was a native of Greenock, Scotland, had been a midshipman in the British navy; his mother traced her ancestry back to Henry Brezier, one of the original settlers in New Amsterdam. Young MacKellar attended McGowan's Classical Academy until he was fourteen, when his father's circumstances suffered a change and the boy had to go to work. He was first given employment in the office of the *New York Spy* as a compositor, but after a year he entered the publishing house of John and James Harper, where he soon was promoted from setting type to reading proof. Although he was fascinated with the work, his eyesight suffered, and he devoted himself during the remainder of his time with the firm to the practical work of printing. Shortly before he had reached his majority he went to Philadelphia and took a position as proof-reader in the type foundry of Lawrence Johnson and George F. Smith who, in addition to manufacturing type, also set and stereotyped composition for books.

In 1845 MacKellar was taken into partnership, as were the two sons of Smith, who had then retired. The business grew extensively and rapidly. After Johnson died, in 1860, MacKellar and John F. and Richard Smith bought out his interest and formed the firm of MacKellar, Smiths & Jordan, Peter A. Jordan having been admitted to the business. MacKellar succeeded in making the foundry the leading manufactory of type in the United States. In 1855 he began the publication of the *Typographic Advertiser*, of which he was editor until 1884, when he was succeeded by his son, William B. MacKellar. In its pages he proposed an asylum for aged printers, which subsequently was endowed by George W. Childs and Anthony J. Drexel [*qq.v.*]. The Specimen Book of the Johnson Type Foundry, which cost $40,000 to produce, was largely the work of MacKellar, and he is said to have "elevated the prosaic theme of a business catalogue into a work of art" (Ringwalt, *post*, p. 289). "The matter was mostly original, and being uniquely adapted to the conformation of the differing styles of the types exhibited, attracted the attention of printers everywhere" (Scharf and Westcott, *post*, III, 2325). In 1866 he wrote *The American Printer*, a book for the craft, which "proved to be the most popular work on typography ever printed" (*Ibid.*). The eighteenth edition was published in 1893.

In his maturer years, MacKellar developed into a graceful poet. His first volume was *Droppings From the Heart* (1844), which was followed by *Tam's Fortnight Ramble and Other Poems* (1847), *Rhymes Atween-Times* (1873), *Hymns and a Few Metrical Psalms* (1883), and *Faith, Hope, Love, These Three* (1893). He wrote with earnestness and fluency, and his poetry is "inspired by a devotional spirit and a tender feeling to the claims of family and friendship, expressive of the author's hopeful and hearty struggle with the world" (Duyckinck, *post,* II, 566). The Memorial Ode read at the unveiling of the Soldiers' Monument, in Germantown, Philadelphia, July 4, 1883, was written by him. He took a deep interest in religious affairs and for twenty-five years was corresponding secretary of the Philadelphia Bible Society; he also established one of the earliest mission schools in that city. He was president of the Type Founders Association of the United States, and of the Philadelphia Book Trade Association. On Sept. 27, 1834, he was married to Eliza Ross, by whom he had two sons and eight daughters.

[J. T. Scharf and Thompson Westcott, *Hist. of Phila.* (1884), vol. III; J. L. Ringwalt, *Am. Encyc. of Printing* (1871); *One Hundred Years: MacKellar Smiths and Jordan Foundry, Phila., Pa.* (1896); R. W. Griswold, *The Poets and Poetry of America,* (1855); E. A. and G. L. Duyckinck, *Cyc. of Am. Lit.* (1875), vol. II; *Public Ledger* (Phila.), Dec. 30, 1899; *Who's Who in America,* 1899–1900.] J. J.

McKELWAY, ST. CLAIR (Mar. 15, 1845–July 16, 1915), editor, was born at Columbia, Mo. His father was Alexander J. McKelway, a physician who had emigrated from Scotland in early childhood, and his mother was Mary (Ryan) McKelway. In 1853 the family removed to New Jersey. The boy's education was chiefly under private tutelage. While his father was absent at the front as a surgeon in the Civil War he was instructed by his grandfather, John McKelway, who lived in Trenton. For a short time he was a student of the New Jersey State Normal School at Trenton. Having an inclination to write, he contributed to local newspapers and at the age of seventeen sent to the *New York Tribune* an account of the activities of Confederate sympathizers in and near Trenton, for which Horace Greeley sent a check and wrote him a letter of appreciation. Yielding to the wish of his family he studied law, but he never practised that profession and on the day after his admission to the bar in 1866 became a reporter for the New York *World.* In 1868 he was sent to Washington as correspondent for the *World* and for the *Brooklyn Daily Eagle.* He was an editorial writer for the *Eagle* from 1870 to 1878 and then became editor of the *Albany Argus,* whose position on public questions helped to pave the way for the election of Cleveland to the presidency.

After the death of Thomas Kinsella in 1884, he was made editor-in-chief of the *Eagle* and held that post during the remainder of his life. His writing gave distinction to the editorial page of the paper. He was fearless and independent in expression, and the influence of the *Eagle* became national. His name and personality were identified in the public mind with his more striking editorials, which were widely quoted. He had for the background of his utterances an extensive acquaintance among public men, insight into national and local affairs, and wide reading. Under his editorship, the *Eagle* became an intensely local paper, presenting fully the news and interests of Brooklyn, yet at the same time neglecting no part of the general news field. It had a long period of financial as well as journalistic success. Both he and the paper became thoroughly identified with Brooklyn. He was active in demanding the prosecution of John Y. McKane for the frauds in the Gravesend election in 1893, for which McKane was sentenced to imprisonment.

He had rare gifts as a public speaker and was called upon to use them often. His speech on the occasion of a dinner given in his honor by the Lotos Club of New York in 1906 is printed in *After Dinner Speeches at the Lotos Club* (arranged by John Elderkin and others, 1911). From 1883 to 1915 he served as one of the regents of the University of the State of New York, being chancellor of the university at the time of his death. He wrote a memorial volume on *William C. Kingsley* (1885), the contractor for the Brooklyn Bridge and one of the owners of the *Eagle.* He was also the author of an introduction to *Random Recollections of an Old Political Reporter* (1911) by William C. Hudson, for many years a staff writer for the *Eagle.* On one occasion he remarked that journalism "is served as loyally, bravely, unselfishly, intelligently and honestly as Church or State, army or navy, university or sovereign" (*Memorial, post,* p. 45). He was chosen by Pulitzer as one of the first members and, after 1913, was chairman of the advisory board of the Columbia University School of Journalism. He was married in 1867 to Eleanor Hutchinson, who died in 1884. There were two sons from this marriage both of whom died before their father. In 1888 he was married to Virginia Brooks Thompson, who survived him.

[St. Clair McKelway, *Regent of The University of the State of N. Y. . . . Memorial* (1915?); D. C. Seitz, *Joseph Pulitzer* (1924); *Outlook,* July 28, 1915; *New York Times,* July 17–21, 1915; *Brooklyn Daily Eagle,* July 17–20, 1915.] A. S. W.

McKENDREE, WILLIAM (July 6, 1757–Mar. 5, 1835), first American-born bishop of the Methodist Episcopal Church, was a native of Virginia, the oldest of the eight children of John and Mary McKendree. At the time of William's birth his father was a small planter in King William County, but in 1764 he removed to James City County, and six years later to Greenville County. Not until he was thirty-one did the future bishop become a preacher. His schooling had been most elementary, and his experience only such as an unimportant planter might acquire, augmented by that which came from service in the Revolutionary War, during which he is reputed to have risen from the ranks to the office of adjutant, and been present at the surrender of Cornwallis. Whatever early religious training he had received had been in connection with the Established Church. When about nineteen he had joined a Methodist society on probation, but it was not until more than ten years later that, under the evangelistic activities of Rev. John Easter in Virginia, he was thoroughly converted. Without consulting him, through the recommendation of Easter, the Virginia Conference, meeting at Petersburg, June 1788, appointed McKendree a helper on the Mecklenburg circuit. Though he undertook the work with many misgivings, the year's experiences convinced him that he was divinely called to spread the knowledge of salvation. In June 1790 Bishop Asbury ordained him deacon, and in December of the following year, elder.

Hardly had his ministry begun when a crisis arose which almost separated him from the Methodist Episcopal Church. Under the influence of James O'Kelly [*q.v.*], later a seceder and founder of a new sect, he became distrustful of Asbury, and at the General Conference of 1792 supported O'Kelly in his attempt to secure a limitation to the powers of the bishops. When the attempt failed he left the Conference with O'Kelly and his followers, and at the succeeding session of the Virginia Conference declined to take an appointment. Soon afterward, however, at Asbury's invitation he accompanied him for a time on his travels, and as a result of this association McKendree's views changed and he accepted an appointment to Norfolk. Scanty as his early advantages had been, he had the character, the whole-souled consecration to his calling, and the natural gifts which his time and place required. He was tall and attractive physically, with all the graces of the gentleman; he preached with a sincerity, simplicity, force of illustration, and evangelistic zeal which were highly persuasive; he had business sense and skill as a parliamentarian, acquiring as the years went on a knowledge of Methodist government and discipline second to none; he was wise and prudent. Never marrying, he had no ties to interfere with complete surrender to the cause he had espoused.

For twenty years he served on circuits as a traveling pastor or as presiding elder. Until 1800 his labors were chiefly in Virginia. Tireless and diligent, he frequently preached every day in the week. It was said of him that he "kept house in his saddlebags," and that "he could pack more in them and in better order than other men." In 1800 he accompanied Asbury and Whatcoat on their journey west of the Alleghanies, and was put in charge of that vast region which included western Virginia, Ohio, Kentucky, and sections of Illinois, Tennessee, and Mississippi. He was an important factor in the Great Revival in the West, and for eight years was the life and soul of the army of itinerants in this pioneer field. Elected bishop at the General Conference of 1808, he was Asbury's only associate until the latter's death, Bishop Coke being out of the country. Although treating his senior with great deference and affection, McKendree was no mere assistant. In spite of Asbury's disapproval, he inaugurated consultation with the presiding elders in the making of appointments, and the "cabinet" has remained an institution of the Conference down to the present time. At the General Conference of 1812, much to Asbury's amazement, he presented a written statement of his views on prevailing conditions, and the episcopal address became a fixed custom. He was a strict constitutionalist, and when the question of how presiding elders should be selected came to a crisis at the General Conference of 1820 he took extreme grounds in opposition to limiting the bishops' power of appointment. Although relieved of the fixed duties of his office after 1820 because of physical infirmities, he continued to make long journeys and contributed to the superintendency of the work until his death. In 1830 he gave 480 acres of land to Lebanon Seminary, Illinois, the name of which was changed to McKendree College (J. M. Buckley, *A History of Methodists in the United States,* 1896). He died at the home of his brother, Dr. James McKendree, Sumner County, Tenn., in his seventy-eighth year, and was buried nearby. Later his body was taken up and re-buried on the campus of Vanderbilt University.

[Robert Paine, *Life and Times of William M'Kendree* (2 vols., 1869); E. E. Hoss, *William McKendree, a Biog. Study* (1914); Joshua Soule, *Sermon on the Death of the Rev. William M'Kendree* (1836); Nathan Bangs, *A Hist. of the M. E. Church* (1840); J. J. Tigert, *A Constitutional Hist. of Am. Episcopal Methodism* (1904); J. M. Buckley, *Constitutional and Parliamentary Hist. of the M. E. Church* (1912); T. O. Summers, *Biog. Sketches of Eminent Itinerant Ministers . . . of the M. E. Church, South* (1858); J. B. Wakeley, *The Heroes of Methodism* (1856); T. L. Flood and J. W. Hamilton, *Lives of Meth. Bishops* (1882); P. D. Gorrie, *The Lives of Eminent Meth. Ministers* (1852); W. B. Sprague, *Annals Am. Pulpit,* vol. VII (1859); *National Banner and Nashville Whig,* Mar. 13, 1835.]

H. E. S.

McKENNA, CHARLES HYACINTH (May 8, 1835–Feb. 21, 1917), Catholic missionary, eighth child in Francis and Anna (Gillespie) McKenna's family of ten, was born in Fallalea, County Derry, Ireland. His mother was a McDonald, her grandfather having assumed the name Gillespie for reasons of prudence, since he had supported the cause of the Pretender. Her husband's death and the famine forced her in 1848 to take five of her children to her brother in Lancaster, Pa. Charles, who was left with an older brother on the farm in Ireland, was tutored by a kinsman, Father John McKenna, and attended a national school until 1851, when he joined his mother. Two years in a public school, where he was ridiculed because of his brogue, corrected his speech, for which benefit he was later thankful. From 1853 to 1859 he labored as an apprentice and journeyman stone-cutter in Lancaster, Philadelphia, St. Louis, and finally in Dubuque, Iowa, near which place the McKennas had settled in an Irish rural colony. McKenna, however, never abandoned the hope of studying for the priesthood as soon as he had provided a competence for his mother. Through his zeal in parochial societies, he became a friend of Bishop Clement Smyth, who tutored him in Latin and brought his case to the attention of the Dominican provincial, Joseph A. Kelly, who sent him to the college at Sinsinawa Mound.

The self-trained artisan learned rapidly, spending his spare time in the study of Latin and hagiology or in labor on the grounds. Completing his novitiate at St. Joseph's Priory, Somerset, Ohio, he was professed as Brother Hyacinth, Apr. 20, 1863. His course in theology was broken and hurried because of the burning of St. Joseph's and the ravages of war, but on his transfer to St. Rose's Priory, Springfield, Ky., he read widely and was ordained priest in Cincinnati, on Oct. 13, 1867, by Archbishop Purcell. Returning to St. Rose's as assistant master of novices, he soon became master and sub-prior as well as pastor of the local congregation. Recognizing his latent possibilities as a preacher, his superiors ordered the young friar to the priory and church of St. Vincent Ferrer in New York, where the mission band made its headquarters. As a missionary, Father McKenna gradually developed into a powerful preacher who appealed especially to the laboring class with whose problems he sympathized. Association with the noted Irish Dominican, Father Tom Burke, schooled him in the orator's devices of dramatic appeal. For forty-four years he preached the fundamentals of Catholicism in Catholic missions throughout the land, led retreats in colleges and seminaries, gave lectures for non-Catholics, and delivered occasional addresses on Irish historical subjects.

A man of deep piety, he compiled a number of religious manuals which passed through several editions: *The Manual of the Holy Name* (1871); *How to Make the Mission* (1873); *The Dominican Manual* (1875); *St. Dominic's Tertiaries' Guide* (1883); *The Angelic Guide* (1899); and *The Rosary, the Crown of Mary* (1900). A Methodist neighbor, writing of Father McKenna's days at St. Vincent Ferrer's, described him as "a holy man entirely separate from the world, night and day either before the altar or among the most miserable of the living and dying" (A. E. Barr, *All The Days of My Life,* 1913, p. 384), while Cardinal Gibbons considered him one of the greatest American missionaries. His special concern was Catholic societies—the Catholic Knights of America, St. Vincent Ferrer's Union in New York, of which he was a founder, the Angelic Warfare Society, and the Junior Holy Name Society. Director general (1900–1906) of both the Rosary Confraternity and the Men's Holy Name Society, he so popularized the latter society at all his missions that he became known as its apostle. Within his order, he received a number of honors, including the appointments of prior (1878–81) and preacher-general of the Louisville priory (1881) and director of Eastern American missions (1880–92); but outside, he sought no honor, though few priests were more widely known or respected. In 1886, he was worried lest he be named bishop of Providence. At various times, as a relief from overwork, he visited the shrines of Europe and the Holy Land; but finally in 1914, he was forced to retire to the Dominican House of Studies in Washington. He died in Jacksonville, Fla.

[V. F. O'Daniel, *Very Rev. Charles Hyacinth McKenna, O. P.* (1917), a full biography based upon community records and memoirs; *Am. Cath. Who's Who* (1911); *N. Y. Times,* Feb. 23, 1917; material furnished by Father McKenna's associates.] R. J. P.

McKENNA, JOSEPH (Aug. 10, 1843–Nov. 21, 1926), jurist, was born in Philadelphia, the son of John and Mary (Johnson) McKenna, of Irish lineage. His parents moved to Benicia, Cal., in the winter of 1854–55. He was chiefly educated in Catholic seminaries and was graduated from Benicia Collegiate Institute in 1865, having turned to law after an original destination for the priesthood. The same year he was admitted to the bar. His practice, begun in Fairfield, Solano County, was varied by two terms as county attorney (1866–70), and by service for one term (1875–76) as a representative in the state legislature, where he was the unsuccessful Republican candidate for the speakership. Politics continued to attract him. Thrice defeated, apparently because he was a Catholic, as a candidate for the national House of Representatives (1876, 1878, 1880), he was thereafter four times successful, serving from Mar. 4, 1885, to Mar. 28, 1892, when he resigned to accept appointment by President Benjamin Harrison as United States circuit judge for the 9th circuit (Pacific coast). Throughout his residence in Washington he was intimate, politically and socially, with Leland Stanford, then senator from California; and during his third term in the House he served on the committee on ways and means under William McKinley, with whom he formed an abiding friendship. These relations—the latter evidently, the former presumptively (for in California his appointment to the circuit bench was generally ascribed to the influence, or insistence, of Senator Stanford)—were determinative of his later fortunes.

In February 1897, President-Elect McKinley announced his selection as attorney-general, and he was nominated and confirmed Mar. 5. He held the office only a few months, then became associate justice of the Supreme Court of the United States, nominated Dec. 16, 1897, and confirmed Jan. 21, 1898, in succession to Stephen J. Field [*q.v.*]. McKenna had practised only in or about Solano County, where he lived, and had apparently appeared very little in the local federal courts or in the supreme court of the state; contrary to a general impression, therefore, he could not have been associated in any important way with the legal interests of the Southern and Central Pacific railways. He had been, however, one of the small minority who voted against the creation of the Interstate Commerce Commission in 1887 (*Congressional Record,* 49 Cong., 2 Sess., p. 881). His appointment as circuit judge was rather long delayed, and his nomination for the Supreme Court (though not that for the attorney-generalship) aroused remarkably violent opposition (the *Examiner,* San Francisco, Dec. 3, 4, 5, 6, 1897, and the *San Francisco Chronicle,* Dec. 5, 1897, Jan. 22, 1898; the *World,* New York, Dec. 4, 7, 1897, Jan. 22, 1898). To a large degree this opposition seems to have been due to the rivalry of certain railway systems, and to his personal differences with other federal judges on the Pacific coast, or to their ambitions; in addition, however, his service as a circuit judge had been marked by dilatoriness, and by indecision in certain cases politically important. On the other hand, he was reversed in but few cases. On the Supreme Court he did not often speak for the Court, but did speak for it in some exceedingly important cases. His mental processes were slow, and, according to his critics, confused. At best he had no clear general legal philosophy that made his attitude on new cases readily predictable. His final opinions, however, were characterized by practical sense and clear expression. On the whole, his record was thoroughly respectable, and special students of constitutional law refer to some of his decisions and enunciations of principle as commendable for political vision and sound social judgment with reference to labor, the development of federal power, and its relation to the states (184 *U. S. Reports,* 540; 194 *U. S.,* 338; 203 *U. S.,* 192; 227 *U. S.,* 308; 233 *U. S.,* 389). He resigned on Jan. 25, 1925, and died in Washington in November 1926. On June 10, 1869, he married Amanda F. Borneman of San Francisco, and he left a son and three married daughters.

[O. T. Shuck, *Hist. of the Bench and Bar of Cal.* (1901); H. L. Carson, *The Hist. of the Supreme Court of the U. S.* (1902); vol. II; A. G. Feather, *The Supreme Court of the U. S.* (1900); *Sunday Star* (Washington), Nov. 21, 1926; San Francisco *Examiner* and the *World* (N. Y.), Nov. 22, 1926; *Biog. Dir. Am. Cong.* (1928); *Who's Who in America,* 1926–27.]

F. S. P.

McKENNAN, THOMAS McKEAN THOMPSON (Mar. 31, 1794–July 9, 1852), congressman, railroad president, was born at Dragon Neck, New Castle County, Del. His grandfather, Rev. William McKennan, emigrated from Ireland about 1730 and lived and died in Delaware. Thomas' father, Col. William McKennan, was a soldier of the Revolution; his mother, Elizabeth (Thompson) McKennan, was a niece of Thomas McKean [*q.v.*], chief justice of Pennsylvania. In 1797 the family moved to western Virginia, and soon thereafter to Washington, Washington County, in southwestern Pennsylvania. In 1810 Thomas graduated from Washington College (later Washington and Jefferson), and afterwards studied law in the office of Parker Campbell, Washington, Pa. He was admitted to the bar in 1814, and the following year, when only twenty-one, became deputy attorney-general for Washington County, holding this office till 1817. From 1818 to 1831 he was a member of the Washington town council. This office he resigned to assume his duties as a member of the federal House of Representatives, in which capacity he served continuously from Mar. 4, 1831, to Mar. 3, 1839. From May 30, 1842, to Mar. 3, 1843, he was again a member of Congress, completing an unexpired term. In politics he was a Whig, and his influence was exerted in furthering typical Whig policies, such as national banking, internal improvements, and protective tariffs. He was particularly active in connection with the tariff of 1842. In 1840 he was a presidential elector on the ticket of Harrison and Tyler, and in 1848 he headed Pennsylvania's presidential electors. His political prominence led to his selection by President Fillmore as secretary of the interior. This post he held, however, only from Aug. 15 to Aug. 26, 1850.

He had long been interested in promoting internal improvements, having been as early as 1831 an official of the Washington (Pa.) & Pittsburgh Railroad Company. The Baltimore & Ohio Railroad Company secured legislative authority to build a line through Pennsylvania to the west at Pittsburgh or Wheeling, but found it necessary to ask for extensions of time. Meanwhile, opposition developed on the part of the Pennsylvania Railroad Company and also on the part of vested interests associated with the National Road. Washington, lying between the Baltimore & Ohio and the Pennsylvania lines, set about securing connections with the main arteries of trade by building the Hempfield Railroad to Wheeling. The company was incorporated in 1850 and in February 1851 McKennan became its first president. In 1871 the line passed, under foreclosure sale, to the Baltimore & Ohio as an important part of its plan, frustrated earlier, for tapping Pennsylvania traffic. McKennan's incidental activities included his life-long support of Washington College, of which he was a trustee from 1818 to 1852, and his promotion of such local enterprises as the Washington Female Seminary and the Agricultural Society of Washington County. On Dec. 6, 1815, he married Matilda Bowman, by whom he had eight children. His death occurred in Reading, Pa.

[Roberdeau Buchanan, *Geneal. of the McKean Family of Pa.* (1890); Boyd Crumrine, *The Courts of Justice, Bench and Bar of Washington County* (1902) and *Hist. of Washington County, Pa.* (1882); *Commemorative Biog. Record of Washington County, Pa.* (1893); *Biog. and Hist. Cat. of Washington and Jefferson Coll.* (1902); *Biog. Dir. Am. Cong.* (1928); *Am. Railroad Jour.*, 1851–52, see index; *Daily National Intelligencer* (Washington, D. C.), July 12, 17, 1852.] W. B—n.

McKENNEY, THOMAS LORAINE (Mar. 21, 1785–Feb. 20, 1859), author and administrator of Indian affairs, was born in Hopewell, Somerset County, Md. He attended school at Chestertown, Md., and, after preliminary experience in his father's counting-house, opened stores in Georgetown and in Washington, D. C. During the War of 1812 he was adjutant and aide with militia and volunteer companies. His first government appointment, made by President Madison in April 1816, was as superintendent of the Indian trade. He continued in this office until that attempt at federal control of the Indian trade was abolished in 1822, largely owing to the opposition of private fur-traders, merchants, and manufacturers who had not profited by the administration. Charges of favoritism and abuse of trust were brought against him at the same time, particularly by Thomas H. Benton, and, although he considered himself triumphant in the congressional investigation, nevertheless, contemporary slanders were long in dying out, and he appears to have been indiscreet in permitting his notes to be indorsed by John Cox, a merchant from whom he bought large quantities of goods, as well as in persuading the Columbian College to take over his own notes to the amount of $11,958 (*House Report 104,* 17 Cong., 2 Sess., n.d., *Sen. Doc. 103,* 20 Cong., 1 Sess., n.d., see also *Sen. Doc. 60,* 17 Cong., 1 Sess., 1822). On Aug. 7, 1822, he began the publication of a semi-weekly newspaper, the *Washington Republican and Congressional Examiner,* devoted to the interests of John C. Calhoun. After some months of bitter attack he gave up the editorship on May 31, 1823.

Disappointed in his desire to be appointed first assistant postmaster-general, he was, on Mar. 11, 1824, given charge of the newly organized bureau of Indian affairs under the War Department. While superintendent of the Indian trade he had been instrumental in obtaining an annual appropriation of $10,000 for the civilization of the Indian tribes adjoining the frontier settlements. Most of this sum was distributed to the mission schools of the various denominations, which developed steadily during the years he was in charge of the Indian bureau so that, when he was forced out of the Indian department in 1830, about 1800 children were in mission schools. As joint commissioner with Lewis Cass, he negotiated the treaty of Aug. 11, 1827, at Butte des Morts on the Fox River with the Chippewa, Menominee, and Winnebago. His *Sketches of a Tour to the Lakes* (1827) described this expedition. Continuing down the Mississippi on a second expedition, he helped to influence the Chickasaw and Creeks to agree to migrate west of the Mississippi, and he negotiated the agreement of Nov. 15, 1827, with the Creek Indians. Although his *Memoirs, Official and Personal* (*post*) are lavish in defense of his own motives and actions and although all of his reports express his philanthropic interest in the Indian, he seems rather to have been a man hard pressed financially, holding desperately to his jobs, promising impossible things from the languishing Indian trade, constantly prating of Indian betterment, yet siding eagerly with politicians in their argument of state rights and in their desire to move the natives westward. Besides other controversial writings he published *Essays on the Spirit of Jacksonism as Exemplified in its Deadly Hostility to the Bank of the United States* (1835), and with James Hall, a *History of the Indian Tribes of North America, with Biographical Sketches and Anecdotes of the Principal Chiefs* (1836–44), three folio volumes chiefly valuable for the 120 portraits, in color, from the Indian gallery in the War Department. He died from typhoid fever in New York City.

[T. L. McKenney, *Memoirs, Official and Personal* (2 vols. in 1, 1846); a different estimate of motives and accomplishment in A. H. Abel, "The Hist. of Events Resulting in Indian Consolidation West of the Mississippi," *Am. Hist. Assoc. Report . . . 1906*, vol. I (1908); *Memoirs of John Quincy Adams*, ed. by C. F. Adams, vols. VI, VII, VIII (1875); *Bibliographical Soc. of America Papers*, vol. XIX (1925), p. 63; spelling of middle name taken from Lib. of Cong. on authority of niece; transcript of death certificate by department of health with date of Feb. 21 but death notice in *N. Y. Times*, Feb. 21, 1859, with date Feb. 20.]

D. A. D.

McKENZIE, ALEXANDER (Dec. 14, 1830–Aug. 6, 1914), Congregational clergyman, was born in New Bedford, Mass., the son of Daniel and Phebe Mayhew (Smith) McKenzie. His father was captain of whaling vessels, a man of dauntless spirit, well-balanced mind, and a gift of eloquent speech. During the War of 1812, when he was nineteen years of age, the whaling ship in which he was serving as boat-steerer was captured by the British and he suffered extreme hardships for many months at Capetown and later in Dartmoor prison. The devoted and courageous wife trained their children during her husband's long absences on the sea. Graduating at sixteen from the New Bedford high school, Alexander found business positions in Cambridge and Boston. His mind turned increasingly, however, to thoughts of an education and the profession of the ministry, and at twenty-three years of age he entered Phillips Academy, Andover, where he made rapid progress and graduated in 1855. Entering Harvard College, he was asked by Edward Everett to be roommate of his gifted son William. He graduated at Harvard in 1859, and at Andover Theological Seminary in 1861, and on Aug. 28, 1861, he was ordained and installed pastor of the Congregational church in Augusta, Me., where James G. Blaine and Lot M. Morrill [*qq.v.*] were among his parishioners. On Jan. 25, 1865, he was married to Ellen Holman Eveleth, daughter of John H. and Martha (Holman) Eveleth of Fitchburg, Mass.

In 1866 he was called to the pastorate of the First (Congregational) Church in Cambridge, Mass. Founded in 1636, this church was a leading one in the Massachusetts Bay Colony and had always exercised a wide influence. Installed Jan. 24, 1867, McKenzie held this pastorate over forty-seven years, the last four as pastor emeritus—a term longer than that of any of his predecessors save one. Of fine physique, never absent from his pulpit because of illness, eloquent in address, often with touches of latent humor, a wise counselor and guide and a public-spirited citizen, he occupied a place comparable to that of the leading ministers of colonial New England. His preaching was not so much argumentative as strongly affirmative, with rich diction, poetic allusion, and penetrating insight. For years during his ministry Harvard students were grouped on Sunday mornings in the east transept of the church.

McKenzie was an overseer of Harvard, 1872–84; and secretary of the board of overseers, 1875–1901. In 1886 he was made one of the first board of preachers to the University. He was also a trustee of Bowdoin College, Phillips Andover Academy, Wellesley College, and Hampton Institute; president of the Boston Seaman's Friend Society and of the Boston Port Society; a trustee of the Cambridge Hospital; and for seven years one of the Cambridge school committee. He was lecturer at Andover Seminary, 1881–82, and at Harvard Divinity School, 1882–83. Besides historical monographs and single sermons, he published *The Two Boys* (1871); *Lectures on the History of the First Church in Cambridge* (1873); *Cambridge Sermons* (1883); *Some Things Abroad* (1887); *Christ Himself* (copr. 1891); *A Door Opened* (1898); *The Divine Force in the Life of the World* (1898), Lowell Institute lectures; *Getting One's Bearings* (1903); *Two Ends of a Houseboat* (1909).

[*Harvard Coll. Records of the Class of 1859* (1896); *Cat. of Officers and Students of the Andover Theological Sem.*, 1881–82; *Proc. Mass. Hist. Soc.*, Feb. 1914; James Schouler in *Ibid.*, Oct. 1914; *Manual of First Ch. in Cambridge, Congl.* (1920); *Who's Who in America*, 1914–15; *Boston Transcript*, Aug. 7, 1914; *Congregationalist and Christian World*, Aug. 13, 1914; letters to the writer from Frank Gaylord Cook.]

E. D. E.

MACKENZIE, ALEXANDER SLIDELL (Apr. 6, 1803–Sept. 13, 1848), naval officer and author, was known as Alexander Slidell until 1838, when, under authorization of the New York legislature, he added Mackenzie to his name out of regard for a maternal uncle. He was a son of John Slidell, a New York City merchant, and a brother of John Slidell [*q.v.*], the Confederate diplomatic agent. His mother, Margery or May (Mackenzie) Slidell, was a native of the Highlands of Scotland. After a period of attendance at a boarding school, he continued his education in the navy, which he entered on Jan.

1, 1815, as a midshipman. Fond of books, he applied himself to the study of literature and the rudiments of his profession. From 1818 to 1821 he was with the *Macedonian* in the Pacific Ocean, and later, obtaining a furlough, commanded a merchant vessel. Returning to the navy, he aided in the suppression of piracy in the West Indies in 1824, being attached to the *Terrier.* In January 1825 he was promoted to a lieutenancy and soon thereafter, on leave from the navy, visited France and made a tour of Spain, the main incidents of which he embodied in a two-volume book entitled *A Year in Spain,* which appeared first in Boston in 1829 and later in London. Favorably noticed by some of the leading American and English reviewers and translated into Swedish, it started its author upon a literary career that henceforth absorbed all the time that he could spare from the active duties of his profession.

In 1830–33 he made a cruise in the Mediterranean on the *Brandywine,* and upon his return home published his second book, *Popular Essays on Naval Subjects* (1833). He next toured England and again visited Spain and gathered the material that appeared in *The American in England* (2 vols., 1835) and *Spain Revisited* (2 vols., 1836). In 1837–38 he served as lieutenant on the *Independence* and visited Russia. Thence he proceeded to Brazil, and, taking command of the *Dolphin,* witnessed the siege and surrender of Bahia and other important events in that region, some of which he described in a pamphlet published at this time. Soon after he returned to the United States in 1839, he wrote a *Life of Paul Jones* (2 vols., 1841). In the previous year his *Life of Commodore Oliver Hazard Perry,* in two volumes, had appeared. He was promoted commander, September 1841, and soon thereafter took command of the steamer *Missouri* of the home squadron. From this vessel he was transferred to the brig *Somers,* then used as a training ship for apprentices, and in September 1842 sailed for the African squadron with dispatches. While on the return voyage, plans for a mutiny were discovered and Midshipman Philip Spencer, a boatswain, and a seaman were executed for their complicity therein. When the brig reached the United States this extreme act of discipline caused much public excitement, and in circles friendly to Spencer, who was a notorious scapegrace but a son of the secretary of war, the feeling against Mackenzie was bitter. A court of inquiry and a court martial that investigated his conduct exonerated him, and all attempts to indict him in civil courts failed. The official judgment has been justified by the verdict of posterity. (Benjamin, *post,* p. 138.) Mackenzie now retired to his home on the Hudson near Tarrytown, N. Y., and occupied himself with writing *The Life of Stephen Decatur* (1846). In May 1846 President Polk sent him on a special mission to General Santa Anna at Havana. In the Mexican War he acted as one of the two representatives of the navy at the surrender of Vera Cruz and as a commander of artillery at the second attack on Tabasco. In 1847–48, he commanded the steamer *Mississippi* of the home squadron, his last naval service.

Mackenzie was a popular writer and several editions of most of his books were published. He had considerable talent for description and wrote readily, in a sprightly, humorous style. On Oct. 1, 1835, he was married in New York City to Catherine Alexander Robinson. Ranald S. Mackenzie [*q.v.*] was his son; another son, Lieutenant Commander Alexander S. Mackenzie, died gallantly in battle on the island of Formosa in 1867.

[Record of Officers, Bureau of Navigation, 1818–58; L. M. Sears, *John Slidell* (1925); Park Benjamin, *The U. S. Naval Acad.* (1900); J. H. Smith, *The War with Mexico* (1919), vol. I; *Mag. of Am. Hist.*, Feb. 1887; *Proc. of the Naval Court Martial in the Case of Alexander Slidell Mackenzie . . . to which is Annexed an Elaborate Review by James Fennimore Cooper* (1844); *Case of the Somers' Mutiny: Defence of Alexander Slidell Mackenzie* (1843); E. A. and G. L. Duyckinck, *Cyc. of Am. Literature* (1875), vol. II; *N. Y. Herald*, Sept. 14, 1848.]

C. O. P.

MACKENZIE, DONALD (June 15, 1783–Jan. 20, 1851), fur-trader, was born in Scotland, a brother of Roderic Mackenzie of the North West Company, and a cousin of Alexander Mackenzie, the explorer. He was educated for the ministry, but instead of entering that profession went to Canada and joined the North West Company. On June 23, 1810, after ten years' experience, he was engaged by John Jacob Astor to be one of his partners in the Pacific Fur Company. With Wilson P. Hunt [*q.v.*], he led a band of adventurers by the overland route to the mouth of the Columbia River. Mackenzie with his group arrived at Fort Astoria Jan. 18, 1812. He later became the head of a large party which engaged in hunting and trapping. His journeys took him to the rivers Willamette, Columbia, and also the Snake, where he established a post. He left Astoria again in March 1813, and in June returned with 140 packs of furs from Okanagan post, and Spokane River. While carrying supplies to the interior that fall he was robbed by Indians. Returning to Astoria, he occupied himself storing salmon until his party learned of the war with Great Britain. Concluding that Astoria would be captured and goods confiscated, he and his partners there sold out to the North West Company the following spring. On Apr. 14, 1814, Mackenzie set out for New York, where he remained for some time seeking reëmployment by Astor. Failing to obtain it, he returned to Canada and again entered the service of the North West Company. In 1816 he was on the Columbia River, spending his time at Fort George and Fort William, and Spokane House. He rendered valuable service to his company in developing the rich trade of southern Idaho. His brigade of 1817 was the first to report a year without casualties, and the quantity of furs obtained was considerable.

Mackenzie was retained when the Hudson's Bay and North West Companies consolidated, and the following year, 1822, established Chesterfield House. In 1824 he was made chief factor at Fort Garry, on the Red River of the North, and the same year was appointed councilor of the governors. Soon thereafter he was made governor of Red River Colony, the highest post in the country next to the governor-in-chief, which vast province he ruled judiciously and with kindness. To him is due credit for the peace and progress which prevailed during the following eight years. He retired in August 1833, and took his family to Mayville, N. Y., where he had an estate. There he lived until his death.

Donald Mackenzie was eminently fitted, both physically and mentally, for life in the wilderness. His knowledge of the Indians was remarkably keen and accurate, and his influence over them was great. His boldness and prompt decision, in times of danger, helped to awe and conquer them. His ways and accomplishments astonished his associates; he weighed over 300 pounds, but was so active that he was called "perpetual motion." In August 1825, at Fort Garry, he married Adelgonde Humbert-Droze, by whom he had thirteen children.

[Mackenzie MSS. in Mo. Hist. Soc.; "Reminiscences by Hon. Roderic McKenzie," in L. R. Masson, *Les Bourgeois de la Compagnie du Nord-Ouest,* vol. I (Quebec, 1889); Alexander Ross, *The Fur Hunters of the Far West* (1855), and *The Red River Settlement, Its Rise, Progress, and Present State* (1856); William Anderson, *The Scottish Nation,* vol. III, Supp. (1863); Elliott Coues, ed., *New Light on the Early Hist. of the Greater Northwest* (1897); E. Cawcroft, "Donald Mackenzie," in *Canadian Magazine,* Feb. 1918; A. W. Young, *Hist. of Chautauqua County, N. Y.* (1875); *Mo. Republican* (St. Louis), Feb. 13, 1851.]

S. M. D.

MACKENZIE, GEORGE HENRY (Nov. 24, 1837–Apr. 14, 1891), chess-player, was born at Belfield House, North Kessock, Ross and Cromarty, Scotland, the youngest of the four sons of John and Ann (Douglass) Mackenzie. The year after the boy's birth, his father died and the family moved to Inverness and later to Aberdeen. George received his early education in the schools of that city and was then sent to a high school in Southampton, England. In 1853 he returned to Aberdeen and afterward went to Rouen, France, where he entered a business office. Subsequently, he served as ensign in the 60th Rifles, a Scottish volunteer regiment, and with the regulars at the Cape of Good Hope, attaining the rank of lieutenant. In 1861 he sold his commission. The following year he competed in the London handicap chess tournament, winning the first prize by defeating Anderssen, the foremost European chess player, at the odds of pawn and move.

In 1863 he emigrated to New York and on Aug. 27 of that year enlisted as a private in Company F, 83rd New York Infantry. On Apr. 20, 1864, he was promoted to a captaincy in the 10th United States Infantry (Colored) and was honorably discharged, June 16, 1864. Taking up his residence in New York City, he became a professional chess player and writer on chess. He won first prize in the tournaments of the New York Chess Club for 1865 to 1868 inclusive. In the second American Chess Congress (1871), at Cleveland, the third, at Chicago (1874), and the fifth, at New York (1880), he took first prize, winning recognition as the American chess champion. In international tournaments he placed fourth at Paris in 1878; tied for fourth-fifth at Vienna in 1882; tied for fifth-sixth-seventh at London in 1883; placed seventh at Hamburg in 1885; won first place at Frankfort in 1887, which victory made him world champion. He was second at Bradford, England, in 1888, and fourth at Manchester in 1890; only at the tournament in London in 1886 did he fail to place among the prize-winners. In match play he defeated such notable American players as Reichhelm (1866, 1867), Stanley (1868), Judd (1881), and Lipschuetz (1886). In matches with English experts he defeated Bird in 1876 and Blackburne in 1882, tied with Amos Burn in 1886, and lost to Blackburne in 1888. He also won three minor matches in Havana in 1887 and 1888.

Mackenzie made a somewhat precarious living by his success in tournaments, matches, and exhibitions in various parts of the United States and Cuba. He was found dead in his room at Cooper Union Hotel, New York, having died apparently of pneumonia. He was tall and handsome in appearance and genial in manner; with his Vandyke beard and slouch hat he resembled more the typical Southern "colonel" than a former British army officer.

[London *Times*, Apr. 16, 1891; *N. Y. Times* and *N. Y. Herald*, Apr. 15, 1891; G. A. MacDonnell, *The Knights and Kings of Chess* (London, 1894); *New York in the War of the Rebellion* (1912), vol. V; *Schach-Jahrbücher*, 1894–1901; *British Chess Mag.*, May 1891.] L. C. K.

MACKENZIE, JAMES CAMERON (Aug. 15, 1852–May 10, 1931), educator, was born in Aberdeen, Scotland, the son of Alexander and Catherine (Cameron) Mackenzie. After the death of his father, the child was brought to America by his mother, who settled in Wilkes-Barre, Pa. For the first twelve years of his life practically all his schooling consisted of one winter term in a public school. He was subsequently a clerk in the town's largest bookstore and by reading and study educated himself. Intending to prepare to teach in the public schools, he entered the normal school at Bloomsburg, Pa., and a year later went to Phillips Academy, Exeter, N. H., where he graduated at the head of his class in 1873. After a year of teaching and administrative work in Wilkes-Barre Institute, a girls' school, he entered Lafayette College, where he graduated as valedictorian in 1878. Several teaching positions were open to him and he accepted the first principalship of the newly founded Wilkes-Barre (later Harry Hillman) Academy. Here his work attracted the attention of the legatees of the estate of John Cleve Green [*q.v.*], who were looking for a man to build a thoroughly equipped academy at Lawrenceville, N. J., along the lines of the schools at Andover and Exeter. On Oct. 5, 1880, he married Ella Smith, daughter of Robert C. Smith of Wilkes-Barre. In 1882 he went to Lawrenceville, where, using the land and buildings of the old proprietary school there which had been purchased by the legatees of Green's estate, he organized the present Lawrenceville School, in accordance with their desires. During the session of 1882–83 he attended Princeton Theological Seminary, and in 1885 he was ordained to the Presbyterian ministry.

Under his far-sighted, revolutionary method of administration the Lawrenceville School attracted much attention in the outer world; it grew in numbers and its graduates distinguished themselves at college. The English house system was established and in 1893, against the determined opposition of the faculty, Mackenzie organized the Upper House, where the older boys should live and have the greater freedom that would prepare them for the transition from school to college. This was a revolutionary step in the administration of boys' boarding schools. Andover and Exeter had always been like colleges in their treatment of their boys, and other schools had kept the pupils under the strictest discipline even through their graduation year. Lawrenceville became, in spite of financial difficulties, a large and famous school, with a modern plant. As a result, Mackenzie was offered many excellent positions. Exeter and Lafayette both wanted him, and he was tendered the superintendency of the Philadelphia public schools.

In 1891 the United States Commissioner of Education appointed him to membership on the Committee of Ten on Secondary Education, and in 1893 appointed him chairman of the congress on secondary education to be held at the World's Columbian Exposition in Chicago. He was president of the Schoolmasters' Association in the early nineties, and in 1893, in Boston, was instrumental in the formation of the Headmasters' Association, of which he was later president. He was also a president of the Association of Colleges and Preparatory Schools of the Middle States and Maryland.

After the death of the last of Green's legatees, and upon certain changes in the board of trustees, Mackenzie resigned from the headmastership of Lawrenceville School in 1899 (*New York Times*, May 11, 1931) and became director of Jacob Tome Institute, Port Deposit, Md. Here he reorganized the school and supervised the erection of new buildings. In 1901, finding that his plans were not approved by the relatives of Tome (*Ibid.*), he resigned and founded a school of his own, the Mackenzie School, at Dobbs Ferry, N. Y., moving it later to Monroe, N. Y. There he remained as director until 1926, when he retired from active work. He made his home thereafter in New York City, where he died.

[Roland J. Mulford, history of Lawrenceville School, soon to be published; *Who's Who in America*, 1930–31; *Who's Who in N. Y.*, 1907; *N. Y. Times*, May 11, 1931; letters and documents in the possession of the family and of T. Dean Swift, N. Y.] M. A. A.

MACKENZIE, JOHN NOLAND (Oct. 20, 1853–May 21, 1925), physician, pioneer laryngologist, was born in Baltimore, Md., of the fourth generation of a medical family. His father, John Carrere Mackenzie, was a physician, as was his grandfather, John Pinkerton Mackenzie; and his great-grandfather, Colin, was a surgeon. His mother, Eleanor (Noland), was the daughter of Lloyd and Elizabeth (Wynn) Noland of Loudoun County, Va. Part of his boyhood was spent in France and England. In 1872 he entered the academic department of the University of Virginia, but two years later transferred to the Medical Department, graduating (M.D.) in 1876. He took a second medical degree from the University of the City of New York in 1877, and was subsequently interne at

Bellevue Hospital, 1877–79. Meanwhile, he sought the instruction of Dr. Clinton Wagner, then at the full tide of his well-deserved popularity as founder of the pioneer school of advanced laryngology at the Metropolitan Throat Hospital. In 1879 Mackenzie went abroad for an extended course of study, devoting himself principally to laryngology, first under Oertel and as assistant to Von Ziemssem at Munich; then under Von Schroetter and Stoerk at Vienna. Finally he spent a year as chief of clinic at the London Throat Hospital, Golden Square, under Sir Morell Mackenzie, the distinguished master of laryngology. Here he rendered material assistance in the preparation of Mackenzie's great *Manual of the Diseases of the Throat and Nose* (2 vols., 1880–84), work which afforded a discipline rich and productive in the development of his literary gifts. He improved his unusual opportunities to the utmost, gaining an amount of knowledge and experience unusual for one of his years.

Returning to Baltimore, he inaugurated a brilliant career. As a practitioner, he was a founder and surgeon of the Baltimore Eye, Ear and Throat Charity Hospital, surgeon to the nose and throat department of the University of Maryland Hospital from 1887 to 1897, and to the Johns Hopkins Hospital from 1889 to 1912; and consulting laryngologist to a number of different hospitals. He was clinical professor of rhinology and laryngology in the University of Maryland, 1887–97, and clinical professor of laryngology in the Johns Hopkins University Medical School, 1889–1912. He was a co-editor of the *Maryland Medical Journal,* American editor of the British *Journal of Laryngology and Rhinology,* and connected in some capacity with various other special journals, American and foreign. As investigator and author, beginning in 1880, he covered the full range of laryngo-rhinology. His most important original contributions were a number of papers upon the vaso-motor neuroses of the nose and upper air passages. In this field he was a pioneer and his writings formed the basis of many of the accepted theories relating to the subject. From 1895 onward his original studies relating to the accessory sinuses were also of great importance. After 1900 he became a leader in the study of laryngeal cancer. He opposed excessive surgery, showing a conservatism in the treatment of nose and throat conditions which was much needed at the time. He contributed a number of special articles to *A Reference Handbook of the Medical Sciences* (8 vols., 1885–89), edited by A. H. Buck, and to other standard publications.

Quickly recognized everywhere as an authority of the first rank, he was elected a fellow of the American Laryngological Association in 1883 and became its vice-president in 1886 and its president in 1889. Widely known and appreciated abroad, he was a corresponding fellow of the leading British, French, and German associations. Attractive in appearance as in intellect, he had a charm of manner and a bouyancy of spirit that made him a beloved companion. He was married, Feb. 2, 1887, to Rachel Pratt Clark, grand-daughter of Thomas G. Pratt, a governor of Maryland and a United States senator for many years. He died at his home in Baltimore.

[Memoir by D. B. Delavan, in *Trans. of the Forty-Eighth Ann. Meeting of the Am. Laryngological Asso.* (1926), with bibliography; *Who's Who in America,* 1924–25; *Jour. Am. Medic. Asso.,* June 13, 1925; the *Sun* (Baltimore), May 22, 1925; personal acquaintance.]

D. B. D.

MACKENZIE, KENNETH (Apr. 15, 1797–Apr. 26, 1861), fur-trader and merchant, was born in the shire of Ross and Cromarty, Scotland, son of Alexander and Isabella (Mackenzie) Mackenzie. He received a good education. In 1816, at the suggestion of Sir Alexander Mackenzie, a kinsman, he went to Canada and entered the employ of the North West Company. In February 1822 he appeared in St. Louis and immediately applied for citizenship. Here he organized the Columbia Fur Company with a rather small capital stock. The principal power of the company was in the personnel—bold, experienced, and energetic men, including several former North-Westerners. Their trade extended north to the headwaters of the Mississippi, east to the Great Lakes, and west to the Missouri River.

When the Western Department of the American Fur Company was organized, its promoters found Mackenzie's outfit such a strong rival in the Sioux and Omaha countries that they could not operate without a loss of at least ten thousand dollars annually. After a bitter fight the American Fur Company tried to buy out the Mackenzie group. For almost a year efforts were made to prevent competition by agreement, and finally, in July 1827, there was an amalgamation of the two companies. Kenneth Mackenzie and two of his partners were given separate shares in the Upper Missouri Outfit of the American Fur Company. By this arrangement Mackenzie and these partners got control of the Upper Missouri and became as independent as if they had remained in a separate company.

Mackenzie carried on the trade in regions made dangerous by hostile Indians, from which other traders had been driven. Within four years he had posts on the Yellowstone, Bighorn, and Marais rivers. He built Fort Union, the best-equipped post west of the Mississippi. Here he reigned, feared and loved by his men and by the Indians, coming to be called "King of the Missouri," "Emperor Mackenzie," and "Emperor of the West." In 1834, he was charged with having erected a distillery at Fort Union, contrary to law. This unfortunate occurrence threatened the Company's charter and forced Mackenzie to leave the country for a time. In the winter of that year he went abroad to study wine making, and while in Germany was the guest of Prince Maximilian. During this same year he joined the firm of Chouteau & Mackenzie, commission and forwarding merchants, which firm dissolved in July 1841. After returning from Europe in the summer of 1835, he went back to Fort Union. His last trip seems to have been made a decade later. Until about 1850, he was connected with Pierre Chouteau, Jr. & Company in the fur trade, although he spent little time at his old post. He continued his business as commission merchant and importer of foreign liquors until 1854, and then, for the rest of his life, dealt solely in liquors. He invested largely in lands in Missouri, Illinois, and Minnesota, as well as in railroads and other industries, and by the time of his death in St. Louis, he had amassed a fortune.

Mackenzie married Mary Marshall, June 26, 1842, at St. Louis. He had six children, two of whom died in infancy.

[H. M. Chittenden, *The Am. Fur Trade of the Far West* (1902); Richard Edwards and M. Hopewell, *Edwards's Great West* (1860), p. 98; *St. Louis Enquirer*, July 19, 22, 1824; *Daily Missouri Democrat* (St. Louis), Apr. 27, 1861; St. Louis Probate Court Records, Estate of Kenneth Mackenzie; Naturalization Papers, Mo. Hist. Soc.; Fort Union Letter Book, Pierre Chouteau Collection, Mo. Hist. Soc.] S. M. D.

MACKENZIE, RANALD SLIDELL (July 27, 1840–Jan. 19, 1889), soldier, elder son of Alexander Slidell Mackenzie [*q.v.*] and Catherine Alexander (Robinson), was born in New York City. He matriculated at Williams College with the class of 1859, but withdrew to go to West Point, where he graduated No. 1 in the class of 1862. Assigned to the Corps of Engineers, he went promptly to the front, taking part, as an engineer officer, in the battles of Manassas, Fredericksburg, Chancellorsville, Gettysburg and the subsequent campaigns, the Wilderness, Spotsylvania, and the siege of Petersburg (June–July 1864), and receiving during that time two wounds and four brevets for gallantry. In July 1864 he was made colonel of the 2nd Connecticut Heavy Artillery Volunteers, with which he helped defend Washington against Early's raid. In command of a brigade during the Shenandoah campaign, he was wounded at Cedar Creek in October, but returned to duty in time to take part in the siege of Petersburg, February–March 1865. With the further brevets of colonel and brigadier-general, United States Army, and major-general of volunteers, he commanded a highly efficient cavalry division with the Army of the James during the Five Forks-Appomattox campaign in the spring of 1865, and was stationed in and about Appomattox while the details of Lee's surrender and the dispersion of the Army of Northern Virginia were carried out. In his *Personal Memoirs* (II, 541), General Grant said, "I regarded Mackenzie as the most promising young officer in the army. Graduating at West Point, as he did, during the second year of the war, he had won his way up to the command of a corps [division] before its close. This he did upon his own merit and without influence."

After the war he was transferred to the South and Southwest in lower rank, owing to the reduction of the military establishment. As colonel of the 4th Cavalry, he took the leading part in the campaigns of the early 1870's against marauding Indians in West Texas and along the Rio Grande, and was severely wounded (1871) while engaged in a cañon of the "Staked Plains," Texas Panhandle. In 1873 he crossed the Rio Grande, made a forced night march, attacked and destroyed an Indian camp, precipitating a situation which was finally settled by diplomatic exchanges with the Mexican government. As a result of these operations and his subsequent military supervision, large areas in Texas—particularly the "Staked Plains"—were opened to permanent settlement. Mackenzie was then transferred to the Indian Territory, where he was equally successful in coping with the hostile Indians of that region.

When, after the Custer fight at the Little Big Horn, June 25–26, 1876, Gen. P. H. Sheridan, commanding the Military Division of the Missouri, planned large-scale operations against the Sioux and Cheyennes, he relieved Mackenzie from command at Fort Sill, Indian Territory, and brought him with six companies of the 4th Cavalry up into Nebraska to form part of the Powder River Expedition. Before starting on that campaign, Mackenzie, with his own companies, two from the 5th Cavalry, and a detachment of Pawnee Indian scouts, surrounded and disarmed the Red Cloud and Red Leaf bands on Chadron Creek, Nebr., Oct. 23, and then became the mounted column of Gen. George Crook's winter campaign into and up through an extensive district in Wyoming Territory. Locating the

Northern Cheyennes in the Big Horn Mountains, Mackenzie thoroughly defeated them in the battle of Nov. 25, 1876, dispersing and breaking the fighting power of Dull Knife's formidable band. This campaign, with corresponding successes by troops operating in Montana under Col. Nelson A. Miles [*q.v.*], led to the surrender of Crazy Horse without further hostilities in Wyoming.

Transferred back to the Indian Territory in 1877, and thence again to Texas, Mackenzie completed the work of pacifying the region extending down to the Mexican border. At the outbreak of the Ute disturbances in Colorado and Utah in 1879 he was sent into that district, and was engaged for about two years in military operations and administration, with marked success. Later Indian troubles in Arizona and New Mexico required short tours of duty in both these territories. After comparatively brief periods of command in the departments of New Mexico and Texas, he was retired on Mar. 24, 1884, for disability incurred in the line of duty; already failing in health, he died at New Brighton, Staten Island, N. Y., as brigadier-general, United States Army, although he had held the brevet rank of major-general of volunteers since Mar. 31, 1865, for gallant and meritorious services during the Civil War.

Mackenzie was slightly above medium height, very active, somewhat nervous, often impetuous and exacting; he had a reputation in the old army for being a severe disciplinarian, but his officers and men became much attached to and had complete confidence in him as a leader. "I really classed him," writes Capt. Robert G. Carter, who served under him in Texas, "as our best, most reliable and dependable Indian fighter. He had an indomitable will, wonderful powers of endurance, and unsurpassed courage." Several times he was in the forefront of battle; one of the three wounds received in the Civil War resulted in the loss of fingers, which led the Indians to call him "Bad Hand." His particular interest was in the tactical handling of troops in the field, of which he was one of the acknowledged masters. He was, withal, a conserver of forces, and several times—notably in the Dull Knife fight—went through to the point of assured victory, without pressing an advantage at too great sacrifice. His fame has been circumscribed by his temperamental aversion to publicity; all of the military operations under his command were followed by brief reports and immediate retirement to his station or other duties. No act of his ever brought censure from his superiors, and the only incident of his career resulting in controversy was his crossing of the Rio Grande with United States troops in 1873, and that was at least tacitly approved by the government. Mackenzie never wrote for publication and was never married, but devoted all of his energies to the profession of a soldier.

[G. W. Cullum, *Biog. Reg. Officers and Grads., U. S. Mil. Acad.* (3rd ed., 1891); J. H. Dorst, in *Twentieth Ann. Reunion, Asso. Grads., U. S. Mil. Acad.* (1889); James Parker, *The Old Army Memories 1872–1918* (1929); D. L. Vaill, *The County Regiment; a Sketch of the Second Regt. of Conn. Vol. Heavy Artillery* (1908); Col. C. A. P. Hatfield, "Army Life on the Texas Plains in the 1870's," MS. in the possession of Robert Bruce, New York; letter from Capt. R. G. Carter, U. S. A., retired, Sept. 27, 1932; *Personal Memoirs of U. S. Grant* (2 vols., 1885–86); J. G. Bourke, *On the Border with Crook* (1891); *Army and Navy Jour.*, Jan. 26, 1889.]
R. B.

MACKENZIE, ROBERT SHELTON (June 22, 1809–Nov. 21, 1881), author, journalist, was born at Drew's Court, County Limerick, Ireland, second son of Capt. Kenneth Mackenzie of the Kaithness Fencibles, later postmaster of the small military town of Fermoy. His mother was Maria (Shelton) Mackenzie. Robert received his early education at Fermoy and taught school there in 1825. Before he reached his majority he had become editor of a county journal at Hanley, Staffordsville, England, thus beginning a career in newspaper work which lasted until his death. In 1830–31 he wrote a large number of biographies for the *Georgian Era.* From 1831 to 1833 he conducted the *Derbyshire Courier* and shortly thereafter became editor of the *Liverpool Journal.* In 1834 he was appointed English correspondent of the New York *Evening Star,* and is said to have been the first paid European correspondent of any American paper (*Ballou's Pictorial,* Jan. 12, 1856). To the *Star* he contributed letters on politics, literature, fashion, and gossip of high life until 1851. During this period he was also connected with the Liverpool *Mail* and (from about 1840 to 1843) with the *Salopian Journal* in Shrewsbury. The statement is made in biographical sketches published during his lifetime that he received the degree of D.C.L. from Oxford in 1844, but there is no record of it at the University. From 1845 to 1851 he is variously stated to have been editor of a railway journal in London and the London secretary of a railway company. In 1848 he was active in securing publicity in the London *Sun* and the weekly *Times* for Lord Brougham's Law Amendment Society, in recognition of which service he was appointed by Brougham official assignee of the Manchester bankruptcy court, an appointment which came to an end in October 1852 (*Law Times,* London, Oct. 30, 1852). In 1851 he married Georgiana Dickinson, by whom he had one child.

Because of financial difficulties, after the premature death of his wife in 1852 Mackenzie came to New York, where for a time he was literary editor and political writer on a daily, and music and dramatic critic for a Sunday paper. In July 1857 he removed to Philadelphia and in August, upon the establishment of the Philadelphia *Press,* became its literary and foreign editor and dramatic critic. This position he retained for over twenty years. In 1858 he married, in Philadelphia, Adelheid Zwissler (the author of several romances), by whom he had three children. In 1862 he was one of the organizers of the Philadelphia Dental College (now a part of Temple University) and became its secretary. Toward the end of his life he was literary editor of the Philadelphia *Evening News.* He died Nov. 21, 1881 (not Nov. 30, 1880, as frequently stated), and was buried in Philadelphia.

His original literary work began with *Lays of Palestine* (1828), and included a three-volume novel, *Titian: A Romance of Venice* (1843); *Mornings at Matlock* (3 vols., 1850) and *Bits of Blarney* (1854), collections of stories; *Tressilian and His Friends* (1859), in part autobiographical; *Life of Charles Dickens* (1870), written in five weeks; and *Sir Walter Scott: the Story of His Life* (1871). The biographies are interesting accounts, enlivened by numerous reminiscences and anecdotes. Mackenzie is probably best remembered, however, for his five-volume edition of the *Noctes Ambrosianae* (London, 1854; 2nd ed., revised, 1863), the first adequate collection of these papers, accompanied by a valuable commentary. He likewise edited R. L. Sheil's *Sketches of the Irish Bar* (1854), William Henry Curran's *Life of the Right Honorable John Philpot Curran* (1855); *Miscellaneous Writings of the late Dr. Maginn* (5 vols., 1855–57), the last volume containing a 110-page memoir; Lady Morgan's *The O'Briens and the O'Flahertys: A National Tale* (1856); and the *Memoirs of Robert-Houdin, Ambassador, Author, and Conjurer* (1859), of which he seems also to have been the translator. Numerous other works appeared, especially after the publication of the *Noctes Ambrosianae,* with brief introductions or memoirs by Mackenzie, among them *Father Tom and the Pope, or a Night at the Vatican* (1868), by Sir Samuel Ferguson, which Mackenzie attributed to John Fisher Murray. Mackenzie seems not to have taken too seriously his relation of literary god-father to these works and the introductions are often perfunctory. They are useful chiefly as indicating that his name on the title-page of a book had commercial value.

[Sketch by D. J. O'Donoghue, in *Dict. Nat. Biog.*; Frederic Boase, *Modern English Biog.* (1897); *Ballow's Pictorial Drawing-Room Companion,* Jan. 12, 1856; *Public Ledger* (Phila.), Nov. 22, 1881; *Notes and Queries,* Sept. 28, 1907, p. 247; occasional references in his books; a few letters in the Pa. Hist. Soc. and the N. Y. Pub. Lib.; certain data from a daughter, Dr. Marion Mackenzie, of Philadelphia.]
A. C. B.

MACKENZIE, WILLIAM (July 30, 1758–July 23, 1828), bibliophile and book-collector, was probably the only child of Kenneth Mackenzie and his wife Mary, daughter of Edward Thomas of Barbados. His parents were married at Christ Church, Philadelphia, on Dec. 12, 1754. It is possible that his father was of Scottish birth, since William later became an active member of the St. Andrew's Society and bequeathed money to it in his will. The fact that he was entered a student at the Philadelphia Academy in 1766 by one Captain Morrell suggests that his father had died before that time. At the Academy he formed a lifelong friendship with his classmate, James Abercrombie, afterwards an associate pastor of Christ Church and principal of the Episcopal Academy for many years. After leaving the school he entered the counting-house of John Ross, one of the most eminent shipping merchants of the city and muster-master of the Pennsylvania navy. Here he acquired an extensive knowledge of mercantile and shipping affairs, in which he never entirely lost interest; at his death he bequeathed one thousand dollars for the relief of distressed ship-masters.

By temperament, however, he was little adapted to a business life, and when about thirty years of age, he inherited an income sufficient to enable him to devote himself to scholarship and the collecting of books. In time he built up a library which, when he died, was one of the largest in the United States. He never married, and by his will bequeathed "to the Library Company of Philadelphia, 500 volumes, to be chosen by the directors, from his English books printed since the commencement of the eighteenth century; to the same, in trust for the Loganian Library all his books printed before the commencement of the eighteenth century, and 300 volumes more, to be chosen by the trustees, from his Latin and French books printed since that period" (*Daily Chronicle,* July 28, 1828). Large bequests to libraries were not common at that time and the generosity of William Mackenzie to his native city attracted much attention. His wishes were punctiliously fulfilled, and furthermore, all of his books which had not been bequeathed were purchased for the libraries, which thus, by purchase and bequest, acquired a total of 7,051 volumes, including examples of printing from the earliest European presses. Many of the important incunabula left to the Loganian Library are listed in the *Census of Fifteenth Century Books Owned in America* (1919) as being the only copies in America. Among these are Gratian's *Decretum,* printed at Nürnberg by Koberger in 1483; *Les Oeuvres de Senecque translatez de latin en francoys* printed by Verard at Paris without date; *Nicolaus Bessarion, Oratzione . . . contra il Turcho, vulgarizate,* Venice, 1471. Included also are a Pliny on vellum printed by Jenson in 1476, and other works from that important press, and the *Biblia latina cum postillis Nicolai de Lyra,* printed by Paganinus at Venice in 1495. The library is rich, moreover, in early English printing, and in this section is included a fine Caxton, the first edition of the Golden Legend in English, printed about 1485 (Seymour De Ricci, *A Census of Caxtons,* 1909, p. 103). There is a vast quantity of miscellaneous literature, both English and European, and much valuable Americana.

Mackenzie's portrait, painted by John Neagle in 1829 and presented to the Library Company of Philadelphia by Dr. James Abercrombie, now hangs in the Reading Room of that institution. It suggests a gentle and scholarly personality. Abercrombie described him as being without an enemy, adding: "at least, from the purity of his principles and correctness of his conduct, I am sure he never deserved one." The author of the short account prefixed to the catalogue of his books in the Loganian Library (possibly Judah Dobson who printed the pamphlet), thus describes him: "His constitution, though vigorous, was not robust, his manners plain and conciliatory, his hand and his purse were ever open and ready to relieve individual and domestic distress, and contribute to public requisitions; in short, in every relation which he bore to society, he exhibited a truly estimable and exemplary character. . . . He was an accomplished Belles Lettres and classical scholar, and the tenor of his life was an uniform illustration of his principles and the benevolence of his heart."

[Official records at City Hall and Christ Church, Phila., and at the Univ. of Pa.; minutes of the Library Company of Phila.; *Catalogue of the Books Belonging to the Loganian Library,* vol. II (1829); *Daily Chronicle* (Phila.), July 24, 1828, and *Democratic Press* (Phila.), July 29, 1828.] A. S. W. R.

MACKEY, ALBERT GALLATIN (Mar. 12, 1807–June 20, 1881), Masonic writer and encyclopedist, was born in Charleston, S. C., the youngest son of Dr. John Mackey, also a native South Carolinian, of Scotch descent. The latter was a physician, editor, and teacher. He conducted *The Investigator* from its establishment in 1812 to 1817, and in 1826 published *The American Teacher's Assistant and Self-Instructor's Guide.* Albert received a good English education and an elementary classical one, which later he extended greatly by private study. After teaching school for a time, he entered the South Carolina Medical College, Charleston, and graduated in 1832, receiving the first prize for his Latin thesis. On Dec. 27, 1836, he married Sarah Pamela Hubbell, daughter of Sears Hubbell, a sea-captain of Connecticut ancestry. He practised medicine in Charleston and became demonstrator of anatomy in the Medical College. In 1854, however, his increasing interest in Freemasonry impelled him to relinquish his profession and devote his entire time to the interests of the Masonic fraternity. When South Carolina seceded from the Union he espoused the latter's cause and remained steadfast throughout the Civil War, although practically all the citizens of Charleston were Southern sympathizers. Confined within the city limits he gave his time, his energies, and his substance to the succor of his brethren, little heeding whether they belonged North or South. After the war he made a journey to the North, where he was received with enthusiastic and substantial manifestations of gratitude and appreciation. In July 1865 he was appointed by President Johnson collector of the port of Charleston.

Mackey was a Mason in St. Andrew's Lodge, No. 10 of Charleston in 1841, shortly thereafter joining Solomon's Lodge, No. 1 of the same city, of which he became master in 1842. He was a member and presiding officer of practically all the subordinate bodies of the various rites of Freemasonry, eventually becoming grand secretary of the Grand Lodge, grand high priest of the Grand Chapter, grand master of the Grand Council, and general grand high priest of the General Grand Chapter of the United States. The last decade of his life was spent in Washington, D. C., where he devoted himself to the continuance of his work as secretary general of the Supreme Council of the 33rd Degree, having held this office since 1844. While Mackey attained high official positions in Freemasonry, it is chiefly through his literary labors for the fraternity that his name has been perpetuated. Most of his writings are still in constant demand, and his *Encyclopædia of Freemasonry* is a standard authority, which, with slight revisions, continues to be republished at frequent intervals. His first book was *A Lexicon of Freemasonry* (1845), after which appeared in quick succession *The Mystic Tie* (1849), *The Ahiman Rezon, or Book of Constitutions of the Grand Lodge of South Carolina* (1852), *Principles of Masonic Law* (1856), *The Book of the Chapter* (1858), *A*

Text Book of Masonic Jurisprudence (1859), *History of Freemasonry in South Carolina* (1861), *Manual of the Lodge* (1862), *Cryptic Masonry* (1867), *Mackey's Masonic Ritualist* (1869), *The Symbolism of Freemasonry* (1869), *Encyclopædia of Freemasonry* (1874), *Masonic Parliamentary Law* (1875). He was the editor of a number of Masonic magazines, a contributor to many others, and some of his many Masonic addresses have been printed.

Mackey was of stalwart and commanding presence with somewhat harsh but striking features, replete with intelligence and amiability; he conversed well and was liked as a genial and companionable man, of cheerful, tolerant and kindly nature, who, if he had quarrels with individuals, had none with the world (Pike, *post*, p. 203). His death occurred at Old Point Comfort, Va., and he was buried in Glenwood Cemetery, Washington, D. C.

[Mackey's *Encyc. of Freemasonry* (1929), revised by R. I. Clegg; T. A. W. Melcher, *A Hist. Sketch of S. C. Commandery, No. 1, K. T.* (1900); Albert Pike, *Ex Corde Locutiones: Words from the Heart . . . 1860–1891* (copr. 1899); *Freemasons' Monthly Mag.*, vols. I–VI, VIII, X, XIII, XXII (1841–63); *Masonic Eclectic* (Washington), July 1881; *Masonic Rev.* (Cincinnati), Aug. 1881; Walter Hubbell, *Hist. of the Hubbell Family* (1915); *Washington Post*, June 21, 27, 1881; *News and Courier* (Charleston), June 21, 1881.]

W. L. B.

McKIM, CHARLES FOLLEN (Aug. 24, 1847–Sept. 14, 1909), architect, born at Isabella Furnace, Chester County, Pa., was the second of the two children of James Miller McKim [*q.v.*] and Sarah Allibone (Speakman) McKim, who made their home in Philadelphia. He was named for Charles Follen [*q.v.*], the first professor of German at Harvard, who lost his position on account of his anti-slavery activities. McKim's father spent his life in promoting the abolition of slavery and the education of freedmen; his mother, a Quaker, was an ardent advocate and helper in the same cause. Yet the rancor and strife of the bitter struggle did not cross the threshold; there was neither plenty nor meagerness; and the amenities of life were cultivated in the home. Trained in the school of that ardent abolitionist, Theodore D. Weld, at Perth Amboy, N. J., and in the Philadelphia public schools, Charles McKim prepared for the Lawrence Scientific School at Harvard, with the purpose of becoming a mining engineer. Entering in 1866, he spent a year in Cambridge and longed for the better training of French schools. His father persuaded him to enter the architectural office of Russell Sturgis, in New York, because he had "a positive talent" for drawing. Still determined to go to Paris, McKim now bent his desires toward the École des Beaux Arts. In September 1867, he entered the Atelier Daumet; there he stayed until the spring of 1870, during which time he visited England, Germany, Austria, and northern Italy.

The threatened outbreak of the Franco-Prussian War sent American students from Paris. The McKim family were now settled in Orange, N. J., and Charles was taken into the New York office of Charles D. Gambrill and Henry H. Richardson [*q.v.*]. He was put in charge of the drawings at $8.00 a week, which meant independence and joy. Trinity Church, Boston, was then the chief work in the office. McKim's proclivities were towards early rather than modern French architecture; and the romantic element in Richardson's work appealed to him. He was bent on establishing a practice of his own, and, when several small commissions came to him, he took rooms near the Richardson offices for his special work. Thither by chance came William Rutherford Mead [*q.v.*], fresh from European study, and for several years they worked together on their individual commissions, until in 1878 a partnership was formed by McKim, Mead, and William B. Bigelow. The next year Bigelow gave way to Stanford White [*q.v.*], who had succeeded to McKim's place in the Richardson office.

Even before the partnership, McKim, Mead, Bigelow, and White had made a walking trip to New England, visiting Boston, Salem, Marblehead, Newburyport, and Portsmouth in order to measure and draw specimens of colonial architecture. They had become convinced that the style of architecture based on classical precedents developed in England by Sir Christopher Wren, brought to America by the English colonists, and practised in New England by Charles Bulfinch [*q.v.*] was fundamentally the style best suited to the life of the American people, in both their homes and their public buildings. From this conviction the firm of McKim, Mead & White has not departed during more than half a century. The further tendency towards the Italian Renaissance came largely from Joseph M. Wells, who entered the office in 1879 and who, in spite of an unsocial nature, became the intimate friend and companion of the three partners and of Augustus Saint-Gaudens as well. Having reached their own conclusions, these men had the ability to win over their clients, for each of whom they created a distinct, individual work of art. It would have been easy and natural to follow the then popular Richardson tradition. McKim has made plain the point of departure from it. He wrote deliberately in 1905 that Richardson, "an artist and a man of genius," finding the methods of the École des Beaux Arts slow and laborious, "coined for himself a style eclectic, personal and romantic—Gothic in spirit, Romanesque in detail—robust, virile, ingenious, but wholly barbaric: remarkable for its absence of proportion and sense of real beauty; in the hands of his followers lawless, and now happily extinct" (Charles Moore, compiler, *The Promise of American Architecture,* 1905, p. 23 note). In Paris, McKim learned the essential value of the plan; he first pondered the problem, the purpose of the structure; when he had mastered that he gave thought to the exterior. The plan of the Century Club, New York, is McKim's; the general design of the unique exterior is Stanford White's; the details, an architectural triumph in themselves, are Joseph M. Wells's. Such coöperation was characteristic of the office.

It took several years, however, for convictions to ripen into actualities. McKim's early predilection for the romantic found vent in the Newport Casino, designed in 1881 at the behest of James Gordon Bennett as the social center of Newport life. The use of the Romanesque marked the McKim group of buildings (1884) at Narragansett Pier, R. I., most of which have disappeared. In 1882, Henry Villard, by marriage a connection of the McKim-Garrison family, commissioned McKim to build the group of houses on Madison Avenue between 50th and 51st Streets. The result (the combined work of McKim, White, Wells, and George F. Babb), designed in the style of the Italian Renaissance, marked a departure in American architecture so novel as to bring to the firm high renown, and led directly to a commission (1887) to design the Boston Public Library, distinctly the work of McKim. The three features of the Boston plan are: a reading room extending across the entire front of the building and giving a maximum of light; an interior arcaded court with pool and accommodations for out-of-doors reading in summer; and a monumental staircase leading from the offices below to the main floor, after the Italian fashion. These elements settled, the exterior design was studied with relation to the picturesque mass of Richardson's Trinity Church opposite and the square-towered New Old South Church at the left, both prominent features of Copley Square. McKim's conviction was that a building based on classical precedents would hold its own in any company, irrespective of size. His direct inspiration for the series of arched windows along the front came from the Coliseum; and in working out the design of the façade the resemblance to the Library of Ste. Geneviève in Paris was immediately remarked in his office when he sent the drawings from Boston. Such resemblance, so far from disturbing McKim, caused satisfaction; it proved that he was working along the lines of the best traditions in architecture. Applying a quotation from Lowell, one may say: "Always he took the coinage of the past and reminted it to suit his own purposes, giving to it his own image and superscription."

As in all McKim's monumental work, the conception of the Boston Library grew both in intensity and extent. He seized the opportunity to create a building that should express the civic consciousness of an old, proud, wealthy city, in which learning was the most valued tradition. So this Library, with its rare collections of books, should give proper setting to these heaped-up treasures, and at the same time provide for the everyday uses of a multitude of readers. Hence the rare marbles, the like of which had never been used in the United States; the obtaining of them in proper sizes and color, and at the proper times, was a triumph in itself. Then he had to surmount the objections to vastly enlarged appropriations as the project grew and expanded, and also criticisms of details so novel as to excite opposition. To McKim the idea of a monumental building without sculpture and painting was unthinkable—painting and sculpture not as mere adornment but as constituent parts, equal to the architecture itself. From the beginning he had the constant advice of Augustus Saint-Gaudens and Stanford White; and it was due to this consensus of minds that John S. Sargent and Edwin A. Abbey were induced to enter the field of mural painting and undertake the works which have come to be among the most important of their achievements. Also, Puvis de Chavannes, greatest of mural painters of his epoch, was brought to decorate the grand stairway with a series of designs of great dignity and beauty. Saint-Gaudens himself was to execute two groups in sculptural harmony with the architecture of the entrance, but, through vicissitudes regrettable but unavoidable, he is represented only by the shields over the doorways. However, Louis Saint-Gaudens, D. C. French, and F. W. MacMonnies contributed vitally to the ensemble. This first masterpiece of McKim embodied characteristic results of his thought and daring afterwards exhibited in many of his works.

For the Chicago World's Fair of 1893 he designed the colossal and highly adorned Agricultural Building and also the exquisite New York State Building (based on the Villa Medici); especially he had to do with perfecting the architectural scheme of the Court of Honor. To this orderly arrangement of monumental buildings and their landscape settings one traces the movement for city planning in the United States, which followed close upon the Chicago Fair. The popular acclaim excited at Chicago by Daniel H. Burnham [*q.v.*] and his associates led Senator James McMillan [*q.v.*] to select Burnham, McKim, and Saint-Gaudens, together with the younger Olmsted, to make the Plan of 1901, according to which the capital of the nation is being developed on a scale previously unequaled. Here McKim's especial part was to design the central composition from the Capitol to the Potomac, including gardens about the Washington Monument, the location of, and tentative sketches for, the Lincoln Memorial (designed by Henry Bacon, for nine years in the McKim office), and for the Arlington Memorial Bridge and the Water Gate, subsequently redesigned and executed by McKim, Mead, and White, under the immediate supervision of William M. Kendall, who began direct association with McKim in 1882. The office of McKim, Mead, and White came to be regarded by young architects as the best training school in America, because of the inspiration that resulted from two such harmoniously different men as McKim and White, and their methods of encouraging and requiring the young men to think for themselves.

McKim's inherent modesty and his respect for the good work of predecessors were manifested in his restoration of the White House (1902–03) at the call of President and Mrs. Theodore Roosevelt. Here he took the work of Hoban and Latrobe, removed from it later excrescences, and carried it on in their spirit to a culmination that the resources at their disposal did not permit. In the design of the Army War College buildings in Washington, about the same time, he took a motive found on the spot (Bulfinch's, as it has since turned out) and developed it as a capable musician develops an indigenous theme, building quite simply in brick and stone. McKim's ingenuity found play in dealing with the problem of locating the new Columbia University on Morningside Heights, in New York. Others would have cut off the top of the hill to make a plateau. McKim built to the height of three stories on the sides of the hill, thereby saving space and creating a platform at the level of the pinnacle. Then he made the central feature a monumental library of stone and built the subordinate buildings of brick, quite in a style of their own, closer to Italy than to England, and designed especially to obtain a maximum of light and air. The Harvard gates and fence, so severely criticized by Charles Eliot Norton at the time of building, have become a standard type for universities. They were a deliberate start "to bring Harvard back to bricks and mortar," now an accomplished feat.

In 1903 it fell to McKim's lot to design at one and the same time the Pierpont Morgan Library, called by President Charles W. Eliot "the most exquisite architectural gem of our country, and among the masterpieces of the world" (Moore, *post*, p. 283), and also the Pennsylvania Railway Station (1904–10), both in New York, the latter the largest building that had ever been erected at one time. The exterior was constructed entirely of pink granite and the interior of travertine from Rome. In both cases, his persuasiveness with his clients overcame obstacles to the creation of structures according to McKim's ideas rather than the original conceptions of the clients. The University Club in New York, considered by many McKim's masterpiece, has, for the decoration of its library, paintings based on those in the Borgia apartments of the Vatican. For the painter, McKim selected H. Siddons Mowbray, with the avowed purpose of having in America an example of the finest decorations in the world.

Feeling keenly his own limitations and lack of early training, and the limitations of the young men who came into his office, McKim was a devout believer in such schools as the French Academy, founded in Rome by Louis XIV. From the time of the Chicago Fair in 1893 till his death his one consuming purpose was to establish an American Academy in Rome, where young men of high promise might have, under competent direction, association with the masterpieces of all time. He felt that such traveling scholarships as he established at Columbia and Harvard were not enough. He aimed to bring into a community of life and endeavor students in architecture, landscape architecture, sculpture, painting, and music, each one sharing with kindred spirits the enjoyment of past achievements as incentives to future mastery of those problems which the increase of wealth and taste in America would inspire. From small beginnings, supported by his own contributions and those of his friends, the school grew year by year, obtained government recognition (but not support) and persisted until it has become the highest embodiment of American training in the fine arts.

McKim was married on Oct. 1, 1874, to Annie Bigelow of New York; one daughter was born to them. On June 25, 1885, he married Julia Amory Appleton of Boston; she died in 1887. The deaths of Stanford White in 1906, and of Augustus Saint-Gaudens in 1907, broke ties that were the essence of McKim's life. In January 1908 he left the office, suffering from overwork;

he retained an intermittent interest in affairs until his death at St. James, Long Island, on Sept. 14, 1909. He was buried with his family in Rosedale Cemetery, Orange, N. J. At the memorial meetings in New York (Nov. 23) and in Washington (Dec. 15) tributes to his work and worth were paid by his friends, Elihu Root, President Taft, and Joseph H. Choate, as well as by his professional associates. He received honorary degrees from Harvard, Columbia, and Princeton, and, in 1903, the gold medal of the Royal Institute of British Architects; he was posthumously awarded that of the American Institute of Architects. An exquisite memorial to him in the American Academy in Rome, an inscription on the pavement in front of the Columbia Library, and a tablet placed by the architects of Boston in their Public Library keep alive the name of a modest man and an architect eminent in the history of his art.

[Photographs and measured drawings of the architectural work of McKim, Mead, and White have been published in a series of sumptuous volumes. The issue of *The Brickbuilder, An Architectural Monthly,* Feb. 1910, is devoted to McKim. It contains a critical sketch by Royal Cortissoz; see also articles by him in *Scribner's Mag.,* Jan. 1910, July 1929. L. G. White, *Sketches and Designs by Stanford White* (1920), shows the contrasting characters of the two sympathetic men. *The Life and Times of Charles Follen McKim* (1929), by Charles Moore, gives the intimate side of his working life, and has lists of the men in the office and the buildings designed by the firm. See also A. H. Granger, *Charles Follen McKim: A Study of his Life and Work* (1913); C. H. Reilly, *McKim, Mead and White* (1924); *N. Y. Times,* Sept. 15, 1909. McKim letters relating to the plan of Washington and the restoration of the White House are in the Lib. of Cong.] C. M.

McKIM, ISAAC (July 21, 1775–Apr. 1, 1838), merchant, congressman, was born in Philadelphia, Pa., the son of John and Margaret (Duncan) McKim. His grandfather, Judge Thomas McKim, came from Londonderry, Ireland, about 1734, and settled first in Philadelphia, then in Brandywine, Del. John McKim established a mercantile business in Baltimore. When Isaac was nine years old, his mother died, leaving two small sons, to whom the father gave his personal care as they grew up. Isaac attended the public schools, and at an early age began to work in his father's office. At twenty-one he went into partnership with his father in the shipping and importing firm of John McKim & Son, and five years later John McKim retired from active business. Under the direction of Isaac McKim the importing business continued to expand and prosper. It was interrupted briefly by the War of 1812, during which he acted as aide-de-camp to Gen. Samuel Smith, commander of the forces defending Baltimore. In this emergency he advanced $50,000 for the city's defenses.

McKim was a leader in the commercial and industrial life of Baltimore. His importing business firmly established, he built in 1822 a large steam flour mill for which he had to import the machinery from England. A few years later he built a great copper rolling and refining works, and was said to be the largest copper importer and manufacturer in the United States. He was one of the organizers of the Baltimore & Ohio Railroad, and was a member of its first board of directors, 1827–31. His ships were on every sea. His life-long passion for them was based on thorough knowledge and early experience. It is said that when he was a young man his father sent him to Europe as a supercargo on one of his ships. After a difficult voyage across the Atlantic, the captain thought the vessel unseaworthy, and had it inspected and condemned. Isaac McKim vigorously protested the judgment; the captain was left ashore, and McKim brought the ship home himself. In his day the fast, small "Baltimore clippers" were famous. After deliberating for some time, in 1832 he took to Kennard & Williamson, a ship-building firm, a plan for a much larger vessel, a "three-skysail-yarder," modeled along the slender lines of the clipper. It was built despite the derision of all the other ship owners, and christened the *Ann McKim* after his wife. He spared no expense upon it. The rails and hatches were mahogany; the cannon were cast of finest brass. For years it was the finest and fastest merchant ship afloat, and though no other ship was ever made just like it, it anticipated the famous Yankee clipper ships which began to appear about a decade later.

McKim gave much time to charitable enterprises and public service. With his brother he established a free coeducational school in 1821, in memory of his father. Later, he built and endowed a second free school. He served on the Baltimore library board and was a charter member of the Protective Society of Maryland, organized in 1816 to protect the liberty of free negroes. In 1821 he was elected to the Maryland Senate as a Democrat, and served from Dec. 4, 1821, to Jan. 8, 1823, when he resigned in order to fill a vacancy in the House of Representatives of the Seventeenth Congress, caused by the resignation of Gen. Samuel Smith. He was elected for the succeeding term, serving Jan. 8, 1823–Mar. 3, 1825, and later returned to the Twenty-third, Twenty-fourth, and Twenty-fifth congresses (1833–38), in which he served on the House ways and means committee. His death, in Washington, followed a brief illness during a session of Congress in 1838, and he was buried in St. Paul's churchyard, Baltimore. His wife, Ann Bowly of Baltimore, whom he married Dec. 21, 1808, survived him some thirty-seven years. They had no children.

[*Biog. Dir. Am. Cong.* (1928); *Baltimore, Past and Present* (1871); *Md. Hist. Mag.*, Dec. 1906, Sept. 1914; A. H. Clark, *The Clipper Ship Era* (1910); Hawthorne Daniel, *The Clipper Ship* (1928); C. C. Cutler, *Greyhounds of the Sea: The Story of the American Clipper Ship* (1930); *Daily National Intelligencer* (Washington, D. C.), Apr. 2, 5, 1838; name of wife and date of marriage from Md. Hist. Soc., Baltimore.]

I. L. T.

McKIM, JAMES MILLER (Nov. 14, 1810–June 13, 1874), anti-slavery leader, born at Carlisle, Pa., was the grandson of James McKim who came in 1774 from the north of Ireland to Carlisle and there married Hannah McIlvaine; he was the son of James McKim (1779–1831) and Catharine Miller (1783–1831), the latter of German descent. Graduating at Dickinson College at the age of eighteen (1828), he studied for a few weeks in 1831 at Princeton Theological Seminary and attended Andover Theological Seminary (1832–33). After ordination by the Wilmington Presbytery in October 1835, he was settled as the first pastor of the Presbyterian church at Womelsdorf, Berks County, Pa., virtually a home-missionary field rather than the foreign field to which he aspired. William Lloyd Garrison's attack on the American Colonization Society led McKim into the movement for the immediate emancipation of the slaves, and in 1833 he represented a Carlisle negro constituency in the Philadelphia convention at which the American Anti-Slavery Society was formed. Being the youngest delegate, he attracted the attention of the leaders, among them Lucretia Mott. His "New School" theology had already closed orthodox Presbyterian doors; his talks against slavery in Carlisle and elsewhere, together with the permanent conversion of the entire membership of his church to the anti-slavery cause, brought him into antagonism with the prevailing public sentiment. Drawn into association and cooperation with James and Lucretia Mott, McKim resigned his charge and, in a letter explaining the growth of his religious convictions, withdrew from the ministry. He became one of the "seventy" gathered from all professions, whom the eloquence of Theodore D. Weld inspired to spread the gospel of emancipation. His stipend of eight dollars a week laid him open to the charge of being bought by "British gold."

In 1838–39 the name of James M. McKim appears on the rolls of the medical school of the University of Pennsylvania. On Oct. 1, 1840, he married Sarah Allibone Speakman (1813–1891), great-grand-daughter of Thomas Speakman, who came in 1712 from Reading, Berks, England, and settled in Chester County, Pa. She was a Quaker beauty who used her feminine attractions to further the anti-slavery cause. They had two children, Charles Follen [*q.v.*] and Lucy, who married Wendell Phillips Garrison; their adopted daughter, McKim's niece, became Garrison's second wife. The McKims found their service mainly in the protection of fugitive-slaves, and in systematic resistance to legalized slave-hunts and slave-captures. William Still wrote from fourteen years' companionship: "James Miller McKim, as one of the earliest, most faithful, and ablest abolitionists in Pennsylvania, occupied a position of influence, labor and usefulness, scarcely second to Mr. Garrison" (*Underground Railroad,* p. 655). At the time of his marriage McKim was publishing agent of the Pennsylvania Anti-Slavery Society, in Philadelphia; he succeeded John Greenleaf Whittier as editor of the *Pennsylvania Freeman*; then as corresponding secretary he had a share in all the anti-slavery work both local and national. These duties were particularly arduous by reason of the fact that, to use his own expression, the Fugitive-slave Law had "turned Southeastern Pennsylvania into another Guinea Coast" (Still, p. 580).

In 1859 McKim and his wife accompanied Mrs. John Brown to Harpers Ferry to take leave of her husband and receive his body. In the winter of 1862 McKim started the Philadelphia Port Royal Relief Committee to provide for the wants of ten thousand slaves suddenly liberated, and the report on his visit to the Sea Islands of South Carolina was used in America and in Europe as the basis of operations (*The Freed Men of South Carolina,* 1862). He urged the enlistment of colored men as soldiers and had part in creating Camp William Penn, which added eleven regiments to the Union army. In 1863 he became corresponding secretary of the Pennsylvania Freedmen's Relief Association, traveling through the South to establish schools and through the North to organize public sentiment. In 1865 he removed to New York as the corresponding secretary of the American Freedman's Union Commission, which he helped to organize with the aim of promoting education among the blacks. On his motion the Commission disbanded (July 1, 1869), its work having been accomplished. In 1865 he raised a portion of the capital required to found *The Nation,* with which his son-in-law Wendell Phillips Garrison was so long connected, first as literary editor and finally as editor-in-charge.

McKim established the family home at Llewellyn Park, Orange, N. J., where he died June 13, 1874.

[William Still, *The Underground Railroad* (1872); Charles Moore, *The Life and Times of Charles Follen McKim* (1929); W. L. Garrison, Jr., *In Memoriam: Sarah A. McKim* (1891), including genealogies; *N. Y. Tribune*, June 15, 16, 1874.] C. M.

McKINLEY, CARLYLE (Nov. 22, 1847–Aug. 24, 1904), journalist, essayist, and poet, was born at Newnan, Coweta County, Ga., the son of Charles G. and Frances (Jackson) McKinley. He was also known as Carl McKinley. He entered the Confederate army with a student company and subsequently saw active service in the battles around Atlanta. After the Civil War he became a cotton broker in Augusta, Ga., and later worked in the United States marshal's office at Savannah, Ga. He entered the Columbia Theological Seminary at Columbia, S. C., where he graduated with distinction in 1874. Shortly after graduation he was married to Elizabeth H. Bryce, the daughter of Campbell R. Bryce. Owing to a change in his theological views he refrained from entering the ministry and became a teacher in the school of Hugh S. Thompson [*q.v.*] at Columbia. During this teaching his interest in literature and writing became aroused, and in 1875 he was made the Columbia correspondent for the Charleston *News and Courier*. In 1879 he went to Washington to be correspondent for the paper and in 1881 went to Charleston to become associate editor. This position he held until failing health just before his death caused his retirement.

He was a brilliant essayist, an editor with a clear insight into public questions, and a poet of considerable ability. His monographs, *An Appeal to Pharaoh* (1889), a powerful analysis of the negro question, "The August Cyclone . . . of 1885," and "A Descriptive Narrative of the Earthquake . . . of 1886," in the *Year Book . . . City of Charleston* for 1885 and for 1886, are noted for their vigorous and highly artistic prose style. His verse, published in *Selections from the Poems of Carlyle McKinley* (1904), is of great beauty. It is mostly subjective and reflective in theme and it exhibits the bravery and the hopefulness of the Southern writers during the Reconstruction period. He sometimes indulged, however, in the romantic, satiric, and humorous types of poetry, but he was always restrained and had a delicate sense of humor. The charm of his expression of his own faith and optimism made for him a place as one of the chief Southern poets of the period.

[*In Loving Memory of Carlyle McKinley*, ed. by W. A. Courtenay (1904); G. A. Wauchope, *The Writers of South Carolina* (1910); W. A. Courtenay, "Carlyle McKinley," in *The Library of Southern Literature*, ed. by E. A. Alderman and J. C. Harris, vol. VIII (copr. 1907); M. L. Rutherford, *The South in History and Literature* (1907); *News and Courier* (Charleston), Aug. 25, 1904.] R. D. B.

McKINLEY, JOHN (May 1, 1780–July 19, 1852), representative, senator, and associate justice of the United States Supreme Court, was born in Culpeper County, Va., the son of Mary (Logan) and Andrew McKinley, a physician. In his early childhood his parents moved to Kentucky, where his mother's family was numerous and well-connected. As a young man, he became a mechanic. After reading law he was admitted to the bar, and practised at Frankfort and at Louisville, Ky. About 1818 he followed the tide of immigration into the Tennessee Valley of Alabama, settled at Huntsville, then the center for a powerful group of planters, lawyers, and politicians, and with his customary vigor plunged into law practice and politics. In 1820 he entered the state legislature, and two years later he was a candidate for the seat in the United States Senate made vacant by the resignation of John W. Walker. The Georgia machine supported him, but his fellow townsman, William Kelly, the leader of the popular cause, defeated him by a majority of one vote. The death of Henry Chambers in 1826 gave him another chance at a much coveted seat in the Senate, and he entered the contest against Clement Comer Clay, of Huntsville, ex-chief justice of the Alabama supreme court and a prominent planter. McKinley had attracted a good deal of popularity by abandoning the moribund Georgia machine after 1824 and attaching himself to the rising star of Andrew Jackson. Even the Huntsville *Democrat*, claiming to be the people's tribune, supported him, though only three years previously it had felt constrained to reject him as an aristocrat. He was victorious over Clay by three votes and served from Nov. 27, 1826, to Mar. 3, 1831. During his senatorial term he moved to Florence, Ala., which had recently been projected on a pretentious scale and promised to become a great city.

When he stood for reëlection he was defeated decisively by Gabriel Moore [*q.v.*] of Huntsville. He represented Lauderdale County in the legislature in 1831, and two years later he was elected to Congress over James Davis of Franklin County. He did not seek reëlection. Instead, he returned to the state legislature in 1836 with a view to succeeding Moore, who had fallen into public disfavor by opposing Jackson's plans to make Van Buren his successor to the presidency. McKinley's own support of Jackson and of Van Buren as his successor had been unflagging, so when Moore made no effort to succeed himself, he was elected to the seat. Before he qualified as senator Van Buren appointed him, on Apr. 22, 1837, as associate justice of the United States Supreme Court. He held this position till his death. He continued to live simply and devoted himself to his work at Washington and on the circuit. He was a conscientious, hard-working judge, and even in his last years when he was ill and increasingly feeble he forced himself to attend to the duties of his office. He died in Louisville, Ky., where he had made his home after his elevation to the supreme bench. He was married twice: first to Juliana Bryan and later to Elizabeth Armistead.

[H. Levin, *The Lawyers and Lawmakers of Ky.* (1897); *The Biog. Encyc. of Ky.* (1878); T. M. Green, *Historic Families of Ky.* (1889); memorial remarks in the Supreme Court in 14 *Howard*, pp. iii–v; T. M. Owen, *Hist. of Ala.* (1921), vol. IV; Willis Brewer, *Ala.* (1872), p. 297; T. H. Jack, *Sectionalism and Party Politics in Ala.* (1919); T. P. Abernethy, *The Formative Period in Ala.* (1922); *The Second Gathering of the Clan MacKinlay at Chicago . . . 1894* (1894), p. 11; *Daily Louisville Times*, July 20, 21, 1852.] A. B. M.

McKINLEY, WILLIAM (Jan. 29, 1843–Sept. 14, 1901), twenty-fifth President of the United States, was born at Niles, Ohio, seventh of the nine children of William and Nancy (Allison) McKinley. A descendant of David McKinley, known as "David the Weaver," who settled in York County, Pa., about 1743, he came of Scotch-Irish stock (F. A. Claypool, *The Scotch Ancestors of William McKinley*, 1897). His father and grandfather, iron-founders on a small scale, followed the ore from the Susquehanna Valley to Columbiana County, Ohio. Schooled at Poland, Ohio, and at Allegheny College, Meadville, Pa., McKinley had taught a rural school before he enlisted at seventeen as a private in the Union army. Short, slight, and serious as a lad, he took on weight and power with years; and like Napoleon, whom the caricaturists thought he resembled, he bore himself so as to make dignity take the place of inches. He served through the Civil War with the 23rd Ohio Volunteer Regiment, under Rutherford B. Hayes, and at Antietam was a commissary sergeant. Shifted to the Shenandoah Valley, he saw duty at Kernstown, and at Cedar Creek where he was a captain. After being mustered out with brevet rank as major, he studied law in the office of Charles E. Glidden in Mahoning County, Ohio, and, for less than a year, in the Albany Law School. In 1867 he opened a law office at Canton, seat of Stark County, where he maintained residence for the rest of his life, and in 1869 he was elected prosecuting attorney. He married, on Jan. 25, 1871, Ida Saxton, daughter of a local banker and a member of a substantial family that had helped to found the town. The marriage was one of devoted affection, with the greater need for devotion when, after the birth and early death of two daughters, Ida McKinley became a chronic invalid (Josiah Hartzell, *Sketch of the Life of Mrs. William McKinley*, 1896; New York *Evening Post*, May 27, 1907).

Major McKinley, as he was generally known, flourished moderately at the Canton bar; and when in 1875 Hayes was for the third time a candidate for the governorship of Ohio McKinley was among his active supporters. The next year he was elected to Congress as representative from the 17th Ohio district. There is a tradition that President Hayes advised McKinley to study the tariff and to grow up with the issue, but there was no need for such advice to a young congressman who was sympathetic with his constituents, in close touch with Republican leaders, and aware that Southern Democrats were talking of tariff revision on the basis of revenue only. A few weeks after he made his first pronouncement upon the tariff (*Chicago Times*, Apr. 16, 1878), his future was threatened by a Democratic gerrymander of the Ohio congressional districts, whereby Stark County was thrown into a new 16th district. Yet he carried the district in 1878, earning distinction when men more prominent than he fell under the Democratic thrust. A Republican legislature restored his old district in 1880, when he was again elected. His plurality in 1882, however, was so low (only eight votes out of 33,000) that a Democratic House of Representatives unseated him (*Congressional Record*, 48 Cong., 1 Sess., pp. 4567–94). In the autumn of 1884 he faced a new adverse gerrymander with success; and in 1886, his old district having been restored, he was again elected. Once more successful in 1888, he had now become a national figure, able to command renomination by acclamation (Chicago *Daily Inter Ocean*, Apr. 18, 1888). His career in Congress was ended with the help of the third Democratic gerrymander that he had to face, and he was overcome in the landslide of 1890 (J. P. Smith, ed., *History of the Republican Party in Ohio*, 1898, vol. I, p. 699).

While McKinley was struggling upon the treacherous footing of Ohio politics, he was growing in public stature. He was made temporary chairman of the Ohio Republican convention in 1880, and at the end of the year Speaker S. J. Randall gave him Garfield's place on the committee on ways and means (*Congressional Record*, 46 Cong., 3 Sess., p. 281). In 1884 he was permanent chairman of the Ohio convention, and chairman of the committee on resolutions of the Republican National Convention (*Cincinnati Commercial-Gazette,* Apr. 25, June 6, 1884). He was active in the state convention that renominated Foraker for governor in 1885. In 1888, with new distinction from his brilliant warfare against the Mills Bill, he was once more made chairman of the committee on resolutions of the National Convention (*Chicago Tribune,* June 20, 1888); he was a Sherman man, but, over his protest, delegates were now voting for him as a nominee for President. He acquired, after the final failure of the Sherman movement in 1888, a loyal friend in Marcus Alonzo Hanna [*q.v.*] of Cleveland, a business man with money to spend for the advancement of protection. With Hanna's active support, McKinley was elected governor of Ohio in 1891, at a time when Republican fortunes seemed low; the governorship was to be his sounding board during two terms beginning in 1892. In that year at Minneapolis he was permanent chairman of the Republican National Convention. Hanna had an organization at work to make him President, but McKinley insisted on the renomination of Harrison and declined to permit a stampede to himself. He had, however, been tried and tested as a party leader, and was becoming "the foremost champion of protection" (*Chicago Tribune,* Jan. 9, 1894).

The Republican party became more closely identified with the protective tariff in each successive year of McKinley's congressional experience. The tariff was to him a national policy and not a cloak for special privilege to favored interests. He sniped continuously at Democratic attempts at revision, and in 1888 he so vigorously backed up the efforts of the venerable William D. [Pig Iron] Kelly, senior Republican on the committee on ways and means, that he outshone him. When a Republican Congress convened in December 1889, McKinley, trained and disciplined by long years in opposition, contested in the Republican caucus for the speakership. Reed, who won, made him chairman of the committee on ways and means, in charge of the new tariff bill (*New York Tribune,* Dec. 11, 1889). McKinley was, throughout the ensuing debate, the moderator and harmonizer. He challenged the influence of Blaine, who now made a plea for reciprocity, and he met the demand of Western Republicans who insisted that something be done for silver before they voted for the tariff. When the McKinley Bill became a law, Oct. 1, 1890, the November elections were so close at hand that there was no time to explain it even to patient constituencies, far less to the exasperated Western voters who resented an increase in retail prices for the benefit of Eastern manufacturers. As a result, a landslide placed the Democrats again in control of the House of Representatives.

Before McKinley was reëlected governor in 1893 his future was brought into hazard by the consequences of his kindness of heart. He had repaid early favors of an old friend, Robert L. Walker of Youngstown, by indorsing notes as an accommodation; so many, indeed, that when Walker failed in February 1893, McKinley was involved for nearly $130,000. This was much more than he possessed, and even with the aid of all of his wife's fortune, which she placed in Hanna's hands at once, the payment of the debt would have reduced them to poverty. His whole property was deeded to a group of trustees, headed by Myron T. Herrick and including Hanna, who raised from unnamed friends the funds needed to meet his deficit, and the estate of Mrs. McKinley was released (Kohlsaat, *post,* p. 10). The misadventure did not injure his political availability; in the congressional campaign of 1894 he was the outstanding campaigner for his party (*New York Times,* Oct. 25, 1894).

The identification of McKinley with the politics of protection, and a personal kindliness of spirit which enabled him to escape the bitter enmities that harassed many of his contemporaries, placed him in a commanding position in the Republican party after the death of Blaine. But as his availability for the presidency as a protectionist candidate increased, the voters turned away from the tariff to discuss free silver; and upon this issue McKinley was worse than unprepared. He did not believe, even after his nomination, that the currency could become a major issue. He had voted for free silver, and for the Bland-Allison Act over the veto of Hayes, in spite of his avowed admiration for Garfield's "greatest effort" of Nov. 16, 1877, against inflation (*Congressional Record,* 49 Cong., 1 Sess., p. 764). When the unrest of debtors was intensified by the depression of 1893 and free silver was urged as a panacea, some of McKinley's speeches might have been interpreted as favoring it. Only by heroic management did Hanna hold together his organization for the nomination of McKinley when the tariff issue yielded to that of silver. Since most of the Democratic state conventions had demanded free coinage of silver, it was clear that the Republicans must oppose this. It was also probable that an open avowal of the gold standard would drive out of the party many Western Republicans whose support would be badly needed. The platform was agreed upon before the convention met in St. Louis, June 16, 1896. Although many of the leaders later claimed the credit of inserting the word "gold" in the currency plank, Hanna was satisfied to have it there, with McKinley as the candidate, and yet to avoid adding to the pain of Western silver Republicans by seeming responsible for its presence. In the remarkable campaign that followed, while his eloquent rival William Jennings Bryan [*q.v.*] toured the country, and his astute manager Hanna collected funds, perfected organization, and distributed literature, McKinley remained in imperturbable dignity at his old home in Canton, reading carefully drafted arguments to the scores of delegations that were brought to his front porch. The fear of loss through payments in a fifty-cent silver dollar intensified Eastern support of the ticket, regardless of party; and a good harvest with an improving price of grain lessened hard times in the West sufficiently to reduce the bitterness of the demand for cheap money as a measure of debtor relief. McKinley was elected President in November 1896, with 271 electoral votes against 176 for Bryan and with more than 7,000,000 popular votes out of about 14,000,000 cast (Edward Stanwood, *A History of the Presidency,* 1898). He was the first President to receive a popular majority since 1872.

The administration that he set up was orthodox in its Republicanism, with little distinction. It did not include Hanna (though McKinley would have welcomed him), because Hanna did not wish an administrative post, and preferred to sit in the Senate in the seat of John Sherman [*q.v.*]. Sherman was accordingly offered the State Department, and invited to make the gesture for international bimetallism that the party had promised to offset its repudiation of free silver. Sherman, in his seventy-fourth year, was willing to make the transfer for he feared the stress of the approaching campaign in Ohio for reëlection, and it was all too possible that Hanna could then take the seat from him by force. He retained the post of secretary of state for a little more than a year, until his physical incompetence grew to be a danger during the war with Spain. In the Treasury, McKinley placed Lyman J. Gage, a hard-money banker who escaped the stigma of Wall Street by coming from Chicago. The remaining departments went to local politicians: Russell A. Alger (War), John D. Long (Navy), Joseph McKenna (Justice), James A. Gary (Post Office), Cornelius Bliss (Interior), and James Wilson (Agriculture). As vacancies later occurred, McKinley brought into his family men of real significance: John Hay as secretary of state, Elihu Root as secretary of war, and Philander C. Knox as attorney-general.

Except for the restoration of the high tariff and the establishment of the gold standard (which had to be deferred), the theory implicit in Republican ideology was that all that was needed was to let business and life alone, and to harmonize the clashing claims of interest with as little loss as possible. For this task McKinley was ideally suited. His long professional career had given him an intuitive knowledge of the psychology of members of Congress. His natural kindliness and consideration had been developed by the need of a protectionist to conciliate everyone in order to attain his own ends. He met angrily insistent men with a smile at his office door, and sent them away beaming, often wearing a red carnation from the presidential desk. He did not pretend to know more than Congress or his party; to him, as to so many in his generation, the Nation and the Republican party seemed merged as one, and he felt that neither could be other than right. He did not surrender his mind to any of his advisers, not even to Hanna, and he could not easily delegate authority to his subordinates, but he rarely allowed himself to stand far in advance of the opinion of his constituents. The new Congress met in March 1897, and carried through at once the tariff measure for which business men were waiting, the Dingley Act (1897).

The choice of Sherman as head of the State Department, "indecent and alarming," the *Nation* thought (Jan. 31, 1897), could be justified only on the score of party balance. Sherman was feeble and failing, and by ignorance and temper had shown unfitness to meet the difficult diplomatic problems growing out of the Cuban insurrection. McKinley soon faced the alternatives of leading the United States into a war which he abhorred, or of fighting the politicians of his party who were yielding to popular clamor and egging war on. He settled the matter when he referred it to Congress, for Congress was incapable of anything but a declaration of war. It directed him, Apr. 20, 1898, to intervene in Cuba in order to establish Cuban independence, disclaiming an intent to aggrandise the power of the United States in so doing. In the short contest with Spain that resulted, "as his own Chief of Staff, McKinley carried on the war" (W. H. Taft, in *The National McKinley Birthplace Memorial,* 1918, p. 78). There was no alternative, for the War Department and the army as erected by law were inadequate, Secretary Alger [*q.v.*] lacked the qualifications of a successful war minister, and there was no available general on the active list upon whom he was willing to rely. In the navy, matters were not so bad, less because of virtue than because any navy, to go to sea at all, must have in time of peace much of the organization that is required in time of war. Secretary John D. Long [*q.v.*] was indifferent to technical matters; but his very indifference gave freedom to his assistant secretary, Theodore Roosevelt, who made an impression upon the training of the fleet and the selection of its commanders. The experiences of mobilization and the management of the army brought mortification to McKinley, while the details of operations occasioned controversies that might have been disastrous had the enemy possessed any capacity for resistance; but before the mind of the government had been adjusted to the fact of war it was turned to the policy of the peace, to the stipulations required for the tutelage of Cuba, and to the situation of that part of the Philippine Archipelago that lay helpless under Dewey's guns. Again McKinley, not desiring annexations and sincere in his philanthropic gesture towards Cuba, was the slave of his technique. When he instructed his commissioners to negotiate peace at Paris (Royal Cortissoz, *The Life of Whitelaw Reid,* 1921, II, p. 226), he was not ready to say whether the Philippines should be returned, released, or kept. At this crisis he turned, as always, to his conscience, for he was devout and earnest; and to his party, which could not well be wrong (J. F. Rhodes, *The McKinley and Roosevelt Administrations, 1897–1909,* 1922, p. 107). From the former he derived a sense of duty to the Filipinos, whom Spain could not recapture, and who lacked the experience in self-government necessary to survive alone in the tempestuous waters of the Far East. From the latter, as he toured the Middle West in the summer, he gathered opinions reminiscent of the traditional Western attitude that expansion was a natural experience. On Oct. 26 he cabled the commissioners to hold the Archipelago. He had once characterized Garfield's determination to decide each question upon its merits, apart from politics, as an "experiment . . . a perilous one" (*Congressional Record,* 49 Cong., 1 Sess., p. 764); he commended its courage without following its example.

Before the treaty was signed at Paris, the voters had strengthened the Republican majorities in both House and Senate, and prosperity had so weakened the lure of free silver as to permit the passage of a gold-standard bill (Mar. 14, 1900). With the return of courage to business had come a renewal of the trust movement, for which no policy was ready, though there is some reason to believe that had McKinley lived he might have turned a constructive imagination upon the problem of the trusts. Congress, in 1900, passed laws for the government of the new insular possessions, knowing that before these could operate their constitutionality would be tested by the opponents of expansion. There could be no delay in the reorganization of the army and the navy, and Elihu Root, who had succeeded Alger in the War Department, guided essential laws through Congress. Nor could there be indifference towards the erection of civil government in the Philippine Islands, whither William H. Taft was sent; or towards the speedy construction of a canal at the Isthmus. John Hay [*q.v.*] negotiated with Great Britain to get rid of the limitations set by the Clayton-Bulwer Treaty (1850), only to be dismayed by a new spirit of nationalism that prevented the ratification of his agreement. He would have resigned in chagrin, but McKinley bade him "bear the atmosphere of the hour" (W. R. Thayer, *The Life and Letters of John Hay,* 1915, II, pp. 226–28), and prepared to negotiate such a treaty as the party leaders in the Senate would approve. While Cuba was working out a constitution under the guiding hand of Leonard Wood [*q.v.*], it was suspected that the Cubans had forgotten their debt to the United States for their existence. Accordingly, there was slipped through as a rider to the Army Act of 1901 the Platt Amendment requiring Cuba to refrain from financial suicide and to concede to the United States a right to protect Cuban independence and good order. The legal beginnings of a new imperialism were laid down in this provision. It was necessary, too, to determine how to hold the Philippines without the use of force, and with this end in view John Hay in 1899 invited the European Powers with interests in Chinese waters to agree to a self-denial of special advantage and to adopt an "Open-Door" policy. Revolution in China soon occasioned a joint intervention which tested the sincerity of all adherents to the new doctrine. Whatever its inclination, the United States could no longer keep aloof from the international issues that were arousing ambitions and jealousies among the Powers of the world.

The campaign of 1900 was noisy but tame; the issue of imperialism which Bryan tried to raise proved less successful in arousing emotion than free silver had been. Had Hobart been living, he would doubtless have been renominated with McKinley (D. Magie, *Life of Garret Augustus Hobart,* 1910); his death brought the nomination for the vice-presidency to Gov. Theodore Roosevelt, for whom McKinley and Hanna had scant liking but who was now too prominent to be openly resisted. McKinley and Roosevelt won easily, and the new administration started Mar. 4, 1901, without a jolt. Its position was strengthened a few weeks later by the decision of the Supreme Court in the Insular Cases, which upheld what had been done respecting the islands and denied the anti-imperialists the constitutional prohibition they sought. A new period of booming prosperity was opening, and the Republican business interests had no fear of adverse interference by the government. There might have developed some concern lest the President should start upon a new course after he announced at Buffalo, Sept. 5, 1901, that "the period of exclusiveness is past," and suggested doubts as to the complete sufficiency of the tariff policy upon which his fame as statesman was grounded. But an anarchist, Leon F. Czolgosz, shot the President during a public reception on the afternoon of Sept. 6, and he died at Buffalo eight days later. On his lips at the end was the phrase "It is God's way. His will, not ours, be done." He believed in "the divinity of Christ and a recognition of Christianity as the mightiest factor in the world's civilization"; and from his youth he had been by conviction a member of the Methodist Episcopal Church. He was buried at Canton, where in 1907 his wife was laid beside him in a great memorial tomb; at Niles, his birthplace, another memorial to his memory was erected. His personal associates maintained for the rest of their lives an affectionate loyalty to his memory such as few American statesmen have inspired; but upon his death the United States passed out of an era in its history.

[The official biography, C. S. Olcott, *The Life of William McKinley* (1916), contains probably as much as can be said about McKinley's private life, for he was not given to expression by the pen and left no private papers of importance. Much of the office file of his administration is in the custody of George B. Cortelyou of New York, who was his secretary. The following are of some value: Thos. Beer, *Hanna* (1929); N. W. Stephenson, *Nelson W. Aldrich, A Leader in Am. Politics* (1930); H. H. Kohlsaat, *From McKinley to Harding: Personal Recollections of Our Presidents* (1923); T. B. Mott, *Myron T. Herrick, Friend of France; An Autobiographical Biography* (1929); C. W. Thompson, *Presidents I've Known and Two Near Presidents* (1929). None of these, however, adds much information to the facts of his early life that were already recorded in the campaign biographies of 1896. The best of these is R. P. Porter, *Life of William McKinley, Soldier, Lawyer, Statesman,* which had fifteen editions before the end of the year. There are no monographs of consequence. The obituaries, long and laudatory, drew their material from the campaign biographies.]

F. L. P.

McKINLY, JOHN (Feb. 24, 1721–Aug. 31, 1796), president of Delaware, was born in the north of Ireland, settled in Wilmington, Del., and began the practice of medicine. In 1747–48 he seems to have been lieutenant of militia and in 1756 was commissioned major in a militia regiment of New Castle County. In three successive years, 1757, 1758, and 1759, he was elected sheriff, and in 1759 he was also elected chief burgess of the borough of Wilmington for a year's term, being reëlected eleven times including the year 1776. Between 1761 and 1766 he was married to Jane Richardson, the twelfth child of John and Ann Richardson, English Friends living near Wilmington. Elected a member of the colonial Assembly in October 1771, he was still a member when, in October 1773, that body appointed a standing committee of correspondence of which he became one of the five members. As chairman of the New Castle County committee he presided over the meeting that, on Nov. 28, 1774, approved the "Association" recommended by the First Continental Congress and over the meeting that in December issued a call for the organization of a county militia the next month. In March 1775 he served on the committee of the Assembly that drew up the instructions for the delegates to the Second Continental Congress. In March 1775 he was chosen colonel of a regiment of the New Castle County militia. At a meeting of the Council of Safety, begun at Dover on Sept. 11, 1775, he was not only elected president of the council but also brigadier-general of the three battalions of New Castle County. In October 1776 he was elected a member of the first state legislature and, when that body assembled in the same month, was elected speaker of the lower house. Although the constitution provided for the election of a governor (called president) by the legislature, no executive was chosen during the fall session of the General Assembly. Instead, the two houses in joint session, in November 1776, elected a Council of Safety to exercise executive authority during the next recess of the General Assembly. He was included in the membership of this council and, when it organized, was chosen its president.

At the following session of the General Assembly he was chosen, in February 1777, president and commander-in-chief of Delaware for a term of three years. He was destined to exercise the authority of the office only a few months, for on the second night after the Battle of the Brandywine several British regiments occupied Wilmington and captured him. He was removed to Philadelphia, kept a prisoner during the British occupation of that city, and then taken to New York. Paroled by General Clinton in August 1778, he proceeded to Philadelphia to obtain the consent of Congress to his exchange for William Franklin, late governor of New Jersey.

In September he returned to Wilmington, resumed the practice of medicine, and took no further part in politics. He assisted in founding the first medical society of Delaware in 1789 and served for a number of years as trustee of the First Presbyterian Church in Wilmington.

[Records of the borough of Wilmington and letters of McKinly in possession of the Hist. Soc. of Del., Wilmington; colonial and state records and letters in Public Archives at Dover; letters from and to McKinly in N. Y. Pub. Lib., Lib. of Hist. Soc. of Pa., Lib. of Cong., and in the private collection of Judge Richard S. Rodney, New Castle, Del.; Minutes of the Privy Council in Lib. of Cong., esp. vol. I, pp 43, 69; *Delaware Archives*, vols. I–III (1911–19); W. T. Read, *Life and Correspondence of George Read* (1870); J. T. Scharf, *Hist. of Del.* (1888), vol. I; *Biog. and Geneal. Hist. of Del.* (1899), vol. I; H. C. Conrad, *Hist. of the State of Del.* (1908), vols. I, III; Richard Richardson, *The Geneal. of the Richardson Family of Del.*, n.d.] G. H. R.

McKINSTRY, ALEXANDER (Mar. 7, 1822–Oct. 9, 1879), lawyer, Confederate soldier, lieutenant-governor of Alabama, was born at Augusta, Ga., the son of Alexander and Elizabeth (Thompson) McKinstry. His father was of Scotch-Irish descent, the great-grandson of Rev. John McKinstry who came from County Antrim, Ireland, to New England in 1718, settling in Connecticut in 1728. Orphaned before he was fourteen, Alexander went to Mobile, Ala., where he had relatives. There he served as clerk in a drugstore, read law in the office of John A. Campbell, and was admitted to the bar when he was twenty-three. He immediately began the practice of his profession and at the same time began to take an active part in local politics. Before 1860 he had held various city and county offices.

Although he was opposed to secession, he accepted the decision of the majority in the state when in January 1861 Alabama withdrew from the Union. Joining the Confederate army, he was commissioned colonel and assigned to the 32nd Regiment of Alabama Infantry when it was organized at Mobile in 1862. This regiment was attached to the Army of Tennessee under Gen. N. B. Forrest. McKinstry was mentioned in dispatches for able service in the field at Bridgeport, Ala., and Battle Creek, Tenn., Aug. 27, 1862, and was in command in Chattanooga in September and October. The following year he was on detached service, acting as provost marshal-general to the Army of Tennessee. On Apr. 6, 1864, he was made colonel of cavalry and assigned to serve on the court of military justice of Forrest's division. He was presiding judge of this court until the end of the war.

Paroled at Gainesville, Ala., May 9, 1865, McKinstry returned to Mobile and resumed the practice of his profession. He continued to take an active interest in politics, identifying himself with the Radical party which was then being formed in the state to oppose the Democratic party. Elected to the state legislature in 1865 and again in 1867, he was chairman of the judiciary committee and largely instrumental in securing the adoption of the Alabama Code of 1867 by the legislature. In 1872 he was elected lieutenant-governor of the state. By virtue of this office, created by the constitutional convention of 1867, he became presiding officer of the state Senate at a critical point in the reconstruction struggle. The Democrats had won a majority in both houses of the legislature, although the Radicals had succeeded in electing their candidates for governor and lieutenant-governor. This situation was particularly displeasing to the Radicals because they were anxious to send one of their number to the United States Senate and it fell to the legislature to elect him in joint session. It was McKinstry who, by the exercise of his authority as presiding officer of the Senate, enabled the Radical group to overcome the Democratic majority and send their candidate to Washington. With the return of the Democrats to power in 1874, McKinstry retired from politics. He died at Mobile in 1879. On Mar. 20, 1845, he had married Virginia Thompson Dade of Mobile, descendant of an old Virginia family; of their eleven children, five lived to maturity.

[T. M. Owen, *Hist. of Ala. and Dict. of Ala. Biog.* (1921), vol. IV; W. L. Fleming, *Civil War and Reconstruction in Ala.* (1905); Wm. Willis, *Geneal. of the McKinstry Family* (1858); *Daily Register* (Mobile, Ala.), Oct. 10, 1879; *War of the Rebellion: Official Records (Army)*.] H. F.

McKINSTRY, ELISHA WILLIAMS (Apr. 11, 1825–Nov. 1, 1901), California jurist, was born in Detroit, Mich., the seventh and youngest child of David Charles and Nancy Whiting (Backus) McKinstry. His great-grandfather, Capt. John McKinstry, had come to America from Armagh, Ireland, in 1740, settling first in Boston and later in Londonderry, N. H.; his grandfather, Charles, served as an officer with the New York troops in the Revolution; through his mother he was descended from Pilgrim ancestors. He was educated in Michigan and New York and at Kenyon College, Gambier, Ohio, and in 1847 was admitted to the bar in New York. The California gold rush of 1849 turned his eyes to the West, however, and he took passage on the S. S. *Panama*, one of the first steamers of the newly organized Pacific Mail Steamship Company, and sailed with her on her maiden voyage around the Horn, arriving in San Francisco June 4, 1849. By 1850 he had opened a law office in Sacramento and was chosen to represent that district in the lower branch of the first California legislature. A year later he removed to Napa, where in the fall of 1852 he again entered public service with his election to the post of district judge for Napa and adjoining counties. He was reëlected in 1858 and served until 1862, when he resigned to become candidate on the Democratic ticket for the lieutenant-governorship. He was defeated, however, and in 1863 moved to Nevada, where in 1864 he was unsuccessful candidate for the position of justice of the supreme court.

After several years' residence in Nevada, he returned to San Francisco (1867), where, as a Democrat, he was elected county judge and served in that capacity from Jan. 1, 1868, until his election as judge of the twelfth district court in October 1869. Four years later, he was chosen justice of the supreme court, in the last two instances having won the election on an Independent ticket. After the reorganization of the supreme court under the new constitution of 1879 he was reëlected and drew a term of eleven years. During his unusually long service on the supreme bench he dealt with some of the most important cases in California's judicial history, among them being the local option case of 1874 (*Ex Parte Wall*, 48 *Cal.*, 279), in which he delivered the opinion of the court, and the great controversy over water-rights, waged in 1886, known officially as the case of *Lux* vs. *Haggin* (69 *Cal.*, 255). On Oct. 1, 1888, he resigned from the bench to become professor of municipal law in Hastings' College of the Law, San Francisco. In 1890 he resumed private practice and was later joined by his son, James C. McKinstry. In 1896, they became members of the firm of Stanly, McKinstry, Bradley & McKinstry, from which in 1899 Stanly was removed by death. McKinstry had an enviable reputation as one of the ablest members of the San Francisco bar. He was a member of the Sons of the American Revolution and in 1900–01 was president of the Society of California Pioneers.

On July 27, 1863, at Marysville, Cal., he had married Annie L. Hedges, and four children were born to them. His death came suddenly at San José, Cal., where he was seeking recuperation in the warmer climate of the Santa Clara Valley.

[Wm. Willis, *Geneal. of the McKinstry Family* (1858); *New-Eng. Hist. and Geneal. Reg.*, Jan. 1859; O. T. Shuck, *Hist. of the Bench and Bar of Cal.* (1901); *San Francisco Chronicle*, Nov. 2, 1901.]

R. G. C—d.

McKNIGHT, ROBERT (*c.* 1789–March 1846), Santa Fé trader, miner, was born in Augusta County, Va., the son of Timothy and Eleanor (Griffin) McKnight. In 1809 he went to St. Louis and joined his brother John and Thomas Brady in a mercantile venture. In May 1812, Robert McKnight and nine others left St. Louis for Santa Fé on a trading expedition. This enterprise was designed to carry goods easy of transport, and expected to derive great profit under the monopolistic conditions then existing in Santa Fé. The descriptions given by Capt. Zebulon M. Pike [*q.v.*] of rich prospects at Santa Fé were attracting general notice to that trade. The McKnight party, greatly enthusiastic, started on their adventure without passports and without arms other than those for defense against the Indians. They proceeded believing that the declaration of independence by Hidalgo, in 1810, had completely removed the previous requirement of a special permit from the Spanish government in cases of foreign intercourse. Unfortunately, they had not learned of the execution of Hidalgo and the restoration of the Royalists, who were suspicious of all foreigners, particularly Americans, and imposed many hardships upon them.

When McKnight and his companions arrived at Santa Fé, they were seized as spies, and their goods confiscated. The captives, destined to be detained nine years, were distributed among several prisons, some being sent to Chihuahua and others to Durango. In 1815, Edward Hempstead, Congressional delegate from Missouri, laid their case before the State Department, but nothing was done in their behalf until Feb. 8, 1817, when Secretary Monroe began an exchange of diplomatic letters with the Spanish minister. John Scott, of Missouri, brought up the case again the following December, and the President addressed a request to the Mexican government for the return of the prisoners, but they were not returned. Although in 1819 a treaty of amity was made between the United States and Mexico, no condition was imposed as to the release of these men, and not until 1821 was their imprisonment ended. McKnight never forgave his native land for this seeming neglect.

He returned to St. Louis in 1822 with his brother John, who had gone to Durango to effect his release. In the fall of that year, Robert and John McKnight and eight others left for the Comanche country on a trading expedition. They joined Thomas James [*q.v.*] and his party of twelve men, by prearrangement, at the mouth of the Canadian River. This expedition was a failure, however; John McKnight was reported killed by the Indians, and Robert McKnight returned to St. Louis in 1824. In the meantime, and thereafter, he sought redress for the wrongs he had suffered in Mexico, but without avail. Thoroughly disgusted, he renounced his allegiance to the United States, and returned to Mexico, where he spent his remaining years. By his wife, a Spanish lady whom he married at Chihuahua, he had two daughters, and a son who died in early youth. In 1828 he gained possession of a rich copper mine, known as Santa Rita del Cobre, in northern Chihuahua. Here he made a fortune, but in 1846 his mining operations were broken up by the Apache Indians. James describes McKnight as very impulsive, courageous, and unyielding in the midst of danger, but lacking that coolness and presence of mind best adapted to leadership.

[Thomas James, *Three Years Among the Indians and Mexicans* (1916), ed. by W. B. Douglas; *Detroit Gazette*, July 23, 1819; *Am. State Papers, Foreign Relations*, IV (1834), 207–09; *House Ex. Doc. 41*, 30 Cong., 1 Sess., p. 58; *Weekly Reveille* (St. Louis), May 18, Aug. 31, 1846; *Santa Fé Republican*, Nov. 20, 1847; D. C. Peters, *The Life and Adventures of Kit Carson* (1858); "The Personal Narrative of James O. Pattie," in R. G. Thwaites, *Early Western Travels*, XVIII (1905), 86, 350; Grant Foreman, *Indians and Pioneers* (1930); McKnight Family History, MSS. in Mo. Hist. Soc.] S. M. D.

MACKUBIN, FLORENCE (May 19, 1861–Feb. 2, 1918), portrait and miniature painter, was born in Florence, Italy, where her parents were living temporarily. Her father, Charles Nicholas Mackubin, and her mother Ellen (Fay), were members of old well-known Maryland families; one of her grandfathers had served as treasurer of the Western Shore in 1839. Developing early in life a talent for drawing and painting, she was placed under the masters of Florence and Nice, later studying in Munich with Herterrich and with Julius Rolshoven and Louis Deschamps in Paris. She also studied miniature painting in Paris with Jeanne Devina. She became thoroughly familiar with the Italian, French, and German languages and read widely in the literature of these countries. Upon returning to America she adopted Baltimore as her home and took a keen interest in its affairs.

Under a commission from the Governor and Board of Public Works of the State of Maryland she made a copy of Van Dyck's portrait of Queen Henrietta Maria, after whom the state of Maryland was named, for the State House at Annapolis. While engaged in this work at Warwick Castle she was asked by Lady Warwick to paint her portrait. She made copies of the portraits of George and Cecilius Calvert, the first and second lords Baltimore, under a special commission from the Baltimore Club. The originals hang in Windlestone Hall, the seat of Sir William Eden at Windlestone, England. She painted portraits and miniatures of several distinguished men of Maryland; among them a portrait of Gov. Lloyd Lowndes for the Maryland State House at Annapolis, a portrait of Prof. Basil L. Gildersleeve for the University of Virginia, which is considered one of her best; another of Prof. Marshall Elliott for the Johns Hopkins University, Baltimore. At the Louisiana Purchase Exposition in St. Louis she exhibited an oil portrait of Cardinal Gibbons which was later taken to the Maryland Historical Society. While staying at her summer home, "Oriole Cottage," St. Andrews, New Brunswick, she painted portraits of several prominent Canadians, among them Sir William Van Horne. She exhibited at the World's Columbian Exposition, Chicago, in 1893; in Paris in 1900, Buffalo in 1901, Charleston in 1902, and St. Louis in 1904. She received a number of awards, including a bronze medal and diploma for miniatures at the Tennessee Exposition in 1897. A number of her miniatures are in the Walters Gallery, Baltimore. Her work won recognition not only in Baltimore but elsewhere for its exquisite quality. Residing in Europe during the early part of the World War, she wrote a number of letters to the Baltimore *Sun* on the war, full always of her Americanism in spite of long periods spent abroad. She was a member of the Maryland Association Opposed to Women Suffrage, and expressed her views on several occasions. She died in Baltimore.

[A portrait miniature of Florence Mackubin appears in the *Century Magazine*, Oct. 1900. See also *Who's Who in America*, 1918–19; *Am. Art Annual*, vol. XV (1918); *Sun* (Baltimore), Feb. 4, 1918; *Baltimore American*, Feb. 3, 1918; *Am. Art News*, Feb. 9, 1918; *Maryland Women* (1931).] H. W.

McLANE, ALLAN (Aug. 8, 1746–May 22, 1829), Revolutionary soldier, father of Louis McLane [*q.v.*], was born in Philadelphia, as he wrote in his diary, of parents "of the midling grade," whose names he failed to set down. Whatever their station in life, his father accumulated an ample property which, on his death in 1775, he left to his son. At the age of twenty-one Allan McLane visited Europe, and several years after his return, in 1769, he married Rebecca Wells, daughter of the sheriff of Kent County, Del. In 1774 he settled in Kent County, near Smyrna. At the outbreak of the Revolution he hastened to aid the Virginians against Lord Dunmore, fighting at Great Bridge and about Norfolk. Returning North, he was commissioned adjutant (Sept. 11, 1775) in Cæsar Rodney's regiment of volunteers, which saw active service at Long Island. When Col. John Patton's Additional Continental Regiment was created, McLane was made one of its captains (January 1777), and in this capacity proved himself an independent and dashing officer of the most gallant type. During the British occupation of Philadelphia he commanded a body of light troops upon the lines for general reconnoitering purposes, but chiefly as "market stoppers," to prevent the smuggling of provisions into the city by Loyalists. Once while scouting for a reconnoitering expedition of Lafayette's he discovered that the enemy were about to surround the General. Acting with celerity, he warned him in time to prevent his capture. When the British evacuated Philadelphia, McLane, being anxious about his properties, and by special permission from Washington, was the first to enter the city. His exceptional scouting abilities were utilized by Benedict Arnold, who was given command in Philadelphia, to follow the enemy movements before and after the battle of Monmouth. In his contacts with Arnold, McLane came to doubt that officer's patriotism, but was apparently unable to convince Washington of the truth of his charges (McHenry to McLane, June 3, 1778, Washington Papers, Library of Congress; W. S. Stryker, *The Battle of Monmouth,* 1927, pp. 58, 64, 236; McLane Papers, see under June 13, 1778).

When Colonel Patton's regiment was disbanded in June 1779, McLane, at his own and Major Henry Lee's request, was given command of the dismounted dragoons in Lee's partisan corps. One of his first assignments under Lee was to reconnoiter the approaches to Stony Point in order to discover the best route for Wayne's celebrated attack (H. P. Johnston, *The Storming of Stony Point,* 1900, pp. 62, 74). The association which both McLane and Lee seemed to desire soon ended in jealousy and discord. Lee's corps, augmented, became the famous "Lee's Legion" and was dispatched South to join Greene, but McLane was detached to purchase supplies in Maryland while a captain, his junior in the same corps, was raised to a majority. McLane wrote in strong terms to Lee, threatening to resign. The letter was forwarded to Washington, who praised McLane highly, saying that he deserved much, but stated that scores of other officers in the army with longer Continental service than McLane also deserved promotion. McLane was then retired on half-pay. Although the subject was a source of bitterness to him for the remainder of his life, he prevailed upon Washington to attach him to Steuben's command in Virginia, which he joined the last of February. In the closing phase of the war his reconnoitering ability was displayed in acquainting the Comte de Grasse and Washington of the movements of the enemy fleet near the Chesapeake.

After the Revolution, his patrimony swallowed up by his war debts, he entered into a trading venture on the Delaware River with Robert Morris [*q.v.*], and in September 1789 was appointed marshal of Delaware, which office was exchanged in 1797 for the more lucrative post of collector of Wilmington. Intercession of powerful friends with Jefferson tided him over the pressure of Republicans for his office in 1801, and he retained the place until his death (*Annual Report of the American Historical Association for the Year 1913,* 1915, II, 128–29; Jefferson Papers, Library of Congress). He also held various state offices, being member of the Delaware House of Representatives in 1785 and in 1791, when he was chosen speaker; member of the Privy Council in 1788; and justice of the peace in 1793. During the War of 1812 he was in charge of the defenses of Wilmington.

[Three bound volumes of letters and papers of McLane, including autobiographical notes, completely calendared, are in the N. Y. Hist. Soc.; about twenty letters of, to, or about McLane are in the Washington Papers, Lib. of Cong. Published sources include W. G. Whitely, "The Revolutionary Soldiers of Delaware," *Papers of the Hist. Soc. of Del.*, No. XIV (1896); H. H. Bellas, "A History of the Delaware State Society of the Cincinnati," *Ibid.*, No. XIII (1895); T. W. Bean, *Washington at Valley Forge* (1876); F. B. Heitman, *Hist. Reg. of Officers of the Continental Army* (1893); H. C. Conrad, *Hist. of the State of Del.* (3 vols., 1908); *Del. Gazette* (Wilmington), May 29, 1829. Signatures in McLane's MSS. give the spelling "Allan."]

C. W. G.

McLANE, LOUIS (May 28, 1786–Oct. 7, 1857), cabinet officer, diplomat, son of Allan [*q.v.*] and Rebecca (Wells) McLane, was born in Smyrna, Del. At the age of twelve he became a midshipman in the navy and cruised for a year on the *Philadelphia* under Commodore Stephen Decatur. He left the navy in 1801, however, and entered Newark College, Delaware, but apparently abandoned his course without taking a degree and began to read law under the direction of James A. Bayard [*q.v.*]. From this preceptor he seems to have acquired federalistic principles which were never fully eradicated. Admitted to the bar in 1807, he practised law in Smyrna, and in 1812 married Catherine Mary, eldest daughter of Robert Milligan.

McLane's political career began in 1817 when he entered the lower house of Congress as a Jeffersonian Republican. He remained for ten years in this branch and was then transferred to the Senate. As a legislator he was sometimes a political non-conformist. Usually he upheld the party program, but he invariably championed the cause of the Bank of the United States. In 1818 he opposed an investigation of its discounts, and he denied the power of Congress to interfere with the operations of the bank. Although he was opposed to slavery, he denied the power of Congress to exclude Missouri from the Union because her constitution permitted slavery; and when the legislature of Delaware instructed him to vote against admission, he refused to obey, on the federalistic ground that he was an officer of the Union and not the agent of his state.

In 1824 he was an ardent supporter of Crawford, and when the presidential election devolved upon the House of Representatives he remarked that "they might as well think of turning the Capitol upside down as of persuading him to vote for Jackson" (E. S. Brown, *The Missouri Compromises and Presidential Politics,* 1926, p. 136). Four years later, however, he supported Jackson and was rewarded by being offered first the position of attorney-general and second, that of minister to England. Resigning from the Senate (1829), he accepted the latter post with reluctance, in order, as he said, "to preserve my chance for what I frankly tell you would make me happier than any other honor—the Bench" (Van Buren, *post,* p. 258). While in London his principal achievement was an agreement regarding trade with the West Indies. In 1831 he was recalled and made secretary of the treasury, because Jackson wished the diplomatic post for Van Buren. McLane's views on finance did not accord with those of the President. He urged Congress to recharter the Bank of the United States, although it was well known that the President was opposed to such action. Jackson overlooked this defection and his friends talked of running McLane for vice-president in 1832; but when the Senate refused to ratify Van Buren's diplomatic appointment, Jackson decided to make Van Buren the presiding officer of the body which had sought to ruin him politically.

Meanwhile McLane's position in the Treasury Department became very uncomfortable when the President, in 1832, vetoed the bill to recharter the bank. His sympathies were with that institution, but he could not hope for the coveted place on the bench unless he could retain Jackson's good will until the first vacancy should occur. He therefore formulated a plan whereby Edward Livingston was to be sent to France, he himself was to succeed to the Department of State and W. J. Duane [*q.v.*] was to take the Treasury portfolio (Van Buren, p. 593). His wishes were gratified in 1833, but within a few months Jackson dismissed Duane for refusing to remove the government deposits from the United States Bank and appointed Roger Brooke Taney [*q.v.*] in his place. Taney removed the deposits, but the Senate refused to confirm his appointment and the "martyred secretary" had prior claim to the first vacant seat on the supreme bench. Foreseeing the success of his rival and the blasting of his own hopes, McLane began to talk of resigning his portfolio and did so when he was overruled on questions concerning the French spoliations.

The principal diplomatic questions which demanded his attention as secretary of state (May 29, 1833–June 30, 1834) were those with Mexico regarding claims and boundaries; with Great Britain on the subject of the Northeast Boundary; and with France concerning spoliation claims. With Mexico he was firm but reasonable. With Great Britain he could accomplish nothing because the views of the two governments were at that time irreconcilable. On the spoliation claims he took a firm stand, and when the French Chambers refused to appropriate the money to pay the claims, he advised the president to ask Congress for authority to issue letters of marque and reprisal against French shipping, but Jackson was dissuaded by Taney and Van Buren from taking so drastic an action. McLane soon resigned from the cabinet in the hope, as Van Buren believed, of becoming the anti-administration candidate for the presidency at the next election (Van Buren, p. 616). His greatest achievement was his introduction of orderly procedure into the operations of the department (Gaillard Hunt, *The Department of State,* 1914, pp. 203–18). He had undoubted ability, but ambition and jealousy ended abruptly what might have been a successful diplomatic career.

After leaving the cabinet, McLane resided for a time in New York, where he was president of the Morris Canal & Banking Company. In 1837 he moved to Baltimore, tempted by what was then considered to be a munificent salary, $4,000 yearly, to accept the presidency of the Baltimore & Ohio Railroad Company, a position which he held for ten years. While still in the employ of this company he was sent as United States minister to England by President Polk to conduct negotiations on the Oregon question (June 1845–August 1846). When Buchanan expressed a wish to relinquish his portfolio for a place on the supreme bench Polk planned to make McLane secretary of state, but the vacillating Buchanan changed his mind and there was no vacancy in that department. McLane retired from the presidency of the railroad in 1847, and a year later refused to go to Mexico as one of the commissioners to procure the ratification of the Treaty of Guadalupe Hidalgo. He performed his last public service as a member of the Maryland constitutional convention of 1850, and died in Baltimore seven years later. Robert Milligan McLane [*q.v.*], his son, attained some distinction in politics and diplomacy.

Louis McLane's principal weakness was his reluctance to cooperate with his fellows. Unless he could dominate, he would refuse to "play the game." His greatest ambition was to be a distinguished jurist; but Jackson doubtless rendered him a service by not elevating him to the bench, for his temperament was far from being judicial. He gave promise as a diplomat, but his precipitate resignation from the cabinet deprived him of an opportunity to demonstrate his abilities in this field of action. He succeeded best as an executive. As such, he could give rather than receive orders, and he was more at liberty to formulate his own plans. As an executive he was capable and systematic. He was an enemy of waste, whether of money or time, and conducted any enterprise entrusted to him with order and efficiency.

[Sketch by E. I. McCormac in S. F. Bemis, *The Am. Secretaries of State and Their Diplomacy,* vol. IV (1928); "The Autobiography of Martin Van Buren," *Ann. Report Am. Hist. Asso. for . . . 1918,* vol. II (1920); J. T. Scharf, *Hist. of Del.* (1888); Beckles Willson, *America's Ambassadors to England* (1928); Edward Hungerford, *The Story of the Baltimore and Ohio Railroad* (1928); *Baltimore American and Commercial Advertiser,* Oct. 9, 1857.] E. I. McC.

McLANE, ROBERT MILLIGAN (June 23, 1815–Apr. 16, 1898), lawyer, congressman, diplomat, was born in Wilmington, Del., the son of Louis McLane [*q.v.*] and his wife, Catherine Mary Milligan of Cecil County, Md. He received his general education in a Wilmington academy, St. Mary's Academy in Baltimore, and the Collège Bourbon, Paris, which he attended for a year while his father was United States minister to England. In 1833 he entered the United States Military Academy, from which he was graduated in 1837. He served in Florida in the Seminole War and in 1838 was with the troops sent to control the Cherokees in connection with their transfer to the region west of the Mississippi. Following this duty, as a member of a corps of topographical engineers he aided in a military survey of the northern lakes. In 1841 he was sent to Europe to study dikes and drainage, and was occupied with the subject for some time in Italy. In the same year he married Georgine Urquhart, in Paris.

McLane did not like military life, and during his winters he studied law in Washington. He was admitted to the bar of the District of Columbia in 1840 and to that of Baltimore in 1843. In the latter year he resigned his commission and settled in Baltimore, where he began the practice of his new profession, quickly gaining distinction. Early in 1851 he went to California as counsel in a contest over possession of the rich quicksilver mines of New Almaden, in the Santa Clara Valley. While in the West he secured other important cases. He was retained by Commodore Vanderbilt in the dispute over possession of the steamship *Pacific* and of the transit route across Nicaragua, and won both cases for his client. For some years, in the fifties and sixties, he was counsel for the Western Pacific Railroad Company, a forerunner of the Central Pacific.

The competence derived from his professional success enabled McLane to devote considerable time to politics, in which, as a Democrat, he began to be active soon after moving to Baltimore. In 1845 he was elected to the Maryland House of Delegates, where he worked hard for the financial reform of the state, then bankrupt. In 1847 he won a seat in the national House of Representatives, and was reëlected in 1849. In Congress he supported and defended Polk in connection with the war with Mexico. During his second term he was chairman of the committee on commerce and stood for tariff for revenue, with protection an incident. A moderate on the slavery question, he favored the compromise measures of 1850, contending that the admission of California as a free state was a proper offset to the admission of Texas as a slave state.

In 1853 he was made United States commissioner to China and accredited also to Japan, Siam, Korea, and Cochin-China. Shortly after he reached Hong-Kong early in 1854 he tried, in cooperation with the diplomatic agents of Great Britain and France, to secure a renewal of the existing commercial treaty with China; but the effort proved futile at this time. Suffering from poor health and discouraged by the situation, in December 1854 he sailed for the United States on sick leave, and resigned his post when he reached Paris.

In 1859 President Buchanan named him minister to Mexico, which was torn by revolutionary factions, with instructions to recognize the Juárez government, then at Vera Cruz, if the extent of its authority seemed to justify such action. McLane recognized Juárez, and labored, but in vain, to make peace between the warring factions. In December 1859 he signed with the Juárez government a treaty of transit and commerce and a convention to enforce treaty stipulations. By request, he went to Washington to explain the measures before the Senate committee on foreign relations, but neither arrangement was ratified by the Senate, and the imminence of civil war at home made him decide not to return to Mexico.

After the Civil War had opened he was a member of the Maryland committee which conferred with President Lincoln regarding the alleged unconstitutional procedure of the Federal authorities in Maryland. For some time following he was chiefly occupied with his law practice, but in 1876 he resumed activity in politics and was a Maryland delegate to the convention which nominated Tilden. The following year he was elected to the state Senate, but resigned in 1878 to take a seat in the national House of Representatives, to which he was reëlected in 1880. In Congress he was especially active in trying to secure the reduction of existing tariffs and endeavoring to bring about laws to prevent the adulteration of foods. He was elected governor of Maryland in 1883, and in that capacity strove to better the conditions of labor, securing the passage of laws in the interest of working women and children. His term was short, however, for he resigned in March 1885, to become minister to France under President Cleveland. In this new office, the last public position that he filled, the most serious question with which he had to deal concerned the rights of naturalized citizens of the United States, born in France, from whom the French authorities tried to exact military service. After being displaced following the election of Harrison, he continued to reside in Paris, where he died.

[McLane's *Reminiscences, 1827–1897* (privately printed, 1903) is the best single authority and forms the basis of the sketch in H. E. Buchholz, *Governors of Md.* (1908). See also G. W. Cullum, *Biog Reg. . . . U. S. Mil. Acad.* (3rd ed., 1891), vol. I; Beckles Willson, *America's Ambassadors to France* (1928); J. J. Conway, *Footprints of Famous Americans in Paris* (1912); *Baltimore Past and Present* (1871); *Foreign Relations of the U. S.*, 1885–89; *N. Y. Herald*, Apr. 17, 1898; Baltimore *Sun*, Apr. 18, 1898.] M. W. W.

McLAREN, WILLIAM EDWARD (Dec. 13, 1831–Feb. 19, 1905), the third bishop of Illinois, and leader of the High-Church party in the Protestant Episcopal Church, was born in Geneva, N. Y., the son of the Rev. John F. McLaren, a Presbyterian clergyman. After graduating from Jefferson College (now Washington and Jefferson), at Washington, Pa., in 1851, he taught for one year and then from 1852 to 1857 was engaged in journalistic work in Cleveland and Pittsburgh. During the years 1857–60 he took a theological course in the Presbyterian Theological Seminary in Pittsburgh with the purpose of becoming a missionary in China. Ordained by the Presbytery of Allegheny City, Pa., in the year of his graduation, he was sent by the Presbyterian Board of Foreign Missions to Bogotá, South America, remaining there a year and a half, until an impairment to health forced him to return to the United States. After acting as assistant minister in the Second Presbyterian Church at Pittsburgh for a few months he was called to the pastorate of the Second Presbyterian Church in Peoria, Ill., where he remained until 1867. In that year he became pastor of the Westminster Presbyterian Church in Detroit, Mich. It was during his ministry in Detroit that he began to question some of the Presbyterian doctrines. He undertook a careful study of the doctrine and worship of the Episcopal Church and was particularly attracted by its sacramental emphasis, as set forth in its Book of Common Prayer and by its leading theologians. Convinced that he should change his ecclesiastical allegiance, he resigned his pastorate and was confirmed at St. John's Church, Detroit. On July 29, 1872, he was ordained to the diaconate by Bishop McCoskry at St. John's and on Oct. 20 at the same place he was ordained by McCoskry to the priesthood.

Following his ordination McLaren received a call to the rectorship of Trinity Church, Cleveland, Ohio. He accepted and served until his election to the episcopate by the Diocese of Illinois in 1875. He was consecrated at the Cathedral Church of SS. Peter and Paul, Chicago, Dec. 8, 1875. Two years after his consecration the agitation to divide the Diocese of Illinois, owing to its growth in population, resulted in the establishment of two new sees, those of Quincy and Springfield. McLaren continued as head of the old diocese, the name of which was changed to the Diocese of Chicago in 1883. He was a gifted executive. In 1881 he founded the Western Theological Seminary in Chicago, which has had a distinguished record as a theological training school in the Episcopal Church, and in 1885 he founded at Sycamore, Ill., Waterman Hall, a school for girls. He became president of the board of trustees of these two institutions, and in addition held the same position in Racine College and at St. Mary's School at Knoxville, Ill. He was also known as a scholar, linguist, and writer, and was a convincing preacher. He possessed marked judicial capacities, which, in combination with his other qualifications, resulted in bringing his jurisdiction into prominence as a leading diocese of the Episcopal Church. It was he who called the first diocesan "retreat" known to the Episcopal Church in this country, thereby establishing a custom which has become increasingly common, adopted by all parties in the church. His writings include *Catholic Dogma: The Antidote of Doubt* (1883) in which he set forth arguments for the so-called "Catholic position"; *Analysis of Pantheism* (1885); occasional sermons, addresses, and charges, and a few ventures in poetry.

[W. S. Perry, *The Episcopate in America* (1895); H. G. Batterson, *A Sketch-book of the Am. Episcopate* (1878); *Biog. and Hist. Cat. of Washington and Jefferson Coll.* (1902); the *Churchman*, Feb. 25, 1905; *Chicago Tribune*, Feb. 20, 1905.] G. E. S.

McLAUGHLIN, HUGH (Apr. 2, 1826?–Dec. 7, 1904), political boss, was born in Brooklyn, N. Y., the son of Hugh McLaughlin, a poor Irish immigrant. He received practically no formal education. At an early age he went to work at rope-making, then handled barrels on the docks, and later ran a fish stand for several years. In 1849 he became a lieutenant of Henry C. Murphy, a local boss, in 1853 attended his first Democratic state convention, and in 1855, as a result of political activity, became master foreman of civilian labor at the Brooklyn navy yard. Here he judiciously disposed of jobs that he controlled and gradually built up a considerable following. Having purchased the "White House," a well-known saloon, he met his followers there until he emerged as boss of the Brooklyn Democracy and established political headquarters on Willoughby Street. In 1860 he was defeated for sheriff of Kings County and sat as a delegate in the National Democratic Convention. The next year he was elected county register, an office that he held, with the exception of three years, until 1873. From 1862 until 1903 he controlled the Brooklyn Democracy, sometimes being absolutely dominant but rather frequently encountering defeat and enjoying only partial control. During this period he gathered around himself a political ring composed of an elder sister, "Aunt Nancy," a nephew, Hugh, and a changeable group of outsiders, among whom W. C. Kingsley, Alexander McCue, solicitor of the treasury and assistant treasurer of the United States under Cleveland, Thomas Kinsella, W. C. Fowler, and Judge Fred Massey stood out. Although definitely preferring local politics to state or national, he maintained cordial relations with Horatio Seymour, Samuel J. Tilden, Grover Cleveland, and especially with David B. Hill. In 1879 and again in 1881 he led the Brooklyn delegation to the state convention. His most successful years in Brooklyn politics were the years 1886 to 1894. In 1881 he had to face a serious revolt led by Thomas Kinsella and handed in one of his famous resignations as boss—there were three altogether. During the years following 1893 Judge William J. Gaynor, John Y. Kane, Patrick McCarren, and Charles F. Murphy proved thorns in the flesh. "Commissioner" Murphy, of Tammany Hall, desiring to control the political affairs of the entire city of which Brooklyn had become a part, inspired McCarren to declare war on McLaughlin and caused the latter's retirement in 1903.

In 1862 McLaughlin married Sarah Ellen Kays, daughter of a Dutch farmer of New Jersey. They had four children. He lived simply and regularly, read the newspapers faithfully, greatly enjoyed the theatre, spoke rarely but fluently, and was unceasingly active, even whittling, and soaking stamps off old letters. Although apparently mild and quiet, he was actually stubborn, stern, and exacting. He devoted himself to fishing, hunting, and fancy dogs, spending from one to six months each year fishing from Maine to Florida and hunting in the Adirondacks. In spite of few visible business connections he had a shrewd business head, particularly in the field of real estate, and accumulated a fortune of almost three million dollars. Both he and his wife gave generously to hospitals, orphanages, and to poor Irish folks, and they were unusually active in the Roman Catholic Church. Shortly before his death he presented Saint James' procathedral with a $15,000 marble altar.

[Harold Zink, *City Bosses in the United States* (1930); *Brooklyn Citizen*, Dec. 8, 1904; *Brooklyn Daily Eagle*, Dec. 8, 1904.] H. Z.

McLAUGHLIN, JAMES (Feb. 12, 1842–July 28, 1923), agent and inspector in the Indian service, was of Scotch-Irish ancestry, the son of Felix and Mary (Prince) McLaughlin, and was born in Avonmere, Ontario. He was educated in the common schools. In 1863 he went to Minnesota, where for eight years he was variously employed. He was married, on Jan. 28, 1864, to Mary Louise Buisson, of French, Scotch, and Sioux ancestry. On July 1, 1871, he entered the United States Indian service as the assistant agent, under Maj. W. H. Forbes, of the newly established Devils Lake Agency, at Fort Totten, in the present North Dakota. Five years later, on the death of Forbes, he was made agent. While in this post he succeeded in abolishing the savagely cruel sun dance of the Sioux. His work attracted official attention, and in the fall of 1881 he was transferred to the important Standing Rock Agency, at Fort Yates, on the Missouri. Here he had the management of some 6,000 Sioux, many of them former hostiles who had been driven back by force or hunger to the reservation. He became greatly attached to Gall [*q.v.*] and Crow King, two of the leaders in the Little

Bighorn battle, and to John Grass [*q.v.*], the outstanding orator and diplomat of the Sioux nation, and was enabled to alter radically the Indian attitude toward peaceful industry and the education of the children. In the negotiations over the proposed agreements of 1882, 1888, and 1889, whereby large land cessions were demanded by the government, he took an active part and was influential both in obtaining concessions for his wards and in persuading the leaders to accept the final proposal. During the Ghost-Dance craze of 1890, when a general Indian uprising was feared, he opposed the use of the military and exerted himself to check the spread of the excitement by peaceful means. He was, however, compelled to order the arrest of Sitting Bull [*q.v.*], an attempt that resulted (Dec. 15) in the death of the chief and eleven other Indians (*Sixtieth Annual Report of the Commissioner of Indian Affairs,* 1891, pp. 325–38).

In January 1895, the office of assistant commissioner of Indian Affairs was offered him. Preferring field service, he declined the offer but accepted instead (Mar. 31) the post of inspector under the personal direction of the secretary of the interior. He traveled widely and thus became acquainted with conditions among the Indians in every part of the country. He was especially valuable in the rôle of negotiator and participated in more than forty formal agreements with the various tribes. He had returned to Washington from a protracted visit to the Dakotas, where he distributed an award to the Santee Sioux, when he suddenly became ill. He died at the National Hotel. The body was taken to his home at McLaughlin, S. Dak. He was survived by his wife, who, by reason of her command of the Sioux tongue, had been of inestimable help to him, and by several children.

McLaughlin was tall, with a dignified bearing and graceful manners. His tastes were refined, and his intellectual interests were broad and varied. It is doubtful whether any one has better understood Indian character. In 1910 he published *My Friend the Indian,* in considerable part an autobiography. Though the composition is largely another's, the substance is all his own, and the book faithfully reflects the man and his work. It is a contribution of high rank to the study of the Indian question, to Sioux history, and especially to the Indian side of the battle of the Little Bighorn.

[An edition of *My Friend the Indian,* published in 1926, contains an introductory appreciation of McLaughlin by Geo. B. Grinnell. See also: the *Washington Post,* July 29, 1923; *Bismarck Tribune,* July 30, 1923; and the *Native American* (Phoenix, Ariz.), Sept. 8, 1923. Information for this sketch was supplied by Charles H. Burke, commissioner of Indian affairs at the time of McLaughlin's death, and others.] W. J. G.

McLAURIN, ANSELM JOSEPH (Mar. 26, 1848–Dec. 22, 1909), senator, governor of Mississippi, was the eldest of the eight sons born to Lauchlin and Ellen Caroline (Tullus) McLaurin. His father, a native of South Carolina, of Scotch descent, was a man of local prominence and represented his county in the legislature of Mississippi four times between 1841 and 1875. His wife was a native Mississippian. Though Anselm was born at Brandon, Miss., the family soon moved to a farm in Smith County. After some training at the hands of local schoolmasters, he entered Summerville Institute. In August 1864 he became a private in Company K, 3rd Mississippi Cavalry, and served through the remainder of the Civil War. He then returned to Summerville Institute and completed the work of the junior class in 1867. The following year he was admitted to the Mississippi bar, having read law at night. On Feb. 22, 1870, at Trenton, Miss., he was married to Laura Elvira Victoria Rauch, and there were ten children born of this marriage.

After serving as prosecuting attorney of the fifth judicial district from 1871 to 1875, he returned the following year from Smith County to his birth place, Brandon. In his legal career he was chiefly notable in criminal cases. In 1879 he was elected to the state legislature. He took part in framing the Mississippi constitution of 1890, and on Feb. 7, 1894, he was elected to the United States Senate to fill the unexpired term of Edward C. Walthall, who had resigned. McLaurin was elected governor of Mississippi in 1895, having defeated Frank Burkitt, Populist candidate, by a vote of three to one. His administration extended from Jan. 21, 1896, to Jan. 16, 1900, a period which included three mild yellow-fever epidemics, the Spanish-American War, and the decline of the Populist movement within the state. The condition of the state treasury was greatly improved during this term. In 1900 he was again elected to the Senate, defeating Congressman "Private" John Allen. He served from 1901 until his death in 1909, having been re-elected for the term extending from 1907 to 1913. He was a member of a number of important senatorial committees, including those on civil service and retrenchment, immigration, and interstate commerce. On Feb. 25, 1908, he was appointed a member of the United States Immigration Commission. His death precipitated a bitter fight in Mississippi over the choice of a successor to his seat in the Senate.

McLaurin was a man of sanity, wisdom, and

genial humor. A close associate, Senator Money, stated that he never knew a man more disinclined to speak ill of others. Nevertheless, he was a shrewd politician. He did not hesitate to advocate the disfranchisement of wife beaters, a minimum pension of seventy-five dollars a year to disabled Confederate veterans, and the popular election of the judiciary of Mississippi as matters proper for incorporation in the Mississippi constitution of 1890. He was also a diligent member of numerous Democratic executive committees.

[Dunbar Rowland, *The Official and Statistical Reg. of the State of Miss.*, 1904, 1908, 1912, 1917, and *Mississippi* (1907), vol. II; *Who's Who in America*, 1908–09; *Biog. Dir. Am. Cong.* (1928); *Anselm J. McLaurin . . . Memorial Addresses* (1911); *Daily Democrat* (Natchez, Miss.), Dec. 23, 1909.] C. S. S.

MACLAURIN, RICHARD COCKBURN (June 5, 1870–Jan. 15, 1920), physicist, born at Lindean, Scotland, was the son of the Rev. Robert Campbell Maclaurin and his wife Martha Joan (Spence) Maclaurin. The family was an ancient one in Scotland, the most famous representative of which was the mathematician Colin Maclaurin, the friend of Sir Isaac Newton and author of the *Treatise on Fluxions* (1742). It was his brother John Maclaurin, one of the leading theologians of his day, who had some communications with Dr. Prince, pastor of the Old South Church in Boston, concerning the founding of the College of New Jersey. Robert Campbell Maclaurin was a minister of the Church of Scotland in a small parish near Edinburgh and a man of literary and scientific tastes. Early in life, finding himself unable to subscribe to the tenets of his church, he resolved to make a new start in New Zealand. With his large family he settled in a country district in Auckland where in the course of a few years he was appointed schoolmaster and had a house with a small farm. Thus from the time he was five years old Richard grew up in New Zealand and got his early training there. Both parents were persons of unusual character and attainments and they and their twelve children made a remarkable household. His mother, who was the daughter of a physician in Lerwick, Shetland, exerted a strong influence over his life.

Although his constitution was never very robust, the boy took kindly to the outdoor life of a country farm and at the same time evinced an unusual aptitude for books and study. At school and afterward at college he was uniformly at the head of his class. When he was seventeen years old he led the list of competitors of the whole colony for a scholarship in Auckland University College, and four years later he had graduated from this college with the highest honors in physics and mathematics. A scientific career seemed to be marked out for him. In 1892 he proceeded to the University of Cambridge. Winning scholarships in both Emmanuel College and St. John's College, he preferred to enter the latter on account of its high reputation in mathematics. He took the degree of bachelor of arts in this university in 1895, obtaining the highest rank in the most advanced mathematical examinations. Throughout his life at Cambridge he held a distinguished place and won the most coveted prizes both in mathematics and in law. He was awarded the Smith prize in mathematics in 1897, which had been won previously by such notable scientific men as Sir John Herschel, Sir G. G. Stokes, James Clerk Maxwell, Lord Kelvin, Lord Rayleigh, and others; and the Yorke prize in law in 1898 for his original essay, *On the Nature and Evidence of Title to Realty* (1901). The strain of these studies told upon his health.

In 1896–97 he spent about a year in Canada where he taught for a short time in the University of Montreal and also began to study law. Returning to England in 1897, he was elected a fellow of St. John's College, Cambridge, and was awarded the McMahon law studentship. During this period he also studied six months in the University of Strassburg. In the autumn of 1898, when he was only twenty-eight years old, he was called to take the chair of mathematics in the newly founded Victoria College of the University of New Zealand at Wellington. He held this post until 1905 and during part of the time he also gave courses of lectures in law without additional compensation. When the law school was established in 1905, he became dean of the faculty of law of the University of New Zealand. As a member of the University Senate he strove to promote the advancement of general education throughout the colony, but his ideas were too far ahead of the rural communities around him. In 1904 Cambridge University conferred on him the honorary degree of LL.D. in recognition of his original contributions in law. At the close of this year, Dec. 27, 1904, he was married to Margaret Alice Young of Auckland.

In 1907 he was invited to Columbia University in the city of New York to take the chair of mathematical physics that had been established for advanced researches in this field. The opportunity of resuming his favorite scientific studies under such conditions was not to be resisted, and in February 1908 he gave his first lectures in Columbia University. His lectures on light given at the American Museum of Natural History during the winter of 1908–09 were published under that title by the Columbia University Press in 1909. Although he was almost immediately made head of the department of physics in Columbia University, he was not destined to remain long in New York. In the following autumn he was chosen to succeed President Pritchett as the sixth president of the Massachusetts Institute of Technology, and on June 7, 1909, when he was just thirty-nine years old, he was formally inaugurated in this office. Here he entered upon a notable career. It was a critical period in the development of the school. It had outgrown its old habitations and was cramped for lack of space and facilities, while the demands for trained engineers in all the fields of industry and commerce were growing every year. The new president grasped the situation from the start and was able to stimulate enthusiasm and win support for his projects, for his wide knowledge, broad culture, and experience in two hemispheres "gave him a cosmopolitan quality that carried him over and through many obstacles." Within the short space of ten years he had transferred the institute to its spacious new home across the river in Cambridge.

Maclaurin had applied to become a citizen of the United States in 1913, but the World War followed in 1914, and he never severed his allegiance to his native country. Four years later when the United States also was in the midst of the war, he was selected by the War Department at Washington to be the director of college training for the huge army that was being sent overseas and also for the select few who were to carry on war work at home in scientific fields. He played a leading part in the prodigious task of organizing the Students Army Training Corps throughout all the American colleges, and it was largely due to his wisdom and tactfulness that the colleges were able to carry on in those distracting times and to resume their normal status practically unimpaired when the war ceased. Doing double duty and beset with problems of the most complex kind, he was under a great strain until several months after the armistice was signed, and it is possible that his health was undermined a year before he died. While he did not live to see the fruition of all his dreams for the Institute of Technology to which he had given the best years of his life, "he saw his great endowment secure, his student body doubled, his faculty growing, and the inception of a plan which should give the school permanent and increasing funds and unexampled opportunities for usefulness" (*Technology Review,* January 1920, p. 13). After an illness of five or six days, he died of pneumonia in his fiftieth year, at the height of his powers of accomplishment. One of the foremost scholars of his day, he was also a man of the broadest human sympathies. While slow to express his own views and eager to hear what others had to say, he formed his own decisions and was quick to detect sham in all its forms.

[There are several articles on the life and work of Maclaurin in the *Technology Rev.,* Jan., Apr. 1920. See also: Ernest F. Nichols, "Dr. Maclaurin as a Colleague," *Ibid.,* July 1920; M. A. DeWolfe Howe, *Later Years of the Saturday Club, 1870–1920* (1927); *Outlook,* Nov. 21, 1908, Jan. 28, 1920; *Boston Transcript,* Jan. 16, 1920. Information as to certain facts was supplied by Mrs. Richard Cockburn Maclaurin.]

J. P. C. S.

McLAWS, LAFAYETTE (Jan. 15, 1821–July 24, 1897), soldier, was born in Augusta, Ga., the son of James McLaws of Augusta and his wife, Elizabeth Huguenin of South Carolina. He entered the University of Virginia in 1837 and West Point the following year. Upon graduation in 1842, he was commissioned in the infantry and soon afterward married Emily Allison Taylor, niece of Zachary Taylor [*q.v.*]. Following service in Indian Territory, Mississippi, Louisiana, and Florida, he entered Texas with Taylor's army of occupation and participated in the defense of Fort Brown and the capture of Monterey. He was transferred to Scott's army before Vera Cruz as a first lieutenant, and was present at the capture of that city. Upon his return from Mexico, he was acting assistant adjutant-general of the department of New Mexico, a member of the Utah expedition of 1858, and in 1859 was engaged in protecting emigrants and escorting Mormons to California.

When the secession movement came to a head, he was on an expedition among the Navajo Indians in New Mexico. Resigning his captaincy in the United States army, he entered the Confederate service as a major, was shortly appointed colonel of the 10th Georgia Regiment, and was promoted to brigadier-general, Sept. 25, 1861. As the result of the excellent manner in which he acquitted himself in the Yorktown campaign, he was made a major-general, May 22, 1862. His division took part in all the larger operations of General Lee's Army of Northern Virginia during 1862–63. In 1862 he cooperated with "Stonewall" Jackson in the capture of Harpers Ferry, effecting the seizure of Maryland Heights, the key position. Arriving on the field of Antietam as Hood's troops were being driven back, McLaws' force was quickly thrown into the fight and helped to restore the situation. He heads the list of those mentioned by Longstreet (*post,* p. 266) as making the best tactical moves at Antietam. At Fredericksburg, McLaws' di vision made a brilliant defense of Marye's Hill against several times its numbers and inflicted appalling losses on the Union troops. After Chancellorsville, it was assigned to Longstreet's corps. At Gettysburg, it fought at the Peach Orchard and the Devil's Den. McLaws went with Longstreet to Bragg's assistance at Chickamauga, and upon the failure of the attempt to capture Knoxville by storm, he was relieved of his command, at the instance of Longstreet, and court-martialed for failing to make proper preparations for the assault. President Davis exonerated him and placed him in command of the district of Georgia and the defenses of Savannah. Because of the exhausted condition of the district, his efforts to oppose Sherman's operations were unavailing. His command was included in the surrender of General Johnston.

McLaws was popular with his men, yet a good disciplinarian; he loyally carried out decisions of higher authority; when assigned a task, he acted with energy and directness. After the war, he engaged in the insurance business in Augusta, and was collector of internal revenue and postmaster of Savannah in 1875 and 1876.

[G. W. Cullum, *Biog. Register of the Officers and Grads. of the U. S. Mil. Acad.* (3rd ed., 1891); *War of the Rebellion: Official Records (Army)*; War Department Records; *Battles and Leaders of the Civil War* (4 vols., 1887–88); W. J. Northen, *Men of Mark in Ga.*, vol. III (1911); *Confed. Mil. Hist.* (1899), vol. VI; James Longstreet, *From Manassas to Appomattox* (1896); *Morning News* (Savannah), July 24, 1897; names of parents from a son, U. H. McLaws, Esq., Savannah, Ga.] J. R. V.

MACLAY, EDGAR STANTON (Apr. 18, 1863–Nov. 2, 1919), author, was born in Foochow, China, the son of the Rev. Robert Samuel Maclay [*q.v.*] and Henrietta Caroline (Sperry) Maclay of Bristol, R. I. Edgar prepared for college chiefly under the instruction of his mother in Japan, and in 1881 entered Syracuse College, at Syracuse, N. Y., graduating four years later with the degree of B.A. In 1888, after a year spent in Europe, where he was engaged chiefly in the study of American history, he received from his alma mater the degree of M.A. After serving as a reporter on the *Brooklyn Daily Times,* he held a similar position with the *New York Tribune,* 1891–93, and for a year, 1893–94, was a member of the editorial staff. The following year he was on the editorial staff of the New York *Sun.* In 1895 he became lighthouse keeper at Old Field Point, L. I., and five years later accepted a minor office in the New York navy yard, with the rating of "laborer." In the meantime, utilizing his spare moments, he had established a considerable reputation as a writer of books, chiefly of a naval character. The rapid succession of their publication is indicative of his unusual industry: *The Maclays of Lurgan* (1889); *Journal of William Maclay* (1890); *A History of the United States Navy from 1775 to 1893* (2 vols., 1894); *Reminiscences of the Old Navy* (1898), and *A History of American Privateers* (1899). His naval books were interestingly written and his *History of the United States Navy* was adopted as a textbook for midshipmen by the United States Naval Academy. They reveal however not a few limitations: want of perspective and proportion, carelessness of statement, unfortunate omissions, and unfamiliarity with the naval art.

In 1901 he published a third volume of his *History,* covering the period of the Spanish-American War and containing a partisan account of the conduct of Admiral Schley in the battle of Santiago. He asserted that the admiral "cravenly declined" to pick up the gauntlet thrown down by Cervera. This account precipitated the Schley court of inquiry and led to Maclay's separation from the New York navy yard. On Dec. 20, 1901, under instructions from President Roosevelt, Secretary Long asked for his resignation. When he declined to comply, the President, four days later, dismissed him. His punishment, judged by its tragic results, was excessive. He was not well adapted to win from a niggard world a livelihood for himself and his family, and the fickle public now showed little interest in his writings, which in the years immediately preceding his death almost ceased. Of this later period he has three books to his credit: *Life and Adventures of "Jack" Philip, Rear Admiral, U. S. N.* (1903); *Moses Brown, Captain, U. S. N.* (1904); and *A Youthful Man-O'-Warsman* (1910). In October 1904 he formed a connection with the Brooklyn *Standard Union.* At the time of his death he was living in Washington, D. C., engaged in research work. He had married, on Dec. 22, 1893, Katherine Koerber, by whom he had four sons.

[E. S. Maclay, *The Maclays of Lurgan* (1889); *Who's Who in America,* 1906–07; *Evening Star* (Wash., D. C.), Dec. 21–26, 1901, Nov. 4, 1919.] C. O. P.

MACLAY, ROBERT SAMUEL (Feb. 7, 1824–Aug. 18, 1907), founder of three colleges and pioneer missionary in China, Korea, and Japan, was born in Concord, Franklin County, Pa., the son of Robert and Arabella (Erwin) Maclay and a descendant of John Maclay who emigrated to Pennsylvania from the north of Ireland in 1734. Graduating from Dickinson College in 1845, he was ordained a Methodist minister in the following year and in October

1847 was included in the first important group of missionaries sent to China, being assigned to Foochow a few weeks after the opening of the Chinese field. Five years later he became secretary and treasurer of the Foochow group and served in this capacity from 1852 to 1872, becoming "practically the founder of Methodist missions in China." He also assisted in the translation of the New Testament into the local dialect and in collaboration with the Rev. C. C. Baldwin published at Foochow *An Alphabetic Dictionary of the Chinese Language in the Foochow Dialect* (1870). Because of his "pre-eminent fitness for responsibility," he was designated to lead the new mission to open Japan to Methodism, and he remained in general charge of the Japanese work from 1872 till his return to the United States in 1888. While serving in Japan, he undertook a special trip to Seoul, Korea, to confer with the ruler of the then "Hermit Kingdom," and in 1884 he secured permission to establish Christian missions in the peninsula. Korea has since been regarded by missionaries as ranking among the regions most responsive to Christian propaganda. As in Foochow, Maclay helped in translating the New Testament into the native language of Japan.

Both in China and in Japan, Maclay was active in educational work. On a temporary furlough in Foochow, in 1881, he organized the Anglo-Chinese College, and two years later he opened the Anglo-Japanese College at Tokyo, serving as its president from 1883 until 1887. He also established the Philander Smith Biblical Institute at Tokyo, in 1884, and was its dean from 1884 until 1887. He served as delegate to the London Ecumenical Conference in 1881, and to the General Conference of the Methodist Church, at New York, in 1888. Upon returning to the United States in 1888, he became dean of the Maclay College of Theology, formerly at San Fernando, Cal., but transferred to Los Angeles when it became the University of Southern California College of Religion. He continued as dean of this institution until it was temporarily closed in 1893. He then withdrew from active church work and lived in retirement at San Fernando until his death in 1907. He was twice married. His first wife was Henrietta Caroline Sperry, to whom he was married at Hong Kong on July 10, 1850. She died in 1879 and on June 6, 1882, he was married to Sarah Ann Barr, at San Francisco. Edgar Stanton Maclay [*q.v.*] was a son by the first marriage. In addition to the works mentioned Maclay's writings include *Life Among the Chinese* (1861); sketches of Japanese Methodist missions for J. M. Reid's *Missions and Missionary Society of the Methodist Episcopal Church* (2 vols., 1879; 3 vols., 1896); and the article on Shintoism for Reid's *Doomed Religions* (1884).

[*Who's Who in America,* 1908–09; J. M. Buckley, *A Hist. of Methodism in the U. S.* (1897), vol. II; L. G. Paik, *The Hist. of Protestant Missions in Korea, 1832–1910* (1929); Matthew Simpson, *Cyc. of Methodism* (1882); E. S. Maclay, *The Maclays of Lurgan* (1889); *Cal. Christian Advocate,* Aug. 29, 1907; *Christian Advocate* (N. Y.), Sept. 12, 1907.] H. E. W.

MACLAY, SAMUEL (June 17, 1741–Oct. 5, 1811), representative and senator from Pennsylvania, was born in Lurgan township, Franklin County, Pa., the son of Charles and Eleanor (Query) Maclay. In 1734 his father and grandfather, John Maclay, had emigrated from the north of Ireland. In 1767–68 Samuel Maclay appears as an assistant to his brother, William Maclay [*q.v.*], who, during a trip to England, had secured the approval of the proprietors of Pennsylvania to his own appointment as deputy surveyor of Cumberland County. In 1769 Samuel began surveying the "Officers' Tract." He became one of the large landowners of this region, settling in Buffalo Valley probably about 1770. On Nov. 10, 1773, he was married to Elizabeth, eighteen-year-old daughter of William and Esther (Harris) Plunket. He engaged in farming and surveying, owned at least one slave, and soon enjoyed a position of leadership in the affairs of the county. On July 29, 1775, he became a justice of the quarter sessions. Being one of the local court circle, he naturally became a member of the local committee of correspondence at the opening of the Revolution. He was commissioned lieutenant-colonel of militia, and on July 4, 1776, was a delegate to the convention of "Associators" at Lancaster, where the state militia was organized.

In 1787 he entered state politics through his election to the lower house of the legislature; he served in this position until 1791. On Feb. 23, 1792, he was appointed an associate judge for Northumberland County. On Oct. 14, 1794, he was elected to Congress as a Republican. Northumberland County, where the noted liberals Joseph Priestley and Thomas Cooper [*qq.v.*], had just settled, was overwhelmingly Republican, and "Samuel Maclay's influence, from his good character and ability, was almost unbounded" (Linn, *post,* p. 296). In 1795, however, the Rev. Hugh Morrison, a Presbyterian minister, led a determined opposition against the Jeffersonians, and, like Father Peto before Henry VIII, he lectured Maclay from the pulpit. Maclay withdrew from the congregation, and most of the members followed him. In 1799 Morrison brought suit for slander, which was finally discontinued. The attack merely increased Maclay's popularity with his own political group. In Congress, with no less ardor than his brother had shown in the Senate in the years 1789–91, Maclay promptly identified himself with the Opposition. The French minister, Adet, wrote that *"nos amis"* in Congress had calculated a plan to defeat the Jay treaty and throw the onus upon the administration. Maclay introduced the resolution, but his strategy failed: "Even the gentleman from Pennsylvania's promptitude failed him," chided one member, adding: "and the promptest man certainly he was he had ever known" (*Annals of Congress,* 4 Cong., 1 Sess., p. 974). But the gesture strengthened his popularity at home.

In 1797 Maclay was again elected to the lower house of the state legislature, and from 1798 to 1802 he held a seat in the state Senate, serving in 1801 and 1802 as speaker of the latter body. On Dec. 14, 1802, he was elected to the United States Senate, but he took little part in the debates. He voted consistently for administration measures, proposed no less than three amendments to the Constitution, and introduced the resolution calling for the investigation of Senator Smith of Ohio, charged with being in collusion with Aaron Burr. In 1809, before his term had expired, he resigned his seat, probably because of ill health. Like his brother, he was an aristocrat of the frontier, an intense individualist who belonged in spirit neither to the "eastern men of property" nor to the frontiersmen. In a speech in Congress he revealed his conflicting leanings (*Annals of Congress,* 4 Cong., 1 Sess., pp. 346–47): he would use the national territory for the advantage of speculators as well as settlers by dividing it into both large and small tracts. He was an expert marksman and a good mechanic, but his frontier environment would no more permit him to embrace Federalist politics than it would allow him to use the handsome coach which he is said to have abandoned when his democratic neighbors objected to such evidences of aristocracy. His training in the classics and his large library also tended to give him less in common with his neighbors. The *Journal of Samuel Maclay* written during a surveying expedition on the western rivers of Pennsylvania in 1790 reveals almost as much of these dual characteristics as the more famous *Journal of William Maclay.* Samuel Maclay had six sons and three daughters. He died at his home in Buffalo Valley.

[*Journal of Samuel Maclay, while Surveying the West Branch of the Susquehanna, the Sinnemahoning, and the Allegheny Rivers in 1790* (1887), ed. by J. F. Meginness; J. B. Linn, *Annals of Buffalo Valley, Pa., 1755–1855* (1877); *Hist. of . . . the Susquehanna and Juniata Valleys* (1886), vol. II; J. F. Meginness, *Otzinachson; or, A Hist. of the West Branch Valley of the Susquehanna* (rev. ed., 1889); F. J. Turner, "Correspondence of the French Ministers to the U. S., 1791–97," *Ann. Report of the Am. Hist. Asso. for the Year 1903* (1904), vol. II; H. V. Ames, "The Proposed Amendments to the Const. of the U. S. During the First Century of Its Hist.," *Ibid.*, for the year 1896 (1897), vol. II; *Hist. Soc. of Pa., Colls.*, I (1853), 94–118; E. S. Maclay, *The Maclays of Lurgan* (1889); P. D. Evans, *The Holland Land Company* (1924); *U. S. Gazette for the Country,* Oct. 7, 1811.] J. P. B.

MACLAY, WILLIAM (July 27, 1734–Apr. 16, 1804), lawyer, senator, diarist, brother of Samuel Maclay [*q.v.*], was the son of Charles and Eleanor (Query) Maclay. His father, a farmer, came to America in 1734 from the north of Ireland, settling first in New Garden township, Chester County, Pa., where William was born, and afterward moving to Franklin County. The Rev. John Blair, successor to his brother Samuel Blair [*q.v.*] as head of a noted school in Chester County, and a prominent guardian of Scotch-Irish discipline in the New World, gave the stalwart youth his classical training.

In 1758 Maclay was a lieutenant with Gen. John Forbes's expedition to Ft. Duquesne; in 1763–64 he participated in the expedition of Col. Henry Bouquet against the Indians. After the French and Indian War, visiting England, he took up the matter of surveys with Thomas Penn; he was engaged in surveying land in 1766, if not earlier. On Apr. 11, 1769, he was married to Mary McClure, daughter of John Harris, founder of Harrisburg, and settled at Mifflintown, where he owned 300 acres of land. He was admitted to the bar of York County in 1760, whether or not he practised there. He held various local offices in the new county of Northumberland, organized in 1772, laid out the town of Sunbury that year, and lived there himself until his removal to Harrisburg in 1786. Though he had been on good terms with the proprietors, he gave his allegiance to the patriot side when the battle for independence opened. He served for a time in the militia, acted as issuing commissary in Sunbury, and played a considerable part in organizing the frontier defense against Indian raids. The successful conclusion of the Revolution carried him to the state legislature, where he represented Northumberland County from 1781 to 1785. He was also a member of the Supreme Executive Council, in 1786 and 1788, a judge of the court of common pleas, deputy-surveyor, and a member of commissions to examine the navigation of the Susquehanna (1783) and to treat with the Indians for the purchase of lands (1784–85).

As United States senator he represented rural Pennsylvania in the first Congress held under the Constitution (1789–91). His colleague was Robert Morris who, in the drawing of lots, secured the long-term seat whereas Maclay got the short term. When he stood for reëlection he lost his seat to a Federalist. His historical significance consequently was lost until 1880, when the publication of a private journal he kept during the time he served in Congress revealed both the extent and nature of the debates in the Senate on the financial proposals of Hamilton and the rôle of Maclay in opposition. His notes are the only continuous report in existence of that early federal period when debates occurred behind closed doors and no official record was prepared for the public. They reveal the diarist as such a stanch antagonist of the Hamiltonian program, such a strong defender of the interests of the small-farming class, such a denunciator of the speculation rife at the time, that Pennsylvania may be called the home of the first Jeffersonian democrat. Jefferson did not reach the seat of government until eleven months after Congress commenced to work and during that time Maclay was at the democratic helm. As his journal discloses, moreover, he was often distressed by Jefferson's attitude when he became secretary of state, particularly with reference to the building up of a navy for an attack on the Algerian pirates and for dealing with the fisheries question. His comments on all the leaders of that critical period, including Washington, are invaluable sidelights on the contest so bitterly fought between the Federalists and their opponents over the interpretation of the new Constitution, the funding of the debt, the tariff, the bank, the excise tax, proper ceremonials and a title for the president, and manners and tastes in the young republic. Since Maclay sat in on conferences with Morris and others relative to the location of the federal capital and attended functions where the ladies of the "republican court" were present, his comments are warm with the personal aspects of the economic struggle. His wit is caustic, perhaps because he suffered from rheumatism, but the journal was meant solely for private release.

His neighbors sent him to the state legislature again in 1795, and in 1803. In the meantime, he had been a presidential elector in 1796 and associate judge of Dauphin County (1801–03). He died at Harrisburg in 1804.

[G. W. Harris, ed., *Sketches of Debate in the First Senate of the U. S., in 1789–90–91, by William Maclay* (1880), with a good biog. sketch in the preface; E. S. Maclay, ed., *Journal of William Maclay* (1890); C. A. Beard, ed., *The Journal of William Maclay* (1927); L. R. Harley, *William Maclay, U. S. Senator from Pa., 1789–1791* (1909); E. S. Maclay, *The Maclays of Lurgan* (1889); J. B. Linn, *Annals of Buffalo Valley, Pa., 1755–1855* (1877); *Pa. Archives*, 1 ser., vols. IV–X (1853–54); E. P. Oberholtzer, *Robert Morris* (1903).]

M. R. B.

MACLAY, WILLIAM BROWN (Mar. 20, 1812–Feb. 19, 1882), lawyer, editor, legislator, was born in New York City, one of twelve children of the Rev. Archibald and Mary Brown Maclay. His father was born in the village of Killearn, Stirlingshire, Scotland; his mother was the daughter of a Glasgow merchant. He matriculated at the University of the City of New York at twenty and graduated with highest honors in the class of 1836, remaining after his graduation to accept a temporary professorship in Latin language and literature. In 1839, having taken up the study of law, he was admitted to the bar and at once formed a partnership with his brother-in-law, Isaac P. Martin. In the same year he was elected to the state Assembly and was reëlected in 1840 and 1841. He, more than any one else, was responsible for the legislation reorganizing the superior court and the court of common pleas of the city and county of New York. He also secured the publication of the *Journals of the Provincial Congress . . . of New York* (2 vols., 1842), covering the years 1775–77 and containing many original unpublished letters of distinguished Revolutionary personages. His most important legislative work, however, related to popular education. As a member of the committee on colleges, academies, and common schools, he obtained the passage of an act which in substance gave the City of New York full benefit of the state law providing for publicly supported, publicly controlled schools. At the time, the Protestants charged that the measure was designed to favor the growing Catholic population of the city, and Maclay was roundly and unjustly denounced, but he was a believer in religious toleration and wished to have the schools of the city and state open on equal terms to all.

In 1842 Maclay was elected to Congress. He served five terms in all, being reëlected in 1844, 1848, 1856, and 1858, after which he declined to be a candidate for reëlection. At Washington he was distinguished for his punctuality and diligent attention to business. He advocated the passage of the bill to aid S. F. B. Morse in demonstrating the practical utility of the telegraph, introduced an unsuccessful bill for the relief of the heirs of John Paul Jones, and was one of those foremost in the movement for the reduction of postal rates. He asserted that the title of the United States to the disputed Oregon territory was "clear and unquestionable," was an earnest advocate for annexation of Texas, and favored the war with Mexico. A pronounced Democrat of the Jacksonian type, he maintained that public lands should be gratuitously conveyed to actual settlers in the form of homesteads rather than be held by the government for sale to private speculators; he did not favor their donation to private corporations for the ostensible purpose of internal improvements. He vigorously opposed the doctrines of the Native Americans or Know-Nothings as contrary to the spirit of republican institutions and incompatible with national unity.

Maclay was a lover of books and libraries, was widely read, could speak or write intelligently and often eloquently on many subjects. His characteristic traits were those of a cultured gentleman. He was proud of his good name, yet modest; he possessed a high sense of honor, loved justice, and was urbane and refined in taste and manner. On Aug. 22, 1838, he married Antoinette Walton, daughter of Mark Walton, a New Orleans merchant. Three children were born of this marriage. In the spring of 1849, at the close of his third term in Congress, he removed with his family to Mount Palatine, Ill. Here, soon after their arrival, his wife died of cholera; he then returned to New York where his youngest daughter died of the same malady. He did not remarry. From 1838 to the time of his death he served as a trustee of the University of the City of New York.

[Orrin B. Judd, *Maclay Memorial Sketching the Lineage, Life and Obsequies of Hon. Wm. B. Maclay* (1884); *Biog. Dir. Am. Cong.* (1928); *N. Y. Times*, Feb. 20, 1882; W. B. Maclay, *Address* [*on civil and religious liberty*] *Delievered at the Democratic-Republican Celebration . . . July 4, 1840* (1840), *A Selection of Letters Written on Various Pub. Occasions* (1859).]

H. J. C.

McLEAN, ARCHIBALD (Sept. 6, 1849–Dec. 15, 1920), clergyman and missionary executive of the Disciples of Christ, son of Malcolm and Alexandra (McKay) McLean, was born on his father's farm near Summerside, Prince Edward Island, Canada. His immediate forebears were of Scotch stock of the island of Skye. His early education was obtained at the near-by Graham's Road public school, which he attended until his fourteenth year. Thereafter he undertook to learn the carriage-builder's trade, first in the service of an uncle, then as apprentice for five years to William Tuplin, a skilful carriage maker of the village of Margate. Afterward he spent one year in Boston as a journeyman mechanic. The spring of 1870 found him again at home, with a desire for a more influential career than that of the tradesman. He had been reared in a strongly religious environment. John Geddie, a Presbyterian minister of New London, P. E. I., who became the first missionary sent abroad from any British colony, made a lasting impression on him, and he also felt the influence of Donald Crawford, a Baptist minister who identified himself with the "Campbellite" movement and founded in 1858 the Summerside Church of Christ. McLean had been baptized by Crawford in 1867 and since then had considered entering the Christian ministry. With this purpose in mind, in the autumn of 1870 he went to Bethany College, West Virginia, an institution founded by Alexander Campbell and conducted by the Disciples of Christ. Here he took the regular four-year classical course and graduated with honors, June 18, 1874. Ordained immediately, he began his ministry on June 21 with the Christian Church of Mount Healthy, near Cincinnati, where after two months he was formally installed. During this pastorate, which continued until 1885, he erected a new church building.

In 1882 he was elected corresponding secretary of the Foreign Christian Missionary Society of the Disciples' brotherhood, and for three years carried on the duties of this office along with his pastorate. In 1885, however, he resigned his pulpit to give the Missionary Society his full time. In 1888 he began the publication of the *Missionary Intelligencer*, first as a quarterly, but soon as a monthly. He represented his Church at the ecumenical conference on foreign missions, held in London June 9–10, 1888. In 1889 he accepted the presidency of Bethany College, in addition to his work as a missionary executive. This office he resigned in 1891—although an emergency required the continuation of his administration through the autumn of that year—and thereafter he devoted his entire time, in one capacity or another, to the work of the missionary society, keeping a connection with the college through a trusteeship.

On July 24, 1895, he left Cincinnati—his headquarters—for a year's tour through all the mission fields, save Africa, in which the Society was working: the Hawaiian Islands, Japan, China, India, Palestine, Turkey, Scandinavia, and England. His observations are admirably recorded in his book, *A Circuit of the Globe* (1897), published soon after his return. He was a delegate to the Ecumenical Missionary Conference held in New York City Apr. 21–May 1, 1900, and in that year was elected president of his Society, in which office he served with distinction until the formation of the United Society in 1919. In 1905 he instituted the policy of missionary "rallies" throughout his denomination, in the interest of missionary education and of support for the missionary enterprise. He served on the committee in charge of arrangements for the centennial of the Church, held in Pittsburgh Oct. 11–19, 1909. In 1910 he attended the Edinburgh World Missionary Conference as a delegate of his denomination. He was chairman of the executive committee of the "Men and Millions" movement (1914–18) of the Disciples, a great financial drive on behalf of missions and the work of the church. He aided in the organization of the Panama congress (1916) on Christian work in Latin America, and attended its sessions as a delegate of his Society. As the movement among the Disciples toward the amalgamation of several of their intra-denominational organizations gathered momentum, he gave it his sympathy and assistance, and on the formation of the United Christian Missionary Society in 1919 he became its first vice-president. As president of the former Foreign Society he had commissioned every missionary sent to non-Christian lands in the entire history of the organization. He died at Battle Creek Sanitarium, Michigan, the best known and most highly esteemed man among the Disciples of Christ. His body was taken first to St. Louis—at that time the headquarters of the United Society—thence to Cincinnati, and finally to Bethany, W. Va., where it was interred in the Campbell Cemetery.

McLean was the author of *Missionary Addresses* (1895); *Handbook of Missions* (1897); *A Circuit of the Globe* (1897), previously mentioned; *Where the Book Speaks* (1907); *Epoch Makers of Modern Missions* (1912); *The Primacy of the Missionary* (1920); *The History of the Foreign Christian Missionary Society* (1921); and many articles in the *Missionary Intelligencer, Christian-Evangelist, Christian Standard,* and other periodicals. Among his tracts were *Intercessory Prayer, Doubling the Preacher's Power,* and *Forty Years of Service for the King.* He was also the author of two memorable addresses, *Alexander Campbell as a Preacher,* and *Thomas and Alexander Campbell,* both of which were published (Cincinnati, no date).

[W. R. Warren, *Archibald McLean* (1923); *Who's Who in America,* 1920–21, inaccurate; *Missionary Review of the World,* Sept. 1921; *Christian Evangelist,* Dec. 23, 1920; *Christian Standard,* Dec. 25, 1920; *Commercial Tribune* (Cincinnati), Dec. 16, 1920.]

J. C. A.

MACLEAN, JOHN (Mar. 1, 1771–Feb. 17, 1814), chemist, educator, was born in Glasgow, Scotland, the son of John and Agnes (Lang) Maclean. His father was a surgeon of the British army, who was present at the capture of Quebec from the French, being the third man to scale the Heights of Abraham. The boy was left an orphan at an early age, and George Macintosh, father of Charles Macintosh who later invented the waterproof cloth, was appointed his guardian. Maclean received his early education in the Glasgow Grammar School and entered the University of Glasgow before he was thirteen years old. He was especially interested in chemistry, natural philosophy, medicine, and anatomy, for it was his purpose to become a surgeon. Under the influence of Charles Macintosh, who was four years his senior, while a student at the university he joined the Chemical Society, before which he read several papers. Leaving Glasgow about 1787, he spent two or three years in study at Edinburgh, London, and Paris, where he was greatly impressed by Lavoisier, Berthollet, and other French scholars. Returning to Glasgow in 1790, he resumed his studies for another year, and then engaged in the practice of medicine and surgery. The diploma authorizing him to practise surgery and pharmacy was dated Aug. 1, 1791, and on the same day he was admitted as a member of the faculty of physicians and surgeons of the university.

Being in sympathy with the political sentiments of the United States, he left Scotland for America in April 1795. In Philadelphia, Dr. Benjamin Rush advised him to settle in Princeton, seat of the College of New Jersey. In the summer of 1795, he delivered there a course of lectures on chemistry, and on Oct. 1 he was chosen professor of chemistry and natural history in the College. Two years later he relinquished his medical and surgical practice to give his full time to his academic duties, which were increased in 1797 by his appointment as professor of mathematics and natural philosophy, with the provision that chemistry and natural history be taught as branches of natural philosophy. He was the first professor of chemistry in any American college other than medical institutions (Benjamin Silliman, Jr., "American Contributions to Chemistry," *American Chemist,* August-September, December 1874), and for a number of years he was the only professor, other than the president, on the faculty of the College of New Jersey. While in Paris, he had been won to the support of the antiphlogistic theory, as the "new chemistry" of Lavoisier was called. In 1797 he prepared *Two Lectures on Combustion: Supplementary to a Course of Lectures on Chemistry Read at Nassau Hall; Containing an Examination of Dr. Priestley's Considerations on the Doctrine of Phlogiston, and the Decomposition of Water*, printed in that year by T. Dobson, at the Stone-House, No. 41 South Second Street, Philadelphia. The lectures displayed ability and learning, and were helpful in the overthrow of the phlogistic theory. The discussion was continued for a time by Maclean, Joseph Priestley, James Woodhouse, and Samuel Mitchill [*qq.v.*] in the New York *Medical Repository*. In 1797, the University of Aberdeen conferred the degree of M.D. upon Maclean. He was elected a member of the American Philosophical Society, Jan. 18, 1805, and two years later became a naturalized citizen of the United States. Meanwhile, in 1802, he had given a reading list to Benjamin Silliman [*q.v.*], who had been appointed professor of chemistry at Yale College despite a scant knowledge of the subject. Silliman (the elder of the name), who later came to be revered as one of the fathers of science in America, left in his diary the following note: "Dr. Maclean was a man of brilliant mind, with all the acumen of his native Scotland; and a sprinkling of wit gave variety to his conversation. I regard him as my earliest master in chemistry, and Princeton as my first starting point in that pursuit; although I had not an opportunity to attend any lectures there" (G. P. Fisher, *Life of Benjamin Silliman,* 1866, I, 109–10).

In 1812, in consequence of certain contemplated changes in the Princeton faculty, Maclean resigned, and shortly thereafter accepted the chair of natural philosophy and chemistry in the College of William and Mary, Williamsburg, Va. After one year, his health being poor, he returned to Princeton, where in February 1814 he died. He was buried in the old cemetery, in a grave adjoining those of the college presidents and professors. On Nov. 7, 1798, he had married Phebe Bainbridge, sister of Commodore William Bainbridge [*q.v.*], and to them were born two daughters and four sons. One son, John Maclean [*q.v.*], became the tenth president of the College of New Jersey at Princeton.

[The chief source is *A Memoir of John Maclean, M.D.* (1876), by his son, John Maclean, privately printed. See also William Foster, "John Maclean—Chemist," in *Science,* Oct. 3, 1924, and "Doctor Maclean and the Doctrine of Phlogiston," in *Jour. of Chemical Educ.,* Sept. 1925, and "Some Letters by Dr. John Maclean," *Ibid.,* Dec. 1929; *Poulson's Am. Daily Advertiser* (Phila.), Feb. 23, 1814. There are in the Princeton University Library seven letters written by Maclean.]

W. F.

McLEAN, JOHN (Mar. 11, 1785–Apr. 4, 1861), congressman, postmaster-general, jurist, was born in Morris County, N. J., the son of Fergus and Sophia (Blockford) McLean. His parents came to America from Ireland, the father being descended from the Scottish clan of McLean. A weaver by trade, he became a farmer, but having a large family and being limited in means, he soon decided to go West. In 1789 the family moved to Morgantown, Va., then to Jessamine, near Nicholasville, Ky., thence to Maysville, Ky., and finally, in 1799, settled on a farm near Lebanon, in what is now Warren County, Ohio. During these wanderings young McLean's education suffered. He attended school as opportunity offered and as the pressing needs of the family permitted. Determined to get further instruction, he worked for wages and at sixteen was able to hire private tutors. Two years later he went to Cincinnati, where he was formally indentured for two years to the clerk of the Hamilton County court. By working part of the day in the office he was able to support himself. Meanwhile, he read law with Arthur St. Clair, one of the best counselors in the West, and the son of General St. Clair. He also joined a debating club, in which he acquired facility of expression.

In 1807 he was admitted to the bar. The same year he married Rebecca Edwards and moved to Lebanon, where he founded the *Western Star,* a weekly newspaper. Commencing to practise in Lebanon, he soon won recognition by his industry and scrupulous care. In October 1812 he was elected as a War Democrat to Congress from the Cincinnati district, which then included Warren County. He was reëlected in 1814 "by the unanimous vote of all the electors who took part in the election. Not only did no one vote against him, but also no one who voted for any office at the election, refrained from voting for him" (Force, *post,* 271–72). He vigorously sponsored the war with England and advocated bills to indemnify persons for property lost in the public service, to grant pensions to officers and soldiers, and to pay congressmen a salary of $1500 per annum instead of the per diem allowance. In 1815 he declined to be a candidate for the United States Senate. The following year he resigned his seat in Congress to become judge of the supreme court of Ohio, to which office he had been elected by the state legislature. He remained upon the bench until 1822, when President Monroe appointed him commissioner of the land office. The next year he was made postmaster-general, and in the direction of this office he acquired a national reputation as an able administrator. Heretofore, this branch of the public service had been inefficient and disorganized. Under his management contractors were held to their agreements and incompetent and unfaithful officials were removed. He was reappointed by President J. Q. Adams and, it is claimed, used his official position to work against the reëlection of his superior (Bassett, *post,* II, 412, 413). McLean was not in sympathy with President Jackson's policy as to removals, and, after declining the portfolios of secretary of war and secretary of the navy, he was nominated by Jackson to be associate justice of the United States Supreme Court. His appointment was confirmed by the Senate on Mar. 7, 1829. "It is a good and satisfactory appointment," wrote Joseph Story, "but was, in fact, produced by other causes than his fitness or our advantage. The truth is . . . he told the new President, that he would not form a part of the new Cabinet, or remain in office, if he was compelled to make removals upon political grounds" (W. W. Story, *post,* I, 564). He was assigned to the seventh circuit, which then included the districts of Tennessee, Kentucky, and Ohio; later, the districts of Ohio, Indiana, Illinois, and Michigan. He took his seat in January 1830 and served until his death. On the bench he was dignified, courteous, painstaking, fearless, and able. Not until his health began to fail, two years before his death, was he absent a single day from his duties. He was not a great judge but his decisions on the circuit were seldom reversed and he was not often in the minority in the Supreme Court. In the celebrated Dred Scott case he dissented from the majority of the court and rendered an opinion of his own, which defined his position upon the slavery question (19 *Howard,* 558, 559). He held that slavery had its origin merely in force and was contrary to right, being sustained only by local law.

During his term on the bench he was frequently mentioned as a possible candidate for the presidency. He maintained that a judge was under no obligation to refrain from the discussion of political affairs and steadfastly defended the propriety of his candidacy. He declined the nomination in the Anti-Masonic Convention of 1831, and was proposed as a candidate by the Ohio legislature in 1836. His name was considered by the convention of "Free Democracy" in 1848 and was before the Whig Convention in 1852. In the Republican Convention of 1856 he received 196 votes, and, although seventy-five years of age, he still hoped for the nomination in the Republican Convention of 1860.

His first wife, by whom he had four daughters and three sons, died in December 1840, and three years later he married Sarah Bella Garrard, widow of Col. Jephtha D. Garrard and the youngest daughter of Israel Ludlow.

[M. F. Force, in *Memorial Biogs. of the New-England Hist. Geneal. Soc.*, vol. IV (1885); Charles Warren, *The Supreme Court in U. S. Hist.* (1922); W. W. Story, *Life and Letters of Joseph Story* (1851); J. S. Bassett, *Andrew Jackson* (1911); B. P. Poor, *Perley's Reminiscences* (1886); *Biog. Dir. Am. Cong.* (1928); 66 *U. S. Reports* (1 *Black*), 8–13; F. H. Hodder, "Some Phases of the Dred Scott Case," in *Miss. Valley Hist. Rev.*, June 1929; *Cincinnati Commercial*, Apr. 5, 1861; *Cincinnati Gazette*, Apr. 5, 1861.] R. C. M.

MACLEAN, JOHN (Mar. 3, 1800–Aug. 10, 1886), president of the College of New Jersey, was born at Princeton, the eldest son of Prof. John Maclean [*q.v.*] and Phebe (Bainbridge) Maclean, a sister of Commodore William Bainbridge [*q.v.*]. His paternal grandfather, a surgeon in the British army, was the third man to scale the Heights of Abraham in Wolfe's attack on Quebec. The boy inherited a strong, active body, great boldness and versatility of spirit, and a scientific turn of mind. His home advantages were such that he entered the College of New Jersey well prepared in the spring of 1813 and graduated, the youngest member of his class, in the autumn of 1816. After teaching for a year at the Lawrenceville preparatory school, he entered the Princeton Theological Seminary. For two years he studied theology, but in 1818 he accepted a position as tutor in the college, and his ordination as a Presbyterian minister did not take place until 1828. He was appointed teacher of mathematics and natural philosophy in 1822 and professor of mathematics in 1823. In 1829 he was shifted to the department of languages and the following year appointed professor of ancient languages and literature; in 1847 he became professor of Greek.

His early and rapid promotions were justified by his natural ability and the ardor of his zeal for teaching. In 1826 he founded the Alumni Association of Nassau Hall, the second oldest college alumni association in America. James Carnahan [*q.v.*], the president of the college, lacked energy, which Maclean possessed in great abundance, and in 1829 the younger man was made vice-president, charged with the duties of a modern dean, with the raising of funds, and with the selection of new members of the faculty. The college was passing through a period of depression. The funds were low; the classes were becoming smaller; the professors were poorly paid. Some of the trustees favored a policy of shrinkage and retrenchment. Maclean, on the other hand, proposed to turn retreat into a bold forward movement. He set forth to raise money for endowment, and came home with a goodly supply. Instead of reducing the faculty, he determined to enlarge it and to offer positions to men of eminence. East College was built in 1832 and West College in 1836. Through his insistence the college calendar was reformed, Commencement being changed from September to June. In 1852 and 1853 he successfully resisted a movement to place the college under the control of the Presbyterian church.

Upon Dr. Carnahan's retirement, Maclean was elected to the presidency on Dec. 20, 1853, and inaugurated on June 28, 1854. His courage was severely tried the next year, when the interior of Nassau Hall, the oldest and largest college building, was ruined by fire, and his task of soliciting money began again. The Civil War caused more loss of students to Princeton than to the New England colleges, but by skilful management Maclean held the faculty together through those years of trial. The students, though amused by his eccentricities, admired and loved the active man, who embodied for them the spirit of the place and time. From 1866 to 1868 he served as professor of Biblical instruction, in addition to his other duties. On Dec. 11, 1867, he resigned the presidency, but remained in office till the Commencement of 1868, when the alumni bade affectionate farewell to him and welcomed his successor, James McCosh [*q.v.*]. No president or professor of Princeton has been regarded with such a harmonious mixture of amusement and affection as "Johnny" Maclean. The men might smile at him as he hurried about in his plaid and, laying aside his dignity, engaged in the performance of some proctorial function; but when they were in trouble he befriended them, when they needed money he gave them his own, when they were sick he visited them.

After his retirement, he employed the rest of his life in works of charity and public service and in writing his history of the college. With the profits from this book he founded scholarships for poor students. He died at Princeton on Aug. 10, 1886; he was never married. Among his numerous pamphlets, sermons, and addresses, may be mentioned his *Lecture on a School System for New Jersey* (1829), and *Letters on the True Relations of the Church and the State to Schools and Colleges* (1853). His chief literary work is his *History of the College of New Jersey*, in two volumes, published in 1877.

[V. L. Collins, *Princeton* (1914); *True American* (Trenton), Aug. 11, 1886; manuscript letters and other records in the office of the secretary of Princeton University; personal recollections.] G. M. H.

McLEAN, WALTER (July 30, 1855–Mar. 20, 1930), naval officer, was born in Elizabeth, N. J. His father was Col. George Washington McLean, who organized, equipped, and commanded a New Jersey regiment in the Civil War; his mother, Rebecca J. McCormick, daughter of James McCormick, whose Maryland estate was Mount Pleasant, now a part of Baltimore, near the site of Johns Hopkins University. Destined by his father for a military career, the boy early decided on the navy, and at fourteen took affairs into his own hands by running away. Going to Washington he called on President Grant, a friend of his father, and applied for an appointment to Annapolis. Though it was necessary for him to spend some time further in study, the appointment was promised, and in June 1872 he entered the Naval Academy.

Graduated in 1876, he had his first duty on the *Trenton*, then fitting out for the European Squadron. After later duty on the North Atlantic Station, he was ordered in 1879 to the Asiatic Station, where he spent three years. On being detached and ordered to Washington for instruction in ordnance, he returned by way of Russia, journeying over the barren wastes of Siberia to Moscow. Varied duties followed, with two assignments in the Coast Survey. In 1891 he received his commission as lieutenant. Four years later he was again sent to the East, and he was there at the outbreak of the Spanish-American War, attached to the old sidewheeler *Monocacy*. Dewey, realizing the need of more officers and men, detached McLean from this ship on Apr. 25, 1898, and ordered him to the *Olympia*. When he reported, May 11, he was placed by Dewey on his staff and became the senior aide. There was need of supplies and also of communications with the United States by way of Hong-Kong. McLean was repeatedly sent in charge of the little supply steamer *Zafiro* to attend to both. Promotion followed rapidly: to lieutenant commander, 1899; commander, 1905; captain, 1908. From 1903 to 1906 he was attached to the Bureau of Ordnance, and then was sent to the Philippines as commandant of the naval station at Cavite and Olongapo. In 1914 he was promoted to the rank of rear admiral. After two years and a half in Washington as a member of the naval examining and retiring boards, he was given a part in the troubled affairs of Mexico by being ordered to relieve Admiral Mayo in command of the fleet off Vera Cruz (1914). The following year he was placed in command of the Norfolk navy-yard and the fifth naval district. When the World War broke out and the United States was finally swept into it, this duty became of great importance. The naval operating base established at Hampton Roads was the scene of intense activity, and large numbers of recruits were there assembled and trained. In addition to this duty McLean was the navy representative in the War Council appointed by the director general of railroads.

On Mar. 15, 1919, after forty-seven years of service in the navy, twenty-two years at sea, he was at his own request placed on the retired list. His last residence was in Annapolis, Md., where he died. He was married in 1887 to Emma Bowne Jarvis of Cooperstown, N. Y., by whom he had a daughter.

[*Register of the Commissioned and Warrant Officers of the Navy of the U. S. and of the Marine Corps* (1901); *The Records of Living Officers of the U. S. Navy and Marine Corps* (7th ed., 1902); *Who's Who in America*, 1928–29; *Army and Navy Jour.*, Mar. 22, 1930; the *Sun* (Baltimore), Mar. 21, 1930; material from friends.] C. S. S.

McLEAN, WILLIAM LIPPARD (May 4, 1852–July 30, 1931), newspaper publisher, philanthropist, was born at Mount Pleasant, Pa. His father, Robert Caldwell McLean, of Scotch ancestry, head of a furniture factory, was an elder in the Middle Presbyterian Church. His mother, Augusta Dorothea (Voigt) McLean, was the daughter of a clergyman. On both sides, the son profited by examples of industry, thrift, and conscientious rectitude. While at public school, he crossed the threshold of journalism by serving as local carrier for the Pittsburgh *Leader.* At twenty he took a position in its circulation department in Pittsburgh, becoming shortly a subscription solicitor in the outlying districts. One of his early tasks was to help compile the first newspaper almanac published in that city, to which may be traced the annual *Bulletin Almanac and Yearbook* he later established and made a standard statistical reference work. After six years of varied experience, McLean, though only twenty-six, was sent to Philadelphia by Calvin Wells, a Pittsburgh manufacturer who had bought the *Press,* to be its business manager; and he was soon credited with reviving the prestige of that famous journal.

In 1895, he struck out for himself by purchasing, at executor's sale, along with associates whose interests he later secured, the *Evening Bulletin,* the oldest afternoon daily in Pennsylvania. In an editorial in his first issue (*Evening Bulletin,* June 1, 1895), he proclaimed his purpose "to present a complete afternoon paper that will be abreast of every improvement in modern journalism." Promising support of the principles of the Republican party, he added that "on the vital issue of the financial integrity of the nation, it [the *Bulletin*] will oppose all attempts to debase the currency with the free coinage of silver or to alter the existing standard of values. It will register the decrees of no leader or faction and it will reserve to itself the right of independent criticism of men and policies." The circulation, which had ebbed below 6,000 a day, reached 33,625 within a year. McLean molded the *Bulletin* to his journalistic ideals: "Avoid scare heads; treat crime as loathesome; guard against exaggeration." He insisted on honesty above all things. Even when the circulation passed 500,000, he refused to drop the word "nearly" from his slogan, "In Philadelphia, nearly everybody reads *The Bulletin.*" To safeguard his independence, he consistently brushed aside public office and corporate directorships, excepting only in organizations of newspapers.

Taking over the *Bulletin* at the height of the bitter news-association war, he was soon active on the side of the victorious Associated Press and shared prominently in its reorganization in 1900. Through him, John G. Johnson [*q.v.*], the noted Philadelphia attorney, was engaged to draft a new charter and bylaws which would stand clear of the court ruling in Illinois that the old Association was "affected with a public interest" and must serve all alike. McLean remained a director of the Associated Press from 1896 until 1924 and was also, for a time, on the Board of the American Newspaper Publishers' Association.

Tall, with a large frame, tireless, deliberate of speech and action, inclined to reticence yet plainspoken on occasion, he was gentle in manner and most considerate of his subordinates, to whom he accorded full confidence and support. He was a lover of nature: hunting, fishing, and camping out filled his vacations. His philanthropy was mostly unobtrusive. In 1919 he established a scholarship at Princeton in memory of his eldest son, who was killed in a military training camp. He presented the "Tudor Room" to the Pennsylvania Art Museum, and gave $100,000 to provide a statue of Benjamin Franklin for the Franklin Memorial Museum. Although a purveyor of publicity, he stubbornly shunned the limelight for himself, refusing interviews and even personal data for biographical compendia. He was married in 1889 to Sarah Burd Warden, daughter of William G. Warden of Philadelphia, who had the same birthday as her husband and died on her fifty-eighth anniversary. Two sons and a daughter survived their parents. McLean had devolved the active conduct of the *Bulletin* gradually upon his sons and, in his closing year, was confined to his home in Germantown, where he died.

[E. P. Oberholtzer, *Phila., A Hist. of the City and Its People* (n.d.), vol. IV; *Who's Who in America,* 1930–31; *Evening Bulletin* (Phila.), July 30, 1931.] V. R.

McLELLAN, ISAAC (May 21, 1806–Aug. 20, 1899), poet and sportsman, was born in Portland, Me., the son of Isaac and Eliza (Hull) McLellan. When he was thirteen his family moved to Boston. With his friend, Nathaniel P. Willis, he attended Phillips Academy, Andover, Mass., and from there he proceeded to Bowdoin, graduating in 1826. He then returned to Boston and devoted his time to law and journalism. He was associate editor of the *Boston Patriot and Daily Mercantile Advertiser,* merged in 1831 with the *Boston Daily Advertiser,* and he began the publication of a monthly magazine which was consolidated with the *Boston Pearl,* previously edited by Isaac C. Pray. For two years in the forties he traveled in Europe. Upon his return he gave up law and journalism, turning exclusively to the life of an ardent sportsman and poet of sport. He never married. After 1851 he made his home in Greenport, L. I., in an unpretentious board house on Barnegat Bay. He became an active member of the group of New York sportsmen which included William T. Porter, of the *Spirit of the Times,* Henry William Herbert ("Frank Forester"), Genio C. Scott, Edward Zane Carroll Judson ("Ned Buntline"), and Harry Fenwood. He had been a frequent contributor of prose and verse to the magazines of the day, and he now wrote for the sporting journals, principally *Turf, Field and Farm*; *Forest and Stream*; *American Angler*; *Amateur Sportsman,* and *Gameland.*

Most of his poetry, though little of his prose, was from time to time reprinted in book form. His first book, *The Fall of the Indian with Other Poems* (1830), with a timid preface, is heavy with youthful, literary melancholy and elegy, strange perhaps in view of the actual devotion to sport. The graveyard strain is continued in *Mount Auburn and Other Poems* (1843), the title poem being a detailed, annotated elegy over the dead in Mount Auburn Cemetery (where he himself was later buried), and in a fugitive broadside, "Paradise Spring," a poem read before the Phi Beta Kappa society of Bowdoin, Sept. 3, 1835. The outward aspects of Nature do enter these poems, often in expressive epithet, but it is not until the appearance of *Poems of the Rod and Gun, or Sports by Flood and Field* (1886), edited by Frederick E. Pond ("Will Wildwood"), that McLellan became, for the reader familiar only with the collected poems, the sportsman's poet. This and his last volume, *Haunts of Wild Game, or Poems of Woods, Wilds and Waters* (1896), edited by Charles Barker Bradford, are true curiosities in American poetry. They are nothing short of natural histories in verse of the United States and other regions. To invest such subjects as "Bison-hunting in the Far West," "Elephant-hunting in the Island of Ceylon," and "My Parker Gun" with genuine poetry is often beyond his power, as it indeed might be beyond that of any poet, but he was the spokesman in verse of a generation of American sportsmen which, like the noble Indian whom he mourned, has passed away.

[There is a memoir of McLellan by F. E. Pond in the latter's edition of *Poems of the Rod and Gun* and one by C. B. Bradford in *Haunts of Wild Game.* See also: R. W. Griswold, *The Poets and Poetry of America* (1850); G. B. Griffith, *The Poets of Maine* (1888); *Who's Who in America,* 1899–1900; *Obit. Record of the Grads. of Bowdoin Coll. . . . 1900–09* (1911).]

A. L. B.
F. E. B.

McLEOD, ALEXANDER (June 12, 1774–Feb. 17, 1833), Reformed Presbyterian clergyman, author, and editor, was the son of Rev. Neil McLeod, pastor of two Scottish Established Church parishes on Mull island of the Hebrides, on which isle Alexander was born. Dr. Samuel Johnson refers to the "elegance of conversation, and strength of judgment" of the elder McLeod, by whom the lexicographer was entertained when he visited Mull (*A Journey to the Western Islands of Scotland,* 1775, p. 357). The father having died when Alexander was five years old, care of the boy fell to the mother, Margaret McLeod, daughter of Rev. Archibald McLean, McLeod's predecessor in the parishes. Before he was seven Alexander had mastered his Latin Grammar and had determined to enter the ministry. His mother died when he was about fifteen.

In 1792 he emigrated to the United States and for a time taught Greek at Schenectady, N. Y. He entered Union College in 1796, and was graduated with high honor two years later. During his first year in the United States, through the influence of Rev. James McKinney, who had arrived from Ireland in 1793, McLeod had united with the Reformed Presbyterian Church. After theological studies under McKinney, he was licensed to preach in 1799. The following year he was called to be pastor at Coldenham, near Newburgh, N. Y., and also of the First Reformed Presbyterian Church, New York City. When he objected to the Coldenham call because among its signers were several slave-owners, the presbytery formally forbade communicant membership to slave-holders. A revised call was accepted, but the New York parish grew so rapidly that the young man soon gave all his time to it, and he remained connected with it until his death. Within a few years he was recognized as a leader in his denomination, and as one of America's foremost pulpit orators.

McLeod entered the controversy with the Episcopal Church regarding validity of presbyterial ordination of ministers when, in 1806, he published his *Ecclesiastical Catechism.* In 1814 his *Lectures upon the Principal Prophecies of the Revelation* appeared; and in 1816, *The Life and Power of True Godliness,* which like his *Catechism* was well received in both America and Great Britain. Among his other publications was a sermon in opposition to slavery, *Negro Slavery Unjustifiable* (1802), which pointed toward his active aid, some years afterwards, in organizing the American Colonization Society. His *Scriptural View of the Character, Causes and Ends of the Present War* (1815) accorded with his vigorous defense of the government's war policy. When his synod founded the *Christian Expositor,* a monthly, McLeod became its editor, continuing as such nearly two years. He frequently contributed to the *Christian Magazine,* edited by John M. Mason and John B. Romeyn. He was a member of the New York City Historical Society, and helped organize the American Society for Meliorating the Condition of the Jews and also the New York Society for Instruction of the Deaf and Dumb. Having been in poor health for a long time, he died of heart disease in his fifty-ninth year.

McLeod was a fearless defender of human liberty, whether individual, civic, or religious. Naturally impetuous, he disciplined himself to restraint and was dignified and urbane in manner. In the pulpit, however, he ordinarily followed his calm and reasoned exposition with an application the eloquence of which was vehement, impassioned, and unconfined. One of his distinguished contemporaries characterized his preaching as that of "a mountain torrent, full of foam, but sending off pure water into a thousand pools." In 1805 he married Maria Anne, daughter of John Agnew.

[W. B. Sprague, *Annals Am. Pulpit,* vol. IX (1869); S. N. Rowan, *Tribute to the Memory of Alexander McLeod, D. D.* (1833); R. E. Thompson, *A Hist. of the Presbyterian Churches in the U. S.* (1895); S. B. Wylie, *Memoir of Alexander McLeod, D. D.* (1855); *N. Y. Standard,* Feb. 19, 1833.]

P. P. F.

McLEOD, HUGH (Aug. 1, 1814–Jan. 2, 1862), military leader of the Texan Santa Fé expedition, was born in New York City, but while he was yet a boy his family removed to Macon, Ga. From Georgia he entered the United States Military Academy on Sept. 1, 1831. Four years later he was graduated and was commissioned as second lieutenant of the 3rd Infantry, but before joining his company at Fort Jessup, La., he visited Macon and accompanied the Georgia batallion on its journey to Texas as far as Columbus, Ga. Fired with a desire to join the Texas revolution, he sent in his resignation, which took effect June 30, 1836. He then went to Texas, where he rapidly advanced to prominence. In December 1837, he became adjutant-general and continued as such until Jan. 18, 1841, playing an important part in the Indian wars, particularly the Caddo expedition of 1838, the expulsion of the Cherokee in 1839, and the Comanche troubles of 1840.

In 1841 President Lamar appointed him military head of the expedition sent to Santa Fé to open a trade route and peacefully extend Texas jurisdiction to the Rio Grande. On June 17 he received his commission as brigadier-general. A few days later six companies of soldiers and a band of merchants commenced the journey, without adequate knowledge or adequate equipment. Though delayed by the illness of McLeod and a shortage of provisions, the expedition pushed steadily across the prairies until the end of August, in spite of geographical uncertainty, the infidelity of their Mexican guide, and trouble with the Kiowa, who had been encouraged by Mexican officials. At the Quintufue (Pease River?), the party divided. Almost one hundred men went ahead; the rest, under McLeod, encamped until a guide arrived from the advance party in the middle of September. Joyously, McLeod advanced, only to meet Armijo's hostile army near Laguna Colorada. Treachery, the starving condition of the men, and his officers' insistence forced McLeod to surrender. The party was marched to San Miguel, where the other Texans, also prisoners, were held. All were then marched to distant Mexico city. McLeod, an important prisoner, was always well treated, even during his weary months at Perote fortress, where he remained until the next summer. Released, he returned to Galveston.

In that year he married Rebecca Johnson Lamar, who was the sister of Gazaway Lamar and the cousin of Mirabeau B. Lamar, president of Texas [*qq.v.*]. They had one son, Cazneau. He settled down to a quiet family life, holding several minor offices. He was a member of the Texas Congress, served again as adjutant-general in 1845–46, and later was a member of the state legislature. He may have been the Hugh McLeod who, when Matamoras was occupied by American troops in 1846, began to edit a newspaper there, the *Republic of the Rio Grande.* The editorials, advocating the establishment of an independent republic in the border states of Mexico, aroused the opposition of the military officials, who forced him to resign the editorship. Whether or not he was that editor he was in

Galveston in November of that year and not taking part in the Mexican War (Lamar, *post,* vols. IV, pt. 1, p. 144, V, p. 22). He was in 1850 a member of the company organized to construct the Buffalo Bayou, Brazos, and Colorado Railroad, the first railroad of Texas. In 1855 he was sent as a delegate to the southern commercial convention in New Orleans. He became interested in the Know-Nothing movement but returned to the Democratic fold in 1858. A fat, jovial man, he was personally popular and highly esteemed locally but was chiefly known in state politics for his violent tirades against Sam Houston. After Texas seceded from the Union he enlisted in the Confederate army. As lieutenant-colonel, he assisted in taking over the United States forts on the Rio Grande. Later, as colonel of the 1st Texas Infantry, he went to Dumfries, Va., where he died in camp. His body was taken to Texas and buried in the state cemetery.

[G. W. Cullum, *Biog. Reg. of the Officers and Grads. of the U. S. Mil. Acad.,* 3rd ed., vol. I (1891); G. W. Kendall, *Narrative of the Texan Sante Fé Expedition* (2 vols., 1844); Thomas Falconer, *Letters and Notes on the Texan Sante Fe Expedition* (1930); *Weekly Telegraph* (Houston), esp. Jan.–Mar. 1862; *The Papers of Mirabeau Buonaparte Lamar,* vols. II–IV, VI (1922–27); G. P. Garrison, *Diplomatic Correspondence of the Republic of Texas,* vol. II, pts. 1, 2 (1908–11). W. C. Binkley, *The Expansionist Movement in Texas* (1925); F. R. Lubbock, *Six Decades in Texas* (1900), esp. pp. 185, 199, 233–34, 380; *War of the Rebellion: Official Records (Army),* 1 ser., vol. LIII (1898), 4 ser., vol. I (1900); Edward Mayes, *Geneal. Notes on a Branch of the Family of Mayes and on the Related Families* (1928?), p. C–34; *Quarterly of the Texas State Hist. Asso.,* July 1897, Apr. 1904; *Southern Hist. Quart.,* Jan. 1917, Apr. 1925, Jan. 1932; *Am. Hist. Review,* Oct. 1932.] W. B—r.

McLEOD, MARTIN (Aug. 30, 1813–Nov. 20, 1860), fur-trader, Minnesota pioneer, was born in L'Orignal, near Montreal, the son of John and Janet McLeod and one of a large family of children. In 1836, impelled by a desire for adventure in the wilds, he resigned a Montreal clerkship and joined a mysterious filibustering expedition under "General" James Dickson, a visionary who planned to cross the continent and establish an Indian kingdom in the Far West. As a major in Dickson's "Indian Liberating Army" of some sixty adventurers, including a few Polish refugees, McLeod endured the rigors of a winter march across northern Minnesota to the Red River colony. Cold, hunger, and fatigue caused the collapse of this fantastic filibuster but failed to break the buoyant spirit of McLeod, who found leisure to study Spanish, to read Xenophon, *The Lady of the Lake, Thaddeus of Warsaw,* and *Scottish Chiefs,* and to keep a remarkable diary, with entries telling of nights when he lay nearly buried in snowdrifts to escape the biting fury of northern blizzards. Late in February 1837, with a guide and some members of the defunct filibuster, he set out from the Red River colony for Fort Snelling. Two of his companions lost their lives on the journey, but McLeod, though he nearly froze to death and so blistered his feet that "at every step," he wrote, "the blood from my toes oozes through my Moccasins," reached his objective.

Soon after his arrival, in April 1837, he engaged in the fur trade, which for two decades led him up and down the Minnesota Valley, braving the perils and loneliness of wilderness winters, equipping Indians, and collecting furs from them at Traverse des Sioux, Big Stone Lake, and Lac qui Parle. He attained great influence over the red men, especially the Upper Sioux, who trusted him. It was due largely to him that the Sioux treaties of 1851 were extremely favorable to the traders. Notwithstanding his growing influence and responsibility and his tireless industry, the evils of the credit system brought him continued losses, and in 1858 he sold his interests.

McLeod identified himself with the frontier commonwealth of Minnesota. He was a member of the territorial council from 1849 to 1853, and president during his last term. As a councilor he worked zealously in behalf of measures for the general welfare and advancement of the territory. Because of his superior education, acquired principally through wide reading, he was made chairman of the committee on schools; and in that capacity, as author of the bill that laid the foundation of Minnesota's school-system, he performed his most important legislative service. He was a vigorous settlement promoter. His letters to Canadian newspapers brought out a considerable number of pioneers. He planned town sites and bought and improved property in various places in the hope that an influx of settlers would enhance its value and bring him fortune. He was one of the founders of Glencoe, and he labored energetically for the development of the county that bears his name. The panic of 1857 dealt a severe blow to these projects, however, and left him heavily in debt and his death three years later forestalled the execution of his plans for the development of the young state.

About 1838 McLeod contracted a union with Mary E. Ortley, the daughter of a trader and a Sioux woman, and they had several children. In 1849 he established his family on a farm at Oak Grove, near Fort Snelling, which remained his home until his death. He is described by a contemporary as "a man of noble form, commanding presence, cultured intellect . . . dignified, eloquent, persuasive, charming" (J. H. Stevens,

Personal Recollections of Minnesota and Its People, 1890, p. 266).

[Further information may be found in McLeod's diary, ed. by Grace L. Nute, in *Minnesota Hist. Bull.,* Aug.–Nov. 1922; see also G. L. Nute, "James Dickson: A Filibuster in Minnesota, in 1836," in *Miss. Valley Hist. Rev.,* Sept. 1923; C. J. Ritchey, "Martin McLeod and the Minnesota Valley," in *Minn. Hist.,* Dec. 1929; papers of McLeod, J. H. Stevens, and H. H. Sibley, in the possession of the Minn. Hist. Soc., St. Paul.]

T. C. B.

McLOUGHLIN, JOHN (Oct. 19, 1784–Sept. 3, 1857), factor of the Hudson's Bay Company on the Columbia River, was born in the parish of Riviere du Loup, province of Quebec, the son of John McLoughlin, a native of Ireland, and Angélique (Fraser), who was born in Canada of Scottish parents. Young John and his brother David were both educated for the profession of medicine under their grandfather Fraser's direction, their father having lost his life early by drowning. David became a physician in Paris. John, after receiving his training in Scotland, returned to Canada and became a partner of the North West Fur Company. At the time of the union of the North West and Hudson's Bay companies in 1821, he was in charge at the important post of Fort William on Lake Superior. In 1824 as chief factor of the Hudson's Bay Company he was given direct supervision of the Columbia District, with headquarters on the Columbia. There he remained in control from 1824 to 1846, the critical period in the history of the Oregon country.

When McLoughlin arrived at Fort George, the former Astoria, there were no American traders regularly established west of the Rockies, notwithstanding John Jacob Astor's attempt—foiled by the War of 1812—to engross the entire commerce of the region, and the fact that the treaty of joint occupation (1818) guaranteed to Englishmen and Americans equal rights to "trade and make settlements" between the crest of the mountains and the Pacific, north of the 42nd parallel and south of the parallel of 54° 40′. The chief factor's duty as manager of the company's affairs in that vast terrain was to monopolize the fur trade as completely as possible, and to exploit it in a way to produce the maximum annual profits for an indefinite period of time. To that end it was necessary to impose permanent peace upon the numerous tribes of Indians and incite them to diligence in collecting furs under strict conservation principles, to keep out rival traders, and to prevent if possible the agricultural settlement of the country. This proved a difficult program for McLoughlin to execute to the satisfaction both of his employers and of his own conscience.

With George Simpson, he fixed upon a location within the present city of Vancouver, Wash., as the most eligible site for the central post, and after 1825 Fort Vancouver was the virtual capital of his far-flung domain. A large farm, gardens, orchards, dairies, a sawmill and flouring mill, a shipyard and mechanics' shops, with the personnel required to man all of these activities, developed around the fort a considerable village. Annual ships from England brought in the supplies of goods for trade, and carried back the furs assembled from all subordinate stations, to the value, it has been estimated, of from $105,000 to $150,000 per year.

McLoughlin was generally successful in keeping peace among the tribes and preventing the murder of white men, whether Englishmen or others. American traders exercised their right of entering the territory, but he succeeded in ruining their business by controlling the Indian customers, underselling, and overbidding. Nevertheless, although his business competition was merciless, he accorded all rivals personally the most generous treatment, furnishing necessaries, entertaining them at his fort, and facilitating their travels. When missionaries began to go to Oregon from the United States in 1834, McLoughlin was their good angel. He encouraged both the Methodist and the Presbyterian missions as well as the later Catholic establishment. He was equally kind to American settlers, whom company policy forbade him to encourage in any way. Being unable to carry more supplies than were imperatively needed on the way, most of the emigrants reached the lower Columbia in a destitute condition. By withholding succor McLoughlin might have delayed the occupation of the country, yet he made it a practice to sell them provisions and wait for his pay till the wheat crop came in the following year. He defended this charitable attitude against the criticism of his superiors on the dual ground of humanity and true policy. He could not let the settlers perish, and had he done so the opposition to the "British monopoly" would have brought upon it swift disaster. Many settlers never paid him, and the Company suffered loss, but not without complaining seriously to him in consequence.

Although through his generosity he gave material aid toward the American occupation of Oregon south of the Columbia, he advised against Americans settling north of that river, thus furthering Canning's policy of making the river itself the future international boundary. When convinced that the 49th parallel and Fuca's Strait were to be the boundary, he quietly prepared to establish the Company's headquarters at Fort Victoria on Vancouver Island. In 1846, the year the boundary treaty was signed, McLoughlin retired from the company under criticism. He had filed with the Oregon Provisional Government a claim embracing the falls of the Willamette, where he built a mill, laid out a town, and proceeded to sell lots. His right to do this was contested by certain Americans, and despite a private adjustment with them and McLoughlin's previous declaration of intention to become an American citizen, Congress in 1850 invalidated his claim under the Donation Land Law, granting the tract to the future state for university purposes. McLoughlin was not ousted, however, and though he died without receiving justice, in 1862 the state released the property to his heirs on the payment of a nominal sum.

This land-claim episode was a *cause célèbre* in Oregon for many years. McLoughlin had gained hosts of friends among the pioneers, notwithstanding his connection with the hated British monopoly. His opponents argued that he was trying to hold his valuable water privilege, with the land adjacent, for his company. Sir George Simpson wrote in 1841 that the claim had been taken in 1829 for the company's benefit (*American Historical Review,* October 1908, p. 80). This seems conclusive, but there is no reason to doubt that McLoughlin later used his own means to develop the tract and that he came to regard it as a support for his old age. How the transfer occurred is not known.

"Doctor McLoughlin," as he was always called, was a man of extraordinary personality. He was six feet four inches tall, splendidly proportioned, dignified and imposing. He had both the air and the gift of command. The Indians called him, on account of his long white locks, the White Eagle. His righteous wrath struck terror to the hearts of his most hardened dependants, whether white or red. He prevailed through character, strict justice, and good judgment, though his personal writings disclose an otherwise ordinary, unimaginative mind. Some manuscripts bearing his signature were written by others possessing higher literary attainments. Probably the "McLoughlin Document" (Holman, *post,* pp. 229–43) was prepared by an attorney, McLoughlin supplying the data for it. Like other traders, he married a half-breed Indian woman, widow of Alexander McKay of the Astoria party, by whom he had four children.

[F. V. Holman, *Dr. John McLoughlin, The Father of Oregon* (1907), which is extremely eulogistic, contains 110 pages of illustrative documents possessing considerable value. Eva Emery Dye's story, *McLoughlin and Old Oregon* (1900), represents much research and supplies an interesting if somewhat idealized picture of life in Oregon under the McLoughlin regime. Three works by Joseph Schafer: "The British Attitude toward the Oregon Question" (*Am. Hist. Rev.,* Jan. 1911), "Oregon Pioneers and American Diplomacy" (*Essays in Am. Hist. Dedicated to Frederick Jackson Turner,* 1910), and *A Hist. of the Pacific Northwest* (1918), and Frederick Merk, "The Oregon Pioneers and the Boundary" (*Am. Hist. Rev.,* July 1924) discuss the political and social backgrounds of McLoughlin's career from somewhat divergent viewpoints. In "Letters of Sir George Simpson," *Am. Hist. Rev.,* Oct. 1908, especially at p. 80, is land-claim testimony. The *Ore. Hist. Soc. Quart.* from 1900 on has valuable material, especially the issues for Sept. 1907 (McLoughlin letter), Mar. 1909 (Warré and Vavasour's report), June 1910 (Minto's recollections), Mar. 1913 (Howison's report), Sept. 1916 (McLoughlin to Simpson, 1844; important), Dec. 1922 (McLoughlin letters), Mar. 1928 (Lieut. Wm. Peel's report). See also Frederick Merk, *Fur Trade and Empire: George Simpson's Jour.* (1931). Letters of McLoughlin, copied from Record Office F. O. Am. 440 and 444, published in the appendix to R. C. Clark, *Hist. of the Willamette Valley* (1927).]
J. S.

MACLURE, WILLIAM (Oct. 27, 1763–Mar. 23, 1840), pioneer geologist, patron of science and education, was born in Ayr, Scotland, the son of David and Ann (Kennedy) McClure. Apparently he was baptized James, but later called himself William and changed the spelling of his family name (Keyes, *post*). He received his elementary education at Ayr, under the tutelage of a "Mr. Douglass, an intelligent teacher, who was especially reputed for classical and mathematical attainments" (Morton, *post,* p. 8). He entered a mercantile house, and at nineteen made his first visit to the United States, to transact some business in New York. Upon his return to Great Britain he became a partner in the London firm of Miller, Hart & Company. He was eminently successful in business, quickly acquiring a fortune which enabled him to retire and devote his life to science and philanthropy.

In 1796 he again paid a visit to America. From boyhood, according to his biographer (Morton, p. 10), the United States "had been to him the land of promise," and at this time he may have taken the first steps toward naturalization. In 1803, having become a citizen of the United States, he was appointed member of a commission to settle spoliation claims between his adopted country and France, a task which engaged him for several years. In 1807 he published *To the People of the United States: A Statement of the Transactions of the Board of Commissioners Appointed in 1803 for the Adjustment of Claims against the French Government.*

During these years in Europe he traveled extensively, studying the geology and natural history of the continent and collecting specimens. Returning to America, he entered upon the task of making a geological map of the United States, the first map of its scope in the history of geology.

The greater part of the country was at this time a wilderness; nevertheless Maclure went forth, for the most part alone and always at his own expense, making observations throughout the entire region east of the Mississippi River. The American Philosophical Society published his colored geological map, with the explanatory "Observations on the Geology of the United States," in Volume I of its *Transactions.* The production was one with which any worker might have been content to rest. Instead, Maclure set about a revision almost at once, completing it in 1817. Published with an accompanying volume, *Observations on the Geology of the United States* (1817), it appeared also in 1818 in Volume I, new series, of the *Transactions of the American Philosophical Society.*

Meanwhile, in 1812, he had become one of the first members of the Academy of Natural Sciences of Philadelphia, and in December 1817 was elected its president, a position to which he was annually reëlected for the remaining twenty-two years of his life. He was heartily interested in the welfare of the Academy and presented to it at different times the greater part of his valuable library, as well as several of his collections of specimens. He supervised the publication of the first volumes of its *Journal,* and by a series of gifts, totaling some $20,000, made possible the erection of a building for its permanent housing. During the winter of 1816–17, with C. A. LeSueur [*q.v.*] as a companion, he visited the West Indies, directing his studies particularly to volcanic phases of their geology, and in the *Journal* of the Academy for November 1817 published his observations.

Another phase of Maclure's activity related to education. In 1805, while in Switzerland, he had visited Pestalozzi's school at Yverdun, and, enthusiastic over what he saw there, had persuaded Joseph Neef [*q.v.*] to come to Amercia to introduce Pestalozzian methods. In 1819 he went to Spain in the hope of establishing a great agricultural school for the common people, in which labor should be combined with instruction. He had purchased some 10,000 acres of land near Alicante and fitted up the necessary buildings when the liberal government of the Cortes was overthrown by revolution, the land was restored to the Church from which it had been confiscated, and he was obliged to relinquish his plan with a complete loss of all the property. This misfortune did not discourage him permanently, however, and after a visit in 1824 to Robert Owen's school at New Lanark, Scotland, he became interested in Owen's projected community at New Harmony, Ind. In his usual whole-hearted manner, he purchased an extensive tract of land in the vicinity and forwarded his library, instruments, and other personal effects that might be useful in carrying out once more, in new territory, his plan for an agricultural school. He succeeded in persuading a number of other scientific men to accompany him to New Harmony, and when he set out, took with him down the Ohio the "boat-load of knowledge," which included LeSueur, Gerard Troost, and Thomas Say [*qq.v.*]. Even after the failure of Owen's venture Maclure persisted in an attempt to organize societies for adult education among the working classes. He founded the New Harmony Working Men's Institute in 1838, and by his will directed his executors to pay $500 to any club of laborers which should establish a library of 100 volumes.

The breakdown of his health led him to spend the winter of 1827–28 in Mexico, with his friend Say. That country, he came to believe, offered a more hopeful field for the realization of the projects near to his heart. Accordingly, after visiting Philadelphia and presiding in November 1828 at the New Haven meeting of the American Geological Society, of which he had been president for several years, he returned to Mexico, in the hope of aiding in the educational uplift of its people. He planned to bring back with him "a considerable number of aboriginal young men" to be trained in his school at New Harmony to "a knowledge of useful arts and the habits that may fit them both to rule and to obey, in a republican government" (*American Journal of Science,* vol. XV, 1829, p. 401), but apparently the design was never carried out. Maclure spent most of the rest of his life in Mexico. Upon the serious failure of his health in 1839 he made an attempt to return to the United States, but was unable to stand the difficulties of the journey and died in the village of San Ángel, near the city of Mexico, early in 1840.

During his residence in Mexico, he had continued to correspond with his scientific friends and contributed a number of letters on political, social, and economic topics to the New Harmony *Disseminator.* These papers were collected and published under the title, *Opinions on Various Subjects, Dedicated to the Industrious Producers* (2 vols., 1831–37). He is described as a man of "above the middle stature and of a naturally robust frame," of conspicuous serenity of mind, singularly mild and unostentatious in manner. He never married.

[Sources include: S. G. Morton, *A Memoir of William Maclure* (1841; 2nd ed., 1844), also pub. in *Proc. Acad. Nat. Sci. of Phila.,* vol. I (1841) and *Am. Jour. Sci.,* Apr.–June 1844; C. R. Keyes, in *Pan American Geolo-*

gist, Sept. 1925. See also G. B. Lockwood, *The New Harmony Movement* (1905); T. J. de la Hunt, *Hist. of the New Harmony Working Men's Inst.* (1927); H. B. Weiss and G. M. Zeigler, *Thomas Say: Early Am. Naturalist* (1931); *A Cyc. of Educ.* (1925), ed. by Paul Monroe; G. P. Merrill, *The First One Hundred Years of American Geology* (1924).] G. P. M.

McMAHON, BERNARD (d. Sept. 18, 1816), Philadelphia horticulturist, was born in Ireland and in 1796 came to America as one of those "Exiles of Erin," driven from Ireland by political motives, who sought and found refuge in the United States. He settled in Philadelphia. William Darlington, the botanist, in a letter written at West Chester, Pa., on June 15, 1857, says: "In the autumn, I think, of 1799, he [McMahon] passed some weeks at my native village of Dilworthtown, in Chester County, in order to avoid the ravages of yellow fever, in Philadelphia, where he resided; and in that rural retreat I first knew him. I renewed the acquaintance in 1802, 3, and 4, while attending medical lectures in the University of Pennsylvania, by which time he had established his nurseries of useful and ornamental plants: and I ever found him an obliging, intelligent, and instructive friend" (*American Gardener's Calendar, post,* p. xiii). These nurseries, including McMahon's greenhouses and experimental gardens, were situated near the Germantown turnpike between Philadelphia and Nicetown. From them "emanated the rarer flowers and novelties such as could be collected in the early part of the present [nineteenth] century," and in them "were performed, to the astonishment of the amateurs of that day, successful feats of horticulture that were but too rarely imitated" (*Ibid.,* p. xi.).

In connection with the nurseries, McMahon had established a seed and general nursery business at 39 South Second Street below Market, on the east side of Philadelphia. Behind the counter was his wife, "with some considerable Irish accent, but a most amiable and excellent disposition, and withal an able saleswoman." The remarkable part of the store was not in its stock, although it was one of the largest seed stores in the United States at that time, but rather the character and prominence of the botanists and horticulturists who were attracted there as a common meeting place for varied scientific discussions. Here Nuttall, Baldwin, Darlington, and other authorities came to impart or receive scientific information. McMahon took an active part in the discussions occurring in his store and his opinion is said to have been greatly respected. As a consequence of his contacts with McMahon, when Nuttall published in 1818 his *Genera of North American Plants,* he named an evergreen barberry *Mahonia,* "in memory of the late Bernard McMahon, whose ardent attachment to Botany, and successful introduction of useful and ornamental Horticulture into the United States, lays claim to public esteem" (vol. I, p. 211, note).

McMahon early began the collection and exportation of American seeds and he was continually soliciting seed and plant exchanges with his many correspondents in the United States and abroad with the purpose of discovering new plants suited for cultivation in the United States. In his catalogue published in 1804, he lists about a thousand species of such seeds. After the Lewis and Clark expedition, Jefferson wrote to La Contesse de Tesse (R. G. Thwaites, ed., *Original Journals of the Lewis and Clark Expedition,* vol. VII, 1905, p. 393): "All Lewis's plants are growing in the garden of Mr. McMahon, a gardener of Philadelphia." According to Bailey (*post,* p. 1586), "M'Mahon and Landreth were instrumental in distributing the seeds which those explorers collected." McMahon was interested in one of the numerous abortive attempts to grow the European wine grape (*Vitis vinifera*) in the eastern United States. In 1806 he gave to America its first notable horticultural book, the *American Gardener's Calendar,* which was a standard cyclopedic work for more than fifty years, the last (eleventh) edition appearing in 1857. After McMahon's death in 1816 his wife conducted his business for a time and then it passed to other hands.

[See Preface to the 1857 edition of the *Am. Gardener's Calendar*; L. H. Bailey, *The Standard Cyc. of Horticulture,* vol. III (1915); *Poulson's Am. Daily Advertiser* (Phila.), Sept. 20, 1816.] R. H. S.

McMAHON, JOHN VAN LEAR (Oct. 18, 1800–June 15, 1871), lawyer and historian, was born in Cumberland, Md. His father, William McMahon, a popular Irish-Presbyterian farmer of Allegany County, was repeatedly elected a member of the Maryland House of Delegates. His mother was a daughter of John Van Lear, a prominent pioneer of Western Maryland. The son was graduated with highest honors, at the age of seventeen, from the College of New Jersey (Princeton). He studied law in his native county, was admitted to the bar in 1819, and began practising in Baltimore the same year. His uncouth manners, unbridled temper, and proud spirit yielded him difficulties with both bench and bar, and in less than two years he closed his office, returned to Cumberland, and took up, in turn, the study of medicine and theology. Resuming the practice of law in Cumberland, he soon won distinction as a public speaker and was elected a representative of Allegany County in the Maryland House of Delegates. He entered this body in 1823 dressed as a mountain huntsman, advocated state aid to the Chesapeake & Ohio Canal, made an effective speech in favor of the removal of the political disabilities of the Jews, was made chairman of the committee on the judiciary, and, before the session closed, won recognition as the House leader. During a second term he supported a measure to allow Baltimore a representation equal to that of a county. Returning, in 1825, to the practice of law in Baltimore he rose rapidly to leadership of the Maryland bar. He represented Baltimore in the House of Delegates for two terms, 1827–28, and subsequently refused to be a candidate for public office.

At a meeting in Baltimore in February 1827, he was appointed a member of a committee to consider a project for the construction of the Baltimore & Ohio Railroad and he subsequently drafted the charter which contributed largely to the success of the undertaking and served as a model for other railroad corporations. McMahon was a leader of the Jackson Democrats of Maryland in the presidential campaign of 1829 but early in Jackson's first administration he affiliated with the National Republicans, alleging dissatisfaction with Jackson's financial and commercial policy. In June 1829, he declined a nomination by his party for a seat in Congress. In November 1837, he could not be persuaded by appeals from every quarter of the state to become a candidate for a seat in the United States Senate. In the presidential campaign of 1840 he was recognized as one of the most powerful speakers in the country. He was rewarded with the offer of a seat in President Harrison's cabinet. This he declined. When Tyler had become president he was urged to accept the post of attorney-general, but again he declined, alleging that he had not the courage to perform duties while the eyes of the whole country were upon him.

At the beginning of his service in the Maryland legislature McMahon undertook the compilation of an elementary treatise on the laws and institutions of the state. The project was revised and expanded and in 1831 he published his *Historical View of the Government of Maryland,* a constitutional history reliable in statement, illuminating in interpretation, and written with some literary merit. After a lapse of more than a hundred years it ranks as one of the most substantial contributions to the historical literature of the state. When, about 1857, McMahon was at the height of his career as a trial lawyer before the Maryland court of appeals he was stricken with partial loss of eyesight. He gradually withdrew from the bar and in 1863 removed to Cumberland where he remained with two sisters until his death, except for an interval with a third sister at Dayton, Ohio. McMahon was known to his friends as a bachelor but he had a son, John A. McMahon (1833–1923), a distinguished lawyer of Ohio, who stated that his mother was Elizabeth (Gouger) McMahon. He possessed an exceptionally retentive memory and a faculty for close observation, and a strong deep voice enhanced his power as a speaker. A mixture of vanity and humility were manifest in his eccentricities.

[John T. Mason, *Life of John Van Lear McMahon* (1879), is a critical review of McMahon's career. Consult also Henry F. Powell, *Tercentenary Hist. of Md.* (1925); J. T. Scharf, *Hist. of Western Md.* (1882), vol. I; and the *Sun* (Baltimore), June 16, 1871. For a sketch of John A. McMahon see Charlotte R. Conover, ed., *Dayton and Montgomery County* (1932), vol. II.]

N. D. M.

McMANES, JAMES (Apr. 13, 1822–Nov. 23, 1899), politician, was born in County Tyrone, Ireland, the son of James and Rebecca (Johnson) McManes. He emigrated with his parents to the United States at the age of eight years, and settled in Philadelphia. Because of his family's poverty, he left school before completing the elementary grades and went to work as a bobbin-boy in the cotton-mills. At the age of twenty-five he began spinning for himself on a modest scale, but his mill burned, and he returned to the older mills as an employee. In 1855 he left to establish a real-estate business. Meanwhile, in 1844 he had received naturalization papers and joined the Whigs. In 1852 he was moderately active in support of Winfield Scott; after Scott's defeat he turned to the People's Republican ranks and got himself elected to the ward school board, and by 1858 he controlled the politics of Philadelphia's Seventeenth Ward. In 1860 he sat as a Lincoln delegate in the Republican National Convention and at the state convention helped nominate Andrew G. Curtin [*q.v.*] for governor. Two years later he ran unsuccessfully for a seat in the national House of Representatives. In 1865 he became one of the trustees charged with the management of the municipal gas works and during his twenty years of service had much to do with making the gas trustees a ring which almost completely dominated Philadelphia politics. In 1866 he received election as prothonotary of the district court and a seat on the city board of education. Thenceforward until 1881 his power in Philadelphia politics exceeded that of any other person.

At the Republican National Convention in 1880 McManes favored Garfield, refusing to support Grant for a third term in spite of the state boss, Senator James Donald Cameron [*q.v.*]. As a reprisal, Cameron invaded Philadelphia in 1881 and with the support of a reform movement inflicted on McManes a bad defeat. The next two years were turbulent and in 1883 McManes even temporarily lost his position as gas trustee. By 1884, however, the uprising had sufficiently receded for him to elect the mayor. During the years following 1885, when Matthew S. Quay [*q.v.*] attempted with considerable success to dominate Philadelphia politics, McManes devoted much of his time to private business and to Fairmount Park, which he served as commissioner.

Although gentle to his family and friends, devoted to his wife, Catherine McNamee, simple in habits, taciturn, and of exemplary private life, McManes possessed an imperious nature which together with a pronounced bluntness of manner alienated many, particularly during his later years. He overcame the lack of a formal education by keen powers of observation, dogged perseverance, and ability to judge men. Withal he dealt generously with the poor and faithfully attended the Presbyterian Church. Thrifty and shrewd, he accumulated a fortune of approximately two and a half million dollars. Starting with real estate, he later became interested in street railways and merged the important lines of Philadelphia into the Union Passenger Railway. After helping organize the People's Bank, he became a director and later its president, and although apparently not personally cognizant of the acts that led to its failure, he felt obligated to the depositors and paid out of his own pocket more than half a million dollars. He died in Philadelphia.

[James Bryce, *The Am. Commonwealth* (1888), vol. II, ch. lxxxix; Harold Zink, *City Bosses in the U. S.* (1930); George Vickers, *The Fall of Bossism,* vol. I (1883); S. W. Pennypacker, *The Autobiog. of a Pennsylvanian* (1918); F. W. Leach, "Twenty Years with Quay" and "Philadelphia Politics," appearing in serial form in the *North American* (Phila.), 1904–05; obituaries in *Phila. Inquirer, Public Ledger* (Phila.), and *North American* (Phila.), Nov. 24, 1899; date of birth and maiden names of wife and mother from a grandson.] H. Z.

McMASTER, GUY HUMPHREYS (Jan. 31, 1829–Sept. 13, 1887), jurist and poet, was born in Clyde, Wayne County, N. Y., the son of David and Adeline (Humphreys) McMaster. About a year after his birth his parents moved to Bath, which was thenceforth the family home. After attending Franklin Academy at Prattsburg, N. Y., McMaster entered Hamilton College, where he enjoyed the friendship of Charles Dudley Warner and Joseph R. Hawley [*qq.v.*]. Soon after his graduation in 1847 he began the study of law, but during the next few years varied the tedium of his preliminary studies by literary work. In February 1849 he contributed to the *Knickerbocker* the lyric "Carmen Bellicosum," which was signed "John MacGrom"; and in 1851, to the *American Whig Review,* a poem entitled "The Northern Lights" (September) and some prose essays. In 1853 he published a *History of the Settlement of Steuben County.* In the same year he married Amanda Church; and in succeeding years they had four children.

McMaster was admitted to the bar in 1852. Associated with a succession of partners, he ultimately formed a partnership with his son-in-law, John F. Parkhurst; and the firm of McMaster & Parkhurst continued to function until McMaster's death. In 1863 he became county judge and surrogate, a position which he held until the close of 1883, when the two offices were separated, and he was elected surrogate. As a lawyer and judge, he was greatly respected both for his knowledge of the law and for the fairness of his decisions. His activities were varied in 1877 by a journey to the Pacific Coast, and in 1885 by a trip to Europe. While on these trips, he wrote for the *Steuben Courier* the "Pacific Letters" and the "Other-Side Letters." A member of the Republican party and of the Presbyterian Church, he was one of the most influential citizens of Bath. For many years he was the organist of his church.

To the American public McMaster is known chiefly as the author of "Carmen Bellicosum," which has appeared in many anthologies, including *The Oxford Book of American Verse* (1927). This poem, which was written to the memory of the Continental soldiers, E. C. Stedman regarded as "the ringing, characteristic utterance of an original man" (*post,* p. 52). A similar vigorous note is struck in the descriptive poem "The Northern Lights." During the Civil War he also published in the *Hartford Courant* (November 1864) the half-patriotic, half-humorous "Dream of Thanksgiving Eve" (reprinted in *Army and Navy Journal,* May 5, 1877). Other poems of his include "The Commanders" (1879), later printed in Frederick Cook's *Journals of the Military Expedition of Major General John Sullivan* (1887); and "The Professor's Guest Chamber," published in the *Utica Herald* in 1880. Although the body of his poetry is small, it is nevertheless important in representing a spirited, forceful note in American verse at a period when many native poets found their chief inspiration in the vapid and sentimental.

[Letters from McMaster's daughter, Miss Katherine McMaster, and from J. D. Ibbotson, librarian of Hamilton College; *Hamilton Literary Monthly*, Oct. 1887; *Medico-Legal Jour.*, Sept. 1887; I. W. Near, *A Hist. of Steuben County, N. Y.* (1911); W. W. Clayton, *Hist. of Steuben County* (1879); M. F. Roberts, *Hist. Gazetteer of Steuben County* (1891); H. Hakes, *Landmarks of Steuben County* (1896); E. C. Stedman, "A Belt of Asteroids," *Galaxy*, Jan. 1869; *Critic*, Oct. 22, 1887.] N.F.A.

McMASTER, JAMES ALPHONSUS (Apr. 1, 1820–Dec. 29, 1886), journalist, son of the Rev. Gilbert and Jane (Brown) McMaster, was born in Duanesburg, N. Y. His strict covenanting Scotch father forced him at an early age to study the classics and Scripture in preparation for the ministry, into which two of his brothers entered. On leaving Union College, 1839, he studied law and commenced its practice. Presumably he preached from a Reformed Presbyterian pulpit and attended the Union Theological Seminary, where he was associated with Isaac Hecker and Clarence Walworth [*qq.v.*] before being received into the Roman Catholic Church by Father Rumpler in 1845. Thereupon, McMaster accompanied Hecker and Walworth to the Redemptorist College at Louvain, Belgium, on the way paying a visit to Newman at Littlemore, England. Here he acquired his vaunted knowledge of Catholic theology, though he agreed with his superiors that he lacked a religious vocation. Returning to New York, he entered journalism as a writer for the *New York Tribune* and the *New York Freeman's Journal*. In 1847 he borrowed enough money from George V. Hecker to buy Bishop Hughes's interest in the *Freeman's Journal*, which he edited until his death. In 1850 he married a Miss Fetterman of Pennsylvania by whom he had four children: Alphonsus, who tried out a vocation at Ilchester, England, and became a New York journalist; and three daughters who entered convents, thus leaving a proud but lonely widowed father to fend for himself.

As an editor, McMaster was honest, able, courageous, and annoyingly frank. Indeed he was a stormy petrel in Catholic circles. A stout supporter of Hughes in the school fight, he so frequently took issue with him that at times the bishop repented of ever selling the journal, though at other times he keenly appreciated McMaster's picturesque service to the Church. A stanch friend of the Redemptorists and Paulists, he was amusingly suspicious of the Jesuits and on occasion violently critical of journalists like Orestes A. Brownson [*q.v.*], Denis Sadlier [*q.v.*], of the *Tablet*, and Thomas D'Arcy McGee, who became a cabinet minister in Canada, and of prelates like Kenrick and Purcell. At times his lack of interest in Irish affairs annoyed extremists, but he made the *Freeman's Journal* the outstanding Catholic organ, which challenged the respect of churchmen and politicians. Without political ambition, and above either flattery or bribery, he was a power in the Democratic party on the side of state rights and against abolition. Even regardless of its nativist associations, Whiggery was detestable to him. While he denounced the South and refuted such clerical "rebels" as Patrick Neeson Lynch and Napoleon Joseph Perché [*qq.v.*], he had little confidence in Lincoln's policies. Criticism of the administration closed the mails to the *Freeman's Journal* and brought about McMaster's arbitrary arrest without warrant or indictment. Imprisoned in Fort Lafayette on Aug. 24, 1861, he was finally freed without trial and resumed the publication of his paper (Apr. 19, 1862) without amending its editorial policy. McMaster to the end gloried in his martyrdom for freedom of the press in war time.

After the war, he paid his compliments to Reconstruction measures, the "godless" schools as he described public schools without training in religion and morals, and to the bishops whose attitude on infallibility he questioned. His journalistic model was Louis Veuillot of *L'Univers Religieux*. He was a stout advocate of the temporal power and a lover of the Eternal City, and he prided himself on his precise Latin and his inauguration of the first American pilgrimage. Archbishop Corrigan he loved; this explained his vicious attacks on Edward McGlynn. He was well characterized by Archbishop Ryan of Philadelphia as "a Scotch Highlander with a touch of Calvinism not yet sponged out of him." Toward the end the *Freeman's Journal* lost influence as more diocesan organs were founded, but its editorials challenged attention even during the last six years when McMaster's fiery rhetoric was toned down by the genial Maurice Francis Egan. Bitter in prejudices, stubborn in support of principles, firm in friendship, and aggressive in religious beliefs, McMaster was a picturesque character. Not until he died was it learned that he had long worn a hair-shirt in mortification.

[M. F. Egan, "A Slight Appreciation of Jas. Alphonsus McMaster," U. S. Cath. Hist. Soc., *Hist. Records and Studies*, vol. XV (1921); J. G. Shea, *Hist. of the Cath. Ch. in the U. S.*, vol. IV (1892); J. T. Smith, *The Cath. Ch. in N. Y.* (2 vols., 1905); *Cath. Encyc.*; files of the *Freeman's Jour.*, especially the issue of Jan. 8, 1887; *U. S. Cath. Hist. Mag.*, Apr. 1887; *N. Y. Herald*, Dec. 30, 1886.] R. J. P.

McMASTER, JOHN BACH (June 29, 1852–May 24, 1932), historian, was born in Brooklyn,

N. Y., the son of Julia Anna Matilda (Bach) McMaster and Theodore James McMaster, a planter and banker. His grandfather, James McMaster, came from England in 1796, apprenticed to a Mr. Titford, importer and seller of drugs in New York. In 1800 he bought the business, opened a shop at 128 Pearl St., and three years later married Elizabeth Watrous of Balston, N. Y. The grandparents on the mother's side were Robert Bach of Hereford, England, and Margaret Cowan of Newry, Ireland. John Bach McMaster was educated in the public schools of New York, graduating with the B.A. degree from the College of the City of New York in 1872 and remaining for a year longer as instructor in English. It was at this time that he became interested in writing a history of the United States. In 1873 he was appointed chief clerk and civil assistant to Maj. George L. Gillespie of the Engineering Corps, and assigned to make a survey of the battlefield of Winchester for use in the memoirs which General Sheridan was preparing. After a year of map-making at Sheridan's headquarters in Chicago, he returned to New York to practise engineering from 1874 to 1877. During this time he published *Bridge and Tunnel Centres* (1875), and *High Masonry Dams* (1876); he wrote a work on "The Struggle of Man with Nature," the manuscript of which was later destroyed. In 1875 his alma mater conferred upon him the degree of C.E., and in 1877 he was appointed instructor in engineering at the College of New Jersey (Princeton), a position which he held until 1883. In the summer of 1878 he had charge of the Princeton scientific expedition to the Bad Lands of Wyoming in search of fossil remains. The colorful drama of the frontier made a deep impression on him and strengthened his resolve to write the history of the nation while the spirit of growth and expansion was still strong. From the active life of the engineer, he turned to history, spending much of his spare time in research in the Library of Congress, the rooms of the American Antiquarian Society, and the Historical Societies of Pennsylvania, New York, and New Jersey. In 1881, after many years of patient work, the first volume of *The History of the People of the United States* was completed. Written entirely in longhand, the bulky manuscript was sent to Appleton & Company who hesitatingly "ventured its publication" in 1883. The second volume appeared in 1885, and others at irregular intervals until the eighth was published in 1913.

Shortly after the publication of the first volume, the University of Pennsylvania offered McMaster a professorship in American history which he accepted, remaining at that institution for thirty-seven years. On Apr. 14, 1887, he married Gertrude Stevenson of Morristown, N. J., by whom there were three children, a son alone surviving his father. In June 1920, having reached the age of sixty-eight, McMaster was retired as professor emeritus. He continued his researches, however, adding to his larger history another volume, *The History of the People of the United States during Lincoln's Administration* (1927). In the autumn of 1931 he moved from Philadelphia to Darien, Conn., where he died of pneumonia on May 24, 1932. He was slight in physique, reticent and retiring in general society, but his quiet dignity and strength of character marked him as a man of distinction in any group, while in more intimate circles his broad range of information, fund of anecdotes, and genial personality won him the admiration and love of his associates.

McMaster's outstanding work is *The History of the People of the United States.* The earlier volumes in particular hold a unique place in the field of social and economic history, until then so largely neglected for war and politics. Scholars and critics acclaimed them not only because of the shift in historical point of view but also because of the author's originality of thought and realistic narrative style. Working independently and at firsthand in contemporary sources, he made much use of newspapers, magazines, memoirs, books of travel, and letters of prominent men, but he soon found that blazing a new path in historical writing, through materials so voluminous and often unreliable, invited pitfalls and much criticism. Similarly the absence of all hero worship led to dissatisfaction in certain quarters despite the fervent patriotism of the volumes and their strong nationalistic spirit. McMaster was the first professor of American history in the United States to combine research and writing with teaching. Through his advanced students and through his textbooks, his influence upon the study and writing of history was widely disseminated. More than two and a half million copies of the texts, which were carefully graded to meet the needs of primary, grammar, and high school pupils, were sold during his lifetime. Penetrating, and keen in their analysis of men and movements, his texts, like his larger works, show originality and breadth of conception. Seventeen volumes and more than a score of articles, some of which were widely quoted in the press of the time, constitute his contribution to history. In addition to his major work, the following may be cited: *Benjamin Franklin as a Man of Letters* (1887); *With the*

Fathers. Studies in the History of the United States (1896); *Daniel Webster* (1902); "The United States" in *The Cambridge Modern History,* Vol. VII (1903); *The Struggle for Social, Political and Industrial Rights of Man* (1903); *The Life and Times of Stephen Girard* (2 vols., 1918); *The United States in the World War* (2 vols., 1918–20).

He belonged to many learned and social organizations. One of the early members of the American Historical Association, he was an associate editor of the *American Historical Review* from 1895 to 1899, and president of the Association in 1905–06. In 1899 he was elected a member of the National Institute of Arts and Letters.

[Brief "Memoirs" (MS.) written in 1931; scattered family papers in the possession of his son, Dr. Philip D. McMaster; reviews of his writings, at the time of their appearance, in the daily press and historical periodicals; W. T. Hutchinson, "John Bach McMaster, Historian of the American People," in *Miss. Valley Hist. Rev.,* June 1929; *Who's Who in America,* 1930–31; an appreciation by E. P. Cheyney in *Am. Hist. Rev.,* July 1932; E. P. Oberholtzer, "John Bach McMaster, 1852–1932," in *Pa. Mag. of Hist. and Biography,* Jan. 1933; obituaries in *N. Y. Times, N. Y. Herald Tribune,* Philadelphia *Public Ledger,* May 25, 1932; J. L. Chamberlain, ed., *Universities and Their Sons. Univ. of Pa.,* vol. I (1901).] W. E. L.

McMATH, ROBERT EMMET (Apr. 28, 1833–May 31, 1918), civil engineer, was born at Varick, Seneca County, N. Y., the son of Alla and Elizabeth (Homan) McMath. He graduated from Williams College with the degree of A.B. at the age of twenty-four. Soon after his graduation, he went to St. Louis and was engaged on surveys, designs, and construction to improve the Mississippi and some of its tributaries. In 1862 he became an assistant engineer in the United States Coast Survey. His first important assignment was in Nicaragua, where he made surveys of the San Juan River and Greytown Harbor in connection with an interoceanic canal proposed by a company which had obtained a grant from the Nicaraguan government. Becoming an assistant engineer in the United States Engineer Corps in 1865, he was engaged until 1883 in improving for navigation the Illinois, Arkansas, and Mississippi rivers. Of principal importance was his work on the Illinois. In 1873 he was made principal civil assistant in charge of special physical investigations. From 1880 to 1883 he was employed by the Mississippi River Commission. At the age of fifty, he left the government service and was appointed sewer commissioner of St. Louis, a position which he occupied for eight years. In 1893 he was elected president of the board of public improvements of St. Louis and served in this capacity until 1901. He then closed his official career, although he remained in practice as a consulting engineer until a few years before his death, which occurred at his home, Webster Groves, Mo. On Dec. 29, 1859, he married at Detroit, Mich., Frances Brodie, a native of Berfield, England, who died Feb. 12, 1867.

McMath was held in high esteem among engineers for his personal as well as his professional qualities. During his connection with the Mississippi River, he was looked upon as the best informed engineer on river hydraulics in America. He was a ready and careful writer and contributed to professional engineering literature. He is best known for the formula which he devised to help in determining the proper size for storm-water sewers. Originally the subject of a paper which was read Dec. 15, 1886, and later published in the *Transactions of the American Society of Civil Engineers* (vol. XVI, 1887, p. 179), it was not the first, nor has it been the last, attempt to provide an economical solution for a difficult and common problem. It has been criticized as an empiric, and not a rational, method; yet, after nearly fifty years, it is used more often than any other to determine the size for storm sewers to carry off the water of the great storms of a given locality with no excess of size or cost. His method in arriving at his formula, under St. Louis conditions, was to note every case where a sewer proved inadequate, determine the rainfall in the tributary area, and plot these on a large diagram. A line drawn to represent sewer capacity somewhat greater than indicated by the incapacities so illustrated gave the proper capacity. The formula is applicable elsewhere if certain local data are available. With the help of tables or diagrams such as those proposed by Allen Hazen and published in the *American Civil Engineers' Pocket Book* and elsewhere, rapid determinations of sizes of sufficient accuracy for preliminary estimates can easily be made.

[F. M. McMath, *Memorials of the McMath Family* (1898); *Trans. Am. Soc. Civil Engineers,* vol. LXXXIII (1921); *Am. Men of Science* (1906); *Am. Civil Engineers' Pocket Book* (1912); L. Metcalf and H. P. Eddy, *Am. Sewerage Practice,* vol. I (1914); Emil Kuichling, in *Trans. Asso. of Civil Engineers, Cornell Univ.* (1893); R. E. McMath, "The Waterway Between Lake Michigan and the Mississippi River by Way of the Illinois River," in *Jour. of the Asso. of Engineering Societies,* Aug. 1888; *Jour. of the Engineers Club of St. Louis,* May–June 1918; *St. Louis Republic,* June 1, 1918.] G. A. S.

McMICHAEL, MORTON (Oct. 20, 1807–Jan. 6, 1879), editor, mayor of Philadelphia, was born in Bordentown, N. J., and educated in the local schools. His family had come to America from the north of Ireland; his father, John McMichael (1777–1846), was employed on the estate of Joseph Bonaparte; his mother was Hannah Maria Masters. Upon the removal of his parents to Philadelphia, McMichael continued his education there. The statement sometimes made that he attended the University of Pennsylvania is apparently an error. He read law with David Paul Brown and was admitted to the bar in 1827. He was already active in journalism, having become editor of the *Saturday Evening Post* the previous year. In 1831 he resigned this position to become editor-in-chief of the newly established *Saturday Courier.* The same year he married Mary, daughter of Daniel Estell of Philadelphia, by whom he had eight children. About this time he began his political career as a police magistrate, displaying early his power of leadership by dispersing a mob in the slavery riot of 1837 and preventing the burning of a negro orphanage. For a number of years he was an alderman and in 1836 was active on the commission for school reform in the city.

The division of his activities between politics and journalism continued throughout his life. He entered upon his career as a newspaper publisher in 1836, when with Louis A. Godey and Joseph C. Neal [*qq.v.*] he started the *Saturday News and Literary Gazette.* Eight years later he associated himself with Neal in editing *Neal's Saturday Gazette.* From 1842 to 1846 he was one of the editors of *Godey's Lady's Book.* In 1847 he became joint owner, with George R. Graham [*q.v.*], of the Philadelphia *North American,* which in July of the same year absorbed the *United States Gazette.* Robert Montgomery Bird [*q.v.*] joined the enterprise at this time. After the withdrawal of Graham in 1848 and the death of Bird in 1854, McMichael became sole owner. He retained his interest in the paper until his death and by a vigorous and progressive editorial policy succeeded in making it the leading Whig journal of the country. During these early years his activity in publishing brought him into intimate association with Leland, Boker, Poe, Richard Penn Smith, and other well-known literary men then in the city. He contributed to the magazines and other occasional publications, and one of his poems was highly praised by Poe in *Graham's Magazine* (December 1841).

From 1843 to 1846 he was sheriff of Philadelphia, again displaying unusual vigor and courage in ending the anti-Catholic or "Native American" riots of 1844. Always active in the cause of civic betterment, he lent his support and that of his paper to the hotly contested movement for the consolidation of various independent districts of Philadelphia under one government, and was in no small measure responsible for the ultimate passage of the Consolidation Act of 1854. As early as 1858 he was mentioned as a possible candidate for mayor and eight years later was elected to that office, filling it from 1866 to 1869. During the Civil War, in which two of his sons served with distinction, he was one of the founders of the Union League, and later became its fourth president (1870–74). When the Fairmount Park Commission was formed in 1867 he was made president and was reëlected repeatedly until his death. He declined the appointment as minister to Great Britain tendered him by President Grant, on the ground that he could not afford to support the office with the proper dignity. In 1872 he was temporary chairman of the Republican National Convention which renominated Grant for president, and at this time was considered for the vice-presidency. He was a delegate at large to the fourth constitutional convention of Pennsylvania in 1873. After a trip to Europe (1874) he was appointed, in 1875, to the board of managers of the Centennial Exposition. In 1876 he declined, on account of ill health, the chairmanship of the Republican National Convention at Cincinnati. In 1877 he was awarded the degree of LL.D. by the University of Pennsylvania.

Although the only public offices McMichael ever held were in Philadelphia, his influence was wide. By concerning himself with issues and refusing to tolerate personal abuse, he did much to improve the tone of the newspaper press. He was a brilliant speaker and hardly a function in Philadelphia passed without finding him its presiding officer or the orator of the occasion. He died in Philadelphia, and was buried in North Laurel Hill Cemetery.

[*North American,* Jan. 7, 8, and *Public Ledger* (Phila.), Jan. 7, 9, 1879; J. T. Scharf and Thompson Westcott, *Hist. of Phila.* (1884); *In re Morton McMichael* (privately printed, 1921), ed. by Albert Mordell; J. W. Forney, *Memorial Address upon the Character and Public Services of Morton McMichael* (1879) and *Anecdotes of Public Men,* vol. II (1881); F. L. Mott, *A Hist. of Am. Mags.* (1930); *Poulson's Am. Daily Advertiser,* Apr. 28, 1831.]

A. C. B.

McMILLAN, JAMES (May 12, 1838–Aug. 10, 1902), United States senator from Michigan, was a grandson of a sea-captain of Stranraer, Scotland, who traded to Philadelphia and Russia, and was one of three sons of William McMillan and his wife, Grace MacMeakin of Wigtown, Scotland, who emigrated to Canada in the 1830's, settling at Hamilton, Ontario. Here James was born and attended the provincially famous school of Dr. Tassie. He came to Detroit in 1855, with excellent letters and some training in the hardware business. After a short service under the leading wholesale hardware merchant of the city, he was employed by a contractor who was building an extension of the Detroit & Milwaukee Railroad. He was so successful in handling men that his employer offered him like work in Spain; but he preferred to remain in Michigan as purchasing agent of the Detroit & Milwaukee road. There he was said to have acquired Aladdin's lamp, from which he never parted. On June 7, 1860, at the age of twenty-two, he married Mary, daughter of Charles Wetmore, one of the dominant merchants of the city. Four sons and two daughters were born to them.

About the time of McMillan's marriage, a group of Detroit capitalists organized the Michigan Car Company to build freight cars, and made McMillan their manager. Owing in part to the demands of the Civil War, the company was highly successful. With the president, John S. Newberry [*q.v.*], the leading admiralty lawyer of Michigan, McMillan established a relation out of which grew the firm of Newberry & McMillan, which made successful adventures in railroads, ship-building, steam-ship lines, and kindred enterprises. They established car plants at Hamilton, Ont.; Cambridge, Ind.; and St. Louis, Mo. With the avowed purpose of uniting commercially the upper and lower peninsulas of Michigan, McMillan promoted the building of the Duluth, South Shore & Atlantic Railroad.

His interest in politics began in 1878 with his successful management of the candidacy of his partner, Newberry, for Congress. In 1886 as chairman of the Republican State Committee he reorganized the party, torn by internal dissensions, and thereby attained a leadership which continued during his life—a sort of benevolent authority based on consultation rather than on dictation. Declining to become a candidate for the United States Senate that year, he was the unanimous choice of the Republican members of the legislature in 1889, and by two reëlections he retained his seat in the Senate until his death in 1902. His previous experience in office had been confined to membership on the Detroit Board of Estimates in 1874 and on the Park Commission in 1881–83. In the latter connection, against strenuous opposition, he secured the purchase, for $100,000, of Belle Isle, and then had Frederick Law Olmsted design what has become one of the three leading island parks of the world.

On entering the Senate, McMillan withdrew from active participation in business. His good judgment, fairness, experience with affairs, absence of self-seeking, and conscientious study of the problems presented led to his appointment to those non-official committees having to do with the management of the business of the Senate. His associations naturally were with the active conservatives, and thus it came about that a group of congenial Republicans used to dine together, usually at his hospitable home, on Thursday evenings. Facetiously they called themselves the S. O. P. C. ("School of Philosophy Club"). The membership, varying with the years, included Senators Allison, Aldrich, Hale, Hanna, Hawley, Manderson, Spooner, and Wetmore, and Vice-President Hobart, with Speaker Reed and General Schofield as customary guests; and on rare occasions President Harrison or President McKinley. While cards, billiards, and stories were the ostensible after-dinner diversions, the real interest was Republican policies. Informally it was agreed by this group that President Harrison's Force Bill and Hanna's ship-subsidy bill were bad politics. They supported President Cleveland's successful efforts to repeal the Bland-Allison Act and opposed the free coinage of silver. Above all they succeeded in keeping out of the public eye, and thus escaped arousing needless antagonisms. Just such another influential group has never existed in the Senate. Not adverse to large appropriations to accomplish large purposes, McMillan was influential in securing the "twenty-foot channel" through the Great Lakes; and as a member of the Committee on Commerce his firm opposition to the small economists secured adequate channels to the harbors of New York, Boston, and Philadelphia.

McMillan was drawn into his most conspicuous and enduring service by his casual assignment to the Senate Committee on the District of Columbia. Concerned at the outset with questions of civic economy, he used his experience in revising railroad terminals, eliminating grade crossings, developing the street-railway system, installing filtration for the water supply, opening cardinal streets, and putting the hospitals and reformatory institutions on an adequate basis. Then, public sentiment being propitious, he secured the creation of a commission to make a comprehensive plan for the future development of Washington. To this commission were appointed only artists: D. H. Burnham and C. F. McKim [*qq.v.*], architects; Augustus Saint-Gaudens [*q.v.*], sculptor; Frederick Law Olmsted, Jr., landscape architect. McMillan authorized and personally advanced the money for the preparation and presentation of the plans.

With premeditation the commission returned to the almost forgotten and sadly mutilated L'Enfant plan of 1792, which they restored and extended to meet the growth of a century. Presented to the Senate by McMillan on Jan. 15, 1902, instantly the plans met public favor; but there was criticism and delay in Congress, largely on account of expense. McMillan himself took up the first and most vital task, the removal of the railroads from the Mall to a union station on a new site, and by dint of persuasion and enthusiasm was able to secure the necessary legislation. Then suddenly, in August 1902, he died. Under the National Commission of Fine Arts, subsequently created, the L'Enfant plan as restored and amplified by the McMillan plan (now so-called) is being carried out with a magnitude of scale and an elegance beyond anything ever before undertaken. A fountain, designed by Herbert Adams and Charles A. Platt, the gift of the people of Michigan in memory of the Senator, stands in McMillan Park, in Washington. Grace Hospital, Detroit, a Shakespeare library at Michigan University, a chemical laboratory at Albion College, are among his permanent gifts.

[*In Memory of Hon. James McMillan, . . . Senator . . . from Mich.* (1903); *Senate Report No. 166*, 57 Cong., 1 Sess.; Park Papers, U. S. Senate, 1900–03; and D. C. Committee reports, 1890–1903; Charles Moore, *Daniel H. Burnham, Architect, Planner of Cities* (1921) and *Life and Times of Charles Follen McKim* (1929); *Detroit Free Press*, Aug. 11, 1902.]

C. M.

McMILLAN, JAMES WINNING (Apr. 28, 1825–Mar. 9, 1903), Union soldier, was born in Clark County, Ky., the son of Robert and Nancy (Winning) McMillan. At the age of twenty-one he enlisted for the Mexican War, serving in the 4th Illinois Infantry and in the 3rd Battalion, Louisiana Volunteers, Fiescas Regiment. Upon being discharged he went to Indiana and engaged in business. Here he was twice married: in 1858 to Olivia Ames at Lawrenceburg, and in 1860 to Minerva Foote of Bedford. A daughter, Minerva, was born of the second marriage. When President Lincoln called for volunteers to preserve the Union, McMillan organized the 21st Indiana Infantry Regiment and was sent as its colonel to Louisiana, where he took part in the operations resulting in the opening of the Mississippi River. General Butler, commanding the Department of the Gulf, had a high opinion of McMillan's ability as a leader and placed him in charge of several independent expeditions. In May 1862 McMillan led forces that captured a large quantity of Confederate stores at Berwick Bay, and a blockade runner, the steamer *Fox*. In June he was wounded in an encounter with guerrillas. September found him back with his men and in command of a reinforced brigade that routed Waller's Texas Cavalry near St. Charles Court House. An expedition to Donaldsonville, La., narrowly escaped destruction by being withdrawn under his excellent leadership. His regiment was now stationed at Baton Rouge and reorganized as the 1st Indiana Heavy Artillery.

McMillan was promoted to brigadier-general in November 1862 and assigned to the command of the 2nd Brigade, 1st Division, XIX Corps. In General Banks's Red River expedition in the spring of 1864 the 1st Division arrived on the battlefield at Sabine's Crossroads, La., as the Union troops were fleeing in confusion. McMillan's brigade did its share in stopping the Confederates and driving them from the field. Later, at Pleasant Hill, McMillan's command broke up the attack on the retreating column. Moved to Virginia in July 1864, his brigade took an active part in the Shenandoah Valley campaign. At Winchester he formed line of battle in the midst of disorganized and panic-stricken troops. By keeping control of his regiments, he was able to maneuver in conjunction with the VI Corps in such manner as to drive the Confederates from that part of the field. When, a month later, General Early succeeded in surprising the left and rear of Sheridan's Army near Cedar Creek, Va., McMillan, now commanding the 1st Division, XIX Corps, deployed it at right angles to his former front. It held the position and gained time for troops in rear to get into line. McMillan's men then gave ground, fighting as they went. McMillan was now placed in command of the 1st Division of the Department of West Virginia with headquarters at Grafton. He was brevetted a major-general of volunteers in March 1865 and resigned from the service May 15, 1865. For a time after the war he resided in Kansas, but in 1875 he moved to Washington, D. C., to become a member of the Board of Review in the Pension Office. He held this position until his death in 1903. He was a man of great personal bravery, a tenacious fighter, and a strict disciplinarian.

[*Mil. Order of the Loyal Legion of the U. S., Commandery of D. C., Circular No. 4, Ser. of 1903*; *War of the Rebellion: Official Records (Army)*, 1 ser., VI, XV, XXXIV, XLIII, pt. 1, XLVI, pt. 3; *Personal Memoirs of P. H. Sheridan* (2 vols., 1888); *Army and Navy Jour.*, Mar. 14, 1903; *Evening Star* (Washington, D. C.), Mar. 9, 1903; Pension Office records.]

J. R. V.

McMINN, JOSEPH (June 22, 1758–Nov. 17, 1824), governor of Tennessee, was born in West Marlborough Township, Chester County, Pa., the fifth of ten children of Robert and Sarah (Harlan) McMinn. Early in life he settled in the region that was to be Hawkins County, Tenn. He was a member of the territorial legislature of 1794 and for more than a quarter of a century thereafter was in public office. In 1796 he was a member of the convention that framed the constitution of Tennessee, and it was upon his motion that a bill of rights was incorporated in that document. He served almost continuously in the first eight general assemblies of the state, and was three times speaker of the Senate. In 1815 he defeated four other candidates for governor, and in 1817 and 1819 was reëlected, thus serving the constitutional limit of six successive years. As governor he advocated public education, from which he thought "advantages incalculable would arise to the citizens of the state," and charged the legislature, unsuccessfully, to guard well the lands allotted by Congress for two colleges. He favored improving the navigation of the Tennessee River and sponsored a plan for a canal connecting the Holston and the Tennessee. He championed a project for penal reform, but to no avail. Neither was he successful in his attempt to solve the currency and banking difficulties by the establishment of loan offices.

One of the major problems of his administration was that constituted by the presence of the Indians within the borders of Tennessee. McMinn desired their removal to a region west of the Mississippi, for he believed it an injustice to withhold lands from the white settlers "with no other object than to serve the Cherokee and Chickasaw Indians for a hunting ground" (*Journal of the Senate . . . of Tennessee,* 1817, p. 9). While he was governor, the Chickasaws ceded their claims to the western third of the state. He himself negotiated a treaty by which the Cherokees ceded vast tracts in East Tennessee. In 1823 he was appointed United States agent to the Cherokees, a position that he retained until his death. To the surprise of friend and foe, white man and redskin, he practised "kindness to those miserable Deluded People," his "Red Brethern, the Cherokee." At the solicitation of the Cherokee chief known as the Path Killer, he served notice on intruders from Georgia "to remove their families without the limits of the Cherokee Nation." Then, without awaiting orders from his superior, the secretary of war, thinking that any delay "would prejudice the Public Interest," he burned their houses and cut down their corn. The luckless squatters answered by firing on McMinn's troops: not until October 1824 was quiet restored.

Despite a crowded public life, the democratic ex-governor maintained "a plain but reputable 'hostelry'" at Rogersville, Tenn. Guests found him "affable, kind, and communicative." He was thrice married: on May 9, 1785, to Hannah Cooper of Pennsylvania, who died in 1811; on Jan. 5, 1812, to Rebecca Kincade of Hawkins County, Tenn., who died in 1815; and some time later to Nancy Williams of Roane County, Tenn., whom he sought unsuccessfully to divorce. His name is perpetuated in Tennessee in McMinn County and the town of McMinnville, county seat of Warren County.

[MSS. in Bureau of Indian Affairs, Dept. of the Interior; *Am. Hist. Mag.* (Nashville), vol. IV (1899) and issue of Oct. 1903; A. H. Abel, "The Cherokee Negotiations of 1822 and 1823," *Smith Coll. Studies in Hist.*, vol. I, no. 4 (1916); *Tenn. Hist. Mag.*, Oct. 1930; *Journals* of the Tennessee legislature, *passim*; A. H. Harlan, *Hist. and Geneal. of the Harlan Family* (n.d.); *Knoxville Weekly Register,* 1817; *Knoxville Reg.*, Nov. 26, 1824.]

M. B. H—r.

McMURTRIE, WILLIAM (Mar. 10, 1851–May 24, 1913), chemist, was born on a farm near Belvidere, N. J., the son of Abram and Almira (Smith) McMurtrie. During his boyhood he acquired an interest in chemistry through listening to some lectures by the village pastor. At school, he was an active, ambitious lad, and in 1867 he entered Lafayette College, Easton, Pa., enrolling in the mining-engineering course. Here he was known as an industrious and faithful but self-contained student who had but small interest in the social side of college life.

After his graduation in 1871, he was made assistant to Dr. R. J. Brown, then chief chemist of the department of agriculture at Washington, D. C., and on Dr. Brown's retirement, two years later, McMurtrie was made chief chemist. Resigning in 1877, he became an agent of the department and special commissioner to the Exposition Universelle at Paris. His account of his work there is contained in *Reports of the United States Commissioners to the Paris Universal Exposition, 1878* (1880). In consequence of this appointment he was made a *chevalier du mérite agricole* by the French government. While abroad he studied the beet-sugar industry and made a report which was instrumental in starting beet root sugar manufacture in this country (*Report on the Culture of the Sugar Beet and the Manufacture of Sugar Therefrom in France and the United States,* 1880). While still a special agent of the department in chemical technology he also made investigations which resulted in the publication of *Report on the Culture of Sumac in Sicily and Its Preparation for Market in Europe and the United States* (1880), *On the Mineral Nutrition of the Vine for the Production of Wine* (1882), and *Report on the Examination of Raw Silks* (1883). Several years later he published *Wool—Its Structure and Strength* (1885), *Report Upon an Examination of Wools and Other Animal Fibers* (1886), and "Wools and Other Animal Fibers," in *World's Columbian Exposition* (1901). In 1882 he became professor of chemistry at the University of Illinois; in 1884, chemist of the Illinois State

Board of Agriculture; and in 1886, chemist of the Agricultural Experiment Station.

In 1888 he went to New York as chemist of the New York Tartar Company, manufacturers of Royal Baking Powder. With his customary determination McMurtrie set about improving and cheapening the product. At that time the argols from which the cream of tartar was produced were put into copper-lined pressure cylinders with water and superheated. The solution thus formed was filtered under pressure, and when the pressure was released, steam was given off and the crude cream of tartar precipitated in fine crystals. Copper, however, was dissolved during the process and contaminated the product. After much experimenting McMurtrie succeeded in getting a pure product at a reasonable cost. He then turned his attention to building and equipping a factory for putting the product on the market, completing it to the entire satisfaction of his employers, by whom he was made manager and vice-president of the company. He was not, however, allowed to disclose the manufacturing methods employed, and an interesting chapter of chemical experience was thus lost.

McMurtrie was much interested in the American Chemical Society and the Chemists Club of New York, and devoted much time to them, serving as president of the latter and of the New York section of the former. He was for a number of years a member of the council of the Chemical Society and in 1900 he became its president. On Apr. 5, 1876, he married Helen M. Douglass. His death occurred suddenly in New York.

[C. F. McKenna, in *The Percolator* (N. Y. Chemists Club), June 20, 1913; *Who's Who in America*, 1912–13; H. W. Wiley, in *Jour. of Industrial and Engineering Chemistry*, July 1913, with bibliography by McMurtrie's son, Douglas C. McMurtrie; Edward Hart, in *Science*, Aug. 8, 1913; *N. Y. Times*, May 25, 1913.]

E. H.

McNAIR, ALEXANDER (May 5, 1775–Mar. 18, 1826), the first governor of Missouri, was the grandson of David McNair, a Scotch Covenanter who emigrated from County Donegal, Ireland, before 1737 and settled in what is now Dauphin County, Pa. He was the son of David and Ann (Dunning) McNair and was born on his father's farm in Mifflin (now Juniata) County, Pa. After his father's death in 1777 his mother took him to live near Pittsburgh, where he grew up and obtained some education. In 1799 he became a first lieutenant in the United States Army. When the army was reduced he was discharged in June 1800, and in 1804 he moved to St. Louis. His marriage, in March 1805, to Marguerite Susanne de Reilhe, the well educated and talented daughter of a prominent French merchant who had died three years earlier, gave him standing within the most influential political circles of the city. At the March 1805 term of the court of common pleas he was appointed one of the associate judges and from that time until his death he held public office continuously. Aside from the governorship, the principal offices he held were those of city trustee, sheriff of St. Louis County, colonel, then adjutant and inspector of territorial militia, United States marshal, register of the St. Louis land office, and federal agent to the Osage Indians. He also engaged in various mercantile pursuits and acquired a good deal of property.

Although he was a member of the constitutional convention, he played an unobtrusive part in its deliberations, except in his opposition to the constitutional provision for a high salary schedule for state officials. Before the convention adjourned he announced himself as a candidate for governor against William Clark [*q.v.*]. He had greater gifts of popularity than Clark, and he conducted an extensive personal campaign. His opponents, led by the St. Louis machine, charged that he lacked education and ability for such an office, that he had used his authority in the land office loosely in order to gain popularity, and, as the campaign grew hotter, that he was using the "greatest exertions in the tippling shops" of St. Louis (Shoemaker, *Missouri's Struggle, post*, p. 264). Nevertheless, he was elected by a majority of 4,020 in a total of 9,132 votes. As governor from 1820 to 1824 he urged no startling policies. He opposed any restriction on slavery, but in order to hasten her admission into the Union he approved Missouri's adroitly worded "Solemn Public Act." He was careful to observe all the proprieties connected with the inauguration of the new state government and took great pains to study and lay before the assembly copies of the laws of the older states. His messages to the legislature were clear, brief, and conservative in tone, and they dealt with subjects appropriate to a new frontier state, such as fiscal affairs, immigration, relations with the Indians, the militia, and the industrial development of the commonwealth.

Although brought up as a Presbyterian and, during his earlier years at St. Louis, an active member of a Masonic lodge, before his death he received the last rites of the Roman Catholic Church of which his wife was a member. She, with eight of their ten children, survived him.

[McNair Papers in Jefferson Memorial Lib., St. Louis; *The Messages and Proclamations of the Governors of the State of Mo.*, ed. by Buel Leopard and F. C. Shoemaker, vol. I (1922); F. C. Shoemaker, *Mis-*

souri's Struggle for Statehood (1916); W. B. Stevens, *Mo., the Center State,* 2 vols. (1915); Louis Houck, *A Hist. of Mo.* (1908), III; Richard Edwards and M. Hopewell, *Edwards's Great West and her Commercial Metropolis* (1860); F. L. Billon, *Annals of St. Louis in her Territorial Days* (1888); E. H. Shepard, *The Early Hist. of St. Louis* (1870); *Mo. Hist. Rev.,* Oct. 1922; *St. Louis Catholic Hist. Rev.,* July–Oct. 1919; *Wis. State Hist. Soc. Colls.,* II (1856); J. B. McNair, *McNair, McNear, and McNeir Geneals.* (1923); *Mo. Gazette and Public Advertiser* (St. Louis), Apr. 26, 1820; *Mo. Intelligencer* (Franklin), Apr. 7, 1826.]

H. E. N.

McNAIR, FRED WALTER (Dec. 3, 1862–June 30, 1924), college president, son of Hugh A. Wilson McNair and Mary Jane (Dorland) McNair, was born at Fennimore, Wis. His father, a farmer and surveyor, kindled an early and permanent interest in mathematics and allied subjects in young McNair, who for two undergraduate years was instructor in mathematics at Wisconsin University, and after graduation in 1891 served as assistant professor of mathematics at Michigan Agricultural College, 1892–93, from which he was called to Michigan College of Mines as professor of mathematics and physics in 1893. In 1899 he was made president of Michigan College of Mines, a position which he occupied with distinction for the rest of his life. He married Berta Philbrick of Fennimore, Wis., in 1886. In June 1924, as he was returning from an engineers' meeting in Boulder, Colo., he was killed in a railroad wreck near Buda, Ill.

The deep copper mines of the Lake Superior country gave opportunity for unique physical research, and in cooperation with the United States Coast and Geodetic Survey McNair measured the force of gravity a mile under ground. He also studied the method of transferring the azimuth of a line on the earth's surface to the bottom of a mine by means of two plumb-lines. Extended observations on pairs of plumb-lines cver 4400 feet long in vertical mine shafts showed that some pairs hung nearly parallel while others were an inch or more farther apart at the bottom than at the top. McNair found that this divergence was produced by air currents and emphasized the necessity of eliminating air circulation wherever long plumb-lines are used (*Engineering and Mining Journal,* Apr. 26, 1902, p. 578). He next sought to determine experimentally, by means of falling spheres, the easterly deviation which a falling body theoretically undergoes because of the earth's rotation, and to study the air resistance of falling spheres. A steel ball was suspended motionless over the center of a deep shaft and the supporting silken thread was burned away. But the ball was invariably deflected laterally in its downward course, lodging in the timbers lining the walls of the shaft, and never reached the bottom. This was an early demonstration of an aerodynamic principle, now widely recognized, that a slight asymmetry in the air flow around a body produces a lateral force.

When the United States entered the war, McNair was temporarily relieved from his college duties in order to join the staff of the Bureau of Standards, where, in cooperation with J. F. Hayford and L. J. Briggs, he engaged in the successful development of an instrument for directing the gun-fire of battleships. The determination of the proper elevation of the guns formerly depended upon the visibility of the sea-horizon, which was often obscured by fog, or smoke of battle. This instrument, based upon gyroscopic action, provided an artificial horizon and could be used below decks regardless of fog, smoke, or the roll and pitch of the ship.

But it was as an educator that McNair did his greatest work. Slender in physique, he was given an effective presence by his keen mentality and wide, sensitive, and sympathetic understanding of men and their problems. For nearly fifty years he was actively identified with the Society for the Promotion of Engineering Education, of which he was president in 1904–05. He was a fellow of the American Association for the Advancement of Science: vice-president of section D, 1904–05; secretary of the council, 1905–06; general secretary, 1906–07. He was a member of the American Institute of Mining and Metallurgical Engineers; the Mining and Metallurgical Society of America; and the American Physical Society. His chief avocation was biology, and in the company of his four children, he took the keenest delight in roaming the forests near his home in search of *Myxomycetes,* a curious group of slime fungi which possess the remarkable habit of crawling slowly over decaying stumps and logs. His valuable collections of *Myxomycetes* is now deposited with the University of Wisconsin.

[*Who's Who in America,* 1922–23; Hugh McNair, "Fred Walter McNair," *Trans. Am. Inst. Mining and Metallurgical Engineers,* vol. LXX (1924); *Engineering and Mining Journal-Press,* July 5, 1924; Mining and Metallurgical Soc. of America, *Bulletin,* no. 172, Nov.–Dec. 1924; J. B. McNair, *McNair, McNear, and McNeir Geneals.* (1923) and supplement published in 1929; *Detroit Free Press,* July 1, 1924; personal acquaintance.]

L. J. B.

McNAIR, FREDERICK VALLETTE (Jan. 13, 1839–Nov. 28, 1900), naval officer, was born at Jenkintown, Pa., just north of Philadelphia, the son of John and Mary (Yerkes) McNair, and a descendant of Scotch-Irish settlers in Pennsylvania. On the nomination of his father, who was then representative from the fifth district of Pennsylvania, he was appointed midshipman Sept. 21, 1853. After four years at the Naval Academy he went to the China station in the *Minnesota,* 1857–59; was commissioned lieutenant Apr. 18, 1861; and during the first months of the Civil War was in the *Iroquois,* West Indies. In this ship he subsequently served through the Mississippi River campaign under Farragut, taking part in the battle with the forts below New Orleans, April 1862, the engagement at Grand Gulf, and the running of the batteries at Vicksburg. At Natchez and Baton Rouge he was the officer sent ashore to demand their surrender. After a brief leave in the summer of 1862 he served in the *Juanita* and the *Seminole* on the East Coast until August 1863, and then in the *Pensacola* on the Mississippi until April 1864. Promoted at that time to lieutenant commander, he was for the remainder of the war executive in the *Juanita,* participating in both attacks on Fort Fisher, Dec. 24–25, 1864, and Jan. 13–15, 1865. In connection with a boat accident in March 1865, the commander of the *Juanita,* J. J. Almy, commended McNair as "a most excellent officer, possessing good judgment and . . . more than usual experience" (*War of the Rebellion: Official Records, Navy,* 1 ser., III, p. 450).

Coming through the war with a notable record for dependability and initiative, he was during his later career assigned to positions of unusual responsibility. In 1866–67 he was executive of the flagship *Brooklyn,* Brazil Squadron, and after a year as instructor at the Naval Academy was executive of the flagship *Franklin,* European Squadron. He was head of the department of seamanship at the Naval Academy, 1871–75, and again, after duty on the Asiatic station, at the academy as commandant of cadets, 1878–82. Promoted to captain in 1883, he was at the Mare Island Navy Yard in California, 1883–86; commander of the flagship *Omaha,* Asiatic station, 1887–90; superintendent of the Naval Observatory, 1890–94; and in command of the Asiatic Squadron, 1895–98, during which service he brought his ships to the efficiency in gunnery proved next year under Dewey at Manila. Promotion to rear admiral came in July 1898, and for the next two years he was at the Naval Academy as superintendent. Owing to failing health he resigned from this position in the spring of 1900 and was living in Washington, senior on the active list, at the time of his death from apoplexy. He was married on Oct. 9, 1862, to Clara, daughter of James W. W. Warren of Philadelphia. His son, Frederick Vallette, also became a naval officer.

[L. R. Hamersly, *The Records of Living Officers of the U. S. Navy* (ed. 1898); J. B. McNair, *McNair, McNear, and McNeir Geneals.* (1923), pp. 227–29; Washington *Evening Star,* Nov. 29, 1900.] A. W.

MACNAUGHTAN, MYRA KELLY [See KELLY, MYRA, 1875–1910].

MCNEILL, DANIEL (Apr. 5, 1748–1833), privateersman in the Revolution and naval officer, born at Charlestown, Mass., was the son of William and Catherine (Morrison) McNeill, and the grandson of Daniel McNeill who emigrated from Ireland in 1683. On Feb. 10, 1770, he married Mary Cuthbertson, whose early death may be assumed, for not later than 1772 he married Abigail Harvey, of Nottingham, England. The eldest of their ten children was born July 20, 1773. McNeill was doubtless bred to the sea. He first comes into notice as commander of the privateer brig *Hancock,* in November 1776. He commanded five other privateers during the Revolution: the *America, Eagle, Ulysses, Wasp,* and, most noted of all, the *General Mifflin,* a ship of twenty guns and 150 men, in which he cruised in European waters in 1778 and 1779. In this vessel he took thirteen prizes and fought an engagement with a British sloop of war. He has been credited by historians with firing a salute in the harbor of Brest, which was returned by the French admiral, causing international correspondence, but this incident occurred in 1777, when the *Mifflin* was commanded by Capt. William Day. McNeill returned to Boston early in 1779. His privateering ventures were successful and before the end of the war he was part owner of two vessels.

Until the outbreak of hostilities with France in 1798 he was probably employed either as master or owner of ships. On July 17 of that year he was commissioned a captain in the United States navy and given command of the ship *Portsmouth,* of twenty-four guns. She was attached to the squadron of Commodore Barry and until the end of 1799 cruised in the West Indies and off the coast of Surinam, where, with the help of a revenue cutter, she blockaded a French man-of-war and forced her surrender. In April 1800, McNeill was sent in the *Portsmouth* with dispatches to France and brought home the American peace commissioners.

After his return McNeill was given command of the frigate *Boston* and was sent again to France, in October 1801, with the new United States minister, Robert R. Livingston. He then proceeded to the Mediterranean under orders to join the squadron of Commodore Dale, engaged in war with Tripoli. During 1802 he was employed in cruising and in blockading Tripoli. Throughout his stay in the Mediterranean he never fell in with either Commodore Dale or his successor, Commodore Morris, and was supposed to have purposely avoided them. He returned to Boston in October 1802 and was dismissed from the navy on the 27th of that month, under the Peace Establishment Act of Mar. 3, 1801. His son, Daniel McNeill, Jr., entered the navy as a midshipman in 1799 and was dismissed in 1807. McNeill's later years were passed in Boston, where he acquired property in real estate and became a man of substance.

[T. B. Wyman, *Geneals. and Estates of Charlestown* (1879), vol. II; *A Vol. of Records Relating to the Early Hist. of Boston, Containing Boston Marriages from 1752 to 1809* (1903); Nathaniel I. Bowditch's abstracts of Boston titles (manuscript) in the library of the Mass. Hist. Soc.; G. W. Allen, "Mass. Privateers of the Revolution," *Mass. Hist. Soc. Colls.*, vol. LXXVII (1927), and *A Naval Hist. of the Am. Revolution* (2 vols., 1913), *Our Naval War with France* (1909), and *Our Navy and the Barbary Corsairs* (1905).]
G. W. A.

McNEILL, GEORGE EDWIN (Aug. 4, 1837–May 19, 1906), leader of American labor movements, and one of the founders of the American Federation of Labor, was born in Amesbury, Mass. He was brought up in the midst of the anti-slavery agitation, of which his father, John McNeill, a friend and neighbor of John G. Whittier, was an active propagandist. His mother was Abigail Todd (Hickey) McNeill. McNeill's formal education came from the public and private schools of Amesbury. He was working in the woolen-mills of his native town at the time of the great strike in 1851. About this time he learned the shoe-maker's trade. He settled in Boston in 1856 and married Adeline J. Trefethen on Dec. 24, 1859. His main renown came through his espousal of the eight-hour philosophy of Ira Steward. As secretary of the Grand Eight-Hour League (1863–64) and president of the Boston Eight-Hour League (1869–74), he was the oratorical, journalistic, and organizing influence which began to place eight-hour legislation on the statute books of state and federal governments as early as 1867, and which, after such legislation was shown to be ineffective, placed the issue at the front in trade-union programs during the eighties. He organized several workingmen's associations, acting as president of one of these, the Workingmen's Institute, from 1867 to 1869. As a member of the school committee of Cambridge, Mass. (1872–75), he succeeded in establishing free evening drawing-schools.

The declaration of principles which was adopted by the Knights of Labor Assembly in 1874 had been written in substance by McNeill for a labor congress at Rochester earlier the same year. It became from this time the platform of the order. Beginning as early as 1865, he was connected in an editorial or associate editorial capacity with the labor papers of the day in New York, Fall River, and Paterson, N. J. On account of his eight-hour philosophy of more leisure for workingmen he opposed vigorously the far more popular greenback and cooperative programs of the labor organizations of his time. While joining with Wendell Phillips in starting a labor party he separated from Phillips when the latter espoused the greenback movement; and with Steward, he organized the hostile Eight-Hour League. The antagonism of the two organizations reached its height in 1872 and meanwhile had much to do with the failure of the political movement led by Phillips. Yet to Phillips and McNeill was due the creation, by the Massachusetts legislature, in 1869, of the first Bureau of Labor Statistics, which has been copied by other states and nations. In 1869 he was appointed the first assistant chief of that bureau but in 1873, on account of his labor activities, he was dropped from the position.

In 1878 McNeill became the president of the newly founded International Labor Union, a precursor in some respects of the American Federation of Labor, in that it eschewed politics and directed its attention to the organization of all classes of labor for strictly economic gains of shorter hours and better wages. It did not reach far beyond the textile industries, but in these industries McNeill showed unusual organizing ability. He was an active member of the Knights of Labor, having joined in 1883, and was treasurer of District 30 of that order, 1884–86. He resigned because he favored the principle of trade autonomy for each trade. When the contest between the Knights and the American Federation of Labor reached its crisis in 1886, it was McNeill, as a member of the Committee on the State of the Order, who, at the special session of the General Assembly of the Knights in May 1886, drafted the plan of cooperation with the Federation. This was destined to failure, and in July of that year he resigned from the Knights and went over to the Federation, whose non-political program fitted his original ideas of labor organization.

Henceforth he was prominent as writer and speaker for that organization, supporting himself as treasurer and general manager of the Accident Insurance Company after 1883. He was successful as arbitrator of differences between employers and employees, notably in the great horse-car strike in Boston in 1885. In 1886 he was the United Labor Party's candidate for mayor of Boston, at which time he was also editor and proprietor of the *Labor Leader,* Boston. From 1886 to 1898 he was a delegate to the conventions of the American Federation of Labor and was sent by it as a fraternal delegate to England in 1898. He served the state of Massachusetts as commissioner of manual training in 1893–94 and on other commissions till his death on May 19, 1906, in Somerville. He edited and wrote the larger portion of *The Labor Movement: the Problem of Today* (1887), the first systematic history of the labor movement in America, wherein he summarized his experiences and views. His other publications include *The Philosophy of the Labor Movement* (1893); *Eight Hour Primer* (1889); *A Study of Accidents and Accident Insurance* (1900); and *Unfrequented Paths: Songs of Nature, Labor, and Men* (1903). In 1903 he contributed to the publications of the American Economic Association a paper on "Trade Union Ideals."

[There is a biography of McNeill, to 1886, in *The Labor Movement,* pp. 611–12. See also: *Who's Who in America,* 1906–07; the *Am. Federationist,* July 1906; John R. Commons and others, *Hist. of Labour in the U. S.* (1918), vol. II, and *A Documentary Hist. of Am. Industrial Soc.* (1910), vol. IX; and the Boston *Transcript,* May 21, 1906.] J. R. C.

McNEILL, HECTOR (Oct. 10, 1728–Dec. 25, 1785), Revolutionary naval officer and privateersman, son of Malcolm and Mary (Stuart) McNeill, was born in County Antrim, Ireland, and came with his parents to Boston in 1737. He was educated in the Boston schools and while still young went to sea, becoming master of a vessel before he was twenty-two. On Nov. 12, 1750, he was married in the Presbyterian church to Mary Wilson. They had four children, three of whom survived infancy. In 1769 his wife died and on Dec. 26, 1770, he was married to Mary Watt, by whom he had one daughter.

McNeill served at the beginning of the French and Indian War as master of a vessel which, in 1755, carried General Monckton to Nova Scotia. Very soon afterward his vessel was captured by Indians and he was sent a prisoner to Quebec. Several years later he was engaged in the coasting trade between Quebec, Boston, and the West Indies. In 1775 he was living in Quebec, but soon entered the service of the United Colonies on the St. Lawrence River. Early in 1776 he returned to Boston and on June 15 was appointed a captain in the Continental Navy. On Oct. 10, 1776, he was placed third on the list of captains (*Journals of the Continental Congress,* Oct. 10, 1776). He was given command of the new frigate *Boston,* of twenty-four guns. On May 21, 1777, the frigate *Hancock,* under Captain John Manley, senior to McNeill, and the *Boston,* accompanied by nine privateers, sailed on a cruise to the eastward. The privateers soon became separated and took no further part in the enterprise. The *Hancock* and *Boston* fell in with and escaped from the British sixty-four-gun ship *Somerset* and the frigate *Mercury.* Soon after this, in June, they captured, after a fight, the British frigate *Fox.* Three small prizes were burned.

On July 7 the little American squadron encountered the enemy's forty-four-gun ship *Rainbow,* the frigate *Flora,* and the brig *Victor.* A severe action followed, first with the *Flora.* The American ships becoming separated, the *Hancock* engaged the *Rainbow* alone and was captured, as was also the prize *Fox.* The *Boston* escaped and went into Wiscasset, later returning to Boston. McNeill was blamed for not coming to the rescue of the *Hancock* when it was attacked by the *Rainbow,* was court-martialed, and was dismissed or suspended from the navy in June 1778. No report of his trial has been preserved. In January 1779, the Marine Committee recommended that the sentence of the court "be not carried into execution." But nothing was done and the captain never again served in the navy. Doubtless one of the contributing factors to the disastrous outcome of this cruise, so auspiciously begun, was the lack of cordial relations between Manley and McNeill; effective cooperation between them was hardly possible.

Later in the war McNeill commanded two privateers—the brigantine *Pallas* and the ship *Adventure*—the bonds of which are dated May 22 and Nov. 22, 1780, respectively. What success, if any, he achieved is unknown. The *Pallas* was supposed to have been lost or captured on her way to Amsterdam, but this is uncertain. After the war the captain returned to the merchant service and on Christmas night, 1785, was lost at sea. McNeill's many letters show strength of character and, despite a somewhat contentious disposition, a kindliness and devotion to the interests of the officers and men who served under him.

[The *Proc. Mass. Hist. Soc.,* vol. LV (1923), contain an article on McNeill by G. W. Allen, an autobiographical sketch dated July 13, 1773, and McNeill's letters, papers, and journal. See also G. W. Allen, *A Naval Hist. of the Am. Revolution* (1913) and "Mass. Privateers of the Revolution," *Mass. Hist. Soc. Colls.,* vol. LXXVII (1927); and E. S. Maclay, *A Hist. of the U. S. Navy* (1894), vol. I.] G. W. A.

McNEILL, JOHN HANSON (June 12, 1815–Nov. 10, 1864), stock-raiser and exhibitor, Confederate ranger, was born in Hardy County, Va., the son of Strother McNeill. His formal education was meager, probably not extending beyond the country schools of the time. In January 1837 he was married to Jemima Cunningham.

and the year following he moved to Kentucky where he became a farmer and stock-raiser. After remaining there about six years, he became dissatisfied and returned to Virginia. Relatives in Missouri in time convinced him of that state's promising future, and, in 1848, with his family and slaves, he settled in Boone County and commenced farming operations. He imported from Kentucky and from Ohio blooded short-horn cattle and developed the finest herd in Missouri. He was one of the first and most successful stock-breeders and exhibitors in the state, winning many premiums at the numerous county fairs. He was also vitally interested in various agricultural associations devoted to the care and breeding of the better types of live stock. From 1848 to 1861 he lived the leisurely life of a Virginia gentleman and landowner, acquiring additional holdings in Daviess County, in northern Missouri, whither he had moved in 1855.

By birth and by conviction a Southerner, McNeill urged that Missouri join the Confederacy, and, in 1861, under the governor's commission, he recruited and became captain of a company in Price's army. He and his three sons fought through the Missouri campaigns of 1861–62, serving with devotion and distinction. Severely wounded and captured, he escaped from the federal prison at St. Louis and made his laborious way to Virginia and to the mountainous region of his boyhood. It was by that time evident that Missouri was irrevocably lost to the Confederacy so McNeill decided to remain in the South. Upon authority of the Confederate Congress he organized, late in 1862, the McNeill Partisan Rangers, cooperating with the Southern army but independent in command. His company included friends and relatives selected from the surrounding territory and familiar with every mountain road and bypath. For two years, "Hanse" McNeill and his rangers wrought great havoc among the Northern forces in several West Virginia counties, destroying numerous supply trains, railroad rolling stock and equipment, and capturing some 2600 prisoners. The terrain was admirably adapted to the method of fighting, which was suddenly to attack the enemy, scatter and destroy his supply and ammunition trains, then retreat to the inaccessible mountain fastnesses. Six feet tall and of aristocratic bearing and manner, McNeill possessed a boldness, bravery, and magnanimity which endeared him to his command. He won the commendation of Lee as being "bold and intelligent" and was characterized officially by Sheridan as the "most daring and dangerous of all the bushwhackers" (*War of the Rebellion: Official Records, Army,* 1 ser. XLIII, pt. 1, p. 30). Other Union generals respected and feared the Partisan Rangers and their commander. On Oct. 2, 1864, while leading a surprise daybreak raid into the Shenandoah Valley, McNeill was accidentally and fatally shot by one of his own company. He died on Nov. 10, at Harrisonburg, Va. A minor figure of the Civil War, this intrepid soldier symbolized the best traits of the men who fought on both sides in that conflict.

[W. D. Vandiver, Columbia, Mo., has considerable material relating to McNeill, including an unpublished account of his life by his son, Jesse, and numerous maps. J. W. Duffy, *McNeill's Last Charge* (1912), describes the events of Oct. and Nov. 1864, while W. D. Vandiver, "Two Forgotten Heroes," in *Mo. Hist. Rev.,* Apr. 1927, gives an account of his career. See also C. A. Evans, *Confed. Mil. Hist.* (1899), II, 116–23, and *War of the Rebellion: Official Records (Army),* 1 ser. XXV, XXIX, XXX, XXXVII, and XLIII.]

T. S. B.

MCNEILL, WILLIAM GIBBS (Oct. 3, 1801–Feb. 16, 1853), civil engineer, was born at Wilmington, N. C., the son of Dr. Charles Donald McNeill. His great-grandfather, a member of a Highland clan, after service at the Battle of Culloden, emigrated to North America with the celebrated Flora McDonald in 1746. His father served with the British Army in the West Indies and eventually settled at Wilmington, N. C., where he was a physician of high repute. William Gibbs McNeill was educated near New York, intending to become a minister, but upon visiting West Point with his friend, Joseph Gardner Swift [*q.v.*], he became interested in a military career and succeeded in obtaining a cadet appointment by President Madison. After service at West Point, in 1817 he received a commission as third lieutenant of artillery. Among his comrades at the military academy was George W. Whistler [*q.v.*], who married his sister Anna, and with whom he was professionally associated in many public works.

McNeill's early work, under the Corps of Engineers, was with the United States Coast Survey in the South, although he served as aide-de-camp to General Andrew Jackson during the war in Florida in 1819. In 1823 he was transferred to the corps of topographical engineers, on the general staff. Here he was employed to ascertain the practicability and cost of constructing a railway or canal between the Chesapeake Bay and the Ohio River—across the Alleghany Mountains. He also made surveys for the James River and Kanawha canals, as well as the location survey for the Baltimore & Ohio Railroad. In recognition of his work, he was made a member of the Board of Engineers and in 1828, with his comrades—Whistler, and Jonathan Knight—was deputed to visit Europe to examine the public works, especially existing railroads and those in course of construction. He came into contact with George Stephenson and other noted engineers of the time and became especially impressed with the advantages of railroads as a new mode of transportation. Upon his return to the United States, he took every means to stimulate activity in this field. As a result, McNeill and Whistler became joint engineers upon a majority of the new railways in the eastern part of the country. Among those upon which he was engaged alone or with Whistler, in addition to the Baltimore & Ohio, were the Baltimore & Susquehanna, Paterson & Hudson River, Boston & Providence, Providence & Stonington, Taunton & New Bedford, Long Island, Boston & Albany, and Charleston, Louisville & Cincinnati. His promotion in rank was rapid and in 1834 he became brevet-major of engineers. In 1837 he resigned from the army and became engineer for the state of Georgia, conducting surveys for a railroad from Cincinnati to Charleston.

In 1842 he was appointed major-general of militia in the state of Rhode Island to aid in suppressing the Dorr rebellion. He helped to quell the disturbances, but his vigorous action in the affair made him enemies and resulted in his removal by President Polk in 1845 from his position as chief engineer of the Brooklyn dry dock, for which he had prepared the plans. The same influences were also active in 1846 in causing the declination of his offer of services for the Mexican War. His close application to work severely tried his physical powers, and in 1851 he again visited Europe for the benefit of his health. At this time he was elected a member of the Institution of Civil Engineers of Great Britain—the first American to receive this honor. While in London he was actively engaged in the interests of several large American mining concerns. He returned in 1853 to America, where he died very suddenly at Brooklyn, N. Y., on Feb. 16. His numerous professional reports comprise some of the early history of railways in the United States. He was connected with many public-improvement works of note in Canada and the West Indies—as well as in the United States. He was married to Maria Matilda Camman of New York and had seven children, with whom his family life was especially happy. It has been said of him (Cullum, *post,* pp. 165–66) that his skill as an engineer lay in his ability to "survey the adaptability of ground to practical purposes," and in his ability to manage a project. For the details of construction he was dependent upon his assistants, who were superior to him in technical attainments.

[*Minutes of Proc. of the Inst. of Civil Engineers* (London), vol. XIII (1854); G. W. Cullum, *Biog. Reg. . . . of the U. S. Mil. Acad.*, vol. I (1890); *The Memoirs of Gen. Jos. Gardner Swift* (1890); *N. Y. Times*, Feb. 17, 1853.]

H. K. B.

MACNEVEN, WILLIAM JAMES (Mar. 21, 1763–July 12, 1841), physician, Irish patriot, was born in County Galway, Ireland, the son of Catholic parents, James and Rosa (Dolphin) MacNeven. His father was a country gentleman who lived on his own estate. The family had formerly possessed large holdings in the North of Ireland, but had been expelled by Cromwell and forced to settle in the wilds of Galway. MacNeven's uncle, William O'Kelly MacNeven, finding it necessary to leave Ireland to obtain a professional education, had gone to Austria, where he rose to the post of physician to the Empress Maria Theresa and was made a baron. When William James MacNeven was ten or twelve, since the penal laws which restricted Catholic education were still in force, he went to live with his uncle in Vienna. Eventually he studied medicine at the universities of Prague and Vienna, and received a degree from the latter institution in 1784. Settling at once in Dublin, he began what promised to be a brilliant career.

An earnest patriot and a member of the United Irishmen, he engaged in political activities which led to his internment first in Kilmainham prison and then at Fort George, Scotland, where Thomas Addis Emmet [*q.v.*] was one of his fellow prisoners. During his incarceration he studied extensively, and upon his discharge in 1802 under sentence of banishment, went almost at once to Switzerland, where he spent several months in a walking tour, described in his first book, *A Ramble through Swisserland in the Summer and Autumn of 1802* (1803). In 1803 he went to France, where he sought an interview with Napoleon in regard to a possible invasion of Ireland, but to no effect. For the next two years he served in the Irish Brigade of the French army, and then, apparently convinced that he could no longer aid the cause of Ireland in Europe, he took ship for America, arriving in New York July 4, 1805, with the intention of beginning life anew.

He found a cordial welcome in New York, and soon established himself in practice. Two years after his arrival he delivered a course of clinical lectures at the New York Hospital, and in 1808 was elected professor of obstetrics in the College of Physicians and Surgeons. Three years later he was transferred to the chair of chemistry, and, in addition to this subject, from 1816 to 1820 taught materia medica. His is said to have been the first chemical laboratory in New York. In 1815 he published a *Chemical Examination of the Mineral Waters of Schooley's Mountains,* and in 1819 an *Exposition of the Atomic Theory of Chymistry.* His last scientific publication was an edition, with emendations, of W. T. Brande's *Manual of Chemistry* (1821). He was also coeditor for a time of the *New York Medical and Philosophical Journal and Review.* In 1823 he was elected a member of the American Philosophical Society. Together with his colleagues Valentine Mott, David Hosack, and John W. Francis [*qq.v.*], he withdrew from the College of Physicians and Surgeons in 1826 to found a rival medical school, affiliated with Rutgers College. Although this enterprise was successful, it was short-lived, being abandoned after four years because of legal difficulties.

Meantime, his expatriation did not end MacNeven's interest in his native land. In 1807 he published *Pieces of Irish History*; he also established an employment bureau to find positions for Irish immigrants; he is said to have published a manual of directions for Irishmen arriving in America; he was an organizer and first president (1828–29) of a society known as the Friends of Ireland. An attack of gout in 1838 obliged him to give up his work and move to the country, and the remainder of his life was spent in the home of his step-daughter and her husband, Thomas A. Emmet, Jr., son of his old friend. His death in 1841 followed a long and painful illness. Throughout his life he was a loyal Roman Catholic and the last rites of his Church were administered to him by Bishop Hughes. MacNeven was married in 1810 to Jane Margaret, daughter of Samuel Riker and widow of John Tom. Most of their children died of tuberculosis, an affection to which the children of Irish emigrants were unusually susceptible. Only two sons and a daughter survived their father.

[*N. Y. Medic. Gazette,* Aug. 11, 1841; sketch by J. W. Francis in S. D. Gross, *Lives of Eminent Am. Physicians and Surgeons* (1861); sketch by MacNeven's daughter in R. R. Madden, *The United Irishmen, Their Lives and Times,* 2 ser. (1843); *Cath. Encyc.,* vol. IX (1910); J. H. McCarthy, *Ireland Since the Union* (1887); Robert Dunlop, in *Dict. Nat. Biog.*; H. A. Kelly and W. L. Burrage, *Am. Medic. Biogs.* (1920); *N. Y. Tribune,* July 14, 1841.] E. P.

McNULTY, FRANK JOSEPH (Aug. 10, 1872–May 26, 1926), labor leader and congressman, was born in Londonderry, Ireland, the son of Owen McNulty, a veteran of the Union Army in the Civil War who had returned to Ireland after his marriage to Catherine O'Donnell in New York. When the boy was four years old the family returned to the United States and settled in New York City where he was educated in the public schools. He became an inside electrical wireman, moved to Perth Amboy, N. J., and there assisted in organizing a local of the International Brotherhood of Electrical Workers. Distinguished in appearance, with an excellent tenor voice, a love of sports, great personal courage, undeviating loyalty to his friends, a reputation as a wit, and considerable personal magnetism and charm, he early became a leader in his organization and in 1901 was elected international vice-president of the Brotherhood, with headquarters in Springfield, Ill. Two years later, in 1903, he became president and held this office until 1919 when, after several months' leave of absence, he resigned to continue in the position, in which he had acted since 1917, of deputy director of public safety in Newark. Here he had long made his home with his wife, Edith H. Parker, whom he married in Jersey City in 1893. Upon his retirement, as a mark of appreciation of his services, he was given the title of "president emeritus"—an innovation in the labor movement—and also became chairman of the international executive council of the Brotherhood, a position which he held throughout the remainder of his life. From 1908 to 1913 he carried the organization successfully through one of the most bitter and hard-fought internal struggles that has ever occurred in any American labor union—a socialistic (industrial union) secession movement which involved over half the membership and threatened the entire American labor movement. In the end, supported by the American Federation of Labor and victorious in a series of legal battles with the rival organization, he succeeded in his diplomatic efforts to win back, on liberal terms, the bulk of the seceders and in further increasing the membership until the Brotherhood became the fourth largest American labor organization.

McNulty's chief constructive policies were the promotion of craft improvement to rescue electrical workers from the condition of an unskilled group and the settlement of disputes by reason and negotiation instead of by strikes. In 1906 he was a member of the commission sent to Great Britain by the National Civic Federation to study public ownership. During the war he served as vice-chairman of the Railway Board of Adjustment No. 2, but resigned this office in August 1918 to go to Italy and France for three months with a government commission of five labor leaders, selected by the American Federation of Labor on the request of President Wilson, to strengthen the morale of the Italian working men by showing them that the American labor movement vigorously supported the war. The delegation traveled through the industrial districts of Italy by automobile, addressing sometimes a dozen meetings a day, visited the battle front, dined with the King of Italy, and was entertained by General Diaz. In 1922, after his retirement in 1921 from the city government of Newark, McNulty was elected to Congress from the eighth congressional district of New Jersey as a Democrat and served from Mar. 4, 1923, to Mar. 3, 1925. Always stronger in dealing with individuals than with large groups, he exerted his chief influence in Congress as a member of the committee on labor, though he made short speeches on prison labor and on the railroad labor bill. Defeated for reëlection in the Coolidge landslide of 1924, he spent the remainder of his life in Washington, to which the headquarters of the International Brotherhood of Electrical Workers had been moved, and in Newark, where he died suddenly on May 26, 1926.

[See *Who's Who in America,* 1926–27; *Biog. Dir. Am. Cong.* (1928); notices in New York, Newark, and other newspapers; the *Jour. of the Electrical Workers and Operators,* June 1926; the *Congressional Record,* 68th Cong.; Michael A. Mulcaire, *The Internat. Brotherhood of Electrical Workers* (1923); and the convention proceedings and reports of officers of the International Brotherhood of Electrical Workers.]

H. S. W.

McNUTT, ALEXANDER (*c.* 1725–*c.* 1811), colonial land promoter, the son of Alexander and Jane McNutt, was probably born in Londonderry, Ireland. He came to America before 1753 and settled near Staunton, Va. In 1756, he was an officer in the militia on Major Andrew Lewis's Shawnee expedition. In 1760 he was captain of Massachusetts militia, raising replacements. Representing Apthorp and Hancock of Boston from 1758 to 1761 he canvassed New England for settlers for Nova Scotia. Having persuaded a number, including some Scotch-Irish of Londonderry, N. H., to go there, he proposed direct immigration of Irish Protestants. In 1761, he went to England, where he was well received. At first his project was favored, and he sent some settlers, but later direct Irish settlement was forbidden. He next encouraged immigration from other colonies and interested prominent people in the north, including Benjamin Franklin and the Rev. James Lyon of Trenton, N. J. In 1765 with his associates he was granted about 1,745,000 acres in Nova Scotia, of which probably 1,600,000 acres were in the ill-defined St. John region. Most of this land was escheated between 1770 and 1788 because the promoters did not comply with the terms, and on account of the Revolution. He established New Jerusalem at Port Roseway, now Shelburne, and brought some settlers from New England and Pennsylvania to the St. John.

He sympathized with the revolting colonies and left Nova Scotia in 1778. He lived at Jamaica Plain, Mass., but visited Philadelphia to urge the Congress to try to draw Nova Scotia into the Revolution. Between 1778 and 1781 he advocated invasion of the province and helped foment rebellion. Probably he was still associated with Lyon, who was in Maine. He obtained a grant of $15,000 from Congress to build a road from the Penobscot River to the St. John. About 1780 he published *The Constitution . . . of the Free and Independent State . . . of New Ireland,* a tract containing promises of democratic government but really advertising his lands. "New Ireland" probably embraced eastern Maine and southern New Brunswick. After the Revolution he lived near Lexington, Va. He died unmarried. To the last he claimed his northern lands and bequeathed 100,000 acres to Liberty Hall Academy, now Washington and Lee University, but the title was not good.

His schemes were too ambitious to be practicable. His enthusiasm ultimately inspired distrust rather than confidence. This may be the explanation of his failure to obtain the support of British and provincial officials for his land schemes and was probably the cause of American distrust of his plans for winning Nova Scotia. He was a man of strong personality, not always scrupulous, but an interesting example of the colonial speculator-patriot.

[A. W. H. Eaton, "Alexander McNutt," in *Americana,* Dec. 1913, a critical examination of other biographies from sources carefully cited; *Proc. and Trans. of the Royal Soc. of Canada,* 3 ser., vols. V, VI (1912–13); Beamish Murdoch, *A Hist. of Nova Scotia,* vol. II (1866); George Patterson, *A Hist. of the County of Pictou, Nova Scotia* (1916); H. H. McCormick, *Genealogies and Reminiscences* (rev. ed., 1897), pp. 57–64.]

R. G. L.

MACOMB, ALEXANDER (Apr. 3, 1782–June 25, 1841), soldier, was born at Detroit. His paternal grandfather, John Macomb, had come to New York from Ireland as early as 1742; his father, Alexander Macomb, had built up a prosperous trading business at Detroit, which he did not relinquish until after the close of the Revolution. He then returned to New York, with his wife, Catharine Navarre, daughter of Robert de Navarre, a former French official at Detroit, and with their son, Alexander Macomb the younger. The boy was placed in school at an academy in Newark, N. J., where he received "the rudiments of a classical, mathematical, and French education." At the age of sixteen he was enrolled in a New York City militia company, and during the period of hostilities with France the recommendation of Alexander Hamilton secured him a commission in the regular army as cornet of light dragoons. In the same year (1799), he was promoted to second lieutenant, and after being honorably discharged at the close of hostilities, he was again commissioned (Feb. 16, 1801), this time as second lieutenant of infantry (F. B. Heitman, *Historical Register and Dictionary of the United States Army,* 1903, I, 680). During his period of service in the dragoons he had been designated as assistant to Adj.-Gen. William North, a thoroughly trained veteran of the Revolution, and from North and Hamilton, near whose headquarters he was stationed, he learned much about the organization and administration of an army. In 1801 and 1802 he was attached as secretary to a commission composed of Generals Wilkinson and Pickens and Colonel Hawkins, appointed to treat with the Indians of the Southeast. The commission traveled extensively in the country of the Cherokee, Choctaw, Chickasaw, and Creek Indians. Shortly thereafter (Oct. 12, 1802), Macomb was commissioned first lieutenant in the Corps of Engineers, the newly created unit which at this time constituted the United States Military Academy. Macomb and another lieutenant (James Wilson of Pennsylvania) were the first student officers to receive formal training at West Point and to complete a course of study there (*American State Papers, Military Affairs,* II, 1834, p. 634). After completing his own course of study Macomb remained on duty at West Point till 1805, when he was commissioned captain in the Corps of Engineers and ordered to duty elsewhere. From 1807 to 1812 he was chief engineer in charge of coast fortifications in the Carolinas and Georgia. He became a major in February 1808 and a lieutenant-colonel in July 1810. In April 1812 he was ordered to Washington as adjutant-general, charged with the duty of preparing the army for impending war. When war was declared, and his position in the Corps of Engineers prevented his holding an active command, he was at his own request transferred to the artillery, commissioned colonel (July 6, 1812), and sent to New York to raise a regiment. The following winter he was in command at Sacketts Harbor; in the spring of 1813 he participated in the capture of Fort George on the Niagara River, and in the fall of the same year took a minor part in Wilkinson's St. Lawrence campaign. He was made a brigadier-general in January 1814 and was stationed with his brigade in the Lake Champlain region. When General Izard with the main army at Plattsburg was ordered to Sacketts Harbor in August 1814, Macomb was left with about fifteen hundred regulars fit for duty, and such volunteers as could be mustered in the neighboring country, to confront an invading force of some fifteen thousand British veterans under Gov. Sir George Prevost (H. Adams, *History of the United States,* VIII, 1891, pp. 100–11). His position at Plattsburg had been strongly fortified under Izard's direction, and Macomb worked energetically to make it stronger and to give the British an exaggerated idea of his resources. His defense against the attack of Sept. 11 was skilfully conducted, but the precipitate retreat of the British was probably due rather to the destruction of their fleet by Macdonough and the resulting danger to their communications than to the prowess of the small American army. Nevertheless, Macomb and his troops were signally honored by Congress and by the state and city of New York, and Macomb was given the brevet rank of major-general. After the close of the war Macomb was a member of a board which worked out the plan on which the army was reorganized. He was stationed for a short time in New York in command of the third military district and was then shifted to the fifth district with headquarters at Detroit. In 1821 he went to Washington as head of the Corps of Engineers. On the death of Gen. Jacob Brown in 1828, Macomb was designated to succeed him as senior major-general and commanding general of the United States army—a position which he filled until his death at Washington, June 25, 1841.

Among Macomb's official papers was a "Memoir on the Organization of the Army of the United States" (1826), in which he urged a plan for bringing the militia under more centralized control and better discipline (*American State Papers, Military Affairs,* III, 1860, pp. 458–65). In a letter of Jan. 27, 1829, replying to an inquiry of Secretary of War Peter B. Porter, he recommended the abolition of the whiskey ration in the army and should share in the credit for the general order issued the next year discontinuing that ancient practice (*Ibid.,* IV, 1860, p. 84; *Subject Index of the General Orders of the War Department, from Jan. 1, 1809, to Dec. 31, 1860,* 1886, p. 180). His ability seems to have been primarily of the organizing, systematizing kind, which the army of his day greatly needed. Macomb was married, July 23, 1803, to his cousin, Catharine Macomb, of Belleville, N. J., who became the mother of a large family. After her death he was married in 1826 to Harriet (Balch) Wilson, a widow. His second wife took a lively part in the "Eaton war" in the first administration of Andrew Jackson—"more to his [Macomb's] amusement than annoyance," says Van Buren, "for he took such things lightly." Macomb was the author of *A Treatise on Martial Law and Courts-Martial* (1809) and *The Practice of Courts Martial* (1840), and edited Samuel Cooper's *Tactics and Regulations for the Militia* (1836).

[In addition to works cited above see *Memoir of Alexander Macomb, the Maj. Gen. Commanding the Army of the U. S., by Geo. H. Richards, Esq., Capt. of Macomb's Artillery in the Late War* (1833), and the *Daily Nat. Intelligencer,* June 28, 1841.] J. W. P—t.

MACOMBER, MARY LIZZIE (Aug. 21, 1861–Feb. 4, 1916), painter of decorative symbolic panels, was born at Fall River, Mass., the daughter of Frederick William and Mary White Poor Macomber. She came of both Pilgrim and Quaker stock. As a child she was fond of drawing. She began to study painting with Robert S. Dunning, an able Fall River painter whose specialty was fruit and flower pieces. Her first efforts were naturally in the same line. After studying with him for about three years she went to Boston and entered the school of the Museum of Fine Arts, where she took up the study of figure painting. In the second year of her course her health failed and for nearly three years she was unable to continue her studies. Later she resumed work for a short time under the direction of Frank Duveneck, and she then opened a studio in Boston. The first of her pictures to be exhibited was "Ruth," in the National Academy exhibition of 1889.

In the early period, that to which the most characteristic works belong, roughly, from 1889 to 1899, she produced a series of symbolic panels which were admirable in a decorative sense and original in conception. Of these perhaps the most interesting example was "Love Awakening Memory" (1892), shown at the Chicago exposition of 1893. Her "St. Catherine" was awarded the Norman W. Dodge prize "for the best picture painted in the United States by a woman" at the National Academy exhibition of 1897. It is now in the permanent collection of the Boston Art Museum. "Love's Lament" (1893) went the rounds of numerous exhibitions. In these early pictures the execution was of a Pre-Raphaelite finish, and the work was essentially decorative. In a period of fourteen years twenty-five of her pictures were seen in the National Academy exhibitions.

In 1898 she made a radical change in her method of painting; she began to stand up while at work instead of sitting. This change of position, with its opportunity for changes of focus, brought about a noticeable broadening of her style. The first work produced in the new manner was "The Hour Glass," exhibited at the Society of American Artists, 1900. "The Lace Jabot," which also made its first appearance in 1900, was a self-portrait. "Night and Her Daughter Sleep," shown at the first exhibition of ideal figure pictures held by the National Arts Club in 1903, is one of the most impressive of her allegories. A fire which occurred in the Harcourt studio building, Boston, in 1903, virtually destroyed Miss Macomber's studio with its contents. Among the paintings ruined was the almost finished "Memory Comforting Sorrow." The artist set to work and painted the motive for the second time, completing it in 1905. This work was bought for $2,500 by the Art and Fortnightly Clubs of Fall River and was hung in the Fall River Public Library.

Coincident with her change of style she began to paint portraits, and, since a number of commissions came to her from New York, she made several lengthy visits to the metropolis. At this period she had her first and only opportunity to go to Europe. She spent a few weeks in England, France, and Holland, and she returned aflame with admiration for Rembrandt, whose work became the most potent influence in her practice. Her portraits showed this dominant influence plainly, more especially in the arbitrary character of the lighting. Her portrait of her mother (1900) is in the Boston Art Museum. A portrait of Dr. Adams, for many years minister of the First Congregational Church of Fall River, hangs in the parish house of that church. Miss Macomber died of pneumonia in a Boston hospital in 1916. At the funeral in the New Old South Church a remarkable company of artists and art-lovers paid homage to her character and achievements.

[W. H. Downes, "Miss Macomber's Paintings," *New Eng. Mag.,* Nov. 1903; A. J. Philpott, article in *Boston Globe,* Feb. 6, 1916; D. M. Cheney, article in *New Bedford Standard,* Feb. 13, 1916; *Boston Transcript,* Feb. 5, 1916; *Fall River Evening News,* Feb. 5, 1916; Mich. State Lib., *Biog. Sketches of Am. Artists* (1916); *Am. Art News,* Feb. 12, 19, 1916; Sadakichi Hartmann, *A Hist. of Am. Art* (1932), vol. I; Boston Museum of Fine Arts, *Cat. of Paintings* (1921); E. S. Stackpole, *Macomber Geneal.* (1908).] W. H. D.

MACON, NATHANIEL (Dec. 17, 1758–June 29, 1837), Revolutionary soldier, speaker of the House, United States senator, was born at "Macon Manor" in Edgecombe (later Bute and now Warren) County, N. C., the sixth child of Gideon and Priscilla (Jones) Macon. He entered the College of New Jersey at Princeton in 1774 and remained there two years. In 1776 he "served a tour" in the New Jersey militia, and late in 1777 left the army and, returning to North Carolina, began to study law. In May 1780 he enlisted as a private in a company commanded by his brother and took part in the battle of Camden. During this period he refused a commission. In 1781 he was elected to the state Senate but ignored the summons until General Greene urged him to accept, on the score of the aid he might render the army.

In the legislature he came under the influence of Willie Jones [*q.v.*], with whom and with whose political doctrines he was thereafter in close accord. He was again elected to the Senate in 1782 and in 1784. On Oct. 9, 1783, he married Hannah Plummer of Warren County, who died leaving three children, on July 11, 1790. In 1786 he was elected to the Continental Congress and declined to serve. He opposed the Federal Convention and advocated the rejection of the Constitution. In 1790 he was a member of the House of Commons, and in 1791 was elected to the federal House of Representatives, taking his seat Oct. 26. He served continuously until December 1815, when he was transferred to the Senate. Here he remained until December 1828, when, having reached the age of seventy, he resigned, giving up at the same time his place as justice of the peace and trustee of the University of North Carolina. He was speaker of the House from 1801 to 1807, and for the last two years of his senatorial service was president *pro tempore.*

A close and devoted friend of Jefferson, except for a period of estrangement after 1806 caused by Macon's support of John Randolph of Roanoke, he was for years the outstanding leader of the Republicans in the House. As such he fought vigorously against the Federalists and their entire program. He detested Hamilton and all his works. He advocated the maintenance of the treaty with France, bitterly opposed the Jay treaty, the Alien and Sedition laws, and the whole movement for war with France in 1798–99. He was a supporter of the purchase of Louisiana and urged upon Jefferson the purchase of Florida as well. Throughout his entire career he opposed building a navy. He supported in its entirety the foreign policy of the Jefferson and Madison administrations, and in 1809 was chairman of the foreign relations committee. In this capacity he reported successively the two bills which bear his name, although he was the author of neither and was definitely opposed to the second. The first, a stroke at British shipping, was defeated, but on May 1, 1810, Macon's Bill No. 2 was passed, giving the president power to suspend intercourse with either Great Britain or France if the other should cease to interfere with United States commerce.

Macon favored the War of 1812, but opposed conscription and the levy of higher taxes. He opposed the recharter of the United States Bank in 1811 and in 1816, uniformly voted against any form of protective tariff, and while favoring road construction by the federal government, opposed the policy of internal improvements. He took part in the Missouri debate and voted against the compromise measure. Throughout his life he was an earnest defender of slavery. Numbered among the opponents of the Adams administration, he fought against the participation of the United States in the Panama Congress. He preferred Monroe to Madison in 1808, and, although he would not enter the caucus, supported Crawford in 1824, in which year he received the electoral vote of Virginia for vice-president. In 1828, while opposing Adams, who wished him as a running mate, he did not want Jackson for president, in spite of their warm personal friendship.

Important and valuable a figure as Macon was in Congress for thirty-seven years, he was not a constructive force. He was a negative radical, and it was said of him that during the entire term of his service no ten other members cast so many negative votes. "Negation was his ward and arm." He was rural and local-minded, and economy was the passion of his public career. "His economy of the public money was the severest, sharpest, most stringent and constant refusal of almost any grant that could be proposed." With him, "not only was . . . parsimony the best subsidy—but . . . the only one" (C. J. Ingersoll, quoted in the *Weekly Raleigh Register,* Sept. 26, 1845). He was a frequent and influential, though not eloquent, speaker. On the floor and in personal intercourse he was genial, human, and inclined to jocularity, and was generally popular in spite of the fact that he was strongly, even dogmatically, opinionated. Of moderate abilities only, he won his way by force of constant integrity, industry, and the entire absence of any personal or selfish motives.

After his resignation from the Senate he spent most of his remaining days in happy retirement at "Buck Spring," his home in Warren County. Constantly asked for political advice, he wrote many letters which are notable for their hard common sense and for their clear revelation of the writer. In 1832, although still a champion of the principles of the Virginia and Kentucky Resolutions, he opposed nullification as unconstitutional, taking the position that secession was the rightful remedy for usurpation of power by the federal government. In 1835 he accepted election as a delegate to the convention called to revise the state constitution, and was unanimously chosen its president. There he opposed such changes as the abolition of annual election of the legislature, and he declined to vote for the amended constitution. The following year he supported Van Buren for president, and as a candidate for elector aided powerfully in winning the last victory the Democrats were to have in North Carolina for many years. He died suddenly at his home the following summer.

["Letters of Nathaniel Macon, John Steele, and William Barry Grove," ed. by K. P. Battle, *James Sprunt Hist. Monograph No. 3* (1902); "Some Unpublished Letters of Nathaniel Macon," ed. by J. S. Bassett, in *Trinity Coll. Hist. Papers,* 6 ser. (1906); "Nathaniel Macon and Bartlett Yancey," in *N. C. Univ. Mag.,* Oct. 1857; E. M. Wilson, "The Congressional Career of Nathaniel Macon," *James Sprunt Hist. Monograph, No. 2* (1900); E. R. Cotten, *Life of the Hon. Nathaniel Macon* (1840); W. N. Edwards, *Memoir of Nathaniel Macon* (1862); W. E. Dodd, "The Place of Nathaniel Macon in Southern History," *Am. Hist. Rev.,* July 1902, and *Life of Nathaniel Macon* (1903); Josephus Daniels, "Nathaniel Macon," in *Proc. . . . State Lit. and Hist. Asso. of N. C. . . . 1912* (1913); *The John P. Branch Hist. Papers of Randolph Macon Coll.,* no. 2 (1902) and *Ibid.,* vol. III, no. 1 (1909); D. H. Gilpatrick, *Jeffersonian Democracy in N. C. 1789–1816* (1931); *Richmond Enquirer,* July 4, 11, 1837.]

J. G. deR. H.

McPHERSON, EDWARD (July 31, 1830–Dec. 14, 1895), member of Congress, clerk of the House of Representatives, author, editor, was born in Gettysburg, Pa., of Pennsylvania colonial stock, the son of John Bayard McPherson and Katharine Lenhart. He attended the common schools of Gettysburg and was graduated from Pennsylvania (now Gettysburg) College in 1848. For a time he studied law, but he left legal studies to enter journalism. From 1851, when he became editor of the *Harrisburg American,* until his death he was connected with various newspapers in Pennsylvania: with the *Independent Whig* of Lancaster, 1851–54; with the Pittsburgh *Daily Times,* 1855; with the Philadelphia *Press,* 1877–80; and as editor and proprietor of the Gettysburg *Star and Sentinel,* 1880–95. In 1862 he was married to Annie Dods Crawford, also a Pennsylvanian. Although he was a member of Congress for two terms and clerk of the House of Representatives for sixteen years, he is best known as a political cyclopedist and statistician. His *Political History of the United States of America During the Great Rebellion* (1864); *The Political History of the United States of America During the Period of Reconstruction* (1871); *Political Manual,* published annually from 1866 to 1869, and the *Handbook of Politics,* published biennially from 1868 through 1894, are invaluable to the student of American history as source books of political material.

McPherson was elected as a Republican to the Thirty-sixth and Thirty-seventh congresses, 1859–63, but was defeated for reëlection in 1862. He was then appointed deputy-commissioner of internal revenue. After six months he resigned to become clerk of the House of Representatives, serving continuously from 1863 to 1875, and again during the years 1881–83 and 1889–91. In fact, he made more of a name for himself as clerk of the House than as member of Congress. His clear knowledge of parliamentary law and his exact command of a wide range of political information made him indispensable to the speaker and to members of Congress. For a brief moment he held the center of the political stage and was the master of destiny of the Southern states. When the Thirty-ninth Congress assembled, Dec. 4, 1865, members from the former Confederate states presented themselves for admission with credentials duly inscribed by the reconstructed governments. The recognition of these representatives from the South was the first trial in the combat now set between Congress and President Johnson. According to the rules of the House, it was McPherson's duty as clerk of the previous House to call the House to order and to call the roll of members. In the midst of the greatest excitement, with floor and galleries of the House crowded, he quickly passed up the aisle, unfolded his papers in a businesslike way, unperturbed by the excitement around him, and began the critical procedure of calling the roll. He had learned his lesson well and carried through completely the agreements reached by the caucus of Republican members of the House two days before. He refused to hear protests from the Southern members whose names were omitted in the roll-call, on the ground that none save those whose names were called had the right to speak. The Civil War was ended, but the Reconstruction battle was only beginning, and in the first skirmish McPherson advanced the standard of the Congressional forces.

McPherson was long an active member of the Republican party. In 1860 he was a member of the Republican National Committee; in 1876 he was permanent president of the Republican National Convention; and in 1880 he was secretary of the Republican Congressional Committee. He contributed a chapter entitled "Rise and Progress of the Republican Party, 1856–88" to *The Republican Party: its History, Principles and Policies* (1888), edited by John D. Long. For a short time in 1877–78 he was chief of the Bureau of Engraving and Printing under appointment by President Hayes. In 1879 he retired to Gettysburg where he bought and edited a newspaper. He also edited the New York *Tribune Almanac and Political Register* from 1877 to 1895, and for several years acted as American editor of the *Almanach de Gotha.*

[*Appletons' Ann Cyc.*, 1895; *Biog. Dir. Am. Cong.* (1928); *The Alumni Record of Gettysburg Coll., 1832–1932* (1932); James G. Blaine, *Twenty Years of Cong.*, vols. I and II (1884–86); E. P. Oberholtzer, *A Hist. of the U. S. Since the Civil War*, vol. I (1917); information as to certain facts from McPherson's son, William L. McPherson.] C. M. T.

McPHERSON, JAMES BIRDSEYE (Nov. 14, 1828–July 22, 1864), Union soldier, was born in Green Creek township, Sandusky County, Ohio, near the present town of Clyde. He was the son of William and Cynthia (Russell) McPherson. Appointed cadet at the United States Military Academy in 1849, he graduated in 1853 at the head of his class, and was assigned to the corps of engineers as brevet second lieutenant. For a year he was retained at the Academy as assistant instructor in practical engineering, and was then assigned to duty in connection with river and harbor improvement and seacoast fortification. Upon duty of this nature he continued, first on the Atlantic and then on the Pacific coast, until 1861; meanwhile, he was promoted second lieutenant, Dec. 18, 1854, and first lieutenant, Dec. 13, 1858.

The outbreak of the Civil War found him in San Francisco. He was ordered East, and employed on fortification work in Boston. Upon the enlargement of the regular army, May 14, 1861, he was offered a commission as captain in the new 19th Infantry, but declined it, and on Aug. 6 reached the grade of captain in his own corps. When General Halleck assumed command in Missouri, he took McPherson with him as an aide-de-camp, with the rank of lieutenant-colonel and later of colonel. He served first as assistant engineer, Department of Missouri, but when General Grant opened his Tennessee campaign in February 1862, he accompanied the expedition as chief engineer, and from that time on was constantly in the field. While before Corinth, May 15, 1862, he was promoted brigadier-general of volunteers; and after the occupation of that place he was made military superintendent of railways in the district of Western Tennessee. Of his services at this period, General Sherman said: "McPherson . . . was one of the most useful staff-officers in the whole army—riding night and day. . . . I think he knew more of the lay . . . of the country around Corinth than any officer of the army" (*Hours at Home,* April 1866, pp. 485–86). His first command, small but unusual in character, resulted naturally from this employment. On Oct. 2, Rosecrans, at Corinth, was heavily attacked by Van Dorn; the situation seemed critical, and Grant, at Jackson, Tenn., made efforts to reinforce him. McPherson, then at headquarters in Jackson, was directed to collect four regiments stationed along the railway between there and Corinth, and report with them to Rosecrans. He moved by rail to within ten miles of Corinth, detrained, and marched the rest of the way, arriving too late to assist in the repulse of Van Dorn, but in time to lead the pursuit. For his conduct in this affair he was made major-general of volunteers, Oct. 8, 1862, and was assigned to command the 2nd Division, Department of the Tennessee; which command, on Nov. 24, became the 2nd Division, XIII Army Corps. Later, Jan. 18, 1863, the army, having been reinforced, was reorganized, and McPherson received command of the XVII Army Corps. He was actively employed throughout the entire Vicksburg campaign, and after the surrender (July 4, 1863) remained in command of the District of Vicksburg until the following March, participating meanwhile in Sherman's raid to Meridian. In recognition of his services before Vicksburg, he was made, Aug. 1, 1863, brigadier-general in the regular army.

On Mar. 18, 1864, Grant went east to assume direction of all the armies; Sherman succeeded him in command of the Military Division of the Mississippi, and began preparations for his Atlanta campaign. McPherson took over Sherman's Army of the Tennessee, assuming command at Huntsville, Mar. 26. At the head of this army he fought the entire campaign, up to the fortifications of Atlanta. At Kenesaw Mountain, the rapid and decisive movements of his force won for it the soldier nickname "the whiplash of the army." On July 22, the armies of the Cumberland and the Ohio were well established north and east of Atlanta. The Army of the Tennessee was directed to connect with the Army of the Ohio on its right, and extend its left to the south. While this movement was in progress, a Confederate turning movement against the left and rear developed. McPherson was at Sherman's headquarters, receiving his orders, and at once started to join his troops. Passing, with a single orderly, through a wood road which had been previously reconnoitered and found clear, he suddenly encountered hostile skirmishers who had penetrated between his XVI and XVII Corps, and was killed.

His death was one of the heaviest individual losses ever suffered by the Union forces. By his superiors, he was recognized as one of the ablest generals in the army. Energetic and ambitious, he welcomed responsibility and active service, but loyally and with no spirit of self-seeking. Grant, in a letter written upon leaving the western army, coupled Sherman and McPherson together as "the men to whom, above all others, I feel indebted for whatever I have had of success" (*Memoirs of Gen. William T. Sherman, post,* I, 399). Sherman was equally emphatic in his praise. In the army at large his talents seemed to be fully recognized, and his advancement to corps and army command gave rise to little or no jealousy. A man of striking and pleasing appearance—over six feet in height, erect and well-proportioned—and possessed in a high degree of the faculty of command, he was able to gain the confidence and loyalty of his subordinates. Young and vigorous, he lived in close association with his troops, and bore his full share of hardship and exposure.

[G. W. Cullum, *Biog. Register of the Officers and Grads. of the U. S. Mil. Acad.* (3rd ed., 1891); *Memoirs of Gen. William T. Sherman* (2 vols., 1875); *Personal Memoirs of U. S. Grant* (2 vols., 1885–86); *Hours at Home,* Mar. 1866; D. R. Keim, "The Life and Character of Maj.-Gen. James B. McPherson," *U. S. Service Mag.,* Oct. 1864; *Biog. Cyc. and Portrait Gallery . . . of the State of Ohio,* vol. I (1883); Basil Meek, *Twentieth Century Hist. of Sandusky County, Ohio, and Representative Citizens* (1909); *Army and Navy Jour.,* July 30, 1864.] O. L. S., Jr.

McPHERSON, LOGAN GRANT (Aug. 11, 1863–Mar. 23, 1925), railway statistician, economist, organizer of railway publicity, was born in Circleville, Ohio, the son of Daniel Workman and Frances Louise (Kinnear) McPherson. The basis for his education, mostly self-directed, was laid in the public schools which he attended until sixteen years of age. After a year's work on a newspaper, he obtained a position with the Pennsylvania Railroad, and remained with the company from 1880 to 1891. Thus began his connection with American railway transportation which was his chief interest for most of his life. In the years from 1892 to 1903 he held various positions with coal companies in Pittsburgh, but he returned to railroading in 1904 when he became statistician for the Rock Island system. At this time the railroads were incurring much public disfavor. They were accused of charging unreasonable rates for unsatisfactory service. Amalgamations and community of interest schemes were denounced as dangerous to the public interest. A greater measure of government control was urged, and bills were introduced into Congress giving the Interstate Commerce Commission wide powers over railway rates, regulations, and practices. It was during this period that the railroad companies were brought to realize the value of well-organized publicity. In 1905 the Associated Railways of the United States was founded by Samuel Spencer, president of the Southern Railway Company, who engaged McPherson as his assistant. In this position he was occupied for two years in collecting railway statistics and in preparing material for use before congressional committees and for dissemination in the public press. The railroads lost their fight, for in 1906 the Hepburn Act was passed.

McPherson's connection with the Associated Railways ended and he was appointed lecturer on transportation at the Johns Hopkins University, 1905–15. For several years he devoted himself to the study of the effects of railway rates on American business conditions and published two books. He had previously published *The Monetary and Banking Problem* (1896). *The Working of the Railroads* (1907) was a modest but distinctly successful attempt to describe the general railroad situation. *Railroad Freight Rates in Relation to the Industry and Commerce of the United States* (1909) contained a wealth of concrete details of rate-making obtained at first hand from traffic officials, but it was not well arranged and it was not an impartial statement of the rate problem from the point of view of public policy. For six months in 1909 McPherson toured Europe making a study of railroads and canals for the National Waterways Commission. After his return he wrote *Transportation in Europe* (1910), an interesting and instructive account of conditions as he observed them. The Bureau of Railway Economics organized by him in Washington in 1910 is a monument to his industry and ability. Its purposes were the exchange of statistics among the cooperating railroads and the creation of public opinion favorable to the railway industry. From 1910 to 1914 he served as director, continuing at the same time his lectures at Johns Hopkins. He also lectured at Harvard and Columbia. After leaving the Bureau he devoted himself to study and writing. He was a frequent contributor to railway journals and to general periodicals; and he also undertook a series of books in the field of general economics: *How the World Makes its Living* (1916), *The Flow of Value* (1919), and *Human Effort and Human Wants* (1923). These books represent an attempt to humanize economics, and to carry its discussions beyond wealth to welfare. They showed wide reading in the literature of economics as well as in history and sociology, but they contributed little to the subject. Lacking the precision of technical works, they also lacked the literary style essential to wide circulation. Their best parts are those drawn from the author's own experience. In 1924 McPherson spent several months in England studying amalgamations of railroads. Shortly after his return to New York City, then his home, he was injured in a street accident, which was a contributing cause of his death a few months later. He never married. Outside his work, his interests were chiefly books which he read constantly and insatiably. Independent, and straightforward in his expressions of opinion, he could be a bitter antagonist in controversies; yet by his thoughtfulness and consideration he attracted the loyalty and affection of those who worked with him.

[The *N. Y. Times,* Mar. 25, 1925; *Railway Age,* Mar. 28, 1925; *Who's Who in America,* 1924–25; E. S. White, *The Kinnears and Their Kin* (1916).]

P. W. B.

McPHERSON, SMITH (Feb. 14, 1848–Jan. 17, 1915), congressman from Iowa and federal district judge, the son of Oliver H. and Polly (Matthews) McPherson, was born and reared on a farm near Mooresville, Ind. Having completed his academic training at the Mooresville academy, he entered the law department at the State University of Iowa in September 1869 and graduated the following June. During the summer of 1870 he worked at Council Bluffs in the law office of his uncle, M. L. McPherson, of whom he many years later wrote a biographical sketch (*M. L. McPherson,* 1913). In November he moved to Redoak, Iowa, where he lived the rest of his life. He was married to Frances H. Boyer of Oskaloosa, on Oct. 2, 1879. They had no children. Beneath his brusque manner was a genial disposition and a sympathetic attitude that attracted many clients and made lifelong friends. Gov. C. C. Carpenter appointed him, in August 1874, to fill a vacancy as prosecuting attorney for the third judicial district. A year later he was elected to the same office and was reëlected in 1878 for a full term of four years. He distinguished himself by winning several important cases and attained sufficient prominence in the Republican party to be elected attorney general of Iowa. Probably the most important episode during his two terms in office, from 1881 to 1885, was the trial of the case of *Koehler & Lange* vs. *Hill* (60 *Iowa Reports,* 543) testing the validity of an amendment to the state constitution prohibiting the manufacture and sale of intoxicating liquor. In spite of his well-reasoned argument before the Supreme Court that the amendment had been adopted in the proper manner and by two successive General Assemblies in substantially identical form, the court decided in favor of the contrary view (*Iowa Journal of History and Politics,* Oct. 1908, pp. 529–33).

Between 1885 and 1900, he established a reputation as an eloquent and aggressive advocate whose services were in great demand, particularly by corporations. Like other successful and conservative lawyers who lived on the Burlington "reservation" in southern Iowa, he was retained as attorney for the Chicago, Burlington, & Quincy Railroad. In 1898 he was nominated for Congress on the 619th ballot after a deadlock that lasted four days (*Iowa State Register,* Des Moines, Aug. 26, 1898, weekly edition). Elected by a majority of nearly 4,000 votes, he found his duties in Congress to be "altogether the most unsatisfactory work in which a public man could engage" (*Iowa Alumnus, post,* p. 18). Consequently when President McKinley offered to appoint him judge for the southern district of Iowa he accepted with alacrity, though he did not resign from Congress until the end of the first session.

During the fifteen years he was on the federal bench, the business of the court increased enormously, particularly in the number of criminal cases, but he had a faculty for expediting procedure and kept his docket fairly clear. His decisions were always influenced by his innate conservatism. He ruled that the Iowa sterilization law as it applied to habitual criminals was unconstitutional (*Davis* vs. *Berry,* 216 *Federal Reporter,* 413). While he was holding court in Missouri, he enjoined the state of Missouri from enforcing maximum freight and passenger rates on the ground that they were confiscatory (*St. Louis & S. F. R. Co.* vs. *Hadley, et al.,* 168 *Federal Reporter,* 317). On appeal the Supreme Court of the United States decided that the Missouri maximum rates were not confiscatory on the basis of assessed valuation of the railroads and reversed the decrees (*Missouri Rate Cases,* 230 *United States Reports,* 474). Meanwhile popular resentment against judicial frustration of statutory rate regulation found expression in a resolution introduced in Congress by Arthur P. Murphy of Missouri calling for an investigation of the official conduct of Judge McPherson (*Congressional Record,* 61 Cong., 1 Sess., pp. 1689, 1801–1805). The charges proved to be unfounded, however, and no further action was taken.

[*Iowa Jour. of Hist. and Pol.,* Jan., Apr. 1915; E. H. Stiles, *Recollections and Sketches of Notable Lawyers . . . Iowa* (1916); *Iowa Law Bulletin,* Mar. 1915; *Law Notes,* Mar. 1915; *Iowa Alumnus,* Feb. 1915; *Register and Leader* (Des Moines), Jan. 18, 19, 1915; *New York Times* Jan. 18, 1915.] J. E. B.

McQUAID, BERNARD JOHN (Dec. 15, 1823–Jan. 18, 1909), first bishop of Rochester, was born in New York of Irish parents, Bernard and Mary McQuaid. His mother died in 1827 and in 1832, following the murder of his father, a laborer in a Paulus Hook glass factory, he found a refuge with the Sisters of Charity. After attending the graded school, he was sent to Chambly College in Canada and then to St. Joseph's Seminary in Fordham, N. Y., where his precarious health kept him apart from fellow-seminarians. He was ordained on Jan. 16, 1848, by Bishop Hughes and assigned to a church in Madison, N. J., from which he worked an area of five counties in addition to teaching in a basement school. Hard and zealous, he sought no ease: he restored isolated Catholics to the fold, instructed the young in doctrine, and built modest chapels at Morristown, Springfield, and Mendham. In 1853 he commenced his long pastorate of St. Patrick's Cathedral in Newark. In 1854 he courageously faced a mob which attacked the German Catholic Church and strove in vain to have the ringleaders brought to justice. He organized relief work in the hungry winter of 1854–55; brought the Sisters of Charity of Mt. St. Vincent to conduct orphanages at Newark and Paterson; developed a cathedral school of 600 pupils; virtually founded and presided over Seton Hall College and Seminary (1857); aided in establishing St. Elizabeth's Convent; organized the Newark branch of the St. Vincent de Paul Society; and promoted a Young Men's Catholic lyceum. During the Civil War he was an aggressive Unionist. In 1864 he rushed to Washington to investigate the care of Catholic soldiers and remained at Fredericksburg to administer the sacraments to the wounded. As a theologian he attended the Second Plenary Council of Baltimore, and as vicar-general (1866–68), he administered the diocese, rigorously handling problems and priests that were wearing out Bishop Bayley.

Named bishop of Rochester, McQuaid was consecrated on July 12, 1868, by Archbishop McCloskey. Immediately he was in conflict with priests who did not relish autocratic discipline and exacting demands. At the Vatican Council he voted against the definition of papal infallibility, July 13, 1870, but he left Rome before the final vote, so anxious was he to reform his diocese. On Aug. 28 he defined and proclaimed the doctrine from St. Patrick's Cathedral. His heart was in Rochester; he had no ambition for elevation but settled down to church-building, giving special attention to educational and charitable institutions. Organizing the Sisters of St. Joseph as a diocesan community, he gave them charge of parochial schools which were built in all well-organized parishes, especially in German centers. In his zeal for Catholic education and in his fear of the "godless school," he drastically refused absolution to parents who failed to send their children to a Catholic school if one was available. Through the East he was regarded as the spokesman for free Christian schools and as such was frequently called upon to lecture. As the diocese grew prosperous, McQuaid established St. Bernard's Seminary (1891), a Catholic Summer Institute (1896) for teacher training, the Nazareth Normal School (1898), a branch of the St. Cecilian Society for the reform of church music, and cathedral schools. His ardor for parish schools accounted in part for his unreasoning bitterness toward Archbishop Ireland, Edward McGlynn, Bishop S. V. Ryan of Buffalo, Sylvester Malone, his successful rival for a regency of the University of New York, and Msgr. Keane of the Catholic University of America, whom he prevented from speaking to the Catholic students of Cornell University lest this give formal sanction to their attendance, which he only tolerated. For girls he did not even tolerate attendance in non-Catholic institutions.

McQuaid rigidly interpreted the ban on secret societies; he was suspicious of the Knights of Labor regardless of Cardinal Gibbons' approbation, and hostile to the Irish Land League, Clan-Na-Gael, and the Ancient Order of Hibernians, who as a body were not allowed to attend Mass in his diocese until 1894. In this respect he emphasized Americanism and boasted of native birth when a majority of the prelates were foreign born. He conducted in 1875 a successful campaign for a chaplain in the Western House of Refuge in Rochester and in 1892 spiritedly aided in the struggle for the law guaranteeing freedom of worship in penal institutions. In addition to building orphanages in Rochester, Canandaigua, and Auburn, he provided chapels at Craig Colony for Epileptics and at the State Soldiers' Home. Toward the end this "venerable but crusty old ecclesiastic who in perfect good faith felt that he alone was fighting the battles of the Church" (Archbishop Dowling of St. Paul in *American Historical Review,* April 1928, p. 702) grew more mild. In an exchange of visits he even found that he had much in common with Archbishop Ireland. In 1908 distinguished guests from the Catholic seminaries of the world attended the dedication of the Hall of Theology at St. Bernard's when McQuaid spoke from an invalid-chair until he collapsed.

The end soon came, and the doughty bishop's remains were consigned to the chapel in Holy Sepulchre Cemetery.

[F. J. Zwierlein, *The Life and Letters of Bishop McQuaid* (3 vols., 1925–27), is a detailed study, biased but startlingly frank. See also J. G. Shea, *The Hierarchy of the Cath. Ch. in the U. S.* (1886), and the *Rochester Democrat and Chronicle*, Jan. 19, 1909.]

R. J. P.

McQUILLEN, JOHN HUGH (Feb. 12, 1826–Mar. 3, 1879), dentist, writer, editor, a son of Hugh and Martha (Scattergood) McQuillen, was born in Philadelphia, Pa., and received his early education in the Friends' schools of that city. At the age of sixteen he became a clerk in an importing house, but in 1847 he began the study of medicine. In 1849 he also became student-assistant to Elisha Townsend, a well-known dentist of Philadelphia, and was shortly enrolled as a member of the Pennsylvania Association of Dental Surgeons. He received the degree of M.D. from the Jefferson Medical College in 1852, and from that year until 1861 he was associated in the practice of dentistry with Daniel Neall. Beginning in 1861, he practised independently in Philadelphia. From 1852 to 1859 he contributed eight articles to the *Dental News Letter*, which periodical was succeeded in the latter year by the *Dental Cosmos*, with McQuillen as one of its editors. He was professor of operative dentistry and dental pathology in the Pennsylvania College of Dental Surgery from 1857 to 1862. In the latter year he severed his connection with this college because of his dissatisfaction with the selection of a new member of the faculty, and in 1863 he founded the Philadelphia Dental College, of which until his death he was dean and professor of anatomy, physiology, and hygiene. During the Civil War he served gratuitously as a surgeon in the military hospitals at Philadelphia, and in that capacity was present at the battle of Antietam.

In 1859 he had been one of the prime movers in the organization of the American Dental Association, for which, under the pseudonym of Junius, he made the original published call, in an article in the *Dental News Letter* (April 1859, p. 184). In 1865 he was president of the association. In 1863 he was one of the organizers and first corresponding secretary of the Odontographic Society of Philadelphia, and served as its president from 1868 to 1870. In 1866 he was the first corresponding secretary of the Association of the Colleges of Dentistry. He also served as president of the Pennsylvania Association of Dental Surgeons, and was a member of several other societies at home and abroad. From 1865 to 1872 he was editor-in-chief of the *Dental Cosmos*, and he contributed many articles to its pages and to other dental journals. His published papers and addresses, some of which were translated into foreign languages, number altogether over one hundred. (See the *Index to Dental Periodical Literature*, vols. I and II.) They relate chiefly to dental anatomy, physiology, pathology, and histology. He was one of the first in America to demonstrate the importance of microscopical knowledge of the human teeth in health and disease, his earliest paper in this connection appearing in 1857, with others following from 1862 to 1874. He was the founder of the biological and microscopical section of the Academy of Natural Science at Philadelphia, of which he was a member for many years.

McQuillen was a skilful practitioner of dentistry and a conscientious teacher. He insisted upon a thorough preliminary as well as professional education for a dentist, and he labored unremittingly in his private practice and at his duties in the college founded by him, until he broke under the strain shortly before his death. He was impulsive and aggressive, but nevertheless generous and hospitable. With liberal religious views, he had due respect for all denominations, but affiliated with none. His one hobby was music, and he enjoyed nothing more than to surround himself with friends for a musical evening. He died in his fifty-fourth year and was interred in Woodland Cemetery, Philadelphia. In 1852 he married Amelia D. Schellenger, and they had five children.

[J. T. Scharf and Thompson Westcott, *Hist. of Phila.* (1884), vol. II; B. L. Thorpe, in C. R. E. Koch, *Hist. of Dental Surgery* (1910), vol. III; *Trans. Am. Dental Asso.*, 1879; *Am. Jour. Dental Sci.*, Mar. 1879; *British Jour. Dental Sci.*, Apr., May 1879; *Dental Cosmos*, Apr. 1879; the *Press* (Phila.), Mar. 5, 1879.]

L. P. B.

McRAE, DUNCAN KIRKLAND (Aug. 16, 1820–Feb. 12, 1888), lawyer, consul, soldier, was born at Fayetteville, (then Campbelltown), N. C., the son of John and Margaret S. Kirkland McRae. His grandfather, Duncan McRae, came to America from Scotland in 1773 or 1774 and became a leader in public affairs in Campbelltown. His father, postmaster and editor in the same city, numbered among his friends many men famous in American history, among them General Lafayette, whom he accompanied through North Carolina on his American tour in 1825 and entertained at his home. Duncan Kirkland McRae was educated at the College of William and Mary, Virginia, and at the University of North Carolina, and was admitted to the bar at twenty-one. As a lawyer he early developed a wide reputation for eloquence and quickness of repartee.

One of the first incidents in his vigorous and varied career was a mission to Mexico city as bearer of dispatches for the Department of State early in 1842. Returning to North Carolina, he was elected to the legislature of 1842, his first and most successful political venture. He subsequently practised law in Raleigh until 1851, when he removed to Wilmington to engage in banking. In 1845 he married Louise Virginia Henry, daughter of Judge Louis D. Henry of Raleigh. In 1853, as an independent candidate for Congress from the third district, he advocated the distribution of the proceeds from the sale of public lands among the states for internal improvements, but withdrew from the campaign to become American consul at Paris under President Pierce. While there he was commissioned to carry the famous Ostend Manifesto from London to Washington. His service at Paris fell in the stirring days of the Second Empire and lasted until ill health compelled his resignation in 1857. A few months after his return to North Carolina, and his establishment of a law office at New Bern, he plunged into politics for the third time, running independently for governor in opposition to John Willis Ellis [*q.v.*] in the campaign of 1858, with the unofficial support of the disorganized remnants of the American or Know-Nothing party. Always individualistic, high-spirited, and undisposed to yield to party restraints or popular sentiment, he favored a positive program of economic development as against what he believed undue emphasis on the slavery question, and was defeated.

At the opening of the Civil War, he was appointed colonel of the 5th North Carolina Regiment by his late political opponent, Governor Ellis. Beginning with the first battle of Manassas, he took an active part in the Virginia and Pennsylvania campaigns of 1861 and 1862. At Williamsburg he led his men in a desperately gallant charge, ranked by an English war correspondent with that of the Old Guard at Waterloo and the Light Brigade at Balaklava. Of this charge General Hancock of the Federal forces said, "The Fifth North Carolina and the Twenty-Fourth Virginia deserve to have the word immortal inscribed on their banners" (Jefferson Davis, *The Rise and Fall of the Confederate Government,* 1881, II, p. 96). Wounded at Williamsburg and again at Sharpsburg (Sept. 17, 1862), he retired from active service. Shortly afterward he was sent by Governor Vance of North Carolina on an important and successful mission to Europe to find a market for Southern cotton and state bonds and to arrange for the purchase of supplies. As a result the North Carolina troops were the best equipped in the Southern army. His European mission occupied almost a year. He then campaigned for a seat in the Confederate Congress, but was defeated. In 1864–65 he edited the *Confederate* at Raleigh, an administration organ to encourage Southern morale. The new political régime in 1865 forced him to leave the state. He practised law for fifteen years at Memphis, Tenn., then, after a few months at Chicago, returned in 1880 to Wilmington, N. C., where he established his last legal practice. He died in Brooklyn, N. Y., Feb. 12, 1888.

[Brief biographical sketches are to be found in Lawrence MacRae, *Descendants of Duncan & Ann (Cameron) MacRae of Scotland and N. C.* (1928), and in the *Confed. Mil. Hist.* (1899), IV, 626–28. His correspondence as U. S. consul at Paris is in the Department of State Archives at Washington (Paris Consulate, vol. X), and military reports by and concerning him are printed in *War of the Rebellion: Official Records (Army).* An article by himself, "The Battle of Williamsburg—Reply to Colonel Bratton," is in *Southern Hist. Soc. Papers,* Aug. 1879. See also Dunbar Rowland, *Jefferson Davis, Constitutionalist, His Letters, Papers, and Speeches* (1923), IX, 329–33, and the *Morning Star* (Wilmington, N. C.), Feb. 14, 1888.]

I. L. T.

MCRAE, MILTON ALEXANDER (June 13, 1858–Oct. 11, 1930), newspaper publisher, was born in Detroit, Mich., the third child of Duncan B. and Helen (Stevenson) McRae, both of Scotch descent. The father had been brought to Canada as a lad; later he went to Detroit, where he engaged in the dry-goods trade. In the public schools, Milton at once manifested noticeable creative talent, particularly in contriving and managing juvenile shows and circuses. After the death of his mother, when he was fourteen, he persuaded his father to let him go to work. For some time he ran a wide gamut—selling groceries, acting on the stage, managing a traveling theatrical troupe, teaching a country school, braking on a railroad, compiling a city directory, newspaper reporting—all the while cherishing an ambition to become a physician, an ambition which he sharpened by industrious reading of books on physiology and anatomy.

The execution of an idea which came to him in connection with his medical studies brought him his first recognition in the newspaper field. A cub reporter on the *Detroit Free Press,* he wormed his way, as an interne, into the pest house during a smallpox epidemic and wrote so realistic a story of his experiences as to cause an increase in his pay. Assigned to help in the promotion of an "Excursions-to-the-Sea" scheme undertaken by the paper, he did so well that he was induced to stay on in the advertising department at a salary which warranted his marriage, in 1880, to Victoria Wallis, of Saginaw, Mich. Closer contact ensued with the publisher, James E. Scripps [*q.v.*], and also with Scripps's brothers, who were interested together in dailies in Cleveland and Cincinnati. McRae was on the point of taking a War Department clerkship at Washington, when Scripps convinced him that a greater opportunity awaited him as advertising manager of the Cincinnati *Penny Paper*, soon renamed the *Penny Post*. He accepted this position and his rise in the newspaper world was thereafter continuous. He became business manager of the *Post* the next year, 1883, and, in 1887, managing director of the *Evening Chronicle*, which Edward W. Scripps [*q.v.*] had started in St. Louis and which McRae consolidated with the *Star*. These papers were the first in each city to sell for one cent. In 1889 McRae entered into a life-partnership agreement with Edward W. Scripps to pool salaries and profits on a division basis of one third and two thirds respectively. They soon began systematic development of their plan for a chain of newspapers of the same popular type as those they had been conducting. Their policy called for the purchase or establishment of papers in many cities. During one period of six months, McRae organized and put into operation six such papers. Not all were successful. Characterizing William R. Nelson as "one of the best newspapermen America has ever produced," he added, "I ought to know—he ran us out of the Kansas City field and cost us several hundred thousand dollars" (Hamby, *post*, p. 68). The enterprise as a whole proved most profitable, however, and, subsequently reorganized, became the Scripps-Howard Newspapers. In 1897 the Scripps-McRae Press Association, with McRae as president, was formed to furnish news to the papers of the Scripps-McRae League. Other evening papers desiring the service were later admitted and the association developed into the United Press Associations, a world-wide news-gathering and distributing agency of the first magnitude.

Forced by ill health into partial retirement at the age of forty-nine, McRae returned to Detroit and directed his energies to civic and philanthropic objects. The Boy Scouts of America, especially, commanded his hearty support and he filled out an unexpired term as its national president. Public office, however, never tempted him. He refused a commission on the military staff of McKinley, when he was governor of Ohio, and was promptly dubbed "Colonel" by his newspaper colleagues. The title thus bestowed clung to him and was proudly borne. His keenest enjoyment came from extensive travels to all quarters of the globe. Newspaper reminiscences and observations abroad constitute the subject matter of his *Forty Years in Newspaperdom*, published in 1924. His death occurred in the Scripps Memorial Hospital at La Jolla, Cal., not far from his winter home in San Diego, in which place he was buried.

[In addition to McRae's book, see W. H. Hamby, "Lifted by Loyalty," in *Sunset: The Pacific Monthly*, Nov. 1919; Victor Rosewater, *Hist. of Cooperative News-Gathering in the U. S.* (1930); *Outlook*, May 12, 1926; N. D. Cockran, *E. W. Scripps* (1933); A. N. Marquis, *The Book of Detroiters* (1914); *Who's Who in America*, 1930–31; *Detroit News*, Oct. 11, 1930.] V.R.

McRAE, THOMAS CHIPMAN (Dec. 21, 1851–June 2, 1929), lawyer, congressman, governor of Arkansas, was born in Union County, Ark., the son of Duncan L. and Mary Ann (Chipman) McRae. His paternal ancestors emigrated from Scotland to North Carolina in the early part of the eighteenth century. Thomas attended private schools, the Soulé Business College in New Orleans, and the law department of Washington and Lee University, from which he graduated in 1872. He opened a law office in Rosston, Ark., in 1873, but moved to Prescott in 1877, when that town was made the county seat. He was representative in the legislature in 1877, a Democratic presidential elector in 1880, chairman of the Democratic state convention in 1884 and 1902, and a member of the national committee from 1896 to 1900.

In 1885 he was elected to Congress. During his first session (1886) he introduced a bill for a graduated income tax, and again in 1888. He was a member of the committee on public lands for ten years and its chairman for four; for a time he was the ranking Democrat on the appropriations committee. He introduced bills for the recovery of lands previously granted to the Pacific railroads, to preserve the timber on public lands, and to safeguard the national forests. He also worked for the return of the cotton tax, which had been collected after the close of the Civil War. Besides serving on important conference committees, he was several times made chairman of the committee of the whole.

On retiring from Congress voluntarily in 1903 he resumed the practice of law at Prescott and engaged in banking. He was elected president of the Arkansas Bankers' Association in 1909 and of the Bar Association in 1917. In 1917–18 he was a member of the constitutional convention. He secured the Democratic nomination for governor in 1920 by a small plurality, but was elected by a good majority and made an excellent record for two terms. The chief planks in his platform were the abolition of useless offices and a systematic and economical financial administration. He secured the substitution of honorary boards for salaried commissions in four instances. The penitentiary board, which was nearly half a million dollars in debt, he reorganized and put on a firm basis. He secured the abolition of the corporation commission, which exercised jurisdiction "from the greatest railroad to the most insignificant light plant" and restored control of local utilities to the local governments. He was much interested in the common schools and particularly in vocational and agricultural education and had the satisfaction of seeing an increase in funds for their support, partly due to the tobacco tax, and a great improvement in educational conditions generally. Road building had been begun on the mistaken policy of improvement districts, which threw the burden upon the owners of the adjacent real estate; McRae proposed that the roads should be built and maintained by the users and suggested higher fees for motor licenses and a gasoline tax. Throughout his four years he advocated a state income tax and the repeal of the state general property tax. Powerful interests blocked the former measure at the time, but he lived to see such a tax in operation before his death. He secured an appropriation for a tuberculosis sanitarium for negroes, a law giving women the right to hold office, and advocated the creation of a forestry commission. At the expiration of his term he again resumed his law practice at Prescott and engaged in banking. He gave freely to charity, and donated two blocks in Prescott for a park for the negroes, the site of the postoffice, and land upon which to build a county court house. On Dec. 17, 1874, he was married to Amelia Ann White, by whom he had nine children. His death was caused by influenza.

[*Biog. Dir. Am. Cong.* (1928); *Jour. of the House of Representatives of the . . . State of Ark.*, 1921, 1925; *Jour. of the Senate*, 1923; *Jour. of the House of Representatives . . . 1925*; *Proc. of the . . . Bar Asso. of Ark.*, 1929; D. T. Herndon, *Centennial Hist. of Ark.* (1922), vol. II; D. Y. Thomas, *Ark. and Its People* (1930); *Who's Who in America*, 1928–29; *Arkansas Gazette*, June 3, 1929; information furnished by a son, T. C. McRae.]

D. Y. T.

MACSPARRAN, JAMES (Sept. 10, 1693–Dec. 1, 1757), missionary of the Society for the Propagation of the Gospel in Foreign Parts, rector of St. Paul's Church in the Narragansett Country, in the extreme southern part of the present township of North Kingstown, R. I., is believed to have been born in Dungiven, County of Derry, Ireland, of Presbyterian parents who had gone there from Kintore, Scotland. He was educated at the University of Glasgow, receiving the degree of master of arts Mar. 5, 1709. He studied for the Presbyterian ministry and received credentials as a licentiate of the Presbytery of Scotland. In 1718 he visited America, stopping at Boston, Barnstable, and Plymouth on the way to the home of the widow Pampelion, a relative, in Bristol, at that time under the jurisdiction of the Colony of Massachusetts. He filled temporarily the vacant pulpit of the Congregational church in Bristol and was invited on Dec. 16, 1718, to become its pastor at an annual salary of £100, an invitation in which the town concurred, Dec. 22, 1718. During his stay in Boston, MacSparran seems to have aroused the enmity of Cotton Mather, who first delayed his ordination and then spread reports that his credentials were fraudulent. He proceeded to Ireland to procure their confirmation but never returned to the Congregational church at Bristol and later wrote that a false charge in his youth had opened the way into the Anglican priesthood for him.

Ordained deacon by the Bishop of London in the chapel of Fulham Palace Aug. 21, 1720, and priest by the Archbishop of Canterbury in the chapel of Lambeth Palace, Sept. 25, 1720, he was licensed to discharge the ministerial office in the province of New England by the Bishop of London on Oct. 3, 1720. The Parish of St. Paul, Narragansett Country, had written to the Bishop of London and to the Society for the Propagation of the Gospel in Foreign Parts, June 15, 1720, asking for a missionary to succeed William Guy, and the Society now sent out MacSparran to officiate there and at Bristol, Freetown, Swansea, and Little Compton at an annual salary of £70. He arrived at Narragansett Apr. 28, 1721, and proved to be one of the ablest of the missionaries sent to America by the Society, serving as rector of St. Paul's and ministering to the surrounding country for a period of thirty-six years. On May 22, 1722, he married Hannah, daughter of William Gardiner of Boston Neck, Narragansett, a sister of Silvester Gardiner [*q.v.*]. He was instrumental in the establishment of an Episcopal church at New London, Conn., in 1725. He entertained Dean Berkeley and John Smibert in 1729, but it was probably at a later date that Smibert's portrait of MacSparran now in the possession of Bowdoin College and that of Mrs. MacSparran now in the possession of the Boston Museum of Fine Arts were painted. During almost his entire ministry at St. Paul's he was involved in a lawsuit to gain possession of three hundred acres of land granted by the proprietors of the Pettaquamscutt purchase to an orthodox ministry but lost the suit by the decision of the Privy Council in 1752. He paid two visits to England; the first, between June 1736 and August 1737, during which the University of Oxford conferred upon him the degree of doctor of sacred theology, and the second, between the autumn of 1754 and February 1756, perhaps to work for the creation of an American bishopric, which he had long favored, and to obtain the office for himself. In the course of this latter visit his wife died of smallpox in London, June 24, 1755.

MacSparran published *The Sacred Dignity of the Christian Priesthood Vindicated* (1752), a discourse delivered at St. Paul's Aug. 4, 1751, intended to correct irregularities among the clergy of his own denomination but which aroused a storm of protest from the non-conforming ministers of New England; and *America Dissected* (1753), an account of the American colonies in a series of letters to friends in Ireland. He contemplated publishing an extended history of New England and is supposed to have written an account of the Narragansett Country, but after his death no trace of the manuscript was found. A diary kept by him during the years 1743, 1744, 1745, and 1751 was discovered and published in 1899. MacSparran died in the present township of South Kingstown at the age of sixty-four. He had no children and bequeathed his farm for the use and support of an American bishop whose diocese should include the Narragansett Country; this provision of his will was not carried out, however, and individuals of the parish of St. Paul bought the farm from his heirs to be used as a perpetual glebe. A monument to his memory was erected in 1869 in North Kingstown, R. I.

[*A Letter Book and Abstract of Out Services, Written During the Years 1743–1751 by the Revd. James MacSparran* (1899), ed. with a sketch of the author and numerous notes by Daniel Goodwin; Wilkins Updike, *A Hist. of the Episcopal Ch. in Narrangansett, R. I., including a Hist. of other Episcopal Churches in the State* (3 vols., 1907), ed. by Daniel Goodwin; *Hist. Colls. Relating to the Am. Colonial Church*, vol. III (1873), ed. by W. S. Perry; *Samuel Johnson, President of King's College, His Career and Writings* (4 vols., 1929), ed. by H. W. and Carol Schneider; A. C. Fraser, *Life and Letters of George Berkeley* (1871); W. S. Perry, *The Hist. of the Am. Episcopal Ch. 1587–1883* (2 vols., 1885); W. B. Sprague, *Annals Am. Pulpit*, vol. V (1859); W. H. Munro, *The Hist. of Bristol, R. I.* (1880); F. M. Caulkins, *Hist. of New London, Conn.* (1852); *Munimenta Alme Universitatis Glasguensis; Records of the Univ. of Glasgow from its Foundation till 1727* (1854), vol. III; Joseph Foster, *Alumni Oxonienses 1715–1886*, vol. III (1888), p. 899; Gordon Goodwin, in *Dict. of Nat. Biog.*]

I. M. C.

McTAMMANY, JOHN (June 26, 1845–Mar. 26, 1915), inventor of the perforated music roll, player-piano, and voting machine, was born in Kelvin Row, a suburb of Glasgow, Scotland, of poor parents, John and Agnes (McLean) McTammany. His father emigrated to America, leaving his two infant sons in the care of their mother, who had to work out, and their grandmother. John enjoyed a few months at school but was soon obliged to help support the family. His ambition was to beome a great pianist when he grew up, but fate decided otherwise. There was not an industry on the Clyde, from rope- and chain-making to ship-building, with which he did not become familiar, and by his work the muscles of his hands permanently lost their pliancy. In 1862 the elder McTammany was able to send for his family. They settled in Uniontown, Ohio, and John, a born inventor, turned his attention to improvements in harvester machinery. According to his own statement he enlisted in 1863 in the 115th Ohio Volunteer Infantry. He was more than once wounded, critically during the fighting around Chattanooga. During his convalescence, at Nashville, while visiting a pawnshop where musical instruments were kept, he volunteered to repair a music box. While thus engaged, the idea of a new musical instrument, to be operated by depressions instead of pins and staples, occurred to him.

Returning to Uniontown, in 1865, he taught music, played in the band, and sold pianos and organs during the day, while he experimented with his piano at night. Within a year he practically mastered his invention. During the next ten years he built, successively, three models of his player and two machines to prepare the perforated sheets. In St. Louis, in the winter of 1876, he gave a public exhibition of his largest model, fitted to an Estey organ (*Boston Herald*, Jan. 28, 1877). Up to that time no instrument had ever been constructed embodying the essential and necessary elements of his invention, such as a flexible sheet on rolls, wind motor, foot pedals, and other important features, suitable for pianos as well as organs. There had been keyboard attachments and other propositions, but even the most pretentious one, of French origin, soon became obsolete.

The musical profession strongly opposed McTammany's innovation from the start. Manufacturers to whom he confided his plans shook their heads but copied his blueprints. In the fall of 1876, considering his invention completed, he had filed a caveat fully describing it. (See illustrated description in McTammany's *Technical History of the Player*, pp. 29–34.) This application gave him two years in which to take out a basic patent. Unfortunately, two years found him in worse difficulties; he let the time in which to obtain his patent go by, and it was declared public property. In due time the manufacturers felt at liberty to apply for and obtain patents. McTammany finally landed in a garret on Tremont Street, Boston, and there, on credit desperately obtained, he built a small instrument embodying his invention, which he named the Organette. After finishing two of these miniature players, which had a special scale of sixteen notes, the inventor tried unsuccessfully to sell them to the music trade. Finally he found buyers for his player and in time he became successful.

Then came a long and costly litigation which once more reduced him to poverty. The patentees of the player stopped him from manufacturing his instrument, but in 1880 he was declared to be the original and prior inventor (*Decisions of the Commissioner of Patents for the Year 1880,* 1881, p. 203). He received three patents on his invention in 1881 and several subsequent patents. Finding themselves defeated in the courts, his competitors, after he had obtained capital to manufacture his player on a large scale, acquired a majority of his company's stock and ousted him. On Sept. 13, 1892, McTammany received a basic patent for a pneumatic registering ballot box, employing the perforated roll. It was the first machine ever used in an election and was adopted in a number of states, but again McTammany was unable to overcome competition. At last the inventor, although of large, robust build, broke down completely and died on Mar. 26, 1915, in the military hospital at Stamford, Conn. The city accorded him a public funeral, at which all the music was played on a grand player-piano. His remains were two years later removed from Stamford, to Canton, Ohio, where elaborate Memorial Day exercises in his honor were held, May 30, 1917, in Westlawn Cemetery, and where the final interment took place near the McKinley monument.

[See John McTammany, *Hist. of the Player* (1913) and *Technical Hist. of the Player* (1915), containing an introduction by Wm. Geppert; W. M. Butler, "Scotch Prodigy's Great Invention," *Presto,* Aug. 23, 1917; *Specifications and Drawings of Patents Issued from the U. S. Patent Office,* June, July, Nov. 1881, Sept. 1892; *Hartford Courant,* Mar. 27, 1915.]

W. M. B.

McTYEIRE, HOLLAND NIMMONS (July 28, 1824–Feb. 15, 1889), bishop of the Methodist Episcopal Church, South, was born in Barnwell County, S. C., and died at Vanderbilt University, Nashville, Tenn. He was of Scotch-Irish ancestry, the son of John and Elizabeth Amanda (Nimmons) McTyeire. His boyhood was spent on the farm in South Carolina. When he was fourteen years of age he began preparation for college at Cokesbury Academy, Abbeville County, S. C., and at twenty he graduated from Randolph-Macon College, Virginia, remaining there one year more as tutor. Admitted to the Virginia Conference of the Methodist Episcopal Church, South, on trial in November 1845, he was appointed pastor of the church at Williamsburg, Va., the seat of William and Mary College. So remarkable was his early intellectual maturity that at twenty-three he was appointed to the St. Francis Street Church, Mobile, Ala., and as a member of the Alabama Conference was ordained deacon Jan. 26, 1848. The preceding year, Nov. 9, he had married Amelia Townsend of Mobile. On Dec. 26, 1849, now a member of the Louisiana Conference, he was ordained elder. He had a large share in pioneering the work of the Methodist Church in New Orleans, and while in charge of a parish there, he also preached regularly to a large negro congregation. In 1851 he founded the *New Orleans Christian Advocate,* through which he became an influential factor in directing the trend of thought in his Church. At the General Conference of 1858 he was elected editor of the *Christian Advocate,* the official periodical of the Methodist Church, South, published at Nashville, Tenn. In this capacity he continued until 1862, when the publication of the *Advocate* was suspended, the Methodist Publishing House being used at that time as an arsenal and hospital by the Federal army.

Transferred to Alabama, he now took charge of the church in Montgomery, with which he remained connected until the General Conference of 1866. In this body he was not only a member, but was probably the master mind. Conditions at this time offered an opportunity for reconstructing the Methodist Episcopal Church, South, and McTyeire was the leader of progressive reforms, winning for himself the name of "fighting elder." The principal reform which he advocated was known as "lay representation." Hitherto the controlling bodies of American Methodism had been exclusively clerical. The measure which McTyeire sponsored provided for laymen in the annual conferences and especially for lay delegates in the General Conferences equal in number to the clerical delegates. At this Conference McTyeire was elected bishop, an office in which he served with statesman-like ability for twenty-three years. It was also decided that in case the negro membership of the Church desired to be organized into an independent body, the bishops should cooperate in providing for such an organization. Four years later Bishop McTyeire was one of the chief commissioners in the formation of the Colored Methodist Episcopal Church as a distinct ecclesiastical body; he shared in turning over to it properties valued at one million dollars, and in committing the mother church to contributing in all possible ways to the support and welfare of the new organization. McTyeire was also one of the chief promoters of the foreign-missionary enterprise of his Church, and when, in 1891, an institution for the higher education of women was founded in China, it was named McTyeire School in recognition of his services. Probably, however, Vanderbilt University will prove the most enduring monument to him, since he was the chief agent in its founding. While he was busy with the plans for establishing such an institution under the auspices of his Church, he was the guest of the elder Cornelius Vanderbilt [*q.v.*], and discussed the enterprise with him. Vanderbilt was so favorably impressed with the plan and with McTyeire's administrative ability that he at once gave him a check for $500,000, and later increased the gift to a million dollars. He insisted that Bishop McTyeire be president of the board of trust and vested with full veto power. During the first fifteen years of the history of the university, therefore, McTyeire had a determining voice in its affairs. He spent his last days in a home especially provided for him on the campus, and there died. He was buried on the campus, and the monument to his memory bears the appropriate inscription:

"A leader of men.
A lover of children."

As an author McTyeire will be known principally for his *History of Methodism* (1884). He also wrote *Duties of Christian Masters* (1859); *A Catechism of Bible History* (1883–84); *A Manual of the Discipline of the Methodist Episcopal Church, South* (1870); *A Catechism on Church Government* (2nd ed., 1880), and a volume of sermons entitled *Passing Through the Gates* (copr. 1890).

[Material for a life of McTyeire is in the custody of his daughter, Mrs. Janie McTyeire Baskerville, Washington, D. C.; published material may be found in the files of the *Christian Advocate* (Nashville), esp. the issue of Feb. 28, 1889; *Jour. of the General Conference, M. E. Ch. South*, 1890; Charles Forster Smith, *Reminiscences and Sketches* (1908); introduction to *Passing Through the Gates*; Gross Alexander, *Hist. of the M. E. Ch., South, in the U. S.* (1894); H. M. DuBose, *Hist. of Methodism* (1916); Richard Irby, *Hist. of Randolph Macon Coll., Va.* (1898), T. L. Flood and J. W. Hamilton, *Lives of Methodist Bishops* (1882); *Daily American* (Nashville), Feb. 16, 17, 1889; records of the proceedings of the Vanderbilt University Faculty, Minute Book, vol. II, p. 190; records of the proceedings of the board of trust of Vanderbilt University, vol. IV, p. 12.] O. E. B.

MACVEAGH, ISAAC WAYNE (Apr. 19, 1833–Jan. 11, 1917), lawyer, diplomat, political reformer, was born near Phoenixville, Chester County, Pa.; his parents were Maj. John and Margaret (Lincoln) MacVeagh. He attended school at Pottstown, Pa., and graduated at Yale, ranking tenth in the class of 1853. Distinction in debate marked him for the law and politics, and he entered the office of J. J. Lewis, prominent lawyer of West Chester, Pa. He was admitted to the bar in 1856 and married Letty Miner Lewis in the same year. He was district attorney for Chester County, 1859–64, adding to his legal duties service during the Civil War in the militia, in which he attained the ranks of captain of emergency infantry (1862) and major of cavalry (1863), attached to the staff of General Couch in reorganizing the local forces. He also became chairman of the Republican State Committee in 1863 and accompanied Lincoln to Gettysburg on the occasion of his address. After the war he transferred his practice to Harrisburg. His first wife had died in 1862 and in 1866 he was married to Virginia Rolette Cameron, daughter of the formidable political boss, Simon Cameron, in alliance with whom he became a figure in the Republican party.

He was appointed minister resident in Turkey, June 4, 1870, reaching his post late in the year. In connection with the Black Sea problem then under discussion among the European powers, he upheld Turkey's right of closure of the Straits against Secretary Fish's disposition to claim freedom of passage for American warships, and warned the Secretary strongly against entangling the United States government in the ulterior designs of other governments in the question. Coming home on leave in June 1871, he found political conditions under the Grant administration so distressing that he resigned his post to begin a lifelong career of "insurgency" by joining the opposition to the Cameron machine in Pennsylvania. He was a delegate to the state constitutional convention, 1872–73. In 1876 he moved to Philadelphia. His opposition to the Grant forces in the Republican National Convention of 1876 marked him for a part in the liquidation of Reconstruction undertaken by President Hayes. He was sent, in 1877, to Louisiana as head of a commission under whose auspices the local Democratic claimants to office were able to make a settlement with their Republican rivals which broke a dangerous deadlock and permitted the withdrawal of Federal troops from New Orleans (*Colonel Alexander K. McClure's Recollections of Half a Century*, 1902, pp. 104, 178). The aftermath of this accomplishment was a classic controversy with Benjamin F. Butler.

MacVeagh's independent position in politics, coupled with his recognized legal ability, won him the post of attorney-general in Garfield's cabinet, in which he was commissioned Mar. 5, 1881. He resigned on the President's death but held office until November, securing the indictment of the assassin, Guiteau, but escaping involvement in the scandalous trial. He then returned to the practice of law in Philadelphia and to his struggle with the powers of darkness in politics. He was especially active in the Civil Service Reform Association, of which he served as state chairman, as well as of the Indian Rights Association. The issues of civil-service reform and tariff reduction finally impelled him to desert the party of his formal allegiance and to support Cleveland's second election to the presidency. On Dec. 20, 1893, he was appointed ambassador to Italy, which post he held for about two years. It imposed upon him the delicate task of helping to preserve good relations in the excitement attending the outrages upon Italians in the United States at the time, although the actual negotiations arising out of these disturbances were conducted at Washington.

In 1897 MacVeagh entered the Washington law firm of McKenney & Flannery, counsel for the District of Columbia and the Pennsylvania Railroad, but he maintained his residence in Pennsylvania and took an active interest in the reform movement which swept the state after the turn of the century. As persistent a non-conformist in his new party as in the old, he opposed the control and policies of Bryan and was on the friendliest terms with Republican presidents and cabinet officers. Roosevelt appointed him chief counsel for the United States in the Venezuela arbitration of 1903. He was intimate with John Hay and Elihu Root and as a conversational foil was found worthy of the steel of Mark Twain. "Rapier-like" he was well called for the spareness of his frame and the penetrating keenness of his wit. By George Harvey, whom he supported against Woodrow Wilson after Harvey's break with Wilson, he was dubbed a "passionate patriot" and compared with Voltaire because of his ardent and tireless warfare against injustice. He was a contributor, chiefly to the *North American Review,* of articles on political reform and international peace. His last literary effort was a plea for the entrance of the United States into the World War ("The Impassable Chasm," *North American Review,* July 1915).

[*Who's Who in America,* 1916–17; *Obit. Record of Grads. of Yale Univ.,* 1917; *Wayne MacVeagh: Proc. of a Meeting of the Phila. Bar* (1917); memoir in *Report of the Twenty-third Ann. Meeting of the Pa. Bar Asso.,* 1917; W. F. Johnson, *Geo. Harvey, 'A Passionate Patriot'* (1929); W. R. Thayer, *The Life and Letters of John Hay* (2 vols., 1915); *Foreign Relations of the U. S.,* 1871, 1894–96; the *Nation,* July 29, 1915; *North Am. Rev.,* Mar. 1917; the *Evening Star* (Wash., D. C.), Jan. 11, 1917; *Pub. Ledger* (Phila.), Jan. 12, 1917.]

J. V. F.

MACVICAR, MALCOLM (Sept. 30, 1829–May 18, 1904), educator, author, was born in Dunglass, Argyleshire, Scotland. When he was six years old his father, John, and his mother, Janet MacTavish, left the Highlands for Canada with their twelve children, settling near Chatham, Ontario. Here frontier conditions and a deeply religious home life gave lasting direction to the boy's future career. His early education was undertaken with a view to his entering the Presbyterian ministry. Since there were no schools in the settlement, the local Presbyterian pastor, a University of Edinburgh graduate, prepared Malcolm for Knox College, Ontario, which he entered in 1850. Three years later he changed his profession of faith and became a Baptist, in which denomination he was ordained in 1856. He never held a pastorate, however, but turned almost immediately to teaching.

After the educational success but financial failure of a private venture in tutoring young men for college, MacVicar left for the United States, where he entered the University of Rochester as a senior. Upon receiving the degree of A.B. in 1859, he engaged in teaching and finally became principal of the Brockport Collegiate Institute, where, excepting for one year at the Buffalo Central High School, he remained till 1867. During this period he so made his mark in secondary education in New York that he was appointed chairman of a committee to report on the operation of the regents' examinations just instituted. He was particularly interested in the "teachers classes" in the academies, which New York State was still utilizing for part of its supply of teachers for the common schools. Believing that the utmost these classes could do was too little, he became largely instrumental in securing in 1866 legislation for four new normal schools. This leadership brought him the principalship of the first normal school under the law, that at Brockport. Owing to the strain of organizing it, his health gave way, but rather than accept his resignation, the state granted him a year's leave of absence. Restored in health by a Western trip, he was appointed, upon his return, to open and organize the Potsdam state normal school. Here from 1869 to 1880 he was at the peak of his normal school career; nevertheless he was glad to accept a call to the Michigan state normal school at Ypsilanti, where he would be free from the unhappy conflict of dual control which characterized New York state educational administration. Again worn out with hard work, he welcomed in 1881 an appointment to the faculty of the Toronto Baptist College, where he might return to his early interest in the philosophy of religion. When this college became the theological department of McMaster University, he reluctantly became its first chancellor (1887–90). After succeeding in its initial organization he resigned to superintend the educational work of the American Baptist Home Mission Society (1890–1900). The last post, and one he held till shortly before his death, was the presidency of Virginia Union University (1900–1904).

His success as an administrator is attested by his succession of offices; his ability as a teacher, however, was no less prominent. His mechanical skill, which had enabled him to earn his college tuition in a ship-carpenter's shop in Cleveland, made him ingenious in inventing mechanical contrivances as aids to classroom exposition, of which his tellurian globe was the most notable. At a later date he was instrumental in instituting a department of manual training in Woodstock College, Canada. Among his publications was *Principles of Education* (1892). Throughout his life he was addicted to hard work without the usual forms of relaxation. Even his year's quest of health in the West was spent in reorganizing the school system of Leavenworth, Kan. In 1865 he married Isabella McKay, a childhood friend, by whom he had three sons and a daughter.

[G. M. Rose, *A Cyc. of Canadian Biog.*, vol. II (1888); *First Quarto-Centennial Hist. of the State Normal and Training School, Potsdam, N. Y., 1869–94* (1895); Daniel Putnam, *A Hist. of the Mich. State Normal School at Ypsilanti, Mich.* (1899); Paul Monroe, *A Cyc. of Educ.*, vol. IV (1913); W. S. Wallace, *The Dict. of Canadian Biog.* (1926); *McMaster Univ. Mo.*, Feb. 1905; *The Baptist Home Mission Monthly*, June 1904; *N. Y. Times*, May 19, 1904; information from a son, John G. MacVicar.] J. S. B.

McVICKAR, JOHN (Aug. 10, 1787–Oct. 29, 1868), Protestant Episcopal clergyman, economist, was the son of John McVickar, born in County Antrim, Ireland, who emigrated to New York in 1780 and there became a wealthy merchant, and his wife Anna, daughter of John Moore of Newtown, L. I. Their son John was born in New York, entered Columbia College, where he ranked at the head of his class throughout his course, and graduated in 1804 at the age of seventeen. Hamilton had died shortly before Commencement, and McVickar's Latin salutatory oration, "Eloquence and Hamilton," was one of the first public eulogies of that statesman. The following year McVickar went abroad with his father, and upon his return began the study of theology with Rev. (afterwards Bishop) John Henry Hobart [*q.v.*], who ordained him deacon in 1811 and priest in 1812. McVickar and Hobart were lifelong friends, and after the bishop's death, McVickar wrote his biography. On Nov. 12, 1809, he married Eliza, daughter of Dr. Samuel Bard [*q.v.*] of Hyde Park, N. Y., and in 1811 he was made rector of the Church of St. James in that town, founded and erected by his father-in-law. He remained there until November 1817, when he was elected to the professorship of moral philosophy in Columbia College. At this time the faculty was composed of the president, three professors, and one adjunct professor; McVickar also gave instruction in rhetoric, belles-lettres, ancient history, and the history of philosophy. He was one of the earliest teachers of political economy in the United States, teaching the subject as a branch of moral philosophy, but the claim that he held the first American chair in that field is not borne out by the records; his title is variously given during his long professorship, some of the changes being official and some his own. In 1857 when Francis Lieber [*q.v.*] was called to Columbia to teach political economy, McVickar was transferred to the more appropriate chair of the evidences of natural and revealed religion, which he held until his retirement in 1864. He died in New York four years later.

During the last illness of President William Harris [*q.v.*] in 1829, and after the resignation of President W. A. Duer [*q.v.*] in 1842, McVickar was acting president of the college. On both occasions, however, he failed to be elected president, due perhaps to "something in his personality which repelled rather than attracted popular approval, an excessive correctness and frigidity, a certain removal from human sympathy" (Dorfman and Tugwell, *post*, p. 371). On the first occasion, his disappointment was so great that he secured leave and took his family to Europe. There he visited Wordsworth, Southey, the Pestalozzis, James Mill, Scott, and other notables; he was particularly impressed by Scott, and upon his death delivered an oration on him in New York (*Tribute to the Memory of Sir Walter Scott, Baronet,* 1833).

Although McVickar is now remembered chiefly as an economist, because of his early teaching of that subject, he was first of all a churchman and a moralist, and his subjects of instruction were merely avenues for the inculcation of sound moral and social precepts. Throughout his career he was active in religious affairs, preaching often, and taking a leading part in denominational activities; in 1835 he issued anonymously *Devotions for the Family and the Closet.* From 1844 to 1862 he was chaplain of the army post at Fort Columbus in New York harbor; there he built the Chapel of St. Cornelius the Centurion, and sent regiments to the Mexican War with individual Bibles and the Church's blessing. In 1860, largely as a result of his labors, St. Stephen's College at Annandale-on-Hudson was established as a training college for Episcopal clergymen.

His biography of Hobart appeared originally in two parts: *The Early Years of the Late Bishop Hobart* (1834) and *The Professional Years of John Henry Hobart* (1836). The two were published together in 1838 under the title *The Early Life and Professional Years of Bishop Hobart.* Other publications, in addition to various sermons and addresses, were: *A Domestic Narrative of the Life of Samuel Bard, M.D., LL.D.* (1822); *Outlines of Political Economy* (1825), a republication of the *Britannica* article of John Ramsay McCulloch, to which McVickar added extensive notes; *Interest Made Equity* (1826), also by McCulloch, with an editorial preface added; *Hints on Banking* (1827), an important tract, reputed to have been responsible for the "Free Banking System" established in New York and elsewhere a decade later; *Considerations upon the Expediency of Abolishing Damages on Protested Bills of Exchange, and the Effect of Establishing a Reciprocal Exchange with Europe* (1829); *A National Bank; Its Necessity and Most Desirable Form* (1841), advocating a national bank fundamentally similar to the second United States Bank. In 1839 he wrote a preliminary essay for the New York edition of Coleridge's *Aids to Reflection.*

[Edward McVickar and W. C. Breed, *Memoranda Relating to the McVickar Family in America* (1906); J. W. Moore, *Rev. John Moore of Newtown, L. I., and Some of His Descendants* (1903); W. A. McVickar, *The Life of the Rev. John McVickar, S.T.D.* (1872); Joseph Dorfman and R. G. Tugwell, "The Rev. John McVickar, Christian Teacher and Economist," *Columbia Univ. Quart.*, Dec. 1931; *N. Y. Times,* Oct. 31, 1868.]

M. H. T.

McVICKAR, WILLIAM NEILSON (Oct. 19, 1843–June 28, 1910), bishop of the Protestant Episcopal Church, was born in New York City, where his great-grandfather, John, an emigrant from County Antrim, Ireland, had been a prosperous merchant and long a vestryman of Trinity Church. One of his sons, John [*q.v.*], was a prominent Episcopal clergyman and professor in Columbia College. William was the grandson of James and the son of Dr. John Augustus McVickar, a well-known homeopathic practitioner, whose wife was Charlotte, daughter of William Neilson, the first president of the New York Board of Underwriters. Young McVickar was prepared for college in private schools and graduated from Columbia in 1865. He entered the Philadelphia Divinity School but later transferred to the General Theological Seminary, New York, where he completed his course in 1868. Ordained deacon in 1867, and priest in 1868, he was for a short time assistant to Dr. Stephen H. Tyng at St. George's Church, New York, but in 1868 became rector of Holy Trinity, Harlem, an infant enterprise with few adherents and no church buildings. During the seven years that McVickar was in charge it became a comparatively large, and well-equipped institution. In 1875 he was called to Holy Trinity, Philadelphia, where he was rector for twenty-two years. Six feet, five inches tall and built on extraordinarily large proportions, of bright and kindly countenance, and possessing a voice of great richness and sweetness, he was impressive in the pulpit and attracted notice and interest wherever he appeared. He and Phillips Brooks [*q.v.*] were intimate friends and kindred spirits, corresponding frequently and traveling abroad together. Like Brooks, McVickar never married. His breadth of sympathies and largeness of heart corresponded with his physical appearance. He exerted much influence in Philadelphia outside the bounds of his parish, and became increasingly prominent in the corporate affairs of the Episcopal Church. He was a deputy to all the General Conventions from 1883 to 1895, and a member of the board of managers of the General Missionary Society. One of those most seriously considered for bishop of Pennsylvania when Dr. O. W. Whitaker was chosen, he was elected coadjutor bishop of Rhode Island in 1897, and became bishop at the death of Bishop Thomas M. Clark [*q.v.*] in 1903. His interest in civic and philanthropic affairs and his catholic spirit soon made him in fact as well as in name one of the first citizens of the state. He was a fearless, yet wise and generous fighter in the cause of righteousness, active in the Watch and Ward Society and president of the Rhode Island Anti-Saloon League, and an outspoken opponent of the political corruption then existing. When his unexpected death from pneumonia at his summer home, Beverly Farms, Mass., was announced, tributes of esteem and affection poured in from people of all classes and faiths.

[*Who's Who in America,* 1910–11; *Providence Daily Jour.*, June 29, 30, and July 2, 1910; *Churchman,* July 9, 1910; *Living Church,* July 9, 1910; *Outlook,* July 9, 1910.]

H. E. S.

McVICKER, JAMES HUBERT (Feb. 14, 1822–Mar. 7, 1896), actor and theatrical manager, was born in New York City, the son of James and Nancy McVicker. With only the most elementary education, he became an apprentice in a printing-shop. In 1837 he went to St. Louis and served for a time as printer on the *St. Louis Republican.* His interest in the theatre, which had been aroused by visits to the local stock company managed by Noah Miller Ludlow [*q.v.*] and Solomon Franklin Smith [*q.v.*], caused him to abandon his trade and go to New Orleans where there was an opening for him at the St. Charles, another Ludlow-Smith theatre. It was there he made his début as an actor, playing the rôle of the old servant in *The Honeymoon,* and it was also under these veteran Western producers that he served his theatrical apprenticeship, at both the St. Charles and the American theatres, in New Orleans. On May 2, 1848, he made his first appearance in Chicago as first low comedian under the management of James B. Rice, prominent political leader and theatrical pioneer of the growing city. For three years he remained a valuable member of Rice's company, becoming eventually stage manager. Having decided, however, to do a more specialized type of acting, McVicker bought from the widow of Danforth Marble [*q.v.*] the rich collection of original Yankee comedies which various authors had written especially for her husband during his lifetime. With a repertory made up of these rôles McVicker built for himself a growing reputation in the Eastern theatres and in London, where with considerable success he opened at the Drury Lane Theatre in 1855. Although throughout his career McVicker continued to appear as an actor in varying rôles, his fame rests much more securely on his activities as manager and producer.

Shortly after his return from England he was invited by George Wood, owner of the People's Theatre in St. Louis, to serve as his manager. McVicker had been in St. Louis but a short time when Wood suggested that they extend their joint activities by opening a theatre in Chicago in opposition to Rice. For most of the financing Wood was to be responsible, while his manager's rôle was that of superintending the construction of a theatre and the assembling of a company. In the midst of carrying out these responsibilities in Chicago, McVicker received word that the financier had withdrawn his support. But overcoming the serious embarrassment which resulted, McVicker was able, with help from other sources, to carry through the original enterprise and in November 1857 to open the New Chicago Theatre with *The Honeymoon* and *The Rough Diamond.* In spite of the many excellent features of the new theatre, McVicker was forced for a number of years to struggle against an accumulation of financial difficulties arising from the panic of 1857 and against rather stiff competition from Rice and others. It was not until the unexpected boom of Chicago during the years after 1862 that the young manager was able to establish his theatre on a profitable basis. In 1864 the building was completely remodeled, and seven years later, thanks to the large receipts which various visiting stars had brought to the box office, McVicker was able to build a still more handsome theatre. Although this was almost immediately destroyed by the great fire of 1871, so firmly was his prestige established that within less than a year, the manager had built his third theatre, which for the next eighteen years, through various developments of the stock, the star, and the combination systems of production, maintained its leadership over its increasingly numerous rivals. This building, remodeled in 1885, was destroyed by fire in 1890, but the following year the final McVicker Theatre opened its doors with a brilliant performance of *The Rivals.*

Owing to ill health, McVicker some years before his death surrendered the direction of this enterprise to the McVicker Company, of which he owned the controlling shares. In Chicago McVicker enjoyed the same prestige as the great New York managers, Lester Wallack, Augustin Daly, and Albert M. Palmer. According to Edward Freiberger, he was "an actor-manager in the fullest and best sense of the word. His stock companies were among the very best in the United States, some of the most accomplished and popular members being members of the same. . . . Mr. McVicker's productions left little to be desired either in the casting of the plays or in the scenic environment. His revivals of *The School for Scandal, A Midsummer Night's Dream* and *The Tempest* were among the most elaborate and correct the American stage has ever known." Imbued with a high civic sense, McVicker was active in numerous phases of Chicago's life, and with outspoken aggressiveness maintained the lofty rôle played by the theatre in the life of society. His first wife was Annie Levering; his second Mrs. Runnion, whose daughter Mary adopted the name of McVicker before her marriage to Edwin Booth.

[N. M. Ludlow, *Dramatic Life as I Found It* (1880); Edward Freiberger, "Theater Beginnings in Chicago," *Theatre Mag.,* June 1911; M. B. Leavitt, *Fifty Years in Theatrical Management* (1912); *Chicago Tribune,* Mar. 8, 1896; *N. Y. Clipper,* Mar. 14, 1896; *N. Y. Dramatic Mirror,* Mar. 14, 21, 1896; A. T. Andreas,

Hist. of Chicago, vols. I and II (1884–85); J. H. McVicker, *The Press, the Pulpit, and the Stage* (1883).]

E. M., Jr.

MACWHORTER, ALEXANDER (July 15, 1734 o.s.–July 20, 1807), Presbyterian clergyman, was born in New Castle County, Del., the son of Hugh and Jane MacWhorter. His father's ancestors, who spelled the family name McWirter or McWhirter, and his mother's as well, had emigrated from Scotland to the north of Ireland. Hugh, a linen merchant in the county of Armagh, came to America and settled in Delaware about 1730. Upon his death in 1748, Alexander went with his mother to North Carolina, where three older children were then living. Here he was awakened to a vivid sense of his sinfulness through the preaching of Rev. John Brown, a "New Light" minister, and for several years experienced great distress of mind. After a time he returned to Delaware and attended an academy in Newark. Later he spent two years at the school of Rev. Samuel Finley [*q.v.*], West Nottingham, Pa., where "he was enabled for the first time to rest his soul on Christ." In May 1756 he entered the junior class of the College of New Jersey, graduating in the autumn of 1757. After studying theology under Rev. William Tennent of Freehold, N. J., in August 1758 he was licensed to preach by the Presbytery of New Brunswick, and in October of the following year he married Mary, daughter of Robert Cumming of Freehold, high sheriff of the county of Monmouth. Ordained at Cranberry, N. J., July 4, 1759, he was soon afterwards installed as pastor of the Presbyterian church, Newark. Here, except for a brief interim, he remained until his death forty-eight years later.

During this period he gathered into his church the fruits of six extensive revivals; rose to leadership in his denomination; and in the days of the Revolution was one of the most conspicuous patriots among the clergy of his locality. While on a visitation to the churches of North Carolina with Elihu Spencer [*q.v.*] in 1764, he developed "a hectick, accompanied with expectoration of blood." After being partially incapacitated for a couple of years, he sought a cure in the climate of Boston, where, strangely enough, he became well, and thereafter was in vigorous health, except for "a paralytick affection in his hands, which he inherited from his father." In 1775, appointed by the Continental Congress, he went to North Carolina to try to win over the Loyalists. His patriotic activities attracted the notice of the British, who, when they invaded Newark in November 1776, inquired for MacWhorter, who had fled, and ransacked the parsonage. In a letter written to Congress Mar. 12, 1777, he describes the unjustifiable conduct of the enemy. When Washington was encamped opposite Trenton, MacWhorter advised with him regarding the safety of New Jersey, and was present at the counsel which recommended the crossing of the Delaware. In the summer of 1778 he became chaplain of General Knox's brigade, but resigned the following year because of the condition of his wife, who had been struck by lightning. Sought by the British and his parish impoverished by the war, in 1779 he accepted a call to the church in Charlotte, N. C., and to the presidency of Charlotte Academy. Scarcely had he settled here, however, when Cornwallis entered the town, and MacWhorter and his family were forced to flee, losing what books and other belongings they still possessed. After a brief stay in Abington, Pa., in April 1781 he resumed his pastorate in Newark.

A man of cool deliberation and sound judgment, never sanguine, always cautious, he was at his best in deliberate assemblies and in the management of large affairs. "He possessed little fancy, but a deep and solid judgment," said the assistant of his later days, Rev. Edward D. Griffin [*q.v.*]. "His genius had no uncommon share of vivacity; it held a stately and even course. It had no wings; but it stood like the pillars of the earth. He never would have gathered laurels in the paths of poetry; but he would have filled with superior dignity the seat of justice" (*A Sermon Preached . . . at the Funeral of the Rev. Alexander MacWhorter, D.D.*, 1807). A member of almost all the important committees of the synod, he was also influential in settling the confession of faith and framing the constitution of the Presbyterian Church of the United States. He was a charter trustee of the General Assembly, serving until 1803. From 1772 until his death he was a trustee of the College of New Jersey, and when the college buildings were burned in 1802, he went to New England and raised $7,000 for their restoration. Yale had conferred the degree of Doctor of Divinity upon him in 1776. On Christmas 1806 he was injured by a fall, and in the following July he died. Several of his sermons were published separately, including one in memory of Washington (1800), and *A Century Sermon* (1807) containing a brief history of the Presbyterian church in Newark; also two volumes of collected sermons, *A Series of Sermons upon the Most Important Principles of Our Holy Religion* (1803).

[J. F. Stearns, *Hist. Discourses, Relating to the First Presbyterian Church in Newark* (1853); Wm. B.

Sprague, *Annals Am. Pulpit*, vol. III (1858); *The Biog. Encyc. of N. J. of the Nineteenth Century* (1877); Jos. Atkinson, *The Hist. of Newark, N. J.* (1878); J. T. Headley, *The Chaplains and Clergy of the Revolution* (1864); S. D. Alexander, *Princeton College During the Eighteenth Century* (1872). MacWhorter's letter to Congress is printed in part in *Archives of the State of N. J.*, 2 ser. I (1901), 350–53. His name is sometimes spelled McWhorter, M'Whorter, or Macwhorter.]

H. E. S.

MACY, JESSE (June 21, 1842–Nov. 3, 1919), prairie philosopher and political scientist, was born, amidst pioneer conditions, near Knightstown, Ind., the son of William and Phoebe (Hiatt) Macy and a descendant of Thomas Macy who emigrated to New England before 1639 and settled later in Nantucket. His parents were Quakers, active in the Underground Railroad. Among the boy's vivid experiences was "hearing stories told by fugitive slaves" at his own fireside. In 1856 the family moved in a covered wagon to another pioneer community near Lynnville, Jasper County, Iowa. Three years later young Macy, "a tall gangling figure in a butternut suit," betook himself to Grinnell, Iowa, to prepare for college. After two years he transferred to a Friends' Institute near Oskaloosa, Iowa, but in September 1864 he was drafted into the army and marched with Sherman to the sea as a non-combatant in hospital service. The war over, he resolved to devote himself to the political reconstruction of his country and, in preparation, spent the years 1866–70 in Iowa (now Grinnell) College. There he encountered Darwin's theory of evolution which completely changed his whole outlook on life. On his graduation he began his forty-two years' career as teacher in his alma mater, first in the academy and then in the college in the chair of political science, created by himself (1884–1912). He believed it "his duty to use every endeavor toward the attainment of a more righteous order in the state and in society, regardless of the prospects of success" (*Autobiography*, p. 25). It seemed to him also that the scientific spirit and method which had accomplished so much in science "would be even more beneficent when applied to political science" (*Ibid.*, p. 33).

He was the first to advocate teaching civil government in the public schools by first-hand observation of the workings of local government. In his college teaching he abandoned textbook and lecture and attempted by the Socratic method to stimulate the students to think for themselves. He was no mere closet-philosopher; he played an active part in local politics and wrote widely in the press and magazines on the tariff, gold standard, public utilities, and woman's suffrage. Isolated in a small college, he worked alone under great handicaps, and his intellectual growth was slow and deliberate. Nevertheless, by the time he was sixty he had won recognition as an original thinker both in America and Great Britain. This achievement was in part due to the devoted cooperation of Mary Maude Little whom he had married on July 25, 1872. The years 1887–88 and 1895–96 he spent abroad, chiefly in England, where he formed a lifelong friendship with James Bryce and was at home in the London Economic Club and the Fabian Society. In his later years he received many honors. He lectured in leading American universities, was Harvard exchange lecturer in the provincial universities of France (1913), and became president of the American Political Science Association (1916).

His political and social philosophies were the fruit of his early pioneer experiences, the study of Darwin and Spencer, and his deep religious convictions. He shared Lincoln's faith in the homely wisdom of the common people and never lost touch with them. He could have as readily doubted "the life-giving air" he breathed as doubt "the continual divine presence" (*Autobiography*, p. 22). To him the "acceptance of evolution and the attempt to carry the scientific spirit and method into the study of politics was a distinctly religious experience" and only the religious motive led him to "persevere against what seemed insuperable obstacles" (*Ibid.*, p. 25). He maintained that science and democracy had come into the world at the same time, that they were mutually related as cause and effect, and that science was fitted to be a determining factor in the establishment of righteousness in government. He was confident too that democracy in the post-war world would achieve a fuller and richer life than it had before achieved and that the democratic nations would "learn to co-operate through a United States of the World" (*Ibid.*, p. 148). His last letter was a plea for the League of Nations as a means of eliminating war.

Tall and erect, with a frank open countenance, Macy had the natural dignity and unconscious simplicity of the pioneer. In an age of theological and political rancor, he remained open-minded and serene. He had the honesty and courage to live his own philosophy while his rich humor and friendliness of spirit disarmed bitterness. Included in his published writings are: *Civil Government in Iowa* (1881); *Institutional Beginnings in a Western State* (1884); *Our Government* (1886); *The English Constitution* (1897); *Political Parties in the United States, 1846–61* (1900); *Party Organization and*

Machinery (1904); *Comparative Free Government* (1915), with J. W. Gannaway; and *The Anti-Slavery Crusade* (1919) in the Chronicles of America Series edited by Allen Johnson.

[The chief source is *Jesse Macy, an Autobiog.* (1933), edited and arranged by Macy's daughter, Katherine Macy Noyes, assisted by Albert Shaw, J. S. Nollen, and Chas. E. Payne. Other sources include: *Who's Who in America,* 1918–19; S. J. Macy, *Geneal. of the Macy Family from 1635–1868* (1868); the *Grinnell Rev.,* Nov. 1919; *Iowa Jour. of Hist. and Pol.,* Jan. 1920; *Annals of Iowa,* July 1920; the *Am. Pol. Sci. Rev.,* Feb. 1920.] C. E. P.

MACY, JOHN ALBERT (Apr. 10, 1877–Aug. 26, 1932), author, literary critic, poet, was born in Detroit, Mich., the son of Powell and Janet Foster (Patten) Macy and a descendant of Thomas Macy who emigrated to New England before 1639 and settled in Nantucket. He was reared in modest circumstances. From Malden High School he entered Harvard in 1895. Dependent largely on his own resources, he achieved a brilliant academic as well as extra-curricular record. Alone in the class of 1899 he received honorable mention on four counts. He won the Phi Beta Kappa key, was editor-in-chief of the *Harvard Advocate* and an editor of the *Lampoon,* was elected to the best clubs, and was chosen class poet. After graduation he was appointed assistant in English at Harvard. Two years later he became advisory master in the Ellet School at Richmond, Va., a connection which he maintained for eighteen years. In 1901 he joined the staff of the *Youth's Companion* and remained as associate editor for eight years. His first serious literary effort, *Edgar Allan Poe* (1907), was followed by *A Child's Guide to Reading* (1909), and *The Spirit of American Literature* (1913). In 1913 he became literary editor of the *Boston Herald.* His articles brought distinction to its book-page, but differences between him and the management brought his retirement after a year.

He had become a Socialist in 1909, "largely through observing the asininities of the present system" (personal conversation). Desiring first-hand experience with what he believed to be the coming social system, he served as secretary in 1912 to the then-Socialist mayor of Schenectady, George R. Lunn. In 1916 Macy published *Socialism in America.* It was this slender volume that caused him to be refused membership in the Harvard Club of New York in 1920 (*Harvard College Class of 1899,* 5th Report, 1924). More gleefully did he record that his views on the folly of war had earned him "the supreme honor of having been reported as a traitor to the . . . fools in Washington, D. C., who were called with unconscious irony the 'Intelligence Department'" (*Ibid.,* p. 428). At the outbreak of the World War in 1914 he had been accepted for an American volunteer ambulance unit, but, as he said, "the armchair patriots . . . were not able to find money for my passage and expenses." He was referring to some of his fellow members of the St. Botolph Club, which for the major part of his Boston residence was in effect his retreat and home. It was here, paradoxically, that he had composed in 1917 his stirring poem "France," read at a banquet in honor of the French military mission to Harvard.

Macy was a vigorous and original thinker. In conservative surroundings he appeared an iconoclast. It was his intellectual pioneering that established his enduring contribution to American letters and criticism. As early as November 1906 in an *Atlantic Monthly* article he extolled Joseph Conrad, then little known. His book, *The Spirit of American Literature,* blazed the trail which has become a well-worn and generally accepted thoroughfare. In lucid and trenchant phrasing Macy pointed out that, excepting Thoreau, Whitman, Mark Twain, and when at their best, Whittier, Lowell, and Emerson, and Mrs. Stowe in *Uncle Tom's Cabin* only, American writers turned "their backs on life" in America. And he plead for and prophesied the subsequent realism. Edith Wharton's *Ethan Frome* and Theodore Dreiser's *Jennie Gerhardt* he signalized as the only contemporary novels that came "to grips with the problems of life."

In 1918 Macy published *Walter James Dodd, a Biographical Sketch,* concerning one of the pioneers and martyrs of roentgenology. This tribute reveals what Macy deemed true service to society. In 1920 he moved to New York. In 1922–23 he was literary editor of the *Nation.* His sympathies for fellow craftsmen in financial distress at times led him to assign books to reviewers against his reasoned judgment. He was impulsively warm-hearted, generous, careless of his own material interests, improvident. A genial sweetness, a deep kindliness, pervaded his personal contacts. His irony and barbed wit he reserved for the shams and injustices of society. From 1926 till his death he was literary adviser to the publishing house of William Morrow & Company. He contributed the article "Journalism" to the symposium *Civilization in the United States* (edited by H. E. Stearns, 1922), and on "Massachusetts" to *These United States* (edited by Ernest Gruening, 1923). He published *The Critical Game* (1922); *The Story of the World's Literature* (1925); *The Romance of America as Told in Our Literature* (1930); *About Women* (1930), and, in collaboration with Blanche Colton Williams, *Do You Know English Literature?* (1930). His last work was editing a symposium, *American Writers on American Literature* (1931), in which he called for "a scholarship which shall be both erudite and animated; an unofficial free-and-easy criticism, irreverent, skeptical, watchful of humbug and stupidity, yet not itself lacking in amenity; a sober, aggressive criticism which sees literature as life itself and does not forget that humor and merriment are essential ingredients." That was his own critic's credo. With it he had for a generation infused new light and lightness into the staid academicism that before him had ruled almost unchallenged.

At the time of his instructorship at Harvard, Macy became profoundly interested in Helen Keller, who had entered Radcliffe in 1900. In 1903 he edited her book, *The Story of My Life.* His devotion to the blind deaf-mute prodigy led to his marriage in 1905 to her teacher and life-companion, Anne Mansfield Sullivan of Wrentham, Mass. He was unhappy in this marriage and a separation followed. Unable to secure a divorce he entered into an intensely happy companionship with a deaf-mute, a woman of talent and charm, a sculptor by profession. She died after five years, but their daughter survived. Macy died suddenly of a heart attack after delivering the third of a series of five lectures on rebellious currents in American literature before a gathering of trade union workers at Unity House, Stroudsburg, Pa.

[*Harvard College Class of 1899,* first report (1902); second report (1905); third report (1909); fourth report (1914); fifth report (1924); *Who's Who in America,* 1930–31; *The Publishers' Weekly,* Sept. 3, 1932; *Nation,* Oct. 4, 1922, Oct. 10, 1923, Sept. 7, 1932; *N. Y. Times,* Aug. 27, 1932; G. E. De Mille, *Lit. Criticism in America* (1931); personal recollections and conversations.]

E. G.

MACY, JOSIAH (Feb. 25, 1785–May 15, 1872), merchant captain, founder of the shipping and commission house of Josiah Macy & Son, was born at Nantucket, Mass., the son of Jonathan and Rose (Pinkham) Macy. He was a descendant of Thomas Macy (or Macie), one of the first settlers of Nantucket. Like the majority of the islanders, the Macys were members of the Society of Friends. Josiah received a common-school education, and at the age of twenty, Feb. 6, 1805, he married Lydia Hussey. Beginning his career under his father in a coastwise trading voyage, he engaged in coastwise trade for fifteen years, becoming a shipmaster when hardly out of his teens. On outbound voyages cargoes of sperm and whale oil, whalebone, and sperm candles were carried; these were sometimes consigned, but frequently were peddled from port to port. The proceeds were reinvested in outfits required by the Nantucket whalemen and in provisions needed in the homes of the islanders.

Macy made his first foreign voyage to Gibraltar, Cadiz, and Lisbon with a Nantucket cargo in 1807. In 1808, word of an intended embargo having been brought to Nantucket, he immediately loaded and cleared his one-hundred-ton ship for Spain and was towed out of the harbor and over the bar by a flotilla of whaleboats, according to the practice of that day. After a voyage of continuous anxiety, he reached the island of Fayal, disposed of his cargo, and returned to Nantucket with a load of wine, oranges, and specie. After an interval of coasting, in 1810 he sailed in the brig *Little William* to the Mediterranean. In 1812 he bought the ship *Prudence,* of 243 tons, and sailed for Spain. On his return he made New York and from there was the first to bring to Nantucket the news of the United States' declaration of war against Great Britain. His ship was laid up until the cessation of hostilities.

Nantucket was an unprotected island town of about 8,000 inhabitants, wholly at the mercy of either force. The islanders were non-combatants. Under the circumstances they preserved a tacit neutrality throughout the war, but their trade was gone and there was great difficulty in securing bare necessities. In October 1813 Macy went to Baltimore and commenced buying flour, shipping it in small schooners to Nantucket. A number of these arrived at their destination, but several were captured. Later he commanded one of three vessels, to which the British gave letters of protection, for the purpose of proceeding to Philadelphia for provisions. By accepting British papers the ships were open to capture by American naval vessels; but the plight of the islanders was well understood and sympathized with by the mainlanders, and the ships were not searched. At the conclusion of the war Macy entered the New York-Liverpool trade with a new ship, the *Edward,* of 346 tons. The next fourteen years he spent on the western ocean, concluding his final voyage as shipmaster in 1827.

The following year he founded in New York the shipping and commission house of Josiah Macy & Son, with William H. Macy, his eldest son, as partner. When they came of age, his two younger sons were admitted to the firm. Retiring from business in 1853, having amassed a considerable fortune, he spent the remainder of his life on his farm in Rye, N. Y. A number of men who afterward achieved distinction have testified to the aid given, and the good influence exerted in their early lives by Macy; among them, Capt. Benjamin Morrell [*q.v.*], who was the first American to explore south of the Antarctic circle. Macy served on many business directorates, and was a worthy citizen; but he does not appear to have been concerned with state affairs. He was the founder of a great fortune at a time when great fortunes in the nation were few.

[A long autobiographical letter, dated Dec. 1867, is printed in S. J. Macy, *Geneal. of the Macy Family from 1635–1868* (1868). See also L. S. Hinchman, *Early Settlers of Nantucket* (2nd ed., 1901); *Vital Records of Nantucket, Mass. to the Year 1850* (5 vols., 1925–28); Benjamin Morrell, *A Narrative of Four Voyages . . .* (1832); files of the *Nantucket Inquirer*; *N. Y. World*, May 16, 1872.] C. W. A.

MACY, VALENTINE EVERIT (Mar. 23, 1871–Mar. 21, 1930), capitalist, philanthropist, and public official, was born in New York City, a son of Josiah and Caroline (Everit) Macy. The progenitor of the family in America was Thomas Macy (or Macie), whose settlement on Nantucket Island is commemorated in Whittier's ballad "The Exiles." Most of the Nantucket Macys and their descendants were Friends. Josiah, an official of the Standard Oil Company, had inherited a fortune, the foundation of which had been laid by a group of Nantucket whalers. His grandfather Josiah [*q.v.*] and his father William H. had established in 1828 the firm of Josiah Macy & Son, New York. When Josiah, Jr., died in 1876, he left a large estate to which the son succeeded on reaching his majority. Meanwhile, his education proceeded chiefly under private tutors at home and abroad. At seventeen he was interested in teaching wood-carving to city boys. Later he entered the Columbia University College of Architecture and received the degree of Ph.B. in 1893, but was never active professionally. For many years he was chiefly occupied with the care of his estate, giving much time, however, to public causes, notably the Teachers College of Columbia University, the Metropolitan Museum of Art, and the National Child Labor Committee.

Macy established a residence at Scarboro, Westchester County. In the fall of 1913 a county superintendent of the poor was to be elected and Macy's friends succeeded in placing his name on the Democratic and Progressive tickets. Though strongly opposed by the old-line Republican leaders, he was elected. Upon taking charge of the poor farm and almshouse he at once installed an accounting and purchasing system that within two years reduced the per capita cost of caring for inmates more than twenty per cent., while at the same time he introduced an improved diet that lowered the number of deaths from diabetes and nephritis sixty per cent. For the first time, able-bodied adult inmates were put to work. Macy's chief concern, however, was for the dependent children. He expanded the system under which they were placed in homes throughout the county, and employed a staff of trained social workers in connection therewith. Since public funds were not available at first, he paid the salaries of these workers out of his own pocket for several years, the entire charge being eventually assumed by the county when the value of the service had been fully demonstrated. After three years of his administration Macy, now a candidate of both Democrats and Republicans, was reëlected by a virtually unanimous vote. The title of his office was changed to commissioner of charities and corrections, and later to commissioner of public welfare. The county hospital was separated from the almshouse and a desirable site was acquired for a modern hospital building, to be known as Grasslands; for the purposes of the department of child welfare eight districts were erected in the county; and a county penitentiary was planned for correctional work with first offenders. The World War, during which Macy served as head of the labor-adjustment commission for the United States Shipping Board, delayed the completion of many of his plans for the expansion of county welfare work, but in 1920 the hospital was opened and within three years was so overcrowded that in 1923 its capacity had to be increased from 350 to 500 beds.

When Macy resigned the commissionership, after more than ten years of service, he had clearly shown how a county government may cooperate with enlightened private effort in attacking the causes of dependency. A paper read by him in 1921 before the Congress of the American Prison Association was subsequently published under the title, *Self-Government on a County Prison Farm* (1922). His wife, Edith W. Carpenter, whom he married Feb. 18, 1896, was actively interested in the Girl Scouts, and after her death in 1925 Macy made generous gifts to that organization as memorials to her. As president of the Westchester County park commission he devoted much time in the last four years of his life to the beautification of the county park system, which was placed upon a practically self-supporting basis. He died of bronchial pneumonia near Phoenix, Ariz. Two sons and a daughter survived him.

[S. J. Macy, *Geneal. of the Macy Family from 1635–1868* (1868); D. W. Hoyt, *The Old Families of Salisbury and Amesbury, Mass.*, vol. I (1897); *N. Y. Times*,

Mar. 22, 1930; *Who's Who in America*, 1928–29; Ruth Taylor, "Child Welfare in Westchester County," in *Proc. of the Nat. Conference of Social Work*, 1919; W. D. Lane, "A Rich Man in the Poorhouse," in *The Survey* (N. Y.), Nov 4, 1916; *Reports of the Westchester County Park Commission*, 1926–29; *Milestones of Ten Years of the Westchester Way* (1924), a summary of Macy's work as commissioner of public welfare.] W. B. S.

MADDEN, JOHN EDWARD (Dec. 28, 1856–Nov. 3, 1929), breeder of race horses, was born in Bethlehem, Pa. He was of Irish descent, his grandfather having been a political refugee who emigrated to the United States with his family. As a boy, after working in the steel mills at Bethlehem, he became a professional athlete, as a foot-racer, broad-jumper, boxer, and oarsman, later retiring to become a manager of other athletes. Having a natural love for horses, he began investing his savings in trotters. His ventures from the first were unusually successful, which he himself attributed to "luck and logic," and he soon accumulated a good working capital. Two of the first horses of note that he acquired, the gelding Class Leader, 2:22¼, and the stallion Warlock, he bought for low prices and sold for $10,000 each.

After establishing himself firmly as a judge of trotting horses, he turned to the thoroughbred. He was not merely interested in race horses because of their financial possibilities but aspired to become a breeder of great horses. Purchasing a farm near Lexington, Ky., in the heart of the blue-grass region, he there embarked in the breeding business, first in a small way; then, by gradual expansion, he became one of the largest breeders in the world, his stud including over four hundred brood mares at one time and a dozen or more famous stallions. He became America's leading breeder of winners in 1916 and remained so annually for eleven years. During the fourteen years preceding his death, horses bred by him had won over 5,000 public races and over $5,000,000 in stake and purse money on both sides of the Atlantic, for many horses of his breeding were sent abroad to race in his own and other colors. Two horses of his breeding were Zev, winner of $313,639, the largest amount of money at that time credited to any horse, in America or Europe, and Princess Doreen, from 1925 to 1931 the leading American money-winning mare, credited with $174,745. He bred also no less than five winners of the Kentucky Derby: Old Rosebud (1913), Sir Barton (1919), Paul Jones (1920), Zev (1923), and Flying Ebony (1925). He continued to breed trotters throughout his career, but on a smaller scale, and produced many famous ones, Periscope, 2:03½, Margaret Parrish, 2:06¼ (the dam of Arion Guy, 1:59½, and grand-dam of Protector, 1:59¼, and The Marchioness, 1:59¼, and others. His sales of both trotters and thoroughbreds for sensational prices were constant and made him facile princeps in the turf world.

Madden was a man of striking personality, combining a Herculean physique with a mentality of great force and acumen. He was celebrated for his epigrams and aphorisms and his quickness in both thought and action. These qualities enabled him to accumulate a tremendous fortune. He was married to Ann Megrue, of Cincinnati, Ohio, from whom he was divorced many years before his death. He died at his hotel in New York City.

[Neil Newman, *Famous Horses of the Am. Turf*, vol. I (1931); L. H. Weeks, *The Am. Turf* (1898); *Daily Racing Form* (N. Y.), Nov. 5, 1929; *Horse Rev.*, Nov. 6, 1929; the *Thoroughbred Record*, Nov. 9, 16, 1929; *Nat. Turf Digest*, Jan. 1930; *N. Y. Times*, Nov. 4, 1929; various manuals of turf statistics, and personal acquaintance.] J. L. H.

MADDEN, MARTIN BARNABY (Mar. 20, 1855–Apr. 27, 1928), congressman, was born in Darlington, England, the son of John and Elizabeth (O'Neill) Madden. At the age of five he emigrated with his parents and settled in Lemont, Cook County, Ill., where he went to public school. Family necessity forced him to start earning money at the age of ten, and his subsequent education was gained in night school and business college. His first position as waterboy in a quarry at Lemont opened a career in the stone business that carried him to an important position in the Western Stone Company, which became one of the largest concerns of its kind in the world. This prominent position brought to him other offices, such as the presidency of the Quarry Owners' Association of the United States, and of the Illinois Manufacturers' Association, and the vice-presidency of the Builders' and Traders' Exchange of Chicago.

Becoming interested in politics he began in 1889 an eight-year period of service in the Chicago city council, of which he was president from 1891 to 1893. Here he affiliated with the dominant Cook County machine so closely that the Municipal Voters' League frowned upon his activities in behalf of so-called "boodle ordinances" alleged to have conferred franchises without adequate compensation to the city. In the early stages of the campaign for a seat in the United States Senate in 1897, he was supported by the Cook County machine which, however, deserted him when it became evident that he could not win the nomination. Promptly swinging his support to William E. Mason, he helped complete the wreck of the machine and started a realignment in the local Republican party. Later joining the Lorimer faction, he made an unsuccessful race for the House in 1902 but was elected in 1904 to the Fifty-ninth and each succeeding Congress through the seventieth. These activities were punctuated by party service on various local committees, as temporary chairman of the state convention in 1896, and as delegate to the national conventions of 1896 and 1900. At the latter convention he was a member of the committee on resolutions and drafted the plank in the platform that committed the party to the construction of a canal across either Panama or Nicaragua.

In the House he evinced a good deal of ability, rather unusual activity, and a high degree of party regularity, the last marked by occasional streaks of intelligent independence. Much of his early work naturally centered around local interests and his committee assignments, and in these days he showed special solicitude for the welfare of postal workers and the postal service as a whole. He was probably the most progressive member of the Chicago delegation on questions of railroad rate regulation, frequently supporting the various measures intended to increase the powers of the Interstate Commerce Commission. He made repeated efforts to obtain a physical valuation of the roads as a basis for a fair assignment of charges. His interests tended to concentrate more and more upon fiscal and financial matters, and he was made a member of the committee on appropriations in the Sixty-sixth Congress and helped to frame the bill to create the bureau of the budget. In that same Congress he also became a member of the "steering committee." As chairman of the powerful committee on appropriations in the Sixty-seventh Congress, he celebrated his elevation by bringing in the first appropriation bill under the new budget system. His chief claim to fame in the later days lay in the fact that his committee position and his natural bent made him one of the long line of "watchdogs of the treasury," being considered by the contemporary press as, perhaps, the grimmest of them all. In 1925 he published in the *Saturday Evening Post* two articles on "Tax Reduction and the Public Debt" and "The Budget to Date" (Oct. 17, Nov. 7), which are popular expositions of his ideas on the relation of the government to the money acquired by federal taxation. He died from a heart attack at his desk in the room of the appropriations committee at the Capitol. He was survived by his widow, Josephine (Smart) Madden, whom he had married on May 16, 1878, and by their daughter.

[E. W. Brent, *Martin B. Madden* (1901); *Memorial Services Held in the House of Representatives* (1929); *Biog. Directory of the Am. Cong.* (1928); *Who's Who in America, 1926–27*; *Review of Reviews* (N. Y.), Nov. 1925, pp. 459–60, Aug. 1926, pp. 161–62; *Literary Digest*, Nov. 14, 1925; *Evening Star* (Washington), Apr. 27, 30, 1928.]

L. E. E.

MADISON, DOLLY PAYNE (May 20, 1768–July 12, 1849), hostess, is said to have been named Dorothea for Dorothea Dandridge, afterward the second wife of Patrick Henry, but she is known to history as "Dolly." The eldest daughter and apparently the third child of John and Mary (Coles) Payne, she was born in what is now Guilford County, N. C., where her Virginian parents were spending a year with an uncle (Hunt, *post*, p. 351). Her paternal grandfather, John Payne, was an Englishman who settled in Goochland County, Va., and married Anna Fleming of Scotch descent. Her maternal grandfather was William Coles of "Coles Hill," Hanover County, Va., and formerly of Enniscorthy, County Wexford, Ireland. Brought to Virginia by her parents, Dolly grew up at "Scotchtown," in Hanover County. A member of a Quaker family, the little maid lived a restrained country life and received slight schooling. It is said, however, that her fair skin was scrupulously protected from the rays of the Southern sun; her eyes were blue and her hair was black; she was destined to grow tall and to be esteemed beautiful.

Finding the atmosphere of Virginia uncongenial and desiring to provide better educational opportunities for his numerous children, John Payne set free his slaves and in the summer of 1783 removed to Philadelphia, where he engaged unsuccessfully in business and died in 1792. Dolly Payne was married on Jan. 7, 1790, to John Todd, Jr., a lawyer and a member of the Society of Friends. Their son, John Payne Todd, was born on Feb. 29, 1792. Another son was born in the summer of 1793, but his life went out, soon after that of his father (Oct. 24, 1793), during the epidemic of yellow fever. Living thereafter with her mother, who had gentlemen boarders, Dolly Todd was too much admired and sought after to remain a widow long. Senator Aaron Burr introduced to her James Madison [*q.v.*], almost a score of years her elder, and on Sept. 15, 1794, at the home of her sister Lucy, Mrs. George Steptoe Washington, at "Harewood," Jefferson County, Va. (now W. Va.), she became the wife of this noted congressman. The marriage proved to be an unusually happy one, but there were no children.

She became a social figure of the first importance when her husband assumed the secretaryship of state in 1801. Jefferson was a widower and Dolly Madison was in effect the "first lady." Almost invariably she assisted the informal President with his "female guests," and, unwittingly, she was a storm-center in the battle for precedence waged by the British minister, Anthony Merry (Henry Adams, *History of the United States,* 1889, vol. II, 369). Mrs. Merry criticized her dinners as being like "harvest-home" suppers, but few others objected to her generous, unassuming hospitality. She undoubtedly contributed indirectly to political harmony and served to relieve the excessive plainness of the Jeffersonian social régime. With the inauguration of her husband as president, in 1809, she blossomed into more glorious raiment, and, to one observer at least, she met all the requirements of royalty (Hunt, *post,* p. 62). Social life in the Executive Mansion became somewhat more elaborate than it had been in Jefferson's day, though the stiff formality of the Federalist era did not return. She was described by Washington Irving as "a fine, portly, buxom dame," and her "elegance" was much remarked. Her charm, however, was chiefly due to her perennial and inherent friendliness, to her remarkable memory of persons and their interests, to her unfailing tactfulness. Her popularity may have been a minor factor in Madison's reëlection, but essentially she was negative. "She was brilliant in the things she did not say and do" (Goodwin, *post,* p. 101). In August 1814 she had to flee before the British invaders, but she managed to save many state papers and a portrait of George Washington before the Executive Mansion was burned. Living after her return in "The Octagon," she again enjoyed the sunshine of popularity.

From the retirement of Madison in 1817 until his death in 1836, she remained at "Montpellier" (now spelled "Montpelier"), in Orange County, Va., caring for his aged mother (until 1829), reading to her husband and writing for him, living the busy, hospitable life of the mistress of a plantation. In 1837 she returned to Washington with her niece Anna Payne, whom she adopted; she lived at the northeast corner of Lafayette Square in a house formerly owned by Richard Cutts, husband of her beloved sister Anna, and, as "the venerable Mrs. Madison," became again a noted and honored figure. Her last public appearance was at a reception in February 1849, when she passed through the rooms of the White House on the arm of President Polk. Financial difficulties and the waywardness of her son clouded her last days. She was forced to sell "Montpellier." Congress had bought Madison's notes on the Federal Convention for $30,000 in 1837; in 1848 a further appropriation of $25,000 was made for the purchase of other manuscripts of his (*United States Statutes at Large,* V, 1846, p. 171; IX, 1851, p. 235). She died in Washington at the age of eighty-one. After ceremonies at St. John's Church, attended by the highest officials of the Republic, she was buried in the Congressional Cemetery, whence her remains were later removed to "Montpellier." Her reign as a queen of official society may have been benign rather than brilliant, but in length and popular acclaim it has had no parallel in American history.

[The Dolly Madison Collection (13 vols.) in the Lib. of Cong. consists chiefly of private correspondence during her last twenty years. It contains some poetry of her own. She signed her will "Dolley," but the more conventional spelling appears on the certificate of her marriage to Madison in the Account Book of Alexander Balmain, 1782–1821, and has been adopted in this article. Among printed sources may be cited: sketch by Mrs. S. H. Smith, in James Herring and J. B. Longacre, *The Nat. Portrait Gallery of Distinguished Americans,* III (1836); L. B. Cutts, *Memoirs and Letters of Dolly Madison* (1886); J. M. Cutts, "Dolly Madison," in *Records of the Columbia Hist. Soc.,* III (1900); A. C. Clark, *Life and Letters of Dolly Madison* (1914); M. W. Goodwin, *Dolly Madison* (1896); E. L. Dean, *Dolly Madison The Nation's Hostess* (1928); Gaillard Hunt, ed., *The First Forty Years of Washington Society Portrayed by the Family Letters of Mrs. Samuel Harrison Smith* (1906). The best-known of her portraits is the one by Gilbert Stuart, reproduced in Dean and other biographies.] D. M.

MADISON, JAMES (Aug. 27, 1749–Mar. 6, 1812), president of the College of William and Mary and first bishop of the Protestant Episcopal Church in Virginia, was born near Staunton, Va. He grew up at "Madison Hall," purchased by his father in 1751, in Augusta (now Rockingham) County. He was the son of John Madison and a cousin of President James Madison. His mother was Agatha, daughter of William Strother of King George County. After early education at home and at a private school in Maryland he entered the College of William and Mary, from which he graduated in 1771 with high honors. He studied law under George Wythe and was admitted to the bar but did not enter upon practice. In 1773 he was elected professor of natural philosophy and mathematics in the college, and in 1775 he went to England for further study and for ordination to the ministry of the Church of England. Returning to Williamsburg and his professorship, he was in 1777 elected president of William and Mary, though lacking two years of the statutory age. He held this office till his death, being relieved of the teaching of mathematics in 1784 and serving thereafter as professor of natural and moral philosophy. Like the great majority of the clergy of the Established Church in Virginia, he supported the patriot cause in the Revolution, even going so far as to speak of Heaven as a republic rather than a kingdom (Tyler, *post,* p. 73). He served as chaplain of the House of Delegates in 1777; on Aug. 18 he was commissioned captain of a company of militia organized from among the students of the college, and he saw active service on several occasions during the war (*Virginia Magazine of History and Biography,* Jan., July 1933). Selected in 1779 as a member of the commission to define the boundaries between Virginia and Pennsylvania, he determined the line "with great astronomical precision" (Goodwin, *post,* p. 129). Later he made the surveys from which *A Map of Virginia Formed from Actual Surveys . . .* (1807) was engraved. Commonly known as "Madison's Map," this was the standard for many years. (A corrected edition was published in 1818; see E. G. Swem, in *Virginia State Library Bulletin,* Apr.–July 1914, pp. 84–86, 88.) He was of note among the scientific men of his day and carried on an extensive correspondence with Jefferson, mostly on scientific subjects. He received the degree of D.D. from the University of Pennsylvania in 1785.

He cooperated with Jefferson in effecting some changes in the organization of William and Mary during the latter's governorship of Virginia. His own position as president of the college became exceedingly difficult toward the close of the Revolution. Classes were disbanded and the college buildings were in the hands, first of the British, and later of the French and American forces. After the Revolution, both the income of the college and the attendance of students were seriously affected. Madison was the guiding, dominating spirit through the difficult years of reorganization and revival. In addition to the administration and discipline he was compelled to hold the chairs of different departments to supply the lack of adequate faculty. In 1784, he taught political economy, using Adam Smith's *Wealth of Nations* as a textbook (Tyler, *post*). Under his leadership the college was brought to a high degree of efficiency and prosperity. He lived on terms of close intimacy with the students. One of his pupils, John Tyler, later president of the United States, said of him: "His manner to the inmates of the College was kind and parental, and his reproof was uttered in the gentlest tones— . . . ; no one who attended the College during the time that he presided over it, hestitates to acknowledge him as a second father" (Sprague, *post,* V, 321). "Under his guidance and instruction," writes a later biographer, "there was trained a body of alumni which included the flower of Virginia's youth, which moulded the destiny of the state and largely of the United States for half a century, and which for exalted character, distinguished statesmanship and commanding influence could hardly have been equalled in any institution of its day" (Goodwin, *post,* p. 134).

Madison took a prominent part in the reorganization of the Episcopal Church in Virginia after the Revolution and in the formation of the Diocese of Virginia. He was president of the first convention of the Church in 1785. Elected bishop in 1790 and consecrated in Lambeth Chapel, Canterbury, on Sept. 19, 1790, by the Archbishop of Canterbury and the Bishops of London and Rochester, he was the third of the three bishops through whom the episcopate of the Church of England was brought to the United States, the other two being Bishops White of Pennsylvania and Provoost of New York. As the first bishop of Virginia, Madison undertook a superhuman task. The Established Church of the Colony had never been permitted to have its own bishop or to legislate for its own affairs. Supported by taxation, it had been the ward of the government which established new parishes as it formed new counties. The Church emerged from the Revolution simply as a group of disestablished parishes with no training in corporate government and no experience of corporate life. It faced the changed conditions and a constantly growing hostility of elements in the population who sought to take away its glebe lands and endowments. The history of the Episcopal Church in Virginia from 1785 to 1814 is a tragic story of inability to solve the problems of the new day and of gradual weakening, almost to the point of death. Tied as Madison was to his duties at the college for ten months of the year, he could give only two months to visitation of the parishes, but this he did year after year. His scientific spirit and political opinions caused some persons to regard him as a deist (Meade, *post,* I, 29), but his convention addresses are noteworthy for their earnestness and devotion to the cause of his Church. There are no existing records of his administration beyond casual references in the convention journals. In his later years sufficient attendance of the few remaining clergy could not be secured to justify the holding of annual conventions and the history of the Church for these years is almost a blank.

Madison died Mar. 6, 1812, and was buried in the college chapel. In 1779 he had married Sarah Tate.

[William Meade, *Old Churches, Ministers, and Families of Va.* (2 vols., 1857); W. B. Sprague, *Annals of the Am. Pulpit,* vol. V (1859); *Addresses and Hist. Papers before the Centennial Council of the Protestant*

Episcopal Church in the Diocese of Va. . . . 1885 (1885); L. G. Tyler, "Early Presidents of William and Mary," *William and Mary Coll. Quart. Hist. Papers*, Oct. 1892; C. E. Kemper, "The Birth-place of Bishop Madison," *William and Mary Coll. Quart.*, July 1922; "Letters of Rev. James Madison . . . to Thomas Jefferson," *Ibid.*, Apr., July 1925; E. L. Goodwin, *The Colonial Church in Va.* (1927); *Addresses Delivered at the Centennial Celebration of the Diocesan Missionary Soc. of the Protestant Episc. Ch. in the Diocese of Va., . . . May 14, 15, 1929*; the *Richmond Enquirer*, Mar. 10, 13, 1812.]

G. M. B.

MADISON, JAMES (Mar. 5/16, 1750/51–June 28, 1836), fourth president of the United States, was the eldest of ten children. He was born at Port Conway, Va., the home of his maternal grandparents, but soon thereafter mother and son returned to the Madison home in Orange County. According to a statement which, if not written by James Madison, was at least indorsed by him, "his ancestors, on both sides, were not among the most wealthy of the country, but in independent and comfortable circumstances" (Gay, *post*, p. 5). We can safely trace the family no farther back than to John Madison, a ship-carpenter of Gloucester County, who received considerable grants of Virginia land in 1653 and succeeding years and who died prior to Apr. 16, 1683 (*William and Mary College Quarterly*, July 1900, pp. 37–40); and this is one generation farther back than James Madison himself traced it. The Madison blood descended through a second John, Ambrose, and James, Sr., whose mother was Frances Taylor. The mother of the younger James Madison was Eleanor Rose (or, as he himself seems always to have spoken of her, Nelly) Conway, who also contributed the Catlett strain derived from her mother.

James Madison began his formal schooling at twelve years of age under Donald Robertson in King and Queen County, where he studied the classics, French, and Spanish. The inadequacy of the "Scotch French" acquired from Robertson was a favorite theme of jest with him in later years. After further tutoring under the Rev. Thomas Martin in his home parish, he entered the College of New Jersey (Princeton) in 1769. There he was a diligent student, especially of history and government, and was one of the founders of the American Whig Society, a debating club. The college was already imbued with the spirit of resistance to British demands (Hunt, *Writings of James Madison*, I, 7). After receiving the B.A. degree (Oct. 7, 1771), Madison continued another year at Princeton, studying Hebrew and ethics under President Witherspoon—a fact which some have thought an indication that he contemplated entering the ministry.

He continued his semi-theological course of study after his return to Virginia, meanwhile undertaking to instruct his "brothers and sisters in some of the first rudiments of literature" (*Ibid.*, I, 12). He passed through a period of melancholy at this time, forming the conviction that he could not "expect a long or healthy life" and therefore taking little interest in things which would be "useless in possessing after one has exchanged time for eternity" (*Ibid.*, I, 10–11). From this depressed state of mind he was aroused to interest and activity by the political struggle with the mother country and the local controversy over religious toleration. On the latter question, despite his rearing in a good Anglican family, he felt with especial keenness. In letters to a friend in Philadelphia he contrasted the religious freedom of Pennsylvania with its reverse in Virginia, where "that diabolical, hell-conceived principle of persecution rages among some," and where, he said, "I have squabbled and scolded, abused and ridiculed, so long about it to little purpose, that I am without common patience" (*Ibid.*, I, 21). That the melancholy youth had by this time shaken off his absorption in the preparation for eternity is indicated not only by this vigorous language but also by his election the same year to the Committee of Safety for Orange County, and in 1776 to the Virginia convention, where he was a member of the committee which framed the constitution and declaration of rights. His chief contribution to this was a resolution, offered from the floor, which made the free exercise of religion a matter of right rather than of toleration and which, had it been accepted in the form in which he offered it, would have resulted at once in the disestablishment of the Anglican Church in Virginia. A member of the first Assembly under the new constitution, Madison was defeated for reëlection because (according to tradition) he refused to canvass or treat for votes. The Assembly, however, elected him to the governor's Council in 1778 and in 1780 made him a delegate to the Continental Congress.

Madison took his seat in Congress Mar. 20, 1780, and served until December 1783. He was, during this time, in almost constant attendance and from Nov. 4, 1782, to June 21, 1783, he kept notes on the debates which are a useful supplement to the official *Journal.* He was a consistent advocate of a federal revenue to be raised by duties on imports for twenty-five years. He wrote the instructions of Oct. 17, 1780, to John Jay, minister to the court of Spain, supplying him with arguments for the free navigation of the Mississippi by the United States (*Ibid.*, I, 82–91). Upon receipt of the draft of the preliminary treaty of peace with Great Britain in March

1783, Madison joined Hamilton in mild criticism of the American commissioners for breaking their instructions and working behind the backs of the French; like Hamilton he believed that the secret clause regarding the Florida boundary should be made known to France (*Ibid.*, I, 415, 417–19). He stood up stoutly for Virginia's claims to western territory against the assaults of the smaller states and was instrumental in working out the compromise of September 1783 by which Congress accepted Virginia's cession of the Northwest with most of the conditions that the state had sought to impose (Rives, *Madison,* I, 445–64; *Journals of the Continental Congress,* Sept. 13, 1783, pp. 559–64). In the debate on a proposal to change the basis of state contributions from land values to population, he broke a deadlock by suggesting that five slaves be counted as three free persons, thereby becoming the parent of the "federal ratio" later to be incorporated in the Constitution (Hunt, *Writings,* I, 400, 434–35). Altogether, he served his state and country well. His state requited his services by a chronic failure to pay his salary. He was continually in money difficulties and was often saved from serious embarrassment by a philanthropic money lender, Haym Salomon [*q.v.*], who made loans to necessitous members of Congress without interest (Gay, p. 25). The last few months of his term in Congress were spent at Princeton, whither Congress had fled out of fear of the mutinous Pennsylvania troops and where, as he wrote, he and a colleague were "lodged in a room not 10 feet square without a single accommodation for writing." In December 1783, he returned to Virginia because of "the solicitude of a tender and infirm parent," abandoning a half-formed plan for a winter of "close reading" in Philadelphia (Hunt, *Writings,* II, 18–22).

At home at "Montpellier" (now spelled "Montpelier"), he threw himself into a variety of intellectual pursuits. He took up the study of law in order, as he wrote Edmund Randolph, to have a profession in which he could "depend as little as possible on the labour of slaves" (*Ibid.*, II, 154). He wrote Jefferson, who was in Philadelphia and later in Paris, to make for him occasional purchases of "rare and valuable books," especially "whatever may throw light on the general constitution & droit public of the several confederacies which have existed" (*Ibid.*, II, 43). He secured through Jefferson a set of Buffon and set about studying the natural history of his county, sending Jefferson detailed measurements and descriptions of moles and weasels, and, confessing to the same friend "a little itch to gain a smattering of chymistry," he requested a treatise on the subject and a set of apparatus, not to cost "more than a couple of Louis" (*Ibid.*, II, 249–53).

His time for such pursuits, however, had to be found in the intervals permitted by public business. Within a few months after his return to Virginia he was elected to the House of Delegates as member from Orange County, and he filled this office to the end of 1786. He became almost at once a leader in the Assembly. His hand is to be seen in nearly every legislative project of the three years—in the efforts to develop the state's resources, improve her commerce, defend her credit against the paper-money craze, and modernize her laws. He defeated a project of Patrick Henry and other conservative leaders to impose a general assessment for the support of religion and followed up his victory by a measure completing the disestablishment of the Anglican Church begun in 1779 by Jefferson. He showed a sympathetic interest in Virginia's western district, Kentucky; favored its admission to statehood under proper safeguards for Virginia's rights; inaugurated a series of surveys for the improvement of transmontane communications; and stoutly defended the "natural right" of the West to the use of the Mississippi outlet. Measures which he advocated in vain would have established a general system of common schools and have made proper provision for the payment of pre-Revolutionary debts to British creditors and of the state's obligations to the federal government. He favored the limiting of Virginia's foreign trade to two ports in the hope of thus securing better regulation and building up "a Philad[a] or a Baltimore among ourselves" (*Ibid.*, II, 148), but he saw steadily and clearly that the effectual regulation of commerce and commercial concessions from foreign nations could be secured only by the adoption by the states of a united commercial policy. In the pursuance of this object he urged in the Assembly a grant to Congress of the power to regulate commerce, and took a prominent part in bringing about the series of interstate conferences which led through the Annapolis Convention of 1786 to the Federal Convention at Philadelphia in 1787. Madison went as a delegate of Virginia to the Annapolis Convention, knowing that many wished to make that meeting "subservient to a plenipotentiary Convention for amending the Confederation." He himself dared not hope for so much; in fact, he almost despaired of the meeting's producing even a commercial reform (*Ibid.*, II, 262), and he was in gloomy apprehension lest the growing friction among the states would result in a breakup of the Confederation. When the few delegates who attended the Annapolis meeting issued a call for a convention of all the states to revise the Articles, and when the Assembly of Virginia resolved unanimously to accept the call, Madison wrote Washington that at last he had "some ground for leaning to the side of Hope" (*Ibid.,* II, 283).

From February to May 1787, Madison was again in Congress. According to his own statement, made many years later, his main object in returning to Congress had been "to bring about, if possible, the canceling of Mr. Jay's project for shutting the Mississippi" (Gay, p. 84). The seven northern states had, in 1786, voted to authorize John Jay, in his negotiations with Gardoqui, the Spanish minister, to agree that the United States would for twenty-five years forego the right to use the Mississippi River, in order to obtain commercial concessions favorable to the maritime states. In a report of Apr. 11, 1787, Jay informed Congress that he and Gardoqui had "adjusted" an article embodying the proposal. Thereupon Madison made two motions, one to transfer the negotiations with Spain to Madrid and send Jefferson from Paris to take charge of them, and one declaring the vote of seven states insufficient to effect the above-mentioned change in Jay's instructions. Neither proposal was adopted, but the ensuing discussion and votes made it plain that two northern states now sided with the South and thus put an end to the proposal to abandon the Mississippi.

Madison had been named one of the Virginia delegation to the Philadelphia convention. While not sanguine as to the probable results of that assemblage, he believed that its failure would be followed by either a recourse to monarchy or, more likely, a breakup of the Confederation into "three more practicable and energetic Governments" (Hunt, *Writings,* II, 319). Determined to use every endeavor to prevent such an outcome, Madison busied himself with preparations for the approaching convention. The results of his years of study of the history of confederacies ancient and modern he embodied in a paper exhibiting the form and failings of each (*Ibid.,* II, 369–90). In another paper, entitled "Vices of the Political system of the U. States," he set down what he had learned through his own experience of the weaknesses of the existing federal system and of the constitutions of the states (*Ibid.,* II, 361–69). His constructive suggestions were set forth in letters to Jefferson, Edmund Randolph, and Washington in March and April 1787. His principal proposals were: (1) a change in the principle of representation which would give the large states a more just influence; (2) the arming of the national government "with positive and compleat [sic] authority in all cases which require uniformity"; (3) "a negative *in all cases whatsoever* on the legislative acts of the States," perhaps to be lodged in the less numerous house of the legislature; (4) the extension of the "national supremacy" also to the "Judiciary departments"; (5) a legislature of two houses with differing terms of office; (6) a national executive; (7) an article "expressly guarantying the tranquillity of the States against internal as well as external dangers"; (8) an express declaration of the right of coercion; (9) ratification "obtained from the people, and not merely from the ordinary authority of the Legislatures" (*Ibid.,* II, 345–49).

Madison's suggestions were, in substance, embodied in the resolutions drawn up by the Virginia delegates and submitted to the Convention on May 29, known thereafter as the Virginia or Randolph Plan. The actual authorship of these resolutions is not claimed for Madison, but his influence is evident. In the Convention, Madison took a prominent part from the first and became the acknowledged leader of the group favoring a strong central government. "Every Person," wrote one delegate of Madison, "seems to acknowledge his greatness. He blends together the profound politician, with the Scholar. In the management of every great question he evidently took the lead in the Convention, and tho' he cannot be called an Orator, he is a most agreeable, eloquent, and convincing Speaker. . . . The affairs of the United States, he perhaps, has the most correct knowledge of, of any Man in the Union" (*Ibid.,* III, 42 note). He held out strongly for representation of the states in Congress according to population, contending truly that the real conflicts of interest were between sections, not between the large and the small states, and voting against the compromise which gave the small states equality of representation in the Senate. He advocated popular election of members of the federal legislature and of the executive, ratification of the Constitution by state conventions popularly elected for that purpose, and grants to the federal government of wide powers, including the authority to create a national bank and to charter corporations of other kinds (Max Farrand, *The Framing of the Constitution of the United States,* 1913). He opposed the clause forbidding for twenty years the prohibition of the slave trade. While many of his ideas failed of adoption, his influence upon the Convention's work was so great that he has been aptly described as "the master-builder of the constitution" (*Ibid.,* p. 196). His most conspicuous quality was perhaps his practical sense which sought solutions in the realm of past experience rather than in untried theory. Madison was not only the dominating spirit of the Convention; he was the chief recorder of its proceedings. From its first sitting on May 25 to its adjournment on Sept. 17, he was daily at his post, not missing "more than a casual fraction of an hour in any day" (Hunt, *Writings,* II, 411). Although not the official secretary of the body, he had resolved to make the most complete notes of its deliberations that time permitted, and he carried out his purpose with an industry that, as he said, almost killed him. The result, his "Journal of the Federal Convention," first published in 1840, is by far the most complete record of the proceedings (*Ibid.,* vols. III, IV).

Though he wrote Jefferson that the new Constitution would neither sufficiently strengthen the national government nor "prevent the local mischiefs" (Max Farrand, *Records of the Federal Convention,* 1911, III, 77), he threw himself energetically into the fight for its adoption. In Congress he was instrumental in overcoming the opposition of Richard Henry Lee and others and in securing the reference of the Constitution unamended to the states. While in New York in attendance upon Congress he cooperated with Hamilton and Jay in the series of essays published in several New York newspapers over the signature of "Publius," later collected and published (1788) under the title of *The Federalist.* (On authorship see *American Historical Review,* April 1897, pp. 443–60; July 1897, pp. 675–87.) While these essays have, from the time of their publication, been accepted as an authoritative exposition of the new Constitution and "regarded as the most important contribution of our country to political science" (E. G. Bourne, *Ibid.,* April 1897, p. 443), the full significance of Madison's contribution has been pointed out only in recent years (see especially C. A. Beard, *An Economic Interpretation of the Constitution of the United States,* 1913). In *The Federalist* (No. 10) Madison depicts the problem of government as primarily that of reconciling the rivalries among the various economic groups which compose society and argues that the form of government provided in the proposed Constitution is more likely than any other to hold the balance even among these groups and to prevent any one economic interest from unduly exploiting its rivals. Thus, to a large degree, he anticipates the views of economic historians of the modern school. Almost equally noteworthy is the wide departure in these essays from the radical democratic philosophy which had marked the literature of the Revolution; for while the political science of *The Federalist* is based upon the idea of popular sovereignty, it places emphasis upon the protection of property interests against the attacks of popular majorities, not the protection of "the people" against the exactions of executives. Perhaps Madison is most remarkable in this combination of faith in popular government with an open-eyed realization that a popular majority can be quite as tyrannical as a monarch. (See C. E. Merriam, *A History of American Political Theories,* 1903, pp. 100–22). Emphasis upon the dual nature of the new government, federal in the extent of its powers, national in their operation (*Federalist,* No. 39); and the idea that to form effective checks upon one another the legislative, executive, and judicial branches must not be entirely distinct but must be interrelated (*Federalist,* No. 48) are other noteworthy points in Madison's exposition of the Constitution. In these as elsewhere there is apparent a determination to see realities, an unwillingness to be bound by the clichés of current political thinking.

Madison had not intended to take part in the contest over ratification in Virginia, but when it became evident that the foes of ratification were developing great strength in the state, he yielded to the arguments of his friends and stood successfully for election to the ratifying convention as a delegate from Orange County. In the convention, which met in June 1788 and was almost equally divided between the advocates and the opponents of ratification, Madison found himself ranged against Patrick Henry and George Mason as leaders of the opposition. In the ensuing debates, Madison's quiet but cogent reasoning was in striking contrast with Henry's rambling and flamboyant oratory. His knowledge of recent events in Congress he used with telling effect when he answered Henry's prediction of the loss of the Mississippi by revealing that two northern states now stood with the South on that issue, thus assuring a majority against surrendering the right of navigation (Hunt, *Madison,* ch. xvi; *Writings,* V, 123–234; Jonathan Elliott, *The Debates . . . on the Adoption of the Federal Constitution,* vol. II, 1828). This assurance allayed the chief fear of the delegates from the Kentucky district, with the result that most of them voted for ratification. The final vote on June 25 showed a narrow majority of 89 to 79 in favor of ratification. Four days earlier, New Hampshire had become the ninth state to ratify, thus completing the number necessary to launch the new venture. The adherence of Virginia, followed a month later by that of New York, made certain the support of all the greater states.

Madison was again chosen by the Virginia Assembly to represent the state in the expiring Congress. His election to the new United States Senate was blocked by Henry, but Henry's attempt to prevent his election to the House of Representatives by what would have been later described as a gerrymander of his district was unsuccessful, and thus Madison from the beginning participated in the new government which he had had so large a share in building (Hunt, *Madison,* ch. xvii). In the first session of the first Congress he took a leading part in the passage of revenue legislation, in the creation of the executive departments, and in the framing of the first ten amendments to the Constitution, sometimes known as the Bill of Rights (*Ibid.,* ch. xviii). In the second session of the same Congress, and thereafter, Madison was increasingly critical of Hamilton's financial measures, and from an ardent Federalist became a recognized leader of the opposition, the Jeffersonian or Democratic-Republican party. He wished to provide compensation for original holders of federal securities who had sold them at a loss. He opposed assumption of the state debts by the federal treasury, though it appears that his opposition was in part silenced by the agreement to locate the capital on the Potomac (*Ibid.,* pp. 184–85, 197–99). He opposed the creation of the United States Bank on constitutional grounds, though his letters show that he was more shocked by the "stock-jobbing" connected with Hamilton's measures and by the profits and power which they gave to northern capitalists than by their questionable constitutionality (Hunt, *Writings,* VI, 55 note, 81 note; Beard, *Economic Origins of Jeffersonian Democracy,* 1915, pp. 51–52). He was also wholly out of sympathy with the pro-British trend of Hamilton's policy. He wished the United States to remain at peace and he roundly condemned the behavior of "Citizen" Genet; but his sympathies in the European conflict were with France, and he believed that Washington, through Hamilton's influence, was unnecessarily subservient to Great Britain. In a series of letters in the *Gazette of the United States* (Aug. 24–Sept. 18, 1793) over the signature "Helvidius" he criticized the form of the President's neutrality proclamation, which Hamilton as "Pacificus" had defended in the same paper (Hunt, *Writings,* VI, 138–88). He advocated harsh measures of retaliation to meet British violations of American rights and voted against the measures for putting the Jay treaty into effect (Hunt, *Madison,* ch. xxiii; Bemis, *post,* III, 5). Down to 1792, at least, his relations with Washington remained cordial. In fact, when Jefferson retired as secretary of state in July 1793, Washington spoke of Madison as a possible successor. Thereafter the relations of the two men became cooler, though there was never an open break.

Madison's marriage to Dolly Payne Todd [see Madison, Dolly Payne], a young widow of Philadelphia, which occurred Sept. 15, 1794, was the beginning of an extraordinarily happy married life. After two years more in Congress he voluntarily retired from public service (Mar. 4, 1797), expecting to devote his time to scientific farming and the pleasures of Virginia rural life. The Federalists were now in full control of the federal government. They signalized their victory by the passage of some rather hysterical legislation against aliens and even against native-born critics of their administration—the famous Alien and Sedition Acts. The chief answer to these ill-advised laws was the resolutions drawn by Madison and Jefferson in 1798 and adopted by the Virginia and Kentucky legislatures, respectively. Both these documents asserted the right of the states, in the last resort, to judge of the constitutionality of acts of Congress; both argued that the Alien and Sedition Acts were unconstitutional. The Virginia Resolutions, penned by Madison, declared that "in case of a deliberate, palpable, and dangerous exercise of other powers not granted by the said compact, the States, who are parties thereto, have the right and are in duty bound to interpose for arresting the progress of the evil, and for maintaining within their respective limits the authorities, rights, and liberties appertaining to them," and invited the other states to join Virginia in declaring the obnoxious acts unconstitutional and "maintaining unimpaired the authorities, rights, and liberties reserved to the States respectively, or to the people" (Hunt, *Writings,* VI, 326, 331). The precise meaning of these Resolutions became a matter of controversy and is even today difficult, if not impossible, to determine. In a report drawn by Madison in 1799 (after his election to the Virginia House of Delegates) in which he defended the Resolutions against hostile criticisms passed by the legislatures of seven northern states, he stated that declarations such as those of Virginia and Kentucky were "expressions of opinion, unaccompanied with any other effect than what they may produce on opinion by exciting reflection" (*Ibid.,* VI, 402). In later years, when the South Carolina nullifiers appealed to the authority of the Virginia and Kentucky Resolutions as supporting their doctrine, Madison took great pains to explain that there was no threat of actual nullification in the

Resolutions drawn by him and by his friend Jefferson; that what they proposed was merely co-operation among the states for securing the repeal of the laws or the amendment of the Constitution. He found it very difficult, however, to place a satisfactory construction upon the assertion that it was the right and duty of the states to maintain "within their respective limits the authorities, rights, and liberties appertaining to them." "The pretext," he wrote (Dec. 23, 1832), "for the liberty taken with those [resolutions] of Virginia is the word *respective,* prefixed to the 'rights' &c to be secured within the States. Could the abuse of the expression have been foreseen or suspected, the form of it would doubtless have been varied" (*Ibid.,* IX, 491). It seems most probable that the strongly partisan spirit of 1798 and the influence of Jefferson led Madison to use language which in a calm moment he would have avoided (Hunt, *Madison,* chs. xxvi, xxvii; Gay, ch. xv).

The overthrow of the Federalists in the election of 1800 and the inauguration of Jefferson brought Madison again into a prominent position in public life. His long friendship with Jefferson and the almost complete accord between the two men on public policies made it only natural that Madison should become the new President's secretary of state and chief adviser. It is evident that Jefferson had offered this post to Madison before the close of the year 1800 and before the outcome of the election was known. Though appointed to the office Mar. 5, 1801, and at once confirmed by the Senate, he did not actually take up its duties until May 2, being detained at home by his father's illness and death (Feb. 27) and the resulting cares. While inexperienced in diplomacy, Madison brought to the office a well-informed mind, a knowledge of men, a quiet dignity, and a good-humored affability which did much to promote his popularity with foreign diplomats in Washington. Since the President and Vice-President were both widowers, Mrs. Madison became the capital's leading lady, and her establishment was conducted on a liberal scale. Her personal charm gave her great popularity in Washington society, which easily survived some embarrassing experiences resulting from the application of Jefferson's democratic rules of etiquette. From the outset, however, a faction within the Republican party distrusted Madison, partly because of his earlier association with Federalists, partly because he, like Gallatin, refused to make sufficient places for political followers by ousting Federalist officeholders (Henry Adams, *post,* I, 236, 261). This hostile faction, headed at first by Duane of Pennsylvania and Senator W. B. Giles of Virginia, came later to embrace the brilliant but erratic John Randolph of Roanoke, and still later, the influential Robert and Samuel Smith of Maryland. The opposition of these men was to be responsible for some bitter defeats during Madison's presidency.

The principal problems of foreign policy confronting the new Secretary of State arose from the relation of the United States to the war between Great Britain and Napoleonic France. Both belligerents had paid scant regard to rights of neutrals on the high seas. For the moment, no crisis with either threatened. The Jay treaty of 1794 had smoothed over the chief sources of friction with Great Britain, and a few weeks before Jefferson's inauguration the Senate had advised ratification (with amendment) of a treaty with France which removed the immediate causes of difficulty with that country. Madison believed the prospects for peace with both to be good, resting that faith in part upon the supposed vital need of both for the services of the United States. "France," he wrote to Jefferson, Jan. 10, 1801, "has sufficiently manifested her friendly disposition, and what is more, seems to be duly impressed with the interest she has in being at peace with us. G[reat] B[ritain], however intoxicated with her maritime ascendency is more dependent every day on our commerce for her resources, must for a considerable length of time look in a great degree to this Country, for bread for herself, and absolutely for all the necessaries for her islands. . . . Besides these cogent motives to peace and moderation, her subjects will not fail to remind her of the great pecuniary pledge they have in this Country, and which under any interruption of peace or commerce with it, must fall under great embarrassments, if nothing worse" (Hunt, *Writings,* VI, 414–15). In this letter, written two months before Jefferson's inauguration, may be seen the germ of the policy of "peaceful coercion" adopted in the Embargo Act of 1807.

The Peace of Amiens (preliminaries signed Oct. 1, 1801) interposed a breathing spell in the European war. The relief afforded the United States by that event gave way to alarm as rumors of a sale of Louisiana by Spain to France were followed by definite confirmation of the transaction and that in turn by the abrogation of the right of deposit at New Orleans, which had been guaranteed to the people of the United States by the Spanish treaty of 1795. In the ensuing negotiations with France, culminating in the purchase of Louisiana in 1803, it would appear that Madison played merely a formal part, penning the instructions which carried out Jefferson's policy. Thus, although one biographer has termed the Louisiana purchase "the only completed act of Madison's term as Secretary of State" (Hunt, *Madison,* p. 298), such credit as is due to American statesmen for accepting what fate and Napoleon placed in their hands should probably be assigned principally to Jefferson and to Robert R. Livingston, minister in Paris. In the subsequent attempts to make the boundaries of Louisiana include portions of Florida and, by dickering with Napoleon, to force Spain to sell Florida to the United States, Madison seems also to have been merely carrying out the ideas of his chief.

With the renewal of the European war in 1803, American commerce and American seamen were again subjected to losses and indignities by the belligerents. Seamen on American ships—of whom some were deserters from British ships, some naturalized American citizens who under British law remained British subjects, and some native-born Americans—were seized on the high seas and even in American and neutral ports and pressed into service in the Royal Navy. Great Britain invoked the "Rule of 1756," which forbade neutrals to engage in the trade between France or Spain and the French or Spanish colonies; and in applying it British courts invented the "doctrine of continuous voyage," under which the rule could not be evaded by stopping at an American port en route. Finally, Great Britain and France launched at each other a series of Orders in Council on the one hand and decrees on the other; the first designed to levy tribute for the British Crown on all neutral trade with France, the second to deprive Great Britain of all trade with the continent of Europe. No neutral incapable of throwing a respectable military weight into the scale could expect much consideration from the great powers. What could be done with the pen to protect American rights Madison did. His diplomatic notes were able presentations of the legal arguments against the British and French practices. The ineffectiveness of such correspondence, however, was aptly summed up by John Randolph in his characterization of a treatise written by Madison against the Rule of 1756 as "a shilling pamphlet hurled against eight hundred ships of war" (Hill, "James Madison," in Bemis, *post,* III, 110). His contentions produced no modification of the belligerent practices. Nor can it be said that history has wholly vindicated Madison's position. Paper blockades and the confiscation of enemy non-contraband property on neutral ships were formally banned by international agreement in the Declaration of Paris (1856). Impressments went out of fashion when they ceased to be advantageous. But arbitrary extensions of the contraband lists, unreasonable and annoying searches and seizures, and the doctrine of "continuous voyage"—against all of which he protested—continued in use by the great naval powers including the United States itself. British policy, while morally no worse than France, came nearer home and was more widely felt in the United States, and hence produced a greater volume of diplomatic correspondence. Rufus King, James Monroe, and William Pinkney labored successively (the two last for a while together) in London in vain efforts to arrive at a settlement with the British government, and one British minister followed another every year or so in Washington with no better results. American exasperation was guided by Jefferson and Madison into the form of the Embargo Act of Dec. 22, 1807, which closed American ports and forbade American ships to go to sea. When this ineffectual measure was repealed, Mar. 1, 1809, the administration party desired measures of war against both Great Britain and France as a substitute, but proposals to that effect were defeated in Congress.

Jefferson had chosen Madison as his successor. There was little opposition to the choice, though James Monroe, offended by what he regarded as the failure of the administration to recognize the merit of his diplomatic service, allowed himself to be offered as a candidate by a group of Virginia malcontents. Monroe's support was feeble. Madison entered upon his new duties Mar. 4, 1809. Observers noted his careworn and aging appearance. At his inauguration he was "extremely pale and trembled excessively when he first began to speak, but soon gained confidence and spoke audibly." At the inauguration ball, where "poor Mrs. Madison was almost pressed to death," and "as the upper sashes of the windows could not let down, the glass was broken, to ventilate the room," Madison, though "he made some of his old kind of mischievous allusions," seemed "spiritless and exhausted" (Mrs. S. H. Smith, *The First Forty Years of Washington Society,* ed. by Gaillard Hunt, 1906, pp. 59–63). Washington Irving, another observer, thought him "but a withered little apple-John" (Hunt, *Madison,* p. 300). A small man, he was never impressive in person. Eight difficult years and considerable tragedy awaited him in the presidency. He made no change in Jefferson's cabinet, except to promote Robert Smith from the Navy to the State Department, making Paul Hamilton secretary of the navy. But an old feud between Smith and Gallatin, secretary of the treasury, produced so much trouble that Madison at length (April 1811) dismissed Smith and named Monroe to his place, thereby securing an abler secretary and a more harmonious cabinet, but adding strength to the Republican faction that already opposed his administration.

When Madison became president, the United States was under a régime of non-intercourse with the British and Napoleonic empires but unrestricted trade with the rest of the world. After holding out for a year a promise to trade with either belligerent which would repeal its obnoxious measures, Congress in May 1810 resolved to trade with both, authorizing the president, if either France or Great Britain should reform its practices, to revive non-intercourse against the other. Madison appears to have fallen into a trap laid for him by the wily Corsican, who pretended that the objectionable decrees were revoked in so far as they affected the United States. Without waiting for adequate proof, Madison assumed that the revocation was genuine and on Nov. 2, 1810, issued a proclamation of non-intercourse against Great Britain. It was assumed by members of the cabinet at the time that this measure would lead to war with Great Britain; and it is true that, despite the able efforts for peace made by Monroe, who became secretary of state in April 1811, relations with that country grew steadily worse until the declaration of war in June 1812. Upon this hypothesis, the war is chargeable to Napoleon's clever stratagem and Madison's naïve acceptance of it. Other causes were, however, tending toward the same result. Indian outbreaks in the Ohio Valley were ascribed to British intrigue, and the West raised a cry that the British must be driven from Canada, and their allies, the Spanish, from Florida. Madison secretly encouraged revolution in Florida—a policy which cannot be justified by the highest ethical standards—and when opportunity arose annexed to the United States as part of the Louisiana purchase the portions of West Florida which had declared their independence of Spain. Pressure for war from the West was at its height from November 1811 to June 1812 and must be added to the failure of Monroe's negotiations with Foster, the British minister, in accounting for the final decision in favor of war. In his message of Nov. 5, 1811, Madison had warned Congress of the danger of hostilities, and had counseled preparation; in a special message of June 1, 1812, he advised a declaration of war against Great Britain, assigning as principal causes the impressment of American seamen, interference with American trade, and the incitement of the Indians to hostilities on the American frontier. The legend that Madison was coerced into recommending war by the threat that otherwise he would not be renominated for the presidency is unsupported by any reliable evidence (Hunt, *Madison*, pp. 316–19). Congress, which acted upon the advice of the June message and declared war June 18, had neglected to follow Madison's counsel of the previous November to put the United States "into an armor and an attitude demanded by the crisis," and the country was unprepared for war. All this he realized. Years later he told the historian Bancroft that "he knew the unprepared state of the country, but he esteemed it necessary to throw forward the flag of the country, sure that the people would press forward and defend it" (*Ibid.*, pp. 318–19). Unfortunately, Madison, despite his admirable qualities, was not the man to lead the country through such an ordeal. "Our President tho a man of amiable manners and great talents," wrote John C. Calhoun, "has not I fear those commanding talents, which are necessary to control those about him" (Pratt, *post*, p. 155). His martial efforts only amused; "he visited in person—a thing never known before—all the offices of the departments of war and the navy," wrote Richard Rush, "stimulating everything in a manner worthy of a little commander-in-chief, with his little round hat and huge cockade" (Henry Adams, *post*, VI, 229). Six months of failure went by before those same departments were cleared of their incompetent executives, and a year more before men of talent in the army could find their way to the top. Responsibility for the failure of incompetent commanders is in the final analysis the president's. Sectionalism and faction, furthermore, paralyzed the nation's energies. Federalists opposed the war *in toto*. Northern Republicans and Madison's personal enemies within the party thwarted the administration's efforts to seize what remained of the Floridas. Southern Republicans, including Monroe, secretary of state, felt little enthusiasm for conquering Canada and thus creating more northern states. Every thrust across the St. Lawrence or the Lakes before the summer of 1814 (except Harrison's brief campaign in 1813) was mismanaged and inexcusably bungled. In the remote struggle for the upper Mississippi valley, William Clark was so badly worsted by his Canadian opponents that, had peace been made on the basis of possession, the United States would have lost not only Wisconsin and Minnesota but also northern Illinois and Iowa. By the time the army became competent it was too late for victory, for Napoleon was on Elba and Great Britain could give undivided attention to the war in America. Efforts at peace had begun a few weeks after the declaration of war, when it was learned that Great Britain had repealed the Orders in Council—seemingly a tardy triumph for Jefferson's and Madison's policy of peaceful coercion. The war might have been halted then (August 1812) had the war-spirit in the West been less powerful. An offer of mediation from the Czar of Russia, precipitately accepted by Madison in March 1813, was declined by the British government, but an offer from the latter to negotiate directly with the United States led in time to the negotiations at Ghent from August to December 1814. At Madison's suggestion the American commissioners were instructed to drop the demand for the abandonment of impressments—formerly regarded as a *sine qua non* of peace—and to demand only the surrender of occupied territory. A treaty on this basis was signed Dec. 24, 1814. Though not a single aim of the war had been attained, though Washington had been captured and the President and his family forced to flee to the Virginia woods, a series of notable victories in the closing months—at Baltimore, Plattsburg, Fort Erie, and New Orleans—brought the struggle to an end in a blaze of glory and sent "Mr. Madison's war" down to posterity in the school-histories as an American triumph.

The war had been opposed throughout by the New England Federalists, who held the Hartford Convention in its closing months. Their conduct weighed heavily upon Madison. He was described in October 1814, as looking "miserably shattered and woe-begone . . . heart-broken. His mind . . . full of the New England sedition" (Henry Adams, VIII, 231). The outcome of the war marked the end of the Federalists as a party but the adoption of many of their principles by the Republicans. Madison shared partially in this conversion. He signed a bill providing for a new Bank of the United States. He signed the tariff act of 1816, the object of which was to protect American "infant industries" from British competition, and he allowed himself to be enrolled in a society for the encouragement of American manufactures, declaring his belief in "the policy of encouraging domestic manufactures, within certain limits, and in reference to certain articles" (Hunt, *Writings*, VIII, 392). He also approved measures strengthening the permanent military and naval establishments. Yet most of these changes on Madison's part were changes in policy rather than in constitutional interpretation, as was shown in his veto of a bill for internal improvements at federal expense. He approved the end sought in the measure, but found no express authorization for it in the Constitution and suggested the propriety of a constitutional amendment giving Congress the power in question (*Ibid.*, VIII, 386–88).

Madison retired from the presidency March 4, 1817, leaving the office to his and Jefferson's friend, Monroe. This brought to a close his political career, except for his participation in the Virginia constitutional convention of 1829. This participation, while unimportant, is interesting in that it gave occasion for a new approach to his favorite theme of the protection of rights of minorities in a democracy. The threatened minority interest in this instance was that of the slaveholders of eastern Virginia, and Madison's suggestion was for a representation of slaves in the Virginia legislature upon the "federal ratio," counting five slaves as three free men (*Ibid.*, IX, 358–64). He was a prominent supporter of Jefferson in the founding of the University of Virginia, of which he became rector after Jefferson's death in 1826. He was interested in the work of the American Colonization Society as the most eligible solution of the negro problem, that "dreadful calamity which has so long afflicted our Country" (*Ibid.*, IX, 469), but declined to become its president. He was consulted by Monroe in regard to the British suggestion of joint action in defense of the independence of Spanish America and advised acceptance of the British proposal. This advice Monroe disregarded in favor of a lone declaration by the United States, the Monroe Doctrine. The controversy over nullification produced an occasion for Madison to review and reappraise his contributions to political thought and constitution making. The situation was precisely of the sort that he had warned against in *The Federalist* (No. 10); a majority in Congress representing the interests of certain economic groups was using its power in a fashion detrimental to the interests of the minority. This Madison saw, but he had slight sympathy with the injured minority, and he had no feasible plan for their relief, merely warning them that their interests would be no more secure outside the Union than in it. On the other hand, he denied the validity of the doctrines of nullification and peaceful secession and maintained stoutly the constitutionality of the tariff, the competence of the Supreme Court to decide questions of doubtful jurisdiction between the federal government and the states, and the general beneficence of the Constitution and Union which he had done so much to create (*Ibid.*, IX, 314–16, 480–82, 513). To the charge of inconsistency brought against him by advocates of the South Carolina doctrine Madison replied at length, maintaining (as has been said) that the nullification theory could not properly be derived from the Virginia Resolutions, and showing that upon all constitutional questions except the bank his position had been unchanged. That he had opposed Hamilton's bank as unconstitutional but had signed the law creating the Second Bank he explained by saying that on this point of interpretation he had yielded to an overwhelming "Public Judgment, necessarily superseding individual opinions" (*Ibid.,* IX, 477). Notably, in regard to the supremacy of the federal judiciary, he asserted that from the beginning he had regarded it as essential. "A supremacy of the Constitution & laws of the Union, without a supremacy in the exposition & execution of them, would be as much a mockery as a scabbard put into the hands of a Soldier without a sword in it" (*Ibid.,* IX, 476).

Apart from minor public service and controversial writing, Madison lived quietly at "Montpellier" (now "Montpelier"), where he was under the necessity of reducing his scale of living and selling part of his farm because of straitened circumstances. Nevertheless, his hospitality to the many visitors who came his way was of the traditional Virginia kind, and his conversation and manner, at least to friends, were charming. Margaret Bayard Smith, who visited "Montpellier" in 1828, described his conversation as "a stream of history . . . so rich in sentiments and facts, so enlivened by anecdotes and epigramatic remarks, so frank and confidential as to opinions on men and measures, that it had an interest and charm, which the conversation of few men now living, could have. . . . His little blue eyes sparkled like stars from under his bushy grey eye-brows and amidst the deep wrinkles of his poor thin face." But she added that "this entertaining, interesting and communicative personage, had a single stranger or indifferent person been present, would have been mute, cold and repulsive" (*First Forty Years,* pp. 235–36). Harriet Martineau, who paid a similar visit to the Madisons in 1835, found him weakened by rheumatism but mentally agile, still given to gay conversation and anecdote, and full of "inexhaustible faith . . . that a well-founded commonwealth may . . . be immortal." Only on the slavery question was he pessimistic, "acknowledging, without limitation or hesitation, all the evils with which it has ever been charged" (Harriet Martineau, *Retrospect of Western Travel,* 1838, I, 191). The most important work of these later years was the arrangement and preparation for publication of his notes on the Federal Convention. Looking back over his busy life, he may have felt, as the historian must feel today, that his work as architect of the Constitution overshadowed in importance and success his labors as secretary of state or even as president. The direction of his political thinking in his last years may be inferred from a note found among his papers after his death under the caption "Advice to my Country." It concludes with the following: "The advice nearest to my heart and deepest in my convictions is, *that the Union of the states be cherished and perpetuated. Let the open enemy of it be regarded as a Pandora with her box opened, and the disguised one as the serpent creeping with his deadly wiles into paradise*" (Hunt, *Writings,* IX, facing p. 610). He died without issue in his eighty-seventh year at "Montpellier," and there he was buried.

[W. C. Rives, *Hist. of the Life and Times of James Madison* (3 vols., 1859–68), was never completed and ends with 1797. Briefer biographies are Gaillard Hunt, *The Life of James Madison* (1902); and S. H. Gay, *James Madison* (1884). Earlier editions of Madison's writings have been superseded by Gaillard Hunt, *Writings of James Madison* (9 vols., 1900–10), which, besides a large amount of private correspondence, includes his "Journal of the Constitutional Convention" (vols. III & IV), his speeches in the Virginia Convention of 1788, his speeches in Congress, and many of his official papers as secretary of state and president. Some letters not printed in this edition are in H. D. Gilpin, ed., *The Papers of James Madison* (3 vols., 1840); the Cong. ed., *Letters and Other Writings of James Madison* (4 vols., 1865); and E. C. Burnett, *Letters of Members of the Continental Cong.* (6 vols., 1921–33). The extensive collection of Madison papers in the Lib. of Cong. contains correspondence, largely covered by printed and manuscript calendars, together with miscellaneous MSS., his famous notes, and some printed matter. Henry Adams, *Hist. of the U. S. of America* (9 vols., 1889–91), is indispensable for the years of Madison's service as secretary of state and president. See also the sketches of Madison and Monroe by C. E. Hill and J. W. Pratt, respectively, in S. F. Bemis, ed., *The Am. Secretaries of State and Their Diplomacy,* vol. III (1927); and J. W. Pratt, *Expansionists of 1812* (1925). For portraits of Madison, see C. W. Bowen, *The Hist. of the Centennial Celebration of the Inauguration of George Washington* (1892).]

J. W. P—t.

MAEDER, CLARA FISHER [See FISHER, CLARA, 1811–1898].

MAES, CAMILLUS PAUL (Mar. 13, 1846–May 11, 1915), Roman Catholic prelate, son of Jean Baptiste and Justine (Ghyoot) Maes, was born in Courtrai, Belgium, of a family which had furnished a number of priests to the diocese of Bruges. Camillus was trained in the local preparatory school of St. Aloysius, in the College of St. Amandus, and in an architect's office. Burning with missionary zeal, fostered by American bishops who were recruiting continuously in the Low Countries, he studied for the priesthood in the seminaries of Roulers and Bruges, and in the American College at Louvain. Ordained at Mechlin, Dec. 19, 1868, he took leave of his family and Bishop Faict, who grudgingly surrendered him to the diocese of Detroit.

Maes was assigned to the mission of Mount Clemens as assistant to the dying Belgian pastor, Van Renterghem, whom he soon succeeded. In building a school and caring for several hundred scattered families of various races, he found opportunity for tactful leadership and practice in speaking French, German, Dutch, Flemish, and English. In 1871 he became assistant to Msgr. Edward Joos of St. Mary's Church at Monroe, Mich. Here he built St. John the Baptist Church for English-speaking Catholics (1873); organized a model parish with school, religious confraternities, and temperance society; and incidentally wrote a brochure, *History of the Catholic Church in Monroe City and County* (printed in part in the *United States Catholic Historical Magazine,* April 1888). In 1880 he was called to Detroit as secretary to Bishop Caspar H. Borgess. In this capacity he improved diocesan finances, acted as theologian at synods, aided in the establishment of the House of the Good Shepherd, for which he acted as chaplain, arranged for a Flemish parish, established the Catholic Club, which was later imitated in other diocesan centers, and wrote a *Life of Rev. Charles Nerinckx* (1880). Named bishop of Covington, Ky., he was consecrated by Archbishop W. H. Elder on Jan. 25, 1885.

Again Maes proved a constructive organizer. He cleared the diocese of a heavy debt; built, with the aid of James and Michael Walsh, philanthropists, a Gothic cathedral on the order of Notre Dame of Paris; established St. Elizabeth's Hospital under the Franciscan Sisters of Aix-la-Chapelle, whom he introduced into the diocese; and established about thirty parishes with chapels, an orphan asylum, a few academies, two homes for the aged, and a House of the Good Shepherd. He administered thirty-seven parochial schools, in which he was an ardent believer, brought the Sisters of Divine Providence from Lorraine (1888), and led an opposition to Archbishop Ireland's Faribault plan and Msgr. Satolli's fourteen propositions, on the ground that they undermined the effectiveness of the parochial system. In harmony with the Paulist idea, he promoted an Evangelist's Home in Richmond, Ky., as a center for missionaries to non-Catholics (1905). With the opening of the Kentucky coal fields, he avoided a racial problem by providing Italian and Slavic laborers with priests of their own race. Nationally, he was prominent as a director of the Federation of Catholic Societies; as a governor of Father Francis C. Kelly's Extension Society; as a founder and director of the Priest's Eucharistic League, whose organ, *Emmanuel,* he established and edited (1895–1903); as permanent president of the various American Eucharistic congresses; as a leading delegate to the World Eucharistic congresses at Namur (1902), Metz (1907), Montreal (1910), and Vienna (1912); as chairman of a board of bishops for the American College, Louvain, which, on his advice, was constituted a part of the university; and as a promoter of the *Catholic Encyclopedia,* for which he wrote a few articles. At the Third Plenary Council of Baltimore (1884), he challenged the hierarchy by a spirited advocacy of a national Catholic University. When this university was established in Washington (1887), he acted as secretary and member of the board of trustees for a score of years, and ultimately bequeathed his library to the institution.

An efficient, industrious man, Maes found time for many things; he preached well; published a number of sound pastorals of marked clarity and force; contributed twelve articles to the Flemish *Rond den Heerd* (1870–76), largely on Belgian life in America, a few articles to the *Ecclesiastical Review,* the *Catholic World,* the *Children's Magazine,* and the *Christian Year,* which he founded in 1912. He might have been appointed to the archepiscopal See of New Orleans in 1897, but, it is understood, President Faure intrigued in Rome for a French appointee. For racial reasons he was not available for Cincinnati in 1907. Urged to write on Flemish Franciscans in North America, he wrote to the *Catholic Historical Review:* "You have evoked a literary ghost snuffed out years ago by a mitre." He commenced the work, however, which his death soon ended. The incomplete article, "Flemish Franciscan Missionaries in North America, 1674–1738," appeared in the *Catholic Historical Review* for April 1915.

[*Records of the Am. Cath. Hist. Soc.,* June 1922; *Cath. Hist. Rev.,* July 1915; *Cath. Encyc.,* IV, 463; C. P. Maes, *Golden Jubilee of the Diocese of Covington* (1903); *The Cath. Encyc. and Its Makers* (1917); *Am. Cath. Who's Who,* 1911; Cath. Directories; *Character Sketches of the Rt. Rev. C. P. Maes* (1917); Joseph Van der Heyden, *The Louvain Am. College. 1857–1907* (1909); *Cath. Telegraph* (Cincinnati), Dec. 21, 1893, May 13, 20, 1915; *Louisville Times.* May 11, 1915.]

R. J. P.

MAFFITT, DAVID (d. May 1, 1838), privateersman in the War of 1812, presumably had earlier followed the sea. When war against England was declared, June 18, 1812, he was one of the first privateersmen to go out in search of enemy vessels. In command of the schooner *At-*

las, of 12 guns and 140 men, he sailed from Philadelphia early in July. Very soon he captured his first prize, the brig *Tulip.* Early in August he fell in with two British ships, the *Pursuit,* of 16 guns and thirty-five men, and the *Planter,* 12 guns and fifteen men. The *Atlas* engaged both of them at the same time and a hard-fought battle followed. When the action had lasted about an hour the smaller vessel struck her colors; not long afterwards the larger ship also surrendered, and Maffitt took possession of both. About a month later the *Atlas* and her prizes were chased by a ship, supposed to be British, which, however, proved to be the United States frigate *Essex.* Maffitt eventually got his prizes safely into port. From the fall of 1812 until the following summer his movements are unrecorded and how much time he spent at sea is unknown, but he seems to have made no more captures. In the spring or summer of 1813 he sailed in the *Atlas* on a cruise which turned out disastrously, for he was captured, July 12, by a British squadron at Ocracoke Inlet, North Carolina.

Later in the year 1813, having been released from captivity, Maffitt was given command of the 16-gun brig *Rattlesnake,* a fine, fast-sailing vessel with a good crew. He devoted his attention thereafter to European waters. For several months he cruised about the British Isles and off the coast of Norway, part of the time in company with the privateer *Scourge,* of New York. They inflicted great injury to British commerce, and sent their prizes into Norwegian ports. The *Rattlesnake* on this cruise took eleven vessels. Early the next spring Maffitt decided to try his fortune in the Bay of Biscay and in March 1814 was at La Rochelle. Capt. George Coggeshall [*q.v.*], a noted New York privateersman who saw much of Maffitt at this time, called him "an excellent seaman, and a brave, honorable man" (*post,* p. 219). The *Rattlesnake* fought an engagement with the British armed transport *Mary,* with many English army officers, soldiers, and French prisoners on board, and captured her. The *Mary* lost three killed, including the captain, and three wounded; one American was wounded. The captive English officers highly praised Maffitt for the treatment they received at his hands. The *Mary* was unfortunately recaptured before she could be brought into port. Soon afterwards the *Rattlesnake* was blockaded in La Rochelle by a British squadron. Maffitt tried to escape, but was driven back, and finally, June 3, 1814, the *Rattlesnake* was captured by the frigate *Hyperion.* This ended the career of Maffitt in the War of 1812. While in command of the *Rattlesnake* he had made prizes of three ships, twelve brigs, and three sloops, most of which reached port in safety.

Whether he pursued a seafaring life, engaged in peaceful commerce, after the War of 1812, is unknown. At all events, in due time he took up his abode on shore and married Mrs. Elizabeth B. Myers, July 21, 1819. During the remainder of his life, about nineteen years, or for the last part of that period at least, he occupied the post of master warden of the port of Philadelphia.

[G. F. Emmons, *The Navy of the U. S. from the Commencement, 1775 to 1853* (1853); George Coggeshall, *Hist. of the Am. Privateers and Letters-of-Marque During Our War with England in the Years 1812, '13, and '14* (1856); *Poulson's Am. Daily Advertiser,* July 23, 1819, May 3, 1838; E. S. Maclay, *A Hist. of Am. Privateers* (1899).] G. W. A.

MAFFITT, JOHN NEWLAND (Feb. 22, 1819–May 15, 1886), naval officer, was born at sea between Dublin and New York. He was the third child of John Newland Maffitt, a native of Dublin, and Ann Carnic. Three years after reaching America the elder Maffitt entered the New England Conference of the Methodist Episcopal Church. Although he later became prominent in the ministry and in 1841 was chaplain of the House of Representatives, he was in such reduced circumstances in 1824 that he permitted his brother, Dr. William Maffitt, of Ellerslie, near Fayetteville, N. C., to adopt John Newland, Jr. After four years in his uncle's home, young Maffitt was sent to school at White Plains, N. Y., where he remained until his appointment as midshipman in the United States Navy, Feb. 25, 1832.

He trained chiefly on the sloop-of-war *St. Louis* (West Indian Squadron) and the frigate *Constitution* (Mediterranean flagship), and was promoted to passed midshipman, June 28, 1838. He remained on sea duty, principally as acting master on the frigate *Macedonian* (West Indian flagship), until the spring of 1842, when he was detached and ordered to the Coast Survey. He spent sixteen years charting the New England and South Atlantic coasts. He was promoted to lieutenant as of June 25, 1843; but in 1857 he was placed on the reserve list on furlough pay by the retiring board, the reasons given being that his prolonged absence from the Navy had impaired his professional fitness. This decision was reversed by a court of inquiry—the evidence showing that his work as a chief of the hydrographic party had demonstrated not only a very high order of scientific ability but unexcelled efficiency as a navigator and disciplinarian. Upon being restored to the active list, he was ordered to the Cuban station (June 1, 1858), on which he remained, except for a brief interlude in the

Coast Survey office, until his resignation, Apr. 28, 1861. He commanded the brig-of-war *Dolphin* and the war steamer *Crusader,* in which he captured the slavers *Echo, Bogota,* and *William R. Kibby* and the pirate brig *Young Antonio.*

On May 8, 1861, he was appointed a lieutenant in the Confederate States Navy. He performed three tours of duty in command of combat ships—the gunboat *Savannah,* Port Royal Squadron (May 9 to Nov. 11, 1861), the cruiser *Florida* (May 4, 1862, to Sept. 17, 1863), and the ironclad *Albemarle,* stationed at Plymouth, N. C. (June 25, 1864, to Sept. 20, 1864); three tours as captain in the blockade-running service —on the transports *Cecile* and *Theodora* (Jan. 7, 1862, to May 4, 1862), on the *Florie* and *Lillian* (Sept. 17, 1863, to June 25, 1864), and on the *Owl* (Sept. 20, 1864, to June 1865); and one detail on shore duty—as engineer officer on the staff of Gen. Robert E. Lee, Nov. 11, 1861, to Jan. 7, 1862. His last trip in the *Owl*—striving to enter Confederate territory with an important cargo of government freight at Wilmington, and traversing the coast to Galveston before gaining a harbor—was a classic in blockade running. His service on the *Florida* won him promotion to commander (Apr. 29, 1863), "for gallant and meritorious conduct . . . in running the blockade in and out of the port of Mobile against an overwhelming force of the enemy and under his fire, and since in actively cruising against and destroying the enemy's commerce" (*Maffitt, post,* p. 306). The citation only faintly suggests the adventure, which insured him an enduring place in naval annals. When he took command of the *Florida* at Nassau she was only partially equipped, and he proceeded to Mobile to complete the equipment and recruiting. Through an inadvertence, no sights, rammers, or sponges had been provided for the guns, and he was unable to return the enemy's fire. The crew, furthermore, was in such a state of decimation from yellow fever that his mad run through the blockading squadron into Mobile was an extraordinary achievement. He later captured twenty-two merchantmen (Mrs. Maffitt in her biography, *post,* adds three not verifiable in official records), and fitted out two tenders, which in turn made twenty-three captures. On July 8, 1863, he put to flight the U. S. S. *Ericsson.* His armament consisted of two 7-inch, and six 6-inch rifles and one 12-pounder howitzer.

For nearly two years after the war he was in command of the British steamship *Widgeon,* which was chartered by Brazil as a transport in the Paraguayan War; and in 1870 he was for a short time in command of the Cuban Revolutionists' cruiser *Cuba* (*Hornet*). The remainder of his life was spent at "The Moorings," near Wilmington, N. C., where he wrote a novel, *Nautilus, or Cruising under Canvas,* privately printed in 1871, and several magazine articles, among which were "The Life and Services of Raphael Semmes" (*South Atlantic,* Wilmington, N. C., November, December 1877), "Reminiscences of the Confederate Navy" (*United Service,* Philadelphia, October 1880), and "Blockade-Running" (*Ibid.,* June, July 1882). He left one uncompleted memoir on piracy in the West Indies.

Maffitt was married three times: to Mary Florence Murrell of Mobile, Ala., Nov. 17, 1840, a marriage which ended unhappily; to Caroline Laurens Read of Charleston, S. C., Aug. 3, 1852, who died in 1859; and to Emma Martin of Wilmington, N. C., Nov. 23, 1870, who survived him. His children by his three wives numbered seven. His second wife was a widow with three children, the youngest of whom was burned to death while the couple were on their bridal trip. His third wife was the sister-in-law of his eldest son.

[Emma Martin Maffitt, *The Life and Services of John Newland Maffitt* (1906); John Wilkinson, *The Narrative of a Blockade-Runner* (1877); J. D. Bullock, *The Secret Service of the Confederate States in Europe* (London, 1883); James Sprunt, *Chronicles of the Cape Fear River 1660–1916* (2nd ed. 1916), and *Derelicts* (1920); *War of the Rebellion: Official Records* (*Army*); *Official Records of the Union and Confederate Navies*; *Morning Star* (Wilmington, N. C.), May 16, 1886.]

W. M. R., Jr.

MAGEE, CHRISTOPHER LYMAN (Apr. 14, 1848–Mar. 8, 1901), politician, philanthropist, was the son of Elizabeth (Steele) Magee, an Englishwoman, and Christopher Lyman Magee, a hatter of Scotch-Irish descent, grandson of Robert Magee who came to Pennsylvania in 1786 from County Derry, Ireland. Born in Pittsburgh, Pa., the younger Christopher first attended a private school, then entered the public schools, but did not complete his high-school course because of the financial crisis caused by the death of his father. Later, however, he attended Western University for a time as a special student. After a brief career as office boy he secured a political appointment in the office of the city controller in 1864, moved on to the city treasurer's office in 1869, and in 1871 received election as treasurer of Pittsburgh. During his service of four years he reduced the city debt from fifteen to eight million dollars. At the expiration of his second term, he decided to abandon public office as a profession, drew up an ambitious plan which involved control of the politics of Pittsburgh and Allegheny County, and for several years devoted himself to its realization. Almost at once he became an important factor in Allegheny County politics. By 1877 he had become influential in city affairs. An advantageous political alliance in 1879 with William Flinn, a public contractor, materially added to his power, which was further increased when, in 1882, Flinn became chairman of the city Republican executive committee, a position which he held continuously for twenty years. Magee next proceeded to safeguard the permanence of his position by firmly entrenching himself with Pittsburgh business interests. Banks, utilities, and other businesses consistently supported Magee and Flinn in return for deposits of public funds, franchises, and other favors. Magee became the political agent of the Pennsylvania Railroad in Allegheny County and finally, it is reported, in the entire state of Pennsylvania. In spite of more or less friction with M. S. Quay [*q.v.*], he and Flinn controlled the politics of Pittsburgh and Allegheny County with scarcely a break from 1882 to 1899. In the latter year Magee's health began seriously to fail, a bitter fight with Quay on the opposite side developed over the award of public contracts, and in 1903, two years after Magee's death, the Magee-Flinn machine disappeared.

Beginning with 1876 Magee sat as a delegate in every Republican National Convention. In 1884 he served as national committeeman and in 1892 led the Harrison forces in the national convention. With two exceptions he attended every state convention from 1872 until his death, twice held the post of secretary to the state committee, and was twice elected to the state Senate. His public-office record also included a ten-year term as fire commissioner of Pittsburgh and a term as treasurer of the Pittsburgh sinking-fund commission. He occupied a prominent place in Pittsburgh business circles, owned considerable real estate, a newspaper, and stock in more than fifty enterprises; served as director of fifteen banks, insurance companies, and traction lines and as president of the thirty-million-dollar Consolidated Traction Company; and left an estate appraised at more than four million dollars. In 1878 he married Eleanor Louise Gillespie and entered into Pittsburgh social life to the extent of listing in the *Social Register*. He possessed more than average physical distinction. Finely poised, tactful, dashing, he was unusually magnetic in personality. He belonged to several prominent clubs, held a rather casual membership in the First Methodist Protestant Church, and served as life trustee of the Carnegie Fine Arts and Museum Fund, trustee of Western University and Pittsburg College of the Holy Ghost, and president of the trustees of Mercy Hospital. He gave $100,000 for a zoölogical garden as a Christmas present to the children of Pittsburgh, a $15,000 pathological laboratory to Mercy Hospital, $10,000 toward a newsboys' home, and left the bulk of his large estate for the establishment of the Elizabeth Steele Magee Hospital.

[Harold Zink, *City Bosses in the U. S.* (1930); Lincoln Steffens, *The Shame of the Cities* (1904); *Proc. . . . Nat. Municipal League*, 1896, 1902; obituaries in *Pittsburgh Commercial Gazette, Pittsburgh Press, Pittsburgh Chronicle Telegraph, Pittsburg Post, Pittsburg Leader, Pittsburg Dispatch,* issues of Mar. 9, 1901.]

H. Z.

MAGIE, WILLIAM JAY (Dec. 9, 1832–Jan. 15, 1917), jurist, was the son of David Magie, a Presbyterian minister who preached in Elizabeth, N. J., from early manhood until his death in 1865. His mother was Ann Frances (Wilson), a woman of considerable wealth, who for many years devoted herself to the needy in her husband's parish. The earliest member of the Magie family, of whom reliable information exists, was John MacGhie who was born in 1659 and died in 1735. He was banished from Scotland, according to tradition, for the part he took in a religious controversy. Arriving at Perth Amboy, N. J., in 1685, he soon settled in Elizabeth, where the family subsequently remained. William Jay Magie attended school and prepared for college in Elizabeth, entered the College of New Jersey (Princeton), and was graduated in 1852. He studied law under Francis B. Chetwood of Elizabeth, and was admitted to the bar as an attorney in 1856, and as a counselor three years later. While studying law he was elected clerk of the court of common pleas of Elizabeth, and continued in this office until the abolition of the court in 1857. He was elected superintendent of schools in Elizabeth in 1857, serving in that capacity until 1861. For two years, 1858 to 1860, he was also a commissioner. The records show that he organized and greatly improved the school system, many of the regulations drafted by him being yet in force. He was married, Oct. 1, 1857, to Sarah Frances, daughter of Jediah and Abby (Johnson) Baldwin. The years immediately following were fully occupied with a rapidly growing law practice. He found time, nevertheless, to serve as prosecutor of the pleas of Union County from 1866 to 1871, and as state senator from 1876 to 1879. He declined a nomination for reëlection to the Senate, and shortly thereafter refused to stand for election to the national House of Representatives. As a legislator he served with distinction upon the judiciary committee and gave much time to the work of drafting bills, in compliance with the constitutional mandate of 1875, providing for the government of municipalities through general laws.

His judicial career began in 1880 with his appointment by Gov. George B. McClellan to the supreme court of New Jersey. He was elevated to the office of chief justice in 1897, and in 1900 was appointed by Gov. Foster M. Voorhees as chancellor of the state to fill out an unexpired term. In 1901 he was elected for the full term of seven years. Thus he sat as a justice of the supreme court for seventeen years, as chief justice for three, and as chancellor for nearly eight years, until his retirement early in 1908, a threefold honor not conferred on any other member of the New Jersey judiciary. His long judicial career was marked by constant attention to duty. If any part of his activities were to be singled out for special excellence, it would be his work at the circuit. From 1891 to 1917 he was a trustee of Princeton University. Upon his retirement from the bench he was chosen trustee of the public library in Elizabeth and became president of the board, a position which he continued to hold by reëlection each year until his death.

[Frank Bergen, "Memorial of the Late Chancellor William Jay Magie," *N. J. State Bar Asso. Year Book*, 1917–18; *Memorial to William Jay Magie by the Board of Trustees of the Free Public Library of Elizabeth, N. J.* (1917); 86 *N. J. Equity Reports*, pp. xxiii–xxviii; *Manual of the Legislature of N. J.*, 1908; *Who's Who in America*, 1916–17; *N. Y. Times*, Jan. 16, 1917; information from a daughter.] W. S. C.

MAGILL, EDWARD HICKS (Sept. 24, 1825–Dec. 10, 1907), teacher, college president, was born in Bucks County, Pa., the son of Jonathan Paxson and Mary (Watson) Magill. He spent his boyhood in a Quaker farmer's household and received his formal education in a "monthly meeting school" and in Westtown Boarding School, both under the control of the Society of Friends. At the age of sixteen, he began his teaching career, but after seven years in elementary-school work he became convinced that he needed more adequate training. Accordingly he spent a year (1848–49) in Williston Seminary, Easthampton, Mass., another at Yale, and in 1852 received the degree of A.B. at Brown University and three years later that of A.M. Following his graduation, he was married to Sarah Warner Beans, by whom he had four daughters and a son. From 1852 to 1859 he was principal of the classical department in the Providence, R. I., high school. His success in this position led to his being engaged as sub-master of the Public Latin School, Boston, in which position he served until 1867. The following year he spent in travel and study in Europe.

At the opening of Swarthmore College in November 1869, he became principal of its preparatory department, and in 1871, president of the college, serving until his resignation in 1889. When he became connected with Swarthmore, there was no coeducational institution of higher learning in the eastern section of the United States. The making of this experiment a success was Magill's life-work and it constitutes his chief service to the world of learning and of citizenship. When he assumed the principalship, the preparatory department included three-fourths of the 170 students enrolled in the institution. As president of the latter, one of his most difficult tasks was to prevent the preparatory school from subordinating the college, and gradually to eliminate the school entirely. By the time of his retirement as president, the preparatory department enrolled only 33% of the total number of students, and three years later it was entirely abolished. This achievement was accomplished in the face of determined opposition on the part of some members of the board of managers and a fraction of the institution's constituency, and not without the loss of some financial support. Magill's insistence on an institution of genuine college rank was all the more remarkable because of his own previous experience in secondary-school work.

His teaching before he went to Swarthmore was devoted chiefly to Latin and French; he varied his administrative labors at the college with the occasional teaching of these languages, and was professor of them for some twelve years after his retirement as president. He published several French grammars and a series of readers, designed for his own method of teaching the language, which met with encouraging success. Almost every year found him devising some new and better way of mastering a foreign language "through eye, ear, tongue and hand." An illustration of the courageous enthusiasm which characterized all his undertakings was his attempt, at the age of seventy, through letters written by his own hand, to persuade the manufacturers of America to solve the labor problem by means of profit-sharing. His introduction of a system whereby American students of French and French students of English exchanged letters, and his founding, in 1887, of the College Association of Pennsylvania, which finally became the Association of the Colleges and Preparatory Schools of the Middle States and Maryland, are noteworthy illustrations of his pioneering spirit and executive ability. He was married a second time, in his seventy-seventh year, Apr. 24, 1902, to Sarah Elizabeth Gardner of New York. During the last part of his life he was occupied with literary labors, including the writing of an autobiography, *Sixty-five Years in the Life of a Teacher, 1841–1906* (1907). His death occurred in New York.

[In addition to Magill's autobiography, see Wm. P. Holcomb, "Swarthmore College," in C. H. Haskins and W. I. Hull, *A Hist. of Higher Educ. in Pa.* (1902); *Who's Who in America,* 1906–07; *Friends' Intelligencer,* Twelfth mo. 21, 1907; *N. Y. Times,* Dec. 11, 1907.] W. I. H.

MAGINNIS, MARTIN (Oct. 27, 1841–Mar. 27, 1919), soldier, Montana politician, congressman, was born in Wayne County, N. Y. His parents, Patrick and Winifred (Devine) Maginnis, had come from Ireland about 1838. In 1851 the family moved to Lasalle, Ill., and in 1853 to Red Wing, Minn. Martin Maginnis attended Hamline University, then at Red Wing. Before graduating, he enlisted in the 1st Minnesota Volunteers and he served throughout the Civil War. He was in most of the battles of the Army of the Potomac and by July 1863 had attained the rank of captain. After Cold Harbor he was sent to Tennessee and assigned to the staff of Andrew Johnson, military governor of the state. At the end of the war he was mustered out with the rank of major. For a while he worked for a newspaper in Red Wing, Minn., but in 1866 he organized a party of about 150 men whom he led from Minnesota along the northern route to Montana. For a year he engaged in mining and then he joined with Peter Ronan in editing the *Daily Rocky Mountain Gazette,* which later became the *Helena Independent* (Henry N. Blake, in *Contributions to the Historical Society of Montana,* vol. V, 1904, p. 255). On Mar. 11, 1868, he was married to Louise E. Mann of Pontiac, Mich.

In a few years he became influential as a politician. His newspaper was the leading Democratic publication of the territory and he was a popular campaign orator. In 1872 he was elected delegate to Congress where he served continuously for six terms. His chief activities in the House were "serving Montana's interests." He persuaded Congress to reduce the size of the Indian reservations and to open the lands to white settlement. He obtained appropriations to build a number of military posts, secured an assay office for Helena, and induced Congress to build a federal penitentiary at Deer Lodge, later turned over to the territory. Through his influence, Congress granted land for a state university and for other state institutions. When the Northern Pacific was under fire on account of the failure of Jay Cooke, he defended its charter and secured an extension of time for the completion of the road. He also took a prominent part in securing legislation granting railways free right-of-way through the public domain and through Indian reservations. He supported appropriations for a large army, and he urged Congress to retain control of the public domain, instead of intrusting it to administrative officials.

After his retirement from Congress in 1885, having been defeated for reëlection, Maginnis engaged in mining but did not lose his interest in politics. In 1889 he was a member of the state constitutional convention. He was again defeated for representative in Congress in 1889 and, in 1890, although chosen for United States senator by one faction calling itself the legal state legislature, he was denied his seat in Washington. Governor Toole appointed him land commissioner, and for the next few years he fought the Northern Pacific's claim to minerals on its land grant, finally winning his suit for independent prospectors and miners. In 1900 he was appointed to fill the unexpired term of William A. Clark in the United States Senate, but he was not seated. A lifelong Democrat, he was delegate to eight successive national conventions. He was quick to comprehend public sentiment and to give it expression, but his popularity outlasted his influence as a politician. He died at Los Angeles, Cal., in his seventy-eighth year.

[*Who's Who in America,* 1918–19; *Biog. Dir. Am. Cong.* (1928); *Progressive Men of the State of Mont.* (n.d.); "A Partial Sketch of the Civil and Mil. Service of Maj. Martin Maginnis," *Contributions to the Hist. Soc. of Mont.,* vol. VIII (1917), and references in *Ibid.,* vols. II–VII (1896–1910); R. G. Raymer, *Montana: The Land and the People* (1930), vol. I; Tom Stout, *Montana: Its Story and Biog.* (1921), vol. I; *Proc. and Debates of the Const. Convention . . . of Mont. . . . 1889* (1921); *Los Angeles Times,* Mar. 28, 1919.] P. C. P.

MAGOFFIN, BERIAH (Apr. 18, 1815–Feb. 28, 1885), lawyer, farmer, governor of Kentucky, brother of James Wiley Magoffin [*q.v.*], was born in Harrodsburg, Ky. His father, Beriah Magoffin, was a native of County Down, Ireland; his mother, Jane McAfee, was a daughter of Samuel McAfee, an early Kentucky pioneer. He attended Centre College at Danville and was graduated there in 1835. Thereupon he began the study of law privately and afterward entered the law department of Transylvania College at Lexington where he finished his course in 1838. Immediately he moved to Mississippi and began the practice of law in Jackson. He remained in Mississippi only about a year, however, returning to Kentucky in 1839 in ill health. He now began the practice of law in his native town, and upon the death of his partner, he succeeded to a remunerative business. In 1840 Gov. Robert P. Letcher, a Whig, appointed him, a Democrat, police judge for Harrodsburg. Ten years later he ran for the state Senate and was elected, but the next year, 1851, he refused to make the race for Congress. He ran for Democratic elector in 1844, 1848, 1852, and 1856, but it was only in the last year that he served since Kentucky was lost by the Democrats in the other years. He was also delegate to the Democratic national conventions in 1848, 1856, and 1860. In 1855 he was nominated for lieutenant-governor, but the Know-Nothings won the state that year.

In 1859 he was nominated for governor and was elected over Joshua F. Bell by a vote of more than 8,000. He took office just on the eve of secession. Realizing the dangers which would beset this strategic border-state, Magoffin did all he could to prevent the disruption of the Democratic party at Charleston. On Dec. 9, 1860, he presented to the governors of the slave states a plan for saving the Union, but it failed to be accepted. He then became an ardent advocate of the Crittenden Compromise. Although a believer in secession as a right, he was opposed to the piecemeal process of leaving the Union. He pleaded for a convention of all the Southern states and declared that a solution could be worked out within forty-eight hours which would suit both sections. Believing that the people of his state should vote on what they wished to do, he called the legislature to meet in January 1861. But the legislature, which had elected John C. Breckinridge United States senator, refused to call a sovereign convention. Magoffin defiantly refused Lincoln's call for troops (Apr. 15, 1861), and a week later he refused Davis' call for troops, though secretly he allowed Confederate recruiting agents to raise their banners in the state. He summoned another session of the legislature in May, which again refused to call a sovereign convention. Instead, it allowed six arbiters, chosen in party caucus, and including Magoffin, to work out a plan which the legislature pledged itself to adopt. This move resulted in the state's declaring its neutrality, the House and Senate passing separate resolutions, and the governor issuing his proclamation on May 20. Magoffin came to terms with McClellan, in command of troops in Cincinnati, and established understandings with both President Davis and President Lincoln. But neutrality was not enough; he sought to secure the adhesion of Ohio, Indiana, Missouri, and Tennessee to a plan for mediation, but the Northern states refused to entertain the idea. Kentucky's position was impossible. By September her neutrality had been broken so many times by both sides that the Confederates decided to march into the state in full force, thereby beating the Federals in by a short time. The legislature passed a resolution (Sept. 11, 1861) calling upon the Governor to order the Confederates out. Magoffin vetoed it, but the legislature, by this time strongly Union in its feelings, passed it over his veto, as indeed it did many other bills looking toward Kentucky's full participation on the side of the Union. Magoffin obstructed this policy wherever he thought the constitution was not being observed and thereby incurred the ill will of the Unionists. Stripped of his power and threatened with assassination he resigned in August 1862, though he was allowed to designate his successor.

He retired to Harrodsburg for the remainder of the war and did not reënter politics except from 1867 to 1869 when he represented his county, Mercer, in the legislature. After the war he took the position that Kentucky should accept with resignation the results of the conflict. He advocated Kentucky's ratification of the Thirteenth Amendment and the granting of civil rights to the negroes. This position lost him the friendship of many Democrats. In 1878 President Hayes appointed him an honorary commissioner to the Paris Exposition. Magoffin had married, in April 1840, Anna Shelby, a granddaughter of Gov. Isaac Shelby, and to them were born five sons and five daughters. Through judicious investments in Chicago, he became one of the wealthiest men in the state. He died on his ancestral estate in Harrodsburg.

[Short sketches of Magoffin can be found in Lewis and R. H. Collins, *Hist. of Ky.* (1874), vol. II, and in *The Biog. Encyc. of Ky.* (1878). For the main facts concerning his public career, see Collins, *supra*, vol. I; R. M. McElroy, *Ky. in the Nation's Hist.* (1909), and E. M. Coulter, *The Civil War and Readjustment in Ky.* (1926). The state archives in Frankfort contain his state papers. Some of the important documents relative to his position in the secession and neutrality movement are in *War of the Rebellion: Official Records* (*Army*) and *Appletons' Ann. Cyc.*, 1861–63.]

E. M. C.

MAGOFFIN, JAMES WILEY (1799–Sept. 27, 1868), trader, American consul, and early pioneer in Texas, was born at Harrodsburg, Mercer County, Ky., the son of Beriah and Jane (McAfee) Magoffin. The family consisted of seven sons, of whom James was the eldest, and three daughters. Some time prior to 1825 James Wiley Magoffin engaged in trading expeditions into old Mexico, and the records of the Department of State contain the bare announcement (his name being spelled McGoffin) of his appointment as American consul at Saltillo on Mar. 3, 1825, the first appointee at that post. This overland trade, beset by many dangers and hazards proved very lucrative. Magoffin, who evidently had the brave frontier spirit combined with inherited Irish buoyancy and joviality, became well known and liked in Mexico, and was called by the Mexicans "Don Santiago." He married Mary Gertrude Valdez, of Chihuahua, in 1830, and several children were born to them there. In 1844 he left Chihuahua with his family and settled near Independence, Mo. His wife died there in January 1845. About this time war was declared with Mexico. Senator Thomas H. Benton of Missouri presented Magoffin to President Polk, and on June 18, 1846, Secretary of War Marcy wrote to Gen. Stephen Watts Kearny saying that the President was so favorably impressed with "Colonel Magoffin" that he had engaged him to assist in the expedition (*House Executive Document 17,* 31 Cong., 1 Sess., pp. 240–41). Thereupon Magoffin went in advance of Kearny to Santa Fé and very cleverly induced Gen. Manuel Armijo to retire, thus enabling Kearny with his small army to enter Santa Fé on Aug. 18, 1846, and take possession of all of the Department of New Mexico without firing a shot.

After this success Magoffin, under directions of Kearny, went forward to Chihuahua to render the same service for Gen. J. E. Wool, but the authorities there arrested him as a spy and cast him into prison. He was saved from execution only through his popularity with Mexican officers, whom he entertained lavishly. He was, however, confined at Chihuahua and afterward at Durango until the end of the war (1847). By a provision of an act of Mar. 3, 1849, Congress authorized the payment of $50,000 for secret service rendered during the Mexican War. Although Magoffin was not named, the sum was designed to compensate him for his expenses and losses. After a change of administration he was finally offered $30,000, which he accepted, preferring patriotically to be underpaid rather than to wrangle over finances. He then settled in Texas, opposite the Mexican town of El Paso, and built up and owned the township of Magoffinsville, which is now a part of the city of El Paso, Tex. During the Civil War he furnished supplies to the Confederates. He died at San Antonio, Tex., in 1868. His sons, Joseph and Samuel, served in the Confederate army, the latter giving his life to that cause. His brother Beriah [*q.v.*] was governor of Kentucky.

[W. E. Connelley, *War with Mexico, 1846–47: Doniphan's Expedition and the Conquest of N. Mex. and Cal.* (1907); Stella M. Drumm, ed., *Down the Santa Fé Trail and into Mexico: The Diary of Susan Shelby Magoffin, 1846–47* (1926); T. H. Benton, *Thirty Years' View* (2 vols., 1854–56); P. St. G. Cooke, *The Conquest of N. Mex. and Cal.* (1878); H. H. Bancroft, *Hist. of Ariz. and N. Mex.* (1889); J. H. Smith, *The War with Mexico* (2 vols., 1919); *San Antonio Express,* Sept. 29, 1868.]

A. E. I.

MAGOON, CHARLES EDWARD (Dec. 5, 1861–Jan. 14, 1920), lawyer, civil administrator, was born on a farm in Steele County, Minn., the son of Henry C. and Mehitable W. (Clement) Magoon. After the family had moved to a homestead in Platte County, Neb., he attended the preparatory department 1876–78 and for one year the college of arts of the University of Nebraska. He studied law in the offices of Mason & Wheeler in Lincoln and later he became a member of the law firm of Wheedon & Magoon, practising law in Lincoln from 1882 to 1899. During this period of his life he became interested in military affairs and served as major and judge-advocate, Nebraska National Guard. He also compiled and published a treatise of considerable local value entitled *The Municipal Code of Lincoln* (1889). In the year 1899, at the instance of Assistant Secretary of War Meiklejohn, Magoon became law-officer of the Bureau of Insular Affairs of the War Department, serving in that capacity until 1904 and specializing in matters growing out of the acquisition by the United States of Cuba, Puerto Rico, and the Philippines. As such, he prepared and submitted to the Secretary of War (Feb. 12, 1900), an exhaustive study, *Report on the Legal Status of the Territory ... Acquired by the United States During the War with Spain.* He also rendered many important interpretations of United States law affecting the country's new possessions, which were ultimately assembled and published under the title, *The Law of Civil Government in Territory Subject to Military Occupation* (1902). In a prefatory introduction to this work, Secretary Elihu Root stated that it was of such value to him in deciding important War Department problems affecting insular possessions, that he ordered the reports printed as a public document for the use of those concerned with the government of the Philippine Islands.

Magoon served as general counsel of the Isthmian Canal Commission, 1904–05, and as a member of the Commission, 1905–06. From May 25, 1905, until Oct. 12, 1906, he served as governor of the Canal Zone and for most of this period also acted as United States envoy extraordinary and minister plenipotentiary to the Republic of Panama. From Oct. 12, 1906, until Jan. 28, 1909, he served as provisional governor of Cuba during a most important period in the Island's recrudescence, in which his administration of affairs was confronted with the difficult problems concerning the maintenance of order, the development of commercial prosperity, and the inauguration of a sound financial system. Not the least of his far-reaching reforms in Cuba was the introduction of adequate sanitary measures throughout the Island and the almost complete elimination of the scourge of yellow fever. Of his administration during this period, Secretary Taft wrote to President Roosevelt, Jan. 14, 1908: "Governor Magoon has conducted matters in a most clear-headed and tactful way. . . . He has successfully handled numerous economic questions. . . . He has had labor troubles which through his conciliatory but impartial attitude have been brought to an end" (Preface to *Annual Report of Charles E. Magoon, Provisional Governor of Cuba . . . 1907*). Withal, Magoon succeeded in winning the high regard and esteem of the Cuban people.

On Feb. 19, 1904, Magoon delivered before the Patria Club of New York City an important address, printed under the title *What Followed the Flag in the Philippines* (1904), dealing in a masterly way with policies governing United States sovereignty over occupied territory, the inauguration in the Philippines of a government of law in which the Filipino people were permitted to exercise certain privileges of citizenship, and the insistence upon a policy of complete religious freedom and tolerance in newly acquired territory. Magoon never married. After his retirement he made his home in Lincoln, Neb., and Washington, D. C., passing away suddenly in the latter city after an operation for appendicitis, in the fifty-ninth year of his age.

[The Bureau of Insular Affairs of the War Department has made available considerable information affecting Magoon's service with the Bureau, up to his incumbency as governor of Cuba. Other sources include: *Who's Who in America*, 1918–19; R. C. Weightman, "Cuba's Am. Gov.," *Rev. of Revs.*, Nov. 1906; *Omaha World-Herald*, and *N. Y. Times*, Jan. 15, 1920; *Evening Star* (Washington, D. C.), Jan. 14, 15, 1920.]

C. D. R.

MAGOUN, GEORGE FREDERIC (Mar. 29, 1821–Jan. 30, 1896), Congregational clergyman, college president, was born at Bath, Me., where his grandfather, Elisha Magoun, a native of Scituate, Mass., was a pioneer ship-builder. His father, David Crooker Magoun, was ship-owner, merchant, bank president, mayor of Bath, member of the Maine legislature in both branches, and one of the authors of the first state prohibitory law; his mother, Hannah (Webb), was the daughter of William Webb, collector of the port of Bath. The Magoun family, of Huguenot descent, had been driven by persecution from France to the North of Ireland, when John Magoun had come to America, settling in 1660 on a farm three miles long on the Massachusetts coast, near Scituate.

George Frederic was graduated from Bath Academy in 1837, received the degree of B.A. from Bowdoin in 1841, and studied theology at Andover and Yale. He is represented in *The Bowdoin Poets* (1840) by a poem on "The Gathering of the Covenanters." In 1844 he went West, serving as principal of a school at Galena, Ill., 1844–45, and of the academy at Platteville, Wis., 1845–46, but then returned to Andover to complete his theological training. He was ordained, Jan. 25, 1848, at Shullsburg, Wis., where he founded a home-mission Congregational church. He was subsequently, for three years, pastor of the Second Presbyterian Church at Galena (1848–51), and served, for five years each, Congregational churches at Davenport and Lyons, Iowa. Between 1851 and 1855 he also studied and practised law.

In 1856 he became a trustee of Iowa College, Davenport, which in 1859 was removed to Grinnell. He was elected president of the college in 1862, but since most of the college men were serving in the Civil War, he continued in his pastorate at Lyons for nearly three years, resigning in 1864 to assume his academic duties. Endowed with superabundant energy, besides carrying on the administrative work of the presidency he taught in the college, wrote many articles, preached and gave public addresses, and spent himself without stint in the raising of funds for the institution after the burning of one of the two buildings in 1871 and the total destruction of all the buildings by a tornado in 1882. He repeatedly declined pastorates and college presidencies at salaries far greater than that paid by the young college at Grinnell. After twenty years' active service, in 1884 he retired from the presidency, but continued for six years longer to teach mental and moral philosophy, a task for which his metaphysical turn of mind peculiarly fitted him.

Magoun was fearless and somewhat combative in temperament, a strong and uncompromising partisan of things be believed in, great-hearted and tender in his affections. A man of large stature, commanding presence, and fine voice, he was recognized, not only as an effective pulpit orator, but also as a powerful advocate of such causes as temperance, anti-slavery, and foreign missions. He was a stanch Republican, having assisted at the forming of the party in 1854. Three times he was a delegate to Peace Congresses in Europe, and in 1882 he represented the Congregationalists of Iowa, Maine, and the National Council at the semi-centennial of the Congregational Union of England and Wales. In 1872 he gave the first of the Boston Lectures, and from 1877 to 1879 lectured on home missions at Andover Theological Seminary. His baccalaureate addresses at Grinnell were events in the life of the community. His publications include contributions to various journals, an address, *The Past of Our College* (1895), and a book on one of the religious and educational pioneers of the West: *Asa Turner, a Home Missionary Patriarch and His Times* (1889). He was twice married: in 1847 to Abby Anne Hyde of Bath, Me., who died at Lyons in 1864; and in 1870, at Waterbury, Conn., to Elizabeth E. Earle.

[*Portr. and Biog. Record of Johnson, Poweshiek and Iowa Counties, Iowa* (1893); B. F. Gue, *Hist. of Iowa* (1903), vol. IV; T. O. Douglass, *The Pilgrims of Iowa* (1911); J. B. Grinnell, *Men and Events of Forty Years* (1891); *Grinnell Herald*, Feb. 4, 1896; *Minutes of the Iowa Congreg. General Assoc.*, 1896, p. 46; *Obit. Record Grads. Bowdoin Coll.*, 1896; *Congreg. Year Book* (1897); *Iowa State Register* (Des Moines), Jan. 31, 1896; also information from family.] J. S. N.

MAGRATH, ANDREW GORDON (Feb. 8, 1813–Apr. 9, 1893), jurist and governor of South Carolina, was born, lived, and died in Charleston. His father, John Magrath, was a soldier in the Irish rebellion of 1798 who, captured by the British, escaped and fled to Charleston; his mother, Maria Gordon, came to Charleston from Scotland in 1792. He received his early education at the private school of Bishop England in Charleston and graduated in 1831 from the South Carolina College. In 1835, after studying law in the office of James L. Petigru and spending a few months at the Harvard Law School, he began the practice of law in Charleston and, with the exception of brief intervals in 1840 and 1842 when he represented the parishes of St. Philip and St. Michael in the South Carolina House of Representatives, continued in this profession until 1856. He insisted on the right of slaveholders to take their property into the newly acquired territory of the United States, and in 1848 he supported Taylor against Cass for president on the ground that the former, although a Whig, was a Southerner and a slaveholder. In 1856 he was elected as a delegate to the National Democratic Convention at Cincinnati, but he resigned before the meeting of the convention to accept an appointment as judge of the United States district court, then in great disfavor in South Carolina and rarely resorted to. He won for the court the confidence of the bar of the state, raised it to a position of commanding distinction, and together with James Connor, the district attorney, won national reputation in the cases of the *Echo* and the *Wanderer*, vessels accused of violating the law against the African slave trade.

He opposed secession as inexpedient when it was advocated by Robert Barnwell Rhett in 1852, but with the election of Abraham Lincoln as president he accepted the view that there were sufficient grounds for separation and that the dissolution of the relations of South Carolina with the Union was necessary to the welfare of the state. On Nov. 7, 1860, he resigned his position as United States district judge with the dramatic declaration that "the Temple of Justice, raised under the Constitution of the United States, is now closed" (*Charleston Daily Courier*, Nov. 8, 1860, p. 1). He was immediately afterward elected a delegate to the secession convention, where he was active in influencing the withdrawal of the state from the Union. On Dec. 30, 1860, he was appointed secretary of state in the executive council of Governor Pickens and directed much of the correspondence of the governor with President Buchanan and Major Anderson regarding the disposition of Fort Sumter. Shortly after the establishment of the Confederate government he was appointed judge of the Confederate district court in South Carolina. Although he upheld the validity of the Confederate sequestration and conscription acts (*Courier*, Nov. 9, 1861, Schwab, *post*, p. 195), some of his decisions, particularly the one declaring the Confederate war tax upon state securities unconstitutional (*Courier*, Apr. 21, 1862), ran counter to the policy of the government at Richmond and appear to have excluded him from its confidence and deprived him of its favor.

In 1864 he resigned from the moribund Confederate court and was elected governor by the legislature, the last governor of South Carolina to be elected in this manner. As governor he took an extreme state-rights position, stating in his inaugural address on Dec. 20 that his efforts would be directed equally toward resisting the invaders from the North and the encroachments of the Confederate government upon the powers of the state. He addressed strong letters to Jefferson Davis criticizing the policy of conscripting South Carolina regiments for the defense of Richmond and even entered into correspondence with Governors Vance of North Carolina and Brown of Georgia with a view to making plans for the defense of their respective states independent of the Confederate government. After the burning of Columbia, however, he was unable to reorganize the state government, and, on May 22, 1865, he issued a proclamation advising submission to the Federal authorities. On May 28 he was arrested and shortly afterward, upon the order of the President, imprisoned at Fort Pulaski. On Nov. 23 the President directed that he be released upon taking the oath of allegiance as prescribed in the amnesty proclamation. He resumed the practice of law and lived quietly in Charleston until his death in 1893. He was a man of unusual personal charm and graciousness of manner. On Mar. 8, 1843, he was married to Emma C. Mikell, by whom he had five children. During his imprisonment at Fort Pulaski he entered into a correspondence with Mary McCord, of Columbia, previously unknown to him, and upon his release they were married. They had no children.

[Leroy Youmans, "A Sketch of the Life of Gov. Magrath," Charleston *Year Book*, 1895, pp. 365–75, is reprinted in U. R. Brooks, *S. C. Bench and Bar*, vol. I (1908). See also: S. W. Crawford, *The Genesis of the Civil War* (1887); J. C. Schwab, *The Confed. States of America, 1861–65* (1901); and *War of the Rebellion: Official Records* (*Army*). The files of the Charleston *Mercury* and the Charleston *Courier* are valuable, and there is an excellent obituary in the *Courier*, Apr. 10, 1893. The Charleston Historical Society possesses copies of several letters written by Magrath to Johnson, Seward, and others while he was confined in Fort Pulaski, and also possesses three large letter-books containing copies of letters and telegrams sent by him while governor.] J. W. P—n.

MAGRUDER, GEORGE LLOYD (Nov. 1, 1848–Jan. 28, 1914), physician, sanitarian, was the son of Thomas Contee and Elizabeth Olivia (Morgan) Magruder. His earliest American ancestor on the paternal side was Alexander McGruder of the Scotch clan Gregor. His father was paymaster with the Washington aqueduct and capitol extension and later disbursing officer under Quartermaster-Gen. M. C. Meigs. Lloyd Magruder had the advantages of both private and public school training and in 1868 received from Gonzaga College, Washington, D. C., the degree of A.B. In 1870 he graduated in medicine at Georgetown Medical School and remained in Washington to follow his chosen profession until his death. Early in his medical career he was appointed professor of chemistry at Gonzaga College (1871–73); afterward the medical faculty of Georgetown selected him prosector of minor surgery. He rapidly rose to the chair of professor of materia medica (1883–96) and was also dean and treasurer of the medical college. During the year 1871–72 he was physician to the poor and from 1883 to 1887 he administered to the police and fire departments.

Magruder was active as a member of the American Medical Society, the Washington Obstetrical and Gynecological Society, the American Public Health Association, and the Washington Academy of Sciences. He was also a member of the Medical Association of the District of Columbia and of the Medical Society of the District of Columbia. In the latter organization he was corresponding secretary, 1876–77, vice-president, 1895, and a member of the executive committee, 1902–03. He wrote several papers, including *Some Practical Observations Made at the Department of Diseases of Children at the Central Dispensary* (1880); *The Milk Supply of Washington* (1907); and *The Solution of the Milk Problem* (1913). He visualized the need for increased hospital facilities and the necessity of prompt treatment for accident cases. In cooperation with Dr. H. H. Barker and others he founded the Central Dispensary (later Emergency Hospital) and was a member of the consulting staff from its opening, May 1, 1871, until his death. He was also eager to increase clinical facilities for Georgetown medical department and was influential in the founding of Georgetown University Hospital, which opened on Aug. 1, 1898. After thirteen years as dean of the medical school he resigned in 1901. In June 1894 the District commissioners assigned Magruder to draw up a bill to regulate the milk supply for the District of Columbia, and he secured an investigation by the Department of Agriculture of the dairy supply (1906–07). In 1907, at his instigation, a permanent milk commission was established by the District of Columbia authorities.

Magruder's great desire was to make the Capital a healthful place in which to live. He devoted considerable time to ridding the community of all sources of typhoid fever, securing pure water, and closing all city pumps which were a source of infection. He conducted a thorough investigation of the milk supply and the management of dairies which resulted in bringing about the effective legislation regarding the sale of milk. His contribution to humanity was strangely his physical undoing, for the lowered resistance occasioned by the strain of his work exaggerated a glycosuria, with later symptoms of myocarditis, which closed his career. He was survived by his wife, Belle (Burns) Magruder, the daughter of Gen. W. W. Burns, whom he had married on Nov. 22, 1882.

[*Who's Who in America*, 1912–13; *Washington Medic. Annals*, May 1914; *Year Book of the Am. Clan Gregor Soc.*, 1914; J. S. Easby-Smith, *Georgetown Univ. in the District of Columbia* (2 vols., 1907); H. A. Kelly and W. L. Burrage, *Am. Medic. Biogs.* (1920); the *Evening Star* (Wash., D. C.), Jan. 29, 1914.] M. D. M.

MAGRUDER, JOHN BANKHEAD (Aug. 15, 1810–Feb. 18, 1871), Confederate soldier, was born in Winchester, Va., the son of Thomas Magruder and Elizabeth Bankhead. The Magruders were originally members of the unfortunate Scotch Clan Gregor. After the McGregor name had been proscribed in 1603, some of the disbanded clan assumed the name of McGruder.

In 1651 one Alexander McGruder was captured at Worcester, and was sent to Maryland where he started the numerous Maryland McGruder or Magruder family, with its Virginia offshoot. John Bankhead Magruder's early education was in preparation for West Point. Here he was graduated in 1830 with the brevet rank of second lieutenant of infantry. The next year he transferred to the artillery, and for the following fifteen years served at scattered garrisons, in the occupation of Texas, and in the Seminole War. In 1836 he was promoted first lieutenant. After the outbreak of the Mexican War he was put in charge of the light artillery of Pillow's division. For "gallant and meritorious conduct" he was thrice promoted, finally being appointed, after Chapultepec, lieutenant-colonel. While other officers showed no eagerness to serve under the "restless and hot-tempered Magruder," Thomas Jonathan Jackson bent all his energies and got command under him, for Jackson knew that "if any fighting was to be done Magruder would be 'on hand'" (G. F. R. Henderson, *Stonewall Jackson and the American Civil War,* 1898, I, p. 41).

Magruder later was stationed in Maryland, California, and at Newport, R. I. During this period he devoted himself largely to society, his courtly bearing and "brilliant ability to bring appearances up to the necessity of the occasion" winning him the title of "Prince John" (*Confederate Military History,* III, p. 633). At Newport his entertainments were the envy of fashionable society. On Mar. 16, 1861, having resigned his commission, he was appointed colonel in the Confederate army and was in May put in command of the troops on the Virginia Peninsula. Not only was he one of the best trained of the Virginia officers, but he was the type to attract attention. At Big Bethel in May he won a small engagement, the much-heralded first battle of the Civil War. After Big Bethel he was made brigadier-general and in October 1861, major-general. Upon McClellan's advance in the spring of 1862, Magruder, commanding about 12,000 men, displayed much energy in building defensive works to delay him and in deceiving him in regard to the smallness of his force. While "keeping up a clutter" to fool McClellan, "Prince John" was in his element; indeed his whole conduct so far on the Peninsula won him considerable fame.

But in the Seven Days' Battle around Richmond Magruder's star went into eclipse. His failure to command efficiently was one of the numerous causes of Lee's failure to injure, if not to crush, McClellan. Magruder's force was placed on the south side of the Chickahominy in front of the enemy's left. On June 28, Lee sent orders for him to use the utmost vigilance, and, if the enemy retreated, to pursue vigorously. But Magruder gave no intimation of the Federal withdrawal that day, and it was only discovered the next sunrise by two of Longstreet's engineer officers (Long, *post,* pp. 174–75, and *War of the Rebellion: Official Records* (*Army*), 1 ser. XI, pt. 2, p. 494). On June 29, though there was a serious gap in the opposing forces, Magruder was not quick enough to take advantage of the opportunity, even sending for reinforcements (Ropes, *post,* pt. 2, pp. 191–92). In the late afternoon he attacked gallantly, first at Allen's Farm and then at Savage Station, but was repulsed with heavy loss, and the Federal rearguard continued its retreat. Lee wrote a firm note regretting his slight progress and urging him to press on vigorously (*Official Records,* 1 ser. XI, pt. 2, p. 687). There was some excuse, however, for Magruder in that he erroneously believed that Jackson had been ordered not to support him. At Malvern Hill on July 1 Magruder marched on the wrong road, but made a natural mistake for which he was unduly censured.

Magruder considered himself mistreated in the official reports. He opened a correspondence with Lee, arguing with vigor and not with literal accuracy. He was a disappointment to Lee, who desired not only good generals but men with whom he could work. On Oct. 10, 1862, Magruder was transferred to the command of the district of Texas, later enlarged to include New Mexico and Arizona. He strove to fortify the defenseless Texas coast, and equipped two cotton-clad steamers; on Jan. 1, 1863, he captured Galveston and the revenue cutter *Harriet Lane,* and drove off the blockading fleet. In March 1864 he sent most of his troops to reinforce R. H. Taylor opposing Banks in Louisiana. Upon the close of hostilities, refusing to seek parole, Magruder went to Mexico and became a major-general under Maximilian. He returned to the United States after the downfall of the Emperor and lectured upon his Mexican experiences. In 1869 he settled in Houston, Tex., where he died. He never married.

[C. A. Evans, ed., *Confed. Mil. Hist.* (1899), III, 632–34; G. W. Cullum, *Biog. Reg. . . . U. S. Mil. Acad.* (3rd ed., 1891); J. C. Ropes, *The Story of the Civil War,* pts. I and II (1894–98); A. L. Long, *Memoirs of Robert E. Lee* (1886), and "Memoir of Gen. John Bankhead Magruder," *Southern Hist. Soc. Papers,* vol. XII (1884); B. P. Lee, "Magruder's Peninsula Campaign in 1862," *Southern Hist. Soc. Papers,* vol. XIX (1891); *War of the Rebellion: Official Records* (*Army*), especially 1 ser. XI; *Year Books of Am. Clan Gregor Soc.,* 1913, 1915, 1923; *Houston Telegraph* Feb. 19, 1871; *Houston Daily Union,* Feb. 20, 1871.] **R. D. M.**

MAGRUDER, JULIA (Sept. 14, 1854–June 9, 1907), novelist and writer of short stories, was born in Charlottesville, Va., the daughter of Allen Bowie and Sarah Magruder. She was the niece of the Confederate general John Bankhead Magruder [*q.v.*]. When she was three her family moved to Washington where her father practised law and where she and her two sisters were educated by governesses under the supervision of the parents. Throughout her childhood the family returned for frequent residence to Virginia. Her early training was true to the old ideals of Southern culture and taste of the mid-century. While still a young girl she began to write fiction. Her first publication in her eighteenth year, was a serial story which won a prize of three hundred dollars awarded by the Baltimore *Sun*. After the Virginia family home was closed, she lived for several years in North Carolina with her sister. Although she later maintained a home in Washington, she spent a large portion of her life in Europe, traveling and visiting her many friends, among whom were her cousin Lady Abinger of Inverlochy Castle, Scotland, and the Princess Troubetskoy (Amelie Rives) who entertained her in Italy at Lake Maggiore. She had a wide social acquaintance and was highly regarded as a friendly, generous woman with a gift of good conversation.

She was earnest and conscientious in all her literary work, giving to it her best efforts. She read carefully and critically other writers, and many references in her work show especially her interest in Emerson, Eliot, and Tennyson. Upholding the traditions of the old South with ardency, she nevertheless desired the obliteration of sectional feeling. This is well illustrated in her early novel, *Across the Chasm* (1885), which was published anonymously and judged one of the best stories of the year. She wrote about twenty novels, some appearing serially in magazines. They include *A Magnificent Plebeian* (1888); *A Realized Ideal* (1898); *A Beautiful Alien* (1900); and *A Manifest Destiny* (1900). She generally used one of two plot patterns: that of a hero and heroine who overcome fragile barriers to matrimony, or that of a heroine who marries the wrong man and after his death or disappearance joins her true love. Her novels are pleasant reading, but lack a sense of actuality and vigor. Her *Princess Sonia* (1895) was most popular, and best represents her work. This and many of her other books were illustrated by Charles Dana Gibson. She also wrote several juvenile books, one of which, *Child-Sketches from George Eliot* (1895, also in *St. Nicholas Magazine*) shows her interest in popularizing the work of the English novelist. Her numerous short stories were accepted by outstanding magazines and, like her novels, were directed at the feminine reader. Her articles likewise related largely to feminine problems and show a serious and responsible attitude of mind. They discuss such topics as the changing social position of woman and child-labor questions. She was awarded the Order of the Palm by the French Academy a week before her death. Six months before she died she knew of her hopeless illness but continued the writing of a novel, *Her Husband,* which was published posthumously in 1911. She died in St. Luke's Hospital, Richmond, Va., June 9, 1907, and was buried in the family plot at Charlottesville.

[A monograph on Julia Magruder, by Alice Archer Graham, is in the library of George Washington University. Other sources include: *Who's Who in America,* 1906–07; *Lib. of Southern Lit.,* vol. VIII (1909); *Book News,* Mar. 1897; M. L. Rutherford, *The South in Hist. and Lit.* (1907); obituaries in the Richmond *Times-Dispatch, Washington Post,* the *Sun* (Baltimore), and *N. Y. Times.*] R. W. B.

MAGUIRE, CHARLES BONAVENTURE [See McGuire, Charles Bonaventure, 1768–1833].

MAHAN, ALFRED THAYER (Sept. 27, 1840–Dec. 1, 1914), naval officer, historian, was born at West Point, N. Y. His father, Dennis Hart Mahan [*q.v.*], of pure Irish stock, was for many years professor of engineering at the Military Academy. His mother, Mary Helena Okill, was the daughter of an Englishman who married into the distinguished Jay family of New York. After two years at a private school in Hagerstown, Md., and two years at Columbia University, the boy entered the Naval Academy, and, though just turned sixteen, was granted a year's advanced standing—a concession unique in academy records. He graduated with second honors in 1859. Letters of this period to his classmate and lifelong friend Samuel Ashe of North Carolina reveal the future grave historian as intensely emotional in friendship, fond of reading, a prolific and delightful letter-writer, shy and reserved, as always, yet not averse to social life nor unaware of his good looks and brilliant mind. Slender and over six feet tall, he had light sandy hair, a clear complexion, and grey-blue eyes. By his father and early environment he was imbued with the highest moral and military ideals, his strict observance of which, in reporting a delinquent classmate, led to his being "put in coventry" by part of his class during his graduating year. Right was on his side, yet this affair may help to explain the lukewarm view of Mahan's professional proficiency among many officers of his time. He himself indorsed his father's opinion that he might have done better elsewhere; but, though he was too much a student to be wholly immersed in ship-routine, it is good evidence of his practical attainments that a fellow officer on his first cruise, in the *Congress* to Brazil, 1859–61, asked him to be his "first lieutenant" in an expected command.

Made lieutenant in August 1861, at the outbreak of the Civil War, Mahan came under fire in the *Pocahontas* at Port Royal, and afterward spent many weary months in blockade duty, first in the *Pocahontas* on the Atlantic coast, and later —after eight pleasant months at the Naval Academy, in Newport, and on a midshipmen's cruise in the *Macedonian* (1863)—in the *Seminole* off Sabine Pass, Tex. During the last year of the war he was on Admiral Dahlgren's staff off Charleston. Promoted to lieutenant-commander in 1865, for twenty years thereafter he followed the routine of sea and shore duty. A long cruise in the *Iroquois* (1867–69), to Japan via Rio, Capetown, Aden, and Bombay, was the realization of "a dream of years," and during six months' leave in Europe on his way home he viewed with eager interest the last days of the Empire in Paris and of papal power in Rome. On June 11, 1872, occurred his marriage to Ellen Lyle, daughter of Manlius Evans of Philadelphia, the fortunate outcome of which is attested by Mahan's later comment, "No man can have had a much happier life than I" (Taylor, *post,* p. 23). There were three children, two daughters and a son. In 1883 he wrote for a series dealing with the naval history of the Civil War a short volume, *The Gulf and Inland Waters.* But in 1885, the year he became captain, he had done no other writing; in his own words, he was "drifting on the lines of simple respectability as aimlessly as one very well could" (*From Sail to Steam,* p. 274), when the opportunity came that determined his later career. This was a call from Admiral Luce, which reached him while commanding the *Wachusett* on the west coast of South America, to lecture on tactics and naval history at the newly established War College in Newport.

After over a year's preparation he delivered the first lectures in the autumn of 1886, and in 1886–89 followed Luce as president, fighting for the college with characteristic persistence against a hostile Secretary and an indifferent service. In 1890 the lectures were published as *The Influence of Sea Power upon History, 1660–1783.* This celebrated book contains the essence of Mahan's teaching, the first hundred pages tracing rapidly the rise and decline of the great maritime nations, and pointing out the elements constituting a nation's sea-power, while the remainder treat in detail, over the period indicated, the inter-relation of naval and political history. It won immediate recognition, far greater in Europe than in America. A thirty-two-page article appeared in the *Edinburgh Review* (October 1890), and Theodore Roosevelt wrote enthusiastically of the book, "I am greatly in error if it does not become a classic" (Alden and Earle, *post,* p. 238). Lectures were suspended in 1889–92, and Mahan was sent on a commission to select a navy-yard site on Puget Sound; but he soon returned and devoted two happy, untroubled years to his second, more carefully prepared work, *The Influence of Sea Power upon the French Revolution and Empire, 1793–1812* (2 vols., 1892). These two books were the basis of his fame. There will always be a question what measure of this was due to the fact that the books afforded perfect propaganda for the naval expansion already under way in Great Britain, Germany, and America. British critics hailed them as the gospel of England's greatness; the Kaiser Wilhelm II declared he was "devouring" them, and had them on all his ships (Alden and Earle, p. 243). Something of their success was due also to the fact that they dealt with a relatively unexploited field. There had been naval histories before, but Mahan's power of generalization, his ability to subordinate details to the central theme, and to trace the logic of events and their significance for later times, made him truly the first "philosopher of sea power." He was again president of the War College in 1892–93. When sea-service was due, he pleaded for opportunity to continue writing, but was told it was "not the business of a naval officer to write books" (*From Sail to Steam,* p. 311) and in 1893 was given command of the cruiser *Chicago,* flagship of Admiral Erben in the European Squadron. Between Mahan and Erben there was some friction, for there were drawbacks to having a distinguished author as captain, and in the enthusiastic reception accorded the author during two visits in England the admiral played a secondary rôle. Mahan's modesty, dignity, and courtesy won British hearts. He was dined by the Queen and the Premier, was the first foreign guest of honor ever entertained by the Army and Navy Club, and within a week received degrees from both Oxford and Cambridge. Subsequent degrees from American universities and the presidency of the American Historical Association (1902), were somewhat tardy recognition of this international fame. His reception abroad greatly ncreased his reputation.

His books as they appeared were translated into many languages, and, as Mahan himself remarks, were nowhere more assiduously studied than in Japan.

He retired in 1896, but during the Spanish-American War was recalled from Italy to become a member of the strategy board directing naval operations, on which he served from May 9 until the close of hostilities. Through his frequent magazine articles and his influence on Roosevelt, Lodge, and others, he undoubtedly had no small share in stimulating the growth of the American expansionist policy throughout this period (J. W. Pratt, "American Expansionists of the Spanish War Period," in MS.). In 1899 he was a delegate to the first Hague Peace Conference, where he stood strongly against immunity of private property at sea and arbitration agreements that would limit American freedom of action under the Monroe Doctrine. Always a conservative, in these and other fields, he defended with great cogency and realism the thought of the school to which he belonged. "When he speaks," wrote the head of the American delegation, "the millennium fades, and this stern, severe, actual world appears" (*Autobiography of Andrew D. White,* 1905, vol. II, 347). Yet only a fanatical advocate of disarmament and universal arbitration would deny the steadying effect of his opposition, based on firm convictions and lifelong study of world politics.

Among books of his not already mentioned were two excellent biographies, *Admiral Farragut* (1892), and *The Life of Nelson* (2 vols., 1897); *Types of Naval Officers* (1901); *Sea Power in Its Relations to the War of 1812* (2 vols., 1905); *Naval Strategy* (1911); *The Major Operations of the Navies in the War of American Independence* (1913); and a number of volumes of collected essays on international politics and naval affairs. A devout Episcopalian, he gave expression to his religious feeling in *The Harvest Within* (1909). *From Sail to Steam* (1907), written just after his promotion to rear admiral, retired, in 1906, is a delightful book of reminiscences, unmarred by the heaviness and over-elaboration into which he was sometimes betrayed in his historical writing by his effort to be perfectly accurate and clear. Of all his books, the sea-power series, covering the years 1660–1815, have the best claim to permanence, not only as sound naval history, but also as affording a definitely new outlook on political history. To future students it may also appear that few other historians by their writings so widely influenced the political thought and policies of their own time as did Mahan.

At the opening of the World War his health suffered from his intense concern in the conflict which he had long foreseen and clearly prophesied. Curbed by governmental restriction from writing on public affairs, he was at Washington engaged in research for a study of American expansion in its relations to sea-power, when his death came suddenly from heart failure. He was buried at Quogue, Long Island, where since 1896 he had made his principal home.

[Aside from the autobiography, *From Sail to Steam* (1907), the chief source is C. C. Taylor, *The Life of Admiral Mahan* (1920), which contains a full list of Mahan's writings and of articles and references relating to him. See also G. K. Kirkham, *The Books and Articles of Rear Admiral A. T. Mahan, U. S. N.* (1929); Allan Westcott, *Mahan on Naval Warfare* (1918), a book of selections with an introduction and notes; C. S. Alden and Ralph Earle, *Makers of Naval Tradition* (1925), pp. 228–46; *U. S. Naval Institute Proc.,* Jan.–Feb. 1915; *Army and Navy Jour.,* Dec. 5, 1914; *N. Y. Times,* Dec. 2, 1914; R. P. Chiles, ed., "Letters of Alfred Thayer Mahan to Samuel A'Court Ashe (1858–59)," *Duke Univ. Lib. Bulletin No. 4,* July 1931. Many of Mahan's letters and papers are in the hands of his family.]

A. W.

MAHAN, ASA (Nov. 9, 1799–Apr. 4, 1889), Congregational clergyman, college president, was born at Vernon, N. Y., the son of Capt. Samuel Mahan and his second wife, Anna Dana, of Worcester, Mass. From his twelfth to his seventeenth year the family lived in western New York, then a pioneer region. Home missionaries from Connecticut were frequently entertained by the Mahans. The mother, who was intensely interested in religious subjects, would propound theological questions to the visitors, and the boy's "heart would leap," he tells us, at the prospect of the discussion. From his eighth year he was much given to religious thought, and as a youth accepted unhesitatingly the high Calvinistic system in which he was trained. When seventeen years old he was appointed to teach a winter school in a district near his home. It was arranged that his father should have the son's wages that winter, after which the latter should be free to apply his earnings to obtaining an education, which it was his consuming desire to secure. During this winter he passed through a period of agony over the question as to whether he was "one of the elect," from which condition he emerged into a free Christian experience, resulting in a radical modification of his Calvinism by the adoption of a doctrine of full moral freedom. Teaching school year after year during the winter months, he pursued his studies at Hamilton College, Clinton, N. Y., graduating in 1824. Entering Andover Theological Seminary, he completed his course there in 1827. He was an active participant in the great revivals from

1824 to 1832. At New Brunswick, N. J., May 9, 1828, he married Mary H. Dix.

He was ordained pastor of the Congregational Church at Pittsford, N. Y., Nov. 10, 1829. Having a naturally weak voice, he subjected it to a self-devised training until it became adequate to the most exacting requirements of public speaking. In 1831 he was called to the pastorate of the Sixth Presbyterian Church, Cincinnati. As trustee of the recently established Lane Theological Seminary, he dissented vigorously from the action of the trustees interdicting discussion of the question of slavery. In 1835 he was elected first president of Oberlin College, founded in 1833. Eighty of the Lane students followed him to Oberlin, which fact led to the establishment of a theological department in the college. For some months the president and his family lived in a log house, the first which had been built in the Oberlin colony.

Mahan threw himself with ardor into the work of the young college, did much speaking and preaching, and taught philosophy with enthusiasm, giving an enduring impetus to this study at Oberlin. In philosophy he was intuitionist of the Scottish "common sense" school. He shared student manual labor, including work on the highway (*Autobiography,* p. 275). His acceptance of the presidency of Oberlin he had made conditional upon its reception of students without discrimination as to color. He was, moreover, always proud of having been the first college president to give degrees to women on the same conditions as to men. A believer in fullest freedom of discussion, he was sometimes suspected of "a greater facility in conviction than in conciliation" (J. H. Fairchild, *post,* p. 278). He was an impressive figure, with solid frame and full-bearded face. His administration in the main was successful; but in 1850 he accepted a call to take the direction of Cleveland University, which friends of his were projecting. Since this enterprise did not succeed, in 1855 he resumed pastoral work, serving Congregational churches, at Jackson, Mich. (1855–57), and at Adrian, Mich. (1857–60). He was connected with Adrian College as professor and from 1860 to 1871 as president. His wife died in 1863 and in 1866 he married Mrs. Mary E. Chase. The later years of his long life he passed in England, preaching to large congregations, advocating Christian perfection, editing a monthly magazine, *The Divine Life,* and issuing volume after volume on philosophy and religion. He died at Eastbourne, England. His published works include *Scripture Doctrine of Christian Perfection* (1839), *A System of Intellectual Philosophy* (copr. 1845), *Doctrine of the Will* (1845), *The True Believer; His Character, Duty and Privileges* (1847), *The Science of Moral Philosophy* (1848), *Election and Influence of the Holy Spirit* (1851), *Modern Mysteries Explained and Exposed* (1855), *The Science of Logic* (1857), *Science of Natural Theology* (1867), *Theism and Anti-Theism in Their Relations to Science* (1872), *The Phenomena of Spiritualism Scientifically Explained and Exposed* (1875), *A Critical History of the Late American War* (1877), *The System of Mental Philosophy* (1882), *A Critical History of Philosophy* (1883), *Autobiography, Intellectual, Moral and Spiritual* (London, 1882).

[In addition to Mahan's *Autobiog.,* see E. H. Fairchild, *Hist. Sketch of Oberlin Coll.* (1868); J. H. Fairchild, *Oberlin, the Colony and the College* (1883); D. L. Leonard, *The Story of Oberlin* (1898), *Oberlin Rev.,* Apr. 30, 1889; *The Times* (London), Apr. 10, 1889.] E. D. E.

MAHAN, DENNIS HART (Apr. 2, 1802–Sept. 16, 1871), educator and soldier, the son of John and Mary (Cleary) Mahan and half-brother of Milo Mahan [*q.v.*], was born in New York City shortly after the arrival of his parents from Ireland, but spent his boyhood in Norfolk, Va. Having begun the study of medicine in Richmond, he wished, also, to take up drawing. Finding no teacher and learning that drawing was taught at the United States Military Academy, he sought and obtained (1820) appointment as cadet. Graduating at the head of his class in 1824, he was assigned as a lieutenant to the corps of engineers. From 1824 to 1826 he was assistant professor, first of mathematics and then of engineering, at the Academy. Because of his native talent and persevering industry he was then sent by the War Department to Europe to study public works and military institutions with a view to improving the course at West Point. He remained abroad four years, during which time he pursued studies at the School of Application for Engineers and Artillery at Metz, France. At the time it was the foremost school of its kind, numbering on its faculty officers who had seen service under Napoleon, and some of the most eminent French scientists.

On his return to the United States he was appointed assistant professor of civil and military engineering at the Military Academy, and in 1832, professor, which position he held until 1871. Instruction at that institution was then in its infancy and as there were no suitable textbooks for his course, he supplied the lack by lectures and lithographic notes, which became the groundwork of subsequent publications. His *Complete Treatise on Field Fortification,* first published in 1836, was the standard work on this subject carried into the field by United States officers in both the Mexican and Civil wars. His *Elementary Treatise on Advance-Guard, Out-Post, and Detachment Service of Troops* (1847) was written during the Mexican War, and utilized by officers in the Civil War. Both were reprinted in Richmond for the use of the officers of the Confederate army. His *Elementary Course of Civil Engineering* was first published in 1837 and, revised from time to time, was a standard text for many years. His other textbooks were *Summary of the Course of Permanent Fortification and of the Attack and Defence of Permanent Works* (1850), *Industrial Drawing* (1852), *Descriptive Geometry as Applied to the Drawing of Fortification and Stereotomy* (1864), *An Elementary Course of Military Engineering* (2 vols., 1866–67). He also edited the American edition (1856) of Henry Moseley's *Mechanical Principles of Engineering and Architecture.*

Though best known as the author of textbooks, he was an accomplished writer in other fields and contributed articles to periodicals on many subjects. His loyalty to his country, its army, and the Military Academy was strong, and his pen was ever ready in their defense. As senior member of the academic board of the Academy his influence in the development of that institution was preëminent through four decades. He was one of the fifty original incorporators of the National Academy of Sciences, a member of the Geographical Society of Paris and many other scientific associations. In 1850 the governor of Virginia appointed him on a board of engineers to decide a controversy between that state and the Baltimore & Ohio Railroad, and in 1871 he was appointed an overseer of Thayer School of Engineering of Dartmouth College. In 1871 the board of visitors of the Academy recommended his retirement. He brooded over the fact and on a trip to New York to visit his physician, he stepped over the side of the boat and was drowned.

In 1839 he married Mary Helena Okill by whom he had three sons and two daughters. His sons all entered either the army or the navy. Frederick A. Mahan graduated at the Military Academy and became an officer of the corps of engineers. Alfred Thayer Mahan [*q.v.*] and Dennis Hart Mahan graduated from the Naval Academy.

[G. W. Cullum, *Biog. Register Officers and Grads. U. S. Mil. Acad.* (3rd ed., 1891); H. L. Abbot, in *Nat. Acad. Sci. Biog. Memoirs,* vol. II (1886); A. T. Mahan, *From Sail to Steam* (1907); *N. Y. Times,* Sept. 17, 1871; names of Mahan's parents from his daughter, Jane Mahan.] G. J. F.

MAHAN, MILO (May 24, 1819–Sept. 3, 1870), clergyman of the Protestant Episcopal Church, educator, was born in Suffolk, Va., the son of John Mahan, a native of Ireland, by a third wife. His father died when Milo was about two years old and his half-brother, Dennis Hart Mahan [*q.v.*], assumed responsibility for the care and education of the boy, leaving him with his mother for some years and at length placing him in the school at Flushing, L. I., conducted by Rev. William Augustus Muhlenberg [*q.v.*], known after 1838 as St. Paul's College. Here he showed unusual intellectual ability, and in his seventeenth year he went to the Episcopal High School, Alexandria, Va., to teach Greek. During the years he spent there he became affected by the Oxford movement to a degree displeasing to Bishop William Meade, and he returned to St. Paul's College as a teacher. Having carried on studies preparatory to the ministry, he was ordained deacon by Bishop Thomas C. Brownell at New Canaan, Conn., Oct. 27, 1845; and priest, by Bishop Levi S. Ives, at the Church of the Holy Communion, New York, on Dec. 14, 1846. After serving as assistant to Dr. Samuel Seabury at the Church of the Annunciation, New York, in November 1848 he became rector of Grace Church, Van Vorst, Jersey City, organized not long before. In two years, under his leadership, it developed into a flourishing parish, and he then went to St. Mark's Church, Philadelphia, as assistant to Dr. J. P. B. Wilmer. In 1851 he published *The Exercise of Faith in Its Relation to Authority and Private Judgment,* in which, from the Anglican point of view, he set forth the errors of the Roman Catholic position. The same year he was appointed professor of ecclesiastical history at the General Theological Seminary, New York. With two or three other clergymen he started and for several years conducted the *Church Journal,* the first number of which appeared Feb. 5, 1853. On Aug. 23, 1853, he married Mary Griffitts (Fisher) Lewis, widow of Charles Smith Lewis. An intimate friend of Bishop G. W. Doane [*q.v.*] of New Jersey, Mahan cooperated in the bishop's educational projects, serving as a trustee of St. Mary's Hall and of Burlington College. He also represented the New Jersey diocese in the General Conventions of 1856, 1859, and 1862. Bishop Doane, shortly before his death in 1859, expressed the desire that Mahan be his successor, but his election was prevented by those who had been hostile to Doane. In the General Convention of 1862 he made vigorous protest against indorsement of the Union cause, on the ground that the issue was political rather than religious (see *Dr.*

Mahan's Speech, 1862). His Southern sympathies made him uncomfortable in New York and this fact, together with the need of more salary, led him to resign his professorship in 1864, and assume the rectorship of St. Paul's Church, Baltimore.

He had previously published *A Church History of the First Three Centuries, from the Thirtieth to the Three Hundred and Twenty-third Year of the Christian Era* (1860), a useful compendium, but without originality and somewhat influenced by the writer's own ecclesiastical views; and a reply to Bishop John William Colenso's conclusions regarding the Pentateuch, *The Spiritual Point of View: or the Glass Reversed, an Answer to Bishop Colenso* (1863). Obsessed with the idea that the Bible contains elaborate and abstruse symbolisms, he had also published in 1863 an ingenious work on the significance of numbers employed therein, entitled: *Palmoni: or, the Numerals of Scripture a Proof of Inspiration.* His *Comedy of Canonization,* called forth by the *Comedy of Convocation,* a caricature of the Anglican position by a convert to Rome, appeared anonymously in 1868; and his *Church History of the First Seven Centuries,* in 1872. He represented the diocese of Maryland in the General Conventions of 1865 and 1868. On June 30, 1870, he was called back to the General Theological Seminary as professor of systematic divinity. The following month he accepted the appointment, but his death occurred before he entered upon its duties. In 1875 *The Collected Works of the Late Milo Mahan, D.D.,* in three volumes, edited by J. H. Hopkins, was published.

[Memoir in *Collected Works,* vol. III; *Churchman's Year Book,* 1871; *Proc. of the Board of Trustees of the Gen. Theolog. Sem. . . .,* vol. III (1866), vol. IV (1875); *No. Am. Rev.,* Oct. 1860; *Southern Rev.,* July 1875; *The Sun* (Baltimore), Sept. 6, 1870; information from relatives.] H. E. S.

MAHONE, WILLIAM (Dec. 1, 1826–Oct. 8, 1895), railroad president, Confederate soldier, senator from Virginia, was born in Southampton County, Va., the son of Fielding Jordan and Martha (Drew) Mahone. In a region of large slaveholders his father kept tavern and "Billie" rode the mail from Jerusalem (Courtland) to Hill's Ford (Emporia). Tradition has it that the youth was deemed a good mixer and clever at the prevalent sport of gambling. Aided financially by friends he graduated from the Virginia Military Institute in 1847. Continuing the study of engineering while teaching in Rappahannock Military Academy, he became engineer of the Orange & Alexandria road-building project and then (1851) of the Norfolk-Petersburg Railroad. Of the latter—a well-built road for that day—he was in 1861 president, chief engineer, and superintendent. Meantime, in February 1855, he had married Ortelia Butler, who in the course of time bore him three children, and had settled in Petersburg. Though he was apparently little interested in politics, on Virginia's secession he was appointed quartermaster-general. Soon, however, as lieutenant-colonel, then as colonel, of his 6th Virginia Regiment of eastern volunteers, he was taking part in the capture of the Norfolk Navy Yard. He commanded the Norfolk District until its evacuation in May 1862, when he was shifted to the Drewry's Bluff defenses of the James River. Thereafter he was continuously with the Army of Northern Virginia except while recuperating from a severe wound received at Second Manassas. D. H. Hill criticized his conduct at Seven Pines; Magruder and Longstreet praised him at Malvern Hill and Second Manassas respectively. Perhaps because he was not a West-Point man, he was not commissioned brigadier-general until March 1864. In July following, because of the flanking movement in the Wilderness which he commanded, he was recommended by Longstreet for the major-generalship; after his action at the Crater this came quickly, and he was a Southern hero besides (*War of the Rebellion: Official Records, Army,* 1 ser. XI, pts. 1–3, XIV, pt. 1, XL, pt. 3). As a commander Mahone was alert, prompt, precise, and contemptuous of indecision or unnecessary self-exposure in other commanders. Perhaps because he was careful of its equipment and condition "Mahone's Brigade" displayed uncommon *esprit de corps* until and through Appomattox; and in post-war days it held enthusiastic reunions. Not improbable is the report that Gen. Robert E. Lee, who had observed him closely, said after the war that among the younger men he thought William Mahone had developed the highest quality for organization and command (Pearson, *post,* p. 69).

Promptly back at railroading, out of three short and largely state-owned lines from Norfolk to Bristol, Mahone, under legislative authorization of 1867 and 1870, created the privately owned Atlantic, Mississippi & Ohio Railroad, with steamer connections at Norfolk and the right to extend to the Ohio. Of this fine road —later the Norfolk & Western—he was president at a salary (men noted) "as big as the President's." In the sane movements of 1869 for mitigating Reconstruction rigors he helped quietly but powerfully; and thereby secured for governor, Gilbert C. Walter, a director of the Norfolk & Petersburg, whose fiscal ideas were Hamiltonian. Through railroad patronage he dominated the *Richmond Whig* and built himself a strong legislative following. The tavern-keeper's son was traveling far and fast. But everywhere he met obstacles, hostilities: he was dubbed "Railroad Ishmael," "King of the Lobby"; Governors Walker and Kemper successively abandoned him; twice at least he forfeited prestige to escape duels; in the crash of the seventies an unfriendly receivership took away his railroad; and in the Conservative (Democratic) convention of 1877 a combination defeated his gubernatorial aspirations though he led the field on his record for material progress. Undaunted, in 1879 he organized and assumed command of the "Readjusters," who advocated a scaling of the state's huge debt and popular social and economic legislation. Favored neither by the regular party machines nor by wealthy and intelligent people generally, this movement swept the state in 1879 and 1881; and important reforms followed. Aided, perhaps coached, by the Pennsylvania Camerons, Mahone in 1880 was elected to the United States Senate. There he traded his commanding vote for offices and committee assignments, bringing upon his head vials of Southern Democratic wrath for his "treason" but winning great applause from Northern Republicans for his "Anti-Bourbonism," which to them meant protecting the negro's vote. Two years later another senator and a majority of Virginia's representatives, elected as "Coalitionists," were with him in Washington. With the state and federal offices thus secured Mahone built a political machine which thereafter dominated the Republican party of Virginia; and of it he was absolute boss. After 1882, however, though a constant threat, he won no more elections—not even when he himself ran for governor in 1889—owing in part to the rejuvenating effects of the Readjuster Movement on the old dominating elements and in part to defections caused by his own imperiousness. He had shown how to break the "Solid South" but not how to maintain the breach. To the end a unique figure—short, spare, and long-bearded, always in gray slouch hat and peg-top trousers, eyes blue and restless, voice thin and piping—he died in Washington and was buried quietly in Petersburg. There the Daughters of the Confederacy later erected a monument to him.

[See: C. C. Pearson, *The Readjuster Movement in Va.* (1917), for political matters and for biographical references; C. A. Evans, ed., *Confed. Mil. Hist.* (1899), vol. III; P. C. Headley, *Pub. Men of Today* (1882); W. L. Royall, *Some Reminiscences* (1909); R. E. Withers, *Autobiog. of an Octogenarian* (1907); the *Richmond Dispatch*, Oct. 9, 1895; the *Hist. Mag. and Notes and Queries* (N. Y.), June 1870; *The Vital Va. Issues: A Speech by Gen. Wm. Mahone . . . Sept. 23, 1889*; *Characteristic Facts in the . . . Career of Gen. Wm. Mahone* (n.d.); *Special Report . . . to the Stockholders of the Norfolk and Petersburg Railroad Company* (1866). The doctor's thesis of N. M. Blake on Wm. Mahone (Duke Univ., 1932), admirably covers the subject.]

C. C. P.

MAILLY, WILLIAM (Nov. 22, 1871–Sept. 4, 1912), Socialist, journalist, and dramatic critic, was born in the poorhouse in Pittsburgh, Pa., the son of John Mailly and Mary McDowell. His Irish father was a heavy drinker who frequently deserted his mother and the seven children of whom only three boys survived childhood. When William was three his mother took the family back to her native Scotland and his earliest recollections were of Lennoxtown and of a Glasgow close. Afterward she started a laundry in Liverpool and at twelve William left school to become her errand boy. Tips received for delivering laundry he spent for theatre tickets and thus began his lifelong devotion to the drama. He also became interested in socialism. In 1889 his father brought the family again to America and William became a section hand in Illinois and later a coal miner in Alabama. His intelligence, gift for friendship, and keen sense of humor, together with his attractive brown eyes and eager, searching expression, almost immediately made him a leader. At twenty-one he was organizer and the next year state secretary of the United Mine Workers of America. For a time associate editor of the Birmingham *Labor Advocate,* in 1896 he went to Nashville, became secretary of the Tennessee Federation of Labor, and edited the Nashville *Journal of Labor.* Having become an admiring friend of Eugene V. Debs he assisted, in 1898, in forming the Social Democratic (now Socialist) party at Chicago. Shortly afterward he was made organizer for that party in New York City and later went to Massachusetts for the "Social Crusaders." There he edited the Haverhill *Social Democrat,* assisted in electing Socialist mayors in Haverhill and Brockton, and in 1902 became secretary of the state party. His success in that office and as secretary of the "Unity convention" in 1901 led to his choice, early in 1903, as national secretary of the Socialist party, with headquarters first at Omaha and later at Chicago. At a time when the movement was in special need of English-speaking leaders Mailly threw into his task executive ability, forthright sincerity, infectious enthusiasm, and a devotion transferred from the Catholic religion which he early discarded. But he was primarily an idealist and writer and in 1905, having more than doubled the number of organized states, got the party out of debt, and managed the campaign of 1904 in which socialism first became a real factor in American politics, he declined reëlection as secretary though for the next year he was a member of the national executive committee. Meanwhile, on May 15, 1903, at the bedside of his dying mother in Haverhill, he married Bertha Howell, a college-educated woman and an active Socialist. For a time he was joint publisher of a Socialist paper at Toledo, Ohio, but from 1907 to 1909 he was managing editor first of the New York *Worker* and later of the *Evening Call.* In May 1909, he resigned to become dramatic critic for the *Twentieth Century Magazine* and to write articles and stories for the *Arena, Independent, Munsey's Magazine,* and other periodicals. At the time of the Triangle fire he was business manager of the Ladies Waist Makers' Union and the burden of relief work and agitation for better fire protection for workers thrown upon him proved too heavy for his strength, already weakened by diabetes. During the last six months of his life he was associate editor of the *Metropolitan Magazine.* His early death cut short a career of much promise as a writer and pioneer in interpreting the effect of the drama upon social ideals.

[W. P. D. Bliss, *The New Encyc. of Social Reform* (1908), contains a biographical sketch. G. D. Herron, *William Mailly as a Socialist Type* (1912) is a memoir reprinted from the *Coming Nation.* Obituaries were published in a large number of Socialist and other periodicals, including the principal New York and Chicago dailies, the *Springfield Republican,* the *New York Dramatic Mirror,* the *Woman Voter,* the *Milwaukee Leader,* and the *Young Socialists' Mag.* Biographical materials are also contained in the newspapers which Mailly edited and the articles and stories which he wrote for magazines. Other information has been furnished by his widow.] H. S. W.

MAISCH, JOHN MICHAEL (Jan. 30, 1831–Sept. 10, 1893), pharmacist, was born in the ancient German town of Hanau, Hesse, the son of Conrad Maisch, a merchant. He attended a private school, then the *bürgerschule,* entered the *realschule* at twelve, and upon its foundation in 1844 was transferred to the *oberrealschule.* Here he received an excellent fundamental training in natural history, chemistry, physics, and mathematics, as well as instruction in Greek and Latin and in microscopy. His parents wished him to study theology, but his bent was toward a scientific calling, and he selected pharmacy as the study of his preference. Before he had the opportunity to secure training in this subject, however, he took part in the Baden Rebellion of 1849 and was forced to leave Germany.

He came to America in his nineteenth year, without money, influence, or friends, but with so much native ability and industry that he soon made contacts that enabled him to gain practical experience in his chosen profession. He worked in pharmacies in Baltimore, Washington, and New York, and then for some time in the employ of Robert Shoemaker, a pioneer wholesale druggist and manufacturing pharmacist of Philadelphia, who was actively connected with the Philadelphia College of Pharmacy. In May 1854 he contributed his first paper, "On the Adulteration of Drugs and Chemical Preparations," to the *American Journal of Pharmacy.* In 1859 he became associated with another well-known pharmacist, Edward Parrish [*q.v.*], who conducted a pharmaceutical preparatory course for students of medicine, and in this year he revised the chemical section of the second edition of Parrish's *Introduction to Practical Pharmacy.* He profited so well by his contacts with these men that in 1861 he was called to the chair of botany and materia medica in the New York College of Pharmacy. Here he remained for two years, spending his spare time in the laboratory of Dr. Edward R. Squibb [*q.v.*] of Brooklyn, another pharmacist of national repute.

In 1863 he returned to Philadelphia to take charge of the United States Army Laboratory, in which medical and pharmaceutical supplies were made for the Union army. He conducted this work in such a conscientious and thorough manner as to save large sums of money for the government. When the laboratory was discontinued at the close of the Civil War, he opened a pharmacy in Philadelphia. In 1866 he became a professor in the Philadelphia College of Pharmacy, with which he was connected thereafter until his death, occupying several chairs in succession, and finally becoming dean. For many years (1865–93) he was permanent secretary of the American Pharmaceutical Association; he was the chemical, botanical, and pharmaceutical editor of the first three editions of the *National Dispensatory* (1879–84), was editor of the *American Journal of Pharmacy* from 1871 until his death, and was a member of the Committee of Revision of the *Pharmacopoeia of the United States* for three successive decades (1870–90). He also edited and revised R. E. Griffith's *Universal Formulary* (3rd ed., 1874), and published a successful work of his own, *A Manual of Organic Materia Medica* (1882). He was an honorary member of many foreign scientific societies, and just before he died was the recipient of the Hanbury Medal, awarded for distinguished services in pharmacy by the Pharmaceutical Society of Great Britain. His wife, Charlotte Justine Kuhl, whom he married in 1859, predeceased him; but he was survived by five sons and two daughters.

[Files of the *Am. Jour. Pharmacy*; *Alumni Report of the Phila. Coll. of Pharmacy*, Oct. 1893; *Proc. Am. Pharmaceutical Asso.*, 1893, 1894; *The First Century of the Phila. Coll. of Pharmacy* (1922), ed. by J. W. England; *Phila. Press*, Sept. 12, 1893.] C. H. L—l.

MAJOR, CHARLES (July 25, 1856–Feb. 13, 1913), novelist, the son of Stephen and Phoebe (Gaskill) Major, was born in Indianapolis, Ind. His father, who came to the United States in 1829 from his birthplace, Granard, County Longford, Ireland, was descended from ancestors who had gone to Ireland from Scotland in the days of Cromwell. At the age of thirteen Charles removed with his parents to Shelbyville where he lived for the remainder of his life. After attending the public schools he read law in his father's office and was admitted to the bar in 1877. He interrupted a lifelong practice only once, when, in 1885, he was elected to the Indiana legislature on the Democratic ticket. At the end of his first term he refused renomination, and, thereafter, declined to reënter public life. On Sept. 27, 1885, he married Alice Shaw of Shelbyville. A man of quiet demeanor and studious habits, he devoted the greater part of his leisure to reading, especially English and French history of the Renaissance period. He took particular interest in diaries, memoirs, and state papers of the Tudor age, with the result that by the time he came to write his first romance he was an important amateur historian. His best novels were the fruit of his enthusiasm for study.

In 1898 he achieved his widest popularity by the publication of his first book, *When Knighthood Was in Flower,* a novel that reached a sale of over two hundred thousand copies in two years and remained a best-seller for fourteen consecutive months. Told ostensibly by Sir Edwin Caskoden, master of the dance, it recounts the love story of Mary Tudor, sister of Henry VIII, and Charles Brandon against a colorful background of sixteenth-century England. Although accurate in detail the historical setting lacks fullness and does not always succeed in giving life to a somewhat sentimental plot. The principal characters, broadly drawn and glamorous, tend to be the usual romantic types. Major had definite views as to the use of history in fiction; he deplored the practice of attempting contemporary speech, stressed the value of original sources, and advocated a knowledge of the whole life of all the people (*Scribner's,* June 1900). In spite of his theories, however, he seems to put his actors into fancy dress rather than into an actual period atmosphere. He returned to the field of his first success with *Dorothy Vernon of Haddon Hall* (1902). Again, using the first person, he presents a pair of amiable though theatrical lovers, who find happiness after typically fictional difficulties; and again he sketches historic personages, this time chiefly Elizabeth and Mary, Queen of Scots. Like its predecessor the book substitutes sincerity and accuracy of fact for a real portrayal either of character or of history. Continuing in the historical vein with less popular and no greater artistic success, Major published: *Yolanda, Maid of Burgundy* (1905); *A Gentle Knight of Old Brandenburg* (1909); *The Little King* (1910) and *The Touchstone of Fortune* (1912). Meanwhile, though he admitted he knew less about them than he did about historical subjects (*Bookman,* June 1902), he attempted local themes in *The Bears of Blue River* (1901), *A Forest Hearth* (1903), and *Uncle Tom Andy Bill* (1908). *When Knighthood Was in Flower* and *Dorothy Vernon* were made into popular plays by Paul Kester.

Although his importance may be said to be entirely in the historical field, Major made no real contribution to the development of the historical novel created by Scott and Americanized by Cooper. He had their faults but seldom possessed their powers. His books are kept in print chiefly by juvenile readers.

[See *Who's Who in America,* 1912–13; *The Cambridge Hist. of Am. Lit.,* vol. III (1921); J. P. Dunn, *Indiana and Indianans* (1919), vol. III, p. 1366; *Book Buyer,* Mar. 1900; *Current Lit.,* May 1900; *Bookman,* Nov. 1900; F. L. Pattee, *The Hist. of Am. Lit. Since 1870* (1915); *Indianapolis News,* Feb. 13, 1913. The Julia Marlowe edition of *When Knighthood Was in Flower* (copyright 1901) contains an article by Maurice Thompson: "The Author and the Book."] D. A. R—s.

MAJORS, ALEXANDER (Oct. 4, 1814–Jan. 12, 1900), freighter and promoter of the pony express, the son of Laurania (Kelly) and Benjamin Majors, a native of North Carolina, was born near Franklin, Simpson County, Ky. His father moved to what is now Lafayette County, Mo., about 1819, and he later acquired an extensive farm with saw and flour mills in Jackson County, where the family lived from 1825 to 1858. The boy worked on the farm and served as a miller's boy. On Nov. 6, 1834, he married Katherine Stallcup, having in the meantime started farming on his own account. The returns from farming were not sufficient for his growing family, and on Aug. 10, 1848, with an outfit of six wagons and teams, he undertook the business of carrying freight from Independence to Santa Fé. He made the round trip in ninety-two days and cleared $1,500. He avoided traveling and all unnecessary work on Sunday, and his men had to take the pledge: "While I am in the employ of A. Majors, I agree not to use profane language, not to get drunk, not to gamble, not to treat animals cruelly, and not to do anything else that is incompatible with the conduct of a gentleman" (*Seventy Years, post,* p. 72). In all his operations he persevered in this discipline. He carried freight on his own account for several years, most of the time transporting government supplies to the various forts in New Mexico, Colorado, and Utah. About 1855 he went into partnership with William Hepburn Russell [*q.v.*] and William B. Waddell and continued as Majors & Russell until 1858, when the firm name was changed to Russell, Majors & Waddell. He took complete responsibility for all the business on the road, while the others managed the purchasing and financing. Their operations required the employment of more than four thousand men, forty thousand oxen, and one thousand mules. The shipments were made in trains of about twenty-five wagons each, stationed several miles apart; each wagon had twelve oxen and a teamster; and each train had thirty oxen in reserve, five mules, wagonmaster, and extra men. The partnership agreement required him to move his home from Jackson County to Nebraska City. Their profits in 1855–56 amounted to about $300,000. The business was very hazardous, and they would sometimes lose the profits of several years in one season.

In 1859 the firm took over the operation of a daily stage-coach line from Fort Leavenworth to Denver, begun independently by Russell and John S. Jones, who were, however, unable to carry it financially. Afterward they included in their schedules, St. Joseph, Mo., Atchison, Kan., Salt Lake City, Fort Kearney, Nebraska Territory, and Fort Laramie in what is now Wyoming. On Apr. 3, 1860, they established the famous pony express, a very daring and romantic enterprise, which lasted about eighteen months, and was a financial failure. Nevertheless at the outbreak of the Civil War it performed an important service in maintaining swift communication between the federal government at Washington and the population of the Pacific Coast, and, before the completion of the telegraph, it carried the news of Lincoln's inaugural address, the fall of Fort Sumter, the call for troops, and the battle of Antietam. The old firm of Russell, Majors & Waddell collapsed in the early part of 1861, and, when liquidation failed to provide funds for the debts, Majors, as did his former partners, surrendered his personal estate for that purpose. He had purchased the interests of his partners in the freighting business, and he continued freighting until 1866. In 1868 he worked on the Union Pacific Railroad and later prospected for silver near Salt Lake City until 1872. From 1869 to 1879 he lived in Salt Lake City. In 1893 he published a volume of reminiscences, *Seventy Years on the Frontier,* which was, however, edited by Prentiss Ingraham [*q.v.*], the prolific writer of dime novels. For several years before his death he lived in Kansas City, Mo., and he died in Chicago.

[F. A. Root and W. E. Connelley, *The Overland Stage to Cal.* (1900); L. R. Hafen, *The Overland Mail* (1926); G. D. Bradley, *The Story of the Pony Express* (1913); W. L. Visscher, *A Thrilling and Truthful Hist. of the Pony Express* (copr. 1908); *Collectors Club Philatelist,* Jan., Apr. 1929; *Mo. Republican* (St. Louis), Nov. 14, 1886; *Kansas City Star,* Jan. 15, 1900; *Rocky Mountain News* (Denver), Jan. 15, 1900.]

S. M. D.

MA-KA-TAI-ME-SHE-KIA-KIAK [See Black Hawk, 1767–1838].

MAKEMIE, FRANCIS (*c.* 1658–1708), Presbyterian clergyman, of Scotch parentage, was born near Ramelton, in Donegal County, Ireland. The severe persecution to which the Scotch-Irish Presbyterians were subjected during his boyhood seems to have deepened his allegiance to the church of his fathers. Graduating from the University of Glasgow during Scotland's bloody killing time, he was ordained by Laggan Presbytery, probably in 1682, as a missionary to America. In 1683 he arrived in Maryland—according to tradition, a blue-eyed, brown-haired, fair-complexioned youth, with an intellectual forehead, and the mien of a true Irish gentleman. It was a number of years before he settled permanently. He labored as an evangelist in North Carolina (1683–84), on the Elizabeth River in Virginia (1684–85), on the Eastern shore of Virginia and Maryland (1690–91), in Philadelphia, for a single sermon (1692), and in Barbados (1696–98). Four letters to Increase Mather, two from Virginia and two from Barbados, and one to Benjamin Colman have been preserved (see Briggs, *post,* Appendix X). During these years he published a catechism, popularizing the tenets of the Westminster Confession, of which he was a stanch adherent. The catechism was violently attacked by the Quaker George Keith [*q.v.*], and Makemie defended Presbyterian beliefs and practices against Keith's animadversions in *An Answer to George Keith's Libel* (1694). More serious opposition came to the nascent Presbyterian Church from representatives of the Church of England. In 1699 Makemie published *Truths in a True Light; or a Pastoral Letter to the Reformed Protestants in Barbadoes Vindicating the Non-Conformists from the Misrepresentations Commonly Made of Them, in That Island, and in Other Places,* written in 1697.

The lack of organized churches, and of any stated support, as well as Makemie's own independent spirit, led him to enter the mercantile business. Sometime before 1698 he married Naomi, the daughter of William Anderson, a rich merchant of Accomac County, Va., who died in 1698, leaving to his son-in-law the bulk of his estate. Successful both as a merchant and as a trader in land, Makemie now settled down on the Eastern Shore of Virginia. In 1699 he secured a license to preach at two of his own houses in Virginia. He thus became the first dissenting minister licensed under the Toleration Act to preach in a colony noted for its intolerance. His main service, however, was given to the churches in Maryland, just across the line, particularly Snow Hill and Rehobeth. He remained the pastor of the latter church until his death.

In 1704–05 Makemie made a journey to England. He published here *A Plain & Friendly Perswasive to the Inhabitants of Virginia and Maryland for Promoting Towns & Cohabitation* (1705), in which he displays an intelligent concern for the material needs of the two colonies, and a keen interest in the relation of material welfare to spiritual well-being. He also persuaded the Presbyterian and Independent ministers of London to send two Presbyterian ministers to America, and to assume their support for two years. These young men, John Hampton and George McNish, became pastors of four of the five churches to which Makemie had ministered in Maryland. The following year Makemie and these two ministers united with four others to form the first American Presbytery. It is generally admitted that Makemie was responsible for the organization. He was also its first moderator.

In January 1707 he was arrested by order of Lord Cornbury, governor of New York, and imprisoned for six weeks, for preaching in that colony without a license. Cornbury described him as "Jack of all Trades; he is a Preacher, a Doctor of Physick, a Merchant, an Attorney, or Counsellor at Law, and which is worse of all, a Disturber of Governments" (*Ecclesiastical Records of the State of New York*, III, 1670). Makemie saw that the rights of non-conformists to the Church of England were at stake, not only in New York, but in other colonies as well. He spoke ably and at length himself, and was defended by William Nicoll, James Reignere, and David Jamison [*q.v.*]. The jury acquitted him but he was required by the court to pay all the costs, including that of the prosecution. Being further hounded by Cornbury, Makemie printed in Boston the sermon which caused his arrest, and also published *A Narrative of a New and Unusual American Imprisonment of Two Presbyterian Ministers and Prosecution of Mr. Francis Makemie* (1707). His vigorous action called attention to the conduct of Cornbury and contributed to his recall in 1709. The next legislature made another such persecution impossible in New York.

Makemie died in 1708, survived by his widow and two daughters. He is regarded as the chief founder of the Presbyterian Church in America. He organized or developed some of its earliest churches; was the foremost expounder of its tenets, and its chief literary apologist; defended its liberties; and secured its initial organization. A monument was erected to his memory, May 14, 1908, on the site of his old home in Accomac County, Va.

[L. P. Bowen, *The Days of Makemie* (1885); A. G. Lecky, *In the Days of the Laggan Presbytery* (Belfast, 1908), appendix, pp. 139–42; *Jour. of the Presbyt. Hist. Soc.*, Mar. 1907–Dec. 1907, Dec. 1908; W. B. Sprague, *Annals Am. Pulpit*, vol. III (1858); C. A. Briggs, *Am. Presbyterianism* (1885); *Ecclesiastical Records State of N. Y.*, vol. II (1901), vol. III (1902); W. H. Foote, *Sketches of Va.* (1850); Alfred Nevin, *Hist. of the Presbytery of Philadelphia and Philadelphia Central* (1888); Irving Spence, *Letters on the Early History of the Presbyterian Church in America* (1838); Richard Webster, *A Hist. of the Presbyterian Ch. in America* (1857); L. P. Bowen, *Makemieland Memorials* (1910).]

E. T. T.

MALBONE, EDWARD GREENE (August 1777–May 7, 1807), miniature painter, was born at Newport, R. I., and died in Savannah, Ga. The painter's grandfather, Capt. Godfrey Malbone, went to Newport from Virginia as a young man. He soon claimed a share of Newport's profits in the rum trade, and with his wife, Katherine Scott Malbone, established himself in the community. The artist's father, John Malbone, was the eighth of ten children. For a time he was engaged in the West-Indies trade. At his death in 1795 he left an estate valued at $5,500. His burial was attended with ceremonies conducted by the Marine Society, and an obituary in the *Newport Mercury* referred to his title of brigadier-general in the Rhode Island militia, to his substantial qualities as a citizen, and to his philanthropy. He had several times served as vestryman in Trinity Church. More obscure is the artist's mother, Patience Greene, to whom, tradition says, John Malbone was never married. By her Malbone had five children: Edward, Henry, Harriet, later Mrs. John Whitehorne; Mary, later Mrs. Benjamin Rathbone; and Sarah, later Mrs. John Knight. Their birth dates are not recorded, and it was not until after their father's death that the three sisters were baptized in Trinity Church with the name Malbone.

Harriet Malbone Whitehorne, writing in 1834, said that the family lived in seclusion in Newport and refers to an "accumulation of evils" not of a pecuniary nature (Dunlap, *post,* II, p. 147).

Edward Malbone numbered among these evils the neglect of his early education. It is possible however that this neglect assisted the development of the painter by throwing him upon his own resources. As a small boy he showed an inventive genius and facile hands in fashioning kites with streamers of fireworks, in cutting moulds and in making little lead toys. He early began to draw, copying any picture or illustration at hand. He made his own brushes and paints and at the age of eleven or twelve he started to draw gods and goddesses in India ink on small pieces of ivory or bone. These he cut himself and framed in twisted wire. At one time the local theatre contributed to his artistic education for in it he learned to paint scenery. He finally painted an entire scene which won him a ticket of admission and local renown. But chiefly he painted heads, soon attempted likenesses, and finally devoted himself entirely to portraiture. He kept much to his own room and was somewhat of a trial to his brother and sisters who thought him unsocial and different. His earnestness and passion for work, amounting to a creative fury, were remarkable in a young boy and figured as a source of power in his later career. He used to visit the fascinating shop of Samuel King who made compasses and quadrants and sometimes portraits, and who lent him engravings to copy and helped him with his painting.

In spite of this help, Malbone must be considered a self-taught artist, for by painstaking and constant copying he taught himself to draw and then learned for himself the difficult technique of miniature painting. When at the age of sixteen he painted a head of Thomas Lawrence on paper which was thought a work of genius, his father sent the picture to a painting master in Philadelphia for criticism, but the master sent word back that the boy would take the bread out of his mouth and named an exorbitant fee for giving him lessons, and the question of a teacher was dropped. In the fall of the next year, 1794, Malbone left home without telling anyone but his sister, Harriet, and went to Providence where he set up as a professional miniature painter, an act of considerable rashness in a lad of seventeen. In a letter to his father shortly after his arrival in Providence, he said he expected to succeed in his project and hoped soon to furnish material aid in support of the family. "I must conclude," he wrote, "with making use of that name which I shall study never to dishonor. Your dutiful son, Edward G. Malbone" (*Scribner's Magazine,* May 1910, p. 560). That his confidence in his ability to paint miniatures was justified is shown by his immediate success in Providence. During his stay of a year and a half he drew commissions from the best families and, if an extant receipt is typical, charged $23.33 for his portraits. The few known examples of his first work in Providence were brought together for the first time in 1929 during an exhibition of Malbone miniatures held at the National Gallery of Art. They show the use of fine stipple for modeling the face, scrupulous regard to detail in finishing face and costume, and careful painting in the background.

In October 1795 Malbone was called home to attend the funeral of his father. He returned to Providence, but in the spring of the following year established himself in Boston. There his ability was quickly recognized and his charming manner won him a circle of friends. He renewed his friendship with Washington Allston, then a student at Harvard, whom he had known at Newport. Too much attention from Boston society might have interfered with his career, had he been less determined to perfect his art. He told Dunlap that his average allowance for work each day was eight hours. His self-portrait painted in 1797 (belonging to R. T. H. Halsey) pictures a serious young man possessed of poise and charm, with powdered hair, and wearing the elegant costume of the day. He was tall and slender and Dunlap says by nature of good constitution.

The next two years Malbone divided between New York and Philadelphia. In the autumn of 1800 he went to Charleston, where new friendships included one with the artist Charles Fraser [*q.v.*]. His technique by this time had changed from a stiff, detailed style to a freer method. He used delicate interwoven lines of color which performed the double function of creating form and giving color. The backgrounds are light and simple, kept entirely subordinate to the subject. The miniature of Thomas Lowndes (belonging to C. S. Green), an excellent example of this second style, illustrates Malbone's masterly use of line.

In May 1801 he and Allston went to London. His judgments on what he saw in the galleries and studios are contained in a letter to Fraser: "Mr. West is decidedly the greatest painter amongst them for history. Mr. Lawrence is the best portrait painter . . . Amongst miniature painters, I think Mr. Shelly [*sic*] and Mr. Cosway the best" (Dunlap, *post,* II, pp. 141–42).

Though Malbone admired Shelley and Cosway he was able even at this time to surpass them in portraying individuality. Benjamin West, the president of the Royal Academy, praised Malbone's ability after seeing one of his miniatures and advised him not to "look forward to anything short of the highest excellence." While in London Malbone painted "The Hours" which is now in the Providence Athenæum. He returned to Charleston in December 1801. From this time another or third style is recognizable in his painting, a development of the second period. He used the same delicate lines of color in painting the face but the stroke is even freer and somewhat broader. Subtle transitions give the effect of smoothness. The size of the ivory becomes larger, the largest known portrait being seven inches by five, a beautiful three-quarter-length portrait of Eliza Mason, painted in 1805 (now belonging to Mrs. Samuel Dunn Parker).

It is said that Malbone sometimes painted on hard wood, inlaying pieces of ivory for the face and hands. He always placed his subject on a seat somewhat higher than his own and while at work never conversed. Latterly he received fifty dollars for his portraits. His signature, sometimes a neat and graceful "Malbone," sometimes "E. G. Malbone" or again "E. G. M." or "E. M.," is usually very delicately painted or scratched in some inconspicuous corner of the ivory. Often the date appears. Altogether hardly more than a third of Malbone's miniatures are signed. Most of the years 1804 and 1805 were spent in Boston and in December 1805 he sailed for Charleston, intending to go again to London in the following spring. But in March he contracted tuberculosis and was forced to give up his painting. Neither horseback riding nor a trip to Jamaica gave him relief, and at the home of his cousin, Robert Mackay, in Savannah, Ga., he died on May 7, 1807, at the age of twenty-nine. He was buried in the Colonial Cemetery at Savannah.

Malbone's genius as a technician and as a portrait painter is undisputed. The great variety resulting from his continual and thoughtful experimentation is one of his chief claims to superiority over other miniaturists. This variety is a result not merely of his inventiveness in method but of his ability in characterization, an ability that lifts his art out of the merely good and places it with the most distinguished. He painted perhaps as many as three hundred miniatures in his short professional career of twelve years. Some of these are lost and most of the known examples are privately owned. There are, however, examples in the Metropolitan Museum, the Boston Museum of Fine Arts, the Pennsylvania Academy, the Rhode Island School of Design, and the Providence Athenæum, which has also two oil paintings by Malbone.

[Trinity Church records, Newport, R. I.; Rhode Island records; copies of Malbone family letters belonging to Mrs. W. S. Lovell; anonymous article in *Analectic Mag.*, Sept. 1815; Wm. Dunlap, *A Hist. of the Rise and Progress of the Arts of Design in the U. S.* (1918), vol. II; R. T. H. Halsey, article in *Scribner's Mag.*, May 1910; M. H. Elliott, "Edward Greene Malbone, Rhode Island's Distinguished Miniature Painter," *Providence Jour.*, Sept. 22, 1926; Theodore Bolton, *Early Am. Portrait Painters in Miniature* (1921); Harry B. Wehle, *Am. Miniatures, 1730–1850* (1927); J. L. Brockway, "Malbone, Am. Miniature Painter," *Am. Mag. of Art*, Apr. 1929; R. P. Tolman, "Newly Discovered Malbone Miniatures," *Antiques*, Nov. 1929, and "Other Malbone Miniatures," *Ibid.*, Apr. 1933; and *The Metropolitan Museum of Art Cat. of an Exhibition of Miniatures Painted in America, 1720–1850* (1927). R. P. Tolman, director of the National Gallery of Art, has in progress a definitive study on the life and works of Malbone.]

J. L. B.

MALCOLM, DANIEL (Nov. 29, 1725–Oct. 23, 1769), patriot, merchant, and sea-captain, was descended from the Scottish Clan Malcolm. He was born in Georgetown, Me., the son of Michael and Sarah Malcolm, who came to America a few years before Daniel's birth. His father was one of the selectmen of Georgetown for many years. Two other sons were Allen Malcolm, who fought on the patriot side in the Revolution, and Capt. John Malcolm, a customs officer under the Crown, who was twice tarred and feathered. Daniel became a sea-captain and owned several vessels. He bought two houses in Boston and was a warden of Christ Church. A leader of the Sons of Liberty, he was associated with Otis, Hancock, Revere, and Adams. Believing that the Revenue Acts were unjust, he became the most active antagonist of the customs authorities. On Sept. 24, 1766, the comptroller of customs, having information that a number of casks of uncustomed wine were concealed in Malcolm's cellar, went to his house armed with a writ of assistance, which was presumed by the superior court to give the right to enter and search. Malcolm refused to unlock an inner cellar. He "solemnly swore it should not be [opened] and if any Man attempted it, he would blow his Brains out . . . and took a Pistol in his hand and soon after another and then put on a sword. . . . He said . . . he knew the Laws and that no Body had a right to Come into his House" (*Proceedings of the Massachusetts Historical Society*, vol. LVIII, p. 27). The defeated officers returned in the afternoon with the high sheriff to find Malcolm's gate locked. They besieged him in his house until sunset, but to no avail. Then fearing for their lives from the crowd which had gathered, they abandoned the siege.

"I only wanted for the good of the Country to know whether they would break open Houses," said Malcolm (*Ibid.*, p. 42). When this case was referred to England, the attorney-general ruled that the courts in America had no right to issue writs of assistance.

In February 1768, a schooner of Malcolm's laden with sixty pipes of wines came into Boston harbor. He ordered her to anchor among the islands five miles out, landed the cargo in the night, and had it carried in drays to safety, each load being guarded by men with clubs. A few days later he called and presided at a meeting of the merchants of Boston, at which they entered into an agreement not to import any goods from Great Britain for a year and a half. Of this event Gov. Francis Bernard wrote to London: "This may be said to be the first movement of the merchants against the Acts of Parliament." On June 10, 1768, John Hancock's sloop *Liberty* was seized by the customs officers because her cargo of Madeira wine had been unloaded at night. Malcolm raised a mob at the wharf and attempted to prevent the seizure which was being made by marines from the *Romney*. Thus he led the patriots in the first clash with the armed forces of England. Malcolm married Ann Fudge, by whom he had several children. He died Oct. 23, 1769, at the age of forty-four. His gravestone on Copp's Hill, Boston, records his services: "a true Son of Liberty, a Friend to the Publick, an Enemy to oppression, and one of the foremost in opposing the Revenue Acts on America." This stone still shows the marks of bullets fired at it by British soldiers.

[Sources include: Georgetown, Me., records; Suffolk Deeds; Suffolk Probate Files, No. 14,571; Christ Church records; Lee MSS., Harvard College Lib., I, 15–23; G. G. Wolkins, "The Seizure of Hancock's Sloop 'Liberty'," *Proc. Mass. Hist. Soc.*, vol. LV (1923), and "Daniel Malcom and Writs of Assistance," *Ibid.*, vol. LVIII (1925); *Letters to the Right Hon. the Earl of Hillsborough from Gov. Bernard, Gen. Gage, and . . . Council for the Province of Mass. Bay* (1769); *A Report of the Record Commissioners . . . of Boston Containing the Boston Town Records, 1758 to 1769* (1886). Malcolm's name was sometimes spelled Malcom or Malcomb.] F. W. C. H.

MALCOLM, JAMES PELLER (August 1767–Apr. 5, 1815), line-engraver, author, and antiquary, who in earlier life signed himself James Peller Malcom, was the son of Moses and Mary (Peller) Malcom and was born in Philadelphia, Pa. He began his education in the Friends' School, then presided over by Robert Proud [*q.v.*]. His great-grandfather, James Peller, came over in the ship with William Penn, returned with him to England, but later settled with his family in Pennsylvania. Malcolm never ceased to remember that he had been born a British subject, and continued Loyalist until his death, spending the last half of his life in England. Because of the dangers expected of the Revolution he was taken to Pottstown, Pa., just before the struggle resulted in open warfare, and there his education was continued. He returned to Philadelphia after the war was ended, in 1784, and there he began to devote himself to the study of art. Having a natural aptitude for drawing, he entered the field of engraving. His first published engraving was the frontispiece for Col. John Parke's *Lyric Works of Horace,* which he engraved in line after a sketch by Peter Markoe in 1786. This example is good neither technically nor artistically, but it displayed promise. Under the patronage of the Rev. Jacob Duché and Thomas Willing of Philadelphia Malcolm went to England. He studied three years in the schools of the Royal Academy. His engraving of a view of Bush Hill, the seat of William Hamilton, was published in the *Universal Magazine,* London, in 1787 (vol. LXXXI, Supp., facing p. 361).

In England Malcolm made illustrations for the magazines, especially for the *Gentleman's Magazine.* He is thought to have returned to Philadelphia in 1792 or 1793, though in his own autobiography in the *Gentleman's Magazine* (May 1815), he makes no mention of ever having visited his native land. Originally he intended to become a painter, but after his course in the Royal Academy schools, he received no encouragement and began to devote himself to engraving plates for the London magazines, and to compiling books. For Daniel Lysons' *Environs of London* (4 vols., 1792–96), he engraved seventy-nine plates. He was himself the author and illustrator of many volumes, among them *Londinium Redivivum* (4 vols., 1803–07); *Anecdotes of the Manners and Customs of London, During the Eighteenth Century* (1807); *Excursions in the County of Kent, Gloucester, Hereford, Monmouth, and Somerset* (1807); *Anecdotes of the Manners and Customs of London, from the Roman Invasion to the Year 1700* (1811); and *An Historical Sketch of the Art of Caricaturing* (1813). When his *Manners and Customs of London in the Eighteenth Century* reached a second edition in 1810, he seized the opportunity to refute his critics (the *European Magazine and London Review,* June 1808) by pointing out that for both text and illustrations he had used the great collection of John Nichols, the antiquary. As an engraver Malcolm was careful and painstaking in the interests of accuracy, but his art lacked inspiration. During the last three years of his life, he was ill, and his funds were exhausted. When he died his widow and aged mother were left destitute.

[The basic source for biographies of Malcolm is the autobiographical sketch in the *Gentleman's Mag.*, May 1815. For other printed references see *Ibid.*, Feb., June 1797, Jan., Apr. 1798, Supp. 1800, Apr. 1815; the *Dict. Nat. Biog.*; W. T. Lowndes, *The Bibliographer's Manual of English Lit.* (1834), vol. III; D. M. Stauffer, *Am. Engravers upon Copper and Steel* (1907), vol. I; T. J. Scharf and Thompson Westcott, *Hist. of Phila.* (1884), vol. II; *Phila. Monthly Mag.*, Apr. 1829. The names of his parents were derived from the manuscript records of Christ Church, Phila.]
J. J.

MALCOM, DANIEL [See MALCOLM, DANIEL, 1725–1769].

MALCOM, HOWARD (Jan. 19, 1799–Mar. 25, 1879), Baptist clergyman, author, educator, was born in Philadelphia, Pa., the son of John J. and Deborah (Howard) Malcom. His father had emigrated from Scotland; on his mother's side he was of Welsh ancestry. After the death of his father, his home was with his grandfather, John Howard, a wealthy merchant. He entered Dickinson College but left in his junior year to take a position in a large commission house in Philadelphia. During the following seventeen months of business experience, he passed through a religious experience which resulted in his joining the Sansom Street Baptist Church, where in 1818 he was licensed to preach. There, also, having spent the intervening time at Princeton Theological Seminary, he was ordained a Baptist clergyman on Apr. 23, 1820. On May 1, 1820, he was married to Lydia Morris Shields, who died in 1833. She was the mother of his eldest son. On June 26, 1838, he was married to Ruth A. Dyer, by whom he had two sons and two daughters.

From 1820 to 1826 he was pastor of a Baptist church at Hudson, N. Y., where his capacity for leadership became so well and favorably known that the American Sunday School Union invited him to give all of his time to the field work of that organization. In this service he visited nearly all the principal towns and cities in the United States. In November 1827 he accepted the pastorate of the Federal Street Baptist Church, Boston, which he had to relinquish in 1835 because of a throat disease which made it difficult for him to speak to large audiences. That same year the American Baptist Foreign Missionary Union sent him abroad to visit missionary stations in India, Burma, and China. As a fruitage of three years of travel he published in 1839, *Travels in South-Eastern Asia,* a work which added to his growing reputation as an author, his first venture in authorship, *A Dictionary of Important Names, Objects, and Terms Found in the Holy Scriptures* (1830), having already become the most popular book of its kind.

In 1840 he became president of Georgetown College, Ky., where he remained nine years. When he voted for an anti-slavery amendment to the state constitution, the trustees of the college asked for his resignation. He had been warned that he would have to leave the state if he so voted. Returning to Philadelphia, he soon became pastor of his old home church, but the large auditorium overtaxed his voice and in 1851 he resigned to become president of Lewisburg University, now Bucknell University, Lewisburg, Pa. For six years he made a valuable contribution to the growth of that institution. His literary interests came to absorb so much of his time and strength, however, that in 1857 he resigned his presidency to give them first place. To facilitate his work as a writer he moved to Philadelphia where he became identified with a wide variety of public interests. He was president of the American Baptist Historical Society, of the American Peace Society, of the Pennsylvania Baptist Educational Society, and from 1874 till his death, of Hahnemann Medical College.

In addition to his *Dictionary* and *Travels,* he published about a dozen other books, among them *Extent and Efficacy of the Atonement* (1833), a discourse; *A Brief Memoir of Mrs. Lydia M. Malcom* (1833); *The Christian's Rule of Marriage* (1834); *Theological Index: References to the Principal Works in Every Department of Religious Literature* (1868; 2nd ed., 1870). He also edited several works, including Thomas à Kempis' *The Imitation of Christ* (1830), Matthew Henry's *Communicant's Companion* (1840), William Law's *A Serious Call to a Devout and Holy Life* (1835), and Joseph Butler's *Analogy of Religion* (1857). As his *Dictionary* passed through successive editions, he continued to revise and enlarge it for thirty years. From his royalties he built a home in Lewisburg, Pa.

[*Bucknell Alumni Mo.*, vol. IX; *Dickinson Alumni Record*; *Baptist Memorial and Monthly Record,* vol. X (1851); *The Am. Cyc.*, vol. XI (1875); William Cathcart, *The Baptist Encyc.* (1881); *Princeton Theological Seminary Biog. Cat.* (1909); *Necrological Report . . . Princeton Theological Seminary,* 1879; J. H. Spencer, *A Hist. of Ky. Baptists* (1866), vol. I; *Public Ledger* (Phila.), Mar. 26, 1879.]
H. T. C.

MALCOM, JAMES PELLER [See MALCOLM, JAMES PELLER, 1767–1815].

MALL, FRANKLIN PAINE (Sept. 28, 1862–Nov. 17, 1917), anatomist and embryologist, was born on a farm near Belle Plaine, Iowa, the son of Francis and Louise (Miller) Mall.

His father had emigrated to the United States from Germany in 1848; his mother, who was born in this country, died when he was a young boy. Having obtained his early education in a boarding school near his home, he entered the department of medicine and surgery of the University of Michigan and received the degree of M.D. in 1883. He showed at this time a strong inclination to get knowledge at first hand, rather than through lectures. Victor C. Vaughan [*q.v.*] and Henry Sewall gave him a special inspiration. After graduating he studied at Heidelberg and then at Leipzig under the physiologist K. F. W. Ludwig and the embryologist Wilhelm His. Returning to the United States, he became fellow in pathology at Johns Hopkins Hospital and later instructor in pathology. When Clark University was opened, in 1889, he became adjunct professor of vertebrate anatomy there, but three years later went to the new University of Chicago, as professor of anatomy, with others of his colleagues at Clark. He was soon called back to Baltimore, as head of the department of anatomy in the Johns Hopkins Medical School. In 1914 he was appointed, in addition, director of the department of embryology of the Carnegie Institution, Washington. He maintained close relations with biologists as well as medical men and was a trustee of the Woods Hole Biological Laboratory and member of the advisory board of the Wistar Institute, a member of the National Academy of Sciences, the American Philosophical Society, and a number of other learned societies.

Mall contributed much to the knowledge of human anatomy and embryology. In 1883 American laboratories were adding little to the results of research in these subjects. An English reviewer of Mall's first volume dealing with the accomplishments of the Carnegie Laboratory referred to the remarkable changes which had taken place in the study of anatomy in America during the past twenty-five years, and added: "In effecting this transformation the chief credit must be assigned to one man—Franklin P. Mall. . . . By his personal influence and example, by pupils and disciples, and by reason of the inherent excellence of the Leipzig traditions, he has succeeded in Germanising the majority of the dissecting rooms and anatomical laboratories throughout the length and breadth of North America" (*Nature,* London, Feb. 3, 1916). In medical education Mall stood for freedom of curricula, concentration of courses, broad electives, and freedom for research by the teacher. His department of anatomy at Baltimore was the first to bring into one discipline as correlated studies cytology, histology, embryology, and adult structure. He rarely lectured, insisting that learning from nature was of primary importance and that students should do their own thinking. He was largely responsible for the founding of the *American Journal of Anatomy* in 1901, and was one of its editors until his death. He played a prominent part in the American Association of Anatomists, of which he was president from 1905 to 1907. In 1912 he formulated a plan for an institute of human embryology which so impressed the president and trustees of the Carnegie Institution that they created the department of embryology for him. To increase his already large collection of human embryos he sent a circular letter to physicians of the United States and as far afield as the Orient. As a result the laboratory has ever since been the world repository for specimens. Their study was systematically begun, new methods of research were invented and perfected, and a series of publications, *Contributions to Embryology,* undertaken, which reached seven volumes during Mall's lifetime.

His own researches were numerous and important. He first traced the embryologic origin of the thymus gland, added to knowledge of the structure and function of the intestines, introduced the idea of histological units in organs, worked out the muscular system of the heart, described with unexampled completeness a human embryo of about twenty-eight days, laid the foundation of the science of the development of organs, and placed the subject of the production of human monsters on a scientific basis.

Though shy and retiring in company, and a little tinged with pessimism, he loved association with scientific men. He was too absorbed in his own ideas to converse fluently; but he had broad human interests and a humor that was occasionally a little biting. Behind his whimsical way of saying things, however, was profound wisdom. In 1895 he married Mabel Stanley Glover, who with two daughters survived him.

[Simon Flexner, "Dr. Franklin P. Mall, an Appreciation," and F. R. Sabin, "Franklin Paine Mall; A Review of His Scientific Achievement," in *Science,* Mar. 15, 1918; G. C. Huber, "Franklin Paine Mall," in *Anatomical Record,* Jan. 20, 1918; "Memorial Services in Honor of Franklin Paine Mall, Professor of Anatomy, Johns Hopkins University, 1893 to 1917," *Johns Hopkins Hospital Bull.,* May 1918; *Jour. of the Iowa State Medic. Soc.,* Mar. 1928; H. A. Kelly and W. L. Burrage, *Am. Medic. Biogs.* (1920); *Who's Who in America,* 1916–17; *Evening Sun* (Baltimore), Nov. 17, 1917.]

C. B. D.

MALLARY, ROLLIN CAROLAS (May 27, 1784–Apr. 15, 1831), congressman from Vermont, was born in Cheshire, Conn., the eldest of seven children of Daniel and Martha (Dutton)

Mallary. In 1795 he moved with his father to Poultney, Vt., from which place he entered Middlebury College, graduating in 1805. He studied law with Horatio Seymour at Middlebury and with Robert Temple at Rutland, and, after serving one year (1806–07) as preceptor of Castleton Seminary, was admitted to the bar of Rutland County in March 1807. He practised law with conspicuous success in Castleton until 1818, when he transferred his office to Poultney. While in Castleton he was state's attorney in the years 1810–13 and 1815–16. He was appointed in October 1807 as secretary to the governor and council and held the position intermittently in 1807, 1809–12, and 1815–19.

In 1819 Mallary was a candidate for Congress against Orsamus C. Merrill, of Bennington, the incumbent. Merrill was declared elected, but Mallary claimed the seat, and the House, after a hearing, decided in his favor, Jan. 13, 1820. He proved to be a very effective business member of Congress, mild in manner and unspectacular, but punctual and industrious. He won some distinction as an opponent of the admission of Missouri with slavery, and later became a conspicuous champion of the protective system. At the opening of the Twentieth Congress he was made chairman of the House committee on manufacture and reported the notorious "Tariff of Abominations" in 1828. He was the leader of the debate in the House on this measure and his pertinacity was largely responsible for its passage. At a notable dinner given in his honor at Rutland, on July 6, 1830, he was enthusiastically lauded for his efforts in behalf of the protective system. He was reëlected for six successive terms. Because of overwork, his health failed during the winter of 1830–31 and, after the adjournment of Congress, he was removed to the home of a relative in Baltimore, where he died. Funeral services were held in Baltimore, but he was buried in the old cemetery at East Poultney, Vt., where a marble monument to his memory was erected by the Rutland County Bar. Mallary had married, on Oct. 29, 1806, Ruth Stanley, eldest daughter of John Stanley, by whom he had three children. He was a trustee of Middlebury College from 1825 until his death. His chief distinction was his advocacy of the protective tariff.

[See: Abby M. Hemenway, *The Vt. Hist. Gazeteer,* vol. III (1877); Walter H. Crockett, *Vt., The Green Mountain State,* vol. V (1923); J. S. Ullery, *Men of Vt.* (1894); J. Joslin and others, *A Hist. of the Town of Poultney, Vt.* (1875); *Biog. Dir. Am. Cong.* (1928); *Cat. of the Officers and Students of Middlebury Coll., 1800 to 1900* (1901); *Niles' Weekly Reg.,* Apr. 23, 1831. Mallary's middle name is variously spelled. This sketch follows the spelling given in the *Biog. Dir. Am. Cong.*]

C. M. F.

MALLERY, GARRICK (Apr. 23, 1831–Oct. 24, 1894), soldier, ethnologist, was born in Wilkes-Barre, Pa., the son of Garrick and Catherine J. (Hall) Mallery. His early education was received in private schools, and since his father was a jurist, the son was naturally destined for the legal profession. Accordingly, after graduating from Yale in 1850, he studied law and in 1853 was admitted to the bar in Philadelphia. At the outbreak of the Civil War he immediately enlisted as a private but on June 4, 1861, he was appointed captain in the 71st Pennsylvania Infantry. At the battle of Peach Orchard, Va., the following year, he was wounded and taken prisoner. After his exchange, he was commissioned, Feb. 17, 1863, lieutenant-colonel of the 13th Pennsylvania Cavalry. He was honorably mustered out July 15, 1864, and brevetted colonel of volunteers on Mar. 13, 1865. The following year, July 28, he was commissioned captain in the 43rd Infantry of the regular army, and on Mar. 2, 1867, was brevetted lieutenant-colonel. When in 1870 the system of meteorological observations, which developed into the Signal Service Bureau, was established, Mallery became acting signal officer and remained with this branch of the service for six years. On duty at Fort Rice, Dakota, in 1876, he became interested in the pictography and sign language of the Indians. Later he was engaged on field work with Maj. J. W. Powell in connection with surveys in the Rocky Mountains. Disability from wounds received in the war caused his retirement from the army, July 1, 1879.

This same year he became connected with the Bureau of Ethnology, under the Smithsonian Institution, with headquarters in Washington, D. C. His first paper, "The Former and Present Number of Our Indians" (*Proceedings of the American Association for the Advancement of Science,* vol. XXVI, 1877), was on the moot question that has been raised so many times and not satisfactorily answered. A paper originating from his observations among the Indians, which foreshadowed his future work with the Bureau, was: "A Calendar of the Dakota Nation" (*Bulletin of the Geological and Geographical Survey,* vol. III, no. 1, 1877). This paper related to the conveying of ideas of events by picture writing. Easily the foremost student of the subject, he published: *Introduction to the Study of Sign Language Among the North American Indians as Illustrating the Gesture Speech of Mankind* (Smithsonian Institution—Bureau of Ethnology, 1880), followed by: "Sign Language among North American Indians Compared with That of Other Peoples and Deaf Mutes" (*First*

Annual Report of the Bureau of American Ethnology, 1881). An important feature of this study was the philosophical discussion of the origin of the communication of ideas by the vehicle of language symbols. Mallery's culminating work, requiring years of assiduous collection of data and original investigation on pictography, appeared in 1893—"Picture Writing of the North American Indians" (*Tenth Annual Report of the Bureau of American Ethnology*). As a monumental storehouse of well classified and digested data it is without peer. Through all its overwhelming mass of necessary illustrations the philosophic mind of the author is evident. In only one instance did Mallery's writing evoke controversy. The paper: "Israelite and Indian: a Parallel in Planes of Culture" (*Popular Science Monthly,* November–December 1889), provoked severe and no doubt justified criticism by one of the races thus brought into juxtaposition. As a man of solid attainments Mallery received many high honors. He was an active member of many scientific societies. A tall, erect, dignified man, always well groomed, he gave the impression of capability and directive force. Unmistakably an army man trained in formality, he was nevertheless a pleasant associate and appreciated by his scientific equals. His influence in promoting scientific methods in the formative period of the branch of anthropology was notable. On Apr. 14, 1870, he married Helen W. Wyckoff of New York.

[*Obit. Record Grads. Yale Univ.,* June 1895; F. B. Heitman, *Hist. Reg. and Dict. U. S. Army* (1903), vol. I; S. P. Bates, *Hist. of Pa. Volunteers,* vols. II (1869), III (1870); J. W. Powell, in *Johnson's Universal Encyc.* (1897); Robert Fletcher, *Brief Memoirs of Col. Garrick Mallery* (1895); *Ann. Report of the Board of Regents of the Smithsonian Institution,* 1895; *Evening Star* (Washington, D. C.), Oct. 25, 1894; personal recollections.] W. H.

MALLET, JOHN WILLIAM (Oct. 10, 1832–Nov. 7, 1912), chemist, was born near Dublin, Ireland, the eldest of six children of Robert Mallet, an engineer and fellow of the Royal Society (see *Dictionary of National Biography*), and Cordelia (Watson) Mallet. After studying chemistry (1848) at the Royal College of Surgeons in Ireland, he entered Trinity College in 1849, publishing about this time his first scientific contribution, "Notice of a New Chemical Examination of Killinite," in the *Journal of the Geological Society of Dublin* (vol. IV, 1848–50). In 1852 he graduated (Ph.D.) under Wöhler at Göttingen and in 1853 received the degree of A.B. at Trinity College, Dublin. Meanwhile he had assisted his father in experiments on the velocity of shock-transmission from gunpowder explosions through rock and loose earth, and had commenced the preparation of a "Catalogue of Recorded Earthquakes from B.C. 1606 to A.D. 1842," which was published in the *Report of the British Association for the Advancement of Science* for 1852, 1853, and 1854 (1853–55).

Coming to America in 1853, he was assistant professor of analytical chemistry at Amherst College for several months in 1854, then became chemist to the state geological survey of Alabama (1855–56) and professor of chemistry at the state university (1855–60). From the papers of Michael Tuomey [*q.v.*] he edited the *Second Biennial Report on the Geology of Alabama* (1858). He also undertook an exhaustive scientific study of the culture of cotton. For this work specimens of plants, soils, and rocks were secured from India, Algeria, Africa, and America; soils were analyzed; density, cohesion, capillarity, and absorption of gases were determined; stems, roots, seeds, fibers were separately analyzed. The resulting treatise was published in book form under the title, *Cotton: the Chemical, Geological, and Meteorological Conditions Involved in Its Successful Cultivation* (1862), and appeared the same year in the *Proceedings of the Royal Society of London* (vol. XI, 1862).

Enlisting as a private in the service of the Confederacy shortly after the outbreak of the Civil War, Mallet became in November 1861 an officer on the staff of Gen. R. E. Rodes [*q.v.*], and in 1862 was given general supervision of the ordnance laboratories of the Confederacy. After the war, for a group of Northern capitalists, he made a survey for petroleum in Louisiana and Texas (1865). He was professor of chemistry in the medical department of the University of Louisiana, 1865–67; at the University of Virginia, 1867–83; in the University of Texas, 1883–84; and in Jefferson Medical College, 1884–85. He then returned to the University of Virginia, where he remained, as professor emeritus after 1908, until his death.

As a lecturer Mallet was systematic, concise, clear in his presentation and explanation of facts. He insisted that each of his students make some investigation and so add his fragment to the sum total of knowledge. His own publications comprised more than one hundred papers on new compounds, minerals, and chemical and physical phenomena. In 1881–82 he made investigations of drinking waters, reporting the results in the *Annual Report of the National Board of Health, 1882* (1883). Three times (1886, 1888, 1896) he was a member of the Assay Commission. In 1877–78 he lectured at Johns Hopkins University. He was one of the founders of the American Chemical Society and its president in 1882, a member of several European chemical societies, and a fellow of the Royal Society of London. He served as member of the International Committee on Atomic Weights, 1899; and of the International Congress of Applied Chemistry in Berlin, 1903, and Rome, 1906. He was married in 1857 to Mary Elizabeth Ormond of Tuscaloosa, Ala., who died in 1886; and in 1888 to Joséphine (Pagès) Burthe of Louisiana. Three children were born of his first marriage. Although he was a resident of the United States for more than fifty years, Mallet never relinquished his status as a British subject. He died in Virginia at the age of eighty.

[F. P. Dunnington, in *Am. Chemical Jour.*, Jan. 1913; W. H. Echols, in *Univ. of Va. Alumni Bull.*, Jan. 1913; full bibliography of Mallet's writings, *Ibid.*, Oct. 1923; *Who's Who in America*, 1912–13; *Times-Dispatch* (Richmond), Nov. 8, 1912.] F. P. V.

MALLINCKRODT, EDWARD (Jan. 21, 1845–Feb. 1, 1928), manufacturer of chemicals, benefactor of educational institutions, was born on a farm near St. Louis, Mo., the son of Emil and Eleanor Didier (Luckie) Mallinckrodt. His father, disheartened by conditions in Germany, had emigrated fourteen years before from Westphalia, home of the grandfather, Arnold Mallinckrodt, a Dortmund publisher. Edward's parents had looked forward to his remaining on the farm, but when he was eighteen Liebig's treatises turned him to chemistry. Accordingly his father, who was then visiting in Germany, made arrangements for Edward and Otto, a younger son, to study the subject there, and Edward spent the next three years in Fresenius' laboratory, Wiesbaden, the De Haën works near Hanover, and the University of Berlin.

Returning in 1867, Edward and Otto joined an elder brother, Gustav, under the firm name of G. Mallinckrodt & Company, in what was a pioneer undertaking in the Middle West, the manufacture of chemicals. The enterprise had an unpretentious start, being housed in a small, rough structure on the parental farm. With the West undeveloped and the South prostrated by the Civil War, St. Louis was an unfavorable location. Since it was necessary, moreover, to send products East to compete with established firms, hardships were many in the first decade. Otto and Gustav died six months apart (1876–77), and in 1882 the business was incorporated as the Mallinckrodt Chemical Works, with Edward as president. Although learned in chemical technology, he now devoted himself to the commercial side of the business and the enterprise grew rapidly. Before he died its output included 1,500 chemical products, and it maintained offices or branches in New York, Jersey City, Toronto, and Montreal. In 1889 he formed the National Ammonia Company with subsidiaries as far away as Australia. The press called him the "ammonia king." He was also active in the Phosphorous Compounds Company at Niagara Falls and the St. Louis Union Trust Company, and was an owner of downtown real estate in St. Louis.

Wealth enabled him to indulge a generous nature. His largest single gift, $500,000 to Harvard for its chemical laboratory, named for him, was made because he felt that although chemistry held more potential benefits than any other science, American facilities for its study were inferior to those in some other countries. Further gifts endowed departments in Washington University Medical School and helped to complete its $1,000,000 Mallinckrodt Radiological Institute. He established a ward in the St. Louis Children's Hospital in memory of his wife, formerly Jennie Anderson of St. Louis, whom he married June 7, 1876, and who died in 1913. St. Luke's Hospital, which he helped direct for twenty-five years, as president part of the time, received numerous grants, and the St. Louis College of Pharmacy, which he headed, funds for a scholarship. His will gave approximately $2,000,000 to such "benevolent, scientific, charitable, literary or educational" agencies as his only son should see fit to benefit. He was a member of the Washington University board, a director of the Missouri Botanical Garden, a president of the Mercantile Library, and vice-president of the City Art Museum, to which he donated paintings. The professional and learned societies to which he belonged included British and German organizations. An expert gardener, he was at eighty still caring for the flowers about his homes. He died soon after his eighty-third birthday, of pneumonia following a heart attack, and was buried in Bellefontaine Cemetery, St. Louis.

[Published sources include: *Industrial and Engineering Chemistry*, news. ed., Mar. 10, 1928; W. L. R. Gifford, "Edward Mallinckrodt," in *Harvard Alumni Bull.*, May 22, 1924; *St. Louis Post-Dispatch*, Feb. 1, 1928; *Who's Who in America*, 1928–29. A biographical sketch prepared by George Dumas Stout, of St. Louis, for private distribution is soon to appear.] I. D.

MALLORY, STEPHEN RUSSELL (*c.* 1813–Nov. 9, 1873), secretary of the Confederate navy, was the son of Charles Mallory, a civil engineer, of Reading, Conn., professionally engaged on public work in Trinidad Island, near Venezuela, where he had met and married the sixteen-year-old Ellen Russell, recently of County Waterford, Ireland. They had two children, John, born about 1811, and Stephen Russell Mallory, born in Trinidad about 1813, though it is worth noting that his tombstone in St. Michael's Cemetery, Pensacola, bears no birth date. About 1814 the parents moved first to the United States, then to Havana for Charles Mallory's health. Before settling at Key West around 1820, they entered Stephen at school on Mobile Bay, where he remained six months or a year. In 1822 the father died of tuberculosis, and John did not long survive him. Stephen and his young mother lived on at Key West. Thus the future naval secretary grew up by the sea, loving and learning about ships. When he was fourteen his mother sent him inland to the Moravian school for boys at Nazareth, Pa. Three years in this institution of about eighty youths completed his meager schooling, but not his opportunities to learn and grow. In 1833 he was appointed inspector of customs at Key West. About the same time he began to study law with Judge William Marvin of the local United States district court. Admitted to the bar before 1840, he forged ahead. In 1845 President Polk made him collector of customs at Key West. Meanwhile he had fought in the Seminole War and married Angela, the daughter of Francisca and Josefa Moreno of Pensacola, Fla.

In 1850 Mallory was sufficiently prominent to be picked by his state as a delegate to the Southern convention at Nashville. Though eleven years later a secessionist, he did not attend this abortive convention. In 1851 the Florida legislature elected him to the United States Senate. His opponent, David L. Yulee, with Edwin M. Stanton for attorney, failed to convince the United States Senate that Mallory had been irregularly elected. Mallory was doubtless genuinely interested in the navy. Active in congressional naval reform, he was reëlected senator in 1857 and appointed chairman of the committee on naval affairs. Possibly his ability to speak Spanish correctly, as well as French, had something to do with President Buchanan's offering to send him (if Scharf, *post,* is correct) as United States minister to Spain in 1858. Mallory refused. When Florida seceded he gave up his seat in the Senate, returned to Pensacola, his home since 1858, and took emphatic stand for peace (J. B. Moore, *The Works of James Buchanan,* IX, 1910, pp. 285–86). But in February 1861 he accepted from President Jefferson Davis the office of secretary of the navy of the Confederacy.

Here was a challenge to all of Mallory's ability. Well versed in the advanced naval experiments of the American, Robert L. Stevens [*q.v.*]; aware that England and France were actually building iron fleets, he saw that the confederacy must instantly stimulate her young naval experts to lead the world in naval invention. As early as May 10, 1861, he wrote that the South should fight wood with iron (*War of the Rebellion: Official Records, Navy,* 2 ser. II, pp. 67–69). He dreamed of securing at once two ironclads from England or France. He hurried Lieut. James H. North in May to London, but he did not wait for North's report, or for Congress to sanction the building of an ironclad at home. Having discovered a brilliant naval inventor in John Mercer Brooke [*q.v.*], by March 1862 he had afloat in Hampton Roads that strange murderous craft, the *Merrimac-Virginia.* He pinned greater hope on the *Mississippi,* an ironclad, more like the European models, which in April 1862 the Tift brothers, eagerly aided by the secretary, were feverishly completing at New Orleans. Within about two weeks of a successful launching of the *Mississippi,* the Tifts were forced to burn her to keep her from falling into the hands of the approaching enemy.

Mallory failed to secure a single up-to-date ironclad, but his wide naval horizon, his grasp of naval construction, and his tireless endeavor so stimulated specialists like Brooke and George Minor, chief of ordnance and hydrography, to naval organization and invention that the Confederacy, which started without ships or navy yards, anticipated modern naval invention in deadly torpedoes and submarines to such extent that it terrorized the Federal navy and effectively delayed it from penetrating the great rivers of Virginia. Insight into Mallory's vehement, unconquerable nature, inherited possibly from his Irish mother, may be seen in his ardent wish (not carried out) to burn the Tredegar Iron Works before the Davis government evacuated Richmond.

Retreating with President Davis in April 1865, Mallory joined his wife in La Grange, Ga., and was hauled out of bed there by armed men just past midnight, May 20, 1865, and hustled off half-clothed, a prisoner of state. Until March 1866 he was held in Fort Lafayette, New York Harbor. Released on parole, he returned to Pensacola with his family and resumed his law practice. But he did not have long to live. On Nov. 9, 1873, about the age of sixty, he died at Pensacola and lies buried there in St. Michael's Cemetery. His family consisted of two daughters and three sons, one of whom, Stephen Russell Mallory, Jr., a bachelor until his death, served for years with distinction in the United States House and Senate.

[Mallory has been meagerly treated by historians, and the brief accounts of him in encyclopedias and dictionaries differ astonishingly as to the facts of his life. His only extant papers, according to his grand-daughter, Mrs. Ruby Mallory Fisher of Pensacola, are unpublished letters to his wife, before and after 1865, and a personal manuscript diary which he wrote at Fort Lafayette. The statements in J. T. Scharf, *Hist. of the Confed. States Navy* (1887), pp. 29–30, were probably gained through correspondence with the Secretary's widow in 1886. See also: *War of the Rebellion: Official Records* (*Army* and *Navy*), especially 2 ser. I and II of the latter; *Senate Miscellaneous Doc. 1*, 32 Cong., Special Sess.; *Senate Miscellaneous Doc. 109* and *110*, 32 Cong., 1 Sess.; *Senate Report 349*, 32 Cong., 1 Sess.; Kathleen Bruce, *Va. Iron Manuf. in the Slave Era* (1931); and the *Mobile Daily Reg.*, Nov. 12, 1873. Contemporary local newspaper files are in the Fla. Hist. Soc. at Pensacola.]

K. B.

MALONE, SYLVESTER (May 8, 1821–Dec. 29, 1899), Roman Catholic priest, son of Laurence and Marcella (Martin) Malone, was born in Trim, County Meath, Ireland, where his father was a surveyor. Trained in a mixed school kept by two graduates of Trinity College, the boy imbibed a spirit of tactful toleration as well as classical lore. Experiencing a priestly call, in 1839 he accepted the invitation of Father Andrew Byrne [*q.v.*] to come to New York, where he entered St. Joseph's Seminary, Fordham. Ordained Aug. 15, 1844, he was assigned to Williamsburg (Brooklyn), then a town of about 5,000 people. Within three years, he paid off the debt of St. Mary's Church, gathered scattered Catholics into the fold, won the good will of even prejudiced citizens, and commenced the construction of the Church of Saints Peter and Paul, the first Gothic structure in the diocese. Caring for hordes of immigrants, he contracted both the smallpox and the ship's cholera (1848–49). On the eve of his journey to Rome in 1854, however, he could point to a congregation of 5,000, and a well-organized parish.

Regarded as a mild abolitionist, Father Malone suffered some inconveniences on this account; yet even his espousal of Republican principles did not lessen his popularity among Irish Democrats. When Fort Sumter was fired upon, he unfurled a flag from his church, which was soon carried to the front by members of the congregation. Public subscription provided a substitute flag, which waved from the steeple until the war ended. An active war-man, he aided sanitary fairs, quieted turbulent draft-rioters, encouraged enlistments, and donated a fourth of his salary to the fund for soldiers' wives. In 1866, as Bishop Loughlin's theologian, he attended the Second Plenary Council of Baltimore, where he was so impressed with reports of Catholic reconstruction in the South that in 1868 he toured that part of the country, contributing to the press descriptive letters of the conditions he found. On his return he urged Catholic activity among the negroes of the South. At Memorial-Day celebrations of the Grand Army of the Republic, he joined in the exercises with Protestant divines; and in 1870, at a Jewish reception, he aroused comment by demanding equal rights for black and white and for Jew and Gentile.

Returning from a tour through Europe and the Holy Land an ardent Irish Land Leaguer, he later became a liberal with strong labor views. He was deeply interested in civic affairs, clean government, temperance, the improvement of public schools, and the Anti-Poverty Society. Greatly disturbed by the break between Archbishop Corrigan and Edward McGlynn [*q.v.*], he courageously wrote to Pope Leo, in December 1886, that a censure of Dr. McGlynn, "the friend of the poor, the eloquent defender of the doctrines of the Church, the advocate of temperance and of every good cause that works for the public good," unless for a grave irregularity, would set the Church back half a century and raise the question of the rights of a citizen (letter reprinted in Zwierlein, *post,* III, 16). In 1894, urged by Hamilton Fish, Malone stood as a candidate for a regency of the University of New York, and, supported by Archbishop Ireland [*q.v.*], Bishop Ryan of Buffalo, and the Republican press, he was elected by a Republican legislature over Bishop McQuaid [*q.v.*]. Even Democratic papers were not personally hostile, though in some quarters his election was described as an affront to the Catholic Church, since Archbishop Corrigan and most of his suffragan bishops favored McQuaid. This year saw the celebration of Father Malone's golden jubilee as a priest. Congratulations came from Leo XIII, Cardinal Gibbons, the apostolic delegate, and many notable citizens as well as members of the hierarchy and priesthood. The event was considered a vindication of the liberal element in the metropolitan diocese of New York. The *Outlook* (Oct. 27, 1894) pertinently asked: "Why should such a man be allowed to remain in one pastorate? Naturally one would suppose that he would have risen to be a bishop or archbishop" (Oct. 27, 1894); while the *Independent* (Oct. 25) believed that his Republican politics prevented promotion. He continued as pastor of the parish which he had created until his death six years later.

[S. L. Malone, *Memorial of the Golden Jubilee of the Rev. Sylvester Malone* (1895); D. R. O'Brien, "The Centenary of Rev. Sylvester Malone, Great Catholic and Great Citizen," *Jour. Am.-Irish Hist. Soc.*, vol. XX (1921); *Father Malone Memorial, Citizens' Committee Report* (1923), on the occasion of placing a bust of Father Malone in the Brooklyn Institute of Arts and Sciences; H. R. Stiles, *Hist. of the County of*

Kings and City of Brooklyn, N. Y. (1884); F. J. Zwierlein, *The Life and Letters of Bishop McQuaid*, vol. III (1927); *Brooklyn Daily Eagle* and *N. Y. Times*, Dec. 29, 1899–Jan. 2, 1900.] R. J. P.

MALONE, WALTER (Feb. 10, 1866–May 18, 1915), jurist, poet, was born in De Soto County, Miss., near Memphis, Tenn., the son of Dr. Franklin Jefferson and Mary Louisa (Hardin) Malone. During the period of his education, which was principally at the University of Mississippi, where he studied law and was graduated with the degree of Ph.B. in 1887, he did much independent studying and writing. At sixteen he published *Claribel and Other Poems*, tramping the countryside to secure subscribers. In this, as in *The Outcast and Other Poems* (1886), there was, amid much that was grandiloquent and derivative, an unusual facility coupled with a serious predilection for the larger forms of verse and some leaning toward native materials.

Admitted to the bar in 1887, he moved to Memphis and practised law with his brother, James H. Malone, meanwhile serving during 1888 as city editor of the Memphis *Public Ledger* and writing poetry. Of a somewhat reserved, but gentle and sensitive temperament, he matured slowly as a poet. In *Narcissus and Other Poems* (1892), *Songs of Dusk and Dawn* (1894), and *Songs of December and June* (1896) his verse did not escape the savorlessness of current models; but it was precise, serious, and profuse in imagery. There were occasional metrical experiments and frank bursts of passion and melancholy, reflecting his loneliness in the contemporary scene. After writing a volume of short stories, *The Coming of the King* (1897), and three years' residence in New York, only partially satisfactory to him in literary achievement, Malone returned to Memphis in 1900, publishing in that year his *Songs of North and South*. In its seasonal poems and verse sketches full of affectionate observation of Southern scenes, richly described, this volume showed Malone at his best; but his poem "Opportunity," which appeared in 1905, captured the public ear and got him popular fame at a level somewhat lower than his own ideal. In 1904 he published *Poems*, containing his work up to that date with revisions.

Appointed judge of the second division of the Shelby County Circuit Court in 1905, he held this position, universally respected and loved, until his death, and conducted his court according to the best traditions of the Tennessee bench. He experimented a little with play-writing and published *Songs of East and West* (1906), a volume of travel poems. Then for some years he gave his whole creative strength to his epic poem, *Hernando De Soto*, which, notwithstanding his ill health and his fears that it could not be finished, was published in 1914. Though illustrating the difficulty of following epic conventions in modern verse, the poem was one of the most ambitious ever written by an American. The Mississippi River and the historic encounters of Spaniard and Indian had fired Malone's imagination. Despite much that was labored and artificial, his ardor infused magnificence of detail and narrative force into the long tale of De Soto's travels, conquests, and death. In its monumental quality it symbolized the grave intensity of Malone's career, as a jurist and gentleman whose beloved avocation was poetry, and who felt that he owed it to himself and his subject to ignore contemporary trivialities, and that, in the perspective of posterity, only epic dignity could do justice to the history and scenes he loved. He died of an apoplectic stroke in the Peabody Hotel, Memphis. He was never married.

[M. W. Connelly, in *Lib. of Southern Lit.*, vol. VIII (1909); Memphis *Commercial Appeal*, May 19, 1915; Frazer Hood, "Walter Malone—His Life and Works," in Malone's *Selected Poems* (1919); J. T. Moore, *Tenn. The Volunteer State 1769–1923* (1923); J. P. Young, *Standard Hist. of Memphis, Tenn.* (1912); *Munsey's Mag.*, Mar. 1905; information furnished by Dr. F. M. Malone and Judge J. P. Young.] D. D.

MALONEY, MARTIN (Dec. 11, 1847–May 8, 1929), industrialist, philanthropist, was born in Ballingarry near Thurles in Ireland. In 1854 his parents, John and Catharine (Pollard) Maloney, famine-refugees to Scranton, Pa., in 1848, were able to send for him. He had little schooling but developed dependable and thrifty ways as a worker in the mines, as a clerk in a grocer's store, and as an apprentice to a metal worker. As a youth he established a grocery store which failed, and later a plumbing business. In the latter connection he obtained some patents from which he improved a gasoline burner which came to be used widely in street-lighting. He retained his rights and manufactured and marketed this lamp and other lighting devices through the Maloney Manufacturing and Lighting Company. In the meantime (1868), he married Margaret A. Hewittson of Carbondale who maintained a harmonious home for him and their three daughters.

Although only twenty-six years of age when he removed to Philadelphia, he was well on the road to success. He obtained contracts for lighting the grounds of the Centennial Exposition and for the street-lighting of Philadelphia, Pittsburgh, Camden, and Jersey City. In 1880 he organized the Pennsylvania Globe Gas Light

Company. He became an authority on the processes of gas production and thus became interested in chemistry as a business rather than as a science. In 1882 he was an organizer of the United Gas and Improvement Company of Philadelphia which acquired local gas companies in various states. Later he promoted the Pennsylvania Heat, Light and Power Company which absorbed a number of electric companies and in 1899 was reorganized as the Philadelphia Electric Company. The success of this organization made Maloney a factor in promoting the Electric Company of America, one of the earliest holding companies. His interests in time included the Standard Oil Company, the Maloney Oil Company of Scranton, the Pennsylvania Railroad, the Pennsylvania Iron Works Company, and even real-estate and hotel ventures.

Maloney lacked a *flair* for politics, but as a self-made man, he felt his importance and liked adulation. Despite a contentious and suspicious nature, he was kindly, generous in a large way, and amusingly penurious in small matters. A fervent Catholic, he was a supporter of the Catholic Church Extension Society, building chapels in Rock Hill and Florence, S. C., and Rome, Ga., and was a quiet donor to charities and hospitals. He built St. Martin's Chapel for the Seminary of St. Charles Borromeo, Overbrook, Pa., the beautiful Italian Renaissance St. Catherine's Church at his summer home in Spring Lake, N. J., as a memorial to a daughter who died at sea, the Martin Maloney Home for the Aged in Scranton, and the elaborate Maloney Chemical Laboratory at the Catholic University of America in Washington. In Rome he paid for repairing the ancient Church of St. John Lateran, and in France he became identified as the wealthy American who took title to a number of convents and religious institutions which were thus preserved from confiscation as a result of the legislation of 1901. On intimate terms with great prelates, he was created a papal marquis by Leo XIII (1903) and a papal chamberlain by Pius X (1904). Outside the church his gifts included a park for Scranton and the Martin Maloney Memorial Clinic at the University of Pennsylvania. His "White House" by the sea at Spring Lake was modeled on Leinster House in Dublin. Here he retired amid surroundings which conformed to his sense of beauty in the rich, ornate, and massive form. His remains were interred in the crypt of the memorial church at Spring Lake.

[*Records of the Am. Cath. Hist. Soc.*, Dec. 1929; S. M. Lyons, *St. Catherine's Church, Spring Lake, N. J.: A Descriptive Booklet* (n.d.); *Cath. Univ. Bull.*, Nov. 1917, Nov. 1925; clippings of obituary notices in files of Cath. University; notes from his associates; obituaries in *Cath. Standard and Times* (Phila.), the *Phila. Inquirer, Pub. Ledger,* and *N. Y. Times.*]

R. J. P.

MALTER, HENRY (Mar. 23, 1864–Apr. 4, 1925), scholar, teacher, was born in the village of Banse, near Sabno, Galicia (at that time in Austria), the son of Solomon and Rosa Malter. He studied rabbinical literature as a youth, took up secular studies in his eighteenth year, spent four years at the University of Berlin, giving special attention to philosophy and Semitic languages, and received the degree of Ph.D. *cum laude* at Heidelberg in 1894. He then entered the Lehranstalt fur die Wissenchaft des Judentums in Berlin and at the same time the Veitel Heine Ephraimsche Stiftung, studying in the latter under the great Jewish scholar Moritz Steinschneider. For one year he was librarian of the scientific library of the Jewish Community in Berlin. On Sept. 30, 1900, he married Bertha Freund. In the same year he was called to the professorship of Jewish philosophy and Oriental languages in the Hebrew Union College, Cincinnati; this post he resigned in 1907. In 1909 he was elected professor of rabbinical language and literature in the Dropsie College for Hebrew and Cognate Learning, Philadelphia, which position he occupied until his death.

He was one of the leaders of the Hebrew Renaissance, translating into Hebrew Steinschneider's work on Jewish literature, which he greatly expanded and published under the title *Sifrut Yisrael* (1897; 2nd ed., 1923). With Alexander Marx, he edited one volume of the collected writings of Steinschneider, *Gesammelte Schriften von Moritz Steinschneider* (1925). His favorite field was Judeo-Arabic philosophy, and being an excellent scholar in both Hebrew and Arabic, he readily commanded the original sources. In this field he published many articles, but his most distinguished contribution was his *Saadia Gaon: His Life and Works* (1921), which exhibited a profound knowledge of Jewish philosophy and medieval literature, and also a creative imagination that vividly restored an important Jewish figure of the tenth century. Ethiopic was another language with which he was familiar. During the last fifteen years of his life, he undertook the beginning of a great project in Talmudic literature, that of establishing a method for the creation of a critical text of the Talmud. At the time of his death he had completed such a text of one tractate of the Talmud, with an English translation and notes, published in 1928 under the title, *The Treatise Ta'anit of the Babylonian Talmud.* The justification for his method in creating this critical text he put into a separate work, entitled *The Treatise Ta'anit of the Babylonian Talmud . . . Provided with Notes Containing the Critical Apparatus as well as Discussions and Explanations of the Text,* published in 1930 by the American Academy for Jewish Research, of which Malter had been secretary. He also left in manuscript a critical text of the Arabic original of *Emunoth we-Deoth* (Beliefs and Opinions), of Saadia.

He was a painstaking and careful scholar, not prolific, but every work he published was a definite contribution to Jewish or Arabic literature. He was a modest man of simple tastes and had a horror of publicity. He had a genuine passion for learning, a wide interest in men and things outside of his own specialty, and a dry sense of humor that often found delightful expression.

[Alexander Marx, in *Am. Jewish Year Book,* vol. XXVIII (1926); *Who's Who in America,* 1924–25; *Jewish Daily Bull.* (N. Y.), Apr. 7, 1925; *Jewish Tribune* (N. Y.), Apr. 24, 1925; *Jewish Exponent* (Phila.), Apr. 10, 1925; *Ha-Doar* (N. Y.), Apr. 24, May 8, 1925.] C. A.

MANATT, JAMES IRVING (Feb. 17, 1845–Feb. 13, 1915), classicist, till middle life Irving James Manatt, was the son of Robert and Jemima (Gwin) Manatt. His family was Scotch and Scotch-Irish; the name may have a Huguenot origin. His father, a pioneer farmer, moved gradually westward from Pennsylvania. Irving was born at Millersburg, Ohio, but was soon taken to Poweshiek County, Iowa. In 1861 he entered the preparatory department of the recently established Iowa (now Grinnell) College. After a discontinuous school life, he enlisted in May 1864, in the 46th Iowa Infantry, a hundred-day regiment, and spent the summer near Collierville, Tenn., as regimental clerk and picketing a railroad. In 1865 he returned to Iowa College and graduated in 1869. On June 28, 1870, he married Arletta Winifred Clark of Grinnell. Of their children, a son and five daughters attained maturity. After a year on the *Chicago Evening Post,* Manatt went to Yale for graduate study, especially under William Whitney, teaching meanwhile at Hopkins Grammar School in New Haven. His Ph.D. degree (1873) was followed by a Greek professorship at Denison University (1874–76), a year at Leipzig, and a Greek professorship at Marietta College (1877–84).

In 1884 he became chancellor of the University of Nebraska. His selections for the faculty were excellent. He realized that the university was part of the state public school system, and did much to bring it into organic relationship with the high schools. Unfortunately, his four years of administration were marked by difficulties common in the formative stages of universities. He was by nature an inspiring teacher, not an administrator. His policies were good, but he lacked the tact necessary to reconcile divergent groups and he was rendered irritable by asthma, a lifelong affliction. Even so, the charges laid before the regents would have collapsed if he had kept silent at the hearings. The closing argument against him rested on the sole ground that his sarcastic treatment of the professors called as witnesses rendered future harmonious action impossible. On July 19, 1888, the regents "found it necessary to dispense with the services" of Manatt. In 1902 the university made him doctor of laws.

The stormy end of a task Manatt never should have undertaken led to one of the happiest events in his life. Nebraska friends procured his appointment by President Harrison as consul at Athens, where he remained from 1889 until 1893. Those four years gave him a vivid sense of the continuity of the Greek countryside since classical times. In 1892 he completed his edition of Xenophon's *Hellenica* (2 vols., 1888–92). Friendship with Dr. Chrestos Tsountas, who was excavating at Mycenæ, brought about their collaboration in *The Mycenæan Age* (1897), the first complete and systematic survey of primitive Greek culture, not yet wholly superseded by later archeological discoveries. In 1892 he was appointed professor of Greek literature and history in Brown University, where he served from 1893 until his death in Providence, just before retirement. He paid three more visits to Greece. He joined the managing committee of the American School of Classical Studies in Athens and helped organize and attended the First International Congress of Archeology there in 1905. A Greek sabbatical resulted in his *Ægean Days* (1914), a charming union of personal reminiscences with Greek scenery and life, present and past.

Manatt's oratorical powers would never have been guessed from his gaunt appearance, with the heavy gray beard which caused the students to nickname him "Zeus." His addresses used to test some phase of contemporary life by Greek standards, and he would pour out ridicule, invective, eloquence, and paraphrases of classical poetry in a rush of splendid words. In teaching, Manatt delighted especially in the lyric poets and the *Odyssey.* He emphasized philology very little. To him it was the men and women in the poems that mattered, and the land. His later years were depressed by constant asthma, small means, and the abandonment of compulsory Greek, which steadily reduced his classes, but the few students who did know him were much closer to him. To one of them he wrote: "My teaching has fallen so far short of my own ideal, of the pattern shown me in the mount, that I wonder every time I find that some elect spirit like yours has got good from it. It is one thing to have the vision, quite another the vitality to communicate it. With old Socrates, I hold it full reward if among my younger comrades I win a good friend now and then—all the more so if the fathers acquit me of corrupting the youth."

[Manatt's address in *Semi-centennial of the Founding of Grinnell, 1854–1904* (1904); *Ninth Biennial Report of the Board of Regents of the Univ. of Neb., Dec. 1, 1888*, p. 6; *Roster and Record of Iowa Soldiers in the War of the Rebellion*, vol. V (1911), p. 1423; G. E. Barber, "J. Irving Manatt," *Semi-centennial Anniversary Book. The Univ. of Neb.* (1919); H. H. Wilson, "Impeachment of Univ. Chancellor," in *Occasional Addresses* (1929); *Brown Alumni Monthly*, June 1912, Mar., June 1915; the *Providence Sunday Jour.*, Feb. 14, 1915; the *Evening Tribune* (Providence, R. I.), Feb. 15, 1915; catalogues of Iowa College and reports of the regents and chancellor of the Univ. of Neb.; information as to certain facts from members of the family; personal reminiscences.] Z. C., Jr.

MANDERSON, CHARLES FREDERICK (Feb. 9, 1837–Sept. 28, 1911), lawyer, Union soldier, United States senator from Nebraska, was born in Philadelphia, Pa., the son of a Scotch-Irish father, John Manderson, and a German mother, Katharine Benfer Manderson. He obtained a high-school education in Philadelphia, then went to Canton, Ohio, where he read law. He was admitted to the bar in 1859 and was twice elected city solicitor of Canton before the outbreak of the Civil War. In that struggle Manderson quickly demonstrated his capacity for leadership. He enlisted at the outset as a private soldier and shortly afterward helped raise Company A of the 19th Ohio Infantry. His advancement in the service was rapid. He was commissioned first lieutenant, then captain of his company, and thereafter he rose through the various grades to be colonel of his regiment. He saw strenuous fighting from the beginning of the war and participated in all the more important battles fought in the Western theatre of action. While with Sherman in the Atlanta campaign, he commanded a demi-brigade composed of his own and two other regiments. He was severely wounded, Sept. 2, 1864, in a charge on the enemy's works at Lovejoy's Station, Ga., and on this account shortly afterward found it necessary to resign from the army. Before he resigned, however, he was brevetted brigadier-general of volunteers "for long, faithful, gallant and meritorious service." After the war he was an active member of the Grand Army of the Republic, and for three years he was commander of the Military Order of the Loyal Legion of the District of Columbia.

After resigning from the army Manderson resumed his practice of law and his interest in politics. For a few years he remained at Canton, Ohio, where he was twice elected district attorney of Stark County, and once almost nominated by the Republicans for Congress. In 1869, however, he removed to Omaha, Neb. In the new environment he quickly became a prominent political figure. He was a member of the state constitutional conventions of 1871 and 1875, and for over six years was city attorney for Omaha. In 1883 he was elected to the United States Senate, and at the conclusion of his first term was reëlected without serious opposition from within his party—an unusual experience for a Nebraska senator, who could ordinarily count on retirement after a single term. In the Senate Manderson served faithfully on many committees, worked and spoke for high pensions, advocated a more efficient organization of the army, and won considerable notice by introducing a measure, then regarded as novel, for nationally built highways. He foresaw in the nineties a revolution in means of travel, and he predicted confidently "the construction ultimately by this government of great highways or boulevards that shall connect metropolitan centers" (Tipton, *post*, p. 353). He was consistently orthodox and conservative in his votes and speeches, and was rewarded in 1891 by election without opposition to the post of president *pro tempore* of the Senate to succeed Senator John J. Ingalls of Kansas.

After he left public office Manderson became general solicitor for the Burlington Railroad west of the Missouri River. In this capacity he served his client well, but there were those in Nebraska who regretted his course. "What a fine influence he might have exerted," wrote one such critic, "if, after retirement, he had used the knowledge and influence gained at Washington as the representative of the people in their behalf, instead of devoting this experience to the service of a great railroad corporation, to gain legal control of which the people were engaged in a mighty and doubtful struggle!" (Morton and Watkins, *post*, vol. III, p. 289). In 1900 he was chosen president of the American Bar Association. He was a man of varied talents and interests. He knew his way in the fields of literature and art, and he was possessed of a strong collector's instinct. He published in 1902 a romance of Civil-War times, *The Twin Seven-Shooters*, the plot and incidents of which were drawn mostly from his own war-time experience and observation. Many of his addresses on political, legal, and military topics were also published. He was an interesting conversationalist, a skilful after-dinner speaker, and an able orator. In general his tastes were urbane and aristocratic, at once a matter of pride and of suspicion to the unsophisticated country constituency which he represented as senator. His death came in the fall of 1911, on shipboard, as he was returning to America after a summer in Europe. His wife, Rebeckah Brown Manderson, to whom he had been married in 1865, survived him.

[The *Sunday World-Herald* (Omaha), Oct. 1, 1911, gives many Manderson anecdotes, and the *Omaha Daily Bee,* Sept. 29, 1911, contains an excellent obituary notice. His political career is traced in T. W. Tipton, *Forty Years of Neb. at Home and in Cong.* (1902), pp. 333–61, and in J. S. Morton and Albert Watkins, *Illustrated Hist. of Neb.* (3 vols., 1905–13). See also *Who's Who in America,* 1910–11; and the *Report of the Thirty-Fourth Ann. Meeting of the Am. Bar Asso.,* 1911.]

J. D. H.

MANEY, GEORGE EARL (Aug. 24, 1826–Feb. 9, 1901), soldier, lawyer, diplomat, born at Franklin, Tenn., was the eldest son of Thomas and Rebecca (Southall) Maney, and a descendant of James Maney, a French Huguenot, who settled in North Carolina. He attended the Nashville Seminary and in 1845 graduated from the University of Nashville. At the beginning of the Mexican War he entered the United States army, May 28, 1846, as second lieutenant of Captain Foster's Company (subsequently designated Company L), 1st Tennessee Infantry, to serve one year; he was honorably discharged Sept. 7, 1846, at Camargo, Tenn., upon tender of his resignation, due to physical disability. On Mar. 6 of the following year he was appointed first lieutenant, United States Infantry, and in April, first lieutenant, 3rd United States Dragoons, and was honorably mustered out on July 31, 1848.

In 1850 he was admitted to the bar and practised law in Tennessee, but upon the outbreak of the Civil War he entered the Confederate service as captain of Company D, 11th Tennessee Infantry. In May 1861, however, he was made colonel of the 1st (Field's) Regiment, Tennessee Infantry. He took part in the Cheat River campaign under Gen. Robert E. Lee and served at Bath and Romney under General Jackson, one of the few officers of the Army of the Tennessee to have that distinction. He distinguished himself at the battle of Shiloh, Apr. 6–7, 1862, and was made brigadier-general on Apr. 18, the appointment to date from Apr. 16, 1862. He commanded a brigade at the battles of Perryville, Stone's River, Chickamauga, and Chattanooga, where he was wounded in the right arm. In the Atlanta campaign he commanded a division and was engaged in the battle of Atlanta, July 22, 1864. He was paroled at Greensboro, N. C., on or about May 1, 1865.

Maney became president of the Tennessee & Pacific Railroad in 1868. He was the Republican nominee for governor of Tennessee in 1876, opposing James D. Porter [*q.v.*], but withdrew before election. He served in the state legislature and being an able speaker took an active part in presidential campaigns. On May 19, 1881, he was appointed minister resident to Colombia. His predecessor had been recalled at the request of the Colombian government, and since it was a critical period in the relations of the United States with Colombia, owing to an attempt by European powers to establish a guarantee of neutrality over the inter-oceanic canal, Maney's duties were both onerous and delicate. He was transferred to Bolivia Apr. 17, 1882, as minister resident and consul general at La Paz. On June 20, 1889, he was made minister resident to Paraguay and Uruguay, and on Sept. 23, 1890, his rank was raised to that of envoy extraordinary and minister plenipotentiary. He remained at that post until June 30, 1894.

He was married at Nashville, Tenn., June 23, 1853, to Bettie, daughter of F. G. Crutcher, and had two sons and three daughters. His death occurred suddenly in Washington, D. C.

[War Dept. records; State Dept. records; *Reg. of The Dept. of State,* Jan. 1894; *Conf. Mil. Hist.* (1899), vol. VIII; *War of the Revellion: Official Records (Army),* 2 ser., 4 ser.; M. J. Wright, *Tenn. in the War, 1861–1865* (copr. 1908); *Washington Post,* Feb. 10, 1901; *Evening Star* (Washington), Feb. 11, 1901; *Nashville Banner,* Feb. 11, 1901; names of parents from James T. Maney, Esq., Nashville, Tenn.]

A. E. I.

MANGIN, JOSEPH FRANÇOIS (fl. 1794–1818), engineer, architect, was of French origin. His letters indicate that he was a cultivated aristocrat, and he may have come to New York as a refugee from the Revolution. He first appears as an assistant to Vincent, another Frenchman, who was engineer-in-chief of the New York fortifications. In 1795 he succeeded Vincent as chief engineer, with another Mangin (probably a younger brother) as his assistant. He was admitted and sworn as a freeman of the city on May 9, 1795, and a week later was appointed one of the city surveyors. As such, in partnership with Casimir T. Goerck, he began in 1797 the preparation of an official city map which was published in 1803. This well-known map, which was a magnificent piece of draftsmanship determined the present shore line and street layout of the entire Corlear's Hook section, of which one street perpetuates his name.

Meanwhile, in 1797 he had designed the monumental prison for the state of New York, on the block now bounded by Washington Street, Christopher Street, and the North River. According to contemporary newspapers (*e.g., New York Daily Advertiser,* Jan. 31, 1798), Mangin Brothers were the architects of the Park Theater, built between 1795 and 1798, the design of which is often credited to Marc Isambard Brunel, who was at this time perhaps a draftsman in their office. During the French war scare of 1798, while Mangin was a technical adviser to Ebenezer Stevens, agent of the War Department in connection with the fortifications of the city, Aaron Burr wrote from Albany to Stevens (Aug. 17) asking that Mangin prepare plans and estimates for an "impregnable castle" two or three stories high, to be erected in about six feet of water and connected with the land by a drawbridge. This is possibly the first appearance of the idea of the fort built later and eventually known as Castle Garden, of which John McComb [*q.v.*] was the architect. Mangin's reports to Colonel Stevens are precise, scholarly, and imaginative.

Mangin is best known for his connection with the New York City Hall. A competition for designs was advertised Feb. 20, 1802, and on Oct. 4, the plan of "Mr. Joseph F. Mangin and John McComb, Jr." was adopted and the premium of $350 awarded to them (Council Minutes, *post*). The plan was curtailed somewhat by request of the committee, and in March 1803 the curtailed plan was approved and McComb appointed architect. When the cornerstone was laid May 26, 1803, McComb, as architect, assisted the mayor, and no mention of Mangin in connection with the building was made in the ceremonies or on the inscribed foundation stone. On June 2, the New York *Evening Post* published a letter signed "Justice," deploring the absence of Mangin from the ceremonies and the denial of credit to him, together with an assertion that a brass plate giving the true state of affairs and naming Mangin as chief designer had been built secretly into the walls. This question of the design of the City Hall is still a matter of controversy. It is significant that certain of the competition drawings now signed "John McComb, Jr., Architect" show unmistakable signs of the erasure of some other name and that, while McComb's work is in every other case distinctly English in feeling, the spirit of the City Hall design is entirely Louis XVI.

Mangin's only other known important work was the design for the first St. Patrick's Cathedral, on Mott Street, 1809–15. This building was famous for its Gothic style, and is without doubt one of the first signs of the beginning of the Gothic revival in America. It was dedicated on Ascension Day 1815, and contemporary views show that the twin towers once intended for the façade were never completed and only carried slightly above the main roof ridge. The original walls and the lower part of the front are still standing (1933). Mangin appears last in the New York Directory for 1818, at Bowery Hill, as a city surveyor. He was probably married, since the Vital Statistics of New York show that a Charles Mangin, aged one year, died on Bowery Hill, Apr. 10, 1818.

[Plans and elevation of N. Y. State Prison in Schuyler Papers, N. Y. Pub. Lib.; McComb Drawings and Papers, Ebenezer Stevens Papers, and Proceedings of the Commissioners for N. Y. and Vicinity, in N. Y. Hist. Soc.; *Minutes of the Common Council of the City of N. Y.* (1917), vols. II–IX, see Analytical Index; I. N. P. Stokes, *The Iconography of Manhattan Island* (6 vols., 1915–28); Thomas Eddy, *An Account of the State Prison or Penitentiary House in the City of New-York* (1801); Montgomery Schuyler, "The N. Y. City Hall," in *Arch. Record,* May 1908; E. S. Wilde, "The N. Y. City Hall," *Century Mag.,* Apr. 1884, and "John McComb, Jr., Architect," in *Am. Architect and Building News,* Aug. 12, 19, 1908.]

T. F. H.

MANGUM, WILLIE PERSON (May 10, 1792–Sept. 7, 1861), senator, was born in Orange (now Durham) County, N. C. He was the son of William Person Mangum, a farmer and merchant, and of Catharine (Davis) Mangum, a native of Pennsylvania. Like that of Willie Jones his Christian name was pronounced Wylie. His preparatory education was received at home and at academies in Hillsboro, Fayetteville, and Raleigh, and in 1815 he was graduated from the University of North Carolina. He studied law under Judge Duncan Cameron, while serving as tutor in his family, and was licensed in 1817. Beginning practice at home he was immediately successful, but his mind was set on public life, and in 1818 and 1819 he was a member of the House of Commons, where he actively supported the cause of constitutional reform, thereby winning great popularity in the western part of the state. In 1819 he was elected a judge of the superior court but was compelled for financial reasons to retire at the end of a year. In 1823 he began a service of two terms in the federal Congress. In 1824 he supported Crawford and voted for him when the election was thrown into the House. He resigned in 1826 and was soon appointed to fill a vacancy as judge, but the appointment was not confirmed by the legislature. In 1828 he was a Jackson elector and was again elected judge, but once more he resigned after a year's service. He was a candidate for the United States Senate in 1828 but withdrew, and in 1830 he was elected.

He entered the Senate a Jacksonian Democrat, a strong opponent of the protective tariff, and a champion of state rights. In the House he had been an opponent of the Bank of the United States, but by this time he was converted to its cause, though he objected to making it an issue in 1832 and voted against the rechartering bill. At this time he was distrustful of Clay and in general disapproved of his policies. While opposed to nullification, he was friendly to South Carolina in 1832 and voted against the Force Bill in 1833. This measure and the removal of the deposits led to a definite break with Jackson, and he voted for the resolution of censure and against the expunging resolution. The North Carolina legislature of 1834, in the hands of the Democrats, passed a resolution instructing him to vote to expunge. Mangum, denying the right of instruction, refused to obey, but the succeeding legislature was also Democratic and he resigned. In 1837 he received the electoral vote of South Carolina for president. Except for service in the state Senate in 1840 he remained in private life busily engaged in the practice of law for several years. He identified himself with the Whig party and became one of its chief leaders in the state. He was a Clay delegate to the Whig convention of 1839, and was offered the nomination for vice-president, but refused it. He was elected to the United States Senate in 1840 and served until 1853. He was active in the Whig quarrel with Tyler, directing the caucus, and he offered the resolution reading him out of the party. He was elected president *pro tempore* of the Senate from May 31, 1842, to Mar. 4, 1845, and was thus acting vice-president of the United States. He seldom spoke in the Senate, but when he did so he proved himself an effective debater. He was a most astute political leader, and his personal charm and magnetism as well as his brilliancy in conversation gave him great strength. In North Carolina he was best known for his power as a campaign speaker. He was the intimate of Webster and, with his colleague, George E. Badger [*q.v.*], persuaded him to make his Seventh of March speech. In 1852 he was a supporter of Scott for the Whig nomination.

He was defeated in 1852 and retired to private life. Although in desperate health, he took an active part for Fillmore in the campaign of 1856 but not long thereafter suffered a stroke of apoplexy from which he never recovered. He was not a secessionist, but after Lincoln's call for troops he yielded the point. After the death of his only son in battle a second stroke proved fatal. On Sept. 30, 1819, he married Charity Alston Cain, the daughter of William and Sarah (Alston) Cain of Orange County.

[Mangum Collection in Lib. of Cong.; *Trinity College Hist. Soc. Papers,* vol. XV (1925); J. H. Wheeler, *Reminiscences and Memoirs of N. C.* (1884); S. A. Ashe, *Biog. Hist. of N. C.,* vol. V (1906).]

J. G. deR. H.

MANIGAULT, ARTHUR MIDDLETON (Oct. 26, 1824–Aug. 16, 1886), soldier and adjutant-general of South Carolina, was born in Charleston, the eighth and youngest child of Charlotte (Drayton) and Joseph Manigault. His father, a wealthy rice planter, was the son of Peter Manigault, the grandson of Gabriel Manigault, and the great-grandson of Pierre Manigault [*qq.v.*]. His mother was descended from an English family that had been prominent in Charleston life from the earliest history of the city. He received an elementary education but instead of attending college set out to learn the export trade in Charleston. He became sergeant-major of a local militia company and received his first military experience during the Mexican War when, as first lieutenant of Company F of the Palmetto Regiment, he served under General Scott. This experience he afterward described as "perhaps the happiest and most romantic period" of his life (unpublished memoirs). Upon his return from Mexico in 1848 he entered the commission business in Charleston and, on Apr. 18, 1851, was married to Mary Proctor Huger, grand-daughter of Daniel E. Huger [*q.v.*]. They had five children. In 1856 he removed to Georgetown County, where, having inherited considerable property from his parents, he began rice planting.

Upon the secession of South Carolina in December 1860 he was elected captain of the North Santee Mounted Rifles, a volunteer company organized in his community, and during the following winter he superintended the construction of several batteries for the defense of Winyaw Bay and the North Santee River. Early in April 1861 he became volunteer aide-de-camp on the staff of General Beauregard. He took part in the attack upon Fort Sumter and shortly afterward was commissioned lieutenant-colonel and assigned to duty as adjutant and inspector-general on Beauregard's staff. He was elected colonel of the 10th South Carolina Volunteers on May 31, 1861, became commander of the first military district of South Carolina, and later was ordered to Corinth, Miss., with his regiment. Throughout the remainder of the war he served in the West. On Apr. 26, 1863, he was advanced to the rank of brigadier-general, a promotion which he thought was unjustly delayed through the influence of certain enemies of his family at

Richmond (unpublished memoirs). He was slightly wounded at Resaca, Ga., on May 14, 1863, but he participated in all of the engagements of the Army of Tennessee until the Battle of Franklin, Tenn., in November 1864, when he received a wound in the head so serious as to incapacitate him for the remainder of the war. At the close of the war he returned to rice planting and pursued that occupation with varying success until 1880, when he was elected adjutant and inspector-general of the state. He held this office until his death at South Island, Georgetown County.

[Unpublished Memoirs in the possession of his grandson, Edward Manigault, Charleston, S. C.; *Trans. of the Huguenot Soc. of S. C.*, no. 4 (1897); *Confederate Military Hist.*, ed. by C. A. Evans (1899), vol. V; C. I. Walker, *Rolls and Hist. Sketch of the Tenth Regiment, S. C.* (1881); *News and Courier* (Charleston), Aug. 17, 18, 1886.] J. W. P—n.

MANIGAULT, GABRIEL (Apr. 21, 1704–June 5, 1781), wealthy South Carolina merchant and planter, the only son of Pierre Manigault [*q.v.*] by his first wife Judith (Giton) Royer, was born and died at Charlestown. He was about twenty-five years old when his father died and had for some time been associated in the well-established trade carried on with the West Indies, England, and France. On Apr. 29, 1730, he married Ann Ashby, the daughter of John Ashby, a cassique of Carolina, and of Constantia (Broughton) Ashby, a sister of Thomas Broughton, at one time governor of South Carolina, thus forming an important social and political connection. In the diary that his wife kept from 1754 to 1781 (*South Carolina Historical and Genealogical Magazine,* July 1919–July 1920) was reflected the social life of the times, the rising prosperity of the colony, and the extensive hospitality of the Manigaults, who entertained all visitors of note, the governors, the members of council, and other local gentry. At a time when rice was the leading staple and indigo a profitable crop, the slave trade offered increasingly large returns, but dealing in slaves did not form an important part of Gabriel Manigault's business. He invested his profits in plantations and in slaves to work them. When the British Parliament undertook to investigate the condition of slaves, the situation on his plantations was cited in defense of slavery since it could be shown that in 38 years the number had increased from 86 to 270 with the addition by purchase of only 12 or 14 slaves. By 1754 he had become the wealthiest merchant in the province. He retired from the active management of his commercial business in order to attend particularly to his rice and indigo plantation, "Silk Hope," which he had bought from the heirs of Gov. Robert Johnson.

He entered public life as a member of the Commons House of Assembly. In 1735 he succeeded Alexander Parris as public treasurer and continued in office until 1743. He labored diligently to reduce to order the confused accounts of the unfortunate expedition of 1740 against St. Augustine. He was for many years vice-president of the Charlestown Library Society, of which the governor of the province was always president, and he leased for twenty-one years without charge a convenient building near his counting-house for the books and the librarian. Interested in helping poor French-Protestant immigrants to South Carolina, he advanced £3,500 for that purpose. He was one of the leaders in the Revolutionary movement. During the war he lent the equivalent of $220,000 to the province, most of which was lost since the amount was repaid by the state in the form of indents on which only about $44,000 was realized. Too old to go into the army he did, however, offer his services, along with those of his grandson, Joseph, then a youth of fifteen and later the father of Arthur Middleton Manigault [*q.v.*], to defend the city of Charlestown against the attack of General Prevost in 1779. Two years later he was buried in the French churchyard. His wife died the next year and their only child, Peter Manigault [*q.v.*], already lay buried in the family tomb. He left, chiefly to his grandchildren, a very large estate, including 43,532 acres of land. Among his bequests was one of £5,000 sterling to the South Carolina Society, the interest of which was used to educate a number of children.

[Registers of the parishes of St. Philips, St. Thomas, and St. Dennis; records from the probate court at Charleston; *Trans. Huguenot Soc. of S. C.*, no. 4 (1889); Edward McCrady, *The Hist. of S. C. under the Royal Government* (1899); W. R. Smith, *S. C. as a Royal Province* (1903); David Ramsay, *The Hist. of S. C.* (1809), vol. II; *S. C. Hist. and Geneal. Mag.*, esp. Oct. 1914, Jan. 1917.] M. L. W.

MANIGAULT, PETER (Oct. 10, 1731–Nov. 12, 1773), speaker of the colonial Assembly, business man, and planter, was born in Charlestown, S. C., the only son and heir of Ann (Ashby) and Gabriel Manigault [*q.v.*]. He was educated at a classical school and under a tutor in Charlestown until 1750, when he was sent to study law in England under the care of Thomas Corbett, who had tutored him in Carolina. He lived with Mr. Corbett for two years, then entered the Inner Temple in 1752, residing in chambers there, and was called to the English bar on Feb. 8, 1754. His letters to his parents (*South Carolina Historical and Genealogical Magazine,* July 1914,

July, Oct. 1930) give interesting pictures of fashionable society, the theatre, and his acquaintances at the Carolina Coffee House. While in London he had his portrait painted by Allan Ramsay, later the Court painter. In 1753 he spent ten weeks in France, Belgium, and Holland, staying most of the time in Paris and showing little interest in La Rochelle, the native city of his grandfather, Pierre Manigault [*q.v.*]. He returned to South Carolina in 1754 and began at once to practise law. He was married, on June 8, 1755, to Elizabeth, the daughter of Joseph Wragg. They had, besides three children who died young, two sons and two daughters. The year of his marriage he was elected to the colonial Assembly and was speaker from 1765 until he resigned in October 1772. He opposed the Stamp Act and, when Parliament repealed it, as speaker he wrote to Charles Garth, South Carolina's agent in London, enclosing an address of thanks to the King and to Parliament. During the struggle over South Carolina's contribution to the Wilkes fund, he was a member of the committee, in 1770, entrusted with the £1,500 sterling that the House voted for the support of the Bill of Rights society in spite of the opposition by William Wragg and William Henry Drayton, who maintained that such funds would be used to pay the debts of John Wilkes.

In 1763 he took over the management of the estates and affairs of Ralph Izard [*q.v.*], including rice and indigo plantations on the Goose Creek and Santee River, and also managed the interests in South Carolina of several London business firms. He bought a small estate at Goose Creek and made frequent visits there. His health, always delicate, had grown very much worse with recurring attacks of fever. On May 16, 1773, he sailed for England in the hope that he might benefit by spending a summer in that climate. His letters to his mother from England report his own continued hopefulness as well as the gradual weakening of a body too sick to withstand the medical treatment of the time (*South Carolina Historical and Genealogical Magazine*, Apr. 1920). He died in London at the home of Benjamin Stead. His body was taken back to Charlestown for burial.

[Edward McCrady, *The Hist. of S. C.* (1899); W. R. Smith, *S. C. as a Royal Province* (1903); E. A. Jones, *Am. Members of the Inns of Court* (1924); *Trans. Huguenot Soc. of S. C.*, no. 4 (1897); *S. C. Hist. and Geneal. Mag.*, esp. Jan. 1902, July 1914, Jan. 1919–July 1920, July, Oct. 1930.] M. L. W.

MANIGAULT, PIERRE (d. December 1729), South Carolina merchant, was a native of La Rochelle, France. The son of Gabriel and Marie Manigault, he was a member of a family of good position that had long been Protestant. Pierre with his brother, Gabriel, left France about 1685, after the Edict of Nantes was revoked. They went to London, where they remained for several years, then to South Carolina, arriving in Charlestown (now Charleston) probably early in 1695 since, on June 28, 1695, Gabriel received a warrant for land for the arrival of himself and a negro man named Sambo. On June 22, 1696, Pierre received a warrant for 100 acres. The two brothers seem to have had some means when they arrived, from their earnings in England and from the sale of lands in France. They first settled on the Santee River but, finding the work of planting uncongenial and the climate unhealthy, removed to Charlestown, where Gabriel pursued the trade of carpenter, and Pierre set up in business as a victualler. Gabriel never married and died about ten years after he came to Charlestown as the result of a fall from a scaffold. Pierre was married in 1699 to Judith (Giton) Royer, who with her first husband, Noe (Noah) Royer, came to South Carolina before the Manigaults. (See her letter describing the sufferings she experienced during the journey from France to England and the first hard years of her life in Carolina in David Ramsay, *The History of South Carolina*, 1809, vol. I, pp. 5–8.) She died in 1711, leaving two children by her second marriage. Her son, Gabriel Manigault, her grandson, Peter Manigault, and her great-great-grandson, Arthur Middleton Manigault [*qq.v.*], as well as numerous other descendants, continued to represent her Huguenot blood in the life of South Carolina. Pierre was married in 1713 to Ann Reason, of English parentage, who died on Aug. 10, 1727, leaving no children.

Pierre identified himself with the English colonists, changed his name to Peter, and, although he still kept a connection with the French Church, attended the English Church. He set up a small distillery to make brandy and, about 1719, also became a merchant, conducted trade directly with England, built storehouses, and sold his goods to the colonists. Unlike so many of the French refugees in South Carolina, who arrived in a destitute condition and suffered for some years from the refusal of the colonial government to grant the rights promised before they left England, he prospered greatly and died possessed of a considerable fortune. He was buried, on Dec. 10, in the French churchyard. His will, written in English (printed in full in *Transactions of the Huguenot Society of South Carolina*, No. 30, 1925), left £10 each, Carolina currency, to the English and to the French Church in Charlestown, for their poor.

[*Warrants for lands in S. C., 1692–1711*, ed. by A. S. Salley (1913); Public Records of S. C. in probate court and mesne conveyance office, Charleston, and in possession of the historical commission, Columbia; St. Philip's Register, no. 1; *Trans. Huguenot Soc. of S. C.*, nos. 4, 5 (1897), no. 5 (1897), p. 35, for mother's name.] M. L. W.

MANLEY, JOHN (*c.* 1734–Feb. 12, 1793), naval officer, was born probably in Boston (Greenwood, *post*, p. 17). He was living there in 1757, his occupation being that of mariner. On Feb. 26, 1763, he married Hannah Cheevers of that city. In 1768–69 he commanded the *Little Fortescue*, trading between Boston and St. Eustatius. When, in the fall of 1775, Washington was fitting out a small fleet to operate against British transports, he chose Manley to command the schooner *Lee* and commissioned him a captain in the army. Sailing on one of the last days of October, he captured, a month later, the first valuable prize taken in the war, the brigantine *Nancy*, laden with a cargo of ordnance and military stores. It was a timely capture, for the army at Cambridge was sorely in need of these supplies. Fortune continued to favor him and in December he seized several other ships. He was widely acclaimed as a naval hero, the first of the Revolution to be thus distinguished. In January 1776 Washington made him commander of the fleet, with the schooner *Hancock* as his flagship. He made several successful cruises in this vessel, but on one occasion was forced to beach her to prevent her capture. On Apr. 17, Congress recognized Manley's services by appointing him a captain in the Continental navy, and later fixed his rank, making him the third officer in the service. Taking command of the new frigate *Hancock*, he sailed from Boston on May 21, 1777, accompanied by the frigate *Boston*, Capt. Hector McNeill [*q.v.*], and a small fleet of privateers. On June 7, he captured the frigate *Fox*, 28 guns, but a month later the *Hancock* and her prize were taken by the enemy. Manley was confined on board a prison-ship in New York harbor until exchanged in March 1778. He was tried by a court martial for the loss of his ship and acquitted.

Since Congress had no naval vessel suitable to Manley's rank he entered the privateer service, and in the fall of 1778 made a successful cruise in the *Marlborough*. Early in 1779 he went to sea in the *Cumberland* and near Barbados was forced to surrender to the frigate *Pomona*. Escaping from prison and returning to Boston, he next made two cruises in the *Jason*, the second of which ended with her capture, after a sharp engagement. Manley was committed to Old Mill Prison, England, and confined there two years before he was exchanged. Returning to the navy, he commanded the frigate *Hague* and made a cruise in the West Indies that was marked by a brilliant escape from a superior force and by the capture of the *Baille* in January 1783, the last valuable prize taken by a Continental ship.

After the Revolution he continued to reside in Boston. His wife Hannah died in 1786, and on Dec. 14, 1791, his marriage intentions to Friswith Arnold, his second wife, were recorded. In the last year of his life, in consideration of the severe injuries he had received in the war, Congress granted him a pension of thirty dollars a month. He was buried with military honors.

[I. J. Greenwood, *Captain John Manley* (1915); R. E. Peabody, "The Naval Career of Capt. John Manley of Marblehead," in *Essex Inst. Hist. Colls.*, Jan. 1909; G. W. Allen, *A Naval Hist. of the Am. Revolution* (2 vols., 1913); Peter Force, *Am. Archives* (4 ser., 6 vols., 1837–46; 5 ser., vol. II, 1851); *Jour. of the Continental Cong.*, Apr. 17, Oct. 10, 1776; *Columbian Centinel* (Boston), Feb. 16, 20, 1793; *Mass. Mercury* (Boston), Feb. 16, 19, 1793.] C. O. P.

MANLEY, JOSEPH HOMAN (Oct. 13, 1842–Feb. 7, 1905), politician and journalist, was born in Bangor, Me., where his parents, James Sullivan and Caroline (Sewall) Manley, were temporarily living. After going to the public schools of Augusta, he entered in 1853 the Abbott Family School for boys at Farmington, which he attended during four years. Since he never fully recovered from a severe illness he had at the age of five, he was compelled to give up the idea of going to college. In 1861 he began to study law in an office in Boston. In 1863 he was graduated from the law school at Albany, N. Y., and returned to Augusta, where he practised law with Hilton W. True for some years. Admitted to practice in the federal courts in 1865, he was appointed commissioner of the district court. He began his political career as a member of the Augusta city council in 1865 and the next year was president of that body. In 1869 he was a special agent for the federal government in the department of internal revenue, resigned in November 1876, and became agent of the Pennsylvania Railroad to adjust its claims with the Treasury Department. He gave up this work in the spring of 1878, when he purchased from Joseph H. Homan, formerly his father's partner, a half interest in the *Maine Farmer*. For several years he was in active charge of its editorial columns. President Garfield in May 1881 appointed him postmaster at Augusta, and President Harrison appointed him to the same office in 1889. He resigned in August 1892 to assume his duties during the presidential campaign as a member of the Republican national executive committee. He was a delegate to the Republican National Conventions of 1880, 1888, 1892, and 1900 and was chairman of the Republican national committee from 1896 to 1904. He was a member of the Republican committee of the state of Maine from 1881 to 1900 and its chairman from 1885 to 1900. He represented Augusta in the state legislature from 1887 to 1890 and again from 1899 to 1902. During the last session he was speaker. He was a member of the state Senate from 1903 to 1904.

He was James G. Blaine's closest political friend; of him the latter is reported to have said, "As a political organizer, and as an astute reader of political conditions and forecasts, I never met Mr. Manley's equal" (*Lewiston Evening Journal,* Me., Feb. 7, 1905). Where Blaine's political observations were general, his were specific. His detailed, acute, and accurate analyses were a great aid to Blaine in his political activities. After his defeat in the presidential campaign of 1884, Blaine personally asked Cleveland to keep Manley in office as postmaster at Augusta. Manley was in charge of Thomas B. Reed's interests at the Republican convention at Saint Louis in 1896. His honest though indiscreet and premature admission that McKinley's nomination was assured brought upon him the wrath of Reed's friends and supporting newspapers, who had planned to fight to the finish for Reed's nomination (S. W. McCall, *The Life of Thomas Brackett Reed,* 1914, p. 224). The opposition of the Reed forces, thus engendered, was much in evidence later when he sought to realize his life's ambition of being governor of Maine. A carefully planned campaign, whose preliminaries were carried on by mail for fifteen months, came to nought when he was forced to withdraw on account of ill-health. Nor could he accept President Theodore Roosevelt's offer of an appointment as first assistant postmaster general. He had numerous other business interests in addition to the *Maine Farmer.* He married on Oct. 4, 1866, Susan H. Cony of Augusta, the daughter of Governor Samuel Cony. They had four children.

[*Biog. Sketches of Representative Citizens of Me.* (1903); *Representative Men of Me.,* ed. by Henry Chase (1893); *Biog. Sketches of the Members of the Senate . . . of Me., . . . 1903,* comp. by Howard Owen (1903); *Geneal. and Family Hist. of the State of Me.,* ed. by G. T. Little (1909), vol. III; *Men of Progress,* ed. by P. W. McIntyre and W. F. Blanding (1897); *Biog. Encyc. of Me.,* ed. by H. C. Williams (1885); *Letters of Mrs. J. G. Blaine,* ed. by H. S. B. Beale (2 vols., 1898); *Daily Portland Press,* Feb. 8, 1905; *Lewiston Evening Jour.,* Feb. 7, 1905.] R. E. M.

MANLY, BASIL (Jan. 29, 1798–Dec. 21, 1868), Baptist clergyman, educator, was born near Pittsboro, Chatham County, N. C., second son of Basil and Elizabeth (Maultsby) Manly. The father was a farmer who had served with some distinction in the Revolution. Two other sons, Charles and Matthias, became men of local distinction, the former as governor of the state and the latter as a jurist. Basil, like his brothers, received his early education at Pittsboro and in the Bingham School. His father was a Catholic, but his mother became a Baptist, and Basil followed her into her church, being baptized Aug. 26, 1816. Soon afterwards he announced his desire to study for the Baptist ministry and, despite the opposition of his father, who refused to assist him toward further education, was licensed to preach by the Rocky Spring Church, Apr. 26, 1818. About this time Rev. W. T. Brantly, pastor of the Baptist church at Beaufort, S. C., and president of a small college located in that town, made a visit to this section of North Carolina. Impressed with the promise of young Manly, Brantly persuaded him to go to Beaufort and enter college there, where he could secure financial assistance.

After eighteen months of study in Beaufort, he entered the junior class of South Carolina College in December 1819, graduating as valedictorian and honor man of his class Dec. 3, 1821. During the later months of his college career, with the encouragement of Jonathan Maxcy [*q.v.*], president of the institution and an able and eloquent Baptist minister, he had begun to preach in the churches of the surrounding country. His ability was at once recognized and his services were much in demand. In January 1822 he settled in Edgefield, S. C., becoming pastor there and at Stevens Creek, a neighboring country church. He joined the Stevens Creek church, where he was ordained Mar. 10, 1822, by John Landrum and Enoch Breazeale. He was everywhere greatly loved as a pastor. His sermons were carefully prepared, packed with pungent thought, delivered with pathos and power.

His efforts soon reached beyond his own narrow field. He was elected secretary of the Baptist State Convention, and in 1823 was a member of the committee of five appointed to select a site, arrange courses of study, and complete all necessary details connected with the founding of Furman Academy and Theological Institution, the forerunner of Furman University. Throughout its early years of struggle he was the steadfast friend and ablest helper of this institution. On Dec. 23, 1824, he married Sarah Murray Rudulph of Edgefield, by whom he had five children. In

February 1826 he accepted a call to the pastorate of the First Baptist Church of Charleston, the oldest and at that time the wealthiest church of his denomination in the Southern states. Here he remained in a happy and prosperous pastorate for about twelve years. In 1835 he declined the presidency of South Carolina College, but in September 1837 accepted the presidency of the University of Alabama, a position which he held till 1855. He was also largely instrumental in founding the Alabama Historical Society and Judson, Howard, and Central colleges.

In 1853 he declined the presidency of Furman University, but two years later returned to South Carolina, to the pastorate of Wentworth Street Church, Charleston. He was an ardent promoter of the Southern Baptist Theological Seminary and president of the three conventions (1856, 1857, 1858) which established that institution. In 1859 he returned to Alabama as state evangelist and then became pastor in Montgomery. He gave whole-hearted support to the secession movement, and on Feb. 22, 1861, was chaplain at the inauguration of Jefferson Davis as president of the Confederacy, riding with the presidential party and delivering the prayer. In 1863 he returned once more to South Carolina. He was partially paralyzed in 1864, and died four years later in the home of his son Basil [*q.v.*], at Greenville.

[T. M. Owen, *Dr. Basil Manly, The Founder of the Ala. Hist. Soc.* (1904), repr. from *Trans. Ala. Hist. Soc.*, vol. IV (1904); Louise Manly, *The Manly Family* (1930); W. J. McGlothlin, *Baptist Beginnings in Education* (1926); B. F. Riley, *History of the Baptists in the Southern States East of the Mississippi* (1898); *Charleston Daily Courier*, Dec. 28, 1868.] W. J. M.

MANLY, BASIL (Dec. 19, 1825–Jan. 31, 1892), Baptist clergyman, educator, son of Basil [*q.v.*] and Sarah Murray (Rudulph) Manly, was born in Edgefield District, S. C. His early years were spent in Charleston, while his father was pastor of the First Baptist Church there, but in 1837 his father became president of the University of Alabama and Basil removed with the family to Tuscaloosa. He entered the University in 1839, at the age of fourteen, graduating four years later with first honors. On Oct. 19, 1840, he had united with the Baptist church of Tuscaloosa; he was licensed to preach May 13, 1844, and entered Newton Theological Institution, Newton Center, Mass., the same year. Increasing bitterness of feeling over slavery led to a split between Northern and Southern Baptists and the formation of the Southern Baptist Convention in May 1845, and this event rendered his position so uncomfortable at Newton that he withdrew and entered Princeton Theological Seminary, where he graduated in 1847. He was ordained by the Tuscaloosa church Jan. 30, 1848, having been called to the pastorate of the church at Providence, Ala. This position he held till Jan. 28, 1849, at the same time preaching at Sumterville, Ala., and in Noxubee County, Miss. He then became stated supply of the Tuscaloosa church, 1849–50, but on Sept. 1, 1850, went to the pastorate of the First Baptist Church of Richmond, Va. This important pastorate he held till Sept. 1, 1854, when he became president of the Richmond Female Institute, which he had assisted in founding. At the same time he supplied the Walnut Grove Baptist Church.

When the Southern Baptist Theological Seminary was being established, Manly was appointed to draw up the articles of faith which each professor is required to sign at his inauguration, and when it was opened at Greenville, S. C., in 1859, he was made professor of "Biblical Introduction" and "Old Testament Interpretation." In addition to his teaching, he preached for a time at the churches of Damascus, Siloam, and Clear Springs. The Seminary opened with bright prospects, but was soon closed by the Civil War, which left it in ruins. Manly returned with the others to the work of rehabilitation in 1865, but seems to have lost hope by 1871, in which year he became president of Georgetown College, Georgetown, Ky. In 1877, however, when the Seminary was removed to Louisville, he was reëlected to his old position, and the remainder of his life was given with singular devotion to the work of ministerial education.

He rendered other important services to his denomination, however. He was a great lover of sacred music and made important contributions to Christian hymnology. With his father he compiled and published *Baptist Psalmody* (1850), which was extensively used; later he prepared *Manly's Choice* (1891), a collection of the great old hymns. He wrote for the first Seminary Commencement an appropriate hymn which has been sung at every Commencement since. His most pretentious literary work, *The Bible Doctrine of Inspiration*, was published in 1888; he was also the author of numerous articles, addresses, and pamphlets. Under his leadership a Sunday School Board was established by Southern Baptists in 1863, of which he was president and John A. Broadus [*q.v.*] secretary. In 1866 they established the periodical *Kind Words*, which continued as an important Sunday-school publication for many years. Manly was singularly gentle, lovable, and versatile; an able scholar and an effective teacher. He was twice married: on Apr. 28, 1852, to Charlotte Elizabeth (Whitfield) Smith, who died in 1867; and on June 10, 1869, to Henrietta Summers Hair, who survived him. He died in Louisville, Ky., at the age of sixty-six.

[Louise Manly, *The Manly Family* (1930); *Necrological Report of Princeton Theological Seminary*, 1892; Minutes of the Southern Baptist Convention, the Baptist State Convention of S. C., and the Baptist Gen. Asso. of Ky.; *Seminary Mag.*, Mar. 1892; *Courier-Journal* (Louisville), Feb. 1, 1892.] W. J. M.

MANLY, CHARLES MATTHEWS (Apr. 24, 1876–Oct. 15, 1927), mechanical engineer, inventor, was born at Staunton, Va., the son of Charles and Mary Esther Hellen (Matthews) Manly. His father, a Baptist minister, was the son of Basil Manly, 1798–1869 [*q.v.*], and the brother of Basil, 1825–1892 [*q.v.*]. Mechanical aptitude was a common heritage in the Manly family, but rose to genius in Charles. Graduating at Furman University, Greenville, S. C., in 1896, he pursued graduate work at Cornell University, from which he received the degree of M.E. in 1898. On the recommendation of Prof. R. H. Thurston, he was engaged by Secretary Samuel P. Langley [*q.v.*] to have charge of the construction of a large aeroplane, then building at the Smithsonian Institution for the United States War Department. Langley had already flown (1896) 13-foot models with light steam engines in flights up to three-quarters of a mile, catapulting the models from a houseboat. The same launching method was to be followed with a large machine, though Manly suggested flying from wheels on land. In the final trials Oct. 7 and Dec. 8, 1903, disaster from the launching device occurred in both instances, and Manly, acting as pilot, narrowly escaped being drowned in the wreckage. His great contribution to Langley's work, and his permanent contribution to aviation, was his design and construction of a 5-cylinder water-cooled radial gasoline engine of fifty-two horsepower, weighing but 125 pounds. This engine performed in an exemplary manner, making continuous runs of ten hours in tests. Charles L. Lawrance, president of the Wright Aeronautical Corporation, speaking before the International Civil Aeronautics Conference at Washington, December 1928, said of it: "When we consider that the most popular type of airplane engine of today is almost identical in its general detail and arrangement with the one evolved by Charles Manly in 1902, we are lost in admiration for a man who, with no data at his disposal, no examples of similar art on which to roughly base his design . . . nevertheless, through the processes of a logical mind, the intelligent application of the science of mathematics, and the use of his surprising mechanical skill, succeeded in constructing [this] . . . engine [which] . . . may in fact be characterized as the first 'modern' aircraft engine in the world" (Lawrance, *post*, pp. 415–16).

While yet in Langley's employ, Manly invented and patented, Oct. 7, 1902, the Manly drive, a hydraulic device for transmitting power at variable speeds from a constant-speed motor. In essentials it comprised a radial multicylinder pump of constant speed delivering oil to a radial multicylinder motor. The throw of the pistons was continuously variable from zero to a maximum, thereby enabling a wide-ranged continuous change of speed of the driven element to be made at the pleasure of the operator. The firm of Manly & Veal, consulting engineers, and the Manly Drive Company developed this device in New York, applying it to heavy trucks and to battleship turrets. Manly was the owner of some fifty patents on automotive transportation and power generation and transmission.

He completed and edited the *Langley Memoir on Mechanical Flight*, published by the Smithsonian Institution in 1911, which was begun by Langley and gives in detail his experiments in aviation. He served as consulting aviation engineer to the British War Office, 1915; to the Curtiss Aeroplane & Motor Corporation, 1915–19, of which from 1919 to 1920 he was assistant general manager; as a member of the United States commission to the International Aircraft Conference, London, 1918; and as consulting engineer to various corporations. He was a member and president (1919) of the Society of Automotive Engineers. In 1930 the Smithsonian Institution, in recognition of the permanent value of his pioneer work on the light radial internal combustion engine, awarded to him posthumously the Langley Gold Medal for Aerodromics. On June 9, 1904, he married Grace Agnes Wishart, who died May 15, 1921, leaving two sons.

[*Who's Who in America*, 1926–27; Louise Manly, *The Manly Family* (1930); unpublished records of the Smithsonian Institution; *Specifications and Drawings of Patents Issued from the U. S. Patent Office*, Oct. 1902, July 1904, Oct. 1905; *Ann. Report of the Commissioner of Patents*, 1913, ff.; C. L. Lawrance, "The Development of the Airplane Engine in the U. S.," in *International Civil Aeronautics Conference, 1928, Papers* . . . (1928); E. C. Vivian and W. L. Marsh, *A Hist. of Aeronautics* (1921); F. A. Magoun and E. Hodgins, *A Hist. of Aircraft* (1931); *Ann. Report of the Board of Regents of the Smithsonian Institution* (1930); *Jour. of the Soc. of Automotive Engineers*, Nov. 1927, Oct. 1928; *World* (N. Y.) and *N. Y. Herald Tribune*, Oct. 18, 1927.] C. G. A.

MANN, AMBROSE DUDLEY (Apr. 26, 1801–November 1889), diplomat, was born at Hanover Court House, Va. He was educated in the Virginia schools and at the United States Military Academy at West Point, whence he resigned just before graduation in order to avoid entering the military profession. He took up the legal profession and soon became interested in politics. In 1842 he was appointed United States consul at Bremen, Germany, and in 1846 he was given diplomatic powers as a special commissioner to the German states for the purpose of negotiating commercial treaties. He drew up commercial treaties with Hanover, Oldenburg, Mecklenburg-Schwerin, and with other German states. Acting on Mann's suggestion, Polk recognized the federal government of Germany at Frankfort in 1848. In 1849 Mann was appointed special agent of the United States to Kossuth's government in Hungary. He was virtually authorized to extend recognition if events seemed to warrant it. After the collapse of this project he was sent to Switzerland as special agent of the United States during the administration of Fillmore. In this capacity he negotiated and signed a general convention of friendship and reciprocal agreements. On his return to America he became assistant secretary of state and served from 1853 to 1856.

With the approach of the Civil War Mann was increasingly identified with the Southern Rights party. He was especially prominent in the advocacy of the economic independence of the South, which, because of his special knowledge of commerce and navigation, assumed the form of championship of a Southern merchant marine. He wrote pamphlets and articles for *DeBow's Review,* 1856–58, urging the establishment of a direct steamship line between the Southern states and Europe. He also advised building fast ships which would be specially fitted for Southern waters. Because of his representations to it, the Virginia legislature in 1858 incorporated a company for establishing the direct trade (*Acts of the General Assembly of Virginia,* 1857–58, ch. 187). The idea was very popular during this period when such men as Yancy, Hammond, DeBow, and others were attempting to convince the South of the necessity of casting off its vassalage to Northern industry and commerce. So when the South withdrew from the Union in 1861 the choice of Mann as joint commissioner with Yancy and Rost and as associate commissioner with Mason and Slidell was not entirely illogical.

But expert knowledge of trade and shipping and experience in arranging commercial treaties apparently constituted Mann's chief qualifications for a position which required diplomacy of the highest skill. He was credulous and lacking in penetration and seems never to have been aware of the real drift of affairs. His diplomatic correspondence is characterized by ponderous and bombastic phrases and sophomoric sentiments. He spent the first year of his mission in London and the last three years in Belgium where he wasted time cultivating the already friendly King Leopold, who it was hoped would exercise moving influence upon Napoleon and Queen Victoria. In two matters, however, he was not a complete failure: he managed to influence the press in both England and Belgium in 1861 at the time when the Confederacy had no regular propagandist agents in Europe; and in the winter of 1863–64 he went to the Vatican to obtain the aid of the Pope in checking the Federal recruiting in Europe of Catholic Irish and Germans. Altogether the Northern cause won large numbers of recruits from Europe, mostly in Ireland and Germany, and it would have been worth a whole series of successful campaigns to the Confederacy if this enlistment of foreigners could have been frustrated. The Pope expressed great indignation and horror when he learned to what extent his subjects were being utilized by the United States as cannon fodder and immediately attempted to put a check to their enlistment. But, while many were restrained by the Pope's objection, there was no appreciable decrease in the number of those who left Ireland and the other Catholic countries and entered the Federal armies to get the bounty. Mann remained in Europe after the overthrow of the Confederacy and lived in Paris until his death in 1889.

[The Pickett papers in the Manuscript Division of the Lib. of Cong. contain all of Mann's diplomatic correspondence during his mission to England and Belgium, 1861–65; James M. Mason's papers contain some private letters from Mann to Mason, 1861–65 (Manuscript Division of the Lib. of Cong.); his consular and diplomatic correspondence while in Germany and Switzerland, 1842–53, is in the Dept. of State. For his reports upon Hungary see *Senate Executive Doc. 43,* 31 Cong., 1 Sess., *Senate Doc. 279,* 61 Cong., 2 Sess., and *Senate Doc. 282,* 65 Cong., 2 Sess. For résumés of his diplomatic career by Lewis Cass, secretary of state, and by a congressional committee, see *House Executive Doc. 17* and *House Report 254,* 35 Cong., 2 Sess. Further sources include: Dunbar Rowland, *Jefferson Davis, Constitutionalist; His Letters, Papers and Speeches* (1923), vol. VII; H. M. Wriston, *Executive Agents in Am. Foreign Relations* (1929); *Journal des Débats* (Paris), Nov. 16, 1889; obituary reprinted from *Galignani's Messenger* (Paris) in the *N. Y. Tribune,* Dec. 1, 1889. Mann wrote the memoirs of his life but the whereabouts of this document is apparently unknown.]

F. L. O.

MANN, HORACE (May 4, 1796–Aug. 2, 1859), educator, one of five children of Thomas and Rebecca (Stanley) Mann, was born on the ancestral farm in the town of Franklin, Mass., a descendant of William Mann, an early settler of

Cambridge, Mass. From his father, who died of tuberculosis in 1809, Horace inherited a frail constitution and a susceptibility to this disease. His parents were people of meager education but of sterling character, and imparted to their children habits of industry and high ideals. Mann's childhood was an unhappy one passed in poverty, unremitting toil, repression, and fear. The studies and methods of the district school were stultifying, the school masters ignorant, and their discipline stern and terrifying. Still more terrifying were the Sunday sermons preached by the Rev. Nathaniel Emmons [*q.v.*], in which were pictured the eternal torments of those damned for the glory of God. Night after night the little lad, filled with grief and horror over the possible fate awaiting his loved ones, sobbed himself to sleep. Although Franklin possessed a town library, it brought little relief to the mind of the harrowed child, made up as it was chiefly of old histories and theological works. Undoubtedly, the immediate influence of school, church, and town library upon this highly sensitive boy were repressive, if not injurious; nevertheless, to the spirit of revolt engendered by their defects can be traced directly many of the most important reform efforts of his later life.

The superiority of Mann's mental gifts was revealed in connection with his preparation for college. Up to the time he was sixteen, he had never attended school more than eight or ten weeks in any one year, and he did not begin preparing for college until 1816. Then, in six months, under the direction of an eccentric but brilliant itinerant teacher named Barrett, he completed a course of study which enabled him to enter the sophomore class of Brown University. Here he made a brilliant record, graduating with high honors in 1819. He now entered a law office in Wrentham, Mass., but after a few months returned to Brown as a tutor in Latin and Greek. In 1821 he left Brown to enter the famous law school at Litchfield, Conn., and in 1823 was admitted to the bar of Norfolk County, Mass. For fourteen years, first at Dedham, Mass., and after 1833 at Boston, he practised with marked success. Meanwhile, he had begun his public career as a member of the Massachusetts state legislature, first serving in the House (1827–33), and then in the Senate (1833–37). During the last two years, he was president of the Senate, and as such signed the epoch-making education bill which became a law Apr. 20, 1837. This bill provided for a state board of education, to consist of the governor, lieutenant-governor, and eight citizens to be appointed by the governor. It empowered the board of education to appoint and employ a secretary at an annual salary of $1,000 (increased in 1838 to $1,500), and to make annual reports to the state legislature.

It had been expected that the board would choose as its first secretary James G. Carter [*q.v.*], the framer of the bill, a man whose services to education undoubtedly eclipsed those of any other citizen of the state up to that time. The selection of Mann, largely through the influence of Edmund Dwight [*q.v.*], was, however, a matter of no greater surprise than Mann's acceptance, involving, as it did, his abandonment of a lucrative legal practice and the prospect of an alluring political career; but his reasons for acceptance are not difficult to discover. Though exceedingly successful, he had never been ardently enthusiastic about his profession; from early childhood he had been possessed with a consuming desire to do something for the benefit of mankind; he saw in the secretaryship, moreover, a means of combating the grief and despair which had held him in clutch ever since the death of his wife, Charlotte Messer, daughter of President Asa Messer [*q.v.*] of Brown University, whom he had married Sept. 12, 1830, and who had died childless, Aug. 1, 1832.

The educational situation awaiting the new secretary offered ample scope for his many talents. The school-district system legalized in 1789 had brought with it a multitude of evils, including disastrous decentralization, a decline in public interest, and a decrease of financial support. Free schools, the one-time glory of colonial Massachusetts, were now regarded with contempt by the well-to-do classes, who more and more patronized private schools. The effects of this attitude were everywhere evident in short school terms, dilapidated and unsanitary schoolhouses, untrained and underpaid teachers, and irrational methods of teaching. To remedy these conditions as far and as soon as possible was the task awaiting Mann. Clothed with almost no authority except to collect and disseminate information, he brought to his new duties such a degree of courage, vision, and wisdom that during the brief period of twelve years in which he held office, the Massachusetts school system was almost completely transformed. His first task was to arouse and to educate public opinion with reference to the purpose, value, and needs of public education. With this end in view, he organized annual educational conventions in every county for the benefit of teachers, school officials, and the public. He not only addressed these meetings himself, but pressed into service distinguished clergymen, lawyers, and college professors. Realizing that there was little hope of any improvement in the schools apart from the improvement of the teaching profession, he rapidly consummated plans which led to the establishment of teachers' institutes and normal schools. During the second year of his office, Edmund Dwight, through Mann, anonymously offered $10,000 to the state of Massachusetts for improving the preparation of elementary teachers, provided the state would furnish a like amount. Dwight's gift and its conditions were accepted by the legislature, and within two years Massachusetts had established the first three state normal schools in the United States.

In 1838, with the avowed purpose of bringing about a better understanding of the problems of the public school, he started a semi-monthly magazine, the *Common School Journal,* which he edited for ten years. A far more important channel through which he disseminated a knowledge of existing conditions and needed reforms were the twelve annual reports which he prepared (1837–48) as secretary of the state board of education. Each contains not only the customary statistical data, but a presentation and discussion of school problems of crucial importance. The needs and remedies growing out of these problems are set forth with convincing clearness and with the fervor of a prophet and reformer.

The results of his labors were remarkable. When he became secretary, elementary men teachers were receiving an average annual wage of $185, and women, $65; one-sixth of the children of the state were being educated in private schools and academies, and approximately one-third were without any educational opportunities whatsoever. In multitudes of districts the school term did not extend beyond two or three months. Under Mann's influence, a minimum school year of six months was established by an act passed in 1839. More than $2,000,000 was spent in providing better schoolhouses and equipment. Appropriations for public education were more than doubled. The proportion of private school expenditure to that of public schools decreased from seventy-five to thirty-six per cent. of total school costs. Salaries of public school masters were increased by sixty-two per cent. and those of women, by fifty-four per cent. The high-school law of 1827, largely a dead letter prior to his time, became effective, with the result that at least fifty new high schools were established during his secretaryship and opportunities for free public secondary education became widely distributed throughout the state. The professional training of teachers was placed on a firm basis, the elementary curriculum was enriched, and improved methods of instruction, including especially the Pestalozzian object methods and the word method of teaching reading, were introduced.

It was inevitable that Mann's aggressive efforts should sooner or later arouse bitter opposition. As a Unitarian, he contended that the Bible should be read in public schools, but without comment. He had scarcely entered upon his progressive educational program when one church after another began to charge him and the board of education with being responsible for creating a godless system of schools. With these charges came the demand that sectarian instruction, which had been excluded from the schools by an act of 1827, should be restored. Mann met these sectarian attacks with vigor, courage, and a final victory of great importance, not only to the schools of Massachusetts, but to the nation at large. Immediately after his marriage to his second wife, Mary Tyler (Peabody) Mann [*q.v.*], on May 1, 1843, he sailed for Europe with two purposes in mind: to recover his health, and to discover what America might learn from European schools. He spent five months studying educational conditions in England, Ireland, Scotland, Holland, Belgium, France, Germany, and Switzerland. His observations and conclusions, embodied in his seventh annual report, drew no comparison between the schools of the United States and those of European countries; nevertheless, his high commendation of German schools was interpreted by a considerable number of Boston school masters as implying a drastic criticism of their own professional preparation and practices. An acrimonious controversy ensued from which, however, Mann again came forth victorious.

In 1848 he resigned his secretaryship, having been elected to the United States House of Representatives as an anti-slavery Whig to succeed John Quincy Adams. Although allied with anti-slavery forces, Mann was not an abolitionist; nevertheless, he was eventually led into open conflict with Daniel Webster, whose friendship and political support he had enjoyed up to this time. In 1852 he met defeat as the candidate of the Free-Soilers for the governorship of Massachusetts. He then accepted the presidency of the recently established Antioch College at Yellow Springs, Ohio. Besides serving as president, he taught political economy, intellectual philosophy, moral philosophy, and natural theology. In 1859, owing to bad management, lack of funds, and internal dissensions, the college was sold for debt and reorganized. Following his delivery of the baccalaureate address of that year, Mann, exhausted and broken by the anxieties and persecution amid which he had labored, retired to his home, where he died within a few weeks. He was survived by his wife and their three sons.

Mann espoused many other causes beside that of the common schools, notably the establishment of state hospitals for the insane and the restriction of slavery, lotteries, and the liquor traffic. Essentially a Puritan without a theology, he denounced not only profanity and intemperance, but smoking and ballet dancing. His lasting place in American history rests, however, upon his services to public education. His influence in this field extended far beyond the boundaries of Massachusetts. Copies of his annual reports and other educational writings were widely disseminated throughout the United States with the result that one state after another sought and followed his advice. Owing to his efforts combined with those of other educational pioneers, there ensued a period so marked by educational progress and reform that it has ever since come to be known as the period of the common-school revival in the United States.

Among the many influences which played an important part in developing the character, philosophy, ideals, and aims of Horace Mann were the writings of Emerson and those of the Scotch philosopher and phrenologist, George Combe. Although Mann acquired from Combe a belief in phrenology, undoubtedly the greatest source of Combe's influence over him was the Scotch philosopher's unswerving faith in the unlimited improvability of the human race through education. The motivating principle of Mann's life was nowhere better or more clearly expressed than in the oft-quoted words with which he closed his last Commencement address at Antioch College: "Be ashamed to die until you have won some victory for humanity." In addition to his twelve annual reports which are included in abbreviated form in Mary Mann's *Life* (*post,* vol. III), and numerous articles in magazines, he published *Lectures on Education* (1845).

[Biographies and biographical sketches of Mann have been published in English, French, and Spanish. Of these the most important in English are: *Life and Works of Horace Mann,* ed. by Mary Tyler Peabody Mann (3 vols., 1865–68), enlarged and ed. by G. C. Mann (5 vols., 1891); B. A. Hinsdale, *Horace Mann and the Common School Revival in the U. S.* (1898); G. Compayré, *Horace Mann and the Public School in the U. S.* (tr. 1907); A. E. Winship, *Horace Mann the Educator* (1896). See also R. B. Culver, *Horace Mann and Religion in the Massachusetts Public Schools* (1929). For a genealogy of the Mann family, consult G. S. Mann, *Mann Memorial: A Record of the Mann Family in America* (1884). For bibliographies consult B. P. Mann, in *Report of the Commissioner of Education, 1895–96* (1897), vol. I, and B. A. Hinsdale, *supra,* pp. 311–19.] F. H. S.

MANN, JAMES (July 22, 1759–Nov. 7, 1832), army surgeon, was born in Wrentham, Mass., the son of David and Anna Mann and a descendant of William Mann, an early settler in Cambridge, Mass. He graduated from Harvard at the age of seventeen and then took up the study of medicine under Dr. Samuel Danforth. At the age of twenty he became surgeon of Col. William Shepard's 4th Massachusetts Regiment. In June of 1781 he was captured by the British and was imprisoned on Long Island during July and August. He left the army because of poor health on Apr. 14, 1782. He settled first at Wrentham but later moved to New York, where he practised until the outbreak of the War of 1812. Entering the army as a hospital surgeon, he was soon put in charge of the medical department on the northern frontier. Upon the establishment of peace in 1815 he apparently left the service, as his name is not in the next army register, but in August 1816 he is again shown as the senior hospital surgeon, on duty at Detroit. The reorganization of 1818, which established the medical corps and consolidated the hospital, garrison, and regimental surgeons on one list of post surgeons, ranked according to seniority, put him number twenty-four on that list. The reorganization of 1821, which reduced the number of surgeons to eight, left him an assistant surgeon. He served in that grade until his death, which occurred at Governor's Island on Nov. 7, 1832.

Mann was a scholarly person and an interesting writer. He published articles on the defeat of the Indians at Wrentham, and on diabetes, cholera infantum, pneumonia, amputations through joints, swelling of the inferior extremities of puerperal women, and on menorrhagia and leucorrhea and their treatment. But his fame rests principally upon his *Medical Sketches of the Campaigns of 1812, 13, 14, to which are added Surgical Cases, Observations on Military Hospitals; and Flying Hospitals Attached to a Moving Army, Also An Appendix . . .* (1816). The sketches, written in good English, reveal striking powers of observation. They describe not only the medical affairs of the Northern army but the country and the frontier villages of that day, when Buffalo, two miles above Black Rock, was a village of less than 200 houses, though rapidly increasing in population and trade. Mann's professional standing is witnessed by the fact that in 1819, while stationed in Boston, he was elected one of the eight consulting physicians of the Massachusetts General Hospital. He was also awarded an honorary degree of M.D. from Brown University in 1815. Unquestionably one of the most notable army surgeons of his day, he was, by an ironical fate, the individual victim of well-meant general legislation, which, though he had ranked next after the head of the department, left him an assistant surgeon at the time of his death at the age of seventy-three. Mann was married, Dec. 12, 1788, to Martha (or Mary) Tyler. They had five children.

[Army registers, 1815–32; G. S. Mann, *Mann Memorial: A Record of the Mann Family in America* (1884); W. I. T. Brigham, *The Tyler Geneal.* (1912), vol. I; *Mass. Hist. Soc. Colls.*, vol. X (1809); *Boston Medic. and Surgic. Jour.*, Nov. 14, 1918; N. I. Bowditch, *Hist. of the Mass. Gen. Hospital* (1881); *N. Y. American*, Nov. 8, 1832.] P. M. A.

MANN, JAMES ROBERT (Oct. 20, 1856–Nov. 30, 1922), lawyer, congressman, was born near Bloomington, Ill., the son of William Henry Mann, Illinois horticulturist, and Elizabeth Dabney (Abraham) Mann. He attended the University of Illinois, where he distinguished himself in student activities and athletics and graduated as valedictorian in 1876. He was also valedictorian of the class of 1881 at the Union College of Law (Chicago), and while a student, began to assist in the editing of certain United States court reports. On May 30, 1882, he was married to Emma Columbia of Champaign, Ill. His real-estate and legal connections with the nearby village of Hyde Park brought him a fortune which permitted him to indulge a taste for politics. He became attorney for the Hyde Park commissioners and the South Park commissioners of Chicago, and master in chancery of the superior court of Cook County. His aid in bringing the Columbian Exposition to the Hyde Park area sent him to the Chicago common council upon the incorporation of his village. Serving from 1892 to 1896, he became known as a hard fighter and a hater of "boodle," a not-unknown commodity in the council of that day. In 1897 his strongly Republican district sent him to Congress and kept him there until his death in 1922.

Mann was connected with much of the important legislation of his period. Seniority made him chairman of the commerce committee for a single congress before the Democratic landslide of 1912. Measures bearing his name or handiwork are: the Mann-Elkins act (railroad rate regulation, anti-rebate law), the pure food and drugs act (1906), the bureau of corporations act, the Mann act ("white slave" law), the wood-pulp tariff, isthmian canal legislation, the resolution providing for the woman-suffrage amendment, and numerous local matters. Cannon's choice of Mann as official "watchdog of legislation" in part explains his rise and his tendency to standpattism. Just at the time (1912) when his talents were coming to their peak the shift of parties threw him into the position of minority leader. Here he came into his own. A rather short, stocky, grizzly-bearded, beetle-browed individual, he made a formidable antagonist to anyone trying to put through loose, unwise, or Democratic legislation. Often on his feet, an able and willing filibuster, for six years he served his party by hectoring the Democratic majority.

After a short retirement in 1914 caused by illness Mann returned in 1915, seemingly with some notion of his own eligibility for the presidential nomination in 1916. Failing this, he lost the caucus nomination for the speakership in 1919, a defeat illustrating if not resulting from his own characteristics as minority leader. His devotion to the Cannonism which gave him his start made him unacceptable to the post-Progressive Republican party, and his very capabilities were a limitation. Better informed on legislation than his fellow Republicans, he tended to shoulder the entire burden, leading an exasperated colleague to accuse him of undertaking "not only to play Hamlet, but the fair Ophelia and the King and the Queen and first grave-digger" (*James R. Mann: Memorial Addresses, post*, p. 45). This hurt his larger usefulness while making him superficially even more valuable to the party. With his health and prestige weakened, he retired into a sort of emeritus position with the return of a Republican majority, ending his career as a sort of peppery oracle delivering opinions on the questions of the day. To his ability, industry, and keen insight into parliamentary intricacies friend and foe bore witness; the former with pride tempered by a somewhat smarting sense of Mann's self-imposed superiority, the latter with envy not untouched with humiliation at the flaws he had found in their legislative armor.

[See *Who's Who in America*, 1922–23; *Biog. Dir. Am. Cong.* (1928); *James R. Mann: Memorial Addresses Delivered in the House of Representatives . . . Jan. 14, 1923* (1924); *Chicago Tribune, Evening Star* (Washington), Dec. 1, 1922. The Mann papers (35 vols.) in the Lib. of Cong. contain a mass of newspaper material and a few letters. He destroyed his personal correspondence.] L. E. E.

MANN, LOUIS (Apr. 20, 1865–Feb. 15, 1931), actor and playwright, was born in New York City, the son of Daniel and Caroline (Hecht) Mann. His first stage appearance was at the Stadt Theatre on the Bowery, New York, at the age of three, when he impersonated a snowflake in a Christmas pantomime. But his parents had no thought of a stage career for him. In youth he worked for a time in a haberdasher's shop, and then was sent to the University of California. After some two years of study, he left the University surreptitiously to join a theatrical stock company in San Francisco. His parents at length traced him to central New York, where the company was playing *East Lynne, Ingomar,* and other old favorites. Unknown to him, the parents saw him perform, and deciding that he had talent, gave him $200 to further his dramatic education; but Louis turned it over to his manager to bolster the shaky finances of the company. For several years he played in support of Tommaso Salvini, Lewis Morrison, E. H. Sothern, Cyril Maude, and Daniel Bandmann. By 1890 he was making ventures at the head of small companies of his own in *Lady Audley's Secret* and other strenuous dramas. In 1892 he scored a hit in the part of Dick Winters in *Incog.* In the following year he again took a company of his own on tour in *The Laughing Girl.* His burlesque of Du Maurier's Svengali in *The Merry World* in 1895 was much praised. In 1897 in *The Girl from Paris* he shared honors with his wife, Clara Lipman, actress and playwright, whom he had married on Oct. 28, 1895.

Throughout the greater part of his career, Mann played dialect rôles—German, Jewish, French, and in *The Red Kloof* (1901) he assumed the part of a South African Boer farmer. In *The Telephone Girl* (1898), *The Girl in the Barracks* (1899), *All on Account of Eliza* (1900), and *Hoch the Consul* (1902) he continued playing these eccentric leading rôles, usually with his wife as co-star. In 1903 he appeared for a time with the Weber and Fields burlesque company. In 1904 he played Baron von Walden in *The Second Fiddle,* and in 1906–07 he appeared in New York and London in *Julie Bonbon,* written by Clara Lipman. *The White Hen* followed in 1907, and then *The New Generation,* later renamed *The Man Who Stood Still,* which continued from 1908 to 1910. In 1910 came his own play, *The Cheater,* and in 1911 *Elevating a Husband,* written by his wife (in collaboration with Samuel Shipman), and utilizing Mann's enthusiasm for baseball. *Children of To-Day* in 1913, *The Bubble* (1915), and *The Warriors* (1917) were not remarkable, but in 1918 he scored one of his greatest successes as co-star with Sam Bernard in *Friendly Enemies,* a war play. When it appeared in Washington, President Wilson sat in a box, and at Mann's invitation arose and spoke a few words in praise of the play—the first time in history that such an incident had occurred. This comedy ran for more than a year in New York and toured the country until late in 1920. In *The Unwritten Chapter,* Mann next appeared as Haym Salomon, Jewish financier of the American Revolution, in whose history the actor was deeply interested. Subsequent appearances were in *The Whirl of New York, Nature's Nobleman,* and *Give and Take.* Mann was a person of strong opinions and intense emotions, qualities which he injected into his stage characters. He was one of the organizers of the Actors' Fidelity League, which fought the Actors' Equity strike in 1919.

[*Who's Who in America,* 1930–31; John Parker, ed., *Who's Who in the Theatre* (1930); Felix Isman, *Weber and Fields* (1924), pp. 291–95; L. C. Strang, *Famous Actors of the Day in America* (1902), second series; the *Theatre,* Apr. 1905; obituaries in New York newspapers, Feb. 16, 1931; Robinson Locke Dramatic Collection, N. Y. Pub. Lib.] A. F. H.

MANN, MARY TYLER PEABODY (Nov. 16, 1806–Feb. 11, 1887), educator, author, was born in Cambridge, Mass., the second of the seven children of Nathaniel and Elizabeth (Palmer) Peabody. The eldest child of the family was Elizabeth Palmer Peabody [*q.v.*], and the third was Sophia Amelia, who married Nathaniel Hawthorne in 1842. Their father, a graduate of Dartmouth College in the class of 1800, was a physician and dentist with varied cultural interests, and the mother conducted a school in which her own children received their excellent training.

In 1832 the Peabodys removed from Salem to Boston and opened a bookstore as a sort of family enterprise. They imported French and German books and periodicals, carried a stock of artists' supplies—chiefly for the personal convenience of Washington Allston—and made their shop one of the focal points of the Transcendental movement. About this time Mary first met Horace Mann [*q.v.*] in the Ashburton Place boarding house kept by the mother of James Freeman Clarke. They were alike in their intellectual ardor and in their devotion to educational and philanthropic work, and she was soon in love with him; but Mann was all but broken by grief for the death of his wife, and some nine years passed before he could bring himself to propose marriage to her. Meanwhile, Mary spent the years 1832–35 with Sophia in Cuba and on her return was Elizabeth's assistant in her school. On May 1, 1843, she and Horace Mann were married, and the marriage, contrary to his forebodings, proved singularly happy. Mrs. Mann was her husband's active collaborator and influenced his life and thought profoundly; she bore him three sons. After her husband's death at Yellow Springs, Ohio, Aug. 2, 1859, she returned to Massachusetts and made her home successively in Concord, Cambridge, and Jamaica Plain, where she died. She had already published a children's book, *The Flower People* (1838; rev. ed., 1875) and a cook book, *Christianity in the Kitchen: A Physiological Cook Book* (1857; 1858), based on the soundest scientific knowledge then available; she now devoted herself to writing her husband's life and editing his works, producing her *Life and Works of Horace Mann* (3 vols., 1865–68; extended edition in 5 vols., ed. by G. C. Mann, 1891). In the *Life* the only reference to herself is at the beginning of Chapter v: "On the 1st of May, 1843, Mr. Mann was again married, and sailed for Europe to visit European schools, especially in Germany, where he expected to derive most benefit." She wrote for various periodicals, made translations from the Spanish, supervised the education of her sons, interested herself actively in philanthropic work among Indians and negroes, and aided her sister Elizabeth in her kindergarten in Boston. Her essay, "Moral Culture of Infancy," was published in 1863 in a single small volume with Elizabeth Peabody's "Kindergarten Guide." *Juanita: A Romance of Real Life in Cuba Fifty Years Ago* (1887) appeared posthumously and exhibits both the limitations and the virtues of her remarkable mind, which kept its vigor to the end. A few hours before her death she called for the Boston *Evening Transcript* and listened with evident pleasure while a review of one of her sister's books was read aloud to her.

[S. H. Peabody and C. H. Pope, *Peabody Geneal.* (1909); Julian Hawthorne, *Nathaniel Hawthorne and His Wife* (1885); *Grandmother Tyler's Book: The Recollections of Mary Palmer Tyler* (1925), ed. by Frederick Tupper and H. T. Brown; G. A. Hubbell, *Horace Mann, Educator, Patriot and Reformer* (1910); Boston *Transcript*, Feb. 12, 15, 1887.] G. H. G.

MANN, NEWTON (Jan. 16, 1836–July 25, 1926), Unitarian clergyman, author, was descended through his father, Darwin H. Mann, from Richard Mann of Scituate, Mass., who emigrated from England about 1644; and through his mother, Cordelia Newton, from Richard Newton, who was a freeman of Marlboro, Mass., in 1645. Born in Cazenovia, N. Y., the first of five children, all surviving, and educated at Cazenovia Seminary, he was obliged to shorten his schooling at the death of his father in 1844 and take up the responsibilities of farming. So successfully, however, did he combine his duties with self-culture that at twenty he was acquainted with the best literature and philosophy of the day, notably Emerson, Renan, and Spencer, and had command of five languages. An inheritance of intellectual independence from his paternal grandfather, a physician, overcame the strongly sentimental orthodoxy of his Baptist mother and kinsfolk. His tendency toward heterodoxy was strengthened by a rebuff from the family minister, who told him that his doubts were a temptation of the devil. As a result Mann decided for "liberty,—liberty to choose, and to follow the good; deliverance from the dominating authority of what has been called the 'written Word'; . . . and the committal of the soul to the guidance of the free Spirit, out of which have come all bibles, all holiest thoughts, all highest things" (*Evolution of a Great Literature,* 1905, p. 371).

While on a visit to relatives in Wisconsin (1856–59) he came in contact with many Mid-west Liberals and was engaged to supply the pulpit of the First Unitarian Church in Cincinnati (1859). A copy of Darwin's newly published *Origin of Species* came into his hands and prompted a sermon on "The Implication of Darwin's Philosophy," containing the first accurate forecast in the American pulpit of the effect of the hypothesis upon religious thought: "*The Origin of Species* marks a determining break in the whole history of thought. The theory of special creations, of man, of everything that falls within the realm of nature is from now on effectually disposed of. . . . Disposing of the special creation of Adam brings the fall of the doctrine of original sin. With the fall of the doctrine of original sin falls the Christian scheme of redemption and atonement." Such avowals made him an undesirable person even in the Unitarian pulpit of the day and he became principal of the school in Alton, Ill., whence, in 1861, he was called to be superintendent of the Western Sanitary Commission's soldiers' home at Vicksburg. Returning to the North and the ministry, he was ordained in 1865 as minister of the Unitarian Church in Kenosha, Wis., which he had organized. Three years later he became pastor of the Unitarian Society in Troy, N. Y., and in 1870 he was called to the Unitarian Church in Rochester, N. Y., where he remained until 1888. His years there were a period of great literary and scientific activity. He interpreted Kuenen in a series of lectures published in 1879 under the title, *A Rational View of the Bible*; he built an observatory on his lawn and computed the orbit of Sirius and its dark companion, the calculations and arguments appearing in *Popular Astronomy,* March 1897. In 1889 he became minister of the First Unitarian Church in Omaha, Nebr. Here he continued the cultural and scientific educational work he had begun in the Fortnightly Club of Rochester by founding Unity Club, the liberal and progressive programs of which exerted a profound influence upon the city. He also founded the Nebraska Humane Society and was its first president. During these years he published *The Evolution of a Great Literature* (1905, 1906), a lucid, scholarly presentation of modern Biblical criticism, and *The Import and Outlook of Socialism* (1910), in which he compared modern socialism with early Christianity, maintaining that "to perfect the great work and really bring peace among men, it needs that Christ come again, and with a more inclusive gospel, reaching to and moulding outward conditions as well as the inward spirit."

In addition to the published prose mentioned, Mann wrote many poems, usually upon religious or philosophic themes, which have never been collected, although his translation and adaptation of the Jewish hymn, "Praise to the Living God," is found in many hymnals. His death in Chicago at the age of ninety closed a life of remarkable mental vigor, independence, and originality. On Aug. 8, 1857, he married Eliza J. Smith, who died in 1908; by her he had four children. On Aug. 20, 1912, he married Rev. M. Rowena Morse of Chicago.

[G. S. Mann, *Mann Memorial: A Record of the Mann Family in America* (1884); *Meadville Theol. Sch. Quart. Bull.*, Oct. 1929; *Who's Who in America*, 1920–21; *Unitarian Yearbook*, 1927; *Christian Reg.*, Aug. 5, 19, 1926; *Chicago Tribune*, July 26, 1926.]

C. H. L—e.

MANN, WILLIAM JULIUS (May 29, 1819–June 20, 1892), Lutheran clergyman, author, was born in Stuttgart, Württemberg, the second son of Johann Georg Mann by his second wife, Auguste Friederike Gentner. His father, a merchant of good education and varied interests, was a founder and treasurer (1812–40) of the *Württemberger Bibelgesellschaft* and was city almoner (1845–58). Mann attended the *Lateinschule* at Blaubeuren (1827–33), the *Gymnasium Illustré* of his native city (1833–37), and the University of Tübingen (1837–41). As a theological student he was more influenced by Christian Friedrich Schmidt, an offspring of the old supranaturalistic school of Tübingen, than by either C. F. Baur or D. F. Strauss. After leaving the university Mann taught in a boys' school at Bönningheim, became assistant pastor there in February 1844, and in December of that year went to a similar position at Neuhausen, near Metzingen.

Meanwhile, in March, Philip Schaff [*q.v.*], whom Mann had first met in his gymnasial days, had gone to the United States and was soon urging his friend to join him at Mercersburg. Despite the sundering of family ties Mann was easily persuaded, for the thought of America had already fired his imagination. In 1843 he had written a children's story, *Die Ansiedler in Amerika* (Stuttgart, 1845), that indicates where his thoughts were wandering. He left Stuttgart Aug. 16, 1845, and arrived at Mercersburg Oct. 24. Having taught history and German at Mercersburg for a few months, he became assistant pastor in January 1846 of Salem German Reformed Church, Philadelphia, and was ordained May 17. In 1849 he married Margaretta Catherine, daughter of John Rommel of Philadelphia who with a son and three daughters survived him. He did not feel at home outside the Lutheran Church and was happy when in 1850, without solicitation on his part, he was called to St. Michael's and Zion's congregation as assistant to Charles Rudolph Demme [*q.v.*].

In 1854 he succeeded Demme as chief pastor of the congregation, the largest of its denomination in America. He ministered to it with untiring fidelity and during the 1860's superintended its division into several independent congregations, himself retaining the pastorship of Zion's. When the Philadelphia Lutheran Theological Seminary was founded in 1864, he was elected to the German professorship, a post for which he was eminently qualified; but his parishioners would not accept his resignation, and for twenty laborious years he filled both offices. He taught Hebrew, ethics, symbolics, homiletics, and New Testament exegesis, and was housefather of the Seminary (1872–84). He took a prominent but dignified part in the controversy that led to the founding of the General Council of the Evangelical Lutheran Church in North America, publishing *A Plea for the Augsburg Confession in Answer to the Objections of the Definite Platform* (1856) and *Lutheranism in America* (1857), but after its organization he took little active interest in it. On the vexed question of pulpit and altar fellowship, and on several other matters of importance, he was in sharp disagreement with Charles Porterfield Krauth [*q.v.*] and other leaders of the General Council. He was president of the Ministerium of Pennsylvania from 1860 to 1862 and again in 1880 and active in all its work. He was a prolific writer in both German and English. He was co-editor, with Schaff, of the *Deutscher Kirchenfreund* from 1848 to 1859 and contributed voluminously, on a large variety of subjects, to ten other church papers. He edited an edition of Luther's *Small Catechism* (1863) in collaboration with G. F. Krotel and *Kohler's Familien-Bibel* (1865), published *Heilbotschaft* (1881), a volume of sermons, and several popular works in history and biography. During the last twelve years of his life he devoted much of his time to the early history of the Lutheran Church in America, producing his admirable *Life and Times of Henry Melchior Mühlenberg* (1887) and, in collaboration with Beale Melancthton Schmucker [*q.v.*], an annotated edition of the *Hallesche Nachrichten* (2 vols., 1886–95). Such work was possible only to a man whose mind and pen moved with equal rapidity, and who was habitually at his desk at four o'clock in the morning.

To his seventy-third year, in spite of not a little illness, he kept the freshness and energy of a young man. Unfatigued by the heavy duties of his profession, he was in his hours of leisure a poet, an artist, and a musician, a student of history and the sciences, a close observer of politics, and a delightful companion. Krotel's comparison of him to the man in the parable to whom the five talents were entrusted was best appreciated by those who knew him most intimately. On Oct. 28, 1891, he was prostrated by a heart attack and never recovered fully. He died the following June in a hotel in Boston and was buried in West Laurel Hill Cemetery, Philadelphia.

[Adolph Spaeth, "William Julius Mann, D.D., LL.D.," *Luth. Ch. Rev.*, Jan. 1893 (also separately printed), and *D. Wilhelm Julius Mann, Ein deutsch-amerikanischer Theologe* (Reading, Pa., 1895); *Memoir of the Life and Work of William Julius Mann* (privately printed, 1893), by his daughter, Emma T. Mann; D. S. Schaff, *The Life of Philip Schaff* (1897); T. W. Kretschmann, "William Julius Mann, D.D., LL.D.," *Luth. Ch. Rev.*, July 1917; G. W. Sandt, "Lutheran Leaders as I Knew Them," *Ibid.*, Oct. 1917; L. D. Reed, *The Phila. Sem. Biog. Record 1864–1923* (1923); *Public Ledger* (Phila.), June 21, 1892.] G. H. G.

MANNERS, JOHN HARTLEY (Aug. 10, 1870–Dec. 19, 1928), actor, dramatist, was one of the many successful writers for the stage who have served an apprenticeship as actors. He was born in London of Irish parentage, and going to Australia, began his career as an actor in Melbourne in 1898, his first rôle being Lord Chetland in *The Squire of Dames*, a once popular play anglicized by R. C. Carton from the younger Dumas's comedy, *L'Ami des Femmes*. Returning to London in the following year, he made his début there with George Alexander at the St. James's Theatre, Apr. 26, 1899, as Nat Brewster in Edward Rose's play, *In Days of Old*. He remained an actor in the London theatres for several years and was at one time a member of Sir Johnston Forbes-Robertson's company, playing Laertes to that star's Hamlet at the Imperial Theatre in 1902. During this period he began to attract attention as a writer of plays, and having completed *The Crossways* for Mrs. Langtry, he supervised its production in London in November 1902, himself playing the part of Lord Robert Scarlett. He came to the United States as a member of her company for its American tour, which began at the Garrick Theatre in New York, Dec. 29, 1902. Not long afterward he abandoned acting and thenceforth was a prolific playwright, the total number of plays that he wrote either alone or in collaboration being more than thirty. During the last twenty years of his life he was closely associated with the American stage, and marrying Laurette (Cooney) Taylor, the widow of Charles A. Taylor, in 1912, he made both her and himself prominent and popular with *Peg o' My Heart*, a simple play, that through the acting of his wife touched the hearts of multitudes of theatregoers. It was produced in 1912 and was acted more than six hundred times consecutively in New York, and for more than five hundred performances in London. Five companies or more were touring in it simultaneously through several seasons in the United States alone, and it even found favor in translation with audiences in France, Italy, and other European countries.

Manners was a playwright with aspirations for something more than mere popularity, but he never achieved it. The success of *Peg o' My Heart* unfortunately dimmed the reputation of his other work and made him scarcely more than a one-play dramatist. "I won't write 'situations' merely for the sake of 'situations,'" he said. "They . . . interest me only as they reveal character" (*Christian Science Monitor*, June 24, 1919). He also asserted that "reality is the curse of the modern theatre. Imagination is its boon!" (*New York Times*, Jan. 13, 1918). Others of his plays were *The House Next Door* (1909), *The Great John Ganton* (1909), *The Girl in Waiting* (1910), *Happiness* (1914), and last of all, *The National Anthem* (1922). He died in retirement in New York City after an illness of several months.

[Dixie Hines and H. P. Hanaford, *Who's Who in Music and Drama*, 1914; John Parker, *Who's Who in the Theatre*, 1925; *Who's Who in America*, 1926–27; article by John Corbin in the *N. Y. Times*, Jan. 13, 1918; interview in *Christian Science Monitor*, June 24, 1919; obituary in Boston *Transcript*, Dec. 20, 1928.] E. F. E.

MANNING, DANIEL (May 16, 1831–Dec. 24, 1887), secretary of the treasury under Cleveland, was born in Albany, N. Y., the second son of John and Eleanor Manning who were natives of Albany of Dutch, Irish, and English ancestry. When Daniel was six years old his father died and at eleven the boy was compelled to leave school to help support the family. In the winter of 1841 he was appointed a page in the state Assembly and held the position for two sessions.

At the end of the legislative session of 1842 he became a route carrier for the *Albany Atlas.* He soon advanced to the position of office boy and messenger, and at fifteen he went to the composing room where he learned the printer's trade. Economic necessity and the desire to better himself led him to study stenography and French; he also tried out as a reporter and on occasion was called upon by the *Atlas* to report proceedings of the legislature. In 1856 when the *Atlas* and the *Argus* combined, Manning was assigned a reporter's desk in the city department. This enabled him to come into contact with men of prominence in Albany County. In 1863 he was chosen by the Associated Press to report the proceedings of the state Assembly, and a few years later he became legislative correspondent of the *Brooklyn Eagle.* From 1858 to 1871 he reported the proceedings of the state Senate for the *Argus.* Meanwhile (1865) he became part owner and business manager of the Argus Company and in 1873 was elected to its presidency. As a newspaper man Manning gained the reputation of being a careful and accomplished writer.

His experience as a journalist proved to be good political training. A close friend and political lieutenant of Samuel J. Tilden, he virtually succeeded him in 1877 as the leader of the Democratic party of the state of New York. For ten years, 1874–84, he was a member of the state Democratic committee and of every state Democratic convention. From 1881 to 1884 he was chairman of the state committee. Like Tilden, he disliked Tammany and fought its repeated attempts to dominate New York state politics. As a delegate to the national Democratic conventions of 1876, 1880, and 1884, he worked indefatigably for the nomination of Tilden and Cleveland. Possibly Cleveland was indebted to Manning more than to any other person for his nomination as governor of New York and for his first nomination to the presidency.

Manning was not a speechmaker nor an office seeker for himself. He was a quiet man, and his power lay in his judgment of men and affairs, and in his abilities as a harmonizer and political manager. His appointment as secretary of the treasury by Cleveland in 1885, at the request of Tilden, elicited considerable surprise and some adverse criticism. During his two years in office, however, he proved to be not only an able treasury chief but a source of strength to the administration generally. His treasury reports are notable for their insight into fiscal affairs and for their recommendations concerning currency and taxation. He agreed with Cleveland that the further government purchase and compulsory coinage of silver should be suspended, and defeated the advocates of silver who made strenuous efforts to force the government to accept a silver basis. He vigorously condemned the proposals to reduce the treasury surplus by means of additional premiums to bondholders, extravagant appropriations, or treasury accumulations. In urging reduction of the tariff and retirement of the greenbacks he emphatically indorsed Cleveland's views. While ill health was a primary reason for his resignation from Cleveland's cabinet, the fact that Cleveland resented Tilden's desire to be "the power behind the throne" and, therefore, proscribed all of Tilden's friends, undoubtedly had much to do with Manning's withdrawal. Indeed, an evidently inspired editorial in *Leslie's Weekly* of Jan. 27, 1887, boldly asserted that Manning was "squeezed out" because of his independence of thought and action. After his resignation as secretary of the treasury he accepted the presidency of the Western National Bank of New York City. He was twice married. His first wife was Mary Little, who died in 1882. Two years after her death he was married to Mary Margaretta Fryer, daughter of William Fryer of Albany.

[Manning's reports as secretary of the treasury together with the detailed obituary in the Albany *Argus* of Dec. 25, 1887, are important. See also A. J. Parker, ed., *Landmarks of Albany County* (1897); Robert McElroy, *Grover Cleveland: the Man and the Statesman* (1923); G. F. Parker, *Recollections of Grover Cleveland* (1909); John Bigelow, *Letters and Lit. Memorials of Samuel J. Tilden* (1908); *Autobiog. of Andrew D. White* (1905); D. S. Alexander, *Four Famous New Yorkers: The Political Careers of Cleveland, Platt, Hill and Roosevelt* (1923); H. T. Peck, *Twenty Years of the Republic, 1885–1905* (1906); H. C. Thomas, *The Return of the Democratic Party to Power in 1884* (1919).]

H. J. C.

MANNING, JAMES (Oct. 22, 1738–July 29, 1791), Baptist clergyman, a founder and the first president of Rhode Island College (Brown University), was born in Piscataway, Middlesex County, N. J., son of James and Grace (Fitz-Randolph) Manning, and great-grandson of Jeffrey Manning, one of the earliest settlers in Piscataway township. His father was a prosperous farmer, and James had good educational advantages. At eighteen he became a pupil in the Latin Grammar School conducted by Rev. Isaac Eaton at Hopewell, N. J. In 1758 he entered the College of New Jersey, from which he graduated in 1762, second in a class of twenty-one. On Feb. 6, 1763, he was licensed to preach by the Scotch Plains Baptist Church, and on Mar. 23 of the same year he was married to Margaret, daughter of John Stites of Elizabethtown. He was ordained Apr. 19, 1763, and proceeded to travel through the colonies with a view to informing himself regarding religious conditions.

About this time the Philadelphia Association of Baptist Churches was discussing the advisability of establishing a college to be principally under the direction of the Baptists. It finally decided that it was practicable to found such an institution in Rhode Island, and Manning was put in charge of the project. Accordingly, in July 1763, on his way to Halifax, he stopped at Newport and laid the matter before a number of influential gentlemen, who gave it their active support. Manning prepared a rough plan for the constitution of the college, and, leaving it in the hands of a committee, who, with the assistance of Ezra Stiles [*q.v.*], were to draft a charter, went on his way. After considerable delay and friction, in March 1764 the Rhode Island Assembly granted a charter, which was signed and sealed by the governor and secretary Oct. 24, 1765. In the meantime, April 1764, Manning had settled in Warren, R. I., opened a Latin School, and become the first pastor of a Baptist church, organized in November 1764. In September 1765 he was elected president of the new college. He conducted both school and college in Warren until 1770, when they were moved to Providence, where the first college building, now known as University Hall, was soon erected.

That Manning should have been chosen by the Baptists when he was but twenty-five years old to lead their movement in behalf of higher education indicates that thus early he had impressive characteristics. They seem to have been both physical and mental. As a youth, we are told, "he was remarkable for his dexterity in athletic exercises, for the symmetry of his body, and gracefulness of his person" (Guild, *post,* p. 503). In his later years he was about three hundred pounds in weight. Among his principal diversions were mowing and laying stone walls. He was invariably cheerful and genial, and was a good conversationalist. His direction of the college through the first twenty-six years of its history reveals that he had administrative ability of a high order. All that had been accomplished previously was well-nigh destroyed by the Revolution, but at his death the institution was in a thriving condition. He was a good all-round scholar, but too busy to be a thorough student. In addition to his college duties, he assumed charge of the First Baptist Church, Providence, in connection with which for years he carried a heavy load of pastoral work.

Although Ezra Stiles, speaking from the Congregational point of view, called Manning a "bigotted Baptist," among Baptists themselves he was regarded as tolerant and broad-minded. He was one of their acknowledged leaders, and with Isaac Backus [*q.v.*] and others took a firm stand against the oppression suffered by Baptists under the "Standing Order" in Connecticut and Massachusetts. He was the moving spirit in the organization of the Warren Association, 1767, for the promotion of harmony and concerted effort among the New England Baptist churches. In 1774, at a conference with members of the Continental Congress, Philadelphia, he presented a memorial citing acts of oppression in Massachusetts and pleading for both civil and religious liberty. His influence in public affairs was considerable. Some apparently thought him not over-enthusiastic in his support of the Revolution. Stiles ill-naturedly accuses him of not praying for Congress or the success of the army until General Washington once attended his church in Providence; and remarks, "He was a Baptist Tory . . . an Enemy to the Revolution here, altho' afterw*ds* he trim'*d* about . . ." (*Literary Diary, post,* II, 23, III, 425). Though with Backus and others he fell under the charge of attempting to sow seeds of discord by presenting to the Continental Congress the previously mentioned memorial in behalf of religious liberty, his patriotism can hardly be questioned. He certainly deplored the war, and wished to have no part in it himself. Writing to an English friend under date of Nov. 13, 1776, he exclaims: "Oh horrid war! How contrary to the spirit of Jesus! . . . I desire to bless God, these scenes of carnage always appeared shocking to me, and I feel no disposition to destroy or injure my fellow-man." To another English friend, however, he wrote, Aug. 3, 1784: "Our blood indeed was wantonly shed. . . . I think I can say that I never in one instance doubted the justice of our cause, but I desire to bless God that I never thirsted for the blood of those who were shedding ours" (Guild, pp. 294, 379). In 1786 he represented Rhode Island in the Congress of the Confederation, and his letters contain strong arraignments of the states for not better supporting that body. He was chairman of a committee appointed by Providence in 1789 to draft a petition to Congress praying that since Rhode Island would probably soon join the Union, her ships be exempted from foreign tonnage and her goods from foreign duties. With Benjamin Bourne he went to New York to present the same. He strongly advocated the adoption of the Constitution. Interested in public education and long a member of the Providence school committee, in the summer of 1791 he drew up a report recommending the establishment of free public schools. This was one of the last acts of his career. While offering prayer in his home, Sunday morning, July 24, he suffered a stroke of apoplexy, and died five days later in his fifty-third year.

[R. A. Guild, *Early Hist. of Brown Univ., Including the Life, Times, and Correspondence of President Manning* (1897); F. B. Dexter, *The Literary Diary of Ezra Stiles* (3 vols., 1901); Morgan Edwards, "Materials for a History of the Baptists in R. I.," *R. I. Hist. Soc. Colls.*, vol. VI (1867); Isaac Backus, *A Hist. of New Eng. with Particular Reference to the Denomination of Christians Called Baptists* (3 vols., 1777–96); *Providence Gazette*, Aug. 6, 1791; Jonathan Maxcy, *A Funeral Sermon Occasioned by the Death of the Rev. James Manning* (1791); W. G. Goddard, "Memoir of the Rev. James Manning," *American Quart. Reg.*, May 1839; W. C. Bronson, *The Hist. of Brown University* (1914).] H. E. S.

MANNING, RICHARD IRVINE (May 1, 1789–May 1, 1836), governor of South Carolina, was born in Camden district of that state. His father was Laurence Manning who emigrated from Ireland to Pennsylvania, served during the Revolution as lieutenant of the Continental legion commanded by "Light-Horse Harry" Lee, and after the war settled in South Carolina. His mother was Susannah Richardson, the daughter of Gen. Richard Richardson, a brigadier-general in the Revolution, who moved from Virginia to South Carolina and became the ancestor of six governors of the state. Richard Manning was graduated from South Carolina College in 1811, during the War of 1812 was captain of a militia company called to the defense of Charleston, and after the war became a planter in Sumter district. In 1814 he married his cousin Elizabeth Peyer Richardson, the daughter of Floride Bonneau (Peyre) and John Peter Richardson and the niece of Gov. James Burchill Richardson. They had five sons and four daughters of whom one son was John Laurence Manning, 1816–1889, who became a political leader and governor of the state, and another son was Richard Irvine Manning, the father of Richard Irvine Manning, 1859–1931 [*q.v.*]. In 1822 the Richard Manning of this sketch entered politics and became a member of the state House of Representatives. From 1824 to 1826 he was governor and when the Marquis de Lafayette made his second visit to America in 1825, it fell to him to entertain this distinguished guest during his stay in South Carolina.

When the question of Nullification divided the state into two well-defined groups, he attached himself to the Union party, which opposed the Nullification doctrines. In 1826 he was defeated as the Union candidate for Congress. In 1830 he was defeated for the governorship by James Hamilton [*q.v.*]. In the bitter struggle that ensued he was one of the leaders of the opposition to Nullification. He was one of the few Unionists elected to the state convention of 1832 and voted against the Nullification ordinance. He was one of the vice-presidents of the Union convention at Columbia in 1832, which adopted an official protest against Nullification as contrary to both state and national constitutions. When the state convention reassembled in March 1833, he was a member of the committee chosen to consider the mediation of Virginia's agent, Benjamin Watkins Leigh. After the death of James Blair in April 1834, Manning succeeded to his seat in the federal House of Representatives. In November 1834 he was reëlected for the full term. When Henry Laurens Pinckney introduced the gag resolution in 1836 he supported it by speech and by vote. He died in Philadelphia while attending Congress, and is buried in Trinity churchyard, Columbia, S. C.

[Information from his grandson, the late Richard I. Manning, Columbia, S. C.; *Journal of the Conventions of the People of S. C., . . . 1832 . . . 1833* (1833); T. D. Jervey, *Robert Y. Hayne* (1909); Yates Snowden, *Hist. of S. C.* (1920), vols. II, III; *Biog. Directory of the Am. Cong.* (1928); J. C. Hemphill, *Men of Mark in S. C.* (1907), vol. I.] J. G. V–D.

MANNING, RICHARD IRVINE (Aug. 15, 1859–Sept. 11, 1931), governor of South Carolina, was the grandson of Richard Irvine Manning [*q.v.*] and the son of Elizabeth Allen (Sinkler) and Richard Irvine Manning, a Confederate colonel who died in service. He was born at Holmesley plantation, Sumter County, S. C. He went to school in the neighborhood, then in Amherst, Va., and entered the University of Virginia, where he was a student from 1877 to 1879, but was not graduated. He married on Feb. 10, 1881, Lelia Bernard Meredith, daughter of John A. Meredith, of Richmond, Va. Farming on poor land, living in a cottage, the husband could proudly give his wife a buggy only after the passage of several years. A capable manager, he prospered, bought plantations, invested in industries, and became president of a bank in the town of Sumter. In 1892 he was elected to the legislature and was one of the small minority opposed to the Democratic faction led by Gov. B. R. Tillman. A student, watchful of legislation, not active in debate, he was a progressive in politics. In 1894 when the Australian ballot was scarcely heard of in South Carolina he offered a bill for its adoption, which was, however, defeated, and he pressed for improvements in education and reforms in taxation. After three terms he was elected state senator in 1898 and served until 1906. As an author of a bill for the complete reform and rebuilding of the "state dispensary" or liquor-traffic system, he defended his plan in the campaign for the governorship in 1906, but he was defeated.

He spent the next years in caring for his interests as planter and business man, as well as for the affairs of the Protestant Episcopal diocese of South Carolina, in which he was perhaps the most prominent layman. In 1914 he ran for governor against eight candidates and was nominated by a large majority in the second primary, in a state where nomination was equivalent to election. He was not an adept politician but was a business man of quiet manner, tenacious purpose, and real courage. His administrations were the most notable in South Carolina since the régime of Wade Hampton after the Reconstruction period. He emphasized law enforcement and the suppression of lynching. He was especially concerned for the rehabilitation of the state hospital for the insane, which was accomplished at cost of more than a million dollars without increasing the state debt. A school for feeble-minded girls and a hospital for tuberculous patients were established, a tax commission, a board of welfare, and a board of labor conciliation were created. The last grew out of textile strikes in which his attitude toward labor cost him the support of some of the cotton-mill executives who had been his friends. A strenuous campaign by the former governor, Coleman L. Blease, was waged against him in 1916, but he was renominated by a decisive majority. During the World War he threw himself into the American cause and worked to administer the resources of the state as effectively as possible. His appointments were such as to make it an honor to serve on a county draft board under him. Six of his own sons, all but the youngest, served as soldiers. He moved from Sumter to Columbia shortly after his retirement as governor and died there, survived by his widow, six sons, and a daughter.

[Personal acquaintance; information from his son, Wyndham Manning, Columbia, S. C.; Yates Snowden, *Hist. of S. C.* (1920), vols. II, III; J. C. Hemphill, *Men of Mark in S. C.* (1907), vol. I; *N. Y. Times*, Sept. 9, 12, 1931; *News and Courier* (Charleston), Sept. 12, 1931.]
W. W. B.

MANNING, ROBERT (July 18, 1784–Oct. 10, 1842), pomologist, was born at Salem, Mass., the son of Richard and Miriam (Lord) Manning. He was of English descent, his great-great-grandmother, Anstice Manning, widow of Richard Manning of Dartmouth, England, having come to Massachusetts with her children in 1679. He received his education in the common schools and as a young man opened a broker's office in Salem. When only twenty-four years of age he took charge of the family of his widowed sister, Elizabeth Manning Hawthorne, afterwards sending her son, Nathaniel Hawthorne [*q.v.*], to Bowdoin College. Later he took over the management of the extensive stage-coach lines with which his father and his uncle were connected. On Dec. 20, 1824, he was married to Rebecca Dodge Burnham.

In 1817 he began in a small way to collect choice varieties of fruits. In 1823 he branched out more widely and established a pomological garden, with the design of securing specimen trees of all the varieties of fruits which were hardy enough to withstand the climate of his section. Getting into touch with many noted fruit men of Europe, he received from them scions and trees of choice varieties. This interest in pomology involved the expenditure of much time and money, for, through the slowness of packet boats and from poor handling, much of the imported stock was ruined in transit. He also spared no pains to secure new varieties from fruit growers and nurserymen in America and even originated a few himself. Having tested all these, he established a nursery for the propagation and sale of the best of them, and, through his wide acquaintance with the fruit men of the country, his varieties were distributed far and wide. His interest and enthusiasm led him also to give away both scions and trees with a liberality that did more for the fruit interests of the country than for his own fortune. At the time of his death he possessed by far the finest collection of fruits in America and one of the best in the world, consisting of over one thousand varieties of pears alone, and nearly as many more of the other fruits combined. The practical importance which was attached to this collection by the men of his day is attested by the fact that when he died the officers of the Massachusetts Horticultural Society, of which Manning was one of the founders, fearing that the family might not be able to maintain the orchards, entered into an agreement by which the society was to contribute a certain amount of money each year for their upkeep, in return for which the family agreed to send to the society each year fruits for exhibition, and in particular to exhibit specimens of any new fruits as soon as they should begin to bear (*Transactions . . . for the Years 1843–4–5–6*, 1847).

Manning read widely and was for many years a regular contributor to various horticultural journals. While modest and unassuming, he was always delighted to give the best information he had regarding fruits to all comers. In 1838 he published the *Book of Fruits*—"Being a descriptive catalogue of the most valuable varieties of the Pear, Apple, Peach, Plum and Cherry for New England culture"; in 1844, two years after his death, a revised edition, *The New England Fruit Book,* was issued, with some additions by John M. Ives. To Manning, more than to any other man of his time, and perhaps more than to all others combined, the fruit growers were indebted for the introduction of new and choice fruits, for correcting the nomenclature of fruits —at that time in a state of great confusion—and for identifying varieties.

[W. H. Manning, *The Manning Families of New England* (1902); *Vital Records of Salem, Mass.* (1918), vol. II; Robert Manning [Jr.], *Hist. of the Mass. Horticultural Soc. 1829–1878* (1880); G. E. Woodberry, *Nathaniel Hawthorne* (1902); *New England Farmer,* Nov. 23, 1842; G. P. Lathrop, *A Study of Hawthorne* (1876); L. H. Bailey, *Cyc. of Am. Horticulture,* vol. II (1900); *Salem Register,* Oct. 13, 1842.] F. C. S.

MANNING, THOMAS COURTLAND (Sept. 14, 1825–Oct. 11, 1887), jurist, son of Joseph and Sarah (Houghton) Manning, was born in Edenton, N. C., where the Mannings, originally from Virginia, had settled. He was educated in the public schools of Edenton and at the University of North Carolina, which, although he did not graduate, conferred the honorary degree of LL.D. upon him in 1878. After leaving the university he taught school in Edenton, studied law, and on Jan. 18, 1848, married Mary Blair. About this time he was admitted to the North Carolina bar, and thereafter practised in his native town until 1855, when he removed to Louisiana, settling in Alexandria, Rapides Parish. He soon had a large and lucrative practice, and when the Civil War broke out he was the acknowledged leader of the bar in his section of the state.

From early manhood he had been a Democrat of the state-rights school, and he took an active part in the political life of Louisiana. In 1861 he was a member of the secession convention. Soon afterward he was made a lieutenant in the first Confederate military company raised in Rapides Parish, but shortly accepted the position of aide-de-camp on the staff of Gov. Thomas O. Moore [*q.v.*], which office he held until 1863, when he was appointed adjutant-general of Louisiana with the rank of brigadier-general. In 1864 he was appointed an associate justice of the state supreme court by Gov. Henry W. Allen [*q.v.*], serving in this capacity until the close of the war, when he returned to Alexandria and his law practice. In 1872 he was a delegate to the Democratic state convention, and presidential elector for the state at large. He was a delegate to the National Democratic Convention of 1876, where he supported Samuel J. Tilden for the presidential nomination. In 1877 he was appointed chief justice of the Louisiana supreme court, and held the office until 1880, when the new constitution of 1879 went into effect and ended his term by the formation of a new court. The following year he was again a presidential elector and was appointed by the Democratic governor to the seat in the United States Senate occupied by W. P. Kellogg [*q.v.*], but was not recognized by that body. In 1882 he was again appointed to the supreme bench of Louisiana, and served until 1886, when he was appointed United States minister to Mexico by President Cleveland. He held this office until his death in the Fifth Avenue Hotel, New York City, soon after his arrival to attend a meeting of the board of trustees of the Peabody Educational Fund, of which he was a member.

Manning was a man of imposing appearance and deportment, cultured, endowed with a large measure of self-esteem, self-reliant, reserved, and somewhat exclusive. He was a lawyer of extensive and varied acquirements and held a distinguished position at the bar of his state.

[Information as to certain facts from a grand-niece, Mary S. Manning of Chapel Hill, N. C.; *Alumni Hist. of the Univ. of N. C.* (2nd ed., 1924); 39 *La. Reports,* p. v; Percy Roberts, *Sketch of the Hon. Thomas Courtland Manning, LL.D., Chief-Justice of La.* (1880); Henry Rightor, *Standard Hist. of New Orleans, La.* (1900); *Green Bag,* Mar. 1891; *Daily Picayune* (New Orleans), Oct. 12, 19, Nov. 8, 1887.] M. J. W.

MANNING, VANNOY HARTROG (Dec. 15, 1861–July 13, 1932), second director of the United States Bureau of Mines, was born at Horn Lake Depot, Miss., the son of Vannoy Hartrog Manning and Mary Zilafro (Wallace). His father was a member of the national House of Representatives from 1877 to 1883. The son attended school at Holly Springs, Miss., and entered the University of Mississippi. Leaving at the end of his third year, he taught school at Holly Springs for a time and then went to Washington, D. C., toward the end of his father's second term in Congress. In 1885 he obtained a position with the United States Geological Survey as topographic aide, and for the next two years did topographic work in Massachusetts. From 1888 to 1894 he was in charge of topographic field parties in Wisconsin and North Dakota and was subsequently assistant to the supervisor of the survey of Indian Territory. In 1904 he became section chief in charge of the survey in Missouri and Arkansas, and in 1906 was placed in charge of the southern section of the eastern division. From 1907 to 1910 he was a member of the Geological Survey Business Committee. In 1908 he had charge of the Tallahatchie drainage work in Mississippi.

When, in 1910, part of the work done by the Geological Survey was transferred to the newly created Bureau of Mines, Manning was transferred to the new organization, with the title of chief clerk, to serve as its executive officer pending the appointment of a director. His title was later changed to assistant to the director, and in 1914 he was appointed assistant director. He was in effect the general manager of the Bureau's administrative work. On the death of Joseph Austin Holmes [*q.v.*], the first director of the Bureau, in 1915, Manning was appointed to succeed him and continued in office until 1920.

His vision and initiative led him to perceive that the special knowledge of the technical staff of his bureau should be utilized in preparing for the possible participation of the United States in the World War. The Secretary of the Interior, at his suggestion, in 1916 offered to aid the War Department in any capacity within his power, noting that the Bureau of Mines could aid in the study of methods and materials necessary for the manufacture of nitrogen products. Much work of this character was done by the Bureau with funds furnished by the War Department, various pilot plants were built, and eventually a $2,500-000 plant for the production of sodium cyanide, by the Bucher process, for gas warfare was constructed and turned over to the War Department in November 1918. Meanwhile the staff of the Bureau, experienced in such problems from its work in mine disasters, had begun work on gas masks. Financial support from the War Department was soon forthcoming and the work expanded into research on different types of poisonous and irritating gases and smokes, smoke screens, gas shells and gas bombs, flame throwers, trench projectors, signal lights, and gas bombs. In June 1918 the staff engaged in this work, including more than 700 chemists, was transferred to the War Department. Regulation of the use of explosives by the civilian population, promotion of the production of needed mineral substances formerly imported, and the study of airplane motor fuels were undertaken and successfully carried out by the Bureau; but the activity that has attracted most attention was the production of helium for use in lighter-than-air craft, which the Bureau initiated in 1917 and subsequently carried on with funds supplied by the Navy Department. The Bureau was one of the most important and efficient agencies in the conduct of the war, and there can be no doubt that its service in this regard was due in large measure to Manning's foresight, initiative, and administrative skill.

After the war, in 1920, the petroleum interests of the country organized the American Petroleum Institute, and he resigned his directorship of the Bureau of Mines to become director of research for the Institute. The industry never raised the necessary funds to initiate research in its own laboratories, however, and after organizing cooperative research with a number of universities and technical institutions, Manning resigned in 1924 to take up special work with the Pan-American Petroleum & Transport Company. In 1928 he became director of engineering and technical research for the Petroleum Research Corporation, which was affiliated with a large petroleum investment trust. The business depression which began at the end of 1929 seriously interfered with this activity and the following year he resigned. Ill health postponed his return to active work, and he died in 1932. In 1898 he was married at Denison, Tex., to Emily S. Stevens, of Washington, D. C. Two sons were born to them.

[*Who's Who in America*, 1930–31; U. S. Bureau of Mines, *Bull. 178* (4 parts, 1919), describing the war work of the Bureau; *Mining Cong. Jour.*, Sept. 1915; *Colliery Engineer*, Oct. 1915; *Hardware Age*, June 7, 1917; *Metallurgical and Chemical Engineering*, May 1, 1918; *Black Diamond*, May 8, 1920; *Engineering and Mining Jour.*, Feb. 21, 1920; *Science*, May 7, 1920; *Oil, Paint and Drug Reporter*, May 3, 1920; *Mining and Metallurgy*, Sept. 1932; *N. Y. Times*, July 14, 1932.]

T. T. R.

MANSELL, WILLIAM ALBERT (Mar. 30, 1864–Mar. 4, 1913), Methodist missionary, the son of Rev. Henry and Annie (Benshoff) Mansell, was born in Moradabad, India. At the age of six he could read the Bible in English, Urdu, and Hindi. At seven, he, along with his two sisters, was taken by his mother to America, where he remained for eighteen years. He made his home with his grandfather in Newark, Ohio, and there attended the public schools. He went to the "mourners' bench" at ten, and took an active interest in religion. Graduating from the Newark high school in 1880, he entered Ohio Wesleyan University in the fall of that year, and upon the completion of his college course in 1884, obtained a state teacher's certificate and was made principal for two years of the schools of Worthington, Ohio. In the fall of 1886 he entered the Boston University School of Theology and graduated therefrom three years later, being chosen one of two speakers representing his class at Commencement. During his senior year he was ordained deacon and applied for and received appointment to service in India under the Methodist Episcopal Church. After a summer's supply of the pulpit of the Methodist Church at Nahant, Mass., he sailed for India and arrived in Bombay on Nov. 19. He began work almost immediately as teacher of philosophy and English literature in Lucknow (later Reid) Christian College. For two years (1890–93) he acted as vice-principal, and was then made principal, serving until 1898. He served, also, as pastor of the local English Methodist church and as preacher on the Hindustani circuit, being ordained elder at Lucknow, Jan. 5, 1890, by Bishop Thoburn. In addition he edited *India's Young Folks.* On Mar. 17, 1894, he was married to Florence M. Perrine, daughter of Rev. W. H. Perrine, of Albion, Mich., who had come to Lucknow after her graduation from Albion College in 1888 to teach in the Isabella Thoburn College. In 1896 Mansell was one of the organizers of the Student Volunteer Movement in India.

In the following year he was appointed superintendent of the Oudh district of his Church, with headquarters in Lucknow, and in 1899 he acted as superintendent of the Sitapur district also. Early in 1900, with his wife, he left India on furlough, journeying to America by way of the Pacific and visiting Methodist conferences at Singapore, Shanghai, Kobe, and Osaka. After his return to Lucknow in March 1901, he served three years as superintendent of the Bijnor district, with headquarters in Bijnor town. During this time he prepared many "Helps" for the use of his associates, was chosen secretary of the India Epworth League, became editor of the mission vernacular periodical, *Kaukab-i-Hind* ("Star of India"), and during the last year acted as head of the Oudh district also.

From 1904 until his death, he was principal of his Church's theological seminary at Bareilly, and spent his unusual talents in the training of an Indian ministry. Having perfect control of Hindustani, he took occasion to visit widely throughout the Bareilly district in connection with ventures in religious education. For one year he acted as district superintendent. He continued to edit the *Kaukab-i-Hind,* and after 1908 was a member of the interdenominational United Council on Work among Young People. In 1909 he was superintendent of the Bijnor district again. In 1910 he was in charge of the open-air evangelism during the World's Christian Endeavor Convention in Agra. He then went to America on furlough, returning in two years to his work at Bareilly. Though in failing health for several years, he had persevered cheerfully in his chosen career, but in 1913 he died, in Bareilly, at the age of forty-nine. His associates had honored him with every important office in their gift save that of bishop—an office which would doubtless have come to him had he lived longer.

[L. A. Core, *The Life and Work of William Albert Mansell* (Madras, 1914); *Indian Witness,* Mar. 11, 25, 1913; *Missionary Review of the World,* May 1913; *Methodist,* Mar. 13, 1913; *Ann. Report of the Mission Stations of the North India Conference of the Meth. Episc. Ch.,* 1889–1907; alumni records of Ohio Wesleyan Univ. and Boston Univ. School of Theol.]

J. C. A.

MANSFIELD, EDWARD DEERING (Aug. 17, 1801–Oct. 27, 1880), author and editor, was the son of Jared [*q.v.*] and Elizabeth (Phipps) Mansfield. He was born in New Haven, Conn., and after spending his earlier boyhood, first at Marietta and later in Cincinnati, Ohio, attended a school in Connecticut and the Military Academy at West Point, where he graduated high in his class in 1819. Deciding to study law, he attended the College of New Jersey, graduating with the class of 1822, studied at the Litchfield Law School, 1823–25, and in 1825 was admitted to the bar in Connecticut. Returning to Cincinnati, he engaged in practice; but his interest lay chiefly in writing and publishing. In 1826, with Benjamin Drake [*q.v.*], he undertook a study of Cincinnati designed to stimulate immigration. To secure information for this work, each author made a house-to-house canvass of his allotted half of the city. Their booklet, *Cincinnati in 1826,* published the next year with the aid of a grant of seventy-five dollars from the city council, is a valuable study of the governmental organization and local economic and social conditions. It was republished in England and in Germany in translation, and undoubtedly greatly affected immigration to Cincinnati.

Mansfield began his editorial career with the *Cincinnati Chronicle* shortly after that paper was launched in 1826. In this enterprise he was again associated with Benjamin Drake. The *Chronicle* was merged with the *Mirror* in 1834, but later reëstablished under its old title. In 1849 it was consolidated with the *Atlas,* and ultimately with the *Cincinnati Daily Gazette.* Somewhat intermittently, Mansfield edited these papers. He was connected with the *Gazette* in one capacity or another from the time he assumed the editorship in 1857 until his death. A number of young writers who later became widely known, among them Harriet Beecher Stowe, first published their contributions in the *Gazette* and the *Atlas* under his editorship. He also edited the *Railroad Record* from 1853 to 1871. For some years, particularly during the Civil War, he was a vigorous writer for the *New York Times* over the signature, "Veteran Observer." His contributions to the *Gazette* over the initials "E. D.

M." were forcible and noteworthy. In politics, he was a strong Whig and later a Republican.

He was an industrious student and a prolific writer. His first book to appear after *Cincinnati in 1826* was *The Political Grammar,* which he published in 1834. This work, entitled *Political Manual* in later editions, was widely used as a textbook in the schools. Other volumes from his pen were: *The Utility of Mathematics* (1834); *The Legal Rights, Liabilities and Duties of Women* (1845); *The Life of General Winfield Scott* (1846); *The Mexican War* (1848); *American Education* (1850); *Memoirs of the Life and Services of Daniel Drake* (1855); and *A Popular and Authentic Life of Ulysses S. Grant* (1868). In 1879 he published his *Personal Memories, Social, Political, and Literary, with Sketches of Many Noted People 1803–1843,* a vivid picture of the times.

He was one of the early advocates of a railway connection from Cincinnati to the South, calling attention to the advantages of such a line in an article published in the *Western Monthly Magazine* in September 1836; and he was secretary of a committee under the leadership of William Henry Harrison which visited the South in the interests of the plan. He also prepared a pamphlet and map entitled *Railroad from the Banks of the Ohio River to the Tide Waters of the Carolinas and Georgia* (1835). He was for a time professor of constitutional law and history in Cincinnati College and was active in forming the College for Teachers. He held but one public office, that of commissioner of statistics for Ohio, 1858–68. He was married twice: first to Mary Wallace Peck of Litchfield, Conn., and second, Apr. 24, 1839, to Margaret Worthington, daughter of Thomas Worthington, a former governor of Ohio. There were two children of the first marriage and four of the second. Mansfield died at his country home near Morrow, Ohio.

[Mansfield's *Personal Memories* (1879); G. W. Cullum, *Biog. Reg. Officers and Grads. U. S. Mil. Acad.* (3rd ed., 1891); C. T. Greve, *Centennial Hist. of Cincinnati* (1904), vol. I; W. H. Venable, *Beginnings of Literary Culture in the Ohio Valley* (1891), ch. xiv; James Landy, *Cincinnati Past and Present* (1872); H. A. and K. B. Ford, *Hist. of Cincinnati, Ohio* (1881); Horace Mansfield, *The Descendants of Richard and Gillian Mansfield* (1885); *Cincinnati Daily Gazette,* Oct. 28, 1880.]

S. G. L.

MANSFIELD, JARED (May 23, 1759–Feb. 3, 1830), teacher, investigator in the fields of mathematics and physics, United States surveyor general, was born in New Haven, Conn., the son of Stephen Mansfield, a sea captain, and Hannah (Beach) Mansfield. He was a descendant of Richard and Gillian Mansfield who settled in New Haven in 1639. Having entered Yale with the class of 1777 he was expelled in his senior year for various "discreditable escapades" (Dexter, *post*), but later regained the esteem of the college, receiving the degree of A.M. in 1787 and being enrolled with his class. In 1825 Yale conferred the honorary degree of LL.D. upon him. In 1786 he became rector of the Hopkins Grammar School, New Haven, resigning in April 1790 because of "brighter prospects" elsewhere. These did not materialize, however, and he soon returned to his former position, in which he remained until 1795. After teaching for a few months in the Friends' Academy, Philadelphia, he was connected with an advanced school for both sexes in New Haven until 1802. On Mar. 2, 1800, he married Elizabeth, daughter of David and Mary (English) Phipps.

While in the New Haven school he wrote his *Essays, Mathematical and Physical* (1801), which is considered to be the first book of original mathematical researches by a native American. The essays deal with problems in algebra, geometry, fluxions (calculus), and with nautical astronomy, giving practical methods of finding time, latitude, and longitude from observations at sea. A chapter on gunnery deals with fundamental problems of ballistics, and in it the importance of air resistance is pointed out, not only as a retarding force (which is considered in the light of our modern molecular theory of matter), but also in its effect on the projectile. That effect, he showed, is a deviation of the projectile from its due course—what is known today as the gyroscopic phenomenon. Prior to his book, projectiles were treated without consideration of the effect of the medium through which they passed.

The *Essays* brought him into prominence as a man of science and in 1802 President Jefferson appointed him captain of engineers in the United States army. From 1802 to 1803 he was acting professor of mathematics in the Military Academy, West Point, but in the latter year he was appointed surveyor general of the United States, with the rank of lieutenant-colonel, to survey Ohio and the Northwest Territory. Until he resigned his office he lived at Marietta (1803–05) and at Cincinnati (1805–12). Mansfield, Ohio, was named for him. While serving as surveyor general, he also made observations (with surveyor's instruments) of the comet of 1807 and calculated its orbit. In 1812 he was appointed professor of natural and experimental philosophy at West Point, but because of the war he was detailed to superintend fortifications at New

London and Stonington, Conn. In 1814 he resumed his teaching at West Point and continued there until 1828, when he resigned and went to live in Cincinnati. He died while on a visit to New Haven and was buried in Grove Street Cemetery. Edward Deering Mansfield [*q.v.*] was his son.

Among his published papers are: "A Calculation of the Orbit of the Comet which Lately Appeared," "On the Figure of the Earth," and "Observations on the Duplication of the Cube and the Trisection of an Angle," all of which were printed in *Memoirs of the Connecticut Academy of Arts and Sciences* (vol. I, pt. 1, 1810); and "On Vanishing Fractions," printed in the *Transactions of the American Philosophical Society* (vol. I, n.s., 1818).

[Horace Mansfield, *The Descendants of Richard and Gillian Mansfield* (1885); E. D. Mansfield, *Personal Memories, Social, Political, and Literary* (1879); L. W. Bacon, *An Hist. Discourse at the Two Hundredth Anniversary of the Founding of the Hopkins Grammar School* (1860); F. B. Dexter, *Biog. Sketches Grads. Yale Coll.*, vol. III (1903); *The Centennial of the U. S. Mil. Acad. at West Point, N. Y., 1802–1902* (2 vols., 1904); *Columbian Register* (New Haven), Feb. 6, 1830.] A.F.K.

MANSFIELD, JOSEPH KING FENNO (Dec. 22, 1803–Sept. 18, 1862), military engineer, the son of Henry and Mary (Fenno) Mansfield, was born in New Haven, Conn. He was a lineal descendant of Richard Mansfield who came from Exeter, England, in 1639, and a nephew of Jared Mansfield [*q.v.*], professor at the United States Military Academy from 1812 to 1828, and a first cousin of Edward Deering Mansfield [*q.v.*]. Joseph Mansfield became a cadet at the Military Academy in 1817, and on graduation in 1822 was commissioned second lieutenant and assigned to the Corps of Engineers. Until the Mexican War he was engaged mainly in the construction of the coast defenses of the South Atlantic states and was specially charged with the construction of Fort Pulaski at the mouth of the Savannah River. He was promoted to first lieutenant in 1832 and captain in 1838.

During the Mexican War, he was chief engineer of the army under General Taylor and as such served with great distinction. At the beginning of operations he designed and constructed Fort Brown on the Rio Grande opposite Matamoras and took part in its defense. George Gordon Meade [*q.v.*], then a subaltern in this army, wrote in a letter that Mansfield "had gained for himself great credit for the design and execution of the work and still more for his energy and bravery in its defence" (*The Life and Letters of George Gordon Meade,* 1913, I, 76). At Monterey, he made the preliminary reconnaissance on which the plan of the battle was based and conducted one of the columns of attack. He was equally active in reconnoitering the ground and selecting the positions for the troops in the battle of Buena Vista. For gallant and distinguished services in the defense of Fort Brown he received the brevet of major, for gallant and meritorius conduct in the battles of Monterey and Buena Vista he received the brevets of lieutenant-colonel and colonel. After the war he was again engaged as a captain in the construction of coast defenses until 1853 when, upon the recommendation of Secretary of War Jefferson Davis, who had also served in Taylor's army, he received an unsolicited promotion to colonel and inspector-general of the army. Under his new commission he traveled extensively, inspecting frontier posts in Texas, New Mexico, California, and Oregon.

Shortly after the outbreak of the Civil War he was commissioned brigadier-general in the Regular Army and assigned to the command of the Department of Washington, which included the capital and surrounding territory. It was on his recommendation that the heights on the south bank of the Potomac opposite the city were promptly seized and fortified. When his department was merged into the Department of the Potomac under McClellan, he was assigned to command under General Wool at Fort Monroe and in 1862 took part in the occupation of Norfolk and Suffolk, Va., being commissioned major-general of volunteers in July. When McClellan reorganized the Army of the Potomac after the Manassas Campaign, Mansfield was recalled from Suffolk where he was in command, and assigned to the command of the XII Corps. He joined the army two days before the battle of Antietam and was mortally wounded in that battle, Sept. 17, 1862, while reconnoitering the enemy's position as his corps was coming into action. On Sept. 25, 1838, he had married Louisa Maria Mather, the daughter of Samuel and Catherine (Livingston) Mather. They had two daughters and two sons, one of whom, Samuel Mather Mansfield, became a brigadier-general in the Corps of Engineers.

[*Memorial of Gen. J. K. F. Mansfield* (1862); J. L. Dudley, *Discourse on the Death of Gen. Joseph K. F. Mansfield* (1862); J. M. Gould, *Joseph K. F. Mansfield* (1895); G. W. Cullum, *Biog. Reg. Officers and Grads. U. S. Mil. Acad.* (3rd ed., 1891), vol. I; Horace Mansfield, *The Descendants of Richard and Gillian Mansfield* (1885); *Battles and Leaders of the Civil War* (4 vols., 1887–88); *War of the Rebellion: Official Records (Army)*; *Hartford Daily Courant,* Sept. 22, 24, 1862.] G.J.F.

MANSFIELD, RICHARD (Oct. 1, 1723–Apr. 12, 1820), Episcopal clergyman, was the son of Jonathan and Sarah (Alling) Mansfield, and great-grandson of Richard Mansfield who emigrated from Exeter in Devonshire, England, to New Haven in New England in 1639, where the younger Richard was born. He prepared for college at the Hopkins Grammar School in that town, entered Yale at the age of fourteen, and graduated with the class of 1741, receiving the Berkeley premium for his high standing in classics. He continued his studies at Yale for a year after his graduation and then served as rector of the Hopkins Grammar School for a period of five years. His father was a deacon of the Congregational Church and the son was brought up in the Congregational faith, but under the influence of Dr. Samuel Johnson of Stratford he accepted Anglicanism. An Anglican church had already been established at Derby, Conn., and in the absence of a clergyman, Mansfield read the services there. On Mar. 17, 1746/7, Johnson, in behalf of the Episcopal clergy of Connecticut, wrote to the Society for the Propagation of the Gospel in Foreign Parts, asking that Mansfield be permitted to go to England for holy orders and for his appointment as missionary to Derby (*Samuel Johnson, President of King's College, His Career and Writings,* 1929, edited by Herbert and Carol Schneider, III, 235). Permission was granted and Thomas Herring, Archbishop of Canterbury, ordained him a deacon Aug. 3, 1748, and a priest Aug. 7, 1748. Appointed missionary to Derby, West Haven, Waterbury, and Northbury, he returned to America, arriving at New York Oct. 23, 1748, and took up his residence at Derby. Here he served as rector of St. James Church for seventy-two years. On Oct. 10, 1751, he married Anna, the daughter of Joseph Hull of Derby, and by her had thirteen children, nine of whom lived to maturity. In 1755 the field of his labors was limited to Derby and Oxford.

At the outbreak of the American Revolution he preached subjection to the King, and under his influence 110 of the 130 families in his charge remained loyal to the Crown. He wrote to Governor Tryon in 1775 that several thousand men from the three western counties of Connecticut would join the King's troops sent to protect the Loyalists. When the contents of this letter became known he was forced to flee to Hempstead, Long Island, but soon returned to Derby. After the conclusion of peace, Mansfield and nine other Episcopal clergymen of Connecticut met at Woodbury to deliberate upon ecclesiastical affairs and organize for the future. He was chosen coadjutor to Bishop Seabury [*q.v.*] in a convention at Wallingford Feb. 27, 1787, but declined the office. In the fall of 1792 he served on a committee to revise the articles of religion in the Book of Common Prayer. He was the first Episcopalian to receive the degree of doctor of divinity from Yale (1792). About 1800 his voice failed and he ceased to preach but continued to hold the office of rector. He presided over a convention of clergy which met at New Haven June 2, 1819, to choose the third bishop of Connecticut. He died at Derby at the age of ninety-six.

[Horace Mansfield, *The Descendants of Richard and Gillian Mansfield Who Settled in New Haven, 1639* (1885); *Vital Records of New Haven, 1649–1850* (2 vols., 1917–24); F. B. Dexter, *Biog. Sketches Grads. Yale Coll.*, vol. I (1885); *Cat. of the Officers and Grads. of Yale Univ., 1701–1924* (1924); *Documentary Hist. of the P. E. Ch. in the U. S. of America* (2 vols., 1863–64), ed. by F. L. Hawks and Wm. S. Perry; E. E. Beardsley, *The Hist. of the Episcopal Ch. in Conn.* (2 vols., 1866–68); W. B. Sprague, *Annals Am. Pulpit,* vol. V (1859); Samuel Orcutt and Ambrose Beardsley, *The Hist. of the Old Town of Derby, Conn., 1642–1880* (1880); A. F. Sherwood, *Memories of Old Derby* (1924); *The One Hundred and Fiftieth Anniversary of the Founding of St. James's Parish, Birmingham, in the Town of Derby, Conn.* (1891); Lorenzo Sabine, *Biog. Sketches of Loyalists of the Am. Revolution* (1864), vol. II; *Columbian Register* (New Haven), Apr. 15, 1820.]
I. M. C.

MANSFIELD, RICHARD (May 24, 1854–Aug. 30, 1907), actor, one of the most vivid artists in the American theatre, was born in Berlin, Germany, while his mother was on an opera tour. His father, Maurice Mansfield, was a London wine merchant with musical proficiency; his mother, Erminia Rudersdorff, daughter of an Amsterdam violinist, was a noted opera singer. His father died in 1859, and Richard passed his boyhood in many places, both in England and on the Continent. He had a variety of schooling, and singing lessons from his mother. She wished him to go to Oxford, but he lacked sufficient scholastic application. In 1872, when Richard was eighteen, Madam Rudersdorff came to Boston, to sing at the Peace Jubilee, bringing her son with her, and she remained in Boston as a singing teacher, also buying a summer residence in Berlin, Mass. Young Richard passed the next few years either in Boston or Berlin (near Fitchburg), uncertain of what he wished to do, and often quarreling with his temperamental mother. For a time he was employed by Eben D. Jordan in the latter's great store in Boston. But trade did not appeal to him. He left his mother's house, took a room on Beacon Hill, and decided to become an artist. He also joined an amateur dramatic group, "The Buskin Club," and acted Beau Farintosh in *School,* Jan. 14, 1876. In June of the same year he gave a one-man entertainment at the Y. M. C. A. Hall on Boylston Street.

Feeling that he was getting nowhere with his painting in Boston, he returned to London in 1877 and there led a precarious existence for many months. To support himself he gave entertainments of song and mimetic skits in private houses, and when he could, in music halls. His painting brought him nothing. Finally he secured an engagement in a touring company of *Pinafore* to sing Sir Joseph Porter, at fifteen dollars a week, and kept the job till he asked for a raise—when D'Oyly Carte dropped him. But in December 1879 he was reëngaged for the part in a more important company and also sang in the copyright performance of the *Pirates of Penzance.* According to Paul Wilstach (*post,* pp. 74-75) the tune of "A Modern Major General" was improvised by Mansfield at the rehearsals, and retained by Sullivan. Until the spring of 1882 he eked out a poor existence playing small parts in London and the provinces, both in plays and operettas. His mother died in Boston in February 1882, and in April his old employer, Eben D. Jordan, found him lonely and discouraged, and persuaded him to return to America.

His first professional appearance in the United States was on Sept. 27, 1882, at the Standard Theatre, New York, as Dromez in the operetta *Les Manteaux Noirs.* He next sang both Nick Vedder and Nick's son in an operatic version of *Rip Van Winkle,* and then, in Baltimore, sang the Chancellor in *Iolanthe.* But a sprained ankle forced his resignation, and he returned to New York determined to break into the spoken drama. He was engaged by A. M. Palmer for the rôle of Baron Chevrial in *A Parisian Romance,* solely because J. H. Stoddart refused to play the part, and he spent hectic hours in lonely rehearsal. With a touch of arrogance that annoyed the older actors, he announced the day before the opening, "Tomorrow night I shall be famous." And he was! Few débuts of an unknown actor have been more sensational. The driveling death of this lecherous old baron was so vivid that the audience could watch nothing else, talk about nothing else. Mansfield toured with the Palmer company across the Continent till the fall of 1883 and then bought the play and with an access of ambition launched himself as an independent star. But he soon found that one success does not make a star. Very early in 1884 he had to disband his company in Cincinnati and borrow money to get back to New York. He at once joined the Madison Square Company, playing von Dornfeld in *Alpine Roses,* and remained there till summer. In January 1885 he was engaged for Wallack's stock company but remained only a month, going back for a time to operetta. In June he dashed to London and acted Louis XI for a single performance, but nothing came of it. In September 1885 he was back in New York supporting Minnie Maddern (later Mrs. Fiske) in *In Spite of All.* Then, in January 1886 he was reluctantly persuaded back into operetta by John Stetson of Boston, and sang Koko in *The Mikado* at the Hollis Street Theatre there—a most solemnly hilarious and perfectly Gilbertian performance it was, too. But his ambition knew no rest; he was determined to be a star in legitimate drama, or nothing, and on Apr. 5, 1886, he appeared at the Boston Museum as Prince Karl, in a play of that name by Archibald C. Gunter. This drama gave him the opportunity to display the romantic side of his art, and was very successful. He took it to New York May 3, where it ran all summer, and that run was followed by a tour of the East and Middle West which lasted until Apr. 25, 1887. He was finally established in the ranks where he had always declared he belonged, and thereafter, to the end of his life, was his own master and manager, whatever the burden and cost.

On May 9, 1887, at the Boston Museum, Mansfield first acted the rôle which was always the favorite with a large element of his public, and which was certainly his most spectacular performance—the dual rôle of Dr. Jekyll and Mr. Hyde in a play made by Thomas Russell Sullivan, from Stevenson's story. There was a considerable element of trickery in his transformations from one character to the other, in view of the audience, as well as considerable physical strain. But the changes were gruesomely spectacular, and the public never tired of staring at them. In August 1888 he took the play to London (Lyceum Theatre), and later acted Prince Karl and Chevrial. In March 1889, at the Globe, London, he made his Shakespearian début as Richard III, and in the autumn brought the production to America. It was always one of his most popular rôles thereafter. His next important production was *Beau Brummell,* by Clyde Fitch, after suggestions by William Winter (Winter, *post,* I, p. 128), at the Madison Square, New York, May 19, 1890. This added a vivid character rôle to his growing repertoire. In May 1891, at the Garden Theatre, New York, he produced *Don Juan,* written by himself. It was not successful, nor was *Nero,* by Thomas Sullivan, produced the next September. In September 1892, his next important production was made—a dramatization by Joseph Hatton of *The Scarlet Letter.* In 1893 he enriched his repertoire by adding Shylock, and now toured the country with at least half a dozen plays, alternately acted.

In 1894, Sept. 17, at the Herald Square Theatre, New York, he produced *Arms and the Man,* the first play by George Bernard Shaw ever seen in America. It considerably puzzled his audiences, accustomed to romantic drama. But when, in April 1895, he opened the Harrigan Theatre, on Thirty-fifth Street, New York (rechristened the Garrick), which he had rented and renovated, he chose the Shaw play for his first bill. The task of keeping open his own theatre was severe, and in midsummer he was stricken with typhoid and narrowly escaped death. He retained the management of the house only till the next December. On Oct. 1, 1897, at Albany, he produced *The Devil's Disciple,* the second Shaw play seen in America, and acted it, as the major item in his repertory, through the country, adding a production of *The First Violin* in the spring. In October 1898, at the Garden, New York, he produced, in an English version by Howard Thayer Kingsbury, Rostand's *Cyrano de Bergerac,* then the theatrical sensation of Europe. The same night, in Philadelphia, Augustin Daly's company produced another version. But Mansfield's Cyrano held the field and became so popular that he acted nothing else for a year. For romantic gusto and tragic pathos, it was a landmark of its era.

At the Garden Theatre, Oct. 3, 1900, he produced very elaborately *Henry V,* and acted it for a year. The care and expense of the company and production, especially on tour, was a severe drain, and the following October he produced Booth Tarkington's pleasant romance, *M. Beaucaire,* with enormous popular success, played it for a year, and recouped his fortunes. The next season—October 1902—found him again engaged in large undertakings—*Julius Cæsar,* with himself as Brutus. This, in 1903, was in turn followed by a light romance, *Old Heidelberg,* in which he gave an astonishing illusion of youth, and then in 1904 (Mar. 1), by another ample tragedy—Alexis Tolstoi's *Ivan the Terrible.* After a year in repertoire, he added (April 1905) Molière's *Alceste* to his rôles, and in October of the same year *Don Carlos,* in his own version of Schiller's play. His repertoire of parts on tour the following year consisted of Jekyll and Hyde, Shylock, Arthur Dimmesdale, Gloster, Alceste, Ivan the Terrible, and Baron Chevrial. In October 1906, he began his season in Chicago with the first American production of *Peer Gynt* —a difficult and baffling work into which he put every ounce of his strength and spirit. The play was warmly received in Chicago, and in February reached New York. Mansfield was warned that he was overtaxing his strength, but continued to act. On Mar. 23, he played Peer in the afternoon, and Chevrial in the evening—and that was his last appearance on the stage. He was taken ill the next day, when starting on a tour, and the tour was canceled. In May he was able to sail for England, but gained nothing by the change, and in July returned to his summer home in New London, Conn., where he died on Aug. 30, 1907. He had, almost literally, burned up his nervous energies.

The passing of Richard Mansfield was felt to be almost the passing of an era, because he had represented more brilliantly and persistently than any actor of his day in America the romantic tradition, the "grand style" in plays and playing, and the tradition, as well, of repertoire. In but few seasons had he devoted all his time to a single play; more often he acted a different part every night; and the plays included the works of Shakespeare, Molière, Rostand, and character rôles of striking picturesqueness or vivid appeal. On the other hand, while he thus represented the theatre of a grander past, he was the first to recognize the genius of Shaw, his performances in the Shaw plays were as mordantly modern as the comedies themselves, and his last work was a devoted production of Ibsen. If he was at the end of a great romantic era in acting, he also helped to usher in a new and different era. Had he lived, it is highly probable that he would have moved forward eagerly with the age. At any rate, the mounting costs of travel and production, and the changing tastes of the public, would have compelled him to abandon his tours with large companies and scenery for half a dozen plays. As it was, he practically killed himself at fifty-three, trying to carry the burden of his ambitious programs.

As actor, Mansfield was highly individual. A wag once said, "There are good actors, bad actors, and Richard Mansfield." He had a splendid voice, under perfect command, yet his inflections of speech were eccentric in the extreme. His listeners thought they were going to be annoying but instead they were curiously thrilling. His face was one of those comparatively rare masks which can, with little artificial aid, look like anybody, and his body was under unusual control. Hence, with his natural mimetic faculty, he was able to play a wide variety of character parts and give to each a superficial verisimilitude which pleased the crowd, though he never could, or tried to, conceal his own vivid personality behind the mask. What made his art unique was a certain electric quality; it gave off sparks, it was strangely exciting. He had no old timer's rant, nor did he follow the new cult of repression. His acting was not entirely naturalistic, even in modern plays. He never forgot the theatre, and in a sense foreshadowed the revolt from naturalism of a later generation. And when the play was poetic, as in Shakespeare or *Peer Gynt,* he could strike the chords of passionate music with sure hand. There was never a dull moment in his acting, least of all when whimsical or ironic or macabre humor was called for.

The story of Mansfield's life is largely confined to his professional career, because his driving and perhaps egocentric ambition kept him at his huge task of production and management. He was not a clubable man, which partly accounted for the acrimonious comments about him frequently made by other actors. And his temper, his outbursts of "temperament," became, before his death, a legend of the American stage. Without question he knew his capacities, and did not meekly minimize them; and, at the same time, he was driven by a deep, artistic urge to realize them fully in his art, and had small place in his mind for other matters. What often seemed arrogance was actually indifference. His temper, also, was really part of the same quality in the man. Highstrung, nervous, always carrying the whole weight of a production, and plunged in agony if anything went wrong, he was a hair trigger in the theatre, and his famous outbursts were not in the least a sign of unkindliness of disposition, but of sensibilities on edge. Actually he was a generous, gracious, and kindly man. In this paradox, he strongly resembled Macready. It is amusing to record that on one occasion, at least, he got a Roland for his Oliver. When he produced *The Devil's Disciple,* he converted Essie into a young girl. Shaw protested that this meant loss of heart interest. "Heart interest be damned," wrote Mansfield. "The same to you," Shaw cabled back. The wonder is that even in those early days, Shaw did not withdraw the play.

Mansfield's stature was below the normal height, a difficulty which he triumphantly overcame by pose and fire, as well as high heels. He always wore his scant hair cropped, displaying a broad and high forehead. His eyes were brown, his jaw aggressive, his neck large, his shoulders broad, and his whole figure athletic and sturdy. When playing young men, he kept his chin up, his face alert, and his heels almost off the ground, giving him a quality of expectation and vitality difficult to suggest, but very appealing. And he ranged from the young prince in *Old Heidelberg,* with his wistful renunciation of youth and happiness, to the horrible evil of Mr. Hyde, or the haunted, half-insane Brutus, after the murder of Cæsar (one of Mansfield's finest studies in psychology), making his face, his postures, even the very aspect of his body, conform to each rôle. It used to be his frequent custom, on the last night of an engagement, to present an act from five different plays, and these exhibitions of versatility were greatly enjoyed. His tastes were quiet, artistic, and fastidious, and centered largely, outside the theatre, about his estate at New London, Conn., and the playing and composition of music. Once, in 1891, in Washington, a concert of his songs was given during his engagement there. On Sept. 15, 1892, he was married in New York to Beatrice Cameron (Susan Hegeman) who had been for some time his leading lady. This marriage was an ideally happy one, and his domestic life absorbed most of his time when he was not professionally engaged. There was one child of the union, a son, who died in training camp when a member of the American Expeditionary Force in 1918.

[Wm. Winter, *Life and Art of Richard Mansfield* (2 vols., 1910); Paul Wilstach, *Richard Mansfield, the Man and the Actor* (1908), with bibliography; Mansfield Scrap Book, Locke Collection, N. Y. Pub. Lib.; Mansfield clippings, Shaw Collection, Harvard Univ. Lib.]

W. P. E.

MANSON, OTIS FREDERICK (Oct. 10, 1822–Jan. 25, 1888), physician, was born in Richmond, Va., the son of Otis Manson and Sarah Dews (Ferrill). His father, a skilled architect, came from a Massachusetts family which had emigrated from Glamis, Scotland. The son attended the public schools of his native city and was graduated in 1840 from the medical department of Hampden-Sidney College, later called the Medical College of Virginia. Shortly after his graduation he settled in Granville County, N. C., for the practice of his profession, and subsequently married Mary Ann Spottswood Burwell, the daughter of a prominent citizen of the county. In this rural community he resided for more than twenty years, building up a large practice and extending his reputation over the state.

The neighborhood was highly malarious and Manson was continually being faced with the problems of this disease. He early recognized the protean character of malaria and its importance as a causative agent and as a complication of other disease conditions. He perceived the relationship between malarial fever and pneumonia and is credited with being the first American writer to recognize puerperal malarial fever. He was an advocate of massive doses of quinine in malarial fever and of the treatment of pneumonia with the same drug. In 1857 he presented to the state society a paper on "Malarial Pneumonia" which aroused a controversy that filled the pages of the *North Carolina Medical Journal* for the two following years. Other notable works in this field, published much later, include *Remittent Fever* (1881), *Physiological and Therapeutic Action of Sulphate of Quinine* (1882), and *Malarial Hematuria* (1886). He was engaged upon an exhaustive "History of Fevers from the Earliest Times" at the time of his death, and left the most complete collection of the literature of malaria then in existence. The independent thought expressed in his writings, together with his aggressive advocacy of the revolutionary application of some of his ideas, brought down upon him the opposition of the leaders of his profession in the state. For years he was bitterly assailed and made to suffer all the trials of the reformer, but many of his bitterest opponents lived to see the complete vindication of his views and practices and to adopt them as their own.

Meanwhile, upon the request of Governor Vance of North Carolina, he went to Richmond in July 1862 to establish a hospital for disabled soldiers from that state. He secured a tobacco warehouse, naming it the Moore hospital, after the Surgeon General of the Confederate army. Though by choice an internist, in this position he showed himself a skilful operator. He held the grade of major in the medical service of the Confederacy until the end of the war. Its termination finding him in Richmond, he settled there to resume private practice. In 1869 he was appointed professor of pathology and physiology at the Medical College of Virginia, filling the position until 1882, when he became professor emeritus. In 1871–72 he was associate editor of the *Virginia Clinical Record*. His first wife died in 1872, and in 1881 he married Helen (Gray) Watson, daughter of William Gray, Esq., of Richmond. The stress of an arduous professional life brought on a nervous breakdown, followed by an apoplectic stroke from which he died, in Richmond.

Though positive in manner, Manson was kindly and gracious. Elegant in dress, he wrote in a florid style then not uncommon, but which has since disappeared from scientific writing. He early became a member of the Medical Society of North Carolina and was a member of the first State Board of Medical Examiners in 1859. He was a member of the Medical Society of Virginia from its origin in 1870, and of the Richmond Academy of Medicine. For several years he was president of the Richmond city council.

[S. S. Satchwell, *Memorial of Prof. Otis Frederick Manson* (1888) with portrait; T. F. Wood in *N. C. Medic. Jour.*, Mar. 1888; *Trans. Medic. Soc. N. C.*, vol. XXXV (1888); *Va. Medic. Monthly*, Mar. 1888; *The State* (Richmond), Jan. 25, 1888; family information.]

J. M. P.

MANTELL, ROBERT BRUCE (Feb. 7, 1854–June 27, 1928), actor, was of Scottish ancestry and birth, the son of James and Elizabeth Bruce Mantell. He was born in the Wheatsheaf Inn, at Irvine in Ayrshire, of which his father was the landlord, and was one of a family of four sons and four daughters. At the age of five he was taken to Belfast, where his father established himself as an inn-keeper, and there after receiving a brief schooling, he made his first tentative experiments in amateur theatricals. His début in a theatre, following appearances in halls, was in 1873 at the Theatre Royal, Belfast, as De Mauprat in *Richelieu.* The law was his first intended destiny, but it was given up soon in favor of an apprenticeship in the wholesale liquor business until he was nineteen, when he made up his mind, in spite of maternal objections, to become an actor. He called himself then, and he was known to the public for some time, as Robert Hudson. In May 1874 he worked his way to America as a steward on a steamship of which his brother was purser, and landing in Boston, he sought ineffectually for an engagement as an actor in the theatres of that city. Only ten days were sufficient to discourage him, and he returned to Belfast.

His career on the stage actually began Oct. 21, 1876, when he secured the small part of the Sergeant in Dion Boucicault's *Arrah-na-Pogue* with a stock company in Rochdale, England. Later he acted in support of Charles Mathews, Alice Marriott, Ellen Wallis, and other English stars, until, in October 1878, he set sail again for the United States under engagement to join Mme. Modjeska's company, making his début in America on Nov. 18, 1878, at Albany, N. Y., as Tybalt to the star's Juliet, playing then for the first time under his own name. At the end of the season he returned to England, where he passed several years of alternate hard work and lack of engagements. Coming back to the Unitd States, he acted variously and with little encouragement for about a year. Then, on Oct. 1, 1883, he played with exceptional acclaim the part of Loris Ipanoff to Fanny Davenport's Fedora in Sardou's play of that name at the Fourteenth Street Theatre in New York, and continued in it for the entire season. He went to Scotland for the summer, and returning in the autumn he was henceforth identified with the American stage for over forty years. In the spring of 1885 he acted the title rôle in Steele MacKaye's *Dakolar* during the opening weeks of the new Lyceum Theatre in New York. A contemporary reviewer said that his characterization, "although rough at present, is a very powerful sketch," and that "the young man's handsome presence, expressive face, fine voice, and physical vigor give him great advantages" (New York *Evening Post,* Apr. 7, 1885). Other engagements followed, including a return to the part of Loris Ipanoff with Fanny Davenport, but his desire to shine as a stellar attraction was soon foremost in his mind, and it did not subside until his ambition was realized. In 1886 he found himself at the head of his own company under the astute management of Augustus Pitou, playing in a romantic drama by John Kellar entitled *Tangled Lives.* The play itself was mediocre, but he gave it a wide popularity, and soon added *The Marble Heart, The Corsican Brothers, Monbars, The Face in the Moonlight,* and other melodramas new and old to his repertory, finally reaching the height of his ambition by devoting himself during his later years almost wholly to Shakespeare, with whose plays he had had abundant experience by acting secondary characters at intervals during many years. He first acted Romeo in 1887, Othello in 1888, Hamlet in 1890, Richard III in 1901, and so on through a Shakespearean repertory that also came to include Macbeth, Iago, Brutus, King John, Shylock, and King Lear. Because of marital difficulties, which involved the payment of alimony, he was little known in the New York theatres for a decade, although he found a warm welcome in other large cities.

In his younger days Mantell was handsome, graceful, and impassioned, his appeal being made more through the superficial phases of character interpretation dependent mainly upon force of action and vigor of voice than through intellectual subtlety. In his later days he became heavy, and he lacked the ability to carry the idea of inspiration and the illusion of reality across the footlights. His Shakespearean impersonations were studious, sturdy, and somewhat slow-moving. He was essentially a melodramatic and a romantic actor, and romance departed from him with the passing of his youth and his transition from middle to old age. In his last days on the stage he was hampered by lameness. He was first married to Marie Sheldon, from whom he was divorced in 1893, second to Charlotte Behrens, third to Marie Booth Russell, and fourth to Genevieve Hamper, who survived him. All were at one time or another actresses and members of his companies, usually playing leading feminine characters in his support. He died at his home in Atlantic Highlands, N. J.

[C. J. Bulliet, *Robert Mantell's Romance* (1918); J. B. Clapp and E. F. Edgett, *Players of the Present* (1900); *Who's Who in America,* 1922–23; John Parker, *Who's Who in the Theatre,* 1925; Francis Wilson, obituary in *The Players Year Book,* 1925–28; interview in *Christian Science Monitor,* Dec. 13, 1921; obituary in Boston *Transcript,* June 27, 1928; Walter Browne and E. De Roy Koch, *Who's Who on the Stage,* 1908.]

E. F. E.

MAPES, CHARLES VICTOR (July 4, 1836–Jan. 23, 1916), agricultural chemist, manufacturer, was the son of James Jay Mapes and the brother of Mary Mapes Dodge [*qq.v.*]. His mother was Sophia, *née* Furman. Born in New York City, where he spent his early boyhood, he moved with his family to a farm near Newark, N. J., in 1847. Possessing a versatile and brilliant mind with his family's characteristic taste for music, painting, and letters, he had also his father's bent toward practical science. He fitted up a laboratory in his own room and there laid the foundations for his future work. At twenty-one he was graduated from Harvard College with the class of 1857. He had intended to study medicine, but the state of his health and other circumstances caused him to abandon the plan and in 1858 he entered the counting room of a firm of wholesale grocers in New York. The following year, in partnership with one of his employers, B. M. Whitlock, who provided most of the capital, he established a factory near Newark and began to manufacture and sell agricultural implements and fertilizers. He also took over the publication of his father's paper, *The Working Farmer,* of which he had been assistant editor since January 1858.

Mapes's chief contribution to scientific agriculture was his pioneer work in developing fertilizers adapted to the peculiar needs of different crops and different soils. In 1874 he prepared a fertilizer especially for potatoes, the first special-crop manure produced in the United States. In 1877 he became vice-president and general manager of the Mapes Formula and Peruvian Guano Company, organized that year with offices in New York and factory at Newark. Becoming president later, he served in that capacity until his death. He was the first president of the New York Chemical and Fertilizer Exchange. He contributed "Some Rambling Notes on Agriculture and Manures" to the *Sixth Annual Report of the New Jersey State Board of Agriculture, 1878* (1879) and "The Effects of Fertilizers on Different Soils" to the *Seventh, . . . 1879–80* (1880), and wrote numerous articles for agricultural journals. For a while he was associated in soil tests with W. O. Atwater [*q.v.*], of the federal Department of Agriculture. He was a member of the American Association for the Advancement of Science, and of the Municipal Art Society. On June 25, 1863, he married Martha Meeker Halsted, and they had five sons.

[*Who's Who in America,* 1914–15; *Report of the Class of 1857 in Harvard College,* 1866, 1882, 1910; *Charles V. Mapes' Illus. Cat. (for 1861) of Plows, and Other Agricultural Implements and Machines* (1861); *N. Y. Times,* Jan. 24, 1916.] L. G.

MAPES, JAMES JAY (May 29, 1806–Jan. 10, 1866), agriculturist, was born in Maspeth, L. I., the son of Jonas and Elizabeth (Tylee) Mapes. His father, descended from Thomas Mapes who came from Norfolk, England, to Southhold, L. I., in 1649, served as major-general of the New York militia in the War of 1812 and for some years was senior partner in a New York firm of importers and merchant tailors. James was sent for a time to a classical school conducted by Timothy Clowes at Hempstead, L. I., but was in the main self-educated. A boy of precocious mind with a turn for the practical sciences, he began his career at the age of eight, when, after hearing a lecture on the subject, he produced illuminating gas with a clay pipe for a retort. In his teens he entered business as a clerk, but upon reaching his majority launched out for himself as a merchant. In this year (1827) he married Sophia Furman, of a Long Island family. About 1832 he invented a process of refining sugar. Acquiring a reputation as an analytical chemist, he abandoned his mercantile pursuits to open an office as consultant and was frequently called upon for expert testimony in patent cases. He made analyses of beer and wines for the New York Senate and temperance societies, and was the author of improvements in distilling, dyeing, and steel manufacture. An amateur miniature painter, he experimented with pigments, and between 1835 and 1838, as professor of chemistry and natural philosophy of colors in the National Academy of Design, New York, gave a course of lectures on the chemistry of colors which displayed both scholarship and a quiet, humorous humanitarianism. From 1840 to 1842 he edited the *American Repertory of Arts, Sciences, and Manufactures* in four volumes, and from January 1842 to June 1843 he was associate editor of the *Journal of the Franklin Institute,* Philadelphia. In January 1845 he became president of the Mechanics' Institute of the City of New York, delivering an *Inaugural Address,* published that year, in which he set forth the delights and advantages of a liberal education. He was also a member of the New York Lyceum of Natural History and in 1847, vice-president of the American Institute of the City of New York. In the latter connection he had a share in founding conversational schools and night schools that were the forerunners of such ventures as Cooper Institute. He was one of the organizers and second president of the Franklin Institute of Newark, N. J.

In 1847 he purchased a worn-out farm near Newark which he converted into productive acres by subsoil drainage, rotation of crops, and judicious fertilization, and there he demonstrated by precept and example the practical application of science to agriculture. His neighbors were invited to observe and benefit by the experiments conducted. Seeds were grown under controlled conditions to produce more hardy and profitable crops, and these were sold and given away with excellent advice for good measure. In February 1849 he founded, and edited until 1863, a journal called *The Working Farmer,* in which he published the results of his experimental farming, making it a point to explain the scientific principles underlying his practice. Through its columns he was an early advocate of a federal Department of Agriculture with a cabinet officer at its head. He took pupils in scientific agriculture on his farm, and advertised his services as consulting agricultural chemist. He invented a subsoil plow, and developed a formula for nitrogenized superphosphate which was probably the first complete plant food among artificial fertilizers used in the United States. This, after considerable litigation, he patented Nov. 22, 1859, and it was subsequently manufactured and sold by his son, Charles V. Mapes [*q.v.*]. Mapes's vigorous personality and winning conversational ability enhanced his influence among all classes and led many to adopt the measures which ahead of his time he advocated. His friend Horace Greeley, writing an editorial on his death, said of him, "American agriculture owes as much to him as to any man who lives or has ever lived" (*New York Daily Tribune,* Jan. 11, 1866). Mapes was for years an officer in the New York militia, and was honored by the presentation of a sword from his company. He died in New York City, at the age of fifty-nine, leaving his widow, three daughters, one of whom was Mary Mapes Dodge [*q.v.*], and his son Charles, who was also an agricultural chemist.

[C. R. Woodward, *The Development of Agriculture in N. J., 1640–1880* (1927); W. H. Shaw, *Hist. of Essex and Hudson Counties, N. J.* (1884), vol. I; *Newark News,* June 5, 1904; *The Family Record,* Jan., Mar., Sept., Oct. 1897; *Report of the Commissioner of Patents for the Year 1859* (1860); T. S. Cummings, *Hist. Annals Nat. Acad. of Design* (1865); N. Y. Directories; *Ann. Report Am. Inst. of the City of N. Y., 1865–66* (1866); *N. Y. Daily Tribune,* Jan. 11, 1866; *N. Y. Times,* Jan. 12, 1866.] L. G.

MAPPA, ADAM GERARD (Nov. 25, 1754–Apr. 15, 1828), soldier, typefounder, and land agent, was born of Dutch parents at Delft, Holland. When he was about twenty he was serving as an officer in the army, moving from post to post in the Netherlands and enjoying the rather stiff and formal society of the middle-class Dutch of that day. Then he fell in love with Anna Adriana Passpoort of Delft, whom, after some delay in obtaining parental consent, he married in 1780. His new responsibilities made army life irksome, and he therefore resigned his commission and became a typefounder, thanks to his father's purchase on his behalf of an established business in Rotterdam which he shortly moved to Delft. Since the management of this enterprise was not onerous, he had ample time to devote to politics. Liberal in political as in religious opinions, he took an active part in the Patriot movement which in that period of ferment aimed to recast the cumbersome and ultra-conservative political institutions of the Netherlands. He had neither the social position, the intellectual gifts, nor the force of character to attain leadership in the movement. Thanks to his military training, however, he became colonel of one of the Patriots' volunteer militia regiments and took part in that revolution which evaporated so ingloriously in the summer of 1787 at the appearance of Prussian troops sent to restore the *stadhouder* to his ancient position.

Exiled with other Patriots, Mappa took refuge in France. He passed two dreary years near St. Omer; then, convinced that no military assistance could be expected from France, decided to begin life anew in America, the country of Patriot inspiration and the home now of several fellow exiles. With his wife and three children he reached New York on Dec. 1, 1789, and there set up the first type-foundry the city had known. His business did not prosper, however. For lack of type-casters he was forced himself to do the manual labor, and apparently lost orders because he was unable to fill them (Thomas Greenleaf's preface to his *Laws of the State of New York*, 2 vols., 1792). Hence he accepted with alacrity an agency with the Holland Land Company. By the spring of 1794 he was installed as assistant land agent at Olden Barneveld (now Trenton) in Oneida County, N. Y.

Life in the backwoods was not easy, but the early years at Barneveld were perhaps the happiest of Mappa's life. There were novelty and interest in the new work, relative prosperity with a good salary and a large farm which his employers had helped him to stock and develop, a prospect of future comfort—especially after his appointment in 1797 as agent in full charge of the settlement—above all, happiness in his family life and in the pleasant society of men of his own stamp. For there were soon nearly a score of Dutch in the little village, some his own relatives, some fellow exiles, among them the learned and kindly Francis Adrian Van der Kemp [*q.v.*], scholar and former clergyman of Leyden. To Mappa the New World at first offered ample compensations for the disappointments of the Old. Reverses were in store, however, which clouded his later years. He lacked the aggressive and energetic character necessary to the successful land agent. Sales were difficult and collections from not over-prosperous settlers still more so. His situation became increasingly embarrassing after 1818, when with a partner he bought the interests of his employers on credit. He fell behind in the payment of installments due on his contract; already his affairs were complicated by the failure of a textile mill which he had helped to finance and by the assumption of the debts of one of his sons. Gentle and kindly as he was, Mappa had little gaiety in his character; he became despondent under the weight of his burdens and died in 1828, feeling that his life had been a failure. He had, however, played a not unimportant part in settling his section of New York State.

[Helen L. Fairchild, *Francis Adrian Van der Kemp* (1903); Nina M. and Francis Tiffany, *Harm Jan Huidekoper* (1904); P. D. Evans, *The Holland Land Company* (1924), being Buffalo Hist. Soc. Pubs., vol. XXVIII; L. C. Wroth, *The Colonial Printer* (1931); *Ars Typographica*, July 1925; dates of birth and death from tombstone, Barneveld, N. Y.; Mappa's correspondence as land agent in the private archives of Van Eeghen & Company, Amsterdam.] P. D. E.

MARBLE, ALBERT PRESCOTT (May 21, 1836–Mar. 25, 1906), educator, author, was the son of John and Emeline Prescott Marble, descendants of old New England stock. He was born at Vassalboro, Me., where he spent most of his early life on the ancestral farm and developed a robust physique. By his own industry he accumulated enough money to send himself to academies at Yarmouth and Waterville and to enter, when past his twenty-first birthday, old Waterville College, now Colby. Here his abilities and maturity brought him distinction both from his classmates and from the faculty, and he graduated in 1861 with Phi Beta Kappa honors. In the same year he was married to Louise Wells Marston. The following year, 1862, Marble took his family to Beaver Dam, Wis., to accept the professorship of mathematics in Wayland University. While there he served as recruiting officer for the Northern army. His career as an educator had commenced even before he completed his undergraduate training; for he had taught in elementary and secondary schools and had been principal of a public school at Eastport, Me., and of a private school at Stockbridge, Mass.

From Wisconsin he returned to Maine for a short while and then (1866) accepted the principalship of Worcester Academy. In two years he raised the institution, then in a state of decline, to a position of success and eminence. The achievement of this feat brought him the superintendency of the public schools in Worcester, Mass., in 1868. Marble did much by personal example to make the city school superintendency a post of professional leadership rather than a pawn of political chieftains. His attention to the construction, sanitation, and equipment of school buildings not only made Worcester notable but through a secondary momentum gave Massachusetts a position of leadership in the nation. In the period when the public high school was wresting leadership from the academies in secondary education he gave it his special attention. He was never swept off his feet by the latest novelties in education, but he saw a place for the "English" high school in contrast to the classical and welcomed other progressive measures.

When the administration of New York City's public schools was reorganized in 1896 into a board of superintendents, Marble was brought from Omaha, Nebr., where he had been for the two years previous, and was put in charge of the city's first three high schools. When the charter of Greater New York was set in operation, he was retained in the same capacity on the new board of superintendents and held the position till his failing health demanded that he be relieved. He found time to take active part in professional associations, being three times president of the Massachusetts State Teachers Association and secretary and later president of the National Education Association. A prize speaker in college, he continued an engaging and fluent speaker in later life. He was also equally active and effective with his pen. His *Sanitary Conditions for School Houses* (1891) was published as a Circular of Information by the United States Bureau of Education. His interest in private education he continued as one of the board of visitors at Wellesley College.

[Clarence E. Meleney, memorial sketch in *Nat. Educ. Asso. Fiftieth Anniversary Vol., 1851–1906* (1907); *Proceedings* of the Nat. Educ. Asso. for the year 1906; Paul Monroe, *A Cyc. of Educ.*, vol. IV (1913); *Bulletin* of the High School Teachers Asso. (N. Y. City), Feb. 1932; *N. Y. Tribune*, Mar. 26, 1906; information as to certain facts from Marble's daughter, Katherine Marble Hodgkins.]

J. S. B.

MARBLE, DANFORTH (Apr. 27, 1810–May 13, 1849), actor of Yankee rôles, was born in East Windsor, Conn., the son of William and Mary Marble. At an early age and with only a very slight education he went to Hartford, where he remained for a number of years, first as errand boy in a dry-goods store and later as apprentice to a silversmith. His interest in the stage, which had been aroused by a company of actors visiting Hartford, prompted him to go to New York City. Thanks to the help of a friend, who was a silversmith, Marble was enabled to secure employment in his trade, and in the evenings gain admission behind stage at the Chatham Theatre. Before long under an assumed name he was playing minor rôles at the Chatham, and in addition became a member of a local Thespian Society of amateurs. Finally he abandoned his trade of silversmith, and on Apr. 11, 1831, made his first appearance under his own name—for which privilege he paid the sum of twenty dollars. In the following year while temporarily stranded in Newark, N. J., he first displayed his skill in Yankee dialect. In the hotel of the landlord for whom Marble was working there was a woman from Maine with an extreme Yankee accent, which the young actor took delight in mimicking. His skill attracted such attention that he was compared by his friends to George Handel Hill [*q.v.*].

During the course of the next four years, while he was on barnstorming tours in Virginia and in the smaller towns of upper New York state, he became increasingly proficient in his Yankee stories. But his reputation was not firmly established until in 1836 Dean and McKinney, enterprising Buffalo managers, presented him in *Sam Patch*, a Yankee play written especially for him by E. H. Thompson. The tremendous popularity of the rôle caused the managers to repeat it in Cleveland and in their newly opened theatre in Columbus, Ohio. During the remainder of his career Marble's most popular character was Sam Patch, and the scene in which the hero jumps from a height of forty feet into the swirling waters of Niagara, although trying to the actor, provided unfailing delight to audiences from Boston to New Orleans, from Savannah to St. Louis. In return for his performances in the Mississippi Valley theatrical centers alone Marble, over a period of ten years, received from the managers forty thousand dollars. "He was hailed with delight and enthusiasm whenever he appeared on the Mississippi," writes his biographer. "He was known to nearly every captain, clerk, and engineer, senator, and landlord from Pittsburg to New Orleans" (Kelly, *post*, p.

145). He was equally popular in the eastern theatres, especially at the Bowery, New York City. In September 1844 he was enthusiastically received at the Strand Theatre in London and afterward gave performances in Glasgow and Dublin. Marble's long list of Yankee rôles included, besides Sam Patch, those in *The Wool-Dealer, Jonathan in England, The People's Candidate, The People's Lawyer, Game Cock of the Wilderness, Down Easter, Home in the West, Next Steamer, Bushwhacker,* and in *Family Ties,* the prize-winning play in a competition sponsored by him. In general his types of characters were akin to those of the other Yankee comedians, but according to the testimony of his biographer he possessed complete individuality of dialect and accent. Marble died in Louisville, Ky., from an attack of cholera. His wife was Anne Warren, daughter of the distinguished Philadelphia actor and manager, William Warren.

[J. F. Kelly, *Dan. Marble* (1851); S. F. Smith *Theatrical Management in the South and West* (1868), pp. 220–21; N. M. Ludlow, *Dramatic Life as I Found It* (1880); J. N. Ireland, *Records of the N. Y. Stage* (2 vols., 1866–67); H. R. Stiles, *The Hist. and Geneals. of Ancient Windsor, Conn.*, vol. II (1892); O. S. Coad and Edwin Mims, Jr., *The Am. Stage* (1929).]

E. M., Jr.

MARBLE, MANTON MALONE (Nov. 15, 1835–July 24, 1917), newspaper editor and publisher, was born in Worcester, Mass., the son of Joel and Nancy Chapin (Coes) Marble. His early education was supervised by his father, and he was graduated from the Albany (N. Y.) Academy in 1853. After two years at the University of Rochester (B.A., 1855) he began newspaper work as a member of the staff of the *Boston Journal.* A year later (1856) he became an editor of the *Boston Traveler* and in 1858–60 was on the staff of the New York *Evening Post.* In 1860 he was made night editor of the New York *World* and in 1862 became editor and owner of that paper. His control of the *World* continued throughout the last two years of the Civil War and the period of reconstruction of the South. During the war he opposed many of the policies of the federal government, although he held that no course but war was open after the firing on Fort Sumter. He was against great extension of the federal power, a federal income tax, the issuing of greenbacks, negro suffrage, and the impeachment of President Johnson.

Early in 1864 the *World* was one of a few New York newspapers which were made the victims of a fraud in the publication of a forged call from President Lincoln for the addition of 400,000 men to the army by draft and enlistment, and appointing a day of national fasting and prayer. The President ordered the arrest of Marble and a military guard was put in charge of the *World* office. Three days later Marble succeeded in resuming publication of the paper and addressed an open letter to Lincoln declaring that the *World* had been imposed upon by methods which it had been impossible to detect. He protested against the President's action, declaring that "for the purpose of gratifying an ignoble partisan resentment you have struck down the rights of the press" (*World,* May 23, 1864, p. 6). The letter, which was long and couched in vigorous language, was reprinted (1867) in pamphlet form by a group of men who sympathized with Marble's stand. He supported the Geneva arbitration treaty and the *Alabama* awards, expressing the view that they constituted a beginning of a period of peaceful policies. In the attacks on the "Tweed ring" in New York he was active. He was credited with having written the New York state platform of the Democratic party in 1874 and the national platform of the party on which Samuel J. Tilden was nominated for president in 1876, as well as much of the national platform of 1884.

In 1876 Marble sold the *World* to a group of men headed by Thomas A. Scott, president of the Pennsylvania Railroad. He was sent abroad by President Cleveland in 1885 to sound European governments on bimetalism, and conferred with Gladstone, Bismarck, Freycinet, and other public men. After extensive investigation he reported to the President that the resumption of bimetallic coinage would not be carried out by any European government without the cooperation of Great Britain, which he saw no prospect of obtaining, since neither the British Conservative nor Liberal leaders were prepared for it. He advised Cleveland against further purchases of silver by the United States Treasury Department. The last years of his life were devoted to literary endeavors and leisure, and he spent much time in England, where he died. He was the author of a pamphlet entitled *A Secret Chapter of Political History; the Electoral Commission* (1878) and of a memoir of the Rev. Alexander G. Mercer, published in the latter's *Bible Characters* (1885). His name also appears as editor on the title page of *Memories of Familiar Books* (1876) by William B. Reed.

[Don C. Seitz, *Jos. Pulitzer: His Life and Letters* (1924); Frederic Hudson, *Journalism in the U. S. from 1690 to 1872* (1873); J. M. Lee, *Hist. of Am. Journalism* (1923); John L. Heaton, *The Story of a Page* (1913); Robt. McElroy, *Grover Cleveland: The Man and the Statesman* (1923), vol. I; *Who's Who in America,* 1916–17; *Worcester Births, Marriages, and Deaths* (1894), ed. by F. P. Rice; obituaries in the *World* and other N. Y. newspapers.]

A. S. W.

MARCH, ALDEN (Sept. 20, 1795–June 17, 1869), surgeon and anatomist, was born in Sutton, Worcester County, Mass., the son of Jacob and Eleanor (Moore) March, of old New England ancestry. His father, a poor farmer with a large family, had a hard struggle with the soil, and the son received little schooling. Upon the father's death in 1814 he took charge of the farm and family for a while. In 1817 he was in Hoosick, N. Y., teaching in a writing school and working in a stone and slate quarry. One year later he was influenced by an elder brother, David, then an army surgeon, to take up medicine, and during 1818–19 attended lectures on anatomy and surgery at Boston, at the same time making up for defects in his early education. In 1820 he graduated from the Medical Department of Brown University (later abolished). Before he was established, he performed an operation for harelip. He settled in Albany in 1820 as a general practitioner and at once opened a private school of anatomy with fourteen pupils. He taught by lectures and dissections, obtaining his first cadaver by freighting it overland from Boston. He also at once began a private collection of anatomical specimens. So much enterprise and originality on the part of a man of twenty-five antagonized the local representatives of his profession, and despite his efforts both practice and school failed to prosper. Sinking further and further into debt, he thought seriously of abandoning his practice in Albany and trying to find a more congenial location, but his landlord, one of his creditors, persuaded him to remain, and by 1824 his circumstances had changed for the better. In that year he married Joanna P. Armsby, and in the following year was made professor of anatomy and physiology in the Vermont Academy of Medicine at Castleton, Vt., with which he was connected until 1838, meanwhile continuing his practice and his school of anatomy. In 1830 he published *A Lecture on the Expedience of Establishing a Medical College and Hospital in the City of Albany,* thus incurring once more the hostility of the profession and notably that of the local Fairfield Medical College and the other medical schools of New York State. He went ahead with his project, however; the new institution was opened, and he served it as professor of anatomy and operative surgery. When the buildings were burned in 1834, however, he resumed his private venture, under the style of Practical School of Anatomy and Surgery. In 1839 the Albany Medical College was formally opened, and March, having resigned his chair at Castleton, became professor of surgery. His free surgical clinics on Saturdays, at which the students were enabled to watch all kinds of operations on a great variety of clinical material, made the College famous. The Fairfield Medical School soon agreed to merge with the new institution and eventually the Albany City Hospital was established. March was made professor of surgery in the consolidated college and retained the chair until his death. He had a farm near the city, and his only recreation was to visit it as often as possible and perform hard farm labor. His great surgical hobby was hip-joint disease. In 1853 he published a pamphlet entitled *Coxalgia or Hip Disease* and in the same year another on an ingenious forceps devised by him for harelip operation. He wrote a number of other papers, published chiefly in the *Transactions of the Medical Society of the State of New York.* In 1863 he was president of the American Medical Association. During the last year of his life he attended the meeting of the Association at New Orleans in apparent health, but his death revealed that for years he had suffered from prostatic obstruction. A controversy (see *New York Medical Journal,* October 1869, January, March 1870) was started after his death as to the correctness of the diagnosis and treatment.

[W. C. Wey, *The Late Alden March* (1869); *Trans. Medic. Soc. of the State of N. Y.*, 1870; *Trans. Medic. Soc. of the County of Albany*, 1870; J. L. Babcock, *Life and Character of Alden March, M.D.* (1871); *Tribute to the Memory of Alden March M.D.* (1870); *Cat. . . . of Castleton Medic. Coll. since 1818* (1854); *Albany Jour.*, June 17, 1869.]
E. P.

MARCH, FRANCIS ANDREW (Oct. 25, 1825–Sept. 9, 1911), philologist, was sixth in descent from Hugh March of Newbury, Mass., who emigrated from England in 1638, and his wife Judith. Their great-grandson Daniel settled by the Blackstone River in Sutton (now Millbury), Worcester County, Mass. Here was born Francis Andrew, the eldest child of Daniel's grandson Andrew Patch March (1798–1874) and Nancy (Parker) March (d. 1830). In 1828 Andrew March removed with his family to Worcester, Mass., and it was in this city that his son grew up. A precocious child, he was well taught in the excellent public schools of Worcester, and entered Amherst College in 1841. His four years at Amherst were among the most pregnant of his life. A brilliant student, he excelled likewise in public speaking and in athletics, and still found time to read philosophy and to ponder the history of his mother tongue. The latter interest, awakened by the lectures of Noah Webster [*q.v.*] and the instruction of Professor William C. Fowler, Webster's son-in-law, was destined to prove a decisive factor in his career.

March was graduated from Amherst in 1845, with first honors; in 1848 he was awarded the degree of M.A. by the same institution. From 1845 to 1849 he served as teacher in New Hampshire and Massachusetts, for two years as tutor at Amherst. During this period he made up his mind to become a lawyer, and devoted his spare time to legal studies, which he pursued under the direction of a Worcester attorney, Francis H. Dewey. In 1849 he became a student in the office of the legal firm of Barney & Butler in New York. The following year he was admitted to the New York bar, and, in partnership with Gordon L. Ford, opened a law office of his own. He had hardly been practising for two years when an ailment of the lungs developed which forced him to leave New York and seek health in a milder climate. In 1853 he secured a post as teacher in a private school of Fredericksburg, Va., and a teacher he remained for the rest of his days. In 1855 he was called to Lafayette College, at Easton, Pa., as tutor. The next year he was made adjunct professor and in 1857 he was appointed professor of the English language and comparative philology. This chair, the first of the kind to be established in any institution of learning in America or Europe, he held thenceforward until his retirement from active service forty-nine years later. On Aug. 12, 1860, he was married to Margaret Mildred Stone Conway (Jan. 25, 1837–Feb. 11, 1911), daughter of Walter P. Conway, of Falmouth, Stafford County, Va. The eldest of their nine children was Francis Andrew March, 1863–1928 [*q.v.*].

March's activities in Lafayette College were by no means confined to the teaching of English. During his earlier years at this institution he was called upon to conduct classes as well in French and German, Latin and Greek, the law, political economy, political science, philosophy, and even botany, and he continued to give courses in some of these subjects almost to the end of his career. His teaching program was so full, indeed, that he would have found time for nothing else had he not been gifted with an almost limitless supply of mental energy and the ability to toil interminably, and this in spite of the long precarious state of his health. His method as a teacher was exegetical, and he seems to have been the first to apply exegesis in all its scientific rigor to the classroom study of English literary monuments. In his hands the success of the method was nothing short of phenomenal. Through it he raised collegiate instruction in English to the dignity of a mental discipline, and gave to it the place which it has since occupied alongside the study of the classics. His influence on the teaching of English spread through his pupils, notably James W. Bright [*q.v.*] of the Johns Hopkins, from Lafayette to many another American seat of learning, and his method was adopted to admirable effect by many (notably George L. Kittredge of Harvard) who had not learned it directly from him. Since March's day the less rigorous method of the formal lecture has gained ground, largely because of its relative cheapness.

March's chief title to fame, however, rests on his researches in the field of English historical grammar. In agreement with the tastes and tendencies of his time, he specialized in the study of early medieval English, then called Anglo-Saxon, and published in 1870 an epoch-making work on the subject, the fruit of nearly ten years of exhaustive research, done under difficulties which would have proved insuperable to a lesser man. The title, *A Comparative Grammar of the Anglo-Saxon Language, in which its forms are illustrated by those of the Sanskrit, Greek, Latin, Gothic, Old Saxon, Old Friesic, Old Norse, and Old High German,* makes plain the nature of the work and indicates the importance of his achievement, which was no less than to show in detail the relationship of the English language to the other languages of the Indo-European group. March's *Comparative Grammar* won instant and general recognition, in America and Europe alike, as a piece of research of the first order. He had laid the foundation on which all future historical grammarians in the field of English were destined to build, and his fame will ever rest secure as in a very real sense the founder of a science. Besides his masterpiece he published *Introduction to Anglo-Saxon: An Anglo-Saxon Reader* (1870), for the classroom instruction of beginners, and numerous articles, addresses, and reviews by his hand appeared in encyclopedias, transactions of learned societies, and journals professional and popular.

In addition to his medieval studies, March did valuable work in English lexicography. He served for some years as director of the American workers for *The Oxford English Dictionary,* and was a guiding spirit in the preparation of the *Standard Dictionary* (2 vols., 1893–95), of which he was consulting editor. He was active in the movement for the reform of English orthography, and published an admirable pamphlet on the subject, *The Spelling Reform* (1881), which went through several editions. His methods of research and instruction alike are revealed with a luminous clarity in his earliest book, the *Method of Philological Study of the English Language* (1865), a work still of more than historical interest. He also found time to edit four volumes of Latin and Greek Christian classics: *Latin Hymns* (1874), *Eusebius* (1874), *The Select Work of Tertullian* (1875), and *Athenagoras* (1876). In sum, his labors were prodigious, varied, and of a uniformly high quality. His services to scholarship were recognized by numerous honorary degrees; by election to the presidency of the American Philological Association (1873–74 and 1895–96), the Spelling Reform Association (1876–1905), and the Modern Language Association of America (1891–93); and by a variety of other distinctions. He received several calls to chairs in other institutions of learning, but consistently refused to leave Lafayette College, loyalty to which was central in his professional career.

[*Addresses . . . in Honor of Prof. Francis A. March, . . . at Lafayette College, Oct. 24, 1895* (1895), containing list of writings to that time (little of importance was written by him thereafter); R. N. Hart, *Francis Andrew March, A Sketch* (Easton, Pa., 1907); D. B. Skillman, *The Biography of a College* (2 vols., 1932); J. W. Bright, in *Pubs. of the Modern Language Asso. of America,* March 1914; *Obit. Record of Grads. of Amherst Coll., for the Academic Year Ending June 26, 1912* (1912); *Who's Who in America,* 1910–11; family letters.]
K. M.

MARCH, FRANCIS ANDREW (Mar. 2, 1863–Feb. 28, 1928), lexicographer, was the eldest son of Francis Andrew March [*q.v.*] and Margaret Mildred Stone (Conway) March. He was born and brought up in Easton, Pa., and lived there all his days. His education was gained under the best possible auspices, since he was trained by his father, one of the most notable Anglicists of the day and professor of English in Lafayette College. Young March was graduated from Lafayette with the B.A. degree in 1881; later he received the degrees of M.A. and Ph.D. (1889) from the same institution. He began his professional career in 1882, when he was appointed tutor in his Alma Mater. In 1884 he was promoted to an adjunct professorship of modern languages, and in 1891 he was made professor of English literature, a chair which he exchanged in 1905 for that of professor of the English language. This professorship he held until his death. He was married on Sept. 4, 1889, to Alice Youngman, daughter of Robert B. Youngman, professor of Greek in Lafayette College. They had three children.

The younger like the elder March was first of all a faithful servant of Lafayette College. His loyalty expressed itself, not only in a lifetime of service as a teacher, but also in a lifetime of devotion to the athletic activities of the institution. Himself an outstanding athlete in his student days, March became in 1890 the member of the teaching staff entrusted with the supervision of the athletic side of student life, and his interest in these matters culminated in a study of the athletic history of the school, published in book form in 1926 under the title, *Athletics at Lafayette College.* March also took an interest in the local political scene, and served from 1905 to 1909 as mayor of Easton. But his chief contribution to American life was to be in the lexicographical field. He served his apprenticeship in this field as an assistant in the etymological department of *The Century Dictionary and Cyclopedia* (1 ed., 1889–91), the most ambitious lexicographical enterprise ever undertaken on American soil. When the staff of the *Standard Dictionary* (2 vols., 1893–95) was made up, March was invited to join it as editor in charge of the etymological department, and his services in this capacity had no little to do with making the dictionary standard in fact as well as in name. This task done, March undertook, in collaboration with his father, the editorship of a thesaurus dictionary. This work came out in 1902, under the title, *A Thesaurus Dictionary of the English Language,* and proved a great success; it has run to five editions. The connection of the elder March with this dictionary was little more than nominal, and to the younger must go the credit for its successful execution. March's interests, in his later years, seem to have shifted over to the historical field, for he wrote two books (popular rather than learned, it is true) about the World War: *History of the World War* (1918) and *America's Part in the World War* (1919), both in collaboration with R. J. Beamish.

[R. N. Hart, *Francis Andrew March, A Sketch* (1907); J. W. Bright, in *Pubs. of the Modern Language Asso. of America,* March 1914; D. B. Skillman, *The Biography of a College* (2 vols., 1932); *Who's Who in America,* 1926–27; (Philadelphia) *Public Ledger,* Feb. 29, 1928; family letters.]
K. M.

MARCHAND, JOHN BONNETT (Aug. 27, 1808–Apr. 13, 1875), naval officer, was born in Greensburg, Pa., the son of Dr. David and Catherine (Bonnett) Marchand. His father, a major-general of militia during the years 1812–14 and a member of Congress from 1817 to 1821, was descended from emigrants from Switzerland. Young Marchand entered the navy as a midshipman on May 1, 1828, and in the years 1829–32 saw his first sea service in the West Indies on the *Peacock* and *Porpoise.* After attending the Norfolk naval school and receiving in June 1834 a promotion to the rank of passed midshipman, he served from 1834 to 1837 with the Mediterranean Squadron, first on the *Potomac,* and later the *John Adams.* Attached to the *Porpoise* he engaged in the survey of the Savannah

River, and then again served in the West Indies. In 1840 he was promoted lieutenant and a year later, while in command of the *Van Buren,* he took part in the war against the Seminole Indians. From 1843 to 1845 he cruised in the East Indies on the *Brandywine.* In the Mexican War he served on the *Ohio* and participated in the bombardment of the castle of San Juan de Ulloa. After the war, a second cruise in the East Indies was followed by a second period of service in the Mediterranean. In 1855 he was advanced to the grade of commander and in 1858–59 he commanded the *Memphis* of the Paraguay expedition. At the outbreak of the Civil War, while acting as lighthouse inspector at Detroit, he was offered the command of a Michigan regiment but declined it, preferring service in the navy. On his application for active duty, he was on Aug. 31, 1861, placed in command of the *James Adger* and was employed in blockading the coast of South Carolina and searching for the Confederate steamer *Nashville.* Promoted captain from July 16, 1862, he was in the following October ordered to the *Lackawanna.* In February 1863 he reported to Admiral Farragut for blockade duty in the Gulf of Mexico. After capturing the *Neptune* and *Planter,* which ran the blockade at Mobile, he was placed in command of the third division of Farragut's squadron operating on the coast of Texas. He returned eastward in time to participate in the battle of Mobile Bay and in the capture of the ram *Tennessee.* In the latter part of 1864 he was detached from the *Lackawanna* and assigned to special duty. His last years of service were spent ashore on duty at Hartford and elsewhere and in command of the Philadelphia navy yard. He was promoted commodore from July 25, 1866, and was retired in that grade on Aug. 27, 1870. He died at his home in Carlisle, Pa. His wife, Margaret Donaldson Thornton, to whom he was married in 1856 or 1857, was the daughter of a naval paymaster.

[Record of Officers, Bureau of Navigation, 1825–78; G. D. Albert, *Hist. of the County of Westmoreland, Pa.* (1882), pp. 444–46; J. N. Boucher, *Hist. of Westmoreland County, Pa.* (1906), vol. III; *War of the Rebellion: Official Records (Navy),* 1 ser. I, XIII, XIX–XXI; *Army and Navy Jour.,* Apr. 24, May 1, 1875.] C. O. P.

MARCHANT, HENRY (April 1741–Aug. 30, 1796), Rhode Island jurist and delegate to the Continental Congress, was born on Martha's Vineyard, the son of Hexford Marchant, a sea-captain. His mother, whose maiden name was Butler, died when the boy was four, shortly after the family had removed to Newport. His father's later marriage to a daughter of Samuel Ward gave young Marchant a useful connection with a leading Rhode Island family. He studied at the College of Philadelphia (later the University of Pennsylvania) from 1756 to 1759, but did not graduate. In 1762, however, he received the degree of A.M. Meanwhile he was reading law with the greatest common lawyer and preceptor in New England, Edmund Trowbridge of Cambridge. This conservative judge hatched a numerous brood of young patriot barristers, among them Francis Dana, a fellow student of Marchant and his close friend.

After settling in Newport Marchant rose rapidly in his profession and in politics. He had stimulating contacts with the Redwood Library circle and was strongly influenced intellectually by his intimate friend and pastor, the erudite Dr. Ezra Stiles, whom he assisted in 1769 in observing the transit of Venus. An ardent Son of Liberty from Stamp Act days he was chosen attorney-general of Rhode Island in 1771 and each year thereafter through 1776. In 1771 when he went to England on private legal business before Privy Council he was designated joint colonial agent to press for compensation for the expenses of the 1756 campaign against Crown Point. He traveled widely in England and was Benjamin Franklin's companion on a visit to Scotland. Stiles noted with pride that his protégé "was personally acquainted with the Men of the first Eminence for Literature in Scotland and England" (*The Literary Diary of Ezra Stiles,* I, p. 304). He was also in close touch with the merchants, nonconformists, and radicals who made up the "friends of America" in Great Britain.

After his return in 1772 he fell under suspicion for accepting a retainer from the collector of customs, but he soon took his place in the leadership of the Revolutionary movement in the colony. In May 1773 he was named on the Rhode Island committee of correspondence, and in December 1774, on the committee to instruct the delegates to the first Continental Congress. At the outbreak of war he removed from Newport to his farm in South Kingstown. He was chosen delegate to Congress, 1777–79, and served on the standing committees on marine, appeals, treasury, and the southern department. He was elected again in 1780 and in 1783, but did not attend in either year, and in 1784 he resigned after reëlection.

From 1784 to 1790 he sat for Newport in the General Assembly and was a vigorous exponent of the commercial interests in those troubled times. He was associated with Varnum as counsel in *Trevett* vs. *Weeden.* In 1787 he signed the minority protest against Rhode Island's abstention from the Philadelphia Convention; in 1790 he introduced the bill for a ratifying convention. As a Newport member of the convention he took a leading part in the debates, and also in the maneuvers which finally brought Federalist success. He was promptly rewarded by President Washington with appointment as judge of the United States district court (July 2, 1790). He continued on the bench until his death at Newport six years later. Marchant married Rebecca Cooke, Jan. 8, 1765. His son, William, was graduated from Yale in 1792 when Marchant himself received the degree of LL.D. from his old mentor, President Stiles.

[See Edward Peterson, *Hist. of R. I.* (1853); W. R. Staples, *R. I. in the Continental Cong.* (1870); W. C. Ford, ed., *Jours. of the Continental Cong.*, vols. VII–XV (1907–09); E. C. Burnett, ed., *Letters of Members of the Continental Cong.*, vols. II–IV (1923–28); J. R. Bartlett, ed., *Records of the Colony of R. I.*, vols. VI–X (1861–65); J. N. Arnold, *Vital Record of R. I.*, vols. X (1898) and XII (1901); F. B. Dexter, ed., *The Lit. Diary of Ezra Stiles, D.D., LL.D.* (3 vols., 1901); and *Theodore Foster's Minutes of the Convention Held at South Kingstown, R. I., in Mar. 1790* (1929). Marchant's manuscript diary of his English journey and numerous letters are in family possession.]

V. W. C.

MARCOU, JULES (Apr. 20, 1824–Apr. 17, 1898), geologist, was born at Salins, France, and received his early education at the *Collège* there and at the *Lycée* of Besançon. He entered the College of St. Louis at Paris when eighteen years old but devoted himself so assiduously to mathematics that he undermined his health and was obliged to abandon his studies and return home in the spring of 1844. His interest and ability in the field of mathematics are demonstrated by the fact that he published three papers in the *Nouvelles Annales de Mathématiques* (vols. II, III, 1843–44) during those undergraduate days. On returning to Salins, he gave himself up to an out-of-door life and became interested in botany, but his family physician, who was an amateur collector of fossils, quickly turned his attention to the field of geology, where he found his life work. He soon became known as an authority on fossils and was visited by Louis Agassiz [*q.v.*], who encouraged him to publish his first geological work in 1845 ("Recherches Géologiques sur le Jura Salinois," *Mémoires de la Société d'Histoire Naturelle de Neuchâtel*).

He joined the faculty of the Sorbonne in 1846 as professor of mineralogy but within two years was made traveling geologist for the Museum in the Jardin des Plantes, and gave up teaching. North America was selected as the field for his first work, largely owing to the presence of Louis Agassiz here, and, coming to the United States in 1848, he accompanied Agassiz on his expedition to Lake Superior that summer. He left the party at Keweenaw Point, Mich., however, and devoted himself thereafter with extraordinary energy to collecting for the Paris Museum. In 1850 he resigned his connection with that institution, but in 1854 returned to Europe to live and in 1856 became professor of paleontology at the École Polytechnique in Zurich, where he remained four years. Returning to America in 1860, he finally settled in Cambridge, Mass., where he made his home until his death. He was at work as a geologist in the field more or less frequently until 1875, when he made his last long excursion, accompanying Lieut. George M. Wheeler's party on a surveying expedition to southern California. In 1862, he was appointed geologist in the Museum of Comparative Zoölogy at Harvard, but his official connection with the Museum seems to have ended two years later.

Marcou was a voluminous writer, 188 titles occurring in a bibliography which he himself compiled towards the close of his life. A large proportion of his publications were written in French and issued in Europe. His most important works, *Lettres sur les Roches du Jura* (1857–60), *Geology of North America* (1858), and *Geological Map of the World* (1862), were all published in Europe. During this brief period of five years Marcou seems to have reached "the acme of his career" (Hyatt, *post*, p. 654). In 1869, he published in Paris a volume, *De la Science en France,* which caused much comment because of its criticism of official methods. His *Life, Letters and Works of Louis Agassiz* (2 vols.), published in New York in 1895, also aroused interest and controversy by its unusual frankness. He was a great lover of books and his library was notable for the number of rare volumes which it contained. He was married in 1850 to Jane Belknap of Boston and had two sons. Throughout his life his health was unreliable and in spite of his extensive field work there were long periods when he was obliged to treat himself as an invalid. Nevertheless he was a man of striking personality, and in later years was a picturesque figure, tall and erect, with long, flowing beard. Energetic in his work, devoted to the truth as he saw it, he was apt to become very positive of the correctness of his own position and quite intolerant of opposition.

[Max Buchon, *Biographie Salinoise: Jules Marcou* (1865); Alpheus Hyatt, "Jules Marcou," in *Proc. Am. Acad. Arts and Sci.*, vol. XXXIV (1899); G. P. Merrill, *The First One Hundred Years of Am. Geology* (1924); bibliog. in *Bull. U. S. Nat. Museum,* no. 30

(1885); Boston *Transcript,* Apr. 19, 1898; information from a former colleague.] H. L. C.

MARCY, HENRY ORLANDO (June 23, 1837–Jan. 1, 1924), surgeon and gynecologist, was born in Otis, Mass., the son of Smith and Fanny (Gibbs) Marcy. He was descended on both sides from Puritan stock and his paternal grandfather, Thomas Marcy, was one of the first settlers of northern Ohio. Smith Marcy was a school-teacher and a veteran of the War of 1812. After attending Wilbraham Academy and Amherst College, Henry O. Marcy was graduated by the Harvard Medical School with the class of 1864. The year before his graduation, however, he entered the Massachusetts militia as a surgeon and served in various campaigns of the Civil War, especially at the siege of Charleston. In the last year of the war he was appointed medical director of Florida. His work was characterized by common sense, for he did much to prevent dysentery among the troops by supplying them with fresh and well-cooked food, and at Charleston his house-to-house cleaning, with a force of five hundred men, made a sanitary city out of one that was pest-ridden. Following the war, he returned to Boston, where he practised for a short time, being greatly influenced by Horatio R. Storer [*q.v.*], a pioneer surgeon in diseases of women. Feeling that his education was incomplete, Marcy spent two years in Europe studying pathology and surgery; in 1869 he was with Virchow, the pathologist, in Berlin; and the next year with the surgeons Paget and Spencer Wells, in London. Later he went to Edinburgh, where he became the first American pupil of Joseph Lister, the founder of antiseptic surgery.

On returning to Boston, he attempted to interest Henry J. Bigelow [*q.v.*] in Lister's methods, but, according to Marcy, Bigelow "declared that it was only another fad, unworthy of consideration" (*Transactions of the Southern Surgical Association* for 1920, p. 32). The younger man could make no headway against the powerful Bigelow, and accordingly retired to Cambridge, Mass., where in 1880 he established a private hospital for diseases of women. Through the use of the Lister methods and many innovations devised by himself, he attained considerable success in abdominal operations. He began to use catgut and other animal sutures, especially of the absorbable type which could be left in the wound, and was a pioneer in the use of antiseptic solutions and the disinfection of the surgeon's hands before operation, as well as in the use of rubber gloves. All these new methods were tested out carefully in Marcy's private hospital. Furthermore, he and his assistants were among the earliest bacteriologists in America.

Marcy was an ardent advocate of the American Medical Association, and year after year, over a long period of time, presented the results of his work before that body. Partly through his persistent efforts, Listerism was accepted in the United States and he should, undoubtedly, receive the credit for introducing the method of antiseptic wound treatment into America. His most important original contribution to American surgery, however, was the development of animal sutures. His publications include a long list of papers covering various aspects of surgery, especially the treatment of hernia, and a few on the history of surgery in America. Notable titles are: *The Radical Cure of Hernia by the Antiseptic Use of Carbolized Catgut Ligature* (1879); *The Best Methods of Treating Operative Wounds* (1882); *Recent Advances in Abdominal Surgery* (1887); *A Treatise on Hernia* (1889); and *The Scientific Rationale of Modern Wound Treatment* (1891). Historical papers that throw light on his own career include: "The Early History of Abdominal Surgery in America" (*Journal of the American Medical Association,* Feb. 19, 1910); "The Surgical Service of the Civil War Then and Now—the Progress of Fifty Years" (*Transactions of the Southern Surgical and Gynecological Association* for 1914, p. 138); and "The Semicentennial of the Introduction of Antiseptic Surgery in America" (*Ibid.* for 1920, p. 25). Never popular with his brother physicians in Boston, he held no hospital or teaching position of importance, but received a number of other honors, including the presidency of the American Medical Association in 1891.

Marcy was married to Sarah E. Wendell of Great Falls, N. H., in 1863. His only son became a physician and was associated for many years with his father. Marcy did much to develop Cambridge and was instrumental in building the Harvard Bridge, the Charles River Basin, with its Esplanade, and the Massachusetts Institute of Technology, of whose site he was chief owner.

[*Jour. Am. Medic. Editors' Asso.,* June 1925; *Am. Doctor,* May 1891; T. F. Harrington, *The Harvard Medic. School, A Hist.* (1905), III, 1513; *Jour. Am. Medic. Asso.,* Jan. 19, 1924; Boston *Transcript,* Jan. 2, 1924.] H. R. V.

MARCY, RANDOLPH BARNES (Apr. 9, 1812–Nov. 22, 1887), soldier, was born at Greenwich, Mass., the eldest son of Laban and Fanny (Howe) Marcy. He was descended from John Marcy, an Irish emigrant who was in Roxbury, Mass., as early as 1685 and died in Woodstock, Conn., in 1724. Marcy graduated at the Military Academy in 1832, as brevet second lieutenant in the 5th Infantry; reached the substantive rank of second lieutenant in 1835, first lieutenant in 1837, and captain in 1846. His service for some thirteen years was entirely on the Michigan and Wisconsin frontier, except for two short periods on recruiting duty in the East. In 1845 he went to Texas, and served there during the military occupation and in the battles of Palo Alto and Resaca de la Palma. He then went on recruiting duty again, but returned to Texas in 1847.

For the next twelve years he remained in the Southwest, much of the time in the field. In 1849 he escorted emigrants from Fort Smith to Santa Fé, reconnoitering and opening a new trail. In 1851 he commanded the escort of General Belknap, who traveled extensively in that region selecting sites for military posts. In 1852 he led an exploring expedition to the headwaters of the Red and Canadian rivers, and in 1854 he surveyed Indian reservations in northern and western Texas. His reports of the explorations of 1849, 1852, and 1854, were published as *Senate Executive Document No. 64* (31 Cong., 1 Sess.), *No. 54* (32 Cong., 2 Sess,), and *No. 60* (34 Cong., 1 Sess.). For a short time in 1857 he was engaged in the campaign against the Seminole Indians in Florida, but returned to the West in time to accompany Col. Albert Sidney Johnston's expedition against the Mormons in Utah. This expedition had to winter at Fort Bridger, under conditions of great hardship, its trains having been seriously crippled by Mormon raiders. Marcy, with a hundred men, made a winter march of nearly a thousand miles through trackless country and over the Rocky Mountains, to the military posts in New Mexico, to obtain animals and supplies; he reached Fort Bridger again in June 1858. Until this time his service had been entirely with his regiment. He was now detailed as acting inspector-general of the Department of Utah. After a few months on this duty he was ordered to New York to prepare a semi-official guidebook, called *The Prairie Traveler,* which was published in 1859 by authority of the War Department. It was an excellent compendium of practical hints for travelers, and included a remarkable collection of detailed road notes covering thirty-four important overland trails.

In August 1859 he was appointed major and paymaster, and served in the northwest until May 1861, when he became chief of staff of his son-in-law, Gen. George B. McClellan [*q.v.*]. In this capacity he served through the Peninsular and Antietam campaigns, holding the rank of colonel and inspector-general from Aug. 9, 1861, and the temporary rank of brigadier-general from Sept. 23, 1861, to Mar. 4, 1863. At the close of the war he received brevet commissions as brigadier- and major-general. From 1863 to 1878 he served as inspector in various departments and on Dec. 12, 1878, was appointed inspector-general of the army, with the rank of brigadier-general. He served in this capacity until his retirement from active service, Jan. 2, 1881. From his retirement to his death he resided at West Orange, N. J.

He was married in 1833 to Mary A. Mann, daughter of Gen. Jonas Mann of Syracuse, N. Y. She died in 1878. They had three children—a son who died in infancy; Mary Ellen, who married Gen. George B. McClellan; and Frances, who married Edward Clarke. Marcy was tall, broad-shouldered, and soldierly in bearing. He was essentially an out-of-doors man, and continued to make big-game hunting trips even after his retirement. At the same time he had some facility in writing and published two volumes of recollections of frontier service: *Thirty Years of Army Life on the Border* (1866), and *Border Reminiscences* (1872), besides the guidebook mentioned above.

[G. W. Cullum, *Biog. Reg. Officers and Grads. U. S. Mil. Acad.* (3rd ed., 1891); L. R. Hamersly, *Records of Living Officers of the U. S. Army* (1884); *Army and Navy Jour.*, Nov. 26, 1887; *N. Y. Times*, Nov. 23, 1887; *New-Eng. Hist. and Geneal. Reg.*, July 1875; *War of the Rebellion: Official Records (Army)*; Marcy's own books; personal and family notes furnished by Hon. George B. McClellan, his grandson.]

O. L. S., Jr.

MARCY, WILLIAM LEARNED (Dec. 12, 1786–July 4, 1857), lawyer and statesman, son of Jedediah and Ruth (Learned) Marcy, was born in Sturbridge (now Southbridge), Mass. He was descended on his father's side from John Marcy, whose name occurs under date of 1685 in the records of John Eliot's church at Roxbury, and on his mother's side from William Learned, who came to Massachusetts probably on one of the vessels of the Winthrop fleet in 1630 and joined the First Church at Charlestown in 1632. The boy's early education was obtained in the village school, in the academy at Leicester then under the preceptorship of Ebenezer Adams [*q.v.*], and—with an interval of teaching at Union, Conn.—at Woodstock Academy. In September 1805, he entered Brown University as a sophomore. Aiding himself during the winter of 1805–06 by conducting a private school in Newport, R. I., with his friend, Eleazer Trevett (*Newport Mercury,* Nov. 16, 1805, Mar. 29, 1806), he was graduated in September 1808, with a place on the Commencement program. After graduation he left Sturbridge, intending to seek his fortune in western New York, but stopped on the way at Troy, and remained there for the next fifteen years.

Quickly identifying himself with local interests, he won friends and the respect of his fellow townsmen. He read law and was admitted to the bar within three years. On Sept. 27, 1812, he married Dolly Newell of Sturbridge, Mass., who died in 1821, having borne him three children. He wrote for the *Northern Budget*, revealing a facility which served later to invigorate the columns of the *Albany Argus*, organ of the "Albany Regency." Interested while at Leicester Academy in Thomas Jefferson, he had developed since then convictions which led him into the Jeffersonian party. His *Oration on the Three Hundred and Eighteenth Anniversary of the Discovery of America*, delivered before the Tammany Society in 1809 and published that year—the first of his literary efforts to be printed—was a defense of the doctrines and policy of President Jefferson, and in view of the bitter attack upon Jefferson made by Stephen C. Carpenter (*Memoirs of the Hon. Thomas Jefferson*, 2 vols., 1809) was especially timely. As a member of the 155th Regiment, Marcy passed from the grade of ensign (May 20, 1812) by successive promotions to that of adjutant-general of the state (Feb. 12, 1821), and thereafter was often addressed as "General" Marcy. During the War of 1812 he took part as a minor officer in the capture of an Indian village at the mouth of the St. Regis River (Oct. 22–23, 1812), and in an engagement (Nov. 19–20) near Lacolle, in the province of Quebec. Afterward, for a time, he resumed his law practice, but returned to the army late in 1814. In April 1816 he was appointed first recorder of the newly organized city of Troy and for two periods (1816–18 and 1821–23) he served as a sort of vice-mayor with sundry judicial duties to perform. For five years (1818–23) he was associated with Jacob L. Lane in the firm of Marcy & Lane.

About 1818, deprived of his position as recorder through the machinations of Gov. De Witt Clinton, Marcy had won the friendly interest of Martin Van Buren, with whom he prepared a pamphlet, *Considerations in Favor of the Appointment of Rufus King to the Senate of the United States* (1819), which aided in securing King's return to the Senate in 1820. In 1821 Van Buren went to Washington as King's colleague, and Marcy was restored to the recordership of Troy. The political group which they had helped to organize came to include such local leaders as Benjamin F. Butler, Azariah C. Flagg, and Edwin Croswell [*qq.v.*], and later, Silas Wright, Jr., John A. Dix, Horatio Seymour, and Samuel J. Tilden. First popularly dubbed the "Holy Alliance," the combination was known for many years as the "Albany Regency." Democratic to the core, it influenced and directed state and federal appointments and as a powerful political machine became famous throughout the country. In 1823 Marcy accepted the state comptrollership of New York and moved from Troy to Albany, which was his home for the rest of his life. Here, about 1825, he married Cornelia, daughter of Benjamin Knower, one of his political associates. Three children were born to them.

In the capacity of comptroller (1823–29), aware that public indebtedness was increasing under the spell of a popular movement favoring canals and roads, Marcy exercised discerningly his power of restraint over the legislature. Late in 1827 (*Memoirs of John Quincy Adams*, VII, 1875, pp. 388, 404) he was considered for the governorship; early in 1829 Governor Van Buren appointed him associate justice of the state supreme court. For the court he delivered about 175 opinions (2–6 *Wendell's Reports*, *passim*). In several cases involving phases of the conspiracy in western New York to abduct William Morgan for his alleged revelations of the secrets of the Masonic order, Marcy displayed erudition and a high sense of justice. His task called for courage and clear thinking, for the popular furor aroused by Morgan's disappearance was so great as to result in the formation of a national Anti-Masonic party.

Resigning from the bench in 1831, he accepted reluctantly an election to the United States Senate. There he remained for a single long session (Dec. 5, 1831–July 17, 1832) and a month (December 1832) of the short session, serving on the finance committee and as chairman of the judiciary committee. On such subjects as the tariff and the bank he spoke briefly. His best effort was made in behalf of Van Buren, then minister in London on a recess commission. Twice (Jan. 17 and 25, 1832) Vice-President Calhoun, embittered toward President Jackson and jealous of Van Buren, used his casting vote in an evenly divided Senate to force the rejection of Van Buren's appointment (*Register of Debates*, 22 Cong., 1 Sess., 1309 ff.). Defending Van Buren against reflections on his alleged introduction into national affairs of the system of rewards and punishments ascribed to the "Albany Regency," Marcy declared that he could see "nothing wrong in the rule that to the victor belong the spoils of the enemy" (*Ibid.*, col. 1325), an expression that caught the attention of the public and gave the phrase "spoils system" to the language. In debate, however, Marcy made little impression against such experienced speakers as Clay, Webster, Benton, and Hayne. On Sept. 19, 1832, he was nominated for governor. Carrying the election, he resigned from the Senate in January 1833.

As governor for three terms (1833–38) Marcy left his mark upon the state. Aided by a gifted young secretary of state, John A. Dix [*q.v.*], he organized the first geological survey of New York's fifty-six counties. In the course of the survey the highest peak in the Adirondacks was given the name Mount Marcy in honor of the governor. He refused assent to the constitutional gloss by which in 1835 Governor Gayle of Alabama made requisition for Robert G. Williams, publishing agent of the American Anti-Slavery Society in New York, under an act of Congress concerning "fugitives from justice"—early evidence of his interest in extradition which later assumed international proportions. He reprobated activities of the Abolitionists (1836) as likely to destroy the Union, and even suggested that states might find it necessary to take action by penal laws against activities tending to promote insurrection in another state—sentiments which strengthened the hopes of Southerners in 1853 that as secretary of state he would uphold state's rights against federal interference with slavery. Under his régime the New York-New Jersey boundary dispute was settled.

From 1840 to 1842, as a member of the Mexican Claims Commission by appointment of President Van Buren, he exhibited skill at conciliation, and, with his colleagues, secured for the American claimants awards totaling nearly $2,400,000, leaving only a few cases unsolved (J. B. Moore, *History and Digest of the International Arbitrations to which the United States has been a Party,* 1898, II, 1209–44). In Washington he met the prominent leaders of the time; he attended public receptions, played whist (his favorite game) with Clay, and dined occasionally with Presidents Van Buren and Tyler at "the Palace." The Marcy Papers (*post,* V–IX, *passim*) show clearly that after 1840 he had set his mind on a high federal post. Early in 1844 Tyler considered him for the United States Supreme Court, and he received a few votes for the vice-presidency in the Baltimore convention of 1844 which selected Polk and Dallas. In November of that year, in a mood of watchful waiting, he declined Governor Bouck's offer of appointment to fill the unexpired term of Senator N. P. Tallmadge, resigned, because he wanted a place, preferably the Treasury, in Polk's cabinet. He accepted the secretaryship of war (*American Historical Review,* October 1924, pp. 76–83). With this position neither Van Buren nor the "Regency" (already losing power) had anything to do; it came to Marcy on his own merits. His acceptance of it marked a breach between him and the "Barnburner" faction of his party, with which Van Buren was now associated.

The war with Mexico involved Marcy in heavy duties. He was subjected to harsh criticism, especially from Gen. Winfield Scott in the field. An exchange of letters between Scott and the Secretary was given wide publicity ("Mexican War Correspondence," *House Executive Document No. 60,* 30 Cong., 1 Sess., pp. 1218–51). There were errors of judgment on both sides, and insubordination on the part of Scott, but when Marcy left the cabinet, he had added to his record of administrative competence. Among those near him able to appreciate his tasks, he had acquired rather than lost prestige. A friendship begun in the thirties between him and George Bancroft [*q.v.*], secretary of the navy, was firmly knit and lasted for the rest of Marcy's life. With Buchanan he kept up an intermittent correspondence—both men watchful of public opinion and eager alike for the presidency. To both, the results of the Baltimore convention of 1852 were disappointing. Neither could be ignored by President Pierce: he sent Buchanan as minister to England and made Marcy his secretary of state (*American Secretaries of State, post,* VI, 161–68, 177–79).

During the next four years Marcy was chiefly responsible for the negotiation of twenty-four treaties, the largest number ratified within an administration up to that time. Four are significant: the Gadsden Treaty with Mexico (Dec. 30, 1853) which added nearly 30,000 square miles to United States territory; the Reciprocity Treaty with Great Britain (June 5, 1854), relating to trade and the fisheries in Canada and the Maritime Provinces; a treaty with the Netherlands (Jan. 22, 1855) which first opened ports in the Dutch colonial possessions to American consuls; and the treaty with Denmark (Apr. 11, 1857) which, though ratified under Buchanan, was a result of Marcy's effort to abolish forever the Danish Sound dues. Eleven extradition treaties led the list numerically. Other treaties were made with the Argentine Confederation, Peru, Russia, Siam, and Persia. With treaties opening Japan (Mar. 31, 1854) and the Lew Choo Islands (July 11), the Pierce administration had nothing to do beyond ratification, since

Commodore Perry had sailed under instructions formulated in November 1852 by President Fillmore's acting secretary of state, but Marcy in 1855 sent to Japan Townsend Harris [*q.v.*], who laid the basis for notable accomplishments in the Far East.

Three cases involving the handling of delicate problems in international relations were settled during Marcy's term: the Koszta case with Austria (September 1853), the *Black Warrior* case with Spain (May 1855), and the Patrice Dillon case with France (August 1855). The "Dress Circular," containing instructions to United States agents abroad regarding dress to be worn on formal occasions, was issued in June 1856, and constitutes the substance of present-day usage as defined by statute Mar. 27, 1867. Marcy's two notes in explanation of the United States' refusal to join in the Declaration of Paris (Apr. 16, 1856) have become famous (Sir Francis Piggott, *The Declaration of Paris, 1856,* 1919, pp. 264–66, 393–404). Toward bringing Central American issues to a head Marcy made little progress, though he would have done so had the British government accepted the Dallas-Clarendon convention (Oct. 17, 1856) which was approved by both President Pierce and the Senate. A matter which created widespread sensation was the publication (March 1855) of the "Ostend Manifesto," a report made to the State Department on Oct. 18, 1854, recommending that the United States acquire Cuba by purchase or, that failing, by force. The document was chiefly composed by Buchanan, aided by Pierre Soulé and John Y. Mason [*qq.v.*], the American ministers to England, Spain, and France. For authorizing these men to advise him in regard to arranging differences of opinion with the Madrid authorities over Cuban relations hinging upon the *Black Warrior* affair, Marcy and the cabinet were at fault. Had Marcy not maintained a neutral attitude toward the rapidly developing issue over slavery, he might have avoided the error of putting trust in Soulé, an unsuitable appointee from Louisiana, who was bent on acquiring Cuba for Southern interests. The "Manifesto" came near to wrecking the solution of the *Black Warrior* case, which was, however, eventually settled to the satisfaction of the United States. Another sensational episode which was shrewdly if somewhat tardily handled (July 1856), was the dismissal of the British minister and three British consuls as the result of a controversy with Great Britain over attempts within the borders of the United States to enlist recruits for the Crimean War.

With the close of the Pierce administration (March 1857), Marcy's public life came to an end and on July 4 following he died, at Ballston, N. Y. He was buried in the Rural Cemetery five miles north of the city of Albany. At the time of his death he was reckoned "among the foremost men of the country" (Moore, *post,* 395), and he stands high on the list of American secretaries of state.

[Marcy Papers (1806–57), 76 vols., in MSS. Div., Lib. of Cong.; Instructions and Despatches (MSS.), 1853–57, Dept. of State; *State of N. Y.; Messages from the Govs.* (1909), vol. III; "Diary and Memoranda of Wm. L. Marcy," *Am. Hist. Rev.*, Apr.–July 1919; H. B. Learned, "The Sequence of Appointments to Polk's Original Cabinet," *Ibid.*, Oct. 1924; W. G. Rice, "The Appointment of Gov. Marcy as Sec. of State," *Mag. of Hist.*, Feb., Mar. 1912, Jan. 1913; J. B. Moore, "A Great Secretary of State: William L. Marcy," *Pol. Sci. Quart.*, Sept. 1915; Mrs. Calvin D. Paige, "The Marcy Family," *Quinabaug Hist. Soc. Leaflets*, no. 11 (n.d.), read 1902; H. B. Learned, in S. F. Bemis, *The Am. Secretaries of State and Their Diplomacy*, VI (1928), 145–294, 420–31, with portrait and bibliography; R. F. Nichols, *The Democratic Machine: 1850–1854* (1923); D. S. Alexander, *A Political Hist. of the State of N. Y.*, vols. I, II (1906); J. B. Brebner, in *Canadian Hist. Rev.*, Dec. 1930; A. A. Ettinger, *The Mission to Spain of Pierre Soulé* (1932); *N. Y. Times*, July 6, 1857; information as to certain facts from Johannes C. Westermann of Hilversum, The Netherlands.]
H. B. L—d.

MARDEN, CHARLES CARROLL (Dec. 21, 1867–May 11, 1932), philologist, son of Jesse and Anna Maria (Brice) Marden, was descended from old Colonial stock, Marylanders on his mother's side and New Englanders on his father's. He was born in Baltimore, his paternal grandfather having in 1829 removed to that city from New Hampshire. Receiving in 1889 his bachelor's degree from the Johns Hopkins University, he taught a year in Virginia at the Norfolk Academy, for another year was instructor in French at the University of Michigan, and then pursued graduate study under A. Marshall Elliott [*q.v.*] at the Johns Hopkins, completing his course in 1894 with a doctoral thesis on the Spanish dialect of Mexico city. While North America had early acquired an honorable name in Spanish studies with the publication in 1849 of George Ticknor's remarkable *History of Spanish Literature,* successors to Ticknor had been lacking, and Elliott, eager to see the interrupted tradition renewed, welcomed his pupil's desire to concentrate upon the domain in which he had made an auspicious beginning, and retained him as instructor at his alma mater, where Marden's work won him successive promotions through the intermediate ranks to the first American university professorship in Spanish, to which he was named in 1905 and which he retained until 1917. He was elected in 1916 to the newly established Emery L. Ford Chair of Spanish at Princeton, but for a year divided his time between the two universities. He also had an important part in another active center of Spanish studies, the University of Chicago, where between 1909 and 1928 he conducted graduate courses during seven of the summer quarters.

Marden's initial interest in Latin-American Spanish was never lost, and his last study in that field was dated 1925; but he early centered his attention on the language and literature of medieval Spain, and few were the years unmarked by some contribution from him in this domain. His text of the *Poema de Fernan Gonçalez,* issued in 1904, was the first critical edition ever issued of a medieval Spanish literary work. It won international commendation, and was followed by his election in 1907 as a corresponding member of the Spanish Academy. An edition of the *Libro de Apolonio* (2 vols., 1917–22) confirmed his standing as an accurate and penetrating interpreter of the early literature. In 1925 he discovered in Madrid a portion of the manuscript of the works of the first known Castilian poet, Gonzalo de Berceo—a priceless treasure which he generously presented to the Spanish Academy. While he was preparing this text for publication, his conviction grew that a systematic search within a circumscribed territory might bring to light other portions of the manuscript. When, in February 1928, he next went to Spain, and as soon as he had acquitted himself of his commission as Carnegie visiting professor to Spanish universities, he thoroughly combed the province of Logroño, and there, just on the eve of his departure, he found and acquired in a remote mountain village thirty-two of the missing folios, which he joined with those already in the Academy's possession. Upon the completion of his edition of the two parts of this manuscript (*Cuatro Poemas de Berceo,* 1928, and *Veintitrés Milagros,* 1929), he began what promised to be the crowning work of his career, an edition of the *Libro de Alexandre,* interrupted before its completion by his unexpected death.

While Marden's published work was limited to the field of Spanish, his influence had a wider reach. Many of his students who later became leaders in kindred subjects bear testimony to the contagiousness of his enthusiasm for scholarship and to the profit they derived from the sound principles which he unceasingly inculcated. Similarly, when after the death of Elliott, founder of *Modern Language Notes,* Marden was for several years managing editor of that journal (January 1911–December 1915), his adherence to those same principles was a stimulus and an example to a wide circle of contributors and readers. To his unbroken activity in research and the training of scholars he joined a live interest in the instruction of beginners in language, for whom he regularly conducted courses, and in *A First Spanish Grammar* (1926), collaborating with F. C. Tarr, he placed at the service of others his own clear and accurate analysis and exposition. He was also during some years chief examiner in Spanish for the College Entrance Examination Board. In addition to his corresponding membership in the Spanish Academy, he was Knight Commander in the Order of Isabel la Católica, fellow of the Medieval Academy and of the Hispanic Society, and at the time of his death, president of the Modern Language Association.

Honesty, clear thinking, and the capacity for taking pains lay at the basis of all Marden's accomplishment. He scrupulously controlled his material and as scrupulously made accessible the data behind his arguments. In analyzing the work of others he applied the same standards, and the reviews he wrote form no small element of his contribution to scholarship. Tender in his human sympathies, rather than voice a dissenting judgment he often kept silent; but if the word came, he was outspoken. Praise from him was highly prized, and the sincerity of his less favorable criticisms was never questioned. He was not effusive in his casual contacts but in company of kindred spirits became expansive and even jovial. Particularly happy in his family life, he was at his best in his home, and it was there by preference that he greeted his friends and that he carried on the work that made of him the leading American hispanist. He was survived by his wife, Mary Talbott Clark, daughter of John L. and Mary Corinne Clark of Howard County, Md., whom he had married on Dec. 2, 1897, and by their four children.

[*Who's Who in America,* 1932–33; H. Seris, in *Gaceta Literaria* (Madrid), Mar. 15, 1928; E. A. Peers, in *Bull. of Spanish Studies* (Liverpool), Apr. 1929; *N. Y. Times,* May 12, 1932; *Times* (London), May 28, 1932; *Princeton Alumni Weekly,* June 2, 1932; *Pubs. Mod. Lang. Asso. of America,* Sept. 1932; *Romanic Rev.,* July–Sept. 1932; *Mod. Philology,* Nov. 1932; sketch by H. C. Lancaster, with bibliography by F. C. Tarr, in *Mod. Lang. Notes,* Dec. 1932; *Hispanic Rev.,* Jan. 1933; G. A. Hanson, *Old Kent* (1876), under "John Brice"; J. D. Warfield, *The Founders of Anne Arundel and Howard Counties, Md.* (1905), under "Marden" and "Dr. Chas. Carroll."]
E. C. A.

MARDEN, ORISON SWETT (1850–Mar. 10, 1924), journalist, writer, the son of Louis and Martha (Cilley) Marden, was born near Thornton, N. H. At seven he was an orphan. As a boy he read Samuel Smiles's *Self Help* and determined that his career should be one of service to mankind. After graduating from New

Hampton Institute, N. H., in 1873, he attended Boston University (B.A., 1877) and then studied medicine at Harvard (M.D., 1882). At the same time he was working his way by catering and by hotel management with such success that on leaving college he had a capital of nearly $20,000. He then made an extensive continental tour through Italy, Austria, Germany, France, and the British Isles. His business career began with the purchase and enlargement of a hotel on Block Island, off Newport, R. I., a resort which Marden did much to develop through effective advertising and judicious investment in real estate. Until 1892 he was very fortunate in his ventures. Retaining his holdings on Block Island, he bought controlling interests in four or five hotels in the Northwest. Attracted by the Nebraska boom of the early nineties, he moved west and made himself proprietor of the Palmer House, Grand Island, and the Midway Hotel in Kearney, where as resident manager he soon became a leading citizen. The soubriquet of "Lucky" Marden seemed justified. But in 1892 he suffered financial reverses and in 1893, heavily in debt, he left Kearney for Chicago where he worked during the Columbian Exposition as manager of the Park Gate Hotel. He then closed his affairs in the West and returned to Boston where he went doggedly about making a fresh start. He devoted his energy toward framing the message of optimism which for so long he had felt it his mission to spread: namely, that the will to succeed is the most vital single factor in success. In 1894 he published his gospel in *Pushing to the Front*. The book was received with enthusiasm and began a phenomenal run of 250 editions. He then decided to found a magazine to be devoted to the teaching of his credo. Louis Klopsch, a New York publisher, agreed to float the venture, and in October 1897 the first issue of *Success* appeared. By 1900 Marden was able to maintain a permanent editorial office in New York City and under his guidance the magazine grew with extraordinary swiftness until 1910, when a somewhat quixotic editorial policy began seriously to impair its credit. In 1912 the venture failed, and Marden was again in financial straits. In May 1905 he had married Clare L. Evans of Louisville, Ky., and had bought a farm at Glen Cove, L. I. With his old tenacity he began at once to plan for the day when a new *Success* should appear. In 1917, in spite of war conditions, he felt that the world would welcome the message he had to offer. He found a financial backer in Frederick C. Lowrey of Chicago and by January 1918 was publishing the new *Success*. When on Mar. 10, 1924, Marden died, his magazine was well on the way to the record circulation he had predicted for that year. Typical of his works are: *Rising in the World* (1896); *He Can Who Thinks He Can* (1908); *Ambition and Success* (1919); and *Masterful Personality* (1921). Thirty of his books were translated into German, and over three million of them, variously translated into twenty-five languages, have been sold.

[Margaret Connolly, *The Life Story of Orison Swett Marden* (1925); R. M. Bayles, *Hist. of Newport County, R. I.* (1888); *Who's Who in America*, 1922–23; *Success*, May 1924; *N. Y. Times*, Mar. 11, 12, 1924.]

E. M. H.

MARÉCHAL, AMBROSE (Aug. 28, 1764–Jan. 29, 1828), Roman Catholic prelate, was born near Orléans, France, of a good family. On graduation from college, he studied law in accordance with parental instructions, although his pronounced inclination was for the ministry. In 1787, as a student in the Sulpician Seminary at Orléans, he received the tonsure and joined the community. Transferred on the eve of the Revolution to the Sulpician Seminary at Bordeaux, he was privately ordained in 1792 and immediately sent to America in company with Abbés Matignon [*q.v.*], Richard [*q.v.*], and Cicquard. Arriving in Baltimore June 24, 1792, he said his first mass on July 8 and was assigned to the Maryland missions. Later he taught at Georgetown College and at St. Mary's Seminary, where his exacting course won the approbation of Bishop John Carroll [*q.v.*]. Recalled by his superior general, who was engaged in reorganizing the French seminaries, he returned to France in 1803 and taught in the theological schools of his community at Saint-Flour, Lyons, Aix, and Marseilles. In 1810, Bishop Concanen of New York, with the approval of Archbishop Carroll, proposed Maréchal as his coadjutor with the right of succession, but nothing came of this plan, presumably because of Sulpician disinclination for an episcopal appointment. When Napoleon withdrew the seminaries from Sulpician control however, Maréchal accepted a reappointment to St. Mary's Seminary, Baltimore (1812). Four years later he was nominated to the See of Philadelphia, but his name was withdrawn at his request. Soon Archbishop Neale [*q.v.*] required a coadjutor and sought Cheverus [*q.v.*], who asked to remain in Boston and urged the selection of Maréchal. Neale acquiesced, and Rome named the Abbé a titular bishop and coadjutor of Baltimore (July 24, 1817). Archbishop Neale died before the papal briefs arrived, however, and Maréchal was elevated to the archbishopric. Consecrated by Bishop Cheverus and Bishop Connolly of New York (Dec.

14, 1817), he zealously undertook the management of his vast diocese.

A mild but firm man, he conducted himself well though confronted with innumerable difficulties: controversies over trusteeism in Norfolk, Charleston, and Philadelphia; a bitter conflict with the Jesuits, over their old manorial estates, which could not be compromised during his rule; malicious suspicions of some Irish-born priests that he favored the French and was intent on establishing a French hierarchy; annoying, though futile, clerical appeals to civil authorities quite in conflict with canonical regularities; and wretched ecclesiastical intrigues intended to discredit him with the Propaganda. While the Archbishop may have been anti-Irish and somewhat anti-Jesuit, he was thoroughly American in sympathy, as men like Jefferson and Carroll readily appreciated. Despite the insistence of Bishop England of Charleston [*q.v.*], a leader of the Irish element, he refused to summon a national synod, apparently feeling that such a move might aggravate rather than settle the racial afflictions of the Church. Assiduous in visiting the diocese, he gained the warm regard of his people, and with the aid of Rev. Enoch Fenwick, he was able to collect sufficient funds for the completion of the Cathedral (1821), then the finest church in the United States, with a great organ and paintings donated by Louis XVIII and French prelates. Soon after his return from an ecclesiastical mission to Canada in 1826, realizing that an incipient disease would soon end his working days, he applied for a coadjutor. Death came before the appointment of his vicar general, James Whitfield, was actually made. Though regarded as a man of superior talents and broad intellectual acquirements, Maréchal left no writings save some remarkable pastoral letters, and a few unpublished manuscripts, a fact explained by his own words to Bishop England in reply to a request for material for the *Catholic Miscellany:* "Such unfortunately have been the austere rules of criticism printed on my institutions in literature . . . that they actually are a torment to myself on a thousand occasions" (Guilday, *John England,* I, 468). It was as a teacher and as an administrator in trying times that he merited contemporary renown.

[R. H. Clarke, *Lives of the Deceased Bishops of the Cath. Ch. in the U. S.,* vol. I (1872); Peter Guilday, *The Life and Times of John Carroll* (1922), *The Life and Times of John England* (1927); J. G. Shea, *A Hist. of the Cath. Ch. in the U. S.,* vols. II, III (1888, 1890); Thos. Hughes, *Hist. of the Society of Jesus in North America* (1910); C. G. Herbermann, *The Sulpicians in the U. S.* (copr. 1916); *Am. Cath. Hist. Researches* (1884–1912), see index volumes and sketch in vol. XXVI (1909); M. J. Riordan, *Cathedral Records* (Baltimore, 1906); *Cath. Mag.,* Jan. 1845; *U. S. Cath. Almanac,* 1836; *Cath. Miscellany,* Feb. 16, 1828; "Diary of Archbishop Maréchal," in *Records Am. Cath. Hist. Soc.,* Dec. 1900.]
R. J. P.

MAREST, PIERRE GABRIEL (Oct. 14, 1662–Sept. 15, 1714), pioneer priest in Illinois, was a native of Laval, where he was baptized in the old Gothic cathedral, seat of the bishop's see. The family was a religious one and two sons entered the Jesuit order, Gabriel and Joseph, both to become missionaries in Canada. Gabriel entered his novitiate Oct. 1, 1681, at Paris, studied there and at Bourges, was instructor at Vannes, and in 1694, then thirty-two years old, was ordered to New France. When he arrived at Quebec, Iberville [*q.v.*] was just setting out on a buccaneering expedition to Hudson Bay and Marest was detailed as chaplain for the expedition, because, as he wrote, he knew no Indian language and could be better employed ministering to Canadians than to aborigines.

Marest has given a thrilling account of his experiences in Hudson Bay, of the cold and storms, of the attack on the English fort and its surrender, of the Indians who visited the post, of the death in his arms of the commander's young brother Chateauguay, and of the final departure of Iberville's fleet in September 1695, leaving Marest to minister to the men of the French garrison (*Jesuit Relations, post,* LXVI, 67–119). Not long after the vessels had gone, an English fleet swooped down on the post and carried the captured garrison off to England. There Marest experienced prison fare, but was shortly permitted to return to France, whence at the earliest opportunity he again set sail for Canada.

In 1698 he embarked on another long journey, this time to the interior of America, where Father Jacques Gravier [*q.v.*] needed reinforcement in the Illinois mission. Marest ministered to the Kaskaskia branch of the Illinois tribe, at first located on the upper Illinois River near the present Ottawa. In 1700 the Kaskaskia determined to remove to the Mississippi, having heard that a French colony had been founded near the mouth of that great river. Marest, learning that his old leader Iberville was the founder of the colony, did not discourage his neophytes' removal. They spent the first years on the west side of the stream at the Rivière des Pères, now a part of the city of St. Louis, then, in April 1703, they crossed to the east side and formed a village on a river called for them the Kaskaskia. At this mission Marest passed the remainder of his life, except for a journey to Mackinac to consult with his Jesuit brother Joseph, whom he opportunely met en route at the

St. Joseph mission. On his return he promised the Peoria to continue their mission; but his Kaskaskia converts and his colleagues would not consent to his removal. His mission was one of the most successful in North America; in 1707 he estimated that all the Kaskaskia, numbering over two thousand, were Christians. He is said to have been an accomplished Indian linguist, but none of his manuscripts has survived. His letters are well composed, artless, and sincere. He was buried in the chapel of his mission of the Immaculate Conception; but on Dec. 18, 1727, his remains were removed to the new church just finished at Kaskaskia.

[R. G. Thwaites, ed., *The Jesuit Relations and Allied Documents,* vols. LXIV, LXV, LXVI (1900), LXXI (1901); G. J. Garraghan, "Earliest Settlements of the Illinois Country," in *Cath. Hist. Rev.,* Jan. 1930; T. J. Campbell, *Pioneer Priests of North America,* vol. III (1911).] L. P. K.

MARETZEK, MAX (June 28, 1821–May 14, 1897), opera impresario, conductor, composer, was born in Brünn, Moravia. He studied music and composition in his youth with the Viennese composer, I. X. Seyfried, a piano pupil of Mozart and conductor at the An der Wien theatre. When he was twenty-one his three-act opera *Hamlet* was produced in Brünn. In the year following he gave up a theatrical conductorship in Agram, then the capital of Croatia, to go to Paris, where he dedicated a series of songs to the Duchess de Nemours and wrote ballet music for Grisi and Grahn. In 1844 he went to Her Majesty's Theatre in London as assistant conductor to Balfe, and in 1847 his ballet "Les Génies du Globe" opened the season at Drury Lane in conjunction with *Lucia di Lammermoor.* In 1848 he emigrated to New York as the conductor of the Italian Opera Company at the Astor Place Opera House, then under the management of Edward R. Fry. When the company failed in 1849, Maretzek reopened the same house as impresario-conductor. Thereafter, until 1879, he was active as an impresario and producer of Italian opera at the Astor Place and Grand opera houses and, notably, at the old Academy of Music, making occasional tours with his company through the United States and beyond. He opened the new Academy of Music in 1867 with Minnie Hauk in Gounod's *Romeo et Juliette.* In 1879 his three-act American opera, *Sleepy Hollow,* was given there.

Maretzek was the only impresario who, after others had failed, managed to establish Italian opera in New York as a permanent institution for a term of years. As he himself says (*Crotchets and Quavers,* p. iv): "During the first three years of my residence in New York, I carried out four regular seasons of Italian opera. This alone was more than anyone had done in this quarter of the world, since Christopher Columbus first discovered it." The first impresario in this country who conducted his own operatic performances, he gave grand opera at prices ranging from fifty cents to two dollars, and his career was marked by the production of many novelties and the introduction to the American public of many notable singers.

Maretzek, "the Magnificent." as he was familiarly known, retired from his managerial activities with the advent of James Henry Mapleson and devoted himself to teaching singing, coaching operatic aspirants, and contributing musical sketches to American, French, and German periodicals. A "golden jubilee concert" given in his honor at the Metropolitan Opera House (Feb. 12, 1889) testified to the esteem in which he was held by his associates. He died of heart disease at his home in Pleasant Plains, Staten Island, N. Y., in his seventy-sixth year. His two books of autobiographic reminiscences, *Crotchets and Quavers: or, Revelations of an Opera Manager in America* (1855), and *"Sharps and Flats": A Sequel to "Crotchets and Quavers"* (1890), a "serio-comic history of opera in America for the past forty years, with reminiscences and anecdotes," offer vivid pictures of operatic life in New York during the fifties, sixties, and seventies of the nineteenth century, and of the adventurous side of touring with an opera company in Cuba and Mexico in those days.

[Waldemar Rieck, "Max Maretzek, Impresario, Conductor and Composer," *Musical Courier,* June 22, 1922; Robt. Grau, article in the *Musical Leader,* Dec. 26, 1912; Clara Louise Kellogg, *Memoirs of an Am. Prima Donna* (1913); H. E. Krehbiel, *Chapters of Opera* (1908); *Music,* Sept. 1897; G. C. D. Odell, *Annals of the N. Y. Stage,* vols. V and VI (1931); *N. Y. Times,* May 15, 1897.] F. H. M.

MARGOLIS, MAX LEOPOLD (Oct. 15, 1866–Apr. 2, 1932), scholar, teacher, author, the son of Isaac and Hinde Bernstein Margolis, was born in Merech, Vilna, Russia. His father was a Rabbi and a descendant of the great Hebrew scholar, Lipmann Halevi Heller. Margolis was educated at Merech and Warsaw, 1873–83; graduated from the Leibnitz Gymnasium, Berlin, in 1889, in which year he came to America and entered Columbia University. He received the degrees of M.A. in 1890 and Ph.D. in 1891, and spent another year at Columbia in further postgraduate studies. He was essentially a philologian and devoted himself to the whole cycle of the Semitic languages. He also had a good knowledge of Latin and Greek. He began his teaching in 1892 at the Hebrew Union College,

Cincinnati, Ohio, where he was assistant professor of Hebrew and Biblical exegesis until 1897. He then was called to the University of California, where he was assistant professor of Semitic languages and literature from 1897 to 1898 and associate professor from 1898 to 1905. He returned to the Hebrew Union College, holding the professorship of Biblical exegesis from 1905 to 1907, and in 1909 was called to the chair of Biblical philology at the Dropsie College for Hebrew and Cognate Learning, retaining that position until his death. In 1924–25 he held the post of annual professor at the American School for Oriental Research in Jerusalem and also lectured at the Hebrew University in Jerusalem that year. In the various institutions in which he gave instruction, he was known as an exact and inspiring teacher and has left many devoted disciples in various parts of the world.

In 1908 Margolis was invited to become the secretary of a board of editors engaged in a Jewish translation into the English language of the Holy Scriptures and had added to this secretaryship the post of editor-in-chief. He labored with his colleagues from 1908 to 1914 and the translation was published in 1917. He was one of the editors of the *Journal of the American Oriental Society* from 1922 to 1932 and an editor of the *Journal of Biblical Literature* from 1914 to 1921. He began his production of scientific publications with two works, published in the early nineties, having to do with the study of the Talmud. Then he principally devoted himself to grammatical work in pure Hebrew and later took up studies in the Greek Old Testament. Some of the most useful and best known of his many works were his *Manual of the Aramaic Language of the Babylonian Talmud* (1910), of great use to students; *A History of the Jewish People* (1927), written in collaboration with Alexander Marx, a remarkably accurate study; *The Holy Scriptures with Commentary: Micah* (1908); *The Story of Bible Translations* (1917); and *The Hebrew Scriptures in the Making* (1922). For a long period of years he had set his heart on the study of the Greek text of the Book of Joshua. Toward this end he published many preliminary papers and before his death there appeared the first part of *The Book of Joshua in Greek* (1931), of which the Second Part followed. This was a most laborious undertaking and was called by Professor James A. Montgomery "the monument to the scholarship of Margolis." Margolis was short, rather solidly built, possessed of few recreations, a man of wide reading. When he wished to change the current in his thought in later years, he read astronomy. He was one of the very foremost Biblical scholars of his period—as a grammarian, as a textual critic, and as an exegete—and a teacher of the very first rank. He was married on June 20, 1906, to Evelyn Kate Aronson, by whom he had three children.

[David J. Galter, "Max L. Margolis—Distinguished Am. Scholar and Author," the *Jewish Exponent*, Apr. 8, 1932; *Who's Who in America*, 1930–31; *Jour. Am. Oriental Soc.*, June 1932; unpublished addresses delivered at a memorial meeting for Max Leopold Margolis by James A. Montgomery, Simon Greenberg, and Cyrus Adler, May 9, 1932; Alexander Marx, "Max Leopold Margolis—In Memoriam," *Proc. of the Rabbinical Assembly of the Jewish Theol. Sem. of America*, vol. IV, pp. 368–79.]

C. A.

MARIGNY, BERNARD (Oct. 28, 1785–Feb. 3, 1868), Louisiana planter, official and social leader, was born in New Orleans and was christened Bernard Xavier Philippe de Marigny de Mandeville. He was the son of Pierre Enguerrand Philippe de Mandeville, Écuyer Sieur de Marigny, Chevalier de St. Louis, whose grandfather, François Philippe de Marigny, the scion of a noble Norman house, was ordered to Canada as an infantry officer in 1709 and was later transferred to Louisiana as *"commandant des troupes,"* where he assisted Bienville in the founding of New Orleans. Bernard's mother was Jeanne Marie d'Estréhan, the daughter of a rich planter, who married Pierre Marigny when he was an officer in the Spanish colonial army in Louisiana. As the value of lands and slaves increased they became the richest family in the colony. Partly owing to Bernard's antipathy to study, and partly to his father's theory that a thorough training in fire arms, fencing, and horsemanship was the most important part of a gentleman's education, the boy did not have more than a common-school knowledge of the three R's.

In 1798 Louis Philippe, Duc d'Orléans, and his two brothers came to New Orleans and were royally entertained by Bernard's father. To prove his hospitality further he lent them a large sum of money on their departure. Two years later Bernard's father died, leaving him an orphan at sixteen. The boy was so wild that his kinsman and guardian, De Lino de Chalmette, finally sent him to England. Here he continued his dissipations, spending much time at Almack's playing "Hazard," a dice game then the rage at the coffee houses. When he returned he taught it to his Creole companions, and the Americans dubbed it the game of the "Johnny Crapauds," their nickname for Creoles. Soon this was shortened to "Crapauds," and finally "craps." Marigny became more and more fantastically extravagant until he was forced to subdivide and dispose of his plantation below New Orleans.

and when he opened up a roadway and sold off the lots on it to pay some pressing gambling debts, he named it Craps Street. Near it was "Rue de l'Amour" on which it was said he housed his mistresses in separate cottages; quite logically Good Children Street came next.

In 1803 when Louisiana was retroceded to France by Spain and later transferred to the United States, Marigny was present at both these historic ceremonies as an aide to the French envoy Pierre de Laussat, and then was appointed aide to General Wilkinson. His political career began with his election to the territorial legislature in 1810, and from then on until 1838 he served continuously in either the upper or lower house of the legislature of his state, and was in addition a member of the convention of 1812 which drafted its first constitution, and of the second one in 1845 which modified it. In 1815 when General Pakenham and his English forces marched on New Orleans, Marigny was chairman of the committee of defense of the House of Representatives and indirectly persuaded Gen. Andrew Jackson to enlist Jean Lafitte and his pirates in the city's defense.

After Louis Philippe had been on the throne of France for some few years, Bernard de Marigny, who had squandered most of his fortune, crossed the ocean to collect the money his father had lent the monarch when as the Duc d'Orléans he visited New Orleans. Louis Philippe received him cordially, made him a guest at the palace, and even asked his advice about the recognition of Texas by France, but he was deaf to every suggestion of repayment, and all Marigny got was the gift of a gold snuff-box and the promise of a cadetship at St. Cyr for his son Mandeville. Bitterly disappointed he returned to New Orleans and in the late forties his friends had him appointed registrar of conveyances to keep him from starving. He lost this position through politics in 1853. In order to make money he wrote a small history entitled *Thoughts upon the Foreign Policy of the United-States* (1854) and the House of Representatives passed a bill purchasing a thousand copies each of the French and English editions.

This remarkable old Creole, who had *"tutoyied"* a king of France and who had lived through the conflicting influences of the five changes in the flag flying over Louisiana, stubbed his toe on the foot-scraper of his humble cottage and, in falling, struck his head. He never regained consciousness and died on Feb. 3, 1868. In addition to his little history Marigny's published works include a few political pamphlets and his *Réflexions sur la Campagne du Général André Jackson en Louisiane* (1848). On May 28, 1804, Marigny was married to Mary Ann Jones, who died after four years, leaving two sons. Within a year he married again—Anne Mathilde, daughter of a former Spanish intendant of Louisiana, Juan Ventura Morales. Two sons and three daughters were the children of this marriage.

[E. L. Tinker, *Les Écrits de Langue Française en Louisiane au XIXe Siècle* (1932); *Bernard Marigny to his Fellow Citizens* (1853); Alcée Fortier, ed., *Louisiana* (1914), vol. II; W. H. Sparks, *The Memories of Fifty Years* (1870); Grace King, *Creole Families of New Orleans* (1921); J. S. Whitaker, *Sketches of Life and Character in La.* (1847); J. W. Cruzat, "Biog. and Geneal. Notes Concerning the Family of Philippe de Mandeville, Écuyer Sieur de Marigny," *La. Hist. Soc. Pubs.*, vol. V (1911); *La. Hist. Quart.*, July 1931; *New Orleans American*, Aug. 29, 1915.] E. L. T.

MARION, FRANCIS (*c.* 1732–Feb. 26, 1795), Revolutionary general, was born probably in St. John's Parish, Berkeley County, S. C. The date of his birth is indicated only by the fact that he died in his sixty-third year. He was the grandson of Benjamin Marion, a Huguenot and a native of Poitou, who came to the province about 1690, and the fifth and youngest son of Gabriel, who married Esther Cordes. Francis spent his youth near Georgetown, his parents' modest property providing him with a country-school education and a small inheritance. About 1755 he returned to St. John's and in 1773 acquired Pond Bluff on the Santee, four miles below Eutaw Springs, where he established himself as a planter. In 1759 and 1761 he served in campaigns against the Cherokees. He was elected to the Provincial Congress of 1775 from his parish, and when that body provided for two regiments of troops, was made a captain in the 2nd Regiment. After five years of service in and near Charleston he commanded this regiment in the assault on Savannah, October 1779. He was then a lieutenant-colonel in the Continental service. A badly injured ankle saved him from capture with the garrison of Charleston seven months later, for with others unfit for duty he was ordered to the country before the surrender. At Camden he again escaped disaster, since the day before the battle he had been detailed by Gates to cut the British communications with Charleston, and, evidently, to take command of the militia between the Santee and Pedee.

The destruction of Gates's army put upon the militia for the second time the entire burden of the war in South Carolina, and for five months Marion could draw upon only the resources of his own district. He was thus placed in a position of peculiar perils and possibilities. In the center of his territory was the strongly Whig population of Williamsburg. From this base, attacks could be made upon Georgetown, or upon the main line of British communications where the road from Camden to Charleston crossed the Santee. On the other hand, there were strong British posts on three sides, and the Loyalists of the Pedee region on the fourth. The militia at times drove him to despair, for with the state's authority in eclipse they came and went at will; sometimes he gathered several hundred for an attack, again his force melted away to a handful. His patience, tact, and military skill, however, enabled him to use these troops as he could not have used regular soldiers. If the odds were favorable the British faced a formidable foe, if the situation changed they pursued a shadow. His first exploit was the release of a party of American prisoners taken at Camden, and a week later he dispersed a force of two hundred Tories on the Pedee. Twice in the next four months he was forced to retire from his district, twice he failed in attacks on Georgetown, but he won three important field assignments, and Tarleton could do no more than drive him to the swamps.

His work in disrupting the British communications and preventing the organization of the Loyalists joined with the battle of King's Mountain and other developments in the Piedmont to bring about the turn of the war in the South. In January 1781 Greene appeared, but retreated immediately, drawing Cornwallis after him. Behind them the reviving Whigs and alarmed British fought with redoubled vigor. Marion now had somewhat larger forces, but only by a masterly series of movements and three hard-fought engagements did he survive a determined attempt to destroy him made by several British detachments. He was in sore need of the rescue which Lee brought when Greene returned to the state. The recovery of South Carolina now began, and as brigadier-general of the militia Marion was brought out of his district into larger and more aggressive movements. Despite his jealousy of authority he was generally prompt and faithful in his cooperation, and his part in two important raids and in the capture of several posts further enhanced his reputation. He commanded the militia in the battle of Eutaw Springs, and from that time to the evacuation of Charleston was Greene's chief dependence for outpost duty.

The last year of Marion's army service was interrupted by a term in the state Senate, to which he was elected in 1781 and again in 1782 and 1784. The war left him little but his land, and in March 1784 the legislature, in gratitude for his "eminent services," provided him with the command of Fort Johnson, one of the harbor defenses, at a salary of £500 a year. After his marriage in 1786 to his cousin, Mary Esther Videau, a wealthy and elderly spinster, his salary was reduced to five shillings a day, but he continued his dual rôle of planter and commandant until 1790. He sat in the state constitutional convention of 1790, and the next year was elected to the state Senate to fill an unexpired term. He died at his home in St. John's in February 1795, and was buried at Belle Isle, St. Stephen's. The personal as well as the soldierly qualities of the plain little man endeared him to his contemporaries. Through a process begun by his friend and most trusted officer, Col. Peter Horry, who in his age aspired to turn author, he became an epic figure, and as the "Swamp Fox" has a distinctive place in Revolutionary legend.

[Horry apparently wrote his life of Marion without access to the General's papers, which were afterwards given to him (*S. C. Hist. and Geneal. Mag.*, Apr. 1924, p. 97). This biography appears to be the manuscript which he turned over to Mason L. Weems [*q.v.*]. The result was the *Life of Gen. Francis Marion* (Phila., Mathew Carey, 1809). Horry seems never to have recovered his manuscript. A memoir of his own career and the Marion papers formed the basis of the *Sketch of the Life of Brig. Gen. Francis Marion* (Charleston, 1821) by W. D. James, and *The Life of Francis Marion* (N. Y., 1844) by William Gilmore Simms [*q.v.*]. Comparison of these, together with Horry's indignant letters to Weems (P. L. Ford, *Mason Locke Weems*, a bibliography, ed. by E. E. F. Skeel, 3 vols., 1929), his manuscript diary for the years 1812–13, and his marginal notes on the first edition, leads to the conclusion that the manuscript which Horry turned over to Weems was a memoir full of anecdotes and interspersed with letters; that Weems omitted the letters, garbled a number of statements of fact, introduced imaginary speeches, and dressed up Horry's style—the process, however, leaving the authorship distinctly Horry's. Sources include the Marion letters, published in R. W. Gibbes, *Doc. Hist. of the Am. Revolution . . . in 1781 and 1782* (1853) and . . . *1776–1782* (1857). *The State Records of N. C.*, vols. XIV (1896) and XV (1898); and the manuscript Journals of the Senate of S. C. *The Southern and Western Monthly Mag. and Rev.* (Charleston), Mar.–Aug. 1845, has the only reliable data on Marion's family and youth. See also *S. C. Hist. and Geneal. Mag., passim.* Horry's diary and the annotated copy of the first edition of the Weems-Horry *Marion* are in possession of the Guignard family, "Still Hopes," Columbia, S. C. The inscription on Marion's tomb gives the day of his death as Feb. 27, but the *City Gazette, or Daily Advertiser* (Charleston), of Tuesday, Mar. 3, 1795, says he died on "Tuesday last," *i.e.* Feb. 26.]

R. L. M—r.

MARKHAM, CHARLES HENRY (May 22, 1861–Nov. 24, 1930), railway president, was the son of Daniel Markham, farmer, and Mary (Reddan), of County Clare, Ireland. His parents emigrated to the United States, living first in Clarksville, Tenn., where Charles was born, and subsequently in Addison, N. Y., where he attended the public schools until he was fourteen years old. He then left school to earn his own way. Three years later he started west, and in 1881 began his first railway work as a section laborer on the Atchison, Topeka, & Santa Fé at Dodge City, Kan. This was the beginning of a career which he was to follow, with a single interruption, until his death.

Leaving the Santa Fé after a few months, he went to work for the Southern Pacific at Deming, N. Mex., as a station helper, shoveling coal for locomotives. He stayed at Deming for six years, finally becoming baggage master. For the next ten years he served as agent for the Southern Pacific successively at Lordsburg, N. Mex.; Benson, Ariz.; Reno, Nev.; and Fresno, Cal. At Fresno he was also in charge of the solicitation of freight and passenger traffic for a district, and worked out an effective carloading plan which attracted the attention of Julius Kruttschnitt, then general manager of the road, who gave him other efficiency problems to solve. In 1897 he was sent to the Willamette Valley of Oregon as general freight and passenger agent of the Oregon lines of the Southern Pacific, charged particularly with promoting agricultural development. In 1901 he was transferred to San Francisco as assistant freight traffic manager, and three months later was elected vice-president of the Houston & Texas Central Railroad at Houston, in which position he was executive head of the Harriman lines in Texas. Early in 1904 he returned to San Francisco to become general manager of the Southern Pacific Company, and three months later was elected vice-president and general manager.

The rapidity of this series of promotions would have satisfied most men, yet Markham, toward the end of 1904, temporarily left railroading to accept the position of vice-president of the J. M. Guffey Petroleum Company at Beaumont, Tex., because this position offered him better opportunities than the railway business for the moment could afford. The change was one of executive responsibility only, since he had no financial interest in any oil property. In 1910 he became president of the Gulf Refining Company, the Gulf Pipe Line Company, and other properties embraced in the Mellon oil interests in Texas, Oklahoma, and Louisiana. In January 1911 he returned to railroad work as president of the Illinois Central Railroad Company; in February of the same year he was also elected president of the Central of Georgia Railway Company and the Ocean Steamship Company of Savannah, both subsidiaries of the Illinois Central; and in April 1914, he became chairman of the boards of directors of the two subsidiary companies. These positions he held until May 1918. Meanwhile, after the entrance of the United States into the World War, he entered the service of the federal Railroad Administration, and acted as regional director of the railroads comprising the Southern Region, with headquarters at Atlanta, Ga., from Jan. 1, 1918, to June 1, 1918, and as regional director of the railroads comprising the Allegheny Region, with headquarters at Philadelphia, from June 1, 1918, to Oct. 1, 1919. On completion of his war service he resumed the presidency of the Illinois Central and the chairmanship of the boards of the Central of Georgia and the Ocean Steamship Company, continuing in active service until Sept. 15, 1926, when illness compelled him to resign his office of president, accepting the less onerous position of chairman of the board of the Illinois Central. He died four years later at his winter home, Altadena, Cal. On Feb. 18, 1884, he had married Anna Eliza Smith, a native of Syracuse, N. Y. His wife died on Sept. 18, 1921. There were three children, of whom only one son survived him.

While Markham never attained great wealth, yet his rapid advance from the position of baggage master on the Southern Pacific in 1887 to that of president of the Illinois Central Railroad in 1911 is sufficient evidence that he possessed unusual executive ability. His record as president, moreover, bore out the promise of his earlier years. Upon his own system his administration was distinguished by a vigorous program of expansion and improvement, as well as by a determined effort to build up the territory in which the Illinois Central operated. The most spectacular part of this program, and perhaps that most generally associated with Markham's name, was the beginning of the electrification and modernization of his company's Chicago terminal, including the construction of a great classification and transfer yard south of Chicago and the first steps in the development of the valuable air rights over Illinois Central property in downtown Chicago. Outside of his activity in improving facilities and service upon his own system Markham was very generally known as a leader in developing improved relations between the railroad industry and the public. He devoted much time and thought to this aspect of the railroad problem, and is credited with successful pioneering work in a field now generally recognized to be important.

[*Who's Who in America*, 1930–31; *The Biog. Dir. of the Railway Officials of America* (1913); *Poor's Manual of the Railroads of the U. S.*, 1901–24; *Railway Age*, Nov. 29, 1930; *Chicago Daily Tribune*, Nov. 25, 1930; correspondence with Markham's family and friends.]

S. D.

MARKHAM, WILLIAM (*c.* 1635–June 12, 1704 o.s.), colonial governor of Pennsylvania and Delaware, was born in England about 1635.

His father was probably William Markham of Ollerton, Nottinghamshire, and his mother was a sister of Admiral Sir William Penn. Since he is called Captain or Colonel Markham in the provincial records, it is believed that he was at one time an officer in the English army. He received a commission as deputy governor of Pennsylvania from his cousin, William Penn, on Apr. 10, 1681, with instructions to assert the proprietor's authority over existing settlements, appoint a council, organize a judicial system, commission sheriffs and justices of the peace, and settle the question of the boundary between Pennsylvania and Maryland. Arriving at Upland (now Chester) in July 1681, he presided over the first provincial council on Aug. 3, reorganized the court, and joined Nathaniel Allen and John Bezar in selecting the site for the city of Philadelphia. He also conferred with Lord Baltimore about the boundary and, on July 15, 1682, purchased from the Indians the site of Pennsbury Manor on the Delaware River. He became an ordinary member of the council when Penn arrived in the province in October 1682, but was almost immediately sent to England to represent the proprietor's interests in the boundary dispute.

He returned to Pennsylvania shortly after Penn's departure (1684) and served as provincial secretary from May 1685 to March 1691, deputy governor of the lower counties (Delaware) from March 1691 to April 1693, and lieutenant-governor or governor of both the province and the lower counties from April 1693 to December 1699. During the latter part of this period, he came into conflict with Edward Randolph, His Majesty's surveyor general of the customs, and with Robert Quary, the judge of the court of vice-admiralty. As a result of their complaints that he harbored pirates and did not enforce the acts of trade and navigation, the Privy Council ordered his removal from office (Aug. 31, 1699). The dispute was finally settled in December 1699, when Penn returned to the province and superseded Markham as chief executive. At Penn's request, Markham was appointed register general of Pennsylvania in 1703, but his title was disputed by John Moore [*q.v.*], the former incumbent, and before the case was decided he died, in Philadelphia. He was survived by his wife, Johannah Markham, and by a daughter.

During the greater part of Markham's career in Pennsylvania, he was Penn's secretary and attended to his private business. He was not as learned or as able a man as James Logan [*q.v.*], who succeeded him as the representative of proprietary interests, but he was devoted to Penn and he worked hard to advance the welfare of the colony. The value of his services was not fully appreciated by the colonists, partly because he represented the prerogative influence in the government and partly because he was a member of the Church of England and could not accommodate himself to the Quaker point of view. His most influential opponents were Thomas and David Lloyd [*qq.v.*], the leaders of the democratic or anti-proprietary party. He opposed the Lloyds in their controversy with deputy-governor Blackwell in 1689 and he also had a dispute with David Lloyd and the Assembly over the question of constitutional reform, which was complicated by a demand for an appropriation to defend the frontiers of New York against the French. A compromise was finally reached in 1696: Markham's "Frame of Government" was adopted (Nov. 7, 1696) and money was voted "for food and raiment" for the Indian allies of New York who had suffered from the French attack. Although Markham was probably the chief author of the "Frame of Government," he does not deserve any special credit for its liberal character. On the other hand, he should not be blamed too severely for his failure to enforce the acts of trade and navigation, because the Quaker Assembly would not sanction the establishment of an adequate police force.

[Penn MSS., Hist. Soc. of Pa.; *Memoirs of the Hist. Soc. of Pa.*, vol. X (1872); *Minutes of the Provincial Council of Pa.*, vols. I, II (1852); "Papers of the Governors," *Pa. Archives*, 4 ser. I (1900); Samuel Hazard, *Annals of Pa. . . . 1609–1682* (1850); J. B. Linn, *Charter to William Penn and Laws of the Province of Pa.* (1879), Appendix B; Robert Proud, *The Hist. of Pa. 1681–1742* (2 vols., 1797–99); W. C. Armor, *Lives of the Governors of Pa.* (1872); W. R. Shepherd, *Hist. of Proprietary Govt. in Pa.* (1896); Isaac Sharpless, *A Quaker Experiment in Govt.* (1898); C. C. Hall, *Narratives of Early Md.* (1910); W. T. Root, *The Relations of Pa. with the British Govt., 1696–1765* (1912).]

W. R. S.

MARKOE, ABRAHAM (July 2, 1727–Aug. 28, 1806), capitalist, patriot, was born on the island of Santa Cruz (or St. Croix), one of the Virgin Islands, then subject to the Crown of Denmark. His grandfather, Pierre Marcou, a Huguenot, had accompanied Count Créqui from France to the Danish West Indies before the revocation of the Edict of Nantes. There he acquired one of the largest sugar plantations on the island of Santa Cruz, and became colonial governor of that settlement. His son Pierre, who seems to have been the first to change the family name to Markoe, married Elizabeth Farrell, and Abraham Markoe was their son. He inherited the rich plantations, traded with Europe and the American colonies, and in 1751 married a widow,

Elizabeth (Kenny) Rogers, who bore him two sons, Peter [*q.v.*], and Abraham. About the year 1770, his wife having died a few years before, he went to Philadelphia, where he established a residence. On Dec. 16, 1773, he was married in Christ Church to Elizabeth Baynton, daughter of John Baynton, a Philadelphia merchant. Seven children were born to this union.

Abraham Markoe became a prominent figure in the business and social life of Philadelphia. From the first rumblings of the Revolution he took the side of the Patriots, and was the founder of the first volunteer military association in what is now the United States. This was the Philadelphia Light Horse, now known as the First Troop, Philadelphia City Cavalry, which was organized Nov. 17, 1774. It was composed of gentlemen of fortune, who provided all their own equipment and paid for their own maintenance. The first active duty of the Troop, of which Markoe was the first captain, was to escort General Washington as far as New York, when, on June 21, 1775, he started for Cambridge to take command of the Continental Army. The standard of the Philadelphia Light Horse was presented to it by Markoe, and although there exists a bill from John Folwell for "drawing and designing the colours for the Light Horse," dated Sept. 16, 1775, Markoe is generally credited with having suggested the design. In the upper left-hand corner of the flag, in what is known as the canton, are thirteen stripes of alternate blue and silver, supposed to be the "earliest instance of the thirteen stripes being used upon an American banner" (Preble, *post,* p. 181). Markoe resigned his command early in the year 1776 because the government of Denmark, of which he was still a subject, had issued an edict of neutrality, and disobedience on his part would have imperilled his family and rendered his estates in Santa Cruz liable to confiscation. He never lost his interest in the cause of the colonies, however, and was present at the battle of Brandywine in October 1777. During the British occupation of Philadelphia he retired to Lancaster, Pa., but returned to the capital in time to witness the evacuation of that city by the King's troops. In 1782–83 he acquired by patents from the state of Pennsylvania a block of ground now bounded by Ninth, Tenth, Market, and Chestnut Streets, in Philadelphia. Upon this ground he erected a mansion, which was one of the wonders of the city being the first house to use marble lintels over its windows. He died in Philadelphia and was buried in Christ Church graveyard.

[C. W. Baird, *Hist. of the Huguenot Emigration to America* (1885), vol. I; *Book of the First Troop, Phila. City Cavalry* (1915), ed. by J. L. Wilson; *Extracts from the Diary of Christopher Marshall* (1877), ed. by William Duane; G. H. Preble, *Our Flag; Origin and Progress of the Flag of the U. S.* (1872); J. F. Watson, *Annals of Phila.* (3 vols., 1884); F. W. Leach, "Old Phila. Families—XVI: Markoe," *North American* (Phila.), Sept. 22, 1907; Joseph Jackson, *Market Street, Phila.* (1918); *Poulson's Am. Daily Advertiser,* Aug. 30, 1806.]

J. J.

MARKOE, PETER (*c.* 1752–Jan. 30, 1792), poet and dramatist, was the eldest son of Abraham Markoe [*q.v.*] by his first wife, Elizabeth Rogers (*née* Kenny). He was born on the island of Santa Cruz (or St. Croix) in the Danish West Indies, probably between Jan. 31 and Feb. 16, 1752, though at his matriculation at Pembroke College, Oxford, Feb. 17, 1767, his age was given as sixteen. The statement that he was educated at Trinity College, Dublin, appears to be without foundation. On May 29, 1775, he was admitted to Lincoln's Inn. It is usually said that he was in England during the period of the Revolution, but in 1775 he is listed as captain of Light Horse, 3rd Battalion, Philadelphia City Militia (*Pennsylvania Archives,* 6 ser. I, 183; 2 ser. XIII, 556). The Danish decree of neutrality (1775) which caused his father to resign from the Light Horse, may have prevented Peter Markoe's further participation in the war. It is possible that he returned to Santa Cruz, perhaps more than once, to transact business for his father after the latter settled in Philadelphia. (One of his brothers was drowned on such a trip.) Among his poems are "Verses Addressed to His Excellency General Van Roepstorf on his arrival in St. Croix, 1771" and "To Her Excellency Lady Clausen, of St. Croix, on Her Birth-Day, 1780." In 1784 he published in Philadelphia *The Patriot Chief,* a tragedy, the scene of which is laid in Lydia. It was offered to Lewis Hallam [*q.v.*], manager of the American Company, but rejected, and apparently was never produced. It called forth, however, an Epistle by Markoe's friend, Col. John Parke, "To Mr. Peter Markoe, on His Excellent Tragedy Called The Patriot Chief" (in Parke's *Horace,* 1786), in which the author urged Markoe to treat native themes and native heroes. On May 17, 1785, he received a lottery warrant for 500 acres of land in Northumberland County, Pa. His name appears in the muster roll of the Philadelphia militia from 1786 to 1789. In 1787 (May 28; cf. *Pennsylvania Packet and Daily Advertiser* of that date) he published by subscription a volume of *Miscellaneous Poems,* "many of them" according to the Preface, "written when I was very young." The following January (1788) he published *The Times,* a satirical poem full of allusions to local personages, only a few of whom can now be identified. Part of it had previously appeared "in one of the public papers" (Preface), and the whole was republished in July (printed for Prichard & Hall) with the addition of several hundred lines. A contemporary review of the poem in Noah Webster's *American Magazine* (September 1788) resents Markoe's criticism of Joel Barlow but adds: "It is but justice to Mr. Markoe to declare, that we think him one of the first poetic geniuses in America." In 1790 he published *The Reconciliation: or, the Triumph of Nature,* one of the earliest comic operas written in America. Charles Evans (*American Bibliography,* VI, 132, 213) attributes to Markoe *The Algerine Spy in Pennsylvania: or, Letters Written by a Native of Algiers on the Affairs of the United States in America, from the Close of the Year 1783 to the Meeting of the Convention* (1787) and *The Storm, a Poem: Descriptive of the Late Tempest, Which Raged with Such Fury Throughout the Southern Parts of North-America, in July, 1788,* issued with the Philadelphia edition of William Falconer's *The Shipwreck,* published in 1788.

Markoe died in Philadelphia, in his fortieth year according to family tradition, and was buried in the graveyard of Christ Church in that city. He seems to have had a reputation for conviviality not to be assumed from the sentiments expressed in his verse. He managed the couplet with ease but without distinction. That he was interested in other arts than literature is to be inferred from the design for a frontispiece which he contributed to Col. John Parke's volume, *The Lyrical Works of Horace Translated into English Verse; to Which Are Added a Number of Original Poems* (1786).

[*Pa. Archives,* esp. 6 ser.; register of Christ Church, Phila.; *Dunlap's Am. Daily Advertiser,* Jan. 31, 1792; Charles Evans, *Am. Bibliog.,* vols. VI, VII (1910–12), which confuses the two editions of *The Times*; F. W. Leach, "Old Philadelphia Families: XVI—Markoe," in *North American* (Phila.), Sept. 22, 1907; A. H. Quinn, *A Hist. of the Am. Drama, from the Beginning to the Civil War* (1923); family papers in the possession of Miss Emily Rivinus, Philadelphia, and Mr. Francis Hartman Markoe, New York.] A. C. B.

MARKS, AMASA ABRAHAM (Apr. 3, 1825–July 19, 1905), inventor, manufacturer, descended from Mordecai Marks, a native of London, England, who died in Derby, Conn., in 1771, was the son of Levi Merwin and Esther Tolles (Tuttle) Marks. He was born in Waterbury, Conn., where his father had established and operated a hauling business between Waterbury and New Haven. He attended the public schools in Waterbury until he was sixteen years old and then joined his father for a year or two, after which he went to farming. At the age of twenty, although he was without experience, he began a small wood-working business in New Haven. By some means he secured a large order for making hubs for carriages and wagons, then rented a mill, hired an expert wood-turner, and succeeded in filling the order with entire satisfaction. At the same time by close observation and practice he mastered the art of wood turning and for about six years carried on a fairly successful business. Shortly after his marriage on Aug. 22, 1850, to Lucy Ann Platt, a second cousin, he transferred his shop to New York.

Two years later he formed a partnership with his elder brother David, a dentist who had given considerable thought to improvements of artificial limbs. Upon the granting of a patent (No. 10,611) to David B. Marks on Mar. 7, 1854, the brothers began with enthusiasm to manufacture and introduce the new products. After several years during which they attained very little recognition, David withdrew from the partnership to resume the practice of his profession, but Amasa, with characteristic tenacity of purpose, carried on alone. He improved the mechanism of the artificial leg in 1856 by providing for knee articulation as well as ankle and toe movements, and further improved the ankle joint in 1858, but still the business made little progress. About 1861 he began to use rubber in the construction of artificial hands and feet, and after two years of active research, on Dec. 1, 1863, was granted Patent No. 40,763. The radical change in artificial limbs which this invention effected was the elimination of all mechanism from the calf of the leg down. Knee articulation was retained, but both ankle and toe movements were eliminated. In 1864 the Federal government awarded Marks a contract for furnishing artificial limbs to the disabled soldiers and sailors of the Civil War, and in a comparatively short time his products were used in practically every part of the world. He personally directed all phases of his rapidly expanding business during the next fifteen years and at the same time conducted experimental work looking toward the further improvement of his products. Eventually a rubber foot consisting of alternate layers of rubber and canvas was perfected which gave the toes greater resilience and forced the foot to return to its proper shape with more certainty. Shortly after securing Patent No. 234,596 (Nov. 16, 1880) for this improvement, Marks retired, leaving his business in the hands of his sons. He then took up his permanent residence in Sound Beach, Conn., where he had owned a country estate since 1872. Here he interested himself in local affairs, particularly in the improvement of schools. For his inventions he received awards in 1859, 1865, 1867, and 1870–78, from the American Institute, New York City. In 1889 he was the recipient, jointly with his son, George E. Marks, of the John Scott Legacy Premium and Medal awarded by the Franklin Institute of Philadelphia. He died at his home in Sound Beach at the age of eighty and was survived by three sons and one daughter.

[*Encyc. of Conn. Biog.* (1917), vol. IX; G. E. Marks, *A Treatise on Marks' Patent Artificial Limbs* (1888, 1894, 1896); E. J. Lines, *Marks-Platt Ancestry* (1902); *House Ex. Doc. 59*, 33 Cong., 2 Sess.; *House Ex. Doc. 60*, 38 Cong., 1 Sess.; *Specifications and Drawings of Patents Issued from the U. S. Patent Office*, Nov. 1880; *Jour. Franklin Inst.*, May 1889; *N. Y. Times* and *N. Y. Tribune*, July 20, 1905; National Museum correspondence with firm.] C. W. M.

MARKS, ELIAS (Dec. 2, 1790–June 22, 1886), physician, educator, founder of the South Carolina Female Collegiate Institute, was born in Charleston, S. C., the son of Humphrey and Frances Marks of Lancashire, who settled in Charleston in 1785. After preparatory training in Charleston, he completed his classical and medical education in New York City, graduating from the College of Physicians and Surgeons in 1815. His dissertation, *A Conjectural Inquiry into the Relative Influence of the Mind and Stomach* (1814), treats of the connection of moral faculties with bodily sense and the influence of mind on bodily functions. His *Aphorisms of Hippocrates from the Latin of Verhoofd* (1818), continues the classical and ethical interests observable in his first work. About 1817, he was married to Jane Barham, of Lincolnshire, a teacher. On account of her health he moved south and resumed practice in Columbia, S. C., where the two also conducted the Columbia Female Academy on Washington Street. After the death of his wife in June 1827, he continued a year longer with his school, in which he had both day scholars and boarders. In 1826 he had attempted to enlist the support of the legislature for what appears to have been a plan for the higher education of women. Failing that, he decided to establish a school of his own in the seclusion of the sandhills, at a place which he named Barhamville.

The prospectus of his South Carolina Female Institute appeared in 1828 as *Hints on Female Education.* The school was formally opened on Oct. 1, 1828. The few annual catalogues now remaining give evidence of systematic internal economy and increasing educational range and efficiency in accordance with Marks's theories. In 1833 he was married to Julia (Pierpont) Warne of Sparta, Ga., a friend and pupil of Emma Willard, who assumed the duties of directress of the Institute on Jan. 1, 1830. Through her influence, according to her daughter, the Institute became collegiate, and in 1835 the word "Collegiate" was added to the name. The reorganization of the school involved a modeling, in some measure, after "similar institutions in Prussia, Germany, and other parts of continental Europe."

The school gained wide popularity and reached an enrolment of 124 students. Marion Sims, writing in 1831, said: "Young ladies were sent there from all parts of the state to school, as it was the first and only school of its character at the South" (J. M. Sims, *The Story of My Life*, 1884, p. 102). Teachers were drawn from wherever talent offered, and the work was intensive and systematic. The curriculum offered four years of collegiate study beyond an academic year sometimes necessary for entrants. Resident graduates could pursue further studies, and the vacation period provided opportunity for private instruction in residence, possibly for making up deficiencies. From the first insistence was placed on thoroughness, thinking rather than memory, and regular reviews. Reliance was placed on the student's honor. Walks, entertainments, visits of approved troupes or singers, and May parties enlivened the routine. In 1855, six years before he gave over the school into other hands, Marks claimed nearly thirty-nine years of professional services during which time he had had in his charge over four thousand young women. Marks relinquished his connection with the Institute on June 15, 1861. He spent his declining years in Washington, cheered in his old age by expressions of love and respect of his former pupils. Throughout his life he had written occasional poems and in 1850 he published *Elfreide of Guldal, a Scandinavian Legend, and Other Poems.*

[J. W. Davidson, *The Living Writers of the South* (1869); Jean H. Witherspoon, "Dr. Marks and the Barhamville School," the *State* (Columbia, S. C.), Mar. 15, 1903; B. A. Elzas, *The Jews of S. C.* (1905).] H. C. D.

MARLING, JOHN LEAKE (Dec. 22, 1825–Oct. 16, 1856), journalist and diplomatist, was born in Nashville, Tenn., the son of Samuel and Charlotte Clara (Leake) Marling. Under the pen-name of "Clara" his mother wrote popular sentimental verses, and Marling inherited and to some extent practised his mother's gift. At seventeen he joined the Baptist church. Beginning his career in a printing office, Marling overcame his lack of a systematic education by reading in leisure moments, and though without wealth or family prestige won his way into public life by a precocious exercise of his talent for political writing. He studied law in the office of A. O. P. Nicholson and Russell Houston and was admitted to the bar, but did not practise. On May 16, 1850, he was married to Mary E. March of Nashville. In the following July he became editor and part-owner of the Nashville *Daily Gazette,* and thus, in the heat of the controversy over the territorial expansion of slavery, entered upon his short, but stormy and brilliant, journalistic career. On taking over the *Gazette* he announced that he would conduct it as an "independent" paper, avoiding partisan quarrels, but he speedily became embroiled in the excitement that attended upon the meetings of the Southern convention in Nashville in 1850. During the second session of the convention he uncompromisingly denounced the secessionist policies it expressed, to such effect that there was an attempt to exclude him from its sessions. In his editorial opposition he undoubtedly reflected a strong element of Tennessee opinion.

In September 1851, leaving the *Gazette,* Marling became part-owner and editor of the Nashville *Daily Union,* a prominent Democratic paper. The young editor soon was hotly involved in the presidential campaign of 1852, strongly advocating the candidacy of Pierce against a powerful Whig opposition, locally centered in the *Republican Banner,* edited by Felix K. Zollicoffer. On Aug. 20, 1852, at the height of the campaign, Marling topped a series of attacks on the *Banner* by openly charging its editor with misrepresentation of Pierce's Southern sympathies, and in effect giving Zollicoffer the lie. Zollicoffer's answer was to call Marling out for personal satisfaction, which Marling immediately tendered. That morning the two editors met on the street in front of the *Union* office and, with little preliminary, exchanged several shots. Marling was seriously wounded and was unable to resume his duties until the campaign was over. It was thought, even by Zollicoffer's friends, that the difficulty was less personal than political and that Marling, who was known as a brave man and a crack pistol shot, had been egged on by Democratic partisans who wished to put Zollicoffer, a strong political opponent, out of the way. At any rate the difficulty between the two was later composed. Marling continued his connection with the *Union* through its consolidation with the *American* in 1853. In 1854 he was rewarded by President Pierce with an appointment as United States minister resident to Guatemala. Less than two years later he became seriously ill and returned to Nashville, on leave, in May 1856, to die there of tuberculosis within a few months.

[John Wooldridge, ed., *Hist. of Nashville, Tenn.* (1890); Nashville *Daily Gazette,* July 30, 1850, Oct. 8–Nov. 19, 1850; Nashville *Daily Union,* Aug. 20, 21, 1850; *Republican Banner,* Aug. 24, 1850, and previous issues; obituaries in Nashville papers at the time of Marling's death; *Clara's Poems* (1861); private papers furnished by Octavia Zollicoffer Bond.] D. D.

MARMADUKE, JOHN SAPPINGTON (Mar. 14, 1833–Dec. 28, 1887), Confederate soldier, governor of Missouri, was born on a farm near Arrow Rock, Mo. His mother was Lavinia Sappington, a daughter of the well-known Dr. John Sappington of Saline County. His father was Meredith Miles Marmaduke, of Westmoreland County, Va. Upon the death of Gov. Thomas Reynolds, the elder Marmaduke, who was lieutenant-governor, served almost a year as governor of Missouri (1844). John S. Marmaduke was educated in the country schools of Saline County, in Masonic College at Lexington, Mo., at Yale (two years), and at Harvard. After attending Harvard less than a year, he left to accept a cadetship at West Point, from which he graduated in 1857. Thereupon commissioned second lieutenant, he was soon assigned to the 7th Regiment of United States Infantry and served in the Mormon War (1858–60) in Utah under Col. Albert Sidney Johnston. When secession began he was stationed in New Mexico.

At the opening of the Civil War Marmaduke came home on furlough and talked over the question of allegiance with his father, who favored the Union but told his son to make his own decision. The latter immediately resigned from the United States army and was made a colonel of state militia by Gov. Claiborne F. Jackson. Disappointed at the poor showing of the state forces at the battle of Boonville (June 17, 1861), Marmaduke resigned his colonelcy and rode to Richmond where he was commissioned a first lieutenant in the Confederate army. For a short time he was on duty in Arkansas and was there made a lieutenant-colonel. Shortly afterward he was placed in charge of the 3rd Regiment under his old commander, Albert Sidney Johnston, and fought so well at Shiloh that he was commissioned a brigadier-general (May 25, 1863, to rank from Nov. 15, 1862). After Shiloh he was sent to Arkansas again, where, although his forces were inadequate for ambitious offensive tactics, he nevertheless gave a good account of himself. Early in 1863 he made a raid into south central Missouri, but his attack on Springfield failed. In April of the same year he invaded southeast Missouri, but after a few minor victories he was forced to beat a hasty retreat back into Arkansas. For his faithful and often brilliant activities around Helena, Fayetteville, and Little Rock he was promoted to a major-generalship in March 1864. In charge of the cavalry in Price's raid (1864), Marmaduke had two horses shot under him at the battle of the Little Blue near Kansas City, and on the retreat a few days later he was captured while conducting a rear-guard action at the Marais des Cygnes River in western Missouri. He was a prisoner at Fort Warren (Mass.) until the summer of 1865.

For about five years after the war Marmaduke was engaged, with moderate success, in the commission and then in the insurance business in St. Louis. From 1871 to 1874 he was editor of the *St. Louis Journal of Agriculture,* and from 1880 to 1885 he served as a member of the newly created Missouri Railway Commission. Although defeated for the Democratic nomination for governor in 1880, he was easily nominated and elected to that office four years later. He died at Jefferson City a year before the expiration of his term. Prominent among the pressing public questions during his governorship was the problem of the regulation of railroads. The bill which he sponsored for that purpose was defeated in the first regular session of the legislature during his administration. Marmaduke immediately called the Assembly into special session, and, when the proponents of the railroads stood ready to adjourn without action, he threatened to continue calling special sessions until some such regulatory measure was passed. The threat was sufficient, and a law satisfactory to him was enacted. During his administration there occurred the first railway strike that seriously affected Missouri. For handling this problem so firmly that there was little loss of property and no loss of life, he was accorded much credit. Marmaduke never married. He was not a member of any religious denomination. He was more than six feet tall, and retained throughout life an erect military bearing.

[*Messages and Proclamations of the Govs. . . . of Mo.,* vol. VII (1926); J. F. Lee, "John Sappington Marmaduke," *Mo. Hist. Soc. Colls.,* July 1906; R. J. Rombauer, *The Union Cause in St. Louis in 1861* (1909); T. L. Snead, *The Fight for Mo.* (1886); W. B. Napton, *Past and Present of Saline County, Mo.* (1910); *Confed. Mil. Hist.* (1899), vol. IX; *Jefferson City Tribune,* July 20, 1883; Sept. 23, Oct. 29, 1884, Dec. 29, 1885, Jan. 13, Mar. 16, Nov. 7, 1886; *Boonville Weekly Advertiser,* Dec. 11, 1874, May 3, 1878, Aug. 4, 1882, July 13, 1883, Sept. 19, 1884, Jan. 16, July 24, Aug. 28, 1885, Dec. 30, 1887, Aug. 29, 1890, Nov. 30, Dec. 7, 1900.] H. E. N.

MARQUAND, ALLAN (Dec. 10, 1853–Sept. 24, 1924), university professor and art historian, was born in New York City, the son of Henry Gurdon Marquand [*q.v.*], a wealthy banker and patron of arts, and Elizabeth Love (Allen) Marquand, who was of old New England origin. Preparing at St. Paul's School, Allan graduated from Princeton in 1874, being Latin salutatorian and class president. As an undergraduate, he was stroke of the crew and a member of the Glee Club. For three years he studied theology, first at Princeton Theological Seminary and later at Union. He was licensed to preach by the New York Presbytery, but was never ordained; his interest had shifted to logic and philosophy. The year 1877–78 found him a student at the University of Berlin. Thence he passed to the new Johns Hopkins University, where he held a fellowship in philosophy and in 1880 received the degree of Ph.D. At Johns Hopkins, he invented an ingenious logic machine, which is preserved in the historical collections of Princeton University.

President McCosh called him to the College of New Jersey in 1881 as lecturer in logic and tutor in Latin, a position which he held for only two years. He was then made professor of history of art, the professorship being designated archaeology and history of art in 1890. That year he became, also, director of the Museum of Historic Art. In 1883, at Rome, he was stricken by a malignant fever, which left him much of a valetudinarian. The disadvantages of such a condition he overcame by a sensible regimen and by extraordinarily persistent and systematic habits of study. Although as a lecturer, because of his hesitant delivery he was at first mildly boring to the bulk of his undergraduate hearers, he made a personal impression through the charm and the kindliness of his manners, and always inspired a few elect students, among them, his later and brilliant colleague, Howard Crosby Butler [*q.v.*]. Quietly, he gained a national reputation through his patient and accurate scholarship. Living in a spacious way as a wealthy bachelor, he gathered personal disciples, entertaining them at his home and taking them on his travels. For a time Arthur L. Frothingham [*q.v.*], a most active and versatile scholar, was his associate. Together they edited and largely wrote the third volume (1887) of the *Iconographic Encyclopedia* (a translation and revision of Moritz Carrière's *Bilder Atlas*) and *A Textbook of the History of Sculpture* (1896). Marquand's willing drudgery on the *Encyclopedia* turned out to be the best possible training for his later work as a cataloguer.

From its beginning, Marquand deeply interested himself in the work of the Archaeological Institute of America, being an editorial contributor to its journal, the *American Journal of*

Archaeology, from the time it was started, in 1885, until his death. For over thirty years with characteristic secrecy he financed traveling fellowships of the Institute. On June 18, 1896, being forty-three years old, he married Eleanor Cross, by whom he had four children. She was much younger than himself, but already interested in his subjects and fitted for the ideal partnership which ensued. After their marriage they went to Rome, where he served as annual professor at the American School of Classical Studies.

Marquand came to what was to be his life work, the cataloguing of the sculpture of the Robbia family, almost accidentally. In 1882 his father bought a fine altar-piece by Andrea della Robbia. The son wrote an elaborate account of it for the *American Journal of Archaeology* (October–December 1891). His interest thus established in Robbia sculpture, he toured Italy for unstudied examples, and published his preliminary observations in the *American Journal of Archaeology* (January–March 1893) and in *Scribner's Magazine* (December 1893). The thoroughness of his methods may be inferred from the fact that it was nineteen years before the first of the Robbia catalogues appeared. Meantime, he wrote many journal articles, gave himself willingly to the drudgery of reviewing, fostered the interests of the Institute, and gradually built up a department of art and Archaeology for Princeton. Its essential apparatus of research was his own library and photograph collection, which he first lent and then gave to the University.

He was fifty-six years old when he published his first independent book, *Greek Architecture* (1909). He soon founded and financed the Princeton Monographs in Art and Archaeology, of which his own Robbia catalogues remain the most distinguished numbers. *Della Robbias in America* (1912) was an *hors d'œuvre* to the series, being an elaborate try-out of methods of classification. The World War brought some retardation of the work, for Marquand gave himself loyally to the drudgery of miscellaneous teaching in a militarized college with a depleted faculty. Since heraldry often meant chronology, he next dispatched that subject in *Robbia Heraldry* (1919). The breadth and wisdom of his long preparation was shown by the quickness with which the remaining volumes appeared: *Giovanni della Robbia* in 1920, *Benedetto and Santi Buglioni,* in 1921, and *Andrea della Robbia and His Atelier,* two volumes, in 1922. His never robust health was now beginning to break, but he left the last of the catalogues, *The Brothers of Giovanni della Robbia* (1928), so far advanced that it could readily be completed by his colleagues after his death. He died in a hospital in New York City.

Marquand was of middle stature and slight build, immaculate in person and dress. His manner was shy and hesitating, but his vivid blue eyes were friendly. His sagacity and his generosity, which he disliked to have mentioned, brought him widest influence. He was extraordinarily helpful to beginners in research. Profoundly the scholar, he was exquisitely the aristocrat and the gentleman.

[MS. material in possession of secretary of faculty and of the chairman of department of art and architecture, Princeton Univ.; C. R. Morey, *Art Studies,* vol. II (1924), preface; *Decennial Record of the Class of 1874 of Princeton Coll.* (1884); *Princeton Alumni Weekly,* Oct. 1, 1924; *Who's Who in America,* 1922–23; *N. Y. Tribune,* Sept. 25, 1924; *N. Y. Times,* Sept. 25, 26 (editorial), 1924.] F. J. M., Jr.

MARQUAND, HENRY GURDON (Apr. 11, 1819–Feb. 26, 1902), capitalist, philanthropist, was born in New York City, the son of Isaac and Mehitable (Perry) Marquand. His father and his elder brother Frederick were connected with the firm of Marquand & Company, silversmiths. The boy received his education in New York and in Pittsfield, Mass. In 1839 Frederick Marquand withdrew from active association with the silversmith firm, and for twenty years thereafter Henry assisted him in managing large real-estate interests. During this time he acquired some knowledge of architecture and criticized the faulty design and poor construction of buildings then being erected in New York. Since he was not a professional architect, these criticisms were not at first kindly received, but ultimately many of his suggested improvements were adopted. From real estate he turned to banking, becoming prominent in Wall Street, and interested in railroad and other corporations. In 1874, with his brother Frederick and other capitalists, he purchased the St. Louis, Iron Mountain & Southern Railroad, serving as its vice-president from 1875 to 1881, and then for a year as its president. He was succeeded by Jay Gould, who had secured control of the road for his Missouri Pacific. Marquand remained a director of both roads for several years, however, and his interest in the company was such that his death occasioned a bear raid on the Missouri Pacific stock.

Retiring from the most of his business activities about 1881, he thereafter devoted much time to philanthropic and civic undertakings. He was one of the ablest and most generous supporters of the Metropolitan Museum of Art. Since the latter part of the eighteenth century there had been a more or less connected series of attempts to found such an institution. Finally, on Oct. 14, 1869, a meeting of the Union League was held to promote the project, after which the president of the League appointed a committee of fifty, of which Marquand was one, to perfect an organization and raise an endowment. From this time on Marquand was actively interested in the affairs of the Museum, serving as its treasurer from 1882 to 1889, and as its president from 1889 until his death. To him in large measure it owes its growth and distinction. Among his many gifts to it was $10,000, in 1886, which made possible the purchase of a collection of sculptural casts; and $30,000 for the endowment fund of the Museum art school. He purchased and presented to the Museum the collection of antique glass made by M. Charvet; the reproduction of many carvings exhibiting the medieval continuance of the art; the collection of Renaissance iron works; the Della Robbia altar-piece; the metallic reproductions of gold and silver objects in the Imperial Russian Museums; as well as a collection of paintings of the English School and old masters. Russell Sturgis said of Marquand, "He bought like an Italian Prince of the Renaissance" (Preface to Catalogue, *post*).

His benefactions were not limited to the Museum alone. He founded and endowed a free library at Little Rock, Ark. With his brother Frederick he gave to Bellevue Hospital the Marquand Pavilion; he gave Marquand Chapel to Princeton University and endowed the professorship of the history of art; with Robert A. Bonner, he also provided a gymnasium for Princeton. He was a member of the New York Historical Society, of the American Geographical Society, vice-president of the Municipal Art Society, and one of the board of managers of the Presbyterian Hospital. On May 20, 1851, he married Elizabeth Love Allen of Pittsfield, Mass. One of his four children was Allan Marquand [*q.v.*].

[*Am. Ancestry*, vol. IX (1894); F. B. Lee, *Geneal. and Personal Memorial of Mercer County, N. J.* (1907), vol. II; W. E. Howe, *Hist. of the Metropolitan Museum of Art* (1913); D. C. Preyer, *The Art of the Metropolitan Museum of N. Y.* (1899); *Bull. of the Metropolitan Museum*, Jan. 1911; Ernest Knaufft, "Henry G. Marquand as an American Art·Patron," in *Rev. of Revs.* (N. Y.), Feb. 1903; T. E. Kirby, ed., *Illustrated Cat. of the Art and Literary Property Collected by the Late Henry G. Marquand* (copr. 1903); H. V. Poor, *Manual of the Railroads of the U. S.*, 1875, 1881, 1882, 1891; *Commercial and Financial Chronicle*, Mar. 1, 1902; *Who's Who in America*, 1901–02; *N. Y. Herald*, and *N. Y. Tribune*, Feb. 27, 1902.] K. S. E.

MARQUETT, TURNER MASTIN (July 9, 1829–Dec. 22, 1894), railway attorney, congressman for two days, was born on a farm in Clark County, Ohio, the son of John T. Marquette and Julia (Wright) Marquette, who had come as pioneers to Ohio from Virginia. His signature does not show the final *e* which was used by all other members of his family. He conceived an early ambition to become a lawyer and with that end in view attended successively the Springfield (Ohio) high school, Wittenberg College, and Ohio University, at Athens. After his graduation from the last-named institution in 1855 he went almost immediately to Plattsmouth, Nebraska Territory, where, to piece out his insignificant earnings as a lawyer, he found it necessary for a time to work in a store.

At the outset of his career young Marquett obviously had strong political aspirations. Beginning in 1857, he served in seven successive sessions of the territorial legislature, first in the House, then for the last four years in the Council. He was an ardent opponent of slavery, and he urged as early as the session of 1859 its definite prohibition within the boundaries of Nebraska. He took a prominent part in the movement for statehood, and in June 1866 was elected to represent Nebraska in the lower House of Congress, should admission be granted. When, on Mar. 2, 1867, Nebraska actually became a state, he took office; but only two days of the term for which he had been chosen remained. During this time, however, he voted on important reconstruction acts. In 1868 he was a candidate for the Republican nomination for Congress, but when this was denied him, his interest in a political career began to wane. Although he remained to the end of his life an ardent Republican, he never again held public office.

As a lawyer, meantime, Marquett's services were increasingly in demand, and when the Burlington Railroad began to build west of the Missouri River it selected him as the principal legal adviser of its corporation in Nebraska. It was in this capacity more than in any other that he distinguished himself. He became an expert on railroad and corporation law when experts in these fields were few, and he smoothed the way legally for the remarkable progress that the Burlington was soon able to make. His counsel was often sought by corporations other than his own, but he made it a point not to take more cases than he could fully master. His part in two cases, one at the beginning and one at the end of his career, won him much distinction. He appeared as counsel for the defense in the impeachment trial of Governor David Butler, and he represented the plaintiff in a suit brought by John Fitzgerald, a railway contractor, against the

Missouri Pacific Railroad, then dominated by Jay Gould. The impeachment case went against Butler, but in the Fitzgerald case Marquett won a notable victory for his client.

For the last twenty years of his life he resided in Lincoln, Nebr., an important western center of the Burlington. The high respect in which he was there held is attested by an unusual series of appreciations printed by court order in the introductory pages of the *Nebraska Reports* for 1894 (43 *Nebr.*, vii–xxix). He was twice married: first, in 1861, to Harriett Borders, who died in 1883, and by whom he had four children; second, in 1885, to Mrs. Aseneth Stetson, who survived him.

[There are useful sketches of T. M. Marquett and of his brother, Rev. David Marquette, a pioneer Methodist preacher, in J. Sterling Morton and Albert Watkins, *Illustrated Hist. of Nebr.* (3 vols., 1905–13), I, 353, II, 523; and in Andrew J. Sawyer (ed.), *Lincoln, the Capital City, and Lancaster County, Nebr.* (1916), II, 756. A good obituary notice appears in the *Nebraska State Journal* (Lincoln), Dec. 23, 1894. The history of the Fitzgerald case is reviewed in 41 *Nebr.*, 475, and in 160 *U. S.*, 556.]

J. D. H.

MARQUETTE, JACQUES (June 1, 1637–May 18, 1675), explorer and missionary, was a native of Laon, France, where his ancestors had been prominent from the fourteenth century. He was the sixth and youngest child of Nicolas and Rose (de la Salle) Marquette. The Marquettes were warriors and officials, but the La Salles were religiously inclined. From his early years Jacques was thoughtful and gentle, and when in 1654 at the age of seventeen he decided to become a Jesuit novice, he had the ready consent of his family. He passed his novitiate at Nancy; in 1656 he went to Pont-à-Mousson to study philosophy; then he taught for several years at Rheims, Charleville, Langres, and Pont-à-Mousson. All this time he cherished the hope that his ultimate calling would be that of a missionary overseas. He chose as his pattern the great Jesuit, Francis Xavier, and wished that it might be his fate to die in the wilderness. In 1666, designated by his superiors for service in New France, he set forth in the royal fleet of that year and on Sept. 20 landed at Quebec. He was not allowed to remain long at the capital, and on Oct. 10 left for Three Rivers, an outpost of the colony, where he became a pupil of a veteran missionary in the difficult Indian languages. He made such rapid progress that in 1668 he was appointed to the mission among the Ottawa Indians, kindred of those tribesmen whose language he had mastered.

The Ottawa mission had been begun in 1660 by Father Ménard [*q.v.*], who the next year was lost in the Wisconsin forests. In 1665 the work had been taken up again by Father Allouez [*q.v.*], who at Chequamegon Bay on the south shore of Lake Superior established the mission of La Pointe de St. Esprit. Here dwelt the fugitive Ottawa from the shores of Lake Huron, and in the vicinity a few refugee Hurons from Georgian Bay. Young Marquette was now ordered to this most difficult and dangerous mission of New France. He spent the first winter (1668–69) at Sault Ste. Marie in comparative comfort. The Indians of that region were friendly, and he baptized many children. Then on Sept. 13, 1669, he went to the mission at La Pointe, Father Allouez having left to visit Green Bay. During the eighteen months Marquette spent at Chequamegon he was visited by many tribesmen from far away, among others the Illinois, who had crossed a great river on their way. Marquette learned the rudiments of the Illinois language, and because these Indians were gentle and courteous he longed to establish a mission among them. The Hurons and Ottawa were less docile; nevertheless he endeavored to teach them by pictures and symbols, and he even sent a holy picture to the fierce Sioux, hoping to open a way to instruct them. His neophytes, the Hurons, had a quarrel with the Sioux, however, and finding themselves outnumbered abandoned their village at La Pointe and fled to Lake Michigan. Marquette accompanied them, and in the summer of 1671 founded the mission of St. Ignace on the north shore of the Straits of Mackinac.

It was at St. Ignace that Marquette's great opportunity came. While at the Sault in 1668 he had met a young Canadian explorer, Louis Jolliet [*q.v.*], then returning to New France. To St. Ignace came Jolliet on Dec. 8, 1672, with the tidings that the governor had commissioned him to find the great river of which the Illinois had spoken and that Marquette was to be his companion on the expedition. All through the winter they studied and planned, drew a map of the countries Jolliet and Marquette knew, gathered the personnel for the expedition, and prepared their simple supplies. It was mid-May before the straits were free of ice and the two explorers could slip their canoes into the waters of the lake. "Indian corn, with some smoked meat," wrote Marquette, "constituted all our provisions; with these we embarked—Monsieur Jollyet and myself, with five men—in two bark canoes, fully resolved to do and suffer everything for so glorious an undertaking" (Thwaites, *post,* LIX, 91). They went by way of Green Bay and Fox River. As far as the Mascouten village on the upper Fox the way was well known, and there they obtained guides to escort them to the portage: That crossed, "we left the waters flowing to Quebeq, four or five hundred leagues from here to float on those that would thenceforward take us through strange lands" (*Ibid.*, p. 107). On June 17, 1673, the two explorers shot out into the Mississippi and, turning their canoes southward, set forth to explore its waterway. In a month they reached the mouth of the Arkansas, where, learning that the river entered the Gulf of Mexico and that white men (Spaniards) were on the lower river, they turned back. They reached Lake Michigan by the Illinois River and the Chicago portage, coasted the lake shore, and came to rest at the mission of St. Francis Xavier at De Pere.

Since Marquette's strength was sadly depleted, he remained here for more than a year, recruiting his health and writing his journal. Then, in October 1674, he set forth to fulfil his long-cherished wish to found a mission among the Illinois. The weather was stormy, the lake rough, and Marquette and his two companions suffered such hardships that when they reached the mouth of the Chicago River the priest was seriously ill. Building a small hut, the three sheltered themselves as best they could from the elements. Parties of Illinois Indians frequently visited them, and by the end of March Marquette thought himself sufficiently recovered to proceed to their village on the Illinois River. There he spent Easter, preaching to a vast concourse; but his disease grew worse, and after a short stay he left for St. Ignace, hoping to reach that place before he died. His strength failed completely, however; he was carried ashore by his attendants, and at the mouth of the river now called the Père Marquette his life came to an end. Two years later some of his neophytes who were passing by carried his remains to the St. Ignace mission, where they were buried in the chapel. Two hundred years later (1877) vestiges of what were thought to be Marquette's bones were unearthed at St. Ignace, where they were reburied except for some fragments which were carried to Milwaukee and given to Marquette University.

Of all the Jesuit missionaries in the West, Marquette is the most renowned, partly because of his early death, partly because of his sweet and saintly nature, partly because he and Jolliet were the first to follow the course of the Mississippi River, a journey made known to the world by the journals, letters, and maps of the explorers. Cities, counties, a river, a university, and a railroad are named for Marquette, a statue of him is in the Capitol at Washington, but his best monument is the account he left of his Mississippi trip and of his last voyage on his way to death in the wilderness.

[The journal of the Mississippi voyage was first published in 1681 in Melchisédeck Thévenot's *Recueil de Voyages*; it was translated and published several times before it appeared, retranslated from the copy at Montreal, in vol. LIX (1900) of *The Jesuit Relations and Allied Documents*, ed. by R. G. Thwaites, which also includes Marquette's journal of his trip to the Illinois, first published by J. G. Shea in his *Discovery and Exploration of the Mississippi River* (1852), as well as Dablon's account of the Illinois mission and Marquette's death. The journal appears also in *Early Narratives of the Northwest* (1917), ed. by L. P. Kellogg. Biographies are R. G. Thwaites, *Father Marquette* (1902), Agnes Repplier, *Père Marquette* (1929). See also L. P. Kellogg, *The French Régime in Wisconsin and the Northwest* (1925), F. B. Steck, *The Jolliet-Marquette Expedition, 1673* (rev. ed., 1928).]

L. P. K.

MARQUIS, JOHN ABNER (Dec. 27, 1861–July 5, 1931), Presbyterian clergyman and college president, was born at Dinsmore, Pa. His father, James Taggert Marquis, lived on the farm which had belonged to his father and grandfather. The family, probably of Huguenot origin, settled in Washington County before the Revolution, and produced many Presbyterian clergymen. John's mother, Mary Campbell Bucher, also came of a line of Washington County farmers. Marquis graduated from Washington and Jefferson College in 1885, and after teaching in Blairsville College for Women (1885–87), studied in Western Theological Seminary, graduating in 1890. While serving as associate pastor of the First Presbyterian Church of Greensburg, Pa., he was ordained by the Presbytery of Blairsville on Jan. 2, 1891. Three Presbyterian pastorates followed, in Westminster Church, Greensburg, from 1892 to 1902, in Redlands, Cal., for three years, and in Beaver, Pa., for four years. Marquis was also associate editor of the *Presbyterian Banner* of Pittsburgh from 1899 to 1909. His original, thoughtful preaching and power of attaching people to himself brought to his churches substantial growth.

In 1909 he became president of Coe College at Cedar Rapids, Iowa. During his administration important advances were made in teaching, buildings, and endowment. His good sense, sincerity, sympathy, and humor gave him a standing with faculty and students which enriched the life of the college. His services to education and his growing reputation in the Presbyterian Church led to his election to be moderator of the General Assembly in 1916. This Assembly reflected some excitement in the church over an early manifestation of the fundamentalist controversy. Marquis' guidance of the meeting much increased his influence, and largely caused his election to be secretary of the Presbyterian Board of Home Missions in 1917. Coe College protested against his leaving, and he spent some time there until 1920. The board which he had undertaken to direct was then in trouble because of conservative opposition to some features of its policy and of disturbing changes in organization which had been imposed upon it. Marquis strengthened it in the confidence of the church, and overcame administrative difficulties by wisdom and friendliness in personal relations and by his gift for winning cooperation. Before long he met even graver problems through the combination of his board with others in the Presbyterian Board of National Missions. Of this he was chosen general secretary in 1923. Out of somewhat discordant elements he fashioned an effective organization, animated by his own high ideal of the board's function. Through these years he exercised a strong progressive leadership in the Presbyterian Church. In interdenominational relations also he was prominent, working energetically in the Home Missions Council of the American and Canadian churches and in the Federal Council of the Churches of Christ in America, of whose administrative committee he was chairman. He was a delegate of the Presbyterian Church at the Stockholm Conference of 1925 and the Lausanne Conference of 1927.

At Vienna, in September 1928, he suffered a stroke of paralysis, and after nearly three years of infirmity and suffering he died in New York City. He was married on Sept. 1, 1896, to Martha Miller Neilson of Greensburg, Pa., who with a son and two daughters survived him. Besides many articles in periodicals he published *Learning to Teach from the Master Teacher* (1913) and *The Christian Conception of Property* (1916).

[*Who's Who in America*, 1930–31; address by H. S. Coffin at memorial meeting Presbyt. Bd. Nat. Miss. (MS.); records of trustees of Coe Coll.; *Gen. Biog. Cat. Western Theol. Sem., 1827–1927* (n.d.); *N. Y. Times*, July 6, 1931; *Presbyterian Banner*, July 9, 1931; information from family.] R. H. N.

MARSH, CHARLES WESLEY (Mar. 22, 1834–Nov. 9, 1918), inventor, manufacturer, editor, was born on the old Marsh homestead near Trenton, Northumberland County, Ontario, Canada, on the north shore of the Bay of Quinte. He was the son of Samuel and Tamar (Richardson) Marsh and was descended from William Marsh of Kent County, England, who emigrated to Connecticut about the middle of the seventeenth century and whose grandson, born in Vermont, became a "United Empire Loyalist" and after the outbreak of the Revolution emigrated to Canada where he invested largely in lands. Marsh received his primary education at home and in the district school and helped in the farm labors after the age of six. When he was eleven his parents sold their farm and moved to Illinois. On the way, at Coburg, Canada, his father was converted to the Second Adventist teachings of William Miller with the result that the family migration was delayed for four years. During this period Marsh attended St. Andrews School for one and one-half years and then Victoria College in Coburg, winning prizes for scholarship in both institutions. When he was fifteen years old his family resumed its journey and after an overland trip by way of Chicago, took up late in 1849 a quarter section of government land near Shabbona and De Kalb in De Kalb County, Ill. During the succeeding decade he lived with his parents and experienced all that pioneer farming entailed, the building of a home, clearing and cultivating the land, and harvesting the crops.

In the course of time agricultural machinery was gradually added to the farm equipment including in 1856 a Mann reaping machine. With this Marsh and his younger brother William [*q.v.*] harvested grain for two consecutive years. The machine was of the side-delivery type with an endless belt which delivered the grain into a receptacle from which it was discharged in gavels onto the ground ready for binding into sheaves. In the course of working with the new machine the brothers were struck with the idea of binding the grain *on the machine,* and throughout the winter of 1857 and the following spring they conducted many experiments toward that end. In June 1858 they applied for a patent. Meantime they refitted their Mann reaper in accordance with their plan and successfully used it in the harvest of that year. Their patent for a "reaping machine" was granted on Aug. 17, 1858, No. 21,207. The machine was the first practical hand-binding harvester, furnishing the foundation for the modern harvesting machine in that it was the first and only machine to which self-binding devices could be successfully attached.

From 1858 to 1863 Marsh divided his attention between the farm and the harvester, refining the latter and taking steps toward its later manufacture. He unsuccessfully undertook the construction of twelve machines in 1860, but he built in 1861 a single machine which had all the qualities required for field work. In 1863, in connection with Lewis Steward, he established a manufactory for the harvester at Plano, Ill., and began building machines in a small way. Twenty-five were made and sold for the harvest of 1864. They performed so successfully that manufacturing licenses were applied for by others and within a few years Marsh harvesters were being made at two establishments in Illinois and at one in Ohio. The plant at Plano was enlarged from year to year and machines were manufactured under the firm name of Marsh, Steward & Company. In 1865 a financial interest in the establishment was secured by Gammon & Deering, which organization finally purchased the entire property. Then in 1869 Marsh established the Sycamore Marsh Harvester Manufacturing Company at Sycamore, Ill., and successfully operated that for seven years. In 1876 he sold a controlling interest in this enterprise to J. D. Easter & Company and retired the following year.

Easter & Company failed in 1877 and deeply involved the Harvester Manufacturing Company at Sycamore. Marsh, who still possessed a large financial interest there, endeavored to prevent a complete collapse of the business. In the course of the succeeding three years, however, matters went from bad to worse. In 1879 the original patents for the harvester expired as did also the manufacturing licenses, so that eventually in 1881 Marsh was compelled to close out the Marsh Company. He then founded the Marsh Binder Manufacturing Company, using the same plant and facilities at Sycamore, and endeavored to develop an automatic binding machine. Inventors were employed and inventions purchased for this purpose, but the attempt failed completely in 1884 and Marsh lost everything. In 1885 he became the editor of the newly formed trade journal *Farm Implement News,* the first number of which appeared in April 1885. The paper was successful from the start and became one of the leading farm machinery trade papers of the world. In the course of time Marsh was made president of the publishing company and continued to serve in this office, though retiring as editor at the age of seventy.

Marsh went abroad in 1870 and demonstrated the machine in Austria and Hungary. He participated in a number of competitive trials and in Hungary won the first prize. In 1868 he had served in the lower house of the Illinois legislature and two years later one term in the Senate. He also served for twenty years as a trustee of the Northern Illinois Hospital for the Insane. He was twice married: first, on Jan. 1, 1860, to Frances Wait, and after her death to Sue Rogers on Jan. 10, 1881. He was survived by his widow and by three children of the first marriage.

[C. W. Marsh, *Recollections, 1837–1910* (1910); *House Executive Doc. 105,* 35 Cong., 2 Sess.; *House Executive Doc. 51,* 38 Cong., 2 Sess.; *House Executive Doc. 52,* 39 Cong., 1 Sess.; *House Executive Doc. 96,* 40 Cong., 2 Sess.; *Specifications and Drawings of Patents Issued from the U. S. Patent Office,* June 18, 1872; *Decisions of the Commissioner of Patents for the Year 1872* (1873); L. M. Gross, *Past and Present of De Kalb County, Ill.* (1907), vol. II; E. W. Byrn, *The Progress of Invention in the Nineteenth Century* (1900); W. B. Kaempffert, *A Popular Hist. of Am. Invention* (2 vols., 1924); R. L. Ardrey, *Am. Agric. Implements* (1894); *Farm Implement News,* Nov. 14, 1918; *Farm Machinery-Farm Power,* Nov. 15, 1918; *Implement and Tractor Age,* Nov. 20, 1918; *Chicago Sunday Tribune,* Nov. 10, 1918.] C. W. M.

MARSH, GEORGE PERKINS (Mar. 15, 1801–July 23, 1882), lawyer, diplomat, and scholar, a first cousin of James Marsh [*q.v.*], was born at Woodstock, Vt. His father, Charles Marsh, an eminent lawyer, was a descendant of John Marsh who settled at Hartford, Conn., in 1636, and the son of Joseph Marsh, a former lieutenant-governor of Vermont; his mother, Susan (*née* Perkins), at the time of her marriage to his father was the widow of Josias Lyndon Arnold. His ancestors on both sides belonged to the intellectual aristocracy of New England. Brought up in a family of Puritan restraint, George was a frail and serious child who played by preference with girls and almost ruined his eyesight when he was seven by too assiduous reading. Unable for long periods to use his eyes, he learned by listening to others read and entered Dartmouth College in 1816 having had only a few months of formal schooling. There he was recognized as the most brilliant scholar in his class. Studious almost to excess, he learned French, Spanish, Portuguese, Italian, and German in his spare time, yet a dry humor made him not unpopular with classmates. In 1820 he graduated with highest honors and immediately tried teaching, but finding it distasteful, studied law in his father's office. Admitted to the bar in 1825, he practised in Burlington, Vt., where he not only became prominent in his profession but also found time to familiarize himself with the Scandinavian languages. On Apr. 10, 1828, he married Harriet, daughter of Ozias Buell of Burlington, and her death in 1833, within a few days of that of the older of their two sons, was a crushing blow. Six years later he married Caroline, daughter of Benjamin Crane of Berkley, Mass. Meanwhile his ability as a lawyer, business man, and scholar had been recognized, and in 1835 he was appointed by the governor to the supreme executive council of the state. In 1834 he was elected to Congress as a Whig, and during two successive terms proved himself a cogent if dry speaker in support of high tariff and in opposition to slavery and the Mexican War.

In 1849 President Taylor appointed him minister to Turkey, and at Constantinople his encyclopedic knowledge of languages was most useful. He cooperated with Sir Stratford Canning in aiding many refugees from the central European revolutions of 1848 and arranged for the departure of Kossuth and fifty compatriots on an American frigate. In the summer of 1852 he was sent to Athens, where the United States had no regular diplomatic representative, to investigate the case of Jonas King [*q.v.*], an American missionary imprisoned by the local authorities. After careful study of the copious evidence in modern Greek, Marsh found him the victim of unscrupulous and bigoted persecution and returned the next spring to demand redress. While the Greek government procrastinated, the minister was recalled to Constantinople by an acrimonious dispute over Martin Koszta, a Hungarian revolutionist half-naturalized in the United States and illegally seized in Smyrna by an Austrian naval commander. Instructed by John Porter Brown [*q.v.*], the American chargé at Constantinople, Capt. Duncan N. Ingraham [*q.v.*] of the American sloop of war *St. Louis* had demanded the prisoner and cleared his ship for action to enforce compliance before the Austrian discreetly delivered him to the French consul. Marsh and the Austrian ambassador pointed out with equal correctness that both naval officers had flagrantly disregarded the sovereignty of Turkey, but the Porte did nothing, and excitement soon died down.

Recalled by a new administration in 1854, Marsh labored to mend his bankrupt fortunes, acted as railroad commissioner for the state of Vermont, and delivered at Columbia University and the Lowell Institute lectures on English philology and etymology which established his reputation as an outstanding authority in those fields. Having joined the Republican party in 1856, he was sent by President Lincoln as the first United States minister to the new kingdom of Italy in 1860. This post he held for the remaining twenty-one years of his life, gaining great prestige with the Italian government through his obvious honesty and sympathy with their aims, and building up a greater reputation as a scholar by his numerous reviews and encyclopedia articles. He died at Vallombrosa, near Florence, and was buried in the Protestant Cemetery at Rome.

A man of great personal dignity and reserve, Marsh was master of a punning humor and could turn a compliment prettily. With interests which ranged from comparative grammar to physiography and from the gathering of reptiles for the Smithsonian Institution to the collection of engravings, which were ultimately acquired by the Smithsonian, he was a sort of universal genius, a conscientious and erudite scholar in many fields. His early interest in Scandinavia resulted in the publication of *A Compendious Grammar of the Old-Northern or Icelandic Language* (1838), largely a compilation from the work of R. K. Rask; while another aspect of the same study showed itself in his preaching a gospel of old Teutonic simplicity and virtue, to which he attributed everything good in the English tradition (*The Goths in New-England,* 1843). His travels in the Near East inspired *The Camel, His Organization, Habits, and Uses, Considered with Reference to His Introduction into the United States* (1856). He was one of the early workers associated with the Oxford Dictionary (J. A. H. Murray, *A New English Dictionary,* vol. I, 1888, Preface, p. v). His *Lectures on the English Language* (1860) and *The Origin and History of the English Language* (1862) were excellent philological and etymological works for their day but have since become antiquated. His *Man and Nature, or Physical Geography as Modified by Human Action* (1864; revised edition of 1874 entitled *The Earth as Modified by Human Action*), embodying the fruit of many years' acute observation during his extensive travels, has been called "the fountainhead of the conservation movement" (Lewis Mumford, *The Brown Decades,* 1931, p. 78). It was a pioneer effort "to suggest the possibility and the importance of the restoration of disturbed harmonies and the material improvement of waste and exhausted regions" (Preface, quoted by Mumford, p. 75), and had a significant influence both at home and abroad.

[H. L. Koopman, *Bibliog. of George Perkins Marsh* (1892); Caroline Crane Marsh, *Life and Letters of G. P. Marsh* (1888), projected as a two-volume work, only one volume published; S. G. Brown, *A Discourse Commemorative of the Hon. George Perkins Marsh* (1883); D. W. Marsh, *Marsh Geneal.* (1895); H. L. Mencken, *The Am. Language* (1919), pp. 8, 144; *Proc. Am. Acad. Arts and Sci.*, vol. XVIII (1883); *Atti della R. Accademia dei Lincei . . . 1882–83* (3 ser. VII, 1883); the *Nation* (N. Y.), July 27, Aug. 3, Oct. 12, 1882; *N. Y. Times,* July 25, 1882.]

W. L. W., Jr.

MARSH, GRANT PRINCE (May 11, 1834–Jan. 2, 1916), steamboat captain, pioneer, was born in Chautauqua County, N. Y., the son of John and Lydia (Dyer) Marsh. A few years later the family moved to Rochester, Pa., on the Ohio River. At the age of twelve young Marsh's schooling came to an end, and he became a cabin boy on a local steamboat plying from Pittsburgh. For more than sixty years thereafter, almost without interruption, he was connected with river transportation. In 1852, as a deckhand, he reached St. Louis, which for a long period was to be his home. As a watchman on the *A. B.*

Chambers, he narrowly escaped with his life in the great disaster of Feb. 27, 1856, when the breaking of an ice jam wrecked or sank some fifty vessels on the St. Louis waterfront. In the following year he became a mate, and in the winter of 1858–59 served with Mark Twain, with whom he formed a lifelong friendship. In 1861, at St. Louis, he married Katharine Reardon. He was the mate of the *John J. Roe* when that vessel, in March 1862, assisted in carrying Grant's army from Fort Donelson to Pittsburg Landing, and on the bloody Sunday of Apr. 6 aided in placing Buell's army on the left bank of the river. In 1864, in the service of transporting supplies for General Sully's army, operating against the Sioux, he had his first experience with the Indian country. He became a master in 1866, taking his vessel, the *Luella,* to Fort Benton, the head of navigation on the Missouri. He soon acquired an exceptional knowledge of the upper waters, and his skill as a pilot (for he always piloted his own vessels) caused him to be frequently employed by the military authorities during the Sioux wars. Early in 1873 he carried Gen. G. A. Forsyth's party of reconnaissance up the Yellowstone to a point near the mouth of the Powder, and on the voyage he gave names to many of the physical features of the valley. In the summer of that year he cooperated with the Stanley-Custer expedition along the Yellowstone, and two years later carried Gen. J. W. Forsyth's expedition nearly fifty miles above Pompey's Pillar. In 1876, in the historic *Far West,* he cooperated with the Custer-Terry expedition, forcing his boat up the tortuous channel of the Bighorn to the mouth of the Little Bighorn. From there he brought down the wounded from the Custer battlefield, and starting from Fort Pease, in the afternoon of July 3, took his vessel to Fort Abraham Lincoln, a distance of 710 miles, in the unparalleled time of fifty-four hours.

The close of the Sioux wars and the advent of railroads to the Upper Missouri had by 1882 paralyzed the steamboat industry in that region. For the next twenty-one years Marsh's service was on the Mississippi. A revival of steamboating on the Upper Missouri brought him again to the region in 1903, at first in the employ of Gen. W. D. Washburn and later of the Benton Packet Company. He made his home in Bismarck, N. Dak. In 1906 his wife died, and about 1910 he retired. He died at St. Alexius Hospital, Bismarck, and was buried, by his own request, on Wagonwheel Bluff, overlooking the Missouri River. Four children survived him.

Marsh was a man somewhat above medium height, of sinewy body and of great strength. He was keen-sighted, alert and quick of movement, and deliberate in speech. His manner was as a rule gentle, though at times he could be aroused to a high pitch of anger. His skill as a pilot and his fearlessness in time of danger were recognized by all. He was, wrote Gen. G. A. Forsyth, "the ideal man of his profession" (Hanson, *post,* p. 167); and Sherman, Sheridan, Custer, Miles, Stanley, and others paid high tribute to his abilities and his character.

[J. M. Hanson, *The Conquest of the Missouri: Being the Story of the Life and Exploits of Captain Grant Marsh* (1909); *Bismarck Daily Tribune,* Jan. 4, 1916; information from Marsh's sister, Mrs. Lydia Gordon, Rochester, Pa.]

W. J. G.

MARSH, JAMES (July 19, 1794–July 3, 1842), philosopher and president of the University of Vermont, a first cousin of George Perkins Marsh [*q.v.*], was born on a farm at Hartford, Vt., the son of Daniel and Marion (Harper) Marsh, and the grandson of Joseph Marsh, first lieutenant-governor of the state. He was destined for the farm; but at the age of eighteen his circumstances changed, and after a brief preparation under William Nutting, a schoolmaster at Randolph, he entered Dartmouth College. Here he became an omnivorous reader, with a special devotion to the classics and to the Cambridge Platonists. In 1815 he was converted during a revival, and in 1817, upon graduation from Dartmouth, proceeded to Andover Theological Seminary. From 1818 to 1820 he was back at Dartmouth as a tutor; then returned to Andover until 1822. In his last year at Andover he contributed to the *North American Review* (July 1822) an article on "Ancient and Modern Poetry," and helped to translate J. J. Bellermann's *Geography of the Scriptures.* He was then out of employment for a year and even thought of settling down as a farmer. In 1823 he became a teacher at the college and theological school at Hampden-Sidney, Va., and in 1824 was appointed professor of Oriental languages there; in the same year he was ordained at Hanover, N. H., as a Congregational minister, and married Lucia Wheelock, niece of the president of Dartmouth. In 1826 he was chosen president of the University of Vermont.

Under Marsh's influence the institution became a leader in educational reform, both in New England and in the Middle West. His views on education are set forth in *An Address Delivered in Burlington upon the Inauguration of the Author to the Office of President of the University of Vermont, Nov. 28, 1826* (1827) and in *An Exposition of the Course of Instruction and Disci-*

pline in the University of Vermont (1829). He made the entrance qualifications less exclusive, allowed students greater freedom to follow their own interests, strengthened the personal contacts between teachers and undergraduates, and based discipline on personal influence rather than on obedience to rules. In 1829 he edited Coleridge's *Aids to Reflection,* with a preliminary essay, and the next year published *Selections from the Old English Writers on Practical Theology.* He also contributed to the *Vermont Chronicle* (Windsor, Vt.), beginning Jan. 16, 1829, a series of articles on popular education; and to the *Christian Spectator,* a review of Moses Stuart's two-volume *Commentary on the Epistle to the Hebrews* (1828–29), in which he defended German methods of Biblical criticism. Feeling that the University needed at its head a man of greater business ability, Marsh resigned the presidency in 1833 and became professor of philosophy. In the same year he published a translation of J. G. Herder's *The Spirit of Hebrew Poetry,* and in 1837, a translation of D. H. Hegewisch's *Introduction to Historical Chronology.* In 1836 during a religious revival in Vermont under one Burchard, who was making converts by arousing mob emotion, Marsh became a vigorous opponent of these "new measures."

He admired the poetry of the Romantic movement in England and Germany, which he considered a natural product of Christian influences; and his romanticism caused him to revolt against the philosophy of Locke and the Scotch school which then dominated New England. In his search for a modification of Calvinism which should "satisfy the heart as well as the head," he adopted the Coleridgean distinction between the reason and the understanding. His edition of *Aids to Reflection* created a ferment among young intellectuals, was read with enthusiasm by Emerson, and had a formative influence upon the transcendentalist movement. Though his voice and manner unfitted him for preaching to large audiences and he was stiff and diffident in society, he was a brilliant conversationalist, and his students found him a sympathetic and inspiring teacher. His wife having died in 1828, he married in 1833 her sister Laura, who died in 1838. He died at Burlington.

[Joseph Torrey, *The Remains of the Rev. James Marsh, . . . with a Memoir of his Life* (1843); John Wheeler, *A Discourse Delivered July 6, 1842 at the Funeral of James Marsh* (1842); G. B. Cheever, *Characteristics of the Christian Philosopher* (1843); W. B. Sprague, *Annals Am. Pulpit,* vol. II (1857); D. W. Marsh, *Marsh Geneal.* (1895); M. H. Nicolson, "James Marsh and the Vermont Transcendentalists," in *Philosophical Rev.,* Jan. 1925; *Vermont Chronicle* (Windsor), July 6, 1842.]

H. B. P.

MARSH, JOHN (Apr. 2, 1788–Aug. 4, 1868), Congregational clergyman, temperance reformer, a descendant of George Marsh who settled in Hingham, Mass., in 1635, was born in Wethersfield, Conn., where his father, Rev. John Marsh, was for many years pastor of the Congregational church. His mother was Ann, daughter of Capt. Ebenezer Grant of East Windsor, Conn. John grew up familiar with the hard drinking of a New England town, where even clerical hospitality was made perfect only by the aid of alcoholic stimulants. In his own home, during the winter seasons, flip was the antidote for the paralyzing chill of the meeting house. "Well do I remember," he says, "crying in meeting from the cold (there were then no stoves), and holding on to my chair after drinking the FLIP till my head became steady" (*Temperance Recollections,* p. 9). When he was ten years old he went to the school of Rev. Azel Backus [*q.v.*] at Bethlehem, Conn. Two years later he entered Yale College, from which he graduated in 1804, no longer able to say truthfully that he had not been drunk at least once in his life. After teaching school and studying theology with his father, in June 1809 he was licensed to preach by the Hartford South Association of Ministers. Having supplied several churches in the meantime, on Dec. 16, 1818, he was ordained to the ministry and installed as pastor of the Congregational church, Haddam, Conn.

The temperance movement, which was just then beginning to gain momentum in the United States, soon enlisted his vigorous support. His activities attracted increasing attention, and when the Connecticut Temperance Society was organized, May 1829, he was appointed secretary and general agent. On Oct. 21 of that year he delivered an address before the Windham County Temperance Society on *Putnam and the Wolf, or the Monster Destroyed,* more than 150,000 printed copies of which were sold. Securing three months' leave of absence from his parish in 1831, he accepted an invitation to promote the cause of temperance in Baltimore and Washington. In order to attract nation-wide attention to the movement he arranged for a congressional temperance meeting, which was held in the hall of the House of Representatives, and had the support of many prominent federal officials. His labors for the cause were now commanding so much of his time and interest that in the spring of 1833 he resigned his pastorate. He was a delegate to the first National Temperance Convention, held in Philadelphia, May 1833, and was one of its secretaries; and on Oct. 1, he began a three years' term of service as agent of the Pennsylvania State Temperance Society. In 1836 the executive committee of the reorganized American Temperance Union determined to establish a national press in Philadelphia, and Marsh was appointed editor, and corresponding secretary of the Union. A monthly publication, the *Journal of the American Temperance Union,* was begun, the first number of which appeared on Jan. 15, 1837; and in October 1839, the office now having been removed to New York, the *Youth's Temperance Advocate* was started. Not until 1865, when the American Temperance Union was superseded by a new organization, did Marsh's tireless editorial and promotional activities come to a close. At this time he had already suffered two attacks of partial paralysis; nevertheless he was engaged in raising money for a building for the Yale Divinity School when in 1868 the last and fatal attack came. His death occurred at his home in Brooklyn, N. Y., and he was buried in Wethersfield, Conn. During his last years he prepared *Temperance Recollections: Labors, Defeats, Triumphs. An Autobiography* (1866). He also published many pamphlets relating to temperance, and *An Epitome of General Ecclesiastical History from the Earliest Period to the Present Time* (1827), which went through numerous editions. His wife, whom he married Oct. 5, 1824, was Frances Fowler, daughter of John and Phebe Talmadge of Warren, Conn.

[In addition to *Temperance Recollections* cited above, consult F. B. Dexter, *Biog. Sketches Grads. Yale Coll.*, vol. V (1911), which lists Marsh's publications; E. J. Marsh, *Geneal. of the Family of George Marsh* (1887); *N. Y. Times,* Aug. 5, 1868; and *Congreg. Quart.*, Jan. 1869.] H. E. S.

MARSH, JOHN (June 5, 1799–Sept. 24, 1856), California pioneer, was the eldest of the seven children of John and Mary (Brown) Marsh and a descendant of John Marsh who emigrated from England to Salem, Mass., about 1633. Born and reared in South Danvers, Mass., he attended Franklin Academy in North Andover, Lancaster Academy, and was graduated from the Phillips Academy at Andover in 1819. Entering Harvard College he graduated with the class of 1823. He was appointed tutor to officers' children at Fort St. Anthony, now St. Paul, and arrived at this frontier post in October 1823. During his two years' service he studied medicine under Dr. Edward Purcell, the fort surgeon, and had almost completed the course mapped out, when his preceptor died. He mingled freely with the neighboring Indians and in 1824 and 1825 served as sub-agent to the Sioux at St. Peter. Here he fell in love with Marguerite Decouteaux, daughter of a French father and a Sioux mother. This romance profoundly influenced his life for it was, perhaps, the principal reason why he stayed in the wilderness instead of returning to the East. For seven years the couple lived together and raised an only son, who survived both parents. In 1826, with the help of Lewis Cass, then governor of Michigan Territory, Marsh was appointed sub-agent for Indian affairs at Prairie du Chien, and he served in that post and also as justice of the peace of Crawford County until the death of Marguerite. During these years he worked on a Sioux dictionary and wrote a brief grammar of the Sioux language, which were published in Caleb Atwater's *Remarks Made on a Tour to Prairie du Chien* (1831, pp. 149–72). His friendship with the Sioux indirectly led to the outbreak of the Black Hawk War of 1832, in which he organized and led a band of Sioux. Dispirited and melancholy over the death of Marguerite, he resigned as justice at the end of the war and had disposed of his fur-trade when he learned of the issuance of a warrant to arrest him on the charge of unlawfully selling arms and ammunition to the Indians. He fled down the Mississippi to St. Louis, located at Independence, Mo., and for two years was engaged in general merchandising. In 1835 he lost all his property and, still fearing arrest, departed secretly for Santa Fé, where he arrived only after escaping death at the hands of Indian captors.

In February 1836 he reached Los Angeles, where he soon received permission to practise as a physician, but in less than a year he had sold his practice and started north in search of a cattle range. In order to obtain a Mexican land title, he was baptized a Roman Catholic and became a naturalized Mexican citizen. Later he bought a rancho ten miles wide and twelve miles long in the San Joaquin Valley, near the site of the present city of Antioch. He resumed the practice of medicine and for many years was the only physician in the San Joaquin Valley. In return for his services he exacted heavy fees, usually in cattle, and soon became the owner of large herds. The discovery of gold drew him into the mines for a time and added greatly to his rapidly accumulating fortune. In June 1851 he married Abigail Smith Tuck of Chelmsford, Mass. She died in a few years, leaving him a daughter, who, with her half-brother, inherited the large estate. Impressed by the results of American infiltration into Texas, he became convinced that the story of Texas might be repeated in California and in Oregon. He wrote letters to friends in Missouri and to his former patron Senator Cass, urging immigration to California and begging for official encouragement of it.

Some of his letters were published in newspapers and seem to have been influential in starting the first American migration to California just before the discovery of gold. In person, he was tall, heavy, athletic, and commanding. He was fond of books and a linguist of no mean ability. As a business man he was adroit, exacting, and not over-scrupulous. Dissatisfied with their wages, three of his *vaqueros* waylaid, robbed, and murdered him not far from Martinez, Cal.

["Doctor John Marsh, Cal. Pioneer," an unpublished thesis by E. J. Ulsh at the University of Cal., with numerous letters from Marsh; G. D. Lyman, *John Marsh* (1930); *Hist. of Contra Costa County, Cal.* (1882); *The Hist. of Contra Costa County, Cal.*, ed. by F. J. Hulaniski (1917); L. B. Marsh, *The Geneal. of John Marsh of Salem* (1888); Joseph Palmer, *Necrology of Alumni of Harvard College, 1851–52 to 1862–63* (1864).]

P. O. R.

MARSH, OTHNIEL CHARLES (Oct. 29, 1831–Mar. 18, 1899), paleontologist, eldest son of Caleb and Mary Gaines (Peabody) Marsh, both of Danvers (now Peabody), Mass., was born in Lockport, N. Y. His father was a brother of John Marsh, 1799–1856 [*q.v.*], and a descendant of John Marsh who was established in Salem in 1637. After the death of his mother, when he was three years old, the boy lived for some two years with a maiden aunt whose interest in him thereafter seems to have had an important influence upon his future. His early education was acquired in the schools of Lockport and the Wilson Collegiate Institute. Graduating from Phillips Academy, Andover, Mass., in 1856, he entered Yale College, where he took a classical course and graduated with the degree of B.A. in 1860. In 1861–62 he pursued graduate studies in the Yale Scientific School and then spent three years in study at Berlin, Breslau, and Heidelberg, Germany. In 1866 he received an appointment to the chair of paleontology at Yale, the first chair of this nature to be established in America. This position he held for the rest of his life.

While but a youth, Marsh had shown more than passing interest in natural history and by the time he was nineteen the study was his dominant concern. His vacations from 1851 to 1862 were occupied with field trips throughout New York, the New England states, and Nova Scotia. In 1855 he found some fossil vertebrae in the coal-measures of the South Joggins, Nova Scotia, and the interest these aroused definitely turned him toward the subject that was to constitute his life work. Soon after his appointment at Yale, he went west over the newly constructed Union Pacific Railroad as far as Nebraska and Wyoming. Here, for the first time, he gained a realization of the almost boundless field to which he was henceforth to devote his major efforts. In 1870 he organized his first Yale Scientific Expedition, consisting of thirteen persons with a military escort to see them safely from post to post. This first year they explored the Pliocene deposits of Nebraska and the Miocene of northern Colorado, crossed over into the Bridger Basin of Wyoming, and pushed southward into the Uinta Basin and thence into California. During the following years similar expeditions were carried on, bringing to light an undreamed of wealth of material and placing Marsh—with the possible exception of Edward Drinker Cope [*q.v.*]—at the head of American vertebrate paleontologists. Until 1880, his expeditions were financed largely through his own private means, which had been augmented by his inheritance of a share of the fortune of his uncle, George Peabody [*q.v.*], who died in 1869. In 1882, following the reorganization of the various federal surveys, Marsh was appointed vertebrate paleontologist to the United States Geological Survey, incidentally, it may be added, much to the chagrin of Cope, who with the exception of Joseph Leidy [*q.v.*] was Marsh's only rival in his field. Between Marsh and Cope there was ever thereafter a warfare to the extreme limit possible to verbal combat.

Marsh's first great discovery was that already mentioned of *Eosaurus* remains in the coal-measures of Nova Scotia. From the beginning of his western trips in 1870 to the close of his active career, he accumulated materials more rapidly than he could study them, and his published bibliography is not as full nor as comprehensive as the opportunities he enjoyed seemed to warrant. Aside from numerous short papers in the *American Journal of Science*, his principal monographic works were *Odontornithes; a Monograph on the Extinct Toothed Birds of North America* (1880), and *Dinocerata; a Monograph of an Extinct Order of Gigantic Mammals* (1884). Several others which were projected were found after his death to be scarcely begun, so far as shown by written manuscript; and thus the expensive work of years of collection and preparation, while not wholly lost, did not yield its full measure of printed matter. His most masterly and comprehensive single paper, according to his biographer, Beecher, was his *Introduction and Succession of Vertebrate Life in America* (1877). He was the first to describe the remains of fossil serpents and flying reptiles in the western part of the American continent.

To Marsh must be given credit for putting the collection and preparation of vertebrate fossils upon a truly scientific basis. It is because of his influence and that of his able assistants that the exhibits of ancient vertebrate life in American museums are no longer limited to isolated fragments of bones, but often include entire skeletons as complete in every part as those of animals now living. It may be added that his interests as a collector were by no means limited to vertebrate fossils. He formed what was at the time of his death one of the most complete osteological collections in America. Minerals, invertebrate fossils, archeological and ethnological materials also came within his domain. "He not only had the means and the inclination, but entered every field of acquisition with the dominating ambition to obtain everything there was in it, and leave not a scrap behind" (Beecher).

Marsh was a man of fairly large frame, robust, and of about medium height. Throughout his youth he indulged freely in outdoor life, and until well past middle age could endure exposure and physical strain to a degree far beyond the ordinary. He was remarkably free from the petty annoyances of ill health, and through the beneficence of his uncle, George Peabody, was economically completely independent. As a man he was strongly self-reliant, inclined to be seclusive, but hospitable and kindly, and of pronounced esthetic tastes. He never married, but lived the life of a wealthy bachelor and patron of science in his fine house in New Haven. He died after a brief illness from pneumonia in his sixty-eighth year. Among the many honors he received were the presidency of the National Academy of Sciences (1883–95), the Bigsby medal from the Geological Society of London (1877), and the Cuvier prize from the French Academy (1898). He was connected with the United States Geological Survey from his appointment in 1882 until his death.

[C. E. Beecher, in *Am. Jour. Sci.*, June 1899, with bibliography; abridgments of the same sketch in *Bull. Geol. Soc. of America*, July 31, 1900, and *Am. Geologist*, Sept. 1899; G. B. Grinnell, in *Leading Am. Men of Sci.* (1910), ed. by D. S. Jordan; *Obit. Record Grads. Yale Univ.*, 1899; L. B. Marsh, *The Geneal. of John Marsh of Salem* (1888); *New Haven Evening Register*, Mar. 18, 1899.] G. P. M.

MARSH, SYLVESTER (Sept. 30, 1803–Dec. 30, 1884), inventor, was born at Campton, N. H., in the sparsely settled Pemigewasset Valley. He was a descendant of Alexander Marsh who was in Braintree, Mass., as early as 1654, and the son of John and Mehitable (Percival) Marsh, who, toward the close of the eighteenth century, had emigrated from East Haddam, Conn., cleared a bit of forest, and begun farming. In this primitive environment (he was nine years old before he saw a wheeled vehicle) Marsh grew to manhood, working on the farm and attending the district school a few months each winter. At nineteen he left home and for the next three years worked about Boston as a farm hand, learned brickmaking, and tended a provision stall in Quincy Market, incidentally learning to cure and pack pork. Early in 1828, in company with a friend, he went to Ashtabula, Ohio, and there began a beef and pork packing business, shipping the products east by way of the Erie Canal. Five years later, in 1833, he moved on to Chicago and on the site of the present Court House established a beef-marketing business. Following the financial crash of 1837, in which he experienced the disastrous fate which overtook many other business men, he began all over again as a grain dealer. This enterprise was successful, and in the course of a quarter of a century, operating both in Chicago and in Davenport, Iowa, he built up a comfortable fortune. Much of his success was due to his inventions, patented between 1855 and 1865, for the mechanical handling of grain, for improvements in grain dryers, and for an improved process of manufacturing kiln-dried meal. This product was marketed as "Marsh's Caloric Dry Meal," the largest part of it being exported to the West Indies. During this period Marsh lived in several places. He moved from Chicago to Jamaica Plain, Mass., in 1855, and five years later returned to Chicago for four years. In 1864–65 he resided in Brooklyn, N. Y., managing his export business.

Some years earlier Marsh had conceived the idea of constructing a railroad up Mount Washington in New Hampshire, and as a first step obtained a charter from the state legislature in 1858. Before he could proceed to realize the project, however, the Civil War began and actual construction was not started until 1866. The road was completed in 1869 at a cost of $150,000. It is two and one-half miles long, the average grade being 1,300 feet to the mile, and one and one-half hours are required to make the ascent. Much of Marsh's mechanical ingenuity was called into play, not only in the construction of the roadway but also in the design of the steam locomotives. He patented an improvement in locomotive engines for ascending inclined planes (Sept. 10, 1861); apparatus for ascending gradients (Nov. 8, 1864); cog rail for railroads (Jan. 15, 1867); atmospheric brake for railway cars (Apr. 12, 1870). His central cog rail driving mechanism proved extremely successful, as did the braking system (there were six ways of stopping the train) and the plan was adopted subsequently in the construction of the railroad on Mount Rigi, Switzerland. The Mount Washington project was not a financial success, however, and up to the time that the Boston & Maine Railroad took over the property some time after Marsh's death, the officers of the company received no salaries. Marsh lived at Littleton, N. H., from 1865 to 1879, and spent the last five years of his life in Concord, N. H. He was married, first, Apr. 4, 1844, to Charlotte D. Bates of Monson, Mass., who died in 1850; and second, in March 1855, to Cornelia H. Hoyt of St. Albans, Vt. He was survived by his widow and four children.

[J. R. Jackson, *Hist. of Littleton, N. H.* (1905), vols. I, III; D. W. Marsh, *Marsh Geneal.* (1895), p. xxi; C. C. Coffin, "Sylvester Marsh," in *Bay State Monthly*, May 1885, repr. in *Granite Monthly*, May–June 1885; J. W. Merrill, "The Mt. Washington Railroad," *The Railway & Locomotive Hist. Soc. Bull.* no. 4, 1923; *Daily Monitor*, Concord, N. H., Dec. 31, 1884; Patent Office records.] C. W. M.

MARSH, WILLIAM WALLACE (Apr. 15, 1836–May 2, 1918), inventor, manufacturer, was the son of Samuel and Tamar (Richardson) Marsh and the younger brother of Charles Wesley Marsh [*q.v.*]. He was born on his father's farm near Trenton, Northumberland County, Canada, and was educated at home and in the district school near his home as well as in St. Andrews School and Victoria College at Coburg, Canada, where he was a student for three years. His schooling ceased when he was thirteen years old and he moved with his parents to De Kalb County, Ill. During the succeeding eight years he worked assiduously with his father and brother to improve the raw land and to make it produce profitable crops. In 1857, while working in the fields with their newly acquired Mann reaper, Marsh and his brother conceived the idea of binding the grain on the machine. Neither youth possessed much mechanical experience but by diligent effort they succeeded in carrying out their idea and patenting their implement on Aug. 17, 1858. The machine changed the farm system from "reaping" to "harvesting" and by this invention one man could do the work formerly required of two.

In the winter of 1860 Marsh built, in connection with a neighbor, a second machine which was ready for the harvest of 1861. He used it on the farm during the next three seasons and harvested over four hundred acres with it. He also staged public demonstrations and participated in public trials, one of which was held at De Kalb in 1863, when he won first prize by binding an acre of heavy grain in fifty-two minutes. While Charles looked after the business details of their venture, William Marsh devoted himself to the mechanical, and during the formative stage of the business he gave considerable study and thought to harvester improvements and details of its manufacture. In 1864 he took charge of the manufacturing plant which had been established at Plano, Ill., in 1863 and for the succeeding twenty years both there and at Sycamore, Ill., where the company established its second factory in 1869, he served in the general capacity of superintendent. Though this work consumed the greater part of his time, he devised a number of improvements on the machine. Patents on these were granted jointly to him and his brother on Jan. 5, 1864, Feb. 15, 1865, Nov. 12, 1867, and June 18, 1872. In addition he designed other farm machinery including a plow, cultivator, corn harvester, corn husker, wire stretcher, and windmill—a total of forty inventions. All of these products were manufactured in the Marsh factories.

After the failure of the Marsh brothers in 1884 with a combined loss in excess of $400,000, they had to separate, each to make his own way thereafter. William went to Lincoln, Neb., in 1887 to superintend a manufacturing plant, and five years later he was sent to Little Rock, Ark., to reorganize and redesign a stave and lumbering enterprise. In his halcyon days he had made purchases in these states of timber lands which after a few years yielded him sufficient income so that in 1895 he was able to retire to his home in Sycamore. He then became interested again in an agricultural machinery business and continued actively in its affairs until 1906. After his retirement he devoted his energies to the betterment of Sycamore. He had married on Jan. 8, 1871, Mary Jane Brown of Chicago. She died in 1891 and on Nov. 9, 1893, he was married to Emma L. Eldredge. At the time of his death in Sycamore he was survived by his widow and two children of his first marriage.

[C. W. Marsh, *Recollections, 1837–1910* (1910); L. M. Gross, *Past and Present of De Kalb County, Ill.* (1907), vol. II; R. L. Ardrey, *Am. Agric. Implements* (1894); *Ann. Reports of the Commissioner of Patents*, 1858 and years following, *Farm Implement News*, May 9, 1918; *Farm Machinery-Farm Power*, May 14, 1918.] C. W. M.

MARSHALL, BENJAMIN (1782–Dec. 2, 1858), merchant, manufacturer, was born in Huddersfield, in the West Riding of Yorkshire, England, the youngest of six brothers who were brought up to manufacturing pursuits. In 1798 he entered the cotton manufacture at Manchester. He brought an invoice of cotton goods to New York in 1803 and here became the friend of Isaac Wright, a Quaker merchant, and Francis Thompson, Wright's son-in-law, the New York representative of a West Riding firm of woollen-cloth manufacturers. He joined Thompson in the business of importing cotton goods and exporting cotton, and spent the winters in Georgia as a cotton buyer. In 1813, he married Niobe, daughter of Capt. John Stanton, commander of Wright & Thompson's fast-sailing transatlantic trading ship *Pacific*. In 1816, Benjamin Marshall, William Wright (Isaac Wright's son), and Jeremiah Thompson (Francis Thompson's nephew) acquired shares in the *Pacific*, and in a new ship, *Amity*. At this time, Benjamin Marshall and Jeremiah Thompson [*q.v.*] were doing business in the same premises at 273 Pearl St., New York. In the spring of 1817, the five partners placed another new ship, *Courier*, in transatlantic trade, and in October 1817 they announced the establishment of a line of American packets, to make regular monthly sailings from New York and Liverpool. This was the Black Ball Line, the first of the famous transatlantic packet lines of New York. The first sailing on a regular schedule was made Jan. 1, 1818. To complete the service a fourth ship, *James Monroe*, was purchased. The management of the line appears to have been principally entrusted to Jeremiah Thompson; there is no indication that Marshall did any special part of this work.

After the enactment of the tariff of 1824, Marshall turned from importing to manufacturing and printing cotton cloths. In partnership with Benjamin S. Walcott, Jr., who was already engaged in manufacturing at Whitestown, N. Y., he established the New York Mills on a waterpower a couple of miles to the west of Utica. In 1827 (or thereabouts), with his brother Joseph, he established the Hudson Print Works, near Hudson (later Stockport), N. Y., one of the earliest cotton-printing works in the United States. Benjamin seems to have left his brother in charge of the store in New York and to have withdrawn to Hudson to manage the enterprise there.

In 1833 he sold his share in the packet line to his brother. It had become by this time the leading shipping service of New York, with a fleet of eight first-class ships and regular sailings twice a month. Early in 1834, Joseph Marshall in turn sold the line to Jonathan Goodhue & Company. Later in that year, the two brothers divided their interests in the various factories they owned, Joseph taking the Hudson Print Works, and Benjamin their share in the New York Mills and some other factories at Troy, N. Y., and elsewhere. From this time onward he seems to have devoted himself principally to the development of the factories at Troy. The cottons produced by the New York Mills near Utica and the Mount Ida Mill at Troy appear to have been clearly the finest goods of their kind produced in the United States at this time. About 1840 Marshall developed the waterpower in the Poestenkill Creek at Troy by a series of tunnels and built a chain of mills down the creek. He became one of Troy's leading citizens, and was president of one of the banks of the city, of the Troy & Schenectady Railway, and of Mrs. Emma Willard's Female Seminary. In 1847 he sold his interest in the New York Mills to the Walcott family. His wife died in 1823, leaving him one son, who developed a mental disease about 1847 of which he died ten years later. To make provision for his and similar cases, in 1850 the father founded in Troy the Marshall Infirmary (now the Marshall Sanitarium), of which he was the first president. He died in Troy in December 1858.

[John Livingston, *Portraits of Eminent Americans*, vol. III (1854); Nathan Crosby, *Annual Obituary Notices . . . for 1858* (1859); C. C. Cutler, *Greyhounds of the Sea* (1930); W. R. Bagnall, *The Textile Industries of the U. S.* (1893), pp. 506–16; A. J. Weise, *Troy's One Hundred Years* (1891); C. P. Wright, "The Packet Ships of New York," unpublished thesis in Harvard Univ. Lib.; *Atlas & Argus* (Albany), Dec. 4, 1858.]

C. P. W.

MARSHALL, CHARLES HENRY (Apr. 8, 1792–Sept. 23, 1865), sea captain, shipping executive, was born on Nantucket Island, the third of the seven children of Charles and Hepzibah (Coffin) Marshall, and the descendant of generations of whaling skippers. With the island's industry ruined by the Revolution, the father abandoned whaling for farming, settling on a tract of virgin forest in the Saratoga Patent at Easton, N. Y. The hundred acres could not support so large a family and the five sons turned to the sea, where all became successful captains. Charles Henry started his career at fifteen on the Nantucket whaler *Lima*, and then made a voyage to England. He spent a winter in school at Johnstown, N. Y., and in 1810 sailed for Riga, being detained for a year in Denmark. During the War of 1812, he taught school for a time, served on the Hudson steamboat *Paragon*, and engaged in trade with his uncle at Sacketts Harbor. In 1815 he was at sea again, as mate in the *Mary* for Oporto, under Capt. Robert Waterman, later a well-known packet captain. By 1816, at the age of twenty-three, Marshall was a captain himself and drove his *Julius Cæsar* at top speed from Charleston to Liverpool to win a hotly contested race. His next voyage was to the East Indies, and in 1822 he married Fidelia Wellman of Piermont, N. H., a "rare beauty." That same year he was given command of a Black Ball packet, one of the most coveted maritime honors of that day.

The Black Ball or "Old Line" made the first successful attempt to provide regular transatlantic service under private auspices, as distinct from the official British mail packets. It was inaugurated in 1817 by Benjamin Marshall [*q.v.*], Isaac Wright, Francis Thompson, and Jeremiah Thompson, of New York, and its continued success was an important element in the rise of the port of New York. Its ships, run with the *élan* and discipline of East Indiamen, sailed from New York for Liverpool on the 1st and 16th of every month with passengers and select freight. It enjoyed a primacy among the various packet lines which developed, until eclipsed by the Cunard and Collins steamships; but even then its sailing vessels continued profitable until after the Civil War. Marshall commanded successively the line's *James Cropper, Britannia,* and *South America* for twelve years, making, altogether, ninety-four Atlantic crossings.

In 1834, he came ashore to make his home in New York as agent of the line for the remaining thirty-one years of his life. It had then passed from its original owners into new control, particularly that of Goodhue & Company, formerly its agents. Marshall soon bought out the company's share, becoming principal owner as well as active manager, with Baring Brothers as Liverpool consignees. He personally supervised the building of all the new ships for the line and raised the standard of sailing packets to a high degree. His principal venture in steam came about 1848 when, with William H. Webb [*q.v.*] and others, he built the *United States,* which was sold to Prussia for a steam frigate after two rather unprofitable years of running between New York and Southampton. Marshall also did some business as a general commission merchant. His wealth was estimated at $120,000 in 1845; $150,000 in 1847; and the same in 1855; but it was probably more by the time of his death. He was prominent in many of the activities of the port of New York, serving for years as a commissioner of pilots, as head of the Marine Society, and as a director of the Sailors' Snug Harbor. From 1851 to 1855, he was a commissioner of emigration. Strongly anti-slavery, he was first a Whig, and later a Republican. He was nominated for Congress in 1854 and defeated while absent in Europe. Early in 1861 he declined to cooperate with naval officials in the proposed relief of Fort Sumter, on the ground that it would precipitate a conflict. Once the war started, however, he was an active Union man, prominent on the local Union Defence Committee and in the Union League Club. In the name of the state Chamber of Commerce, he urged upon the navy a tightening of the blockade and energetic pursuit of the *Alabama,* suggesting privateers for that purpose. His picture shows a strong, square, rugged face with chin whiskers, tight lips, piercing eyes, and something of a permanent scowl. Even a eulogistic obituary states that he had "an air of sternness about him that was somewhat repulsive to strangers" (*New York Herald, post*), but he was a perfect gentleman and a delightful companion with his intimates. He was noted for his independence of spirit and fearless exposing of abuses.

[W. A. Butler, *Memorial of Charles H. Marshall* (1867), with portrait and autobiog. story of his first voyage; J. A. Scoville, *The Old Merchants of N. Y. City,* vols. I (1863), IV (1866); C. G. Davis, *Ships of the Past* (1929); C. C. Cutler, *Greyhounds of the Sea* (1930); *Vital Records of Nantucket, Mass.,* vols. II (1926), IV (1927); M. Y. Beach, *Wealth and Biography of the Wealthy Citizens of N. Y. City* (6th ed., 1845); *War of the Rebellion: Official Records (Navy),* 1 ser., I, 545, IV, 225, 246; *Confidential Correspondence of Gustavus Vasa Fox,* vol. I (1918), ed. by R. M. Thompson and Richard Wainwright; W. A. Butler, in *Portrait Gallery of the Chamber of Commerce of the State of N. Y.* (1890), compiled by George Wilson; *N. Y. Herald,* Sept. 24, 1865.]

R. G. A.

MARSHALL, CHRISTOPHER (Nov. 6, 1709–May 4, 1797), pharmacist, Revolutionary patriot, diarist, was born probably in Dublin, Ireland. He received a classical education in England, left his home in that country at the age of eighteen, and came to Philadelphia. There he became a noted pharmacist, conducting his business at the sign of the Golden Ball, one of the largest establishments of its kind in the city. By 1774 he had acquired considerable wealth and retired from active participation in his business, the control of which he transferred to his sons. From the beginning of the Revolution he heartily embraced the American cause, John Adams finding him, Sept. 20, 1775, "a fine, facetious old gentleman, an excellent Whig" (C. F. Adams, *The Works of John Adams,* vol. II, 1850, p. 425). As a member of the Philadelphia committee of inspection and observation he was active in enforcing the non-importation agreements, in collecting supplies for the army, in ferreting out inimical and suspected persons, and in other patriot undertakings. He was one of the managers of a factory established in 1775 for making woolens, linens, and cottons, and was a delegate to the provincial conference in Philadelphia (1776) which set the wheels in motion for a new state government. On Dec. 5, 1776, he was appointed by the Council of Safety to assist in procuring housing and other necessaries for sick and wounded soldiers returned to Philadelphia. In 1777, owing to ill health, and to escape the difficulties of imminent British invasion of Philadelphia, he moved to Lancaster. On Oct.

13, 1777, he was appointed to the Council of Safety, serving from Nov. 17 until Dec. 6 following. While in Lancaster he served as chairman of a price-fixing committee (1779), assisted in providing clothing for Pennsylvania troops, and in securing wheat and flour for the state. Although of a moderate temperament, he aligned himself with the Constitutional party which supported the state constitution of 1776.

Marshall is best known for the "Remembrancer," or diary, which he kept during the Revolution. One of the most valuable sources of the period, it contains, in addition to its observations on politics, illuminating data on food, crops, prices, customs, *et cetera.* It is the account of a conscientious Whig who in those troublous times was aware of only the serious side of life and constantly deplored seeing so many fellow Whigs engaged "in monopolizing, gaming, drinking, dancing" and other frivolities. To this ardent patriot, Howe's army was "that handful of banditti" or "a parcel of poltroons" and Howe, "that monster of rapine" (*Diary,* 1877 ed., pp. 152, 169). A comprehensive edition of the diary, containing matters of public interest, *Extracts from the Diary of Christopher Marshall, Kept in Philadelphia and Lancaster, during the American Revolution, 1774–1781,* was edited and published in 1877 by William Duane, who had previously issued *Passages from the Remembrancer of Christopher Marshall* (1839), covering the period 1774–76, and *Passages from the Diary of Christopher Marshall* (1849), covering the period 1774–77. A man of great moral courage, Marshall was thoroughly imbued with Quaker doctrine, and except in his support of the Revolution, for which he was read out of the Society of Friends, he adhered rigidly to its principles. He was married twice, his first wife dying prior to the Revolution, and his second, Abigail, in 1782. Three sons of his first marriage, two of whom survived him, followed his footsteps in business, Charles, the second, attaining considerable rank as a pharmacist. Marshall died in Philadelphia.

[Marshall's Letter Book and the six manuscript volumes of his "Remembrancer" are in the Hist. Soc. of Pa., Phila. See also *Minutes of the Supreme Exec. Council in Pa.,* XI (1852), 34, 325–53; *Pa. Mag. of Hist. and Biog.,* Oct. 1893, Jan. 1904; J. T. Scharf and Thompson Westcott, *Hist. of Phila.* (1884), vol. I; Henry Simpson, *The Lives of Eminent Philadelphians Now Deceased* (1859); Claypoole's *Am. Daily Advertiser,* May 6, 1797.] J. H. P—g.

MARSHALL, CLARA (*c.* 1848–Mar. 13, 1931), pioneer leader of women in medicine, was born in West Chester, Pa., of Quaker family, the daughter of Pennock and Mary (Phillips) Marshall. She attended the Woman's Medical College of Pennsylvania, graduating in the class of 1875. Although the college had been in existence since 1850, it was still small and had been able to achieve little standing in medical circles. Clara Marshall became identified with the faculty immediately after graduation and worked for the improvement of the college and the recognition of its graduates throughout a long career. It was largely through her efforts and those of the group with which she was associated that success was attained. Her entry in 1875 opened to women the doors of the Philadelphia School of Pharmacy and Science. She was so successful as a student that she was assigned the task of arranging the pharmaceutical display at the Centennial Exhibition in Philadelphia. During the year 1875–76, she served the Woman's Medical College as demonstrator of pharmacy. The following year she was made professor of materia medica and therapeutics, a post she held for thirty years. She acted as dean from 1888 till 1917, and continued at the college as emeritus professor until 1923.

In all her activities, she was noted for energy and enthusiasm. She was responsible for the addition of many new departments to the college, and at the beginning of the century, when it became necessary for a standard medical college to have its own hospital, she secured funds to add a hospital building to the Woman's Medical College. It is largely to her credit that the school received a rating of Grade A when the medical colleges of the country were inspected and classified in the years 1905–09. In addition to her teaching, she practised medicine in Philadelphia for many years. In 1882 she acted as obstetrician at the Philadelphia Hospital, and in 1886 she was appointed attending physician to the girls' department of the Philadelphia House of Refuge. In 1893 she was lecturer at the Nurses Training School of the Jefferson Hospital. She was the first woman to address the graduating classes of nurses at the St. Agnes Hospital and at Bryn Mawr Hospital. Because of her interest in politics she was asked to address a convention of women suffragists that met in Richmond in 1898. Her lecture, "Fifty Years in Medicine" (printed in the *Virginia Medical Semi-Monthly,* Jan. 27, 1899), bears upon the place of women in the profession and their contribution to the science. Well known as a writer on medical subjects, she contributed many short articles to professional journals and also prepared *The Woman's Medical College of Pennsylvania; An Historical Outline* (1897). She died in March 1931, at the age of eighty-three. A woman of decisive and energetic character, she made a choice of her career early in life and carried out her plans with thoroughness.

[*Who's Who in America*, 1910–11; *Woman's Who's Who of America*, 1914–15; *Evening Bull.* (Phila.), Mar. 14, 1931; *Pub. Ledger* (Phila.), Mar. 13, 14, 1931; *Bull. of Woman's Medic. Coll. of Pa.*, Apr. 1931; information from the registrar of the Woman's Medic. Coll.]
F. E. W.

MARSHALL, DANIEL (1706–Nov. 2, 1784), one of the pioneer Baptist preachers of the South, was born in Windsor, Conn., the son of Thomas and Mary (Drake) Marshall and the grandson of Samuel Marshall who was settled at Woodbury in 1637. Converted at the age of twenty, he joined the Congregational Church. He took his religious duties with such seriousness that he was soon elected deacon, a position which he held for twenty years. He became a prosperous farmer, and on Nov. 11, 1742, married Hannah Drake, who died after she had given birth to one son. When Marshall was thirty-eight years of age he came into contact with George Whitefield [*q.v.*], under whose influence he was completely transformed and incited to spend the remainder of his life in religious work. Convinced that the second coming of the Lord was at hand, he left his comfortable farm and rushed off, with others, to preach the gospel to the Mohawk Indians located on the upper reaches of the Susquehanna. With him he took his second wife, Martha Stearns, whom he had married on June 23, 1747, and his three children. He remained in the Indian country for some eighteen months, but was finally driven out by strife among the Indians. After a short time spent elsewhere in Pennsylvania, he went southward into Virginia, settling near Winchester, where his brother-in-law, Shubael Stearns [*q.v.*], had preceded him. Stearns had been a Congregationalist, but as a result of Whitefield's influence he had become a "New Light," or "Separate," and finally a "Separate Baptist." Marshall and his wife, the latter a remarkable woman, full of energy, herself an excellent preacher or exhorter, now accepted Baptist views, and joined a Baptist church. Marshall was soon licensed to preach and henceforth devoted himself with consuming zeal to extensive evangelism.

There were already Baptists of the Philadelphia type, later known as "Regulars," in northern Virginia, but they were rigidly Calvinistic in theology, and dignified and orderly in their preaching and methods; consequently they were not altogether friendly to these newcomers from the North who were highly emotional, noisy, suspected of Arminianism, and disposed to allow women prominence in religious work not generally sanctioned. Accordingly, the "Separates" moved southward again to Guilford County, N. C., where in 1755 they established the Sandy Creek church. Marshall and his wife were among the constituent members. The former soon established Abbott's Creek church, some thirty miles distant, over which at the age of fifty-two he was ordained pastor by his brothers-in-law, Stearns and Ledbetter.

From this center the "Separate Baptists" spread with wonderful rapidity over much of Virginia, the two Carolinas, and Georgia. Marshall, who was but poorly educated and not highly endowed, made up for all other deficiencies by zeal and activity. Churches sprang up and men were called into the ministry wherever he went. In a few years he moved to South Carolina, settling a few miles north of Augusta, on Horse Creek, where he very quickly formed a church. His eyes were on Georgia, however, into which colony he extended his itinerating tours. On one of these trips he was arrested for preaching "in St. Paul's parish" contrary to a law of 1758. When haled into court at Augusta he defended himself with such meekness and firmness that both the constable and the magistrate were soon afterwards converted. In January 1771 he removed to Georgia and settled on Kiokee Creek about twenty miles northwest of Augusta, where he spent the remainder of his life. He soon founded the Kiokee church, the first Baptist church in the state, organized in 1772 and in 1789 formally incorporated as "The Anabaptist Church on Kioka." During the Revolution many of the preachers fled from the state, but Marshall remained with the people, sharing their hardships and dangers and affording the comforts and encouragements of the gospel. After the Revolution the Baptist cause flourished, and before his death Marshall saw six churches formed, and presided at the organization of the Georgia Association in 1784.

[H. R. Stiles, *The Hist. and Geneals. of Ancient Windsor, Conn., 1635–1891*, vol. II (1892); "Abraham Marshall," in *Ga. Analytical Repository* (1802); W. B. Sprague, *Annals of the Am. Pulpit*, vol. VI (1860); J. B. Taylor, *Lives of Va. Bapt. Ministers* (1837); A. H. Newman, *Hist. of the Bapt. Churches in the U. S.* (1915); B. F. Riley, *A Hist. of the Baptists in the Southern States East of the Mississippi* (1898); W. M. Gewehr, *The Great Awakening in Va., 1740–1790* (1930); W. J. Northen, *Men of Mark in Ga.*, vol. I (1907); J. H. Campbell, *Ga. Baptists: Hist. and Biog.* (1874).]
W. J. M.

MARSHALL, HENRY RUTGERS (July 22, 1852–May 3, 1927), architect, psychologist, and writer, the son of Henry Perry and Cornelia (Conrad) Marshall, was born in New York City, a descendant of Edward Marshall who came thither from Barbados in the latter part of the seventeenth century, and of his son John, who married Elsie, daughter of the well-known brewer, Harman Rutgers 2nd. Henry Rutgers Marshall was therefore related to the famous Rutgers family of New York City and New Jersey. He was educated at private schools in New York, and then at Columbia College, where he received the degree of B.A. in 1873 and that of M.A. in 1876. After a year in business, he turned to architecture. His practice, begun in 1878, was widely scattered and included Rudyard Kipling's house in Brattleboro, Vt., the Storm King Club at Cornwall, N. Y., a Congregational church at Colorado Springs, Colo., and the old building (since destroyed) of the Brearley School in New York.

On May 18, 1881, he married Julia Robbins Gilman and after her premature death in 1888 his interest turned more and more toward psychology, philosophy, and aesthetics. He published "The Field of Aesthetics Psychologically Considered" (*Mind,* July, October 1892), *Pain, Pleasure, and Aesthetics* in 1894, and a year later, *Aesthetic Principles.* His aesthetic ideas were further clarified in *The Relation of Aesthetics to Psychology and Philosophy* (1905), and in *The Beautiful* (London, 1924). Marshall's aesthetic theory is mainly the result of the application of common sense to aesthetic speculation; he makes a sharp distinction between the aesthetic processes of the creator and those of the observer; and his psychological study led him to be suspicious of easy generalities like those of Bernard Bosanquet (see his review of Bosanquet's "Three Lectures on Aesthetic" in *The Nation,* July 29, 1915). He also lays great stress on the pleasure and pain factors of aesthetics. His philosophical interests widened continually. To academic psychology and philosophy he brought a refreshing and unconventional directness of speculation; *Instinct and Reason* (1898) and *Mind and Conduct* (1919) show the breadth and the basic simplicity of his approach. The more daring type of metaphysical speculation (yet governed by his typical persuasive common sense) is well illustrated in *Human and Other Types of Consciousness* (1905). Obviously humanistic in the broad sense, his philosophy led him to generally conservative ideals. He was an idealistic pacifist, and in *War and the Ideal of Peace* (1915) his hatred of war found expression. Yet, as the World War drew on his war-hatred gradually yielded to fear of German victory. When the United States finally entered the war, therefore, he, like so many other pacifists of his age and background, became enthusiastically patriotic, and in *The Atlantic Monthly* for May 1918, he published an article, "The Pacifist at War," which was perhaps the most forceful apologia for what was at best an illogical stand.

He was a member of the American Psychological Association and its president in 1907, and a member of the American Philosophical Association. He lectured an aesthetics at several universities and gave the principal address on aesthetics before the St. Louis International Congress of Arts and Sciences in 1904. With all his philosophic interests, Marshall never forgot his original profession. He was a fellow of the American Institute of Architects, and president of the New York Chapter from 1902 to 1904. He was also one of the committee of the Fine Arts Federation which elaborated the idea of a municipal art commission and procured its inclusion in the New York city charter. He was the architect member of that commission from 1902 to 1905, and from 1914 till his death he was its executive secretary, giving to it the greater part of his time and energy. During his later years he lived almost entirely at the Columbia University Club and at his summer home in Woodbury, Conn., spending his leisure hours at the Century Association, of which he was a much loved member. He was buried in Woodbury, Conn. His only child, a daughter, predeceased him.

[*N. Y. Times,* May 4, 1927; *The Nation* (N. Y.), May 18, 1927; *Who's Who in America, 1926–27*; *Am. Art Annual, 1927* (1928); William Cothren, *Hist. of Ancient Woodbury, Conn.* (2 vols., 1854, 1872); E. H. Crosby, "The Rutgers Family of New York," in *N. Y. Geneal. and Biog. Record,* Apr. 1886; J. M. Strong, *The Town and People, . . . Woodbury, Conn.* (1901), pp. 188–89.] T. F. H.

MARSHALL, HUMPHREY (1760–June 26, 1841), senator and historian of Kentucky, the son of John and Mary (Quisenberry) Marshall, was born in Fauquier County, Va. His father was a younger son in humble circumstances but was a member of a distinguished family. There is a tradition that the boy was sent to be educated at the home of his uncle, Thomas Marshall [*q.v.*], and that there in company with his first cousins he was instructed by members of the family and by their tutors. Among these cousins were John, Louis, and James Markham Marshall [*qq.v.*] and Mary (christened Anna Maria), to whom he was married on Sept. 18, 1784. In 1778 Humphrey Marshall enlisted in the Virginia forces, and in 1781 he was captain-lieutenant of the Virginia artillery. In 1782 he settled in Kentucky and became deputy surveyor of Fayette County in the office of his uncle Thomas Marshall. In December of that year he received from Virginia a warrant for 4,000 acres of land for his Revolutionary services, and before his death he had become one of the greatest landholders in Kentucky and one of its wealthiest citizens, according to tradition measuring his money by the peck. He studied law and attained a position of eminence as an attorney. Like most of the Marshalls he became a Federalist and doggedly remained so, in spirit, to the end of his days. In Kentucky, where Jeffersonians greatly predominated, such perversity was unforgivable. An additional provocation to his neighbors was his scorn for any revealed religion. He had an extreme amount of candor and very little tact. He did not believe in the rule of the masses and often publicly stated his contempt for them. He had a blistering tongue and a cutting pen, and though he spent all of his public life in the midst of bitter political warfare and personal contentions, he claimed never to have provoked them.

He first attracted public attention, when he began in 1786 to oppose the schemes of James Wilkinson to separate Kentucky from Virginia. He was elected a delegate from Fayette County to the Danville convention of 1787, where he came into collision with Wilkinson. The next year as a delegate to the Virginia convention he voted for ratification of the federal Constitution. In 1789 he was a delegate to the Danville convention that was attempting to advance Kentucky to statehood. Having moved to Woodford County he became surveyor there in 1790, and in 1793 and 1794 he was elected to the Kentucky legislature. Suspecting a plot he opposed the movement of George Rogers Clark [*q.v.*] to attack the Spaniards at New Orleans, under the direction of Genet, and he accused Governor Isaac Shelby of complicity. Jeffersonian Republicanism was so weakened by these Spanish and French schemes that the Kentucky legislature in 1795 elected Marshall to the United States Senate over John Breckinridge, 1760–1806 [*q.v.*]. By voting for the Jay Treaty in the Senate Marshall brought down upon himself in Kentucky hostility that did not stop short of mob violence. He was dragged to the Kentucky River and was only by a trick prevented from being ducked. He was actually stoned out of Frankfort. In 1806 he suspected Aaron Burr's motives and was instrumental in exposing him. At this time John Wood and Joseph M. Street [*q.v.*] set up their *Western World* and with Marshall's aid began to pry into the dealings of some prominent Kentuckians with Spain. Writing over the signature of "Observer" Marshall soon drove from the bench of the highest court in the state Benjamin Sebastian, and he began an onset upon Harry Innes [*q.v.*] that ran its course through lawsuits instituted by both parties and finally ended by both signing an agreement to cease attacking each other. Marshall was elected to the lower house of the legislature in 1807, 1808, and 1809. Already in conflict with Henry Clay in the Burr exposure, Marshall, in 1809, insulted him over a resolution that Clay had introduced calling for the wearing of homespun, and at Louisville the two crossed the Ohio into Indiana to fight a duel, in which both were slightly wounded.

Marshall has been remembered by subsequent generations largely for *The History of Kentucky,* which was first published in 1812 in one volume, and revised and republished in 1824 in two. It was the first formal history of the state. In it he vindicated himself and made havoc of his enemies. Notwithstanding the agreement he had signed, his second edition repeated the earlier attacks on Innes, who had died in 1816. He also wrote a large number of communications to the newspapers of Kentucky and now and then wrote verse. In 1810 he set up the only Federalist newspaper in the state, the *American Republic,* and as an act of defiance to his enemies, flew a rattlesnake from its masthead. He soon changed the name to the *Harbinger* and sold it in 1825. He had a daughter and two sons, Thomas Alexander [*q.v.*], and John Jay, who was the father of Humphrey Marshall, 1812–1872 [*q.v.*]. In his old age becoming paralyzed, he moved back to Lexington to live with his son Thomas Alexander Marshall and died there.

[A. C. Quisenberry, *The Life and Times of Hon. Humphrey Marshall* (1892); T. M. Green, *The Spanish Conspiracy* (1891); Lewis and R. H. Collins, *Hist. of Ky.*, revised ed. (2 vols., 1874); J. M. Brown, *The Political Beginnings of Ky.* (1889); Wm. Littell, *Political Transactions in and Concerning Ky.* (1806); R. M. McElroy, *Ky. in the Nation's Hist.* (1909); W. M. Paxton, *The Marshall Family* (1885); date of death accepted from *Louisville Daily Journal,* July 9, 1841, though date of July 3 officially reported to pension office, Quisenberry, *ante*, p. 13.]

E. M. C.

MARSHALL, HUMPHREY (Jan. 13, 1812–Mar. 28, 1872), soldier, minister to China and member of the United States Congress and of the Confederate Congress, was a son of John Jay and Anna Reed (Birney) Marshall. He was born in Frankfort, Ky. His father was a son of Humphrey Marshall (1760–1841), and his mother was a sister of James G. Birney [*qq.v.*]. At the age of sixteen he received an appointment to the Military Academy at West Point, where he was graduated in 1832, and he became lieutenant of the mounted rangers. On Jan. 23, 1833, he was married to Frances, the daughter of Charles McAllister of Franklin, Tenn., by whom he had six children. He resigned his commission in April 1833, studied law, and the same year began practice in Frankfort. In 1834 he moved to

Louisville, where he practised law until 1846. He developed political inclinations, served in the city council in 1836, and the following year was unsuccessful in the election for state representative. In 1836 he raised a company of Kentuckians and prepared to lead them to Texas, but on the arrival of news of Houston's victory at San Jacinto he disbanded the company. Taking an active part in the development of the state militia, from 1836 to 1846 he held successively the ranks of captain, major, and lieutenant-colonel. On the outbreak of war with Mexico in 1846 he raised the 1st Kentucky Cavalry and, on June 9, was commissioned its colonel. He took a prominent part in the battle of Buena Vista, in which he executed some brilliant cavalry charges. For a short period after the war he carried on farming operations in Henry County.

After a hard fight for election, in 1849 he entered Congress as a Whig and was reëlected two years later. Receiving a few votes for the speakership in the strenuous contest of 1849, he immediately took a position of prominence in the debates that developed around the many questions growing out of the Mexican War. He upheld the orthodox position of the Southern Whigs and spoke in favor of various points in Clay's compromise scheme. So prominent did he become in Whig affairs that in 1852, when a vacancy occurred in the Supreme Court, he was urged for the position. Since geographical considerations prevented his appointment, President Fillmore offered to appoint him minister resident to Central America, but he refused the honor. Thereupon Fillmore offered to send him to China. He accepted and resigning from Congress on Aug. 4, 1852, he arrived in China in January 1853, where he spent the next year in dealing with the details of American shipping in the free ports of China. He was also busied with the increasing Chinese emigration to the United States as well as with the delicate problems arising from China's unwillingness to be drawn into the maelstrom of western commercial and political relations. On his return to America early in 1854, finding the Whig party disrupted, he joined the Know-Nothings and became an important force in their national councils. Serving from 1855 to 1859 in Congress, he again took a prominent part in the proceedings. He tried to evade the slavery issue wherever possible, but he insisted on the rights of slave-holders and the South's right to equality in the Union. By 1859 he refused to run for Congress again; instead he settled down in Washington to practise law. In 1860 he supported Breckinridge for the presidency (*Speeches of Hon. Humphrey Marshall & Hon. B. F. Hallett . . . on the Nomination of Breckinridge and Lane,* 1860).

With the coming of war, he returned to Kentucky and sought to hold the border states to a peaceful course. Failing, he retired to Nashville, Tenn., in the fall of 1861 and, on receiving a commission as brigadier-general in the Confederate Army, set out for Eastern Kentucky. He was obsessed with the idea that he could swing Kentucky into line if he were given a free hand and proper support. During the winter of 1861–62 he fought a few engagements in the Big Sandy region and then retired into southwestern Virginia, where in May 1862 he surprised the Federals at Princeton, W. Va., and defeated them. He took part in Bragg's invasion of Kentucky in the autumn of 1862, after which he retired into southwest Virginia. He always wanted an independent command and never found conditions quite to his liking. In 1863 he resigned from the army, went to Richmond to practise law, and the next year was elected to the Second Confederate Congress in which he served to the end. When the war was over he fled to Texas and in November 1865 got permission to go to New Orleans. The next year he returned to Kentucky and practised law in Louisville until his death.

[Lewis and R. H. Collins, *Hist. of Ky.*, revised ed. (2 vols., 1874); J. S. Johnston, *Memorial Hist. of Louisville* (2 vols., 1896); *The Biog. Encyc. of Ky.* (1878); W. H. Perrin, J. H. Battle, and G. C. Kniffin, *Ky. A Hist. of the State* (1886); *Battles and Leaders of the Civil War*, ed. by R. N. Johnson and C. C. Buel, vols. I–III (1887–88); *War of the Rebellion: Official Records (Army)*, esp. ser. 1, vols. IV, VII, XII, XVI (pt. 1), XX (pt. 1); *Sen. Doc. 234*, 58 Cong., 2 Sess. (1905), for service in Confederate Cong.; *House Exec. Doc. 123*, 33 Cong., 1 Sess. (1854), for dispatches from China.]

E. M. C.

MARSHALL, HUMPHRY (Oct. 10, 1722 o.s.–Nov. 5, 1801), botanist, was a cousin of John Bartram [*q.v.*] and belonged to a family of botanists. His father, Abraham Marshall, was born in Derbyshire, England, became a Friend, and about 1697 emigrated to Pennsylvania, where he settled near Darby and married Mary Hunt, the daughter of James Hunt, who had been a companion of William Penn. Soon after his marriage he moved to what is now Chester County, took up a large tract of land on the west branch of the Brandywine, and acquired a considerable fortune. Humphry was born there and after 1748 managed this farm. The eighth child in a family of nine, he is quoted as saying that "he never went to school a day after he was twelve years of age; and consequently, was instructed only in the rudiments of the plainest English education" (Darlington, *post*, p. 486). In the course of a long life he gave himself, however, an excellent education and became one of the best-read men of his times, specializing in all branches of natural history and astronomy. He was early apprenticed as a stone mason and followed the trade for a few years. On Sept. 16, 1748, he married Sarah Pennock of West Marlboro, Chester County. In 1764 he enlarged his father's house, doing all the work himself, even to making the bricks. He added a small conservatory for rare plants, probably the first conservatory in Chester County. In 1773 he built with his own hands the house at Marshallton, which is still standing, and not only included a hot-house but also a small observatory.

A considerable fortune left him by his father in 1767 enabled him to move to his own house at Marshallton in 1774. There he planned and laid out a botanic garden, which in time came to include not only many foreign specimens but also a noteworthy collection of native plants, shrubs, and trees and was only less celebrated than that of his cousin, John Bartram [*q.v.*]. Both men were correspondents of two enthusiastic English collectors, Peter Collinson and Dr. John Fothergill. Some time about 1767 Marshall began collecting and shipping to Fothergill in London plants, birds' nests and eggs, and other specimens of animal life. In return Fothergill sent him many books, a reflecting telescope, and, through the good offices of Benjamin Franklin, a microscope and a thermometer. In 1785 he published his *"Arbustrum Americanum, the American Grove,"* a list of native forest trees and shrubs. This is arranged in alphabetical order and the descriptions, which are still extraordinarily vivid, follow the Linnean system. It was according to his biographer "the first truly indigenous Botanical Essay published in the Western Hemisphers" (*Ibid.*, p. 489). He also wrote a a paper on agricultural botany in which he called attention to the instinct that animals show in choosing or rejecting different kinds of fodder as a subject worthy of study in animal husbandry (*Ibid.*, pp. 582–85). As early as 1772 he submitted to the American Philosophical Society a paper on his "Observations upon the spots on the Sun's Disk from Nov. 15, 1770 to Dec. 25, 1771," and was later elected to membership in that society.

After his first wife's death he married Margaret Minshall on Jan. 10, 1788. There were no children by either marriage, and in his later years the place of a son seems to have been taken by his nephew, Dr. Moses Marshall, the botanist, for whom J. C. D. Schreber, in his 1791 edition of the *Genera Plantarum* by Linnæus, named a genus of plants of the Compositae family, *Marshallia*. Toward the end of his life his eyesight was affected, though he never became totally blind. His interest in botany remained active, and his philanthropic zeal is evidenced by his activity in founding the Chester County alms house and the Westtown boarding school, one of the many educational foundations established by the Society of Friends.

[Wm. Darlington, *Memorials of John Bartram and Humphry Marshall* (1849); R. H. Fox, *Dr. John Fothergill and his Friends* (1919); J. W. Harshberger, *The Botanists of Philadelphia* (1899); *Hazard's Register of Pa.*, ed. by Samuel Hazard, vol. I (1828); *Early Proceedings of the Amer. Philosophical Soc.* (1884); *Bulletin of the Chester County Hist. Soc.*, Sept. 27, 1913.]

M. P. S.

MARSHALL, JAMES FOWLE BALDWIN (Aug. 8, 1818–May 6, 1891), merchant, diplomat, and educator, was born in Charlestown, Mass., son of Thomas, a prosperous banker, and Sophia (Kendal) Marshall. One grandfather, Christopher Marshall, had fought at Bunker Hill in a regiment commanded by his brother, while the other, Samuel Kendal, had been a noted preacher. James was sent to Harvard College in 1834, but during his sophomore year trouble with his eyes—a lifelong weakness—forced him to drop out. In 1838 he went to the Hawaiian Islands and engaged in business at Honolulu. When Lord George Paulet, commander of a British frigate, in February 1843 used the specious claims of an ambitious consul as grounds for provisional annexation of the islands, young Marshall was secretly appointed an envoy to put the Hawaiian case before the British government and the world. His instructions and commission as minister plenipotentiary to the Court of St. James's were made out on a coffin for a table in the royal tomb at Honolulu, where the native government was functioning in hiding, and signed by King Kamehameha III, who had taken refuge in mountain fastnesses.

The youth of twenty-four set out ostensibly as agent of the American firm from which Paulet had chartered a vessel—the only one permitted to sail—to carry his dispatches to England. Leaving Honolulu on Mar. 24, he traveled with the unsuspecting British messenger to San Blas and thence across Mexico to Vera Cruz, where the two parted company. Thence Marshall sailed to New Orleans, and on his journey from that place to Boston broadcast the news from Hawaii. In the interests of his mission he interviewed Daniel Webster, then secretary of state, who said: "We will await the result of your mission. If England does not then disavow the acts of Lord George Paulet and restore the group, *we'll make a fuss.*" (*Harper's Magazine,* September 1883, p. 516.) Hurrying to London, Marshall joined other Hawaiian envoys, with whose help he succeeded during the month of July in persuading Lord Aberdeen, the foreign secretary, to review the whole subject. An admission was finally obtained that the situation had been misrepresented to the British government and that justice would be done. Satisfied with this answer, which led eventually to joint recognition of Hawaiian independence by England and France in November, he sailed for America on Aug. 20, married Eunice S. Hooper in Charlestown, Nov. 9, 1843, and set out immediately for Honolulu. Reaching there in April 1844, he learned that at the very time when he was negotiating in London, Admiral Thomas, Paulet's superior officer, had restored the sovereignty of the islands to the native king. The incident has recently been explained as a move to prevent French occupation.

Marshall now returned to business and for a number of years was a partner in one of the largest trading firms of Honolulu. Deeply interested in public affairs, he was elected to the Hawaiian legislature, and there advocated the protection of native rights and the substitution of land-tenure in fee simple for the ancient feudal system. He was active also in encouraging agricultural improvements and temperance legislation. Shortly before 1860 he returned to Boston with a considerable fortune, and during the Civil War served as paymaster general of the Massachusetts troops and as agent of the state Sanitary Commission in charge of a hospital train. After the war he joined Gen. Samuel C. Armstrong [*q.v.*] at Hampton Institute (Va.), an industrial school for negroes and Indians, where from 1870 to 1884 he was resident trustee, assistant principal, treasurer, and instructor in bookkeeping. To his business reputation and able management of its finances the school owed much of its early growth in public confidence. Forced by failing eyesight to retire, he spent the last years of his life on his estate at Weston, Mass., where he died, only two days before the death of his second wife, Martha A. T. Johnson, daughter of John Johnson of Charlestown, Mass., whom he had married Oct. 4, 1848.

[Marshall's "Reminiscences," in *Twenty-Two Years' Work of the Hampton Normal and Agricultural Institute* (1893) and "An Unpublished Chapter of Hawaiian History," *Harper's Mag.,* Sept. 1883; portrait in *New Eng. Mag.,* June 1892; Josephine Sullivan, *A Hist. of C. Brewer and Company, Ltd.* (1926); *Town of Weston; Births, Deaths, Marriages 1707–1850* (1901); *Records of the Church in Brattle Square, Boston, 1699–1877* (1902); T. B. Wyman, *The Geneal. and Estates of Charlestown . . . Mass.* (1879); *Boston Daily Advertiser,* Nov. 11, 1843; Boston *Transcript,* Oct. 5, 1848; *Boston Post,* May 7, 9, 1891.] W. L. W., Jr.

MARSHALL, JAMES MARKHAM (Mar. 12, 1764–Apr. 26, 1848), land proprietor, was the fifth child of Mary Randolph (Keith) and Thomas Marshall [*q.v.*] and a brother of John and Louis Marshall [*qq.v.*]. He was born in Fauquier County, Va., and died there, though much of his life was spent elsewhere. He was educated at home by his parents, both of whom were of high intellectual attainments. When he was fifteen years of age, he joined the 1st Virginia Artillery, State Line, in which his father was colonel and in which he became captain. His father removed to Kentucky in 1785, but he did not follow until about three years later. When he arrived the district was in a state of excitement over problems of statehood and the unfolding schemes of Spanish plotters to join Kentucky to Louisiana. He became a strong partisan of the central government and joined the Federalist party as soon as it was crystallized. In 1790 he opposed John Brown, 1757–1837 [*q.v.*], for Kentucky's seat in Congress. He charged that Brown had plotted with Gardoqui, the Spanish minister, to deliver Kentucky to Spain, and as proof he cited a letter Brown had written Judge George Muter on July 10, 1788. Marshall forced the publication of the letter to substantiate his contention, but not before he had so embroiled himself with James Brown, a younger brother of John, that a duel was averted only through a trick by Humphrey Marshall, 1760–1841 [*q.v.*], his cousin and brother-in-law. He was defeated for Congress, but soon he was selected as a delegate to the ninth convention held by Kentucky in her quest for statehood. Here he drew up the memorial to the president of the United States and to Congress, declaring Kentucky's warm attachment to the federal government and reiterating her desire to enter the Union. He returned to Virginia, and he lived for a short time in Philadelphia, where he was married in April 1795 to Hester, the daughter of Robert Morris, who was considered one of the richest heiresses in America. In the meantime he had joined a group made up of his brother John Marshall, his brother-in-law Raleigh Colston, and General Henry Lee, 1756–1818 [*q.v.*], to buy up the large Fairfax estates in Virginia, and in January 1794 he had gone to England to negotiate the purchase from the Fairfax heirs. As the purchase price of £14,000 was much more money than his group could command at the time, at the instigation of his father-in-law, he was sent to Europe again in October 1795 in order to obtain the necessary loans. The money was finally borrowed and the Fairfax heirs were satisfied, but the situation in America had become considerably complicated with Virginia confiscation laws, squatters, and other disturbances. Finally an agreement with the Virginia legislature and the decision in the case of *Martin* vs. *Hunter's Lessee* (1 *Wheaton*, 304), resulted in clearing the title. About 180,000 acres were secured, confined to the Northern Neck, and through trading and purchase he personally acquired half of this estate. While in Europe he witnessed some of the excesses of the French Revolution, and, when Lafayette was arrested and thrown into prison in Berlin, he was appointed to bring about his release, which was obtained, however, before Marshall could act. When trouble developed with France in 1798, Marshall offered his services as aide-de-camp to Washington. Being in the good graces of John Adams, he was chosen by the president near the end of his term as assistant judge of the District of Columbia. Though he had been appointed before the judiciary act of 1801 had been passed, he went out with the "midnight judges." In Winchester, Va., he then took up the practice of law, which he had studied years before. He also gave time to the management of his estate. Long before his death he divided most of his great landholdings among his six children.

[There is considerable confusion as to the simple facts in the life of Marshall; the most reliable short sketch may be found in T. M. Green, *The Spanish Conspiracy* (1891), p. 175; for the Fairfax affairs see A. J. Beveridge, *The Life of John Marshall* (4 vols., 1919), E. P. Oberholtzer, *Robert Morris* (1903), L. C. Bell, "John Marshall: Albert J. Beveridge as a Biographer," *Va. Law Register*, Mar. 1927, for a critical view of the matter; see also W. M. Paxton, *The Marshall Family* (1885); J. M. Brown, *The Political Beginnings of Ky.* (1806); R. M. McElroy, *Ky. in the Nation's Hist.* (1909); A. C. Quisenberry, *The Life and Times of Hon. Humphrey Marshall* (1892).] E. M. C.

MARSHALL, JAMES WILSON (Oct. 8, 1810–Aug. 10, 1885), discoverer of gold in California, was born in Hunterdon County, N. J., the son of Philip and Sarah (Wilson) Marshall. His paternal grandmother was Rebecca Hart, the daughter of John Hart [*q.v.*]. In his boyhood Marshall received a fair education, learned to use a rifle, and learned from his father the trade of wheelwright. When of age he started west, seeking adventure and fortune. Stopping for brief periods in Indiana and Illinois, he settled for a longer time on the Platte Purchase, near Fort Leavenworth. Here he took up land, planted it in grain, and devoted two or three years to building up a homestead. But fever and ague attacked him, causing him great misery, and on the advice of his physician he decided to join an emigrant train for the Far West. The wagon train started across the Indian Country on May 1, 1844. Their route was along the Oregon Trail to Fort Hall on the Snake River, where they spent the winter of 1844–45. Although the main party continued toward California by way of the Humboldt River, Marshall and about forty others, without wagons, followed the Oregon Trail to the Willamette Valley. Here they joined a group traveling across the Klamath Mountains to California under the leadership of James Clyman [*q.v.*]. By this means Marshall arrived at Sutter's Fort, the site of the present city of Sacramento, early in July 1845.

John A. Sutter [*q.v.*] welcomed all immigrants to his establishment, and especially Marshall, who was a very useful man because of his technical skill. Soon Marshall acquired some live stock and enough means to purchase two square leagues of land in the Sacramento Valley in the present Butte County. When the Bear Flag war broke out in 1846 Marshall joined with the American settlers and afterward became a member of Frémont's California Battalion. He was a member of the party that marched to the relief of Kearny after the battle of San Pasqual in December of 1846. The next March he was mustered out of service, at San Diego, without pay. Making his way on foot, he reached Sutter's Fort again after an absence of about a year, only to find that his cattle had disappeared. In order to secure needed funds he was required to sell his ranch. Seeking to regain his meager fortune, he sought employment from Sutter and the two entered into a partnership for the construction and operation of a sawmill near Sutter's Fort. Sutter was to furnish the money, while Marshall agreed to superintend the construction and operation of the mill, the profits to be divided equally. In due course a site was selected on the South Fork of the American River at Coloma, Eldorado County. Early in 1848, when the mill was ready to begin operation, it was found necessary to deepen the tail race to enable the wheel to rotate freely. It was there, on Jan. 24, 1848, that gold was discovered during the excavation of the raceway. The discovery was kept quiet for a short time, but such important news could not be long suppressed. By May or June San Francisco and other California towns were deserted; by the end of the year settlers had poured in from Oregon and neighboring regions, and the gold rush of 1849 followed.

The discovery of gold by Marshall was an epoch-making event, but to Marshall himself it brought only misfortune. The sawmill venture failed for lack of laborers, since most able-bodied men were feverishly panning gold. The first comers paid a small fee for the right to dig gold, but later arrivals refused to pay and the claims of Sutter and Marshall were swept aside in the onrush of gold seekers. Marshall resented this treatment and became despondent and misanthropic, bringing to himself other misfortunes. In 1872 the California legislature voted him a pension, but this was discontinued in 1878. Marshall spent his later years as a gardener in the vicinity of Coloma, where he was buried in 1885. Near his cabin at Coloma, now preserved in a state park, a large monument with a bronze figure of Marshall was erected in his honor in 1890.

[P. B. Bekeart, "Jas. Wilson Marshall," *Quart. of the Soc. of Cal. Pioneers,* Sept. 1924; J. S. Hittell, "The Discovery of Gold in Cal.," *Century Mag.,* Feb. 1891; "The Discovery of Gold in Cal.," *Hutchings' Cal. Mag.,* Nov. 1857; G. F. Parsons, *The Life and Adventures of Jas. W. Marshall, the Discoverer of Gold in Cal.* (1870); H. H. Bancroft, *Hist. of Cal.,* vol. VI (1888); T. H. Hittell, *Hist. of Cal.,* vols. II and III (1885–97); C. C. Upton, *Pioneers of El Dorado* (1906); J. W. Revere, *A Tour of Duty in Cal.* (1849); O. C. Coy, *Gold Days* (1929); T. J. Schoonover, *Life and Times of Gen. John A. Sutter* (1907); M. A. Kelley, "Jas. W. Marshall, Life and Reminiscences of California's Gold Discoverer," *Grizzly Bear Mag.,* Jan.–May 1919; the *Morning Call* (San Francisco), Aug. 11, 1885.] O. C. C.

MARSHALL, JOHN (Sept. 24, 1755–July 6, 1835), chief justice of the United States and principal founder of judicial review and of the American system of constitutional law, was born in a log-cabin in the wilderness on the Virginia frontier. His birthplace, near Germantown, Va., lay in the western part of Prince William County, which in 1759 became Fauquier County. About 1765 the Marshall family, increasing steadily in size and prosperity, removed thirty miles westward to a small inlet of the Blue Ridge called "the Hollow," and a second removal some miles eastward occurred in 1773. The frame dwelling erected on the latter site, commodious and even elegant for the time and place, still stands as a wing of "Oak Hill," the residence which was built many years later by Marshall's eldest son Thomas. Until his twentieth year, "John Marshall was never out of the simple, crude environment of the near frontier" for more than a year (Beveridge, *post,* I, 33; autobiographical letter to Story, *post*). The circumstance necessarily rendered parental influence and immediate home environment factors of inestimable importance in his development.

Marshall on his father's side was of humble origin. The first American Marshall of the line appears to have been a Welsh immigrant. His descendant John, a small farmer of Westmoreland County, married Elizabeth Markham and became the father of Thomas Marshall [*q.v.*] and the grandfather of the Chief Justice. Little more is known of the family. On the side of his mother, Mary Randolph (Keith), the story is a very different one. Of the famous William Randolph of "Turkey Island" [*q.v.*] and his wife Mary Isham, ancestors also of Thomas Jefferson, of Robert E. Lee, and of many noted Randolphs, John Marshall was the great-great-grandson. Both the Randolphs and the Ishams traced their descent from English county gentry, while the Keiths, descended from hereditary earls marischal of Scotland, supported even greater pretensions in the motherland. Marshall's grandfather William Keith, a clergyman of the Church of England, owed his residence in Virginia to a youthful indiscretion in taking sides with the Pretender, and when he wed Mary Isham Randolph, he was already well past middle life. Surprisingly enough, Marshall's early biographers make no reference to his more distinguished lineage on his mother's side. The explanation, it may be surmised, is to be found in the tradition that Mary Isham Randolph had been married, following an elopement, before she met Keith, that the husband had disappeared, having been—as it was believed—slain by her brothers, but that late in life she received a letter purporting to come from him (Paxton, *post,* pp. 25–26). From these circumstances the validity of Mary's marriage with Keith and so the legitimacy of Marshall's mother have been challenged. Unfortunately, an assured evaluation of the tradition seems today impossible. Even Beveridge, in apparent despair, consigns the story virtually without comment to a footnote.

A portrait survives of each of Marshall's parents—testimonial again to the fact that this was a rising family. That of the mother shows an intelligent and winsome face with much sweetness and humor about the eyes and lips. The countenance of the father is of sterner mold; it is an unusually long face, and the compressed lips show stubbornness and determination; friendliness nevertheless, as well as shrewdness, light the dark eyes and intellectual brow. If one can read these portraits aright, Marshall's temperament was a happy combination of his mother's amiability and his father's resoluteness of purpose. For the rest, John appears to have been distinctly a father's boy. From the first the relations between the two were those not merely of natural affection but of entire congeniality, and the Chief Justice's most cherished memory was of his father's superior ability and force of character. "It was," says Story, "a theme, on which he broke out with a spontaneous eloquence," attributing to his father "the solid foundation" of all his own success in life (Joseph Story, *post,* p. 9; autobiographical letter). Nor was his son peculiar in appreciating the virtues of Thomas Marshall. Between 1761 and 1776 at various times the latter represented Fauquier County in the House of Burgesses, exercised the lucrative office of sheriff of the county, became principal vestryman of his parish, and was made clerk of Dunmore (now Shenandoah) County. These offices brought him, and through him in due course his son, into touch with the great questions which were increasingly agitating the best minds of the colony and of America, a tremendous stimulation to a boyish mind. Another consequence of the elder Marshall's participation in public life was that he conceived an ever increasing admiration for his former neighbor and employer, George Washington, which he duly shared with his son. In young John's life this too was a formative influence of great importance.

Of the more usual tools of education there was, naturally, in the wilderness a considerable dearth. "The only book," says Beveridge, "which positively is known to have been a literary companion of John Marshall" in his early youth was a volume of Pope (Beveridge, I, 44); and, according to Story, he had "at the age of twelve . . . transcribed the whole of Pope's *Essay on Man,* and some of his moral essays; and had committed to memory many of the most interesting passages of that distinguished poet" (Joseph Story, p. 10; autobiographical letter). The effect of so early and intensive cultivation of a single author was unavoidable. Pope's optimistic outlook and his sententious style both affixed their hallmark on Marshall's mind. The *Essay on Man* depicts the universe as a species of constitutional monarchy which is governed "not by partial, but by gen'ral laws," and where, with reason to restrain it, "self-love" lies at the basis of all human institutions, the state, government, laws. Pope was, moreover, but the first of a succession of writers of similar outlook with whom Marshall would later become acquainted —Blackstone with his proprietarian legalism, Burke with his reasoned abhorrence of revolution, Adam Smith with his philosophy of *laissez faire.* For all these Pope's iambics had prepared receptive ground.

At the age of fourteen John was placed under the tuition of the Rev. Archibald Campbell of Westmoreland County, where he remained one year. The following year he was taught at home by a young Scotch clergyman, named Thompson, who during this period lived in the Marshall household. Under him, John "commenced reading Horace and Livy," studies which he later continued "with no other aid than my Dictionary" (autobiographical letter to Story). But his principal tutor was his father, who directed his reading in English literature, thus inculcating in him his most pronounced taste, the law aside, and one of his chief sources of pleasure in after life. Then in 1772 occurred the first American publication of Blackstone's *Commentaries,* one of the subscribers for which was "Captain Thomas Marshall, Clerk of Dunmore county, Virginia" (Beveridge, I, 56). As he had been "destined for the bar" from infancy ("Autobiography," Oster, *post,* p. 197), it is not unlikely that John now began his self-education in the law.

Though a child of the wilderness and reared amid its simple homespun conditions of life, Marshall was sheltered from the frontier's usual barbarism by parents who possessed uncommon gifts of character and entertained definite ideals for the advancement of their offspring. Frugality and helpfulness were watchwords of the small colony; for in time John's advent was followed by that of fourteen brothers and sisters, in whose daily upbringing he had a constant hand. All these children were reared to maturity and several of them attained distinction. From joyous youth spent largely out of doors Marshall derived that resiliency and health of body which he retained unimpaired till near the end of life itself, and a serenity of mind that never deserted him. To the same source are also to be traced his fondness for out-of-door relaxations, especially the primitive sport of tossing horseshoes, his love of wild nature, and his fondness for companionship—a much sought boon on the frontier. His "lax lounging manners," too, were not as Jefferson asserted, "affectations"; they were the habitual alertness at ease of the frontiersman which is stamped on all his portraits. Neither was his notorious carelessness of dress an artifice; it was due to the ingrained thrift of one of a family of seventeen most of whose apparel must have come from the family loom. With access to comparatively few books but living in a period of wide-flung and excited debate on the most profound topics of politics, he came naturally to fall into that category of mankind whose flow of mind is most readily started along the auditory nerve. His judicial opinions reveal this idiosyncrasy very strikingly. Marshall usually prepared these following hard upon the close of argument by counsel, sometimes even before it was concluded, and they betray the debater in every line, in the strength of their phrasing, in the sweep of their conclusions, and sometimes even in a point-by-point refutation of a rejected argument.

Further than this, Marshall was a leader of men. The group which he led was a small one, but its rôle in the country's government became of immense importance because of his leadership, and it was often exerted upon men of a divergent political faith, as well as upon men of professional attainments much surpassing his own. The raw stuff of leadership is, no doubt, a fact of nature rather than of nurture; yet nurture may give it shape. The distinctive feature of Marshall's leadership of the Supreme Court was its easy avoidance of anything suggestive of the strong hand. Its implement was not assertion but insinuation. In the words of a contemporary, John Marshall had the knack of "putting his own ideas into the minds of others, unconsciously to them" (George Gibbs, ed., *Memoirs of the Administrations of Washington and John Adams, . . .,* 1846, vol. II, p. 350). Any competent nursemaid has the same knack and Marshall had been nurse to a whole squadron of younger brothers and sisters. Marshall's political creed, which embraced nationalism and individualism as twin values, combined with distrust of the too-immediate democracy of the state legislature and its proclivity to interference with anything not within its own narrow experience and comprehension, is sufficiently explicable by his own participation in and observation of events during and following the Revolution, and by his personal interests. Yet it also drew sustenance from his early reading, from reverence for Washington, from the sense of superiority that a rising, well-disciplined family like the Marshalls must inevitably have felt for the generality of their frontier neighbors.

Young Marshall was propelled from the family nest by "the shot heard round the world." His politics were those of his father, which were those of Henry, the dominant voice in the Virginia revolutionary convention of the same year. The news of Lexington and Concord found the two Marshalls already self-instructed in the manual of arms, and they now began putting their neighbors through the prescribed evolutions. John's own active service began at Greatbridge, Va., in the autumn of 1775. He then went to the siege of Norfolk, as a member of the Culpeper Minute Men; and on July 30, 1776, he was mustered into the Continental service in the 3rd Virginia Regiment. Successively as lieutenant, captain-lieutenant, and captain, he fought at the Brandywine, Germantown, and Monmouth, shared with characteristic cheerfulness the rigors of Valley Forge, and participated in the capture of Stony Point. What the import of his experience was for his subsequent career was stated by himself years later: "I was confirmed in the habit of considering America as my country and Congress as my government" (Joseph Story, p. 20; autobiographical letter). Like his great leader, on whose outlook the French and Indian War had affixed a like impress, he became an American before he ever had time to become a Virginian. His regiment's term of enlistment running out in 1779, Marshall returned home to await a new command, and when this was not forthcoming he was mustered out of service in 1781. Meantime, in May–June 1780, he attended a course of lectures on the law given by Chancellor George Wythe [*q.v.*] at the College of William and Mary, on a foundation which his cousin Governor Jefferson had just created by converting to it funds which originally endowed a chair in theology. Altogether he must have spent at least a month under the learned Chancellor's tuition—his only institutional instruction of any sort; and during the same interval he contrived to fall in love with Mary Willis Ambler, the state treasurer's daughter. Nevertheless, on Aug. 28, 1780, he was admitted to the bar in Fauquier County.

In the autumn of 1782 Marshall was elected to the state Assembly from the family bailiwick, an event which transferred him to Richmond, Mary Ambler's home. On Jan. 3, 1783, they were married, and soon afterward he hung out his shingle in the new capital, thereby throwing down the gauntlet to the most brilliant bar in America. At the beginning things moved slowly, and during his first year he and Mary were glad to have his official salary. Perhaps his frontiersman's carelessness of attire hampered recognition fully as much as his exiguous professional equipment; to an even later period appears to belong the anecdote of an old farmer, who had at first engaged an empty-headed, showily powdered bigwig in preference to Marshall, but speedily repented his choice once he saw the two men in action (Beveridge, II, 166). At any rate, prosperity was not unduly delayed. Within two years, Marshall was recording considerable losses at whist and backgammon, generous contributions to churches, horse-races, festivals, card games, and balls, liberal purchases of wines and other drinkables, sundry entry fees to the Masons, "The Jockie Club," and "Farmicola's." He was also a frequent purchaser of books, though not often of law books; he bought an occasional slave, and in 1785 he made repeated purchases of "military certificates" which were redeemable in land. The same year he was presented with the Fauquier County estate by his father and was made city recorder (Beveridge, I, 148–99).

From this point Marshall's emergence both political and professional was swift. It is the latter which most demands explanation. One thing that greatly aided him in his struggle with his better-equipped competitors was the fact that following the Revolution English precedents were out of favor, while of American precedents there were as yet none. What was chiefly demanded of counsel was consequently not acquired learning, but just what Marshall had to a remarkable degree: a spider-like capacity, as it were, of rapidly absorbing material suited to the immediate occasion and then of spinning it out in his own silk—wrought, forsooth, into a web of argumentation which his opponents would find exceedingly baffling. Indeed, Marshall developed much ingenuity in making his daily practice in open court educate him in the law. As Beveridge has shown, he "preferred to close rather than open an argument," and so "informed himself from the knowledge displayed by his adversaries" (Beveridge, II, 177). He cited few authorities, thus anticipating a striking feature of his judicial opinions.

Marshall's emergence into political prominence proceeded with the crystallization of his political convictions. This was the period when governmental power was concentrated in the state legislatures; and they speedily forfeited the confidence of those elements of society whose views or interests transcended state lines, playing fast and loose with the treaty obligations of the Confederation, starting commercial wars among the states, and finally becoming in the majority of instances the abject tools of the numerous but bankrupt small-farmer class. To this course of policy in Virginia, Marshall himself, as a member of the Assembly and of the Executive Council from 1782 to 1784, was direct witness, and he did not hesitate to announce his disgust for it, as well as for the body responsible. The news from other states impelled him in the same direction, especially that of Shays's Rebellion, which he thought drew into question man's capacity to govern himself and so "cast a deep shade over that bright prospect which the Revolution in America and the establishment of our free governments had opened to the votaries of liberty throughout the globe" (to James Wilkinson, Jan. 5, 1787, *American Historical Review,* January 1907, p. 348). Accordingly, when Washington and Madison raised the banner of constitutional reform looking to a strengthened Union, they found in Marshall an eager recruit. In order to forward the ratification of the Constitution in Virginia, Marshall again entered the Assembly in the autumn of 1787, and it was through his skill that that document was submitted to the state-ratifying convention without hampering instructions with respect to amendments. Nor was his rôle in the ratifying convention, while comparatively inconspicuous, unimportant. Whether by accident or preference, he gave his chief attention in the debate to the judiciary article and in that connection championed the idea of judicial review. Should Congress, said he, "make a law not warranted by any of the powers enumerated . . . they [the judges] would declare it void" (Jonathan Elliott, *The Debates . . . on the Adoption of the Federal Constitution,* II, 1828, p. 404). But he also expressed the opinion that Bills of Rights were "merely recommendatory. Were it otherwise . . . many laws which are found convenient, would be unconstitutional" (*Ibid.,* p. 409).

A champion of Washington's administration and of Hamilton's financial measures from the first, Marshall gradually became the recognized leader of the Federalist interest in Virginia. In 1795 Washington offered him the attorney-generalship, which he declined. In 1795–96 he won more than a local reputation by his vigorous defense of the Jay Treaty, so that when, in the latter year, he appeared in Philadelphia to argue *Ware* vs. *Hylton* (3 *Dallas,* 199), his first and only case before the Supreme Court, his effort drew interested auditors from other states. One of these was Rufus King of Massachusetts, whom a year later we find declaring that "his head" was "one of the best organized of anyone that I have known" (C. R. King, *The Life and Correspondence of Rufus King,* II, 1895, p. 235). In 1796 he again refused appointment under the federal government, as minister to France; but in 1797 he was finally induced by President John Adams to become one of the famous X. Y. Z. mission to the same government. His immediate motive, it is to be suspected, was largely mercenary. In 1793 or 1794 he had become one of a syndicate to purchase the remnant of the great Fairfax estate in the "Northern Neck," and this investment, owing to an act of confiscation which had overhung it from the days of the Revolution and to the bankruptcy of Robert Morris, who had financed the deal, was now in desperate case. At any rate, from this single year's employment Marshall as commissioner obtained nearly $20,000, which, says his biographer, "over and above his expense," was nearly "three times his annual earnings at the bar" (Beveridge, II, 211). The Fairfax investment was thus saved from its creditors. The act of confiscation, however, still remained to be reckoned with.

In 1798 Marshall was offered James Wilson's place on the Supreme Court but declined. The following year, nevertheless, at Washington's warm insistence, he stood for Congress and was elected. Here his most conspicuous act was his successful defense of Adams against the charge of having usurped a judicial function in surrendering, under the Jay Treaty, an alleged fugitive from the justice of Great Britain. Adams, who had now split with the Hamiltonian elements of his party and cabinet, needed defenders outside of Congress too; and he soon concluded that John Marshall was his best reliance. On May 7, 1800, without consulting him, Adams nominated him secretary of war, to succeed James McHenry [*q.v.*], who had been forced to resign, and he promptly declined. Nothing daunted, the President a few days later asked him to become secretary of state (appointment May 12, 1800) in succession to Timothy Pickering [*q.v.*], who had just been dismissed. After a fortnight's pondering Marshall accepted, and by so doing won the harassed President's eternal gratitude.

The actual circumstances of Adams' nomination of Marshall to the chief justiceship on Jan. 20, 1801, are recounted by Marshall himself in the autobiographical sketch which he prepared for Story in 1827, and which has only recently been recovered (see bibliography). "On the resignation of Chief Justice Ellsworth," Marshall there wrote, "I recommended Judge Patterson [William Paterson] as his successor. The President objected to him, and assigned as his ground of objection that the feelings of Judge Cushing would be wounded by passing him and selecting a junior member of the bench. I never heard him assign any other objection to Judge Patterson, though it was afterwards suspected by many that he was believed to be connected with the party which opposed the second attempt at negotiation with France. The President himself mentioned Mr. Jay, and he was nominated to the Senate. When I waited on the President with Mr. Jay's letter declining the appointment he said thoughtfully 'who shall I nominate now?' I replied that I could not tell, as I supposed that his objection to Judge Patterson remained. He said in a decided tone, 'I shall not nominate him.' After a moment's hesitation he said 'I believe I must nominate you.' I had never before heard myself named for the office and had not even thought of it. I was pleased as well as surprised, and bowed in silence."

The nomination, as Beveridge, with pardonable litotes, remarks, "was not greeted with applause from any quarter" (Beveridge, II, 554–55). The Republicans bitterly resented Ellsworth's too-opportune resignation, which had snatched from their very grasp the highest of appointive offices, while the more rabid Federalists, resenting Marshall's practice of kicking over the party traces, wanted Paterson. The President, however, was adamant; on Jan. 27 the Senate gave its consent; and on Feb. 4, Marshall, with customary lack of haste, accepted and took his seat, thereby opening court for the first time in the new Capital on the Potomac. He continued as secretary of state till the end of the administration, though he did not draw the salary of that office. He was thus able to lend a helpful hand in the so-called "midnight appointments," one of which went to a certain William Marbury.

For all the lack of enthusiasm attending his elevation, the new Chief Justice possessed a personality to capture attention and then to captivate it. The contemporary pen of William Wirt pictures a man "tall, meagre, emaciated," loose-jointed, inelegant in "dress, attitudes, gesture," of swarthy complexion, and looking beyond his years, with a countenance "small in proportion to his height" but pervaded with "great good humour and hilarity; while his black eyes—that unerring index—possess an irradiating spirit, which proclaims the imperial powers of the mind that sits enthroned therein" (William Wirt, *The Letters of the British Spy,* 1803, p. 46). Marshall enjoyed, Wirt asserts, "one original, and, almost, supernatural faculty," that "of developing a subject by a single glance of his mind. . . . Nor does the exercise of it seem to cost him an effort." He determined immediately on which side a question was to be most advantageously assailed; and "his premises once admitted, the demonstration, however distant, follows as certainly, as cogently, as inevitably, as any demonstration in Euclid" (*Ibid.,* p. 47). In brief, he was a supreme debater. Another contemporary, Speaker Theodore Sedgwick, coming from the sterner atmosphere of Boston harbor, had previously been struck by his "very affectionate disposition," his "great simplicity of manners," his attachment to pleasures and "convivial habits strongly fixed." He was "indolent therefore" (King, *ante,* III, 1896, p. 237). The word is hardly the just one. Marshall led a leisurely life, but he did not permit his intellectual powers to corrode. On the contrary, the fresh energy of mind with which he usually met the larger occasions of his career is one of his most striking characteristics.

There being no causes to be heard in the February term of 1801, Marshall's first official duty as chief justice was to administer the presidential oath of office to Jefferson. In the August term, there was one case, *Talbot* vs. *Seeman* (1 *Cranch,* 1), and Marshall signalized the occasion to put into effect a significant reform. Hitherto the justices had frequently delivered *seriatim* opinions; henceforth for some years "the unanimous Court," or simply "the Court," was to speak generally through its Chief Justice. Of the reported opinions to the February 1805 term, Marshall delivered all except two, and those in causes over which he had presided on circuit. But one dissenting opinion was given, although the justices were not always agreed at other times. That the new procedure signified at this date Marshall's domination of his associates may be questioned; rather it betokened their appreciation of a common peril.

One of the last acts of the Federalists had been to enlarge the lower federal judicial establishment, and one of the early acts of the Jeffersonians was to abolish the new courts (Apr. 29, 1802). At the same time, in order to prevent a judicial test of the constitutionality of the repeal act, Congress postponed the next term of the Supreme Court to February 1803, by doing away permanently with all but the February term. Although Marshall was thus probably presented by his foes with several years of vigorous life, since in the warmer months Washington at this period was a malarial swamp, what he saw in their action was a dangerous challenge to the prestige of the Court, to the security of the lower federal judiciary, and to the principle, which had come to be generally accepted previous to the debate on the repealing act, that the Supreme Court was the final authoritative interpreter of the Constitution. It was, therefore, no wonder that he should make the most of the opportunity that soon offered to vindicate all these causes at one stroke. When the Court reconvened in February 1803, after its enforced vacation of fourteen months, the first case to claim its attention was that which appears in the *Reports* under the style of *Marbury* vs. *Madison* (1 *Cranch,* 137). Marbury and other "midnight appointees" to the office of justice of the peace in the District of Columbia were asking for a *mandamus* to the secretary of state, James Madison, to compel him to deliver their commissions, the basis of their application being section thirteen of the judiciary act of Sept. 24, 1789, which authorized the Court to issue this writ "to officers of the United States." Marshall, for "the unanimous Court," conceded that Marbury was entitled to the remedy he sought, but held that the Supreme Court could not award it, since to do so would be to assume original jurisdiction in a case not within the categories enumerated by the Constitution, and that section thirteen was unconstitutional and void.

A more cleverly contrived document for its purposes than Marshall's opinion in *Marbury* vs. *Madison* it would be impossible to imagine. By "backing into" the case, Marshall was able to read Jefferson a lecture on his legal duty, while by ultimately declining jurisdiction of it he avoided all danger of a direct clash with his antagonist. By holding the constitutional enumeration of cases in which the Supreme Court has original jurisdiction to be exclusive (wherein he had been anticipated by Ellsworth; 3 *Dallas,* 327), he put a spoke in Republican projects to abolish the lower federal judiciary and parcel out its jurisdiction between the Supreme Court and the state courts. Most important of all, by holding section thirteen unconstitutional, on the basis of an argument that Jefferson himself did not venture to traverse, he brought to the support of the Union, while the memory of the Virginia and Kentucky Resolutions was still green, the ineffably important proposition that the Constitution has one final interpreter, at the same time seizing for the Court its greatest prerogative. Nor is this to say that, considered as a judicial pronouncement, the opinion in *Marbury* vs. *Madison* is flawless. Section thirteen, by the logic of later cases, was not intended to increase the Court's original jurisdiction, but only to give it power to issue certain writs when it had jurisdiction; and in the recent case of *Myers* vs. *United States,* Jefferson's claim that he had removed Marbury, who was consequently not entitled to his commission, appears also to have been ratified by the Court. Besides, it was Marshall who had countersigned and sealed that commission, a circumstance which, by a nicer view of judicial propriety, should have disqualified him from sitting in the case at all.

The Federalist Court had drawn first blood in its feud with the Republican administration, but the decisive battle was still to be fought. Not all the justices shared their Chief's "wise as serpents, harmless as doves" disposition, least of all Justice Samuel Chase [*q.v.*]. Early in May 1803, Chase, to whom the Republicans had already succeeded in fastening something of the reputation of a "Bloody" Jeffries, had the unwisdom to assail "our late reformers" in a charge to a Baltimore grand jury, and on Mar. 12, 1804, the House voted articles of impeachment against him. What was even more alarming, the exponents of "judge-breaking" were now pressing the theory that impeachment was historically not a punitive process at all but "an inquest of office," talk which was at once interpreted by contemporaries as indicating that the entire bench of the Supreme Court was to be swept clean. For once in his life John Marshall was obviously perturbed. This was shown not only by his timid manner of testifying before the court of impeachment, ostensibly in Chase's behalf, but also by a letter to his brother James at this time in which he broached the remarkable suggestion that "the modern doctrine of impeachment should yield to an appellate jurisdiction in the legislature" (Beveridge, III, 177). In other words, if Congress would only leave John Marshall in office they might reverse such of his legal opinions as they "deemed unsound" to their heart's content, and thereby consign both judicial review and the principle of the separation of powers to the scrap-heap.

But Chase was not convicted, and in due course Marshall recovered his composure, so much so indeed that he was presently ready to tilt against the administration all by himself. The opportunity offered when Aaron Burr [*q.v.*] was brought, early in 1807, before his court at Richmond to be tried for treason. These proceedings began Mar. 30 and ended Sept. 15, and Marshall's conduct of them from start to finish was one prolonged baiting of the President, whose unholy zeal to see Burr hanged fairly exposed him to such treatment. In only one instance did Jefferson score, when he ignored a *sub poena duces tecum* which Marshall was incautious enough to send him. On the main point Marshall got his way: Burr's neck was saved, albeit in the process the whole common-law view of treason as a conspiracy, a view which the Constitution was undoubtedly intended to embody and which Marshall himself had accepted in the Bollman Case (4 *Cranch,* 75), was junked, with the "monstrous" result—as Wirt rightly urged —that it becomes impossible to convict the procurer of a treason who is canny enough to leave to his dupes the rest of the business—the "overt acts." Three years later Edward Livingston brought his famous "Batture Case" before Marshall at Richmond, in which he sued Jefferson for $100,000 damages on account of the latter's seizure when president of certain lands of Livingston in New Orleans. Fortunately a renewal of the vendetta between the two cousins was obviated when the case was dismissed on the point of jurisdiction (1 *Brockenbrough,* 203).

Meantime, Marshall had been busying himself for some years in hours off the bench with *The Life of George Washington* (5 vols., 1804–07). The work was doubly disappointing to its author. His hopes of large profits were blasted when Jefferson forbade the federal postmasters to take orders for it, and much of it was hastily written and badly proportioned. Yet it does not lack even to a present-day reader flashes of insight, especially in its treatment of the period immediately preceding the Convention of 1787. Furthermore, this part of the work stands in an important relation to Marshall's own later labors. Its preparation undoubtedly contributed not a little to that confidence which his famous constitutional opinions breathe of his knowledge of the intentions of the framers of the Constitution, as well as to his resolution that these should prevail. Indeed, the first half of his chief justiceship was largely a period of preparation for the greater achievement to follow. With the appointment of Duval and Story, in November 1811, the personnel of the Court became what it was to remain for twelve years and, with two changes, for eighteen years. As there was but one term of court annually and that, till 1827, rarely more than seven or eight weeks in length, none of the justices resided in Washington but they took lodgings, sometimes all in the same boarding-house, living, as Story wrote, "in the most frank and unaffected intimacy" (W. W. Story, *Life and Letters of Joseph Story,* 1851, I, 215). "Our social hours when undisturbed with the labors of law, are passed in gay and frank conversation, which at once enlivens and instructs" (*Ibid.,* p. 217). Circumstances could not have been better contrived to enable Marshall to bring to bear upon his associates, all of them except Washington Republican appointees and most of them his juniors, his charm of personality and his superiority in face-to-face discussion, or to win them with "the inevitability of gradualness" to his own constitutional faith. In the case of Story himself the process was not even gradual; he fell under the spell of "the Chief" at once. A uniquely fruitful friendship resulted. As Story testifies, Marshall's bias was "to general principles and comprehensive views, rather than to technical and recondite learning" (Joseph Story, *Discourse,* p. 70); while his own was that of the student and delver. The familiar legend that Marshall was accustomed to say to Story, "that, Story, is the law; now you find the precedents," is at least "well found." Nor should the Court under Marshall be thought of apart from the bar which practised before it. The membership of this body was almost as constant as that of the Court itself and included talent of the first order —William Pinkney, William Wirt, Luther Martin, Joseph Hopkinson, Daniel Webster, Jeremiah Mason, to mention only the most illustrious. Again Marshall's debt is discernible, even in the sphere in which he was supreme, although as regards Webster, this has been exaggerated. Indeed, one gains the impression that when it came to constitutional law, Marshall was often more grateful to counsel whose views he rejected than to their opponents, because of the stimulation they imparted to his own powers of analysis and statement.

His most important opinion during this early period, after that in *Marbury* vs. *Madison,* was in *Fletcher* vs. *Peck* (6 *Cranch,* 87), where he held that the "obligation of contracts" clause stood in the way of a state's rescinding a grant of public lands, although it had been induced by notorious bribery and corruption. The result is the more remarkable inasmuch as the "obligation" attributed to the fraudulent grant was manifestly not a legal but a moral one. The opinion indeed smacks of predetermination, and the case was probably a moot one. Could Marshall have been thinking of that act of confiscation which still overhung the Fairfax estate? Four years later this act too was before the Court (*Fairfax's Devisee* vs. *Hunter's Lessee, 7 Cranch,* 603). Quite properly Marshall declined to sit in the case, but his circumspection profited him little with his critics; if Story's opinion disallowing the measure was the voice of Esau, the hand that penned it was that of Jacob. Aside from those in *Marbury* vs. *Madison* and *Fletcher* vs. *Peck,* Marshall's foundational constitutional opinions are to be read in the following cases: *McCulloch* vs. *Maryland* (4 *Wheaton,* 316), *Sturges* vs. *Crowninshield* (17 *U. S.,* 122), and *Dartmouth College* vs. *Woodward* (17 *U. S.,* 518), all three delivered at the single term of 1819; *Cohens* vs. *Virginia* (6 *Wheaton,* 264), given in the 1821 term; *Gibbons* vs. *Ogden* (9 *Wheaton,* 1) and *Osborn* vs. *U. S. Bank* (22 *U. S.,* 738), rendered in 1825; *Brown* vs. *Maryland* (25 *U. S.,* 419) and *Ogden* vs. *Saunders* (25 *U. S.,* 213)—the latter Marshall's sole dissenting opinion in the constitutional field—rendered in 1827.

Herein is set forth a corpus of constitutional doctrine which possesses internal consistency to a notable extent, however open to attack some of its premises may have been on other grounds. The Constitution was the act of the people of the United States, although in bringing about its establishment they naturally made such use of existing governmental machinery as convenience dictated. It springs therefore from the ultimate source of authority in the country and possesses such characteristics as this authority chose to stamp upon it. By its own terms it is law and supreme law, wherefore its provisions control all governments and governmental agencies within the territory of the United States. Furthermore, being law, it is directly enforcible by courts in the decision of cases. Indeed, its clear intention is to designate the Supreme Court as the one final authoritative expositor of its terms; and while the Court has no will of its own apart from that of the law, it is none the less under obligation always to remember that "it is a constitution" which it is expounding, and that this Constitution was "intended to endure for ages to come" and hence to be "adapted to the various *crises* of human affairs." Especially should a narrow rendition of its terms be avoided when questions of the advancement of national unity and power or of the security of private, especially property rights, are involved. These were the interests which had suffered most acutely at the hands of the states during the period of the Confederation and concern for which had brought about the convention that framed the Constitution. By the same token must state power be sternly repressed whenever it entrenches upon the field of powers delegated by the Constitution to "the government of all" or when it menaces the principles on which public and private faith depends. The designated organ to effect these ends is the Supreme Court.

The immediate target, indeed, of all Marshall's great opinions following 1809 was furnished by the pretensions of the state legislature, the seat then as in 1787 of localizing and democratic tendencies. His system of constitutional doctrine thus becomes the vehicle to the present time both of his ingrained conservatism and of his love of the Union. But meantime a dilemma has arisen which, because of the then-particularistic outlook of democracy, Marshall did not have to face. Present-day American democracy is nationalistic, and at the same time it is more strongly inclined to regard government as an instrument of social betterment than ever before. By other preconceptions, too, his fellow citizens came to Marshall's assistance, even when perhaps they might have desired it otherwise. Natural science was still in its infancy, and intellectual method was deductive. Even the common law had not yet discovered that it was "inductive." Most intellectual enterprise set out accordingly from a safe base of agreed premises, and its chief weapon was the syllogism, of which Marshall was an acknowledged master. Furthermore, his age was willing to concede Marshall his three most vital premises. It acknowledged that the upright judge had no will of his own save that of the law. It acknowledged, too, that the meaning of the Constitution—like that of Scripture—was perfectly plain when the document was approached from the proper angle and with good intentions. Finally, it acknowledged that the proper angle in the case of the Constitution was furnished by the purposes of the framers.

Yet in the face of all this a constantly increasing consensus of his fellow countrymen found Marshall's reading of the Constitution less and less acceptable. The slogan of the day was "state rights" or "state sovereignty"—high-sounding phrases which not infrequently boiled down to a claim of right for some state legislature to foster "wild-cat" banking or to promote expedients of less than doubtful honesty for meeting public and private obligations. In Virginia, however, where the uprising started, it was based on grounds almost altogether personal and doctrinal. Here its spokesmen were Spencer Roane, chief judge of the court of appeals, and John Taylor of Caroline [*qq.v.*]. The latter's *Construction Construed, and Constitutions Vindicated* (1820) applies to some of Marshall's great opinions a dialectic worthy of the Chief Justice's best steel; and what Roane, who would have been chief justice if Jefferson had had the naming of Ellsworth's successor, lacked in subtlety he more than made up for in vehemence. Nor was Jefferson himself at all averse to shying a missile now and then from the leafy boscage of his voluminous correspondence at the "subtle corps of sappers and miners" which was "constantly working underground to undermine our confederated fabric" (P. L. Ford, Federal Edition, *The Works of Thomas Jefferson,* XII, 1905, p. 177). To the standard hoisted by Virginia soon repaired Ohio and Kentucky, whence the agitation spread to Congress. From 1821 on, hardly a congressional session intervened for some years which did not witness some proposal for weakening the Court or at least Marshall's weight on it; and by the act of Mar. 3, 1837, the Court was in fact enlarged by two additional justices. Marshall himself was now dead, but the measure guaranteed that the members who had survived him and whom he had presumably indoctrinated should be in a safe minority.

These proceedings did not leave Marshall altogether unmoved. Especially do his opinions in *Providence Bank* vs. *Billings* (4 *Peters,* 514) and in *Barron* vs. *Baltimore* (7 *Peters,* 243), in the latter of which he rejected a most persuasive invitation to make the Bill of Rights restrictive of state power, appear very like concessions to the spirit of the hour, and his announcement in 8 *Peters* that decisions setting aside state laws must be supported by a majority of the entire Court was unmistakably so. But to intellectual honesty there is, after all, a limit to concession, and in *Craig* vs. *Missouri* (4 *Peters,* 410) and *Worcester* vs. *Georgia* (6 *Peters,* 515) Marshall quite justly felt that this limit had been reached and passed. Never were state acts more palpably unconstitutional than those involved in these cases. Yet in the former the Chief Justice's opinion divided his associates three to three, and in the latter the Court's judgment was defied openly, while the word ran round that President Jackson had declared "John Marshall has made his decision, now let him enforce it" (Horace Greeley, *The American Conflict,* I, 1864, p. 106).

With these developments and the contemporary Nullification movement in South Carolina before him, Marshall saw the Union crumbling: it had been "prolonged thus far by miracles" (Oster, *post,* p. 143) and these could not continue. His hold upon the Court, too, was weakening; a new generation was rising with "new aspirations of power" and bent on finding "new versions of the Constitution" to meet these; his life's achievement was seemingly being engulfed before his eyes. One reassuring voice there was, however, for in 1833 Story published his *Commentaries on the Constitution of the United States* (1833). There Marshall saw his version of the Constitution systematized and given its historical setting, and in the dedication of the work to himself, he read: "Your expositions of constitutional law enjoy a rare and extraordinary authority. They constitute a monument of fame far beyond the ordinary memorials of political and military glory. They are destined to enlighten, instruct, and convince future generations; and can scarcely perish but with the memory of the constitution itself" (*Ibid.,* I, iii). That was it precisely—Marshall's fame was linked with that of the Constitution.

It has been observed that Marshall's judicial life was a somewhat leisurely one, although it became gradually less and less so. In his first three terms the Court decided, on the average, eight cases; in his last term of active service it decided sixty (8 *Peters,* 834). Meantime, beginning with 1827, the opening of Court had been moved up to the second Monday in January, with the result of lengthening the term from about nine weeks to twelve or thirteen. The Court's leisurely procedure, none the less, still continued, and in important cases counsel took their own time. In the argument of *Fletcher* vs. *Peck* the Court adjourned to enable Luther Martin to sober up; while on another occasion it permitted William Pinkney to go back and repeat part of an argument in order that some ladies who had just entered the courtroom might not miss some especially choice tropes. Marshall's own part in the labors of the Court were apparently considerably heavier than those of his associates. "Of a total of one thousand two hundred fifteen cases during that period [1801–1835], in ninety-four, no opinions were filed; in fifteen, the decision was by the Court; and in the remaining one thousand one hundred six cases, Marshall delivered the opinion in five hundred nineteen," of which thirty-six involved constitutional questions and eighty involved questions of international law or kindred questions (Warren, *post,* II, 273 note). The Chief Justice was free to lean on the learning of his associates, and doubtless often had their assistance in the preparation of opinions which he delivered, but the unmistakable *imprimatur* of his own style is on the opinions which support his fame.

In one respect Marshall had a distinct advantage over most of his brethren, in that he lived in his own circuit and near the seat of government. Altogether, his annual journeyings to and from court came to less than 900 miles, while the justice assigned to the seventh circuit had to travel more than 3,300 miles and over mountains. During the Burr trial Marshall was kept at Richmond continuously for nearly seven months, but usually his judicial labors on circuit both at Richmond and Raleigh could hardly have occupied more than three months. It thus appears that, except for opinion writing, Marshall had nearly half the year to devote to his duties and pleasures as householder, neighbor, and citizen. In all these capacities he appears in a singularly engaging light. For many years his wife was a nervous invalid, a fact which cut him off from society in the more formal sense, but far from repining he found in her conversation and their common fondness for good reading one of his chief satisfactions in life. When he eulogized to Story those qualities of womanhood which "make up the sum of human happiness and transform the domestic fireside into an elysium" (Oster, p. 125), he was voicing his own contentment. Bereavement, too, drew them together. Of the ten children born to them, four died early in life—"three of them," he informed Story, "bidding fairer for health and life than any that have survived them" (*Ibid.,* p. 135). Of the survivors five were sons—one of whom predeceased Marshall; his wife died Dec. 25, 1831. But with all his domesticity, Marshall never lost his intense delight in the companionship of men—in eating and drinking with them, frolicking with them, debating with them. A favorite resort of his when in Richmond was the famous Barbecue Club which had grounds just outside the city and was celebrated for its excellent repasts of roast pig and its generous supplies of choice drinks. The *raison d'être* of the organization, however, seems to have been furnished by the game of quoits, and more than one account remains of Marshall's boyish zest in this bucolic sport, in which he excelled. Besides the club, he had a farm nearby; while in summer he often retreated to his estate in the mountains out of the way of malaria—also, perhaps to refresh boyhood associations.

While official propriety forbade that Marshall should express himself publicly on political issues, in his correspondence he could be less reticent. A letter written in 1812 in criticism of the war with Great Britain suggests between the lines that he would not have regarded with aversion the Federalist nomination that year (Beveridge, IV, 35); and twenty years later he was hoping against hope for the election of Clay so that Jackson would not have the appointment of his successor, and when fate ruled otherwise, determining to stick it out to the end. Meanwhile, in 1829, he had accepted election, though with strong professions of reluctance, to the Virginia constitutional convention of that year. He at once took a leading rôle, and it was due in no small part to his and Madison's efforts that manhood suffrage was defeated and that the oligarchic system of county justices was fastened upon the state more tightly than ever.

Till his seventy-sixth year Marshall had scarcely known a day's illness. That year he underwent, at the hands of the celebrated Dr. Physick of Philadelphia, operation for stone. It proved successful and his health was restored. Three years later a more serious ailment appeared, an enlarged liver, and it was rendered critical by contusions received in a stage-coach upset. Again he went to Philadelphia, but this time surgery was impracticable. He died with his sons about him July 6, 1835, in the thirty-fifth year of his chief justiceship and the eightieth of life.

[A. J. Beveridge, *The Life of John Marshall* (4 vols., 1916–19), reproducing the notable portraits by Chester Harding and Inman; L. C. Bell, "John Marshall: Albert J. Beveridge as a Biographer," *Va. Law Register,* March 1927; Edward S. Corwin, *John Marshall and the Constitution* (1919); R. E. Cushman, "Marshall and the Constitution," *Minn. Law Review,* Dec. 1920; W. M. Paxton, *The Marshall Family* (1885); E. J. Lee, *Lee of Virginia 1642–1892* (1895); Joseph Story, *A Discourse upon the Life, Character and Services of the Honorable John Marshall, LL.D.* (1835), republished with eulogy by Horace Binney in J. F. Dillon, *John Marshall, Life, Character and Judicial Services* (3 vols., 1903); U. S. Supreme Court *Reports* from 1 *Cranch* to 9 *Peters,* inclusive; J. M. Dillon, ed., *John Marshall: Complete Constitutional Decisions* (1903); J. P. Cotton, ed., *The Constitutional Decisions of John Marshall* (2 vols., 1905); J. W. Brockenbrough, ed., *Reports of Cases Decided by the Honourable John Marshall . . . in the Circuit Court of the U. S., for the Dist. of Va. and N. C., from 1802 to 1833 Inclusive* (2 vols., 1837); *Reports of the Trials of Colonel Aaron Burr for Treason . . . and for a Misdemeanor,* by David Robertson, stenographer (2 vols., 1808); Charles Warren, *The Supreme Court in U. S. History* (3 vols., 1922). Most of Marshall's published letters, as well as his will and a brief autobiography which he evidently prepared for Delaplaine's *Repository* in 1818 will be found in John E. Oster's absurdly entitled and still more absurdly arranged *The Political and Economic Doctrines of John Marshall* (1914). The *Repository* was discontinued before the Marshall sketch could be published (see Oster, pp. 197–99). In 1931 William Wetmore Story's widow died in Rome, and among her papers was found the "letter written long afterwards to a friend" which is referred to in Joseph Story's *Discourse.* Actually the letter was written to Story himself, at his request, in 1827 and is the principal source of the portion of the *Discourse* covering Marshall's early life. It concludes with the passage quoted above about the circumstances of Marshall's appointment to the chief justiceship—circumstances regarding which the *Discourse* maintains a discreet silence. The letter has been acquired by the William L. Clements Lib., at the Univ. of Mich., and the writer of this sketch was permitted to see a photostatic copy of the document through the courtesy of Dr. Randolph G. Adams.]

E. S. C.

MARSHALL, LOUIS (Oct. 7, 1773–April 1866), physician and teacher, was the youngest of the fifteen children of Mary Randolph (Keith) and Thomas Marshall [*q.v.*]. He was a brother of John and of James Markham Marshall, a cousin of Humphrey Marshall, 1760–1841, and of the mother of Duff Green [*qq.v.*], and was related to many other distinguished men of Virginia and Kentucky. He was born on the family estate, "Oak Hill," in Fauquier County, Va. In 1785 he went with his family to Kentucky and settled at "Buckpond" in Woodford County. Here he was given his early educational training principally by his father and by Scotch tutors, among whom was Dr. Ebenezer Brooks. In 1793 he went to Philadelphia and spent a year with his brother, James Markham Marshall, and soon thereafter went abroad for study. After pursuing literary studies in Edinburgh he went to Paris, where he took courses in medicine and surgery. During the Revolution he was sent to prison and was in danger of execution when his brothers, John and James Markham Marshall, obtained his release. He returned to America, and in 1800 at Frankfort he married Agatha, the daughter of Francis Smith, a Virginian who had moved to Kentucky. They had five sons and one daughter. His father gave him the "Buckpond" estate, but, being by nature unsuited to the business of planting, he devoted his attention to the practice of medicine.

He was, however, much more interested in education than he had ever been in anything else, so he soon set up a classical school for boys at "Buckpond," which became celebrated not only for the fame afterwards attained by some of its graduates, but also for its rigid discipline and standards. Becoming president of Washington College (now Washington and Lee University) at Lexington, Va., in 1830, he entirely deserted the system of discipline and education he had employed at "Buckpond." According to his new methods there were no classes in groups unless a group so desired. Instead, individuals came at any time to the professor to recite or to obtain aid. Rules were discarded, and a state of nature was declared. His purpose was to develop an untrammeled individualism in the college, but he devastated the time and enthusiasm of the members of his faculty and raised up bitter opposition. The students, however, made of him a hero of the first magnitude. He played with them on the terms of the most complete familiarity; and in his class room, fitted up with a great arm-chair and a bed, pipe in mouth he received them as he lounged. Yet when his students began to take too many liberties, he began to meet them with sneers and sarcasm. Having lost the applause of his students and the support of his faculty, he set out for his Kentucky home in the summer of 1834 and never returned.

In Kentucky he began teaching boys again, and in 1838 Transylvania University elected him professor of languages and president *pro tempore* for two years. In 1844 his wife died, and thereafter he wandered among his kinsmen, spending a considerable part of his time in Covington, Ky., where he did some teaching. During the Civil War he was a Unionist with many reservations. He died at "Buckpond" and was at first buried there but was later removed to Frankfort. In France he had changed his name from Lewis to Louis, and had become an agnostic. On returning to America, however, he seems to have become genuinely religious and was long an elder in the Presbyterian Church. He expounded the Bible much to his students and gave especial attention to the prophecies. He actually set the date when the world would be destroyed. He was bitterly opposed to whiskey. He had an irregular temper, which got him into many duels in France, the scars from which he carried through life. In Kentucky he killed a person in a duel, and contemptuously refused to shoot at Gen. Thomas Bodley in another. He was eccentric in manners and speech, singular in his views, arbitrary and impatient of contradiction, yet a man of great intellectual attainment and force of character.

[Washington and Lee Univ., *Hist. Papers,* nos. 5, 6 (1895–1904); Louis and R. H. Collins, *Hist. of Ky.,* revised ed. (2 vols., 1874); Robert Peter, *Transylvania University* (1896); W. M. Paxton, *The Marshall Family* (1885).] E. M. C.

MARSHALL, LOUIS (Dec. 14, 1856–Sept. 11, 1929), lawyer, publicist, and civic and Jewish communal leader, was born in Syracuse, N. Y., the son of Jacob and Zilli Strauss Marshall, who emigrated from Germany to the United States in 1849 and 1853 respectively. They were of extremely modest means. Louis graduated from the Syracuse high school in 1874. His schooling had been interfered with even before he was in his teens, but his zest for knowledge was prodigious, and he acquired a knowledge of the leading modern languages, besides Latin, Greek, Hebrew, and Yiddish. After studying in a law office for a year, he took the two-year course at Columbia Law School in a single year (1876–77) and was admitted to the bar in January 1878. He was immediately made a junior member of the Syracuse law firm of which William C. Ruger, later chief judge of New York state, was the head. In February 1894 he moved to New York City to become a member of the law firm of Guggenheimer, Untermyer & Marshall, with which he was associated until his death.

Marshall is said to have argued no fewer than 150 cases in the New York court of appeals, before his removal to New York City, involving every branch of jurisprudence. It has also been said that he appeared in more cases in the United States Supreme Court than any one else, excepting the representatives of the government. Certainly no contemporary succeeded so frequently in striking down measures as violative of the federal or state constitutions. Among the leading cases in which he appeared were *People ex rel. Tyroler* vs. *Warden of Prison* (157 *N. Y.,* 116; 1898), in which the New York railroad ticket scalping act was adjudged unconstitutional, and in 1927 the Tyson case (273 *U. S.,* 418), in which the New York theatre ticket resale law was adjudged unconstitutional. His arguments were also sustained in the case of *Ives* vs. *South Buffalo Railway Company* (201 *N. Y.,* 271), in which the New York workmen's compensation act was held unconstitutional, before an express constitutional amendment authorized such measures. Similarly, he secured an adjudication (231 *N. Y.,* 465) invalidating New York's soldiers' bonus law. He was of successful counsel in *Pierce* vs. *Society of Sisters of the Holy Name* (268 *U. S.,* 510), adjudging the Oregon anti-parochial school law unconstitutional, and secured a favorable opinion in *Nixon* vs. *Herndon* (273 *U. S.,* 536), adjudging a state statute excluding negroes from political primaries unconstitutional. He also argued the Pacific Coast anti-Oriental land cases (263 *U. S.,* 225, 313, 326).

While he was unsuccessful in his efforts in the Leo Frank case (237 *U. S.,* 309) to secure a holding that a verdict in a capital case induced in the state courts by mob intimidation was a ground for reversal, under the Fourteenth Amendment, the dissenting opinion of Justice Holmes in that case was later adopted by the court in 261 *U. S.,* 86. In *Engel* vs. *O'Malley* (219 *U. S.,* 128), as counsel for the state of New York, he was upheld by the court when the New York private banking law which he had drafted was declared constitutional. He also argued in favor of the constitutionality of the migratory bird laws (252 *U. S.,* 416). He was of counsel successfully attacking the act enlarging the jurisdiction of the New York city court (207 *N. Y.,* 290), and was successful in the Onondaga County senatorial election case of 1891 (129 *N. Y.,* 395). He was of counsel in the case involving the constitutionality of the New York subway contracts (*Admiral Realty Company* vs. *City of New York,* 206 *N. Y.,* 110) and in the New York special franchise tax law case, as special counsel for New York state (199 *U. S.,* 1), in the Pennsylvania anthracite coal tax case (260 *U. S.,* 245), in the interstate commerce act railway valuation cases (252 *U. S.,* 178, leading up to the O'Fallon case, 279 *U. S.,* 461), and in the cases involving the right of municipal operation of buses in New York City under the home-rule amendment of the constitution (229 *N. Y.,* 570; 241 *N. Y.,* 96).

In cases involving aliens he secured holdings that naturalization is a judicial function, reviewable on appeal, and not merely administrative (*Tutun* vs. *United States,* 270 *U. S.,* 568), and that naturalized citizens enjoy rights equal to natural-born citizens (*Luria* vs. *United States,* 231 *U. S.,* 9). He also frustrated administrative efforts to prevent the naturalization of aliens whose families were still abroad (*American Jewish Year Book,* 1925–26, pp. 450–59, 1914–15, pp. 19–89, 1929–30, pp. 347–52). He was of counsel in the Sampson Simpson will case (133 *N. Y.,* 519), in the Gottlieb immigration case (265 *U. S.,* 310), in the case involving the constitutionality of the call for the New York constitutional convention of 1915 (212 *N. Y.,* 520), and in that involving the validity of the New York literacy test for voters (236 *N. Y.*, 437). He served as a member of the New York constitutional conventions of 1890, 1894, and 1915, and was a member (1903–22), and chairman after 1911, of the New York City Bar Association Committee on Amendment of the Law. In the constitutional convention of 1894 he was influential in the shaping of the judicial and charitable appropriations provisions and prepared the amendments to the judicial provisions of the civil and criminal codes thereby necessitated. He also drafted important amendments to the New York Civil Rights Law and was active in the revision of New York corporation laws.

In 1902 Marshall accepted Mayor Low's appointment as chairman of a committee to investigate the Rabbi Jacob Joseph funeral riot, and the committee report led to the checking of discrimination against Jewish and other immigrants on the part of the police and petty magistrates of New York City. In 1908 he became chairman of Governor Hughes's state immigration commission whose work culminated in a notable printed report recommending constructive measures for the benefit of the immigrants. He was active in the American Jewish Committee, and served as president from 1912 until his death. It was in this capacity that much of his best work after 1906 was rendered. The annual reports of the Committee from 1912 on were drafted mainly by him and displayed a comprehensive knowledge of Jewish and world affairs. On behalf of the American Jewish Committee he was a consistent and vigorous champion of liberal immigration laws. He argued before committees of Congress and drafted party platform planks, and it was largely due to his influence that adoption of a literacy test for immigrants was prevented until 1917, and that discriminatory measures were defeated.

As mediator in the New York cloak-makers' strike of 1910, involving seventy thousand people, Marshall effected a settlement, framing a protocol later used as a model in labor adjustments in several industries. In 1919 he was arbitrator in the clothing-workers' strike. He was one of the founders of the Jewish Welfare Board and was chairman of the American Jewish Relief Committee, which, in conjunction with two associated organizations, raised approximately sixty-five million dollars for the relief of Jews in the war zone. Soon after moving to New York he became a director of the Educational Alliance, and thereafter deeply influenced its work for the Americanization and improvement of the Jews on the East Side. He was also a founder of the Jewish Protectory, seeking to redeem youthful delinquents. He served as one of the reorganizers of the Jewish Theological Seminary of America and was chairman of its board of directors until his death. As a memorial to his wife, Florence Lowenstein, whom he married in 1895 and who died in 1916, he established a foundation to promote the religious education of Jewish girls. He served for many years and until his death as president of Temple Emanu-El of New York City. He was also for many years president of the New York State College of Forestry and at Governor Franklin D. Roosevelt's instance the building of the College at Syracuse University bears Marshall's name.

One of his most important achievements was his leadership of the movement for the abrogation of the Russian-American treaty of 1832, because of Russia's refusal to accord right to enter Russia to American Jews and American clergymen of certain other denominations. Marshall delivered an address demanding abrogation on Jan. 19, 1911, before the Union of American Hebrew Congregations, and subsequently when President Taft showed unwillingness to approve abrogation Marshall and his associates appealed to the American people. Mass-meetings were held all over the country. Marshall delivered masterly arguments before the House committee on foreign affairs on Feb. 15 and Dec. 11, 1911, and before the corresponding Senate committee on Dec. 13, 1911. Later in the month the abrogation of the treaty was effected.

Even more important was Marshall's championship of minority protective clauses at the Peace Conference of 1919. When he reached Paris on Mar. 2, 1919, he found that an unsatisfactory clause regarding Roumania's minorities had been approved by a committee for insertion in the peace treaties. Aided by Judge J. W. Mack he drafted a substitute in conjunction with the legal advisers of the United States. When this had been approved in principle by the "Big Four" of the Conference, it was referred to a newly constituted committee on new states, and Marshall cooperated with this body in drafting new clauses which were inserted into the treaties with Poland, Roumania, and other East-European states, primarily at the instance of the United States. Provisions forbidding all discriminations as to civil, religious, and political rights should, it was agreed by all these countries, be inserted in their constitutions, *ipso facto* nullifying all abridgments of minority rights, and infractions of these rights were made a "matter of international concern" and "placed under the guarantee of the League of Nations." Some of the most important decisions of the World Court have borne upon these provisions.

For years after the Balfour declaraton of 1917, Marshall worked to secure united Jewish support to establish a "national Jewish home" in Palestine for persecuted Jews. He attended a meeting in Zurich in August 1929 which adopted a constitution (largely drafted by him) of this enlarged "Jewish Agency." Practically all of world-Jewry united in the enlarged plans. Barely was this conference over when he was suddenly stricken down, and he died at Zurich Sept. 11, 1929. By his last will he left a tithe of his large personal estate to charitable organizations. In an interesting study published in the *New Yorker,* Sept. 21, 1929, many apparent anomalies in Marshall's character were described, such as his large philanthropies and his trifling personal economies, his refusal to accept assistance in the preparation of his numerous briefs, the contrast between his briefs and addresses and his sonnets and humorous dialect sketches, and his kindly, jovial nature, in contrast with his fearless and earnest denunciations. On the occasion of his seventieth birthday, an address of congratulation was presented to him, signed by more than eight thousand representatives of organizations throughout the world. On that occasion Benjamin N. Cardozo characterized Marshall as "a great lawyer; a great champion of ordered liberty; a great leader of his people; a great lover of mankind."

[*Louis Marshall: A Biog. Sketch by Cyrus Adler and Memorial Addresses by Cyrus Adler, Irving Lehman, Horace Stern* (1931), pub. by the Am. Jewish Committee; the *Am. Jewish Year Book,* 1929–30; *Jewish Tribune,* Dec. 10, 1926, Sept. 20, Oct. 4, 1929; *N. Y. Times,* Jan. 12, 1930; *Who's Who in America,* 1928–29; supplementary American chapters in Luigi Luzzatti, *God in Freedom* (1930), ed. by Max J. Kohler; Oscar I. Janowsky, *The Jews and Minority Rights (1898–1919),* (1933); personal acquaintance.]

M. J. K.

MARSHALL, THOMAS (Apr. 2, 1730–June 22, 1802), surveyor, legislator, soldier, was one of the ten children of John Marshall "of the forest," a small planter of Westmoreland County, Va., and his wife, Elizabeth Markham, daughter of Lewis Markham, one-time sheriff of Westmoreland County. Though heir to his father's acres, on his marriage in 1754 to Mary Randolph Keith, the sixteen-year-old daughter of an Episcopal clergyman, James Keith, and Mary Isham Randolph, a descendant of William Randolph of "Turkey Island," Thomas Marshall moved to Prince William County. He built a log-cabin near Germantown. Here John Marshall, eldest of their fifteen children and destined to be chief justice of the United States was born in the next year. There followed in steady succession, as the family constantly moved westward, the other fourteen sons and daughters, all of whom lived to reach maturity and position. Besides John, James Markham and Louis, 1773–1866 [*qq.v.*] attained special distinction. In later years, Chief Justice Marshall said of his father, "My father was a far abler man than any of his sons. To him I owe the solid foundation of all my own success" (J. F. Dillon, *John Marshall, Life, Character and Judicial Services,* 1903, III, p. 330).

Thomas Marshall was a man of great stature. He shared with his wife a deeply religious outlook and unusual hardihood. Although he was a frontiersman for most of his life, he had a liking for books, possessed some of his own, and followed intellectual interests. He became a land surveyor and was brought into close contact with his contemporary George Washington for whom he developed an intimate and lasting friendship. For a time he was engaged by Washington as assistant surveyor of the Fairfax estate. Like Washington he had close associations with Lord Fairfax. After some years at Germantown he moved farther westward and built in a valley in the Blue Ridge a more pretentious house of four rooms with a small stone meat house, a cabin for his two slaves, and a log stable. Here he lived for twelve years, moving in 1773 to seventeen hundred acres adjacent to North Cobler Mountain, a short distance from his earlier location. He built a seven-room house, "Oak Hill," which attested his steadily increasing property. His active service as an officer in Fauquier County began at the first court in that county in 1759 when he was sworn in as a justice of the peace, justice of the county court in chancery, and was given a commission as county surveyor. He was the leading citizen in Fauquier County in the succeeding years. He was a member of the House of Burgesses from 1761 to October 1767, when he became sheriff of Fauquier County. From 1769 to 1773 he again served as a Burgess from Fauquier and in the latter year was appointed clerk of Dunmore, later Shenandoah County. In 1775 he returned to the Burgesses. When Leeds Parish, embracing Fauquier County, was established in 1769 he was made the principal vestryman.

Marshall attended the Virginia Convention of 1775 and when Culpeper, Orange, and Fauquier counties raised regiments of minute men he was named their lieutenant in view of his prominence, his adherence to the Revolution, and his previous military experience as lieutenant and captain in the militia and a participant in the Indian wars. He fought with the Culpeper minute men at Great Bridge, the first battle of the Revolution in Virginia. While there he was appointed by the Virginia legislature major of the 3rd Virginia Regiment. With his son Lieut. John Marshall, he joined the Continental forces and had distinguished service at Trenton and at the Brandywine, where he had two horses shot under him. He had been promoted lieutenant-colonel on Aug. 13, 1776, and colonel on Feb. 21, 1777. The Virginia legislature rewarded him for his bravery at the Brandywine by electing him colonel of the Virginia State Regiment of Artillery. He served in this capacity until Feb. 16, 1781, when his men were discharged and he became a reduced officer. In 1780 he rode to Kentucky under special permit from the Virginia governor to locate land warrants. In November 1780 he was appointed surveyor for a part of Kentucky. The next year he was appointed on a commission to examine and settle the public accounts in the Western country. Though he had already acquired considerable property in Virginia, owning at least 2,000 acres in Fauquier and twenty-two negroes, he was embarrassed for lack of money at the close of the Revolution. He opened his surveyor's office in Kentucky and in 1783 moved his large family to their new home across the mountains. He acquired large tracts of land. In 1785 he gave his son John 824 acres of the best land in Fauquier County. He took prominent part in Kentucky affairs, represented the district of Kentucky in the Virginia legislature, and became "Surveyor of Revenue for the District of Ohio," resigning that office on June 30, 1797, because of age and infirmity. He had great faith in the Union and steadily opposed disaffection in Kentucky and feared foreign influence as the gravest danger to the young republic. Thomas Marshall died in 1802. His widow survived him until Sept. 19, 1809. He left in his will immense quantities of land to be divided among his children, including his home farm in Kentucky, "Buckpond."

[A. J. Beveridge, *The Life of John Marshall,* vols. I and II (1916), has the best material on Thos. Marshall. See also: Humphrey Marshall, *The Hist. of Ky.* (2 vols., 1924); "Thos. Marshall," *Bull. Fauquier Hist. Soc.,* July 1922, and "The Genesis of Fauquier," *Ibid.*; W. M. Paxton, *The Marshall Family* (1885); *Reg. of the Ky. State Hist. Soc.,* Jan. 1921, pp. 93–96.]

M. H. W.

MARSHALL, THOMAS ALEXANDER (Jan. 15, 1794–Apr. 17, 1871), jurist and congressman, was born in Kentucky, the son of Humphrey Marshall, 1760–1841 [*q.v.*], and of his wife Mary, who was a sister of John, Louis, and James Markham Marshall [*qq.v.*]. Thomas profited much from the position of influence and wealth of his father. He was sent to the celebrated school in Mercer County conducted by Joshua Fry and was there prepared for college. He was then sent to Yale College, where he received the B.A. degree in 1815. Returning to Kentucky, he read law and the next year established himself in Frankfort. On Nov. 26, 1816, he was married to Eliza Price, a sister-in-law of Henry Clay and a grand-daughter of Thomas Hart, one of the proprietors of Transylvania. Since Frankfort at this time had a full supply of able lawyers and was besides not particularly friendly to the Humphrey Marshall tradition, he removed to Paris, Bourbon County, in 1819. In 1827 he was elected to the lower branch of the legislature and served for two years. Finding that the Whig party came closest to the doctrines his father had advocated, he acted with it. He was elected to the Twenty-second and Twenty-third congresses, from 1831 to 1835, but was defeated for the Twenty-fourth. At Washington he attained a position of some influence. He served first on the committee on private land claims and then as chairman of the committee on Revolutionary claims. He spoke frequently and sometimes at great length, upholding the orthodox Whig position. He was active in the tariff debates of 1832 and often advocated rates higher than were obtained. He also spoke in favor of the United States Bank. He showed, perhaps, his greatest interest in the veterans of the Revolution who were seeking pensions or adjustments of claims.

He had a judicial turn of mind that could be better satisfied elsewhere than in the excitement of active politics. Following his defeat for a third term in Congress he was offered an appointment to the Kentucky court of appeals, which he readily accepted and was commissioned in March 1835. When his position became elective under the state's new constitution of 1850 he was elected and continued to serve until 1856. During his uninterrupted term of twenty-one years he was twice chief justice, once through appointment, 1847–51, and the second time through the operation of the provision in the constitution that provided each justice should serve his last two years as chief justice. Shortly after becoming a justice he accepted in addition a professorship of the law of pleadings, evidence, and contracts in Transylvania University, which he held from 1836 to 1849. On retiring from the court, he went to the rapidly developing city of Chicago, but, failing to be satisfied there, he soon returned to Kentucky. He settled in Louisville, where he spent the period of the Civil War. He became a Union man and took an inconspicuous part in the politics of the times by serving as a Louisville representative in the lower house of the legislature from 1863 to 1865. Eschewing the radicalism that gripped some of the Kentuckians after the war he joined the Conservatives. On Feb. 12, 1866, Gov. Thomas Bramlette appointed him chief justice of the court of appeals to fill the vacancy caused by the death of William Sampson. In the following August at the regular election he ran for the full term of six years, but his Unionism during the war was too much for Kentucky now turned Confederate so he was defeated. His active career ended with this reverse. He died at his home in Louisville, but his remains were buried in Lexington.

[Lewis and R. H. Collins, *Hist. of Ky.*, revised ed. (2 vols., 1874); *Green Bag*, Aug. 1900; F. B. Dexter, *Biog. Sketches of the Grads. of Yale College*, vol. VI (1912); W. M. Paxton, *The Marshall Family* (1885); Robert Peters, *Transylvania Univ.* (1896); *Cincinnati Commercial*, Apr. 19, 1871; *Courier-Journal* (Louisville), Apr. 17, 1871.] E. M. C.

MARSHALL, THOMAS RILEY (Mar. 14, 1854–June 1, 1925), governor of Indiana, vice-president of the United States, was born at North Manchester, Ind. His father, Daniel M. Marshall, was an old-fashioned country doctor, himself of Hoosier birth, but the son of a Virginia couple who had emigrated to Indiana when the state was still frontier. Thomas' mother, Martha (Patterson) Marshall, and his mother's parents, were natives of Pennsylvania. When Thomas was about two years old, he was taken by his parents to Illinois, remaining there long enough to acquire a distinct recollection of having attended the Freeport debate between Lincoln and Douglas. Soon the Marshall family went on to Kansas, but, finding the political situation there too tense for comfort, they moved again, first to La Grange, Mo., and later, back to Indiana.

After attending the public schools, young Marshall entered Wabash College, Crawfordsville, Ind., and was graduated in 1873 with Phi Beta Kappa honors. During his college years he made up his mind to study law, and, taking the advice of some lawyer friends, he read law in the office of Judge Walter Olds of Ft. Wayne. He was admitted to the bar on his twenty-first birthday at Columbia City, Ind., where he practised continuously for more than a third of a century, acquiring both a comfortable living and an enviable degree of contentment. Until well after his fortieth birthday he remained a bachelor, but on Oct. 2, 1895, Lois I. Kimsey of Angola, Ind., became his wife—a most felicitous marriage. As a typical "prominent citizen," Marshall was a member of the Presbyterian Church, taught a Sunday-school class, served on the local school board, and became a thirty-third degree Mason (*Review of Reviews*, August 1912, pp. 185–90).

"Democrats, like poets," said Marshall, "are born, not made." Like his father before him, Marshall was always a Democrat, and he served his party well. To his way of thinking, the fundamental principle of the Democratic creed was the right of every man to "his chance in life, unhampered and unaided by legislative enactment" (*Outlook*, Sept. 28, 1912, p. 221). For many years his interest in politics did not seem to extend to a desire to hold office; but once when he was importuned to run for Congress and refused on the ground that he "might be elected," he hinted that he would like to be governor. At length, in 1908, this nomination came to him, as he insisted, "through the inability of the leading candidates to obtain a majority of the votes of the convention" (*Recollections*, p. 161).

During this campaign the Republicans came out for county option on the licensing of saloons, and indeed actually put a county-option law on the statute books. The Democrats favored township option, a system by which cities would have the chance to vote their preference apart from the strongly dry rural population. The anti-saloon forces promptly denounced the Democratic stand as "wet," but in spite of this opposition Marshall won after a vigorous campaign, although the electoral vote of the state went to Taft. Not until 1911, however, were there enough Democrats in the legislature to make possible the enactment of a township-option law. Marshall himself believed that prohibition could be effective only when local sentiment was behind it, and that the substitution of township for county option was "of immense advantage to temperance" (*World's Work*, Oct. 1912, p. 633).

As governor for four years, Marshall also pushed to enactment an extensive program of labor and social legislation; and he attempted to secure in an unusual way the adoption of a much needed new constitution for the state. The "Tom Marshall Constitution," so-called because Marshall was credited with having written it himself, failed to materialize because of hostile action by the state supreme court (*Ellingham* vs. *Dye*, 178 *Ind.*, 336). While Marshall believed this judicial veto to be a "clear usurpation of authority," he yielded to it gracefully lest the respect properly due the court by the people should be diminished (*Recollections*, p. 213). It was Marshall's record as governor that led to the presentation of his name to the Democratic national convention of 1912 as Indiana's favorite son for president. When the nomination went to Wilson, Marshall was given second place with little opposition. His election followed, and four years later he was renominated and reëlected—the first vice-president in nearly a century to succeed himself.

As vice-president, Marshall was of greater consequence in the government than most of his predecessors. He made it his business to master the rules of the Senate, over which he presided with grace and tact. While scrupulously careful not to exceed his constitutional and legal powers, he exerted his personal influence most effectively on behalf of many administration measures. Nor did he deem it improper to speak his mind occasionally on public matters. Once, in 1913, his remarks on the subject of inheritances aroused much criticism in conservative circles (*Literary Digest*, May 3, 1913), but ordinarily what he had to say was well received. During his second term, when the President was for much of the time absent from the country or ill, Marshall often acted as ceremonial head of the nation, welcoming royal visitors to the United States, and discharging with democratic simplicity many other unwonted duties. Had he countenanced the idea, it is probable that he might have been declared president during the time that the stricken Wilson was incapable of carrying the full responsibilities of his office (*Outlook*, June 10, 1925).

Marshall was perhaps the most popular vice-president that the country ever had. His clear blue-gray eyes, his plentiful iron-gray hair, his genial smile, and his well-groomed appearance marked him out as a man of note, in spite of his instinctive modesty and his none too impressive physique. "Lovable, generous, kindly, keenly observant and always tolerant," he was above all else possessed of a never-failing sense of humor. Once during a tiresome debate in the Senate on the needs of the country, he let drop his most frequently quoted remark: "What this country needs is a really good five cent cigar." A devoted admirer of the original constitution, he paid his respects to some of the later changes by the observation that "it's got so it is as easy to amend the Constitution of the United States as it used to be to draw a cork" (*Literary Digest*, June 20, 1925, p. 45). Late in life he put much of his quaint humor and homely philosophy into a book of *Recollections*, "in the hope," so his foreword declared, "that the Tired Business Man, the Unsuccessful Golfer and the Lonely Husband whose wife is out reforming the world may find therein a half hour's surcease from sorrow." It may be that Marshall's love of fun led some undiscerning people to set too low an estimate on his ability. After leaving office in 1921, Marshall returned to Indiana, making his home in Indianapolis. He died four years later, in Washington, D. C., while on a business trip to the Capital.

[Marshall, as he said, "was never able to accumulate the note-making or the diary habit"; hence his book, *Recollections of Thos. R. Marshall, Vice-President and Hoosier Philosopher—A Hoosier Salad* (1925), is precisely what its title implies. Chas. Kettleborough, *Constitution Making in Ind.*, vol. II (1916), gives the history of the "Tom Marshall Constitution" and prints many documents, including the Constitution itself and the court decision which set it aside. Marshall's sketch of himself in the *Cong. Directory*, 63 Cong., 2 Sess., p. 3, is characteristically brief. Appreciative remarks on Marshall by John McSweeney of Ohio are in *Cong. Record*, 69 Cong., 1 Sess., p. 11548. Of the numerous periodical references to Marshall's career, the more important have already been cited.] J. D. H.

MARSHALL, WILLIAM EDGAR (June 30, 1837–Aug. 29, 1906), portrait painter, engraver, was born in New York City of Scotch parents. His father, Francis Marshall, coming to the United States a stone-mason, founded the contracting firm of Marshall, Bates & Company, builders. The son got his education at a public school in Varick Street. At seventeen he began his engraving in a watchcase factory. His free hours, he devoted to ambitious portrait ventures in line. He was encouraged by a friendly engraver, Cyrus Durand [*q.v.*], at whose suggestion the youth executed plates of both presidential candidates in the Buchanan-Frémont campaign. Submitted to the American Bank Note Company, these won Marshall, in 1858, a coveted chance to engrave portrait vignettes. He worked for this company several years and became one of its best engravers. Meanwhile, he published large portrait plates, two of which, Washington after Stuart, and Fenimore Cooper after Elliott, had wide circulation. He also tried his hand at painting original portraits. Finding that he had talent, he went to Paris about 1863 for study under Couture. Two of his student canvases won admission to the Salon. News of the assassination of Lincoln brought him home to paint, from photographs and descriptions, a portrait of the martyred President, which is now at Yale University. His engraving from this picture had an enormous sale. During a period spent in Boston, Emerson, Hawthorne, Longfellow, and Holmes sat for him.

About 1866 he returned to New York, taking up his permanent abode in Broadway, near Washington Square, where during the days when artists swarmed in that vicinity his studio became a rendezvous. He had an engaging, humorous personality and in conversation could draw from a wealth of entertaining anecdotes concerning his famous sitters, who, as the years went by, included Grant, whom he painted six times, Sherman, Blaine, Beecher, John Gilbert, Mark Hanna, Harrison, McKinley, and Roosevelt. He helped many a struggling painter, notably Albert P. Ryder [*q.v.*], whose talent he was among the first to recognize. When Clemenceau was in exile in America, he renewed a friendship with Marshall begun in the Latin Quarter, making the studio his headquarters.

About 1871, having engraved a head of Christ after Da Vinci, Marshall was fired with ambition to paint his own conception of the Galilean. To the project he devoted vast research, producing at length a colossal canvas depicting a dark-eyed, Greco-Arabian type, which he exhibited widely but refused to sell. During his later years he lived in retirement in his attic studio, 711 Broadway, keeping so aloof from currents of art life that many believed him dead, but happy with his engravings, his autograph letters, and the great head of Christ, which covered one whole wall. Here, cared for by a second wife, Florence Rogers Garrison, a widow whom he married in 1900, he died. From his first wife he had been divorced. Marshall is represented in the National Gallery of Art in Washington by his portrait of Longfellow, and one of himself painted at the age of twenty-three.

[Interview in Illus. Supp. to *N. Y. Tribune*, June 3, 1906; obituary articles in *N. Y. Tribune* and *N. Y. Times*, Aug. 30, 1906; D. M. Stauffer, *Am. Engravers upon Copper and Steel* (1907); Frank Weitenkampf, *Am. Graphic Art* (1924); W. S. Baker, *The Engraved Portraits of Washington* (1880), and *Am. Engravers and Their Works* (1875); F. J. Mather and others, *The Am. Spirit in Art* (1927); *Shields Mag. of Art*, Jan. 1908.]

M. B. H—t.

MARSHALL, WILLIAM LOUIS (June 11, 1846–July 2, 1920), soldier and engineer, was born in Washington, Ky., the son of Col. Charles A. and Phoebe A. (Paxton) Marshall. His grandfather, Thomas, was a brother of Chief Justice John Marshall [*q.v.*]. William attended the grammar school of Kenyon College, Ohio, from 1859 to 1860, and then entered the collegiate department. At the outbreak of the Civil War, however, he enlisted in the 10th Kentucky Cavalry, serving from Aug. 16, 1862, until Sept. 17, 1863, when ill health prevented further service. The following year he received an appointment as cadet at the United States Military Academy, from which he graduated in June 1868 and was assigned as second lieutenant to the corps of engineers.

His first important service was from 1872 to 1876, when he was engaged as assistant to Lieut. G. M. Wheeler [*q.v.*] in the exploration of the Rocky Mountain region of the West. It was during this period, 1873, that he discovered the Marshall Pass, now traversed by the Denver & Rio Grande Railroad, and, in 1875, the gold placers in the Marshall Basin of the San Miguel River, Colorado. From 1876 to 1884 he was assistant engineer on various river improvement projects in Alabama, Georgia, and Tennessee and in charge of a section of the Mississippi River. He was then placed in charge of river and harbor improvements in Wisconsin and Illinois, on which assignment he was engaged for fifteen years. Part of this time, 1890 to 1899, he was employed in constructing the Hennepin Canal, connecting the Illinois River at Lasalle with the Mississippi River at Rock Island, which was to be a part of an inland waterway from the Mississippi to Lake Michigan. This canal with its thirty locks has practically every type of structure employed in canal construction. "Begun in the early nineties before the art of concrete construction had become well known among engineers, all of its masonry is concrete. This courageous departure from the then existing practice was due entirely to . . . Marshall's sound judgment and bold initiative, and he then developed the details of methods which were subsequently adopted by the entire engineering profession and have continued in force practically unchanged to the present day" (Keller, *post*, p. 111). While constructing the canal, he patented several improvements connected with it, including a combined breakwater and beach, May 12, 1890; an automatic movable dam or sluiceway gate, Mar. 23, 1897; and an automatic dam, weir, or gate, Dec. 28, 1897, and Jan. 4, 1898. During this period, he also served on many important commissions and boards, among them a board to advise on the water supply of Washington, D. C., of which he was president; the Missouri River Commission; and the Lincoln Park Board, Chicago, for which he was consulting engineer.

In 1899 he was sent to New York City to take charge of both fortification and river and harbor work. Here he completed the Ambrose Channel, planned and completed the extension of Governor's Island, and displayed great originality in the construction of coast defenses. In the meantime he had been advanced through the various grades and on Aug. 27, 1907, commissioned colonel. In 1908, July 2, he was commissioned Chief of Engineers with the rank of brigadier-general, which position he held until his retirement from active service on June 11, 1910. In 1909, in addition to his other duties, he served on a board to report on the necessary defenses of the Panama Canal. Shortly after his retirement he was appointed by the President consulting engineer to the Secretary of the Interior, and as such served on various boards dealing with projects of the United States Reclamation Service and made reports on possible hydro-electric power development projects in different parts of the country. He held this position until his death, which occurred in Washington, D. C. On June 2, 1886, he married Elizabeth Hill Colquitt, daughter of Alfred H. Colquitt [*q.v.*], by whom he had one daughter.

[W. M. Paxton, *The Marshall Family* (1885); G. W. Cullum, *Biog. Reg. Officers and Grads. U. S. Mil. Acad.*, vols. III (1891), IV (1901), V (1910), VIa (1920); Charles Keller, in *Fifty-third Ann. Report Asso. Grads. U. S. Mil. Acad.* (1922); *The Official Gazette of the U. S. Patent Office,* May 12, 1891, Mar. 23, 1897, Dec. 28, 1897, Jan. 4, 1898; *Army and Navy Jour.*, July 10, 1920; *Who's Who in America*, 1918–19; *Evening Star* (Washington, D. C.), July 3, 1920.]

G. J. F.

MARSHALL, WILLIAM RAINEY (Oct. 17, 1825–Jan. 8, 1896), Union soldier, governor of Minnesota, was the son of Joseph and Abigail Black (Shaw) Marshall and the descendant of Joseph Marshall who emigrated from the north of Ireland about 1746 and settled near Carlisle, Pa. He was born in Boone County, Mo., and spent his boyhood in Quincy, Ill. For several years after 1841 he and his brother worked in lead mines of Illinois and Wisconsin, and during this time he obtained a practical knowledge of surveying. While living at St. Croix Falls in 1847 he went to the Falls of St. Anthony, where he staked out a claim, which he could not, however, make legal until 1849. In 1848 he was elected to the Wisconsin legislature but was disqualified because his residence was west of the St. Croix River. He was one of the leaders in the movement for the erection of Minnesota Territory and after 1849 was identified intimately with the development of Minnesota. He surveyed and plotted parts of the town at the Falls of St. Anthony (now part of Minneapolis), opened a hardware store, and was elected a member of the first territorial legislature. In 1851 he removed to St. Paul, where he plunged into a variety of activities, each of which seemed to him to promise greater possibilities than the last, for "his was the sanguine temperament in excess" (*Min. Hist. Soc. Colls.*, VIII, 510). He established and ran for a time a hardware store, was county surveyor, and in 1853 with his brother and Nathaniel P. Langford, whose sister, Abby, he married in 1854, set up a bank which prospered until the panic of 1857. He was chairman of the convention that founded the Republican party in Minnesota, sought unsuccessfully the office of delegate to Congress, and in 1861 started the *St. Paul Daily Press,* which soon absorbed the *Minnesotian.*

He soon sold his interest in the newspaper to his assistant editor, Joseph A. Wheelock, and entered upon that brief period of soldiering that probably brought him more satisfaction than any other experience. When the 7th Minnesota Infantry was recruited he was made lieutenant-colonel. He served with Sibley against the Sioux in the Minnesota Valley and participated in the punitive campaign of 1863. The 7th Infantry was then transferred to the South and attached to the XVI Army Corps. He was colonel in November 1863, and he campaigned in Arkansas, Missouri, Mississippi, and Tennessee. He was cited for distinguished skill and bravery in the fighting about Nashville in December 1864, and he was brevetted brigadier-general. Commanding his brigade at the siege of Mobile, he was wounded at the attack on Spanish Fort. The regiment was mustered out at Fort Snelling in August 1865, in time for him to capitalize his military prestige in the biennial gubernatorial campaign. He was nominated, elected by a narrow margin, and reëlected in 1867. No significant events marked his career as governor. He vetoed a bill to move the seat of government from St. Paul, and he vainly urged the legislature to redeem the credit of the state in the matter of the "Five Million Loan." A number of enterprises occupied him after his term as governor ended. He was one of the first railroad and warehouse commissioners in the state, holding the office from 1874 to 1882. Banking, farming, stock-raising, and other ventures engaged his attention but in none of them was he very successful, and he died poor. He was one of the founders and a life-long member of the Swedenborgian Church of St. Paul. He took an interest in the state historical society, being its president in 1868 and nominally its secretary from 1893 to 1895, but his health was failing and in 1894 he went to Pasadena, where he died.

[M. D. Shutter and J. S. McLain, *Progressive Men of Minn.* (1897); W. W. Folwell, *A Hist. of Minn.*, vols. II, III (1924–26); E. V. Smalley, *Hist. of the Republican Party* (1896); *Minn. Hist. Soc. Colls.*, vols. IV, VIII, IX, XII, XIII (1876–1908), esp. J. F. Williams, "Hist. of St. Paul" (vol. IV) and J. K. Baker, "Lives of the Governors of Minn." (vol. XIII); T. M. Newson, *Pen Pictures of St. Paul* (1886); *Daily Pioneer Press* (St. Paul), Jan. 10, 1896.]

L. B. S—e.

MARTIN, ALEXANDER (1740–Nov. 2, 1807), Revolutionary soldier, governor of North Carolina, United States senator, was the son of Hugh and Jane Martin of Hunterdon County, N. J. He received the degree of A.B. from the College of New Jersey in 1756 and soon thereafter moved to the village of Salisbury, N. C., where he was merchant, justice of the peace in 1764, deputy king's attorney in 1766, and judge in 1774–75. Incurring the hostility of the Regulators, he was severely whipped by them at the Hillsborough superior court in 1770 and was one of the signers of an agreement with them in Rowan County in 1771 to refund all fees taken illegally and to arbitrate all differences. He represented Guilford County, to which he had recently moved, in the North Carolina House of Commons (1773–74) and in the second and third provincial congresses (1775) as a supporter of the Patriot cause. Appointed lieutenant-colonel of the 2nd North Carolina Continental Regiment, Sept. 1, 1775, he participated in the "Snow Campaign" against the Loyalists in upper South Carolina late in the year; in the Moore's Creek campaign of February 1776; and, after promotion to a colonelcy, in the defense of Charleston in June. In 1777 he joined Washington's army in the North, but having been arrested for cowardice in the battle of Germantown, tried by court martial, and acquitted, he resigned his command on Nov. 22 and returned to North Carolina.

He represented Guilford County in the Senate, 1778–82, 1785, 1787–88, being speaker at every session except those of 1778–79; was a member in 1780–81 of the powerful Board of War and its successor, the Council Extraordinary; and acted as governor during the captivity of Governor Burke in the autumn and winter of 1781–82. The General Assembly elected him governor in 1782 over the conservative Samuel Johnston [*q.v.*], in 1783 over Richard Caswell [*q.v.*], and in 1784 without opposition. In December 1786 he was elected to the Continental Congress, but resigned the next year. He was the least strongly Federalistic and a relatively inconspicuous member of the North Carolina delegation to the Federal Convention of 1787. He left the Convention late in August and did not sign the completed Constitution. Nevertheless, his Federalism caused his defeat in the election of delegates to the Hillsborough Convention in 1788. He was again elected governor in 1789 and, by reëlections, completed in 1792 the constitutional limit of three consecutive terms.

Martin was not a public speaker or a man of remarkable ability. Suave, upright, moderate, faithful, an excellent parliamentarian, and a master of the art of conciliation, he courted with great success the favor of the powerful General Assembly by magnifying its ascendency over the governorship and drifting with the current of its opinion, in divining which he was an adept. In courteous gubernatorial messages he suggested clemency toward the Tories; encouragement of education; public support of ministers, regardless of denomination; greater power for the Continental Congress; stimulation of agriculture, commerce, and manufactures; and the construction of a system of internal improvements by convict labor. In public life he sought to placate both sides. A moderate Federalist before 1790, he inclined toward Republicanism thereafter. In 1792 the Republican legislature elected him to the United States Senate. Here his most conspicuous rôle was that of advocate of open legislative sessions. He voted for the Alien and Sedition acts, and probably for that reason failed of reëlection in December 1798. In 1799 he returned to his plantation, "Danbury," in Rockingham County, whither he had moved his residence prior to 1790, when he was reported as the owner of forty-seven slaves. He represented Rockingham County in the state Senate, 1804–05, serving as speaker during the session of 1805. He was a trustee of several academies and of the University of North Carolina, 1790–1807. He never married. On Nov. 2, 1807, he died at "Danbury," closing a public career unusual in length and popularity.

[*Colonial Records of N. C.* (10 vols., 1886–90); *State Records of N. C.* (16 vols., 1895–1905); Governors' Papers and Letter Books (MSS.), in N. C. Hist. Commission; *Journals of the House of Commons and Senate,* 1792, 1798; G. J. McRee, *Life and Correspondence of James Iredell* (2 vols., 1857–58); *Raleigh Register and N.-C. State Gazette,* Nov. 19, 1807; *The Papers of John Steele* (2 vols., 1924), ed. by H. M. Wagstaff; Francis Nash, *Governor Alexander Martin: An Address* (1908); R. M. Douglas, "Alexander Martin," in S. A. Ashe, *Biog. Hist. of N. C.,* vol. III (1905).]

A. R. N.

MARTIN, ARTEMAS (Aug. 3, 1835–Nov. 7, 1918), mathematician, was born on a farm in Steuben County, N. Y., the son of James Madison Martin and Orenda Knight (Bradley) Martin. During his early childhood the family moved to Venango County, Pa. His formal education consisted of three winters in the district school and a few months in the Franklin Academy when he was seventeen. As a boy he worked at farming and gardening in summer, and at woodchopping during the winter. Later he taught a district school for four winters, but for the most part, until he was fifty, he earned his living at farming, woodchopping, and oil-well drilling. His meager leisure he spent in the study of mathematics. Early in life he had begun to contribute mathematical problems and solutions to various journals, and in 1877, while making a bare living in market gardening on a small rented place in Erie County, Pa., he began to edit and publish the *Mathematical Visitor* (1877–94). In 1882 he began to publish the *Mathematical Magazine* (1882–1913). For financial reasons he found it necessary to do the typesetting as well as the editing, and he became an expert mathematical typesetter. His mathematical abilities received wide recognition: Yale conferred upon him the honorary degree of A.M. in 1877; Rutgers honored him with a Ph.D. degree in 1882; and in 1885 Hillsdale awarded him an LL.D. degree. Numerous learned societies in the United States and abroad honored him with membership.

In 1885 Martin joined the United States Coast and Geodetic Survey, first as librarian and later as computer. All of his spare time he still devoted to work in pure mathematics, to the editing of his mathematical journals, which did much to foster a love for mathematics on its less academic side, and to the preparation of papers which appeared in various journals at home and abroad. His writings dealt chiefly with the properties of numbers and of triangles, diophantine analysis, average, probability, elliptic integrals, and logarithms. He was an authority on early mathematical textbooks, of which he had a notable collection, and collaborated with J. M. Greenwood in the preparation of *American Text-Books on Arithmetic,* issued by the United States Bureau of Education in 1899.

Personally, Martin was a man of simple tastes but of prepossessing appearance. Although he exhibited some of the limitations imposed by pioneer life, he at the same time exemplified most of its robust virtues. He was fond of home life and of children, but he denied himself marriage that he might care for his parents and sisters. He died in Washington. His memory is perpetuated in the Artemas Martin Library of the American University. This library, consisting principally of mathematical works, was during Martin's lifetime considered one of the finest private mathematical collections in America. At the same university Martin also endowed an Artemas Martin Lectureship in mathematics and physics.

[The *Illustrated Buffalo Express,* Feb. 12, 1899; *Who's Who in America,* 1918–19; J. M. Cattell, *Am. Men of Sci.* (ed. 1910); *Science,* Nov. 22, 1918; the *Evening Star* (Wash., D. C.), Nov. 8, 1918; personal information.] H. A. M.

MARTIN, FRANÇOIS-XAVIER (Mar. 17, 1762–Dec. 10, 1846), jurist and author, was born at Marseilles, France. He received an excellent education and was, it has been said, intended for the priesthood. At seventeen or eighteen, however, he joined an uncle in Martinique, and, after a short stay there, came to New Bern, N. C., seeking, so the story goes, a lost shipment of molasses. He is said, too, to have served a short time in the Continental Army, but the story is highly unlikely. In New Bern he taught French for a living and learned English. He secured a position in a printing office and, although he had never been in one before, held his place as a typesetter, finally becoming foreman of the shop and, ultimately, its owner. He began a publishing business which became extensive, handling school books, novels, and translations made by himself from the French. In the meantime he studied law and was admitted to the bar in 1789. Soon afterwards he wrote and published several volumes dealing with the duties of local officers, executors, and administrators, which had a wide sale. The legislature employed him to collect the Parliamentary statutes in force in the state—a task which he did very inaccurately (1792)—and later to collect the private laws of North Carolina (1794). Still later he was employed to make his well-known "Revisal" of the *Laws of the State of North Carolina.* Meanwhile he published reprints of North Carolina statutes, translations of *Latches Reports* (1793), Pothier, *A Treatise on Obligations* (1802), *Cases in the Court of King's Bench during the Reign of Charles I* (1793) and *Notes of a Few Decisions of the Superior Courts of the State of North Carolina* (1797). He served in 1806 as a borough member of the House of Commons, and was in active practice in the state for twenty years, during which time he acquired command of English, became a master of common and statute law, with a familiar acquaintance with Roman and French law, and laid by a comfortable estate.

Never a notable advocate, he was, nevertheless, admirably prepared for the career as a jurist into which he was ushered in 1809 when President Madison appointed him a federal judge for the Mississippi Territory. A year later he was transferred to the Territory of Orleans, then just moving toward statehood. His knowledge of French language and law was of immeasurable value here. He was the first attorney general of Louisiana (1813), and two years later, Jan. 31, 1815, he became a judge of the state supreme court. In 1836 he became chief justice. Retiring in 1846, when the new constitution abolished the court, he died a few months later.

When Martin came to the supreme court, Louisiana law was in apparently hopeless confusion, with both French and Spanish law in operation. The coming of English-American law only added difficulty. By act of Congress the common law was made the basis of criminal jurisprudence, and in 1808 a civil code had been adopted which did not repeal other law not in conflict with it. It was, therefore, necessary for the courts to study and compare Spanish and

French codes, to be familiar with Roman law and the essentials of the English common law. In other words, a jurisprudence had to be created, and Martin played a notable part in doing it, applying deep learning to the solution of the countless knotty problems with which the court was confronted, reconciling the conflicting systems, and bringing order out of chaos. Justly he won a great name in constructive jurisprudence, particularly for his skilful blending of the best principles of the English and Roman law. His numerous opinions run through fifty-one volumes of the *Louisiana Reports.* His first opinion, *Johnson* vs. *Duncan* (3 *Martin's Reports, Old Series,* 530), written during the War of 1812, is distinguished by its masterly and unanswerable argument sustaining the doctrine that neither the executive nor any subordinate had the power to suspend the regular operation of the laws or the writ of *habeas corpus,* holding such suspension a legislative power, and declaring that the legislative power could never be capable of impairing the obligation of private contracts.

Not alone as a judge did Martin acquire reputation. He began in 1811 to publish reports of cases decided by the courts, and continued them until 1830. He also published *A General Digest of the Acts of the Legislature of the Late Territory of Orleans and of the State of Louisiana and the Ordinances of the Governors under the Territorial Government* (1816). In 1827 his *History of Louisiana* appeared and two years later, his *History of North Carolina.* His total output amounted to thirty-four volumes, among which the *Reports* are much the most valuable. His histories, the result of tremendous research and labor, were poorly written, badly arranged, "as lifeless as the minutes and records of proceedings in a court of justice" (Gayarré, *post,* p. 246), and scarcely as valuable. At best they are collections of facts.

As a speaker Martin was neither eloquent nor pleasant, and was described as "dry as a hard-baked brickbat" (*Ibid.,* p. 245). Personally, before age and blindness made him hopelessly eccentric, he was a quiet, agreeable little man. His life was utterly cheerless, his French thrift combining with his recollection of poverty to make him a complete miser. "He lived, so to speak, on nothing, and heaped up his savings with compound interest" (Howe, in *History of Louisiana, post,* p. xxiv). He never married and left an estate of nearly half a million dollars to a younger brother. In 1838 he became quite blind, but continued his work easily and efficiently. In 1844 he visited France hoping for a cure, but met with failure. He died in New Orleans in December 1846.

[Memoirs by W. W. Howe, in Martin's *Hist. of La.* (2nd ed., 1882) and in W. D. Lewis, *Great Am. Lawyers,* vol. II (1907); sketch by H. A. Bullard in B. F. French, *Hist. Colls. of La.,* vol. II (1850); S. A. Ashe, *Biog. Hist. of N. C.,* vol. IV (1906); Charles Gayarré, *Fernando de Lemos* (1872); *State Records of N. C.* (16 vols., 1895–1905); *The Jeffersonian* (New Orleans), Dec. 12, 1846.]

J. G. deR. H.

MARTIN, FREDERICK TOWNSEND (Dec. 6, 1849–Mar. 8, 1914), author and philanthropist, the son of Henry Hull and Anne (Townsend) Martin, was born in Albany, N. Y. His father was a leading Albany lawyer and banker, and his mother was a woman well-established in the most fashionable Newport and New York society. From the first, therefore, young Martin had every material advantage. He was educated at the Albany academy and later the Albany Law School, where he studied law and in 1872 received the degree of LL.B. He was for eleven years active in the affairs of the Zouave Cadets, 10th Regiment of the New York state national guard. He traveled extensively and in the course of his world tours met an astonishing number of notables. At the same time he was a deeply interested observer of the conditions of labor and of poverty. He drew heavily upon his large fortune in helping the unfortunate both in the United States and abroad. He was particularly interested in the work of the Bowery mission in New York City, where each Christmas-time he gave a dinner; and he was also well-known and well-loved by the poor of London's East End.

In time his observation led him to entertain theories that were considered radical in his own day. He became convinced that the age of great individual fortunes was passing and that, with it, the reign of the old social order was drawing to a close. These beliefs he stated very clearly in *The Passing of the Idle Rich* (1911) which appeared also in serial form in *Everybody's Magazine* (Feb.–Apr. 1911). In this book he set himself the task of illustrating the theory that decay always follows idleness and extravagance. His self-imposed mission was to call to the attention of other well-to-do members of society the dangerous foundation upon which their order rests. The work had an immense vogue and, being dramatized, appeared at the Garden Theatre in New York on May 1, 1913. In 1913 he published *Things I Remember,* and he wrote many magazine articles of a miscellaneous character. At the time of his death he was at work on another book, "Snobs." These books took the form of rather delightful descriptions of the earlier days of the Astor-McAllister dictatorship in New York society and of a variety of fashionable coteries in France and England, to which Martin, as a bachelor clubman and cosmopolitan society man, had *entrée*. Closely associated with his zest for travel was the hobby of Martin's latter days, his work as one of the founders and vice-president of the American Embassy Association. In 1909 he was struck by the fact that, with the exception of Constantinople, there were no permanent residences for American Ambassadors in the capitals of the world. With E. Clarence Jones, therefore, he toured the United States in an attempt to win public favor for an appropriation bill for embassy purchases. To further this aim and to manage the funds collected, they founded the association. His principal business connection was with the Metropolitan Trust Company of which he was a director. While in London arranging for the housing of an art bequest from his friend Henry Sands, he died of angina pectoris.

[*Who's Who in America,* 1912–13; *New York Times,* Mar. 9, 10, 21, 22, 1914; autobiographical references in published works.] E. M. H.

MARTIN, HENRY AUSTIN (July 23, 1824–Dec. 7, 1884), vaccinator and surgeon of Roxbury, Mass., the eldest son of Henry James Martin, was born in London. The Martins were descended from a distinguished Huguenot family, and his great-grandfather, Gen. James Agnew, was in command of the British troops in Boston at the outbreak of the American Revolution. Martin was also descended from the Earl of Eglinton, and was a cousin of Lord Kingsale. He came to America when a boy and graduated from Harvard Medical School in 1845. Immediately after graduation he settled in Roxbury, Mass., where he enjoyed a large practice for nearly forty years. Although primarily a physician, he was skilful both as an accoucheur and surgeon. At the outbreak of the Civil War he was made staff surgeon at Fort Monroe and was subsequently transferred to Southeastern Missouri. Here he became ill and was forced to return to Norfolk, Va., where he served as medical director; later he was at Portsmouth in the same capacity, and finally at Newbern. Eventually he was appointed surgeon-in-chief of the 1st Division of the II Corps of the Army of the Potomac under General Miles. At the end of the war he was dismissed with the brevet rank of lieutenant-colonel, with special citation for his services. He then returned to Roxbury, where he practised until his death.

Martin's great service to American medicine arose from his energetic investigation of vaccination and the conditions essential for standardizing the procedure. After Jenner had convinced the world in 1798 that vaccinia (cowpox) gave permanent protection against smallpox, cases of spontaneous cowpox became rare, and many accidents had occurred through careless vaccination and the use of an attenuated humanized virus. On Apr. 26, 1866, a spontaneous case of cowpox occurred at Beaugençy, a town near Orléans, France. The strain was transmitted to a heifer and a strong virus was in this way produced. The heifer-transmitted Beaugençy virus was brought to America by Martin in 1870, and in a memorable report on animal vaccination in the *Transactions of the American Medical Association* (vol. XXVIII, 1877) Martin introduced the modern method of vaccination and of standardization of the vaccine virus. He was bitterly attacked both in the profession and out, as is evidenced by the following: "I gave them every aid in my power freely, frankly, and fully, and was repaid by ingratitude, slander, and an effort, as futile as it was earnest and persistent, to rob me of the scrap of professional honor and reputation I had worked so hard to win and deserve, in introducing and firmly establishing in America a system which has already conferred infinite though hardly fully appreciated blessings" (*Ibid.*, pp. 199–200). Martin was well known for his rubber bandage, used in treatment of ulcers of the leg ("Surgical Uses of the Strong Elastic Bandage other than Haemostatic," *Ibid.*, vol. XXVIII, 1877). He also advocated, and practised professionally, tracheotomy without tube (*Ibid.*, vol. XXIX, 1878).

Though a finished writer, Martin liked controversy, and few were more skilful in literary invective. He was a handsome, well-formed man—impatient, proud, quick to denounce, but loyal always to his friends. He collected books and works of art, and was widely read in the history of medicine. He died in Boston on Dec. 7, 1884, of diabetes. In 1848 he had married Frances Coffin Crosby, a daughter of Judge Nathan Crosby of Lowell, Mass. They had five children, two of whom, Stephen Crosby and Francis Coffin, became physicians.

[H. A. Kelly and W. L. Burrage, *Am. Medic. Biogs.* (1920); T. F. Harrington, *Harvard Medic. School* (1905), vol. III; *Boston Medic. and Surgic. Jour.*, Jan. 8, 1885; H. O. Marcy, article in *Jour. of the Am. Medic. Asso.*, Jan. 10, 1885; *N. Y. Medic. Jour.*, Dec. 13, 1884.] J. F. F.

MARTIN, HENRY NEWELL (July 1, 1848–Oct. 27, 1896), physiologist, was born in Newry, County Down, Ireland, the eldest of twelve children. His father was a Congregational minister and later a schoolmaster, and young Martin was not able to enjoy the advantages of school life, his early training being obtained mainly at home. When about sixteen years of age, he matriculated at the University of London, and attended the Medical School of University College, being at the same time apprenticed to a physician in the neighborhood. Later, in 1870, he went to Cambridge on a scholarship, becoming at the same time demonstrator to the prelector of physiology at Trinity College, Michael Foster. Both at London and Cambridge he made a brilliant record for scholarship in natural science, gaining eventually the degree of B.Sc. at Cambridge and the degree of M.B. at London. He was the first to take the degree of D.Sc. in physiology at Cambridge. He thus had the advantage of instruction under Foster in physiology and also under Huxley in biology, and in 1874 he served as assistant to Huxley in the latter's course in elementary biology. Under Huxley's supervision he prepared a textbook, bearing both names, entitled *A Course of Practical Instruction in Elementary Biology* (1875), which had wide use for many years.

In 1874 Martin was made fellow of Trinity College at Cambridge, and with his broad preparation in natural science was admirably fitted to carry on biological instruction and research at that University. His activities, however, were destined to be transferred to America, for on the founding of the Johns Hopkins University he was selected as the occupant of the chair of biology, and thus he came to Baltimore in 1876 as one of that small group of professors who were to give character to the new institution. Coming as he did at a time when biological problems were assuming large importance in the scientific world of Europe and Great Britain, Martin with his training was able to introduce at Baltimore the new conceptions of "the genetic relationships of living things," and to arouse a general and deep interest in the study of biology by the experimental method.

While Martin was primarily interested in physiology and his own research work lay in that field, during his seventeen years at the Johns Hopkins University he laid down broad foundations for instruction and research in the biological sciences, which brought distinction to the University and furnished inspiration to other institutions. In physiology, it is easy to trace the influence of Martin's work on the development of this branch of biology in the United States. He was in a sense a pioneer in the United States, helping to put physiology in its proper relation to the science and art of medicine. He held that physiology should be studied without regard to its applications to medicine; "that it should be cultivated as a pure science absolutely independent of any so-called practical affiliation" (Sewall, *post,* p. 328). At the same time he realized quite well that all knowledge of function must in time contribute to a fuller understanding of medicine. His own researches were mainly in the field of cardiac physiology, especially noteworthy being his discovery of a new method of studying the isolated mammalian heart, which paved the way many years later for extended researches by others on the functions of the heart, yielding results of great value to medicine. One of his researches, on the influence of temperature on the heart-beat, was the basis of the Croonian lecture of the Royal Society of London for 1883 ("The Direct Influence of Gradual Variations of Temperature upon the Rate of Beat of the Dog's Heart," *Philosophical Transactions of the Royal Society of London, for 1883,* pt. 2, 1883). The papers containing the results of his various researches were republished in 1895 by his friends and pupils in the form of a memorial volume entitled *Physiological Papers.*

Martin found time to write several textbooks which had wide use, notably *The Human Body* (1881), which became very popular and did much to arouse interest in physiology. He also founded and edited the *Johns Hopkins University Studies from the Biological Laboratory* (5 vols., 1877–93). The eminence attained by many of his pupils testifies to his ability as a teacher. He was endowed with a pleasing personality, always interested in the welfare of his pupils, sympathetic and with a joyous outlook on life that made him an interesting as well as a helpful companion. In 1878 he married Hetty (Cary) Pegram, the widow of an officer who served in the Confederate army. After the death of his wife, in 1892, his health, which during his later years was far from robust, broke down and he became unable to carry on his work. He resigned his position in 1893 and returned to England, hoping there to regain his health and the strength to continue his physiological investigations. This, however, was not to be and he died in 1896 at Burley-in-Wharfedale, Yorkshire.

[Henry Sewall, "Henry Newell Martin, Prof. of Biology in Johns Hopkins Univ., 1876–93," *Johns Hopkins Hospital Bull.,* Sept. 1911; *Proc. Royal Soc. of London,* vol. LX (1897); the *Johns Hopkins Univ. Circular,* May 1908; E. F. Cordell, *The Medic. Annals of Md.* (1903); the *Sun* (Baltimore), Nov. 2, 1896.]

R. H. C.

MARTIN, HOMER DODGE (Oct. 28, 1836–Feb. 12, 1897), landscape painter, was born in Albany, N. Y. His father Homer Martin, a carpenter, was of good plain New England stock; his mother, Sarah Dodge, was of an old Albany family and better educated. The desire to draw and make pictures manifested itself in his early boyhood. After a trial in his father's shop, and episodes as a clerk in a store and as a draftsman in an architect's office, young Martin, encouraged by the venerable sculptor Erastus D. Palmer, was allowed to follow his bent. Aside from a few weeks of instruction from the landscape painter James MacDougal Hart, Martin was self-schooled. At sixteen he was making a modest living from the sale of little landscapes of the lake and mountain scenery of New York and New England, pictures which were often garish in color and feebly slicked up, but already remarkably tasteful as compositions. He followed Thomas Cole's predilection for wild scenery and large spaces. For a matter of twenty years he tramped the Adirondacks, the Catskills, the Berkshires, and the White Mountains, bringing back sheaves of pencil sketches usually touched with white on tinted paper, very dry in method, but accurate in form and compositionally excellent. This constituted much of his apprenticeship, and after 1870 he sketched little.

In 1857, at twenty-one, he exhibited two Connecticut landscapes at the National Academy. On June 21, 1861, he married Elizabeth Gilbert Davis, a young woman of cultivation and ability, whose facile pen for years helped out the always scanty family budget. She was one of the early reviewers for the *Nation.* Martin was headed for a larger field, and after an essay in New York, in 1862 and 1863, as the studio mate of James Smillie, in 1865 he moved his family to the metropolis. He got ahead, had his passing mention in Tuckerman's *Book of the Artists* (1867) and the next year was elected an associate of the National Academy. In 1866 an election to the Century Club had made him free of the best literary and artistic society of the town, but his Bohemian and convivial tastes made him offish to those general social relations which were almost essential to any financial success.

Meanwhile his style had changed perturbingly. Under a closer study of nature and observation of good pictures the tight handling loosened up, instead of the conventional browns, recondite colors appeared, the compositions were simplified, with much elimination of needless detail. No American painter, with the exception of George Inness and John La Farge, was painting so well in landscape, but Martin's difference and distinction passed for eccentricity, and his patronage fell off. And the harmony of his home was at least qualified by his wife's conversion to Roman Catholicism, he himself being an agnostic. This is the period of the "Lake Sanford," in the Century Club, and the first pictures of the sand dunes on Lake Ontario, pictures grandly spacious and fraught with a noble melancholy. Within three years he made the firm friendship of John Richard Dennet of the *Evening Post,* and of William C. Brownell, the future critic. Among artists he saw few but Winslow Homer and John La Farge, whose studios were in the same building as his. And although the National Academy elected him to full membership in the seventies, he remained somewhat of an outsider —a position enhanced by his incorrigible, witty, and sometimes bitter tongue, as it was by his personal disfigurement in a permanently inflamed nose.

In 1876 a trip to England brought him the friendship of Whistler and the sight of fine pictures. The few pictures painted in the three or four following years, perhaps somewhat under Whistler's influence, are of great refinement in handling and tonality. "Andante, Fifth Symphony"—a forest brook opening gracefully into a pool—an eloquent record of Martin's musical enthusiasms, is perhaps the finest picture of this period, and the culmination of what may be called the American Martins. Practically none of the pictures of this period, which some prefer to the more popular canvases later painted in France, have found their way into museums. To eke out an always poor living, Martin had occasional recourse to illustration. It was paradoxically this gift that was to bring him the few years of tranquillity he ever enjoyed and the fulfilment of his genius. In *Scribner's Monthly* for February 1879 appeared certain illustrations made at Concord for Frank B. Sanborn's "The Homes and Haunts of Emerson." These with other cuts figured in *The Homes and Haunts of Our Elder Poets,* by Sanborn and others. The success of this venture incited the *Century* to send Martin to England to sketch in George Eliot's country. The immediate results of this expedition may be seen in Rose G. Kingsley's article in the *Century* for July 1885. The ulterior and unexpected results were an excursion to Normandy, in 1882, to visit an illustrator friend, William John Hennessy [*q.v.*].

By the winter of 1882 the Martins were settled at Villerville, on the estuary of the Seine, and there or at neighboring Honfleur they stayed for some four years. There were occasional trips to Paris, but generally the Martins let friends come to them. For the first time Martin caught the penetrating charm of a more intimate scenery, immemorially inhabited and cultivated. His scale is no longer panoramic but intimate. His method grows richer. There is more body of paint, more carefully adjusted flicks of tone to make the surface "twinkle." Possibly he was being influenced by that moderate impressionist, Boudin, who was painting in the same region. Some of Martin's most famous pictures were painted, or at least begun, in these years: "The Church at Criqueboeuf," "Mussel Gatherers," "Low Tide—Villerville," "Ontario Sand Dunes," and "Blossoming Trees." But the finest fruits of this experience were characteristically garnered in after years in America. With an eminently contemplative talent, he was at his best when working from remote and well-matured memories.

The Norman idyl closed with Mrs. Martin's decision to resume the struggle in America. By the new year of 1887 they were again in New York. At fifty Martin was already breaking. His eyesight, always defective, grew progressively worse. But he had nine amazing years before him still. His command of his mood and of his material was now complete. He drew at will from recent Norman memories or from American memories of his young manhood. To celebrate his return he finished "Sand Dunes, Lake Ontario," begun in France, painted "The Sun Worshippers," and that gravest of his American subjects, "Westchester Hills." Nothing much sold. The family moved uncomfortably from lodging to lodging.

To the early nineties belong such masterpieces as "Honfleur Light," "Criqueboeuf Church," the "Old Manor," and "View on the Seine." Still little sold except as groups of friends now and then bought a picture for a club or a museum. His eyesight grew so feeble that the contour had to be drawn for him on the canvas. His wife's nerves broke, and she took refuge late in 1892 with their eldest son Ralph at St. Paul. Within a few months he followed her. Then in an isolation he had never known he finished the "View on the Seine," the "Normandy Farm," and "Adirondack Scenery," perhaps his richest work. By the early days of 1896 it was clear that he had cancer of the throat. He lived on for a year, still worked, was cheered by the unexpected and favorable sale of a picture, and died in February 1897 in St. Paul. Within a few years of his dying deeply in debt his erstwhile unsalable masterpieces had become the sensation of the art market and he received the posthumous honor of being forged.

Martin was a painter of sentiment. He lacked the vigorous construction of Inness in his best estate and of Winslow Homer. Poet as much as painter, drawing from the contemplation of nature a gentle soothing and noble melancholy, Martin is the most distinguished American artist in that imaginative tradition of landscape panting which was splendidly inaugurated by Thomas Cole.

[In *Harper's Weekly* for Mar. 27. 1897, on the occasion of a memorial exhibition at the Century Club, Martin's friend Montgomery Schuyler published what remains one of the best personal appreciations. A valuable obituary, probably by S. G. Champlain, is in *Appletons' Ann. Cyc.*, 1897. To the *Art Interchange*, Oct. 1899, John J. A'Becket contributed an intimate appreciation. There is some suggestive but capricious criticism in Sadakichi Hartmann's *Hist. of Am. Art* (1902). The first elaborate critique is that of C. H. Caffin in *Am. Masters of Painting* (1902). Mrs. Martin's *Homer Martin, a Reminiscence* (1904) will remain classic as an interpretation, but offers relatively few biographical details. Samuel Isham's *Hist. of Am. Painting* (1905) gives an excellent technical analysis of Martin's two styles. Ann Nathan Meyer's article in the *Internat. Studio*, Oct. 1908, adds an anecdote and one or two genealogical details derived from correspondence from Martin's wife. The press reports of the Evans-Clausen trial (1907), in the matter of forgeries, gives the opinions of artists and critics cited as witnesses. See also: Frank Jewett Mather, Jr., *Homer Martin: Poet in Landscape* (1912).] F. J. M., Jr.

MARTIN, JAMES GREEN (Feb. 14, 1819–Oct. 4, 1878), Confederate soldier, was the grandson of James Green Martin, a Methodist minister of Norfolk, Va., and the son of William Martin, a physician. The latter moved to Elizabeth City, N. C., where he became a prominent planter and shipbuilder, and was elected a member of the North Carolina General Assembly. He married Sophia Scott Daugé, a daughter of Gen. Peter Daugé of Camden County. Their eldest son, James Green, born in Elizabeth City, received his early education at St. Mary's in Raleigh, then a boys' school. He entered the United States Military Academy in 1836 and graduated in 1840, number fourteen in his class. Appointed second lieutenant of artillery, he did duty chiefly in Maine until 1846. At Newport, R. I., on July 12, 1844, he was married to Marian Murray Read, great-granddaughter of George Read [*q.v.*] of Delaware, a signer of the Declaration of Independence.

During the Mexican War, Martin commanded a battery which distinguished itself at the assault of Monterey and was later sent to reinforce Scott at Vera Cruz. He was promoted first lieutenant Feb. 16, 1847, and captain, Aug. 5. His battery participated in the severe fighting during the march on Mexico City. At Churubusco Martin's right arm was shattered by grape shot, necessitating amputation, and on Aug. 20 he was brevetted major for gallant and meritorious conduct here and at Contreras. After his discharge from hospital, he was stationed at Fortress Monroe, Va., at Schuylkill Arsenal, Pa., and at Nebraska City on the frontier. During this last assignment his wife died, leaving him with four young children. On Feb. 8, 1858, he was again married, to Hetty King, daughter of Charles King [*q.v.*], president of Columbia College. Soon afterwards he served as quartermaster under Albert Sidney Johnston [*q.v.*] in Johnston's Utah expedition.

When North Carolina seceded in May 1861, Martin was stationed at Fort Riley, Kan. He resigned his commission in June and went to Raleigh, where on Sept. 20 he was made adjutant-general of the ten regiments of state troops then being raised and on Sept. 28, was commissioned major-general of militia and given command of all the state forces and supervision of the entire defense of the state. He prepared all the North Carolina regiments for service; the militia laws were revised at his suggestion; instruction camps and powder, shoe, and clothing factories were established; horses were ordered from Kentucky, saddles and harness material from New Orleans; forts on the coast were erected and strengthened. At Martin's suggestion, blockade-running ships were first employed to bring supplies from Europe. He raised 12,000 more troops than the state's quota, which were of much service during McClellan's advance in 1862. It is chiefly for this brilliant administrative work that Martin will be remembered. North Carolina could with good reason claim that her troops were better trained and supplied than those of any other Confederate state.

When this task was done, Martin asked for active service and in May 1862 was promoted brigadier-general, Confederate States Army. On June 2, he was given command of the district of North Carolina, with headquarters at Kinston, and in the fall of 1863 he was commanded to organize a brigade for duty in the field. In the summer of 1864 his brigade was ordered to Petersburg, Va. After a gallant charge at Howlett's House, where he displayed conspicuous bravery, his men "carried him around on their shoulders, shouting: 'Three cheers for Old One Wing'" (Clark, *post,* IV, 531). Martin's health broke down under the strain of this campaign and he was transferred to the command of the district of Western North Carolina, where he served until the end of the war. He surrendered at Waynesville, May 10, 1865. After the war he took up the study of law, and practised in Asheville from 1866 until his death. During this period he was a prominent Episcopal layman, serving as a delegate to both Diocesan and General conventions of his Church.

[Walter Clark, *Memorial Address upon the Life of General James Green Martin* (delivered at Raleigh, 1916; privately printed), and *Hists. of the Several Regts. and Battalions from N. C. in the Great War* (1901); *Confed. Mil. Hist.* (1899), vol. IV; D. H. Hill, *N. C. in the War between the States* (2 vols., 1926); F. B. Heitman, *Hist. Reg. and Dict. U. S. Army* (1903), vol. II; *War of the Rebellion, Official Records (Army)*; G. W. Cullum, *Biog. Reg. Officers and Grads. U. S. Mil. Acad.* (3rd ed., 1891); *Morning Star* (Wilmington, N. C.), Oct. 9, 1878.] R. D. M.

MARTIN, JOHN ALEXANDER (Mar. 10, 1839–Oct. 2, 1889), journalist, Union military officer, and governor of Kansas, the son of James Martin and Jane Crawford, was born at Brownsville, Pa. He received his education in the common schools and in the printing office. Late in 1857 he went to Kansas and in February 1858, when he was not yet nineteen, he bought an Atchison newspaper, which he renamed *Freedom's Champion* (subsequently the *Champion* and still later the *Atchison Champion*). Within three years he was recognized as one of the political leaders of the younger generation in Kansas Territory, serving, among other positions of honor, as secretary of the Wyandotte constitutional convention and as state senator in the first state legislature. He resigned political office to become, Oct. 27, 1861, lieutenant-colonel of the 8th Volunteer Infantry. On Nov. 1 he was promoted to the rank of colonel, serving as provost-marshal of Nashville, Tenn., and later as brigade-commander during the Chattanooga campaigns. He was mustered out Nov. 17, 1864, and returned to the editorship of his newspaper. Martin had three ruling passions; the Old Soldier interest, the Republican party, and Kansas. During the period 1865–84 he was an active leader in the editorial organization of the state, and in the management of the affairs of the Republican party, local, state, and national. He was chairman of the Atchison county central committee, 1859–84, except during the war, a member of the state committee, beginning in 1870, and of the national committee almost continuously, beginning in 1868. He was secretary of the national committee during the early eighties and sponsored a plan for reapportioning representation in the national convention in order to recognize partially the growing Republican vote in the West.

Martin's major political ambition was the governorship of Kansas. He was elected in 1884 and reëlected in 1886. Among the chief issues of his administration was the enforcement of the prohibition law. He had been an opponent of prohibition at the time of the adoption of the constitutional amendment of 1880, but by 1883 he indorsed it and was nominated and elected on a platform containing a prohibition plank. He was convinced by the experience of the state and especially of his home town of Atchison that "the saloon-keepers, as a rule, were a lot of shameless ingrates, who were not only opposed to prohibition, but to any and all restraint on their dirty business" (Martin to Sol Miller, Dec. 4, 1885: Correspondence of the Governors of Kansas, Letterpress Books, personal, Vol. V, pp. 61–67). He felt that the only way to deal with them was to stand squarely on prohibition of the liquor traffic and thereby to eliminate its influence from politics. Prohibition under his administration became the settled policy of the Republican party in the state and of the state of Kansas. He advocated revision of legal procedure, the modification of the judicial system, both an enlargement and a reform in line with progressive practices adopted in some other states, and the codification of state law. He took great interest in penal reform, and was quite successful in dealing with railroad labor troubles, 1885–88. A state law providing for arbitration of labor disputes was enacted in 1886, and he urged the passage of a federal law in this field, as well as the federal licensing of locomotive engineers.

Martin's administration came in a period of unusual railroad building and of the settlement of the western part of the state. Local government units were induced by various means to issue excessive amounts of bonded indebtedness to finance railroad building. These practices were opposed by Martin, and he urged repeatedly, but without success, the adoption by both state and national governments of a program which might forestall the collapse of the boom in Kansas and elsewhere, and bring about a public control of big business. He advocated a comprehensive state corporation law designed to meet the abuses prevalent in the conduct of business, and attacked the monopoly question in its national aspect from the standpoint of the discriminative practices of the railroads: "They are monopolizing a dozen branches of business—the coal trade, the grain trade, the elevator business, the express business, etc." (Martin to Senator John J. Ingalls, Jan. 20, 1887: Correspondence of the Governors of Kansas, personal, Vol. IX, pp. 290–92). After four strenuous years as governor, he retired again to the editorship of his newspaper. He had married, on June 1, 1871, Ida Challiss, the daughter of Dr. W. L. and Mary (Harres) Challiss. In 1869 he published a *Military History of the Eighth Kansas Veteran Volunteer Infantry,* and in 1888 he printed, for private distribution, a volume of *Addresses.*

[The Wis. Hist. Soc. Lib. has the most complete file of the Atchison *Champion* for the period of Martin's editorship. This file includes the years 1865–89. The Kan. State Hist. Soc. Lib. has a file of the paper for 1858–63 and for 1876–89, together with some broken files for the middle years. The same library has his correspondence as governor, both the official and the confidential or personal files. This correspondence contains, in addition to state matters, information on such national matters as Indian defense, control of livestock diseases, quarantine for protection of public health, railroad labor strikes 1885, 1886, and 1888, national Republican party politics, press-association problems, and the National Soldiers' Homes. Except for the Civil War letters (in process of printing for private distribution) in possession of the family, all of Martin's correspondence prior to the governorship has been lost. Other sources include: D. W. Wilder, *The Annals of Kan.* (rev. ed., 1886); W. E. Connelley, *A Standard Hist. of Kan. and Kansans* (1918), vol. II; *Trans. Kan. State Hist. Soc.,* vol. IV (1890); the *Evening Standard* (Leavenworth), Oct. 2, 1889; the *Topeka Weekly Capital,* Oct. 3, 1889.] J. C. M.

MARTIN, JOHN HILL (Jan. 13, 1823–Apr. 7, 1906), lawyer and author, was born in Philadelphia, Pa., the son of William Martin, a lawyer and business man, and Sarah Ann (Smith) Martin. As a boy John lived with his grandmother on a farm in Chester County, Pa., but about 1836 he returned to his parents, then living in Chester, Pa., in order to attend school. On July 1, 1838, he entered the United States Military Academy at West Point, but he failed in his work and resigned in July 1841. He then studied law in the office of George L. Ashmead of Philadelphia and was a member of the Law Academy. On Nov. 13, 1844, he was admitted to the Philadelphia bar and for thirty-seven years he engaged in his profession. His practice was largely confined to cases in the Orphan's Court and to cases in Admiralty. He retired in 1881. He was always greatly interested in literary work and in June 1857 became the legal editor of the *Insurance Intelligencer,* later the *Philadelphia Intelligencer,* which post he held throughout his life. He spent his summers at Bethlehem, Pa., and in 1872 published his *Historical Sketch of Bethlehem in Pennsylvania, with Some Account of the Moravian Church,* which ran into two editions (Philadelphia, 1872 and 1873). In the same year, 1872, he wrote a series entitled "Sketches in the Lehigh Valley" which appeared in the Bethlehem *Daily Times.* In 1873 he edited and published a book by Rufus A. Grider: *Historical Notes on Music in Bethlehem, Pa.,* and also published *Martin's Bench and Bar of Philadelphia* which had appeared serially in the *Philadelphia Intelligencer* beginning in December 1876. In 1877 he published *Chester (and Its Vicinity) Delaware County, in Pennsylvania.* Besides these publications he compiled and edited many papers in history, genealogy, and marine insurance. In the spring of 1861 he was elected captain of an independent artillery company but saw no field service. He was a very active member of the Pennsylvania Historical Society and bequeathed a large collection of manuscripts of his books and other historical and genealogical data to that organization. He never married.

[J. W. Jordan, *Colonial and Revolutionary Families of Pa.*, vol. III (1911); *Reg. of the Officers and Cadets of the U. S. Mil. Acad.*, 1838–41; Martin's *Chester* and his manuscript autobiography in the possession of the Pa. Hist. Soc.; *Pub. Ledger* (Phila.), Apr. 9, 1906; the *Legal Intelligencer*, Apr. 20, 1906.]
J. H. F.

MARTIN, JOSIAH (1737–1786), colonial governor of North Carolina, was the son of Col. Samuel and Sarah (Wyke) Martin of Antigua, West Indies, and one of twenty-three children. He was an army officer from 1757 until ill health induced him to sell his lieutenant-colonelcy in 1769. In 1761 he married his cousin Elizabeth, daughter of Josiah Martin at whose country seat, "Rockhall," on Long Island he resided at various times. To this union were born eight children. Commissioned by the Crown as governor of North Carolina early in 1771, he sailed from Long Island in July and took the oath of office before the council at New Bern on Aug. 12.

Though reports of his amiable character preceded him, he soon became involved in protracted conflicts with the sensitive assembly, first, over the sinking-fund tax, whose discontinuance in 1771 he disallowed as illegal and violative of public faith; and, beginning in 1773, over the right of the courts to attach property in North Carolina for debts of non-residents to North Carolinians. The assembly, dominated by the eastern planters and merchants, would pass no new court law without the "foreign attachment clause"; and Martin, who was under positive instructions from the Crown, would not assent to a law containing the clause. Consequently, the judicial system of the colony collapsed in 1773, and the ensuing confusion and resentment was accentuated by the emergency creation by royal prerogative of criminal courts whose expenses the assembly in December refused to bear. The sinking-fund tax was not collected generally, and the province remained without courts for the trial of civil cases involving more than £20. The survey of the North Carolina-South Carolina boundary line in 1772, as decreed by the Crown, deprived the colony of much claimed territory and created dissatisfaction. In bold defiance of the governor, the Patriot leaders convened at New Bern in August 1774 a revolutionary provincial congress which elected delegates to the first Continental Congress and inaugurated a system of county committees of safety which gradually superseded the royal government as the source of authority. With his authority and influence gone and fearing personal violence from the local militia after the battle of Lexington, Martin fled from New Bern, arriving at Fort Johnston on June 2, 1775. In July he was driven aboard a British vessel in the Cape Fear River.

Though a military man without previous political experience, somewhat stubborn and insistent on prerogative, and unappreciative of the colonial position, Martin was accomplished, energetic, able, honest, faithful, as well as sincere and patient in his efforts to promote the public welfare and to conciliate the colony without violating his positive instructions and his conception of the duties of his office. He sought to become informed of conditions in the colony, to eliminate abuses in administration, and to pacify the Regulators, but he was not able to reconcile the tempers, aims, and political philosophies of colony and mother country. Aboard ship in the Cape Fear, he formulated a plan for the subjugation of the Southern colonies which was approved by the British government; but the Loyalist Scotch Highlanders, assembled under his direction, were defeated at Moore's Creek Bridge, Feb. 27, 1776, before the British reënforcements arrived off the Cape Fear. In May, Martin departed with the British for an attack on Charleston; he returned in the summer to "Rockhall," and in 1779 joined the Clinton expedition against South Carolina, serving with usefulness and credit as a volunteer with Cornwallis in the campaign of 1780–81 in the Carolinas.

Declining health caused him to leave Cornwallis at Wilmington in April 1781, and sail via Long Island for London, where he died in the spring of 1786. He drew his salary as governor until October 1783, and was granted compensation for his confiscated North Carolina property by the American Loyalist Claims Commission, before which he testified in behalf of the claims of many North Carolina Loyalists.

[*Colonial Records of N. C.* (10 vols., 1886–90); *State Records of N. C.* (16 vols., 1895–1905); *Journal of a Lady of Quality* (1921), ed. by E. W. Andrews; M. deL. Haywood and S. A. Ashe, "Josiah Martin," in S. A. Ashe, *Biog. Hist. of N. C.*, vol. III (1905); William Betham, *The Baronetage of England*, vol. IV (1804); transcripts of British records in N. C. Hist. Commission.]
A. R. N.

MARTIN, LUTHER (*c.* 1748–July 10, 1826), first attorney-general of the State of Maryland, member of the Continental Congress, member of the Federal Convention, and an eminent lawyer, was born near New Brunswick, N. J. The date of his birth is generally given as Feb. 9, and in some accounts is assigned to the year 1744. There is uncertainty also about the names of his parents, but it is probable that he was the third in a family of nine children of Benjamin Martin, a farmer, and his wife Hannah. His ancestors, who were of English stock, had been farmers in America for several generations. After attending the grammar school of the College of New Jersey (now Princeton University), he entered the college in 1762 and was graduated with honors in 1766. He went to Maryland to seek a position as teacher, and obtained a school at Queenstown, Queen Anne's County. Among his pupils were the children of Solomon Wright, a lawyer, in whose home he became a frequent visitor and whose library he was permitted to use. In 1769, after teaching nearly three years at Queenstown, Martin gave up his position and left for Somerset County, Md., to devote a year to the study of law with friends there. Shortly afterward, while making a brief visit in Queen Anne's County, he was served with five writs of attachment for debts; but Wright, acting as his attorney, succeeded in striking off the writs in the spring of 1770. In the summer of that year Martin left Somerset County to become superintendent of the grammar school at Onancock, Accomac County, Va. Here he served one year, continuing the study of law in the meantime. In 1771 he applied at Williamsburg for admission to the Virginia bar, was accepted, and in September qualified as an attorney in Accomac County. After practising a short time in Virginia, he decided to settle in Somerset County, Md., where his practice was lucrative until the outbreak of the Revolution.

In the fall of 1774 Martin was named on the patriot committee of Somerset County, and in December was a delegate to the convention of the Province of Maryland at Annapolis. In 1777 he published a reply to the appeal issued from the British fleet by Lord Howe; and his address, *To the Inhabitants of the Peninsula between the Delaware River and the Chesapeake to the Southward of the British Lines*, was circulated in handbills. On Feb. 11, 1778, Martin was appointed by Gov. Thomas Johnson, upon the recommendation of Samuel Chase, as attorney-general of Maryland; and qualifying on May 20 he took up his residence in Baltimore. During the remaining years of the war he prosecuted the Loyalists with great vigor. In 1785 he was a delegate to the Continental Congress. He was also a delegate to the Federal Convention at Philadelphia, where he opposed the plan of a strong central government. Before the convention was over, he walked out with John Francis Mercer [*q.v.*] and returned home without signing the Constitution. He assailed the proposed form of government before the Maryland House of Delegates in 1787 in a speech which attracted wide attention. In 1788, as a member of the Maryland convention, he made a futile effort to prevent the ratification of the federal Constitution.

On Dec. 25, 1783, Martin married Maria (sometimes referred to as Mary) Cresap, eldest daughter of Capt. Michael Cresap [*q.v.*], Maryland frontiersman. Cresap was charged with the murder of the family of the Indian chief, Logan; and Thomas Jefferson, in his *Notes on the State of Virginia,* quoted Logan's speech. To defend Cresap's character, Martin published letters (1797–98) in the Baltimore newspapers in reply to Jefferson (John J. Jacob, *A Biographical Sketch of the Life of the Late Capt. Michael Cresap,* 1826). Jefferson refused to make any reply in the newspapers, holding that Martin's object was to gratify party passions (P. L. Ford, *The Writings of Thomas Jefferson,* vol. VII, 1896, p. 137). Martin's domestic life was unhappy. His wife died young, leaving two daughters. He courted a wealthy client, the widow of Jonathan Hager, of Washington County, Md., but she married another man. (The letters of entreaty written by him to Mrs. Hager in 1800 and 1801 are in J. T. Scharf, *History of Western Maryland,* 1882, vol. II, pp. 1013–15.) Martin's daughters married when very young, against his will, and both of the marriages ended tragically. Maria married Lawrence Keene, a naval officer, but soon separated from him and died insane. Eleonora eloped with Richard R. Keene (unrelated to Lawrence), son of a Queen Anne's County farmer, who had entered Martin's office in 1799 and became a member of the bar in 1801. Martin condemned Keene in a series of five pamphlets entitled *Modern Gratitude,* printed in 1801 and 1802. The son-in-law replied in a pamphlet of fifty printed pages, *A Letter from Richard Raynal Keene to Luther Martin, Esq.* (1802). Martin later became infatuated with the beautiful Theodosia Burr [*q.v.*], who was already married; his "idolatrous admiration" for her doubtless served to blind him to the faults of her father's character (W. H. Safford, *The Blennerhassett Papers,* 1861, p. 469).

Martin, now allied with the Federalist party because of his hatred of Jefferson, went to the aid of Justice Samuel Chase [*q.v.*] in the impeachment trial before the United States Senate in 1804. In 1805, after twenty-seven years of service, he resigned as attorney-general of Maryland. In 1807 he was one of the lawyers who came to the rescue of Aaron Burr at his trial for treason in Richmond, where he attacked the Administration with so much bitterness that President Jefferson in a letter dated June 19, 1807, wrote to George Hay, United States district attorney for Virginia: "Shall we move to commit L[uther] M[artin], as *particeps criminis* with Burr? Graybell will fix upon his misprision of treason at least. And at any rate, his evidence will put down this unprincipled & impudent federal bull-dog, and add another proof that the most clamorous defenders of Burr are all his accomplices" (P. L. Ford, *The Writings of Thomas Jefferson,* vol. IX, 1898, p. 58). After the trial, Burr, and Harman Blennerhassett were entertained by Martin in Baltimore; a mob threatened to do violence; but Martin's house was guarded by the police, and the mob spent the force of its indignation on the hanging of effigies (*American Law Review,* January 1867, p. 278). In 1813 Martin became chief judge of the court of oyer and terminer for the City and County of Baltimore and served in this office until the tribunal was abolished in 1816. In February 1818, forty years after the date of his first appointment, he was reappointed attorney-general of the state. His last important case was *McCulloch* vs. *State of Maryland* (4 *Wheaton,* 316), wherein as attorney-general of Maryland in 1819 he opposed Daniel Webster, William Pinkney, and William Wirt on the question of state rights, and Chief Justice Marshall held that a state tax on the Bank of the United States was unconstitutional. In 1820 Martin was incapacitated for active service by a stroke of paralysis, and although an assistant attorney-general was appointed he was obliged to resign in 1822. Always of a convivial disposition, he had become increasingly addicted to the use of intoxicants; his brilliant faculties had decayed and he now faced the world broken in health, worn out in mind, and financially destitute. His plight led the legislature to pass a resolution compelling every practitioner of law in the state to pay an annual license fee of five dollars to be turned over to trustees for the use of Martin (*Acts of Maryland,* December Sess., 1821, Resolution No. 60). During the time the resolution was in effect only one protest was made against it; and it was repealed in 1823 before its constitutionality could be tested (*Ibid.,* December Sess., 1822, Resolution No. 16). Martin, wrecked by misfortunes, drunkenness, extravagance, and illness, was now welcomed into Burr's home in New York, where he was permitted to remain until the time of his death. He was buried in the Trinity Churchyard in New York.

Martin's chief faults were his intemperance and his improvidence in financial affairs. He was a stanch opponent of slavery, and was known for his generosity and his loyalty to his friends. While not a polished orator, he became a leader of the American bar because of his thoroughness and extraordinary memory. Blennerhassett, following Mercer, called him the "Thersites of the law." Chief Justice Taney said that Martin was "strong in his attachments, and ready to make any sacrifice for his friends" (Samuel Tyler, *Memoir of Roger Brooke Taney,* 1872, p. 68). He has been described as "the rollicking, witty, audacious Attorney-General of Maryland; . . . drunken, generous, slovenly, grand; bull-dog of federalism, . . . the notorious reprobate genius" (Henry Adams, *John Randolph,* 1882, p. 141). At the time of the Chase impeachment trial, Martin was "of medium height, broad-shouldered, near-sighted, absent-minded, shabbily attired, harsh of voice . . . with a face crimsoned by the brandy which he continually imbibed" (A. J. Beveridge, *The Life of John Marshall,* vol. III, 1919, p. 186).

[No definite biography of Luther Martin has been written. An autobiographical sketch of his early life is included in the last pamphlet of his *Modern Gratitude* (1802), in which he states that he was eighteen years old in 1766. On the other hand, an obituary in the N. Y. *Evening Post,* July 11, 1826, states that he died in his eighty-second year. An early sketch of his life, in *The Nat. Portrait Gallery of Distinguished Americans,* vol. IV (1839), pp. 167–74, was followed by a sketch in *Am. Law Review,* Jan. 1867, pp. 273–81; an article in *Biog. Cyc. of Representative Men of Md. and D. C.* (1879); "Luther Martin: The 'Federal Bull-Dog,'" by H. P. Goddard, published by the Md. Hist. Soc. in *Fund-Publication No. 24* (1887); and "Luther Martin," by E. L. Didier, in *The Green Bag,* Apr. 1891. Later sketches include those by A. M. Gould, in W. D. Lewis, ed., *Great American Lawyers,* vol. II (1907); H. H. Hagan, *Eight Great American Lawyers* (1923); T. C. Waters, in *Am. Bar Asso. Jour.,* Nov., Dec. 1928; and J. F. Essary, in *Md. in Nat. Politics* (1915), pp. 59–78. An article, "The Influence of Luther Martin in the Making of the Constitution of the United States," by E. D. Obrecht, appeared in the *Md. Hist. Mag.,* Sept.–Dec. 1932.

Martin's address, *The Genuine Information, Delivered to the Legislature of the State of Maryland, Relative to the Proceedings of the General Convention, Lately Held at Philadelphia,* published in 1788, is included in *American Eloquence,* edited by Frank Moore (1859), vol. I, 373–400; and in Jonathan Elliot, *The Debates . . . on the Adoption of the Federal Constitution* (2 ed., 1836); a different draft of the speech, from a MS. in the Lib. of Cong., appeared in the *Md. Hist. Mag.,* June 1910, pp. 139–50. Charles Warren, *The Making of the Constitution* (1928), p. 792, refers to newspaper letters of Martin. See also Max Farrand, *The Records of the Federal Convention* (3 vols., 1911); E. S. Delaplaine, *The Life of Thomas Johnson* (1927).]

E. S. D.

MARTIN, THOMAS COMMERFORD (July 22, 1856–May 17, 1924), author, editor, was born in London, England, the son of Thomas and Catherine (Commerford) Martin. He attended an academical school at Gravesend, England, continued his early education under private tutors, and then became a student in divinity at the Countess of Huntingdon Theological College. Being of a naturally active and adventuresome nature, and intensely interested in physics, although not a trained physicist, he left England at the age of twenty-one and came to the United States with letters to men of prominence here. At that time America offered splendid opportunities for the advancement of a young man interested in scientific research. Alexander Graham Bell, Charles J. Brush, Elihu Thomson, Thomas A. Edison, and others were converting electrical energy from a school-room curiosity into the channels of industrial application in many fields. Martin entered the Edison laboratory at Menlo Park in 1877 and remained there until 1879. Some of the experimental work on which he was engaged during this period had to do with the early phonograph, the electric pen, printing and embossing telegraphs, and the carbon telephone transmitter.

He soon developed special aptitude for clear and concise description of mechanical and scientific subjects. In 1878 he began to contribute articles to various New York papers, pointing out in graphic and dramatic style the interesting developments which were taking place or anticipated in the Edison laboratory. Soon this reportorial work became of greater interest to him, or as he put it, he found it "more agreeable than laboratory work with Wheatstone's Bridge, grimy carbon telephone buttons, inky electric pens and rebellious tinfoil." Late in the year 1879 he received an invitation to act as editor of a daily newspaper in Kingston, Jamaica, W. I., and being in ill health by reason of his combined experimental and journalistic labors, he eagerly accepted the opportunity, and served on the *Daily Gleaner* from 1880 until the end of 1882. While in Jamaica he married Elizabeth Gould of Kingston.

In 1882 Martin returned to the United States and after serving for a time as editor of the *Operator,* in 1883 became editor of the *Electrical World.* In 1890 he became editor of the *Electrical Engineer,* which in 1899 merged with the *Electrical World.* From that date until 1909 Martin and W. D. Weaver were joint editors of the journal. During this time the publication became the largest and best known magazine in the electrical field. In the year 1919 he became secretary of the National Electric Light Association, composed of practically all the public service corporations in the country, and continued in active service with that organization until 1921, and in an advisory way until his death. During the years from 1900 to 1915, he acted as special agent for the United States Census Bureau, writing an exhaustive report covering the electrical industries of the United States, published in 1902, and during his career he contributed special electrical articles to the *Encyclopædia Britannica, Chambers's Encyclopedia,* and *The Encyclopedia Americana.* Besides these activities, he prepared numerous articles, principally upon electrical subjects, for the *North American Review, Century,* and other publications.

Among the books of which he was author or co-author are: *The Electric Motor and Its Applications* (1887); *The Inventions, Researches and Writings of Nikola Tesla* (1894); *Edison, His Life and Inventions* (2 vols. 1910); *The Story of Electricity* (2 vols., 1919–22); and *Forty Years of Edison Service, 1882–1922* (1922). He was a frequent lecturer before electrical and engineering societies, including the Royal Institution of Engineers, Great Britain, and the Société Internationale des Électriciens, France, as well as various American Colleges and Universities. During the Great War he took an active part on behalf of the allied nations and frequently spoke before and assisted in organizing societies for the successful prosecution of that tragic enterprise. In this special work he became chairman of the Marconi Fund for Italian War Relief, and secretary of the Florence Nightingale Hospital for the training of nurses in France. He was a founder of the American Institute of Electrical Engineers (president, 1887–88), a member of other scientific, commercial, and charitable societies, and a trustee of the engineering college of George Washington University. He died at the House of Mercy Hospital in Pittsfield, Mass., survived by his second wife, Carmelita Beckwith, whom he had married in 1910.

[*Jour. Am. Inst. Electrical Engineers,* May, June, 1924; *Electrical World,* May 24, 1924; *Who's Who in America,* 1924–25; *N. Y. Times,* May 18, 1924; letters and memoranda from Edison employees; Martin's autobiographical notes.]

F. L. D.

MARTIN, THOMAS STAPLES (July 29, 1847–Nov. 12, 1919), senator from Virginia, was born in Scottsville, Va., the son of John Samuel Martin, a merchant and manufacturer, and Martha Ann (Staples) Martin. He entered the Virginia Military Institute at Lexington on Mar. 1, 1864, and served for a year in the Confederate army with the famous New Market Corps of cadets. He then attended the University of Virginia from 1865 until 1867. In 1869 he was admitted to the bar and began the practice of law in Albemarle County, Va. Before many years had passed, he had built up a large clientele.

His first important political activity came as a Democratic leader during the heated contests of the eighties, when Gen. William Mahone [*q.v.*], a "Readjuster," took advantage of the problems presented by the state debt to make himself a power with the aid of the negro vote. Then in 1893, although he was comparatively unknown, Martin announced his candidacy for the United States Senate. It was the first time he had ever run for public office, and many believed that he stood little or no chance of success. His opponent was the popular and magnetic Fitzhugh Lee [*q.v.*], nephew of Gen. Robert E. Lee, who had served as major-general of cavalry in the war and had been governor of Virginia. To the surprise of thousands, Martin was elected by the General Assembly. He took his seat in the Senate on Mar. 4, 1895.

This was the beginning of a service in that body which lasted without interruption until his death in 1919. Martin was never a fluent or polished speaker, and he made few addresses while in Congress, but those who predicted that he would be a failure in politics found that they had misjudged their man. He soon revealed unusual political astuteness, and shortly after the turn of the century, he came to be regarded as the leader of the Democratic "machine" in Virginia, which leadership he retained for the remainder of his life. At the same time his influence in the Senate increased steadily, and he was majority floor leader for the two years beginning in March 1917. He also served as chairman of the committee on appropriations during the war period, when billions were spent by the government.

Martin was what is known as a "business senator." He was notable for his industry, common sense, and knowledge of men, and for his willingness to go to almost unlimited trouble to accommodate a constituent. He belonged to the school of thought which believes in always "standing by your friends," and in that ancient Jacksonian principle, "to the victor belong the spoils." During the last ten years that he was boss of the Democratic "machine" in Virginia he was in alliance with the Anti-Saloon League. This combination was generally unbeatable. Unfortunately, Martin was a conservative, and the state made comparatively little progress under his régime. On the other hand, he rendered conspicuous services to his country during the World War, when as majority floor leader of the Senate and chairman of the appropriations committee he had charge of much of the important war legislation. Warned many times that he was working to excess, he refused to spare himself, and his life is believed to have been shortened as a result. His absolute personal honesty is attested by the fact that despite the vast sums which he handled, he died a poor man.

On Oct. 10, 1894, he married Lucy Chambliss Day, of Smithfield, Va. They had two children, a daughter and a son.

[Sketch in *Biog. Directory of the Am. Congress, 1774–1927* (1928); in *Men of Mark in Va.*, vol. I (1906); *Register of Former Cadets, Va. Mil. Institute* (1927); obituaries in Richmond *Evening Journal*, Nov. 12, 1919, in *Richmond Times-Dispatch*, Richmond *Virginian* and *N. Y. Times*, Nov. 13, 1919; editorial in Richmond *News Leader*, Nov. 13, 1919.] V. D.

MARTIN, VICTORIA CLAFLIN WOODHULL [See WOODHULL, VICTORIA CLAFLIN, 1838–1927].

MARTIN, WILLIAM ALEXANDER PARSONS (Apr. 10, 1827–Dec. 17, 1916), missionary, educator, and author, was born in Livonia, Ind., the son of William Wilson Martin and Susan Depew, both of frontier Scotch-Irish stock. His father was a Presbyterian minister, and all of the three sons were named for foreign missionaries. Given such an environment, it is not strange that he early decided to devote his own life to the missionary enterprise. He was graduated from Indiana University in 1846 and for three years thereafter studied theology in the Presbyterian seminary at New Albany, Ind. In 1849, the year of his graduation, he married Jane Vansant (who died in 1893) and was ordained to the ministry by the Presbytery of Salem, Ind. As a boy he had had his attention drawn to China by the first war between that country and Great Britain (1839–42), and now, his preparation completed, he sought appointment under the foreign mission board of his church to one of the ports which that struggle had opened to foreign residents. In the spring of 1850 he and his brother Samuel Newall and their wives arrived in China. He was assigned to Ningpo and early proved himself both energetic and able. Before he had been six years in China he had worked out, through public lectures and discussions before Chinese audiences, a series of studies on evidences of Christianity which sought to present the Christian gospel convincingly to Chinese. These he put into the literary language and had published. They became very popular, and went into many editions in both China and Japan.

Martin learned not only the local dialect and

the literary language, but Mandarin, and it was his knowledge of the latter colloquial which helped to open to him the opportunity which led him away from Ningpo and into the region where the major part of his life was to be spent. During the second war between Great Britain and China, he was appointed, on his own application, as an interpreter to William B. Reed [*q.v.*], who obtained for the United States the treaty of 1858 with China. Martin had a share in the negotiations and the following year went north again, this time to Peking, to assist in the exchange of ratifications of the treaty. After a well-earned furlough in America, in 1862 he returned to China and for a short time was connected with the Presbyterian Mission Press in Shanghai. While there he translated into Chinese Wheaton's *Elements of International Law.* The following year he removed to Peking, founding in that city a mission of his denomination which later grew to large proportions.

In Peking his contact with officials, begun during the negotiation of the Treaty of Tientsin, continued, and his interest increased in the diplomatic relations with Western powers into which China was so reluctantly and awkwardly entering. In 1868, accordingly, he accepted a position as teacher of international law in the T'ungwên Kuan, a school which had recently been formed by the government to train in Western languages and learning Chinese youths who were to serve in intercourse with foreign countries. After spending a few months in America in further preparation for his new work, in 1869 he assumed his duties, not only as teacher, but as head of this institution. In these positions he continued until 1894, and through his translations and original works in Chinese, his contacts with officials, and his teaching, he had a significant part in introducing Western learning to China. In 1898 he was made president of the imperial university which the reform movement of that year had brought into existence. The Boxer outbreak (1900) caught him in Peking, and, although then past seventy years of age, he was active in the defense of the legations. After the raising of the siege he was in the United States for a time, lecturing on China, and then, at the invitation of the Viceroy Chang Chih-tung, he once more returned and lectured on international law in an institution which that dignitary was attempting to establish in Wuchang. With the transfer of Chang Chih-tung to Nanking, Martin deemed it advisable to withdraw. Most of the remainder of his life was spent in Peking. Here he taught individual Chinese students, wrote, and, about 1911, rejoined the staff of the Presbyterian mission, serving on it until his death.

Martin's literary output was voluminous. It included many works in Chinese on international law, natural science, and Christianity, and a number of works on China in English, among them *Hanlin Papers* (two series, Shanghai, 1880, 1894); *The Chinese* (1881), a reprint of the first series of *Hanlin Papers*; *A Cycle of Cathay* (New York, 1896); *The Lore of Cathay* (1901); and *The Awakening of China* (1907). He received many honors, both in China and in the United States.

[Martin's book, *A Cycle of Cathay* (1896); *Gen. Cat. Presbyt. Theol. Sem., Chicago* (1928); *Who's Who in America,* 1914–15; *Chinese Recorder,* Feb. 1917; *Reports of the Board of Foreign Missions of the Presbyt. Ch. in the U. S. A.,* 1911–17.] K. S. L.

MARTIN, WILLIAM THOMPSON (Mar. 25, 1823–Mar. 16, 1910), Confederate soldier, railroad builder, was the eldest son of John Henderson and Emily Monroe (Kerr) Martin. Born at Glasgow, Ky., he graduated from Centre College in 1840, shortly after the family had moved to Vicksburg, Miss. Following the death of the father he moved to Natchez in 1842 and was there admitted to the bar as soon as he reached his majority. As district attorney, he made an enviable reputation as a vigorous prosecutor and as an eloquent and forceful speaker. On Jan. 5, 1854, he married Margaret Dunlop Conner, whose mother lived near Natchez. He was a man of moral as well as physical courage, and he did not hesitate to take unpopular stands in following his own best judgment. He was a Whig and opposed secession in 1851 and again in 1860, when he was accused of unfaithfulness to the South and of untrustworthiness. Though a Unionist he prepared for the conflict, after becoming convinced that it was inevitable, by organizing in the spring of 1861 the Adams County troop of cavalry, of which he was elected captain. After the firing on Fort Sumter he led his men to Richmond. He proved himself a resourceful and daring cavalry leader, was soon given command of the Jeff Davis Legion, and participated in all the battles against McClellan in the Peninsular campaign. When J. E. B. Stuart made his famous raid around McClellan's army, Martin commanded the rear third of the detachment. Upon the battlefield at Sharpsburg (Antietam) he acted as personal aide to Robert E. Lee. In December 1862 he was made brigadier-general and in November 1863 major-general. After the failure of Lee's Maryland campaign, Martin was ordered to the West. He was in the battle of Chickamauga and a number of other important engagements, commanding a division of Wheeler's cavalry during the Atlanta campaign. Toward the close of 1864 he was transferred to northwest Mississippi and ordered to protect that region from lawless bands.

After the war he took an active interest in politics, education, and railroad building. He was a delegate to the state constitutional convention of 1865. In the Mississippi constitutional convention of 1890, he was one of three members who did not sign that document. He followed this course because the constitution contained a provision forbidding the legislature to pay principal or interest of the Union Bank bonds and the Planters' Bank bonds. Before the war he had opposed repudiation and had advocated the payment of these bonds. He was a delegate to Democratic national conventions between 1868 and 1880, and was a member of the state Senate from 1882 to 1894. In 1884, under his sole presidency a railroad line between Natchez and Jackson, known as the Natchez, Jackson & Columbus Railroad, was completed. For twelve years he was a trustee of the University of Mississippi, and for a time was president of the board of trustees of Jefferson College, Washington, Miss. He was survived by his wife, four sons, and five daughters.

[Manuscript sketch by his son, W. C. Martin, Natchez; *Who's Who in America*, 1906–07; C. A. Evans, *Confederate Military Hist.* (1899), vols. III, VII; *War of the Rebellion: Official Records* (*Army*), esp. ser. 1, vols. V, XI, XXX (1881–90); Douglas Walworth's sketch of military career prepared for J. F. H. Claiborne's second volume of the history of Mississippi, in *Daily Democrat* (Natchez), June 8, 1908; *Ibid.*, Mar. 17, 1910.] C. S. S.

MARTINDALE, JOHN HENRY (Mar. 20, 1815–Dec. 13, 1881), lawyer, soldier, was born at Hudson Falls (formerly Sandy Hill), N. Y., the son of Henry C. Martindale. His father was a prominent member of the community and served several terms in Congress as a Whig. Martindale entered West Point in July 1831 and upon graduation in 1835 was commissioned a brevet second lieutenant of Dragoons, to his great disappointment, for he had hoped to become an engineer. While on leave of absence, he had the opportunity of joining the engineering staff of the Saratoga & Washington Railroad of New York, and he resigned his commission (Mar. 10, 1836) without ever having served with troops. He soon turned to the study of law, was admitted to the bar of New York in 1838, and launched on the career that was to bring him prominence. Establishing a residence in Batavia, he practised there until 1851, meanwhile serving as district attorney of Genesee County for two terms. He continued his law practice in Rochester during the decade preceding the Civil War.

When war between the North and South became a certainty, Martindale took an active part in organizing volunteer regiments. He believed that by utilizing officers of the regular army as instructors, the volunteer organizations would be greatly improved and the military strength of the North brought to bear on the South more quickly. In addition, he proposed to the War Department that the first and second classes at West Point be graduated immediately and sent to their respective homes to drill and aid the people. With considerable vision, he wrote to the secretary of war on Apr. 25, 1861: "We can have a long and exhausting war, or we can conquer a peace before the end of another winter if we will only organize and use our power promptly" (*War of the Rebellion: Official Records, Army,* 3 ser. I, p. 111). He was commissioned a brigadier-general of volunteers in August 1861 and was stationed in the defenses of Washington during the following winter. Commanding a brigade in the Army of the Potomac, he was in the field from March until July 1862, taking part in the engagements at Yorktown, Hanover Court-House, Mechanicsville, Gaines's Mill, Malvern Hill, and Harrison's Landing.

While convalescing from an attack of typhoid fever, he was the subject of an investigation by a court of inquiry looking into charges preferred by Maj.-Gen. Fitz John Porter to the effect that Martindale had influenced men to surrender at Malvern Hill. He was exonerated by the court and restored to duty as military governor of the District of Columbia. This position required tact, firmness, and legal ability, involving as it did the control of a large civilian population as well as the masses of troops in Washington. Martindale distinguished himself in the performance of this duty, but again desiring a field command, he was given a division in the Army of the James in 1864 and took part in the battle of Bermuda Hundred and in the operations south of Richmond. Transferred to the Army of the Potomac, he led his division in the Cold Harbor and Petersburg campaigns. In the latter, he commanded the XVIII Corps for a short time. Again overtaken by sickness, he resigned from the army because of ill health in the fall of 1864. On Mar. 13 of the following year he was brevetted a major-general of volunteers for gallant and distinguished service at the battle of Malvern Hill.

Martindale returned to his law practice at Rochester, N. Y. He was an interesting figure of the bar of New York and gained prominence especially in his handling of cases against the New York Central Railroad involving personal damages. He was elected attorney-general of the state of New York for the term of 1866–68. From 1868 to 1879 he was vice-president of the board of managers of the National Asylum for Disabled Volunteer Soldiers. He died in 1881 at Nice, France, where he had gone for his health. He had married on June 16, 1840, Emeline M. Holden at Batavia, N. Y. They had two sons and three daughters.

[G. W. Cullum, *Biog. Reg. . . . U. S. Mil. Acad.*, vol. I (1891); *War of the Rebellion: Official Records (Army)*, 1 ser. V, XI, pts. 1, 2, and 3, XIX, pt. 2, XXI, XXXIII, XXXVI, pts. 1, 2, and 3, XL, pt. 1, and LI, pt. 1; War Dept. records, *Thirteenth Ann. Reunion, Asso. Grads. U. S. Mil. Acad.*, 1882; F. W. Beers, *Gazetteer and Biog. Record of Genesee County, N. Y.* (1890); *Army and Navy Jour.*, Dec. 17, 1881; information as to certain facts from Martindale's daughter, Mrs. James B. Perkins.] J. R. V.

MARTINY, PHILIP (May 19, 1858–June 25, 1927), sculptor, son of Philip and Kathrine (Blacke) Martiny, was born in Strasbourg, Alsace, France, and as a boy often hid in the cellars during the Franco-Prussian War. He claimed lineal descent from the Sienese painter Simone Martini, who died in Avignon, France, in 1344. Whether or not this claim is just, much of what the critic J. Addington Symonds wrote of the Italian painter is strikingly true of the American sculptor: "full of delicate inventiveness, and gifted with a rare feeling for grace," an "ingenious and delightful master" (*Renaissance in Italy, The Fine Arts,* 1877, p. 218). Foreign sources state that Martiny was a pupil of Eugen Dock, who was born in Strasbourg in 1827, who studied at the Beaux-Arts in Paris, and who became in 1860 the foremost decorative sculptor in his native town. American accounts state that as a boy Philip worked as a carver with his father, and that he studied in various French ateliers. Certain it is that he came to New York as a young man thoroughly well grounded in old-world technique and tradition.

In the early eighties, Augustus Saint-Gaudens was superintending the wood-carving in the important scheme of decoration he had planned for the Vanderbilt house. "I had noticed," he wrote in his *Reminiscences* (vol. II, pp. 5–6) "that one of my carvers reproduced models with an artistic felicity so markedly superior to any of the others that I asked him to come and help me in my studio. This was Philip Martiny," who during his first period of a year or so in the Saint-Gaudens studio, worked on the figure of the "Puritan." Saint-Gaudens often recalled Martiny's boundless skill and inventiveness, then displayed with a fervor which the master was no doubt obliged to curb, in order to keep the integrity of his own design. At this period Martiny came into contact with Saint-Gaudens' close friends, McKim, Mead, and White. The young Frenchman's instinct for the decorative aspect of sculptural form met appreciation from this famous firm, and indeed from other architects, with the result that when he started out for himself, he had plenty of work. For the Chicago world's fair of 1893, in which McKim, Mead, and White were actively interested, Martiny received a fifty-thousand-dollar contract to execute an ambitious scheme of sculptural decoration for McKim's Agricultural Building. The design was to include figures of eighty-three great angels, forty towering eagles, and sixteen large groups. No wonder that in 1891, McKim wrote to Saint-Gaudens, in the whimsical vein customary between the two, "Martiny is 'clean bust' as usual, and if you can come down and . . . make an estimate of what is due him, you will save him from the poorhouse and McK., M. & W. from the lunatic asylum" (Charles Moore, *The Life and Times of Charles Follen McKim,* 1929, note p. 119).

This first large commission of Martiny's was typical of others to follow. It called for exuberant imagination, a consummate understanding of sculptural light and shadow, a power of quick decision, and an ability to make the best use of assistants. Deities, angels, men, women, infants, oxen, horses, goats, fruits, flowers—all were stuff for his undaunted designs. In the roof decorations for McKim's building, with their "Groups" and "Seasons," he triumphed as the foremost decorative sculptor of the day. His impassioned improvisations of *putti* and *frutti,* of trumpery trumpets and papery drapery supplied every demand of the sculptural pageantry. He juggled with his plaster, apparently creating a figure by assembling parts once belonging to another. It would seem that in some such manner he put together the study for the central motive of his "Fountain of Abundance" for the Pan-American Exposition at Buffalo in 1901—a garlanded figure surrounded by dancing cherubs. The method was dubious, the result delightful. For the St. Louis world's fair of 1904 he made the group of "Apollo and the Muses," crowning the main entrance to Festival Hall, and two massive quadrigae, "Progress of Art" and "Progress of Commerce," flanking the dome of the New York State Building. Apparently no subject baffled his imagination or exceeded his capacity.

Martiny's technique was suitable for world's fairs, but at times unpleasing traces of this facility appear in his more lasting productions—

perhaps in his bronze "Lampbearers" on the newel-posts of the famous double staircase in the entrance hall of the Library of Congress, but not in his idyllic high-relief marble carvings of the balustrade. Only a pedant could find fault with those twenty-six panels, in which babes astride garlands disport themselves at various genial trades, such as the "Hunter with a Rabbit," and the "Vintager with Grapes." Other works by Martiny in this building are cartouche and tablet figures for ceiling and dome. Adequate to their purpose, they display that "papery drapery" in which he was at times all too skilful, for monumental ends. To the same period, yet in different vein, belongs one of the most impressive productions of his career, the Soldiers and Sailors' Monument in Jersey City, N. J., 1899. A seated female figure, draped and helmeted, holding a sword in her left hand, an olive branch in her right, surmounts a high pedestal of beautiful design. The ensemble is monumental rather than decorative. Both monumental and decorative, as well as perfectly adapted to its architectural purpose, is Martiny's south pair of bronze doors, with limestone frieze and marble tympanum, for Saint Bartholomew's Church, New York City. The frieze of the "Road to Calvary" is fine, the marble tympanum less so. As a whole, his contribution to the St. Bartholomew façade is notable for actual richness of surface rather than for suggested depth of religious feeling.

Between 1903 and 1908, an enormous volume of architectural sculpture in granite, and of heroic size, was executed in the Martiny studio for the New York City Hall of Records. The list includes eight cornice statues of New York worthies, from the seventeenth century onward; sixteen symbolic cornice statues; two seated entrance figures, "Justice" and "Authority"; two entrance groups of three figures each, "New York in its Infancy," and "New York in Revolutionary Times." Of earlier date are his two groups for the New York Chamber of Commerce, with their central figures of John Jay and Alexander Hamilton, and his marble statue of Confucius for the appellate court (1899). He made sculpture for the residences of Senator Clark and Charles T. Yerkes, New York City; for the Carnegie Library, Washington, D. C.; for the Courthouse at Elizabeth, N. J.; for the Kunhardt Memorial, Moravian Cemetery, Staten Island; for a tympanum over the doors of the Shepherd memorial chapel, Scarboro-on-the-Hudson; for the Cullum Memorial at West Point. His statue of Vice-President Hobart, erected in Paterson, N. J., in 1902, is considered excellent. His McKinley monument at Springfield, Mass., with its familiar French motive of a draped female figure of Fame, reaching upward to adorn with a palm branch a portrait bust on a lofty pedestal, has dignity and beauty, yet on the whole is decorative rather than monumental. In 1919, for New York's celebration of the return of American troops from overseas, his vigorous staff group, "Our Allies," had a prominent place on the Flatiron Building. His last public works of importance were two World-War memorials for New York City. The monument to the soldiers from Greenwich Village is on a high pedestal in Abingdon Square, and shows a single bronze figure of an American soldier defending the flag. The tribute to the soldiers from the Chelsea district is in Chelsea Park. Here a lofty, well-designed stele of granite is used as a background for a bronze figure in a resolute attitude. Both these memorials are simple, dignified, eloquent, though their monumentality is slightly impaired by Martiny's characteristic "papery" rendering of flag and uniform.

In view of his amazing fecundity, his list of portrait busts is not long. He was no solitary worker; from boyhood he had the habit of gregarious endeavor. He spent little time in soul-searching, either of himself or others, and so has left behind none of those vivid records of contemporary personalities, such as Grafly's portraits of his artist friends, or Saint-Gaudens' bust of Sherman. Of the countless heads his nimble fingers shaped, all decorative, all somehow suited to his purpose of the moment, few or none awake in the beholder a new and poignant sense of human beauty or of human greatness. Yet both as to inner meaning and outward expression, he brought a new note into American sculpture. In his creations it is vain to seek for what he never set out to disclose, a feeling for the profounder issues of life. It would be equally wrong to call his contribution to our art a superficial one. On the contrary, his spontaneous grace of color and rhythm, supported by unlimited technical resources, indicated to American sculptors at least one way to avoid a Puritanic drabness in expression. His work might set a standard for the wise as well as a snare for the foolish.

Martiny's temperament was jovial. In the words of one of his assistants, he earned largely, and spent everything twice—once before he had it, and once after. He was twice married, first to Hermine Horning, a German, afterward to a young French woman, Yvonne E. Flouret. His closing years were clouded by illness; a stroke incapacitated him. He died in New York, of paralysis, leaving a widow as well as four children of the first marriage and eight of the second.

[U. Thieme and F. Becker, *Allgemeines Lexikon der Bildenden Künstler*, vol. XXIV (1930); *The Reminiscences of Augustus Saint-Gaudens* (2 vols., 1913), ed. by Homer Saint-Gaudens; Lorado Taft, *The Hist. of Am. Sculpture* (1930); C. H. Caffin, *Am. Masters of Sculpture* (1903); C. R. Reynolds, *Washington Standard Guide* (1924); Sadakichi Hartmann, *A Hist. of Am. Art* (1932), vol. II; *Cat. of the Works of Art Belonging to the City of N. Y.* (1909); *Who's Who in America*, 1926–27; *Architectural Record*, Apr. 1904; *Am. Architect*, Feb. 5, 12, 1898; the *Art Digest*, July 1927; *Am. Art Annual*, 1927; *N. Y. Times*, June 27, 1927; private information.] A. A.

MARTY, MARTIN (Jan. 12, 1834–Sept. 19, 1896), prelate and Indian missionary, the son of Jacob Alois Marty, a shoemaker and church sexton, and of Elizabeth (Reichlin) Marty, was born and baptized as Aloysius at Schwyz in Switzerland. He attended a local preparatory college until the Jesuit fathers were banished in an anti-clerical campaign. In 1848 he transferred to the Benedictine college of Einsiedeln, where he translated into German a French edition of the "Annals of the Propagation of the Faith," thus acquiring a youthful zeal for missionary labors. In 1854 he pronounced his monastic vows as Brother Martin, O.S.B., and on Sept. 14, 1856, was ordained priest together with a life-long friend, Frowin Conrad, later abbot at Conception, Mo. He continued at Einsiedeln as a teacher and wrote an essay on the manner of teaching in monastic institutions a thousand years ago, which won commendation from the University of Berlin. In 1860 he volunteered for American service and joined the monastery at St. Meinrad, Ind., which had been established by a colony of monks from Einsiedeln in 1854. In 1866 he became prior, and, when St. Meinrad's monastery was made an abbey by Pope Pius IX four years later, he was chosen its first mitred abbot. In answer to appeals for Indian missionaries, about 1873 he led a group of Benedictines to the Standing Rock agency of the Sioux. His activities extended over the Dakotas, where he soon acquired a wide acquaintance with the natives and pioneers who trusted him as a counsellor. He became proficient enough in the Siouan tongues to translate hymns and prayers. In recognition of his influence with the Indians, he was appointed a member of the Indian commission established by the plenary council at Baltimore.

In 1879 when the territory of Dakota was created into a vicariate, as titular bishop of Tiberias, he was named vicar apostolic with headquarters at Yankton. Consecrated by Bishop Francis Silas Chatard on Feb. 1, 1880, he became an ideal frontier bishop, traversing the vast region in a wagon or on horseback, fighting the cause of temperance in wigwam and camp, and often rolling himself up in furs to spend the night on the snow-covered prairie. Not unmerited was his title of "Angel of the West." In 1884 he was an active participant in the council of Baltimore and thereafter he went to Europe in the interest of his vicariate. As the region grew he saw his priests increase from twelve to ninety, his churches from twenty to about 130, and the Catholic population from 14,000 to about 80,000. When the vicariate was divided he was selected as first bishop of Sioux Falls. He had built, or at least fostered, a score of schools, ten industrial institutes for boys and girls, and three academies. He introduced the Jesuits into the diocese and several communities of nuns, who managed academies and hospitals at Fargo, Grand Forks, Yankton, and Deadwood, as well as Indian schools at the various agencies. While at Sioux Falls for only five years, his success was marked especially in the creation of mission schools. He found time to write a life of the first bishop of Milwaukee, *Dr. Johann Martin Henni* (1888), and in 1890 he published his revision of *Katolik Wocekiye*, the ritual in the Siouan language composed by Father Augustin Ravoux. In 1895 he was transferred to the quiet diocese of St. Cloud, Minn., where he died among his Benedictine brethren of the St. John's University.

[Marty's papers and letters were burned by a family in ignorance of their value; material supplied by Ignatius Forster, O. S. B., of Yankton, S. D., who is planning to write a biography; a careful, detailed biography is in *Paradies-Früchte*, Dec. 1914–Oct. 1916. See also *Acta et Dicta*, July 1917; Hoffmans' *Catholic Directory*, 1897, p. xxxi; J. H. O'Donnell, "The Catholic Hierarchy," *The Catholic University of America Studies in Am. Church Hist.*, vol. IV (1922); J. G. Shea, *The Hierarchy of the Catholic Church* (1886), p. 396; *Dakota Catholic*, 1889–90.] R. J. P.

MARTYN, SARAH TOWNE SMITH (Aug. 15, 1805–Nov. 22, 1879), author, was born in Hopkinton, N. H., the daughter of the Rev. Ethan and Bathsheba (Sanford) Smith, both descendants of seventeenth-century settlers in New England. Her early education was directed by her father, a scholarly clergyman, who, as a youth, had served in the Revolution, and afterward graduated from Dartmouth College. Under his tutelage she studied Greek and Hebrew and learned to translate readily from modern languages. She spent a brief period at a school for young ladies in New York City, where her considerable talent for music received some training. As she grew older she shared with her father his ardent interest in the temperance and anti-slavery movements. She was warmly sympathetic with Oberlin College in its early efforts and was invited to act as one of the first principals of its "female department." This honor she declined, feeling that her work lay in another direction. She was active in the Female Moral Reform Society of New York after 1836 and assisted in editing its journal, the *Advocate of Moral Reform,* until 1845, when dissension within the society caused her to secede from it with the disaffected minority. In March 1841 she married her brother-in-law, Job H. Martyn, a clergyman in New York City. She lived in New York until 1868, with the exception of three years (1850–53) spent in Waukesha, Wis., while her husband was in charge of a church in that place. Three sons and a daughter were born of this marriage, the eldest, William Carlos, becoming a well-known minister and writer.

After her marriage Mrs. Martyn continued her devotion to religious and reform movements. In 1842 she acted as editor for a few weeks of the *Olive Plant and Ladies' Temperance Advocate.* Following her separation from the *Advocate of Moral Reform* she was connected for a short time with a rival, the *True Advocate.* In April 1846 she began the publication of the *White Banner,* an undertaking that gave place the following month to the *Ladies' Wreath,* "a magazine devoted to literature, industry, and religion." This periodical she edited from 1846 to 1850, writing a large part of its decorous contents herself. In addition to these editorial ventures she wrote for the American Tract Society many unpretentious volumes designed for juvenile readers and a number of more ambitious works dealing with historical subjects. Among these are *Margaret, the Pearl of Navarre* (1867), *The English Exile, or William Tyndale at Home and Abroad* (1867), *Daughters of the Cross* (1868), and *Women of the Bible* (1868). She was known among the literati of New York as a gracious hostess in whose home well-known writers and reformers frequently assembled. After the death of her husband in 1868, she divided her time between New York and Connecticut, living with her children and sharing their interests. She died in New York City and was buried in Cheshire, Conn.

[*New-Eng. Hist. and Geneal. Reg.,* Apr. 1847; J. Q. Bittinger, *Hist. of Haverhill, N. H.* (1888); files of the *Ladies' Wreath* and of the *Advocate of Moral Reform*; obituary notices and personal information in possession of family; John S. Hart, *A Manual of Am. Lit.* (1874).]

B. M. S.

MARVEL, IK [See MITCHELL, DONALD GRANT, 1822–1908].

MARVIN, DUDLEY (May 29, 1786–June 25, 1852), congressman, the son of Elisha and Elizabeth (Selden) Marvin, was born in Lyme, Conn., where his ancestor, Reinold Marvin who emigrated from Essex County, England, before 1638, finally settled and died. He attended the Colchester Academy in Connecticut and then followed the path of New England pioneers westward into New York and settled in Ontario County at Canandaigua. With a general education such as was afforded by a small New England academy of that time he studied law and was admitted to the bar, probably in 1811. At the outbreak of war with Great Britain the following year he took active military duty with the state militia and served as lieutenant. After peace had been declared he continued to take a prominent part in the militia, rising eventually to the rank of major-general. He was married on Jan. 31, 1818, to Mary Jepson Whalley, the daughter of Joseph and Hannah (Saltonstall) Whalley of Canandaigua. They had one child.

Marvin practised law successfully and was recognized as one of the ablest barristers in the western counties of the state. In 1822 he was elected to Congress, as an Adams Democrat, and was reëlected in 1824 and in 1826. He came under the influence of Henry Clay's leadership and espoused the Whig cause. In Congress he advocated with distinction the dominant interests of the rising industrial power of the North, a protective tariff and the limitation of slavery. During his first term he became a member of the committee on manufactures and was an ardent advocate of a protective tariff. In the debate over the celebrated tariff of 1824 he defended against Southern opposition the cause of the Northern manufacturing interests, then slowly developing. He maintained that the tax that falls in the first instance upon the cotton planters "is paid back again by all other States, in the various proportions in which they are consumers of cotton" (*Annals of Cong.,* 18 Cong., 1 Sess., col. 1527). The fact that two-thirds of the cotton crop was consumed abroad did not in his mind disturb the logic of the Northern position. After completing his third term in Congress, he went to Maryland and to Virginia for a time and then removed to New York City to practise law there and in Brooklyn. About 1843 he again removed to the outlying districts of the state and settled in Ripley, Chautauqua County. In 1847 he returned to Congress as a Whig and served for one term. The stirring controversy over slavery in the territory newly acquired from Mexico brought him once more into the sectional debate. "It will not be denied," he asserted, "that the introduction of slavery equally excludes from a participation in the enjoyment of these acquisitions the free laboring men of the North" (*Congressional Globe*, 30 Cong., 1 Sess., App., p. 1211). The right of the federal government to exclude slavery from the territories he declared to be derived from the sovereign rights of the nation, the territories having been acquired in the first place "by the act of war—an act of sovereignty in which the respective sovereign States in the Union neither were nor could be known" (*Ibid.*, p. 1209). The remainder of his life was spent in Ripley. He interested himself in community affairs, was active in the temperance movement, and in the Presbyterian Church.

[A. W. Young, *Hist. of Chautauqua County* (1875); *Biog. Dir. Am. Cong.* (1928); G. F. and W. T. R. Marvin, *Descendants of Reinold and Matthew Marvin* (1904) as authority for dates of birth and death.]

G. L. R.

MARVIN, ENOCH MATHER (June 12, 1823–Nov. 26, 1877), bishop of the Methodist Episcopal Church, South, was a descendant of Reinold Marvin, born in Great Bentley, England, who emigrated to America about 1637 and settled in Hartford, Conn. In 1817 Wells Marvin married Mary Davis, of Welsh ancestry, in Pittsfield, Mass. The young couple immediately set out for the West, and established themselves near Peruque Creek, in what is now Warren County, Mo. There in a log-cabin Enoch Mather Marvin was born. Until he was twelve years old he was taught in a school conducted by his mother for her own and her neighbors' children. So far as is known, he attended school only six months thereafter; yet, as time went on, he acquired a good knowledge of history, an acquaintance with the scientific lore of his day, and enough Latin and Greek for his professional needs.

His father had little concern for religion, but his mother was a Baptist. In Missouri, however, the Baptists were so thoroughly Antinomian that she was never a member of a church there. Methodist circuit-riders came early to the Peruque Creek community, and Enoch was converted under their preaching when he was seventeen. A year later he was licensed to preach and admitted on trial in the Missouri Conference. At this time he was so homely and awkward that, dressed in ill-fitting homespun, he attracted no little attention. His first circuit covered three hundred miles along the Missouri-Iowa border, and his salary for the year was fifteen dollars. He soon demonstrated that he was a preacher of unusual power, especially among the common people, by whom he was always beloved. In 1854–55 he served as financial agent for St. Charles College, in which capacity he raised an endowment for that institution. From 1855 to 1862 he was pastor of some of the larger Methodist congregations in Missouri. During the Civil War he was chaplain in the Confederate army, serving with forces operating in Arkansas and the West. Some of the greatest preaching of his career is said to have been his sermons to soldiers in the camps. Hundreds were converted as a result of his appeals. He was also successful in organizing religious activities among the men. Following his term as chaplain he was transferred to Texas and stationed at Marshall. Though he was not a delegate, and not even present until after his election, the General Conference of 1866 chose him as one of the bishops of the Methodist Episcopal Church, South. "He was too rudely dressed to enter the church where he was to be received as bishop-elect, so several ministers . . . insisted on presenting to him a clerical suit becoming the occasion. He was the first man of his church who had been elected to the episcopacy with a full suit of beard" (*Frank Leslie's Sunday Magazine*, April 1878, p. 506).

Two achievements mark his eleven years in the episcopacy: upon his own responsibility he secured a sum of $5,000 for want of which, apparently, the whole work of the Methodists in the Indian Territory would have failed; and during the year preceding his death, he undertook a visitation to the East, during which he made a careful survey of all the foreign mission work carried on by the denomination, presenting the result of his observation in a series of articles in the church papers. He was author of *Errors of the Papacy* (1860); *The Work of Christ* (1867); *Life of William Goff Caples* (1870); *Sermons* (1876); *The Doctrinal Integrity of Methodism* (1878); *To the East by Way of the West* (1878). In 1845 he was married to Harriet Brotherton Clark, who with five children survived him.

[G. F. and W. T. R. Marvin, *Descendants of Reinold and Matthew Marvin* (1904); T. M. Finney, *Life and Labors of Enoch Mather Marvin* (1880); D. R. McAnally, *The Life and Labors of Rev. E. M. Marvin* (1878); *The Centennial Vol. of Mo. Methodism* (1907); *Cyc. of Methodism* (1882), ed. by Matthew Simpson; *Meth. Rev.* (Nashville), Nov.–Dec. 1895; *St. Louis Globe-Democrat*, Nov. 28, 1877; *To the East by Way of the West*, Appendix.]

R. W. G.

MARWEDEL, EMMA JACOBINA CHRISTIANA (Feb. 27, 1818–Nov. 17, 1893), apostle of Froebelianism and the kindergarten movement in Germany and the United States, particularly on the Pacific Coast, was born in Münden, near Göttingen, Germany. Little is known of her education; whether or not she was a pupil of Froebel, of his widow, or whether her training as a kindergartner was entirely self-acquired are still mooted questions. She was one of five children born to Captain Heinrich Ludwig Marwedel and his wife Jacobina Carolina Christiana Maria (Brokmann) Marwedel. The death of her mother placed a large share of the household work and the care of her brothers and sisters upon her shoulders. It may be that this early experience laid the foundation of her life-long interest in the welfare of little children and in the training of mothers. On the death of her father, left without sufficient means, she was obliged to go to work, thus breaking with the traditions of the social class to which by birth she belonged, but at the same time acquiring an interest which continued throughout her life in the welfare and education of working women.

At this time educational facilities for women were meager in Germany and it is certain that what she became was due largely to self-instruction. It was even more difficult for a woman to gain public recognition. Yet in 1864 she was elected to the board of directors of an association for the promotion of public education in Leipzig, and in 1865 she became a member of the first German association for the advancement of women. In 1867–68 she was directress of the Girls' Industrial School in Hamburg during the first year of its existence. At the same time she conducted a kindergarten of which Elizabeth Palmer Peabody wrote, "It was Miss Marwedel who, in 1867, first introduced me to Froebel's genuine Kindergarten in the city of Hamburg, and inspired me with the courage to make the main object of the remainder of my life to extend the Kindergarten over my own country" (Marwedel, *The Missing Link, the Continuation of the Three-fold Development of the Child from the Kindergarten to the Manual-Labor School*, p. 37). While in Hamburg Emma Marwedel spent over a year visiting female industrial schools in France, Belgium, and England, an account of which she published in 1868 under the title, *Warum bedürfen wir weibliche Gewerbeschulen? und wie sollen sie angelegt sein?* (reviewed by E. P. Peabody, *Harper's New Monthly Magazine*, May 1870). Soon after this, at the earnest request of Miss Peabody, she emigrated to America. Failing to find the opportunity she had expected for kindergarten work, she established in 1870 near Brentwood, Long Island, a women's cooperative industrial training school. Following the speedy failure of this institution, she went to Washington, D. C., where for four years she conducted with great success a school of industrial arts, a German-American kindergarten, and a Froebelian training school.

Under the combined auspices of the Froebel Union of New England, the United States Bureau of Education, and Caroline Seymour Severance [*q.v.*] she moved to Los Angeles in 1876 and established there a kindergarten and the first kindergarten normal class conducted in California. Her normal class, which numbered only three pupils, included Katherine Douglas Smith (Kate Douglas Wiggin), Mary Hoyt, and Nettie Stewart. At the end of two years, dissatisfied because of the lack of interest her work had aroused in Los Angeles, she moved her schools to Oakland in 1878, to Berkeley in 1879, and to San Francisco in 1880. She played an important part in the establishment in 1878 of the Silver Street Kindergarten of San Francisco, and in 1879 organized and became the first president of the California Kindergarten Union. In connection with her Pacific Kindergarten Normal School she conducted a primary department and a model kindergarten. After her retirement from active teaching about 1886 until the close of her life, she devoted herself to writing, lecturing, and the improvement of her system of kindergarten materials. In her latter years she suffered increasing financial difficulties and declining health. She died at the German Hospital (later the Franklin Hospital) in San Francisco and was buried in the Mountain View Cemetery, Oakland, Cal.

Emma Marwedel represents the traditional, sense-training type of Froebelianism. Her life was animated by the belief that through the kindergarten and the extension of Froebelian principles to the home and to the higher levels of education, particularly through the industrial arts, lay the path to the prevention of crime and the regeneration of human society. These ideas she embodied not only in her teaching activities but in numerous writings, most notably in *Conscious Motherhood, or the Earliest Unfolding of the Child in the Cradle, Nursery and Kindergarten* (1887) and in *The Connecting Link, to Continue the Three-Fold Development of the Child from the Cradle to the Manual-Labor School* (1891). The recognition which California early gained as one of the foremost leaders of the kindergarten movement was largely the result of her work. By her educational writings and by addresses delivered throughout the United States she promulgated the ideas not only of Froebel but of Seguin, Preyer, and other educational philosophers and psychologists of her day, and thus became one of the most important leaders in education. Her writings, in addition to those mentioned, include *An Appeal for Justice to Childhood* (n.d.), and *Games and*

Studies in Life Forms and Colors of Nature for Home and School (n.d.).

[The data in the present account concerning Emma Marwedel's birth and parentage have been taken directly from the birth and baptismal register of the church of St. Blasius, Münden. See Earl Barnes, "Emma Marwedel," in *Pioneers of the Kindergarten in America* (1924); "Kindergarten Work in Cal.," *Barnard's Am. Jour. of Educ.*, Sept. 1880; W. S. Monroe, "Emma Marwedel and the Kindergarten," *Education*, Feb. 1894; E. P. Peabody, "Industrial Schools for Women," *Harper's New Monthly Mag.*, May 1870; and F. H. Swift, *Emma Marwedel, Pioneer of the Kindergarten in Cal.* (1931), Univ. of Cal. Pubs. in Educ., vol. VI, no. 2, in which attention is called to inaccuracies in previous accounts. Important papers, filed in the matter of the estate of Emma Marwedel, are in the superior court for Alameda County, Cal.] F. H. S.

MARZO, EDUARDO (Nov. 29, 1852–June 7, 1929), composer, organist, and teacher, was born in Naples, Italy, the son of Carlo Marzo, a journalist and author, and Angiola Bertolè-Viale. After studying in his native city with Guglielmo Nacciarone and Giorgio Miceli he came to New York in 1867 as a boy pianist but soon returned to Italy to complete his studies in composition with Salvator Pappalardo. In 1869 he came to the United States to stay. For several years he toured the country as a musical director of opera troupes and concert companies and was the accompanist of many of the great solo artists then appearing in America, among them Carlotta Patti, Giuseppe Mario, Tom Karle, Giorgio Ronconi, Ernest de Munck, Gaetano Braga, Louise Carey, Émile Sauret, and Pablo Sarasate. In 1878 he definitely established himself in New York where in 1882 he married Clara L. Philbin, daughter of Eugene A. Philbin. He devoted himself to composition, voice teaching, and his work as a church organist. The constructive value of his work in music was recognized in Italy as well as in the United States, and he was made knight of the Crown of Italy (1884); member of the Royal Academy of St. Cecilia (1892), and knight of the Order of St. Sylvester (1914)—an honor conferred by Pope Benedict XV.

Marzo's secular compositions include songs, duets, operettas, piano pieces, some fugues for stringed quartet, and orchestral preludes. His sacred music, which is considerably more important, includes fifteen masses, four vespers, and over forty songs for Catholic services, as well as anthems and songs for the Protestant church. He also compiled various collections: *Songs of Italy* (1904); *Neapolitan Songs* (1905); *Dance Songs of the Nations* (1908); *Fifty Christmas Carols of all Nations* (1923); *Children's Carols* (1925); and *Sixty Carols of all Nations* (1928); and arranged a series of voice studies in *The Art of Vocalization* (18 vols., 1906), and *Preparatory Course to the Art of Vocalization* (1908). His *Collected Works* were published in twenty volumes (1870–1917).

Marzo filled a number of organ positions in New York, at the churches of St. Agnes, All Saints', St. Vincent Ferrer, and Church of the Holy Name. At the time of his death he was the organist of the Church of the Holy Spirit in the Bronx. He was one of the founders of the American Guild of Organists. During his long and successful career as a voice teacher he numbered among his pupils members of well-known New York families. In various articles contributed to musical magazines he gave interesting pictures of musical life in New York in the seventies and eighties of the nineteenth century. On Nov. 7, 1917, a number of the composer's friends tendered him a banquet at the Waldorf-Astoria Hotel in commemoration of his completion of fifty years of musical activity in the United States.

[Marzo's "Memoirs" and a "Sketch of Eduardo Marzo" by Otto Kinkeldey are in the N. Y. Pub. Lib. For printed sources see: *Musical America*, Dec. 15, 1917, July 13, 1918; *Who's Who in America*, 1928–29; *Il Carroccio* (N. Y.), Nov. 1917; the *Cath. Choirmaster*, July–Aug.–Sept. 1929; the *Am. Organist*, July 1929; *N. Y. Herald Tribune* and *N. Y. Times*, June 8, 1929.] F. H. M.

MASCHKE, HEINRICH (Oct. 24, 1853–Mar. 1, 1908), mathematician, was born in Breslau, Germany, where his father was owner of the Raths-Apotheke and had a position of considerable importance in the medical profession. As a student Heinrich showed marked ability in the Gymnasium of that city, and in 1872 he entered the University of Heidelberg, where he came under the influence of Königsberger. After serving his required term of one year in the army, he went to Berlin and here studied under Weierstrass, Kummer, and Kronecker. Proceeding to Göttingen, he received his doctor's degree there in 1880. After teaching for a few years in the Luisenstädtische Gymnasium in Berlin, he returned to Göttingen for a year's work (1886–87) under the direction of Prof. Felix Klein. He then resumed his position in Berlin, also taking up the study of electrotechnics at the Polytechnicum in Charlottenburg. In 1890, however, he resigned his position in the Gymnasium in order to do practical work in the Berliner Allgemeine Electricitätsgesellschaft. The following year he completed his technical training in the Polytechnicum at Darmstadt, under Professor Kittler.

Feeling at this time that there were greater opportunities for him in America, he came to the United States in the spring of 1891, did some work for a year with the Western Electrical Instrument Company, Newark, N. J., and in 1892 was called to the University of Chicago as assistant professor of mathematics. He devoted the remainder of his life to the training of mathematicians and to assisting in building up and maintaining a strong department in that university. He was a teacher of great ability and his courses were made more valuable by his all-round culture, by his originality of thought, and by his personal interest in the large numbers of young mathematicians who attended his lectures. Among those of foreign birth who have contributed notably to the advance of mathematics in the United States, he holds high rank.

Maschke's original work in pure mathematics may be said to have begun with his memoir *Ueber die quaternäre endliche, lineäre Substitutionsgruppe der Borchardtschen Moduln* (1887), developed under the inspiration of Klein's courses in Göttingen. This carried him extensively into the theory of finite groups of linear substitutions, a subject already attracting attention in this country through the translation of Eugene Netto's work on the theory of substitutions by Frank Nelson Cole [*q.v.*] and the latter's work at Ann Arbor and Columbia. His second line of major activity lay in the theory of quadratic differential quantics and led to the development of a symbolic method for the treatment of differential quantics, a study which occupied his attention during his later years. His wife, Theresa, survived him; they had no children.

[Oskar Bolza, "Heinrich Maschke: His Life and Work," in *Bull. Am. Mathematical Soc.*, Nov. 1908; *The Univ. Record* (Chicago), Apr. 1908; *Chicago Tribune*, Mar. 2, 1908.] D. E. S.

MASON, CHARLES (Oct. 24, 1804–Feb. 25, 1882), jurist, was born in Pompey, Onondaga County, N. Y., the son of Chauncey and Esther (Dodge) Mason. He entered the United States Military Academy at West Point in 1825 and was graduated in 1829 at the head of his class, with Joseph E. Johnston and Robert E. Lee as classmates. For the next two years he was assistant professor of engineering at West Point. His interest in law, already manifest at West Point, led him to devote his whole time to its study. He read law in New York City, was admitted to the bar in June 1832, and began practice at Newburgh, N. Y. Within two years he returned to New York City, where he contributed to the *Evening Post* and during the temporary absence of its regular editor, William Cullen Bryant, served for a short period as acting editor. In 1836 he went West on a tour of observation and, in April 1837, was appointed by Gov. Henry Dodge as an aide and as public prosecutor of Des Moines County in Wisconsin Territory. On Aug. 1, he was married to Angelica Gear, of Berkshire, Mass., the aunt of John Henry Gear [*q.v.*], and in November he established himself in Burlington.

When the new Territory of Iowa was organized in 1838, he was appointed chief justice of the supreme court. He was twice reappointed to this position and retained his seat for several months after the organization of the state of Iowa in December 1846. Among his notable decisions was the one relating to the legal status of the negro, Ralph (1 *Iowa Reports,* 1). His view in this case was that a slave going into a free territory by the consent of his master was thereafter to be treated not as a fugitive and chattel but as a free man—a theory in conflict with a later pronouncement of the Supreme Court of the United States in the case of Dred Scott. In 1847 he was attorney for Iowa in the Iowa-Missouri dispute that was submitted to the Supreme Court of the United States and decided in favor of Iowa (*Annals of Iowa,* Oct. 1866–Jan. 1867). As a member of the commission to draft the first code of the state, *The Code of Iowa . . . 1851* (1851), he exercised a marked influence on the laws of the state and subsequently on the codes of other states. In the interval between his work on the Iowa code commission and his election, in 1851, to the position of county judge of Des Moines County, he was in law partnership with Samuel R. Curtis and John W. Rankin at Keokuk. Appointed federal commissioner of patents in 1853, he laid down certain precedents that are followed by the agriculture department to the present time. He resigned this office in 1857 and became a member of the first Iowa state board of education. Two years thereafter he was legal adviser to Munn & Company in their patent agency, effecting, among other things, the extension of the Morse telegraph patent in the face of vigorous opposition.

Later he went to Washington, D. C., where he engaged in the practice of patent law. He was active in efforts to provide for the city of Washington a more efficient system of drainage and was able to draw upon his own knowledge of engineering for the plans. He declined the Democratic nomination for the governorship of Iowa in 1861, was defeated in 1863 for a position on the supreme court of Iowa, and in 1867 was defeated for the governorship. In 1864 he was chairman of the national central committee of his party and was a delegate to the nominating conventions of 1868 and 1872. He wrote various pamphlets on financial subjects, drainage, and sanitation. Among these were: *Articles on the Currency* (1858), *A Plan for Specie Resumption* (1874), and *What Shall Be Done with the Surplus Funds of the Patent Office?* (1870). The last years of his life were spent partly in Washington and partly in Iowa, where he continued his connections with the financial and industrial interests of the community. One of his three daughters, the wife of George Collier Remey [*q.v.*], survived him.

[Diaries in the possession of the historical department of Iowa; information from his grandson, Charles Mason Remey, Washington, D. C.; letter from Mason in E. H. Stiles, *Recollections and Sketches of Notable Lawyers* (1916); *Iowa Hist. Record,* Oct. 1893; *Annals of Iowa,* July–Oct. 1864, July–Oct. 1895, Oct. 1896, Jan. 1901, Jan. 1902, Apr., Oct. 1926, Apr. 1929; J. C. Parish, *Robert Lucas* (1907); Walter Geer, *The Geer Geneal.* (1923); *Iowa Jour. of Hist. and Politics,* Jan. 1914.] B. F. S.

MASON, CLAIBOURNE RICE (Nov. 28, 1800–Jan. 12, 1885), builder of bridges and railroads, the son of Rev. Peter Mason, a Baptist minister, was born in Chesterfield County, Va. (Waddell, *post*), but spent at least part of his early boyhood in Richmond. His ancestors had removed on account of religious persecution from the south of England to Holland and from there came to America. His mother, Elizabeth, died when the lad was very young, and at the age of eight he ran away from home and made his living for a time doing chores on a farm in Pennsylvania. Later he carried mail in Maryland, and at the age of sixteen or seventeen worked in Washington as apprentice to a ship's carpenter. In 1829 he began his career as a contractor in connection with the construction of the Midlothian Railway of Virginia, one of the earliest in the country. In 1836 he began the Louisa Railroad, the oldest part of the line that later became the Chesapeake & Ohio, and for a time he acted as its superintendent. An interesting feature in the operation of this railroad was the stable car containing four horses which were used for the purpose of helping the engine pull the train up hill. He was also a contractor, perhaps the largest, on the Virginia Central Railroad.

At the outbreak of the Civil War, though he was past sixty years of age, he raised a company of Confederate volunteers, mainly at his own expense, and was chosen captain. He saw his chief service under "Stonewall" Jackson, and in the army came to be known as "Jackson's bridge builder." Jackson's brilliant successes were unquestionably due in part to the short cuts made possible by Mason's resourcefulness. Not an engineer by training, he possessed many of the attributes of the engineer. He had an uncanny mathematical ability, and it was said of him that he could look at a hill and declare immediately how many cubic yards of material it contained. His special talent lay in his ability to plan and execute jointly. A story is told that once when Jackson needed a bridge quickly in order to cross the Shenandoah River he instructed his engineers to prepare plans for Mason, but before the plans were finished the bridge was built.

After the war Mason returned to railroad contracting. In 1872, when the Chesapeake & Ohio Railway completed its line from Richmond to Huntington, he drove the last spike at Hawks' Nest, thirty-six years after he had turned the first shovelful of earth for the old Louisa Railroad at Doswell. Among his notable achievements on the Chesapeake & Ohio were the construction of Jerry's Run Fill, 575 feet high, and the Lewis Tunnel. He had contracts also on the Valley Railroad of Virginia, the Baltimore & Ohio, the Cincinnati Southern, the Kentucky Central, the Richmond, Fredericksburg & Potomac, the Richmond & Allegheny, the Richmond & Mecklenburg, the Kentucky Union, and the Virginia & North Carolina Extension. The last large contract executed under his personal supervision was for the Southern Pennsylvania Railroad.

Mason was a man of mild deportment, good physique, and tireless energy. Believing in the policy of a protective livelihood other than contracting, some time before the Civil War he bought a farm at Swope's Station, Augusta County, Va., which was his home thereafter until his death. Here he cared for his horses and mules during off seasons and stored his surplus contracting equipment. On Mar. 13, 1838, he married Drucilla W. Boxley, who bore him eleven children, three of whom died young. Through the Mason Syndicate and the Mason & Hanger Company, Inc., of New York, of which he is considered the founder, two of his sons and their sons and grandsons were carrying on construction activity a hundred years after Mason took his first contract. He died at his home in 1885.

[Dixon Merritt, *Sons of Martha* (1928); a history of the Mason & Hanger Company; *War of the Rebellion: Official Records* (*Army*), 1 ser. V, XII, XXXVII, LI, 2 ser. 1; J. A. Waddell, *Annals of Augusta County, Va.* (1902); J. P. Nelson, *The Chesapeake and Ohio Railway* (1927); *Richmond Dispatch,* Jan. 13, 1885; information as to certain facts from the Mason & Hanger Company, Inc.] W. T. L.

MASON, FRANCIS (Apr. 2, 1799–Mar. 3, 1874), Baptist missionary, was born in York, England. His father, Thomas Mason, was a cobbler by trade, a radical in politics, and a lay preacher of a local Baptist society; his mother's maiden name was Hay. The son acquired a rudimentary education at the parish school (for the children of workers) and served as errand-boy in a shoe-factory. Too poor to pay the apprentice's fee in the factory, he finally went to work with his father. Because of a strike in York, the family moved to Hull, where the boy became interested in geography and mathematics, and studied Euclid in a night school conducted by a retired naval officer. From Hull the family moved to Leeds, the mother's native city.

In 1818 at the age of nineteen, Francis emigrated to the United States, his passage money being provided by a maternal uncle already in America. He landed in Philadelphia and worked his way as a journeyman shoe-maker to Pittsburgh, thence went by boat down the Ohio and the Mississippi rivers to Cincinnati, St. Louis, and New Orleans, and finally by sea to Boston, where he arrived in 1824. Soon thereafter he settled at Randolph, Mass., boarding at the home of the Baptist minister, Rev. Benjamin Putnam, working at his trade, and teaching school. In 1825 he married Lucinda Gill (died 1828), daughter of a farmer living in Canton, Mass., to which place Mason now removed and opened a shoe shop of his own. Influenced by his wife and by the reading of Butler's *Analogy,* he professed conversion and joined the Canton Baptist Church. By this church, on Oct. 1, 1827, he was licensed to preach, and in the following November he entered Newton Theological Institution to prepare for the ministry. He had previously begun privately the study of Hebrew and Greek, and had read widely in literature, science, and theology. During his senior year at Newton, Dec. 7, 1829, he received appointment from the Baptist missionary society to service in Burma. On May 23, 1830, he was ordained to the ministry, and on the same day was married to Helen Maria Griggs (died 1846). Three days afterward he and his bride sailed from Boston for Calcutta, arriving in October, and passing on to Maulmain in the following month. Stationed in Tavoy for work among the Karens, he began his duties in January 1831, and spent in all twenty-two years there. He was superintendent of the station several years; conducted a training school for mission workers, which was later moved to Maulmain and finally to Rangoon; engaged in extensive evangelism; and made translations, especially of the Christian Scriptures, into the Sgau and Pgho Karen dialects. He published at Tavoy in 1837 a Karen version of the Gospel of Matthew—on a press established that year, which was removed to Rangoon in 1853. In 1843 his Sgau Karen New Testament appeared and also, in English, *The Karen Apostle, or Memoir of Ko Thah-byu,* edited by H. J. Ripley. These were followed by *Synopsis of a Grammar of the Karen Language* (1846), *The Natural Productions of Burmah, or Notes on the Fauna, Flora, and Minerals of the Tenasserim Provinces of the Burman Empire* (1850), a memoir of his second wife, Helen Griggs, entitled *A Cenotaph to a Woman of the Burman Mission* (1851), and his Karen Bible issued in 1853.

In 1847 he was married to Mrs. Ellen Huntly Bullard, widow of the Rev. E. B. Bullard, formerly of Maulmain. On the completion of the Karen Bible, he turned for a time to evangelism, taking up residence in Toungoo, where he established a new station. His health was failing, however, and in January 1854 he set out for the United States, journeying by way of India, South Africa, Europe, and the British Isles, where he visited his aged mother in Leeds. He sailed again for Burma on July 2, 1856, and reached Toungoo on Jan. 2, 1857. In 1860 he published in Rangoon his valuable *Burmah, its Peoples and Natural Productions.* For this and other researches and literary works he was admitted to membership in the Royal Asiatic Society and the American Oriental Society. There was a time (Apr. 25, 1865, to July 11, 1871) when both Mason and the mission suffered much from the effects of a form of dementia which afflicted his wife and led to the temporary establishment of a cult. She claimed to have found in the Karen women's dresses and in various objects connected with Buddhist worship, the language in which God spoke to Adam, and believed that she had the key by which she could read it. Mason was asked to sever his connection with the mission for a time, and during that period he published a Pali grammar (Toungoo, 1868), and an autobiography, *The Story of a Working Man's Life* (New York, 1870). He was later reinstated and died a member of the mission which he had served so conspicuously. He was buried in Rangoon.

[In addition to Mason's autobiography, see article on "Burmah" in Harvey Newcomb, *Cyc. of Missions* (2nd ed., 1856); *Baptist Missionary Mag.,* June 1874; S. F. Smith, *Missionary Sketches* (6th ed., 1879); William Cathcart, *Baptist Encyc.* (1881); *Encyc. of Missions* (1904).]
J. C. A.

MASON, FRANK STUART (Oct. 21, 1883–Oct. 25, 1929), musician, was a son of Frank Hale and Lucretia Augusta (Chipman) Mason, of Weymouth, Mass. He was of Pilgrim and Puritan lineage. Early disclosing musical talent, Stuart, as he was always called, was sent, after his graduation from the Weymouth schools, to the New England Conservatory of Music in Boston, where he had as his principal instructor J. Albert Jeffery. While still a music student he made many public appearances of local note. Graduated in 1907 at the head of his class, he continued his professional education at Paris where he studied the pianoforte with Isidor Philipp, Raoul Pugno, and André Wormser, and composition with André Gedalge. He began at this time researches in old French music which he pursued throughout his career with scholarly thoroughness and an artist's enthusiasm.

Mason returned to Boston singularly well equipped for professional success. His training had been of the best. He possessed remarkable physical energy and mental buoyancy. No struggle was needed to establish him in a city where he was already well known. A place was at once offered him on the Conservatory faculty, with a full teaching schedule. Because of his reputation and the charm of his personality pupils were eager to attend his classes in pianoforte, harmony, harmonic analysis, canon, fugue, composition, and instrumentation. When Louis C. Elson [*q.v.*] died Mason took over his celebrated course in the history of music and maintained its popularity. While teaching long hours at the Conservatory he multiplied his contacts in the community. His début as a pianist with the Boston Orchestral Club in 1910 was followed by many engagements. In 1919 he was invited by Emil Mollenauer, conductor, to be assistant conductor of the newly organized People's Symphony Orchestra of Boston, of which he himself later became conductor, showing marked ability in arranging unusual programs and in inspiring a band containing both professional and amateur players. As a composer he made a most auspicious start toward eminence with his "Rhapsody on a Persian Air" and the orchestral suite, "Bergerie," both which were produced by several symphony orchestras. His published work also included pianoforte and chamber music compositions and several songs. He continued to give programs of ancient French music at frequent intervals, and accounts of them, sent to his friends in France, led to his being twice decorated by the French government. He was invited in 1923 to be guest conductor of the Boston Symphony Orchestra, an unusual honor for a resident musician.

Mason meantime lectured on the history and appreciation of music throughout the state under the university extension division of the Massachusetts department of education. He gave courses in the summer school of Boston University, ranking as assistant professor. He wrote music criticism for the *Christian Science Monitor,* "always," according to a contemporary, "with admirable clarity, discrimination and avoidance of meaningless eulogy and puff." He was married on Dec. 25, 1925, to Margaret C. Mason, formerly of Clarinda, Iowa, who like himself was a high-honor graduate of the New England Conservatory and a member of its faculty. Mason was often warned by friends that he was doing too much, but his reply was always that of a vigorous and genial man who took his responsibilities seriously, himself not at all so. A breakdown occured in October 1929, from which he appeared to be recovering when he was fatally stricken in his classroom.

[Obituary in the *New Eng. Conservatory of Music Bull.,* Nov. 1929; tribute by Philip Hale, *Boston Sunday Herald,* Nov. 3, 1929; notes on Mason as conductor of the People's Symphony Orchestra, *Musical Courier,* Dec. 4, 1924; biographical sketch in the program notes in *Boston Symphony Orchestra: Forty-Third Season: Ninth Programme,* Dec. 21, 22, 1923.] F. W. C.

MASON, GEORGE (*c.* 1629–*c.* 1686), colonist, progenitor of the fourth George Mason [*q.v.*], author of the Virginia Declaration of Rights, was traditionally one of the cavalier emigrants to Virginia during the rule of Cromwell. The first known mention of him in the colonial records is in a patent of March 1655 for land in Westmoreland County, headrights for eighteen persons brought into Virginia. In 1664 and again in 1669 he secured large tracts of adjacent lands on Potomac Creek at the mouth of Accoceek, where he had his dwelling. In a deposition dated Aug. 20, 1658, he declared his age to be twenty-nine, thus establishing approximately the date of his birth. From another record of Westmoreland (1655) his wife is known to have been named Mary. His son, George, was active in Stafford County affairs. A will of the date of 1686, known to have been on file in Stafford before 1840, is assumed to be that of the first George Mason, and it is therefore inferred that his death occurred in that year.

In 1667 Mason was active on the Northern Neck committee charged with the defense and local government of that region, and a member of the committee representing the counties of Westmoreland, Northumberland, and Stafford to carry out an act of the Assembly providing for the erection of a fort on Yeocomico River. He was sheriff of Stafford County in 1669, clerk of the court in 1673, and was sent as a burgess to the Assembly of 1676, which passed the measures known as "Bacon's Laws," democratic in tone and designed to correct certain abuses of the administration. He held the office of county lieutenant, and, doughty and daring, he and his aggressive neighbors often took the law in their own hands in defense of northern Virginia against the Indians. In 1661–62, with Col. Gerard Fowke, Capt. Giles Brent, and John Lord, he was subjected to disciplinary measures imposed by the Assembly for what it considered unjust treatment of Wahanganoche, king of the Potomac Indians. Mason was ordered to pay damages to the Indian king and to the public treasury for contempt of the Governor's warrant and was suspended from all civil and military power until he could clear himself of Wahanganoche's charges. He and his recalcitrant neighbors, however, formed the governing group in northern Virginia, and they were returned to official favor.

It is as an Indian fighter and precipitator of events culminating in Bacon's Rebellion that Mason is chiefly remembered. When, in 1675, a band of Doegs made raids in his community and finally killed a neighbor, Mason and Col. Giles Brent gathered about thirty men and pursued the murderers into Maryland. There Brent attacked the Doegs, who had taken refuge in a cabin among the Susquehannocks, and Mason with his men pursued the Indians who fled from a neighboring cabin. When he discovered the Indians were the friendly Susquehannocks, Mason cried out, "for the Lords sake shoot no more, these are our friends the Susquehanoughs." Unwittingly, however, he had set loose a chain of circumstances that provoked the Susquehannocks to take the war path and resulted in Bacon's Rebellion. Mason agreed to fight under Bacon's command against the Indians, but he had no sympathy with the young radical's democratic program. When, therefore, it was clear that Bacon's leadership meant opposition to the established government, Mason took no part in the campaigns. It is significant that the troops from Stafford were loyal to Berkeley and helped to put down the young rebel's forces. With his neighbors of position and power, among them Col. William Ball and Col. John Washington, Mason served in 1677 on the committee ordered by the Assembly to lay a levy in the Northern Neck for the costs of suppressing "the late rebellion." In his later years he continued to be a successful landholder and official, carving out an inheritance for his heirs and giving dignity to the family name.

[Peter Force, *Tracts and Other Papers, Relating Principally to the Origin, Settlement, and Progress of the Colonies in North America*, vol. I (1836); W. W. Hening, *The Statutes at Large; Being a Collection of All the Laws of Virginia*, vol. II (1823); H. R. McIlwaine, *Executive Jours. of the Council of Colonial Va.*, vol. I (1925); H. R. McIlwaine, *Jours. of the House of Burgesses of Va., 1659/60 . . . 1693* (1914), p. 14 (suspension), and *passim*; *Va. Mag. of Hist. and Biog.*, July 1893, Oct. 1896, Jan. 1898, Oct. 1904, Oct. 1909, Jan. 1915; *William and Mary College Quart. Hist. Papers*, July 1893; *William and Mary College Quart. Hist. Mag.*, July 1895, Apr. 1901, Jan. 1905; Kate Mason Rowland, *The Life of George Mason 1725–1792* (2 vols., 1892); Fairfax Harrison, *Landmarks of Old Prince William* (2 vols., 1924); T. J. Wertenbaker, *Va. under the Stuarts, 1607–1688* (1914); E. D. Neill, *Va. Carolorum* (1886).] M. H. W.

MASON, GEORGE (1725–Oct. 7, 1792), planter, Revolutionary statesman, constitutionalist, was the fourth of his name and line in Virginia. The first American George Mason [*q.v.*], who probably emigrated from England soon after the battle of Worcester, settled in the Northern Neck on 900 acres near Pasbytanzy; he and his descendants added to this original grant so that when the fourth George Mason came of age and settled at Dogue's Neck, on the Potomac below Alexandria, he controlled some 5,000 acres in the region. Because of the death of his father, the third George Mason, when he was ten, the boy grew up under the guardianship of his mother, Ann (Thomson) Mason, and his uncle by marriage, John Mercer of "Marlborough," an exceptionally able lawyer. Mrs. Mason's account books show payments to private tutors during the years 1736–39, but Mason found his education in Mercer's library. It numbered upwards of 1,500 volumes, a third of them on law, and at the time of his guardianship Mercer was at work among them. This association accounts for the fact that while Mason was never licensed as an attorney he was called in as a notably competent counsel on questions of public law throughout his later life. On Apr. 4, 1750, he married Anne Eilbeck of "Mattawoman," Charles County, Md.; soon afterward, their portraits were painted by John Hesselius. In 1758 their new home, "Gunston Hall," begun in 1755, was completed; its architect was William Buckland, a skilled craftsman from Oxford whom Mason's younger brother Thomson brought back with him under indenture in 1754. In the course of the twenty years after their marriage, five sons and four daughters were born.

Mason persisted in regarding himself as a private gentleman, even during his most intensive periods of public service. Without the aid of a steward, he personally managed his large and practically self-sufficient plantation. He served as trustee of the recently founded town of Alexandria from 1754 until its incorporation in 1779; Alexandria was also the seat of Fairfax County, and he was one of the gentlemen justices of the county court from his early manhood until his resignation in 1789. Parallel to the jurisdiction of the county ran that of the parish, which under the Establishment was vested with governmental duties in respect of the moral and charitable obligations of the community; Mason was a vestryman of Truro Parish from 1748 until 1785, serving as one of the overseers of the poor after relief became a lay function. As the executor of Daniel French, the original contractor, he supervised the building of Pohick Church, some of whose details repeat the carvings at "Gunston." This triple experience in local government formed an important part of his political apprenticeship.

Complementary to Mason's familiarity with the tidewater section of the colony was his association with the problems of the West. He became a member of the Ohio Company in 1752, and served as its treasurer until 1773. His initial interest in it was merely as a speculation, but as the company changed from a private economic venture into the lever which upset the political balance, first between French and British forces in the New World, and then, after the Peace of Paris, between Crown and Colony across the Alleghanies, the constitutional aspect of Virginia's claims to the Northwest Territory engaged his attention; when the Crown, in 1773, abrogated the Ohio Company's rights and regranted the area they covered to the Grand Company organized by a group of Pennsylvanians, Mason produced his first major state paper, *Extracts from the Virginia Charters, with Some Remarks upon Them* (1773, reprinted in Rowland, I, 393–414).

Prior to midsummer, 1775, Mason's part in the Revolution was in the wings of the public stage. Various reasons have been adduced for his reluctance to accept office; on the one hand his chronic ill-health, on the other the death of his wife early in 1773, leaving him, as he wrote in 1775, with a sense of "the duty I owe to a poor little helpless family of orphans to whom I must now act the part of Father and Mother both" (*Ibid.*, I, 198). It is true that after his marriage, on Apr. 11, 1780, to Sarah Brent he accepted a seat in the Federal Convention in Philadelphia (1787), but by far the most probable cause of his persistent refusals to serve was the low rating which he put upon human nature in committee. In 1759 he and Washington had served together in the House of Burgesses; at the end of his first term he withdrew with an opinion of that body which did not change when he went to take the place of the newly-elected Commander-in-chief in the July convention of 1775. Writing Washington on Oct. 14, 1775, in regard to the session he said: "I never was in so disagreeable a situation and almost despaired of a cause which I saw so ill conducted. . . . Mere vexation and disgust threw me into such an ill state of health, that before the Convention rose, I was sometimes near fainting in the House. . . . However, after some weeks the babblers were pretty well silenced, a few weighty members began to take the lead, several wholesome regulations were made" (*Ibid.*, I, 210–11). Off-stage, however, Mason had played a highly important part ever since 1765, when, at the instance of Washington and G. W. Fairfax, he contrived a method of replevying goods under distress for rent without the use of stamped paper. His open letter of June 6, 1766, to a committee of London merchants (*Ibid.*, I, 381–89) tersely summarized the mood of the colonists in its balanced profession of loyalty and independence: they were ready wholeheartedly to welcome the repeal of the Stamp Act as an act of justice; that repeal was a favor they would never admit. When the Townshend duties revived the trade dispute, Mason prepared the resolutions which Washington presented to the dissolved House of Burgesses and which, adopted by them as a non-importation association, were passed on for subsequent approval by the Continental Congress. After the Boston Port Act brought matters to a head, he wrote the Fairfax Resolves of July 18, 1774 (*Ibid.*, I, 418–27), stating a version of the constitutional position of the colonies *vis-à-vis* the Crown which was successively accepted by the county court in Fairfax, the Virginia convention in Williamsburg, and the Continental Congress in Philadelphia; some weeks later his plan for the organization of troops led to the creation of the Fairfax Independent Company of volunteers.

During the period in which he was writing these important papers, Mason was exerting a parallel influence on the consolidation of public opinion by word of mouth. Philip Mazzei, in his memoirs, and Edmund Randolph, in his manuscript history of Virginia, both emphasize this aspect of his effectiveness. Randolph said: "Among the numbers who in their small circles were propagating with activity the American doctrines, was George Mason in the shade of retirement. He extended their grasp upon the opinions and affections of those with whom he conversed. . . . He was behind none of the sons of Virginia in knowledge of her history and interest. At a glance he saw to the bottom of every proposition which affected her" (Quoted, *Ibid.*, I, 178). Washington's diary bears witness to the frequency of his collaboration with Mason in the years before his departure to lead the army, and the letters of the three younger colleagues who succeeded him as the Virginia dynasty all testify specifically to the influence upon them of conversations at "Gunston Hall."

In 1775 Mason emerged from retirement as a member of the July convention, and served on the committee of safety which took over the executive powers vacated by the flight of Governor Dunmore. In 1776, as a member of the May convention, he achieved his outstanding contribution as a constitutionalist by framing the Declaration of Rights (reprint of original draft, *Ibid.*, I, 433–36) and the major part of the constitution of Virginia. The former was drawn upon by Jefferson in the first part of the Declaration of Independence, was widely copied in the other colonies, became the basis for the first ten amendments to the Constitution of the United States, and had a considerable influence in France at the time of the French Revolution. The latter was notable as a pioneer, written "constitution," prepared with a view to permanence, and used by a commonwealth over a period of years. The years 1776–80 were occupied in implementing the various provisions of the two documents, with Mason in the forefront of legislative activity, closely collaborating with such men as Jefferson, Henry, and Wythe. He was a member of the committee of five entrusted with the revision of the laws, and while he resigned after the general plan had been agreed on, he continued to contribute his share of the new drafts, particularly those relating to the western lands. He was among the liberal churchmen who effected disestablishment. He was active in the organization of military affairs, particularly in the West. Mason's connection with the Northwest Territory is worthy of special note. His relation to George Rogers Clark was as close as that of father to son; he was one of Governor Henry's secret committee that authorized Clark's conquest, and it was to him that Clark sent his full account of the campaign. Since it was his *Extracts from the Virginia Charters* that had convinced Virginians of the western extent of their sovereignty, he was in some measure responsible for the fixing of the British-American boundary, in the treaty of 1783, at the Great Lakes rather than the Ohio, and it was he who sketched the plan out of which grew the cession by Virginia of her western lands to the United States, and Jefferson's ordinance for their government (Letter to Joseph Jones, July 27, 1780, Rowland, I, 360–67).

During the early eighties Mason was among those whom disgust at the conduct of public affairs drove into retirement; not until 1786 could he be again prevailed upon to go to the Assembly. His return to active life was motivated by his desire to prevent Virginia from indulging in a further orgy of inflation, and his growing conviction, in spite of his lifelong attachment to doctrine of state rights, that the Articles of Confederation were an inadequate basis for the central government. He was an active member of the Virginia delegation at the Mount Vernon meeting of 1785; he was appointed to but did not attend the Annapolis meeting of 1786 which grew out of it; in the debates at Philadelphia he was one of the five most frequent speakers. An examination of Madison's notes on the Federal Convention shows the extent of the constructive influence which Mason exerted on the Constitution. His decision not to sign the document was made during the last two weeks; until the final days of the convention he struggled for the inclusion of certain clauses and the exclusion of others which he regarded as respectively essential and iniquitous. In several instances his "Objections to the Federal Constitution" (reprinted in P. L. Ford, *Pamphlets on the Constitution*, 1888), on the basis of which he conducted his campaign against ratification in the Virginia convention of 1788, though negative in their immediate application, proved in the long run to have been well-founded. In two cases, his justification is written into the Constitution. His insistence on the necessity of a Bill of Rights bore fruit in the first ten amendments. The eleventh amendment, in 1798, testified to the correctness of his strictures on one part of the judiciary article, when his prophecy that suits would be brought against states was ridiculed by a young lawyer named John Marshall. In a third case his justification is written into general American history. Mason's outstanding reason for refusing to sign the Constitution was that it incorporated the compromise between the New England states and those of the extreme South on the tariff and the slave trade. His opposition to the institution of slavery was perhaps the most consistent feature of his public career. His first political paper opens with a paragraph on the advantage of settling land with free as contrasted with slave labor; his final speeches in the Richmond convention reiterate his opinion that "such a trade [in slaves] is diabolical in itself and disgraceful to mankind."

Mason's constructive proposals for the situation in which a century and a half of slave-owning had left his community, proposals which run curiously parallel to the solution of the problem effected by the British Parliament in 1833, can be taken as illustrative of his general philosophical attitude. More than perhaps any other

American statesman of the period, he represented the rationalist spirit, the Enlightenment in its American manifestation. He believed in the existence of a rule of right reason, and in the possibility of giving it concretion in terms of the problem at hand. He believed life, liberty, and the use of property to be central human rights. Applying those criteria to slavery, he favored manumission, so that one man's life should not be at the mercy of another, preceded by education, so that liberty might be given a positive content; at the same time he desired recognition of the property rights of the owner, so that the termination of an undesirable economy might take place without the confiscation of a large part of the community's capital. His conclusions were thorough, impersonal, convinced. They may stand as indicative of the mental fiber of Mason the gentleman, the representative of the Enlightenment, and the statesman.

[MS. materials include the George Mason Papers and other collections, and the Truro Parish Book in the Lib. of Cong.; Mason letters in the Emmet Collection, N. Y. Pub. Lib.; Minute Book of the Alexandria Trustees, City Hall, Alexandria, Va.; Fairfax court records, Courthouse, Fairfax, Va. K. M. Rowland, *The Life of George Mason, 1725–1792* (2 vols., 1892), reprints valuable correspondence, writings, and speeches. See also H. B. Grigsby, *The Va. Convention of 1776* (1855), and *The Hist. of the Va. Federal Convention of 1788* (2 vols., 1890–91); James Madison, reporter, *The Debates in the Federal Convention of 1787* (1920), ed. by Gaillard Hunt and J. B. Scott; H. R. Connor, *Gunston Hall, Fairfax County, Va.* (1930), the Monograph Series, No. 3, vol. XVI; R. W. Moore, "George Mason, the Statesman," *William and Mary Coll. Quart.*, Jan. 1933. Other items in Virginia publications may be located through the checklist prepared by E. G. Swem. A biography by Helen Hill is in manuscript.] H. H.

MASON, HENRY (Oct. 10, 1831–May 15, 1890), piano manufacturer, fourth son of Lowell Mason [*q.v.*] and Abigail (Gregory) Mason, was born in Brookline, Mass., and educated in the Boston public schools. Like his brother William [*q.v.*] he completed his education abroad, studying at the universities of Göttingen, Paris, and Prague. On his return to America he entered the music store of Sylvanus B. Pond in New York and at the same time served as a church organist. In 1854 he left New York for Boston and with Emmons Hamlin [*q.v.*], founded the Mason & Hamlin Organ Company, though he continued for a time as a church organist in Cambridge and was active as a music critic for various Boston newspapers. Mason's partner, who had an inventive mind, was very successful in improving the reed quality and tone-color of their instruments. In 1855 the firm brought out an Organ-Harmonium, an improvement on the existing reed-organ. It was provided with double bellows, making possible a greater volume of sound and the production of a continuous tone. With further improvements the instrument became the American Cabinet Organ, introduced in 1861, and under that name it became widely known. In 1882 the firm branched from organ construction to piano manufacturing, reorganizing as the Mason & Hamlin Organ and Piano Company. Insisting upon the maintenance of high standards of workmanship, the firm produced a piano of excellent quality. In the illustrious musical family of which he was a member, Henry Mason represented the creator of musical values in the mechanical and commercial fields, as his brother William did in those of concert pianism and pedagogy. He died in his home in Boston at the age of fifty-nine. In 1857 he had married Helen Augusta Palmer. One of his sons, Henry Lowell Mason, became the head of the firm of Mason & Hamlin in 1906.

[H. L. Mason, *The Hist. and Development of the Am. Cabinet Organ* (n.d.), reprinted from *Presto*, June 4, 1903; Alfred Dolge, *Pianos and Their Makers* (2 vols., 1911–13); the *Folio*, June 1890; Boston *Evening Transcript*, May 15, 1890.] F. H. M.

MASON, JAMES MURRAY (Nov. 3, 1798–Apr. 28, 1871), representative, senator, Confederate diplomatic commissioner to Europe, was born in Georgetown, D. C. A grandson of George Mason [*q.v.*] of Revolutionary fame, and the son of Gen. John Mason and Anna Maria Murray, he had five brothers and four sisters all of whom lived to maturity. His early education was obtained in the schools of Georgetown and the neighborhood, and he graduated from the University of Pennsylvania in 1818 after four years of study. He then studied law at the College of William and Mary. After spending a short time in the office of Benjamin Watkins Leigh of Richmond, he did an unusual thing for a Tidewater aristocrat by moving to the Valley and establishing a practice at Winchester (1820). On July 25, 1822, he was married to Elizabeth Margaretta Chew, daughter of Benjamin Chew, Mason's devoted friend and counselor during his college days in Philadelphia and until Chew's death.

Just on the outskirts of the town of Winchester the young couple bought a modest home which they called "Selma." Here their eight children were reared. Devoted to his family, Mason was destined to spend a great part of his life away from them. Except for the term of 1827–28, he represented his county in the state legislature from 1826 to 1831. In 1829, as a delegate to the Virginia constitutional convention, he proved himself once again unorthodox, from the point of view of the Tidewater, by favoring the white basis of representation, as advocated by the back country. It was good politics for him to champion the interests of his constituents, but there is evidence that he followed convictions of long standing. In 1832 he was an elector on the Jackson-Van Buren ticket, a fact which is rather interesting in view of his later friendship with Calhoun. In 1837 he was elected to Congress and represented his district one term. In 1847 he was sent to the United States Senate to fill the unexpired term of Senator Pennybacker. Reëlected in 1849 and 1855, he was in the Senate when Virginia seceded.

At Washington, Mason was intimately associated with the most prominent Southern-Rights Democrats. Calhoun and R. M. T. Hunter were for years his mess mates during the session of Congress and he fell especially under Calhoun's influence. It is not surprising, therefore, that he drafted the famous fugitive-slave law of 1850 and that it was he who read the speech of John C. Calhoun to the Senate on the proposed compromise measures. When Lincoln was elected, Mason, unlike many border state leaders, believed that compromise was not possible and that the South must withdraw from the Union or be submerged and exploited by the North. To him, as to Calhoun, the "irrepressible conflict" was between two social and economic systems, or civilizations, one of which was agrarian and the other industrial. Slavery while strongly upheld by Mason was only one of the elements of the Southern system.

With his clear stand upon Southern rights, his restrained and conciliatory demeanor, his high social connections, his ten years as chairman of the Senate's foreign relations committee, and his friendship with Davis, Mason was well qualified to go to England as Confederate diplomatic commissioner and a colleague of John Slidell who was dispatched to France in the same capacity. The seizure of Mason and Slidell while on board the *Trent* by Captain Wilkes of the United States navy nearly caused a war between Great Britain and the United States and helped create an atmosphere favorable to the Confederacy. The prisoners were held at Fort Warren, Boston Harbor, until Jan. 1, 1862. Upon arriving in England Mason was received as one born of the manor. He shared the universal conviction of the South that Great Britain would recognize the Confederacy or actually intervene in its behalf in order to obtain cotton. The hostility to a strong American Union and the prospect of practically free trade with the South he thought would likewise be inducements for British intervention. He probably did all that could have been done. He cultivated the friendship of the leading members of the Lords and Commons, of the great merchants and manufacturers, and of the newspaper men. He acted as central agent for the various naval and military purchasing agents of the Confederacy, and cooperated with the Confederate propagandists. He aided in the raising of money and the sale of Confederate bonds and entered into communication, chiefly written, with members of the British government over such matters as recognition, the Federal blockade, and the Confederate iron-clads. But the British government never received him officially and refused with two or three exceptions to hold interviews with him as a private citizen. The government was friendly enough to the Confederacy, but there was a two-year surplus of cotton in the country out of which great profit was realized. Profits in munitions, linen, and woolens, and the great expansion of the merchant marine made Great Britain prosperous as a result of war. As for her desire to see the United States divided, the dread of a war with the possible loss of her merchant marine and her war profits counteracted any inclination to intervene.

In April 1866 Mason repaired to Canada where he remained nearly three years because of his fear of being arrested by the federal government as an important Confederate official. After Johnson's second proclamation of amnesty in 1868 he returned to Virginia, though not to his old home, "Selma," for that had been burned by Sheridan during the war. On Apr. 28, 1871, he died at "Clarens" near Alexandria, Va.

[See Virginia Mason, *The Pub. Life and Diplomatic Correspondence of Jas. M. Mason, with some Personal Hist. by his Daughter* (1903); R. K. Crallé, ed., The *Works of John C. Calhoun* (6 vols., 1854–60); Dunbar Rowland, ed., *Jefferson Davis, Constitutionalist: His Letters, Papers and Speeches* (10 vols., 1923); F. L. Owsley, *King Cotton Diplomacy* (1931); *Evening Star* (Washington), Apr. 29, 1871. The Pickett Papers, Manuscript Division, Lib. of Cong., contain all of Mason's diplomatic correspondence, most of which has been published in *War of the Rebellion: Official Records (Navy)*, 2 ser. III. The Mason Papers, Manuscript Division, Lib. of Cong., contain unofficial papers, for the most part written while Mason was commissioner. His private papers were burned with his house.]

F. L. O.

MASON, JEREMIAH (Apr. 27, 1768–Oct. 14, 1848), lawyer, United States senator, was born in Lebanon, Conn., the sixth of nine children of Col. Jeremiah Mason and his wife, Elizabeth (Fitch) Mason, and fifth in direct descent from Maj. John Mason, 1600–1672 [*q.v.*], the famous Indian fighter and conqueror of the Pequots. His father, except for some years in the Revolutionary army, was a farmer, occupying land originally deeded to his family by Uncas, the Mohican chief. The boy, after two years of preparation under Nathan Tisdale, entered Yale College in 1784, graduating with distinction in 1788. A year of legal study with Simeon Baldwin [*q.v.*], in New Haven, was followed by two years in the office of Stephen Row Bradley [*q.v.*], in Westminster, Vt. After several years of practice in small towns in Vermont and New Hampshire, he moved in 1797 to Portsmouth, N. H., then the largest city in the state. In November 1799 he married Mary Means, daughter of Col. Robert Means of Amherst, N. H. Five sons and three daughters were born to them.

Within a brief period, Mason became one of the acknowledged leaders of the New Hampshire bar. It has been said that, from 1805 to 1808, the number of original entries made by him at any court session was larger than that of all the other attorneys in Portsmouth together. With the arrival of Daniel Webster [*q.v.*] in Portsmouth in 1807, Mason had keener competition, and the two men were soon retained on opposite sides in nearly every important case in Rockingham County. Webster, who was inclined to be rhetorical and grandiloquent, learned much from Mason, who was direct, colloquial, and economical of speech. Furthermore, Mason, through his thoroughness and earnestness, compelled Webster to exert himself to the utmost. The latter often testified to his indebtedness to Mason for what he had learned from him in courtroom pleadings, and more than once expressed the opinion that he was the greatest lawyer he had known.

Although Mason, like Rufus Choate [*q.v.*], really preferred law to public life, he was drawn inevitably into political affairs. In 1802 he was appointed attorney-general of New Hampshire, serving acceptably in that capacity till 1805. Elected in 1813 to the United States Senate by the Federalist party, he joined with Webster—who was then in the House of Representatives—in opposing the War of 1812 and criticizing the policies of the administration. A conservative by temperament, he disliked Jefferson's theories of government and found congenial friends in such senatorial colleagues as Rufus King [*q.v.*] and Christopher Gore. He resigned his seat in June 1817, disgusted with the hopeless decline of his party and unwilling to be longer separated from his family. For several terms (1820, 1821, 1824) he sat in the New Hampshire legislature, where he assisted in revising the legal code of that state. In 1824 he was again a candidate for the United States Senate, but was defeated in the legislature. He declined several important positions on the bench, including that of chief justice of the highest court of New Hampshire (1816), choosing instead the more active life of the courts.

Mason was associated with Webster and Jeremiah Smith [*q.v.*] in the earlier stages of the so-called Dartmouth College Case, and his arguments were used freely by Webster before the United States Supreme Court in 1819 (Fuess, *Webster, post,* I, 221–24). During the summer of 1828, he reluctantly accepted the presidency of the Portsmouth Branch of the United States Bank. Some of his policies aroused the antagonism of certain strong adherents of President Andrew Jackson, notably Isaac Hill [*q.v.*], then assistant comptroller of the treasury through a recess appointment, and a movement for Mason's dismissal was initiated; but President Nicholas Biddle [*q.v.*] of the Bank refused to listen to the partisan protests of the Jacksonians and reappointed Mason.

He removed in 1832 to Boston, where he practised actively for six years, accumulating a considerable fortune. He retired at the age of seventy. Mason was of unusual stature, being six feet, six inches in height. His stooped shoulders, awkward manner, and slow movements made him appear sluggish, and his handsome face, except for his piercing and vigilant eyes, was not immediately impressive. In the courtroom, however, he was transformed. His homely phrases and provincial pronunciation, to a large extent deliberately adopted, caught the attention of the jury, and he held them by the clearness and sincerity of his arguments. He had a gift for cross-examination, and was a master of sarcasm. It has been said of him that "no other man ever tried so many cases and lost so few, in proportion to the whole number that he tried" (Hillard, *post,* 1917 ed., p. 368). The testimony of Webster, Choate, and Joseph Story [*q.v.*] bears evidence to the energy and sagacity of his mind and places him among the greatest lawyers of his time. In character he was generous, high-minded, scrupulously honest, and deeply religious. Retaining his intellectual powers almost to the last, he died in his eighty-first year and was buried in Mount Auburn Cemetery. His wife survived him by almost ten years.

[*Memoir, Autobiography and Correspondence of Jeremiah Mason* (1873), ed. by G. S. Hillard, repr. in 1917, with notes and additions by G. J. Clark; J. C. Gray, in W. D. Lewis, *Great Am. Lawyers,* vol. III (1907); C. H. Hill, in *Am. Law Rev.,* Jan. 1878; A. P. Stokes, *Memorials of Eminent Yale Men* (2 vols., 1914); F. B. Dexter, *Biog. Sketches Grads. Yale Coll.,* vol. IV (1907); *Boston Transcript,* Oct. 16, 1848; references to Mason in biographies of Webster and Choate, esp. J. B. McMaster, *Daniel Webster* (1902); C. M. Fuess, *Daniel Webster* (2 vols., 1930); Joseph Neilson, *Memories of Rufus Choate* (1884); C. M. Fuess, *Rufus Choate* (1928).]

C. M. F.

MASON, JOHN (*c.* 1600–Jan. 30, 1672), colonial soldier and magistrate, was born in England and saw service in the Low Countries. Coming to Massachusetts before July 2, 1633, he was soon made captain of militia for Dorchester (*Records of the Governor and Company of the Massachusetts Bay Colony,* vol. I, 1853, pp. 106, 110), and was one of the leaders in the migration thence in 1635 to found Windsor on the Connecticut (*Massachusetts Historical Society Collections,* 2 ser. IX, 154 and note; 4 ser. VII, 411).

In the ensuing Indian troubles Mason won his chief claim to distinction. The powerful Pequots had been latently hostile to the colonists for some time when, in the autumn of 1636, open strife was precipitated by a fruitless expedition sent against them by Massachusetts. Their outrages then became so flagrant that in May 1637 the Connecticut authorities were obliged to take the offensive (Orr, *post,* p. 19). Mason was dispatched with eighty white men and one hundred Indian auxiliaries led by Uncas [*q.v.*] to invade the heart of Sassacus' domain. At Saybrook Fort, Capt. John Underhill [*q.v.*] joined him with nineteen Massachusetts men, who relieved twenty of the original company for home defense (*Ibid.,* p. 20). According to his commission Mason was to proceed by water to Pequot River (now the Thames) and begin operations directly. Disregarding these instructions, he boldly decided upon the more strategic course of going first to Narragansett Bay and then marching overland to strike where he would be less expected. This plan was followed with great success. After a brief delay among the Narragansetts, who provided a large addition to his native cohorts, he advanced toward the enemy's stronghold near the Mystic River. By a combination of good judgment and good fortune he took the Pequots completely by surprise. Attacking their fort before dawn, his soldiers effected an entrance from two sides almost unopposed. The slaughter began with musket and sword; but Mason, to bring a more speedy termination to the battle, fired the wigwams and gave orders to encircle the place and cut down any who tried to escape. The number killed, including women and children, was probably six or seven hundred (*Ibid.,* pp. 21–31). The power of the Pequots was broken. All that remained was to accept the submission of those who yielded and to hunt down the few that fled. In this work Mason cooperated with the Massachusetts troops under Capt. Israel Stoughton (*Ibid.,* pp. 34–40).

After the war Mason was promoted to the rank of major. On Oct. 2, 1656, at a meeting of the General Court, he was requested to write a history of the Pequot War. It was printed without the preface in *A Relation of the Troubles that Have Hapned in New England* . . . (1677), by Increase Mather, who was apparently unaware that Mason was the author, and was reprinted with an introductory sketch of Mason's life by Rev. Thomas Prince, under the title *A Brief History of the Pequot War,* in 1736. For over thirty years after 1637 Mason took a prominent part in Connecticut affairs. He served as deputy, 1637–42; magistrate, 1642–60; deputy governor, 1660–69; and assistant, 1669–72. During most of the period he was chief military officer of the colony, and handled Indian relations both for it and for the New England Confederation. In 1660 he was one of the founders of Norwich, where he spent the last twelve years of his life. His first wife died in Windsor, prior to Mar. 16, 1638, leaving a daughter, and in July 1639 he married Anne Peck. He left seven children by his second wife.

[The four classical contemporary histories of the Pequot War are Mason's, John Underhill's *Nevves from America* (1638), Philip Vincent's *A True Relation of the Late Battell Fought in New-England Between the English and the Pequet Salvages* (1638), and "Leift Lion Gardener his Relation of the Pequot Warres," first printed in *Mass. Hist. Soc. Colls.,* 3 ser. III; these have been collected in a single volume by Charles Orr under the title, *Hist. of the Pequot War* (1897). An important variant of Mason's account appears in William Hubbard's *A Narrative of the Troubles with the Indians in New England* . . . (1677). See also *Records of the Colony of New Plymouth in New England,* vols. IX, X (1859), ed. by D. Pulsifer; William Bradford, *Hist. of Plymouth Plantation* (2 vols., 1912), ed. by W. C. Ford; *Winthrop's Journal* (2 vols., 1908), ed. by J. K. Hosmer; "Winthrop Papers," in *Mass. Hist. Soc. Colls.,* 4 ser. VI, VII (1863–65), 5 ser. I, VIII (1871, 1882); biog. of Mason by George Ellis in Jared Sparks, *Library of Am. Biog.,* 2 ser. III (1844); H. R. Stiles, *The Hist. and Geneals. of Ancient Windsor, Conn.,* vol. II (1894); F. M. Caulkins, *Hist. of Norwich, Conn.* (1845); *Pub. Records of the Col. of Conn.,* vols. I, II (1850–52); information as to certain facts from L. B. Mason, Esq., New York City.]

G. P. B.

MASON, JOHN (Oct. 28, 1858–Jan. 12, 1919), actor, was born in Orange, N. J., the son of Daniel Gregory and Susan W. (Belcher) Mason, and grandson of Lowell Mason [*q.v.*], the musician and teacher. His full name was John Hill Belcher Mason. He lived and studied for a time during his youth in Germany, and upon his return to the United States attended Columbia University (1876–77) but did not graduate. His beginnings on the stage were in the acting of small parts in Philadelphia, New York, and other cities, including a tour as a singing actor with Maggie Mitchell, but his first distinctive engagement was at the Boston Museum, where he made his début as a member of its stock company in the rôle of Careless in *The School for*

Scandal on Aug. 25, 1879. He remained there, with a few intermissions, for more than ten years and gradually rose from general utility parts to the position of leading man, succeeding to many of the principal old comedy rôles and other characters that had been acted by Charles Barron. He appeared in many new plays, including *The English Rose, Sweet Lavender, Harbor Lights,* and *Held by the Enemy,* and in such familiar rôles as Eliot Grey in *Rosedale,* Captain Absolute in *The Rivals,* Young Marlow in *She Stoops to Conquer,* Charles Surface in *The School for Scandal,* Dazzle in *London Assurance,* Littleton Coke in *Old Heads and Young Hearts,* Zekiel Homespun in *The Heir at Law,* and Harry Dornton in *The Road to Ruin.* During the interruptions to these seasons at the Boston Museum, he played the Duc de Villafour in Steele MacKaye's *Dakolar* on the opening night at the Lyceum Theatre in New York in April 1885, and for a time he acted in support of Nat Goodwin.

After his engagement at the Boston Museum had ended, Mason went to London and in February 1891 he played the American character of Simeon Strong in *The Idler* with George Alexander at the St. James's Theatre. He starred for a time in comic opera and in plays with Marion Manola, and in a later London engagement in 1895 he played Colonel Moberly in E. S. Willard's production of Augustus Thomas' *Alabama.* He became in his middle age an extremely accomplished and finished actor, his skill at impersonation increasing notably with the passing years. He won wide-spread praise for his acting of Horatio Drake in *The Christian,* following that with a series of important characters in Daniel Frohman's Lyceum Theatre company, and later appearing successively in support of Elsie DeWolfe, Annie Russell, and Mrs. Fiske. He won new laurels for his acting with Mrs. Fiske as Rawdon Crawley in *Becky Sharp,* Eilert Lovborg in *Hedda Gabler,* John Karslake in *The New York Idea,* and Paul Sylvaine in *Leah Kleschna.* Beginning in 1907, he acted Jack Brookfield in Augustus Thomas' drama, *The Witching Hour,* more than a thousand times, and he had no less success some years later as Dr. Seelig in the same playwright's *As a Man Thinks.* Among the plays in which he appeared during his final years on the stage were *Liberty Hall, The Attack,* and *Big Jim Garrity.* After the first performance of *The Woman in Room 13* he was stricken suddenly and died at Stamford, Conn. Mason was an actor of exceptional native and acquired ability, with an assurance and a poise that were especially effective in their realization of men of distinction. He was, says Augustus Thomas, "one of the best actors that America has ever produced. . . . His power lay in his great self possession and a wonderful sense of time. . . . His voice was deep and resonant, modulated and trained. . . . He never showed a consciousness of his audience" (*The Print of My Remembrance,* pp. 444–45). His first wife was Marion Manola, from whom he was divorced. His second wife was Katharine Grey, who survived him.

[Augustus Thomas, *The Print of My Remembrance* (1922); J. B. Clapp and E. F. Edgett, *Players of the Present* (1900); Kate Ryan, *Old Boston Museum Days* (1915); Dixie Hines and H. P. Hanaford, *Who's Who in Music and Drama,* 1914; *Who's Who in America,* 1918–19; Wm. L. Mason, *A Record of the Descendants of Robt. Mason* (1891); interview in *N. Y. Dramatic Mirror,* Apr. 16, 1898; *Boston Herald,* Mar. 10, 1912; obituary in the *Morning Telegraph* (N. Y.), Jan. 13, 1919; *Boston Globe,* Jan. 19, 1919; Walter Browne and E. De Roy Koch, *Who's Who on the Stage,* 1908.]

E. F. E.

MASON, JOHN MITCHELL (Mar. 19, 1770–Dec. 26, 1829), clergyman and educator, was born in New York City, the second child of Rev. John Mason and Catharine (Van Wyck) Mason. In 1761 his father had been sent by the Associate Synod of Scotland to be pastor of the Scotch Presbyterian church on Cedar Street. He was a man of vigorous mind and notable scholarship, and he gave his son most of the boy's earlier education. At Columbia College, from which the younger John graduated in 1789, he revealed a versatile and profound mind. His theological training was received from his father and at the University of Edinburgh, from which he graduated in 1792. A tribute to his nascent reputation was the call he received to become successor to his father shortly after the latter's death in that same year. He was licensed to preach on Oct. 18 and in April 1793 was ordained and installed as pastor. Five years later he published *Letters on Frequent Communion,* a successful appeal to his denomination, the Associate Reformed Church of North America, to observe the Lord's Supper oftener and more simply. Early feeling the need for elevating the educational standards of the American ministry, after some years' thought he outlined a plan for establishing a theological seminary. In 1804 it was opened in New York with Mason as its first professor. It was the forerunner of Union Theological Seminary. To obtain a library for it he had spent more than a year in Great Britain, where he gathered about 3,000 volumes. The intellectual quality of his addresses abroad made a deep impression on the British public. Several printings were required to meet the demand for his sermons, *Living Faith* (1801) and *Messiah's Throne* (n.d.).

In 1806 he founded *The Christian's Magazine,* and for several years he wrote much of its contents, which were mainly polemic. One of his most notable publications was the indirect result of a change in pastorates. In 1810 he resigned his first charge for the purpose of forming a new congregation, which in 1812, as Murray Street Church, occupied its new edifice. In the interim his people had worshipped in the Cedar Street Presbyterian Church, and had joined with its congregation in the communion service. Though the General Synod declined to censure him for this departure from denominational regularity, criticism was general and severe. He responded in 1816 with *A Plea for Sacramental Communion on Catholic Principles,* a book which produced keen interest in America and abroad.

From 1795 until 1811, and from 1812 to 1824, he was a trustee of Columbia College. In 1809 he became a member of a committee on raising the standards for college admission, and spent much time on the problems involved. The trustees in 1811 adopted a final report, providing for a new curriculum. The same year the office of provost was created, and Mason was elected thereto. His duties were to exercise "the like general superintendence with the president" (*An Historical Sketch of Columbia College,* 1876, p. 54), to occupy the president's position in the latter's absence, and to teach classics to the senior class. The office evidently was created specially for his occupancy. His work on the committee and as provost definitely enhanced the reputation of the college.

Ill health caused his resignation as provost on July 11, 1816; even his strong physique could not long endure the strain of his many duties in college, seminary, church, and public affairs. Despite several rest periods, during one of which he spent four months in Europe, his vigor was so evidently impaired that in 1821 he resigned his other positions in New York and, hoping that change of climate and responsibilities would benefit him, accepted the presidency of Dickinson College, Carlisle, Pa. His health failed to rally, however, and in 1824 he returned to New York, where, in moderate physical health, he remained until his death. While at Carlisle, in 1822, he left the Associate Reformed Church and became a member of the Presbyterian Presbytery of New York. At his best period he nad no superior in America as a preacher (C. F. Himes, *A Sketch of Dickinson College,* 1879, p. 52), and in all the English-speaking world he was "one of the greatest pulpit orators of a period which produced Robert Hall and Thomas Chalmers" (John DeWitt, "The Intellectual Life of Samuel Miller," *Princeton Theological Review,* April 1906, p. 175). He was handsome, with patrician features, graceful gestures and carriage, and had a manner attractive and sympathetic. His quick perceptions, power of rapid analysis, extensive vocabulary, and forceful, original speech gave him command of his hearers both in conversation and in public address. His wife was Ann, only child of Abraham Lefferts of New York, whom he married May 13, 1793. He had five sons and two daughters. *The Complete Works of John M. Mason, D.D.,* edited by his son Ebenezer, was published in four volumes in 1832.

[Jacob Van Vechten, *Memoirs of John M. Mason, D.D., S.T.D.* (1856); W. B. Sprague, *Annals of the Am. Pulpit,* vol. IV (1859); W. D. Snodgrass, *The Victorious Christian Awaiting His Crown* (1830), a memorial sermon; *N. Y. Mercury,* Dec. 30, 1829.]

P. P. F.

MASON, JOHN YOUNG (Apr. 18, 1799–Oct. 3, 1859), congressman, jurist, diplomat, son of Edmunds Mason and Frances Ann (Young) Mason, and grandson of Capt. James Mason of the 15th Virginia line, was a native of Greensville County, Va. Educated at the University of North Carolina (A.B., 1816) and at the law school at Litchfield, Conn., he was admitted to the Virginia bar in 1819 and began the practice of law at Hicksford (Greensville County), but removed to Southampton County in 1822. From 1823 to 1831, he was a member of the General Assembly; in 1830, he represented a Tidewater district in the constitutional convention. In this distinguished assembly, Mason did not participate in the discussions but was an opponent of the extension of the suffrage and of the establishment of the white basis of representation. He served in Congress from Mar. 4, 1831, to Jan. 11, 1837, and during his congressional career was a supporter of the Jacksonian measures, with the exception of the "force bill." He refused to vote for the rechartering of the National Bank, even at the request of the Virginia General Assembly. As chairman of the House committee of foreign affairs, he advocated naval preparedness in the face of France's dilatory attitude over the spoliation claims, and introduced the bill recognizing the independence of Texas. Resigning from Congress, he held a federal judgeship until his appointment, Mar. 14, 1844, by Tyler as secretary of the navy. He was the only member of Tyler's cabinet retained by Polk, who made him attorney-general. He served from Mar. 4, 1845, to Sept. 9, 1846, when he succeeded Bancroft as secretary of the navy. Under him the naval affairs in the Mexican War were conducted. Though an expansionist, Mason opposed in the cabinet the incorporation of Mexico into the United States and advocated the acceptance of the treaty signed by Nicholas P. Trist with Mexico.

After his retirement from the cabinet, he resumed the practice of law in Richmond. At the same time, he became president of the James River & Kanawha Company, being elected in May 1849. He realized the economic and political importance of a transportation system connecting eastern and western Virginia and urged the rapid extension of the canal to the Ohio. In the meantime, in 1850, he was elected without his solicitation to represent his old constituency in the constitutional convention of 1850–51 and was chosen unanimously by this body as its presiding officer. The *Richmond Whig* for Nov. 6, 1850, said of him: "Fat, ruddy, and fifty-five [*sic*], comes the President of the Convention, a fair, pleasant speaking man, with one of those voices Shakespeare so much commends in women. . . . He has the habit of success. . . . Judge Mason is a very influential man. He is a great Democrat, a transcendental Democrat, passionately fond of the people, but votes against the free basis." Although he voted against the final engrossment of the constitution, after its adoption by the convention, he expressed the hope that the new constitution would allay sectional strife and promote a cordial feeling among the people. He was a member of the Democratic state central committee in the presidential contest of 1852 and urged the South "to cherish and defend Northern men like Pierce who had risked so much for the maintenance of Southern rights and honor" (*Richmond Enquirer,* Oct. 9, 1852). From Oct. 24, 1853, until his sudden death from apoplexy in 1859 he was envoy extraordinary and minister plenipotentiary to France. His career as a diplomat was inglorious, though with Buchanan and Soulé he signed on Oct. 18, 1854, the Ostend Manifesto. Courteous, generous, and popular, Mason was a loyal Virginian, devoted to the institutions and to the social and political ideas of the state. He married Mary Anne Fort, Aug. 9, 1821, and was the father of eight children.

[S. F. Bemis, *The Am. Secretaries of State and Their Diplomacy,* vols. V and VI (1928); Kemp P. Battle, *Hist. of the Univ. of N. C.,* vol. I (1907); *Jour., Acts and Proc. of a Gen. Convention, of the State of Va.* (1850); E. I. McCormac, *James K. Polk, A Pol. Biog.* (1922); *Proc. and Debates of the Va. State Convention of 1829–30* (1830); annual reports of the James River and Kanawha Company, 1850–54; *Richmond Enquirer,* Oct. 9, 1852, Mar. 30, 1853, Oct. 17, 18, 1859; Justin H. Smith, *The War with Mexico* (2 vols., 1919); L. G. Tyler, *Letters and Times of the Tylers,* vol. II (1884); A. A. Ettinger, *The Mission to Spain of Pierre Soulé, 1853–55* (1932); M. B. Field, *Memories of Many Men* (1874); information as to certain facts from Mason's grand-daughter, Miss Mary Mason Heath, Washington, D. C.]

W. G. B.

MASON, JONATHAN (Sept. 12, 1756–Nov. 1, 1831), United States senator from Massachusetts, was born at Boston, Mass., the son of Jonathan and Miriam (Clark) Mason. His father was a prominent merchant, a Son of Liberty, a deacon of the Old South Church, a selectman of the town of Boston (1769–71), and one of the witnesses of the Boston Massacre. Mason attended the South Grammar or Latin School, but unlike most of his schoolmates he went to the College of New Jersey (now Princeton) instead of to Harvard for his higher education. He received the degree of A.B. in 1774 and then read law with John Adams and in the office of Josiah Quincy. On Dec. 3, 1779, he was admitted to the bar of Suffolk County, and in 1780 he delivered the annual oration to commemorate the Boston Massacre. From 1786 to 1796 he was a member of the Massachusetts House of Representatives; in 1797 and 1798, a member of the Executive Council; and in 1799 and 1800, state senator. When Benjamin Goodhue [*q.v.*], United States senator from Massachusetts, resigned from office in 1800, Mason was chosen to fill his place and served in that capacity from Nov. 14, 1800, until March 1803. Though not a member of the Essex Junto, he was a strong Federalist; his career as senator was notable chiefly because of the part he took in the debates on the repeal of the Judiciary Act of 1801. Returning to Boston in 1803 he resumed the practice of the law, was elected to the state Senate for the year 1803–04 and to the Massachusetts House of Representatives 1805–08. At a special town meeting at Boston, Aug. 9, 1808, he moved that President Jefferson be requested to remove the Embargo, and the motion was carried.

After this time he "refused every office of every kind" and rarely even talked politics (Letter to Wilson C. Nicholas, Nov. 26, 1814, in *Massachusetts Historical Society Collections,* 7 ser. I, 1900, p. 214). Nevertheless he was elected to the Fifteenth and Sixteenth congresses, serving from March 1817 until his resignation in May 1820. Like all orthodox Federalists of his time he took a very gloomy view of the political situation, and in the letter cited above he predicted: "We shall not be destroyed today or tomorrow, but it will come, and the end of these measures will be disunion and disgrace" (p. 220).

Besides his law practice, Mason was interested to a considerable extent in Boston real estate. He and Harrison Gray Otis, Joseph Woodward [*qq.v.*], and Charles Ward Apthorp formed the syndicate which bought the southwestern slope of Beacon Hill in 1795 and turned it into the fashionable residential district of the town. A later venture, probably not so successful, was the development of Dorchester by the South Boston Association, of which Mason was a prominent member. He was also a director of the Boston branch of the United States Bank. In 1779 he married Susannah, daughter of William Powell of Boston. They had two sons and four daughters, one of whom married the elder John Collins Warren [*q.v.*]. Mason died at Boston and was buried in Mount Auburn Cemetery, Cambridge. A portrait of him painted by Gilbert Stuart in 1805 shows a face of striking intelligence and good breeding.

[Biographical sketches have often confused Mason with his father, who bore the same name. For date of birth see *A Report of the Record Commissioners of Boston*, 1894, p. 289, and *Columbian Centinel*, Nov. 5, 1831. There are frequent glimpses of him in S. E. Morison, *The Life and Letters of Harrison Gray Otis, Federalist* (1913). His diary of a journey to Savannah in 1804–05 is printed in *Proc. Mass. Hist. Soc.*, 2 ser. II (1886); his Boston Massacre oration is in *Orations Delivered . . . to Commemorate the Evening of the Fifth of March, 1770* (1785). See also J. S. Loring, *The Hundred Boston Orators* (2nd ed., 1853); C. F. Adams, *Works of John Adams*, IX (1854), 422, 432; *Proc. Mass. Hist. Soc.*, 1 ser. XIX (1882), 152–57, 161–64; H. A. Hill, *Hist. of the Old South Church* (1890), vol. II, *passim*; *New-Eng. Hist. and Geneal. Reg.*, Apr. 1884, pp. 235, 236; Lawrence Park, *Gilbert Stuart* (1926), II, 512, and IV, 321.] L. S. M.

MASON, LOWELL (Jan. 8, 1792–Aug. 11, 1872), musical educator and hymnwriter, was born in Medfield, Mass., the son of Johnson and Catharine (Hartshorn) Mason and a descendant of Robert Mason who emigrated to Salem in 1630. He described himself as "a wayward, unpromising boy" (Seward, *post*, p. 4). His father, besides being a manufacturer of straw goods and a member of the state legislature, was a good 'cellist, and his son, beginning at an early age, learned to play on "all manner of musical instruments that came within his reach" (Thayer, in *Dwight's Journal*, Nov. 22, 1879). At twenty he went as a bank clerk to Savannah, Ga. He had already been leading a church choir in his native town, and in Savannah he taught singing and played a church organ. With F. L. Abel, a teacher of harmony, he made a collection of psalm tunes based upon William Gardiner's *Sacred Melodies*. The Handel and Haydn Society of Boston sponsored the publication of the work and at Mason's request, because he did not wish to be known as a musician, issued it as the work of the Society. It was published in 1822 under the title: *The Boston Handel and Haydn Society's Collection of Church Music*. Republished in many later editions, it proved astonishingly profitable both to Mason and to the Society.

Mason remained in Savannah until 1827, when he was invited to take charge of the music for six months, successively, at three Boston churches. He did not carry out the original plan, but he became definitely connected with the musical life of Boston. After serving for five years (1827–32) as president of the Handel and Haydn Society he organized in 1833 the Boston Academy of Music which established a music school and promoted the introduction of music instruction in the public schools. The Academy's normal class for teachers was the origin of the musical "convention," an institution which, under the leadership of Mason and George J. Webb, spread from Boston to New England and farther west. At these gatherings, which offered a variety of musical activity, musical and pedagogical training was offered to adults.

In developing a system of instruction for children, used at the Academy, Mason had taken up a study of Pestalozzian methods and developed his system in accordance with its principles. Thus his *Manual of Instruction* (1834) emphasized the teaching of singing prior to the teaching of symbols—"the thing before the sign." He was aided in his efforts to introduce music training into the public schools by Samuel Atkins Eliot [*q.v.*], first president of the Academy and a member of the Boston School committee. In 1837, after Mason had visited Pestalozzi in Zurich and had made a study of teaching methods abroad, he was permitted to teach music in one of the Boston schools, but he was obliged to conduct his classes without pay and to supply his own materials. His efforts met with the approval of the school authorities and in 1838 he was appointed to teach in all of the Boston schools. This work he continued until 1841, when he left to devote himself to music conventions. In 1851 he moved to New York City. After 1854 he lived in Orange, N. J., where he died in 1872. He had married, in 1817, Abigail Gregory of Westboro, Mass. They had four sons: William and Henry [*qq.v.*], pianist and piano manufacturer, respectively, and Daniel Gregory and Lowell Mason, Jr., music publishers. In the last years of his life Mason continued his musical activities and devoted himself to the enlargement of his library, the nucleus of which was the musical library of Johann Rinck, the German organist, which Mason had purchased in 1852. In its entirety Mason's collection comprised over eight thousand printed works and several hundred manuscripts. It included some seven hundred volumes in hymnology and valuable sixteenth and seventeenth century works in theory, some of which were rare first editions. After Mason's death the library was presented to Yale College.

Mason was not a great composer. Many of his tunes were adaptations of melodies from Händel, Haydn, and Mozart, and from earlier church music, but they came to replace the "fugue tune" of the earlier nineteenth century and gained great popularity throughout the United States. Beginning with the Handel and Haydn collection, Mason published more than fifty books of tunes, sacred and secular. His chief works, aside from the first collection, are: *The Juvenile Psalmist* (1829); *The Juvenile Lyre* (1830); *Lyra Sacra* (1832); *Boston Academy's Collection of Church Music* (1835); *Sabbath-School Songs* (1836); *Boston Anthem Book* (1839); *The Psaltery* (1845); *Cantica Laudis* (1850); *The New Carmina Sacra* (1850); and *The Song Garden* (3 parts, 1864–65). Among his best-known tunes are the "Missionary Hymn" ("From Greenland's Icy Mountains"); "Olivet" ("My Faith Looks up to Thee"); and "Bethany" ("Nearer, My God, to Thee"). It has been well said (C. A. and M. R. Beard, *The Rise of American Civilization*, 1927, I, p. 801): "A compiler of church music, an organizer of choral societies . . . and an originator of conventions for the training of music instructors in the public schools, Mason impressed himself indelibly on the democracy of his times."

[T. F. Seward, *The Educ. Work of Dr. Lowell Mason* (n.d.), with bibliography of Mason's works; F. J. Metcalf, *Am. Writers and Compilers of Sacred Music* (1925); Wm. Mason, *Memories of a Musical Life* (1901), especially App., pt. 1; C. C. Perkins and J. S. Dwight, *Hist. of the Handel and Haydn Soc. of Boston, Mass.*, vol. I (1883); Wm. L. Mason, *A Record of the Descendants of Robt. Mason* (1891); *Dwight's Jour. of Music*, Nov. 22, Dec. 6, 1879; *Music*, Feb. 1892, Sept. 1893, and Feb., Apr. 1896; *New Music Rev.*, Nov., Dec. 1910, Jan. 1911, Jan. 1927; *Musician*, Nov. 1911; *Etude*, Mar. 1910; "The Rise and Fall of the Fugue-Tune in America." *Musical Quart.*, Apr. 1930; the *N. Y. Times*, Aug. 13, 1872.] F. H. M.

MASON, LUTHER WHITING (Apr. 3, 1828–July 14, 1896), musical educator and teacher, was born in Turner, Me., the son of Willard and Mary (Whiting) Mason. His father died in 1834 and the boy was apprenticed to his step-brother to learn the trade of last-making. At the same time he studied Greek, Latin, and music. He gave up his plan of becoming a missionary in favor of a career as a musician. He was practically self-taught in music, having acquired his knowledge, in part, by teaching his pupils. His talent as an instructor was such, however, that at the age of twenty-five he was superintendent of music in the Louisville, Ky., schools. Some years later, in Cincinnati, where he filled the same office, he prepared the "National System" of music-charts and books, the success of which established his fame in the school-music field. Called to Boston in 1865, he settled there and, as supervisor of music, improved musical instruction in the primary schools of the city.

In the late seventies, when experts in education were invited by the Japanese government to bring Western ideas into Japan, Mason was asked to organize music education in the Japanese schools. He went to Japan and introduced a modification of his music system in the public schools, as well as establishing a school of music with an orchestra that played both Japanese and European music. As governmental music supervisor he procured the introduction of the diatonic scale, and was so successful in his educational efforts that Western school music in general in Japan came to bear his name. He also gave piano lessons in the homes of the Japanese nobility, and taught singing to Kalakaua, King of Hawaii, who was visiting in Japan at the time. When Mason left Japan in 1882 after three years, the University of Tokyo, which had opened its doors in 1877, bestowed its first doctor's degree to be awarded a musician upon him. Returning to Boston with the increased reputation gained by his successful educational adventure in the Far East he compiled, in collaboration with George A. Veazie, Jr., *The National Music Course* (4 vols., 1887–97). His studies in Germany made in connection with this work, led him, with the approval of the faculty of the University of Leipzig, to issue it in a German version. Mason died in Buckfield, Me., at the age of sixty-eight.

[W. S. B. Mathews, "Luther W. Mason and School Music," *Music*, Sept. 1892; *The Mason Testimonial: Addresses at the Reception of Luther Whiting Mason, Dec. 3, 1879*; *Lewiston Evening Jour.* (Lewiston, Me.), July 15, 1896.] F. H. M.

MASON, OTIS TUFTON (Apr. 10, 1838–Nov. 5, 1908), ethnologist, was born in Eastport, Me. At the time of his birth his parents, John and Rachel Thompson (Lincoln) Mason, were affected by business reverses, and for a while could give few opportunities for education to their children. During Otis' boyhood they moved to Philadelphia, then to Haddonfield, N. J. Here the boy, with able teachers, laid the foundation for his future activities. Removing again, to Woodlawn, Va., in 1851, Mason in his later teens had the opportunity to enter Columbian College (now George Washington University), where he graduated in 1861. In the next year he became principal of its preparatory school, and taught there for more than twenty years. Meantime he became interested in ethnology and in 1872 was appointed collaborator in ethnology in the Smithsonian Institution. In 1884 he gave up his teaching to become curator of ethnology in the Smithsonian, and from that time, for the rest of his life, he devoted his attention to the classification and regulation of the newly founded National Museum. He was one of the leaders in American museum science, his disciplined mind and gospel of hard work carrying him far. In 1902 he became head curator of anthropology.

His proficiency in all branches of anthropological science is evident in his publications, which cover a great variety of subjects. The history of human culture—especially the technological aspect, concerned with the tangible evidence of man's progress—was his specialty, and the elucidation of aboriginal technology is regarded as his most valuable contribution to his science. Noteworthy papers in this field include: "Basket-work of the North American Aborigines," *Report of the United States National Museum, 1884* (1885), greatly elaborated in "Aboriginal American Basketry: Studies in a Textile Art without Machinery," *Ibid., 1902* (1904); "Cradles of the North American Aborigines," *Ibid., 1887* (1889); "Aboriginal Skin Dressing," *Ibid., 1889* (1891); "The Ulu, or Woman's Knife, of the Eskimo," *Ibid., 1890* (1891); "The Man's Knife Among the North American Indians," *Ibid., 1897* (1899); "Aboriginal American Harpoons," *Ibid., 1900* (1902); and "North American Bows, Arrows, and Quivers," *Annual Report of the . . . Smithsonian Institution . . . 1893* (1894). Always with the idea of instructing in the background, his papers conveyed a message in an intelligible, even a literary form, thus reaching a wide audience. Papers of broader scope are: "What is Anthropology?," in *The Saturday Lectures Delivered in the Lecture Room of the United States National Museum* (1882); "Resemblances in Arts Widely Separated," *American Naturalist* (March 1886); "The Birth of Invention," *Annual Report of the . . . Smithsonian Institution . . . 1892* (1893); "Technogeography, or the Relation of the Earth to the Industries of Mankind," *American Anthropologist* (April 1894); "Mind and Matter in Culture," *Ibid.*, (April–June 1908). Mason was also the author of two books of popular science: *Woman's Share in Primitive Culture* (1894) and *The Origin of Inventions* (London, 1895). In 1879 he was one of the founders of the Anthropological Society of Washington and for years contributed to its organ, the *American Anthropologist*. For many years he was anthropological editor of the *American Naturalist* and the *Standard Dictionary*. His knowledge of American Indian nomenclature gave him a place on the United States Board of Geographic Names, in which connection he served for eighteen years. Mason had pleasant features and a most attractive manner, which inspired confidence. In 1862 he married Sarah E. Henderson. He died in Washington, D. C.

[Walter Hough in *Am. Anthropologist*, Oct.–Dec. 1908; Aleš Hrdlička, in *Science*, Nov. 27, 1908; *Popular Science Mo.*, Jan. 1909; *Who's Who in America*, 1908–09; *Evening Star* (Washington), Nov. 5, 1908.]

W. H.

MASON, RICHARD BARNES (Jan. 16, 1797–July 25, 1850), soldier, first military and civil governor of California, was born in Fairfax County, Va., in the environs of Mt. Vernon. He was the son of George Mason VI by his second wife, Eleanor Patton, and a great-grandson of George Mason [*q.v.*] of "Gunston Hall." The boy was carefully educated, principally by tutor. On Sept. 2, 1817, he was commissioned a second lieutenant in the 8th Infantry of the regular army. Owing to the temporarily rapid promotion in that branch of the service, he was immediately advanced to the grade of first lieutenant, and on July 31, 1819, was made a captain of the 1st Infantry, which participated in the Black Hawk War. In the same regiment with Zachary Taylor, he took part in the successful battle of the Bad Axe, Aug. 2, 1832. Two days after Congress created the First Dragoons on Mar. 2, 1833, he was elected as its major, a distinction heightened by the fact that the unit later became the first regiment of Cavalry in the United States army. He rose to be its lieutenant-colonel on July 4, 1836, and its colonel on June 30, 1846. When Gen. Stephen Watts Kearny, who had just commanded the regiment, went on his memorable conquest of New Mexico and California at the outset of the War with Mexico, he took Mason and some of the dragoons with him. They reached and occupied Los Angeles in January 1847. Shortly thereafter, when Kearny was called to other fields, Mason again relieved him and became the military commander of that region, authorized to establish temporary civil government in California.

Although Mason understood the supreme power of the province to be vested in himself, he assumed a conservative attitude and continued the alcalde. In view of the situation, he decided that it would be unwise to establish a government on the old Mexican basis. Accordingly he and his staff prepared a code of laws "for the better government of California." But on the news that Mexico had ceded the territory to the United States, Mason felt that the responsibility for its government had shifted to Congress and withheld the distribution of the code. Meanwhile, lacking a uniform and understood law, the settlers chafed and became restless. The discovery of gold in 1848, with its consequent influx of "forty-niners," made the situation more tense. Mason delayed in providing standard laws in the faith that Congress would act, but in neither the session of 1848 nor that of 1849 was any measure taken. As a consequence the citizens began to take the initiative to the extent of forming the Legislative Assembly of San Francisco. At this juncture Brig.-Gen. Persifor F. Smith relieved Mason as military commander, and in April 1849, Brig.-Gen. Bennet Riley relieved him as acting-governor of California.

Though Mason had given painstaking attention to the civil affairs of the territory, he had allowed technical impediments to outweigh emergency needs. Altogether his command, though negative, was constructive. He was brevetted a brigadier-general, May 30, 1848, for meritorious conduct. During his tour of duty he visited with Lieutenant (afterward General) W. T. Sherman the initial operations of the gold collectors in the El Dorado. His report at Monterey, Aug. 17, 1848 (copy in Revere, *post*), remains today the most authentic and descriptive story of the discovery of the gold deposits in California, especially at Sutter's Fort. It was copied in all parts of the world, published everywhere in the newspapers, and distributed in thousands of pamphlets. After his relief in California, Mason returned to the headquarters of the First Dragoons at Jefferson Barracks, Mo., where he died. He was survived by his wife and two daughters.

[R. D. Hunt, *Cal. and Californians* (1926), vol. II; *Ann. Report of the Secretary of War*, Dec. 1, 1848; J. W. Revere, *A Tour of Duty in Cal.* (1849); H. E. Hayden, *Va. Geneals.* (1891); F. E. Stevens, *The Black Hawk War* (1903); W. A. Ganoe, *The Hist. of the U. S. Army* (1924); *Daily Mo. Republican* (St. Louis), July 27, 1850; Old Files Section, Adj.-General's Office, War Department.]

W. A. G.

MASON, SAMUEL (*c.* 1750–July 1803), desperado and river pirate, was born in Virginia and is believed to have been a member of the distinguished Mason family. By one chronicler he is said to have "grown up bad." He served with distinction, however, as a captain in the Ohio County (Va.) militia during the Revolutionary War. Letters and receipts written by him show that he had obtained some schooling. He seems to have married at an early age. After the war he moved with his family to Washington County, in eastern Tennessee, but was soon driven out for petty thieving. He next appeared in Russellville and later in Henderson, Ky., where several acts of outlawry compelled another exodus. During most of the year 1797 he made his home in the once famous Cave-in-Rock, on the Illinois side of the Ohio, and with his two older sons and several other outlaws preyed upon passing boatmen.

About the end of the year he disappeared. He and his band are next heard of as robbers of travelers along the Natchez Trace and of boatmen on the lower Mississippi. Daring and shrewd, he was almost uniformly successful. The fame of his depredations spread throughout the western country, and many efforts were made to capture him. In January 1803, near New Madrid in the present Missouri, Mason, his four sons, a man variously known as Setton, Taylor, or Wells, and the wife and three children of one of the sons were arrested by the Spanish authorities. Examined at length before the local commandant, they were sent under guard to the governor general at New Orleans. Convinced that none of the crimes was committed west of the Mississippi, that official ordered the outlaws turned over to the American officials at Natchez. On the way, Mar. 26, Mason shot the commander of the boat and with the remainder of the party made his escape. In July he was waylaid and killed by Setton and a companion, James May. Bringing in his head in expectation of a reward, they at once came under suspicion. May was identified as a former member of the band and Setton as the notorious Wiley (Little) Harpe, former accomplice and reputed brother of Micajah (Big) Harpe, perhaps the bloodiest ruffian in frontier annals, who in August 1799, after a series of murders in Kentucky and Tennessee, had been killed and decapitated. The hanging of these two outlaws, Feb. 8, 1804, at Old Greenville, Miss., marked the end of Mason's band.

Mason was a large man, described as "fine looking." His manner was agreeable, and his favorite pose was that of an injured innocent diligently seeking the men guilty of the crimes falsely attributed to himself. Unlike Harpe, he was primarily a robber; and he killed only when killing was thought to be essential for safety.

[Otto A. Rothert, *The Outlaws of Cave-in-Rock* (1924), contains an extensive bibliography on Mason, the Harpes, and other desperadoes of the region and period.]

W. J. G.

MASON, STEVENS THOMSON (Dec. 29, 1760–May 10, 1803), United States senator from Virginia, was a member of one of the most distinguished of Colonial families. His original American ancestor, George Mason [*q.v.*], emigrated to Virginia in the seventeenth century. The family established itself in the Northern Neck, acquired considerable property, and named the county of Stafford in memory of the English shire of its origin. Stevens Thomson Mason was a lineal descendant of this emigrant. The son of Thomson Mason [*q.v.*] and his first wife, Mary King Barnes, he was born at "Chippawamsic," Stafford County, was educated at the College of William and Mary, and prepared himself in Virginia for the practice of law. His first real contact with life came when his father, who had reared him with strictness, sent him, during the Yorktown campaign, to General Washington with a tender of his services. He was now little more than twenty years of age, but the General made him an aide on his staff (Kate Mason Rowland, *The Life of George Mason,* 1892, II, pp. 20, 39).

Returning home after this experience, the young man began to take an active interest in politics, and in 1783 served his first term in the House of Delegates, sitting with his father, who was serving his last. After this service in the lower house of the Assembly, he was, in 1787, elected to the state Senate. In 1788 he was a member of the Virginia ratification convention and there sided with his more famous uncle against the adoption of the Constitution. Later in the Assembly he opposed the amendments proposed by Congress on the ground that they were inadequate. In 1794 he was elected to the United States Senate to succeed James Monroe, and at the commencement of his career in that body achieved notoriety by publishing an abstract of the articles of Jay's treaty when its fate was still in the balance. The rules of the Senate forbade such a violation of its secrecy, and the proponents of the treaty were loud in condemnation. Its opponents applauded, as did the Virginia Assembly. There can be no doubt but that Mason's motives were honorable. The strength of his partisan feeling was manifest by the aid and comfort he gave to Thomas Cooper (Dumas Malone, *The Public Life of Thomas Cooper,* 1926, p. 133), James Thomson Callender (*The Writings of Thomas Jefferson,* Monticello Edition, X, 1904, pp. 330–33), and Matthew Lyon (J. B. McMaster, *A History of the People of the United States,* II, 1885, p. 401) when they were prosecuted under the Sedition Act. From this beginning he became a consistent opponent of Federalism and a steady friend of Jefferson and his cause (*The Writings of Thomas Jefferson,* X, 1904, p. 61).

Mason was an able jurist, and his last speech in the Senate, delivered in support of the bill to repeal the Judiciary Act of 1801, shows that he was a debater of no mean powers. He married Mary Elizabeth Armistead of Louisa County and lived at "Raspberry Plain," the country seat in Loudoun County which had been left him by his father (Robert A. Lancaster, *Historic Virginia Homes and Churches,* 1915, pp. 377–78). His two sons, Armistead Thomson and John Thomson, won distinction in public life, the former becoming a United States senator, and the latter secretary of Michigan Territory. His grandson, Stevens Thomson Mason [*q.v.*], was the first governor of the state of Michigan. Mason died in Philadelphia while still a member of the Senate. There is an account of his funeral in that city in the *Aurora* for May 14, 1803. His remains were later reinterred at "Raspberry Plain."

[There are brief sketches of Mason in the *Biog. Dir. Am. Cong.* (1928) and in L. T. Hemans, *Life and Times of Stevens Thomson Mason,* 1920, pp. 13–15. There is a more detailed account in H. B. Grigsby, "Hist. of the Va. Fed. Convention of 1788," *Va. Hist. Soc. Colls.,* n. s. X (1891).] T. P. A.

MASON, STEVENS THOMSON (Oct. 27, 1811–Jan. 4, 1843), first governor of the state of Michigan, was born in Loudoun County, Va., probably at Leesburg, where his father was practising law, the second of the eight children of John Thomson and Elizabeth (Moir) Mason, and a grandson of Stevens Thomson Mason [*q.v.*]. In 1812 the family migrated to Kentucky, settling first at Lexington and later at Owingsville and Mt. Sterling. At one time they were tenants of Henry Clay's "Ashland." John Mason was a brother-in-law of William Taylor Barry and counted Andrew Jackson and Richard Mentor Johnson among his friends. In 1828 Stevens—or Tom, as he was usually called—left Transylvania University and became a grocer's helper, for his father was in financial straits. Two years later President Jackson rescued the sinking fortunes of the family by appointing John Mason secretary of Michigan Territory. Father and son arrived at Detroit together July 18, 1830, but a year later the Secretary resigned and set out for Texas and Mexico, ostensibly on private business but conjecturally on a mission for the President, who promptly named Stevens Thomson Mason to the vacant secretariat. The appointment excited general indignation and protest, for Mason was only nineteen years old. Ignoring the furore, he took the oath of office July 25, 1831, and conducted himself so discreetly that he gained acceptance. He was modest, courteous, and affable, spoke and wrote intelligently, and was precocious in his political sagacity.

During most of the next five years he was acting governor *ex officio.* He seized the leadership of the movement for statehood and vigorously prosecuted the boundary dispute with Ohio, calling out the militia to guard the disputed area. According to the Ordinance of 1787, the northern boundary of Ohio, Indiana, and Illinois should have been a line running east and west from the southern bend of Lake Michigan, but in carving these states out of the Northwest Territory, this stipulation of the Ordinance had been disregarded. Mason's insistence on Michigan's right to the "Toledo strip" was a serious embarrassment to President Jackson and the Democratic party. Congress refused to admit Michigan as a state until the dispute was settled in Ohio's favor, but as compensation the Upper Peninsula was added to the state of Michigan. Mason was elected the first governor of Michigan in 1836 and served two terms. He appointed an able superintendent of public instruction, used his veto to protect the university lands, and proved himself a friend of education. He opposed imprisonment for debt and solitary confinement in the penitentiary, advocated a geological survey, and in general showed an enlightened attitude toward public problems. Unfortunately, he was too inexperienced to perceive the danger lurking in the banking law of 1837 or to negotiate successfully with Eastern bankers for the flotation of $5,200,000 of state bonds. In consequence the state suffered severely from the financial stringency that set in in 1837, and Mason was held accountable for much of the trouble. Declining to run again for governor, he retired in January 1840. At the invitation of his successor, a Whig, he wrote a farewell message to the legislature, which refused to receive it.

Mason had been married Nov. 1, 1838, to Julia Elizabeth Phelps of New York, who with three children survived him. In 1841 he removed to New York, where he practised law until his death in 1843 after a short illness. As the "boy governor" he became a romantic hero in Michigan, and in 1905 his body was reinterred, with fitting ceremony, in Capitol Square, Detroit.

[Mason's private letters 1833–42, his executive correspondence and documents 1831–40, and his father's family correspondence 1831–49 are in the Burton Hist. Coll., Detroit Pub. Lib. L. T. Hemans, *Life and Times of Stevens Thomson Mason* (1920) is the standard work; see the review, *Am. Hist. Rev.*, July 1921. See also: J. V. Campbell, *Outlines of the Political Hist. of Mich.* (1876); "Letters of Hon. S. T. Mason to his father, John T. Mason," *Wm. and Mary Quart.*, July 1908; L. T. Hemans, "Michigan's Debt to Stevens T. Mason" and D. E. Heineman, "The Portraits of Gov. Mason," *Mich. Pioneer and Hist. Soc. Colls.*, vol. XXXV (1907); numerous minor references in same series (see index vols.).]

G. H. G.

MASON, THOMSON (1733–Feb. 26, 1785), Revolutionary patriot, legislator, was born in Prince William County, Va., the third and youngest child of Col. George and Ann (Thomson) Mason. He was eight years younger than his famous brother, George Mason [*q.v.*] of "Gunston Hall." The father met his death by drowning when Thomson was two years old, and George eventually assumed a measure of guardianship over him, helping defray part of the cost of his education. After some preparation under private tutors, Thomson went to England and was admitted to the Middle Temple in 1751. On his return from London he began the practice of law in his native state. He represented Stafford County in the Virginia Assembly from 1758 to 1761 and from 1765 to 1772; Loudoun County, from 1772 to 1774, and from 1777 to 1778. In the last named year he was elected one of the five judges of the general court, but in 1779 he was again in the Assembly as representative from Elizabeth City County. He resigned his seat that year, but his resignation was not accepted. He vacated it, however, by accepting a coroner's commission.

His vigorous defense of American liberties came to a climax in the nine letters of a "British American," which he wrote in the summer of 1774. In the concluding paragraph of the last letter he disclosed his identity. The theme of the letters was that Parliamentary Acts after 1607 were not binding on Virginia, a theme he developed by a copious use of references to English legal and constitutional documents. He suggested that the first Continental Congress be held in a Virginia or Maryland frontier town, where the members would be amply protected by the excellent marksmanship of the frontier riflemen. Throughout all of the letters he cautioned against rash moves and radical tendencies. America was to save England from the madness of her Parliament. Mason's best contribution to the reorganized Virginia government was his leadership in the move to conserve the work of George Rogers Clark [*q.v.*], in the Northwest Campaign. In this connection he was the author and champion of the bill through which the Virginia Assembly organized the Northwest as the County of Illinois.

During the Revolutionary period Virginia claimed the services of an array of lawyers unique in American annals. From the standpoint of legal knowledge and sheer ability, Mason was probably the chief among them. His independence and fearlessness and his unwillingness to sponsor measures merely on the basis of their popularity undoubtedly stood in the way of his political advancement. In 1783 he was again a member of the General Assembly. He advocated the exclusion of Loyalists from citizenship, and sought to regulate the payment of foreign and domestic debts, by canceling interest during the war and allowing for depreciation of the currency. He also opposed granting a permanent fund to Congress, but was willing to grant funds collected by state officers. Any inclination to assume that he benefited from the prestige and echoed the sentiments of his more famous elder brother is dispelled by the poignant appraisal of Jefferson, "T. Mason is a meteor whose path cannot be calculated" (P. L. Ford, *The Writings of Thomas Jefferson,* vol. III, 1894, p. 318). A hint of his political and social philosophy may be derived from a peculiar but emphatic provision in his will for the rearing of his minor children under such conditions that they would not "imbibe more exalted notions of their own importance than I could wish any child of mine to possess."

Mason died when only a few years beyond middle age. He was twice married, first, in 1758 or 1759, to Mary King Barnes; and second, to Elizabeth (Westwood) Wallace. From the earlier of these unions there was born Stevens Thomson Mason [*q.v.*] who achieved greater distinction than his father, though he was probably no more able. It is perhaps worthy of note in view of Thomson Mason's interest in the Northwest, that the grandson of Stevens, also named Stevens Thomson Mason [*q.v.*], was the "boy governor" of Michigan Territory, in its critical years, and the first governor of the state.

[The best account of Mason is to be gathered from the frequent references to him in K. M. Rowland's *Life of George Mason, 1725–1792* (2 vols., 1892); his "British American" letters, IV–IX, are in Peter Force, *Am. Archives*, 4 ser., vol. I (1837); information as to his political activities must be gleaned from *Jours. of the House of Burgesses of Va., 1758–1776* (5 vols., 1905–08); *Jour. of the House of Delegates,* 1777–83, and H. R. McIlwaine, *Legislative Jours. of the Council of Colonial Va.*, vol. III (1919); see also, H. B. Grigsby, *The Hist. of the Va. Federal Convention of 1788,* vol. II (1891); E. A. Jones, *Am. Members of the Inns of Court* (1924).] F. H. H.

MASON, WILLIAM (Sept. 2, 1808–May 21, 1883), inventor, manufacturer, was the son of Amos and Mary (Holdredge) Mason. He was born at Mystic, Conn., but when he was six years old his parents moved to Stonington, where his father cultivated a small farm and worked as a blacksmith. William spent his boyhood helping in his father's shop and going to school occasionally in the winter time. When he was thirteen he began an apprenticeship in the spinning room of a cotton factory at Canterbury, Conn., but three years later entered a cotton-thread factory in Lisbon, Conn. He was here only a year, but in that time he won a reputation as a skilled mechanic by repairing complicated machinery, and, though he was but seventeen years old, his services were requested to start the machinery in a new mill at East Haddam. This mission accomplished, he returned to his first employer, whose machine shop he now entered, and finished his apprenticeship at twenty.

During the succeeding four years, from 1828 to 1832, he engaged in various occupations. Going to New Hartford, near Utica, N. Y., he went to work for a company that failed a few months later. While there, however, he turned his attention to machinery for making diaper cloth, and after going back to Canterbury he designed and built the first power loom in the United States for the manufacture of this material. He next constructed an ingenious loom for weaving damask table cloths. Thereafter, as he told a friend, "I was fooling about for some time painting portraits, making fiddles, and one thing and another" (*Railroad Gazette, post,* p. 341). In 1832 he was surprised to receive an order for some diaper looms, which he proceeded to fill by renting space in a shop in Willimantic, Conn., and having the frames made there. The making of these looms brought him a handsome profit. In 1833 his services were requested in Killingly, Conn., to work on a new device for spinning cotton since known as the ring frame. The device had been patented in 1828 but had ruined the manufacturer who tried to make it of practical use. Mason remodeled and perfected it within two years and brought about its extensive use in the textile industry.

In 1835 he went to Taunton, Mass., to operate the shop of Crocker & Richmond, taking his ring frame machinery with him. The company failed in 1837, but Mason continued as foreman for Leach & Keith, the firm that succeeded it, and concentrated his attention on improvements in cotton machinery. He patented a speeder for cotton roving machines on May 4, 1838, and on Oct. 8, 1840, secured the patent for his greatest invention, the "self-acting mule," for spinning cotton and other fibrous materials. Two years later Leach & Keith failed and Mason purchased the establishment with the aid of a cotton machinery commission house of Boston. The prosperous times which succeeded the tariff of 1842 were favorable to Mason and his business grew rapidly, so that in 1845 he was able to build a new plant. Competition called for improvements on the self-acting mule, and on Oct. 3, 1846, he received a second patent on this device. Gradually he added to the products of his plant and besides cotton and woolen machinery he made tools, cupola furnaces, blowers, gears, shafting, and Campbell printing presses, the methods of manufacture and the machinery used being chiefly of his own invention. In 1852 he began the building of locomotives, the first of which was completed Oct. 11, 1853, and the seven-hundreth, just a week after his death. The Mason locomotives were recognized the world over for their beauty and symmetry of design and for the excellence of their workmanship; they exerted a great influence on locomotive construction in the United States, especially with respect to harmony of the visible outlines. As an outgrowth of locomotive building, Mason began the manufacture of car wheels with tubular spokes, in contradistinction to the "plate" or "disc" wheel generally used. During the Civil War he produced a large quantity of Springfield rifles. Ten years before he died he reorganized his company as the Mason Machine Works and, with the assistance of his sons, directed its affairs until his death. At that time the plant covered ten acres of land; a thousand people were employed; and the firm did more than a million dollars' worth of business annually.

Mason was a founder and first president (1847–57) of the Machinists' National Bank of Taunton, and a director of the Taunton Gas Company. He was interested in art, and found recreation in portrait work and playing the violin. On June 10, 1844, he married Harriet Augusta Metcalf of Cambridge, Mass., and was survived by two sons and a daughter.

[*Railroad Gazette,* June 1, 1883; J. L. Bishop, *A Hist. of Am. Manufactures from 1608 to 1860* (1868), vol. III; *Railway and Locomotive Hist. Soc. Bull.,* no. 15, Nov. 1927; Angus Sinclair, *Development of the Locomotive Engine* (1907); *Taunton and the Machinists' National Bank* (1928); J. D. Van Slyck, *Representatives of New England: Manufacturers* (1879); S. H. Emery, *Hist. of Taunton, Mass.* (1893); Edward Hungerford, *The Story of the Baltimore and Ohio Railroad, 1827–1927* (1928), vol. II; *Report of the Commissioner of Patents,* 1828, 1838, 1840, 1846; *Boston Daily Advertiser,* May 22, 1883; date of birth from tombstone.] C. W. M.

MASON, WILLIAM (Jan. 24, 1829–July 14, 1908), pianist, teacher, and composer, was born in Boston, Mass., the third son of Lowell Mason [*q.v.*] and his wife Abigail Gregory. He evinced his inherited musical talent at an early age. He studied the piano with Henry Schmidt in Boston and made his début as a boy of seventeen at a concert at the Boston Academy of Music on Mar. 7, 1846. In 1849 he went to Germany to complete his studies. In Leipzig he was the pupil of Ignaz Moscheles, Moritz Hauptmann, and Ernst Friedrich Richter; in Prague he took piano lessons of Alexander Dreyschock, and in Weimar (1853–54) he studied with Franz Liszt. It was Liszt who probably exerted the greatest influence on his development, and from whom he largely derived the rich tone-color and variety in expression that marked his playing. While at Weimar Mason associated with Rubinstein, Von Bülow, Klindworth, Pruckner, and other music students, appeared as a concert-pianist in Weimar, Prague, Frankfurt, and London, and returned to America with the prestige attaching to a brilliant young disciple of Liszt.

Upon his return in 1854, he toured the country as a concert-pianist, playing with success in various cities from Boston to Chicago. He then (1855) established himself permanently in New York City where, besides teaching, he devoted much time to public performance, and was the first pianist to introduce the "Hungarian Rhapsodies" and other Liszt compositions to American audiences. He was possibly the first pianist to tour the United States giving piano recitals exclusively; Gottschalk and others always toured with a singer or another instrumentalist. During the winter of 1855–56, with Theodore Thomas, Carl Bergmann, Joseph Mosenthal, and George Matzka, he founded the Mason-Thomas Soirées of Chamber-Music, a series of concerts of high quality which were continued until 1868. At these concerts many notable works, including compositions by Schumann and Brahms, were performed for the first time before American audiences.

After 1868 Mason devoted himself principally to teaching, at which he was very successful. In collaboration with E. S. Hoadly he wrote *A Method for the Pianoforte* (1867) and *A System for Beginners in the Art of Playing Upon the Pianoforte* (1871), and with W. S. B. Mathews he compiled *A System of Technical Exercises for the Pianoforte* (1878). His most widely popular piano textbook, however, was his *Touch and Technic* (*opus* 44), the sum of his more than forty years experience, which Paderewski pronounced the best piano method known to him. It undoubtedly played an important part in stabilizing the piano technique of his day.

Mason wrote about forty pieces for the piano, refined in style and poetically imaginative, among them "Silver Spring" (*opus* 6); the mazurka-caprice "Spring Dawn" (*opus* 20); "Rêverie Poétique" (*opus* 24); "Serenata" (*opus* 39); and "Capriccio Fantastico" (*opus* 50). But his chief importance lies in his work as a teacher. Liszt had praised him for rising above mere finger virtuosity; this higher outlook upon piano playing he sedulously inculcated in his pupils. He was generous in his sympathy and encouragement to young composers, and always a gentleman. He died in his home in New York at the age of seventy-nine. He had married, on Mar. 12, 1857, Mary Isabella Webb, by whom he had three children.

[The principal source of information is Mason's autobiographical *Memories of a Musical Life* (1901). See also: H. C. Lahee, *Famous Pianists of To-Day and Yesterday* (1901); L. C. Elson, *The Hist. of Am. Music* (1925); *Dwight's Jour. of Music,* Sept. 30, 1854; the *N. Y. Musical Gazette,* July 1873; the *Musician,* Sept. 1908; *Musical Observer,* Dec. 1928; *Etude,* Sept. 1908, Nov. 1914; *Musical Courier,* July 22, 1908.]

F. H. M.

MASON, WILLIAM ERNEST (July 7, 1850–June 16, 1921), representative and senator from Illinois, the son of Lewis J. and Nancy (Winslow) Mason, was born at Franklinville, N. Y. When he was eight years old his family took him to Bentonsport, Iowa, where he attended school. Four years of teaching led him to the study of the law, and in 1872 he was admitted to the Illinois bar from Chicago. A relatively short residence in his adopted state gave him some local prominence, and he obtained a seat in the state House of Representatives in 1879 and in the Senate from 1881 to 1885. He served in the Fiftieth and Fifty-first federal congresses from 1887 to 1891. His reputation as a stump speaker was enhanced by a stirring campaign against Bryan in 1896, which resulted in his election to the Senate, where he served from 1897 to 1903, as an avowed opponent of the Lorimer machine that had been dominant in Chicago politics for some time. Sympathy with the downtrodden, possibly inherited from a father who was an ardent abolitionist, led him to champion the Cuban revolt against Spain. It also led him into conflict with the administration, at the moment in a temporizing mood (*Congressional Record,* 55 Cong., 1 Sess., pp. 1130–35). His resolution of Feb. 9, 1898, requested the president to declare and maintain peace in Cuba and was designed to force McKinley into action (*Ibid.,* 2 Sess., pp. 1578–85, 3294–95, 4035). His supporting speech came on the same day that de Lome, the Spanish minister, admitted writing derogatory statements about the president and caused a sensation that placed Mason among the insurgents who flayed executive inaction. With these he demanded intervention coupled with recognition of Cuban independence. Early in 1899 he proposed a resolution "that the Government of the United States of America will not attempt to govern the people of any other country in the world without the consent of the people themselves, or subject them by force to our dominion against their will" (*Ibid.,* 55 Cong., 3 Sess., p. 528). This might be taken as the text of his many speeches and occasional filibusters against the increasingly evident imperialistic trend of the administration and of the country at large. His efforts to prevent the acquisition of the Philippines failed, and, after voting at his constituents' instance for the treaty provisions concerning the islands, he turned his efforts toward obtaining self-government there.

This double defiance of the administration and of the party sent him into retirement. During those years he practised law in Chicago and in 1910 published a religious novel, *John, the Unafraid,* which was an expression of his own faith in the power of revealed religion. In 1917, although he lacked both an organization and money, he was returned to Washington as congressman-at-large. Here he rounded out his career, serving until his death. Again it was his convictions that forced him to oppose American entry into the World War and the selective draft (*Ibid.,* 65 Cong., 1 Sess., pp. 326–28, 1190–93, 3850–55). So bitter was his hostility that he was at one time made the object of a proposed investigation by Senator Heflin (*Ibid.,* pp. 5756–57, 7711–15; *Chicago Tribune,* Sept. 28, Oct. 4, 7, 1917). Cessation of hostilities found him, for once, with his own party, in fighting the League of Nations, but he championed one more lost cause by pleading for the recognition of the Irish republic. On June 11, 1873, he was married to Edith Julia White of Des Moines. At his death one of their daughters was chosen to serve the rest of his unexpired term in the House.

[*Wm. E. Mason, Memorial Addresses Delivered in the House of Representatives* (1924); *Who's Who in America,* 1920–21; *Biog. Dir. of Amer. Cong.* (1928); *Chicago Tribune,* July 11, 1886, Jan. 20, 21, 1897, June 17, 1921.]

L. E. E.

MASQUERIER, LEWIS (b. Mar. 14, 1802), pioneer in phonetic spelling and reformer, was born in Paris, Ky. His father, Lewis Masquerier, a son of French Huguenot parents, and a brother of John James Masquerier, the English painter, was educated in England, emigrated to Java, and during the French revolution returned to England and later went to Haiti. Narrowly escaping a general massacre of whites at Santo Domingo, he took ship for Philadelphia and about 1800 emigrated to Kentucky, where he married Sarah Hicklin. Their son, Lewis, received the meager schooling of a frontier community, read the few books in his father's house, and worked on the farm. As a boy he was more fond of spending his Sundays in the forest than in learning Old Testament stories, which even then shocked his moral sense and his ideas of human rights. After his father died, his mother married again, and in 1818 the family moved to the Boonslick settlement on the Missouri River. Lewis soon returned to Paris, Ky., where he went to work in a printing shop. Ambition to be an orator led him to study law. He was licensed and began practice in Quincy, Ill., but there he discovered that he was too shy to succeed as a trial lawyer and that office work bored him. Neglecting his practice, he indulged a "thirst for promiscuous learning" (*Appendix, post,* p. 29). Meanwhile he made a living by land speculation. Among the subjects that aroused his mental curiosity was phonetic spelling. In 1830 he invented a new alphabet of eleven vowels and twenty-two consonants, and in 1834 he published in St. Louis a pamphlet on the subject. He went to New York to obtain better facilities for popularizing his phonetic system. A special font of letters was cast and specimens of a small dictionary were published, which included a treatise on scientific orthography. In 1867, he published *The Phonotypic Spelling and Reading Manual.* In this field Masquerier was a pioneer, preceding by more than twenty years Smalley in the United States and Ellis in England.

In New York Masquerier's attention was soon diverted by schemes for general social reform. He became one of the first disciples of George Henry Evans [*q.v.*] and, with characteristic disregard of practical considerations, pushed Evans' doctrines of individualism to their logical conclusion, which was anarchism. In lectures, delivered in New York and Boston, and in pamphlets he developed the outlines of an agrarian Utopia. The entire surface of the earth was to be divided into townships six miles square with villages in the geometric centers. The townships were to be subdivided into homesteads of forty acres each. Thus landlordism, rent-paying, and the wage system were to be abolished. Although his ideas attracted no important following, he lived to see the adoption of one principle of agrarianism, the distribution of the public domain to actual settlers, in the Homestead Act of 1862. In his passion for individualism he would have abolished not only organized government but also organized religion, which he regarded as an additional means of enslaving humanity. In 1877 his writings, comprising newspaper articles, pamphlets and poems on phonetics, land reform, and theology, were collected in a volume entitled *Sociology, or the Reconstruction of Society, Government, and Property. An Appendix to Sociology* was published in 1884. About 1840 he married Anna Taber of Bradford, Vt. The date of his death has not been found.

[J. R. Commons, *Hist. of Labor* (1918), vol. I; autobiog. material in *Sociology* (1877), esp. pp. 132–36 and in *Appendix to Sociology* (1884); G. L. Randall, *Taber Geneal.* (copr. 1924), p. 35.] P. W. B.

MASSASSOIT (d. 1661), "great chief," or more properly Ousamequin, "yellow feather," has appeared under many names with great variance in spelling. He was chief of the Wampanoags, making his main home at Pokanoket, or Mount Hope, near Bristol in Rhode Island. Even the approximate date of his birth is unknown but in 1621 he was described as a "very lusty man, in his best years, an able body, grave of countenance, and spare of speech" (Drake, *post,* book II, p. 22). His sway is said to have extended over Cape Cod and all of Massachusetts and Rhode Island between Massachusetts and Narragansett Bays, with somewhat indefinite boundaries westward. Just before the Pilgrims arrived at Plymouth, however, his tribes had been almost decimated by some illness and their strength greatly reduced.

He had already become acquainted with white men. It is likely that he was the "king of the country" whom John Smith met when cruising the New England coast, and Capt. Thomas Dermer was in communication with him in 1619, recovering from him two Frenchmen who had been cast away. On Mar. 22, 1621, Massassoit and his brother Quadequina, with sixty warriors, accompanied Samoset and Squanto to Plymouth and there met the Pilgrims. After the proper preliminaries, and a drink of whiskey that "made him sweat all the while after" (Young, *post,* p. 191), the chief negotiated a treaty of peace and amity with the whites, which he never broke. The following July Edward Winslow and Stephen Hopkins paid him a visit at Pokanoket to forward the relations and spy out his position and strength. They found many skeletons of his followers still lying on the ground, the dead having been so many in the "great sickness" that the living could not bury them. The same year, when John Billington was lost, Massassoit located him with some Indians and returned him to Plymouth. In 1623 he sent word to his new friends that he was very ill if not dying, and Winslow and others went to see him. Owing to their treatment he recovered and disclosed to them the facts of an Indian conspiracy to destroy Weston's plantation (Bradford, *post,* I, 292).

In 1632 the Narragansetts tried to capture him and he fled to Plymouth for protection. Winslow went to see him in 1634 and Massassoit returned to Plymouth with him. He had frightened the Pilgrims by sending word that Winslow was dead and when they both arrived, he explained his act by saying it was an Indian custom to make them more glad of his arrival when he came safely (*Winthrop's Journal,* I, 131). The next year Roger Williams made peace between Massassoit and Canonicus in order to have quiet in Rhode Island. In 1638 Massassoit went to

Boston with eighteen beaver skins, saying he understood the English were provoked with him, and sued for peace. Apparently he had no cause for his anxiety. He again visited Boston in July 1642 with many men and some sagamores and was entertained by Winthrop. Seven years later he sold the site of Duxbury to the English. Some of the earlier histories state that he died in 1656 but it is known from the New Plymouth Colony records that he was alive in or shortly before May 1661 when he complained of an attack by other Indians; a letter of Roger Williams, Dec. 13, 1661, refers to him as deceased (*Publications of the Narragansett Club*, vol. VI, 1874, p. 316). His son Metacomet became famous as King Philip. Always inclined to peace, even among his own race, Massassoit remained a faithful friend to the English throughout his entire life.

[F. W. Hodge, *Handbook of American Indians*, pt. I (1907); S. G. Drake, *The Book of the Indians* (8th ed., 1841); *Winthrop's Journal* (2 vols., 1908), ed. by J. K. Hosmer; William Bradford, *Hist. of Plymouth Plantation, 1620–1647* (2 vols., 1912), ed. by W. C. Ford; Alexander Young, *Chronicles of the Pilgrim Fathers* (1841); David Pulsifer, *Records of the Colony of New Plymouth . . . Acts of the Commissioners of the United Colonies of New England*, II (1859), 268–69.]

J. T. A.

MASSEY, GEORGE BETTON (Nov. 15, 1856–Mar. 29, 1927), physician, born near the village of Massey, Kent County, Md., was the son of Benjamin Hemsley Clinton Massey and a descendant of James Massey who came from Guernsey, Channel Islands, in 1644, to settle in Maryland. Under the instruction of his intellectually gifted mother, Bersheba (Betton) Massey of Tallahassee, Fla., the boy developed a taste for scientific studies, especially physics. After the Civil War he attended an academy at Galena, Md., and later taught school for a year. In 1873 he began his preliminary medical studies at Tallahassee, under the guidance of his maternal uncle, Dr. George W. Betton. He attended the Medical College of South Carolina in 1874, receiving a prize for proficiency in chemistry, and in 1876, before he was twenty years of age, graduated with the degree of M.D. from the University of Pennsylvania, submitting a thesis entitled "Salicylic Acid."

His first experience in private practice was in Tallahassee; but he was soon called to the position of assistant physician in the State Hospital for the Insane at Danville, Pa., where he served for some two years, resigning in 1879 to enter private practice in Philadelphia. For a time he was assistant to Dr. William Goodell of the University of Pennsylvania. Meantime, he continued his studies of nervous disorders in the Orthopedic Hospital and Infirmary for Nervous Diseases, where he became associated with Dr. S. Weir Mitchell [*q.v.*] and his staff. For seven years he was electrical assistant to Mitchell, who was one of the first specialists to advocate the use of electrotherapy, and from 1881 to 1887 he was electrotherapist in the institution, a position created for him. Resigning from the Infirmary in 1887, he was appointed attending physician to the department of diseases of the mind and nervous system in Howard Hospital, but the next year was transferred to the gynecological clinic of that hospital, where he demonstrated electrotherapeutics in the diseases of women until 1898.

When the International Electrical Exposition of the Franklin Institute was held in Philadelphia, in 1884, Massey served on the board of judges. He participated in the affairs of numerous local, state, and national medical societies and of the Pan-American Medical Congress, and represented the United States at the Third International Physiotherapeutic Congress held in Paris in 1910. The American Electro-Therapeutic Association, the first national association of its kind, owed its establishment largely to the stimulus which Massey gave it as a founder and as president in 1891. His zeal for the advancement of electrotherapeutics was further shown by his share in founding the American Oncologic Hospital, in Philadelphia, for the treatment of cancerous affections, with which institution he was connected as attending surgeon from 1904 to 1912. His writings on medical subjects were voluminous; his work as one of the pioneers in the field of electrotherapeutics and his reports and clinical observations therein placed him in the front rank as an investigator and gave him an international reputation. He was one of the editors of *An International System of Electro-therapeutics* (2nd ed., 1901), collaborator in the *American Journal of Electrotherapeutics and Radiology* from 1917, and the author of *Electricity in the Diseases of Women* (1888; 2nd ed. 1890), *Conservative Gynecology and Electro-therapeutics* (1898, 6th ed. 1909), *Ionic Surgery in the Treatment of Cancer* (1910), *Practical Electrotherapeutics and Diathermy* (1924), and joint author with Frederick H. Morse of *Galvanic Currents and Low Voltage Wave Currents in Physical Therapy* (1927). Massey was married, Mar. 25, 1885, to Harriet Louise Stairs of Philadelphia, who with three children survived him. He died in his seventy-first year.

[*A Sketch of the Life of George Betton Massey, M.D.* (4 pp., n.d.), and other family papers in the possession of Massey's daughter, Mrs. George L. Winslow, Pittsburgh, Pa.; records of the School of Medicine, Univ. of Pa.; *Index.-Cat. of the Lib. of the Surgeon-General's Office*, 2 ser. X (1905), 3 ser. VII (1928); *Who's Who in America*, 1926–27; *Jour. Am. Medic. Asso.*, Apr. 16, 1927; *Evening Bulletin* (Phila.), Mar. 30, 1927.]

R. L. B.

MASSEY, JOHN EDWARD (Apr. 2, 1819–Apr. 24, 1901), Baptist clergyman, politician, was born in Spotsylvania County, Va., son of Benjamin and Elizabeth (Chewning) Massey. In 1836, from the old-field school near his home, with his belongings packed in a pillowcase, he journeyed on foot the sixty miles to the Virginia Baptist Seminary, now University of Richmond, for a year's study. Further work in private schools and another year at the Seminary followed, after which he read law while working in his father's shop to pay for his lawbooks. In 1843 he was admitted to the bar. The youngest in a very religious household, however, he had from infancy successfully "exhorted" at revivals, and now men said that he ought to be a preacher. Accordingly, the next year he was licensed, and for eight years thereafter as the Virginia Baptist Association's missionary he energetically carried his message to the people of the heterogeneous Valley region from Winchester to Lexington, meeting considerable success and learning much about the psychology of plain men and the arts of dialectic and side-stepping. He was a pastor in Albemarle and Nelson counties from 1854 to 1862; and then, alleging ill health, he purchased the "Ash Lawn" farm in Albemarle and thither retired with Margaret Ann Kable, his wife since 1847.

He had originally been a Whig, but a trip through New England about 1854 made him a Democrat; by 1860 he was an ardent and argumentative secessionist; and during the Civil War he raised "grain and provender" for the army and bought Confederate bonds. During Reconstruction he was resentful but quiet. Then, after he had passed his fiftieth birthday, he began a career of thirty years as a "champion of the people." Asserting that, through the corrupt collusion of Carpet-baggers, bankers, and brokers, taxes and interest rates had become excessive while the state's schools and charities were neglected and farming languished he declared that the recent "funding act" ought to be undone and the state's enormous debt "readjusted" to the state's diminished capacity to pay. Accordingly, notwithstanding his opposition to ministers' participating in politics, since other capable and trustworthy men were lacking because of the penalties of Reconstruction, he announced himself as a candidate for the legislature. Elected to the House in 1873 and 1875 and to the Senate in 1877, he was ere long dubbed "Father of the Readjuster Movement," through which the various elements of discontent eventually compelled a definite settlement of the debt issue. The movement was strongly disapproved by the "best people," however, and when Massey found his gubernatorial aspirations thwarted and his group being led into the Republican party by William Mahone [*q.v.*], he revolted and aided powerfully in the restoration of a liberalized Democratic régime. His unsuccessful campaign for the place of congressman at large (1882), his election as lieutenant-governor (1885), and his election as superintendent of public instruction (1889) were incidents in this "redemption" of the state. As state auditor under the Readjusters (1879–81), he had rendered important service, though not without an eye to politics; as superintendent he desired that schools for negroes should receive only such taxes as had been paid by negroes for that purpose. Always a temperance advocate, he distinctly aided the local-option movement but vigorously opposed any identification of the anti-liquor agitation with a party. There were many stories reflecting upon his personal financial integrity, but most of these he disproved to the satisfaction of a jury in 1895; and shortly before his death he was elected to the constitutional convention of 1901–02.

Massey's strength lay in the common man's conviction of his honesty and sympathy and in his remarkable skill as a rough-and-tumble debater. Thoroughly understanding the shallower aspects of finance and the deep needs of his people, he was so full of anecdote and Scriptural quotation, so ready at repartee, so self-confident and poised, that few public men could boast of a successful encounter with him. In 1890 he married Mattie E. McCreary of Alabama.

[E. H. Hancock, *Autobiog. of John E. Massey* (1909); Ida B. Patterson, "John E. Massey" (1929), unpublished master's thesis, Univ. of Va.; C. C. Pearson, *The Readjuster Movement in Va.* (1917); *Richmond Dispatch*, Apr. 25, 1901; *Times* (Richmond), Apr. 25, 1901.] C. C. P.

MAST, PHINEAS PRICE (Jan. 3, 1825–Nov. 20, 1898), inventor, manufacturer, was born in Lancaster County, Pa., the son of John and Elizabeth (Trego) Mast. His father, also born in eastern Pennsylvania, was a farmer and school teacher. When young Mast was five years old his parents moved to Ohio and established themselves on a farm near Urbana, where the boy grew to manhood. He helped in the farm work, attended the public schools, and with the assistance of his father prepared for college. When he was twenty years old he entered Ohio Wesleyan University and graduated in 1849, having given especial attention to scientific and Biblical studies. He then returned to his home where he remained for a number of years, teaching school in the neighborhood, assisting his father in the farm work, and devoting his spare time to the grain and stock business. On Jan. 4, 1850, he married Anna M. Kirkpatrick and six years later moved to Springfield, Ohio, where, with capital given him by his wife, he formed a partnership with John H. Thomas, bought the patent rights to the cider-mill invention of T. J. Kindelberger, and began its manufacture.

Within a short time the partners undertook the manufacture of farm implements, their first products being a Buckeye grain drill and a corn plow. Seeing many opportunities for improvements in agricultural machinery, they began developing ideas of their own and within two years began making implements of their own invention, the first one being a seed planter, patented July 27, 1858. This was followed by other inventions, twelve in all, including improved seeding machines, cultivators, and fertilizer distributors. In 1871 Thomas retired from the firm, Mast purchasing his interest and organizing the corporation, P. P. Mast & Company, of which he was president throughout his life. He associated with him men of inventive minds and carried forward his development work. Between 1872 and 1880 a number of patents were issued to him as a co-patentee, and assigned to his company. Most of these were for improvements in grain drills, and all were incorporated in the machines manufactured by his company. About 1880 he became interested in the improvement of lawn mowers and windmills and organized Mast, Foos & Company for the manufacture of these devices with novel features of his own invention. Still later, he purchased the Driscoll Carriage Company and reorganized it as the Mast Buggy Company. At the time of his death he was the directing head of all three concerns.

Mast was also financially interested in the publishing business. In 1879 he organized the firm of Mast, Crowell & Kirkpatrick and began the publication of *Farm and Fireside,* one of the most extensively circulated agricultural journals in the United States; the firm also published the *Woman's Home Companion.* Mast was president of the Springfield National Bank, established Mar. 31, 1882, and took an active part in the municipal affairs of Springfield, serving on the city council for twenty-two years. In 1895 he was mayor of the city. In addition to his manufacturing interests, he had large holdings of real-estate in Ohio, Kansas, California, and Georgia. At the time of his death in Springfield he was survived by three adopted daughters who were the children of his deceased brother.

[C. Z. Mast, *A Brief Hist. of Bishop Jacob Mast and other Mast Pioneers* (1911); W. M. Rockel, *20th Century Hist. of Springfield and Clark County, Ohio, and Representative Citizens* (1908); *Farm Implement News,* Nov. 24, 1898; *Farm Machinery,* Nov. 22, 1898; *Implement Age,* Dec. 1, 1898; *Report of the Commissioner of Patents,* 1858, 1862, 1865, 1866, 1868, 1869, 1870, 1871; *Ohio State Jour.* (Columbus), Nov. 21, 1898.]

C. W. M.

MASTERSON, WILLIAM BARCLAY (Nov. 24, 1853–Oct. 25, 1921), frontier peace officer, sports writer, familiarly known as "Bat" Masterson, was the son of Thomas and Catherine McGurk Masterson and was born in Iroquois County, Ill. Little is recorded of his youth. In 1871 the family moved to a farm near Wichita, Kan., and in the following fall young Masterson and his brother Edward joined a party of buffalo hunters which set out from Fort Dodge. With a partner, in the summer of 1872, he undertook a grading contract on the Atchison, Topeka & Santa Fé railroad. Two years later he was again with a party of buffalo hunters, and on June 27, 1874, in the desperate battle with Indians at Adobe Walls, won distinction for coolness and bravery. For a time he was a scout under General Miles. In the spring of 1876 he served as a deputy-marshal of Dodge City, but in July he resigned and joined in the gold rush to Deadwood. He returned in the fall and in November 1877 was elected sheriff of Ford County. Early in 1878 he won an added distinction by surprising and capturing the noted outlaw, Dave Rudabaugh, and on Apr. 9, when his brother Edward, then the acting marshal of Dodge City, was shot down by two gunmen, he arrived on the scene in time to kill one and mortally wound the other.

At some time in 1880 he went to Tombstone, then considered the most lawless town in the world, and on several occasions assisted Wyatt Earp in his duties as a federal marshal. He left Tombstone in 1881, was for some months in Trinidad, Col., and was apparently back in Dodge City in 1883. By 1885 he seems to have established himself in Denver, where on Nov. 21, 1891, he married Emma Walters. In the main his occupation was gambling, a mode of livelihood which in those days on the frontier was generally deemed quite as reputable as any other gainful employment. He became deeply interested in athletics, especially pugilism. In May 1902 he moved to New York City, and within a year became a sports writer on the *Morning Telegraph.* President Roosevelt, by whom he was greatly admired, appointed him a federal deputy-marshal early in 1905, but finding the intermittent calls to duty in conflict with his newspaper work he resigned the post within two years. At the time of his death he was the sports editor of the *Morning Telegraph* and the secretary of the company. He died suddenly, while working at his desk. His funeral, on Oct. 27, 1921, was largely attended, and the interment was at Woodlawn Cemetery. He was survived by his wife.

Masterson usually dressed well and was something of a dandy. He was genial and easy of approach, had many friends, and was highly respected. As a frontier peace officer he ranks with Earp, Hickok, and Tilghman, a fearless company of whom it has been strikingly said that they "shot their way to heaven" by subduing the lawless, protecting the weak, and establishing peace and order.

[Robert M. Wright, *Dodge City, the Cowboy Capital* (1913); Olive K. Dixon, *Life of Billy Dixon* (revised ed., 1927); Fred E. Sutton and A. B. Macdonald, *Hands Up!* (1927); N. Y. *Morning Telegraph, Times, World,* and *Tribune,* Oct. 26, 1921; information from Kirke Mechem, Topeka, Kan., Thomas Masterson, Wichita, Kan., and Mrs. Emma Masterson, New York.]

W. J. G.

MASTIN, CLAUDIUS HENRY (June 4, 1826–Oct. 3, 1898), surgeon, was born at Huntsville, Ala., to Francis Turner Mastin and Ann Elizabeth Caroline (Levert). His paternal grandfather had emigrated from Wales to Maryland; his maternal grandfather was chief surgeon of Rochambeau's fleet. Mastin attended Greenville Academy at Huntsville and later the University of Virginia. Returning to Huntsville, he began the study of medicine under Dr. John Y. Bassett, an accomplished physician and anatomist. He received the degree of M.D. in 1849 from the University of Pennsylvania. After brief periods of practice at Huntsville, and Nashville, Tenn., he went to Europe where he attended lectures at the University of Edinburgh, the Royal College of Surgeons, London, and the University of France in Paris. In 1854 he settled for practice in Mobile, Ala., in association with an uncle, Dr. Levert. From the first he devoted himself to surgery and in time became the leading operator of his section. Although a general surgeon, he was particularly interested in genito-urinary surgery, for which purpose he devised a number of instruments. He was a pioneer in the employment of metallic sutures and is credited with being the first to use silver wire for ligating the external iliac artery for aneurism of the femoral artery. This operation was performed in June 1866. About the same time he employed silver wire for the closure of a vesico-vaginal fistula. From 1854 to 1857 he was employed by the United States Marine Hospital Service in Mobile and in 1855 he was appointed surgeon to the Mobile City Hospital. In 1861, at the outbreak of the Civil War, he was commissioned as a surgeon in the Confederate army and served as medical director, first on the staff of Gen. Leonidas Polk and later with Gen. Braxton Bragg and Gen. G. T. Beauregard. He was the chief medical officer at the battle of Shiloh. Returning to Mobile after the war, he resided there until his death.

Mastin was an organizer of the Congress of American Physicians and Surgeons, which held its first meeting in 1888 (*Transactions . . . First Triennial Session, 1888,* 1889). He was an original fellow of the American Surgical Association and its president in 1890–91, and was a member of the Southern Surgical and Gynecological Association. One of the organizers of the American Genito-Urinary Association, he was president in 1895–96. He was active in the affairs of the alumni association of the medical department of the University of Pennsylvania and in 1874 delivered the annual address. To him is largely due the credit for the erection of the monument to Dr. Gross in Philadelphia. He made a notable address upon the unveiling in 1895. His writings are mainly journal articles published in the transactions of the societies to which he belonged. Among the more notable are: *Inguinal Aneurism: Successful Ligation of External Iliac Artery by Means of Silver Wire* (1866), *Internal Urethrotomy as a Cure for Urethral Stricture* (1871), *Chronic Urethral Discharges* (1872), *New Method of Treating Strictures of the Urethra* (1873), *Causes and Geographical Distribution of Calculous Diseases* (1877), and *Hernia, a Comparison of the Various Methods Employed for its Cure* (1889).

Mastin was a scholarly man, a facile writer, and an effective public speaker. Physically he was tall, slight, and erect. He was married Sept. 20, 1848, to Mary Eliza, daughter of William McDowell of Huntsville. Two sons followed him in the practice of medicine.

[*Ala. Medic. and Surgic. Age,* Apr. 1896, portr.; *Trans. Am. Surgic. Asso.,* vol. XVIII (1900); *Trans. So. Surgic. and Gynecol. Asso.,* vol. XV (1903); portr.; H. A. Kelly and W. L. Burrage, *Am. Medic. Biogs.* (1920); *Memorial Record of Ala.* (1893), vol. II; J. H. McDowell, *Hist. of the McDowells and Connections* (1918); *Medic. Record* (N. Y.), Oct. 8, 1898; *Daily Register* (Mobile, Ala.), Oct. 5, 1898.]

J. M. P.

MASURY, JOHN WESLEY (Jan. 1, 1820–May 14, 1895), manufacturer, inventor, was born in Salem, Mass., the son of John and Priscilla (Carroll) Masury and a descendant of the French Huguenot family of Le Mesuriers. After receiving a good secondary education he worked in various capacities in Salem until 1842, when he went to Brooklyn, N. Y., which was his home for upwards of forty years. Here he became a clerk in the retail paint store of John D. Prince. A few years later, at the suggestion of Masury, Prince established a factory for the making of ground dry colors under the firm name of John D. Prince & Company, with Masury as partner.

The business was imediately successful and in a short time a third partner, to serve as salesman, was admitted and the company name changed to Prince, Masury & Weeks. Subsequently, Masury and Weeks bought out Prince and the two partners continued the business until the death of the latter in 1857. In order to buy his deceased partner's holdings Masury secured as a partner Frederick L. Whiton, and the firm was known as Masury & Whiton. On the death of Whiton in 1871, Masury took his son-in-law, F. L. Miller, into the business, changing the name of the concern to John W. Masury & Son.

A short time after Prince and Masury began the manufacture of dry colors, the latter conceived the idea of making ready-mixed paints as well. The greatest problem involved was that of securing a suitable metal container, and Masury began experimenting with this object in view. As early as 1857, Apr. 28, he patented a "metallic paint canister," and on July 5, 1859, he secured a second patent for an "improved paint can"; but it was not until 1873 that he perfected a paint can with a top so thin that it could be cut with a pocket knife. The use of this type of can as a container for ready-mixed paints marked the beginning of a very successful business for Masury, since his company enjoyed a monopoly of the invention for twenty-one years. Another important invention of Masury was an improved paint mill, patented Oct. 4, 1870, for grinding colors to an impalpable fineness in quick-drying varnish. Such grinding required that the millstones be held in close contact, and in the ordinary mill the frictional heat developed was sufficient to spoil the thinning material. Masury, however, devised a method by which a stream of cold water was passed over the outer surfaces of both the upper and lower millstones, thus preventing a destructive temperature. This invention alone permitted the manufacture of the so-called coach colors, which, prior to this time, had been made wholly in individual shops. Within two years after he began making coach colors, ground in Japan, with his improved mill, the demand for them called for more than three hundred tons a year per color.

Masury wrote a number of books and pamphlets on paints and painting, the best known of which is *House-Painting, Carriage-Painting and Graining,* published in 1881. He was twice married: first, Oct. 15, 1844, to Laura A. Carlton of Salem, and, second, to Grace Harkins of Brooklyn. He died at his residence in New York and was buried at Center Moriches, L. I.

[*Vital Records of Salem, Mass.,* vol. IV (1924); *Report of the Commissioner of Patents,* 1857, 1859, 1870–73; Henry Hall, *America's Successful Men of Affairs* (1895), vol. I; *N. Y. Tribune,* May 15, 1895, *Salem Daily Gazette,* May 16, 1895.] C. W. M.

MATEER, CALVIN WILSON (Jan. 9, 1836–Sept. 28, 1908), Presbyterian missionary to China, was born in Cumberland County, Pa., a few miles west of Harrisburg. His parents, John Mateer and Mary Nelson (Diven), were both of Scotch-Irish stock, and, true to that tradition, reared their family on the Bible and the Shorter Cathechism. His mother, especially, instilled in the children a love of education and an admiration for missionaries. Mateer made his way through country school, academy (at Hunterstown and then at Menittstown), and Jefferson College (later Washington and Jefferson), taking his bachelor's degree in 1857 with one of the two highest scholastic averages of his class. For two years after graduation he taught school with marked success, and then, having decided to enter the ministry, went to Allegheny (Western) Theological Seminary, graduating in 1861. While in seminary, he determined to be a missionary, but since the mission board at first lacked funds to send him, for two years he held a pastorate at Delaware, Ohio. In 1863, however, he was appointed to the mission in the recently opened port at Tengchow, in the province of Shantung, China, and there he spent most of his life.

Quiet, persevering, indefatigable, scholarly, with an aptitude for and an interest in mechanics amounting almost to genius, unyielding in his religious convictions, but possessing beneath his reserved exterior a tender heart for children and his students, he had a versatile and rather noteworthy career. He traveled extensively through the rural districts of Shantung, preaching, distributing literature, and helping to found churches, often in the face of persecution and personal danger. Early he established a school for boys, and under his patient and skilful management in time it became a college, one of the institutions that were eventually merged into what was later Shantung Christian and then Cheeloo University. He was president of the college until 1895 and retained his connection with it until 1907. He emphasized teaching in Chinese rather than in English. Largely with his own hands he built laboratory equipment for the college and examples of Western mechanical appliances which he collected into a museum for the purpose of educating the Chinese in Occidental science. In 1871–72 he was in charge of the Presbyterian Mission Press in Shanghai. He achieved a noteworthy mastery of the Chinese language and engaged in extensive literary activity in that medium. His voluminous *Mandarin Lessons* (first edition, 1892) was for many years the standard text for introducing Protestant missionaries to the various forms of Mandarin. He prepared many textbooks in Chinese and served as chairman of a committee on textbooks appointed by the Missionary Conference (of Protestant missionaries in China) of 1890. That conference also appointed him on committees for the revision of the translations of the Bible into Mandarin and the literary language. He labored on these for many years, especially on the Mandarin version of the New Testament. He also wrote numerous articles and brochures in English. He died at Tsingtao, whither he had gone for medical care. He was married twice: on Dec. 27, 1862, to Julia A. Brown, who died Feb. 16, 1898; and on Sept. 25, 1900, to Ada Haven, who for years had been a missionary in China under the American Board of Commissioners for Foreign Missions.

[D. W. Fisher, *Calvin Wilson Mateer, Forty-five Years a Missionary in Shantung, China* (1911); R. M. Mateer, *Character Building in China: The Life Story of Julia Brown Mateer* (1912); *Who's Who in America*, 1908–09; F. W. Baller, in *Chinese Recorder*, Nov. 1908; W. A. P. Martin, in *Ibid.*, Dec. 1908; *Ann. Reports of the Board of Foreign Missions of the Presbyt. Ch. in the U. S. A.*, 1863–1908.] K. S. L.

MATHER, COTTON (Feb. 12, 1662/63–Feb. 13, 1727/28), Puritan clergyman, scholar, and author, was the eldest son of Increase [*q.v.*] and Maria (Cotton) Mather, and the grandson of Richard Mather and John Cotton [*qq.v.*]. His schooling he received partly at home and partly at the Boston Latin School, but the greatest influence in his early years was that of his family. He came to see himself as by birth appointed to carry on its tradition of leadership in the church and of championship of Congregational ideals. Sensitive and self-conscious as a boy, and given to fits of melancholy, he felt increasingly that he was predestined to a kind of priesthood. By the time he was twelve and entered Harvard as the youngest student who had ever been admitted there, he had already tried his hand at correcting his less pious comrades. At college he was at first "hazed," and, justifiably enough, apparently, regarded by some as a prig. More popular with his tutors than with his classmates, he showed a definite interest in science. After his graduation in 1678 he was so handicapped by stammering that he feared he could not enter the pulpit, and undertook the study of medicine. By 1680, however, he was able to preach, and soon began to assist his father at the Second Church in Boston. He took the degree of M.A. at Harvard in 1681, and refused a call to a church in New Haven. In 1685 he was finally ordained at the Second Church, where he held office for the rest of his life, serving as his father's colleague until 1723. Once regularly settled in Boston he became an Overseer at Harvard.

In 1686 he married Abigail Phillips, daughter of John Phillips, a prosperous citizen of Charlestown. Two years later his father's departure for England in order to plead for the restoration of the Massachusetts charter left to Cotton Mather the whole responsibility of conducting the Second Church as well as the task of working at home, as his father was working abroad, in the interests of what many colonists believed were their rights in opposition to the will of James II, expressed in Massachusetts through the royal governor, Sir Edmund Andros [*q.v.*]. When open rebellion against Andros broke out, Mather was a ringleader, and wrote *The Declaration of the Gentlemen, Merchants, and Inhabitants of Boston,* published in 1689 (W. H. Whitmore, *The Andros Tracts,* vol. I, 1868, pp. 11–20), which served as the manifesto of the insurgents. This increased his reputation, which his ability as a preacher and his skill as a writer, evidenced thus far in about a dozen printed works, had already made great. By 1690, when he was elected a fellow of Harvard, he was recognized, in spite of his youth, as one of the most eminent divines in New England. When his father came home in 1692, bringing a new royal charter for Massachusetts and accompanied by the new governor, Sir William Phips [*q.v.*], whom he had nominated, Cotton Mather rejoiced at the chance for political influence which was now offered him. Phips was a disciple of the Mathers and had been baptized by Cotton Mather not long before. He wrote much to defend both the charter and Phips's acts as governor. Two works of this character are his "Political Fables," circulated in manuscript in 1693 (*Andros Tracts,* vol. II, 1869, pp. 324–32), and his *Pietas in Patriam* (1697), a life of Phips.

One of Sir William's first official acts was the appointment of a court to try certain suspected witches who had been arrested at Salem Village. This was the beginning of the famous Massachusetts witchcraft prosecution of 1692. Cotton Mather's connection with the affair has provoked much debate, but the facts, so far as they can now be ascertained, are easily summarized. Very early Mather adopted the theory that persons molested by the Devil might best be treated by fasting and prayer, and he seems to have decided that it was his duty to study cases of supposed diabolical possession in order to combat Satan's wiles. His fervent introspection, coupled with his taste for scientific investigation, led him not only to scrutinize everything which might tend to demonstrate the reality of the world of spirits but also to exaggerate the importance of his observations. In 1688 he took into his house a child believed to be a victim of witchcraft, in order that he might study her case. He published the result of his observation in his *Memorable Providences, Relating to Witchcrafts and Possessions* (1689). In 1690 and 1691 he printed in at least two other works his views on witchcraft. Just before the Salem witch court began its work he warned one of the judges against putting on so-called "spectral evidence," unfavorable to the accused, as much emphasis as had been usual in many earlier trials in England, and suggested that punishments milder than execution might be imposed (*Massachusetts Historical Society Collections,* 4 ser. VIII, 397 ff.). He then wrote a statement of advice to the judges, signed and issued by him and other leading ministers, in which he repeated the same warning, though he urged careful examination of the accused and vigorous prosecution of those safely to be suspected of guilt. In 1693 he published *Wonders of the Invisible World,* a narrative of a few of the Salem trials, written at the request of the judges. In this work he argued for the justice of the verdicts in the trials he described, since in each there was evidence enough, by contemporary standards, English and American, to convict a witch. He attended no one of the trials, but appeared at one execution and there publicly defended the sentence of the court. Throughout the summer of 1692 the judges did not heed his advice and that of the other ministers, and put to death many persons who by Mather's tests were not proved guilty. During the trials, however, Mather, like the others who doubted the justice of what was being done, uttered no public protest. In 1693, after the last execution, he eagerly investigated the case of a girl whom he believed to be bewitched, but made no attempt to start a new prosecution. He wrote an account of the affair, and entered into controversy with Robert Calef [*q.v.*], a man unusual in his time for his scepticism about witchcraft. Much recrimination resulted—Calef endeavoring to show that the Mathers, especially Cotton, were in some ill-defined way responsible for the injustice done at Salem. He published his views in *More Wonders of the Invisible World* (1700), including in the volume, apparently without permission of its author, Mather's narrative of the "bewitched girl" of 1693, hitherto unprinted. The publication of Calef's book was sponsored by those who opposed Mather's influence in the church and in politics and saw that by 1700, when it was generally admitted that wrong had been done at the Salem trials, even vague insinuations against Cotton Mather as an agent in the execution of the accused might undermine his power. When the book appeared, however, Mather had already declared his belief that the methods of the court had been unfair, and had sent to press his *Magnalia Christi Americana* (published in London in 1702), in which he quoted with approval John Hale's view of the trials, which went as far as Calef in asserting that innocent persons had been condemned. Although it may be said that he helped, through his talking and writing of the reality of witchcraft, to make possible the tragedy at Salem and to keep alive the excitement out of which it came, there is no evidence that he sought to accomplish what came to pass. The only cases of witchcraft with which he was directly concerned he endeavored to treat not by legal action but by fasting and prayer, and like many of his brethren he advocated principles in respect to evidence, which, if the court had accepted them, would have prevented most of the executions.

After 1692 his popularity waned somewhat, partly because of his identification with Phips's policies and the new charter, both of which had critics, partly because of his aggressiveness in controversy and his too frequent arrogance of tone, and, especially, because changed conditions had lessened religious ardor in Massachusetts and had weakened the old Puritan ideal of the dominance of the clergy. His hot temper made matters worse. He was not a skilful politician, and when Joseph Dudley [*q.v.*] became governor in 1702, Mather, who had urged his appointment, found that he could not hope to influence political action as he had done during Phips's régime. His efforts by correspondence with English friends and by pamphleteering to oust Dudley were unavailing; his zeal in keeping the loyalty of Massachusetts nonconformists before the eyes of English royalty bore little fruit, and after 1706, when he finally broke with Dudley, he must have seen that his dream of holding power in the state as well as the church could not come true.

He met defeat at Harvard also. His father was forced to give up its presidency in 1701, and Cotton Mather, mourning that the college was in the hands of the less orthodox, longed to be president himself. His name was considered at least twice, but he was not chosen. In 1703 the House of Representatives did appoint him president of Harvard, but their action was overruled. In the same year he gave up his fellowship. He soon came to look upon Yale, not Harvard, as the hope of the Congregational education in which he believed. He virtually committed the founders of the Connecticut College to naming it after Elihu Yale, thereby securing benefactions from him, and in other ways did what he could for the new seat of learning. In 1721 he was invited to become its president (*Colonial Society of Massachusetts Publications,* XXVI, 388–401).

In spite of frustrated ambitions, failure in politics, and the loss of some of the popularity which he once had, he remained a leader in the church, and his fame steadily increased. He projected societies for various "good causes," the maintenance of peace, the building of churches in poor communities, the relief of needy ministers, the distribution of tracts, Indian missions, and the like, imitating in part the many reform societies springing up in England. He worked much with children, and seems to have been popular with them. He set up and supported a school for the education of the slaves, and to others of the poor and afflicted he gave generously both of his time and money. His tireless activity as a writer won him unique eminence among his countrymen, and many of his works extended his reputation abroad, where also his learning, his scientific communications to the Royal Society (to which he was elected in 1713), and his correspondence with such men as Lord Chancellor King, William Whiston, John Desaguliers, Sir Richard Blackmore, Dr. Woodward, and August Hermann Francke made his name more familiar than those of other Americans. When smallpox broke out in Boston in 1721, he interested Dr. Zabdiel Boylston [*q.v.*] in inoculation, of which he had learned some years before, and—opposed by other physicians, by the people generally, and by some of the clergy—he defended ably in print what seemed to him a beneficent medical practice and by his zeal made possible its successful use in Boston.

There was much tragedy in Mather's life. His first wife died in 1702; his second, Elizabeth (Clark) Hubbard, mother of his son Samuel [*q.v.*], in 1713, and his third, Lydia (Lee) George, became mentally unbalanced. Of his fifteen children all but six died young, and only two lived until his death. One of his sons was a scapegrace. Three widowed sisters became largely dependent on him. He was himself far from robust nervously; he was a prey to a morbid love of introspection and, perhaps, the victim of hallucinations. It is impossible now to estimate finally either his character or the quality of his accomplishment. Some of his faults, his vanity, his instability, his occasional intemperance in speech, and his too great acerbity in debate, may have been produced by his craving to realize an ideal too great for him, which led him by indefatigable industry to overtax nerves always irritable and made more so by disappointments and bereavements. His honesty in money matters and even his sexual morality have been questioned, but no such charges have been substantiated. It is difficult, however, to acquit him of self-seeking, though it is fair to remember that his ambition for power and rank may have been determined at least in part by his desire to preserve orthodoxy and piety as he conceived of them, as well as by love of worldly position for its own sake. Essentially a conservative, he was always torn between allegiance to inherited ideals and realization that a newer day demanded new standards. He was often bitter in his denunciation of other sects, but he was consistently more tolerant in deed than in word, and his tolerance grew as he aged. By 1726 he boasted in print that he had seen admitted to communion in his own church not only Anglicans but Baptists, Presbyterians, and Lutherans, and urged upon candidates for the ministry certain highly tolerant principles (*Manuductio ad Ministerium,* pp. 116–121, 126–127). Though bred in Calvinism he expounded in his *Christian Philosopher* (1721) doctrines which represent a step toward deism. Neither a thorough-going reactionary nor a thorough-going liberal, he reflected in his life much of the conflict of a period in which ideas were changing rapidly and the colonists' attitude toward this world and the next was being radically modified. Much in his nature seems repellent; his religious transports appear too often to be deliberate efforts to imitate saints of whom he had read rather than genuine expressions of his own emotion; his erudition sometimes carried him over the line into pedantry; his missionary zeal misled him into something perilously like dishonest casuistry, and his constant efforts to derive religious meaning from every experience, however small, savor today of artificiality. But, however unlovable he may appear, he commands a measure of respect for his studiousness, his industry, and for the self-forgetfulness in his work for what he believed were the best means of serving his generation.

Of his numerous books—more than 450 in all—the most were published after 1692. They reveal Mather as an able editor and compiler, a historian, a well-bred amateur of many fields of knowledge, and a *prosateur* with a definite theory of style. This theory, as he explained (*Manuductio ad Ministerium,* 1726, pp. 44–46) was that of a lover of allusions and quotations and of prose made ornate by them, and that of a man who set richness of content above mere elegance of expression. Much that he wrote is dull; some of it is too hastily written to succeed, but the most, probably, however far from literary greatness in the narrow sense and however out of accord with modern conventions, is artistically more worthy than the bulk of American literature prior to 1728. Of his books, those having the greatest interest for today are, first, the *Magnalia Christi Americana: or the Ecclesiastical History of New England from its First Planting* (1702), a more considerable literary achievement than any previously produced in Massachusetts, and then, in addition to the others previously mentioned: *A Poem to the Memory of . . . Mr. Urian Oakes* (1682); *The Present State of New England* (1690); *Eleutheria: Or an Idea of the Reformation in England: And a History of Non-Conformity* (1698); *Pastoral Letter to the English Captives in Africa* (1698); *A Family Well-Ordered* (1699); *La Fe del Christiano* (1699), an effort in Spanish; *Reasonable Religion* (1700); *Some Few Remarks upon A Scandalous Book . . . By one Robert Calef* (1701); *Le Vrai Patron des Saines Paroles* (1704); *A Faithful Man . . . Michael Wigglesworth* (1705); *The Negro Christianized* (1706); *Corderius Americanus . . . The Good Education of Children* (1708); *Bonifacius* (1710), which under its later title of *Essays to do Good* had great popularity and was praised by Franklin; *Fair Dealing between Debtor and Creditor* (1716); *Brethren Dwelling together in Unity* (1718), a sermon preached at a Baptist ordination; *Psalterium Americanum* (1718), a translation of the Psalms for use in singing; *The Accomplished Singer* (1721), a tract to aid the movement for better congregational singing; *Sentiments on the Small Pox Inoculated* (1721); *An Account . . . of Inoculating the Small-Pox* (1722); *The Angel of Bethesda* (1722), the same title having been used for another book by Mather preserved in manuscript at the American Antiquarian Society; *Parentator* (1724), a biography of his father, and *Ratio Disciplinae* (1726), still a valuable exposition of Congregational polity. His *Biblia Americana,* a work which the author considered his greatest, is in manuscript at the Massachusetts Historical Society.

[The best biography is Barrett Wendell's *Cotton Mather* (1891, 1926). A. P. Marvin, *The Life and Times of Cotton Mather* (1892) is fuller but less valuable as a character study. The most recent biography is R. and L. Boas's *Cotton Mather* (1928). Mather's diary so far as it is preserved has been printed, ed. by W. C. Ford, in *Mass. Hist. Soc. Colls.,* 7 ser. VII, VIII (1921–22). Of the other biographical works the following are useful: Benjamin Colman, *The Holy Walk* (1728); Samuel Mather, *The Life of the Very Reverend and Learned Cotton Mather* (1729); K. B. Murdock, "Introduction," in *Selections from Cotton Mather* (1926), and chapter on Cotton Mather in A. B. Hart, ed., *Commonwealth Hist. of Mass.,* vol. II (1928); W. B. O. Peabody, in Jared Sparks, *Lib. of Am. Biog.,* vol. VI (1836); A. H. Quint, "Cotton Mather," in *Congreg. Quart.,* July 1859; Chandler Robbins, *A Hist. of the Second Church . . . in Boston* (1852); and J. L. Sibley, *Biog. Sketches of Grads. of Harvard,* vol. III (1885), which contains the most nearly complete bibliography. *The Cambridge Hist. of Am. Lit.,* I (1917), 407–23, contains a check-list of brief titles which adds many items to Sibley's list. For notable treatments of special phases of Mather's life and work, see esp. Robert Calef, *More Wonders of the Invisible World* (1700), the basis of later attacks upon Mather's attitude toward the witch trials; S. G. Drake, introduction and notes in *The Witchcraft Delusion* (3 vols., 1866); Kuno Francke, "The Beginning of Cotton Mather's Correspondence with August Hermann Francke," in *Philological Quart.,* July 1926, and two articles on this correspondence in *Studies and Notes in Philology and Literature,* V (1896), 57–67, and *Americana Germanica,* vol. I, no. 4 (1897), pp. 31–66; C. N. Greenough, "A Letter Relating to the Publication of Cotton Mather's Magnalia," in *Col. Soc. Mass. Pubs.,* vol. XXVI (1927); T. J. Holmes, "Cotton Mather and His Writings on Witchcraft," in *Papers of the Bibliog. Soc. of America,* XVIII (1924), 30–59, and "The Surreptitious Printing of One of Cotton Mather's Manuscripts," in *Bibliog. Essays: A Tribute to Wilberforce Eames* (1924); G. L. Kittredge, "Cotton Mather's Election into the Royal Society," in *Col. Soc. Mass. Pubs.,* XIV (1913), 81–114, "Further Notes on Cotton Mather and the Royal Society," *Ibid.,* 28–92, "Introduction," in the Cleveland, 1921, reprint of Increase Mather's *Several Reasons,* "Cotton Mather's Scientific Communications to the Royal Society," in *Proc. Am. Antiq. Soc.,* n.s., XXVI (1916), "Notes on Witchcraft," *Ibid.,* n.s., XVIII (1907), 148–212, and "Some Lost Works of Cotton Mather," in *Proc. Mass. Hist. Soc.,* XLV (1912), 418–79; K. B. Murdock, "Cotton Mather and the Rectorship of Yale College," in *Col. Soc. Mass. Pubs.,* XXVI (1927), 388–401; W. F. Poole, *Cotton Mather and Salem Witchcraft* (1869); I. W. Riley, *Am. Philosophy, The Early Schools* (1907); C. W. Upham, *Salem Witchcraft* (2 vols., 1867); "Salem Witchcraft and Cotton Mather," in *Hist. Mag.,* Sept. 1869. See also T. J. Holmes, *The Mather Literature* (1927); H. E. Mather, *Lineage of Rev. Richard Mather* (1890); "The Mather Papers," in *Mass. Hist. Soc. Colls.,* 4 ser. VIII (1868); Albert Matthews, introduction and notes to the early Harvard records printed in *Col. Soc. Mass. Pubs.,* vols. XV, XVI (1925); K. B. Murdock, *Increase Mather* (1925); Josiah Quincy, *The Hist. of Harvard Univ.* (1840); J. H. Tuttle, "The Libraries of the Mathers," in *Proc. Am. Antiq. Soc.,* n.s., XX (1910), 269–356; M. C. Tyler, *A Hist. of Am. Lit. . . .* (1878), vol. II; Williston Walker, "The Services of the Mathers," in *Papers of the Am. Soc. of Ch. Hist.,* V (1893), 61–85. The Am. Antiq. Soc. owns two paintings of Cotton Mather, both by Peter Pelham, who also did a mezzotint of Mather in 1727.] K. B. M.

MATHER, FRED (Aug. 2, 1833–Feb. 14, 1900), pisciculturist, writer on outdoor life, was born in Greenbush, now Rensselaer, N. Y. His parents were Joseph and Chianna (Brockway) Mather of Lyme, Conn., and he was a descendant of Rev. Richard Mather [*q.v.*] of Toxteth, England, who came to Massachusetts in 1635 and settled in Dorchester. After the removal of his family to Albany in 1850, Mather studied at the Classical Institute of Prof. Charles Anthony. In 1854 he married Elizabeth McDonald. During boyhood he had exhibited a strong interest in outdoor pursuits, particularly hunting and fishing, and it was probably this that impelled him, soon after his marriage, to join the great Western migration. He located temporarily in Wisconsin, where he was interested in lead mines at Potosi, also engaging in hunting and trapping. He participated in the government surveys in Minnesota and passed some time in Kansas prior to the Civil War. In 1862 he enlisted in the 113th New York Volunteers and served with credit throughout the Civil War, being discharged with the rank of captain in the 7th New York Artillery.

What led him to adopt fish culture as a life work is not clear, but he may have been influenced by the activities of Seth Green [*q.v.*] and other pioneers in this field between 1860 and 1870. In any case, he experimented with the hatching of perch eggs in the rooms of the State Geological Survey at Albany in 1867. The following year he established himself at Honeoye Falls, Monroe County, N. Y., initiating the more extensive piscicultural work in which he rapidly gained distinction. With the establishment of the United States Fish Commission in 1872 he was called upon for various services, being entrusted with the shipment of live shad to Europe in 1874. He repeated the trip in 1877, carrying eggs of the California salmon in a case of his own designing, and bringing back a few European sole for planting in American waters. In 1874 and 1875 he experimented with the hatching of Michigan grayling and made some efforts to propagate the sea bass. His first wife had died in 1861 and in 1877 he married Adelaide Fairchild. He supervised the American representation at the International Fisheries Exhibition at Berlin in 1880, and gained European recognition. In 1883 he was placed in charge of the state hatchery at Cold Spring Harbor, N. Y., holding the position until 1895. During this period he conducted many of the experiments which were the basis of his numerous technical reports and articles on fish culture. Here he developed methods for the propagation of cod, lobsters, smelt, and other marine forms. The Mather hatching cone, a device for suspending fish eggs in a current of water, in the originating of which he was assisted by Charles Bell was one of his earlier inventions (1875), and embodied a new principle in fish culture.

In his literary activities he was prominently identified with *Forest and Stream,* serving as a member of its editorial staff and furnishing frequent contributions. His work also appeared in *Rod and Gun and American Sportsman,* and in the *Chicago Field* now the *American Field,* the fishing department of which he edited from March 1878 to April 1880. The latter periodical alone published over three score short articles from his pen. A compilation of his writings shows over seventy titles of a technical nature in addition to the foregoing. As a prominent member of the American Fish Cultural Association and its successor the American Fisheries Society he wrote extensively for their annual *Transactions.* Other works, such as *Men I have Fished With* (1897), *In the Louisiana Lowlands* (1900), and *My Angling Friends* (1901), consisted largely of anecdotes and reminiscences of his experience during his travels and numerous field investigations. He was author of *Memoranda Relating to Adirondack Fishes* (1886) of some scientific value, and a technical handbook, *Modern Fish Culture* (1901). His contributions as a developer as well as originator of technical methods in fish culture were of marked value. He died near Lake Nebagomain, Wis.

[Mather's writings constitute the most prolific source of information regarding his activities as a pisciculturist; see also *Bull. of the U. S. Fish Commission,* vols. III (1883), IV (1884); *Report of the U. S. Commissioner of Fisheries,* 1882–87 inclusive; *Report of the Am. Fish Cultural Asso.,* 1879, 1881; *Trans. Am. Fisheries Soc.,* 1890, index; *Am. Field,* Mar. 3, 1900; *Forest and Stream,* Feb. 24, 1900; *Albany Evening Jour.,* Feb. 15, 1900; *Who's Who in America,* 1899–1900; H. E. Mather, *Lineage of Rev. Richard Mather* (1890).]

M. C. J.

MATHER, INCREASE (June 21, 1639–Aug. 23, 1723), Puritan clergyman, politician, author, was the youngest son of Richard [*q.v.*] and Katherine (Holt) Mather. He was born in Dorchester, Mass., and was brought up there in the strict Puritanism of his father's household. His early education he received at home and in a free school in Boston. In 1651 he entered Harvard, but during most of his course he lived in Ipswich or in Boston, studying under the tutorship of the Rev. John Norton. In 1656 he graduated with the degree of A.B. On June 21, 1657, he preached his first sermon. A few weeks later he went to England and thence to Ireland, where he entered Trinity College, Dublin, and received the degree of M.A. in 1658. The Irish climate disagreed with him, and, refusing an academic post at Trinity, he returned to England. There John Howe, one of Cromwell's chaplains and one of the most famous English Puritans, delegated the young Bostonian to preach in his stead at Great Torrington, Devonshire. In 1659 Howe came back to his own flock, and Mather went as chaplain to the garrison at Guernsey. Thence he was called to Gloucester, where he would have been content to stay, but the signs of the impending Restoration led him once more to leave England for Guernsey. He arrived there in April 1660, and on the last day of May Charles II was proclaimed king. Mather refused to rejoice or to express confidence in the Stuarts. His attitude was not tolerated, and, early in 1661, he went to Weymouth and Dorchester, in Dorset, where he worked to establish Congregational churches. But, although he found England more to his taste than Massachusetts, he saw that unless he accepted Anglicanism, to which he was tempted by substantial offers, his only opportunity as a minister lay in the land of his birth.

He arrived in Boston in September 1661. At once half a dozen churches called him, but he stayed in Dorchester with his father. In March 1662 he married Maria Cotton, his step-sister, the daughter of the Rev. John Cotton [*q.v.*]. Later in the same year he made his first important public appearance as a delegate from Dorchester to an ecclesiastical synod. In its councils he opposed his father and most of the clergy by arguing against the Half-Way Covenant, which, he believed, weakened the pristine strength of Congregationalism by relaxing the tests for admission to church membership. Practical experience soon convinced him, however, that the churches could not prosper unless their standards made possible the obtaining of new members; and he became an advocate of the Half-Way Covenant. In 1675 he published two books defending it.

He became teacher of the Second Church in Boston in 1664; in 1674 he was appointed one of the licensers of the press, and fellow of Harvard College. Seven years later he was elected president of that institution, but, adhering to a principle from which he never deviated, he put his duty to his church before all else, and declined the offer from Cambridge because his Boston congregation was not willing to release him. By 1683 he had published more than twenty-five books, which, together with his skill as a preacher, brought him recognition as one of the foremost divines of the time and place. He organized in Boston a society for the discussion of scientific matters, and his interest in such topics is displayed also in his *Essay for the Recording of Illustrious Providences* (1684). Superficially the book is like many other collections of pious tales of God's intervention in human affairs, but it differs from them in its more scientific method, and in the devotion of some space to the exploding of superstition and the treatment of purely scientific subjects.

The crisis produced late in 1683 by the *quo warranto* against the Massachusetts charter drew him into politics. He exhorted the citizens of Boston not to submit to the king's behests, and his words had great influence. In 1685 he was appointed acting president of Harvard, and, a year afterwards, definitely took charge with the title of Rector. Without relaxing his care of his church, he managed to guide the college through troublous days. He encouraged the study of science and showed willingness to make the institution something more than a ministerial training school, but at the same time resisted successfully all efforts to undermine its Congregationalism. He won the enmity of advocates of the royal policy in Massachusetts, but when, in 1688, it seemed desirable to try to regain the charter by an appeal to James II, Mather was chosen to take to the king petitions from the Congregational churches in the colony. Naturally Edward Randolph [*q.v.*] and the royal officials in Boston opposed his going. They had charges brought against him, based on a libelous letter which he was said to have written. The letter was a forgery, and he was acquitted, but Randolph again threatened him with arrest, so that in April 1688, when he set out for England, he was forced to steal away in disguise.

In London he enlisted in his cause many of the nonconformists who had for the moment political influence. He gained a hearing with Sir Nicholas Butler, Lord Culpeper, the Earl of Sunderland, William Penn, Lord Bellasis, Powis the attorney-general, and others of the powerful at court. He was aided, too, by the Countess of Anglesey and Mrs. Blathwayt, whose husband, the clerk of the privy council, was by no means well disposed toward Mather's cause. The first stage of his quest ended with the fall of James II, who had no time to carry out the large promises he had made. Mather had had five interviews with him, and William III was hardly in London before the colonial emissary obtained an audience. His assurances of New England's loyalty to the new king and his censure of Governor Andros [*q.v.*] were heeded, and when a royal order confirmed in power most of the colonial governors—an order which would have made Andros' position impregnable—Massachusetts was expressly excepted. Later in 1689 Boston citizens revolted against the royal governor, and Mather explained this action to the king not as disloyalty to English authority but simply as defiance of James II, the tyrant. Until 1690 Mather was not an official representative of the colonial government, but he was then appointed one of four agents from Massachusetts. His colleagues were two Bostonians, Elisha Cooke [*q.v.*] and Thomas Oakes, and Sir Henry Ashurst of London. Plans for restoring the charter by parliamentary act came to nothing, and in spite of the agents' exertions it became evident that a new charter would be issued. Mather and his fellow agents had to decide whether by refusing to accept a new charter framed by William III they should escape blame for any of its clauses which might prove unpopular at home, or whether they should meet the king half way in order to try to win concessions for their countrymen. Cooke chose the former course; Mather and Ashurst, the latter.

The wisdom of Mather's policy was proved by its results. Although the new charter took away the colonists' right to elect their own governors, his entreaties helped to preserve most of the power of the representative assembly elected by the voters. Instead of objecting to the provision —which he may well have regretted—removing the old restriction of the franchise to church-members, he argued for more power for the people's representatives and against the king's authority to veto their acts. Knowing that by accepting the new charter he gave up what was dear to the narrower Congregationalists and in other ways ran the risk of popular hostility, he knew also that even if the old charter could have been regained many of the "rights" once enjoyed under it could no longer be exercised, and that William III's plan had the merit of giving for the first time legal sanction to certain "liberties" dear to the colonists. Mather was accorded by the king the privilege of nominating the governor, who was to rule during the royal pleasure, and also all the other officers to be appointed for the first year of the new government. The slate he drew up was accepted and he was thus given unique influence in Massachusetts politics.

During his agency his inexperience and one or two unfortunate outbursts of temper were largely atoned for by some diplomatic skill and much personal persuasiveness. Anthony Wood, the antiquarian, who hated Puritans, remarked that among them Mather alone was unfailingly courteous to him—a comment which helps to explain the colonial agent's success. He knew no law, but he took the advice of eminent English lawyers; the pamphlets he wrote and published in London showed adroitness in political debate. Political negotiation, however, was not his only interest. He made friends of Robert Boyle, the scientist, and Richard Baxter, the famous Puritan. The latter dedicated his *Glorious Kingdom of Christ* (1691) to Mather, testifying to his respect for the New Englander's learning. For Harvard he did much, persuading several Englishmen to make bequests and planting the seed which eventually bore fruit in Thomas Hollis' generosity to the college. In nonconformist circles he was welcomed and respected, and he had a large share in the plan for union of Presbyterians and Congregationalists, drawn up in 1691. Furthermore, he took advantage of opportunity by buying in London many books, of which a considerable number dealt with science and with politics.

He came back to Boston in May 1692, with Sir William Phips [*q.v.*], the royal governor whom he had nominated. Officially they were well received, and Mather's work in England was praised. But Cooke and the others who regarded the old charter as the foundation of Massachusetts liberties, together with those who resented the political influence of Mather and other orthodox Congregationalists, soon mustered a considerable party which was eager to discredit him. His policy was to defend the new charter, and, now that the government was no longer solely in the hands of church-members, to educate the voters to elect only the pious. As rector of Harvard he tried also to bring up colonial youths to revere the old standards. In order to safeguard its Congregationalism and to provide for its stability he tried to secure a charter for Harvard, and wished to go to London again to plead for one from the king. His enemies prevented this maneuver, and centered their attack in an attempt to oust him from office at the college. In spite of them he held the rectorship until 1701, and even then had he been willing to compromise by neglecting what he believed was the prior claim of his church, he might have held his post.

The outbreak of suspected witchcraft at Salem Village occurred while Mather was in England, and when he landed in Boston many reputed agents of the devil were under arrest. A court appointed by Phips to try them gave to "spectral evidence," damaging to the prisoners, more weight than Mather and most of the other ministers believed to be just. Except for signing the ministers' statement of advice to the court, written by his son, Cotton [*q.v.*], and issued in June, Increase Mather made no public protest against the trials until autumn. During the summer, however, Thomas Brattle [*q.v.*], also an opponent of the judges' methods, expressed his views in a private letter and listed Mather as one of those who agreed with him. In October the ministers put out an explicit statement of their opinion. This was written by Mather, and published as *Cases of Conscience Concerning Evil Spirits.* The printed version is dated 1693, but the manuscript was circulated and perhaps even printed before the end of 1692. The book was definite in its disapproval of the emphasis put on "spectral evidence" during the Salem trials. Cotton Mather maintains that it ended the executions for witchcraft in Massachusetts. Phips reported to England that Increase Mather's opinion led him to stop the carrying out of sentences imposed on the convicted "witches." Both statements are true, at least in part. *Cases of Conscience* was the most outspoken, and almost certainly the earliest, public utterance issued in New England in opposition to the practice of the court.

More cautious than his son, Increase Mather, though he never questioned the reality of witchcraft, wrote and preached on the subject comparatively rarely and during the trials did nothing to increase the excitement. He summed up his attitude when he said that he felt that it was better for a guilty witch to escape than for an innocent person to die. Robert Calef [*q.v.*], in his *More Wonders of the Invisible World* (1700), accusing Cotton Mather of responsibility for the death of innocent victims at Salem, also attacked Increase Mather, but criticized him chiefly for his political course as representative of the colony in England.

Mather's political prestige, like his son's, declined after 1692, and for the same reasons. He was committed to the new charter, which he had helped to obtain, and a supporter of Governor Phips, whom he had nominated. Wherever the charter and the governor were unpopular, Mather was censured; his opposition to the polity proposed by the founders of the Brattle Street Church also won him their enmity and that of their friends. His opponents succeeded by 1701 in making it impossible for him to continue as president of Harvard unless he neglected his church and lived in Cambridge, and he chose to give up his office. Thenceforth he mingled less in politics, though he partook in his son's unsuccessful campaign against Governor Dudley. He continued to write, of course, and to pursue his ministry. He interested himself in Yale, which he hoped might remain a stronghold of orthodoxy, and in the councils of Massachusetts Congregationalism he was to the end a leader. In 1721 his lifelong openmindedness toward scientific progress bore fruit in his championship of the highly unpopular cause of inoculation for smallpox.

Two years later he died, and the extent of the mourning and the tributes paid to him then prove that he had lost neither his fame nor the approbation of his people. One of his former enemies said: "He was the patriarch and prophet among us, if any one might be so called" (Benjamin Colman, *The Prophet's Death,* 1723, p. 32), and the comments of his contemporaries and of later historians agree in picturing him as unequaled in reputation and power by any native-born American Puritan of his generation. His hot temper, his confidence in his own wisdom and in his right to lead others, and his liking for power, all tend to estrange sympathy. As the spokesman of Massachusetts Congregationalism and, during a short period, of a political party, he was often embroiled in controversy; but with few exceptions he managed his debating with less personal virulence than did his adversaries. What seems like ambition in him may have been in part the product of his belief that only in places of authority could he make his voice heard in defense of the ideals which he sincerely felt were for the public good. He was by no means implacable toward those who disagreed with him: he preached at a meeting of reconciliation between the orthodox Boston congregations and the Brattle Street Church; in 1718 he helped to ordain a Baptist minister. He leaned away from the democracy of the original Independents toward a somewhat Presbyterianized ecclesiastical system, and seems always to have preferred an oligarchy dominated by the most learned and devout, yet in civil affairs he argued for the preservation of democratic institutions. He gave much to charity, and the young Bostonian who saw his last appearance in the pulpit and declared that the old preacher's face was to his audience "the face of an angel" no doubt voiced an affection shared by others of the townsfolk (*Colonial Society of Massachusetts Publications,* vol. XXVI, 1927, p. 390).

As an author he mastered a style strong in its simplicity and directness though usually without brilliance; and the number and variety of his publications—there are about one hundred and thirty books or pamphlets and some sixty-five prefaces or contributions to books by others —made him deservedly renowned. The most interesting of them today are his political tracts, written in connection with his agency; his two histories, *A Brief History of the Warr with the Indians* (1676) and *A Relation of the Troubles Which Have Hapned in New-England by Reason of the Indians There* (1677); his *Life and Death of that Reverend Man of God, Mr. Richard Mather* (1670), and two sermons, *The Great Blessing, of Primitive Counsellours* (1693) and *The Surest Way to the Greatest Honour* (1699), which outline his political position after 1692.

By his first wife he had three sons and seven daughters. Of these one died young. His eldest son, Cotton, became famous in his turn and was always his father's close ally. The third son, Samuel, also became a minister, spending most of his active life in England, preaching at Witney, Oxfordshire; and a daughter, Elizabeth, became the mother of the Rev. Mather Byles [*q.v.*]. In 1714 the first Mrs. Mather died, and in the next year her husband married Ann (Lake) Cotton, his nephew's widow.

[T. J. Holmes, *Increase Mather; a Bibliog. of His Works* (2 vols., 1931), with intro. by G. P. Winship and supplementary material by K. B. Murdock and G. F. Dow, is complete. K. B. Murdock, *Increase Mather* (1925), the only detailed biography, contains a full list of sources. Mather's manuscript autobiography and diaries covering many years are in the Am. Antiq. Soc. Another diary is in the Mass. Hist. Soc., and some of Mather's entries for 1674–87 are printed in the Society's *Proceedings,* 2 ser. XIII (1900), 339–74, 397–411. Cotton Mather's *Parentator* (1724) is a life of his father. An abridgment of it, *Memoirs of the Life of the Late Rev. Increase Mather* (1725), was made by Samuel Mather of Witney, and contains an introduction by Edmund Calamy. The best brief sketches are those by J. L. Sibley in his *Biog. Sketches of Grads. of Harvard,* vol. I (1873) and by Williston Walker, in *Ten New England Leaders* (1901). See also Samuel Palmer's edition of Edmund Calamy's *Nonconformist's Memorial* (1802), II, 245–49; Enoch Pond, *The Lives of Increase Mather and Sir Wm. Phipps* (1870); H. E. Mather, *Lineage of Richard Mather* (1890); Chandler Robbins, *A Hist. of the Second Ch., or Old North, in Boston* (1852); and Barrett Wendell's *Cotton Mather* (1891, 1926). The *Calendar of State Papers, Colonial Series, America and West Indies*; W. H. Whitmore, *The Andros Tracts* (3 vols., 1868–74), and R. N. Toppan and A. T. S. Goodrick, *Edward Randolph* (7 vols., 1898–1909), are valuable authorities on Mather's political activities. For his connection with Harvard see especially the early records of the college, printed with an invaluable introduction by Albert Matthews, in *Colonial Soc. of Mass. Pubs.,* vols. XV and XVI (1925). The best study of the inoculation episode is G. L. Kittredge's Introduction to the Cleveland, 1921, reprint of I. Mather's *Several Reasons.* On other special topics consult St. J. D. Seymour, *The Puritans in Ireland* (1921), and R. H. Murray, *Dublin Univ. and the New World* (1921). K. B. Murdock, *The Portraits of Increase Mather* (1924), reproduces and discusses all the known pictures which have any claim to be considered authentic likenesses of Mather.] K. B. M.

MATHER, RICHARD (1596–Apr. 22, 1669), Puritan clergyman, author, was born at Lowton, in Lancashire, the son of Thomas and Margaret (Abrams?) Mather (*New-England Historical and Genealogical Register,* July 1900, pp. 348–49). During his boyhood he lived in Lowton, attending school at Winwick, a few miles away. At fifteen he was ready for the University, but his parents were poor and he went instead to Toxteth Park, now part of Liverpool, as master of a grammar school. He lived in the household of Edward Aspinwall, whose influence and that of various preachers brought about Mather's "conversion" in 1614. In May 1618, he was admitted to Brasenose College, Oxford, but in November was called back to occupy the pulpit at the Toxteth Park Chapel. He was ordained by Bishop Morton of Chester, but his Puritan tendencies developed rapidly, so that when he wooed Katherine Holt (or Hoult) of Bury, her father, one of the local gentry, "not being affected towards Non-conformable Puritans," opposed his suit (Increase Mather, *post,* ed. of 1850, p. 51). In 1624, however, Richard Mather and Katherine Holt were married, and went to live in Much Woolton. He continued to preach at Toxteth, and occasionally at Prescot, Liverpool, and other Lancashire towns. As his influence widened, his Puritanism attracted attention from the ecclesiastical authorities, and in 1633 he was suspended from his ministry. Friends had the sentence revoked after three months, but in the next year visitors from Archbishop Neile of York haled Mather before them, and once more he was forbidden to preach.

He drew up a series of arguments for emigration, which, together with what he had heard from John Cotton and Thomas Hooker [*qq.v.*], who were already in the colonies, led him to sail with his family from Bristol in May 1635. After a narrow escape from shipwreck, he landed at Boston on Aug. 17. Invited to preside over several of the churches in Massachusetts, he chose to go to Dorchester, whence most of the original congregation had moved to Connecticut. On Aug. 23, 1636, the church in Dorchester was formally reorganized with Mather as teacher. His ministry there continued till his death.

From the first he was a leader of Massachusetts Congregationalism, and to it he devoted his energies as writer and preacher. His *Church-Government and Church-Covenant Discussed* (1643) was "the first elaborate defense and exposition of the New England theory of the Church and its administration to be put forth in print" (Walker, *post,* p. 115). It was printed without his name, as was his *Apologie of the Churches in New-England for Church Covenant* (1643), an argument for the Congregational principle as to the basis of the church in a covenant of members; but both works are surely his. With the Rev. William Tompson he collaborated in *A Modest & Brotherly Answer to Mr. Charles Herle* (1644) and *An Heart-Melting Exhortation* (1650). The former was another defense of the Congregational scheme, as was Mather's *Reply to Mr. Rutherfurd* (1647). With the Rev. John Eliot and the Rev. Thomas Welde he translated the Psalms in meters adapted for singing in the meeting-houses, the result being *The Whole Booke of Psalmes* (1640), better known as the "Bay Psalm Book." Mather, in his preface, shows that he was in no doubt as to the book's literary shortcomings, declaring that its object was "Conscience rather then Elegance, fidelity rather than poetry." But the most important of Mather's works was the original draft of the famous "Cambridge Platform," which, amended and adopted by a synod at Cambridge in 1646 and printed as *A Platform of Church Discipline* (1649), was for many years the basic document of New England Congregationalism.

He took an active part in all the church controversies of his day, especially that concerning admission to membership in Congregational churches. Originally only those who could offer evidence of sincere faith and genuine conviction were admitted, but a question soon arose about the status of such of their children as had not experienced "conversion." Might they be members of a church, and might their children in turn be baptized? A compromise was proposed: the Half-Way Covenant, which provided that those who had been granted baptism by virtue of their parents' church-membership might enter into covenant relations with the church and have their children baptized, but could not sit at the Lord's table or vote in the business meetings of the church. In 1657 a ministerial convention at Boston advocated the Half-Way Covenant, and its conclusions were drawn up by Mather. Five years later a synod approved the decision of the convention, and in its debates he championed the cause which prevailed.

It is as an expositor of Congregational doctrine and organizer of Congregational polity that Mather is important. He wrote forcefully, though without literary distinction, and his contemporaries must have relied principally upon his works for authoritative statements of the New England ecclesiastical system. He was a practical teacher and minister rather than a theorist, and the reasons for his advocacy of the Half-Way Covenant show his fundamental attitude. To him, a system which denied to many of the younger members of the community any connection with the church seemed impracticable; he believed that in them lay the only hope for the continued development of Congregationalism, and he saw the Half-Way Covenant as a means of causing "the Rising Generation in this Country" to be "brought under the Government of Christ in his Church" (I. Mather, p. 79). Similarly certain Presbyterian elements in the system which he favored were probably recommended to him by the chance that they might strengthen the organization of the colonial church and lessen the differences between some of the more powerful English Puritans and their brethren in Massachusetts.

A portrait owned by the American Antiquarian Society and reproduced in a woodcut by John Foster in 1670 shows Mather to have been bearded, and apparently florid in complexion. It suggests also that he was of moderate stature. More vivid is the impression to be derived from Hooker's statement, "My brother Mather is a mighty man" and from his grandson's comment on his preaching: "His voice was loud and big, and uttered with a deliberate vehemency, it procured unto his ministry an awful and very taking majesty; nevertheless, the substantial and rational matter delivered by him, caused his ministry to take yet more" (C. Mather, *Magnalia,* 1702, Bk. III, pt. 2, ch. xx, §14). For the rest we know of his personal characteristics only through the eulogies of his descendants, who emphasize his diligence, his patience, and his zeal for learning. By his first wife he had six sons, one of whom died in childhood. Of the others all but one became ministers. The two eldest, Samuel and Nathaniel, returned to England after graduating from Harvard; the others, Eleazar and Increase [*q.v.*], occupied Massachusetts pulpits. Shortly after the death of his first wife in 1655, Mather married Sarah (Hankridge or Hawkridge) Cotton, widow of the Rev. John Cotton.

In addition to the works already mentioned, Mather is known to have published the following books: *A Catechism* (1650); *An Answer to Two Questions* (1712); *A Defence of the Answer ... of the Synod* (1664), with Jonathan Mitchell; *A Disputation Concerning Church-Members* (1659); *A Farewel-Exhortation* (1657), an Election Sermon (1660); *The Summe of Certain Sermons* (1652), and a few shorter pieces printed in books by others.

[The best authority is Increase Mather, *The Life and Death of that Reverend Man of God, Mr. Richard Mather* (1670), reprinted with Mather's journal of his voyage to America in *Dorchester Antiq. and Hist. Soc. Colls.*, no. 3 (1850). Other early biographies based on Increase Mather's book are by Cotton Mather, in his *Magnalia Christi Americana* (1702), Bk. III, Pt. 2, ch. xx; and by Samuel Clarke, in *The Lives of Sundry Eminent Persons* (1683). The best modern study is in Williston Walker, *Ten New Eng. Leaders* (1901). See also K. B. Murdock, "Richard Mather," in *Old-Time New Eng.*, Oct. 1924; H. E. Mather, *Lineage of Richard Mather* (1890); *Records of the First Ch. at Dorchester* (1891); William Beamont, *Winwick* (n.d.); Benjamin Brook, *The Lives of the Puritans* (1813), III, 440–45; V. D. Davis, *Some Account of the Ancient Chapel of Toxteth Park* (1884); S. A. Green, *Ten Fac-simile Reproductions Relating to Various Subjects* (1903); *Hist. of the Town of Dorchester* (1859); T. J. Holmes, "Notes on Richard Mather's 'Church Government,'" in *Proc. Am. Antiq. Soc,*, n.s., XXXIII (1924), 291–96; W. B. Sprague, *Annals Am. Pulpit,* vol. I (1857); John Winthrop, *Hist. of New Eng.* (2 vols., 1853), ed. by James Savage; and Anthony Wood, *Athenae Oxonienses,* vol. II (1692].

K. B. M.

MATHER, SAMUEL (Oct. 30, 1706–June 27, 1785), Congregational clergyman, author, son of Cotton Mather [*q.v.*] and his second wife, Elizabeth (Clark), was born in Boston, attended the North Grammar School, and received the degree of A.B. from Harvard in 1723. During his college course he was granted financial aid from the gifts of Nathaniel Hulton and Thomas Hollis, which his grandfather had helped to obtain for the college. In August 1724 he began preaching at Castle William, where he remained chaplain till 1732. In October 1724 he delivered a sermon at the Second Church of Boston, where his father was minister. He became an assistant to the Rev. Joshua Gee at the Second Church in 1731 and on Jan. 28, 1732, was chosen pastor by sixty-nine out of one hundred and twelve votes. On Aug. 23, 1733, he married Hannah Hutchinson, sister of Thomas [*q.v.*], later royal governor of Massachusetts. By 1741 some of Mather's flock challenged his doctrines and accused him of improper conduct. An ecclesiastical council called to investigate the charges failed to effect a reconciliation, and on Dec. 12, 1741, the church dismissed Mather with one year's salary. Ninety-three of his congregation withdrew with him and established a new church, where he ministered until his death. The charges against him do not seem to have seriously damaged his reputation in the community, and are not precisely defined. An enemy in 1773 wrote of "the fair Daughters of Liberty on whose account you have already suffered a dire flogging at an ecclesiastical council," but this is insecure evidence, even if it refers to the affair of 1741 (Timothy Prout?, *Diana's Shrines Turned into Ready Money,* 1773, p. 7).

Mather published about twenty books or pamphlets and some contributions to books by others, which display erudition rather than distinction in style or marked intellectual strength. His *Life of the Very Reverend and Learned Cotton Mather* (1729) is a useful though unsatisfactory biography. His *Attempt to Shew That America Must Be Known to the Ancients* (1773) reflects his patriotic views. He wrote verse, and his poem, *The Sacred Minister,* was printed by itself in 1773.

His eldest son, Samuel, became a Loyalist and left Boston; Thomas, the second son, died in 1782; and Increase, a third, was lost at sea. Samuel Mather was, therefore, the last of the "Mather dynasty" in the Boston pulpit. Respected, apparently, as a scholar, minister, and owner of a great library of books and manuscripts, he had neither wide public influence nor as great power as his ancestors or many of his contemporaries. He was not a successful preacher, and late in life he is said to have had "an audience of not more than twenty or thirty." A contemporary says that, "though a treasury of valuable historical anecdotes," he was "as weak a man as I ever knew" (*Proceedings of the Massachusetts Historical Society,* vol. XXXVII, 1903, p. 335). His enemies twitted him with "an itch of writing" and ambition to be president of Harvard (*Diana's Shrines,* p. 7). Against this must be weighed the recognition of his talents shown in an honorary degree of D.D. from Harvard in 1773, of M.A. from Glasgow in 1731, and of D.D. from Aberdeen in 1762. In his will he asked that there be no "funeral encomiums" for him, and that only one bell be tolled for five minutes, lest, as he said, "sick and infirm persons should be disturbed . . . at the carrying of the body of my humiliation to the silent grave."

[Most of the library which Mather inherited or accumulated was given to the Am. Antiq. Soc. by his daughter, Hannah Mather Crocker [*q.v.*]. Albert Matthews, "Samuel Mather (H. C. 1723) His Honorary Degrees and Works," in *Col. Soc. Mass. Pubs.,* vol. XVIII (1917), contains biog. data and a bibliog. of Mather's writings. See also records (MSS.) of the Second Church, Boston, and some MSS. by Mather at the Am. Antiq. Soc., the Mass. Hist. Soc., and the Boston Public Library; W. B. Sprague, *Annals Am. Pulpit,* vol. I (1857); H. E. Mather, *Lineage of Richard Mather* (1890); Chandler Robbins, *A Hist. of the Second Church, or Old North, in Boston* (1852); "Diary of Cotton Mather, 1681–1700," *Mass. Hist. Soc. Colls.,* 7 ser. VII, VIII (1911–12); J. H. Tuttle, "The Libraries of the Mathers," in *Proc. Am. Antiq. Soc.,* n.s. XX (1910); *Col. Soc. Mass. Pubs.,* vol. XVI (1925).]

K. B. M.

MATHER, SAMUEL (July 13, 1851–Oct. 18, 1931), iron merchant, financier, and philanthropist, was born in Cleveland, Ohio, the eldest son of Samuel Livingston Mather [*q.v.*] and Georgiana Pomeroy (Woolson) Mather. His mother was a grandniece of James Fenimore Cooper (Clare Benedict, *Voices Out of the Past: Five Generations, 1785–1923,* 1930, p. 71); his father was descended from the Rev. Richard Mather [*q.v.*]. Samuel attended the Cleveland high school and Saint Mark's School, Southboro, Mass., and intended to enter Harvard College in 1869. During the summer of that year he was time-keeper and payroll clerk in his father's business, the Cleveland Iron Mining Company, at Ishpeming, Mich. Seriously injured in an explosion at the company's mines, July 14, he was an invalid for nearly two years, an experience which probably prepared the way for many of his charitable interests. He then traveled in Europe for a year and a half, slowly recovering his health and acquiring an intimate knowledge of European culture.

On his return to the United States late in 1873, he entered the employ of the Cleveland Iron Mining Company, to learn the business his father had made extraordinarily successful. Following his marriage, Oct. 19, 1881, to Flor-

Amelia Stone, youngest daughter of Amasa Stone and only sister of Mrs. John Hay, he spent another period in extensive travel abroad. In 1883, with Col. James Pickands and Jay C. Morse, he organized Pickands, Mather & Company, dealers in iron ore, coal, and pig iron. On the death of Pickands in 1896 Mather became senior partner, and the business grew enormously under his guidance. The company became one of the two or three largest shippers of iron ore from the Lake Superior ranges, operated coal mines in Pennsylvania and West Virginia, blast furnaces at Chicago, Toledo, Duluth, and Erie, and a large fleet of freight carriers on the Great Lakes. Through stock ownership in the Lackawanna Steel, the Youngstown Sheet and Tube, and United States Steel concerns, the partners in Pickands, Mather & Company were assured of a market for their products. Mather's brother, William G. Mather, became president of the Cleveland Cliffs Iron Company in 1890, the successor of the old family property, the Cleveland Iron Mining Company, and Samuel was a director in this organization and also in the United States Steel. The industrial history of Northern Ohio, and to a considerable extent of the United States, is the record of the achievements of the Mathers in the iron and steel business.

Mather amassed a large fortune, and gave of it liberally and discriminatingly in varied ways. A list of his charities, like one of his corporation directorships and institutional trusteeships, would be very long. His most notable benefactions were his gifts to Kenyon College and to Western Reserve University and its affiliated hospitals; his most notable public service was his share in the establishment of the Cleveland Community Fund. The latter grew out of the Cleveland Red Cross War Council, of which Mather became chairman in 1917. Of the Community Fund he was honorary chairman from its origin (1920) until his death, eleven years later, and its largest contributor. His will provided for the continuation of his support of this fund and of some fifty-six other annual subscriptions to as many educational or charitable institutions. For forty-five years he gave invaluable service as a trustee and, from 1914, as vice-president of Western Reserve University. In 1920 the government of Serbia honored him with the Cross of Mercy for his generous gifts to its people during the Great War; France, in 1922, awarded him the Cross of the Legion of Honor for similar benefactions. In 1924 he became the first recipient of the Cleveland Chamber of Commerce medal for conspicuous service in his own community. In the view of Mather's closest friends his first interest was his church, the Protestant Episcopal. He was senior warden of Trinity Cathedral, Cleveland, an active officer in the diocese of Ohio, an annual delegate to the diocesan convention, and regularly a deputy to the General Convention. He was also a member of the National Council of the Episcopal Church. His vigorous, dominating personality impressed all who were associated with him. He grasped the details of complex situations whether in business, charitable, or educational affairs; remembered these details when others thought them forgotten; and reached decisions with promptness and finality. His wife, who was actively interested in all his charities, died in 1909; three of their four children survived him.

[H. E. Mather, *Lineage of Rev. Richard Mather* (1890); *Who's Who in America,* 1928–29; *Who's Who in Finance,* 1911; E. M. Avery, *A Hist. of Cleveland and Its Environs* (1918), vol. III; *Cleveland Plain Dealer, Cleveland News,* and *Cleveland Press,* Oct. 19, 1931; notes collected for use in a biography by T. J. Holmes, librarian of the W. G. Mather Library, Cleveland.]

E. J. B.

MATHER, SAMUEL HOLMES (Mar. 20, 1813–Jan. 14, 1894), lawyer, banker, the second of the two sons of Dr. Ozias and Harriet (Brainard) Mather, was born in Washington, N. H. His father was the son of Dr. Augustus Mather of Lyme, Conn., and a descendant of Rev. Richard Mather [*q.v.*] of Dorchester, Mass.; his mother, the daughter of Jabez Brainard of Washington and Lempster, N. H., was also a member of an old New England family of English ancestry. Ozias Mather died the same year Samuel was born. The boy attended the academy of his native town, and Kimball Union Academy, Meriden, N. H. He graduated with high honors from Dartmouth College in the class of 1834. For fifteen months after graduation he studied in a law office in Geneva, N. Y. Attracted to Cleveland, Ohio, in December 1835, by reports friends gave him of the opportunities in that growing city, he continued his study of law there and was admitted to the bar in 1836.

In 1849 he joined with others who had formerly lived in New England in establishing the Society for Savings, modeled after an organization then popular in New England, the name being suggested by that of a similar society in Hartford, Conn. Mather was from the first its secretary and chief officer, and soon began to devote practically all his time to the institution. In 1884 he became its president, an office he held until his death, Myron T. Herrick [*q.v.*] succeeding him. Mather described the Cleveland Society for Savings as "a benevolent institution, without capital, managed by trustees without salary, in the interest of the depositors only, to whom profits are paid, or for whose benefit they are accumulated and reserved." Under Mather's direction it came to be a powerful, conservative banking house. Its policies, and particularly the high rate of interest it could pay on time savings deposits, benefited savings accounts in all the Cleveland banks. At the time of his death, one in six of the population of Cleveland was a depositor in the Society for Savings, and the total deposits amounted to $23,000,000.

Mather's record as a business man was above reproach. Fairness and trustworthiness won him the confidence of his community. From 1854 to 1857 inclusive he was a member of the board of education, and for the first three years secretary, or acting business manager, of the schools. In the latter capacity he was charged with much of the detail work which fell to the board, the selection of teachers, and the supervision of the construction of buildings. On May 9, 1842, he married Emily W. Gregory, daughter of Uriah M. Gregory of Sand Lake, N. Y. His interests, aside from his business, were centered in the Second Presbyterian Church, of which he was an elder. He was survived by two children.

[H. E. Mather, *Lineage of Rev. Richard Mather* (1890); L. A. Brainard, *The Geneal. of the Brainerd-Brainard Family in America* (1908); G. T. Chapman, *Sketches of the Alumni of Dartmouth Coll.* (1867); obituary in *Cleveland Leader*, Jan. 14, 1894, reprinted in the *Annals of the Early Settlers Asso. of Cuyahoga County, Ohio* (1894); *Cleveland Weekly Leader*, Jan. 20, 1894; *Three Score Years and Ten: The Story of the Rise of the Society for Savings* (1919); *The Banker's Mag.*, Feb. 1894.] E. J. B.

MATHER, SAMUEL LIVINGSTON (July 1, 1817–Oct. 8, 1890), capitalist, was born in Middletown, Conn. His father, Samuel, was descended from the Rev. Richard Mather [*q.v.*] of Dorchester, Mass.; his mother, Catherine (Livingston), was a daughter of Abram Livingston of Stillwater, N. Y. Samuel Livingston Mather's grandfather, Samuel, was a lawyer of Middletown, and a stockholder in the Connecticut Land Company which purchased the Western Reserve Tract along the south shore of Lake Erie. His son, Samuel Mather, Jr., graduated from Yale College in 1792 and went into the commission business in Albany, N. Y. Samuel Livingston graduated from Wesleyan University, Middletown, in 1835. He was in his father's employ for a time and later, until 1843, was in the commission business in New York City on his own account. During these years he twice visited Europe. He was subsequently sent to Cleveland to dispose of the family's Western Reserve holdings and to act as agent for other eastern interests with land in Ohio. Soon after his settlement in Cleveland he was admitted to the bar, but never practised law.

The discovery of iron ore in the Lake Superior region determined his life interest. About 1850 several Cleveland business men, of whom he was one, organized the Cleveland Iron Mining Company to conduct exploration for iron ore and to purchase ore lands. In 1853 Mather became secretary-treasurer, and the driving force in the organization. Within a year the company began shipping ore. For a short time the ore was hauled by wagons to the lake shore, transferred to small wooden sailing vessels, unloaded for portage at "The Soo," loaded again for lake passage to Cleveland, and there transferred to canal and railroads for distribution to the furnaces of Ohio and Pennsylvania. Under Mather's guidance the Cleveland Iron Mining Company, later known as the Cleveland Cliffs Company, steadily improved the means of shipping iron ore, building railroad lines and larger ore boats. The construction of the canal at Sault Sainte Marie greatly facilitated the company's ore trade. The foresight and business ability of Mather and a few others revolutionized the iron industry in the United States; gave it a bountiful supply of raw material; and drew it toward northern Ohio, and the lake ports. The beginning of Cleveland's industrial prominence may be attributed to the Cleveland Iron Mining Company more than to any other single enterprise. In 1869 Mather became president and treasurer of the company, offices which he held until his death. As the iron industry developed he extended his personal activities and investments into allied fields. He was secretary and manager of the Marquette Iron Company, a director of the Bancroft Iron Company, president of the Cleveland Boiler Plate Company, of the American Iron Mining Company, and of the McComber Iron Company. After his death his sons, Samuel, 1851–1931 [*q.v.*], and William G. Mather, carried on and developed further their father's manifold iron interests.

On Sept. 24, 1850, Mather married Georgiana Pomeroy Woolson, who died Nov. 2, 1853; on June 11, 1856, he married Elizabeth Lucy Gwin. He gave liberally of his abundant means to charitable and religious objects.

[H. E. Mather, *Lineage of Rev. Richard Mather* (1890); *Alumni Record of Wesleyan Univ.* (1883); *Cleveland Leader* and *Cleveland Plain Dealer*, Oct. 9, 1890; E. M. Avery, *A Hist. of Cleveland and Its Environs* (1918), vol. III; *The Cleveland Cliffs Iron Company, An Hist. Rev.* (*c.* 1920); MSS. in the W. G. Mather Library, Cleveland.] E. J. B.

MATHER, STEPHEN TYNG (July 4, 1867–Jan. 22, 1930), organizer and director of the

National Park Service of the Interior Department, was a descendant of Rev. Richard Mather [*q.v.*], who became teacher of the church at Dorchester, Mass., in 1636. The son of Joseph Wakeman Mather of Connecticut and Bertha Jemima (Walker), he was born in San Francisco and graduated from the University of California in 1887. After graduation, he was a successful reporter on the New York *Sun* until 1893, when he went into the New York office of the Pacific Coast Borax Company, of which his father was manager. In 1894 he planned and established the company's distribution center at Chicago, and became its manager. In 1903, he helped organize the Thorkildsen-Mather Borax Company of Chicago in competition for the business of the continent, and about 1920 became president of its successor, the Sterling Borax Company. He was also president of the Brighton Chemical Company of Pennsylvania.

It was not, however, as a business man that he achieved nation-wide repute, but as organizer and upbuilder of the system of national parks. In order to bring the fourteen national parks into cooperation under a bureau to be created for the purpose, he accepted in 1915 Franklin K. Lane's invitation to become assistant to the secretary of the interior, and upon Lane's insistence, two years later, he became first director of the new National Park Service. During his twelve years' administration of this office, he brought the national park system into a high degree of development, differentiated it from land systems of lesser scenic standard, and made it celebrated over the world.

Since Congress had never verbally defined national parks to distinguish them in kind and use from state parks and others, Mather at the very outset of his administration sought warrant for his idealistic views in the national parks already created by Congress. A study of these authorized their official defining as areas of unmodified primitive condition, scenically the finest—each of its kind—in the country, preserved forever from industrial use. This view, agreed to by the Interior Department and accepted in Congressional practice, became his measure for park selections. The fourteen national parks in unrelated existence at the time he assumed office had become twenty-one closely related cooperating units of a highly developed system when failing health forced his resignation in 1929. Several had been eliminated, while those added under his promotion included Rocky Mountain, Hawaii, Lassen Volcanic, Mount McKinley, Grand Canyon, Zion, Bryce Canyon, Grand Teton, and Great Smoky Mountains. His opposition in Congress to many local bills for proposed national parks of lesser scenic importance performed excellent service in educating both Congress and the people in national park ideals. His establishment and maintenance of the national park standards were the greater achievement because during the period of his administration long-distance motor touring spread over the country a mesh of surfaced highways and filled the parks to overflowing with motoring explorers. For a decade, recreation became the nation's fetish to the exclusion from public recognition of the parks' major uses of education and inspiration.

Mather probably owed his popularity as much to his personality as to the dignity and sincerity of his public service. Modest, simple, and friendly in manner and speech, he was fearless and untiring in the prosecution of what he conceived to be a high mission of civilization. A profound lover of beauty in nature in its simplest as well as its sublime manifestations and an uncompromising defender of wild life, he nevertheless saw all in terms of human enjoyment and inspiration. He was a constant traveler and a ready and frequent speaker on national park policies, but though he was an able writer made little use of his pen, even in private life preferring the telegraph or long-distance telephone. His bibliography consists of signed reports of park progress and planning from 1915 to 1930 inclusive, together with articles and letters to be found in the files of the National Park Service. Those who were closely associated with him during his public career found him devoid of political and personal ambition of any kind. His defender, he used to say, would always be his record, and the story of the National Parks in the process of organization is his biography.

Mather was married, Oct. 12, 1893, to Jane Thacker Floy of Elizabeth, N. J. They had one child, a daughter. Mather's residence from the time of his connection with the National Park Service was in Washington, D. C., but the old Mather place at Darien, Conn., was his summer home for many years. He died in Brookline, Mass.

[*Who's Who in America*, 1928–29; H. E. Mather, *Lineage of Rev. Richard Mather* (1890); *Survey*, July 1930; *Saturday Evening Post*, Feb. 23, 1929; *Nature Mag.*, Mar. 1930; *Playground*, Mar. 1930; *Science*, Feb. 26, 1932; *N. Y. Times*, Jan. 23, and editorial, Jan. 24, 1930; files of the Nat. Park Service; information as to certain facts from Mrs. Mather; personal acquaintance.]

R. S. Y.

MATHER, WILLIAM WILLIAMS (May 24, 1804–Feb. 26, 1859), geologist, son of Eleazar and Fanny (Williams) Mather, was born in Brooklyn, Windham County, Conn. His father was of English descent, through Timothy, son of Richard Mather [*q.v.*], who came to Massachusetts in 1635 and settled in Dorchester the following year. It is said that William was at first inclined toward the medical profession and went to Providence, R. I., to study; but in 1823, when not quite nineteen years of age, he sought and secured admission to the United States Military Academy at West Point, and was graduated and brevetted second lieutenant of the 7th Regiment of Infantry in 1828.

He early showed a bent toward the sciences. During his West Point career he made experiments to determine the temperature at the bottom of an ice-coated stream and is said to have aided in the preparation of Webster's textbook of chemistry (Austin, *post*), and in the year of his graduation (1828) he published in the *American Journal of Science* an article, "On the Non-conducting Power of Water in Relation to Heat." After a brief service on the Louisiana frontier, he was acting professor of chemistry and mineralogy in the Military Academy, 1829–35, and meantime, with permission of the Secretary of War, acted during 1833 as professor of chemistry, mineralogy, and geology in Wesleyan University, Middletown, Conn. In this year he published *Elements of Geology for the Use of Schools,* which seems to have been fairly well received. Promoted first lieutenant in 1834, he served as a topographical engineer with G. W. Featherstonhaugh in a geological survey from Green Bay, Wis., to the Coteau de Prairie, June–December 1835, and was then assigned to frontier duty in Indian Territory. On Aug. 31, 1836, he resigned his commission to enter upon the profession of geology.

For a short while he was professor of chemistry at the University of Louisiana (Cullum, *post,* p. 412). From 1836 to 1844 he served as geologist of the first district in the geological survey of New York; during 1837 and 1838 he served also as director of the geological survey of Ohio, and in 1838–39 as state geologist of Kentucky. Of his work with the several state surveys, that in New York was most important. His report (*Geology of New York,* Pt. I, 1843), comprising 639 quarto pages with forty-five plates and a geological map, was the most voluminous of the series, but while highly creditable was not the most valuable. His views on causes of folding, uplift, and depression of portions of the earth's crust seem to have excited little interest, and he assigned the glacial drift to ice-laden currents from the north, a not uncommon explanation at that period. In general, he made too large an appeal to oceanic currents to account for sundry effects possibly ascribable to other causes. His work with the contemporaneous Ohio and Kentucky surveys was necessarily limited in large degree to administration. The Ohio survey lasted but two years and yielded two annual reports, both bearing the date of 1838. His personal contribution had to do mainly with economic questions. He estimated that there were within the state limits coal resources "not only sufficient for domestic use for any reasonable time, but to supply the country around the lakes, and throughout the valleys of the Ohio and Mississippi, for as long a time as it is proper to calculate" (*Second Annual Report of the Geological Survey of the State of Ohio,* p. 8). His work in Kentucky was purely in the nature of reconnaissance and yielded no direct results (*Report on the Geological Reconnoissance of Kentucky Made in 1838,* 1839).

From 1842 to 1845 he was professor of natural science in Ohio University at Athens, and after 1847 vice-president and acting president of the same institution. He was at various times elected to scientific and literary organizations, and for fifteen years was a trustee of Granville College, Ohio. He died in Columbus, quite unexpectedly, in his fifty-fifth year.

Mather was a man of powerful frame and robust health, with resolute will and enthusiastic devotion to his chosen calling. He was twice married, first to his cousin, Emily Maria Baker, who died in November 1850, leaving six children, and second, in August 1857, to Mrs. Mary Curtis (*née* Harry), by whom he had one child, a son.

[I. J. Austin, in *Memorial Biogs. of the New-Eng. Hist. Geneal. Soc.,* vol. III (1883); W. J. Youmans, *Pioneers of Science in America* (1896); *Am. Jour. Sci.,* May 1859; G. W. Cullum, *Biog. Reg. Officers and Grads. U. S. Mil. Acad.* (3rd ed., 1891); H. E. Mather, *Lineage of Rev. Richard Mather* (1890); *Ohio Statesman* (Columbus), Mar. 1, 1859.] G. P. M.

MATHESON, WILLIAM JOHN (Sept. 15, 1856–May 15, 1930), chemist, financier, and philanthropist, was born in Elkhorn, Wis., the son of Finlay and Anna Meigs (Lighthall) Matheson. After a boyhood in British Guinea, he was educated at St. Andrews, Scotland. His interest in chemistry began during his school days, and when twenty years old he opened a laboratory in New York City. Little was then known in America regarding the production of synthetic colors, and in the development of the processes of dyeing he found his greatest opportunity. He secured, first, an appointment as representative of A. Porrier, Paris, but by 1880 he had joined Leopold Cassella & Company, beginning an association which covered a period of forty years. Though in time he organized his own companies, among them the W. J. Matheson Company, Ltd., the Matheson Lead Company, and the Hamolin Company, it was the Cassella Color Company, distributors of synthetic hydro-carbons, to which in later years he gave almost his entire attention. At the outbreak of the World War, he devoted his energies to stabilizing the dye industry, and when the entry of the United States into that conflict cut off the American importation of German dyes, he used his experience and ability in meeting his country's needs. As president and chairman of the board of the National Aniline & Chemical Company, he was a leader in the development of the practical as well as the scientific aspects of the dye industry. He was also instrumental in organizing the Allied Chemical & Dye Corporation, usually regarded as the climax of his business career of fifty years, covering almost the entire history of American synthetic dyes. In 1920 St. Andrews University, Scotland, bestowed upon him the degree of LL.D. in recognition of his achievements.

His interests were by no means confined to his chosen profession. He was a pioneer in real-estate projects in Florida, where he made his winter home for twenty-five years, beginning operations there in 1904. To the Long Island Biological Association, which he served as president from 1905 to 1923, he gave freely of his time and resources. One of his important achievements, it is said, was the extermination of mosquitoes from the north shore of Long Island. Occasionally he turned antiquarian, and in 1918 published *An Historical Sketch of Fort Hill, Lloyd Neck, Long Island.*

Though many philanthropic enterprises gained his attention from time to time, perhaps his greatest service to mankind was the establishment of a fund, in 1927, for an international study of epidemic encephalitis, popularly known as "sleeping sickness." A committee of eminent physicians representing the laboratory, clinical, and epidemiological viewpoints was appointed for the purpose of collecting and tabulating the work being done throughout the world on this subject. The first report of the Matheson Commission, *Epidemic Encephalitis,* was published in 1929. The commission was deprived of his personal assistance by his sudden death on board his yacht, the *Seaforth,* while returning from a cruise in the Bahama Islands, but the continuance of its work was assured by the terms of his will, which established a fund of two million dollars for the organization and maintenance of the William J. Matheson Foundation for charitable and educational purposes, its first work to be in encephalitis research. In 1881 Matheson married Harriet Torrey, and to them two sons and one daughter were born.

[*N. Y. Times,* June 5, 1927, Nov. 17, 1929, May 16, 27, 29, 1930; *Miami Herald,* May 16, 1930; *Chemical Markets,* June 1930; *Textile Colorist,* June 1930; *Who's Who in America,* 1930–31; *Who's Who in Finance, Banking, and Insurance,* 1929–30; preface to *Epidemic Encephalitis* (1929).] I. V–F.

MATHEWS, ALBERT (Sept. 8, 1820–Sept. 9, 1903), author, the son of Oliver and Mary (Field) Mathews, was born of a well-to-do family in New York City and there received his early education. Entering Yale College he graduated in 1842 and devoted the next three years to the study of law, first at the Harvard Law School and later in New York. In 1845 he was admitted to the bar and immediately went into partnership with Augustus L. Brown. The new firm of Brown & Mathews became attorneys for the sheriff, and Mathews found himself launched almost at once into a lucrative practice. He was married twice, first on Dec. 12, 1849, to Louise Mott Strong, who lived only a few years, and, on Mar. 20, 1861, to Mrs. Cettie (Moore) Gwynne, who died in 1884. All through his early years as a practising lawyer, he had contributed essays and articles to the periodical press, but not until a few months before his second marriage, and perhaps in connection with his courtship, did he begin to take authorship very seriously. In 1860 he published his first book, *Walter Ashwood, A Love Story.* This novel is altogether a very wooden performance having a faintly Byronesque hero and the approved sentimental flavor of the day. As his *nom de plume* he continued to use Paul Siogvolk, the same name under which his earlier essays and legends had been written and which he used for all subsequent writing of a non-legal character. His essays and legends are the best of the work he has left and are of creditable literary quality, though, of course, outmoded as regards technique and style. In the main their tone is rather grave than gay, and their appeal was limited to the thoughtful and reflective few. He figured prominently in the foundation of the New York City bar association. In 1879 he became a member of the bar association of the state of New York. In the same year he brought out a collection of essays under the title *A Bundle of Papers.* Other writings of a mixed character followed in rapid succession: *Thoughts on Codification of the Common Law* (1881); *Memorial of Bernard Roelker* (1889); *Ruminations* (1893); *A Few Verses* (1896). By 1897 both his partners A. L. Brown and G. W. Blunt were dead, and he, himself, had virtually retired. To his friends he was known as an amiable and genial character, and among them he acquired a degree of celebrity by the enticing way in which he was able to word legal forms of a content intrinsically grim. Though nicknamed after the Prince Consort because of his stately bearing, he could unbend when occasion demanded and beam very winningly through his antique gold spectacles upon judges and juries who failed to respond to impersonal logic. In a purely professional way, he was distinctively a court lawyer and dealt for the greater part in the trial of causes and the arguing of appeals. As he specialized closely in no single branch of the law, he has left no work of a permanently valuable character. In the proceedings of the bar associations of the city and of the state he was active to the end of his life and to the city association he left a generous legacy when he died. His death occurred at Lake Mohonk, N. Y.

[*Who's Who in America*, 1903–05; *Biog. Record of the Class of 1842 of Yale College* (1878); *Green Bag*, Jan. 1897; *Asso. of the Bar of the City of N. Y. Reports . . . 1904* (1905); *N. Y. State Bar Asso. Reports*, vol. V (1882); *N. Y. Times*, Sept. 10, 12, 1903.]

E. M. H.

MATHEWS, CORNELIUS (Oct. 28, 1817–Mar. 25, 1889), author, was born in Port Chester, N. Y., the second son of Abijah and Catherine (Van Cott) Mathews. He was descended from Annanias Mathews an early settler in Long Island. During the years 1830–32 he was enrolled in Columbia College, but in the fall of 1832 he matriculated at the University of the City of New York (now New York University), which had just opened for instruction, and in July 1834 he received his A.B. degree at the first Commencement of the new university, delivering an oration on "Females of the American Revolution." He was, apparently, related to the first chancellor of the University, Rev. James M. Mathews; this relationship may have had some connection with his transfer from Columbia to the new university. His membership in the college literary society, the *Adelphic*, which published a magazine (under the inspiration of Professor Henry B. Tappan, afterward chancellor of the University of Michigan), may possibly have affected his later career. To please his father he studied law and in 1837 was admitted to the New York bar, but he soon abandoned this profession and turned to literary production and editorial work.

He had since 1836 contributed regularly to the *American Monthly Magazine*, the *New York Review*, and the *Knickerbocker Magazine* articles in both prose and verse, mostly humorous in character. In 1839 appeared his first romance, *Behemoth: a Legend of the Mound Builders*, an imaginative story of which it can at least be said that the plot is original. In 1840, with his friend Evert A. Duyckinck [*q.v.*], he founded and edited a monthly magazine, *Arcturus, a Journal of Books and Opinion*, of which three volumes appeared, and in which Mathews wrote numerous articles, mostly critical, but including a novel, "The Career of Puffer Hopkins" (June 1841–May 1842) on the theme of New York politics. He had already turned to the drama, and in 1840 brought out *The Politicians*, a comedy on New York electioneering life, which had no success. In 1846 his tragedy, *Witchcraft, or the Martyrs of Salem*, met with unusual success, and was even translated into French. Its blank verse is often excellent, and it possesses considerable dramatic power. Two other plays, *Jacob Leisler* (1848), a tragedy, and *False Pretences* (1855), a satire on social parvenus, met a less popular response.

His *Poems on Man in His Various Aspects under the American Republic*, published in 1843, was favorably received by critics, especially by James Russell Lowell, whose remarks upon them in the *Fable for Critics*

> "(which contain many verses as fine, by the bye
> As any that lately came under my eye)"

give Mathews today perhaps his chief claim to fame. Lowell, be it added, has several other less complimentary references to Mathews in the *Fable for Critics*, particularly with regard to the copyright issue and in association with E. A. Duyckinck. Perhaps the reader of today will best sympathize with Lowell's caustic judgment of *Yankee Doodle*, a comic magazine edited by Mathews in 1846–47:

> "That American Punch, like the English, no doubt,
> Just the sugar and lemons and spirit left out."

Mathews in his earlier years, at any rate, was a vigorous nationalist in his literary ideals and insisted that the United States needed a literature which should not be imitative of Europe, but original and American in its essence. At the same time he was always an enthusiastic champion of international copyright, and welcomed the occasion of speaking on that topic at the dinner given to Charles Dickens in 1842. Elizabeth Barrett Browning, also, found his friendship of assistance in first securing American attention to her verse.

After 1855 he published little. The *Indian Fairy Book*, which was compiled by Mathews from material supplied by Henry R. Schoolcraft, is the only book to bear his name. It was issued first in 1856 and was republished in later editions, in 1877 as *The Enchanted Moccassins*. Mathews appears, however, to have continued his association with the world of journalism and after 1882 was regularly until his death a contributing editor of the *New York Dramatic Mirror.* He never married.

[E. A. and G. L. Duyckinck, *Cyc. of Am. Lit.* (2 vols., 1875); C. Mathews, "Temple Court," in the *Manhattan,* July 1883; *N. Y. Dramatic Mirror,* Apr. 6, 1889; *N. Y. Times,* Mar. 27, 1889; A. H. Quinn, *A Hist. of the Am. Drama from the Beginning to the Civil War* (1923); manuscript records of N. Y. Univ., manuscript recollections of Mathews' niece, Frances A. Mathews.] T. F. J.

MATHEWS, GEORGE (Aug. 30, 1739–Aug. 30, 1812), Revolutionary soldier, congressman, and governor, son of John Mathews, a recent Irish immigrant, was born in Augusta County, Va., and fought the Indians at Point Pleasant (Oct. 10, 1774). During the Revolution he took part in the campaigns around Philadelphia, spent some months in a British prison ship, and later served with distinction as colonel of Virginia troops in Greene's Carolina campaigns. Removing to Georgia in 1785, he became brigadier-general in the militia of that state, governor in 1787, and its representative in Congress, 1789–91. As governor of the state again, 1793–96, he opposed the filibustering operations of Elijah Clarke [*q.v.*] and his associates and signed the notorious Yazoo Act. In 1798 President Adams nominated him as first governor of Mississippi Territory, but within a month was obliged to withdraw his name because of his dubious land speculations and suspected connection with the Blount Conspiracy (Cox, "Border Missions," *post,* p. 309). Mathews journeyed to Philadelphia, according to reports, to chastise the President, but desisted from his purpose when his son was given a federal appointment (Gilmer, *post,* pp. 73–82). He appears to have been married three times; his first wife, *née* Woods, was of Albemarle County, Va.; his second, Mrs. Reed of Staunton, whom he divorced; and his third, Mrs. Flowers of Mississippi. He had four sons and two daughters.

In the fall of 1810 he was employed, evidently on the initiative of William H. Crawford [*q.v.*], to sound Vizente Folch, the Spanish executive of West Florida, on the question of delivering that province to the United States. In this he failed (Cox, *op. cit.,* pp. 310–12), but his observations around Mobile and St. Augustine convinced him that both Floridas should at once be brought under the control of the United States. During the following winter he was at Washington when the administration received from Folch a belated but conditional offer to deliver his province. Congress having authorized its acceptance and also, in certain contingencies, the occupation of East Florida, Mathews and John McKee, the bearer of Folch's offer, were authorized to take the necessary steps in the transfer. When, however, the commissioners interviewed Folch at Mobile in March 1811, that executive refused to make the proffered delivery (*Ibid.,* 312–17).

This refusal evidently convinced Mathews that in respect to East Florida, where he believed his instructions empowered him to continue irregular activities, he must employ more direct if dubious methods. He had already (1810–11) sought to stir up insurrection there and by an interview with Crawford in October 1811 was further confirmed in his tortuous course, although the administration left him without further instructions. His method of procedure was to organize the English-speaking Spanish subjects of East Florida, draft recruits in nearby Georgia, and when these irregular contingents were ready, secure "volunteers" from among the American regulars. Thus he hoped to bring about the surprise and capture of St. Augustine. This plan failed through the opposition of the American military commander, but the "insurgents" declared independence of Spain and on Mar. 17, 1812, aided by recruits from Georgia and by the intervention of the American gunboats on the St. Marys, forced the surrender of Fernandina. On the following day Mathews took formal possession of that smuggling center in the name of the United States. Following this initial success the "insurgents" successively occupied outlying portions of the province and then turned each over to Mathews, who, with his regulars, followed them closely. In this piecemeal fashion the two contingents, early in June, came within sight of St. Augustine. Here Mathews was halted by Secretary Monroe's tardy but complete disavowal of his course. The Secretary in a private letter praised his agent's zeal, but regretted that he had not used more "restrained" methods.

For some weeks the repudiated commissioner preserved silence; then, the rôle of silent martyr becoming unbearable, the impulsive old man started northward, fell ill at Augusta, and fulfilled Crawford's presentiment that he would "die of mortification and resentment" (Pratt, *post,* p. 114) over his repudiation. By his demise the authorities at Washington escaped the consequences of his threat that he'd "be dam'd if he didn't blow them all up" (*Ibid.,* p. 115), and he carried to the grave much evidence that might explain his debatable conduct.

[The foregoing account is largely based on manuscript material found in *Papeles procedentes de la Isla de Cuba,* Archivo General, Seville; in the Pickering Papers at the Mass. Hist. Soc.; and in the various collections of the Division of Publications, Dept. of State, and of the Lib. of Cong. Consult I. J. Cox, "The Border Missions of General George Mathews," in *Miss. Valley Hist. Rev.*, Dec. 1925; J. W. Pratt, *Expansionists of 1812* (1925); and I. J. Cox, *The West Fla. Controversy* (1918). An article based on printed material is R. K. Wyllys, "The East Florida Revolution of 1812–1814," in *Hispanic Hist. Rev.*, Nov. 1929. Some details of Mathews' early life are found in *Cyc. of Ga.* (1906), vol. II, and in G. R. Gilmer, *Sketches of Some of the First Settlers of Upper Ga.* (1855). An obituary notice appeared in the *Republican and Savannah Evening Ledger*, Sept. 3, 1812.] I. J. C.

MATHEWS, HENRY MASON (Mar. 29, 1834–Apr. 28, 1884), governor of West Virginia, the eldest son of Mason and Eliza Shore (Reynolds) Mathews, was born in Greenbrier County, Va., now W. Va. His mother was a sister of Alexander Welch Reynolds [*q.v.*]. The elder Mathews was a successful merchant and was able to give his son good opportunities for schooling. Young Mathews was prepared for college at the Lewisburg academy and in his eighteenth year entered the University of Virginia. He was a student there from 1852 to 1856 and received the A.B. degree in 1855 and the A.M. degree in 1856. After leaving the university he studied law for one year in the school conducted by Judge John W. Brockenbrough, of Lexington, Va. In 1857 he began the practice of the law at Lewisburg, the county seat of Greenbrier County, and on Nov. 24 of that year he married Lucy Clayton Fry, the daughter of Judge Joseph L. Fry, of Wheeling. They had two daughters and a son. For a short period before the Civil War he added to his duties as an attorney the teaching of modern languages and history in Allegheny College, a school for boys at Blue Sulphur Springs. When hostilities broke out he enlisted in the Confederate service and by the end of the war had attained the rank of major.

At the close of the war he returned to Lewisburg, but for a while was debarred from the practice of his profession by the proscriptive laws against former Confederates. In like manner he was also excluded from the state Senate, although he had been elected by an overwhelming majority. In 1872 he was a member of the state convention that framed the present constitution of West Virginia. He was in this same year also elected attorney-general of the state. Four years later, in 1876, he was nominated by the Democratic party for governor and was elected by a very large majority. He became governor at a time when passions born of civil war and reconstruction ran high. He was well qualified by temperament, education, and experience for the task of allaying strife and of mediating between the opposing parties. His genial disposition and gentle demeanor enabled him to make contacts with his political opponents with a minimum of friction. The keynote of his inaugural address was harmony, and the policy of his administration was characterized by the same spirit. He appointed representatives of both parties on all important governmental boards, a practice that was unusual for that period. The most dramatic event of his four-year term was the great railroad strike, which was caused by a ten per cent. reduction in the wages of employees of the Baltimore & Ohio Railroad. It started at Martinsburg in July 1877 and soon spread to other points in West Virginia and to other states, since the same reduction in wages had been made by other railroad systems. The mob violence that attended the strike at Martinsburg was beyond the control of the police authorities, and at other places outbreaks were threatening. He insisted that grievances, however great, must be redressed through legal means alone, and so he promptly ordered out the state militia, but the force at his command was too small to cope with the riot. Thereupon he called upon the president for federal troops. This request was complied with, and order was promptly restored. Mathews showed the same firmness in dealing with the coal strike that broke out along the Chesapeake and Ohio Railway three years later, in January 1880. The strikers, who were threatening injury to persons and the destruction of property, were moving toward the Ansted mines in Fayette County to compel the miners there to cease work. At the request of the sheriff of the county he promptly sent a battalion of infantry and all disorder was quickly put down. The last few years of his life were spent at Lewisburg in the practice of his profession.

[Information from his daughter, L. Josephine Mathews, and from the registrar of the University of Virginia; Phil Conley, *The W. Va. Encyc.* (1929); R. E. Fast and Hu Maxwell, *The Hist. and Government of W. Va.* (1901); G. W. Atkinson and A. F. Gibbens, *Prominent Men of W. Va.* (1890); *Jour. of the House of Delegates of . . . W. Va.*, 1879, pp. 32–34, 1881, pp. 23–24; *Wheeling Daily Intelligencer*, Mar. 6, 7, July 17–21, 1877, Jan. 12–17, 1880; *Wheeling Register*, Apr. 30, 1884.] O. P. C.

MATHEWS, JOHN (1744–Oct. 26, 1802), delegate to the Continental Congress, governor of South Carolina, was born at Charlestown (now Charleston), S. C., the son of John and Sarah (Gibbes) Mathews. In 1760 he was ensign and then lieutenant in the expedition against the Cherokee. On Oct. 27, 1764, he was admitted to the Middle Temple in London to study law and on Sept. 22, 1766, was admitted to the bar of South Carolina. In December of that year he was married to Mary Wragg, the daughter of William Wragg and the half-sister of Charlotte

Wragg who married William Loughton Smith [*q.v.*]. In the quarrel between Great Britain and the colonies he early took the colonial side, served in the first and second provincial congresses from St. George's, Dorchester, was elected as associate justice of the court of general sessions in 1776, and became speaker of the General Assembly under the temporary constitution of 1776 and the first speaker of the House of Representatives under the constitution of 1778. From 1778 to 1782 he represented South Carolina in the Continental Congress, where he voted against the motion privately to instruct the minister to Spain that he might recede from the claim to free navigation of the Mississippi River, bitterly opposed Samuel Huntington of Connecticut, the president of Congress, bent his whole efforts to defeating the proposal to make a separate peace between Great Britain and the other colonies at the price of abandoning the Carolinas and Georgia, and signed the Articles of Confederation. On the committee at headquarters in 1780 he was most active in his efforts to strengthen Washington's authority and greatly injured the Congress' sense of its own dignity by his outspoken expression of impatience at its failure to act. In 1782 he was elected governor by the Jonesborough Assembly. Through the next year of the war, he transacted the business of his office from various places, part of the time from his plantation of "Uxbridge" on the Ashley River, which had been a part of the Ashley barony. He negotiated with the British on the difficult questions of sequestration, confiscation, and destruction of property, struggled with the conflicting interests of the inhabitants and the army that had been impressing the foodstuffs of which it stood in urgent need, and, when at last the British troops sailed out of Charlestown harbor, took possession of his own capital city. He has been accused of the abuse of men and property left behind by the British evacuation and even of permitting the hanging of several Tories, but a recent examination of the evidence seems to indicate that such charges were unfounded (J. W. Barnwell, "Evacuation of Charleston by the British," *South Carolina Historical and Genealogical Magazine,* January 1910).

When the court of chancery was established on Mar. 21, 1784, he was appointed by the legislature as chancellor and, after the organization of the courts of law and equity in 1791, continued to serve as a judge of the court of equity. His decisions show his legal capacity and learning as well as his grasp of the principles of fundamental justice (1 *S. C. Equity Reports,* especially the case of *Deveaux* vs. *Executors of Barnwell,* pp. 497–98). He resigned in November 1797. He was one of the original trustees of the College of Charleston and he helped found the St. George's Club of St. George's Parish, Dorchester, for the encouragement of the breeding of good horses. After the death of his first wife he married, on May 5, 1799, Sarah, the sister of John and Edward Rutledge [*qq.v.*]. No children survived him.

[A few MSS. in the Lib. of Cong.; R. W. Gibbes, *Documentary Hist. of the Am. Revolution,* vols. II (1857), III (1853); E. C. Burnett, *Letters of Members of the Continental Cong.,* vols. IV–V (1928–31); Wm. Moultrie, *Memoirs of the Am. Revolution* (1802), vol. II, esp. pp. 330–36, 343–51, 359; J. B. O'Neall, *Biog. Sketches of the Bench and Bar of S. C.* (1859), vol. I; Edward McCrady, *The Hist. of S. C. under the Royal Government* (1899) and *The Hist. of S. C. in the Revolution* (1901); David Ramsay, *The Hist. of S. C.* (1809), I, pp. 468, 471–75, II, pp. 135, 146–47, 155, 384; E. A. Jones, *Am. Members of the Inns of Court* (1924); *S. C. Hist. and Geneal. Mag.,* Oct. 1902, Apr. 1906, Jan., Apr. 1907, Apr. 1910, Jan. 1916, Oct. 1917, July 1919, July 1924, Oct. 1925, Jan., Apr. 1926; *Carolina Gazette,* Nov. 4, 1802.]

K. E. C.

MATHEWS, SAMUEL (*c.* 1600–January 1660), colonial planter and last governor of Virginia under the Commonwealth, was born in England, coming to Virginia in 1622 and forthwith engaging actively in the colony's affairs. The next year, after serving in the Assembly and commanding an expedition against the seat of the Pamunkeys, he became a member of the council, in which body he served intermittently until his election as governor. In 1624 he was one of the four commissioners—"certayne obscure persons," Sandys acrimoniously designated them later—appointed by the Privy Council to investigate conditions in the colony. Industrious and forceful, he rapidly acquired a fortune through planting and trading, and added to his standing as well as his acreage by his marriage in 1629 to Frances, daughter of Sir Thomas Hinton, and widow successively of Capt. Nathaniel West and of the wealthy Abraham Piersey. With William Claiborne he built the palisade between the York and James rivers for protection against Indian attack, and he contracted alone to rebuild the fort at Point Comfort but expended so liberally of his own resources in this enterprise that Governor Harvey sought his favor by recommending him to King Charles for special privileges in compensation. Mathews, however, was not to be bought; "a man of a bold spiritt, turbulent and strong" (C. C. Hall, ed., *Narratives of Early Maryland,* 1910, p. 59), he was soon alienated by the executive's usurpations and abuses of power, and led the council in the revolt which culminated in Harvey's deposition. When Harvey was returned to office by the King, he sent the chief rebels to England under accusation of treason and seized their estates.

The leaders of this first American uprising in defense of popular rights were never called to trial, but so rancorous was Harvey that he despoiled and ransacked Mathews' property and delayed obeying the Privy Council's order to make complete restitution to him (T. J. Wertenbaker, *Virginia under the Stuarts,* 1914, ch. iii). Mathews regained his seat in the council in 1642 and again busied himself in the contention with Baltimore over the Maryland territory. Himself a Puritan and an early convert to the Parliamentary cause—although named by John Hammond the chief persecutor of the 'Independents' in Virginia—from 1652 to 1657 he was in England as agent to recover Maryland to Virginia; but before returning from his unsuccessful mission, he signed, November 1657, an agreement with Baltimore settling the differences between the two colonies. On Mar. 13, 1658, he succeeded Digges as governor, and shortly became involved in a controversy with the Assembly. When the burgesses, disregarding precedent, refused the governor and council seats in the House, Mathews declared the body dissolved. The burgesses refused to disperse, claiming supremacy as representatives of the people; whereupon the Governor offered certain concessions. These the Assembly rejected and deposed Mathews and his councilors, but upon their recognizing the authority of the House reëlected them as responsible to it alone. The remainder of his term, until his death in office, was uneventful; but he governed with efficiency, honesty, and liberality, and under him Virginia prospered. Posterity has overlooked both the passionate striving for justice and the sturdy independence of this "most deserving Common-wealth's-man," who, according to a contemporary, kept a good house, lived bravely, and was a true lover of Virginia (Peter Force, *Tracts and Other Papers,* II, 1838, pp. 14–15); but for a time he was perhaps the leading and most influential citizen of the colony, distinguished little less for his extensive holdings of land and his comfortable, self-sufficing plantation at Blunt Point than for his unquestioned ability and character.

[See P. A. Bruce, *Econ. Hist. of Va. in the Seventeenth Century* (2 vols., 1895); J. H. Claiborne, *Wm. Claiborne of Va.* (1917); E. D. Neill, *Va. Carolorum* (1886); W. W. Hening, *The Statutes at Large,* vol. I (1823); *Va. Mag. of Hist. and Biog.,* July, Oct. 1893, Apr. 1894, Apr. 1906. Mathews' name is variously spelled. His signature, given in the *Va. Mag. of Hist. and Biog.,* Apr. 1894, gives the form adopted in this sketch.]

A. C. G., Jr.

MATHEWS, WILLIAM (July 28, 1818–Feb. 14, 1909), journalist, teacher, and author, was born in Waterville, Me., the eldest son of Simeon and Clymena (Esty) Mathews. After preparation in various academies in Maine, he was ready at the age of thirteen to enter Waterville (now Colby) College. He received the A.B. degree in 1835. He then studied law in the office of the Hon. Timothy Boutelle of Waterville and in the Harvard Law School. In 1838 he was admitted to the bar of Kennebec County and in 1839 received the degree of LL.B. from Harvard. He taught school for a time and in 1841 began the practice of law in Waterville. He also launched in May 1841 a literary and family weekly known as the *Watervillonian,* devoted to "Literature, Morals, Agriculture, News, Etc." Within two years the newspaper enterprise required all of his time, and he abandoned the practice of law, moved the paper to Gardiner, Me., and changed its name to the *Yankee Blade.* In 1847 the *Blade* was moved to Boston, where in 1856 Mathews sold the enterprise to the *Boston Mercantile Journal.* It was then merged with an existing periodical published by the owners of the *Journal* under the title of the *Portfolio.*

Freed from editorial responsibilities, Mathews moved in 1856 to Chicago, where for three years he edited a financial weekly, conducted a department in the *Daily Tribune,* and gave public lectures. In 1859 he was made librarian of the Chicago Y.M.C.A. and continued to contribute to various periodicals. From 1862 to 1875 he was professor of rhetoric and English in the University of Chicago. A series of articles which he wrote for the *Tribune* in the early part of 1871 on the general subject of success in life proved so popular that he revised and issued the essays in 1873 in a volume entitled *Getting on in the World.* The book was well received, reaching a sale of 70,000 copies. It was followed in 1874 by *The Great Conversers and Other Essays.* The success of these two ventures encouraged Mathews to give up his professorship and devote his time to literary work, and in 1876 he published *Words: Their Use and Abuse,* of which 25,000 copies were sold. A volume of literary essays, *Hours With Men and Books,* appeared in 1877, and in the same year he published a translation of Sainte-Beuve's *Causeries du Lundi* under the title *Monday Chats. Oratory and Orators* followed in 1879.

In 1880 Mathews returned to New England and for the rest of his life made his home in Boston, devoting himself to the writing of essays, to lecturing, and to prolonged travel abroad. His later works include: *Literary Style and Other Essays* (1881); *Men, Places, and Things* (1887); *Wit and Humor: Their Use and Abuse*

(1888); *Nugae Litterariae* (1896); and *Conquering Success* (1903). In 1896 he supplied critical notes and introductions for an elaborate edition of Bulwer-Lytton. He also contributed largely to Appletons' *Cyclopædia of American Biography*. Mathews was thrice married; in 1845 to Mary Elizabeth Dingley, of Winslow, Me.; in 1850 to Isabel I. Marshall, of China, Me., and in 1865 to Harriet M. Griggs of Chicago. In 1907 he was injured by a fall and confined to his bed for two years, but he continued his literary work by dictation. He died in the Emerson Hospital at Forest Hills.

[E. C. Whittemore, *The Centennial Hist. of Waterville, Kennebec County, Me.* (1902); "Senior Colby Graduate," *Boston Sunday Globe*, Jan. 24, 1909; the *Colby Echo*, Jan. 27, 1909; *Who's Who in America*, 1908–09; obituary in the *Boston Herald*, Feb. 15, 1909.]
J. C. F.

MATHEWS, WILLIAM SMYTHE BABCOCK (May 8, 1837–Apr. 1, 1912), teacher, musician, and writer on musical subjects, was born in Loudon, N. H., the son of Samuel S. Mathews, a Methodist minister, and Elizabeth Stanton Babcock. His mother encouraged the development of his musical talent from an early age. After studying piano with local teachers, he attended the Lowell, N. H., Conference Seminary, and then continued his studies in Boston. At the age of fifteen he was already a teacher of music at the Appleton Academy, Mount Vernon, N. H. From 1857 to 1860 he was professor of music at the Wesleyan Female College of Macon, Ga. Later he taught piano in Greensboro, N. C., and in Marion, Ala., but he left the South for Chicago where, from 1867 to 1893, he was organist of the Centenary Methodist Episcopal Church. During this period also he wrote most of his books on music. In 1866 he had become a contributor to *Dwight's Journal of Music*, and he continued to write for the journal until its discontinuance in 1881. From 1869 to 1871 he edited Lyon and Healy's *Musical Independent*, and at various times he acted as music critic for the *Chicago Record, Times*, and *Daily Tribune*. On Nov. 1, 1891, he issued the first number of the magazine *Music*, which he edited until it merged with the *Philharmonic* in 1902.

Mathews' books on music, popular and educational in character, include: *An Outline of Musical Form* (1868), with William Mason [*q.v.*]; *Emerson Organ Method* (1870), in collaboration with L. O. Emerson; *A System of Technical Exercises for the Pianoforte* (1878), with William Mason; *How to Understand Music* (2 vols., 1880–88); *One Hundred Years of Music in America* (1889); *A Popular History of the Art of Music* (1890); *Pronouncing and Defining Dictionary of Music* (1896), with Emil Liebling [*q.v.*]; *Music, Its Ideals and Methods* (1897); *The Masters and Their Music* (1898); and *The Great in Music* (3 vols., 1900–03), each volume designed to cover a year's work in study and appreciation for music-student extension clubs. He also published various compilations of instructive technical studies for the piano, notably the *Studies in Phrasing* (2 vols., 1883–88); *Standard Graded Course of Studies for the Pianoforte* (1893) in ten grades; and the supplementary eight volumes of *Graded Materials for Piano Teaching* (1895).

Mathews did much to raise the general level of music education in the West. He was a zealous advocate of the cultural value of music in the community and continually preached the need of organization among teachers and musicians. In 1910 he removed from Chicago to Denver where he died two years later. Just before his death he spent several months in Dallas, Tex., revising the correspondence courses of the Columbian Conservatory of Music. Mathews' first wife was Flora E. Swain, of Nunda, N. Y., to whom he was married in 1857. His second wife was Blanche Dingley, whom he married in 1902.

[See *Who's Who* in America, 1912–13; the *Musician*, May, June 1912; the *Etude*, May, June 1912; *Musical America*, Apr. 6, 1912; *Musical Courier*, Apr. 10, 1912; *Rocky Mountain News* (Denver), Apr. 2, 1912. In a letter to the Lib. of Cong., relative to the spelling of his name, Mathews spelled his second name as it is given in this sketch.]
F. H. M.

MATHEWSON, CHRISTOPHER (Aug. 12, 1880–Oct. 7, 1925), baseball player, son of Gilbert B. Mathewson and Minerva J. (Capwell) Mathewson, was born at Factoryville, Pa. His father was a gentleman farmer. At the age of fourteen Christopher entered Keystone Academy, graduated in 1898, and having won a scholarship at Bucknell College, Lewisburg, Pa., entered that institution. To pay his living expenses, he did the catering for the student eating club. He had played baseball from childhood and at Bucknell became the star pitcher of the college nine. He was interested, also, in student activities in general and was popular with his fellows.

The lure of professional baseball drew him from college, however, before he had completed his course. He had played professionally during summer vacations, being with the Taunton team of the New England League in 1899, and with the Norfolk team of the Virginia League until midsummer of 1900, when he was sold to the New York Giants. With them he remained for sixteen years, becoming one of the greatest pitchers that baseball has ever known, and setting numerous records, some of which have stood down to the present time. He aided his team in winning many pennants and in capturing World's Series championships. In the World's Series of 1905 he pitched three winning games against the Philadelphia Athletics without allowing the opposing team a single run. During his career in the National League he won 511 games, and was famous for his "fadeaway" delivery, a ball that dropped deceptively and on the "inside" for a right-handed batter.

In 1916, after his long and honorable career with the Giants, he became manager of the Cincinnati Reds, a position he held until he enlisted in the United States Army in 1918 and became a captain in the gas and flame division of the American Expeditionary Force in France. On his return from the war, he joined his old team, the Giants, as a coach, and remained in that capacity until 1920. Symptoms of pulmonary tuberculosis were apparent in his later years with the Giants and he spent many rest periods at Saranac, N. Y. His precarious state of health brought an end to his coaching career but there was a popular interest in keeping such a famous figure in baseball, and in 1923 he was asked to accept the presidency of the Boston Braves, with the understanding that he would give that club as much attention as his health permitted. For two years he did what he could, spending part of the time in baseball work and part at Saranac. It was a vain fight and he died at Saranac during the playing of the World's Series of 1925 at Pittsburgh. His death cast a gloom over the series and, with many baseball officials attending, he was buried in Lewisburg, Pa., the town in which he had gone to college and which for many years he considered his home. His grave is in the cemetery below the Bucknell Stadium, the entrance to which is the Mathewson Memorial Gateway. There is also a bronze memorial tablet to him on the outfield wall of the Polo Grounds in New York, and a memorial building at Saranac, commemorating his sports career and his war service. He was survived by his wife Jane (Stoughton) Mathewson and their only child, Christopher Mathewson, Jr.

"In addition to physical ability, Mathewson had the perfect temperament for a great ball player. Always he sought to learn something new, and he never forgot what he had learned in the past. He had everything—strength, intelligence, courage and willingness" (John J. McGraw, *post*, p. 221). It was the character as much as his accomplishments of Mathewson, known all over the country as "Matty," "Christy," and "Big Six," that brought him lasting fame and wide recognition. A college man, a gentleman, a soldier, and an outstanding athlete, he was an inspiration to the younger lads of the country, a sportsman that educators could point to as a model for college athletes to emulate. He had scholarly interests as well, and during his days at Saranac he took up the study of natural history and became acquainted with all the birds, trees, and flowers of that region. Because of a promise made to his mother, he never played baseball on Sunday through his whole career. He was much in demand as a speaker before boys' clubs and college gatherings. By his example and his success, he became the leader of the "college element" in big-league baseball and did much to improve the tone of the game.

[F. C. Richter, *Richter's Hist. and Records of Baseball* (1914); J. B. Foster, *Spalding's Official Baseball Guide* (1926); J. J. McGraw, *My Thirty Years in Baseball* (copr. 1923); C. H. Claudy, *The Battle of Baseball* (1912); *Baseball Mag.*, Dec. 1925; *Literary Digest*, Oct. 24, Dec. 26, 1925; *Collier's Weekly*, Apr. 11, 1925; *N. Y. Times*, Oct. 8, 9 (editorial), 10, 11, 1925; family records.]

J. K.

MATIGNON, FRANCIS ANTHONY (Nov. 10, 1753–Sept. 19, 1818), Catholic priest, was born in Paris of a good family. Early in life he displayed talents of a high order and was prepared for the Seminary of Saint Sulpice, from which he received the bachelorate in divinity. As a Sulpician, he was ordained (Sept. 19, 1778), and on the completion of four years as a curate, he entered the Sorbonne, from which he received a doctor's degree in theology (1785). Assigned to the chair of theology in the College of Navarre, he continued teaching until 1789, when, through Cardinal de Brienne, he obtained an annuity from Louis XVI. As a royalist, he was compelled to flee the wrath of the Revolutionists and sought refuge in England. Returning later to Paris, he set out from there in 1792 for Baltimore with three distinguished Sulpicians, Abbés Richard, Maréchal [*qq.v.*], and Francis Cicquard. Bishop Carroll assigned him to the small Catholic church in School Street, Boston, where the over-zealous convert, John Thayer [*q.v.*], had aroused rather than allayed Puritan hostility.

A scholar and a gentleman, the French abbé with kindness, humility, and quiet demeanor disarmed even the most captious critics. In 1795 he invited another French refugee, John Louis Ann Magdalen Lefebre de Cheverus [*q.v.*], then in England, to be his assistant, and with him he worked in perfect harmony and brotherly friendship. The epidemic of the year 1798 gave Matignon a wider opportunity for service. In 1799, since the old church was outgrown, he commenced the collection of funds for Holy Trinity Church in Franklin Square. Fully a fifth of the amount was subscribed by Protestant friends, including President Adams; Charles Bulfinch [*q.v.*] donated his services as architect. Recognizing the epochal character of the occasion in New England, Bishop Carroll accepted Father Matignon's invitation and consecrated the edifice (1803). Renewing their efforts, the inseparable priests gathered a congregation of about a thousand communicants. Bishop Carroll petitioned Rome to have Boston made a see with Matignon as bishop, and when the latter learned of the fact he offered strong protest, even threatening to leave for France, and urged that Father Cheverus be named. Appointed bishop in 1808, Cheverus retained Matignon as pastor and served as his curate when not on missions. In 1813, while on his way to New York, Matignon was forced by a Sunday anti-traveling law to remain in Hartford, where he experienced the unusual courtesy of being permitted the use of the First Church of Christ, Congregationalist, of which Dr. Nathan Strong was pastor, for Catholic services. On his death, Boston thronged to pay respect to the humble priest, over whose funeral services Bishop Cheverus presided, and to follow his remains to the Granary burial ground, from which they were soon removed to the new St. Augustine's Cemetery in South Boston.

[J. G. Shea, *Hist. of the Cath. Ch. in the U. S.*, vol. II (1888); Peter Guilday, *The Life and Times of John Carroll* (1922); Jas. Fitton, *Sketches of the Establishment of the Church in New England* (1872); W. Byrne and others, *Hist. of the Cath. Church in the New England States* (2 vols., 1899); W. F. Kenny, *Centenary of the See of Boston* (1909); *Memorial Volume, One Hundredth Anniversary Celebration of the Dedication of the Church of the Holy Cross, Boston* (1904); *Am. Cath. Hist. Researches*, 1884–1912, index vol.; *U. S. Cath. Hist. Mag.*, Apr. 1890; *Cath. Encyc.*, II (1907), 704; *Records of the Am. Cath. Hist. Soc.*, Mar. 1904; C. A. Place, *Charles Bulfinch, Architect and Citizen* (1925); *Boston Monthly Mag.*, June 1825; *Columbian Centinel* (Boston), Sept. 23, 1818.]
R. J. P.

MATLACK, TIMOTHY (d. Apr. 14, 1829), Revolutionary patriot, state official, was the son of Timothy and Martha (Burr) Matlack, members of the Society of Friends, who in 1745 or 1746 removed from Haddonfield, N. J., to Philadelphia, where Timothy followed in his father's footsteps as a merchant. Varying dates are given for his birth: a family record (Stackhouse, *post*, p. 4) says it occurred "At Haddonfield, . . . the 28th day of 3rd month [May] 1736 O.S."; his tombstone gives Apr. 26, 1734 (*Publications of the Genealogical Society of Pennsylvania*, May 1902); but in the notice of his death (*National Gazette*, Philadelphia, Apr. 15, 1829) his age was given as ninety-nine years. He early found irksome the restraints which the Quaker discipline imposed, being fond of convivial company and interested in horse racing, cock fighting, and other sports of the day. He was married, Oct. 5, 1758, to Ellen, daughter of Mordecai Yarnall, a leading Quaker preacher, but was disowned by the Quakers in 1765 for "frequenting company in such manner as to neglect business whereby he contracted debts, failed and was unable to satisfy the claims of his creditors" (quoted by Stackhouse, p. 6).

In May 1775, shortly after the news of the battle of Lexington reached Philadelphia, he joined the Philadelphia Associators, and in the same month was employed as an assistant to Charles Thomson, secretary of the Continental Congress. A few of the minutes of Congress are in Matlack's handwriting and he wrote the commission for Washington as commander in chief (May 20, 1775). The following year, it is probable, he was employed to engross the Declaration of Independence. Congress appointed him a storekeeper for military supplies. He was elected colonel of a battalion of Associators raised early in 1776 and in the same year was a member of the constitutional convention for Pennsylvania, in which he served on the committee to prepare the draft. On July 24, 1776, he became a member of the Council of Safety and on the adoption of the new state constitution, when the executive functions were assumed by the Supreme Executive Council, he was made its secretary (Mar. 6, 1777), which office he filled with great zeal until the end of the war. In the military operations around Trenton and Princeton, he took the field with other Pennsylvania militia as colonel of a rifle battalion. Returning from this campaign he devoted himself to the various offices of secretary of the council, keeper of the great seal, and keeper of the register of persons attainted.

In 1779, he was designated a trustee of the newly created University of the State of Pennsylvania. In 1780, he was elected a member of the Continental Congress, in which he was active and influential, serving for two years. On the formation of the Bank of North America by Robert Morris in 1781, he was one of the first members on the board of directors. A member of the American Philosophical Society from about 1780 until his death, he was one of its secretaries, and delivered numerous addresses before that body. In 1782, he was removed as secretary of the Supreme Executive Council on charges of irregularities in his accounts. Judgment was obtained against him and for a time he was imprisoned for debt. He vigorously resented these charges and in 1783 the Council of Safety of Philadelphia, as a mark of confidence, presented him with a silver urn for the many valuable services he had rendered the cause of Independence. After a brief residence in New York in 1784 he returned to Philadelphia. He was one of the commissioners appointed under the act of Sept. 28, 1789, "to view the navigable waters" of Pennsylvania, being assigned with two others to the Delaware River. Later he resided in Lancaster, Pa., as a minor official of the state government, serving as clerk of the Senate and master of the rolls. After the death of his wife, he married on Aug. 17, 1797, Elizabeth, sister of David Claypoole the printer and widow of Norris Copper. He was appointed prothonotary of the United States district court at Philadelphia, Mar. 14, 1817. In 1813 he had been elected an alderman of the city, and served till 1818, when he retired from public life. He was active in forming, in 1781, the Society of Free Quakers, composed of those who had been disowned, or who had resigned from the Society of Friends on account of their wartime activities. Of this society he was a member for the rest of his life, and on his death he was buried in the Free Quaker burying ground in Philadelphia, the bodies from which were later removed to Matson's Ford across the Schuylkill River from Valley Forge. By his first marriage he had five children; through the three daughters and one son who lived to maturity, he left numerous descendants.

[A. M. Stackhouse, *Col. Timothy Matlack* (privately printed, 1910), contains footnote references to sources. See also Lincoln Cartledge, "Timothy Matlack—Penman of the Declaration of Independence," *Papers Read Before the Hist. Soc. of Frankford*, vol. II (1922); J. H. Martin, *Martin's Bench and Bar of Phila.* (1883); J. T. Scharf and Thompson Westcott, *Hist. of Phila.* (1884); Charles Wetherill, *Hist. of the Religious Soc. of Friends Called by Some Free Quakers in the City of Phila.* (printed for the society, 1894). Charles Wilson Peale's portrait of Matlack painted in 1826 hangs in Independence Hall. Peale made two earlier portraits, one of which is now in the Clark Collection of American portraits.] C. F. J.

MATTESON, JOEL ALDRICH (Aug. 2, 1808–Jan. 31, 1873), governor of Illinois, the son of Elnathan and Eunice (Aldrich) Matteson, was born in Watertown, N. Y., where he worked as a boy on his father's farm and attended the local schools. He then worked in a store in Prescott, Ontario, taught school and engaged in business in Brownsville, N. Y., and in 1831 went South and worked as foreman on the first railroad in South Carolina. At the age of twenty-five he established himself on a farm in Kendall County, Ill. During the speculative boom of 1836 he sold his land and moved to Joliet, where he went into business. The period was one of rapid development and of great enthusiasm for internal improvements, the legislature authorizing some 1,300 miles of railroad, the construction of canals, and the distribution of a cash bonus to those counties which did not share in the improvements. Matteson secured large contracts for work on the Illinois and Michigan canal in 1838, which he executed with great ability.

In 1842 he was elected to the state Senate on the Democratic ticket and was reëlected in 1844 and 1846. In his private affairs and as chairman of the Senate committee on finance he showed himself a practical business man and, although he lacked the art of public speaking, was put forward by his party on account of his executive ability. In 1852 he was elected governor of Illinois, serving from 1853 to 1857. He favored internal improvements and liberal banking laws, and belonged to the moderate anti-slavery group. During his administration he did much to restore the credit of the state, which had been sadly strained by the excesses of the internal-improvement era, and to liquidate its debt. For the fiscal years 1853–54 principal and interest to the amount of $3,950,037 were paid on the state debt, and in four years the payments aggregated $11,129,236. The system of free schools was first introduced into Illinois during Matteson's administration, and the cause of education in general received impetus. While in office (1855) he was a candidate on the Democratic side for the United States Senate against Abraham Lincoln, the Whig candidate, and others. A deadlock ensued and Lincoln withdrew in favor of Lyman Trumbull, who was elected. Upon the conclusion of his term Matteson retired to private life a popular and respected man.

The following year, however, a grave scandal developed in connection with the theft and refunding of certain canal scrip, in which Matteson was unfortunately implicated. In 1839 a large number of ninety-day warrants had been issued by the canal commissioners, payable at the Chicago branch of the State Bank; these had been paid and the vouchers had been packed in a box without being cancelled or destroyed. In the same box were the original check books of the canal commissioners, in which a number of blank checks had been signed but never used. Governor Matteson had ordered the box containing these papers conveyed to his office, and later presented $107,450 of the old canal scrip and $10,100 of the unused checks, properly filled out, to the canal commissioners, receiving in return state bonds as provided for by an act of 1847. He testified that he bought the warrants at sundry times and of sundry persons, but could not tell who they were or where they lived. The evidence of Matteson's guilt seemed conclusive, but he was permitted to turn over to the state for its indemnification property to the value of nearly $250,000, which was practically the amount of the stolen securities together with the accumulated interest paid on them.

Matteson had become interested in the railroad construction then rapidly going on and in 1847 had been associated with H. N. Ridgley and James Dunlap of Springfield in the purchase of the Northern Cross Railroad. He was for many years a lessee and president of the Chicago & Alton Railroad, and had a controlling interest in several Illinois banks. During his later years his home was in Chicago, where he died. On Oct. 7, 1832, he married Mary, daughter of Calvin Bacon and Clarissa (Sterling) Fish. They had three sons and four daughters.

[A. M. Sterling, *The Sterling Geneal.* (1909); Newton Bateman and Paul Selby, *Hist. Encyc. of Ill.* (1900); John Moses, *Ill.: Hist. and Statistical,* vol. II (1892); D. W. Lusk, *Politics and Politicians* (1884); A. C. Cole, *The Era of the Civil War, 1848–1870* (1919); *The Diary of Orville Hickman Browning, . . . 1850–1864* (1925), ed. by T. C. Pease and J. G. Randall; *Memoirs of Gustave Koerner, 1809–1896* (2 vols., 1909), ed. by T. J. McCormack; *Governors' Letter-Books, 1840–1853* (1911), ed. by E. B. Greene and C. M. Thompson; *The Governors of Ill. 1818–1918* (1918); *Chicago Daily Tribune,* Feb. 1, 1873.]

E. L. B.

MATTESON, TOMPKINS HARRISON May 9, 1813–Feb. 2, 1884), historical and genre painter, born at Peterboro, N. Y., is remembered chiefly for his popular patriotic pictures, which were widely known through reproductions. His father, an astute Democratic politician, named him for Governor Tompkins of New York, and having been appointed deputy sheriff for Madison County, he permitted his son to take his first lessons in art from a clever Indian prisoner in the Morrisville jail, who was awaiting trial on a charge of murder. Several other incidents showing the boy's zeal in the pursuit of knowledge are recorded. He copied prints, cut out silhouettes, obtained a paint-box, and experimented assiduously in the intervals of work in a pharmacy and a tailor's shop. He ran away from home and started for Albany, hoping to be able to support himself on the way by making crayon likenesses. With an occasional lift on a canal-boat, he finally reached his destination, but his cash and courage were exhausted and he was forced to return home. Then he wandered for a while, making portraits in Manlius, Cazenovia, Hamilton, and other towns near his birthplace. In 1834 he found his way to Sherburne, making his first appearance there as Othello in a company of strolling players whose star performer had been prostrated by sickness in Hamilton. Soon after this he went to New York. He drew from the antique in the National Academy school, opened a studio, and in 1839 went back to Sherburne, where he was married to Elizabeth Merrill.

After a move to Geneva, N. Y., in 1841 Matteson made his second invasion of the metropolis. This time he was prosperous, and much of his best work was done in this period. His "Spirit of Seventy-six" was received with enthusiasm and was bought by the Art Union. Among his other works were "Signing the Compact on the Mayflower," "The First Sabbath of the Pilgrims," "Perils of the Early Colonists," "Washington's Inaugural," and "Eliot Preaching to the Indians." He was made an associate of the National Academy and exhibited frequently up to 1869. In 1850 he retired to Sherburne, and the rest of his life was passed there. He had a large family. Elihu Vedder, who was one of his pupils, says: "his good wife . . . presented him with the yearly child,—one, no more, no less." He was a useful and respected citizen, serving in various public offices—as a member of the legislature, as president of an agricultural society, as president of the school board, as foreman of the fire department, and in other capacities. He was always busy; he painted many portraits; had a group of students; and conducted drawing classes in the schools. After his death at Sherburne in 1884, the National Academy paid a tribute to his character and talents. The Sherburne Public Library owns his "King Lear" and "Washington Crossing the Delaware." His "Trial of George Jacobs for Witchcraft" belongs to the Essex Institute, Salem, Mass. Matteson's drawing is more spirited than accurate. He had a knack of suggesting action, however. His color is rather dry. His most successful motives were drawn in black and white for reproduction.

[H. T. Tuckerman, *Book of the Artists* (1867); Elihu Vedder, *The Digressions of V.* (1910); F. J. Mather, Jr., and others, *The Am. Spirit in Art* (1927); *Sherburne Illustrated* (1896); the *Sherburne News,* Dec. 6, 1866, Apr. 2, 1868, May 24, July 26, 1873, Dec. 5, 1874, Mar. 27, 1880, Feb. 9, 1884.] W. H. D.

MATTHEW, WILLIAM DILLER (Feb. 19, 1871–Sept. 24, 1930), vertebrate paleontologist, was born at St. John, New Brunswick, the son of George Frederic and Katherine Mary (Diller) Matthew. His father, who was connected with the Canadian Customs, was an amateur geologist and invertebrate paleontologist of high rank, and to his tutelage Matthew's interest in the earth sciences can be attributed. His education began in the public schools of St. John; later he entered the University of New Brunswick, where he received the degree of A.B. in

1889; and then, going to New York, he enrolled in the School of Mines at Columbia University. Here he received the degree of Ph.B. in 1893, the master's degree in 1894, and the following year, the degree of Ph.D.

At Columbia he came under the influence of Prof. James F. Kemp [*q.v.*], the head of the department of geology, and for a time Matthew's interests were in that science, nearly all of his earliest published studies being on geologic or petrogeographic subjects. His inspiration for vertebrate paleontology came during his last year at Columbia. Prof. Henry F. Osborn had just established, in the department of biology, a course on the evolution of the vertebrates and Matthew, with his geological knowledge as a background, became a deeply interested and brilliant student in this field. After Matthew had finished his work at Columbia, Osborn, who had also just founded the department of vertebrate paleontology at the American Museum of Natural History, appointed him an assistant there. His rise in the department was gradual; in 1911 Osborn relinquished the curatorship to him; and eleven years later he became curator-in-chief of the division which embraced paleontology and geology, a position which he held until his resignation in 1927. During the thirty-two years of his association with the American Museum he published about two hundred and forty papers, nearly all of which deal directly or indirectly with his chosen science. While the majority of these papers are highly technical, he had a facility for popularizing a difficult subject and the pages of *Natural History* contain many of his articles on extinct creatures written in an entertaining and instructive style. Probably no one knew the fossil vertebrate faunas of the world so well as did Matthew. He was familiar with the great American collections, and several trips to Europe and one around the world gave him an excellent acquaintance with foreign collections. Arising out of this extensive knowledge, coupled with his early geologic training, came his greatest work, "Climate and Evolution" (*Annals of the New York Academy of Sciences*, vol. XXIV, 1915), in which he argued for the relative permanency of the great ocean basins and the continental masses, and against the existence of former land bridges across what are now abyssal depths. The population by terrestrial mammals of such islands as Cuba he attributed to transportation by means of natural rafts. One of the main theses of this important contribution to science was that the majority of the orders and families of mammals had their origin in the Northern Hemisphere, subsequently spreading to southern areas, and that long isolation in the more remote southern areas, such as Australia, accounted for the extraordinary primitive faunas found there. Other important publications were "The Evolution of the Horse" (*Quarterly Review of Biology*, April 1926) and "Evolution of the Mammals in the Eocene" (*Proceedings of the Zoological Society of London*, 1927).

In 1905 Matthew married Kate Lee of Brooklyn who with two daughters and one son survived him. His home for over twenty years after his marriage was at Hastings-on-Hudson. In 1927 he accepted the professorship of paleontology in the University of California. He was brilliantly successful there and in the three years before his death he had established himself as a most popular instructor of large and enthusiastic classes of undergraduates, and had gathered about him a group of promising advanced students. By previous arrangement he returned to the American Museum for two months each summer to complete important studies which he had under way at the time of his resignation. It was while he was putting the finishing touches on the first and most important of these memoirs, "The Paleocene Faunas of New Mexico," that he was stricken, in the summer of 1930, with his final illness. He was taken immediately to the Pacific Coast and died in San Francisco three months later.

[H. F. Osborn, "Memorial to William Diller Matthew," in *Bull. Geol. Soc. of America*, Mar. 1931; A. S. Woodward in *Nature*, Oct. 11, 1930; W. K. Gregory in *Natural Hist.*, Nov.–Dec. 1930, and *Science*, Dec. 26, 1930; *Am. Museum Novitates*, May 14, 1931; Walter Granger, in *Jour. of Mammalogy*, Aug. 1931; *Who's Who in America*, 1930–31; *San Francisco Examiner* and *N. Y. Times*, Sept. 25, 1930.] W. G.

MATTHEWS, BRANDER [See MATTHEWS, JAMES BRANDER, 1852–1929].

MATTHEWS, CLAUDE (Dec. 14, 1845–Aug. 28, 1898), stock-breeder, governor of Indiana, was born at Bethel, Ky., the son of Thomas and Eliza Ann (Fletcher) Matthews. His maternal grandfather was Thomas Fletcher, who represented a Kentucky district in Congress, 1816–17. Matthews graduated from Centre College, Danville, Ky., in 1867, and the following year, Jan. 1, married Martha Renwick Whitcomb, daughter of Senator James Whitcomb [*q.v.*], a former governor of Indiana. Leaving Kentucky shortly after his graduation, he settled on a farm near Clinton, Ind., where he became intensely interested in the breeding of fine live-stock, and soon attracted much attention by his success with shorthorn and Jersey cattle, and with trotting horses. He was largely instrumental, also, in the formation of the National Association of Breeders of Short Horn Cattle in the United States and Canada. Acutely conscious of the difficulties that confronted the rural classes in the United States, he became an active member of the Farmers' Mutual Benefit Association.

Matthews was a stockman rather than a politician, but he spoke well in public, and sometimes campaigned for Democratic candidates. In 1876 he was elected to the Indiana legislature from a strongly Republican district, and thereafter was much in demand for political speeches. In 1882 he stood for election to the state Senate, but was defeated. In 1890, however, when the influence of the Farmers' Alliance demands was being felt throughout the country, he was nominated for secretary of state on the Democratic ticket, and was elected. His long interest in farming made him an available candidate for governor in 1892, and with him at the head of their state ticket the Democrats won a notable victory.

His term of office, from January 1893 to January 1897, coinciding as it did with one of the worst periods of depression the nation had known, was far from tranquil. The election of a Republican legislature in 1894 increased his difficulties. From April to June 1894, a coal-miners' strike occasioned much disorder in the vicinity of Terre Haute, Fontenet, and Farmersburg. Militia had to be used freely to insure the passage of coal trains. The coal strike was scarcely settled when the Pullman railroad strike spread into Indiana. At Hammond the disorders were so serious that Federal troops were sent from Chicago to maintain order until the state militia should arrive on the scene. Matthews promptly called out eight companies of militia, including a section of artillery, later relieved by eight more, and in a short time had the situation in complete control. When the state auditor, on advice of the attorney-general, held that there was no state money available to pay these troops, the Governor promptly borrowed the necessary sum, $40,962, on his own personal credit. A later legislature voted payment of the bill. His vigorous handling of the Indiana situation contrasted sharply with the methods used by Gov. John P. Altgeld [*q.v.*] in Illinois. Matthews' administration was also notable for his contest with a corporation that carried on winter races, prize-fighting, and similar amusements at Roby, Lake County, Ind. Claiming that the law was being deliberately evaded, the Governor asked the courts for an injunction against the Roby gamesters, which he finally secured. Less spectacular, but probably more important, was the enactment of amendments to the tax law during his administration. Matthews' prominence as governor of Indiana, together with his adherence to free-silver views, led to the presentation of his name for the Democratic presidential nomination at the Chicago convention in 1896. He received the vote of his own state on several ballots, in spite of the strong Bryan sentiment that finally overcame the convention. He did not long survive his term of office as governor.

[Matthews' career as governor can be traced in the volumes of *Appletons' Ann. Cyc.*, 1893–96, inclusive, under the caption, "Indiana"; there is a brief sketch of his life in *Ibid.*, 1898, pp. 557–58. See also, J. P. Dunn, *Indiana and Indianans* (1919), vol. II; Charlotte Whitcomb, *The Whitcomb Family in America* (1904); *Indianapolis Sentinel*, Aug. 29, 30, 31, Sept. 1, 1898.]

J. D. H.

MATTHEWS, FRANKLIN (May 14, 1858–Nov. 26, 1917), journalist, the son of J. H. and Mary (Force) Matthews, was born in St. Joseph, Mich. He was named Albert Franklin Matthews but dropped the first name in his adult life. After receiving his secondary education in the local schools he matriculated in 1879 at Cornell University. In 1883 he received the degree of B.A. and after a year of graduate work joined the staff of J. B. Pond's lyceum bureau. During his two years with the bureau he traveled as lecture agent for many notables, one of whom was Clara Louise Kellogg [*q.v.*], whose cousin, Mary Crosby of New Haven, he married in 1886. In this year he met Talcott Williams, the managing editor of the Philadelphia *Press*, who employed him as a reporter. With his wife, he settled in Philadelphia, and by 1890 he was editor of the *Press*. After a short service with the New York *World* he began to write for the *Sun*. With this paper for twenty-two years, he worked variously as reporter, copy reader, telegraphic editor, city editor, and special correspondent. Through his association with Charles A. Dana and S. Merrill Clarke he gained an unrivaled knowledge of practical newspaper technique. He traveled widely as correspondent for the *Sun* and for *Harper's Weekly* and in a series of articles having the title "Bright Skies in the West" described the return of prosperity to the drought-ridden western states. At the time of the American occupation of Cuba, he was sent by the *Weekly* to report conditions at Havana and Santiago de Cuba. In 1899 these dispatches were collected and issued in book form as *The New-Born Cuba*. About the same time he brought out a popular naval history, *Our Navy in Time of War* (1899). The continued popularity of this book justified its revision fifteen years later (1915). With the outbreak of the Russo-Japanese War he sailed for the Orient and followed the southward drive of the Japanese down the Liaotung peninsula toward Port Arthur, assisting Dr. Louis M. Seaman in gathering material for his medical history of the war. His last and most memorable experience as a correspondent came in 1907 when he accompanied the Atlantic fleet on its cruise round the world, as special correspondent for the *Sun. With the Battle Fleet* (1908) is the literary log of the first half of the cruise, enlivened with a wealth of seagoing anecdote. *Back to Hampton Roads* (1909) deals in a similar way with the return cruise from San Francisco through Australasia, the Suez Canal, and the Mediterranean, and home again across the Atlantic. After his return he lectured extensively upon his war experiences and on the navy, contributing articles on the same subjects to the *Century,* the *Atlantic Magazine,* and to Frank Leslie's periodicals. In 1912 he joined the staff of the *New York Times* as Sunday editor and the next year was night city editor. In 1912, at the invitation of Talcott Williams, he had accepted a teaching post in the Pulitzer school of journalism at Columbia University, and in 1914 he was made associate professor. He was serving in this position at the time of his death.

[*Who's Who in America,* 1916–17; *Cornell Alumni News,* Nov. 29, 1917; *Columbia Alumni News,* Nov. 30, 1917, Jan. 11, 1918; *Sun* (N. Y.), Nov. 27–28, 1917; *New York Times,* Nov. 27, 29, Dec. 12, 22, 1917.]
E. M. H.

MATTHEWS, JAMES BRANDER (Feb. 21, 1852–Mar. 31, 1929), university professor and man of letters, was born in New Orleans, La. His father, Edward Matthews, of a family which had, since the seventeenth century, lived on Cape Cod, could, on the maternal side, claim descent from William Brewster, leader of the Pilgrims on their voyage to New England, as well as from Thomas Prince, twice governor of the Plymouth colony. His mother, Virginia Brander, was daughter of James S. Brander, a Scotsman who settled in America and married Harriet McGraw of Chesterfield County, Va. Thus, Brander Matthews came of American stock that might be rated as of the sturdiest and the best. Though born in New Orleans he became a devoted citizen and lover of New York City.

Since the business ventures of the elder Matthews carried him north and south, east and west, the first years of Brander Matthews' life found him in various cities of the United States, and once on a long trip abroad. The father's wealth and fine taste allowed him to surround his children with luxuries and with beautiful objects of art. Brander Matthews passed a happy boyhood, among refined home influences, at school, in attending plays, and in wandering about the city that he grew to love. From the windows of his father's home in lower Fifth Avenue he saw the torchlight parade of Lincoln's supporters, and, shortly thereafter, regiment after regiment marching to the war.

In 1866 the family again went to Europe and for a year and a half the growing boy saw at close range exciting affairs in France and viewed the art of Italy. In those lands he met notable persons, leaders in all walks of life. On his return to New York in 1867, he prepared for entrance to Columbia College and in 1868 was admitted to the sophomore class, graduating in 1871. His best training for literary and professional pursuits was gained outside of college walls. After graduation he entered, at the age of nineteen, the Columbia Law School, attaining the degree of LL.B. in 1873. On May 10, 1873, before commencement, he married Ada S. Smith, an English actress well known under the stage name of Ada Harland. In consequence of the financial panic of 1873, the father's fortune dwindled, and in 1887 was found to be almost without assets. From the mid-seventies Brander Matthews devoted himself to literature, contributing to such periodicals as the *Galaxy,* the *Nation,* the *Critic, Appletons' Journal, Puck,* and others. A bibliography of those early, fugitive pieces would fill many pages. An early success was an article on "Actors and Actresses of New York," in *Scribner's Monthly,* April 1879. Thereafter he published stories in that and other magazines, soon dropping from his name the baptismal James. But he was chiefly experimenting in playwriting, then the object of his ambition.

During the decade of the eighties, he was prominent among the literary men and the artists of New York. He was of the group which, in 1882, founded the Authors' Club. Almost as an outcome of this was organized in 1883 the American Copyright League, known later as the Authors' League, in the activities of which he was prominently associated. With Laurence Hutton and others he founded in 1885 the Dunlap Society, devoted to printing important works relating to the theatre. The Kinsmen, a social club of international membership, with affiliations in London, was started in 1882, with E. A. Abbey, Lawrence Barrett, Laurence Hutton, W. M. Laffan, Frank D. Millet, and Brander Matthews as earliest members; W. D. Howells, Thomas Bailey Aldrich, Joseph Jefferson, and Charles Dudley Warner were elected later. Matthews was, in 1889, one of the fifteen founders of The Players, that royal gift of Edwin Booth to his fellow actors. His London associates were also notable. His first intimate acquaintance in that city was Austin Dobson, through whom he met Andrew Lang, Edmund Gosse, and Frederick Locker-Lampson. He became a member of the Savile Club and The Athenæum. Fleeming Jenkin, Thomas Hardy, William Black, W. E. Henley, and, somewhat later, Rudyard Kipling came, in greater or less terms of intimacy, among those he met in his London visits. In September 1883, Walter Pollock invited him to become a contributor to the *Saturday Review,* for which thereafter he wrote frequently.

In this same decade, 1880–90, his interest in the theatre definitely shaped his writings. A volume on *The Theatres of Paris* (1880), since treasured by collectors, and another on *French Dramatists of the 19th Century* (1881), were followed in 1885 by his edition of *The Rivals* and *The School for Scandal,* the introduction to which threw light on several problems, hitherto unsolved, in the life of Sheridan. In 1884, his comedy, *Margery's Lovers,* was played in London, and three years later it was presented at a special matinée in New York, followed by subsequent performances in Chicago. With Laurence Hutton he edited in 1886 five volumes of essays, *Actors and Actresses of Great Britain and the United States.* In collaboration with George H. Jessop he wrote the comedy *A Gold Mine,* produced in 1887 by John T. Raymond in Memphis, and in 1889 by Nat C. Goodwin, in New York. In 1889, also, William H. Crane staged Jessop and Matthews' farce, *On Probation.* Both of these plays were successful, as were the one-act comedies of the same period by Matthews—*The Silent System,* adapted from the French for Coquelin and Agnes Booth, and *The Decision of the Court* (1893), also played by the accomplished Mrs. Booth. Meanwhile, in the eighties, Matthews had written in conjunction with H. C. Bunner some short stories, collected under the title *In Partnership.* To *St. Nicholas* (November 1891–October 1892) he contributed a serial story for boys, "Tom Paulding," published in book form in 1892. These are only the more striking of his writings of that time.

When Thomas R. Price, professor of English at Columbia College, spent the academic year of 1891–92 in Europe, he arranged to have Matthews, as a man of letters, lecture to the students during his absence. Matthews undertook the work with some hesitation but was so successful that he was appointed, in 1892, professor of literature in Columbia, a position he held till 1900, when he was created professor of dramatic literature, the first man, he always proudly asserted, to hold a chair of that title in an American university. His account in *These Many Years* (1917) of his earliest experiences in teaching shows him demanding from his classes more reading than they could perhaps digest, but he felt that "if they were exposed to the contagion of literature, some of them might catch it." His success is shown by the large number of playwrights, critics, and novelists, once his students, who proclaim the inspiration of his lectures and his personality. Trained for his professorship by constant intercourse with many of the most stimulating minds of Europe and the United States, he brought to the classroom a wealth of personal experience, of anecdotes of great men, that was nothing short of a revelation to his listeners.

Thenceforward Matthews' books were, to a great extent, by-products of his courses at Columbia. He wrote, to be sure, several volumes of fiction, all founded on life in the New York that he knew and loved: *Vignettes of Manhattan* (1894); *His Father's Son, a Novel of New York* (1895); *Outlines in Local Color* (1897); *A Confident To-Morrow* (1899); *The Action and the Word* (1900); and *Vistas of New York* (1912). But his major interests—in subjects relating to the theatre (especially to dramaturgy) and to questions of English language and literature—bore fruit in *Americanisms and Briticisms* (1892); *Studies of the Stage* (1894); *Bookbindings Old and New* (1895); *Aspects of Fiction* (1896); *An Introduction to the Study of American Literature* (1896); *Parts of Speech* (1901); *The Historical Novel* (1901); *The Development of the Drama* (1903); *Inquiries and Opinions* (1907); *A Study of the Drama* (1910); *Molière: His Life and His Works* (1910); *A Study of Versification* (1911); *Gateways to Literature* (1912); *Shakspere as a Playwright* (1913); and *A Book about the Theater* (1916). He inspired and directed the volume of *Shakspearian Studies* produced by the members of the department of English at Columbia University, in 1916, the tercentenary of Shakespeare's death. His autobiography, a striking gallery of pictures of life, here and abroad, among professional men and artists of the last half of the nineteenth century, appeared in 1917. Remaining volumes were compilations of mellow essays that he had contributed to various periodicals: *The Principles of Playmaking* (1919); *Essays on English* (1921); *Playwrights on Playmaking* (1923), and *Rip Van Winkle Goes to the Play* (1926)—the last his final production, and one of those most widely discussed. In it he treats of the theatre of that day, to which, after an enforced abstention, he returned with zest and enjoyment in 1924. Unlike most praisers of past times, he found that much of the new was better than the old, and he won young actors by sympathetic understanding of their aims and their accomplishment.

Honorary degrees came fast during the later years of his academic life. In 1902 he delivered before the Brooklyn Institute of Arts and Sciences seven of his lectures on the development of the drama; three of these he repeated in the same year at the Royal Institution in Albemarle Street, London. In 1908 he gave before the Lowell Institute, Boston, six lectures on Molière. In 1907 he received from France the decoration of the Legion of Honor, in recognition of his services in making French literature known more widely in the United States. In 1910 he served as president of the Modern Language Association of America. In this same period he was actively writing, lecturing, and administering as chairman of the Simplified Spelling Board—a cause which he took deeply to heart. He was one of the original members, in 1898, of the National Institute of Arts and Letters (president, 1913–14); in 1904, a central group from that organization was formed as the American Academy of Arts and Letters, a select body to which he was, in time, elected. From 1922 to 1924 he was chancellor of the Academy, and in 1922 officer of the French Legion of Honor. Ill health forced his resignation from his prized professorship at Columbia; he resigned, formally, on the anniversary of his birth, Feb. 21, 1924, less than a month, as it happened, after the death of his wife. Their only child, Mrs. Nelson Macy, had died a few years previously.

In his last years he found great pleasure in attending the dinners of The Round Table, a group of notable men who met and dined and talked, at intervals, during the winter. At the very end, before his last protracted illness, his keenest delight was in meeting kindred spirits at this club, or at The Century, or at The Players, or in his own home, or in the offices and in the Faculty Club of his beloved Columbia. To all these gatherings he brought an ardent friendship, an unwearied intellect, and a wit that had suffered no diminution with the passing of time. He died on Mar. 31, 1929, an unforgettable figure in American life and letters.

Brander Matthews was perhaps the last of the gentlemanly school of critics and essayists that distinguished American literature in the last half of the nineteenth century. His style is exact, fastidious, and founded on close study of French and English masters, yet easy and apparently spontaneous. His influence was felt most in the drama. His oft-repeated dictum that a play "is something written to be acted before an audience in a theatre" implied, of course, that playwriting is an art with rules of its own adapted to the medium in which it works. His best years coincided with the rise and acceptance of the "well-made" play as exemplified in the works of the Jones-Pinero school in England; of the theories and principles of that school he was a chief expounder for America. A comparison of the loosely constructed plays produced in this country before 1890 with the well-knit plays of subsequent years will show what he and his disciples largely helped to effect. He was a great personality, intolerant of affectation or pretense, but stimulating and helpful to all who aimed at genuine literary or artistic expression. His genius for friendship has seldom been equaled; a choice spirit, a wit, master, and inspirer of brilliant talk, he has become a tradition.

[This essay is founded upon Matthews' autobiography, *These Many Years*, and on an intimate personal and professional friendship of nearly forty years. There are, as yet, no trustworthy biographies and but few trustworthy critical estimates of Matthews. A lengthy unpublished bibliography of his works is at Columbia Univ.]

G. C. D. O.

MATTHEWS, JOHN (1808–Jan. 12, 1870), inventor, manufacturer, was born in London, England. He is said to have been christened John Henry, but apparently never used the middle name. After gaining a common-school education he became an indentured apprentice in the machine shops and manufactory founded in London by the distinguished engineer Joseph Bramah. After completing his apprenticeship and working as a machinist for a few years in the Bramah establishment, he emigrated to the United States at the age of twenty-four. Settling in New York, he immediately opened a modest shop and began general machine repairing. In England he had gained a thorough knowledge of the Bramah system of manufacturing soda water and of the apparatus with which to make it. Within a year after coming to New York he began to manufacture these products. At the time soda water was commonly made by individual druggists in copper fountains. One of Matthews' first improvements was to construct his fountains of cast iron and line them with tin. At first he had considerable difficulty in marketing his apparatus because of the druggists' prejudice, but by manufacturing soda water for use in his fountains and peddling them, filled, about the city, he gradually built up a prosperous business, and at the time of his death, soda water manufactured by him was sold at more than five hundred places in New York alone.

Matthews, however, was much more interested in improving the manufacturing and dispensing machinery. Leaving the fountain peddling to others, he devoted his whole time and a large portion of his income to experimental work looking toward the improvement of the apparatus, though he never patented any of his inventions. In his generators, which were made of cast iron lined with lead, the carbonic acid was produced from marble dust and oil of vitriol. After being purified by passing through water in a purifying chamber it was conducted to the fountain where it was combined with water by means of a revolving agitator. The dispensing apparatus was a simple draft-tube projecting up from the counter, beneath which the fountain lay incased in ice. The flavorings were kept in glass bottles on the counter. Matthews' manufacturing business grew by leaps and bounds, his products were used all over the world, and in 1865 when he retired and turned over the business to his sons, his plant at First Avenue between Twenty-sixth and Twenty-seventh streets was of immense proportions. He had married in 1830, before coming to the United States, Elizabeth Chester of Bristol, England, and at the time of his death was survived by his widow and two sons. He was buried in Brooklyn, N. Y.

[Henry Hall, *America's Successful Men of Affairs*, vol. I (1895); C. M. Depew, ed. *One Hundred Years of Am. Commerce* (1900), vol. II; *Am. Artisan*, Jan. 26, 1870; *N. Y. Times*, Jan. 14, 1870.] C. W. M.

MATTHEWS, JOSEPH MERRITT (June 9, 1874–Oct. 11, 1931), chemist, textile expert, was born in Philadelphia, Pa., the son of Joseph Merritt and Blanche (Fowler) Matthews. He attended the University of Pennsylvania, receiving the degrees of B.S. in 1895 and Ph.D. in 1898. Appointed professor of chemistry and dyeing in the Philadelphia Textile School in 1898, he became interested in textile chemistry and dyestuff application and during the next few years he combined with teaching intensive study and writing. In 1904 he published *The Textile Fibres, Their Physical, Microscopical and Chemical Properties,* which, enlarged and republished in later editions, was a standard work of reference. In 1907 he resigned his position at the Philadelphia Textile School and for three years was manager of the dyeing department of the New England Cotton Yarn Company. In 1910 he entered a broader field, establishing himself as a consulting expert to the textile and dyestuff industries. He was regularly retained by a number of prominent textile and dyestuff interests and through this consulting practice, which involved a vast amount of industrial research, he gained recognized standing in his profession. In 1916 he became interested in the publication of the *Color Trade Journal,* an interest which he maintained first as editor and later as publisher. An extended development of his *Laboratory Manual of Dyeing and Textile Chemistry* (1909) appeared in 1920 under the title *Application of Dyestuffs to Textiles, Paper, Leather and Other Materials,* and in 1921 he published *Bleaching and Related Processes.*

Matthews possessed a mild and genial disposition. Of a retiring nature, he did not have many close friends, but he had innumerable friendly acquaintances. His services were almost without exception sought rather than offered. He was a member of the Chemist's Club in New York and for many years maintained a research laboratory and office in their building. He was also an active member of many technical and scientific societies, among them the American Chemical Society, the Society of Chemical Industry, the Society of Dyers and Colourists of England, a charter member of the American Association of Textile Chemists and Colorists, and a fellow of the American Association for the Advancement of Science. As a hobby he made a study of Japanese prints and of these he had a notable collection. During his later years he was greatly handicapped by failing health and in 1925 he found it necessary to retire from all active work. The remaining years of his life were spent on the French Riviera, in Bermuda, and finally in San Diego, Cal., where he died. His wife was Augusta Spalding Gould, to whom he was married on May 15, 1903.

[J. M. and Jaques Cattell, *Am. Men of Sci.* (1927); *Who's Who in America*, 1930–31; *Am. Dyestuff Reporter*, Oct. 26, 1931; *N. Y. Times*, Oct. 13, 1931; information from Matthews' associates; personal acquaintance.] L. A. O.

MATTHEWS, NATHAN (Mar. 28, 1854–Dec. 11, 1927), municipal official and reformer, was born in Boston, lived in Boston practically all his life, served his city actively for over forty years, and died there. He came from an old New England family that, ever since the English immigrant, James Matthews, settled there probably as early as 1638, had had a record of public service in the little town of Yarmouth on Cape Cod. His father, Nathan Matthews, moved to Boston at the age of nineteen. His mother, Albertine (Bunker) Matthews, is credited with giving to her son much of his cultural interest and devotion to ideals. The father's fortunes fluctuated between the extremes of wealth and bankruptcy; but, although the son saw his father fail three times, he also saw him each time resolutely turn to the task of paying back every cent of his debts. The impression made by such an attitude must have been very deep, for instances show that the son throughout his life "leaned backward" in the honesty of his dealings. The young man's education was of a varied character, somewhat unusual for the times. From Epes Sargent Dixwell's Boston school he entered Harvard College at eighteen. He was graduated from the college in 1875 and from the law school in 1893 as of the class of 1880. During the years from 1875 to 1877 he traveled and studied in Europe, chiefly at the University of Leipzig. His chief interests there, as always, were in political economy and jurisprudence, but he found time also to indulge in numerous canoe trips. His love of forests, stream, and garden never left him, and, joined with an antiquarian tinge, made him a devotee of the New England country side and its old homesteads. He was admitted to the bar in 1880 and practised law in Boston. On Apr. 5, 1883, he married Ellen Bacon Sargent. They had two children.

His public life dates from his activity in the Cleveland-Blaine campaign of 1884. In 1888, with others, he helped to form the Young Men's Democratic Club of Massachusetts, and by 1889 this group was in control of the state Democratic party, with Matthews as the president of the state convention. The next year he was chairman of the state executive committee and under his leadership the Democrats elected William E. Russell as governor. Up to this time his interests had been largely in the realm of state and national politics. Because of his eminent services to his party he became the logical candidate for mayor of Boston and was elected without difficulty. He served four terms and retired voluntarily in 1895. Choosing the municipal field as he did, his public life, on the surface, does not appear to be as important as that of many of his contemporaries who have probably left much less permanent imprint. Together with Seth Low [*q.v.*] he must be credited with revealing to students of municipal government the practical possibilities of the strong mayor type of municipal character and with thus indicating the course of municipal reform for many years. Before this time the council had been the center of power if not of prestige. The 1885 Boston charter had nominally given the chief power to the mayor, but not until his vigorous administration had that power received effective use. As early as the 90's he advocated the small, unicameral council, election at large, consolidation of city departments, longer terms of office, and nonpartisan civil service. During his later life he continued these interests. From 1907 to 1909 he was chairman of the city finance commission, which resulted in a remodeling of the Boston charter, and he served on other commissions later. From 1909 to 1917 he lectured on municipal government at Harvard. His published works include *The City Government of Boston* (1895) and *Municipal Charters* (1914) in addition to a number of articles and addresses. He was ever an indefatigable worker, outspoken, almost brutal at first, but developing a tenderness with the years, a man of strong will and courage who "had no boss but himself."

[Letter from his brother, Albert Matthews, Boston; *Harvard College Class of 1875 Secretary's Rept.*, nos. IV, VI, VII, X (1884–1925); *Harvard Graduates' Mag.*, Mar. 1928; New England Hist. and Geneal. Register, July 1928; *Proc. Mass. Hist. Soc.*, vol. LXI (1928); *Proc. in the Supreme Judicial Court at Boston in Memory of Hon. Nathan Matthews, Oct. 26, 1929* (1929); *Boston Herald* and Boston *Evening Transcript*, Dec. 12, 1927.] E. S. G.

MATTHEWS, STANLEY (July 21, 1824–Mar. 22, 1889), jurist, was born in Cincinnati, Ohio, the eldest child of Thomas Johnson Matthews and his second wife, Isabella Brown. He was named Thomas Stanley, but dropped the name Thomas in early manhood. His father, a native of Leesburg, Va., spent his youth in Alexandria, Va., and in Philadelphia, and emigrated with his family to Cincinnati in 1818. His mother was a daughter of William Brown, a pioneer of the Miami country, who settled in Columbia, Hamilton County, Ohio, in 1788. Thomas Johnson Matthews was for several years Morrison professor of mathematics and natural philosophy at Transylvania University, Lexington, Ky., but he returned to Cincinnati as president of Woodward College, later Woodward High School, which his son attended. Stanley Matthews entered Kenyon College as a junior, graduating in the summer of 1840. After two years spent in the study of law in Cincinnati, he went in 1842 to Maury County, Tenn., to assist the Rev. John Hudson in the conduct of Union Seminary. In the same year he was admitted to the Tennessee bar, commenced the practice of law at Columbia, and in February 1843 was married to Mary Ann, daughter of James Black. He edited a weekly political paper, the *Tennessee Democrat*, in the interests of James K. Polk. In 1844 he returned to Cincinnati to practise law and soon came before the public through his appointment as assistant prosecuting attorney, and as editor, for about a year, of the *Cincinnati Morning Herald*, an anti-slavery paper. The latter activity resulted in his election as clerk of the Ohio House of Representatives for the session of 1848–49.

Upon the adoption of the constitution of 1851 in Ohio, Matthews was elected one of the three judges of the court of common pleas for Hamilton County, but soon resigned the position because of the inadequacy of the salary and resumed the practice of law. He served one term in the Ohio Senate and was appointed by President Buchanan in 1858 United States attorney for the southern district of Ohio, a position which he resigned after the inauguration of President Lincoln. While United States attorney, he prosecuted a reporter, W. B. Connelly, under the Fugitive-Slave Law for assisting two negro slaves who were trying to escape. Connelly was convicted, but the feeling ran high against Matthews and this incident contributed to his defeat as a candidate for Congress in 1876 in a very close election, and was used later in opposing his confirmation as justice of the Supreme Court.

During the war Matthews served as lieutenant-colonel in the 23rd Ohio Infantry and later as colonel of the 51st Ohio Volunteers. While in camp in 1863, he was elected to serve with Bellamy Storer and George Hoadly [*qq.v.*] on the superior court of Cincinnati. He resigned from the army to take his place on the bench, and two years later resigned from the bench for the more lucrative practice of the law. By this time he had reached a position of eminence as a lawyer. He attracted national attention in 1877 as one of the counsel before the electoral commission that passed upon the disputed returns in the Hayes-Tilden contest for the presidency. He made the opening argument in the Florida contest and the principal argument in the Oregon case. The decision of the commission in the Florida case followed the line of argument which Matthews advanced, namely, that Congress should not go behind the returns of the state electors, but that the action of the duly constituted state authorities should be final. Matthews later joined Congressman Charles Foster of Ohio in a letter to Senator John Brown Gordon of Georgia and Congressman John Young Brown of Kentucky, leading Southern Democrats, which was of great importance in alleviating fears of a continuation of federal interference in South Carolina and Louisiana.

In March 1877 the Ohio legislature elected Matthews to the United States Senate to fill the vacancy caused by the appointment of John Sherman as secretary of the treasury. His short term of two years was marked chiefly by the passage on Jan. 25, 1878, of the "Matthews resolution" for the payment of the principal and interest of the United States bonds in silver and making silver legal tender. Upon the resignation of Justice Noah W. Swayne, President Hayes submitted the name of Matthews as his successor. Hayes had known Matthews first as a student at Kenyon College, then as a fellow lawyer in Cincinnati, and as a fellow officer in his regiment during the war. Matthews had campaigned actively for Hayes and had made the most important arguments in his behalf before the electoral commission. Matthews' name had been considered by President Grant before he nominated Morrison R. Waite to succeed Chief Justice Chase. But the Senate refused to confirm the appointment of Matthews, and there was criticism of Hayes for submitting the name as a reward, it was alleged, for Matthews' earlier support.

The vacancy on the bench was still unfilled when Garfield became president, and Matthews' name was again submitted to the Senate. The opposition to the confirmation of the appointment continued. It was partly political and partly due to the belief that, as a former attorney for railroads and large corporate interests, he might favor them in suits before the court. The Senate's committee on judiciary, with the single exception of Senator Lamar, opposed confirmation, but the Senate approved the nomination by a majority of one. The doubts regarding Matthews' ability and fairness as a judge proved unfounded. He was a member of the Supreme Court from May 12, 1881, until his death in 1889. It was a period in which the powers of the federal government were greatly extended by a liberal interpretation of the constitution, particularly the commerce clause and the clause empowering Congress to borrow money. Matthews wrote the majority opinion in the Virginia Coupon Cases (114 *U. S.*, 269) in which it was held that when a state had issued bonds the passage of a subsequent statute forbidding the acceptance of coupons of these bonds for taxes was void as impairing the obligations of contract, and delivered the opinion of the court in the case of *National Bank* vs. *Insurance Company* (104 *U. S.*, 54), in which he laid down the rule that money deposited by one in a fiduciary capacity is not subject to a banker's lien for debts the depositor owes the bank. In *Bowman* vs. *Chicago and North Western Railway Company* (125 *U. S.*, 465) he declared that a state statute prohibiting the carrying of intoxicating liquor into the state by common carriers amounted to a regulation of interstate commerce and was repugnant to the constitution of the United States. In *Yick Wo* vs. *Hopkins* (118 *U. S.*, 356) he held that a law though fair on its face and impartial in appearance, was nevertheless a denial of the equal justice the Fourteenth Amendment guarantees if administered in such a way as to make unjust discriminations.

Politically, the career of Stanley Matthews showed independence and courage. He was a Douglas Democrat before the war but took a leading part in the abolitionist movement. His actions in the Connelly case showed his willingness to prosecute the violation of the unpopular Fugitive-Slave Law, as required by his oath of office, even at personal sacrifice. A Republican after 1863 and a presidential elector on the Lincoln and Johnson ticket in 1864, and on the Grant and Colfax ticket in 1868, he joined the Liberal-Republican movement in 1872, and as temporary chairman of the convention declared that since the war was over, so should military rule end. He did not support Greeley, however, the nominee of the convention for president. Matthews' first wife died in 1885, and in 1887 he married Mrs. Mary Theaker of Washington. He had eight children by his first marriage, five of whom survived him.

[C. T. Greve, "Stanley Matthews, 1824–1889," in *Great Am. Lawyers*, vol. VII (1909), ed. by W. D. Lewis; C. R. Williams, *The Life of Rutherford Birchard Hayes* (2 vols., 1914) and *Diary and Letters of Rutherford Birchard Hayes* (5 vols., 1922–26), ed. by C. R. Williams; Charles Warren, *The Supreme Court in U. S. Hist.* (1922), vol. III; James Landy, *Cincinnati Past and Present* (1872); the *Green Bag*, May 1889; *Cincinnati Enquirer*, Mar. 23, 26, 1889.]

S. G. L.

MATTHEWS, WASHINGTON (July 17, 1843–Apr. 29, 1905), ethnologist, the son of Dr. Nicholas Blayney and Anna (Burke) Matthews, was born in Killiney, County Dublin, Ireland, and was named Washington as an American appreciation. While the child was still an infant, his mother died and his father brought him to America, settling in Wisconsin. Later the elder Matthews moved to Dubuque, Iowa, where Washington was brought up. After a common-school education, he began the study of medicine with his father, took a course of lectures in the University of Iowa, and received the degree of M.D. in 1864. Immediately he volunteered in the United States army and was assigned to the post at Rock Island, Ill., as acting assistant surgeon. Mustered out in 1865, he was appointed post surgeon at Fort Union, Mont. His many assignments in the West acquainted him with various tribes of Indians and incited him to investigate their languages and mythology. Few of the old army had more extended opportunities to become acquainted with the Indians and few knew better how to handle the Indian. Especially at Fort Berthold, where he remained six years in contact with the Hidatsa, was his work productive, yielding three important studies: *Grammar and Dictionary of the Hidatsa (Minnetarees, Grosventres of the Missouri)*, in Shea's American Linguistics (ser. II, no. 1, 1873); *Hidatsa (Minnetaree) English Dictionary,* in the same series (ser. II, no. 2, 1874); and *Ethnography and Philology of the Hidatsa Indians* (United States Geological and Geographical Survey, Miscellaneous Publications, no. 7, 1877).

Following his transfer to the Southwest Matthews wrote several papers on the Navaho. Of these Indians he was the first and foremost student. "Navajo Silversmiths" in the second (1883) and "Navajo Weavers" in the third (1884) annual report of the Bureau of American Ethnology were the initial papers on these Indians. In 1887 "The Mountain Chant: a Navajo Ceremony" appeared in the fifth annual report. His book entitled *Navaho Legends* was issued as a memoir of the American Folk-Lore Society (vol. V, Boston, 1897). "The Night Chant," his last important work, was published in the *Memoirs of the American Museum of Natural History* (vol. VI, 1902). This monograph shows Matthews' insight into Navaho mythology.

In 1885 Matthews took up the study of physical anthropology, then a comparatively new science, and designed apparatus for making measurements. His chief paper on the subject was "Human Bones of the Hemenway Collection in the United States Army Medical Museum" (*Memoirs of the National Academy of Science,* vol. VI, 1893). He published in all fifty-eight papers, each of which required careful research. He was a member and presiding officer of a number of learned societies. Outside of his profession he was interested in botany, mathematics, poetry, and art. He died in Washington, D. C. He had married, in 1877, Caroline Wotherspoon. Because of his scientific methods of work, his results are regarded as of permanent value in the study of the American Indian.

[Jas. Mooney, "Washington Matthews," *Am. Anthropologist,* July–Sept. 1905; *Who's Who in America,* 1903–05; I. A. Watson, *Physicians and Surgeons of America* (1896); *Jour. of Am. Folk-lore,* July–Sept. 1905; personal recollections.]

W. H.

MATTHEWS, WILLIAM (Mar. 29, 1822–Apr. 15, 1896), bookbinder, writer on bookbinding, was born at Aberdeen, Scotland. Before the child was a year old his father died, and when he was seven his mother took him to London, where he was sent to school and later apprenticed to a bookbinder. Employed in one of the largest binderies at the time of the great strike of 1841, young Matthews remained faithful to his employers and advanced rapidly to a responsible position and a broad and thorough knowledge of the business. In 1843 he emigrated to New York, where his ability was promptly recognized. Three years later he established a bindery of his own, at 74 Fulton Street, winning the highest award given for binding for his exhibit at the International Crystal Palace Exhibition in Reservoir Park in 1853. This attracted the attention of the firm of D. Appleton & Company, and the following year he became the head of their bindery, retiring in 1890, when he was succeeded by his son, Alfred. Among the large editions issued by the firm was an annual output of one million copies of Webster's spelling book. Matthews was preëminent in his art, his name becoming a synonym for good workmanship, while his advice and his bindings were alike eagerly sought by fellow-workers and by collectors. While thoroughness was to him the highest essential, he added a scholarly knowledge of the history of his craft, and the taste that is necessary to elevate it to the status of an art. For special work he could use to advantage all the resources at his command, but he denounced the "story-telling cover of commerce," holding to restrained decoration for commercial binding. The forwarding of a book was always, to him, as important as the finishing. He regarded Francis Bedford as the greatest modern English binder.

Matthews' winning personality, admirable qualities, and public spirit made him an active force in the charitable, religious, social, and commercial life of the city, and his hospitable home in the Flatbush section of Brooklyn was a center for the friends who sought his well-filled library and listened to his talk of the books and the bindings which he loved. Aside from his bookbinding interests, he was president of the Flatbush Water Works Company. In 1895 he moved to Brooklyn Heights, where his death at the age of seventy-five resulted from the shock of being run down by a bicycle. He left a widow (*née* Marle), two sons, both bookbinders, and three daughters. Interested in many and varied associations, he was an active member of the Grolier Club and a cherished friend of that group of book-lovers of the eighties and nineties who worked so effectively to stimulate and improve all phases of bookmaking. In 1885 he delivered before the Club a lecture, "Modern Bookbinding Practically Considered," which was published in 1899 as the Club's tenth publication. He was also the author of the article upon bookbinding in Appletons' *American Cyclopædia* and of professional contributions to magazines. He collaborated with William Loring Andrews in *A Short Historical Sketch of the Art of Bookbinding* (1895) and contributed "Suggestions how to Bind our Books" to *The Book-Lover's Almanac for 1895.* His memories of James Lenox, in the form of a letter to Samuel P. Avery, appeared in *Harper's Weekly* on Aug. 1, 1896. When Matthews' library was sold at auction on Feb. 10 and 11, 1897, the catalogue described many books bound by him.

[S. P. Avery, tribute in *The Book-Lovers Almanac for 1897*; Brander Matthews, *Bookbindings Old and New* (1895); the *Critic*, Apr. 1896; J. C. Derby, *Fifty Years Among Authors, Books, and Publishers* (1884); *N. Y. Times*, *N. Y. Tribune*, and *Evening Post* (N. Y.), Apr. 16, 1896; reminiscences of Thomas M. Moore, a pupil of Matthews.] R. S. G.

MATTHIESSEN, FREDERICK WILLIAM (Mar. 5, 1835–Feb. 11, 1918), metallurgist, manufacturer, philanthropist, was one of the pioneers who developed the zinc industry in the United States. He was born at Altona, in Schleswig-Holstein, Germany. A graduate of the Bergakadamie (school of mines) at Freiberg, Saxony, he came to the United States in 1857 in company with E. C. Hegeler, who was afterward his partner in their joint enterprises. Landing in Boston, they went to New York, where they were engaged by Joseph Wharton, to design for him a zinc-smelting plant to treat the zinc ore mined at Friedensville, near Bethelehem, Pa. The project was abandoned, partly through Wharton's failure to agree with the designers and partly for financial reasons. Matthiessen and Hegeler then went West to build a plant to smelt the zinc ores from the Platteville district of Wisconsin, locating it at La Salle, Ill., because of the coal there. Work was started Dec. 24, 1858, and the plant was running successfully (the first commercial production of zinc in the United States) when the outbreak of the Civil War caused a temporary shutdown for lack of market. In 1862 a lively demand developed for zinc to be used in making the brass for cartridges. Together Matthiessen and Hegeler, though the latter was the chief technical man of the partnership and invented most of the improvements, built the first zinc rolling-mill in America at La Salle in 1866 and it has been continuously in operation, ever since, though many times redesigned and rebuilt. They began mining their own coal in 1874 and in 1881 Matthiessen started a sulphuric acid manufacturing plant.

In 1864 he married Fannie Clara Moeller, of Mineral Point, Wis. There were five children. Matthiessen's contact with the public has a broad, though generally unrecognized phase, since he started at La Salle the Western Clock Manufacturing Company, which produces the widely-known "Big Ben" alarm clock. The growth of its business to large proportions from small beginnings was the more remarkable because the manufacture of brass clocks had for so long been practically monopolized by Connecticut. Matthiessen had many other technical and business interests, among them the La Salle Short Railway and the La Salle Machine & Tool Company.

In his later years his contributions to education and philanthropy made his name well known. As a gift to the cities of La Salle, Peru, and Oglesby, Ill., he endowed the Tri-City Hygienic Institute, which maintains a staff of health officers and facilities which include an isolation hospital, an infant-welfare station, and a free dental clinic as well as a milk station, a bacteriological laboratory, and a medical library. He made the La Salle-Peru township high school a model for secondary education in the United States, and he converted Deer Park into a model scenic resort, turning over the profits from its operation to the charities of La Salle. He was three times elected mayor of La Salle and contributed to the welfare and development of the city in many ways in addition to those already mentioned. His death occurred in February 1918, toward the close of his eighty-third year.

[*Bull. Am. Inst. Mining Engineers*, Apr. 1918; *Trans. Am. Inst. Mining and Metallurgical Engineers*, vol. LXI (1920); *Engineering and Mining Jour.*, Feb. 23, 1918.]
T. T. R.

MATTICE, ASA MARTINES (Aug. 1, 1853–Apr. 19, 1925), mechanical engineer, naval officer, the son of Frederick Martines Mattice and Melissa (Driggs) Mattice, was born in Buffalo, N. Y., and received his preliminary education in the public schools of that city. Graduating in 1874, at the head of his class, from the separate course for engineers at the United States Naval Academy, he was assigned to sea service as cadet engineer and assistant engineer (Feb. 26, 1875) on the *Brooklyn, Vandalia,* and *Trenton* until 1879. He was then instructor in engineering at the Naval Academy, 1879–82, and with John C. Kafer [*q.v.*] developed a course in mechanical drawing which was one of the best in the country. Sea service (1882–85) on the *Miantonomoh* and the *Juniata* followed. While on the *Juniata* he was engaged in relief work (August 1883) following the eruption of Krakatoa in the Strait of Sunda. Assigned then to the Bureau of Steam Engineering, he performed special duty with Chief Engineer George W. Melville [*q.v.*] in designing machinery for new vessels. When Melville became engineer in chief of the Navy Mattice was made chief designer, in which capacity he was responsible for some excellent work, including the machinery of the original *Maine,* blown up in Havana Harbor in 1898. The specifications for this machinery were the most complete ever prepared up to that time and served as a model for many years. Granted leave of absence in 1889, he became principal assistant to E. D. Leavitt [*q.v.*], a prominent consulting engineer, and on June 30, 1890, resigned from the Navy.

During the next ten years he designed engines and other machinery for the Calumet & Hecla Mining Company, the Bethlehem Steel Company, Pope Tube Company, and various other concerns. The machinery for the Calumet & Hecla Mining Company has received especial commendation from competent judges. After leaving Leavitt, Mattice conducted an office of his own for about a year and then became chief engineer of the Westinghouse Electric and Manufacturing Company, and three years later, of the Westinghouse Machine Company. At the invitation of B. H. Warren, an old friend and classmate, who had become president of the Allis-Chalmers Company, he joined that concern in 1904 as chief engineer and manager of manufacturing. In 1906, he formed a partnership for consulting practice with John C. Kafer and Warren; but after the death of both partners that same year he closed the office and became works manager of the Walworth Manufacturing Company of Boston. In 1911 he resigned this position to retire from active business. Purchasing a farm in Lockport, N. Y., he began to raise poultry and fruit. At the Westinghouse and Allis-Chalmers plants, however, he had formed a warm friendship with Charles C. Tyler who later became vice-president of the Remington Arms Company, and with the great expansion of that organization during the World War, Tyler persuaded Mattice to resume active work as its advisory engineer. He took up the new duties in 1915 and continued with the Remington company until his death, which occurred at the Engineers' Club, New York, ten years later.

Mattice's mind worked with great quickness and accuracy; his information was encyclopedic as to scope and readiness. With all his ability he was very modest and willing to receive suggestions. He was also very practical, and it was his habit, with important designs, to have the work of the drawing office examined and criticized by the shop foremen who would later be responsible for the actual work of construction.

This practice resulted often in suggestions for changes which would expedite and reduce the cost of the work. Mattice was inclined to be retiring, especially in his last years, but was by nature affectionate and devoted to his intimate friends. His naval service came before the era of good feeling, when there was strife between the line and the staff. His prominence in the engineer corps made him active in this controversy, but he was universally respected and had many warm friends in the line. He was never married.

[*Jour. Am. Soc. Naval Engineers,* Aug. 1925; *Army and Navy Jour.,* Apr. 25, 1925; *N. Y. Times,* Apr. 21, 1925; Navy Registers; personal acquaintance; information as to certain facts from the family.]

W. M. M.

MATTISON, HIRAM (Feb. 8, 1811–Nov. 24, 1868), Methodist Episcopal clergyman and reformer, was born at Norway, Herkimer County, N. Y., one of the twelve children of Solomon and Lydia W. Mattison. His parents, natives of New England, were poor, high-minded, and devoted Methodists. In his infancy the family removed to a wilderness farm near the site of Oswego, N. Y. The boy's education was derived chiefly from his mother. He was of a serious and reflective temperament and displayed much mechanical ingenuity. At the age of twenty-four, after a transforming religious experience, he left the farm to become a Methodist minister in the Black River Conference (1836), although the weakness of his lungs several times interrupted his pastoral work. In 1840–41 he represented the American Bible Society in New Jersey, showing notable gifts as a preacher, but soon returned to northern New York, where he preached and edited an outspoken paper, the *Primitive Christian* (at first called *Tracts for the Times,* and later *The Conservative*). From 1846 to 1852 he was again disabled, but found congenial occupation in the study of astronomy, writing lectures and a school textbook, *Elementary Astronomy* (1847), revised as *A High-School Astronomy* (1853), which achieved wide popularity. In 1850–51 he taught the subject in Falley Seminary, Fulton, N. Y. From 1852 to 1858 he served New York City churches (John Street and Trinity) as a supply pastor.

As a member of the General Conference in 1848, 1852, and 1856, he displayed power in debate. In the General Conference of 1856 he ardently but unsuccessfully advocated the exclusion of slave-holders from church membership. Transferring to a pastorate in Adams and Syracuse, N. Y., he continued to agitate the question of slave-holding, and, though defeated for membership in the General Conference of 1860, bombarded that body with petitions signed by 100,000 Methodists of Central New York and Great Britain praying the church to sever all connection with slavery. When that prayer was disregarded, he lost hope for his denomination, resigned from the Conference, and founded St. John's Independent Methodist Church in New York City. This body was denounced as a nest of abolitionists; his house was ransacked and his life threatened by the draft rioters in 1863. In 1864, however, when the Methodist Episcopal Church tardily took the action for which he had fought, he was welcomed back to its ministry, entering as a local preacher in August 1865 and being assigned to a Jersey City pastorate. Later he was admitted to Newark Conference. In Jersey City he became involved in a vigorous controversy with one Father Smarius, a Jesuit missioner, which led to his employment by the American and Foreign Christian Union (1868), to which he devoted the last of his failing energy, speaking, writing, and printing against "Romanism." His endeavor to rescue Mary Ann Smith, a convert alleged to have been abducted by Catholics to save her from Protestantism, used up his strength, and he died of pneumonia in Jersey City at the age of fifty-seven.

Mattison was by nature controversial, and he fought slavery, intemperance, and pernicious amusements as fiercely as he did "Romish superstitions and idolatries" and doctrines which he believed to be erroneous or heretical. He was twice married. His first wife, Melinda Griswold, died young, leaving four children. By his second wife, Elizabeth S. Morrison, who survived him, he had five children. Throughout his career he wrote much for publication in books, pamphlets, and church periodicals. Among his works were *A Scriptural Defence of the Doctrine of the Trinity; or A Check to Modern Arianism* (1846); *Spirit Rappings Unveiled* (1853); *The Resurrection of the Dead* (1864); *Popular Amusements* (1867); *The Abduction of Mary Ann Smith* (1868).

[Nicholas Vansant, *Work Here, Rest Hereafter; or the Life and Character of Rev. Hiram Mattison* (1870); *Minutes of Ann. Conferences of the Meth. Episc. Ch.,* 1869; *Christian Advocate* (N. Y.), May 1856, May 1860, Dec. 3, 1868; I. S. Bingham, "History of Black River Conference," in *Minutes of Northern N. Y. Ann. Conf. of the Meth. Episc. Ch.,* 1878; L. C. Matlack, *Anti-Slavery Struggle and Triumph in the Meth. Episc. Ch.* (1881); *Daily Evening Times* (Jersey City), Nov. 25, 1868.]

J. R. J.

MATTOCKS, JOHN (Mar. 4, 1777–Aug. 14, 1847), congressman and governor, was born in Hartford, Conn., the youngest son of Samuel Mattocks. Originally a farmer, the father moved in 1778 to Tinmouth, Vt., where he served in the state legislature, became a judge and chief justice of the Rutland county court, and was long state treasurer (1786–1801). At the age of fifteen, his son went to live with a married sister, Rebecca Miller, in Middlebury. Largely self-educated, he studied law first with Samuel Miller and later at Fairfield, with Judge Bates Turner, and was admitted to the bar in February 1797. In the same year, he opened an office at Danville, Caledonia County, Vt., but moved three years later to Peacham, in the same county, where he was soon engrossed in politics.

In 1807 he was sent to the legislature, where, in all, he sat five terms—1807, 1815, 1816, 1823, and 1824. In 1820, he was elected to the national House of Representatives, and later served for two other terms—in 1825–27 and 1841–43. He was a vigorous opponent of negro slavery, and his most noteworthy appearance in debate was in a speech on the presentation of a petition for abolishing slavery in the District of Columbia. He was chosen in 1832 as judge of the supreme court of Vermont, but resigned within a year. In 1843, running as a Whig, he was elected governor of Vermont, but declined a reëlection. He was proud of the fact that he was never defeated for any office for which he was a candidate. While governor, he made an unsuccessful effort to establish Thanksgiving on Dec. 25. The people at large objected to having New England Thanksgiving "disgraced by . . . Popish nonsense," and Churchmen objected to Christmas being merged into a "Pumpkin pie Holiday" (Chandler, *post,* p. 37).

In 1806 he was made a director of the Vermont State Bank. During the War of 1812 he was a brigadier-general in the Vermont militia. He married, Sept. 4, 1810, Esther Newell, of Peacham, who died, July 21, 1844, leaving three sons and one daughter. Of the sons, one became a clergyman, one an attorney, and one a physician.

Mattocks was perhaps best known as a lawyer. During nearly fifty years of practice, he became the most important figure at the Vermont bar. It was said that he was frequently engaged in every jury trial at a session of the county court and won every case. He adopted an easy, conversational manner, with no rhetorical flourishes, making his appeal mainly on the basis of common sense. He was a large and robust man, somewhat inclined to corpulency, and of a sanguine temperament. To his younger colleagues at the bar he was exceedingly kind and helpful. In his own time he was notorious, like Rufus Choate, for his crabbed and illegible handwriting. His witty stories and clever repartee were frequently quoted. He was an orthodox Congregationalist, of firm religious principles.

[W. H. Crockett, *Vermont* (1921), vol. III; A. M. Hemenway, *The Vt. Hist. Gazetteer,* vol. I (1868); J. G. Ullery, *Men of Vermont* (1894); O. P. Chandler, in *Vt. Bar Asso. Constitution, Proceedings, Papers, and Addresses, 1886,* vol. II (1887); *Vt. Patriot* (Montpelier), Aug. 26, 1847.] C. M. F.

MATTOON, STEPHEN (May 5, 1816–Aug. 15, 1889), Presbyterian clergyman, was, with his co-worker Samuel Reynolds House [*q.v.*], the founder of the Presbyterian mission in Siam. He was born at Champion, Jefferson County, N. Y., the son of Gershom Mattoon and Anna Nancy (Sayre). With his parents he removed to Geneva, N. Y., where he obtained his early schooling. Deciding to enter the ministry, he set about acquiring the necessary education, earning his way by teaching. At the age of twenty-two he entered Union College, and graduated in 1842. After a year as principal of the academy and minister of the Presbyterian church at Sandy Hill (now Hudson Falls), N. Y., he went to Princeton Theological Seminary, where he graduated in 1846. In February of that year he was ordained by the Presbytery of Troy, and on June 3 married Mary, daughter of Hon. George Lowrie of Coila, Washington County, N. Y.

Very soon, with his wife and his associate, Dr. House, he sailed for Siam, reaching Bangkok in March 1847. At once he gave himself to the study of Siamese and eventually gained a thorough mastery of the structure and difficult pronunciation of the language. It fell to his lot to supervise nearly all the building operations during his term of service. When in 1851 King Maha Mongkut (Rama IV) provided the mission with a permanent location, Mattoon designed and superintended the erection of the buildings, although in order to erect a permanent brick house he had not only to learn the principles of architecture but also to teach his workmen new trades. In ecclesiastical affairs he was the leader. In 1849 he became the pastor of the first Presbyterian church organized in Bangkok. He baptized the first convert in 1851. When in 1858 the first Presbytery was organized, since he was about to sail for the United States, he was chosen the first commissioner to represent the Presbytery in the General Assembly. Because of his proficiency in both the native and the Bible languages he was assigned the task of making a new translation of the New Testament. Excellent as was the previous version of Rev. John Taylor Jones [*q.v.*], the growth in the understanding of Siamese idiom on the part of the Americans made a new translation desirable

Mattoon gave nearly fifteen years to the task, his version being published in 1865.

His mastery of both the written and spoken language brought two appointments of honor. When Sir John Bowring, the British ambassador, reached Siam in 1855 to accomplish the revision of a treaty, the King desired to appoint Mattoon and House as official interpreters "because of his express confidence in their integrity," and when the ambassador objected on account of their American citizenship, circumvented the objection by having them serve privately. In the following year an American embassy, headed by Townsend Harris [*q.v.*], also came seeking a treaty revision. Mattoon was appointed official interpreter for the embassy, and by his knowledge of the language and of the British negotiations was an invaluable aid to the Americans.

Upon completion of the treaty, Harris appointed Mattoon the first United States consul at Bangkok. Concerning this appointment Dr. W. M. Wood, surgeon-general of the East India squadron, who accompanied Harris to Siam, said in his book *Fankwei* (1859): "It was very evident that much of the apprehension they felt in taking upon themselves the responsibilities of a treaty with us would be diminished if they could have Rev. Mr. Mattoon as the first United States Consul to set the treaty in motion" (p. 194). How well he discharged the delicate duties is indicated by the testimonial which was tendered him when he resigned from the consulship in 1859 before taking a furlough in America. The King and high officials gave him distinguished marks of their esteem; the English and American residents extended public honors to him, and the Americans presented him with a purse for the purchase of a silver table service to be inscribed with a laudatory legend prepared by the committee.

Resigning from the mission in 1865, Mattoon returned to the United States in 1866, was pastor of the Presbyterian Church at Ballston Spa, N. Y., for nearly three years, and then served as president (1870–85) of Biddle Institute (now J. C. Johnson University) at Charlotte, N. C. After resigning from the presidency he continued as professor in the theological department until his death. He died at the home of a daughter in Marion, Ohio.

[Biographical sketch (MS.) by Mattoon's daughter, in archives of Presbyt. Bd. Foreign Missions, N. Y.; G. B. McFarland, *Hist. Sketch of Protestant Missions in Siam* (1928); G. H. Feltus, *Samuel Reynolds House of Siam* (copr. 1924); *Siam and Laos as Seen by Our American Missionaries* (copr. 1884); *Necrological Report . . . Princeton Theol. Sem.*, 1890; *Morning Star* (Wilmington, N. C.), Aug. 20, 1889.] G. H. F.

MATTSON, HANS (Dec. 23, 1832–Mar. 5, 1893), Swedish pioneer in Minnesota, publisher, emigration agent, was born in Önnestad parish, Skåne, Sweden, the son of Matts and Elna (Larson) Mattson. His father was a well-to-do land-owning farmer and gave his studious and ambitious son the advantages of an education above the average for that time. After two years in the Latin school of Kristianstad, Mattson became an artillery cadet in 1849, but at the age of eighteen abandoned the life of a soldier and emigrated to America, landing in June 1851 at Boston. His experiences in Boston, Buffalo, Albany, New York, and Contoocook, N. H., and as a ship's boy, belong rather to the pages of fiction than to the sober pages of history. In the summer of 1852 the young immigrant was joined by his father and brother, and the party made their way to the West, where they won a living by engaging in the drudgery that usually fell to the lot of immigrants. Among the Swedes in Moline, Ill., Mattson found a number who were agitating the establishment of a settlement where land could be acquired on liberal terms. Since he was the only one among them who spoke English, he was appointed the leader of a party that took passage on a Mississippi River steamboat to find a location in Minnesota Territory in the summer of 1853. About twelve miles from the present Red Wing Mattson and two companions established claims by writing names on trees. This was the beginning of the Vasa settlement, for a long time known as "Mattson's settlement," which gained publicity through the leader's letters in *Hemlandet* describing the attractions of the new country.

Mattson soon found the life of a pioneer farmer somewhat cramped and fell victim to the fever of speculation that preceded the panic of 1857. In consequence, he and his young wife were compelled to start life anew. He was admitted to the bar and held several local political offices; but with the outbreak of the Civil War he recruited a company of his countrymen, served for the period of the war, and was mustered out with the rank of colonel. With the prestige of a military title and endowed with the qualities of a leader and organizer, he remained to the end of his life a power among the Swedish-Americans. He was a mediocre speaker and had no literary style, but these shortcomings were more than balanced by his imposing appearance, kindliness, generosity, honesty, and interest in the welfare of the plain people. In 1866 he was appointed special emigration agent by the governor of Minnesota and the following year a member of the state board of immigration, a position he retained *ex-officio* in his capacity as secretary of state, 1870–72. In the sixties and seventies he resided for some time in Sweden as agent for the Northern Pacific Railroad, land companies, and the Canadian government. He was one of the few emigration agents to win the good will of the newspapers in Sweden in spite of his outspoken criticism of the bureaucracy and class distinctions of his native land. As a newspaper editor and publisher he cast his lot with the more liberal element, although he always remained within the Republican fold. From 1866 to 1867 he was editor of *Svenska Amerikanaren* (Chicago); in 1877 he established *Minnesota Stats Tidning* in Minneapolis, which he edited until 1881; during the same period he was business manager of *Svenska Tribunen* (Chicago), dividing his time between Chicago and Minneapolis. He served as United States consul general in India from 1881 to 1883 and again as secretary of state in Minnesota, 1887–91. On Nov. 23, 1855, he married Cherstin Peterson. Toward the end of his life he wrote an autobiography, published in Swedish as *Minnen af Öfverste H. Mattson* (Lund, 1890, 1891) and in English as *Reminiscences: the Story of an Emigrant* (1891).

[A number of Mattson's letters, pertaining chiefly to the Civil War, are in the manuscript collection of the Minn. Hist. Soc.; a few are printed in the *Year-Book of the Swedish Hist. Soc. of America*, 1923–24. An account of the settlement of Vasa by Carl Roos, which appeared originally in *Minnesota Stats Tidning*, Feb. 1, 1877, is printed in translation in the *Year-Book*, 1924–25. Mattson's work as emigration agent is explained in T. C. Blegen, "Minnesota's Campaign for Immigrants," *Ibid.*, 1926. See also Mattson's letters and advertisements in *Svenska Amerikanaren, Kristianstads Bladet, Nya Verlden* (Gothenburg), and *Swerige och Amerika* (Jönköping), 1867, 1868, 1871–73. For brief sketches see C. F. Peterson, in *Valkyrian* (New York), Sept. 1897; Luth Jaeger in A. E. Strand, *A Hist. of the Swedish-Americans of Minn.* (1910), I, 80–89; and Malte Persson, *Överste Mattson* (Kristianstad, 1932). An obituary appears in *Minneapolis Tribune*, Mar. 6, 1893.] G. M. S.

MATZELIGER, JAN ERNST (1852–1889), inventor, was born in Dutch Guiana. His father was a Dutch engineer engaged in important government work in the colony; his mother, a native black woman. At the age of ten, Matzeliger was put to work in the government machine shop, where, in the course of a long apprenticeship, he developed a keen interest in mechanics and showed a natural aptitude for machine work. When about twenty years old, he emigrated to the United States and for five years worked at the machinist's trade in various places.

In 1877 he went to Lynn, Mass., and there secured employment in the shoe factory of Harney Brothers, operating a McKay stitching machine for turned shoes and a burnishing machine. While thus occupied, he directed his attention to possible improvement which he might make in these machines, and decided to attempt the perfection of a complete turned-shoe sewing machine. While considering this project, however, he overheard, with considerable disgust, the hand lasters at the factory boasting that no one would ever devise a machine to supersede hand lasting of shoes. Matzeliger thereupon forgot his earlier idea and closely observed the lasters' motions with a view to imitating them by machinery. He rented a room over the old West Lynn Mission and with pieces of wood, old cigar boxes, and similar material, worked alone and at night for six months on a model of a machine incorporating his ideas. This, when completed in September 1880, indicated to Matzeliger that he was on the right track and he then proceeded with the construction of a full size working machine. Though roughly made, it proved capable of pleating the leather around the toe. His efforts became known and, in spite of the fact that he was extremely poor, he refused an offer of $1,500 for the toe pleating device and with renewed energy went to work on a third machine. This he completed and patented in 1883, receiving patent No. 274,207 on Mar. 20, two-thirds interest being assigned to M. S. Nichols and C. H. Delnow. Shortly afterward, the Consolidated Hand Method Lasting Machine Company was formed by the several Lynn men who had helped Matzeliger financially, and he began the construction of a fourth machine. When completed this could simultaneously and in a minute's time hold the last in place to receive the leather; move it forward step by step so that the other coaching parts might draw the leather over the heel; properly punch and grip the upper and draw it down over the last; lay the leather properly at the heel and toe; feed the nails and hold them in position for driving; and then discharge the completed shoe from the machine.

Unfortunately Matzeliger developed tuberculosis, and his plans for the further improvement of his machine and for the development of his company were frustrated. After a lingering illness he died at the age of thirty-seven years. His patent and the stock of his company were exchanged for stock of the United Shoe Machinery Company and the Matzeliger laster eventually completed the series of machines now required for making shoes. Some years before his death Matzeliger became a member of the North Congregational Church at Lynn and he bequeathed to this society a block of the stock of his original company. By 1904 these shares had more than doubled in price and enabled the church to pay off a mortgage.

[M. N. Work, *Negro Year Book*, 1921–22; D. W. Culp, *Twentieth Century Negro Literature* (1902); *Pamphlet of Consolidated Hand-Method Lasting Machine Company*, Boston, Mass., privately printed; Patent Office records; Waldemar Kaempffert, *A Popular Hist. of Am. Invention* (1924); information as to certain facts from the pastor of North Church, Lynn, Mass.] C. W. M.

MAURY, DABNEY HERNDON (May 21, 1822–Jan. 11, 1900), Confederate soldier, was born in Fredericksburg, Va., the son of Capt. John Minor Maury of the United States Navy, and Eliza (Maury) Maury. His parents were first cousins, descendants of Jean de la Fontaine, Huguenot, said to have been burned at the stake by French Catholics, whose great grand-daughter married in Dublin Matthew Maury, also of Huguenot descent, and came with him to America in 1718. From this stock sprang all the Virginia Maurys, including Dabney, his paternal uncle, Matthew Fontaine Maury [*q.v.*], and his great-grandfather, the Rev. James Maury, whom Patrick Henry [*q.v.*] opposed in the "Parson's Cause."

Maury received the degree of A.B. from the University of Virginia in 1842 and studied law there and at Fredericksburg. Disliking the law, he obtained an appointment to the United States Military Academy, where he was graduated in 1846. As second lieutenant of the Mounted Rifles, later the 3rd Cavalry, he went to Mexico, was mentioned in general orders for gallantry at the siege of Vera Cruz, and was brevetted first lieutenant for bravery at Cerro Gordo. From 1847 to 1850 he was assistant professor of geography, history, and ethics and from 1850 to 1852 assistant instructor of infantry tactics at West Point. He then served four adventurous years on the Texas frontier, hunting buffalo and deer, and chasing Indians. In 1856 he married Nannie Mason of King George County, and was appointed superintendent of the cavalry school at Carlisle, Pa. Here he remained until 1860, when he was promoted captain and appointed assistant adjutant-general of the Department of New Mexico. In 1859 he published a standard manual, *Skirmish Drill for Mounted Troops*.

At Santa Fé, in May 1861, telegrams forwarded by mail brought the news of the fall of Fort Sumter and of the secession of Virginia. Maury immediately resigned his commission, bade a sorrowful farewell to his brother officers, and went to Richmond, where he was appointed captain of cavalry in the Confederate States Army. Early in 1862 he was promoted colonel and made assistant adjutant-general and chief of staff to General Van Dorn, commander of the Trans-Mississippi Department. For his conduct at Pea Ridge, Ark., Mar. 7–8, 1862, he was promoted brigadier-general. This was after Van Dorn had highly praised his courage and patriotism, and his readiness "either with his sword or his pen" (*Official Records,* 1 ser. VIII, 286). Later Maury fought with the Army of the West at Iuka, Corinth, and Hatchie Bridge; at Corinth he commanded the center, driving the enemy through the town and fighting doggedly in the subsequent retreat. In November 1862 he was promoted major-general, and, after brief service in East Tennessee, in July 1863 was made commander of the district of the Gulf with headquarters at Mobile. In this capacity he served for the rest of the war, losing the harbor defenses to Farragut in August 1864 and in the following year, with about 9,200 effectives, defending the city against Farragut's fleet and Canby's army of 45,000 from Mar. 27 to Apr. 12, when after heavy loss he retired to Meridian, Miss.

The end of the war found him penniless and unfitted by training and temperament for a business career. After teaching at Fredericksburg, Va., and holding various positions in Louisiana, he made his home in Richmond. There he is remembered as a small, spare man, socially, and, at least in his younger days, even convivially inclined, but with a sense of duty and honor worthy of the best of the traditional Virginia gentleman officers. When old and impoverished, he declined to be a supervisor of drawings for the Louisiana Lottery at a yearly salary of $30,000, and once he gave up his business in order to serve as a volunteer nurse in a New Orleans yellow-fever epidemic. In 1868 he organized the Southern Historical Society, opening its records to the United States war records office in return for free access by former Confederates to records of the latter. He was chairman of the executive committee of the Society until 1886 and contributed a number of articles to its *Papers.* He was also the author of *A Young People's History of Virginia and Virginians* (1896; 2nd ed., 1904) and the entertaining *Recollections of A Virginian* (1894). In 1873 he assisted in organizing the Westmoreland Club of Richmond. During the critical year of 1876 he started the movement for the improvement of the United States volunteer troops, and served as a member of the executive committee of the National Guard Association until 1890. From 1885 to 1889 he was United States minister to Colombia. He died at the home of his son, in Peoria, Ill.

[Maury's *Recollections* (1894); *Battles and Leaders of the Civil War* (1887–88), vols. II–IV; C. A. Evans, *Confed. Mil. Hist.* (1899), vol. III; *Richmond Dispatch,*

Jan. 12, 14, 1900; *So. Hist. Soc. Papers*, vol. XXVII (1899); *War of the Rebellion: Official Records (Army)*; G. W. Cullum, *Biog. Reg. Officers and Grads. U. S. Mil. Acad.* (3rd ed., 1891); *Thirty-first Ann. Reunion Asso. Grads. U. S. Mil. Acad.* (1900); James Fontaine, *Memoirs of a Huguenot Family* (1853); R. A. Brock, *Docs. Rel. to the Huguenot Emigration to Va.* (1886); information as to certain facts from Dabney H. Maury, Jr., Chevy Chase, Md.] R. D. M.

MAURY, FRANCIS FONTAINE (Aug. 9, 1840–June 4, 1879), surgeon, was born near Danville, Boyle County, Ky., and spent his boyhood days on the farm which was the scene of the research of Dr. Ephraim McDowell [*q.v.*], who gave to surgery the operation of ovariotomy. Maury's parents were Matthew Fontaine Maury, an Episcopal clergyman, and Eliza (Chipman) Maury, of Middlebury, Vt. His grandfather, for whom he was named, was a first cousin of the distinguished naval officer, Matthew Fontaine Maury [*q.v.*].

Maury received the degree of bachelor of arts from Centre College on June 28, 1860, and entered the medical department of the University of Virginia the same year. He continued his medical studies at Jefferson Medical College, graduating Mar. 8, 1862. In that year he was appointed to an unexpired term as resident interne to the Philadelphia Hospital (now Philadelphia General Hospital). Here he proved himself possessed of abundant energy, acuity of observation, a retentive memory, and astuteness in evaluating a patient's ability to withstand surgery. On Apr. 1, 1863, he was commissioned acting assistant surgeon in the United States Army, with duties at the South Street General Hospital, which position he occupied until Apr. 15, 1865. In October 1863 he was elected clinical assistant to Prof. S. D. Gross [*q.v.*] in the department of surgery at Jefferson Medical College, and here conducted private teaching until 1864, when he became chief of the surgical clinic at Jefferson Medical College. On Nov. 27, 1865, he was appointed chief surgeon to the Philadelphia Hospital. His private practice in surgery grew with unusual rapidity. He became a member of the American Dermatological Association and Pathological Society of Philadelphia in 1865; of the College of Physicians in 1866, the Academy of Natural Sciences in 1868, and the Philadelphia County Medical Society in 1877.

Among his notable feats in surgery were ligation of the common carotid and subclavian arteries for aortic aneurism; gastrotomy for relief of syphilitic stricture of the esophagus (he was the first to perform this operation in America; see *American Journal of the Medical Sciences*, April 1870); resection of a portion of the brachial plexus to relieve the pain in neuroma of the skin of the upper extremity (*Ibid.*, July 1874; the first operation of this nature on record); the removal of cystic goiters; and his special plastic operation for exstrophy of the bladder, using the flap from the perineum and scrotum. He had the first recovery following amputation of the hip joint, in America; and was dexterous at lithotomy and lithotrity. He edited conjointly with Dr. Duhring, the *Photographic Review of Medicine and Surgery* (1870–72). His last literary contribution was a paper written in collaboration with C. W. Dulles on "Tattooing as a Means of Communicating Syphilis" (*American Journal of the Medical Sciences*, January 1878). Dr. Samuel W. Gross, in a memoir of Maury (*post*) read before the College of Physicians, characterized him as a cool, dextrous, cautious surgeon, of sound judgment.

[Memoirs by S. W. Gross in *Trans. Medic. Soc. of the State of Pa.*, vol. XIII, pt. I (1881), and repr. in J. W. Croskey, *Hist. of Blockley* (1929); J. H. Adams, *Hist. of the Life of D. Hayes Agnew* (1892); H. A. Kelly and W. L. Burrage, *Am. Medic. Biogs.* (1920); *Phila. Medic. Times*, June 21, 1879; *N. Y. Medic. Jour.*, Aug. 1879; *Boston Medic. and Surgic. Jour.*, June 13, 1879; *Public Ledger* (Phila.), June 5, 1879.] L. N. B.

MAURY, MATTHEW FONTAINE (Jan. 14, 1806–Feb. 1, 1873), naval officer, oceanographer, the fourth son in a family of five sons and four daughters of Richard Maury and Diana (Minor) Maury, came of Huguenot, Dutch, and English stock long settled in Virginia. [See sketch of Dabney Herndon Maury for ancestry.] He was born near Fredericksburg, Va., but in his fifth year the family emigrated to Tennessee, settling on a farm near the frontier village of Franklin. The country schools of the region furnished his schooling to the age of twelve, when he entered Harpeth Academy, near Franklin. Since an elder brother had become a naval officer, Maury looked forward to a career in the navy. In 1825 he secured a midshipman's warrant and in the following nine years made three extended cruises. The first was to Europe on the war vessel that took Lafayette back to France after his memorable visit to the United States; the next, around the world in the *Vincennes*; and the third, to the Pacific coast of South America. Returning in 1834 he applied for leave of absence, and on July 15 was married to Ann Hull Herndon of Fredericksburg, Va. Establishing his residence there, he used his leisure in the publication of a work on navigation which he had begun during the last part of his recent tour of sea duty. This appeared in 1836 under the title *A New Theoretical and Practical Treatise on Navigation* and met with immediate favor.

Promoted to the rank of lieutenant in 1836, he was attached the following year, as astronomer, to the Exploring Expedition to the South Seas which was being organized by the navy. Objecting to what he thought an exhibition of favoritism in the final selection of the commanding officer, Maury asked to be detached from the expedition, and was then assigned to surveying duty in the harbors of the southeastern states. Meanwhile, under the pseudonym of Harry Bluff, U. S. Navy, he published five articles in the *Richmond Whig and Public Advertiser* in which he criticized the former Secretary of the Navy for inefficiency and called upon his successor to restore the navy to its earlier prestige. These appeared in the summer of 1838; and in December of that year he followed them up with seven more articles in the same paper, inscribed "From Will Hatch to his old messmate Harry Bluff." In these he went into further detail regarding inefficiency in the administration of the navy and suggested specific reforms. In the fall of 1839, while returning from a visit to his parents in Tennessee, Maury sustained a severe injury to his right knee in a stage-coach accident, which resulted in permanent lameness. He made use of the enforced leisure in writing a series of articles under the title "Our Navy: Scraps from the Lucky Bag," published in the *Southern Literary Messenger* during the years 1840 and 1841. These articles also dealt with the need of reform in the conduct of naval affairs, and were written under his former pseudonym, Harry Bluff, but in July 1841 a sketch of Maury appeared in the *Messenger* which connected him with the authorship of the series.

In the following year he was appointed superintendent of the Depot of Charts and Instruments of the Navy Department at Washington, succeeding J. M. Gilliss [*q.v.*]. The post included the superintendency of the new Naval Observatory and in 1854 the institution was officially designated United States Naval Observatory and Hydrographical Office. Maury, however, gave little attention to the astronomical part of the work, being much more interested in its hydrographic and meteorological aspects (G. A. Weber, *The Naval Observatory, Its History, Activities, and Organization,* 1926, p. 17). Soon after his appointment he began his researches on winds and currents, and in 1847 issued his *Wind and Current Chart of the North Atlantic,* which was followed in the next year by explanatory sailing directions under the title *Abstract Log for the Use of American Navigators,* issued in subsequent editions as *Notice to Mariners* (1850) and *Explanations and Sailing Directions to Accompany the Wind and Current Charts* (1851). So confident was he of the practical utility of his charts and sailing directions that he predicted a saving of from ten to fifteen days in the passage from New York to Rio de Janeiro by their use. The fulfillment of his prediction created great interest in the new charts on the part of mariners, and Maury turned this interest to account by securing the cooperation of the mariner in noting the winds and currents encountered in various regions. The success of these cooperative oceanographic observations made Maury conceive of extending the system universally. As a result of his labors an international congress was held at Brussels in the fall of 1853; Maury was the United States representative and leading spirit; and the uniform system of recording oceanographic data he advocated was adopted for the naval vessels and merchant marine of the whole world.

Back again in Washington, he threw himself into his oceanographic work with renewed enthusiasm. On the bases of the data now coming in from all quarters of the earth, he revised his wind and current charts of the Atlantic and Pacific oceans and drew one up also for the Indian Ocean. The gold rush to California which had begun several years before made the sailing time between the Atlantic ports of the United States and San Francisco a most important matter. Prior to the use of Maury's charts the passage from New York to San Francisco averaged 180 days; but by 1855 this time had been reduced to 133 days. Other passages were shortened in like measure, resulting in savings amounting to millions of dollars annually. During this period, also, Maury was busily engaged in lecturing and writing on scientific subjects connected with the sea, and in 1855 he published *The Physical Geography of the Sea,* now recognized as the first textbook of modern oceanography. The sea, for the first time, was here viewed as the subject matter of a distinct branch of science with problems of its own. The importance of these problems Maury discussed in engaging and stimulating fashion. The book went through numerous editions and was translated into half a dozen different languages. In the early fifties the idea of a trans-Atlantic cable was being actively discussed, and aroused Maury's interest. He prepared a chart representing in profile the bottom of the Atlantic between Europe and America, calling attention to the existence of what he termed "the telegraphic plateau," and stated definitely that in so far as oceanographic conditions were concerned "the practicability of a submarine telegraph across the Atlantic is proved" (Corbin, *post,* p. 100). His wide knowledge of the sea was called upon in selecting the most advantageous time for undertaking the laying of the cable; Cyrus Field [*q.v.*] consulted him frequently and publicly expressed his indebtedness to Maury.

His attainments now received wide recognition. Foreign governments vied with one another in bestowing honors and medals upon him; several universities awarded him honorary degrees; and he was elected to membership in various learned societies at home and abroad. In 1853 the merchants and underwriters of New York presented him with a fine silver service and a purse of $5,000 in recognition of the benefits he had conferred on the commerce of that port. With his scientific reputation secure, however, he was placed in a humiliating position by a board of naval officers convened by act of Congress in 1855 to "promote the efficiency of the navy." Meeting in secret, the board recommended that certain officers be dropped from the navy, others be placed on furlough, and still others on leave of absence. Maury's name was included in the third list, ostensibly because the injury to his leg unfitted him for sea duty. It is not improbable, however, that his fame, gained on shore, did not endear him to many officers who found themselves assigned to less pleasant service afloat. Maury appealed to his friends to help him secure justice; several newspapers took up his cause; resolutions in favor of his restoration to active service were passed by the legislatures of seven states; and in 1858 the president restored him to active service, promoting him at the same time to the rank of commander, retroactive to the date when he was placed on leave of absence.

While engaged in his oceanographic pursuits, he was also deeply interested in the development of Southern commerce. He cherished as a favorite project the opening of the Amazon Valley to free trade, hoping that one effect of such a measure would be to draw the slaves from the United States to Brazil. He was keenly interested in the Amazon expedition of his brother-in-law, W. L. Herndon [*q.v.*], and used material from Herndon's report to support his own arguments (see Maury's articles in *De Bow's Southern and Western Review,* February 1852, May–June 1853, and *The Amazon and the Atlantic Slopes of South America,* 1853, a collection of letters originally contributed to the *National Intelligencer and Union*). In the growing antagonism between North and South, his sympathies were naturally with his section, but in regard to the questions at issue he favored conference and conciliation. On the day of Lincoln's inauguration he wrote: "The line of duty, therefore, is to me clear—each one to follow his own State, if his own State goes to war; if not, he may remain to help on the work of reunion" (Corbin, p. 186). On Apr. 20, 1861, three days after the secession of Virginia, he tendered his resignation and proceeded to Richmond, where he soon was commissioned a commander in the Confederate States Navy.

Assigned to harbor defense, he began experimenting with electric mines, but in the fall of 1862 was sent to England as special agent of the Confederate government. Here his world-wide reputation made him an effective spokesman for the Southern cause. He was instrumental in securing ships of war for the Confederacy and he also continued his experiments with electric mines. With the purpose of making use of these mines in the war, he set out for America in the spring of 1865, but when he reached the West Indies the Confederacy had collapsed, and he found himself in a precarious situation; for the representatives of the Confederacy abroad were excluded from the pardon of the amnesty proclamations that were issued upon the close of the war.

Maury now offered his services to the Emperor of Mexico, laying before him a scheme for the colonization of former Confederates and their families, and in August 1865 he was appointed imperial commissioner of immigration. Some progress in colonization was made, but the troubled political conditions in Mexico, coupled with the failure of a large exodus from the Southern states to materialize, caused the scheme to be abandoned the following year: Maury meanwhile returned to England, where for the next two years he busied himself with his electric mines and with writing a series of geographies for school use, at the request of a New York publishing house. His *First Lessons in Geography* (1868), *The World We Live In* (1868), and *Manual of Geography* (1870) went through many editions, under varying titles. During this time he was presented with a purse of 3,000 guineas raised by popular subscription in appreciation of his services to the maritime world, and Cambridge University honored him with the degree of LL.D.

Urged now by his friends at home to return to the United States, he left England in 1868 to accept the professorship of meteorology in the Virginia Military Institute at Lexington. Here he spent the last four years of his life. He undertook a survey of the state, publishing a preliminary report, *Physical Survey of Virginia,*

No. I, in 1868. Even before the war he had stressed the importance of a system of telegraphic meteorological observations in the interests of agriculture; and now he took this subject up again in a number of addresses delivered before various organizations. While on such a lecture tour in the fall of 1872 he fell ill, dying four months later. After temporary interment at Lexington he was finally laid to rest in Hollywood Cemetery at Richmond, between the tombs of Presidents Monroe and Tyler.

Maury's name is commemorated in a long list of memorials. The Pilot Charts of the oceans, published monthly by the Hydrographic Office of the United States Navy, bear a caption stating that they are founded upon Maury's researches. At the Naval Academy, Annapolis, there are Maury Hall and the annual Maury Prize. In 1916 the State Board of Education designated Jan. 14—the day of his birth—as Maury Day in the schools of Virginia, and in 1923 the State of Virginia placed a bronze tablet in his honor at Goshen Pass on the North Anna River. A monument erected through the efforts of the Maury Memorial Association was unveiled in Richmond in 1929. There are minor memorials in various places, both at home and abroad.

Personally, Maury is described as a stout man about five feet six inches in height, with a fresh and ruddy complexion; and, despite the many honors showered on him, of a modest and reserved nature. He was happy in his family life, devoting considerable time to the teaching of his five daughters and three sons. Himself largely self-educated, he had definite ideas regarding education. As against Latin and Greek he urged mathematics and the sciences. West Point he is said to have considered "the only tolerable institution in the United States because of the absence there of the humbuggery of the Learned Languages" (Lewis, *post*, p. 131). He thought little of female seminaries, regarding them as "downright cheats" because of the superficiality of the knowledge taught there. An indefatigable worker himself, he stressed the importance of industry, declaring: "It's the talent of industry that makes a man" (Corbin, p. 161).

[Diana Fontaine Maury Corbin, *A Life of Matthew Fontaine Maury* (1888); J. A. Caskie, *Life and Letters of Matthew Fontaine Maury* (1928); C. L. Lewis, *Matthew Fontaine Maury: The Pathfinder of the Seas* (1927); J. W. Wayland, *The Pathfinder of the Seas: the Life of Matthew Fontaine Maury* (1930); R. M. Brown, "Bibliography of Commander Matthew Fontaine Maury," *Bull. Va. Polytechnic Inst.*, vol. XXIV, no. 2 (Dec. 1930); W. H. Beehler, "The Origin and Work of the Division of Marine Meteorology, Hydrographic Office," *Proc. U. S. Naval Inst.*, vol. XIX (1893); R. L. Maury, *A Brief Sketch of the Work of Matthew Fontaine Maury During the War, 1861–65* (1915); *Richmond Daily Dispatch*, Feb. 3, 1873; *Richmond Times-Dispatch*, Nov. 12, 1929.]

H. A. M.

MAUS, MARION PERRY (Aug. 25, 1850–Feb. 9, 1930), soldier, was the son of Isaac Rhodes and Mary Malvina (Greer) Maus, and was born at Burnt Mills, Montgomery County, Md. His maternal grandfather, James Greer, was a Presbyterian minister, born in Scotland, who settled in Georgetown, D. C., probably about 1800. On the paternal side, his first ancestor in America was Frederick Maus, an Alsatian, who arrived in early colonial times. A great-uncle, Philip Maus, sacrificed his fortune in aiding the Revolutionary cause and also served as a soldier; another relative, Matthew Maus, was a surgeon in the ill-fated Montgomery expedition to Quebec (1775–76). Young Maus attended the local public schools and later Charlotte Hall Academy. In 1870, through the influence of Montgomery Blair, he was appointed a cadet at West Point. Graduating in 1874, he was assigned to the 1st Infantry, at Fort Randall, in the present South Dakota, and for the next two years took part in a series of actions against bandits and Indians and in the work of expelling prospectors from the Black Hills. He served under Gen. Nelson A. Miles [*q.v.*] in the winter campaign (1876–77) against Lame Deer's band; in the following autumn, as commander of the white and Indian scouts, in the Nez Percé campaign ending in the surrender of Chief Joseph, he won a silver citation for gallantry in action.

In 1880, a first lieutenant (Sept. 29, 1879), he was transferred to Texas, and in May 1882, to Arizona, where for several years he rendered notable service against the Apaches. In the fall of 1885 he succeeded Britton Davis as commander of the Apache scouts, and for his conduct in an attack on Geronimo's band and a defensive action against a body of Chihuahua troops (Jan. 10–11, 1886), near the Aros River, Mexico, was awarded the Congressional medal of honor. Further frontier service took him to Colorado and to the theatre of the Ghost Dance troubles which culminated in the battle of Wounded Knee, S. Dak., Dec. 29, 1890. In November of that year he became a captain. In 1897, as aide-de-camp to Miles, he witnessed some of the operations of the war between Greece and Turkey, and in the following year, in the same capacity, took part in the Cuban and Porto Rican campaigns of the Spanish-American War. He was promoted major, June 16, 1899. In July of that year he was appointed inspector-general of the department of California and the Columbia. Three years later he accompanied Miles in an official tour of the island possessions of the United States. On June 28, 1902, he was made lieutenant-colonel. From 1903 to March 1906, he was on active duty in the Philippines. His next station was Monterey, Cal., and from there, on receipt of the news of the earthquake and fire of Apr. 18, 1906, he was transferred to San Francisco to take command of the troops guarding the financial district. He had become a colonel Jan. 24, 1904, and in 1909 he attained the rank of brigadier-general and was assigned to the command of the department of the Columbia. On Aug. 20, 1913, he retired. He died at New Windsor, Md., and was buried, with full military honors, at Arlington.

At Skaneateles, N. Y., on June 28, 1899, Maus was married to Lindsay, the daughter of Charles H. Poor, who survived him. His long career of exceptionally varied duties was marked by efficient performance, and in his frontier campaigns he displayed a courage, resourcefulness, and endurance that rank him among the most noted of the Indian fighters.

[G. W. Cullum, *Biog. Reg. Officers and Grads. U. S. Mil. Acad.* (1891), vol. III, and succeeding supplements; *Sixty-First Ann. Report Asso. Grads. U. S. Mil. Acad.* (1930); N. A. Miles, *Personal Recollections and Observations,* chs. XX–XXI (1896); Britton Davis, *The Truth About Geronimo* (1929); *Who's Who in America,* 1920–21; the *Evening Star* (Washington), Feb. 10, 1930; information as to certain facts from Mrs. M. P. Maus and Capt. R. G. Carter.] W. J. G.

MAVERICK, PETER (Oct. 22, 1780–June 7, 1831), engraver, was born in New York City, the son of Peter Rushton and Anne (Reynolds) Maverick. He was the grandson of Andrew Maverick, a painter, born in Boston in 1728/29 and admitted a freeman in New York in 1753, and a descendant of Elias, brother of Samuel Maverick [*q.v.*]. Peter was a pupil of his father in copper-plate engraving and began to engrave at an early age. The frontispiece of the *Holy Bible Abridged* (New York, 1790) is signed "P. Maverick sct. Æ 9 years." For some time he was occupied in New York City but later he went to Newark, N. J., where Asher B. Durand [*q.v.*] served an apprenticeship (1812–17) and then went into partnership with him. "The preference which Trumbull gave to Durand," says Sumner (*post,* p. 175) "by employing him to the exclusion of Maverick, broke up the business connection." Maverick returned to New York, where he established himself as a general engraver and copper-plate printer; he eventually added lithographic printing, as did more than one other engraver. This "general graphic business" covered "bank-notes engraved on copper or steel, with all the variety of die work and machine facilities now in use" (Weitenkampf, *post,* p. 80). He engraved a number of portraits in line and in stipple, notably that of Cadwallader D. Colden, after Waldo and Jewett, signed "Peter Maverick & Durand & Co.," as well as views, historical scenes, many book illustrations after British designers, and also bookplates, cards, college commencement tickets, and similar objects. One of his lithographs was "Daughter of Charles B. Calmody," after Lawrence (1829); among the lithographs he printed was a view of Wall Street, as rare as it is artless.

Maverick was one of the founders of the National Academy of Design, which had a number of engraver members in the early days. He died in New York City. Stauffer reports that his portrait was painted by John Neagle, though it did not figure in the exhibition of portraits by Neagle held by the Pennsylvania Academy of the Fine Arts in 1925; Sumner names Jarvis as the painter of a portrait. Maverick's son Peter, Jr., is listed in the New York directories (1832–45) as "engraver and lithographer," which appears to be all that is known of him. Augustus, the son of his second wife, Matilda Brown, whom he married in 1828, became an assistant editor on the staff of the *New York Times.* His brothers Samuel and Andrew were engravers and plate-makers; his daughters Maria and Emily are likewise said to have engraved.

[The chief sources of information are D. M. Stauffer, *Am. Engravers upon Copper and Steel* (2 vols., 1907) and Mantle Fielding's supplement to the same (1917); Wm. Dunlap, *A Hist. of the Rise and Progress of the Arts of Design in the U. S.* (ed. 1918), vol. II, p. 370; Frank Weitenkampf, *Am. Graphic Art* (1912); W. H. Sumner, *A Hist. of East Boston* (1858), pp. 173–75; *New-Eng. Hist. and Geneal. Reg.,* Apr. 1894; and *Names of Persons for Whom Marriage Licenses were Issued by the Secretary of the Province of N. Y. Previous to 1784* (1860). The *Evening Post* of June 8, 1831, and the *Morning Courier & N. Y. Enquirer* of June 9 carry death notices, but no obituaries.] F. W.

MAVERICK, SAMUEL (*c.* 1602–*c.* 1676), colonist, came of a Devonshire family which gave a number of clergymen to the Church of England. His father, Rev. John Maverick, later teacher of the church at Dorchester, Mass. (1630–36), was the son of Peter, vicar of Awliscombe, Devon, and the nephew of Radford Maverick, rector of Islington, where John was married in 1600 to Mary Gye and may have served for a time as his uncle's curate. Samuel apparently received a good education and became a man of culture and gentle manners. About 1624 he came to America, settling on Boston Bay. He seems to have been connected with the Gorges plans for colonizing, owned lands in Maine, and about 1628 married Amias (Cole), widow of David Thompson, one of the settlers sent out by Gorges in 1623, who later established himself on an island in Boston Harbor. About 1625 Maverick built a fortified house at Winnisimmet (Chelsea), where he was living in 1630 when Winthrop and his party arrived. To the newcomers he was generous and courteous. He took the oath as freeman of the colony of Massachusetts Bay in October 1632. An entry in Governor Winthrop's journal in December of the following year (*post,* I, 115), speaks of his kindness to the Indians during an epidemic of smallpox: "Among others, Mr. Maverick of Winesemett is worthy of a perpetual remembrance. Himself, his wife, and servants went daily to them, ministered to their necessities, and buried their dead, and took home many of their children." He engaged in commerce and had several vessels on the coast. In 1635–36 he spent about a year in Virginia, returning "with two pinnaces," bringing "some fourteen heifers, and about eighty goats" (*Ibid.,* p. 185). He had negro slaves (Sumner, *post,* pp. 90–91) as well as other servants and was noted for his hospitality. At his house on Noddle's Island he entertained Henry Vane and Lord Ley at dinner, during the controversy of 1637, and John Josselyn [*q.v.*], who visited him in 1638, later characterized him as "the only hospitable man in all the Country" (*An Account of Two Voyages to New England,* Veazie reprint, 1865, p. 13).

Although himself a freeman of the colony and apparently held in considerable respect, Maverick came into conflict with the Puritan authorities over the matter of civil and religious rights for settlers who were not of the Congregational fold. In 1646 he was one of those who signed the petition of Dr. Robert Child which described the Massachusetts government as an "ill compacted vessel" and prayed for admission to full civil rights or exemption from taxation and military service, for permission to maintain a church and minister of their own, since they were not admitted to baptism and the sacrament of the Lord's supper in the New England churches, and for the establishment of the body of English law as the law of the colony. As a result of his connection with this petition and the subsequent controversy in 1647, Maverick was fined £150 (later reduced by half). He professed himself willing to pay, but not an excessive amount, and deeded Noddle's Island to his son to prevent its confiscation. He seems to have left Massachusetts about 1650. After the restoration of the Stuarts he returned to England, where he pressed a plan for a more rigid supervision of the colonies. While here he wrote (1660) "A Briefe Discription of New England and the Severall Townes Therein," probably for the use of Clarendon in regulating the New England government. In 1664 he returned to Massachusetts as one of four royal commissioners sent out to hear and determine complaints. His duties took him to New York and for his services there he was granted a house on Broadway by the Duke of York in 1669. Maverick had two sons and a daughter. His death occurred between 1670 and 1676.

[Maverick's "Briefe Discription" in *New Eng. Hist. and Geneal. Reg.,* Jan. 1885, and in *Proc. Mass. Hist. Soc.,* 2 ser. I (1885), 231; letters to the Winthrops in *Mass. Hist. Soc. Colls.,* 4 ser. VII (1865), and to the Earl of Clarendon in *N. Y. Hist. Soc. Colls. . . . 1869* (1876), being Pub. Fund Ser., vol. II; C. F. Adams, *Three Episodes of Mass. Hist.* (1892), I, 328–35; W. H. Sumner, *A Hist. of East Boston* (1858); *New Eng. Hist. and Geneal. Reg.,* Apr. 1894, Apr. 1915; *Proc. Mass. Hist. Soc.,* 2 ser. I, 366; *Winthrop's Journal* (2 vols., 1908), ed. by J. K. Hosmer; *Records of the Governor and Company of the Mass. Bay,* vols. I–IV (1853–54).]

J. T. A.

MAXCY, JONATHAN (Sept. 2, 1768–June 4, 1820), college president, was born in Attleborough, Mass., son of Levi and Ruth (Newell) Maxcy, and a descendant of Alexander Maxcy who moved to Attleborough from Gloucester, in 1721. Virgil [*q.v.*] was a younger brother of Jonathan. The latter prepared for college at Wrentham Academy under William Williams, who was a member of the first class that graduated at Rhode Island College (now Brown University), which institution Maxcy entered in 1783. After his graduation in 1787 he remained at the college as tutor, acting also as librarian. He was licensed to preach Apr. 1, 1790, and succeeded James Manning [*q.v.*], president of the college, as pastor of the First Baptist Church of Providence, being ordained Sept. 8, 1791. While in charge of the church he also served the college as its first professor of divinity, and as a trustee. President Manning died suddenly in 1791, and Maxcy succeeded him in the presidency, resigning his pastorate and being elected president *pro tempore* in September 1792. It indicates the esteem in which he was held that at this time he had just passed his twenty-fourth birthday. In September 1797 he was chosen president. The college "flourished under his administration, and his fame was extended over every section of the Union" (Elton, *post,* p. 14). His chief service to the institution was his teaching of oratory and belles-lettres, and the widening of its fame by his personal reputation as an orator and divine (Bronson, *post,* p. 132). Naturally, in the state of Roger Williams and in a college the charter of which required that the trustees be of several denominations, Maxcy developed breadth of sympathy and a catholicity of view in religion.

After having served Brown for fifteen years as tutor, professor, and president, he resigned in 1802 to become president of Union College, Schenectady, N. Y. Here he was remarkable for diligent and persevering labor. As a result, his health became impaired, and, wishing to live in a milder climate, he was glad to accept, in 1804, a call to become the first president of the University of South Carolina (then South Carolina College). Richard Furman [*q.v.*], a strong advocate of education in South Carolina, recommended him for the position, since through his students he had become favorably known in the South. Both Furman and Maxcy were Federalists. The college opened in January 1805 with Maxcy and one professor as faculty. The former taught belles-lettres, criticism, and metaphysics.

While it is clear from the "rules and regulations," which he no doubt drew up, that the college he launched was of the ordinary classical type, it is significant that in the year 1811 a chair of chemistry was established, paving the way for a succession of eminent scientists on the faculty. Maxcy also recommended the establishment of chairs of law and political economy. Mineralogy was added to the department of chemistry, and natural philosophy was joined to mathematics. Some provision was made for students who did not wish to take Latin and Greek. In 1813, probably as a result of student uprisings due to lax discipline, Maxcy was censured by the trustees and asked to show cause why he should not be removed from office. The matter was ultimately dropped, however.

While the extant sermons and orations of Maxcy have little interest for our more practical and scientific age, Robert Henry records that he seems to have had no superior in his time as an orator. His sermon, *The Existence of God Demonstrated from the Works of Creation* (1795), delivered at Providence, "produced the most lively and striking effect on the audience," and was frequently spoken of at the end of half a century. The power of his personality is to be judged from the reverence in which he was held by such of his students as James L. Petigru and George McDuffie [*qq.v.*]. He was a man of medium stature, but "had a peculiar majesty in his walk." "His features . . ., when they were exercised in conversation or public speaking, were strongly expressive, and exhibited the energy of the soul that animated them" (Elton, p. 21). A central principle of his life was religious freedom. "I am not . . . disposed," he said, "to be so rigidly tenacious of my own sentiments, as to imagine I may not be in an error. All men have full liberty of opinion, and ought to enjoy it without subjecting themselves to the imputation of heresy" (*Ibid.*, p. 149). In his funeral sermon for Dr. Manning he coupled the "great theological champions" Edwards and Hopkins, with Priestley and Price, "preeminent in virtue," and asked if the former were to engross heaven while the latter sank to regions of darkness and pain (*Ibid.*, p. 151).

On Aug. 22, 1791, he married Susan Hopkins, daughter of Commodore Esek Hopkins [*q.v.*], of Providence, R. I. Of this union there were born four sons and several daughters. He died in Columbia, S. C. A monument to his memory stands upon the campus of the University of South Carolina, erected by the Clariosophic Literary Society, of which he was an honorary member.

[Romeo Elton, *The Lit. Remains of the Rev. Jonathan Maxcy, D.D. . . . with a Memoir of His Life* (1844); J. C. Hungerpiller, "A Sketch of the Life and Character of Jonatnan Maxcy, D.D.," with bibliography, *Bull. of the Univ. of S. C.*, July 1917; Robert Henry, *Eulogy on Jonathan Maxcy* (1822); W. B. Sprague, *Annals Am. Pulpit*, vol. VI (1860); W. C. Bronson, *The Hist. of Brown Univ.* (1914); E. L. Green, *A Hist. of the Univ. of S. C.* (1916); Maximilian LaBorde, *Hist. of the S. C. College* (2nd ed., 1874); John Daggett, *A Sketch of the Hist. of Attleborough* (1894); *City Gazette* (Charleston) and *Charleston Courier*, June 10, 1820.] S. C. M.

MAXCY, VIRGIL (May 5, 1785–Feb. 28, 1844), lawyer, legislator, diplomat, was born in that part of Attleborough, Mass., which was later annexed to Wrentham. He was the son of Levi and Ruth (Newell) Maxcy, and a younger brother of Jonathan Maxcy [*q.v.*]. The boy grew up in a home of the best New England tradition, and matriculated at Brown University two years before his brother Jonathan resigned as president of that institution to become head of Union College, Schenectady, N. Y. At nineteen Virgil graduated from Brown with the degrees of A.B. and A.M. After an interlude as tutor in the home of a Southern family, he studied law in Baltimore under Robert Goodloe Harper [*q.v.*], and was admitted to the Maryland bar. He married Mary Galloway, the grand-daughter of Chief Justice Benjamin Chew [*q.v.*] of Philadelphia. Samuel Galloway, her paternal grandfather, had built an estate at "Tulip Hill," near Annapolis, and this became the home of the Maxcys.

An able scholar, a persuasive speaker, and a fluent writer, Maxcy was not long in establishing a reputation for himself as a lawyer in Anne Arundel County. In 1811 he published in three volumes *The Laws of Maryland, with the Charter, the Bill of Rights, the Constitution of the State and Its Alterations . . . 1692–1809*. Politics, however, claimed his chief interest. He was chosen a member of the Maryland executive council in 1815, and afterward served as a member of the state Senate and of the House of Delegates, where he vigorously supported the interests of the rural districts. He campaigned actively for Andrew Jackson for president, speaking tirelessly and writing innumerable newspaper articles and pamphlets. He took a leading part in the calling and transactions of the state Jackson convention early in 1827, the first to be held in the United States. When Jackson was elected Maxcy vainly hoped for an appointment as First Comptroller of the treasury, but on May 29, 1830, the office of solicitor of the treasury was created by act of Congress as recommended by President Jackson in his first annual message, and Maxcy, nominated May 29, 1830, had the distinction of becoming the first solicitor. He held office until 1837. On June 16 of that year he was appointed by President Van Buren American chargé d'affaires at Brussels, capital of the new Kingdom of Belgium, and the appointment was confirmed Sept. 18.

The political situation in Belgium, following its secession from the Kingdom of the Netherlands in 1830, was much unsettled. Maxcy, the second representative of the United States at Brussels, witnessed the critical period accompanying the negotiation and signing of the "Twenty-four Articles" and the Treaty of London. During his term of service he tried to accomplish two things. One was to negotiate a treaty of commerce between Belgium and the United States; the other, to bring to a settlement the claims of American merchants whose goods were destroyed when the *Entrepôt Royal de libre re-exportation,* a government warehouse at Antwerp, was burned during the revolution in 1830. In neither endeavor was he successful, but in both he made material progress. He was a conscientious representative of the United States and the interests of its citizens. He made careful and frequent reports on political and economic conditions, the first of which was written at Liverpool, en route to his station, scarcely two hours after he had landed. He resigned his post on June 17, 1842, and later returned to Maryland, where he again took up his private law practice. On Feb. 28, 1844, while he was a guest of President Tyler on the *Princeton,* a gun (called the "Peacemaker") exploded, killing him instantly, with several others. He was buried at "Tulip Hill."

[*Vital Records of Wrentham, Mass., to the Year 1850* (1910), vol. I; Romeo Elton, *Am. Eloquence; . . . Being the Literary Remains of Rev. Jonathan Maxcy, D.D., with a Memoir of His Life* (1845); John Daggett, *A Sketch of the Hist. of Attleborough from Its Settlement to the Division* (1894); a long letter from Maxcy to Calhoun, reviewing his political activities in support of Jackson, in "Correspondence of John C. Calhoun," ed. by J. F. Jameson, *Ann. Report of the Am. Hist. Asso. for the Year 1899,* vol. II (1900); U. S. Dept. of State Archives: Belgium, Diplomatic Correspondence, vol. I; *Baltimore Clipper,* Mar. 2, 1844.]

I. L. T.

MAXEY, SAMUEL BELL (Mar. 30, 1825–Aug. 16, 1895), Confederate general and senator from Texas, was born at Tompkinsville, Monroe County, Ky. His father, Rice Maxey, came of a Virginia family of Huguenot extraction, and his mother was the daughter of Samuel Bell of Albemarle County, Va. In 1846 he was graduated from the United States Military Academy at West Point and was immediately assigned to the 7th Infantry as second lieutenant. He served during the Mexican War, was brevetted first lieutenant for gallant conduct in the battles of Contreras and Churubusco, and was present at the capture of the City of Mexico. When the war was over he soon wearied of the monotony of garrison life and in 1849 resigned his commission. His father was a lawyer and within a year the young man had learned enough law to begin practice at Albany, Clinton County, Ky. On July 19, 1853, he was married to Marilda Cassa Denton. Four years later the Maxeys, father and son, removed to Texas, where they practised at Paris until the outbreak of the Civil War. Originally a Whig, Maxey became a Democrat, voted for Breckinridge, and advocated secession. In 1861 he declined election to the Texas legislature in order to join the forces of the South.

Organizing the 9th Texas Infantry, he entered the war as a colonel but was soon made a brigadier-general and later a major-general. He was actively engaged in the campaigns of 1862 and 1863 in Tennessee and Mississippi, and on Dec. 11, 1863, received his most important assignment as commander in the Indian territory. For the next year he was responsible for the security of this western outpost of the Confederacy. Finding the prospects of the South at a low ebb he used tact and energy in organizing three brigades of Indians, respecting fully the tribal loyalties of the Creek, Cherokee, and Choctaw. His ability as an orator, for which he was already well known, served him in good stead. He also established a printing-press in order to reach a larger audience. Both at the council-fire and through printed propaganda he persuaded the Indians that victory for the South was essential to their safety. He had soon gained their almost pathetic good will as no other Texan had done since the days of Sam Houston. A recent writer sums up the account of his activities,

"Behind all this virility was General Maxey. Without him, it is safe to say, the war for the Indians would have ended in the preceding winter" (Abel, *post*, p. 329).

The war over, he practised law for ten years. In 1873 he declined the appointment as federal judge of the 8th district of Texas. In 1875, at the end of Reconstruction, he was sent to the United States Senate, where he served for twelve years. In the Senate he was not unlike other members of the group known as the "Confederate Brigadiers." He advocated economy but did not fail to obtain appropriations for Texas rivers, harbors, and postroads. His most notable speeches, and he made many, were on Indian relations. Maxey was among the first to favor individual farms as the ultimate solution of the Indian question. On constitutional grounds he was opposed to the prevailing policy of protective tariffs. Defeated for reëlection he retired to practise law in Paris. He died at Eureka Springs, Ark.

[*The Encyc. of the New West*, ed. by W. S. Speer and J. H. Brown (1881); J. H. Brown, *Indian Wars and Pioneers of Texas* (189?); *Biog. Directory Am. Cong.* (1928); *Confederate Military Hist.*, ed. by C. A. Evans (1899), vol. XI; A. H. Abel, *The Slaveholding Indians*, vol. II (1919); *War of the Rebellion: Official Records (Army)*, 1 ser., vols. X, pt. 2, XVI, pt. 1, XXII, pt. 2, XXXIV, pts. 1–4 (1884–1902); *Galveston Daily News*, Aug. 17, 1895.] R. G. C—l.

MAXIM, HIRAM STEVENS (Feb 5, 1840–Nov. 24, 1916), inventor, engineer, was the eldest of the eight children of Isaac Weston and Harriet Boston (Stevens) Maxim and was born at Brockway's Mills, near Sangerville, Piscataquis County, Me. The region was still sparsely settled: bears outnumbered the men; money and the common comforts were scarce; and survival depended on strength, endurance, frugality, and resourcefulness in making a few devices serve many ends. The Maxims, however, were fitted to survive. According to family tradition they were of Huguenot origin and had been domiciled at Canterbury before coming to America, but from Isaac the direct line could be traced back only four generations to a Samuel Maxim of Rochester, Mass. The father was a farmer and wood-turner with a taste for philosophic speculation and a talent for invention. Among the ideas that he tinkered with were an automatic gun and a flying machine. Hiram, because of his precocious strength of body and application to business, early became the paragon of the household. At the age of fourteen he was bound out to a carriage-maker, Daniel Sweat, at East Corinth. He studied whatever scientific books came in his way, and with a faculty for drawing and painting and an uncanny facility in handling tools quickly became an adept at several trades. Deciding, on the advice of a friendly physician, not to waste any time on pugilism or the Civil War, he went to Montreal and thence to several towns on either side of the international boundary—Malone, N. Y.; St. Jean Chrysostome, Que.; Brasher Falls, N. Y.—where he worked as carriage-painter, cabinet-maker, and mechanic; discovered, but utilized for only a few days, some profitable innovations in the art of bar-tending; and won renown as a practical joker and tamer of bullies. Having satisfied his *Wanderlust* in the North, he returned home and secured employment in the engineering works of his uncle, Levi Stevens, at Fitchburg, Mass. During the next few years he studied hard and was deeply influenced by Oliver P. Drake, a scientific instrument maker of Boston. His genius for invention, nurtured from childhood by his environment, now came to fruition. In 1866 he took out his first patent, an improvement in irons for curling hair, although he already had several useful inventions to his credit. For the next few years he lived in New York and occupied himself chiefly with machines for generating illuminating gas, but also invented a locomotive headlight. In 1878 he was appointed chief engineer of the United States Electric Lighting Company, the first enterprise of its kind in the country. He therefore turned his attention to the incandescent carbon lamp and devised the method of "flashing" the filaments in a hydrocarbon atmosphere so as to even them up by a deposit of carbon on the thinner places. This invention was of fundamental importance to the electric lighting industry, but through a combination of accident and machination it became public property both in England and the United States.

In 1881 he went to the Paris Exposition to exhibit an electric pressure regulator that brought him the decoration of the Légion d'Honneur. A little later he set up a laboratory in Hatton Garden, London, and though at first disgusted with the ways of English workingmen he soon came to like the country and remained there permanently. He formed the Maxim Gun Company in 1884 and effected a merger in 1888 with the Nordenfeldt Company, and in 1896 the firm was absorbed into Vickers Sons and Maxim, of which Maxim was a director. On his retirement in 1911 the name was shortened to Vickers, Ltd. He became a British subject in 1900 and was knighted by Queen Victoria in 1901. He received numerous decorations from other governments.

Maxim was the equal of any mechanician of

his day. His knowledge of physics and chemistry and his ingenuity in tool-making were always available to him: he could use no machine or process without seeking to improve it. In all he took out 122 patents in the United States and 149 in Great Britain. His range of invention included an improved mouse-trap, automatic gas-generating plants, automatic sprinkling apparatus for extinguishing fires, automatic steam pumping-engines for supplying houses with water, feed-water heaters, steam and vacuum pumps, engine governors, gas motors, and an inhaling apparatus for medicating the throat. His international fame was gained by his invention of the Maxim gun, which completely changed the technique of modern warfare, and by his experiments with flying machines. Though it had been preceded by the Gatling gun (1862), the mitrailleuse (1867), and the Nordenfeldt (1877), his automatic gun of 1883 was the first efficient weapon of its class. It fired eleven shots a second from a single barrel, the loading, firing, extracting, and ejecting of the cartridges being effected automatically by utilizing the recoil of the barrel as each shot was fired. Subsequently he made various improvements in it, some of which were suggested by Lord Wolseley, who also pointed out the necessity of using a smokeless powder. Maxim himself discovered a smokeless powder of the cordite type and made numerous other contributions to gunnery.

His interest in flying began about 1889, when he reached the conclusion that "if a domestic goose can fly, so can a man." His experiments culminated in 1894 with the trial at Bexley, Kent, of a machine that was technically successful, since it actually lifted itself from the ground. Unfortunately, as Maxim himself expressed it, he had no time to invent an internal combustion engine and therefore had to make use of steam. His two compound steam engines and the water-tube boiler were marvels of lightness, weighing about six pounds per horse-power, but the weight of the fuel and water made the machine impracticable.

Maxim was twice married: first, to Louisa Jane Budden, by whom he had a son, Hiram Percy Maxim, inventor of the Maxim silencer, and two daughters; and second, to Sarah Haynes of Boston, who survived him. He was about six feet tall and well built, with fluffy hair and beard, jet black in early life, and snow white in his later years. Unlike so many inventors, he was fastidious about his appearance. A philosophic nihilist and a citizen of the world, he retained to the last many of the traits of the Maine Yankee and of the successful self-made man. Lawyers and labor leaders—classes with which he had had much experience—were his special abominations. Despite an active sense of humor he was distinctly vain and jealous of other inventors, especially of Thomas A. Edison, his rival in electric lighting, and of his own brother, Hudson Maxim [*q.v.*], his rival in ammunition making. But his boastfulness was happily accompanied by a personal charm totally disarming. He died at his home at Streatham after a short illness, having kept his vigor and his scientific interests to the end.

[H. S. Maxim, *My Life* (1915); P. F. Mottelay, *The Life and Work of Sir Hiram Maxim* (1920); Clifton Johnson, *Hudson Maxim: Reminiscences and Comments* (1924); Brysson Cunningham, article in *Dict. Nat. Biog. 1912–21* (1927); London *Times*, Nov. 25, 1916; J. F. Sprague, "Sir Hiram Maxim," *Sprague's Jour. of Me. Hist.*, Apr. 1917.] G. H. G.

MAXIM, HUDSON (Feb. 3, 1853–May 6, 1927), inventor and expert in explosives, was born in Orneville, Piscataquis County, Me., and was the sixth child of Isaac Weston and Harriet Boston (Stevens) Maxim. He was named for his father but disliked the name so much that he dropped it when eighteen years old and took that of Hudson. His father was a wood-turner, millwright, and miller, impoverished in worldly goods but a philosopher, lover of poetry and history, a gifted story teller, and the source of abounding inspiration to his children. Maxim's early life, accordingly, was a difficult but happy one. He rarely had decent clothing and obtained his first pair of shoes when thirteen, but he developed into an unusually strong and healthy boy, full of ambition and determination to amount to something. He attended the district schools occasionally between the ages of nine and seventeen and then worked for a year for his brother Hiram [*q.v.*], the machine-gun inventor, in New York. During the next seven years he alternately worked a few months and attended Maine Wesleyan Seminary, Kent's Hill, Me., completing there the course in chemistry and the natural sciences.

For the next decade he was engaged in job printing and book publishing with a schoolmate, Alden Knowles, who was an expert ornamental penman. The first part of this period was spent in the vicinity of Columbus, Ohio, where the partners enjoyed considerable success canvassing with their chart of writing styles and their colored ink powders; but in Pittsfield, Mass., where they later established themselves and began publishing their own book, *Real Pen-Work Self-Instructor in Penmanship* (copr. 1881), their success was phenomenal. In five years, through canvassers and mail orders, over a half-million copies of the book were sold. It was followed by a family record book, the sale of which reached more than a million copies. With the advent of the fountain pen and the typewriter, however, their business stopped.

Maxim then hired a number of mechanics for his brother Hiram, and went with them to England to work in the latter's gun factory. There Hudson had his first opportunity to examine some smokeless powder of French manufacture, and after a few simple experiments he determined its composition. This work proved fascinating, and upon returning to Pittsfield, Mass., in December 1888, as the American representative of the Maxim-Nordenfeldt Guns and Ammunition Company, Limited, he began the serious study of explosives. Although he had a two-years' contract with his brother's company, business difficulties soon arose and Hudson felt bound to look to his own future. He continued his studies, began experimenting, and occasionally contributed articles to the newspapers on his favorite subject. He secured a patent on the production of high explosives, Sept. 17, 1889, and another for a detachable gas check for projectiles, May 20, 1890. Early in 1891 the contract between the Maxims expired, and shortly thereafter Hudson, known chiefly through his newspaper writings, became chief engineer of the Columbia Powder Manufacturing Company, makers of dynamite at Squankum, N. J. He thereupon moved to New York and for a year or more worked on the problem of making a safer dynamite. He assigned two patents, issued May 10 and Aug. 2, 1892, to the company; and when it failed in 1893, he organized the Maxim Powder Company and took over the plant at Squankum. He then began serious work on smokeless powder and secured a number of patents between 1893 and 1895. He was unsuccessful in selling these to his brother in England but in 1897 sold them, together with his plant, to E. I. du Pont de Nemours & Company of Wilmington, Del. He now became a consultant for this company, which position he held throughout his life. From 1895 to 1900 Maxim worked on the perfection of a shock-proof high explosive for guns of large caliber and finally produced an explosive, which he named "Maximite," that could propel a projectile through the heaviest armor plate and was fifty per cent. more powerful than dynamite. For this invention Maxim received $50,000 from the United States government in 1901. That year the Du Pont Company established an experimental laboratory for him at Lake Hopatcong, N. J., and from that time until his death he worked there. He invented "stabillite," a smokeless powder that could be used as soon as produced and gave much better ballistic results. He also devised the machinery to manufacture smokeless powder and invented a number of gun cartridges as well as the United States service projectiles. He was a consultant for E. W. Bliss Company of Brooklyn, N. Y., manufacturers of torpedoes for submarines and destroyers, and secured a number of patents for torpedo-boat improvements; for "motorite," an explosive compound for driving torpedoes; and for apparatus for propelling torpedoes. Interspersed with his inventions in the explosive field, Maxim invented an automobile in England as early as 1895; a process of manufacturing calcium carbide, patented Oct. 8, 1901; and a game of skill in 1912, patented June 25. During the World War he served as chairman of the committee on ordnance and explosives on the Naval Consulting Board in Washington.

He was a fluent public speaker, a frequent contributor to newspapers and periodicals on current topics, and the author of *The Science of Poetry and the Philosophy of Language* (1910). A man of decisive opinions, he was no respecter of persons or reputations and voiced his likes and dislikes with great freedom and emphasis. In 1915 he published *Defenseless America,* a vitriolic denunciation of pacifism; in 1916, *Leading Opinions Both for and Against National Defense*; and *Dynamite Stories.* He was greatly interested in aviation and became president of the Aeronautical Society of New York. He was also a member of the Navy League and the Chemists Club of New York. He was married, first, in 1888, to Jane Morrow of Pittsfield, Mass., from whom he was soon afterwards divorced; second, on Mar. 26, 1896, to Lilian Durban, of London, England. No religious services were held at his death and his body was cremated. He was survived by his widow and a son by his first wife.

[Clifton Johnson, *Hudson Maxim: Reminiscences and Comments* (1924); *Who's Who in America,* 1926–27; *N. Y. Times,* May 7, 8, 1927; Pat. Office records.]

C. W. M.

MAXWELL, AUGUSTUS EMMETT (Sept. 21, 1820–May 5, 1903), United States representative, Confederate senator, Florida jurist, was born at Elberton, Ga., the son of Simeon and Elizabeth (Fortson) Maxwell. His parents were natives of Georgia, but the family came from Virginia. In 1822 the Maxwells removed to Greene County, Ala., and there the boy received his elementary education. He attended the University of Virginia from 1837 to 1840. Returning to Alabama he was admitted to the bar in 1843 and began the practice of law at Eutaw, but in 1845 he removed to Tallahassee, Fla. Aided by the influence of his brother-in-law, William H. Brockenbrough, he entered into the political life of the new state and began a public career that lasted almost until the time of his death. He was a member of the state legislature in 1847, was attorney-general in 1846 and 1847, secretary of state from April 1848 to July 1849, and state senator from 1849 to 1850. In the latter capacity it is evident that he exerted considerable influence, holding the chairmanship of both the judiciary and the federal relations committees as well as being a member of the committees on schools and colleges and on amendments and revisions of the constitution. His election to the federal House of Representatives seemed to promise him a national career, but his two terms, from 1853 to 1857, evidently did not add much to his reputation. He seems to have taken little part in legislation except to forward the passing of local bills. He retired from Congress at the end of his second term and took up the practice of law at Pensacola. Appointed navy agent at Pensacola in 1857 he held the position until Florida seceded in 1861. He was elected to the Confederate Senate and served throughout the war.

Although he had been educated in law and had a reputation as a lawyer of ability, his public career had been chiefly in legislative positions, but after the war he devoted himself more closely to the law and made a second career for himself as a jurist. Immediately after the war he was appointed associate justice of the Florida supreme court, but, finding it impossible to go on with his work under the Carpet-bag rule, he resigned in 1866 and resumed the practice of law at Pensacola in partnership with Stephen R. Mallory [*q.v.*], the former secretary of the navy in the Confederacy. When the Democrats regained control of Florida in 1877 he was appointed judge of the 1st judicial circuit. He held this position until his resignation in 1885. In 1887 he was appointed chief justice of the supreme court of Florida. The new constitution of 1885 provided that the chief justiceship should be filled by lot from the justices, and as a result of this arrangement, in 1889, he became associate justice and served until 1891. Retiring to Pensacola he practised law in partnership with his son until the latter was appointed circuit judge in 1896. At this time he gave up his law practice and retired from active life after a public career of over half a century. In 1896 he was a candidate for elector on the Palmer and Buckner ticket but was defeated. He was married twice. His first wife was Sarah Roane Brockenbrough, whom he married at Charlottesville, Va., in 1843. After her death he married, in 1853, Julia Hawks Anderson of Pensacola, the daughter of Walker Anderson, the chief justice of the state supreme court. In 1902 he removed to Chipley, where he died. He was buried from the Christ Episcopal Church of Pensacola of which he had long been a member. He was survived by two of the three children of his first marriage and three of the five children of the second.

[Information from his son, E. C. Maxwell, Pensacola; Journal of the General Assembly of Florida, 5 Sess.; H. C. Armstrong, *Hist. of Escambia County* (1930); R. H. Rerick, *Memoirs of Florida* (1902), vol. I; *Who's Who in America*, 1901–02; *Pensacola Daily News*, May 6, 7, 1903.] R. S. C.

MAXWELL, DAVID HERVEY (Sept. 17, 1786–May 24, 1854), physician, legislator, born in Garrard County, Ky., the son of Bazaleel and Margaret (Anderson) Maxwell, came of the Scotch-Irish Presbyterian stock which figured conspicuously in the making of early Indiana. Reared in a pioneer environment, he had meager opportunities for early schooling, but at the age of eighteen he went to Danville, Ky., an educational center, where he became proficient in mathematics and well read in English. He then studied medicine at Danville under Ephraim McDowell [*q.v.*], a noted surgeon of the day. In 1809 he married Mary E. Dunn of Danville, and settled down to the practice of his chosen profession. Emigrating a year later to Indiana, then a new and promising country, he settled in Jefferson County about the time the town of Madison was founded. There he practised medicine for nine years, serving for part of the time as military surgeon during the War of 1812.

In 1816 Indiana became a state, and at this time Maxwell first appeared in a public capacity, as a delegate to the convention which framed the state constitution. A dynamic member of that convention, he introduced the clause prohibiting slavery in the state, and though not a member of the "committee relative to education," was probably a supporter of the clause which provided for "a general system of education, ascending in a regular gradation, from township schools to a state university, wherein tuition shall be gratis and equally open to all" (Art. IX, sec. 2). This theoretical system was so far in advance of what was possible at that time and place that more than thirty-five years elapsed before it actually existed.

From the time of his activity in the constitutional convention, Maxwell was concerned in educational affairs, his chief interest being in the establishment of a state university. In the federal enabling act which paved the way for statehood, a township of land had been donated for the benefit of a "seminary of learning," the exact tract to be designated by the president of the United States. The land chosen chanced to be in Monroe County, on what was then the state's frontier, and to Maxwell's mind this was the logical place for the state university provided for by the constitution. In 1818 the little backwoods town of Bloomington, Monroe County, was in its first struggle for existence, and thither he moved to lay his plans for a school campaign. The legislative assembly of 1819–20 found him on hand as a lobbyist for a bill to establish a state seminary at Bloomington, and so effective was his influence that the law was passed Jan. 20, 1820, with Maxwell as one of six members of a board of trustees. He proved to be the leading member and for many years was the president of that board. To further his influence in promoting the welfare of the university and of education generally he several times sought election to the state legislature, serving in the House during the sixth, eighth, and ninth sessions (1821, 1823–25), and in the Senate during the years 1826–29. In the eighth session he was speaker of the House. Throughout his legislative service he was recognized as a champion of education, and his name is repeatedly found on educational committees. An unexpected honor that fell upon him in 1836 was his nomination by Governor Noble to the State Board of Internal Improvements and his unanimous election to the presidency of that board. He was also twice postmaster at Bloomington. It is for his long and unflagging interest in higher education, however, that he is chiefly remembered. Indiana University's memorial to him is Maxwell Hall, named for him and his son, Dr. James Darwin Maxwell. Maxwell died in Bloomington, in his sixty-eighth year.

[Sketch by Louise Maxwell in *Ind. Quart. Mag. of Hist.*, Sept. 1912; J. A. Woodburn, in *Ind. Univ. Alumni Quarterly*, July 1916, p. 355; Logan Esarey, "Internal Improvements in Early Indiana," *Ind. Hist. Soc. Pubs.*, vol. V (1912); "Ann. Reports of the State Board of Internal Improvements" in *Documentary Jours. of Ind.*, 1836; *Jour. of the Conv. of the Indiana Territory* (1816); Charles Kettleborough, *Constitution Making in Ind.*, vol I (1916); *Ind. Univ. 1820–1920 Centennial Memorial Vol.* (copr. 1921); F. W. Houston and others, *Maxwell Hist. and Geneal.* (copr. 1916).]

G. S. C.

MAXWELL, GEORGE TROUP (Aug. 6, 1827–Sept. 2, 1897), physician and legislator, was born in Bryan County, Ga. His father, John Jackson Maxwell, was a planter who served a number of terms in the state Senate; his mother was a daughter of Col. John Baker, an officer in the Revolutionary War. After obtaining his preliminary education at Chatham Academy, Savannah, he entered the medical department of the University of the City of New York, from which he obtained the degree of M.D. in 1848. He settled in Tallahassee, Fla., for practice and remained there until 1857, when he was appointed surgeon to the Marine Hospital at Key West. In 1860 he was appointed professor of obstetrics and diseases of women and children in Oglethorpe Medical College, and moved to Savannah. At the outbreak of the Civil War he enlisted as a private in the 1st Florida Cavalry. He was later commissioned major of cavalry, and colonel in 1862. In that grade he commanded a brigade of Florida troops in the Army of the Tennessee under General Bragg, until he was captured at the battle of Missionary Ridge. His capture prevented his acceptance of a commission as brigadier-general which was on the way to him. He was a prisoner until March 1865, when he returned to Tallahassee. Shortly thereafter, as a representative of Leon County, he took an active part in the proceedings of the convention held under the proclamation of President Johnson for the purpose of rewriting the constitution and reorganizing the state government of Florida. The next winter he was elected a member of the state legislature. In 1866 he moved to Jacksonville, where he practised his profession until 1871. In that year he went to New Castle, Del., where he conducted a daily paper in addition to the practice of medicine. Here he was prominent in Democratic politics and in Masonic activities. He was vice-president of the Delaware Medical Society in 1874 and secretary in 1875–76. From Delaware he moved to Atlanta where he practised for a brief time, after which he accepted a professorship at the State Agricultural College, Lake City, Fla. In 1888 an outbreak of yellow fever took him to Jacksonville, where he remained during the epidemic and afterward until his death, which resulted from a stroke of apoplexy.

Maxwell was always a prolific contributor to medical periodicals. While in Delaware he wrote "An Exposition on the Liability of the Negro Race to Yellow Fever," "A Demonstration of the Non-digestive Powers of the Large Intestine" and "The Laryngoscope, an American Invention." The last-named paper, published in the *Medical Record,* New York, Jan. 1, 1873, described an instrument which Maxwell had perfected in 1869. Though the credit for the first laryngoscope goes to Manuel Garcia, the Spanish music teacher, Maxwell's instrument showed originality, and he is credited with being the first American physician to see the vocal cords of a living subject. After his return to Jacksonville he published pamphlets on *Malarial Hæmoglobinuria* (1892), *Municipal Hygiene* (1894), and a paper on "Hygiene in Florida" (*Proceedings of the . . . Florida Medical Association,* 1896). The Florida Medical Association, of which he had been president, adopted resolutions upon his death which not only reviewed his career but made note of his exceptional social qualities and conversational powers. He married Augusta Jones of Tallahassee shortly after his graduation in medicine. She died of yellow fever while he was serving at the Marine Hospital in Key West.

[*Twenty-fifth Ann. Session Fla. Medic. Asso.* (1898); R. F. Stone, *Biog. of Eminent Am. Physicians and Surgeons* (1894); W. B. Atkinson, *Biog. Dict. of Contemporary Am. Physicians and Surgeons* (1880); H. A. Kelly and W. L. Burrage, *Am. Medic. Biogs.* (1920); *Florida Times-Union* (Jacksonville), Sept. 3, 1897.] J. M. P.

MAXWELL, HUGH (1787–Mar. 31, 1873), lawyer, was born in Paisley, Scotland. About 1790 the family emigrated to New York where his father, William Maxwell, operated a distillery and a tallow chandlery. Hugh was educated at Columbia College, graduating in 1808, nineteenth in a class of twenty-one members. Owing to his participation in the "riotous commencement" of 1811, the A.M. degree in course which he was to have received at that time was withheld until 1816. Maxwell, at the commencement of 1811 held in Trinity Church, took the part of one of the candidates who had been refused his degree, and addressed the audience on behalf of the student. Gulian C. Verplanck, a distinguished alumnus, supported Maxwell and moved a vote of thanks. Faculty supporters intervened and the ceremonies were adjourned in disorder. Both Maxwell and Verplanck were indicted by a grand jury, arraigned before Mayor Clinton, and fined. As a consequence, Maxwell joined Verplanck in his attacks upon Clinton.

In 1814 Maxwell was appointed assistant judge-advocate-general of the United States army. In 1817 he was appointed district attorney for the twelfth district (New York County). After the passage of the law of 1818, under which an attorney was named for each county, he was appointed district attorney for New York County, serving from 1821 to 1829. In 1826 he conducted the prosecution of Jacob Barker [*q.v.*] and others on charges of fraud and conspiracy, following the failure of the Life and Fire Insurance Company. Barker fought the indictment bitterly and Fitz-Greene Halleck, who had been in Barker's employ, attacked Maxwell as "Billingsgate McSwell" in a privately circulated poem.

Maxwell was active in the Whig party, largely in the capacity of a party manager, in association with Thurlow Weed. From 1849 to 1853 he held the post of collector of the port of New York. At the age of seventy he gave up his successful law practice and retired from business and politics. His death occurred in 1873. He had married Agnes Stevenson, by whom he had four children.

["The Riotous Commencement of 1811," *Columbia Univ. Quart.*, June, Sept. 1901; *The Trial of Gulian C. Verplanck, Hugh Maxwell and Others for a Riot in Trinity Church* (1821); W. M. MacBean, *Biog. Reg. of St. Andrew's Soc. . . . of N. Y.* (2 vols., 1922–25); E. A. Werner, *Civil List and Constitutional Hist. . . . of N. Y.* (1889); David McAdam, *Hist. of the Bench and Bar of N. Y.*, vol. I (1897); D. R. Fox, *The Decline of Aristocracy in the Pol. of N. Y.* (1918); J. G. Wilson, *The Life and Letters of Fitz-Greene Halleck* (1869), pp. 313–19; I. S. Clason, *Horace in N. Y.* (1826), pp. 31–34, *The Conspiracy Trials of 1826 and 1827* (1864) with an introduction by R. D. Turner; *N. Y. Tribune*, Apr. 1, 1873.] P. W. B.

MAXWELL, LUCIEN BONAPARTE (Sept. 14, 1818–July 25, 1875), frontiersman, rancher, was one of the twelve children of Hugh B. and Marie Odille (Menard) Maxwell and was born in Kaskaskia, Ill. The mother was a daughter of the noted Pierre Menard [*q.v.*], the first lieutenant-governor of Illinois. The son seems to have had a fair degree of schooling. Probably before he was twenty he accompanied a trading caravan or a trapping party to Taos, N. Mex. Here he met Kit Carson, with whom he formed a close friendship that lasted until death separated them. For a time, about 1840–41, he was employed at Fort St. Vrain, on the South Platte. He was the hunter for Frémont's first expedition (1842), of which Carson was the guide. In the same year, at Taos, he married Luz, the daughter of Charles Beaubien, one of the two owners of the vast Beaubien-Miranda tract granted by the Mexican government. With Carson he joined Frémont's third expedition, which left Bent's Fort in August 1845 and arrived at Sutter's Fort on Dec. 9, and he was an active and valuable member of the Pathfinder's force in the events culminating in the conquest of California. He was one of the party of fifteen, led by Carson, that started from Los Angeles in September 1846 to carry dispatches to Washington; and on Oct. 6, near Socorro, N. Mex., where they met Kearny's expedition, westward bound, rendered a notable service by persuading the angry Carson not to ruin his career by defying Kearny's order that he give up his dispatches and return as guide to the army.

He now settled down to the management of

his father-in-law's estate. Beaubien had become the sole owner of the grant, a tract of 1,714,764 acres, the largest single holding in the United States, and Maxwell energetically applied himself to its development. Under the American rule the products of his fields found a ready market with the government purchasing agents, and he prospered. At the town of Cimarron, in the present Colfax County, N. Mex., he built a large dwelling, with an encircling veranda and a central patio, where he entertained with princely hospitality. In the spring of 1853 he and Carson set out from the Cimarron for California with two large herds of sheep, some 12,000 head. By way of the Oregon Trail and the Humboldt River they reached Sacramento in September. Selling their animals at a good profit, they returned by the southern route and on Christmas eve were again in Taos.

Beaubien died in 1864, and Maxwell, by purchasing the holdings of the other heirs, became the sole owner of what has ever since been known as the Maxwell Grant—a tract that in later years was to be the subject of much litigation and the scene of occasional settlers' wars. In 1870 he founded the First National Bank of New Mexico, but soon tiring of his plaything disposed of it. In 1871 he sold his entire estate to a Colorado syndicate headed by Jerome B. Chaffee [*q.v.*]. A series of reverses followed. For a time he engaged in mining, and he was one of the founders of Silver City, N. Mex. His last days were spent at Fort Sumner, and he was buried there in the government cemetery. He was survived by his wife and several of his nine children. As a trapper, hunter, and Indian fighter Maxwell was brave and self-reliant. He was improvident, and he seems to have had more than his share of eccentricities; but he was a kindly, generous, and dependable man, who was universally liked and whose friends were devotedly attached to him.

[R. E. Twitchell, *The Leading Facts in New Mexican Hist.*, vol. II (1912); E. L. Sabin, *Kit Carson Days* (1914); C. L. Camp, "Kit Carson in California," *Quart. Cal. Hist. Soc.*, Oct. 1922, also pub. separately; *Daily New Mexican* (Santa Fé), July 29, 1875; information from the Rev. G. J. Garraghan of St. Louis Univ., and from Maxwell's daughter, Mrs. Odila Abreü, Fort Sumner, N. Mex.]

W. J. G.

MAXWELL, SAMUEL (May 20, 1825–Feb. 11, 1901), Nebraska jurist, congressman, author of legal treatises, was born in Lodi, N. Y., the son of Robert Maxwell, a well-to-do farmer, and Margaret (Crosby) Maxwell, a woman of education and refinement. During his boyhood, financial reverses caused the family to move to Michigan, and here young Maxwell, following a well-worn western formula, worked on a farm, taught school, and studied law. In 1856 he pushed farther west, to Plattsmouth, Nebr., where he took and improved a "claim." Within two years, however, he returned to Michigan, read law in a brother's office at Bay City, and was admitted to the bar. The year 1859 found him once again in Nebraska.

His political career was early under way. He was a member of the territorial legislatures of 1859–60, 1865, and 1866, of the first state legislature, June 1866, and of the constitutional conventions of 1864, 1871, and 1875. The first of these conventions was opposed to statehood, and refused to draw a constitution. In the others Maxwell, thanks to his knowledge of legal fundamentals and his skill as a debater, took a prominent part. In 1870 he was an unsuccessful candidate for the Republican nomination for governor. In 1872 he was elected justice of the state supreme court, and by successive reëlections was a member of the court continuously from 1873 to 1894, serving much of the time as chief justice. His influence over the court during this formative period was tremendous. He served longer than any other judge who sat with him, and he wrote far more than his share of the court's opinions. One of his outstanding characteristics was an impatience of legal technicalities. If substantial justice could be done, he was content, and as "Substantial Justice" Maxwell he was generally known. This pleased the public, but lawyers who saw well established rules of law treated with little respect did not always approve. Moreover, Maxwell was never an ardent party man, and some of his decisions failed to find favor with the Republican machine. His renominations, therefore, were conceded somewhat grudgingly, and finally in 1893 a Republican convention rejected him. This defeat undoubtedly was meant as a rebuke to the Chief Justice for his attitude in two important cases. In one, an election contest with the governorship of the state at stake, he had held against the majority of the court that the Democratic candidate was entitled to the office (31 *Nebr.*, 682). In the other, which involved the impeachment of some faithless Republican state officials, he had again deserted his colleagues and had written a blistering dissenting opinion (37 *Nebr.*, 96 and 38 *Nebr.*, 584).

Maxwell now went over to the Populists, in whose doctrines he had come to believe. He was their unsuccessful candidate for the supreme court in 1895, and as a fusionist won a seat in Congress by the election of 1896. Here he did his share towards carrying on the losing fight for free silver, but he failed of renomination, and in 1899 retired to private life. He died at Fremont, Nebr., and was buried at Plattsmouth. Three times married: first to Amelia A. Lawrence of Michigan, second to Jenette M. McCord of Cass County, Nebr., third to Elizabeth A. Adams, also of Cass County, he was the father of eleven children, nine of whom survived infancy. He was in comfortable financial circumstances at the time of his death in 1901, and left a small legacy to his family.

Maxwell's best-known book is *A Treatise on Pleading, Practice, Procedure, and Precedents in Actions at Law and Suits in Equity* (1880). He also wrote or compiled *Digest of the Decisions of the Supreme Court of the State of Nebraska* (1877), *A Treatise on the Powers and Duties of Justices of the Peace, Sheriffs, and Constables* (1879), *A Practical Treatise on Criminal Procedure with Directions and Forms* (1887), and *A Treatise on the Law of Pleading under the Code of Civil Procedure, Designed for All the Code States* (1892). Most of these books are handy manuals of great value to the practising lawyer. They have gone through many editions and have continued in use through much of the Middle West.

[Maxwell correspondence, 1853–1901, in State Hist. Soc. of Nebr.; J. M. Klotsche, "The Political Career of Samuel Maxwell," in *Nebr. Law Bull.*, May 1928; R. D. Rowley, "The Judicial Career of Samuel Maxwell," manuscript thesis in Univ. of Nebr. Lib.; J. S. Morton and Albert Watkins, *Illus. Hist. of Nebr.* (3 vols., 1905–13); *Biog. Dir. Am. Cong.* (1928); *Nebr. State Jour.* (Lincoln), Feb. 12, 1901.] J. D. H.

MAXWELL, WILLIAM (*c.* 1733–Nov. 4, 1796), Revolutionary soldier, was born of Scotch-Irish ancestry near Newtown Stewart, County Tyrone, Ireland. His parents, John and Ann Maxwell, with four children, of whom William was the eldest, came to America about 1747, settling in Greenwich township, Sussex (now Warren) County, N. J. William was brought up as a farmer's son, with only ordinary educational advantages. When twenty-one he entered military service in a British regiment to take part in the French and Indian War, and was with General Braddock at the battle of Fort Duquesne in 1755. Later he became an ensign in Col. John Johnston's New Jersey regiment, and, later still, lieutenant in Col. Peter Schuyler's New Jersey regiment. In 1758 he was in the army under General Abercromby [*q.v.*] in the expedition against Fort Ticonderoga, and he is believed to have fought under Wolfe at the capture of Quebec in September 1759. Toward the close of the French and Indian War, he became attached to the British commissary department at Mackinac, with the rank of colonel. He was there until 1774, when, learning that New Jersey was nearly ripe for a revolution against Great Britain, he returned to his home in Sussex County, N. J.

He was a member of the Provincial Congress at Trenton, which met in May 1775. In August he was chairman of the Committee of Safety of his county, and in October, when again a member of the Provincial Congress, was recommended by that body to the Continental Congress for appointment as colonel of the Western Battalion of New Jersey Continental troops, and elected to that office Nov. 7, 1775 (*Journals of the Continental Congress*). He at once raised what became the 2nd Battalion, 1st Establishment, of the troops named, and in February 1776, with five full companies, started on the expedition against Canada, under the command of Gen. John Sullivan. He was at the battle of Three Rivers, June 8, 1776. Because of his bravery in this campaign the Continental Congress commissioned him brigadier-general, Oct. 23, 1776, and he was placed by Washington in command of four battalions in the 2nd Establishment of New Jersey Continental troops. From Dec. 2, 1776, to the summer of 1777, he harassed the enemy in New Jersey at Elizabethtown, Rahway, and Springfield; on Sept. 11, 1777, he fought in the battle of Brandywine, Pa.; then in the battle of Germantown, Oct. 4. He spent the winter and spring, 1777–78, at Valley Forge. On June 28, 1778, his brigade took an active part in the battle of Monmouth, and during the rest of that year and the following winter was stationed chiefly near Elizabethtown, N. J., again harassing the enemy, interfering with foraging parties from New York and Staten Island. When the Sullivan expedition left Easton, Pa., June 18, 1779, to proceed against the Six Nations in Western Pennsylvania and New York, Maxwell's brigade was with it, and continued with it until the return in October, when the brigade went into winter quarters near Scotch Plains, N. J. In June 1780, Maxwell fought at the battle of Springfield and the skirmish at Connecticut Farms. This ended his army service, since he resigned his commission in July. Washington, in forwarding the resignation to Congress, spoke of him as "an honest man, a warm friend to this country, and firmly attached to her interests" (to Samuel Huntington, July 20, 1780, Washington Papers, Library of Congress).

In 1783 Maxwell was elected to the New Jersey Assembly. He died in November 1796 while on a visit to an army friend at Lansdown, N. J. He was buried in the graveyard of the old Stone Church (Presbyterian) near his home, where a monument, describing his virtues, marks his grave. He never married. Maxwell is said to have been a "tall, stalwart man" with a "florid complexion." Because of his Scotch accent his soldiers, by whom he was greatly beloved, called him "Scotch Willie." The state of New Jersey has always considered him one of its foremost soldiers.

[H. D. Maxwell, *The Maxwell Family* (1895); *Archives of the State of N. J.*, 1 ser. IX (1885); *Selections from the Corresp. of the Executive of N. J., 1776–86* (1848); J. H. Griffith, "William Maxwell of New Jersey," *Proc. N. J. Hist. Soc.*, 2 ser. XIII, no. 2 (June 1897); W. S. Stryker, *Official Reg. of the Officers and Men of N. J., in the Revolutionary War* (1872), and *Gen. Maxwell's Brigade of the N. J. Continental Line in the Expedition against the Indians in the year 1779* (1885); B. J. Lossing, *The Pictorial Field-book of the Revolution*, vol. II (1852); *The First Sussex Centenary* (1853); Sullivan's Orderly Book (1779), in the possession of the N. J. Hist. Soc.; Wm. Nelson, *N. J. Biog. and Geneal. Notes* (1916).]

A. V–D. H.

MAXWELL, WILLIAM (*c.* 1755–1809), pioneer publisher, born in New York or New Jersey, was the son of William Maxwell, an emigrant from Scotland. In 1792 he started for the West, and before the close of that year was engaged in the printing business in Lexington, Ky. In this enterprise he evidently had partners. The title page of *A Process in the Transilvania Presbytery*, by Adam Rankin, bears the imprint: "Lexington: Printed by Maxwell & Cooch. At the sign of the Buffalo, Main-Street." The copyright date of this pamphlet is Jan. 1, 1793. Another pamphlet, *A Narrative of Mr. Rankin's Trial*, bears the imprint: "Lexington: Printed by W. Maxwell & Co. M,DCC,XCIII."

Later in 1793 he arrived in Cincinnati, where, on Nov. 9, 1793, he issued the first number of *The Centinel of the North-Western Territory*. It was published at the corner of Front and Sycamore streets. A four-page, three-column sheet, it was a brief chronicler of the times and contained little local news. In it, however, were discussed from its beginning questions that were claiming the attention of the small frontier village in which it was published. In the first issue appeared an account of an attack by the Indians near Fort St. Clair and a contribution on local taxation filling a column and a half. The paper was issued regularly on Saturday of each week through practically all the years of its existence. In the summer of 1796 its founder, who had been appointed postmaster of Cincinnati, sold the *Centinel* to Edmund Freeman who changed the name to *Freeman's Journal*. Before Maxwell disposed of his printing office, however, he published a compilation, *Laws of the Territory of the United States, Northwest of the Ohio*, which has since been known as the "Maxwell Code." It bears the date of 1796 and was the first book published in the Northwest Territory. In 1799, he moved to Dayton and later in the same year to a tract on the Little Miami River in what is now Beaver Creek Township, Greene County, but was then a part of Hamilton County.

He was elected to the House of Representatives of the first General Assembly of Ohio which convened in Chillicothe, Mar. 1, 1803. At its first session the Assembly passed a law for the erection of Greene County and elected Maxwell as one of its first associate judges. On Dec. 7, 1803, he was chosen sheriff of Greene County, and through reëlection served till 1807. He was also active in the organization of the state militia; was commissioned captain, June 19, 1804, and lieutenant-colonel, Jan. 1, 1806, and was thereafter generally addressed as Colonel Maxwell. After his arrival in Cincinnati he met and married Nancy Robins, and of this union were born eight children. Maxwell died and was buried on his farm in Greene County in 1809. His widow, who later married John White, died Nov. 9, 1868, in the 108th year of her age.

[Files of the *Centinel of the North-Western Territory* still exist; the only known copy of the first issue is in the Library of the Ohio State Archaeol. and Hist. Soc., Columbus. Sources include Maxwell's Salutatory in the *Centinel*, Nov. 9, 1793; interview with Mrs. Nancy Maxwell White, former wife of William Maxwell, reprinted in the *Xenia Gazette*, Jan. 26, 1869; manuscript records from the office of the Governor of Ohio, 1803–06; manuscript journal of the legislature of the Northwest Territory, 1795; C. B. Galbreath, "The First Newspaper of the Northwest Territory," *Ohio Archaeol. and Hist. Quart.*, July 1904; "Legislature of the Northwestern Territory, 1795," *Ibid.*, Jan. 1921; *The Ohio Newspaper*, vol. X, no. 4, pp. 9–10; D. C. McMurtrie, "Antecedent Experience in Kentucky of William Maxwell, Ohio's First Printer," *The Filson Club Hist. Quart.*, July 1931; R. G. Thwaites, "The Ohio Valley Press Before the War of 1812–15," *Proc. Am. Antiq. Soc.*, n.s., XIX (1908); W. H. Venable, *Beginnings of Literary Culture in the Ohio Valley* (1891).]

C. B. G.

MAXWELL, WILLIAM (Feb. 27, 1784–Jan. 10, 1857), lawyer, college president, was born in Norfolk, Va., the son of James and Helen (Calvert) Maxwell, natives of Scotland. The father was "general superintendent" of the Virginia fleet. William prepared for college chiefly under the tutorship of Rev. Israel B. Woodward of Wolcott, Conn., and graduated from Yale in 1802 at the age of eighteen. He studied law in Richmond, Va., and in 1808 was admitted to practice at the Norfolk bar. His brilliant talents soon gave him a leading position among the attorneys of Virginia and a reputation beyond the borders of the state. He was noted also for his keen wit and oratorical abilities. His readiness was remarkable; his addresses were never written; and if he was "knocked up at midnight and requested to speak, he would make a finer speech than anyone else could have done after deliberate preparation" (Grigsby, *post*, p. 39). Having literary tendencies, he published in 1812 a small volume entitled *Poems.* Although attributed to Maxwell, *Letters from Virginia,* a translation from the French issued anonymously in 1816, was probably the work of George Tucker. In 1827 Maxwell was elected editor of the *New York Journal of Commerce,* but he retained his home in Norfolk, and held the position for only about a year. In 1828 he presented to his native town a lyceum for lectures and scientific experiments.

From 1830 to 1832 he was a member of the Virginia House of Delegates. Elected to the state Senate for an unexpired term, he was returned for the following term, serving in all from 1832 to 1838. During this period, 1835, he published his most ambitious library work, *A Memoir of Rev. John H. Rice, D.D.,* valuable not only as a biography but also as a sidelight on Presbyterian history. In 1836 Hampden-Sidney College conferred on him the degree of LL.D., the third it had awarded in a period of more than sixty years. He was at the same time elected a trustee and in 1838, president of the college, a position which he held until 1844. While president he married Mary Robertson.

Upon his resignation he removed to Richmond where he practised and taught law. He was an active member of the Virginia Colonization Society and of the Virginia Bible Society. With others he reëstablished the Virginia Historical Society, and from 1848 to 1853 was editor of the *Virginia Historical Register.* Of his many addresses, only one was published, *An Oration on the Improvement of the People,* a plea for better education in Virginia, delivered at the anniversary of the Literary and Philosophical Society of Hampden-Sidney, September 1826. An unpublished manuscript of his, now in the Virginia State Library, Richmond, "My Mother's Memoirs," which records events of Revolutionary days, is of historical value. He died near Williamsburg, Va., and was buried in Hollywood Cemetery, Richmond.

[F. B. Dexter, *Biog. Sketches Grads. Yale Coll.,* vol. V (1911); H. B. Grigsby, in *Bull. of Hampden-Sidney Coll.,* Jan. 1913; W. H. T. Squires, *William Maxwell, A Virginian of Ante-Bellum Days* (n.d.), and article in *Union Seminary Rev.,* Oct. 1918, supplemented and corrected by J. D. Eggleston, *Ibid.,* Jan. 1919; *Southern Argus* (Norfolk), Jan. 15, 1857; *Richmond Enquirer,* Jan. 16, 1857.] J. D. E.

MAXWELL, WILLIAM HENRY (Mar. 5, 1852–May 3, 1920), educator, was the son of John and Maria (Jackson) Maxwell and a descendant of John Knox, the great Scotch reformer. The second of three children, he was born at Brigh Manse, Stewartstown, County Tyrone, Ireland. His father, a Presbyterian clergyman of more than parochial reputation, tutored him in the classics after the local national schools had grounded him in the common branches. Later the Rev. George MacCloskie taught him mathematics and modern languages, ultimately sending him to the Royal Academical Institution at Belfast. Thence he proceeded to Queen's College, Galway, where he took his bachelor's and master's degrees with honors (1872 and 1874), especially distinguishing himself in metaphysics and English and classical literature. His last two years he supported himself by teaching, being concurrently sub-master in the Royal Academical Institution and lecturer in the Ladies Collegiate Institute. Originally he planned to read law, but when he failed by a single vote of the secretaryship of the "Liberal Association" with its annual stipend and when no further financial assistance from his family was in sight, he decided to seek his fortune in the United States.

Arriving in America (1874) armed only with a letter to President McCosh [*q.v.*] of Princeton, Maxwell found entrance into the public schools barred because he lacked the patronage of a ward boss. This initial discouragement and a letter of introduction to Whitelaw Reid [*q.v.*] led him to try journalism. Work as reporter for the *New York Tribune* and the *New York Herald* and as associate editor of the *Metropolitan Weekly* was followed by five years spent as managing editor of the *Brooklyn Times.* From this vantage-point he returned to his interest in education with a series of powerful articles on the needs and future development of the public-school system. He succeeded in gaining an appointment as teacher and lecturer in the evening schools of Brooklyn; in 1882 was appointed associate superintendent of schools; and in 1887, superintendent. To this office he was thrice reëlected. When the greater city of New York was chartered, Manhattan desired Andrew S. Draper [*q.v.*] for the new joint superintendency of schools, while Brooklyn demanded Maxwell. On Draper's recommendation Maxwell was chosen (1898). Here in three stormy terms he achieved his greatest successes. Once on motion of the opposition his salary was raised. When his health failed in 1917 the city charter was amended so that he could retire as superintendent emeritus with full pay.

Few professional educators have been so frequently criticized or so consistently vindicated as was Maxwell. Among other struggles, he contended for vocational education and the enrichment of the elementary-school curriculum in social content, but insisted always upon a curriculum hacked and hewed down to fundamentals. He aided in the diversification of the educational ladder to permit of kindergartens, summer, and continuation schools, and schools for the atypical. He helped to organize the public high-school system and even conducted some early experiments in intermediate schools. Overcrowding of school buildings with consequent part-time attendance presented a problem which he never quite solved. Playgrounds, free meals and eyeglasses for poor children were all part of his program. To gain all these he had to spend the public's money generously. Fought by the board of estimate and apportionment, he became an advocate of financial independence for city boards of education. He placed the city's teaching personnel on a high plane by securing the passage of a law requiring high and normal school preparation for all teachers of the city's schools. The achievement in which he took the greatest personal pride, however, was his placing the appointment and promotion of teachers on a merit basis, beyond the reach of politicians.

His leadership, later demanded in regional, state, and national educational associations, was finally crowned with the presidency of the National Education Association in 1905. An anniversary collection of excerpts from his more important educational pronouncements was published in 1912 under the title, *A Quarter Century of Public School Development.* On his death the *Educational Review,* of which he was a founder and editor, rated him, together with William T. Harris and Andrew S. Draper, as among the three greatest American educators since the time of Horace Mann. Although he was not the equal of Harris as an educational philosopher, he was unsurpassed in the skill with which he managed lay boards and politicians. Though both his lay and professional enemies charged him with autocratic tactics, the courage and fierceness with which he fought for his high standards was an inspiration to those despairing of efficient public service in American democracy. Over six feet in height and of vigorous frame, he made an impressive appearance. In 1877 he married Marie A. Folk. A son and a daughter were born to them.

[Extensive obituary notices appeared in *N. Y. Evening Journal,* May 3, 1920; *N. Y. Times, N. Y. Tribune, Sun, N. Y. Herald,* and *Brooklyn Eagle,* May 4, 1920; the *Sun* and *Times* included editorials on May 4 and 5 respectively. A pamphlet, *The Election of William H. Maxwell as City Supt. of Schools Emeritus* (1918), sketches his career, while the *Educ. Rev.,* June 1920, and *School and Society,* May 15, June 26, 1920, contain estimates of his life. M. I. MacDonald, "Dr. Maxwell as Educator," unpublished doctor's dissertation at N. Y. Univ., is a mediocre evaluation of his educational labors but contains a nearly complete catalogue of his writings. A letter, July 26, 1930, from his sister, Mrs. A. M. Browne, a resident of Ireland, gives a full account of the Irish setting of his life.]

J. S. B.

MAY, EDWARD HARRISON (1824–May 17, 1887), historical and portrait painter, was born in Croydon, England. He was brought to the United States as a boy of ten by his father, the Rev. Edward Harrison May, a Reformed Dutch clergyman, who had been called to a pastorate in New York. The May family was one of culture and talent. Edward himself had unusual ability as a draftsman, a mathematician, and civil engineer, but he abandoned engineering for the art of painting and took up training under Daniel Huntington. His early work met with some success in New York. Aided by other young painters, he made a panorama of "The Pilgrim's Progress," which was exhibited in several cities and proved profitable. He soon left for Europe, and thereafter most of his life was spent abroad.

In 1851 he was working in Thomas Couture's studio in Paris. Later he made several trips to Italy to study the work of the old masters. He also made several visits to England, where he painted a number of portraits. In Paris he made exceptionally good copies of some of the old Italian works in the Louvre, including Titian's "Entombment" and Murillo's Madonna. As early as 1855 he began to exhibit pictures at the Salon. His "Death of a Brigand," which received a medal, is now the property of the Pennsylvania Academy of the Fine Arts. Couture thought highly of his "Cardinal Mazarin Taking Leave of his Pictures in the Louvre," and Théophile Gautier warmly praised his "Francis I Lamenting the Death of his Son." These typical Salon canvases, with a score or more of other elaborate historical compositions, were hung in the Salon between 1855 and 1885. Notable examples were the "Last Days of Christopher Columbus" (1861) and "Milton Dictating to his Daughters" (1883). The French critics were more than merely respectful in their comments on his work. The *Annales Historiques* alluded to the exactitude and firmness of his drawing, the harmony and depth of his color, and his striking veracity of expression.

Among May's many portraits were those of Gen. John Meredith Read, United States consul-general in Paris, Edouard de Laboulaye, the historian, Anson Burlingame, United States minister to China, Jerome Bonaparte, Count A. E. de Gasparin, William Lewis Dayton, United States minister to France, and other personages of the time. His large picture of Lady Jane

Grey taking leave of the constable of the Tower as she went to her execution was acquired by Joseph Harrison, Jr., of Philadelphia. Other important historical and genre pieces came to the United States. "Mary Magdalen" and "The Brigand" are in the permanent collection of the Metropolitan Museum, New York.

May's pictures were unquestionably academic, and they had the excellences and defects of the type. Like Hunt, he mastered the method of work taught by Couture, but, unlike Hunt, he continued to use it throughout his career. He was a first-rate draftsman, and his compositions are very well organized in the conventional manner of the old painters. Isham remarks that there is no intensity of personal emotion in his work; on the other hand they make no appeal to the gallery by excess of sentiment. During the Franco-Prussian War of 1870 May served as captain of an American ambulance corps at the front, for which he was awarded a medal by the French government. He died at Paris in his sixty-fourth year.

[Samuel Isham, *The Hist. of Am. Painting* (1905); H. T. Tuckerman, *Book of the Artists* (1867); *Illustrated Cat.: Paintings in the Metropolitan Museum of Art* (1905); *Galignani's Messenger* (Paris), May 19, 1887.] W. H. D.

MAY, SAMUEL JOSEPH (Sept. 12, 1797–July 1, 1871), Unitarian clergyman and reformer, was born at Boston, Mass., the son of Col. Joseph May and Dorothy (Sewall) May, and brother of Abigail May who became the wife of Amos Bronson Alcott [*q.v.*]. His father was descended from John May of Mayfield, Sussex, who was admitted a freeman of Roxbury, Mass., in 1641; his mother was a descendant of Judge Samuel Sewall [*q.v.*]. Their home was a place where cheerful and practical piety was much in evidence. The father stanchly supported the rational teachings of Dr. James Freeman of King's Chapel, and May himself never felt anything but horror for "the heart-withering theology of . . . Calvin" (*Brief Account*, p. 6). After graduating from Harvard in 1817 and teaching in small schools, he read divinity under Norton and Ware in Cambridge, gladly adopting the liberal doctrines now known as Unitarian. For some months he assisted Dr. William Ellery Channing at his Boston church. In 1822 he was ordained, and three years later, June 1, 1825, he married Lucretia Flagge Coffin.

May's energetic life was spent in pastoral duties and in humanitarian services. As a pastor, he served churches at Brooklyn, Conn., 1822–36; South Scituate, Mass., 1836–42; and Syracuse, N. Y., 1845–67. He had small interest in expounding systematic theology, but an unflagging ambition to convert men to the life of personal righteousness, marked by "the spirit of true goodness, active benevolence, stern integrity, moral courage." His gentle and cheerful nature did much to disarm the hostility of his orthodox critics. As a humanitarian, he worked ardently in the service of many reforming causes. He was a disciple of the venerable Noah Worcester in the movement for universal peace, writing and speaking much in its favor. He organized the Windham County (Conn.) Peace Society in 1826, and twelve years later called the convention of the American Peace Society which gave birth to the New England Non-Resistance Society. This association was too extreme for May to support, however, although he was always a friend of peace. When the Civil War began, he modified his views somewhat, but could not bring himself to urge men to enlist. As an advocate of temperance, he persuaded many retailers to cease selling liquor, converted scores of persons to abstinence, drilled youngsters in a Cold Water Army, and preached effectively on the theme for a generation. But he preferred the pledge system and individual self-control to prohibitory laws. In vigorous fashion, he championed equal rights for women, and wrote and spoke much in defense of his position. He cooperated heartily with Lucretia Mott [*q.v.*] and gave the public sentiment of the times a rude shock by inviting Angelina Grimké to occupy his pulpit and address his congregation on abolitionism. In his widely circulated sermon-pamphlet, *The Rights and Condition of Women* (1846), he asserted that "if the people have the right of self-government, then I am unable to see why a half of the people have a right to govern the whole." He played a part in promoting the cause of efficient popular education and while at Brooklyn called a convention (May 1827) to discuss the improvement of the common-schools in Connecticut; later, at Horace Mann's earnest request, he served from 1842 till 1844 as principal of the Normal School at Lexington, Mass. At all times he did much to soften the asperities of American educational practice. May took great pride in his service as an abolitionist. He knew Garrison well, attended the Philadelphia Convention of 1833, acted as general agent and secretary of the Massachusetts Anti-Slavery Society for more than a year, gave substantial aid to Prudence Crandall [*q.v.*] in her time of need, counseled resistance to the Fugitive-slave Law, and in 1851 took part in the public rescue of a slave. He helped negroes to reach Canada, his house being a station on the Underground Railroad. Kindly and brave, with a rich fund of sympathy, he gave of himself without stint to so many humanitarian tasks, great and small, that he thoroughly earned Bronson Alcott's epithet: "the Lord's chore boy."

[May gave his collection of anti-slavery material to Cornell University. His literary remains consist of sermons, addresses, reports, etc., on humanitarian themes. Of special interest are his autobiographical discourse, *A Brief Account of His Ministry* (1867); and *Some Recollections of Our Anti-slavery Conflict* (1869). See also *Samuel Joseph May* (1871); *Memoir of Samuel Joseph May* (1873), prepared by G. B. Emerson, S. May, and T. J. Mumford; *New-Eng. Hist. and Geneal. Reg.*, Apr. 1873; *Autobiog. of Andrew Dickson White* (2 vols., 1905); *Christian Register*, July 8, 15, 1871; *N. Y. Times*, July 3, 1871.] F. M.

MAY, SOPHIE [See CLARKE, REBECCA SOPHIA, 1833–1906].

MAYER, ALFRED GOLDSBOROUGH [See MAYOR, ALFRED GOLDSBOROUGH, 1868–1922].

MAYER, ALFRED MARSHALL (Nov. 13, 1836–July 13, 1897), physicist, nephew of Brantz Mayer [*q.v.*], was born in Baltimore, Md. His parents were Charles F. Mayer, a distinguished member of the Baltimore bar, and his second wife, Eliza Blackwell. The father, expecting his son to follow the law, sent him for schooling in the classics to St. Mary's College, Baltimore, but the boy early showed that his bent was toward science, and at sixteen became a machinist in the shop of a Baltimore engineer. Here and in the drafting-room he worked for some two years, then began to acquire a small practice as analytical chemist, and before he was nineteen published his first scientific paper, on a new apparatus for the determination of carbonic acid (*American Journal of Science*, no. 57, 1855). This early work won the approval of Joseph Henry [*q.v.*], through whose influence Mayer was appointed assistant professor of physics and chemistry in the University of Maryland at the age of twenty, and two years later, to a similar position at Westminster College, Fulton, Mo. From 1863 to 1865 he studied physics, mathematics, and physiology at the University of Paris, being a pupil of the distinguished physicist Regnault. In 1865 he became professor of physical sciences in Pennsylvania College, Gettysburg, and two years later was called to the chair of physics and astronomy at Lehigh University. Here he designed and equipped the astronomical observatory given to the university by Robert H. Sayre [*q.v.*]. Chosen to accompany the expedition sent out by the office of the United States Nautical Almanac to make observations of the solar eclipse of Aug. 7, 1869, he directed the taking of some forty photographs with results accounted as remarkable in those early days of photography (*Journal of the Franklin Institute*, October 1869; *Proceedings of the American Philosophical Society*, vol. XI, 1871). He published observations of Jupiter (*Journal of the Franklin Institute*, August 1870) and a number of papers on electricity, heat, and magnetism.

In 1871 he was invited to the newly founded Stevens Institute of Technology to organize and conduct the department of physics, and was identified with that institution thenceforth until his death. The exceptional instrumental equipment provided for him, together with proximity to New York, afforded him intellectual stimulus, and he began here the series of experiments on acoustics, reported in the *American Journal of Science*, 1872–96, which made him "decidedly the leading authority on this subject in America" (Stevens, *post*, p. 263). During his quarter-century at Stevens he published, in a dozen or more of the leading scientific magazines in America and Europe, fifty-four papers embodying the results of original research on subjects dealing mostly with sound, heat and light, gravity, and electricity. In addition he devised a number of measuring instruments; wrote three books of a popular character: *The Earth a Great Magnet* (1872), *Light* (1877), with Charles Barnard, and *Sound* (1878); and prepared several articles for cyclopedias and technical journals.

Between 1881 and 1889 he achieved a reputation as an amateur of outdoor sports. In 1884 he won first prize at the amateur Minnow-Casting Tournament of the National Rod and Reel Association with a rod of his own invention; he contributed a number of articles on sporting subjects to the *Century Magazine*, and edited *Sport with Gun and Rod in American Woods and Waters* (1883). In 1890, moving from his country place near Maplewood, N. J., into the city, he resumed his activity in science and published some sixteen or seventeen papers before his death. He was married in 1865 to Katherine Duckett Goldsborough, by whom he had one son, Alfred Goldsborough Mayor [*q.v.*], who changed the spelling of the family name. After the death of his wife he was married, in 1869, to Louisa Snowden. Two sons were born of the second marriage. Among the honors accorded Mayer for his scientific work were the degree of Ph.D. granted by Pennsylvania College in 1866—his only academic degree—and election to the National Academy of Sciences.

[A. G. Mayer and R. S. Woodward, in *Nat. Acad. Sci. Biog. Memoirs*, vol. VIII (1919), with biblog.; W. Le Conte Stevens, in *Science*, Aug. 20, 1879; *Morton Memorial: A Hist. of the Stevens Inst. of Technology* (1905), ed. by F. DeR. Furman; *N. Y. Times*, July 14, 1897.] F. DeR. F.

MAYER, BRANTZ (Sept. 27, 1809–Feb. 23, 1879), lawyer, author, was born in Baltimore, Md. His father, Christian Mayer, a native of Ulm, Württemberg, came to Maryland in 1784 and became a trader—later president of a local insurance company and consul-general of Württemberg in the United States. He married Anna Katerina Baum of Kutztown, Pa. Their son, named for Lewis Brantz, his father's partner, was educated partly in the Baltimore schools and at St. Mary's College (Sulpician), but largely by a private tutor. At eighteen he traveled to China and India, studying law by the way. He completed his law course at the University of Maryland, and, on admission to the bar in 1832, visited Europe, stopping for a while at Ulm. After his return he practised law until 1841, when he went to Mexico as secretary of the United States legation.

Evidently his mind turned to history, for in 1844 on his return to Baltimore he was instrumental in founding the Maryland Historical Society, of which he subsequently became president (1867–71). In this year he published *Mexico as It Was and as It Is* (1844), which ran through three editions. It was well-timed, for the United States was on the verge of the Mexican War. Though the book was on the whole a scholarly work, its references to the Catholic Church caused heated controversy. In 1845 Mayer edited, for the Historical Society, the *Journal of Charles Carroll of Carrollton, during His Visit to Canada in 1776,* a valuable record which was republished by the Society in 1876. As president of the Library Company of Baltimore, he directed the erection of the Atheneum Building in 1846. In 1851 he published *Tah-Gah-Jute: or Logan and Captain Michael Cresap* (rev. and enl., 1867), defending Cresap [*q.v.*] from the charge of murdering the family of the Indian, James Logan [*q.v.*]. This was followed by *Mexico, Aztec, Spanish and Republican* (2 vols., 1851) and *Calvert and Penn* (1852). In 1854, he edited and published *Captain Canot; or Twenty Years of an African Slaver,* illustrated by his nephew, Frank Blackwell Mayer. It was a highly colored account, though evidently based on fact; seventeen thousand copies were sold, and it was republished in London and Paris, with a New York edition as late as 1928.

In 1851 and again in 1855 Mayer was called to Louisiana as executor of the will of John McDonogh [*q.v.*], and in this capacity drew the plan and charter of the McDonogh School near Baltimore. Retiring from practice in 1855, he continued to interest himself in writing, contributing articles to the *Baltimore American,* of which he was an editor. Other works of his include: "Observations on Mexican History and Archaeology," in *Smithsonian Contributions to Knowledge,* vol. IX (1857); *Outlines of Mexican Antiquities* (1858); *Memoir of Jared Sparks* (1867); *Baltimore: Past and Present* (1871); and *Memoir and Genealogy of the Maryland and Pennsylvania Family of Mayer Which Originated in the Free Imperial City of Ulm, Wurtemberg, 1495–1878* (1878). In 1866 he urged the state to create an archive commission and depository, and eventually the state records were placed with the Historical Society under whose auspices publication of the *Archives of Maryland* has been carried on ever since, fifty volumes of this important series having appeared by 1933.

On the outbreak of the Civil War Mayer was elected chairman of the Maryland Union Central Committee, where his spirit of conciliation was valuable. He was appointed in 1862 a brigadier-general of Maryland volunteers, was active in recruiting troops, and in 1863 was appointed an additional paymaster. On Jan. 17, 1865, he was made a major and paymaster in the regular army, and the following year was brevetted lieutenant-colonel, to date from Nov. 24, 1865, for his services during the war. He continued in the pay department of the army until 1875, the last five years in California, and then retired with the rank of colonel.

He was an untiring student and an able writer; his work on local history is still considered authoritative. His writings on Mexico, still referred to, contain numerous errors, due, no doubt, to the vast extent of his subject, and the unreliable government statistics of the time, but he was a pioneer in encouraging the study of local material, especially on social history. By his first wife, Mary Griswold, whom he married Sept. 27, 1835, at St. Mary's, Ga., he had five daughters. She died Oct. 30, 1845, and on Nov. 15, 1848, at Baltimore, he married Cornelia Poor. Three daughters were born to this union. He was a member of the Unitarian Church.

[B. C. Steiner, "Brantz Mayer," in *Md. Hist. Mag.,* Mar. 1910, with many references; Mayer's *Baltimore: Past and Present* (1871), and *Genealogy*; John Bigelow, *Retrospections of an Active Life,* I (1909), 300–14; *Army and Navy Jour.,* Mar. 1, 1879; *Baltimore American,* Feb. 24, 1879.]

J. L. W.

MAYER, CONSTANT (Oct. 3, 1829–May 12, 1911), genre and portrait painter, was born at Besançon, Doubs, France. His father, Salomon Mayer, merchant, was a native of Durmenach, Haut Rhin, and his mother, Joséphine Mayer, was born at Verdun, Meuse. He was educated in the schools of Besançon and at an early age went to Paris and entered the École des Beaux-

Arts. He also studied under Léon Cogniet, an able instructor, whose school was celebrated. Mayer lived and worked in Paris until 1857, when he came to the United States, opened a studio in New York, became a naturalized citizen, was elected an associate of the National Academy of Design, and met with considerable success. His genre pictures, usually rather large canvases, with life-size figures, were exhibited in the Academy; many of them were reproduced in black-and-white; and they made a strong appeal to the popular taste. His "Maud Muller" was exhibited in New York in 1867 and at the Paris Salon of 1870. The remark of a critic of 1867 to the effect that the girl's whole story was told by her eyes explains the painter's ability to catch facial expression as well as his shrewdness in capitalizing Whittier's sentiment. In 1869 the artist received the cross of the Legion of Honor from the French government. He was *hors concours* in the Salon, where he was a frequent exhibitor during his several visits to his native land.

In his "Song of the Shirt" and "Evangeline," Mayer showed his predilection for pathetic or mildly melancholy subjects, which, illustrating Hood's and Longfellow's familiar ballads, supplied perfect pictorial equivalents of the original poetic images, and thus made an easy conquest of the public. Less obviously sentimental were such scenes from everyday life as "The Organ Grinder," "Street Melodies," "The Knitting Lesson," and "The Vagabonds," but in "Love's Melancholy," shown at the Centennial exposition in 1876, he reverted to his most romantic vein. "A thoroughly competent painter," wrote Isham, "with a tendency to commonplaceness." The verdict is not unjust. His "Orphan's Morning Hymn," first exhibited in 1875, made a favorable impression on several subsequent occasions, especially at the first exhibition of American pictures held by the Art Institute of Chicago in 1888. The *Art Journal* (May 1875, p. 158) spoke of his work as being "invested with an expression of sentiment which reflects the highest credit upon his genius" and added that it showed no evidence of sentimentalism. "The First Communion," painted in 1886, was reproduced in an etching by Thomas Hovenden. "The Knitting Lesson" was prominent in the Prize Fund exhibition held in New York in 1885. "Dimanche," a young Quakeress with a Bible on her lap, was exhibited at the National Academy of 1883, and at the Paris Salon of 1897. In the field of portraiture Mayer met with a fair degree of success. Among his best-known sitters were Generals U. S. Grant and Philip H. Sheridan. About 1895 Mayer returned to France, and the remaining years of his life were spent in Paris, where he died in the spring of 1911. One of his pictures, "Femme iroquoise de l'Amérique du Nord," is in the art museum of his native city of Besançon. It was shown in the Paris Salon of 1869.

[C. M. Kurtz, *Am. Acad. Notes*, 1881, 1883, 1885; *Aldine*, Nov. 1875; Samuel Isham, *The Hist. of Am. Painting* (1905); *La Chronique des Arts et de la Curiosité*, May 29, 1911; *Am. Art News*, June 17, 1911; *Boston Transcript*, May 16, 1911; Bulletin de Naissance de la Ville de Besançon; information from the *conservateur* of the public library of Besançon.]

W. H. D.

MAYER, EMIL (May 23, 1854–Oct. 20, 1931), laryngologist, was born in New York City, the son of David Mayer, a native of Prussia, and of Henrietta (Rosenbaum), of Bavaria. After receiving his preliminary education in the public schools and the College of the City of New York, he graduated in 1873 from the College of Pharmacy of the City and County of New York. He then took up the study of medicine and graduated from the Medical Department of the University of the City of New York in 1877. After serving as an interne at the hospital on Blackwell's Island he began the practice of medicine in New York City. From the outset he devoted himself particularly to diseases of the nose and throat, working after 1880 with Dr. Morris J. Asch [*q.v.*] at the New York Eye and Ear Infirmary. From 1893 to 1904 he was chief surgeon to the clinic for diseases of the throat in that institution, and then became attending laryngologist at the Mount Sinai Hospital. In 1919 he was appointed consulting laryngologist at the Mount Sinai Hospital.

Mayer was a pioneer in the performance of the operation of submucous resection of the nasal septum. In the *New York Medical Journal*, June 13, 1896, he described his method in this operation, and the instruments devised by him for the purpose. During the World War he served in the medical intelligence bureau of the American Red Cross. He was chairman of the section of laryngology of the American Medical Association in 1920; from 1915 to 1918 he was abstract editor of the American Laryngological Association, and was president of the Association in 1922. He also served as chairman of the section of laryngology of the New York Academy of Medicine and as president of the Academy of Ophthalmology and Oto-Laryngology. The Laryngological Society of Berlin elected him a corresponding fellow, and he was American correspondent of the *Centralblätt für Laryngologie*. When the Therapeutic Research Committee on Pharmacy and Chemistry of the American Medical Association undertook to investigate the advantages and dangers of local anesthetics, Mayer was chosen as chairman and as such submitted the report presented by the committee to the American Medical Association (*Local Anesthesia in Otolaryngology and Rhinology by James Joseph King . . . with Supplement on the Toxic Effects of Local Anesthetics . . . edited by Emil Mayer, M.D., Chairman, Research Committee on Local Anesthesia,* 1926). This report constitutes a most valuable contribution to the subject. Mayer was a frequent contributor to the periodical literature of his specialty. The papers which he read before the various societies of which he was a member were remarkable for their originality and for facility of expression.

In 1884 he married Louise Blume, who died several years before his decease. They had no children. Mayer suffered in his later life from organic heart disease and had retired from active practice some years before his death, which occurred at his home in New York City in October 1931. His genial disposition, kindness—especially toward the younger men—and wide erudition won him well-deserved popularity and respect among his professional colleagues.

[D. B. Delavan, in *Trans. . . . Am. Laryngological Asso.,* 1932; *Laryngoscope,* Nov. 1931; *Jour. Am. Medic. Asso.,* Oct. 31, 1931; bibliography of Mayer's writings in *Annals of Otology, Rhinology, and Laryngology,* Dec. 1931; *N. Y. Times,* Oct. 21, 1931; information from Dr. Delavan and Dr. M. C. Myerson, of New York; personal acquaintance.] F. R. P.

MAYER, LEWIS (Mar. 26, 1783–Aug. 25, 1849), German Reformed clergyman, was born at Lancaster, Pa., the third of the seven children of George Ludwig Mayer, a prosperous, well-educated tradesman, by his second wife, Maria Barbara Haller, and the seventh in descent from Melchior Mayer, who was made *Stadthauptmann* of the Free Imperial City of Ulm in 1550. Lewis' father had emigrated with his parents from Ulm to Frederick, Md., in 1751–52 and settled later in Lancaster. His death in 1793 interfered seriously with his son's education. At Frederick, Md., where Lewis was employed for a time, he attended an academy and was converted to the Reformed faith by the Rev. Daniel Wagner, who prepared him for the ministry. He was licensed in 1807 and ordained in 1808 by the Synod of the United States, and was pastor at Shepherdstown, Martinsburg, and Smithfield, Va. (now W. Va.), 1808–21, and at York, Pa., 1821–25. On Nov. 5, 1809, he married Catharine Line of Shepherdstown, who bore him a son and three daughters and died in 1820. Later he married Mary (Gonder) Smith of York, who survived him for almost sixteen years. In 1818, despite threats of violence, he preached the first English sermon ever delivered in the Second Street Reformed Church of Baltimore.

He was by this time one of the leaders of his denomination and especially prominent in the movement to secure an official theological seminary. In 1824 the Synod authorized the establishment of a seminary, which was to be affiliated with Dickinson College. Neither Philip Milledoler [*q.v.*] nor Samuel Helffenstein would accept the professorship; money and moral support were almost entirely lacking; and the prospect that the seminary would ever open was dark until Mayer himself agreed to undertake the work. His qualifications as a teacher of theology were probably as adequate as those of any other German Reformed minister of the time. He had a very respectable command of Greek and Latin, had mastered Dutch, and could read French and Hebrew; he was an excellent preacher in both German and English; and he was more than merely well-read in Reformed theology. To his courage and unselfishness at a critical juncture his denomination owes much.

After visiting the seminaries at Princeton and New Brunswick to obtain information about books and courses of study, he opened the seminary at Carlisle, Pa., to five students in the spring of 1825. The seminary failed to attract many students, partly because of opposition to it among the conservative German congregations and partly because of its location in a region chiefly Scotch-Irish. In 1829 Mayer, acting on his own initiative, moved it to York, where it began to prosper. Daniel Young was called in to assist him, and a preparatory school was started with the brilliant Frederick Augustus Rauch [*q.v.*] as principal. In 1835 the school was moved to Mercersburg and was reorganized as Marshall College; when the seminary was also removed there in 1837 Mayer resigned. Since no one was available to take his place, he resumed his professorship in 1838. His doctrinal position had by this time become somewhat low-church; he found himself in sharp disagreement with the high-church Rauch, who was preparing the way for the "Mercersburg theology," and in 1839 he resigned again. He spent the rest of his life in York, where he died. He was the author of *Expository Lectures, or Discourses on Scriptural Subjects* (1845), *The Sin against the Holy Ghost* (1867), and *History of the German Reformed Church* (1851), which brings the story of the Swiss Reformation down to the close of the year 1525. He was editor of the *Magazine of the German Reformed Church* from its first publication in 1827 until 1835. He accumulated much material relating to the German Reformed Church in Pennsylvania, and also published some sermons.

[Elias Heiner, "Life of the Rev. Lewis Mayer, D.D.," *Mercersburg Rev.*, May 1851, and prefixed to Mayer's *Hist. of the German Ref. Ch.* (1851); Henry Harbaugh, *The Fathers of the German Ref. Ch.*, vol. III (1872); Brantz Mayer, *Memoir and Geneal. of the Md. and Pa. Family of Mayer* (1878) and H. H. Mayër, *The Mayër Family* (1911); J. H. Dubbs, "The Ref. Ch. in Pa.," *Proc. Pa. Ger. Soc.*, vol. XI (1902); J. I. Good, *Hist. of the Ref. Ch. in the U. S. in the 19th Century* (1911).]

G. H. G.

MAYER, PHILIP FREDERICK (Apr. 1, 1781–Apr. 16, 1858), Lutheran clergyman, was born in New York, the son of George Frederick and Mary Magdalene (Kammerdiener) Mayer. His father was a Swabian, his mother a native of New York State. Mayer graduated from Columbia College with first honors in 1799 and studied for the ministry under John Christopher Kunze [*q.v.*], teaching meanwhile to support himself. The habit of early rising and morning study, formed in these years, remained with him through life and assisted his vigor of body and mind. One of his most treasured books was a Cruden's *Concordance,* inscribed in Latin, which Kunze presented to him on Trinity Sunday, 1801, to commemorate the preaching of his first sermon. He was licensed Sept. 1, 1802, by the New York Ministerium. On May 24, 1804, he married Lucy W., daughter of Daniel Rodman of New York, who with six of their eight children survived him. After serving the Lutheran congregation at Loonenburg (Athens), N. Y., 1803–06, he accepted a call to the newly organized St. John's Church in Philadelphia, the second strictly English Lutheran congregation in the country. Of this large and influential church he was pastor for fifty-two years. Although at this time his denomination was generally committed to parochial schools, he was an earnest advocate of public education. He was one of the founders of the Pennsylvania Bible Society, a trustee of the University of Pennsylvania, and the president of the Philadelphia Dispensary and of the Pennsylvania Institution for the Deaf and Dumb. In 1814 he declined the degree of D.D. from Harvard College on the ground that he was too young to receive such a distinction; later he accepted it from Columbia and from the University of Pennsylvania. He was indefatigable in visiting the sick and the afflicted of his immense congregation, refused to have an assistant, and took only a brief yearly vacation, when he would visit his mother and attend the meetings of the New York Ministerium. He was a close student of Biblical criticism and laid the exegetical foundation of his sermons with scholarly care. His reputation as a preacher was great and lasting, but like his German contemporary, Charles Rudolph Demme [*q.v.*], he would not allow his sermons to be published. With his master, Kunze, and his step-father, Frederick Henry Quitman [*q.v.*], he edited *Dr. Martin Luther's Catechism Translated from the German* (Hudson, N. Y., 1804); in 1806 he prepared another edition, with numerous changes, for his own congregation; and his final version of Luther's Short Catechism, with even greater revision, formed the chief part of his *Instruction in the Principles and Duties of the Christian Religion for Children and Youth* (1816; last edition, 1846). "It is doubtful whether any Lutheran pastor has surpassed him in purity and elegance of style in English writing. In literary culture he was thoroughly competent for the task. . . . Nine-tenths of this translation remains to-day as the accepted and enduring version; not more than one-tenth has been superseded in later revisions." (B. M. Schmucker, *post,* p. 105.) The dignity for which he was noted was not incompatible with his sallying forth to market every morning with a capacious basket under his arm. He conversed easily in Latin and German. His death occurred after an illness of several months. His daughter Mary became the wife of Robert Montgomery Bird and the mother of Frederick Mayer Bird [*qq.v.*]. His successor at Old St. John's was Joseph Augustus Seiss [*q.v.*].

[M. L. Stoever, *Memorial of Rev. Philip F. Mayer, D.D.* (1859), also in *Evangelical Rev.*, Oct. 1858; J. G. Morris, *Fifty Years in the Lutheran Ministry* (1878); B. M. Schmucker, "Luther's Small Catechism," *Luth. Ch. Rev.*, Apr., July 1886; *Press* (Phila.), Apr. 19, 1858.]

G. H. G.

MAYES, EDWARD (Dec. 15, 1846–Aug. 9, 1917), chancellor of the University of Mississippi, author, was born at "Montverde," near Jackson, Miss. His parents, Daniel and Elizabeth (Rigg) Humphreys Mayes, both natives of Virginia and the former a descendant of the Reverend William Mayes (or Mease) who had emigrated to America in 1611, moved from Kentucky to Mississippi in the late 1830's. In Kentucky Daniel Mayes had attained distinction in the state legislature, on the bench, and as professor of law in Transylvania University. The beginning of the Civil War found Edward at Bethany College, located in what is now West Virginia. He at once returned to Jackson and, though very young, assumed charge of a clothing store. In April 1864 he volunteered for service, became a private in the 4th Mississippi Cavalry, and served until the end of the war. When the University of Mississippi again opened its doors to students in October 1865, he was one of the youthful veterans in the freshman class. He received the liberal arts degree in 1868 and the law degree probably in 1870. On May 11, 1869, he was married to Frances Eliza Lamar, the daughter of L. Q. C. Lamar, and the granddaughter of Augustus Baldwin Longstreet [*qq.v.*]. He remained one year at the university as tutor in English and then practised law for several years, first at Coffeeville and then at Oxford.

From 1877 through 1891 he was professor of law in the University. From 1886 to 1889 he was chairman of the faculty, acting virtually as chancellor, and then filled the office of chancellor from its reëstablishment in 1889 until his resignation on Jan. 1, 1892. During his administration there were a number of material improvements and a reorganization of the curriculum. His legal training stood the university in good stead when he defeated J. Z. George [*q.v.*] in a controversy over the endowment act of 1880. As a result of his success the state continued to pay to the university the interest on the endowment lent the state. In the Mississippi constitutional convention of 1890 he was chairman of the committee on bill of rights and general provisions, and he was particularly noted for having originated the plan to aid in the maintenance of white supremacy by electing the officers of the state by the county electoral votes. The active practice of law in Jackson, including the district attorneyship for the Illinois Central Railroad, engaged his attention after he retired from the university, though he found time also to perform the duties of professor of law and dean of the law school in Millsaps College at Jackson. His prominence in religious affairs is indicated by the fact that in 1891 and in 1901 he was a delegate to the ecumenical conference of the Methodist Episcopal Church, South. He was an able and scholarly writer. He was the first president of the Mississippi Historical Society and contributed to the *Publications of the Mississippi Historical Society* (esp. vols. VI, XI, 1902–10). His chief writings were *Lucius Q. C. Lamar: his Life, Times and Speeches* (1896) and the *History of Education in Mississippi* (1899). He also prepared a short outline of legal study for the use of law students entitled, *Ribs of the Law* (1909), and *Genealogical Notes on a Branch of the Family of Mayes* (1928?).

[Biog. material in Edward Mayes, *Geneal. Notes on a Branch of the Family of Mayes* (1928?), p. 42, b–112, c–56; *Biog. and Hist. Memoirs of Miss.* (1891); *Report of the . . . Miss. State Bar Asso. . . . 1918* (1918); Dunbar Rowland, *Miss.* (1907), vol. III; *Who's Who in America*, 1916–17; *Who's Who in Miss.* (1914); *Hist. Cat. of the Univ. of Miss.* (1910); *Vicksburg Herald*, Aug. 10, 1917.] C. S. S.

MAYES, JOEL BRYAN (Oct. 2, 1833–Dec. 14, 1891), Cherokee chief, son of Samuel and Nancy (Adair) Mayes, was born in the old Cherokee Nation near what is now Cartersville, Ga. His father was a white man and his mother a Cherokee who was the daughter of Walter Adair and the grand-daughter of John Adair. Young Joel went to that part of Indian Territory which is now Oklahoma with his family in 1838, when the Cherokee were driven westward from Georgia. He attended the Cherokee public schools and in 1851 entered the seminary near Tahlequah, where he graduated in 1855. From 1855 to 1857 he taught school and then left the school room to engage in live-stock raising until the outbreak of the Civil War. Enlisting as a private in the 1st Confederate Indian Brigade, he was soon promoted to the office of paymaster and later to that of quartermaster, which he retained until the close of the war. He returned to his home in 1865 and resumed the business of farming and stock raising. He was appointed clerk of the district court and was elected judge of the northwestern circuit of the Cherokee Nation. During the next four years he was successively clerk of the commissioners court, clerk of the national council, associate justice, and chief justice of the Cherokee supreme court. In 1887 he was elected principal chief to succeed Dennis Wolf Bushyhead and was reëlected in 1891, but soon afterward he was stricken with influenza and died. He was married in 1857 to Martha J. Candy. Upon her death a few years later he married Martha M. McNair. She also died after some years, and he married Mary Vann. He was a Methodist, a Royal Arch Mason, and a man of highest character. For nearly forty years he worked hard for the educational and material advancement of the Cherokee people and few men have contributed more to their welfare.

[Letters and papers of Mayes in Cherokee Archives, Charles Eldred Papers, manuscript hist. of Mayes Family by J. M. Mayes, all in the Univ. of Okla. Manuscript Coll.; Emmet Starr, *Hist. of the Cherokee Indians* (1921), esp. pp. 184, 232, 263, 284, 293; J. B. Thoburn and M. H. Wright, *A Hist. of Okla.* (1929), vol. II.] E. E. D.

MAYHEW, EXPERIENCE (Feb. 5, 1673 N.S.–Nov. 29, 1758), missionary, translator, author, was the eldest son of John and Elizabeth (Hilliard) Mayhew, the grandson of Thomas Mayhew, Jr. [*q.v.*], and the great-grandson of Gov. Thomas Mayhew [*q.v.*], patentee of Martha's Vineyard. John Mayhew was minister to the churches of Tisbury and Chilmark, Martha's Vineyard, and also preached to the Indians. Experience was born at Chilmark (*Vital Rec-*

ords of Chilmark, Mass., 1904). Of the five Mayhews who engaged in missionary work he was preëminent. As a boy he became a master of the Indian tongue of the Vineyard and later studied other dialects (Letter to Paul Dudley, Mar. 20, 1721/22, published as *Observations on the Indian Language,* 1884, ed. by J. S. H. Fogg). In March 1693/94 he began preaching to the Indians and in October of that year was asked to be "teacher" of the English church in Tisbury. It is not known whether or not he accepted (Banks, *post,* I, 249). From this time until his death he was employed by the Society for the Propagation of the Gospel in New England (*Ibid.,* p. 253). Cotton Mather said of him that "in the evangelical service among the Indians, there is no man that exceeds that Mr. Mayhew, if there be any that equals him" (*Magnalia,* 1853 ed., II, 665, note). A lecture by Cotton Mather, *The Day Which the Lord Hath Made,* was translated into the Indian tongue by Mayhew in 1707. The Society employed him to make a new Indian version of the Psalms of David and the Gospel of St. John, which he did in the *Massachusee Psalter* (1709). Of this work J. H. Trumbull says: "Next to Eliot's Indian Bible, this is the most important monument of the Massachuset Language. His version has some of the peculiarities of the dialects of Martha's Vineyard, . . . but in literal accuracy and its observance of the requirements of Indian grammar, it perhaps surpasses even Eliot's" (*Proceedings of the American Antiquarian Society,* October 1873, pp. 60–61). An account of his visit to the Indians on the mainland, authorized by the Society, is preserved in "A Brief Journal of My Visitation to the Pequot and Mohegin Indians, 1713–1714." In 1720 Harvard College conferred upon him the honorary degree of A.M. It is probable that the *Indiane Primer* of 1720 was revised by Mayhew (J. C. Pilling, *Bibliography of the Algonquian Languages,* 1891, p. 252). He wrote *Indian Converts* (1727), probably the best known of his writings, to show that the Indian work was not in vain. His theological writings, of which *Grace Defended* (1744) was the most important, show him to have been a moderate Calvinist who deviated, as he himself realized, from the strictly orthodox. He seems to have spoken for a measure of free will against the doctrine of total depravity, and it has been said that he wrote in opposition to Jonathan Dickinson and Whitefield (Alden Bradford, *Memoir of . . . Jonathan Mayhew,* 1838, pp. 14–15). He was twice married: first, in 1695, to Thankful Hinckley, daughter of Governor Thomas and Mary Hinckley of Barnstable; and second, in 1711, to Remember Bourne, daughter of Shearjashub and Bathsheba Bourne of Sandwich. He preached until the last week of his life and died of apoplexy in 1758. Jonathan Mayhew [*q.v.*] was a son of his second marriage.

[There is an account of Mayhew in C. E. Banks, *The Hist. of Martha's Vineyard* (3 vols., 1911–25), I, 249–54, with genealogy, III, 305; and one by Thomas Prince, in *Indian Converts,* pp. 306–07. A number of MSS. are in the possession of the Mass. Hist. Soc., including a letter to Cotton Mather, 1723; Sermons in Indian and English, 1714–28; and the following papers: "Key to the Indian Language," "Of the Trinity," "Covenant of Grace," and "A Discourse on Human Liberty" (1752). Inserted in a copy of *Indian Converts* in the Boston Public Library is a manuscript by Zachariah, son of Experience, which contains a few facts about the father.] R. F. F. T.

MAYHEW, JONATHAN (Oct. 8, 1720–July 9, 1766), clergyman, was born at Chilmark, Martha's Vineyard, the son of Experience [*q.v.*] and Remember (Bourne) Mayhew. After graduating with honors from Harvard in 1744, he was called to the pastorate of the West Church, Boston, in 1747, and there remained till his death. A volume of sermons published in 1749 won him favor abroad and soon procured him the degree of D.D. from Aberdeen. A vigorous thinker and ready writer, he was theologically in advance of his time; years afterward James Freeman [*q.v.*] of King's Chapel declared that Mayhew had anticipated him in all his theological conclusions. He preached a rational and practical Christianity based on the Scriptures and not on Calvin; he defended the right of private judgment, rejected the Trinitarian view as early as 1755, and affirmed the doctrine of free will (Eliot, *post*). With the American followers of Whitefield he had small patience. A true Puritan, he detested prelatical institutions and worked and wrote vigorously against them. As Dudleian Lecturer at Harvard in 1765 he delivered a sermon on *Popish Idolatry.* He roundly condemned the Society for the Propagation of the Gospel in Foreign Parts for its policy of sending Anglican missionaries into the settled parts of New England, and censured in strong terms the much-discussed scheme of introducing an American episcopate. He composed three controversial discourses in support of his position, one of them being a reply to a pamphlet by Archbishop Secker (A. L. Cross, *The Anglican Episcopate and the American Colonies,* 1902, ch. vi). When aspects of his theology were attacked by a neighboring minister, he replied with *A Letter of Reproof to Mr. John Cleaveland* (1764), in tone so disdainful and caustic that after a century and a half its pages still sting.

He was a stanch upholder of civil liberty against arbitrary rule; his mind fed upon Milton, Locke, Sidney, and the Bible, and from these writings derived liberal theories in government. His *Discourse Concerning Unlimited Submission and Non-Resistance to the Higher Powers* (1750) defended popular disobedience in cases where commands contrary to God's laws were enjoined (Baldwin, *post,* 44–45). After the repeal of the Stamp Act, he preached a sermon, *The Snare Broken* (1766), in which he counseled the people to observe the laws, but at the same time to have a watchful care for their rights. Though the sermon bore a dedication to William Pitt, Mayhew did not scruple to write: "I will not meddle with the thorny question, whether, or how far, it may be justifiable for private men, at certain extraordinary conjunctures, to take the administration of government in some respects into their own hands. Self-preservation being a great and primary law of nature ... the right of so doing, in some circumstances, cannot well be denied" (p. 42). Ten years afterward that "extraordinary conjuncture" which he had envisaged occurred, and he was not the least of those whose preparatory labors had helped to bring about the event. In June 1766 he had proposed that the Massachusetts lower house send out circular letters to draw the colonies closer so that they might the more effectively defend their liberties.

Mayhew's friendship was sought by Thomas Hollis of London, and by other distinguished Englishmen, and he was the intimate of such provincial leaders as Otis, Quincy, and Samuel Adams. John Adams had a high regard for him, said he was a "transcendent genius," and that "To draw the character of Mayhew, would be to transcribe a dozen volumes" (*The Works of John Adams,* vol. X, 1856, p. 288). He had great learning and boundless industry. His enemies charged him with vanity and harshness and there is no doubt that he had a good deal of severity in his character, but since he was championing great causes, his friends largely glossed over these faults, and he was accounted a social and gracious person by those who knew him well. Worn out by heavy labors, he died at Boston in his forty-sixth year, survived by two daughters and his widow, Elizabeth (Clarke) Mayhew, whom he had married Sept. 2, 1756.

[Hollis Papers 1759–1771, and Belknap Papers, in the Mass. Hist. Soc. library; Francis Blackburne, *Memoirs of Thomas Hollis* (2 vols., 1780), with many letters and an engraved portrait of Mayhew; *Mass. Hist. Soc. Colls.,* vol. LXXIV (1918); William Tudor, *The Life of James Otis* (1823); J. W. Thornton, *The Pulpit of the Am. Rev.* (1860); A. M. Baldwin, *The New England Clergy and the Am. Rev.* (1928); F. H. Foster, *A Genetic Hist. of the New England Theology* (1907); Alden Bradford, *Memoir of the Life and Writings of Rev. Jonathan Mayhew, D.D.* (1838), eulogistic, poorly arranged, but containing much excellent source material; S. A. Eliot, *Heralds of a Liberal Faith* (1910), vol. I; C. E. Banks, *The Hist. of Martha's Vineyard,* vol. III (1911–25).]
F. M.

MAYHEW, THOMAS (1593–Mar. 25, 1682), patentee and first governor of Martha's Vineyard, missionary to the Indians, was baptized at Tisbury, Wiltshire, England, Apr. 1, 1593. His parents were Matthew and Alice (Barter) Mayhew. After apprenticeship, he became a mercer in Southampton (Banks *post,* I, 108, 110; III, 300). Before 1632 he settled in Medford, Mass., as factor for Matthew Cradock, London merchant, for whom he built a mill at Watertown, later acquiring and operating it himself. On May 14, 1634, he was admitted a freeman of the Bay Colony. He engaged rather unsuccessfully in mercantile ventures, acting also as agent for Cradock who, becoming dissatisfied, ended this relationship about 1637. From the first, Mayhew served on responsible committees appointed by the General Court. He was deputy from Medford in 1636, and between 1637 and 1644 from Watertown, where he served locally as selectman and commissioner and built a bridge across the Charles River.

In September 1641 he purchased, under Lord Stirling's patent, Martha's Vineyard, Nantucket, and the Elizabeth Islands, also securing under the Gorges patent a more valid title to the Vineyard, where his son Thomas [*q.v.*] settled with others about 1642 (Dukes County Deeds, VIII, 83; Experience Mayhew, *post,* p. 80; see also R. C. Winthrop, *Life and Letters of John Winthrop,* vol. II, 1867, p. 152). Thomas the elder followed about 1646, and thereafter acted as magistrate. The younger Thomas converted the Indian Hiacoomes [*q.v.*] to Christianity in 1643, and developed the work of Christianizing the natives until his death at sea in 1657. Thereafter his father continued and extended it throughout his own life. All the Vineyard, and many Nantucket, Indians became professed Christians, acknowledging Mayhew's rule. Their first church was organized in 1670, Mayhew refusing the pastorate because of his age and his magisterial duties. He governed first as magistrate in the Massachusetts manner, but a later tendency to govern as patentee through himself and his family was confirmed in 1671, when Lovelace, governor under the Duke of York, proprietary successor to Stirling and Gorges, commissioned him governor for life (New York Colonial MSS.; Deeds, III, 70). In 1673–74, when the Dutch again held New York, Mayhew's paternal rule was challenged by the Vineyard settlers, but not overthrown. His commission was afterward confirmed by Andros. During King Philip's War the Vineyard Indians, then the most fully civilized and Christianized in New England, remained entirely loyal to the English. Mayhew formed and armed an Indian guard, to which the common safety was entrusted. He died (1682) just short of eighty-nine years of age (Banks, I, 109, 247 note), active to the last as governor and father to the Indians, the first of five generations of Mayhews who were Indian missionaries. He was succeeded as missionary and chief magistrate respectively by his grandsons John and Matthew. Thomas Mayhew was married first, in England, to the mother of his son Thomas Jr., and second, about 1635, to Jane (Gallion?), widow of Thomas Paine, a London merchant. Four daughters were born of this second marriage.

[N. B. Shurtleff, ed., *Records of the Governor and Company of the Mass. Bay in New England* (1853), vols. I, II; account by Thomas Prince in Experience Mayhew, *Indian Converts* (1727); "Winthrop Papers," *Mass. Hist. Soc. Colls.*, 4 ser. VII (1865), 30–43; letters from Thomas Mayhew, Jr., on the Indian work in four of the "Eliot Tracts," *Mass. Hist. Soc. Colls.*, 3 ser. IV (1834), 69–260; Cotton Mather, *Magnalia Christi Americana* (1702); Matthew Mayhew, *A Brief Narrative*, etc. (1694), dealing with Vineyard politics; W. B. Sprague, *Annals Am. Pulpit*, vol. I (1857); C. E. Banks, *The Hist. of Martha's Vineyard* (3 vols., 1911–25), vol. I; L. C. M. Hare, *Thomas Mayhew, Patriarch to the Indians, 1593–1682* (1932).]

J. G. K., Jr.

MAYHEW, THOMAS (*c.* 1621–1657), Congregational clergyman, first English missionary to the Indians of New England, was the only son of Gov. Thomas Mayhew [*q.v.*] of Martha's Vineyard. The name of his mother is not known and few of the details of his early life are recorded. He was born in England and it is supposed that he came to America with his father in 1631 and that his boyhood days were spent at Medford and Watertown in the Massachusetts colony. With his father he was in 1641 granted the ownership and government of Martha's Vineyard, Nantucket, and the Elizabeth Islands. A settlement was planted on Martha's Vineyard in 1642 by a group of colonists under the leadership of the younger Thomas, at what is now Edgartown. A church society was early formed and the plantation's youthful leader, who had shortly before attained his majority, was called to its pastoral office.

His pity was aroused by the poverty and ignorance of the Indian inhabitants of the Vineyard and the islands adjacent. Acquiring a knowledge of their language, in which he became a recognized proficient, he undertook to convert them to Christianity. His first convert was Hiacoomes [*q.v.*], who accepted the white man's faith in 1643, three years before missionary work was begun on the mainland by John Eliot. Mayhew trained Hiacoomes and another Indian to preach to their fellows on Sundays, and himself conducted fortnightly services, spending more time in "familiar reasoning" than in the sermon itself (Prince, *post,* p. 286). In 1652 he opened a school to teach the Indian children to read. His labors progressed in spite of the early enmity of powwows and sagamores, who were generally against the new way. In time Indian priests and noblemen alike were converted.

The expenses of the mission were for many years borne by Mayhew out of his private purse. Devoting almost his entire time to the Indian service, he neglected his personal estate, which in consequence became so seriously impaired that " 'twas bare with him for food & rayment" (Thomas Mayhew, Sr., to John Winthrop, Jr., *Massachusetts Historical Society Collections,* 4 ser. VII, 1865, p. 35). The Indian mission at Martha's Vineyard was one of the first Protestant missions in the world to have more than ephemeral existence. Shortly before the founder's death the work came under the financial patronage of the Society for the Propagation of the Gospel in New England, an organization of philanthropists in London incorporated by Parliament to support the work of Mayhew and Eliot.

Mayhew sailed for England in 1657, accompanied by an Indian convert, with the double purpose of stimulating interest in missionary work and attending to matters of business connected with the patrimony of his wife, whose father had died seized of estates in Northamptonshire. The ship in which he took passage was lost at sea and the missionary was never heard of again. By his wife, Jane Paine, daughter of Thomas Paine, a London merchant, and Jane (Gallion?) Paine who married as her second husband the elder Thomas Mayhew, Thomas the younger had three sons, one of whom, John, became minister at Tisbury and Chilmark, Martha's Vineyard, and was the father of Experience Mayhew [*q.v.*]. In conjunction with John Eliot, Thomas Mayhew, Jr., was the author of a number of Indian tracts published in London. These included *The Glorious Progress of the Gospel* (1649) and *Tears of Repentance* (1653).

[Matthew Mayhew, *A Brief Narrative*, etc. (1694); Cotton Mather, *Magnalia Christi Americana* (1702); Daniel Gookin, "Historical Collections of the Indians in New England," *Mass. Hist. Soc. Colls.*, vol. I (1792); C. E. Banks, *The Hist. of Martha's Vineyard* (3 vols., 1911–1925); biography by Thomas Prince in Experience Mayhew, *Indian Converts* (1727); Mayhew's writings and other material in *Mass. Hist. Soc. Colls.*, 3 ser. IV (1834); L. C. M. Hare, *Thomas Mayhew, Patriarch to the Indians, 1593–1682* (1932).]

L. C. M. H.

MAYNARD, CHARLES JOHNSON (May 6, 1845–Oct. 15, 1929), taxidermist and naturalist, was born in West Newton, Mass., the son of Samuel and Emeline (Sanger) Maynard and a descendant of John Maynard who emigrated from England about 1638 and settled in Sudbury, Mass. When Charles was but twelve years of age his father died and the boy was forced within a few years to leave school and work on his mother's farm. Later he engaged in watchmaking, but from early youth he had been deeply interested in natural history, especially ornithology, and having learned something of taxidermy he soon turned his attention to this more congenial occupation.

As early as 1866 he did work for the Boston Society of Natural History, thus becoming acquainted with T. M. Brewer [*q.v.*], Henry Bryant, Alpheus Packard, and F. W. Putnam, and the association with these leaders in science undoubtedly brought him much inspiration and valuable knowledge. He was also employed by E. A. Samuels to secure natural history specimens for the Massachusetts state collection while he likewise furnished bird skins to such leading ornithologists as J. A. Allen, William Brewster, and Henry W. Henshaw [*qq.v.*], with whom he became well acquainted. In 1881 he moved his taxidermy shop and the natural-history establishment which he had developed to Boston, where it remained for many years. During all this time he was making collecting trips to various parts of the country. He made nine expeditions to Florida and five to the Bahamas, as well as visits to Grand Manan and the Magdalen Islands. All told his field work covered a period of fifty years.

He was a keen observer and did not hesitate to publish his observations. His first note, which appeared in the *American Naturalist* for December 1869, described the occurrence of the Baird's Sparrow at Ipswich, Mass., and commented on sexual differences in the painted turtle, the latter remarks being cited in Darwin's *Descent of Man* (1871; II, 28). The sparrow proved to be in reality a new species, the Ipswich Sparrow, which he subsequently described and named. These first papers were followed shortly by *Naturalist's Guide* (1870), a work that went through several editions and served as a first textbook for many a budding naturalist. Maynard published "A Catalogue of the Birds of Coos Co., N. H., and Oxford Co., Me.," with notes by William Brewster, in the *Proceedings of the Boston Society of Natural History,* vol. XIV (1872), and various notes in other standard journals, but most of his literary work consisted of books published by himself, even to the setting of the type and the making of the woodcuts which served as illustrations, as well as the tools with which they were cut. His most important works were *The Birds of Florida* (6 parts, 1872–78); *The Birds of Eastern North America* (16 parts, 1872–81; rev. ed., 1881); *Eggs of North American Birds* (1888), a monograph of the genus *Strophia,* in his *Contributions to Science* (three volumes covering a wide range of subjects, issued in parts, 1889–96); *Manual of North American Butterflies* (1891); *Handbook of Sparrows, Finches, etc. of New England* (1896); *The Warblers of New England* (1905); *Methods in Moss Study* (1905). There are also twelve volumes entitled *Walks and Talks with Nature,* published between 1908 and 1921.

While Maynard's observations were voluminous, often original, and covered a wide field, his lack of early scientific training was frequently evident in his publications and he fell short of the accomplishments that might have been his had he had a thorough foundation in science. Nevertheless, as one of his biographers has said, "It is possible this would have spoiled his independence and originality, and made a narrow specialist of him" (Townsend, *post,* p. 7). In addition to his business activities and his publications he conducted bird and nature walks which became very popular and served to stimulate the young people who made up his classes, as well as the adults, to a real interest in nature. He also prepared comprehensive school collections, gathering and preparing the specimens himself and constructing models of the more minute or perishable forms of life. He was an early member of the Nuttall Ornithological Club, its vice-president in 1876, and one of the editors of the first number of its *Bulletin.* In 1912 he became an associate member of the American Ornithologists' Union and was president of the Newton (Mass.) Natural History Society. He was married at Somerville, Mass., in 1883, to Elizabeth B. Cotter, by whom he had one daughter, who survived him. His death occurred at West Newton, in his eighty-fifth year.

[C. W. Townsend, in *Bull. Boston Soc. Nat. Hist.,* Jan. 1930; *Who's Who in America,* 1928–29; *Vital Records of Newton, Mass.* (1905); *Am. Ancestry,* vol. IX (1894); *Boston Transcript,* Oct. 15, 1929; slight personal acquaintance.] W. S.

MAYNARD, EDWARD (Apr. 26, 1813–May 4, 1891), dental surgeon, inventor, was the son of Moses and Chloe (Butler) Maynard, both of English descent. He was born at Madison, N. Y., where his father, a farmer, was county sheriff and in later life a member of the New York legislature. After taking a preparatory course at

Hamilton Academy, Maynard entered the United States Military Academy at West Point when he was eighteen years old, but frail health caused him to resign during his first year there. He then began the study of dentistry, completing the course in 1835, and in 1836 settled in Washington, D. C., where he practised his profession, except for short intervals, for the rest of his life. From the very beginning of his career he was a profound research student and as early as 1836 announced the existence of dental fevers. This discovery was much discussed by the American Society of Dental Surgeons and was subsequently proven correct by the aid of microscope. He was the first to fill teeth with gold foil (1838), filling also the nerve canals in molars and bicuspid teeth, and he introducd the practice into Europe in 1845. He invented many improvements in dental instruments. From 1843 to 1846 he was co-editor of the *American Journal of Dental Science*. In 1846 he announced before the faculty of the Baltimore College of Dental Surgery the great diversity of situation, form, and capacity of the large cavities of the superior maxillaries, a discovery which proved of great importance in the treatment of these cavities. From 1857 until his death he held the chair of theory and practice in the Baltimore College of Dental Surgery and from 1887 to 1891 a like position in the National University, Washington.

In spite of his notable work in dentistry, however, Maynard is probably best known for his improvements in firearms. In 1845 he patented a system of priming consisting of a coiled, tape-like paper strip containing fifty fulminate caps spaced at equal distances apart, and a mechanism which automatically fed the tape, a cap at a time, from the recess of the gun in which it was protected, into position for firing. The Maynard tape primer, as it was called, was adopted by the federal government and generally used by the governments of Europe. In 1851 he patented an improvement in breech-loading rifles which, with subsequent improvements made by him in the succeeding fourteen years, brought about the general adoption of the Maynard rifle by governments and sportsmen throughout the world. Prior to 1886 he patented also a number of minor improvements in firearms, including a method of converting muzzle-loaders into breech-loaders; a method of joining two rifle or shotgun barrels to permit longitudinal expansion or contraction; and a device to indicate the number of cartridges in a magazine of a repeating firearm. For his work in the advancement of the science of dentistry and for his inventions in firearms he received many honors: he was designated court dentist to Emperor Nicholas I of Russia, was made a chevalier of the military order of the Red Eagle by the King of Prussia, and received from the King of Sweden a gold medal of merit. He held several honorary degrees and was an honorary member of the American Academy of Dental Sciences and the European Society of American Dentists, and a member of the International Medical Congress. He was twice married: in 1839 to Ellen Sophia Doty at Sherburne, N. Y., and in 1869 to Nellie Long of Savannah, Ga. At the time of his death in Washington he was survived by eight children, one of whom was George Willoughby Maynard [*q.v.*].

[E. W. Byrn, *Progress of Invention in the Nineteenth Century* (1900); Patent Office records; *A Coll. of Ann. Reports and Other Important Papers Relating to the Ordnance Dept.*, vol. II (1880); *The Maynard Rifle* (Mass. Arms Co., Chicopee Falls, Mass., 1886); V. D. Stockbridge, *Digest of Patents of Breech-loading and Magazine Small Arms* (1875); C. B. Norton, *Am. Inventions in Breech-loading Small Arms* (1880); obituaries in many dental journals, notably: *Dental Cosmos*, June 1891, *Am. Jour. Dental Sci.*, May 1891, *Archives of Dentistry*, July 1891; *Forest and Stream*, May 7, 1891; *Evening Star* (Washington), May 5, 1891; correspondence with family.]

C. W. M.

MAYNARD, GEORGE WILLIAM (June 12, 1839–Feb. 12, 1913), mining engineer, was born in Brooklyn, N. Y., and in 1855 became a student in Columbia College, registering under the name of George William Toy. Before he reached his majority, however, his name had been changed to Maynard, and the names of his parents, as given in *Who's Who in America* (1910–1913), are George Washington and Caroline Augusta (Eaton) Maynard. He graduated from Columbia in 1859, having earned a large part of his expenses. In the following year he was employed as assistant by the professor of chemistry, and in 1860 he went abroad to study at Göttingen, where he specialized in chemistry, physics, and mineralogy, under Wöhler and other distinguished teachers. Later he went to the school of mines at Clausthal to study mining and mineralogy. His first professional engagement (1863–64) was to devise a suitable process for the treatment of pyritic ores at Wicklow, Ireland. This he successfully accomplished. Returning to the United States, he opened an engineering office and chemical laboratory under the firm name of Maynard & Tiemann. In 1864 he received the degree of A.M. from Columbia College. Being sent to Colorado the same year to examine a gold mine, he was so much impressed with prospects there that he established an engineering and assay office in Gilpin County which he maintained some three years. On June 12, 1865, he married Fannie Atkin of New York City.

Returning to the East in 1867, he took charge of a small plant for manufacturing sulphuric acid, on Staten Island, but in 1868 accepted the professorship of metallurgy and practical mining at Rensselaer Polytechnic Institute, Troy, N. Y. Four years later, since the Institute was without the means to establish an adequate school of mines, he returned to New York, and on his retirement the course was discontinued. In 1873 he went to England to endeavor to negotiate the sale of an iron property in the Southern states, and, to occupy himself in the intervals of the protracted negotiations, opened an office in London, becoming consulting engineer for sundry steel works in England and Wales. Sidney Gilchrist Thomas was then developing his modification of the Bessemer steel-making process which permits steel to be made from pig iron that is too high in phosphorus to be used in the ordinary or "acid" Bessemer. Maynard directed the first test in England, on a large scale, of the Thomas process. He remained abroad for six years, part of the time in Russia, where he erected a copper smelting plant at Vosskressensk for a British company.

During this time he had maintained his friendship with Thomas, and on returning to the United States in 1879 he succeeded in selling the American rights to the Thomas process, which never proved of any importance in this country, although it became the principal basis of the German iron industry, making available for use the extensive ore deposits of Alsace-Lorraine. Maynard wrote a careful historical account of the development of this process which was published in the *Transactions of the American Institute of Mining Engineers* (vol. XLI, 1911). The remainder of his life was spent in practice as consulting engineer with offices in New York, although his work took him to Nova Scotia, Newfoundland, British Columbia, the Yukon, Mexico, and Cuba. He was active in the development of technology, and in addition to being for two years a vice-president of the American Institute of Mining Engineers, he contributed to its *Transactions* a half-dozen technical papers, most of them dealing with iron and steel, and was a frequent contributor to other technical journals. He was interested in art and natural history and was active in organizations in those fields. Attacked during a professional journey with the disease of which he died, he was taken to the home of his daughter in Boston and died in that city in his seventy-fourth year. The notices of his death quite generally referred to him as "the dean of American mining engineers."

[*Bull. Am. Inst. Mining Engineers*, Apr. 1913; *Engineering and Mining Jour.*, Feb. 22, 1913; *Who's Who in America*, 1912–13; *Boston Transcript*, Feb. 13, 1913.] T. T. R.

MAYNARD, GEORGE WILLOUGHBY (Mar. 5, 1843–Apr. 5, 1923), portrait, figure, and mural painter, born at Washington, D. C., was the son of Edward [*q.v.*] and Ellen Sophia (Doty) Maynard. At the age of twenty-three he began to study drawing and modeling under Henry K. Brown, the sculptor, and a year later he entered the school of the National Academy of Design, New York. Soon after this he became the pupil of Edwin White, historical painter, with whom he went to Florence in 1869. He subsequently visited Rome and thence found his way to Antwerp, where he continued his studies under J. H. F. Van Lerius at the Royal Academy of Art in that city. In 1873, in company with his friend Francis D. Millet, he went on a long journey through southeastern Europe. After an absence of five years he returned to New York in the spring of 1874. He exhibited a picture, "The Angelus," at the National Academy of Design in 1875, and thenceforth became a regular exhibitor of portraits and figure pieces. Among his subjects were "The Strange Gods," the "Ancient Mariner," and the "Bachelor's Breakfast." He was elected associate of the National Academy in 1882, and academician in 1885.

In 1876 Maynard sent to the Centennial exposition in Philadelphia "Vespers in Antwerp" and "1776." "In Strange Seas," a group of mermaids at play, was shown at the Paris exposition of 1900 and later hung in the Metropolitan Museum of Art, New York. "Sirens" and "A Sea Witch," similar motives, appeared at the Chicago exposition of 1893, and a composition entitled "Mermaids and Marines" was in the National Academy exhibition of 1890. At the St. Louis exposition of 1904 he exhibited "Surf" and "Sport." For a time he taught drawing classes at the Cooper Institute and at the National Academy. Among his portraits were those of William M. Evarts, Francis D. Millet, Kate Field, Chester Chapin, Judge Addison Brown, and C. C. Beaman. His numerous honors included the award of the Temple gold medal of the Pennsylvania Academy, 1884; a gold medal at the prize fund exhibition in New York, 1886; the Evans prize of the American Watercolor Society, 1889; the Shaw prize of the Society of American Artists, 1897; and a special medal for decoration at the Chicago exposition, 1893.

Maynard made his first essay in mural painting as one of the assistants of John La Farge in the decoration of Trinity Church, Boston, in 1876. At the close of this undertaking, having become deeply interested in this branch of the art, he went abroad in 1877 and made a special study of the most important mural decorations in Italy, France, and England. He then took a studio in Paris (1878) but returned to New York before the end of that year, to find his services in great demand for decorative work in public and private buildings. His productions in this field include two panels in St. James' Church, Jamaica Plain, Mass.; figures on each side of the proscenium in the Metropolitan Opera House in New York—"The Chorus" and "The Ballet"; a large part of the interior decoration of the Ponce de Leon Hotel at St. Augustine, Fla.; parts of the entrance hall of the Boston Public Library; decorations in Keith's Theatre, Boston, in the houses of Whitelaw Reid and William Rockefeller at Tarrytown, N. Y.; in Sherry's ball-room and in the Waldorf-Astoria, the Manhattan, the Plaza, the Savoy, and the Imperial hotels, New York. His most important commission was that for the exterior decoration of the Agricultural Building at the World's Columbian exposition at Chicago, 1893. This, like many of his other decorations, was in the Pompeian style. According to Samuel Isham it was probably the most effective of any on the grounds, and it was for this work that he was awarded the special medal before-mentioned. Especially fine were the classic themes of the great main portico, with the figures of "Abundance" and "Fertility," the Greek frieze, and the side panels showing Cybele, the mother of all the gods, seated in a golden chariot drawn by lions, and King Triptolemus, sent forth in Demeter's car with its team of winged dragons, to instruct all the nations of the earth in farming. This was his *magnum opus.*

Less impressive though still felicitous are his Pompeian panels in the north and south corridors of the second floor of the Library of Congress, Washington. Here he chose for his designs eight floating female figures typifying "The Virtues"—clad in classic drapery and relieved against the rich red background of the wall. In his decorations of the southwest pavilion he was given four tympanums and the disc in a domed ceiling, and selected for his subjects in the tympanums "Adventure," "Discovery," "Conquest," and "Civilization" and for the disc appropriate qualities—"Courage," "Valor," "Fortitude," and "Achievement." The ingenuity of the conceptions and the excellent workmanship are in a measure nullified by the awkward shape of the spaces, especially in the tympanums. In his adaptations of the Pompeian style and color scheme he was eminently successful; moreover he manifested intelligent realization of the principles governing mural work. His decorations are rich in classical ideas treated with dignity and distinction and in pertinent historical allusions, though it is true that his symbolism is at times of a stereotyped order. Maynard was married on Dec. 26, 1907, to Louise Brownell of Brooklyn, N. Y. He died in New York City.

[W. A. Coffin, "The Artist Maynard," *Century Mag.*, Dec. 1890; Pauline King, *Am. Mural Painting* (1902); Herbert Small, *Handbook of the Lib. of Cong.*; *Who's Who in America*, 1922–23; Mich. State Lib., *Biog. Sketches of Am. Artists* (1916); *Cat. of Paintings in the Metropolitan Museum of Art* (1905); *N. Y. Times*, Apr. 7, 1923.]

W. H. D.

MAYNARD, HORACE (Aug. 30, 1814–May 3, 1882), congressman and Unionist, was the son of Ephraim and Diana Harriet (Cogswell) Maynard. Born in Westboro, Mass., he was prepared for college at Millbury Academy and was graduated with high honors at Amherst College in 1838. He went immediately to Knoxville, Tenn., where he had been appointed tutor in the preparatory department of East Tennessee College (now the University of Tennessee), and where he made his home for the remainder of his life. He was soon advanced to a professorship of mathematics. On Aug. 30, 1840, he was married to Laura Ann Washburn, the daughter of Azel Washburn of Royalton, Vt. They had seven children. In 1844 he deserted teaching for the practice of law and entered political life as a Whig. More than six feet tall, thin, straight, with a swarthy complexion, dark and piercing eyes, and long, black hair that fell to his shoulders, he was popularly supposed to have Indian blood in his veins and was commonly referred to as "the Narragansett." In his political campaigns he displayed oratorical powers and made effective use of invective and sarcasm. He was able and successful, but he never was an idol of the people. One explanation for this can perhaps be found in the fact that as a university professor he wrote an article in which he characterized the masses as "the common herd," with whom he desired "no fellowship" (Temple, *post,* p. 147). Certainly this was used to defeat him in his first campaign for a seat in Congress in 1853. Four years later, however, he was elected as a candidate of the Whig and American parties and two years later was reëlected.

In 1860 he campaigned for the Bell and Everett ticket in Massachusetts and in Tennessee. In the following year, when secession threatened, he joined forces with Andrew Johnson, Thomas A. R. Nelson, Oliver P. Temple, and William G.

Brownlow to fight bitterly against the withdrawal of Tennessee from the Union. His section of the state, the eastern, remained loyal to the Union, however, and he was returned in the August election to a third term in the federal Congress. In Washington he was an ardent but unsuccessful advocate of immediately sending a federal army to the relief of the Unionists of East Tennessee. In 1863 he became attorney-general of Tennessee under the military governorship of Andrew Johnson and held this office, much to the dislike of conservative Unionists, until the reëstablishment of civil rule under Governor Brownlow. He was then reëlected to Congress and took his seat in the House, on July 24, 1866, when Tennessee was readmitted to representation in that body. Here he broke with his fellow Unionist of Civil War days, President Johnson, and aligned himself with the radical Republicans. Consequently, he was thoroughly hated by the conservatives of his state, who took advantage of the first opportunity to gerrymander his district. He refused to retire to private life, however, and as a candidate for Congress from the state at large in 1872 defeated his two Democratic opponents, Andrew Johnson and Benjamin F. Cheatham [*qq.v.*]. Two years later he was the Republican party's unsuccessful candidate for the governorship. In 1875 his long and able services to his party were rewarded by President Grant, who appointed him minister to Turkey. After five years in Constantinople he returned to the United States to succeed David M. Key as postmaster-general in the cabinet of President Hayes. In the following year he retired to private life.

[*Vital Records of Westborough, Mass.* (1903); James Park, *Life and Services of Horace Maynard* (1903); *Report of the Proc. of the Numismatic and Antiquarian Soc. of Philadelphia . . . 1882* (1883); O. P. Temple, *Notable Men of Tennessee* (1912); *Amherst College Biog. Record of the Grads. and Non-Grads.* (1927); *War of the Rebellion: Official Records (Army)*, ser. 1, vols. VII, XVI (pt. 2), XX (pt. 2), ser. 2, vols. I, IV (1882–99); *Knoxville Daily Chronicle*, May 4–6, 1882.]

P. M. H.

MAYO, AMORY DWIGHT (Jan. 31, 1823–Apr. 8, 1907), Unitarian clergyman, educator, was born in Warwick, Franklin County, Mass., the son of Amory and Sophronia (Cobb) Mayo, and a descendant of John Mayo of Roxbury who emigrated to Massachusetts with his mother and her second husband in 1632. Educated in a district school and the Deerfield Academy, he entered Amherst College at the age of twenty but because of ill health was unable to complete the freshman year. For a time he taught school and then studied theology with Hosea Ballou, 1796–1861 [*q.v.*]. He was ordained in 1846 and settled over the Universalist church in Gloucester, where he remained until 1854. There followed pastoral service in each of the following churches: Independent Christian Church, Cleveland, Ohio, 1854–56; Division Street Unitarian Church, Albany, N. Y., 1856–63; Church of the Redeemer, Cincinnati, Ohio, 1863–72; Church of the Unity, Springfield, Mass., 1872–80. Appointed in 1863 as non-resident professor of church polity and administration in Meadville Theological Seminary, he served this institution for thirty-five years, delivering usually a course of twelve or fifteen lectures on the principal denominations in the United States, at first annually and after 1883, triennially. During the year 1897–98 he also delivered lectures on the Ballou Foundation entitled "The New Education."

His interest in education, which began when he lived in Albany, developed strongly during his life in Cincinnati and Springfield. He was an active and able member of the school board in each of these cities. He was a leader of the "Christian Amendment Movement," which had for its purpose the incorporation in the federal Constitution of a provision guaranteeing the right to teach the Bible in public schools. When he moved to Boston in 1880 his greater ministry of education began. From 1880 to 1885 he was associate editor of the *Journal of Education*. From 1880 to 1900 he devoted himself as a private citizen to the development of education in the Southern states. During these twenty years he traveled two hundred thousand miles, visiting schools in the South and conferring personally with school committees and state legislatures. He gave freely his lectures, sermons, and counsel, his expenses being cared for by a few friends interested in education and by an annual grant, for some years, from the American Unitarian Association. Everywhere he was received with great cordiality and there was general recognition that he had contributed largely to the building up of the public-school systems of the South.

During his career as a clergyman he published *The Balance; or, Moral Arguments for Universalism* (1847); *Graces and Powers of the Christian Life* (1853); *Selections from the Writings of Mrs. Sarah C. Edgarton Mayo: With a Memoir by her Husband* (1849); *Symbols of the Capital or Civilization in New York* (1859). Educational publications include *Religon in the Common Schools* (1869); *The Bible in the Public Schools* (1870), with Thomas Vickers; *Talks with Teachers* (1881); and *Industrial Education in the South* (1888). From 1900, at the instance of the United States Commissioner of Education, Dr. William T. Harris, he devoted himself to writing a history of the American common-school. Many chapters had been published in the annual reports of the commissioner of education from 1893 on, but the work was not completed at the time of his death. Besides this series, he also published in both reports and Circulars of Information many articles on education, especially in the South.

Mayo's first wife, whom he married July 28, 1846, was Sarah Carter (Edgarton) Mayo [*q.v.*] of Shirley, Mass. She died July 9, 1848; on June 7, 1853, he married Lucy Caroline Clarke of New Brighton, Pa. His death occurred in Washington, D. C.

[C. G. Mayo, "The Mayo Family in the U. S." (1927), 2 vols., typewritten, in Library of Congress; *Jour. of Education*, Mar. 14, 28, Apr. 18, 1907; *Unitarian Year Book*, July 1, 1907; *Christian Reg.*, Apr. 18, 1907; *Evening Star* (Washington), Apr. 9, 1907; memoranda furnished by son, W. S. Mayo, Washington, D. C.]
D. A. R—n.

MAYO, FRANK (Apr. 18, 1839–June 8, 1896), actor, was born on Essex Street, Boston, and at the age of fourteen went to California with his parents by way of Cape Horn. When he became an actor he discarded his family name, McGuire. His first speaking part was the waiter in *Raising the Wind*, at the Adelphi Theatre, San Francisco, July 29, 1856. He lost his next job, at Maguire's Opera House, when as a super in *Pizarro*, he ruined a scene by mistaking a cue and cheering Rolla too soon. Junius Brutus Booth, Jr., the Rolla of the production, was so enraged that he insisted on Mayo's dismissal. Then Mayo acted for five weeks in George Chapman's company at Sacramento, but quit when no pay was forthcoming, went the rounds of the towns and mining camps with Charles Wheatleigh's troupe, and fell in with Edwin Booth, for whom he played De Mauprat in *Richelieu*. Finally, in 1863, he returned to Maguire's as leading man in the same company from which he had been so ignominiously expelled. He finished his San Francisco engagement June 14, 1865, sailed for New York by the Panama route, and made his Eastern début Aug. 8, 1865, as Badger in *The Streets of New York*, a part that he had originated on the Coast. Theatre-goers were astonished and delighted by the artistry with which he transformed Boucicault's crude sketch into something theatrically fine, and from then till his death Mayo was one of the most popular actors on the American stage.

His first New York appearance was as Ferdinand in *The Tempest*, at the Grand Opera House, Mar. 31, 1869. He appeared often, and with much satisfaction, in the leading rôles in Münch-Bellinghausen's *Ingomar*, Sheridan Knowles's *Virginius*, Bulwer Lytton's *Richelieu*, and other favorites of that class, of which his own *Nordeck* (1883), written in collaboration with John G. Wilson, was a characteristic example. *Hamlet* and *Macbeth* were in his regular repertory, and he was also an excellent Iago and Richard III. He was most popular, however, and was probably at his best, in American character parts. Two of these are inseparably associated with his interpretation of them. *Davy Crockett*, which was written for him by Frank Hitchcock Murdoch [*q.v.*], was first put on Sept. 23, 1872, at the Opera House, Rochester, N. Y., of which Mayo was the manager (*Rochester Democrat and Chronicle*, Sept. 23, 1872). It was then hardly a success, but Mayo tried it again from time to time, and after a few years it became extremely popular. On June 9, 1879, he began an English tour with it at the Alexandra Theatre, Liverpool. After its 2,000th performance Mayo lost track of the number of times he appeared in it. In its final form the play may have been as much his work as it was Murdoch's. Mayo was the author, also, of the stage version of Mark Twain's *Puddin'head Wilson*, which was first played at Proctor's Opera House, Hartford, Apr. 8, 1895. His interpretation of the title rôle was a masterpiece of restrained humor and mellow realism. He gave his last performance of the play at the Broadway Theatre, Denver, June 6, 1896. Two days later he died of heart disease on a train near Grand Island, Nebr. He was buried in West Laurel Hill Cemetery, Philadelphia. His wife and three children survived him.

[A. H. Quinn, *A Hist. of the Am. Drama from the Civil War to the Present Day* (1927), vol. I; Katherine Goodale, *Behind the Scenes with Edwin Booth* (1931); *Harper's Weekly*, June 22, 1895; *Phila. Inquirer*, June 9, 10, 13, 1896; *Public Ledger* (Phila.), *N. Y. Daily Tribune*, *Boston Herald*, *Boston Daily Advertiser*, and *Boston Transcript*, June 9, 1896; *N. Y. Clipper*, June 13, 1896; John Drew, *My Years on the Stage* (1922), pp. 98–99.]
G. H. G.

MAYO, MARY ANNE BRYANT (May 24, 1845–Apr. 21, 1903), pioneer Grange and Farmers' Institute worker, was born in Convis Township, Calhoun County, Mich., near Battle Creek. She was the eldest child of James Bryant and Ann (Atmore) Bryant. Her mother was born near Norwich, England, and came to America in 1840. Her father's family came originally from New England and New York. She was tutored while very young in a private school taught by two maiden aunts from New England. Later she graduated from the Battle Creek High School and began to teach a district school at seventeen. On Apr. 14, 1865, she was married to Perry Mayo, soon after his return from service in the Union army. He and his young wife purchased a farm and began their home-making in a log house in Marshall Township. As the years went by they continued their education through home study and Mrs. Mayo completed the four years' course of the Chautauqua Reading Circle. They were active in their home neighborhood organizations, and early in their married life they identified themselves with the Grange movement. They became officers in the county Grange and were early sent as delegates to the state Grange. In the latter Mrs. Mayo acted first as lecturer, and for twelve years as chaplain, holding this office at the time of her death.

Seeing what was being done for city and town women through social and study clubs, Mrs. Mayo believed that the Grange and kindred organizations offered corresponding opportunities to isolated farm women. She visited nearly every township in the state, talking at farmers' picnics, institutes, and other gatherings. As chairman of the woman's work committee of the State Grange, she introduced the "Fresh Air" feature by which many children of the poor in the cities were sent into the homes of the Grange for a few weeks' enjoyment of country life. She was also responsible for the origin and development of children's day in the Grange. In the activities of the Farmers' Institute she was a pioneer in holding separate women's sections at the meetings, a feature that later became permanent and accomplished much good. She was the leader and champion from the farm for a woman's department at the Michigan State Agricultural College. Her labors in this direction covered a period of from ten to fifteen years and culminated in the introduction, in 1897, of a course for women and in the erection in 1900 of a woman's building. In recognition of her services the Michigan state board of agriculture on Sept. 11, 1931, named the new dormitory for women at the Michigan State College the Mary Mayo Hall. She was closely identified with many charitable and reformatory organizations in her state, particularly with the Michigan State Industrial Home for Girls at Adrian, which she served for several years as a member of the Board of Control. As a public speaker she was a general favorite wherever she went. Her writings were principally articles contributed to the *Michigan Patron* and the *Michigan Farmer*. At the time of her death probably no woman was more widely known and loved throughout her state, particularly among farm women. She was survived by her husband and two children.

[Jennie Buell, *One Woman's Work for Farm Women, the Story of Mary A. Mayo's Part in Rural Social Movements* (1908); articles in the *Michigan Farmer*, May 2 and 9, 1903; a manuscript "Hist. of the Mayo Family," written by Mrs. Mayo's son, Nelson Slater Mayo of Highland Park, Ill.; a manuscript letter by Dr. F. C. Kedzie, dated Jan. 6, 1931, and addressed to the dean of women, Mich. State Coll.] C. R. B.

MAYO, SARAH CARTER EDGARTON (Mar. 17, 1819–July 9, 1848), author, daughter of Joseph Edgarton and his second wife, Mehitable (Whitcomb), was born in Shirley, Mass., and spent there all but two of her brief twenty-nine years. She was a descendant of Dennis Edgarton who lived in Bridgewater, Mass., and died in 1734. Her grandfather, John Edgarton, had marched from Shirley on Apr. 19, 1775, to serve his country, and had returned to become a prominent man in local politics. Her father played an important part in the industrial development of the village. She grew up in a pleasant home, one of a large family, assisting with domestic duties and reading eagerly whatever books the neighborhood afforded. Her limited educational advantages were supplied by the district school and by fourteen weeks at the academy of Westford. With an intense desire for self-improvement, however, she taught herself several languages and read widely in history, fiction, and poetry. "I do believe," she wrote in 1840, "that there is nothing in life so beautiful and elevating as the cultivation and improvement of the intellect in connection with moral sentiments" (A. D. Mayo, *post*, p. 42).

When she was about seventeen she began to write for publication, moved by a desire to contribute to the family income, then much reduced by reverses in her father's business. An ardent Universalist, she sent her first offerings to a periodical which had been devoted to the improvement and instruction of the women of her denomination since 1833—*The Universalist and Ladies' Repository* of Boston. She promptly became identified with this paper, supplying it regularly with sketches, poems, and short tales. From 1839 to 1842 she acted as its associate editor, and continued to write for it after withdrawing from this connection. By 1842 she had published two little books for children—*The Palfreys* and *Ellen Clifford*, and two volumes made up of her magazine articles—*Spring Flowers* and *The Poetry of Woman*. Her best work, both in prose and verse, appeared in the ten volumes of a Universalist annual called *The Rose of Sharon: A Religious Souvenir*, which she edited from 1840 until her death. In addition to this she published *Poems, by Mrs. Julia H. Scott, Together with a Brief Memoir* (1843), *The Flower Vase* (1843), *Fables of Flora* (1844), and *The Floral Fortune Teller* (1846).

On July 28, 1846, she married the Rev. Amory Dwight Mayo [*q.v.*] and accompanied him to his parish in Gloucester, Mass., where she spent the last two years of her life. The illness of her husband and the death of a talented younger brother with whom she had planned further literary ventures saddened these years, although the serenity of her religious faith enabled her to write of life even at this time, "I see no mysteries, and hear no discords" (Mayo, p. 116). After the birth of a daughter in September 1847, her health failed rapidly, and she died the following July.

[Seth Chandler, *Hist. of the Town of Shirley, Mass.* (1883); E. S. Bolton, *Shirley Uplands and Intervales* (1914); A. D. Mayo, *Selections from the Writings of Mrs. Sarah C. Edgarton Mayo: With a Memoir* (1849); Mrs. E. R. Hanson, *Our Women Workers* (1882); Phoebe A. C. Hanaford, *Daughters of America; or, Women of the Century* (1882); R. W. Griswold, *The Female Poets of America* (1849); *The Rose of Sharon: A Religious Souvenir for 1849*; *Boston Transcript,* July 13, 1848.]
B. M. S.

MAYO, WILLIAM (*c.* 1684–1744), surveyor, son of Joseph and Elizabeth (Hooper) Mayo, was christened at Poulshot, Wiltshire, England, Nov. 4, 1684. Prior to 1712 he went to Barbados, and made a survey of that island which appears to have been accepted as standard. William Byrd, 1674–1744 [*q.v.*], attests its accuracy, and in April 1722 the board of trade ordered its secretary to subscribe "for the use of the Board, for one of the maps of Barbados, which Mr. Mayo is about to publish" (*Journal of the Commissioners for Trade and Plantations . . . 1718 . . . 1722,* 1925, p. 348). He married in Barbados Frances Gould, and about 1723 removed with his family to Virginia.

When Goochland County was erected in 1728 he was appointed justice of the peace and county surveyor. In 1728, also, he helped to run the boundary line between Virginia and North Carolina. The task was not easy. At the Great Dismal Swamp the other surveyor "was excus'd from the Fatigue, in complement to his Lungs," but Mayo won through. William Byrd, one of the Virginia commissioners, was impressed by his skill, and wrote of him: he "endured the same Hardships and underwent the Same Fatigue that the forwardest of the Men did, and that with so much Cheerfulness as if Pain had been his Pleasure, and Difficulty his real Diversion" (*post,* p. 253). One of the rivers encountered was named in his honor. Byrd's high opinion of Mayo, who was appointed major of militia in 1730, led to their being associated in later enterprises. An expedition in 1731 was prevented by Byrd's illness, but Mayo was not idle, the council directing him to run the boundary between Goochland and Hanover counties. His first wife having died, he now (August 1731) wrote to induce Anne, daughter of John Perratt of Barbados, to come to Virginia as his bride; and she consented. In 1733 Mayo accompanied Byrd on his "Journey to the Land of Eden," and with him "laid the foundation of two large Citys. One at Shacco's, to be called Richmond, and the other at the Point of Appamattuck River, to be nam'd Petersburgh. These Major Mayo offered to lay out into Lots without Fee or Reward" (*Ibid.,* p. 292). Both sites were shrewdly located at the falls line. Within four years Mayo laid out the city of Richmond in a rectangle eight squares long and four wide. Each square was divided into four lots, which were advertised for sale in the *Virginia Gazette,* and each lot brought seven pounds Virginia currency. Meanwhile, in 1732, Byrd had been appointed a commissioner for the crown to determine the southern boundary of Lord Fairfax's proprietary, the Northern Neck. Mayo was selected chief engineer, and when the surveyors had completed their work he combined their plats into a general map "in a Masterly Manner," a comparison with modern surveys demonstrating the almost uncanny accuracy of his work. The duties of the surveyor of Goochland having perhaps grown too onerous for a man of advancing years, in 1739 the council permitted Mayo to employ Ambrose Smith as assistant. Time had prospered him, and his surveys included many broad acres of his own. His will was proved Nov. 20, 1744, and he is said to have died Oct. 20, preceding (*Virginia Magazine of History and Biography,* January 1924, pp. 55–57). He had eight children, four by each marriage.

[J. S. Bassett, ed., *The Writings of "Colonel William Byrd, of Westover in Virginia Esqr"* (1901); M. N. Stanard, *Richmond, Its People and Its Story* (1923); *William and Mary Coll. Quart. Hist. Mag.,* Jan. 1924; Alexander Brown, *The Cabells and Their Kin* (1895); E. G. Swem, "Maps Relating to Va.," in *Va. State Lib. Bull.,* vol. VII (1914), no. 263.]
L. D.

MAYO, WILLIAM KENNON (May 29, 1829–Apr. 9, 1900), naval officer, was born at Drummondtown (or Accomac), Va., son of Peter Poythress and Leah Custis (Upshur) Mayo, and a descendant of William Mayo [*q.v.*], an English civil engineer who came to Virginia about 1723. His mother was a sister of Abel P. Upshur [*q.v.*], secretary of the navy and secretary of state under Tyler. Appointed midshipman from Virginia Oct. 18, 1841, Mayo made his first cruise in the frigate *United States* of the Pacific Squadron, and was in charge of the boats of the landing party at the temporary occupation of Monterey, Cal., October 1842. The following year he was transferred to the *Cyane*. In the sloop *St. Mary's* he saw active duty throughout the Mexican War, including the blockades of Tampico and Vera Cruz and service of the naval battery during the attack on the latter port. He attained the grade of passed midshipman, Aug. 10, 1847, and after study at the newly established Naval Academy, 1847–48, he was for several years engaged in survey and scientific work, returning to Annapolis in 1854 as instructor in seamanship and gunnery. While on this duty he prepared a manuscript, "System of Naval Tactics and Fleet Sailing," used for the instruction of midshipmen. Promoted to lieutenant Sept. 15, 1855, he was on the Asiatic station in the *Minnesota*, 1857–59; instructor in ethics and English at the Naval Academy, 1859–60; and in the *St. Mary's*, Pacific Squadron, from December 1860 to January 1862. Service on this remote station doubtless facilitated his decision to remain loyal to the Union in the Civil War. He was the only member of his family to do so; his younger half-brother Wyndham Mayo joined the Confederate navy.

Early in 1862 he was transferred to the East Coast and became executive of the *Housatonic* off Charleston. After promotion to lieutenant commander, July 16, 1862, he commanded the *Kanawha* of the West Gulf Squadron from November 1862 to November 1863, capturing six blockade-runners and receiving commendation from Commodore H. K. Thatcher [*q.v.*] for gallantry in a sharp action, Oct. 12, 1863, with Fort Morgan (*Annual Report of the Secretary of the Navy*, 1864, pp. 478–79). He commanded the monitor *Nahant* off Charleston from July 1864 until the evacuation of Charleston in February 1865, and then until the close of the war was ordnance officer of the South Atlantic Blockading Squadron, retaining his command of the Bay Point Depot until May 1866. Commissioned commander July 25, 1866, he was engaged during the next three years in technical navigation work at Boston, during which time he designed a new type of navy binnacle. Subsequently, he commanded the *Tuscarora* and the *Congress* of the North Atlantic Squadron, 1870–71; the *Omaha* in the Pacific, 1872–74; and the *Hartford* in the South Atlantic, 1877–79; and was commandant of the Norfolk Navy Yard, 1882–85. He was promoted to captain Dec. 12, 1873, and to commodore July 2, 1882, but failed of promotion to rear admiral owing, it is said, to "infirmity of temper," and retired voluntarily May 18, 1886. His home thereafter was in Washington, D. C., where his death occurred after a brief illness. He was twice married, first to Virginia Kendall of Hartford, Conn., and second to Nannie Glover, who survived him. There were no children by either marriage.

[L. R. Hamersley, *The Records of Living Officers of the U. S. Navy* (6th ed., 1898); *Army and Navy Journal*, Apr. 14, 1900; *Washington Post*, Apr. 11, 1900; *Who's Who in America*, 1899–1900; information from family sources.] A. W.

MAYO, WILLIAM STARBUCK (Apr. 15, 1811–Nov. 22, 1895), physician and author, son of Obed and Elizabeth (Starbuck) Mayo, was descended in the seventh generation from the Rev. John Mayo, first regular minister (1655–72) of the North Church in Boston, and, on his mother's side, from the Starbucks of Nantucket, whalers and merchantmen. His father, it is said, went to sea first as a stowaway, but very soon earned for himself a position on a merchantman. At the instigation of his wife, however, who had an aversion to the sea, he abandoned the calling, settled in Ogdensburg, N. Y., and became a builder of lake and river boats. In that town William Starbuck Mayo was born. Eight years after his birth his father died, and about three years later the boy was sent to the academy in Potsdam. From there he turned to the study of medicine. After studying under two local physicians, he attended the College of Physicians and Surgeons in New York and graduated in 1832. He practised for a few years in Ogdensburg; then he was forced by ill health to travel. His subsequent tour of Spain and the Barbary States left upon him an indelible impression which colored his novels. Upon his return he settled in New York City and resumed medical practice. In 1851 he married Helen Stuyvesant, daughter of Nicholas Warren Stuyvesant. He began writing with minor contributions to a number of periodicals, but it was his fiction which brought him prominence.

The success of his first novel or tale was astonishing, even to the author. *Kaloolah, or Journeyings to the Djébel Kumri* (1849), purporting to be an autobiography of Jonathan Romer edited by W. S. Mayo, M.D., went through not less than nine editions, of which the latest bears the date 1900. Critical notices classed the novel with Melville's *Typee*, a relationship which Mayo disavowed, affirming in the Preface to the fourth edition (1850) that *Kaloolah* was written before *Typee* issued from the press. It is a rollicking tale of Yankee prowess, cunning, and self-reliance in love and adventure on the high seas and in Africa. Its prolonged popularity may be explained by the author's extraordinary versatility in ranging without discrimination from improbable heroism and delicately romantic love, through satire and common sense to practical joking and buffoonery. Only slightly less popular was his novel *The Berber; or, the Mountaineer of the Atlas* (1850, 1873, 1883). In it Mayo set himself to tell an agreeable story which should provide an illustration of Moorish manners, customs, history, and geography—and an exemplification of Moorish life as it actually was in Barbary in that day. Unlike *Kaloolah, The Berber* has a plot, complicated but well controlled, and although its incidents are romantic, the character types, the manners, and the settings are clearly the result of study and first-hand observation.

Mayo's last novel carries out the promise of a portion of *Kaloolah* by returning to the American scene. *Never Again* (1873) pits a Yankee somewhat less impetuous than Jonathan Romer but just as shrewd and self-reliant, against the moneyed society of New York. In addition to the novels mentioned Mayo wrote *Romance Dust from the Historic Placer* (1851), republished in 1855 under the title *Flood and Field,* a collection of short tales not essentially different in type from the novels. He has also been credited with scientific interests, indicated by his *Illustrations of Natural Philosophy* (1850), and by a letter, *To the Hon. Gideon Welles* (1862), on the construction and design of warships. With his generous background of catholic reading, his independent observation, his penetration of character and sanity of view he might, had he written with more singleness of purpose and control, have achieved a much less temporary distinction. He died in New York City.

[C. G. Mayo, "The Mayo Family in the U. S." (1927), vol. II, a manuscript genealogy of which there is a copy in the Lib. of Cong.; obituary in *Report . . . of the Century Asso. for the Year 1895* (1896); the *Internat. Mag. of Lit., Art and Sci.,* July 1851; *Blackwood's Edinburgh Mag.,* Aug. 1849; the *British Quart. Rev.,* Feb. 1851; *N. Y. Tribune,* Nov. 23, 1895.]

A. L. B.

MAYO, WILLIAM WORRELL (May 31, 1819–Mar. 6, 1911), physician, surgeon, was born in Manchester, England, of well-to-do parents, in a family many of whom had been physicians. He attended Owens College, Manchester, where he studied physics with John Dalton. Coming to America when twenty-six years of age, he taught physics and chemistry in New York for some two years. In 1847 he took up the study of medicine with Dr. Eleazer Deming of Lafayette, Ind., and two years later entered the Medical School of the University of Missouri in St. Louis, where he gave instruction in chemistry while completing his medical course. Here, in 1851, he married Louise Abigail Wright, who had been born Dec. 23, 1825, in New York. After receiving his medical degree from the University of Missouri in 1854, he returned to La Porte, Ind., and began the practice of medicine.

In the spring of 1855 Mayo removed with his family, consisting of his wife and two daughters, to St. Paul, Minn., then on the extreme frontier of civilization. His experiences in the next ten years were typical of those of the pioneer physicians of the period. The habit he acquired during this time of failing to collect his professional accounts became fixed for the rest of his life. Besides treating the sick he took part in the further organization of the territory, serving as chairman of the first board of county commissioners of St. Louis County. He located the county seat at a point where the city of Duluth is now built. He took the census of 1855 in St. Louis County. In 1856 he settled on a farm near Le Sueur, Minn., and a year later became a resident of Le Sueur. During this year and the next he also engaged in steamboating on the Minnesota River with James J. Hill.

In 1862 Mayo served as a surgeon with a relief force sent to quell the Sioux Indian outbreak in the vicinity of New Ulm, and in the spring of the following year was appointed provost surgeon for southern Minnesota with headquarters in Rochester, where he soon became the leading physician and surgeon of Olmstead County. In 1871 he took a postgraduate course in medicine at Bellevue Hospital in New York. When in 1883 a cyclone killed twenty-two persons and injured many others in the town of Rochester, Mayo was placed in charge of an emergency hospital for the injured and was assisted by the sisters of the Order of St. Francis. Two years later this Order began the erection of a forty-bed hospital on the edge of town. This original building is still the central nucleus of an institution (St. Mary's) now grown to a capacity of more than eight hundred beds.

Mayo was an untiring practitioner of medicine at a time when country practice in Minnesota was a very laborious task. His fierce struggle to wrest a precarious living from adverse nature in the wilderness developed a rugged manhood which formed a stable setting for, without burying, his scholarly and professional training. He was one of the earliest physicians in the West to use the microscope for diagnostic work. He was a surgeon as well as a physician of keen observation and professional skill. In 1871 he performed his first of thirty-one laparotomies for ovarian tumor. One of the founders of the Minnesota State Medical Society in 1868, he was its president in 1873, and contributed numerous technical articles to its *Transactions* (1871–87). He organized the Olmstead County Medical Society in 1882 and was a member of the American Medical Association for nearly fifty years. From the time they were twelve years of age, his two sons, William James Mayo and Charles Horace Mayo, were his companions and assistants whenever possible.

Mayo took an active interest in politics, serving as mayor of Rochester several times and as state senator twice, in spite of the fact that he was a liberal Democrat living in a Republican state and community. He died in Rochester in his ninety-second year, after an illness which was the result of an accident.

[*Sketch of the Hist. of the Mayo Clinic and Mayo Foundation* (1926); L. B. Wilson, "Wm. Worrell Mayo: A Pioneer Surgeon of the Northwest," *Surg., Gynecol., and Obstetrics*, May 1927; *The Jour. Minn. State Medic. Asso. and the Northwestern Lancet*, Mar. 15, 1911; *Minneapolis Morning Tribune*, Mar. 7, 1911; personal acquaintance.] L. B. W.

MAYO-SMITH, RICHMOND (Feb. 9, 1854–Nov. 11, 1901), statistician and economist, was born in Troy, Ohio, the third child of Preserved and Lucy Richards (Mayo) Smith. He was a direct descendant in the ninth generation of a distinguished Puritan family of clergymen established in America in 1641 when the Rev. Henry Smith, who had come from England some years earlier, became the first settled pastor in Wethersfield, Conn. His mother was the daughter of Seth Mayo of Medford, Mass., also of old New England stock. Preserved Smith emigrated to Ohio in 1839 where he became a successful railroad man and car manufacturer. The family moved from Troy to Dayton in 1856, and there Richmond spent an uneventful childhood. He was graduated from a Dayton high school in 1871 and the same year entered Amherst College. During his college course, under the influence of Prof. John W. Burgess, he became interested in economics and allied subjects. He was graduated in 1875 and went to Europe for further study at the suggestion of Burgess, who offered him a chair in economics and statistics in the new faculty of political science at Columbia, contingent upon his study abroad. After two years of study at the universities of Berlin and Heidelberg, Mayo-Smith returned to the United States in 1877 as an instructor in history and political science at Columbia, beginning a connection with the university that terminated only with his death. From 1878 to 1883 he was assistant and adjunct professor of political economy and social science; in 1883 he became a full professor. In 1880 he was named as one of the five original instructors in the graduate School of Political Science, simultaneously carrying on his teaching of undergraduates. At the reorganization of the university in 1890 he was selected as a member of the council and was continued as such until the year of his death. He had marked success as a teacher in both graduate and undergraduate departments. His course in statistics, said to be the first given in an American university, attracted numbers of able graduate students, many of whom subsequently became distinguished statisticians.

His most significant contributions to American thought and scholarship were in the kindred subjects of economics and statistics in which he became a recognized authority. Desiring to place statistics on an adequate scientific basis, he published many scholarly papers which gained him immediate and gratifying recognition from official statisticians as well as from his academic colleagues. In 1889 he assisted in the revival of the then dormant American Statistical Association and became one of its vice-presidents, a position he retained until his death. In 1890 he was made a member of the National Academy of Sciences, an honor hitherto usually reserved for pursuivants of the pure and natural sciences. He was one of the most active American members of the International Statistical Institute, to which he was elected in 1889; contributed to its bulletins; and attended several meetings (Vienna, 1891; Chicago, 1893; St. Petersburg, 1897; and Christiania, 1899). In 1890 he was elected honorary fellow of the Royal Statistical Society. His best-known writing on statistics is the two-volume work, *Science of Statistics*. Volume I, *Statistics and Sociology*, appeared in 1895 and contained one of the first systematic applications of statistics to social problems; Volume II, *Statistics and Economics*, published in 1899, was designed to show what economic problems could be treated by statistical inquiry. The author was well aware of the limits of the then new science and made no extraordinary claims in its behalf. Both volumes were used as standard texts for years and still remain sources of the first importance.

Though subordinated to his statistical investigations, his study of economics was no less vigorous and sound. His writings in the economic journals cover a range of subjects, but his only book in this field was *Emigration and Immigration* (1890), a treatise largely devoted to the effects of population movements on the ethnical and ethical standards of communities. This book is perhaps the least significant of the three, since he argues from the *a priori* assumption that American political ideals may be treated as a standard. He was one of the founders of the American Economic Association in 1885 and a member of its council, contributing freely to its meetings and publications. When the *Political Science Quarterly* was founded in 1886, he was a member of the original editorial board and supported the publication with indefatigable zeal by his frequent articles, reviews, and skilful editing. In 1895 he read a paper before the American Economic Association on the "Desirability of a Permanent Census Bureau." As a result of his constructive opinion, the Association, conjointly with the Statistical Association, prepared memorials and reports for Congress, and after the joint committee was disbanded, the Economic Association on its own responsibility appointed him chairman of a committee to report on various ways of improving census work. This committee presented a five-hundred-page octavo volume, *The Federal Census, Critical Essays by Members of the American Economic Association,* which was published in March 1899.

Mayo-Smith married Mabel Percy Ford of Brooklyn in June 1884, and had four children. Following a boating accident, he suffered a nervous collapse, and died suddenly in New York City a few months later as the result of a four-story fall.

[E. R. Seligman, in *Memoirs Nat. Acad. Sci.,* vol. XVII (1924), with portrait and bibliography, also in *Columbia Univ. Quart.,* Dec. 1901; W. F. Willcox, "The Development of the American Census Office since 1890," *Pol. Sci. Quart.,* Sept. 1914; *N. Y. Times,* Nov. 12, 1901.] W. R. L.

MAYOR, ALFRED GOLDSBOROUGH (Apr. 16, 1868–June 24, 1922), biologist, the son of Alfred Marshall Mayer [*q.v.*] and his wife, Katherine Duckett (Goldsborough), was born near Frederick, Md., at the home of his grandfather, Dr. Charles H. Goldsborough, a beloved and self-sacrificing physician. Alfred G. Mayor (whose name was legally changed in August 1918 from Mayer) studied engineering at Stevens Institute of Technology, where his father was professor of physics, took the degree of M.E. in 1889, was assistant to Prof. A. A. Michelson [*q.v.*] at Clark University, 1889–90, and then to Prof. L. I. Blake at the University of Kansas, 1890–92. He was strongly attracted toward zoology, however, and in 1892 left Kansas abruptly to study at Harvard. Here his artistic capacity attracted the attention of Alexander Agassiz [*q.v.*], whom he thereafter accompanied on marine voyages to the Atlantic and Pacific, making colored drawings of jellyfish, on which organism he later published several beautifully illustrated volumes. From 1895 to 1900 he was assistant in charge of radiates at the Museum of Comparative Zoology, Harvard, and in 1897 received the degree of D.Sc. In 1900 he became curator of natural science in the new Museum of the Brooklyn Institute of Arts and Sciences, and, in 1904, curator-in-chief.

As an experimental naturalist he found museum work too static, however, and, accordingly, accepted the appointment of the Carnegie Institution of Washington to organize and direct their proposed marine laboratory at Dry Tortugas, Florida Keys. For eighteen years he conducted this laboratory and he edited the fifteen large volumes of researches that issued from it during his lifetime (*Papers from the Tortugas Laboratory of the Carnegie Institution,* vols. I–VI, 1908–14; *Papers from the Department of Marine Biology of the Carnegie Institution,* vols. VII–XV, 1915–22). His own researches included studies of the development, function, and significance of coloration of the wing and wing scales of butterflies; the reactions of butterflies both in larval and imaginal stages; the physical nature and chemical basis of muscular contraction, especially rhythmical pulsation as seen in jellyfishes; the method of formation of coral reefs, based on analytical studies in Torres Straits and American Samoa, in which latter studies he showed that Darwin's theory of coral-reef formation does not apply universally. With those associated with him at Tortugas and elsewhere, he made many additions to scientific knowledge relating to the growth of corals, the formation of limestone deposits through bacterial action, the nature of phosphorescent light, and the significance of the diversity of island faunas.

Mayor's achievements were the outgrowth of a remarkable personality. Like his father he had the fondness of a physicist for precise experimentation. He used a wide range of physical instruments in the study of heat, light, and friction in relation to organisms; and he made extensive use of mathematical analysis. He utilized his facility in mathematics during the World War when he wrote a book on navigation (*Navigation, Illustrated by Diagrams,* 1918) and taught this subject to naval recruits, being commissioned as captain. His interest in the sea was a trait which appeared in several of the Goldsboroughs—notably Charles and Louis M. [*qq.v.*], naval officers—as well as in the merchantmen among the early Mayers. Mayor was slightly below average stature, of athletic build, and with deep-set, blue eyes capable of the liveliest expression. His traits of generosity, companionableness, love of conversation, and sense of humor made him generally adaptable to the drawing room, to marine usage, or to the hut of Papuans. He had the concern for the well-being of his associates that characterized his grandfather, the rural physician. Mayor seemed to have a wiry constitution, but a hereditary weakness in the ciliary muscles of the eyes prevented too close application to the microscope; and when, following influenza, tuberculosis of the lungs became active in 1920, despite a sojourn in Tucson during the winters, he grew rapidly worse while conducting the laboratory at Tortugas and died there at the scientific workshop he had created.

On Aug. 27, 1900, Mayor married Harriet Randolph Hyatt, a sculptor, the daughter of Prof. Alpheus Hyatt [*q.v.*], paleontologist. Artistic talent reappeared in all their four children. Mayor was president of the American Society of Zoologists, and a member of the National Academy of Sciences and other scientific organizations. His published technical works include seventy-five scientific papers, four volumes, *Medusae of the World* (3 vols., 1910) and *Ctenophores of the Atlantic Coast of North America* (1912), also eighteen reports as director of the Tortugas Laboratory, and numerous popular papers.

[C. B. Davenport in *Memoirs Nat. Acad. Sci.*, vol. XXI (1926); *Science*, July 21, Aug. 4, 18, 1922; *Papers from the Dept. of Marine Biol., Carnegie Inst. of Washington*, vol. XIX (1924), containing posthumous papers by Mayor and a bibliography; *Carnegie Inst. of Washington: Year Book No. 21* (1923); *Brooklyn Museum Quart.*, Oct. 1922; Brantz Mayer, *Memoir and Geneal. of the Md. and Pa. Family of Mayer* (1878); supplemented by H. H. Maÿer, *The Maÿer Family* (1911).] C. B. D.

MAZUREAU, ÉTIENNE (1777–May 25, 1849), lawyer and state official, was born in France in 1777. He began school at the age of nine and after his father died, four years later, entered a lawyer's office. When war was declared in 1793 he enlisted in the navy and saw service on *L'Entreprenant* and *Le Formidable.* The latter ship was captured at the battle of Groces off the coast of Ireland during the winter of 1794 and Mazureau was taken prisoner. He was exchanged after four months' incarceration in England and accompanied Delatouche on a legal mission for the French government to Spain, where he remained long enough to acquire a thorough knowledge of the language and law of the country—most useful to him in later years.

After various adventures he found himself at the age of twenty-two inspector of agriculture of French Guiana, but he returned to Paris when the Directorate fell. One evening he was told that Napoleon was about to crown himself Emperor of France, and indiscreetly replied that although he greatly admired Napoleon, he would regard him in that position as the usurper of the throne of the Bourbons. The remark was reported to the authorities and brought about his imprisonment. As soon as he was released he sailed for New York, and after fifteen months spent in New Jersey, in March 1804 went to New Orleans and was soon after admitted to the bar. His industry and his familiarity with both French and English were of great assistance to him in this bilingual city where most of the jurors and witnesses spoke only one of these languages, and where the law required an interpreter to be present in every court room.

For a time he was a partner of the well-known attorney, Edward Livingston [*q.v.*], and in 1815 was appointed attorney-general of Louisiana, a position he repeatedly occupied later. He also served two terms in the state legislature. In his day, he appeared on one side or the other in every important case tried. The best known were the famous Batture Case, in which he argued against his former partner, Edward Livingston, who was conducting a long-drawn-out litigation to obtain possession of a valuable piece of ground formed by accretions from the river; and the case of *The State* vs. *Hyppolite Truette* in which the defendant was charged, under a new law prohibiting duelling, with the murder of Paulin Prué. Mazureau was the prosecutor and his attack upon the *code duello* aroused a great furore in a day when gentlemen considered this method the only one by which a personal disagreement could be settled. Mazureau was short and stout, with a head much too large for his body. As an orator he was fiery, adroit, convincing, and eloquent. His knowledge of the law was encyclopedic, and the income from his practice was great, but his generosity and extravagance were greater, and he died in New Orleans in 1849, a very poor man.

[Edward L. Tinker, *Les Écrits de Langue Française en Louisiane au XIXe Siècle* (1932); E. Mazureau, *Aux Électeurs de l'État de Louisiane* (1827); H. S. Foote, *The Bench and Bar of the South and Southwest* (1876); W. H. Sparks, *The Memories of Fifty Years* (1870); Alcée Fortier, ed., *Louisiana* (1914), vol. II; Chas. Gayarré, "The New Orleans Bench and Bar in 1823," *Harper's New Monthly Mag.*, Nov. 1888; *L'Abeille de la Nouvelle-Orleans,* May 26, 1849.] E. L. T.

MAZZEI, PHILIP (Dec. 25, 1730–Mar. 19, 1816), physician, merchant, horticulturist, agent of Virginia in Europe during the American Revolution, author, was born at Poggio-a-Caiano, Italy, the fourth child of Domenico and Elisabetta Mazzei. Having received there and in Prato an elementary education, he studied surgery at Santa Maria Nuova in Florence. In 1752 he accompanied a Dr. Salinas to Smyrna to practise medicine. Three years later he went to London, where he was a wine merchant for about eighteen years. In 1773 he sailed for Virginia to introduce the culture of grapes, olives, and such other fruits as might be expected to flourish there. Early in 1774 he married Marie (Hautefeuille) Martin.

Mazzei's agricultural experiment was carried on at "Colle," a few miles east of Charlottesville, adjoining "Monticello." It was not a success, mainly on account of the American Revolution, to which Mazzei devoted most of his time and energy. He was an ardent supporter of both religious and political freedom in Virginia. In June 1779, Gov. Patrick Henry sent Mazzei abroad to borrow money from the Grand Duke of Tuscany for the Commonwealth of Virginia. He, his wife, and his step-daughter were captured by the British and imprisoned for about three months on Long Island. To destroy evidence against him, Mazzei had thrown overboard his instructions and commission from the Governor, so when he finally arrived in Europe he found himself without the authority to act. Benjamin Franklin, believing that the federal government alone should make foreign debts, blocked at every turn Mazzei's attempt to borrow for the individual state of Virginia. So Mazzei busied himself gathering useful political and military information which he sent to Governor Jefferson. For his services the State of Virginia paid him six hundred luigi a year from Jan. 8, 1779, to Apr. 8, 1784. Late in 1783 Mazzei returned to America in quest of a consulate, but he was disappointed.

On June 16, 1785, Mazzei sailed from New York for Europe, never to return to America. He published in Paris his *Recherches historiques et politiques sur les États-Unis de l'Amérique septentrionale* (4 vols., 1788). Based in part on materials furnished by Jefferson, this was the most accurate work on America that had appeared in French, but, because of its very lack of extravagance, it failed to gain popularity (Bernard Faÿ, *L'Ésprit Révolutionnaire en France et aux États-Unis,* 1925, p. 136). He had previously written several pamphlets on America. In 1788 he was appointed "Intelligencer to the King of Poland," with a salary of 8,000 livres annually. In 1792 Mazzei went to Warsaw, where he was private adviser to Stanislas II, until the second division of Poland forced his retirement.

His first wife having died in Virginia in 1788, Mazzei remarried in Pisa about 1796, and in 1798 had a daughter, Elisabetta. In 1802 the Emperor of Russia began paying him the pension of 1,200 rubles a year, which the Polish government had granted him on his retirement. This pension continued until his death. In 1813 he completed his *Memorie della Vita e delle Peregrinazioni del Fiorentino Filippo Mazzei.* He died in Pisa and is there buried. This extraordinarily versatile man lived in twenty-odd cities of importance in the old and new worlds, was a naturalized citizen of Virginia, and later a naturalized Pole. He carried on an active correspondence with Madison, Jefferson, Thomas Adams, and other Virginians. A letter to him from Jefferson, written on Apr. 24, 1796 (see article on Jefferson, and P. L. Ford, *Writings of Thomas Jefferson,* VII, 72–78), became famous in the history of American political controversy.

[Filippo Mazzei, *Memorie della Vita e delle Peregrinazioni del Fiorentino Filippo Mazzei* (2 vols., 1845–46); *William and Mary Coll. Quart.,* July, Oct. 1929, Jan. 1930; R. C. Garlick, Jr., *Philip Mazzei, Friend of Jefferson; His Life and Letters* (in press) and article on Mazzei in *Italy and the Italians in Washington's Time* (1933); MSS. in archives of Va. State Lib., and in Va. Hist. Soc., Richmond, and in Dept. of State, Washington, D. C.; P. L. Ford, *The Writings of Thomas Jefferson* (10 vols., 1892–99).] R. C. G., Jr.

MAZZUCHELLI, SAMUEL CHARLES (Nov. 4, 1806–Feb. 23, 1864), Roman Catholic missioner, architect, and schoolman, was born in Milan, Italy, to Luigi Mazzuchelli and Rachele Merlini. The father was a member of an affluent family of bankers long prominent in the financial circles of the Lombard capital. Educated first by tutors at Milan, Samuel then studied at Faenza and at Rome, and in the former city became a novice of the Dominican order in 1823. He left for the American missions in 1828, going first to Bardstown, Ky., and then to Ohio, where on Sept. 5, 1830, he was ordained to the priesthood in the Cincinnati Cathedral by the Dominican bishop, Edward Fenwick.

He departed immediately for the island of Mackinac to commence his missionary endeavors, but three years later made Green Bay his headquarters. From these points he made frequent visits to Arbre Croche, St. Ignace, Sault Sainte Marie, and Fort Winnebago, and also labored a short while in Detroit. He worked among the French Canadians and half-breeds, but principally among the Indians—the Menominee, Ottawa, Chippewa, and Winnebago. He mastered their languages with facility; numerous conversions crowned his efforts; and in 1833 he printed a prayerbook and catechism in the difficult Winnebago tongue. Though accustomed to the polished society of Old-World capitals, he lived cheerfully amid the squalid savages and primitive pioneers of the rough Northwest.

Early in 1835 he crossed the snows on his second journay to Prairie du Chien and commenced the first church for that entire area. He then visited the fast growing villages of Galena and Dubuque and hastened down the valley to St. Louis to make a report of his missions. That same spring, by steamboat, coach, horseback, and foot he traveled seven hundred miles to visit his Dominican superiors in Ohio, and thirteen hundred more to return to Galena and Dubuque. Here he found himself for several years the only priest among Indians and whites for a distance of hundreds of miles in some directions and thousands of miles in others. His *Memoirs* recount his experiences among the rough, hard-drinking, but sincere pioneers. When Dubuque was created a diocese in 1837, he was the sole representative of Bishop Loras [*q.v.*] until the latter's arrival and then for several years acted as his vicar general and missioner extraordinary. Among his daring excursions was a visit in February 1843 to Nauvoo, where he interviewed Joseph Smith [*q.v.*], the Mormon leader, and attempted to convert him. In that year he participated in the Fifth Provincial Council of Baltimore, acting as the theologian of Bishop Loras. He visited his native land, finished his *Memoirs*, written in Italian, and had them printed in Milan in 1844.

Returning to America, he commenced in 1845 the erection of Sinsinawa Mound College for the education of young men, at Sinsinawa, Wis. Of this institution he was the first president and chief teacher. Later he confided its direction to his fellow Dominicans from Ohio, while he devoted himself, after 1847, to the founding of a congregation of teaching sisters, the Dominican Congregation of the Most Holy Rosary. He was chaplain of the first territorial legislature of Wisconsin. He persuaded the first Senate of the Iowa Territory to hold its sessions in his yet undedicated church in Burlington. He was the architect of the county courthouse at Galena; he built the bishop's residence in Dubuque; and he designed the first capitol of Iowa at Iowa City. While acting as pastor of the church at Benton, as chaplain of the sisterhood, and as director of the Benton Academy which he had founded, Father Mazzuchelli died from exposure to a severe blizzard while on a sick-call to a dying parishioner.

[Mazzuchelli's memoirs are available in English translation as *Memoirs Historical and Edifying of a Missionary Apostolic of the Order of St. Dominic among the Various Indian Tribes and among the Catholics and Protestants in the U. S. A.* (1915). See also Rosemary Crepeau, *Le Père Samuel-Charles-Gáetan Mazzuchelli* (Paris, 1932); *Freeman's Jour.* (N. Y.), June 10, 1876; *Golden Bells in Convent Towers, the Story of Father Samuel and St. Clara* (1904); J. D. Butler, "Father Samuel Mazzuchelli," *Wis. Hist. Soc. Colls.*, vol. XIV (1898); "Who Designed Iowa's Old Capitol?," *The Witness* (Dubuque), June 21, 1928; letters and documents in the St. Louis Archdiocesan archives, and in St. Clara Convent, Sinsinawa, Wis.]

M. M. H.

MEAD, CHARLES MARSH (Jan. 28, 1836–Feb. 15, 1911), Congregational clergyman, biblical scholar, was born in Cornwall, Vt., youngest of the nine children of Rufus and Anna (Janes) Mead. His father, a descendant of John Mead who came from England and settled in Greenwich, Conn, about 1650, was a farmer who placed high value on mental training. Charles completed his preparation for college under his brother Hiram in Flushing Institute, New York, and entered Middlebury College, graduating as valedictorian in 1856. He taught in the classical department of Phillips Academy, Andover, Mass., 1856–58, then entered Andover Theological Seminary. He was tutor in Middlebury College, 1859–60, and graduated at Andover Seminary in 1862. He studied in Germany, 1863–66, mainly in Halle and Berlin, taking the degree of doctor of philosophy at Tübingen in 1866. While in Germany he was appointed in 1865 to the Hitchcock professorship of Hebrew in Andover Seminary.

Returning to America in 1866, he was ordained to the Congregational ministry, Aug. 10, at Cornwall, Vt., and in the autumn was inaugurated at Andover. On Aug. 2, 1867, he married Caroline, daughter of Joseph H. and Martha S. Thayer of Boston. In 1871–72 they spent sixteen months in Europe and the Near East, and made a study of Palestine. Shortly after their return, Mead began serving as a member of the American committee cooperating with the English committee in Bible revision, an undertaking in which he was engaged for nearly thirty years. He resigned the Andover professorship in 1882, and the following ten years were spent abroad with his wife, mainly in studies at Bonn and Berlin. In 1889 he was temporarily in America, lecturing in Princeton Theological Seminary. From 1892 to 1898 he was Riley Professor of Christian Theology in the Hartford (Conn.) Theological Seminary. For several years thereafter he gave his entire time to Biblical revision. The American committee did not disband, as the English committee had done when their revision was published in 1885, but continued to work on the projected American revision. Mead was the youngest of the American revisers, and an increasingly large share of the labor devolved upon him. He was deputed to go through the Old

Testament, making notes and suggestions to be sent to the other members for their votes. He prepared the topical page-headings, a large part of the Scripture references, the preface, and an appendix for the first edition; he also revised the paragraph divisions of the English revision. The reading of the proof of the Old Testament fell to him, an exacting labor by which his health was impaired for several years. His work of Biblical revision, for which he had exceptional equipment, stands probably as his most distinctive service in Christian scholarship.

Mead was of slender physique, with quiet, kindly manner. His learning was extensive, his thought well-balanced, his expression clear, often trenchant, with a vein of subtle humor. He translated from the German the volume on Exodus (1876) in the J. P. Lange *Commentary on the Holy Scriptures,* and, in part, I. A. Dorner's *System of Christian Ethics* (1887). He was the author of *The Soul Here and Hereafter* (1879); *Supernatural Revelation* (1889); *Romans Dissected* (1891)—employing an ironic use of conjecture in Biblical criticism; *Christ and Criticism* (1893); *Irenic Theology* (1905). Besides various addresses and lectures he wrote many articles, some of which were reprinted separately.

[G. N. Boardman, "Tribute to Charles Marsh Mead by His Friends," in *Bibliotheca,* Apr. 1912, with bibliography of Mead's writings; *Congregationalist,* Feb. 25, 1911; *Congregational Year-Book* (1912); *Hartford Times,* Feb. 16, 1911; personal recollections of the writer; letters from Prof. Arthur L. Gillett of Hartford Seminary and others.] E. D. E.

MEAD, LARKIN GOLDSMITH (Jan. 3, 1835–Oct. 15, 1910), sculptor, son of Larkin Goldsmith and Mary Jane (Noyes) Mead, was born at Chesterfield, N. H., and was of distinguished colonial stock. He was brought up in Brattleboro, Vt., where his father was a prosperous lawyer. His mother was a sister of John Humphrey Noyes [*q.v.*], founder of the Oneida community. Brattleboro had unusual cultural advantages. Partly because of a water cure established there by Dr. Wesselhoeft, a German political refugee, it was visited by famous persons. The Mead home was a scene of intellectual and artistic activity, and several of the nine children were skilful in drawing and painting. Larkin's sister Elinor was an artist, and became the wife of William Dean Howells. A younger brother, William Rutherford Mead [*q.v.*], was long the central partner in the firm of McKim, Mead & White, architects.

From 1853 to 1855 Mead received excellent training in the studio of Henry Kirke Brown, who was at that time working on his equestrian statue of Washington. In 1856 he established himself in Brattleboro, and on the evening of Dec. 31, built up at a crossroads in Brattleboro a colossal snow figure called "The Recording Angel," which astonished the townsfolk, and later was celebrated in James Russell Lowell's poem, "A Good Word for Winter." This picturesque exploit came to the attention of Nicholas Longworth, of Cincinnati, Ohio, who encouraged him by giving him his first order. In 1857 he completed a nineteen-foot figure, "Vermont," for the dome of the capitol at Montpelier, and in 1861 a marble statue, "Ethan Allen," for the interior of the same building. For six weeks during 1861 he was at the battle front and sent to *Harper's Weekly* graphic sketches of camp life. In 1862 came the long-desired voyage to Italy for study. On the way he escorted his sister Elinor to Paris and gave her in marriage to Howells, then United States consul at Venice. Encouraged by Hiram Powers, the young sculptor established himself in Florence, occasionally going to Venice, there to act as vice-consul in the absence of Howells. On Feb. 26, 1866, he married a beautiful Venetian girl of impoverished noble family, Marietta di Benvenuti. The courtship had begun before she could speak English, or he Italian. Their married life was spent in Florence, where later he became honorary professor of sculpture in the school where Michelangelo had taught.

At about the time of his marriage he had returned to New York, where he showed four popular pieces in marble, "Echo," "La Contadinella," "Thought of Freedom," and "The Returned Soldier, or the Battle Story," a life-size statue representing a soldier and a listening child. What was more important, he brought also a plaster study in competition for the proposed Lincoln monument for Springfield, Ill., the most extensive undertaking of the kind then known in the United States and destined to cost over $200,000. His elaborate design had a professional look and was chosen. It included a bronze figure of Lincoln, with four great groups. To execute the whole in plaster Mead returned to Florence. The bronze casting was done at Chicopee, Mass. The work at Springfield dragged. Foundations were begun in 1869; the statue of Lincoln was dedicated in 1874; the infantry and navy groups were placed in 1877; the artillery group came in 1882, and the cavalry group in 1883, completing a conscientious design, doubtless the best to be had at the time. But from 1865 to 1884, American sculpture experienced a profound change. Younger sculptors, disdaining pseudo-classicism, were seeking inspiration from France instead of from Italy. Mead kept his old allegiance and did his work in Florence, returning home at times for business reasons. In 1876 his large marble statue of Ethan Allen, a vigorous, carefully carved work of its generation, sent by the state of Vermont, was placed in Statuary Hall in the Capitol at Washington, D. C. His "Triumph of Ceres," a pedimental group for McKim's Agricultural Building at the Columbian Exposition of 1893, was carried forward with enthusiasm in his Florence studio, and had many beautiful passages. Its chief lack was what the occasion demanded, a striking decorative effect; he was already listed as "sculptor of the old school." His last important public work was a heroic reclining marble figure, "The Father of Waters," which after many vicissitudes, found a place in Minneapolis, Minn.

Mead died in Florence, leaving a widow but no children. One of the last of the American expatriates, he was not only a "sculptor of the old school." He was a kindly, cultivated gentleman, honorably displaying in a foreign land some of the finest traits of the American character.

[Lorado Taft, *The Hist. of Am. Sculpture* (1930); H. T. Tuckerman, *Book of the Artists* (1867); Chas. Moore, *The Life and Times of Chas. Follen McKim* (1929); *Life in Letters of Wm. Dean Howells* (2 vols., 1928), ed. by Mildred Howells; Mary R. Cabot, *Annals of Brattleboro, 1681–1895* (2 vols., 1921–22); Chas. E. Fairman, *Art and Artists of the Capitol of the U. S. of America* (1927); *Am. Art News*, Oct. 22, 1910; *N. Y. Times*, Oct. 16, 1910.] A. A.

MEAD, WILLIAM RUTHERFORD (Aug. 20, 1846–June 20, 1928), architect, was born in Brattleboro, Vt., the son of Larkin Goldsmith and Mary Jane (Noyes) Mead. He spent two years at Norwich University, Northfield, Vt., and graduated from Amherst College in 1867. Having been influenced toward architecture by his admiration for the classical Capitol of Vermont at Montpelier, he spent a year in an engineer's office, and, in July 1868, entered the office of Russell Sturgis, architect, in New York as a paid student. There he was under the guidance of George Fletcher Babb, who afterwards became a formative influence in the firm of McKim, Mead & White, and a life-long friend of the three partners. In 1871 Mead went to Florence for a year and a half, living with his brother, Larkin G. Mead [*q.v.*], the sculptor, and continuing his studies in the Academia de Belle Arte, where his interest in Renaissance architecture developed. Returning in the autumn of 1872, Mead fell in with C. F. McKim [*q.v.*]. For five years they shared an office at 57 Broadway and helped each other. In 1878 they formed a partnership under the name of McKim, Mead & Bigelow; in 1879, Stanford White [*q.v.*] took the place of William B. Bigelow. In the firm of McKim, Mead & White, Mead managed the office, often conceived the basic scheme of the plan (as in the Capitol at Providence), and acted efficiently as critic of the designs of both his creative partners, who were bent primarily on producing works of art. The association was a companionship both in and out of business hours and Mead's influence was potent. He was especially helpful to the multitude of young men who got their early training in that office.

On the death of McKim in 1909, Mead took up his partner's work as president of the American Academy in Rome, an institution founded after the World's Columbian Exposition (Chicago, 1893) to give to American students of the fine arts opportunity to become familiar, under competent direction, with the masterpieces of all time, and thus to prepare them to solve the problems their own practice would present, and especially to train their appreciation of beauty as the fundamental requirement in works of dignity and permanence. For eighteen years, Mead was the stabilizing influence in this fast-growing and expanding institution for the training of architects, painters, sculptors, landscape architects, and musicians.

A loyal alumnus of Amherst, he had a large part in replanning and rebuilding the college along the lines of effective amenity; he left a considerable fund to foster the artistic side of education. On Nov. 13, 1884, he married, at Budapest, Olga Kilyeni, whom he had known in New York. They had no children. Mead died in Paris and his body was placed with his brother Larkin's in the American Cemetery in Florence.

[M. R. Cabot, *Annals of Brattleboro 1681–1895*, vol. II (1922); *Amherst Grads.' Quart.*, Nov. 1928; L. G. White, *Sketches and Designs by Stanford White* (1920); Charles Moore, *Life and Times of Charles Follen McKim* (1929); C. C. Baldwin, *Stanford White* (1931); *A Monograph of the Work of McKim, Mead & White 1879–1915* (n.d.); *Who's Who in America*, 1928–29; *Jour. Am. Inst. of Architects*, July 1928; *N. Y. Herald Tribune*, June 21, 22, 1928.] C. M.

MEADE, GEORGE (Feb. 27, 1741–Nov. 9, 1808), merchant, was born in Philadelphia, Pa., the son of Robert and Mary (Stretch) Meade. His father, who was probably born in Ireland, went to Philadelphia about 1732 from Barbados and was a shipping and commission merchant with extensive interests in the West Indies. The son was educated under the supervision of his uncle, George Stretch, in Barbados, and at an early age was captain of a vessel trading between the island and Philadelphia. He then established a firm with his brother in Philadelphia under the name of Garrett and George Meade, engaging in importing, freighting, and shipping. They built up an extensive business, became prominent merchants of Philadelphia, and were among the signers of the Non-Importation Resolutions of 1765. Upon the retirement of Garrett Meade the firm became George Meade & Company, with Thomas FitzSimons, Meade's brother-in-law, as a partner. This connection lasted for some years until FitzSimons' public duties forced his retirement. Meade was an ardent patriot and contributed large sums from his private fortune toward the cause of the colonies. During the Revolution he was a member of the 3rd Philadelphia Battalion (1775–76) but did not take part in any military engagements. He served, however, on various relief, correspondence, and other committees and was a member of the Public Defence Association. In 1780 his firm subscribed a large sum toward organizing the Pennsylvania Bank, which was to supply Washington's army with food and clothing.

Meade was a prominent citizen though he was not drawn to public office. He was, however, a member of the common council of Philadelphia in the years 1789–91 and in 1792 was chairman of the board of management of Philadelphia prisons. He was a stanch Roman Catholic and was instrumental in the building of Saint Mary's Church, one of the oldest Catholic churches in Philadelphia. He was also one of the original members of the Society of the Friendly Sons of St. Patrick, established about 1771, and one of the incorporators of the Hibernian Society in 1792. About 1795 he invested largely in undeveloped land in various parts of the country, but he failed in the financial crisis of 1796. He continued to manage his affairs until he was forced in 1801, because of his increasing age and declining health, to go into bankruptcy. His son Richard Worsam Meade, 1778–1828 [*q.v.*], was appointed as his assignee. He had married Henrietta Constantia Worsam, the daughter of Richard Worsam of His Majesty's council, Barbados, on May 5, 1768, and they had ten children. He died in Philadelphia.

[Meade family manuscript in possession of the Pa. Hist. Soc.; R. W. Meade, "Geo. Meade: A Patriot of the Revolutionary Era," *Records of the Am. Cath. Hist. Soc. of Phila.*, vol. III (1891); Geo. Meade, *The Life and Letters of Geo. Gordon Meade* (1913), vol. I; R. M. Bache, *Life of Gen. George Gordon Meade* (1897); *Poulson's Am. Daily Advertiser*, Nov. 11, 1808.]

J. H. F.

MEADE, GEORGE GORDON (Dec. 31, 1815–Nov. 6, 1872), soldier, the victor of Gettysburg, was born in Cadiz, Spain, where his father Richard Worsam Meade, 1778–1828 [*q.v.*], was naval agent for the United States. His mother, Margaret Coates (Butler) Meade, was the daughter of Anthony Butler, of Perth Amboy, N. J. His grandfather, George Meade [*q.v.*], a merchant of Philadelphia, contributed generously to the American cause in the Revolution. His father, after having lived in affluence in Spain, died in Washington, D. C., in poverty, through the failure of the government to pay a just debt. Because of this financial loss, young Meade had to be withdrawn from Mt. Airy School near Philadelphia and sent to one conducted by Salmon P. Chase in Washington. Afterward he attended a Mt. Hope school in Baltimore. Though his tastes pointed toward a collegiate education, lack of funds turned his attention toward West Point, where he became a cadet, Sept. 1, 1831, having received an appointment upon his second application. While at the Academy he was not a particular admirer of the course, and determined to resign from the military service as soon as he could properly do so. He was graduated number nineteen among the fifty-six members of the class of 1835. During his graduation leave he helped with the survey of the Long Island Railroad. As brevet second lieutenant of the 3rd Artillery, he was ordered to Florida. Though he was advised not to go to that climate because of the weakness of his health, he arrived at the outbreak of the Seminole War. After serving a year in southern Florida, where he was stricken with fever which rendered him unfit for duty, he was ordered to Watertown Arsenal, Mass., on ordnance work. There he resigned from the army, Oct. 26, 1836, along with many others who foresaw little promotion in the service. He at once became assistant engineer of the Alabama, Florida, & Georgia Railroad. In 1839 he acted as principal assistant engineer on a survey of the mouths of the Mississippi. In 1840 he was one of the assistants to the joint commission for establishing the boundary between the United States and Texas. During the same year he returned to Washington, where he was married on his twenty-fifth birthday to Margaretta Sergeant, daughter of John Sergeant.

At work now as one of the civil assistants of the survey of the northeastern boundary, he determined with the new responsibilities of matrimony to apply for reinstatement in the army. Accordingly, on May 19, 1842, he was appointed a second lieutenant of Topographical Engineers, his classmates already having attained the rank of captain. As a military engineer he was continued on the northeastern boundary survey until the end of 1843, when he was transferred to Philadelphia in the work of designing and constructing lighthouses in the Delaware Bay. He was on this duty when, in August 1845, he was ordered to Aransay Bay, Tex., with Taylor's army of occupation. He arrived at Corpus Christi

Sept. 14, 1845, a young man in robust health, tall, gaunt, with a hatchet face and prominent aquiline nose. During the Mexican War he was engaged in the battles of Palo Alto and Resaca de la Palma, and was brevetted a first lieutenant (Sept. 23, 1846) at Monterey for performing daring reconnaissances. He was then transferred to Scott's column, participating in the siege of Vera Cruz, whence, because of the superfluity of topographical engineers and the lack of opportunity for further active service, he was returned to Philadelphia. There he was presented by a body of citizens with a sword for his services in the war. From 1847 to 1849 he was employed in the construction of lighthouses in Delaware Bay and in making surveys and maps of the Florida reefs. In 1849 and 1850 he was in Florida in active service against the Seminoles. In 1850 and 1851 he was again in the Delaware Bay at work upon lighthouses and the Delaware breakwater. On Aug. 4, 1851, he was promoted a first lieutenant of Topographical Engineers. In 1851 and 1852 he was in Florida at work upon the Iron Screw Pile Lighthouse on Corysfort Reef; and from 1852 to 1856 at Sand Key. He was promoted a captain of Topographical Engineers, May 17, 1856. He was then ordered to Detroit, Mich., on the geodetic survey of the Great Lakes, his report of which was of such value as to place him in charge of the Northern Lake Surveys from 1857 to 1861.

When the Civil War broke out, Meade, through the efforts of Gov. Andrew G. Curtin of Pennsylvania, was made a brigadier-general of volunteers, Aug. 31, 1861, and given one of the three Pennsylvania brigades with Reynolds and Ord. It was at this time that the close friendship between Reynolds and Meade began, to end only when Reynolds was killed early in the battle of Gettysburg. Meade's first active service in command of his brigade was in the defenses of Washington, D. C., where he assisted in the construction of Fort Pennsylvania, near Tennallytown. In March 1862, he was transferred with his command to McDowell's army, and after the evacuation of Manassas went into the Department of the Shenandoah. In June 1862 he was ordered to the Peninsula under McClellan, when (June 18) he was promoted to major in the Topographical Engineers of the regular army. His brigade took part in the battles of Mechanicsville, Gaines's Mill, and Glendale. At Glendale he received the wound which was to trouble him the remainder of his career and which was to be the indirect cause of his death. The ball entered just above the hip joint, indented his liver, and passed out near his spine. Simultaneously another ball hit his arm. In spite of these wounds he stuck to his horse, directed his subordinates in the action, and was forced to quit the field only through loss of blood. Though afterward his hat was riddled with bullets, his mounts were killed, and his leg was numbed by a shell, he was never again actually wounded. Before he was fully recovered at Philadelphia, he rejoined his command and participated in the Second Bull Run, Aug. 29–30, 1862. When Reynolds' division at South Mountain, Sept. 14, 1862, was without its leader, Meade was placed in temporary command. His successful and skilful advance elicited written praise from his superiors. At Antietam, on Sept. 16–17, he again pressed forward with intrepidity until the ammunition of his troops was exhausted. When Hooker was carried off the field, Meade was placed in temporary command of the I Corps, which he led for the remainder of the battle. He was then engaged under McClellan in the pursuit of Lee to Falmouth, Va., in October and November 1862, during which time he was given the old division of Reynolds, who succeeded by rank to the command of Hooker's Corps. On Nov. 29 Meade was made a major-general of volunteers, and on Dec. 25 was given the regular command of the V Corps, after the disastrous battle of Fredericksburg. On Jan. 26, 1863, he was placed in command of the Center Grand Division, composed of the III and VI Corps. On Feb. 5, when Hooker abolished the grand divisions, Meade reverted to the command of the V Corps, which in the battle of Chancellorsville, May 24, 1863, gave an excellent account of itself in so far as Hooker used it.

It was because of Meade's insight and advice in this battle that Couch and Reynolds both recommended him to Washington as the next commander of the Army of the Potomac, though this act may not have affected the appointment. While leading his corps northward paralleling Lee, he was awakened in the early morning of June 28 by a messenger from the President, who delivered a letter placing him in command of the Army of the Potomac. Thoroughly surprised and displeased, he protested against his selection. Nevertheless, even with his handicaps and his unfamiliarity with Hooker's plans, he quickly adjusted himself to his new office and began at once to carry out his sudden and complicated mission. He at once issued orders for taking up a position on the line, Emmitsburg-Hanover, for the protection of Baltimore and Washington, thus concentrating his forces but making no attempt to destroy Lee's army. The Gettysburg position was an accident induced by a meeting engagement of advance elements. Though Meade generally handled his troops well, he has been criticized for not strengthening his flanks, for holding out no reserve, and for failure on July 2–3 to counter-attack and to pursue in exploitation of his success. His was no Napoleonic victory, nor did he display—doubtless because of the same heckling that had beset all early commanders of the Army of the Potomac—the aggressiveness that he had urged at Chancellorsville. But it must be remembered he had been given the command only five days before, that his troops were exhausted, and that the topography of the country favored an orderly retirement by the master soldier, Lee. On Jan. 28, 1864, he received the thanks of Congress "for the skill and heroic valor which, at Gettysburg, repelled, defeated and drove back, broken and dispirited, beyond the Rappahanock, the veteran army of the Rebellion"; and after the battle he was promoted a brigadier-general in the regular army to rank from July 3, 1863. He was continued in sole command of the Army of the Potomac through the Rapidan campaign and the Mine Run operations. However, when Grant who had been made a lieutenant-general in command of all the Union forces, Mar. 12, 1864, decided to accompany the main army in Virginia, Meade's powers were mechanically curtailed. It was an anomalous situation for both Grant and Meade, which, even with the deference Grant displayed, relegated Meade's work to the tactical rather than the strategical realm. But notwithstanding tense moments, when Meade's high-strung, scholarly nature grew irascible and petulant, he was unswervingly loyal to his superior and carried out the orders given him with skill and fidelity. He was retained in command of the Army of the Potomac continuously from Gettysburg to Appomattox, during which time he was promoted a major-general in the regular army, Aug. 18, 1864.

At the close of the war he was placed successively in command of the Military Division of the Atlantic, and the Department of the East with headquarters at Philadelphia. On Jan. 2, 1868, he was transferred to Atlanta, Ga., in command of the third military district of the Department of the South, comprising the states of Georgia, Alabama, and Florida. He served there until Mar. 12, 1869, when he was transferred to the command of the Military Division of the Atlantic with headquarters in Philadelphia. His work in the South was unusually trying and responsible, because of the almost impossible task of administering the unjust reconstruction laws. His uncompromising attitude and sense of fairness were able to make tolerable a most difficult situation (C. M. Thompson, *Reconstruction in Georgia,* 1915, pp. 179–85). From 1866 until his death he acted as commissioner of Fairmount Park, Philadelphia, the plan and beautification of which are ascribed to his energies more than to those of any other. On Oct. 31, 1872, while taking his daily walk from his office with his wife, he was attacked with a violent pain on the side of his old wound. It was the second time since the war that pneumonia had overtaken him. He died Nov. 6, 1872. There had been six children from his marriage, four sons and two daughters.

Meade's outstanding qualities were soundness and steadfastness. His mind was scientific, and his convictions were deep-seated. These traits, coupled with an intense honesty and unswerving adherence to what he believed to be the truth, often brought him into heated contentions with inferiors and superiors, regardless of person or place. He was not a popular type, but in the field of efficiency his rugged, lofty character outweighed any possible defects of tact.

[George Meade, *The Life and Letters of George Gordon Meade* (2 vols., 1913); R. M. Bache, *Life of Gen. George Gordon Meade* (1897); I. R. Pennypacker, *General Meade* (1901); G. W. Cullum, *Biog. Reg. of the Officers and Grads. of the U. S. Mil. Academy,* vol. I (1891); *War of the Rebellion: Official Records* (*Army*); *Battles and Leaders of the Civil War* (4 vols., 1887–88); Civil War Pamphlets, War College Library, Washington, D. C.; obituary in Philadelphia *Press,* Nov. 7, 1872.]

W. A. G.

MEADE, RICHARD KIDDER (July 14, 1746–Feb. 9, 1805), Revolutionary soldier, was born in Nansemond County, Va., the son of David Meade and his wife Susannah, daughter of Gov. Richard Everard of North Carolina. He was educated in England at Harrow, and later in a small private school. One of his masters declared that while he would never make a learned scholar, he would make what was far better, *vir probus.* His subsequent career justified the prediction. He threw himself zealously into the struggle between England and the colonies, and was chosen (May 8, 1775) member of a "committee of intelligence" in Prince George, the function of which was "to convey any alarm as speedily as possible to the adjacent counties." On June 24, 1775, he helped to remove certain arms from Governor Dunmore's palace at Williamsburg. In the battle of Great Bridge, Dec. 9, 1775, he served as captain of a company under Colonel Woodford. Writing shortly afterward to his friend Theodorick Bland [*q.v.*], he vowed that he would see the controversy with England through to the end or die in the attempt.

He at once sold his estate at Coggins' Point,

Prince George and tendered his services to the patriot cause. He was appointed (Jan. 12, 1777) aide-de-camp to Washington, with the rank of lieutenant-colonel. Highly esteemed by the General, he thenceforth accompanied him on all his campaigns. Being an excellent horseman and possessed of a rugged physique, he was especially useful in carrying orders and reconnoitering; his fine black mare was a sight familiar to both British and American armies. At Monmouth he narrowly escaped capture. He assisted in making the arrangements for the execution of Major André, although confessing that he could not contemplate the event "without a tear" (letter to Bland, *Bland Papers,* II, 34). At the close of the war, Washington counseled him: "Friend Dick, you must go to a plantation in Virginia; you will make a good farmer and an honest foreman of the grand jury of the county where you live" (William Meade, *post,* I, 295).

With part of the proceeds from the sale of his former estate, he acquired a thousand acres of land in Frederick County, then a wild, backwoods region. The enterprise proved so successful that the estate became known as "Lucky Hit." As often as his health would permit, he served as foreman of the grand jury. In 1798 Washington, whom he sometimes visited at Mount Vernon, consulted him regarding the choice of officers for the army it was proposed to raise in view of possible war with France. Meade was twice married. In 1765 he espoused Jane Randolph of "Curles," aunt of John Randolph of Roanoke. In 1780, after her death, he married Mary Fitzhugh (Grymes), widow of William Randolph of "Chatsworth." In a time of great need she had contributed handsomely to the patriot cause. He died "at the seat of Matthew Page, Esq., in Frederick County," of gout aggravated by the hardships of military life. Of his eight children, four were sons and four, daughters. One of the sons, William [*q.v.*], became eminent as the third Protestant Episcopal bishop of Virginia.

[*The Bland Papers* (2 vols., 1840–43), edited by C. Campbell; William Meade, *Old Churches, Ministers, and Families of Va.* (2 vols., 1857); Charles Campbell, *Hist. of the Colony and Ancient Dominion of Va.* (1860); John Johns, *A Memoir of the Life of the Rt. Rev. William Meade* (1867); "Meade Family History: Autobiography of David Meade," *Wm. and Mary Coll. Quart., Hist. Mag.,* July–Oct. 1904; W. C. Ford, *The Writings of George Washington,* vol. XIV (1893); P. H. Baskervill, *Andrew Meade of Ireland and Va.; His Ancestors and Some of His Descendants* (1921).]

E. E. C.

MEADE, RICHARD WORSAM (June 23, 1778–June 25, 1828), merchant, was born in Chester County, Pa., where his parents, George [*q.v.*] and Henrietta (Worsam) Meade were residing during the British occupation of Philadelphia. He attended private schools in Philadelphia and then entered his father's business and while so employed made several voyages to the West Indies. In 1795, as supercargo on board one of his father's vessels, he went to Europe and subsequently toured through England and France, returning in 1796. He then went to the island of Santo Domingo in the West Indies and established a business on his own account. At the end of three years he had accumulated a considerable fortune. After his return to Philadelphia he was married in 1801 to Margaret Coates Butler and went into business, at the same time taking charge of his father's affairs which had become seriously complicated. While on a visit to Spain he decided to establish a commercial house in Cadiz, and in 1804 his family took up residence there. Two years later he was appointed naval agent for the United States at the port of Cadiz, a position which he held until 1816. He resided in Spain for seventeen years, living luxuriously and occupying a favored social position. He gathered a choice collection of pictures and statuary which later formed the basis for one of the first private collections in America. He also took an active interest in the exportation of merino sheep to the United States.

Meade was in Spain during the Peninsular War. At the time of the French invasion he entered into many contracts with the Spanish government involving quantities of supplies of all kinds. In one year alone his vessels brought some 250,000 barrels of flour to Cadiz. In this way he contributed materially to the support of the Spanish cause and Spain became greatly indebted to him for funds and merchandise. In recognition of his services he was offered, but declined, full citizenship of the country. In the confusion which followed the return of Ferdinand VII to the throne, he was greatly embarrassed and delayed in obtaining a settlement of his claims. He also became involved in legal difficulties arising out of his efforts to settle the affairs of an insolvent English mercantile firm doing business in Cadiz of which he had been appointed assignee. He was ultimately arrested and imprisoned in May 1816 in the fort of Santa Catalina at Cadiz. After nearly two years he was released by a royal order, demanded by the United States minister to Spain. In the meantime he had sent his family to America and immediately upon his release moved to Madrid to continue his efforts to obtain payment of the amounts due him. On May 9, 1820, a special tribunal appointed by the Spanish government awarded him a certificate of debt amounting to $491,153.62. Under the Treaty of Florida, signed in 1819, all just claims of American citizens then existing against Spain, to the amount of five million dollars, were assumed by the United States. Meade returned to Philadelphia and later moved to Washington in order to prosecute his claim more vigorously. In 1822 the claims commission refused to consider the certificate of debt which he had received from the Spanish government, demanding original vouchers. Before these could be presented the session of the commission terminated and the fund which had been provided was exhausted. Meade retained some of the most famous lawyers in the country in an effort to obtain a rehearing of the claim and the passage of a bill for its payment by Congress, but was unsuccessful, as were his heirs in later attempts to prosecute the claim. Meade's disappointment undermined his health and he died in Washington, D. C., at a comparatively early age. Richard Worsam, 1807–1870, and George Gordon Meade [*qq.v.*] were his sons.

[Meade family manuscript in the possession of the Pa. Hist. Soc.; R. W. Meade, "Geo. Meade: A Patriot of the Revolutionary Era," *Records of the Am. Cath. Hist. Soc. of Phila.*, vol. III (1891); Geo. Meade, *The Life and Letters of Geo. Gordon Meade* (1913), vol. I; *The Case of Richard W. Meade, . . . Imprisoned 2nd of May, 1816, by the Govt. of Spain, and Still Detained* (1817); *The Claim of Richard W. Meade upon the U. S. . . . with all the Documents . . . Connected with It* (1825); *Daily Nat. Intelligencer* (Wash., D. C.), June 26, 1828.]

J. H. F.

MEADE, RICHARD WORSAM (Mar. 21, 1807–Apr. 16, 1870), naval officer, was born at Cadiz, Spain, son of Richard Worsam Meade [*q.v.*], United States naval agent at that place, and Margaret Coates (Butler) Meade. He was a brother of George Gordon Meade [*q.v.*]. Returning with his mother to Philadelphia in his tenth year, Richard received a good education at Constant's School, Philadelphia, and at St. Mary's College, Baltimore. He was appointed midshipman Apr. 1, 1826, made his first cruise in the *Brandywine* in the Pacific, 1827–30, served in the *St. Louis* in the West Indies, 1833–35, and was promoted to lieutenant Dec. 20, 1837. After varied service afloat and ashore, including active duty during the Mexican War in the *Scorpion* and *Potomac* and a Pacific cruise as commander of the *Massachusetts,* 1853–55, he was still lieutenant when the selection board of 1855 made a drastic overhauling of officer personnel. Meade was dropped, but in 1857 secured reinstatement with the rank of commander as of Sept. 14, 1855. The testimony in his appeal (*Defense of Richard W. Meade before the Court of Inquiry,* 1857) indicates a man of chivalrous spirit, high character, great abilities and energy, but also of an intractable temper which involved him in difficulties with superiors and subordinates. Despite his reinstatement, sea assignments went to others, and for the first three years of the Civil War he was kept chafing as commander of the receiving ship *North Carolina* in New York. At last, in his own words, he "floored all his enemies" (*Army and Navy Journal,* Apr. 23, 1870, p. 566), gained his captain's rank (dating from July 16, 1862), and sailed in May 1864, commanding the *San Jacinto* of the East Gulf Squadron. Misfortune followed him. On Jan. 1, 1865, his ship grounded on No Name Key, Bahama Islands. Though all lives and stores were saved, largely through the commander's exertions, the ship was abandoned. Meade suffered a severe attack of brain fever. In May following he was suspended for three years, and a second trial in February 1866, after appeal to the President, confirmed the suspension. On Dec. 11, 1867, he was retired for physical disability. From his illness, the strain of the litigation preceding, and a paralytic stroke, his mind became clouded, and for a short time in the autumn of 1868 he was under confinement. Secretary of the Navy Welles (*Diary, post*) complained of the powerful influence exerted in Meade's behalf and of Meade's alleged threats of violence. The claims of his father's estate, of which he was executor, were also under litigation at this time, and his death from apoplexy was hastened by an adverse judgment of the Supreme Court two weeks before. Meade was married, Dec. 5, 1836, to Clara Forsyth, daughter of Congressman Henry Meigs of New York and grand-daughter of Josiah Meigs [*q.v.*]. He was survived by two daughters and three sons—Richard Worsam [*q.v.*], Henry Meigs, a naval paymaster; and Robert Leamy [*q.v.*], who rose to the rank of brigadier-general in the Marine Corps.

[H. B. Meigs, *Record of the Descendants of Vincent Meigs* (1901); L. R. Hamersly, *The Records of Living Officers of the U. S. Navy and Marine Corps* (1st ed., 1870); *Defence of Capt. Richard W. Meade, Tried for the Loss of the U. S. Str. San Jacinto on the Bahama Banks, Jan. 1, 1865* (1866); *War of the Rebellion: Official Records (Navy)*; *Diary of Gideon Welles* (1911), vols. II, III; George Meade, *The Life and Letters of Geo. Gordon Meade* (1913), vol. I; *Army and Navy Jour.*, Apr. 23, 1870; Rebecca P. Meade, *Life of Hiram Paulding* (1910), pp. 259–64; *N. Y. Tribune*, Apr. 18, 1870; information from family sources.]

A. W.

MEADE, RICHARD WORSAM (Oct. 9, 1837–May 4, 1897), naval officer, son of Capt. Richard Worsam Meade, 1807–1870 [*q.v.*], and Clara Forsyth (Meigs), was born at his maternal grandfather's home, Fourth and Perry streets, New York. Following study at Fordham School and Worcester Academy, he entered the Naval Academy at thirteen, and after six years' training, four of them at sea, graduated fifth in the class of 1856. Two years later, Jan. 23, 1858, he was promoted to lieutenant. In 1860 he was court-martialed and reprimanded for calling Lieut. Thomas Field of the Marine Corps "a liar and a coward." In the Pacific Squadron at the opening of the Civil War, he was invalided home with fever, August 1861; served as ordnance instructor in the receiving ship *Ohio* at Boston; and after brief assignments in the *Dacotah* and *Conemaugh,* and promotion to lieutenant commander (July 14, 1862), was in command of the *Louisville* on the Mississippi, September–December 1862. Detailed to ordnance work in New York after a recurrence of illness, he had charge of the naval battalion which preserved order in the lower section of New York during the Draft Riots, July 13, 1863. He next commanded the *Marblehead,* September 1863–May 1864, on the Charleston blockade. Admiral John A. B. Dahlgren [*q.v.*] commended him in general orders following his action with shore batteries while supporting the flank of Gen. Quincy A. Gillmore [*q.v.*] in Stono Inlet, Dec. 25, 1863, during which his ship was hulled thirty times in a two-hour bombardment. Afterward, until the end of the war, he commanded the *Chocura* in the Gulf, capturing seven prizes, and on Jan. 22, 1865, cutting out and destroying the blockade runner *Delphina* in the Calcasieu River, Louisiana. He was head of the seamanship department, Naval Academy, 1865–68 (promoted to commander Sept. 20, 1868), and prepared for midshipmen's use *Manual of the Boat Exercise at the U. S. Naval Academy* (1868) and *A Treatise on Naval Architecture* (1868). Subsequently, he also published several translations of French naval articles, and wrote frequently on professional subjects. The famous yacht *America,* used as a training ship at the Academy after war service, was under his command, though he did not actually sail her, in the second America's Cup race off New York, Aug. 8, 1870, in which there were eighteen entries; she finished fourth, and the British yacht, tenth. The year before he had commanded the *Saginaw* on an Alaskan cruise. Admiral Seaton Schroeder [*q.v.*], then under him, describes him as a "well-known, daring, and skillful seaman," naturally kind of heart, but "disconcertingly frank in both look and spoken expression" (*A Half Century of Naval Service,* 1922, p. 15). He had indeed great energy, emotional temperament, aggressiveness, and also combativeness. In 1871–73 he took the *Narragansett* on an extraordinary Pacific cruise —60,000 miles, chiefly under sail, in 431 days—during which he protected American interests in innumerable places, made the first treaty with Samoa (see *Report of the Secretary of the Navy . . . 1872,* pp. 14–15), and according to the Secretary of the Navy (Hamersly, *post,* p. 82), "accomplished more professional work than any other ship afloat for the past two years." After ordnance duty in Brooklyn, he commanded the *Vandalia,* North Atlantic Squadron, 1879–82, Admiral Robert H. Wyman [*q.v.*] declaring that "as a commanding officer he has no superior" (*A Tribute, post,* p. 28). With the rank of captain (Mar. 13, 1880), he was commandant of the Washington Navy Yard, 1887–90; as commodore (May 5, 1892), was naval representative at the World's Columbian Exposition, Chicago; and as rear admiral (Aug. 1, 1894) was selected to command the North Atlantic Squadron. After a very active cruise in the West Indies, during which he was thanked by the British government for the services of the fleet in preventing the destruction by fire of Port of Spain, Trinidad, Meade became dissatisfied with his relations with the Navy Department under Secretary Hilary A. Herbert [*q.v.*], resigned his command, and voluntarily retired, May 7, 1895. Thereafter, he lived at Germantown, Pa. His death from appendicitis occurred in Washington, and he was buried at Arlington. In appearance he was strikingly handsome. He was married, June 6, 1865, to Rebecca, daughter of Admiral Hiram Paulding [*q.v.*], and had a son and four daughters.

[L. R. Hamersly, *Records of Living Officers of the U. S. Navy* (4th ed., 1890); *Army and Navy Jour.*, May 8, 1897; W. F. Brown, *A Tribute of Respect by Lafayette Post No. 140 . . . Grand Army of the Republic in Memory of Commander Richard Worsam Meade* (1898); *Evening Star* (Washington), May 4, 1897; information from family sources.]
A. W.

MEADE, ROBERT LEAMY (Dec. 26, 1841–Feb. 11, 1910), officer of the United States marine corps, was born at Washington, D. C., the son of Richard Worsam Meade, 1807–1870 [*q.v.*], of the United States navy, and Clara Forsyth (Meigs) Meade. Gen. George Gordon Meade [*q.v.*], commander of the Union forces at Gettysburg, was his uncle, and Richard Worsam Meade, 1837–1897 [*q.v.*], a rear-admiral in the United States navy, was his brother. He received his early education at Mt. Saint Mary's College, Emmitsburg, Md., and was graduated from the United States Naval Academy on Sept. 30, 1856, with the rank of acting midshipman. Some months later he resigned his commission in the navy and until the outbreak of the Civil

War served as watch-officer on the United States coast survey steamer, *Bibb*. Seeking active war service, he was on June 4, 1862, appointed a second lieutenant, United States marine corps, from the state of Tennessee, and in July of the following year commanded a company of marines engaged in quelling the New York draft riots. In August he accompanied the Federal expedition of combined land and naval forces against the forts guarding the city of Charleston, S. C., and volunteered his services for the unsuccessful night attack upon Fort Sumter, Sept. 8, 1863, in which he, with a number of others, was taken prisoner by the Confederates (D. D. Porter, *The Naval History of the Civil War,* 1886, pp. 447–49). As a prisoner of war, Meade remained in Charleston for some fifteen months, suffering the hardships of prison life until exchanged. For gallant and meritorious services in storming the forts, he received the brevet of first lieutenant. His regular promotion to that grade followed on Apr. 2, 1864.

The Civil War ended, Meade served on board the *Shenandoah* during an extended cruise to the Orient (1865–69), visiting India, China, Japan, and Korea in the interest of better international relations. During this cruise he surveyed some 2,100 square miles of Korean territory, surveys later utilized by Admiral John Rodgers and his naval command in the occupation of the Korean capital (*Boston Transcript,* Feb. 11, 1910). He was promoted captain, Jan. 22, 1876, and served at Brooklyn and Philadelphia, on lake duty attached to the *Michigan,* as fleet marine officer on board the *Hartford,* at Boston, and at Pensacola, Fla. In April 1885 he accompanied the naval expedition to the Isthmus of Panama, having for its object the protection of the lives and property of American citizens endangered by the revolution. He commanded the marine barracks, Washington, D. C., 1890–92, and on Sept. 6, 1892, was promoted major. His lieutenant-colonelcy followed, Aug. 10, 1898.

During the Spanish-American War Meade served as fleet marine officer, on board the *New York* of Admiral Sampson's North Atlantic Squadron, and participated in the battle of Santiago-de-Cuba. Later he commanded a prison camp at Camp Long. He became a colonel, Mar. 3, 1899, and the year following took part in the China Relief Expedition for the relief of the allied legations at Peking at the time of the Boxer Rebellion. For gallant conduct at the battle of Tientsin, China, he received the brevet of brigadier-general. He was retired from active service with the rank of brigadier-general, Dec. 26, 1903, and died at his home, Lexington, Mass., some years later, after a prolonged illness. He was married in New York City, Feb. 6, 1865, to Mary, the daughter of Admiral Hiram Paulding, who with two sons and two daughters survived him. Interment was at Huntington, Long Island.

[*War of the Rebellion: Official Records (Navy),* 1 ser., XIV; R. S. Collum, *Hist. of the U. S. Marine Corps* (1890); *Army and Navy Jour.,* Feb. 19, 1910; *Boston Post* and *N. Y. Times,* Feb. 12, 1910; personal records on file in the Historical Section, Headquarters Marine Corps, Washington, D. C.] C. D. R.

MEADE, WILLIAM (Nov. 11, 1789–Mar. 14, 1862), third bishop of the Protestant Episcopal Church in the Diocese of Virginia, was born in Frederick (later Clarke) County, Va., the son of Col. Richard Kidder Meade [*q.v.*], aide on Washington's staff during the Revolution, and his wife, Mary Fitzhugh (Grymes), widow of William Randolph. The father was a descendant of Andrew Meade who emigrated from County Cork, Ireland, about 1685, lived in New York for some five years, where he married Mary Latham, a Quakeress, and finally settled in Nansemond County, Va. William attended a private school and entered the junior class of the College of New Jersey in 1806, graduating in 1808 as valedictorian. In preparation for the ministry of the Episcopal Church he studied under Rev. Walter Addison of Maryland, was ordained deacon by Bishop James Madison of Virginia in 1811; and priest, by Bishop Claggett of Maryland in 1814.

The situation of the Episcopal Church in Virginia was then wellnigh hopeless. In spite of the notable devotion of both clergy and people to the American cause in the Revolution the Church had been unable, because of inadequate organization and intense opposition, to meet the changed conditions and had steadily declined, until at the General Convention in 1811 the fear was expressed that the Church in Virginia was dead. Meade entered the ministry expecting to serve in his own community while supporting his family by manual labor on his farm; but the movement of events and his innate ability soon made him a leader in the little group still loyal to the church of their fathers. He was largely influential in securing as second bishop of Virginia, in 1814, Richard Channing Moore [*q.v.*], of New York, to whom is chiefly due the beginning of the revival of the Episcopal Church in Virginia. Recognized as a strong and notable preacher, Meade was such a leader as Virginia needed. Widespread infidelity fostered by the French Revolution and paralysis of the Church for many years had produced a condition of godlessness and license for more than a generation. Meade's character and leadership made him a power for good throughout not only the Episcopal Church but the entire state.

In 1829 he was unanimously elected assistant bishop of Virginia, and from 1841 until his death in 1862 he was bishop of the diocese, which included the present states of Virginia and West Virginia. The revival of the Church begun under Bishop Moore had extended in 1829 to about half of the former colonial parishes; under Bishop Meade it extended throughout the state. Meade was intensely interested in the spiritual condition of the negroes, preaching to them constantly and seeking to arouse interest in their welfare. Early in his ministry he liberated his slaves, although afterwards he believed that this was a mistaken kindness. The American Colonization Society and the establishment of Liberia owed much to him. One of the most influential men in the House of Bishops, he was regarded as a leader of the Evangelicals in the contest between the High Church and Low Church parties. Like many leading Virginians he was strongly opposed to secession, but went with his state when the die was cast. As senior bishop he was the presiding officer of the convention in Columbia, S. C., Oct. 16, 1861, which formulated the constitution of the General Council of the Protestant Episcopal Church in the Confederate States, of which he became presiding bishop. In March 1862, although ill, he was a consecrator of Rev. Richard H. Wilmer [*q.v.*], elected at that General Council as Bishop of Alabama. Meade died eight days later; his body is buried at the Theological Seminary in Alexandria, Va., which he helped to establish in 1823 and to guide throughout his lifetime.

He published many addresses, tracts, charges to the clergy, and sermons delivered upon special occasions. Of more extended works his *Family Prayers Collected from the Sacred Scriptures, the Book of Common Prayer, and the Works of Bishop Wilson* (1834), had a wide circulation. In 1846 he published *Companion to the Font and the Pulpit,* and three years later, *Conversations on the Catechism.* His *Lectures upon the Pastoral Office* (1849), a series of lectures delivered annually for several years to students at the Virginia Theological Seminary, was long in use as a textbook upon pastoral theology; another of his publications is *The Bible and the Classics* (1861). By far the best known of his writings, however, is his *Old Churches, Ministers, and Families of Virginia* (2 vols., 1857). In spite of numerous slight errors and a too sweeping characterization of the unworthiness of the colonial ministers, denied by later students of Virginia history, this book remains an indispensable storehouse of information about the ecclesiastical history of Virginia during the colonial period. He was twice married, first, Jan. 31, 1810, to Mary, daughter of Philip and Sarah Burwell Nelson of Clarke County, who died in 1817; and second, Dec. 2, 1820, to Thomasia, daughter of Thomas and Frances Page Nelson of Yorktown, both grand-daughters of Gov. Thomas Nelson, signer of the Declaration of Independence and major-general of Virginia militia at the siege of Yorktown.

[P. H. Baskervill, *Andrew Meade of Ireland and Va.* (1921); John Johns, *A Memoir of the Life of the Rt. Rev. Wm. Meade, D.D., etc.* (1867); E. L. Goodwin, *The Colonial Church in Va.* (1927); W. A. R. Goodwin, *Hist. of the Theol. Sem. in Va. and its Historical Background* (2 vols., 1923–24); *Addresses and Hist. Papers Before the Centennial Council of the Protestant Episcopal Church in the Diocese of Va.* (1885); Philip Slaughter, *Memoir of the Life of the Rt. Rev. William Meade, D.D.* (1885); Robert Nelson, *Reminiscences of the Rt. Rev. William Meade* (1873); *Richmond Enquirer,* Mar. 15, 1862.] G. M. B.

MEAGHER, THOMAS FRANCIS (Aug. 23, 1823–July 1, 1867), politician, lawyer, soldier, was born in Waterford, Ireland, the son of Thomas Meagher, a wealthy merchant in the Newfoundland trade, who for a time represented his district in Parliament. His mother, of the well-known family of Quan, died while Thomas Francis was yet an infant. He attended the Jesuit college of Clongowes-Wood, Kildare (1833–39), and the English college of Stonyhurst, near Preston, Lancashire (1839–43). He joined the Young Ireland party in the year 1845 and in 1846 made his first appearance as a public speaker at the great national meeting at Kilkenny, over which Daniel O'Connell presided. In the following year he became one of the founders of the Irish Confederation and a member of the so-called "War Directory," and in April 1848 went to France in its interest, bringing back to the city of Dublin an Irish tri-color. Meagher made presentation of the flag the occasion for an incendiary speech, and was arrested July 11, 1848, charged with sedition. In October he was tried for high treason at Clonmel and condemned to death. The sentence of the court was commuted and in July 1849 he was banished to Tasmania, where on Feb. 22, 1851, he was married to a Miss Bennett, daughter of a farmer. Escaping in January 1852, he arrived in the United States in the following May, took out citizenship papers in August, and became the virtual leader of the Irish element in New York City. He lectured throughout the East with considerable success, studied law and was admitted to the bar in 1855, became editor of the *Irish News* in 1856, and practised law from 1856 to 1861. His first wife had died in Ireland in

1854, and on Nov. 14, 1855, he was married to Elizabeth Townsend of Southfield, N. J.

With the outbreak of the Civil War, Meagher organized in 1861 a company of Zouaves which became part of the 69th Volunteers. With his regiment he took part in the first battle of Bull Run, where he had a horse shot under him while acting as a field-officer. In the winter of 1861–62 he organized in New York City the Irish Brigade, and became its commander, Feb. 3, 1862, participating in the battles of the Peninsular Campaign, Second Bull Run, Antietam, Fredericksburg, and Chancellorsville. When his brigade was so decimated as to be non-effective, Meagher resigned his commission and returned to New York City where, June 25, 1863, he was banqueted by a number of leading citizens and presented with a gold medal. Early in 1864 he was reappointed a brigadier-general and in November took over command of the district of Etowah. In the following January he joined General Sherman's army at Savannah, where he was mustered out of the service with the coming of peace. Later in 1865 he was appointed territorial secretary of Montana, and after his arrival in October served for a year as temporary governor in the absence of Gov. Sidney Edgerton. He encountered many obstacles in the administration of his office. In July 1867, while engaged in a reconnoissance on the Missouri River near Fort Benton, he fell from the deck of a steamer and was drowned. Meagher published *Speeches on the Legislative Independence of Ireland* (1853), *The Last Days of the 69th in Virginia* (1861), and other letters and papers.

[Michael Cavanagh, *Memoirs of Gen. Thos. Francis Meagher* (1892); W. F. Lyons, *Brig.-Gen. Thos. F. Meagher* (1870); C. G. Bowers, *The Irish Orators* (1916); J. C. O'Meagher, *Some Hist. Notes of the O'Meaghers of Ikerrin* (1893); *N. Y. Times,* July 8, 1867.] C. D. R.

MEARNS, EDGAR ALEXANDER (Sept. 11, 1856–Nov. 1, 1916), naturalist, army surgeon, was born at Highland Falls, Orange County, N. Y., the son of Alexander and Nancy (Carswell) Mearns. His family was of Scotch descent on the side of the father and of New England descent on the side of the mother. At a very early age he began to take interest in birds and other animals, and this interest, intelligently directed by his parents, was destined to dominate his entire career. He received his formal education at Donald Highland Institute, Highland Falls, and at the College of Physicians and Surgeons, New York City, graduating from the latter in 1881. Having passed the examinations for entrance into the medical department of the United States army, in December 1883 he received his commission as assistant surgeon with the rank of first lieutenant. Among the several stations that were open for his choice, he selected the arid and desolate Fort Verde in Central Arizona as the one that offered the greatest interest to the naturalist. After remaining nearly four years in Arizona he went to Fort Snelling, Minn., where he served for about three years.

Late in the year 1891 Mearns (now captain) was appointed medical officer of the Mexican-United States International Boundary Commission. Through cooperation between the authorities of the commission and those of the United States National Museum and the American Museum of Natural History, he was enabled by September 1894 personally to explore the entire boundary line, from El Paso, Tex., to the Pacific Coast, and he brought together not less than 30,000 specimens representative of the animal and plant life of the region. During the next eight years he collected in the Catskills, at Fort Clark, Tex., at Fort Adams, R. I., in Florida, and in the Yellowstone National Park. He received his advancement to surgeon, with the rank of major, in 1901. Two terms of service in the Philippines, 1903–04 and 1905–07, gave him an opportunity to become acquainted with tropical life. With the cooperation of many associates and in particular of Gen. Leonard Wood, he was enabled to make important collections, especially of mammals, birds, and plants. At considerable personal risk he ascended all three of the highest peaks in the Philippines, something that no naturalist had previously done.

In 1908 Mearns, with two assistants, Edmund Heller and J. Alden Loring, was selected to act as naturalist for the Smithsonian African Expedition. He retired from the army with the rank of lieutenant-colonel on Jan. 1, 1909, and immediately reported for duty on the expedition. He was in the field with the explorers nearly a year, traversing parts of British East Africa (now Kenya), Uganda, and Lado Enclave, returning by way of the White Nile and Egypt. In 1911 he again successfully visited Africa, this time as the guest of Childs Frick. The objective was Abyssinia and some of the less-known parts of eastern Africa. Mearns finally returned in September 1912 and began to prepare a report on the birds obtained by the two expeditions. But the disease, diabetes, from which he had known he was suffering since 1907, so sapped his strength that the task could not be completed. He died in Washington, leaving a widow, Ella Wittich Mearns, whom he had married in 1881, and a daughter. Diphtheria had already taken his son, Louis DeZeraga Mearns, a gifted young astronomer, in April 1912. His busy life as an army surgeon and his extraordinary activity as a collector prevented him from making any large contribution to scientific literature, but he printed more than a hundred articles in technical journals and in publications of the National Museum. His most important study, *The Mammals of the Mexican Boundary of the United States*, Part 1, was published as a bulletin of the Museum (no. 56, 1907). As a gatherer of material for the use of specialists in systematic zoölogy and botany, Mearns made his great contribution to the advance of learning, and unquestionably outdid every other American in his particular field of activity. His zoölogical additions to the national collections number approximately: mammals, 7,000; birds, 20,000; reptiles, 5,000; fishes, 5,000. Other important material that he gathered went to the American Museum of Natural History in New York City. At the time of his death his contributions to the National Herbarium were greater than those made by any other one man.

[Notice in *Report on the Progress and Condition of the U. S. Nat. Museum for the Year Ending June 30, 1917* (1918), pp. 92–94; C. W. Richmond, "In Memoriam: Edgar Alexander Mearns," the *Auk*, Jan. 1918; *Who's Who in America*, 1916–17; *Evening Star* (Washington, D. C.), Nov. 3, 1916.] G. S. M.

MEARS, DAVID OTIS (Feb. 22, 1842–Apr. 29, 1915), Congregational and Presbyterian clergyman, eldest son of David and Abigail (Burnham) Mears, was born in Essex, Mass., a town of shipbuilding fame. His father was a manufacturer of cotton line for the rigging of ships, a quiet man of sterling integrity and business shrewdness. The mother, well-educated for that day, was deeply religious and a fine singer. In 1858 David entered Phillips Academy, Andover, of which the famous "Uncle Sam" Taylor was then principal. Graduating in 1861, he entered Amherst College and received the degree of A.B. in 1865. His years of preparation for the ministry were spent as the special personal student of Dr. Edward N. Kirk [*q.v.*], a noted Boston pastor. On Oct. 2, 1867, he was ordained pastor of the North Avenue Congregational Church, Cambridge, Mass. During the following nearly ten years the church had marked growth and the pastorate was distinguished by outspoken Sunday-evening addresses on the duties of citizens and on social questions, as well as by the effective interest of the pastor in the improvement of church music. He was a founder of the "Monday Club" of ministers in Boston and vicinity. In 1877 he became pastor of the Piedmont Congregational Church, Worcester, Mass. During the first years of this pastorate he led the successful effort to clear off the heavy debt with which the house of worship was encumbered. His advocacy of moral reform was continued. In 1886 a No-license League was formed in the church, and the movement spread to other churches and cities, until a Massachusetts Anti-Saloon League was organized in 1892, of which Mears was the first president. In 1888 he made an extended journey in England and on the Continent.

In 1893 he accepted an invitation to the Calvary Presbyterian Church of Cleveland, Ohio, notwithstanding the determined opposition of his Worcester people. The Cleveland pastorate was marked by activities and results similar to those characterizing his preceding pastorate. In 1893 the Anti-Saloon League of Ohio was organized and Mears, who was one of the founders, became its first president. He accepted in 1895 a call to the historic Fourth Presbyterian Church of Albany, New York. Here for fourteen years, while devoted to the upbuilding of the church, he actively participated in the movement to secure temperance instruction in the schools, in the effort to amend the Raines law in the interest of temperance, and in the sound-money campaign of 1896. After the close of his active ministry he lived at "Orchard Home" on the ancestral estate in Essex, Mass.

Mears was of medium height, of vigorous physique and had a resonant voice. For one of such strong convictions he had unusual ability to recognize the sincerity and appreciate the views of those differing with him. His power of effective speech, his musical gifts, deep pastoral feeling, and capacity for lasting friendships were elements of his strength. He married, Sept. 11, 1867, Frances J. Bentley of Amherst, Mass., who died Mar. 26, 1879; on Sept. 6, 1882, he married Mary Chapin Grinnell, daughter of Hon. Josiah B. Grinnell [*q.v.*], of Grinnell, Iowa. Besides single addresses, articles, and sermons, he published *Life of Edward Norris Kirk* (1877); *The Deathless Book* (1888); *Oberlin Lectures of 1892; The Pulpit and the Pews* (1892); *Inspired Through Suffering* (1895).

[*David Otis Mears, D.D. An Autobiog.* (copr. 1920), with memoir and notes by H. A. Davidson; *Biog. Record of the Alumni of Amherst Coll. 1821–1871* (1883); *Who's Who in America*, 1912–13; *Albany Evening Jour.*, May 1, 1915, editorial; *Albany Argus*, Apr. 30, 1915; *Congregationalist and Christian World*, May 13, 1915; *Continent* (New York), June 24, 1915.] E. D. E.

MEARS, HELEN FARNSWORTH (Dec. 21, 1872–Feb. 17, 1916), sculptor, third daughter and youngest child of John Hall Mears and Mary Elizabeth (Farnsworth) Mears, was born in Oshkosh, Wis., of Scottish ancestry on both sides. Her father was a native of Hawkesbury, Ontario.

and her mother, of Groton, Mass. Both parents were well endowed mentally; the mother had attained modest fame as a writer. In early childhood, Helen shaped figures in any plastic stuff she could find—mud, dough, putty, tar—until her father gave her clay. Later he guided her attempts, and since he had studied to be a surgeon, taught her something of anatomy. At the age of nine, she exhibited at the county fair a clay head of Apollo, baked in her mother's oven. When she was sixteen, photographs of her kneeling figure called "Repentance" were shown to Ward and to Saint-Gaudens, both of whom expressed interest by inviting her to their workshops.

During a few weeks of study under Lorado Taft at the Chicago Art Institute, she received an order for a nine-foot statue, "The Genius of Wisconsin," to represent that state at the World's Columbian Exposition in Chicago (1893). This work, cut in marble, was later placed in the rotunda of the Capitol at Madison, Wis., and won from the Milwaukee Women's Club a prize of $500. With her prize money Helen Mears went to New York for study at the Art Students' League. Here her modeling met approval from Saint-Gaudens, who accepted her as assistant in his private studio. Under this uncompromising but friendly master, her progress was real. Aided by a wealthy woman, she went to Paris and broadened her horizon by seeing museums and monuments, as well as by studying under the painters Raphael Collin and Luc Olivier Merson, and the sculptors Alexandre Charpentier and Denys Puech. While Saint-Gaudens was in Paris, engaged on his Sherman equestrian group and other undertakings, she again acted as one of his assistants. She exhibited in the Salon, and visited Italy.

In 1898, she received in competition the commission for the marble statue of Frances E. Willard, gift of the State of Illinois to the national Capitol at Washington, D. C. Both the first and second blocks of marble revealed bad faults after much work had been spent on them, and were discarded for a third. The statue was unveiled in Statuary Hall in 1905. At the St. Louis Exposition of 1904, her monumental three-paneled wall fountain, "The Fountain of Life" (a work in which it was her good fortune to have the collaboration of Henry Bacon, architect of the Lincoln Memorial), received praise from distinguished critics and won a silver medal. It was the most ambitious project of her lifetime. Saint-Gaudens' faith in her ability appears in the thoughtful letters of counsel he wrote to her about these two efforts, the Frances Willard statue and the fountain, her main endeavor during five years. In 1907, she became a member of the National Sculpture Society.

Among her works are bronze busts, "General George Rogers Clark" in the Milwaukee Public Library, and "Dr. William T. G. Morton," pioneer in anaesthesia, in the Smithsonian Institution. Her bronze bas-relief portraits include those of her mother, Mary Elizabeth Mears, in the possession of the Madison Art Association; her master, Augustus Saint-Gaudens, at Peabody Institute, Baltimore; the composer Edward MacDowell, in the Metropolitan Museum. She created many imaginative figures and groups, mainly in private ownership. Her command of the monumental is shown in the "Adin Randall Fountain," erected in Eau Claire, Wis., 1914. Although competent criticism had already pointed her out as a figure of unusual promise, it is recorded that privation hastened her end. She died suddenly in her studio in Washington Square, New York, surrounded by a quantity of good work in many stages, bearing witness to her spiritual outlook, her intellectual grasp, and her tireless self-dedication. Memorial exhibitions of her works were held in Milwaukee, 1917, in Baltimore, 1918, and at the Brooklyn Museum, 1920.

[*The Reminiscences of Augustus Saint-Gaudens* (1913), II, 29, 30, 185; *Wisconsin History Bulletin*, Mar. 1927; *Am. Art Annual*, vol. XIII (1916); *Catalogue, International Exhibition of Contemporary Medals* (Am. Numismatic Soc., 1911); Catalogue, *Helen Farnsworth Mears Memorial Exhibition* (Milwaukee Art Inst., 1917); C. E. Fairman, *Art and Artists of the Capitol of the U. S. of A.* (1927); P. V. Lawson, "Mary Elizabeth Mears," in *Proc. Wis. Hist. Soc.*, 1916; *Art Rev.*, Mar. 1908; *Biog. Sketches of Am. Artists* (1924), pub. by Mich. State Lib.; *N. Y. Times*, Feb. 18, 19, 1916; *N. Y. Herald*, June 4, 1916. The year of birth is variously given as 1872, 1874, 1876, and 1878, but the weight of evidence seems to rest with 1872.] A. A.

MEARS, JOHN WILLIAM (Aug. 10, 1825–Nov. 10, 1881), Presbyterian clergyman, educator, author, son of Henry Haller Mears and his wife, Ann Barbara (Birkinbine) of Reading, Pa., was a descendant in the fifth generation from William Mears, who emigrated from Everton, England, about 1735, and settled in Georgia. John Mears, son of the emigrant, settled in Philadelphia about 1754. Although identified with the Society of Friends, he was during the Revolutionary War one of the "fighting Quakers." Later he removed to Reading, and then, possessed of the pioneer spirit, pushed on over the mountains and laid out and built the road connecting the valleys of the Schuylkill and Susquehanna rivers, founding the town of Catawissa. His grandson, Henry Haller Mears, was a successful business man in Philadelphia and an elder in the Presbyterian Church. John Wil liam Mears was born in Reading, and graduated from Delaware College in 1844, studied at the Yale Scientific School, 1846–48, and in the Divinity School, 1848–49. Three years later, on Apr. 15, 1852, he was ordained to the Presbyterian ministry. On Sept. 2, of the same year, he married Phebe A. H. Tatem. He was pastor at Camden, N. J., 1852–53; at Elkton, Md., 1854–57; and at Milford, Del., 1857–60. As a representative of the views of the "new school" of the Presbyterian Church he was one of the editors of the *American Presbyterian* of Philadelphia from 1860 to 1865, and thereafter was editor and publisher until 1870, when the periodical was merged with the *New York Evangelist.*

On Mar. 6, 1871, he was appointed to the Albert Barnes Professorship of Intellectual and Moral Philosophy at Hamilton College, Clinton, N. Y., in which connection he continued until his death, at Clinton, ten years later. His inaugural address (*American Presbyterian Review,* October 1871) reveals his attitude as that of an idealist, in opposition to materialistic types of philosophy. He was recognized by his colleagues and students as "a thorough scholar, possessed of a mind that was inquisitive and keenly analytical." On the platform and with the pen he was master of a vigorous style. He was successful in securing important accessions to the college library, of which he had charge for a time. He also gave instruction in German and French. Out of his classroom instruction in the philosophy of Kant came the plan of celebrating the centennial of the publication of the Critique of Pure Reason. On that occasion he delivered an address at Saratoga, N. Y., July 6, 1881, which was later given before the Concord School of Philosophy and printed in the *Journal of Speculative Philosophy* (January, July 1881). He was interested in public questions and identified himself with the Prohibition party, standing as their candidate for Congress in 1878, and for governor of New York in 1879. Through his active efforts the sentiment that existed in central New York against the institution of "complex marriage" as practised at the Oneida Community found effective expression, with the result that in 1879 that feature of the Community system was voluntarily abandoned. In 1878 he was president of the New York State Teachers' Association.

His earliest published work, *The Bible in the Workshop* (1857), dealt with the relation of Christianity to labor. Later works, published by the Presbyterian Board, were: *The Martyrs of France* (1860); *The Beggars of Holland and the Grandees of Spain* (1867); *The Story of Madagascar* (1873); *Heroes of Bohemia* (1874); *From Exile to Overthrow* (1881). His address, "The Presbyterian Element in our National Life and History," delivered before the Synod of Central New York in 1876, was published in the second part of P. H. Fowler's *Historical Sketch of Presbyterianism within the Bounds of the Synod of Central New York* (1877). In 1879 his *Brief English-French Compend of the Grammar of the French Language* appeared.

[*Notice of Henry Haller Mears, with a Geneal. of the Mears Family* (1873); H. C. Kirk, *A Hist. of the N. Y. State Teachers' Asso.* (1883); *Am. Socialist,* Aug. 28, Sept. 4, 1879; *Utica Herald,* Feb. 15, Aug. 30, Sept. 1, 1879, Nov. 11, 14, 1881.] E. F.

MEARS, OTTO (May 3, 1840–June 24, 1931), Colorado pioneer and roadbuilder, was born in Courland, Russia, of mixed English and Hebrew stock. Orphaned at the age of two, he was taken into the family of an uncle who had thirteen children. When ten years old, he emigrated to California, where he was to have met an uncle, but failed to find him. In a strange land, unable to speak English, the boy was thrown upon his own resources. He began selling newspapers and later took odd jobs of various kinds. At the outbreak of the Civil War he enlisted in Company H of the 1st California Volunteers and saw service in the New Mexico region. When his term expired he became a store clerk in Santa Fé, then he began business for himself at Conejos, Colo., in 1865. With a partner he established a pioneer sawmill and a gristmill, and to increase the grists of the flourmill, he began to grow wheat. He brought the first mower, reaper, and threshing machine into the region, much to the astonishment of his Mexican neighbors.

Mears found a demand for flour in the mountain mining camps to the north, but there was no wagon road to this market. He therefore built a road over Poncho Pass. This incidental project inaugurated the great road-building projects that were to become his chief contribution to the development of Colorado. When rich mines were discovered in the inaccessible San Juan Mountains, he organized a company and built a toll road to the region. To aid in promoting the district he published newspapers at Saguache and Lake City. He extended his system of toll roads until they embraced 300 miles of road. After the Meeker massacre of 1879, Mears assisted in rescuing the women captives. He then accompanied an Indian delegation to Washington where a treaty was negotiated, further reducing the Indian reservation. The Utes at home refused at first to accept the treaty, but Mears secured their acceptance by privately paying each Indian two dollars. Charges of bribery were preferred against him, but were dismissed by the secretary of the interior, who reimbursed him for the $2,800 he had paid the Indians.

Mears continued his toll-road building and operated freighting outfits and pack trains. Then he began railroad construction, building the Rio Grande Southern and the Silverton Northern railroads in southwestern Colorado. He also acquired an interest in certain mining and smelter properties in the district. In 1884 he was elected to the Colorado legislature and continued for many years thereafter as an important influence in the Republican party of the state. He accumulated a fair-sized fortune, much of which was lost in the panic of 1893. His last railroad venture was the building of the Chesapeake Beach Railroad in Maryland. He spent his last years in California where he developed ranch and hotel property. In 1870 he had married Mary Kampfschulte, by whom he had two daughters. His portrait appears in one of the stained-glass windows of the Colorado Capitol and a historical tablet is set in the granite wall of the mountain beside one of his picturesque pioneer roads in the San Juan Mountains near the present town of Ouray, Colo. He died at Pasadena, Cal.

[Sidney Jocknick, *Early Days on the Western Slope of Colo. and Campfire Chats with Otto Mears, the Pathfinder* (1913); *The Colo. Blue Book*, 1891; *Ann. Report of the Commissioner of Indian Affairs . . . for the Year 1881*; W. F. Stone, *Hist. of Colo.*, vol. IV (1919); J. C. Smiley, *Hist. of Denver* (1901); J. H. Baker and L. R. Hafen, *Hist. of Colo.* (1927), vol. V; *Daily Press* (Montrose, Colo.), Aug. 30, 1926; *Denver Post*, June 24, 1931; *Rocky Mountain News*, June 25, 1931; information as to certain facts from Mears's daughter, Mrs. J. R. Pitcher, and from his associates.]

L. R. H.

MEASE, JAMES (Aug. 11, 1771–May 14, 1846), physician, scientist, and author, the son of John and Esther (Miller) Mease, was born in Philadelphia, Pa. His father was a wealthy shipping merchant and a Revolutionary patriot. James entered the University of Pennsylvania in 1784 and after graduating in the College in 1787, began a course in the medical school of the same institution, receiving the degree of M.D. in 1792. In August 1790, while he was still a student, he published an article on hydrophobia in the *American Magazine*. When he prepared his thesis for his medical degree, he enlarged the same subject in his *Inaugural Dissertation on the Disease Produced by the Bite of a Mad Dog or Other Rabid Animal* (1792). The essay was dedicated to Benjamin Rush, who had been one of his professors. In 1808 he published in the *Philadelphia Medical Museum* (vol. V, no. 1) a paper revealing the quackery practised in connection with diseases produced by the bites of snakes and mad dogs. During the War of 1812 he served as a hospital surgeon (Sept. 2, 1814–June 15, 1815). He became identified with many of the organizations of Philadelphia. He was one of the managers of the "Company for the Improvement of the Vine," in connection with which he developed a vineyard, and he was a leader in the organization of the Pennsylvania Horticultural Society. Many of his papers were read before the American Philosophical Society to which he was elected in 1802 and which he served from 1824 to 1830 as curator and from 1832 to 1836 as councilor. He was one of the founders and first vice-president of the Philadelphia Athenæum.

Mease wrote, edited, or compiled several medical works, although he is principally remembered for his contributions to literature unidentified with his profession. Of his printed works, his *Picture of Philadelphia* (1811) is best known, but his *Geological Account of the United States* (1807), a physical and commercial geography, was a valuable compilation and a pioneer work in its field. He edited *The Surgical Works of the Late John Jones, M.D.* (1795); the first American edition of *The Domestic Encyclopædia* of A. F. M. Willich (1803–04); and *Archives of Useful Knowledge* (2 vols., 1811–12). In addition, he wrote *An Address on the Progress of Agriculture* (1817); *Address on the Subject of Establishing a Pattern Farm in the Vicinity of Philadelphia* (1818); "Description of Some of the Medals Struck in Relation to Important Events in North America," published in the *Collections of the New York Historical Society* (vol. III, 1821); *Observations on the Penitentiary System and Penal Code of Pennsylvania* (1828); *On the Utility of Public Loan Offices and Savings Funds by City Authorities* (1836); and *Thermometrical Observations as Connected with Navigation* (1841). He married Sarah, daughter of Pierce Butler [*q.v.*], United States senator from South Carolina in the First Congress, July 3, 1800, and their two sons, in order to secure an inheritance, later had their names changed to Butler. One of these, Pierce Butler, married Frances Anne Kemble [*q.v.*], actress and poetess. Mease died in Philadelphia and lies buried in the ground of the Third Presbyterian Church in that city.

[J. T. Scharf and Thompson Westcott, *Hist. of Phila.* (1884), vols. I and II; H. A. Kelly and W. L. Burrage, *Am. Medic. Biogs.* (1920); Henry Simpson, *The Lives of Eminent Philadelphians* (1859); *Univ. of Pa.: Biog. Cat. of the Matriculates of the Coll., 1749–1893* (1894); *The Athenæum of Phila.* (1884); *Poulson's Am. Daily Advertiser*, July 7, 1800; *North American* (Phila.), May 15, 1846.]

J. J.

MEASON, ISAAC (1742–Jan. 23, 1818), pioneer ironmaster west of the Alleghanies, came from Virginia before 1771 and settled upon a 323-acre tract of land called "Mount Pleasant," in what is now Fayette County, Pa. In some records his name appears as Mason, and he was probably a member of a well-to-do family of that name in Sussex County, Va. He took steps to secure his land in southwestern Pennsylvania within one year after purchase of the land from the proprietors had become legal. Since a definite boundary line between Pennsylvania and Virginia was not determined until October 1786, for a number of years the uncertainty of allegiance caused legal confusion in the Western country. Although Isaac Meason had bought his land from Pennsylvania, he was recommended in 1775 as a proper person to be added to the commission of the peace for Augusta County, Va. There is reason to believe that in 1776 he served in the Continental Army under Col. Anthony Wayne (*Pennsylvania Archives,* 5 ser., II, 1906, p. 150). On Apr. 28, 1778, Thomas Gist swore that, being a magistrate, in April 1772 he had "solemnized the wrights of Matrimony between Isaac Meason and Catharine Harrison," whose father was Lawrence Harrison (Yohogania County Court Records, quoted by Crumrine, *post,* p. 217; Ellis, *post,* p. 527). Other witnesses said that at the time all parties, including Catharine, were required by Isaac Meason to swear "not to divulge said marriage." Isaac and Catharine became the parents of two sons and two daughters. In October 1779, Meason was elected to the Pennsylvania Assembly from Westmoreland County. During the Revolution he was among those who wrote to the state government of the dangers threatening western settlements; in 1782 his brother-in-law, William Harrison, was captured, burned, and cut in pieces by the savages. In October 1783, Meason was elected by Westmoreland County to the Supreme Executive Council of Pennsylvania.

The first recorded reference to iron ore in this section of Pennsylvania occurred in 1780 when Col. William Crawford, one of Meason's neighbors, surveyed a farm on the Monongahela "to include a bank of iron ore" (Ellis, p. 233). By 1791 Meason had established Union Furnace on Dunbar Creek, the first successful iron works west of the Alleghany Mountains. Two years later he formed a partnership with Moses Dillon and John Gibson as Meason, Dillon & Company, and built a larger furnace. Here were manufactured in great numbers the "castings, stoves, pots, sugar kettles, salt kettles and other articles" needed by the thousands of immigrants who at that time began to flock over the mountain and down the Ohio River to the country further West. The trade brought Meason such wealth that in 1803 he erected a splendid Georgian mansion of limestone at Mount Braddock.

In 1816, despite those who urged him "not to impose upon the old gentleman," one Thomas C. Lewis, a Welshman, persuaded Meason to finance a mill for puddling and rolling bar iron. Lewis, who had learned the process in Wales, had tried without avail for more than a year to convince Eastern iron masters that iron could be rolled into bars. Meason, by financing Lewis's project, contributed one more step to the development of the Western Pennsylvania iron and coal industry in which he had been the first to achieve success. When he died he left to his heirs over 20,000 acres of the best coal land in Western Pennsylvania, in addition to Middleton Iron Works, Dunbar Furnace, Mount Vernon Furnace, Union Furnace, Maria Forge and Union Forge, toll ferries and bridges, gristmills, rolling-mills, salt works, the town of New Haven, and lands in other parts of Pennsylvania and Kentucky.

[Account books of Union Ironworks, Mount Vernon Forge, etc., in the Uniontown, Pa., Public Library; *The Jour. of the Rev. Francis Asbury* (3 vols., 1821); court records, deeds, wills, etc., of Fayette County, Pa.; *Pa. Archives,* 1 ser. IX (1854), 5 ser. II (1906); gravestone inscriptions; Boyd Crumrine, *Hist. of Washington County, Pa.* (1882); Franklin Ellis, *Hist. of Fayette County, Pa.* (1882), esp. pp. 502–03.] E. A.

MECHEM, FLOYD RUSSELL (May 9, 1858–Dec. 11, 1928), lawyer, teacher, author, was born at Nunda, N. Y., the son of Isaac J. and Celestia (Russell) Mechem. He attended the public schools at Battle Creek, Mich., and Titusville, Pa. While he was still a boy, his father died leaving him to assume part of the responsibility of supporting the family. Deprived of opportunity to attend college, he completed his education outside. At the age of twenty-one he was admitted to the Michigan bar and for the following few years devoted himself to the practice of law, first in Battle Creek (1879–87), then in Detroit (1887–93). In 1891–92 he held a professorship at the Detroit College of Law and from that time on devoted the greater part of his time to legal education. In 1892 he became a member of the faculty of the University of Michigan and remained there, teaching and writing, until 1903 when he moved to Chicago to assume a professorship in the newly organized law school of the University of Chicago. He remained in this position until his death. He was married to Jessie Collier, Dec. 4, 1884, and they had two sons. He was president for several years of the University of Chicago Settlement; a member of the district appeal board, number 1, northern district of Illinois; and a member of the summer-session law faculty of Columbia University (1919, 1920), the University of Colorado (1922), and Stanford University (1923).

Mechem was internationally known as an authority on agency, partnership, sales, and corporations, and his published treatises and his numerous articles in law reviews illustrate the precision of his writing and his broad conception of legal problems. Any writing to him included the labored exhaustion of all the contributory subject matter, and his citations were strengthened by his intimate knowledge of the allied cases. The portion of the world of knowledge he had made his own lay in his mind in orderly array. One of his outstanding characteristics was his complete independence of thought, his habit of reëxamining for himself opinions however confidently they might be entertained even by those whose judgment he most respected. He was wont to say that although almost everybody's believing a thing may not create a presumption of its being false, it certainly does not prevent its being so. His basic political outlook was occasionally reflected in his teaching to the great advantage of his students, who were coming to maturity during a period when contemporary thought was submerging the individual for the "social good" without pointing out that this, like everything else, costs something. His conviction that the more important ultimate values were individual, not social, served to warn students of the half-truth of contemporary thought which all but completely lost sight of the individual. Nor was his view on this matter the result of an uninformed conservatism; it was a thoughtfully developed philosophy.

Mechem's most notable work was his *Treatise on the Law of Agency* (1889), revised and republished in 1914, which more than any other single work shaped the law of agency in the United States. Next in importance was his *Treatise on the Law of Sale of Personal Property* (2 vols., 1901), an exhaustive study, which has been widely cited by the courts. His other works, *A Treatise on the Law of Public Offices and Officers* (1890); his edition (1891) of Robert Hutchinson's *Treatise on the Law of Carriers*; and his *Elements of the Law of Partnership* (1896), as well as his case books in agency, partnership, and damages, exerted a strong influence in shaping contemporary legal education. In November 1923 he undertook the task of directing the "Restatement of the Law of Agency" for the American Law Institute. Without neglecting his heavy teaching program, he worked continuously on this project. It was a gigantic undertaking and he had hoped to be able to complete it, but he was taken suddenly ill and died of influenza before the work was finished.

[H. A. Bigelow, memoir in *Am. Bar Asso. Jour.*, Mar. 1929; *Ill. Law Rev.*, Feb. 1929; *Ann. Report of the Ill. State Bar Asso.*, 1929, pp. 403–04; *Who's Who in America*, 1928–29; *Chicago Daily Tribune*, Dec. 12, 1928.]

H. O.

MECOM, BENJAMIN (b. Dec. 29, 1732), printer, born at Boston, Mass., was the third of the twelve children of Edward Mecom and Jane, youngest sister of Benjamin Franklin. He was apprenticed to James Parker of New York City, whose business had been established by Franklin in 1742 as a copartnership. Franklin also established the first printing office in Antigua with a manager, in 1748, who died in midsummer of 1752; whereupon Franklin appointed his nephew as his new manager on shares. Mecom sailed from Philadelphia on Aug. 20, 1752, and at St. John found an equipped printery, the only one in the Leeward Islands, with an established, though sometime suspended, newspaper, the *Antigua Gazette,* which he revived, with a new serial numbering, in November. It was a weekly until January 1755 and thereafter came out thrice a week, until June 26, 1756, or later. Franklin had planned to give this business to his nephew, but in view of his youth, and to steady him, held him under strict terms, which irked Mecom because he wished to be independent. Mecom made the fact known and was offended when his uncle long delayed an answer, and notified him of his decision to quit Antigua. The printing outfit was shipped to Franklin, with whom he later settled all accounts honorably, thereby becoming its owner. He sent it to Boston and there set himself up as a printer and bookseller at Cornhill, before June 1757.

Mecom printed editions of *The New-England Primer Enlarged* (1757) and *The New-England Psalter* (1758) for the Boston booksellers on terms so low as to be unprofitable. Among a variety of pieces printed during his Boston career, the most interesting were the first separate collection of Franklin's Poor Richard proverbs, brought out in 1758 as *Father Abraham's Speech* (2nd ed., 1760), and the *New-England Magazine,* which in three numbers ran from August 1758 to March 1759. His business career at "The New Printing-Office" at Boston ended in 1762, probably because he was a very poor business manager. Thomas (*post,* I, pp. 32, 260) credits him, so far as he knew, with being "the first person in this country . . . who attempted stereotype printing." Mecom moved his outfit to New York early in 1763, and there established the "Modern Printing-Office on Rotten-Row." He attempted to issue a newspaper, the *New-York Pacquet,* with a zero trial number appearing on July 11, 1763. The only other extant issue is Number 6, for Aug. 22, 1763.

He failed in New York. Among his creditors was Parker, with whom, by Franklin's consent, the book stock and old Antigua printing outfit were stored as security. Mecom rented Parker's New Haven printery, which was really Franklin's property, and arrived at New Haven early in 1765 to print books and pamphlets, and also to serve as Parker's deputy in the post-office. On July 5, 1765, he revived the *Connecticut Gazette,* which he carried on till Feb. 19, 1768. Failure in liquidating debts and paying rent to Parker forced his resignation from the postal service in February 1767. But as the press was his uncle's property, he continued to use it until he took it to Philadelphia in 1768 to start anew. Here, in January 1769, he began the *Penny Post,* a diminutive news sheet, issued thrice a week, which died after only nine issues. In September 1770 he petitioned for a license to sell spirituous liquors in Philadelphia, in order "to support a Number of young growing Children." However, instead of becoming a rum seller, he got work at his trade with William Goddard, and when the latter removed to Baltimore in 1774, Mecom took his family to Burlington, N. J., where he was employed by Isaac Collins. A sad last notice remains of him in a letter from William Smith of Burlington to Franklin, on July 19, 1776, saying that Mecom was often *non compos mentis* and dangerous, and bidding that he be put in a hospital or incarcerated.

[The best source is Wilberforce Eames, "The Antigua Press and Benj. Mecom, 1748–65," in *Proc. Am. Antiquarian Soc.,* n.s., vol. XXXVIII (1929), and separately reprinted (1929). See also: Isaiah Thomas, *The Hist. of Printing in America* (2nd ed., 2 vols., 1874); C. S. Brigham, "Bibliog. of Am. Newspapers," *Proc. Am. Antiquarian Soc.,* n.s., vol. XXIII (1913); vol. XXX (1921); C. R. Hildeburn, *Sketches of Printers and Printing in Colonial N. Y.* (1895); H. S. Hall, article in the *New England Mag.,* Jan. 1906; Parker's letters to Franklin in *Proc. Mass. Hist. Soc.,* 2 ser., vol. XVI (1903).] V. H. P.

MEDARY, MILTON BENNETT (Feb. 6, 1874–Aug. 7, 1929), architect and architectural consultant, was born in Philadelphia of parents native to that city, Milton Bennett and Mary Emma (Cregar) Medary. Trained at the University of Pennsylvania, where he graduated (B.A.) in 1894, he was steeped in Philadelphia traditions, which he broadened but did not transcend. A year of travel in Europe preceded his architectural apprenticeship in the office of Frank Miles Day [*q.v.*], whose example of public service the pupil ever followed. For ten years (1895–1905) he was a member of the firm of Field & Medary; for five years he practised alone; in 1910 he entered the firm of Zantzinger, Borie & Medary, in which association he continued until his death. On Dec. 27, 1900, he married Hannah Leech Stadelman, of Bala, a suburb of Philadelphia, where they made their home and reared a family.

Gothic architecture appealed to his nature. Infinite detail within clearly defined structural form delighted his sensitive soul. In his art, as in his life, he sought first the pattern and, that determined, he filled it with richness and beauty. Endowed with the faculty of clear thinking and direct, forceful, and picturesque expression, he became a leader among his fellows and a convincing and persuasive advocate with clients in national as well as in private enterprises.

Early in his practice he undertook the Washington Memorial Chapel at Valley Forge, carrying on the work through the years as money came, and putting into the design the evidences of his own expanding and ripening thought. There, where as nowhere else the soul of the Revolution revealed itself and where today the natural scenery imposes a sense of tragic solemnity, the intricately wrought Gothic chapel wins a response which a structure historically more appropriate might fail to evoke. The Divinity School, Philadelphia, the Foulke and Henry dormitories at Princeton, the Penn Athletic Club, and hospitals in Philadelphia and Bryn Mawr are distinctly his conceptions. All show the influence of his Gothic predilections. His preliminary sketches for Penn Charter School in Germantown, however, give abundant evidence of a fine feeling for the colonial type of architecture with its good proportions, flexibility, simple straightforwardness, and economy of construction—traits for which he himself was conspicuous, and which he repeatedly expressed in city-planning problems. The culminating work of his career is the carillon tower designed for Edward A. Bok at Mountain Lake, Fla., on which he spent infinite time and patience. He had the collaboration and sympathetic cooperation of Frederick Law Olmsted in the landscape setting. The resulting structure, so individual in conception, in service, and in isolation, will stand apart during the generations as a memorial to the donor and to the designers. If the completed work, which endeavored to incorporate the ideas of another, did not altogether satisfy Medary's fastidious sense, he but experienced the fate common to architects, as expressed in the epitaph of Framinio Vacca in the Pantheon: "He never did anything which completely satisfied him."

The intensely practical, common-sense portion of his nature found expression during the World War in the government buildings on Neville Island, Pittsburgh, hastily constructed but thoroughly planned for effective administration. He was vice-president and predestined president of the American Institute of Architects when the National Commission of Fine Arts recommended to President Harding the appointment of Medary as one of the three architectural members of that body. The first problem to engage attention after his appointment (1922) was the disputed location of the Arlington Memorial Bridge, and to the resulting satisfactory solution his contribution was significant. After the expiration of his term (1926), he continued his work on the development of the National Capital as a member of the National Capital Park and Planning Commission, by successive appointments of President Coolidge and President Hoover; and then the Secretary of the Treasury made him one of the architectural consultants on the so-called Triangle group of public buildings (1927), assigning to his firm the designing of the Department of Justice building. On this work he was engaged at the time of his sudden death, which occurred in Philadelphia.

He was president of the American Institute of Architects in 1926–28, and the bestowal upon him of the gold medal of that body in 1929 marked the culmination of a career of widespread public usefulness cut short at the time of his greatest power in stimulating and directing public taste. The last works of his pencil were three studies for dormitories at the University of Chicago, dated by him four days before he died.

[*The Year Book of the Ann. Arch. Exhibition, Phila.*, 1929, dedicated to M. B. Medary, contains reproductions of his sketches and photographs of his work, with a sketch of his life by J. I. Bright, and a portrait. See also *Proc. of the Ann. Conventions of the Am. Inst. of Architects*, 1926–29; *Who's Who in America*, 1928–29; *N. Y. Times*, and *Public Ledger* (Phila.), Aug. 8, 1929.] C. M.

MEDARY, SAMUEL (Feb. 25, 1801–Nov. 7, 1864), editor, was born of Quaker parentage in Montgomery County, Pa., where he spent his youth. He attended the academy at Norristown, though he never graduated, and taught school in Montgomery County to earn money to pay for his education. At the age of sixteen he was contributing prose and poetry to the *Norristown Herald and Weekly Advertiser*. In 1820 he went with his father and mother to Montgomery County, Md., in 1823 to Georgetown, D. C., and in 1825 he moved to Batavia, Ohio, where he became a co-worker with Thomas Morris in the Democratic party. Two years later he was a school trustee, county surveyor, and soon afterward, auditor of Clermont County. A born agitator, he with Morris established the *Ohio Sun* at Bethel in 1828 to support Andrew Jackson for president. The people of Clermont County sent him three times to the state legislature and in 1837 his party elected him supervisor of public printing, a post which he held for a decade while he ran the Democratic organ entitled the *Ohio Statesman*. In 1844 he was chairman of the Ohio Democratic delegation to the Baltimore convention. It was in the capacity of editor of a party paper that he became almost a party dictator in Ohio. He ardently supported the movement for the annexation of Texas, the reoccupation of Oregon, and the Mexican War. He also supported the popular cry of "Fifty-four Forty or Fight," but the generally accepted belief that he originated it is without substantiation. His interests were not limited to politics of a local and national character. He advocated sanitation, helped to organize and promote the Ohio Horticultural Society, became an incorporator and director of four railroads, aided Louis Kossuth in his attempt to raise money in America, sympathized with the Cuban revolutionists in 1851, and did more than any other man to cause the adoption of the new constitution of Ohio in 1851. Believing that a constitution should be changed when the people willed it, he devoted his time and energy in 1849 to the publication of a newspaper which he headed with the caption, *The New Constitution*.

Medary supported the Kansas-Nebraska Act and at the National Democratic Convention of 1856, where he served as temporary chairman, he worked for the nomination of Douglas. President Buchanan appointed him to serve as governor of the Minnesota Territory (1857–58), and of the Kansas Territory (1858–60), and he held a brief appointment as deputy postmaster of Columbus, Ohio, from February to December 1858. He assisted in the formation of the state constitution of Minnesota, and he favored the Lecompton Constitution for Kansas. While in Kansas he made a futile attempt to capture John Brown, begged the citizens of Kansas to be peaceable, contributed to the *National Democrat* of Lecompton, Kan., and vetoed a bill to prohibit slavery. He returned to Columbus in 1860 where he founded and edited the *Crisis* (first number, Jan. 31, 1861). As a "Peace Democrat," a supporter of Clement Laird Vallandigham, and of Gen. George B. McClellan for president in 1864, he was one of the most hated men in Ohio by the loyal supporters of the Lincoln administration. He opposed war from the beginning because he believed it might cause the dissolution of the Union and leave the people in debt and misery. He believed that influential editors could have prevented the war, and that no power outside of the individual states of the united confederacy could legally abolish slavery. He made himself so obnoxious to the Unionists that his paper was officially denied circulation in some places, and his press was wrecked by an infuriated mob in 1863. He died the following year in Columbus, Ohio. His wife was Eliza Scott, a Quakeress; they had twelve children.

[C. B. Galbreath, *Hist. of Ohio* (1925), vols. II and III; G. H. Porter, *Ohio Politics during the Civil War Period* (1911); O. C. Hooper, *The Crisis and the Man* (1929); *Proc. of the Democratic State Convention* (Columbus, 1862); R. C. McGrane, *Wm. Allen: A Study in Western Democracy* (1925); E. O. Randall and D. J. Ryan, *Hist. of Ohio* (1912), vol. IV; the *Ohio Statesman*, 1837–57; *Crisis*, 1861–64; *Cincinnati Daily Enquirer*, Nov. 9, 1864; Medary papers in the library of the Ohio Archæol. Soc. at Columbus; scattering letters in the Van Buren and Jackson papers at the Lib. of Cong.; and the Wm. Allen papers at Chillicothe, Ohio.] W. E. S.

MEDILL, JOSEPH (Apr. 6, 1823–Mar. 16, 1899), journalist, was born in a village near St. John in the province of New Brunswick, Canada. He was of Scotch-Irish stock, and for generations his ancestors had been shipbuilders in Belfast. His father, William Medill, emigrated to America in 1819 and settled in an area that was later awarded to Canada by the Webster-Ashburton treaty of 1842. When he was nine his parents moved to Stark County, Ohio, and there he worked on the farm and received such education as the district schools and an academy in Massillon afforded. Upon reaching the age of twenty-one, he determined to enter a law office and after several years of study was admitted to the bar in 1846; but as law practice was at best uncertain, he turned to journalism. With three younger brothers he purchased the *Coshocton Whig* in 1849 and immediately renamed it the *Republican.* Within two years he moved to Cleveland and established the *Daily Forest City.* A year later he consolidated it with a Free-Soil journal and established the *Cleveland Leader.* Accepting the election of 1852 as foreshadowing the end of the Whig party, he labored diligently for the organization of a new party to be called Republican. In March 1854 a secret meeting was held in the office of the *Cleveland Leader* and plans adopted for the new anti-slavery party. There is evidence to show that he was the first man to advocate the name Republican even before the Kansas-Nebraska bill was passed (A. J. Turner, "Genesis of the Republican Party," *Wisconsin State Register,* Mar. 1898; Cleveland, *post,* p. 85).

In the winter of 1854–55 he visited Chicago and with Dr. Charles Ray bought an interest in the *Chicago Tribune,* which was experiencing financial difficulties. He was at that time thirty-two years of age and fired with enthusiasm for the Republican party and the cause of freedom. In the campaign of 1856 he played an important part in the welding of discontented political groups into a compact Republican party and during the Lincoln-Douglas debates threw the resources of his paper behind the Republican candidate. He was a close friend of Abraham Lincoln, and more than once Lincoln conferred with him in the office of the *Tribune.* Although at first in favor of Salmon P. Chase, he soon arrived at the conclusion that Lincoln was the most available candidate and urged him on that ground. He always told with pleasure how he urged Carter of Ohio to change several votes to Lincoln in the Chicago convention, with the result that a landslide was started in favor of the Illinois candidate (Cleveland, *post,* p. 85). At the outbreak of the Civil War, he was opposed to any compromise with the South and at all times demanded an active prosecution of the war. Taking his stand in favor of emancipation and confiscation of southern property, he continually urged the administration to adopt a more radical course of action. He was among the first to advocate the arming of the slaves and insisted from the beginning of the conflict that the soldier in the field should not lose his right to vote. It was largely due to his efforts that several states in the Northwest passed laws to that effect in 1864 (*Chicago Tribune,* Jan. 8, 21, Feb. 4, 1864; *Graphic,* Dec. 19, 1891; Andreas, *post,* vol. II, p. 51). He was also one of the organizers of the powerful and influential Union defense committee, which became the mainstay of the government during the uncertain days of civil strife. In the reconstruction of the South following the war, he supported Congress and was heartily in favor of the radical policies of the Republican party.

He was elected to the Illinois constitutional assembly in 1869, and was the chairman of the committee on electoral and representative reform that wrote the minority-representation clause (*Debates and Proceedings of the Con-*

stitutional Convention . . . Ill. . . . 1869, 1870, vol. I, pp. 560–61). He served as one of the first civil-service commissioners under President Grant. Following the great fire which swept over Chicago in 1871, he was elected mayor and during his term of office labored diligently to remove the municipal government from politics. He greatly enhanced the appointive and removal power of the city administration. In 1874 he bought a majority of the stock of the *Tribune* company and during the remainder of his life controlled the policy of his paper. He had able colleagues, but it was he who gave the paper its impetus and direction. Until the day of his death he was actively in charge of the paper. While in San Antonio, Tex., he was taken ill with heart disease and died at the age of seventy-six. The day before his death he had written a short editorial, which appeared in the same issue of the *Tribune* that carried the news of his death. His last words were, "What is the news?" (*Chicago Tribune,* Mar. 17, 1899). He was married on Sept. 2, 1852, to Katharine Patrick, the daughter of James Patrick of New Philadelphia, Ohio. During the Civil War she took part in the labors of the sanitary commission and was active in all phases of war work. There were three children.

[Lyman Trumbull MSS. in Lib. of Cong.; miscellaneous MSS. in Chicago Hist. Soc. Lib.; manuscript biography written in 1907 by M. Dodge in the office of the *Chicago Tribune*; H. I. Cleveland, "A Talk with . . . the Late Joseph Medill," *Saturday Evening Post,* Aug. 5, 1899; *The W. G. N.; a Handbook of Newspaper Administration* (1922); *Pictured Encyc. of the World's Greatest Newspaper* (copr. 1928); W. J. Abbot, "Chicago Newspapers," *Review of Reviews,* June 1895; A. T. Andreas, *Hist. of Chicago,* 3 vols., 1884–86; *Chicago Times-Herald,* Mar. 17, 1899, *Chicago Tribune,* Mar. 17, 1899.] T. E. S.

MEEHAN, THOMAS (Mar. 21, 1826–Nov. 19, 1901), botanist, horticulturist, author, was born in England, the son of Edward and Sarah (Denham) Meehan. He spent his boyhood on the Isle of Wight and learned gardening from his father, who was an expert gardener. He made experiments on his own initiative and while still young was elected to membership in the Royal Wernerian Society of Edinburgh. After several employments as gardener and nurseryman, including two years at Kew Gardens, he emigrated to America in 1848 and was hired by Robert Buist of Philadelphia. He was in Buist's employ for about a year, then he was made superintendent of Bartram's Garden, at that time owned by Andrew M. Eastwick. In 1852 he took charge of the grounds and conservatories of Caleb Cope, near Holmesburg, Pa. Here he gave special attention to raising the *Victoria regia* from seed which Cope had received from Kew Gardens, and he succeeded in producing blossoms. He was married in 1852 to Catherine Colflesh, daughter of a farmer and florist in Kingsessing. While with Eastwick, he had made a catalogue of the trees growing in Bartram's Garden. He was persuaded by William Darlington [*q.v.*] to enlarge the scope of the work and in 1853 published *The American Handbook of Ornamental Trees.* At about the same time he established his own nurseries in Upper Germantown which grew to large proportions and were successful as a business venture.

From 1859 to December 1887 Meehan was editor of the *Gardner's Monthly.* In 1891 he established *Meehan's Monthly,* which was continued after his death by his sons. For many years he was agricultural editor of *Forney's Weekly Press* and at one time or another he was editor or contributor to various magazines and papers. After his election in 1860 to the Academy of Natural Sciences of Philadelphia he took great interest in its herbarium and spent much time in studying its dried plants from various parts of the world. He published in the *Proceedings* of the Academy a series of "Contributions to the Life History of Plants" (March 1900) in which he blended his botanical observations with philosophic speculation and thought, and shortly before his death he presented a paper, "Bending of Mature Wood in Trees," which was the result of years of observation. In 1868 he was made a member of the American Association for the Advancement of Science (fellow, 1875), and in 1871 he was made a member of the American Philosophical Society. In 1877 he was appointed by Governor Hartranft botanist on the state board of agriculture and held the position until his death. His *magnum opus, The Native Flowers and Ferns of the United States,* a series of descriptions of plants, with colored plates, appeared in four volumes (1878–80).

In 1882 Meehan was elected a member of the Philadelphia Common Council. He fostered the movement for small parks and as a result the City Parks Association was formed. Mainly through his efforts twenty-eight small parks were added to the city, one of which was Bartram Park.

[See *Meehan's Monthly,* Jan. 1902; John W. Harshberger, *The Botanists of Phila. and Their Work* (1899); the *Gardeners' Chronicle* (London), May 11, 1901; "Gardens and Gardeners of Germantown" in *Germantown Hist.* (1915); *Who's Who in America,* 1901–02; *Country Life in America,* Feb. 1902; and obituaries in the Philadelphia newspapers at the time of his death. For details of his publications on flowers and flower pollination see *Handbook of Flower Pol-*

lination (3 vols., 1906–09), I, 307, translated by J. R. A. Davis from the German of Paul E. O. W. Knuth.]

J. W. H.

MEEK, ALEXANDER BEAUFORT (July 17, 1814–Nov. 1, 1865), author, the son of Anna (McDowell) and Samuel Mills Meek, a physician and Methodist minister, was born in Columbia, S. C. The family removed to Tuscaloosa, Ala., when he was about five years old. He had the advantages of a cultured home and apparently received the best educational opportunities available. In 1833 he was graduated from the University of Alabama. He was admitted to the bar in 1835 and began practice in Tuscaloosa. In 1836 he served as a non-commissioned officer in the Indian war in Florida and, later in the year, was appointed by Governor Clay attorney-general of the state to fill a vacancy. In 1841 he published *A Supplement to Aiken's Digest of the Laws of Ala.* He was appointed in 1842 to fill out a term as probate judge of Tuscaloosa County, but he was defeated in the election to succeed himself. He supported Polk for the presidency and obtained an appointment in the federal treasury department. Later he was appointed federal attorney for the southern district of Alabama. This appointment carried him to Mobile, where he lived for many years in a congenial literary atmosphere. After the end of Polk's term he became associate editor of the Mobile *Daily Register,* contributing poetry and essays as well as editorials to this notable paper.

In literature and service to education he won his right to recognition in Alabama history. His literary efforts covered the fields of journalism, oratory, history, essays, and poetry. He was a frequent contributor to newspapers and to magazines, and he was for a short time on the editorial staff of the *Flag of the Union* at Tuscaloosa and on that of the *Southron.* Some thought he was superior in oratory to either William L. Yancey or Henry W. Hilliard. A pioneer worker in Alabama history, he contributed *The Southwest* (1840) and *Romantic Passages in Southwestern History* (1857). He wrote numerous lyrics, the best of which he published in *Songs and Poems of the South* (1857). He is best known for "The Red Eagle" and "Balaklava." The latter, an imitation of the "Charge of the Light Brigade," met with popular acclaim in America and in England. His leadership in the founding of Alabama's public-school system is his most distinguished service. Distressed by Alabama's backwardness in public school legislation, he entered the legislature in 1853 determined to make the Mobile system of public schools statewide. As chairman of the committee on education he reported a bill to establish a public-school system for the state, and the voluminous and compelling report on education which he drew up helped him succeed where others had failed. His bill became law and became the basis for future development.

In 1859 he returned to the legislature and was made speaker of the House. He was a delegate to the Charleston convention in 1860. As a conservative Democrat he joined the secession movement with a good deal of unwillingness. During the war he served from 1862 to 1864, as trustee of the University of Alabama and wrote occasional lyrics. In 1856 he was married to Mrs. Emma (Donaldson) Slatter, who died in 1863. In 1864 he was married to Mrs. Eliza Jane Cannon, the widow of William R. Cannon. He had no children.

[T. M. Owen, *Hist. of Ala. and Dict. of Ala. Biog.* (1921), vol. IV; Wm. Garrett, *Reminiscences of Public Men in Ala.* (1872); Wm. R. Smith, *Reminiscences* (copr. 1889); *Trans. Ala. Hist. Soc.,* vol. V (1906); *Library of Southern Literature,* ed. by E. A. Alderman and others, vol. VIII (copr. 1907); W. Brewer, *Ala.* (1872); B. F. Riley, *Makers and Romance of Ala. Hist.* (1915); *Flag of the Union,* Sept. 5, 1835, May 21, 1836; *Advertiser and State Gazette* (Montgomery), Mar. 25, 1852; H. C. Nixon, *A. B. Meek* (1910).]

A. B. M.

MEEK, FIELDING BRADFORD (Dec. 10, 1817–Dec. 21, 1876), paleontologist, was born in Madison, Ind. His father, a lawyer, had migrated thither from Hamilton County, Ohio, where his parents, Irish Presbyterians who came to America about 1768, had settled prior to his birth. When Fielding was but three years of age his father died. The boy was educated in the public schools of Madison, but was greatly hampered by ill health, which handicapped him throughout his life. During this early period, however, he began to show an inclination toward the sciences. As soon as he was grown he undertook a mercantile venture which proved a failure and was followed by a second, equally unsuccessful. For several years thereafter he struggled with poverty, gaining a meager livelihood by accepting any employment that was offered. He had already conceived an interest in the invertebrate fossils which abounded in the rocks of his vicinity, and throughout this period of hardship persistently seized every opportunity to further his studies of the subject. His first public recognition was from David Dale Owen [*q.v.*], who employed him during 1848 and 1849 as one of his assistants in the United States Geological Survey of Iowa, Wisconsin, and Minnesota. In 1852 Meek entered the employ of the distinguished paleontologist James Hall [*q.v.*] and moved to Albany, N. Y., where he remained until 1858, though absenting himself for three summers: one, that of 1853, spent in the Bad Lands of Nebraska in association with F. V. Hayden [*q.v.*], also employed by Hall, and two, 1854, 1855, spent in work with the Geological Survey of Missouri.

In 1858 Meek took up his residence in Washington, having rooms in the Smithsonian building, where he remained for the rest of his life. The association first formed with Hayden in 1853 was renewed and continued for the most part until Meek's death, though in the meanwhile he accepted occasional employment with other organizations. The names Meek and Hayden became inseparably linked through their joint labors during the existence of the Hayden Survey. Perhaps their most notable publication was *Paleontology of the Upper Missouri* (Smithsonian Contributions, vol. XIV, no. 172, 1865). Meek was a skilled, careful, and conscientious worker and became recognized as one of America's leading paleontologists. Had he possessed the robust frame and mental vigor of some of his fellows he might have outranked them all, but he was never in robust health, he was modest and retiring to a marked degree, and asked in return for his labors only a sum barely sufficient for the most meager and commonplace existence. His first scientific publication was an important memoir on the Cretaceous fossils of Nebraska published in *Memoirs of the American Academy of Arts and Sciences* (new series, vol. V, pt. II, 1855). This was prepared in collaboration with James Hall. Meek's complete bibliography runs to 106 titles, including works of which he was sole author as well as the results of collaboration with Hayden, Worthen, and others. His most important publication was his "Report on the Invertebrate Cretaceous and Tertiary Fossils of the Upper Missouri Country," comprising 629 quarto pages and forty-five full-page plates, published in 1876 as one of the monographs of the Hayden survey (*Report of the United States Geological Survey of the Territories,* vol. IX).

Meek was of tall and slender build, his height being at times somewhat exaggerated by the tall black silk hat he persistently wore. He was naturally diffident, and a growing deafness which began in early manhood gradually cut him off from all associations but those with personal and scientific friends. "Gentleness and candor were apparent in every lineament of his face and in every word he uttered; yet he was eminently self-reliant and rigorously circumspect in all his actions" (White, "Memoir," *post,* p. 80). He never married and died of tuberculosis, with no near relatives, in his room in the Smithsonian.

[C. A. White, "Memoir of Fielding Bradford Meek," *Nat. Acad. Sci. Biog. Memoirs,* vol. IV (1902) and "In Memoriam: Fielding Bradford Meek," *Am. Jour. Sci.,* Mar. 1877; J. B. Marcou, "Bibliographies of American Naturalists, III: Bibliography of Publications Relating to the Collection of Fossil Invertebrates in the United States National Museum," *Bull. U. S. Nat. Museum,* no. 30 (1885); *Ann. Report . . . of the Smithsonian Inst. . . . 1877* (1878); *Evening Star* (Washington), Dec. 21, 1876; *Nat. Republican* (Washington), Dec. 22, 1876; reminiscences of personal friends.]

G. P. M.

MEEK, JOSEPH L. (1810–June 20, 1875), trapper, pioneer settler, was born in Washington County, Va. In after years he spoke of his father as a slaveholding planter and claimed relationship to President Polk. As a boy he was headstrong and lazy, refusing either to work or to learn, and at sixteen he could not read; but he had an inexhaustible fund of animal spirits, and he loved field sports. At eighteen, a strong and athletic youth, he started for the West. He reached St. Louis in the fall, and on Mar. 17, 1829, set out with W. L. Sublette's expedition for the mountains. For eleven years, at various times in company with Bridger, Carson, Fitzpatrick, Milton Sublette, and other noted mountain men, he was employed as a trapper, and in his many wanderings he traversed almost every part of the West. Though adventurous and brave to the degree of foolhardiness, he was best known as a wag and practical joker, whose bubbling humor never left him even in times of extreme peril.

In 1840 he and his friend Robert Newell, convinced that the trapping era was over, journeyed to Oregon and settled as farmers on the Tualatin plains on the Willamette, where later the town of Hillsboro grew up. He was an active spirit in the Americanization movement and a dominating influence in the Champoeg convention of May 2, 1843. On the completion of the provisional government, July 5, he was made sheriff of the territory, and in 1846 and again in 1847 elected to the legislature. After the Whitman massacre he was elected a special messenger to Washington to ask for protection for the colony. Setting out on Jan. 4, 1848, he reached Washington in May. Fond of notoriety, he had loudly announced himself on the way as "envoy extraordinary and minister plenipotentiary from the Republic of Oregon to the Court of the United States," and though "ragged, dirty and lousy" on his arrival, acted his rôle with a spectacular impressiveness. He was warmly welcomed and by popular voice was dubbed "Colonel"—a title that ever afterward clung to him. Congress, on the last day of the session, Aug. 14, passed the Oregon bill, and Polk on the same day appointed Gen. Joseph Lane governor and

Meek United States marshal. One of the acts of his marshalship was the hanging of the five chiefs convicted of the Whitman murders. He lost his office when the Pierce administration came in, and though he served as a major in the Indian war of 1855–56 his remaining days were mostly spent as an indifferent farmer on his Hillsboro tract, where he died. He was thrice married, each time to an Indian woman.

Meek was six feet two in height, well-formed, with a round, jovial, and well-bearded face and twinkling dark eyes. His voice was melodious and well modulated. As a story-teller he had few equals, though in his speech he never overcame the backwoods dialect of his youth. He was a natural leader, and with a better education and something less in his make-up of the wag and the showman he might have attained high office. His autobiography, written from his dictation by Mrs. F. F. Victor and published as *The River of the West* (1870), is a fascinating story, a blend in about equal parts of fact and fiction.

[Mrs. F. F. Victor, *The River of the West* (1870) and "Col. Joseph L. Meek," *Trans. . . . Ore. Pioneer Asso.* for 1875 (1876); J. C. Alter, *James Bridger* (1925); H. W. Scott, *Hist. of the Ore. Country* (1924), vols. I, II; L. A. Long, "Joe Meek, Oregon's Pioneer Politician," *Morning Oregonian* (Portland), Sept. 17, 1905; Osborne Russell, *Jour. of a Trapper . . . 1834–43* (2nd ed., 1921); W. F. Wagner, *Leonard's Narrative: Adventures of Zenas Leonard* (1904); G. W. Ebbert, in *Ore. Hist. Soc. Quart.*, Sept. 1918; *Morning Oregonian* (Portland), June 22, 23, 1875.]

W. J. G.

MEEKER, EZRA (Dec. 29, 1830–Dec. 3, 1928), Oregon and Washington pioneer, was born near Huntsville, Butler County, Ohio, the son of Jacob Redding and Phoebe (Baker) Meeker. His father's ancestors came from England in 1637, and his mother was of mingled English, Welsh, and German blood. In 1837 the father moved his family to Covington, Ind., and later to the outskirts of Indianapolis, where he found employment as a miller. The boy had a few months at school but, disliking its restraint, went to work at an early age. A gift from his mother's father in 1845 enabled the parents to buy a small farm, which for several years the youth operated, the father remaining at his trade. On May 13, 1851, Meeker married a neighbor's daughter, Eliza Jane Sumner, and in October of that year the young couple set out in an ox-drawn covered wagon for Iowa. Near the present Council Bluffs, the following spring, with his wife and infant child, he joined the emigrants for Oregon, and on Oct. 1 reached Portland. Early the following year, in company with his brother Oliver, he journeyed to the north of the Columbia in search of a site for a home. He settled on McNeil's Island, in Puget Sound, later removing to the site of Puyallup, where he built the first cabin. For the greater part of fifty-three years he remained in this region as a farmer and hop-grower, though he spent four winters in London and made several prospecting trips to the Yukon.

Well versed in the history of the Pacific Northwest and deeply impressed with the significance of the emigration movement, he resolved, in his seventy-fifth year, to devote the rest of his life to the commemorative marking of the Oregon Trail. On Jan. 29, 1906, with an ox-team drawing a covered wagon, he started from Puyallup, following such parts of the Trail as were still open, painting inscriptions on various landmarks and urging the citizens of the various settlements to set up inscribed stones and monuments. From the end of the Trail he continued on a tour of the East, everywhere attracting great attention. In 1910 he repeated this performance; in 1915 he traveled over a considerable part of the Trail in an automobile, and in 1924, at the age of ninety-three, he followed its course for 1300 miles in an airplane. Two years later he founded the Oregon Trail Memorial Association, Inc., with headquarters in New York City. From the Atlantic Coast, in the summer of 1928, he started in an automobile to follow the Trail again; but on the way he was taken ill, and after remaining for a time in a Detroit hospital, was conveyed to Seattle, where, two months later, he died.

Below medium height, of somewhat slender build, his head and face framed in a luxuriant snowy shock of hair and bushy beard, Meeker became, in his later years, a familiar figure throughout a great part of the country. He also became widely known as an author. In 1870 he published a descriptive pamphlet, *Washington Territory West of the Cascade Mountains,* which was followed during the next thirty-five years by a number of minor writings. In 1905 he published *Pioneer Reminiscences of Puget Sound*; in 1906, *The Ox-Team; or the Old Oregon Trail, 1852–1896* (revised and reissued in 1922 as *Ox-Team Days on the Oregon Trail*); in 1909, *Ventures and Adventures of Ezra Meeker, or Sixty Years of Frontier Life* (revised and reissued in 1916 as *The Busy Life of Eighty-Five Years of Ezra Meeker*); in 1915, *Story of the Lost Trail to Oregon* (pamphlet); in 1921, *Seventy Years of Progress in Washington*; and in 1926, *Kate Mulhall, a Romance of the Oregon Trail.* During his last years he was engaged on a revision of his autobiographical writings, but the work was not finished. Despite his loose and disconnected style and his carelessness with dates and incidents, his work will remain valuable as a picture of the migration and settlement period. His persistent efforts, in spite of many discouragements, to popularize the study of pioneer history have borne fruit, and to him more than to any other person is due the credit for the nation-wide celebration of 1930 of the first use of wagons on the Oregon Trail.

[In addition to Meeker's writings, see C. B. Galbreath, "Ezra Meeker, Ohio's Illustrious Pioneer," in *Ohio Archaeol. and Hist. Quart.*, Jan. 1927; *Who's Who in America*, 1926–27; *Seattle Daily Times*, *Post-Intelligencer* (Seattle), Dec. 3–4, 1928.] W. J. G.

MEEKER, JOTHAM (Nov. 8, 1804–Jan. 12, 1855), missionary and printer, was born in Hamilton County, Ohio, trained in youth as a printer in Cincinnati, and became a Baptist missionary to the Indians in 1825, serving as teacher and preacher among the Potawatomi, the Ottawa, and later the Chippewa or Ojibway, at missions in what is now Michigan. He mastered the closely related languages of the three tribes and, while at a mission at Sault Sainte Marie in 1832, began his experiments in using the characters of the English alphabet to create an orthography for writing the Indian languages. In 1833 he was ordered to remove to the newly created Indian Territory and to take printing equipment with him. In October 1833 he arrived at the new Shawnee Mission, just beyond the western boundary of Missouri and near the present Kansas City, Kan. On Mar. 8, 1834, he did the first printing in what is now Kansas, in the form of a leaflet containing the text of a hymn in Shawnee. The first book printed in the territory, a twenty-four-page primer in the Delaware language, he completed on Mar. 21. In all, he printed some 65 works, in ten Indian languages, including a Shawnee "newspaper," using his orthographic system, and also in English. Most of the works printed were of a religious character.

In May 1837 he moved to a mission of his own, among his old charges, the Ottawa, near the present city of Ottawa, Kan. There for eighteen years he devoted himself to the temporal and spiritual welfare of his Indians, upholding and guiding them in drought, flood, fire, pestilence, and famine, and helping them to become, before his death, a fairly well organized and self-respecting agricultural community. He was their preacher, teacher, physician, banker, broker, and attorney, their model and instructor in farming, building, and other basic industries of frontier life, and, above all, their friend in whom they learned to have unshakable confidence. In 1849 he took the mission printing plant to Ottawa and for a time resumed printing, producing among a few other things a code of the Ottawa tribal laws in the native language and in English. He died at the Ottawa mission. The diary that he kept reveals him as a practical person not given to expressions of sentiment, devout in his earlier years but toward the close of his life much more a man of practical interests than a missionary, an earnest, honest, sincere man, devoted to his work, with tenacious will advancing in the face of discouragements and reverses and in spite of the handicap of a slight physique and recurring illness. In September 1830 he married Eleanor Richardson, a fellow teacher at the Ottawa Indian mission on Grand River. They had three children.

[Journal in possession of Kan. State Hist. Soc.; D. C. McMurtrie and A. H. Allen, *Jotham Meeker* (1930), for biography, bibliography, and extracts from journal; Isaac McCoy, *Hist. of Baptist Indian Missions* (1840); *Missionary Mag.*, Apr., July 1855.]

D. C. M.

MEEKER, MOSES (June 17, 1790–July 7, 1865), pioneer lead-miner, physician, was born in Newark, N. J., and educated in his native state. In 1817, following the migration westward, he settled in Cincinnati, Ohio, and engaged with success in manufacturing white lead. The following year he married Mary R. Henry. In 1822, while in St. Louis in search of a supply of raw material, he learned that lead was to be found in great abundance in northwestern Illinois, near the present city of Galena. Returning to Cincinnati, he closed out his business, and in the fall of 1822 made a trip by boat and on horseback to the Fevre River region. His inspection convinced him of the value of the lead deposits there, and he returned to Cincinnati to secure the necessary concession from the federal government. After correspondence with John C. Calhoun, secretary of war, and upon the execution of the ten-thousand dollar bond offered by Meeker in accordance with the law, he was given authority "to build furnaces, operate mines, and make other improvements, with no interference until some action on the part of Congress should determine the procedure for the lead-mining region." He thereupon loaded a seven-thousand dollar outfit onto a keelboat, and with a party of forty-two other persons, including women and children, made the eighty-nine day trip down the Ohio and up the Mississippi to the Fevre River. Here he engaged in lead mining, to his great profit, the first year's output of smelted ore from the region amounting to 425,000 pounds. He went back to Cincinnati in 1824, returning to the lead mines with his family and a year's supply of provisions.

In the Black Hawk War (1832) he became a captain and at the close of the conflict removed to Iowa County, Wis., also a lead-mining region, where in 1837 he began the erection of one of the first smelting furnaces in the territory of Wisconsin—a four-blast furnace, the largest thereabout, which cost him $25,000. In this year, his first wife having died in 1829, he married Eliza P. Shakelton. In 1842 he was elected from Iowa County to serve in the territorial legislature, and was reëlected in 1843. In 1846 he moved to Mineral Point, in the same county, and was there chosen a delegate to the constitutional convention of that year. While living in Cincinnati he had undertaken the study of medicine, although he had not regularly practised, and because of the lack of doctors in the whole lead-mining region, his services were often commandeered, and he became known far and wide as "Dr." Meeker. In 1854 he removed to a farm near Benton, Lafayette County, Wis. Having retired from active life, he became a corresponding member of the State Historical Society, and wrote in 1857 an entertaining and valuable account of the early settlement of the Illinois and Wisconsin lead region as he knew it—an account which is a source for the years (1822–25) which it covers. He was an active Freemason and for several years an officer of the Grand Lodge of Wisconsin. He died at Shullsburg, Lafayette County, in July 1865, a few months after taking up his residence there, and was buried at Galena, Ill. He was the father of five sons and three daughters.

[Moses Meeker, "Early History of the Lead Region of Wisconsin," with brief sketch of Meeker by L. C. Draper, in *Report and Colls. State Hist. Soc. of Wis.*, vol. VI (1872; repr. 1908); M. M. Quaife, "The Convention of 1846," *Wis. Hist. Soc. Colls.*, vol. XXVII (1919); Joseph Schafer, *The Wisconsin Lead Region* (1932); *The U. S. Biog. Dict. and Portrait Gallery of Eminent and Self-Made Men: Wis. Vol.* (1877); H. A. Tenney and David Atwood, *Memorial Record of the Fathers of Wis.* (1880); C. W. Butterfield, *Hist. of LaFayette County, Wis.* (1881).] L. K. M. R.

MEEKER, NATHAN COOK (July 12, 1817–Sept. 29, 1879), newspaper writer and Indian agent, founder of the Union Colony of Colorado at Greeley, was born in Euclid, near Cleveland, Ohio, the son of Enoch and Lurana (Hulbert) Meeker. He attended school in Oberlin and in Hudson. From his seventeenth year to 1870 he was a wanderer, changing his home and vocation so rapidly that even his wife could not remember accurately, after his death, when and why the changes had taken place. We read of newspaper work in New Orleans, of teaching in Euclid, of literary labors in New York, of teaching at Allentown, Pa., in 1842, and at Orange, N. J., in 1843, and of a small business store at Euclid in 1844. At this time he married Arvilla Delight Smith who accompanied him on his later wanderings and survived him. While in Euclid, he became interested in the teachings of François Marie Charles Fourier and began to lecture on the subject. Because of this interest he joined the Trumbull phalanx at Braceville, Ohio, where Fourierism was being practised. He worked on a farm, lectured, taught school, prospered, and, as he said later, "learned how much co-operation people would bear" (Boyd, *post,* p. 15). Three years' experience sufficed him, and in 1849 he reëntered the business world in Euclid. Early in the fifties he was invited to open a store in Hiram, where a group of Campbellites were preparing to start a college. While there he wrote a novel, "The Adventures of Captain Armstrong," which was an interesting commentary upon the final phase of his own life, for the captain, wrecked on an island in the South Seas, tried to educate the savages in the ways of civilized life (*Ibid.,* pp. 15–16). The panic of 1857 brought this Hiram venture to a close. He opened a store in southern Illinois, became a newspaper correspondent, and about 1865 joined the staff of the *New York Tribune*. As agricultural editor of Greeley's paper he became a well-known man. More and more interested in cooperation as one means of economic deliverance, his series of articles on the Oneida Community attracted wide attention. A book, *Life in the West* (1868), though largely a collection of stories about the people of the Mississippi Valley, shows where his heart lay. In 1869 he was sent west to survey the work of the Mormons. While he did not reach Utah he learned much about their cooperative plans and still more about the conditions in the Territory of Colorado. Out of this trip grew his plan to organize an agricultural colony in the West.

With the support of Horace Greeley and of the *Tribune* he launched the Union Colony in December 1869. Early the next year he set out, with two others, to choose a suitable site for the colony and, on Apr. 5, selected a site on the Platte River, north of Denver and on the Denver Pacific Railway. His call for settlers proved successful and his earlier wish, to form a community of the people whose interests were in moral and intellectual development, was about to be realized. He returned for a time to New York in order to arrange for the transportation of settlers at reduced fares and to attend to many necessary details. By early May about 12,000 acres of land had been bought from the railroad and from individuals, while agreements had been made with the railroad and with the government to obtain 111,000 acres more. The colony was cooperative, a new type of organization in Colorado. Yet the little settlement was eager to have it understood that it was not a community in the sense of the Oneida Community. Instead it recognized private ownership of land and individual control of activity (*First Report, post,* p. 6). No saloons and no billiard halls were tolerated. A school was opened at once, a library started, and a lyceum founded. The inhabitants of Colorado looked upon the colonists as cranks and as led by a chief crank, Meeker, the president of the colony, tall, awkward, slow of speech, and tactless. On Nov. 16, 1870, he published the first issue of his paper the *Greeley Tribune,* in which his editorials were wise and idealist admonitions to the people who lived in the little town of Greeley set in the center of their irrigated fields. Even though it must have been hard for such a wanderer, he remained in Greeley for eight years. In 1878, however, he accepted the appointment as Indian agent at the White River reservation and proceeded to attempt to carry out his ideas of the proper method of managing Indians. Like the Captain Armstrong of his novel he believed in the civilizing effect of work. He thought to induce the Utes to live in log houses, to plow the fields, to raise crops, and to support themselves. His lack of tactful understanding led him into difficulties. The Utes, hostile to his plans, rose and killed him with all the rest of the white men in the agency.

[Manuscript sketch of life from his wife's dictation in the Bancroft Lib.; articles by his son, Ralph Meeker, in *Tribune-Republican* (Greeley) in the year 1910; *First Ann. Report of the Union Colony of Col.* (1871); J. F. Willard, *The Union Colony at Greeley* (1918); David Boyd, *A Hist.: Greeley and the Union Colony* (1890); T. F. Dawson and F. J. V. Skiff, *The Ute War* (1879).]

J. F. W.

MEERSCHAERT, THÉOPHILE (Aug. 24, 1847–Feb. 21, 1924), Catholic missionary and prelate, was the eighth of ten children born of sturdy parents in Russignies, Belgium. On the mother's death, the family was reared by an elder sister who set aside her religious vocation. Educated in the village school, at the College of Renaix (1859–64), and at the College of Audenarde, from which he was graduated in 1868, Meerschaert, under the inspiration of a clerical professor, Charles Van Quekelberghe, who had labored in the Mississippi Valley, determined to prepare himself for the American missions. With this objective, he continued his theological studies at the American College, Louvain, until his ordination (Dec. 23, 1871), and then spent several months perfecting his knowledge of English. He then sailed for New York and reported to Bishop Elder of Natchez (October 1872), who assigned him to missionary work in Hancock and Harrison counties, Miss., where the scattered Catholics faced some hostility and post-war poverty. As pastor at Ocean Springs, he broke down prejudices by a self-sacrificing service in the yellow-fever epidemic of 1875, until his own life was despaired of. For such ministrations he was well qualified by his collegiate experiences as a St. Vincent de Paul agent among the lowly. In 1878 when he learned that his people were confronted with another epidemic, he immediately returned from Europe whither he had gone to enlist missionaries. Since six priests out of twenty-six in the diocese had succumbed to the fever, Father Meerschaert assumed additional parochial duties in Biloxi and Pascagoula. A year later, he was transferred to Bay St. Louis and in 1880 to the rectorship of St. Mary's Cathedral, Natchez. Here as vicar general (1887), he was Bishop Janssens' main reliance, and on the latter's translation to New Orleans, he was named administrator by the Holy See (1888), serving as such until the appointment of Bishop Thomas Heslin, who reappointed Meerschaert to the vicar generalship.

On June 2, 1891, he was elevated to the titular see of Sidyma as vicar apostolic of Indian Territory. Consecrated at Natchez by Archbishop Janssens on Sept. 8, he set out for Guthrie, where he learned that his territory had only 6,000 white Catholics and sixteen priests of whom about one half were stationed at the Indian school of Sacred Heart. A good pioneer, the bishop won popularity among Indians and settlers as he journeyed in a wagon from station to station and accepted gratefully the humble accommodations of the region. As the territory developed rapidly, Oklahoma was erected into a diocese (1905) with Meerschaert as first bishop. Rome again rewarded him with an appointment as assistant at the pontifical throne in 1916. Five years later, he celebrated his golden anniversary as a priest, which was made the occasion of an elaborate religious function attended by a score of prelates, two hundred priests, and a large body of citizens who honored him as a state-builder as much as a churchman. At the time of his death the diocese had over a hundred priests, including Benedictines and Carmelites, 150 churches and fully as many missions, 60,000 communicants, hospitals at Oklahoma City, Tulsa, and McAlester, an orphanage at Oklahoma City, and several academies and junior colleges.

[J. B. Thoburn, *A Standard Hist. of Okla.* (1916), vol. V; annual Catholic directories; *Who's Who in America,* 1922–23; *Daily Am. Tribune* (Dubuque),

Oct. 11, 1921; *Catholic Advance* (Wichita), Oct. 1, 15, 1921; *Tulsa World*, Feb. 22, 1924; *Nat. Cath. Welfare Conference News Service*, Feb. 25, 1924.] R. J. P.

MEES, ARTHUR (Feb. 13, 1850–Apr. 26, 1923), choral and orchestral conductor, organist, teacher, was born in Columbus, Ohio, the second of three sons of a Lutheran minister, the Rev. Konrad Mees and Elise (Adam) Mees. The family showed an unusual literary tendency and the sons were educated both in America and in Europe and were chosen for high places in the field of education. The eldest, Theophilus Martin Konrad, an ordained Lutheran minister, was professor of Latin, Hebrew, and of mental and moral philosophy in Capital University, Columbus, Ohio; the youngest, Carl Leo, became president of Ohio University at Athens, Ohio. Little is known of Arthur's early training in music except that he began playing the organ in his father's church when very young and that when he later took up instrumental study, he also tried to write anthems. In 1870 he was graduated from Concordia College, Fort Wayne, Ind., with the degree of A.B. He had evidently decided early to make music his life work, for after his graduation he accepted a position in Wesleyan Female College, Cincinnati, Ohio, as teacher of piano and theory. He was also organist of various Cincinnati churches and conductor of singing societies. In 1873 his work as choral accompanist attracted the attention of Theodore Thomas, who appointed him accompanist of the first Cincinnati May Festival. During the same year he went to Berlin, and upon the advice of Rubinstein he studied piano with Theodore Kullak, theory with Carl Friedrich Weitzmann, and score-reading with Heinrich Dorn. He remained in Europe for several years, the last of which he spent at the Leipzig Conservatory.

In 1880 Mees returned to Cincinnati as teacher of harmony and composition at the College of Music, continuing as organist of the May Festivals and trainer of the chorus. In 1886 Thomas called him to New York to become assistant conductor of the chorus of the National Opera Company. This company was short-lived, and when it disbanded, Mees became director of the Orpheus Society of New York, the Albany Festival Chorus, and of the Orange (New Jersey) Mendelssohn Union and numerous smaller organizations. From 1896 to 1898 he was in Chicago as assistant conductor of the Theodore Thomas Orchestra and conductor of an auxiliary choral organization, and from 1898 to 1904 he was conductor of the New York Mendelssohn Glee Club. In 1913 he conducted the Bridgeport (Connecticut) Oratorio Society and in 1918 the Worcester (Massachusetts) festivals and the Cecilia Society of Boston. From 1900 to 1916 he was assistant conductor to Richmond Peck Paine in the Norfolk (Connecticut) festivals, succeeding the latter as conductor in 1916. He became an experienced and gifted director of choral and orchestral organizations but notwithstanding his strenuous work as a conductor he found time to write *Daily Studies for the Piano* (1877) and *Choirs and Choral Music* (1901), the latter a valuable work. He also edited the program books of the New York Philharmonic Society, 1877–96, and of the Chicago Symphony Orchestra, 1896–98. He introduced many novelties to American audiences, such as Granville Bantock's *Omar Khayyám*, Gabriel Pierné's *St. Francis of Assisi*, and Percy Grainger's *Marching Song of Democracy*. He was married on Jan. 28, 1897, to Susan Marguerite Howell of Alfred, N. Y., but they had no children. He died at his home in New York City after a long illness.

["Arthur Mees' Work for Music in America," *Musical Courier*, Oct. 30, 1907; *Who's Who in America*, 1922–23; *Internat. Who's Who in Music* (1918); *Musical Digest*, May 1, 1923; *N. Y. Times*, Apr. 27, 1923.] F. L. G. C.

MEGAPOLENSIS, JOHANNES (1603–1670), Reformed Dutch clergyman, first minister of the church at Rensselaerswyck, in New Netherland, was the son of Catholic parents and adhered to their faith until he was twenty-three years of age. "When I relinquished Popery," he wrote late in life, "I was thrust out at once from my inherited estate" (*Ecclesiastical Records State of New York*, I, 602). He became a minister of the gospel, serving in a couple of parishes in Holland from 1634 to 1642. In the latter year he signed a contract with Kiliaen van Rensselaer by which he bound himself for a period of six years to minister to the patroon's colony at Rensselaerswyck at an annual salary of 1,000 florins for the first three years and of 1,200 for the remainder. He sailed with his wife Machtelt, daughter of Willem Steengen, and four children from The Texel on June 14, 1642, and arrived at New Amsterdam on Aug. 4. Thirteen days later, he preached his first sermon in the *packhuys*, the patroon's storehouse, to an audience of about one hundred. In the following year he began to preach to the Indians, with whose language he had somewhat familiarized himself at great pains. Letters that he wrote to correspondents in Holland about the Mohawk Indians, their country, language, religion, and government, were printed there without his consent. The University Library of Ghent, Belgium, possesses the only extant copy known of this pamphlet (*Een Kort Ontwerp van de Mahakvase*

Indiaenen . . .), which was published at Alkmaar in 1644. Megapolensis, in this booklet, shows himself entirely free from that haughty scorn for the ignorant Indians that Jonas Michaelius [*q.v.*] expressed in his letters. He lived with them on friendly terms, he let them come to his services, which sometimes ten or twelve would attend, each smoking a long tobacco pipe, and had, at one time, "eight at once lying and sleeping upon the floor near my bed." He frankly admitted his failure to convert them; they never would be converted, he said, "until they are subdued . . . and reduced to some sort of civilization; and also unless our people set them a better example" (*Ecclesiastical Records,* I, 398). He found fault with his Catholic fellow missionaries for baptizing the Indians in their ignorance of what baptism meant, and his refusal to follow their example may account for the confidence that the Indians showed him; for they looked upon the christening ceremony as a form of magic that would do them harm. Thanks to these good relations with the Indians, Megapolensis was able, in 1642, to rescue Father Isaac Jogues [*q.v.*], of the Society of Jesus, from their hands. When his six years' term had expired, he arranged, in 1649, for his return to Holland, but Governor Stuyvesant and his Council persuaded him to accept a call to New Amsterdam as successor of the Rev. J. C. Backer. Here he maintained his reputation as a humane Christian, though he was far from being a tolerant man. He requested the authorities in Holland to put a stop to the immigration of Jews; yet he took pity on the twenty-three who, in 1654, arrived at New Amsterdam from Brazil and had his consistory appropriate a few hundred guilders for their immediate needs. He also opposed and prevented the establishment of a Lutheran church at New Amsterdam. In 1657 he received a visit from the Jesuit missionary Simon le Moyne; a sequel to this call was a Latin treatise which the latter sent to Megapolensis urging him to return to the Mother Church. Le Moyne's plea is lost, but its contents may be guessed from the domine's acrimonious Latin reply, which has been published with English translation in *Reply of Rev. Johannes Megapolensis . . . to a Letter of Father Simon Le Moyne* (1907). On Aug. 29, 1664, Megapolensis and his son Samuel, with two of the city magistrates, acted as messengers between Stuyvesant and Col. R. Nicholls, but their names do not appear in the "Remonstrance," signed by ninety-three citizens, urging capitulation. On Oct. 2, however, he swore the oath of allegiance to the King of England, and he continued to minister to his congregation until his death. His attitude at the time of the surrender was evidently criticized in Holland, for on Aug. 27, 1668, Peter Stuyvesant and three members of his former Council signed a certificate in which they declared that Megapolensis had acted no otherwise "than it was the duty of a faithful subject, and as was proper for a godly and pious preacher to act on such an occasion" (*Ibid.,* I, 593).

[*Ecclesiastical Records State of New York,* vol. I (1901); *New York State Lib. Van Rensselaer Bowier Manuscripts* (1908), translated and ed. by A. J. F. van Laer; *Narratives of New Netherland 1609–1664* (1909), ed. by J. F. Jameson; Albert Eekhof, *De Hervormde Kerk in Noord-Amerika 1624–1664* (2 vols., 1913); I. N. Phelps Stokes, *The Iconography of Manhattan Island,* vols. II (1916), IV (1922), VI (1928); W. B. Sprague, *Annals Am. Pulpit,* vol. IX (1869).]

A. J. B.

MEGRUE, ROI COOPER (June 12, 1883–Feb. 27, 1927), dramatist, was born in New York City, the son of Frank Newton and Stella Georgiana (Cooper) Megrue. He studied at Columbia University, from which he was graduated in 1903, and his first contacts with the professional stage were made in a clerical position in the play-brokerage offices of Elizabeth Marbury. His first play to be acted, after many discouragements and disheartening delays, was *White Magic,* which he completed from an unfinished dramatization of David Graham Phillips' novel of that title. It was produced at the Criterion Theatre in New York on Jan. 24, 1912, with Gertrude Elliott as the star, and although it met with but little popularity, it was really the starting point of his brief career. His first successful play was *Under Cover,* a sensational drama involving a smuggled necklace, a mysterious secret-service quest, and New York Custom-House graft. It was first acted in Boston in 1913, and was followed in succession by *It Pays to Advertise* (1914), written in collaboration with Walter Hackett; *Under Fire* (1915), one of the first plays dealing with the World War, and having for its crucial scene the German troops entering a German city; *Potash and Perlmutter in Society,* first called *Abe and Mawruss* (1915), written in collaboration with Montague Glass; *Seven Chances* (1916); *Under Sentence* (1916), written in collaboration with Irvin S. Cobb; *Where Poppies Bloom* (1918), from the French; and *Tea for Three* (1918), taken from a play by Carl Slaboda. Several of these plays were acted in London, but they attracted little notice there.

Megrue was a typical playwright who wrote always with his finger on the public pulse, with his eye on the footlights, and with his mind on events as they were recorded on the first page of the daily newspaper. After passing through some five years of popularity, he was unable to keep up with the demands of those play-goers who had grown enthusiastic about *Under Cover.* He found that he had exhausted his vein, and that he could not attract the public indefinitely by means of ephemeral sensation. His view of the dramatist's technique was unblushingly revealed by him in an interview in which he declared that the only kind of art he knew was the ability to get his plays over the footlights. For some years prior to his death he was little heard of by the play-going public except through an occasional stock-company revival of one or two of his best-known plays. He never married.

[Dixie Hines and H. P. Hanaford, *Who's Who in Music and Drama,* 1914; John Parker, *Who's Who in the Theatre,* 1925; *Who's Who in America,* 1926–27; interviews in the *Sun* (N. Y.), Dec. 1, 1918 and Apr. 20, 1919; Burns Mantle and G. P. Sherwood, *The Best Plays of 1900–11* (1933); *The Nineteen Hundred and Three Class Book: A Record of the Senior Class of Columbia Coll.* (1903); *N. Y. Times,* Feb. 28, 1927.]

E. F. E.

MEIGGS, HENRY (July 7, 1811–Sept. 29, 1877), builder of South American railroads, was born in Catskill, N. Y., the second son in a family of nine children. Elisha and Fanny (Williams) Meiggs, his parents, were both of old New England stock, the father descended from Vincent Meigs who settled in New Haven, Conn., about 1644. After receiving a common-school education, Henry worked at the lumber trade in Catskill, Boston, and New York. In 1837 he opened his own yard in Williamsburg, N. Y., and the confidence which he usually inspired is shown in his soon being elected a member, and then president, of the village board of trustees. Yet he was insolvent in 1842 and his fortunes continued uncertain until 1848, when news of the gold discovery led him to load a vessel with lumber and sail by Cape Horn to San Francisco. Arriving when the town was booming he sold at a large profit. He invested heavily in lumbering, erecting the largest sawmill in the territory and sending hundreds of men into the woods to cut timber. He donated to the city an imposing music hall, was elected to the board of aldermen, and interested himself in many civic improvements. His success and confidence impressed every one and he had no difficulty borrowing capital. When the boom slowed down, however, he found he had over-reached himself. In a frenzied effort to cover his loans he was tempted to forge warrants purloined from the office of the city treasurer. When discovery became inevitable he placed his family and personal property on board the barque *America,* and, under cover of darkness, Oct. 5, 1854, sailed out into the Pacific, leaving behind him obligations of over $800,000.

During the whole of his subsequent career Meiggs was a fugitive from justice. Landing in Chile, he had, by 1861, gained a reputation by his record as construction superintendent of certain stretches of the Santiago al Sur Railroad. The Chilean government then contracted with him to complete for $12,000,000 the Valparaiso and Santiago line which had already ruined several contractors. Allowed four years, he finished it in less than two years and made a profit of $1,320,000. He built a $500,000 home in Santiago, had surveys made for a road across the Andes, planned railroads in Bolivia, dealt extensively in Bolivian guano, and founded a bank in La Paz. His chief theatre of action, however, was furnished by the Peruvian government, which was planning an extensive system of railways to be financed from its nitrate and guano monopolies. Beginning in 1868 with the contract for a line from Mollendo to Arequipa, Meiggs in the next five years, by a system of bribery which paralyzed all opposition, secured contracts totaling at least $120,000,000 for some 1,015 miles of standard gauge road. Completion of the Arequipa line in 1870 was celebrated by an entertainment attended by the Peruvian president and 2,000 other guests, which lasted two weeks and cost $200,000—a typical Meiggs gesture. He continued the Arequipa road to Puno on Lake Titicaca, crossing the Andes at 14,665 feet, and he also built a branch to Cuzco, the old Inca capital. His executive genius was best shown, however, in his construction of the famous Callao, Lima & Oroya railroad, the highest in the world, which, tunneling under Mount Meiggs at 15,658 feet, "broke the backbone of the Andes." This line, with its dizzy viaducts and its sixty-seven tunnels, built in the face of incredible difficulties, remains one of the engineering wonders of the world. Before it was complete Peru was bankrupt, and Meiggs, having sunk his fortune in the construction of the road, looked about desperately for the means to extricate himself. He persuaded the government to give him a new contract to complete the line, with the right also to drain and operate the famous Cerro de Pasco silver mines. He issued new notes on this contract, the workers were recalled, and confidence again reigned until it was found the notes were returned from England unhonored. A succession of paralytic strokes carried Meiggs to his death, and with elaborate ceremonies he was buried on his hacienda at the side of the Oroya railroad, his grave looking out to the Pacific.

A man of commanding presence, admirable tact, and untiring activity, Meiggs was also vain, impetuous, and an incurable prodigal. He repaid most of his San Francisco debts, and did much to improve the environs of Lima with parks and boulevards. In 1874 he secured the passage of a law by the California legislature, over the governor's veto, making it illegal for a grand jury to indict him for offenses committed before 1855 (Hittell, *post,* III, 441, citing *California Statutes,* 1873–74). He was married Apr. 9, 1832, to Gertrude Burns of Catskill, who died in 1833, and in 1837 to Caroline Doyle of Ulster County, N. Y., who died in 1861. Two sons and a daughter survived him.

[H. B. Meigs, *Record of the Descendants of Vincent Meigs* (copr. 1901); T. H. Hittell, *Hist. of Cal.,* III (1897), 434–41; Samuel Nuñez Olaechea, *Los Ferrocarriles del Estado* (Santiago, 1910); Federico Costa y Laurent, *Reseña Historica de los Ferrocarriles del Perú* (Lima, 1908); F. M. Halsey, *Railway Expansion in Latin America* (1916); E. W. Middendorf, *Peru* (3 vols., 1893–95); *Colección de Leyes, Decretos, Contratos y demas Documentos Relativas a los Ferrocarriles de Perú* (1871), collected by Meiggs's order; articles in *The Pioneer* (San Francisco), Nov. 1854, p. 297, Jan. 1855, pp. 16–22; *Overland Monthly,* Aug. 1871; *Scribner's Monthly,* Aug. 1877; and *Engineering News,* Oct. 20, 1877; *N. Y. Tribune,* Oct. 11, 1877; *San Francisco Chronicle, Daily Morning Call* (San Francisco), and *N. Y. Times,* Oct. 12, 1877.]

O. W. H.

MEIGS, ARTHUR VINCENT (Nov. 1, 1850–Jan. 1, 1912), physician, author, was born in Philadelphia, a grandson of Charles Delucena Meigs [*q.v.*] and a son of John Forsyth Meigs [*q.v.*] and Ann Wilcocks (Ingersoll), his father being thirty-two years old. William Montgomery Meigs [*q.v.*] was a younger brother. When Arthur was six years of age he had the misfortune to lose his mother, but he received the affectionate care of his father's mother, and spent much of his time in childhood at his grandfather's beautiful country place at Hamanassett. As a boy he attended the Classical Institute of J. W. Faires, from which he entered the Academic Department of the University of Pennsylvania in 1866. His father was so anxious to have him begin his medical studies, however, that he took him from college at the end of his second year and entered him in the Medical Department, from which he was graduated in the spring of 1871. Since he was not yet twenty-one years of age, he did not receive his diploma until some months later. After spending parts of the year 1871–72 abroad, chiefly in Vienna, he returned to become a resident physician in the Pennsylvania Hospital. Here he remained until 1874, when he began the practice of medicine which he continued to the time of his death. His success was assured on account of his excellent preparation, distinguished ancestry, and social position. In 1878 he married Mary Roberts Browning. Their family consisted of three sons, one of whom became the fourth physician in the direct line of family descent.

Arthur Vincent Meigs was made a visiting physician to the Pennsylvania Hospital, to succeed his father, in 1881. He also became a visiting physician to the Children's Hospital and to the Sheltering Arms (a home for foundlings). He was an active fellow of the College of Physicians and its president from 1904 to 1907. He was also much interested in the Philadelphia Pathological Society, of which he was president in 1891–92. He was for a time a consulting physician to the Eastern Penitentiary and to the Pennsylvania Institute for the Instruction of the Blind, and in 1899 he was elected a member of the American Philosophical Society. He was also for a time a trustee of the University of Pennsylvania and of the Wistar Institute.

He represented the most conservative type of medical practitioner, by whom ideas not their own are always regarded with caution, yet who cling tenaciously to any they themselves have originated. Meigs was not lacking in originality. He conceived it strange that infants should thrive upon their mothers' milk, but often pine and die when fed upon cow's milk, and believed that it was the result of chemical difference in the composition of the foods. This idea was scouted by his contemporaries, to whom milk was milk. Nevertheless, he spent much time in analyzing milks both human and bovine and succeededed in "modifying" the cow's milk so as to make it practically as wholesome for babies as their mothers'. This was his most important contribution to medical science, and it is the one for which he should be remembered. In his own eyes, however, it was probably of less value than his belief that he had demonstrated that the capillary blood-vessels of the heart actually penetrate into the muscle cells. His chief writings are: *Proof that Human Milk Contains Only about One Per Cent of Casein; with Remarks upon Infant Feeding* (1883); *A Study of the Arteries and Veins in Bright's Disease* (1888); *The Artificial Feeding of Infants* (1889); *The Microscopic Anatomy of the Human Heart, Showing the Existence of Capillaries within the Muscular Fibres* (1891); *The Origin of Disease, etc.* (1897); *Analysis of Human Milk the Basis of the Artificial Feeding of Infants* (1902).

Meigs was a thorough gentleman, good to look at, pleasant to talk to, well-groomed, cultured and refined to the highest degree. He was very sensitive and so extremely sympathetic with pain that he could scarcely endure seeing it in others. He was so highly conscientious that he was continually telling his patients that they could help themselves more than he could help them. He was fond of the open air, and especially of horses and boats. His death occurred at his home in Philadelphia, in his sixty-second year.

["Memoir of Arthur Vincent Meigs, M.D.," by his son Edward B. Meigs, in *Trans. Coll. Phys. of Phila.*, 3 ser. XXXVI (1914); H. B. Meigs, *Record of the Descendants of Vincent Meigs* (1901); T. G. Morton and Frank Woodbury, *The Hist. of the Pa. Hospital* (1895); *Public Ledger* (Phila.), Jan. 2, 1912.]

J. M.

MEIGS, CHARLES DELUCENA (Feb. 19, 1792–June 22, 1869), physician, author, son of Josiah Meigs [*q.v.*] and Clara (Benjamin) Meigs, the fifth of ten children, was born at St. George, Bermuda, and there passed the first four years of his life. The next four years were spent in New Haven, Conn., where his father was professor of mathematics in Yale College. These years probably had great influence in the formation of his moral and mental character, and it may have been then that "honesty, honor, love of country, inflexible uprightness, liberality of mind and love of knowledge were there implanted in him" (J. F. Meigs, in *Quarterly Summary, post,* p. 421). Later his father became president of the University of Georgia, at Athens, whither the family moved in 1801. Here the boy made the intimate acquaintance of an intelligent and cultivated *émigré,* M. Petit de Clairvière, and from him learned the French language and also perhaps the gentle and courteous manners that characterized his long professional career. He was graduated from the University of Georgia in 1809, at seventeen years of age, and immediately began to read medicine with Dr. Thomas Hanson Marshall Fendall, to whom he became apprenticed and under whose roof he lived for three years. In 1812–13 he pursued a course of medicine at the University of Pennsylvania, then, as he wrote later, "went home to set up for myself, and practice on that stock in trade" (*Ibid.*, p. 426). In 1814–15 he returned to Philadelphia to study for another year. He was graduated from the University of Pennsylvania, apparently *in absentia,* in 1817, and the subject of his thesis was *Prolapsus uteri.*

In Philadelphia, in 1814–15, he met Mary Montgomery, whom he married Mar. 15, 1815, and took with him to Georgia, where he set up practice in Augusta. But since Mrs. Meigs was made unhappy by slavery as she saw it in the South, and the doctor suffered repeated attacks of the "bilious fever," they left Georgia after a couple of years and took up their residence in Philadelphia. Meigs worked hard at his profession and soon became intimate with a number of the best physicians of the city. On the death of his wife's mother, the family moved to the Montgomery home on Arch Street above Sixth Street, after which his practice grew and success began to arrive. His family also grew; there were ten children, among whom were John Forsyth and Montgomery Cunningham Meigs [*qq.v.*]. In 1826 Meigs became one of the editors of a new periodical, the *North American Medical and Surgical Journal,* and continued in this capacity as long as the publication continued, which was until 1831.

In 1830 he began to lecture in midwifery in what was called the "School of Medicine." This probably led him into a more careful study of the subject, for in that same year he made a translation from the French A. A. L. M. Velpeau, which appeared the next year under the title, *Elementary Treatise on Midwifery* (1831). In 1838 he published his first independent work in the form of an octavo volume of 370 pages, entitled *The Philadelphia Practice of Midwifery.* It at once became popular, and a second edition in 1842 was increased to 408 pages. His practice grew and became more remunerative, and consequently, in 1835, he moved to Chestnut Street above Tenth Street, where he continued to live until 1850. With his success in practice and in authorship his reputation also grew, and in 1841 he was elected professor of obstetrics and diseases of women in the Jefferson Medical College, which position he filled with great satisfaction to both faculty and student body until 1861, when he voluntarily retired.

After retiring from his professorship he ceased to be any longer interested in medical subjects, and spent his remaining years enjoying life in the country at Hamanassett, where he died at the age of seventy-six. He was, perhaps, not an original thinker, his one important contribution being to call attention to cardiac thrombosis as a cause of sudden death in childbirth. His only invention was a form of ring pessary. He strenuously opposed the probability of puerperal fever being an infectious disease. As a lecturer, however, he was eloquent, polished, and entertaining, presenting his subject clearly and forcibly. With his superb education and high sense of morality, he influenced his students profoundly. He was far in advance of his times in believing that the standards of medical education should be raised, and that "a young man, destined to the study of medicine, should begin by obtaining a knowledge of Latin and Greek, the French, German and Italian languages" (J. F. Meigs, *op. cit.,* p. 439). He brought his sons and grandsons up to a knowledge of the family history and a sense of "the rigid duty incumbent upon them, to do whatever might be in their power to promote its honorableness" (*Ibid.*, p. 6). Besides the books already noted he wrote *Woman, Her Diseases and Remedies* (1847), *Obstetrics; the Science and Art* (1849), *Treatise on Acute and Chronic Diseases of the Neck of the Uterus* (1850), *Childbed Fevers* (1854), and published *A Treatise on the Diseases and Special Hygiene of Females* (1845), translated from the French of Marc Colombat de l'Isère.

[J. F. Meigs, *Memoir of Charles D. Meigs, M.D.* (1876), published also in *Quart. Summary of the Trans. of the Coll. of Phys. of Phila., 1872* (1873); John Bell, in *Proc. Am. Phil. Soc.*, vol. XIII (1873); *Boston Medic. and Surgic. Jour.*, May 23, 30, 1849; H. B. Meigs, *Record of the Descendants of Vincent Meigs* (1901); *Public Ledger* (Phila.), June 23, 1869.]

J. M.

MEIGS, JAMES AITKEN (July 31, 1829–Nov. 9, 1879), physician, teacher, and anthropologist, was born in Philadelphia, the son of John G. and Mary A. Meigs. His parents were of English, Scotch, and German descent; his father, known as "Honest John," was a shoe merchant. After preparation at the Mount Vernon Grammar School and at the Boys' Central High School, James entered Jefferson Medical College, from which he graduated with high honors in 1851. He then began general practice and became especially noted for work in obstetrics. From 1854 to 1862, he served as professor of climatology and physiology in the Franklin Institute and, from 1856 to 1859, as librarian of the Academy of Natural Sciences of Philadelphia. During these years, most of his papers on medical and scientific data appeared. His interests seem to have touched a wide range of subjects; in 1855 he contributed a paper entitled, "Relation of Atomic Heat to Crystalline Form," to the *Proceedings of the Academy of Natural Sciences;* and to the *North American Medical and Chirurgical Review* for 1859, "Some Remarks on the Methods of Studying and Teaching Physiology." Outside of the medical profession, he is perhaps best known for his anthropological work, which reached its climax in the "Catalogue of Human Crania in the Collection of the Academy of Natural Sciences of Philadelphia"; this formed a special supplement of 103 pages to the *Proceedings* for 1856. He also contributed an article on "The Cranial Characteristics of the Races of Men" to J. C. Nott and G. R. Gliddon, *Indigenous Races of the Earth* (1856), and edited the American edition of W. S. Kirkes's *Manual of Physiology* (1857). Papers by him were also published in the *Medical Examiner* and in the *American Journal of Medical Sciences.*

After several years' assistantship to the professor of physiology at the Philadelphia College of Medicine, he was appointed in 1857 to the chair of Institutes of Medicine in that school. In 1859, he transferred to a professorship on the same subject at Pennsylvania Medical College and was appointed physician and clinical lecturer in the Philadelphia Hospital at Blockley, but resigned his teaching position at the outbreak of the Civil War. For thirteen years, beginning in 1855, he was also physician in the department of pulmonary diseases at Howard Hospital and Infirmary for Incurables. In 1868 he became professor of the Institutes of Medicine and Medical Jurisprudence at Jefferson Medical College, and appears to have been especially successful in physiological demonstrations and in lectures on the eye and ear. The same year, he was chosen as physician to the Pennsylvania Hospital. In 1871, he was elected president of the Philadelphia County Medical Society, in which he had successively acted as secretary and vice-president. He also served several years on the board of trustees of the Polytechnic College of the State of Pennsylvania. During the latter years of his life, his duties as a teacher and practitioner occupied the most of his attention. He never married but lived with his aged father, and, after a short sickness which was diagnosed as malaria, died of blood poisoning.

[George Hamilton, "James Aitken Meigs, M.D., 1829–1879," in *Trans. of the Medic. Soc. of the State of Pa.*, vol. XIII, pt. 1 (1880); H. C. Chapman, "Memoir of James Aitken Meigs, M.D.," in *Trans. Coll. of Physicians of Phila.*, 3 ser., vol. V (1881); E. J. Nolan, "Report of Librarian," *Proc. Acad. Nat. Sci. Phila., 1895*, vol. XLVII (1896); *Phila. Medic. Times*, Nov. 22, 1879; *Medic. and Surgic. Reporter*, Nov. 15, 1879; *Boston Medic. and Surgic. Jour.*, Nov. 20, 1879; *Medic. Record* (N. Y.), Nov. 22, 1879; *Phila. Times* and *Phila. Record*, Nov. 11, 1879.]

H. B. B.

MEIGS, JOHN (Aug. 31, 1852–Nov. 6, 1911), educator, son of Rev. Matthew K. Meigs and Mary Morton (Gould), both of New England ancestry, was descended from Vincent Meigs who settled in New Haven about 1644. His father served as a Presbyterian pastor in Michigan and Virginia and later was president of Delaware College. Determining on account of his health to retire from his college position, he bought an old stone house on a hill near Pottstown, Pa., and in it established a small day school where he planned to train his own boys. In this house John Meigs, the fifth child and fourth son, was born. He entered Lafayette College at fourteen, but upon the death of a brother in December, was taken from college and spent the rest of the year in Europe, returning to Lafayette in the fall of 1867. Graduating in 1871 with honors, he began to teach under his father, but in 1872 became tutor in Latin and Greek at Lafayette, and in 1875, adjunct professor of modern languages. He was awarded the degree of doctor of philosophy in 1876.

In the fall of that year, in response to his mother's urging, he reluctantly went home to take charge of the school, from which his father wished to withdraw. With The Hill School he was identified for the rest of his life. He found the institution established in extemporized quarters with meager and primitive equipment, a faculty of three teachers, and an enrollment of sixty boys. Giving evidence at once of his extraordinary energy and tenacity, he assumed the responsibility of direction and at the same time conducted as many recitations as any one of the other teachers—about twenty-five a week. In addition, he kept the accounts; wrote all the letters with his own hand, saw to all matters of discipline; kept the general records; and received all the visitors. The school had no endowment, nor any wealthy friends. By his management, he provided the funds with which to improve and enlarge the buildings according to the rapidly rising standards which he partly created for himself and partly accepted from the general progress of educational ideas. Three disastrous fires, one in 1884, the second in 1890, and the third in 1901, though entailing great immediate loss, became in each case the occasion for bolder plans. Year by year he put back into the school whatever profit there had been from the year before, and by the time of his death the institution was one of the most extensive and completely equipped schools in America.

Of his qualities as a man and as a schoolmaster, most notable were his own extraordinary capacity for work, and his ability to require and to gain the utmost energy of those who worked with him. He set and exacted high standards of industry and thoroughness both for masters and for boys. Vehement and impetuous and quick to anger, he was quick also to tenderness and able to inspire loyalty. He reflected Thomas Arnold of Rugby in his passionate moral purpose and Edward Thring of Uppingham in his emphasis upon beauty and dignity in equipment and surroundings, and in his concern not only for the brilliant but for the ordinary boy.

Like his mother before him, John Meigs was instinctively and strongly religious. In 1882 he married Marion Butler of New York, and as "Mrs. John" her influence was linked with his in creating the general tone of the school and in developing the religious interest of individual boys. Although an Evangelical in spirit, John Meigs stood among the theological liberals in his beliefs and sympathies. As a member of the Presbyterian General Assembly which in 1893 conducted the ecclesiastical trial of Charles Augustus Briggs [*q.v.*] he did his utmost to prevent Briggs's condemnation for heresy. An epidemic of typhoid fever of which nearly one hundred, boys and masters, fell ill in the early summer of 1902, laid John Meigs under such a strain physically and emotionally that in the following years his great vitality began to wane. In 1906 it was evident that he had serious heart-trouble. With intervals of seeming improvement, this grew worse in the next five years; and in 1911 he died of a heart attack at The Hill School, in the house in which he was born.

[H. B. Meigs, *Record of the Descendants of Vincent Meigs* (1901); W. R. Bowie, *The Master of The Hill, A Biography of John Meigs* (1917); *Outlook*, Nov. 18, 1911; *Who's Who in America*, 1910–11; S. J. Coffin, *Record of the Men of Lafayette* (1879); *Public Ledger* (Phila.), Nov. 8, 1911.] W. R. B.

MEIGS, JOHN FORSYTH (Oct. 3, 1818–Dec. 16, 1882), physician, pediatrician, author, brother of Montgomery C. Meigs [*q.v.*], was the son of Charles Delucena Meigs [*q.v.*] and Mary (Montgomery) Meigs, and the third of ten children. He was born in Philadelphia, soon after his father, aged twenty-six, had arrived in that city to start upon the practice of medicine. Being by nature quiet and sober-minded, and having before him the example of his cultured and industrious father, from early childhood he desired to become a physician and never departed from this purpose, which was early recognized and accepted in the family. He first attended a "dame's school" in Cherry Street, and later went to the Classical Institute of Mr. Samuel Crawford, a notoriously harsh and cruel man who is said to have used his rattan unmercifully. Since his father was impatient to have him begin his medical studies, he was taken from school before he was sixteen and began attending lectures "upon two of the elementary branches at the University of Pennsylvania, and at the same time studying music and having a tutor who gave him some further instruction" (A. V. Meigs, *post*, p. lxxiv). He was graduated at the University of Pennsylvania in 1838, when less than twenty years of age, and almost immediately became a resident physician to the Pennsylvania Hospital, a position to which he had been appointed before graduation.

With the completion of his service, in 1840, he sailed for Europe to spend some six or seven months in Paris, where he enjoyed the lectures and clinics of Velpeau and Louis. In 1841 he began to practice medicine in his father's house on Chestnut Street, in his native city, with the latter's great reputation and large clientele to aid him. Success came at once. Following his father's example he began, in 1843, to teach obstetrics and later the practice of medicine and diseases of children, in the Philadelphia Association for Medical Instruction—an enterprise whose function was to provide supplementary courses for medical students in the spring and autumn. He continued to teach here until 1854, when his practice absorbed too much of his time.

On Oct. 17, 1844, he married Ann Wilcocks Ingersoll, daughter of Charles Jared Ingersoll [*q.v.*], by whom he had eight children, six of whom survived. The union was terminated by his wife's death after about twelve years, and he never remarried. At the age of thirty, in 1848, he completed his book, *A Practical Treatise on the Diseases of Children,* published as a volume of the Medical Practitioner's and Student's Library. It was an immediate success and became a standard work upon the subject in all English-speaking countries. Other editions were soon called for, but as he reaped justified rewards for his labors in an ever increasing practice, he found himself too busy to prepare the fourth edition. He, therefore sought a worthy young associate to collaborate with him, finally selecting Dr. William Pepper, to whom he gave one-half the rights of ownership. Under the names of Meigs and Pepper appeared the fourth, fifth, sixth, and seventh editions (1870–86).

In 1859 Meigs was elected one of the physicians to the Pennsylvania Hospital, which position he held until 1881, when he resigned. He was also at various times a visiting physician to the Children's Hospital, a consulting physician to the Women's Hospital and to the Blind Asylum, a fellow of the College of Physicians, and a member of the American Philosophical Society. He is described as gentlemanly, modest, and correct in all things; a keen observer, an accurate medical diagnostician, and a physician loved and revered by patients and friends. His life was so simple as to have been almost austere. He lived for his family and his work, dying in December 1882 after a short illness from pneumonia, at the age of sixty-four years. One of his sons, Arthur Vincent Meigs [*q.v.*], carrying on the family tradition of medical distinction, was his father's successor as physician to the Pennsylvania Hospital; another, William Montgomery Meigs [*q.v.*], was noted for his scholarly biographies and studies in constitutional law.

[A. V. Meigs, "Memoir of J. Forsyth Meigs, M.D.," *Trans. Coll. of Phys. of Phila.*, 3 ser. VII (1884); Wm. Pepper, "Obituary of John Forsyth Meigs, M.D.," *Proc. Am. Phil. Soc.*, vol. XXI (1884); T. G. Morton and Frank Woodbury, *The Hist. of the Pa. Hospital* (1895); H. B. Meigs, *Record of the Descendants of Vincent Meigs* (1901); *Medic. News* (Phila.), Dec. 23, 1882; *Public Ledger* (Phila.), Dec. 18, 1882.]

J. M.

MEIGS, JOSIAH (Aug. 21, 1757–Sept. 4, 1822), lawyer, editor, educator, and public official, was a native of Middletown, Conn., the thirteenth child of Return Meigs, a hatter, and Elizabeth (Hamlin) Meigs. He was a descendant of Vincent Meigs, or Meggs, who came from England and finally settled in New Haven about 1644. One of Josiah's brothers, Return Jonathan, 1740–1823 [*q.v.*], rendered distinguished service in the War of the Revolution, and his son, Return Jonathan, 1764–1824 [*q.v.*], had a notable political career. Josiah graduated from Yale in 1778. Among his classmates were Joel Barlow, Noah Webster, Zephaniah Swift, and Oliver Wolcott [*qq.v.*]. He was teaching at Claverack, N. Y., when, in 1781, he was elected tutor in Yale College. That year he delivered an oration at the New Haven celebration of the victory over Cornwallis, which was published in 1782. On Jan. 21, 1782, he married Clara, daughter of Col. John Benjamin of Stratford, Conn. He was admitted to the bar in April 1783, and in February 1784, at the first election following the establishment of city government, was chosen city clerk of New Haven. After resigning as tutor in 1784, with Daniel Bowen and Eleutheros Dana he opened a printing office and established *The New Haven Gazette,* a weekly newspaper, the first number of which was issued May 13, 1784. In February 1786 Bowen retired, and the name of the publication was changed to *The New Haven Gazette and the Connecticut Magazine.* After Aug. 2, 1787, Meigs was sole proprietor until its discontinuance at the close of 1788. It supported the adoption of the Federal Constitution, and among the literary contributions which appeared in its columns was "The Anarchiad," written by Joel Barlow, John Trumbull, David Humphreys, and Lemuel Hopkins [*qq.v.*]. Keenly interested in scientific subjects, in 1787 Meigs delivered lectures at Yale on natural philosophy and astronomy.

He retained his position as city clerk until 1789, and at the Fourth of July celebration of that year delivered an oration which was described as "replete with benevolence and Federal ideas" (*Connecticut Journal,* July 15, 1789, quoted by Meigs, *post,* p. 26). A few months later he left New Haven for St. George, in the Bermuda Islands, to care for the interests of Connecticut clients. During the latter part of his sojourn there, which lasted until 1794, he advocated the causes of American claimants of captured property in the Court of Vice-admiralty so successfully as to incur the enmity or those who were directly or indirectly engaged in privateering. Furthermore, he was a man of hot temper and occasional recklessness of speech. As a result of his unpopularity and unguarded statements, he was arrested on the charge of treason, and was acquitted and released only through the exertions of Gov. Henry Hamilton.

After his return to the United States, he was appointed, Oct. 8, 1794, professor of mathematics and natural philosophy in Yale College, of which his friend Ezra Stiles [*q.v.*] was then president. He had by this time become an ardent Jeffersonian. In a Federalist stronghold, and with the inexorable Federalist Timothy Dwight [*q.v.*] as president of Yale—Stiles had died shortly after Meigs's appointment—it was inevitable that he should get into trouble. Consequently, after several years of friction, in December 1800 he resigned to accept a professorship in the University of Georgia—"exiled" from his native state "to the backwoods of Georgia only twelve miles from the Cherokee Indians," his wife declared with bitterness years later, "for no earthly reason but his stern democracy" (Meigs, *post,* pp. 42–43).

Chartered in 1785, this institution was as yet unestablished. Abraham Baldwin [*q.v.*] was its titular president, and it was at his instigation that Meigs had been called there. Baldwin now resigned and Meigs was elected in his place. He gathered students out of the academies of the state, and instructed them under the trees, in a tavern, and in his own dwelling, until a temporary log building was erected. In 1806 Franklin College, a substantial, three-story brick structure, was ready for occupancy. There were now some seventy students and the institution had acquired reputation throughout the state. Meigs's political pronouncements, however, his ill-concealed contempt for Georgians, whom he considered rude and uncivilized, and his frankness of speech soon made him enemies. The number of students decreased; his salary was reduced; and in August 1810 he resigned the presidency. He continued as professor for a year, and at the end of that time was charged with gross criticism of the trustees, and was dismissed. He published *A Statement of the Causes of the Removal . . .* (1811).

In November 1812 the President appointed him surveyor-general of the United States, and he took up his residence in Cincinnati. Two years later, October 1814, he was made commissioner of the General Land Office of the United States, at Washington. In this city he lived pleasantly for the remainder of his life. From 1819 until his death he was president of the Columbian Institute. He was one of the original corporators and trustees of Columbian College (now George Washington University), and professor of experimental philosophy there. His daughter Clara married John Forsyth [*q.v.*], later secretary of state under Jackson and Van Buren; Charles Delucena Meigs [*q.v.*] was his son; Montgomery C. Meigs and John Forsyth Meigs [*qq.v.*], were his grandsons.

[Wm. M. Meigs, *Life of Josiah Meigs* (1887) contains many references to source material. See also H. B. Meigs, *Record of the Descendants of Vincent Meigs* (copr. 1901); F. B. Dexter, *Biog. Sketches Grads. Yale Coll.,* vol. IV (1907); E. M. Coulter, *College Life in the Old South* (1928); A. L. Hull, *A Hist. Sketch of the Univ. of Ga.* (1894); C. E. Jones, *Education in Ga.* (1889); *Daily National Intelligencer* (Washington, D. C.), Sept. 5, 1822.]

H. E. S.

MEIGS, MONTGOMERY CUNNINGHAM (May 3, 1816–Jan. 2, 1892), soldier, engineer, was born in Augusta, Ga., the son of Dr. Charles Delucena Meigs [*q.v.*] and of Mary (Montgomery) Meigs of Philadelphia. He was an elder brother of John Forsyth Meigs [*q.v.*]. During his childhood the family moved from Georgia to Philadelphia, where he matriculated at the University of Pennsylvania in 1831. He later entered the United States Military Academy, graduating in 1836, fifth in his class. After temporary assignment to the artillery, he was transferred to the engineer corps of the Army, and thereafter, for a quarter of a century, his conspicuous ability was devoted to many important engineering projects. Of these, his favorite was the Washington Aqueduct, carrying a large part of the water supply from the Great Falls of the Potomac to the city of Washington. This work, of which he was in charge from November 1852 to September 1860, involved not only the devising of ingenious methods of controlling the flow and distribution of the water, but also the design of the monumental bridge across Cabin John Branch which for some fifty years remained unsurpassed as the longest masonry arch in the world. To this task was added from 1853 to 1859 the supervision of the building of the wings and dome of the national Capitol, and from 1855 to 1859, of the extension of the General Post Office building, as well as the direction of many minor works of construction. In the fall of 1860, as a result of a disagreement over certain contracts, Meigs "incurred the ill will of the Secretary of War, John B. Floyd," and was "banished to Tortugas in the Gulf of Mexico to construct fortifications at that place and at Key West" (Abbot, *post,* p. 317). Upon the resignation of Floyd a few months later, however, he was recalled to his work on the aqueduct at Washington.

Here, in the critical days preceding the actual outbreak of the Civil War, Meigs and Lieut.-Col. E. D. Keyes were quietly charged by President Lincoln and Secretary Seward with drawing up a plan for the relief of Fort Pickens, Fla., by means of a secret expedition; and in April 1861, together with Lieut. D. D. Porter of the Navy, they carried out the expedition, embarking under orders from the President without the knowledge of either the Secretary of the Navy or the Secretary of War. On May 14, 1861, Meigs was appointed colonel, 11th Infantry, and on the following day, promoted to brigadier-general, he became quartermaster-general of the Army, in which capacity he served throughout the war. Of his work in this office James G. Blaine remarked: "Montgomery C. Meigs, one of the ablest graduates of the Military Academy, was kept from the command of troops by the inestimably important services he performed as Quartermaster-General. . . . Perhaps in the military history of the world there was never so large an amount of money disbursed upon the order of a single man. . . . The aggregate sum could not have been less during the war than fifteen hundred millions of dollars, accurately vouched and accounted for to the last cent." (*Twenty Years in Congress,* vol. II, 1886, p. 30.) William H. Seward's estimate was "that without the services of this eminent soldier the national cause must have been lost or deeply imperilled" (letter, May 28, 1867, from the Secretary of State, asking the good offices of diplomatic officers for General Meigs during a tour of Europe; in possession of the family). His brilliant services during the hostilities included command of Grant's base of supplies at Fredericksburg and Belle Plain (1864), command of a division of War Department employees in the defenses of Washington at the time of Early's raid (July 11–14, 1864), personally supervising the refitting and supplying of Sherman's army at Savannah (Jan. 5–29, 1865), and at Goldsboro and Raleigh, N. C., reopening Sherman's lines of supply (March–April 1865). He was brevetted major-general July 5, 1864.

As quartermaster-general after the Civil War, Meigs supervised plans for the new War Department building (1866–67), the National Museum (1876), the extension of the Washington Aqueduct (1876), and for a hall of records (1878). In 1867–68, to recuperate from the strain of his war service, he visited Europe, and in 1875–76 made another visit to study the government of European armies. After his retirement on Feb. 6, 1882, he became architect of the Pension Office building. He was a regent of the Smithsonian Institution, a member of the American Philosophical Society, and one of the earliest members of the National Academy of Sciences. In 1888, although he "was not a literary person and had no taste for writing except of official reports of work done," at the request of the editors of *Battles and Leaders of the Civil War* he submitted an article on the relations of Lincoln and Seward to the military commanders during the war which was apparently intended as a reply to some of the statements in *McClellan's Own Story* (1887). It was not printed, however, until long after the author's death, when it appeared as a "document" in the *American Historical Review* (January 1921).

Meigs died in Washington after a short illness and his body was interred with high military honors in the National Cemetery at Arlington. The General Orders (Jan. 4, 1892) issued at the time of his death declared that "the Army has rarely possessed an officer . . . who was entrusted by the government with a greater variety of weighty responsibilities, or who proved himself more worthy of confidence." In 1841 he had married Louisa Rodgers, daughter of Commodore John Rodgers, 1773–1838 [*q.v.*]. Four of their seven children lived to maturity, but one of these, John Rodgers Meigs, a lieutenant of engineers, was killed in action during the Civil War.

[G. W. Cullum, in *Asso. Grads. U. S. Mil. Acad. Ann. Reunion,* 1892; H. L. Abbot, in *Nat. Acad. Sci. Biog. Memoirs,* vol. III (1895); the *Times* (London), Jan. 4, 1892; H. B. Meigs, *Record of the Descendants of Vincent Meigs* (1901); G. W. Cullum, *Biog. Reg. Officers and Grads. U. S. Mil. Acad.* (3rd ed., 1891); *Battles and Leaders of the Civil War* (4 vols., 1887–88); *War of the Rebellion: Official Records (Army)*; J. G. Nicolay and John Hay, *Abraham Lincoln: a History* (1890), esp. vols. III, IV; *Am. Hist. Rev.,* Jan. 1921, containing many other references; *Washington Post,* Jan. 3, 1892; information as to certain facts from Meigs's grandson, Col. J. R. M. Taylor.]

C. D. R.

MEIGS, RETURN JONATHAN (Dec. 17, 1740–Jan. 28, 1823), soldier and pioneer, was born at Middletown, Conn., the son of Return and Elizabeth (Hamlin) Meigs and the descendant of Vincent Meigs, who emigrated from Dorsetshire, England, about 1635. His brother was Josiah Meigs [*q.v.*]. His father, a hatter, was a member of the Connecticut General Assembly. In Feb. 14, 1764, he married Joanna Winborn, who died in 1773. She was the mother of his son, Return Jonathan Meigs, 1764–1824, and the grandmother of Return Jonathan Meigs, 1801–1891 [*qq.v.*]. On Dec. 22, 1774, he married Grace Starr, who died in Tennessee in 1807. In 1772 he was commissioned by Governor

Trumbull of the Connecticut colony as lieutenant in the 6th Connecticut Regiment. Two years later he was made captain. After the battle of Lexington he swiftly assembled his company and marched to the aid of Boston. He was commissioned major and, in September, with his command joined Arnold's ill-fated expedition to Quebec, during which he kept a diary, written with ink made by mixing powder and water in his palm, which was afterward published ("Journal," *Massachusetts Historical Society Collections,* ser. 2, vol. II, 1814, and privately printed 1864). At the assault of the city he was one of those who scaled the walls and was made prisoner of war. He was paroled and the following January was exchanged. He reëntered the Continental service and was commissioned lieutenant-colonel. In 1777 he led the brilliant Sag Harbor expedition in reprisal for Tryon's Danbury raid. Taking about 160 men from General Parson's forces, in thirteen whaleboats he crossed Long Island Sound under convoy of two armed sloops, not forgetting to take an extra sloop in which to bring back the prisoners. Landing on Long Island he marched across to Sag Harbor, surprised the garrison, burned eleven or twelve vessels, destroyed a large quantity of military stores, killed several of the enemy, and took about ninety prisoners, without losing a man. For this exploit he was voted a sword by Congress. Soon afterward he became colonel and reported at Peekskill with his 6th Connecticut Infantry, "the Leather-Cap Regiment." During the summer and fall he took part in all the principal engagements along the Hudson. At the storming of Stonypoint under Gen. Anthony Wayne, which did so much to raise the morale of the American army, he led a regiment and was one of the first to storm the fort. In May 1780 he received a personal note of thanks from Washington for his prompt action in suppressing a mutiny among the Connecticut troops. Upon the discovery of Arnold's treason in September his regiment was one of those sent to West Point to meet any consequent attack by the British. When the Connecticut regiments were reorganized in 1781 he was retired.

Becoming interested in the organization of the Ohio Company, he was appointed one of its surveyors, and in April 1788, he landed at the mouth of the Muskingum with the small group of other settlers from New England. He drew up a code of rules, which were adopted by the colony, and posted them on a big oak tree. In 1801 he was appointed Indian agent to the Cherokee, who named him "The White Path." He was commissioner to negotiate treaties in 1804, 1805, and 1807, and in 1808 he was given authority to negotiate a convention between the state of Tennessee and the Cherokee. When he was eighty-two years old, having given up his quarters to an elderly visiting Indian chief and moved into a tent, he contracted pneumonia and died. He was buried at the Cherokee agency in Tennessee.

[MSS. in Lib. of Cong.; H. B. Meigs, *Record of the Descendants of Vincent Meigs* (1901) with facsimiles of Revolutionary documents; S. P. Hildreth, *Biog. and Hist. Memoirs* (1852), pp. 195–96, 258–78; *Am. Archives,* ed. by Peter Force, ser. 5, vol. I (1848); *The Record of Conn. Men in the Military and Naval Service during the . . . Revolution,* ed. by H. P. Johnston (1889); *Am. State Papers: Indian Affairs* (2 vols., 1832–34); G. H. Hollister, *The Hist. of Conn.* (1855); T. J. Summers, *Hist. of Marietta* (1903).] I. L. T.

MEIGS, RETURN JONATHAN (Nov. 17, 1764–Mar. 29, 1824), governor of Ohio, senator, and postmaster-general, was the son of Joanna (Winborn) and Return Jonathan Meigs, 1740–1823 [*q.v.*], and the uncle of Return Jonathan Meigs, 1801–1891 [*q.v.*]. He was born in Middletown, Conn., graduated from Yale College in 1785, studied law, and was admitted to the Connecticut bar. In 1788 he married Sophia Wright. The same year he moved to Marietta, Ohio, a settlement so near the frontier that he, along with other settlers, narrowly escaped death at the hands of Indians. In 1798 he was appointed one of the judges of the territorial government. With the organization of the territorial legislature in 1799 he was elected to represent the Marietta region. He supported the cause of statehood in 1801 and, upon the creation of the new state, was appointed chief justice of the supreme court. In October 1804 he resigned this position to accept an appointment as commandant of United States troops and militia in the St. Charles district of Louisiana. In 1805 he was appointed a judge in Louisiana Territory. He returned to Ohio in 1806 and was called to Richmond, Va., on business relating to Burr's trial. He was transferred to serve as a judge in Michigan Territory but resigned for he became a candidate for governor of Ohio in opposition to Nathaniel Massie. He won the election by a considerable majority but was declared to be constitutionally ineligible because of his prolonged absence from the state. He was elected to the federal Senate to fill the vacancy created by the resignation of John Smith, who was alleged to have been an accomplice of Burr. He was reëlected the next election and sat in the Senate from Dec. 12, 1808, to May 1, 1810. In 1810 he ran again for governor with Thomas Worthington as his opponent. Worthington represented the ardently democratic Scioto settlements, while Meigs, on account of his conservatism and New England connections, gained the support of the conservative Republicans and of the Federalist minority. He was elected by the strength of this combination.

Although the governors under the first constitution were almost powerless, the imminence of war with Great Britain gave him an opportunity for real leadership. Largely through his efforts 1,200 state militiamen were recruited and equipped in time for Hull's rendezvous at Dayton in 1812. The war spirit in Ohio was dampened by Hull's defeat, however, and for a time Meigs suffered severe criticism. Nevertheless he was again elected in 1812, and in the following year again was active in raising men and supplies for the war. In March 1814 he resigned as governor to accept the position of postmaster-general, an appointment that was a recognition of his vigorous support of the war. During his administration of the post office department the number of post offices increased from approximately 3,000 to 5,200 and the mileage of post-roads from about 41,000 to 85,000. Consequently he experienced difficulty in maintaining the department on a self-supporting basis. Occasional deficits and alleged irregularities in the awarding of mail-contracts led to an investigation of the affairs of the department by Congress in 1816 and again in 1821. Neither investigation resulted in more than a charge of inefficiency against him. He resigned from office in June 1823 because of ill health and returned to Marietta, where he died. His wife and their only child, Mary, who married John George Jackson [*q.v.*], survived him.

[MSS. in the Lib. of Cong. and in the Ohio State Lib. at Columbus; F. B. Dexter, *Biog. Sketches of the Grads. of Yale College,* vol. IV (1907); *Biog. Sketches with other Literary Remains of the late John W. Campbell* (1838); for reports of post office *Am. State Papers: Post Office Department* (1834), pp. 46–113; H. B. Meigs, *Record of the Descendants of Vincent Meigs* (copr. 1901); *Green Bag,* Mar. 1893.] W. T. U.

MEIGS, RETURN JONATHAN (Apr. 14, 1801–Oct. 19, 1891), lawyer, the son of John and Parthenia Clendinen Meigs, was born near Winchester in Clark county, Ky. He was the grandson of Return Jonathan Meigs, 1740–1823, the nephew of Return Jonathan Meigs, 1764–1824, and was related by marriage to John George Jackson [*qq.v.*]. After his father died in 1807 he lived part of the time with his uncle, James Lemme, in Bourbon County. In the schools of the community he acquired the fundamentals of a classical education. He studied law and was admitted to the bar in Frankfort in 1822. He moved to Tennessee where, on Nov. 1, 1825, he married Sally Keys Love. For some ten years or more he practised law in Athens, Tenn. On account of popular prejudice against lawyers he was defeated in 1834 for a seat in Tennessee's constitutional convention. Soon he moved to Nashville, the capital of the state, where for a quarter of a century he was a distinguished and highly respected member of the bar. In 1838 and 1839 he was attorney-general of the state and reporter of its supreme-court decisions (19 *Tenn. Reports,* 1839). In 1841 he was appointed United States attorney for the Middle Tennessee district. In 1848–50 he published a two-volume *Digest of all the Decisions of the Former Superior Courts of Law and Equity, and of the Present Supreme Court of Errors and Appeals in the State of Tennessee.* In 1858 he and William F. Cooper published their compilation of the *Code of Tennessee,* the only one legally adopted by the legislature until 1931. As a Whig he served one term in the state Senate from 1847 to 1848. In this body he sponsored a free banking bill, based upon New York's banking laws, that was defeated at this time but subsequently enacted. He was also an advocate of public education and state and local aid to internal improvements. As early as 1831 he had supported proposals for the building of railroads to connect Tennessee with the Atlantic seaboard. He took a prominent part in the encouragement of the educational, cultural, and humanitarian development of his adopted state. He was the first president of the Tennessee society for the diffusion of knowledge, a corresponding secretary of the Tennessee historical society, a member of the Nashville board of education, a trustee of the University of Nashville and of the state school for the education of the blind, and an incorporator of the Tennessee society for the colonization of free negroes. He was a patron of public lectures, the theatre, and music. He was said to have declined a position on the state's supreme court because the salary, $1,800, was too small, but in 1856 he accepted appointment as state librarian at a salary of $500. He was one of the few prominent inhabitants of Middle Tennessee who remained loyal to the Union after the Civil War began. In 1861, severely censured by his neighbors for his Unionism and in danger of mob violence, he resigned the office of librarian and went to New York. When Andrew Johnson became military governor of Tennessee, he gave him legal advice regarding the government of the state. He is said to have declined election to the United States Senate in 1865 and an offer of appointment to the United States Supreme Court (statement of son in *Record of Descendants, post,* p. 250; see *Star, post*). In 1863 he was appointed clerk of the supreme court of the District of Columbia. He continued in the active discharge of the duties of this office until almost the day of his death at the age of ninety. He was survived by his five sons.

[J. T. Moore, *Tenn.* (1923), vol. II; J. W. Caldwell, *Sketches of the Bench and Bar of Tenn.* (1898); H. S. Foote, *The Bench and Bar of the South and Southwest* (1876); H. B. Meigs, *Record of the Descendants of Vincent Meigs* (copr. 1901); *Evening Star* (Washington), Oct. 20, 1891.] P. M. H.

MEIGS, WILLIAM MONTGOMERY (Aug. 12, 1852–Dec. 30, 1929), lawyer and historian, was one of the eight children of Dr. John Forsyth Meigs [*q.v.*] and Ann Wilcocks (Ingersoll) Meigs. Arthur Vincent Meigs [*q.v.*] was his brother; their progenitors included Chief Justice Benjamin Chew [*q.v.*] of Pennsylvania, Professor Josiah Meigs [*q.v.*] of Yale and the University of Georgia, and Charles Jared Ingersoll [*q.v.*], historian, playwright, and member of Congress. After the death of their mother, the children were cared for in part by their paternal grandmother, while their grandfather, Charles Delucena Meigs [*q.v.*], taught them the family history and the "duty incumbent upon them . . . to promote its honorableness." William attended John W. Faires's Classical Institute (1862–68) and the University of Pennsylvania (A.B., 1872; A.M. and M.D., 1875), read law in the office of George W. Biddle, and in 1879 was admitted to the Philadelphia bar. Unhappily, after this preparation for several sorts of useful citizenship, he remained handicapped by persistent ill health; but by adjusting his activities to his limitations he achieved a life of singular unity. Selecting two fields of historical interest, he explored them in parallel lines thenceforward: legal problems of the relationship between constitutions and courts; biographical problems of certain men whose lives spanned the septennial of 1780–1850.

American legal origins and practice, concerning the powers of federal and state courts, were the objects of careful study, which he summarized in numerous articles contributed to the *Southern Law Review, American Law Review, American Law Register*, and *Constitutional Review* (see *Index to Legal Periodicals*). When federal courts were called upon to determine questions arising from state laws, Meigs concluded, they should, generally, follow the laws of the states and the decisions of state courts thereon. But the power of supreme courts to declare laws unconstitutional and to refuse to enforce them was sound and eminently beneficial, if not abused. Contrary arguments, that this power was in itself "a great usurpation," aroused his amazement. He edited Brinton Coxe's *Essay on Judicial Power and Unconstitutional Legislation* (1893); and produced his own topical summary of the debates waged in the Constitutional Convention and the action finally taken in *The Growth of the Constitution in the Federal Convention of 1787* (1900; reprinted in W. M. Meigs and T. H. Calvert, *The Constitution and the Courts*, 3 vols., 1924).

In biography, the semi-invalid found "an occupation that could be taken up or dropped at will." In the course of his travels in search of health he searched for distant source materials. Sick or well, he kept to the rigorous standards of his first book in this field, *Life of Josiah Meigs* (1887). "I have made every effort," he wrote in the preface, "to be accurate and to avoid writing a sentence . . . which would not be easily capable of proof . . . while not hesitating at the same time to speak in plain language" (p. vii). He then turned to a study of "Pennsylvania Politics Early in this Century," published in the *Pennsylvania Magazine of History and Biography*, December 1893. Next, another ancestral biography, *The Life of Charles Jared Ingersoll* (1897), developed the thesis that the men who agitated against slavery, with disregard for the Union, were not necessarily right. Thereafter for some time Meigs concentrated his efforts upon *The Life of Thomas Hart Benton* (1904), producing an able and scholarly biography of a character in whom he had long been interested. Years of industrious examination of sources next were devoted to *The Life of John Caldwell Calhoun* (2 vols., 1917), a work accepted by J. S. Bassett as "the long-desired complete and impartial life of the Great Nullifier" (*American Political Science Review*, February 1918, p. 139). Its breadth of treatment and sense of proportion, its discussion of economic causes behind nullification, were especially commendable. Southerners found in it an indication of Northerners' improved understanding of the South's predicament (*Virginia Law Review*, October 1919, pp. 73–75), and although W. E. Dodd thought that it had certain defects as history, he commended it as biography unsurpassed for thoroughness of research (*American Historical Review*, July 1918, pp. 872–74). Meigs never married. Despite his frail health he lived to a ripe age, dying four months after the completion of his seventy-seventh year.

[*Who's Who in America*, 1928–29; H. B. Meigs, *Record of the Descendants of Vincent Meigs* (1901); C. J. Cohen, *Memoir of Rev. John Wiley Faires* (1926); *Phila. Inquirer, Public Ledger, N. Y. Times*, Dec. 31, 1929; information as to certain facts from Miss A. I. Meigs.] J. P. N.

MELCHERS, GARI (Aug. 11, 1860–Nov. 30, 1932), painter, probably received the germ of his proficiency by transmission from his father, Julius Theodore Melchers, a Westphalian who had a Franco-Dutch mother. The elder Melchers was himself a sculptor and decorator, who had studied under Carpeaux and Étex in Paris. On coming to America—and marrying Marie Bangetor—he made his home in Detroit, where the son, named Julius Gari, was born. From the start there seems to have been complete sympathy on the father's part for his son's gravitation toward an artistic career. The boy was only seventeen when he was permitted to go abroad to study painting, not amid the beguilements of Paris, to be sure, but in either Munich or Düsseldorf, as he chose. Melchers selected Düsseldorf and entered the Royal Art Academy there under Professor Von Gebhardt. His sojourn was indicative of future contacts. He was always to have ties with the artistic side of Germany. But in his youth the lure of Paris was not to be withstood. He visited the great exposition there in 1878. Returning to Düsseldorf he remained for three years but at the end of that period he entered the École des Beaux-Arts, where he received instruction and criticism from Boulanger and Lefebvre. It was the turning point in his career. Paris completed what Düsseldorf had begun and he had a picture accepted for the Salon of 1882.

A brief period of work in Italy followed and after that a visit to his home, but in 1884 he was in Europe again, with studios in Paris and at Egmond, in Holland. Thenceforth he was active on both sides of the Atlantic down to the time of his death. He achieved an international repute through the solidity of his gift and through the wide range covered in its exercise. Religious as well as secular motives came within his scope. He was skilled alike in portraiture and in the painting of landscape and flowers, and his works in the Library of Congress at Washington and elsewhere testify to his aptitude in mural decoration. He was in a rare degree the thoughtful practitioner, working in all the categories and functioning therein with a full-rounded equipment of both mind and hand. In 1903 he married Corinne Lawton Mackall, of Savannah, Ga., and in 1916 they established themselves on a delightful estate above the Rappahannock at Falmouth, near Fredericksburg, Va. It was there that he died, childless, very soon after the American Academy of Arts and Letters, of which he was a member, had opened a retrospective exhibition of his works and the National Institute of Arts and Letters had awarded him its gold medal. He was president of the Century Association in New York at the time. He died literally "full of years and honors." All his life fortune had smiled upon him, appreciation had met him upon every side. It was as a distinguished artist that he was in 1909 invited by the Grand Duke of Saxe-Weimar to occupy one of the park pavilions at Weimar. His colleagues in America and in Europe recognized his powers. He was a member of the Royal Academy of Berlin, the International Society of Sculptors, Painters, and Gravers in England, the Société Nationale des Beaux-Arts in Paris, the Institute of France, the Royal Society of Austrian Painters, and the National Academy of Design in his own land. He was an officer of the Legion of Honor and was the recipient of more than one European Order. The enumeration of these honors has no merely conventional significance. It points rather to the character of his art.

His early training had much to do with the felicity of his painting, for it grounded him in habits of fine draftsmanship and sound design which he never lost. The retrospective exhibition mentioned above made this last circumstance impressively manifest, illustrating as it did with equal brilliance the diverse aspects of a long career. In his early manhood at Egmond he inscribed over the door of his studio the Dutch words "Waar en Klaar," and he pursued those qualities with unremitting ardor and astonishingly even success. His art was, indeed, true and clear, true to nature, and invested with the clarity only attainable by an expert technician. Nothing offers better evidence of his poise than the unforced nature of that quality in his work to which the word "picturesque" must be applied. He long had a keen interest in the humble life of Holland, the milkmaids in the fields, the peasant girl dressed for Communion, the villagers at worship, and he loved both the distinctive dress they wore, and the background against which they moved. But his most ambitious design was never the set "costume piece." On the contrary it was a page from life, singularly direct and sincere. So when he chose "The Last Supper" for a theme he treated it imaginatively, tenderly, but above all things humanly.

Melchers was a forthright, candid man, pungent in speech, frank in action, and of altogether generous and genuine traits. His character, as lovable as it was virile, passed into his work. There is nothing fumbling or uncertain about his stroke. The drawing in a picture of his is firm and flowing, the touch of the brush forceful, the color pure, strong, and charming. As a colorist, indeed, he was exceptionally dowered, making a note of white, or green, or violet, or orange, sing with equal plangency and beauty. He had deep feeling. It comes out in the earnest countenances of the men and women assembled in one or another of his Dutch church interiors. It is perceptible in his "Last Supper," a composition of noble dignity and warm emotional content. His insight is disclosed by his portraits, which are vivid characterizations. His rank is determined by these imponderables and by his ability as a painter pure and simple, a master of his craft who was devoted to the integrity of art.

[*Gari Melchers: Painter* (1928) is a book of plates containing a Foreword by Henriette Lewis-Hind. See also: *Who's Who in America*, 1932–33; *Am. Art Annual*, 1931; Christian Brinton, *Modern Artists* (1908); *Biog. Sketches of Am. Artists* (1924), pub. by the Mich. State Lib.; *Internat. Studio*, Mar. 1907, Dec. 1912; *World's Work*, Apr. 1908; *Mag. of Art*, Feb. 1900; obituaries in *N. Y. Herald-Tribune*, *N. Y. Times*, *Boston Transcript*, and other papers. This spelling of Melchers' mother's name is correct, although the form Bangertor appears in *Who's Who in America*.] R. C.

MELISH, JOHN (June 13, 1771–Dec. 30, 1822), geographer, traveler, merchant, was born in Methven, Perthshire, Scotland, where he spent his early years and attended the parish school. He was apprenticed to a wealthy cotton factor in Glasgow who permitted him to take the examinations at Glasgow University with his own son, and in time he became a member of his employer's firm. In 1798 he voyaged to the West Indies and on the trip began to study geography and navigation. In 1806 he sailed to Savannah, Ga., and there established a mercantile house of his own through which passed manufactured goods from abroad and raw cotton from the South. He traveled extensively through the cotton states, taking numerous notes as he went with the intention of publishing later a work on the geographical, social, and political character of the United States. In 1807 he returned to Scotland, but in 1808 his business suffered from the effects of the Orders in Council and the Non-Intercourse acts, and in 1809 he again sailed to the United States to look after his affairs, bringing his family with him. For a time he was in New York, engaged in the importing business, then he resumed his travels in America, this time through Upper Canada and the West.

In 1811 he settled in Philadelphia, which was thereafter his home. He decided to write the narrative of his travels in America, hoping that it would encourage British subjects to emigrate to the United States, and in 1812 he published in two volumes *Travels in the United States of America, in the Years 1806 & 1807, and 1809, 1810 & 1811*. The work was republished, with a slight variation in title, in 1815 and 1818. Melish displayed his talent for draftsmanship in the eight maps which illustrated the work. "Here is a kind of phenomenon," said a reviewer in the *Port Folio* (February 1813, pp. 114, 132), "two whole volumes of travels in America; without any material errors; with no palpable falsehoods; no malignant abuse of individuals; no paltry calumnies on the institutions of the U. S. . . . A singular example of the good temper, the sound sense, and the candid feelings which a sensible foreigner has brought to the examination of our country."

While Melish was engaged in drawing the maps for his first work, it was suggested to him that a map of the seat of the War of 1812 would be useful, and from his own and two British army maps he compiled *A Military and Topographical Atlas of the United States, Including the British Possessions & Florida* (1813), which was republished in enlarged form in 1815. Melish was listed in the Philadelphia directory in 1813 as a merchant, in 1814 as a map and print seller, in 1816 as a map publisher, and in 1818, in association with Samuel Harrison, as a geographer, engraver, and map publisher. He built up an establishment which at one time employed thirty persons. He continued to publish his own works. His most notable undertaking was *The State Map of Pennsylvania* (1822) for which the state legislature made provision in 1816. Much of the data for the chart was collected by Melish. Some geological data was supplied by William Maclure [*q.v.*]. His other works include: *A Statistical Account of the United States* (1813); *A Description of East and West Florida and the Bahama Islands* (1813), with map; *A Description of the Roads in the United States* (1814); *The Sine Qua Non: A Map of the United States, Shewing the Boundary Proposed by the British Commissioners at Ghent* (1814); *A Geographical Description of the United States with the Contiguous British and Spanish Possessions* (1816), to accompany a map; *A Geographical Description of the World* (1818), to accompany a map of the world; *The Necessity of Protecting and Encouraging the Manufactures of the United States* (1818); *Information and Advice to Emigrants to the United States* (1819); and *Views on Political Economy* (1822). Melish died in Philadelphia and, although he was not a Quaker, was buried in the ground of the Free Quakers. He had married, in Scotland, Isabella Moncrieff.

[There is some autobiographical information in Melish's *Travels*. Other sources include: R. B. Beath, *Hist. Cat. of the St. Andrew's Soc. of Phila.*, vol. II (1913); *A Cat. of Maps and Geog. Works Published and for Sale by John Melish* (1822); W. H. Egle, *Notes and Queries*, I (1894), 361; *Poulson's Am. Daily Ad-*

vertiser, Jan. 1, 1823; manuscript register of the Philadelphia board of health.] J. J.

MELL, PATRICK HUES (July 19, 1814–Jan. 26, 1888), Baptist clergyman, teacher, author, born in Walthourville, Liberty County, Ga., was the eldest surviving son in a family of eight children. His father was Benjamin Mell, whose ancestors were among the early settlers of Charleston, S. C., and his mother, Cynthia Sumner, a descendant of New England Puritans who went to Georgia in the migration of 1754. When Patrick was still in his teens, both his parents died. The estate having been lost on a surety bond, Mell was obliged to provide for the family. Having received some educational training before the death of his father, he continued his schooling at the academies of Walthourville and of Darien, teaching in the primary department to pay his tuition. His industry attracted the attention of George Walthour, who provided funds for his education at Amherst College, and Mell enrolled there in 1833. His independent disposition caused him to accept this financial aid with reluctance, and disagreement over his expenses together with a distaste for some of his instructors caused him to leave college in 1835. He immediately found a teaching position in a West Springfield school and in 1836 became associate principal of the high school in East Hartford, Conn. In 1837 he returned to Georgia and was thereafter identified with that state.

For two years he taught successively at Perry's Mill in Tatnall County and at Ryall's in Montgomery County. From 1839 to 1841 he was the principal of a classical and English school at Oxford. He had joined the Baptist Church in 1832, abandoning an inclination to study law, and in October 1839 he received a license to preach. He now began preaching to the destitute congregations in the countryside. In 1841 he was elected professor of ancient languages at Mercer College, an institution which the Baptists had established a few years previously at Penfield, and he continued in this position for fourteen years. Following a rather common practice of teaching and preaching at the same time, he was ordained Nov. 19, 1842, and took charge of the Baptist congregation at Greensboro. After serving this congregation for ten years, he accepted calls from two churches, one at Bairdstown and the other at Antioch, continuing his ministry to the latter for twenty-six years. At Mercer College a conflict developed between him and the president on the question of the respective rights and duties of each, which resulted in his forced resignation. Much bitterness resulted which a faction of the Baptists long kept alive.

By this time Mell's influence had become so widespread that he was offered various pastorates in the state and the presidency of several Baptist colleges. In 1856 he accepted the professorship of ancient languages at the University of Georgia, Athens, and when in 1860, the University was reorganized with a chancellor and vice-chancellor at its head, he accepted the latter position. At the same time he was transferred to the professorship of ethics and metaphysics. He remained vice-chancellor until 1872 when the office was abolished, but retained his professorship for the rest of his life. At the outbreak of the Civil War he was made captain of a company known as the Mell Rifles. Because of the death of his wife on July 6 following, he resigned; but in 1863, when the state was in danger of invasion from the Tennessee border, he raised a regiment, made up in part of students and professors of the university, and became its colonel. He remained in the service until the end of the war.

His strenuous work as teacher and preacher broke down his health in 1871 and it was not fully restored until after a trip to Europe two years later. In 1878 he was elected chancellor of the university, which position he held until his death. He was an able educator and a strict disciplinarian, erect in figure, austere in manner, independent in disposition, reserved and distant generally, though courteous and punctilious. As a preacher he was powerful though not eloquent, and as a parliamentarian he was unequaled in the state. He was moderator of the Georgia Baptist Association for twenty-nine years, president of the Georgia Convention for twenty-five years, and of the Southern Baptist Convention for fifteen years. The best known of his numerous writings are *Baptism in Its Modes and Subjects* (1852); *Manual on Corrective Church Discipline* (1860); *A Manual of Parliamentary Practice* (1868); and *Church Polity* (1878). He was married twice: first, June 29, 1840, to Lurene Howard Cooper of Montgomery County, who died July 6, 1861, and by whom there were eight children, one of whom was Patrick Hues Mell, 1850–1890 [*q.v.*]; second, Dec. 24, 1861, to Eliza Elizabeth Cooper of Scriven County, who bore him six children.

[The most satisfactory and complete account is P. H. Mell, Jr., *Life of Patrick Hues Mell* (1895). His record as chancellor of the University of Georgia may be found in the Minutes of the trustees and of the faculty, in the University Library. See also Dr. and Mrs. P. H. Mell, *The Geneal. of the Mell Family in the Southern States* (1897); *Amherst Coll. Biog. Record of the Grads. and Non-Grads.* (1927), ed. by R. S. Fletcher and M. O. Young; A. L. Hull, *A Hist. Sketch of the Univ. of Ga.* (1894), and *Annals of Athens, Ga., 1801–1901* (1906); E. M. Coulter, *College Life in the*

Old South (1928); *Proc. Thirty-third Session of the Southern Bapt. Convention* (1888); B. D. Ragsdale, *Story of Ga. Baptists* (copr. 1932); *Atlanta Constitution*, Jan. 27, 1888; W. J. Northen, *Men of Mark in Ga.* (1911), vol. III.] E. M. C.

MELL, PATRICK HUES (May 24, 1850–Oct. 12, 1918), scientist, educator, was born in Penfield, Ga., the son of Patrick Hues Mell [*q.v.*] and Lurene Howard (Cooper). He was reared in an atmosphere of discipline, scholarship, and culture, which left its stamp upon him. Entering the University of Georgia in 1866, he received the degree of A.B. in 1871 and that of M.E. in 1872; eight years later he was awarded the degree of Ph.D. In 1874, he became chemist for the Georgia Department of Agriculture. Resigning in 1877 because of ill health, he tramped and rode through the mountains of Alabama, Georgia, and North Carolina collecting specimens of clays and other minerals. These and magazine articles which he wrote attracted attention, and in 1878 he was elected professor of natural history in the State Agricultural and Mechanical College (Alabama Polytechnic Institute) at Auburn, Ala.; later his title was changed to professor of geology and botany. In 1884, in addition to his teaching, he had charge of the state weather service for Georgia, Florida, and Alabama, and when separate bureaus were formed in these states he became director of the Alabama weather service. In the latter work, which he carried on until 1893, he originated the system of weather signals long in use by the United States Weather Bureau (*Who's Who in America*, 1918–19). From 1888 to 1902 he was also connected with the Alabama Agricultural Experiment Station, serving as botanist and meteorologist and from 1898 as director. He declined the presidency of Mercer University, Georgia, in 1893, and of the North Georgia Agricultural College in 1897, but in 1902, accepted the presidency of the Clemson Agricultural College, South Carolina. The institution was then only nine years old, and Mell's experience was most valuable in directing its affairs, his enthusiasm and ability as a teacher of science making themselves distinctly felt. Resigning in 1910, he made his home thereafter in Atlanta, and gave his time to the work of treasurer of the board of missions of the Southern Baptist Convention.

Mell was a pioneer in several lines of science. His collections of fossils was one of the best in the South; his work in hybridizing cotton was extensive for his day and of suggestive value to plant breeders; and his work on the climatology of Alabama was of permanent value. Among his publications were "Auriferous Slate Deposits of the Southern Mining Region" (*Transactions of the American Institute of Mining Engineers*, vol. IX, 1881), "The Southern Soapstones, Kaolin, and Fireclays and Their Uses" (*Ibid.*, vol. X, 1882); *Wild Grasses of Alabama* (1886), issued by the Alabama Department of Natural History and Geology; *Climatology of Alabama* (1890), *A Microscopic Study of the Cotton Plant* (1890), *Experiments in Crossing for the Purpose of Improving the Cotton Fiber* (1894), all bulletins of the Alabama Agricultural Experiment Station; and *Report on the Climatology of the Cotton Plant* (1893), a bulletin of the United States Department of Agriculture Weather Bureau. He also contributed extensively to periodicals, revised several works by others, and published a biography of his father, *Life of Patrick Hues Mell* (1895).

Probably his most distinctive contribution, however, was his service as a teacher. The agricultural and mechanical colleges of the South were in their infancy when he went to Alabama, and in the development of two of these he was an important agent. "He was a very modest man and an extremely courteous one, but his influence was not to be resisted. In this he was a fine type of the Southern professor of the old days. He was not a specialist; he was a scientist with broad sympathies and attractive personality" (Calhoun, *post*, p. 45). On June 15, 1875, he married Annie R. White of Athens, Ga. He died in Fredericksburg, Va., while visiting a brother-in-law.

[Dr. and Mrs. P. H. Mell, *The Geneal. of the Mell Family in the Southern States* (1897); F. H. H. Calhoun, "Memorial of Patrick Hues Mell," in *Bull. Geol. Soc. of America*, Mar. 1919; *Bulls. of Ala. Agric. Experiment Station*, 1888–1902; P. H. Mell, *Life of Patrick Hues Mell* (1895); *Reports* of the board of trustees of Clemson Coll., S. C., 1906–11; *Science*, Nov. 22, 1918; *Who's Who in America*, 1918–19; *Atlanta Constitution*, Oct. 15, 1918; information from associates; date of death from a brother.] E. W. S.

MELLEN, CHARLES SANGER (Aug. 16, 1851–Nov. 17, 1927), railroad executive, son of George K. and Hannah M. (Sanger) Mellen, was born at Lowell, Mass. He was educated in the public schools of Concord, N. H., graduating from the high school in 1867. He began his career in the cashier's office of the Northern New Hampshire Railroad (1869), and then rose in his profession through successive positions on the Central Vermont (1872–73), Northern New Hampshire (1873–80), and the Boston & Lowell (1880–88). He became general purchasing agent for the Union Pacific in 1888 (*Railroad Gazette*, Aug. 31, 1888, p. 580), and was later advanced to general traffic manager. In 1892 he was made general manager of the New York & New England Railroad and then second vice-president of the New York, New Haven & Hartford. During this period he was married twice: first, to Marion Beardsley Foster of St. Albans, Vt., on Sept. 23, 1875; and second, to Katharine Lloyd Livingston of Brooklyn, N. Y., on Nov. 15, 1893.

Mellen's advance from 1892 on, was due largely to the influence of J. P. Morgan, who was instrumental in obtaining for him in 1897 the presidency of the Northern Pacific. Mellen's term of office was during a significant period in the history of the Northern Pacific, but he had little to do with the financial affairs of the company. He acquired feeders, improved the road, and produced a favorable operating ratio. His competition with the Great Northern was objectionable to James J. Hill [*q.v.*], and as Hill's power increased, a change became inevitable. In 1903 Mellen returned to the New York, New Haven & Hartford Railroad as president. By this time he had a national reputation. In 1904 he was a delegate to the Republican National Convention. During the same year President Roosevelt consulted him about railroad affairs and quoted him extensively in the annual message to Congress (See *Congressional Record,* 58 Cong., 3 Sess., p. 12).

Mellen's policy with the New Haven was similar to that which he had followed with the Northern Pacific. Leaving the financial affairs largely in the hands of the road's directors and bankers, he improved the rolling stock, added new track, built stations, beautified the yards, installed safety devices, electrified the entrance to New York City, and joined the Pennsylvania Railroad in constructing the Hell Gate route. He nearly succeeded in monopolizing the transportational system of New England by buying trolley lines, steamships, and railroads (he was president of both the Boston & Maine and the Maine Central from 1910), and by preventing the Grand Trunk from entering Providence. Mellen was a hard worker and had a driving personality, but he tended to be glacial in his human contacts, dictatorial to his subordinates, and subservient to his superiors. Furthermore, he had marital troubles during the years 1912–13. A series of very serious train accidents in these same years brought to a climax the growing resentment against a virtual monopoly of New England transportation. The Interstate Commerce Commission, after an investigation, called the Mellen management "one of the most glaring instances of maladministration revealed in all the history of American railroading" (31 *Interstate Commerce Commission Reports,* 33). Most of the charges against Mellen can be read in this report. The bad financial practices were probably only slightly his fault, but as president he had to assume the responsibility. The failure to maintain proper equipment and service must be laid at his door, although he had made some improvements and was handicapped by a conservative board of directors. No matter where the fault lay, the popular outcry plus a long series of governmental investigations finally caused his resignation in 1913. After rumors of other possible positions, he retired from practically all his business interests to live at his home at Stockbridge, Mass. Later he returned to Concord, N. H., where he died.

[Newspapers and magazines, particularly during the years 1912–13, contained a great amount of material about Mellen; among the magazine articles may be mentioned E. P. Lyle, Jr., "C. S. Mellen, Master of Traffic," *World's Work,* May 1905; G. W. Batson, "Charles S. Mellen: Railroad Organizer," *Rev. of Revs.* (N. Y.), Aug. 1907; B. J. Hendrick, "Bottling Up New England," *McClure's Mag.,* Sept. 1912; Garet Garrett, "Things That Were Mellen's and Things That Were Cæsar's," *Everybody's Mag.,* July 1914. The best adverse analysis of the Mellen régime is L. D. Brandeis, *Financial Condition of the New York, New Haven & Hartford . . .* (1907), and the most extensive defense is J. F. Moors, "Betraying New England!" in *New Eng. Mag.,* Mar. and Apr. 1913. Mellen's testimony before the Interstate Commerce Commission was reprinted as a pamphlet, *Official Stenographer's Report of the Testimony of Charles S. Mellen . . . at Boston, Mass., May 2, 1913*; see also *Sen. Doc. 543,* 63 Cong., 2 Sess. Among Mellen's public utterances may be mentioned *Letter of C. S. Mellen . . . to the Public on Dec. 20, 1912* (n.d.) and an interview by F. C. Leupp in the *Outlook,* Feb. 3, 1912. For biographical details see *Who's Who in America,* 1924–25; and obituary in *N. Y. Times,* Nov. 18, 1927.]
R. E. R.

MELLEN, GRENVILLE (June 19, 1799–Sept. 5, 1841), author, the son of Prentiss Mellen [*q.v.*] and Sarah (Hudson) Mellen, was born at Biddeford, now in the state of Maine, before his father's removal to Portland. He attended Portland Academy and entered Harvard in 1814. In college he cultivated his interests in poetry and oratory and was class poet at graduation in 1818. He next attended the newly established Harvard Law School until 1820, spent another year in his father's law office, was admitted to the Maine bar, and practised his first year at Thomaston. In the autumn of 1823 he settled at North Yarmouth, Me., where he was married, Sept. 9, 1824, to Mary King Southgate, and lived happily, much in demand as a local orator and poet. The first of many occasional poems, his "Ode" for the two-hundredth anniversary of the landing at Plymouth, Dec. 22, 1820, was followed by another for the dedication of the Bunker Hill Monument in June 1825. Together with his fellow townsman, Henry W. Longfellow, he contributed poems, prose sketches, and tales to the *United States Literary Gazette* and to the annuals, the *Atlantic Souvenir* and the *Legendary.* His volume of *Sad Tales and Glad Tales,* by "Reginald Reverie," published at Boston in 1828, is interesting chiefly as pioneer work leading up to the short story as later developed by Hawthorne and Poe. His tales show the influence of Irving, but are more diffuse, sentimental, and mystifying.

The deaths of Mellen's infant daughter in September 1828, and of his wife in the following May were blows from which he never recovered. His own health was undermined; he lived an unsettled life at North Yarmouth, Portland, and Boston; tried vainly for a diplomatic post in the Netherlands; and for a few months in 1829 acted as editor of the *Portland Advertiser.* At Boston he delivered in 1830 the Harvard Phi Beta Kappa poem, "The Age of Print," and in September 1833 published a volume of verse, *The Martyr's Triumph; Buried Valley; and Other Poems.* His poetry, largely influenced by Byron, has at its best a delicacy of which Byron was seldom capable. Unfortunately however, John Neal, his friend, was justified in saying: "He dealt too much in mystery—the mystery of language, not of thought" ("The Unforgotten Dead," in *Brother Jonathan,* Jan. 1, 1842, p. 25). After 1836, Mellen lived mostly at New York, in the household of Samuel Colman, for whom he acted as co-editor of the *Monthly Miscellany* in 1839. He also delivered the Yale Phi Beta Kappa poem for that year. He devoted his last days to historical and statistical compilations, *A Book of the United States* (1838), and "General View of the American Continent," left in manuscript at his death. A voyage to Havana in the winter of 1839–40 failed to benefit his health, and he died at Colman's home late in the following summer.

[The authoritative account of Mellen is Joy L. Nevens' "Grenville Mellen, a Study of his Life and Works" (1925), University of Maine master's thesis, with bibliography. His works in manuscript, carefully edited by himself, with a notebook "Bibliography" containing valuable information regarding the composition and reception of his productions, are preserved in the Maine Hist. Soc. Lib. An unfinished autobiography in Byronic stanzas called "Something" sheds much light upon his early years. For printed sources see L. B. Chapman, *Monograph on the Southgate Family of Scarborough, Me.* (1907); E. A. and G. L. Duyckinck, *Cyc. of Am. Lit.* (1875), vol. II; *N. Y. Tribune,* Sept. 6, 1841.]

M. E.

MELLEN, PRENTISS (Oct. 11, 1764–Dec. 31, 1840), senator, chief justice of Maine, eighth of the nine children of the Rev. John and Rebecca (Prentiss) Mellen, was born in Sterling, Mass. His father, a graduate of Harvard in the class of 1741, prepared his sons Henry and Prentiss for his own college, which they entered in 1780, graduating in 1784. Prentiss then spent a year as tutor in the family of Joseph Otis of Barnstable, later studying law with the eccentric lawyer, Shearjashub Bourne, of that place. In after years Mellen used to refer semi-humorously to the inadequacy of his professional preparation. Admitted to the bar in Taunton in October 1788, he practised for about eight months in Sterling, then he removed to Bridgewater. Not being as successful here as he had hoped, he left in November 1791 and spent the winter with his brother Henry who was practising law in Dover, N. H. Upon the advice of his friend, George Thacher, a lawyer and at that time a representative in Congress from the District of Maine, he removed to the nearby town of Biddeford, now in the state of Maine. Here with a meager law library, but with an unbounded ambition, he opened his humble law office in Squire Hooper's tavern. By 1806 his law practice in the adjoining county, Cumberland, had grown so extensive that he moved to Portland, where he became a leader in what was commonly considered to be the ablest bar in the commonwealth of Massachusetts. In 1808, 1809, and 1817 he was a member of the executive council of Massachusetts. In 1818 he was chosen senator from Massachusetts, thus becoming a colleague of Harrison Gray Otis. In 1820, when Maine became a state, he left the Senate to accept appointment as chief justice of the supreme court of Maine, an office which he held until October 1834, when, having reached the age of seventy, he was required by law to retire.

As chief justice Mellen wrote a majority of the court's decisions and thus left an indelible impress upon the law of his state. Tall and imposing, fervid and impassioned in speech, he was an effective lawyer. Perhaps the most famous case in which he appeared was that in 1809 when he, with Samuel S. Wilde, successfully defended seven men accused of the murder at Malta, Me., of Paul Chadwick, who was engaged in surveying land (*Trial of David Lynn .. for the Murder of Paul Chadwick,* 1810). As a judge, Mellen was conscientious, and his opinions are careful and pointed. His long service was crowned, Jan. 1, 1840, when he with two colleagues appointed by the governor in July 1838 submitted their report containing the revision and codification of the statutes of Maine (*Revised Statutes of the State of Maine,* 1841). Mellen died at Portland, Me. He had married, on May 5, 1795, Sarah Hudson of Hartford, Conn., by whom he had six children. His son, Grenville [*q.v.*], after studying law, deserted that profession for literature. In this he may well have been influenced by his father's lifelong interest in and practice of the composition of verses.

[Simon Greenleaf, "Memoir of the Life and Character of the Late Chief Justice Mellen," in 17 *Maine Reports*, 467; Wm. Willis, *A Hist. of the Law, the Courts, and the Lawyers of Maine* (1863); H. C. Williams, ed., *Biog. Encyc. of Me. of the Nineteenth Century* (1885); *Biog. Dir. Am. Cong.* (1928); "Presentation of Portrait of Prentiss Mellen to the Town of Sterling . . . Nov. third 1911," typed MS. in the Lib. of Cong.; Willis Papers, Me. Hist. Soc. Lib., Book Y; *Eastern Argus* (Portland), Jan. 1, 1841; and *Portland Advertiser*, Jan. 5, 1841.] R. E. M.

MELLETTE, ARTHUR CALVIN (June 23, 1842–May 25, 1896), first governor of South Dakota, born in Henry County, Ind., is said to have been descended from Jean de Mellet, a sub-lieutenant in the Régiment de Bourbonnais, a French military organization that sailed for America in 1780 and at the close of the Revolution returned to France. De Mellet is said to have emigrated to Virginia with his family after resigning his commission. Charles Mellette, father of Arthur Calvin, was born in Monongalia County, Va. (now W. Va.), and removed in 1830 to Henry County, Ind., where he spent the remainder of his life and where he was married on Apr. 14, 1836, to Mary Moore; she bore him five children. Arthur spent his youth as a farmer lad with an insatiable desire for education, and in his elementary learning he was almost self-taught. He attended Marion Academy and entered the sophomore class of Indiana University, where he received the A.B. degree in 1864. After graduation he served as a private until the end of the Civil War. He returned to the university and completed his law studies in 1866, received the LL.B. degree, and was admitted to the bar. He was married, on May 29, 1866, to Margaret, the daughter of Theophilus Adam Wylie, long associated with Indiana University. He settled in practice at Muncie but was soon diverted from the law by journalism. He conducted the *Muncie Times* with success and acquired influence in politics. He was a member of the state House of Representatives from Delaware County in the session of 1872 and 1873 and was largely responsible for the development of the Indiana township school system, which has become the model system for many states.

In 1879, when his wife's health failed and a change of climate was imperative, he removed to Dakota Territory, where influence from Indiana soon obtained for him an appointment as register of the United States land office, then located at Springfield but soon removed to Watertown, where he lived for the remainder of his life. When he retired from the land office in 1882 he resumed the practice of law, but having acquired a competence his attention was chiefly devoted to his personal affairs. He was a member of the first constitutional convention of 1883 and was chiefly responsible for the provisions in the constitution placing a limit on the legal indebtedness of the state and on tax levies for state purposes, fixing salaries of state officers at a very low figure, and providing that the state should engage in no work of internal improvement. These limitations were carried over to the second and to the third constitution, under which South Dakota was admitted to statehood. In 1885 he was chosen provisional governor of the "State of Dakota," to which admission was denied. He was the original advocate in the Northwest of Harrison's nomination for president, in 1888 was successful in obtaining for him the support of Dakota and some adjacent states, and was made national committeeman of the Republican party for Dakota. Among the first appointments made by President Harrison, was that of Mellette to be governor of Dakota Territory, and at the election of 1889 he was elected the first governor of the state of South Dakota. As the first governor he took infinite pains to establish precedents of simplicity and economy. He was himself philanthropic by nature, and he spent himself and his fortune in benevolence. When he left the governorship, in January 1893, his health was seriously impaired, and he was never again strong. The tragic death of his eldest son and the loss of his fortune through the treachery of a friend added to the burden of his declining years. It was characteristic that, upon the defalcation of the state treasurer for whom he had become surety, he immediately turned over to the state all of his possessions. He was hoping to devote himself to experimentation in the field of physics when broken health and broken fortune brought his useful years to a close. He died at Pittsburg, Kan., and was buried at Watertown, S. D.

[Doane Robinson, *South Dakota* (1930), vol. I; *S. D. Hist. Colls.*, vols. I, X (1902–20); *Les Combattants Français de la Guerre Américaine* (1903); T. A. Wylie, *Indiana University* (1890), esp. pp. 107, 236.] D. R.

MELSHEIMER, FRIEDRICH VALENTIN (Sept. 25, 1749–June 30, 1814), Lutheran clergyman, entomologist, was born at Negenborn, near Holzminden, Duchy of Brunswick, the son of Joachim Sebastian and Clara Margaretha Melsheimer. His father was superintendent of the ducal forests. Melsheimer attended school at Holzminden, matriculated in 1769 at the University of Helmstedt, and in 1776 was appointed chaplain of the Dragoon Regiment of Brunswick Auxiliaries commanded by Major-General Friedrich Augustus Riedesel, which was hired by the British Crown to help subdue the rebellious colonies in America. His journal for the period Feb. 22–Sept. 21, 1776, published in that year, displays an admirable talent for topographical writing (*Tagebuch von der Reise der Braunschweigischen Auxiliär Truppen von Wolfenbüttel nach Quebec,* Minden, 1776, including an *Erste Fortsetzung*; another edition with identical pagination, Frankfurt and Leipzig, 1776; translated by William Wood and W. L. Stone in *Transactions of the Literary and Historical Society of Quebec,* no. 20, 1891, pp. 133–78). He was wounded in the arm at the battle of Bennington, Aug. 16, 1777, and was taken prisoner (*Letters from America 1776–1779,* translated by R. W. Pettengill, 1924, p. 96). He was one of a party of captured German officers who arrived at Bethlehem, Pa., Jan. 26, 1779, and were quartered there pending their exchange.

While his friends were enlivening the village with their musical serenades, Melsheimer fell in love with Mary Agnes Mau, daughter of Samuel Mau, a former redemptioner. He meanwhile was exchanged for W. Cardelle, chaplain of the 11th Virginia Regiment, received permission to travel (U. S. R. Miscellaneous Papers, Jan. 18, 1779, Library of Congress), was married to Agnes Mau on May 10, 1779 (J. M. Levering, *A History of Bethlehem, Pennsylvania,* 1903, pp. 492–93), and applied unsuccessfully for the pastorate at Lebanon, which had been left vacant by the death of John Caspar Stoever, Jr. (T. E. Schmauk, *Old Salem in Lebanon,* 1898, pp. 111–12). Presumably he never intended to rejoin his regiment. That autumn he assumed the pastorship of five small Lutheran congregations in Dauphin County and attended the Tulpehocken convention of the Ministerium of Pennsylvania, into which, however, he was not received as a member until 1785. Later he served for three years as secretary of the Ministerium, was officially designated as an instructor in theology, and was chairman of the committee on English congregations. He was pastor at Manheim, Lancaster County, 1784–86; at New Holland, 1786–87; professor of Greek, Latin, and German in Franklin College, 1787–89, working manfully to keep the college alive; and finally pastor of St. Matthew's, Hanover, York County, from 1789 until his death.

Besides being a faithful pastor he was an enthusiastic friend of education and a careful student of natural history, his *Catalogue of Insects of Pennsylvania, Part First* (Hanover, 1806) being the first volume published on the entomology of North America. It lists 1,363 species of beetles, of which over four hundred have been identified. He was not a mere collector but paid considerable attention to food habits and mode of occurrence; his notes are few and brief but occasionally telling, as the description of the rose-bug—*"Habitat praecipue in rosarum floribus quas misere destruit."* Until the year of his death he maintained a correspondence with his school friend, August Wilhelm Knoch, who mentions him in his *Neue Beyträge zur Insectenkunde, Erster Theil* (Leipzig, 1801), and sent him hundreds of specimens of American insects. He is said to have contributed a description of Pennsylvania to the *Schleswig'sche Journal* of 1792 and geographical essays to the same periodical in 1794. Some notes of his *"Über bisher Unbekannte Käfer"* appeared in Oken's *Isis* (vol. XXII, 1830, cols. 608–10). He was also the author of *Gespräche zwischen einem Protestanten und Römischen Priester* (Hanover, 1797) and *Wahrheit der Christlichen Religion für Unstudirte* (Frederick, Md., 1811). He was elected to membership in the American Philosophical Society in 1795. Melsheimer was short in stature and frail of body, suffered for many years from a disease of the lungs, but remained active till shortly before his death. He died at Hanover and was buried in the yard of his church. Two of his sons, Johan Friedrich and Ernst Friedrich, were Lutheran ministers and carried on his studies in entomology.

[*Evangelisches Magazin,* IV (1817), 62–63; J. H. C. Schierenbeck, *Lebensbeschreibungen von Lutherischen Predigern in Amerika* (Selingsgrove, Pa., *c.* 1864); *Doc. Hist. Ev. Luth. Ministerium of Pa., 1748–1821* (1898); J. H. Dubbs, *Hist. of Franklin and Marshall Coll.* (1903); J. G. Morris, "American Zoology, No. 1," *Lit. Record and Jour. Linnaean Asso. of Pa. Coll.* (Gettysburg), Aug. 1845, and "Contributions toward a History of Entomology in the U. S.," *Am. Jour. Sci.,* Jan. 1846; G. R. Prowell "F. V. Melsheimer," *Proc. Hist. Soc. York County, Pa.,* vol. I (1903), reprinted in *Pa.-Ger.,* May 1908; H. A. Hagen, "The Melsheimer Family and the Melsheimer Collection," *Canadian Entomologist,* Oct. 1884; E. A. Schwarz, "Some Notes on Melsheimer's Catalogue of the Coleoptera of Pennsylvania," with a note by C. V. Riley, *Proc. Entomol. Soc. Wash.,* III (1895), 134–38; H. B. Weiss, "First Book on Insects in America and its Author," *Am. Collector,* Oct. 1927.] G. H. G.

MELTZER, SAMUEL JAMES (Mar. 22, 1851–Nov. 7, 1920), physician, physiologist, was born in Ponevyezh, Courland, Russia, the son of Simon Meltzer, of Hebrew ancestry. He received his early training at Königsberg, Prussia, going from there in 1875 to the University of Berlin, where he devoted himself to the study of philosophy and medicine, receiving the degree of M.D. in 1882. The following year he came to the United States, defraying his expenses by serving as ship's surgeon. He engaged in his profession in New York, gradually building up a practice sufficient to support himself and his family; but his chief interest was in the advancement of clinical medicine through knowledge of physiology. To this end he worked early and late, whenever he could find time from his medical practice, carrying on experimental work in physiology with such success that he soon gained for himself wide recognition in the field of scientific medicine and became ultimately, in 1906, the head of the department of physiology and pharmacology of the Rockefeller Institute for Medical Research. Having attained that position, he was able to devote all his time and energies to research work in physiology and kindred fields, although by so doing he was compelled to relinquish the larger income derived from his medical practice. This sacrifice, however, was for Meltzer a small matter compared with the wider opportunity of enlarging the boundaries of knowledge in physiology and medicine. Endowed with a clear mind, tireless energy, and a devotion to high ideals, he became one of the leading American physiologists of his generation.

Meltzer's career as a research worker in the field of physiology was determined while he was still a student in Berlin, through his association with Professor Hugo Kronecker. Under the latter's supervision, he carried on a series of experiments to determine the mechanism of swallowing, from which came the Kronecker-Meltzer theory of deglutition, published prior to Meltzer's graduation and constituting his first contribution to medical science ("Ueber die Vorgänge beim Schlucken," in *Archiv für Anatomie und Physiologie,* 1880, pts. IV, V). The extent of his productive work is indicated by a list of nearly two hundred and fifty scientific papers covering a wide range of physiological and medical research on such subjects as excitation and inhibition, theory of shock, the action of adrenalin, the anaesthetic effects of magnesium salts, and artificial respiration through intratracheal insufflation. He founded and was the first president of the Society for Experimental Biology and Medicine, and its vigorous growth and wide influence constitute a testimonal of his ability to arouse interest in research, and justify his vision of the part experimental study and investigation were destined to play in the development of scientific medicine. During the latter years of his life he was troubled by a disease that curtailed his activities somewhat, but he pursued his research work to the very end, his active mind constantly suggesting new problems for solution. His life was one of service, devoted to the progress of the art and science of medicine, through experimental methods; and his work made an indelible impression upon American physiology. When twenty years old he married, in Russia, Olga T. Levitt, by whom he had two children.

[W. H. Howell, "Biog. Memoir, Samuel James Meltzer, 1851–1920," in *Memoirs Nat. Acad. Sci.*, vol. XXI (1927); *Memorial Number for Samuel James Meltzer, Founder and First President of the Soc. for Experimental Biology and Medicine* (1921); *Science*, Feb. 4, 1921; *Lancet* (London), Sept. 17, 1921; *Medic. Record* (N. Y.), Mar. 12, 1921; *Who's Who in America,* 1920–21; *N. Y. Times,* Nov. 8, 1920.]

R. H. C.

MELVILLE, DAVID (Mar. 21, 1773–Sept. 3, 1856), pewterer, inventor, son of David and Elizabeth (Thurston) Melville, was born in Newport, R. I. He was descended from David Melville who came to Boston, Mass., from Scotland during the last decade of the seventeenth century and later married Elizabeth, daughter of Rev. Samuel Willard, 1640–1707 [*q.v.*], pastor of South Church and vice-president of Harvard College. While little is known of Melville's environment, it is believed that he was of a family of metal craftsmen and that after securing a common-school education he learned this trade. By the time he was thirty years old he was established in Newport as a pewterer, maker of household utensils, and the proprietor of a hardware store, as indicated by his advertisement in the *Rhode Island Republican* of June 4, 1803.

About this time there was considerable interest in France and England in public demonstrations of illuminating gas. It is probable that Melville took note of these but was not aware of the processes involved. He was an ingenious individual, however, and having his curiosity aroused, he began experimenting and in 1806 succeeded in lighting his house on Pelham Street in Newport with coal gas. Encouraged by the public interest, he continued experimenting for upwards of seven years, constantly improving the process, and on Mar. 18, 1813, obtained the first United States patent for apparatus for making coal gas. He then formed a partnership with Winslow Lewis [*q.v.*] of Boston and advertised in the newspapers for business in the lighting of "manufactories, mines, mills, streets, theatres, lighthouses and other buildings" by gas. During the year he succeeded in lighting a cotton factory at Watertown, Mass., and a factory of the Wenscott Manufacturing Company near Providence, R. I. The cost of installation and operation was almost prohibitive, however, and he soon realized that the opportunities for general gas lighting were extremely limited. With the help of his partner, therefore, he concentrated his attention on interesting the government in using gas for lighthouses and in 1817 obtained a contract to install his gas light in the Beaver Tail Lighthouse at Newport and demonstrate it for a year. Melville fulfilled the terms of his contract, but the government declined to adopt gas lights, owing chiefly to opposition by persons who had contracted to furnish oil, including his own partner, and by those engaged in whale fisheries. Wholly discouraged, he abandoned his project and for the balance of his life gave his attention to his trade and to the hardware business. The defection of his partner and the latter's attempt to deprive him of his patent rights were a bitter disappointment to him. To clarify his position he published in 1819 the whole story of his relationship with Lewis under the title *An Exposé of Facts Respectfully Submitted to the Government of the U. S. Relating to the Conduct of Winslow Lewis.* He married Patience S. Sherman of Newport on Mar. 4, 1812, and was the father of seven children. He was buried in Newport.

[E. M. Tilley, "David Melville and his Early Experiments with Gas in Newport," *Bull. Newport Hist. Soc.*, no. 60, Jan. 1927; R. M. Bayles, *Hist. of Newport County, R. I.* (1888); Waldemar Kaempffert, *A Pop. Hist. of Am. Invention* (1924), vol. I; J. N. Arnold, *Vital Record of R. I., 1636–1850*, vol. IV (1893); Am. Gas Institute, *Lectures on the Centenary of the Introduction of Gas as an Illuminant* (1912); *Newport Advertiser*, Sept. 10, 1856; *Newport Mercury*, Sept. 13, 1856.] C. W. M.

MELVILLE, GEORGE WALLACE (Jan. 10, 1841–Mar. 17, 1912), naval officer, was born in New York City, the son of Alexander and Sarah Douther (Wallace) Melville, and the grandson of James Melville of Stirling, Scotland, who emigrated to America in 1804. Manifesting a taste for mechanics, young Melville went from the public schools to the Brooklyn Collegiate and Polytechnic Institute, and from there to the engineering works of James Binns of East Brooklyn. On July 29, 1861, he entered the Engineer Corps of the navy as third assistant engineer and served on various vessels throughout the war. He was on board the *Wachusett* at Bahia, Brazil, when she captured the *Florida.* Previous to the engagement he attempted to board the *Florida* in broad daylight in civilian clothes for the purpose of obtaining information respecting her fighting strength, thus taking the risks of a spy. At the capture of Fort Fisher he served on torpedo boat *No. 6* in Admiral Porter's fleet. In October 1863 he was promoted second assistant engineer; 1865, first assistant engineer; and 1881, chief engineer. After the Civil War he served in various positions at sea and at the navy yards and shore stations. In 1867 he was on board the *Tacony* during the French evacuation of Mexico; from 1869 to 1871 on the *Lancaster,* the flagship of the South Atlantic Squadron; and from 1875 to 1878 on the *Tennessee,* the flagship of the Asiatic Squadron. For his successful performance of the routine duties of his profession he was often commended by his superior officers. Thus it was said officially that he exhibited as an officer of the *Lancaster* an "amount of mechanical ability, energy, and engineering skill rarely found" (Cathcart, *post,* p. 466).

Ambitious and enterprising, Melville was not content to rest on the laurels that might be won in ordinary naval occupations. In the spring of 1873, when the *Tigress* was chartered for the rescue of the missing members of the crew of the *Polaris,* originally commanded by Capt. Charles F. Hall [*q.v.*], Melville volunteered to serve as her chief engineer. At the end of the search he was strongly commended for his "great fertility of resource, combined with thorough practical knowledge" (Cathcart, *post,* p. 466). Fascinated by polar exploration, six years later he again volunteered for Arctic service, this time as the chief engineer of the *Jeannette,* Lieut. George W. De Long [*q.v.*]. Held in the ice almost two years as she drifted in the Arctic Ocean westward of Alaska, the *Jeannette* was kept afloat largely by reason of the energy and skill of Melville. His taking possession of Henrietta Island in behalf of the United States was described by De Long as a "brave and meritorious action." After the *Jeannette* sank, for many days he led the working force on its fearful march to Bennett Island. He commanded one of the three boats upon which the expedition embarked when it came to the open sea. His boat was one of the two that reached Siberia, and he was the only boat commander to survive and bring his crew to safety. After a few weeks of rest, although still feeble, he again turned northward and led a fruitless expedition in search of De Long. A few months later he was once more in the field and finally found his dead shipmates and gave them a respectable burial. Recognition by the government of his extraordinary efforts was tardy and inadequate, owing to jealousies largely within the navy. In 1882 his friends introduced a resolution in the Senate tendering him the thanks of Congress, advancing him forty numbers, and giving him a pecuniary reward. Eight years later (Sept. 3, 1890) a law was passed omitting the "thanks," advancing him fifteen numbers, and giving him a medal. In the meantime, in 1884, as the chief engineer of the *Thetis* in the Greely Relief Expedition, he had brought to a close his Arctic services, being among the first to reach the dying explorers at Cape Sabine.

On Aug. 9, 1887, Melville was appointed by President Cleveland, over forty-four senior officers, chief of the Bureau of Steam Engineering. He remained in that office sixteen and a half years, an epoch-making period in the construction of the new navy. He superintended the designing of the machinery of 120 ships. Among the innovations that he introduced, often in opposition to conservative opinion, are the water-tube boiler, the triple-screw system, vertical engines, the repair ship, and the "distilling ship." He designed the machinery of the *Columbia* and *Minneapolis,* two vessels that held the record for speed among warships for almost a decade. He was influential in obtaining the amalgamation of the Engineer Corps with the Line and the establishment of a post-graduate school in naval engineering. On Mar. 3, 1899, he was made a captain with the rank of rear admiral, and on Jan. 10, 1903, was retired in the latter grade. He received many honors from governments, scientific societies, and universities, and in 1899 served as president of the American Society of Mechanical Engineers. He wrote many technical articles and one book, *In the Lena Delta* (1885), which contains accounts of some of his Arctic experiences. Sometimes gruff and irascible, he possessed a dauntless and masterful spirit, which suited his massive frame, leonine head, and great dome-like forehead. Melville was divorced from his first wife. On Oct. 18, 1907, he was married in New York City to his second wife, Estella Smith Polis. He died in Philadelphia.

[Record of Officers, Bureau of Navigation, 1859–88. *Who's Who in America,* 1912–13; F. M. Bennett, *The Steam Navy of the U. S.* (1896); W. L. Cathcart, "Geo. Wallace Melville," *Cassier's Mag.,* Apr. 1897; Emma De Long, ed., *The Voyage of the Jeannette* (2 vols., 1883); *Army and Navy Jour.,* Mar. 23, 1912; *Pub. Ledger* (Phila.), Mar. 18, 1912.] C. O. P.

MELVILLE, HERMAN (Aug. 1, 1819–Sept. 28, 1891), author, was born at No. 6 Pearl Street, New York City, the second son and third of the eight children of Allan Melville, a merchant, and Maria Gansevoort, daughter of General Peter Gansevoort [*q.v.*] of Albany. His ancestry was distinguished on both sides, for his father's father was Major Thomas Melville of Boston, celebrated by Oliver Wendell Holmes in "The Last Leaf," one of the "Indians" in the Boston Tea Party, and a direct descendant of John Melville, Lord of Raith in Fifeshire, who was beheaded during the reign of Mary, Queen of Scots, "becaus," as an old record stated, "he was known to be one that unfainedlie favoured the truthe," and of a numerous race of Scottish worthies of whom the earliest known was one Sir Richard de Melvill, who flourished in the reign of Alexander III and was compelled in 1296 to swear allegiance to King Edward I of England when the latter overran Scotland. Both of Melville's grandfathers served with distinction in the Revolutionary War, General Peter Gansevoort having been in command of Fort Stanwix, for his gallant defence of which he received a vote of thanks from Congress; and both families were among the earliest and most aristocratic settlers of the country. Harmen Harmense Van Gansevoort was well known as a brewer in Beverwyck in 1660 and his descendants intermarried during the following generations with the Van Rensselaers, the Van Schaicks, and most of the other leading colonial Dutch families.

Melville himself took a great and natural pride in the stock from which he sprang and which had left its traces in the magnificent bearing and physique and the high adventurous courage that characterized him. His family, however, was falling on evil days at the time of his birth. His father, a widely traveled and cultivated man, underwent many financial ups and downs, finally went into bankruptcy, and died when Herman was twelve years old, leaving his wife and eight children virtually destitute. Herman was thus left in the care of his mother, a cold, "haughty" woman, whose portrait he is said to have drawn in Mrs. Glendinning in *Pierre,* and whose unsympathetic attitude towards her son may have had something to do with his leaving home at the age of seventeen, "driven out an infant Ishmael into the desert, with no maternal Hagar to accompany and comfort him" (*Pierre,* 1930, p. 101). Of her he is said to have remarked years later: "She hated me." He was described by his father as "very backward in speech" in his early boyhood, and "somewhat slow in comprehension," though "docile and amiable" (Weaver, *post,* pp. 62, 66). His only schooling he received at the Albany Academy, where he is said to have been a favorite pupil, distinguished especially for his writing, but he received no formal education after the age of fifteen. In 1834 he became a clerk in the New York State Bank. There were, however, certain compensations in his childhood: the fine library which his father had left and in which he browsed to the good effect revealed in his later style, the vacations passed at his uncle's farm, "Broadhall," near Pittsfield, the summers spent at the country home of the Gansevoorts in Saratoga County, N. Y., which he describes so poetically in *Pierre* under the name of "Saddle-Meadows."

In 1837, at the age of seventeen, Melville, after experimenting with his clerkship, with a small post in his brother's fur and cap store, with farming, and even school-teaching, suddenly decided to go to sea and shipped as cabin-boy on the *Highlander,* bound for Liverpool, on the voyage described in *Redburn.* After a month on the sea, which left in his mind experiences and characters that he was never to forget, he spent six weeks in Liverpool, returning to New York, with a taste for the sea that was never to leave him, to engage in various activities, school-teaching again, at Pittsfield and East Albany, and writing with the passionate zest he describes in *Pierre,* taking ship again at Fairhaven (opposite New Bedford) on his famous voyage on the whaler *Acushnet,* on Jan. 3, 1841, for the South Seas. This was the beginning of the great adventure of his life. On the *Acushnet* he spent the eighteen months which he recreated imaginatively years later in *Moby Dick,* escaping finally (July 9, 1842), when he could no longer endure the hardships of a whaleman's existence, at the Marquesas Islands, where, in company with his shipmate, Toby (Richard Tobias Greene), he experienced the adventures described in *Typee.* They struggled for five days through the jungle, reaching at length the valley of Typee, which Melville remembered ever afterwards as an earthly paradise. There he dwelt among the friendly cannibals, with the lovely Fayaway as his constant companion, chatting and smoking with the bachelors of the Ti, or men's club, an idyllic existence of which recollected traces are to be found in *Mardi.* Then, finding the savage life irksome, he escaped by a clever ruse from the warriors who were holding him captive and succeeded in getting aboard an Australian whaler, the *Lucy Ann* (called by Melville the *Julia*), where he slowly regained his health and formed the famous friendship with Doctor Long Ghost, celebrated in *Omoo.* He was very glad to escape again when the *Juila* sailed into the harbor of Papeete (Sept. 9, 1842). At Tahiti he hired himself out for a time as a field-laborer, studied the island life with all the charmed and amused interest that is reflected in the pages of *Omoo,* and enlisted Aug. 17, 1843, as an ordinary seaman on the frigate *United States.* Here he spent the year pictured in *White-Jacket, or The World in a Man-of-War,* from which he was discharged Oct. 14, 1844, on the vessel's return to Boston. He had passed nearly four years wandering and accumulating memories that were to furnish material for the whole of his literary life.

He came home, a romantic figure indeed, "the man who had lived among the cannibals," and immediately set to work writing out his experiences. *Typee* (1846) was finished and the manuscript bought by John Murray within scarcely more than a year after his return. *Omoo* (1847) followed a year later. Melville found himself immediately both famous and notorious, for his attacks on the missionaries had stirred up a hornet's-nest of criticism. Meanwhile, on Aug. 4, 1847, he had married Elizabeth, the only daughter of Lemuel Shaw [*q.v.*], Chief Justice of Massachusetts, an old friend of his family, and had established a household at 103 Fourth Avenue, New York, where he continued industriously writing, preparing *Mardi* (1849), *Redburn* (1849), and *White-Jacket* (1850) for the press. His first child was born in February 1849; and in October of that year he sailed for England to interview his publishers and try to make better terms with them. He visited Paris also at this time, gathering impressions that served him well later in the composition of *Israel Potter*; then, returning home, he moved with his family to Pittsfield, where he bought the farm "Arrowhead," which became his home for the next thirteen years. It was there that he formed his intimate friendship with Hawthorne, who was living close by at Lenox and writing *The House of the Seven Gables.* Melville finished and published *Moby Dick* in 1851, dedicating it to his friend, and immediately followed this with the composition of *Pierre: or the Ambiguities* (1852), which revealed the strain and torment through which he had passed and marked the decline of his powers, for his great book, as he put it, had been "broiled in hell-fire." Thereafter his talent passed slowly into a sort of eclipse that was never, however, to result in actual extinction. Broken with overwork, he set out in 1856 for a tour to the Holy Land, visiting Hawthorne on the way at the latter's consulate in Liverpool and remarking that he had "pretty much made up his mind to be annihilated" (Weaver, *post,* p. 331). He was in search of he knew not what, the philosopher's stone, some secret of religious faith; and on his return he tried to describe his quest in the long metaphysical-narrative poem *Clarel,* published many years later in 1876. Fortune had turned against him. His great book, *Moby Dick,* was a complete practical failure, misunderstood by the critics and ignored by the public; and in 1853 the Harpers' fire destroyed the plates of all his books and most of the copies remaining in stock. After failing to obtain a consulship for which he had applied he continued to write as well as he could out of a depleted imagination. He published in 1855 *Israel Potter,* a story of the American Revolution, remarkable for its portraits of John Paul Jones and Benjamin Franklin. *The Piazza Tales* followed in 1856, containing among other stories the sombre narrative of "Benito

Cereno"; and in 1857 appeared *The Confidence Man,* the first volume of an abortive satire, as we may assume, though the precise significance of the work is not clear, on the over-developed commercial smartness of the period. Thereafter Melville wrote no more prose except *Billy Budd,* completed during the last year of his life and only published in 1924, a story based on the character of Jack Chase, the "handsome sailor" who appears in *White-Jacket.* He turned to the composition of poetry, and published, besides *Clarel,* three volumes, *Battle-Pieces and Aspects of the War* (1866), *John Marr and Other Sailors* (1888) and *Timoleon* (1891), the two latter privately printed, most of this verse being undistinguished. He tried lecturing as a mode of supplementing his income, going as far west as San Francisco, his subjects being the South Seas and "Statuary in Rome." In 1861 he was introduced to Lincoln at Washington, where he was again applying unsuccessfully for a consulship. His literary life had died of inanition, overstrain, and excessive subjectivity, as well as of neglect on the part of the reading public.

Melville's later life was marked by a complete withdrawal from society. In 1863 he moved with his family to New York, and in 1866 he received an appointment as out-door customs inspector on the wharf at the foot of Gansevoort Street, which he held for nineteen years; but he had passed so entirely out of public notice that Robert Buchanan wrote in 1885: "I sought everywhere for this Triton, who is still living somewhere in New York. No one seemed to know anything of the one great writer fit to stand shoulder to shoulder with Whitman on that continent" (*Academy,* Aug. 15, 1885, p. 103). But amid the obscurity there are evidences of a certain surviving geniality in the old writer. He carried on a friendly correspondence with W. Clark Russell, who wrote to him in gratitude for his "delightful books" and informed him of the high regard in which his work was still held in England (New York *World,* Oct. 11, 1891; see also *North American Review,* Feb. 1892). He devoted his leisure hours to reading and study, and continued to write poetry at intervals, returning in memory to his early experiences on the sea. He completed the manuscript of *Billy Budd* three months before his death. He died at his home 104 East Twenty-sixth Street, and was buried in Woodlawn Cemetery.

As Clark Russell said, Melville's fame never passed into obscurity in England. But he was virtually ignored in the literary histories of his own country until about 1920, when his greatness came to be recognized for the first time, largely as an indirect result of the sudden vogue of books dealing with the South Seas. *Typee* and *Omoo,* which had enjoyed a brief romantic reputation on their first appearance, came back into popular favor, but are overshadowed now by the mighty bulk of *Moby Dick* and with close rivals in *White-Jacket* and *Redburn.* Even *Pierre* and *Mardi* came in for a measure of popular interest. During the years immediately following, a sumptuous complete edition of Melville's works was published, and it was generally recognized that at his highest moments Melville is one of the great masters of English prose and one of the two or three supreme writers of America. Allowing for certain excesses of enthusiasm due to so sudden a re-discovery, this position which Melville has assumed will probably never again be challenged, for it is based on certain substantial realities of thought, and especially of style and feeling.

Undoubtedly *Moby Dick* will continue to be regarded as Melville's masterpiece; but all of his books published before his thirty-third year are sterling contributions to literature, notable for their clear, firm, classical style, their gusto, their vivid portraiture and their wealth of keen-eyed and well-organized observations. *Typee* and *Omoo* are models of romantic narrative, written with all the exuberance of the young man who could have contrived such unsuual adventures, adventures that were almost unprecedented at the time, for Melville was among the first white men to explore certain parts of the South Sea Islands and the very first literary artist to do so. He may be considered in some respects, in these books, a disciple of Rousseau, for no one has ever glorified more than he the virtues of the natural man, the primitive man, as against such specimens of the civilized man as found their way to those parts, the missionaries whose narrow Protestantism was destroying all joy of life in the islanders, and the visiting sailors who brought with them only the vices of their countrymen. And certainly no other author has celebrated with a greater charm and exuberance the engaging natural features of the islands and the pagan ways of the islanders, an exuberance that led Stevenson to characterize Melville as a "howling cheese." His portrait of Fayaway, in various attitudes and scenes, swimming, smoking, floating in a canoe or, as on one occasion, standing upright in the bow of the canoe with arms upraised and her tappa robe stretched out like a sail, is one of the best-known of its kind in modern literature. Memorable also are the figures of Kory-Kory and his mother, among the natives; and, among the white men, those of

Toby, that "strange, wayward being, moody, fitful and melancholy," and especially Doctor Long Ghost, the ship's doctor of the *Julia,* who quoted Virgil and repeated "Hudibras" by the canto and in company with whom Melville hired himself out as a farmer-laborer on the island of Imeeo.

These two books will probably always remain the most popular, aside from *Moby Dick,* that Melville wrote. *Redburn, the Sailor-Boy Confessions and Reminiscences of the Son-of-a-Gentleman,* deserves a place beside them for its youthful high spirits, for the swiftness of its narrative and the vividness of its portraits. Although the book was written twelve years after the adventure took place, Melville seems to have forgotten none of the details, perhaps because, as he says, he loved ships as he loved men, and the bizarre characters whom he describes do not seem to be fictitious: rather we may suppose that he had a gift for encountering types that were never seen before on sea or land. As he was only seventeen at the time, everything that passed before him was etched on his memory as with acid, the miseries of the forecastle, the phosphorescent corpse of the dead sailor, the demoniacal figure of Jackson, as well as the dismal sights of Liverpool, all of which he describes with biting realism. *Redburn* may survive most properly perhaps as a boys' book, but it must always hold a distinguished if minor place in the literature of the sea.

White-Jacket is more ambitious, though not so lively as a composition. Its purpose was to "give some idea of the interior life in a man-of-war," and it must always remain as a standard document illustrating a phase of American naval history. Here we find also several powerful bits of writing, such as the macabre account of the amputation of the seaman's leg, and the splendid figure of "noble Jack Chase," the ideal sailor, the frank and charming Jack, idol of his fellows, who could speak five languages and was indeed "better than a hundred common mortals," a character as vivid in its virtue, its manifestation of all the manly virtues, as Jackson's is vivid in its viciousness. The atmosphere of the book fairly shines with the fresh and jubilant spirit of the days when American shipping ruled the seas.

Mardi and *Pierre* retain certain powerful features, energetic passages of writing and, above all, traces of deep feeling. In *Pierre,* especially, Melville has given us much of himself: the book is plainly autobiographical, especially in the account of the author's childhood, of his forbidding mother and the aristocratic traditions of the Glendinning family, the beautiful, idyllic life at "Saddle-Meadows," Pierre's preparation for authorship and especially the composition of the "great work," that "Inferno," composed in the midst of "clamourous pennilessness," which is evidently no other than *Moby Dick.* If the love-story is fantastic and improbable to a degree, the pages dealing with the struggles of the writer's soul have a splendid passion and veracity, equal to those of *Moby Dick* itself. And there are many chapters of *Mardi* of an ethereal beauty, many pages of profound speculation, and the book contains two or three characters, such as Anatoo and Jarl, that are highly successful as grotesque portraits. In its general scheme it is reminiscent of Rabelais, being a voyage in search of happiness, in this case represented by the girl Yillah instead of the oracle of the Bottle, conducted by the narrator and his three companions, Mohy the chronicler, Babbalanja the antiquary, and Yoomy the minstrel, who set out in their three canoes for a tour of the isles, here of course the South Sea Islands which had left such glorious impressions in Melville's memory; and we can find in the "ontological heroics" that formed the substance of their conversation direct reminiscences not only of the talk that must have passed between Melville and Hawthorne in the Berkshires but more especially of the cheerful confabulations during the Feast of Calabashes at the Ti, in the valley of Typee. And the thatched huts, the verdurous arbors, the luxuriant glens that form the local color of the book are all those of the Marquesas. The whole composition is a curious compound of Rabelais, the earlier Melville, and Thomas Moore, for there is a certain faint Oriental aroma lingering over the scene that distinctly recalls *Lalla Rookh.*

Nothing that Melville wrote is wholly without quality, though *The Confidence Man* virtually touches the absolute of incomprehensibility. *Israel Potter,* a minor work, contains, besides the portraits of Franklin and John Paul Jones, a remarkable picture of a naval engagement, for Melville seldom fails completely when he touches the sea. In *The Piazza Tales* one finds "Benito Cereno," the most successful of his shorter pieces, and "The Encantadas," a grim and powerful sketch of certain deserted volcanic islands that Melville had visited in his voyages. *Clarel,* his longest poem, is extremely involved and obscure; he described it himself as "a metrical affair, a pilgrimage or what not, of several thousand lines, eminently adapted for unpopularity," but Frank Jewett Mather had reason for saying that it was "about all America has to show for the poetical stirrings of the deeper theological waters which marked the age of Matthew Arnold, Clough, Tennyson and Browning" (*The Review*, Aug. 16, 1919, p. 300). But Melville's permanent fame must always rest on the great prose epic of *Moby Dick,* a book that has no equal in American literature for variety and splendor of style and for depth of feeling. No doubt the story would flow with more consistency if many of the sections dealing with whaling were omitted, for Melville's sense of form was very defective; but there is not a page of the book that is not richly rewarding. The heroic figures of Captain Ahab and Father Maple, the fantastic figures of Queequeg, Tashtego and the gigantic Negro, Daggoo, are almost of Homeric proportions. "Give me a condor's wing!" exclaims Melville in the midst of his inspiration. "Give me Vesuvius' crater for an inkstand!" And he is justified in his enthusiasm; for the mighty rhythm of the book recalls that of the great Scandinavian sagas.

[R. M. Weaver, *Herman Melville, Mariner and Mystic* (1921), and Lewis Mumford, *Herman Melville* (1929), are full biographical studies; the only complete edition of Melville's writings was published by Constable, London, 1922–24. Among the biographical and critical studies the most useful are: "Notes on Herman Melville," in Van Wyck Brooks, *Emerson and Others* (1927); Lincoln Colcord, "Notes on Moby Dick," *Freeman*, Aug. 23, 30, 1922; Carl Van Doren, "Lucifer from Nantucket," *Century Mag.*, Aug. 1925; H. H. Scudder, "Melville's Benito Cereno and Capt. Delano's Voyages," *Mod. Lang. Asso. Pubs.*, XLIII (1928), 502–32; Russell Thomas, "Melville's Use of Some Sources in the Encantadas," *Am. Lit.*, Jan. 1932; W. S. Gleim, "A Theory of Moby Dick," *New England Quarterly*, July 1929; Michael Sadleir, *Excursions in Victorian Bibliog.* (1922); D. H. Lawrence, *Studies in Classic Am. Lit.* (1922); V. S. Parrington, *The Romantic Revolution in America 1800–60* (1927); John Freeman, *Herman Melville* (1926); R. M. Weaver, intro. to *Shorter Novels of Herman Melville* (1928); R. S. Forsythe, intro. to *Pierre, or The Ambiguities* (1930); Henry Chapin, ed., Melville's *The Apple-Tree Table and Other Sketches* (1922) and *John Marr and Other Poems* (1922); Meade Minnigerode, *Some Personal Letters of Herman Melville and a Bibliog.* (1922). See notes by A. H. Starke and R. S. Forsythe, *Am. Lit.*, Nov. 1929 and 1930; "Family Correspondence of Herman Melville," *N. Y. Pub. Lib. Bull.*, July and Aug. 1929; O. W. Riegel, "The Anatomy of Melville's Fame," *Am. Lit.*, May 1931; J. N. Reynolds, *Mocha Dick or the White Whale of the Pacific* (1932), with intro. by L. L. Balcom (reprinted from *Knickerbocker Mag.*, May 1839). Robert S. Forsythe and John H. Birss have in preparation a bibliography of Melville, including all imprints of his works, a calendar of letters pub. and unpub., a description of existing manuscripts, a list of portraits, catalogue of books that Melville is known to have possessed, and a list of biog. and critical articles on him.] V. W. B.

MEMBRÉ, ZENOBIUS (1645–1687?), Recollect missionary, was born of good family in Bapaume, department of Pas-de-Calais, France. He was a cousin of Chrétien le Clercq, who was the historian of the Recollects in New France. It is supposed that the name Zenobius was taken by Membré upon entering the Recollect convent at Artois, where he was the first novice in the newly created Franciscan department of St. Anthony. In 1675 Le Clercq and Membré were sent to Canada, where the latter tarried two or more years at the Recollect convent at Quebec.

In 1678 he was ordered to Fort Frontenac on the north shore of Lake Ontario, whence he accompanied La Salle's men to their shipyard on Niagara River near Buffalo. Membré ministered to the shipwrights and the men preparing the *Griffon,* and in the summer of 1679 he sailed around the Great Lakes to Green Bay. There the *Griffon* was loaded with peltry and sent back, while Membré accompanied La Salle's party in small boats around Lake Michigan to St. Joseph River. The party tarried at Milwaukee River, the name of which first appears in Membré's account. Late in the year, La Salle's party reached its destination on the Illinois River, built Fort Crêvecoeur, and laid the keel of a small vessel. La Salle was called back to Fort Frontenac, because of the loss of the *Griffon*; Tonty was left in charge with the two priests, Membré and La Ribourde. Before La Salle's return a party of Iroquois attacked the Illinois Indians; Tonty, the two priests, and three other men made a retreat through the woods to Lake Michigan. In this flight Father de la Ribourde was killed; Membré and the others, after suffering great hardships, finally reached the mission at De Pere (L. P. Kellogg, "A Wisconsin Anabasis," in *Wisconsin Magazine of History,* March 1924). Membré met La Salle at Mackinac in the summer of 1681 and again accompanied him to the Illinois. Thence, late in December, they set forth to explore the Mississippi and descended to its mouth, where, Apr. 9, 1682, La Salle took possession for France of the Mississippi Valley and named it Louisiana. Father Zenobius signed the act of taking possession (*Collections of the State Historical Society of Wisconsin,* vol. XI, 1888, pp. 33–35). When on the return journey La Salle was taken ill, the Recollect priest cared for him tenderly and on his recovery accompanied him to Canada and finally, at his request, to France.

Arrived in the Old World, Membré was sent to the convent of the Recollects at Bapaume, his birthplace, where he was warden for several months. Thence he was summoned by La Salle to join a new expedition for the founding of a colony at the mouth of the Mississippi and was made superior of the group of Recollect missionaries that La Salle took with him. Missing the mouth of the Mississippi, the expedition landed in Texas, where a settlement was made on the Garcitas River in Lavaca Bay. There, at the colony named St. Louis, Membré and his companions passed two years. At one time a mission was attempted for the Cenis Indians, but because of threatened hostilities Membré and Maximus le Clercq retreated to Fort St. Louis There La Salle left them in 1687, and subsequently the entire colony perished; how or why is not known.

Membré was a voluminous writer and his journals of his expedition were embodied in the history of his order in the New World, compiled by his cousin Chrétien le Clercq, under the title *Premier Établissement de la Foy dans la Nouvelle France* (Paris, 1691). His style is plain and simple, not that of a learned man. He had great physical hardihood and seems to have been adaptable to his surroundings and on good terms with his companions. His writings give certain details of La Salle's expedition not found elsewhere.

[J. G. Shea translated and edited Le Clercq as *First Establishment of the Faith in New France* (2 vols., 1881); I. J. Cox, in *The Journeys of Réné Robert Cavelier Sieur de La Salle* (2 vols., 1905) includes Membré's narrative and a brief biography of him; for the site of La Salle's colony in Texas see H. E. Bolton, in *Miss. Valley Hist. Rev.*, Sept. 1915; *Early Narratives of the Northwest* (1917), edited by L. P. Kellogg, p. 292, gives a note on Membré.] L. P. K.

MEMMINGER, CHRISTOPHER GUSTAVUS (Jan. 9, 1803–Mar. 7, 1888), South Carolina legislator and secretary of the treasury of the Confederacy, the son of Christopher Godfrey and Eberhardina (Kohler) Memminger, was born in Nayhingen, in the Duchy of Württemberg, Germany. His grandfather, Johann Friedrich Memminger, was an official of the University of Babenhausen. Soon after the child's birth his father, an officer in the army of the duke, was killed, and the mother, with her parents, emigrated to Charleston, S. C. She died there, and the boy, four years of age, was placed in the Charleston Orphan House. At the age of eleven he was taken into the home of Thomas Bennett, later governor of the state. A year or so later he was sent to the South Carolina College, where he graduated in 1819. Returning to Charleston, he studied law, acquired a license, and began to rise in his profession. He opposed nullification and wrote a satirical booklet in biblical style, called *The Book of Nullification* (1830) against the leaders of that movement. In 1836 he became a member of the state house of representatives and soon afterward, as chairman of the committee on finance, began a long struggle to disassociate the state from banking corporations and to force the banks to maintain specie payments on pain of forfeiture of their charters. In these contests he won considerable reputation as a sound financier (but see F. H. Elmore, *Defense of the Bank of . . . S. C.*, n.d.). In 1855 he became a commissioner of schools for Charleston, a position he held for more than thirty years, and began constructive work on the public-school system of the city. He also served for thirty-two years on the board of the South Carolina College. Although he was fully convinced of the righteousness of slavery and was apprehensive of the designs of the northern antislavery element, he acted with the conservative Democrats of South Carolina. During the period from 1850 to 1852 he opposed separate action on the part of his state as dangerous and fruitless, although he was himself dissatisfied with the compromise measures of 1850. In January 1860, in consequence of the John Brown raid, he was sent as commissioner to address the Virginia legislature on the necessity for joint defensive measures (*Address . . . before the Assembled Authorities of . . . Va., . . . Jan. 19, 1860*, 1860). By December he was won over wholly to secession. He was an active member of the secession convention of South Carolina and was one of the delegates to the southern convention at Montgomery, where he was chairman of the committee that drafted the provisional constitution of the Confederate States.

Put forward by his delegation for the office of secretary of the treasury and appointed by Jefferson Davis, he faced a difficult and, as it proved, a hopeless task. He seems to have hoped to use treasury notes sparingly, for he was well aware of the danger in them, but the new bonds issued for the absorption of the notes were taken slowly, while the obligations of the government for the support of the war accumulated rapidly. There was no means of meeting requisitions except by issuing more treasury notes. Hoping to stimulate the sale of bonds, he advised a "produce loan," by which the cotton and tobacco planters would exchange the proceeds of their crop sales for bonds, but the result was disappointing. The first effort at a direct tax was unsuccessful, for most of the states assumed the burden and paid in their own notes, thereby swelling the flood of paper. Congress passed no comprehensive tax law until April 1863, when it was too late. Meanwhile, military reverses and redundant notes had caused rapid depreciation of the currency. Prices rose alarmingly, increasing governmental expenditures that could be met only by more treasury notes. Bonds were taken sparingly. His various funding schemes failed, partly because of business conditions and partly because of the tinkering of Congress. The blockade prevented the exportation of cotton, the only resource that could command cash. That he was fully aware of the causes of the derangement of the finances is clear from his reports and correspondence, but it is equally clear that he saw no way to remedy the situation. In 1863 he recommended a stringent reduction of the volume of the currency through compulsory funding in bonds, and Congress responded with the famous funding act of February 1864, which varied materially from his recommendations and was unquestionably a worse measure than the one he had proposed. When the credit of the government collapsed completely he was generally held responsible for the disaster. Most students of the subject have severely criticized his handling of the treasury and have attributed his failure to lack of constructive imagination. There is some ground for the criticism, but it is hard to see how even a gifted financier could have coped successfully with the difficulties that beset him. On June 15, 1864, he resigned and retired to his country home at Flat Rock, N. C., where he remained until after the war. In 1867 he received presidential pardon, returned to Charleston, and began once more the practice of law. In 1868 he organized a company for the manufacture of sulphuric acid and super-phosphates. His chief public service in the post-war years was in behalf of the public schools for both races. He was married in 1832 to Mary Wilkinson, a daughter of Willis Wilkinson. After her death he was married, in 1878, to her sister, Sarah A. Wilkinson. Eight children survived him.

[H. D. Capers, *The Life and Times of C. G. Memminger* (1893); M. C. Kneece, "The Contributions of C. G. Memminger to the Cause of Education," *Bulletin of the University of South Carolina*, No. 177 (1926). Ernest A. Smith, *The History of the Confederate Treasury* (1901), and J. C. Schwab, *The Confederate States of America* (1901). *News and Courier* (Charleston), Mar. 1, 8, 10, 1888.] C. W. R.

MENARD, MICHEL BRANAMOUR (Dec. 5, 1805–Sept. 2, 1856), Indian trader and founder of Galveston, Tex., was born at Laprairie, Lower Canada, the son of Michel B. and Marguerite (deNoyer) Menard. When he left home at about the age of fourteen he had received little, if any, formal education, but during the next four years, while in the service of a fur company with headquarters probably at Detroit, he gained a mastery of woodcraft, the technique of the Indian trade, and an insight into Indian psychology that was to make possible his career. In 1823 he arrived at Kaskaskia, Ill., to take employment under his uncle, Pierre Menard [*q.v.*], as a trader among the Delaware and Shawnee in the vicinity of Sainte Genevieve, Mo. Humiliated by the contrast between his own untutored state and the comparative elegance of his cousins, he applied himself diligently to study and in three months he learned not only to speak but to read English. It was his custom thereafter to read while on trading expeditions, and eventually he passed as a well-informed man. He lived among the Shawnee on the White River in the Arkansas territory, by whom he was adopted and elected a chief. Years later he is reported to have said that he almost succeeded in uniting the northwestern tribes into an Indian nation, making himself their king, and moving them to California and Utah. However that may be, he moved southward with the Shawnee and in 1826 was in the vicinity of Shreveport.

When the Indians pushed into the region between the Trinity and Red rivers in Texas, he received permission from the Mexican officials to settle at Nacogdoches, where he traded with Mexicans as well as Indians and became prominent as a land operator. In 1833, with Thomas F. McKinney and Samuel M. Williams, he established a sawmill on Menard Creek, forty miles above Liberty on the Trinity River. There he also maintained a trading-post and continued to acquire lands in various parts of Texas. As a representative of the municipality of Liberty in the consultation at Washington-on-the-Brazos, he signed the Texas Declaration of Independence on Mar. 2, 1836, and was a member of the committee that drafted the constitution of the Republic. President Burnet selected him to make sure the neutrality of the Shawnee and other Indians in northwest Texas during the struggle with Mexico. After two missions to the Indians with A. J. Yates he tried unsuccessfully, as Texas commissioner, to negotiate a five-million-dollar loan for Texas in the United States.

The First Congress of Texas validated, for $50,000, Menard's claim to a league and a labor of land, about six square miles, which he had located in 1834 on the east end of Galveston Island (*Laws of the Republic of Texas,* 1838, I, pp. 70–72). In 1838 he organized and became president of the Galveston City Company, which issued one thousand shares of stock at a book value of $1,000 each. Generous terms were offered to attract settlers and donations of land were liberally made for public and charitable purposes. Shares, which at one time sold for ten cents on the dollar, were at par at the time of his death and fourteen years later were worth $10,000. He was also president of the wharf company and actively engaged in various commercial enterprises. He lived to see the population of the city he founded approach 7,000. He represented Galveston county in the Fifth Congress of Texas from 1840 to 1842 and was considered one of the best authorities in that body on the vexed question of Texas land titles. He also advocated the scheme of public finance known as the "exchequer system," which was adopted after he retired from Congress. He held no other political office. In the 40's he erected, on a ten-acre lot in Galveston, a large residence, where he dispensed a lavish hospitality to his white and Indian friends. He was four times married: first, in 1832, at Sainte Genevieve, Mo., to Marie Anne (Diane) Leclere, who died the next year; second to Adeline Maxwell, of Kaskaskia, his second cousin, who did not long survive; third to Mary Jane Riddle, of St. Louis, who died in 1845; and fourth to Mrs. Rebecca Mary Bass, of Georgia, who, after Menard's death, married Colonel J. S. Thrasher. Menard was a useful, though not a spectacular figure in the development of Texas. He was primarily a business man and the success that attended his commercial ventures attests his practical sagacity. He was a man of powerful physique and was counted a delightful raconteur. After his death, which resulted from a carbuncle, his body was buried in the old Catholic Cemetery at Galveston. A county, created in 1858, was named in his honor.

[MSS. in Rosenberg Lib. of Galveston; information from the archives of Mo. Hist. Soc. through the courtesy of Stella M. Drumm; *Galveston Directory, 1866–67* (1866), pp. 42–45; Joseph Tasse, *Les Canadiens de L'Ouest* (1878), vol. II; *Galveston Daily News*, Dec. 9, 1906; *Hist. of Texas, together with a Biog. Hist. of the Cities of Houston and Galveston* (1895); S. C. Griffin, *Hist. of Galveston* (1931); F. W. Johnson, *A Hist. of Texas* (1914) ed. by E. C. Barker, vol. II; his Christian names were sometimes spelled Michael Brindamour.] H. P. G.

MENARD, PIERRE (Oct. 7, 1766–June 13, 1844), fur-trader, merchant, and statesman, was born at St. Antoine, Quebec, the son of Jean Baptiste and Marie Françoise (Cirée) Menard. His father, a native of Languedoc, France, sided with the colonists in the Revolution and is said to have served under Montgomery at Quebec. His mother, a woman of superior intelligence and education, was a Canadian. The youth, according to Gov. John Reynolds (*post*, p. 242) received a "common, plain education." About 1787 he moved to Vincennes, Ind., where he was employed by the Indian trader, Col. François Vigo [*q.v.*]. In 1789 he accompanied Vigo to Carlisle, Pa., to consult Washington regarding the protection of the frontier. Two years later he moved to Kaskaskia and with Toussaint DuBois as a partner opened a store. He was married, June 13, 1792, to Thérèse Godin. On the organization of Randolph County he was appointed by Gov. Arthur St. Clair (Oct. 7, 1795) major of the county's first regiment of militia, and was recommissioned five years later. In February 1801, Gov. William Henry Harrison appointed him a judge of the county court of common pleas, a position he retained for ten years. In 1803 he was elected a delegate to the Indiana legislature (serving until the separation of Illinois in 1809) and in 1806 he was appointed lieutenant-colonel commanding the county militia.

His wife died in 1804, and on Sept. 22, 1806, he married Angélique Saucier, whose sister was the wife of Jean Pierre Chouteau [*q.v.*]. He was one of the organizing partners (Mar. 7, 1809) of the St. Louis Missouri Fur Company, and, as a captain of infantry on special service, commissioned by Gov. Meriwether Lewis, he accompanied its first expedition, which restored the Mandan chief, Big White, to his people. From Fort Mandan, the trading-post established by the company, he and Andrew Henry [*q.v.*] led the first organized invasion of trappers to the Three Forks of the Missouri, where they arrived Apr. 3, 1810; but on being driven out by the Blackfeet he returned to his home in Kaskaskia. At the beginning of 1811 he resigned his judgeship. He was elected in 1812 to the first Illinois senate (legislative council), of which he was made the first president, continuing to serve until statehood was attained. Until 1816 he had held his various offices without having been formally naturalized. In 1818 he was the general choice for the state's first lieutenant-governor; and the constitutional convention, in order to permit his election, altered the requisite period of citizenship, which it had placed at thirty years, making eligible for office a citizen who had resided in the state two years preceding the election. Elected by acclamation, he served with ability. At the end of his term he retired to his home, a place famous throughout the West for its hospitality. In 1828, on the appointment of President John Quincy Adams, he served with Lewis Cass on a commission to treat with the Winnebagos at Prairie du Chien; and in the following year, reappointed by President Jackson, he served with Caleb Atwater and Gen. John McNeil on a like commission to treat with other tribes of the region. No further public duty seems to have called him from his retirement. His later days were spent quietly in the care of his many business interests, in the dispensing of aid to the needy, and in the companionship of his family. He had four children by his first wife, and six by his second, who died in 1839. He died at his home.

Menard won the high esteem of all with whom he came in contact. Gov. Reynolds praised him in unstinted terms. "An honorable, high minded gentleman," is the tribute of Gen. Thomas James, who heartily detested the other officials of the St. Louis Missouri Fur Company whom he knew. An Illinois county, organized in 1839, is named for him, and a statue of him, presented by Charles P. Choutou and unveiled on Jan. 10, 1888, stands in the capitol grounds at Springfield.

[John Reynolds, *The Pioneer Hist. of Ill.* (1852); *Chicago Hist. Soc. Colls.*, vol. IV (1890); "The Governors' Letter-books 1818–1834," ed. by E. B. Greene and C. W. Alvord, *Colls. of the Ill. State Hist. Lib.*, vol. IV (1909); Thomas James, *Three Years Among the Indians and Mexicans* (1916), ed. by W. B. Douglas.]
W. J. G.

MÉNARD, RENÉ (Sept. 7, 1605–August 1661), the first Jesuit missionary in the upper Great Lakes region, was Parisian born and entered the Jesuit order as a novice, at Paris, Nov. 7, 1624. He completed his novitiate after studying in Paris, La Flèche, Bourges, and Rouen. Subsequently he was an instructor at Orléans (1629–32) and at Moulins (1636–39). He had long cherished a desire to enter the missionary field and was ordered in 1640 to reinforce the Jesuits in Canada, where he arrived about the last of June.

The new missionary was detailed to learn the Algonquian language and was registered at Sillery for the first year. In 1641 he accompanied co-workers to Huronia, where he was expected to evangelize the outlying tribes of Algonquian stock. In April 1642 Pijart and Ménard opened a mission for the Nipissing, north of the lake of that name. Because of this tribe's wandering habits, the mission was abandoned eighteen months later and Ménard ministered among the Huron until 1649, when he withdrew to Canada. For several years he was stationed at Three Rivers, acting for a time as superior at that center. In 1656 he was one of the Jesuits chosen for the hazardous experiment of founding a French colony among the Iroquois. During the somewhat less than two years of this mission he suffered the indignities and torture heaped upon the emissaries of the gospel by this fierce race. When, in March 1658, the entire colony fled to Canada and Ménard "was compelled to forsake that fair harvest it was like tearing his heart out of his bosom" (*Jesuit Relations,* XVIII, 141).

In 1660 the first mission to the Ottawa country was undertaken. Bishop Laval wrote to the pope that he was sending Father Ménard thither. Ménard himself knew it was his death warrant; but frail and worn as he was in body, his spirit was indomitable. He gloried in the opportunity, like St. Francis Xavier, to seek the wilderness alone. The Indians who promised to care for the missionary broke their promise; he was forced to paddle and portage with the strongest of them; he was nearly starved; and finally on the shore of Lake Superior a tree fell upon and crushed his canoe. At last, on Ste. Thérèse's day (Oct. 15), he reached a village in a cove now called L'Anse. The chief was brutal and turned him out of his hut; he then dwelt in a hut made by himself of fir branches. Fortunately, the winter was mild; wine did not congeal until February. In March some traders came for him and escorted him to the main Ottawa village on Chequamegon Bay. There he learned that some fugitive Hurons were starving in the interior, and against the advice of his trader friends, he insisted on visiting them. With one helper he set forth and somewhere en route was lost in the forest. Older historians, ignoring his visit to Chequamegon Bay, placed the site of his death on the upper Wisconsin River. It is now thought that it took place on a tributary of the Chippewa in Taylor County, Wisconsin, even yet a region of dense woodlands. His companion endeavored to persuade the Hurons to go in search of the father, but they refused. Since he had some provisions with him, it was thought he might have kept alive until the day of the Assumption of the Virgin, Aug. 15. His effects were reported to have been seen in an Indian cabin, but the rumor was not verified. An old, frail man he no doubt became confused in the forest paths and died from exhaustion. His saintly character, his high courage, and earnest zeal were extolled by his superior and have given him a place in the history of the Northwest.

[R. G. Thwaites, ed., *The Jesuit Relations and Allied Documents* (73 vols., 1896–1901), esp. vols. XVIII, XLIII–XLIX, LXXI; T. J. Campbell, *Pioneer Priests of North America,* vol. I (1908); L. P. Kellogg, *The French Régime in Wis.* (1925).]
L. P. K.

MENDENHALL, THOMAS CORWIN (Oct. 4, 1841–Mar. 22, 1924), physicist, administrator, educator, was born on a farm near Hanoverton, Ohio, the youngest of five children of Stephen Mendenhall and Mary (Thomas) Mendenhall. Of Quaker stock, he grew up in a community intensely anti-slavery in sympathy during a period when grave public questions were matters of wide and earnest discussion. He was largely self-educated, his formal education being limited to the local public schools and to a short period in the Southwest Normal School at Lebanon, Ohio, from which he graduated in 1861.

Following his graduation he taught mathematics and science in various high schools of his native state, meanwhile studying physics and higher mathematics privately. Possessed of the power of lucid presentation and imbued with enthusiasm for experimentation, he met with such success as a teacher that he was elected in 1873 to the chair of physics and mechanics in the newly founded Ohio Agricultural and Mechanical College (later Ohio State University) at Columbus. In addition to his teaching, he was active in popularizing science through the organization of scientific societies and through popular lectures. At this time, scientific education in the Middle West was in its infancy, and by his ability as a teacher, his interest in research, and his charm as a lecturer he was instrumental in furthering to a marked extent the spread of science.

In 1878 he was called to the chair of physics at the Imperial University at Tokyo, Japan. Here he remained three years, during which time he established a physical laboratory and a meteorological observatory. He was also influential in organizing a seismological society and in inaugurating a system of popular lectures. While in Japan he measured the absolute force of gravity at Tokyo and the relative force of gravity between Tokyo and Fujiyama. From these measurements he determined the mean density of the earth, his result representing the best value obtained by this method at that time.

Returning to the United States in 1881, he again occupied the chair of physics in the Ohio State University until 1884, at the same time organizing and directing the State Weather Bureau. In the next two years he served as professor of electrical science in the United States Signal Corps at Washington, in which connection he organized and equipped a physical laboratory, made systematic observations on atmospheric electricity, and established the systematic collection of data relating to earthquakes. In 1886 he left Washington to assume the office of president of Rose Polytechnic Institute at Terre Haute, Ind., remaining there three years, during which time his book *A Century of Electricity* (1887) was published.

In 1889 President Harrison appointed him superintendent of the United States Coast and Geodetic Survey, in which position he made his influence felt both as scientist and as administrator. As scientist he was responsible for the development of an improved portable apparatus for the measurement of gravity, which permitted the determination of the relative force of gravity with greater facility and accuracy, and under his plans a transcontinental series of gravity measurements were made. He was the first to propose the use of the ring pendulum for the measurement of the absolute force of gravity, a method which is now receiving considerable attention. As administrator he was responsible for inaugurating and maintaining high standards of scholastic attainment as a prerequisite to entrance into the technical force of the Coast Survey, and this at a time when the ideals of civil service were not yet firmly established. During this period he was also an active member of various important boards and commissions such as the United States Lighthouse Board, the United States Board of Geographic Names, the first Bering Sea commission, and the Alaska boundary commission.

After five years as head of the Coast and Geodetic Survey, he left in 1894 to accept the presidency of Worcester Polytechnic Institute. In 1901 ill health compelled his resignation and he went to Italy to recuperate, remaining eleven years in Europe. Returning to the United States in 1912, he settled in Ravenna, Ohio, where he died in 1924 in the eighty-third year of his age. On July 12, 1870, he had married Susan Allen Marple of Columbus, Ohio. Happy in their family life for forty-six years until the death of Mrs. Mendenhall, they had the further happiness of seeing their only son become a distinguished physicist.

Mendenhall's principal scientific contributions were to the subjects of electricity, gravity, seismology, and atmospheric electricity, but his labors covered a much wider field, evidenced by numerous monographs, reports, and papers. His scientific attainments received wide recognition. Although not a college graduate, he was awarded honorary degrees by many American universities. He was elected to the National Academy of Sciences (1887), and to the presidency of the American Association for the Advancement of Science (1889); and various other scientific societies honored him with membership. In 1901 he was awarded the Cullum Geographical Medal by the American Geographical Society; in 1911 the National Educational Society of Japan bestowed a gold medal on him; and in 1918 the Franklin Institute awarded him a Franklin Medal at the same time that a similar medal was awarded Marconi. In the High School at Salem, Ohio, in which he taught early in his career, a bronze tablet has been erected to his memory, and at the Ohio State University the physics building has been named the Mendenhall Laboratory of Physics in his honor.

[*Who's Who in America*, 1922–23; *Science*, July 11, 1924; *Jour. of the Franklin Inst.*, July 1918; *Ohio State Jour.*, Mar. 23, 1924; W. H. Siebert, *Thomas Corwin Mendenhall: Teacher, Scientist, Administrator* (pamphlet, repr. from History, Columbus High School, 1847–1910); *Hist. of the Ohio Sate Univ.* (3 vols., 1920–26), ed. by T. C. Mendenhall.] H. A. M.

MENDES, FREDERIC DE SOLA (July 8, 1850–Oct. 26, 1927), rabbi, son of the Rev. Abraham Pereira and Eliza (de Sola) Mendes, was born in Montego Bay, Jamaica, British West Indies, where his father was minister. He was a descendant of David Pereira Mendes, who, after fleeing from Spain to Bayonne, settled in Jamaica in 1768. His mother's mother, Rica Meldola, traced her ancestry to Isaiah Meldola of Toledo, who was born in 1282. When Frederic was a year old, his family went to England, and spent the next seven years in Birmingham. From there they moved, in 1858, to London, and young Mendes received his education at his father's private school, at University College School, London, and at London University (B.A. 1869). Proceeding to Germany, he studied at the University of Breslau, receiving the degree of Ph.D. at the University of Jena in 1871. At the same time, he obtained his rabbinic training in the Jewish Theological Seminary, Breslau, 1870–73. Returning to England, he was licensed to preach in 1873 by the Sephardic Chief Rabbi, Benjamin Artom. After serving as preacher for a few months in the New Synagogue, London, in December 1873 he accepted the call to become assistant to Rev. Samuel M. Isaacs [*q.v.*], minister of Congregation Shaaray Tefila in New York, taking office on Jan. 1, 1874. Isaacs, who had served the congregation since its organization in 1845, retired in 1874, whereupon, Mendes was elected preacher, and after the death of Isaacs, on May 19, 1878, he became the rabbi of the congregation, a position which he held until elected rabbi emeritus on Oct. 1, 1920. On Feb. 14, 1877, he married Isabel, daughter of Aaron N. and Isabel Frances Cohen, who bore him two sons and four daughters. His death in New Rochelle, N. Y., closed a career of almost fifty-four years with the one congregation.

Mendes belonged to the generation of scholarly rabbis who came to America from Europe in the last third of the nineteenth century. He inherited from his father, and from his maternal ancestors in the learned De Sola and Meldola families a tradition of scholarship which influenced him towards a literary rabbinate. In 1876 he helped to found and conduct the *Independent Hebrew,* a magazine which lived for only three months. He took the lead in establishing the *American Hebrew* in 1879, and was its editor from 1879 to 1885. He edited two volumes of *The Menorah Monthly,* 1901–02; he was revising editor of the *Jewish Encyclopedia* and chief of its translation bureau until September 1902; and was a contributor to *Johnson's Encyclopedia* and the *Encyclopedia Americana.* Among his other writings may be mentioned *The Child's First Bible* (1877; 4th ed., 1887); *Defence, not Defiance, a Hebrew's Reply to the Missionaries* (1876); *Jewish Family Papers; Letters of a Missionary* (1875), a translation from the German of Gustav Meinhardt (Wilhelm Herzberg); *The Life of Menasseh ben Israel* (London, 1877), a translation from the German of Meyer Kayserling; and *Outlines of Jewish History* (1886).

Mendes took part in the development of the Jewish community of New York in its critical years of prodigious growth at the end of the nineteenth and beginning of the twentieth centuries. After the massacres of Jews in Russia in 1881 and the promulgation of the May Laws in 1882, Russian Jewish refugees began to find their way in large numbers to the United States. Mendes was actively interested in trying to keep them out of the cities, and gave much time to the founding and the administration of the agricultural village alliance near Vineland, N. J. He was also one of the founders and a president of the New York Board of Jewish Ministers, and one of the founders of the Young Men's Hebrew Association in New York.

In the weekly magazine, the *American Hebrew,* which for decades was devoted to the conservation of historical Jewish tradition, Mendes expressed his religious views. Though in later years he reluctantly moved with his congregation more towards reform Judaism, he always remained a conservative Jew. He was strongly opposed to the radical reform Judaism of his day, and was one of those who in 1885 uncompromisingly denounced the Pittsburgh Program of Reform Judaism. His interests were broad, including such subjects as chemistry, poetry, anatomy, music, Semitic languages, scientific farming and gardening. He was small in stature, but his geniality, tolerance, culture, and humane scholarship gave him an unvarying dignity, and commanded general respect.

[*The Jewish Encyc.*; *Am. Hebrew,* Apr. 10, 1914, Oct. 28, 1927; Nathan Stern in *Yearbook: Central Conf. Am. Rabbis,* vol. XXXVIII (1928); *Who's Who in America,* 1926–27; *N. Y. Times,* Oct. 27, 1927.]

D. deS. P.

MENEELY, ANDREW (May 19, 1802–Oct. 14, 1851), bell-founder, was the son of Andrew Meneely and Eleanor Cobb. His father came to the United States from the north of Ireland in 1795 and settled in West Troy (now Watervliet), N. Y., where the younger Andrew was born. At the age of seventeen, after an elementary education, Meneely was apprenticed to Julius Hanks, who, with his brother Oscar, was engaged in making bells, clocks, and scientific instruments. Their father, Benjamin Hanks, had come to West

Troy from Mansfield, Conn., and had established his foundry there in 1808. He was one of the first founders in the country to cast church bells and brass cannon, and he is said to have made the first tower clock and surveying instruments produced in this country. In 1826 Meneely established in West Troy a bell foundry of his own, and at about the same time he married Philena, daughter of Rodney Hanks, the brother of his employer. Bell-making had been only one of several enterprises in which the Hanks family had engaged. Meneely, on the other hand, devoted himself to this work, and by constant experimentation he greatly improved upon the methods used by his former employers. He was, after a few years, able to predict with accuracy the weight and tone of each bell he cast. Such precision had not previously been attained in America, and it had been common, both in the United States and abroad, to secure the desired tone by chiseling off portions of the bells after they were cast.

As Meneely was one of comparatively few foundrymen specializing in bell-metal bells, that is, bells made of copper and tin, usually in the proportion of four to one, and inasmuch as his preëminence was easily established, his foundry was soon sending bells not only throughout the United States but also throughout the world. His chimes were particularly sought after and won many prizes at fairs and expositions. The business grew rapidly, and Meneely came to be regarded, in the words of a contemporary newspaper, as "one of those who have done most for the general advancement of the industrial arts in all their branches." Though he devoted himself unsparingly to his business, even to the detriment of his health, he took an interest in his community and was twice, in 1839 and again in 1843, president of the village of West Troy. His chief interest, however, was the local Reformed Dutch Church of which he was a ruling elder. To this church he gave generously both of time and money, contributing also to the support of other religious institutions. After his death the business was carried on by his sons, who further improved the technique of bell-making, and still later by his descendants.

[Sources include: O. H. Gregory, *Memoir of Andrew Meneely, Esq., a Ruling Elder in the Reformed Dutch Church of West Troy, N. Y.* (1852); J. T. Myers, *Hist. of the City of Watervliet, N. Y., 1670–1910* (n.d.); J. L. Bishop, *A Hist. of Am. Manufactures from 1608–1860*, vol. II (1864); and information as to certain facts from the Meneely family. The date of Meneely's birth was taken from the family Bible in the possession of his great-grand-daughter.] G. H.

MENÉNDEZ DE AVILÉS, PEDRO (Feb. 15, 1519–Sept. 17, 1574), Spanish naval officer, founder of St. Augustine, was a member of a noble but somewhat impoverished Asturian family. At an early age he sought his fortune at sea. All the rest of his life he followed the sea, seldom finding opportunities to return to his wife, Ana María de Solís, and his children. At thirty he distinguished himself fighting pirates off the French coast, and at thirty-five he was appointed by Charles V captain-general of the Indies fleet. Between 1555 and 1563 he made three voyages to the New World and served Philip II ably in Flanders and in England; during these years he demonstrated his honesty, his seamanship, and his capacity for vigorous and intelligent action. Early in 1565 the king selected him to resist the encroachments of the French in Florida. By contract of Mar. 20, 1565 (translated in Connor, *Pedro Menéndez de Avilés,* pp. 259–70) he was given the title of *adelantado* of Florida, and in return for various privileges undertook at his own expense to explore and colonize the Florida coast; and he was ordered to drive out by any means he saw fit any "settlers who are corsairs, or of any other nations not subject to Us" (p. 261).

He sailed with his fleet from Cadiz in June; late in August he found Jean Ribaut's fleet at anchor off the St. John's River whither it had come to reinforce the French port of Fort Caroline. He scattered it with a bold night attack, and then took his fleet south to the harbor of St. Augustine, where on Sept. 6th a fort was started. Five days later Ribaut's fleet, about to attack the new fort, was driven south by a violent storm. Menéndez seized the chance for an overland attack on Fort Caroline. Leading a force of 500, he surprised and took the badly guarded French fort, killed or captured three-quarters of the 240 occupants, and, leaving a garrison, returned at once to St. Augustine. Ribaut's fleet had been wrecked. Twice in the next three weeks Menéndez faced the problem of dealing with large parties of Frenchmen, trapped at Matanzas Inlet in their attempt to win their way back to Fort Caroline. On each occasion, after a parley in which Menéndez promised no mercy and forced an unconditional surrender, those who accepted his terms were disarmed, ferried across the inlet in small groups, and slaughtered behind the sand dunes. Over 200 Frenchmen, including Ribaut himself, were thus put to the knife. Menéndez wrote the king that such treatment of heretic interlopers was "necessary for the service of God Our Lord and of Your Majesty" (Ruidíaz, *post,* II, p. 103). Perhaps doubts as to his ability to feed and guard so many captives played a part in his decision. But in his letter to the king (Oct.

15, 1565) he did not disguise his satisfaction that the able Ribaut had been put out of the way.

The later capture (on a promise of mercy, which he kept) of the few Frenchmen who had not surrendered at Matanzas, ended the French danger. Menéndez now proceeded with his plans for posts on both coasts of Florida, at Port Royal and in Chesapeake Bay, and searched for a water route from the Gulf of Mexico through the peninsula. (See map in Lowery, *post,* p. 210, for location of settlements.) In all his explorations he dealt honorably with the Indians, tried to pacify them and to save them from exploitation, and worked, though handicapped by a scarcity of missionaries, to implant the rudiments of Christianity. In May 1567, unable to get sufficient support in the West Indies, he returned to Spain to seek help from the king, but Philip's response was disappointingly small. Menéndez made his fifth voyage to the west in 1568–69 and may have visited Florida. In 1570 he was at sea protecting Spanish commerce from pirates; not till 1571 could he return to St. Augustine. Conditions in Florida were deplorable. Only a handful of discouraged colonists and mutinous soldiers in the three posts of St. Augustine, San Mateo, and Santa Elena was the result of his efforts over the past six years. Leaving such aid as he could, he sailed again for Spain in April 1572. In 1573 he asked permission to wage war on the Florida Indians and to export as slaves any who should be taken alive (Connor, *Colonial Records of Spanish Florida,* I, pp. 30–81). Later he asked to be allowed to take his two daughters and sons-in-laws and fifty settlers with their households to Florida. But while in command of a large fleet at Santander he died, Sept. 17, 1574. In 1591 his body was taken for final burial to his native city of Avilés.

Menéndez was a man of honor and of strong religious feeling, an expert seaman and a bold and resourceful leader. His early dealings with the Indians, before he not unnaturally lost patience, are a refreshing contrast to the conduct of many early explorers. Like most adventurers in colonization, he overestimated the results to be expected and underestimated the difficulties; his plans were too large for his resources; he scattered his forces too widely, perhaps because of the scanty food supply. Nevertheless he did succeed in establishing Spanish power in Florida. He will be chiefly remembered, however, as the author of the slaughters of Matanzas; these can be explained but never excused.

[Andrés Gonzáles Barcia, *Ensayo Cronologico para la Hist. General de la Fla.* (1723); J. T. Connor, ed., *Pedro Menéndez de Avilés* (1923), a translation of the biography by Solis de Merás, Menéndez' brother-in-law, which is no. 3 of the Publications of the Fla. State Hist. Soc.; J. T. Connor, ed., *Colonial Records of Spanish Fla.,* vol. I (1925), which is no. 5 of the Publications of the Fla. State Hist. Soc.; Genaro García, *Dos Antiguas Relaciones de la Fla.* (1902), containing a biography of Menéndez by Bartolomé Barrientos; C. M. Vigil, *Noticias Biográfico-genealógicas de Pedro Menéndez de Avilés* (1892); Woodbury Lowery, *The Spanish Settlements within the Present Limits of the U. S., 1562–74* (1905); translation of letters of Menéndez to the King in 1565 in *Proc. Mass. Hist. Soc.,* 2 ser., vol. VIII (1894); Eugenio Ruidíaz y Caravia, *La Fla., Su Conquista y Colonización por Pedro Menéndez de Avilés* (2 vols., 1893–94), containing the biography by Solís de Merás, many letters written by Menéndez, and documents relating to his life.]

F. P.

MENETREY, JOSEPH (Nov. 28, 1812–Apr. 27, 1891), educator and missionary, was born in the Swiss canton of Freiburg, where he probably attended the University. On Sept. 29, 1836, he entered the Society of Jesus and passed through the regular Jesuit training prior to ordination late in 1846. As a volunteer for the American missions, he sailed on a ten months' voyage via Cape Horn for Oregon, where he arrived Aug. 13, 1847, and set about learning the Indian dialects in which he ultimately gained fluency. From St. Paul's, Ore., he passed to other mission stations in Idaho, Montana, and Washington, working among the Kalispel, Blackfeet, Flathead, Spokane, Coutenais, and Coeur d'Alène tribesmen. Monuments to the activity of "Pel Leméné," as he was known to the natives, were found everywhere. In 1854, along with Adrian Hoecken, S. J., he founded the model mission of St. Ignatius with a church, barracks, shops, and farms, in the heart of the Pend d'Oreilles country in the Siniélemen Valley. This, as a center on occasions of feasts, attracted the various tribesmen for two hundred miles around. In 1874 a printing press was brought from St. Louis and religious tracts and an Indian dictionary (*A Dictionary of the Kalispel or Flat-head Indian Language,* 2 vols., 1877–79), were printed. For a time, Menetrey was located at the Sacred Heart Mission among the Pointed Hearts Indians (*c.* 1859). Later he was the first pastor of Frenchtown, from which he ministered to scattered white and half-breed Catholics in Hell's Gate Valley and visited the gold gulches of a wide area.

In 1874, he was sent to Last Chance Gulch or Helena, where he built a church and attended stations as far-flung as Crow Creek, Gallatin Valley, Boulder, and the Missouri River settlements. Transferred to Missoula in 1877, he established a flourishing congregation and built St. Patrick's Hospital and St. Francis Xavier Church. In 1888, broken in health, he retired to St. Ignatius Mission, where, three years later, he died on the feast of St. Peter Canisius whom he especially revered. His funeral services were attended by a concourse of Indians of various tribes, of whom 1,000 are said to have received communion for the repose of his soul. Few missionaries were more widely known or labored more successfully for the conversion of the Indians.

[Annual Catholic directories; L. B. Palladino, *Indian and White in the Northwest* (1894); S. J. Sullivan, *The Golden Jubilee of St. Joseph's Church, Canton, Mont.* (1926); H. M. Chittenden and A. T. Richardson, *Life, Letters, and Travels of Father Pierre-Jean De Smet, S. J.* (1905); *Helena Herald*, Apr. 29, 1891.] R. J. P.

MENEWA (fl. 1814–1835), Creek chief, was born probably about 1766 with white and Indian blood in his veins. He was called Hothlepoya, "the crazy war hunter," in his younger days, when he was famous for the skill and effrontery of his plundering expeditions across the Tennessee border. His notoriety was so great that there grew up around his name a body of frontier tradition comparable to the stories told of such figures as Robin Hood and Rob Roy. As he grew older he adapted himself to the more lucrative economic system of the white man, kept large herds of cattle, and traded with the Indians for furs and skins. He sent to Pensacola heavily laden trains of horses, perhaps fifty to a hundred at a trip. By the time Tecumseh [*q.v.*] went south to preach confederation, he had risen to the rank of second chieftain of the Oakfuskee villages in what is now Alabama and was known as Menewa, "the great warrior." He had scant sympathy with Georgia's efforts to possess the lands of the Indians, was the bitter enemy of William McIntosh [*q.v.*], and led the warriors of his villages into the Creek War. Superstitious faith in the advice of the first chief of his people, a medicine man, betrayed him into placing his troops in a vulnerable position at the battle of Horseshoe Bend in 1814. When he saw his defenses attacked by Andrew Jackson he realized his terrible mistake, for vengeance killed the false prophet, and rushed into hopeless battle. Wounded and left for dead, after the battle he saved himself only by incredible exertions. Although stripped of his wealth by the war, he assumed again the leadership of what remained of his band of warriors, who chose him in 1825 to execute their death sentence on McIntosh for ceding tribal lands against tribal law. The next year he was one of the delegation to Washington to protest against the treaty signed by McIntosh. There he smoked the pipe of peace and had his portrait made for the gallery of the War Department. Ten years later when the Creeks joined the Seminoles in war he served with the Alabama troops and for his services was promised the privilege of remaining to die in his native land. The promise was broken, however, and he was transported with the rest of his tribe across the Mississippi.

[T. L. McKenney and James Hall, *Hist. of the Indian Tribes of North America*, vol. I (1836); F. W. Hodge, *Handbook of Am. Indians*, vol. I (1907); James Pickett, *Hist. of Ala.* (1851), II, 343–44.] K. E. C.

MENGARINI, GREGORY (July 21, 1811–Sept. 23, 1886), Catholic missionary and educator, was born in Rome of a distinguished family. He entered the novitiate of the Society of Jesus, Oct. 28, 1828; and on completion of his philosophical training, he taught in Jesuit colleges in Rome, Modena, and Reggio. In 1839, while in the Jesuit seminary in Rome, he was much affected by the public reading of a letter from Bishop Joseph Rosati of St. Louis, which appealed for missionaries to the Flathead Indians, who were petitioning for a "black robe." Ordained a priest in March 1840, he volunteered for the Indian missions and sailed in July from Leghorn to Philadelphia. After spending a few months at Georgetown College, he went to St. Louis, from which he accompanied Fathers Pierre de Smet, Nicholas Point, and three Alsatian and Belgian lay brothers to Fort Hall, Idaho (Aug. 15, 1841). Escorted by a party of Flatheads, the missionaries went to St. Mary's Mission in the Bitter Root Valley. Here in a log-cabin with windows of thin beaten skin, Mengarini, despite suffering from bitter cold to which he was unacclimated, served the Indians, composed hymns in various dialects, trained a native choir, and compiled a *Selish or Flat-head Grammar; Grammatica Linguae Selicae,* which was published from his third manuscript, in 1861, as the second volume of J. G. Shea's Library of American Linguistics. It is said that he became so fluent in the Selish or Kalispel dialect that in speech he could pass for a tribesman. About this time he wrote a Kalispel Indian-English dictionary, which was ultimately published with an English-Indian supplement by the Indians and missionaries of the St. Ignatius Mission in Montana (*A Dictionary of the Kalispel or Flat-head Indian Language,* 2 vols., 1877–79).

In spite of Mengarini's entreaties to his superiors at St. Paul, Ore., St. Mary's Mission was ordered closed because of trouble with the Blackfeet tribesmen in 1850. Two years later, the repentant Blackfeet appealed for his return. Their petition was not granted, but the Jesuits reëstablished the St. Ignatius Mission. In the meantime, Mengarini had been ordered to the Santa Clara mission in California, where he assisted in the foundation of the College of Santa Clara, the first collegiate institution on the Pacific slope. Here serving as director of studies, as professor of modern languages, as treasurer, or as vice-rector, he continued his work until stricken by apoplexy. He had not only a deep affection for the Indians but a scientific interest in their language and customs. He furnished vocabularies of the Colville, Coeur d'Alène, Flathead, and Santa Clara dialects in John Wesley Powell's *Contributions to American Ethnology* (vols. I, III, 1877). Toward the end of his life, he dictated personal reminiscences which appeared in the *Woodstock Letters* (1888).

[*Cath. Encyc.*, X, 189; annual Catholic directories; *Woodstock Letters* (1887); *Jour. of the Anthropological Institute of N. Y.*, vol. I (1871–72); *Records of the Am. Cath. Hist. Soc.*, II (1889), 174 f.; H. M. Chittenden and A. T. Richardson, *Life, Letters, and Travels of Father Pierre-Jean De Smet, S. J.* (1905); L. B. Palladino, *Indian and White in the Northwest* (1894); *Morning Call* (San Francisco), Sept. 25, 1886.] R. J. P.

MENKEN, ADAH ISAACS (June 15, 1835?–Aug. 10, 1868), actress and poet, was born probably in Milneburg, a suburb of New Orleans, La. Accounts of her birth and early life, most of which are based on her own statements, are conflicting. These declarations, naming her father variously as Josiah Campbell, James McCord, Richard Irving Spenser, and Ricardo Los Fiertes, are fabrications and were made for purposes of publicity. It is true, however, that she was born a Jewess, and that her given name was Adah Bertha. Her father (whose surname was probably Theodore), died when she was about two years old, and her mother married again. Of this union, two children were born. Adah studied the classics, knew French, Hebrew, German, and Spanish, could ride, sing, and dance, and in later years became an amateur painter and sculptor. About 1853 the stepfather (probably named Josephs) died, leaving the family in straitened circumstances.

In 1856, she is said (probably incorrectly) to have privately printed a volume of verse entitled *Memories,* under the pseudonym "Indigena." In Livingston, Tex., on Apr. 3 of that year, she married Alexander Isaac Menken, son of a Cincinnati dry-goods merchant. In March 1857 she appeared at James Charles' theatre in Shreveport, La., as Pauline in *The Lady of Lyons*; on Aug. 29 she made her début in New Orleans, at Crisp's Gaiety as Bianca in *Fazio.* On Sept. 25 she published a poem in the Cincinnati *Israelite,* and subsequently contributed regularly to this paper until Apr. 22, 1859.

With her husband as her manager, she appeared in the principal Southern and Western cities during the next year, meeting with moderate success. On Mar. 1, 1859, she made her New York début at Purdy's National Theatre as Widow Cheerly in *The Soldier's Daughter.* In July, she left Alexander Menken, and believing herself to have been divorced by him, married John Carmel Heenan [*q.v.*] in New York on Sept. 3 (Heenan divorce bill presented before the circuit court, McHenry County, Ill., October 1861, by Adah Isaacs Menken). At Pfaff's, New York's Bohemian rendezvous, she met Ada Clare, Walt Whitman, Fitz-James O'Brien, and other American writers and critics. In January 1860 the news of her marriage to Heenan became public. Subsequently a scandal arose when Alexander Menken announced that he had never divorced his wife but that he would now proceed to do so. In the summer of that year, Adah Menken bore Heenan a son who died within a short time. Heenan, returning from England in July after his fight with Tom Sayers, repudiated his wife. To add to her unhappiness, she received word in September from her half-sister, Annie Campbell Josephs, telling of her mother's death in New Orleans. Her poems written in this year, twelve of which were later included in *Infelicia,* reflect her depression of spirit.

With the new year, however, she resumed her theatrical activities, meeting especial success in Milwaukee and Pittsburgh. On June 3, 1861, she made her first appearance as Mazeppa at the Green Street Theatre, Albany, before the largest audience in the history of that theatre. In April of the following year she received her divorce from Heenan, and on Sept. 24, married Robert Henry Newell [*q.v.*]. In November, an amazing success in Baltimore was accompanied by a gift of diamonds worth $1,500. She declared herself a secessionist and was promptly arrested and brought before Provost-Marshal Fish, who released her on parole. On July 13, 1863, she sailed for San Francisco with her husband, appearing at Tom Maguire's Opera House on Aug. 24. To the literary group including Mark Twain, Bret Harte, Artemus Ward, Joaquin Miller, and others that met in Joe Lawrence's *Golden Era* office, she was a strange, beautiful goddess.

On Apr. 23, 1864, she sailed for England. Newell, who accompanied her as far as the Isthmus, returned to New York. Opening in *Mazeppa* at Astley's, London, on Oct. 3, she created a tremendous sensation. At her salon in the Westminster Palace Hotel such men as Dickens,

Reade, Swinburne, Rossetti, Burne-Jones, Purnell, and Charles Fechter were among her guests. On Aug. 24, 1865, she arrived in New York, but her stay was short, and on Oct. 9, she opened at Astley's in *Child of the Sun* by John Brougham [*q.v.*]. The play was withdrawn after six weeks and *Mazeppa* revived. In March 1866 she returned to New York, where on Apr. 30, at Wood's Broadway Theatre, she played before a house jammed to suffocation. She had divorced Newell in 1865, and after a triumphal tour of the larger cities, she was married, on Aug. 19, 1866, to James Barkley by Alderman John Brice at her home, 458 Seventh Avenue. Three days later she sailed alone for Europe. Barkley later went to California, where he died in 1878.

In Paris, "la Menken" went into retirement until the birth early in November of her son, who was christened, in honor of George Sand, his godmother, Louis Dudevant Victor Emanuel Barkley. On Dec. 30, she opened in *Les Pirates de la Savane* at the Théatre de la Gaité to the greatest triumph that had ever been accorded an American actress. Her apartment at the Hôtel de Suez was crowded with admirers, including Gautier and Dumas *père.* After a short engagement in Vienna, she returned to Paris. Astley's recalled her to London in the fall. At Sadler's Wells Theatre, on May 30, 1868, she gave her last performance. On July 9, in Paris, while rehearsing a new version of *Les Pirates,* she collapsed; on Aug. 10, she died and was buried in the Jewish sector of Père Lachaise. Edwin James removed the body, Apr. 21, 1869, to Montparnasse, where a marble monument bearing the inscription "Thou Knowest" (from Swinburne's *Ilicet*) had been erected. A collection of her poems, *Infelicia,* edited by John Thomson, Swinburne's secretary, and dedicated to Charles Dickens, was published in London, Aug. 18, 1868. Twenty-five of these poems had appeared in the New York *Sunday Mercury* in 1860 and 1861, and one in the *Israelite* of Sept. 3, 1858.

"The Royal Menken" was probably not a great dramatic figure, but her acting was as free from the platitude of the stage as her poetry was from its language. Swinburne, in his extravagant manner, wrote across a copy of *Infelicia,* "Lo, this is she that was the world's delight." Volatile, fearless, and uninhibited, she scandalized the staid Victorians of her day by her unconventional conduct, and, after her death, biographers accepted as fact her rumored immoralities. She possessed a keen intellect that recognized the genius of Walt Whitman as early as 1860. Under his stimulus she developed her own technique in the "rolling rhythms" of her poems. Dante Gabriel Rossetti called them "really remarkable." Driven by an insatiable ambition, and aided by her vivid personality and strange beauty, she climaxed a meteoric career with the fame she so ardently desired.

[Collection belonging to Alfred F. Goldsmith of New York City; Album of Adah Isaacs Menken (MS.), owned by Richard Gimble; H. S. Gorman, *The Incredible Marquis: Alexandre Dumas* (1929); Edmund Gosse, *The Life of Algernon Charles Swinburne* (1917); Harvard College Library Theatre Collection; Edwin James, *Biog. of Adah Isaacs Menken* (1881?); marriage records, N. Y. City Board of Health; "Ada Isaacs Menken, the Wife of John C. Heenan," *N. Y. Illustrated News,* Mar. 17–Apr. 14, 1860; Richard Northcott, *Adah Isaacs Menken* (1921), unreliable; *Dante Gabriel Rossetti: His Family-Letters* (1895), ed. by W. M. Rossetti; Constance Rourke, *Troupers of the Gold Coast* (1928); highly colored "autobiographical" fragment, ed. by Augustin Daly, in *N. Y. Times,* Sept. 6, 1868; C. W. Stoddard, "La Belle Menken," *Nat. Mag.,* Feb. 1905; T. E. Welby, *A Study of Swinburne* (1926); obituaries in *N. Y. Tribune, N. Y. Times,* Aug. 12, 1868; A. F. Lesser, "The Romantic Vagabond: Adah Isaacs Menken," dissertation in preparation at N. Y. Univ.]
A. F. L.

MENOCAL, ANICETO GARCIA (Sept. 1, 1836–July 20, 1908), civil engineer, was born in Cuba, the son of Gabriel Garcia Menocal, a wealthy planter, and his wife, Carmen Martin Monte Rey. He came to the United States to attend Rensselaer Polytechnic Institute, where he graduated in 1862 with the degree of C.E. Almost immediately he became assistant engineer and later chief engineer in charge of construction at the waterworks of Havana. On June 16, 1866, he married Elvira Martin, who survived him. They had four children.

In 1870 Menocal left Cuba, returning to the United States. After two years in the Department of Public Works of New York City, he entered the service of the United States Navy Department, being commissioned chief engineer in the navy on July 15, 1874. During his connection with the Navy Department, he was chief engineer of all the surveys made at Panama and Nicaragua, with a view to the construction of an interoceanic canal, but he is chiefly remembered as an early and persistent advocate of the Nicaraguan route. This he mapped in 1872–74; and in 1874–75 he pointed out the impracticability of a sea-level canal at the Isthmus. Convinced of the merits of his first proposals, he induced General Grant and others to organize the Provisional Interoceanic Canal Society (1880), which was later (1887) merged in the Maritime Canal Company of Nicaragua. Although, as chief engineer, he secured the necessary concessions, the project came to nothing because Grant's failure led to that of the Company. Unable to obtain further support in the United States, Menocal turned to the government of

Nicaragua, under whose auspices he carried out improvements at Grey Town, on the Rio San Juan, and at Lake Managua. He also investigated conditions at Panama. At length, in 1887, he became chief engineer of the newly organized Maritime Canal Company of Nicaragua and again secured concessions from Nicaragua, as well as from Costa Rica. Although work, beginning propitiously, continued until 1890, he was once more thwarted by a financial panic; and, in spite of his efforts to obtain capital in Europe or to secure government aid for the undertaking, it ended in disastrous failure. Nevertheless, his activities were not without fruit. Through his reports he kept the advisability of a canal before important groups; and through his papers read at the International Conference at Paris (1879), before the American Association for the Advancement of Science, at the Fourth International Conference on Inland Waterways at Manchester, England (1890), and at the World's Columbian Water Commerce Congress (1893), he appealed to a wider audience. His efforts helped to awaken the public interest which eventually made possible the construction of the interoceanic canal, though the route adopted, through Panama, was not that he had favored.

In 1881 as consulting engineer for the bureau of yards and docks he had designed the naval gun plant at Washington. After his retirement from the navy, Sept. 1, 1898, with the rank of commander, he continued to be called upon for assistance. He served on the board appointed to take charge of the properties surrendered in Cuba; he went to the Philippines to aid in the establishment of a naval base; and, in 1902, he investigated the sites available for a coaling station in Liberia. He was also retained by the government of Cuba and in the last two years of his life developed an irrigation system for the northern provinces of that country. He died in New York City.

[Menocal's activities are reflected in his reports and papers, especially in those contributed to the *Proceedings* of the United States Naval Institute and the *Transactions* of the American Society of Civil Engineers. See also memoir in *Trans. Am. Soc. Civil Engineers,* vol. LXXXIV (1921); H. B. Nason, *Biog. Record Officers and Grads. Rensselaer Polytechnic Inst.* (1887); R. P. Baker, *A Chapter in Am. Educ.: Rensselaer Polytechnic Inst.* (1924); *Who's Who in America,* 1908–09; *Army and Navy Jour.,* July 25, 1908; *N. Y. Times,* July 21, 1908; Navy Registers.]

R. P. B—r.

MENOHER, CHARLES THOMAS (Mar. 20, 1862–Aug. 11, 1930), soldier, came of Scotch-Irish colonial stock. His parents, Samuel and Sarah Jane (Young) Menoher, moved from Ohio to Johnstown, Pa., where Charles was born while his father was a soldier in the Civil War. He attended the borough schools, was interested as a boy in local literary and musical organizations, taught school for a while, and in the year 1882 was selected from among fifteen applicants to enter the United States Military Academy. Upon graduation in 1886, he was assigned to the artillery, and rose through all intermediate grades to become colonel, July 1, 1916. Meanwhile, he had graduated from the Artillery School (1894) and the Army War College (1907), and had been selected for the original General Staff Corps.

With the advent of the World War, he was appointed brigadier-general, National Army, Aug. 5, 1917; and while in command of the School of Instruction for Field Artillery at Saumur, France, was advanced to the grade of major-general, National Army, Nov. 28, 1917. His assignment to the 42nd (Rainbow) Division followed, with service in the Lunéville and Baccarat sectors; in repelling the critical German Champagne-Marne offensive; in the Allied offensive across the Ourcq River; in the attack on the St. Mihiel salient; and in the Meuse-Argonne offensive. His brilliant services were recognized, Nov. 7, by appointment as brigadier-general, Regular Army, and his assignment, Nov. 10, 1918, to command the VI Army Corps. For his conspicuous record in the World War, he was awarded the Distinguished-Service Medal, the citation stating in part that "The reputation as a fighting unit of the Forty-Second Division is in no small measure due to the soldierly qualities and the military leadership of this officer." He received also many foreign decorations, and was entitled to wear the American Victory Medal with five clasps.

With the signing of the Armistice, Menoher was appointed by the president to be director of the Air Service at Washington, Jan. 2, 1919, and was commissioned major-general, chief of Air Service, the next year, July 3, 1920. His successful administration of this office was impaired by friction with his principal assistant, Col. William Mitchell, over questions affecting the adequacy and conduct of the Air Service, and although upheld in the main by the Secretary of War, Menoher finally requested and received duty with troops. He commanded the Hawaiian Division, 1922–24, and then the Hawaiian Department until February 1925, after which he was in command of the IX Corps Area at San Francisco until the date of his retirement by operation of law, Mar. 20, 1926.

An officer of sterling character, high professional attainments, and strong sense of duty, Menoher was characterized by Secretary of

War Weeks as "a man of fine fighting record in France, a man of good judgment and level head, and a very capable executive" (*New York Times,* Aug. 12, 1930). He was married early in life to Nannie Wilhelmina Pearson, daughter of Maj. William H. Pearson, U. S. A. She died in 1919, and on Jan. 17, 1923, at Honolulu, he married Elizabeth Painter, who survived him, as did three sons by his former marriage, all of whom entered the military service.

[G. W. Cullum, *Biog. Register Officers and Grads., U. S. Mil. Acad.,* vol. III (3rd ed., 1891), and supplements; *Who's Who in America,* 1930–31;; *Ann. Report, Asso. Grads. U. S. Mil. Acad.,* 1931; *N. Y. Times,* Aug. 12, 1930; *Army and Navy Jour.,* Sept. 28, 1918, July 24, 1920, Feb. 17, 1923; Mar. 27, 1926, and Aug. 16, 1930; information furnished by the Secretary, Asso. Grads. U. S. Mil. Acad., and by a son, Maj. Pearson Menoher, U. S. A.] C. D. R.

MERCER, CHARLES FENTON (June 16, 1778–May 4, 1858), congressman from Virginia, was born at Fredericksburg, Va., the youngest son of Eleanor (Dick) and James Mercer [*q.v.*]. His mother died when he was two years old and thirteen years later his father died leaving heavy debts, which the son later undertook to pay. The boy entered the College of New Jersey (Princeton) in 1795 and graduated in 1797 at the head of his class. In college he began his lifelong friendship with John Henry Hobart [*q.v.*] and became a devout Episcopalian. From 1797 until 1802 he read law at Princeton and at Richmond, Va. When war with France threatened in 1798 he volunteered and was twice offered a commission in the army, but since the threat of war had already passed he declined. In 1802 he was licensed to practise law. Soon afterward he went to England on business and also visited France. On his return he settled at Aldie, Loudoun County, Va., and began the practice of his profession. He became a member of the House of Delegates of Virginia in 1810 and served until he resigned in 1817 to enter Congress. While a member of the legislature he took a leading part in efforts to increase the banking capital of Virginia, to found a new bank, to promote the colonization in Africa of free negroes from the United States, and to build roads and canals. He offered a bill to provide for a complete system of public education, from common-school to state university, which was defeated in the Senate in the spring of 1817 after having passed the House (see his *Discourse on Popular Education: Delivered in . . . Princeton . . . Sept. 26, 1826,* 1826). He was also the author of the act by which a sword and pension were given to George Rogers Clark. During the War of 1812 he served with the Virginia troops, rising to the rank of brigadier-general.

His enthusiasm for internal improvements, the suppression of the slave trade, and the colonization of free negroes gave direction to his efforts when he became a member of the federal House of Representatives in 1817. He was chairman of the committees on roads and canals and on the District of Columbia. Though a member of the Federalist party until its dissolution and then a Whig, he was never an ardent party man. He enjoyed the friendship of Monroe and of John Quincy Adams. He disliked Jackson and Van Buren and on Jan. 26, 1819, delivered an address in Congress in which he assailed Jackson's course in the Seminole War (*Annals of Congress,* 15 Cong., 2 Sess., cols. 797–831). He was a strong Unionist but was alarmed at the rapidly increasing power of the president and was opposed to the executive's control over federal patronage. He was active in the movement that resulted in the building of the Chesapeake and Ohio Canal and was for five years, from 1828 to 1833, president of the company. He was a leader in the Virginia constitutional convention of 1829–30, in which he advocated manhood suffrage, equal representation, and the popular election of important officers with the whole power of his distinguished oratorical ability.

Resigning from Congress on Dec. 26, 1839, he became cashier of a bank in Tallahassee, Fla. He was original grantee, partner, and agent of the Texas association, a company which obtained a contract to settle colonists in Texas and to receive pay from the Republic in land. When the convention in 1845 declared colonization contracts unconstitutional he and his associates brought suit to force payment, but the case was decided against them in the United States courts. In 1845 he published *An Exposition of the Weakness and Inefficiency of the Government of the United States.* In 1847 he built a house near Carrollton, Ky., which he made his home until 1853, when he disposed of his property there. For three years he traveled in Europe, working in the interest of the abolition of the slave trade. Ill with cancer of the lip, he returned to Fairfax County, Virginia, where he was nursed by relatives until his death. He was never married.

[J. M. Garnett, *Biog. Sketches of Hon. Charles Fenton Mercer* (1911); W. F. Dunaway, "Charles Fenton Mercer," manuscript thesis in the lib. of Univ. of Chicago; *Wm. and Mary College Quart.,* Jan. 1909, p. 210; *The Correspondence of John Henry Hobart,* esp. vol. III (1912); John McVicar, *The Early Life and Professional Years of Bishop Hobart* (1838); *Memoirs of John Quincy Adams,* ed. by C. F. Adams, vols. IV-X (1875–76), esp. X, p. 360, for Adams' explanation of Mercer's becoming a bank cashier at Tallahassee.] C. F. A.

MERCER, HENRY CHAPMAN (June 24, 1856–Mar. 9, 1930), archeologist, antiquarian, inventor, was born at Doylestown, Pa., and was the son of William Robert and Mary Rebecca (Chapman) Mercer. He attended the Tennent School near Hartsville, Pa., and Harvard College, receiving the degree of A.B. in 1879. He then read law in Philadelphia and was admitted to the bar in 1881, but his rapidly developing enthusiasm for archeology outweighed his interest in law, and after a few years he gave up the legal profession. As early as 1885 he published a monograph on *The Lenape Stone,* in recognition of which Spain later conferred a decoration upon him. He was an honorary member of the United States Archeological Commission at Madrid in 1893 and that same year became editor for anthropology in the *American Naturalist.* In 1894 he was made curator of American and prehistoric archeology for the University of Pennsylvania and filled that position until 1897. During this time he explored many caves and Indian mounds in the United States and Mexico. In the caves he identified the remains of several extinct animals, some of them hitherto unknown, including the prehistoric tapir, mylodon, peccary, and sloth. He explored the caves and ruins of Yucatan, fixing a geological date for the latter, and published his *Hill Caves of Yucatan* in 1896. He studied aboriginal remains in the Delaware, Ohio, and Tennessee valleys, discovering Indian stone-blade quarries and workshops along the Delaware, and giving much time to a study of technical comparison of these stone blades with the supposed geologically ancient human implements found in America (in drift gravels in New Jersey, for example) and with those of the Pleistocene Age in Europe, particularly around Abbeville and in the Dordogne Valley, France, and in Spain and Belgium, where he did much work in drift gravels and flint quarries. His study of human remains in the American river valleys aided in tracing the lines of early migrations. His *Researches upon the Antiquity of Man in the Delaware Valley and the Eastern United States* appeared in 1897.

The possession of ample private means enabled Mercer to drop his curatorship and editorial connection with the *American Naturalist* in 1897 and pursue his favorite studies at will. From that time until his death he made his headquarters at Doylestown, his birthplace. He was never married. He had been one of the founders of the Bucks County Historical Society at Doylestown in 1880, and it was with that society that he began depositing his growing collection of utensils and implements illustrating the colonial history of the United States. He published a monograph on the subject entitled *Tools of the Nation Maker* in 1897, and that name came in time to be applied to the collection itself. He was president of the society from 1911 until his death. In 1916 he built and endowed with his own funds a large concrete building to serve as museum for the collection and as a home for the society. Here, each in its own compartment, are complete sets of tools of varied metal, wood, clay, and textile working industries, as carried on by American pioneers, and other unusual yet kindred exhibits, as for example, an original Conestoga wagon, a "Democrat" wagon and a Norse gristmill, brought from a North Carolina mountain glen, but of an ancient type found in the northern Scottish isles and Scandinavia. Here also is a collection of the remarkable stove plates of the Pennsylvania Germans, regarding which Mercer wrote his monograph, *The Bible in Iron,* in 1914. He likewise studied the other artistic remains of the early German settlers, developing their processes of making and decorating pottery, until he finally invented in 1899 a new method of making mural decorative tiles, and in 1902 a new process for mosaics. He established a factory for the production of these tiles and designed many of them himself, taking his subjects from the Bible, history, literature, and mythology. In 1904 he invented a process for printing large designs in color on fabrics and paper, and was awarded a grand prize on it at the Louisiana Purchase Exposition in St. Louis that year.

He made a number of other excursions in pursuit of his researches, meanwhile writing numerous articles on scientific and antiquarian subjects, and for several years prior to his death men under his guidance were employed in various parts of the world, such as China, southern Europe, and the near East, mostly in search of ancient implements, from which he was tracing the descent of modern tools. In this field he published *Ancient Carpenters' Tools* in 1929. He had made an intensive study of old houses and was often able to determine the age of a building by examining the door hardware, nails, screws, lath, and shaping of timbers. During the years 1906–08 he erected his own residence, "Fonthill," a unique monolithic structure of sixty-six rooms near Doylestown, portions of it embellished with his own tiles, other rooms illustrating American colonial interiors. This, by his will, was endowed and bequeathed to the public as a museum, the ground around it to be an arboretum and bird sanctuary. He also left $100,000 to finance an expedition to the Far East to collect tools and utensils used in the daily life of those countries. He was a fellow or member of a number of learned societies.

[*Who's Who in America*, 1928–29, and articles in the *Doylestown* (Pa.) *Intelligencer* of Mar. 10 and 14, 1930, furnish notices of Mercer's life and his will. A partial idea of the scope of his work may be gained from his articles and books. The papers of the Bucks County Historical Society from 1917 to 1930 contain numerous articles by him which show his interest in antiquarian subjects. Information for this sketch was also gained through Mercer's associates and by the author's acquaintance with the archeologist.]

A. F. H.

MERCER, HUGH (*c.* 1725–Jan. 12, 1777), Revolutionary soldier, was born in Aberdeenshire, Scotland, the son of the Rev. William Mercer and his wife, Anna Munro. Educated as a physician at Marischal College, University of Aberdeen (1740–44), he joined the army of Prince Charles Edward as a surgeon's mate, and was present at the battle of Culloden. The collapse of the Pretender's cause led him to emigrate to America, and after a brief sojourn in Philadelphia, where he landed in 1746 or 1747, he settled near the present site of Mercersburg, Pa.

For about ten years he practised his profession in the Conococheague settlement, winning the esteem of the frontier community by his skill and courage. At the outbreak of the French and Indian War, he abandoned the lancet for the sword, becoming an officer of the Pennsylvania Regiment, a provincial corps. After having ranked as captain, major, and lieutenant-colonel, he was commissioned colonel of the third battalion, Apr. 23, 1759. Many daring escapes from the Indians are ascribed to him. It is said that he took part in Braddock's expedition in 1755 and was wounded in the action of July 9. He participated in the attack upon the Indian village of Kittanning in September 1756, and for gallantry was awarded a vote of thanks and a medal by the corporation of the city of Philadelphia. He accompanied the expedition of General Forbes to Fort Duquesne in 1758, and on its successful termination was appointed commandant at Fort Pitt, where in the following year he conducted important negotiations for peace with chiefs and warriors of the Six Nations and other tribes. During the course of the war he made the acquaintance of Washington, and at his suggestion, it is said, removed from Pennsylvania to Fredericksburg, Va., where he took up once more the practice of medicine and also conducted an apothecary shop. He attended the same Masonic lodge as Washington, and was an occasional visitor at Mount Vernon. He married Isabella Gordon of Fredericksburg, and had four sons and a daughter.

When the colonies rebelled against Great Britain, Mercer again deserted the medical for the military profession. On Sept. 12, 1775, he was elected colonel of minute men for the counties of Caroline, Stafford, King George, and Spotsylvania. He presently relinquished this position for the colonelcy of the 3rd Virginia Regiment, to which he was elected by the Virginia Convention on Jan. 11, 1776. Previously he had been nominated for the colonelcy of the 1st Regiment, but had been defeated in a close contest by Patrick Henry.

At Williamsburg he set about organizing and drilling his battalion. On June 5, he was elected brigadier-general by the Continental Congress. Washington directed him to repair to Paulus Hook, and placed him in charge of the Flying Camp, comprising militia from Pennsylvania, Delaware, Maryland, and New Jersey. Its function was to hover between Howe's forces and Philadelphia, at the same time protecting northern New Jersey against attack by the British troops on Staten Island. Mercer experienced difficulty in holding his command together. Despite his patriotic appeals, scores of his men went home on the expiration of their enlistments, or deserted outright. He accompanied the army in its retreat across New Jersey, and was employed for a time in guarding the ferries of the Delaware against passage by the British. If he did not exclusively originate the plan of recrossing the river and surprising the Hessians at Trenton, he helped to execute it. His brigade was assigned to the left wing under General Greene, and was one of the first corps to enter Trenton on the morning of Dec. 26, 1776.

The claim that he suggested to Washington the stroke which resulted in the subsequent victory at Princeton has been challenged, but there is no doubt as to his part in the battle. On the morning of Jan. 3, 1777, in accordance with the orders of the commander-in-chief, he attempted to seize the bridge over Stony Brook on the American left, but his men were driven back in disorder and his horse was shot from under him. As he was attempting to rally his brigade on foot, he was surrounded by redcoats, clubbed on the head with the breech of a musket, forced to the ground despite his efforts to defend himself with his sword, and bayonetted in seven places. After the battle he was carried by his aide to a neighboring farmhouse, where he died. His remains were buried with civic and military honors in Christ Churchyard, Philadelphia, and in 1840 were transferred to Laurel Hill Cemetery. The Continental Congress voted to erect a monument in his honor (not accomplished, however, until 1902), and to educate his youngest son.

Washington, who repeatedly lauded his judgment and experience, in a letter to the President of Congress, Jan. 5, 1777, characterized him as "the brave and worthy Gen'l Mercer."

[J. T. Goolrick, *The Life of Gen. Hugh Mercer* (1906) is invaluable. See also Peter Force, *Am. Archives,* 4 ser. (1837–46); I. D. Rupp, *Early Hist. of Western Pa.* (1846); W. S. Stryker, *The Battles of Trenton and Princeton* (1898); J. S. Keene, "Hugh Mercer," in *The John P. Branch Hist. Papers of Randolph-Macon Coll.*, vol. II (1908); W. E. McCulloch, *Viri Illustres Universitatum Abredonensium* (1923); *Va. County Records,* I (1905), 31; *The Writings of George Washington* (1932), ed. by J. C. Fitzpatrick; *Journals of the Continental Congress,* 1775–77; W. B. Blanton, *Medicine in Va. in the Eighteenth Century* (1931); *Pa. Evening Post,* Jan. 18, 1777.] E. E. C.

MERCER, JAMES (Feb. 26, 1736–Oct. 31, 1793), Revolutionary patriot, member of the Continental Congress, was one of the foremost men of his day in Virginia. His father, John Mercer, emigrated from Dublin, Ireland, in 1720, settled at "Marlborough," Stafford County, Va., acquired a considerable fortune as a successful lawyer and business man, and was secretary of the Ohio Company, in the affairs of which his two sons, James and George, were also active. By his first wife, Catherine Mason, the aunt of George Mason, *c.* 1629–*c.* 1686 [*q.v.*], he was the father of James, and by his second wife was the father of John Francis Mercer [*q.v.*]. James Mercer was educated at the College of William and Mary. He served in the French and Indian War and was in command, with the rank of captain, of Fort Loudoun at Winchester, Va. In 1762 he was elected to represent the nearby county of Hampshire, now in West Virginia, in the Virginia House of Burgesses. He continued to serve this county, not only in that position, but also as a member of the Revolutionary conventions of 1774, 1775, and 1776.

He joined with his neighbors at Fredericksburg in drafting resolutions against the oppressive acts of the British government and was appointed, on June 1, 1774, a member of the committee of correspondence. He was active in bringing about the first Virginia Revolutionary convention of August 1774 and was elected by the convention on Aug. 17, 1775, to the first Committee of Safety, which governed Virginia until the state government was inaugurated in 1776. Reëlected to the committee upon its reorganization on Dec. 16, 1775, he aligned himself with the progressive group. As a member of the committee of the convention of 1776 that was appointed to draft a declaration of rights and a new plan of government for Virginia he was very active; he was considered one of the best speakers of the period. On June 18, 1779, he was elected by the General Assembly to the Continental Congress and took his seat on Sept. 9, 1779.

In 1779 he was appointed to the General Court and served also as a member of the first court of appeals. On Nov. 18, 1789, he was elected one of the five judges of the state's highest court, the reorganized court of appeals, to succeed John Blair, who resigned. He died in Richmond, while attending a session of the court, and was buried in St. John's church yard. A brief sketch in *Call's Reports* (IV, p. xx) thus describes him: "He possessed a sound understanding; was an honest man, a learned lawyer, and an impartial and upright judge." He was married on June 4, 1772, to Eleanor, the daughter of Charles Dick of Fredericksburg, Va., commissary in the French and Indian War and associated with Fielding Lewis in manufacturing arms and ammunition for the Revolutionary army. The youngest of their two sons was Charles Fenton Mercer [*q.v.*] and their only daughter was Mary Eleanor Dick Mercer, who married James Mercer Garnett, 1770–1843 [*q.v.*], her first cousin.

[Account of destruction of Mercer papers by Federal troops in *Wm. and Mary College Hist. Quart.*, Apr. 1893; J. M. Garnett, "James Mercer," *Ibid.*, Oct. 1908, Jan. 1909; *Ibid.*, July 1898, Oct. 1909, Jan. 1912, Oct. 1918; *Calendar of Va. State Papers,* vols. V, VI, VIII (1885–90); sketch of Mercer family, *Va. Mag. of Hist.*, Jan. 1907.] R. L. M—n.

MERCER, JESSE (Dec. 16, 1769–Sept. 6, 1841), Georgia pioneer preacher and philanthropist, was born in Halifax County, N. C., the great-grandson of a Scotch emigrant who settled in Virginia about the end of the seventeenth century. His father Silas Mercer was reared a devout Episcopalian, but shortly after his removal from North Carolina to Wilkes County, Ga., about 1775, he became a Baptist and later a minister, the founder and pastor of several prominent churches of the original Georgia Association, constituted probably in 1784. Jesse, the eldest of eight children, was brought up on the frontier with scant opportunity for an education in books, but after he began to preach he was able to go back to school from time to time. After passing through a depressing religious struggle of some twelve years, he was baptized in 1787 by his father. In 1789 he was ordained a Baptist minister in Phillips' Mill Church. A tall, slender youth, rather unprepossessing in appearance, mainly on account of his oddly shaped head with an unusually high crown and slanting forehead, he went the next year to be pastor at Sardis in Wilkes County and, on his father's death in 1796, succeeded to his place as pastor of the churches at Phillips' Mill in Wilkes County, at Bethesda in Greene County, at Powelton in Hancock County, and later he became pastor at Eatonton in Putnam County. On his marriage to his second wife he removed to Washington, Ga., to minister to a newly organized church there. He purchased the *Christian Index* and, having transferred it from Philadelphia, Pa., to Washington, was its editor from 1833 to 1840, when he resigned and donated it to the Baptist State Convention.

He was an important figure in the councils of the Baptists of America. In Georgia he was a kind of bishop, without the prerogatives of that office, over a body that by 1840 had grown to number 30,000 members. For almost the whole period from 1795 to 1816 he was clerk of the Georgia Baptist Association, and, becoming moderator of the body in 1816, he served in the office until 1839. In 1838 he published *A History of the Georgia Baptist Association.* He was for eleven years a member of the board of managers of the Baptist general convention for missionary purposes, a national body organized in 1814. When, in 1822, a general state association was formed as the General Baptist Association of the State of Georgia, later the Baptist Convention of the State of Georgia, he became the first moderator and served until 1841. His leadership was owing to his frank democracy, modesty, and devotion to the support of benevolent enterprises, especially foreign missions and higher education. In meeting dissension in churches and associations he practised conciliation and tact. He was reluctant to participate in politics unless what he considered the fundamental Christian principles lying at the base of the government were threatened. As a delegate to the state constitutional convention of 1798, he was instrumental in defeating a motion to make ministers ineligible to the legislature, though he advised against their taking part in "every-day politics of the country" (*Memoirs, post*, p. 102). He was not a scholar, but his writings show simple strength and beauty. He was exceptionally cogent in expounding matters of church discipline and doctrine.

His own efforts to obtain an education lasted throughout his lifetime, and he contributed largely to making possible an education for others. Very early in his life he began to give his time to teaching, in his own home, young men too poor to afford other means of advancing their education. In his honor the Baptist school near Greensboro was named Mercer Institute, when it was opened in 1833 to combine a classical and theological training with agricultural labor and study. He devoted great effort to the project for founding a Baptist college at Washington, Ga., but, when the plan was given up in spite of his earnest advice, he lent his aid to obtaining the transfer of most of the subscriptions and himself subscribed $5,000 to the enlargement of Mercer Institute, which was renamed Mercer University in 1837. In later years and by his will he gave to the university a sum of more than $40,000. On Jan. 31, 1788, he was married to Sabrina Chivers, a member of the church in which he was ordained. She bore him two daughters and died in 1826. On Dec. 11, 1827, he was married to Nancy Simonds, a wealthy widow of Washington, Ga., formerly Nancy Mills of Virginia. It was through the wise management of her properties that he was able to give generously to benevolent causes. He died in Butts County, Ga.

[C. D. Mallary, *Memoirs of Elder Jesse Mercer* (1844); *Hist. of the Baptist Denomination of Ga.* (1881); S. G. Hillyer, *Reminiscences of Ga. Baptists* (1902); J. H. Campbell, *Ga. Baptists*, 2nd ed. (1874).]

W. J. B.

MERCER, JOHN FRANCIS (May 17, 1759–Aug. 30, 1821), soldier, congressman, and governor of Maryland, belonged to the distinguished Mercer family of Virginia. His father, John Mercer, its founder, came of a family which originated in Chester, England. Born in Ireland, he emigrated in 1720 to Virginia, where he became known as an able lawyer and wealthy man of affairs. By his first wife, Catherine Mason, he had ten children, one of whom was James Mercer [*q.v.*]. His second wife, the mother of John Francis, was Ann Roy of Essex County, Va. The son, fifth of her nine children, was born at "Marlborough," his father's estate in Stafford County, Va., and received his higher education at the College of William and Mary. Since war with England seemed inevitable, early in 1776 he enlisted as lieutenant in the 3rd Virginia Regiment. He was promoted to a captaincy Sept. 11, 1777, and in the following year became aide-de-camp to Gen. Charles Lee [*q.v.*]. When, after the battle of Monmouth, the latter was court-martialed and disgraced, Mercer resigned his commission (October 1779) and returned to Virginia. In the fall of 1780 he reëntered the war as lieutenant-colonel of infantry under General Lawson; and the following May he recruited a small group of cavalry to aid Lafayette, under whom he served for a short time. He then raised a corps of militia grenadiers, whom he commanded, with the rank of lieutenant-colonel, at the surrender of Cornwallis at Yorktown.

During the first interval in his military service (1779–80) Mercer studied law for a year at Williamsburg under the direction of Thomas

Jefferson, then governor of Virginia; and between his service under Lawson and that under Lafayette he practised law at Fredericksburg. This appears to have been the extent of his experience as an active practitioner. Subsequently, he devoted most of his time to politics. He was a member of the Virginia House of Delegates in 1782 and in 1785–86. In December 1782, he was elected member of Congress from Virginia, to succeed Edmund Randolph who had resigned; and the following year he was reëlected. Early in 1785 he married Sophia Sprigg of Maryland, and soon thereafter took up his residence at "Cedar Park," an estate in Anne Arundel County inherited by his wife from her father. He was a member from Maryland of the Federal Convention of 1787, and was so strongly opposed to the centralizing character of the document drawn up that he left before the gathering finished its work. As a delegate to the Maryland ratification convention, he spoke and voted against the Constitution; and after it was adopted, aligned himself with the Republicans. He was a member of the Maryland House of Delegates in 1788–89 and 1791–92. Elected in 1791 to the federal House of Representatives to take the place of William Pinkney, resigned, he was reëlected, but resigned his seat in April 1794 and retired to "Cedar Park." This terminated his career in national office.

He was again a member of the state House of Delegates in 1800–01, and in November 1801 was chosen Republican governor of Maryland by the state Assembly. The term of governorship was one year, and in the following autumn he was reëlected. During his incumbency a constitutional amendment providing for manhood suffrage and vote by ballot was adopted, but Mercer appears to have had no special part in bringing this action about. His second term as governor ended, he served in the House of Delegates, 1803–06. When the trouble with England began in Jefferson's administration, he broke with the Republicans, virtually allied himself with the Federalists, and worked hard to avert war. During his last few years, because of poor health, he lived quietly at "Cedar Park." Death came to him in Philadelphia, where he was seeking medical aid. Margaret Mercer [*q.v.*] was his daughter.

[The biographical sketch in H. E. Buchholz's *Governors of Maryland* (1908) contains many errors, but the article by James Mercer Garnett in *Md. Hist. Mag.*, Sept. 1907, is dependable and quotes some rare documents. See also, in addition to the *Annals of Cong.* and Md. legislative journals: J. M. Garnett, *Geneal. of the Mercer-Garnett Family of Essex County, Va.* (1910); W. C. Ford, *The Writings of George Washington*, vols. XI, XII (1891); *The Writings of Thomas Jefferson* (Memorial Ed.), vols. VIII, IX, XI (1903–04); Gaillard Hunt, *The Writings of James Madison* (9 vols., 1900–10); S. M. Hamilton, *The Writings of James Monroe* (7 vols., 1898–1903); Max Farrand, *The Records of the Federal Convention of 1787* (3 vols., 1911); E. G. Swem and J. W. Williams, *A Reg. of the Gen. Assembly of Va.* (1918); F. B. Heitman, *Hist. Reg. of Officers of the Continental Army* (1893); *Baltimore Patriot and Mercantile Advertiser*, Sept. 8, 1821.]

M. W. W.

MERCER, LEWIS PYLE (June 27, 1847–July 6, 1906), Swedenborgian clergyman, was born at Kennett Square, Chester County, Pa., the son of Pennock and Ann (Pyle) Mercer, both Quakers. He was educated in the common-schools of Chester County, in the Normal School, and at Taylor's Scientific and Classical Academy, Wilmington, Del., where he also taught. At Wilmington, in 1865, he became interested in the teachings of Swedenborg, and after hearing lectures on the subject by the Rev. Abiel Silver, he sought out the lecturer and began with him a study of Swedenborg's doctrines. With the New Church ministry in mind he continued his studies with the Rev. Willard H. Hinkley and the Rev. Nathan C. Burnham, going finally for a term to the New Church Theological School, Waltham, Mass. In 1868 he married Sarah Taylor Pennock of Chester County, Pa., by whom he had six children.

In this year he went West to teach at East Rockport near Cleveland. Here he found an opportunity to preach and in 1870 was licensed, taking charge of the New Church society there and also later for a short time of the society in Cleveland. In 1872 he accepted a call to Detroit and was ordained to the ministry of the General Convention of the New Jerusalem in the United States of America. In Detroit he quickly attained popularity, with the result that in 1877 he was called to Chicago. Here a difficult task awaited him. After a prosperous beginning, the society had been weakened by the great fire of 1871 and the panic of 1873. The wide extent of the city and internal friction had led to dissatisfaction and division. The result was the formation of a separate body, the Union Swedenborgian Church, to the pastorate of which Mercer was called. Under his leadership the new society was immediately successful. His sermons were published regularly in the newspapers and helped spread the teachings to which he was devoted. It was his conviction that these doctrines were divinely provided to meet the needs of the age, and he preached them as such, but he did not believe that assent to elaborate doctrinal definition should be a basis for organization. In 1881 the Union Swedenborgian Church united with the original Chicago society under Mercer's leadership. From a membership of 175 in 1880 the society had grown to 484 in 1900, and in 1894 had been organized into four strong parishes. In 1884 Mercer became president of the Illinois Association of the New Church and in 1895, general pastor, resigning his Chicago charge in 1900 to devote his whole time to this wider field. In 1901, however, he accepted a call to Cincinnati, where he continued in active service till his death. In 1903 he was consecrated as the general pastor of the Ohio Association.

While still in Chicago he had been instrumental in organizing the Western New Church Union (1886), for missionary, educational, and publication purposes in the West. He also took an active part in the organization of the World's Parliament of Religions in connection with the Columbian Exposition, was editor of *The New Jerusalem in the World's Religious Congresses of 1893* (1894), and author of *Review of the World's Religious Congress* (1893). He possessed considerable literary talent, and wrote *The Bible, Its True Character and Spiritual Meaning* (1879) and other expositions of New Church Doctrine which at the time were highly valued. He edited the shortlived *New-Church Review,* 1882–84, and in 1893 founded *The Sower,* the first New Church Sunday-school paper. Always interested in science, he became a member of the Swedenborg Scientific Association, organized for the study and publication of Swedenborg's scientific works, and when this body adopted as its organ *The New Philosophy,* he became the managing editor, serving from July 1900 to April 1902. In 1905 he was chosen president of Urbana University, Urbana, Ohio, a New Church college. He began the raising of an endowment fund which has grown to considerable proportions.

Mercer was of a very devout nature, sanguine, generous, capable of evoking deep friendship and enthusiastic cooperation. On these qualities rather than on his considerable intellectual gifts depended his success. He was a man of strong convictions, yet never anxious to force them on others. His willingness to work with anyone who would work with him held him aloof from party strife. His greatest contribution to the New Church was his talent as organizer and administrator.

[*The New Church and Chicago* (Western New Church Union, Chicago, 1906); *New-Church Messenger,* July 11, 18, 1906; *Jour. of the Eighty-Seventh Ann. Sess. General Convention of the New Jerusalem in the U. S. A.* (1907); E. C. Silver, *Sketches of the New Church in America* (*c.* 1920); *New Church Life,* Aug. 1906; *Cincinnati Enquirer,* July 7, 1906.]

F. R. C.

MERCER, MARGARET (July 1, 1791–Sept. 17, 1846), anti-slavery worker and educator, was born in Annapolis, Md., the daughter of John Francis Mercer [*q.v.*] and his wife, Sophia Sprigg. Most of her childhood was spent in Annapolis, while her father filled various public offices, or at "Cedar Park," the estate of her maternal grandfather in Anne Arundel County, Md., which was the country home of the Mercer family for many years. She had a superior mind and a strong scholarly bent, and her education, carefully supervised by her father, was exceptional for a woman of her period.

From a religious motive, she began in her early youth to devote herself energetically to altruistic service. To Sunday schools—which then offered elementary education to the poor, as well as religious instruction—she gave time and money, working in connection with her church, the Protestant Episcopal. For the Greeks, then struggling for independence from Turkey, she also helped raise funds. Through many years, however, her chief interest was probably the anti-slavery cause as represented by the activities of the American Colonization Society, which aimed, through the removal of free negroes to Liberia, to encourage manumission and thereby ultimately to eliminate slavery from the United States. She urged emancipation upon others and after her father's death set an example by freeing her share of the family slaves and sending to Liberia those who were willing to go. She also raised money to purchase the freedom of other slaves, and for educational work in Liberia.

Much of the later part of her life was given to teaching. Cedar Park Institute, her first school, was conducted in her home; but later she moved her school to Franklin, near Baltimore; and, finally, settled at Belmont, near Leesburg, Va., where, on a run-down farm, she started a new boarding-school for girls which soon became noted for its high academic standards and strong religious and moral influence. In the interest of spiritual and ethical training, she wrote two books: *Studies for Bible Classes,* published some time before 1841, and *Popular Lectures on Ethics or Moral Obligation for the Use of Schools* (1837). The Belmont school soon developed into what was virtually a social settlement, including a little church built from money she had raised. The humble inhabitants of the region brought their problems to the leaders of the school, and sent their children to the free classes which it offered in primary subjects and agriculture. During most of Margaret Mercer's busy life she was handicapped by frail health, due to a tendency to tuberculosis; and from this disease she died in the home which she had developed in Virginia.

[Caspar Morris, *Memoir of Miss Margaret Mercer* (1848), which is a eulogy rather than a biography, contains many of her letters, and is the fullest account of her life; her *Popular Lectures on Ethics*, referred to above, throws light upon her ideals and intellectual ability; obituaries appeared in the *Md. Colonization Journal*, Nov. 1846, and the *Daily National Intelligencer* (Washington, D. C.), Sept. 22, 1846. See also J. M. Garnett, *Geneal. of the Mercer-Garnett Family of Essex County, Va.* (1910).] M. W. W.

MERCIER, CHARLES ALFRED (June 3, 1816–May 12, 1894), Creole author, was born in McDonogh, a surburb of New Orleans, the son of Jean Mercier, a native of Louisiana, and Éloise Le Duc, a Canadian. Intended for the law, he was sent to France at fourteen to study at the Collège Louis-le-Grand, where he read extensively both the classical and romantic writers. Not finding law to his taste, he turned to literature. In 1838 he returned to Louisiana for a short stay; then went to Boston to perfect his English; but soon crossed to Paris again, where he published *La Rose de Smyrne; L'Ermite du Niagara; Erato Labitte* (1840). The first is an Oriental tale in verse; the second a mystery play, telling the story of an Indian girl and her white lover; the third, a series of short poems redolent of Louisiana. After the appearance of this volume Mercier traveled far and wide in Europe. In Paris he composed a drama, *Hénoch Jédésias,* which was lost during the Revolution of 1848. A novel of the same name written at this time, a gruesome tale of miserliness, he later rewrote and published in New Orleans (*Comptes Rendus de l'Athénée Louisianais,* March 1892–November 1893). In 1848 he published in Paris *Biographie de Pierre Soulé,* a study of the career of his brother-in-law [*q.v.*]. On May 10, 1849, he married Virginie Vezian.

His interest in literature yielded somewhat to medicine, and in 1855 his dissertation appeared in Paris under the title, *De la fièvre typhoide dans ses rapports avec la phtisie aiguë.* He returned to New Orleans to practise his profession but in 1859 was again in Paris, then sojourned in Normandy for several years. Although he disapproved of slavery, when he saw in the American Civil War the approaching triumph of what he called Anglo-Saxon civilization, he broke his silence in *Du Pan-Latinisme—Nécessité d'une Alliance entre la France et la Confédération du Sud* (n.d.). After the war he returned to New Orleans to seek a livelihood in medicine. The rest of his life was divided between the arduous duties of a family physician and the profitless pursuit of literature. In 1873, *Le Fou de Palerme* was issued, with its gypsies and daggers. On Jan. 12, 1876, he founded the Athénée Louisianais, an organization devoted to the perpetuation of the French language in Louisiana, in whose *Comptes Rendus* he created a vehicle for his prose and verse. The following year he published *La Fille du Prêtre,* a novel in three parts attacking the celibacy of the priesthood. Of his numerous poems found in the *Comptes Rendus,* the best are "Tawanta" (November 1887) and "*Les Soleils*" (March 1889); of his travelogues, "*Excursion dans les Pyrénées*" (July–September 1889) is typical. Along scientific lines, "*Sommeil, Rêves, Somnambulisme*" (March 1889) best represents his thought; in philology, "*Étude sur la Langue Créole en Louisiane*" (July 1880). His best novelettes are *Lidia* (1887), a Parisian and Sicilian idyll, and *Émile des Ormiers* (1891), the pathetic tale of a Parisian painter. Mercier also wrote a long drama, *Fortunia* (published in *Comptes Rendus,* November 1888), whose purpose was to teach that fate rules the world. A long philosophical poem entitled *Réditus et Ascalaphos* (1890) described the efforts of the hero to attain studious solitude. A novel, *L'Habitation Saint-Ybars* (1881), was written to show that Louisiana masters were not all cruel; its local color is heightened by its French negro dialect. A second novel, *Johnelle* (1891), was a condemnation of infanticide. The French government rewarded the author's efforts with its *Palmes académiques* in 1885.

Mercier belonged to that generation of French Creoles of Louisiana who wished to be primarily Louisianians; to be identified as Latins rather than Anglo-Saxons, but as Americans in France. His was a cultivated mind. His talent was best at narration in prose; his style was clear and elegant; but he was too much inclined toward romanticism and he was prone to preach. He remains perhaps the leading French Creole writer of Louisiana; and the Athénée Louisianais, his proudest creation, is a monument to him. After a long illness, bravely borne, he died of cancer in 1894, survived by his widow and three children. Services were held in the Catholic church of Ste. Rose de Lima and interment was in Metairie Cemetery, New Orleans.

[Eulogy by Alcée Fortier, in *Comptes Rendus de l'Athénée Louisianais,* July 1894, offers a good pen picture. In *Louisiana Studies* (1894), Fortier reviewed thoroughly Mercier's literary effort. E. J. Fortier in *Mémoires, Premier Congrès de la Langue Française au Canada* (1914) summarized his father's appreciation. See also R. A. Caulfeild, *The French Literature of La.* (1929); E. L. Tinker, *Les Écrits de Langue Française en Louisiane au XIXe Siècle* (1932); Cyprien Dufour, *Esquisses Locales* (1847), the article on Mercier being translated in *La. Hist. Quart.,* Apr. 1932; Charles Testut, in *Portraits Littéraires de la Nouvelle-Orléans* (1850); Bussière Rouen, "*Les Poètes Louisianais,*" in *Comptes Rendus de l'Athénée Louisianais,* Apr. 1921; *The Louisiana Book* (1894), ed. by Thomas M'Caleb; *Lib. of Southern Lit.,* vol. VIII (1909); obituaries in the *Times-Democrat* and *l'Abeille,* of New Orleans, May 13, 1894, and in the *Daily Picayune* the next day.]

L. C. D.

MERCUR, ULYSSES (Aug. 12, 1818–June 6, 1887), congressman, jurist, a son of Henry and Mary (Watts) Mercur, was of Austrian ancestry. His father, who was educated abroad, returned to America and settled in 1809 at Towanda, Bradford County, Pa., where Ulysses was born. His early life was spent on a farm and in the common-schools of the vicinity. When sixteen years old he became a clerk in his brother's country store. His father intended to establish him as a farmer, but because of the boy's desire to go to college, he sold his farm in order to finance his son's schooling. Ulysses entered Jefferson College at Canonsburg, Pa. (later merged with Washington College at Washington, Pa., to form Washington and Jefferson College), and graduated in 1842. He read law with Judge William McKennan and in 1843 began his career as a lawyer at Towanda. On Jan. 12, 1850, he married Sarah Simpson Davis. In 1856 he was a delegate to the Republican National Convention in Philadelphia. He had been a Democrat, but he favored free-soil doctrines and opposed the repeal of the Missouri Compromise. In 1860 he went so far as to serve as a presidential elector on the Lincoln and Hamlin ticket. He was associated with the group which was led by Galusha A. Grow and David Wilmot, and upon the election of Wilmot to the Senate in 1860 was appointed to fill his place as presiding judge of the thirteenth judicial district of Pennsylvania. At the election for the next full term as judge, he was chosen without opposition, and he served in this position till Mar. 4, 1865.

Mercur was elected to Congress in 1864 and served continuously as a member of the lower house from Mar. 4, 1865, to Dec. 2, 1872. In Congress he was particularly active as an advocate of the extreme measures in dealing with the Southern States, and as an opponent of luxury taxes, especially the taxes on tea and coffee. In connection with Reconstruction, he once said that if the Southern states "will not respect the stars they must feel the stripes of our glorious flag" (Heverly, *post,* II, p. 123). He resigned as a member of Congress to become associate justice of the supreme court of Pennsylvania. He held this position from 1872 till 1883, and from 1883 till his death in 1887 he was chief justice of the court. He died at Wallingford, Pa., and was buried at Towanda. Just as the distinctive policy of his group in Congress in connection with Reconstruction was reversed and discredited, so his conception of the judiciary was soon regarded as antiquated. As a judge, he was described by an associate as "conservative and cautious, looking to the old landmarks" (116 *Pa.,* xxiii). By the end of his career the old landmarks were rapidly being destroyed by the necessity of adjusting government and law to conditions alien to his generation.

[Sources include: *Biog. Dir. Am. Cong.* (1928); 116 *Pa. Reports,* xix-xxxi; *Legal Intelligencer* (Phila.), June 10, 17, 1887; *Pittsburgh Legal Jour.,* June 8, 15, 1887; H. C. Bradsby, *Hist. of Bradford County, Pa.* (1891); C. F. Heverly, *Pioneer and Patriot Families of Bradford County, Pa.,* vol. II (1915); the *Press* (Phila.), June 7, 1887. Mercur's judicial opinions are in 73–116 *Pa. Reports.*]

W. B—n.

MEREDITH, EDWIN THOMAS (Dec. 23, 1876–June 17, 1928), journalist, publisher, secretary of agriculture, was born on a farm near Avoca, Iowa, the son of Thomas Oliver and Minnie Minerva (Marsh) Meredith, who were of English and Welsh ancestry. He attended the country schools until he was sixteen years of age when he entered the business school of Highland Park College (later Des Moines University) at Des Moines, Iowa, meanwhile assisting his grandfather, "Uncle Tommy" Meredith, on the *Farmers' Tribune* which was a weekly county farm paper devoted to the cause of Populism. During the next two years he devoted all of his time to the paper, serving in the capacity of bookkeeper, conducting the correspondence, and selling advertising. On Jan. 8, 1896, when he was nineteen years of age, he was married to Edna C. Elliott of English and Irish ancestry. His grandfather gave him as a wedding present the *Farmers' Tribune* which he transformed into a non-partisan farm paper with a state-wide circulation. Tobacco and liquor advertisements were refused. Profiting in this venture, in 1902 he embarked upon a greater project, founding *Successful Farming,* and two years later he sold the *Farmers' Tribune* in order that he might devote his entire time and attention to the new publication. In 1922 he purchased the *Dairy Farmer,* and in the same year he founded *Fruit, Garden and Home,* which in August 1924 became *Better Homes and Gardens.* Meanwhile the publishing plant was greatly enlarged and the circulation of his periodicals increased.

Meredith created an innovation in the publication of farm papers which was generally adopted by other editors. In the first number of *Successful Farming* he announced that he would make good any loss to paid subscribers sustained by trusting any deliberate swindler advertising in his columns and that any such swindler would be publicly exposed. Soon afterward he made this guarantee more effective by the promise that if the purchaser of any article advertised in *Successful Farming* found it to be otherwise than represented, his money would be returned. In the days when patent medicine was the backbone of most advertising revenues, he closed the advertising columns of *Successful Farming* to it, thus making a noteworthy contribution to the cause of "truth in advertising." He devoted his publications to farming in the Middle West, and to better homes in all parts of the country.

Meredith first voted as a Republican but early became affiliated with the Democratic party. He was the party's candidate for United States senator in 1914 and for governor in 1916 but was defeated in both contests. In January 1920 he was appointed secretary of agriculture by President Wilson, succeeding David F. Houston and serving with distinction until the end of the Wilson administration. His name was mentioned as a possible presidential nominee of the Democratic party in the campaigns of 1924 and 1928. He was an ardent prohibitionist, a champion of "farm relief," tariff reform, adequate military preparedness, tax reform, and the World Court and the League of Nations. He held a number of positions on various boards and commissions. He was a member of the Board of Excess Profit Advisors appointed by Secretary McAdoo in 1917, a member of the Labor Commission to the British Isles appointed by President Wilson in 1918, a director of the Chicago Federal Reserve Bank from 1918 to 1920, and a director of the United States Chamber of Commerce from 1915 to 1919 and from 1923 to his death. He was interested in the boys' and girls' club movements and was an active and enthusiastic supporter of the 4-H Club. Independent, resourceful, and public-spirited, he was a born leader.

[*Who's Who in America*, 1928–29; *Ann. Report of the U. S. Dept. of Agric.*, 1920, and the *Yearbook* for the same year; *Better Homes and Gardens*, Aug. 1928; *Dairy Farmer*, Aug. 7, 1928; *Successful Farming*, Aug. 1928; *Independent*, Mar. 10, 1928; *Des Moines Reg.*, June 18, 1928; manuscript materials prepared by Edwin T. Meredith, Jr., and Peter Ainsworth.]

L. B. S—t.

MEREDITH, SAMUEL (1741–Feb. 10, 1817), financier, was born in Philadelphia, Pa., the son of Reese Meredith, a merchant, and Martha (Carpenter) Meredith. He attended private schools in Philadelphia and Chester, Pa., then entered his father's business. He took an active part in ante-Revolutionary affairs, was one of the signers of the non-importation resolutions adopted in Philadelphia on Nov. 7, 1765, and attended, as a deputy from Philadelphia, the Provincial Convention held in that city from the 23rd to the 28th of January, 1775. During the war he served as a major and then as lieutenant-colonel of the 3rd Battalion of Associators, known as the Silk Stocking Company. He distinguished himself in the battles of Trenton and Princeton and on Apr. 5, 1777, was promoted to brigadier-general of Pennsylvania militia for gallant services in the battles of Brandywine and Germantown. He resigned from the army Jan. 9, 1778, and resumed his business connections. He served three terms in the Pennsylvania Colonial Assembly (1778–79, 1781–83) and on Nov. 26, 1786, was elected to the Congress of the Confederation, serving until 1788. In August of the following year he was appointed surveyor of the Port of Philadelphia. He resigned this post to accept an appointment, urged upon him by George Washington, as treasurer of the United States, the first appointed under the Constitution.

Meredith entered upon his new duties Sept. 11, 1789, at a time when the treasury needed conservative management. He lent the government more than a hundred thousand dollars which it was unable to repay upon his retirement from office. He remained in office until Oct. 31, 1801, when, owing to the state of his health and finances, he retired. With his brother-in-law, George Clymer [*q.v.*], he had purchased large amounts of wild lands in western Virginia, eastern Kentucky, Delaware and Sullivan counties, N. Y., and in all the northeastern counties of Pennsylvania. In 1796 he began to make improvements at a place in the township of Mount Pleasant, Pa., which he afterward named Belmont. In 1802 he moved to this place and devoted the last years of his life to the management of his land, dying in the manor house of the estate. He had married, on May 19, 1772, Margaret Cadwalader of Philadelphia, daughter of Dr. Thomas Cadwalader [*q.v.*]. They had seven children.

[*Biog. Dir. Am. Cong.* (1928); Chas. Lanman, *Biog. Annals of the Civil Gov't. of the U. S., During its First Century* (1876); C. P. Keith, *Provincial Councillors of Pa.* (1883); S. M. M. Graham, *A Short Hist. of the Three Merediths* (n.d.); Wharton Dickenson, "Brig.-Gen. Samuel Meredith," *Mag. of Am. Hist.*, Sept. 1879; F. W. Leach, "Old Phila. Families," the *North American* (Phila.), Feb. 4, 1912; Samuel Whaley, *Hist. of the Township of Mount Pleasant, Wayne County, Pa.* (1856); *Poulson's Am. Daily Advertiser*, Feb. 22, 1817.]

J. H. F.

MEREDITH, WILLIAM MORRIS (June 8, 1799–Aug. 17, 1873), Pennsylvania lawyer and official, secretary of the treasury, was born in Philadelphia, Pa., the son of William Meredith and Gertrude Gouverneur Ogden and the grandson of Jonathan Meredith who emigrated from Wales about 1755. His father was a prominent lawyer and bank president who so educated his precocious son that he was able to graduate from the University of Pennsylvania at the age of thirteen. Five years later, in December 1817, he was admitted to the bar and then was forced to pay the penalty of his rapid advance. He had to wait a long time for a successful practice. Finally he became associated with John Sergeant and Horace Binney [*qq.v.*] in the famous Girard will case and thereafter his fame grew until he became one of the leaders of the Philadlphia bar. While waiting for legal opportunity, he entered politics. He served in the legislature, 1824–28, and from 1834 to 1849 was president of the select council of Philadelphia. When the Whig party was formed he became a member and allied himself with the faction opposed to Thaddeus Stevens and to the anti-Masonic element. In the state constitutional convention of 1837 he attracted considerable attention by a vigorous attack upon Stevens. On June 17, 1834, he married Catherine, daughter of Michael Keppele.

When the Whigs triumphed in 1840, Harrison appointed Meredith (Mar. 15, 1841), United States attorney for the eastern district of Pennsylvania, an office which he held only a year. In 1849 he was defeated for the United States Senate by a fellow Whig, James Cooper, but shortly thereafter his greatest honor came to him. President-Elect Taylor wished a Pennsylvanian for his cabinet, a wish complicated by a factional war in the party. In March 1849 he chose Meredith, a moderate Whig, for his secretary of the treasury, in spite of the fact that the Whig congressmen recommended Andrew Stewart. In this office Meredith's principal achievement was his annual report in which he set forth an elaborate argument for a protective tariff (*Senate Executive Document 2,* 31 Cong., 1 Sess.). He shared Taylor's disapproval of the compromise measures of 1850 and when the President died joined his colleagues in retiring (July 1850).

When the opponents of the Democratic organization in Pennsylvania formed the Opposition or People's party in the days before the Civil War, Meredith joined the new group. He acted as a delegate to the Peace Convention of 1861 and Governor Curtin made him attorney-general of the state, 1861–67. When the Union League Club formed in Philadelphia, he became its first president. He was appointed one of the counsel of the United States in the *Alabama* claims case, but, after aiding in the preparation of the briefs, retired, not wishing to go to Geneva. His last service was as president of the state constitutional convention (November 1872–June 1873) when, in spite of ill health, he remained in this trying position till a few weeks before his death. He died in Philadelphia.

[The available materials on Meredith's life are meager. A sketch of himself and his family by Frank W. Leach in his series on "Old Philadelphia Families" appeared in the Philadelphia *North American,* Feb. 4, 1912. An obituary notice and the proceedings of the Philadelphia bar are found in *Ibid.,* Aug. 18, 21, 1873. See also: J. T. Scharf and Thompson Westcott, *Hist. of Philadelphia* (1884), vols. I and II; *Proc. and Debates of the Convention of . . . Pa. to Propose Amendments to the Const. . . . 1837,* vol. II (1837), pp. 76 ff.; *Proc. of the Const. Convention and Obit. Addresses on the Occasion of the Death of Hon. Wm. M. Meredith* (1873); and H. R. Mueller, *The Whig Party in Pa.* (1922). A few of Meredith's letters are in the collections of the Historical Society of Pennsylvania.]

R. F. N.

MERGENTHALER, OTTMAR (May 11, 1854–Oct. 28, 1899), inventor of the linotype, was born in Hachtel, Germany, the son of Johann George and Rosina (Ackermann) Mergenthaler. He came from a family of teachers and it was expected that he would follow the family calling. After an ordinary grade-school education, however, he showed a decided leaning toward mechanics and accordingly, at the age of fourteen, began an apprenticeship in watch and clock-making under the brother of his stepmother at Bietigheim, Württemberg. Here he applied himself diligently for four years, meanwhile attending night and Sunday schools. Upon the completion of his apprenticeship he sailed for the United States to avoid being drafted into the army. Landing in Baltimore, Oct. 26, 1872, he proceeded to Washington, D. C., where he began work immediately in the scientific instrument shop of August Hahl, son of his former master.

For the next four years Mergenthaler was wholly engrossed in the interesting work of instrument making, especially for the United States Signal Service. His ingenuity, skill, and ability to grasp quickly an inventor's ideas were soon recognized, and his services were much sought after. When Hahl transferred his business to Baltimore in 1876 Mergenthaler went with him and shortly thereafter they were called upon to correct defects in the model of a newly devised writing machine made by Charles Moore of West Virginia. The purpose of the machine was to produce print by typewriting and to multiply the work by the lithographic process. Mergenthaler soon corrected the defects, whereupon James O. Clephane of Washington, who was the originator of the idea, ordered the construction of a full-sized machine. This was completed in 1877 but could never be made to yield satisfactory results. Mergenthaler, however, now definitely launched upon the devising of a machine to eliminate type-setting, enthusiastically took hold of Clephane's next suggestion: a machine which would substitute stereotyping for lithography. Such a machine, incorporating the rotary stereotypic system, was completed late in 1878, but again many troubles were experienced, particularly in obtaining clean type from the papier-maché. After working during most of the year 1879 to correct the difficulties, Mergenthaler and Hahl abandoned the project.

During the next four years they continued with general instrument making, Mergenthaler becoming a partner in the establishment in 1880 and taking up permament residence in Baltimore. He never fully dismissed the idea of a type-setting machine, however, and in spare moments devised a plan calling for an invariable spacing between the lines and the use of regular type as a means of getting perfect impressions into the matrix. Shortly after opening his own shop in Baltimore on Jan. 1, 1883, he communicated this new idea to Clephane and his associates and received an order to proceed with the construction of a machine possessing these features. It was completed in the fall of 1883 and was satisfactory except for the paper matrix. Shortly afterward Mergenthaler hit upon the plan of stamping matrices into type bars and casting type metal into them in the same machine. From this idea the linotype was developed. By July 1884 the first direct-casting linotype was completed. It worked with entire success, but had no provision for automatic justification of the line. On Aug. 26, 1884, Mergenthaler received his first patent on the new machine and shortly thereafter Clephane and his associates organized the National Typographic Company of West Virginia for its manufacture. Not content with his product, Mergenthaler proceeded in his enthusiastic way to improve that which seemed already perfect, and by February 1885 a second machine with automatic justification was completed. On July 3, 1886, the first of twelve machines made by the company for the *New York Tribune* was used to compose a part of that day's issue of the paper. Before all the machines had been delivered, Mergenthaler had devised nine patented improvements, including the single or independent matrix, all of which were incorporated in the last of the twelve. Meanwhile the control of the National Typographic Company and its subsidiary Mergenthaler Printing Company, organized in 1885, passed into the hands of a group of newspaper owners and an entire change in policy for the conduct of the business was put into effect. This caused a break between the board of directors and Mergenthaler, resulting in his resignation in 1888. His pride and passion was the linotype, however, and notwithstanding the rupture with the company he continued to add to its value by devising more than fifty patented improvements. Constant application and never ending anxiety undermined his health, and he succumbed to tuberculosis after a desperate fight of five years. Some years before his death he was awarded a medal by Cooper Union, New York, for his great invention, and the Franklin Institute, Philadelphia, awarded him the John Scott medal and the Elliott Cresson medal. He commenced an autobiography which he was unable to complete because of failing health. Mergenthaler was naturalized in Baltimore, Oct. 9, 1878, and was married there on Sept. 11, 1881, to Emma Frederica Lachenmayer. At the time of his death, in Baltimore, he was survived by his widow and four children.

[*Biog. of Ottmar Mergenthaler and Hist. of the Linotype* (1898); Waldemar Kaempffert, *A Popular Hist. of Am. Invention* (1924); George Iles, *Leading Am. Inventors* (1912); E. W. Byrn, *The Progress of Invention in the Nineteenth Century* (1900); *Ottmar Mergenthaler, 1854–1929, Der Moderne Buchdrucker* (Berlin, 1929); *The Big Scheme of Simple Operation* (Mergenthaler Linotype Co., Brooklyn, N. Y., 1923); the *Sun* (Baltimore), Oct. 16, 30, 1899; Patent Office records; correspondence with family.] C. W. M.

MERGLER, MARIE JOSEPHA (May 18, 1851–May 17, 1901), physician, was born in Mainstockheim, Bavaria, youngest of the three children of Dr. Francis R. and Henriette (von Ritterhausen) Mergler. Her father brought his family to America when Marie was two years of age, settling in Illinois, where he practised until his death. At the age of seventeen Marie graduated from Cook County Normal School and three years later from the State Normal School at Oswego, N. Y., having completed a classical course. For four years she taught in Englewood High School, and then entered the Woman's Medical College at Chicago, graduating as valedictorian of her class in 1879. She took the examinations for interne in Cook County Hospital and stood second, but was barred from service on grounds of sex. Feeling the need of further experience, she studied for a year (1880) in Zurich, Switzerland, specializing in pathology and clinical medicine. In 1881 she took up the practice of medicine in Chicago. She was immediately made adjunct professor of gynecology in the Woman's Medical College under Prof. William Heath Byford [*q.v.*] and served in that capacity until 1890, when she was made professor of gynecology to fill the vacancy left by his death. She acted as secretary of the faculty of the Woman's Medical College from 1881 to 1892, when it became the Northwestern University Woman's Medical School, then continued as secretary until 1899, when she was made dean. This position she held until her death two years later. In 1882 she was appointed attending physician on the staff of the Cook County Hospital, being the second woman to receive such an appointment; in 1886 she became attending surgeon to the Woman's Hospital of Chicago, in 1890 attending gynecologist to Wesley Memorial Hospital, and in 1895–97 she was head physician and surgeon at the Women's and Children's Hospital of Chicago. From 1895 to 1901 she was also professor of gynecology in the Post-Graduate Medical School of Northwestern University. Her activities during the last year of her life were greatly curtailed on account of her suffering from pernicious anemia, of which she died in Los Angeles, Cal., at the age of fifty.

Marie J. Mergler's professional life of only a score of years was of an intense and highly specialized character. Few medical men or women attained such proficiency or occupied positions of such responsibility and importance as early in life as did she. She was notable among women operators for her success in abdominal surgery; she contributed a number of papers to medical journals, wrote a student's classbook: *A Guide to the Study of Gynecology* (1891), and was joint author with Charles W. Earle of "Diseases of the New Born" in *An American Textbook of Obstetrics* (1895), by J. C. Cameron and others. An earnest and able teacher, she left a distinct impression upon her pupils. By her will she bequeathed a generous sum to the Woman's Hospital and founded a medical scholarship in the University of Chicago.

[H. A. Kelly and W. L. Burrage, *Am. Medic. Biogs.* (1920), in which, strangely, the name is misspelled Meigler throughout the article; *Northwestern Univ., A Hist., 1855–1905* (1905), vol. IV; *Woman's Medical School Northwestern Univ.* (*Woman's Medical Coll. of Chicago*), *the Institution and Its Founders* (1896); *Jour. Am. Medic. Asso.*, May 25, 1901; *Chicago Medic. Recorder*, July 1901; *Revue de Chirurgie* (Paris), July 1901; *Woman's Jour.* (Boston), June 15, 1901; *Chicago Tribune*, May 22, 1901; *N. Y. Tribune*, June 13, 1901.]

B. V–H.

MERRIAM, AUGUSTUS CHAPMAN (May 30, 1843–Jan. 19, 1895), philologist and archeologist, the youngest of thirteen children of Ela and Lydia (Sheldon) Merriam, was born at "Locust Grove," in Leyden, Lewis County, N. Y. His ancestor, Joseph Merriam, had come to Massachusetts from Kent, England, in 1638, settling near Concord; his grandfather, Judge Nathaniel Merriam, had moved from Meriden, Conn., to Leyden, N. Y., shortly after 1800. The boy was prepared for college at the Columbia Grammar School, and both there and in Columbia College, to which he was admitted in 1862, had the advantage of the stimulating teaching of Dr. Charles Anthon [*q.v.*]. He was graduated at the head of his class in 1866, and after some months spent in Topeka, Kan., returned to New York City to teach in the Columbia Grammar School. In 1868 he was appointed tutor of Greek and Latin in Columbia College, and for eight years gave instruction in both languages. Beginning with 1876, however, he was able to devote all his energies to Greek, and in 1880 was advanced to the post of adjunct professor of the Greek language and literature. His notable edition of *The Phaeacian Episode of the Odyssey*, published in that year, revealed at once his insight into Homer, the rare charm of his style, and his appreciation of the illuminating contribution to the enjoyment of great poetry which can be made by art and archeology. In fact, from this time on he was more and more captivated by research in archeology and epigraphy, and his published work was such as to gain for him before his death a high international reputation in these fields.

In 1883 he wrote a masterly monograph, *The Greek and Latin Inscriptions on the Obelisk-Crab in the Metropolitan Museum, N. Y.* (published 1884), in which, by establishing a new date, he succeeded in bringing for the first time every detail of the inscriptions into accord with already known history. He was then drawn on, by his inability to accept Mommsen's ascription of the temple in front of which this obelisk had formerly stood, to write a brilliant paper on "The Caesareum and the Worship of Augustus at Alexandria" (*Transactions of the American Philological Association 1883*, vol. XIV, 1884, pp. 5–35). The presence of solid scholarship and the absence from his demeanor of everything that could suggest self-adulation greatly endeared him to his associates and helped to make him president of the American Philological Association for the year 1886–87. His presidential address dealt with the inscriptions published during that year from Naucratis, Crete, Epidaurus, Athens, and Peiraieus (*American Journal of Archaeology*, July–December 1887, pp. 303–21), but he was unable to read it in person, having already sailed for Greece (accompanied by his wife, Louise Oley, whom he had married July 23, 1869) to assume the directorship of the American School of Classical Studies at Athens. There, during the year 1887–88, he conducted successful excavations at Sicyon and at Dionyso, definitely proving the latter place to be the site of the deme Icaria, the birthplace of Thespis, founder of Greek tragedy (*Seventh Annual Report of the Managing Committee of the American School of Classical Studies at Athens, 1887–88,* 1889, pp. 39–98). His distinctive power had by this time been so strikingly shown that in 1890 he was appointed to the newly created chair of Greek archeology and epigraphy at Columbia. From 1888 to 1894 he was chairman of the committee on publication of the School at Athens, and from 1891 to 1894 was president of the New York Society of the Archaeological Institute of America.

Merriam was by nature a productive scholar. In addition to the titles already cited the following works of his deserve especial mention: "A Greek Tunnel of the Sixth Century B.C." (*School of Mines Quarterly,* March 1885); *The Sixth and Seventh Books of Herodotus* (1885), an admirable textbook; "Aesculapia as Revealed by Inscriptions" (*Gaillard's Medical Journal,* May 1885), a most interesting description of the sanctuaries of Aesculapius at Athens and Epidaurus and of the cures believed to have been wrought there by the god; "Law Code of the Kretan Gortyna; Text, Translation, Commentary" (*American Journal of Archaeology,* October 1885, January–March 1886), an interpretation of permanent value, written shortly after the discovery in 1884 by Halbherr and Fabricius of that remarkably humane code; "Telegraphing among the Ancients" (*Papers of the Archaeological Institute of America, Classical Series,* vol. III, no. 1, 1890). His last articles were three papers contributed to *Classical Studies in Honour of Henry Drisler* (1894). In his classroom, through the play of a constructive and delightful imagination, the past lived again, and the beauty and music inherent in great poetry and prose were engagingly made clear. Death came to him in the fulness of his powers, while he was in Athens on sabbatical leave. A severe cold developed into pneumonia, and the end came swiftly. He was buried in his beloved "City of the Violet Crown," where a beautiful monument marks his grave.

[For partial lists of Merriam's writings consult the Index to *Am. Jour. Archaeol.,* vols. I–XI, 1885–96, and to *Trans. and Proc. Am. Philological Asso.,* vols. I–XX, 1869–89. For his life and character consult the account of the memorial meeting at Columbia in the *Univ. Bull.,* Mar. 1895; also the obituary by Dr. C. H. Young, a favorite pupil, in *Am. Jour. Archaeol.,* Apr.–June 1895. See also C. H. Pope, *Merriam Geneal. in England and America* (1906); *N. Y. Tribune,* Jan. 21, 1895. Some additional details are on file in the Columbiana Collection at the University.]

N. G. M.

MERRIAM, CHARLES (Nov. 31, 1806–July 9, 1887), publisher, descended from Joseph Merriam who came to America in 1638, settling near Concord, Mass., was born at West Brookfield, Mass., the second of nine children of Dan and Thirza (Clapp) Merriam. In 1797 his father and uncle founded a newspaper in that village and under the firm name of E. Merriam & Company continued until 1823 to do miscellaneous printing and publishing. Among their books were several editions of William Perry's *Royal Standard English Dictionary* (1801, 1806, 1809), and thus the Merriam name was associated with the publication of dictionaries from an early date. During his boyhood Charles attended district school and worked on his father's farm. At the age of fourteen he was apprenticed to a printer in Hartford, Conn., where he remained until the death of his father in 1823. After completing his apprenticeship in the shop now conducted by his uncle and his elder brother, George (Jan. 19, 1803–June 22, 1880), he spent a year in the academies at Monson and Hadley, taught school through the next winter, worked in Philadelphia for a few months, and then for several years in Boston as journeyman and foreman in the well-known printing shop of T. R. Marvin. On the recepit of an invitation from Rev. Samuel Osgood to come to Springfield and start a newspaper, he left Boston, and with his brother George went to Springfield to look over the prospects. The time did not seem to be propitious for a newspaper, but the two brothers with another relative established a printing house and bookshop in 1831, which in 1832 became G. & C. Merriam. A third brother, Homer, became a member of the firm in 1856.

Although all three brothers connected with the firm as partners were exceptionally capable, Charles appears to have had the greatest literary bent. In the early days he was in charge of the bookstore, and in later years concerned himself with the publishing end of the work, even trying his hand at writing verse. The firm was successful from the start, but its great fortune came after the death of Noah Webster [*q.v.*] in 1843, when it purchased from J. S. & C. Adams of Amherst the unsold copies of Webster's two-volume *American Dictionary of the English Language* and the right to publish it in the future. Securing the editorial services of Dr. Chauncey Allen Goodrich [*q.v.*] of Yale, Webster's son-in-law, the Merriams had the book revised along more conservative lines, printed it in one volume, and reduced the price to six dollars. Extensive advertising and large sales of the Unabridged helped promote the sales of the various abridged editions and the firm quickly bought up the rights of these also. Charles Merriam himself read the complete proof of one edition. The firm also published school books, law books, Bibles, and other volumes, but the business connected with the dictionary became so great that they eventually withdrew from their bookstore and general printing. Charles retired from active participation in the firm at the age of seventy and sold his interest in the business in 1877. Although his main interest was in the publishing venture, he was also a director of the Springfield Fire and Marine Insurance Company and of the old Springfield Bank. He was a man of intense and unremitting industry, of unassuming demeanor, and of simple and scholarly tastes. An ardent and strictly orthodox Congregationalist, he taught a Bible class for many years and was one of the founders in 1842 of the South Church of Springfield. He gave liberally to the church and church institutions, particularly to home and foreign missions. For his native town of West Brookfield he built a public library and endowed it; in the Springfield library he took a lively interest, serving as one of the first members of the association and using his best efforts to establish a free system. When the government of the city of Springfield was organized in 1852, he was a member of the Common Council. He was married twice: on Aug. 11, 1835, to Sophia Eleanor Warriner, who died Apr. 26, 1858; and on May 8, 1860, at Detroit, Mich., to Rachel White (Capen) Gray, a widow. By his first marriage he had three daughters and two sons, one of whom died in infancy; by his second marriage he had one daughter.

[*Springfield Republican*, Nov. 13, 1880, July 10, 1887; *Springfield Daily Union*, July 9, 1887; material on the Merriams in the Conn. Valley Hist. Soc. library at Springfield, particularly a ninety-page manuscript, "Memorial of Charles Merriam" (1892), by Mrs. Rachel Merriam; *Vital Records of Brookfield, Mass.* (1909); C. H. Pope, *Merriam Geneal.* (1906); J. C. Derby, *Fifty Years Among Authors, Books, and Publishers* (1884); *100th Anniversary of the Establishment of G. and C. Merriam Company, Springfield, Mass., 1831–1931* (n.d.); *Biog. Review . . . of Hampden County, Mass.* (1895); Moses King, *King's Handbook of Springfield, Mass.* (1884).] H. U. F.

MERRIAM, HENRY CLAY (Nov. 13, 1837–Nov. 18, 1912), soldier, was a descendant of Joseph Merriam of Kent, England, who came to Concord, Mass., in 1638. He was born at Houlton, Me., the son of Lewis and Mary Ann (Foss) Merriam, and received his early education at Houlton Academy and Colby College, where his law studies were interrupted by the outbreak of the Civil War. Colby College granted him the degree of B.A. in 1864, however, and that of M.A. in 1867.

He left college in 1862 to become captain in the 20th Maine Volunteers, and participated in the battle of Antietam, where he was brevetted lieutenant-colonel for gallantry, and in the battles of Shepherdstown and Fredericksburg. As captain in the 80th United States Colored Infantry, he led in the assault on Port Hudson, La., May 27, 1863, and was promoted lieutenant-colonel. At Fort Blakely, Apr. 9, 1865, he again led in the assault on the enemy's works, an attack resulting in the capture of some 6,000 prisoners. For this achievement, he was awarded the Congressional Medal of Honor and the brevet of colonel in both the Regular and Volunteer services. Mustered out of the military service Oct. 24, 1865, he resumed the study of law until recommissioned a major in the Regular Army, July 28, 1866. Subsequently, he commanded Fort McIntosh, Tex., during prolonged border troubles. On Apr. 10, 1876, he assumed responsibility for firing upon Mexican federal forces in reprisal for outrages committed against American citizens; and on Aug. 22, crossing the Rio Grande, he rescued the American commercial agent, held prisoner by revolutionists. He was promoted lieutenant-colonel, 2nd Infantry, June 10, 1876, and took part in the Nez Percé Indian campaign of the year following, receiving high commendation from Generals Oliver O. Howard and Nelson A. Miles [*qq.v.*] and from the territorial authorities of Idaho and Washington. He was promoted colonel, 7th Infantry, July 10, 1885. During the Sioux Indian War of 1890–91, he was instrumental in disarming some three hundred of Sitting Bull's followers. He was promoted brigadier-general, Regular Army, on June 30, 1897. Appointed major-general of volunteers May 4, 1898, after the outbreak of the war with Spain, he had charge of organizing and equipping the Philippines Expeditionary Force. The following year, while in command of the Department of Colorado, he was in charge of the troops sent at the request of the Idaho authorities to help suppress the labor riots at the Coeur d'Alène lead mines. Here he acted with vigor and good judgment; martial law was declared and order was restored. A subsequent investigation, ordered by the president to satisfy public opinion aroused by the labor agitators, resulted in Merriam's conduct being officially approved.

On Nov. 13, 1901, he was placed on the retired list by reason of age, but by Act of Congress in February 1903 he was advanced to the grade of major-general. He died at his home in Portland, Me., after an illness of nearly two years, and was interred at Arlington with high military honors. He was the inventor of a successful pack for infantry soldiers which bore his name, and for which he was awarded a gold medal by the French Academy of Inventors. He was twice married: on Jan. 16, 1866, to Lucy J. Getchell, who was drowned with an infant daughter, in a cloudburst at Staked Plains, Tex., Apr. 24, 1870; and on June 4, 1874, to Una Macpherson-Macneil of Kingston, Jamaica, who survived him, together with three sons and two daughters.

[*Official Army Register*, 1903; F. B. Heitman, *Hist. Reg. and Dict., U. S. Army* (1903), vol. I; *Army and Navy Jour.*, Nov. 23, 1912; *N. Y. Herald*, *N. Y. Times*, Nov. 19, 1912; *Report to the Gov. of Idaho on the Insurrection in Shoshone County, Idaho, by Samuel H. Hayes, Atty. Gen.*, June 30, 1900; *Sen. Doc. No. 142*, 56 Cong., 1 Sess.; C. H. Pope, *Merriam Geneal.* (1906); information as to certain facts from a son, Col. Henry M. Merriam, U. S. A., retired.] C. D. R.

MERRIAM, WILLIAM RUSH (July 26, 1849–Feb. 18, 1931), banker, politician, and director of the Twelfth Census, was born at Wadham's Mills, N. Y., the son of John Lafayette and Mahala Kimpton (De Lano) Merriam. His father was descended from Joseph Merriam who came to Massachusetts in 1638 and settled near Concord. In 1861 the family moved to St. Paul, Minn., where the elder Merriam became prominent in the business and civic life of the frontier city and of the state. Young Merriam was sent, at the age of fifteen, to Racine College, Wisconsin, where he remained until 1871, completing both preparatory and college courses and becoming valedictorian of his class.

After an apprenticeship as clerk in the First National Bank of St. Paul, in 1871 he was made cashier of the newly organized Merchants' National Bank, and subsequently became vice-president (1880) and president (1884). Banking and other business activities, and even a rather lively participation in various civic and community enterprises, did not satisfy him, however; he cherished definite political ambitions. In 1883 he was elected as a Republican to the state legislature and had a considerable part in bringing about the defeat of the veteran Senator Windom for reëlection and the selection of Dwight M. Sabin for his place. In 1886 he was again elected from his district and was made speaker of the House, where his "good-nature, gracious manners and attractive personality" (Folwell, *post*, III, 184) stood him in good stead and made him especially *persona grata* to the rural members of the legislature. This fact contributed to his election as vice-president (1887) and president (1888) of the State Agricultural Society, honors which in turn had a bearing on his later political career.

In 1888 Merriam sought the gubernatorial nomination from the Republican convention and secured it despite the unwritten rule that an incumbent had an almost vested right to renomination. Gov. A R. McGill's stand for high license and the fear of some Republicans that a strong Democratic candidate with the backing of liquor interests stood a chance of winning the election undoubtedly contributed to Merriam's choice. But the episode caused resentment which had after results. The election gave Merriam a substantial majority. In 1890 he was renominated practically without opposition and was elected by a small plurality over Democratic and Farmers' Alliance candidates. Issues of paramount significance were lacking during his governorship, although it was then that Minnesota adopted the Australian ballot, refunded the state debt, and made provision for leasing iron-ore lands which formed a part of the school fund.

As his term drew to an end Merriam aspired to the United States Senate. His friends worked up a sentiment which was calculated to throw the nomination by the Republican caucus to him instead of to Cushman K. Davis [*q.v.*], the incumbent; their zeal diminished, however, and Davis was nominated, although subsequent investigation showed that, if they had stood firm, they probably would have carried their plan through (C. B. Cheney in *Minneapolis Journal*, Aug. 13, 1922). Davis was elected by a majority of one vote in the legislature; he evidently looked upon Merriam as the principal cause of opposition and his resentment was probably responsible later for McKinley's failure to designate Merriam to a diplomatic post, a reward that might have been expected from Merriam's part in the campaign of 1896, both as a delegate to the Republican National Convention and as a worker in the state canvass.

Davis' animosity did not, however, block McKinley's selection of Merriam as director of the Twelfth Census in 1899. To this new position Merriam took the organizing ability, and the willingness to delegate authority to competent persons which had served him in his business career. According to S. N. D. North, his successor as director, the Twelfth Census "was not only the best census ever compiled in the United States, from the point of view of accuracy and comprehensiveness, but it was also the most economical, tested on the per capita basis, and what is even more important, the most expeditious in publication of the results" (Baker, *post*, p. 319). North also gave Merriam credit for securing the establishment of the permanent Bureau of the Census (*Ibid.*, p. 320).

In 1903 Merriam resigned his position as director and from then to the end of his life sought no further political preferment. He continued to reside in Washington, being active in business; for some years he was president of the Shenandoah Coal and Iron Company and of the Liberty Furnace Company; later he was president of the Tabulating Machine Company. The last years of his life were spent in retirement and he died at Fort Sewall, Fla. On Oct. 2, 1873, he married Laura E. Hancock, niece of Gen. Winfield Scott Hancock [*q.v.*], and to them were born five children.

[J. H. Baker, "Lives of the Governors of Minnesota," *Minn. Hist. Soc. Colls.*, vol. XIII (1908); W. W. Folwell, *A Hist. of Minn.*, vol. III (1926); *N. Y. Times*, Feb. 19, 1931; *St. Paul Pioneer-Press*, Feb. 19, 1931; *Minneapolis Jour.*, Aug. 13, 1922; *Western Mag.*, Sept. 1919; *Who's Who in America*, 1918–19; C. H. Pope, *Merriam Geneal. in England and America* (1906).]
L. B. S—e.

MERRICK, EDWIN THOMAS (July 9, 1808–Jan. 12, 1897), jurist, was born in Wilbraham, Mass., the eldest son of Thomas and Ann (Brewer) Merrick and a descendant of Thomas Merrick who emigrated from Wales in 1636 and settled later in Springfield. On his mother's side he was of English descent. Left fatherless while yet a mere boy, he was brought up by his uncle, Samuel Brewer of Springfield, Mass. At the age of nineteen he entered Wesleyan Academy at Wilbraham and graduated in 1832. While in the academy he began the study of law in the office of William Knight, and after his graduation he went to New Lisbon, Ohio, where he completed his law studies in the office of his uncle, Alonzo L. Brewer. He was admitted to the bar of Ohio in 1833 and began to practise at Carrollton. A year later he took charge of his uncle's business at New Lisbon and formed a partnership with William E. Russell. In 1838 he formed a partnership with James H. Muse to practise law in Louisiana and opened an office in Clinton under the firm name of Muse & Merrick. Inasmuch as the civil law instead of common law was the basis of Louisiana jurisprudence, Merrick was obliged to make special preparation for admission to the bar. He is said to have passed a very brilliant examination and was admitted to the bar in 1839. With his knowledge of both categories of the law he soon acquired a large practice at Clinton and was retained in nearly all the important litigation in that part of the state. In 1854 he was elected judge of the seventh judicial district of Louisiana which included East and West Feliciana parishes. He was frequently called upon to act in adjoining districts. In 1855 he was elected chief justice of Louisiana for a term of eight years on the Whig ticket. One of his most famous decisions (1856) was that in *Succession of Daniel Clark* (11 *Louisiana Reports*, 124), involving the legitimacy of Myra Clark Gaines, the plaintiff.

When Louisiana withdrew from the Union, although Merrick was opposed to secession, he remained loyal to her cause. After the capture of New Orleans by the Federals in 1862, he moved to the western part of the state and held court at Opelousas and Shreveport. He was reelected chief justice in 1863 but was removed from office at the close of the war under the Reconstruction régime. He returned to New Orleans, but as he declined to take the "iron-clad oath," he was debarred from the practice of law. He was finally pardoned for giving aid and comfort to the Confederacy and was allowed to resume the practice of law and also to recover his home in New Orleans and his plantation in West Feliciana which had been taken from him during the war. He was active in carrying appeals to the United States Supreme Court from Louisiana in cases arising out of the system of administration in the state during the Reconstruction period, and was very successful in these appeals. In later years he associated his second son Edwin Thomas Merrick, Jr., with him, under the name of Merrick & Merrick. He had married, Dec. 3, 1840, Caroline E. Thomas, of Jackson, La. He died at his home in New Orleans. He was the author of several legal treatises, notably *The Laws of Louisiana and their Sources* (1871).

[Alcée Fortier, *Louisiana* (1909), vol. II; G. B. Merrick, *Geneal. of the Merrick-Mirick-Myrick Family of Mass., 1636–1902* (1902); biographical sketch and editorial in the *Times-Democrat* (New Orleans), Jan. 13, 1897; information as to certain facts from Edwin Thomas Merrick, Jr., New Orleans, La.]
E. M. V.

MERRICK, FREDERICK (Jan. 29, 1810–Mar. 5, 1894), Methodist Episcopal clergyman and educator, was born on the ancestral farm in Wilbraham, Mass. His father, Noah, a first cousin of Pliny Merrick [*q.v.*] was in the fifth generation from Thomas Merrick who came to Massachusetts from Wales in 1636, settling first in Roxbury and then in Springfield; his mother was Statira Hays, of Hartford, Conn. His parents were pious Congregationalists, his grandfather having been a minister of that communion, but the novelty and vitality of the Methodist meetings attracted the boy, who was of an introspective turn. From his fifteenth year he worked as a clerk in a store in Springfield, Mass., becoming a partner before he was twenty. In 1829, after a joyous and transforming spiritual experience he joined the Methodist Society. Feeling called to be a minister, he attended the Wesleyan Academy in Wilbraham, and entered Wesleyan University at Middletown, Conn. He left college (1834) to teach in Amenia Seminary (N. Y.), a Methodist secondary school of which he was principal until 1838, when he was elected professor of natural science in Ohio University at Athens. While in college he had been licensed as an exhorter and local preacher, and at Amenia he had married, in 1836, Sarah Fidelia Griswold of Suffolk, Conn.

At Athens he achieved marked influence and popularity and was much sought as a teacher by the Methodist colleges springing up in what was then the West. In 1841 he joined Ohio Conference on trial and in 1842–43 was pastor at Marietta. He was ordained elder in 1843. The churches of the state had embarked on the ambitious enterprise of founding a college at Delaware, and in that year Merrick became one of its financial agents. The Ohio Wesleyan University then consisted of a sulphur spring and the buildings and grounds of a bankrupt sanitarium, without faculty, students, or endowment. From that year until his death he was identified with the school, coming to be venerated as one of its "Great Five" founders. The college opened its doors in 1844 and in 1845 he began to teach natural science there, later (1851) transferring to the chair of moral philosophy. For a brief period he was acting president, and for forty years he was auditor, financial watchdog, and emergency man in several crises. Chapel, library, laboratories, museums, endowments, were largely the fruit of his personal influence and untiring zeal. Merrick Hall was named for him. From 1860 to 1873 he was president, continuing as lecturer on natural and revealed religion after ill health compelled him to relinquish the executive office. At his death, leaving no issue, he willed his small property to the institution to found the Merrick Lectureship on experimental and practical religion.

Merrick's diary reveals him as a man of intense devotion, who sought divine guidance through prayer for every action, great or small. One of his critical decisions was called for in 1845 when he was asked to lead a Methodist Mission in China, an offer which he did not decline without a struggle. Although he was zealous to build up the University in buildings and funds, his first care was the character and religious life of its students, and his precept and example made the school a prolific mother of ministers and missionaries. He was a vigorous advocate of total abstinence and a militant foe of the liquor traffic. He opposed slavery and helped to operate the "underground railway." In 1860, 1864, and 1876 he was a delegate to the General Conference of his denomination, and at the centennial conference at Baltimore in 1884, which commemorated the founding of the Methodist Episcopal Church, he gave the closing message. Though he preached on many occasions, he lacked the greater gifts of pulpit eloquence. He lectured frequently and his only published volume, *Formalism in Religion* (1865), is a series of lectures. He had a singularly serene and steady habit of mind, based on a supreme faith in a loving and wise providence, and in his later years he came to enjoy in the college community a unique reputation for saintliness. He died at Delaware, Ohio, at the age of eighty-four.

[W. G. Williams, "Frederick Merrick," *Meth. Rev.*, May-June 1895 (also reprinted separately); J. W. Bashford, "Frederick Merrick," *Ann. Report of President to Trustees of Ohio Wesleyan Univ.*, 1894; *Fifty Years of Hist. of the Ohio Wesleyan Univ.* (1895), ed. by E. T. Nelson; Isaac Crook, *The Great Five: The First Faculty of the Ohio Wesleyan Univ.* (1908); Diary of Frederick Merrick, 1843–88 (MS.), in Library of Ohio Wesleyan University ("mostly personal experiences relating to my religious life. F.M."); G. B. Merrick, *Geneal. of the Merrick-Mirick-Myrick Family of Mass., 1636–1902* (1902); *Cincinnati Commercial Gazette,* Mar. 6, 1894.]

J. R. J.

MERRICK, PLINY (Aug. 2, 1794–Jan. 31, 1867), Massachusetts jurist, counsel for Prof. John White Webster in his trial for the murder of Dr. George Parkman, was descended from Thomas Merrick who emigrated to America in 1636 and later settled in Springfield. His parents, Pliny and Ruth (Cutler) Merrick lived at Brookfield where the father, a Harvard graduate, was a respected lawyer and public servant. The son attended Leicester Academy and Harvard, graduating in 1814. He read law at Worcester in the office of Levi Lincoln [*q.v.*], son of Jefferson's attorney-general. His preceptor was a distinguished lawyer and judge and subsequently governor. After three years Merrick was admitted to the bar. Now heavily in debt, the young lawyer cast about for a practice without immediate success. He had an office in Worcester, then at Charlton and at Swansea in Bristol County, then at Taunton where for a while he was a partner of Marcus Morton. In 1824 he returned to Worcester, where he was appointed district attorney for Worcester and Norfolk counties and served from 1832 until his appointment to the court of common pleas in 1843. While his service as a prosecuting officer made him a master of the criminal law, his civil practice increased until it sometimes happened that he was retained as senior counsel in every case to be tried at a term of court.

In these earlier years Merrick was active in politics. Like Caleb Cushing, whom he succeeded on the supreme court, he was somewhat inconstant in party affiliations. In 1834 he appears to have favored a National Republican-Antimasonic alliance in Massachusetts to oppose the Jackson administration; yet on Jackson's death he pronounced his eulogy at Faneuil Hall. (Speech in J. S. Loring, *The Hundred Boston Orators,* 1852, pp. 635–38.) As a leader of the minority party, he received few of the rewards of office: four years a selectman of Worcester, in 1827 a representative in the legislature; in 1850 a senator. He was active in local affairs and for a time he edited the Worcester *National Aegis.* In 1848, after five years of service on the common pleas bench he became president of the Worcester & Nashua Railroad, then in a precarious situation financially. When Merrick relinquished the presidency in 1850 the road was operating on a sound financial basis.

At this time he became engaged in one of the *causes célèbres* of American criminal law. Professor Webster of Harvard Medical School, becoming hopelessly indebted to Dr. Parkman, had killed his creditor but was detected before he had completed the destruction of the body. He was indicted, convicted before the supreme court, and hanged on Aug. 30, 1850. So erratic was the accused toward the line of defense to be pursued that Rufus Choate declined to take the case (Joseph Neilson, *Memories of Rufus Choate,* 1884, pp. 15–21), and Merrick was retained as senior counsel. The evidence was overwhelming and the accused an untrustworthy client, yet the defense was conducted with ability and eloquence. In 1851 Merrick was reappointed to the court of common pleas, and in 1853, when Caleb Cushing resigned from the supreme judicial court to become attorney-general in Pierce's cabinet, he was promoted to fill the vacancy. Two years later he moved to Boston. In the spring of 1864 he was stricken with paralysis and was forced to give up his work, resigning on Aug. 15 following. A subsequent stroke caused his death. In character and style his opinions showed a marked improvement during his years of service. On the bench he was "kind, courteous, and dignified; and if his quickness at any time outran the slower development of the cause before him, thereby sometimes disturbing the sensitiveness of counsel, no one ever doubted that his convictions were unbiased, though to the losing party they sometimes may have seemed to have been hastily formed" (*American Law Review,* April 1867, p. 585). Merrick had married, on May 23, 1821, Mary Rebecca Thomas, whose brother Benjamin became one of his associates on the supreme court. She died childless in 1859. On his death the judge left bequests to the public library at Brookfield and to the orphanage at Worcester.

[*Am. Law Rev.,* Apr. 1867; Wm. Lincoln, *Hist. of Worcester, Mass.* (1837); D. H. Hurd, *Hist. of Worcester County, Mass.* (1889), vol. I; G. B. Merrick, *Geneal. of the Merrick-Mirick-Myrick Family of Mass., 1636–1902* (1902); A. B. Darling, *Pol. Changes in Mass., 1824–48* (1925); Geo. Bemis, *Report of the Case of John W. Webster* (1850); Geo. Dilnot, *The Trial of Prof. John White Webster* (1928); Pliny Merrick, *A Letter on Speculative Free Masonry* (1929), and the rejoinder, by an anonymous author, *Strictures on Seceding Masons* (1830); *Boston Evening Transcript,* Feb. 2, 1867.] C. F.

MERRICK, SAMUEL VAUGHAN (May 4, 1801–Aug. 18, 1870), manufacturer and railroad executive, was born in Hallowell, Me., the son of John and Rebecca (Vaughan) Merrick. His father, an emigrant from England in 1798, had been educated as a Unitarian minister but spent most of his life as a student and writer (D. R. Goodwin, *Memoir of John Merrick, Esq.,* 1862). The boy attended the schools of his native town and in 1816 entered the employ of his uncle, John Vaughan, a wine merchant of Philadelphia, Pa. In 1820 he left his uncle and joined John Agnew in the firm of Merrick & Agnew, to manufacture an improved type of fire-engine. His knowledge of mechanical engineering was slight at this time but through constant study he gained a good practical knowledge of engineering and developed an innate talent for mechanics. On Christmas day 1823 he was married to Sarah Thomas, by whom he had six children. In 1836, with John H. Towne [*q.v.*] as junior partner, he established the Southwark Foundry for the manufacture of heavy machinery and boilers. Upon Towne's retirement in 1849, Merrick took his son, J. Vaughan Merrick, into partnership. As Merrick & Son, and after 1852 as Merrick & Sons, the firm continued until the retirement of the senior partner in 1860. Among their notable achievements were the construction of the engines of a number of naval vessels, notably those for the steam frigate *Mississippi.* They also built the iron lighthouses along the coast of Florida and the *New Ironsides,* a pioneer armor-clad vessel.

Merrick was an early advocate of the use of gas for street lighting in Philadelphia, and in order to bring about its adoption ran for and was elected to the City Council. He was appointed chairman of the committee to investigate the matter and was sent abroad to study European methods of gas manufacture. Upon his return in 1834 he was given charge, as chief engineer, of building the gas works and distributing the gas throughout the city. This work was completed on Feb. 8, 1836, and on Feb. 8, 1837, he resigned his official position in order to devote himself to his private business.

Realizing the importance to Philadelphia of a railroad connection with the interior, he was an early promoter of the Pennsylvania Railroad Company, which was organized, Apr. 13, 1846; and on Mar. 31, 1847, he became its first president. While not possessing technical training, he was well fitted to manage and inspire confidence in the enterprise. He held this position until Sept. 1, 1849, when, with the construction of the road progressing satisfactorily, and the prospect that sufficient capital would be raised for its completion, he tendered his resignation. He remained as a director, however, until Feb. 2, 1852. In 1856 he was prevailed upon to accept the presidency of the Sunbury & Erie Railroad, then on the verge of bankruptcy, and held this post until December 1857, when he resigned because of ill health. During this time he saved the road from failure by advancing large sums from his private funds. He was also a director of the Catawissa Railroad and was connected in various official capacities with other corporations. A founder of the Franklin Institute of Pennsylvania in 1824, he was its president from 1842 to 1854. In 1833 he was elected to the American Philosophical Society. After the Civil War he became interested in the problems of education in the South and made large gifts toward the maintenance of schools in that section. He was also a liberal giver to other agencies, particularly the Episcopal Hospital in Philadelphia. He died in Philadelphia.

[J. T. Scharf and Thompson Westcott, *Hist. of Phila.* (1884), vols. I, III; E. P. Oberholtzer, *Phila.—A Hist. of the City and Its People* (n.d.), vol. II; H. W. Schotter, *The Growth and Development of the Pa. Railroad Company* (1927); W. B. Wilson, *Hist. of the Pa. Railroad Company* (2 vols., 1899); D. R. Goodwin, in *Proc. Am. Philosophical Soc.*, vol. XI (1871); Ellwood Hendrick, *Modern Views of Physical Science; Being a Record of the Proc. of the Centenary Meeting of the Franklin Inst. at Phila., Sept. 17, 18, and 19, 1924* (1925); E. T. Freedley, *Phila. and Its Manufactures . . . in 1857* (1858); *Public Ledger* (Phila.), Aug. 19, 1870; name of wife and date of marriage from a descendant, J. Hartley, Esq.]

J. H. F.

MERRILL, DANIEL (Mar. 18, 1765–June 3, 1833), Baptist clergyman, was the son of Thomas and Sarah (Friend) Merrill of Rowley, Mass., and a descendant of Nathaniel Merrill, who emigrated to America in 1635. At fifteen he enlisted in the 3rd Massachusetts Infantry and served until the end of the Revolution. He decided to become a Congregational minister and entered Dartmouth College, from which he graduated in 1789. After studying theology, probably with Dr. Spring of Newburyport, he was licensed to preach in 1791. He went to Sedgwick, Me., where his first sermon started a revival in which nearly one hundred were converted. He preached at Sedgwick for five months, then after an absence of eighteen months, when he was preaching elsewhere, he returned to Sedgwick and was ordained pastor of a new Congregational church on Sept. 17, 1793. He led revivals in 1798 and 1801, and by 1805 his church had one hundred and eighty-nine members and was the largest in Maine.

In 1803 part of his congregation began to have doubts about the efficacy of infant baptism. Merrill studied to confute them, but was himself converted to their opinion. In February 1805 a majority of the church agreed to become Baptists, and in May Merrill and eighty-seven of his congregation were baptized by three ministers from southern New England in the tide-waters of Benjamin's River. The next day he was re-ordained as a Baptist. In the same year he published seven sermons under the title *The Mode and Subjects of Baptism Examined* (1805) in which he argued that the Baptists had been the uninterrupted church of Christ from the days of the apostles, whereas all other Protestant churches sprang from the Church of Rome.

The Baptist ministers in Maine were for the most part uneducated farmers, and in 1810 the Bowdoinham Association elected a committee, of which Merrill was one, to consider the foundation of a college. Merrill, chiefly in order that he might help the cause of education, had been elected to the General Assembly of Massachusetts, and in 1813 he took the lead in securing a charter and a grant of land for the "Maine Literary and Theological Association," and was named one of the twenty-one trustees. The institution was established at Waterville and its name afterward changed to Waterville College (now Colby College). In 1814 Merrill moved to Nottingham West (now Hudson), N. H. Seven years later he returned to Sedgwick, of which church he remained pastor until his death. In 1805 he published *Eight Letters on Open Communion,* in 1807 *Letters Occasioned by the Rev. Samuel Worcester's Two Discourses,* and in 1815 a Thanksgiving sermon entitled *Balaam*

Disappointed. He was twice married: on Aug. 14, 1793, to Joanna Colby of Sandown, N. H., who died in three months; and on Oct. 14, 1794, to Susanna Gale, of Salisbury, N. H., by whom he had thirteen children. In appearance Merrill was short and stout. He was an old-fashioned puritan, simple, straightforward, and outspoken, who worshiped the Bible and drew a very distinct line between the saved and the damned.

[G. T. Chapman, *Sketches of the Alumni of Dartmouth Coll.* (1867); Samuel Merrill, "A Merrill Memorial" (1917–28), 2 vols., mimeographed, in Lib. of Cong.; H. S. Burrage, "The Beginnings of Waterville Coll.," *Colls. and Proc. of the Me. Hist. Soc.*, 2 ser., IV (1893); E. C. Whittemore, *Colby Coll., 1820–1925* (1927); W. B. Sprague, *Annals Am. Pulpit*, vol. VI (1860); Joshua Millet, *A Hist. of the Baptists in Me.* (1845).] H. B. P.

MERRILL, GEORGE EDMANDS (Dec. 19, 1846–June 11, 1908), Baptist clergyman, president of Colgate University, was born in Charlestown, Mass., the son of Nathan and Amelia (Edmands) Merrill and a descendant of Nathaniel Merrill, an early emigrant to Massachusetts. His father had been a successful teacher in Portsmouth, Charlestown, and Boston. His mother had a brilliant mind and a keen sense of humor which seem to have been transmitted to her three sons. His father died when George was about ten years of age. An elder half-brother, J. Warren Merrill, of Cambridge, Mass., cared for him and his younger brother, supplying them a home and education. George was graduated from the Cambridge High School in 1865 and from Harvard College in 1869. He was elected to Phi Beta Kappa and was class poet. He spent the next three years in Newton Theological Seminary and was ordained on Oct. 3, 1872. He was pastor of the First Baptist Church in Springfield, Mass. (1872–77), and of the First Baptist Church in Salem, Mass. (1877–85). Failing health demanded rest for an over-worked body, and he spent the summer of 1885 in Europe. In the following November he was compelled to leave the East to regain his broken health and spent five years in Colorado, during which time he steadily recovered. For two years he was pastor of the First Baptist Church in Colorado Springs. He returned to New England in 1890 to become pastor of the Immanuel Baptist Church of Newton, Mass. From there he was called to the presidency of Colgate University at Hamilton, N. Y., in 1901. Here he achieved honor and rendered a notable service. He gave his life to the work, dying in office there on June 11, 1908.

Merrill was a man of wide interests and varied avocations. He was fond of carpentry and was proficient as an architect. Besides his sermons he wrote many poems, stories, and essays. Among his published books were *The Story of the Manuscripts* (1881); *Crusaders and Captives* (1890); *The Reasonable Christ* (1893); and *The Parchments of the Faith* (1894). He had a keen appreciation and understanding of music and art. In all his pastorates he was successful, but his outstanding achievement was his contribution as president of Colgate University. His plans for that institution included the renovation and remodeling of old buildings, the erection of new buildings, better equipment, a broader curriculum, a larger faculty, a beautified campus, and the organization of a strong body of alumni who should be influential in forming the future policies of the university. He lived long enough to see all of these features of his vision well under way. Merrill was married three times. Florence A. Whittemore accompanied him as a bride to his first pastorate in Springfield. Her early death left him with a baby daughter. On Apr. 5, 1877, he married Carrie A. Beebe, who died during his pastorate in Salem. On Sept. 19, 1882, he married Emma M. Bateman of Springfield, who with his daughter Elinor survived him.

[*Who's Who in America*, 1908–09; *The Inauguration of the Rev. Geo. Edmands Merrill, D.D., as President of Colgate Univ.* (1901); *The Colgate Univ. Centennial Celebration, 1819–1919* (1920); Samuel Merrill, "A Merrill Memorial" (1917–28), 2 vols., mimeographed, in Lib. of Cong.; *Tenth Report of the Class of 1869 of Harvard Coll.* (1908); article in *N. Y. Educ.*, May 1899; the *Utica Observer*, June 12, 1908; the *Watchman* (Boston), June 18, 1908; information as to certain facts from Miss Elinor Merrill.] F. H. A.

MERRILL, GEORGE PERKINS (May 31, 1854–Aug. 15, 1929), geologist, was born at Auburn, Me., one of seven children, and died there suddenly at the age of seventy-five while on his way to collect beryl crystals. His father, Lucius Merrill, a carpenter and cabinet maker, was a descendant of Nathaniel Merrill, a settler of old Newbury, Mass., in 1635, who traced his ancestry to the Huguenot, De Merles, driven out of France after the massacre of St. Bartholomew's Day; his mother, Elizabeth Anne (Jones), was the daughter of the Rev. Elijah Jones, of the First Congregational Church at Minot, Me., and it was this grandfather who influenced Merrill toward science. Prepared in the schools of Auburn, he worked his way through the University of Maine, graduating in 1879 with the degree of B.S. He was married in November 1883 to Sarah Farrington of Portland, Me., to whom were born one son and three daughters. She died in 1894, and in 1900 he married Katherine L. Yancey, of Virginia, who became the mother of one daughter.

As a small boy and as a student Merrill collected natural-history specimens. At college he specialized in chemistry, and after graduating was assistant to Prof. W. O. Atwater [*q.v.*] at Wesleyan University (1879–80). Meeting here America's greatest pioneer in museum administration, G. Brown Goode [*q.v.*], then in charge of the United States National Museum, he was later (1881) given a position on the staff of that Museum, where he remained the rest of his life. He was at first assistant to George W. Hawes, in charge of geology, and was influenced by him to become a geologist. He soon rose to the rank of curator (1887) and finally to that of head curator (1897). Under his care the department of geology and paleontology grew from insignificant size to include one of the great collections of the world.

Aside from this work of organization, Merrill was a pioneer in research along three lines: on building stones and the processes of rock-weathering, on meteorites, and on the history of American physical geology. His most widely known book, *Stones for Building and Decoration* (1891, with subsequent editions, 1897, 1903), treats of the building stones of the United States, their physical and chemical properties and weathering qualities. The volume that gave him an international reputation was, however, *A Treatise on Rocks, Rock-weathering and Soils* (1897). The first book of its kind, it is the source from which American textbooks on soils have drawn their materials, and its contribution to scientific agriculture is beyond estimate. A third book, *Non-metallic Minerals* (1904, 2nd ed., 1910), is a classic in its field.

In later life, his chief interest lay in meteorites, "the chips of other worlds." He built up at Washington the sixth most important collection of these celestial bodies, and described the microstructure of forty new falls. Meteorites, he concluded, are a result of explosive activity. The stony meteorites he was at first inclined to regard as the solidified molten drops of a "fiery rain" or world-making mist, but later he gave up this idea and held that they were originally tuffaceous or volcanic in character and that they owe their crystalline condition, where such exists, to "heat and pressure in a non-oxidizing or even reducing atmosphere" ("On Chondrules and Chondritic Structure in Meteorites," *Proceedings of the National Academy of Sciences,* 1920, vol. VI). Detailed by the Smithsonian Institution in 1906 to study the so-called Coon Butte or Meteor Crater in Arizona, a crater-like hole 4,000 feet in diameter and 600 feet deep, about the origin of which there were conflicting opinions, Merrill concluded that it was formed by the impact of a huge meteorite, which plowed deeply into the underlying water-bearing Coconino sandstone and converted its moisture into steam, with a resulting explosion which might well have disrupted the meteor and built up the crater rim.

As pioneer historian of American physical geology, Merrill published three books that portray the rise of this science in North America up to the close of the nineteenth century. These are "Contributions to the History of American Geology" in *Annual Report of the Board of Regents of the Smithsonian Institution: Report of the United States National Museum, 1904,* published in 1906; *Contributions to a History of American State Geological and Natural History Surveys* (Bulletin 109, United States National Museum, 1920), and *The First One Hundred Years of American Geology* (1924). He was the author of numerous encyclopedia articles and wrote many of the sketches of geologists for the *Dictionary of American Biography,* to which he also contributed invaluable counsel. His complete bibliography includes more than two hundred titles. From 1893 to 1916 he was professor of geology and mineralogy at George Washington University. He was elected to the National Academy of Sciences in 1922, and in that same year received its J. Lawrence Smith gold medal.

Physically, Merrill was tall and sturdy, with sandy hair and keen blue eyes. Alert and active, he was always occupied, possessing, in addition to his scientific bent, a love for poetry and music. Always critical and reserved, he was nevertheless fond of humor and apt quotation. In science he was rarely speculative, preferring, as he said in James Dwight Dana's words, to be "always afloat in regard to opinions in geology."

[Samuel Merrill, "A Merrill Memorial" (1917–28), 2 vols., mimeographed, in Lib. of Cong.; Marcus Benjamin, "George Perkins Merrill," *Am. Jour. Sci.,* Oct. 1929; J. H. Benn, in *Science,* Aug. 2, 1929; O. C. Farrington, "Tribute," in *Bull. Geol. Soc. of America,* Mar. 1930; Charles Schuchert, "George Perkins Merrill," *Ann. Report . . . Smithsonian Inst. . . . 1930* (1931); *Bull. Geol. Soc. of America,* Mar. 1931, with complete bibliography; *Portland Press Herald,* Aug. 16, 1929.]

C. S.

MERRILL, JAMES CUSHING (Mar. 26, 1853–Oct. 27, 1902), army surgeon and ornithologist, was born in Cambridge, Mass., the son of James Cushing and Jane (Hammond) Merrill and a descendant of Nathaniel Merrill, an early settler in Massachusetts. Following preliminary studies in his native town he spent some time in Dresden and other German schools. His medical education was obtained at the University of Pennsylvania where he graduated in 1874. His graduation thesis was entitled *Anomalies of Human Osteology.* In 1875 he was appointed assistant surgeon in the United States army and for the following twenty years he served in posts in the West and Southwest. During this period he developed into one of the best-known naturalists of the country. He made extensive studies of the fauna of Texas, Oregon, Idaho, and what is now Oklahoma. He was primarily interested in birds, but he made collections of insects, mammals, and fishes, most of which he contributed to the collections of the National Museum. He was an active member of the American Ornithologists' Union, attended its first Congress in 1883, and for twenty years he was one of the leading American contributors to the literature of ornithology. His "Notes on the Ornithology of Southern Texas," published in the *Proceedings of the United States National Museum* (vols. I and II, 1879–80), was the result of two years' observation of birds in and around Fort Brown, Tex. "Notes on the Birds of Fort Klamath, Oregon," was published in the *Auk* (April, July, October 1888), and "Notes on the Birds of Fort Sherman, Idaho," in the same journal (October 1897, January 1898). He made many interesting contributions to *Forest and Stream* and other publications of a popular nature. He also wrote an article, "On the Habits of the Rocky Mountain Goat," for the *Proceedings* of the National Museum for 1879 (vol. II, 1880).

In the meantime Merrill had reached the grade of major and in 1897 he was named to succeed Col. David L. Huntington as librarian of the Library of the Surgeon-General in Washington. He occupied this position for five years, giving to medical bibliography the same enthusiasm that he had spent on nature study. He edited volumes III to VII of the second series of the *Index Catalogue of the Library of the Surgeon-General's Office.* Merrill was singularly well fitted for his work as librarian. He read thirteen languages and was adding Russian at the time of his death. During this time, however, his health gradually broke down and he was a semi-invalid for a year or more before his death at his home in Washington. He was tall and slender, alert and active in movement, and always scrupulously well dressed. To a distinguished appearance he added an attractive personality which gave him a host of friends. In his western days he developed into an ardent hunter of big game. In this connection he formed a friendship with President Theodore Roosevelt, who speaks of Merrill's prowess in his *Hunting the Grisly and Other Sketches* (1900). While in Washington he found diversion in duck shooting at the Dedlo Island Hunting Club.

[Sources include: *The Alumni Reg., Univ. of Pa.,* Feb. 1903; H. A. Kelly and W. L. Burrage, *Am. Medic. Biogs.* (1920); Samuel Merrill, "A Merrill Memorial" (1917–28), 2 vols., mimeographed, in Lib. of Cong.; *Proc. of the Washington Acad. of Sci.,* vol. V (1903–04); the *Auk,* Jan. 1903; *Boston Medic. and Surgic. Jour.,* Jan. 22, 1903; the *Evening Star* (Washington, D. C.), Oct. 28, 1902.] J. M. P.

MERRILL, JAMES GRISWOLD (Aug. 20, 1840–Dec. 22, 1920), pastor and educator, was born in Montague, Mass., the son of the Rev. James Hervey and Lucia (Griswold) Merrill and a descendant of Nathaniel Merrill, an early emigrant to Massachusetts. In 1863 he received the degree of A.B. from Amherst, then studied for a year in Princeton Theological Seminary, then transferred to Andover Theological Seminary, where he graduated in 1866. On Oct. 11, 1866, he married Louisa W. Boutwell of Andover, Mass. In January 1867 he was ordained a minister of the Congregational Church and was accepted for service by the Congregational Home Mission Society. His first assignment was at Mound City, Kan., where he continued for two years (1866–68). He then went to Topeka, Kan. (1868–69), and for the following three years he was the superintendent of home missions in the state of Kansas. Following this period of service he was in the regular Congregational pastorate for some twenty-two years. From 1872 to 1882 he was at Davenport, Iowa, and during this time he published two volumes of children's sermons. For seven years (1882–89) he was pastor of the First Congregational Church in St. Louis, and for five years (1889–94) of the Payson Memorial Church at Portland, Me.

In 1874 Merrill left the pulpit to become the editor of the *Christian Mirror,* which was subsequently absorbed in the *Congregationalist.* He left editorial work to accept in 1898 the chair of logic and ethics at Fisk University and also became dean of the institution. In 1899, owing to the failing health of Erastus Milo Cravath [*q.v.*], the first president of Fisk, Merrill was named acting president. On the death of Cravath, Merrill was elected president of the university and served in that capacity for seven years (1901–08). Three features characterize his service in that institution. He put the finances of the university on a more substantial basis by raising a building and endowment fund; he confirmed the policy of the institution in having a bi-racial faculty, a policy which has been an important contributing factor in the growth of the University, and he was instrumental in helping to create a very wide-spread interest in the work of the "Fisk Jubilee Singers." He contributed the chapter on Fisk University to a volume entitled *From Servitude to Service* (1905). He was honored by the National Congregational Council (1907) at Cleveland, Ohio, by being elected first assistant moderator of that body. Primarily owing to the failing health of his wife, in 1908 he resigned as president of Fisk University but continued his active interest in the University by service on the board of trustees during the remainder of his life. On leaving Fisk, for three years (1909–12) he was pastor at Somerset, Mass., and following that for five years (1912–17) was pastor at Lake Helen, Fla. In 1917 he retired from active work and spent the remaining three years of his life at Winter Park, Fla., Andover, Mass., and Mountain Lakes, N. J. He died at Mountain Lakes, in his eighty-first year and was buried at Andover, Mass.

[Sources include: W. L. Montague, ed., *Biog. Record of the Alumni of Amherst Coll. . . . 1821–71* (1883); Samuel Merrill, "A Merrill Memorial" (1917–28), 2 vols., mimeographed, in Lib. of Cong.; *Who's Who in America*, 1920–21; files of the *Christian Mirror* and the *Congregationalist*, especially the latter for Jan. 6, 1921; files of the *Nashville Banner*, especially June 10, 1901; files of the *Nashville Tennessean*, especially June 10, 1908; *Fisk University Herald*, vol. VIII, p. 1, vol. XIX, pp. 6–11; catalogues of Fisk University, 1901–08.] O. E. B.

MERRILL, JOSHUA (Oct. 6, 1820–Jan. 15, 1904), chemist and pioneer oil refiner, was born at Duxbury, Mass., the sixth child and fourth son of Abraham Dow Merrill and his first wife, Nancy (Morrison) Merrill. On his father's side he was descended in the eighth generation from Nathaniel Merrill who settled in Newbury, Mass., in 1635, and on his mother's from John Morrison who emigrated from Scotland to Londonderry, N. H., around 1720. His grandfather, Joshua Merrill, served in the War of 1812, and his father was a successful Methodist minister, who served charges in Massachusetts, Rhode Island, and Vermont. Merrill's formal education, which he received in the grammar school at Lowell, was short, for he left school at the age of fifteen to work for an elder brother who was engaged in Boston in the manufacture of paper hangings. During the next few years he was employed by both Luther Atwood and Samuel Downer [*q.v.*], oil merchants, who were to become pioneers in the development of mineral oils. In 1852 the first coal-oil made for sale in the United States was produced by Luther Atwood and manufactured as a lubricant by the United States Chemical Company at Waltham. This product was known as "Coup Oil," and Merrill was engaged in 1853 to introduce it to the market. He continued in this capacity after Downer secured control of the company in 1854. In 1856 George Miller & Company of Glasgow, Scotland, appealed to Downer for assistance in the manufacture of coal tar, and Luther Atwood and Joshua Merrill were sent to aid in the erection of a factory. While in Scotland they discovered new methods of obtaining oil from coal and succeeded in purifying it of its offensive odor. This opened up the possibility of hydro-carbon oils for illumination, and Atwood and Merrill, who had gone to Scotland to manufacture lubricating oil, returned to manufacture illuminants. In the years following 1856 Merrill carried on ceaseless experiments in the production of both lubricants and illuminants from a hydro-carbon base, manufacturing them from Trinidad asphaltum, Cuban chapapote bitumin, and particularly, in the years 1857 and 1858, from albertite, a bituminous coal obtained from Albert County, New Brunswick.

While Merrill and his associates were in the midst of their experiments with albertite, turning out large quantities of various kinds of hydro-carbon oils, and rapidly developing the business into a position where it was endangering the prestige of whale and sperm oil, there came the news of the discovery of petroleum in Pennsylvania. Downer reorganized his business into the Downer Kerosene Company and set out for the oil regions to insure a supply of raw materials, while Merrill and his assistants turned their talents to the problem of refining the new product. After the trying experiences which he had encountered with albertite and other bituminous products, he found the problems of refining petroleum relatively easy, especially after Luther Atwood's process of distillation, known as "cracking," was successfully applied to the new material. Many of the most important technological processes and discoveries in the early days of the oil business were worked out in the laboratories of the Downer Kerosene Oil Company. Among these should be particularly noted Merrill's invention in 1869 of a method of distilling by steam at so low a temperature that the partial decomposition, which usually takes place in oil distillation at high temperature, might be avoided, thereby producing less odorous paraffine lubricating oils (patent no. 90,284, May 18, 1869). In 1869 also Joshua patented a rosin oil and in 1870 Rufus S. Merrill received a patent (no. 100,915) which was assigned to his brothers, Joshua and William, for a process and burner for "the production of light from heavy hydro-carbons." So important was the work carried on in the Downer company that a reliable expert said in 1872 that he found it "generally acknowledged" that to Merrill "more than to any one else, belongs the honor of bringing this manufacture to its present advanced state" and that "an account of his labors and discoveries in this connection would provide a nearly complete history of the art" (Hayes, *post,* p. 7). When Downer disposed of much of his interest in the company in 1871, Merrill and his three brothers took over the management and Joshua became president. He was also senior partner in the firm of Joshua Merrill & Son, dealers in petroleum. For almost half a century Merrill was a generous benefactor of the Tremont Street Methodist Episcopal Church, and one of the most prominent Methodist laymen of Boston, serving for many years as president of the Boston Wesleyan Association and as trustee of Boston University. He married on June 13, 1849, Amelia S. Grigg, who with three daughters and one son survived him.

[For biographical and genealogical details see: Samuel Merrill, "A Merrill Memorial" (1917–28), 2 vols., mimeographed, in Lib. of Cong.; *Biog. Encyc. of Mass. of the Nineteenth Century,* II (1883), 442–47; *Boston Transcript,* Jan. 15, 1904. On his contributions to the oil industry see: S. D. Hayes, *On the Hist. and Manuf. of Petroleum Products: A Memoir, Communicated to the Soc. of Arts, Mass. Inst. of Technol., Mar. 14, 1872*; Merrill's account of his work in *The Derrick's Hand-Book of Petroleum: A Complete Chronological and Statistical Rev. of Petroleum Developments from 1859 to 1898* (1898), pp. 880–90; *Ann. Report of the Commissioner of Patents,* 1869–71.] H. U. F.

MERRILL, SAMUEL (Oct. 29, 1792–Aug. 24, 1855), Indiana official, was the second of nine sons of Jesse and Priscilla (Kimball) Merrill of Peacham, Vt. His first American ancestor, Nathaniel Merrill, settled at Newbury, Mass., in 1635. Samuel Merrill attended an academy at Peacham and studied for a year, 1812–13, as a sophomore at Dartmouth College. He then taught school and studied law for three years at York, Pa. In 1816 he settled at Vevay, Switzerland County, Ind., in the next year was admitted to the bar, and soon took his place as an active member of the community. Appointed tax assessor, he made the round of the county on foot for necessary economy; he was a contractor in the erection of a stone jail; superintendent of a town Sunday school started as early as 1817; and a representative of the county in the General Assemblies of 1819–20, 1820–21, and 1821–22. The General Assembly elected him state treasurer on Dec. 14, 1822, and he held the office for four terms, till 1834. In 1824 he moved the state offices from Corydon to Indianapolis, one wagon sufficing for all the records and money. It took eleven or twelve days to cover the distance (125 miles by present highways); the road through the wilderness was impassable in some places, and a new way had to be cut through the woods.

He lived henceforth at the capital. In the absence of teachers, he personally conducted a school; he acted for a time as captain of the first military company, served as a commissioner for the erection of the state capitol building, which was finished in 1835, was an early president of the Temperance Society, a manager of the State Colonization Society, a trustee of Wabash College, and the second president of the Indiana Historical Society, 1835–48. He was active in the organization of the Second Presbyterian Church (New School) and an intimate friend of Henry Ward Beecher during his pastorate. On Jan. 30, 1834, the General Assembly elected him president of the State Bank of Indiana. In this capacity he personally examined each of the thirteen branches twice a year. An excellent law and the efficient service of such officers as Merrill, Hugh McCulloch, and J. F. D. Lanier [*qq.v.*] combined to develop one of the best of all the state banks. After two terms in the office, Merrill was replaced by the choice of a Democratic legislature. From 1844 to 1848 he was president of the Madison & Indianapolis Railroad, during which time it was completed to Indianapolis. He spent the next two years compiling a third edition of the *Indiana Gazetteer* and in 1850 he bought Hood and Noble's bookstore, which later, under the name of the Merrill Company, undertook some publishing and eventually entered into the Bowen-Merrill (now the Bobbs-Merrill) publishing company. He also, with others, constructed a mill on Fall Creek.

On Apr. 12, 1818, Merrill married Lydia Jane Anderson of Vevay, daughter of Capt. Robert and Catherine (Dumont) Anderson. Ten children were born to them. After his wife's death in 1847, he was married, second, to Elizabeth Douglas Young, of Madison, Ind. Throughout his life he was the personification of traditional New England Puritanism: conscientious, industrious, and devout. He is said to have read the entire Bible every year after he reached the age of twelve. The square-cut features, tightly-closed lips, and clean-shaven face shown in most of his portraits reveal a sober, straightforward, uncompromising character. A bitter, twenty-four-page pamphlet which he published in 1827 attacking Gov. James Brown Ray illustrates the thoroughness with which he performed "an unpleasant task." During the existence of the Whig party, he adhered to it—with a strong anti-slavery leaning—and was an active party worker. He died in Indianapolis and was buried in Greenlawn Cemetery, though his remains were subsequently removed to Crown Hill Cemetery.

[Unpublished memoirs of Mrs. John L. (Jane Merrill) Ketcham; Samuel Merrill, "A Merrill Memorial" (1917–28), 2 vols., mimeographed, in Lib. of Cong.; *Ind. Mag. of Hist.*, Mar. 1916; Perret Dufour, *The Swiss Settlement of Switzerland County, Ind.* (1925); G. I. Read, *Encyc. of Biog. of Ind.* (1899); J. H. B. Nowland, *Early Reminiscences of Indianapolis* (1870); J. P. Dunn, *Ind. and Indianans*, vol. I (1919).]

C. B. C.

MERRILL, SELAH (May 2, 1837–Jan. 22, 1909), Congregational clergyman, archeologist, consul, was born at Canton Center, Hartford County, Conn. His parents, Daniel Merrill and Lydia (Richards), sprang from old New England stock; an ancestor, Nathaniel Merrill (or Merrell, as the name was then spelled), is known to have been at Newbury, Mass., in 1635. After preparing for college at Westfield, Mass., as well as at Williston Seminary, Easthampton, Merrill entered Yale with the class of 1863, but left college before graduation to study at the Yale Divinity School. In 1864 he was ordained as a Congregational minister, and was appointed chaplain of the 49th United States Infantry, a colored regiment, with which he served at Vicksburg, 1864–65. After the war he preached in Le Roy, N. Y., 1866–67, San Francisco, 1867–68, and Salmon Falls, N. H., 1870–72.

Though he received the honorary degree of A.M. from Yale "for special services in Biblical learning," and spent two years (1868–70) at the University of Berlin, his lack of an adequate academic training was later to affect the value of his work very seriously. His interest in the Holy Land was whetted by an extended tour through Egypt, Palestine, and Syria, in 1869, but it was not until 1874 that his archeological career began. Before it was well under way he had been thrice married: first, Mar. 15, 1866, to Fanny Lucinda Cooke, who died the following year; then, Sept. 16, 1868, to Phila (Wilkins) Fargo, who died in 1870; and on Apr. 27, 1875, to Adelaide Brewster Taylor, a direct descendant of Elder Brewster of the *Mayflower.*

In 1870 a large group of American scholars launched the American Palestine Exploration Society, formally organized the following year. In 1873 an expedition was sent to Palestine to carry out a geographical and archeological survey of Eastern Palestine (Transjordan), parallel to the Survey of Western Palestine which had just been begun by the English Palestine Exploration Fund, but the expedition was a total failure, both from the standpoint of cartography and from that of archeology. In 1874–75 a new expedition was organized, with Col. J. C. Lane as leader and Merrill as archeologist. After an initial trip into Eastern Palestine Lane saw that the task was too difficult for the limited resources of the society, and resigned, whereupon it was decided to give up any attempt to make a complete survey and to restrict the work to archeological exploration. Merrill was placed in charge of the expedition, and in three extended trips (1876–77) collected a mass of archeological, topographical, and ethnographical data. His most important results were published in popular form in his *East of the Jordan* (London, 1881). Such success as he had was undoubtedly due, in large measure, to his practical ability and his skill in dealing with the natives. He possessed a respectable knowledge of the documentary and philological material, and indeed surpassed his English colleagues of the Palestine Exploration Fund in this respect. Had he been able to follow in the footsteps of Edward Robinson, the founder of the scientific study of Palestinian geography, and to combine a sound European philological and critical training with his New England endurance and practicality, his work might easily have been epoch-making.

After two years as teacher of Hebrew in the Andover Theological Seminary, he secured appointment as American consul at Jerusalem, a position which he occupied during all the Republican administrations from 1882 to 1907, his tenure being interrupted only by Cleveland's two terms. He took his duties very seriously, and administered his post efficiently, as might be expected from a man of his practical bent. Being, however, a man of strong prejudices, he became involved in a most unfortunate feud with the American religious community founded by Spafford and generally called "The American Colony." He was also drawn into an attack on the authenticity of the Holy Sepulchre, in which he took a narrow Puritan attitude, as may be seen from his big book, *Ancient Jerusalem* (copyright 1908), a work almost entirely devoted to the problem of the ancient northern walls of the city and their relation to the site of the Holy Sepulchre. Aside from his prejudiced approach and the lack of critical training which the book manifests, it was a most useful production, anticipating some much more recent discoveries and conclusions. While consul in Jerusalem, he aided greatly in the establishment and later success of the American School of Oriental Research, founded in 1900. After retiring from his post at Jerusalem, he was appointed consul at Georgetown, British Guiana (1907–08), and only two years later he died, near East Oakland, Cal.

In addition to his two important works, mentioned above, Merrill also published *Galilee in the Time of Christ* (1881), *Greek Inscriptions Collected in the Countries East of the Jordan* (1885), *The Site of Calvary Identified* (1885), and collaborated in *Picturesque Palestine, Sinai and Egypt* (2 vols., 1881–84), edited by Sir Charles William Wilson. He lectured extensively, and wrote numerous popular articles on Palestine and the Bible; he was also an enthusiastic collector of antiquities, birds, and animals.

[*Annual of Am. Schools of Oriental Research*, vol. VIII (1928); Merrill's own books, especially *East of the Jordan*; Samuel Merrill, "A Merrill Memorial" (1917–28), 2 vols., mimeographed, in Lib. of Cong.; *Congreg. Year-Book*, 1910; *Who's Who in America*, 1908–09; *Congregationalist*, Jan. 30, 1909; *San Francisco Examiner*, Jan. 23, 1909.] W. F. A.

MERRILL, STEPHEN MASON (Sept. 16, 1825–Nov. 12, 1905) Methodist Episcopal bishop and writer, was born near Mount Pleasant, Jefferson County, Ohio, the fifth in a family of eleven children. His father, Joshua, was a farmer and shoemaker of New Hampshire birth and Revolutionary ancestry, descended from Nathaniel Merrill who settled at Newbury, Mass., in 1635; his mother, Rhoda (Crosson), was the daughter of a Revolutionary soldier of Bedford, Pa. Both were plain pioneers, with small school-learning, but characterized by sturdy moral fiber and strict Methodist piety. Stephen grew up in Clermont County, Ohio. His schooling ceased after a term or two in the rural academy at South Salem. He learned his father's trade of shoemaker, but did not stick to his last, for having "experienced religion," after the thorough Methodist manner, he joined the Methodist Society at Greenfield, Ohio, in 1842, and resolutely set about preparing himself to preach the gospel, working at his bench by day and toiling over his books far into the night. In his twentieth year, when he was teaching school, he was licensed to preach. Two weeks before he was twenty-one he was admitted to Ohio Conference on trial and appointed to Georgetown, a "hard-scrabble" circuit of twenty-two preaching places. On July 18, 1848, he married Anna Bellmire, who survived him by only a few days. They had one son.

Ordained deacon in 1849 and elder in 1851, Merrill rode hard circuits, read hard books, and meditated for eleven years. His salary was $216 and "table exercises." Then he was advanced to be pastor of a church, and from that position rose to the captaincy of a district, as presiding elder. In 1859 he was transferred to Kentucky Conference, but in 1863 returned to Ohio Conference. During these years he conquered a tendency to pulmonary disease and acquired rugged health. He also developed unusual gifts as a close student of the doctrines and especially the discipline of his denomination, and won recognition for power of lucid and logical statement in the public forum and in the church press.

Nor was he solely concerned with defending Arminian theology and Methodist polity against polemic Calvinists, Universalists, and others. In that seething ante-bellum period, his sound judgment, deep conviction, and knowledge of constitutional law were thrown into the discussions that sprang up wherever men gathered. Merrill, though not a radical agitator, was against slavery and for the Union. In his first General Conference (1868) he made his reputation as a Methodist leader, when his unanswerable argument defeated the popular project for admitting laymen to the Methodist legislature without duly amending the constitution. The General Conference was so impressed with his ability, "mental equipoise, mastery of constitutional principle and clearness of expression" that it elected him, though a new-comer, to the editorship of the *Western Christian Advocate* (Cincinnati). After four years in the editorial chair, where he gave ample demonstration of his intellectual resources, he was elected a bishop (1872). For eight years he resided in St. Paul, Minn. He was then assigned to Chicago, where he made his headquarters thereafter. In 1904 he retired from active duty at his own request, and died suddenly the following year while on a visit in Keyport, N. J.

Merrill's talents were rather solid than showy, and he had not the imaginative qualities essential to popularity as a preacher or occasional orator. He was no revivalist or stump speaker, but his power of massive argument, which his admirers likened to that of Daniel Webster, bore down all opposition. His knowledge of Methodist law was encyclopedic, and all his resources were at instant call. Physically he was tall and gaunt, with head of unusual size and the features of a Roman senator. He had a voice whose heavy tones were under complete control, and he pursued the course of his thought to its conclusion unruffled by contrary argument. As a bishop his calm judgment and dispassionate attachment to known principles of law made him a useful counselor. Only one man, Joshua Soule [*q.v.*], is rated his superior as an expounder of the Methodist constitution. In 1888 Merrill wrote the Episcopal Address to the General Conference, out of which came in substance those sections of the present constitution of the Methodist Episcopal Church which treat of the composition, powers, and limitations of the General Conference. He shone as a parliamentarian, and was a model presiding officer. In his handling of men in the appointive function of the episcopacy he was wise, sympathetic, and just. His quiet humor eased many difficult situations. His most valuable book was *A Digest of Methodist Law* (1885). Other works included: *Christian Baptism* (1876); *The New Testament Idea of Hell* (1878); *The Second Coming of Christ* (1879); *Aspects of Christian Experience* (copyright 1882); *Outline Thoughts on Prohibition* (1886); *The Organic Union of American Methodism* (1892); *Mary of Nazareth and Her Family* (1895); *The Crisis of This World* (1896); *Sanctification* (1901); *Atonement* (copyright 1901); *Discourses on Miracles* (copyright 1902).

[R. J. Cooke, "Bishop Stephen Mason Merrill," *Meth. Rev.*, May 1907; *Western Christian Advocate*, Sept. 2, 1896; *Christian Advocate* (N. Y.), Sept. 17, 1896; autobiographical statement in *Journal of the Twenty-fourth Delegated Gen. Conf. of the Meth. Episc. Ch.* (1904); *Minutes of the Ann. Conferences of the Meth. Episc. Ch., 1846–51* (1854); Samuel Merrill, "A Merrill Memorial" (1917–28), 2 vols., mimeographed, in Lib. of Cong.; J. B. Doyle, *20th Century Hist. of Steubenville and Jefferson County, Ohio* (1910); *N. Y. Daily Tribune*, Nov. 14, 1905.]

J. R. J.

MERRILL, STUART FITZRANDOLPH (Aug. 1, 1863–Dec. 1, 1915), poet, was born at Hempstead, L. I., the eldest of three children. His father, George Merrill, a lawyer in New York City, came of a New England family. His name was originally Tibbetts, but he was adopted by an uncle by marriage, Nathaniel Wilson Merrill (Samuel Merrill, "A Merrill Memorial," 1917–28, mimeographed copy, in Library of Congress). Stuart's mother, Emma FitzRandolph Laing, was the daughter of William L. Laing of Virginia, who went north with his family about 1840 and settled at Hempstead. Her grandmother is said to have been French. In 1866 George Merrill was appointed counsellor to the American Legation in Paris. He was a man of strict and gloomy religious principles, and he obliged his family to lead in Paris, as far as possible, the same order of life they would have led in a New England village. When Stuart was twelve years old he was sent as a boarder to the Lycée at Vanves, a suburb of Paris. He stayed here till 1879, when he was removed to the Lycée Fontaines (now Condorcet). Here as at Vanves he proved a good scholar and obtained a high rank in his classes. He joined certain of his schoolfellows in starting a little magazine called *Le Fou*. One of the contributors was René Ghil, destined to be a leader of the Symbolist movement and to have some influence on Merrill's development as a poet. Merrill's contributions to the magazine reveal a poetic temperament and prove that he already possessed the technique of French versification.

He took his degree (*bachelier ès lettres*) in 1884. But whatever plans he had made to lead an artist's life in Paris were frustrated by his father who decided that the family must return to New York. There he became a very unwilling student at the Columbia Law School. His main interest was in literature, and in Washington Square, where he lived, he prepared his first book of poems, *Les Gammes*, and sent it to Paris. It was published in 1887 by Léon Vanier, and was dedicated to René Ghil, who saw it through the press, distributed it to the critics, and wrote a notice of it himself.

When he wrote *Les Gammes* and *Les Fastes*, which followed four years after, Merrill was interested only in exteriors and decoration, and for him to accept the noise and turmoil and passion of life at all they must come to him in symbols. It was not till much later that he gave expression to his vision of the world and to the love and anguish of his heart. In these two early books are some poems which he never surpassed. The influence of English poetry, which may be remarked in them, came principally from William Morris' "Defence of Guenevere," and in a much less degree from Rossetti and Swinburne and Wilde. Morris was Merrill's ideal man, and Morris' brand of socialism, with artistic beauty as a cure for all ills, Merrill kept all his life, though in his later years it became tinged with Tolstoyism. The youth of twenty had arrived in New York with his socialist convictions already strong. He campaigned for Henry George, and took up the defense of the eight Chicago anarchists condemned to death in 1886. Merrill's devotion to Henry George provoked his father to disinherit him; if he enjoyed easy financial circumstances all his life, he thenceforth owed it to his mother.

George Merrill died in 1888. The next year Mrs. Merrill and her sons went to Europe. From Vienna Stuart sent to America the only book he ever wrote in English, *Pastels in Prose* (1890), translations of short pieces by twenty-three French writers. The volume doubtless owed such trifling sale as it had to the preface by W. D. Howells. In the autumn of 1890 he returned to America to please his mother. On the way home he spent some weeks in London, where he came to know Oscar Wilde, then at the height of his fame. Their friendship continued till Wilde's downfall in 1895.

Merrill remained only five months in New York. Here he prepared his new book, *Les Fastes*, which was published in Paris at the end of

1891 with a dedication to Howells. During this winter he was an unfailing attendant upon Wagnerian opera. Wagner was one of the great influences of his life, as he was for most of the Symbolists. Another great influence was Walt Whitman. With him Merrill had an interview at a New York hotel. Whitman's humanitarian theory, his respect for individual freedom, Merrill entirely adopted. He returned to Paris in May 1891, and became one of the managers of the New Théâtre d'Art, founded as a protest against the commercial and realist theatres. He was back again in New York in the autumn, but in 1892 left America for the last time. As he was sailing, a letter from Howells was put into his hands, urging him to be an American poet and to write in English. Merrill did write some verses in English, but they have none of his special merits.

Upon his return to Paris, he fell in love with an artists' model known to her friends of the Latin Quarter as "Bob," and she became his wife in all but name. He now furnished an apartment on the Quai Bourbon which became famous in the annals of Symbolism, for therein gathered many of the young writers and painters. He began to lead the life of a poet of the Latin Quarter, and whenever this life became too much for him he retired to the country or traveled; fashionable social life he sedulously avoided. He lost all contact with America and in his later years had almost the same views about the United States as a Frenchman who has never been there. He had a house at Marlotte in the Forest of Fontainebleau. There he wrote *Petits Poèmes d'Automne* (1895) and *Les Quatre Saisons* (1900), which show a complete alteration in his conception of poetry and poetic expression.

In 1905 the woman who had lived with him so many years left him to marry another man. This departure threw Merrill into a state of demoralization. He cut himself off from general life. For some time he was hardly ever sober. He traveled at random. But out of this morbid condition arose his greatest work, *Une Voix dans la Foule* (1909). The section called *"Les Cris dans la Nuit"* contains some of the best poetry of the kind in French literature. Here he made what is perhaps the most stirring appeal for the wretched which had been heard in France since Victor Hugo. Pity for all who suffered had become the keynote of his life.

His wanderings took him to Belgium where he was extremely well received by the young writers, who regarded him as a master. He made the acquaintance of a family named Rion, who lived at Forêt, a suburb of Brussels, and in the summer of 1908 he married Claire Rion, who was about eighteen years old. After traveling for a while they settled permanently at Versailles in a beautiful house at 22 Boulevard de Roi. After his marriage Merrill published little, but his papers show that he had many projects, and he kept up a considerable correspondence with his friends. In 1913 he engaged in an unfortunate controversy with Guillaume Apollinaire concerning the morals of Walt Whitman, in which he made ferocious onslaughts on puritanism (*Mercure de France,* 16 avril, 16 novembre 1913).

The World War was the second crisis in his life, and this time he did not recover. It is necessary to realize Merrill's idealism, his dreams of human fraternity, to understand what the war meant to him. He thought of joining the French army, but his state of health made that impossible. He aided as he could several whom the war had reduced to misery, and wandered inconsolably in Versailles and Paris. The sight of the funeral of a British soldier at Versailles inspired his poem "Tommy Atkins," an entirely new expression of his art, which was published after his death, which occurred rather suddenly on Dec. 1, 1915. He had left instructions that he was to be buried without religious ceremonies.

In 1925 appeared *Prose et Vers,* an interesting volume containing some of his prose sketches and criticism and some hitherto unpublished poems. A great many of his prose contributions to magazines have never been reprinted. In 1929 a memorial tablet was placed on the outer wall of his house in Versailles, and the same year the Paris municipality gave the name of the American poet to a wide street near the Porte Champerret—*Place Stuart Merrill.*

Merrill performed the incredibly difficult feat of wringing out of French versification the soft far-away music of the English Pre-Raphaelites. More than any other he produced the nearest thing in words to Debussy's music. His amiable personality has become a legend. Not long before his death the great Belgian poet Verhaeren wrote to him: "For me you are as a flame and a glowing hearth at which I warm my hands." Although he spoke French like a Frenchman and German quite well he was generally recognized as an American.

[Marjorie Louise Henry, *Stuart Merrill* (Paris, 1927), written in French by an American, the chief authority on the subject; *Poètes d'Aujourd'hui* (1900), ed. by Adolphe Van Bever and Paul Léautaud, biographical notice by Léautaud; *Commemoration de Stuart Merrill à Versailles* (Paris, 1929), containing reminiscences by friends; Remy de Gourmont, *Promenades Littéraires 4me Série* (1912), and *Le Livre des Masques*

(1896); René Ghil, *Les Dates et les Œuvres* (1923); Ernest Raynaud, *La Mêlée Symboliste* (1918), André Barré, *Le Symbolisme* (1911), André Fontainas, *Mes Souvenirs du Symbolisme* (1928), and other books on the Symbolist period; scattered articles on Merrill in French magazines: by Charles Maurras in *Revue Encyclopédique*, Jan. 22, 1898, by Pierre Quillard in *Mercure de France*, Oct. 16, 1909, and many others listed in the bibliog. to Henry's *Stuart Merrill*; *Mercure de France*, Jan. 1, 1916, and July 15, 1929; T. B. Rudmose-Brown, *French Lit. Studies* (London, 1917); private information. V. O.

MERRILL, WILLIAM BRADFORD (Feb. 27, 1861–Nov. 26, 1928), newspaper editor and manager, descended from Nathaniel Merrill who settled at Newbury, Mass., in 1635, was born at Salisbury, N. H., the son of the Rev. Horatio Merrill, a Congregationalist minister, and Sarah Bradford (Whitman) Merrill. He studied at the Boston Latin School, 1874–76, preparing for Harvard, but instead of entering that institution he went to Paris, where he finished his education, devoting especial attention to art. While in Paris he wrote news letters for Philadelphia papers and on his return to the United States he took up newspaper work in Philadelphia, becoming a reporter for the *North American.* Within a year he was made its telegraph editor, despite his youth, and in another year became its dramatic critic. He gave up newspaper work for a time to make a study of American railroads, which took him into every part of the country and gave him an insight into railroad finance which was useful to him later, although the resulting publication, *Guide to Railways of the United States* (1881), was of temporary value only.

Returning to journalism, he became at the age of twenty-three managing editor of the Philadelphia *Press.* In a few years he developed to a marked degree the scope of the *Press* as a powerful and enterprising newspaper, gathering around him a staff of unusual efficiency, one of whose members was Richard Harding Davis [*q.v.*]. His success in Philadelphia attracted attention and at the age of thirty years he was called to be managing editor of the *New York Press,* being the youngest managing editor in the city which was the center of American journalism.

Merrill's versatility developed rapidly. His grasp included the problems of a publisher as well as those of an editor and in 1895 he became financial manager of the *Press.* In 1901 he transferred his services to the New York *World* and was made managing editor of the paper, then under the active control of Joseph Pulitzer. Later he became financial manager of the *World,* in which capacity he attracted the attention of William Randolph Hearst, who engaged him in 1908 as manager of the *New York American.* In 1917 he became general manager of all the Hearst papers, which was said to have been the fulfilment of an early ambition he had formed to be the director of a number of newspapers, at a time when newspaper "chains" did not exist. His favorite maxim was that "vigilance, enterprise and accuracy are the keynote of the successful newspaper," and he impressed that view upon editors and reporters.

As a member of the New York Publishers' Association, in which body he represented the *New York American* and the *New York Evening Journal,* he was active in negotiations with labor unions whose members were employed by newspapers, attaining a reputation for fairness to both sides. At the conclusion of a strike of pressmen, the publishers presented to him a memorial expressive of their appreciation, and the Pressmen's Union made him an honorary member. His zeal was centered intensely upon newspaper work, and only rarely could he be persuaded to take a vacation. A remark which he often made was that "all the rewards of life come in the day's work."

In his early days as a dramatic critic Merrill formed a lasting friendship with Charles and Daniel Frohman. He was one of the first to detect the latent abilities of Theodore Roosevelt and brought him to the attention of Mayor William L. Strong of New York City, who appointed him head of the police board, a stepping stone to his subsequent career.

Merrill continued active in the management of the Hearst papers until failing health caused him to give up work a year before his death. In appearance, he was slender and of medium height, with an expression of keenness and alertness. From his early twenties his hair was almost snow white. He married in 1882 Sara Louise Taylor, of Georgetown, D. C., who died in 1913. In 1922 he married Mrs. Josephine H. Bissell.

[Some information about Merrill may be found in J. K. Winkler's *W. R. Hearst* (1928) and Don C. Seitz's *Joseph Pulitzer, His Life and Letters* (1924). Other sources are *Who's Who in America,* 1928–29; Samuel Merrill, "A Merrill Memorial" (1917–28), 2 vols., mimeographed, in Lib. of Cong.; and the files of newspapers in Philadelphia and New York. A full obituary account prepared by one of his associates appeared in the *N. Y. American* of Nov. 27, 1928.]

A. S. W.

MERRILL, WILLIAM EMERY (Oct. 11, 1837–Dec. 14, 1891), soldier, engineer, was born at Fort Howard, Wis., the son of Capt. Moses E. Merrill and Virginia (Slaughter) Merrill. His father, born in Maine, was of New England ancestry, being descended from Nathaniel Merrill who settled at Newbury, Mass., in 1635; his mother came of an old Virginia family. When William was not quite ten, his father was killed while leading his troops in an attack at the battle of Molino del Rey, Mexico. Because of the father's services, President Pierce, in 1854, appointed the son a cadet at the United States Military Academy. He graduated at the head of his class in 1859 and was assigned to the Corps of Engineers.

Throughout the Civil War he served as a military engineer, first in the Department of the Ohio, subsequently in the Army of the Potomac and the Army of Kentucky, and finally, Jan. 27, 1864, to June 27, 1865, as chief engineer of the Army of the Cumberland. During McClellan's campaign in West Virginia he was captured (Sept. 12, 1861) and was a prisoner until the following February, except for two days in November when he escaped and was recaptured. Wounded in an engagement near Yorktown, Va., in April 1862, he was brevetted captain for gallantry. Subsequently, he served under Pope in the Cedar Mountain and Manassas campaigns, and was then transferred to the West to fortify Covington and Newport (September–October 1862) when threatened by Kirby-Smith's invasion of Kentucky. Promoted captain, Mar. 3, 1863, he served under Rosecrans in the Chickamauga campaign, under Thomas in the battle of Missionary Ridge, and under Sherman in the advance on Atlanta. He was specially charged with the construction of fortifications for the protection of the railways supplying Sherman's army. For his services in the battles of Chickamauga, Lookout Mountain and Missionary Ridge, and Resaca and New Hope Church, he received the brevets of major, lieutenant-colonel, and colonel. His military services closed in 1870 after three years of duty on Sherman's staff as chief engineer of the Division of the Missouri. As a military engineer he was excelled by none.

The second half of his career was devoted mainly to the river and harbor improvement work carried on by the Corps of Engineers. He originated one of the greatest projects for the development of American inland waterways—the canalization of the Ohio River from Pittsburgh to its mouth. In 1870 he was charged with the improvement of this river and in 1878, at his own request, he was sent to Europe to study the improvement of non-tidal rivers by means of locks and movable dams. On his return he advocated this method of improving the Ohio and, after overcoming great opposition, in 1879 succeeded in securing from Congress an appropriation for the Davis Island lock and dam below Pittsburgh. These were completed in 1885 and led to the approval of his project, with some modifications, for the entire river. He lived long enough to build only the first lock and dam; the entire project was not completed until 1929, when the President of the United States took part in the celebration which announced its accomplishment.

In 1870 Merrill published *Iron Truss Bridges for Railroads* and later he published studies of the improvement of non-tidal rivers and of inland navigation in France and the United States. In 1889 he was the United States representative at the Congress of Engineers in Paris. He was married in January 1873 to Margaret Spencer of Cincinnati. Two of their sons became officers of the United States Army.

[G. W. Cullum, *Biog. Reg. Officers and Grads. U. S. Mil. Acad.* (3rd ed., 1891); reports of the Chief of Engineers, U. S. Army, 1874–85, in annual reports of the Secretary of War; *Twenty-second Ann. Reunion Asso. Grads. U. S. Mil. Acad.* (1892); *Proc. Am. Soc. Civil Engineers*, vol. XVIII (1892); Samuel Merrill, "A Merrill Memorial" (1917–28), 2 vols., mimeographed, in Lib. of Cong.; *Army and Navy Jour.*, Dec. 19, 1891; *Cincinnati Enquirer*, Dec. 16, 1891.] G. J. F.

MERRIMON, AUGUSTUS SUMMERFIELD (Sept. 15, 1830–Nov. 14, 1892), jurist, was born at Cherryfields, in Buncombe (now in Transylvania) County, N. C. His father, Branch H. Merrimon, a Methodist minister and farmer, was a native of Virginia; his mother was Mary Paxton of North Carolina. His boyhood, spent in Haywood County, was one of hard labor on the farm and in a sawmill, with limited educational opportunity; but he "studied between the plow handles," and was able later to have more than a year at school in Asheville, serving part of the time as a junior teacher. He then began to study law, and in 1852 married Margaret J. Baird, the daughter of Israel Baird of Buncombe County. Receiving his license in 1853, he began practice at Asheville and was soon made a county attorney. In 1860 he went to the House of Commons and, as a Union Whig, opposed the secession movement, voting against submitting the question of a convention to the people and against all military preparation. After Lincoln's call for troops, however, he voted for calling the secession convention and at once enlisted. In May 1861 he was commissioned captain in the commissary department and was stationed successively at several posts in the state, but when later in that year he was appointed solicitor of a western district he accepted and served until 1865. The position was no sinecure during those years of war, with lawlessness flagrant and sedition common, and the performance of its duties took, perhaps, more courage than those of the field. He filled it with much credit and stanchly upheld the civil authority as superior to military power or to mob rule. He was instrumental in securing the candidacy of Vance for governor in 1862 and supported his administration loyally. In 1865 he was defeated for the "Johnson" convention, but the legislature elected him judge of the superior court. Here his task was perhaps as difficult as during the war, but he again proved his courage, decision, and initiative. He chafed under the interference of the army in judicial matters, and in 1867, when he was ordered to disregard the law and enforce military orders, he resigned, and moving to Raleigh began again the practice of law.

He vigorously opposed congressional reconstruction, cooperating with the Conservative party. For a short time he was chairman of its executive committee and was offered the nomination for governor in 1868, but declined and instead accepted one for associate justice of the supreme court. Defeated, he was quietly active in politics during the next four years. In 1871 he was one of the counsel of the board of managers in the impeachment trial of Gov. William Woods Holden [*q.v.*] and had charge of the examination of witnesses. The following year he was nominated for governor and covered the entire state in his campaign. North Carolina had the first state election that year and both national parties made a determined effort to win, sending their leading men to participate in the contest. Against Merrimon was employed the whole power of the Grant administration as well as that of the state, and, while he drove his opponent from the stump, he was defeated by a small majority.

He was promised by political leaders election to the Senate, but Vance was a candidate and secured the caucus nomination, which some of Merrimon's supporters in the legislature disregarded. After a deadlock both withdrew, but the caucus again nominated Vance, and the Republicans voted with Merrimon's supporters and elected Merrimon. He served until 1879 when he was defeated by Vance, who had, in the meantime, been elected governor. In 1883 Governor Jarvis appointed Merrimon associate justice of the supreme court, and he filled the place until 1889, when he was appointed chief justice. He served in this capacity until his death.

Merrimon was a straightforward, forceful, and magnetic man, a good speaker, and a warmly human person. He was an excellent trial judge and was highly regarded as an appellate judge, although he was in no sense a great one.

[Merrimon's decisions appear in 89–110 *N. C. Reports*. For estimates and biographical material see 111 *N. C. Reports*, 735 and 114 *N. C. Reports*, 930; S. A. Ashe and others, *Biog. Hist. of N. C.*, vol. VIII (1907); *News and Observer* (Raleigh, N. C.), Nov. 15, 16, 1892. See also *N. C. House Journal*, 1860–61; *Congressional Record*, 1873–79; J. G. deR. Hamilton, *Reconstruction in N. C.* (1914).] J. G. deR. H.

MERRITT, ANNA LEA (Sept. 13, 1844–Apr. 7, 1930), painter and etcher, was born in Philadelphia, Pa. The daughter of Joseph and Susanna (Massey) Lea, she was descended through her father from John Lea, a Quaker who came from England to Philadelphia in 1699, and from Andrew Robeson, first chief-justice of Pennsylvania. She was educated privately. At the early age of seven she began the study of drawing under William H. Furness. After leaving school she traveled abroad for four years, and about 1865 she was studying painting under Heinrich Hoffman in Dresden. In 1871 she went to London, where she continued her training under Henry Merritt (see *Dictionary of National Biography*), artist and author, whose interest in his pupil was more than academic, for on Apr. 17, 1877, they were married.

Before this event took place she had begun to exhibit portraits and figure pieces at the Royal Academy, and had received some recognition. When she married she intended to give up her career as an artist, but her husband died soon afterward, and she then resumed painting. She was a fairly regular exhibitor at the Royal Academy exhibitions for nearly thirty years, and sent occasional contributions to exhibitions in Philadelphia and New York. She won a medal at the Centennial Exposition, Philadelphia, 1876; was elected a member of the Royal Society of Painter-Etchers; and wrote a memoir of her husband which was published with selections from his writings in *Henry Merritt: Art Criticism and Romance* (2 vols., London, 1879). She also made a series of twenty-three small etchings as illustrations for the same book. At a later period she etched a number of portraits, her subjects including likenesses of Sir Gilbert Scott, after the original by George Richmond; and Ellen Terry as Ophelia.

Among her more important paintings shown at the Royal Academy were "The Pied Piper of Hamelin," "Eve Overcome by Remorse" (which brought her a medal at the Chicago Exposition of 1893), "Camilla" (which appeared at the Paris exposition of 1889), and "Love Locked Out" (1890), which was purchased by the Chantrey Fund and hung in the National Gallery of British Art, commonly known as the Tate Gallery—the first work by a woman artist to be thus honored. Love, shown as a little boy, stands pushing at a golden door which is barred against him.

After 1890 she made her home in a tiny Hampshire village, Hurstbourne Tarrant. She made this village the theme of a book, illustrated by herself, called *A Hamlet in Old Hampshire* (1902); and her garden there was the subject of a magazine article published in 1908. The summers of 1893 and 1894 were devoted to mural paintings for St. Martin's Church, near Wanersh, Surrey. Another mural painting which she did was the large decoration in the vestibule of the Women's Building at the Chicago Exposition of 1893, for which she was awarded a medal. Her "Piping Shepherd" (1896) was bought by the Pennsylvania Academy of the Fine Arts, Philadelphia. Her portrait of James Russell Lowell belongs to Harvard University. Among other distinguished sitters were Gen. John A. Dix, United States minister to France, Lady Dufferin, General the Earl of Dundonald and Countess Dundonald, and Lord Walter Campbell. The group portrait of two children, Justine and Bayard Cutting, exhibited at the National Academy, New York, 1883, was entitled "Taming the Bird."

Mrs. Merritt was a versatile and accomplished woman; but her work lacks spontaneity. In the case of the etchings this defect is especially noticeable. When her death occurred, in London, she was eighty-five years old and for some time had been blind.

[Autobiographical data in *Henry Merritt . . .* (1879); J. H. and G. H. Lea, *The Ancestry and Posterity of John Lea* (1906), in which Anna Lea's name is given as Anna Massey Lea; K. H. Osbourne, *An Hist. and Geneal. Account of Andrew Robeson* (1916); *Who's Who* (British), 1920; *Who's Who in America*, 1920–21; *Am. Art Rev.*, Apr. 1880; *Art News*, Apr. 12, 1930; *Boston Transcript*, Apr. 9, 1930; the *Times* (London), Apr. 15, 17, 1930.] W. H. D.

MERRITT, ISRAEL JOHN (Aug. 23, 1829–Dec. 13, 1911), wrecker, inventor, eldest child of Hamilton and Elizabeth Merritt, was born in New York City. His father, seventh in descent from Thomas Merritt who came to America in the seventeenth century, was a merchant in moderate circumstances and had every intention of giving his son a good education, but in 1841 he was lost at sea and the boy was compelled to find work in order to help support his widowed mother and her family of children. After doing a number of odd jobs, including driving mules on a canal, Merritt went to sea until he was fifteen, then became associated with Capt. Thomas Bell salvaging wreckage from Long Island Sound and the waters about Manhattan Island. At the age of twenty he obtained command of a coasting schooner and some four years afterward was appointed agent for the Board of Marine Underwriters. In 1860 he became the general agent of the Coast Wrecking Company and from that time on his whole attention was given to salvage. In connection with this work Captain Merritt, as he came to be known, originated and employed many novel ideas and methods which to this day are successfully used by the company which bears his name. His greatest contribution probably was the pontoon patented by him in 1865. This was a specially constructed device for raising sunken vessels by displacement. Making possible the recovery of large vessels sunk with all decks submerged, it completely revolutionized the salvage business. In its various forms the pontoon is still an important and useful adjunct of modern salvage equipment. Merritt continued with the Coast Wrecking Company until 1880, when he organized the Merritt Wrecking Organization, with his eldest son as partner. The new company's operations quickly assumed immense proportions. Its fleet was one of the largest of the kind in the world, doing practically all the marine salvage on the Atlantic Coast. Offices were established in New York with storehouses and docks on Staten Island, and a similar establishment was set up at Norfolk, Va. In 1897 Merritt's organization and the Chapman Company, engaged in derrick and lighterage business about New York, united as the Merritt & Chapman Derrick & Wrecking Company, with Merritt as president and his son as treasurer. Merritt was active at the head of the combined organizations until his death. During the Civil War he took charge of the fitting out of many expeditions with surf boats and served under the secretary of the navy in an advisory capacity. He was for years an active volunteer fireman in New York City, and for many years foreman of Engine No. 17. He was married in March 1853 to Sarah L. Nichols of New York, who died on June 11, 1879. In 1890 he married Caroline Elizabeth Bull. He died in New York, survived by his widow and four children of his former marriage.

[Henry Hall, *America's Successful Men of Affairs*, vol. I (1895); Douglas Merritt, *Revised Merritt Records* (1916), pp. 121, 131; correspondence with Merritt & Chapman Holding Corporation, New York; Patent Office records; *N. Y. Times*, Dec. 15, 1911.] C. W. M.

MERRITT, LEONIDAS (Feb. 20, 1844–May 9, 1926), prospector, discoverer—with his brothers—of the Mesabi iron-ore deposit in Minnesota, was born on a farm in Chautauqua County, N. Y. His parents, Lewis Howell and Hepzibeth (Jewett) Merritt, later moved their family to Warren County, Pa., then to Ohio, and finally, in 1856, shortly after the opening of the canal at Sault Ste. Marie, to Duluth, Minn. They settled on a homestead claim at Oneota, a suburb of Duluth, where the father worked at his trade of millwright and sawyer. Of the ten children, eight sons survived to maturity and of these Alfred, Napoleon, Louis, and Cassius were actively associated with Leonidas in his iron-mining exploits. Although Leonidas, in his later years, was fond of writing narrative poems in the meter made popular by Longfellow's "Hiawatha," his formal education seems to have been limited to attendance upon the common-schools afforded by the frontier community and a brief term at Grand River Institute, Ashtabula, Ohio. In his late teens he enlisted in the Minnesota cavalry for service in the Civil War, and remained in the army through some of the Indian campaigns that followed.

From 1856 until 1890 the family was engaged in the usual pioneer ways of making a living, chiefly in connection with the lumbering industry, though Leonidas and Alfred built a sloop to engage in the carrying trade, wrecked it, worked as lumberman to pay off debts incurred, and built a schooner and operated it. Their most profitable adventures were in timber lands and at times they possessed considerable funds. After the first discovery of rich iron-ore fields in the Lake Superior region, nearly everyone who traversed the woods hoped to discover iron ore and thereby achieve a fortune. Lewis H. Merritt was early convinced that the Mesabi region was rich in iron-ore. Beginning in the seventies, it was repeatedly investigated, but without success because the explorers supposed its deposits would exhibit the same characteristics as those previously discovered, which were found in bold outcrops, whereas they were actually quite different, lying flat, buried beneath the surface. In 1887 the Merritts, who in connection with their work as "timber cruisers" had several times explored the field, made another survey, "running diagonals across the formation and mapping the lines of attraction with a dip-needle" (Van Brunt, *post*, p. 398). Their map conforms closely to later maps of the deposits. Leonidas Merritt filed claims for the land thus located, and in July 1890 the brothers organized the Mountain Iron Company to exploit the Mesabi range.

On Nov. 16 of that year, J. A. Nicols, who with a gang of men was working for Leonidas and Alfred Merritt in depressions, discovered high-grade ore at the bottom of a test pit. Other discoveries followed, and the Merritt family embarked on a program of mining and railroad and ore-dock building that required more capital than their local associates could provide. They therefore sought and secured the participation of John D. Rockefeller, who was shrewd enough to safeguard his own interests carefully, while the Merritts, engaging in enterprises that were of a magnitude entirely beyond their business and financial ability, were not so astute. As a result of the financial crisis of 1893 they lost their control of the mining and transportation enterprises they had initiated. Litigation ensued (1895), and, ultimately (1912), a congressional investigation. Leonidas apparently suffered a mental breakdown, at any rate he was not able to give the congressional committee any clear statement of what happened or even clearly to remember how and why, in 1897, he and some other members of the family transferred their holdings to Mr. Rockefeller for something over $500,000 in order to meet their other obligations. Louis Merritt took advantage of Mr. Rockefeller's offer to permit them to buy back their holdings at the price he paid, plus interest, and became very wealthy through their subsequent appreciation. During his later years Leonidas was commissioner of public utilities (1914–17) and commissioner of finance (1921–25) for the city of Duluth. He died there in May 1926, aged eighty-two years. On May 8, 1873, he had married Elizabeth E. Wheeler of Oneota, Minn. Three children survived him.

[*Who's Who in America*, 1924–25; Walter Van Brunt, *Duluth and St. Louis County, Minn.* (1921), vol. I; *Am. Mag.*, Sept. 1923; *Hearings before the Committee on Investigation of United States Steel Corporation* (8 vols., 1912), esp. III, 1885–1934, for Merritt's testimony; F. T. Gates, *The Truth about Mr. Rockefeller and the Merrits* (1912); Paul de Kruif, *Seven Iron Men* (1929); *Minneapolis Morning Tribune*, May 10, 1926; *Ely Miner* (Ely, Minn.), May 14, 1926.]

T. T. R.

MERRITT, WESLEY (June 16, 1834–Dec. 3, 1910), soldier, seventh in descent from Thomas Merritt who came to America in the seventeenth century, was the fourth of eleven children born to John Willis Merritt and his wife Julia Anne (de Forest). The father was a lawyer, but in 1841, after financial reverses suffered during the crisis of 1837, abandoned his profession, and moved his family West to Illinois. After a few years of farming he turned to journalism, editing the Bellville *Advocate* and then the Salem *Advocate* and eventually being elected to the legislature. Wesley Merritt attended the school of the Christian Brothers and studied law with Judge Haynie in Salem, but when the opportunity came to him, in 1855, entered the United States Military Academy. The appointment had been tendered first to his younger brother, Edward, who did not wish to accept it, and it is the year of Edward's birth that still stands on the army records.

Upon graduation in 1860 Merritt was commissioned second lieutenant of dragoons. The following year, promoted first lieutenant, he served as aide-de-camp to Gen. Philip St. George Cooke [*q.v.*], commanding the cavalry of the Army of the Potomac. He was promoted captain in 1862, and on June 29, 1863, was commissioned brigadier-general of volunteers. He commanded the reserve cavalry brigade at Gettysburg, and received the brevet of major in the regular establishment for bravery there. Following continuous service in Virginia, he was brevetted major-general of volunteers in 1864, and commissioned in the same rank in 1865. In the meantime he was successively brevetted lieutenant-colonel, colonel, brigadier-general and major-general, United States Army, for meritorious services. He was present at Appomattox, then became chief of cavalry in the Department of Texas, and was mustered out of the voluntary service Feb. 1, 1866, resuming his regular rank. Later that year he became lieutenant-colonel, 9th Cavalry, and ten years later colonel, 5th Cavalry. Until 1879 his service was principally in the West in connection with Indian disturbances.

From Sept. 1, 1882, to June 30, 1887, he was superintendent of the United States Military Academy. Commissioned brigadier-general Apr. 10, 1887, he assumed command of the Department of the Missouri in July. He later commanded the Department of Dakota, and then the Department of the Missouri, with headquarters at Chicago from 1895 to 1897, being promoted to the grade of major-general, Apr. 25, 1895. The post at Chicago was considered a territorial command second in importance only to that of the Department of the East, and in 1897 Merritt succeeded to the latter command with headquarters at Governor's Island, New York.

The war with Spain brought larger responsibilities. On May 16, 1898, he was given command of the first Philippine Expedition. Sailing from San Francisco June 29, he arrived at Cavite, Manila Bay, July 25, where Dewey's fleet was anchored. Landing immediately, he assumed command of the American forces investing Manila, July 27, 1898. These forces, about two miles from the Spanish defenses, extended from the Bay to a point not far therefrom where the Philippine insurgents, under command of General Aguinaldo, continued the investment. The insurgents also had other forces between the American and Spanish lines. Since the American officers had been instructed to avoid all appearance of an alliance with the insurgents, and at the same time were hardly disposed to treat them as enemies, the situation presented extraordinary difficulties. On Aug. 6, Merritt and Dewey entered into communication with the Spanish commander, with a view to preventing suffering to non-combatants in case an attack should be necessary. Meanwhile, through one of his officers, Gen. F. V. Greene [*q.v.*], Merritt had tried to persuade the insurgents "to move out of the way" (Dewey, *post*, p. 270). On Aug. 9 a formal joint demand was made for the surrender of Manila. When this was refused Merritt decided, after consultation with Dewey, to try to carry the extreme right of the Spanish line of entrenchments without bombarding the city. Early in the morning of the 13th, after a short naval bombardment of the Spanish entrenchments, the attack was opened and was almost immediately successful, although there were numerous casualties on both sides. An exploitation of the attack brought the whole city into American possession, with the exception of the Walled City, which shortly after surrendered. Merritt's official report summarizes the operations as follows: "I submit that for troops to enter under fire a town covering a wide area, to rapidly deploy and guard all principal points in the extensive suburbs, to keep out the insurgent forces pressing for admission, to quietly disarm an army of Spaniards more than equal in numbers to the American troops, and finally by all this to prevent entirely all rapine, pillage, and disorder, and gain entire and complete possession of a city of 300,000 people filled with natives hostile to the European interests and stirred up by the knowledge that their own people were fighting in the outside trenches, was an act which only the law-abiding, temperate, resolute American soldier, well and skillfully handled by his regimental and brigade commanders, could accomplish."

On Aug. 14, the day after the capture of the city, Merritt issued a proclamation to the people of the Philippine Islands establishing military government therein, and entered on duty as military governor. Two days later he received the president's proclamation directing the cessation of hostilities. During his short governorship, in addition to setting up an administrative machine, he was under the necessity of conducting negotiations with Aguinaldo with regard to the location and conduct of the Philippine insurgents, who were much dissatisfied at not being permitted to occupy Manila. On Aug. 28 he was ordered to France, for conference with the Peace

Commission, and on completion of this duty, Dec. 10, returned to America, arriving Dec. 19. Relieved as military governor of the Philippines, he resumed his old command of the Department of the East, returning to Governor's Island, where he completed his military career. He retired at the statutory age of sixty-four, in June 1900.

In appearance as in character, Merritt was representative of the best in the United States Army of his day. A fine looking man of strong will and wide experience, he was highly competent, and at the same time modest and agreeable. He was twice married: in 1871, to Caroline Warren of Cincinnati, Ohio; and in 1898, at London, to Laura Williams of Chicago. He died at Natural Bridge, Va., and was buried at the United States Military Academy.

[Personnel files, War Dept.; files Army War College; G. W. Cullum, *Biog. Reg. Officers and Grads., U. S. Mil. Acad.* (3rd ed., 1891), and supplementary volumes; *Forty-Second Ann. Reunion Asso. Grads. U. S. Mil. Acad.* (1911); *Who's Who in America,* 1910–11; Douglas Merritt, *Revised Merritt Records* (1916); *Autobiog. of George Dewey* (1913); *Army and Navy Jour.*, Dec. 10, 1910; information as to certain facts from a cousin, Mrs. J. M. Chance, Kensington, Md.]

J. N. G.

MERRY, ANN BRUNTON (May 30, 1769–June 28, 1808), tragédienne, theatrical manager, was the daughter of John Brunton, a tea-dealer of London, and his wife, formerly a Miss Friend. In 1774 her father turned to the stage and after a few years joined the company at Bath and Bristol. Ann was educated by her mother's instruction and her father's Shakesperian readings, but no effort was made to direct her ambition toward the theatre. When, however, her father discovered that she had memorized several tragic rôles, he resolved to bring her before the public, and within a week she made her début at Bath, Feb. 17, 1785. She at once captured the town. Thomas Harris, manager of Covent Garden, engaged her for the coming season, and London bestowed on her its high favor until her retirement in 1792 after her marriage in August 1791 to Robert Merry, the Della-Cruscan poet.

In a few years Merry's extravagant living had so diminished his fortune that when Thomas Wignell, the Philadelphia director, made Mrs. Merry an offer in 1796, she readily accepted it and on Dec. 5 faced her first American audience as Juliet. Philadelphia remained the scene of her major efforts, though she occasionally played in other towns, especially New York, where she was a tremendous favorite. On Jan. 1, 1803, having been a widow for four years, she married Wignell, but his death followed seven weeks later. The theatre was now conducted by Mrs. Wignell and her late husband's partner, Alexander Reinagle, until, on Aug. 15, 1806, she married William Warren, a prominent comedian, to whom she committed the management of her affairs. When the company started its summer tour in 1808, Mrs. Warren, though pregnant, accompanied her husband, contrary to her physician's advice. At Alexandria, Va., she gave birth to a still-born son and died four days later. One child, the daughter of Wignell, survived her.

Mrs. Merry (by which name she is usually designated in theatrical histories) was one of the really notable players on the early American stage. As late as 1832 William Dunlap described her as one "who will long be entitled to the character of the most perfect actor America has seen" (*A History of the American Theatre,* 1832, p. 173). Despite her low stature and her lack of positive beauty, she made an irresistible appeal through gentleness, simplicity, and grace. John Bernard, the English comedian, found her less majestic than Mrs. Siddons but "equally perfect, and equally gifted to enrapture an audience. With a voice that was all music, and a face all emotion, her pathos and tenderness were never exceeded" (*Retrospections of America,* 1887, p. 269). Her character was as distinguished as her art. Her associates abundantly testified to the charm and beauty of her personality, and to the scrupulous honor of all her professional dealings. She was adored by her inferiors in the theatre and was on terms of social equality with some of the first families of Philadelphia. After her death her husband wrote in his diary "she has not left a better woman behind" (G. C. D. Odell, *Annals of the New York Stage,* II, 1927, p. 301).

[In addition to the works cited above, see: *The Thespian Dict.* (1802), which has been relied upon for the birth date; an anonymous article in the *Mirror of Taste,* Feb. 1810; Chas. Durang, "The Philadelphia Stage," published serially in the *Philadelphia Dispatch* (1854–60); W. B. Wood, *Personal Recollections of the Stage* (1855); J. N. Ireland, *Records of the N. Y. Stage,* vol. I (1866); John Genest, *Some Account of the English Stage* (1832), vols. VI and VII; *Gentleman's Mag.*, Sept. 1791, Aug. 1808.]

O. S. C.

MERRY, WILLIAM LAWRENCE (Dec. 27, 1842–Dec. 14, 1911), sea-captain, merchant, diplomat, was prominent as a supporter of the Nicaragua Canal project. He was born in New York City, the son of Thomas Henry and Candida Isbina (Xavier) Merry. His parentage helps to explain his interests and career, for his father came from a line of New York sea-captains and merchants of English descent, while his mother was a Latin American, apparently from Rio Grande do Sul in Brazil. At the age of seven he accompanied his father around Cape Horn to California, but returned east for an education in the schools of Massachusetts and at the Collegiate Institute of New York City. His maritime career was associated with the route between New York and San Francisco by way of Central America. At sixteen he was a junior officer on the steamship *George Law* between New York and Central America, and in 1862 he was commanding the New York clipper *White Falcon* on the Pacific Coast. In this year he visited Lake Nicaragua for the first time. Subsequently he had ample opportunity to study the rival canal routes of Panama and Nicaragua. In 1863 he was agent for the United States Mail Steamship Company on the Panama isthmus, making frequent trips over the Panama Railroad between Aspinwall and Panama City. A year later, he was given command of the steamship *America,* plying between San Francisco and Nicaragua. In 1867, he became general agent in charge of Nicaraguan transit for the Central American Transit Company and the North American Steamship Company, of which his father's old friend, William H. Webb [*q.v.*], of New York, was president. For three years Merry "practically lived" on the line of the projected Nicaragua Canal, passing over it "night and day, in steamers, boats and canoes" (*The Nicaragua Canal,* p. 46) and making a thorough study of the canal possibilities, which impressed him as superior to those of Panama. In the early seventies, he was with the Pacific Mail Steamship Company, and in 1874 he moved to San Francisco. There he engaged in business, becoming president of the North American Navigation Company, a Pacific Coast line, and serving as consul general of Nicaragua on the west coast. He was president of the San Francisco Chamber of Commerce for seven years.

"Captain Merry" was an active supporter of a strong navy and the maritime development of the Pacific ports, but he attracted particular attention between 1890 and 1895 as a protagonist of the Nicaragua Canal. He claimed credit for having *"first introduced the Canal question to the merchants of the United States from a commercial standpoint"* (*The Nicaragua Canal,* p. 46). It is said that his enthusiasm for the Nicaragua route arose partly from his financial interest in lands in that country, but the sincerity of his belief in its advantages was not questioned. He was appointed by McKinley on July 17, 1897, as minister to Nicaragua, Costa Rica, and Salvador. Residing at San Jose in Costa Rica, he held that position until, in 1907 and 1908 respectively, the increasing importance of Caribbean problems led to the appointment of separate ministers to Salvador and Nicaragua. Merry remained minister to Costa Rica until ill health forced him to resign in 1911. Though he was in such an important position when "dollar diplomacy" was spreading into Central America his printed dispatches in the *Papers Relating to the Foreign Relations of the United States* bear little trace of such methods, dealing mostly with perfunctory matters. Most of the important transactions seem to have been carried on at Washington. Merry's views, however, are set forth in several canal propaganda pamphlets including *The Nicaragua Canal, the Gateway between the Oceans* (1895), reprints of an article in the *California Bankers' Magazine,* October 1890, and a speech before the Trans-Mississippi Commercial Convention at St. Louis, Nov. 28, 1894. He argued that the nation that with the Nicaraguan Government on a joint agreement should control Lake Nicaragua, would then control the destiny of the Western Hemisphere. The decision in favor of Panama naturally thwarted his lifelong ambition to sail through a Nicaraguan canal before he died. His death occurred at the Battle Creek Sanitorium, shortly after he had retired from his post. He had married Blanche, daughter of William S. Hill of Scarsdale, N. Y., and he was buried in Scarsdale. He has been described as a "pure Yankee skipper" with quaint speech and ways, who spoke abominable Spanish with a nasal accent. He was generally liked and respected as an honest old gentleman who wanted to do his best both for his country and for Central America. In appearance he was undersized, spare, nervously built and wiry, acquiring some dignity from a remarkable pair of long, pointed side-whiskers.

[*Who's Who in America,* 1910–11; *Register* of the U. S. Dept. of State, 1897–1911; *Bull. Pan-Am. Union,* May 1912; *San Francisco Examiner,* Dec. 16, 1911.]

R. G. A.

MERVINE, WILLIAM (Mar. 14, 1791–Sept. 15, 1868), naval officer, was born at Philadelphia, Pa., the son of John and Zibia (Wright) Mervine. His grandfather, Philip Mervine, who wrote his name in German, "Marvine," although believed to be a Huguenot, settled in Germantown Township, near Philadelphia, before 1746. William was appointed midshipman from Jan. 16, 1809, and was assigned to duty at the Philadelphia naval station. Serving on board the *John Adams* at the outbreak of the War of 1812, he was on September 30 of that year transferred to the Black Rock flotilla on Lake Erie, and he remained on the Lakes until the end of the war. After the battle of Black Rock, in which he was wounded, he was transferred to the *Hamilton*. He was promoted to an acting lieutenancy on Aug. 25, 1813, and to a lieutenancy on Feb. 4, 1815. A tour of duty at Sacketts Harbor, N. Y., was followed by cruises on board the *Cyane* on the west coast of Africa, in the West Indies, and in the Mediterranean from 1820 to 1825. In 1827–28 he served with the *Natchez* of the West India Squadron. Having been promoted master-commandant in June 1834, he commanded the *Natchez* in 1836–37 during a cruise in the West Indies. From 1838 to 1845 he was on waiting orders. He saw his first sea service as captain, to which rank he was promoted from Sept. 8, 1841, in command of the *Cyane* from 1845 to 1846, and of the *Savannah* from 1846 to 1847, both of the Pacific Squadron. On July 7, 1846, with a detachment of sailors and marines he landed at Monterey, Cal., and took possession of the town, serving later as its military commandant. In October he commanded a landing party that engaged the Mexicans near Los Angeles with a loss of about a dozen men on each side and then retired.

From 1855 to 1857 he commanded the Pacific Squadron. During the last year of this tour of duty he was employed on the coast of Panama and Central America on account of the filibustering expedition of William Walker [*q.v.*]. He was on waiting orders when, on May 6, 1861, he was chosen to command the Gulf Blockading Squadron. With the *Colorado* as his flagship anchored off Fort Pickens, Fla., he established a blockade extending from Key West to Galveston. The destruction of the *Judah* by a boat expedition from the flagship was warmly commended by Gideon Welles, the secretary of the navy. Mervine, however, who was now more than seventy years old, impressed the secretary as lacking in energy and initiative, and he was therefore, in September 1861, relieved of his command. Later during the war he performed special duty at Washington and Philadelphia and served as president of the retiring board at New York. He was promoted commodore from July 16, 1862, and rear admiral from July 25, 1866, both on the retired list. He died at his home at Utica, N. Y. On Jan. 12, 1815, he was married to Amanda Maria Crane at Litchfield, N. Y.

[Letters of June 17, Sept. 2, 1930, from Mrs. Wm. M. Mervine; records of officers, bureau of navigation, Navy Department; records of the bureau of pensions; *War of the Rebellion, Official Records (Navy)*, ser. 1, vols. XVI, XXVII (1903–1917); *Register of the Commissioned and Warrant Officers of the Navy of the U. S.*, 1814–69; *Rept. of the Sec. of Navy*, 1855–57, 1861; H. H. Bancroft, *Hist. of Cal.* (1890), vol. V, esp. pp. 230–31, 318–20; *Diary of Gideon Welles* (1911), vol. I; *Utica Daily Observer*, Sept. 16 (misdated 15), 1868.]

C. O. P.

MERZ, KARL (Sept. 19, 1836–Jan. 30, 1890), musician, was born in Bensheim, Hesse, near Frankfort-on-the-Main. He was the third of nine children of Johannes Merz and Katharina (Werle). The father, a native of Steinheim, Prussia, was an excellent all-round musician who taught school and music for fifty years. He gave Karl his first lessons in violin and organ, enabling him to become a church organist at the age of eleven. The boy's schooling was not confined to music, however, but included excellent literary discipline; nor did his father continue long to teach him, but placed him with Franz Joseph Kunkel, a good musician though a less able schoolmaster.

Karl was graduated from the Gymnasium (in arts) in 1852 and the following year received a government appointment as school-teacher in a small town near Bingen-on-the-Rhine. His devotion to music caused him to weary of teaching school in so small a town and he remained only a year, coming to America in September 1854 and settling at once in Philadelphia. Since he could not speak English, he met with many obstacles. Through his friend Johann Heinrich Bonawitz he secured a position as violinist in a theatre orchestra and also an organ position in the Sixth Presbyterian Church of Philadelphia, where he remained for one year. From 1856 to 1859 he taught in a ladies' seminary near Lancaster, Pa., and played the organ associated with the school. Here he had much time for furthering his own study and growth, and for testing himself in musical composition. During the next two years, he was successively in Salem, Roanoke County, in Harrisonburg, at Hollins Institute, and at Botetourt Springs (all in Virginia), teaching music in schools for girls. While he was away on vacation in 1861 the Civil War began and he was obliged to seek another position. This circumstance was not really a misfortune, for he secured a much better place at Oxford Female College, Oxford, Ohio, where he remained twenty-one years. When this institution closed its doors temporarily in 1882 he was immediately called to Wooster University as director of the department of music and the arts, and here he remained until his death. He was a gifted lecturer, possessing personal charm which, combined with his thorough knowledge of his subject, won wide favor.

Besides his success as a teacher and lecturer, he achieved considerable reputation as a writer on musical topics. His "Musical Hints for the Million," published serially in *Brainard's Musical World* beginning in April 1868 (and in book form in 1875), gained immediate attention. He became a regular contributor to that journal and was made associate editor in 1871 and editor in 1873. His other works—useful in their time—include *The Modern Method for the Reed Organ* (1876); *Karl Merz' Piano Method* (1885), probably the best instruction books of the period; and his textbook, *The Elements of Harmony and Musical Composition* (copyright 1881). Probably his work most widely read by musicians is the posthumous volume, *Music and Culture* (1890), a collection of essays and articles, some of which were given as lectures before the students at Wooster University and some of which had appeared in musical periodicals. These writings were compiled by his son, Charles Hope Merz, in response to many requests for them made while the father was still living. Merz's compositions, now little remembered, included a trio for piano, violin, and 'cello, the three movements bearing the titles *"L'inquiétude," "Éloge," "La Belle Américaine"*; two nocturnes for piano entitled "Bitter Tears" and "Tranquility"; a piano sonata in C minor; and three operettas: *The Runaway Flirt* (1868), *The Last Will and Testament* (1877, produced at Oxford), and *Katie Dean* (1882, Oxford). He also wrote numerous quartets and choruses, organ and piano pieces, and songs. After his death, which occurred at Wooster, his valuable library was purchased and presented to the Carnegie Institute Library, Pittsburgh, Pa. His wife, whom he married in 1858, was Mary Louise Riddle of Paradise, Pa., a pupil. Their daughter, Bessie C. Merz, was, until her death in 1921, a well-known music teacher in New York City.

[W. S. B. Mathews and Granville Howe, *A Hundred Years of Music in America* (1889); letters from Merz's son, Charles Hope Merz, M.D.; *Grove's Dictionary of Music and Musicians, Am. Supp.* (1930); M. T. MacMillan, "The Wisdom of a Great Teacher, Karl Merz," *The Etude*, June 1930; *N. Y. Times*, Jan. 31, 1890.]

F. L. G. C.

MESERVE, NATHANIEL (*c.* 1705–June 28, 1758), colonial soldier, was the son of Clement Meserve (spelled variously), a carpenter of Newington, N. H., and of his wife, Elizabeth Jones. Shortly after his marriage in 1725, to Jane Libby, Nathaniel moved to Portsmouth, and during the next twenty years acquired a considerable fortune, a reputation as a prominent shipwright, and a character for probity and honesty which caused him to be named on numerous occasions as appraiser and executor. In 1746 he was one of the twelve chief inhabitants who purchased from Mason's heirs their claims to New Hampshire territory. After the death of his wife Jane on June 18, 1747, he married Mary (Odiorne) Jackson, a member of a leading Portsmouth family. He had eleven children, ten of whom survived him.

Meserve turned his carpentry training to good account in the siege of Louisbourg in 1745, when, as lieutenant-colonel of Moore's New Hampshire regiment, which he had helped to raise, he constructed sledges for the transportation of artillery across Cape Breton marshes. In compensation for his services he was selected, through the instrumentality of Sir Peter Warren and Sir William Pepperrell, to build a British frigate, one of the rare occasions when the British navy employed colonial shipyards. This vessel, the *America*, 44 guns, was launched from Portsmouth in 1749. In the trying summer of 1756 he served at Fort Edward as colonel of the New Hampshire regiment, and his readiness to obey all orders, the vigor which he instilled into his men, not scrupling himself to wield an axe when work did not progress to his satisfaction, his skill in constructing blockhouses, and perhaps his good-natured simplicity, marked him out definitely from the majority of provincial officers and gained him the esteem of his British superiors. Loudoun wrote of him in highest terms to Governor Wentworth and to the secretary of state, made him a present of a valuable piece of plate, properly inscribed, and later, with Pitt's authority, expressed to him "the gracious sense the King has of the Zeal and Diligence he has shewed the Service." In 1757 he was commissioned as captain of an independent company of sixty carpenters, paid, as were the ranging and Indian companies, out of British contingencies, and in that capacity, though still a New Hampshire colonel, he accompanied Loudoun to Halifax in the summer, where he built barracks and storehouses. Though Loudoun reëngaged him in 1758 for duty in New York, Pitt expressly ordered that he collect eighty carpenters to serve under Amherst at Louisbourg, and that he be urged to resign the command of the New Hampshire troops in order to devote his whole attention to the more essential service. Of his company of 108 men, ninety-two caught the smallpox at Louisbourg, and he and his son Nathaniel died there of the disease; "a very great loss," wrote Amherst, "to this Army." Another son, George, who as distributor of stamps was the target of Portsmouth rioters in 1765, petitioned for lands on account of his father's services, and put in claims as a Loyalist during the Revolution.

[Nathaniel Adams, *Annals of Portsmouth* (1825); *New Hampshire State Papers*; *Dover, N. H., Hist. Soc. Colls.*, I (1894), 130; *New-Eng. Hist. and Geneal. Reg.*, Oct. 1868, Apr. 1869; *Généalogie de la Famille Messervy* (Jersey, 1899); C. E. Potter, *The Mil. Hist. of the State of N. H.* (1866), also pub. in *Report of the*

Adjutant Gen. of . . . N. H., 1866; J. B. Meserve, in *Granite Monthly*, Jan. 1927; *Correspondence of William Pitt* (2 vols., 1906), ed. by G. S. Kimball; *Acts of the Privy Council of England, Colonial Ser.* (5 vols., 1908–12); the Loudoun Papers in the Henry E. Huntington Library; *N. H. Geneal. Record*, July 1903.]

S. M. P.

MESSER, ASA (May 31, 1769–Oct. 11, 1836), educator, for thirty-five years officially connected with Brown University and for twenty-four years its president, was born in Methuen, Essex County, Mass., the son of Asa and Abiah (Whittier) Messer. He grew up on his father's farm until he was thirteen years old, when he went to the nearby town of Haverhill and became a clerk in a wholesale grocery. Relinquishing this position, he prepared for college, partly, it is said, at an academy in Windham, N. H., but also under Rev. Hezekiah Smith [*q.v.*], pastor of the Baptist Church, Haverhill, who wrote in his diary under date of June 2, 1788, "Then Asa Messer quit his learning with me to go to college" (Guild, *post*, p. 455). Smith had labored zealously for the establishment of Rhode Island College, and presumably turned his pupil's footsteps toward that institution. At all events, Asa sought admission there, and so well prepared was he that he was admitted to the sophomore class in June 1788 and graduated in 1790. The following year he was elected tutor of the college; in 1798, professor of the learned languages; and in 1799, professor of natural philosophy. He had been licensed to preach by the First Baptist Church, Providence, in 1792 and was ordained in 1801, but never was a pastor. Upon the resignation of Jonathan Maxcy [*q.v.*], Sept. 2, 1802, Messer, at the age of thirty-three, was made president of the college *pro tempore* and two years later, president. He continued in this office until September 1826.

Although never attaining eminence in the field of scholarship, he was a most capable college president and as one of the leading citizens of the state came to be highly esteemed. His physical height and breadth were suggestive of the general solidity and catholicity of the man. He was hard-headed, sagacious, and practical, but withal kindly, not easily thrown off his balance, a good judge of men, and an excellent financier. His attainments were substantial and varied, but his taste was for mathematics, natural philosophy, and mechanics. Several inventions are credited to him, two of which were patented: "Flumes for Mill," Nov. 19, 1822, and "Water-wheel and Flume," May 18, 1826 (H. L. Ellsworth, *A Digest of Patents Issued by the United States from 1790 to Jan. 1, 1839*, 1840). The confidence people had in his judgment and honesty was evinced by the fact that he was offered a seat on the bench of the supreme court of Rhode Island. While he was no orator, his addresses were effective because of their common sense, sound reasoning, and terse, homely sayings. Under his wise leadership Rhode Island College made quiet but sure progress. Nicholas Brown [*q.v.*] became its generous patron and its name was changed to Brown University; a commodious dormitory was built; the number of students, professors, and courses increased; a medical school was established in 1811, for which an able faculty was secured. The students found Messer a good friend but a strict disciplinarian, and one difficult to outwit. He kept a bottle of picra in his office and anyone asking to be excused on account of a headache was obliged to take a dose.

Messer's breadth of mind and insistence on freedom of thought and speech finally brought his academic career to an end. He offered prayers in the First Congregational Church, Unitarian. Heretical Harvard conferred the degree of doctor of divinity upon him in 1820. While he held that Christ was preëminently the Son of God, he believed that he was such of himself and not from God. This alleged Arianism created much controversy and aroused such antagonism, variously expressed, that on Sept. 23, 1826, he presented his resignation with the accompanying remark that when his last hour came he hoped he might feel that he had served his God as faithfully as he had served Brown University. Through his business sagacity he had acquired one or two farms and an interest in a cotton-mill. He continued to reside in Providence, was for many years an alderman, and in 1830 was a candidate for governor of the state, but was defeated. On May 11, 1797, he married Deborah Angell, by whom he had a son who died in infancy and three daughters. One of the latter married Horace Mann [*q.v.*].

[*Vital Records of Methuen, Mass.* (1909); W. B. Sprague, *Annals Am. Pulpit*, vol. VI (1860); *The Brunonian*, July 1871; Romeo Elton, *The Lit. Remains of Rev. Jonathan Maxcy* (1844); R. A. Guild, *Early Hist. of Brown Univ., Including the Life, Times, and Correspondence of President Manning* (1897); W. C. Bronson, *The Hist. of Brown Univ., 1764–1914* (1914); E. M. Snow, *Alphabetical Index of Births, Marriages, and Deaths Recorded in Providence* (1879).]

H. E. S.

MESSLER, THOMAS DOREMUS (May 9, 1833–Aug. 11, 1893), railway official, sometimes regarded as the founder of the modern system of railway accounting, was born in Somerville, N. J., the first son of Rev. Abraham Messler and Elma (Doremus) Messler. He was of Dutch ancestry on both sides, his paternal ancestor, Jan Adamsen Metsalaer, having settled in New

Netherland about 1649. Educated at the Somerville Academy, he spent three years (1849–52) in a wholesale dry-goods house in New York City, then entered the auditor's office of the New York & Erie Railroad Company, now the Erie Railroad. In 1856 he became secretary and auditor at Pittsburgh of the Pittsburgh, Fort Wayne & Chicago Railway Company, whose line was then being completed between Pittsburgh and Chicago. He at once found that his department, like other railway departments of that time, was conducted with but little method and exactness. He thereupon evolved a system of railroad accounting having for its object simplicity, comprehensiveness, and classification, a system which subsequently became generally known as the "Messler System."

The principal object of this system was to consolidate in one department a uniform classification of revenues, expenses and operating statistics. The plan was outlined in the first annual report (1857) which Messler, as auditor, submitted to the president of the Pittsburgh, Fort Wayne & Chicago Railway Company. This system of accounts and statistics was carried out by the accounting department, the freight and passenger transportation departments, the treasurer of the company, and the general department, whose records and reports were interrelated. The chief accounting officer was made responsible for collecting all accounts due the company, and for making settlements with other companies. All operating expenses were classified, and a system of checks and balances was maintained, to furnish an accurate record of all transactions. The report was a model for its day, and many of its features have become standard practices in the uniform railway accounting system of today.

Messler continued with the Pittsburgh, Fort Wayne & Chicago Railway until July 1869, when it was leased to the Pennsylvania Railroad Company. At this time, by successive promotions, he had become assistant to the president. He was made comptroller of the Pennsylvania in 1871, and was promoted in 1876 to third vice-president. He was also chief executive officer of several auxiliary corporations controlled by the Pennsylvania company in the interest of the Pennsylvania Railroad. At his death, which occurred at Cresson, Pa., his total railroad service had covered a period of forty-one years. He was married on June 3, 1857, to Maria Remsen Varick of Poughkeepsie, N. Y. They had three sons, one of whom died in infancy.

[*Railroad Gazette*, Aug. 18, 1893; *The Biog. Dir. of the Ry. Officials of America*, 1887; *First Ann. Report . . . of the Pittsburgh, Fort Wayne & Chicago Railway Co.* (1857); J. B. Brittain, *A Financial Hist. of the Pa. Lines West of Pittsburgh . . .* (n.d.); L. F. Loree, *Railroad Freight Transportation* (1922), p. 211; R. V. Messler, *A Hist. or Geneal. Record of the Messler (Metselaer) Family* (1903); *Pittsburgh Post*, Aug. 12, 1893.]

J. H. P—e.

MESSMER, SEBASTIAN GEBHARD (Aug. 29, 1847–Aug. 4, 1930), Roman Catholic canonist and prelate, son of Sebastian Gebhard and Rosa (Baumgartner) Messmer, was born at Goldach, Switzerland. In 1866, after classical studies at the Seminary of St. George in St. Gall, he commenced to read philosophy and theology at the University of Innsbrück, Austria. Ordained to the priesthood July 23, 1871, he sailed for America in the fall, on the invitation of Bishop Bayley [*q.v.*], to take the chair of theology and canon law at Seton Hall College, South Orange, N. J. Here, during a professorship of eighteen years, he kept in touch with pastoral ministry, serving the German parish of St. Peter's in Newark for a number of years, St. Mary's Orphan Asylum, Newark, for eight years, and St. Leo's Church in Irvington for two. In the meantime, as assistant secretary of the Provincial Council of New York, he published *Praxis Synodalis* (1883). He was one of a commission of eight theologians who prepared a draft of decrees for consideration by the Plenary Council of Baltimore in 1884, acted as secretary of the Council, and in collaboration with Dr. Denis O'Connell edited the published decrees (1886). In recognition of his ability, in 1885 he was awarded an honorary doctorate in divinity by Pope Leo XIII. During the following year he edited an English translation of a German work by Franz Droste, *Canonical Procedure in Disciplinary and Criminal Cases of Clerics* (1887), which still remains an authoritative treatment of the subject. When the Catholic University of America was established in Washington he was called to the chair of canon law, and assumed his duties after two years of graduate work in Roman civil law at the Collegio Apollinare, Rome, where he earned the degree of D.C.L. Two years later, Dec. 14, 1891, he was appointed bishop of Green Bay in Wisconsin. Consecrated in St. Peter's Church, Newark, by Bishop Otto Zardetti of St. Cloud, Mar. 27, 1892, he served his diocese for ten years, during which a dozen parochial schools were established, as well as four academies, an Indian school, several asylums, and a number of hospitals.

On Nov. 28, 1903, he was translated to the prosperous archbishopric of Milwaukee. There was no modification in his democratic tastes. He continued to play the German card games of *skât* and *schafskopf* for relaxation and to chop wood for exercise. Approachable to priests and people to the extent of being easily imposed upon by place-seekers, he had no desire for luxuries. In traveling he sat bolt-upright in the smoking car, where his powerful physique, full beard, and affability made him a marked man. Racially broad-minded, alive to the problems of his people and his state, sympathetic with labor and trade unionism and with most of the progressive reforms though fearful of woman suffrage and of prohibition, he was a power in Wisconsin. His discreet pro-Germanism prior to 1917 and his loyalty after the United States entered the World War had a deep influence on Germans in America in general and German and Polish Catholics in particular. An active administrator, at least before old age left its mark upon him, he saw his archdiocese advance rapidly, although its extent was curtailed in 1905 when the separate diocese of Superior was created. Forty parochial schools, ten hospitals and sanitariums, and about fifteen additional charitable institutions for dependents were built during his régime; St. Francis Seminary was so developed in equipment and in staff that it attained first rank as a training school for priests; Marquette University became non-sectarian and one of the most progressive of Jesuit schools; and Mount Mary College for girls was established with a lay chancellor. While this growth cannot be directly ascribed to the archbishop, little could have been done without his active leadership and unstinted patronage.

Outside of his diocesan labors, he was a promoter of the American Federation of Catholic Societies, the National Catholic Welfare Conference, and the Deutsch Römisch Katholische Centralverein, and after 1925 an honorary president of the Catholic Hospital Association of the United States and Canada. His interest in the Catholic University continued till the end of his life; he was an active patron and trustee, rarely missing a meeting of the board even in his advanced years. His episcopal burdens did not end his scholarly activities. He edited *Spirago's Method of Christian Doctrine* (1901), *W. Devivier's Christian Apologetics* (1903), and the *Works of the Right Reverend John England* (7 vols., 1908), and contributed a number of articles to the *Catholic Encyclopedia, Ecclesiastical Review, Pastoral Blätt,* and *Catholic Historical Review.* At times, he permitted important diocesan matters to sleep in unanswered letters while he was busy with researches in county courthouses. The honors he earned included appointment as an Assistant at the Pontifical Throne (Nov. 16, 1906) and an elaborate religious and civic celebration to mark his golden jubilee (1921).

Death overtook him in his native Goldach, and here he was buried in his father's grave with religious services by local ecclesiastics, by representatives of the Vatican and Switzerland, and by Cardinal Pifff of Vienna in gratitude for his philanthropies on behalf of the starving Viennese after the war. By his will, which limited the cost of casket and grave marker, he bequeathed a small estate in books and life insurance to his diocese.

[*Am. Cath. Who's Who,* 1911; *Who's Who in America,* 1930–31; *Cath. Herald* (Milwaukee), Apr. 20, 1922, Apr. 25, 1929; official annual Catholic directories; *Cath. Citizen* (Milwaukee), Aug. 9, 1930; *N. Y. Times,* Aug. 5, 8, 1930; bulletin of Nat. Cath. Welfare Council news service, Aug. 4, 1930; *Milwaukee Jour.,* Aug. 4, 5, 1930; information from personal acquaintances.]

R. J. P.

METCALF, HENRY HARRISON (Apr. 7, 1841–Feb. 5, 1932), author and editor, son of Joseph P. and Lucy (Gould) Metcalf, was born at Newport, N. H., and received his early education at various public schools in his native state and at Mount Caesar Seminary. He graduated from the law school of the University of Michigan in 1865 and studied for the New Hampshire bar in the office of Edmund Burke, one of the prominent Democratic leaders of the state. He was admitted in 1866, but was too deeply interested in journalism and politics to continue in the profession. The next year he began his editorial career in charge of the *White Mountain Republic,* founded at Littleton partly at his suggestion by Chester E. Carey. In December 1869 he married Mary Jane Jackson of that town. During the next twenty-five years he conducted five different journals and acquired an encyclopedic knowledge of New Hampshire people and affairs. His most important editorship was that of the *New Hampshire People and Patriot* (Concord), 1882–92. He also acted for many years as New Hampshire correspondent of various New York papers. He was an active Democratic leader, rendering devoted service on sundry party committees and running several times for public office, though unsuccessfully, since his state was too strongly Republican during his active career to offer many opportunities for opposition candidates. As an editor he was intensely partisan and a vigorous critic of men and measures which aroused his antagonism.

In 1877 he founded the *Granite Monthly,* one of the pioneer state magazines, which he published until 1919, acting during several periods as editor. To its pages he contributed many articles on New Hampshire, historical, biographical, and descriptive. He was an organizer and active worker for the Patrons of Husbandry, and constantly endeavored to stimulate interest in agriculture and the rural life of the state. A life-long member of the Universalist Church, he was one of the outstanding laymen of that denomination, his influence extending far beyond the state boundaries.

In 1913 he was appointed state historian, and assisted in publishing some of the early records of New Hampshire, notably the second and third volumes of *Probate Records of the Province of New Hampshire* (1914, 1915), found in volumes XXXII and XXXIII of the State Papers. He also edited *New Hampshire Women* (1895), *Laws of New Hampshire* (vols. III–V, 1915–16), *One Thousand New Hampshire Notables* (1919), and wrote *New Hampshire in History* (1922) and several other historical articles or monographs. While he was neither a trained historical investigator nor a scholarly writer, his work in the field of state and local history was of considerable merit and his interest and loyalty to the social and educational interests of his state exercised a wholesome influence in its affairs.

[*Exercises at the Centennial Celebration of the Incorporation of the Town of Littleton, July 4, 1884* (1887); J. R. Jackson, *Hist. of Littleton, N. H.* (3 vols., 1905); Edmund Wheeler, *The Hist. of Newport, N. H.* (1879); *Manchester Union*, Feb. 6, 1932; *Concord Daily Monitor and N. H. Patriot*, Feb. 5, 6, 1932; *N. Y. Times*, Feb. 6, 1932; information from personal acquaintances.]
W. A. R.

METCALF, JOEL HASTINGS (Jan. 4, 1866–Feb. 21, 1925), Unitarian clergyman, astronomer, was born in Meadville, Pa., the son of Lewis Herbert and Anna (Hicks) Metcalf. He graduated from the Meadville Theological Seminary in 1890, pursued graduate work for a time in the Harvard Divinity School, and continued at Allegheny College, where he obtained the degree of Ph.D. in 1892. In 1891 he married Elizabeth S. Lochman, of Cambridge, Mass. For ten years (1893–1903) he served a pastorate at Burlington, Vt., then went to England for rest and study at Oxford University. On his return, in much improved health, he assumed the duties of a pastorate in Taunton, Mass. From 1910 to 1920 he was minister of the Unitarian Society at Winchester, Mass., and from 1920 to the time of his death, of the First Parish, Portland, Me. Possessing "a wide tolerance side by side with an intense faith," he "met each man on his own plane and took him at his best" (Bailey, *post*, p. 493). Soon after the United States entered the World War, he took service in the Young Men's Christian Association, working by preference at the front, sharing the perils and privations of the soldiers, and distinguishing himself in getting food and supplies to men in exposed positions. He was cited for special courage at Château Thierry and later rendered commendable service during the reconstruction of Rumania.

Throughout his life, almost as deep as the interest in men that led him into the ministry was his devotion to astronomy. At the age of twelve he selected Proctor's *Other Worlds than Ours* to bring home from the Sunday-school library. An eclipse of the sun about the same time stimulated him to further investigation; he found a lens in an abandoned house and did odd jobs to earn the sixteen dollars needed to pay for materials for mounting. During his pastorate at Burlington he bought a second-hand photographic telescope and dome in New York State and brought it across Lake Champlain in winter on sledges, although the cost of the outfit—five hundred dollars—was a serious item in the budget of a minister on a small salary, with a wife and two children to support. While he was at Oxford, in addition to attending lectures on philosophy and religion, he became a frequent visitor at the observatory and spent much time on astronomical problems. Upon his return he built himself a private observatory at Taunton and both here and at Winchester made many astronomical observations of great value, discovering six comets, forty-one asteroids, and a number of variable stars. His observations are published in *Astronomische Nachrichten, Popular Astronomy,* and *Harvard College Observatory Bulletins.* His finest scientific work, however, was in applied optics. He combined in a remarkable degree the abilities to compute the lens curves necessary to perfect performance and the manual dexterity and skill to do the actual grinding. He made the telescope with which he himself observed; a ten-inch telescope and one of sixteen inches aperture of his make are in regular use at the Harvard College Observatory, while a thirteen-inch triplet, started by him shortly before his death and finished by C. A. R. Lundin the younger, was used in January 1930 at the Lowell Observatory in the discovery of the Trans-Neptunian planet. Metcalf was a fellow of the American Academy of Arts and Sciences and an active member of the American Astronomical Society. For many years he was chairman of the Committee to visit the Harvard Observatory, and a member of the Visiting Committee of the Ladd Observatory. He died in his sixtieth year, survived by his wife and two children.

[S. I. Bailey, "Joel Hastings Metcalf," *Pop. Astron.*, Oct. 1925; *Observatory*, May 1925; *Pubs. of the Astron. Soc. of the Pacific*, Apr. 1925; *Who's Who in*

America, 1924–25; *Press Herald* (Portland, Me.), Feb. 22, 1925.] R. S. D.

METCALF, THERON (Oct. 16, 1784–Nov. 13, 1875), Massachusetts jurist, was born in Franklin, Mass., the son of Hanan and Mary (Allen) Metcalf. The family was descended from Michael Metcalf who emigrated to New England and settled in Dedham. After graduating from Brown University in 1805 as valedictorian of his class, Metcalf studied law at Canterbury, Conn., then at Tapping Reeve's law school at Litchfield, Conn., and finally under Seth Hastings at Mendon, Mass. He was admitted to the bar of Litchfield County in 1807 and the following year began to practise in Massachusetts, first at Franklin and then at Dedham near-by. The region was one of Shaysites and Jeffersonians, with enough Federalists like Fisher Ames to keep politics boiling. Among these agrarian levelers Metcalf cast his lot and here in 1809 he brought his bride, Julia, daughter of Senator Uriah Tracy of Connecticut. Then and later, in the ferment of Jacksonian democracy, he was mistrustful of the "approaching reign of popular opinion, and the triumph of popular rights" (*An Address to the Phi Beta Kappa Society of Brown Univ. . . . 1832,* 1833, p. 24).

For many years Metcalf was county attorney. For two years, 1833–34, he sat in the lower house and in 1835 was a member of the state Senate He edited the *Dedham Gazette* (1813–[illegible]) and in 1828 opened a law school. His *Law of Contracts* (1867) originated in one of his lecture courses. Every year a number of articles and reviews appeared in law journals over his name. He edited Sir Henry Yelverton's *Reports* (1820), Thomas Starkie's *Evidence,* and Sir William O. Russell's *Crimes.* But his chief claim to recognition lies in his *Reports of Cases Argued and Determined in the Supreme Judicial Court of Massachusetts* (13 vols., 1841–50), compiled when he was reporter to the court from 1840 to 1847, and in his indexes to the state statutes. On Feb. 25, 1848, he was appointed to the supreme bench. In his self-deprecating way he explained "that he was taken to fill a gap in the Court as people take an old hat to stop a broken window" (Hoar, *post,* II, p. 395). He retained his position until his resignation in August 1865, some ten years before his death. His opinions appear in 55–92 *Massachusetts Reports.* He was a quaint character, whose *bon mots* were repeated with zest. He enjoyed society, but was not especially given to hospitality. He was so steeped in the common law that he detested statutes and procedural innovations such as the abolition of special pleading. As a trial judge he was thought "fussy and interfering" (Hoar, *post,* II, p. 397), and by his misapplication of principles to facts he was often overruled, but his memory was a digest of the common law, and his opinions were clear and proverbially compact.

[G. S. Hale, "Memoir of the Hon. Theron Metcalf, LL.D.," *Proc. Mass. Hist. Soc.,* vol. XIV (1875–76); W. T. Davis, *Hist. of the Judiciary of Mass.* (1900); D. H. Hurd, *Hist. of Norfolk County, Mass.* (1884); G. F. Hoar, *Autobiog. of Seventy Years* (2 vols., 1903); *New-Eng. Hist. and Geneal. Reg.,* Apr. 1852, Oct. 1876; *Am. Law Rev.,* Jan. 1876; *Boston Evening Jour.,* Nov. 15, 1875.] C. F.

METCALF, WILLARD LEROY (July 1, 1858–Mar. 9, 1925), landscape and figure painter, born at Lowell, Mass., was the son of Greenleaf Willard and Margaret Jane (Gallop) Metcalf. His early education was obtained in the public schools of Lowell and Newton. At the age of twelve he went to Boston and found employment in a wholesale hardware store; in 1875 he was apprenticed to a wood engraver, then entered the studio of George L. Brown as an art student and remained there two years (1876–77), at the same time attending the life classes in the Lowell Institute. Later he continued his art studies at the Massachusetts Normal Art School, the school of the Museum of Fine Arts, and finally (1883) at the Académie Julien, Paris, studying under Boulanger and Lefebvre. Meanwhile he had spent two years in New Mexico and Arizona. The earlier years of his professional life were passed in Boston, and his first exhibition was held there in Chase's Gallery, about 1882, although he had previously sent his works to the exhibitions of the Boston Art Club and the Paint and Clay Club.

In these early years his paintings found few buyers, though his work was good from the first. In 1889, on his return to Boston from France, an exhibition of his pictures was held at the St. Botolph Club, which contained, besides landscapes painted in France, a number of excellent paintings from Tunis and Biskra. Shortly after this time he moved to New York, where he taught at Cooper Institute and the Art Students' League. He was subsequently an instructor at the Rhode Island School of Design. In 1892 he collaborated with William Hole in illustrating *The Wrecker* by Robert Louis Stevenson and Lloyd Osbourne.

Beginning in the nineties, fortune favored him; his paintings met with a brisk demand from private collectors and museums alike, and an impressive list of medals and prizes attest the high esteem in which his work was held. At the time of his death he was represented in fifteen public collections, including the museums of Philadelphia, Chicago, Boston, Washington, Pittsburgh, Cincinnati, St. Louis, and Buffalo. He became a member of the Ten American Painters, the National Institute of Arts and Letters, the American Society of Water Color Painters, and the Century Association.

Never surrendering his independence as an artist, Metcalf cannot be classified as a member of any esthetic sect. His personal talent was developed naturally, along congenial lines, unaffected by passing fashions in painting. He was not an impressionist; nor could he be fairly called a realist without some qualifications. He got very close to nature, however, and his point of view was modern, yet modest. His innate sensibility was kept in poise by his good sense; and he never erred in the way of extravagance or excess. His landscapes are noticeably free from mannerisms. His paintings were mostly of New England scenes, and he chose to depict the charm and beauty of his native region rather than its harsher aspect. The kind of subject that especially appealed to him, and in the treatment of which he was peculiarly felicitous, was an evanescent effect such as that in his "May Pastoral." This painting, now in the Boston Art Museum, is a landscape of great delicacy in which the signs of spring with its various hints of new life are indicated with rare and exquisite veracity. He was also happy in depicting the twinkling foliage of breeze-shaken birches and other delicate trees.

On Sept. 14, 1901, he was married, in New York, to Margaret Beaufort Hailé, and in 1911 he married Henriette A. McCrea of Chicago. Two children of his second marriage survived him.

[*Who's Who in America,* 1906–07, 1924–25; E. V. Lucas, in *Ladies' Home Journal,* June 1927; *Museum of Fine Arts Bull.* (Boston), Aug. 1908; W. H. Downes, in *Boston Sunday Courier,* Mar. 5, 1882; *Art Rev.,* Feb. 1912; Royal Cortissoz, in *Appleton's Booklovers Mag.,* Oct. 1905; Christian Brinton, in *Century Mag.,* Nov. 1908; F. W. Coburn, in *New Eng. Mag.,* Nov. 1908; C. B. Ely, in *Art in America,* Oct. 1925; Bernard Teevan, in *International Studio,* Oct. 1925; *Art News,* Mar. 14, 1925; *N. Y. Times,* Mar. 10, 1925.]

W. H. D.

METCALF, WILLIAM (Sept. 3, 1838–Dec. 5, 1909), metallurgist, steel manufacturer, was born in Pittsburgh, Pa. His father, Orlando Metcalf, was an attorney whose ancestor came from England in 1637; his mother was Mary Mehitabel (Knap) Metcalf. After attending the public schools of Pittsburgh, William went to Rensselaer Polytechnic Institute at Troy, N. Y., graduating in 1858. His first position was that of assistant engineer and draftsman at the Fort Pitt Foundry in his native city. Within a year he had become general superintendent of the company, a post he held until 1865. During this time, although not yet thirty years of age, he produced the largest castings and the heaviest machinery then known in the United States, and, perhaps, in the world. His foundry supplied more than three thousand heavy guns and projectiles for the United States during the Civil War. Two of the guns, the largest in the world, were of the twenty-inch variety and weighed eighty tons each. Not only were his deliveries prompt (in one instance General Grant received guns ordered only forty days before) but the quality was of the finest. His modest boast, many years later, was that "not one gun of Fort Pitt make was ever reported as failing in service" (Raymond, *post,* p. 866).

Following the war he entered the firm of his uncle, Charles Knap, which leased and operated the Fort Pitt foundry until late in 1867, when the firm became the Knap Fort Pitt Foundry Company. Then he became associated with Miller, Barr, & Parkin (after 1869 Miller, Metcalf, & Parkin), owners of the Crescent Steel Works, which was incorporated in 1889 as the Crescent Steel Company. As managing director of this organization he specialized in fine crucible steels, but after the company was taken over by the Crucible Steel Company of America in 1895 he left to become director of the Braeburn Steel Company (1897), a position he held at the time of his death.

Metcalf was not only a manufacturer of steel —one "of the generation of great steel-makers who made Pittsburg the Sheffield of America" —he was "one of the first practical experts to emphasize the importance of mechanical treatment and heat-treatment, as compared with chemical composition, and also the different effects of different kinds of tests of strength" (Raymond, p. 865). He read numerous papers before scientific societies on this subject. He was president of the Engineers' Society of Western Pennsylvania, 1880, and of the American Institute of Mining Engineers, 1881; vice-president of the American Society of Mechanical Engineers, 1882–84; and president of the American Society of Civil Engineers, 1893. He was also the author of a book, *Steel: A Manual for Steel Users,* which appeared in 1896 and served as a textbook in several technical schools.

Metcalf was married on Dec. 1, 1864, to Christiana, daughter of Aram Fries of Whitemarsh, Pa. They were the parents of three sons and three daughters. At the time of his death, Metcalf had been the senior warden of St. Peter's Protestant Episcopal Church, Pittsburgh, for thirty-five years. He was one of the most unassuming of men and it is for this reason, perhaps, that his name is not a household word. Greatness in his field came to him in spite of himself. He combined business ability with a love of research and knowledge but he found time for manifestation of character outside of his chosen field as well. He remained young in spirit in spite of age and was in the front ranks of those who welcomed change in a basic industry.

[*Trans. Am. Soc. of Civil Engineers,* vol. LXXIV (Dec. 1911), with portrait; R. W. Raymond, in *Trans. Am. Inst. of Mining Engineers,* vol. XLI (1911); *Trans. Am. Soc. Mech. Engineers,* vol. XXXII (1911); H. B. Nason, *Biog. Record Officers and Grads. Rensselaer Polytechnic Inst.* (1887); *Pittsburg Dispatch,* Dec. 6, 1909; *Pittsburgh Post,* Dec. 7, 1909.] A. I.

METCALFE, SAMUEL LYTLER (Sept. 21, 1798–July 17, 1856), chemist and physician, eldest of eleven children of Joseph and Rebecca (Littler or Sittler) Metcalfe, was born near Winchester, Va. Late in 1802 the family moved to Shelby County, Ky., and settled on a tract of land adjacent to an old Indian fort on Hickory Run, near Lynch's Station. In this primitive locality the boy received his early education. He entered the Medical School of Transylvania University, Lexington, Ky., in 1819, and four years later graduated with the degree of M.D., presenting a thesis entitled "The Malignant Fever of Louisville." While at Transylvania he wrote two books. The first was a choice collection of sacred music called *The Kentucky Harmonist,* which contained 130 pages of hymns and a long account of the origin, nature, and moral tendency of music. Two editions were issued within a short time (2nd ed., 1820). The success of this book enabled him to pay part of the cost of publishing the second, which was *A Collection of Some of the Most Interesting Narratives of the Indian Warfare in the West* (1821). It contained a description of every severe Indian fight which had taken place in Kentucky since its settlement by white men.

During the next seven years Metcalfe practised medicine, first at New Albany, Ind., and later at several places in Mississippi, though he lived most of the time at Natchez. From the latter place as a starting point, he walked over the greater portion of east Tennessee and North Carolina, and wrote several articles on the chemistry, geology, botany, and zoölogy of these regions. In 1831 he went to England where he continued his studies, specializing in chemistry and geology. On his return to the United States he settled in New York City, and for several years devoted himself to writing articles and books on chemistry and other sciences. Several of his scientific articles (signed merely "M") were published in the *Knickerbocker Magazine.* In 1835 he went to England again in order to conduct some researches in chemistry and geology. During this visit he was invited to become a candidate for the Gregorian chair in Edinburgh University, but declined in order to complete certain scientific books on which he had worked for several years. One phase of his chemical-geological studies is recorded in *A New Theory of Terrestrial Magnetism* (1833). Like many of his contemporaries he was attracted by the nature of heat, and after spending several years on the subject, expanded the views first set forth in his *New Theory* in a much more elaborate study, *Caloric: Its Mechanical, Chemical, and Vital Agencies in the Phenomena of Nature.* A portion of this work was issued in 1837; later it was enlarged into two volumes under the title given above and published in London in 1843; in 1853 a revised edition was issued in Philadelphia.

While in Mississippi Metcalfe was married, but his wife died after four years. In 1846, during a visit to England, he married Ellen Blondel of London, by whom he had one daughter. He died at Cape May, N. J.

[Personal communications from Transylvania College, Lexington, Ky.; E. M., "Dr. Metcalfe's Life," in *Caloric,* etc. (ed. of 1859), vol. I; H. A. Kelly and W. L. Burrage, *Am. Medic. Biogs.* (1920); J. N. McCormack, *Some of the Medical Pioneers of Ky.* (1917); *North American Medico-Chirurgical Rev.,* May 1857; *Pub. Ledger* (Phila.), July 18, 1856.] L. C. N.

METCALFE, THOMAS (Mar. 20, 1780–Aug. 18, 1855), Kentucky governor, representative, and senator, was born in Fauquier County, Va., the son of Sally and John Metcalfe, a militia officer in the Revolutionary War. About 1784 the family moved to Fayette County and later to Nicholas County, Ky. After attending the common-schools, young Thomas learned the trade of the stone-mason, which he followed for some years. About 1806 he married Nancy Mason. Entering politics, he served in the lower house of the legislature from 1812 to 1816. During the War of 1812 he raised a company of volunteers and led them at the battle of Fort Meigs. He served in Congress from 1819 to 1828, where he was a strong exponent of Western democracy. He opposed the banks, advocated making a two-thirds vote of the federal Supreme Court necessary to declare a state law unconstitutional, and disapproved of the discontinuance of credit to purchasers of public land. In 1821 he proposed to grant preëmption rights to squatters. He also favored protective tariffs and internal improvements, and he opposed restriction upon slavery in Missouri or in other parts of the Louisiana Purchase.

In 1825 he followed Henry Clay in voting for Adams for president and in 1827 was nominated for governor by the Adams-Clay convention, the first ever held in Kentucky. After an active contest with William T. Barry, the Jacksonian candidate, he was elected by a close vote, 38,940 to 38,231. He promised to disregard party affiliations in making appointments, but the Jacksonians asserted that he did not do so. As governor from 1828 to 1832, he indorsed protective tariffs and federal aid for internal improvements, and he denounced nullification, the spoils system, and Jackson's veto of the bill for federal aid for the Maysville-Lexington turnpike. He also favored the American Colonization Society, protection of the occupying claimants of Kentucky lands, simplification of the judicial system, district schools and additional aid for education, abolition of the branches of the bank of the commonwealth, improvement of rivers and roads, and prison reform. Most of his recommendations to the legislature became law. Later he was state senator from 1834 to 1838, president of the Kentucky board of internal improvements, and a member of the national Whig convention of 1839. During the debates over slavery, while he was United States senator from 1848 to 1849, he denounced secession and declared that Kentucky would uphold the Union. He retired to his farm in Nicholas County, Ky., where he died.

[Some of Metcalfe's letters and papers in Ky. State Hist. Soc. Coll.; *A Sketch of the Life of General Thomas Metcalfe* (1828?); Lewis Collins and R. H. Collins, *Hist. of Ky.*, revised ed. (1874), vol. II; W. E. Connelley and E. M. Coulter, *Hist. of Ky.* (1922), vol. II; *Biog. Directory Am. Cong.* (1928); J. T. McAllister, *Va. Militia in the Revolutionary War* (copr. 1913); *Register of the Ky. State Hist. Soc.*, Jan. 1904; *Niles' National Register*, Dec. 14, 1839.] W. C. M.

METTAUER, JOHN PETER (1787–Nov. 22, 1875), physician and surgeon, was the son of Francis Joseph Mettauer, an Alsatian surgeon, who came to America under Rochambeau and after the Revolution settled in Prince Edward County, Va., near Farmville. He married Jemimah Gaulding, probably *née* Crump. Their son, John Peter, born in Prince Edward County, attended the grammar school of Hampden-Sidney and in 1805 entered Hampden-Sidney College, but left before graduating and in 1807 entered the medical school of the University of Pennsylvania. There he heard the last lecture of the great Dr. Shippen and was a pupil of Rush, Wistar, and Physick. He received the degree of M.D. in 1809, and returned to Virginia to practise. During the War of 1812 he lived in Norfolk, and for one term, 1835–36, he was professor of surgery at Washington Medical College, Baltimore; but except for these brief intervals his long medical career was carried on entirely in his native county.

A daring and original surgeon, he soon became conspicuous for his skill, and patients flocked to him from all parts of the United States. He kept from forty-five to sixty surgical cases constantly under his care. Over 800 operations for cataract and over 200 for stricture of the urethra are recorded to his credit. A pioneer in genito-urinary surgery, he was also among the first in America to extirpate the parotid, ligate the carotid, and resect the superior maxilla. In lithotomy he was second only to Benjamin W. Dudley [*q.v.*], having operated seventy-nine times by 1853. His operation for cleft palate (1827), the third by an American surgeon, received widespread recognition (Smith, *post,* I, 407). Most of his work was done before the day of anesthesia, and most of his instruments he made himself. His chief technical innovation was the use of lead sutures in the treatment of vesico-vaginal fistula, an operation which he first performed, successfully, in August 1838, ten years before it was done by J. Marion Sims (*Boston Medical and Surgical Journal,* April 1840; *American Journal of the Medical Sciences,* July 1847). Sims [*q.v.*] himself called Mettauer one of two men who "stand out in bold relief amongst those who have devoted some time to this subject," the other being the famous French surgeon, Jobert (*Ibid.,* January 1852, p. 61).

Articles by Mettauer, appearing in nearly every medical journal in the country, prove that his interests extended beyond surgery. He wrote frequently on puerperal fever, and is said to have first suggested the use of iodine in scrofula. His paper on *Continued Fever in Middle Southern Virginia from 1816 to 1829* (1843) shows that he early recognized typhoid fever as a distinct disease. A scholarly 3,000-page manuscript work on surgery, in existence as late as 1905, is now lost. Most of his articles were signed "John Peter Mettauer, M.D., LL.D., of Virginia," but the source of the LL.D. is not known. In 1837 he organized the Prince Edward Medical Institute, which in 1847 became the Medical Department of Randolph-Macon College, with himself and his two elder sons constituting the faculty. His clinic was one of the most noted in the country. The prospectus for 1851–52 advertised a "handsome and chaste edifice," a ten months' course recognized by leading medical schools, and an infirmary where "surgical operations are frequently performed." The school was suspended at the outbreak of the Civil War, and never reopened.

Tall and austere, never attending either social or religious functions, Mettauer was eccentric but respected. He wore on all occasions, even while at meals and while operating, a high stovepipe hat. His daughter said she had never seen him without it, and he left instructions that he be buried in it. In spite of his peculiarities, four women married him: Mary Woodard, of Norfolk, by whom he had two sons; Margaret Carter, of Prince Edward County, Apr. 14, 1825; Louisa Mansfield, of Connecticut, 1833, who died in 1835; Mary E. Dyson, of Nottoway County, Va. He had at least ten children; three of his sons studied medicine. In the last week of his life, in his eighty-eighth year, he performed three successful operations: for cataract, stone, and amputation of the breast. He died of pneumonia and was buried in the College Church Cemetery at Hampden-Sidney.

[G. B. Johnston, *A Sketch of Dr. John Peter Mettauer* (1905), also pub. as presidential address in *Trans. Am. Surgic. Asso.*, vol. XXIII (1905); J. D. Eggleston, in *Wm. and Mary Coll. Quart.*, Apr. 1928; W. L. Harris, in *Va. Medic. Mo.*, Nov. 1926; A. M. Willis, in *Surgery, Gynecol. and Obstetrics*, Aug. 1926; *Va. Medic. Mo.*, Dec. 1875; *Richmond Dispatch*, Nov. 23, 1875; H. H. Smith, *A System of Operative Surgery* (2nd ed., 1855, I, 114, 407, II, 228, 273, 291, 297; A. J. Morrison, *College of Hampden-Sidney, Dict. of Biog., 1776–1825* (1921); Prince Edward County, Va., Deed Books 7, 15, 22, 26; Will Books 4, 14; files of medical journals, 1825–75.]

L. F. C.

METZ, CHRISTIAN (Dec. 30, 1794–July 27, 1867), religionist, a spiritual leader of the Community of True Inspiration, was born at Neuwied, Prussia, and with his parents removed to Ronneburg, Hesse, at the age of seven. His grandfather, Jakob Metz of Himbach, was a member of one of the early congregations of Inspirationists who traced their origin to the German Mystics and Pietists of the sixteenth and seventeenth centuries. By the close of the eighteenth century the Community of True Inspiration had suffered a spiritual decline: the founders, Gruber and Rock, were dead, and the gift of inspiration had ceased. But in 1817, when Christian Metz was twenty-three years old, the Community experienced a spiritual awakening and three members were recognized as "endowed with the miraculous gift of Inspiration," namely, Michael Krausert of Strassburg, Christian Metz of Ronneburg, and Barbara Heinemann of Leitersweiler, Alsace. Soon, however, Krausert "fell back into the world," and Barbara Heinemann, having married in 1823, temporarily lost the gift of inspiration. Thus spiritual guidance and temporal leadership devolved solely upon Christian Metz, who remained to the time of his death the recognized head of the Community. He was a man of profound piety and great sincerity, a successful organizer, and an executive of unusual ability. He it was who first conceived the idea of leasing estates in common as a refuge for the faithful; and while the original intention had been to live together simply as a Christian congregation or church, he foresaw that a system of communism would be the natural development of the mode of life which his people had been forced to adopt. He foresaw, also, that exorbitant rents and unfriendly governments would one day require them to seek a home in the New World.

Accordingly, with three other brothers he made the voyage to America in 1842 and purchased the Seneca Indian Reservation, a tract of five thousand acres near Buffalo, N. Y. This site, which he named Ebenezer, was the home of his people until 1854, when he led the brothers westward in search of cheaper and more abundant lands and greater seclusion. A tract of eighteen thousand acres was purchased in the frontier commonwealth of Iowa, and through inspiration Christian Metz christened it Amana. During the thirteen years of his leadership here he successfully organized and molded the community along the lines of his long-cherished hopes and dreams. In 1859 it was incorporated under the laws of Iowa as the Amana Society, with a constitution and by-laws which, with only minor changes, remained its fundamental law until the Reorganization of 1932, by which church and state were separated, ending spiritual authority in temporal affairs.

Christian Metz is remembered as a man of commanding presence and of great personal magnetism whose natural dignity and spiritual poise challenged admiration and respect everywhere. His voluminous writings, collected and preserved in the archives of the Community, reveal a penetrating mind, an earnest, eager spirit, an unusual patience with human frailties, toleration and a fine sense of justice in dealing with men and measures, a practical philosophy of life, a genuine feeling of humility, and a deep sense of the responsibility of his high office. He died at Amana in his seventy-third year and was buried in the cedar-bordered cemetery there. Only a tiny headstone marks his grave. His real monument is the Amana Society with its seven villages, its twenty-five thousand acres of land, its mills, factories, and stores, its barns and sheds, orchards, vineyards, and gardens, its homes and schools and churches—the most successful experiment in communism in America.

[MSS. in the *Archiv* at Amana; Bertha M. H. Shambaugh, *Amana, the Community of True Inspiration* (1908), "Amana the Church and Christian Metz the Prophet" (*The Midland*, Aug. 1915), "Amana Colony" (*The Midland Monthly*, July 1896), "Amana" (*The Palimpsest*, July 1921), "Amana," in James Hastings' *Encyc. of Religion and Ethics*, vol. I (Edinburgh, 1908), and *Amana That Was and Is* (1932); W. R. Perkins and B. L. Wick, *Hist. of the Amana Soc.* (1891); C. F. Noe, *A Brief Hist. of the Amana Soc., 1714–1900* (1904), also pub. in *Iowa Jour. of Hist. and Politics*, Apr. 1904.]

B. M. H. S.

MEYER, GEORGE VON LENGERKE (June 24, 1858–Mar. 9, 1918), diplomat and cabinet officer, was born on Beacon Hill of a good Bostonian family. Both his father and paternal grandfather had borne the name of George Augustus Meyer and both had been merchants in overseas trade. The elder, a native of Germany, had emigrated to New York in early manhood; the younger had moved to Boston and there married Grace Helen Parker. George von Lengerke Meyer was the eldest of his parents' three children. He prepared privately for college and was graduated from Harvard with the class of 1879. In 1885 he married Marian Alice Appleton. Within two decades after his graduation he stood near the center of the closely related inner group which dominated the banking and commercial activity of Boston, and at the same time he participated heartily in the social activity of Boston and Essex County. In 1890 the Meyers acquired "Rock Maple Farm" at Hamilton, which remained their dearest residence and was developed through a lifetime of attention into a show place of the region.

Although possessed of all that one of his group might consider sufficient for a full and contented life, Meyer was as much disturbed by the ambition and will "to make something out of life" as was his later chieftain, Theodore Roosevelt. Entering politics, he was elected as a Republican to the Boston Common Council, serving 1889–90, and in 1891 was chosen alderman. From 1892 to 1896 he was in the legislature, holding the speakership of the House during the last three years. Always a regular Republican and a conservative, he felt that government should be administered as efficiently as a paying business. He was probably especially useful to his party in his contacts with the business leaders who formed so important an element in Republican success (Roosevelt-Lodge *Correspondence*, *post*, II, 69, 136). In 1899 he was made national committeeman from Massachusetts.

His diplomatic career began with his appointment in December 1900 by President McKinley as ambassador to Italy. At Rome the King and the American Ambassador became warm friends, and the effective Meyer raised his embassy to a high standard of influence and popularity. He also formed valuable contacts in important circles throughout Europe. Especially with Emperor William II of Germany he made an acquaintance surprisingly intimate in nature. All the while he corresponded regularly with Henry Cabot Lodge and somewhat less frequently with President Roosevelt, assuming gradually the rôle of an important listening post in Europe for these two formulators of American foreign policy. During the Russo-Japanese War, when President Roosevelt was essaying the part of peacemaker, "I wish in St. Petersburg," he wrote, "a man who, while able to do all the social work, . . . can do, in addition, the really vital and important things" (Howe, *post*, pp. 110–11). Meyer was the man he selected and in March 1905 his Russian mission began. Cutting through the red tape of Russian bureaucracy without causing offense, he reached the Czar himself and effectively presented Roosevelt's proposals (Roosevelt-Lodge *Correspondence*, II, 187, *et passim*). It is said Meyer's skill at bridge did not prove a liability to his diplomacy.

Meanwhile Lodge as well as others were urging his appointment to the cabinet and Meyer himself was anxious for a cabinet post. On Mar. 5, 1907, he took office as postmaster-general under Roosevelt. Here again he gave evidence of efficient administrative ability. The department was conducted smoothly, postal savings banks were established, the parcel-post system was extended, a special-delivery system was started, and a two-cent postage convention was arranged between the United States and Great Britain and Ireland. Retained in the cabinet by Taft, who appointed him secretary of the navy, he held that office until 1913. He instituted naval aids to the Secretary to keep him more responsibly informed; he improved the gunnery and the direction of the active fleet; navy yards were administered to meet the needs of the fleet rather than as mere work-providers for local constituencies; engineering problems were better solved by his greater reliance upon naval engineers. Navy men speak of his tenure as one greatly increasing the efficiency of the department.

Meyer remained loyal to Taft in the political crisis of 1912, but his personal attachment to Roosevelt continued and after the World War began he was soon campaigning under Roosevelt's lead for preparedness and then for American participation. In 1916 he championed Roosevelt for the Republican nomination for the presidency. He died Mar. 9, 1918, in his sixtieth year.

[M. A. DeWolfe Howe, *George von Lengerke Meyer* (1919); *Selections from the Correspondence of Theodore Roosevelt and Henry Cabot Lodge, 1884–1918* (2 vols., 1925); *The Letters and Friendships of Sir Cecil Spring-Rice* (2 vols., 1929), ed. by Stephen Gwynn; *Taft and Roosevelt, The Intimate Letters of Archie Butt* (2 vols., 1930); *Harvard Coll., Class of 1879, Fiftieth Anniv., Ninth Report* (1929); *Harvard Grads. Mag.*, June 1918; *Boston Transcript*, Mar. 11, 1918.]

P. H. B.

MEYER, MARTIN ABRAHAM (Jan. 15, 1879–June 27, 1923), rabbi, Semitist, was born in San Francisco, Cal., the son of Charles and Louisa B. (Silberstein) Meyer. He attended the public schools of his native city, then entered Hebrew Union College, Cincinnati, having been prepared by Rabbi Jacob Voorsanger of San Francisco. He received the degree of A.B. in 1899 from the University of Cincinnati, and in 1901 graduated as rabbi from Hebrew Union College, honor man and valedictorian. Having won a fellowship in the American School of Oriental Study and Research in Palestine, he spent the winter 1901–02 in Jerusalem specializing in archeology, ethnology, and Semitic philology. Several articles which he contributed to American newspapers during that period indicate his disgust with Jewish conditions in the Holy Land. In 1902, he was elected rabbi of Congregation Beth Emeth at Albany, N. Y., where he remained four years. On June 19, 1905, he married Jennie May Haas of Cincinnati; two children, a son and a daughter, were born to them. He registered as a post-graduate student at Columbia University, majoring in Semitics, and received the degree of Ph.D. in 1910. His dissertation, *History of the City of Gaza* (1907), was a scholarly work in Arabic Semitic culture. In 1906, he was called to Temple Israel, Brooklyn, N. Y., and served there four years. As rabbi of the leading congregation in that large borough he wielded a wide influence along civic and philanthropic as well as religious lines. During this time he helped organize the Brooklyn Federation of Jewish Charities.

In 1910, he accepted the unanimous call of Temple Emanu El, the leading Reform congregation in San Francisco, where he served the remaining thirteen years of his life. He soon became an outstanding figure of the Pacific Coast. His scholarly training led to his appointment in 1911 as lecturer in Semitics at the University of California, a post he held with distinction until his death. He was in popular demand for lectures at western colleges, where he discussed scientific as well as religious topics. In addition to his doctoral thesis, he wrote the article "Jerusalem—Modern" for the *Jewish Encyclopedia* (1904); an introduction to *Sermons and Addresses by Jacob Voorsanger* (1913), edited by O. I. Wise; a noteworthy pamphlet, *Jew and Non-Jew* (1913), published by the Central Conference of American Rabbis; and a sketch of "The Jews of California," which appeared in A. W. Voorsanger's *Western Jewry* (1916). As a preacher, Meyer was direct, forceful, and effective. He brought his scholarly attainments into the preparation of his sermons, which were based invariably on the Bible and upon Jewish commentaries interpreted in the light of modern events. He was fearless, though usually tactful in discussing vital issues, and was one of the few Reform rabbis who openly spoke for and worked on behalf of Zionism.

He was most active in civic affairs along non-partisan lines. Appointed in 1911 a member of the State Board of Charities and Corrections, he became chairman in 1912 and served with great credit until a reluctant governor accepted his resignation in 1920. Deeply interested in social-service problems and following reform ideas without being impractical, he became a recognized leader in western philanthropies. The most constructive achievement to his credit is the Jewish Committee for Personal Service in State Institutions, a society which he organized in cooperation with I. Irving Lipsitch, to care for Jewish wards under state supervision and to help them after their release. Another monument to him is the Martin A. Meyer Memorial Fund for needy Jewish students of the University of California, a sum of $25,000 collected by friends shortly after his death. In 1918 he volunteered for war service under the American Red Cross and returned in 1919 a chastened man, eager to uphold the principles of World Peace. He died in San Francisco.

[Files of *Emanu El* (San Francisco), esp. issues of June 29 and July 6, 1923; *The Am. Jewish Year Book*, vol. XXVII (1925); *Who's Who in America*, 1922–23; *Central Conf. of Am. Rabbis*, Yearbook, vol. XXXIII (1923); *San Francisco Examiner*, June 28, 1923; personal acquaintance.]

R. I. C.

MEZES, SIDNEY EDWARD (Sept. 23, 1863–Sept. 10, 1931), educator, was born at Belmont, Cal., the only son of Simon Monserrate and Juliet Janin (Johnson) Mezes. His father was a native of northern Spain who settled in California during the winter of 1849–50, was successful in business and became a large landowner. His mother, born in Florence, Italy, was the daughter of Sidney Law Johnson of New Haven, Conn. A graduate of Yale and a descendant of the second president of Yale College, this grandfather was a lawyer by profession, practising in New Orleans and San Francisco. Sidney Edward Mezes became an accomplished linguist at an early age, both through the help of his parents and in the course of protracted visits to Europe. Completing his preparatory studies at St. Matthew's Hall in San Mateo, he entered the University of California, from which he graduated in 1884 with the degree of B.S. In the early winter of 1884 his father died. For some years thereafter the son gave most of his attention to the affairs of his father's estate, meanwhile carrying on studies in the humanities at the universities of California and Berlin. Convinced at length that his major interest was in philosophy and attracted by the fame of Royce, James, and Palmer, he entered Harvard University as a senior in 1889.

At Harvard he remained four years, receiving the degrees of A.B. in 1890, A.M. in 1891, and Ph.D. in 1893. During the year 1893–94 he taught at Bryn Mawr and the University of Chicago. In the autumn of 1894 he was called to the University of Texas as adjunct professor of philosophy. He became associate professor in 1897, professor in 1900, dean in 1902, and president of the University in 1908. At the close of 1914 he resigned to accept the presidency of the College of the City of New York. It was at the University of Texas that Mezes spent the happiest years of his life. He was married at Austin (Dec. 10, 1896), to Annie Olive Hunter of that city; he formed at the University and in Austin many of his closest and most valued friendships; and his steady and rapid advancement bears witness alike to his ability and his popularity. In 1929, fifteen years after he left Texas, he had the honor of being elected president emeritus of the University.

The College of the City of New York under his administration entered upon a period of extraordinary growth, during which its development was carefully and skilfully guided, its internal organization nicely adjusted, its services to the community made more direct and valuable. Mezes was responsible for the establishment of the schools of Technology, Business, and Education, and for the expansion of evening, summer, and vocational courses; but he was responsible also for strengthening the discipline of the institution and raising its scholastic standards. It was his conscious aim to preserve and improve what was best in the old plan of instruction while introducing, with cautious moderation, what seemed to be good in the new.

While still at Texas he had declined the position of United States commissioner of education; but when in 1917 he was asked by his brother-in-law, Col. Edward M. House, at President Wilson's request, to gather a body of experts to collect data which might be needed eventually at the Peace Conference, he undertook the task at once. A first result of the studies carried on by this body, called The Inquiry, was the submission of a report "on the main outlines of an equitable settlement," which became "the basis from which the President started in formulating his Fourteen Points" (*What Really Happened at Paris,* p. 2). At the Paris Conference the members of The Inquiry were constituted into a Section of Territorial, Economic and Political Intelligence; still under Mezes, who was styled director of specialists and was also appointed United States delegate on the Central (*i.e.,* international) Territorial Commission. His great contribution to this enterprise was the selection and training of his staff of experts; to him belongs a considerable part of the credit for the able service which they rendered at Paris. In the summer of 1927, because of failing health, he retired from active service as president of the College of the City of New York. He died at Altadena, Cal., four years later.

Mezes contributed many articles dealing with philosophy or questions of college policy and administration to various scientific periodicals and was also the author of *Ethics, Descriptive and Explanatory* (1901), and of portions of *The Conception of God* (1895), by Josiah Royce, and *What Really Happened at Paris* (1921), edited by Charles Seymour and E. M. House. He was a tall, spare man, dark in complexion, dignified in his bearing. His most noteworthy qualities of mind and character were clarity in thought and speech, keenness in judgment whether of men or questions, an unusual range of learning and interest, cautious deliberation in planning combined with vigor and courage in execution, fairness, tolerance, and charity, and a modesty which almost reached the point of self-effacement.

[Papers and records of the Mezes family; letters and other writings of S. E. Mezes; records, faculty, and trustee minutes, etc., at Yale, the Univ. of Tex., College of the City of New York; *Who's Who in America,* 1930–31; Harvard classbooks, Class of 1890; E. M. House and Charles Seymour, *What Really Happened at Paris* (1921); *The Intimate Papers of Col. House* (4 vols., 1926–28); articles in *City Coll. Alumnus,* Oct. 1931; record of the City College Memorial Meeting, Nov. 12, 1931 (privately printed); *N. Y. Times,* Sept. 12, 1931; unpublished personal recollections of Mrs. Carmelita Mezes Wynne, Hon. D. F. Houston, Col. E. M. House, Dr. John H. Finley, Presidents H. Y. Benedict (Texas) and F. B. Robinson (C. C. N. Y), Provost Charles Seymour (Yale), Prof. W. J. Battle (Texas), Hon. Adolph C. Miller, and others, including the writer.]

C. L. B.

MIANTONOMO (d. 1643), Indian chief, was the son of Mascus and the nephew of Canonicus [*q.v.*]. Although he was presumably considerably younger than his uncle, the two divided the government of the Narragansett tribe between them. In 1632 Miantonomo visited Boston and was received by the governor. Two years later, when Stone and Norton were killed by the Indians, and again in 1636 when Oldham was killed, he did all he could to help the English catch the murderers. Nevertheless he was suspected by them and had to appear again at Boston in the latter year, when he cleared himself. In 1637 he joined the English and rendered them aid in the Pequot War. The following year both he and Uncas [*q.v.*] were summoned to Hartford to answer complaints regarding the Pequots in their charge and with the hope of bringing about peace between the two chiefs. As Miantonomo would have to cross the hostile Mohegan and Pequot territory, Roger Williams urged him not to risk his life, but, with his family and 150 warriors, he made the trip to Hartford and back in safety, although 600 Pequots were said to have lain in ambush for him. On the other hand, Uncas at first refused to appear, pleading lameness, but the English recognized the excuse as a subterfuge and forced him to come. Miantonomo agreed to a reconciliation but Uncas declined. On Sept. 21, 1638, however, the two chiefs signed a treaty of peace with the English and with each other.

In their Indian relations the English of Connecticut, and more particularly those of Massachusetts, were inclined to oppose the Narragansetts and favor the other tribes. In spite of his dissolute character, Uncas was less subject to suspicion than Canonicus and Miantonomo. Possibly the main reason was that the Rhode Island colonists were anathema to Massachusetts, and the stronger colonies, regardless of the faithfulness of the Indians, preferred to cultivate those on their own borders and to antagonize those who were closer to the Rhode Islanders. Miantonomo had signed a deed for Warwick to Samuel Gorton and his associates, whereupon in Massachusetts he was declared a usurper and the Indian Pumham was instigated to claim his territory. In March 1638 Miantonomo also signed a deed to William Coddington and his associates for the island of Rhode Island. In 1642, when it was said that he was plotting the destruction of the English, he was asked by the magistrates of Massachusetts to answer the charges through a hostile Pequot interpreter. He properly refused but offered to go to Boston if Williams should be allowed to go with him. Williams had tried to convince Winthrop of the Indian's friendliness. When this request was refused Miantonomo went to Boston alone. There, under duress, his accusers insisted upon his answering through the Pequot. He was insulted and forced to say that he had been at fault. In August 1643 Uncas made war on one of the Narragansett undersachems, Sequasson, and in the war following between the tribes, Miantonomo was taken prisoner by Uncas through treachery. He was delivered to the English at Hartford. In Boston the Commissioners of the United Colonies and a body of clergy considered the case and decided that Uncas might murder him within his own jurisdiction. The unfortunate Miantonomo was surrendered to Uncas for that purpose and killed with a hatchet near Norwich. He was buried where he fell, at Sachem's Plain. His wife, Wawaloam, survived him and was alive in 1661. A monument was erected to him in 1841.

[F. W. Hodge, *Handbook of Am. Indians*, pt. 1 (1907); S. G. Drake, *The Book of the Indians* (1841), which is the eighth edition of the *Indian Biography*; J. W. DeForest, *Hist. of the Indians of Conn.* (1851); J. K. Hosmer, *Winthrop's Jour.* (2 vols., 1908); "Acts of the Commissioners of the United Colonies of New England," vol. I (1859), which is vol. IX of the *Records of the Colony of New Plymouth*; J. R. Bartlett, *Letters of Roger Williams* (1874).] J. T. A.

MICHAËLIUS, JONAS (b. 1584), first minister of the Dutch Reformed Church at New Amsterdam, was a son of the Rev. Jan Michielsz, one of those fighting preachers who fanned the hatred of Spanish rule and popery among the Reformed in Holland and Flanders. But he was also a man of affairs, for he was repeatedly employed in matters of state, both in England and Holland, by William of Orange, the Earl of Leicester, and Prince Maurice of Nassau. The son was born in 1584 in the village of Grootebroek in the north of the Province of Holland, to which Jan Michielsz had accepted a call in 1582. After the father's death in 1595, his widow moved to Hoorn, the town nearest to Grootebroek. Here the boy attended the Latin school until, at fifteen, he entered the Theological College at Leyden with a scholarship awarded him by the burgomasters of Hoorn. He graduated in 1605, and thereafter, for a period of twenty years, he ministered to various parishes in Brabant and Holland. In 1624, however, he asked to be transferred to Brazil, where the Hollanders were then trying to oust the Portuguese from their possessions. In March 1625 he sailed for his new destination in the fleet that was to clinch the Dutch hold on Bahia. During the voyage the commander, hearing from home-bound ships that the Portuguese had recaptured Bahia, changed his course and made for More on the coast of Guinea, West Africa.

They arrived on Nov. 19, 1625, and Michaëlius

went on shore and remained in the fort. By the end of the year 1627 he was again in Holland, for on Jan. 24, 1628, he sailed with his family from The Texel for New Netherland. They landed at New Amsterdam on Apr. 7. Five weeks later his wife died in childbed, leaving him three little children, one of whom, an only son, had stayed behind in Holland. Soon after his arrival he organized a church community, the beginning of the Collegiate Church in the City of New York and of the Reformed Church in America, of which Michaëlius may justly be called the founder. The Sunday services were held in Dutch, as the number of those who did not understand the language was very small, but for the benefit of those few he administered the Lord's Supper in French.

Michaëlius had a missionary's zeal to convert the Indians, whom he found to be "strangers to all decency." Two years later he wrote with greater bitterness about the men of his own congregation, including the Director-General Peter Minuit, an elder of his church, and the members of the Council, whom he condemned wholesale as a "pestilent kind of people." He accused them of defrauding the Company, of oppressing the innocent, and of leading immoral lives. Having returned to Holland in 1632, he repeated these charges in person before the Consistory of Amsterdam. The Directors of the West India Company, however, apparently did not appreciate the vehemence with which he had defended their interests. In 1637 the Classis of Amsterdam recommended Michaëlius for reappointment to the ministry in New Netherland, but the Assembly of the Nineteen unanimously rejected him. Their curt reply to the Classis contains the last record of his name. Three of the many letters that he sent from Manhattan to correspondents in Holland have fortunately been preserved. Two of these are written in forceful Dutch, the third is in somewhat florid Latin. They are among the earliest and most interesting records of New Amsterdam in its infancy. His character sketch of Peter Minuit and his Council, contained in the Latin letter to Joannes van Foreest, must be taken with reservations. Michaëlius was one of those who, not content with the care of souls, strove to meddle with things political and to sway the minds of the magistracy. He was, no doubt, an honest man, a fervid Christian, and a good Latin scholar, but intemperate in asserting his superiority in these respects over men of less conscience and less culture.

[*Ecclesiastical Records: State of N. Y.*, I (1901), 48–73; Albert Eekhof, *Jonas Michaëlius, Founder of the Church in New Netherland* (Leyden, 1926), *De Hervormde Kerk in Noord-Amerika* (2 vols., 1913), and an article in P. C. Molhuysen and P. J. Blok, *Nieuw Nederlandsch Biografisch Woordenboek*, vol. I (1911); *Narratives of New Netherland, 1609–1664* (1909), ed. by J. Franklin Jameson; I. N. P. Stokes, *The Iconography of Manhattan Island*, vol. IV (1922); Dingman Versteeg, *Manhattan in 1628* (1904).] A. J. B.

MICHAUX, ANDRÉ (Mar. 7, 1746–November 1802), explorer, silviculturist, and botanist, was born in the park of Versailles, France, at Satory, a royal domain which had long been managed by his ancestors. When ten years old he was sent to a pension but remained there only four years because his father wished to train him for the family tenancy. In October 1769 he married Cécile Claye, the daughter of a rich farmer near Beauce; she died eleven months later after the birth of their son, François André [*q.v.*]. To relieve his despondency, the young widower began the intensive study of botany and came under the instruction of Bernard de Jussieu. In 1779 he moved nearer the Jardin des Plantes and during the next two years herborized in England, the Auvergne, and the Pyrenees. Subsequently he was appointed secretary to the French consul at Ispahan, Persia, but, spurred by that zeal for exploration which was his most salient characteristic, he abandoned this connection in order to wander (1782–85) over much of the region between the Tigris and Euphrates rivers, in which he collected many seeds and plants. On his return to France his government directed him to make a study of the forest trees of North America, in order to ascertain the advisability of their introduction into France and their utility for naval construction.

On the first of October 1785 he arrived in New York with his young son and Paul Saulnier, a journeyman gardener who later brought the Lombardy poplar to the United States. The next year and a half he spent in a study of the local flora and in the establishment of a nursery near Hackensack, N. J. In 1787 he moved to Charleston, S. C., purchased a plantation about ten miles from the city, and continued his search for interesting plants, especially for those which might be successfully cultivated. In the same year he traveled extensively in the southern Appalachians and, during the next, invaded Spanish Florida. In 1789 he visited the Bahamas and also continued his explorations in the Carolina mountains. During this period he was interested in the distribution of ginseng and introduced among the mountaineers the idea of its commercial exploitation. Shortly afterward the French Revolution cut off his support from the home government although, despite family traditions, he appears to have espoused the republican cause. Perhaps the report of his son, who had previously returned to Paris, influenced him to some extent; half of the sixty thousand young trees which the Michaux had sent back had been presented by the Queen to the Austrian Emperor and the rest had been largely scattered or neglected. In 1792 the elder Michaux botanized in Canada and even visited the vicinity of Hudson Bay. On his return he interested the American Philosophical Society in a project for the exploration of the Far West by way of the Missouri; some money was subscribed for the purpose, and he received instructions for the proposed journey from Thomas Jefferson. But during these negotiations, Edmond Charles Genet arrived in Charleston and entrusted Michaux with a commission for George Rogers Clark [*q.v.*]. Genet had asked Jefferson to grant permission to Michaux to act as consul in Kentucky, but Jefferson declined to grant an exequatur, giving him instead letters of introduction as a traveling scientist.

On July 15, 1793, Michaux left Philadelphia for his famous mid-western travels; his manuscript journals were published almost a century later. In April 1796 he returned to Charleston, rich in botanical data but exhausted in finances. Four months later he sailed for France but was shipwrecked off Egmont, Holland, where some of his manuscripts were lost and his herbaria suffered damage. Despite a favorable reception in Paris, he failed to interest his government in further American explorations and finally accepted a commission as naturalist on the Australian expedition of Capt. Nicolas Baudin. They sailed from France on Oct. 18, 1800, visited Teneriffe, and reached Mauritius on Mar. 15, 1801. Michaux decided to leave the expedition in order to explore Madagascar. After some difficulty, he attained the larger island but trusted too well the physique which had withstood hardships in more temperate countries and succumbed to a tropical fever. His great contributions to botany were his explorations and collections. Neither adventures among Arabian bandits nor arduous travel by foot and canoe with only Indians or backwoodsmen as companions gave favorable training for literary attainment, and his journals (or field notes) are crudely laconic. Although largely based on his collections and data, the *Flora Boreali-Americana, sistens caracteres Plantarum quas in America Septentrionali collegit et detexit Andreas Michaux* (Paris, 1803) was prepared by Claude Richard, and Sargent has suggested that the *Histoire des Chênes de l'Amérique, ou descriptions et figures de toutes les espèces et variétés de Chênes de l'Amérique Septentrionale* (Paris, 1801) must have been the result of similar collaboration. His other publication is the "Mémoire sur les Dattiers," published in the *Journal de Physique, de Chemie et d'Histoire Naturelle* (vol. LII, 1801).

[J. P. F. Deleuze, "Notice Historique sur André Michaux," *Annales du Muséum National d'Histoire Naturelle*, vol. III (1804); Asa Gray, "Notes of a Botanical Excursion to the Mountains of N. C.," *Am. Jour. of Sci.*, Oct.–Dec. 1841; Ovide Brunet, *Notice sur les Plantes de Michaux et sur son Voyage au Canada et à la Baie d'Hudson* (1863); C. S. Sargent, "Portions of the Jour. of André Michaux, Botanist, written during his Travels in the U. S. and Canada, 1785 to 1796: With an Introduction and Explanatory Notes," *Proc. Am. Philos. Soc.*, vol. XXVI (1889); R. G. Thwaites, *Early Western Travels*, vol. III (1904) and *Original Jours. of the Lewis and Clark Expedition, 1804–06* (7 vols., 1904–05); F. J. Turner, "Correspondence of the French Ministers to the U. S., 1791–97," *Ann. Report of the Am. Hist. Asso. for the Year 1903* (1904); "Correspondence of Clark and Genet," *Ann. Report of the Am. Hist. Asso. for the Year 1896*, vol. I (1897); *North Am. Rev.*, July 1821; *S. C. Hist. and Geneal. Mag.*, Jan. 1928.] H. B. B.

MICHAUX, FRANÇOIS ANDRÉ (Aug. 16, 1770–Oct. 23, 1855), silviculturist, traveler, and botanist, was born on the royal domain of Satory in the park of Versailles, France. His father was André Michaux [*q.v.*]; his mother, Cécile Claye, who died in the month after his birth. At the age of fifteen he accompanied his father to New York and later (1787) to Charleston, S. C. He also went on the trip to the sources of the Keovee River, Fla., but was mainly entrusted with the management of the nursery. On Sept. 20, 1789, he was accidentally shot in the left eye, which never entirely recovered. Early in 1790 he returned to France and entered ardently into the French Revolution, but he also found time to study medicine with Corvisart. In 1801 he was commissioned by his government to strip and sell the two tree-plantations which his father had established in the United States and to appoint instead native correspondents in the principal seaports; he reached Charleston Oct. 9 and spent the winter on the Atlantic seaboard. On June 27, 1802, he left Philadelphia for the summer of travels that are described in his *Voyage à l'ouest des monts Alléghanys dans les états de l'Ohio, et du Kentucky, et du Tennessée, et retour à Charleston par les Hautes-Carolines* (Paris, 1804), which went through several editions and was translated into English (London, 1805) and German (Weimar, 1805). After a winter in Charleston (Oct. 18, 1802–Mar. 1, 1803), he returned to France. In 1804 he published his report *Sur la Naturalisation des Arbres Forestiers de l'Amérique du Nord.* On Feb. 5, 1806, he again started for Charleston but was captured by the British and detained in the Bermudas, which resulted in his "Notice sur les Iles Bermudes, et particulièrement sur l'Ile Saint-

Georges" (*Annales du Muséum d'Histoire Naturelle*, vol. VIII, 1806). In May he reached the United States and spent three years in travel and study, mainly along the Atlantic Coast. Incidentally, he and another Frenchman were the only passengers on Robert Fulton's trial trip up the Hudson. On his return to France he published the *Histoire des Arbres forestiers de l'Amérique Septentrionale* (Paris, 3 vols., 1810–13), which is better known in this country as *The North American Sylva, or a Description of the Forest Trees of the United States, Canada, and Nova Scotia, Considered Particularly with Respect to their Use in the Arts and their Introduction into Commerce* (Paris, 3 vols., 1818–19), later supplemented by Thomas Nuttall [*q.v.*]. Parts of the larger work were also monographed separately. The remainder of his life was largely spent in the administration of an estate and experimental farm which belonged to the Société Centrale de l'Agriculture, although he published several short papers on a variety of subjects. When advanced in age, he married his housekeeper, a relative; they left no issue. He died quite suddenly from apoplexy. Part of his fortune was bequeathed to the American Philosophical Society. He was a chevalier of the Legion of Honor, a correspondent of the French Institute, and a member of the American Philosophical Society. Apparently he was far better known in the United States than in his native country.

[See Elias Durand, "Biog. Memoir of the late François André Michaux," *Trans. Am. Philos. Soc.*, vol. XI (1860); Michaux's account of his trip with Fulton in the *Bull. de la Soc. d'Encouragement pour l'Industrie Nationale*, Sept. 1848, reprinted in translation in the *Jour. of the Franklin Inst.*, July 1849; and the *Am. Jour. of Sci.*, July 1856. See also the bibliography of André Michaux.] H. B. B.

MICHEL, WILLIAM MIDDLETON (Jan. 22, 1822–June 4, 1894), physician, was born in Charleston, S. C., the son of Dr. William and Eugenia (Fraser) Michel. His father was of French ancestry and was educated entirely in France; his mother was of a family prominent in the colonial history of South Carolina. He was known familiarly by his second name which until about Civil War time he spelled Myddleton. For two years (1835–37) he studied at the Pension Labrousse in Paris. In 1842 he began to study medicine under eminent French instructors and for two years dissected for Jean Cruveilhier. After receiving a diploma in 1845 from the École de Médecine he returned to the United States and in 1846 was graduated from the Medical College of the State of South Carolina. The following year he opened the Summer Medical Institute of Charleston in which he lectured on anatomy, physiology, and obstetrics. The school attracted students from all over the South and continued in operation until 1860. In 1852 he had been offered a chair in Crosby Medical College of New York and was urged by his friend, Dr. Marion Sims, to accept the offer, but he refused it to remain in Charleston. In 1862 he was placed in charge of a Confederate hospital at Manchester, Va., and later became one of the consulting surgeons of the staff of the Richmond Hospital. He was the personal physician of Gen. Joseph E. Johnston.

Michel was professor of physiology and histology in the Medical College of South Carolina from 1868 until his death in 1894 and from 1880 until his death he was a member of the Charleston board of health. He was prominent in the Medical Society of South Carolina, serving as president from 1880 to 1883. He was a member of the Academy of Sciences of Philadelphia, of the American Association for the Advancement of Science, and a corresponding member of the Imperial Society of National History of Paris. For a time during the war (1863–64) he edited the *Confederate Medical and Surgical Journal*, in which he published a number of important case records. After the war he became associate editor, with Dr. F. Peyre Porcher, of the *Charleston Medical Journal and Review* and was also an associate editor of the *Boston Medical Journal*. His contributions to these and other medical magazines were numerous and considered of great value in his time. His study of the embryological development of the opossum, published in the *Proceedings of the American Association for the Advancement of Science* (vol. III, 1850), was the subject of much scientific discussion. In April 1866, Michel was married to Cecilia S. Inglesby, who with four children survived him.

[R. F. Stone, *Biog. of Eminent Am. Physicians and Surgeons* (1894); I. A. Watson, *Physicians and Surgeons of America* (1896); H. A. Kelly and W. L. Burrage, *Am. Medic. Biogs.* (1920); *Charleston News and Courier*, June 5, 1894.] A. R. C.

MICHELSON, ALBERT ABRAHAM (Dec. 19, 1852–May 9, 1931), physicist, was born at Strelno, a small Prussian town near the frontier of Poland. His parents, Samuel and Rosalie (Przlubska) Michelson, came to America in 1854. After a short stay in New York the family went by boat via Panama to San Francisco; thence the gold rush took them first to Murphy's camp in Calaveras County, Cal., and later to Virginia City, Nev., close to the bonanza silver mines. Michelson received his early schooling at Virginia City and, when his parents returned to San Francisco, completed his primary and secondary education in the schools of that city. Because of his evident interest and talent in science, his high-school teachers urged him to continue his education. He took the competitive examinations for congressional appointment to the United States Naval Academy, resulting in a tie between himself and another boy. The latter, through political influence, got the appointment. On the suggestion of the examining committee, Michelson then decided to try for one of the ten appointments at large, and, although only seventeen, set out for Washington to interview President Grant. He was successful in obtaining the interview, but unsuccessful in getting one of the appointments available. On the eve of Michelson's departure from Annapolis again to interview the President, the Commandant, in recognition of his ability and tenacity of purpose, made a place for him as an eleventh appointment.

He graduated from the Naval Academy in 1873. After the usual period of required service, he was appointed instructor in physics and chemistry there (1875–79). This service was followed by study in the University of Berlin in 1880, at Heidelberg the following year, and in Paris at the Collège de France and the École Polytechnique in 1882. Called to the Case School of Applied Science as professor of physics in 1883, he held this position until 1889. Thence he went to Clark University as professor of physics (1889–92). With the organization of the new University of Chicago in 1892 he was called by President Harper to be head of the department of physics, and this position he held until retirement to emeritus professor in 1931. He was made a "distinguished service" professor of physics at Chicago in 1925. He was Lowell lecturer in 1899, his lectures being later published under the title, *Light Waves and Their Uses* (1903); served on the Bureau International des Poids et Mesures, 1892–93; and on the International Committee of Weights and Measures in 1897. He was exchange professor at the University of Göttingen in 1911. On Apr. 10, 1877, he was married to Margaret McLean Heminway, from whom he was later divorced. By this marriage there were two sons and a daughter; one son predeceased him. On Dec. 23, 1899, he was married to Edna Stanton of Lake Forest, Ill., who bore him three daughters.

His career was rather unique in that, although he never received an academic degree in recognition of the completion of any course of study, he was the recipient of eleven honorary degrees from American and European universities. He was awarded the Rumford Medal of the Royal Society of London in 1889; the Grand Prize of the Paris Exposition in 1900; the Mattencci Medal of the Società Italiana, Rome, in 1904; the Copley Medal of the Royal Society and the Nobel Prize in 1907; the Cresson Medal of the Franklin Institute in 1912; the Draper Gold Medal of the National Academy of Sciences in 1916; the Franklin Medal in 1923; the Gold Medal of the Royal Astronomical Society in 1923; the Gold Medal of the Society of Arts and Sciences, New York, in 1929; the Duddell Medal of the Physical Society of London in 1930. In the war period in 1918 he was appointed lieutenant-commander, United States Naval Reserve. He was president of the National Academy of Sciences (1923–27); he served the American Association for the Advancement of Science as president in 1910; the American Physical Society as president (1901–03), and as a member of its editorial board (1915–17). He was vice-president of the American Philosophical Society during the years 1910, 1911, and 1913. Nearly all of the great scientific societies claimed him for membership. He was an honorary fellow of the Physical Society of London, foreign member of the Royal Society of London, honorary fellow of the Royal Society of Edinburgh, corresponding member of the British Association for the Advancement of Science, fellow of the Royal Astronomical Society, honorary member of the Royal Institution of Great Britain, honorary member of the Royal Irish Academy, foreign associate of the Académie Française, and also of the Académie des Sciences (Paris), and honorary fellow of the Optical Society of America. He was foreign member of the Reale Accademia dei Lincei (Rome) and held memberships in the American Astronomical Society, the American Academy, the Société Française de Physique, the Société Hollandaise des Sciences, the Deutschen Physicalische Gesellschaft, the Kungliga, Fysiografiska Sällskapet, Lund, and the Russian Academy of Sciences.

In *American Men of Science* Michelson's official field is succinctly summarized in one word, "Light." His entire scientific career, begun while a student at Annapolis and continued without pause until in his seventy-ninth year he suffered a cerebral hemorrhage that caused his death at Pasadena, Cal., on May 9, 1931, is summed up in some seventy-nine published papers. The first of these, printed in *The American Journal of Science* (May 1878), when he was twenty-six years of age, bears the title, "On a Method of Measuring the Velocity of Light"; the last, written shortly before he lost consciousness, but as yet unpublished, is on the same subject. In some aspect or other, light was the topic of all but twelve of these papers. His work in this field can be divided into two main categories, the first being the problem of the accurate determination of the velocity of light, and the second the study of optical interference. With respect to his work on the velocity of light, neither the young man of twenty-six nor the old man of seventy-nine ever had a rival. World-wide confidence in his ability, his judgment, and his honesty is indicated by the fact that, in this important work, no one ever attempted to repeat his experiments or check his results, excepting himself. In his first experiments, carried on at the Naval Academy, he conceived the idea of slightly modifying the optical path of an apparatus which had been used earlier by Léon Foucault. Foucault's unmodified experiment was at that time being carried on under the leadership of Prof. Simon Newcomb, of the Naval Academy, on a very elaborate scale supported by thousands of dollars of congressional appropriation. Michelson, by changing the position of one mirror, was able, with equipment designed and built by himself and costing less than ten dollars, to achieve precision equal to or superior to that of the official apparatus. This was the first instance of his ingenuity with respect to physical phenomena. In his last determination of the velocity of light, which embodies many refinements of his original plan, an accuracy of about three parts in a million is expected, which means that the journey of more than one hundred and eighty-six thousand miles made by light in one second will be known to within half a mile.

Michelson's work on the interference of light was also begun rather early in life, the first paper being published in *The American Journal of Science* in August 1881, under the title, "The Relative Motion of the Earth and the Luminiferous Ether." This title explains the fundamental object of all of this work, which was to detect, if possible, the absolute motion of the earth as, trailing along with the rest of the solar family, it follows the sun's plunging course through space. In common with his distinguished predecessors, and his contemporaries, Michelson held the idea that light consists of an electro-magnetic wave motion carried through a luminiferous ether, with respect to which, as a fixed system of reference, cosmical motions might be measured. It is well known now that these experiments and all others which have been designed to determine absolute motion have given completely negative results. It is equally striking testimony to confidence in his work that Michelson's first disclosure of the abortive character of this experiment was accepted without question by experimental and theoretical physicists the world over, and that a new philosophy with respect to the fundamentals of physical science was immediately attempted. This new philosophy reached its highest development in the hands of Einstein, first as the special theory of relativity, and later as the general relativity theory. Only within comparatively recent years when a somewhat more modern design of apparatus and many thousands of observations by another worker appeared to give a minute residual effect, was the experimental problem subjected to another rather widespread attack, not only by Michelson himself, but by other experimenters in America and Europe. The upshot of these latest experiments has been a complete confirmation of Michelson's earlier assertion. The constancy of the velocity of light, irrespective of the motion of either source or observer, is perhaps the keystone of the structure of modern physical theory.

As by-products of the interference experiments on ether drift, in which Edward W. Morley cooperated with Michelson, should be mentioned his contributions to fundamental apparatus and fundamental theory in spectroscopy. His echelon spectroscope was one of the earliest forms having sufficiently high resolution to disclose direct optical evidence of molecular motion which is identified with temperature. This same apparatus also, when used to study the effect of a magnetic field upon a source of radiation, did much to lay the foundation for the future of a field of investigation which even in the swiftly changing world of modern physics has maintained the same fundamental and important position with respect to new theories that it held with respect to the old. In July 1890 he published in *The London, Edinburgh, and Dublin Philosophical Magazine* a paper, "On the Application of Interference Methods to Astronomical Measurements." Thirty years later, this method was used by the astronomers in the attempt to measure the diameter of a star, and it achieved such striking success that it became front-page news, in the public press throughout the world.

Other by-products of his work in interference were his adoption of the wave length of cadmium light as a fundamental standard of length, and his calibration of the international meter which he found to contain 1,553,163½ wave lengths of the red radiation from this source. In collaboration with Thomas Chrowder Chamberlin and one or two other colleagues, Michelson applied the delicate methods of measurement by means of interference to the problem of the rigidity of the earth, using for this purpose the ebb and flow of such tiny tides as are engendered in a six-inch iron pipe five hundred feet long, filled with water and buried underground. This investigation confirmed early provisional estimates by Kelvin, based on celestial mechanics, that the earth possessed a rigidity of the same order of magnitude as that of steel. These experiments showed in addition that the earth's viscosity also was not much different from that of steel. In the ruling of diffraction gratings, which are of primary importance in the study of spectra, not only of terrestrial sources but also of the stars, Michelson laid noteworthy contributions on the foundations of work along these lines of his distinguished predecessor, Henry A. Rowland of Johns Hopkins. While failing to achieve his ideals in this direction, he established at the University of Chicago one of the very few centers in the world from which high-grade diffraction gratings may be produced for the benefit of scientific workers elsewhere.

No account of this great figure is complete without some reference to a few aspects of his personality, other than scientific. His life was a magnificent exhibition of singleness of purpose, unruffled by winds of favor or disfavor. Even the cosmic forces of love, hate, jealousy, envy, and ambition seemed to move him little. Possessed of an astonishing indifference to people in general because of his absorption in his scientific pursuits, he nevertheless had the capacity of making and cherishing a few devoted friends. As a teacher, his lectures were models of acute organization and clarity of exposition. Comparatively few students in his classes aroused his personal interest, but those who did found no end of patience and sympathetic and intelligent consideration for their scientific or their personal problems. As the executive head of a large and important department in a great university, it was his practice to delegate full responsibility with respect to all details to others. However, whenever his colleagues or his staff needed his support, no one was ever more quick to champion their cause as his own. In such situations his clarity of vision, fearlessness, and swift assumption of initiative usually won the desired results with little effective opposition.

Michelson's primitive simplicity of character showed itself in his intuitions with respect to natural phenomena and in the boldness and the brilliance of his attack upon those citadels wherein nature keeps her most carefully treasured secrets. His inquiries were of highly fundamental character. The man's artistic side might have been regarded as exhibiting versatility. He was a musician of some talent on the violin, and the musical instructor of some of his children; in water color and in oil he was an artist of unusual skill and feeling, for an amateur. All who knew him well realized that the feeling of the artist was the keynote of his scientific work as well. On one occasion in Chicago he had been prevailed upon to exhibit some of his water colors in one of the university halls. Physical force had been almost necessary to get him there in person. A lady came up to him and said that she felt he must have made a great mistake when he abandoned art for science. Michelson, with that characteristic grave courtesy that he always achieved when disagreeing with another's opinion, replied that he hoped she was mistaken; to his own way of thinking, he said, he felt he had never abandoned art. He said it was his conviction that in science alone was art able to find its highest expression.

F. R. Moulton, in an appreciation of Michelson published in *Popular Astronomy* (June–July 1931), admirably expresses the spirit of his work: "He was unhurried and unfretful. He was never rushed by University duties; he never drove himself to complete a laborious task; he never feared that science, the University, or mankind was at a critical turning point; he never trembled on the brink of a great discovery. . . . If I have correctly caught the dominant note of his life, Michelson was moved only by the æsthetic enjoyment his work gave him. In everything he did, whether it was work or play, he was an artist. . . . He pursued his modest serene way along the frontiers of science, entering new pathways and ascending to unattained heights as leisurely and as easily as though he were taking an evening stroll."

[J. M. and Jaques Cattell, eds., *Am. Men of Science* (4th ed., 1927); "Proc. of the Michelson Meeting of the Optical Soc. of America," in *Jour. of the Optical Society of America*, March 1929, containing an almost complete list of his published papers; R. A. Millikan, in *Science*, May 10, 22, 1931; F. R. Moulton, in *Popular Astronomy*, June–July 1931; H. G. Gale, in *Astrophysical Jour.*, July 1931; *N. Y. Times*, May 10, 11, 28, 1931, the last containing a letter signed Margaret Heminway Shepherd about his first marriage; *Who's Who in America*, 1930–31.]

H. B. L—n.

MICHENER, EZRA (Nov. 24, 1794–June 24, 1887), physician and botanist, the fourth and youngest child of Mordecai and Alice (Dunn) Michener, was born on a farm in London Grove Township, Chester County, Pa. The Micheners were Quakers and Ezra was brought up in this faith. His education began with reading lessons from the Bible taught by his maternal grandmother as she worked at her spinning wheel and was continued at the country school, where he learned writing and arithmetic. A neighbor, John Jackson, was an enthusiastic florist and botanist and taught the child much about the various plants. Young Michener responded eagerly and made good use of his friend's teaching and library. He pored over Rees's *Cyclopaedia* seeking familiar plants which he collected and classified—the beginning of his herbarium. Physically he was not robust. Realizing that he would not be able to carry on the heavy work of the farm he decided to study medicine and at the age of twenty-two entered the University of Pennsylvania at Philadelphia. In recognition of his ability and diligence he was chosen to be house student in the Philadelphia Dispensary and in his second year was given almost entire charge of the out-patient department. On Apr. 10, 1818, he received his diploma and began the practice of medicine in Chester County. He was married on Apr. 15, 1819, to Sarah Spencer. She died in 1843, and in the following year Michener was married to Mary S. Walton. He died at the age of ninety-two at his home near Toughkenamon, Pa.

Michener was one of the first medical men to use ergot as a uterine tonic. He invented an apparatus for the treatment of fracture of the femur which he used successfully for more than sixty years. In addition to his large practice he continued his investigations in botany, attending lectures, collecting specimens, and writing. He was an honorary member of the Medical Society of Pennsylvania; a correspondent of the Academy of Natural Sciences; and a founder of the Chester County Medical Society. His natural history collection included more than five hundred species of birds, animals, and reptiles. It was presented to Swarthmore College in 1869 but was destroyed in the fire occurring there some years later. An extensive herbarium of flowering and cryptogamous plants which he prepared by means of a press of his own invention was left to his heirs. His work brought him to the notice of the eminent scientists of his time, with many of whom he carried on a voluminous correspondence. His autobiography reveals him as a humorless, inflexibly upright man. He was an active member of the religious Society of Friends, and slavery, war, and the use of alcohol and tobacco were abhorrent to him. He overlooked no opportunity to denounce these evils and was one of the founders of the Guardian Society for Preventing Drunkenness. This was said to be the first temperance society in Pennsylvania and perhaps one of the first in the United States. His writings consist of fifteen books, twenty-three medical reports, and contributions to various publications. The more important of his works include the *Manual of Weeds* (1872); *Conchologia Cestrica* (1874), in collaboration with W. D. Hartman; *Handbook of Eclampsia* (1883); *Retrospect of Early Quakerism* (1860), and *The Christian Casket* (1869).

[*Autographical Notes from the Life and Letters of Ezra Michener, M.D.* (1893); J. S. Futhey and Gilbert Cope, *Hist. of Chester County, Pa.* (1881); J. W. Harshberger, *The Botanists of Phila. and Their Work* (1899); *Medic. and Surgic. Reporter,* Aug. 20, 1870; the *Friends' Intelligencer and Jour.,* Seventh Month 2, 1887; the *Phila. Press,* June 26, 1887.] F. E. W.

MICHIE, PETER SMITH (Mar. 24, 1839–Feb. 16, 1901), soldier, educator, son of William and Ann D. (Smith) Michie, was born at Brechin, County Forfar, Scotland. His family came to America in 1843 and settled in Cincinnati, Ohio. After graduating with honors from the Woodward High School he was appointed a cadet at the United States Military Academy from which he graduated second in his class in June 1863 and was assigned to the Corps of Engineers. A short time thereafter he received orders to report at Hiltonhead, S. C., where an army under General Gillmore was engaged in the siege of Charleston. As assistant engineer he was engaged for six months in the construction of batteries for the reduction of Fort Sumter and in the attack on Fort Wagner. In the latter operation he was employed in the hazardous work of laying out and constructing the parallels and approaches which caused the Confederates to abandon the fort. In the early part of 1864 he was selected as chief engineer of a division under General Seymour sent to Florida where he took part in the battle of Olustee and fortified various points on the Florida Coast. When, in the spring of 1864, Gillmore with his corps was ordered to southern Virginia to join the Army of the James under General Butler, he took Michie with him. Later Michie became its chief engineer. He took part in all the operations of this army during 1864 and 1865 and was present in its final advance upon Appomattox under General Ord.

For his services while still a lieutenant he received the brevets of captain, major, lieutenant-colonel, and brigadier-general. General Grant said he was "one of the most deserving young officers in the service" and that his services eminently entitled him to "substantial promotion" (*War of the Rebellion: Official Records, Army,* 1 ser. XLVI, pt. 2, pp. 947, 880). From 1867 to 1871 he served as instructor at the Military Academy and in 1870 as a member of a board of engineer officers sent to Europe to collect information on the development of sea-coast defenses to meet the increased power of artillery. In February 1871 he was appointed professor of natural and experimental philosophy at the Military Academy, which position he held until his death. By his engaging personality and genial manners he made many friends in military, political, and civil life and through them was able to win support for the Military Academy which he loved. He was largely instrumental in securing the necessary legislation for the enlargement of the reservation at West Point in 1889 which made possible the expansion of the Academy after the Spanish-American War. He was the author of textbooks on mechanics, physics, and astronomy and in addition wrote *The Life and Letters of Emory Upton* (1885), *The Personnel of Sea Coast Defenses* (1887), and *General McClellan* (1901). From 1871 to 1901 he was one of the overseers of the Thayer School of Civil Engineering of Dartmouth College. He died at West Point. In 1863 he had married Marie Louise Roberts of Cincinnati, Ohio. They had two sons and a daughter. His younger son, Dennis Mahan Michie, was killed in the battle of San Juan, Cuba, in the Spanish-American War.

[G. W. Cullum, *Biog. Reg. . . . U. S. Mil. Acad.*, vol. II (ed. 1891); *Thirty-second Ann. Reunion: Asso. Grads. U. S. Mil. Acad.* (1901); *N. Y. Times*, Feb. 17, 1901.] G. J. F.

MICHIKINIKWA [See Little Turtle, *c.* 1752–1812].

MIDDLETON, ARTHUR (1681–Sept. 7, 1737), acting colonial governor, was the son of Edward Middleton and his second wife, Sarah Middleton, who had been the widow of Richard Fowell of Barbados. The elder Middleton was born in England, emigrated to Barbados, and thence to Carolina, where he became a lord's proprietary deputy, member of the council, and assistant justice. His son, Arthur, was born in Charlestown to the prestige surrounding a wealthy and enterprising father and was probably educated in England. He inherited estates in Carolina, England, and Barbados. He was not only born to public life but, in 1707, married into it, taking as his wife, Sarah, the daughter of Jonathan Amory, speaker of the South Carolina House of Commons. She was the mother of his son, Henry Middleton, 1717–1784 [*q.v.*]. After her death in 1722 he was married, on Aug. 3, 1723, to Sarah (Wilkinson) Morton, the widow of Joseph Morton, a landgrave of Carolina. They had no children. Middleton began his public career early. From 1706 to 1710, he was a member of the South Carolina House of Commons. He became Lord Carteret's deputy and a member of the council. During the Yemassee War in 1715 he was sent as an agent to obtain aid from Virginia and, successful in his mission, was voted a pipe of wine by a grateful House. A year later he left the council for the House of Commons, where he led a movement against the proprietors, became president of the convention into which the Assembly resolved itself when dissolved by the governor, and helped overthrow proprietary control in 1719. After the Crown, in 1720, accepted the revolution and appointed Sir Francis Nicholson to be governor, Middleton became president of Nicholson's council and administered the government after the governor sailed for England in April 1725. In this capacity he met representatives of Spain in a conference to settle the southern boundary of Carolina but accomplished nothing. Like his predecessors he was concerned with Indian relations, so vital to a border colony, and when the Yemassee were harassing the border he had them subdued and severely punished. He also followed the usual policy against the French by efforts to counteract their influence with the Creeks and Cherokee. However, he found it difficult to maintain amicable relations with his legislature. In 1726 he checked the lower house in its attempt to issue paper money for rebuilding a fort burned on the Altamaha. Rioting followed, the council was threatened, and arrests had to be made before order could be restored. The paper-money party later sent representatives to the council, were denied an audience, and rioted again. Disputes over this question, constantly recurring, persisted throughout his administration and prevented the proper functioning of government. Six times he tried the expedient of dissolving the legislature and ordering new elections only to find the new assembly as hostile as the last. He was accused of corruption and of denying a writ of *habeas corpus.* Alexander Hewatt (*post,* I, p. 312) characterized him as a man "of a reserved and mercenary disposition . . . a sensible man, and by no means ill-qualified for governing," who, however, found it difficult as an erstwhile revolutionary leader to inculcate loyalty to the king and who had as his principal ambition the accumulation of property. After the arrival of Governor Johnson to take over the tangled affairs of the colony he became a member of Johnson's council and again became president of the council, in which position he was serving when he died.

[*S. C. Geneal. and Hist. Mag.*, July 1900, Oct. 1903; Alexander Hewatt, *Hist. Account of . . . S. C.* (2 vols., 1779), esp. I, pp. 312–19; *S. C. Hist. Soc. Colls.*, vol. I

(1857), pp. 236–46, 291–307; Edward McCrady, *The Hist. of S. C. under the Proprietary Government* (1897) and *The Hist. of S. C. under the Royal Government* (1889); W. R. Smith, *S. C. as a Royal Province* (1903); A. H. Middleton, *Life in Carolina and New England* (1929), p. 66, for death date from tombstone.]

H. B—C.

MIDDLETON, ARTHUR (June 26, 1742–Jan. 1, 1787), Revolutionary leader and signer of the Declaration of Independence, the son of Mary (Williams) and Henry Middleton, 1717–1784 [*q.v.*], was born at "Middleton Place" on the Ashley River, near Charlestown, now Charleston, S. C. He was educated in the colony and in England, part of the time probably at the academy in Hackney. On Apr. 14, 1757, he was admitted to the Middle Temple to read law. In 1763 he sailed for home and arrived in time to spend Christmas with his family, in which many changes had taken place since his departure, the birth of at least three of his sisters, the death of his mother, and his father's remarriage. The next summer, on Aug. 19, he was married to Mary, the daughter of Walter Izard. That year he became a justice of the peace and in October was elected to the colonial House of Assembly, in which he soon became a member of the committee to correspond with the colonial agent in London, and served until 1768. In May 1768 he took his wife to London, where their son Henry was born, and where Benjamin West painted a charming portrait of the little family. Visiting southern Europe, they spent some time in Rome, and in September 1771 they returned to South Carolina to settle down at "Middleton Place," which he inherited through his mother.

The next year he was again elected a member of the Commons' House of Assembly. In the anxious days before the Revolutionary War actually broke out he sat in the first provincial congress. He served on the general committee, on the secret committee of five that arranged and directed the action of the three parties of citizens who seized powder and weapons from the public storehouses on the night of Apr. 21, 1776, and within a few days raised 1,000 guineas to support colonial resistance, and on the special committee appointed on May 5 after the receipt of a letter from Arthur Lee in London intimating the possibility of British instigation of insurrection among the slaves of the American colonies. After the arrival of the news of Lexington he continued his activity and on June 14 became a member of the first Council of Safety, upon which devolved the executive power of the colony already in the midst of revolution. In the second provincial Congress he was elected to the new Council of Safety, on Nov. 16, 1775. As a leader of the extreme party he advocated the excommunication of all those who refused to sign the Association and the attachment of the estates of those who fled the colony, and he looked without disfavor on such activities as the tarring and feathering of Loyalists. Constantly he urged the preparation of Charlestown harbor against attack. On Feb. 11, 1776, he was appointed to the committee of eleven to prepare a constitution for South Carolina. A few days later he was elected to the Continental Congress, but not until South Carolina's constitution was written and adopted and the council of safety superseded by a new government did he travel northward to claim his seat. The first record of his presence is for May 20, and he was present to sign the Declaration of Independence. In January 1777 he was reëlected and continued in the Congress until October of that year. He left little imprint on the records of that body and absented himself from sessions to which he was elected. He was reëlected in 1778 but declined the election, and he failed to attend in 1779 and in 1780, although he had been elected on Feb. 5, 1779, and on Feb. 1, 1780. In 1775, when President John Rutledge [*q.v.*] vetoed the bill to enact the new constitution for South Carolina and resigned his office, Middleton was chosen as successor, but declined. During the siege of Charlestown in 1780 he served in the militia, was taken prisoner at the capture of the city, and was sent to St. Augustine as a prisoner of war. Exchanged in July 1781, he presented his credentials to the Continental Congress on Sept. 24, was reëlected by the Jacksonborough Assembly, and sat in the session of 1782.

After the war he repaired the damages suffered by his properties, devoted himself to planting, became a member of the racing club and of the hunting club of St. George's parish, and was an original trustee of the College of Charleston. He died at Goose Creek, survived by his wife and eight of their nine children. His daughter Isabella married Daniel Elliott Huger [*q.v.*], and his two sons, Henry and John Izard Middleton [*qq.v.*], carried on the family tradition of distinguished achievement.

[A. S. Salley, Jr., "Delegates to the Continental Congress from S. C.," *Bull. Hist. Com. of S. C.*, no. 9 (1927); E. A. Jones, *Am. Members of the Inns of Court* (1924); John Hutchinson, *A Cat. of Notable Middle Templars* (1902); Langdon Cheves, "Middleton of S. C.," *S. C. Hist. and Geneal. Mag.*, July 1900; "Correspondence of Hon. Arthur Middleton," *Ibid.*, Oct. 1925, Jan., Apr., July 1926; *Ibid.*, Jan. 1905, Jan. 1914, Apr. 1916, Jan. 1917, Jan. 1920, Apr. 1927, Apr. 1928, July 1929; John Drayton, *Memoirs of the Am. Revolution* (1821), esp. vol. I, pp. 175, 221–22, 231, 255, 268–71, 273, 285, 304–07, 318, 320, vol. II, pp. 15, 18,

23, 174, 180; E. C. Burnett, *Letters of Members of the Continental Congress,* vols. I–V (1921–31); *Journals of the Continental Congress,* vols. IV–XXII (1906–14).]

K. E. C.

MIDDLETON, HENRY (1717–June 13, 1784), president of the Continental Congress, was the son of Sarah (Amory) and Arthur Middleton, 1681–1737 [*q.v.*]. It is probable that he was born at his father's plantation "The Oaks" near Charlestown, now Charleston, S. C., and that he was educated in England. At his father's death he inherited "The Oaks" and a good deal of other property in South Carolina as well as in England and Barbados. Through his marriage to Mary Williams he added the estate afterward known as "Middleton Place," where he made his home, laying out the beautifully proportioned grounds and gardens, which have been enjoyed and embellished by later generations and which remain a delight to the residents and visitors of Charleston. He became one of the greatest landowners in South Carolina, owning nearly twenty plantations with a total of 50,000 acres and about 800 slaves. His wealth was so great that tradition credits him with having raised and supported at his own expense an entire regiment to fight in the Revolution.

Like many other members of prominent Southern families of this period, he held many official positions, of which the most important were, perhaps, justice of the peace, member of the commons house, speaker in 1747 and again in 1754 and 1755, and member of His Majesty's council for South Carolina. In 1769 he was in accord with the rest of the council in opposition to the action of the Assembly in voting £1,500 sterling to the John Wilkes fund. Nevertheless, although a churchman and a conservative with social and political position as well as a fortune at stake, he resigned his seat in the council in September 1770 to become a leader of the opposition to the British policy. In July 1774 a mass convention in Charlestown chose him to represent the province in the Continental Congress. When Peyton Randolph resigned he became the second president of the Congress and served from Oct. 22, 1774, to May 10, 1775. He did not wish for independence but hoped that moderate resistance would hasten the arrival of British commissioners to make a reasonable peace. When the radicals began to obtain control, he resigned from Congress, in February 1776, and was succeeded by his son Arthur Middleton [*q.v.*], who was more radical than he. After his resignation from the Continental Congress he became president of the South Carolina Congress and a member of the Council of Safety after Nov. 16, 1775. On Feb. 11, 1776, he and his son Arthur were appointed members of a committee to frame a temporary constitution for the state, following the adoption of which he was made a member of the legislative council, and in January 1779 he became a member of the newly created state Senate.

After the surrender of Charlestown, he was among those who accepted defeat and "took protection" under the British flag. Although the triumph of the Revolutionists was followed by numerous confiscations of the estates of Loyalists, he did not suffer for his abandonment of the struggle, nor is there any evidence that his fellow citizens regarded him in any less favorable light. His public spirit is shown not only in the offices he held but in the deeds he performed. When, at the outset of the Revolution, there was a lack of money in the province he and four other wealthy citizens "issued joint and several notes of hand in convenient denominations payable to the bearer, and these readily went into circulation at face value" (Allan Nevins, *During and After the Revolution, 1775–1789,* 1924, p. 487).

He was a generous benefactor of the church and was active in advancing the agricultural, commercial, and educational interests of the state. His contributions to the new colleges in New Jersey, Rhode Island, and at Philadelphia were large. In 1741 he married Mary, the only daughter of John Williams, member of the House of Commons from St. George's. She died on Jan. 9, 1761. In 1762 he married Maria Henrietta, daughter of Lieut.-Gov. William Bull, who died on Mar. 1, 1772. In January 1776 he married Lady Mary Mackenzie, who was the daughter of George, third earl of Cromartie, and was the widow of John Ainslie. Of his five sons and seven daughters, all the children of his first wife, Arthur was the eldest and the heir, Thomas became a Revolutionary patriot and a generous public servant, Henrietta married Edward Rutledge [*q.v.*], and Sarah married Charles Cotesworth Pinckney [*q.v.*].

[*S. C. Hist. and Geneal. Mag.,* July 1900, Apr. 1919, pp. 118–19, July 1926; Edward McCrady, *The Hist. of S. C. under the Royal Government* (1901) and *The Hist. of S. C. in the Revolution* (1902); W. R. Smith, *S. C. as a Royal Province* (1903); "An Old-Time Carolina Garden," *Century Mag.,* Oct. 1910; A. H. Middleton, *Life in Carolina and New England* (1929), esp. pp. 65–66.]

J. G. V—D.

MIDDLETON, HENRY (Sept. 28, 1770–June 14, 1846), South Carolina Unionist, the son of Mary (Izard) and Arthur Middleton, 1742–1787 [*q.v.*], was born in London, reared in South Carolina, and educated there and in England. He traveled extensively both in Europe and America. On Nov. 13, 1794, he was married to Mary Helen Hering of Heybridge Hall, England. He inherited "Middleton Place," on which he lavished money and labor. Although the azaleas, so much a feature of the modern gardens, were set out by his son, it was he who planted the first of the camellias, the gift of his friend, André Michaux [*q.v.*]. He served in both houses of the state legislature for ten years and then as governor of South Carolina from 1810 to 1812. One of the accomplishments of his administration was the passage of an act to establish a system of free schools, which, however, failed of a part of its purpose in that no means were found to enforce the provisions of the law and to select able and conscientious officials. As governor and after the expiration of his term, he supported a war policy in 1812. He represented his state in the Fourteenth and Fifteenth congresses, from 1815 to 1819, and then became minister to Russia. With a good deal of skill he negotiated with Russia the convention of 1824 to regulate trade and fisheries in the Pacific.

In 1830 he returned to America with the thought that his days of public service were over, but the nullification controversy soon called him from his retirement. He was among those who disagreed with Calhoun as to the wisdom and the constitutionality of nullification and became one of the leaders of what was called the Union party. He was a delegate to an anti-tariff convention that assembled at Philadelphia on Sept. 30, 1831, and submitted a memorial to Congress proposing the rates of 1816 as a satisfactory compromise. When, in the fall of 1832, the South Carolina Nullifiers obtained the two-thirds of the state legislature constitutionally necessary to call a state convention, he was one of the few Union men elected to this convention and sought in vain to prevent the adoption of the Nullification Ordinance. In the December convention at Columbia, representing the strong Unionist minority, he became one of the vice-presidents, and he was appointed to solicit the legislature of Tennessee to attend a convention in which the other Southern states should participate in order to consider possible constitutional measures of resistance. He died at Charleston survived by eight of his twelve children. Of his children the most distinguished was Henry Middleton (1797–1876), who devoted his attention to writing on political and economic subjects; in *The Government and the Currency* (1844, 2nd ed., with alterations, 1850) he denied the right of the federal government to issue paper money, in *Four Essays* (1847) he advocated free trade, and later touched the vital problem of the South in *Economical Causes of Slavery in the United States, and Obstacles to Abolition* (1857).

[*S. C. Hist. and Geneal. Mag.*, July 1900, Apr. 1919, p. 119; *Life, Letters, and Speeches of James Louis Petigru*, ed. by J. P. Carson (1920); *Hist. of S. C.*, ed. by Yates Snowden (1920), vol. I; Mrs. St. Julien Ravenal, *Charleston* (copr. 1906); C. S. Boucher, *The Nullification Controversy in S. C.* (1916); *The Am. Secretaries of State*, ed. by S. F. Bemis, vol. IV (1928); "An Old-Time Carolina Garden," *Century Mag.*, Oct. 1910; *Charleston Courier*, June 15, 16, 1846.]

J. G. V—D.

MIDDLETON, JOHN IZARD (Aug. 13, 1785–Oct. 5, 1849), archeologist, was born at "Middleton Place" near Charleston, S. C., the son of Mary (Izard) and Arthur Middleton, 1742–1787 [*q.v.*]. His father died soon after the son's birth and John is said to have been educated in England at the University of Cambridge. Having inherited his mother's large fortune he was able to devote his time to painting, for which he had no small talent and in which he attained some reputation. He took up his residence in Italy and spent most of his life there and in France. Endowed by nature with uncommon gifts, which he had cultivated to advantage, he found ready access to good society and "was received on terms of intimacy in circles into which foreigners seldom gained entrance" (Norton, *post*, p. 4). He married on June 11, 1810, Eliza Augusta Falconet, the daughter of Jean Louis Theodore de Palazieu Falconet. By her he had three children, all of whom died young. Two years after his marriage, in 1812, he published in London a volume with numerous colored plates, *Grecian Remains in Italy, a description of Cyclopian Walls and of Roman Antiquities with Topographical and Picturesque Views of Ancient Latium*. In his introduction he wrote that in such a work as his the artist was perhaps more important than the scholar. Therefore, he had made a collection of very accurate drawings, which were published in the book not merely to accompany the text but as the principal object of the publication. He said that he wrote the book because he had drawn the pictures. He had made the sketches while traveling in Italy during 1808 and 1809 with two English gentlemen, one of whom was Edward Dodwell later distinguished as an archeologist. Appearing as it did in a year crowded with events and at a time when scholarly communication between the United States and Europe was interrupted by war, Middleton's volume received little notice. Some of the drawings were used in later work on archeology without acknowledgment to the investigator who produced them, and his name has been largely forgotten. Nevertheless the work deserves to be remembered not only for its pioneer place in the early history of the study of antiquity but also because the accuracy and precision of its detail are notable even in a later day. He died in Paris and his body was brought to America and laid in the family vault at "Middleton Place."

[*S. C. Hist. and Geneal. Mag.*, July 1900; Chas. Eliot Norton, "The First Am. Classical Archaelogist," *Am. Jour. of Archaeology*, vol. I (1885); A. H. Middleton, *Life in Carolina and New England* (1929).] E. L. G..

MIDDLETON, NATHANIEL RUSSELL (Apr. 1, 1810–Sept. 6, 1890), fifth president of the College of Charleston, was born in Charleston, S. C., the eldest son of Arthur and Alicia Hopton (Russell) Middleton. His paternal grandfather, Thomas Middleton, was the son of Henry Middleton, 1717–1784, and the brother of Arthur Middleton, 1742–1787 [*qq.v.*]. His maternal grandfather, Nathaniel Russell, a wealthy Charleston merchant, was born in Bristol, R. I., the son of Joseph Russell, for a time chief justice of Rhode Island. He thus united two representative but very diverse strains in early American life, that of the Southern planter and the New England man of business. In 1824 he entered the College of Charleston and graduated in 1828. Following a sojourn in Europe he was married, on Jan. 18, 1832, to Margaret Emma Izard by whom he had three sons. After her death in 1836 he was married, on Sept. 20, 1842, to Anna Elizabeth de Wolf, of Bristol, R. I., by whom he had four daughters and one son. For many years he managed "Bolton-on-the-Stono," a plantation of about 3,000 acres near Charleston, which he had inherited from his father. The property, however, had financial encumbrances, a result probably of his father's generous and lavish way of life, and in 1852 he found it advantageous to sell the plantation with its slaves. He was then appointed treasurer of the Northeastern Railroad Company and later served for several years as treasurer of Charleston. His interests, however, had always been literary and artistic, and he found very tempting the prospect that was offered in 1857 by the call to the presidency of the College of Charleston. His extreme conscientiousness made him hesitate since he thought that his experience as a planter had not prepared him for such a position. In reality he was admirably fitted for the post. The College of Charleston, founded in the eighteenth century and later transferred to the control of the city council, was largely patronized by the planters' families. Its calendar was made to accommodate the schedule of the planters; Commencement always took place the last week of March; there followed a spring vacation, after which work was resumed and continued till Aug. 1; and the holidays and session days for the rest of the year fitted into the planter's life. Its ante-bellum prosperity was the result of the interest and patronage of this influential section of the community represented by such men as Elias Horry, Langdon Cheves, James L. Petigru, William Aiken, and many others.

The historical and social prominence of his name and family and his sympathetic understanding of plantation life were recognized in ante-bellum Charleston as important considerations in the choice of Middleton as president of the college, but the records of the institution give evidence that his qualifications as an executive went far beyond this. His reports to the trustees are characterized by sound good sense and by a grasp of the true essentials of collegiate training. His sincere love of learning, his appreciation of art, and his firm religious convictions are reflected in the addresses, essays, and fugitive poems that were collected and published after his death by his son (*The Allegory of Plato and Other Essays*, 1891, and *Education*, 1893). It was these characteristics and interests that caused him to be put at the head of the Carolina art association and the Charleston Bible society. As president of the latter he was instrumental during the Civil War in importing Bibles from England for distribution among the men in the service of the Confederate armies. The College remained open throughout the Civil War, except for a few months following the evacuation of Charleston by the Confederate forces in 1865. This is an unusual record among the Southern colleges of the period, and attests the ability, tact, and resourcefulness of the president. As early as 1862 he so arranged the college curriculum that many of the students were able to enter the military service and to perform their duties in the hours free from college work. Throughout the stormy days of Reconstruction the work of the institution proceeded uninterruptedly and he remained in active service until 1880, when he retired at the age of seventy. He continued to divide his time between his winter home in Charleston and his summer residence in Bristol, R. I., and died ten years later at Charleston in the eighty-first year of his age.

[Minutes of the Trustees of the College of Charleston; Journal of the Faculty of the College of Charleston; *S. C. Hist. and Geneal. Mag.*, July 1900; A. H. Middleton, *Life in Carolina and New England* (1919); Wm. Way, *Hist. of the New England Soc. of Charleston* (1920); *News and Courier* (Charleston), Sept. 8, 1890.] H. R.

MIDDLETON, PETER (d. Jan. 9, 1781), New York physician, left no known record of his ancestry, though his obituary places his birth in "North Britain." His first appearance is on the records of the University of St. Andrews, Feb. 27, 1752, when Prof. Thomas Simson represented to the university that "one Peter Middleton, a practitioner of physick, had been with him, and desired the Degree of Doctor of Medicine." After an examination, "the University, being satisfied with his performances," conferred the degree on him. Although the date usually given is 1750, it seems probable that it was in 1752 or later when Middleton and Dr. John Bard [*q.v.*] made in New York one of the first dissections of a human body for purposes of medical instruction on record in America. It was not long before Middleton was one of the chief physicians of New York, with an extensive and remunerative practice among the rich, and a large gratuitous practice among the poor. During the French war he had the rank of surgeon-general of the provincial forces in the Crown Point expedition, and in 1770 he received a grant of five thousand acres of land on the Susquehanna (*Third Annual Report of the State Historian of the State of New York, 1897,* 1898, p. 766). In 1756 he was one of the founders of the St. Andrew's Society of New York City, and from 1767 to 1770 its president; he was also a prominent Freemason, holding the office of deputy grand-master of the province under Sir John Johnson.

On Aug. 14, 1767, letters were presented to the governors of King's College from Middleton and five other New York physicians, proposing "to institute a Medical School within this College for instructing Pupils in the most usefull and necessary Branches of Medicine," and offering to give a course of lectures the following winter. The governors thereupon established the medical school and appointed the six physicians to professorships, Middleton securing the chair of physiology and pathology, to which materia medica was added in 1770 (manuscript minutes of the governors). The school was opened Nov. 2, 1767, with "a very elegant and learned Discourse" delivered by Middleton in the college hall in the presence of the governor of the province and other notables (*New-York Mercury,* Nov. 9, 1767). The discourse was published in 1769 with the title *A Medical Discourse, or an Historical Inquiry into the Ancient and Present State of Medicine*; it is an able work, displaying considerable familiarity with medical history, but gives little on the American situation. His only other known publication is a letter on the croup to Dr. Richard Bayley (R. Bayley, *Cases of the Angina Trachealis,* 1781, pp. 19–23; *Medical Repository,* vol. XIV, 1811, pp, 345–50).

Middleton became a governor of King's College, Nov. 11, 1773 (manuscript minutes). In June 1771 a charter was granted to the New York Hospital and his name headed the list of incorporators. He was one of the first physicians elected to the staff in 1774, but the destruction of the building by fire, and the war postponed the opening of the hospital until ten years after his death. He was a Tory, and in April 1776, "from prudential motives," sailed suddenly for Bermuda, returning to New York when the British occupied the city (*Medical Register of the City of New York and Vicinity,* 1868–69, p. 306). Middleton married (marriage bond, Nov. 25, 1766, *Names of Persons for Whom Marriage Licenses were Issued by the Secretary of the Province of New York,* 1860, p. 262) Susannah, daughter of Richard Nicholls and widow of John Burges of New York, merchant. She died Dec. 6, 1771. They had one child, Susannah Margaret Middleton. The doctor left a large estate and a month after his death his "large valuable library" was sold at auction.

[See the *N.-Y. Gazette and the Weekly Mercury,* Jan. 15, Feb. 5, 1781; Robt. W. Reid, "Peter Middleton, M.D.," *Masonic Outlook,* May 1932; and Middleton's will in the *N. Y. Hist. Soc. Colls. for the Year 1901* (1902), pp. 20–22. The articles by Geo. A. Morrison, in *Hist. of the St. Andrew's Soc. of the State of N. Y.* (1906), pp. 61–64, and Wm. M. MacBean, in *Biog. of St. Andrew's Soc. of the State of N. Y.,* I (1922), 19, abound in errors.] M.H.T.

MIDDLETON, THOMAS COOKE (Mar. 30, 1842–Nov. 19, 1923), educator, was born in Philadelphia, Pa. The eldest of the nine children of Joseph and Lydia (Cooke) Middleton, he was reared in strict Quaker simplicity, although his father as a contractor and president of the Wissahickon Turnpike Company lived a manorial life at "Monticello" near Chestnut Hill. Somewhat unsettled in religious belief, the family turned to Catholicism and was received into the Church in 1854 by the Rev. Michael Domenec, later bishop of Pittsburgh. Joseph Middleton became a devout Catholic. He was instrumental in the erection of a church at Chestnut Hill, sold his estate to the Sisters of St. Joseph for a mother-house, and rejoiced when two daughters became Mercy nuns and his son, Thomas, entered the Augustinian order. After graduation from Villanova College in Pennsylvania (1858), Thomas entered the Italian novitiate at Tolentino and later made his theological studies in San Agostino, Rome, where he gained a reputation for scholarship and linguistic proficiency. Ordained in St. John Lateran's by

Cardinal Patrizi (Sept. 24, 1864), he was recalled the following autumn to Villanova College where he spent the remainder of his life as a teacher, prefect of discipline, vice-rector, rector (1876–81), associate provincial and secretary of the American province of the Augustinians (1878–1914), librarian, and historiographer of the order.

Middleton was a founder and first president (1884–90) of the American Catholic Historical Society and for many years he edited the *Records* of the society. Every moment spared from official duties he devoted to a study of the history of his order and to researches in the Catholic history of Pennsylvania. He delved into parish and local records as he industriously compiled a voluminous manuscript of notabilia of community life from 1866 to 1923 and contributed numerous articles and scrupulously exact abstracts from parochial registers to the *Records,* to Griffin's *American Catholic Historical Researches,* to the *American Catholic Quarterly,* and to the *Ecclesiastical Review.* Among his most serviceable brochures are the *Sketch of Villanova, 1842–92* (1893), *Augustinians in the United States* (1909), *Some Notes on the Bibliography of the Philippines* (1900), and a list of Catholic periodicals published in the United States from 1809 to 1892 (*Records of the American Catholic Historical Society of Philadelphia,* September 1893, March 1908).

[*Am. Cath. Who's Who* (1911); *Who's Who in America,* 1920–21; *America,* Dec. 1, 1923; *Records of the Am. Cath. Hist. Soc. of Phila.,* especially Mar.–Dec. 1901 and Mar. 1924; the *Evening Bulletin* (Phila.), Nov. 19, 20, 1923; information from Middleton's associates.] R. J. P.

MIELATZ, CHARLES FREDERICK WILLIAM (May 24, 1860–June 2, 1919), etcher, was born in Breddin, Germany, the son of Charles and Wilhelmine (Wolff) Mielatz. He came to America at the age of six, attended the schools of Chicago, and studied drawing at the Chicago School of Design and Painting with Frederic Rondel, the elder. About 1880 he went to New York and thence to Newport, where he was employed with the United States engineer corps for about five years. He then returned to New York, where he married Mary Stuart McKinney on Feb. 25, 1903, and where he remained until the day of his death. Active as an etcher in the days of the New York Etching Club, of which he was secretary for a number of years, he was also a prominent figure in the revival of original etching which set in about the turn of the century. He formed a link between the older and the younger men and remained one of the latter. His influence on etching was exerted both through his work and through his teaching at the National Academy, of which he became an associate member. A tireless experimenter, he advanced steadily and did some of his best work in his later days. His "Georgian Courts" (Lakewood, N. J.) series, among his best prints, were of a freedom, even vivaciousness, quite in contrast to the "firm, virile, lean, even ascetic" line which James G. Huneker found in his etchings. The definiteness in treatment which Huneker had in mind appeared especially in his scenes in New York, and this fact may serve to illustrate his aim to select the medium and handling best suited to the particular problem on hand.

In three series of views, in aquatint, lithography, and monotype, respectively, done for the Society of Iconophiles, Mielatz showed his judgment in choosing the proper medium and adapting himself to it. With a rich command of resources, subordinating the craft to the purpose, he occasionally combined various accessories of the etching process to gain results. He was his own printer and knew also the effect of variation in shades of ink. Technical problems and difficulties absorbed him, and he experimented in color-printing. Generally, when he departed from black-and-white, he applied color by way of suggestion, or at most in flat tints, but in his remarkable plate after "Woman and Macaws," by George B. Luks, over which he labored long, he strove for complete color rendition. The technical aspect of his plates makes perhaps the most immediate claim on the interest of students of prints. He was honest always in his intentions and in his work; there was no parade. His subjects were invariably American, and while he did at times seek them outside of Manhattan, it was with that city's picturesqueness that he was particularly identified and to which he gave most of his effort. He was held mainly by the interesting locality or structure, not by the general sweep of urban view, and such aspects of the city he presented with a sure eye for effect and for the spirit of old New York. Much that he showed might easily be passed unnoticed; even the familiar was seen with a freshness of view that gave his work an air of novelty. When he placed the old "Poe Cottage" in a setting of sombre night, E. C. Stedman avowed that he had caught some of "the quality of Poe's own mood and utterance." His plates include pictures of tarpon fishing and of yacht races, which showed swing of action, but as one writer pointed out, he was probably "best in static themes."

[The chief sources of information are "Etchings of New York City by C. F. W. Mielatz, with commentary by Frank Weitenkampf" (75 etchings), a manuscript in the N. Y. Pub. Lib., intended for early publication, and articles by F. Weitenkampf, *Internat. Studio*, Sept. 1911, and G. W. Harris, *Internat. Studio*, July 1922. See also: *Who's Who in America*, 1918–19; the *Am. Art News*, June 14, 1919, *N. Y. Tribune*, June 4, 1919, and *N. Y. Times*, June 5, 1919. With the last was a portrait from a photograph, and the *Evening Post* of Nov. 8, 1919 (magazine section), commented upon a brilliant portrait of Mielatz painted by George B. Luks.] F. W.

MIELZINER, MOSES (Aug. 12, 1828–Feb. 18, 1903), rabbi, teacher, and author, was born in Schubin, province of Posen, Germany, and died at Cincinnati, Ohio. His father, Benjamin Leib Mielziner, rabbi of Schubin, belonged to a long line of Jewish savants, and his mother, Rose Rachel Caro, was descended from the celebrated Jewish ritualistic authority, Joseph Caro (1488–1575). Moses Mielziner naturally obtained his elementary Jewish education from his father, to which additions were made by Moses' brother at Tremessen and by the Yeshivah at Exin. His subsequent secular and Talmudic knowledge was acquired in Berlin, whither he went in 1844. In the fall of 1848 he matriculated at the University of Berlin, where he studied philosophy and philology.

After having served as religious head at Waren, Mecklenburg (1852–54), with David Einhorn as chief rabbi, Mielziner, in 1854, went to Copenhagen, Denmark. In 1855 he became principal of a school. During this period he wrote, in both Latin and German, a dissertation, *Die Verhältnisse der Sklaven bei den Alten Hebräern, nach Biblischen und Talmudischen Quellen Dargestellt* (1859), for which he received the degree of Ph.D. at the University of Giessen (1859). This work, published in English under the title *Slavery among the Ancient Hebrews* (1861), proved of special interest in America during the Civil War. All of Mielziner's writings had a timely message. They were prompted by prevailing needs; but they were marked also by literary grace, clarity, and, above all, reliability. At Copenhagen, on May 19, 1861, he married Rosette Levald, by whom he had seven children.

By heredity and environment Mielziner had been made a conservative liberal. Owing to the dissensions between orthodoxy and liberalism in his Copenhagen constituency, he came to the United States in 1865. His first position was the pulpit of Anshe Chesed, then the oldest German Jewish congregation in New York. On account of internal congregational wrangles, he gave up his office and the congregation merged with Beth-El, of which his friend, David Einhorn [*q.v.*], was rabbi. For a few years Mielziner conducted a private school for boys. In 1879 he was called by Isaac M. Wise [*q.v.*], founder and president of the Hebrew Union College, to Cincinnati, where, in the first American rabbinical seminary, he held the chair of the Talmud until the time of his death. From among his writings growing out of his professional Jewish associations—more especially his particular professorial office—and including essays, reviews, sermons, Hebrew poems, and expert opinions, the following are worthy of note: *Jødisk Almanak for Skudaaret 5622* (1861, reprinted 1928); "A Paper on Neginoth: Hebrew Accents" (*Hebraica*, February–April, 1879); "On Translations of the Talmud" (*Hebrew Review*, vol. I, 1880); "The Talmudic Syllogism" (*Ibid.*); *The Jewish Law of Marriage and Divorce* (1884); *A Selection from the Book of Psalms for School and Family Use* (1888, 1890); *Introduction to the Talmud* (1894, 1903, 1925); and "Marriage Agenda" (*Year Book of the Central Conference of American Rabbis*, vol. I, 1891). The first edition of the *Union Prayerbook* (2 parts, 1892–94) was edited in 1891 by a committee of the Central Conference of American Rabbis, with Mielziner as chairman. He contributed the English translation of Chronicles to the English Bible projected by the Jewish Publication Society under the supervision of Marcus Jastrow [*q.v.*], in 1894. In 1901 he was appointed consulting editor of *The Jewish Encyclopedia*, and himself contributed articles to the first volume of this work.

In 1882, after the death of its rabbi, Dr. Max Lilienthal [*q.v.*], the B'nai Israel Congregation of Cincinnati elected Mielziner temporary rabbi until a regular successor could be appointed. He often occupied the pulpit of Isaac M. Wise in Temple B'nai Jeshurun, Cincinnati. From 1888 to 1889 he was president of the Hebrew Sabbath School Union. When Dr. Wise died, Mielziner was elected, Apr. 5, 1900, president of the Hebrew Union College, and served as such until his death.

[*Year Book of the Central Conference of Am. Rabbis*, vol. XIII (copr. 1904); William Rosenau, "A Tribute to Moses Mielziner," in *Am. Israelite*, Apr. 5, 1928; E. M. F. Mielziner, *Moses Mielziner, 1828–1903* (1931); Kaufmann Kohler, in *Hebrew Union Coll. and Other Addresses* (1916); *Who's Who in America*, 1901–02; *Jewish Comment*, Feb. 20, 1903.] W. R.

MIFFLIN, LLOYD (Sept. 15, 1846–July 16, 1921), painter and poet, was born in Columbia, Pa. His father, John Houston Mifflin, was a descendant of the John Mifflin who emigrated to the colonies from Wiltshire, England, before 1680 and settled on land now included in Fairmount Park, Philadelphia. His mother, who died while he was a child, was Elizabeth Anne

Bethel (Heise) Mifflin, daughter of Solomon Heise, a native of Frankfort, Germany. John Houston Mifflin was an artist by profession, having studied in the Pennsylvania Academy of the Fine Arts and in Europe. He was also the author of a small volume of poems privately printed in 1835. Lloyd attended the public schools of Columbia and completed his education at the Washington Classical Institute in the same town and at a private school conducted by Howard W. Gilbert. He was never robust and was encouraged to engage in horseback riding and rowing in the hope of improving his health. At fourteen he began to draw and sketch, and although his father at first endeavored to divert him from the pursuit of his own profession, he was sent to Philadelphia for instruction by Isaac Williams and then by the well-known artist Thomas Moran. In 1869 he went to Europe and continued his studies with Henry Herzog at Düsseldorf, Germany. He also traveled widely in Italy, France, and Great Britain, sketching and painting industriously. Another period of European travel and study followed in 1871–72. He exhibited in America and continued an active interest in his art until forced in 1872 to abandon it because of a decline in health, induced, it is said, by the fumes of paint.

Having been long an eager student of poetry he now turned to literary work, adopting the sonnet as his favorite form. His *At the Gates of Song,* a volume of 150 sonnets, was published in June 1897 and was so well received that a second edition was called for in the same year and another in 1901. For the next decade he devoted himself chiefly to the sonnet-form and published a succession of volumes, of which the most important are: *The Slopes of Helicon, and Other Poems* (1898); *Echoes of Greek Idyls* (1899), consisting of versions of Bion, Moschus, and Bacchylides; *The Fields of Dawn and Later Sonnets* (1900); *Castalian Days* (1903); *The Fleeing Nymph, and Other Verse* (1905), a volume containing a long blank-verse poem and some lyrics not in sonnet-form; *My Lady of Dream* (1906); *Toward the Uplands* (1908); and *Flower and Thorn* (1909). In 1905 Mifflin gathered into a volume entitled *Collected Sonnets,* a selection from his previously published works with some new verse, amounting to 309 sonnets in all. A second edition of this work appeared in 1907. In 1916 he issued his last book, *As Twilight Falls.* In November 1915 he had suffered a stroke of apoplexy, which kept him in bed for six months and left him in precarious health for the rest of his life. He died July 16, 1921, at his home "Norwood" in Columbia and was buried in Mt. Bethel Cemetery. He was never married. He was unique among American poets in his devotion to a single poetic form, and his work, which faithfully represents the poetic ideals of his period, was distinguished by serious and lofty purpose.

[E. H. Sneath, *America's Greatest Sonneteer* (1928); *Who's Who in America,* 1920–21; J. H. Merrill, *Memoranda Relating to the Mifflin Family* (1890); *N. Y. Times* and *Pub. Ledger* (Phila.), July 17, 1921.]

J. C. F.

MIFFLIN, THOMAS (Jan. 10, 1744–Jan. 20, 1800), merchant, member of the Continental Congress, Revolutionary soldier, governor of Pennsylvania, first son of John Mifflin and Elizabeth Bagnell, was born in Philadelphia, Pa., of a Quaker family. He was of the fourth generation in descent from John Mifflin who emigrated to Pennsylvania from Warminster, Wiltshire, England, before 1680. John, the father of Thomas, was a wealthy merchant, and during his lifetime held the public posts of councilman, alderman, justice of the peace, provincial councilor, and trustee of the College of Philadelphia. Thomas attended a Quaker school and graduated from the College of Philadelphia, now the University of Pennsylvania, at the early age of sixteen. On leaving college he spent four years in the counting-house of William Coleman, prosperous Philadelphia merchant, preparing for a mercantile career. At twenty he visited Europe for a year. The effects of this broadening experience in no wise diminished his ardor for America, for he wrote from London, Nov. 23, 1764: "I find myself as great a patriot for America as when I first left it" (J. H. Merrill, Memoranda Relating to the Mifflin Family, 1890, p. 18). The next year he entered business as a merchant in partnership with his brother, George, the connection continuing until after the outbreak of the Revolution. Their enterprise was thoroughly successful, but Thomas's ambition and talent as a speaker drew him into politics. Recognized as a champion of colonial rights, beginning with 1772 he was elected to the provincial assembly four successive years, in 1774 receiving 1,100 out of 1,300 votes, despite Quaker opposition to his ardent Whiggism. Conspicuous in opposing the Stamp Act, in fostering nonimportation agreements, and in organizing sentiment for a colonial congress, he was one of the youngest and most radical members of the First Continental Congress, and helped to draft the Association of 1774. During the Congress his large and luxuriously furnished home was a rendezvous for its principal delegates. He was elected to the Second Continental Congress, but after the battle of Lexington turned his attention to the more active business of recruiting and training troops. On his appointment as major, May 1775, John Adams declared that he "ought to have been a general" because he was the "animating soul" of the revolutionary movement (C. F. Adams, *Familiar Letters of John Adams and his Wife Abigail Adams during the Revolution,* 1876, p. 59). The Quakers, however, frowned upon his military activities and read him out of meeting because he refused to reform his conduct.

On June 23, 1775, Mifflin was appointed Washington's aide-de-camp and on Aug. 14 following, quartermaster-general of the Continental Army, holding the latter post, except for a brief period, until March 1778. At first he was a faithful and efficient quartermaster, though he preferred the front line to administrative duties. An eye-witness declared he "never saw a greater display of personal bravery" than Mifflin exhibited in his "cool and intrepid conduct" in leading an attack on a British foraging expedition at Lechmire's Point, Nov. 9, 1775 (Rawle, *post,* p. 111). In the following month, on Dec. 22, he was commissioned colonel. He was appointed brigadier-general, May 16, 1776, was relieved as quartermaster shortly thereafter, at his own request, and commanded the covering party in the withdrawal from Long Island. Despite his unusual activity for the patriot cause, he was slow to commit himself on independence and steadfastly opposed the overthrow of Pennsylvania's provincial charter by the radicals, though when separation was achieved he appeared enthusiastic. In the gloom of late 1776, when he was sent by Washington to Philadelphia to rouse the authorities and the people to the need for reinforcements, his spirited appeals in the city and back country bore good fruit. In the following year his animated speeches kept many men in the army after their terms had expired. He was present at the battles of Trenton and Princeton, was appointed major-general, Feb. 19, 1777, and assisted in the defenses at Philadelphia. Meanwhile dissatisfaction developed with his conduct as quartermaster, the duties of which he had reluctantly resumed in October 1776 at the urgent request of Washington and Congress. Chafing under criticism and at congressional interference he went home in the summer of 1777 pleading ill health, and, disappointed at his diminishing influence with the commander-in-chief, resigned both as quartermaster and major-general, Oct. 8, 1777. Congress pressed him to continue the quartermaster's duties temporarily, but, complaining and malcontent, he neglected them, and gross confusion characterized the affairs of the department until a successor was appointed in March 1778. He continued, however, to retain his rank of major-general without salary.

Mifflin was deeply involved in the cabal to advance Horatio Gates over Washington, intent apparently on his own advancement. A severe critic of Washington's "Fabian tactics," when the board of war was reorganized in November 1777 he was appointed a member by Congress ostensibly to weaken the commander-in-chief. It was largely because of his recommendations that Gates became president of the board (W. C. Ford, "Defences of Philadelphia in 1777," *Pennsylvania Magazine of History and Biography,* April 1896, pp. 90–92). On the exposure of the plot he sought cover, solemnly disavowed all connection with it, and is reported to have said publicly at a later date that he considered Washington "the best friend he ever had in his life" (G. W. Greene, *The Life of Nathanael Greene,* vol. II, 1871, p. 37). On Apr. 18, 1778, he left the board of war and rejoined the army, but, with his quartermaster's record under fire, took little active participation. His enemies accused him of peculation and a committee of Congress recommended that he be held responsible for the acts of his subordinates, to which he strenuously objected on the ground that congressional interference had prevented his proper direction of the department's affairs. Washington was directed to order an inquiry and to hold a court-martial if it appeared that the deficiencies were chargeable to him or to his assistants. Mifflin invited the investigation, but waiting vainly for it, indignantly insisted that Congress accept his resignation as major-general, Aug. 17, 1778. His wish was finally granted, Feb. 25, 1779. Thereafter Congress continued, nevertheless, to call upon him for advice, notably in 1780 when he assisted in framing recommendations for reorganizing the staff departments. While his negligence as quartermaster seems inexcusable, and his carelessness in money matters is a matter of record, the charge of peculation has never been sustained.

Out of the army, Mifflin turned to state politics. In the assembly, 1778–79, he advocated amendment of the constitution of 1776, opposed paper-money issues and measures to regulate prices, and fought to save the charter of the College of Philadelphia. From 1782 to 1784 he was again in Congress, was elected president in his absence, Nov. 3, 1783, actually serving in this capacity from Dec. 13, 1783, to June 3, 1784. Through the irony of fate, when Washington returned his commission, Dec. 23, 1783, it became Mifflin's duty as president to accept it. His felicitations showed no trace of his earlier feelings toward the commander-in-chief, and Washington's visits to his home in later years indicate a restoration of their friendship. He was a member of the Federal Convention in 1787, and though participating little in its debates, was in full sympathy with the new Constitution. He was elected to the supreme executive council of Pennsylvania in 1788, serving as its president until 1790, and in 1789–90 was chairman of the state constitutional convention. Displeased at his appointments while president of the state, the Republicans in selecting a gubernatorial candidate in 1790 passed him by for Arthur St. Clair. His friends, however, put him at the head of another ticket, and, supported solidly by the Constitutionalists and by many Republicans, he carried the state by the overwhelming majority of 27,118 to 2,819. During his three terms as governor, 1790–99, the limit set by the constitution, many laws were enacted for the construction of roads and the improvement of inland navigation, and others reforming the judicial and penal establishments and strengthening the militia. He sympathized with the rising tide of Jeffersonianism in Pennsylvania, sat at the banquet table with Genet, and openly favored war with England in 1793 (J. T. Scharf and Thompson Westcott, *History of Philadelphia,* I, 1884, p. 475). In the Whiskey Insurrection, 1794, apprehensive of endangering his influence with the Jeffersonians, he first evaded Washington's plea for support but later called the legislature into special session, urged speedy action against the insurgents, and harangued the militiamen as of old. Despite his pro-French and Jeffersonian sympathies, in 1798 he trimmed his sails to the popular breezes by encouraging preparations for the anticipated French war. His last three years as governor were marked by increasing negligence and moral laxity, his secretary of commonwealth, Alexander James Dallas, constituting the real head of the administration. After retiring from the governorship he was in the legislature until his death.

Mifflin was of medium height, athletic frame, and handsome. He dressed in the height of fashion. Of unusual refinement, he possessed a warm temperament and agreeable manners, his martial and dignified bearing revealing little trace of his Quaker education. In money matters he was extravagant and careless. Borrowing heavily in later life, he was, nevertheless, excessively generous, and entertained lavishly at his home at the falls of the Schuylkill and at his farm, "Angelica," near Reading. An action brought against him by one of his creditors in 1799 obliged him to leave Philadelphia. This unfortunate occurrence preying on his mind hastened his death. When he died he was penniless, and the state of Pennsylvania paid the expenses of his burial in the Lutheran graveyard at Lancaster. His wife, Sarah, daughter of Morris Morris, whom he married on Mar. 4, 1767, and whom John Adams described as "a charming Quaker girl" (*Familiar Letters,* p. 45), died in 1790.

[Mifflin is one of the important Pennsylvanians of whom an adequate study remains to be made. William Rawle, "Sketch of the Life of Thomas Mifflin," in the *Memoirs of the Hist. Soc. of Pa.,* vol. II, pt. 2 (1830), is unsatisfactory. Many Mifflin letters and other manuscripts are scattered through various collections in the Hist. Soc. of Pa., Philadelphia, and in the "Papers of the Continental Cong.," Library of Congress. Other more important sources are: *Autobiog. of Charles Biddle* (1883); E. C. Burnett, *Letters of Members of the Continental Cong.,* vols. I–V (1921–31); W. C. Ford and Gaillard Hunt, eds., *Jours. of the Continental Cong.,* vols. I–XXVII (1904–28); Alexander Graydon, *Memoirs of a Life, Chiefly Passed in Pa.* (1811); *Pa. Archives,* ser. 1, vols. I–XII (1852–56), ser. 4, vol. IV (1890); *Pa. Colonial Records* (16 vols., 1852–53); scattered references in the *Pa. Mag. of Hist. and Biog.*; and contemporary newspapers.] J. H. P—g.

MIFFLIN, WARNER (Oct. 21, 1745–Oct. 16, 1798), Quaker reformer, son of Daniel and Mary (Warner) Mifflin, was born in Accomac County, Va., whither his grandfather, Edward, had removed from Philadelphia, Pa. He was a descendant of John Mifflin who emigrated from Wiltshire, England, sometime before 1680 and finally settled at "Fountain Green," now a part of Fairmount Park, Philadelphia. On May 14, 1767, Warner married Elizabeth Johns, of Maryland, by whom he had nine children, and on Oct. 9, 1788, Ann Emlen, of Philadelphia, by whom he had three. During most of his mature life he lived on his farm, "Chestnut Grove," near Camden, Del. (Justice, *post,* pp. 16–19).

He was a man of mild manner, always charitably inclined, yet of intense convictions. As early as 1775 he was arguing against "the pernicious use of ardent spirits." During the American Revolution he adhered to the Quaker peace principles and shared in the obloquy thereby entailed. He refused to have the least part in supporting the war, even to the use of Continental paper money. Consequently, he was dubbed a Tory, and his patriot neighbors made serious threats against him. While General Howe was in Philadelphia and General Washington on the outskirts of the city, Mifflin was one of a committee of six appointed by the Friends' Yearly Meeting in 1777 to visit both commanders-in-chief and present printed copies of the "Testimonies" against participation in war. They went without passports through the lines of both armies and accomplished their mission.

When he was fourteen years old, on his father's plantation in Virginia, one of the younger slaves, talking with him in the fields, had convinced him of the injustice of the slave system. He soon determined never to be a slave-holder. Later, however, he came into possession of several slaves through his first wife and from his father and mother. After a period of indecision, in 1774–75 he manumitted all his slaves (Justice, p. 39). Supersensitive to the promptings of conscience, he even paid them for their services after the age of twenty-one years. Thereafter, he traveled much in Quaker communities urging Friends to free their slaves. In the same cause he appeared before various legislative bodies including, in 1782, that of Virginia, where a law was passed in May of that year removing the former prohibitions against the private manumission of slaves (W. W. Hening, *Statutes at Large*, vol. XI, 1823, p. 39). Between 1783 and 1797 he helped to draw up, or to present to the Congress of the United States various petitions against slavery and the slave trade. One, dated 1789, helped to start an important debate on the powers of Congress over slavery and the slave trade under the new Constitution. In 1793 he published over his own name, *A Serious Expostulation with the Members of the House of Representatives of the United States* (Phila. 1793 and various reprints), in which he presented with no little force the anti-slavery case. In 1796, his motives and methods having been attacked by his opponents, he published in Philadelphia *The Defence of Warner Mifflin against Aspersions Cast on Him on Account of his Endeavors to Promote Righteousness, Mercy and Peace, among Mankind.* In this pamphlet he sketched the activities of his life and defended his stand on such subjects as slavery, peace, and temperance.

In 1798 he attended the Yearly Meeting of Friends held in Philadelphia and at that time, apparently, contracted the yellow fever which was then so prevalent in that city. He died of the disease soon after returning to his home in Delaware, aged about fifty-three years.

[The most accessible and fullest source of information is Hilda Justice, *Life and Ancestry of Warner Mifflin* (1905), containing reprints of Quaker records and other important documentary material; the most important manuscript Quaker records for the period are at 304 Arch Street, Phila.; about a dozen letters by Mifflin are in the Hist. Soc. of Pa. The most reliable of contemporary accounts of Mifflin's life are his own memoir in *Defence of Warner Mifflin*, cited above, and a "Testimony" by his friend George Churchman, in *Friends' Miscellany*, June 1832. See also J. H. Merrill, *Memoranda Relating to the Mifflin Family* (privately printed, 1890).]

R. W. K.

MIGNOT, LOUIS REMY (1831–Sept. 22, 1870), landscape painter, born at Charleston, S. C., was probably the son of Remy Mignot, a confectioner, who for a time conducted the French Coffee House in Charleston. The Mignots had been ardent Bonapartists and had left France at the time of the restoration of the Bourbons in 1815. Louis Mignot's boyhood was spent in the home of his wealthy grandfather near his birthplace. He manifested a marked love of art while a mere child, and at seventeen he had definitely chosen his career. He passed through a course of drawing with credit, and in 1851, at the age of twenty, he traveled to Holland and became the pupil of Andreas Schelfhout, the landscapist, at The Hague. His progress was rapid. He soon began to work from nature, making trips to several European countries for sketching purposes, and remained about four years. Returning to the United States in 1855, he opened a studio in New York, where his success was immediate and complete.

At that time Frederick E. Church's spectacular pictures of the Andean peaks and jungles were in high favor. He had made one trip to Ecuador in 1853 and was planning to make another in 1857. Mignot, whose admiration for the work of his senior colleague was fervent, and who was deeply interested in tropical scenery, gladly accepted the opportunity offered him to accompany Church on this second voyage to Guayaquil. The two painters, actuated by the same enthusiasm for the stupendous scenes among the Andes, made the most of their time in Ecuador, and brought home studies made at Quito and Riobamba which were destined to bring both of them notice. It was not unnatural that Mignot should have worked much in the spirit of Church, and that some of his tropical landscapes should have resembled those of the elder man. His own native talent and facility, however, appear to have been quite generally recognized by his contemporaries on both sides of the Atlantic.

Mignot was made an associate of the National Academy of Design in 1858 and a year later became an academician. He collaborated with his friend T. P. Rossiter, the historical painter, in making one of the latter's series of Mount Vernon scenes, "Washington and Lafayette at Mount Vernon," in which it is evident that Mignot's part consisted of the landscape background. The picture belongs to the Metropolitan Museum of Art, New York. On the outbreak of the Civil War, Mignot's Southern sympathies made his further stay in New York so repugnant to his feelings that on June 26, 1862, he set sail for England on board the *Great Eastern*. A few days prior to his departure he had sold a collection of his paintings at Leeds' auction-room for a total of something over $5,000. He made his way to London, where he remained, for the most part, during the remainder of his life, and where he was as successful as he had been in New York. He was a frequent exhibitor at the Royal Academy, and among the landscapes shown there in the sixties were several noteworthy Ecuadorian subjects painted from the studies made in 1857—the "Lagoon of Guayaquil," "Evening in the Tropics," "Under the Equator," and "Mount Chimborazo." In 1870 he was in France, and, either by accident or design, was shut up in Paris during the siege. He died of smallpox at Brighton, shortly after his return to England. He was only thirty-nine years old. His collected works were exhibited in London soon after his death and elicited favorable attention.

[*Art Jour.* (London), Nov. 1, 1870, Jan. 1, 1871; T. S. Cummings, *Hist. Annals of the Nat. Acad. of Design* (1865); H. T. Tuckerman, *Book of the Artists* (1867); S. G. W. Benjamin, *Art in America* (1880); Clara E. Clement and Laurence Hutton, *Artists of the Nineteenth Century* (1880); U. Thieme and F. Becker, *Allgemeines Lexikon der Bildenden Künstler,* vol. XXIV (1930).] W. H. D.

MILBURN, WILLIAM HENRY (Sept. 26, 1823–Apr. 10, 1903), Methodist Episcopal clergyman, son of Nicholas Milburn, was born in Philadelphia. The Milburn family came from the Eastern Shore of Maryland. William's early education was obtained in his native city and in Jacksonville, Ill., to which place, after financial losses, the family removed in 1838. When he was five years old, the sight of his left eye was destroyed by a piece of glass thrown by a playmate. Inflammation spread to the right eye, and after several years of bleeding, cupping, leeching, and burning with caustic, he was almost blind. He attempted, however, to secure an education, though able to read only by holding a book very close to his eye. In Jacksonville, while his father kept a store, he helped his mother with housework and studied. He entered Illinois College in 1841 but was obliged to leave in 1843 on account of ill health. Pioneer Methodist preachers frequented his father's house, among them the famous Peter Cartwright [*q.v.*]. From them he heard tales of circuit riding in the backwoods, with its dangers from weather, wild animals, and Indians, which strengthened his conviction, early reached, that it was his duty to become a preacher.

In 1843 he went as an exhorter with Rev. Peter Akers, to cover a 500-mile circuit with a dozen charges. Each week they held services from Saturday noon until Sunday evening, and the remainder of the time traveled on horseback, sleeping at night upon shuck mattresses laid on cabin floors, and partaking of the food those they tarried with could supply. Milburn said that he never thereafter liked fried chicken, hog, hominy, or corn bread. On Sept. 13, 1843, he was admitted to the Illinois Conference on trial and assigned to the Winchester circuit, with thirty charges extending over 300 miles, which he visited every four weeks. His yearly salary was $100 and presents of clothing. His own comment on his circuit life was: "The terms of tuition in Brush College and Swamp University are high, the course of study hard, the examinations frequent and severe, but the schooling is capital" (*Ten Years of Preacher-Life,* p. 82). In 1844 the trouble with his eye became worse and, though almost penniless, he went for treatment to St. Louis, where he lived for nine months in the home of a friendly lawyer. On Sept. 17, 1845, he was ordained deacon and appointed agent to raise money for a "Female Seminary" and for McKendree College. Traveling from Wheeling to Cincinnati by boat, he met a group of congressmen whom he reproved for drinking, card playing, and profanity. They raised a purse for him and shortly after secured his election as chaplain of Congress on the part of the House of Representatives (1845). He retained his position as church agent and after his marriage, Aug. 13, 1846, in Baltimore, made that city his headquarters.

Poor health sent him South in 1848 and he became pastor of a church in Montgomery, Ala., where he remained two years. A like term as pastor of St. Francis Street Church, Mobile, and two years as Mobile city missionary followed. At the Alabama Conference of 1852 he was under investigation for questionable conduct (he had attended a New Year's ball) and for heresy. The latter consisted in a sympathetic attitude toward the higher criticism, which he later deplored. The Conference was satisfied with his explanations and no action was taken. In 1853, at thirty, poor, totally blind, with four children to support, he broke down physically and nervously and returned North, settling in New York City. He supplied churches for longer or shorter periods, lectured widely throughout the country, and visited Canada and England. About 1862 he took orders in the Protestant Episcopal Church, but in 1878 was readmitted to the Illinois Conference of the Methodist Church. He was again elected chaplain of Congress (1853), later of the House of Representatives (1885), and finally of the Senate (1893). In 1902 he resigned this office because of failing health. He died in Santa Barbara, Cal.

Milburn was the author of *The Rifle, Axe, and*

Saddle-Bags, and Other Lectures (1857); *Ten Years of Preacher-Life: Chapters from an Autobiography* (1859); *The Pioneers, Preachers, and People of the Mississippi Valley* (1860); *The Lance, Cross, and Canoe; the Flatboat, Rifle, and Plough in the Valley of the Mississippi* (1892). His style as speaker and writer was simple and undecorated, but enlivened by humor and illustration. He was at his best when telling of the backwoods life he knew well. Philosophic cheerfulness and courage marked his spirit and he indulged in no complaints or pathetic allusions to his misfortune.

[John McClintock, D. D., introduction to *The Rifle, Axe, and Saddle-Bags and Other Lectures* (1857); C. M. Eames, *Historic Morgan and Classic Jacksonville* (1885); Anson West, *A Hist. of Methodism in Ala.* (1893); *Minutes of the Ill. Ann. Conference of the M. E. Church* (1903); *Who's Who in America*, 1901–02; *Congressional Record*, 57 Cong., 2 Sess., p. 13; *Zion's Herald*, Apr. 15, 1903; *Christian Advocate* (N. Y.), Apr. 16, 23, 1903; *Evening Star* (Washington, D. C.), Apr. 11, 1903.] S. G. B.

MILES, EDWARD (Oct. 14, 1752–Mar. 7, 1828), miniature painter, was born in Yarmouth, England, and, as an errand boy for Dr. Giles Wakeman, was found to have a remarkable talent for drawing, which his employer encouraged. Receiving enough patronage among his friends in Yarmouth, at nineteen he set off for London, where he received an introduction to Sir Joshua Reynolds, who was favorable to his plan to copy some of the great painter's pictures. Quite early he directed his talents to the field of miniature painting and soon achieved a reputation. He set up a studio in the fashionable Berkeley Street, Berkeley Square, and was rewarded by the patronage of the aristocracy of London. His contributions appeared regularly at the Royal Academy exhibitions from 1775 to 1797 and he attracted the attention of the Court. In 1792 he was appointed miniature painter to the Duchess of York, and in 1794, Queen Charlotte regularly appointed him "Our Miniature Painter during our pleasure." Either before or after this appointment he painted a portrait of his royal mistress, as well as many of the princesses. In 1797 he went to St. Petersburg, where he became court painter during the reign of the Emperor Paul. After the murder of his original patron, he remained as court painter to the succeeding Czar, Alexander I., whose portrait he painted very beautifully, as he did that of the Empress, Maria Louisa of Baden. His miniatures were distinguished for their good drawing and for the delicacy and exquisiteness of their finish.

In 1807 Miles arrived in Philadelphia, where he remained until the end of his life. He took an active interest in the artistic and social life of the city and became a fellow and one of the founders of the Society of Artists of the United States which was organized in 1810. He did not exhibit in the society's first annual exhibition in 1811, but he was represented in the third annual display, in 1813, by which time the organization was known as the Columbian Society of Artists. He was an academician of the society and probably a drawing master in its schools, for he was so described in the Philadelphia Directory for 1813 and continued to be so designated thereafter, as he was also in the exhibition catalogues.

After Miles came to the United States, his son is said to have lost considerable money. Apparently he then began to give instruction to a few chosen pupils. His work as a miniature painter in Philadelphia seems to have been confined to painting portraits of his friends. He is known to have painted a portrait of Bishop White. In 1809 he was described as "portrait painter in crayons." As the exhibited work of pupils in the schools of the Columbian Society was entirely in this medium, it is probable that Miles literally taught drawing, for which profession he was especially gifted, and not painting. Although his name appears as an exhibitor in the annual exhibition catalogues, no work by him is indicated. One of his pupils, who became noted as a portrait painter, was James Reid Lambdin [*q.v.*], who subsequently learned painting in the studio of Thomas Sully. Lambdin is said to have painted a portrait of Miles as his first exhibition piece. Sir William Beechey, who had been one of Miles's warmest friends in England, painted a portrait of him in 1782. Miles also was on intimate terms with Sir Thomas Lawrence, to whom Thomas Sully carried a letter of introduction from the miniaturist in 1809.

[See Anne Hollingsworth Wharton, *Heirlooms in Miniatures* (1898); Wm. Dunlap, *A Hist. . . . of the Arts of Design in the U. S.* (ed. 1918), vols. II and III; J. J. and Ethel M. Foster, *A Dict. of Painters of Miniatures* (1926); Theodore Bolton, *Early Am. Portrait Painters in Miniature* (1921); *Poulson's Am. Daily Advertiser*, Mar. 8, 1828. In the sketch of Miles, in the *Dict. Nat. Biog.* it is assumed that Miles died in 1798.] J. J.

MILES, GEORGE HENRY (July 31, 1824–July 24, 1871), poet, playwright, and teacher of English literature, was born in Baltimore, Md. On his father's side he was of English ancestry, the great-grandson of Col. Thomas Miles, of the British army, who lies buried at Wallingford, Conn. The poet's father, William Miles, a native of New York, was a Baltimore merchant, at one time a commercial agent of the United States to Haiti. His mother, Sarah Mickle

Miles, was the daughter of a Scotch settler in Baltimore, and his maternal grandmother, Elizabeth Etting Mickle, of Philadelphia, was of Hebrew ancestry. At the age of nine Miles was sent to Mount Saint Mary's College, Emmitsburg, Md., and graduated *summa cum laude* in 1843. After graduation he studied law with J. H. B. Latrobe in Baltimore, was admitted to the bar, and practised for a time in partnership with Edwin Henry Webster. On Feb. 22, 1859, he was married to Adaline Tiers, daughter of Edward Tiers, a New York merchant. Having found the law uncongenial, he abandoned practice and a few months after his marriage accepted appointment as a professor of English literature in Mount Saint Mary's College. There like his brother poet and coreligionist, Father Tabb, he combined teaching with literary work, with the exception of two years, 1863–65, until in 1867 he retired to give his whole time to writing. His residence was a pleasant country place, "Thornbrook," about four miles from Emmitsburg, built for the poet and his wife by his father-in-law, who had an estate in the neighborhood.

The literary aspirations that tempted Miles into academic life were encouraged by early successes. His first tragedy, *Michael di Lando, Gonfalonier of Florence,* was begun in September 1844. His novel *The Truce of God* appeared anonymously in the *United States Catholic Magazine* in 1847, and in 1850 and 1851 *Loretto, or The Choice* and *The Governess* appeared in the *Catholic Mirror.* In 1849 the actor Edwin Forrest offered a prize for the best original tragedy in five acts. Miles was awarded one thousand dollars for *Mohammed, the Arabian Prophet.* Forrest did not use the play but it was performed in 1851 at the Lyceum Theatre in New York. When in 1866 the *Ave Maria* announced a prize of one hundred dollars for the best poem on the Blessed Virgin, Miles competed and was again successful (*Ave Maria,* June 23, 1866). His *Mohammed,* though published in 1850 in Boston and highly praised as poetry, was not successful as an acting play. With other dramas, however, Miles achieved a certain degree of success on the stage. His *Hernando de Soto,* written for J. E. Murdock in 1850, was produced acceptably at the Chestnut Street Theatre in Philadelphia for the first time on Apr. 19, 1852. A comedy, *Señor Valiente,* written at the request of John T. Ford, owner of Ford's Theatre in Baltimore, was produced in Baltimore and New York in 1859, and on Feb. 11, 1861, "Uncle Sam's Magic Lantern" was added to a production of Laura Keene's called *The Seven Sisters* which enjoyed a long run in Laura Keene's Theatre in New York City.

Besides the three novels, already mentioned, Miles wrote numerous lyrics and narrative poems. Of these latter the most ambitious is *Christine,* a romantic legend of the time of the Crusades. His "Inkerman," published in October 1856 in *Brownson's Quarterly Review,* is a spirited description of a battle of the Crimean War. His lyrics are marked by lightness of touch and notable facility in rime. In 1866 he published a collection of his verse under the title: *Christine, A Troubadour's Song, and Other Poems.* He was deeply religious and his faith tinged all of his literary work. In 1870 in the *Southern Review* appeared unsigned Miles's most important critical work, a detailed study of Shakespeare's *Hamlet.* A projected series of similar critiques on other Shakespearean tragedies remained incomplete. He died at "Thornbrook," after a lingering illness, of nephritis, and was buried in the churchyard of Mount Saint Mary's at Emmitsburg.

[Information about Miles is scanty and widely scattered. See an editorial in the *Sun* (Baltimore), July 26, 1871; Esmerelda Boyle, *Biog. Sketches of Distinguished Marylanders* (1877); Thomas E. Cox, *Gems from George H. Miles* (1901), with introduction; Mary M. Meline and E. F. X. McSweeny, *The Story of the Mountain: Mount St. Mary's Coll. and Seminary, Emmitsburg, Md.* (1911), vol. II; A. H. Quinn, *A Hist. of the Am. Drama from the Beginning to the Civil War* (1923) and *A Hist. of the Am. Drama from the Civil War to the Present Day* (1927), vol. I; J. C. Collins, Introduction to Miles's *Said the Rose and Other Lyrics* (1907); *Current Lit.,* Jan. 1898; the *Magnificat,* May, June 1908, Jan. 1933.]

J. C. F.

MILES, HENRY ADOLPHUS (May 30, 1809–May 31, 1895), Unitarian clergyman, historian, was the sixth child of Rev. John and Mary (Denny) Miles, and a descendant of John Miles who in 1639 was a freeman of Concord, Mass. Born in Grafton, Mass., where his father was pastor, Henry graduated from Brown University in 1829. Espousing Unitarian doctrines, he attended the Harvard Divinity School, and was ordained at Hallowell, Me., Dec. 19, 1832. On May 28, 1833, he married Augusta Holyoke Moore of Cambridge, Mass. After serving as minister at Hallowell for four years he was called in December 1836 to be the second pastor of the South Congregational (Unitarian) Church, Lowell, Mass. An address to the people commending the young minister was delivered by Rev. John Pierpont [*q.v.*], of the Hollis Street Church, Boston, which was subsequently published as a model of its kind (*An Address to the People, Delivered at the Installation of H. A. Miles as Pastor of the South Congregational Society, Lowell, 1837*).

In the first years of his Lowell pastorate Miles wrote a history of that then new factory city, entitled *Lowell as It Was and Is.* The little book, published in 1845, went through several editions. It provoked a local controversy, in which the author's critics charged him with drawing an unduly roseate picture of industrial conditions at Lowell, presumably for the purpose of gaining the favor of the mill owners. "It was to repel the charge that large corporations led to oppression, corruption and nepotism, that Dr. Miles seems to have written his history. Fully half of the book is devoted to showing that the mills of Lowell were managed by wise and benevolent men, and in a manner calculated to promote the moral welfare and the highest good, not only of the operatives, but of the community at large" (Chase, *post,* p. 30). Later historians, however, have found in Miles's work a valuable sourcebook, even though it may be admitted that he was disposed to discover mainly what is right in any given social picture.

Miles remained at Lowell until 1853 when he became secretary of the American Unitarian Association, with headquarters at Boston. At this same time he began to edit the *Quarterly Journal,* a denominational periodical, of which he continued in charge until 1857. In 1859 he relinquished his secretarial service in order to have leisure for independent literary work and for travel. Periods of European residence occupied about ten years. From 1865 to 1871 he was settled over the Unitarian church at Longwood, Mass., and from 1876 until his death he was pastor and pastor emeritus at Hingham. He compiled *Genealogy of the Miles Family* (1840), and published a number of religious works, which reflect a gentle and optimistic spirit. Notable among them are: *Gospel Narratives* (1848); *Grains of Gold* (1854); *Channing's Thoughts* (1859); *Words of a Friend* (1870); *Traces of Picture Writing in the Bible* (1870); and *Birth of Jesus* (1877). He was buried in Mount Auburn Cemetery, Cambridge, Mass.

[C. C. Chase's sketch of Lowell, in D. H. Hurd, *Hist. of Middlesex County, Mass.* (1890); F. W. Coburn, *Hist. of Lowell and Its People* (1920); *Boston Herald,* June 3, 1895; *Year Book of the Unitarian Congregational Churches* (1896).] F. W. C.

MILES, MANLY (July 20, 1826–Feb. 15, 1898), agriculturist, naturalist, and physician, was born at Homer, Cortland County, N. Y., the son of Manly and Mary Cushman Miles. On his father's side he came from a long line of soldiers; through his mother he was a lineal descendant of Miles Standish and Thomas Cushman. When he was eleven the family moved to a farm near Flint, Mich. His common-school education was supplemented, through his own efforts, with studies covering the subjects of mathematics, history, and science. His interest at this time in birds, fishes, insects, and other living forms was the starting point of his exceptional work as a naturalist. As a young man he entered Rush Medical College and in 1850 received the degree of M.D. In 1851 he married Mary E. Dodge. He established himself in Flint, but even while practising medicine he roamed in the fields and woods collecting specimens and making accurate observations. In 1858 he became the zoölogist of the new State Geological Survey. During his two years' incumbency he made a remarkable collection of the fauna of the state with excellent descriptions. In 1861, four years after the founding of the Michigan State Agricultural College, he was appointed professor of zoölogy and animal physiology. He was an enthusiastic teacher, was thoroughly interested in what he taught, and was most resourceful in devising apparatus and making the subject matter intelligible.

In 1865 when it seemed imperative that an agricultural college should have a course in agriculture, he was urged to become the head of the department for he had had considerable practical farm experience. He accepted and thus has the distinction of being the first professor of practical agriculture in the first agricultural college in the United States. In 1874 he was given a leave of absence and spent some of the time in England with the celebrated field-crop experimenters, Lawes and Gilbert. Soon after his return to America, in 1875, he accepted the offer of the professorship of agriculture at the University of Illinois. Later, in 1878, he became experimentalist at the Houghton Farm, Mountainville, N. Y., and in 1883 became professor of agriculture at the Massachusetts Agricultural College. In 1886 he returned to Lansing, Mich., and established his office and laboratory in three large rooms over a drug store and took up once more, with vigor, the favorite pursuits of his earlier days in Michigan. This was the period in which his scientific writings were most prolific. He published several books, chief among which were *Stock Breeding* (1879), *Silos, Ensilage and Silage* (1889), and *Land Drainage* (1892). Besides writing for the popular press he was a regular contributor to scientific journals. Three extended reports on the fauna of Michigan appeared in the publications of the Michigan Geological Survey. As President Snyder said in his report of 1906, much of Miles's work was a quarter of a century in advance of his time. His ability was recognized widely throughout the United States and abroad. He kept up his habits of reading, studying, and experimenting until the time of his death.

[W. B. Barrows, "Dr. Manly Miles," *Bull. Mich. Ornithol. Club*, Apr. 1898, and "A Sketch of Dr. Manly Miles," *Second Ann. Report of the Mich. Acad. of Sci.* (1901); W. J. Beal, *Hist. of the Mich. Agric. Coll.* (1915); *Hist. Colls. . . . Mich. Pioneer and Hist. Soc.*, vol. XXVIII (1900); the *Detroit Tribune*, Feb. 16, 1898.] R. P. H.

MILES, NELSON APPLETON (Aug. 8, 1839–May 15, 1925), soldier, came of New England ancestors descended from a Baptist clergyman and educator, John Myles, who emigrated from Wales to New England, settled in Swansea, Mass., in 1664, and fought in King Philip's War in 1675. His son, Rev. Samuel Miles, received a degree from Oxford and was for twenty-nine years rector of King's Chapel, Boston. His son and grandson, Daniel and Joab Miles, fought in the Revolution from Bennington to Yorktown. Joab's son Daniel, a farmer, married Mary Curtis, a descendant of William Curtis who arrived in Boston harbor from England in 1632. Nelson Appleton Miles, son of Daniel and Mary, was born on his father's farm near Westminster, Mass. After attending the district school and a local academy, he ventured to Boston when he was seventeen years old, and, through the good offices of his uncles, George and Nelson Curtis, secured employment in John Collamore's crockery store. He attended night school and incidentally received the rudiments of a military education from Col. M. Salignac, a former officer of the French army.

When the Civil War broke out Miles recruited a company of one hundred volunteers which formed part of Col. Henry Wilson's 22nd Massachusetts Regiment. He was commissioned captain of infantry, but his superiors considered him too young to exercise command in battle, and he served through the Peninsula campaign as a member of Gen. O. O. Howard's staff. His opportunity came at the battle of Fair Oaks (May 31–June 1, 1862), where under heavy fire he led reinforcements to the aid of the 61st New York Volunteers, receiving his first wound and official commendation for gallantry in battle. He was rewarded with promotion to the lieutenant-colonelcy of this regiment, and at Antietam, on Sept. 17, when Colonel Barlow was carried from the field wounded, Miles assumed command, becoming colonel, Sept. 30, 1862. At Fredericksburg, Dec. 13, where he was shot through the throat, his conduct was characterized by General Hancock as "most admirable and chivalrous" (*Official Records*, 1 ser. XXI, 230). For distinguished gallantry at Chancellorsville (May 3, 1863), where he was shot from his horse while desperately holding a line of abattis and rifle-pits against the enemy in advance of the II Army Corps, he was awarded the brevet of brigadier-general (Mar. 2, 1867) and the Congressional Medal of Honor (July 23, 1892). For his services in the battles of the Wilderness and Spotsylvania, he received the Thanks of Congress; he was mentioned for gallantry at Reams's Station, and at Petersburg sustained his fourth wound. On May 12, 1864, he was promoted to the grade of brigadier-general of volunteers. He and his division took a prominent part in the final campaign, which culminated at Appomattox, and he received high praise from General Grant for his services. On Oct. 21, 1865, he was made major-general of volunteers, commanding the II Army Corps of some 26,000 officers and men when but twenty-six years of age. With one exception, he had fought in every important battle of the Army of the Potomac.

After the close of hostilities he became for a time custodian of Jefferson Davis at Fort Monroe. Despite his tactful handling of a difficult situation, and the fact that he was acting on the orders of superiors, he was censured by Southern sympathizers for alleged ill-treatment of the former President of the Confederacy. From these charges he was ultimately vindicated when the true facts became known and the bitterness engendered by the war had passed (*A Statement of Facts Concerning the Imprisonment and Treatment of Jefferson Davis While a Military Prisoner at Fort Monroe, Va., in 1865 and 1866*, 1902).

Appointed colonel, 40th Infantry, in the regular establishment, July 28, 1866, he was mustered out of the volunteer service, Sept. 1, and on Mar. 15, 1869, was transferred to command the 5th Infantry, a regiment which he made famous through long-continued field service. For some fifteen years following, he was constantly associated with difficult but successful campaigns against various hostile Indians west of the Mississippi. He accomplished the defeat of the Cheyennes, Kiowas, and Comanches on the border of the Staked Plains in 1875, and subsequently took a leading part in the pacification of hostile Sioux Indians in Montana, driving Sitting Bull across the border into Canada, and dispersing the bands of Crazy Horse [*q.v.*], Lame Deer, Spotted Eagle, Broad Trail, and other chiefs. In the fall of 1877, while in command of the District of the Yellowstone, he intercepted and captured Chief Joseph [*q.v.*] and his band of Nez Percé warriors after a forced march of more than one hundred and sixty miles, an exploit considered one of the most brilliant feats of arms in Indian warfare. Later, in 1878, he succeeded in pacifying Elk Horn and his band of Bannocks near the Yellowstone Park.

He was appointed brigadier-general, United States Army, Dec. 15, 1880, and until 1885 was in command of the Department of the Columbia. During 1885–86 he commanded the Department of the Missouri and until 1888, the Department of Arizona. In 1886, he succeeded Gen. George Crook [*q.v.*] in the arduous and difficult military operations against the bloodthirsty Chiricahua Apaches under Geronimo [*q.v.*] and Naiche, whom popular opinion credited with twenty-five hundred homicides and with holding back the development of Arizona for many years. Miles accomplished the surrender of these Indians and their incarceration at Mount Vernon, Ala., after a chase which involved occupations of Mexican soil. As a token of appreciation of his service in the cause of Indian pacification he received the thanks of the state legislatures of Kansas, Montana, New Mexico, and Arizona; and in November 1887 the citizens of Arizona presented him with a sword of honor. He commanded the Division of the Pacific, with headquarters at San Francisco, during the years 1888–90, and was promoted major-general Apr. 5, 1890. In a winter campaign in Dakota, 1890–91, he suppressed a serious outbreak of Sioux Indians, inflamed by the supposed coming of a Messiah, and effected their return to government control after but one serious engagement at Wounded Knee. In 1894, while commanding the Department of the Missouri with headquarters at Chicago, he was in command of troops charged by President Cleveland with quelling the industrial riots and disorders accompanying the Pullman strike. In 1894–95 he was commander of the Department of the East, with headquarters at Governor's Island, New York.

Upon the retirement of Maj.-Gen. John M. Schofield, Sept. 29, 1895, Miles became by seniority the commander-in-chief of the Army (order dated Oct. 2). In 1897 he represented the United States at the Jubilee Celebration of Queen Victoria—visiting as an observer the theatre of war between Turkey and Greece and witnessing the autumn maneuvers of the Russian, German, and French armies. The following year, with the declaration of war against Spain, he took a directing part in the organization and training of the regular and volunteer forces, and although not permitted to command the expeditionary force dispatched to Santiago de Cuba, he joined later with reinforcements and dictated the terms of the surrender of the Spanish garrison following the battles fought by Shafter's army. He then proceeded to Porto Rico with United States troops, landed successfully at Ponce and Guanica, and after a few engagements with Spanish troops attended by trifling losses among American units, succeeded in the complete pacification of the island. By appointment of President McKinley, confirmed Feb. 11, 1901, he was advanced to the grade of lieutenant-general, a rank hitherto rarely held. In December of the same year he was officially censured by President Theodore Roosevelt through the Secretary of War for public expressions of approval in connection with Admiral Dewey's report upon the case of Admiral Schley (*New York Tribune,* Dec. 17, 22, 1901). In 1902 he visited the Philippine Islands, then in a state of insurrection, and after an official inspection of troops and an investigation of complaints by Filipino officials, caused much controversy by his report of alleged abuses on the part of American officers and soldiers in their relations with Filipino insurgent forces (*The Philippines: Reports by Lieutenant-General Nelson A. Miles,* Anti-Imperialist League, Boston, 1909; reprinted from *Army and Navy Journal,* May 2, 1903).

On Aug. 8, 1903, having reached the age of sixty-four, Miles was retired from active service by operation of law. He thereafter made his home in Washington, D. C. In 1896 he had published *Personal Recollections and Observations of General Nelson A. Miles.* This was followed, after his trip abroad in 1897, by *Military Europe* (1898). He published a second autobiographical volume, *Serving the Republic,* in 1911. In 1912 he became head of a short-lived patriotic organization known as the Sons of Liberty, and in the ensuing years held office in many societies and associations. From 1918 until his death he was local commander of the Military Order of the Loyal Legion. In his eighty-sixth year, while he was attending a circus performance at Washington, he suffered a heart attack of which he died. His funeral was attended by the President and many distinguished officials as well as several thousand soldiers and sailors and the representatives of numerous patriotic societies. His body was laid to rest, with the highest civic and military honors, in a mausoleum, the erection of which he had supervised many years before, in Arlington Cemetery.

Miles was married, June 30, 1868, while serving in the West, to Mary Hoyt Sherman, daughter of Judge Charles Sherman of Ohio, and niece of Senator John Sherman and Gen. William T. Sherman [*qq.v.*]. He was survived by a son and a daughter. A natural soldier, suddenly transferred, while yet a young man, from the hum-drum of mercantile life to the cataclysm of a great war, and without the benefit of many signal advantages possessed by his military contemporaries, he attained outstanding leadership through his indefatigable industry, sound judgment, and personal bravery.

[Many details of Miles's life are to be found in his two volumes of memoirs, *Personal Recollections* and *Serving the Republic.* See also *War of the Rebellion: Official Records (Army)*; *Battles and Leaders of the Civil War*, vols. III, IV (1888); *Personal Memoirs of U. S. Grant*, II (1886), 451–53; *Personal Memoirs of P. H. Sheridan* (1888), II, 172–73; and H. E. Davies, *General Sheridan* (1895), pp. 235–36; J. M. Schofield, *Forty-six Years in the Army* (1897); J. H. Wilson, *Under the Old Flag* (1912), II, 440–72; H. L. Scott, *Some Memories of a Soldier* (1928); *Who's Who in America*, 1924–25; *Army and Navy Jour.*, May 23, 1925; *Evening Star* (Washington), May 15, 19, 1925.] C. D. R.

MILES, RICHARD PIUS (May 17, 1791–Feb. 21, 1860), Catholic prelate, son of Nicholas and Ann (Blackloc) Miles, both descendants of old Maryland planter families, was born in Prince George's County, Md. His parents moved to Nelson County, Ky., in 1796, and Richard was reared in pioneer surroundings and inured to frontier privations. At the age of fifteen he entered the Dominican school connected with the priory of St. Rose of Lima near Springfield, Ky., where he came under the influence of Fathers Samuel Wilson, W. R. Tuite, and E. D. Fenwick [*q.v.*]. Upon the completion of a collegiate course in which French, Italian, and music were not neglected, he took final vows in the Order of St. Dominic on May 13, 1810. He then studied theology at St. Thomas' College and in September 1816 was ordained a priest. The young friar was retained as a teacher at the academy, where Jefferson Davis studied two years, as a master of novices, and as an assistant on the missionary circuit. In 1828 he was sent to Zanesville, Ohio, where he built a new church and one of the first parochial schools in the state and from which he ministered to a parish which comprised several counties. An agreeable person and a gentle controversialist, he found little difficulty in obtaining court rooms and Protestant meeting-houses in which he preached to Catholics and curious visitors. In 1833 he was named superior at St. Rose's Priory, Springfield, Ky., and in this capacity he established the Convent of St. Catherine nearby, the sisters of which soon founded an academy for girls. Three years later, he was selected as prior of St. Joseph's Priory in Somerset County, Ohio, remaining there until elected provincial by a chapter of his order (Apr. 22, 1837). A council of the Catholic hierarchy at Baltimore urged Rome to erect the diocese of Nashville and honored Miles as its nominee for bishop. Gregory XVI made the appointment, July 28, 1837, which Miles accepted only under obedience; for both he and his religious brethren believed that as provincial he could perform a greater service than as bishop of a destitute see.

Frontier and missionary work on horseback had no terrors for him, however, and as soon as he was consecrated at Bardstown, Ky., by Bishop Joseph Rosati (Sept. 16, 1838), he rode to Nashville, Tenn., on a horse donated by the Dominicans. Well received by the 300 Catholics in the state and by the Protestant people also, he found a boarding house, repaired a dilapidated church for his cathedral, and commenced an arduous visitation of his diocese, during which he attended Irish laborers on public works, drew isolated Catholics together, established mass stations, and preached everywhere. Soon Joseph Stokes, rector of the seminary at Cincinnati, volunteered as an aide; and in time Miles attracted a group of able, self-sacrificing priests of various nationalities, willing to serve in a primitive diocese where ease was unknown. In 1840, as one of the bishops who brought the decrees of the Council of Baltimore to Rome, he had an opportunity to seek aid in Vienna from the Leopoldine Association and in Paris and Lyons from the Society for the Propagation of the Faith. Toward the end of his life, he could point to the Seven Dolors Cathedral (1847), a Dominican church at Memphis, other churches and chapels, several thousand Catholics, a small seminary, St. John's Hospital and Orphanage in Nashville (1849), Catholic colonies of German and Irish immigrants which he founded in Morgan and Humphreys counties, several girls' academies, and a negro school. Even in the trying Know-Nothing days he retained the general good will of the community. Somewhat broken in health, he sought to have Father N. R. Young, O.P., as coadjutor bishop, but in 1858 James Whelan, Archbishop Purcell's candidate, was named. Miles's death occurred two years later.

[V. F. O'Daniel, *The Father of the Church in Tenn.: The Rt. Rev. Richard Pius Miles* (1926) is a detailed biography based on archival and printed materials; see also R. H. Clarke, *Lives of the Deceased Bishops of the Cath. Ch. in the U. S.*, vol. II (1888); *Guardian* (Louisville) and *Cath. Telegraph* (Cincinnati), Feb. 25, 1860; *Freeman's Journal* (N. Y.), Mar. 3, 1860; *Republican Banner* (Nashville), Feb. 23, 1860; *Nashville Union and American*, Feb. 22, 1860.] R. J. P.

MILES, WILLIAM PORCHER (July 4, 1822–May 11, 1899), United States and Confederate States congressman, was born at Walterboro, Colleton District, S. C., the second son of Sarah Bond (Warley) and James Saunders Miles. After spending a year at the noted Willington academy in Abbeville District, he entered the College of Charleston, where he graduated in 1842 with highest honors. He studied law in the office of Edward McCrady but soon abandoned the law to become a teacher. He was assistant professor of mathematics in the College of Charleston from 1843 to 1855. During this period his elegant manners, handsome appearance, and reputation for learning won him a notable position in the polite circles of Charleston. In 1855 an event occurred that changed the course of his career. He excited the admiration of the public by his heroic services as a volunteer nurse during the yellow-fever epidemic at Norfolk, Va. That city presented him with a medal, and the conservative faction of Charleston, seeking an available candidate for mayor to stem the tide of Know-Nothingism, offered him the nomination. He accepted and was elected by a good majority. During his administration the police force of the city was reorganized, and a system of tidal drains was inaugurated. In 1857 he was elected to Congress, where he served until his withdrawal in December 1860, championing slavery and secession in a series of impressive addresses. He took a prominent part in the Washington phase of the negotiations over the status of the Charleston forts and joined other Southern congressmen in signing a manifesto announcing that the organization of a Southern confederacy was necessary. He was active in the Southern independence movement. He was chairman of the committee on foreign relations of the South Carolina secession convention and signed the ordinance of secession. Beauregard made him one of the three to arrange with Anderson the terms of the surrender of Fort Sumter. He represented the Charleston district in the Confederate Congress during its entire existence. In that body he was chairman of the committee that devised the Confederate flag and chairman of the important committee on military affairs.

In 1863 the course of his career was again changed. He married Betty, the daughter of Oliver Beirne, a rich Virginia and Louisiana planter. From 1865 until his death, with one interruption, he was able to play the rôle most congenial to him, that of a country gentleman with the means and leisure to entertain distinguished guests, collect books, and attract attention by his polished addresses. For fifteen years he lived at Oakridge, Nelson County, Va. In 1874 he was an unsuccessful candidate for the presidency of The Johns Hopkins University. In 1880 he became the first president of the University of South Carolina on its reorganization under white control. In 1882 he resigned from the university to become manager of the plantations of his father-in-law located in Ascension Parish, La. There he became one of the largest planters in the state, controlling thirteen plantations, which produced twenty million pounds of sugar annually. He became president of the Ascension branch of the Louisiana Sugar Planters' Association, and he was one of the founders of a sugar-experiment station and of *The Louisiana Planter and Sugar Manufacturer,* a weekly newspaper published in New Orleans. "Houmas House," his home, was noted for its hospitality and for its collection of rare and beautiful books. Although he took no active part in the public life of his adopted state, he frequently delivered orations on public occasions and expressed himself positively on controverted questions. He opposed the state lottery and the tendency of the sugar planters to favor high tariffs, a sugar bounty, and other measures of the Republican party. He died at "Houmas House."

[Newspaper clippings from his daughter, Mrs. Henry Middleton, Hendersonville, N. C.; *Cyc. of Eminent and Representative Men of the Carolinas* (1892), vol. I; *Letters and Testimonials Recommending Mr. Wm. Porcher Miles for the Presidency of Hopkins Univ.* (1874); *Biog. and Hist. Memoirs of La.* (1892), II, pp. 253–54; *Hist. of S. C.*, ed. Yates Snowden (1920), vol. II; E. L. Green, *Hist. of the Univ. of S. C.* (1916); *News and Courier* (Charleston), May 12, 1899.]

F. B. S.

MILHOLLAND, INEZ [See BOISSEVAIN INEZ MILHOLLAND, 1886–1916].

MILLEDGE, JOHN (1757–Feb. 9, 1818), Revolutionary patriot, governor of Georgia, representative, senator, was associated with most of the noteworthy events in his state from the Revolution to the War of 1812, but is remembered today chiefly because of his connection with the founding of the University of Georgia. His father, John Milledge, was one of the passengers on the brig *Ann,* Capt. John Thomas, which brought Oglethorpe and his little band of colonists to the port of Charleston in January 1733. He is said to have enjoyed the advantage of friendship and close association with Oglethorpe, and later became one of the prominent citizens of the colony. In 1751 he was one of the four representatives of the Savannah district in the first Provincial Assembly held under President Henry Parker. Young John's mother was the daughter of Mrs. Frances Robe of Savannah. When he was about ten his father was married again, to Mrs. Anne Rasberry.

The boy had the best advantages the little colony afforded. Probably the greater part of his education was gained at Bethesda, the school founded by the evangelist George Whitefield [*q.v.*] and still in existence as an institution for orphan boys. His intimate associates were the leading young men of the colony. He studied law in the office of the King's Attorney, but at the opening of the Revolution threw in his lot with the patriots. In the excitement caused by the news from Lexington and Concord he joined Joseph Habersham, Noble Wymberly Jones, Edward Telfair, and two others in breaking into Governor Wright's magazine and carrying off six hundred pounds of powder, some of which is said to have been used at Bunker Hill. A few weeks later he aided in an attack on Governor Wright in person, making him a prisoner in his own home. After this episode Milledge served gallantly in various capacities throughout the Revolution. He took part in the defense of Savannah, escaped with James Jackson to South Carolina, where they narrowly missed being hanged as British spies, and later served at the siege of Augusta and in Benjamin Lincoln's attempt to retake Savannah.

In 1780 he became attorney-general, and was later a member of the General Assembly during several sessions. In 1792 he was elected to Congress, succeeding Anthony Wayne who had been ousted after defeating James Jackson [*q.v.*]. He also served in the Fourth, Fifth, and Seventh congresses, resigning in 1802 to become governor. After two terms, in 1806 he was sent to the United States Senate to fill the vacancy caused by the death of James Jackson. Reëlected for a full term in 1807, he resigned while president *pro tempore* in 1809 and retired, respected and admired by all, to a life of elegant leisure.

Milledge's service to the University of Georgia probably seemed to him a small and relatively trivial incident of his eventful life. In 1785 a charter was granted by the General Assembly, and forty thousand acres of land in two newly created counties carved out of the wilderness were set aside as an endowment. The grant, princely in prospect, proved disappointing in product—Gov. Wilson Lumpkin relates that his father once swapped four hundred acres of such land for a shotgun—and the building of the university was deferred. In 1800 a renewed effort was made, and a committee appointed to select a site. Its members included Milledge, Abraham Baldwin [*q.v.*], George Walton, John Twiggs, and Hugh Lawton, all prominent in local annals. The land upon which their choice fell lay outside the bounds of the state grant and had passed into private ownership, but Milledge now immortalized himself by buying it outright for four thousand dollars and presenting it to the university. The tract embraced more than six hundred acres, including land now occupied by the campus of the university as well as a large part of the city of Athens which gradually grew up around the college. The imagination of posterity, struck by the impulsive generosity of the gift, has identified Milledge with the origin of the state's highest institution of learning, and has honored his name in Milledgeville, the state capital from 1807 to 1867, in Milledge Avenue, the principal residence street of Athens, in the Milledge Chair of Ancient Languages at the University of Georgia, and in Milledge Street in the Sand Hills, the aristocratic suburb of Augusta where his declining days were spent and his mortal remains entombed.

Milledge was married twice. His first wife was Martha Galphin of Silver Bluff, S. C., daughter of George Galphin. She bore him one daughter and died in November 1811. In May of the following year he married Ann, daughter of Thomas and Ann (Gresham) Lamar, by whom he had three children.

[George White, *Hist. Colls. of Ga.* (1854); W. J. Northen, *Men of Mark in Ga.*, vol. I (1907); L. L. Knight, *A Standard Hist. of Georgia and Georgians* (1917), I, *passim*, VI, 3200, and *Georgia's Landmarks, Memorials and Legends* (2 vols., 1913–14); T. U. P. Charlton, *The Life of Maj. Gen. James Jackson* (1809), reprinted in 1897 with valuable letters of Jackson to Milledge; C. C. Jones, Jr., *The Hist. of Ga.* (2 vols., 1883); W. B. Stevens, *A Hist. of Ga. . . . to . . . MDCCXCVIII* (2 vols., 1847–59); H. C. White, *Abraham Baldwin* (1926); E. M. Coulter, *College Life in the Old South* (1928); *Biog. Dir. Am. Cong.* (1928); *Daily Savannah Republican*, Feb. 13, 1818; Record of Bonds, Bills of Sale, Deeds of Gift for the Years 1765–72 (Ga. State Archives), p. 418; information as to certain facts from Mrs. A. S. Salley, Columbia, S. C., a descendant.]

J. H. T. M.

MILLEDOLER, PHILIP (Sept. 22, 1775–Sept. 22, 1852), clergyman, educator, son of John and Anna (Mitchell) Muhlithaler, was born at Rhinebeck, N. Y., whither his parents had fled from their home in New York City at the time of its occupancy by the British. His father was a native of Bern, Switzerland, and had come to America about 1751; his mother's parents had emigrated from Zurich. The family was connected with the German Reformed Church and Philip early showed unusual religious tendencies. He was graduated from Columbia College in 1793 and began at once the study of theology under the pastor of his church, John D. Gros [*q.v.*], and of Hebrew under a Lutheran pastor. His proficiency and personal promise were such that, after only a year, having been examined by the German Reformed Synod at Reading, Pa., he was ordained to the ministry (May 21, 1794).

His pastor and preceptor desiring that he succeed him, and the congregation also desiring it, Milledoler became pastor of the Nassau Street German Reformed Church in 1795 when he was but twenty years old, his preaching to be in both German and English. In 1800 he became pastor of the Pine Street Presbyterian Church of Philadelphia. Other churches called him; his former parish in New York repeatedly sought his return; and in 1805 he became pastor of the Rutgers Street Presbyterian Church, New York City. In all these pastorates his ministry was deeply spiritual and very effectual. His preaching was fervid, he was especially gifted in prayer, and his churches were notable for their evangelical interest, for their growth in membership, and for their large congregations. From early in his ministry he was in sympathy with the Reformed (Dutch) Church and for a short time, about 1800, his ministerial membership was in that body. In 1813 he became pastor of the Collegiate Dutch Reformed Church of New York City, to remain with the denomination for the rest of his life. During these years of devoted and distinguished pastorate he was active and influential in many religious associations. He held various important offices under the General Assembly of the Presbyterian Church and was moderator of the Assembly in 1808. He was concerned in the forming and managing of the American Bible Society, the Society for Evangelizing the Jews, and the United Foreign Missionary Society.

He was learned in theology and positive in his convictions. His opposition to Hopkinsianism had something to do, no doubt, with his changing from the Presbyterian to the Dutch Reformed body. In 1811, before Princeton Theological Seminary was organized, he was appointed by the Presbytery of New York to instruct students in theology. The General Synod of the German Reformed Church, in 1820, chose him its professor of theology, an appointment which he finally declined. In 1825 the General Synod of the Dutch Reformed Church elected him professor of theology in its theological seminary at New Brunswick, N. J., and at the same time the trustees of Rutgers, up to that time known as Queen's College, chose him president. He accepted the two offices. The college, which had been weak and even inactive for some years, began at once an era of prosperity, strength, and distinguished service, and the enrollment of students in the seminary also greatly increased. A remarkable number of graduates of this period became leaders in church, state, and education. Remaining in these exacting and important offices for fifteen years, he resigned them both in 1840 and returned to New York City. During his career he delivered many sermons and addresses which were published. On Mar. 29, 1796, he married Susan, daughter of Lawrence Benson of Harlem; she died in 1815 and on Nov. 4, 1817, he married Margaret, daughter of General John Steele of Philadelphia. He had ten children. The day after his death, on Staten Island, his wife also died, and the two were buried in one grave.

[E. T. Corwin, *A Manual of the Reformed Church in America* (4th ed. 1902); W. B. Sprague, *Annals Am. Pulpit*, vol. IX (1869); W. H. S. Demarest, *A Hist. of Rutgers Coll., 1766–1924* (1924); *Centennial of the Theological Seminary of the Reformed Church in America* (1885); *Mag. of the Reformed Dutch Church*, Mar., Apr. 1827, Aug. 1828; *Christian Intelligencer*, Sept. 30, Nov. 4, 30, Dec. 23, 1852; *N. Y. Observer*, Sept. 30, 1852; *N. Y. Times*, Sept. 23, 1852.]

W. H. S. D.

MILLER, CHARLES HENRY (Mar. 20, 1842–Jan. 21, 1922), landscape painter, etcher, born in New York, was a descendant of Fernandus de Muldor, who came to New Amsterdam from Holland in 1664. His parents were Jacob and Jane (Taylor) Miller. He exhibited his first picture at the National Academy of Design when he was eighteen years of age, but it was not until some years later that he adopted painting as his profession. Meanwhile he attended the Mt. Washington Collegiate Institute and later the New York Homeopathic Medical College, graduating with the degree of M.D. in 1863. Upon graduation he made a voyage to Europe as ship's doctor on the Black Ball liner *Harvest Queen* which enabled him to pay brief visits to Paris, London, and Scotland. The impressions he received there strengthened his love of art, and on his return to New York he abandoned the medical profession. His earliest studies from nature were made on Long Island; Bayard Taylor called him "the artistic discoverer" of the island. In 1867 he went to Munich to take up the serious work of preparation for the career of a painter. He became a pupil of Adolf Lier (a pupil of Jules Dupré), at the Bavarian Royal Academy, and later continued his studies in Vienna, Leipzig, Dresden, Berlin, and Paris. After three years abroad he returned to New York. He became an academician in 1875; was president of the New York Art Club in 1879; member of the Society of American Artists, the Art Union, Municipal Art Society, New York Etching Club, Century, Lotos, and Republican clubs; and a welcome contributor to all the important exhibitions, including the Centennial, 1876, and two or three of the international expositions in Paris.

Miller's etchings, like his paintings, were Long Island motives. Five of his prints were in the Boston Art Museum exhibition of etchings in 1881, among them "Home, Sweet Home," the birthplace of John Howard Payne. As the direct expression of a painter of great power, said S. R. Koehler, every one of his plates has some point of interest to the lover of art, though many of them are but hasty memoranda, jotted down rudely, reminding one of Jongkind. His paintings are warm in tone, rich in surface, and of handsome pattern, somewhat reminiscent of the Barbizon school. His Long Island subjects constitute a record of the changing aspect of nature in the suburbs of a metropolis. A typical example is "A Bouquet of Oaks," given to the Metropolitan Museum, New York, in 1907, by W. T. Evans. It was painted in 1883 at Stewart's Pond, near Jamaica, L. I., in the autumn. The region about Queens, where Miller found most of his motives, comprises Jamaica, Garden City, Mineola, Creedmoor; its rural character is a thing of the past; thus his "Oaks at Creedmoor" (Paris exposition of 1878) and his "Sunset at Queens" (Paris exposition of 1882) are not merely effective landscapes, but historic documents as well. Under the pen name of Carl De Muldor the artist published in 1885 a book entitled *The Philosophy of Art in America.* He wrote occasional essays in criticism and lectured. On Oct. 3, 1900, he married Mrs. Elizabeth Dorothea Mosback. He died at his New York home in his eightieth year.

[S. R. Koehler, article in the *Am. Art Review,* vol. II (1881); C. M. Kurtz, *Nat. Acad. Notes* (1884); Samuel Isham, *The Hist. of Am. Painting* (1905); "The Works of Chas. Henry Miller," *Art-Jour.* (London), Dec. 1877; G. W. Sheldon, *Am. Painters* (1881); *Cat. of the Thos. B. Clarke Coll. of Am. Pictures* (1891); *Am. Art News,* Jan. 28, 1922; *N. Y. Times,* Jan. 22, 1922.]

W. H. D.

MILLER, CHARLES RANSOM (Jan. 17, 1849–July 18, 1922), editor, newspaper director, was born at Hanover Center, N. H. His father, Elijah Tenney Miller, a farmer, was descended from early Massachusetts stock. His mother was Chastina Hoyt Miller. As a boy he showed no liking for farm work and in 1863 he became a pupil at Kimball Union Academy at Meriden, N. H., from which he was expelled in 1865 for hilarious conduct. He spent a year in helping his father on the farm and then entered Green Mountain Liberal Institute, South Woodstock, Vt., where he prepared for Dartmouth College. At the end of his sophomore year at Dartmouth he was expelled again for youthful exuberance but after working in a printing office during the summer he was allowed to reënter and was graduated in 1872. Both in preparatory schools and college he showed no zeal for regular studies, preferring private reading and being considered inattentive in classes.

At Dartmouth he had been a contributor, especially of verse, to the college monthly and had acquired a taste for writing which led him to seek a place on the staff of the *Springfield Daily Republican,* for which he was a reporter for three years under the elder Samuel Bowles. Through a college friend he learned of an opening with the *New York Times* and was engaged in July 1875 by George Jones as assistant telegraph editor of that paper. He was in charge of the telegraph news on election night in 1876 but did not participate in the act of John Reid, the managing editor, who persuaded the Republican National Committee to claim victory for Hayes when other newspapers conceded it to Tilden. Miller was then and remained throughout his life an independent Democrat. On Jan. 1, 1876, he was put in charge of the weekly edition of the *Times.* Later in the same year, on Oct. 10, he was married to Frances Daniels, of Plainfield, N. H., who survived until 1906. While in charge of the weekly edition he had begun to write occasional editorials, which he continued to do when he became foreign editor of the *Times* in 1879. He was made a regular editorial writer in 1880. On Apr. 13, 1883, at the age of thirty-four, he became editor in chief in succession to John Foord and retained that post until his death.

The *Times,* as a Republican paper, had exposed Tweed and the Star Route frauds and had developed independent tendencies. In 1884 it supported Cleveland for president. Miller and Cleveland became close friends. Jones having died in 1891, Miller raised $950,000 in subscriptions for the purchase of the paper from the Jones heirs and took control in 1893. Circulation and advertising had been declining and the panic of 1893 hastened that process. Through a complete reorganization in 1896 control and management of the paper were acquired by Adolph S. Ochs, proprietor and publisher of the *Chattanooga* (Tennessee) *Daily Times.* Miller continued as editor in chief and became vice-president of the new company. Freed from heavy financial burdens and in the prime of his intellectual powers, he then began his most productive period as an editorial writer. He had studied deeply after leaving college and became proficient in Latin, Greek, French, German, and Russian, besides acquiring a wide knowledge of history and international affairs. At the outbreak of the World War, he forecast future developments with insight, predicting sure defeat for Germany. When the United States entered the war, the editorials in the *Times* gave vigorous support to the cause of the Allies. A notable editorial appearing in the issue for Dec. 15, 1914, entitled, "For the German People, Peace with Freedom," attracted wide attention, and was republished in many languages in newspapers all over the world. The opening paragraph was most prophetic: "Germany is doomed to sure defeat. Bankrupt in statesmanship, overmatched in arms, under the moral condemnation of the civilized world, befriended only by the Austrian and the Turk, two backward-looking and dying nations, desperately battling against the hosts of three great Powers to which help and reinforcement from States now neutral will certainly come should the decision be long deferred, she pours out the blood of her heroic subjects and wastes her diminishing substance in a hopeless struggle that postpones but cannot alter the fatal decree." On Sept. 16, 1918, an editorial by Miller advised acceptance of the Austro-Hungarian proposal for a non-binding discussion of peace terms, for which public opinion was not then prepared. It created quite a furore, but later it was regarded as wise and judicious. Miller's style in editorials was marked by strong conviction, clarity of expression, and forceful reasoning. He was of medium height, heavily built, and had a large head. He enjoyed his friends, and in his personal relations he was unusually gracious.

[The principal source of information about Miller is the biography, *Mr. Miller of "The Times"* (1931) by F. Fraser Bond who was his editorial secretary. There is also valuable material in the *Hist. of the N. Y. Times* (1921) by Elmer Davis, who was an editorial writer on his staff. His personal letters in the possession of his family and those addressed to George Fred Williams, his classmate, and Solomon Bulkley Griffin, his former associate on the staff of the *Springfield Republican,* throw light upon his character. His editorials are preserved in the files of the *Times.* An account of his death accompanied by a full sketch of his career may be found in the *N. Y. Times,* July 19, 1922.]

A. S. W.

MILLER, CINCINNATUS HINER (Mar. 10, 1839–Feb. 17, 1913), poet, son of Hulings and Margaret (Witt) Miller, was born in Liberty, Ind. His middle name was given in honor of the country physician who was in attendance at his birth; the form "Heine" which appeared in his early books, may or may not have been a printer's error. His father, a Quaker schoolmaster, wandered ever westward, seeking a land of peace and plenty, from Ohio to Indiana, thence to Illinois, and finally, in 1852, across the Rockies and Cascades to Oregon. He settled near the forks of the Willamette not far from the present Eugene. At about the age of seventeen his son "Nat," as he was called, ran away from home in company with another boy. They found their way to one of the mining camps in Northern California where Miller obtained employment as a cook. Being a rather delicate lad, he fell seriously ill with the scurvy as the result of the bad food and his own cooking. He was nursed back to health by a Dr. Ream in Yreka, Cal., and was subsequently befriended by a gambler named James Thompson, who figures attractively in his writings as "The Prince." Despite Miller's lifelong assertion that he was wounded in the battle of Castle Rocks against the Modocs, on June 15, 1855, residents of that vicinity scouted the claim that he had taken part in the skirmish. Probably in 1856 Miller made the acquaintance of Joseph De Bloney, known as "Mountain Joe." According to Miller's story, the mountaineer proposed to establish an Indian republic at the base of Mount Shasta. If so grandiose a scheme was planned, it went no further than the building of a road-house in which Miller did the cooking. In the spring of 1857 he went to live with an Indian tribe, the Diggers, and married one of their women, who bore him a daughter, Cali-Shasta. His native associates were noted horse-thieves, and Miller, as a preliminary to establishing the republic, fell in with their ways. He was captured, after an exciting chase, on July 8, 1859, but was rescued the same night by a friend who sawed through the bars of the jail window. Although he had no share in the Pit River massacre of this year, the Shasta region became very unsafe for any Indian sympathizer, and Miller, soon after it, wisely returned to Oregon.

He then for a time attended an academy named "Columbia College" in Eugene, taught school for a while in Clarke, Washington Territory, studied law on the side, and was admitted to the bar in Portland, Ore., in 1861. Instead of practising, he established in 1862, in company with one Isaac Mossman, a pony express between Washington Territory and Idaho. With its proceeds, he purchased in 1863 the *Democratic Register* in Eugene and became an editor. His first appearance in print had been a letter in defense of the Mexican bandit, Joaquin Murietta [*q.v.*], which had resulted in his friends nick-naming him "Joaquin"; the name pleased him better than his own more burdensome one and in time he adopted it as his pen name. Some verses of his attracted the attention of a poetically minded girl in Port Orford, Ore., named Minnie Theresa Dyer, who wrote to him enthusiastically about them. After some correspondence, Miller rode over to Port Orford and returned the same week with Minnie Myrtle, as he called her, as his bride. His newspaper being suppressed by the government because of its support of the Confederacy, the editor moved to Canyon City, Ore., where he soon won the favor of his fellow-townsmen by successfully leading a party of them against a band of hostile Indians. He was rewarded by being elected judge of the Grant County court in 1866. A little later his wife, now the mother of two children, separated from him. Miller solaced his loneliness by bringing out two volumes of poetry, *Specimens* (1868) and *Joaquin et al* (1869). These attracted some attention, and in 1870 he went down to San Francisco to enjoy his réclame and was there admitted to the circle which included Bret Harte, Charles Warren Stoddard, and Ina Coolbrith.

Thence he started on a literary pilgrimage to England. After visiting the Burns and Byron shrines, he attempted to find a London publisher for a compilation of his own verse, some of which had already appeared in newspapers, under the title, *Pacific Poems*. Failing in this, he printed the book privately and succeeded in gaining the attention of the critics. William Michael Rossetti took him up and introduced him to London literary circles, where his striking appearance in chaps and sombrero, which he wore indoors and out, soon made him the sensation of the season. In 1871 Longmans published his *Songs of the Sierras,* which in spite of its cheap rhythms and Byronic imitations was loudly acclaimed by the British. Its reception in America was less favorable, critics refusing to accept its romanticism as a genuine expression of the Far West. Attention was also unkindly called to the author's lack of learning which had led him into sundry errors in his poems, such as riming "Goethe" with "teeth." A brief visit to America convincing the poet of his unpopularity, he sought consolation in foreign travel. During the next few years he visited South America, Europe, and possibly the Near East. In 1873 he published *Songs of the Sun-lands,* and, in prose, *Life Amongst the Modocs* (republished with variations under other titles), regarded by Stuart Sherman as "his most interesting book." These were followed by *The Ship in the Desert* (1875), *The Baroness of New York* (1877), *Songs of Italy* (1878), showing the influence of Browning, and a prose Indian romance, *Shadows of Shasta* (1881). He also published several dramas, of which *The Danites in the Sierras* (1881), a Mormon play, was the most successful. In 1884 appeared *Memorie and Rime,* an autobiographical miscellany, and in 1886 *The Destruction of Gotham,* an unsuccesful novel. His last prose works were *An Illustrated History of Montana* (1894), a typical subscription history, and *The Building of the City Beautiful* (1897), showing Miller as a Utopist. In 1897, also, he published the *Complete Poetical Works of Joaquin Miller.* His narrative poem, *Light,* which was published in 1907, was his last bid for fame and represents his closest approach to full maturity as a poet.

Meanwhile, Miller had returned to America and tried living in New York, Boston, and Washington, all of which were too crowded for his taste. In 1883 he married Abbie Leland, and in 1886 he settled permanently in Oakland, Cal. There on the hills above the town he purchased an estate, known as "The Heights" (in Miller's spelling usually "The Hights"), which he adorned with trees and stone monuments to Frémont, Browning, and Moses, and with a funeral pyre to be used at his own death. For many years he was one of the landmarks of California. As a bearded sage and advocate of the simple life he was looked upon with a respect which was mingled with amusement at his eccentricities and horror at his theories of free love. In 1897–98 he found renewed adventures as correspondent of the New York *Journal* in the Klondike. By the time of his death in 1913 the West that he loved had vanished. The best of his work remains of significance as an attempt, never wholly successful, to celebrate on a heroic scale its freedom and its beauty.

[Miller's autobiographical writings mentioned above and his *Overland in a Covered Wagon* (1930), ed. by Sidney G. Firman, are useful but untrustworthy. See also: Harr Wagner, *Joaquin Miller and His Other Self* (1929); Stuart P. Sherman, introduction to *The Poetical Works of Joaquin Miller* (1923); the *Frontier,* May 1931, Jan.–May 1932; *Sunset,* June 1913; *Am. Mercury,* Feb. 1926; *San Francisco Examiner,* Feb. 18, 1913. Information as to certain facts was supplied by Dr. Martin S. Peterson of the University of Nebraska, who has prepared a doctoral dissertation on Miller.]

E. S. B.

MILLER, EDWARD (May 9, 1760–Mar. 17, 1812), physician, brother of Samuel Miller, 1769–1850 [*q.v.*], was the son of Rev. John and Margaret (Millington) Miller, and grandson of John Miller, a Scotchman, who emigrated to Boston in 1710, and married Mary Bass of *Mayflower* ancestry. Born near Dover, Del., where his father was pastor of the Presbyterian church, Edward received a good academic education and began the study of medicine with a local practitioner, Dr. Charles Ridgely. Two years later, in 1780, dissatisfied with his lack of clinical opportunities, he began to serve as surgeon's mate in the colonial military hospitals, being stationed chiefly at Basking Ridge, N. J. In 1781 he became surgeon on an armed ship sailing for France, and during 1782–83 pursued his medical studies at the University of Pennsylvania. At the close of the Revolutionary period, he settled at Frederica, Del., removing later to Somerset County, Md., and in 1786 to Dover, Del. He had been accustomed to spend a part of each year in Philadelphia in order to keep in touch with medical advance, and in 1785 he received the degree of bachelor of medicine, and in 1789, that of doctor from the University of Pennsylvania. He appears to have studied the epidemic of yellow fever in Philadelphia in 1793, and about this time he wrote a letter to Dr. Benjamin Rush [*q.v.*], with whom he had formed a friendship, in which he indorsed the latter's belief that the disease was not imported and not contagious from person to person. In 1796 he removed to New York City and at once began to identify himself with the life of the future metropolis. With Drs. Samuel L. Mitchill and Elihu H. Smith [*qq.v.*], he founded what is classed by some authorities as the earliest medical periodical of the United States—the *Medical Repository,* the first number of which appeared in August 1797. He was active in connection with the yellow-fever epidemic of 1798, and on account of his familiarity with the disease was made physician to the Port of New York in 1803.

In 1805 there was a new outbreak of yellow fever and Miller made a report on it to the governor of the state (*Report on the Malignant Disease which Prevailed in the City of New York in the Autumn of 1805: Addressed to the Governor of New York,* 1806), which was reprinted in England and translated into French and German. He rendered valuable aid in the establishment of the College of Physicians and Surgeons (1807), "joining with Dr. Romayne in extending his credit for the procurement of the funds needed" (John Shrady, *The College of Physicians and Surgeons, New York,* vol. I, 1903–04, p. 42). He became its first professor of the practice of physic, and in 1809 was made one of the physicians to the New York Hospitals, where he inaugurated the custom of holding clinical lectures. His death took place in the midst of an active career, due to an acute respiratory affection.

He was evidently a man with unusual vision or intuition. He advocated lengthening the period of undergraduate studies, clinical advantages, and the study of pathology. He correctly recognized an enlarged spleen as the best evidence of chronic malaria and was the first to prescribe small doses of calomel for the summer complaints of early childhood. He wrote no major work but his articles and pamphlets were collected by his brother, Rev. Samuel Miller, and published in a volume of more than 300 pages, entitled, *The Medical Works of Dr. Edward Miller* (1814). At the time of his death he was a member of the American Mineralogical and Philosophical societies and of the Friendly Club, limited to a dozen members. He never married.

[A biog. sketch of Miller is included in *Medical Works* mentioned above; see also, F. B. Lee, *Geneal. and Personal Memorial of Mercer County, N. J.* (1907), vol. I; *Am. Medic. and Philosophical Reg.,* July 1812; L. P. Bush, *Address Before the Medic. Soc. of Del.,* June 1855; *No. Am. Medic. and Surgic. Jour.,* Jan. 1828; *N. Y. Gazette and General Advertiser,* Mar. 18, 1812.]

E. P.

MILLER, EMILY CLARK HUNTINGTON (Oct. 22, 1833–Nov. 2, 1913), author, editor, educator, daughter of Dr. Thomas and Paulina (Clark) Huntington, was born in Brooklyn, Conn. Her father, clergyman and physician, and a graduate of Middlebury College, was the son of Jedediah Huntington [*q.v.*]. Emily Huntington was graduated from Oberlin College, Ohio, with the degree of A.B. in 1857. In September 1860 she was married to John Edwin Miller, a teacher, of Greentown, Ohio. She became the mother of four children, a daughter who died in infancy and three sons. After her marriage she lived in Granville, Ill., where her husband was principal of an academy, then in Plainfield, Ill., where he was professor of Latin and Greek in Northwestern College, then in Akron, Chicago, and Evanston. Her husband was prominent in Sunday-school and Y.M.C.A. activities, in which Mrs. Miller helped him. She also shared his work in connection with a juvenile magazine, the *Little Corporal,* which he published in coöperation with Alfred L. Sewell, and in 1871 she became its editor. In April 1872 the *Little Corporal* absorbed *Work and Play* and in 1875 it was merged into *St. Nicholas.* She had begun to write while she was still in school and her stories and verse were printed in religious papers and magazines. Throughout her life she continued to write, even when domestic affairs absorbed her and during the years when she was connected with Northwestern University. She contributed to leading magazines and was at one time an associate editor of the *Ladies' Home Journal.* Her published volumes include: *The Royal Road to Fortune* (1869); *The Parish of Fair Haven* (1876); a series of stories published by the Kirkwood Library in 1877; *Kathie's Experience* (1886); *Thorn Apples* (1887); *The King's Messengers* (1891); *For the Beloved* (1892), a book of poems; *Home Talks about the World* (1894); and *From Avalon* (1896).

poems. Her stories are of the type known as Sunday-school stories. They are clearly and simply written, with natural conversation, some humor, bits of good description, and inevitable moral lessons. Her verse is usually spiritual in thought, not lacking in imagination, conventional in form, but possessing occasional lyrical values.

In 1871 Mrs. Miller was one of a group which secured a charter for the Evanston College for Ladies, at Evanston, Ill. For the two years of its existence as a separate institution she was a trustee and corresponding secretary. In 1873 the college, of which Frances Willard was president, was united with Northwestern University, and Mrs. Miller was a trustee of the University from 1873 to 1885. Friction arose over the question of separate control of the social life of the women students and Frances Willard resigned. Mrs. Miller was one of a committee to decide whether the resignation should be accepted. She was dean of women and assistant professor of English literature from 1891 to 1898. At that time the position of dean of women was not an administrative office. It involved little more than being at the head of a hall and implied no very important advisory contact with students. The years of her deanship were harmonious. She always believed that women should be considered as part of the general student body, without special treatment and rules on account of sex. Many university occasions were celebrated by her in poetry. Her later years were passed in St. Paul, Minn., and at her summer home in Englewood, N. J. She was always actively interested in temperance, missionary, and Sunday-school work and in the Chautauqua movement. She died at the home of her brother at Northfield, Minn.

[*Who's Who in America,* 1912–13; Frances E. Willard, *Woman and Temperance* (1883); Frances E. Willard and Mary A. Livermore, *Am. Women* (1897), vol. II; A. H. Wilde, *Northwestern Univ.: a Hist., 1855–1905* (1905); *The Huntington Family in America* (1915); obituaries in *N. Y. Times,* Nov. 5, 1913, and *St. Paul Pioneer Press,* Nov. 3, 1913.] S. G. B.

MILLER, EZRA (May 12, 1812–July 9, 1885), engineer, inventor, was born near Pleasant Valley, Bergen County, N. J. He was the son of Ezra Wilson Miller, a native of Westchester County, N. Y., and Hannah (Ryerson) Miller of Pompton, N. J. During his boyhood the family moved to New York City, then to Rhinebeck, and finally to Flushing, L. I., where he received his preparatory school education. His parents wished him to study medicine but Ezra preferred to take up topographical, mechanical, and hydraulic engineering, and became a civil engineer. For upwards of ten years he practised his profession in and about New York. As an avocation he engaged in military studies and was active in the state militia. In 1833 he enlisted in a company of artillery belonging to the 2nd New York Militia and became, by promotion, adjutant in 1839, lieutenant-colonel in 1840, and colonel in 1842. After his marriage in May 1841 to Amanda J. Miller of New York, he settled at Fort Hamilton, N. Y., where he continued the practice of his profession until 1848, when he removed to Rock County, Wis., to take part in the survey of public lands. After a period with the State Survey he engaged in railway survey and construction work.

While so employed in 1853 he became interested in the improvement of existing methods of coupling railway cars, and for some ten years studied and experimented quietly with the problem. His work resulted in the perfection of a car coupler for which he obtained patent No. 38,057 on Mar. 31, 1863. Continuing his experiments, he improved his basic idea and on Jan. 31, 1865, secured patent No. 46,126 for his combined railroad-car platform, coupler, and buffer. Two years later he succeeded in placing his coupler arrangement on three cars being built in the railroad shops at Adrian, Mich. It proved an immediate success and soon replaced the dangerous old railroad car platform with its loose-link coupling throughout the United States and was widely adopted in Europe. The Miller coupler continued in favor for about twenty years before it was superseded by the Janney coupler [see Janney, Eli Hamilton], and provided its inventor with a large income.

In 1867 Miller returned to the East and lived for three years in Brooklyn, N. Y., then purchased a farm near Mahwah, N. J., where he spent the rest of his life, devoting his time mainly to raising prize livestock. He had a natural capacity for making friends which led to his election to public office both in Wisconsin and in New Jersey. He was commissioned colonel in the Wisconsin militia in 1851, and in 1852 was elected to the Wisconsin Senate, serving one term. Under President Buchanan he was deputy postmaster of Janesville, Wis., for two years, and at another time was justice of the peace in Magnolia, Wis. After taking up his residence in New Jersey, he was elected to the state Senate in 1883, and held his seat at the time of his death. He was several times a candidate for Congress. He died in Mahwah, survived by his widow and five children.

[Henry Hall, *America's Successful Men of Affairs,* vol. II (1896); C. M. Depew, *One Hundred Years of Am. Commerce* (1895), vol. I; W. W. Clayton, *Hist. of Bergen and Passaic Counties, N. J.* (1882); *Manual of the One Hundred and Eighth Session of the Legis-*

lature of N. J. (1884); *Railroad Gazette*, July 17, 1885; *Sun* (N. Y.), July 10, 1885; *N. Y. Tribune*, July 10, 1885; Patent Office records.] C. W. M.

MILLER, GEORGE (Feb. 16, 1774–Apr. 5, 1816), Evangelical preacher, was born in Pottstown, Pa., the son of Jacob and Elizabeth Miller. He grew up in Alsace Township, Berks County, lost his father when he was ten years old, was much influenced by his devout Lutheran mother, and attended a Lutheran catechetical class in Reading. Revivalism was then spreading through backwoods Pennsylvania like a grass-fire, but the educated German clergy were relatively incombustible, and for some years Miller's yearning for experimental religion was kept in check. A millwright by trade, in 1798 he bought some land in Brunswick Township, Schuylkill County, and built himself a gristmill. In 1800 he married Magdalena Brobst, whose father was proprietor of an iron forge in Albany Township, Berks; and in the same year he heard Jacob Albright [*q.v.*] preach and was deeply moved by him. It was not until June 3, 1802, however, that he felt himself assuredly converted. Thereupon he identified himself with Albright's followers, later known as the Evangelical Association, was made a class leader, and became the object of attention of his orthodox neighbors, who filled his mill flume with rubbish, took their custom away from him, leaving their bills unpaid, and at times pelted him with clubs and stones. In April 1805, under the guidance of Albright and John Walter, he became an itinerant preacher. His preparation for the ministry, like that of the other leaders of the movement, was of the scantiest: he had had almost no schooling, he knew no language except his Pennsylvania-German dialect, he had read few books except the Bible. In person he was an uncouth countryman, large of limb and feature, his red eyebrows contrasting oddly with a mat of black hair; but he was earnest and courageous, developed rapidly as a preacher and leader, conducted many satisfactory revivals, and made some converts wherever he went. During four years of circuit-riding he traveled through nineteen counties in Pennsylvania, but this heroic labor proved too much for him. On Dec. 26, 1808, he became seriously ill, returned to his home in Albany Township, Berks, and never regained his health. In his enforced leisure he became the first author of the denomination. Basing his work on the German version of the Methodist Discipline, which Ignatius Roemer had made in 1808 under the direction of Martin Boehm [*q.v.*], he compiled the Book of Discipline for the "Albright people" (1809) and did most of the work on the second edition (1817). In consequence his influence on the Evangelical Association has been great and lasting. He also wrote a devotional book, *Thätiges Christenthum* (1814), the earliest life of Albright (1814), and a revealing autobiography. For the four years before his death he lived on his farm at Dry Valley, Union County, a few miles below New Berlin, where he is buried.

[*Jacob Albright and his Co-laborers* (1883), compiled by Reuben Yeakel, contains a translation of Miller's autobiography. See also R. Yeakel, *Hist. of the Evangel. Asso.*, vol. I (1894), and A. Stapleton, *Annals of the Evangel. Asso. of North America* (1896).] G. H. G.

MILLER, HARRIET MANN (June 25, 1831–Dec. 25, 1918), author, naturalist, better known under the pseunonym Olive Thorne Miller, was the daughter of Seth Hunt and Mary Field (Holbrook) Mann, and was born in Auburn, N. Y. Her father was a banker; her grandfather, James Mann, was an importing merchant of Boston. During her childhood the family removed to Ohio, where she was educated in private schools. She was married in 1854 to Watts Todd Miller, at Rock Island, Ill. For twenty years after marriage she lived in Chicago, then in Brooklyn, N. Y., and, after the death of her husband, for the last fourteen years of her life in Los Angeles. For many years she devoted herself to the care of her four children. It was only after they were fairly well grown, while she was still living in Chicago, that she began to write stories for young people, under her pseudonym. She was interested in birds and commenced writing magazine articles and books and lecturing about birds and their habits. Her summers were spent almost entirely out doors, where she studied birds in their natural surroundings. In her Brooklyn home she equipped a room as an aviary, and there she studied the life of her bird pets during the winter. She was a copious note-taker and filled many notebooks with her observations. Her published volumes include: *Little Folks in Feathers and Fur, and Others in Neither* (1875), always one of her most popular books; *Queer Pets at Marcy's* (1880); *Bird-Ways* (1885); *In Nesting Time* (1888); *A Bird-Lover in the West* (1894); *The First Book of Birds* (1899); *The Second Book of Birds: Bird Families* (1901); *True Bird Stories from my Note-book* (1903); *With the Birds in Maine* (1904); and *The Children's Book of Birds* (1915). Her other stories for children are pleasantly free from didacticism and full of informed interest in nature, but her books on birds are her best work. They are results of personal observations rather than of much study and are fairly free from scientific errors. They are written with so much enthusiasm and interesting detail that few children fail to enjoy them and many adults have found them instructive and readable. She retained mental activity throughout her long life and continued writing until within a short time of her death. She was a member of many organizations, among them the American Ornithologists' Union, the Linnæan Society, and the Audubon Society of California. She believed in the educational and social value of women's clubs and wrote a book on the subject, *The Woman's Club* (1891). As a bird lover, she strongly opposed the wearing of birds or plumage for adornment. She died at her home in Los Angeles.

[*Who's Who in America,* 1918–19; Frances E. Willard and Mary A. Livermore, *Am. Women* (1897), vol. II; G. S. Mann, *Geneal. of the Descendants of Richard Mann of Scituate, Mass.* (1884); obituaries in *N. Y. Times,* Dec. 27, 1918, and *Los Angeles Times,* Dec. 26, 1918.] S. G. B.

MILLER, HEINRICH [See MILLER, JOHN HENRY, 1702–1782].

MILLER, HENRY (Nov. 1, 1800–Feb. 8, 1874), pioneer Kentucky physician, was born in the town of Glasgow, Barren County, Ky. His father, Henry Miller, of German descent, came from Maryland as one of the first settlers of that village. His education, he says, "was not acquired in academic halls, but in the primitive schoolhouses of his native state, and upon the ample sward, shaded by forest trees, appurtenant thereunto." He began the study of medicine in his native town with Doctors Bainbridge and Gist and received his degree of M.D. in 1822 from the recently organized Transylvania University at Lexington. His dissertation, *An Inaugural Thesis: Relation between the Sanguiferous and the Nervous Systems* (1822), was deemed worthy of publication by the faculty. Shortly after his return to Glasgow he was offered the position of demonstrator of anatomy in his alma mater and in preparation for this duty he went to Philadelphia by horse-back, where he spent several months in the dissecting-room. Faculty opposition developing, he resigned from Transylvania and took up his practice at Glasgow where he remained until 1827, removing then to Harrodsburg. After nine years at this popular health resort he moved to Louisville, where he had been offered the chair of obstetrics and diseases of women and children in the projected Medical Institute of Louisville. It was not until 1837 that the school was opened and Miller was made professor of obstetrics in the reorganized faculty. In 1846 the Institute became the medical department of the University of Louisville. Miller remained until 1858 when he resigned. In 1867 he returned to the school as professor of medical and surgical diseases of women, but resigned after one year. In 1869 he accepted the corresponding chair in the newly established Louisville Medical College which he held for the rest of his life.

Starting as a general practitioner, Miller developed into one of the leading obstetricians of his state and an able gynecologist. He was a pioneer in the use of ether in obstetrical practice and always a strong advocate of anesthesia in labor. He is credited with being the first in Louisville and one of the first in the United States to make use of the vaginal speculum in gynecological practice. He was a clear forcible writer. In 1849 he published his *Theoretical and Practical Treatise on Human Parturition.* A larger and more complete edition was published in 1858 under the title *Principles and Practice of Obstetrics.* This work has a place among the standard treatises on obstetrics. It is characterized by independence of thought and sound judgment. Notable among his journal articles are those in support of obstetrical anesthesia and of the operation of ovariotomy. In contrast to his facility with the pen were his limitations as a speaker. He had a poor voice and a worse delivery. He spoke haltingly and only his great reputation and a proverbial punctuality with his classes made possible his undoubted success as a teacher. Physically he was tall and slight. He practised up to the time of his death in Louisville from chronic nephritis. Miller was married on June 24, 1824, to Clarissa Robertson (or Robinson). Two sons became physicians. The elder, William, lost his life in the Civil War and Edward followed his father in the practice of surgery.

[*Richmond and Louisville Medic. Jour.,* Jan. 1872; *Trans. Am. Medic. Asso.,* vol. XXVI (1875); J. N. McCormack, *Some Medic. Pioneers of Ky.* (1917); *Trans. Ky. State Medic. Soc.,* 1875; H. A. Kelly and W. L. Burrage, *Am. Medic. Biogs.* (1920); the *Louisville Commercial,* Feb. 11, 1874.] J. M. P.

MILLER, HENRY (Feb. 1, 1860–Apr. 9, 1926), actor-manager, was born in London, England, the child of John Miller, a railroad contractor, and Sophia (Newton) Miller. The family moved to Toronto, Canada, before Henry was thirteen, and he was but fifteen when he attended, in Montreal, a performance of *Romeo and Juliet* which determined his career. There and then he decided to be an actor; by eighteen he was on the stage; within thirteen years thereafter he had become "leading man" in support of such established "stars" as Helena Modjeska, Adelaide Neilson, Clara Morris, Mme. Janauschek, and Dion Boucicault. He then received from the best players and directors in America a thorough training both in the older classical tradition and in the heavily emotional, or sentimental, drama then in vogue. It was, however, to Dion Boucicault that he looked back with the truest admiration and affection almost as pupil to master, regarding him as the great example of all-around "man of the theatre"—actor, manager, director, playwright. It can hardly be questioned that Boucicault's varied career was the immediate inspiration of his own. Henry Miller was a "man of the theatre" in the fullest and most honorable sense of that phrase; his love for the theatre was as deep as his knowledge of it was profound. His career falls naturally into three main divisions: his connection as leading man with the Empire Theatre Stock Company of New York, in the early nineties; his period of stardom; and, finally, the fulfilment of his life's ambitions as an actor-manager.

As leading man of the Empire Theatre Stock Company, he first became nationally known as a forceful and finished actor, scoring one personal success after another in plays of such varying value as *The Younger Son, Sowing the Wind, The Masqueraders, Sweet Lavendar, The Importance of Being Earnest,* and *Michael and His Lost Angel.* The reputation thus gained could, in those days, when the individual "star" ruled the American stage, lead to but one result. In 1899, at the Herald Square Theatre, the name "Henry Miller" appeared in electric lights as star of *The Only Way,* a drama extracted from *A Tale of Two Cities,* in which Miller's performance of the romantically tragic rôle of Sidney Carton was widely admired. The play ran for three years, in New York and on the road, and was followed by other, less impressive, stellar vehicles, such as *D'Arcy of the Guards* and *Heartsease.* Up to this point Miller's career, while successful, had followed conventional lines; but he was now, in his maturity, to prove that his love for the theatre (and, more specifically, for the American theatre) was a deeper thing than the normal stellar desire for continued personal popularity in "vehicles" specially manufactured for him and his too easily contented public. In the autumn of 1906 he entered upon his final phase as actor-manager and director, producing at the Princess Theatre the first prose play of an American poet, William Vaughn Moody's *The Great Divide.* Never was play more happily named, for its production marked a new era in the history of the American stage. Leaving ultimate values out of the question, *The Great Divide* was an enormous advance artistically upon contemporary American play writing; it took insight and courage and taste to back and produce and direct it successfully; and if the American theatre owes much to William Vaughn Moody, it owes hardly less to his manager, director, and "star."

The amazing popularity of this play—then considered so daringly unconventional—firmly established Miller as actor-manager and made possible his excellent production of other dramas. In 1908 he dared greatly again, and brought forward Charles Rann Kennedy's symbolic drama *The Servant in the House*—which made, at the time, a profound impression and scored an emphatic popular success, and in 1910 he produced Moody's far less successful, though possibly more valuable, second play, *The Faith Healer.* The production of *The Great Divide, The Servant in the House,* and *The Faith Healer,* form unquestionably the climax of Henry Miller's career. He was to produce and appear in many another successful play—*The Rainbow, Daddy Longlegs, The Famous Mrs. Fair, The Changelings*—but he will be remembered longest and most justly and gratefully for his faith in and successful championship of *The Great Divide.* He made his first appearance in London in 1909, when he presented both *The Great Divide* and *The Servant in the House.* His last productions were made at the Henry Miller Theatre, designed and built under his personal supervision in 1918. His last illness, pneumonia, struck him down suddenly on the eve of a new production at this theatre; he rose from bed, hoping to play his part, but collapsed on reaching his dressing-room. Death followed within the week. He was survived by his wife, Helen (Stoepel) Miller, whom he married on Feb. 1, 1884, and by three children.

[*Who's Who in America,* 1924–25; J. B. Clapp and E. F. Edgett, *Players of the Present,* pt. 2 (1900); John Parker, *Who's Who in the Theatre* (1922); *N. Y. Times,* Apr. 2, 7, 1918, Apr. 10, 12, 18, 1926; *N. Y. Herald Tribune,* Apr. 18, 1926.]

L. W. D.

MILLER, JAMES RUSSELL (Mar. 20, 1840–July 2, 1912), Presbyterian clergyman, editor, author, was born at Harshaville, Beaver County, Pa., the eldest of the seven children of James Alexander and Eleanor (Creswell) Miller who survived infancy. His father was a country miller and devout elder in the Associate Reformed Church. His mother's grandfather, Thomas McCarrell, a Scotch resident of Ireland, visited America in 1777 on his uncle's ship and remained to serve in the American army during the Revolution, and later to live in Washington

County, Pa., as an elder in the "Seceder" Church. Among McCarrell's descendants were seven clergymen. James Russell Miller attributed to his boyhood home the religious impulses which signally characterized his life. A significant influence was his parents' lifelong habit of visiting the homes of neighbors far and near on every occasion of trouble and sorrow.

His education was received at district schools in Beaver County, Pa., and near Calcutta, Ohio, to which state the family removed when he was about fourteen years old; at Beaver Academy; at Westminster College, New Wilmington, Pa., from which he was graduated in 1862; and at Allegheny Theological Seminary of the United Presbyterian Church, where he completed the course in 1867. Early revealing a deep religious nature, in 1857 he united with the Associate Reformed Church, which in 1858 joined with other groups in forming the United Presbyterian Church. During his academy course he taught a term of school at Industry, Pa., and one at Calcutta, Ohio. His seminary course was interrupted, 1863–65, by work among the soldiers for the United States Christian Commission, eventually as general field agent with scores of workers under his direction. Ordained a minister in 1867, he was in charge of the First United Presbyterian Church, New Wilmington, Pa., 1867–69, and of the following Presbyterian churches: Bethany, Philadelphia, 1869–78; Broadway, Rock Island, Ill., 1878–80; Hollond, Philadelphia, 1881–83 and 1886–97; and St. Paul's, Philadelphia, which he organized, 1898–1912. His work was marked by unusual success with young people, by building weak churches into strong organizations, by remarkably effective and numerous pastoral calls, most of which were made at night, and by extensive personal correspondence, which required the writing of thousands of letters during his lifetime.

In 1880 he began editorial work for the Presbyterian Board of Publication, Philadelphia. As the board's editorial superintendent from 1887 until his death, he edited hundreds of books and all the periodicals, to many of which he contributed regularly; he increased the number of Sunday-school publications from five to eighteen, and founded and edited the magazine *Forward*, which at his death had a weekly circulation of nearly half a million copies. His *Week-Day Religion*, published in 1880, was the first of more than sixty devotional books from his pen. One of the best known of these was his eight-volume *Devotional Hours with the Bible* (1909–13), which attained a sale of more than two million copies during his lifetime and was translated into many languages. He was widely regarded as the most popular religious writer of his day.

In all his activities he was known for his manifold and tireless labors, his sound judgment, simplicity, sympathy, and boundless faith. On June 22, 1870, he married Louise E. King of Argyle, N. Y.

[J. T. Faris, *The Life of Dr. J. R. Miller* (1912), includes a list of Miller's published books and the names of periodicals he edited; see also *Action of the Presbyterian Board of Publication—Life and Service of J. R. Miller, D.D.* (1912); *Who's Who in America*, 1910–11; the *Presbyterian*, July 10, 1912.] P. P. F.

MILLER, JOAQUIN [See MILLER, CINCINNATUS HINER, 1839–1913.]

MILLER, JOHN (Nov. 25, 1781–Mar. 18, 1846), congressman and governor of Missouri, was born in Berkeley County, Va. (now W. Va.). At the age of twenty-two he went to Steubenville, Ohio, where he became editor and publisher of the *Western Herald*, developed a superior literary style, and became deeply interested in all frontier problems, especially in military matters. Shortly before the War of 1812 he was appointed general in the Ohio militia, and then served during that war as colonel of the 19th United States Infantry. His regiment won special commendation for courage and discipline from General William Henry Harrison. At the close of the war he was ordered to duty in Missouri. In 1818 (Heitman, *post*) he resigned from the army and in 1821 (Houck, *post*, p. 184) became register of the land office at Franklin, Howard County, Mo., a position which he held until 1825.

On the death of Gov. Frederick Bates in 1825, he was elected to serve the unexpired term, and was reëlected in 1828 without opposition for the full four-year term. Thus he became the only governor of Missouri to serve more than one term. Although he deplored narrow partisanship he was ordinarily classed as a Jacksonian Democrat. He brought to the office of governor talents of a high order. His public policies and addresses manifested a grasp of frontier problems, social forces, legal principles, educational needs, and financial affairs. It was also his good fortune to be able to express his thoughts in clear and vigorous English. During his administration David Barton and Thomas H. Benton labored to draw party lines more closely and aspired to the political leadership of the state. Miller, however, disliked this emphasis on partisanship, and was, for several years, able to assert a leadership superior to theirs. Placing ability above political considerations, he appointed such men as Spencer Pettis, John C. Edwards, and Hamilton R. Gamble to the highest state offices. Among the major policies advocated by Miller were: a well-organized and trained militia, the withdrawal of state paper money from circulation, combined state and federal protection of trade and travel on the Santa Fé trail, the establishment of a state library and college, and the exclusion by the federal governments of all British traders from the Rocky Mountain fur-trading region. During his administration thousands of immigrants settled in the state, and Missouri grew prosperous. He proved to be an unusually faithful guardian of the state treasury.

After he retired from the governorship, he spent four years of quiet private life at Fayette. In 1836 he was elected to congress, and served three consecutive terms, at the end of which he voluntarily retired. Aside from advocating federal improvement and maintenance of the navigation facilities of the Missouri and the Mississippi rivers, and consistently opposing the growing tendency toward sectionalism and bitter partisanship, his congressional career was inconspicuous. He died near Florissant in St. Louis County. He was never married.

[*The Messages and Proclamations of the Gov. of . . . Mo.*, ed. by Buel Leopard and F. C. Shoemaker, esp. biog. by P. S. Rader, vol. I (1922); F. B. Heitman, *Hist. Register and Dict. of the U. S. Army* (1903), vol. I; H. L. Conard, *Encyc. of the Hist. of Mo.* (1901), vol IV; *Biog. Dir. Am. Cong.* (1928); Louis Houck, *A Hist. of Mo.* (1908), vol. III; *Jeffersonian Republican* (Jefferson, Mo.), Aug. 31, 1833, Jan. 30, 1836, Feb. 10, Sept. 22, 1838, June 4, 1842; *Jefferson City Inquirer*, Mar. 25, 1846; *Boonville Weekly Observer*, May 29, July 17, 1844, Mar. 24, 31, 1846; *Boonville Western Emigrant*, Jan. 24, 1839; *Boonville Weekly Advertiser*, Mar. 16, 1923, all of Missouri.]

H. E. N.

MILLER, JOHN (Apr. 6, 1819–Apr. 14, 1895), Presbyterian clergyman, son of Rev. Samuel [*q.v.*] and Sarah (Sergeant) Miller, was born at Princeton, N. J. On his father's side his ancestry went back to John Miller, a native of Scotland, who came to America in 1710 and married Mary Bass, great-grand-daughter of John and Priscilla Alden. It included a number of scholarly clergymen. On his mother's side he was descended from a line of patriots, his maternal grandfather being Jonathan Dickinson Sergeant [*q.v.*], a member of the Continental Congress and attorney-general of Pennsylvania. His father was the renowned first professor of church history at Princeton Theological Seminary. Consequently, the son was brought up in surroundings of earnest Christian piety, yet with intimate knowledge of the many forms in which that piety has been expressed through the ages. He secured his preparatory education at the Edgehill Boarding School, Princeton, and graduated from Princeton College in 1836. For a year he served with ability as an assistant to Prof. Joseph Henry [*q.v.*] in preparation for becoming a professor of natural philosophy. In later years he was the first person to urge the creation at Princeton of a research university, thereby initiating a movement out of which has grown the Princeton Graduate College.

As the result of his conversion at a revival, he decided to go into the ministry and in 1838 entered Princeton Theological Seminary, graduating in 1841, but remaining another year for special study. On Oct. 30, 1843, he was ordained by the Presbytery of Baltimore and served for five years as pastor of the Presbyterian Church at Frederick, Md. From 1850 to 1855 he was in charge of the West Arch Street Presbyterian Church, Philadelphia, and then for eight years he supplied churches in the Valley of Virginia while he devoted himself to study and writing, serving also in 1861–62 as captain of artillery and chaplain in the Confederate army. From 1863 to 1871 he was pastor of the Second Presbyterian Church of Petersburg, Va. In the latter year he took up his residence in Princeton, where he remained the rest of his life. As the result of his views on immortality, the human nature of Christ, and the nature of the Godhead which he expressed in *Questions Awakened by the Bible* (1877), he was suspended by the Presbytery of New Brunswick and the synod of New Jersey, and after the General Assembly refused to sustain an appeal he withdrew from the Presbyterian Church (1877). His defense at the Assembly was considered a masterpiece of argument and eloquence and he succeeded in retaining the personal friendship of his stanchest theological opponents because of the humility of his character and benevolence of his life.

In 1880 he built at Princeton an independent church, and later established several mission stations in connection with it, of which he served as pastor till his death in 1895. In 1893 he was received into the ministry of the Cumberland Presbyterian Church, giving to it his Princeton church and its missions. This denomination united with the Presbyterian Church in 1906, thus by implication restoring Miller to good standing in the latter. His tombstone in the cemetery at Princeton is a recumbent cross made of great blocks of stone on each of which is chiseled one article of his creed, carefully supported by a subsidiary statement.

Miller was a prolific writer, his chief works being: *Fetich in Theology* (2nd edition 1922); *Is God a Trinity?* (3rd edition 1922); *The Design of the Church* (1846); *A Commentary on Proverbs* (1872); *Metaphysics* (1875); *The Old*

Church Creed (1879); *Commentary on Romans* (1887); "Seven Failures of Ultra-Calvinism," *Cumberland Presbyterian Review*, 1892. In these works he taught the following doctrines: (1) that although Jesus Christ was incorrupt, yet, having the sin of Adam imputed to him, he needed for salvation a ransom as all sinners do—even that of his own death on the cross; (2) that Jesus Christ and Jehovah are one person, and the Godhead is not a Trinity; (3) that Jesus Christ has two consciousnesses—one omniscient and the other ignorant, and two wills—one sovereign and one dependent,—although they interact harmoniously in the execution of his work as one redeemer; (4) that God saves and damns not for his own glory, but for the sake of righteousness—why one sinner should be selected to accept salvation in Christ and be saved rather than another being left a mystery when viewed as an act of God, but as the result of the gradual improvement in the moral character of the sinner when viewed as an act of man; (5) that every soul goes out of existence between death and the return of Christ to judge the world, when misery and happiness will be proportioned to the characters of the souls. These doctrines he upheld by a great array of Biblical proof-texts, at times as translated by himself; by references to the great symbols of the Reformed faith of the Presbyterian Church, to which symbols he considered himself essentially loyal; and by a careful exposition of the contradiction inherent in the Reformed faith as set forth in the *Systematic Theology* of Dr. Charles Hodge [*q.v.*], then professor of systematic theology at Princeton Theological Seminary, the most authoritative exposition of that faith in the Presbyterian Church at the time. Unfortunately, Miller was not aware of the contradictions inherent in his own doctrines and often wrote in a style made obscure by condensations and by passion.

He was twice married: first, Sept. 24, 1844, to Margaret Benedict, who died Sept. 5, 1852; and second, Nov. 3, 1856, to Sally Campbell Preston McDowell, daughter of James McDowell [*q.v.*], governor of Virginia.

[*Necrological Report . . . Princeton Theological Seminary*, 1896; letters from Miller's daughter, Miss Margaret Miller, in the files of the Princeton University Alumni office; F. B. Lee, *Geneal. and Personal Memorial of Mercer County, N. J.* (1907), vol. I; *Records of the Presbytery of New Brunswick in the Case of Rev. John Miller* (1877); *Minutes of the General Assembly of the Presbyt. Church in the U. S. A.*, 1877–79, 1903–06; *Daily True American* (Trenton), Apr. 16, 1895.] G. Y. R.

MILLER, JOHN FRANKLIN (Nov. 21, 1831–Mar. 8, 1886), United States senator, was born at South Bend, Ind., the eldest son of William and Mary (Miller) Miller. His father was of Swiss stock, which had established itself in Virginia in search of religious freedom as early as 1800. On the mother's side he came of Scotch ancestry, identified with American affairs as early as the War of 1812, in which his grandfather served as colonel. His boyhood was spent in South Bend where he entered the academy at the age of fourteen, devoting his summers to work on the farm. In 1848 he became a student in the Hatheway Mathematical and Classical School in Chicago and a year later returned to South Bend, where he began to read law with Judge Elisha Egbert. His law studies were continued in the State and National Law School at Ballston Spa, N. Y., and in 1852 the degree of LL.B. was conferred upon him. He was admitted to the bar and opened his first law office in South Bend in partnership with Joseph Defrees. When ill health made a change advisable Miller joined the emigrants bound for California by way of Nicaragua. In March 1853, he arrived in Napa where his legal ability won him much prestige and a partnership with Judge John Currey of San Francisco. Six months after his arrival in California he was made county treasurer, an office which he held for two years. In 1855 ill health again forced him to make a change, and he returned to South Bend. Here affiliating himself in his profession with Norman Eddy, he continued his practice until 1861, when he became state senator, and was with one exception the youngest member of that body. In 1857, during this period of residence in South Bend, he married Mary Chess of Pennsylvania. One son and one daughter were born of the marriage.

With the opening of the Civil War Miller resigned his seat in the legislature, and on Aug. 27, 1861, received his commission as colonel of the 29th Indiana Volunteers. He was wounded in the battle of Stone River and again at Liberty Gap, Tennessee, in both instances distinguishing himself by his ability and courage. On Jan. 5, 1864, he was made brigadier-general of volunteers, and later, following the battle of Nashville, in which he had been in command of a division, was brevetted a major-general "for gallant and meritorious services." At the close of the war he was offered a colonelcy in the United States army, but declined and returned to California. For the next four years he served under appointment from President Johnson as collector of the port of San Francisco, refusing reappointment to accept the presidency of the Alaska Commercial Company. For a period of twelve stormy years, beginning with its incorporation in 1869, he led this very active organization in its program of control of the fur industry of the Pribilof or Seal Islands. In spite of strong competitors, who fought the monopoly of the Alaska Commercial Company with bitter opposition, this company paid into the federal treasury more than twice the amount expected under the agreement and apparently complied scrupulously with the stipulations of its contract.

Miller served as a member of the California state constitutional convention of 1878–79. His eminence in his profession, coupled with his active interest in political affairs, led to his election as United States senator from California (Republican) in 1880, in which capacity he served until his death. He is chiefly known for the active part he took in the anti-Chinese legislation which reached its culmination during his term of office. His name is closely linked with the successful effort to modify the Burlingame Treaty with China and also with the Exclusion Bill of 1882. He died in Washington, D. C., in March 1886. His body was interred in Laurel Hill Cemetery, San Francisco, but in 1913 was removed to Arlington Cemetery, Virginia.

[*Biog. Dir. Am. Cong.* (1928); *Biog. and Geneal. Hist. of Wayne, Fayette, Union and Franklin Counties, Ind.* (1899), vol. II; *A Biog. Hist. of Eminent and Self-Made Men . . . of Ind.* (1880), vol. II; H. H. Bancroft, *Hist. of Alaska, 1730–1885* (1886); "The Alaska Commercial Company," *House Report 623*, 44 Cong., 1 Sess.; *Cong. Record*, 49 Cong., 1 Sess.; W. H. Miller, *Hist. and Geneals. of the Families of Miller, Woods, Harris* (1907); *Evening Star* (Wash., D. C.), Mar. 8, 1886.]

R. G. C—d.

MILLER, JOHN HENRY (Mar. 12, 1702–Mar. 31, 1782), printer, editor, and publisher, was born at Rheden in the principality of Waldeck, Germany, where his parents then resided. When they returned to their native town, near Zürich, Switzerland, in 1715, young Miller was apprenticed to a printer in Basel. Completing his apprenticeship, he went to Zürich as a journeyman, but soon opened a printing office of his own there and began the publication of a newspaper. Abandoning the business after a few years, he spent some time in travel. In 1741 he accompanied Count von Zinzendorf [*q.v.*] to Pennsylvania and for a short period worked as a journeyman in Franklin's printing shop in Philadelphia. He was back in Europe in 1742, and in 1744 opened a printing office in Marienburg, West Prussia, marrying there in that year Johanna Dorothea Blanner, a Swiss. He was a scholarly man and a good printer; his wife was equally gifted, being a woman of culture, who "spoke French fluently and was an excellent painter in water-colors" (Thomas, *post*, p. 255).

In 1751 he made a second visit to America and associated himself with Samuel Holland in Lancaster, Pa. The two founded *Die Lancastersche Zeitung*, a bilingual paper, the second of its kind in America, the first being Franklin's *Deutsche und Englische Zeitung*. Soon afterward, however, Miller went to Philadelphia where he found work in the printing house of William Bradford, 1721/22–1791 [*q.v.*]. He was again in Europe in 1754, and remained until 1760, when he recrossed the Atlantic, bringing with him equipment with which to set up a printing establishment in Philadelphia. In 1762 he began the publication of a newspaper, *Der Wöchentliche Staatsbote*, which he edited under the successive titles *Der Wöchentliche Philadelphische Staatsbote, Der Wöchentliche Pennsylvanische Staatsbote,* and *Henrich Miller's Pennsylvanische Staatsbote* until 1779. From his shop, also, a German almanac was issued each year. He printed a few books in both the German and English languages, chief among those in English being *Juvenile Poems* (1765), by the younger Thomas Godfrey [*q.v.*], which included "The Prince of Parthia," the first native play to be produced professionally in America.

In 1765, when the Stamp Act became operative, Miller announced that he would suspend his newspaper "until it would appear whether means can be found to escape the chains forged for the people and from unbearable slavery" (Daniel Miller, *post*, p. 27). This suspension continued from Oct. 31 to Nov. 18. On July 5, 1776, *Henrich Miller's Pennsylvanische Staatsbote* had the privilege of being first to announce to the world the adoption of the Declaration of Independence. Through the accident of circumstances it was the only newspaper then published in Philadelphia on Fridays, and July 4th that year fell upon Thursday. Unfortunately Miller was not able to give the text of the historic document until the following Tuesday, but on that day he printed it in large type as an extra leaf to his journal. From Sept. 17, 1777, to Aug. 5, 1778, the occupation of Philadelphia by the British troops forced suspension again. The British seized his press and materials and removed them to New York, but after the enemy left Philadelphia Miller succeeded in reëstablishing himself and his paper. On May 26, 1779, he retired from business and removed to the Moravian settlement of Bethlehem, Pa., where he died. He was a pedestrian of note; even when he was advanced in years he would occasionally walk from Philadelphia to Bethlehem, a distance of fifty-three miles.

[C. S. R. Hildeburn, *A Century of Printing: The Issues of the Press in Pa., 1685–1784*, vol. II (1886); Daniel Miller, "Early German-American Newspapers," *The Pa.-German Soc., Proc. and Addresses*, vol. XIX (1910), Augustus Schultze, "The Old Moravian Cemetery of Bethlehem, Pa.," *Ibid.*, vol. XXI (1912); C. F. Dapp, "The Evolution of an American Patriot: Being an Intimate Study of the Patriotic Activities of John Henry Miller," *Ibid.*, vol. XXXII (1924); "William McCulloch's Additions to Thomas's Hist. of Printing," *Proc. Am. Antiquarian Soc.*, vol. XXI, pt. 1 (1922); Isaiah Thomas, *The Hist. of Printing in America* (2nd ed., 1874), I, 253–55; Oswald Seidensticker, *The First Century of German Printing in America, 1728–1830* (1893); C. F. Dapp, "Johann Heinrich Miller," *German American Annals*, May–Aug., 1916.] J. J.

MILLER, JOHN PETER (Dec. 25, 1709–Sept. 25, 1796), German Reformed clergyman, later head of the Ephrata Community of Seventh Day Baptists, was born in Germany, probably at Zweikirchen, near Zweibrücken, where his father, Johann Müller, was the Reformed pastor. In America he is best known by the anglicized form of his name, as given above; in the Ephrata Community he was called Brother Jabez. He matriculated Dec. 29, 1725, at the University of Heidelberg, his father then being pastor at Alsenborn, and on Aug. 29, 1730, he arrived at Philadelphia on the ship *Thistle* from Rotterdam.

The circumstances of his emigration are unknown, but it is likely that he was already somewhat heterodox, and that he had been in friendly relations with George Michael Weiss, who had come over earlier in 1730. Almost immediately on his arrival he was engaged as minister by the Reformed people of Philadelphia and Germantown and by the anti-Boehm faction at Skippack, and applied for ordination to the Presbyterian Synod. The Synod referred his case to the Presbytery of Philadelphia, the members of which were astonished by Miller's learning, especially by his ability to speak Latin and by the erudition displayed in his answer to a question on Justification. Meanwhile, on Oct. 19, Miller called on John Philip Boehm [*q.v.*], who curtly advised him to seek ordination from the Dutch Reformed clergy of New York; Miller, however, was in a hurry and denied that the Dutch church authorities had any jurisdiction in Pennsylvania. He was ordained Nov. 20, 1730, by three Presbyterian ministers, Jedediah Andrews, Adam Boyd, and Gilbert Tennent [*q.v.*]. In the fall of 1731 he withdrew into the interior and began ministering to the Reformed congregations at Goshenhoppen, Tulpehocken, and along the Conestoga. From the beginning he and Boehm were antagonistic.

Very early he came under the influence of Johann Conrad Beissel [*q.v.*], who was eager to make a convert of him. In May 1735 Miller publicly renounced the Reformed Church and was rebaptized by trine immersion. This event, which came as a surprise to everyone except Boehm, created a huge sensation, seriously threatening for a while the existence of the Reformed Church, for Miller was reputed to be the most learned theologian in the province, and his prestige was great. A number of families and individuals followed him into Beissel's society, among them no less a person than Johann Conrad Weiser [*q.v.*]. From May to November 1735 Miller lived as a hermit on the bank of the Mühlbach, a tributary of the Tulpehocken. Like the other solitary brethren, he was called in by Beissel as soon as the cloister at Ephrata was ready for occupancy, and from then till his death sixty-one years later he lived in the Ephrata Community. In the autumn of 1744 he went to Connecticut and Rhode Island to visit several groups of Rogerines. On Beissel's death July 6, 1768, he succeeded him as head of the Community. Apparently he acted as editor of the various books issued by the cloister press, translated J. T. V. Braght's famous work on the Mennonite martyrs from Dutch into German as *Der Blütige Schau-Platz oder Martyrer Spiegel* (1748), perhaps the largest book to come from the colonial press, and may have been part-author of the *Chronicon Ephratense* (1786). He became a member of the American Philosophical Society, counted Francis Hopkinson, Benjamin Franklin, and George Washington among his acquaintances, and was highly regarded for his attainments and character. He was engaged by the Continental Congress to translate the Declaration of Independence into several European languages. The Ephrata Community gained no new members under his régime, and as the infirmities of age crept upon the brethren it steadily declined. Miller died in his eighty-seventh year and was buried beside Beissel in the cloister cemetery.

[J. F. Sachse, *The German Sectarians of Pa., 1708–1800* (2 vols., privately printed, 1899–1900) is the fullest account, but for Miller's career prior to 1735, see W. J. Hinke, *Life and Letters of the Rev. John Philip Boehm* (1916). For autobiographical material, see *Chronicon Ephratense . . . Zusamen getragen von Br. Lamech u. Agrippa* (1786), tr. by J. Max Hark (1889), and Miller's letter in the *Hallesche Nachrichten*, vol. I (new ed., ed. by W. J. Mann and B. M. Schmucker, 1886). See also "Letter of Peter Miller . . . to James Read, 1776," *Pa. Mag.*, XXXVIII (1914), 227; "Description of the Grotto at Swatara," by the Rev. Peter Miller, communicated by Wm. Barton, *Trans. Am. Phil. Soc.*, II (1786), 177–78; "A Method of Preserving Pease from the Worms," . . . communicated by Charles Thomson, *Ibid.*, I (1789), 313–14; "Original Letters of Peter Miller," Samuel Hazard, *Hazard's Reg. of Pa.*, Mar. 28, Oct. 17, 1835.] G. H. G.

MILLER, JONATHAN PECKHAM (Feb. 24, 1796–Feb. 17, 1847), Greek sympathizer and anti-slavery advocate, was born in Randolph, Vt., the son of Heman and Deimia (Walbridge) Miller (Vital Records, Office of the Secretary of State, Montpelier, Vt.). Upon his father's death in 1799 he was taken in charge by an uncle, Jonathan Peckham, and on the latter's death, about 1805, by Capt. John Granger of Randolph. In 1813, having completed his common-school education, young Miller went to Woodstock, Vt., to learn the tanner's trade, but ill health soon caused him to return to the Granger home where he remained for the next four years. A love of adventure and military life, as well as patriotism, led him to join the town volunteers under Capt. Libbeus Egerton who marched to repel the British invasion that ended at Plattsburg. The Randolph forces arrived too late, however, to take part in the fighting. In 1817, he enlisted as a private in the United States army, in which he served for two years, being stationed on the northern frontier. A recurrence of ill health then caused his return to Randolph, where he attended the local academy and fitted for college. In the fall of 1821 he entered Dartmouth, but a few weeks later removed to the University of Vermont, where he pursued his studies until May 24, 1824, when fire destroyed the college buildings. Rather than wait to finish his college course at Vermont, or transfer elsewhere, he now determined to offer his services to the Greek revolutionists, inspired, no doubt, by his classical studies, by the wave of sympathy for Greece then at its height in western Europe and the United States, and by his own spirit of adventure. From Governor Van Ness he secured a letter introducing him to the Greek Association of Boston, which in turn gave him letters to the Greek government at Missolonghi, as well as $300 for his expenses.

He sailed for Malta Aug. 21, 1824, and from there made his way to Missolonghi, where he reported to Dr. Mayer and Gen. George Jarvis, on whose staff he became a colonel in the Greek service. During the next two years Miller's military exploits won for him the name of "The American Dare Devil." He was among those who took part in the valiant but futile defense of Missolonghi, escaping in the last sortie. A few months later he returned to the United States to lecture throughout the northern and middle states in the Greek cause. In February 1827, he returned to Greece as principal agent of the New York Greek Committee. In this service he spent about a year, turning over to the Greeks food and clothing to the value of more than $75,000. On returning to America, he published *The Condition of Greece in 1827 and 1828* (1828), being his journal as kept by order of the Greek Committee. At this time he brought back with him a Greek youth, Lucas Miltiades, whom he adopted and educated. He also brought to the United States the sword worn by Lord Byron in Greece, now in the possession of the Vermont Historical Society.

After his second return from Greece, he settled in Montpelier, Vt., studied law, was admitted to the bar, and opened a law office in company with Nicholas Baylies. For three years, 1831, 1832, and 1833, he served in the Vermont legislature, and in 1833 initiated the anti-slavery movement in the legislature by introducing a resolution calling upon the Vermont representatives in Congress to urge the abolition of slavery and the slave trade in the District of Columbia. From this time on, Miller devoted much of his energy and money to the anti-slavery cause, lecturing throughout the state. In 1840, as one of the two Vermont delegates, he attended the World's Anti-Slavery Convention in London where he took a prominent part in the debates.

As a public speaker, he was off-hand, bold and earnest. His private life was characterized by a fearless utterance of opinion and a straightforward, unstudied frankness. To these qualities he added a vigorous physical constitution and a soldierly bearing that some thought bordered on roughness. As a citizen he was public-spirited and benevolent. Samuel Gridley Howe [*q.v.*], with whom Miller was closely associated, describes him as "rather superficially than well educated, with an immense deal of good common sense, an acute mind, but self-opinionated, and bigoted in religion, which he reads and argues about rather to confirm his belief than to examine the subject" (Richards, *post*, p. 120). He died prematurely in Montpelier as the result of an accidental injury to his spine, leaving a wife and one child. He had married Sarah Arms, daughter of Capt. Jonathan Arms, on June 26, 1828.

[Material for the above was drawn in part from the sketch of Col. Miller's life found in D. P. Thompson, *Hist. of the Town of Montpelier* (1860); the same sketch appears in A. M. Hemenway, *Vt. Hist. Gazetteer*, vol. IV (1882), p. 457. For further light on Miller's Greek adventure consult his *Condition of Greece in 1827 and 1828* (1828) mentioned above, and *Letters from Greece* (1825) by Miller and others. See also L. E. Richards, *Letters and Journals of Samuel Gridley Howe: The Greek Revolution* (1906); M. A. Cline, *Am. Attitude toward the Greek War of Independence* (1930); E. M. Earle, "American Interest in the Greek Cause 1821–1827," in *Am. Hist. Rev.*, Oct. 1927; *Vt. Patriot* (Montpelier), Feb. 18, 1847.]
W. R. W.

MILLER, LESLIE WILLIAM (Aug. 5, 1848–Mar. 7, 1931), educator in the field of industrial art, was born in Brattleboro, Vt., the son of Nathan and Hannah (Works) Miller. He was a descendant of James Miller, a Scotsman, who was admitted to the First Church, Charlestown, Mass., in 1676, and made a freeman in 1677. His grandson, Isaac, laid out the town of Dummerston, Windham County, Vt. Leslie went to work in his father's harness shop at the age of twelve, but continued his education by reading and study, acquiring a good knowledge of Latin and other high-school subjects. His early interest in art manifested itself in spirited drawings with which he decorated the pages of his textbooks.

Upon attaining his majority, he found work in a japanning factory in Orange, Mass., where he painted baby carriages and decorated sewing machines. This occupation marked the turning point in his career, and he soon went to Boston where he could work during the day and attend drawing school at night. He enrolled in the first classes held in the School of the Museum of Fine Arts, and in 1875 graduated from the Massachusetts Normal Art School. The year preceding, Oct. 29, he had married Maria Persons of Boston. His original intention was to devote himself to portrait painting and he did some excellent work in this field, but circumstances drew him into teaching. While still pursuing his studies he became connected with the Boston schools, and later was instructor in the Salem Normal School and in Adams Academy, Quincy. In 1879 he joined the staff of the Summer Institute, Martha's Vineyard, as teacher of painting.

In Boston he had been closely associated with Walter Smith who had come from London to start a school of industrial art under the auspices of the state of Massachusetts. In 1880 the trustees of the School of Industrial Art, Philadelphia, established four years before, asked Smith to name some one who could reorganize the institution along broader lines and Smith recommended Miller. In the fall of 1880 he took charge of the school, which then had but a handful of students and little equipment. During the forty years he was at its head, it became one of the leading institutions in its field, and he left it with a faculty of forty and some thirteen hundred students. He made occasional contributions to periodicals and in 1887 published *The Essentials of Perspective.* His enthusiasm not only for industrial but also for municipal art led him to assume leadership in various city organizations. He was a member of the Municipal Art Jury of Philadelphia from the time of its organization in 1912 until his retirement in 1920, serving as its secretary during its formative period and thereafter as vice-president, By addresses, articles, and personal labors he furthered many of the important improvements effected in the municipality during his long residence there. He was secretary of the Fairmount Park Association from 1900 to 1920, and "the present Fairmount Parkway and the improvements on the banks of the Schuylkill . . . are in large measure a monument to his devotion to the cause of civic betterment" (*Proceedings of the American Philosophical Society, post,* p. 401). For fourteen years he was secretary of the Art Club of Philadelphia, of which he was one of the founders, and for twelve years its vice-president. In 1899 he was elected to the American Philosophical Society and was long one of its curators. The Art Club of Philadelphia awarded him, in 1920, its gold medal for "distinguished services," and the University of Pennsylvania, the unusual degree of doctor of fine arts.

After his retirement in 1920, he made his home on Martha's Vineyard Island. Here before the fireplace of his home hidden among the pine trees, surrounded by his books and his pictures, he spent his last days, maintaining his interest in public affairs and his genial, philosophic spirit to the end. He died in his eighty-third year, survived by two sons, and was buried in Oak Grove Cemetery, Vineyard Haven.

[A. M. Hemenway, *Vt. Hist. Gazetteer,* vol. V (1891), pt. 2; *Pa. Museum Bull.,* Oct. 1920; *Proc. Am. Phil. Soc.,* vol. LXX (1931); *Who's Who in America,* 1928–29; *N. Y. Times,* Mar. 8, 1931; information from a son, P. C. Miller.] D. G.

MILLER, LEWIS (July 24, 1829–Feb. 17, 1899), inventor, manufacturer, philanthropist, a founder of the Chautauqua, was born in Greentown, Ohio. His grandfather, Abraham Miller, emigrated from Zweibrücken in the Palatinate about 1776 and settled in Maryland. He served in the Continental Army during the Revolutionary War, engaged in many battles, and was at Valley Forge under Washington. In 1813 he bought land in Stark County, Ohio, near Canton, and became a farmer there. His son, John Miller, was a farmer and also a carpenter and cabinet-maker. In 1823 he married Mary Elizabeth York (Jorg), who died at the age of twenty-two, after the birth of their son Lewis. Although he did not have a college education, Lewis Miller was early interested in education and read widely. He taught school and built up a Sunday school of which he was superintendent for forty-five years. Following his mechanical inclinations, he entered the employment of the Ball brothers in Greentown who were manufacturing mowing machines and reapers. In 1852 he became a member of the firm, which, as Ball, Aultman & Company, established its plant in

Canton, Ohio. On Sept. 16, 1852, Miller was married to Mary Valinda Alexander and for the next eleven years they made their home in Canton. Upon the withdrawal of Ephraim Ball the firm became C. Aultman & Company. Miller's inventive genius enabled him to design several improvements in the implements manufactured by the company. Probably the most important were the double-jointed cutting-bar of the mowing machine, the "low down" binder, and a device for binding reaped grain with twine. Thanks to these and other inventions, the "Buckeye Machine" became popular and the business expanded rapidly. In 1863 an additional plant was built in Akron, Ohio, known as Aultman, Miller & Company. Miller managed this plant and maintained his residence in Akron until his death.

Miller displayed his creative and administrative powers in all his activities in business, civic, and religious affairs. As an employer, he anticipated some of the later reforms in industrial relations. As a citizen he was active in the municipal affairs of Akron, serving as president of the board of education, in which capacity he introduced a number of new and now commonly accepted ideas both in public school-house design and in teaching methods. In religion he was a Methodist, and as a member of the church he organized a large teachers' class and introduced normal training and an organized course of instruction for the Sunday school. Although not a trained architect, he originated the so-called Akron plan for church buildings, which was widely adopted in the construction of churches making special provision for Sunday schools. He promoted Mount Union College both financially and educationally, by serving as a member of the board of trustees from 1865 until his death in 1899.

But it was in the development of the Chautauqua Institution in New York that he made his most original contribution to the cause of popular education. He had conceived the idea of combining recreation and some form of education and in 1874 invited John H. Vincent [*q.v.*] to join in organizing a general assembly, as distinct from a Sunday-school teachers assembly, to meet in a grove on Lake Chautauqua. Under the creative influence of the two men, the Assembly became a pioneer in the establishment of adult education. In it were combined summer study, correspondence work, supervised reading, and the combination of recreation, physical training, popular lectures, religion, and music. In the development of this institution the two founders supplemented each other and refused to claim any but joint credit for its development. Miller was especially responsible for its financial support and administration, but he was by no means limited to such activity. He was constantly suggesting new plans and methods. The respect in which he was held by all those with whom he came into contact contributed not only to the success of an institution, but to the general development of educational theory and practice. The pressure of all these enterprises proved too much for even his exceptionally vigorous health, and he died, in New York City, in February 1899. He was survived by his wife and nine of his eleven children. One of his daughters married Thomas Alva Edison.

[Ellwood Hendrick, *Lewis Miller: A Biog. Essay* (1925); J. H. Vincent, *The Chautauqua Movement* (1886); J. L. Hurlbut, *The Story of Chautauqua* (1921); *The Biog. Cyc. and Portrait Gallery . . . of Ohio*, vol. I (1883); the *N. Y. Times*, Feb. 18, 1899; Patent Office records; information as to certain facts from members of the family.]

S. M.

MILLER, OLIVE THORNE [See MILLER, HARRIET MANN, 1831–1918].

MILLER, OLIVER (Apr. 15, 1824–Oct. 18, 1892), jurist, was born in Middletown, Conn., the son of Clarissa Miller (G. T. Chapman, *Sketches of the Alumni of Dartmouth College*, 1867). He received his elementary education in the public schools of that place and at the age of twelve entered the academy at Frederick, Md., of which his brother-in-law, Mr. Converse, was principal. At that time he became closely attached to the Converse family and, in later years, during his sister Emily's widowhood, he supported her as long as he lived and educated her children. In 1845 he entered Dartmouth College, graduating with distinction in 1848. He began reading law in the office of Alexander Randall in Annapolis soon afterward, and in 1850 was admitted to the bar. His career as a practising attorney was brief however, for by nature he preferred more exacting though less remunerative public service. In 1850–51 he reported four volumes of Maryland chancery decisions and mastered the technique of the profession. In 1852 he became reporter of the court of appeals and, in the following decade, edited volumes III–XVIII of the *Maryland Reports, Containing Cases Argued and Determined in the Court of Appeals of Maryland* (1853–1862). His peculiar fitness for such tasks now evinced itself, and these *Reports*, marked by logic, vigorous language, and directness, and still regarded as models, brought him to the favorable attention of lawyers throughout the East.

Miller was chosen a member of the Maryland constitutional convention of 1864 and played a prominent part in drafting the new organic law of the state. He represented Anne Arundel County in the House of Delegates from 1865 to 1867 and became speaker of that body in the latter year. Political life, with its intrigues and harassments by constituents, proved uncongenial to him, however, and in the election of November 1867, the first held under the constitution of 1867, he became candidate for the position of chief judge of the fifth judicial circuit (Anne Arundel, Howard, and Carroll counties), which automatically brought membership in the state court of appeals as associate judge. He was an easy victor and, upon the expiration of his term in 1882, was reëlected. It was during his quarter of a century on the bench that Miller won lasting distinction. He possessed a robust and virile intellect, a coldly analytical mind, an amazing memory, and was a master stylist; his opinions are among the best known in the judicial annals of Maryland and contributed in a marked degree to the high reputation which the decisions of the state court of appeals enjoy throughout the nation. Although he was of stern and forbidding exterior, the justice rendered by him was always tempered with mercy. Dignified, patient, independent, and inflexibly just, he exerted a profound personal influence upon the younger members of the bar, among whom his memory has continued a living force through four decades.

In 1874, he married Adeline Dewees (Piper) Green, widow of Lieut. Charles Green of the United States Navy, and opened a second home in Ellicott City, because of its central location on his circuit. They had no children. His wife died there in 1890. In September 1892, while at Ellicott City, Miller was stricken with paralysis and, resigning as of Oct. 1, died three weeks later.

[*The Debates of the Constitutional Convention of the State of Maryland . . . 1864* (3 vols., 1864); *Proc. of the State Convention of Md. to Frame a New Constitution* (1864); M. R. Hodges, *General Index of Wills of Anne Arundel County, Md., 1771–1917* (n.d.), p. 89; *Baltimore American*, Sept. 29, Oct.19, 1892; the *Sun* (Baltimore), June 20, 1890, Sept. 29, Oct. 18, 19, 20, 22, 1892; *Ellicott City Times*, issues for June 1890 and Oct. 1892; *Anne Arundel Advertiser* (Annapolis), Oct. 6, 20, 27, 1892; *Evening Capital* (Annapolis), Sept. 28 and Oct. 19, 20, 22, 1892; Dartmouth College records; legal and legislative manuals.] L. J. R.

MILLER, PETER [See MILLER, JOHN PETER, 1709–1796].

MILLER, SAMUEL (Oct. 31, 1769–Jan. 7, 1850), Presbyterian clergyman, educator, author, was a son of Rev. John and Margaret (Millington) Miller, and a brother of Edward Miller [*q.v.*]. His grandfather, John Miller, a Scotchman, had emigrated to America in 1710 and was later a sugar refiner and distiller. Samuel's paternal grandmother was a great-grand-daughter of John Alden. He was born near Dover, Del., received his education chiefly at home from his father and brothers, pursued the studies of the senior year in the University of Pennsylvania (1788–89), and then studied theology under his father and after his death in 1791, under Rev. Charles Nisbet, first principal of Dickinson College. On June 5, 1793, he was ordained to the Presbyterian ministry and became associated with Dr. John Rodgers and Dr. John McKnight in a collegiate pastorate of the Presbyterian congregations of New York City. For years he urged a separation of the three churches—Wall Street, Brick, and Rutgers Street—and he regarded his efforts to this end, achieved in 1809, as his most important service in New York. Thereafter, until 1813, he acted as sole pastor of the Wall Street congregation, which later became the First Presbyterian Church. After 1813 he was professor of church history and government in Princeton Theological Seminary, of which he had been one of the founders.

He owed much of his fame to his extraordinary energy and activity. For many years he delivered several long addresses a week, made frequent and prolonged pastoral calls, conducted a voluminous correspondence, and in addition contributed to the religious press and published dozens of books and pamphlets. His success in preserving his never robust health during these labors is ascribed to his exact and systematic ordering of every detail of each day. His literary activities made him widely known in America and Great Britain. Following the appearance of his *Brief Retrospect of the Eighteenth Century* (1803), a scholarly two-volume work published before he was thirty-five years old, he received the honorary degree of doctor of divinity from Union College and from the University of Pennsylvania, and was made a corresponding member of the Philological Society of Manchester, England. Though his larger literary productions were mainly historical and biographical, his writings covered a broad range. His early pamphlets discussed slavery, suicide, novel-reading, education of students for the ministry, and other diverse topics. At Princeton he wrote on such multifarious subjects as Free Masonry, sea kale, social amusements, religious fasting, domestic happiness, temperance, and the theatre. Notable among the books published by him during this period are *The Medical Works of Edward Miller, M.D.* (1814); "Life of Jonathan Edwards," in Sparks's *Library of American Biography,* vol. VIII (1837); *Memoir of the Rev. Charles Nisbet, D.D.* (1840); *Letters from a*

Father to His Sons in College (1843), and *Thoughts on Public Prayer* (1849).

In 1809 he became chaplain of the first regiment of New York State artillery, and he was long official historian of the Presbyterian General Assembly, which in 1806 made him its moderator. He was a trustee of Columbia College and of the College of New Jersey, a founder and later a president of the New York Bible Society, a founder and corresponding secretary of the New York Historical Society, and a corresponding member of the Massachusetts Historical Society. He impressed his contemporaries by his cultured and urbane manner; he was at home in any circle. Somewhat lacking in imagination, he had a quick perception, a retentive memory, sound judgment, and much common sense. He was an acceptable but not a striking preacher; his sermons were well considered and evenly balanced. At Princeton he left a tradition of clear and intelligent teaching and of ability to retain the confidence and affection of his students. On Oct. 24, 1801, he married Sarah, daughter of Jonathan Dickinson Sergeant [*q.v.*], attorney-general of Pennsylvania. They had ten children, one of whom was Rev. John Miller [*q.v.*].

[F. B. Lee, *Geneal. and Personal Memorial of Mercer County, N. J.* (1907), vol. I; Samuel Miller, *The Life of Samuel Miller, D.D., LL.D.* (1869); W. B. Sprague, *Annals Am. Pulpit*, vol. III (1858) and *A Discourse Commemorative of the Rev. Samuel Miller, D.D.* (1850); John DeWitt, *The Intellectual Life of Samuel Miller* (1906), reprinted from the *Princeton Theological Rev.*, Apr. 1906; Margaret Miller, "A List of the Writings of Samuel Miller," *Ibid.*, Oct. 1911; *No. Am. and U. S. Gazette* (Phila.), Jan. 9, 1850; *Christian Observer* (Phila.), Jan. 12, 1850.] P. P. F.

MILLER, SAMUEL (Oct. 4, 1820–Oct. 24, 1901), horticulturist, was born in Lancaster, Pa. While a young man, he moved to Avon, Lebanon County. Here he served as justice of the peace in 1840 and 1845, and in 1847 married Martha Isabel Evans, who became the mother of nine children. His horticultural work was begun probably several years before the Concord grape was introduced in 1854 (U. P. Hedrick, *Grapes of New York,* 1908, p. 488). Miller later stated that he was the first man in Pennsylvania to fruit the Concord grape before it was offered to the public, as well as the well-known seedling grapes introduced by Edward S. Rogers of Salem, Mass. (*40th Annual Report of the State Horticultural Society of Missouri, 1897,* 1898, p. 70).

In 1867, he moved to Bluffton, Montgomery County, Mo., where he lived until his death. Here his horticultural experiments were carried on with increased energy, and from his gardens many plants were disseminated, either of his own breeding or from selections he had made. His best known plant contribution is perhaps the Captain Jack strawberry, a chance seedling found on his farm about 1870 (U. P. Hedrick, *The Small Fruits of New York,* 1925, p. 411). Captain Jack soon became a standard sort, especially in the Rocky Mountain states. It was not only a hardy, drouth resistant variety but commonly served as a pollinizer for the much more famous strawberry Crescent. Most of his plant-breeding work was practised with grapes, and about a half-dozen varieties which he developed found a degree of prominence in the horticultural lists of the times. One particularly, Martha, was for a time the most popular of the green grapes. He also originated or introduced several minor sorts of raspberries. At the time of his death he was engaged in an attempt to improve the native persimmon and had selected a number of promising varieties.

His greatest contribution to horticulture and to the welfare of mankind lies not in the plants he bred so much as in his extensive testing of various types and varieties of fruits and ornamental plants sent him by their owners. His knowledge of varieties and values was considerable and his carefully considered opinions were frequently sought, particularly in the states adjacent to Missouri, concerning varietal adaptabilities to that region. Miller apparently was not concerned with attempting to secure either fame or financial gain from his plants. A contemporary observed in an obituary notice: "It never occurred to him to see 'if it would pay' in any of his experiments. . . . I really believe that he took more genuine enjoyment in finding a new flower or in the ripening of some new fruit which he was testing, than he would in the finding of a thousand dollars. He often said 'that he had no time to make money'" (*44th Annual Report of the State Horticultural Society of Missouri, 1901,* 1902, pp. 277–78). For about thirty years, Miller was an officer of the State Horticultural Society, but steadfastly declined to accept the presidency, which was often tendered him. The annual reports of the society contain many papers by him on all phases of horticulture. He was also a regular contributor, for a third of a century, to the horticultural column of *Colman's Rural World.* He was survived by seven of his children.

[In addition to sources cited above see *Colman's Rural World,* Oct. 30 1901; *Am. Gardening,* Nov. 23, 1901; *Trans. Iowa Hort. Soc.,* 1897; L. H. Bailey, *The Standard Cyc. of Horticulture,* III (1915), 1588; W. H. Egle, *Hist. of the Counties of Dauphin and Lebanon* (1883), p. 121.] R. H. S.

MILLER, SAMUEL FREEMAN (Apr. 5, 1816–Oct. 13, 1890), associate justice of the

United States Supreme Court, was born at Richmond in the blue-grass region of Kentucky. His father, Frederick Miller, was a Pennsylvania German who had gone west in 1812. His mother was Patsy Freeman, whose family had emigrated from North Carolina. In 1836, without formal education, Miller entered the medical department of Transylvania University, at Lexington. He attended lectures for one year and then settled at Barbourville, county seat of Knox County, on the road leading down from Cumberland Gap. The autumn of 1837 found him back at Transylvania, where on Mar. 9, 1838, he was "examined and received" for the degree of M.D. For the next twelve years he practised medicine in the mountain community about Barbourville. Here he married Lucy Ballinger, whose family was locally prominent. In the spring of 1837 the young men of the town formed a debating society. From the start Miller was its most active member. Here current political questions were threshed out, and Miller came to recognize that he had a *flair* for statecraft. He became a justice of the peace and a member of the county court. Surreptitiously he studied law, and on Mar. 22, 1847, he was admitted to the bar of Knox County.

Like most of his neighbors, Miller was a Whig. He favored the gradual abolition of slavery in Kentucky, and aspired, unsuccessfully, to membership in the constitutional convention of 1849 where slavery was to be a leading issue. When the peculiar institution was fastened more firmly upon the state, he decided to seek a more congenial sphere of action. In 1850 with his wife and children he moved to Keokuk, Iowa, and formed the law partnership of Reeves & Miller. Shortly afterward he was left a widower, and in 1857, his partner having died, he was married to the latter's widow, Elizabeth (Winter) Reeves. While his practice was increasing he found time to engage in the organization of the Republican party, and in projects for building plank roads and railroads. He was a candidate for the nomination for governor in 1861. During the early months of the war he drew upon his meager resources to advance funds to meet the state's unforeseen needs. In 1862 President Lincoln was under the necessity of making nominations for the Supreme Court. To him a sound view on public questions was a better recommendation than profundity of legal learning, and Miller was actively suported by the Iowa delegation, which circulated a recommendation among the members of both houses of Congress, and by the lawyers of several western states. On July 16, 1862, he was nominated and unanimously confirmed as an associate justice. He was at the time the chairman of the district Republican committee at Keokuk.

The development in power and authority of this self-made jurist is interesting. His training had been woefully unsystematic but was such as tended to develop independence of judgment and capacity for hard thinking. In later years he came to recognize the superiority in education and training enjoyed by leading eastern jurists. Yet with a certain self-satisfaction he insisted that it was "from some western prairie town . . . that future Marshalls and Mansfields shall arise and give new impulses and add new honor to the profession of the law" (*Albany Law Journal,* July 5, 1879, p. 29). His first term was Taney's last but one, and though Miller had cherished a hatred of the author of the Dred Scott opinion, the newest and the eldest of the justices parted fast friends. Throughout the war and reconstruction no judge was more stanch than Miller in the support of national authority. When in *Ex parte Garland* (4 *Wallace,* 333) the Court held that the requirement of a test oath of former loyalty from lawyers, teachers, and ministers amounted to an *ex post facto* law and a bill of attainder, Miller and the other Republicans argued that the measure was constitutional and proper. He was with the majority in the Legal Tender Cases (12 *Wallace,* 457) when by the advent of Justices Strong and Bradley this feature of the war program was narrowly saved from judicial repudiation.

A characteristic opinion is that in *Crandall* vs. *Nevada* (6 *Wallace,* 35). The legislature had imposed a tax on every person leaving the state. The Court was unanimous in holding the tax unconstitutional. Miller, as its spokesman, relied upon the broadest considerations of policy: "The people of these United States constitute one nation. They have a government in which all of them are deeply interested. . . . That government has a right to call to this point [the capital] any or all of its citizens to aid in its service. . . . The citizen also has correlative rights. He has the right to come to the seat of government to assert any claim he may have upon that government, or to transact any business he may have with it." Thus the tax was objectionable in that it conflicted with these implications of the nature of the union and of federal citizenship. In *Loan Association* vs. *Topeka* (20 *Wallace,* 655), a question of great contemporary importance was raised: Might a state or municipality grant public funds to aid a private enterprise? Miller approached the problem not in the light of constitutional provisions, but of his conception of natural law. "It must be conceded that there are . . . rights in every free government beyond the control of the State. A government which recognized no such rights, which held the lives, the liberty, and the property of its citizens subject at all times to the absolute disposition and unlimited control of even the most democratic depository of power, is after all but a despotism. . . . There are limitations on such [public] power which grow out of the essential nature of all free governments. Implied reservations of individual rights, without which the social compact could not exist, and which are respected by all governments entitled to the name. . . . There can be no lawful tax which is not laid for *a public purpose*."

A courageous and emphatic dissent was that in *Gelpcke* vs. *City of Dubuque* (1 *Wallace*, 175) in Miller's second year on the bench. The city had issued bonds for the purchase of railroad stock, under the authority of a state law which had been held good at the time of the issue. Subsequently the state supreme court reversed itself and held the statute *ultra vires*. A foreign bondholder brought suit on the bonds in the federal courts. Would the Supreme Court, as in most other cases, accept the jurisprudence of the state court as the rule of decision? The mischief seemed so great that the majority upheld the validity of the bonds. Two of Miller's deepest convictions united in compelling his dissent. First, he was always opposed to any tendency to allow a state to grant away its taxing power. Time and again in the next twenty years he dissented on this score. Then again, though a nationalist, he was impressed with the importance of maintaining an ample autonomy for state governments. He was strong in his belief that it was not the function of federal courts to sit in judgment on state courts expounding state law.

The latter conviction appears more maturely in the Slaughter House Cases (16 *Wallace*, 36). The Carpet-bag government of Louisiana granted a monopoly of the slaughtering business at New Orleans. Rival butchers contended that this action abridged their privileges and immunities as citizens of the United States and was a denial of due process of law and equal protection of the laws. Thus the Fourteenth Amendment came to receive its first authoritative construction at the hands of the Court. A majority of five, speaking through Miller, started from the proposition that there is a distinction between those rights which inhere in state citizenship and those which inhere in federal citizenship. It was only the latter with which the new amendment dealt. The monopoly might deny the plaintiffs some right conferred by the state constitution; but no federal privilege or immunity had been abridged. To hold otherwise, said Miller, "would constitute this court a perpetual censor upon all legislation of the States." The argument on due process and equal protection of the laws was briefly answered with the prophecy that "we doubt very much whether any action of a State not directed by way of discrimination against the negroes as a class . . . will ever be held to come within the purview of this provision."

This was not a scholastic discussion of state rights: it signified that the majority of the Court refused to read into the words of a Reconstruction amendment a promise of federal protection of vested property rights against the exertions of state power. Thus the nationalizing purposes of some of the Radical Republican authors of the amendment were frustrated. In the long run Miller's effort was somewhat unsuccessful, for those implications which he severed from the "privileges and immunities" clause were later grafted on to the "due process" clause of the same amendment.

Miller was more concerned with the practical result of a decision than with its doctrinal basis. Mere precedents were unimpressive aside from the authority of the judges who made them. He was disposed to let no technicalities stand in the way of what seemed right or just. Thus in *United States* vs. *Lee* (106 *U. S.*, 196) he held that "no man in this country is so high that he is above the law," adding that, notwithstanding a government's immunity to suit, an action of ejectment may be maintained against an officer who holds the possession of property under an invalid title claimed by the United States. In the case involving a federal marshal who was being held for the killing of a citizen who had attacked Justice Field on circuit (*In re Neagle*, 135 *U. S.*, 1), Miller held that it is an obligation of the President, fairly inferrible from the Constitution, to protect federal judges, and that the marshal had been acting in pursuance of "a law" of the United States, and was therefore entitled to be liberated on a writ of *habeas corpus* from the custody of the state authorities. Notwithstanding this tendency to view legal questions in the large, Miller could, on occasion, engage in minute hair-splitting (*Kring* vs. *Missouri*, 107 *U. S.*, 221; *Medley, Petitioner*, 134 *U. S.*, 160).

Of the nobility and generosity of Miller's nature there is ample evidence. Yet he felt that he was, as Chief Justice Chase said, "beyond question, the dominant personality . . . upon the bench" (Strong, *post*, p. 247). With this confidence came a certain blunt impatience with lesser minds and with futile arguments. The reference to him as "that damned old Hippopotamus" by one attorney in his circuit court was not unnatural (Gregory, *post*, p. 60). Miller was anxious to accelerate the administration of justice, and advocated a curtailment of the appellate jurisdiction of the Court (*United States Jurist*, January 1872, *Western Jurist*, February 1872). He never achieved the chief justiceship, though he was more than once considered for the position.

On the bench Miller retained his interest in the Republican party. He was one of the majority in the Electoral Commission of 1876. Yet he was content to rely upon his judicial labors to win his name immortality, and unlike Chase and Field refrained from gazing toward the presidency. Yet he would have been quite willing to become a compromise candidate if the convention of 1884 had become deadlocked. In stature he was tall and massive. He looked, dressed, and acted the part of a great magistrate. He enjoyed good living and bright company. In the midst of this satisfying life he found no opportunity to save money and died almost penniless. He was in active service on the supreme bench and as circuit justice until the day of his death, which occurred at his residence in Washington. During his tenure of office he participated in more than five thousand decisions of the Court. In more than six hundred cases he was its spokesman. Of 478 cases which required a construction of the federal Constitution, he was the organ of the Court in almost twice the normal quota for one justice.

[See C. N. Gregory, *Samuel Freeman Miller* (1907); Horace Stern, "Samuel Freeman Miller, 1816–1890," in W. D. Lewis, *Great Am. Lawyers*, vol. VI (1909); Henry Strong, "Justice Samuel Freeman Miller," in *Annals of Iowa*, Jan. 1894; *Proc. of the Bench and Bar of the Supreme Court of the U. S. in Memoriam Samuel F. Miller* (1891); *Miss. Valley Hist. Rev.*, Mar. 1931; Charles Warren, *The Supreme Court in U. S. Hist.* (1922), vol. III; the *Evening Star* (Wash., D. C.), Oct. 14, 1890. Information as to certain facts was supplied for this sketch by members of Miller's family. In 1891 a series of *Lectures on the Constitution* by Miller was posthumously published.] C. F.

MILLER, STEPHEN DECATUR (May 8, 1787–Mar. 8, 1838), representative and senator from South Carolina, Nullifier, was the son of William and Margaret (White) Miller. His ancestors were Scotch Presbyterians who emigrated to South Carolina from the north of Ireland and were among the first white settlers in Lancaster District, where he was born at the Waxhaw settlement. His father died early leaving little wealth. The few slaves the boy inherited were sold to pay for his education. He received the usual classical preparation of the time, in 1808 was graduated from the South Carolina College, and then studied law in the office of John S. Richardson of Sumter. He was admitted to the bar in 1811, was known as a good lawyer, and had a large practice. From 1817 to 1819 he was a member of the South Carolina delegation in the national House of Representatives. His next public service was as state senator for the Sumter District from 1822 to 1828. Then he became governor for two years. At the conclusion of his term he was elected, against William Smith, to the United States Senate and took his seat on Dec. 5, 1831. During this period he opposed most of the measures of President Jackson although, like Jackson, he was an enemy of the Bank.

When he entered Congress he was an anti-Calhoun Democrat, but repeated demands of the protectionists converted him to Calhoun's nullification doctrine. When the tariff of 1827 was under consideration, he was a member of a special committee of the state Senate that reported a series of resolutions announcing the compact theory of government and condemning the tariff acts of 1816, 1820, and 1824, federal appropriations for roads and canals, and federal support of the American Colonization Society as violations of the Constitution. As governor his speeches did much to crystallize nullification sentiment. There were, he insisted, three ways of reforming unequal congressional legislation, the ballot box, the jury box, and the cartridge box. It was the prerogative of the people to elect a convention to nullify the federal tariff laws, which all South Carolinians admitted were unconstitutional and oppressive. If the laws were once nullified, juries, regardless of the opinions of federal judges, would not sustain them. Yet, if all other means failed, there still remained the right of resistance. In the United States Senate he spoke and voted against the tariff of 1832, and, when it passed, he and nearly all the other members of the South Carolina delegation united in an "Address to the People of South Carolina." The addressers rejected the lower rates of that act as unsatisfactory, since protection still remained "the settled policy of the country." All hope of fair dealing from the federal government seemed to them to have vanished. The remedy, they declared, was in the sovereign power of the state. He was a member of the state conventions of 1832 and 1833, called to consider nullification. He voted for the nullification ordinance in 1832. In the convention of 1833 he opposed the measure to require of all office holders the test oath of paramount allegiance to the state, which was, nevertheless, passed with a good majority.

He resigned from the Senate on Mar. 2, 1833, on account of ill health and retired to Mississippi, where he had removed three years earlier and had set up as a cotton planter. He died at his nephew's house in Raymond, Miss. He was married twice. His first wife was a Miss Dick of Sumter whom he married about 1814. She died in 1819. Their three sons died in youth. In May 1821 he married Mary Boykin of Kershaw, S. C., who survived him with their son and three daughters.

[J. B. O'Neall, *Biog. Sketches of the Bench and Bar in S. C.* (1859), vol. II; *Cyc. of Eminent and Representative Men* (1892), vol. I; *Biog. Directory of the Am. Cong.* (1928).] J. G. V—D.

MILLER, WARNER (Aug. 12, 1838–Mar. 21, 1918), paper manufacturer and United States senator, of German descent, was born at Hannibal, Oswego County, N. Y., the son of Hiram and Mary Ann (Warner) Miller. In 1839 his parents moved to Millertown (now North Pittstown) and later to a farm near Northville, in Fulton County, where Warner grew up. He attended an academy in Charlotteville, in Schoharie County, N. Y., and for a time taught school near New Brunswick, N. J. From here he entered Union College at Schenectady and was graduated in 1860. He began to teach at Fort Edward Collegiate Institute in New York but upon the advent of the Civil War enlisted in the 5th New York Cavalry. His military experiences were varied and brief, as he was captured, paroled, and honorably discharged by September 1862. Not being able to reënter the army, and having lost interest in an academic career, he took a position in a paper-mill at Fort Edward, where he advanced to a foremanship and was sent to Belgium to study a new process for making paper. In 1865 Warner Miller & Company purchased the paper-mill of A. H. Laflin in Herkimer. In the same year, on July 13, Miller was married to Caroline Churchill. In his business he developed new processes for making paper from wood pulp and gained considerable reputation as a leader in the industry.

His financial success brought him to public notice and directed him into politics. For many years he was the leading Republican of Herkimer County, and in 1872 he was a delegate to the Republican National Convention at Philadelphia. During the next three years he served as state assemblyman. In 1878 he was chosen to represent his district in Congress, a position which he held until July 26, 1881, when he resigned to become United States senator. His election to this office came as the result of a split in the Republican party of his state. Miller became the successful candidate of the "Half Breeds," against the "Stalwarts," for the seat vacated by Thomas C. Platt. He remained in the Senate until Mar. 3, 1887, being denied reëlection because of the political adroitness of Platt, who rather than see Miller triumph over his own candidate, Levi P. Morton, threw his votes to a third candidate, Frank Hiscock. In the Senate Miller served on many committees, at one time being chairman of the committee on agriculture. He was particularly nationalistic in his attitudes and strongly favored Chinese exclusion, the development of the merchant marine, and the protective tariff. He also supported the Nicaraguan canal proposals. He had a simple though effective style of oratory which won for him a considerable reputation.

In 1884 Miller supported Blaine for the presidency and at the National Convention in 1888 was partly responsible for the nomination of Benjamin Harrison. His ability and service to his party were rewarded in August 1888 by his nomination by acclamation as the Republican candidate for governor of New York. During the campaign which followed he supported Harrison and spoke frequently on the merits of a protective tariff. It has often been stated that it was due to his opposition to the liquor interests that he lost the election, being defeated by David Bennett Hill, the Democratic candidate, by 19,171 votes. In 1892, as delegate at large at the Republican Convention, Miller worked for the nomination of Blaine, but he returned to work equally hard for the election of Harrison. In 1894 and 1895 he was an active leader at the state conventions and warmly approved of McKinley in 1896. After this date he gradually retired from politics, although in 1906 he was chairman of a special tax commission in New York. He was a leading and public-spirited citizen, a member of the Herkimer County Historical Society, and an active participant in the affairs of the local Methodist Episcopal Church. He died in New York City.

[*Biog. Dir. Am. Cong.* (1928); J. L. M'Millan, "Printing and Its Development in This Country," *Papers Read Before the Herkimer County Hist. Soc. During the Years 1896, 1897, and 1898* (1899); "Herkimer County People at the Nat. Capitol," *Ibid.*, vol. II (1902); C. M. Depew, *One Hundred Years of Am. Commerce* (1895), vol. I; R. Van V. Raymond, *Union Univ.* (1907), II, 56–59; G. A. Hardin, *Hist. of Herkimer County, N. Y.* (1893); R. B. Smith, *Pol. and Gov. Hist. of the State of N. Y.* (1922), vols. III and IV; D. S. Alexander, *Four Famous New Yorkers* (1923); *N. Y. Times*, Mar. 22, 1918.] W. F. G.

MILLER, WILLIAM (Feb. 15, 1782–Dec. 20, 1849), leader of the Adventist movement, the son of Capt. William Miller, a veteran of the Revolutionary War, was born at Pittsfield,

Mass., and grew to manhood in Low Hampton, Washington County, N. Y. His mother, Paulina, was the daughter of Elnathan Phelps, a Baptist preacher. His early education was limited to that afforded by a frontier school, but his deep thirst for further learning was partially satisfied by reading books borrowed from men of learning in the neighborhood. On June 29, 1803, he married Lucy P. Smith of Poultney, Vt., settled in the bride's home town, and became a farmer. Availing himself of the public library, he became a constant reader and student. His mother had taught him to revere the Bible as the word of God to man, but perplexed by certain apparently contradictory passages and influenced by his reading and certain skeptical friends, he became a deist. In his new home he grew into prominence, filling numerous offices of public trust, including those of justice of the peace and deputy sheriff. During the War of 1812 he served in the army, rising to the rank of captain.

Upon his return to civil life he settled in Hampton, N. Y., on a farm, where, in 1816, after great mental and spiritual struggle, he experienced conversion. Taunted by deist friends, he began a prayerful study of the Bible in an effort to meet their gibes. By pursuing a study of the prophecies, he discovered to his own satisfaction that the Bible revealed the return of Christ to earth about 1843. Fifteen years' further study only deepened this conviction. Along with it came a call to present his views. This he resisted for several years, fearing his calculations might be incorrect. In 1831, however, he accepted an invitation to give a public interpretation of the prophecies. Filled with the theme, and master of his subject, he soon became a power in the pulpit. Invitations poured in upon him and great crowds attended his lectures. Before long he was unable to answer half the calls for his services. In 1833 the Baptist church of which he was a member granted him a license to preach. In 1836 he published the chief Adventist writing of his time, a volume of sixteen lectures entitled *Evidence from Scripture and History of the Second Coming of Christ, about the Year 1843. Exhibited in a Course of Lectures.* Everywhere the Baptist, Methodist, and Congregational churches were thrown open, and pastors requested him to address their congregations. Hundreds were converted in the revivals that followed his work.

In 1839 Joshua Vaughan Himes [*q.v.*] accepted Miller's teaching and became one of the greatest publicity men of his day. Through his activities Adventist papers were published in the chief cities of the country and millions of pages of literature were circulated. A great tent was purchased for a tabernacle and Miller and his associates traveled over the country warning the people to prepare for the great day of the Lord. At least 120 camp meetings were held during the summer months of 1842, 1843, and 1844, with an estimated attendance of half a million. Miller expected Christ to come some time between March 1843 and March 1844. Consequently, his followers began to name different dates as probable times for the advent. Signs in the heavens of its coming were reported; a great meteoric shower which occurred in 1833 was regarded as an omen; strange rings were seen around the sun; crosses were discerned in the sky; and a great comet appeared at high noon and for days hung ominously over the earth like a huge sword threatening a guilty world. The entire country was astir. People began to lose their reason, Miller's followers were accused of donning ascension robes and assembling in graveyards and on high places to await their Saviour. These charges, according to the best evidence, are not based on facts, although tradition to this day readily affirms them. Certain other forms of fanaticism, such as speaking with strange tongues and possessing discerning spirits, did appear. These extravagances, although confined to a small minority, were sharply rebuked by the leaders. Disappointed in their expectation in 1843, the Millerites, as the Adventists were called by their enemies, again looked for Christ on Oct. 22, 1844. The intensity of their anticipation rose to flood tide at this time. Crops were left unharvested, stores closed, and positions were resigned. Men prepared, as though on their death beds, to meet their God. Again disappointed, Miller continued steadfast in the faith, looking for Christ in the immediate future but setting no date.

When he began preaching, he had no thought of forming a separate church. Bitter opposition to his followers, who were members of the principal Protestant churches, arose, however, and they began to withdraw from their several sects in 1843. Two years later the Adventist Church was organized with Miller at its head. Although nominally the leader, he handed over the reins to younger hands and spent the remainder of his days in comparative inactivity, going forth occasionally to preach or to grace a conference with his sage-like presence. His rise had been rapid. From the position of an obscure country preacher to that of a religious teacher of national prominence he rose in three years. Possessing a commanding personality and genial disposition, together with pious scholarship and the deepest sincerity, he was a mighty force in the religious world. In his old age he lost his eyesight and his career closed in darkness. He died at Hampton surrounded by his family.

[Everett Dick, "The Adventist Crisis 1831–1844," doctoral dissertation presented at the University of Wisconsin, 1930, is the most comprehensive study of Miller's work; see also Sylvester Bliss, *Memoirs of William Miller* (1853); I. C. Wellcome (*History of the Second Advent Message and Mission, Doctrine and People* (1874); James White, *Sketches of the Christian Life and Public Labors of William Miller* (1875); C. E. Sears, *Days of Delusion* (1924); *Littell's Living Age*, Jan. 19, 1850, *Advent Herald*, Jan. 1850; O. S. Phelps and A. T. Servin, *The Phelps Family of America* (2 vols., 1899); Crisfield Johnson, *Hist. of Washington Co., N. Y.* (1878).] E. N. D.

MILLER, WILLIAM HENRY HARRISON (Sept. 6, 1840–May 25, 1917), attorney-general of the United States, was born at Augusta, N. Y., the son of Lucy (Duncan) and Curtis Miller, a farmer. His ancestors were Scotch and English. After being graduated from Hamilton College in 1861, he taught school at Maumee, Ohio. In May 1862 he enlisted in the 84th Ohio Infantry but was mustered out in September with the rank of second lieutenant. He then began the study of law in the office of Morrison R. Waite [*q.v.*]; this he continued at Peru, Ind., while serving there as superintendent of schools. He was married to Gertrude A. Bunce in December 1863. In 1865 he was admitted to the bar and in 1866 moved to Fort Wayne. He attracted the attention of Benjamin Harrison at whose invitation he became a partner in the firm of Harrison and Hines at Indianapolis. He was a man of great industry, inclined to be somewhat impulsive at times, and well versed in the law. He took no active part in politics but was the trusted adviser of those Republicans who did; when cases came before the state supreme court involving political questions, he often argued the Republican side. The most dramatic case of this type was the lieutenant-governorship contest in 1886 (*Robertson* vs. *the State, ex rel. Smith,* 109 *Ind. Reports,* 79).

When Benjamin Harrison became president Miller became his attorney-general and one of his most trusted personal advisors. The appointment was a surprise to Republican leaders, for Miller was unknown outside of his state and had had practically no administrative experience. As attorney-general he endeavored to enforce the laws vigorously and impartially with a disregard of political influences that was often disconcerting to Republican leaders. His careful investigation into the records of men suggested for federal judicial appointments was responsible in part for the excellence of Harrison's judicial appointments. Among the more important cases that came before the United States Supreme Court and to which Miller gave his personal attention were those involving the anti-lottery law, the interstate commerce act, the Sherman anti-trust act, and the constitutionality of the McKinley tariff. In the spectacular case *in re Neagle* (135 *U. S. Reports,* 1) his position that it was the duty of the executive to protect federal judges against physical injury while on duty was upheld by the Supreme Court. (See article on Stephen Johnson Field.) Among his most able assistants was the solicitor-general, William Howard Taft. When Taft resigned to become United States circuit judge, he wrote of Miller: "To serve under a chief whose only requirement is that one shall do right and enforce the law without fear or favor is as delightful as it is exceptional" (draft of letter of resignation, *Taft Papers*). When Harrison's term ended in 1893, Miller rejoined his old law firm and engaged in active practice until 1910. He died in Indianapolis, survived by his wife and three of their seven children.

[Benjamin Harrison Papers and William Howard Taft Papers in the Lib. of Cong.; Letter Books and Registers of the firm of Harrison, Hines, and Miller and its successors at Indianapolis; *Indianapolis Star,* May 26, 1917; *Indianapolis News,* May 26, 28, 1917.] A. T. V.

MILLER, WILLOUGHBY DAYTON (Aug. 1, 1853–July 27, 1907), dentist, a son of John H. and Nancy L. (Sommerville) Miller, was born on a farm near Alexandria, Licking County, Ohio. His education began in the county public school; but in 1865 his parents removed to Newark, Ohio, where he graduated from the high school in 1871. In the same year he entered the University of Michigan at Ann Arbor, and received the degree of A.B. in 1875. He then took special courses in chemistry, mathematics, and physics at the University of Edinburgh, and in 1876 entered upon further study along these lines at the University of Berlin. Overwork resulted in a nervous breakdown in 1877, but during his convalescence he mingled in the social life of the American colony in Berlin and collaborated in some chemical researches with F. P. Abbot, a pioneer American dentist in Germany. Miller shortly became engaged to marry Abbot's daughter, and decided to adopt dentistry as his profession and settle in Berlin, so that his future wife could be near her parents. He served a few months as student assistant to Abbot, then, late in 1877, entered the Pennsylvania College of Dental Surgery, which became the Dental Department of the University of Pennsylvania in 1878 and graduated Miller with the degree of D.D.S. in 1879. Returning immediately to Berlin, he married Caroline L. Abbot on Oct. 26, 1879, and began the practice of dentistry with her father, at the same time continuing his studies at the University of Berlin.

From the beginning of his professional career to the time of his death, Miller was especially interested in bacteriology and chemistry as related to dental and oral diseases. The first of his many articles on micro-organisms in the etiology of dental caries appeared in German in 1881 and in English in 1882. In 1884 he was appointed professor of operative dentistry in the newly organized Dental Institute of the University of Berlin. In 1887 he graduated with the degree of M.D. from the medical school of the University of Berlin with the predicate *magna cum laude*. In 1894 he was made a professor extraordinary on the medical faculty of the same university, an honor rarely conferred upon a foreigner and never before upon a dentist; and about the same time he became a state examiner for dentistry in Berlin. His elevation to these coveted positions at first aroused much opposition from German dentists, some of whom repeatedly petitioned the minister of education to give the offices to Germans; but this opposition was soon overcome, and Miller was recognized everywhere as one of the leading dental authorities and bacteriologists of his day. As a practitioner of dentistry he stood second to none in Berlin, the Empress Augusta and other members of the imperial family being included among his many distinguished patients, while in 1906 the Emperor in a personal letter appointed him privy medical councilor. He served as president of the National Dental Association of Germany, the Association of Dental Faculties of that nation, the American Dental Society of Europe, and the Fédération Dentaire Internationale. He was also an honorary member of some forty dental societies in America and abroad.

Miller published more than a hundred articles in professional journals. The majority were in German, while some were in English, but many of the former were translated into English. In America, most of his contributions to dentistry appeared in the *Dental Cosmos* and the *Independent Practitioner*. He also published two extensive works in book form, the more notable of which is *Die Mikro-organismen der Mundhöhle* (1889 and 1892), translated into English as *The Micro-organisms of the Human Mouth* (1890). This was followed by his *Lehrbuch der Conservirenden Zahnheilkunde* (1896 and 1898). In his laboratory experiments, he produced caries in extracted human teeth by means of bacteria from the mouth, and demonstrated that tooth tissue is destroyed by fermentative acids formed by these micro-organisms. This is now generally accepted as the basic truth of the "chemicoparasitic theory"; but neither Miller nor his followers claimed that this theory could explain all the phenomena of dental caries. Miller's researches and writings also relate to various other subjects, such as the use of antiseptics in dentistry, diseased teeth and oral tissues as foci of infection, and the etiology of dental erosion and abrasion.

His practice was confined to Berlin; but such was his loyalty to his native land that he declined to become a naturalized citizen of Germany. In 1907 he accepted the position of dean of the Dental College of the University of Michigan, his alma mater. Efforts were made to have him remain in Berlin, a wealthy merchant even offering to build, equip, and support a research laboratory for him in that city; but he severed his connection with the University there and brought his family to the United States, expecting to begin his duties at Ann Arbor in October 1907. In the summer of that year however, while on a visit with his family to relatives in Alexandria, Ohio, near the place of his birth, he was stricken with appendicitis, and died after an operation at the City Hospital of Newark, Ohio. He was survived by his wife and their three children, one son and two daughters. Miller was of slight build and never robust. His life was devoted to his family, his professional duties, his researches, and his writings. For some years he was secretary of the non-sectarian American Church in Berlin, and he was an ardent golfer. In 1915 a life-size bronze statue of him was unveiled on the campus of the Ohio State University at Columbus.

[The chief sources are *Dental Cosmos*, Sept. 1907; *Index of Dental Periodical Literature*, and family information. See also *Dental Summary*, Apr. 1916, and *Detroit Free Press*, July 30, 1907. The biography of Miller by B. K. Thorpe in C. R. E. Koch's *Hist. of Dental Surgery* (1910), vol. III, is incomplete and unreliable.] L. P. B.

MILLET, FRANCIS DAVIS (Nov. 3, 1846–Apr. 15, 1912), painter, author, war correspondent, illustrator, was born in Mattapoisett, Mass., the son of Dr. Asa and Huldah A. (Byram) Millet. In July 1864 he enlisted as a private in the 60th Massachusetts Militia Infantry and served as a drummer until Nov. 30, when he was honorably discharged. He graduated at Harvard in 1869 with the degree of M.A. in modern languages and literature. While working on the *Boston Advertiser* he learned lithography and so earned money to take him in 1871 to the Royal Academy, Antwerp, where in two years he won all the prizes the academy offered and was publicly crowned by the King. In 1873, as secretary of the Massachusetts commission to the Vienna exposition he formed a lasting friendship with Charles Francis Adams, cemented by travel and work together. He wandered through the Near East, becoming acquainted with the peoples of Turkey, Greece, and Hungary. Then he studied painting in Rome and Venice and returned to act as correspondent of the *Boston Advertiser* at the Philadelphia Centennial, where he was an exhibitor. He helped John La Farge decorate Trinity Church, Boston, and painted a portrait of Mark Twain.

In 1877 the *New York Herald* sent Millet as correspondent with the Russians in their war against Turkey. Later he succeeded Archibald Forbes on the *London Daily News* and as artist for the *London Graphic.* Whistling bullets gave vividness to his pencil, and hard rides to post dispatches taught him the country. So it happened that he daringly broke military etiquette and told the Russian officers of a ford unknown to them by which they might avoid crossing a deep river to attack the Turks. The flank movement succeeded. No notice was taken of Millet's temerity until he was summoned by the Russian general, who "dealt with an unprecedented action of a civilian in proffering advice on military matters" by presenting to him in the name of the Czar the Cross of St. Stanislaus. Next came the Cross of St. Anne for valuable and exceptional service to the Russian government. With his friend, General Gurko he rode into Adrianople and received the Iron Cross of Roumania. Of these decorations he spoke only to point some robust or pithy story.

In 1878 Millet was a member of the fine arts jury at the Paris exposition and an exhibitor in both the Salon and the British Royal Academy. On Mar. 11, 1879, he married Elizabeth Greely Merrill, the sister of William Bradford Merrill [*q.v.*]. For a time they lived in Boston, then New York. In 1884, Millet, with E. A. Abbey, J. S. Sargent, and Alfred Parsons made a Bohemian colony at Broadway, England. In *Picture and Text* (1893) Henry James has written of Broadway and Millet: "He has made pictures without words and words without pictures. He has written very clever ghost stories and drawn and painted some very immediate realities. . . . He has draped and distributed Greek plays at Harvard . . . and given publicity to English villages. . . . The old surfaces and tones, the stuffs and textures, the old silver and mahogany and brass—the old sentiment too, and the old picture-making vision are in the direct tradition of Terburg and DeHoogh and Metzu" (pp. 9–12). In 1891, for *Harper's Magazine,* he made a trip of seventeen hundred miles down the Danube with Poultney Bigelow. Their narratives, which appeared in *Harper's* from February to May 1892, later took book form (*From the Black Forest to the Black Sea,* 1893). Also he printed a sheaf of short stories, which still bubble up in anthologies. In 1887 he had published a translation of Tolstoi's *Sebastopol.* At the World's Columbian Exhibition of 1893 he was director of decorations of the White City and ended as master of ceremonies. His humorous ingenuity brought the fair to a brilliant end, notwithstanding the financial panic. *The Expedition to the Philippines* (1899) represents his war-correspondence for the *London Times, Harper's Weekly,* and the New York *Sun.* A journey through the Far East brought him back to the Paris Exposition of 1900 as representative of his country. Then he painted historical murals for the Minnesota and Wisconsin capitols, the Baltimore Custom House, the Cleveland Trust Company. In 1908 Secretary Root sent him on a special mission to Tokyo, whence he returned with the First Class Order of the Sacred Treasure. France had made him a chevalier of the Legion of Honor.

Millet was the creative spirit of the American Federation of Arts and of the National Commission of Fine Arts (1910). Reluctantly he accepted the directorship of the American Academy in Rome at a time of an academy crisis in 1911. In 1912 he and his Washington companion, Maj. Archie Butt, President Taft's aide, were in Rome, Millet on urgent Academy business. They took return passage on the *Titanic* and went down with the ship. Millet was last seen encouraging the Italian women and children to go into the lifeboats. In a shaded nook in the President's Park (White Lot) in Washington, stands a modest monument to Millet and Butt, the design a tribute of friendship by Daniel Chester French, sculptor, and Thomas Hastings, architect. Elihu Root said of Millet: "He never pushed himself forward. He never thought or cared where the spotlight was. . . . Yet from somewhere among his forbears in old New England there came into his make-up a firmness of fiber which made him modest, sensitive, beauty-loving as he was, a man of strength and force, decision of character, and executive capacity" (*Francis Davis Millet, Memorial Meeting, post,* p. 8).

[*Eleventh Report of the Class of 1869 of Harvard Coll.* (1919); *Harvard Grads.' Mag.,* Sept. 1909; *Francis Davis Millet: Memorial Meeting* (1912), published by the Am. Federation of Arts, and containing a bibliography of Millet's paintings and literary work; *Art*

and Progress, July 1912, Sept., Nov. 1913; *Internat. Studio,* Oct. 1907, Dec. 1912; Leila Mechlin, "A Decorator of Public Buildings," *World's Work,* Dec. 1909; James Hunt, *A List of Paintings, Drawings, Mural Decorations and Designs . . . and Lit. Works of Francis Davis Millet* (n.d.); Thos. Hastings, "La Farge, Abbey, Millet," *Proc. Am. Acad. Arts and Letters,* vol. I (1913); Charles Moore, *Daniel H. Burnham, Architect, Planner of Cities* (2 vols. 1921) and *The Life and Times of Chas. Follen McKim* (1929); *Am. Art News,* Apr. 20, 1912; *N. Y. Times,* Apr. 16, 1912.]
C. M.

MILLIGAN, ROBERT (July 25, 1814–Mar. 20, 1875), minister of the Disciples of Christ, educator, was born in County Tyrone, Ireland, the son of John and Margaret Milligan, who with their children emigrated to the United States about 1818 and settled in Ohio not far from Youngstown. Robert attended academies in Zelienople and Jamestown, Pa., and in 1837 opened a classical school of his own at Flat Rock, Bourbon County, Ky. He was at that time a member of the Associate Presbyterian Church, but a thorough study of the Greek New Testament resulted in his accepting the views of the Disciples of Christ as Scriptural, and in 1838 he united with that body. Entering Washington College, Pa., in 1839, he received the degree of A.B. the following year, and at once became professor of English in that institution. In 1842 he married Ellen Blaine Russell.

Milligan was ordained to the ministry in 1844 by Thomas Campbell, but although he preached frequently he held no regular pastorate. Among the Disciples he occupied a position of leadership, but his influence was exerted chiefly as an educator and writer. He was connected with Washington College for some twelve years, where, after teaching English and the classics, he became professor of chemistry and the natural sciences. In 1852 he was called to Indiana University, but two years later became professor of mathematics at Bethany College. While here he also served for some time as co-editor of the *Millennial Harbinger.* Becoming president of Kentucky University in 1859, and also professor of sacred history and mental and moral philosophy, he managed the institution successfully through the difficult days of the Civil War. When, after its removal from Harrodsburg to Lexington, it was united with Transylvania University in 1865, he voluntarily relinquished the presidency and became head of the College of the Bible, which position he held until his death. During the last decade of his life he published a number of religious works which include *Reason and Revelation, or the Province of Reason in Matters Pertaining to Divine Revelation Defined and Illustrated* (1868); *An Exposition and Defense of the Scheme of Redemption* (1869); *The Great Commission of Jesus Christ to the Twelve Apostles* (1871); *Analysis of the New Testament* (1874). A commentary on Hebrews (*The New Testament Commentary,* vol. IX, 1876), appeared after his death.

[W. T. Moore, *The Living Pulpit of the Christian Church* (1869); J. T. Brown, *Churches of Christ* (1904); G. T. Ridlon, *Hist. of the Families Millingas and Millanges . . .* (1907); W. T. Moore, *A Comprehensive Hist. of the Disciples of Christ* (1909); *Christian Standard,* Mar. 27, Apr. 10, 1875.] H. E. S.

MILLIGAN, ROBERT WILEY (Apr. 8, 1843–Oct. 14, 1909), naval officer, was born in Philadelphia, Pa., the son of James and Mary (Thornton) Milligan and a grandson of Robert Milligan who emigrated from County Down, Ireland, to Pennsylvania, sometime before 1840. After attending Philadelphia grammar and high schools he entered the navy as third assistant engineer, Mar. 3, 1863, and served through the remainder of the Civil War in the *Mackinaw,* participating in both attacks on Fort Fisher, the fall of Wilmington, and the subsequent campaign on the James River. Engineering duty on many ships and stations in the ensuing thirty years was broken by two assignments as Naval Academy instructor, 1879–82 and 1885–89, and service on the Board of Inspection and Survey, 1893–96. He went to the *Oregon* as chief engineer in January 1897, and was in this ship during her famous cruise around South America and her outstanding work at Santiago in the Spanish-American War. Both were essentially feats of engineering, justifying in a measure Admiral C. F. Pond's statement, made on "The Battleship Oregon Day" at the Panama-Pacific Exposition, that to Milligan, "more than to any other one man, was due the wonderful success of this . . . ship" (*Army and Navy News,* San Francisco, November 1915, p. 6).

Leaving San Francisco on Mar. 19, 1898, the *Oregon,* with a trial speed of 16.7 knots, averaged 11.16 on the fourteen-thousand-mile cruise, making Florida in sixty-eight days, fifty-four under way. That no machinery accidents or delays occurred was due primarily to the chief engineer and his devoted assistants, who both at sea and during the brief overhauls worked under great strain. On the Santiago blockade, Milligan "ran a sweat-shop" (J. R. Spears, *Our Navy in the War with Spain,* 1898, p. 294). As during the cruise, he insisted on fresh water only for the boilers, and his was the only ship to keep all four boilers constantly under steam. As a result, the *Oregon* in the battle shot "like an express train," in Capt. Robley D. Evans' words, past all her consorts but the *Brooklyn,* averaging 12.9 knots, whereas the 21-knot *Brooklyn* averaged only 13.2. The last spurt, which brought her in range of the *Cristobal*

Colon, was made with superior coal which Milligan brought from San Francisco and kept under lock and key. Milligan was advanced five numbers and after a year as fleet engineer was stationed at the Norfolk Navy Yard from July 1899 until his retirement as rear admiral on Apr. 8, 1905. He had been made captain in 1902 after the amalgamation of engineers with the line. He was a well-built man above medium height, slow-spoken, thoughtful, and whole-hearted in his work. He was married on Feb. 17, 1870, to Sarah Ann Du Bois of Annapolis, Md., and was survived by two daughters. His death occurred at Annapolis, where he had made his home after retirement, and he was buried there in the naval cemetery.

[F. F. Hemenway, "An Interview with Chief Engineer Milligan," *Machinery,* Oct. 1898; C. A. E. King, "Recent Performances of the U.S.S. Oregon," *Jour. Am. Soc. Naval Engineers,* Aug. 1898; C. E. Clark, *My Fifty Years in the Navy* (1917); L. R. Hamersly, *The Records of Living Officers of the U. S. Navy and Marine Corps* (7th ed., 1902); *Who's Who in America,* 1908–09; *Army and Navy Jour.,* Oct. 16, 1909; the *Sun* (Baltimore), Oct. 15, 1909.] A. W.

MILLINGTON, JOHN (May 11, 1779–July 10, 1868), engineer, scientific writer, and teacher, was born in Hammersmith, near London, the son of Thomas Charles Millington, an attorney, and his wife, Ruth Hill. Millington entered Oxford University but because of his father's poverty withdrew without a degree, studied law, and in the years following 1803 had a considerable practice as a patent agent. In some way, time and place unknown, he apparently acquired the degree of M.D. He never practised medicine, nor did he ever engage in general legal practice, but devoted himself to engineering and teaching. In 1806 he was admitted a fellow of the Society for the Encouragement of Arts (later the Royal Society of Arts). He is said to have been associated with McAdam in road-building, to have been engineer of the West Middlesex water works, and to have served as superintendent of "the royal grounds in London, or at Kew." In 1815 the Royal Institution engaged him to give a course of about twelve lectures on natural philosophy at three guineas a lecture. From this time until 1829, he gave annual courses of lectures on natural philosophy, mechanics, and astronomy before the Institution, and on July 7, 1817, was appointed professor of mechanics there. In 1820 he became one of the original fellows of the Astronomical Society of London and served as secretary for the three years 1823 to 1826. In December 1823 he was elected a member of the Linnean Society of London. Upon the organization of the University of London, he was appointed first professor of engineering but resigned before the university was opened (H. H. Bellot, *University College, London,* 1929, pp. 28, 40, 135).

During these busy years in London, Millington married Emily, daughter of Sir William Hamilton, the painter; invented and patented a ship's propeller; published in 1823 his *Epitome of the Elementary Principles of Mechanical Philosophy,* which had a second edition in 1830; taught chemistry in Guy's Hospital; and was vice-president of the London Mechanics' Institution. At the age of fifty, as an engineer and teacher of science in his native London, he had approached greatness, though at a respectful distance. He now set out upon a career of almost forty years of restless wandering. In 1830 and the year following he was in Mexico, employed by an English company as superintendent of a group of mines and of a mint. Here his wife Emily died leaving a number of small children. A few years later he was in Philadelphia, marrying Sarah Ann Letts and conducting a shop which professed to supply "all the various machines, instruments, apparatus and materials, required for mechanical, philosophical, mathematical, optical and chemical purposes" (Holmes, *post,* p. 28). In 1835 he accepted the chair of chemistry, natural philosophy, and engineering in the College of William and Mary at Williamsburg, Va. While there he wrote his *Elements of Civil Engineering,* published in 1839, possibly the first American textbook on the subject. In 1848 he was elected the first professor of the natural sciences in the newly organized University of Mississippi at Oxford, Miss. He also served as head of the geological survey of the state, though B. L. C. Wailes did the work. In 1853 he became professor of chemistry and toxicology in the Memphis Medical College. At the age of eighty he retired to his new home at La Grange, Tenn. The Civil War reduced him to poverty. He fled to Philadelphia, seeking a livelihood, and finally found a haven at the home of his daughter in Richmond, Va. He died in July 1868 and was buried in the churchyard of Bruton Parish in Williamsburg. In youth the friend of Herschel, Faraday, and Davy, he spent his old age teaching the natural sciences to the restless sons of the Old South.

[G. F. Holmes, "Prof. John Millington, M.D., 1779–1868," *William and Mary Coll. Quart.,* Jan. 1923; S. C. Gladden, "John Millington (1779–1868)," *Ibid.,* July 1933; sketch by R. B. Prosser in the *Dict. Nat. Biog.*; Bennett Woodcroft, *Alphabetical Index of Patentees of Inventions . . . 1617–1852* (1854), p. 380; *Richmond Enquirer,* June 23, 1848; *Daily Enquirer and Examiner* (Richmond), July 11, 1868.]

T. C. J., Jr.

DICTIONARY OF AMERICAN BIOGRAPHY
AMERICAN COUNCIL OF LEARNED SOCIETIES